Personally Oriented Guide

JAPAN

千里之行始於足下

*"journey of one thousand leagues
begins with but one single step..."*

—Confucius, c.500 BC

Dedicated in Loving Memory
to
Isabel Tozzer, 'Tarzan's mother'
Friend and Mentor

JAPAN INSIDE OUT

Jay & Sumi & Garet Gluck

1341 Pages

135 Maps & plans

85 Sketches

2099 Festival dates

PERSONALLY ORIENTED Ltd Ashiya, Japan

– 1992 –

First published 1964, Hiroshima and Kobe, Japan
in set of five regional volumes;
Reprinted various volumes 1965, 1966, 1967, 1968

Second Edition fully revised and enlarged single-volume 1992

by **Personally Oriented** (Publishers) Ltd
13-5 Yama Ashiya-cho, Ashiya City 659, Japan
Cable PERSIANART ASHIYA JAPAN
☎ & Fax [country 81] - (797) 22-3256
local (0797) 22-3256

ISBN-4-89360-035-4

Printed in The United States of America

Library of Congress 88-92781

CONTENTS

INTRODUCTION

CENTRAL JAPAN

YAMATO HEARTLAND OF JAPAN

KYOTO CITY OF CITIES

SOUTH & WEST JAPAN

NORTH JAPAN

TOKYO

MAPS

FESTIVAL CALENDAR

FESTIVALS are year-round in Japan, check page nº. next to dates you'll be here for fete during that time. *Note:** denotes event worth planning itinerary around.

JANUARY
1-Sunrise: 219, 1043 & most everywhere
Dec-New Year, 507, 1086
Early: 1109
1st Sun: 512, 612
1st Fri: 612
1st Tiger Day: 664
1: 321, 327, 507, 664, 709, 822, 934
1-3: 219, 862, 880-1
1-5: 1265
1-15: 366, 390
2: 609, 664, 1265
2-5: 507
2-6: 895
3: 295, 321, 390, 507, 664, 708, 956, 1223, 1265
3-5: 1045
4: 219, 507, 709
5: 219, 319, 390, 664, 1045, 1265
6: 295, 881, 934, 1265
6-Feb 3: 881
7: 256, 298, 609, 709, 934, 1043, 1265
2d Sat/Sun: 950
2d Sun: 1265
8: 295, 1201, 1224, 1265
8-11: 708
8-12: 507, 609
8 pm to 9th am: 295
9: 507
9-10: 609
Sun nr 10: 1204, 1265
10: 1043
11: 298, 321, 954
12: 1043, 1265
13: 952
13-14: 295
13-15: 1045
14: 390, 507, 609, 934, 950, 986, 1043, 1045
3d Sat/Sun: 934
Mid: 934
15: 194, 219, 256, 298, 375, *390, 422, 507, 709, 908, 934, 1045, 1223, 1265
15-16: 1265
15-20: 1045, 1265
15-Feb 15: 256

15-Apr 15: 1122
16: 1045
17: 1043, 1045
18: 1265
19: 507, 934
20: 934, 994, 1045, 1265
21: 440, 555, 507, 513, 612
1-22: 934
4th Sun: 612
23: 194, 634, 934, 952
23-26: 881
24: 921
24-25: 709, 934
25: 507, 513, 555, 881, 1265
25-27: 1122. 1221
26: 1045
27: 194, 954
28: 194, 256, 934, 1224
31: 194, 1228
Late: 507
Last wknd: 788
Thru mid-Feb: 934
Lunar 1: 208, 800
Lunar 1-3: 609
Lunar 7: 1045
Lunar 13: 310
Lun 15: 310, 746, 1045
Lunar 16: 746
Lunar 17: 310
Lunar 18: 321
Sun nr Lun 18: 762
Lunar 20: 788
Late Lunar: 507

FEBRUARY
All: 211, 950
Thru early Mar: 950
Early: 219, 788, 1085, 1091, 1122
1st Horse: 634, 818, 1266
1st wknd: *1078
1st Sat: 1045
1st Sun: 390, 513, 612, 1043, 1086
1st Fri: 612
1st/2d wknd: 1086
1-2: 983, 1043
1-5: 422
2: 422, 952
2-13: 1045

3: 358, 375, 385, 390, 507, 881, 895, 950, 1193 1223, 1233
3-4: 194,*507, 508, 731
3-Mar 17: 1122
4: 609, 881, 1045, 1266
4-13: 1045
5: 139, 319, 741
5-11: 1078, 1086
6: 194, 422, 609, 895, 956
7: 194
7-14: 910, 934
8: 422, 609, 1224, 1233, 8-11: 1104, 1122
2d Wknd: 950, 1043-5
9: 985
10: 194, 256
11: 295, 321, 375, 390, 508, 709, 895, 954, 1043, 1045, 1223
11, 13: 1266
12: 295, 390, 1045
13: 952, 1028
13-15: 1045
14: 340, 390
Mid: 1086, 1266
" – mid-Mar: 508
15: 194, 664, 950, 1043
15-16: 1046
3d Sat: *634, 804
16: 194, 321
16-17: 1046
17: 321, 822, 1046, 1157
17-20: 1046
19: 194
21: 466, 555, 513, 612
4th Sun: 612
22: 950
23: 634, 952
24-25: 709
24-26: 728
25: 508, 513, 519, 555, 965
25-26: 1043
27: 954
28: 1221, 1224
Last Sun: 508
Last wknd: 853
Sun/Hol thru April 3: 1233
– Early Mar: 1233

MARCH
Sun, Hol thru: 1233
Early: 612,814,950,1233
1st Sun: 246, 513, 612, 1266
1st or 2d Wknd: 310
1: 308, 508
1-3: 881
1-14: 390
3: 194,422,609,950,1266
3-4: 1266
5: 319
6: 950
8: 390, 1224
2d Sun: 319, 814, *1266
10: 989, 1043
11: 954
12: 194
13: 390, 508, 952
Mid-End: 508
14-16: 508
15: 194, 310, 508, 1043
15-Apr 16: 256
15-Nov 15: 889
3d Sun: 934, 1266
17: 405, 950
18: 1193, 1266
18-23: 895
18-24: 508, 609
20-week: 664
21: 211, 321, 390, 405, 466, 513, 555, 609, 612-2, 1043, 1223
21-May 20: 390
22: 390
4th Sun: 612
23: 634, 952
24-25: 709
25: 513, 555, 956
27: 249, 256, 954
28: 1223, 1266
30: 390
Late: 674
– mid-Apr: 1266
Lun 3: 640, 788, 844
Lunar 15: 709

APRIL
All: 956
Early 1992, 1998, 2004, 2010: 942
Early: 280, 508, 664, 692, 788, 942, 1223, 1233, 1266

Note: this list only partial, other minor fetes mentioned in text. Check English dailies or regional info magazines, Tourist Information Centers [TICs], hotel or ryokan host, local friends. Small fetes may switch to weekend, even fade completely due to population loss.

ILLUSTRATIONS & CHARTS

Open then the door
You know how little time we have to stay
And once departed may return no more
—Omar Khayyam, *Rubbaiyat*, d.1133

FOREWORD
THRU JAPAN'S RED TORII

MOST VISITORS HAVE ENTERED JAPAN along that same route followed by Commodore Perry some fourteen decades ago. In 1854 his 'Black Ships', Japanese term for those then-fearful fire-belching nautical dragons, steamed into Edo-Tokyo Bay to present President Millard Fillmore's demands for intercourse. For one whole century from arrival 15 days later of first tourist, San Franciscan Silas Burrows, liners followed his route almost exactly, docking just inside bay at Yokohama off which then-tiny fishing village his fleet had sat at anchor. For four more decades airliners brought us some few miles closer to Tokyo, letting us down on ex-tidal flats of Haneda, "Wing Field", approximate point of Perry's closest approach to Tokyo, then called Edo. Since 1970s we have come in further to Narita, air industry's presagement of our future of inconvenience—at least until rebuilding of old in-city Haneda airport is completed.

In those first 88 years succeeding Perry, Japan had far greater contacts with America than with any other Western nation, just as America's physical association with Japan exceeded that with any other Asian culture. Pearl Harbor brought shocking awareness that this contact had been for greater part superficial, that in over 88 years we in fact had learned little of each other (if much *from* each other), established few bonds of mutual understanding or compassion.

This ignorance has been expensive experience for both parties. Many of us have come to recognize magnitude of this ignorance thru that immense

* Torii above at Miyajima (p.665) near Hiroshima

price we have had to pay, and are still paying in trade misunderstanding, and that our only means to reduce these costs is to reduce our ignorance. Yet, despite this noble resolve, those most vocal in "people-to-peopleness" persist in perpetuating errors of foreign policy in their own personal behavior as tourists, or caterers to tourists.

But these are abstractions; it is annoying to deal with abstractions on vacation. Let us get down to specifics...why have we done this book? who are we to have done it? what have we done (or tried to do)?

We've written this book to introduce to you this Japan we have come to know over these past four decades, and to love; to introduce you to tricks of getting around so that you might come to know Japan as well.

We have seen Japan change from veritable tourist paradise of moderate prices and superb service, to what was period of price gouging, phoney service charges for cold soup and rude service, to what it is now balanced delicately between both. We have spent pleasant evenings drinking and dining at reasonable rates we feel we could not match in America or Europe, only to open mail to our then-column next morning to complaints of hundred-dollar beer bills, dinner-priced breakfasts of stale toast and coffee. We have seen tourist influx swelled by wise and generous airline ticket price cuts, only to see each such reduction more than cancelled out by inflationary rises in land rates. All this accelerated with Japan's being awarded (maybe penalized is better word) Olympics of 1964. Dollar falls from '64's $=¥360 and oil shocks next decade; further yen value doubling from $=¥263 when we started this rewrite in early '85, to early '91 near ¥125 accentuated inflation, as planned heating of Japan's domestic economy may do further.

Yet with all this, we still believe that Japan offers one of those truly different, truly fascinating, truly worthwhile travel experiences in our world today. Back then when Japan was "tourist paradise" it took some doing to get around, transportation was not yet geared to strangers and information was sparse, special facilities for those past age of ready-adaptation were lacking. It took considerable planning to set out on any tourist expedition, many places we cover now were inaccessible then. Today, such problems have been largely overcome, but to avoid falling into new pitfalls other preparation is necessary. We believe this planning and study is part of fun and reward of travel. We have enjoyed doing it for ourselves for our travels thru Europe, across Asia and most intensively throughout Japan. We feel much we have learned will make your preparation easier, more complete.

Travel anywhere is partly matter of overcoming language barriers. In Japan (and Far East) there is this extra language barrier of not being able to read simple signs, names of streets, shops, etc. This requires more detailed description in any guide book, almost like treating reader-traveler as child. It also multiplies information required, which accounts for our book's bulk. We partly compensate for this by writing tightly in almost telegram language and hope it does not interfere with clarity.

Our book also may appear to be put together backward, in that Tokyo, which leads off all other travel books and takes up bulk of their pages, is here at our tail end and proportionately far shorter. Tokyo at first meeting is hopeless chaos and, to most, not attractive. Only by seeing how it and Japan have evolved does it—can it—make sense and be pleasant.

Tracing this national evolution is made easier by our discovery of tour route that takes us to most ancient sites first and progresses thru time along with geography. From Japan's first modern city, Yokohama, we step back into feudal times at nearby Kamakura, then to quintessential Mt Fuji and on to reconstructed stone age village at Toro, Shizuoka. Next we visit most ancient shinto palace-shrines at Ise and thru beautiful countryside on to oldest imperial tombs and transition to continental culture with arrival of Buddhism and literacy and building and rebuilding of succession of first cities culminating in still-exciting Nara. Then we make hour train or taxi hop across cradle of Japan to city next in line chronologically and which could easily absorb all one's time here, illustrious Kyoto. Here we can rest, and see that great city, again older sites first in archaeologically stratified order for its thousand-year history. Then we are ready to take on some more of Japan, main-line and offbeat, ending in Tokyo—which hopefully is now better understandable and more appreciable. This itinerary also saves money as well as being more exotic, for as with most capitals, outside-Tokyo tends to be less expensive and less Westernized, tho modern facilities are now everywhere for those not up to adventure of life on *tatami*-mats. (Young Japanese prefer beds and chairs and Western johns, too).

JIKO SHOKAI INTRODUCING OURSELVES

IN ANCIENT Japan, before joining fray, each samurai announced his family pedigree. (He did it, incidentally, in third person. This book was originally dual-authorship and has become triple- in this revision. But where one is 'talking' or being mentioned by others, third person is used).

SUMI, née Hiramoto, Californian of Japanese descent, nisei (Japanese for "second generation") born one unspecified autumn day during grape harvest while her folks were too busy picking to get around to register this bundle. She learned magnitude of Japan-America mutual ignorance in relocation camp in Arkansas during World War II. Later started as stitcher, took time out whenever possible to attend Hunter College and meantime rose to be right hand to Charles James, haute couturier, dressing several women ranked among best-dressed ten. She came to Japan to learn about her ancestral culture ("It seemed expected of me that with slant eyes I knew automatically everything about Japan") and enrolled in Gakushuin Peers College (where she was classmate of then-Crown Prince Akihito, now Emperor Heisei), then started writing distaff and travel for *The Japan Times* and *The Mainichi Daily News* under two different bylines, co-founded and co-edited first postwar travel magazine in Japan, *Anoné* (pronounced *ah-no-nay* and meaning *hey there*), worked with Jay on various architectural restorations from Narenjestan Palace of The Asia Institute in Shiraz, Iran, to American House (1920s middle class US residence for sightseers) and Persia House (19th century Colonial) in Kitano-cho foreigners' quarter of Kobe, and in converted 18th century traditional rice warehouse as Orient-kan Museum in Nara. Two latter house part of our Persian art collection. And awhile raising two multilingual-bicultural sons.

JAY, native New Yorker born out of town while his parents were traveling, has never settled since. Educated in New York, England, five US universities (he was at UC Berkeley while Sumi was at Hunter in New York) majoring in anthropology-Asian studies. In 1951, as youngest matriculated student at The Asia Institute (graduate) School for Asian Studies he was appointed acting director, pioneering popular educational programs on Asia. One of first two 'free-lance' Yankee students to come to Japan, to Kyoto, he was for half year house guest of tea ceremony masters we introduce you to later. Also one of four *gai-jin* (foreigners) in all of wonderful Kyoto those closing days of American Occupation to whom Geisha 'pleasure districts' of Gion, Pontocho and others were not off-limits. Moved to Tokyo as cartoonist–journalist–magazine editor and some time after being joined by Sumi and his sister, founded magazines *Orient Digests* and *Anoné* that were in effect start of decade of work on this book's first edition. Subsequent to and based on our first edition, Jay drafted overall plan for tourism in Iran that became Iranian National Tourist Organization, then lived and traveled extensively there, as deputy director of The Asia Institute now in Shiraz, 1964-70, and then as Publisher of *A Survey of Persian Art* and coauthor with Sumi of its supplementary *Persian Handicrafts* immediately preceding 1978 Islamic revolution. Since then they have created two antique art museums with their Persian collection, in Kitano-cho, Kobe and 'old town' Nara where Persian cultural influence was felt 1200 years ago.

GARET was born while original edition was in preparation, traveling incognito during some of our research. In school he used our book on class tours. In 1976 joined his folks and elder brother for summer in Iran as gofer-photographic porter on expedition that resulted in our book on Persian handicrafts. In this he earned his first byline (as did brother Cellin) at 15 for photos. Educated in Japan and Iran thru high school, he is bilingual-plus. This theater buff did 7 years in junior high-high school in only non-Japanese troupe to perform kabuki in Japanese. His BA in International Relations from Pitzer College, where he also started Chinese, taught him that he wanted to remain footloose *ronin*, masterless samurai. He has since been accepted into membership in Film Editor's Guild in Hollywood.

What this trio has tried to do is to show Japan as it has developed over millennia so that one might come to understand, thus perhaps appreciate, one of truly unique cultures of our world. First, most-isolated non-Western nation to enter 20th century and, among great nation-cultures, perhaps most distantly removed from our own. Yet with all its exotic difference, one which perhaps today holds greatest fascination for us. And being '20th century' is best able to receive even most inflexible of us on familiar physical terms to permit our leisurely, comfortable examination of this 'other' half. For those more youthful or flexible, Japan's own aesthetic of comfort welcomes examination and more than deserves it.

This historical view is made possible by Japan's cult of preservation, whereby art is secreted away for posterity, wooden structures faithfully rebuilt in exact replica when they show signs of decay, old and "impractical" folkways, crafts, rites and what-have-you preserved by subsidization. As you will see in our novel itinerary, quite by coincidence, historical development (and preservation) of culture has occurred along geographical chain which today makes ideal tour itinerary.

Japan today is dynamic, crowded cities with their own not-immediately evident charm; we have lived in several, in comfortable middle-class Japanese neighborhoods, not foreign ghettos. But more, Japan is that Japan of her peculiar past, as still lived in villages; we lived in one for two years, to which we returned whenever we could to recharge. Japan's future is on her college campuses; this book was first written at one radical, provincial, 'characteristic' college where we taught our native language and culture (and learned far more of it, as well as of Japan and of ourselves) for 7 years, where Garet was born. We take you to these 'three states of mind', these three versions of our 'Pagoda Japan', that you yourself might learn how to get in among them.

We have traveled over every lick of Japan, by every means and at every budget level imaginable. Sumi has traveled as one of those hordes of student groups you will certainly become entangled with; we have hoboed and hosteled, luxuriated in royal suites and fine inns; we have used country buses, crowded rural trains, air-conditioned sleepers and planes; we have traveled on foot where no transport ran and by bike, motorbike, midget car, old clunk, air-conditioned Cadillac and sports car; we have traveled alone or together, au pair and with groups of friends exploring unknown or introduced by friends to their old favorite haunts. Garet has continued our traditions and hitch-hiked most of Japan. We prefer to travel on tight budget, saving for that occasional extravagance.

We love travel. We have written this book for our many friends who do also, who have often asked us to present to them, as we do here, our choices variously of superb luxury, thru many stages of comfort to fit varied pockets, including detailed data as well for true student pilgrims.

JAPAN IS NOT CHEAP. *Cost of Living Index* for 1990-91 based on New York=100 put Tokyo at 179, Osaka 157 (dowm from '88's 203-201) vs London 109 and Melbourne 103—yet our long-held belief that Japan is within any budget is borne out by 1990 *Cost of Travel Index* based on Tokyo (world #6)=100, which put New York as 115 and London 148. Taxis and steak dinners are rated especially high here. In 1966 average tour cost in Pacific area was $20 (then ¥7,200) per day, with most luxury tours in Japan $30-35 per day (¥10,800+). In 1991 average group tours cost $100-200 (¥13,-26,000) per day land arrangements only. (Some cheaper ones don't include all meals). On your own in regular international 'luxe' hotels, couple in basic twin, eating buffet breakfast, table d'hote lunch and dinner plus service charge-tax runs ¥65,000 per day (R+B only, transport extra) or with '91 $ bottom at 125 = $520 (but with Bush-projected $ @ ¥100 = $650!) ...vs 1964's $20, or about matching Japan's 25-fold increase in $GNP.

But this inflation is matched by European travel costs, with London's 30-bob Bed & Bkfst of '64 soaring to £50+. Swiss travelers, whose currency has also soared in value, find Japan no more expensive except perhaps for cost of beef—but then how much does one pay for sushi in Geneva? Our once-almighty dollar is all mighty low, where for some decades it was equally artificially high to help war-torn countries export. But holding steady is ¥en price of this book—¥2,500 in 1964 for 5 small volumes at only about half our present single-volume wordage.

JNTO surveys show average visitor 1983 spent daily $148.14 (then ¥34,806) vs '86 $181.19 (but less ¥en at ¥29,949) of which ¥12,939 or two thirds went for accommodations alone, over half that again or ¥7,203 for food and drink—but adventurers will find that by following our tips for budgeteers and eating popular native food that dining here is fun, tasty and cheap with cheaper often tastiest, all home-made. Dollars get lots less distance now and tourist industry suffers despite rise in $ expenditure—actual tourists declined by 22% in each of '86,'87, with attrition more from US-Canada (620,000 > 575,000) and UK (182,000 > 148,000), balanced in part by increase in visitors from NICs, newly-rich Newly Industrializing Countries, like Korea, Singapore, Taiwan. By '90 visitors were back up to over 2,800,000 (US-Can 592,000, UK 177,000), *vs* outbound-tourism of 10,000,000, mostly to USA, bolstering economy of Hawaii.

At this budget, palatial *ryokan*-inns are well within purvey. We will show you how to take it more leisurely, still luxuriously, with $200 (half) per 1991-day, covering *couple* traveling, using fine facilities, frequent taxis.

Using good, comfortable, usually Japanese *ryokans* off main line, trains, occasional taxi, one couple can average out on $160/¥20,000 (@$=¥125, or at 1991 low ¥160=$125). Backpack pilgrim might almost halve this again by bus, train, minshuku and noodle-shop. We stress travel au pair is cheapest and doubled to quartet makes taxi tour cheaper than tour bus. All posted prices of course will change and are intended only as guide.

One 'invisible' expense that particularly hurts budgeteer is admissions (*nyu-jo-ken*) to museums, sights, temples and shrines which run ¥200 to ¥500 each, no college student or senior citizen discounts, and you hit several per day. Package tours of course include this prepaid, taxi-touring usually does not and you pay at each gate.

Group tour is what we highly recommend for first-timer or less-adventurous, its extras are worth it. Next would be pre-booked package, everything scheduled to your design (*see* p.98). Ideal, we feel, is tour or package with basic itinerary then free time at end with open-date return within 45-day limit (if any) of your excursion ticket. Ask your agent. For student traveler suffice it to say we led pioneer USNSA group of American students thru Japan, using comfortable inns, good food (and plenty), entertainment, chartered minibuses on budget of $8 per day, which also covered our own expenses, as well as offset some expenses of 7 Japanese students accompanying us who could not of course afford any such prince's ransom! This was when vogue was for magic formula "...*on $5 a Day*"–no insignificant sum as double room at Imperial Hotel was $8). Indeed "*Japan on...*" was originally pre-advertised as authored by Jay & Sumi.

"*Ah...*" says Garet longingly as he scrounges by on ¥10,000/$66-to-80 per day total. In 1964 few Japanese could afford travel, but today most can. $GNP is up 25 times, so real costs are down, and more mid-level facilities are available. In those old-edition times, if you had double your transPacific airfare, you could travel—this equivalent extra fare meant 3-4 *weeks* land costs in major luxe hotels. Now airticket equivalent buys you 3-4 *days* in same major hotel, or 10-14 days budget touring. Hotels are way up, yes— but airfares are proportionately way way down!

We imagine that most of you will mix your budgets as we have, varying spartan fare with spicing of occasional extravagance. We think this is more interesting way to travel, no matter what your budget. We have tried to cram in for you all detail required of traditional *Baedeker* yet keep it all as personalized as travel diary. While trying to organize all logically to meet guide requirements, we avoid drab (really not useful) listings and catalogings, with equal efforts to avoid dramatization of personal diary which can so often result in let-down.

Travel posters show many exotic scenes of Japan and her customs. For us actually finding when and where these events occur was often imposing. It was sweat and fun finding out about them, and we proudly pass this product of four decades' work-play on to you in our PERSONAL DATEBOOK for each region (*see* index page xxi). You'll find that to many Japanese tourists, most exotic sight is you. We use our own experience as frame of reference to prepare you for what, we hope, you will find.

In sum, we try to help you get what we like to call, Personally Oriented.

Ashiya, December 24, 1991

Jay's 40th anniversary in Japan

*Now when Chaos had begun to condense,
but force and form were not yet manifest,
and there was nought named, nought done
—who could know its shape.* — Kojiki, 712 AD

PERSONAL ORIENTATION
OUR PAGODA OF JAPAN'S HISTORY

EVERY NATION has its own characteristic architecture. That most fittingly associated with Japan is pagoda. These four main isles are stacked one upon another pagoda fashion. This culture has been built up like one, set upon native earth, each new wave of influence comprising one new storey never obliterating what came earlier, just building on and adding to it. Each new level is physically limited by that base formed from what came before and ultimately by conditions inherent in this native ground.

SITE OF PAGODA: *Geotectonics* Pagoda is man's first skyscraper, which structure today characterizes crowded conditions and limited space. That Japan is small and crowded nation we might better appreciate if we move country eastward 140 degrees, almost halfway round world, and superimpose it over same latitude on American eastern seaboard. Four main islands, running north to south, are Hokkaido, main isle of Honshu with Tokyo at its center, and southern isles of Shikoku and Kyushu.

Tokyo, 36°, overlaps Raleigh, North Carolina. Half main isle of Honshu above Tokyo, corresponds almost identically to America's Atlantic Coast, northernmost city on Honshu, Aomori, 41°, overlapping New York. Not far below Tokyo, Japan's coastline turns west to follow south border of North Carolina-Tennessee as far west as Nashville, corresponding to west bottom end Honshu city of Shimonoseki, 34°, so important in recent history.

1

Honshu is narrow. Never are you more than 97km/64mi from sea. Up north, at 38° latitude of Sendai/Washington, DC, Japan is as slim as New Jersey. Matsushima on Japan's scenic east coast just outside Sendai overlaps Cape May southernmost Jersey, while Washington lies submerged off west coast Japan. Lower (western) Honshu, that is Osaka-Kobe thru Hiroshima-Shimonoseki, is as narrow north-south as Tennessee it overlaps. So much for Honshu's 235,000km²/87,293mi².

Shikoku overlaps Georgia's north quarter with cocky Atlanta, 32°, playing host to Kochi of long-tailed cocks. Kyushu is midvertical-third of Alabama placing Madame Butterfly's Nagasaki 33° in Birmingham; southmost main city Kagoshima 32°, between Pensacola-Mobile. Thus Pacific isle portion of Japan would cover 295,000 km² strip of densest populated part of America: 123,600,000 (1991) Japanese crammed into area 1/4 as many Americans find crowded. If this were not enough, only 15% of Japan is arable, rest steep mountains which in most places even defy road and railway builders. While Atlantic coast has great American West to feed it, Japan long fed herself, tho now it is world's largest importer of foodstuffs, US agriculture's best customer.

We haven't mentioned Hokkaido, 2nd island in size. North of Honshu, on our overlay map covers east New York State-west New England to touch Montreal. This wild west of Japan has aboriginal reservations, open spaces, territorial government. Yet in this relatively uninhabited isle as many folk as in populous nonmetropolitan New York State live on 2/3s as much space.

If comparing Japan with gigantic America overemphasizes its smallness, then compare her with two European nations of similar size and shape: Great Britain (60% area or equal to Honshu alone) and Italy (85%). Total population of both is less than Japan's. Japan ranks 7th, after China, India, USSR, USA, Indonesia, Brazil; with Bangladesh gaining fast.

Move Japan east 130° to overlay Europe and it covers southwest Europe and Mediterranean North Africa with westernmost Fukuoka at 34° about at Rabat near Atlantic, Strait of Gibraltar overlaps Strait of Chosen between Tsushima Isle and Korea, while northerly Sendai 13° is east near Isle of Majorca, so north Honshu floats in Tyrrhenian Sea between Sardinia and Spain, Japan Sea coast is as long as and parallels Spain's west coast. Central-western Japan overlaps Mediterranean coast of North Africa: Tokyo at Algiers, Kyoto west at Oran, Nagoya to Kobe and Shikoku overlap Atlas Mts above Sahara. While northern tip of Hokkaido at Cape Soya facing Russian Sakhalin is near Lyon, easternmost Hokkaido's Nemuro Point is at Milan, Sapporo is just above Marseille. Thus we see Japan as Mediterranean in latitude, but while equally hot in summer it is cold winter: area overlapping west of Majorca is snowiest land in entire temperate zone.

If islands of Japan viewed from sea appear as mountain peaks rising from sea bottom, it is because they are just that. Archipelago is confluence of 3 mountain chains: Sakhalin, Fuji and Kyushu systems. Sakhalin is oldest, Paleozoic, running north-south from Arctic isle of Sakhalin, now Soviet, thru Hokkaido and down center of Honshu back of Tokyo, fading off into sea as Shizuoka Peninsula. Its hills are worn smooth and low with age so great that these mountains are all Hokkaido and Honshu share in common in their otherwise contrasting physical geography. Southern Kyushu chain is east extremity of Pamir-Himalayan system fading east into China Sea, to erupt as isles, emerging in Kyushu to form main elevations of that island as well as Shikoku and west Honshu up Wakayama thru Kyoto, almost to Shizuoka. Blocking meeting of these 2 chains is younger violent Fuji range, running east-west, centered on Fuji's volcano and Hakone *kan*,

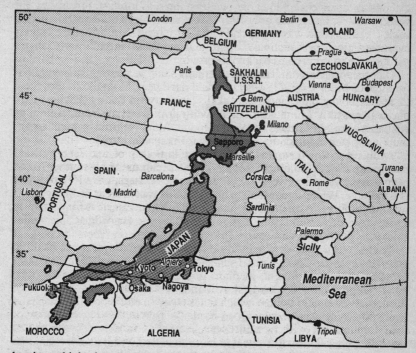

barrier, which gives two main regions of Japan their names: Kan-*sai* = kan-west, centered on greater Kyoto-Osaka-Kobe, and Kan-*to* = kan-east, Tokyo plain. Japan Alps are this young Fuji range's incursion into Sakhalin chain, having risen only 10,000 years ago, perhaps witnessed by men who started legend that Fuji rose in one nite leaving cavity of Lake Biwa. Fuji hills fade into sea as Izu Peninsula to reappear sporadically as volcanic isles of Izu, still rumbling, which we can visit from Tokyo. Other volcanic concentrations punctuate Kyushu and Sakhalin chains thruout archipelago.

Paleozoic era seas covered these lands. During 60,000,000 years of Mesozoic Age of Dinosaurs, land rose, joining Korea, perhaps in south with Java and Philippines. In Miocene-Pliocene Age of Mammals it sank again, perhaps counteracting mountain-raising, or even rolling over from west to east, so that today fishermen in Inland Sea often net fossil skeletons of elephants. There were giraffes in much of Japan, mammoths in Hokkaido. Land bridges must have existed well into Pleistocene epoch for Paleolithic man lived here and these Old Stone Age people had no boats.

FOUNDATION OF PAGODA: Japan's prehistoric anthropology is deep in mist. We do not know what first Japanese looked like; he left only one bone fragment so far known. Stone tools found in volcanic loess of Fuji resemble Middle-Paleolithic Patjitanian 'gigantoliths' found with Peking Man (Pithecanthropus Pekinensis/Sinanthrop) and in Java perhaps linked with Pithecantropus Erectus. Elsewhere, recent find of 106 hand axes, blades etc in Nakamine north of Sendai at 5 meters depth, well below 140,000 year old volcanic stratum, show possible thermoluminescence ages of 170,000-370,000 years. Site in Oita, Kyushu is over 100,000 years old. Late Paleolithic looks blank in east Asia as much of China was desiccated. Ice Age descended upon Europe and Central Asia at this time but brought no glaciers to Japan, except in highest valleys, tho seas rose and fell as they did worldwide. In fact it was only 1947 that first evidence of habitation dating back 100,000 years was found and these were hand axes and stone knives, characteristic of, respectively, south and north Asian cultures—Japan's mixture, dichotomy, dates back to its origins.

Oldest Japanese skull dates back perhaps 8,000 years (tho undated pithecanthropus hip fragment is older). Could have been Mongoloid. But then, three much older pithecanthropoid skulls from cave in Peking (Peking man), one was possibly Mongoloid but showing primitive European (Ainu?) as well as Australoid features; second could be Ainu, Negroid or Melanesian; third resembled Eskimo. Race mixture? Common ancestry?

At this period, when seas were rising and both time and scenery were becoming 'today', dominant population of Japan as of all northeast and central Asia was primitive white. In south and southeast were Negroids and Australoids. While somewhere in northern Siberia "nucleus of Mongoloids was beginning to spread east and south". This 'classic Mongoloid' is known by stocky build, short extremities, flat face, fat-padded epicanthic-shielded (slant) eyes and coarse straight hair sparse on face and body, all traits ideally suited to evolve in frigid clime: no nose to freeze nor beard to ice, slant eyes providing natural sun-snow glasses, fat insulating, etc. Add to this yellow-brown skin, medium to dark-brown eyes, infantile (flat) nose, predominant B-blood, shovel incisors (buck teeth), sacral spot (birthmark on baby's bottom which fades away in childhood) and cephalic index 80+ (brachycephalic or broad-headed). This sounds like caricature of modern Japanese and you will find just this fellow driving your cab or managing your hotel. But you will more than likely find people who, like our Peking fossil trio, might be most anything. For New Stone, Iron and Modern Ages saw, besides this invasion of Mongoloids, migrations of many other races: Polynesians and Melanesians to Turks and Aryans, all of whom have fused to create this fascinating amalgam, Japan.

This Arctic-originated Mongol, incidentally, entered from tropic south after loop thru China, to push white Ainu, with his cold-sensitive nose, north where we visit him in Hokkaido. 'Pure' Mongol still exists now solely in isolated groups outside Japan—Inuit (Eskimo) or Siberian Gilyak.

Neolithic traits of pottery, new stone-working techniques, food producing, appear in Japan by 4,500BC (possibly 8,000?), over 2,500 kilometer arc from north of Hokkaido thru Okinawa—except that true farming is lacking in this rare nonagricultural pottery-producing culture. This era is called *Jomon*, Japanese for 'rope-pattern' which decor distinguishes this pottery form. Jomon man set brush 'teepee' over pit in ground, traces of which found in Osaka '86 date back 22,000 years into Old Stone Age. Unknown people, basically north Asian hunter-fisher similar to men found across world from Scandinavia to American great plains, seem to have centered in north and east Japan. Some of his pottery resembles northwest American and Andean Indio. Radiation dating techniques indicate it to be as old as any on earth, perhaps 8,000BC. He was no primitive as much of his pottery and clay sculpture is fine art, already showing that aesthetic flair his descendants are famed for to this day. (Reproductions make fine gifts; real originals rare.) He dressed in woven hemp: we know his costume from clay idols, and textile from 3,000BC grave-scrap recently analyzed, resembles cloth used in rural north Japan till this century.

Southern Jomon shares cultural traits with South Korea, South China and Southeast Asian temperate belt thru Nepal. His language was probably Polynesian. This *Laurilignosa Culture* worshipped laurel leaf evergreens and mountains as links to deity, evolved from nut gathering for flour, thru root gathering, to slash-and-burn agriculture to dry-, then to wet-rice, with Japan lagging in its wake. As temperature changes, laurel and worshippers now work way up Japan's isles. (Temperate Europe, hot-dry in summer, saw different evergreens evolve—olive, etc). Basic Shinto ritual today is still offering of shiny laurel leaf evergreen branches.

Jomon seems to have contributed to modern Japan: from Southeast Asia, *mochi*-cakes, sake, *nattoh* fermented bean (all basic to popular nite-cuisine); from south Korea, female shamanism (Shinto priestesses and New Religion foundresses), matriarchy (don't take that "man's country" line seriously); from pre-laurel north Asia, bear veneration (as we see among Ainu), fox myths (Inari fox shrines ubiquitous) and pit dwellings (we'll see some on archaeological sites at Toro and Gamagori... but maybe this new Japanese fad for subway arcades...)

BUILDING OUR PAGODA

THERE ARE many variations in pagoda forms. That most popular in Japan is *go-ju-no-to*, five-storey tower. Japan's history divides into five major past periods, with modern century providing *sorin*-finial, TV-antenna-like adornment that soars from pinnacle. Wherever you go there will be antiquities and each will enhance your enjoyment if you are acquainted with names and what they indicate. From base up: Yamato, Nara, Heian-Fujiwara, Kamakura, Ashikaga-Muromachi, Tokugawa-Edo, crowned by modern era. Paragraph on each is in order. We detail them again later following our historical itinerary. We repeat: most convenient itinerary quite coincidentally follows main line of historical development of culture. But quick history first, with handy reference chart for easy location of names met constantly.

What sets pagoda construction apart, what enables it to attain such height yet retain such stability, what makes it earthquake-proof, is its peculiar feature of each level being not just stacked one upon another, but of being hung hat-rack-style from central floating spinal pole. Hidden away beneath or behind visible facade of historical remains, is Japan's...

SPINAL POLE: *Shimbashira* in Japanese architecture. This new era opens about 300BC when enigma of mixture and isolation comes fully into its own. Our stone age Jomon are isolated, two millennia behind China in technology, Philippines in agriculture, perhaps 6,000 years behind West Asia, but developing decidedly own aesthetic base. Now new peoples come in from southwest, whom today we lump as *Yayoi* (after site in Bunkyo-ku, Tokyo where their painted pottery was first found, 1884): south Pacific islanders into south Kyushu, southeast Asians direct and via Korea into north Kyushu —but all of whom were advanced *Laurellignous Culture*, plus Tungusic north Asians via Korea, indicating mix had taken place there.

Some of these southerners called themselves *Wa*. Yayoi man came in longboats of Indonesian isles and Hong Kong festivals to introduce dragon myths and boat races which are highlights of modern Japanese summer fetes, as we'll see in Nagasaki and Miyajima. He venerated sacred mountains like Tibetans of his day: we'll see shrines and 'Shangri-las' atop peaks today and climb sacred Fuji. He tattooed himself as both Central Asians and Maori did, as Okinawans and Ainu did till recently; wore Polynesian-like bark cloth, ancestor of modern summer *yukata*. He had great spring and autumn festivals of mating, which are still around if much expurgated (Nagoya Mar 15, Nov 15; Nara first sat Feb; etc.), worshipped fertility images we visit in Nagoya and near Nara, stumble across at roadsides. Over his pit houses he built more ornate thatched roofs with lovely high gables, still trademark of rural thatched roof home or sophisticated aesthete's tea room.

Technologically he set in action mixture similar to what occurred in China 1,300 years earlier: introduced advanced agriculture, wet-rice or paddy, irrigation, terracing of hills about 300BC, all still basis of local farming. But these were already known in SE Asia and Philippines at least 2,000 years. Early tombs give forth hard greyware, first kiln-fired pottery here—earlier were open-hearth-fired. Tho they didn't make bronze themselves, imported bronzes are found in first century BC Kyushu tombs. They were culturally Bronze Age people politically organized into kingdoms: *Kuna* in Kumamoto -Kagoshima, *Na* Fukuoka, *Ito* North Kyushu, *Yamaichi*, *Yamatai* (possibly Yoshinogari, excavated 1989, sole known walled town—for unlike China, Mid East and Europe, Japan did not fortify civil areas) in Kyushu moving to Yamato later near Nara. Some were known in China 57AD (*see* FUKUOKA) and 239 when called collectively "Kingdoms of Wa", some were ruled by priestess-queens, shamans or popularly mislabeled 'witches'.

More important, he (or she?) established aesthetic still peculiar to Japan, based on *Yorishiro*. This simple belief, in some way basic to all Stone Age peoples, holds that deity links to earth, usually in waterfall, mountain, large boulder or tree, especially evergreen, and in this cultural area particularly in laurel-type glossy broad-leafed trees. Basic Shinto ritual today is still to offer shiny laurel leaf evergreen branches.

We suggest two possibilities, neither of which excludes other. First is that after mankind's Stone Age spiritual awakenings, West and East develop apart. Europe evolves towards monotheism, which in its simplistic popular form does not allow thought of other spirit or even that universal sacredness to which *yorishiro* is living link. East develops toward Buddhism, which is not polytheistic despite its seeming plethora of gods, but truly pantheistic in that our entire universe is seen as itself deity, as totally sacred.

Secondly, it may also have to do with left-brain/right-brain dominance in West and East respectively. European languages and culture are left-brain, thus, more logic-directed. Japan, like its Polynesian roots and perhaps southeast Asia, seems right-brain, more emotion-directed. This may have led as well to Western 'logical' cause-effect concepts of creation, versus Japan's more sentimental ideas of origins: thus, to monotheism in West, and in East overall sacredness—as notably Japan.

Yayoi man began moving up from Kyushu, to Hiroshima thru Inland Sea, reaching Kyoto area within century, by 200BC. He next worked overland up coast to Shizuoka by 100BC, where he built extensive settlement at Toro—excavated, reconstructed, preserved, we visit fittingly on first leg of our itinerary. By 100AD he'd passed Tokyo to reach his northernmost limit, Tohoku. This is more than scattering of people. It is true base of national state, recognized as such in China annals.

Myth of descent from heaven of grandson of Sun Goddess probably refers to original landings in Kyushu—but from where? Legendary first emperor Jimmu, presumed to be north Asian immigrant on father's side, but mother was "daughter of Sea Goddess"—thus, Polynesian? Sea-oriented words, names for fish etc, relate to Malay, Polynesian, even Hawaiian; private parts of body; terms like *denka*, prince, have equivalents only in Malay *tenku* or Hawaiian *tiki*; shrines and palaces are surrounded by gravel areas as in Polynesia, etc. Legendary migration of Jimmu in "660 BC" up Inland Sea to Kansai may be this movement uncovered by archaeology, tho at least five, seven, even ten centuries later than legend.

Relations with China are established by at least 57AD when Han Emperor
Kuang-wu grants gold seal of authority to King of Wa (probably very seal
found near Hakata now in its City Museum). Coins of China Hsin dynasty
(9-23AD) have been found on Iki isle, which we visit by ferry from Fukuoka.
Thus we leave dark of prehistory to enter pre-dawn haze of protohistory.

FIRST STOREY: *KOFUN* — GREAT TOMB PERIOD (250?-552AD) approximates Yamato era (300-710) designating period of rise of power of
Imperial clan in Osaka-Nara area. But in Chinese eyes power was still in
Kyushu (Fukuoka). Chinese records say Himiko, Queen of Wa, in 239
sent tribute mission to patron state in Korea which referred it on to Loyang,
capital of China's Wei Dynasty. Chinese annals are praiseworthy of Wa
traits and qualities in these early contacts. But China's view changes.

For millennium since first saddling of horse somewhere in Central Asia,
pressure of fierce, hard-riding nomads (Aryans and later Huns) determined
histories of Greece, Rome, Egypt, Persia, India, China alike. Century or so
after Christ, small kingdom was set up by such horsemen (Puyo or Fuyu
from Manchuria) in SE Korea, parts of which were culturally Yayoi having
received same sea migration from south. First 'baronial' wave was pedestrian and moved into north Kyushu, enhancing small kingdoms like Na, etc,
in first centuries our era, introducing big tombs and likely fueling their
extension to Nara by 4th century. Content of tombs of early type I: Han
Chinese bronze mirrors (80% in all Japan from Kyushu tombs), *magatama*-
comma-shape beads and other magical items—all mark agricultural SE Asian
types. But N Asian Altaic links of new migrants are also evident early.
Korean folk literature recounts tale of folk hero Yong Gil Dong: hot-head
estranged from family, flees overseas with comrades, comes to rule lovely
land beneath ash-spewing volcano that sounds like ever-erupting Mt
Sakurajima, Kagoshima, Kyushu. Other migrations were chronicled in
Korean *Kandan-koki*, which Japanese authorities during their 1904-1945
occupation tried to hunt down all copies of to burn.

Second wave is quite different. In 5th century Nara sudden change in
tombs from type I to II is evidence of perhaps violent arrival. Contents of II
and III are mostly weapons, armor, horse trappings (by III), realistic items
indicating baronial horse riders of NE Asia. Also in wake of earlier foot
migrations, new invasions of Puyo from Manchuria land around Izumo
(which we visit its Grand Shrine of Storm God) with deities like Paekche-Korea. It
soon developed another center in Yamato near Nara-Kyoto, already Yayoi
area enriched by rice-raising migrants from Kyushu. They brought high
technology, metallurgy, West Asian feudalism, organization, divine kingship, Scythian art styles with Altaic, perhaps Turkic and Aryan, linguistic
elements and smattering of other Indo-Aryan traits like bigger tumuli similar
to those across Asia west to beehive tombs of Homeric Greece, with Aryan
house-shaped sarcophagi identical in form to pre-Christian coffins of Central
and West Asia, even to silver reliquaries of their contemporary Byzantium.

Emperor #10, Sujin, first historical ruler late 4th century AD (trad.97-30BC).
His giant tomb is in Kashiwara #2 between Osaka and Nara, *see*. Said to
have invented taxation (of men's hunt, women's weaving— ramie, raw silk,
cotton—no rice mentioned), developed agricultural irrigation. He may have
come from Mimana, Korea and be real-life prototype for legendary Jimmu.

#15 is Homuda, c400AD, posthumously Ojin God of War, conceived
after father's death during mother Empress Jingu's invasion of Korea, believed interred in giant tomb in Sakai (which we fly over into Osaka airport).
Culturally he is most Scythian-like of all (which hints at violent invasion)

changing Imperial succession to central Asian brother-to-brother. During
his reign Kyushu-Yamato reunite, various *kika-jin*, immigrants, arrive.
Older oral records published 799-815 as part of *Shinsen Shoji-roku* 'Newly
Compiled List of Family Names' list 1177 noble families grouped according
to: (1) descent from Sun Goddess (imperial), (2) from other 'gods' (mostly
Jimmu comrades), and (3) 324 families of recent immigrants of 400AD-on.
These 'immigration records' list Aya & Hata tribes, both names supposedly
indicate royal Chinese origins via Korea. Hata totaled perhaps 180,000
households in original group pre-cleared for migration, but not all made it
across. Major Hata subtribe of Yu-zuki (bow-moon people) can be traced
back centuries, west of China into area of Turks and East Iranians.

Immigrants include weavers, (name *hata* remains as term for loom)
clerks, tax experts, smiths and other such high-tech folk. Aya settled in
Nara, allied with Soga clan of early king-makers: Hata in nearby Kyoto
where they formed economic power base for Fujiwara, later dynasty of
prime ministers. By 800AD fully one third of technocrat-literati "houses of
rank" claim descent from these later immigrants of post-400, differentiating
themselves from scions of "first royal migration from High Plain" (groups 1
and 2) but claiming equal rights. Emperor Kwammu (r.781-806) who moved
capital from Nara to Kyoto, boasted descent from royal Korean–Paekche
thru his Hata-Fujiwara mother.

These *kiba minzoku*, 'horse-archer people' were technologically superior
to original Yayoi, if far outnumbered. Two seem to have fought to negotiated truce in both Kyushu and Nara, linking both regions, resulting in blend
which gave birth to imperial Japan. Beautiful, fertile Nara plain chosen as
their home has remained hub of Japanese culture since.

Their great tombs (some are more voluminous than Egypt's great pyramids) are in area convenient to half-day itinerary, as we see around Nara-
Osaka. Their grave goods, clay *haniwa* figurines, are still popular today in
modern souvenir imitations for their superb design-artistry and humor.

Dichotomy of this mixture remains basic feature of Japan's subsequent
history. Yin and yang unite: feminine-receptive Yayoi with masculine-ag-
gressive horsemen. Early 500s horse-archer dynasty is evidently edged out
by native matriarchal rule with reemerging empresses-cum-high priestesses.
Patriarchal society of knights is to evolve into samurai warrior class
culminating in Shogun dictators of Edo-Tokyo. Matriarchal Yayoi absorbs
best this invasion has to offer materially, but uses it in its own framework
which remains basically that of imperial line coming to flower in Kyoto
culture. Renovationists constantly force door open to new influence: con-
servatives of older Yayoi tradition again absorb and react. Thus Buddhism
now comes in as Chinese, but soon becomes Japanese as Yayoi wooden
floor covers cold stone paving, and steep, homey Yayoi thatch replaces imperious Chinese tile.

This Japanese trait of quick-change, of flip-flop just in time; this judoist
rolling with attacker to come up on his back, evinces Japan's intrinsic Yayoi
soul, its firm, flexible spinal pole of our pagoda. Japan's cultural strength
(until today) is based on homogeneity of which they brag so much—but
homogeneous doesn't mean all-same but well-mixed, implying diverse elements in original mix. Then by dawn's early light we enter historic era...

SECOND STOREY: *NARA* (552-794)—built in image of China marked
by import of Buddhism. There had been growing contact via Korea between
China and local Wa rulers since first century, thru Kyushu and then Nara.
Unification of main power centers of Kyushu-Yamatai and Nara-Yamato,

then this enlarged Yamato absorbed Izumo, which still extended into Korea, enabled new nation to look outward. First Buddhist image is received 552 (now in Zenkoji, Nagano). 562 Yamato loses last colony in Korea, Kaya, tho not until naval battle off Kunsan River, Korea, 663, when Yamato fleet supporting Paekche is sunk by Chinese-Silla fleet, is bond fully severed. Internal strife resumes for half-century between old-line Shintoists vs new Buddhists. Despite early setbacks Buddhists finally prevail led by Prince-Regent Shotoku—whose portrait graced bank notes till recently and whom we meet again in Yamato-Nara at his great monument, Horyuji Monastery. Japan, now one nation under one leading house, emulates mainland.

Korean scribes show how to take down recitations of tribal memorizers to compose official histories: *Tennoki* (Emperors' Annals) and *Kokki* (National Annals) 620, under aegis of Shotoku. Maliciously burned—tho questionable remnant called *Kujiki* has attracted attention lately—then recreated from reciters as *Kojiki* (Ancient Annals) 712, and *Nihon Shoki* (Nippon Chronicle) 720, (both in English). Stories passed down by such reciters understandably confuse, as each would favor his patron. With familial rivalries and spats between main centers of Yamato, Kyushu (with its own internal strife) and Izumo (which has its own contradictory record, *Izumo-fudoki*, 733AD), there was more than one line of succession. As with horse-riding tribes of north Asia, as well as sailors of Polynesia, *uji*-clan chiefs chose emperors by consensus from brothers or cousins of principal 'Sun Line' family, until #26 Keitai Tenno (trad 507-531, actually first to enter Yamato from Osaka) chose his own successor, and fixed imperial regalia of sword, jewel and mirror.

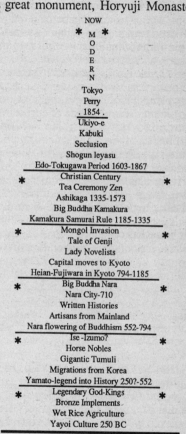

NOW

MODERN

Tokyo
Perry
. 1854 .
Ukiyo-e
Kabuki
Seclusion
Shogun Ieyasu
Edo-Tokugawa Period 1603-1867
Christian Century
Tea Ceremony Zen
Ashikaga 1335-1573
Big Buddha Kamakura
Kamakura Samurai Rule 1185-1335
Mongol Invasion
Tale of Genji
Lady Novelists
Capital moves to Kyoto
Heian-Fujiwara in Kyoto 794-1185
Big Buddha Nara
Nara City-710
Written Histories
Artisans from Mainland
Nara flowering of Buddhism 552-794
Ise -Izumo?
Horse Nobles
Gigantic Tumuli
Migrations from Korea
Yamato-legend into History 250?-552
Legendary God-Kings
Bronze Implements
Wet Rice Agriculture
Yayoi Culture 250 BC

Wa-folk from South   Yayoi pillar   Mongols from North
Basic Jomon Stone Age   250 BC- Native Ainu hunter gatherers

Pagoda of Japanese History

Except for our recent century, succession father-to-son was exception. Imperial clan now decides to build Chinese-style capital. Artisans flood in, refugees from downfall of two Korean kingdoms and Japan's last colonies (or former homelands from which power base had shifted?). They swell tide of priests, artisans, artists from as far away as Tibet, India, Persia who set in motion one of mankind's most highly productive art periods. They lay out one large grid-city, Fujiwara or Asuka, in 687. (At which time Tang Empress Zetian Wuhou sends Nara Emperor Temmu pair of giant pandas, their first known export). This soon proves too small for Think Big Japan, so in 710 they start another nearby, Heijo or Nara, dismantling and moving buildings. Nara at its height around 750 was several times area of today with then-population of 200,000—some assay 500,000. They build great monastery-colleges; second of which, Horyuji (607-670AD), still stands, world's oldest extant wooden buildings, tho some neighbors almost match. Much of what we know of Chinese architecture of era we know only from these Nara relics. As staggering to even Chinese imagination of that day as it is to ours, is colossal bronze Buddha of Nara, p376—tho only half-height of bronze Colossus of Rhodes of millennium earlier. It is era of grandness, of life in grand manner perhaps never since equalled.

Parts of era have own names which you may hear when art is identified: *Asuka* 552-645, and its central portion *Suiko* 593-628; *Hakuho* or White Phoenix 645-710; and *Tempyo* 724-748, heart of *Late Nara*, 710-794, when great city itself, originally called Heijo, was built and blossomed.

These parts have each its own characteristic as seen in religion and its art. Asuka Buddhism is at first personal, masculine, worshipping human being *Sakyamuni*, central image of earliest Asuka-dera. Then abstract, as cult of intermediary Holy Ghost-like *Yakushi-nyorai*, bodhisattva of medicine (*see* BUDDHISM, p23) dominates next Suiko decades at Horyuji, p357, femininely emulating reigning empress of same name. Next as state organizes around immense centralized metropolis, so faith focuses on macho-universal heavenly state around Ultimate Buddha of Light *Dai-nichi nyorai*, as in *Dai-Butsu*, Great Buddha statue of Nara.

China makes major name shift during Hakuho. Till 648 Chinese said Yamato or Wa. From 703 all annals list island kingdom under Ji-pen (Marco Polo later pronounced Chipan, thus Japan)—or Nihon/Nippon, same ideograms. Earlier records praised openness of Wa, then Chinese write in 703 of Wa: "Tribute bearers arrogant...do not answer our questions with facts,... therefore suspicious of these people"–shift from Kyushu to Kansai type.

Itinerary Tip: Main giant tombs, first Buddhist remains in convenient clump— easy half-day tour out of or en-route Nara. Early Sakyamuni image at first temple ASUKA-DERA, mid-era medicine bodhisattva at usually-passed HORYUJI, TOSHODAIJI, SHIN-YAKUSHIJI monasteries, 2nd half-day. NARA itself pleasant half- to full-day, tho full week possible. Can do hilights in single busy day in and around Nara.

THIRD STOREY: *HEIAN* (794-1185) after original name for Kyoto, seat of power for this era; also called Fujiwara after ruling family. Emperor Kwammu (whose name we'll hear again, as fabulous *Jidai Matsuri*, Festival of Ages, **October 22** Kyoto, honors him, p.445) decided Nara had too many power lobbies to work as capital. His own support group, Fujiwara—2-day march distant among settled, rich immigrant technocrats, Hata—he moved every-thing lock, stock and barrel to them to build Kyoto. Nation's population 9th century variously estimated 1 to 4 million, of whom 5,000 titled aristocracy (incl clergy, as in Europe), rest serfs. If Nara emperors 'Thought Big', Kwammu thought colossal. Heiankyo-Kyoto was planned from start to be world's greatest city—several times in its 1200-year history it has been perhaps just that. Few cities can boast of being great continuously as long as has Kyoto. For details of era it is easier, more pleasant to see remains themselves and discuss in situ.

New city and era started out again as mirror of China, with Chinese red pavilions and Chinese-style court and government. Indeed Kwammu proudly traced his ancestry from Paekche-Korea royalty thru mother. But reaction sets in. Even tall, thin Chinese style Buddha images soon develop round faces, plump necks, short arms and legs. In 894 relations with China are cut and island empire becomes isolated. New hybrid culture of late Heian takes best from each parent (Yamato and China) to flower profusely.

We see this dichotomy in literature available in English: exquisite peaceful effeminacy of Lady Murasaki's novel of 1000AD, *Tale of Genji*, and fierce warfare and tragedy in annals of this era *Heike Story*. It is period when men read abstruse Chinese and Buddhist tomes and write poetry as billets doux, acquire fine hand at calligraphy and season it at fighting. Many poetry collections come down to us, as one, *Manyoshu*, survives from Nara. Women write diaries (most translated) about what follows receipt of those romantic poetry notes, first 'true-life romances' including first true novel, *Genji Monogatari* (above). It is epitome of decadence. Its feminine blossom chopped by paired samurai swords wielded by Spartan frontiersmen of Kamakura. Until now, predominant form of marriage in Nara-Kyoto area was husband's (or lover's) romantic nocturnal visit to wife's residence, living apart otherwise. Samurai culture brought cohabitation into style, a la North Asian immigrants, and with it drop in wife's status to that of mother-in-law's housemaid, and concurrent rise of samurai machismo.

Itinerary tip: Kyoto & environs, and in easily chronologically visited groupings.

FOURTH STOREY: *MEDIEVAL* (1185-1613), which has 3 sections...
(1) *KAMAKURA* (1185-1335) for which best visual history book is city of same name (pp215-41) hour south of Tokyo. Macho samurai frontiersmen now take over after winning battles recounted in *Heike Story*, period of upheaval, of discarding old ways. Rulers are Spartans, with Athenian appreciation of culture. One trait marks era: systematization. Excessively esoteric Buddhism, gotten out of hand, is now taken in hand, reduced to popular formulae. Old Great Buddha of Nara symbolized infinite variety of time and space: new Kamakura Great Buddha simply concentrates faith into one's self. These are protestant movements, nationalistic: pop religion. Zen is imported, stripped of much Chineseness, for those who don't need giant idol as focal point for introspection. Key adjective for Kamakura is virility, which is best seen in great explosive sculpture of master Unkei, as his guardians in gate of Nara's great Buddha. Mongols of Kublai Khan invade twice, 1274 & 1281; virility (and luck of *Kamikaze* 'God Wind' typhoon) save Japan, as we see in Kyushu p718. After this purgation, in isolation, Japan again re-examines what of Heian ways she wishes to preserve, and power shifts once more to Kyoto.

(2) *ASHIKAGA* (1335-1573) or *Muromachi*. Kamakura feudalism takes on flowery ways of old Kyoto and new imports from China, central Asia. Systematization now spreads to art as schools of painting become fixed basic styles: names like Tosa, Kano, later Korin art dynasties appear. Flower arrangement, ikebana, evolves as disciplined art form. Literary war correspondent reports of Heike & Mongol wars spawn warrior fiction; Zen hermits write introspective diaries (like translated *Records of Ten-foot Square Hut & Leisure Thoughts*). Era of internal violence as hundred-year Onin War erupts 1467, dispersing courtiers from capital into provinces, with them art/culture—more importantly, interest in learning which stimulates economic growth and regional development. Then violence of war novels seems ingested by introspective Buddhist hermit writing, to be draped onto newly-systematized older folk and imported theater forms, to give birth to *noh* dance-drama (much translated, performed). In architecture cold Spartan conciseness of Kamakura is systematized to degree that with birth of domestic *shoin* style becomes prefab, as today, of fixed elements, dimensions, proportions, then gilded Kyoto style as great Gold and Silver Pavilions.

Then on porch of this storey of our pagoda we see cast-off crucifix...

(3) *CHRISTIAN CENTURY* (1543-1637) is closing century of medieval Japan. Christians arrive 1543. By 1580 there are some 300,000 converts in 18,000,000 populace (compare 1990=1,000,000 in 120,000,000). Century also called *Sengoku*, 'era of warring states' (1490-1600); or latter part as *Azuchi-Momoyama* (1573-1613) referring to 2 castles of successive unifiers of nation, ODA Nobunaga and Napoleonic-peasant-warrior TOYOTOMI Hideyoshi. Christians introduce castle (few thousand built in few decades, of which Himeji best remaining), flintlock guns (300,000 improved models turned off local assembly lines in 12 years after first import taken apart 1543) and etchings showing geometric perspective (which sparks development of ukiyo-e woodblock prints). Christians are at first favored, both for their early modesty and their science, while Buddhists are persecuted, mostly for politico-military power they wield with very un-Buddhistic ego. Then after 1600 are themselves persecuted, in 1637 native converts virtually exterminated, for mainly non-religious—but no less repressive—reasons as we see when we visit Nagasaki area.

Japan is first non-European culture treated with respect by Europe as equal, its language, religion and culture studied intensively and without prejudice by church scholars. "Best people so far discovered". European languages and arts are taught here by these same accomplished men. Ambassadors and savants are treated by Nobunaga and Hideyoshi with respect, listened to, engaged in open exchange. Priest introduces movable-type printing press, writes and publishes bilingual dictionary of 30,000 entries. Mutual impact immense—but peaceful contact and this epochal true internationalism are, alas, short-lived.

Converts took Christian principles, love etc, seriously, as did few if any Portuguese or Spanish nobles or monks. They cooperated, which was threat to central government, and contributed to its fall from official favor and rise of new Confucianism mixed with Shinto and especially Zen discipline. There were numerous true Christians in Japan, at least as many as perhaps anywhere else.

Japan received numerous foreigners, from first Portuguese shipwreck which introduced guns (copied superbly by bell casters of Tanegashima isle almost immediately), to Spanish trading-missionizing expeditions, then Dutch and English traders set up 'factories', old term for trading posts. Spaniards were kicked out, Dutch stuck it out, English failed dismally and left. One Englishman who left his mark was Armada-fighter Will Adams (*see* IZU, p.246), while his contemporary and head of English trading group Richard Cocks was typical born-loser. Respective success and failure of these two contemporaries holds valuable lesson for modern businessmen. Adams wrote (1611): "People of this land of Japan are good of nature, courteous above measure and valiant". Cocks in 1613 writes, "Have especial care not to trust any man with goods without making ready payment, *for I am informed* these country people are not to be trusted". Adams trusted his own experience, Cocks went on hearsay, stayed blind. You get back what you put in.

Era is great castles and palace gardens with tremendous sweep and scope: exquisite Zen hermit shacks and Zen 'gardens' of stone and gravel. It is ponderous, brilliant landscapes painted lightheartedly on gold: somber black ink used for witty Zen cartoons. It ends not in decadent decay, but in simply passing into hands of family which controlled...

Itinerary tip: most rewarding period for tourist, best seen, of course, in Kyoto.

FIFTH STOREY: *TOKUGAWA* (1613-1868) clan ruled from *Edo*, then-name for Tokyo (pp1123-1274): either of which denote this era. Characteristics most evident today form at this time. Characteristic art is lacquerware: exquisitely perfect but just surface; beauty skin deep but skin as thin and hard as Gillette blue-blade. Era began in war which brought total freedom from war for 250 years (world record?). *Ukiyo*, 'floating world' of every-day experience and observation, is key term of arts of era. Arts are plebeian: popular theater 'song-dance-performance' *ka-bu-ki*, popular pictures printed by woodblocks, pop paperback pulp novels mass produced by woodblock. Items are seasonal, ephemeral, throw-away, of paper and biodegradables. In short, world's first consumer society, first true art market, dictated by common consumer of lowest Confucian class (merchants, now economic dominant) rather than noble or church patron. Patronage moved to founding true public schools (*see* p20). But lords are not wealthy as in Europe, for Edo holds each personally (Confucianly) responsible for common weal.

Fine arts now so refined as to be lifeless, uninteresting; higher literature is Confucian state-dialectic, while master poets thrive on popular support. Tea arts, *ikebana*-flower arrangement, bonsai flourish: arts of exquisite aesthetic which so easily degenerate into random ritual, arbitrary arrangements. Absolute state control is attained, maintained by total seclusion from world, thought police system so thoro that Hiroshima historian said "If any farmer here stole radish, someone in Edo castle burped". Time is frozen by legal ban on progress and invention. People become like puppets they so admire in Bunraku theater of Osaka (*see*). Student of ours once replied, "There was no true peace in warless Edo era: there was no peace of mind".

We date temple or palace paintings by their movement or compositional sweep. Momoyama painted screens show verve, freedom: golden clouds, shaped pines, waves, are rolling, sensuously curvaceous; Tokugawa curves steadily become smaller, finer, near perfect, mechanically refined, drafts-manship excels. Were they women, Marilyn Monroe would be 'peach-mount' Momoyama-1600; Edo-Tokugawa is by 1650 bawdy, painted, fun-loving B-girl parody of former self; 1750 cold, calculating Lucretia Borgia; by end of era ideal women's magazine model for cosmetics and Dior cock-tail suits: superficial visual perfection but nothing one could live with.

After victory at Sekigahara 1630, Ieyasu remarks, "After victory, tighten helmet straps". In 1637 country closes itself off intellectually from outer world (*see* KYUSHU) to avoid political entanglements of Portuguese-Spanish imperialism. As most early European tracts were religious, books banned except for Dutch tribute copies to Shogun of new scholarly works. Thus informed of rise of modernism in north Europe, by 1720 book ban is lifted and Daimyo started centers for Dutch language and learning, *Rangaku*, from Holland>Oranda>Ran+*gaku*, study—using homophone for *ran* , orchid. Shogunal school for translation of Western works moves from Nagasaki to Edo in 1811, foundation for later Tokyo University.

Despite all, Shogun system of political feudalism no longer fits reality of rising commercial system. Samurai and Daimyo hold political power, atop which shaky pyramid, held in place by counterbalancing personalities, sits Shogun. However *chonin*-merchants control economy, hold pocketbook. Rice production fails to keep up with population and taxes (which cities avoid) press farmers dearly, chonin playing rice futures market aggravate hardships of farmers. Rural riots proliferate, new religions arise promising salvation (like Tenri-kyo, which we visit p352). This new religiosity helps pro-mote imperial cause, as much sacred-nationalist as political.

This is where Commodore Matthew C. Perry, USN enters Tokyo Bay.

NINE RINGS OF AURIOLE: *1854-1945*. TV antenna atop pagoda has, count them, nine rings one atop another, topped by flaming jewel of essence of existence. Our historical pagoda of Japan now brings us to nine decades between Perry welcoming local officials on board black-painted man-o'war *USS Susquehanna*, and MacArthur receiving black-draped Japanese officials aboard *USS Missouri*. That topmost flaming orb is now.

Tokugawa shoguns reason that seclusion cannot be maintained so seek to approve Perry's demands. Would-be opposition sees this as chance to topple them, raise cry *"Sonno-joi*, Honor Emperor: Expel Barbarian"–good meaningless slogan couched in classical terms so that few understand it (even emperor asks for translation), rather like football cheer. Musical chairs again becomes national sport as daimyo maneuver for position. Samurai chop down Englishman for not showing deference to their lord, so avenging British bombard samurai's hometown Kagoshima, south Kyushu, which is so impressed that samurai welcome them ashore amidst rubble and buy British fleet. What is to become Imperial Navy is born.

In melee that follows Tokugawa clan elects new 15th shogun, believer in sanctity of imperial line who begins reform, offers to abdicate and share rule in 1868 but is overthrown within year anyway. As historian Father Cooper succinctly notes, shogun's full title meant "Queller of Barbarians...allowing barbarians to enter was his undoing". Buddhism is purged from power, for Tokugawas ruled thru local temples while shinto supported Imperial myth. Imperial house and civilian government regain power after millennium of dualism. But end of power dualism is not end of dichotomy.

Thus ends strangest political revolution in history. "Emperor honored" by use of war tools of "barbarian" to expel opposition. Then instead of "expelling barbarian" they look over at what happened to China and wisely agree "if you can't lick 'em, join 'em". Samurai cut off top knots, slip into trousers, voluntarily renounce nobility, put aside sword for monkey-wrench and proceed to build new nation, accomplishing in decades what has taken Europe centuries. Quiet socio-economic true revolution, so astounding that it totally eclipses earlier political revolt.

Itinerary tip: We meet its heroes in JAPAN SEA town of Hagi, pp.805-20.

Strangely enough this is one revolution that keeps most of its promises. Equality is one, and samurai abolish themselves. Many become soldiers, many sword-wielding police (but unable to change their old authoritarian personalities), many bureaucrats in new prefectural system replacing old feudatory realms, and others even merchants. Parliament is promised by revolutionaries and promise kept by emperor with constitution of 1889 (which set base for rebuilding postwar Japan). Education was made universal satisfying craving partially salved by old daimyo and *terakoya* temple schools and sets basis for reasonably-classless meritocracy.

New state turns outward in quest for more means to maintain traditions.

Most important event of first decade must be what has been justly termed "one of most remarkable journeys in world history" that 21-month, 50-man (plus attached students) Iwakura Mission led by several top leaders circumnavigating world to visit dozen heads of state who had signed treaties with Japan (only Kingdoms of Hawaii, Spain, Portugal were omitted). Caretaker government honors pledge not to make major moves, waives chance for coup. Mission blazed and set path for future development of nation and above-mentioned Meiji constitution.

In quick summary lest we all expect any Asian or African nation can emulate Japan: Tokugawa Japan attained high agricultural productivity thru centralized control of production (they ordered modernization and all obeyed) and marketing; thus, in 1867 country has capital base. Strict control enables head to yell "about face...quick step" and 50,000,000-man body snaps-to. Coincidentally, Japan has literacy rate at least as high as any in Europe on which to build. Samurai encouraged to educate himself to keep him peaceful, read orders or file intelligence reports, commoners emulate in local temple schools, *terakoya*. Capitalist consumer society already existed, perhaps as early as Europe, as well documented in popular 17-19th century pulp literature. 'Built-in obsolescence' was basis of seasonal-disposable paper and bamboo crafts (yet exquisitely handcrafted) 'hi-tech'. Old feudal family system of shopkeepers and crafts become family-run small and medium enterprises. Clan establishments, which had never been based on blood but on residence, transfer lock, stock and gun barrel into great interlocking monopoly systems of big industrial-capital concentration. Profit is not much distributed to workers, nor even to leaders, but plowed back into expansion of production. Men who had built palaces in images of China, castles in emulation of Europe, and gold pavilions on blueprints from dreams, now build factories and ships and new chimneyed-dreams. Less leap forward than great leap to parallel track.

We ourselves in West maintain: give chap good classical foundation and he can handle any job...Yep. Leading these chaps during our nine rings are:

KOMEI, born 1831, emperor 1846-67, 121st by traditional count; reigns when Perry and Harris arrive, grudgingly agrees to gradual opening, supports Tokugawa, giving own sister as bride to shogun Iemochi, 1862. Then gives in to *Sonno-joi* wild men and orders "expel barbarians" 1863, but movement collapses later in year after battles in Kyoto, much sword fighting taking place in geisha districts. Favors collaboration with shogun, but dies of smallpox (or poison?) 1867 before matter settled. His reign years carry names Ansei 1854-60, Bunkyu 1861-3, Genji 1864, Keio 1865-7. Son-successor will abolish this custom of changing year names mid-reign for lark or luck and henceforth emperor's reign name covers all years of that rule. But era name changes day after death of ruler, so that Hirohito-Showa 1 runs only Dec 26-31, 1926 and final Showa 64 just Jan 1-7, 1989.

Antiquity of Imperial line not all that singular. Inheritance rarely ran father to son, or parent to child with empresses, but more often to brothers, nephews or cousins, just keeping it within clan. European main royalty can all show common descent from Persia's Cyrus the Great (6th century BC, long pre real Jimmu), further linked by intermarriage especially among Anglo-German royals and spawn.

MEIJI, b. 1852, crown prince 1860, ascends throne as Mutsuhito #122 as boy 14 under tutelage of west-Japan clique who hate Tokugawas. Year 2 of reign sees overthrow-abdication of last shogun Yoshinobu. Capital moves to Edo, renamed <u>To</u>kyo, Eastern Capital, in contrast to Kyoto (a.k.a. <u>Sai</u>kyo) in west, relating to China's <u>Nan</u>king-south, <u>Pe</u>king-north. Endorses modernization on traditional base, as against "westernization" but is unable to control militarists in government, reluctantly goes to war with Korea, China then Russia, paving way for eventual domination of army over parliamentarians and World War II. Dies July 1912, succeeded by son—

TAISHO, b. 1879 Yoshihito, r.1912-26, sickly even as child, son Hirohito regent 1921-6. First prince to attend open school, Gakushuin, now traditional royal school. Enters World War I with allies, provided needed winter supplies, gains ex-German colonies. Reign sees flowering of 'Taisho Democracy', modern party system 1918, rise of House of Representatives, universal manhood suffrage 1925—same year as foreboding Peace Preservation Law, final failure of civil government to control military.

SHOWA 'Enlightened Peace', b. April 29, 1901 **Hirohito**, enthroned Dec 26, 1926 as 124th Emperor, d. Jan 7, 1989. Putting aside Methusalehs of legend, longest-reigning, longest-lived monarch in Japanese history. After tragic emulation of worst aspects of westernization brought military defeat which many thinking natives welcomed, led country into era for which he had prophetically, long seemingly ironically, taken his reign name. Denounced by some as ogre-king who planned world conquest, acclaimed by others as humanist-prince powerless to control his underlings. Asked by shogun MacArthur about renouncing divinity he said he'd never considered himself special in any way. Most revealing story of this quiet marine biologist told that in his study he kept three portrait busts: Lincoln, Einstein, Napoleon. He explained: Lincoln for humanity as ruler; Einstein for science; and Bonaparte?—it seems on his trip to Europe as crown prince, one day in Paris when he should have been midday napping he sneaked his chamberlain's coat, slipped out back exit of hostel and strolled to Seine banks among riverside stalls, first time in his life jingling money in pocket of borrowed clothes. Commotion from behind told him his absence was known, his new freedom was to be short-lived. He had to buy something for himself, by himself as memento of liberty. He spoke no French. He went up to stall and held out handful of change. Pedlar just saw another tourist…"every tourist wants plaster bust of Napoleon" so took his money and handed him bust just as 'rescuers' ended his solo flight of freedom. Napoleon reminded him of that brief episode of early humanization. Just before his death poll revealed 25% of Japanese held him at least partially responsible for war, equal number felt him powerless, remaining half non-committal. Okinawans—who suffered horrendous casualties in invasion, many by own troops—particularly outspoken and he was never able to visit this one prefecture. Asked by US reporter if he ever dreamed of being common man, replied "Constantly". Posthumously simply 'Showa'.

AKIHITO, born December 23, 1933, fifth child after string of daughters, ascended as #125 **Heisei**, 'Peace-perfecting', at 6:33am, Jan 7, 1989—taken to Imperial Palace where at 10:01 he stood at throne before cabinet and notables, flanked by his sons and sole uncle to 'receive' symbolic Sacred Treasures of office: Sword rushed up from Nagoya by Shinkansen, and Magatama-jewel (always in palace) and Imperial and National Seals to frank documents (Mirror stayed in Ise). Rite lasted 4 minutes, no word spoken. New *gengo*, era name, from Confucius, announced 2:30pm. Coronation Nov 12, 1990, in Tokyo. Raised from age 3 by proxies, spent war years in mountains of Nikko. Major influences on him were 'proxy-father' internationalist educator Dr KOIZUMI Shinzo, and high school English tutor Elizabeth Gray Vining, US Quaker. Attended Gakushuin University 'Peers College' (where for one year visitor-Sumi was classmate and sole non-Japanese, but too old-fashionedly modest to speak to him). As his father was first in millennium to marry non-Fujiwara, he was first to marry non-noble, fellow Karuizawa tennis-player who attracted his attention by trouncing him, SHODA Michiko, by whom two sons (elder Hiro is heir as **Naruhito**), both recently attended college in England, and daughter. They trashed tradition and raised children themselves, instead of farming out. Their reign promises to be revolutionary in terms of either further 'humanization' of throne, *vs* reactionary tendency of many in ruling party to return to 'good ole days' of high-flown internal exile and bunraku-style puppet manipulation from below with offstage proxy-voice.

We put our money on quiet, determined ichthyologist-emperor, Akihito.

*Wealthy we do not at all think [Japan] will ever become: the
advantages conferred by nature, with the exception of climate, and
the love of indolence and pleasure of the people themselves, forbid it.
The Japanese are a happy race, and being content with little,
are not likely to achieve much.* —Japan Herald, 1881

FLAMING ORB ATOP PAGODA 1945-NOW

TWO EDITIONS of this book span almost half Showa reign, have seen nation rise from underdeveloped status as poor in 1945 as in 1881, to second biggest economy surpassing GNP of Germany and Russia, individual product of USA. Yet dichotomies persist: world's top automobile product rolls off robot assembly lines into maze of alleys that make London's lanes seem like boulevards. World's #2 GNP reigns where most people still live in near-third world housing, so cramped that domestic consumption is limited less by touted non-tariff barriers than by lack of space to put material purchases. Little of Japan's booming export earnings seem to filter down to populace, who live in buildings which would devolve into slums anywhere else but for this blessed peculiarity of Japanese mass mentality or psyche that prevents them from thinking or feeling poor.

Most Japanese profits from US sales remain in USA to finance US debt at higher interest rates than available locally (Jan 1989 prime interest 3.5%) —besides which domestic economy could never absorb such billions without blowing up. Tho it could absorb far more for public capital outlay to bury overhead wires, widen roads, build better homes, allow 2-day weekends and summer holidays to build family vacation industry (which could redevelop decrepit rural areas), beef up social security for aged. Life expectancy since war has risen from society with compulsory retirement at 55 (which few men reached) to longest-lived with women to 84 years, men 74. World's fastest aging population of 6.6 people age 15-64 supporting every 65-over (level reached in France, etc, in 1940s) which ratio by 2013 will be staggering 2.8:1 as population peaks at 130,-136,000,000. Children per family now 1.75 *vs* replacement rate of 2.09—under 15s now under 20%, beating out US & France at 22+%. Average age of Japanese now 36 years, or less than Jay's time in Japan, for what that's worth.

Postwar Constitution (memorialized annually during Golden Week with National Holiday May 3) often attacked as having been American-imposed, but recent scholarly survey shows overwhelming popular support: "Joint product of Americans and Japanese...like cultured pearl, wonderful albeit alien stuff was inseminated into shell of Japanese milieu...people more than welcomed this and covered it with respect and care for last 40 years...most accept 'no war, no arms' clause wholeheartedly because they had suffered so much from the war and its devastation".

FLICKERS OF ORB FLAMES: *TODAY*

AGRICULTURE: Japan expanded overseas as she could not feed her then-35,000,000 people despite highest agricultural output in Asia. At war's end 72,000,000 faced starvation, MacArthur cabled HST, "Send guns or rice". America sent its famed long grain rice—local is glutinous short grain, but they liked it anyway. When Japan bought extra rice from US in late '50s–60s, locals wondered why US rice then was so bad, rep it still has. Simple: US *gave* top grade rice: Japanese bureaucrats *bought* cheapest animal feed grain, age-yellowed unfit for human consumption—which, had HST sent MacArthur, would have scandalized them, not to say ourselves.

Under Nipponese empire rice culture was raised to science in experimental farms in undeveloped Taiwan. Thus, Japan could upgrade rice strains and technology at home after war. Ancient 8-year cycle of one year bumper crop, 4 years later drought, so-so years between, was broken and since mid-'50s it's been bumpers only. Still, food was short. US Army in Kyushu developed way to break up hard volcanic layers for agricultural land—most later went to housing, as much prime farmland goes. Real estate so valuable that farmer cannot buy more fields: value of harvest doesn't equal interest on purchase price, farm gross income less than 5% land value. Tax-assessed value of Tokyo and 'bedroom' suburban real estate exceeds US total value. Better to sell when can for development, as money invested without labor earns far more than farming—but tradition, emotion...

Agriculture 1950s had 47% of work force, now under 10%, 2.6 million households at 1+ hectare each doing work 150,000 or less can do on viable farm size of 15ha; most part time who work in city, leave upkeep to wife or aging parents, half over 60. Poor farmer works as labor far away, returns seasonally to help. But as electoral base of long-ruling Liberal Democratic Party is farmer and merchant...rice price is protected. Rice retails over 6x world price yet consumers support import ban. State buys all to store for years, sells old. New uses for rice researched—beer, bread, etc.

Rice alternates with wheat or truck. Productivity per acre long highest in world, but per man far below US or Europe, and per acre California now reaps 10% more. Where US rice is seeded broadcast from aircraft, Japanese is planted in nursery then transplanted (by hand until recently as in June festivals, now by special hand-operated garden tractor) in neat rows for ease of weeding and harvesting. Still, most farmers are relatively well off, own more subsidized equipment than small plots can efficiently use, have cars (mamma drives too), household appliances, far more than rabbit hutches. Rice price to farmer 8 times world price, yet 85% of his income is nonfarm other jobs. Gov't spent '85 on farm supports ¥10trillion (then over $65billion, '88 exchange rate $80billion—almost then-US-Japan annual trade deficit): vs salaryman income taxes which generated only ¥7trillion.

Farmer also benefits from income tax breaks and gross undervaluing of agricultural land which keeps much of Tokyo in unproductive 'farmland' and short of housing space. Conversion of this farmland in city limits would double housing area, lower prices and not harm food supply. Housing accounts for only 2.5% all land, less than railroads and inadequate roads 2.8%, while commerce takes 9.3% plus factories 0.4%. Amazingly, forests cover 70% and are strictly protected, while they rape SE Asian rain forests for plywood, disposable chopsticks. World food prosperity will hit them when market opens, as it is doing at this writing, but development of land can more than make up and generate construction boom.

Vegetables are forced-grown under plastic hot houses (driving between cities you see rows of tubular-shape plastic dragons in fields) ultraviolet-starved, low in calcium so dietary deficiency is endemic. School medics complain too many kids break bones too easily; new-recruit sumo wrestlers magnificently obese but bones break or worse, ligaments separate from bones permanently crippling. Other serious nutrient deficiencies in foods due to loss of natural mulch (human 'nite soil' now goes to sewage), excessive use of chemical fertilizers, nitrates, hybrid seeds dependent on chemicals, etc. Agricultural 'miracle' has its prices. But we prophesy that official concern will lead to Japan's using American-developed natural additive technology and solutions before US does, creating market for US hi-tech-ag—or its tools and patents if not its produce.

WORK FORCE: High productivity due not so much to better workers. Don't tell frequent fliers on Boeings or Lockheeds US worker isn't tops. Think of it: no defense industry to sap economy or drain brains, so after war companies like Honda gather idled aircraft .engineers. (Japan's flying matchboxes among best aircraft for much of war, outflew US planes, had to be fought two of ours on one of theirs as Zero could dive and turn inside arc of even Spitfire, which no German could match). Our top engineers build great Buck Rogers armaments and space ships while counterparts in Japan with Honda convert washing machine motor to drive bicycle and give 19th century peasantry transport, evolving into world's best motorbikes, then into cars which must be breakdown-proof because without tradition of teen-tinkering with engines as in UK, US there is no natural pool of mechanics. Our brightest miniaturize electronics for space satellites: counterparts in Japan shrink ponderous US-invented TV studio tape deck to fit under living room TV, shrink clunky tabletop audio tape recorder to fit into pocket. Miniaturization is old tradition in finely crafted doll furniture, live bonsai trees. And as there is nothing else to do, one might as well work—no room at home to go spend weekend with hobby or wife.

Companies don't burn money on takeovers, but put it into research. Management isn't as highly paid relative to workers, eat in same cafeteria or order-in same noodles, wear same smocks at work, sit in same offices with ordinary white collars or on factory floor for access. QC-Quality Circles and such 'Japanese' gimmicks of democratic management were US-invented, often developed in US military, ignored by US companies. Much product is American-designed (all was for some time) for US market. We need not emulate them, but should ape ourselves like they do us.

Unions are in-house, part of system rather than adversarial balance. It is nice to be in big company assembling cars or VCRs on lifetime pay. But what of guy in small pop-owned company who makes parts with non-union labor as no industry-wide unions protect little shopworker—not from pop-owner, but from big assembly company who keeps his prices down when dollar falls not just by streamlining or robotizing, but mostly by forcing down price of part from pop-shop. If pop can't meet new price, someone will: so much for highly touted code of loyalty ('loyal' subcontractor will 'bite his lip', not complain). However, pop still has to meet contractual standards, this honesty remains on both sides—unless exporting substandard high-carbon bolts to US engineering firm, who knows it.

Unions were gift of US Occupation, concept never fully digested or evolved. For decades annual strike more rite of spring than call for better conditions. Craft and industry-wide unions will be forestalled as long as management gives labor fair break in realizing rising expectations.

Despite high prices most working families can still get by on one income, which helps familial and societal stability. High % of women in work force mostly singles or elderly. 'Oppressed' Nippon woman polled as to which rather be reborn, answer over 80% "female again". Family standard of living low by US-European rating, but so far better than of yore, and quality of life self-adjudged tops. Personal income 1989/90 (exchange rate $1=¥140): Japan $23,700 vs US $21,100—tho factory worker hourly wage 20% lower in Japan. Engel's law: US expends 15% on food, Japan 26% (and at what prices, ¥400 per kg/$1.40 per lb for rice). Savings rate high, as also house payments, which far exceed old ideal of 25% income. Middle class apartment rent double-plus for half our floor space, hour+ commute. So, less cash to buy imports, yet savings rate astoundingly high. And 'free' education costs—in this America is coming to emulate Nippon, it seems.

EDUCATION enjoys long popular tradition. Samurai, like Jew, had to pass literacy test to graduate into adulthood, thus was ready to leap into new trade and technology. Talented man with drive could often rise thru apprenticeship in crafts or military arts or temple thru inheritance when blood line failed and void filled by adoption of loyal underling, directly or by marriage to boss' daughter. Noting Peter Drucker in *The New Realities*, mid-18th century (contemporary with Comenius' advocacy of universal literacy, invention of textbook, Thomas Jefferson's first US university [Virginia], Austro-Hungarian emperor Joseph II open university for commoners) *bunjin* (literati) of far-away Japan used education to create new vision and new social class. Rejected official hierarchy based on birth with its 3 hereditary classes, replacing it with meritocracy in which nothing mattered except performance as scholar, calligrapher and artist, laying foundations for modern Japan. While these fief schools run by lords trained samurai in literacy and Confucian philosophy, Buddhist priests emulated this with *terakoya* schools for farmer or merchant in literacy and some Buddhism. 100 years later in 1867, when shogunate fell and Meiji Restoration began, every new leader was graduate of academy founded 70 years earlier by bunjin like NUKINA Kaioku and RAI Sanyo. Japan built basis for modern meritocracy while England was founding Rugby school to 'educate gentlemen' to thus fossilize their feudal social system in modern age.

Meiji at start (1867) had 45% school attendance for boys, 15% for girls. State compulsory education took over with new curriculum and teachers. Unlike most feudal societies in which education was tool of repression by ruling class, mass education was introduced with modernization as great social leveler opening way to top for all—with rare exceptions (minorities, untouchables). It also served poor small country as engine of production, intangible capital, whereas similar mini-countries like England and Holland had built more on profits of empire trade and false economy of conquest. (Not that Japan didn't try this path, too, and like Dutch and British, its economy boomed when they got rid of anchor stone colonies).

Education now universal, compulsory, mostly coeducational for 6-year *sho-gakko* 'small' or primary school, then sorting-out exams for 3-year *chu-gakko* middle school (JHS), after which some who fail repeat exams graduate to work force, 85% go on 3 more years *koto-gakko* high school. This is so-called 6-3-3 system introduced by US Occupation in 1945, replacing more limited elite European-style system. Skipping or accelerated study is considered unequal. Proportion of those continuing on to *dai-gaku* 'big-school' or college now similar to USA. School week includes half-day saturday, far fewer annual holidays than US, Europe—announced to go to "5-day week" by 1992 "...at least biweekly". At all levels *yobi-ko, juku* or cram schools supplement gov't-free or private-fee schools after class. All of which adds up to much-lamented Examination Hell.

Learning complicated *kanji* ideographic writing system supplemented by two sets of syllabic systems (cursive hiragana, square katakana), *romaji* roman-letters, more than makes up time difference in elementary school. Junior high grad should know at least 1800 ideographs on graduation, enough for functional literacy, read newspaper or newsweekly beyond sports page, but needs much more for literary mag or novel. (But how many in US read *New Yorker*?...or can?) High school grad has 2,000 ideograph target, must exceeds it if going on to college where he won't read much anyway unless in 'elite' school. Jay taught at Wakayama National University (near Osaka). Chancellor, ex-aesthetics prof, told him right off there was little he could do for 8 classes of 60 students each for 45 minutes weekly, so just muddle by but devote extra time to English Speaking Society (ESS kids often volunteer as guides for foreign tourists) and any student who might ask for help. Jay came away from 7-year teaching stint with respect for students and utter disdain for lack of professionalism of native faculty. Such students, politically vociferous, demonstrative, hungry, grew up to captain Japan's phenomenal economic boom. School entry far more democratic than UK, matched only by US city or state schools—you don't enter if you don't make grade no matter who poppa is or pays. Notable exception, perhaps, medical school—and medical care is coming to show it.

Before war there were only six National and several private (including Christian mission-run) Universities. US Occupation decreed national free-tuition 4-year *daigaku* in each of 47 prefectures—but we prefer to translate *daigaku* as college rather than university as concept of universality in education is lacking and most are more like trade schools, based on rote memorization of boring lectures (unchanged until prof's notes yellow beyond readability) and light reading assignments, no questioning, much time on teamwork-building extra-curricular activities often at cost of class. Would-be student applies to one department, examined for that one and if admitted not only cannot transfer schools but can't even change department or major within same school. Overseas grads usually return to find selves outcasts, unless dad owns company or unless sent to overseas grad or special school by employer, corporate or government. Beijing language school full of well-paid Japanese company men on study assignment with orders to master Chinese or else; US students mostly on own, poor, struggling and fewer. So who will control China market in 2,000 AD?

Post-baccalaureate studies minimal, perhaps 70,000 students including medical, dental, legal and all other specialties. Scholarly meetings held on campus, tho open to all, rarely attract any students unless one's prof is giving paper. There is little interest in learning per se, beyond class assignment. US graduates as many lawyers annually as Japan has total, but Japan graduates more engineers now than US—and mostly in basic production. Thus, Japan is now doing to world what first Germany did, then postwar US (thanks to GI Bill): turning out men (few girls in professional courses) who can build things and make them work. Aristocratic Europe long invented gizmos which Americans in backyard garages adapted, engineered to become product of basic economy, as Japanese now "copy"—i.e adapt, apply, engineer. Here corporation, not lone-wolf entrepreneur, pays for garage. Research budgets (mostly in applications, little 'pure') far exceed US in proportion to gross sales, % of GNP. Postgraduate engineering studies are done in-company, sometimes in secret country estates, since '60s campus upheavals discouraged US-style on-campus company-financed research. American W.E.Demming developed Quality Control. Ignored in US, lionized here. QC added to feudalistic Confucian code of shared-resposibility spawned Japanese management philosophy.

GRAVEL AROUND FOOT OF PAGODA: Swiss statistics have Tokyo most expensive to live in world, Osaka #2. Spring '87 saw Tokyo replace New York as world's largest stock market, with highest fixed commissions and broker profits. World's largest company is newly denationalized Nippon Telephone-Telegraph, with US-GM now #2. Biggest bank in deposits is Japan Postal Savings system, 10 richest trading banks also locals. World's #3 and #4 automobile makers are Toyota and Nissan; largest ad agency Dentsu. Matsushita electronic (locally National, overseas Panasonic, Quasar, etc) bigger than GE. Insurance firms top gross.

Industrialist friend of ours, postwar American-educated, compares today's youths with pre-1945. "Then government would send out draft notices to 10,000 to report and all but 4 or 5 would obediently show up on time, and those few would be tracked down by feared *kempeitai*-thought police and dragged in for torture. Today such notice to similar 10,000 of our *shin-jinrui* 'new kind' might net 500 or so, rest would laughingly ignore it. What suffering we and our international neighbors would have avoided had my generation been more like this, ah…"

1983 poll by NHK showed 89% thought selves "superior to other races" while "Japan should learn from other nations" were only 29%—same question of Americans saw 49% of them believe they could learn from others (but, will we?). Poll analyst concluded "Once discredited wartime self-image and nationalism seems to be reemerging". We agree, feel it intensified '83-'90, but feel confident public education can also reverse it as people learn more about overseas besides crime rates.

"Even though Japanese read more foreign news and translated books than any other nationality, they are reluctant to become involved with foreigners except when doing business"…Businessweek.

To paraphrase European historic remark about Holy Roman Empire, in Japan's party system Liberal Democrats are neither liberal nor democratic, Socialist parties are downright anti-social. None are even parties, just assemblages of personal claques. But perennially-ruling LibDems are pragmatic to their core and will change, cautiously, however they must. 'Left' parties are so only in their seeming determination to be left behind.

Average income of 38.6 million households (3.2 people ea) 1986 topped ¥5,000,000 = US$40,000, yet half found it difficult to make ends meet. 63% are 2-paycheck families—but only 11% wives in full-time jobs, 22% part- and 30% self-employed or working at home at piece-work. Most girls and wives work in service jobs at ¥500 per hour ($4), work at take-home for less. Male college grad ('90) gets $1000 per month, but with overtime not paid for it comes to ¥400 or so per hour. Dad as manufacturing laborer worked 2,192 hours in 1985, 500 more than average in 15 other industrialized nations; projecting reduction to 1,800 by '93 to hold unemployment under 3%. But it takes him 2hrs26min to earn pound (454g) of beef (US imports are improving this), vs 71min in Germany or 17min in USA. More significant, to earn kilogram (2.2 lb) of fish took 2hrs47min vs French 1hr26min, UK 66min, W German 60min, or US 26min.

City worker pays over double for apartment half-size of US counterpart plus immense deposit-cum-purchase of rental right (key money). Of all houses only 37% connect to sewers, around new Osaka International Airport area only 20%: vs UK 95%. Japan has per registered vehicle, 1/2 expressway mileage of Germany, 1/3 that of UK. Urban expressways world's most expensive to build as land acquisition takes 95% of budget.

He pays more for many Japan-made consumer goods than in USA—but import of Japan-brands from NICs (newly industrializing countries) is suddenly changing this ('89-90). No wonder these purportedly best-paid-in-world workers say, sadly, "How come we don't feel rich?" At household buying power of Yen, exchange should probably still be $ = ¥300.

Local professional: "I like more casual and open American life-style, but I don't want to become an American". What better influence can US be? And for British influence, imperial family prefers Oxbridge education for its scions, even next emperor, which attracts little attention in Nippophobic London press.

*... in the old temples of this country
we see without comprehending clearly,
the meaning of the symbols escapes us.*
—Pierre Loti

NATIVE RELIGIONS
BUDDHISM & SHINTOISM

BUDDHISM: religious system whose followers hope to attain eternal bliss, their ultimate goal, that great desire to end desires, become buddha, become one with past buddhas in buddhahood, *nirvana*. This may be accomplished by obeying 8 commandments to follow 8-fold path of right views, intent, speech, action, livelihood, effort, mood, concentration. Any who fail at this find subsequent hell or purgatory in rebirth for 2nd or 3rd or infinite chances.

Two basic schools of Buddhism: Mahayana, literally 'Great Vehicle', is common to NE Asia: Tibet, China, Korea, Japan. Older form is Hinayana, 'Lesser Vehicle', but called by themselves Theravada 'Older Teaching', common to SE Asia. Buddhism was introduced to Japan with first image received 552 (now reputedly in ZENKOJI, Nagano, *see* p.944).

In turn, Mahayana has numerous sects, from Tantric Shingon, 'True Teaching' closely related to Tibet and practiced at KOYA MONASTERY near Osaka which we visit; various other older esoteric sects some with but one major temple today; thru purely Japanese 'new sects', mostly 12-13th century revivalist like Nichiren-shu (and its modern development Soka Gakkai and SGI), HONGANJI 'Pure Land' sects centered in KYOTO and popular among older Japanese-Americans; to stoic Zen meditative sect (we can join its sitters at several of temples we visit).

Art is Buddhism's principal medium to educate observer towards this goal, providing him with focal points in form of portraits of beings exemplifying desired qualities, illustrations of certain tenets. It is, by its very nature, enigmatic and, by this same nature, nearly impossible to explain just what these statues or paintings portray.

In brief, there have been and will be, infinite buddhas, but there is one ultimate Buddha of which all are manifestations. That Buddha is *Dai-nichi* (Great Light), perfect gnosis. Earth exists thru five kalpas (epochs). Each has its own essential buddha, who is motionless in demonstration of total end of desire, end of action, final rest. Each epoch's buddha has his active manifestation, bodhisattva (or *bosatsu* in Japanese) who is in turn incarnated in one being of flesh, blood and suffering: earthly Buddha.

We are now in kalpa number four, Buddhist quaternary. Essential buddha of our era is Amida (of KAMAKURA great statue), whose bosatsu is Kannon (goddess of mercy in popular parlance), and earthly buddha of flesh and blood is he whom we know as Buddha (tho this was his 'title' not name) whom Japanese call *Shaka-sama*, Indian Sakyamuni (?567-488BC), born as Siddhartha Gautama Prince of Saka, in what is now Nepal.

Japanese popular Buddhism sluffs over business of five epochs, lumping everything up in just saying there have-been/will-be 10 (or 13) *nyorai* (*tathagata*, epithet of Buddha, literally one who has Followed the Path). Essential and terrestrial buddhas are classed together as nyorai so 5x2=10, so let's not bother either. Sometimes Trinity of each of 4 past-present kalpas is, plus Coming Messiah=13. Guides to Tibetan or Chinese Buddhism won't work well here, nationalization has so changed various sects.

Nyorai, whether human or abstract, is shown as simple human who has gone beyond all material desire, thus is unadorned. Highest rank of *jugo*, ten earthly attributes or stages of Buddha, not much used in popular Buddhism except for highest nyorai and lowly *rakan* (below). We see paintings or statues of them seated or standing, dressed only in plain toga, displaying no wealth. However, there will be certain peculiarities: curly hair looking rather like snail shells (heritage of statues of curly moppet Greeks, or older Persians at Persepolis); 'bump of knowledge', actually topknot on which he wore now-discarded crown when he was human king-become-bodhisattva; long ears, elongated by weight of since-discarded jeweled earrings; 'third eye' in forehead, probably originally Indian caste mark. There are other signs of esoteric nature like webbed fingers, peculiar footprint, etc. Popular nyorai are Dai-nichi alias Roshana, Amida, Yakushi 'Healing' or 'Medicine' Buddha, Shaka and Miroku—one big hodge-podge of rankings.

Telling nyorai apart is something else again:

Dainichi Trinity
Asuka Great Buddha,
Asuka-dera; reconstruction

Amida
Kamakura Great Buddha

Dai-nichi (Great Sun or Great Light), being ultimate, may be shown with crown and jewels, or may be shown in simple ascetic garb. If former, as buddha of all buddhas, he will usually have pointed crown. If represented as ascetic his halo is studded with innumerable subsidiary, self-begotten, buddhas, as Nara Great Buddha, *see*, or earlier Asuka Great Buddha, *shown here* in reconstruction. He may be called by his alias, Roshana, Sanskrit for 'Light' related to Latin *lux*, or 'day' as Persian *ruz*, or Hebrew *rosh*. His secondary job is as essential buddha of first kalpa.

Amida is usually, as in Kamakura Great Buddha, *here*, seated with hands in lap, palms up in position of total rest and inactivity. Essential buddha of our kalpa, fourth. Also on crucifix as 'secret savior' of Nagasaki Christians.

Yakushi is usually shown right hand raised in casual "Hi", left hand out palm up as offering advice, often proffering jar of medicine, *yaku-*.

Miroku, a.k.a. Maitreya, Messiah or Coming Buddha, often in position similar to Rodin's 'Thinker', *as here*, bejeweled or not, pondering reality of being. Historic buddha Shaka/Gautama/Siddhartha as child was one Miroku. Next Messiah is due about 4512AD (Shaka's nirvana plus 5,000): in Buddhism his fifth, not second, coming. Miroku is also called...

Bodhisattva (Jpn *bosatsu*)—easily differentiated for 'he' or 'she' (there is no sex as all desire has been left behind) has attained all earthly success and is ready to become buddha. Having attained success, he wears all status symbols of king, crown, jewels, etc, but wears them lightly for they don't matter. But bosatsu remains bosatsu, does not become buddha, for she/he is martyr to her/his own infinite mercy and makes ultimate sacrifice, refraining from passing on to nirvana to remain behind to help and guide other mere mortals.

With such infinite qualities and infinite mercy, there are infinite possible representations and you will hear title bosatsu affixed to many images, even

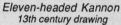

Eleven-headed Kannon
13th century drawing

Miroku
Koryuji Temple, Kyoto

historical great priests like Nichiren (by his followers, only), or shinto deities as Hachiman Dai-Bosatsu (*dai*=great as further rank). And as there's lots of saving to be done in our quaternary time-world, our era bosatsu...

Kannon, who has infinite variations: should have crown in which spiritual father Amida is represented. You'll find him/her with horse head ('horse sense'?); crown of ten heads (for ten nyorai), or three faces plus crown of eight small heads atop his own, thus called eleven-headed Kannon *here* (rear head, almost always unviewable, laughs—Zenists say at foolishness of supplicant who begs instead of acting himself); with several arms; or 1,000 arms (commonly just 42) for infinite mercy; etc, ad inf, ad nirvana. Always ornately bejeweled, face and mien expressing infinite mercy, his major attribute, characterized as 'feminine' trait so that he is popularly feminized as 'Goddess of Mercy'. Also used as Secret Christian 'Maria'.

Jizo, most common, ubiquitous roadside icon (guardian of children, mothers, travelers in time and space, of birth and death) usually lovingly clothed in real red bib carrying staff. Sometimes seated but more commonly standing. Breaks rules again in usually being not bejeweled, but perhaps in simplification as folk sculpture. Probably Buddhafication of primeval earth deity.

If it isn't one of these, it's probably **Shaka**, historical buddha, *below*.

Note use of "usual" and "probably". What by all "rules" might be, say, Amida, might seemingly arbitrarily be attributed as Dai-nichi—as we note in travel text where relevant.

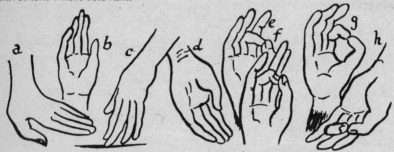

Mudra — Hand Symbolism
a. suppress earthly evil.   c. earthly proof.   e,f. variants of discussing; both hands=preaching.
b. fear not.   d. giving.   g. Amida welcomes to Nirvana.   h. enumerate+e,f.

HAND SIGNS, *mudra*, distinguish some nyorai, comprise special language, each posture with its own meaning. Several of most common are illustrated *above* with 'translation' so that you might get part of message of particular nyorai.

You might also identify puzzling nyorai by identifying attendants usually found with him, but this gets us into complicated families of 'gods' and guards, further complicated by styles in different periods, as well as by temple having lost parts of original set. Even experts falter. Some more popular of these lieutenants are:

Manjusri (Jpn *Monju*), one of attendants (with lotus-bearing **Fugen**) of Shaka. Apotheosis of transcendental wisdom, also worshipped alone in Zen temples for he was historical follower of Shaka who understood his unspoken deathbed message. Holds wordless sutra scroll and sword to cut away delusions. Often shown riding lion. His 8th descendant was...

Fugen

Manjusri

Bodhidharma, *Daruma*, rare except red papier-maché rolly-bottom dolls with beetle-browed blank eyes (to be filled in by purchaser, one at supplication, second at fulfillment). Also painted asquat with legs withered having sat for nine years (few recall he willed legs back, self determination). Brought Indian *dhyana* to China as *ch'an*. Pictured standing on palm frond asea, freed of weight of being, drifting back to India. He epitomizes zen.

Myo-O, eight terrifying Brilliant Kings, most popular of whom is **Fudo**, fierce bolo-wielding bearer of upright 'terrible swift sword' who admonishes reluctant to accept peacefully-presented teachings; also patron of contracts. Often sited alone at mystic places of popular tantric worship: such as waterfalls where midwinter bathing practiced, caves, etc.

j. Dainichi "All is One".   l. invisibility.   o. adoration of word.
     k. moment of enlightenment.   m. meditation.   p. adoration of power.
               n. total stillness (Amida). q. (inverted) nothing is unattainable.

Beyond this there are seven more classes of supernatural beings, such as **Asuras** and **Garudas**, all Indian in origin, found in Japan usually only in earliest temples. Then there are actual historical persons, saints and sages, usually of early Japanese Buddhism, custom revived in Kamakura era, whose portraits were sculpted from life; identified by their evident humanity and obvious saintliness. Most common all over Japan is Kukai, a.k.a. **Kobo Daishi**, (774-834) founder of Shingon 'True Teaching' and of Koya Monastery, (*see*, as also SHIKOKU for his pilgrimage).

Unsympathetic-looking caricatures of grouches are **rakan** (variants Chin *lohan* or Sanskr *arhat*), crotchety old men broadcasting by facial expression: "we have it made", have attained qualities of buddhas, are ready to be raised to nirvana. They differ from buddhas or bosatsu in that while enlightened, they seem concerned only with self, are not teachers, are not themselves enlighteners, have subdued ego but not 'self'. Exceptional group in pagoda of HORYUJI near Nara (flashlight necessary), 7th century.

Bodhidharma

Kobo Daishi

Tennin "angel"

Fudo   Shishi 'lion dog'

Also among such portraits will be several of...
Buddha himself, at various times during twelve stations or stages of his
historical life: born in Lumbini, present-day Nepal, about 567BC— roughly
contemporary with Confucius, Lao-tse, Zoroaster, Cyrus the Great and
Periclean Athens. His father was minor king, he was prince–thus kingly
symbolism in his images. Immaculately conceived, 'born educated', gave
his first sermon to midwives delivering him: icon standing hand upraised is
bathed at nationwide **Apr 8** *Hana-Matsuri*, his birthday. Given name was
Siddhartha, but soon came to be known as Sakyamuni, sage of Sakya (Lion)
tribe. Statues at this stage show him pensive as Maitreya, Messiah or Coming Buddha, which of course he was. He married, had son, led idyllic life,
then discovered harsh reality and renounced life to become ascetic, known as
Gautama, at about age 25. Fasted and tormented himself, but gave this up
as futile, self-defeating extremes to follow simple meditation which brought
enlightenment while sitting under Bo tree, reputedly still there in Bodh Gaya
outside of Benares, India. At 35 he was Living *Buddha*, 'Enlightened One'.
Wandered preaching for half-century, gathered followers (including son
Rahula), 'died' age 81. Scene of demise of his physical body—Ascension
to **nirvana**, or release from cycle of rebirths—shows all his followers,
various deva, other beings, animals of woods and dreams, even insects, in
torment (one elephant-like critter **amano-jaku**, forefront, seems to be
laughing but that's because he does everything in reverse). His earthly birth,
enlightenment, death are feted together **Apr 8** (some sects divide them).

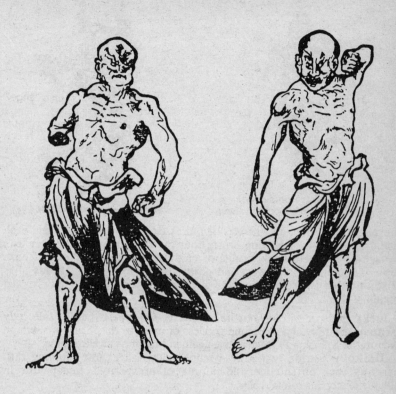

Ni-O guardian karateists, Kofukuji temple, Nara, 7th century

2500th anniversary of 3 events was feted across Asia 1957.

Vatican heard of this miraculous Indian saint in 12th century, thought him follower of lost Christians of St Thomas, canonized him under mispronunciation of *bodhisat* as St Josaphat, feast day **Nov 27**. (Patron Saint of at least one long-time Jesuit in Japan). About same time Chinese Buddhists heard of **Jesus** and acclaimed him as bodhisattva, known in Japanese as *Inro Bosatsu*, manifestation of Jizo, and commonly found outside crematoria blessing newly dead. Essentially ecumenical, buddhism accepts all bearers of sacred messages as at least holy men if not bodhisattvas.

Ni-O, deva kings *Indra* and *Brahma*, are guardians in temple gates: oldest bare-bellied like Persian *zur-khaneh* wrestlers and probably of Manichaean origin as in China's Tun Huang caves; later are armored à la Chinese. He on left has mouth closed, obviously nose-inhaling, tensing *yin*, while right's open mouth implies explosive exhalation and activity, *yang*. Heavenly karateists (above). Often likened to Gog and Magog.

Tennin or *Apsaras* (opposite), heavenly beings, are angels, girls floating in space about altars without wings (Muslim angels like Judaeo-Christian are winged), but robed and beribboned like their Partho-Sasanian Persian boy predecessors, have become feminized in their geographical extremes east and west. Usually shown with musical instruments up on clouds.

Heaven King Komokuten,
whose brush is mightier than sword   Bishamonten   *-by Hokusai*

Devas 12, *ju-ni-ten*, all suffixed *-ten*, dressed in Chinese armor and each
wielding weapon or writing brush, four of whom may be together as...
Shiten-O Four Heavenly Kings of cardinal directions: *Jikoku* of east,
Komoku south, *Zocho* west and north guard **Tamon** who in his alias
Bishamonten is also popular both alone and as one of folk deities, mixed
buddhist-shinto, of...

7 lucky gods or *shichi-fuku-jin*—other 6, *facing page,* being: sole lady
Benten, sea deity and sometime goddess or muse of music and arts, whom
we meet at Kamakura's Bentenjima, again in Miyajima nr Hiroshima;
—**Daikoku** astride two straw-wrapped rice bales (note nibbling rat),
carrying sack on shoulder and hammer of prosperity, often phallic in
silhouette atop his scrotal bales;
—**Ebisu**, happy fisherman with pole and great *tai*-sea bream, ancient
fishing deity, patron of Osaka merchants;
—**Jurojin**, old man with staff and deer;
—**Fukuroku-ju**, high bald-domed, whiskered 'Dr Huer' popularized
version of Lao-tse, founder of Taoism, but here god of longevity; and
—**Hotei**, characterized by smile and big bare belly, symbols of contentment
and good nature, 'laughing buddha'—actual historical Chinese priest Pu-tai.
   Some were local fertility deities, often appear in erotic or suggestive form
—like Daikoku who originates in fertility-tribal god of immigrants to Izumo,
Okuni-nushi-no Mikoto; or Lady Benten on her own island-shrine near
Kamakura, nude image clothed in silks, realistic when viewed from below.

Gongen take no special form but are Buddhism's recognition when
Buddhism and shinto united, of saintly status of shinto predecessors;
Buddhist avatars of shinto deities, usually local *genus locii*, Latin for 'spirit
of that locale', many of which in Europe were similarly absorbed into
Christianity as local Saints. Major example is **Hachiman Dai Bosatsu**,
shinto deity of sword and scythe, deification of Emperor Ojin, 3rd century
or later, a.k.a. Yawata, patron of early immigrant wave from North Asia and
especially sacred to sword-carrying samurai. 'Purified' of Buddhist aspects
in 1868, such as statuary, Hachiman's most numerous shrines (main at Usa,
Kyushu, major in Kamakura) still retain Buddhist architecture and he still
retains Bodhisattva title. Shingon Buddhism in local worship still retains
much shinto flavor, often encompasses local shrines.

Early Buddhism came to terms with native shinto thru explanations that new deities were avatars, or versions, of old: thus Roshana 'Sunlight' Buddha was one with Sun Goddess Amaterasu. Buddhist statues of avatars decorated major shinto shrines until nationalistic Meiji Restoration modernism purged shinto of Buddhist elements, and deprived Buddhism of shinto-state patronage.

Swastika 卍 ancient Indo-Iranian (a.k.a. 'Aryan') sun symbol, auspicious sign to Shakyamuni's people and adopted by buddhists—but in reverse of nazi version, which buddhists consider inverted, even symbolic of negative or adverse power.

Swastika 卍 is key on maps for temple site, while miniature torii 卄 denotes shrine.

That some of these concepts seem capable to multiply selves like amoeba; that these in turn generate other beings and concepts, demons, gods and angels and kings, with different ways of worshipping in turn to beget proliferation of sects and subsects from stark stoic Zen to ornate tantric Shingon; that nothing is at all clear, might seem pagan or primitive or what?

It also might suggest that all is illusion, that these images are meant to puzzle, to get one thinking; or get one counting Shakas instead of sheep to slip off into ultimate sleep. Buddhism cannot simply be defined as polytheistic worship of many gods, certainly not atheistic tho it is called thus as it recognizes no single God Almighty, and probably not even as theistic as it has no individualized gods. Its whole number system all folds back on itself like some möbius band or klein bottle in finite infinity, one ongoing big bang.

No mere matter of one god versus many, not simple pantheism in worshipping all gods, but truly, simply recognition of infinite holographic godliness of everything.

Not just space-matter as hologram, but time, too.

ZEN 禅

MEDITATIVE SECT of Mahayana Buddhism, name from antecedent Chinese Ch'an and Sanscrit Dhyana, meaning 'meditation'. Claiming ancestry of personal follower of Historical Buddha, Manjusri or (Jpn) Monju (see above), who, present at his earthly demise/*nehan*, was sole disciple to 'understand' his unspoken last commandment. Its ultimate origins are in Yogic technique as introduced to China by organizer-cum-first patriarch Indian monk Bodhidharma (popularly Daruma) early 500s. There blended with Taoism to develop particular system based on meditation (Jpn *za-zen*) and pondering of quixotic queries (*koan*)—"What is sound of one hand?" etc.

In China its discipline was reputedly incorporated at famed Shao-lin (Jpn Shorin-ji) Monastery to develop ancestral form of Korean and Japanese martial arts, karate etc. In Japan was found adaptable to all arts and, whether in formal training or informal adaptation, became inseparable from any art calling itself -*do*, Way (see SPORTS, etc). Little of its details of teachings are not found in Western philosophies of art ("to paint tree, become tree"), but West never systematized these ideas. 5 schools evolved in China of which two rooted in Japan: Linji (Rinzai) and Cao-dong (Soto).

Chinese monks brought it to Japan repeatedly 8-12th centuries, but never took root. Under revivalism of late 12th century Kamakura, with Nichiren and others developing popular Buddhism and nation threatened by double danger of decadence and Mongol invasion, local monks Eisai and Dogen travelled to China. They brought back teachings usable in reviving military discipline, and teachers fleeing from Mongols who provided important intelligence both theoretical, tactical, practical to help (thru such as *kyu-do* 'archery-way') rearm debased samurai and develop Kamakura shogunal grand strategy which eventually defeated invasion (see KYUSHU-FUKUOKA). Live fountainhead of zen training continues to be KAMAKURA (see).

Rinzai relies mostly on koan-solving using zazen as unthinking time with koan held in mind till solution suddenly suggests itself, often non-rationally —but not irrationally. Big Bang solution may be *satori*, enlightenment, becoming one with all. Soto stresses meditation, zazen, performed in Yogic 'perfect position', lotus (full=legs entwined, half=one leg pretzeled thru other, insist back straight, chin in, hands in lap). Good posture is stressed more than in any other sitting system.

Promoted in West not so much as religion or even philosophy, but as metaphysics. Its techniques appeal to mystic searchers of other faiths and traditions, who include Christian clergy. Its other-reality reliance on 'nonsense' and 'fool-ness' has great appeal to fans of Gimpel the Fool—likely Jewish bodhisattva in tradition of patriarchs Kanzan-Jitoku.

Recent decades indicate zen future is in America or West in general. Ego-quelling individuality, freedom thru discipline, squat are all too strange to young Japanese. Besides, 'bushi' of late, non-lamented Japanese army proved they couldn't handle it here at all since Meiji times, confusing then— as in local school sports clubs today—discipline with sado-masochism.

BOOKSHELF: Greatest exponent in English is late SUZUKI Daisetsu, 1870-1966— himself not Zen but Nishi Honganji. Brought to New York in 1950 from Chicago by AU Pope to teach at Asia Institute. No students enrolled except for scholarshippers (freebies) and course offering dropped, he gave individual lectures. Columbia picked him up on life-saving retainer. Any Suzuki book fine to start. Ignore Christmas Humphries and his zeny-dime-store trifles, as well as arch(ery) nazi Herrigel.

See INTRODUCTION: LEARNING ABOUT JAPAN p86. For training, zazen see temples: KAMAKURA p223, KYOTO, OKAYAMA p628, FUKUYAMA p641, EIHEIJI p852, etc.

SHINTO

DIVINE-WAY

NATIVE belief system prior to
introduction of Buddhism, with
minor regional variations. Amalgam of
various neolithic beliefs from mountain
worship, earth fertility, fisherman's luck
and safety at sea to worship of sun,
moon, North Star and storm. Many
such original aspects are preserved today
in major shrines, or continuing regional
variations in locals. In short, it has no
overall ideology or church. Thus it is not
legally 'religion', not in eyes of Japanese
law nor our churches—Catholics are free
to enter and respect sanctity of shrines,
Jews or Muslims may worship in own
manner in or at shrine as it is sanctified
ground and there are no idols.

Japanese describe selves as being
religious without religion. Pre-1945 all
Japanese were by law shinto, but free to
practice any religion in addition. Late
1990 head of Shrine Assoc called it "not
religion, but folk custom". Many today
adhere to two faiths, even Christians; as
some reject, especially recently with
resurgent Yasukuni shinto.

With no ideology it has no code of ethic or morality, no good or evil, no
sense of sin. Judgment is made on basis of clean or unclean: cleanliness is
sacred. Thankfully, simplistically, there are no special forms of ritual
cleanliness beyond common-sense 'clean' or clean acts, no way to inadver-
tently step on people's toes—at least as long as your shoes are off.

Object of worship, *kami* (Ainu *kamui*), is translated in English as god,
which in its frequently used English plural (no singular-plural in Japanese)
implies it to be polytheism. Written with ideograph made up of two elements
'indicate' & 'announce'—thus something set aside or above. Sacred objects
are often marked with, or enfolded in, white paper (also *kami* spelled with
different ideograph), and sometimes labeled with still another homonym
meaning 'above'. This latter we believe is key to meaning of original pre-
writing term: similar to our 'lord above', 'heaven above', 'on high'.

Kami is also used for any supernatural spirit, benevolent or malevolent.
Homonyms 'paper'–'deity' lend selves to pun valid to anyone who deals
with officialdom, that 'paper = god' or bureaucracy = priesthood.

Kami are basically heavenly or earthly, former associated with Imperial
family and allied-clans as their progenitors, reside in shrines associated
prewar with State Shinto, modern statist aberration. Latter are earthly gods,
probably heroes and deities of pre-Yamato inhabitants, from this folk shinto
evolved most Meiji period new shinto sects, known collectively as 'new
religions'. Many opposed State Shinto 1930-1945, were persecuted by state.

We do not consider shinto to be polytheistic as commonly labeled, but
pantheistic where everything is part of deity, of total sacredness: thus every
ritually clean object is 'god', each part reflects whole. More holy hologram.

PANTHEON: On High Plain of Heaven 3 deities come to be: Center, Male & Female Forces, in mankind's most surreal creation myth beget 6 generations till in 7th couple Izanagi (m) and Izanami (f) dip their spear in muckworld, create Japan from its dribblings. After much dabbling beget various forces, son Fire causes mother's death. Izanagi, Orpheus-like, visits her in netherworld of Yomi, comes up, bathes, and from his left eye is born Sun Goddess Amaterasu (*see* ISE), from right Moon deity and from nose stormy Susano-o (*see* IZUMO). Men now appear. Amaterasu's grandson Ninigi descends to Central Reed Plain, Japan. One of his 3 sons weds daughter of Sea Goddess to beget (*see* YAMATO) first earthly emperor Jimmu.

PRACTICE is simply matter of occasional visit to one's patron shrine, or pause at any in passing. Perhaps only at outer torii where stand at attention, clasp hands, bow, or just nod, clap. Coins might be tossed into slotted *saisen bako* box, or not. Beyond that, see ISE as pilgrimage for more serious practices. No 'church services', no assemblages (other than *matsuri*). Similar respect to sacred spot, whether straw-banded tree, shrine on department store roof, or other faith's temple. Observing small shrine in corner of large Tokyo building from window across street, Jay noted more stop-&-bow traffic in quarter hour than weekday traffic at St Pat's, New York.

HOUSE OF WORSHIP: *Jinja* or -*gu*, Englished as 'shrine' as aspect of deity is therein enshrined, one does not enter it but worships at. House of worship of Buddhism is *tera* or -*ji*, Englished as 'temple' as one enters to worship in (usually shoes off) tho may contain smaller edifice with sacred object enshrined for worshipping at, also called shrine in English.

Shrine is divided into Inner and Outer, latter in local *jinja* may be just small foyer, or in major shrines separate complex, sometimes apart as with mountain shrines with Outer at foot of hill and Inner on peak, or on island shrines like Miyajima with Outer on mainland, Inner on isle. Simple form resembles Old Testament temple, rather basic to ancient Near East. Torii marks outer limits of approach or any transitional point, often flanked by…

'LION DOGS' on pedestals (ill p.28): *koma-inu* (Korean dog) or *kara-shishi* (Chinese lion) are Taoist origin being yin-yang (Jpn *in-yo*). Female-former is passive-mouth-closed, male active-mouth-open, like *nio* power-lords at Buddhist temple gate (horned-lion palace-temple guardian in Biblical Sumer was *shir-shi*). Also at some temples. Where guardian is fox it is Inari (rice) Shrine, passive one holds in its jaws rolled-scroll *tora-maki*. *Tora* is ancient mystery word implying 'law'—every martial- or esoteric-art has its own *tora-maki*; *maki* is scroll thus 'tora-scroll of ultimate law'. Any ideas?

TORII: Every shrine is fronted by one or more *torii*, written with descriptive ideograph 'bird perch', resembling door frames 冊—most typically Japanese architectural form but also found in certain Hindu sites in India and phonetically perhaps Indo-European in origin, as English 'door', German *tor*. Buddhist temples often have them, too, relics of millennial union in *ryobu-shinto* 'combined Buddhist-Shinto', ended by Meiji nationalist purge.

Two basic styles, whatever material. 'Pure Shinto' is Bauhaus-clean, two uprights topped by overlapping horizontal of similar girth, below which and parallel between uprights is 2nd bar: as giants at Ise or Yasukuni or forests of small red ones at Inari shrines. 'Ryobu-shinto' at simplest has inward-slant to uprights, which often taper, topped by complex crossbar with upturned ends, lower bar protrudes thru uprights, vertical plaque in center links crossbars: as giant at Heian Shrine Kyoto, or even more ornate with extra supports as most famous torii in water at Miyajima (illustrated page1).

Torii may be of wood, shaped or natural, stone, even metal or, new giants are concrete. Most are natural, some painted vermilion. Thru final torii we enter inner shrine, usually gravel-surrounded, often also fenced, occasionally closed off. Structure is standard Japanese on elevated platform, usually all wood, some newer are ferro-concrete. Fat rope, usually braided cloth, will hang in middle—grab with both hands and shake to ring bells or rap gong, to call attention to self. Now bow, clap, drop some coins in box (no free lunch). To go on (if no barrier), doff shoes.

There will be small altar beyond, perhaps with tray-stands with offerings in front, as elaborate as shrine is large, and small neighborhood shrine may just have tall house-shaped box fronted by plate with few grains of rice in it. In or before altar is often wooden stand with zig-zags of folded paper, *gohei*, representing deity. If priest is present (in white robe usually with tall black horsehair hat, in black lacquer clogs if on ground) he may pick up large similar one and wave it with snap over your head—slight bow please, you are being purified.

Gohei

If altar does not hold gohei, there may be mirror of polished metal—possible element of self-determinism. Said to be sacred play on words as mirror-*kagami* is made up of syllables *ka* and *–k(g)ami*, 'self' and 'deity'—thus in seeking god one must look within oneself.

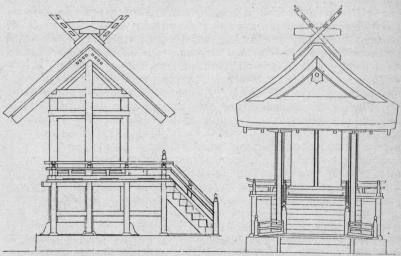

Myojin, southern roof style, female   Izumo Shrine, northern style, male

Roof of shrine tells us if resident kami male or female: *chigi* (horn-like cross-boards extending above roof at both ends) indicate if oblique-cut end is flat edge up female tenant (L above); *chigi* point upwards shows masculine (R above). Frequent exceptions to this, as at most shrines at Ise, indicate old evictions, probable cultural revolutions, invasion.

Roof and entry also tell us which of two main streams of shinto we are dealing with: At presumably older from south we approach side with entry under shade of eaves as in equatorial architecture (*see* above L). Entry end-on under 'A' of roof line as protecting from snow indicates northern stream from Asian mainland, as in Izumo (above R) and Nara's Asuka.

SACRED SCRIPTURE is absent in shinto. Annals *Kojiki* and *Nihongi* are national, rather than sectarian, collections of legends as history to establish identity. Prince-regent Shotoku Taishi may have tried to compose national sacrament in his lost books, but this is highly conjectural.

Shamanism is important in shinto from earliest times: drums and masks excavated from Jomon era neolithic sites indicate antiquity. Shaman usually female (as today): high priestess of Ise Grand Shrine is imperial princess. Shrine maidens also legacy of this tradition: name *miko* derives from Korean for shaman. Significantly, new religions prove their basis in antique feminism as all founded by charismatic women who, like modern messiahs or Old Testament prophets, attract followers by their 'possession' by deity; often proclaim monotheism, promoting faith to Creator-god who created universe, mankind and lesser deities-cum-spirits. Succession should run mother-daughter, but many have been usurped by men.

Art is Mother of Religion is strong aesthetic in folk- (as opposed to imperial- or late state-) shinto. Sacred reality is reflected in beauty, which man's mission is to create and preserve. Our path to enlightenment lay in practice and appreciation of art. These religions—Oomoto near Kyoto (p.456), MOA at fabulous Atami museum (p.244), Shinji Shumeikai's Sacred Garden in Shiga, P[erfect] L[iberty] of Osaka—support traditional fine and martial arts, noh, tea, international art exchange. Even classic shrine shinto uses dance as main rite of worship in *matsuri*–festival around music-dance offerings, general fun (*see* area DATEBOOKS). Architecturally stage-in-round (roofed except where for bugaku as at Miyajima, Tennoji, where balustraded open platform center front of worship hall) and covered painting-offering gallery are basic to shrine compound. Aesthetic of nature-adoration (more apparent than in most new 'Art-is...' sects) is attributable to fact that original shrine, *yashiro*, was not structure but open area in woods left untouched but for cleaning or care. Like similar primeval European sacred glade.

There is no established church, tho 19th century forms of some of oldest folk aspects (Oomoto, Tenri, etc) as well as Meiji era sects that rose under new 19th century nationalism and 20th century fascism (Yasukuni–p.1147– and Go-koku shrines to military dead) took on establishment organization and trappings. Latter, state-supported, exercised authoritarian exclusivity to impose themselves on others with brutal if infantile naivety.

Shinto revival of Meiji Restoration culminated religio-nationalist movement growing thru entire Edo era—never dead since import of 'foreign' Buddhism—promoting idea of return to 'original purity' under imperial paternalism. Espouse innate superiority of *kokutai*—unique national polity of linguistic-ethnic homogeneity first formed to repel foreign invasion. But it succumbed to Japanese practicality in recognizing impossibility to stand up to West and converted to absorbing usable 'material aspects' of West to graft onto 'spiritual values of East'. In this same way for over millennium shinto had absorbed Buddhist, (perhaps Zoroastrian), Taoist, Confucian elements till new State-Imperial Shinto bore little resemblance to agriculture-based original—and often conflicted, in earliest times as now.

Said to be 800-myriads (8,000,000) shrines in country, each with its own kami, mostly *uji-gami*—genus locii, spirit of that locale. Largest number are probably Inari shrines to rice-deity fox, easily spotted by entry arbor of multiple red torii. Not organized sect, biggest is in Fushimi (we visit on p.464). Largest sect organized, however loosely, is probably Hachiman god of scythe and sword, whom we visit at Kamakura (p.216), tho main shrine is Usa (p.771) Kyushu. Largest actively organized sect is Izumo (p.821), one of two Taisha or Grand Shrines, dedicated to concurrent earth-storm god.

Central national shrine is Ise (p.313) twin shrines to rice and sun goddesses, latter ancestral to imperial family. Christian prime minister HATOYAMA Ichiro reinstituted prewar custom of PM 'report' to goddess on his installment—which did not create furor like 1987-8 PM and cabinet 'worshipping' at militarist-associated Yasukuni Shrine in Tokyo (judged illegal '91).

Primordial Ise is not laden with political baggage nor associations with repression as is modern Yasukuni. For reputed "uniquely sensitive" polity like this, latter is uniquely insensitive, acting in bad taste, and internationally self-destructive. (We visit all, with further details on worship etc, in ISE).

Dowser or water-witch, try your pendulum or rod for power points.

ANCESTOR WORSHIP—honoring one's father, mother, antecedents—associated with shinto is adaptation in recent centuries from Confucianism. Dead are deities, or one with deity, but ritual of death, funeral, is unclean and so left for Buddhism to tend to. There are shinto funerary rites, used especially for Imperial family members but rarely for others. Until Meiji's father even emperors were cremated in Buddhist rite. Emperor worship is aspect of family worship as 'father of nation' developed under Meiji into part of German-like military machine-cum-cult.

Great Iwakura Mission of 50 intellectuals and leaders traveled world 1871-73 (under truce with opposition not to upset things in their absence), interviewing world leaders and thinkers to design this new national polity. Concluded to forego military expansion, concentrate on domestic production —which when announced ticked off revolt of samurai under SAIGO Takamori of Kyushu, tragically defeated. Expansionism resumed when nation thought itself sufficiently strong generation later. English advised constitutional monarchy, rule of parliament. But Prussia and Russia impressed more: former for efficiency and standard of living, latter for glorious Court pomp. Bismarck advised retaining god-emperor philosophy (appealed to his Cæsar-vision of Kaiser?) with emperor at top of all systems military and political as unifying principle. England, US, France, Prussia impressed best as role models, Russia least. But St Petersburg Tsarist Court so dazzled YAMAGATA Aritomo, another leader who made similar journey, that its flamboyant and supercilious court system right down to its gilt brass buttons was adopted, rather than originally preferred Court of St James—probably most tragic error of Meiji Restoration.

Emperor now at last becomes that god on earth early strategists had toyed with 12 centuries earlier when Shotoku Taishi changed term for emperor from Dai-O, 'great king', to Tenno, 'heavenly ruler'.

Trappings for aberration so intimately associated as shintoism, that of Emperor Worship, were developed. Yasukuni Shrine was built in 1879 in its present location, with no native precedent, to enshrine militant souls who had died for HIM's personal sake since first anti-shogunal revolts of 1853. To date 2,460,000 souls have been interred, at least symbolically. But only military dead—civilians are not Yasukuni gods, even air-raid or A-bomb dead. Meiji's grandson, Hirohito-Showa, in 1945 renounced deity status to SCAP MacArthur: "Never have I considered myself sacred or in any way special". His going on radio at New Year, moving among people, saved imperial institution every bit as much as did Allied agreement to retain system by not indicting HIM as war criminal.

First time any but Court insiders ever heard his voice was broadcast of Imperial Rescript on Surrender August 15, 1945 (*see* opening TOKYO–IMPERIAL PALACE, p.1139). No one questioned high voice speaking hard-to-follow Imperial dialect was his. With rare exception, entire nation complied as one.

TIPS ON TOURING TEMPLES AND SHRINES

EXCEPT for few older temples with Chinese style flagstone floors where shoes may be worn, those on wooden platforms call for slipping off shoes, leave there or in nearby box, proceed in stocking feet—use slippers if there, pass up if size problem. In winter we carry ski-sox or snuggies of some sort—not slippers as they must be removed on tatami-mats.

No sacrilege in Buddhism or shinto, just good or bad manners. Show respect to others' beliefs in whatever way comfortable to you. Head cover neither prescribed nor proscribed. Follow lead of host or that of crowd. Don't stand out or speak loudly.

Photos in local temple are usually OK, even flash, annoying as it is (refrain, show restraint), but most *fee-charging temples ban photos* for no known reason, *even most public museums*. Always good art-print postcards available, usually in sets: but probably not of what you wanted. So if no one around sneak off shot—if caught feign innocence, apologize profusely-sincerely. Ban is understandable as Japanese tourists will stand in front of anything and pose for souvenir shot — even you, usually fingers raised in 'victory-mudra'. European, US museums allow photography but restrict flash, tripods for obvious reasons.

Flashlight: must for art-lovers, much best poorly under- to totally un-illuminated.

Many sects, but no basic difference that forbids visit of believer to another temple. Older Japanese-American temples stateside mostly Jodo Shinshu with Zen and Nichiren gaining, Shingon and most other sects represented. Main temple function today funerary-memorial.

Weddings usually in shinto shrine, or Christian church that needs fee, preferably one with stained glass and/or tall steeple like in our tourist brochures, blond preacher preferred. Sole legal troth is licence fee-registry at city hall.

Worship is highly personal, individual, usually merely visit to altar; clasp hands, bow prayer, sometimes just stand outside. Buddhist equivalent of Sabbath sermon and song rare, but English dailies carry notices of English-Buddhist sermons, meditations.

At altar or internal shrine simple bow or nod of head will suffice, tho handclasp of any sort is highly appreciated. Incense or candle may be bought honor system. Jesuit priests we know offer memorials according to their own rite. If admission not charged, cash offering is in order according to your conscience or aesthetic appeal of temple based on what you know big places 'charge'. Such, ¥10 OK, toss noisily into slotted-box for maintenance—*no poor box*.

Funeral condolence money, only crisp new bills, in special banded-envelope available stationers, sign, hand to treasurer at table outside—shares cost of funeral among deceased's friends. You get small envelope: before entering home or hotel room open, toss contents, salt, over shoulder in purification. Sit on floor at rite cross-legged, on heels, however is comfortable—try not to look pained as many occidentals seem when on floor other than at some party.

Most temples & shrines sell *omikuji*-lucky fortune slips ¥100 or ¥50, usually thru attendant, simple slot machine, or little robot shrine maids; out-of-way temples have honor system. Look for octagonal tall box like 2-quart milk container, hole on flat top near edge. Look for attendant to pay or box to drop coin in. Pick up, turn over, shake upside down to get bamboo rod to pop out hole. Stick has Japanese number, someone will undoubtedly read for you, get relevant fortune slip: size of large admission ticket, with sketch, your number; key—L to R:

大吉、吉、小吉、凶

BIG LUCK - LUCK - SMALL LUCK - BAD LUCK

True custom: keep good, fold poor longway, knot on tree with others to have winds blow away bad luck. Nowadays Japanese dispose of all that way. Similar custom OT, Islam.

Talismans-*Omamori* at temple desk for traffic safety, fire prevention, easy birth, good business, etc; nice souvenir. Some are works of art priced accordingly, some folk art, some trinketry. Zen derides such 'superstition', sells most of any sect. Fun, if rare, not sacrilege, are at fertility shrines (p.350).

Most temples, tourist sites, have postcard-size rubber stamp with which you stamp diary, pilgrim pad, T-shirt, anywhere.

Roof tiles sold at temples—inscribe in eternal sumi-ink your, loved one's names for roof at next repair: Daibutsu sold them 20 years before Great Showa Repair, still is for lesser out-buildings. Freely inscribe even your own religious symbol or message: Buddhism is open-minded. Hopefully we are too. Buddha loves you, too, yes he does as does Inro-bosatsu, Moses-bosatsu—and in China there *is* Mohammad-bosatsu.

' THE JAPANESE AND THE JEWS '

—vernacular best-seller in early '70s (English edition Weatherhill), purportedly by mystery Jewish scholar of Japan, 'Ben Daisan'—actually written by Japanese with rather good knowledge of Judaism. Noted many cultural similarities, parallels between two education-driven peoples. For all its faults created good will, healthy curiosity in Japan for Jews.

In World War II 15,000 Jews from Riga, Estonia, were saved by transit visas for Japan (consul who issued them is enshrined in Israel among Noble Men). Most crossed USSR to Kobe, relocated to Shanghai, protected from Japan's nazi ally's insistence on applying 'final solution'. Some mistreatment occurred, yet less than native Japanese felt at hands of their own police. Most emigrated postwar to Israel & USA. (*Fugu Plan* by Rabbi Tokayer)

Japanese interest in Jewish affairs goes back to Paul Yoshiro SAEKI, D.Litt OBE. Japan's oldest Christian at death 1967 at 95, conversion at 16 necessitated sneaking away from home in middle of night to avoid persecution. Became eminent scholar of Roman Law, Central Asia Nestorian Christians; postwar mayor (until age 88) of Sumi's ancestral town near Hiroshima. He wrote pre-1930 of his ideas on Lost Tribes of Israel, that Jews migrated east thru China to Korea and Japan—their antiquity in China well-documented. Similarity in layout of ancient Jewish temple as rebuilt in China, into inner- and outer-like Shinto-shrine; biblical description of shoulder-carried 'Ark of the Lord' sounds like festival *mikoshi*; odd headband worn by *yamabushi* resembles phylacteries; alike names of pre-Buddhist religious personages; ancient finding of infant prince in river reeds, etc. Before he developed his thesis it was plagiarized in wild book claiming earlier pre-Yamato emperors were Jewish. This threw whole idea into scholarly disrepute and set back Near-Far East intercultural studies by 50 years. But it could not erase Near Eastern elements from early Far East culture. 1952 Jay visited Shosoin Repository in Nara (*see*)—commenting on its West Asian 'feel', director advised him to hush up. NOGUCHI Yone, sculptor Isamu's poet-father, made similar comments prewar, was not taken seriously.

Late 1950s Japanese began archaeology in Iran and Iraq. TV touted West Asian origins of much Japan culture. 'Silk Road boom' took off in books, music, art, TV. Emperor's uncle HIH Prince MIKASA, who had studied Jewish History, toured Iran-Iraq excavations, wrote book of his observations—Jay reviewed it, noting author's photo with prominent nose, in full bedouin robes "looked like some less well-fed Saudi prince". HIH became doyen of Mid East Studies, Vice Patron of Asia Institute in Iran (of which Jay was deputy director), his Society for Near Eastern Studies in Japan includes every opinion, as scholarship should—tho Mid East specialists in Japan are notably anti-Jewish, not just anti-Zion. Spring '87 in Kobe he visited mosque, Jaina temple, and synagogue Passover service where he kissed his fingers that touched Torah. 1988 he was nominated for Doctor of Humane Letters from Yeshiva University for "Advancement of Hebraic culture...and scholarly interests in Middle Eastern culture", but could not attend due emperor's illness.

His fairness is not emulated here. Japan accepts Arab boycott, sells to Israel thru third countries, bans JAL to Israel, El Al here (contrast Tehran airport under neutral Shah with El Al parked with Saudi, Jordan planes). 1987 announced Jerusalem Museum exhibit at Tokyo National Museum, till Arabs pressed museum to replace with Egypt show.

In mid '80s new viper: *han-Yudaya* anti-Jewish books. Best sellers by 'Prof' UNNO, so-called Christian scholar: bilious variations on *Understand Jews–Understand World* rehash *Protocols of the Elders of Zion*, antique Czarist forgery about Jewish plot to rule world, used by nazis, now by Iranian fanatics in London, from whom venom probably entered.

FUJITA Den, prexy of McDonald Japan franchise, touted as "exemplary success of US business in Japan", often pens Jew-bait diatribes, calls dirty business "Jew business". Recently announced hatred of all foreigners, Americans, most things US (burgers too?). In summer '87 he published newest paperback venom *Jewish Way of Money-making Horn-blowing* with cover 'typical' voracious business-Jew—rusty complexion, thin sandy hair, blond brows over steel-blue eyes and sneering squint holding gold monocle! Talk about mixed metaphors. Thus, in Japan we forego Macs—after 'monocle' came out, blond Jay went to US, did without usual homeland Mac there, too. Readers who think as we and who must have burger have A&W for quicky, burgeoning but not inferior local chains, like **Mos Burger**, and in Kobe, **Attic** whose burger platter better than Kobe steak.

Fiddler on the Roof in Japanese broke all modern theater run records—Japanese can relate to family-rooted tradition. Worth billion Big Macs here, kosher or non.

*Were works of art placed in a directly human context in
popular esteem, they would have much wider appeal
than they can have when pigeon-hole theories of art
win general acceptance.* —John Dewey, *Art as Experience*

ART

OCCIDENTAL AESTHETIC evolved from Greek, essentially based on
geometry and prose literature. Principal plastic art in Greece was sculpture,
formed by sketching geometric design on slab of stone and then chiseling
away to form figure. Literature in Greece was prose—scientific observation,
chipping away at observed reality to form new realities; or literary observation cutting away observed situations for analysis. Poetry was rare.
Pottery was formal in profile derived of lathe-turned alabaster shapes, even
its decoration was mainly resist-painted in style where not actually so. All
'subtractive', creating by taking away.

Our observation is that Japan's art differs essentially: it is more algebraic,
poetic. This is no simple matter of Orient vs Occident. Jay's teacher Dr John
Shapley who expounded this idea, used it to differentiate geometric-prosaic
Greece from algebraic-poetic Persia, and he lined up Egypt with Greece as
being geometric (so much of Greek math and science is actually Egyptian,
Pythagoras studied in Egypt). We would suggest that China in this way resembles Classical Greece, Japan resembles Persia.

Sculpture in earliest prehistoric Japan was in clay, adding and building
up form. Wooden sculpture was introduced with Buddhism from China
where wood played part of Greek stone to be cut down to final form—
which technique was short-lived here—never replaced older additive technique of dry lacquer (weaving skeleton of bamboo strips adding on clay-
lacquer paste to be molded); was itself replaced by wood joinery wherein
small carved blocks of wood are pieced together like Lego.

Pottery in China was even more formal than Greece, based mainly on
carved wood or hammered metal prototypes, quickly developing into industry of mass production, each small step performed by one specialist, each
repetitive step prosaically analyzed in minute detail, every technical non-
essential chipped away. In Japan free-form pottery is preferred as 'art'—
created by single craftsman, from initial kneading of clay to its forming,
glazing and loading into kiln. Here even use of potter's wheel defers to
more 'primitive' building-by-hand from coils of clay on tournet.

Where Greek and Chinese excelled at philosophical analysis, Japan ex-
udes asymmetrically rhythmic syllables emulating frog plopping into still
water. Japan's early literature is not analytical or researched history such as
both Greece and China raised from art to science. It is spiritual-poetic fable
(*Kojiki, Nihon-shoki*) retold more as art, and one almost as antique anthology of short poems, *Manyoshu*. In Greece and China history is matter of
record: in Japan it is nostalgic memorialization in poetry, even by emperors.
Modern publishers grind out amateur and professional 17-syllable *haiku* and
35-syllable *tanka* journals like comic books.

Greek theater was drama, heavily judgmental, analytical. Japanese stage
is dance, poetically 'descriptive', emotional, impressionistic. All her stage
forms evolve from dance, are built on it, any scripts are poetic. Even sport
is dance, its excuses 'poetic'–"We lost 36-0 but won spiritual victory".

In **cuisine**, Europe banquet starts with carving side of beef, while Japan
kaiseki feast is accumulation of dozen or more small dishes to pick at.

Top art, artists, are all protected by designation as 'National Treasure' or 'Important Cultural Asset', abbreviated NT and ICA. Live artist may be hailed 'Intangible Cultural Asset' alias 'Living National Treasure'.

SCULPTURE of primitive sort was known pre-Sinification, pre-Buddhism. *Dogu,* shamanistic idols of fired clay, look like bean-eyed Martians, from late Jomon era, late BC. Grave goods from great tumuli include funereal proxy figures of men and horses in low-fired clay; these *haniwa* are more potter's art than sculptor's. In 1988 it was discovered that great tombs at one time also included simple wooden carved planks, rather than sculpture, probably talismanic. Mainland Buddhists introduced cast-bronze, dry-lacquer and carved-wood icon sculpture, longtime high arts in Korea and China. For iconography of Buddhism *see* preceding chapter.

Despite introduction from Korea of such masterpieces of solid wood sculpture as Miroku in Koryuji, KYOTO, Japanese—true to aesthetic we note above—preferred cast-bronze (based on modeled-clay core) and dry lacquer, both additive. TORI-Busshi (latter title = 'Buddhist image-maker') grandson of Chinese immigrant, cast bronze masterpieces ca603-23: Daibutsu of Asuka-dera (603, head only remains), Shaka Trinity in Horyuji (623–both *see*).

TO SEE ABOVE: for haniwa archaeological research center at KASHIHARA (p.345), and for icons Nara's older outer temples ASUKA-DERA (p.349), HORYUJI (p.357), YAKUSHIJI (p.365), then city itself (p.371–) with fabulous sculpture museum of KOFUKUJI treasure hall and of course GREAT BUDDHA OF TODAIJI. Stone sculpture definitely minor art here, unlike great caves of China and India, even Korea. Some folk-lithics can be seen in hills above Nara park on pleasant hike (p.375), minor modern folk version in Yufu-in Caves OFUNA (p.212) near Yokohama.

Auguste Rodin was major influence in modern sculpture (cast of his *Thinker* fronts Kyoto City Hall), his views on art translated 1915-20— encouraged individual expression.

Buddhist icons sole major traditional sculpture. Minor work is decorative like netsuke, ivories, seals, dolls, sword and building accessories are all *horimono*, 'carved and engraved objects' according to *Encyclopedia of Japan* (tho all but dolls fit this description, and are additive like pottery). Netsuke are true sculpture, but totally subtractive, and in their nit-picking miniaturization and bourgeois use are epitome of Edo-Tokugawa feudal art. Sword fittings: *tsuba*-sword guards and *menuki*-hilt decorations (conceal rivets and enhance nonslip grip) are also masterworks of sculpture, but combine additive (they are cast in iron, additive) then enhanced with carving (subtractive) and inlay (additive). Best public collections of these are overseas, especially USA, some fabulous, but most minor castle museums here have some; curio shops usually have some of fair quality for sale. Dolls best seen in Kyoto shops, especially along Shijo-dori St, or in far western Hakata-Fukuoka (p.701).

PAINTING, purely additive in nature, was also introduced from mainland, with no known graphic art here premain migrations other than perhaps facial tattooing, and early in migration period geometric patterns on some Kyushu tomb walls. Earliest extant examples are door panels on Tamamushi Shrine in HORYUJI treasure house (*see* p363) mid-7 cent, and nearby murals in TAKAMATSU TOMB, ca700, in contemporary Korean-style based on century older Sui Chinese. From earliest times thru today painting is illustrative of balanced dichotomy between imported and native culture as perhaps no other art. Next come murals on plaster walls of HORYUJI Kondo ca 670, almost destroyed in fire 1949. These are fully internationalized T'ang-Buddhist paintings mixing styles of Pre-Islamic Persia, Central Asia,

India and China. From this first example on, murals (including pillar and ceiling decoration) in Japan are exclusively Buddhist in subject.

Painting on *fusuma* sliding wall panels or doors come under screen painting. *Byobu*, folding screens, originated in China 300BC, introduced to Japan from Korea 7 cent. Over 100 stored in SHOSOIN, 752AD (*see*). This became quintessential Japanese form as bulky mainland wooden-framed panels were modified here to lightweight papered honeycomb lattice construction allowing wide single painting surface where desired, as still today —easily hefted even when sextet of 90x180cm (3x6ft) panels. Painting styles on byobu and fusuma have been limited mostly to secular subjects intended mostly for residential use. Byobu come in 2-, 4- or 6-panels, barely meter (yard) tall to over double, and 6-panels customarily come in pairs (tho often sold singly, as who has enough room?). Subjects range from sweeping landscapes in monochrome or lightly tinted or full brazen colors, to brilliant gardenscapes, to fantastically detailed genre paintings, usually colored.

Best collection of top byobu probably Boston Museum, but most traditional art museums and all great mansions visited in Japan have some. Temples abound in superb fusuma paintings—most subjects cover 'wall' of 4, 6 or 8 panels, others run around most or all of one room and some, as in MT KOYA MONASTERY p.397, encompass several rooms. Subject may be single tree, landscape or illustration of ethical tale, either monochrome sumi ink or polychrome. Byobu, both antique and modern reproduction, are available in antiquarians. Noted for fine screens, and expensive as they deserve to be, is dealer David Kidd in KYOTO (*see* p.544).

Scroll-mounted paintings are most common. 7-8th century scrolls were Chinese narrative type, *e-maki-mono* rolling out on horizontal to tell story in series, text running below pictures like comic book in Chinese style, *kara-e*. Then by 12th cent text disappeared, or came in intermediate sections. Acme was reached in early 12th cent *Genji Monogatari Emaki* pictorial rendition of great 11th cent novel. Contrasting with these *onna-e* feminine style scrolls, are masculine *otoko-e* as we find on Osaka's Mt Shigi (p.568) in its *Legends* scroll triptych. These culminated late 13th cent in battle scrolls for which artist and reporter went into battle to report it in support of daimyo-lord's claim for recompense and in these we have firsthand account of Mongol invasion picturing first use outside of China of gunpowder-powered weapon including interview with samurai who survived grenade blast.·

These two feminine and masculine scroll styles became further popularized and eventually evolve into mass art of 17th century ukiyoe vivid polychrome paintings and woodblock prints (below).

Mongol aggression caused another wave of influence from China as Zen priests and intellectuals fled to Japan to introduce strong wave of Sung influence. One aspect was *suiboku*, sumi ink painting. Chinese paintings of this era are treated as Japanese preserved as national treasures—in effect naturalized. It was used, as above, for fusuma and also on hanging scrolls, with vertical composition usually on paper, sometimes silk (paper lasts longer) mounted on vertical scroll matted in silk brocade. As Zen became broader-based in Ashikaga era when shogunal capital moved back to Kyoto, ink painting became secularized into quintessential Japanese style. Somber mountainscapes and humorous zen 'cartoons' predominate, so interlocked with calligraphy that 'draw' and 'write' are same word.

Greatest name of this era and style is Sesshu (1420-1506), best seen in Kyoto National Museum and new Okayama Prefectural Art Museum (p.627) which has constantly rotating display of works by native sons including him and staggering array of other local greats.

In Ashikaga era (1335-1573) art and aesthetics evolved into what we recognize now as peculiarly Japanese classicism. Development of national interior styles (tokonoma and tatami, etc) encompassed display of art wares and development of minor arts like *chado* tea-way or *ikebana* flower arrangement. Painting, both screen or hanging scroll, still fell into original Chinese divisions of figure painting, landscape and birds-and-flowers.

Perspective in all these paintings is different than in West where composition is centripetal: eye falls anywhere on edge and is drawn to center and main theme. Here eye falls on edge to be coaxed to stroll thru landscape as if walking thru actual site—in fusuma falling to side to meander across, in vertical hanging scroll usually starting bottom corner meandering upward.

Buddhist subjects, in figure painting, commonly seen include *nehan-e* or earthly death of Buddha, his passing from this incarnation (*see* BUDDHISM). *Raigozu* is Amida Buddha's descent from paradise with entourage to receive deceased believer's soul, older ones in gold-applied cut gold or colors, also on temple walls, notably most beautifully on BYODOIN of Uji, Kyoto (1053). Then there are countless icons of various buddhas and attributes from Mary-like Kannon 'Goddess of mercy' to ferocious Fudo, singly and in trinities. Also portraits of saints and great teachers. All are popular in modern curio shops, as in Kyoto's Furumonzen antiquarian street, or still made as modern decoration.

Great names Kano, Tosa, Korin, Rimpa stand out. KANO dynasty of master painters starting with Masanobu (1434-1530) from village of Kano in Shizuoka, migrated to Kyoto to study Sung-style painting favored by Ashikaga shoguns. Established first secular school of Japanese art which dominated painting for 250 years. Son Motonobu (1476-1559) established studio system, assuring dynastic professionalism and setting up its political base, prototype for other art schools in all disciplines.

Other great names, not necessarily blood descendants but including those adopted for their ability: Eitoku (1543-90), Sanraku (1559-1635), Sansetsu (1588-1651), Tan'yu (1602-74). There were dozens of others, working in ink and colors, on vertical hanging and horizontal hand scrolls, screens, fusuma panels, fans, and even walls–of which latter none survive. We come across their work in numerous temples, palaces and museums.

TOSA: school of Yamato-e, or Japanese-style painters, mostly on courtly themes, classical literature. Scrolls of *Genji Monogatari* are Tosa-style. Traces lineage to 11th century Fujiwara artists resisting Chinese incursions. But in Edo period saw much interinfluence with stronger Kano school. 16-17th cent turned out brightly illustrated manuscript books *Nara-ehon* which greatly influenced rise of ukiyoe and cheap story books. No outstanding names but great corpus of good work.

Ogata KORIN (1658-1716) rich playboy dilettante, trained in Kano-style, took up painting seriously to survive bankruptcy. Painted some of Japan's greatest and most original byobu, best in MOA museum, Atami.

RIMPA, style of painting rich assemblages of flowers, all face-on and compositionally flat. Developed 1600 by SOTATSU, contemporary KO'ETSU, revived 18th century by Korin (and since renamed after him *Rin*, from Ko*rin* plus *ha*, style), again century later by SAKAI Hoitsu, last great Kano master. Declared in 1905 by OKAKURA Kakuzo "impressionism of Japan". Revived again by OHARA Houn in 1980s adapted to grand ikebana style.

WOODBLOCK PRINTS, *ukiyoe* 'floating world pictures'. Genre painting evolved out of story-scrolls and figure painting (above) into tall hanging scrolls often of popular beauties (*bijin-ga*), and meticulously detailed scenes of famous places, festivals on gold screens in Kyoto, of type shown nites of July 14-16 before Gion Festival at downtown open houses in Kyoto today. Pictures became more popular with fast-rising urban bourgeois. Then using woodblock print technology that came from China in 7 cent to print Buddhist texts and votive pictures in simple outline popular with pilgrims, led to printing popular literary texts, novellas, some of which included illustration. Kyushu edition of *Ise Monogatari* in 1608 led to mass-produced editions of 'paperbacks'. Then popular single-sheet pictures in simple line emulating bold Zen brush strokes, 1660. Soon *beni* red was brushed in by hand, then by second block 1745 later up to 6 colors *(benizuri)*, and full colors *nishiki-e* 1764. This became major art form.

Woodblock print involved four parties. #1 printer-publisher financed, oversaw and distributed what he contracted #2 artist to draw. Artist drew single line drawing on fine paper, which #3 carver pasted face down onto cherry block and carved away undrawn areas leaving raised impression— like modern printing plate not engraving. Several impressions were made and original artist now prepared one with color in or color notes for block maker to prepare color blocks. Next, #4 printer inked blocks in order of color lightness usually, or of dominance, with vegetable base ink, placing dampened paper face down and rubbing back with flat *baren*-pad to force paper against block. This was repeated for each block or color, sometimes same color block used more than once with different intensity of inking to attain special effects. At times dry block was used to impress texture pattern. Powdered mica or metallic dust might be added. Using more than 6 colors was technique for so-called *nishiki-e* or brocade print. Edition sizes are not recorded, but probably ran 100-200. Center of production was Edo-Tokyo, more and more so, but also some in Osaka and Kyoto, later Nagasaki and Yokohama schools arose. Reprints with same blocks were common. At times publisher or artist changed color details so great prints are known in different editions. Blocks were often recarved smaller or larger for new editions. Popular mounted on scrolls as wall hangings, especially 1690s— on. From 1720s prints freed themselves of subservience to schools of painting and led in artistic innovation.

Optimum numbers of blocks and separate impressions realized in early 1950s by French artist in Japan, Paul Jacoulet, using traditional carver and printer. His two New Year prints of Shimabara geisha incorporate 365 and 366 pulls respectfully.

Great names were all in Edo era (family name first, art-name SMALL CAPITALS): Hishikawa MORONOBU, first artist known by name, black ink prints hand-colored, 1660s-70s. Suzuki HARUNOBU developed first full-color style 1764; Torii KIYONOBU I & Torii KIYOMASA I, Torii-school firsts led in field of kabuki prints and posters, 1690s–on; Torii KIYONAGA 1780s, long-bodied svelte beauties and scenes in European geometric perspective adapted from imported Dutch engravings; UTAMARO beauties against mica and textured backgrounds, most notable of *nishiki-e* artists; Utagawa TOYOKUNI, similar; SHARAKU, fl-1794, and his marvelously caricatured *nishiki* actor prints which infuriated his subjects, in at last looking like them instead of being drawn from imagination and simply labeled; Ando HIROSHIGE, 1797-1858, one of greatest of landscape artists especially noted for his travel albums especially his 1834 *53 Stages of Tokaido Highway*—down which we follow (p.201–). And greatest of all, one of mankind's superlative artists, superb landscapist, its greatest cartoonist, student of all classical schools of painting and Dutch engravings, HOKUSAI, 1760-1849, known by many art names but in his 80s self-branded 'Old man mad with art'.

See, my woodblock printers can print anything!

EROTICA, officially then as often now 'pornography', early on became major subject. Not so much single prints, but sex manuals, 'bridal books'. These *shunga* 'springtime pictures', or *iro-e*, 'color' pictures as opposed to our term 'off-color'—little known outside of Japan—were done by all known print artists except Hiroshige and Sharaku (perhaps latter excepted only because his real identity is unknown as he flourished only 10 months in 1794). They are exquisite as art, seeming to have inspired most artists to their best work—Hokusai is his most hilariously ribald. 'Censored' editions exist wherein undress is concealed by frame of window thru which we surreptitiously observe scene, so that action is suggested only by flow of clothes or bedding—full nudes rare and most unnatural—and enraptured facial expressions, perhaps sole incursion of personal individualism into Japanese painting aside from Sharaku's caricatures.

Sosaku-hanga: in modern prints, still on woodblocks, wherein designer-artist-carver-printer are one person as in most Occidental woodblock prints.

Prints best seen in TOKYO: **Riccar Art Museum** behind Imperial Hotel across tracks. Also for buying, opp rear of Imperial Hotel at **Sakai**; or in Kanda at **Ohya Shobo**; top name moderns at **Tolman Collection**, appt ☎434-1300. KYOTO: Nishimura/Nishiharu, Sanjo-dori; on Furumonzen **Red Lantern**, modern prints; and 2 blocks E at **Yamada Gallery** for originals, newer editions, top selection moderns.

CALLIGRAPHY in most of Asia is major art form, its practice acme of intellectual achievement. Basic strokes, its 'graphic alphabet', are basic also to sumi ink painting. It is ultimate additive art in that, tho nothing further may be added once strokes are completed, no corrections, 'adding' process takes place mentally before first stroke is committed. Like tea and dance, (it is form of dance thru brushwork) it is martial art in that it is *ki*-projecting exercise—in modern terms alpha (brain wave) generating exercise.

CERAMICS, ultimate additive art, is country's premier art today. Potters rate like major oil painters in West, command similar star billing and prices.

Historically perhaps oldest pottery, some wares are dated by thermo-luminescence 10,000 years old. Artistic wares based on *jo-mon*, 'rope-pattern', followed by painted pottery in late-arriving upper-neolithic 300BC.

From then on art is marked by series of cultural invasions mostly from Korea, some from China, even Persia, these mostly thru Korea. Major influx from Hideyoshi's invasion of Korea 1589, when Tycoon and several daimyo brought back masses of potters to set up new kilns, hi-tech of its time. We visit these, mostly in KYUSHU: Arita (a.k.a. Imari), Karatsu etc. But kilns of Nagoya area TAJIMI and SETO (which gave Japan term *seto-mono*, Seto-ware, meaning what we call Chinaware) mostly Korean started. Other kilns started subsequently by migrants from these original Korean kilns, like Kutani at KANAZAWA on Japan Sea Coast.

20th century *mingei* movement, instigated by Crafts movement in Europe and US, was inspired by rediscovery of Korean handicrafts and pottery.

But Japan's appreciation of ceramic art, thru its importance in arts of tea, flower and aesthetic of dinner-table setting, is without equal elsewhere.

Terminology of types of ceramic differs with producing culture. Persians call (literal translation) earthenware that made of river earth clay even if fired at near-porcelain temperatures, 1150°C, but not porcelain material or result; stoneware is made of ground stone; *chini* is China-like stoneware, more descriptive of style. Japanese earthenware, *doki*, is low-fire, 700-900°C, of earthen clay and usually glazed (coated with glass material). *Han-jiki*, half-porcelain, is harder silicate (ground stone + earth-clay) fired at higher temperatures, glazed (usually in second firing) and giving off good clink when tapped, but opaque to light. *Ji-ki*, porcelain (a.k.a. chinaware, after its inventors) is delicate silica balance of 'china-earth' and 'china-stone', *petun-tse*, generally fired over 1200°C (earth-clays alone collapse at this heat) which results in fusion of glaze and body, good ring when tapped, good translucency. 'New Ceramic' covers new type materials, still higher fired (1300°C-up), harder, but of little artistic interest so far.

Color may be 'underglaze', usually cobalt blue as in 'blue-and-white', *somé-tsuké*, and high-fired; or overglaze of colored enamels fired lower, for optimum results each color in spectral order blue down to red, gold lowest. But definitions are inexact and vary.

Japanese pottery is highly individualistic tho adhering to strict rules: within local or usage strictures there is much room for improvisation. It is mostly earthenware made, as we have noted, by one craftsman from start to end, unlike most tablewares (predominantly stoneware and porcelain) which are mass-produced. Softest of biscuit is low-fired *raku-yaki*, thrown by coil or on simple tournet, not on wheel. Suffix *-yaki* refers to product of kiln or fire used as we use -ware—but also used for cookery, as suki-yaki, robata-yaki. Numerous-*yaki* refer to local kilns with characteristics dictated by peculiarities of local clays and glazes as well as original source of tradition.

Making of bowls for drinking *matcha* thick green tea of 'tea ceremony', most prized and pricey (tho nice ones are available for small change) of any ceramic anywhere, is strictly delineated art peculiar to Japan, tho prototypes are all Sung Chinese and Korean folkware. Any bowl fitting these specifications and considered beautiful can be used. We have seen in use ancient Persian wine bowls or penny yogurt bowls, American colonial period handleless coffee cups (which in that period of artistic revolt from England were based on Japanese prototypes).

One peculiarity of Japanese style is that its 'foot', raised ring base, is not glazed as potter holds bowl by foot when dipping in glaze. Persian bowls have similar 'bare foot': Chinese and Occidental wares always glaze foot.

Modern art ceramics getting gimmicky—twisted bottles like bad rejects, cracked sinks, distorted toilet bowls—aping junk in US pot contests but at least 4 often 10 years behind. Criterion of successful beauty is still its function: 1971 first national contest Mainichi Newspaper-Education Minister prize for traditional Japanese work went to resident German Gerd Knapper (whom we visit after NIKKO, p.1042).

MARKETPLACE: *See* shops in kiln areas especially at kiln, as described locally; city department stores in household goods and art floor, *mingei* folk art section—much alas diminishing, but tops in **Tenmaya DS OKAYAMA**; **Takumi** folkcraft shop, Nishi Ginza TOKYO and **Yamatoya** in KYOTO. MUSEUMS in general, especially **Museum of Far Eastern Ceramics** OSAKA, **Hyogo Ceramics Museum** KOBE, Folk Art museums KURASHIKI, OSAKA (2), less so TOKYO, numerous local crafts museums.

ARCHITECTURE, like sculpted buddha image, is pieced together—but from roof down. Traditional wooden building is prefabricated, often at another site, all lumber parts precut to size, from pillars down to intricately pieced roof-overhang elements of temple or shrine, mortices and tenons minutely sized and all moved when ready to construction site. There framework is erected on prepared and ritually-purified site, and roof (whether tile, shingle or thatch) is laid on before any walls or in fact anything beyond basic supporting pillars go up.

Buildings here carry their weight on skeletal pillars, unlike European and Islamic architecture where brick or stone walls bear load. With walls bearing weight, tall construction was limited. Ancient Rome had 6-storey tenements of concrete, which periodically collapsed with horrible loss of life. When American architects and engineers in 1860s discovered Japanese pillar-construction it was perfect timing as steel I-beam had been developed for railway bridges and were soon being turned out by steel mills faster than rivers and gullies could be found to bridge. Wedding of I-beam to pillar construction gave birth to modern architecture, and old Roman concrete technology combined with steel frames for ferroconcrete construction. Our Persia House museum in Kobe is in Victorian colonial style house, built by Japanese carpenters, it is European clapboard shell and Japanese tile roof on traditional Japanese framework. Popular American 'balloon house', frame pillars bearing weight but shared with skin, is sophisticated development of Sino-Japanese pillar house, harking back to our own Tudor.

Carpenters traditionally came from HIDA (p.912) above Nagoya in heavily forested mountains. Architects were, until Westernization late 18th century, these carpenters themselves. From Nara times government corvée had each so many families in Hida send carpenter for 300 or more days per year to Nara, later to Kyoto and Kamakura, to work. Priest might lay out specifications, show pictures of Chinese or Korean prototype–tho first carpenter-architects were certainly Korean emigres, possibly Chinese; or daimyo-lord dictate his needs and wants, tea-aesthetician spell out his strictures. We visit many great buildings built and rebuilt over millennium-plus by generations of Hida carpenters, highest rank of whom is *miya-daiku*, 'shrine carpenter' such as work near-continuous reconstruction of ISE GRAND SHRINE (p.313).

But perhaps more interesting is that these men made for themselves and local merchants and farmers, superb homes which today are treasured, highly accessible to us with many utilized for tourism as restaurants, shops, museums and inexpensive (1990=¥5,000 or less per person w/2 fine meals, =¥-B) *minshuku* inns serving local delicacies. Probably nowhere else on earth have common builders who raised world architectural masterpieces built such beauty for their personal private use. Major modern construction companies were founded by or using these men: one, Takenaka Komuten, has **Carpentry Museum** in Kobe (p.593), which no woodwork-lover, carpenter or architect should miss passing hour in. (Read *The Way of the Carpenter*, by WmH Coaldrake, Weatherhill).

To buy and rebuild one of these houses, *see* KAMAKURA SHOPPING p.241.

Today large logs are rare here despite strict forestry control and 67+% of nation forested. Most house lumber comes from NW USA and Canada, plywood from Philippines or SE Asia. But perhaps principal consumer of wood imports is restaurant industry for *wari-bashi*-disposable chopsticks, for which forests of Nepal etc are being leveled—tho from '88 Wisconsin is biggest supplier. Some Japanese conservationists we know when eating out carry own lacquer chopsticks to use to 'spare that tree'.

Oddity of tools—Japanese saw and plane cut on pull, *vs* W on push.

INTERIOR DESIGN came of age, became what we know today as Japanese, during Ashikaga shogunate (1335-1573), a.k.a. Muromachi. Systematization spread to all types and schools of art: ikebana, tea-serving, court painting, architecture, all of which now irretrievably interrelated.

Tatami mats, standard size to accommodate one body, began to be used as flooring instead of as freely-placed 'studio couch' mats-sleeping pads. They were fit into traditional modular Wa-style, as seen even in oldest wooden-floored shrines IZUMO, ISE. Henceforth all rooms measure in tatami as so-many-*jo*, two jo side by side being one *tsubo*—area measure of 6x6 feet, 36 square feet, 3.3 mtr^2. Modern tatami tend to be slightly smaller. Doors standardized at same height as tatami length, sliding panels replace hinged doors interior and rising shutters externally. *Tokonoma* honorary alcove on elevated base, variously fine wood or one or more tatami, set off by framework of rare natural wooden pillars, becomes focus of main room, place to display art which encourages development of all arts henceforth.

With this tradition so avidly emulated elsewhere today, it is special wonder that local modern architecture is so pitiful—'rabbit hutches' or more like egg crates. And considering how superb is Japanese art of packaging and boxing it is especially puzzling that they do so poorly packaging people.

MINOR ARTS
IKEBANA, 'living flower' form of sculpture—additive in being assemblage of parts, mostly flowers, but including with equal importance its container (often work of art itself), other associated works of art–painting or sculpture and architecture-like setting of whole. Derived from formal buddhist altar flower offering and small natural 'bouquet' in primeval Shinto marking sacred place. Buddhism introduced trinitarian rank of Heaven–Earth extremes with man midway, used as physical composition of placement of elements in arrangement. Also used in composition of Chinese type paintings, along with similar triune balance of ink tones from black thru greys to white space known in European languages by Japanese word '*notan*', all basis for compositional system of triangulation of Rembrandt—who imported his Japan vellum sketch paper *tori-no-ko* thru compatriot Dutch at Nagasaki and probably Chinese-Japanese artwork, which he obviouly knew firsthand.

By Ashikaga times (late 1300s) ikebana was becoming secularized as aesthetic pastime of retired shogun Yoshimitsu. He built KINKAKUJI Golden Pavilion as atelier for poetry and flower arrangement competitions. Ikebana were presented, often in fine imported vases, matching paintings hanging behind them. Princely diary, 1418-48, mentions ikebana and tea at court; 1499 saw first instruction book. Interior arrangers, *doboshu*, set flowers, paintings and art works around new *shoin* style rooms, sun-lit thru paper shoji replacing shutters, tatami now room-wide with tokonoma alcove and shelves to hold art in setting in which entire room including spectator were compositional whole, all following strict rules. Among doboshu were IKENOBO Senkei (fl.1462), and Senno (-d.1543) who published philosophy of flower art. Grandson Senko established Ikenobo school, 1620, still run in Kyoto by direct descendant and well worth visiting (*see* KYOTO MUSEUMS p.503). Daimyo competed with each other to patronize aesthetic masters, practicing tea and flower arts, noh dance and poetry. Hideyoshi was major patron who set Japanese aesthetics on its particular course, thru such as SEN Rikyu (*see* KYOTO-TEA p.502), as was emperor Go-Mizuno-o.

During Edo-Tokugawa era 17-19th centuries this and other noble and priestly arts made their way down thru samurai class and wealthy farmers and merchants and manufacturers to influence entire culture, as today.

English architect Josiah Conder late 1800s introduced to world thru book *Floral Art of Japan*. Mid '70s 41% gals did flower or tea, by '90 fell to 33%. Main schools: original **Ikenobo** (KYOTO p.503), **Ohara** (KOBE p.594), **Sogetsu** (TOKYO p.1159)—latter both 20th century. Many mid-size, 100s minor both new and ancient. Most teach both classic and modern styles tho stress one. If member of any school, visit your headquarters here. 3 main schools have museums and demonstration galleries worth visiting by anyone interested.

TEA CEREMONY or **CHADO**, 'tea-way', prime aesthetic discipline unifying (by making use of) all arts and crafts. Today commonly studied by young girls, but originally formal meditative art discipline for men, ultimate martial art because of its innate pacifism and strength thru gentleness based on *ki*. *See* KYOTO p.480, visit main school center teaching art of serving *matcha*-thick green tea. Experience basic form of 'ceremony' in most ¥-S, all ¥-L hotels, often in classic tearoom. Tea itself, tasty but nonsweet, served with sweet cake at many tourist sites from temple garden to tea shop: usually ¥300—500. Great pick-me-up any season, high caffeine.

SEALS: 57AD seal of Na (*see* Fukuoka Museum p.705) awarded by Han China; 701 first local gov't use but 10th cent to late 16th *kao*, signature (much like Ottoman Turk) used by officials, not seals—which began rise among priests and samurai slowly; 12th century on Zen paintings while kao still reserved for documents. Late 1400s seals used by daimyo; by general populace since 1640s with rise of commercial paper. To avoid counterfeiting, government in 1694 ordered all personal seals registered, as they still are today.

Required for certain transactions, personal or legal-person, like buying car—easily proxied. To minimize forgery, important transaction must be accompanied by notarized copy of seal registry. Nationals of nonideograph-using nations may not use ideographs, just either kana syllabary or roman alphabet or picture—Jay's seal is kanji homonym, as most bureaucrats unaware of this law. Common personal seal looks like pencil stub, of ivory or imitation, no decor. Seals of artists larger, stone with sculpted top, often quite beautiful. Printing surface is raised like print-block or rubber stamp, not depressed like European wax-impression seal, or seal-ring. Special ink is seal-red, tho any stamp-pad may do, but because of hardness of seal surface water-base ink rarely works.

POETRY: Earliest literary form in so many cultures as to be almost universal, was poetry. First written native creative literature was 8th century poem anthology *Manyoshu*, with many paeans to beautiful places—travelers in Asuka-Nara still stroll, poetry in hand, looking for original spots described. We visit these places, but sans-poems. Most of its poems are short, ephemeral, extemporized, many linked in series—but also including love and drinking poems lacking in later ages when it seems it was fine for macho samurai to extol fluttering blossoms or mist-enshrouded mountains but not that pretty hand pouring for him or nectar being poured. Perhaps world's first true novel is *Genji Monogatari*, ca1000AD, and that is full of poetry parties. We visit many of its settings, even very room near Kyoto in Ishiyama where it was supposedly penned. No import has had as much impact on world poetry in recent decades as haiku, poem polaroids meant to capture one instant of feeling in three lines of 5-7-5 syllables, or thereabout. Easiest of all forms to enjoy playing at, hardest to accomplish anything in. Basho (1644-94), developed it as major form, with his frog pond, which we visit, and follow in his steps recorded in his poem-travel book (for many over centuries, travel guide) *Narrow Road to the Deep North*. We visit his home town and monument in Iga Ueno (p.333), between Ise and Nara.

MANHOLE COVERS: Indicative of Japanese fetish for good design everywhere, these cast-iron orignals are spreading from Kobe area nationwide. We prophesy tourists will take rubbings of them as of English church brass.

*It is ever the way in houses of China
to learn the state of the country by watching
the dancers and listening to the songs....*
— Fujiwara Moronaga, 12th cent.

ON STAGE

JAPAN IS GREAT THEATER, inhabited by 120,000,000 delightful addicts who spend their lives alternating between roles of audience and actors. Small town traffic cop on his podium (as Tokyo cops worked till not long ago) whirls thru his ballet to four directions simultaneously conducting his own accompaniment of auto horns and bicycle bells, whose players are themselves at once orchestra and audience and at nite provide his footlights. Troubador tour bus conductors serenade their passengers with operatic descriptions of and apologies for road and traffic conditions, announcements of coming stops and all connecting lines, transfer to which is less change of bus than change of channel.

At nite Gay Quarters of any city or town are like super-size pinball machines gone wild, human pinballs careening against score-cushions with tilt mechanism shorted. Then quiet shop and residential streets list to chamber music of wooden clogs of nite strollers, rhythmic clack of fire patrol's sounding sticks and his lullaby of "All's well, don't smoke in bed", and toodle of noodle man's floodle brings nite owls and insomniacs out to his pushcart, not so much for bowls of hot noodles in soup, as to encourage him to return next nite with his soft-voiced tin flute, or now, tape recording.

Theatricality is everywhere, and not surprising has hoary base. At foot of pagoda in most old temples was stage for offering of entertainment. You'll still see such in some temples and most Shinto shrines; you'll still see them in use, for dance-theater is most popular of Japanese arts. *Kabuki, bugaku, bunraku* puppets, all-girl troupes, have entertained America (Jay saw Takarazuka girls at New York World's Fair of 1939), and classical *noh* has impressed France's avant-garde, and elsewhere. These are old theater but they still have great following in Japan. All derive from folk theater. Japan's "Genesis" relates how Sun Goddess locked herself in cave, thus darkening world, and how she was lured out by Goddess of Ritual Dance doing parody of her own rite so that all gods assembled "laughed until high plain of heaven shook"—which indicates that stage art, dance, hoochy kooch and comedy are deeply rooted in local psyche.

This antique, actually neolithic or New Stone Age, ceremonial theater still is popular. Called *kagura*, "gods' fun", it is of two main types. Done by young girls as simple shrine dance it is called *mi-kagura* (maiden kagura) evolved from Korean *miko* lady-shaman ritual—may be seen on request for fee at many Shinto shrines, as we note where relevant. Done by men, it is simply called *kagura*, far more virile affair, using masks and extravagant costumes, usually recounting folk tales or episodes from origin legends, to accompaniment of wildly primitive drum and flute music—performed at festivals, especially in autumn at harvest rite. We take you into mountains of Hiroshima for best troupes and mention many fetes where it's part of entertainment (*See* area PERSONAL DATEBOOK). Each region has its specialty, so if you see several performances you won't see much duplication.

Original labor dances are still performed in rice-planting *ta-asobi*, field play festivals of June (at Ise, Osaka, Hiroshima, etc, *see* DATEBOOKs). Villagers assemble in ornate costumes, usually uniform, as men tote great drums and flutes, and barrels and bellies full of wine. They strike up work rhythm, dancing to it themselves, women swing into work transplanting seedlings. Back-breaking job, bent over, placing seedlings at even intervals (now done by small tractor) to contribute to once-greatest rice-productivity per acre in world (California now 10% higher). Music makes burden lighter, certainly active sympathy of menfolk also helps. Until recently it was done this way everywhere, last rice chore to be mechanized. But now there is garden tractor attachment to do it: less scenic but far more humane. Occasionally villages will compete in contests of their rice-planting songs and dances and music. In Ise, full cycle of rice culture is imitated in dance at grand shrine. Television sometimes makes it all less distant.

GIGAKU
Processional masked mime to music of flutes, drums, cymbals, probably first imported early 7th century, extinct by 18th century. Brought via Paekche Korea, probably from Wu-China, ultimate origins in India, as surviving masks are all of Indians or West Asians. Best masks, some costumes, in Nara's Shosoin Imperial Repository left over from Big Buddha's dedicatory 'eye-opening' rites 752AD. Gigaku-like procession in Taima-dera temple between Nara-Osaka, *Nerikuyo matsuri* May 14, 4pm.

BUGAKU
Which you may have seen when Imperial Court troupe toured US and Europe, simply means dance+music. Stately but highly-charged ballet, essentially visible orchestral music, musicians playing world's oldest symphonic music called *ga-gaku* (elegant music, Chinese term for music by which world order is seen) while dancers dance (*bu-*) weaving intricate living scores upon elevated, red-railinged stage, now moving in harmony, now interweaving in physical fugue. Their costumes are symphonies in silk and masks are justly protected as national treasures (*see* var Nara, Kyoto collections). Imperial Court musicians must master at least two instruments, one gagaku, one Western orchestral, some appear with symphonies.

Among court dances, epics of ancient heroes such as Ran-ryo-o Dragon King are imports. Those from North China, Korea, Mongolia and Persia enter right (*u–mai*, right dances or *koma-gaku* Korean), use drum decorated with three comma-like symbol in frame of dragon, and costumes of green and blue (animal and colors of north); while those from South China T'ang court, Annam, India enter left (called *saho-no-mai*, left-dance also *togaku* or T'ang music), use great drum, yin-yang 'two commas' framed with phoenix and predominantly red costumes (creature and color of south). Specific national origins are fuzzy: any Persian came via North China where it had already mixed with other imports or even Chinese, where these were court ritual dances, and further editing would have taken place en route in Manchuria or Korea. (Persian crown, as on 5th century Sasanian coins, obvious on some masks.) Japan in receiving this art, immediately choreographed dances of their own, cut once lively Central Asian tempos down by at least half, possibly quartered to present funereal beat—tho Korean bugaku similarly slow. Native Japanese, *saibara*, are mixed in repertoire, mostly agricultural work dances whose rhythms of labor and nature need only slight adaptation to be pure dance. One is of four Japanese scarecrows, their paper masks wafting on wind, as you will see real, very same scarecrow masks doing, suspended across rice paddies from high wires—which on dancers are outstretched arms. *Bugaku* performers are men, tho occasionally shrine maidens do butterfly dance, called both *kagura* and *bugaku*, while mixed-sex children's troupes perform *dogon*.

BUGAKU MAY BE SEEN AT:

TOKYO: Imperial Household Musicians best seen at Imperial Court MUSIC BLDG in Tokyo mid-April and mid-October; for which ✍ ahead to **Imperial Household Office**, Kunaisho, Music Dept, Chiyoda-ku, Tokyo 100—request entry (free), enclose international postal reply coupon or Japanese stamps. MEIJI SHRINE during Taisai Festival (no set day), 4/29-5/5, 10/31-11/3; YASUKUNI SHRINE during Matsuri (no set day), 4/21-23, 7/13-16, 10/17-19. Gagaku concerts occasional **National Theater**, check *TJ* or TIC. Occasional performance sponsored by daily newspapers such as Asahi. ONOTERUSAKI SHRINE Taito-ku, Shitaya 2-13 (☎3872-5514), free, musicians practice almost every day, 19-20:30, X-Aug.

NAGOYA: ATSUTA SHRINE ****May 1**,10:30-14:00; **Mid-Oct 10:00, 13:00.

ISE: GRAND SHRINE Naiku ****Apr 5-7**; Sept 20-22 (pre-, equinox, after-), 11am.

KYOTO: HEIAN SHRINE ****Apr 16**; Spring bugaku day, o-kagura, etc. from noon; YASAKA SHRINE **June 14**, 19:30 (Ninjo-no mai); **June 15**, 10:00 (Azuma Asobi) and 17-18:00 mikagura with gagaku music; also **mid-Nov. ICHIHIME SHRINE practice sessions every wed, thur, sat afternoon; YASAKA practices 4th sun, not public but professional musicians welcome. KYOTO KAIKAN, in Sept Nihon Gagaku Hozon-kai (preservation soc) festival (*see* KTO).

Kyoto has many groups centered around respective shrines. Partial listing: contact, *Heian Jingu Gagaku-bu*, Mr. Murakami ☎(075)-761-0221; *Yasaka Gagaku-kai*, Mr. Hida, head priest ICHIHIME SHRINE, ☎361-2775; *Kyoto Bugaku-kai* (girl troupe), SAGI-NO-MORI SHRINE, Mr Ishi, ☎781-6391; *Nihon Gagaku Hozon-kai*, Mr. Nakagawa, ☎525-0005; *Kyoto Kogaku Hozon-kai*, SUGA JINJA, ☎771-1178.

GION CORNER, Yasaka Hall, Gion, Kyoto, nitely theater demos alternate *bugaku* and 'J' *bunraku* (puppets) plus other, 19:40 & 20:40, ¥2,100; Mar 1-Nov 29 only—worthwhile, pleasant evening.

NARA: KASUGA SHRINE **Jan 15**, 13:00; **Feb 3-4 (Setsubun), 18:30 (famed 3,000 lanterns lit); **Mar 13** 11:00, *Yamato-mai*; **Apr 5** 13:00, *Kagura*, **Mar 5 13:00 on MANYO SHOKUBUTSUEN GARDEN stage built over pond; **Aug 14**, 19:00 lighting of 3,000 lanterns; *Nov 3, 13:00 SHOKUBUTSUEN; ***Dec 17, 13:00 to midnite, day-long living historical museum of Japanese dance (*see* NARA DATEBOOK, p.397). Also HIMURO SHRINE Oct 1, 19:00.

KASUGA SHRINE group practices every sat 19:00pm in their shrine practice hall at Mochi-i-dono cho.

TENRI: Oct 26 *Annual Festival*, young men's troupe, also travels for special shows.

OSAKA: SHITENNO-JI: noon **Apr 22 & Oct 22, Aug 8**, by torch light 18:00-20:00.

MIYAJIMA: ITSUKUSHIMA SHRINE **Jan 1**, 5:00; **Jan 2**, 13:00; *Jan 3, 13:00; *Jan 5, 5:00; **Apr 15, 18:00; *May 18, 10:00; Lunar **May 5**, 13:00 (Jigozen village outer shrine across strait); *Lunar **June 5** and **17**, music only, nite (*see* MIYAJIMA for W- calendar dates); **Oct 15, 18:00; *Oct 23, 10:00; *Nov 23.

*Indicates usually 5 dances; **8 dances or more; ***many dances, hours-long program.

Instruments used are aforementioned large standing drums mounted in hoop on pedestal used with small metal gong for main slow beat, while faster beat is kept on intermediate drums of which smaller two-ended hour-glass-shape *kakko* is leader. Strings are 4-string *biwa*-lute, zithers 13-string koto and 6-string *wa-gon*; only for primeval Japanese tunes, plus *sho*-pipes of pan and three types of *fué* -horizontal flutes and one *hichiriki*-short reed. Korean bugaku, performed in May 1990 for first time in Imperial Palace music room to mark state visit of their president and great reconcilliation, is seen to use wider variety of instruments, with more long reeds, fiddles and racks of hanging bronze bells as well as sets of ancient Chinese stone-slab gongs. Women also dance, while that characteristic funereal tempo Chinese scholars believed was Japanese innovation, is already obvious.

Dengaku: *Bugaku* was for imperial court; *ta-asobi* was for old-time 4-H clubs. Farmers wanting something fancier at agriculture rites called for *den-gaku*, 'field pleasure' dancers in brocade versions of farm clothes, haunting but weird instruments (including odd bone rattle that looks like dinosaur spine) and fantastic hats with tableaux on them, like Rose-Bowl Parade floats. *Dengaku* is deceptively simple, but basis seems to be special engrossing weaving of complicated patterns upon raised earthen mound stage, like meanderings of shaman in trance which might be its continental origin. There is nothing like it in Chinese records, but costumes resemble Korean 'bugaku'.

It is best seen at Nara *On-Matsuri* such great fete that it has no name other than 'Honorable Festival', often mistakenly translated as equally apt 'sound festival'. There, midnite **Dec 16-17** magnificent offertory ritual is held (*see* NARA; DATEBOOK also ISE Transfer of Spirit rite, p.317), followed near 2am by ancient dance offerings. For theater buff, PM procession of theatrical costumes followed by hours of performances by torchlight upon earthen stage; of ancient theatrical morality plays, dances and mystic ritual dances all ancestral to modern Japanese theater. Strange pattern and antic dance, *sarugaku,* because of its homonymous name called monkey-play in Japan, but over millennium ago called in China *san-gaku*. By rights all should have long since become extinct but for Japanese cult of conservation. Costumes of performers are, strangely, like those of Persian Zoroastrian fire-rite priests.

These plays and dances were often brought to Japan by Buddhist priests and used as Buddhist ritual. Some, such as *bugaku*, were taken over by Shinto, now performed at both shrines and temples. Others further evolved by Buddhists into morality plays in which epic tales so loved by farmers were adapted to moral tales, and rough, outhouse humor of farmer also turned to teaching. MIBU TEMPLE Kyoto preserves one such masked morality show, heavy on slapstick and natural functions, *Mibu Kyogen*, **Apr 21-29**. Other temples and shrines preserve other antique forms, too numerous to mention here, many of which are listed in our area DATEBOOKS where practical (*see* Nara, Osaka, Miyajima).

Gigaku processional from mainland mixed with kagura; now simplified version seen **May 14** near Nara at TAIMA-DERA (*see* p.370). Movement pattern of early gigaku probably simply linear procession, but unknown. Movement pattern of bugaku centrifugal, quartet moving from center to four directions, accelerating then stopping suddenly, rising up on toes, slowly ebbing back. This pattern of movement culminates in noh, where it is, to us, secret of power on such small stage. Noh and Persian miniature paintings are only two art forms we know of with this centrifugal composition, motion outwards from center—Western dance and painting is centripetal, moving inwards to center. Centrifugality allows performance in restricted space (precisely as with microscopic scale of miniature paintings and chicken-coop proportions of nōh-*butai*), with projection of energies surging outwards to audience.

T'ang dynasty Chinese court was full of exiled Persian courtiers, artists and intellectuals, in situation of Persian diaspora much like that of today. Masks preserved in Nara include 'Persian king and drunken companions', with definitely Persian schnozzles. Gigaku and bugaku masks are preserved at many temples and shrines, many are mentioned in text. Fine reproductions are available in Nara shops and at kiosk inside near exit from Great Buddha pavilion.

NOH

PROFESSIONAL actors (no actresses) got hold of these theatrical gimmicks and competed for shrine and temple patronage. Started as medium to convey Buddhist message to farmer audience at festivals, but was so polished by its principal renovator Zeami that he confessed their meaning sometimes eluded even him. Competition and devotion of professional aesthetes gave us one of most exquisite theatrical forms on earth. Often compared with Greek drama for power of its literature and use of mask and chorus. They are different, but equal excellence always invites comparison. Whereas Greek drama (at least as performed today) confuses caterwauling with power, noh relies on understatement and tight control. Voice control of noh and kyogen is form of martial art, must be heard to be believed. *Trojan Women* seen side by side at Shiraz (Iran) Arts Festival with noh *Sumida-gawa* was sudden enlightenment—worst defeat for Greek culture since Roman invasion.

Product of 14-15th century, most great noh plays were written by father-son team Kan'ami and Zeami (1354-1455) whose descendants, Kanze family, still perform, as do other schools of almost equal antiquity. They have invited translation by Arthur Waley, Ezra Pound, others and in print rank as great literature. As performance art it holds more possibility for modern use than any else we've seen, attracting our young artists at long last, as well as some avant-garde Japanese.

Of course you won't understand dialogue—even most locals take printed librettos. Overall sound of flute and drums, mystic deep-voice styles, chanting chorus interplaying with sight of movement patterns of dances, more-real-than-life masks, hypnotizes—drawing you into stage in near-round on which it is played, which is itself great drum (great empty pottery urns underneath) deftly played by feet of dancers. Sets are almost non-existent, except for skeletal representational objects; great pine tree painted on backdrop recalls tree in Nara Kasuga Shrine courtyard where Kan'ami first performed, pine boughs on entry-bridge roof-posts recall same sacred glade common to our heritages, West and East.

Nothing is allowed to detract attention from hypnotic masks, of which best are national treasures; simplest, even newest, of which are treasured by anyone lucky enough to find one for sale. Each has 3 to 5 expressions carved into it to portray changes from gaiety to deep grief, horror, unearthliness by way actor tilts his head in relation to light. He enters trance during play, absorbed into personality of mask whose representation he is enacting, until mask comes to life, actor and mask becoming one. Mask perspires, seems to flush in agony of its performance. Time-space totally dissolve, fuse in process. Great climactic action is effected by gradual, purposeful slowing of all stage action, of metabolism of theater, reflected in slowing of observer's pulse, so that sudden return to normal speed at climax comes as acute physical shock—unless your metabolism has so slowed that you are asleep, as many aficionados. Record your pulse before & during play.

You may, as many travel writers have been, be bored stiff by noh. Most of our friends—young students, traveling school marms, fellow artists or traveling salesmen—find it exciting. With noh and kabuki you usually either like one or other. We love both. Japanese of old realized *noh* is pretty heavy stuff and 3 to 5 plays on program (you needn't stay for all, best are usually later ones) are interspersed with hilarious slapstick blackouts called–

Kyogen, 'wild words'. Quintessential comedy only matched by jewel-like precision of early Chaplin, Stan Laurel or Buster Keaton, who like kyogen blended dance with restrained slapstick. Kyogen are fun to watch even if you can't understand its language; many translated into English and are side-splitting even secondhand, would make good scripts for our TV— much use of actual slapstick. Usually involve straight man–goof combo, but some require pair of clods—usually named Jiro and Taro. Scripts based on such situations as old blind man 'baby-sitting' mischievous deaf-mute; two alcoholic servants tied up by master so they won't get into his wine cellar, but feeding each other stolen hootch with their bound hands; usual 'moron' jokes found in all cultures. Mostly it is lowest making fool of high-born in democratic rural tradition of kagura—regarded as so dangerous by Tokugawa shoguns and jack-boot successors that they effected its total isolation from public by subsidizing whole noh establishment, making it exclusive theater of effete nobility, out of reach of populace until 1945.

Shigeyamas perhaps finest family of actors on earth, unbelievable versatility and volume of voices. At Shiraz (Iran) Arts Festival 1975 performed in old Persian garden, Sengoro's powerful voice mesmerized. One critic asked "I know Japanese are masters of miniaturization and I can see how they can hide tiny amplifiers in kimono, but how about speakers?"

There are troupes, mixed amateur and pro, which perform regularly and often, sometimes guesting visiting masters. Best, of course, are ancient professional families in Tokyo and Kyoto, some also doing avant-garde.

English dailies carry scheds of main performances, also *TJ* for Tokyo & *KTO*, Kansai. Best reviews: Don Kenny's in *Japan Times* & *TJ*, of both noh and kyogen—which latter he performs frequently in English in mixed troupe with professional kyogen families. Tix, at ubiquitous *PlayGuide* booths; or almost always at door, var ¥2,500–10,000.

Takigi (bonfire) *noh* is presented as of yore, most dramatically on: **May 11, 12**, 16:00, NARA Kofuku-ji Temple; after 11:00 *noh* offerings at Kasuga Shrine on **11, 12** at its Wakamiya subShrine. **Jun 1, 2**, 17:30 KYOTO Heian Shrine. **Aug 11, 12** 17–21:00 OSAKA Ikutama Jinja nr Tanimachi-9ch subway; ¥1500. **Sept** at various TOKYO outdoor park stages, watch papers. **Noh theaters:** *see* KYOTO and TOKYO.

PUPPETS
TOYS in West, serious art in East. CHIKAMATSU Monzaemon (1653-1724) is, not without justification, likened to Shakespeare. Wrote for *bunraku* puppets then as now, based in Osaka—at new National **Bunraku-za** Theater, with beautiful new stage in Tokyo next to National Kabuki Theater. Classics preferred, 50 new postwar plays rarely re-run. Puppets run Charley McCarthy size to 2/3rd human, those in full armor may weigh almost 100 pounds. No threads would hold this, no one man could handle one. 3 men work each doll, stand right behind it—master handling head and right hand, one black-robed assistant on left hand and trunk and 3rd man on legs. Voice, *joruri* reciter, is 4th man sitting upstage, like Greek chorister, with 5th *samisen* accompanist. It all has hypnotic effect and you soon become unaware of three interlopers behind each 'actor'. In fact puppet masters boast of their ability to so capture you that greatness of master is proportionate to colorful, seemingly distracting clothes he will wear to show to all that he is good enough to project attention away from even himself.

Late lamented great handler and friend, KIRITAKE Monjuro, said he fused with puppet on stage and with his two aides—when 'sent' he could feel his left puppet-arm and legs, as all three men become one in their doll.

Amateur puppets, some folk originals of *bunraku* and some imitations, are maintained in various rural areas of Japan; noted in relevant PERSONAL DATEBOOKS. Others, such as famed *Awa puppets* in Tokushima City and nearby Naruto Park on Shikoku, or *Awaji puppets* on Awaji Island off Kobe, perform frequently or to prior reservation.

Kyoto's nitely **Gion Corner** gives short *bunraku* every other nite, 20:00 and 21:00.

KABUKI

STARTED out as highly polished *kagura* dance-drama by mixed troupe under tutelage of female temple-dancer invading realm of male *kagura* and *noh*. One Izumo-no-Okuni about 1600, performed at fairs and on dry river beds, notably Kamo (duck) River in Kyoto near Shijo bridge where **Minamiza** Kabuki Theater now stands. Later came into its own in Tokyo after prostitution control, 1629, barred women performing. As plebeian theater, nobility and warriors were banned from audience, just as public banned from noble noh. It developed beyond splashy review when plays written by CHIKAMATSU Monzaemon—much-translated—originally for Osaka puppet theater (*above*), were adapted to human actors.

Kabuki uses super 'wide-screen' stage with *hanamichi* (flower path) elevated runway thru audience from house rear to stage, on which major dramatic entries and exits occur. It also uses *mawari-butai* (revolving stage), various trick trapdoors and elevators, overhead cables for flying entrances, which with its striking stage sets and brilliant costumes make it most flamboyant of world stage arts.

Characteristic of stage gimmicks is revolving stage which is rear portion of stage used for grand scene shifts. Trick scene changes are made before your eyes without bothering to drop curtain, sometimes on hanamichi to distract from main stage with change written into script, sometimes with partial blackout and done openly on stage just to show off technique. Also various trap doors and elevators for dramatic entrances on hanamichi or parts of stage proper. All this gadgetry is original kabuki invention, preceding similar European techniques. Then there is lighting, projection on cheesecloth forescreens of snowstorms, typhoons, raging infernos and fireworks to simulate conflagrations of epic proportions. Amid all, inimitable little man who isn't there, *kurogo*, in black leotards, skullcap and veil flits around stage, ignored by all, as he arranges long flowing robes into dramatic folds, picks up discarded weapons or props, moves small scenery —ideal hero for Kafkaesque tale. Like so many little people one meets here, he finds his identity in anonymous service to others.

Plays themselves are of several types. Basic to repertoire are **juhachiban** or 18 best plays, also known as **aragoto**, 'rough words' or masculine plays, after their basic quality, and at which Garet excelled in sole foreign troupe performing in Japanese: *Sukeroku, Kanjincho, Shibaraku* and *Yanone* top list. *Jidai-mono*, period plays, are based on literary rendition of some actual event, which if close in time to period in which it was written will be thinly disguised by setting it in some older era, different province, as with famed *Chushingura* or vendetta of 47 ronin which is often excerpted and in late 1986 actually shown in 13-hour entirety as trilogy, monthly over 3 months. *Sewamono*, plays of domestic affairs, often love tragedies with high suicide rate, often adaptations from old Osaka puppet theater—best written by CHIKAMATSU Monzaemon for puppets. *Kizewa-mono* are in same story tradition but later—having been written by 19th century Tokyo playwrights and, while rarely literary stature of Chikamatsu, are often better staged and more realistic. *Jidaimono* and *sewamono* use *joruri* or accompanying chorus who wail story line, background commentary between on-stage actors' dialogue.

There is **neo-kabuki**, a.k.a. **shin-kabuki**, plays written this century, most realistic of all, mix kabuki tradition, western-style reliance on dialogue. Usually on mixed program with classical, but only rarely as good— not to be confused with new versions of 'international' kabuki-ballet.

Dance plays round out repertoire, as short dances alone, dance climaxes to other plays, or adaptations, ancient or recent of dances from other theatrical forms such as noh, kyogen, folk theater, which for us are usually most exciting offerings of kabuki. Then starting 1986 is new, grander than grandiose *Super Kabuki* of avant-garde joining classicists for new stagings of old fables with costumes by such as couturier Issei Miyake, hi-tech to further expand traditional tech-tricks, acting by energetic young traditional kabuki scions—'stage-mafia' families who have controlled for centuries.

Some minor keys to understanding: costumes are color-coded, white of course means pure character, but black indicates strong character, pastel-blue or pink on male is hero, rust is his adversary. Some robes drop away on stage at tug of thread to change character. Costumes are very heavy—with headdresses, moving calls for athletic prowess; dance verges on martial art.

In smaller theaters will be other experimental forms or interpretations of classical plays, by young actors who have split from feudal main troupes because of lack of opportunity to advance, not being born into great houses.

Usual program includes at least one 'heavy' in several scenes and representation from each of two or three other classifications. Formal program planning is less and less followed as master actors choose program to fit season or their mood of experimentation. Recently plays not seen for decades, even century, are revived as master actors constantly experiment with new interpretations of old plays, as in above Super K. Comic parodies of standard repertoire will be created to fill in where light plays are called for. Summer accents ghost plays, to chill viewers' spines, with weird otherworld stage effects created by lighting and projection tricks, ghosts sailing down from rafters on guy wires. Kabuki traditionally is all male, but in fact female bit parts are now sometimes played by women, dance students of kabuki stars being rewarded, or make up scarcity of minor actors. Top heart-throb for gals, youngest NT, female impersonator BANDO Tamasaburo.

Best seen: Tokyo, monthly X-26-30 when sets changed for next month; also Kyoto kabuki theater 3-4x-yr. Best atmosphere TOKYO **Kabukiza** (*see* ON STAGE TOKYO details), followed by **National Theater, Meiji-za** (being rebuilt, reopens '93), **Shinbashi Embujo**; occasionally at **Nissei** theater. NAGOYA **Misono-za**. like Shin Kabuki-za OSAKA alternates with wishy-washy modern; **Minami-za** KYOTO, where best is December *Kao-mise*, 'face showing', marking promotions, new name-grantings—followed one month by worthwhile amateur show, back after long lapse. KOBE now has superb **Shin Oriental Theater** where anything good goes.
See *Japan Times* for excellent reviews. *Mainichi Daily News* final tuesday reviews month's kabuki scene. *TJ* for Tokyo, *KTO* for Osaka-Kyoto cover regional productions.

DRAMA: Western type, *shimpa* or *shingeki*, dates back only to 1925. Both translations from European languages and original Japanese plays, shows strong resurgence. Main troupes *Haiyu-za*, 'actor's theater', theater of same name; *Bungaku-za*, 'literature theater' at small Bungaku-za **Atelier**; and *Gekidan Shiki*, modern translations like *Cats*, based in Nissei Theater. 1965 experiments in performing in English, importing casts and whole shows took root, Broadway shows, usually musicals, now make it here regularly—some translated, some original cast. Japanese *Fiddler on Roof* all time record-breaker, its 'orientalism' readily and sympathetically comprehensible locally; fueled boom in books on Jewish themes and strong public sympathy for Jewry and Israel despite official wimpish subservience to third world anti-Semitism (no landing rights to El Al, accept Arab League boycott rules, etc). *Cats* had own tent theaters built Tokyo, Osaka. Modern Japanese plays tend to be verbose, stand-up oration, exercises in emoting before shaving mirror and of little if any interest to nonlinguist.

Shimpa, modern drama, derives from modern European stage, heavy on translation, will little interest non-linguist, best in Tokyo; also seen at Kyoto and Osaka kabuki theaters when kabuki not on boards. Between it and kabuki is *modern kabuki*; sometimes shown alone, or with either parent, relatively weak, talky; more costume soap than kabuki, if with some notable exceptions. Melodrama, more mellow than drama.

Staging had been dull until opening of **Nissei Theater** (short for **Nippon Seimei**, Japan Insurance whose building it is in) with its Gaudyesque acoustic architecture giving near-perfect sound (permitting performance of plays, opera and music in one theater) and highly advanced stage gimmickry. *Kikutaphone*, private attachment of shirt-pocket transistor radio earphone enables simultaneous interpretation of dialogue in English—new at time of our '64 edition but now in wide use, as at conferences, for multilingual simultaneous translations.

AVANT-GARDE

Best known with recognition internally due to international acclaim, is **Butoh** (archaism for 'dance', *buyo*). "Hallucinatory visionary dance theater... out of German dance expressionism thru Japanese experimentation", in '60s by late HIJIKATA Tatsumi, still-active OHNO Kazuo. Virtually unknown at home until introduced overseas 1982 by *Dai Rakuda Kan* troupe, 'Great Camel (or 'Flunk') Battleship', at US Pepsico Festival; made headlines '84 when 4 nearly nude men slid down cables from skyscraper in Seattle enacting rebirth and one fell to death. Attempts to derive beauty out of hideousness, lotus blooming in muck, dancer become primeval slug from which evolution will flower, chaos which gives forth geos-order. Purposely childish ape-dancing, mugging in slow motion, facial or body expression changing shape imperceptibly, like dance with terminal Parkinsons. Success seems to be freeing–ridding?–it of its once-essential element of protest.

Best seen in Tokyo. **Reading** Mark Holborn, *Butoh, Dance of the Dark Soul*.

Several avant-garde troupes earn international acclaim, usually pre-local recognition. Singular was TERAYAMA Shuji: his **Tenjo Sajiki** dissolved when brilliant young originator died. His people continue in other troupes, often seen in numerous excellent small theaters in Tokyo, *Eiga-Mura* stage Kyoto. Even if they don't appeal much to you, characteristic that sets them all aside from caterwauling European and US avant-garde is their respect for discipline in training, dance in motion no matter how trivial, familial-teamwork, foregoing star syndrome. Noh and like tradition lives on in such— indeed there is avant-garde noh by traditional families including international **NOHO** troupe, which gives workshops. Edinburgh and Shakespeare fetes in UK, such as **Ninagawa troupe** stunned audiences with "perfect point of convergence between W- imagination and J- noh..." to add new dimension to Shakespeare. And there is stunning Franco-Japanese **The Kabuki**....

Hottest director now working, in individual style that aptly fits loosely-bandied term 'fusion', is **Ninagawa**, reworking kabuki with mixed W-style–kabuki casts, women in women's rolls, tuxedo-clad baritones replacing gidayu 'criers', Shakespearian theater-within-theater (play-within-play), Greek chorus, mixed W-/J-style musical instruments, you name it. Wowed Edinburgh Festival 3 times by 1988, *Media* in Athens brought audience to their feet. ASARI Keita-**Shiki group** who also builds modern syncretic theater on tradition. Watch for them, anywhere.

With much theatrical experimentation going on, theater connoisseur is in for fun. Butoh has been exported from Japan so successfully that it even attracts audiences in its native land. Tokyo's Shinjuku and Aoyama-Shibuya areas are alive with little theater groups experimenting.

Summer workshop in traditional Japanese theater works with modernists as well (*see* LEARNING ABOUT JAPAN). Butoh and giant drum troupes have accepted sincere foreign trainees, but it must be done on your own, soul over mind.

ALL-GIRL REVIEWS

DEITY of Japanese theater is female, kabuki started by woman. While stage arts of bugaku, noh, kabuki are now male monopolies, gals still draw top crowds. Geisha dances spring and autumn (best in Kyoto, but also Tokyo and Osaka) combine bits of everything for few hours of fast, fanciful fun.

TAKARAZUKA: modern all-girl review from town of same name near Osaka-Kobe (*see*) with theater of same name downtown Tokyo; original for Mitchener's *Sayonara*, which wanted to sue him for slander till Jay revealed writer-friend USAF Major dating star, just like 'slanderous' novel. Troupe started in 1914 by Hankyu rail (formerly owned Hankyu Braves baseball team) tycoon KOBAYASHI Ichizo to create traffic to suburbs, and pep up lazy Osaka culture scene by 'infusing Western style pizazz and sparkle into traditional stage'. 4 troupes—Flower, Moon, Star, Snow—each of 100 actresses and 20-25 interns in 2-year school, alternate 6-week runs at home theater, Tokyo, rehearsals, while one splits between smaller theater, tours and rest for some.

Takarazuka "Girls' Operatic School" is run like lady-marine boot camp. There are several applicants for each opening, gals enter at 15-18 after JrHi or Hi-school, and long private tutoring, start retiring after 4-5 years usually into TV or stage or film careers. Even stars rarely stick long, turnover is encouraged, wages minimal, but stage education is priceless. Favored stars tend to be male impersonators, *otoko-yaku*, casting somewhat lesbian tint on theater. Many female role-players (more accurately female-impersonators—fascinating in that in kabuki, *onnagata*–female-impersonator also draws female mobs) make it big later as singers, dancers and actresses in TV, movies.

Show usually features one Western-style play, which Jay equates to US Hi-school production, but his dancer-sister thought was marvelous especially for infectious spirit of actresses. This may be translation-adaptation of US or European classic, or specially-written original highly influenced by specific plays or operas. Half of program is based on traditional Japan theater, and Jay fondly recalls seeing young geisha being teased by others playing catch with her clog in snow flurry—at New York World's Fair of 1939. Worth whole ticket just for Japanese portion, skip 'Western'.

Acting aside, musicals reach acme of stage presentation, if weak voices —but less so than straight band crooners, most of whom even amps can't help. Staging is phenomenal, state-of-stage-art, lighting etc—and visual impact of hundred flamboyantly costumed dancers twirling together...

Tickets ¥600 to ¥3,200 top—eminently affordable, as fans mostly school kids and nostalgic housewives. English earphones available. Takarazuka theater ☎(0797)-85-6272, Hankyu electric out of Osaka or Kobe 30min; Tokyo theater ☎(03)-3591-8100.

Alas, old **Kokusai** and **Nichigeki** super chorus-lines of Tokyo, reminiscent of great Zeigfield frolics of granny's day, are no more. Some shadow of them occasionally at Shinjuku's lively **Koma Gekijo** theater. Osaka still has **OSK Review**. Sacred hoochy-kooch still popular, *sutorippu* is modern living art, without much tease, still in smaller cities.

Successful corporations like **Suntory** and **Wacoal** and fabulous real estate developer Mori in his **La Forêt** (French for *mori*) museum-buildings, have built superb little multi-use spaces and theaters in their new buildings. *Tokyo Journal*, *Japan Times* and Monday *Mainichi Daily News* carry good listings. International theater appreciation groups like **International Noh Club** occasionally providing programs in English. **International Friends of Kabuki** meet mid-month, frequent special programs, announced in papers, welcome all (usually ¥2,000); tel Oshima ☎(03)-874-3879.

PLAY GUIDE Japlish name for agencies where tickets for all theater, music, sports events can be had. Branches in most dept. stores of all cities; most theaters have ticket booth for others. English often spoken. Hotel desks handle for you, some travel agents. **Japan Times Ticket Center** expanding, Tokyo ☎(03)-3769-4134 in English.

ENGLISH LANGUAGE STAGE

SLIGHT but of great variety, almost exclusive to Tokyo. *Kabuki* etc usually have English available by rental earphone. *Kyogen* comic *noh* in translation has frequent stagings by Don Kenny, *Japan Times* theater columnist, with traditional actors from ancient families, many of whom are western educated. Umewaka noh school's rising young Naohiko (Garet's schoolmate) carries on his late father's crusade to introduce noh to world so that it may both influence and be influenced and thus stay viable as contemporary traditional theater. English slapstick has taken foothold (in its own mouth) with **Albion Za**, 2 Limies + 1 Yank, mostly satire on life in Japan, successfully appreciated by both visitor and native, large Japanese following — alas leader died during proofs. Successor group, **Za Gaijin**, ☎(03)-3281-7270. Amateur group, **TIP**, Tokyo International Players, play Tokyo once-twice annually. Kyoto-Kobe had fine amateur troupe **KIDS** (Kinki-area International Drama Society) performing US & UK plays disbanded when leader left.

Not in English, but all native English-speakers, Kobe has sadly-named **Kabuki-Japonesque** which grew out of fabulous Canadian Academy international school student kabuki, sole non-Japanese performers of *hon* (real thing) *kabuki*—made up, wigged and costumed by people who do pros. Performs perhaps annually, autumn, watch KTO. Garet played it 7 years, elder brother 4.

CONCERTS

ATTRACT good audiences and there is solid diet of symphony and smaller combinations and soloists in classical and modern music, both local and top-flight import. Especially at music festivals, best being Osaka's **May** *Arts Festival*. Major big-name performers will be covered in newspapers, especially when sponsored by them. Some superb concerts by local and lesser imported talent never get into press, because papers don't bother and impresarios don't know how to handle press.

This is especially true of what would be most exciting for music-loving foreign visitor—experimental modern music with traditional Japanese and other Oriental instruments, or mixtures of Oriental and Occidental instruments and forms. Practitioners are both foreign masters of Japanese traditional instruments, like Hawaiian musicologist 'Kaizan' Neptune on *shakuhachi*, as well as numerous native artists of traditional schools and families. Record shops (enough English spoken) have good selection, from MIYAGI Michio's decades-old classic Oriental potpourri *Eitenraku*, thru modern 'Bach on *shakuhachi*' to some rather far-out avant-garde mixes, dixie on bamboo flute, etc.

As we close this book, newest theater is Daiei–New Oriental Hotel super theater in Kobe built for operas and musicals and with no qualms about red ink or late hours. Bodes nothing but good for theater in Kansai.

BOOKSHELF

Nothing in English on *kagura*, or shrine and temple dances, or modern theater, except some photo essays on Butoh.

Bugaku, fine little illustrated *Bugaku* by TOGI Masataro, translated Don Kenny, in Weatherhill series *Performing Arts of Japan.*

Bunraku—near homonym puppets also PAJ series volume; but best descriptive detail with summaries in paperback *Bunraku* by HIRONAGA Shuzaburo, (Bunraku Theater, Dotombori, Osaka). Add beautiful *Voices and Hands of Bunraku* by Barbara Adachi (KI).

Noh essential is *Guide to Noh* by PG O'Neil, pocketbook of brief summaries of plays (*noh* bookstore Hinoki Shoten, 2-1, Kogawa-cho, Kanda, Tokyo); *Japanese Noh Plays, How To See Them* by NOGAMI Toyoichiro, (Nogaku-Shorin *noh* bookstore, Jimbocho 5-3, Kanda, Tokyo); *Japanese Noh Plays*, Vol. 16, (JTB Tourist Library); *Noh Plays of Japan*, Arthur Waley 19 translated plays, 14 others summarized (Evergreen paperback), worth hunting; *The Classic Noh Theater of Japan*, "poetic" translations, summaries by Ernest Fenollosa and Ezra Pound (New Directions paper); several volumes superb translations with stage sketch instructions à la real librettos, 10 plays per large volume, *Japanese Noh Drama* by Japan Classic Committee (Tuttle).

Kyogen essential is *Guide to Kyogen* by Don Kenny, performer; pocket-size 300+pp synopses of all 275 plays in present day repertoire, (Hinoki Shoten Tokyo ☎(03)-3291-2488 or Kyoto ☎(075)-231-1990 if not easily available); translations by SAKANISHI Shio, (Tuttle).

Kabuki essential is paperback *Kabuki Handbook*, A.S. & G.M. Halford, summaries of many plays, (Tuttle); *You Mean To Say You Still Don't Know Who We Are?* ed Cellin Gluck (our #1 son), colloquial translations of seven commonly performed selections, with summaries of portions not translated, incl only true kabuki comedy *Hokaibo*, plus *Chushingura, Benten Kozo, Bancho Sarayashiki, Death of Yoritomo, Sukeroku, Tale of Shuzenji*, all by sole non-Japanese troupe performing in original language (*see* above) of these same plays printed, paperback (US distrib Tuttle). Ruth Shaver's *Kabuki Costume* (Tuttle) handy for telling good guys from bad, and much else for better understanding snd enjoyment, but bulky and ¥8,240. Also *JTB Tourist Library* vol 7; several superb coffee table books with summaries, but not what you need on your lap at theater.

- J.P. Maroon

Applying the make-up

Garet in kabuki make-up

defeated sumo wrestler
reviews his day's battles
in bed with his wife
    — senryu, *comic haiku*

SPORT

JUST AS DANCE started in Japan as ritual of offering to deity, so in rural areas do you see *sumo* ring adjoining stage in shrine courtyard. Traditional sports of Japan are still very much alive, generally easiest seen in Tokyo.

Sumo holds 3 of 6 annual 15-day meets in Tokyo (check hotel desk for ticket info). *Judo, karate, aikido, kyudo-*'zen' long-bow archery are introduced below. Most high schools and colleges also have clubs for *kendo-*fencing, *karate, judo, kyudo*, perhaps *aikido* and *sumo*, and on visit to school request to see their *dojo*, 'way-place', or traditional gym.

Certain other ancient sports which have not gained popularity are seen performed at festivals or on special occasions and are listed in relevant area DATEBOOKs. These include: *yabusame*, or samurai archery from horseback (notably Kamakura); *kemari*, soccer-like (except no heading due to tall horse-hair hats) 'pepper' game similar to Siamese *takraw* except that it's played in ancient court costume, usually in Kyoto palace; *toh-gyu* or *ushi* (bull)-*sumo*, bloodless fight between bulls, best seen in Shikoku where also bloodless dog-fighting is dying sport. Boat races and water polo are also features of shrine fetes in summer, as also tugs-of-war and ceremonial free-for-all, often midwinter. Windy seasons see aerial dog-fighting of giant kites in southern Nagasaki, central Hamamatsu and northern Niigata. Odd traditional races, water sports, etc, are dealt with in local DATEBOOKs.

SUMO

BEHEMOTHS clash and crash at **Kokugikan**, 10,000-seat Sumo 'National Sport Pavilion' in olde-Edo Tokyo Ryogoku area (*see* TOKYO: ASAKUSA). Great coliseum is modern steel, but air is still that of feudal era Japan. We enter thru alleys lined by eating stalls run by retired gladiators, to great arena. Diminutive feudal throwback in oversized pantaloons mounts stage and operatically announces match. Two giants lumber forth nonchalantly, rinse mouths at team bucket (as worshipper does before shrine), scatter salt in ritual purification, engaging in crotch-splitting calisthenics in rite which makes as much sense, really, as it does good theater. Spontaneity is keynote of sumo, nonevident as it may be. Even, perhaps especially, during clinch when both opponents seem frozen in interlocked embrace is spontaneous action of high-speed sport in subtle evidence. No muscle twitches, no movement is apparent. Yet each wrestler is constantly alert for iota of shift of balance, for slightest indication of instant's relaxation on part of other.

TOURNAMENTS are Tokyo mid-January, May (which emperor visits), September, with others in Ōsaka March, Nagoya July, Fukuoka November. Each, of 15 days, begins sunday nearest 10th of month, ends sunday. NHK TV covers them live daily 15:30-18:00, replays hilites 23:00. Kokugikan also hosts college championships November, amateur playoffs December. Smaller tourneys of visiting stars, and *jungyo* demonstrations, are held all over country and may be stumbled on, where champion may shove-of-war with whole classroom of jock-strapped toddlers, to general hilarity. *Jungyo* road tours of 2-3 weeks are held after each main tournament except January (too cold), with entourage on one-nite stands in town halls, tented fields etc,

Shokkiri

organized like road circus complete from *gyoji* referees and *oyakata* (retired champions now trainers) down to *yobidashi* announcer-sweepers and souvenir hawkers. Start 8:00, go till 16:00 when camp struck. Rikishi earn no points during tours, must be goaded to avoid slacking, but playing hometown of even lowest rassler sees him 'helped' by mates to elevate his 'face' at home. Lower ranks, as usual, perform all necessary services on tour—from cooking to packing and cleaning.

Sport dates back to legendary epoch, perhaps 2,000 years. Similar, less ritualized wrestling styles exist on mainland among Koreans and Mongols. Was sometimes used as divination, in medieval age martial art reserved to warriors. In peaceful age of Edo, 1600-on, became professional sport evolving into what it is today most popular spectator sport. Still based on Edo-era feudal structure, entry is as unpaid apprentice, to live monastic life in *heya* or stable, do all tasks for group, wait on seniors—makes English boarding school seem freer than US campus, marine boot camp like summer camp. It is, like sport elsewhere, best way out of pits for poor boys, who start at 15 after compulsory middle school (occasional collegiate star). Non-Japanese used to less-regimented life seems can't seem to make it. One half-Russian, born and raised Japanese, made top. Korean Rikidozan quit to be pro-wrestling star. Three Americans, Hawaiian, made it to higher levels (Konishiki to ozeki, May '87). In 1991 22 low rank foreigners (11 are American) fighting up. Several Pacific islanders dropped out, but took sport to Samoa. One Caucasian Canadian, muscular rather than tubby, broke all records in entry division winning every fight for several seasons, but couldn't take sumo's limitations on his love life so quit for grunt and groan. Life is rough, apprentices start practice 4am, don't eat till noon, main meal of *chanko-nabé* —and they eat after seniors, get leftovers.

Rikishi, power-men, 1988 number recorded high of 818, ranked: lowest *jonokuchi* at 'arena mouth', 118; *jonidan* 2nd step, 316; *sandanme* 3rd step 200; *maku-shita* 'curtain-below' still outsiders, 120; *juryo*, literally '10-units' (old weight and coin unit, like lb/£) junior pro rank fixed at 26; top *maku-no-uchi* or pros 'curtain-within', up to 38 (full '88-91). Latter, with whom tournaments mostly concerned, again subdivided *mae-gashira*, 'before pillar' or seniors, about 25; *komusubi* champion 3rd class; *sekiwaké* champ 2nd class; *ozeki* champion, grand champion-*yokozuna*, with perhaps dozen in these 4 top ranks. Whole is divided into East and West camps, not fixed team designation, wrestlers move from one to other each tournament.

Also have numerical ranks so top men ranked "East/West maegashira number-X", raised or dropped each tournament even down to juryo. Rank determines monthly base salary (pre-juryo no pay), paid by Sumo Association. Add to this individual bout prizes, fan gifts, commercial endorsements (now banned—how we miss their humorous TV ads).

Bouts begin 10:00 with shaggy-headed teenage *mae-zumo* apprentices, then 11:00 long-haired lower four divisions thru *maku-shita* parade in to grapple, progressing to pompadoured *juryo* rank at 15:00, when main juryo wrestlers parade in *doyoiri*, East first, then West, fancy embroidered aprons like walking art exhibition or fashion show of Goliaths, each introduced by costumed announcer in sumo-operatic voice in brief ritual. This repeats with more ornate *maku-uchi* wrestlers parade hour later, immediately joined by great pomp of *yokozuna doyoiri*. Enter each Grand Champ with escort of two champs, one with broom 'sweeping dew' away, one carrying ceremonial sword, in matching *keshomawashi* aprons costing some $25,-30,000 each, but which supporters vie to present. Then maku-uchi fight. *Yokozuna* wear great 13kg/29lb white rope bow *yoko-tsuna* 'horizontal rope' exclusive rank chevron, bedecked with five *gohei*, zig-zag-fold paper tassels. Trio mount mound on west, face east, squat so champ can show he's unarmed—spread arms, clap hands, turn palms to all. Then strut ring center, face north, Emperor's box (North Star?), perform purification *shiko* so dearly associated with sumo: legs spread, arms and hands dance gracefully, one leg raises and stomps down with great force exploding as it were among crowd simultaneously to their spontaneous cheer, 3 times. Other yokozuna follow and repeat. Then final match series begin in reverse rank, yokozuna last to fight, meet each other final days. 16th duel may be called for end of last day to break any top-rank tie.

Juryo and maku-uchi 60-odd wrestlers wear traditional oiled topknot, *oichonmage*, receive regular salary—very modest, but sponsors help and top bouts earn individual purses, advertised before bout by pantalooned ushers parading banners around ring and handed out to squatting winner after bout. Popular stars used to make good fees in TV and periodical commercials. Below juryo busily grow hair long enough to knot if and when honor is bestowed. Makushita fight alternate days, best of 7. Juryo-up fight daily, next day's opponent decided by their results keeps bouts evenly matched.

WEIGHT CLASSIFICATIONS don't exist. New hopefuls enter Osaka Spring tourney, which in '87 admitted record 135, including some 10 non-Japanese, and another Hawaiian Goliath, who fight from 2nd day. Smallest to start must be 173cm/5'8" and 75kg/165lbs, but pros run 100kg/222lbs-up. All-time scale-tippers are Hawaiian Americans: recent retiree 'Jesse' Takamiyama (High-View-Mount) 200kg/440lbs and protégé 'Sally' Konishiki (Little Glory) 250+kg/qtr ton and still teething; newer Akebono (Dawn) is tallest in history at 204cm/6'8". (Jesse retired with all-time records for consecutive bouts, perseverance; changed name and citizenship to become stable-master Azumazeki). Hairiest must be Jewish-Argentine with poetic name Hoshi-tango (Star Tango). Win 8 of 15 or better earns upping: lose 8 and slide down in number, as well as in rank if several minus tournaments. Certificate of new top rank reads, "You are recommended to rank of yokozuna on account of your *dignity*, competence and skill". These are not mugs but gentle giants and disciplined craftsmen. Ozeki or yokozuna are not demoted, but once performance drops resign with great pomp, topknot is cut off in grand *dampatsu-shiki* ceremony. At hair-cutting retirement rites of champion there is satirical sumo, *shokkiri*, by makushita juniors.

BOUT begins with entry onto *dohyo* (squared circle), truncated pyramid mound 54cm/21" high by 5.54m/18' square, with circle 4.55m/15' across outlined by 20 buried rice bales rising ankle high out of pounded specially-prepared clay, enshrining under center earthenware vase of kelp, nuts and cuttlefish. At center two parallel white lines 90cm/3ft, some 120cm/4ft apart are starting lines. Whole is roofed with *shinmei-zukuri* shinto-style remnant of primeval shrine structure, suspended from domed ceiling. Until late '50s this sat atop corner pillars against which rikishi were often injured.

In fight great apron is put aside, each strips down to broad belt 10-13m/32-42ft long by 80cm/31" wide, wrapped around waist and folded in 6 over privates, decorated with silk-cord tassels which frequently fly off in contest. Band is colored silk for champions, blue denimish *aizomé* cotton for lower. In early days of US Occupation also wore boxer shorts to shield shy US officers' wives of view of brawny broad buttock.

Each bout averages 5 minutes, mostly preparatory ceremony—sip water, toss salt in purification, stamp out (*shiko*) bad luck—all to center oneself to make *ki* energy flow, and evil-eye opponent to rattle him. '89 star Chiyonofuji (string of 53 successive wins, 1,000+ total, tops of century) 'Wolf', pure muscle, handsomest yokozuna ever, half Sally's heft, is noted for stare which can only be described in US teen term 'stink-eye'. Lovable Hawaiian comic Takamiyama could curdle coconut milk. This *shikiri naoshi* in bout Wolf vs Jesse always Oscar-winning performance of sneers. Great psychological, almost psychic duel goes on for some minutes—limited since TV but till '50s yokozuna might take quarter hour to go. Medieval-costumed ref-*gyoji*, who always inherits personal name KIMURA Shonosuke, raises battle fan to signal end of prep time as rikishi gather more salt, crowd claps, tension builds—they stoop last time, knuckles touch clay and they are off at each other spontaneously. If simultaneity fails, either may pull back and they restart. Each slaps other's hands away from grabbing arm or belt to gain one of 70 listed throws, lifts and pushes. First to touch clay in dohyo with any part but soles of feet, or touch clay beyond straw circle, loses. It is all-out, no holding back, full steam for several seconds or few minutes. But no bawdy free-for-all. One UK sumo-scribe writes: "Ring decorum and sportsmanship are of highest order, making even cricket seem somewhat rowdy by comparison". Usually honest, fixes are rare—especially since rash of falls, *yaocho*, in '60s imperiled sport (not gambling instigated, but rikishi 'lending' win repaid by reciprocal fall later to keep score majority of wins to avoid demotion). Konishiki took several early in his rocketing career to calm racist 'pureblood' colleagues who can't accept success of gook—here this category includes us honkies, brother.

On rare occasion pair grapple to stalemate, ref will call bout for *mizu-iri*, water-taking break, to resume after next bout. Saw record-breaker Tokyo 1955 when took 3 rounds to conclude match. '88 saw rarer 3 ties. Both may fly out of ring together, at which ref decides or calls on black-kimonoed judges in front rows to come up for confab. TV gives instant replay from alternate angles after each bout, but refs can't use this. Wonder that rikishi are not seriously injured more often is less than wonder at rarity of injuries of front-row *sunakaburi*, 'covered with sand' seats. Day ends about 6pm with graceful long-bow dance (rite shared with Persian *zur-khane* grapplers) except last day when prizes awarded with, of course, more pomp—parchments with each gigantic silver chalice or bowl. Most wins in 15 gets several awards, from Emperor's to Pan Am's (don't fly here anymore!), so numerous, obviously self-serving, as to be worthless. 'Fighting spirit' goes to lesser but fast-rising champ who dumps yokozuna; one for best technique etc. Can win multiple prizes. Top winner then gets open car parade thru city, few days later returns to hometown, usually farm village in north, like triumphant Caesar. Only return of high school baseball team from annual Nishinomiya championships can match it in hoopla and TV coverage.

All wrestlers are on salary-contract to Sumo Association, which controls their lives—Canadian couldn't take it. Salaries range from subsistence at initiates to Yokozuna Chiyonofuji's 1988 monthly ¥967,000 plus allowance of ¥200,000 per tournament. Then ¥5,000,000 to tournament winner (Chiyo 25x), ¥35,000 *kensho* for each bout won, plus special prizes awarded main bouts by supporters whose banners are thus paraded in ring. Fans invite to parties for good *orei*–Chiyo gets ¥1,000,000 for autographs.

Tickets 3 months ahead: hotel desk, arena (TOKYO ☎(03)-623-5111, OSAKA ☎(06)-647-6301) or **PlayGuide**, few tix on sale early same day at arena. Boxes for 4, ¥36,-75,000 w/bento-lunch most fun, sgle from ¥7,500 in pairs tho cramped on tatami. Discomfort salved by camaraderie, food and drink hawked, passed around. Arena entry thru foodstall-lined alley, *chaya*, run by retired rikishi—who run boxes, so if speak Japanese, check with one of men in medieval costume if any open. If no box, settle for bleachers, eat and drink into mood of crowd. Fans skip early matches so you can quietly, politely squeeze into empty box, alert to withdraw with bows or nods of thanks and apologies when owner appears—sometimes never in early days, as most are reserved for season by supporter-company for possible out-of-town business guests. Tickets different system Tokyo, Osaka. **Tokyo** boxes for 2 & 4, charge per person ¥7,500-9,500 (no bento); rsved seats ¥2,300, ¥5,-7,000; ¥1,500. **Osaka** boxes for 4, ¥70,-82,000 w/bento, souvenir; rsved ¥15,-16,000 w/bento, souvenir; SRO ¥500.

Bookshelf for fan-to-be: basically Andy Adams' edited bi-monthly mag *Sumo World* published for each tournament, full background on sport, profiles on stars, past scores etc. Don't go to bouts without it. Best books: Adams & Hatano *Sumo History and Yokozuna Profiles*; Sumo Association's *Sumo*; Patricia Cuyler's *Sumo from Rite to Sport*; David Benjamin's *Joy of Sumo* from fan's viewpoint in Dohyo, and John Wheeler's wonderful as-told-to *Takamiyama*. Gem by super-science scribe Lyall Watson, *Sumo* (Channel 4 Book, London), who brought full-fledged 5-day tournament to London for '91 Japan Festival, also hosts sole outside-Japan sumo program in seasons on TV Channel 4—surprisingly high audience ratings, why doesn't some US sports cable pick it up.

I cannot tell a lie, hon. father...I did it with my bare hand, karate style!

MARTIAL ARTS OF EMPTY HAND.

FOR AGES important weapon in Asia. Far Eastern fisticuffs were set apart from all others about 525AD when Indian monk Daruma came to China. Formalized meditation sect of Zen (Chinese *Ch'an*, Indian *Dhyana*) which influenced thinking of China for centuries, was important factor in shaping Japanese civilization. China then was split into warring kingdoms and bandit baronies. One local war lord disarmed people but failed to protect them. Tradition holds that Daruma assembled his followers and announced:

> "War and killing are wrong, but so is it wrong not to be prepared to defend oneself. We may not have knives, so make every finger unto dagger...every fist, unto mace...every arm unto spear, and let every open hand be one's sword."

He drew upon ancient 'shadow boxing' and war dance calisthenics, put Taoist scientific principles to them, yoga techniques, and Buddhist pacifism, inaction—use aggressor's strength against him, help him destroy himself. Resulting discipline was two-edged weapon: enabled peaceful unarmed to remain secure; also educate young hot-heads by physical discipline leading to varying degrees of enlightenment. Admittedly, often misused.

Numerous variations on this basic art include: *jujutsu*, gentle technique, *judo* or gentle way; *karate* empty hand; *yawara* plasticity; *aikido* spirit-uniting-way; and China's *tai ch'i chuan* "shadow boxing"; and *kung-fu*, Okinawan *te* or fist; Korean *subag*, *taikwan-do*—to mention but few names known in West. In general we can group these into grappling or wrestling types exemplified by judo, and boxing types like karate, kung-fu.

JUDO, Olympic sport, is 80-year-old refinement on 50-odd varieties of military jujutsu prevalent in Japan at end of feudal period. These were 'secret arts' taught only to samurai class warriors. Their copyright, so to speak, expired with expiration of feudalism and they became public domain. Suffix-*do* (Way), implies discipline, return to some of old Chinese fair play and chivalry that had been somewhat neglected by samurai in feudal Japan. This development was intrinsic part of modernizatio after Perry. Many enlightened warriors anticipated new era, which would see restoration of Imperial power and facing up to outside world as well.

These progressives tended to congregate in Kan-da, 'God field' (*see* TOKYO P.1174)...so called because fields there produced rice for Edo's offerings to Ise Grand Shrine. There were numerous training halls here for *bu-do* or warrior arts. One was founded by ISO Matayemon who developed advanced form of jujutsu by combining best from many schools. One of his students was KANO Jigoro, who founded judo and **Kodo-kan**, located to this day in Kanda. As aside, progressive warriors were probably attracted to Kanda as it was right next to Surugadai, cultural center of Edo.

Kodo-kan judo center (for traditionalists), or recommended alternate, **Budo-kan**, in early morning can also be first stop on singularly macho day's pilgrimage, one that can be done properly only in Tokyo. We start with judo, then to aikido, most esoteric of several jujutsu forms, actually combat yoga; visit mecca of karate 'masters of bare-hand kill'; archery goods shop of one of 'Zen archery' grand masters; end up with alchemist in steel, one of last of ancient sword makers (now makes steak knives). If lucky, sumo in season.

Kodo-kan visitor's gallery opens 6am. Always classes going on; classes for foreigners, directed in English 6-7pm, with use of dojo 4-8pm to grapple freely with any student. Costs ¥7,000 per month for 6 days per week, costume runs about ¥10,000 depending on quality and size; ☎(03)-3818-4172 in English. But something has happened to judo—now sport for giants, men as big or bigger than pro rasslers and sumo-tori. Kano himself was featherweight. Perhaps last of grand old gents was master Mifune. **Reading** on judo his *Cannon of Judo* best. Also fine is Lindy Avakian's *Secrets of Judo* (Tuttle paperback). Many books for those interested only in flips and tricks. From Kodo-kan go to...

Budo-kan, Hall of Martial Arts (*see* TOKYO-IMPERIAL p1142) is good single stop for overall view of warrior arts outlined herein. Architecture interesting from outside, but inside rather standard, if large, gym...which makes for less authentic atmosphere than visiting dojos themselves—and Budo-kan teachers, while experts, are not those more individually interesting masters. Lacking time or special interest, take in Budo-kan—if really interested, go out of your way and go to dojos of masters. Budo-kan starts 6am, continuous all day, several martial sports in session simultaneously: judo, kendo, year-long course start April, **write** for info **Budo Gakuen,** Budokan, Chiyoda-ku, Tokyo. For other -*do* they now refer you to special dojos nationwide; ☎3216-0781. Dorm for full timers available pilgrim rate due to government subsidy, or instructors can introduce budget ryokan. Nearby **Fairmont Hotel** offers generous discount to budo-ka.

KARATE like judo is for use against aggressor physically superior in size, equipment or number. Both work on turning antagonist's own strength back against him. Both are for defense. Both involve, at least in abstract theory,

strict code of chivalry. Here similarity ends. Judo works on bamboo principle that tho enough snow to break oak tree may also fall on bamboo, supple stem gives way with load, causing snow to tumble off by its own weight. Karate follows bamboo principle that tho heavy object may be propelled against bamboo with enough force to smash stone wall, supple stem gives way with attack, to spring back and smash attacker with cumulative force of attacker's forward inertia and bamboo inherent strength. Latter two are duplicated in man–strong tubular shape is bone, flexibility is muscle.

DOJO, or gym, of OYAMA Masatatsu. Mas has been written up often in USA, including first by Jay in *True*, has taught there on periodic visits. Many karate groups in US, UK affiliated with his *Kyokushinkai* group.

Karate-*ka*, practitioners, condition parts of body to be weapons Daruma said to develop, use own variety of punching bags—wooden posts. Famed knife fingers are trained by jabbing sand, beans, then gravel. High jump-kick attack begins by skipping rope with barbells tied to feet. But most important, Zenist breathing training is undergone, and meditation.

Rhythm is developed...sole entrance test to Mas' gym is question, "Do you like music?" Mas says person who doesn't dig music can never learn karate. Mas is Korean, worked his way thru prewar Japanese college as ricksha puller. Example of second purpose of self-defense arts, enlightening of hotheads—he was, he admits, rather nasty-punk-type before karate master, great Funakoshi who introduced technique from Okinawa, got him.

Breaking bricks and boards bare-handed just show-gimmick he confesses—not true karate—tho he seems to think full-contact drill is? Developing inner peace is: originally trained for match alternately drilling and reading poetry—techniques recently abandoned for splash.

Bookshelf: Oyama's *What Is Karate & This Is K...*; Tuttle-published several Karate lesson books various levels; karate chapter Jay's *Zen Combat* introduces Mas.

Getting There: Dojo hard to find, worth hunt: 5min into maze from Ikebukuro Stn, Nishi Ikebukuro 3-3-9, Toshima-ku; spk-Eng, ☎(03)-964-7421; practice tue, thur, sat, sun 6–9pm. **Japan Karate Assoc**–Int'l Ebisu-Nishi 1-6-1, Shibuya-ku; ☎3462-1415.

AIKIDO doesn't really fit into either wrestling or boxing category. Its own principle of bamboo could be said to be that when heavy snow falls it's better for bamboo to be in sunny clime. Art of evasion, attempt to reduce all action to quintessentials. It is, more than any other -*do*, physical mysticism. Even more so than karate, its basic calisthenics are pure dance. It trains one to overcome one's own inertia, to become 'bodyless'. Thus muscle unimportant. Basis is inaction-reaction. There can be no aiki match—two aiki-ka facing each other would sit down to tea and laugh. Pure yogic way, pure Zen, higher stage than turn-other-cheek Christianity as it turns cheek before taking hit, saves everyone hurt or guilt.

Amazing feats of strength by adherents are performed, champion weight-lifter cannot budge tiniest aiki-ist, as Jay saw 240-pounder try futilely to lift 90-pound Sumi...accomplished by internal hydraulic system which can only be described as sexual, whereby even one's little finger can become rigid, yet pliant, totally unbendable. All really so basically simple that most adherents laugh while at practice.

Ueshiba Morihei

Two major schools (plus independents—martial arts politics worse than sororities): 'original' **Ueshiba Aikido** (© name) headed now by son, Kisshomaru, and **Shinshin-toitsu-Ki-do**, 'mind and body blending spirit-way' led by Tohei, long-time UESHIBA Morihei top disciple. Disregarding back-biting counter-claims, Morihei originated Aikido distilling elements from many martial arts he studied (including Sumi's family feudal era *Kiai-do*, same ideograms reversed) to develop sole philosophically pure martial art, impossible to use for aggression, almost as impossible to teach. Tohei's great contribution is brilliantly systematized teaching with testable basic 'postures', which every good teacher uses now regardless of school or what he says he does. Have even seen judo taught with it—which becomes more like what Kano taught.

Many aiki students are artists, dancers, doctors, who study it, as Jay did, as calisthenic to encourage creative self. Note numerous dummy weapons on racks—swords, rifles, bayonets—used for defense training. Aiki-ka is invulnerable to all. Late Founding-Master Morihei, tiny, grinning, bearded sage out of ancient Chinese painting, tuned up catching arrows midair, demonstrated invulnerability to guns to Japanese generals (Houdini-dodged, "but no defense against chaos"). Yet unlike karate and judo, aiki trainees are almost never injured—would reflect on one's teacher.

Grand Master Tohei, speaks English (as do several instructors), tours his affiliated US dojos, his book *Aikido in Daily Life* (var edition *Ki in...*) is clear and comprehensible. Ueshiba also speaks some English, has instructors who do. In USA look up Aikido or Ki in phone yellow pages under 'Karate', see local school. If interested, look up its main school here—or 'comparison-shop' both. Individual teacher important, not style.

Ueshiba Aikido Hon-dojo Wakamatsu-cho 102, Shinjuku-ku; ☎(03)-3203-9236. Get there on bus from Shinjuku W exit, to stop for bus #76, 15min to Benten-cho (walkable from Waseda). In maze of alleys on R, facing Shinjuku; signs. **Shinshin-toitsu Ki** is same bus few stops on, Ushigome Yanagi-cho; ☎3353-3461.

Classes by month, as with judo. Private lessons for short-time visitors, hour daily. Best times betw dawn—9am, or after 4pm, also some weekends. Phone for time to visit. Both highly receptive to sincere foreigners, we think Tohei still has edge on teaching style, now has some good foreign assistants to tutor beginners.

ARCHERY was dropped by Olympic committee from '64 Tokyo fete—chauvinists screamed that sure-fire gold medal had been thus forfeited as archery was Zenist discipline dating back ages in Japan, superior to other ways.

"We'd have been massacred" said traditional archery Grand Master Hideharu Onuma. "Century ago our bows were world's best, perhaps, but today's are antiques, made and used in fine traditional ways, but cannot compare with fabulous atomic age modern bows of glass and plastics using scientific sights. Western bow is made for deadly accuracy in sport. Ours is philosophical-calisthenic instrument". Onuma was both top instructor of Western archery, as well as 15th generation master of centuries-old Heki military school of traditional archery, and one of highest-ranking aces of ceremonial Ogasawara style, or so-called 'Zen archery'.

Kyu-do, 'bow-way' or calisthenic Zen archery, is also based on dance. Develops

Zen archer

great poise, popular with both sexes in college, is, with aikido, best ki-generating exercise, thus of greatest use to general athlete or seeker after spiritual-physical techniques adaptable to other arts or applications. Equipment are works of art—full set of 7+ft bow, yard-plus bamboo arrows, deer-skin arrow glove, wicker quiver, string roll and outfit of kimono-fold blouse, split skirt and belt runs from about ¥75,000. Bows alone start at ¥19,000 in fiber glass, ¥28,000 traditional multi-layer bamboo-&-yew, while masterpieces of lacquered bows run to artware prices. Off-center bow has short bottom arc, long top (usable from horseback as in *yabusame*), is called compound recurve, made of sandwich of several strips of bamboo & yew, that curves back on itself when strung—modern cheaper practice bows are glass fiber. Too long to mail; must, and can, carry back as baggage, set weighs some 3 pounds, goes on plane as check-in or even carry-on baggage as we've done often—it's too unwieldy to use for hijacking. Lay it down along outer wall.

Daughters Takako and Tsutako, adept kyudoists, carry on his **Asahi Archery Shop** (about 400m along Kasuga-dori from Shin-Otsuka stn of Marunouchi subway, or Toden tram from Waseda to Mukohara stop, moderate walk from either aiki dojo, above); at Minami-Otsuka 3-23-3, Toshima-ku, Tokyo 170; ☎(03)-3986-2301. Contact in-house *deshi* assistant, Dan Deprospero, for supplies or to see or take lessons nearby at dojo with English instruction; or **Budo-kan** or archery clubs in any university for shooting or information on meets.

Asakusa Kyudo Kai, in Taito-ku, ☎3672-3181; open 7am-10pm; no English. **Zen Nippon Kyudo Renmei**, 1-1-1 Jin-nan, Shibuya-ku, Tokyo ☎3467-7949. Onuma has good basic book in English; also Jay's *Zen Combat* covers traditional archery in some detail. Term 'archery' used in Japanese means western bow only, J-style is just *kyudo*, which means only Japanese longbow ritual archery, 'bow-way'.

Zen - ken - shu; Zen = sword = brush — Japanese proverb

SWORD is most justly famed Japanese weapon, called *Nihon-to*, above. So fine in ancient times they were even exported to China, hi-tech center of world. **Ueno Museum** for fine collection of old swords, bookshop has excellent handbook on subject; also **sword museum** *To-ken bijutsukan* near Meiji Jingu, (*see* TOKYO-WEST). One of last of old swordsmiths is **Japan Sword**, Toranomon 3-8-1, Minato-ku (☎3434-4321), *see* p.1282. Has fine sword, armor collection, 2nd floor. He doesn't supply samurai today. Main store has old swords for sale, men's jewelry of sword decorations, both antique and modern imitation. (Purely weapon-grade old swords *illegal*, each blade must have police registry, granted only for its cultural worth). If fine sword is being made for US military dress, ancient smithy's ritual is again performed.

KENDO, so-called 'way of sword', best seen at aiki dojo when practicing evading sword wielders; or at Budo-kan. When college in session, visit can take in kendo gym, still popular in schools. Kendo, Jay's 9th-rank master claimed, bears little resemblance to actual swordplay. Now body-building calisthenic, good for developing alacrity. Bamboo 'swords' used in kendo bear no resemblance in balance or feel or use to real thing—unlike Western fencing which uses only slightly modified true weapon. Kendo, with its masks and armor and *ki-ai* shouting, is weird thing to see. *I-ai-do* is sort of sword dance-cum-fast-draw drill with real sword: snap out, slice and return to scabbard in single sweep without slicing oneself. For advanced kendo-ka, rarely seen except at special events, done solo; slight slip, and...

Women fence with *naginata* (long spear—at which chief aiki female instructress, SUNADO-MARI Fukiko, is ace), far more graceful, more interesting.

Kendo match with bamboo sword

All Japan Kendo Federation, *Zen Nihon Kendo Renmei* c/o Budokan, ☎3216-0781; will refer you to dojo convenient to your locale, suggest lessons run ¥5,-6,000/month 2/week, proportionately more for intensive; language not needed, taught by example and puppet-like manipulation. Equipment varies from budget to pentagon-budget, some can be borrowed, but require basic *dogi*. E-lessons **Kyomeikan dojo** ☎3930-4636, any age,sex.

Sole shop in Tokyo specializing in *kumi-himo* braided sword cords is **Domyo**; *see* UENO. In front of Asakusa Kannon toy store **Koyama Shoten**, sword reproductions, once sole manufacturer-supplier of swords for TV and samurai flicks. Also at nearby Kototoi-dori and Hisago-dori sword shop deals in real swords, ornamental replicas are fine.

Bookshelf: on archery or kendo: ✍ **Tuttle** Oriental Book distributors, Rutland VT-05701-410 and ask by subject so they will also send you Weatherhill and other lists as well. However, all of above arts are dealt with, and others besides, in Ballantine paperback *Zen Combat*, by Jay, with detailed instructions for basic drills.

Characteristic shared by all martial arts is *ki-ai*, soul shout to focus energy—best accomplished by parallel study of noh or kyogen.

ORIENTAL HEALING

KI is vital energy: its bodily development thru Oriental martial arts is what sets them apart from Occidental sports—tho there is nothing to prevent western sport using ki-techniques. Wilhelm Reich approached it thru his Orgone energy. Others have called it Life Force, etc. Hemingway described its creative art-force simply as "juice". Many artists and writers have devised their own techniques to 'turn it on', much in same tradition of ancient China which evolved graceful effortless exercises for just this purpose—*ch'i gung* and*tai-ch'i chuan* etc.

Ki flows thru parallel nervous system, thru meridians past various *tsubo* or points at which this system is accessible. Main meridian-systems and their basic vessels or organs are: governing (central-spinal), conception (central-frontal), lung, pericardium, heart, large intestine, triple-heater, small intestine, stomach, gall-bladder, bladder, pancreas, liver and kidney— (see *Tsubo–Vital Points for Oriental Therapy* by SERIZAWA Katsusuke, MD, pub JPT).

Illness according to Chinese Medicine (we don't call it 'Oriental–' as we don't know what principles of Indian medicine are, or old Persian etc) is caused by diversion of natural energy flow in one's body. Acupuncture and *shiatsu* massage (and even more esoteric form *ki-atsu* taught in aikido) are techniques to enable healer to inject his self-generated surplus ki into patient at point/s relevant to malfunction to enable patient to recharge and heal self. Chemical drugs act on electrolytic system of body, may interfere with this healing process, so cannot be taken in parallel—herbals usually OK.

Practitioners differ as to what they can treat. Fever was long considered untreatable by shiatsu till recent Chinese research reached Japan and we have seen raging fever reduced to norm in minutes. Some acupuncturists will not treat viral ailments, some will work to enhance immune systems. Both conflicting opinions prevail in AIDS research.

'Alternative Medicine' has attracted much attention in recent years, with restrictions relaxed in most countries to allow other medical systems to be practiced—tho supervision and regulation is as strict, as it should be. Better term, now used officially in England, is *Complementary Medicine*—as all medical systems should complement one another, work together, exchange. 'Alternate…' implies confrontation competition. Hippocratic Oath expresses universal practitioner goals — "heal…above all…do no harm".

ACUPUNCTURE: *kyu* or *hari*, 'needle', in Japanese. Chinese science of great antiquity, undergoing constant research and updating. Anesthesia only minor aspect. Diagnoses by reading three pulses in wrist (vs Western single pulse)—pulsology has full-time practitioners in China's dual-system hospitals. Effective on nervous-system-related ills. Have seen it work on severe stroke, but only within 36hrs; on shock-induced childhood deafness, prostate and on some real puzzlers. And have seen it not work. Usually requires multiple treatments. Degree takes several years of study.

Most acupuncturists also use moxibustion—apply heat to *tsubo* point.

Needles are fully sterilized, usually three times by boiling, ultra-violet and alcohol; many now use disposable one-time needles. Some use electric stimulation, treatments longer, usually hour—others disdain this and use personal ki-stimulus, shorter 20min. Some leave needles in while you rest, some manipulate seconds and take out. Needles are hair-thin, painless— you will probably only be aware of doc's finger tapping you.

Most charge ¥3,000-4,000 ('90), work mon-fri till 5pm (enter by-), later so noted; half-day sat, X-sun, hols. Reservation usual.

SHIATSU likened to acupuncture without needles. Same theory, works on same critical *tsubo* points. Some believe massaging point is all important, others inducing ki thru point. Aikido-*kiatsu* is latter, recent development from China *ki-ko* (Jpn) or *ch'i-gung* (Chin) is high-energy version of same. Highly effective for headaches, stress, pain relieving. Many shiatsuists include chiropractic techniques, some occidental—some get effect by acting on nerves to cause muscles to perform 'adjustment'—so both theories are probably valid. All theory aside, it is effective and easily enough learned that it should become adjunct to modern Physical Therapy.

MASSAGE in hotel (☎ room svce) and sauna (main feature) is legit here, no hanky panky—except in Soaplands where hank is what you bank on. May include light shiatsu, but take care: if hotel masseuse asks if you want hard massage or soft, if first time ask for soft or ordinary, *futsu*, or can end up with ki-overdose hangover, shaken nerves that take 2-3 days to wear off.

Practitioners, several where (at least enough-) English is spoken: All, from hotel masseuse to shiatsuist-acupuncturist, take gov't exam, license—guaranteeing results no more than does Ivy League MD on wall. J-health insurance won't cover, cash.

ACUPUNCTURE Tokyo: NAGAYA Yoshio Clinic; Heights Bldg, Ginza 7-8-17, 4–fl ☎(03)-3573-5563. Average treatment 1hr, till 7pm, ¥3,000. **Kyoto:** James Jones, setting up, check KTO–if not him, some foreigner is usually in practice. **Osaka:** FUJIBAYASHI Clinic (also W-chiro & Chinese herbals). Rear Osaka Stn, cross St front of New Hankyu Hotel, R, 3rd bldg 5-fl, ☎(06)-373-3815. First exam-visit no appt.

SHIATSU Tokyo: NAMIKOSHI Toru, author of top English **book:** *Shiatsu* (JPT), downtown area Capitol hotel, call ☎(03)-3583-9618. AKAHIGE-DO ☎3370-5015 for rsve and directions, convenient in Yoyogi. (**Learn** ask re seminars, Aug mountain-recluse intensive, or full course). **Kyoto:** E-spkng RYOKU Endo ☎075-712-7132.

MODERN SPORTS

MOST JAPANESEY of sports today, however, are *ya-kyu*—literally 'field-ball' but also known in vernacular as *besuboru*—and *gorufu* (golf).

BASEBALL: Two major ball leagues, Central and Pacific, 6 teams each, play to tremendous crowds at stadiums in major cities.

CENTRAL LEAGUE (*Sé Rigu*): Yomiuri's gigantic Giants, Tokyo Dome, Korakuen; Yakult Swallows, Jingu Stadium, Tokyo; Taiyo Whales, Yokohama; Chunichi Dragons, Nagoya; Hanshin Tigers, Nishinomiya Koshien Stadium, Osaka; Toyo Carps, Hiroshima.

PACIFIC LEAGUE (*Pa Rigu*): Nippon Ham Fighters, Tokyo Korakuen Dome (share w/Giants); Seibu Lions, Seibu Stadium, Saitama (exurb Tokyo); Lotte Marines, Chiba (Tokyo suburb); Orix Blue Waves, West Kobe Stadium; Kintetsu Buffaloes, Nissei Stadium, E Osaka; Daiei Hawks, Heiwadai Stadium, Fukuoka.

Ownership is interesting Japanese phenomenon: 3 owned by railways: Seibu in Tokyo, and Hanshin, Kintetsu around Osaka; 2 by newspapers, Yomiuri-Tokyo Giants & Chunichi-Nagoya Dragons; 1 by chain store Kobe-Daiei; 1 by soft drink, Yakult Swallows (pun?), 1 by chewing gum, Lotte; 1 loan co, Orix; 1 whaler Taiyo Whales of Yokohama, and meat-packer Nippon Ham; 12th is sole independent, Hiroshima Carps.

English dailies heavy on local coverage, scheds. **Reading:** *Japanese Baseball—A Fan's Guide* by Brian Maitland (PB-Tutbook). Niters rank with rooftop beer gardens as top midsummer sport. Local boy OH Sadaharu (actually Chinese) world home run king, 868, tops Aaron (755) and Ruth. 1987 season saw Hiroshima Carp's KINUGASA break Lou Gehrig's half-century iron-man record 2,130 successive games played. Size works against them (Oh under 5'10", 174 lbs). Majors use imported US players, limit 2 per team, but Japanese alone on several recent occasions clobbered visiting US majors. Top native players get movie star salaries topped only by novelists.

Collegiate big games, like Keio-Waseda crosstown Tokyo duel, draw mobs, rambunctious rooters like US collegiate football big games. High school championship at Koshien Stadium betw'n Osaka-Kobe, draw World Series crowds, victorious teams return home like conquerors. Cabbies fortnite in April or August as 40-odd teams play off drive to it on radio, coffee shops are packed for TV viewers. Whole world stops for finals. Their anthropological ritual value is worth viewing even if you don't like game. Some playing is so bad it's hilarious, but no way can spirit of players or rooters be doubted. With organized rooting sections, fields of pompons and placards, it's cross between US football and Democratic convention—wild! But no crowd savagery like English footer. Even pro-ball rooters are fun. In pro-Japan Series, if winning team is railroad-department store-owned, store calls grand sale inciting shopper-stampede, with massive genuine great buys beating D.C.'s Washington's Birthday madness. 1991 Autumn try-outs, Orix Blue Waves opened to women, no one passed.

Tix reasonable, tops about ¥2,500 reserved except big play-offs, ¥700 bleachers, usually available at stadium pre game (except Tokyo Giant home games), or PLAYGUIDES. Visit Kobe restaurant-bar Attic, ask if commentator-owner Marty Kuenert there, now managing US farm team bought in '90 by Japanese.

GORUFU: May very well be answer to inhibitions, repressions of this society. At least, everyone is taking swing at it. Introduced 1903 in Kobe, now 1100-odd courses nationwide—we mention few located major tourist spots. Some 40,000,000 tee-offs per year mean average course (6-day week, X-mon) sees 138 per day swing thru. Yet, many welcome foreign visitor, who need pay only guest fee over standard green fee.

Rural clubs have top hotels handy, as several easy-to-get-to courses around Lake Ashinoko–Hakone, foot of Fuji, Izu spa towns of Kuwana (internationally most popular course) and Shuzenji, Ise National Park's Kokubu, Kobe's Mount Rokko & Takarazuka, Shirahama Spa in Kii out of Osaka, to mention only some of over 1,100—plus some 2,500 driving ranges, many of Tokyo's 500+ being on office and restaurant rooftops. Chemical pollution from fertilizers, etc, causing backlash. Many new links canceled.

TOURS: JAL offers Super Golf Tour to Hokkaido, all fares incl from ¥99,000 2nites/3days, May–mid-Oct. Nippon Air Service offers full menu of golf tours to some 36 courses nationwide, all fees, hotels transportation included; with NAS J-pamphlet FLY Gorufu, good agent could route you around country sightsee-golfing from Hokkaido to Amami Oshima southern isles.

Sun Route Hotels also offer packages to their hotel in TOYOOKA in Hyogo Pref on Japan Sea Coast N of Kobe: half day at any of 4 fine links within 30min cab, ¥12,-15,000 weekday, varies with course, +30% sat, +50-60% sun, plus their ¥-T rate hotel; ☎(06)-341-1605 main Osaka office, or travel agent. Other links welcome guests, fees run anywhere from ¥20,000 to ¥100,000 for day. Best to go with member.

Need not bring your own basic equipment as local goods now to international standards—imported gear commanded top prices here until started licensing name brands locally. But US cheaper for same. 1,500 pros of both sexes, some regulars on world tournaments. Caddies excellent and reasonable. Many places they are local peasant girls in pleasing blue-pattern cottons—who do not chew gum, whistle or skylark. Main distractions are scenery, or in some seaside courses enhanced by diving girls working nearby.

RESERVATIONS at courses and nearest hotels or inns, contact Asahi Golf Center, 8-9 Nishi-Ginza, Chuo-ku, Tokyo ☎(03)-3251-1168, or in Osaka, ☎(06)-648-0011; also Mizuno Sports Goods, Yodoyabashi (on Mido-suji Blvd), Higashi-ku, ☎(06)-202-1171. Handle all for token service charge ¥1,000 weekday, ¥3,000 weekends-hols per rsvt'n, which they add to posted course fees and basic hotel charges, bill you for whole and issue coupons. Carry directory and excellent Asahi Golf mag (Japanese). Advise that golf courses generally full weekends, require at least 2 weeks advance reservation; most courses X-mon. They will help you with any golf problems, shopping.

BOWLING, or Japanese *boh-ringu*, spread like pins scattering in strike. Long (s'help us) considered here cultural pastime. Tokyo restaurants and companies have teams, pin by pin accounts of meets run with *boh-ringu* regularity in English press. Good alleys most major towns, some villages —prosperous fishing village in south Izu even put one in—tho many when boom burst late 70s, converted to super marts. Girls love it, miniscule typist looked like she'd fly down alley with ball bowled 179. Alleys open till late.

BOXING, large following, lighter weight classes dominated by Far East champs. International bouts here always use third country refs, as string of bad decisions in early 60s made advisable. Kick boxing popular, imports hapless Thai amateur kids as punching bags for local sadists.

WRESTLING of grunt & groan school here is big money, TV standby with large arena dedicated to *'puro-'* in Meiji Park sports complex. All shades available, from legit collegiate greco-roman to usual farce to lady-mud rasslin' and specialty *Rezu-puro* foreign 'lesbian' pro-wrestling. Local gal-groaners lead nun-like private lives in dorms, chaperoned like girl scouts to "set example for adulatory fans". Remember, here honkie is boo-able villain, Oriental baddy in USA comes back home as knight-hero.

But this brings us full circle, back to theater and ritual entertainments.

RACE COURSES for horses *kei-ba*, bicycles *kei-rin*, **motorbikes & motah-kurossu**, **motorboats** *motah-boto*, ubiquitous. Scheds are in buses & trains. Nags run often in summer. Racing association puts card scheds in major international hotels. Bikes, boats popular in major cities or nearby resorts, now limited to weekends & holidays because of *yakuza* infestation —and still harshly limit automobile access and parking to discourage them, as these gentlemen out of old George Raft movies don't like to be elbowed on public transportation. Grand Prix **auto circuit** for both sport and road cars was opened in 1963 by speed-god Honda, between Nagoya and Kyoto near Ise (*see*). Sport caught on, still roaring, but not as much as expected.

TOKYO RACING: *See* in hotel *Japan Yellow Pages* phonebook for more.
BICYCLE: *Keirin*: info; Kanto Cycle Race Association, ☎(03)-3436-3921. Most fri, sat, sun, hol; **Kawasaki Midway** main JR to Yokohama; **Tachikawa,** nr USAF Base, hour on Tachikawa line from Shinjuku Stn; **Sayama,** 1hr out from Ikebukuro Stn.

HORSE: *Keiba*; info, Japan Racing Association, *Nihon Chuo Keiba-kai*, ☎(03)-3591-5251; central off-track betting—**Ginza Service Station,** Ginza 2-2; also Korakuen, Shinjuku, Shibuya, Kinshi-cho, Asakusa (*see*), Shimbashi.
Nakayama track: Chiba Prefecture, taxi; train Sobu line from Ochanomizu Stn: main events—mid-April, Satsuki-Sho Stakes; early Apr and mid-Oct, Nakayama Grand Steeplechase; late Dec, Arima Memorial Stakes; late Jan, American Jockey Club Cup.
Funabashi track: Beyond Nakayama, taxi, or Sobu line from Ochanomizu.
Tokyo (Fuchu) track: 30min from Shinjuku on Keio line, near USAF Base at Fuchu, taxi 7-12x-mtr from hotels; main events—late May, Yushun Himba Stakes (Japan Oaks); late May, Tokyo Yushun (Japan Derby); late Nov, Tenno-Sho (Emperor's Cup); mid-May, Argentine Jockey Club Cup Race.
Hachioji track: W of Tokyo, beyond Tokyo track, Chuo JR line from Shinjuku.
Urawa Racecourse: On way to Nakayama, Keihin Tohoku JR to Minami Urawa.
Oi track: Most convenient, on Tokyo Bay halfway out to Haneda Airport, taxi 5x-mtr, or airport monorail to Keiba stn, short walk with crowds.
Kawasaki track: btwn Tokyo–Yokohama, taxi 8-10x-mtr, or Keihin Tohoku JR to Kawasaki stn, follow crowd.
Kinuta track: Setagaya, within Tokyo, taxi, or take Kamagawa line out of Shibuya.

HOW TO BET ON HORSES: Japan Central Racing Association sells four types of pari-mutuel tickets... *tansho* win, place, show and either-order forecast. Pari-mutuels with face values of ¥100, ¥200, ¥500 and ¥1,000 are sold for each betting system. System and face value may vary some according to racecourse. Off Track Betting sell ¥500up only, except Korakuen and Kinshi-cho for ¥100. Pari-mutuel tickets may be purchased at racecourse and 22 OTB shops, called *jogai baken uriba* or WINS, as in Ginza 2-10-13, ☎(03)-3543-3531 and Asakusa (*see*).

WIN **pool**, horse in 1st pays off. Win ticket is purchased at window by indicating horse number and number of tickets required.

PLACE **pool**, *fuku-sho*, is operated only on races of 9 or more starters. Bet on horse to place 1st, 2nd or 3rd. If 5 to 8 starters, horses 1st and 2nd pay off. In event of 9 or more starters, 1st, 2nd and 3rd pay off.

FORECAST, *rensho* or *focusu*, system: select pair of horses to place 1st and 2nd in race of 5–8 starters. Purchase forecast mutuel tickets by forecast or bracket numbers, same as gate number, **not** horse numbers—were horse nos used, in large field of starters possible combinations would be too numerous. Thus horses all grouped into simple 8- or 6-bracket systems.

In National Racing Tokyo, Nakayama, Kyoto and Hanshin tracks sell only either-order forecast (8 bracket system). Oi (or Ohi) Racetrack (Local Racing) also sells only either-order forecast tickets. For example, any horse coming in 1st or 2nd within forecast bracket number is considered winner.

Here is **8 BRACKET SYSTEM** in event of 12 starters:

Horse Numbers	1	2	3	4	5 6	7 8	9 10	11 12
Gate Numbers	1	2	3	4	5	6	7	8
Bracket Combinations	1—2	1—3	1—4	1—5	1—6	1—7	1—8.	
		2—3	2—4	2—5	2—6	2—7	2—8.	
			3—4	3—5	3—6	3—7	3—8.	
				4—5	4—6	4—7	4—8.	
Tracks:				5—5	5—6	5—7	5—8.	
Tokyo *see* preceeding					6—6	6—7	6—8.	
						7—7	7—8.	
							8—8.	

Purchase '3-5' either-order forecast ticket: If horse #3 is 1st and either 5 or 6, 2nd, or vice versa, 3-5 either-order forecast mutuel ticket wins. In either-order forecast systems, official dividends calculate on basis of ¥100. So, with ¥200 mutuel ticket, above dividend is multiplied by 2. Bets close 5mins before race. Tipsters have kiosks on track, as in UK.

Free bus from nearest station, private cars banned to discourage yakuza gangsters— who don't like crowded trains. Niigata, Fukushima, Sapporo, Hakodate run in June. Oi, downtown Tokyo, runs niters June-Sept.   —*thanks to Sei & Sandra Mori*

PACHINKO truly national gambling addiction-cum-noise pollutant. Ono-matopoea for pinball game introduced from US 1934. Presumably to save space, simple children's pinball game set on end. Centered in Nagoya (p296) as demilitarized ball bearing plants searched for new products to develop. Played in brightly over-lit parlors with blasting music, oft wartime marches total milieu of distraction from loneliness. Player sits before vertical set, drops steel ball in, flips plunger with thumb, tries to gauge power needed to get it to best holes. Can't tilt, as fixed in wall. Legally not gambling, game of skill—main skill is to figure which games fixed that day to allow overall wins (look for full ashtray). Balls won redeemed for foods, cigs, soap electric goods, which take outside around corner, rap twice and slot opens to turn in for cash. 'How to' book: *Winning Pachinko* by Sedens, new '91.

*Superior man reads ten thousand books
then travels ten thousand leagues...*
—Confucius

YOUR TRIP
PREFLIGHT PLANNING

Perry had no transportation problem. He had whole fleet of ships at his disposal. But Perry did some private intelligence work before he came, he studied his target destination. In this he was not as fortunate as you or I — he didn't have sources of information open to him which we now have. Enjoy yourself more, save money, take advantage of some of these.

SOURCES OF INFORMATION

YOUR TRAVEL AGENT costs nothing and can save you much; or lose you much if lazy. Agent is your sole safe source for **discount** tickets–more next chapter. S/he makes money from air, ship or bus lines, hotels and others for whom acting as booking agent, but is working for you–if he doesn't, switch! This is very simple, basic fact, but it is surprising how many people are not aware of it. He stands to make fair commission for your tickets and other bookings, so don't hesitate to make him work for it. You'll find that many in travel game got into it out of love of travel. If your agent doesn't impress you, then find another who does; use him fairly and don't treat him like sucker, pumping info, changing your mind, perhaps even booking somewhere else. Get your info and make your bookings! Stick to your plan. Plan well, plan once!

Pick yourself good travel agent, then work *together*. Don't leave it all up to him–for two reasons. *First,* by showing that you know what you want, that you are discerning, you challenge to really serve you up top itinerary; you make his work that joy everyone thinks travel work is, but isn't with so many crotchety bores playing Marco Polo. *Second*, it's easier to *dis*-satisfy people than to satisfy. You'd be surprised at how many people want to go to exotic places and see strange and exciting things, then once there spend most of their time complaining about how things are better back home. True, ratio of such people is small, but with so many traveling (and so many of these first-timers) small percentile of sour apples adds up to lots of individuals, and transPacific expects to increase 10% annually, indefinitely (vs 5% domestic US). Your agent can easily be ruined by hitting unfortunate combination of putting potential grumps into out-of-way place just when plumbing goes out, storms break and local railways strike (*every* year late-April or May in Japan–usually half-day). Any business is always calculated gamble and gamblers play safe: in tours book into regular fool-proof rut.

RECOMMENDED READING: Your agent will load you down with lots of good reading, free. Unfortunately, he won't have most of best available: guide periodicals published here. You have time to write for some. Regardless of factual information you pick up from them, just leafing thru will give you good feeling of tempo of places, feeling of familiarity works wonders in overcoming first impression of helpless, bewildering foreignness that so often ruins one's first days in strange, new places. Even experienced travelers suffer this imbalance of expectation vs preparation. Write (✍) letters enclosing *International Reply Coupons* available at local post office—they can go long way toward inoculating you against this feeling lost on arrival.

Best: *Tokyo Journal* & *Kansai Time Out*, slick *Time*-size monthlies, ✍ & enclose int'l postal reply coupon requesting back issue or most recent:

Tokyo Journal (TJ) is city mag covering greater Tokyo in good special articles plus superb *CityScope*-guide insert of events, festivals, shows etc (best since our pioneer *Anoné* guide-mag of 1954-5). ✍ *Tokyo Journal*, 1F Cross Cultural Enterprises Bldg, 27-10 San'ei-cho, Shinjuku-ku, Tokyo 160, send $7.00 international postal coupons for latest issue airmail; or phone LA office ☎(213)-617-2039, $4.00 posted. Sold at LA New Otani Hotel Kinokuniya bookshop $2.95.

Kansai Time Out (KTO) is regional for *Kansai*–Kyoto-Osaka-Kobe 500km/300mi from Tokyo, is or *should* be your main target area—covered intensively by staff of nit-picking fact-natics; ✍ *Kansai Time Out*, Ikuta-cho 1-chome-13-10, Chuo-ku Kobe 651, enclose $5 postal coupon for latest, airmail.

Once in Japan at major hotels (sometimes Japan-owned hotels overseas) JNTO etc, you can pick up worthwhile freebie tabloids like *Tour Companion*, Tokyo edition weekly; in Tokyo, *Tokyo Weekender*, mostly gossip for residents. In Kansai, colorful freebie *Kinki*. All carry good scheds, but rarely as comprehensive as above *TJ–KTO*. Kyoto also has freeby-colorgravure *Kyoto Visitor's Guide*, available shops & hotels.

JAPAN NATIONAL TOURIST ORGANIZATION (JNTO) is ubiquitous public relations cum 'research' group to help you and travel industry. They concern us here only as source of information and literature. Their actual value to you varies with personnel, who vary with seasons.

JNTO offices overseas:
USA: New York, Rockefeller Plaza, 630 5th Ave, 10111 ☎(212)-757-5640; Chicago, 401 N. Michigan Ave, 60611 ☎(312)-222-0974; Dallas, 2121 SanJacinto, Suite 980, 75201 ☎(214)-741-4931; San Francisco, 360 Post St, Suite 401, 94108 ☎(415)-989-7140; Los Angeles, 624 South Grand Ave, 90017, ☎(213)-623-1952.
Canada: 165 University Ave, Toronto, Ont M5H 3B8 ☎(416)-366-7140.
Australia: 115 Pitt St, Sydney N.S.W. 2000 ☎(02)-232-4522.
England: 167 Regent St, London W.1. ☎(071)-734-9638.
France: 4-8 rue Sainte-Anne, 75001 Paris ☎(1)-42-96-20-29.
Switzerland: Rue de Berne 13, 1201 Geneva ☎(022)-731-81-40.
Germany: Kaiserstrasse 11, 6000 Frankfurt am Main 1 ☎(069)-20353.
Mexico: Temistocles 248-PB, Col Reforma Polanco, Mexico, D.F. ☎(05)-254-6666.
Brazil: Av. Paulista, 509-S/405, 01311-Sao Paulo ☎(011)-289-2931.
Thailand: WALL ST TOWER 33/61 Suriwong Rd, Bangkok ☎(02)-233-5108.
Korea: 10 Da-Dong, Chung-ku, Seoul ☎(02)-752-7968.
Hong Kong: Suite 3606, 2 Exchange Sq, 8 Connaught Place, Central ☎5-255295.

Publications you should certainly get from JNTO: *Condensed Japan Rail* (JR) *Schedule* in English, latest edition of Japanese Inn directory *Ryokan* (also *Japan Hotel Guide* or K&D *Timetable* pocket-size air and Shinkansen scheds plus price list of members of Japan Hotel Assoc) and *Economical Japanese Inn Group*, listing by city, name, address, phone number, type of accommodation and latest prices of better-to-middle class for former, tourist class for latter, of their member J-style inns (many with W-style rooms as well for those preferring half-dose). *All free.* Can save you problems later. JNTO-TIC **Welcome Inn Reservation Service** can book you into rooms under ¥10,000w/bkfst; no fee or deposit—*see* p138.

Or, ⚏ **Ryokan-Federation of Japanese Tourist Hotels** 1-8-3 Marunouchi, Chiyoda-ku, in Tokyo phone ☎(03)-3231-1857; & **Economic Japanese Inn Group** Hiraiwa Ryokan, 314 Hayao-cho Kaminoguchi-agaru, Ninomiya-cho dori, Shimogyo-ku, Kyoto 500, or Tokyo liaison **Sawanoya Ryokan** ☎(03)-3822-2251.

Prefectural and city governments have English pamphlets (Hiroshima, Ashiya, etc), free monthlies (Yokohama, Nagoya, Kyoto, Fukuoka). Some beautiful picture albums, source of what to look for, tho lacking specifics. Also answer your letter queries, in time. Address **Tourist Office** of either prefecture or city: Tourist Office, Kyoto Municipal Government, Kyoto; or Tourist Office, Nara Prefectural Gov't, Nara City; or Nagasaki, Hiroshima, etc, any city or area which interests you, or where going to be assigned. If residence planned, mention so, as they have special booklets to help you get settled in.

Brochures available at travel agents and JNTO you'll find include info on various tours of from half-day to several days' duration. Get briefed on them. You can book most of these from USA or Europe. Those you can book from home often cost less than if booked in Japan, especially if part of package. Or book these tours once in Japan at your hotel. Larger hotels have good tourist information and booking counters in their lobbies with up-to-minute info on seasonal and special offerings. Overseas offices of JTB and JNTO also carry sale stock of JTB books. Many are worthwhile.

Your city or school library has books on Japan and Orient. There is fascinating reading just in standard encyclopedias. Scores of Japanese novels in English translation are in any decent bookstore, most, plus numerous other Oriental works are in paperback (PB)—*Mentor, Meridian, Grove, Pocket Book, New Directions, Ballantine, Universal* and that fantastic old bird whose beak can hold more books than most voracious reader can belly-up to, *Pelican*—but most especially *Tutbooks.* ⚏ **Asia Society**, 725 Park Avenue, New York for *Asia in Paperbacks*, or special book, odd lapses, but paragraph summary of each entry, *Japan for Westerners* $5.95 from **Yes Bookshop**, 1035 31st St NW, Washington DC.

Educated/educatable tourist who wants half-dozen all-encompassing titles...
GLUCK'S **five-inch shelf of paperbacks** for your personally oriented historical study of Japan thru its arts and lives of its people.

Origins of Oriental Civilization by Walter A. Fairservis (Mentor): well-written survey tying in all Asian cultures and showing those links common with our own. For general factual historical outline, follow up with *Japan Past and Present* by Ambassador-Prof Edwin O Reischauer (Tuttle) and flesh this out with two brief, superbly written 'technical' books: *Enduring Art of Japan* by Langdon Warner (Grove)—hard to find, but if you read one book on Japanese history, this is it—traces development of Japan thru her artisans of 6th thru 16th centuries. Taking up where this leaves off, *Floating World in Japanese Fiction,* by Howard Hibbett (Tuttle), poignant and hilarious translations of 18-19th century J-pulp lit interspersed with historical analytical essays. Warner, credited with persuading US Air Force to spare Kyoto-Nara art cities, is enshrined in Horyuji, Nara. *Japanese Inn* by Oliver Statler (Hawaii) is finely produced reportage of 17th century thru present—alas, his inn closed 1986. His recent *Japanese Pilgrimage* is pregnant with medieval ideas for modern travel in one of Japan's last tourist frontiers, rural Shikoku. Some books never die: like Ruth Benedict's *Chrysanthemum and Sword.* To bridge old and new Japan, Richard Storry's *History of Modern Japan*

(Pelican). For postwar miracle of rebirth as seen thru eyes of those who did it *Ukiyo, Stories of Floating World of Postwar Japan*, edited & selected by Jay Gluck (Vanguard & Universal Library PB). To fill out classical picture, add UNESCO *Anthology of Japanese Literature* by Donald Keene. Update with Howard Hibbett's *Contemporary Japanese Literature* (PB Knopf). There is planeload of good modern literature in translation in PB sections of big bookshops, baggage compartment of it from Tuttl.

Equivalent college course in Japanese history is found **hard-bound** in: *Japan Before Buddhism* by J.Edward Kidder (Praeger), good detail outline of prehistory from earliest times thru Korean-Chinese influx of 6th century, but unfortunately no links with neighbor cultures (for this, *see* Fairservis, above), and while generation of active archaeology out of date, there's still no better.

Japan A Short Cultural History by Sir George Sansom (PB: Stanford), beautifully written so as to shield its faults (which in turn are much repaired in his more recent longer books) covers 6-19th centuries. *Western World and Japan* by Sir George (Knopf) and *Japan Story of a Nation* by Ambassador Reischauer (Knopf) bring us up to present era.

If not these, other fine general histories in **PB** are: John Whitney Hall *Japan–from prehistory to modern times* (Delta) & W.G. Beasley *Modern History of Japan* (Praeger). Add one biography, antique but timely because of subject, A.L.Sadler *Life of Shogun Tokugawa Ieyasu*–that very same 'Shogun' (Tuttle). Occupation era at last is fairly treated in *Sheathing the Sword*, by Meirion and Susie Harries (Hamish Hamilton UK & Macmillan US), or in novel with John Toland's *Occupation* (Tor), with side dish of spicy relish in Kaplan & Dubro's fascinating study, *Yakuza* (Futura PB).

But to understand how Japan exploded into modern age, how feudal agricultural society modernized and mechanized in one single generation, missing link of books on Japan is Thomas C Smith's well-written, concise *Agrarian Origins of Modern Japan* (Stanford-cloth), which sets foundation for recent flood of books analyzing business and industry like Ezra Vogel's *Japan as Number 1* (Harper-PB) or Endymion Wilkinson *Misunderstanding Europe vs Japan* (Chuo Koron-PB). If balance is desired, Japan-bashing tomes (too light themselves to hurt) are plentiful: most argumentatively informative Karel vanWolferen's *The Enigma of Japanese Power*. But most new books lack 'heart', for which Lafcadio Hearn is still incomparable (Tuttle reprints).

Successful grafting of modernization onto its traditional base is brilliantly analyzed in series of richly illustrated books by YOSHIDA Mitsukuni: *Hybrid Culture–What Happens When East and West Meet, Compact Culture*, and *Culture of Anima–Supernatural in Japanese Life*, if not in bookshop hound local Mazda auto dealer, as they published them. To bring us up to date on social science research in Japan is gem: *Guides to Japanese Culture* (Japan Cultural Institute) edited Murakami & Seidensticker, translation-digest of 45 books, major articles by modern Japanese scholars.

For more detailed reading above books carry specialized bibliographies, we add recommendations, where pertinent, discussing subjects or places. Japan Society has its revised *Japan, A Reader's Guide* $3.50 postpaid. Probably no country is as much written about. Several local publishers issue library on Japan annually–most especially Tuttle, Weatherhill, Kodansha International, University of Tokyo and smaller houses like Lotus, Yohan, or ourselves. Most are distributed in USA by **Charles E Tuttle**, PO Box 410, Rutland VT 05701-0410 from whom catalogue and in-print list. UK available most major bookshops. Continent suggest **Boxerbooks** of Zurich, or that Orientalia treasure house **Otto Harrassowitz**, attn Horst Rackow–Asia Dept, Taunusstrasse 5, PO Box 2929, D6200 Weisbaden Germany. Australia, **Paul Flesch** & Co Pty Ltd, Melbourne.

One last question might be, "What book did certain travel writers carry?" There weren't any contemporary travel books then, we carried everything available on art and history with special suitcase just for books. Garet, of course, relied on our first edition of 1964, plus new Japanese-language books. Doing original edition generation ago only guide Sumi and Jay found of use was *Murray's Guide to Japan* by B.H. Chamberlain, Lafcadio Hearn, etc. We used 1904 edition; except for transportation data ("...bullock cart in this area, take extra puller for ricksha in steep Hiroshima mountains") far more accurate and informative than successors and imitators. It was original research. We believe we are first really new travel book on Japan since *Murray's* and 1964-91 hasn't dampened our ego. Chamberlain was outstanding translator and scholar who could write, and who took admonition of Confucius to "read 10,000 books and travel 10,000 leagues".

Many travel books since have been written by semi-literates, or from Tokyo Press Club bar (or both). One famous creation-by-committee of 1964 had several chapters written by authors who never got near their subject, and its editor's 1987 forage into travel books usurped our name as his subtitle. Venturing beyond standard bar circuit of Japan's capital with one of these is (to put it kindly) fraught with adventure. Exceptions are recent good books on Tokyo alone (*TJ*'s editors' *Best of Tokyo* (Tuttle) or anything bylined Jean Pearce), some specialized rural areas by devoted denizens, mostly Weatherhill, which we cite locally. One other comprehensive book do we know of done by solo author who wore out shoes, and we consider it as 'No. 2'—*Japan Handbook* by JD Bisignani (Moon publishers, Chico, Cal). Different kind of travel book, of travel modes long lost, is Alan Booth's fine *The Roads to Sata: A 2,000 mile walk through Japan* (Weatherhill).

For readers with **specialized interests**, some further short lists:

Theater buffs: list is endless, for pocket synopses *see* ON STAGE.

Birdwatchers and nature lovers, we quote our favorite expert Mark Brazil, whose excellent column *Wild Watch* appears Friday in *Japan Times*: "...to know more about bird watching in Japan, where to go and what to see", *Field Guide to Birds of Japan* (¥2,900 if in print), *Birds of Japan–a Checklist* (¥500), *Finding Birds in Japan–Tokyo Area* (¥600) and *Finding Birds in Japan–Honshu* (¥1,000), from Mark Brazil, Wild Bird Society of Japan, 5th fl Flower Building, 1-1-4 Shibuya, Tokyo.

Flower Arrangers who'd like to visit *iemoto-* grand masters in their headquarters: start with KUDO Masanobu's *History of Ikebana* (profusely illustrated; Shufu-no Tomo), translated & edited by Sumi and Jay. Get book on your own school and arrange visit to your HQ–then do what Japanese socially cannot do, visit other schools, even take day workshops. Members of Ikebana International get list of master schools from Tokyo HQ.

Garden buffs who want greater coverage of historical gardens than we give: anything by Kuck, especially *World of Japanese Garden* (Weatherhill, cloth); whatever you can find by Shigemori Kanto, expert par excellence; *Invitation to Japanese Gardens* and follow-up *Japanese Gardens Revisited* by Takakuwa (Tuttle) rare good photos.

Martial arts, *Zen Combat* (Ballentine), Jay's pioneer introduction to most Ways; master TOHEI's *Aikido* (var edition says *Ki-*) *in Daily Life*, or his *Book of Ki*, (JPTC) regardless of whichever Way you practise; Ratti & Westbrook *Secrets of Samurai*, (Tuttle); OYAMA Mas's several karate books; and Don Draegger's endless-if-soulless series on mechanics (Weatherhill). Add SERIZAWA Katsusuke's *Tsubo* (JPTC); or NAMIKAWA's *Shiatsu* (JPTC)– and when in Tokyo visit his studio in downtown Akasaka Hotel district for *shiatsu* massage, magic of martial arts healing ☎(03)-3583-9618.

Plan to stay on, settle to work, we highly advise Peter Hadfield's *Sixty Seconds That Will Change the World—The Coming Tokyo Earthquake* [expects 4 whoppers].

British reader refresh yourself with local guide to 230 sites of older J-UK relations when two were allies and UK taught hi-tec modernization and Japan enriched UK art: *Companion to Japanese Britain and Ireland*, by Pearse & McCooey (In Print £10).

True, interest of authors and publishers seems monopolized by abstruse and exotic (Zen Buddhism, Noh Drama, Medieval Literature, martial arts) but it is this exotic and different which add spice to travel. It's very nice to know, and even comforting, that people over our world are basically similar, but is it worth all that expense and bother of long trip just to find this out? It's fun and romantic to see and experience exotica, downright exciting to get to know people and *then* come to realize that despite all our surface differences, despite strange color and flow of costume, flamboyance of festivals and rituals, that underneath all this is unity in beautiful diversity.

PERSONAL CONTACT: Once you've got bit of reading under your belt, might try something one traveler tried on Jay when he was undergraduate in Near Eastern Studies at Berkeley. Mr Traveler got Jay's name thru prof in department, whose name he had in turn gotten from school catalogue or by calling school. Mr T– invited Jay to dinner. Now good dinner is built around main course of conversation. More satisfied our animal appetites, more relaxed our physical body and thus freer our intellect. Over dinner, Mister T-, who proved to be quite well read, outlined his plans, told of interests and drew on Jay's better-disciplined book knowledge of area to answer questions his reading aroused, but did not answer and to help tie his miscellaneous knowledge into organic whole. College students always welcome few dollars and meal and chance to test one's own knowledge. (Or, as happened in Jay's case, be asked what memento he'd like brought back. Months later, Jay got his much longed-for illuminated Koran from bazaar of Marrakech.)

With so many foreign students in America, so many thousands from Japan, you have far better opportunity to invite educated native. Call nearby university, ask for person in charge of hospitality to foreign students. In New York, Chicago, Berkeley, Washington, call *International House*, dormitory and hangout for internationally-minded foreign and US students. Many big cities have *Japan Societies* with main offices in New York (333 E 47th Street, New York, NY 10017) or *Asia Societies* (main: 725 Park Ave, New York, NY 10021). They are happy to act as go-between in bit of person-to-person diplomacy which will enable foreign guest to enjoy good American home hospitality, at same time help Americans better understand distant land and culture. You'll probably receive bonus of personal invitation to visit your foreign guest's home when you become guest in his country. J.S. has fine list of educational tour packages, marvelous newsletter, calendar of Japan-related events–especially films–that makes us envious here in Japan. J.S. of Boston publishes fine *Guide to Japan in New Englsnd*, chock full of info:

✍ **Japan Society** 22 Batterymarch St, Boston MA 02109.

Where there is *Japan* or *Asia Society* you'll not only have college and post-graduate students to choose from, but more than likely mature men and women in your own field. These societies can help you visit your Japanese or other Asian professional counterpart, factory, office or campus similar to your own at home, just as they arrange for Asian guests visiting US.

HOME STAY best arranged if you're active in your town's Sister City group–if not one of 191 US towns with one in Japan (or other nations) why not get started: ✍ Sister City (c/o Japan Society, 333 E. 47 St, New York, NY 10017). Home stay can be arranged for next day in 14 cities, on arrival or writing ahead–we list local numbers which can help in English; or check TIC Tokyo, Kyoto, tourist info offices other towns.

SCHOOL VISITS for teachers ✍ **Kyoiku Iinkai** (board of education) of city of interest to you–do not go direct to school due to teacher union rules, unless you have personal introduction (in which case upon arrival in town best to visit city hall and present letter to education officer, have him fix visit –repeat, problem is not with city officials but with teachers' union). Write ✍ ahead in simple, clear English, paragraph on self, interests, and grade level or type of school or class you'd like to see. If in session (summer vacation short, starts mid July, schools function part time summer, vacation ends early Sept) when you get there be almost certain of warm welcome. Bring mementos–school emblem, pennant, local goods, video or pix of school; during visit arrange penpals, swap videotapes, student paintings (of own life, or how they think other side lives), handicrafts, teacher visits.

SENIOR CITIZEN special deal, must be 50+. Can apply to receive senior Japanese guest at your home first, before you go, as well as apply to visit in Japan. Makes excellent combo: visit your recent guest in one town, next town visit stranger introduced by this volunteer group. ✍ **Seniors Abroad** c/o Ms Evelyn Zivetz, 12533 Pacato Circle North, San Diego CA 92128.

SUPPORT YOUR MISSION fundraisers pass hat at church. Well, now's time to see where your dimes have gone. Ask your priest or parson to put you in contact with your overseas missions. Most Protestants are head-quartered centrally at 775 Riverside Drive, New York, NY, where you can obtain names and addresses. If sincerely interested in mission work, some missionaries can put you up. **Write ahead,** they will be glad to show you their area and tell you of their work (perhaps find reasonable inn for you if they can't offer hospitality). It's custom to recompense them for room and meals at about same as average for hotel level you are using, left in plain envelope as gift. If you are student, discuss matter with them–it's not impossible to work part of it off teaching English or scraping paint. Your arrival will be welcomed by student parishioners eager to try their English.

Catholics will find active missions of international flavor, Order-supported universities (Sophia in Tokyo, Nanzan in Nagoya, and other smaller ones, several girls' schools), and monastery in Hokkaido where one may enter retreat, nunnery. Whatever your faith, missions welcome your visit. Your insight into their work will be of value to all concerned. Perhaps more intelligent, personal involvement by folks at home might help restore missions to their former role in intellectual vanguard of emerging Asia.

Jews find synagogues in Tokyo and Kobe, latter mostly Sephardic, with welcome mat always out for possible tenth worshipper for their shrinking congregation. (*See* Rabbi Tokayer's book *Fugu Plan* about Kobe rescuing European Jews in WWII). Islamic mosque now only in Kobe, near schule–old Tokyo mosque recently razed, being rebuilt.

If curious about or have interest in **Buddhism,** you'll find at least one Buddhist church or temple in every large city in Pacific Coast states, Colorado and Utah, as well as any city with sizable Japanese (or Chinese) population: Chicago, Detroit, New York, Philadelphia, Seabrook Farms, N.J. where Ghenghiz Khan's descendants farm. City without church may have Young Buddhist League chapter. Older priests may be Japanese immigrants, with limited English, but most churches now have American-born priests, including several Caucasians. Los Angeles has Tenri-kyo, Konko-kyo and Oomoto Shinto groups. Buddhism neither proselytizes nor evangelizes, tho passively (except for active Soka Gakkai) seeks converts, which means that visiting temple, even for service, neither commits one nor exposes one to sales pitch. It is purely intellectual experience. Buddhist meditation techniques–Zen and other–are often used by modern Christian as tool.

WHY USE AGENT..." you ask, "...if I have to do all this myself?" Good question...equally good answer. What you do when you get to Japan is up to you. There's so much to do and see that agent is helpless (as you will be if you land unprepared) to know where to steer you. We've been in Japan 40 years, have traveled over every part of country and still have hard time choosing which place or event to see next—so many to choose from. Then, too, your biggest single problem is transportat; in this field your agent is expert. Of course, if you know exactly what you want to do, how to go about it and desire only to be transported in comfort to Tokyo and left alone, then by all means go to any airline office or ticket booker and book fare. They'll also help with general information, literature and advice. Any airline can arrange combined ship-air and air-surface which preserve RT discounts.

With deregulation, there are now various rates available and JAL won't tell what Northwest offers and to either Singapore is what you sling at bars. **Discount tickets** not sold retail by airlines, only thru hypocritical system of subagents to absolve airlines of rate-cutting, so can raise list-price again to make discount look even better. Why?—most travelers are businessmen moving on short notice, not paying own bills anyway (especially up front in exec/1st class). Some 'bucket-shops' specialize in cheapies, allow major lines to offer prices competitive with pioneer cut-raters Korean, Singapore, China; including Ist class tix at Y-class price. (*See* GETTING THERE next chapter).

Good agent, however, offers extras that save money or trouble, especially important to first-timer. When selecting your agent, ask about these services, use as criterion for selection. Some agents handle passport and any visa work, simple, but not detailed here as regulations change toward greater simplification. Japan and US mutually waived visas for tourists, grant 90 day automatic but non-extendable permit-to-stay on arrival. UK, Canada, N.Z. get different periods, respectively 180, 90, 30 days, but extendable 'working-vacation' allowing 20hrs weekly declared employment. Aussies need consul-issued visa, ask for 'working-vacation' (great diplomatic idea). Look for softening of US- or Aussie-Japan requirements–if US moves first. Remember, consular visa desks are open only in office hours, usually only mornings—hours you work. Continuing on to several countries this can be quite some chore, expense—tho many Asian destinations stamp automatic tourist visa on entry. China requires visa as self-arranged travel difficult — few hotels, inadequate transport, no profit from budgeteer. (*See* VISA, below).

FINDING A GOOD AGENT: Just how does one find this mysterious one? Most veteran travelers say you get more for your money, or for less money, from smaller agents, independents. There are many small fly-by-niters, too, so this isn't blanket recommendation. If you need itinerary help, first thing to look for is, we think, if agent takes *personally* conducted tours. If yes, he's traveler him/herself, up on latest conditions in way no trade journal, no matter how good, can keep him. We think little agencies (New York or West Coast) with Japanese names do best all-around job at fairest rates. Tho we fondly recall late friend-adventurer-writer-agent Harrison Forman looked at Jay's airline-issue Round Worlder, rewrote it, got $107 (8% of total) refund by reticketing component legs. That's true agent—we miss him.

INSURANCE: *Warning* your health insurance usually not valid overseas, UK National Health not valid. Buy travel insurance—**not** flight insurance. Planning long stay, get special insurance, join American Citizens Abroad, c/o Dr D.Carol, Im Antsee 13, W-6080 Gross Gera, Germany; Fax 0049-6152-81185. But don't be too conscientious about detailling past medical history.

VISA: TOURIST: New reciprocal 'no-visa protocol', 'free' 4-1-4 permit to stay issued at arrival: UK-180days, Canada-90, NZ-30 (not Australia), all extendable or convertible to other status; US 90days, absolutely nonextendible, requiring quickie to Korea or Hong Kong to revalidate new stay, nonconvertible except to marry. No Yankee-bash, just reciprocal—took US years to agree to no-visa deal as is. Any J-ancestry qualifies better visa.

Americans hopng to stay on in Japan over 90days, perhaps after finding interesting places to study or job, should go to Japanese consul in old way, apply for tourist visa (also 4-1-4, 90days) and if asked say you may stay over 90days and say no more. Extendible for 2nd 90days—more important can be changed to cultural 4-1-l6-3. *Check*—in 1988-91 rule changed 5x!

Warning: can't work (teach, model, anything earning ¥en) on tourist visa. Minor infraction usually overlooked as long as don't work in topless-bar, porn model etc.

BUSINESSMAN on short trip get this 'free' tourist visa. If need other, your office should get it—use agent. If going for employment, J-side host takes care of it, Japan Consul can advise you as needed; sent by US company it's their hassle in which case travel agent handles. If you change jobs while in Japan, must notify immigration—usually old boss must release, new one take up your guarantee. In teacher racket, if old boss gets nasty, out you go —so keep fences mended, and check with immigration before switch.

Visa experts handle all this for reasonable fee per visa plus consul fee. In US, see yellow pages for *Visas Arranged*. (NYC, Boston, DC, San Francisco, LA etc). In Japan, agent selling ongoing tix handles other country visa/s at cost or minimal fee.

NIKKEI, US-Canada J-descent may get special '-other' visa—visit family, work, 180 days multiple. Also seems at arbitrary discretion of consul.

MARRIED to Japanese, should qualify for 4-1-16-1 visa up to 3-year stay, no multiple entry (must apply reentry each exit). Also arbitrary issuance.

CULTURAL VISA or 'other' 4-1-16-3 (valid 4yrs, 6-12mos each stay, extendible) limited, adequate work privilege to 20hrs weekly (but permit "case by case") which is full-time teaching (12-20hrs), earn enough to live in comfort, allow time for required 20+hrs weekly study. Consul in New York may demand you be PhD candidate, have US, Japan college guarantors, practically be pal of PM before they'll issue one. If you arrive as tourist and want to stay on to study, visa extension officers (immigration office, branch Justice Ministry) are more amenable outside Tokyo—which office impossibly understaffed. (Kyoto, Kobe, Hiroshima best, Osaka fair). Ask straight, they *usually* answer straight, telling what documents you need (letters from guarantor and school/s as proof of studying X-hrs weekly at one or more schools of language, tea, pottery, ikebana, weaving, aikido, karate, etc). If serious about study, avoid Tokyo. BA Lit or Ed, advanced degree, certificate (espec TOEFL) or teaching experience can get job at school which gets you proper visa— don't let them run life. Many jobs for less-qualified won't qualify for visa.

Advice: to apply for visa or extension dress conservatively. Balance beard or long hair with necktie, jacket. Pays for man to own necktie as uniform to visit government offices, anywhere. Be polite, ask "kind advice". Dealing with any bureaucrat, even US, pays to stroke his/her ego (boring unrewarding job, you'd probably be as grumpy), tho most needn't be so feisty. And why do US consuls of Asian descent sting more than WASPS? US visa for refugee in most places still lucrative racket of US lawyer-consul consortium.

In Japan regard Immigration Officer as ally—he is as long as you so treat him. He can be generous with prior advice before you screw up, steer you away from temptation of error. 'Obligate' him—deferentially ask advice.

STUDYING ABROAD LEARNING ABOUT JAPAN

"QUITE UNCONSCIOUSLY I had acquired the habit of looking at things two different ways–from the Japanese angle of vision as well as from our own," writes Ambassador Prof Edwin O Reischauer in *My Life Between Japan and America*, "...this proved to be the key to my career and, extended worldwide, is the only hope I can see for world peace and human survival."

Jay & Sumi pioneered **educational tours** here in 1961 when Garet was born and Reischauer was ambassador. For United States National Student Association summer tour we paired 8 Americans one on one with English-speaking students of Jay's from Wakayama National University, then hit boondocks in chartered buses to see places tourists still can't get to easily, drink tea in ancient teahouse with Head Master Sen, interview Shingon Buddhist Abbot in Mount Koya 'ShangriLa', round table rap with radical Zen-Gakuren students who had just rioted and blocked Eisenhower's state visit, stay with demon dancers in hills of Hiroshima, and more. Effective? One of 8 Americans started with Asian major; 7 ended up in work relating to Asia, all Japanese took self-designed overseas tour next year and all ended up in international work. Much of what we learned that summer ended up in our original edition, is repeated, retreated and expanded herein.

Japan's educational strength is in its primary schools, kids first 4-6 years —not highly-touted JrHi or High schools to which US press gives credit rightfully due superb kindergartens and elementary grades. Japan's postwar college system (hard to call them 'universities' as no universality in concept or curricula, they're postgrad high schools as name *dai-gaku*-big school implies) is based on sad imitation of America's postwar assemblyline-worst wherein teacher stands before students to read from yellowed lecture notes, students take notes—where not sleeping, if even present. There is no exchange. Sumi at Gakushuin Peers College once raised her hand to ask question, class and teacher gasped in unison—this just wasn't done. Jay as Prof used zen-slap shock tactics to instigate. College is clerical trade school, easy-going after passing rat-race entry exams licensing to 4 years of easy life, almost no need to work outside or study or read more than single book per year-long-hour-weekly course till automatic graduation. Ideal for mass-producing educated office clerk to cram, follow, never question authority. Then, dumped into *sarari-man* rat-race, little wonder most look back on this brief period of freedom and ease with *nostarujia*.

Into this we now dump our eager would-be Japanologues who soon find many Japanese lecturers in English are xenophobes, incompetent except as poor translators, pre-convinced no *gai-jin*-foreigner can ever 'understand' Japan. No attempt is made to even introduce basics of this very different culture, sole non-Western 20th century civilization—thus depriving students of valid Western-style tools for proper analysis, our most essential educational technique. These rote-factories benefit only exceptional student who can make own way, or lucky proctor sent over from US campus for free ride to do own research for year, so long as no ward gets in trouble. Any student in one is strongly advised not to take classes seriously, but to join student activity (club, etc) of special interest. These 'international exchange' farces earn credits (with much money taken at high mark-up). We have rescued students from such, introduced them to specialized teachers they came in search of, but were never told by colleges or proctors even existed.

We believe 2 basics to education on Japan are: **language** & **tradition**. Language is not for everyone, but should be for most; understanding tradition, or at least comprehending its existence, is, especially if one is going to

do business here. You may not like bitter taste of thick tea, but acquaintance with its 'ceremony' will help you understand (or at least ready you for) why things in front of you suddenly get turned around (besides that seemingly coarse, yet perhaps priceless, tea bowl). Language alone is useless without savvy of traditional usage. Jay studied arts before 'osmosing' language.

We advise, despite our plaints above, that one go easy on analysis (for now), 'understanding'. Don't even 'like-dislike'. Black-American aesthetic gives us our key term: 'soul'–more important than mind–it in fact enhances, enriches mind: closer to what Japanese call *kokoro*, written with ideograph 'heart' and encompassing both heart and mind, ultimate repository of our humanity. Way there starts with feeling. Don't try to understand tea or noh or even physics of martial arts–just feel, do. Start being *simpatico*, or at least sympathize (not quite same, but place to start). Eventually you may even get to empathize, finally to feel that blessed schizophrenia with Reischauer. Prepare to suffer–who stands midroad gets hit by car from both directions.

Back to basics–we stress, repeating here *ad naus*–if coming to Japan to study Japan come to Japan, not Tokyo. This truly great city is too big, consumes one–only makes sense when you understand traditional base on which it built, on which premise this entire book is built. *Get out of Tokyo!*

Oomoto Seminar in Traditional Japanese Arts, (Oo- pron as in b*oa*t, not as in f*oo*d) hot–but not hottest–June-July weeks **near Kyoto** in old castle town at religious (folk-Shinto) foundation HQ (*see* p456), for non-religious training in religiously intensive two hours daily each of noh-dance, martial art, brush calligraphy and painting, *chado*–all complementary *ki* generators basic to understanding why and how Japan makes good cars. Highly recommended preface to any further serious study of Japan.

Shinto meditation (not that different from Zazen), Tantric Shingon-Buddhist 'Moon Meditation', evening lectures and much interaction by students who have ranged ages 16 to 70. Work in teams of 6-10 students. Room (2 per, couples together, single option extra), spartan western and Japanese board, uniform kimono and martial arts gear included, $1,750 for 4 weeks (1990). Non-sectarian–Catholic priest, Protestant clergy, (no rabbi yet), Zenis, Sufis, Tibetan lamas have done. Science-mystic Lyall Watson did it as boot camp before taking on Tokyo establishment to end whaling, beat them at their own game peaceably, effectively. Originated by China author-Japan esthete David Kidd with Oomoto family scion DEGUCHI Kyotaro; David captained for 10 years, now Kyotaro-sama directs.

This is program by which all others must be judged:

✍ **Traditional Arts Seminar**, Oomoto Foundation, Kameoka-shi Kyoto-fu 621. They prefer hand-written application letter with brief bio, intent, enclose snapshot.

Zen Arts Seminar (are arts zen or is zen art?) patterned after Oomoto,
above–US domestic sampler by Oomoto alumna, May (first session '87) at Green Gulch Zen Center near San Francisco. Good preview to your intelligent tour of Japan.
✍ **Kenner**, 526 Ashbury Ave., Santa Rosa CA 95404; ☎(707)-578-8014.

Ura Senke Tea Study with *Midori-kai* (green group) at 400-year-old
teahouse complex, **Kyoto** under direct tutelage 15th master Sen Hounsai. *Chado* (*see* p483) basic to arts of Japan (fine sample at Oomoto above). Year course in English with Japanese, can lead to advanced courses for total 3 years, annual certificates, or if good Japanese, transfer to parallel native course. Consult alumni working in Ura Senke (phone book 'Ura-') centers 153 E.69 St New York 10021; 4 Langton Way London SE3 7TL; San Francisco; Epping Sydney; etc. Scholarships available.
✍ Ms Mori, International Division, Ura Senke, Ogawa-gashira, Kamikyo-ku, Kyoto; in Japan, ☎(075)-431-3111 ask for *Kokusai-bu-cho, Mori-san*.

Kanazawa Summer Program, customized curricula one to 4 weeks in-
struction in language, ikebana, tea, calligraphy, etc in traditional Japan Sea art town, **Kanazawa**, mini-Kyoto, and more beautiful, walkable.
✍ Ms Sonoko Matsuda, Social Education Center, **Society to Introduce Kanazawa to World**, 3-2-15 Honda-machi, Kanazawa C, Ishikawa-ken 920, Japan.

Home Stay with Cultural Studies and language, mid-July, 3 weeks
$1,100, by outfit who bring us *Tokyo Journal*–don't leave Tokyo hotel without it!
✍ **US-Japan Cross Culture Ctr**, 244 SanPedro St, Ste 305, LosAngeles CA 90012.

Decorative Arts of Japan, end June, 3 weeks Nara, Kyoto, Tokyo, ('89)-
$2,150 incl air fare but "*not* tuition–?" ✍ Prof Jaimee Uhlenbrok Director, **On-Site Studies in Art History Abroad**, State Univ of New York, New Paltz NY 12561.

Traditional Theater Training (TTT), obvious spin-off from Oomoto
idea, but, fully structured to own specific needs, apparently as successful. Mid-July–thru August, 6 weeks, daily noh, kyogen & buyo dance drill under traditional masters in AM, option mask-carving, noh-drum etc, PM; study trips, all lead to live performance in traditional recitals and 'fusion' experiments with NOHO theater group; tuition ¥125,000, includes dance-tabi, fan, scripts, trips, etc; room extra about ¥50,-100,000, meals advised ¥150,000, in comfort, but can scrimp on much less.
✍ Director **Jonah Salz**, PO Box 079, New York, NY 10003, or 109 Shimo-Ikeda-cho Kitashirakawa, Sakyo-ku, Kyoto 606; or if already in Japan, phone noh-man John McAteer ☎(075)-751-8389 re off-season activity, introductions, much-etc.

Friends World College East Asia Center branch of 7-country 4-year
school headquartered New York, which offers regular BA requiring time in two cultures plus one's own, chosen from New York, Costa Rica, London, Israel, Kenya, India and here in **Kyoto**. Varies 15-25 bodies with 2 co-director-proctors, small English library on Japan (anything helps in this land of total literacy yet lousy libraries with no subject indexes!). After 2-week indoctrination including intensive language, student guided to find own hands-on teachers in arts or do own research. Treach-erous for immature, great for some. Tuition (1987) $5,700 plus fare and room-board (¥15,-30,000 room only, cook alone or eat out); some home stay with Japanese family about ¥40,000 R&B–but beware vastly different life style often causes friction, US 'kids' far more adult and used to responsibility than locals, not used to early lockout, *mon-gen*. Also accept 'visiting' students from more conventional colleges, usually Jr Year Abroad, for 8-week 3-course core/language plus field projects for 15 crs.
✍ **Friends World College**, Plover Lane, Lloyd Harbor, Huntington LI, NY 11743; –or if already in Japan phone ☎(075)-672-6260.

Preparatory Course to Enter Japanese University: intensive language and culture program (interesting as native student knowledge of own culture is nil) at old-line Buddhist church-established (1639) non-sectarian college in ancient **Kyoto**. Morning full time 20 hrs weekly language study, Afternoon optional lectures and seminars on Japanese history, way of life, customs, art, etc. Fees ¥537,000 (c.$3,600) per annum payable in two halves; typical local room-board off campus runs about ¥80,000 monthly, home stay poss, dorm abuilding; enclose non-refundable fee of ¥25,000 with application, deadline February 28 for April start. Student visa issued 4-1-4 or 4-1-16-3 issued with acceptance, also 80% coverage medical-*dental* insurance, student discount JR, movies, etc.

For excellent literature–✍ Bukkyo University, 67 Tsukamoto-cho Fukakusa, Fushimi-ku Kyoto 612; in Japan ☎(075)-642-1111 ext 719.

ARTS & CRAFTS: Of course major offering of Japan, over years attracting numerous art pilgrims seeking teachers, 'gurus'–but too often, expecting instant perfection. 'Traditional art' implies time to absorb, become part of tradition; involves mastering by physical rote basics of technique–repeating act of making something so many times it becomes automatic, part of one's self. Traditional apprenticeship starts with sweeping floors, or even with sitting outside master's workshop waiting for recognition of your existence, and possible admission. Would you welcome total stranger, probably not speaking your language, to join your family? Show seed of professionalism by not expecting to receive what you would not give. Would you expect to go to grad school straight from kindergarten? Master basics of your craft. Look for school if you haven't got basics. Then travel-study in spare time visiting craftspeople you hear about from classmates and teachers, maybe you'll find your life's master–who might even accept you. Start with Oomoto, above, for instant intro to concept of, philosophy of, tradition and discipline. Get some language under your headband. Get some tea— to be said to "have no tea" in Japan means to have no culture, no taste... no soul.

Tekisui Museum Art School: (between **Osaka-Kobe**, 15min from either on mainline JR or suburban commuter electrics). Minor private museum, frequent changing exhibits, but with fine attached culture center devoted to teach traditional and western arts, from pottery to piano. We recommend pottery or weaving: variety of 'Sunday artist' options, which we advise. Good teachers, top equipment, advance at own rate.

Pottery sign up for 8x/month, ¥5,000 registry plus ¥6,000 month, try for month or two on tourist visa. Then switch to full time eligibility paid for in 6 month commitment at ¥5,000+30,000; plus clay+kiln charges, to attend any days at any hours, X-mon, tues.

Weaving, waiting list ✍ ahead; ¥30,000 registry, ¥8,000 month for 2x-week. But remember, for student visa (school won't guarantee, too many goofs before) must average minimum 20 hrs weekly–including hours in language school or dojo, other, in total.

✍ Tekisui Museum, Yama Ashiya-cho 13-3, Ashiya 659; ☎(0797)-22-2228.

Kawashima Textile School: Founded 1973 to mark top company's 130 years. Attached to their excellent research center, located in city of weavers offering unlimited opportunities for observation-study–not least their factory and 90,000 item museum. Introductory courses of 3, 10 or 20days held monthly, 2 year full time or your own sched. Enough English spoken by instructors, but hands teach best. Everything from natural dye to hi-tech, 50 spinning wheels, 100 various looms.
✍ Kawashima Textiles, Ichihara-cho 418, Shizuichi Sakyo-ku, Kyoto 601-11; ☎(075)-741-3151

ZEN MEDITATION and Introduction: countless would-be tourist bodhisattvas seek crash enlightenment. If that's you, stay home and change
channels. Chapter on Kamakura lists several temples where casual to sincere
zazen is possible (*see* INDEX). How far you go is purely up to you. Kyoto
has long had regular instruction groups. Those functioning '91 include:

Myoshin-ji 'cathedral', Kyoto, longest-running English Zen group (*see*
Kyoto, p472) still meets for overnite lecture-sit, sat 5pm-sun AM; or 2nd Sun 2-
3:30pm sit + 30min lecture, contact Homobu or Kyoku Ctr, ☎(075)-463-3121, no fee;
much of old international activitylessness has moved out of Kyoto tourist belt to...

Sogenji, YAMADA Mumon of Myoshinji of Kyoto – late Rinzai master with
international following, was his main dojo for training non-Japanese. Midway
Kobe-Hiroshima (p628). Sit year-round Sun, 8-9am, arr 7:30. Several-day *sesshin* often,
consult resident Hojo, or asst Priscilla or monk George. Accept greenhorn if think you
have right stuff, or may refer you elsewhere to fit your needs. **Bus** from Okayama
Tenmaya or JR stn (far R end tunnel under hotel to back) bound → SAIDAI-JI, 20min.

Shinshoji Kokusai Zendo, excellent in Hiroshima Pref, ☎(0849)-88-1200.

Kyoto Soto Zen Center, Sosenji Temple zazenkai & Shorinji sesshin.
Sosenji is at Shimogyo-ku Takakura-Gojo-sagaru, 5min walk E from Gojo subway,
☎(075)-351-4270 or 6823, first and 3rd mons except Jan and Aug, English lecture 6pm
followed by two periods zazen 7-8:50; free. Hardier, try *sesshin* or several days straight
sitting, at Shorinji dojo (outside Kyoto) Okabana-4, Sonobe-cho Shishi-udo, Funai-gun
622; ☎(07716)-2-3310. **Get There** by JR Sanin line Kyoto → Sonobe, then Kyoto
Kotsu bus → Shishiudo and 5min walk → Shorinji Temple. Held almost monthly (X–
Feb, Aug and Nov, Dec when latter two conflict with really serious *rohatsu* winter sitting
Dec 1-8), fri–tues around 4th sun; free: rise at 4am, sit 50min, stretch, sit again 5 periods
interspersed with bkfst, clean, then lunch, work and 6 more sits of 50min each, sleep at 9
with "no unnecessary talking during sesshin (4days)"–must do all sits, dozen daily.

Zenjoji Gesshukai Sesshin, between Ishiyama and Uji. Keihan tram, bus
→Ichumae, 30min walk to temple. Fri thru tue, 2nd sun monthly, X-Feb & Aug; fee
¥1,000 per day, same sched as Shorinji. Sesshin not to be attempted without breaking-in
at Sosenji Zazenkai. ✍ or phone **Okumura Shohaku** at Shorinji, Zenjoji, Ujitawara-
cho, Tsuzuki-gun, Kyoto-fu 610-02; ☎(0774)-88-4450; or Daitsu Tom Wright, Awata
Horiike-cho 373-27, Higashiyama-ku, Kyoto 605; ☎(075)-752-0421.

Bukkyo (Buddhist) **University** extension offers frequent free seminars in
English on all aspects; check Shijo Center, Mitsui Bldg 4F, Shijo Karasuma
Higashi, Shimogyo-ku, Kyoto, ☎(075)-231-8004. In Tokyo watch back-page *Japan
Times* for notice of zen meets, lectures, sesshin; or almost weekly talks on various
aspects of Buddhism at **Tsukiji Honganji** (Jodo-shinshu sect); ☎(03)-3541-1131.

Sole Caucasian head of Zen temple in Japan, John Toler, in exquisite
converted 200-year-old manor house, 4 bldgs with 6th century tumulus on
4,000 tsubo (1,200m^2). Can put up sincerely interested, donate according to
your regular budget, minshuku or Hilton, but no hotel-type guests—18 bells
ring at 6am, rise, put up bedding, sit thru chanting or clean and weed for
half hour, then zazen 40min, breakfast, clean up own mess and chip in
doing daily chores. By appointment only, contact **Shogen-in,** Ouda-cho, Uda-gun
Nara-ken 633-21, ☎(07458)-3-0384; after Hase-dera Stn on Kintetsu line from Nara,
Haibara Stn, from which taxi. (*See* Ise to Hase-Nara, p.339). Ideal place for college to run
intensive program, or execs to consult for personalized zazen training like Japanese CEOs
and politicos get.

In passing, we mention numerous temples, mostly Zen, where meditation
or further study is possible. Our lst edition pioneered such introductions but
for other lists of opportunities, Roth & Stevens' *Zen Guide* (Weatherhill); ✍ author
John Stevens, **Zen Art Soc,** 1-37-2 Tsurugaya, Sendai-shi 983; ☎(0222)-51-5580.

LANGUAGE: for those serious about learning what is probably most difficult modern (as opposed to merely contemporary) language, with 2 to 17 seemingly arbitrary variations on pronouncing each of few thousand necessary ideographs (1850 to read paper, much more for effective literacy); considerable status difference in usage worse than French *tu-vous*–but not really that hard, it's how Japanese use it that's complicated. Go intensive or forget it, total immersion! Judging by results we've seen, by far best program is...

International Christian University Intensive Japanese summer session, exurban **Tokyo**, July, 6 weeks (can link with Oomoto seminar), various levels, placement exam on arrival, all day in small classes, hours of homework. Many students make mistake of coming with this as excuse for summer vacation, expect to get ahead without sweat, hopping ride nites into Shinjuku Tokyo to play–forget it, you hold back serious students, play weekends or when session ends. Those who do it right really learn lingo, we've met them, some now work for Japanese or international firms.

(Continues year-round regular college curriculum; if work-studying later, continue with same teachers eve **Asahi Culture Centers**). Class ¥119,000, dorm ¥15,000, cafeteria meals average ¥500. Due to excess applicants, apply early. Unfortunately, we can only advise this fine program to student enrolled in regular college, as ICU itself now prefers.
🖎 **Japanese Course at ICU**, Osawa 3-10-2, Mitaka-shi Tokyo-181;☎(0422)-33-3131

Osaka Foreign Language University, suburb **Osaka**, where gov't sends foreign scholarshippers for intensive language. 🖎 Foreign Student Dean, **Osaka Gaikoku-go Daigaku**, Oaza Aomadani 2734, Mino-o-City 562.

Kobe YMCA Japanese School: Summer Intensive: 4wks about July 13-Aug 7, fine teachers with good system several hours daily in small classes 3-15, various levels, catered to individual, placement after interview. Registry ¥5,000, tuition ¥49,000, books ¥3,000 (approx $400 total). Good textbooks with supplementary tapes. Year course **Regular Language School**, in 5 'steps', morning or evening twice weekly, ¥44,000 per step, add extra parallel reading seminar, ¥22,000 per 1/5. **Full Time** year course, ¥30,000 + ¥235,000 tuition and fees, qualify for cultural visa. Small-town **Kobe** better for study than Tokyo, cooler summer, cheaper digs, and not least, convenient to traditional Japan. 🖎 Japanese Course, **Kobe YMCA College**, Kano-cho 2-chome-7-15, Chuo-ku, Kobe 650; ☎(078)-241-7204.

Asahi Culture Center Japanese Course: eve courses for residents, well done, most big cities–**Tokyo, Osaka, Kobe**. Look up after arrival, good post-summer continuation with job; with art, martial art, etc classes for cultural visa. (*see*).

Berlitz battle cry 'total immersion' gets results, one-on-one or small groups, schools in Tokyo business subcenters, Osaka, Kobe. Angled at executive, priced accordingly, highly effective, worthwhile. Inquire nearest US/UK Berlitz or 🖎 **Berlitz Schools**, DIC Bldg Ist Fl, Nihonbashi 3-7-20, Chuo-ku Tokyo 103.

Japan Times School of Languages, considering quality of daily newspaper, assured to be superb program; small groups, vary 9:30am-9:30pm, 🖎 JT Language Schools, CPO box 144, Tokyo 100-91.

Naganuma School of Japanese Language, oldest and still one of best: new intensive 6 week summer sessions, early July, for all levels 🖎 **Naganuma School**, Nampeidai-machi 16-26, Shibuya-ku, Tokyo 150.

Shibusawa International School language boarding school in old estate of great internationalist family, men's dorm in converted *kura* storage women's in old farmhouse; intensive; 3mos w/R&B ¥451,000; 🖎 **Shibusawa** 247 Chiarai-jima, Fukaya-shi, Saitama-ken 366; ☎0485-87-2100; Tokyo off ☎03-3432-0561.

Others in Tokyo ads in *Tokyo Journal, Japan Times*– **Kyoto-Kobe** *KTO.*

Up-to-date list available in Japan Society *Newsletter*–✍ requesting *Newsletter* with course offerings, 333 E. 47 St, New York, NY 10017; enclose $1 post. Often has good tour list and what's on where in US and Japan–if in New York, join!

SELF STUDY under proper visa is possible. We can envisage individual program here in Kobe which qualifies for Cultural Visa 4-1-16-3: morning/evening language plus reading seminar, YMCA; pottery or art free schedule Tekisui Museum; Aikido or karate dojo; other art to total minimum 20hrs weekly. Time for part-time work if necessary. Same could be done in any of several cities–Nara, Kyoto, etc, even Osaka or Tokyo, where plenty of martial arts dojos, Asahi Culture Centers or Ys for language, independent flower, tea, weaving, pottery. Teachers can give you letter confirming your spending so many hours–which immigration will spot check!. Such would work best starting with summer warm-up at Oomoto (tourist visa) followed by few weeks touring, looking around for teachers you have feel for, and honest consultation with immigration officer–as tourist visa not extendable.

STUDENT RIGHTS & PRIVILEGES: matriculation full-time *should* entitle you to student ID, good for discounts on JR, theater admissions, standby rate domestic air. **Medical insurance** available to students low rate–if school doesn't handle, take Alien Registration, student ID if one, to city office and enquire about *kokumin-hoken*, citizens' insurance: 80% coverage, includes most dental.

JOB is best way for young to see and study country leisurely. *Jobs in Japan*, "...complete guide to living and working in the land of rising opportunity", by John Wharton, Global Press 1510 York St, Suite 204, Denver Colorado 80206 (1986), many refer to it but several young friends who used it insist it not be taken seriously, misrepresents living conditions, etc.

YMCA English Schools nationwide 24 cities recruit full time English teachers overseas, BA required as is 'strong Christian commitment'; pay housing allowance, ¥180,000 monthly salary plus small supplement for higher degree or certificate or pro experience. Study Japanese same place off hours, and you have wonderful cities to choose from like Hiroshima, Kanazawa, Nagasaki. ✍ **Overseas Personnel Program**, YMCAs of USA, 101 N.Wacker Drive, Chicago, Ill 60606; or your National YMCA office London, etc. **Deadlines** Oct 31 and Mar 15 for Feb and Sept starts.

Japanese Education Ministry is importing 800 native speaking teachers of English from English-speaking countries for high schools, require BA minimal, prefer some experience or special training in teaching, good pay of $23,000 plus housing, fare, fogies, full insurance etc, plenty of holidays for travel. While jobs gone by this reading, partially restaff yearly, plan increase. ✍ **Japanese Embassy**, educational attache, your capital city.

Job hunters need *Japan Times* monday edition with its several pages of classified help wanted ads. Check at JNTO, Japan Society library or friend's company who has airmail subscription. ✍ **Japan Times,** CPO Box 144, Tokyo 100-91, for next monday ed, encl $3 international postal reply coupon.

Coming with hopes of hunting teaching job after arrival, bring along well-produced curriculum vitae, plus photocopies (preferably notarized) of any degrees and certificates, copies of publications or title pages, letter of recommendation from professor or professional employer, on official or impressive letterhead. Japan Justice Ministry will issue teacher visa only to citizen of English-speaking nation with BA, or at least English college grad with 10 year-residence in English nation – this is non-negotiable.

This chapter has been kindly checked by Justice Ministry status officer, tho not endorsed.

WHEN TO GO

WEATHER: lots of all kinds, as table of Tokyo temperature records states:

WEATHER IN TOKYO—Lat N35°42'—Alt 30ft/9mtrs–

Temp-°F/°C	JAN	FEB	MAR	APR	MAY	JUN	JUL	AUG	SEP	OCT	NOV	DEC
Low	30/-1	31/0	36/2	47/8	54/12	63/17	69/20	72/23	66/19	54/12	43/6	33/1
High	47/8	47/8	53/12	63/17	70/21	76/24	83/28	85/29	79/27	69/	60/16	47/8
Average	39/4	39/4	45/7	55/13	62/17	70/21	76/24	79/27	73/23	62/17	52/11	42/6
Days of Rain	7	8	13	14	14	16	15	13	17	14	10	7
						(rainy season)			(typhoons)			

Note that number of rainy days is about same all year round except slightly drier winter months. Six-week 'official rainy season' sets in June 6. This is being written on 5th day of rainy season: first day it poured just as gods promised, 3 days of sparkling weather followed, 5th day-rain. 1984, as 1952, first rain of rainy season fell final day, continued pouring for week of 'dry season'; '63 saw floods May, '67 & '83 deluges in July. Real meaning of season is that farmers hope for of moisture during period rice is planted in mire, and May is often lovely dry month—but almost as often not. Expect high humidity June thru till typhoons pass—but not as hot as NY, DC.

People recommend spring cherry time, say weather lovely, sparkling. We say come prepared for 3 drizzly days weekly and you can't be disappointed. Rainy season is awful time to visit: we say come prepared for 3 sunny-ish days weekly, see gorgeous planting festivals and rites. Say summer awful, hot and sticky: we say great improvement over New York, can always sleep nites here, summer evenings are loveliest of year for strolling, shopping (many shops open, except department stores, arcades catering to foreigners), just sitting in rooftop beer gardens, seeing lovely festivals or adventuring forth into fairyland of summer restaurants. Even local eateries not to mention taxis, are air-conditioned, even in sizzling offbeat west.

If any time is best, it's autumn, October-November. Then expect 2 to 3 light showers weekly, perhaps stuffy day of typhoon winds which may cause suffering to fishing villages but little inconvenience to you, and some adventure. Main disadvantage: often sweater-chilly. But maples are lovely. Winter definitely uncomfortable—but not in hotels or better Japanese inns, and there are so many good ways to keep warm (sake, baths, snuggling) and so many good dishes to try, so many exciting events, and, best of all, hot springs even in skiing areas. Main disadvantage is cloudy weather.

KYOTO is 2-3 degrees colder in winter than Tokyo, 2-3 hotter summer; being more humid seems even colder, or much hotter. OSAKA-KOBE are 4 degrees warmer than Kyoto winter, just bit warmer summer—statistically, but humid Kyoto earns higher discomfort index, and Kobe's hillside locale guarantees standing breeze. NAGASAKI, in far Kyushu, averages dim 40s winter, no hotter summer than Osaka, breezier.

Always have light raincoat available, can not get them easily in Japan: ready-made only for women in miniature; and as Japanese arms are short, 5'7" American male in largest plastic raincoat generally available sees 2 inches of bare sleeve get soaked. What do tall Japanese do?–wear imports.

At any time of year, be prepared for highly changeable weather, generally more humid than you are used to at home. Ground damp makes legs uncomfortable winter unless you wear good sox and shoes, preferably stockings if going out much. Almost no fog, however. It's 'shoes off' in private homes, inns, temples, (shrines usually wooden floor, if even entered), so advise carry ski-socks or mukluks for cold season. In summer wear socks as bare feet not appreciated, or must wipe them before entering.

*Ítalo Balbo descended from his plane...in the desert and asked the sheikhs,
who had gathered to do him homage, how long it took them to get to Tripoli.
"Twenty-eight days." ......"And I have come here in three hours!"
"Then, what do you do with the other twenty-seven days?*

GETTING THERE

PERFUNCTORY GLANCE at any map should make it evident that there are two routes to Japan: sea and air (tho friend drove Japan-Alaska in amphibious jeep). Air fares barely changed in 20-odd years since last edition of this book—'official' airline rates are higher than 1963's IATA-posted $825 LAX-TYO r.t.; but similar or even less if thru agent—while ships almost disappeared as their prices escalated drastically.

DISCOUNTS & TOURS

AIR: Increasing competition of newly added Pacific carriers United, Delta, All Nippon Airways (ANA, but *Zen Nikku* in Japanese), bodes nothing but good for us passengers. And more will be added, as flights are often full in all classes–tho this could encourage discount eliminations.

With deregulation, trans-Pacific fares are as difficult to keep track of as domestic US. We warn you **not** to call airlines direct as they will only quote official overcharge; agent gets you same trip for much less. Example: 1989 basic r.t. LA or SF–Tokyo, one year open validity thru any major airline economy Y-class is $1,610; same ticket thru agent costs $520 to 950, with another Asian country as final destination to avoid Japanese price controls. So as well as getting cheaper fare, you get either Taiwan, Manila, Hong Kong, Seoul, Bangkok or Singapore at no extra.

Also look for ads for **Courier Service** whereby you act as commercial courier to carry registered documents or package, or just 'sell back' your baggage allowance for another courier to use.

Real travel costs are way down in total when you consider airline costs, down in simple dollars since 1964, and way down since Jay came by ship in 1951 ($350 o.w. Charleston-Osaka) when Northwest transPacific SFO-Tokyo cost $650 single class o.w., which is about what we sometimes pay r.t. now in greatly depreciated dollars. Similar cut rate fares by first rate airlines available from New York. Nissan 1961 cost $1616 delivered New York...at 1991 car prices r.t. air LA-Osaka should cost $6,000! OK, that was first class in unnatural times. Tourism only started early '60s with jets, when r.t. west coast-Tokyo was US$682. If latter were pegged to hotel rates (Imperial '64 $8.90 double+svce, tax VS ¥29,500+% for $185+, '89 $245+) r.t. economy would be absurd $14,176! OK, 60% of this is exchange loss, but it would still be at least $5,670, over 8 times. Who would? who could pay it? Point we want to make is that we all owe debt of gratitude to true business acumen and efficiency of our airlines. But what do we "owe" those hotels and car makers? Yet hotels are full and cars sell. So what is true value?

APEX (official short validity discount) fares good for minimum 2 weeks to maximum 2 months stay, averages $620 (high-season fares Jun–Oct; low-season Nov–May 10-20% less). Contrary to what some airlines may tell you, Christmas season rates are not higher, just crowded and require book months in advance. Those wanting cheapest fare over Xmas are lucky to find any left after mid-November. But friend got LA-TYO-LA economy-class APEX mid-Oct 1986 for $520, confirmed for travel during Xmas. And confirm return or risk being stranded.

Some airlines serve Osaka direct, from/to Honolulu, west coast, rest of Asia. While some tourists claim Osaka city is not as much fun as Tokyo, it is as least good place to start touring Japan (Jay fumes at suggestion it isn't infinitely better). In heart of old Japan of Nara-Kyoto, international Kobe next door, rugged Kii Peninsula with Shangri-La Koya Monastery, sacred Ise Grand Shrine close. Shikoku is right across bay, Hiroshima only 2 hrs by fast train, 1-4 more hrs puts you anywhere on Kyushu. Half-day train journeys get you to backwoods Japan Sea Coast from Hagi to Kanazawa, or to grand escapes of mountainous antique Hida area. Kobe-Osaka also has ferries down to South Pacific isles of Amami, Okinawa.

US fares cheapest, quickest (8-9hrs) if direct to Japan from Los Angeles, San Francisco or Seattle; stop-off Hawaii, going or (preferably) returning, may add $50 to cheap fares. New York has non-stop trans-polar, most other east coast and mid-west departures either via above west coast cities or Anchorage. Best to use agent to see if direct ticket to Japan cheaper than using domestic line to west coast and switching to international carrier.

Thru agent, JAL often cheapest one-year-open r.t. fare. Flyers from/to Osaka will find JAL convenient as JAL Narita-Osaka link timed to JAL overseas flights and other airline users can blow hours or even overnite at Narita—but this can change suddenly as lines juggle rates. JAL for some time didn't 'discount' at all, then when PanAm stopped, JAL '86-87 became most aggressive. APEX often cheapest on Singapore, Korean, and China; in order of preference Singapore, best airline transPac for food and service; we sighingly recall when all lines were as eye-smilingly conscientious. China Air's service not as good, but convenience of landing Haneda instead of Narita is priceless. Don't recommend Korean unless lots cheaper (varies) since you backtrack to spend hours in Seoul—but Korea itself is tourist sleeper, cheap, exciting sights, great food and great people, good aside.

If Japan is just one stop on your tour of Asia, your ticket buying can get even more complicated, especially for bargain hunter. If Japan is first stop, get ticket that ends elsewhere in Asia: Hong Kong is good, for you can find bargain fares to other Asian cities once there, and inexpensive place to stay. Depending on season and state of air fares, it may be cheaper to buy tickets piecemeal for trips around Asia, or might get cheap fare on something like SA with Japan stop to end Singapore, then add stopovers like Hong Kong, Bangkok, Manila and Jakarta; usually $50 per stopover; good agent will find cheapest way. Continental and Air Nauru sometimes have cheap rates island-hopping across South Pacific.

From Australia or New Zealand, long little in way of bargains, as APEX fares ran abt A$1,000 from Melbourne or Sydney, NZ$1,800 from Auckland. Agents now offer better deals, 'stopover in Japan', than from US.

Those from Europe will also do better to have Japan as stopover; budgeteers get multi-stop tickets as far as Hong Kong or Singapore, where get discount tickets to Japan from either. London is still discount capital of Europe, but deals can be found in Amsterdam, Brussels, Zurich.

Several airlines have AROUND-THE-WORLD (ATW) tix, which for some reason are poorly advertised in US. PanAm pioneered them back when it was great airline. Now usually 2 lines join forces for maximum coverage—good for one year, lets you stop often as long as no major directional backtracking, and can pass thru main air junctions (like Hong Kong) twice. Average cost $2,000 (as low as $1349); extra $500 adds Southern Hemisphere stops Australia, New Zealand, sub-Saharan Africa, South America. Usually only allow one major itinerary change once travel started, but don't have to use every leg of planned itinerary, so get tix made out to everywhere possible before starting, then go where you want, tossing away or doubling leafs. Since you don't have to use each leg, can do things like land Tokyo to travel all over Japan then ferry to Taiwan via Okinawa, or Shanghai or Korea then continue by air, taking trains or boats around Asia wherever you wish (one train ride not to be missed for those with time is to chug along peninsula Bangkok–Singapore). Like APEX, ATW tix have many picky regulations, like purchase 30-days prior to departure: so check carefully to compare itineraries of different companies. CIRCLE PACIFIC is another economy route from $1299 NY-TYO thru SE Asia, Hawaii, LA.

Another consideration whether buy only to Japan or around Asia or world is FREQUENT FLYER PROGRAMS (FFP) of various airlines. Most US lines join foreign carriers. Major line at even full fare (tho discounts count equally as mileage) may pay off in accumulated miles for free trips. United's FFP often has seasonal bonus for travel to Asia; Western joins with JAL, just to mention few of your choices. ANA plans an all-inclusive packet for flying around Japan, nothing yet—worth checking.

Children 2–12 years old half- on full-price but discounts less, infant under 2 yrs not occupying own seat 10% adult fare. Ask airlines what facilities they have for babies (special cribs), request front-row seat any section or bulkhead seat for leg room. Adults with children board first. Most planes have toys to keep kid occupied, good idea to bring own—if electronic game make sure sound can be turned off. Ask if might interfere with plane radio.

Warning: future no lack of discounts, but shortage of seats. *Reserve*.

SEA travel once attracted leisurely, but no more regular passenger lines between Japan and US or Europe since wiped out by convenient air. Jay came in '51 by slow 11,000-ton Japanese freighter from Charleston S.C.; first passenger on Japanese ship thru Panama Canal postwar, to Osaka in 67 days, $350 o.w. 'Captain's Courtesy'; read everything on board including cereal boxes. Sumi came '52 Marseilles-Yokohama on *SS Marseillaise*, 30 days with 7 stopovers, dorm room, $400 o.w. Now, when you can find boat, it is 3-4 times air fare. Cheapest afloat is 'Floating University' of Pittsburg U, aboard *SS Universe*, two sailings annually Feb (E-bound) and Sept (W-bound), about 13 weeks, several days stop in ports; whole cost about same as semester in private college; full credit and accepts elderly auditors. Some **cruise ships** (incl QE-2) visit Japan (Yokohama, Kobe, Kagoshima, Nagasaki) for few days, usually after visiting Southeast Asia or Pacific isles. We know of no agents specializing in sea travel, but most handle cruises. *Travel Sections* of most sunday papers list cruises–work from there. Most do not begin US ports, but Australian or SE Asian. Prices vary depending on if they set your air fare to start of cruise and back, or if do by yourself (often cheaper). Negotiate to end cruise in Japan–most sell single legs–or stay over to catch later ship out. All luxury class; any cruise will be way over limited budgets. Japan in '86 announced, or laid keels for, several new liners–exciting possibilities in near future.

Freighters willing to take passengers now are scarce, offer little in savings over cheap air, unless able to work for fare over. Agents specializing in freighters hard to find; most info passed among network of freighter buffs. Info in US **Freighter Travel Club of America** PO Box 12693, Salem, Oregon, or *Ford's Freighter Travel Guide*, PO Box 505, 22151 Clarendon St, Woodland Hills, Cal.

This doesn't mean sea approach to Japan isn't possible, you just can't do it cheaply from US. However, especially for budget travelers, regular passenger lines link Japan to her four Asian neighbors:

Frequent r.t. Kanpu Ferry between Shimonoseki (west Honshu) and **Pusan South Korea** is most used as it is cheapest way out of Japan (¥8,000 2nd class B), popular with those needing visa renewal. But immigration officials on return at Shimonoseki have reputation for being up-tight and least helpful. They can turn you away if they feel like, but should have less problem on your first crossing from Korea, have proof of continued ticket out of Japan. To renew Japan visa, advise fly excursion to Seoul for about ¥50,000 r.t., less than rail Shimonoseki plus boat crossing, or combi JR ticket train-ferry-train Tokyo-Seoul (28hrs, ¥28,000 o.w.)–much easier on your sanity. Cheapest air to Korea is Fukuoka-Pusan ¥11,500, but boat is good and cheap way to see beautiful Korea, and since you're already this far East, why not? For stay over 15 days get visa for Korea in Tokyo or Osaka, shorter don't need. Ships dep Shimonoseki daily 17:00; arr Pusan 8:30 next day. Dep Pusan 17:00 daily; arr Shimonoseki 8:30 next day. Budget 2nd class should go about 3hrs early to ensure ticket and get sleeping area. Rsv at any large Japanese tourist agent, JTB, or direct thru Kanpu Ferry Co, Shimonoseki ☎(0832)-24-3000, Tokyo ☎(03)-3567-0971. Osaka also serves Pusan: Dep Osaka Nanko (south port) mon, wed, fri, sat 12:00 for scenic coastal run; arr Pusan 10:30 next day. Dep Pusan mon, wed, thur, sat 17:00; arr Osaka 15:30 next day. 2nd class ¥18,000; Osaka Kokusai ferry ☎(06)-263-0200. Return scheds often change, check.

Taiwan is another popular route. Arimura Sangyo lines runs weekly between Naha on Okinawa and Keelung (Chi-lung), N shore near Taipei. Dep Naha wed 19:00, reach Keelung fri 7:00am, stop en route Ishigaki isle (*see*) 1-6pm thur. Return from Keelung mon 10:00, direct to Naha tue 8am. Cheapest 2nd class ¥15,600; check visa requirements, if needed get from Taiwan rep **Assoc of East Asia Relations** (*A-to Kankei Jimusho*), Tokyo at 5-20-2 Shirogane-dai, Minato-ku, ☎(03)-3280-7803. Allow time for long queues. Return schedule often changes last minute, check.

China has recently inaugurated ferry linking Kobe–Shanghai, but visas can be complicated especially from Japan–tho picture brightens constantly. Also sea or air to Shanghai thence train Peking, and on across Russia to Europe.

Russia 4th choice, 51-hour Far East Line ferry links Yokohama-Nakhodka E coast of USSR, extension of trans-Siberian Rail. Frequency of ships diminished over years, only 35% of people reaching Nakhodka board ship, rest fly to Niigata. Latest sched is '89 (should be OK for few years) 2 runs monthly May, June, Sept, & Oct, 4 July-Aug. FESL agent **United Orient Shipping Agency**, Tokyo ☎(03)-3475-2831-3. Also **Japan-Soviet Tour Bureau** ☎(03)-3432-6161, Osaka ☎(06)-531-7416. Or Intourist.

AGENT: Essential for cheap fares, buys blocks from airlines so can cut-rate even with commission. How does one choose or find good agent? You get more for your money, even for less money, from smaller agents, independents, but there are small fly-by-nites, too, so this is no blanket recommendation. We think small agencies (New York, west coast, London) with Japanese names do best all-around at fairest rates. Our favorite in LA is Mr **Torizawa**, best by tel, ☎(714)-557-2100, 'match anyone'. NEW YORK: **Nippon Travel** 551 5th Ave, ☎(212)-986-7393; **Sudo Tours** 500 5th ave; **Eastern Travel Plaza** 45 Rockefeller Plaza suite 554, ☎698-4971-4; **Japan Budget Travel** 9 E 38 St ☎(212)-686-8855 or ☎1-800-722-0797 (branches Boston, Chicago, Houston, Atlanta). LONDON: **New Japan Express** in Middlesex, but London ☎081-430-1911, abt £600. CLUBS like **OC Tours** LA & SF take token member fee to get you budget group-rate.

Specialist in off-beaten-path self-made tours in Japan is **Tozai Travel**.
Started in Amsterdam, Holland ☎(020)-256052, spread to US: San Francisco
☎(415)-421-4511, parent company **Cross Cultural** LosAngeles ☎(213)-617-2039
(where you can get *Tokyo Journal*). We learned of them thru solo budget travelers
(mostly European) we'd run into in most off-beat areas. Arrange all air-
surface travel, book rooms at great inns used to foreign guests (any budget)
without compromising any of true Japanese touch such inns justly famed
for. Tell them where you want to go, or if not sure then what you're looking
for, they'll send you. If you make your own way to Japan but still want
help getting around, office in Tokyo (always native English-speaker on
hand) can help. Short walk from Yotsuya JR loop stn, or subway Marunouchi red line;
☎(03)-3205-8011 for exact directions. Sister company publishes *Tokyo Journal*, which
while in Tokyo area you should never leave hotel without.

In Australia, we have used **Skylink Travel**, Abdul Ahmadi, great money saver:
Suite 402/10 Martin Place, Sydney NSW 2000, ☎223-4277.

DISCOUNT TICKETS: Sunday travel sections of *New York Times* and
Los Angeles Times carry wealth of ads for 'bucket seat' operators. We've
used some satisfactorily for Europe. Also look for discounted **1st class**
and **Executive** Frequent Travel bonus coupons selling to 70% off: NY-
Tyo-China from $1200 First Class, equal to posted tourist class. If in small
town, get *NY-* or *LA-Times*. Many of these outfits are wholesalers or will
cooperate, split commission, with local agent you use for land arrangement.
By 1988 'bucket seat' wholesaling was computerized—we checked friendly
little local **Claremont Travel**, who dialed their fixer, quoted us LA-TYO via
Korean or Varig to match best *Times* ads. Advise use local agent when you
can, as you have better control over them, bad trip can ruin. They'll handle
any land arrangements you need in single package which also may involve
additional savings—they give you more time and personal attention. Can
book most tours advertised at same retail prices. Arrange what we think is
best deal: basic tour (group or individual), plus free time at end with open
return—may require $50+ extension to Hong Kong or Taiwan which you
need not use. If your agent won't, find one who will, or contact these big
city agents direct by phone, save…to spend later where you need it.

ESCORTED TOURS: Top source of offerings, Japanese-American
weekly *Pacific Citizen*. Advertises "cheapest transPac fare–$480 r.t.",
others, varies annually. ✍ P.C., 941 East 3rd St #200, Los Angeles, CA 90013;
☎(213)-626-6936. Send $1, ask for latest issue plus most recent special travel issue.

Here we note occasional offerings such as package to "Japan anywhere,
anytime 9 days" incl air fare, 7-nites hotel, 7-day Rail Pass, from LAX or
SFO, $898—[varying], less than posted airfare. Similar from New York thru
Kintetsu International ☎(212)-307-0827 or ☎1-800-422-3481. 1990 offered NY-
TYO plus Rail Pass & 6 nites hotel $1099 ($1199 summer). Get open or extended return
on this to spend longer freetripping at own expense, or add extra packages thru same
agent. Other deals other agents incl American b'kfsts, airport xfer, sightsee, Hong Kong
extension or Hawaii stopover etc, similar rates. Prices, details vary annually—but buys
will be buys! Best in '90 were to offbeat sights, avoiding expensive centers (better done
alone) which, reckoning $700 for air fare, average $100-150-land costs per day.

Asia Society offers luxe China and Asia tours, with Japan Option almost
$300per day ('90)—high as it seems, it's only about flat cost of room &
meals at top hotels they use, plus ground tours & transfers; fair buy.

JAPAN HOTEL PASS is to be considered while booking Rail Pass, save
10-25% on hotels: runs ¥5,-6,000/$44 ea of 2 traveling (*See* WHERE TO STAY, p129).

IRRASSHAI-MASSE WELCOME TO JAPAN

WHICH MAY NOT seem so welcoming once you have to deal with 'fortress' NARITA NEW TOKYO INTERNATIONAL AIRPORT, which handles most international arrivals. Annoying 60km (36mi) out of town, count on minimum 60min to town by train or bus (cabs at nite can do it in 45min, but for $150+); more to xfer to Haneda which handles most domestic flights to/from Tokyo—only 10 or so daily domestic runs use Narita. Landing here one wonders where megalopolis Tokyo is, since you only see lush fields of one of most prosperous rice baskets of Japan. Old name was Naruta, 'Thundering Fields'; then Buddhist deity Fudo was credited with driving away thunder to make rice grow abundantly, so name changed to Narita 'Plentiful Field'. Many joke (half seriously) that it should again be called Naruta, what with thunder of riots against airport. Until plans for airport materialized, area was used by Imperial Household Agency as pasture and for annual ambassadorial duck-hunt, with big nets.

Plagued with problems since its early stages when government tried to purchase farms at cheap prices without telling farmers why, virtually stealing their land. Early '70s saw violent confrontations as radical students and Red Army sided with farmers trying to regain land, or protect any who refused to sell. During construction Narita resembled armed camp as riot police fended off sporadic attacks by radicals. Giant steel towers rose overnite at end of runway, often shielded by piles of burning rubber tires. Formal opening delayed as few days prior gang slipped by 'impenetrable' security to trash control tower. Fear of sabotage, local clamor against fuel pipeline pushed cost of transporting jet fuel so high that Narita is most expensive airport for airlines. (Most expensive airport in world designed without any allowance to get fuel or passengers to it!) Also ranked most dangerous, as inability to get all originally sought-after land prevents completion of secondary runways. Narita finally opened May 1978, unfinished. Foreign lines would not move out of Haneda, so government coerced them. Most consistent gripes come from visitors who must use Narita, especially frustrating as cab or bus into town can take as long as flight to Hong Kong or Taiwan, longer than flight 500km on plus taxi into Kyoto or Osaka hotels. Kyoto top hotels cheaper than Tokyo's.

GETTING TO TOWN: Much-touted hi-speed train levitating above magnetic guides to Tokyo is still but dream (see test runs along Kyushu's coast near Miyazaki). Exit customs at North or South Wing, JR/Keisei station in basement, or bus and cab stands in front of each. JTB, TIC, other information centers (*see* TRAVEL AIDS p103) in mid section of terminal.

RAIL: Transport into town at last getting better: '91 saw start of direct hi-speed **Narita Express** JR train NARITA–TOKYO or SHINJUKU STNs in 53min, 3+x per hour, all reserved seats (unsolds sold on spot, if sold out usually can get on next train), 2cl ¥2,890, 'green'-1cl ¥4,110, 4-psgr compartment available; also to YOKOHAMA in 84min, ¥4,100/6,720. If on **railpass** get validated here at JR counter before reserving seat—but *not* if staying in Tokyo before heading on our historical itinerary (p201-).

Skyliner, Keisei Narita private rail for budgeteers heading to Ueno stn for Tokyo's Shitamachi (or NIKKO [p1029] or far north) – 55min by non-stop, 67min *tokkyu* (ltd exp), 83min *kyuko* (exp). Porters at Ueno, ¥200 per bag fixed fee, no tip. Skyliner ¥2,170, seats must be rsvd at airport terminal or station, dep track #3 about every hour+. Tokkyu or kyuko ¥730, frequent, tracks #1,#2. Ueno allows easy transfer to JR (for lines to far NORTH); Hibiya and Ginza subway lines, latter terminates W-Tokyo at Shibuya, whence non-railpass bugeteers start our historical route of Japan out of Tokyo (p201) buzz to Yokohama or Kamakura under 1 hour. E-terminus Ginza Line 3 stns on at Asakusa, whence speedy, budget pvt Tobu Rail zips to NIKKO in 100min. Also midst of our favorite part of Tokyo–old downtown SHITAMACHI (p1177).

Warning—send heavy luggage ahead by *takkyu-bin* (page bottom).

CAB: don't even bother: with expressway tolls, fare runs over 40x-basic meter rate (¥20,000-plus, $150 in '91), or about 6-7x-comfortable 1st cl train, or hotel shuttle bus—and for mid-size *chugata* (small by US standards) which normally take 4-5 psgrs, but count on 3 with bags. If lucky you'll find rare **wagon-cab** (8 psgr microbus, same rate, loads of room). Large 5-6-psgr US sedan-*ogata* has big trunk, softer ride, costs about 15% more.

HELICOPTER: Narita → Haneda (domestic airport), Haneda → Tsukuba, Tsukuba → Narita 20-30min each, several-x-daily by Nippon Air, Shin Nihon & Asahi Kobo. Reserve in advance o'seas. More routes to come.

LIMOUSINE BUS: Airport→hotel, most convenient, easiest to use. 'Limo' so-called just for fancy sound, for tho comfortable nothing special except free 'in-flight' mag. 8 lines serve main centers of Tokyo: *Shinjuku Line #1* (Keio Plaza, Century Hyatt hotels, Shinjuku stn); *Shinjuku #2* (Washington, Hilton International, Shinjuku stn); *Akasaka Line* (New Otani, Akasaka Prince, Akasaka Tokyu); *Ginza Line* (Palace, Imperial, Tokyu); *Shiba Line* (Tokyo Prince, Okura); *Shinagawa Line* (Takanawa Prince, New Takanawa Prince, Pacific); *Ikebukuro Line* (Grand Palace, Sunshine City Prince, Ikebukuro stn (arr only)). Also direct to JR Tokyo Stn. All ¥2,600 (child half).

Anyone can get on these buses, but unfortunately, they run only every hour or so; only Tokyo Stn and both Shinjuku runs operate all day (1st from Narita about 6:50); others start around 16:00 with last run 21:00. Earlier runs may improve. Last to Tokyo stn 22:30, last on both Shinjuku lines about 22:35. 80-90min generally accepted time to get into town by bus; traffic can easily add 30min. *May be discontinued or reduced.*

More frequent **bus** (every 5-15min, ¥2,500) to **Tokyo City Air Terminal** (TCAT) at Hakozaki, isolated corner of Tokyo far from JR, subways, near new hotels. All but budgeteer might avoid this route as only way from TCAT is 10min bus or meter basic cab fare to Tokyo stn, or 10min walk to Ningyo-cho subway stn on Asakusa and Hibiya Lines or little further to Kayaba-cho stn on Hibiya and Tozai Lines (*see* TOKYO for subway details). If staying some place not near hotel bus lines, with lots of luggage, bus to TCAT is good since cabs abound; many at TCAT are roomy wagon-cabs. Porters (rare) or U-push carts get bags from customs to *near* bus; unload bags for you at TCAT and pick up at turnstile with carts, cab stand just around corner. Average in good traffic is hour, easily doubles in rush hour; getting to other than Tokyo stn area from TCAT takes time and money, so Hotel Bus ends up costing less in about same time. TCAT good for leaving Tokyo as can do airline check-in, most exit procedures (incl ¥2,000 airport tax, which helps cover cost of extra army of police—no tax other airports). Similar buses leave Narita at every 30min for **Yokohama (YCAT)**, some via domestic Haneda airport. Narita–YCAT 2hrs to 2hrs30min unless bad traffic, JR train faster.

Tip: starting travel right off, travel light and **forward luggage**, *takkyu-bin*, to first main stop. Main floor desk near exit are freight forwarders, send on luggage: small bags overnite (never late), larger extra day, mostly ¥1,-2,000 each. Do same when leaving, send from hotel to departure terminal (*see* p.1225). Service available any hotel front desk. Some airlines will handle, free or reduced, for their Business & First class clients.

While most associate Narita with its annoying airport only, it is actually pleasant rural town with some fine sites nearby. Many fine old traditional Japanese inns are located within walking distance of JR Narita stn, make Narita comfortable alternative to long trip from/to Tokyo (*see* p1225).

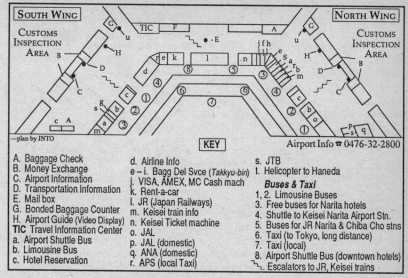

SOUTH WING

NORTH WING

CUSTOMS
INSPECTION
AREA

CUSTOMS
INSPECTION
AREA

TIC

—plan by JNTO

KEY

Airport Info ☎ 0476-32-2800

A. Baggage Check
B. Money Exchange
C. Airport Information
D. Transportation Information
E. Mail box
G. Bonded Baggage Counter
H. Airport Guide (Video Display)
TIC Travel Information Center
a. Airport Shuttle Bus
b. Limousine Bus
c. Hotel Reservation

d. Airline Info
e – i. Bagg Del Svce (Takkyu-bin)
j. VISA, AMEX, MC Cash mach
k. Rent-a-car
l. JR (Japan Railways)
m. Keisei train info
n. Keisei Ticket machine
o. JAL
p. JAL (domestic)
q. ANA (domestic)
r. APS (local Taxi)

s. JTB
t. Helicopter to Haneda
Buses & Taxi
1, 2. Limousine Buses
3. Free buses for Narita hotels
4. Shuttle to Keisei Narita Airport Stn.
5. Buses for JR Narita & Chiba Cho stns
6. Taxi (to Tokyo, long distance)
7. Taxi (local)
8. Airport Shuttle Bus (downtown hotels)
⤴. Escalators to JR, Keisei trains

Narita New Tokyo International Airport arrival area

Especially good for arrival late in day, and/or if skipping thru Tokyo and leaving megalopolis for tail-end of Japan tour as we suggest. Airport TIC (close 8pm, sun) should be able to get you rooms at Narita, can call yourself (have Japanese speaker around), or good agents in US may be able to book in advance for you. Most Japanese inns do not like to take people too late since they cannot give you full hospitality, so if showing up after supper call ahead and inform them.

See NARITA (TOKYO, p.1225) for what to see, do around there, and where to stay.

HANEDA, name for **Tokyo**'s original airport, means 'wing field'—but association with wings of modern travel is pure coincidence. Tidal flats were called 'wing-field' long before man had taken wing; open marshy fields were home of abundant game birds from ancient times—but advance of civilization and encroachment of city had scared most of it off before man nested his own winged vehicles there. Landing here you see Tokyo sprawled below you, but only if flying China AirLines (CAL). When Japan recognized Beijing as sole government of China, Taiwan was thrust into political limbo, its carrier 'exiled' to Haneda as non-country—much to financial benefit of CAL for their planes are almost always full of people who prefer Haneda's proximity to Tokyo as well as cheaper CAL fares. (Other competitive airline countries might sever diplomatic relations with Tokyo to get their flag-carriers advantageously exiled to Haneda).

From here cab affordable into town, or 15min monorail [¥300] to Hamamatsu-cho stn, JR Yamanote Loop. Some Narita-YCAT buses stop here for direct access to Yokohama and on to Kamakura, Hakone or Izu (as we suggest in our first leg Down Tokaido p.201). Haneda is domestic hub to fly to other parts of Japan. For several years there has been persistent and widely-held rumor about Haneda once again becoming Tokyo's main international airport. Just-completed renovated facilities better than at Narita. While some offer purely economic and practical reasons for doing so, others feel government seeking to move back to Haneda to use Narita for under-financed Air Self Defense Forces & airfreight terminal. Back here in December '86, Garet was out at Narita with people from airfreight business who said they can't wait until Haneda re-opens as international port. Even local cabbies seem to think it will happen before too long.

24-hr Kansai Int'l Airport scheduled to open 1994 on man-made island in SE Osaka. New trains, hiways planned to ease access.

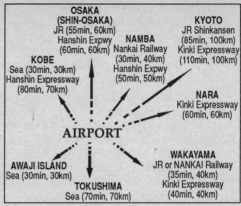

—Kansai Time Out   *Projected Kansai Int'l Airport*

ITAMI Osaka International Airport also serving **Kobe** and **Kyoto**. Busiest airport after Narita, ideal for plunging into heart of Japan. Most international flights landing here are from west coast, Hawaii, Southeast Asia, Pacific Isles. If from Hong Kong or SE Asia, definitely enter Osaka —not Tokyo—for ideal itinerary, save at least $50, one extra day, one hour less flight time. Itami far less frustrating than Narita; its officials much nicer. Most flights from US land first in Narita, some xfer to domestic there, often long wait. West Coast–, Honolulu– flights nonstop–Osaka; others will when traffic merits—go thru immigration, customs at Itami. Using Korean Air with mandatory Seoul leg, arrival/departure Osaka better, cheaper.

Center OSAKA only 15km away, KOBE 26km, KYOTO 45km. Cab to all affordable; '91 fares incl tolls, respectively, 8x-basic mtr-¥4,500, 13x-mt-¥7,500 & 23x-mtr-¥13,000. **Airport Buses** every 10-20min to Osaka either JR stn (Hilton, Terminal Hotels etc) or OBP (New Otani) or Namba (Holiday Inn, Nikko) 40min, or Shin-Osaka Shinkansen stn 20min; downtown Kobe (Sannomiya) 45min and Kyoto JR stn in 1hr—roughly 10% cab, ¥350 Osaka stn, ¥680-Kobe, ¥830-Kyoto. Cabs in front of terminal, marked in English, buses 100m L at domestic terminal. Hotel reservation desk in lobby.

Budgeteers without much baggage can save few hundred yen on private Hankyu rail from Hotaruga-ike stn, 15min walk or quick frequent bus (¥170) from Itami. Take train toward Osaka-Umeda; to terminus if staying in Osaka, or if destination Kyoto or Kobe get off 5min earlier at Juso stn to catch *tokkyu* ltd express to either town, both 30min away, or catch same trains 5mins on at terminus Umeda-Osaka. JR Rail Pass users go into Osaka JR stn Travel Center to validate pass. Hankyu's Osaka terminus, Umeda stn, is 5min walk from adjoining JR Osaka stn—directions, platforms well marked in English.

NAGOYA most international flights xfer Narita; direct WESTCOAST Delta; HAWAII America AirWest, via SOUTH PACIFIC Continental; EUROPE Lufthansa; more soon. If goal Nagoya area, Chubu, our favorites Kiso-kaido & Hida Takayama. Entry here and train on to Tokyo faster than thru Narita.

Those coming from Southeast Asia or Korea can also fly in to...

KYUSHU at two points, FUKUOKA and KAGOSHIMA. Latter is better, has many interesting sights and can accommodate everyone from budget Youth Hostelers to luxury resort hotelers, and it's not too far from international Nagasaki. Fukuoka (whose hotels for some odd reason match Tokyo rates) takes some flights originating in Europe; Kagoshima takes many island-hopping from Nauru, Ponape and other Pacific Islands. Nearby KUMAMOTO handles flights from Korea. All are expanding.

NIIGATA, in north, linked to Khabarovsk, Soviet Siberia; for travelers on Trans-Siberian Railway who can't get ship from/to Yokohama.

Jitoku (Shih-te) asked, *"What is the true Way?"*
Kanzan (Han-shan) answered, *"Every way is the true Way."*

GETTING AROUND

TRAVELERS' AIDS for foreign visitors have improved greatly over past few years especially for English-speakers—having been dismally poor to start. You will still find yourself mostly on your own outside main cities. Like all rules, there are many exceptions; odds are you'll run across extremely helpful bilingual (at least partially) info people out in middle of nowhere. English literature is more readily found once out of major cities, but often squirreled away in station info offices and to be asked for.

JNTO (Japan National Tourist Organization) leads English, other language info on Japan. Have series of 4-8 page pamphlets on various areas and cities. Basic coverage limited mostly to main sites, usually have good maps, detailed transportation to/from and around areas, and short list of lodgings (¥-Budget as well as ¥-Tourist to ¥-Standard). Slightly more detailed are fold-out color brochures of larger areas like Hokkaido, Tohoku, Izu-Fuji-Hakone, Nara, Kyushu, Okinawa, etc. Both types take almost no space in your luggage and make handy secondary references. Can pick up free at overseas offices (*see* p78), all TICs, sometimes at various local info centers. Best stock up when you can get them, even lugging from overseas.

Good walking guides, which we pioneered in 1964, they have improved on since and we unblushingly borrow back and again (hopefully) improve.

JNTO also has numerous other pamphlets: *Budget Travel in Japan*, but only briefly covers Tokyo, Nagoya, Kyoto, Osaka, Kobe. *Your Guide to Japan* and *Travelling Companion Japan* briefly touch upon everything from toilets and phones to food and lodging. JNTO puts out solo traveler's guide; in bookstores, good basic maps, scant info on sites & towns.

JNTO offices overseas are listed in our preceding PREFLIGHT PLANNING p78—with JTB branches in most major foreign cities, worth visiting.

JNTO headquarters is in cylindrical-topped Tokyo Kotsu Kaikan Bldg, at E exit of JR Yurakucho stn one stop W of Tokyo central, by Yurakucho subway stn Yurakucho line, or subway Ginza line's Ginza stn. Every imaginable pamphlet is there and you're welcome to pick thru, but staff can't give practical travel tips.

For that, best is...

TIC (Tourist Information Centers)—in Tokyo, Narita airport, Kyoto—main JNTO offices in Japan where English and some other languages are spoken. Unfortunately, they are sole places with info on all Japan, so stock up. TIC open 9:00-17:00 (Narita till 20:00) weekdays, 9:00-12:00 sat, X-sun & nat'l hol. Narita TIC in mid section of terminal by exit Customs South Wing. Tokyo TIC 6-6 Yuraku-cho 1-chome, ☎(03)-3502-1461; go off JR Yurakucho W exit (facing Imperial Palace), go L few dozen meters to next major street and it's on other side; subway Ginza stn exit A-4. Kyoto TIC 100m up from JR stn main exit, main floor Kyoto Tower Bldg. Plans for more offices in other cities, but who knows when. JNTO or TIC can now help you book cheaper lodgings under ¥10,000 only (*see* p138) thru Welcome Inn Reservation Center. We recommend TIC as first stop in Japan, get anything and everything they have on places you plan to visit. They have spawned series of locally-supported and -staffed City TICs, some as in Asakusa manned by volunteer local officials who work free on their own time. These may lack professionalism and efficiency of parent JNTO-TIC, but they more than make up for it in fervor and good intentions and refusal to give up on hard questions. Check local airport or JR stn on arrival.

JNTO-affiliated TIC right across from main Kaminari-mon gate at Tokyo's **Asakusa**; marked by big English sign, you can't miss it. Volunteers from local Taito-ku Ward Office run it in their spare time, just to help out—marvelous since we first used in 1954. Have lots of great info on Taito-ku ward, better known as Shita-machi, 'downtown' commoners' district—one of our favorite sections of capital. With Tobu line to Nikko nearby, this TIC also has lots of info on Nikko and other sites in that area of country. Open all year, 9:00-17:00 just as long as there are people to staff it (no problem to date). While their English may not be as polished as those at Yurakucho main TIC, their volunteer spirit and sincere desire to help more than make up for it.

TRAVEL-PHONE, nationwide toll-free line operating every day of year, 9:00-17:00, to get info from other places in Japan. Public pay phone, use only green or yellow phones, reds won't connect. Put in ¥10 coin to dial, refunded. From E & N areas ☎(0120)-222-800, W/S ☎(0120)-444-800. In Tokyo (03 area code) dial direct TIC ☎3502-1461; or Kyoto (075 area code) ☎371-5649; ¥10 for 3min. If you can speak Japanese, don't!—it's only to help visitors who need it.

TELE-TOURIST SERVICE, Tokyo & Kyoto TICs, 24hr taped info events each city: ☎(03)-3503-2911 (Eng), ☎3503-2926 (French); Kyoto☎(075)-361-2911 (Eng).

GOOD-WILL GUIDES pioneered by JNTO, bilingual volunteers ready to show you their town. Some 32,000 registered with JNTO, which runs some, advises rest run by local gov't. Denoted by circular blue badge, white dove atop globe. TICs list places with Goodwill Guides, or ask at local tourist bureaus. Best to arrange day in advance. Most are students, thus hard to get during January final exams, but enough are housewives, often with o'seas experience. Excellent are Kamakura, Nara, Imari.

More often than not, help comes from unexpected quarters like average citizen or passing student eager to help. Even in remote parts we run into such people who offer to guide us. Unless agreed upon before start, money rarely expected or accepted; you should, however, cover their expenses (admissions, transportation, food) while with you. Nice idea to carry cheap souvenirs of your home town, school, even your business matchbooks, etc.

JTB (Japan Tourist Bureau) for foreign language literature not as good as JNTO (separated when JTB became commercial agency pre our 1st edition), but they have own brochures. Slowly expanding series of guide books (red paperbacks) for all-Japan, Tokyo, Kyoto. Coverage of tourist sites not in-depth. JTB in most cities and towns, in or near stations, but rarely English-speaking staff. Many places have something in English, often kept in back, ask. JTB as agent arranges lodgings, transport, as will nation-wide **Nippon Express, Nippon Travel, Fujita** etc, and regional railroad-owneds like **Kintetsu, Hiroden**, etc.

Each town also has several other local travel agents, but most helpful are...
KANKO-ANNAI-JO (Tourist Info-office): usually small booth or counter in or around main JR station, bus center or airport. Carry all sorts of pamphlets on local area; English ones sometimes available, occasional staff member will speak some English. If you speak some Japanese, local *kanko-annai* are treasure troves of info. Even if you can't speak or read Japanese, many have well-labeled illustrated brochures with maps of local sites. Prime tourist spots, even in boondocks (like central Hida Takayama, nearby beautiful village of Shirakawa-go) have English material, sometimes English scheds for local bus lines to main sites. They are mentioned in text, but with more and more places catering to foreign visitors, chances are you'll find many new places which were inadequately equipped for foreign visitors when we passed thru. For adventurer wandering thru Japan, we highly recommend seeking out nearest *kanko-annai* and asking for all material available, as they supply great secondary info.

PUBLIC TRANSPORTATION

DOMESTIC AIR: For most part convenient, except when dealing with Tokyo & international connections. All domestic lines use Haneda airport not far from heart of city, while international flights use white elephant Narita, and hell to get from one to other. Aside from inconvenience to Tokyo, its endless security checks & airport taxes, Narita will try your patience. For that, and other reasons, we recommend Osaka for overseas connection, but Osaka gets equally inconvenient international airport by end of century (they say '93, but don't bet).

Japan Airlines (JAL) and All Nippon Airways (ANA—*Zennikku*) dominate domestic routes but Toa Domestic Air, changed name to cumbersome Japan Air System (JAS), growing, with possibly more following deregulation. Air Nippon (ANK) minor line, covers outlying areas; Nippon Air Commuter (JAC) and Southwest Airlines (SWAL) island-hop all over from Kyushu down to Okinawa. There are numerous local lines, usually made up of 12-30 passenger planes servicing nearby islands. Air fares roughly equal top reserved express trains over same span; budgeteers would do well to avoid flying. If full-time student in Japan with proper school ID, get **Sky-mate pass** which gets you on standby at considerable savings (20%), tho virtually useless at peak seasons of New Year and O-bon. Check JAL or ANA office overseas before coming as at one time international student IDs were OK. Late '86, ANA (just acquired trans-Pacific rights) sounding out possibility of Rail Pass-like deal in which those flying over on ANA would be eligible for all-inclusive domestic pass; '91 nothing concrete yet, but ask.

Charter aircraft for sightseeing per hour: Cesna 3psgr ¥60,000, **Shin Chuokoku** ☎(0297)-62-1271. Helicopters fixed rate, 3-4 times US, suggested as negotiable: 3psgr ¥260,000, 4-5psgr ¥299,300 **Asahi-kogyo** ☎(03)-3988-1012; or thru hotel desk.

Most convenient schedule is pocket-size, *K&D Timetable*, available hotels etc *free*, includes all domestic air, Shinkansen trains (not old lines), airport transportation, subway maps and price list of members of Japan Hotel Assoc, but no ryokan.

TRAIN: Most convenient way to get around is on extensive Japan 'National' Railway (JNR)—once great state monopoly, '87 broken up into 6 monster area systems: one each for Hokkaido, Kyushu and Shikoku islands and main island of Honshu's Tokyo-north, Central, Kyoto-southwest systems, plus 7th for freight. But as far as we are concerned, system will still be single interlocked Japan Rail, known now to Japanese solely as *JR*, and as money-eager as same initials in *Dallas*.

Other than during typhoons and blizzards JR can be counted on to stick to schedule—exact enough that if train time and clock don't coincide, reset your watch. Rail system of Japan legendary for its coverage and reliability. Also noted for its deficit (reason it was denationalized), greater than most national debts—1985's $85 billion exceeded Mexico's, equaled total Japan trade surplus '86. But first year '87-'88 as business all lines ran in black. As result its annual price rise will end (we expect other cheaper private lines will now rise) and train frequency increase. Will get you anywhere in land. Frequency of service is probably world's highest. We cannot stress too strongly, do not think you are limited to main cities: it is easy to travel rapidly, quite comfortably anywhere at any time. Station you arrive at has **Kanko-annai** for info and room booking, and **Station Rental Car.** Bullet expresses often fastest in world—and most expensive, tourist-2nd class matches air ticket, and Ist class Green Car adds 40%, private 1-4 seat compartments available some Green Cars, further surcharge.

No fear of wildcat labor strikes either. Ever so Japanese as not to inconvenience others or upset society's rhythm, JR and all private rails set certain dates (posted well in advance) for united 'Spring Offensive'. Disputes usually worked out by then, but if strikes called, rarely last longer than one day (tho we have seen bad years when most service halted for few days), or sometimes limited to major urban areas. If in Japan for spring, check to see what's planned thru JR, newspapers, tourist info places.

'87 breakup of JNR into multiple private JR affecting ticketing system. Deals like Rail Pass or local *shuyu-ken* regional passes as we thought would are getting better, more plentiful, with special package deals multiplying and possibly, oh so very Japanesely, more hospitably lower rate package deals for overseas visitors, especially foreign students. Check **JR InfoLine** ☎(03)3423-0111 for English scheds, fares, discounts—new svce, to expand.

RAIL PASS: vouchers can only be bought overseas at JAL offices or thru travel agents. They are sold in dollars, converted from their set yen price; must be started within 3 months of purchase. Airline-ticket-like voucher is traded in for actual Rail Pass at any of designated Travel Centers once in Japan, and you must show your passport (non-resident visa only) at time of transfer. Present validation spots are: Tokyo's Central, Ueno, Ikebukuro, Shinjuku, Shibuya stations, and Yokohama, Nagoya, Osaka, Kyoto, Hiroshima, Shimonoseki, Kokura, Hakata, Kumamoto, Kagoshima, Sapporo, Sendai and Niigata, as well as Narita International airport for those ready to rail right away. But don't validate to start from Narita if spending time in Tokyo; or in Osaka station if spending time Kyoto-Osaka-Kobe area—using pass for intracity travel wastes money, subways & private lines are cheaper.

Validate to start at your convenience from first day of use to anytime in advance, great for those early morning departures before Travel Centers open (9:00). For long trips thru rural Japan, can validate two or more passes back to back, with or without settle-down break between, knocking out need to return to major city. If planning to spend few days in one condensed area or traveling thru areas where JR is minimal (like back-country bus treks), or areas with better local transport (such as greater Nagoya area's Meitetsu bus-rail, Ise-Yamato's Kinki bus-rail, Kobe-Osaka-Kyoto megalopolis), try not to do it on costly Rail Pass—have one pass end as you reach such area where you want to dally and have next one validated to start few days later when ready to move on, or validate new one when ready.

Rail Pass **rates** '90 (at $1=¥133, add 10% $=¥120): 1-wk Regular ¥27,000 ($200), Green-car ¥37,000 ($275); 2-wk Reg ¥43,000 ($319), Grn ¥60,000 ($445); 3-wk Reg ¥55,000 ($408), Grn ¥78,000 ($578). (Compare 1987 Eurailpass 1st-class: $280 for 2 weeks, 3-wk $350). Single Shinkansen bullet train round-trip Tokyo-Kyoto about equals 1-wk Rail Pass, so good buy if doing much long distance bullet travel—but plan carefully. Pass is good on all JR trains, buses & boats—any JR ferries replacing those discontinued Spring '88 with opening of Honshu-Hokkaido Seikan tunnel and Honshu-Shikoku Great Seto Bridge—plus of course short shuttle from/to sacred Miyajima Isle.

Green-car pass seats you in roomy 1st-class car. Luxurious on Shinkansen also worth it on trunk line long distance express, but not on lesser lines, many of which older trains do not have Green Cars, those that do not much better than regular seats, except for green cloth. Even if fully booked for holidays, Green Car less crowded since usual standing in aisle not allowed.

SUNRISE SUPER SAVER complements Rail Pass, **Hotel Discount Coupons** get you discounts in hotels running ¥13,-16,000 incl tax/svce for 2 (standard), at flat tourist ¥12,000. Apply thru JTB overseas office or your agent, buy book of at least 5 nites. (*See* WHERE TO STAY, p.129).

Rail Pass is convenient as it avoids all ticketing hassles, especially so for fun aimless wandering to let your train take you wherever. **Reserved** seats must be dealt with before boarding, but are mostly unnecessary except on high season long runs. Rail Pass not cheap, based on express train rates. Example: 1-week regular pass about equals r.t. bullet Tokyo–Osaka or Ueno–Morioka. Savings, if you go far using mostly bullet and express, can be astronomical. Old friends home for summer rushed up to Sapporo (14hrs) for beer fest, returned Tokyo via few choice Tohoku stops and still had 2 weeks left on pass to bum around rest of Japan. Regular fare Tokyo-Sapporo-Tokyo would have run about ¥35,000, they even made it to Nagasaki (normally ¥48,000 r.t. Tokyo) while they paid ¥55,000 whole 3 weeks. But budgeteers with time, sticking to locals or at least staying off bullet should consider how far you will cover in pass' time span to see if really saving. Remember, any private rail alternative (below) is cheaper by up to half, often more convenient.

JTB RAIL-HOTEL PACKAGE: Hotel Plan: 20% off train travel (201+ km) plus special hotel rates (about 10% off) w/bkst or w/2. Mostly ¥-S (Standard) facilities, 2 to room; expanding, specials. Check JR, JTB.

REGIONAL PASSES, *shuyu-ken*: sold only in Japan mostly to locals or expats, little publicized for foreign tourists. Cover various regions, all sorts of shuyu-ken often include local private bus lines for better access. In general, *Wide-o* (Japlish for 'wide') *shuyu-ken* cover entire areas (Hokkaido, Tohoku, Chubu, San-In, Shikoku, Kyushu etc) are valid longer, prices vary according start/end point & duration; *'Mini' shuyu-ken* cover sub-sections, valid only few days, don't include from/to fare—others give 20% off from/to. Either basic type pass allows free multiple journeys within set area at 10-20% below single journey cost. On top of these are seasonal passes, special group deals for couples, retired people, 2-3 women together totaling over certain age (25 or so average, others for older), families, etc; buy 3 same tix % off, use together or in succession; short validity times.

10,000km club gives % off all tix around Japan. Buy *Shuyu-ken* any time from 30 days prior, up to day before departure. Stateside travel agents specializing in Japan can get shuyu-ken info, but must buy yourself once in Japan. If already here, JR Travel Centers (English-speakers always at Tokyo, Kyoto; sometimes other main cities), JTB or other major local travel agent will help; if you can't speak Japanese, best to have someone with you who can. TIC may also be of help.

Full Moon elder-couple (total age 88+) passes (only October-June). **Nice Middy** (Mar-Sept) for older *nice* girls of *middle* age in pair or trio. **Silver** for couple one of whom over 70–free pass 5,7,12 days. Will proliferate with JR's new-found acumen, hunger to succeed.

Check Monday *Mainichi Daily News* **Japan-o-file** for seasonals, special tours, cheapy Japanese tour groups, some share rooms. Also *TJ.*

DISCOUNT TICKETS abound for expensive Shinkansen. Best deal is Green Car (1st class)—Tokyo-Osaka lists ¥18,400, discounts abt ¥14,500, bit more than 2nd class. Smaller % discount on 2nd. All lines have similar deals. Tix available in small stores, grocers, teashops etc. Tho they look like black market stalls, fully legal: JR sells blocks of tix to companies that do much travel; dealers buy these and sell at markup, still well under list. In Tokyo, at small shops in front of main stations, plastered with yellow price slips with 2 or 3 name ideographs and Yen-price. Shimbashi stn area has obvious ones. Many mid-range, cheaper hotels sell at desk. Smaller towns usually only have to/from Tokyo or other major stop, as in Kobe where above Hankyu Sannomiya in teashop next door MacD's, also Fuji Coin Shop in Shimbun Kaikan bldg E of Sannomiya stn. Some also sell discount air, ferry boats tix, etc. Fast spreading to smaller station plazas, feeder lines.

TYPES OF TRAINS & FARES. SHINKANSEN or **BULLET** trains are pride of JR, at 230 kph upping 1972 to 270 (Tokyo-Osaka 2hr-30min). Utopian ideal of JNR saw nationwide bullet system snaking out of Tokyo: up Honshu to Aomori and thru Tsugaru Straits Tunnel to Sapporo; another up Japan Sea Coast to join at Aomori; down Honshu and Kyushu to end Nagasaki, with branch line from Kobe, island-hops across to Shikoku and along its Inland Sea Coast to Takamatsu; planned leg up San-In Japan Sea Coast between Shimonoseki and Kyoto. Red tape and red-ink budget dashed these goals. Present lines: oldest Tokaido Line Tokyo–Osaka, continuing Sanyo Line to Kyushu's Hakata (onward Nagasaki link still 'planned'); Tohoku Line Ueno–Morioka (200km leg to Aomori under way; new masterpiece Seikan tunnel to Hokkaido runs narrow gauge, tho triple rails make both gauges possible, allow later change); Joetsu Line Ueno-Niigata is probably as far as it will get up Japan Sea Coast. One reason for slow-down of Shinkansen plans are politicians who decide where stations to be built, based personal decisions mostly on wishes of constituents and less on practicality—so we find stations in middle-of-nowhere rice paddies.

Limited express & 'local' bullet trains: on Tokaido-Sanyo Line ltd express is *Hikari*, local is *Kodama;* on Tohoku Line *Yamabiko* and *Aoba;* on Joetsu Line *Asahi, Toki.* Fares set by basic distance fee *josha-ken*, plus *tokkyu-ken* express fee (about 2/3rds of josha-ken); *shitei-seki-ken* reserved-seat ¥500 fee for such on any trains. 'Local' runs have more *jiyu-seki* free-seating cars. All bullets now have non-smoking cars, stand-up buffets, telephones (card only), vendors with box lunches & drinks; ltd-*Hikari* have sit down dining cars. Wider selection food-drink at **station vendors** where sample boxes show what's in Japanese lunches—curries, cutlets, most W-lunches OK, but avoid sandwiches. 1-3 person private compartments available some Tokyo-Osaka-Hakata runs, ¥8,000 extra, expanding. Some runs have doubledeck vista-dome cars, or 'international' buffet rather than usual greasy chopstick counter.

Regular JR lines run 3 basic trains: *futsu* local non-reserved only *josha-ken* needed; *kyuko* express calls for added *kyuko-ken* fee; *tokkyu* limited express needs surcharge *tokkyu-ken*. Metropolitan areas also have *kaisoku* and *shin-kaisoku* limited express, which don't require extra fee. *Shitei-seki ryokin* reserved seat fee on trains are ¥300 all year on Hokkaido, Kyushu; and slow season (weekdays mid-Jan thru Feb, Jun, Sept, Nov thru Dec 20) on Honshu and Shikoku; ¥500 for Honshu and Shikoku rest of year.

Sleeper-car *shindai-sha* late-nite expresses run only on old trunk lines. For these, you need josha-ken, either kyuko or tokkyu-ken, & *'A' shindai-ken* or *'B' shindai-ken* (A or B sleeper fee). Shindai-sha great to cover distance while asleep, but don't save money over staying at inns, as surcharge comparable to inns and sleepers don't include two meals; few have seating-only cars where you travel at nite without added cost (or comfort). 1990 fees: 'A' car ¥16,850 for private room; ¥10,300 for 4-person-cabin lower bunk, ¥9,630 upper. ¥5,000 for any of 3-tiered 'B' car one-star bunks and upper and middle bunks of two-star cars; ¥6,000 for lower bunk of two-star cars, and any bed of three-star 4-person semi-private cars. 'B' trains also have *ko-shitsu* private cars for 4-persons on long runs like Tokyo–Nagasaki or Kumamoto for slightly more. Of course, all overnite runs aren't sleepers. Many long-runs, such as to Hokkaido, are late nite, but prepare for hard ride on too-small seats.

However, new *Hokutosei* express Tokyo-Ueno to Sapporo thru new Seikan Tunnel is luxurious with sleepers, cabins with TV and VTR, convenient scheds, prices competitive with air. Osaka → Hokkaido has new Twilight express, 20hr, dep Osaka noon. Recommend go by train, ret by plane; best scenes at nite on ret trip.

B-class sleeper cars for **women only** introduced 1990 for privacy and freedom from worry of possible minor harassment. Will spread.

PRIVATE RAIL LINES cover areas bypassed by JR, sometimes overlap. Were cheaper, better, but late '91 announced en masse 11-20% hike for '92. **Last train** abt midnite, so plan accordingly. Many of these names also appear on baseball teams, department stores, zoos and parks. To encourage use rails developed tourism in their jurisdiction, building parks at ends of otherwise little-used commuter branch lines. When Hankyu (now Orix) Braves baseball team won pennant 3 years running, their fares didn't go up while rival team line of parallel Hanshin rose. All are dealt with as we come across them, so let us just briefly mention them here:

TOKYO Metropolitan Area has intricate web of subways, mostly private, (*see* GETTING AROUND TOKYO). NY Mayor Ed Koch rode, said, "Tokyo subways...you can read book, have conversation, even hear yourself speak...New York subways depressing but getting better because we bought your cars, now all we need is to buy some Japanese station walls". Subways link to private rail lines at terminals—**Tobu** line starts from Asakusa for Nikko; **Odakyu** line from Shinjuku covers Hakone area; resort area of Izu Peninsula has **Izu Kyuko** line. **Keisei** Narita line links airport–Ueno.

NAGOYA is also major hub of private lines: extensive **Meitetsu** system convenient around greater Nagoya; equally fine **Kintetsu** system curves down to Ise Grand Shrine then across to Osaka passing thru central Yamato-Nara prime tourist area.

KYOTO-OSAKA-KOBE or *kei-han-shin* area has several fine private lines: **Keihan, Hankyu, Hanshin, Sanyo**, and each of 3 cities have subways.

Other private lines range from super-modern rubber-wheeled silent subways **Sapporo** & **Kyoto** to fun Eno-den toonerville of **Kamakura**, snail-paced funiculars of **Hakone**.

SUBWAYS: all above have undergrounds, as do, S-to-N, Fukuoka, Yokohama, Sendai, Sapporo—all, but one of Tokyo's 10 lines, one Osaka, built in high-labor recent years. Route maps readily available at kiosks, all together in bilingual *K&D Timetable*.

BUS: LONG DISTANCE *Chokyori basu* popular, growing. For budgeteer 30-50% off rail and most run by nite, saving hotel. Competition has made buses deluxe—reclining seats, free tea & coffee, blanket, stereo headsets, toilets. Most popular Tokyo-Osaka on Meishin Expressway has overnite Dream Express ¥8,450. Chugoku Exp'wy from Osaka down center spine of Honshu to Hiroshima ¥4,030, -Fukuoka ¥9,000, -Nagasaki, etc. JR runs numerous routes, railpass accepted. Proliferating rapidly: 17 routes in '88, by end '89 quadrupled to 97. Check TIC, JTB, JR for new runs.

REGULAR BUS: best alternative to train, especially in more remote areas wherever rail lines end. Traveling between towns also served by rail often takes longer and costs more on bus: glaring exception is crossing Honshu between southern Ogori and Hagi where direct bus saves hours over round-about rail route. Even most remote runs on outermost isles have 3-4 runs daily, most hourly or so; frequent on main routes and in towns. Most rural buses relatively easy to figure out and usually stop right at rail stations.

Know your destination and someone will get you on right bus; if not passerby, ask station people or at police box, *koban*, found at almost every station. Once on, tell driver your destination and he'll make sure you get off at right stop (helps to sit up front near driver). Rare towns considerate to foreign visitors have English bus schedule for most popular routes, like at Hida Takayama station-front info office which has schedule for run to gorgeous Shirakawa-go village; and big sign board at Nara's Horyuji monastery stop; others. However, we have found such schedules to be accurate for times, but often out-dated for new fares.

INTERCITY BUS is pay-as-you-go. Enter, look for number-tag dispenser (on either side of entrance), take one. As bus goes on, numbered panel up front shows changing fare, getting off pay fare matching your number. If forget to take one, tell driver name or number of where boarded; nonticket holders liable to pay maximum fare, but we've never heard it applied unless they catch you trying to cheat (remember that as foreigner you stand out, any driver will know where you got on). Another method used on long rural runs or express buses is flat fee ticket bought at terminal window before boarding. Rule of thumb to figure frequency on rural lines—more runs (& crowds) AM & late aft when people going to/from work or school.

INTRACITY BUSES go everywhere, but drawback is often convoluted routes marked only in Japanese. Save time and trouble by writing down destination, ask for route, and any *norikae* (transfers) involved. Short runs 4-5 people as economical by **cab**, far quicker; check availability of 8-12-passenger van-taxi (microbus), same rate, for real bargain. Bus fares are simple: most intracity lines flat fee, clearly marked, drop into coin box as you get on (front entry) or off (mid or rear entry). Most have ¥500 coin and ¥1,000 bill changers, pop in and right change comes out, fare paid. Some long runs like intercity, above, take tag on entry.

TAXI: Found in just about every corner of country, can easily pick up on street (flag, don't whistle) or have restaurant, etc, phone dispatcher. Expensive, especially if visiting Japan after any other Asian nation: rate over double New York, but cars clean, well kept. Basic meter covers 2km in clear traffic, each click of meter thereafter is abt 300m, so that each 2km costs roughly same as first 2km. This way you can estimate your ride if you know how far you're going. With periodic raises in cab fees making printed rates obsolete, we have chosen this method to give general idea of cab rides. Example: 10km would be '5x-mtr', at new 1991 base rate ¥540—it cost roughly ¥2,700, $18.50-no tip (slightly less in some tight-fisted towns) *vs* New York at $1.50/25¢ per 1/5th=$11.00 for 6^1/5 miles plus tip=$12.50, or 30% less. This rate doesn't apply in traffic moving under 10kph, when it clicks 1/6 each 2min. *Shin-ya* 'late-nite' surcharge of 30% from 23:00 to 5:00; and 20% may be added for phone summons, tho meter usually turned on from taxi origin. Announced 10-20% rise end '92 (¥640?), then every 2 yrs.

FOUR TAXI SIZES: small *kogata* (4 passenger plus driver), medium *chugata* most common (also maximum 4, sometimes 5 OK), and large *ogata* (5), usually US car. Newest addition is *wagon-sha*, 8-12 passenger station wagon van, great for airport to hotel run—loads of baggage space. Most taxis have little luggage space as run on LPG gas with tank in trunk. No baggage surcharges. Wagon-sha rates same as chugata, but not many available. You are lucky to get any out at Narita Airport, but if taking airport limo-bus to TCAT, many there. Plenty Osaka-Itami, **OK Taxi** ☎(06)724-8181.

Beside company drivers, drivers who own their cars, *ko-jin*, private drivers, have better reputation than company ones for helpfulness, and are more likely to negotiate better rates on long tours as driver is own boss. Car marked with ideograms ➤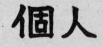

If your hotel desk cannot be of help, go out to taxi line in front of hotel, assuming major hotel, for we assume that smaller hotels will be of help—walk down taxi line and look for two large ideographs illustrated above on side of taxi door. Doorman can help you negotiate with taxi driver, (tho it isn't easy to pick cabby before his time comes on queue) who may very well have heard about our suggestion thru owner-driver's association. If taxi ferries you around on meter only, because time meter is meant for moving delays, his waiting time is, for most part, loss to him. However, Kyoto drivers themselves suggest that they will be more than happy with ¥2,600 *kogata* per hour in town, ¥3,300 *chugata* or meter charge, whichever comes out higher—and meter charge for running and waiting in town will rarely approach this time charge. Tokyo runs ¥3-,4,000, check with hotel desk. Out-of-town run, straight meter, but our local Kobe private taxi will go to Kyoto or elsewhere all (12hr-long) day for ¥28,000+toll. **Budgeteers** find taxi for 4 often cheaper than tour bus, twice as fast, never mind convenience of freedom of choice—competitive even with city transport.

We suggest that you show owner-driver map page in relevant major section (Nara, Kyoto, Osaka, Tokyo) and he will understand what you want. Then take pencil and check off places on map you wish to see, placing "√" next to those at which you wish to stop and disembark for short period. Taxi driver will take you to them in order he thinks most economical and scenic, with variation for traffic conditions. Leave it up to him, he knows his city and is professional with years of experience. You can place your trust in owner-driver completely, in most any driver. You do not tip taxi driver in Japan, but we do suggest at end of your trip if you are fully satisfied and think price has been reasonable, small gratuity of up to top of 10% would here be in order and justly deserved, but by no means mandatory, or even expected.

Rates vary only slightly nationwide, main areas around Tokyo, Nagoya, Kobe-Osaka at top, Kyoto, Hiroshima and rural cities about 4-5% less, and another 4-6% less in some far-off corners. Use cabs as little as possible unless budget is substantial. For long-touring runs, you can often strike flat-rate deal rather than pay meter fare; it's midrange single rides that really cost. You do not tip cabby here, unless he does some *very* special service for you (above), tho sometimes on late-nite basic-meter rides some people leave their change. When getting in/out curbside (left) rear seat, don't open door yourself, it is automatic, operated by driver. Front seat passenger(s) now must fasten seat belt.

Many visitors, and particularly in Tokyo, complain of impossibility of flagging cab late at nite. First of all, most cabbies are in it for money, and not for social service. If you are stuck in Ginza, Roppongi or any other expensive night life area of Tokyo after last subways and JR, cabs are at premium and highest bidder wins. Many cabbies pick Japanese over foreigners because most of us only go to nearby hotel, not much of fare, and local trying to get home is good for ¥3-,5,000, often much more. Trying to get cab and more than 5 people (4 if you're large), split up. Many cabs won't stop for group of 5 foreigners—afraid all will pile in at once, and law strictly limits number of passengers (4 small cabs, 5 mediums). Worst after last trains, many cabbies recommend if out that late wait until at least 2:00am —seems to be magic hour by which everyone wants to be home. Foul weather makes getting cab even worse, so plan to get last train or pick comfortable bar to wait it out. Another resort is to find nearest luxury hotel, catch cab there. Many cold wet nites in Tokyo we trudged past endless lines of people waiting for cabs that rarely come, to reach hotel to find endless line of cabs waiting for people that rarely come. Major Tokyo nite spots (Akasaka, Ginza, Roppongi, Shinjuku, etc) have luxury hotels nearby.

SHIP: From creaky fishing skiffs to giant car ferries and ultramodern hydrofoils, carry passengers thruout myriad Japanese isles. Adventurers floating around Inland Sea like nomad-pirates of feudal times, will often find that passing fisherman or weekly mail run is only way to get to/from some isles; across Ryukyus, fishermen rent selves out as sea-taxis, but for average tourist let's dwell on scheduled runs. Most likely to be used short runs (all frequent times daily) are Honshu to Shikoku thru Inland Sea, Ise to Gamagori, Shikoku to Kyushu at closest point, and across Kyushu's Ariake Sea, linking International Tourist Route stops of Unzen's Hell and feudal castle town Shimabara to modern Kumamoto. Most runs carry cars, passenger only are always hydrofoil, hovercraft or some other enclosed speedboat. Tho time-saving, we prefer slower, open, car ferries which lets you enjoy sea breeze and view at far below speedboat rates. Aomori-Hakodate link up north is all car ferries, dozens daily. Runs to main ones of smaller islands such as Fukuoka-Iki-Tsushima, Matsue-Oki, Niigata-Sado, Wakkanai-Rishiri-Rebun, are considerably cheaper than doing same by plane. Plane fare roughly 3x cheapie 2nd-class ferry, slightly above special 1st-class, and flying only saves few hours at most. People venturing out to these lesser islands are apt to be budgeteers with time who should boat.

Then there are long-distance giant ferries plying Pacific and Japan Sea coasts from Hokkaido to furthest reaches of Okinawa. Fares are also much cheaper than doing same by plane, but time factor, with Tokyo to Hokkaido or Okinawa by boat taking several days instead of hour+ by air. Budgeteers on long hauls ought to bring on own food and drinks, since prices on board somewhat inflated; you'll probably be traveling in open-space 2nd-class; much fraternizing goes on to break monotony and sometimes all pitch in for feast. Budget *ni-to* (2nd class) are large common-rooms with carpeted sections where people sleep on claimed portions of floor, blankets and pillows supplied; students with proper ID get 20% off. *Tokubetsu Ni-to* (special 2nd class) is similar, but smaller sections. *It'to* (1st class), family-size cabins; *Tokubetsu It'to* (special 1st), private cabins. Tho comfortable, ferries, even long distance are far from luxury liners. Rates for cars on ferries are clearly posted (incl driver's 2nd-cl accommodation); motorcycles are lower rates; bicycles are often free, or at most few hundred yen.

Japan Long Distance Ferry Association, Nihon Chokyori Ferry Kyokai, 9th floor Iino Bldg, 2-1-1, Uchisaiwai-cho, Chiyoda-ku, Tokyo, has all sorts of info on boat runs exceeding 300km. They have good English brochure *The Arterial Network of Sea Traffic,* listing all major runs, and which can be gotten thru TIC. While all long runs between 4 main islands of Honshu, Hokkaido, Shikoku and Kyushu are listed, it does not list all. Most obvious are lack of any runs to Okinawa and other south China Sea isles, runs out to Pacific isles of Izu-Oshima chain. Still valuable for frequency, time, distance, name and numbers of each ferry company, and how to get to each pier.

During much of summer (July-Aug) & winter holiday (late Dec-early Jan) recommend show up good hour prior to sailing; reservations absolute must.

DRIVING: Great way to see this country, but it can also be harrowing, frustrating experience if unprepared. Japanese visitors to States are always amazed at width and well-posted directions of US roads. Here streets are notoriously narrow, winding and usually poorly marked; even expressways are only 2 lanes each way. You will often find signs in Latin, or *roma-ji,* lettering, especially on expressways. Exception is long-time home of foreigners Kobe-Osaka area, which road authorities only '86 announced plan to undertake study to put up clear English signs for 'internationalization'. This one of few countries not using international symbol of airplane pointing to airport; Osaka Itami International airport had no sign at all, started some '88 after Jay's article in Japanese paper. However, all other international signs used—often in confusing profusion. Even natives get confused driving. Once off expressways, Latin-letter signs random. Some places loaded with good English signs while others have nothing.

EXPRESSWAYS in Japan are all **toll** roads, and not cheap. Gasoline tax goes into general treasury, not set aside for roads. Toll to drive 500km Osaka-Tokyo for one car is same as one person on Shinkansen. Most roads are long stretches owned by one company and you pay only once at exit (get ticket on entry), but you may find stretches of many locally-owned sections patched together, in which case you end up paying ¥100-300 every so often. You end up paying same per kilometer in long run, but constant stopping to pay is annoying. We find such imbecilic network going west from Osaka-Kobe to Okayama along Inland Sea.

Tomei-Meishin Expressway links Tokyo-Nagoya-Osaka along Pacific Coast; **Chuo** Expwy also links Tokyo-Nagoya, curving via central Japan. From Nagoya, **Higashi-meihan** Expwy crosses Kii Peninsula to Nara and Osaka, branch to Ise. For quick road to Hiroshima from Kobe-Osaka area, avoid coast, take inland **Chugoku** Expwy with branch to Hiroshima. Chugoku Expwy continues to western tip Shimonoseki, tunnels strait to **Kyushu** Expwy, presently ends past Kumamoto, but soon to reach Kagoshima, branch planned to Nagasaki. **Hokuriku** Expwy branches from Meishin at Maibara (east shore Lake Biwa) to cut up to Japan Sea Coast up to Unazuki, soon to reach Niigata, eventually Aomori. **Tohoku** Expwy begins at Tokyo's Omiya, shoots straight up to Aomori. New Tsugaru Straits Tunnel carries expwy on car-trains to Hokkaido, which really has no need for toll roads but system is rapidly growing there. While speed on expressways often justifies high toll, Hokkaido is one place we prefer regular roads—excellent, scenic and so far not too crowded. Many expressways are fenced in by opaque noise barriers, blocking any view.

Driving on ordinary roads is where problems can occur, particularly in boondocks where web of numbered roads often doesn't match numbers in map books, but numbering system is getting better every year, roads being constantly improved and expanded. This rush to pave has some drawbacks, especially if using newest map books which sometimes show extensions of roads which are not quite finished yet, or behind schedule, sometimes show bridges still in planning. On one trip around Shikoku in 1979, Garet and friend found one such newly paved 4-lane road, only to turn last corner and find road end, necessitating carrying their bicycles over last two miles of hilly footpath passing over almost-finished tunnel. Of course, things are nothing like our travels for first edition of this book when much of National Hiway Rte 1 from Tokyo to Kyoto was unpaved, pot-holed and barely wide enough for two cars. Meeting bus or truck in small town often saw us backed into front entrance of private home to make room to pass.

Don't let size fool you either. Extensive and usually well-kept *koku-do* (national hiways) are drain on central government, buying ricefield right-of-way as expensive as buying in US city (90+% of road cost, '91) so usually just 2-lane. Prefectures have more money for *ken-do* (Pref Hiway) often better kept and wider. Much like bullet train stations, you find superb 4-lane hiways going from nowhere to nowhere; symbol of local politician thanking faithful constituents. Once off numbered *kokudo* & *kendo* you're on your own. Some local roads are great, provide scenic shortcuts, but others are poor and suddenly end. Road repair signs also confusing. Sometimes, sign will 'X' out one road at fork and show alternate route. Other signs list days and/or hours when road impassable, but often so confusing that even if you can read Japanese passably you're still not sure if posted times are when you can or can't pass. We do not write this with intent of discouraging driving. On contrary, we recommend driving some places, especially if you have time to explore. Just keep eyes peeled and sense of humor tuned.

We cannot stress enough that driving in cities of Japan is just not worth trouble of bad traffic, bad directions and near total lack of parking space. Tokyo, Osaka and Kobe in particular should be avoided by driving tourist; Kyoto unwary drivers must especially avoid. Nagoya is not so bad with its wide roads. Nara bans private cars in Nara Park area in high season. Large cities up north with lots of space, such as Sendai, Aomori, Toyama, Niigata, Sapporo, are not too bad for driving, but those down in crowded southwest are crisscrossed with typical maze of alleys.

Driving in Japan is most pleasant and convenient for exploring back-country where public transport not so good. Some favorite areas to drive are: narrow winding but beautiful and hard to get-lost-on mountain roads of Koya-san and Kii Peninsula (beware impossible mazes of nearby Yamato Plain where 'roads' disappear into trails requiring dangerous backup); off-beat mountains of Okayama; mountain hotspas, rural villages of central Hida and Shinano; and last but not least, wide open spaces of Hokkaido.

DRIVING LICENSE: Japan & US signed *Convention on Road Traffic of 1949* whereby tourists of signatories "may drive...using own national license plates and personal driver's licenses...." (quoting US Customs publication #520). This is **not** reciprocated in Japan. 'International' Kobe cop arrested US student-friend for driving with valid California permit, fined him ¥45,000–$300+. Longtime resident heard this and checked with 'old-fashioned' Kyoto police who said his US license was valid for year after each entry to country. Most policemen don't know, may accept it or arrest you, but are quite likely to ticket you for *mu-menkyo-unten*, driving without license, order you off road, costs as above plus hours of paperwork. *Get...*

International Drivers License issued by AAA at home (about $15 and as many minutes, bring 2 photos and regular license); it **is** recognized even in Kobe despite fact it is only translation certificate supplementing 'real' license, and of 16 lingos in booklet, Japanese is **not** one—yet reason Japanese cops insist on it is because they say ordinary license poses language problem (oh, Red Queen). Rent-a-car might rent you car on state license (not Hertz or Nissan) but that doesn't mean cops won't bug you at some random roadblock. US now seems to be following Japan since Japan tourists caught using health club cards, license-size with undecipherable script and photo, claiming to be licenses. Jay uses his Japan license in US & Europe to rent car, Garet can't seem to. *Staying on, get...*

Japanese Drivers License by *kiri-kae* (transfer) of your home license —but you need proof of residency (Alien Registration) and cannot be done by casual tourist passing thru. It costs several thousand yen and takes most of day, tho you get license same day. Best take along Japanese-speaking friend to help you figure out system, but test is easy, simple eye exam, preceded by hopping up and down on one leg to show you have basic coordination. Then 20 vague broken-English questions—read them very carefully. Car license in Japan (local or International) also lets you ride scooters 50cc-under. While Japanese license may make great souvenir, don't bother with one if here for only few months. IDL saves hassle; if pulled over with Japanese license, police assume local license-bearer knows what is going on and launch off at you, but IDL usually gets you better treatment, just smile and bow muttering *sumi-masen*—some long-time residents keep IDL just for this. Don't even think of trying to get license in Japan thru normal road examination process as it takes months and several thousand dollars, off-road 'road test' unrelated to real driving.

If by some miracle of patience or good connection you get your own vehicle over here (Forbes of *Forbes* magazine cruised country '86 on fleet of
crowd-catching Harley 74s & 81s, but we're sure he didn't use patience
alone) you will, like Forbes, use your own state plates for up to year. Check
current practice—forget written regulations, find out what they are *doing*.

DRIVING TIPS: obviously, drive on left. American and European drivers
will find Japan painfully slow. Top legal **speed-limits** on expressways
range from 80 to 100kph (50-62mph), urban elevated roads 60kph
(36mph), most city streets are snail's pace 40kph (24mph) as posted, with
rest rare 50kph (32mph) usually not posted. (Osaka's relatively superior
streets are only 40kph even tho unposted which nationally should mean 50
but local cops hauling over out-of-towner says he should know anyway—
different reality.) Red lights much longer, 60 to 140 seconds.

Most locals zip along over speed limit, but watch where they slow down
—usually radar **speed trap**. "Nail that sticks up invites hammer" is old Jpn
saying, speed cops nab only first car in gaggle of speeders—always follow
local if driving fast. Some expressways, usually in large cities, have permanent speed traps set up (many post kindly notice of coming trap—in
Japanese) which triggers camera to take photo of car's front license plate
and driver and ticket is mailed to you while computer debits master record.
Japanese police love to set up speed traps in cities and countryside, but you
will rarely, if ever, see them in bad weather, or cold or hot; but look out on
clear days especially after run of bad weather. Many locals use radar
detectors. US-Escort detector in Japan costs over $1,000, 5 times Stateside
price, prestige toy. Local radar not sophisticated, short range, cheap local
detector is fine and not illegal. If stopped, smile excruciatingly; being bel-
ligerent goes over worse with cops here than it does with CHP. As in US,
following truckers keeps you out of most trouble.

Stoplights are synched to hinder steady movement—official cure for '70s
gas crunch was to discourage driving by making road too miserable. Gas
roughly triple US, oil even more.

Gas stations all full service, brigade of medic-uniformed attendants
rush out yelling *irasshai-mase*, fill you up, check oil, radiator, all else,
change burned out bulb at cost, wash *all* windows, empty ashtrays, run out
to stop traffic to let you out to send you off with chorus of *arigato*.

If in trouble on road, **Japan Automobile Federation** (JAF) has 24-
hour road service, but you must tell them where you are in Japanese. Free to
members, fair fee nonmembers. Many Service Stops (SS) on expressways,
but if can't make it to one, constantly patrolling safety crews in yellow
trucks, many roadside emergency phones.

RENT-A-CAR: abundant, rates comparable most Western countries, but
double other Far East. Several nationwide agencies accept major credit cards
such as Hertz-affiliated Nippon Rent-a-Car, Toyota, Nissan, Mitsubishi,
Japaren. Red-logoed Eki-mae (Station-front) agencies can be found at
almost every place from major towns down to rural villages, as long as there
is rail station—rates lower but may not take credit cards. Often 20% off in
combo with JR ticket. Countless local regional agencies as well. Rates
vary slightly thruout Japan, cities more expensive and rural areas cheaper.
Rather than basic body size like US (subcompact, compact, midsize, etc),
rates in Japan set according to make and engine size.

Can rent for 6hrs, 12hrs—good for local touring—as well as usual mul-
tiples of 24hr; first day rates for Nippon (about same for others) range from ¥6,000 for
1,200cc Charade, 5 folks including driver, up to ¥21,500 for 2,000cc Toyota Crown

saloon car 6-psgr. Additional days each cost 2/3rds first day rate. **Insurance** included in rental fee. Some agencies limit free-mileage, but if possible go for unlimited mileage option as cheaper for long trips. Nippon has 'No. 1 Club' which you can join at time of rental which gives you discounts on any Nippon rental anywhere; other firms may start similar deal. As in any country, return with full tank to avoid exorbitant charge if they fill up. 2 largest firms, Nippon and Toyota, have English brochures at their offices at Narita and at all TIC. Budget Rentacar recently opened branches in Japan, some at gas stations, and you should be able to arrange in US before coming over. Rumor has it more US rental agencies will be entering market in near future, so you may want to see if your favorite company has one yet—if so, how extensive and how much.

On tight budget 3-5 traveling off beaten path or areas with limited rail can save money and time with rent-a-car. Cheapest subcompact 2-door hatch-back fine for 3-4 people with not much luggage (legally cram 5 small folks), average about ¥6,000 per day; whereas one person can easily spend ¥2,-5,000 daily on long rural bus rides. One time we particularly found car to be worth its weight in gold was exploring eastern Hokkaido around Daisetsu-zan, Shiretoko and Akan National Parks. With total freedom to wander thru natural wonders, we ended up saving enough over bus fares we would have otherwise paid to cover hotel. Advise plan all rental car itineraries to finish at starting point to avoid stiff drop-off charge. We list such circular driving routes when rental car options given.

BUYING CAR is possibility for those spending at least few months here— and there is car ferry to Korea, simple procedures. Good **2nd-hand** cars (*chuko-sha*) are abundant and can be bought for relatively little. Official de-preciation is 30% annual, if kept in top shape, and market follows this with special consideration for validity remaining on biannual inspection. Bought 8-year-old Toyota station wagon from returning resident, 6 months *sha-ken* left, $100, used it to teach Garet to drive, then gave it away—but there are difficulties in getting your hands on one. First and foremost is finding one at suitable price, especially if you can't speak Japanese. One solution is to send ad to English newspapers in Japan, *Japan Times, Mainichi Daily News*, for any departing foreigners (or English-speaking Japanese) with cheap car for sale. This will also make wading thru red tape of registration easier. Most cities require *shako-shomei* (proof of off-road parking space) before accepting registration, and don't know how they would deal with tourist buying. You might buy from departing foreigner with understanding it be kept in his name after he leaves, but then you can't resell as his signature certificate only valid 3 months. Or buy from car lot with resale agreement (verbal), using his address. Or phone (even international, now cheap) old-style grease-monkey 'Douglas' (Aussie-Japanese) at his New Ocean Motors, ask him to line up car—local area code ☎078-(from USA 011-81-78-) 861-1247.

Don't be afraid of getting clunk as all cars must undergo *sha-ken* mandatory full inspection in which strict guidelines require car to be almost as good as new, with compulsory 3rd party insurance paid up before being issued two-year road permit (displayed as matchbook-size sticker top center windshield showing number of month of expiration, different color each year). If car you are planning to buy has expired sha-ken, it will cost you at least ¥100,000 even if no work needed, since it also includes registration fees, road tax, and two year insurance premium (latter bought by buyer, prorated). Sha-ken every 2 years regardless of change in ownership, and buying car with enough sha-ken time remaining is well worth extra search. 5-year-old car with few months sha-ken left is scrap-metal cheap.

Once you are done with it, what to do? If real cheap (our Toyota above, or recent like-new 7-year-old Mazda RX-7, 40,000mi, bought by new arrival for blue book

¥100,000, $800!), do what some expats leaving on short notice do—drive to airport, park in lot, leave key in, board plane. Or place ad in English papers when you reach Japan, stating car will be available upon your departure.

If you happen to see really nice car in Japan and plan to take it home, check US import rules before leaving. US Customs pamphlet #520, *Importing A Car*—you may bring in 'wrong side' steering wheel (right-hand side as in UK) 'once in your lifetime', pollution standards pretty much same, bumper may not meet US rule and have to be replaced later. Don't bother getting new car in Japan expecting to get deal as in Germany. Japanese cars, like almost everything else Japanese sold in US, are cheaper overseas than same sold in Japan—and they claim no dumping.

MOTORCYCLE offers mobility, added savings on gas, tolls, ferries, easy parking, going where cars can't. **Drawbacks**—less comfort (June rainy season), less carrying space, *no passenger on expressways*, dangers inherent in riding—Jay is old Harley-61 survivor, Garet had Suzukis. But these are problems bikers experience anywhere. If you aren't licensed biker for at least one year before coming to Japan, we do not advise it, as biking here can get hairy, tho lower speeds make it somewhat safer. Helmet is required by law on anything. Bikers should also get IDL at home as it has only one designation for motorcycles, allowing you to drive anything here with two wheels. Japanese law divides bike licenses into categories according to size: *gentsuki* to ride up to 50cc and is included in car license; *kogata* (small) 51 to 125cc; *chugata* 126-400cc; *ogata* 401cc-up.

License even harder than for car if applying here—start small and work up to larger bikes. Tho J-makers export giant speed demons, 750cc largest sold here; anything larger—Suzuki, Kawasaki or Honda— has been re-imported from overseas. While we prefer midsize bikes (360-550cc), most practical for is 250cc—largest not needing *sha-ken*, smallest allowed on Expwy, powerful enough since slow speed, road conditions make larger not worth hassle, especially since you can't find luxury 1,000cc+ touring bikes of US, Europe. But 1991 imports of Harleys booming, look into bringing one. Many places rent scooters, larger motorcycles hardly ever rented. Japanese physically too small for 750s, as is country, with almost-new bikes often available thru garages for few hundred bucks—worth bringing home. Buying 2nd-hand, same procedures as car. Unlike almost anything in this ultimate throw-away-if-worn land 2nd-hand small to medium bikes are expensive, $1,000-1,500 average. Prices bizarre: 400cc isn't lcheaper than 750cc since less demand for hard to handle larger; 250cc cost same since doesn't need *sha-ken* inspection. Often 750 can be had almost free from sorry over-eager buyer. Check compulsory 3rd party insurance validity, on month-numbered sticker.

BICYCLE is best for healthy, time-insensitive budgeteer; most rewarding way to see Japan, meet its people. Bringing bicycle in is simple—just dismantle, put in box or carrying case, check in as baggage. Some airlines don't even require disassembling, so call your carrier. Should get carrying case, required on trains here. All rails (JR & private) surcharge bikes ¥150-200, but not all stations enforce, especially in boondocks. Bike on any ferry also only few hundred yen. Trains great for getting you out of cities, across boring stretches of road, or over steep mountains. On bike trip we often camp out at any quiet spot; also budget lodgings specially set up for bikers. Very much nation of cyclists (just look around any station), you can get all sorts of repair kits in Japan, almost any village has local repairman. But if you own special mountain bike (not many here) or US-large-sized bike,

bring spare tire/s; local bikes not as big. Be careful, bikes get stolen here—
motor or pedal, we've lost both, including 250cc while camped 6 feet away.
Bicycle Culture Center opp US Embassy knows everything to know about bikes;
videos of itineraries, travel info, maps, extra gear, old bike museum ☎(03)-3582-3311.
Oikaze cycling mag, Eng; stories & want ads: 2-24-3 Tomigaya, Shibuya, Tokyo 105.

HITCHHIKING: Cheapest way to get around, really helps you meet
people. Japan is probably safest place to hitch, with most considerate rides.
Many Japanese who pick up foreign hitchhikers feel fully responsible for
you while you are with them, may go out of way to get you to your
destination, often buying you meals and drinks along way and even putting
you up at their homes. Garet and high school chums hitched up to Hokkaido
every summer break, some of their encounters include being picked up by
bored college student in Tokyo who decided long saturday drive would be
fun and took them whole way to Aomori; or another pal who'd caught cold
was picked up by doctor who took him home "to get healthy sleep, hot bath
and good meal", then chauffeured him back to expressway next morning.

We could fill entire volume with such tales and not one would tell of one
single bad experience. Girls hitching solo or in pairs have had no problems.
Should offer to pay for meals as common courtesy, but many (especially
truckers) will get somewhat offended if you don't accept their hospitality.
We drew line when one trucker offered us cash because he thought we were
too poor to take trains. Return some of kindness by hitching with snacks
which can be shared with your ride. Cigarettes, especially foreign brand,
big hit with chain-smoking truckers. Always try talking to your ride, even if
your Japanese is minimal, for many truckers appreciate company, especially
to keep them alert on overnite hauls. It is easy for paired hitchers to talk
among themselves, so special effort should be made not to exclude driver
who may feel slighted after having stopped for you. If you speak Japanese,
you will discover that truckers are not mere dumb trailer-jocks, they end up
discussing everything from international politics to sports. We have run into
many who have driven trucks overseas, mostly Asia and Middle East, some
spent time in Canada, US. Pocket English-Japanese-English dictionaries
come in handy. Music is universal language, much appreciated (on your
portable cassette player) most of time as long as not heavy metal, hard rock
or punk. Freighters live up to title of knights of road (and dump-truckers
usually conform to international standard bull-headed hooligans), and are
best for long hauls. If they're not going as far as you want, many will use
CB to find another trucker headed your way, ask around for you at service
area or rest stop. Drivers in trouble find express freighters saviors.

Tho we have had limited success with 3 people, optimum is travel solo
or paired. Trucks legally fit 2 passengers plus driver in cab, any more and
truck not allowed on expressway. Few Japanese hitch, so thumbing is still
not well-known sign, tho many urban youths becoming
familiar with it as another piece of 'American culture'
being slowly introduced here. Best bet is to hold out
large sign with your destination written out in Japanese
kanji characters. When going long distances like Kobe—
Tokyo you might want to add ideogram "in direction of—" *-homen* ↑ to one
side, since literal-minded drivers may not stop as they aren't going whole
way. You could also beat them to punch by first asking (many speak simple
English) "where you going?" or if going your way. Advisable to ask where
they are going anyway, especially if ride is from farmer in boondocks—we
have gotten on mini-truck only to be let off few kilos down at their home.

方面

Another choice is to break up trip, writing name of next big town: so from Kobe, one side of card could have Nagoya for first leg and Tokyo on other side. Cardboard is easy to find, especially at expressway rest areas. But most essential tool for hitchhiker is thick black magic marker: ask stationer for *majiku*. And SMILE!

Despite what some policeman may tell you, hitchhiking is **not illegal** as long as you are not pedestrian on actual expressway. We have often gotten directions to nearest expressway ramp from stationside police box. Stand near on-ramp or toll booth, and once on expressway have trucker let you off at Service Area (SA) rather than at his exit if he isn't taking you all way. SA has restaurant and gas, so if your ride isn't able to find you connection, waiting at return to expwy usually gets quick response. Don't get off at Toilet-only Rest Stops as you'll spend hours waiting there; your chances are better at on-ramp. Just ask driver to be let off at SA and they usually take you to best one around. Keep in mind that there are fewer long-distance drivers on sunday, and more family cars which rarely stop for hitchers, unless foreign-experienced, or inquisitive (and generous) students.

Hitching regular roads has its special points for care. First, make sure there is enough space for ride to pull off road (which in rural Japan is not quite as easy as it sounds) as many drivers may want to stop, but can't as most rural hiways are only one lane in either direction with little or no shoulder. This makes it particularly hard to get out of small towns. One option is to wait at stoplight, run along stopped cars and flash your sign. Another choice is to walk out to edge of town where there is more space. If your ride is stopping at some town before your destination, ask to be let off at bypass, if there is one. In large city you may have to take public transportation to nearest expwy ramp or to outskirts...

TOKYO is every hitchhiker's nightmare. Even passing thru on single ride, unless late at nite. Usually quicker to exit expressway at one side and take train to other. **Tohoku Expwy** N-bound out of Tokyo starts at Omiya, 30km N of Tokyo—easiest way there is JR Keihin-Tohoku Line to Omiya, exit front of train and stairs L down to Tobu-sen Line, which take 5 stops to Iwatsuki; from front of stn, head down main street to 2nd large street, R leads to expwy entrance after 10min or so. Entrance wide, well used so ride should come quite easy. Heading N from Narita airport is **Higashi Kanto Expwy**, ends up-coast at Kashima, from where Rte51 to Mito and alternate entry to Tohoku—has entrance near airport, but you will probably be chased off by edgy security police there. In which case bus to Narita City and try your luck on Rte51. W-bound central **Chuo Expwy** down mountain spine of Honshu officially starts on Rte20 near Shinjuku Chuo Koen park and you can try there, but best place to get ride is at first toll-gate Mitaka, 10km W and 15-20min walk N from Senkawa stn on private Keio Line. S-bound **Tomei Expwy** to Nagoya–Kyoto is extension of intracity Expwy #3 passing just next to Shibuya stn, but almost impossible to get rides at ramps in town, so best head out few km to first toll-gate. Take private Shin-Tamagawa Line (extension of subway Hanzomon Line) from Shibuya stn (down steps near Hachiko dog statue) 5 stops to Yoga, from where 5min walk S is overhead expwy. Pass under it and on-ramp is short way to R. Hitching from Tokyo to Yokohama or Kamakura is more trouble than it's worth, train is cheap, far faster.

NAGOYA where Tomei from Tokyo becomes **Meishin** to OSAKA-KOBE (just name change, no need to exit), and **Chuo Expwy** joins both. Several choices here for on-ramps depending on where you are in town. Closest downtown is Nagoya Interchange (IC), short walk from Hongo stn on Higashiyama subway (2nd to last stop) 20min E of town. N of town is Kasugai IC, also good for Chuo Expwy, almost 3km from JR Kasugai stn (many trains as it's on Chuo Trunk Line): W down main road 800m you come to Rte19, little further to parallel big road where R (N) 2km to on-ramp. Could check at stn for buses headed this way. Incidentally, heading inland Rte19 better than Chuo Expwy as used by more truckers. Several km W of Kasugai is similar main IC of Komaki, also good for Chuo Expwy. More trucks use Kasugai and Komaki over Nagoya IC, chances are you will be let off at one or other if coming into Nagoya. Komaki IC is about 3km from Komaki stn on private Meitetsu Rail's Komaki Line: head W on Rte155 about 2km till you come to Rte41 (which goes S into heart of Nagoya City, or N to Hida area) and go R (N) about 1km to ramp. **Higashi-meihan Expwy** to Ise or Nara starts at Taiji's Nishi-Nagoya IC, few km W of Nagoya stn; hard to get to.

MAIBARA midway Nagoya-Kyoto on Meishin Expressway, is where **Hokuriku Expwy** branches off to Japan Sea Coast. You can't wait at junction, but try nearest SA, or get off at Maibara IC and try at on-ramp.

KYOTO is relatively easy, just take bus #19 or #20 and keep eyes open for expwy; ramps nearby. About 12km E of Kyoto at tip of Lake Biwa is city of Otsu (11min JR) with largest SA on road, overhead bridge linking E- and W-bound sides of **Meishin**. If your ride is ending anywhere near Kyoto but you're not, this is best place to be let off. On-ramps near SA, adventuresome types can clamber up to SA. If heading to San-In region of Japan Sea Coast from Kyoto, easiest is to take JR San-In Line to KAMEOKA then hitch on ordinary Rte9.

KOBE-OSAKA area is as bad as Tokyo for trying to hitch thru or out of, and when combined with Kyoto (Kei-han-shin district) whole area is not worth hitching around, what with confusing roads and excellent all-covering cheap private rails. Passing thru Kobe-Osaka isn't too hard as long as one ride takes you thru. To Tokyo direction, best bet is end of **Meishin** at Nishinomiya IC, for from here to Kobe or Osaka on local expressways is expensive and most truckers use lower nontoll Rte43. Take private Hankyu (Kobe-Osaka commuter) Line to Nishinomiya, change to Imazu Line, S to last stop; short walk to Rte 43 and Meishin on-ramp. Nearest stn on parallel private Hanshin (Kobe-Osaka commuter) Line is Koshien-guchi. W from Kobe, towards Hiroshima, is primarily on main Rte 2, which easiest is to take Hankyu out to Suma, Tarumi or Akashi stns and short walk down to Rte2. You can start from Sannomiya (downtown Kobe) on Rte43 but little difficult due to almost constant heavy traffic, tho anywhere between Rokko and Nishinomiya on Rte43 is not as bad, and Hanshin Rail lines run parallel, almost just next to Rte43.

HIROSHIMA is not too hard once out of heart of town; if going W to Miyajima and beyond, in-town start is hard, take tram out to Nishi-Hiroshima and try there. Hiroshima's link to spinal **Chugoku** Expwy is Itsukaichi IC, few km W of Nishi-Hiroshima, near JR Araiguchi stn; or on local coastal Hiroden tram, Rakuraku-en.

OTHER TRANSPORT includes all imaginable. There are hi-tech wheels like Haneda Airport-Tokyo monorail, or Osaka's—built for Expo '70, scrapped, now putting back up at ten times original cost. Linear motor subway in Osaka March '90 for short 5 stations out of Kyobashi on JR loop (¥190); Maglev (no-wheels magnetic levitation) planned for Sapporo to airport. Funiculars and cable cars. Puffing steam trains have been revived on scenic offbeat rail routes, in season. In Kurashiki, other tourist towns, healthy athletic types tired of desk work have gone on own as *jinrikisha*, manpower-vehicle entrepreneurs for short sightsee-hauls at what is for both passenger and puller, fair rate, highly photogenic. Mt Kompira Shrine near Takamatsu, Tsushima, some other scenic spots have brought back old samurai era limo, *kago*, basket-box suspended on carrying rod heaved by 2 muscular porters. Fishermen run sea taxis. Pack-horses carry you across Mt Mihara's smoking crater on Oshima isle off Tokyo (blew its top while writing this, and some mounts were sent to glue factory, alas).

There are more, equally photogenic, transporters we can't recall just now but we mention them where relevant.

my love and i
setting out on journey
left hands banded
with other hands with hearts
entwined, enamored
— Furu Tamuke, 7th cent. *Manyoshu*

WHERE TO STAY

Herein we learn three important words: *ryokan*, Japanese inn; *ofuro*, honorable hot bath, origin of California hot tub; *onsen*, hot spring spa, and spate of minors like *rotenburo*, outdoor bath, often mixed; *minshuku* mom'n-pop-run people's inn; *fasshon hoteru*, new more stylish version of **love hotel** or older *avec*, French 'with' as you go there 'with someone'. In these we learn that Japan was designed for romance, albeit illicit, thus easily adaptable for honeymoony-tourist use. This illicit flavor lingering on in atmosphere adds that tang lacking in even tastiest travel feasts tourist trade at home is able to serve up. Bars and taverns are dimly lit, designed for indiscretion. Japanese-style restaurants are private rooms, ideal for rendezvous; hotels cozily obscure as required for liaison, their main use. No matter how long married, travel together should be resumed honeymoon, even if tax-deducted business trip by day.

No amount of kids in entourage can really get in way, especially in Japan where there's so much harmless mischief for older kids to get into, so many eager maids around waiting to run off with your toddlers. Traveling in duet we go Japanese and use *ryokan*–famed 'Japanese Inn'. You'll certainly explore *onsen*, hot spring spas. Romantic love has scored good arrowhead hold in Japan among younger folk, who have taken to these hideaways and spas, in '80s undergoing great renaissance with *rotenburo* 'hot tub' so placed for fantastic views of ocean, gorges, valleys, waterfalls or whatever.

RYOKAN FOR HONEYMOONERS OF ALL AGES

Staying at Japanese inn is one experience found nowhere else. Not just some place to spend overnite, but hermitage to totally relax mind and body. No place is more romantic. Let's draw into one as we have so many times. We enter to operatic chorus of *"irrashaimasseh"* greetings, have our bags whisked away (service charge, no tip), kick off our shoes and don slippers and be led down corridors thru series of sliding doors (never try to swing one open) to be shown to our room–almost certainly with view either of magnificent vista or small garden, so designed that we seem to have it all for ourselves. Our view is unobstructed, yet someone passing thru our garden (unlikely) would find it almost impossible to look in. After long hard day, there is nothing like sprawling out on wide tatami-matted floor, sipping tea and munching light snacks. Furnishing is bare, typically one low table with *zabuton*-cushions to sit on, perhaps backrests. Most inns have small verandah with regular chairs and small table. One end of veranda usually has wash basin; other side will almost always have...

Small **refrigerator** stocked with soft drinks, juice, beer, other alcohol, and tiny bottles of Japanese 'health' drinks, overpriced but oh, so convenient, and old-fashioned hotel room service used to cost +30%. In morning they see if you had anything, restock. Some fridges now keep track of drinks taken automatically: each item is clamped into place and removing sends message to lobby computer. If your fridge is not one of old ones with simple shelves, take care not to pull drink out if you don't want it. This also means no one can tamper with locked-in drink. Ice box in room started with love hotels, now worldwide at all levels.

If **TV** is pay type, insert ¥100 in box for 2-3 hours viewing. Some have second money box with higher price marked (often ¥300) for 'adult' films. Most have adult channel, international hotels have extra control on it at source, so if you want to keep kids away, just phone front and instruct.

All ryokan rooms will have *tokonoma*-sacred alcove placed back into one wall and small step above tatami floor level. There will always be scroll or some picture hanging there, often with flowers in vase, figure, or some other art item. Every Japanese-style house will have *tokonoma*, for that is where treasured art pieces are displayed. Don't put your bags up in there or sit on raised part. Maid enters, quietly, discretely, to bring our *yukata* and robes and ask us when we wish our bath, what we want for dinner and when it should be served. She hands us Japanese form to register. Just fill in name and nationality, we don't turn in our passport or even show it. She will offer to check our valuables or cash, thus her large envelope. Until recently, Japanese never thought to have doors with locks, but with rare reports of theft (most famous international hotel had murder few years ago), some have installed locks while others stick to time-honored custom of holding valuables for you. Then, some inns will have small safe in each room—many traveling businessmen carry wads of cash. If we haven't set our price in foyer (advised if going for lower rates) or with booking agent, we do so now. If you have prepaid coupon, surrender it now. She will confirm our menu desires: we make clear that we want true Japanese dinner (*jun wa-shoku*) and that we eat anything. It's better to do this and leave food, there's plenty, than to mention what you don't want which only gets them confused, and gets you cold fried pork. If finicky, *sukiyaki* is always available, always good, or its chicken version *mizu-taki*.

With our *yukata* and flat clothes tray we follow her to bath, tho Japanese often change in room. We both follow, for bath is roomy and we both want our backs scrubbed. We enter dressing foyer, strip, place clothes in baskets and go in, carrying our wash-towels. Larger inns have several baths. They will have at least one large public bath and/or some medium-sized ones, perhaps restricted to one sex, but if not, dressing rooms are separate, bath-hall lights are dim and mist, alas, considerable. Then there are 'romance baths'—small affairs with tub 4 to 10 ft long, reserved for your private use. Ordinary inns will, as we have stated, restrict bath to your exclusive use unless, as is rare, they have only one large tub, by large we mean enough to swim in, given bit more depth. Newer 'standard rate' *ryokan* often have private, attached western bath-toilet, tho luxe inns have exquisite traditional private baths matched in hotels only in Hotel Okura's royal suite.

Luxe hotel users have **Bay Sheraton** off Disneyland hotel complex with picture-window onsen bath, Yokohama **Inter-Continental** suites private jacuzzis with view of bay and sometimes Mt Fuji.

OFURO, Japanese bath, is taken according to time-honored rules: douse, soap up, scrub, rinse thoroughly and only then get in. This is observed more in abuse and common Japanese way, minimally, is to **douse, wash** feet and privates, **rinse** then get in to **soak** and meditate, come out to soap and scrub, douse and get in again (and perhaps repeat whole ritual once more). Just don't get any soap or dirt in tub—and don't scrub in there either. In times past, you rinsed off using water from bath, but nowadays there are spigots of hot and cold water along wall and you sit on your stool and wash. Many inns and public baths also now have standing showers, or at least telephone-showers at wall faucets–used squatting only. In classic inns or out in boondocks, if there is shower it is probably cold only, even if there are two spigots. Newer inns usually do have hot-cold showers.

In communal tubs, back-washer has pretty well disappeared, man for women and woman for men–except in *saunas* and *soaplands* (*see* GOING IT ALONE—HIM). In our private bathroom old tradition should be observed and we do each other's back. (Stag may have maid or even madame of house pop in on him unannounced to do job.) Beauty of Japanese bath–whether monster pool of Hokkaido hells, outdoor spas of rural areas, wooden pots of private homes–is this soak. Just sit and soak and listen to tension evaporate (makes light *snap* like one hand slapping afar). Even small tub is big enough for two. Four visiting symphony musician friends floated small tub lid as table in their Tokyo inn big bath for floating poker game.

Many Westerners will find bath to be excruciatingly hot–don't feel bad, so do many young urban Japanese nowadays. However, New York Mayor Ed Koch visiting Tokyo said baths were not as hot as he was used to–but he was usually in hot water anyway. If too hot for you, as is likely, add cold (Japanese do) but be careful not to add too much–it's not all that hot once you get in and soak. In small *kazoku-buro*, family bath, stir brew with bucket or oar usually there for this purpose. In large pools, turn on cold, don't stir, but get in by cool stream which you turn off when you can take it. Small tub can be heated again easily for next people, larger pools reheat themselves with constant running hot water–heating you with them. True, you may turn nice red, but it won't harm or even burn skin and once you get used to that first immersion, after-effects of total relaxation and cold-cream advertisement complexion are worth that first teeth-gritting. Getting feet in is hardest: put one in, pull it out, then other, then get in, exhaling from pit of stomach with each advance into vat. In winter, you can walk naked in snow after bath–which is why Japanese always bathed so often, no better 'central heating'. Cooling in summer, too. Post-WW II Occupation and Korean War GIs brought custom home as Hot Tub.

Baths come all sizes, shapes. Many inns will have large communal baths —alas almost all now segregated—and those in rural hot spring areas have equally large one outdoors, used mainly for soaking and enjoying nite sky, whether along coast with waves pounding nearby or in quiet wooded vales along rivers or streams. Often not segregated, but towels are always carried with remarkable aplomb. There's nothing like soak amid deep woods with snow blanketing whole area, bottle of sake and cup at pool edge. Some hot-spring spas may have several different types of mineral water, thus, several pools in one large hall. All large inns have private *kazoku-buro* 'family baths'; and that is all you will have in some small inns, where each group of guests take their turn in bath (now you see why no one washes in tub). At some popular mountain *onsen* (hot springs), even smallest inns have outdoor baths *roten-buro*—ro-with long O like 'rote-memory', *not* like 'rotten'. Central Japan Oku-Hida onsen cluster abounds in such bathing holes.

Indoor baths are often landscaped, with mineral waterfalls and rocks (*iwa-buro*, rock-bath), oddly shaped like natural pools, red lacquer bridges across their narrows. Some modern hot spring resorts have taken it one step too far, creating enormous bathing pavilions with dozens of tubs, with milk, lemons, mud or what have you, others gaudily decorated, others as large as swimming pools; there are often shows going on. We feel that at that point all relaxation value is gone, but it is something you will not find anywhere else and you may want to check it out to see what hoopla is about.

ONSEN, SENTO, SAUNA are other bath related terms you'll hear. *Onsen* is hot spring spa, with various types of mineral waters basically volcanic-heated but sometimes slightly reheated. Japan has 2,237 onsens to US's 1,003 or steamy Iceland's 516. We are addicted to them and guide you to them where possible. Many have reputed healing value, as in Europe, tho less antiseptic-appearing and more old-shoe comfortable. Prices range from some top ¥-LL to ¥-Pilgrim minshuku. Most top inns allow access to bath from smaller inns or to passers-by, fee ¥200 to ¥2,000. Many now actively invite daytime drive-in trade, bath and rest in room.

Sento is neighborhood bathhouse—we often used them driving in old pre-paved roads days, Garet as student used as in-town spa with pals. Cheap, few hundred yen. Old institution, many look more like temples except for broad curtained entrance with character *yu*, 'hot water'. Entry divided in two—usually males L, females R—where you remove shoes and put in box-locker. To most city folks at time of our first edition it was basic bath, with at-home tubs luxuries: 1964 Tokyo had 2,700+, today still reputedly 2,182. Neighborhood social center, many 19th century woodblock prints (un)cover it as subject. Dressing and bathing areas segregated by sex.

Move of white collar to suburbs, depopulation of nite-time downtown and rise of private baths (now in 87% of homes in Tokyo main ward) and skyrocketing land prices encouraging high rise development is dooming them. However many are holding out, adding improvements that are in keeping with their traditions of friendliness and comfort, like saunas, even full 'health club' with gym, or mineral tub, snack bar, *rotenburo* in garden as at **New Ebisu** in Arakawa ward, Tokyo. **Azabu Juban** (1-chome 5-22) **Onsen** 10min SE of Roppongi subway stn, 3-11:30pm, X-tue, ¥295; also sauna, 11am-9pm, ¥1,200. **Asakusa Kannon Onsen** located by temple, 6:30am-6pm, ¥500.

Shitamachi downtown Tokyo famed for *sento* and new development trying to conserve, with high rise apartment houses built with sento downstairs as luxury-leisure supplement to private baths. Somehow sento will survive. Adventurer sees fascinating aspect of local life in trying one. Folks friendly, if language student great to practice colloquial conversation.

Sauna were called Turkish baths in '64 edition, but varieties evolved. It is our European word and mainly for men (big cities have some for women, both in same building so go together) dealt with in GOING IT ALONE—HIM. Name is European but institution strictly Japanese, and great. Note, all are sexually 'straight'. Spa boom generating new drillings and developments in downtowns. Underway is hot well and large multi-bath pleasure dome right in Osaka Kita-Shinchi fun area by Umeda stn, and elsewhere in town.

In spa, it is usual to take several baths or soaks—one before dinner, one after and perhaps again very late. (Stags note: about midnite housemaids go in.) Either summer (cool off) or winter (thaw out), morning soak is nice.

Regardless of type of bath, when finished, drying off is done with same small towel, which we have rinsed in our bucket and squeeze-dried. Damp towel dries one amazingly well after hot bath. Ring out often. Most inns supply larger towel, too, but this small towel, with their name and emblem and phone, you are expected to take home—good advertising for them.

After dressing in *yukata*, with *tanzen* padded robe in cool weather; (women emulate men and fold left-over-right, right-over is for corpses only) we carry clothes-filled tray back to room. Maid may rush up and take them as we step out. We carry damp towels back, too, and hang on small rack or over porch rail. Common practice is to bathe first to get rid of all road grime, then dine. Applies equally in posh ¥-LL ryokan or ¥-B-minshuku.

DINNER is ready in our room, arranged rather than set, table landscaped in odd-shaped dishes, picturesquely decorated in savory edibles. Maid bows us in, serves us, scoops our rice, pours our beer (about ¥500 per big bottle) or *sake* in half-pint china bottle (which we have ordered separately before bath when dinnertime agreed on). It starts to put us in mellow soft glow and, realizing we'd rather be alone, maid gracefully bows herself out. In some inns, hostess will drop in for few minutes, perhaps to show off her English and tell of some local specialty, explain cuisine.

In one bowl you will probably see what appears to be coarse paste; your chopsticks will draw it out in one endless, viscous blob. It is *yama-imo* (wild potato) very tasty (Jay thinks so, anyway) and Japanese attribute to it those qualities we reserve to manly oyster, some even consider it to be mildly aphrodisiac. We finish dinner, stretch out on *tatami* floor. Maid, allowing time for leisurely meal, returns and cleans up. Perhaps we order some more *sake* and pour for each other (never pour your own), sit over it, or over tea, at small table and chairs on our private veranda with its vista backdrop. Maid asks when we want *futon* (bedding) spread. Perhaps we go for stroll, down to shops if resort town, among other people shopping for souvenirs, promenading in their hotel kimono, as we do. Each hotel is distinguishable by its own pattern, no fear of getting lost. Another sure way back, especially in towns with many winding streets, is to take book of matches from your inn with its name, address and phone number.

We *hashigo* (**pubcrawl**). If we can't maneuver in *geta* clogs offered us, we ask for our shoes. To Garet, nothing looks more out of place than western shoes peeking out from under yukata–but when Jay first came Kyoto saw many Taisho-era ('20s) elderly men in full kimono, fedora and leather shoes. Of course, nothing says you can't go out in your own clothes–you may find wind whistling up your legs and bare feet somewhat too cold, especially in snow. Whatever you wear, there is always another hot bath waiting for you back at our inn. *Hashigo*, literally 'ladder climbing' is favorite Japanese pastime, and it becomes immediately apparent why there are so many drinking and eating joints in Japanese towns. Japanese nite-on-town usually consists of visiting several establishments. Choices are many, ranging from traditional *yakitori* (meat-on-spit tidbits with drinks) stalls to quiet bars, pubs (sometimes live bands) and discos complete with too-loud sound system and strobe lights. You will see many Japanese men wandering to small 'clubs'. Here, mama-san or one of her girls will serve them drinks and listen sympathetically to their problems, psychiatric services which are dearly paid for. We do not recommend soloing to these. Unwary foreigner wandering into such club may discover too late that small ¥500 bottle of beer has just cost ¥2,000 or more, once all extra charges have been added. Many largish onsen towns have hidden in back streets strip joints, 'adult toy' stores (lacking sweaty-smell of New York or London toy stores), and such ilk. Also, at many onsen towns famed for *rotenburo*, there will be at least one outdoor public bath in some pleasant natural setting which you can slip into during hashigo rounds.

In duet, slum anywhere without worry. Bar girls are sure to fuss over her, stroke her hair or ask to touch it–for Mongoloid hair is generally much coarser than Caucasian–especially if she is blonde or red-haired. (And most especially if it is silver or distinctively flecked, they are amazed at how youthful our grand-dames are). Blacks are popular thanks to good old GI reputation and numerous fine musicians, popular baseball stars among men, and recently dance and aerobics teacher gals–and seen too rarely. They will admire her fashions in sincerity, no matter how drably she thinks she is dressed. They will gasp in utter awe at her *daiya* (diamond) even if it is by our standards submicroscopic. (Japan now world's largest diamond mart). They will plead with you to dance for them and if there is no dance floor will move some tables and play tunes of your choosing, with many old slow favorites now available again on *karaoke* tapes of band music. You'll be asked to sing your favorite song to accompaniment of ever-present *karaoke* (music tapes without vocals–which you provide).

Give vent to your hearts and stroll, arms entwined, her head on his shoulder. Heads will turn and lips will curl into smiles for Japanese have come to appreciate romance and especially appreciate honest guidance on how to be in love in public, with discretion. You may go on, oblivious to world around you, they will honor your confidence in them and not intrude with stares. Or we stroll in our garden. 'Modern' type spa resorts may have dancing to records or even band, and often cozy bar. Most larger ones have amusement centers in imitation of movie resorts, even bowling.

Back to our room, we find low table has been removed, *futon* spread all ready to plop down on–more than likely foam mattresses, 'twin beds' placed together. Light in room is low, table-height floor lamp of Japanese room, its soft light filtered thru antique rice paper or modern fiberglass, casts mysterious shadows into corners and cozy dark spots across comforters, heightening silence, making our room island of isolation in timeless void; thin spider webs of sounds from crickets or song-frogs or water course in garden, our sole contact with universe beyond.

Then you notice why Japanese have so stubbornly kept to *yukata* and kimono, for this costume is tailored for romance.

Staying at Japanese inns has its advantages. First of all you can travel light—very important in this age of plane travel. All *ryokan* provide complete nitewear, freshly starched cotton *yukata* kimono and light *haori* (half-coat) for sitting around or strolling in cool weather, and additional wool kimono and padded *tanzen* (dressing gown) in cooler weather. Packaged towel, disposable toothbrush, individual soap and toothpaste are given guests by most inns; men are provided with one-use safety razors (rarely smooth on iron beards, US razor makers should attack this market), hair oil (alas, usually too 'sweet'), and women with basic cosmetic needs, clean comb and plastic brush. Incidentally, first-class sleepers on trains provide above, as well as slippers. Western-style hotels are having to provide these services, too, for increasing number of Japanese patronizing them ask "whoever heard of carrying sleeping gear?...should we bring sheets, too?". Phone to front desk for them if not provided. Many large hotels will have yukata out for you and will offer to sell one of theirs for about ¥2,000 or so, cheaper than store price, discourages souvenir hunting.

MASSEURS, *anma-san* or *massaji* (massage) on call at all ryokan (¥3,500+ till 10pm), also most hotels (from 11am-1am in large cities). We prefer ryokan-anma, usually traditionally trained, where hotel's are more like Swedish muscle-renders. There's nothing like good nerve massage (as opposed to Swedish-style) after straining day at museum- or sight-seeing, head ready to split, shoulders aching from cameras. Ask desk or phone Room Service to get you *massaji* (price runs about ¥4,-5,500 per person in Tokyo, session about 45min, slightly more in big hotels, less out of town)-perfect for tired nerves and muscles. In country inn old *anma-san* may be blind or lame, this work was reserved as form of social security in feudal days and until recently, and Jay's suggestion to would-be youthful emigrants to USA that they earn national government masseur license was greeted with stony silence.

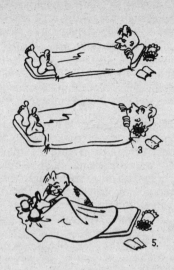

JAPANESE BREAKFAST is usually rice with raw egg which you crack over to be poached by heat of rice, *miso* (soy bean-paste) soup, broiled fish and pickled vegetables–is certain to come as shock to your half-awake system, but it really hits spot on cold, crisp winter morning at ski spa. Most ¥-T *ryokan* can serve up decent W-style breakfast of fried egg, thick toast and coffee–don't order boiled egg as usually comes hard. Younger locals prefer Western coffee, toast and eggs. In ¥-B–T *ryokan*, ask that egg be brought hot, *yakitaté*. Here food is served convenient to server, usually tepid–thus, courses to be kept hot, such as soups, are served in covered lacquer bowls, excellent insulators. No one has yet thought to cover ham and eggs.

Of course, this scene will change somewhat as you go further down price range, but even budget ryokan is great experience. Some cheap inns will turn out to be classy old traditional inns, cheaper because of their age and being little worn looking, but aging gracefully. As original wooden inns age and tourists increase, many tear down old buildings and replace with larger ferroconcrete–many of which manage to be quite attractive. Some merely add larger modern annex (*bekkan*) to take more guests. In most cases, new annex rooms are cheaper than those in original main building (*honkan*), and sometimes aging main is less, but old rooms are as nice or better, as is food and overall service. Bath halls multiply in size and number. We prefer traditional wood-built inns, which abound in countryside. While most remaining wooden inns are high priced, there are those for modest budgets.

Conditions in Tokyo and outside differ greatly—capital is no longer easy place to find good ryokan, government inhospitable to wooden buildings and 'non-intensive' use of land–but we list some, even budget. Kyoto, tourist attraction for world's most addicted tourists for over thousand years, has no dearth of *ryokan*. It is one place where we most insistently recommend you 'go native', go *ryokan*.

In each area we list *ryokan* when discussing sights themselves. Ryokan have widest spread in rates, from luxurious private villas in spacious gardens for ¥50,000 ($390) each with 2 meals–we saw one on TV at ¥500,000!–down to modest but good finds at ¥5,000w/2, even less.

Ryokan have rep for being expensive thanks to few top ones which are—and are worth every yen they charge. Note that ¥-S ryokan ¥13,-15,000 each for couple is ¥25,-30,000—what top international hotels (Hilton, Otani) charge just for room alone and ryokan includes breakfast, gourmet dinner!

International ¥-L Hotel 1992 basic twin and 3 meals table d'hôte, all tax-svce incl, runs minimum ¥65,000 per couple!—for which sum you could laze in luxe ryokan. (However, for busy businessman, nothing matches international luxe hotel for familiar comforts and business amenities).

LUXE RYOKAN FOR TRUE TASTE OF JAPAN: We select here some elegant ryokan–classic wood architecture, serenity with tasteful modern amenities. Beautiful rooms, neighbor river or surrounding mountains 'incorporated' in classical garden: quiet retreat. Instead of highly-touted *kaiseki-ryori* dinner in city for few hundred dollars each, hold treat for luxe ryokan where for price of restaurant dinner, enjoy watching blue Pacific, tantalizing waterfall in mountains, dip in private out-door natural onsen–for same price. Generally small inns with 8 to 20 rooms, cater to you personally. Following routing of our book, head for Hakone mountains to:

HAKONE MIYANOSHITA: Naraya was *honjin* official HQ for *daimyo* lords and royalty. Classic magnificent interiors expound skill of ancient artisans and craftsmen. Huge wooded estate. ¥28,-35,000w/2, ☎(0460)-2-2411.

ATAMI: Horai, faint incense greets you to exquisite inn high on cliff overlooking sea. Known for cuisine, hand calligraphy 'mat' for each dish, personal attention of madam owner, isolated enclosed flowing bath w/seascape. ¥40,-70,000w/2 ☎(0557)-80-5151.

IZU NAGAOKA: Sanyo-so, ex-villa of Baron Iwasaki, Mitsubishi founder: luxurious suites, o-hanare units face expansive lawn incorporating traditional stone lanterns, tea house, iris pond. ¥30,-130,000w/2. ☎(0559)-48-0123.

SHUZENJI: Asaba Kansuikaku, 350-year-old huge gate, garden noh stage overlooks pond (perform Oct). ¥23,-35,000w/2, ☎(0558)-72-7000. **Yagyu-no-sho**, all detached *o-hanare*, bkfst cooked over open hearth in room. ¥36,-90,000w/2 ☎(0558)-72-4126.

GERO ONSEN: Yunoshima-kan, 50-yr-old in 100s of ancient cedars, nestled in Mt Fuji of Gero, luxurious rooms–one, old Shunkei lacquer. ¥-lo-Lw/2, ☎(05762)-5-4126.

KYOTO: Tawaraya ¥36,-63,000w/2 ☎(075)-211-5566, **Sumiya** ¥30,-70,000w/2 ☎221-2188, **Hiragiya** ¥35,-150,000w/2 ☎221-ll36 are tops in every way–been catering to foreign guests for generations. All start ¥-Lw/2, lo or hi or ¥-LL depends on room and amount of food. Following 3 readily accept room-only guests. **Yachiyo** ¥15,-40,000w/2, ☎771-4148, rm only 20% off. Kiyomizu temple area, **Sakaguchi**, huge waterwheel in lovely garden, ¥-hi-Lw/2 ☎561-3160. **Kyo Yamato**, huge garden, ¥50,000w/2, ☎525-1555. More listed in KYOTO, p431.

BEPPU, KYUSHU: Tamanoya, Yufuin Onsen, 14 hanare cottages, rustic. Madam in kasuri pants. Bungo steak rec. ¥-lo-Lw/2, ☎(0977)-84-2158.

NOTO, WAKURA ONSEN: Kagaya, fascinating combination of old and new. Shopping arcade of Kaga crafts next door. ¥-24,-76,000, ☎(07676)-2-2111.

KANAZAWA: Kincharyo ☎(0762)-43-2121 and **Asadaya** ☎31-2228 both ¥-LLw/2, latter has small *hako-niwa*, box-garden. However, **Miyabo** is in Meiji era mayor's huge garden, ¥-S-lo-Lw/2, ☎31-4228.

SENDAI-MATSUSHIMA, AKIU ONSEN: Zuiho, ☎(022)-387-1111, exception as big resort ¥-LLw/2 ¥-24,-76,000; W-rm option, ask Daimler pick-up; serve lady guests in room by young man in formal kimono, var baths; E-spkn, golf avail; *See* p988.

WESTERN HOTELS

THIS COUNTRY is for your every mood, from ultra modern to simple farm homes, or wonderful blend of both. Those who prefer sights, strangeness of foreign country by day and customary bed by nite, good array of W-style hotels is in every city, US facilities at US price plus ('no-tip') mandatory 10% service, 6% tax, which adds up, often, to more than they are worth–as do most hotels worldwide as so many guests now seem to have bottomless pockets or handsome tax dodges. In all fairness, as prices soared more so has quality of service–and have cheaper alternative hotels risen to fill gap.

What we once simply called **International Level** is now truly **LUXE**—**Hilton**s in US to us were big business hotels, but here since their inception they've been tops (4 new ones: 2 Tokyo, palatial Osaka, Nagoya). They are far from alone–**Okura** Tokyo always ranked with us as top so we are proud to see it acclaimed one of world best–tho Garet's generation find clientele old fogeyish, rates **Hyatt Regent** top. Our other favorites are **Otani** chain, monstrous size but maintaining quality (money-saving membership system), and **Prince** chain, evolved from converted princely mansions, still noble. **Miyako** Kyoto is old favorite, not to be confused with lesser namesakes (chain), except co-owned **Nara Hotel**–another favorite blessedly luxe in quality but in price ¥-S. For true European-posh, Tokyo's small 80-room **Seiyo**, with more staff than guests, best of all worlds from personal concierge to VCR and personal computer in room.

Same-day laundry, cleaning normal–in by 10am back at nite. Majors do it in hour. In smaller hotels or inns, perhaps not, but they'll at least direct you to local. In Tokyo **Hakuyosha** ☎3460-1111 pick up, deliver (in before 10am, standard int'l custom) or overnite; budget conscious should walk it to nearest branch, ask bell hop. Anything you can think of, **front-desk** (Jpn) *furonto*, can almost certainly do for you at any level hostelry: theater, sports tix, travel reservations, sightseeing tours. Most boast gift shops of some sort, while international majors have complete arcades where almost anything and everything may be purchased at fair price and shipping home arranged–at atrocious local postal rate. Particularly true in Tokyo, where these arcades are good shopping, goods geared for foreign tastes conveniently concentrated, tax-free where relevant.

TOURIST: Those who want W-beds at reasonable price (dble under ¥15,000 or $100) will find family-style chains, like Sun Route, Washington, Chisan, Seibu Inns, Miyako Inns (English 'inn' suggests travelers' comfort, tho Tokyu Inns we find small, overpriced), Green Hotels (using Green or Sun in name projects youth, modernity), other new chains in most cities are usually near stations. Where Tokyo in '64 had only one hotel in this most-needed category, there are now droves, more a-building. Most popular scenic areas, spas, beaches will have family-style hotels, some finest will have grand ones, many of which date prewar. Below these are Business or Family Hotels, vacationland Pensions, (*see* SANDAL THONG).

Hotel Discount Coupons: *Sunrise Super Saver* available only back home, thru JTB or your agent. Assure you tourist rate (¥12,000 tw/dble incl %) buying in advance at least 5 coupons, making first confirmed reservation– rest may be used freely within 30 days of first. Nontransferable, non-replaceable if lost. Good ('91) at 89 hotels in 52 cities; 23 inns which are 2x-rate as w/2 meals. Single, triple rooms available, pro rata. JTB or agent.

...if you love your son—send him on a journey....

SHOESTRING & SANDAL THONG

THAT OLD JAPANESE PROVERB is gaining popularity in America, Europe and even Australia, where sons and daughters add "...to Japan". American students, traditionally oriented towards Europe, are turning Orientwards. Many who've already seen Europe on shoestring budgets also turn eyes longingly to *"Go West, young 'un"*, go farther West to this farthest East, and ponder how to travel on shoestring in land where traditional pilgrims never wore shoes. Simple: do it on sandal thong. That is, by using excellent budget facilities developed for these travel-crazy local folks.

Can someone who wants to keep his or her budget down to under $50 per day for basic room and board (1964 edition we said $10-total and could then even do it for under $5) set out in this land reputed worldwide as being its most expensive? We still say, 'yes'. Many 'tourist' class ryokan, and all *minshuku* easily make it under this limit. (Our old $10 per day of '64 covered everything, but now we hedge somewhat and follow other books in covering only basic room and board). Taxis are up 7-fold in yen, or about 20x-dollar price, most other prices follow. However, US hotels are up over 20-fold ('64 Sheraton single $8)–and London, laddy we've run out of fingers since bed and breakfast (real sausage) was under one quid.

Again, as then, just few dollars more allows for luxury splurges occasionally, which is way we have always liked to travel and advise you to do so. Occasional roughing it by those who don't have to adds spice to travel (as opposed to tourism). And who needs to explain that occasional deluxe day rests bones and soul and refuels one for setting out again on pilgrimage. New dress codes (or lack thereof) make all this easier. This is still land of inveterate sightseers who generally earn less than we do–nonpermanent jobs here for youths pay $4-5 per hour, starter jobs even less. For old folks, merchants or farmers clubs and such, group tours are continuation of old tradition of pilgrimage at purely lay level, which most of olde were also. Food and water are safe anywhere, infectious disease rates world's lowest, police die of boredom sitting in little kiosks amid houses burglar-proofed with scotch tape. Hardest part of budget travel here may be starting day with breakfast as bad as you get in Paris, but first-terrifying language barrier can be more of aid than hindrance, if you keep your sense of humor–in real crunch someone always seems to materialize to help out.

So let's look at lower-priced facilities.

MINSHUKU are low-end Budget (¥-lo-B), family-run guest home inns, best buys in this land–except in Kyoto where ¥-lo-T. This is as close as most visitors will get to living in Japanese home, since that is what minshuku are. Originally run by families with extra rooms available as kids moved out, many now have been built specifically as inns–still strictly family operation as basically budget ryokan. Sole difference is in elegance or style, factor budget travelers can easily sacrifice. Sculpted garden, amenities, maid service, may be lacking, but often get them nonetheless. Like budget ryokan minshuku can range from grand to bland, but always are good deals. We often use minshuku as savings far outweigh differences in service, and with savings we stay at grand ryokan when we feel like being pampered. JNTO-TIC have brochures of minshuku accustomed to dealing with foreign guests; best info is excellent English booklet with huge 100+ list (and how to get to each) and description of minshuku etiquette.

Available thru TIC or **Nihon Minshuku Association** Shinjuku ☎(03)-3232-6561, no-Eng. Separate outfit is **Nihon Minshuku Center**, reservations ☎(03)-3216-6556; near TIC at NE of Yuraku-cho el-stn, Kotsu-kaikan bldg basement. *Minshuku in Kyoto* lists 40 just in city usually said not to have any, '90 top ¥7,500w/2; some offer cha-do, others pottery making, traditional music, whatever hobby owner-manager plays at. Free, ✍ **Kyoto Minshuku Reservation** Center, ON Bldg 7-fl, Kyoto-eki-mae, Shimogyo-ku, Kyoto 600; ☎(075)-351-4547–it's near JNTO-TIC, who can direct you.

Atmosphere is homey. You may spend enjoyable hours with owners (meals often in main room family-style), tho once in your room privacy is respected. In most, make your own futon at nite, and should fold up (triple) and store back in closet. Minshuku ideal for budgeteers; recently upped rates, w/2, average **¥5,-7,000**. Deep in back-country or hard-to-reach isles, as low as ¥3,000; in historic Edo era houses of Magome near Nagoya, Hida-Takayama, or rural National Cultural Asset village Shirakawa-go, cost ¥5,000w/2–still cheap and you stay in most interesting houses we've ever seen. Minshuku found most anywhere, tho not many new onsen towns have one, nor most large cities–tho Kyoto has scores. Many countryside minshuku are seasonal: on beach or high in central mountains may close winter, ski area ones open only when snow–unless area also popular for onsen or hiking. But you rarely come across place where none are open. That is, as long as you're not heading to some isolated mountain onsen.

To combat ill-earned aura some 76 tourist ryokan banded to form...
Hospitable and Economical Japanese Inn Group–they fit name. Well located in Tokyo (9), down Tokaido (22) & Kyoto (11), our favorite in Nara, **Seikanso**, near our own museum *Orient Kan*, as well as most of country, and growing. Rates listed split: room only w/ or w/o pvt bath, sgle, dble or multiple occupancy, extra for meals. Most offer Continental (¥300-400), if not American, bkfst as well as Japanese (¥500-800). Many in cities don't serve dinner. Average for couple w/o bath (use common pool, usually not mixed), no meals runs ¥7,-8,000, w/2 ¥15,000, ¥-lo-Tw/2. Some offer special dinners, features like occasional ceremonies you are invited to. All are American Express, who helped publish fine pamphlet of individual entries, detailed maps, all are trained to use simple English conversation for rsvtns, and can be reserved by Amex assured reservation system for safe late arrivals. Booklet revised regularly, available from JNTO, TIC, Amex, or ✍ **Japanese Inn Group**, Hiraiwa Ryokan, 314-Hayao-cho, Kaminoguchi-agaru, Ninomiya-cho-dori, Shimogyo-ku, Kyoto 600; ☎(075)-351-6748, Fax 351-6969.

JEAF, JAPAN ECONOMY ACCOMMODATION FEDERATION (Nihon Ekonomii Kanko Ryokan Renmei), '¥-B' ryokan, linked nation-wide to encourage foreign visitors (70-odd mid '89 and growing). Most are quite nice, none are bad. Professional inns in *minshuku* price-range, often larger (9-15 rms), less homey. As their name implies, room w/2 meals start **¥6,500** each, ¥8,000 average. Rare *sudomari* (no meals) room only ¥3,000+ each. Updated list of these inns can be found in special JNTO brochure, available at all TIC. While at TIC, check side wall-racks lined with English brochures of inns wishing for foreign guests. These are not limited to main tourist spots and are in all price ranges. Ryokan rates remain quite stable for many years; have been creeping up slowly but steadily thru late '80's JEAF ☎(075)-561-3025.

KOKUMIN-SHUKUSHA, Peoples' Lodges, not to be confused with *minshuku*, are economical, **government-run** inns. While most are not particularly attractive outside (simply blockish) inside is clean; rooms J-style. Room w/2 average ¥-B, ¥5,-6,000; almost all offer various dinner choices to fit taste and budget. There are simple one-dish meals like curry, noodles for few hundred yen each, multi-course Japanese dinners can range ¥500-2,000. Budget travelers can try for room only at cheap rate (set by Assn) tho most refuse, and get noodles or similarly cheap food if eateries nearby. Dinners served in communal dining room or (sometimes) brought to your room. Breakfast almost always served in dining room and always basic Japanese one of tea, soup, rice, raw egg, pickles and fish, tho many give option of ham, eggs, toast and coffee. Service minimal but always courteous. All have grand baths. Being government backed, and intended for relaxation at affordable costs, Kokumin-shukusha often have prime location, usually little outside of town or at some spectacular natural hideaway. TIC has full list of Kokumin-shukusha, about 340 nationwide, but no regular pamphlet, so must ask for it. Easiest to book by phone, just as long as done in Japanese. Popular with Japanese, are full most holidays and weekends, but worth trying. No membership requirements so foreign visitors more than welcome to use Kokumin-shukusha. *Same goes for...*

KOKUMIN KYUKA-MURA, Peoples' Rest-villages ¥-Pilgrim rate, often set in National and Quasi-national Parks, also government-backed. There are some 30 such villages: compounds with Western and Japanese style accommodations, about 2/3rds have camping facilities, some bungalows, and half have sports facilities. Room-only average **¥2,000**, or w/2 meals matches minshuku rate.

Similar set-up at...
SEI-SHONEN RYOKO-MURA, Youth Travel Villages, ¥-Pilgrim as you can get, 50-odd scattered across rural Japan, as close to nowhere as you can get in cramped Japan. Usually main lodge with campsites.

TIC can give list of both these types of villages; book yourself by phone, most local booking places will not book into either type of village, but may refer you personally and if you know it's there will at least direct you to it.

BUSINESS HOTELS, same *bijiness* in both languages, are ¥-Budget or lo-end ¥-Tourist, mainly for traveling small businessmen, will be found clustered around stations and/or convenient to center of town. Spartan rooms (tiny by US standards) barely fitting bed, cabinet and TV, start as low as **¥4,000** singles, ¥500 or so extra with shower/bath unit. All have communal bath for budgeteers, and some even dedicate entire floor for grand baths and saunas. Some cities have 24hr sauna-hotels, for which you pay few hundred yen for use of baths, and can get simple room with bed for another thousand yen or so. Some places classified as business hotels are quite nice, good for families, even call selves **Family Hotel**; average about **¥6,-8,000** for twins. Most in any price range are clean and safe; if booked thru kanko-annai or other local agents (*see* below) you can't be stuck in that rare bad one.

Business hotels either have adjacent budget restaurant coffee shop for simple meals, and/or will prepare you set meals for low costs; dinners usually ¥800-1,000, breakfast, few hundred yen. Japanese dinners are best bet, simple but good and large; breakfast usually choice of Japanese style (raw egg on hot rice with some sort of meat and vegetables) or Western style (ham, eggs, toast). If you know where to look for cheap food (also often around stations), you can get meals for few hundred yen. Toiletries and drinks, often snacks, available cheap in plentiful vending machines.

Perhaps best known or notorious, business hotels are **Capsule Hotels**, honeycomb set-ups of clean but tiny cubicles found at few major stations, for business**men** who want just place to sleep at cheapest possible prices (probably missed last train). With these, ¥-B, you're on your own for food, unless you consider vending machine packets food (instant noodles, etc).

If you're not in town with much in way of nitelife or dining, best bet is Japanese style lodging (above) which includes two meals with room. Inns make money off food, thus are good 'buy' when taken with two meals (w/2) included. No matter what price range of inn you stay at, you won't be able to get comparable meals at restaurants for amount of money saved if staying room-only (*sudomari*). For example, we stayed at budget minshuku in Northern Japan town of Aizu-Wakamatsu where meals were served at their adjacent diner; dinner multi-course affair of fish, tempura, all fixin's and breakfast was equal feast. Had we paid regular menu prices for those two meals, it would have cost almost as much as room-with-2-meal rate.

Only place to get reasonable rate for *sudomari* is in cities famed for food, with abundance of cheap eateries, such as Sapporo in far north or Hakata-Fukuoka at bottom, and Kyoto where most small Budget inns are *sudomari* —as are many fine old Budget inns in *sh'tamachi* old downtown Tokyo.

PENSIONS, which name and style borrowed from European counterpart, are relatively new (but spreading) phenomena in Japan—over 2,000, of which over 600 in Pensione System Development Association, call center ☎(03)-3295-6333 X-sun/hols; English info Mr NAKAMURA Shiro ☎3293-0469. W-style accoms, usually commons room for dining and parties. Open to anybody, but more popular with younger crowd as atmosphere conducive to mingling. Mostly located in countryside skiing and/or hiking areas, beaches, such pleasant settings. Owner—often refugee from big city rat race, many show-biz folks in semi-retirement following gourmet hobby—will probably be your guide there, at least have great ideas on what to do. Room w/2 meals, often local gourmet, all incl, average ¥6,-7,500, ¥-B, some ¥-lo-T.

LOVE HOTELS: Young couples will find luxury-budget accommo-dations in those 'avec hotels'—*avec* from French 'with' means 'with' someone, be it one's girlfriend or boyfriend, any romantic couple. Also called *romansu*, love (*rubbu*), or *tsurekomi*-hotel ('bring along'). These rent out not on day basis, but by hour. Check-in time for overnite is usually 10pm, checkout 10am. Come earlier or leave later adds hourly rate to overnite. All rates on basis of couple, all inclusive, sometimes payable in advance—but they have your shoes. These places are fun, facilities fair to fantastique. Many are themselves surprised at frequency of man checking in with what is obviously his own wife—for rates are ¥-Tourist.

Luxury found within is caricature of Hollywood movie set: bath with picture window and false glass bottom with goldfish swimming below; multi-channel cable hi-fi (try for US news), cable-TV, well-stocked refrig-erator with hors d'oeuvres, beer, mix and hootch (pay extra on leaving for any consumed, at moderate prices—since first edition this feature picked up by whole hotel world), heat or air-conditioning, ornate chandeliers, stained glass windows (church wedding), and such generous mirrors that one with electric razor may easily shave in bed in morning no matter which side or end you sleep at—even lying on your back. Gynecologists may find, as we did in Shikoku '85, interesting furniture that looked like either delivery couch or torture rack. Many finer ones now advertise on midnite TV, whole programs have been devoted to visiting some. Entrance often hard to find, but lobbies can make Versailles look like shanty, tho all plaster or pastry. New fashion is to call these newer ones *fashin hoteru*, and each will have theme (amazing what some fetishes can involve—some are full torture cham-bers, anyway racks are common). One seen on TV we hunted for since in Kobe, is all *art-deco*, superb (Japanese invention anyway) would make good show at Museum of Modern Art in New York or Paris! We will men-tion where some of these are, especially in Kyoto.

In general, they are marked by garish architecture for older ones, smartly out-of-place for *fashin hoteru*. Prices posted outside, usually on electrically-lighted glass in Japanese, but there will always be at least two figures in numerals: higher and 25-40% lower, respectively overnite and basic 2 hours daylight or pre-10pm. You find some as low as ¥2,000 per couple overnite, but these are simple clean Japanese inns or Western cells, in side streets.

'Movie sets' look made for Hans Christian Andersen in technicolor, with architecture by some mad French pastry chef who got drunk on Disneyland. Names are always Occidental or Near Eastern, but outside of Tokyo or Osaka, Hilton isn't Conrade or -International. Those along Expressways or other highways often use gaudy architecture (best collection along Tomei-Meishin Expwy around Nagoya, Aladdinesque palaces, ships and turreted castles). Approach to Tokyo boasts Queen Mary, even Statue of Liberty. By their very nature these 'Hotels' are not often given as alternate lodgings, but they do offer cheap nite's room. If outside lights are on, they have vacancy, no need to ask. Of course, you probably won't get normal room. Can sometimes get cheap overnite rates showing up late. Set price and time of departure (usually early, 10am) before getting room to avoid possible overcharge when you wake up. Rates are per room, not per person like everywhere else in Japan, so your room is quite cheap if more than one person. No surcharge for trios, Jay and Sumi and friend-couple checked into one in Shikoku and surprised them asking for two separate rooms—which were both different and equally wild. Gender mixes don't matter. Particularly convenient for that long drive on family trips—we have checked in with Garet and brother and their pals in their school days, and rooms are bound to keep kids amused (but oh, that icebox bill!).

Rates posted outside will usually be ¥2,000 to ¥4,000 as minimal figure, and ¥3,500-7,000 maximal, but once inside some 'wilder' rooms go up to ¥-Luxe levels. Former is rate between 10am and 10pm for 2 hours *kyukei* (rest), latter post-10pm–10am overnite. They do make good *kyukei* (*see* DAY HOTELS *follows*). Fashion hotel frequently has big illuminated photo-transparency board at entry showing room interior with key hanging out of box—pull key of your choice, pic's light goes out, lady shows you to room. Parking always discrete, always in building, license plate covered.

If you would prefer to check in earlier and then go out for while, reserve room, ask to leave your baggage, but don't check into room before 10.

They change bedding with every client, as any good hotel. Also provide luxurious pajama, bathrobe, towel, toothbrush and personal effects packet to each, hermetically sealed—they must have learned their service from old movies. You can have dinner sent in, menu in Japanese and English usually available, Western, Japanese and Chinese offerings delivered from local restaurants at reasonable rates, all listed, so that extra time charge for early check-in, added to meal, still makes total reasonable. Meals available till wee hours of nite usually, but not breakfast—so bring milk etc, put in refrig, there will usually be cup-size hot water boiler.

If planning to stay several days, do not keep room but check luggage thru day at desk. Note that until recently most Japanese *ryokan* also worked on this system, charged more for 2 days than twice one, as you were billed 2 overnites plus *kyukei*.

We use these movie sets often ourselves and like them. In 1964 we wrote "...standard hotels would do well to emulate many of their services". Since then they have: full line of toiletries and full refrigerator now standard hotel furnishing worldwide. All other special needs there in small packets.

DAY HOTELS: Useful accommodation offered by hotels and inns all over Japan that you might need to know. Called *kyukei* or rest, and rest is what it provides. You can rest your weary body with plunge into their spa pools or take nice hot bath. Under this arrangement you are provided regular room, given *yukata* to change into, and you may take bath. If you wish, *futon* (quilts) will be put down so you can nap, or...

Kyukei is popular for day trips to hot spring spas, where you can enjoy mineral water baths, have dinner, then head home; likewise for skiing, fishing, hunting or sight-seeing. Lovely idea for few hours rest when passing thru spa areas, especially if driving: Unzen or Beppu in Kyushu; Hakone-Atami-Ito near Mt. Fuji; and Kinugawa, Nasu or Shiobara up north near Nikko. Blessed relief when reaching your destination at ungodly hour (as does Tokyo to Oshima Island ship at 5am) or for train layovers. Convenient for member of group who doesn't feel up to sightseeing to wait at inn, lie down, or call in masseur to relieve those tired muscles–in which latter case in big city, visit to sauna might be better.

Kyukei usually means 2 or 3 hours at set rate; in small inns, about ¥1500+. Longer rests negotiable at about ¥1,000 per hour. Some first class W-style hotels have special rate but most get away with full charge, thus, rack up over 100% occupancy records. One Kobe ¥-L on holiday weekends runs 140% capacity, one mid-rank hotel Osaka runs over 250%– but maybe they have science fiction situation of keeping one room in three time warps...Better inns, plan on about double. Dinner or lunch at inn does not require *kyukei* surcharge, unless you dally too long after simple meal. However, much depends on place and type of meal: if expensive, usually no surcharge. Most inns, especially *ryori-ryokan* which are predominantly restaurants with only occasional overnite guests, expect you to take bath, then spend entire afternoon or evening eating and relaxing, all incl.

In crowded land where many families share one paper-walled house or concrete rabbit hutch, *kyukei* is accepted escape for young marrieds.

YOUTH HOSTELS (*Yuusu Hosteru*) all over Japan, often inconvenient (but Kyoto in town), with strict hours for curfew and lights-out. Cheapest accommodations you will find, YH often full of students, whose constant childish (in Western eyes) antics can get frustrating if you plan to use YH for main means of lodgings. We do not, in most cases, advise them for anyone looking for anything other than saving money. Most have segregated bunk-rooms, but every now and then–don't count on it–they have private room for traveling couple. House-parents range from iron-fisted despots to some of nicest people you meet. There are gov't subsidized Japan Youth Hostels (JYH) & privately run ones. JYH account for some 50 of total 550 YH–veteran hostelers avoid these if possible. YH may be temple, shrine or ex-ryokan, which can be great experience. Temple may awaken you at dawn for service (optional) or help clean grounds (not optional, sweep).

Most require International Youth Hostel Card. USA 🏠 **American Youth Hostels National Office**, PO Box 37613 Washington DC 20013, ☎(202)-783-6161, or JYH Assoc member card which can be purchased (¥1,800) at National HQ in Tokyo, **JYH Inc**, 2nd fl. Hoken Kaikan Bldg, in Ichigaya, ☎(03)-3269-5831. Many private YH let you stay without card (may charge ¥200-300 extra)–if planning much hosteling, get card. JNTO-TIC English pamphlet *Youth Hostels in Japan* lists every hostel with simple directions. Also *Youth Hostel Handbook* ¥350 at JYH-HQ or at many hostel desks. Written mostly in Japanese, but easy to use with simple system of symbols, maps give towns in Roman letters, hostels shown on map are listed numerically by region. If map directions confuse, they are written out in Japanese so passersby can help.

Even budget travelers in Japan plan vacations months in advance, so don't count on getting bed without prior arrangement, especially peak travel times (school vacation April 28-May 5, mid-July to Sept). YH recommend reservations at least 2 weeks advance by self-addressed return confirmation card or phone, but that puts crimp into free-wheeling wandering. Few times we have used YH, it was always on spot and got lucky. Average rates are

¥1,300 for room, ¥400 breakfast, ¥700 dinner and ¥100 sheet fee (which you can avoid by carrying own sheet–no, sleeping bag doesn't count). JYH hostels get ¥50-100 more per category; non-members charged at least ¥300 extra, if accepted at all. Some have cooking facilities (coin-op burners) for small charge if you want to cook own meals (*ji-sui*). As you can see, room w/2 meals costs ¥2,500, not much less than some minshuku which gets you much more comfort, freedom, better food, and traveling couples can have private rooms without hassle–so extra ¥1,000 or so well worth it.

CAMPING isn't as widespread in Japan despite all hiking that goes on here, but campgrounds are found all over country. Range from vaguely marked plots with pit toilets to well-kept areas with rental cabins, hot and cold running water, and various other facilities from swimming, boating, full sports areas to hot spas. Good list in English available from Kyoto or Tokyo TIC. Many rent out tents from burgeoning rental companies, but if camping to save money, bring your own. Camping is not allowed in National Parks unless so designated, but almost any other place is fair game: countryside, beaches, even open plots of land in towns. If latter, best to first eat and bathe (cheap public baths abound) then set up; and depart early. You're not doing anything illegal, but chances of being surrounded by curious kids diminishes with setting sun.

While some tourist towns have nearby campgrounds, average tourist will not have many chances to camp. If budget bumming around San-In Coast, Tohoku or Hokkaido, or island-hopping Okinawa, tent sees much use and it's worth bringing one over. Good, lightweight tents available in US for $40-80, similar or lower UK, Australia, airline baggage almost unlimited, tent isn't much of burden physically or financially. Cheaper to buy at home rather than Japan; can sell to newfound camper friend before leaving. For sudden urge to camp, get most gear here at **rental** shops. Many campgrounds have full rental services, or cheap (¥2,000 way up) bungalows.

Announced summer of '87: **Vacation Camp Parks**, family-oriented, spot like landscaped house plot to park camper or car with tent in integrated 29,000m^2 'estate' with fishing, sports etc. First 20 spring '88, will soon be 20 for each prefecture mostly in scenic undeveloped areas, for grand total of 1,000. Total cost 24,000 *oku*, Japanese number for ¥2,400,000,000,000 =16billion bucks. Of little interest to foreign tourist, possible use to resident families–and it will draw some traffic away from other over-crowded areas.

TEMPLE INNS, *shukubo* (like old 'shoe'), offer unique lodging, usually ¥-Budget. 50-odd are YH listed in all booklets; rest privately run by temple with accommodations ranging from ¥-Pilgrim all-in-one-large-tatami-mat-room to princely private rooms with beautifully painted paper doors and view of landscaped garden. These are remnants of one of two types of inn original to 10th century (not so hoary tradition as China, Persia or even Rome) for religious pilgrims, with at opposite scale of luxury for travelling officials who often just commandeered room in best home. 17th century saw formal divisions into *honjin*-digs for noble families to-and-froing annually between home and Edo as shogun hostages; *hatagoya* for common travellers (see in woodblock prints harrassing passers-by), with different levels again offering services ranging from home comfort down to bare bedding with optional wood to cook dinner. All were noted for their female room service–and as reported by 19th century foreigners, fleas. And things really didn't change all that much till 1960s

Average shukubo rate ¥3,500-5,000w/2, Mount Koya higher (worth it) ¥6,-8,000. Suggest taking meals-included whenever you can, or even go just for meal, as most are traditional *shojin-ryori* vegetarian priests' fare. However, not all are purely vegetarian, some use eggs, others fish. Some offer shojin-ryori which must be reserved by prior arrangement (we list)—cost anywhere ¥1,500-5,000 meal only. Food differs from standard Japanese only in that no meat, fish or fowl used, but looks pretty much same, especially with tofu and other meat substitutes.

Many shukubo are Zen. Hark to strict Zen custom: 'take all you can eat but eat all you take'—especially rice, for which rice bowl may be swilled with tea at end of meal to drink down last grain. Join in dawn zazen meditation—non-sectarian. Some offer longer zazen sessions, those wishing to can arrange extended stays. At best you stay in part of temple itself; lovely rooms in grand, centuries-old wood pavilions. Others are annexes merely within compound, can be lovely wood building or modern concrete box. Most temple facilities listed in this book are former type, and you should try at some time to spend at least one nite—tho Eihei-ji (p852) wisely requires minimum two nites.

Okayama Pref (*see* p627, between Kobe-Hiroshima) Apr '91 opened 6 (more to come) **International Villas** for foreigners and J-escorts only, ¥2,500.

COMMUNES are reputedly widespread, many have philosophical credos for all sorts of lifestyles. Best source is 240-page English book listing all communes in Japan and their various philosophies, by Moshe Matsuba, who, despite Hebrew-Japanese name, is Englishman with much kibbutz time under his yarmulka. (¥1,000 each, rarely stocked at shops). *To order,* ✍ **Japan Commune Movement**, c/o Moshe Matsuba, Kibbutz Akan, Shin Shizen No-en, Nakasetsuri, Tsurui-mura, Akan-gun, Hokkaido, 085-12. From overseas, enclose equivalent postal coupons to about US $8, allow 6wks delivery.

In Kyoto area, you might try **Itto-en Commune**, established 1905, also has much info on other communes. Call them at ☎(075)-581-3136.

For other 'alternate lifestyle' there are some 30 **Yamagishi-kai** organic farms, where all chip in, feed animals, put up building, guests add ¥2,000 to cover bed and board for full weekend. Longer participatory study-stay can be negotiated. In English ✍ **Hans** or **Fumie Wiithrich**, c/o Yamagishiism Seikatsu, Suizawa Utsubegawa Jikkenchi, 2682 Suizawa-cho Yokkaichi-shi, Mie-ken 510-11; or phone ☎(0593)-29-3027.

As we see preceding, Japan has no lack of lodgings, even in her most remote villages. But ¥-Pilgrim-rate lodgings for budgeteers like those which abound thruout rest of Asia, and which could be found in Japan until '70s, hardly exist anymore except to some degree in Kyoto or Tokyo's *Gaijin Houses*—Okubo House, English House and International House (not famed Rockefeller I-House) at ¥900-1,800 (cheaper yet by week or month) for pad in dorm and small lockable locker. Cheapest you'll find are **Youth Hostels** around ¥1,300-1,500, cheapest perhaps ¥1,000 (sheet incl) in Miho Shizuoka. Or in cities near stations are infamous, rather silly, **Capsule Hotels** in which last-train missers entomb themselves overnite in sarcophagus with bedding + TV for ¥1,500-2,000, often sauna on other floor (extra), cheapie eatery or at least vending machines for hot noodles and drinks. Tho Kyoto has some pretty basic share-digs around ¥1,200-1,600, which scruffy as they are, are superior to Tokyo's simplest digs.

Then again, you have no worry about rip-offs (except from fellow foreign 'pilgrims' in dorms) or filthy conditions—bedding is clean, baths ubiquitous. Worst you will find (still risk-free and clean) are cheapest Business Hotels, some only old pilgrim inns relabeled, not bookable thru usual channels, only at front-desk and usually cash on check-in.

BOOKING ROOM can be chore, even total frustration—but nothing like in China. For adventurer of any level, ¥-Luxe to ¥-Pilgrim, we note local tourist offices—*kanko annai-jo*, TICs, etc—at or near stations that can help. Booking into better hotels and ryokan can be done thru many travel agents at home or JTB, hotel/inn desks, *or...*

Welcome Inn Reservation Center new free service of JNTO-TICs, no deposit; will arrange rooms under ¥10,000w/bkfst. Must appear in person, or o'seas write nearest JNTO (p78). This service will enlarge if we don't abuse by excess no-shows and no-calls. ☎ in Tokyo 3502-1461; in Kyoto 371-5649; toll-free E-Jpn 0120-222-800, W-Jpn 0120-444-800.

Almost every rail station or bus terminal has booth or window counter for local reservations. Can be part of *kanko-annai* tourist information, or separate entity (often adjacent) called *ryokan-annai-jo* ryokan information place, or *shukuhaku-annai-jo* room-&-board info. Most annai-jo keep regular business hours, so pulling late into town can be problem. Nara's Sanjo-dori *kanko-annai-jo* is open till 9pm. Some stations have touts–some are official agents who book into any place, others each from one inn, but most can be trusted (except in Atami). Late nite is when business hotels are handy. Most inns won't accept walk-ins much after 18:00 as they need time to prepare your meal. If planning to come in late and already have booked room, call early (or at time of booking) to let inn know approximate arrival.

Tell attendant at annai-jo your price range (minshuku or ryokan) and any preferences in location choice and they will get you good inn, give accurate directions or even put you in cab or bus. Sometimes you may be asked to pay partial deposit or full fare, keep voucher and hand it over at inn, either as you enter or when filling in registration in your room. In smaller towns where inns cluster in same general area, you can walk streets poking into various inns until you find suitable one. Annai-jo quicker and easier, and if you have some specific place you want, they can call it for you.

In this book phone numbers are almost always listed after recommended inns, but unless otherwise specified reservation must be made in Japanese. Last re-standardization of phones occurred over 10 years ago and everyone seems satisfied so phone numbers (☎) won't change—except in boondocks which, like UK, have long area codes (in parentheses)—even then, total digits don't change, area code shortens and extra digits become part of local exchange, change local dial only but not affecting dial from out of town.

If someone calls for you, have him tell innkeeper you can handle ryokan or minshuku conditions; many Japanese are convinced that foreigners can't deal with their ways (especially food). Marvelously located budget inn at Horyuji monastery banned foreigners after Frenchman soaped up in lovely new cypress-wood bath,...maybe problem is real, not just cartoon situation.

Luxury traveler has international and resort class W-style hotels or traditional Japanese inns, where guests are treated like *honjin* nobility. Average traveler will find everything in between, both W- (fine selection of mid-rate hotels since '64 edition when they just weren't), and J-styles.

In short, your choices are Western-style hotels of various levels from world leaders to closets, *ryokan* tradition-on-tatami with even greater range of choice to family-run *minshuku*, *kokumin-shukusha* People's Inns, *kokumin kyuka-mura* People's Rest Villages, *shukubo* temple inns, *pensions* family-run W-style bed & board, newest and cheapest gov't-subsidized International Villas, Youth Hostels, Business Hotels, Capsule Hotels, *gaijin*-houses and tent- or cabin-camping.

...Quite some choice.

*True, you need a certain amount of appetite,
and a certain capacity for adaptation.
But if you travel you don't lack the former,
and if you lack the latter you don't travel.*
—Fosco Maraini, *Secret Tibet*

CHOPSTICKS
WHAT & HOW TO EAT

SITTING down to our first Japanese-style meal–now more than likely, with *wa-shoku* boom worldwide, in our home city–we are struck by its sculptural or flower-arrangement quality, aesthetic of color. Eye combines with taste buds, to sensitize them in basic principle of Japanese cookery–while Occidental cuisine relies on olfactory sense to initiate appetite.

Western table setting gets by with one main dinner plate for main course, while Japanese uses at least two to four smaller dishes, and full course *kaiseki* requires dozen or more. Great care is given to preparing each dish–each artistically composed to blend into whole. Touches of color added with tiny orchids, dozens of red and green edible grasses, sprigs of green; all types of delicately cut raw vegetables garnish most dishes. New 'traditions' are 'discovered' or at least extemporized out of old ones. Different traditions are wed, like serving immense variety of finest French cuisine but with cooking times, sauces (we have refrigeration now so no need to camouflage rotting meat), and portion sizes (health-conscious) reduced and served as decorously as it is cooked, that is to say as decorously as *wa-shoku*. Result is *nouvelle cuisine*, as much Japanese as French and equally at home in brocade-textile capitals of Kyoto or Lyons, both of which claim parentage.

Those so-called Japanese dishes *sushi*, *sukiyaki* (pron s'ki-yaki) and *tempura* (temp'ra or even temp'lla according to one purist) long exemplified local cuisine to many westerners–and justifiably so, for that's all those rare overseas restaurants served. Meat in Japan was considered food only for 'barbarians' until Meiji Reformation of 1868, and tempura was introduced into Nagasaki by early Europeans in 1600s–yet local chefs have developed them into native masterpieces. Tray of arranged sukiyaki raw meats and vegetables brought to your table is suitable model for still life painting, while none but Japanese chefs can give such light crispy coating to deep-fried fish or shrimp tempura–diametrically contrasting to its original newspaper-served fish'n chips.

A FEAST FOR YOUR EYES TOO

HERE, LET'S LOOK at what kind of cuisine Japan offers. Top of line is *kaiseki*: exquisite food, magnificent ceramics, subtle incense, art piece and flowers in tokonoma, best of specific season. If you don't want full course, they have *mini-kaiseki*, fewer dishes, or still smaller lunch would be their *o-bentoh*. There are specialty houses that serve **beef** as steak, *teppanyaki* grill, *shabu-shabu* in broth, *sukiyaki* with veggies, Korean barbecued slices; **chicken** *mizutaki* with vegetables in broth, *yakitori* grilled on skewers; **seafood** as *sashimi* fresh raw hors d'oevre, *sushi* with *sashimi* slices on lightly vinegared rice patty; *fugu* poisonous blowfish, *tempura* deep fried in batter, *chiri* fish in soup, in *nabe* as *chiri* or *yosenabe* with fowl, veggies and *unagi* barbecued or steamed eel. We cover each of above then go into **BUDGET** dining including **noodles** hot, cold and ethnic; *donburi* rice in large bowl with toppings; *robata yaki* many things cooked in front of you; *kushi katsu* seafood, meats, veggies skewered, deep fried; **oden** stew.

In ordering, **teishoku** often 'modernized' to *setto*, 'set', is table d'hote of entré usually with soup, rice (or bread if W-style), side dishes—good buy.

Ippin-ryori, 'one bit' cuisine, or ordering individual portions á la carte, some mere tidbit samplers, to eventually make up multi-course meal. Ranges from gourmet repast in exquisite little geisha-type *ita-mae* counter restaurants off Kyoto alley to nibbles at little more than covered pushcart. Usually mainly as accompaniment to sake, *shochu* or beer.

KAISEKI, loosely used term, originally referred to special meals served at formal tea ceremony. However, it has come to mean any epicurean treat with finest and tastiest of season, at times also rarest. Japanese say *"shun no aji"*, taste of season. But that is not enough, its entire atmosphere is clothed with elegance, faint scent of incense, lights just so, flowers and hanging scroll to fit mood and then quiet efficient service as first tray with *kuchi-tori* tid-bit in translucent porcelain, chopstick holder may be beautiful mini camellia with stem; tiny *sakazuki* sake cup poised on tray; pale green leaf-shaped dish with domino-sized portions of different vegetables, fish cakes, salmon roe; deep square pottery dish reveals rose formed from lily-white slices of squid sashimi; peek into covered deep round bowl for cooked vegetables to see tiniest eggplant you've ever seen, single rare large bean, and lily root that melts in your mouth; next comes oval-shaped blue and white dish with delicate white fish carefully marinated with special wine sauce, broiled, with pink-tinted root ginger. By this time sake cups have been exchanged, conversation is flowing, and exotic dishes one after another in equally enchanting ceramics, baskets and lacquer, have quietly come and gone. One begins to feel more than satiated and wonders why because each has been such tiny serving.

Such dinner could cost $250-$500 per person, but we recommend that it is not necessary to go to special restaurant, and ideal is to combine it with overnite stay at *ryori ryokan* ('cuisine-inn'). Choose where you'd like to spend nite—Kamakura, hot springs like Hakone or Izu-Nagaoka, ancient capital Kyoto, or feudal splendor Kanazawa and choose one of ¥-L or LL. Here, after you're ushered into your rooms, go for stroll, or if dinner time is near, you are guided to large bath especially lavish in hot spring areas after dipping in which you change into comfort of fresh cotton kimonos provided to dine in complete relaxation.

However, there are many other representative Japanese dishes and hasty examination of eight to ten dishes that comprise rather elaborate meal discloses that basically dinners follow this Kaiseki tradition.

Wonderful custom that we should adopt worldwide: hot or cold *o-shibori* towel to wipe hands—men use it freely to wipe face, head, even neck. Small individual towels, usually on own trays and slightly perfumed, are brought to each guest—piping hot in winter and refreshingly cool in summer.

Japanese food "is not as different as all that": but it is different enough to make comparison with what we are used to difficult. Maurice Dreiser, culinary expert, was in Japan while our first edition was in writing. As we have done so often, we went to expert for advice and while sampling his *sake* martinis, asked his opinion of Oriental cuisine. He stressed that it is all (especially Japanese) so different in preparation from anything Western that it can not be given relative rating on our accepted standards. In short, there will be "some as likes it and some as don't". And among former, some will care for it only as taste sensation, and others will "go bamboo" (*i.e.* native) and swear off sitting in chairs for life. Whichever you are, to whatever degree, you will find satisfaction.

If you don't like Japanese food as steady diet you'll find international cuisine available everywhere at every price range.

Word of Warning Many people seem squeamish about ingredients used, "what, seaweed?...raw fish?...octopus?" Well 'seaweed'–called more politely kelp–is staple on many New England health menus; New Yorkers eat far more raw shellfish than Japanese; Germans and Dutch savor same raw tunny as Japanese lovingly call *maguro*; while *tako* (octopus) and *ika* (squid) are major items in Italian, Greek and other Mediterranean menus, etc, ad inf. Don't ask "What is it?" before you eat it, just eat and enjoy.

Neighbor of ours, for years master chef at Voisin in New York, was told by epicure-client that he could tell by taste every item that went into any dish, and that he could never be tricked into eating horse. Next time in he called chef out again, not merely to congratulate him for customarily superb meal, but to rave about never-surpassed entré and to demand to know what mystery treasure it was. Yep, you guessed it.

Another time while at Asia Institute graduate school in New York bunch of us students went out together to eat–five nationalities and colors in group of seven. Jay sat down to self-made Howard Johnson super chocolate-pecan-banana split, and as he raised his spoon, friend Lee Sun Bok of Korea gasped, "You're going to eat that?", turned green and ran out.

Some major dishes you will find yourself dipping into, usually with relish and satisfaction, are...

TEMPURA: May be easier to pronounce if you keep in mind that it comes form our word 'temple' (often spelled temp'lla by specialty houses) in its Portuguese version, for Japanese learned it from friars in Catholic 'temple' in Kyushu. It is, in short, fish and chips gone refined. Its oil is exceptionally fine rapeseed. Each house has its 'secret' mix, most change oil frequently. Most popular with Occidentals and most expensive is shrimp or prawn. In tempura bar, full dinner consists of series of deep-fries, several varieties of white fish, devilfish, lotus, vegetables, fried in front of you. Good tempura not cheap; dinner ¥3,500–20,000. Tho for lunch *teishoku* table d'hote is available at most J-restaurants ¥1,200+, and *tempura-udon* or *tempura-soba* might run ¥700-1500.

Ton-katsu (and following kushi-katsu are not strictly tempura, but are deep-fried, both also budget) is Japanization of deep fried pork (*ton*) breaded cutlets, by far tastiest of cutlet offerings of *bifu-katsu*, *tori-katsu*. In ¥-Budget house it may not be much more than ordinary cutlet, but -*katsu* specialty shops take succulent pork and clothe it delicately in soft breaded negligee. Order *hi-re* filet, no fat; dinner ¥-Tourist to ¥-Standard.

Kushi-katsu is ton-katsu and small bites of other meats, shellfish, shrimp and vegetables breaded, skewered, and deep-fried. Without skewer these become *furai* like *kaki furai* (fried oyster). Order by skewer or *setto*.

SHOJIN RYORI is simply Buddhist vegetarian fare. Standard side dishes, seemingly endless succession without entrée. Tempura is vegetable only, not even fish or fowl is permitted. Nourishing, filling and tasty and served in temple or temple-like surroundings. Variety of cooked dishes and range of taste amazes–not tasteless fodder we might expect. If 'meat' looks like beef, it is tofu soy bean 'steak'. Most use white rice (macrobiotic dieters have hard time here getting natural rice except in health food *shizen-shoku* restaurants). We take you to several, we advise budgeteers choose from lower two price offerings, those with good appetite take middle–only true trenchermen attempt top. Akin is **Fucha Ryori**, temple vegetable cuisine in Chinese style. Well known in Kansai is that by Uji's Obaku Temple.

SASHIMI & SUSHI. **Sashimi** is infamous raw fish fillet served as part of most every decent Japanese dinner. **Sushi** really means vinegared rice mixed with or served with something like fish or vegetable, and at its best sushi is bite-size blob of rice capped with sashimi, which most westerners think word means only this. **Nigiri-zushi**, "fistful"-sushi, is right name and of varieties, **Edo-zushi** (Tokyo style) refers to what everyone thinks of when they hear "sushi". Usually one sits down to counter of pure white cypress with lacquer tray before you, **sushi-ya-san** (sushi-house-master) grinning opposite behind array of fresh fish steaks and shellfish. You point to what you want and he slices off two fillets and makes up pair, of: **maguro*** (red tuna meat), white fish varieties **tai** (red snapper), **hirame** (flounder), which are generally not as tasty, then great array of shellfish: **aka-gai** (clam), redder and tastier than best cherrystone; **himo**, best part of aka-gai, **tori-gai** (cockle clam); and **uni** (succulent sea-urchin paste) which is best **uni-maki**, wrapped in laver (connoisseur's name for seaweed wafers); **ika** (squid); **tako** (octopus, boiled, never raw); and of course **ebi** (boiled shrimp). Others are: **mirugai** (clam), **kai-bashira** (scallop), **saba** (mackerel), **iwashi** (sardine), **ama-ebi** (raw sweet shrimp), **odori** (live & still 'dancing' shrimp), **anago** (broiled sea eel), **unagi** (broiled lake eel), **ikura** (salmon roe, red caviar), **kazunoko** (herring roe), **ume-jiso** (plum and beefsteak-plant leaves) and **shinko** (pickles). To show your expertise, first ask for **tamago**, which is little paddy of steamed egg omelet and its delicacy indicates quality of sushi-ya-san's hand. Sake or beer go perfectly and meal is popular as **sake no tomo** (friend of wine).

(* Tuna has different names by age-size: up to 1m long is *shinko*; 1-2m 'teenage virgin' *yokowa* is supreme taste experience, too delicate for vinegared-rice of sushi; over 2m is *hissage* and full-grown monster is all-popular sushi delicacy *maguro* while *toro*, also sushi delicacy, is fatty white meat from maguro underbelly).

oshi-zushi	rice in odd shapes like fans, flowers, made in molds.
hako-zushi	made in one rectangular box abt 10 inches long, topped with vinegared fish, e.g. saba zushi.
maki-zushi	rolled in seaweed with unagi, eggs, etc. in center. When cut, from 11/2 to 4 inches in diameter.
chirashi-zushi	vinegared rice 'pilao' in bowl, mixed w/ various condiments.

Recently, te-maki hand-roll or cone of laver around rice, with carifoniya-maki California roll, avocado & shrimp in laver cone, is popular new form.

Sashimi is placed on rice ball with dab of *wasabi*, green horse radish, sandwiched between to play part of our tabasco. You dip it (properly with fingers rather than chopsticks) into shallow dish of soy (called *murasaki* by sushi gourmet) and to get most out of it flip onto your tongue upside-down—fish down. Before changing to another type take nip of ginger served you to clear your tongue. Fish is safe. Dangers you hear of apply to river fish, which Japanese don't eat raw. Clams are taken from clear water area. Jay eats everything, anywhere and has nibbled at sidewalk stalls from Mount Ararat to Mount Fuji and never got ill—until in New York had seven dozen cherrystones in gov't-inspected clamhouse and on second day back in Japan several weeks later turned pure mongol color with Raritan Bay hepatitis.

If you like sushi, as most of us who try it find we do, you will find it hard to move away from counter before you have polished off several thousand yen worth and you can easily work your bill up over ¥10,000— especially at sushiya in ¥-L hotel, in one of which trio of newly arrived unwary friends ran up bill of over $400—and it was only good but not great. Best, and rather reasonable, for real sushi gourmets is in Tokyo's Tsukiji fish market area (which see p.1209) and go early. Sushi can be expensive if you eat at counter and select a la carte. Good way is to order by tray of 7-10 pcs: *Jo-nigiri* (¥2,500+); *nami* (¥1,000-2,000); or *moriawase* mix of nigiri, maki, and hako-zushi (under ¥l,000). In small shops, station and department store arcades, budgeteer can order it by tray as usually shown in plastic models in window, between ¥1,-¥3,000 nice and tasty lunch portion.

Cartoon in *New Yorker* on 'Sushi Spinoffs' suggests: '*Grashi*, grass and leaves in season'–joke's on them for grass and leaves (as sashimi without rice) is served regularly; and '*Chishi* raw chicken' is available as sashimi at our favorite Kyoto hole-in-wall **Sankaku** (stuff yourself multi-course *ippin* chicken dinner under ¥2500), both as white meat and liver (cock and hen quite different). Red beef and liver sashimi at Korean restaurants; *sakura* is horsemeat sashimi for which see TOKYO SHITAMACHI (old town). But bear sashimi sometimes offered up north is to be avoided for possible trichinosis.

Tea is free, unlimited, with all Japanese, Chinese and Korean food.

> "*Happiness derives from the verb 'to happen'.*
> *Happiness is to be found simply from observing what happens.*
> *If you cannot be happy at the prospect of lunch,*
> *you are not likely to find happiness anywhere.*
> *What happens is happiness.*" —Robert Johnson, *Transformation*

COOK IT YOURSELF

SUKIYAKI: **and other meat dishes cooked at table, seasoned with salt or soy sauce.** Large platter of colorful array of meat and vegetables; soy sauce seasoning. Basic ingredients: thinly sliced beef, preferably marbled, tofu, Japanese leeks, mushrooms, *shirataki*-vermicelli, *mitsuba*-water cress.

As soon as ingredients are cooked in iron pan with light sauce, everyone helps self to own taste–rare, medium or well done. Hostess adds more meat, vegetables, seasoning, sweetening to taste.

Raw egg is placed in small bowl for each guest. Beat egg and dip your hot food in it. Many may have aversion to raw egg, but it is cooked by heat of meat and serves to cool off, as well as flavor hot beef. Warm *sake* is usually served with *sukiyaki*. Rice in individual bowls comes after few rounds of *sukiyaki;* but many prefer to have rice from beginning.

Meat dishes have become Japanese in past century, done here in ways derived from whale cooking and 'illegal' game cookery of sportsmen hunters. To our taste, best sukiyaki by far is wild boar, *ino-shishi*. On menu as *botan-nabe* and available November thru March only, tho some places now serve domesticated boar year-round.

-YAKI: most dish names so suffixed (*note*, not prefixed) are broiled or barbecued meat, and predominantly beef.

Teppan-yaki is choice beef chunks grilled, usually in front of you to your beef preference. Rocky Aoki made famous in U.S. with his chain of fancy knife-wielding cooks at Beni Hana who give grand show as they cut up steaks being grilled. Besides tender piece of steak, one can order shrimps, scallops, fish and vegetables, seasoned with salt, prepared on large grill with chef on one side and guests facing. Dip in sauce with citron. Price also ranges ¥2,-7,000, with lower in small teppan-yaki specialists, higher in foreigner-catering steak houses, hotels. *Bata-yaki* (butter), *oil-yaki* are pan-broiled variations on teppan-yaki, using butter or cooking oil respectively. *Ami-yaki* is broiled over *ami* (screen), and *shio-yaki* is same rubbed with salt rather than dipped in barbecue sauce.

Okariba-yaki involves various game fowl, is probably original of all
-*yaki*. Restaurants specializing in it go in for gamey decor and special
cooking utensils such as novelty spades and plowshares for pans and grills.
Most offerings are seasonal and best variety comes November thru March.

Okonomi-yaki is true exception to -*yaki* family. Literally 'as you like
it-yaki', is simply do-it-yourself chow mein-omelet. Popular with drinkers
and young folk apartying. Sit around grill table in bibs, chuck on noodles,
or pancake-mix, plus vegetables, scrambled egg, then basic taste of *buta*
(pork); or *niku* (beef); *ebi* (shrimp); *ika* (squid); *tako* (octopus); *yasai*
(vegetable), heavy on Chinese cabbage; *modan* 'modern' W-style and play
house. Inexpensive and generally tasty no matter what you do to it. Kansai
is better than Kanto; best is Hiroshima–thin and light like crepes.

Genghis Khan is Mongol shish kebab. But where Persian Warriors
shivved their meat on rapiers, Mongols took their helmets off, capped fire
with them and while burning out chiggers, broiled sheep slabs on outside.
It is popular barbecue dish now in Japan, sometimes done over special
"helmet" broilers, often just over grid, using both sheep and beef and in
some places very unMuslim pork. Local variations vary as much as spelling
of Gh/Ch/Jingis, but local pronunciation is Chingis. From ¥2,000 healthy
portion in beer halls, to ¥4,-7,00 for dinner in hotels and specialty houses.

YAKI-NIKU means **Korean** cooking, almost nationalized it's so popular
–tasty field in itself involving spicy-sauces with barbecues, yaki-tori variations and original hormone cookery. Cook it yourself at your table on grid
over open flame. Rice and noodle dishes look like Japanese or Chinese but
are highly seasoned. And famed Korean pickle, *kimchi*, is experience in
itself–try some and henceforth kosher dills something to put on banana split.
More and better for your money than any other national food, from budget
on up–especially for carnivores. Best with stein of *nama-beeru*, draft beer.

Rice dish advised is *bibimba*, rice with chopsuey of vegetable topping,
served with small bowl of clear soup with kelp, which some like Sumi drink
separately, but most Koreans and Jay pour over rice to eat Korean style with
spoon, not sticks.

Meats come raw, BBQ them yourself at table, order in portions of type:

rosu	roast beef, lean	*jo-rosu*	roast beef, fatty
mino	tripe	*jo-mino*	better quality
shinzo	heart	*calbi*	rib meat
reba	liver–also often available delectably raw		
yuké	steak tartar, best anywhere, with raw egg or quail egg, eat as is.		

YAKI-TORI means 'broiled bird' on small bamboo spit in individual
portion. Usually chicken, but traditionally poor man's dish of sparrow, as
still at expensive tatami restaurants where served whole as delicacy–like
froglegs in France going from starvation ration to Rue de la Paix. But can be
almost any meat, BBQ'd. Most yaki-tori-ya are counters where gas flame-
or charcoal-broiled in front of you. Always tasty, dipped in sauce of soy
and spices or plain salted. In choice shops gorge yourself, with sufficient
beer or sake on side, for under ¥3,000. Where ordinary Japanese office
gang goes, down back alleys or in drinking areas, you'll pay ¥100-150 per
stick, find it hard to pack away one hotel dinner tab's worth for whole gang.

Kashira (head), *kawa* (skin), *nankotsu* (cartilage), *reba*, *kimo* (liver), *shiro*
(intestine), *tan* (tongue), *shinzo* or *hatsu* (heart), *hinadori* (chicken), *negi* (with
scallions), *ginnan* (gingko nuts); ¥300 for *wakadori-no-momoyaki* (roast chicken
leg), ¥180 *tomorokoshi* (corn-on-cob), priced between last two are non-flying sit-
down dishes *maguro*-(tuna)*sashimi*, *hiyashi*-(cold) *tomato*, *eda-mame* beans
(often served alone with beer), *shitake* (mushrooms); *nama-yasai* (raw veggies).

Hormone-ryori, hormone cookery, is private parts of pig, tripe, etc.
There are some places which specialize in literally, yaki-tori and they spit whole sparrow in ancient style, as still seen as far afield as Afghanistan.

Kaba-yaki doesn't taste like exception, but like some oil-rich game or fowl. It is one of tastiest summer pick-me-up dishes anywhere, and it's eel. Lacquer-box portion will run ¥1,200-4,000. *Unagi-don* comes on bowl of rice (¥1,000-2,500). *Unagi-teishoku*, dinner built around kaba-yaki entre, runs ¥1,500-5,000 depending on size of eel portion and extra dishes.

NABE or earthen-pot cookery is entire class of original dishes which are cold weather favorites, usually cooked right at table enabling hostess to join party, or when eating out makes it more like house party.

Mizutaki is favorite chicken nabe in private homes, autumn and winter. With Chinese cabbage, *shitake* mushroom, tofu, bamboo shoots, shredded *konyaku* (vermicelli) cooked in *konbu* (kelp) *dashi* (sauce). When cooked, dip into sauce of grated daikon and ponzu citron-soy sauce.

Yosenabe: *yose* means to bring together. Starting with mizutaki ingredients, best from land, usually fowl and sea—prawns, oysters, clams, scallops, squid (or abalone, crabs, lobsters)—are skillfully mixed in this chowder. When it starts to simmer, help yourself, dipping in sauce. Soup is delicious. Keep adding ingredients to pot. Electric cooker may be used.

Special variations may rate their own names: *chanko-nabe* is heavy on calories, vegetables, meant for sumo wrestlers who want to pile on pounds. *Chiri-nabe* uses only fish, light meat, and vegetables; adds name of main fish, as *fugu-chiri (tet-chiri)*, which uses 'poisonous' blowfish; *tai-chiri* with tai (sea bream). *Ishikari nabe* uses salmon, specialty of north Japan. All are filling, tasty and moderate, running ¥3,-7,000 at first class restaurants and *mizutaki* specialists for full dinner. Neighborhood noodlery will turn out amazingly tasty yose-nabe portion, ala carte, for under ¥1500.

Shabu-shabu dip paper thin slices of beef into pot of seasoned stock, in which mushrooms, tofu, and other vegetables are cooking. Almost always served at teppanyaki, sukiyaki and mizutaki houses. If we're having good beef, it seems waste to be 'washing' in stock, tho it has subtle taste.

ORIGINAL FASTFOODS   BUDGET & PILGRIM

PLASTIC MODELS grace windows (prices accompany, usually in Arabic numerals but sometimes Japanese) outside cheaper budget or tourist restaurants. New family-style adaptations of US chains are replacing these with photo-menus. All of which make us instant literates: for models, signal waitress outside and point, and for menu pix just point and smile

NOODLES: Cheapest food in Japan, old '30s movie *Marco Polo* saw Gary Cooper-as-Marco Polo introduced to this poor man's food in China, rice being far more expensive–and thus Italia got spaghetti. Supposedly, he also brought back chopsticks, tied them together to make dinner fork. (Ancient Romans, like Persians, ate with flat spoon). *Soba* is brown buckwheat noodles; *udon,* refined white wheat noodles, thicker, and *somen* is either material, extra fine. *Ramen* is Chinese style noodles, in soup with toppings, mainly pork. *Te-uchi-* prefix means handmade (*te-*) on premises, any type of noodle. *Cha-soba* is tea-green, tea-flavored.

Soba, udon available universally, even on many train platforms for quick snack, ¥170-600, business districts, station undergrounds, department store gourmet alleys, and in bar areas at nite from pushcarts (hot only), etc. Cheapest on or in or under JR stations.

Soba is served cold to be dipped in *dashi*-sauce, or hot in *dashi*-soup. *Dashi* is mix of kelp (Kansai-style), or *katsuobushi* bonito flakes (Tokyo-Kanto), with soy sauce and *mirin* sweet sake, adding to taste bit of *wasabi* hot green radish, chopped scallion, grated *daikon* white radish and raw quail egg, etc. Noodle shop's dashi is its main capital, secret passed down thru generations of chefs. And if you come across place selling *shinshu-soba,* noodles of North Japan, they are best–as we will see visiting Shinshu.

Cold soba is served *seiro* plain, more commonly *zaru-* on bamboo slats topped with slivers of *nori* seaweed, dip in *dashi* sauce, above; as cheap as ¥200 at station stand, or ¥500 better places. *Tororo* or *yama-kake* grated mountain potato, like poi, said good for energy and male virility, and may be ordered hot as well, taken only with spot of wasabi and quail egg. *Ten-zaru,* cold zaru with side of tempura, with its own dip, usually most expensive on menu, often ¥1200-1800; *chikara* means 'strength' and is good pick-me-up; *hiyashi somen* cold thin wheat & buckwheat noodles, finest called *haru-samé,* spring rain; *hiyashi ramen* is cold 'China' or chow mein, and *hiya-mugi* cold medium wheat noodle–either taste best splashed with vinegar.

Hot soba or *udon* in dashi-soup, to which you may sprinkle bit of *shichimi,* seven spices, from shaker, is prefixed in name by topping, thus:

arare-	scallops
kake -	green onions, simplest and cheapest hot noodle dish
kamonan-ban	literally 'duck' but actually chicken chunks
kare-	mild curry topping
kitsune-	'fox', wafers of deep-fried tofu slices (same enveloping sushi-rice is *inari-zushi*)
nameko-	mushroom, specialty houses only
natto-	fermented soybean, smelly & local Tokyo, 'health food'
nishin-	herring, generous dried-broiled fillet whole fish, no end
niku-	pieces of thin sliced beef
okame-	fish cake, and veggies
sansai-	mountain vegetables & herbs, superb topped extra with *tororo* mountain potato.
tanuki-	with strips of fried tofu
tempura-	deep-fried whole shrimp, tail sticks from batter as handle
tsukimi-	'moon viewing', egg lightly poached by heat of noodles
yama-imo-	grated mountain yam (potato).

Good soba shop offers teapot of *soba-yu,* very hot water in which your soba was boiled, to pour into remaining dashi for cold soba, drink as soup–delicious & nutritious. *Yaki-soba* is fried chop suey-style, mixed seafood vegetable topping. Many now offer larger *teishoku* of noodle dish plus rice side, or combination of several smaller noodle dishes–*see* showcase outside..

Ton-katsu is Japanization of deep-fried pork (*ton*) breaded cutlets, by far tastiest of cutlet offerings of *bifu-katsu, tori-katsu.* Even in ubiquitous back alley ¥-Budget house it is usually good. But *-katsu* specialty shops take succulent pork and clothe it delicately in soft breaded negligee; dinner ¥-Tourist to ¥-Standard.

Kushi-katsu is ton-katsu and small bites of other meats and vegetables skewered, breaded and deep-fried. Without skewer these same foods become *"furai"*, like *"kaki furai"* (fried oyster).

ROBATA-YAKI is another great budget cuisine, where worker can dine on fine foods prepared before him and wash down with mug of draught beer. But it is highly appreciated now by gourmets and some simple robataya-sans have taken on airs and prices, so before entering judge probable price by neighborhood. Not budget, superb robataya are **Inakaya** shops in Roppongi, Tokyo–no working man's haunt–they are as expensive

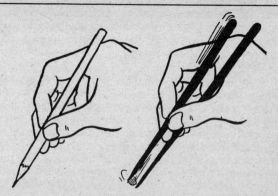

CHOPSTICKS used on most foods–sushi, yakitori, oden fingers ok. Simple to handle. Grasp one as you would pencil, but well back. This is one you will manipulate. Then insert other in base of crotch between thumb and forefinger and press rigid with your ring finger. Tap ends on table to line up tips and you're ready to go. Don't tense or squeeze, relax.

Most young natives cannot use them correctly: at home may use oversized sugar tong on spring; at school use ridiculous *spork*, soup spoon with shallow tines cut in end –too short to use as fork and leaks as spoon.

Japanese fumble too, use rice bowl held in left hand as safety net for food to drop into harmlessly, which in pinch is raised to lips to shovel food in with chopsticks–which in Japanese are *hashi* (hurriers, after Chinese *gwai-tse* or quick-fellows), pidgin *chopchop* means hurry, also food, thus chopsticks.

Also used in this text as section title for WHERE TO EAT.

as any luxe hotel restaurant, but still worth every yen for superb quality and infinite selection, showman-like sonorous service–and English menu, some waiters. Other station area or drinking area robata-yá absurdly cheap yet good and great fun for operatic service.

age-tofu	deep-fried bean curd		
eda-mame	soy bean in pod; pop and munch, best with beer		
korokke	croquette		
moro-kyu	cucumber topped with miso paste		
niku-jaga	meat & boiled potatoes		
sanma	charcoal broiled (smoked) mackerel		
shishamo (komochi)	smelt with roe		
hiya-yakko	cold tofu	horenso	spinach
hiyashi-tomato	cold tomato	yasai	vegetable(s)
yaki-tofu	fried tofu	hirame	halibut

RICE DISHES: Following are all budget and easy to get at neighborhood restaurants and soba shops; *o-nigiri* rice balls can also be bought at convenience stores and department stores.

Gohan means cooked rice, but can also be used to mean meal. When wanting second helping at meal ask for '*okawari*'.

Donburi is large donburi bowl of steamed rice topped with tempura (*ten-don*), unagi (*una-don*), or pork cutlet (*katsu-don*) with tasty sauce or with sukiyaki-like mix of vegetables and other ingredients: (*oyako-don*) parent-child, chicken & egg; (*tanin-don*) strangers, meat & egg; (*niku-don*) beef & veg etc.

Kamameshi is like Mexican paella without so many ingredients and each person's order is cooked and served in individual iron pots with thick wooden lids–mini-*kama* just like one grandma used over her old wood-burning oven. It takes some time since it is cooked to order. Enjoy essence of best in season: fresh chestnut (*kuri-meshi*), bamboo (*takenoko-*), others. Our favorite places, ¥-T, **Suishin** in Hiroshima & Tokyo, its girls in *kasuri* kimono, order sashimi and other dishes while waiting for rice to cook; in Tokyo, **Torigin** in Nishi Ginza is tops for atmosphere & taste.

Ocha-zuke is just steamed rice on which you plop your brine pickles (served with all Japanese food, even cheapest domburi) and pour your tea over it. Order this in nicer places and you get various sliced seaweed and kelp toppings and other condiments for rice.

Zosui is boiled rice cooked in broth; often part of mizutaki or other nabe dishes using liquid stock left in pan after.

O-nigiri (*o-musubi*), different from sushi as is not vinegared, but 'rice ball' plain or wrapped in *nori* seaweed lavers and filled with *umeboshi* (pickled plum), *kombu* (kelp); *katsuo* (shavings of dried bonito), excellent for budget picnic lunch, mostly about ¥100 each 'ball'.

ODEN: Stew pot full of tempura, steamed fish patties and vegetable chunks. Usually at sidewalk pushcart or tiny hole-in-wall, also in weekend campgrounds or hiking parks (we hike up to Koza-no Taki falls from our house sunday morns to breakfast on oden, 5 or 6 big chunks each at ¥80 apiece). Just point and mine host will serve into plate, or some are smaller with toothpicks or bamboo skewers stuck in, which you reach over and help yourself to. Well-cooked, thus hygienic even off pushcart.

NATURAL FOODS: Japan is slowly recognizing need to change and organically grown foods are becoming increasingly available with even some department stores opening up organic food (*shizenshoku*) sections. Shizenshoku restaurants are few and difficult to find. Being inexpensive and with rents what they are, many seem to give up after year or so. We list some that we know of in each locality, but always telephone to make certain they still exist. Good book in English published in 1983, now out of print is *Dining Naturally in Japan* by D Bruce Walker. Ms Yasuko Torii worked with him, has since published her own *Matomona Tabemono Guide* (Guide to Real Eating) Japanese, revised 1989. Two health food chains—Natural House, often with restaurant, and Anew are fast multiplying.

Some terms that you might need are: natural food restaurant or shop, *shizenshoku no restoran* or *o-mise*; brown rice, *genmai*; organic farming, *yuuki nogyo*; no pesticide used, *mu-noyaku*.

This only scratches surface of Japan's epicurean world. But if you got down this far you'll have no problem going on yourself.

COFFEE HOUSES

UNIQUE LOCAL development of old world import, written in ideographs *Kissa-ten* for red-tea shop (as opposed to local green tea). Tho ideographs 'coffee' sometimes used, katakana *ko-hi* more common. Brazil shipped quantities of free coffee to initiate addiction. First coffee house **Brazil** opened off Ginza by 1912 Berkeley alumnus HATA Kanzo, later prof of English, aesthetics in Kobe. Our '64 edition had numerous coffee houses featuring programmed record concerts, even live string quartets, jazz combos—one offered 5 combos daily–coffee menus of many pages to choose your own bean or mix to be ground before you. Always relatively expensive, cuppa cost as much as lunch, and no free refills (tho Morning Service with mild 'American' free refills catching on). Cakes often excellent, but sandwiches soggy midgets.

Ko-cha 'red' tea (after color of liquid, not leaf) also served, order 'milk tea' or 'lemon tea', former darker as to be cut with 'milk'–as often mini-pitcher of pure cream as sealed-plastic eyecup of artificial *Creap*.

Still great institution, still expensive except at breakfast '*morning service*' when full syphon of tea or 'bottomless' cup of coffee plus thick toast with jam, perhaps hard-boiled egg or cereal, some fruit, cost about same as normal cuppa alone: ¥250–500. Commonly found in business districts, cheapest near stations, good ones near now-ubiquitous Sports or Health Centers where office workers work out from 6:30 before going to jobs.

Coffee in ¥-L international hotel lobby will run over $10 per cup, not that good. Many use lobbies for business or marriage negotiation rendezvous, so it is space charge mostly.

Menus list variety. Local specialties are 'blend' which means house blend of their favorite beans brewed rich; 'American' is simpler and brewed lighter, US-style. Others will be bean name: Blue Mountain so popular in Japan that Kobe coffee company bought whole mountain. Espresso and Capuccino not popular yet, just becoming known; Turkish notably absent. Bad cup hard to find. Coffee House **Hanafusa** in Kyoto (from Shijo-Kawaramachi, first alley W up, first bend L) old style coffee menu as thick as Chinese menu, 350, all great–'American' here means w/ice cream, mocca is chocolate mix, ¥400-700.

ABOUT SAKE

PRONOUNCED *sah-kay*, 'tween 'whacky ' and 'hockey', but *socky* is close enough. Properly called *nihon-shu* or *sei-shu* to differentiate from other alcoholic drinks all of which can be called sake. Western hooch is called *yo-shu* W-sake. You've heard much about this notorious rice wine, which technically is beer. Or have you already tried some at home? If so, you probably drank it cold—which despite what some 'experts' say is strictly postwar style, tho only best natural brews should be so taken. Traditionally drunk warmed to avoid hangover, quite hot for cheaper alcohol-added stuff, tepid about body temperature for better brews, best OK cold.

There are three common grades: *tokkyu* (special), *ikkyu* (first class) and *nikyu* (2nd). Difference is alcohol content, 16 to 12%, and thus tax. Some of best rural sake is only 2nd class; country folk are thrifty and in no hurry. When ordering, specify grade. Also differs in taste by brand and region–not to concern you here beyond saying there are 2 'tastes', like wines: *amakuchi* sweet mouth and *karakuchi* dry. Specify that much, or in small town ask for *ji-zake*, local brew, always rewarding as usually naturally fermented *jun-mai-shu*, real rice sake–most big brands now artificial blends with industrial alky. New super-grades, usually of limited circulation, include top two differing in being made from inner 'seed'of grain, *ginjo* from inner 40% and *daiginjo* from center 20%–outer part used for regular sake. Found in special restaurants. By 1.8 litre bottle *daiginjo* runs ¥10,000-up.

As we travel, especially offbeat, we find local brews, often served in old breweries, and guide you to where old cedar ball hangs outside, sign that new batch is ready to be drunk. Yes 'new'. Sake brews 20 days, is not aged beyond next crop. Sooner drunk is better, smoother. Chinese age it. We closed up house in Iran 1969, put household in storage. Came back in '75, hauled all out; found 0.7 liter porcelain bottle of best *tokkyu* Kiku Masamune from Nada-Kobe. Served it warm in proper *saka-zuke* thimbles, soon had friends giggling, staggering. It was high, tinted yellow like Chinese *bai-gar*, just as potent. It is said that stored in clear glass it wouldn't mellow thus. 1987 Japan saw first aged vintage sake on sale in new style sake bars offering *ji-zake* from all over.

Nada area E-end of Kobe, traditionally best, but not all old trads live—most big brands now assembly line blends. Top are little family brands from Shikoku and northernmost Tohoku—aficionados draw swords in favor of either. We take you to local breweries where cedar ball hangs. Tokyo has bars specializing in local brews: best is **Sasashu**. Jay was led here many years ago by Japanese writer friend, lost it, rediscovered it thru Rick Kennedy's great *Good Tokyo Restaurants*. JR Yamanote el or Marunouchi subway to Ikebukuro, big intersection with Marui OIOI, cross N, up, first alley to L past first alley in, it's on R. Till 10, X-sun, hol.

Prepare at home, fill half-pint or smaller bottle (Japanese use chinaware, sold abroad with matching thimble-cups for use as, s'help us, set of flower vase and salt cellar), place bottle in pot of water, as double boiler, heat on low fire till barely hot for wrist, like fixing baby bottle. Cools to perfection as poured. Drink before it cools. If no *sake* cup, use shot glass.

Sake is camaraderie drink, never imbibed solo. Japanese are not solitary drinkers. Friends drinking together pour for each other, even with beer, so they never let one get glass half empty–tough on sociable teetotaler who wants to fake it all nite with half-full glass. Japanese acquaintance or host, if over 50 years old, may offer you his *sake* cup for one drink in which case you hold it, have it filled, slurp-drain it, wipe lip point, return it and fill it for him. Japanese used to do this in days of first edition much as we tip glasses together, tho most today realize many 'furriners' consider custom 'dirty' or 'barbaric'. What the hell, it's alcohol. Now everyone tips glasses, making great to-do about first glass so take it easy on start. If dealing with elderly gentleman-type, or senior geisha, offer your cup first and you'll conquer crowd. And never let companion's cup go empty; grab bottle and serve. If he is much senior, defer by using two hands. Same when receiving hold cup with two hands–but only I repeat for senior, and not to gals. *Never* allow your glass to be filled just setting on table, if you don't hold it up at least quickly place forefinger against it. Some bars use sake in cocktails, Martini variations. It packs slow, smooth, accumulative karate-chop wallop.

SHOCHU is another native drink. When Jay worked in Tokyo in '50s it was mostly laborer's drink, as hardest workers come from Kyushu, its home. Drunk often in *shochu*-beer boilermaker. It's sort of primitive vodka, like Korean soja, made of variously rice grain or sweet potato, most anything, but fermenting agent is rice. In '64 we advised keep clear of it, makes for smelly drunk. Now it has been much refined, is cutting into W-style whiskies and wines in yukky yuppy drink mixed with sweeteners, called *chu-hai,* or shochu-highball. We'd rather be depth-bombed. Good drink is *oyu-wari,* diluted with hot water and slice of lemon.

WINES of local grape run fine to horrid. Most ancient *sake* records–which are as old as oldest historical records, being one and same–tell us it was once made from both rice and various fruits. Latter phased out 1,000 years ago. Now Japan makes fine wines, especially in Yamanashi area (where we visit some good tastin'-tables), but nowhere in enough quantities, nor as cheap as California, etc. Imports dominate market, but not brands you'll know, as *Mise en botteil dans notre caves* on label (and almost no one here reads French) can just mean our old hole was where it was bottled (and if "you knows a better 'ole, go to it"). Legally any bottle containing as little as 5% local vintage can be labeled 'domestic', no further details on label. Much of it is cheapest Algerian squeezins hauled in by tanker, topped with local scent. Decent to good imported brands readily available at good restaurants, but not at prices reflecting strength of yen. Improving, however slowly.

In all, in 1990 Japanese averaged 102 litres of alcohol per person.

*Being married in Japan is like
keeping a cow for a pet in Texas*
— Wally Gayda, nite club proprietor, in *View*

GOING IT ALONE
—FOR HIM (*by* Jay)

BACK IN FIRST or second century of our era, Chinese ambassador visiting this land of Wa left us what is probably first written account of Japan. He seemed impressed, among other things, that "women are faithful and not jealous" and that they far outnumbered men. Another Chinese traveler century or so later registers in Chinese Imperial Annals that Wa women "are not loose in morals or jealous" while another states that "Wa are not lewd". All early travelers mention women favorably, seem well conversant with simplicity of their costume, which was then but slip-on belted poncho or sack dress. All also note general Japanese fondness for liquor and absence of theft. And all stress that when woman was ruling, as often happened, there was also absence of violence and war.

Liquor brands have changed in ensuing two millennia, but that's about all, for women are back in control—except of course that there are more foreign men visitors all of whom seem to be writing. (And what all seem to miss is that in international marriage there appear to be more foreign women marrying Japanese men now than our men getting Japanese gals.)

Basically, Japanese are more South Pacific island culturally than Asian and their morals are classic Polynesian. Where we lived in Hiroshima area Inland Sea village was straight out of *Coming of Age in Samoa*. They were not appreciably affected by later import of puritanical Chinese Confucian superstructure. Japanese have usually taken licentiousness in stride. This does not mean that dashing young bachelor can expect to land in Japan with his "*How To--*" book for studs and within hours be lolling in some Tea House of Crescent Moon buried in sloe-eyed nymphomaniacs. Wa woman is compliant when she cares to be, but notoriously independent. She may be noted for her sylph-like figure and this she can attribute to her Spartan diet. But no matter how spare her diet, she still eats. In these tightest little islands property is scarce and expensive, which means her rent is high if she can afford to live away from family. As she usually can't, there are adequate well-furnished quarters available by hour or overnite.

If this sounds crassly commercial, materialistic—it is. Suave, debonair man of world might with some luck chance upon fair damsel in USA or Europe of standing and tastes similar to his own. (But even this is going to cost money.) Here he has almost no chance, for such gal must be financially independent. It's not so much that few young women in Japan are that independent—it's just that almost no one of her sex is. And younger gals are finding, according to late nite TV, that such independence comes only by mixing business with pleasures. Japan is poor, housing is third-world class —trade surplus stays outside in US T-notes, CDs, Hawaiian hotels.

You may not think so judging from prices of drinks and hotels and fantastic number of cabarets, bars, restaurants and other places of commercialized pleasure—numerous, true, but small. All these places are stage settings, actually built of plasterboard and paper. Our young stud hopes to buy things requiring large sums. But he cannot afford house with swimming pool and limousine to live like some movie star. Thus he flings away his pennies on those things pennies can buy; he is voracious consumer of nicknacks, souvenirs and perishable goods. He can afford nites out in bars with papier-maché décor copied from papier-maché décor of latest movie set, and he can hail clean taxi or even chauffeured limousine (with tiny letters discretely noting it is 'for hire') and dress in snazzy suit and for just one evening imagine he is *"Aran Deron"*—that all this world's his stage.

Most theatrical of Japanese arts is woodblock print, in Japanese, *Ukiyo-e* (floating world-pictures). As floater yourself you may wonder what has happened to conspicuous settings for these prints, **Gay Quarters**—('gay' in its classical usage, with no sense of homosexuality, which latter meaning has taken over only since our first edition)—and their lovely women. Most famed of these quarters was Tokyo's Yoshiwara, next to Asakusa, almost completely leveled by WW II air raids. There were many such areas. Those in Kyoto retained their woodblock-print qualities. However, more destructive to its architecture than air raids has been anti-prostitution law which went into effect in three stages in 1950s. Significantly each degree of enforcement took effect on consecutive April Fool's Days, 1955,6,7. New equal rights for women law took effect same date 1986... tradition.

Law has had little effect on nitelife. True, many girls were 'reformed' with much publicity. But for most part law only served to force trade underground and, at least in Tokyo, largely into hands of thugs. Many girls married—they could bring handsome dowries to their farmer or small shopkeeper husbands as well as knowledge of world men valued—for were they not actresses from romantic big city. Besides, there's old saw even in English that "whores make good wives."

Many girls however were not so lucky, especially younger ones, who 'reformed' into waitresses in restaurants, bars and inns, often in their very same old houses. Since that generation passed on to domesticity, new recruits have flocked in, openly interviewed on TV admitting to wanting money to buy their own condo flat or get set up in business while they can still put down some natural capital. Exchange one type of short term real estate for longer term. Big Brother helps keep it under control, tho. Best clients of those famous special massage parlors are big businesses, even government offices, which must entertain VIP visitors in highly personalized style. These gals reputedly take good care of themselves. Flashier-dressed English speakers often seen in top international hotel lobbies. At other end of spectrum, high school girls are highly experimental and rarely have enough cash to buy doodads fashion dictates, so... And older men have certain charisma, especially teachers etc.

Old Gay Quarters have little changed. Tokyo's Asakusa is still theatrical center, olde Broadway. It's exciting, worth visit. Being lower class, economically, most bars post their prices outside. This proved so effective that more and more bars nationwide took to do so till it became almost universal except for expense account bars. Cabarets also advertise price of "one set," which includes specified drink, usually beer or local whisky and water (in 1964 called *high-borru* but in '80s *mizu-wari*, 'with water'), ubiquitous peanut platter and tip to hostess. Usually this also includes her lemonade, but if she asks you for drink that's extra. Note time limits on sets, *sahvisu taimu* is early eve and prices rise as it gets later: look for smaller numerals like time schedule figures, for time limits. "Set" is higher of course in place with English-speaking girls. Education and skill must be rewarded. In recent years it has been outstripped (sorry) by Shinjuku's Kabuki-cho area.

Asakusa is theater. It is full of movie houses and stage shows. Japanese claim to have imported burlesque, which they call *sutorippu* (obvious loan word), after war. Well, as we discuss in ON STAGE, according to Shinto book of genesis when Sun Goddess hid away in cave she was enticed out by sound of other gods enjoying themselves over raunchy hoochy-kooch being wriggled by goddess of ritual dance. Connoisseur of strip tease *must* experience kimono-strip. It is hilarious. As for western-costume strip, gal rips everything off sans 'tease', or just as often starts out bare.

Walking around Asakusa or any hot spring spa town, you'll undoubtedly be approached by dashing young theatrical agent (note his dark glasses) representing some experimental 'off Broadway' troupe. He will offer limited reservations at some sort of checkerboard affair (black and white squares and talk like that), slightly extra if you care to unlimber your camera. He may even offer to sell you some spare film, either unexposed or fully developed. 'Shows' and 'Photo Studios' are safe. But such invitations to 'Special Bar' are better left alone, where audience is invited to drop trousers and join show. In latter cases gals are usually Filipinas or Southeast Asians on cultural or tourist visas. After one in '87 was discovered with AIDS, which she shared with some 50 rural sports before being deported, cops swore to clamp down on. Situation unchanged '91.

But "every cloud" and all that. New free lance trade surfaced, according to JT writer Bob Horiguchi, called **Fashion Health** (like new and better Love Hotels are now called Fashion Hotels). This is highly erotic massage sans sexual consummation. He offers no gory details: insufficient field research? So maybe some *Japayuki*, as such import is called, will come up with some new forms of bamboo-dance or Thai head-twisting.

GAY WORLD

HERE WE use term in modern international sense, not woodblock print title as above. New exotic diseases can be expected to fuel xenophobia, against both imported gals and tourist guys, of any persuasion. End '86 saw 21 cases of AIDS reported, 13 had died; 11 hemophiliacs and 10 homosexuals —who reported contacting from gaijin gays. 1991 saw 371 cases according to Nat'l Health Dept. Hemophiliacs got it from blood imported from US— 90% of local hospital blood as locals are reluctant to give blood. '89 saw estimated 11,000 virus carriers, 10,000 gay, mostly men. This projected to yield sick call of 15,000 by 1991–tho official figures '91 admit only 1627. Gay Support Group estimates 300,000 mostly closeted 'supporteds' believe AIDS is white man's disease and are 'complacent'—but one in 30 already infected leaves little room for complacency. Nonetheless, pregnant source for racial bias. Gay Support reports gay bathhouses turn away foreigners. Many bars, clubs long have both gay or straight, this just another excuse.

There is more homosexual activity in Japan than figure of 300,000 can account for. Few years ago when yen boomed, overseas travel by Japanese equally boomed so that foreign residents were having trouble getting reservations home for vacation. Then newspapers ran articles about herpes epidemic among US gays. Suddenly travel agents were phoning US business families and teachers, flights home were available due to rash of cancellations of 'official trips' by native businessmen and executive class tix had to be discounted at ¥-economy prices. Exclusive homosexuality frowned on –but if you give your parents at least one grandson, who's to say... Many local chauvinists blame this 'infection' on decadent Yankees. But read Saikaku's *Five Men Who Loved Love* (sequel to famed *Five Women Who Loved Love*–both translated) for revelations of samurai gays. Was big snickering matter in 18th century commoners' teahouses.

But Gay-Way was accepted, at least when introduction of Buddhism saw clerical sodomy come in with celibacy, which prohibited relations with women only, tho some early reformers preached total abstinence). In delicate Kyoto it reputedly spread to nobility along with other arts, then with Zen in Kamakura times to samurai. Still major pastime in zen monasteries. Saint Francis Xavier noted its open practice, one of, if not only, thing he disapproved of here. Early kabuki theater was by female troupes who dallied in prostitution on side, for which women were soon banned from stage—then female impersonators took over, prostitution aspect included. Thus it would appear banning women was less matter of morality than punishment for impinging upon traditional male turf.

Japanese proper term is *doseiai*, alike-love, but old term for male homosexuality is *nanshoku*, man-love, differentiating from *joshoku*, lady-love, which have never been mutually exclusive. There was no term for lesbian, no mention in literature, so modern language simply uses japlish *rezu*, as in widely advertised *rezu-sutorippu* and lady wrestling. This lesbianism is almost solely associated with imported talent, tho it is more than just suggested among nunnery-like all-girl theater troupes.

AC-DC friend of ours visited from US and consulted our acupuncturist about his herpes. Needles cured it, or at least all annoying symptoms. But he was told if he ever took so much as one drink of alcohol he would be scratching again. Three years later: still dry, still itchless. But no miracles even rumored here for AIDS, acupuncturists claim they at least enhance immune system. And forget fear of contracting by acupuncture—needles have long been scrupulously sterilized, or disposable.

For other VD, surveys indicate 70% of disease in men is contacted at red-light bathhouses ('Soaplands' or Turkos) and thru bar contacts. Condoms are readily available, often served free on tea tray at love hotels, or available in room in slot machine, or in hall vending machine of many tourist hotels. Acclaimed world's best, 'skinless skin' has 65% of national market and big export to Europe where importers compare them with local 'one-finger rubber kitchen gloves'. Size is problem—18cm long vs standard US 20, almost inch shorter.

One hopes that upper class baths, so important to trade and diplomacy, are better maintained. 1986 saw 50 *Soaplands* in Yoshiwara, third of total, change hands from AIDS scare, with Osaka and Sapporo reporting similar.

OUT ON THE TOWN   FOR ALL

ONE OF NICEST THINGS about Japanese bars, except some especially catering to foreigners, are lovely bar girls and waitresses. In States they are usually so soured on life that their very features are transposed into portraits of bitterness. Somehow in Japan this doesn't happen. They're happy-go-lucky lot. Life at home is dull, and dorm-home is more than likely pad in attic right over where you're drinking. Work is adventure. Foreigners' bars use poker-faced bartenders almost exclusively so you have little chance to get anywhere with bar girls. Girls in cabarets are better mark—or in those small bars with cabaret airs, tape deck and dancing (rare, as cops think it immoral unless you pay extra—can hardly find place to dance with your wife). If there's language barrier just keep smile and steady chatter of romantic nonsense. "Love", "kiss", "I, you", "beautiful" are all words they know from movies. Practically all girls know few simple sentences, studied English in jr hi for 3 years, or more in hi and college.

Bars change fast. There's little use in listing those we like now, girls and conditions and even owner will be different in year or two. In general, beware bars around Tokyo's Shimbashi. This was once one of more pleasant prowls, but today clip joints abound. And clip in Japan can be full karate chop in pocket-book of few hundred dollars for couple of rounds. If you feel you are being "took" feign loss of wallet and smilingly ask someone to accompany you back to your hotel. We have known member of recognized international credit card system to "clip"—which is where your credit card can help insure. In case this happens, sign with comment of dissatisfaction and report joint immediately to credit club by phone.

If on budget, get used to Japanese hooch, tho imports now often as cheap. *Suntory* is local stab at Scotch (Wa don't care for bourbon, tho Suntory, monster conglomerate, promotes their Jack Daniels import). Originator actually studied in Scotland with Scotch brewer and brought formula home supposedly in exchange for having left in Scotland Japanese formula—highland rice?. They are easier on head morning after than most bourbons. *Suntory* comes in 5-, 8-year (which contain additives to rush aging, as does our cheap hooch) and even 12- and up ages; tho '*Old*' being most common, general house hooch, no longer carries age on label, just notice "best blended whiskies...86 proof". *Nikka*, headquartered in Hokkaido (where we visit for tasting), continues original Scot adopted-tradition and all their whiskies are malt. Domestic drinks are reasonable–but now exchange rates make imports almost same. Suntory runs, or concessions out, small bars using name and brands. Here you can get slug for as little as ¥400 as posted outside: look for prices even if you can't read drinks. Even then, it is rare to pay much except in posh bar.

Beer is major domestic drink, available in summer rooftop beer gardens, local noodleries and 24hr roadside vending machines. Bottled and canned, even small aluminum 'barrels', of draught beers are common. 'Dry' is latest fad of late '80s, as is "non-alcohol" (actually 0.5%). Most are high in chemical additives like US beers, some even 'enhanced' with MSG. *Ebisu* and *Suntory Malt's* meet ancient German standards for pure beer. Price of 'domestic' is double same bottle in US, where it's 'import'.

Foreign drinks, remember, are imported, Japanese liquor taxes were long graduated on quality basis and all imports rank as top quality, even Four Feathers. New 1989 tax law equalized this. Suntory really pushes imports as agent of Haig as well as Jack Daniels, so Haig straight or *mizu-wari* can cost as little or less than domestic, ¥600/$4+. Making import taxes fair is bringing some drinks down to local prices and future will see further drops. Brandies run more and local drinkers appreciate fine brandies, readily pay prices for Napoleons that could refinance nouvel Empire Francaise. *Hermes* local brandy palatable in proper bubble, often warmed to breast heat by lovely walking bubble-warmer. Locals often drink it on rocks as it has less aroma to be brought out by warmth. When Jay ordered brandy-on-rocks in US bar years back, silence roared–as well it should with good stuff.

Guide publications carry up to date lists of dozen or so of clubs with E-speaking hostesses, with notes on their charges, whether minimums or "sets". Check *Tokyo Weekender* or *Tokyo Journal* for timely tips. Most clubs close around midnite, but periodic slacking off of law enforcement usually permits them to stretch this (as at this writing, as, conceivably, in future). Other clubs license as restaurants and limit entertainment features, chase own gals home at midnite (not if you bring your own) to comply with labor laws, thus are able to stay open much later. Hostesses know where these are and there's nothing wrong with your asking her to accompany you to one after she's thru. You'll have to settle up at her cabaret of employment, of course, for all charges to that time. After hours she's on her own.

Rose of Sharon club advertised in English newspapers way back in 1962 "If requested our hostesses will be your sightseeing companions during your stay in Tokyo..."—were closed down in '63 for "fleecing foreigners". No one has tried that tack openly since. Many E-speaking hostesses (or J-speaking, if you speak it) are also available as guides—make your own arrangements. Good way to learn language: Prof-Ambassador Reischauer's famed teacher Elissieff took his graduate language seminar in geisha houses of old Shimbashi, Tokyo. But another seminarian, Charlie Chaplin, didn't learn much beyond how to imitate wiggly local pine tree. Just keep in mind, in Japan as elsewhere specialists demand good fees.

You might take advantage of chance to arrange for package tour on ensuing days, exploring hotspring spas and romantic byways. It will cost more than JTB package, but it has its extras. If you make it to spa solo you'll find that most, despite laws, still offer very individualized room service. Ask for "massage" and grin. (If you really want massage, ask for "Anmah-san" and don't grin – perhaps look pained and point to pain.) True massage runs ¥2,500 to 5,000 depending on rank of hotel. But super extra, if opted for (different practitioners),will double your hotel tab—not available as room service in better hotels, but check out lobby for free-lancers.

SPAS are near volcanos and there are lots of volcanos in Kyushu. Edo-Tokyo was center of world's most efficient police state for almost three centuries and for another century, until 1945, police state was only slightly less efficient, distorted by import of Prussian pseudo-efficiency. Kyushu was beyond area of direct control of old Tokugawa dictatorship. It paid only token obedience, staying in line only because it was too weak to seriously challenge central authority, yet strong enough to keep outsider Edoites at arm's length. Area was still noted for some quaint old ways until last generation—like bride stealing thru ritual rape (rites closed to outsiders, sorry) and others more of interest to anthropologist than tourist. These have greatly decreased since last edition thru series of women's-libber lawsuits. Seems even Kyushu gals can't appreciate machotude of rape, especially when followed by life sentence of marriage.

Out of reach of police state, Kyushu was also out of reach of its attempted puritanizations. To this day new puritan laws are more openly flouted here than anywhere in this flouting land. In Hakata-Fukuoka housewives in downtown entertainment section hand out scented leaflets inviting you to see town under lovely escort. Rates reasonable. In Tokyo or Kyoto leaflets are slipped under car windshield-wipers. Or gals themselves operate with their own chauffeured cars. Kyoto is more flamboyantly wide-open as befits its respect for old traditions, and we will deal more in detail with this most fascinating of towns in its proper place.

And of course you have to phone for help, so you go to phone booth. Dial information? No, just pick number from dozens if not hundreds of printed advertising cards pasted all over booth – which was cleared off only hours ago. Lovely young nymph in tanktop in color picture card on my desk from Tokyo booth simply says in ideographs atop photo, "Very top class" and below photo in characters anyone can read: "¥40,000 TEL404-6254 ELEGANS". But then, you really have to speak Japanese unless you are some sort of telephonic wizard at onomatopoeia.

If this essay has left you yet puzzled about geisha, it's because we are saving her for her hometown— Kyoto.

As for those fabled ...

BATHHOUSES — YES AND NO

DURING Korean War, **Tokyo Onsen**, aka Ginza Turkish Bath, opened in Tokyo and its services so impressed even Turkish contingent with UN forces that some of them liked being walked on by other than sergeants, and deserted to stay clean. It still operates today 3rd street E of Ginza nr Seiryu Hotel, overhead hiway; ☎3541-3021, 6am-11pm, ladies section 10am-11pm; no public pool but 42 pvt rms with tub, steam-cabinet, massage table, own bath girl, 70min sauna & tub, scrub self ¥2,500; w/ scrub and body masssage ¥8,000. After that *Turkos* sprouted all over, each new one outdoing predecessors in gaudy decor and range of services. New varieties of washing evolved, most famous being 'Miss Turko-human washcloth'. Japan's bathing styles influenced visitors, and in US hot tubs developed, along their own lines undreamed of in Japan. But back to our Miss Turkos. Finally in 1984 Turkey had had enough and made representations thru its embassy to ban name Turkish Bath in Japan as defamatory to Turkey. Somewhat strange, as they never complained about what US-European gay Turkish baths have done to great Osmanli manly rep. Baths here, by whatever name, are all basically 'straight', if divided into play- and non-play or Turko vs Sauna—tho gays have their own places less obvious than straight baths. Anyway, by good ole native consensus arrived at by QC of association of bathhouse owners, name was officially changed: *Turko* became, s'help me, *Soapland* with conotation of prostitution (*reminder* bring your own condoms from o'seas, J- while thinner, more sensual, are smaller and appreciably narrower: p,154). But Sauna still means sauna and clearly legit-baths only.

Outside major cities there are soapland towns. Walled-in like old gay quarters (but subtler) and brightly lit like gigantic juke boxes. Biggest in Kansai is on shores of Lake Biwa at **Ogoto** 45min/10x-mtr taxi from **Kyoto**. Approach from afar looks like some apparition from Star Wars special effects or Disneys, with more light outside than inside.

TOKYO'S happy satellite is in **Kawasaki** City, towards Yokohama, where in nearby shipyards big keels get laid. Keelwork on humans runs basic ¥3,-10,000 scrubdown, with skilled labor follow-thru extra ¥15,-20,000 'tip' with extra shift available, prorated. 'Famous people' get taxied out here (¥10,000 o.w.) to avoid problems downtown, like recognition etc. But Edokko (native Tokyoites) are returning to old haunts in **Yoshiwara**, ¥2x-mtr taxi from Ueno, recently spiffed up to modern equivalent of its ancient woodblock-print days of glory. Stroll main street and choose your own pleasure palace, prices posted from ¥3,000+ for bath only; old style 'full service' will run another ¥15,-20,000, some budget places ¥7,000, with super-keel hauling by larger crews to ¥50,000. About half of surcharge goes to girl(s). Or you can settle simply for bath and visual experience of special architecture, which still awaits recording for posterity.

But Japan's big sex trade moves overseas. 1990 saw 1,500,000 J- males take 'sex tours' to SE Asia. With Aids epidemic in Bangkok brothels, Japan has little reason to be smug about present low Aids rate.

Late '86 AIDS threat seriously damaged Soaplands business, so they've come up with new ploys: grander scale like great marble bathtubs full of wine (import, cheaper) catering to expense account crowd—local companies you deal with. Now even take payment in plastic, at 20% surcharge. Grander gimmicks will be invented as necessities require, faster than edition revisions are possible. So play it by ear, or whatever you play with.

Meanwhile good reputation of old Korean war-era Turkish baths was continued by more 'legit' bathhouse now called *sauna*. Expanded on popular steam-boxes of old Turkos, built fine new sauna rooms, big hot and cold and jacuzzi baths but retained great macho feature of brief-clad bather girl and masseuse. These are straight, so reputable you can bring your wife to most bigger ones, tho she goes into separate section, usually on its own floor. (No she isn't washed or massaged by guy, *wumanzu-ribbu* hasn't gotten that far yet, tho old baths did). Missus bathes herself but has exotic choice of tubs and massages. Mister gets washed except for harder to reach areas for which soapy washcloth is handed you. Many major hotels have saunas, open fairly late, usually men only, less fun than big specialists.

TOKYO Yoshiwara new baths all good, taken sans 'special service'. And of course, there's above original **Tokyo Onsen**.

In **OSAKA** we have *all* especially enjoyed—Jay and Garet even going father-son skinny dipping, Jay and Sumi took guest couples, alas to separate floors—**Sauna New Japan** ☎(06)-211-0832) down at Namba in *Minami* fun area, across boulevard from Holiday Inn Hotel, block in on brightest-lit cross street, taxis all know it. Even advertises on TV. Big bath and sauna cabinet for *sarari-man* without massage ¥1,800, open 24 hours; 2 other pool areas with scrubdown and massage ¥4,800 and ¥6,000 all incl, enter before 11pm; after-massage lounge sections are open all nite, bar and snack (hors d'ouevres to sushi) in lounge; have laundry, cleaning done while you bathe (extra); all credit cards. Sumi advises ladies shouldn't miss oil massage, so take Ms and arrange to meet downstairs in, say, 2 hours. Next door **Rubia** not quite as nice, but couples share big private bathroom.

KOBE doesn't offer much—due to heavy lowbrow yakuza presence? and despite sign in entry that *tattoos not permitted* (do you check them at desk?). **Kobe Sauna** opp Washington Hotel just above Sannomiya is fairly good, has shown much improvement over last few years. **Kobe Ladies Sauna** nearby frequently offers special promotional deals.

Smaller cities ask hotel front for sauna; we never got bum steer.

Then there are fabulous *onsen*, covered in detail with *ryokan* few chapters earlier and mentioned thruout book. Many in country offer mixed bathing, especially at *rotenburo* outdoor baths, great experience for moon-viewing with bottle of sake. We all love them. Were fading away, quite rare when we did first edition. Now seeing great renaissance, especially favored by young college and working gals, travelling usually in pairs—not bashful these days as lovely young actresses commonly appear in hot spring interview PR shows on late nite TV (that's *in* program, *in* tub on location and *in* buff) have made it respectable to show off what gals have, with volume no requisite. Be coy yourself, carry flimsy hotel-provided towel held casually hanging below navel. Once submerged, you can hold it out of water and wring dry (your towel) to use to wipe brow or drape over head as locals do. And never stare. It's OK to start up conversation, but play it cool. Artists, writers, teachers are admired and many young things have thing going for older *sensei* (teacher, intellectual)-types.

In summary, it's great place to practice to be Dirty Old Man (DOM Juan), gracefully.

Skinship is Japlish term. One aspect of it is family bath; another aspect is nude bathing together by straight men at city sauna or country onsen. Japanese often go with business colleagues so don't be shocked if invited (they probably won't, as they think we have hang-ups on nudity), tho they never go coeducational. Great way to discard superficial differences.

*There's a house in New Orleans they call
the House of the Rising Sun
It's been the ruin of many a poor girl
And Oh, by God, I'm one...*
　　　　—New Orleans folk song

GOING IT ALONE
FOR HER (*by* Sumi)

"ROMANCE AND ADVENTURE"—eye-catcher used on travel brochures to lure young women to 'idyllic retreats'. What woman, single or other, isn't flattered with attention of flirtation. Who hasn't come back from France without stories of some charming Frenchman inviting you to dinner, entertaining you royally, or visited Italy and wasn't "annoyed" by warm-blooded Italians popping up in unexpected places with words of admiration and attention? It may be so with men in West, but ah, this stoic gent of Orient. What thoughts hide behind their attentive, but reserved politeness? Men are men all over, but in Japan they are rather restrained when it comes to foreign women. It isn't language differences: does that stop Latins or French? But if coming for romance, many say 'forget it'—gay poet James Kirkup claims blonde nymphomaniacs can't make out here—while others smile.

Before going further, you should know most everyone agrees how safe it is to travel alone. No need for chemical spray gun, money belts. Can take last train at night, walk home down neighborhood alleys. Occasionally one encounters 'touchy hands' on crowded rush-hour trains (men do too).

This whole idea of openly approaching women is modern concept that is slowly being mastered here. Collegiate crowd is cramming in lots of field-work. Then what about this so-called freedom that men here have? Well, in olden days, there was time and place for it all. Wealthy had it simple. They picked their pleasure women from proper place, geisha house. Mistresses and extra wives were taken by any who could afford to do so and this brought men status. Today, with tastes—but not basic drives—undergoing change, it is bars and restaurants of certain types. Yes, men have always had great freedom and license. However, standard has been double one of most schizophrenic extremes. One might sell his daughter or even his sister into life of what we consider "shame", but he would never tolerate unsold daughter or sister doing any flirting. Therefore, these very free men had no outlet for their flirtatious drives except recourse to professional ladies. They therefore, never developed anything even remotely resembling that noble Italian art of flirtation or American collegiate sport of sparking.

However, with this great social revolution that has occurred here since World War II and new opportunities liberation of women (and necessities passing of anti-prostitution act) have brought, Japanese are learning fast.

Quick glance backwards tell us much. Just before WW II, girls and boys went to separate schools after primary school. Girls going to high schools did not dare speak to any male in public, even though he were her cousin. They wouldn't have dreamed of being seen going to movies together, for school boys and girls weren't supposed to go to movies at all. How did authorities know they were students? By uniforms which had to be worn at all times. And in universities it was similar. So, boys-becoming-men went to cabarets for any female diversions. There were no such things as teen-age parties, no saturday night dances, no meeting at drugstore counters, no youth fellowship meetings.

When girls came of marriageable age, family elders held council and decided that some arrangements for *miai* (face-seeing, or by homonymous entendre, face-loving) should be made with some suitable young man. Or if family thought their son should wed, then similar council was held for same arrangements. At this *miai* man had chance to look over prospective bride, but she had to keep her eyes cast demurely down, thus really never spoke with him until after their wedding ceremony. This arrangement was for most couples who are now grandparents and great grandparents. Many now in their fifties and sixties followed similar patterns, except that they had good look at photographs and perhaps few opportunities to eat together at some sweetshop, in most cases accompanied by chaperone. Nowadays, 'proper' way is still exchange photographs, have first meetings with parents of both sides and go-between. Many couples choose own mates and then have go-between for formality sake, but surprising number go thru 'miai'.

Postwar saw large increase in coeducational colleges and gradual change in outlook of adults towards girl-boy relationships. Walking arm in arm, holding hands and falling asleep on his shoulder in trains have become commonplace. Since Pacific War, women working in public offices have increased tremendously. So if she doesn't find partner in school, then there's chance at her place of work or thru friends.

There are now nearly two generations of men and women who have spent some few years in foreign countries, predominantly America. Many are businessmen, their families, and lots of students. Latter have had close foreign friends and observed and experienced girl-boy, male-female relationships. Most have come back and settled and often miss those casual friendships so easily cultivated in West. So, here is corps that would be happy to befriend you. Where will you find them? Almost anywhere, you have to keep open attitude, when approached by stranger, male or female.

Some older people may have sons and daughters overseas and are anxious to strike up conversation with you and take you to lunch, dinner, outing or to their home to reciprocate for kindnesses shown their loved ones. Check into 'Home Visit' programs run by city tourist offices. So, be open. Where? In hotels, on trains, buses, restaurants, theaters, parks, etc. Don't forget, there's been large influx of 'foreign' young men—bilingual or now studying Japanese—who realize that knowing Japanese can help them get good job either here in Japan or back home. These fellahs are great because they usually know their way around, happy to have chance to squire you about, someone they can speak English, not 'Anguish' with.

GOING OUT & ABOUT

THERE ARE AREAS in Tokyo where expatriates gather—Roppongi and Shinjuku with lively discos and quiet coffee shops—which Garet covers. Friends say in Roppongi its **Hard Rock Cafe** with Tony Roma's famous spareribs downstairs, **Java Jive** for dancing (basement of Square Bldg), **Henry Africa's** bar for bit older crowd, bar **Mistrial** where yuppies of investment crowd gather. Osaka has **Studebaker, Pig & Whistle** with branch in Kyoto. Kobe's Kitano-cho has baseball addict Marty Kuehnert's bars **Attic** and **Attic Jr.** Places with live music all in Kitano-cho—**Charlie's** with him at piano and Sho with guitar; and Dixieland fans will like **Honky Tonk,** and after 2 yrs in NY owner Eriko's **Albatross** opened on 2nd fl Elephant Bldg. Great dining and dancing at **Casablanca** with mostly American entertainers, host Winston, and owner Natsuko Dama. Then there are fast-food houses where 'Mericans seem to gather. Hotel bars, restaurants, tours, buses and trains for special tours, are likely places to meet someone interesting, someone in same boat as you are, alone in exotic land.

But if you want to see Japan, then traveling solo has its rewards. People are more apt to invite you to special events, treat you, invite you home, etc. Even at home, it's not easy to find romance, so settle for romance of new adventure, new scenes and see how people here work and play. Stroll thru parks, relax in tea shops, sit in hotel lobbies (particularly on Sundays) and watch for kimonoed-lady guests of wedding parties, follow them down to banquet floor and see beautifully decked-out bride and groom.

SOURCES OF INFORMATION: Learn what's going on–special events, lectures, plays, festivals, hiking trips, zazen session–in *Mainichi Daily News'* **Japan-o-file** pages Mon, *Tokyo Journal's CITYSCOPE*, *Kansai Time Out* or *Kyoto Visitors' Guide* or *Kinki*.

TREATING YOURSELF TIPS

RIGHT NOW young women are affluent, are travelers, for they now work in offices, live at home (no need to contribute to family upkeep) and this country's tourism is geared to them. Special menus at top hotels such as 'patisserie hour' of buffet desserts and afternoon tea, ladies' lunch. Hotels for women only are few, spartan, catering to younger girls, with 2-4 per tatami room or bunk beds; many self-service, fix own bedding. ¥-Bw/2.

Warning: most luxe ryokan are limited in number of rooms available, so politely refuse singles, especially in season, as their profit is on meals. In many larger ¥-T, ¥-S ryokan and family type ryokan you are most welcome. Pick area you want to visit, quiet one for relaxation. You've seen enticing scenes of outdoor onsen hot spring baths. All have separate baths for men and women (can arrange for you to have it alone–be prompt), and often picturesque outdoor pools, usually separate. JNTO has onsen booklet. We suggest old favorite **Fujiya Hotel** at Miyanoshita or neighboring **Taiseikan** perched on verdant hillside, ☎(0460)-2-2281, ¥-Sw/2 with its own 300m cable car from Dogashima stn of Hakone Tozan RR. Popular rural village area Takayama has cluster of hot springs, especially at **Gero Onsen**—or to stay on main line **Gifu** by Nagoya, or near Osaka in Wakayama Pref where bit south at Katsuura is **Hotel Urashima** with great outdoor onsen right out in the rocky cliffs or nearby **Koshinoyu Ryokan**.

Reminder: Bring what cosmetics & toiletries you use, they are outrageously priced here; this includes bras, briefs.

SAUNAS, BATHS: Many hotels boast saunas, but most do not have one for ladies. Top hotels do. In Tokyo **Tokyo Onsen**, Ginza, ☎3541-3021, ¥2,500-8,000; Osaka, **New Japan Sauna**, ☎211-0832, just off Midosuji nr Shinkabuki-za theater–top ¥10,000 buys complete relaxation 40-min body oil-massage; shorter course ¥6,300, while sauna alone ¥1,800. (If with hubby, go while he goes to men's floor and meet, say 2 hours later). No tipping here or at beauty shop or anywhere else. Have laundry, pressing done while soaking.

BEAUTY SHOPS with excellent services in all leading hotels. **Shiseido** on Ginza 7-chome ☎3572-5111 is old standby. Tokyo has many foreign beauticians. Most can rush you thru in hour or less for shampoo, set and dry (¥4,500). For permanent, find one used to working with Westerners as hair texture is so different from Orientals' (¥6,-¥13,500) Top beauticians go abroad for study and outstanding hair-stylists from France or USA are regularly invited for workshops. Most beauty shops give facials, and many other body treatments, calling it 'esthetic course'–and great massages.

RETURN TREAT: For your local companion, appreciated would be being taken to 'exotic' place–one of ¥-L hotels with their special treats—such as 'Top-of' restaurants, like Kobe's **Portopia Hotel** 30th fl where buffet breakfast before 10am is ¥1,600, and afternoons until 6pm no cover charge for drinks and wonderful view; music w/ surcharge after 6pm. Also, there's ladies lunch or afternoon coffee and fabulous dessert buffets for reasonable set fee. Or go all out with full meal at some thoroughly Western place, like Kobe's **Casablanca**, exciting, yet inexpensive, under ¥4,000.

Going it alone can be wonderful, in this country so friendly and safe.

as for me, I can take
travels as they come
but my poor wife with the children
she must be falling thin with care.
— Tamatsukuribe, c 753, in *Manyoshu*

"—AND BRING YOUR KIDS"

IN 1964 WE WROTE, "With great American aid and advisory programs certain to continue for years, our diplomatic corps swelling, Okinawa semi-permanent outpost, and our expanding foreign trade calling for more experienced representatives, transfer of whole American families to Far East has brought new element into Japan travel picture...."

Well we have no more aid programs here, diplomatic corps shrinks under Gramm-Rudman, Okinawa is still there and our expanding foreign deficit brings more US families here to relocate our industry overseas — maybe by hiring some "experienced representatives" from among Japanese-speaking kids of last generation residents we might start to try to sell here someday. (Or at least begin to think about getting around to starting to initiate studies to try to sell, maybe...).

Children as travel companions can be problem, but don't let this scare you into leaving them behind or turning down assignment. We can't emphasize enough how safe it is for children, teens and adults. Garet & big brother started travels in crib stage, logged tens of thousands of miles before 'returning' to US for college, with no problems. Coming to Japan, you now have jets, welcome relief for moms. Sumi crossed by slow prop with 4-month-old: total flying time each way was about 24 hours so we broke our trip with stopover in Hawaii. 4-month-old is easy to manage because he sleeps most of time. Even at 10-months of age Morpheus helps out. If basic rule of full tummy and dry bottom is observed, there's no problem.

These few hints may help. Book night-time flight so child can follow normal sleeping routine for most of flight, and midweek when not crowded. To make things easier for you if traveling alone with children, suggest pack-carrier, such as *Snugli*, or *Gerry* so handy when standing in line to check in, immigration, customs.

There are only limited number of snap-on cots on planes, so be sure to make reservation in advance for baby, as well as for any special formula or other needs. Give baby pacifier or bottle, children some hard candy to suck on during landing to counter pressure change in plane.

Travel is always adventure for energetic youngster. You can enlarge on this spirit of adventure and role it can play. Explain to child various things going on in plane. Tell stories of lands he'll see. Have books or magazines, toys or games and favorite sweets, tho airlines supply most of these, too.

Make sure he has good nite's sleep before flight. And you too!

Brief him on simple courtesies of "thank you's" and "excuse me's" to your hostesses and others around, if possible in local language: *arigato* And *gomen-nasai*. Well-mannered child can relieve monotony of trip with pleasant conversations with bored passengers. In confinement of plane, boisterous child can become terrible annoyance to all. Some foresight and planning will make your trip pleasant for child, mother, hostesses and fellow passengers. Those with small children get check-in, boarding and seating priority. Ask for 'Family Service' in advance, if not offered.

FLIGHT TIPS FROM SUMI, FOR SOMEONE THAT YOUNG

1. Write formula and name on index card, give to stewardess. Always carry more than sufficient formula. You never know when plane might be delayed for hours.
2. Always keep three sterilized bottles handy.
3. Don't ask to have baby's formula made at mealtime or just before landing when stewardesses have million things to do.
4. Have pacifier or bottle handy for take-off and landing to ease air pressure change. Adults are given candy or chewing gum, babies shouldn't be neglected.
5. Airlines provide disposable diapers, so convenient and improved from my crossing in 1958 with son Cellin. Many brands are now available at department stores, neighborhood supers and pharmacies. Ask for *kami-no-omutsu*.
6. Dress him comfortably. Planes are air-conditioned so even in summer keep sweater or wrap handy. Change direction of air vent so does not blow directly on child. My doctor advised that infants be protected from chilled air in planes and air-conditioned trains, especially asleep. Take couple receiving blankets or baby sheets, drape over cot or seat like tent.
7. Planes usually have bassinets that hook onto walls but occasionally, not enough. Experience taught me to carry totebag with all baby's things — easy to get into, no need to pull it up to get things out: just reach in and feel. I also had another little grip (or used same tote bag) about height of our seat. Have piece of cardboard about 30x45cm (12x18in). Put it on seat, rest one end on this grip, fold airline blanket on it and *voila*, a bed. Always carry piece of rubberized sheeting or pad about 30x45cm. These must slide under seat for takeoff and landing. Baby paraphernalia need not be weighed in, it's free-allowance .
8. Under **no** circumstances allow children on plane within 48, perhaps even 72, hours of receiving inoculation of any sort: inoculation shock **deafness** can result, for which only known help is probably acupuncture. Check your Dr predeparture.

MISCELLANEOUS TIPS

TRAVELING WITH children in Japan is lightened by national indulgent attitude toward children. Department stores and shopping centers provide little beds in spotless rest rooms for changing baby's diapers, strollers with package baskets for mothers with children, playland on roof. Breast-feeding in public is accepted as well as most of baby's other needs. Japanese dote on children. Foreign children always attract attention and cries of *kawaii*, *neh* (cute, isn't he) will be heard. They above all want to hold child. If your child is extrovert, then you'll have easy time. Whenever we went anywhere whether by car or train, we always took collapsible stroller that folds up compactly. In England we found excellent one that folded up smaller than portable typewriter and introduced it to Japan. Japan now makes fine light strollers—before which baby was carried piggy-back by mom or big sis: 'skinship', Japlish term we should adopt, is big element in child rearing here and probably accounts for why otherwise loose-rearing system works.

FRESH MILK is good all over country, safely pasteurized and homogenized. You'll find *Carnation* brand evaporated milk (*eba-milku*) in large cities, but local *Meiji* and *Yuki* (Snow) brands are excellent. Small cans holding enough for one feeding are handiest. Popular prepared baby foods put out by Wakodo, Meiji, and Yuki brands come in 3 forms: in jars, flakes and freeze dry, while Meiji has new *Aka-chan Restaurant* series of *Tasty Pack* in handy ready-to-eat packages. Flakes or freeze dry have to be added to rice gruel or milk or hot water. Powdered milk (*kona-miruku*) is in all drug stores. Always carry thermos of hot water as short line trains don't have diners. Inexpensive thermos with shoulder strap easily available as

Japanese kids go on outings often. Long distance lines have diners—no problem. Hotels, from minshuku to Hilton, provide *o-yu* (hot water) in thermos as standard service.

BABY PRODUCTS: We personally boycott *Morinaga* brand products (milk, cookies etc) as just before first son was born they accidentally dropped sack of arsenic into milk mixer, leaving many dead and, perhaps more even tragic, horde of human vegetables: they have yet to make proper amends or even accept responsibility, even proffer apology. There was out-of-court settlement which we feel was inadequate, and section chief was found guilty of criminal negligence, yet no company guilt was admitted. We also forego MacDonald's Macs for reasons of its xenophobia and bigotry, as detailed elsewhere.

Bland cookies for tiny tots available at any candy counter. Best is *Karuketto* put out by Meiji or Glico's *Bisco*. Always carry some toys; sweets and mandarin oranges in season are available at any railway station platform, or street corner shop. Good multivitamin for children is Takeda Pharmaceutical *Panvitan* or Shionogi *Shin Popon-S*. Johnson's baby products are found in most local drug (*yakkyoku*) and department stores. But best bring adequate supply of your regular medicines. Another important item—disposable diapers. No need to take up precious baggage space with them for Japan has caught up with *Pampers*, which are relatively expensive here. My friend recommends *Moony* put out by Unicharm particularly for boys and *Pampers* by Proctor & Gamble for girls. Now, they're made for him and her. Many new brands appear on the market and friends report *Merry* put out by Kao Soap is more economical and practical.

We took 3-week trip to Hokkaido taking elder, Cellin, with us when he was 18 months old. Stroller was blessing: we left him in it and we each carried one end of it going onto platform and train and hung miscellaneous small luggage from it.

STAYING: There's no charge for infants at inns; however, there is 50% charge for older child, and those older taking regular meal will be charged full rate. Some minshuku and family hotels are improving on this, slowly. In case just dish or two is ordered, or he shares parents', there will be at most nominal charge. In our case, we were never charged for Cellin except when I ordered something special that they had to go out and buy, like can of mixed fruit or fresh milk. At some inns maids will do baby's laundry. Give it to them as soon as you reach where you'll be overnite and most of next day, allowing sufficient time to dry. Usually there's no charge for this at most inns, so tip your room maid, she must do it on her time. At *minshuku*, cheaper inn, there's washing machine available for guests.

If child is good-natured, you'll find maids want to play with him. Easy to arrange for maid to baby-sit for few hours. At hotels, no extra charge for children except when extra cots are ordered. No other hotel has copied Hilton's intelligent family policy of children free no matter how old, which made us great Hilton fans.

BABY-SITTING available at top hotels; many have nursery with trained staff. Accept 1-month to 5-year olds, hours usually daytime only. Reservation must be made previous day. **Hotel New Otani** has nursery with trained staff: ¥3,500 for 1st 2hrs, addit 30min ¥700. Food, diapers provided; 9:00-22:00. Overnite is ¥15,000, noon-noon. **Hilton** or others without nursery call **Domestic Service Center** (Mrs Sakamoto) who come to hotel room and babysit. Chge 3hr ¥5,000, ¥1,000 each addit hr plus transportation, meals, ☎(03)-3584-4769, 8-7pm, can arrange later hours. Sakamoto-san says one of her English-speaking girls could accompany you and kids on shopping or sightseeing tour for same fee. Also **Baby Harbor** Rm 935, Wein Aoyama bldg, 2-2-15 Minami Aoyama (☎3479-0238); and **Tokyo Maid**, 1-54 Jimbo-cho, Kanda (☎3291-3595).

Children under 6 are free on trains, buses, streetcars; to 12 pay half-fare. As for air, usual international regulations apply: under 3 years accompanied by adult and not occupying separate seat is free; between 2 and 12 years or infants requiring separate seat are carried at 50% of adult fare. But age rulings are lax on domestic, especially for undersizeds.

SHOPPING: What can you get for your little ones? Toys, gadgets, food, books, clothes! Make it toys and gadgets and watch their eyes sparkle as they open toy package. Less reaction with clothes, unless they're girls and bit older. Large department store has whole floor devoted to toys, every shopping arcade will have one or two toy shops. Cuddly dolls way over-priced here, so you might bring your child's favorite with you. There's been revolution in clothes for kids, especially for small fry. Japan now has really imaginative shoes for children—colorful, well-styled and practical, no struggling with shoe laces as 'magic tape' velcro has taken over. Lots of ideas detailed in ORIENTAL MARKETPLACE, *following*.

THINGS TO DO: Rooftops of *depahto* have rides, games, pet shop to keep kids entertained while adult shops. For activities, *Tokyo Journal*'s 'For Kids' in Cityscope guide, Festivals & Events has excellent up-to-date coverage. There's **Disneyland** near Tokyo and every reasonably sized city has some amusement park nearby. Downtown Tokyo has **Korakuen** with rides galore. In fact most private train lines nationwide have amusement park or zoo at end of line. For example, Tokyo's Tobu has fabulous **Insectopia**, home to 700 butterflies of 14 species, plus water striders, migratory locusts, crickets, rhinoceros beetles, all living in natural environment at Tama Zoological Park in Hino; Ikebukuro has **Toshima-en**; while Osaka to its west has Hanshin rail's **Hanshin Zoo** famous for its leopon (half lion, half leopard), to north Hankyu **Takarazuka Familyland** and Takarazuka 'teenybopper' **All-girl Revue**, to south Nankai rail's **Misaki Koen** park and zoo. New Osaka **aquarium** and Tokyo-Kasai's **Rinkai** are fabulous.

TOKYO has two well-equipped havens: kids make things, paint, play instruments, etc, free-of-charge at its Metropolitan **Children's Museum** (*Tokyo-to Jido Kaikan*), with assistants on 5 floors: outdoor playground; science museum, art room; 3fl electrical workshop, make radios; 4fl library, hobby workshop; 5fl music room, meteorological observatory. Two traffic lights E of Shibuya Stn on Meiji-dori. 9am-4pm, daily. X-2nd mon. ☎3409-6361.

National **Children's Castle** (*Kodomo no Shiro*) on Aoyama-dori, opp Aoyama Gakuin Univ. (Ginza Line, Omote Sando Sta exit 2B) 5 storeys; 1&2fl restaurants & tea shop. 3fl hobby fl with crafts, 17m long wall for 'grafittying' what you like, slideshows, computer games; 4fl choose your video rooms; 5fl bicycles, frizbies & other action games. Open tue-fri 1-5:30pm and sat, sun, hol 10:00-5:30pm, X-mon; adults ¥400, kids ¥300; ☎3797-5666.

And **Children's Land** (*Kodomo no Kuni*) in Yokohama city. Midori-ku, Nara-cho. ☎(045)-961-2111. Odakyu line–Tsurukawa, transfer to bus 90 to Kodomo no Kuni. Playgrounds, free cycling, 9 children's pools, zoo, model farm, ice skate rink, lake. 9:30-4:30pm. X-mon. Adults ¥450, 150, 50.

Matsushita P/N, 'Experimental Lifestyle Theater' in 'Human Electronics Environment' for computer nut dads or kids, hands-on educational fun in OA or future home gadgetry, by makers of National, Panasonic etc, owners of MCI. ☎5568-0461; E of Shimbashi stn; no-X 11am-10pm, *free*.

Similar but smaller showplace for **Sony** off middle of Ginza on corner of Harumi-dori St betw Ginza and Yurakucho stn.

Good **guidebook** to keeping kids happy in Tokyo, available any hotel bookstore, we recommend *A Parents' Guide to Tokyo* coauthored by Nancy Harlzenbusch & Alice Shabecoff (pub Shufunotomo).

But most of all, especially in summertime, there are children's heaven, *matsuri*—**traditional festivals** (*see* area DATEBOOKS). Give kids money and turn 'em loose safely. Better yet, stay with them for we had as much fun with our kids at these as they had (and have marvelous photos to jog our memories). Games to play. Lots of toys to buy, some folk toys not elsewhere seen, like masks, ball games, tricks, dolls, plus usual store junk.

And lots to eat, most of it less damaging to digestion than our fairground fare—certainly soy-flavored roasted squid is easier on belly (if not on parents' eyes) than nitrate-saturated hot dog and more photogenic to get rise out of folks back home. Every neighborhood has them spring, summer and autumn, and where you stay or live will be no exception, even near hotels. Buy your kid happi coat and white shorts or *yukata* and sash and let him or her join in carrying shrine or riding on float (plenty of neighborhood big brothers on hand to take loving care—and most festivals carry reasonable accident insurance, ours does, and have security guards). If just sightseeing, passing thru, your kids will be just as welcome on spot as if you'd planned ahead. Kids love other kids and language for them is no barrier.

Most are shinto fetes and are not sectarian religious, even Catholics have ruled on this. There are no 'pagan gods' involved. If you believe in one god, what else can conflict: And if you don't believe in much or anything what is there to be afraid of? If you get to lovely livable Kobe, come join our *Kitano Kokusai Matsuri* international festival last weekend of July (*see* p.588). You and/or kids can entertain on shrine stage or sell old clothes at charity booths or run your own booth. We've had local Sephardic synagoguers stand enscarfed and yarmulkaed in shrine holy of holies and recite traditional saturday prayer for health of national leaders—only time in Japan emperor is mentioned in formal prayer—and when they turned away from shrine to face Jerusalem, shinto priests in formal robes shuffled in their big black-lacquered clogs to turn with them and bow in mutual respect towards that distant sacred wall: *shema israel adonai ehod*, 'god is one'. And Baptist choir visiting from Pensacola serenaded here, local resident Hindus and Sufis danced and sang their prayers, Mother Theresa sent her Peace Prayer to be translated and introduced to Japan, etc.

Hey, bring your kids…

Zipangu....so vast indeed are the riches....
it is impossible to convey an idea of them....
there are pearls also in large quantities
of pink color, round in shape and of great size.
— Marco Polo

ORIENTAL MARKETPLACE
OUR PERSONAL SHOPPING GUIDE

SOMEWHERE in this gigantic Oriental marketplace that is Japan, you'll find "just what I was looking for". Strolling streets in any city is like wending your way thru some huge emporium. Exotic wares spill out from shops with no glass fronts, clerks busily waving their magic dusters. In most cities main shopping streets are covered arcades for pedestrians only, except for Tokyo, tho local areas have their *ichiba* marketplace arcaded. Traditional shopkeepers such as paper-hanger, cabinet maker, lacquer artist, kimono silk designer-dyer, *okaki* and *namagashi* sweet shops carry on today as they have done for generations next door to modern high-rise department stores, American-style fast food shops, fashionable boutiques carrying imported perfumes, designer clothes and accessories, lavish patisseries.

There's no local black market in yen-dollar exchange, which is handled only at authorized stores, hotels and banks. Travelers checks are preferred, credit cards universal (Visa, Amex, Mastercard, Diners most acceptable in that order). Some discount shops may hedge on credit cards since they work on low margin of profit, and will give best discount only for cash purchases. Personal checks seldom accepted—high cashing fees.

Shopping in strange lands is adventure in itself and in Japan you'd think it would be harrowing experience not being able to speak or read Japanese. Language is no barrier if you do your shopping in downtown areas in Tokyo or Kyoto or large hotel arcades. Most department stores have English-speaking personnel to assist you (ask at information booth on main floor), all have directory of floors in English, and progressive ones like Seibu's Yurakucho and Shibuya stores, Isetan Shinjuku, Matsuya Ginza have section with Westerner in charge to help with shopping needs.

You are free to browse without any clerks to bother you. You are their guest and until you ask for some assistance you may be left undisturbed. Oftentimes you can walk into shop, spend hour looking around and leave with no word being offered except possible *"arigato"* when you leave. Don't feel slighted. You can get attention of clerk by saying *"chotto"* or *"onegai shimasu"* in firm voice or just wave article you want until you catch one's eye. Some other handy phrases: *ikura des'ka?* (how much is this?); *okii desu* (too large)—*chiisai desu* (too small); *hoka-ni arimasu ka?* (do you have any others); *onegai-shimasu* I'll take it, or even just say "OK"); *okutté kudasai* (please send it), for more *see* SAY IT IN NIHONGO, p178.

No haggling or bargaining to speak of. Unlike most of Asia where haggle is in order, prices are pretty standardized here. Experienced shopper soon learns that when making large purchase it is custom—except in name shops or department stores—to get discount (exception to exception, in department store art gallery special exhibits, discounts are expected). If you hit it off right with shopkeeper he'll offer discount or throw one or two articles in free and if he doesn't, then OK to ask smilingly *"sukoshi benkyo dekimasu-ka?"* Invariably this will bring some reduction, perhaps large, or just token so as not to embarrass you. But don't haggle or push point.

Shopkeepers are quite honest so shop with no fear of cheating. Prices almost always marked and even if they are not there's no danger of their asking exorbitant price—¥-$ exchange makes them exorbitant enough and all are painfully aware of this. And of fact whole retail system is against consumer: even 'America Basher' ISHIHARA Shintaro admits "Absurd anomolies…typical consumer goods average 40% higher in Tokyo than New York". Items like chinaware, pottery and textiles are standard here in both price and quality, tho cheaper in their home towns, but items like pearls are of infinite range in quality and styles. For antiques and curios in which this country abounds, best judge is yourself—just ask self, "Do I like it and is it worth that much to me?" You'll find both fabulous bargains and Madison Avenue prices mixed in one shop. Advice, if odd piece seems cheap, trust youself—'in style' means high price, 'out'=cheap.

HINTS FOR SHOPPING

JAPAN HAS INITIATED VAT system with all other special taxes cancelled, and overall consumers' 3% tax replacing them. Former tourist tax-free provisions now apply only to this 3%, still applicable at special shops only. Possibility is that 3% may be raised. First of all familiarize yourself with monetary exchange. Make list of what you're looking for and jot down what best buys are and where to find them.

BAGGAGE ALLOWANCE: US residents can send home via parcel post items under $50 fair retail value (up to one package *arriving* per day per addressee) duty-free marked "Unsolicited Gift";—date processed in US, so if 2 or more arrive in customs same day tho postmarked different days, you lose. These are over and above your customs-free $400 limit. This also solves overweight problems for plane travel. With postal charges so high from Japan, we recommend for those traveling to US and Canada, to do what we always do both ways. Just take extra baggage. Baggage allowance is 2 pieces (1st class 3pcs) each maximum wt 32kg(70lb) and 150cm total W+H+D for one, or 280cm for 2—in practice airlines usually enforce only larger size. Extra baggage of same maximum size and weight is ¥20,000 to West Coast, ¥23,000 East Coast on same plane and clears custom with you; no special paperwork. Other way, from US to Japan is about $75. Just check in as your baggage. No need to go thru rigmarole of unaccompanied baggage. Other countries do not have such generous allowances, still max 20kg/44lbs. Check **Shipping and Mailing** in CHERRY BLOSSOMS p189 for other countries, postal, air freight, etc.

Finding something exciting is easy except that dollars do not go very far today. High rate of yen dropped number of travelers (tourists and business-men) 1986 by 11.4% and '87 4.5%, and per capita daily shopping from ¥9,310 in '83 (then $35.80) to ¥5,072 '86 ($31.70) or 45.5% less in yen, if only slightly less in dollars. But this also reflects rise in student and longer-term budget tourists, who both spend less in total and spend it slowly, over more days.

Prices of many Japanese goods are so much cheaper overseas that in 1985 there began odd phenomenon of reverse-import, re-importing Japan-made goods from Hong Kong, then USA. Paying two-way freight, import taxes at both ends (Japan re-imports mostly pay 15% commodity tax), shops can still sell at discount and make profit. This is part exchange ploy, but also reflects difference in export and domestic ex-factory prices.

ELECTRONIC EQUIPMENT: If planning to shop for **camera** or **electronic** equipment, study prices at home first, check your camera and audio mag mail order ads, bring some clippings so you don't forget. If going on think about shopping in Hong Kong, but with great care. *Asiaweek* magazine runs regular features on shopping for travelers, with news of latest cons. Switching Nikon-like for Nikon is common over East Asia beyond Japan. Published comparative price lists over past 2 years show Hong Kong to have at best 15% price advantage over Tokyo, plus another 10-15% haggle margin. But in many top brands Tokyo matches. And this does not include discounters like **LAOX** in Akihabara, or **Yodoyabashi Camera** in Shinjuku, or Nihonbashi electronic district of Osaka or Kobe's Motomachi camera shops, especially our favorite, **Yoshida Camera.** Buying in Japan, too, is absolutely safe, no switches or fakes, satisfaction guaranteed, product warrantees effective. But you will probably do better for electronics in any US shopping mall, and certainly for most cameras or computers at New York's 47th Street Camera and their ilk.

MISCELLANEOUS ITEMS: What will it be—pearls, silks, ceramics, textiles, paintings, handicraft items, books, electronic goods, photography equipment, etc, just to mention some popular categories. Of these silk yard goods are definitely best in China or Hongkong, being imported here.

At this moment with our dollar being what it is, many Japanese things are cheaper at home in United States, or even UK, or in neighboring stops such as Hong Kong or Korea. Silk fabrics, cheap pearls and garments may be better buys in Hong Kong, China, Thailand and now in Korea where export designer garments are made as in Hong Kong, and overage on orders and rejects for slight flaws are great bargains.

There is no place like Japan for fine quality craft wares, notably ceramics —good quality commercial ware or those by artists, semi-antique and antique pieces, woodblock prints and handicraft items such as baskets and paper products which are in great demand by devotees of tea ceremony, flower arrangement, calligraphy, etc. Where these are local specialties, and thus good buys, we cover them in detail as we visit their native areas.

WHERE TO SHOP

COMBINE SHOPPING with sightseeing. Having covered Kyoto shopping since my arrival in 1952 for my shopping columns in Japan Times and English Mainichi, and living just an hour away, I've covered it quite fully. And since everyone goes to Kyoto, you might check *Kyoto Shopping* for almost anything, especially things unusual. For **short-time tourist,** we suggest visit to largest **department store** in town, where we suspect you'll love household floor. I usually head for ceramic section for boxed sets of beautiful dishes, all sizes and shapes, in sets of 5 (traditional number of place settings here) from as low as ¥2,-3,000; kimono floor (cotton yukata, textiles) and art floors. Next most convenient would be **hotel arcades,** or specialized shopping centers geared to foreigner's tastes, such as International Arcade in Tokyo, Yokohama's Motomachi Shopping Street. We'll cover these and special products of each region as we travel around. We mention some in passing: for electronics it's TOKYO's Akihabara, OSAKA's Nihonbashi; wholesale toys, dolls, novelties in TOKYO's Kappabashi, Asakusabashi, as also ceramics; antiques—temple fairs in TOKYO, KYOTO; clusters of antique shops as TOKYO's Aoyama, KYOTO's Shinmonzen and Teramachi-dori; folk arts-only shops *mingei-ten*; and 3-day pottery fairs in KYOTO, SETO, ARITA; *washi*-papermakers; kimonos old and new at temple fairs; gold foil lacquerware in KANAZAWA.

DEPARTMENT STORES called *depahto* are unique institution here: festive air permeates them. They not only fill family's need for merchandise, but serve as entertainment and educational center, combined with recreation to provide everything even for family sunday outing.

Main department stores devote entire floor to exhibits, lasting only one week, of calibre even New York's Met would envy: full-scale reproductions of Tunghuan frescoes with over 326 paintings, many over 6ft wide, some 30ft (Tokyo's Takashimaya Department Store and Kyoto Museum of Art). Archaeological treasures of Iran, Iraq, USSR etc. Every week sees some outstanding exhibit at one or more department stores in town—major ones like Buddhist Sculpture of Heian Era; New Archaeological Discoveries in China; All-Japan Ikebana Artists Exhibition; ceramics by some Living National Treasure. At times, almost entire floor may be rented by secondhand book shops (great woodblock prints); art and curio dealers; groups for flower arrangement, painting, calligraphy, or pottery exhibitions.

Depahto usually 7–9 storeys tall, with rooftop playground for children complete with mini-train rides, and evening beer gardens in summer. Huge, larger than most department stores in US, surprisingly always crowded (Tokyo's Ikebukuro Seibu was largest in world, till Sogo in Yokohama). Open daily 10am - 7:00 (Sogo set new trend staying open daily until 7pm); X-one day in midweek. English-speaking personnel available, take credit cards, free delivery locally, gift-wrap, ship overseas and domestic at cost, have gift certificates, accept returns and exchange goods. Major old chains: Mitsukoshi, Takashimaya, Daimaru, Matsuzakaya, Sogo, Hankyu, Isetan with latecomers Seibu, Daiei.

Newer ones rise 9–12 floors, while older ones spread sideways taking over buildings next door, even across streets, joined by bridges. Many are at terminals of train lines which own them. Setup is similar: **basement** 2fls foods (closes 30min later), delicatessen, prepared Japanese gourmet dishes (from top restaurants), sushi, meats, seafood, fruits, vegetables, groceries, sweets all outlets of leading shops, imports–great place to sample exotic tidbits you may never have seen before. From trays of samples set out fresh every few minutes, toothpicks handy for sticky stuff–just munch, nod smile and go on–unless you want to buy as visiting gift; **Street Fl** jewelry, cosmetics, handbags, shoes; **2nd-4th Fl** ready-to-wear for entire family, designer boutiques both foreign and local; **5th-6th Fl** kimonos, bedding, household, children's goods; **7th Fl** art gallery (or 6), art goods, stationery, toys, furniture, musical instruments; **8th Fl** bargain floor, photo salon, exhibition space, restaurants, special exhibits. Lunch at branches of well-known restaurants here (both W- and J-cuisine) or snack at tea shops scattered throughout store. Restaurants in many open until 9pm, separate entrance also available from street after store hours.

New-type *depahto* or complex of specialty shops doing away with food, furniture and ordinary household goods, etc sprang up, and in Tokyo it started with **Axis**, revolutionary concept featuring design be it in smart fashion both imports and locals, accessories, photos, stationery, gift items; nationwide **Tokyu Hands**, great hobby shop (3 sections with 8 floors each) with everything to do with home and garden. And now conglomerates **Parco I** (9fls), **II** (6fls), **III** (7fls), each open till 8pm; **Hanae Mori Bldg**, first of spectacular architectural masterpieces (this by TANGE Kenzo) for showing off designer clothes, antiques, accessories.

Short of space, shops go **underground**, especially at linked subway-train terminals. No longer just sweets and souvenirs as at first, but discount to high fashion boutiques, restaurants. Tokyo JR always had big one; now amazing underground towns exist at Shinjuku, Ikebukuro and Shibuya—all keep later hours for commuters. Osaka Umeda is another maze of designer boutiques, discount shops, sportswear, shoes, diamonds, books, etc., and eating places many of which are branches of top restaurants.

It's convenient to shop here because small shops stay open almost every day of year and until late. Banks earliest to close, at 3pm; offices 5; name and department stores generally at 6pm, with trend to open until 6:30 or even 7pm daily and later on weekend and holiday. **New specialty** (family- and youth-oriented) stores open till late.

WHAT TO BUY

USED TO BE cameras and hi-fi, but high yen makes you think twice. Clothes are possible if you're 5ft 6in or so; didn't fit well, Japanese physique being different; but younger generation is growing taller. Men's wear, extremely conservative, is changing, particularly for younger male. There is no gay syndrome here—nice to see men taking to clothes more daringly different, flambouyant. Designer garments in demand by many foreign women as they are cut larger, and distinctive, especially sweaters. As we travel along good buys will be listed by area, so have fun browsing.

I'll list at random some things I'd like to take either unique or better made in Japan. Top on list is ceramics–antique, new artists' works or manu-factured–gold foil lacquer, woodblock prints, handmade *washi* paper, paper goods, secondhand kimono and obi, new silks in kimono cloth rolls 36cm/15in x 12.5m/40ft. Old Sendai-type chests, bamboo ikebana baskets, good pearls.

TAKE OR SHIP?: So, you bought too much. Flying to US or Canada it's easy—take it with you, cheapest, as mentioned above, no charges for handling, customs clearance at both ends or delivery; you can have many cases or boxes as long as each is under 32kg/70lb wt limit; pay by piece.

To **Europe** or **Australia** it becomes expensive to take it with you. Your choice is **unaccompanied baggage**, half cost of basic air freight, much less than excess baggage. Allow 3hrs at check-in before flight and have agent like **Kinki Tsukan** in Osaka–Itami airport handle it for you: present passport and airplane ticket. Otherwise advise one day before or earlier to be at destination when you arrive as it takes time for custom clearance and documentation in air freight area far from passenger terminal. This holds for air cargo especially. But check your airline few days ahead, as at least one European line has weird ideas about what can constitute personal excess baggage. Sample rate London unaccompanied bag is ¥3,320/kg; air cargo is ¥7,035; excess baggage is 1% of first class fare. To Australia (Sydney), unaccompanied ¥1,062/kg; air cargo ¥2,134; excess ¥4,400. Post Office **SAL**—Surface Air Lifted, sending package consolidated air to continue by surface. Cost about 40% less than airmail; ex.: to US 3kg by SAL ¥4,700, air ¥7,400, sea ¥2,950; 10kg max. Reduces delivery time over sea by 2/3.

Air parcel post has increased weight limit to 20kg for some countries, tho rate has not changed. Example: Europe 15kg ¥24,000, 20kg ¥29,700. (10kg still ¥18,700).

Federal Express now here, but due to customs rules not convenient for us tourists.

Nippon Express (*Nittsu*), **Kintetsu**, other Express agents door-to-door services for smaller parcels; Max 20kg: to LA 20kg ¥32,000—incl all. Remember, regular air cargo customs clearance-, handling-, delivery-charges mount up, doubling basic freight bill.

KIDS: Dad will have just as much fun as his kids in toy shops. It's custom to have demo models of all items, so test that barking dog, super electro-robot, radio-controlled racing car... In fact, it's good place to leave well-behaved child while Mom does her shopping. Many imported toys line shelves at usually twice price of back home, so local toys are better buys. There are wholesale areas, but if only visiting, savings not worth hassle.

For tots, educational toys, new here, improving; great Japanese toys in States mostly made for export. But good selection in clever wooden toys, imported and traditional, with latter making comeback at impetus of Scandi-navians. Preschool age has cuddly animals tho not cheap and dolls, usually safe hair—tho new imports from cheaper-labor neighbors causing quality problems once so common to 'Made in Japan'. Future mommies have great playhouse items—cooking, serving sets, mini sewing machines. Japanese dolls were made to be admired, not played with. So today's dolls are mostly Western-style. No end to toys that walk, talk and what have you.

For fellahs, no end. Mechanical toys, battery-run, gadgets, games, no end to electronic toys, robots, dinosaurs, Godzillah—who is of American descent, evolved admittedly of King Kong. Do-it-yourself kits for inquisitive, excellent opticals: microscopes still cheap w/ prepared specimen slides; junior astronomer kits; binoculars from toys to pro; cameras cheaper USA. Pocket crystal radio kits to snap-together radio and computer components, entomologist and botanist kits, artist's adjustable easels and oil or watercolor paint kits and colored pencils in attractive kiddy-design cases.

In general *depahto* have best selection, except in TOKYO with its multistorey all-toy shops, as well as bargain areas under JR tracks known as Ameya-yokko-cho, Okachimachi by JR UENO, covered in our TOKYO. In OSAKA, there is Matsuyama (to locals *Matcha-machi* 'toy-town'), blocks of wholesale toys and gadgets. If you live here, then these latter are great, but when passing through stick to *depahto* unless you happen to be in Tokyo and near following. **Kiddyland** was first all-toy shop to open more than 35 years ago during Occupation, in Harajuku at Jingumae on Omotesando-dori in 5-storey bldg, now has basement and five floors filled with toys to play with and look at, games, computers, party favors & goods, hobbies, books, greeting cards, robot toys and hundreds of gadgets. They set up there long before it became fashionable as Hanae Mori's home. **Familiar** at 6-chome has 4fl toy section (*see below*), and 2 short blocks away at 8-chome is largest toy shop in Japan **Hakuhinkan Toy Park**—bit of everything on Ifl; 2fl games and hobbies; 3fl toys; 4fl dolls; 5-7fl restaurants; 8fl theater.

For fashion conscious, there's been complete changeover and youngsters are being catered to by top designers: Mori Hanae, Yves St. Laurent, Ikeda Nobuo's Mini K line, Kenzo even has infants' line; other lines Comme ca du mode, Diable, Crill, etc. **Familiar** is children's wear shop started in Kobe by 3 enterprising housewives 38 years ago. 25-30 years ago when we lived in Wakayama, I used to get wonderful handknits in local marketplace for our kids, nieces and nephews and discovered they were Familiar rejects made by group of ladies near us. Could never see what was wrong, they were great. Their motto is quality first and they've lived up to it. They may not be ultra chic, but you know it's well made—and healthy: infants' and toddlers' wear are strictly 100% fine cotton. They shy away from synthetics and stick to natural fibers; good buys. **Familiar** is found nationwide now in *depahto* and shopping main streets, including Tokyo's Ginza 6-chome, where they have 4-storey building: Ifl clothing for toddlers; 2fl garments up to children 160cm/5'4" tall, plus tea shop, beauty shop; 3fl infants' wear, furniture; 4fl toys, video room. Flagship store in Kobe on Motomachi Shopping Arcade, 1-chome; branch almost as large few blocks W at W end Sentah-gai Arcade. Children's shoes are great, colorful, stylish and sturdy, but best of all are velcroix fasteners on most. Of course, in Japan, everyone takes shoes off as they enter own home or friends'.

Festival happi coat with belt and headband or cotton *yukata* kimono with *shibori* tie-dye sash makes happy souvenir. Synthetic-silk mixture *koshoku* kimono and padded vest sets affordable—pure silk (*honken*) expensive. Child's kimono looks large but vertical tucks at shoulders adjust sleeve and horizontal tuck at hip for length are elements of proper kimono—grow with tot. Don't forget *obi* sash, *geta* wooden clogs, and for her, small purse.

FOR HIM: Dress in Japan is rather informal. You won't have need for tux even if you plan on hitting diplomatic do's. Dinner jacket may be advisable in summer mainly because of its comfort compared to regular jacket. Tux coming into fashion with J- now in 1920s art deco *retro*-boom.

Tokyo is not place to buy clothes, nothing off rack much over size 37, tho' some reasonably-priced local Indian tailors, one we've used with satisfaction is **Riki Sarani**, advertises regularly in tourist papers. Hong Kong, of course, is better, Korea now perhaps best. But, of course, you may not be going on to either. If you like wild vests then look into Japanese silk brocade: ready-made at number of stores in Kyoto and Tokyo. Ah, those days of $5 custom-made silk shirts—best now, Bangkok, but Hong Kong offers fair selection of ready-mades, mostly from mainland, especially summer styles. And India, if going that far.

For something different in summer sports shirts, one *yukata* bolt, best material ¥4,-7,000, makes 2 shirts. Catching on, now sold ready-made in department stores. Slightly higher handwoven *kasuri* weave in linen, silks, cottons in miniscule white dots on blue, or bold 'Italianesque' stripes which Japanese have been wearing for eons. Shikoku, Kyushu best, department stores there push as local *meibutsu*, name-goods. Wears forever, easy care.

If you have precious or semi-precious gems, Japan's fairly good place to have them mounted. It is *not* place to buy gems since only pearls are native. You can however buy fine synthetics cheap. For mounting and special work, silver miscellany and special order mounting see **Mori Silver**, out in big **Oriental Bazaar** at Jingu-mae 5-chome. Wife of maker is blue-eyed, flaming-red-haired Yankee columnist for *Nippon View* and 30 years for major English-language dailies on shopping and festivals, our once leg-gal on our old tourist magazine, Sandy Martine Mori—helped us update our shopping in Tokyo and how to bet on horses. For magnificent gifts, religious paraphernalia including whole mass sets, personal friend Mas SHIMIZU, **Aloha Silver**, bit hard to find, phone ☎(03)-3328-7439, English.

Most hotel shops carry repetitious line. Don't let it get you down with its gaudiness. Hunt and you'll find some little masterpieces of craftsmanship in silver, damascene, cloisonne, Satsuma china or countless other techniques. Japanese don't wear it—they want Champs Elysee or Fifth Ave brands.

For shoes, pass Japan. For custom-made, Hong Kong and Korea (with care). However sizes 8 or smaller may find some casual footwear. Best shoes are all imports from Italy or Switzerland—in Hong Kong.

Hats are out, also gloves. High fashions here still depend on Europe. Some young (Jpn *yongu*) styles originate here now, but pricey. Hong Kong and Korea keep up to date as they manufacture for export, cut labels out of surplus designer clothes to sell locally as 'Brand X'.

FOR HER: There's so much to choose from, where do we start. We'll concentrate on things Japanese. Silk products for one. Modern silks, yard or meter wide, best in Hongkong or China, and perhaps back home, but subtle colors, different textures, hand-painted designs with or without embroidery in oriental motifs can be found inexpensively here in exquisite secondhand kimonos. Japanese women want new washable synthetic kimono materials in *tanmono* rolls (excellent selection in department stores). For blouses two *furoshiki* squares in solids, prints or scenes. Visit kimono fl of DS, for feast for your eyes–rolls and rolls (37.5cm/15in x 12m/13yds). Narrow width may be drawback, but clever bodice design with seam in center or 3-panels and panelled skirts should make up lovely dress. In solid colors there's texture range from thin crepe de chine to heavy rippled chirimen silk, delicate creams thru deep sea blues, unusual colors made from flowers, herbs, trees; classical processes of *katazome* stencil, yuzen paste-resist, *shibori* tie-dye and batik dyeing; machine-woven on jacqard looms, hand-woven intricate ikat. Choice of pure silk, silk with wool, linen, synthetic (*koshoku*), synthetic textured like silk, and cotton. *Obi* sash come in two basic styles—*nagoya* worn by older women, is shorter and narrower, and *fukuro-obi*, longer and wider material folded lengthwise.

My shopping list for $200 in silk products (prices quoted are for inexpensive, but good quality, because there is no limit to price for quality in fabric and workmanship).

2 beautiful silk kimono (secondhand) to make blouses & skirts...	$50.00
1 gorgeous wedding kimono (") for wall hanging...	$70.00
1 old kimono sash (maru-obi) 12'x27" when opened, for cushion covers...	$80.00

Available at shops geared to foreign customers as Japanese shun secondhand articles in general. Best buys in Tokyo: **Hayashi Kimono**, main shop in International Arcade under tracks behind Imperial Hotel. Temple antique fairs have good secondhand kimono stalls: Kyoto monthly temple sales at **Toji** (21st) and **Kitano** (25th), and **Kikuya** (see p.559) with stacks of kimonos from ¥500+. Visit kimono floor any *depahto* for gay washable cotton *yukata*, available generally only in spring and summer except in hotel and shopping arcades geared to tourists—where often cheaper as at Imperial basement magazine counter. Fair selection reasonably priced these and happi-coats in most sizes even XL, airport lobby shops OSAKA, TOKYO.

For your house: Utilitarian ceramics, beautiful sets of tea cups, bowls and dishes with exquisite painting, Western dinnerware like Noritake, and decoratives items, all of these easy to find. However one item which we love, noh masks, are not that easy to find—department stores carry on *bijutsu* (art) floor. Finely carved of females (*ko-omote, waka-onna*), old man (*okina*), demon (*hannya*) ¥120,000+. Osaka **Hankyu** DS decorative ones from ¥20,000 of compress. **Kyoto Handicraft Center** clay ¥5,-12,000 at Nakayama Doll; Uchida unpainted compressed wood ¥4,500. We carefully combed Kyoto shops for them— outstanding are few real at **Satake** Ancient Musical Instrument shop on Teramachi-dori.

'Made in Japan' now signifies well-made, stylish and usually expensive. If you have favorite designers, have fair idea of what their clothes cost at home and then compare prices here. Japanese designers have made their mark overseas, pioneered by such as Hanae MORI in NY, Kenzo TAKADA (Paris), Issey MIYAKE (NY), Gunyuki WATANABE (London) over decade ago. Meantime, in haute couture circles Ichiro KIMIJIMA, Jun ASHIDA, KOSHINO sisters, Hiroko, Junko & Michiko join Dior, Chanel. Then SHIMADA Junko with sports line, YAMAMOTO Yoji, KAWAKUBO Rei (Comme des Garcons) and YAMAMOTO Kansai just begin our list of designers in more popular price range. In Tokyo, Harajuku is fashion center (Omote Sando at Aoyama-dori) where most of these have salons. Depahto are becoming extremely fashion conscious and have boutiques of top designers. Younger fashion conscious have Takeshita-dori off Harajuku stn, latest trendy and far-out clothes, including recycled, ethnic, and nostalgic Roaring '20s and '50s.

It's not possible to cover much here, so if really intent on shopping here pick up *Born to Shop* (*Tokyo*) by Suzy Gershman & Judith Thomas, excellent guide, shows which overseas designers' clothes are sold where, whether cheaper here or home, and discuss clothes by local designers.

Just short mention here on **jewelry**. Only pearls are native to Japan, so we say avoid other gems. At present best quality pearls are better buys here in Japan than elsewhere, but for lower quality Hong Kong, China or elsewhere may be better. However, shell pearl looks and feels like pearl, weighs same at not fraction of cost, is good buy. With dollar exchange as it is, pearl dealers have difficult time and are happy to make sacrifice sales. We have our favorite small shops in Tokyo and cover it more fully there.

Shopping is great fun—only trouble being "there's too much to choose from" and "I'll get it later" and we never find it again. *C'est la vie!*

*Wee spent fortie days in learning the Elements
of the Japanese language with great labour.*
                              —Francis Xavier 1549

*Japanese ... extremely difficult,
yet easy to acquire smattering of.*
          — B.H. Chamberlain, *Handbook to Japan*, 1900

SAY IT IN NIHON-GO

IT'S TRUE what they say–everything goes (some) other way. There is no language spoken in any even moderately advanced society in our world today that differs more from English or other Western languages, than does Japanese. It is not just vocabulary (in fact, Japanese is said to have absorbed over 10,000 English words postwar), but rather its entire concept of expression, concept of intercommunication. Basic trouble is social, and that has, as you may suspect in having read this far, historical cause–three centuries of seclusion and total thought-control. This is not going to be historical or socio-psychological essay any more than it is going to be quickie mastery course in language.

Japanese language is not meant, as western languages, as medium of intellectual communication–it trades on its fine shades of meaning as being aesthetically sensitive and rich in nuance. However, other than art or nature terms it is probably poorer in nuance than English or French, while also clumsy at expressing direct thoughts. Chinese can be more indirect than Japanese, but it can also be as almost jarringly direct and concise as English. Japanese occupies middle ground, less 'diplomatic' than these others, also far less direct. This is not intrinsic to structure of language but purely social. Modern Japan is facing this problem, which reflects on trade imbalance as much as it does on culture shock for tourists–Japanese as well as foreign–on educational and social problems, on youth's reinventing privacy. Expect problems, but expect strong effort by other side to help solve these. Language is medium of expressing intent to help, if also inability. Smile is important, as are patience and good will. It is sincerely reciprocated.

'Yes' is translated in dictionaries as Japanese *'hai'* (pronounced as in 'hi-there'). This does not mean 'yes', it means 'I agree with–', or perhaps just 'understand, what you say' so that if you ask, 'Isn't it raining?' when it isn't raining, answer may be *'hai'*, meaning 'yes, it isn't raining'. It might also be *'hai'*, meaning 'yes, it is raining'–so better look for yourself. This carries over into Japanese-speaker's use of English.

'No' is impolite statement (never be impolite to guest); thus it is more often expressed by silence or changing subject (which gentlemen on prowl should keep in mind). If you get blank stare in answer, rephrase your affirmative question to negative, so response can agree with it and thus tell you 'no' by confirming your negative supposition.

This tight social system has formalized system of fixed responses to set situations, so that if you know proper trigger, you entitle yourself to natural response. And same social system makes 'pidgin' impossible. You simply cannot get by with Japanese version of, 'Hey you fellah b'long shop, you speak how much'. You use different type of language depending upon relative status of yourself and your communicant, with variations for gender (sorry feminists, this is status) and familiarity. If *tu* and *vous* of French annoys or amuses or confounds you, just try mastering minimal half-dozen Japanese terms for 'you', plus their parallel vocabulary changes. This is not as bad as it sounds, as Japanese confuse further by ignoring pronoun almost entirely in both speech and literature. However, situation is reflected in fact that there are at least two ways to phrase every question, simple and refined, with latter almost always complicated construction. You and we, as honorable guests, rate most refined, polite circumlocutions. Our use of few simple phrases will often be met with wide-eyed amazement, total non-reaction (we have seen this happen with Americans who speak fluent Japanese), or other extreme, with answers in English–variously horrid to perfect. Part of this is understandable–Japanese has very subtle musical stress and entire intonation pattern is physically different from any Aryan tongue, tho vowel system is closest to Italian and Spanish.

You will get along just as well, if not better, with very simple English–you will get along better yet if you write it down. English is compulsory for three years in junior high, three years of high school, and two years university minimum. All this is usually limited to translation of written passages or grammatical parsing. Result is only few in tourist-affiliated service industry who can speak decent English (except professionals in major hotels, interpreters, almost never taxi-drivers), yet large number of people who can read simple phrase and understand it. Young English teacher's speech may be barely comprehensible, but fluent English is often spoken by kimonoed old men, fading with those old silk marvels.

Key is also good humor and patience. Don't show annoyance even if you'd like to murder, it only flusters and befuddles, or turns them off. Worst goof-up must be laughed off just as they will allow you–nay, expect you–to smile away your own master faux-pas when you try Japanese.

We have added some key words and expressions in relevant sections. If you are going to leave beaten path (as we certainly hope you will–if you don't, we have failed), there are numerous phrase books and dictionaries. We have tried them all, ourselves, or on friends with varying degrees of language and travel experience.

BOOKS TO CARRY

FOR SPEAKING Japanese, we recommend Berlitz' *Japanese for travellers*–small, handy, well organized ($4.95). Expressions are also written in Japanese so you can show it, if not understood. Simplified dictionary with words in kanji ideographs is included.

Phrase book available at even airports is easy to use *Just Enough Japanese*, series by Passport Books pocketbook, $3.95, with Japanese script for pointing at, under which is raw romanization, under that preferred romanization, intelligently grouped. Problem still is to understand response.

JNTO issues useful, free, shirtpocket-slim *Tourist's Handbook* also intelligently organized, but Japanese in Japanese script only so useful only for pointing at–as inside front cover says in headline-size script for your introductory attention-catching (with slight bow, smile and supplicant *onegai-shimasu*). Then try to figure out response!

Numerous language texts–growth industry. But best current book for learning to read is *Remembering the Kanji* by JW Heisig, JPT Publ., vol 1 –writing and meanings (¥4,000); vol 2–readings (¥3,500). Uses round about novel approach that seems to work with less pain, but no less sweat.

For getting into nitty gritty of conversation, we can't speak too highly of *How to be Polite in Japanese* by eminently readable *Japan Times* language columnists MIZUTANI Osamu and Nobuko, Japan Times Ltd, ¥1,800.

Yes bookshop *Japan for Westerners* best directory of language texts, dictionaries: ✍ Yes Bookshop, 1035 31st St NW, Washington DC.

SOME HINTS FOR PRONOUNCING JAPANESE

IN PRONOUNCING Japanese do not stress any syllable, (don't draw it out or drawl, it is very staccato) but flatten it all out. There is stress, musical, which you will certainly muff. Unstressed Japanese is understood; wrong stress might as well be Swahili. Syllables are always consonant-vowel or vowel alone. Don't mouth, lips should be frozen open in slight smile. All consonants are pronounced clearly; *G* is always hard, as in girl; *J* hard English style, jet; *C* not used except in combination *ch*, when pronounced as in English–any *C* seen alone in nonstandard use will be as *K*. *F* is said lips slightly apart like lightly blowing away feather. Only *N* stands alone as consonant to close some syllables, nasalized in real New York style.

VOWELS are 'as in Spanish', that is in their simple short form with no variations, and are simply *a, e, i, o, u*––in Japanese order–*a, i, u, e, o* (pronounced clipped *ah, ee, oo, eh, oh* as in m<u>a</u>ma, <u>eat</u>, p<u>u</u>t, g<u>e</u>t, <u>or</u>). Two vowels together are pronounced separately, even if double. Vowel may be lengthened with simple alternate (which we use when necessary) of added *h*, instead of scholarly diacritical mark; often as not it is ignored in writing in Latin letters (Tokyo should be Tohkyo, var Tôkyô).

Double consonant results from melding two syllables and should be pronounced harder than single–*tt* is like tonguing off hair, *t-t;* but this will give little trouble in comprehension.

In rendering foreign words they may be written as pronounced by Japanese, with extra vowels thrown in between consonants, and *L* changed to *R* (or *R* to *L* by someone showing off his *L*s), *V* to '*Bu*'. Thus, your mispronouncing English word a la Japanese rules will often be understood as Japanese: *hoteru* for hotel, *moteru*-motel; *runchi* for lunch; *teki* for steak (from French *bif-tek*); *resutoran* for restaurant; *duraibu, d'raibuwei, d'raibu-in* for drive, driveway, drive-in; *sutoppu,* stop; *bakku, raito, refuto* for back, right, left; *orai* (usually *orai-orai*) for all right, and *okeh* for okay; *basu* for both bus and bath and *bosu* for boss; *toi-re* for toilet and *takushi*-taxi, *haya*-hire car, etc ad inf, from *harro* to *guddo-bai.*

More trouble may come from signs in Latin alphabet (*romaji* in Japanese, Roman letters), for there is special Japanese use of our letters wherein they write *tu*, pronounce 'tsu', *ti* for 'chi', *si* for 'shi' (Japanese cannot pronounce our 'si', so don't be surprised to be invited to enter living room for defecation and tea), *hu* for 'fu' and *zi* for 'ji'. Both systems are used chaotically interchangeably on menus and railway stations, so be prepared: Fuji may be distorted to Huzi, halfway to Fuzi, or spelled clearly Fuji.

Nihon-go, like any living language–Academie Francaise au contraire–is replete with foreign words as hundreds enter annually, some to die but most to become naturalized. 8th century Japan absorbed Korean and Chinese terms so much that most ideographs have at least two totally different 'readings', pronunciations–*on* or 'sound' meaning Japanese, and *kun* or 'meaning' being mispronounced Chinese, sometimes more than one as versions entered at different eras as Chinese evolved, or from different dialects of Chinese. Anthropologists are finding earlier incursions of Turkic and even Aryan words. Odd words continued to immigrate. Portuguese *obligato* wet-backed in during 16th century to naturalize as *arigato*, thank you, while 19th century Germanophile intellectuals adopted *arbeit* to mean work, originally for students, thus now being Japanese for 'part time work' –more recently showing contemporary national preferences thru its synonym *pahto-taimu* or *pahto-*, as adjective or noun.

178   SAY IT IN NIHONGO

Academicians can discuss creating new words, especially nouns, from classical native roots. But people decide which will be used. Chauvinistic French chefs still eat *biftek* and Ge̅mans never connected with *farspreckers* but speak afar on 'telefones'. Thus in mid-'50s debate roared as to what to call that new home amusement box: *den-ei* 'electric-picture' like *denwa* 'electric-talk' (telephone, now also commonly understood). Scholars never came up with new term, but people just called unnamed baby *terebijon*, then *terebi* or *t-b*, always written in roman letters 'TV'. And so it goes.

It is said that over 10,000 English words have entered Nihon-go since 1945. You could carry on simple Japanese conversation using only English words, with some proper verb endings and parts of speech–assuming you knew the proper local word order and 'correct' mispronunciation.

HANDY EXPRESSIONS: Few quickie life-saver terms are in order. These 'open sesame' phrases combined with gestures and appropriate nouns will save you much time. These few trigger phrases eliminate need for large vocabulary, but most important they ready your communicant to size up situation and give active response which would be next natural step. You'll find that in stores, stations, anyplace, 1–*chotto* with beckoning motion brings someone to you, as does **sumi-masen** (more polite). Then 2–**sumi-masen ga** readies them to hear what you want, and your 3–*onegai-shimasu* presents your request, ending with 4–*domo-arigato* or *sumi-masen deshita* as your 'thank you' or just all-around *domo* with nod of head, or by itself either *arigato* or *sumi-masen.* Thus these magic words: *Chotto sumi-masen* -pause-; *sumi-masen-ga* -action-; *onegai-shimasu* will get you thru dozens of situations.

Chotto is used to catch one's attention; like 'Sir' or 'Madam' or simply 'say, there,' and also means 'just a minute', 'little bit,' 'slightly'.

Sumi-masen is used to catch attention, too, and also to express regret or apology as when you step on someone's toes. 'I'm sorry, excuse me'.

Sumi-masen-ga (with additional postposition -*ga*) is useful to prefix anything as good trigger meaning, 'Look, I'm going to ask you something, so please prepare to help me...switch on your listen and help attitude'.

Onegai-shimasu is used to ask for something, polite request. Means 'Would you please help me...' and action is required on part of listener.

Now putting these together, we have as an example—at station you want redcap to carry your bags but you don't know how to say 'Would you carry these bags for me.'

Chotto! (hey there!) *sumi-masen-ga* (excuse me). However, it is enough to know *sumi-masen-ga.* Just substitute *kore* (these), point to your bags and *onegai-shimasu.* Just say: '*sumi-masen ga, kore, onegai-shimasu'.*

Dozo is often listed as 'please', along with onegai-shimasu, but it is different in that it implies 'if it pleases you (communicant) then, 'please'. And it also takes care of natural action to follow gesture or situation. So - *dozo* 'please enter'; *dozo* 'please shut door if you'd like it shut', but— *onegai-shimasu* 'I want you to shut door'. It doubles for *dozo, kudasai* (give me), many verbs, for it covers action required in given situation.

Thus **one phrase** *onegai-shimasu* with appropriate gesture is as:
in train or bus: 'Please, let me off', or pointing, palm up, to seat 'Would you kindly move over some so I can sit down';
in store: 'Show me this'; handing object 'Wrap this up, please';
restaurant: 'May we be seated', 'I want to have...', '...check please';
to redcap at station: 'Would you please take these bags and ...' **(entering)** '...show me where to buy tickets', or also proffering tickets '...take us to proper platform', or **(exiting)** '...to taxi stand'. (Cont'd p181)

HANDY TEAR-OUT VOCABULARY

AMENITIES

Yes	*Hai*
No (– no, don't do that)	*Iie (– damé desu)*
Thank you	*Arigato (alone or + gozaimasu)*
Please	*Dozo; onegai-shimasu*
Thank you very much	*Domo arigato gozaimasu*
You're welcome	*Doitashimashite*
Excuse me; (on leaving)	*Sumimasen; shitsurei-shimasu*
I'm sorry	*Sumimasen; gomen-nasai*
Good morning (til l0am)	*Ohayo (alone or + gozaimasu)*
Good day, – afternoon	*Konnichiwa*
Good evening	*Konbanwa*
Good bye	*Sayonara*
Good night	*O-yasumi-nasai*
See you later (tomorrow)	*Dewa mata (ashita)*
Please come in	*Irasshai mase*
Thanks for everything	*Iro-iro arigato gozaimasu*
'..., I troubled you much	*Gomeiwaku o okake shimashita*
Just a minute	*Chotto matte (alone or + kudasai)*
I am _____	*Watakushi wa (name) desu*
This is my friend Mary	*Kochira wa tomodachi no Mary-san desu*
How do you do?	*Hajime mashite*
How are you?	*Ikaga desu ka; O-genki desu ka?*
Fine, thank you	*Hai, arigato gozaimasu*
And you?	*Anata wa?*
Fine	*Genki desu*
Do you speak English?	*Eigo ga deki masu ka?*
I don't speak (much) Japanese	*Nihongo wa (amari) deki masen*
Speak more slowly please	*Motto yukkuri hanashite kudasai*
Could you repeat that	*Mo ichido itte kudasai*
Please write it in English	*Eigo de kaite kudasai*

QUESTIONS

Where, *doko* Where is it (are they)?   _____*wa doko desu ka?*
  Where are you going?   *Doko e iki masu ka?*
  Where did you put it?   *Doko ni oki mashita ka?*
  Where do they sell it (them)?   *Doko de utte imasu ka?*

When, *Itsu* —can be used interchangeably with *nan-ji* (what time)
  When shall we go?   *Itsu iki masho ka?...nan-ji ni iki masho ka?*
  When shall we come?   *Itsu ki masho ka?*
  When did you come?   *Itsu ki mashita ka?*
  When does it open?   *Itsu aki masu ka?*

What, *nani* (*nan*) What is it?   *Nan desu ka?*
  What are you doing tonight?   *Konban nani o shimasu ka?*
  What will you have?   *Nani ni shimasu ka?*

Why, *naze* or *doshite* Why are you going?   *Naze iki masu ka?*
  Why is it ¥600 yen?   *Naze/Doshite 600 yen desu ka?*
  Why did you go?   *Naze/Doshite ikimashita ka?*

Who, *dare/donata* Who is it?   *Dare/donata desu ka?*
  With whom are you going?   *Dare to ikimasu ka?*
  Whose is that?   *Sore wa dare no desu ka?*

Which, *dore/dochira* Which do you want?   *Dore ga hoshii desu ka?*
  Which bus is for Kyoto?   *Kyoto-yuki no basu wa dore desu ka?*
  Which are the cheap ones?   *Dore ga yasui no desu ka?*

How, *donokurai*

How far? or How long?	*Donokurai kakarimasu ka?*
How many (in number)?	*Ikutsu (donokurai) arimasu ka?*
How much (in quantity)?	*Ikura (donokurai) arimasu ka?*

CHOPSTICKS

May I have a menu please?	*Menyu kudasai (onegai-shimasu)*
I want this	*Kore o kudasai (onegai-shimasu)*
Come with me please (to sample in case)	*Chotto kite kudasai*
I'd like more <u>water</u>	*Mo sukoshi <u>omizu</u> onegai-shimasu*
'....(tea / coffee / rice)	'...(*o cha / kohi / gohan*)
(or ask for refill)	*Okawari onegai-shimasu*
Where is the toilet?	*Toi-re (ote-arai) wa doko desu ka?*
May I have the <u>check</u> please?	<u>*O-kanjo*</u> *onegai-shimasu*

GETTING THERE

Where is the <u>train (bus) stn</u>?   *JR no eki (bus sentah)* **wa doko desu ka?**

Ticket booth	*Kippu-uriba*	Gift shop	*Bai -ten*
Platform	*Ho-mu*	Lockers	*Rokkah*
Exit	*De-guchi*	Taxi stand	*Taxi noriba*
Entrance	*Iri-guchi*	Redcap	*Akabo*
End of line/last stop	*Shu-ten*	Dining car	*Shokudo sha*
Information booth	*Annai-jo*	No-smoking car	*Kin-en sha*
Hotel info booth	*Ryokan annai-jo*		
Lost and found	*Wasuremono atsukai-jo*		
Baggage checkroom	*Tenimotsu azukarisho*		

A ticket to Kyoto, please, <u>ordinary</u>	*Kyoto yuki o onegai-shimasu,* <u>*futsuu*</u>
express (*kyuko*) spec express (*tokkyu*)	sleeper (*shindai sha*)
first class (*green sha*) one-way (*katamichi*)	round-trip (*o-fuku*)
I have a rail pass	*JR reiru pasu arimasu*
Where do I <u>change</u> trains?	*Densha wa doko de <u>norikai</u> desu ka?*
Which track is it?	*Densha wa nan ban sen desu ka?*

STAYING THERE

Do you have any <u>vacancies</u>?	<u>*Aita heya*</u> *ga arimasu ka?*
I would like a <u>single room.</u>	<u>*Shinguru rumu*</u> *ga hoshii no desu.*
'...room only	(*heya dake; sudomari*);
w/breakfast	(*choshoku tsuki*);
w/2 meals	(*ni shoku tsuki*);
with bath	(*basu tsuki*);
larger room	(*motto okii heya*);
Does it include tax?	*Zei-komi desu ka?*
How much is it per night?	*Ippaku (or ryokin, charge)wa ikura desu ka?*
I will leave at 3pm.	*San-ji ni dekake masu (shuppatsu shimasu).*
When is there a bus for ___?	*___-yuki no basu wa nan-ji ni arimasu ka?*

SHOPPING

Is there a D.S. nearby?	*Chikaku ni depahto ga arimasu ka?*
Where is the food section?	*Shokuryo hin uriba wa doko desu ka?*
Do you sell shampoo?	*Shanpu arimasu ka?*
I would like to buy a camera	*Kamera ga hoshii no desu ga*
" " " a cheaper one	*Motto yasui no ga hoshii no desu ga*
Show me that one, please	*Are o misete kudasai*
How much is it?	*Ikura desu ka?*
May I test it?	*Tameshite mite mo ii desu ka?*
Do you deliver?	*Haitatsu dekimasu ka?*
About when will it arrive?	*Itsu goro ni tsukimasu ka?*
Can you C.O.D. it?	*Chaku barai dekimasu ka?*
Do you take credit cards?	*Kaado yoroshii desu ka?*

Addition of noun broadens possibilities. Thus in taxi, mentioning name of **hotel** + *onegai-shimasu* = 'Please (take me) to Okura Hotel.'

Pronoun 'this' or *koré* is handy to know, others listed later.

Domo sumi-masen expresses gratitude, encompasses more than *arigato* (thank you—16th century mispronounced import of Portuguese *obligato*). Perfect for when someone has gone to extra trouble for you. *Domo sumi-masen* plus **deshita** (past tense) covers all facets–'Sorry to have bothered you; thank you very much for all your help; sorry it didn't turn out' etc ad inf.

Combine these phrases with international language of gestures, pronounce slowly, simply, clearly–shout is not clear–smile, and you'll get along all right. If all this has been too confusing, *domo sumi-masen*.

Now that you know what it's all about, just tear out the previous page leaf and try out some basic phrases, generally in colloquial usage.

EMERGENCY: You may hear someone shout *abunai*, which means 'watch out, danger'. Noun for danger, not so much used, is *kiken*. Greatest fear here is house-fire, *kaji*, which will electrify people to cooperative action as nothing else. If someone, unlikely as it may be, accosts you, vigorous *kaji* will bring help running–and silliness of your fiery reaction is also bound to send him fleeing in confusion. 'Help' is *tasukete*, or commonly slurred *tas'keteh*.

STUDYING JAPANESE HERE

FOR GOOD **language programs**, which are proliferating and getting better *see* LEARNING ABOUT JAPAN. On arrival Japan see *Japan Times* Monday ed also *Tokyo Journal* for ads for Tokyo programs, and *Kansai Time Out* ads for Kyoto-Osaka-Kobe area programs. We suggest intensive Japanese classes, especially the International Christian University program in Tokyo held in summer, 6 weeks of highly intensive work. Japan Foundation opened in July 1989 its institute in Urawa, Saitama Pref, to train language teachers–foreigners to become qualified Japanese-language teachers, and Japanese to teach Japanese overseas.

Most old bilingual dictionaries were designed for Japanese, or conversation only. For more serious students of language there is at last one handy dictionary designed not for native speakers but for illiterates who mean well: *Basic Japanese-English Dictionary*, Japan Foundation, publ by Bonjinsha, ¥2,500; with idiomatic examples, plenty of romaji and *furigana*. Or their distributed *Romanized English-Japanese Dictionary*, publ Taiseido, ¥4,000. Available **Bonjinsha** bookshop; and for their free *Guide to Japanese Language Teaching Materials*, write or phone their mail order svce:

JAC Bldg 5-5-35 Minato-minami, Minato-ku Tokyo-100;   ☎(03)-3472-2240.

Other good pocket-size phrase books or dictionaries include: hard to find classic *English-Japanese Conversation Dictionary* by Arthur Rose-Innes; *Say It In Japanese* by KAI Miwa (Dover Say It Series, New York); *Japanese in Three Weeks* by S. Sheba (40+th edition), Tokyo; less useful, only due to odd size, is Japan Society's *Useful Japanese* by Hyman Kublin.

WRITTEN JAPANESE instructions and directions for taxi drivers will be jotted down for you gladly by hotel clerks and such who speak English. Good idea is to carry some index cards or blank name-cards available in any stationers, ask for *meishi-yo-no-kami*. Keep name-cards (*meishi*) given you, as taxi drivers can use these to find place again. Restaurants, coffee shops, bars and such give out matches (*matchi*) with address and often map, so take this great source of light even if you don't smoke.

P.O. **T POST**   On red pillar or box indicates **Mailbox** (*Posto*); Shop, **Stamp Seller** (*Kitte-uriba*), usually near mailbox; on any building, **Post Office** (*Yubin-kyoku*).

バスのりば   **Bus Stop** (*Basu Noriba*)

タクシーのりば   **Taxi Stand** (*Taxi Noriba*)

地下鉄   **Subway** (*Chikatetsu*)

駅   **Station** (*Eki*)

特急   **Special Express** (*Tokkyu*)

急行   **Regular Express** (*Kyuko*)

準急   **Semi Express** (*Junkyu*)

普通   **Local** (*Futsu or Kaku-eki*)

Above 4 signs distinguish types of non-Shinkansen trains. Often left-hand character appears alone. Local lines have variations.

Written language consists of some 45,000 ideographs, *kanji*, of which most common use is limited to 1870, most modern literature to some 4,000. Add two supplementary systems of sound writing syllabary of 77 letters each (cursive *hiragana* for Japanese endings, words, many first names, and square *katakana*, like our italics, for foreign words), and you have quite some system. Yet close to 100% literacy is attained–was already over 50% by end of feudal era, above most European nations.

But this is not book for teaching *kanji*–meaning 'Han- or China-character' or our ideogram or ideograph, 'idea-writing'.

Note: Japlish redundancy in our book, sorry, *gomennasai*.. Japanese language has for millennium and half–at least when absorbing foreign terms–used new foreign word followed by translation until well-enough accepted that translation could be dropped. We follow this tradition in place names. Thus Temple in Japanese is -*tera* ,-*dera*, or -*ji*–all alternate pronunciations of same ideograph–and when we direct you to such as Kiyomizu-dera Temple or Engaku-ji Temple we consciously redund. Kiyomizu Temple is correct, but may not be understood when you ask simple directions with mixed sign language, whereas with Kiyomizu-dera Temple your listener will catch proper Japanese term (even if he mentally discards 'temple') and respond. We could drop 'temple', or after -*gu* 'shrine' and let you learn Japanese, but you might sometimes get confused. So...

There are, however, some signs you will want to be able to read or recognize, especially if adventuring. These we illustrate on these pages....

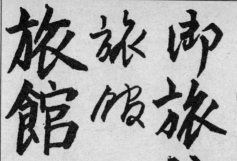

Inn (*Ryokan*)
3 variants

Spa (*Onsen*)
Originally inn with mineral water bath; now also cheap hotel or inn.

ホテル
Hotel (*Hoteru*)

便所

御手洗
Rest Room (*Benjo, O te-arai, W.C.*)

男　女
Fancy Variants:

key
Men (*Otoko*)　**Ladies** (*Onna*)

バス　トイレ
Bath (*Basu*)　**Toilet** (*Toi-re*)
Above 2 signs together outside,
usually signify budget or love hotels

入口
Entrance (*Iriguchi*)

出口
Exit (*Deguchi*)

たばこ
Cigarettes (*Tabako*)

食堂　喫茶　寿し　生そば　バー　クラブ

Restaurant　**Tea Parlor**　**Sushi Shop**　**Noodlery**　**Bar**　**Club**
(*Shokudo*)　(*Kissa*)　(*Sushi-ya*)　(*Soba-ya*)　(*Bah*)　(*Kurabu*)

Note: Characters may be written either from top to bottom or left to right.

184

*One of the pleasant things about life in Japan
is the unexpected complications...*
— John Fujii, *Ukiyo*

CHERRY BLOSSOMS
or SEASONAL & TRIVIAL

BAGGAGE & CHECKING: In so many lands
you don't dare take your eyes off your luggage, can't
check it unless it's in armored coffin. Here we check un-
locked camera bags, all sorts of things wrapped only in
furoshiki square cloth in which objects or shopping are
wrapped as in hobo's kerchief. Everybody used them until
shopping bag worked its cultural revolution. They were part of
Japanese costume. We still carry one or two as spare luggage. We
leave packages few hours with shopkeepers, restaurant cashiers:
makes for carefree travel. Naturally, you don't leave camera on your
train seat or do equally irresponsible things. But if you do, report it
to stationmaster when you get off, odds are you'll have it back by nitefall. As long as
individual *accepts responsibility* (key to understanding much about Japan) have no worry.
Jay, running for last train with too many big bags, left one on Tokyo platform, told
conductor who telephoned back from next station about hour later, it was still there and
got sent on next day.

Buy *furoshiki* or several: make fine gifts, handiest standby luggage. Great for gathering
shopping into one bundle; leftovers you can't squeeze into any bag go into *furoshiki*.
Sumi carries one in purse, out it comes as babushka in sudden chills or showers. Jay
sometimes wears as scarf or ascot, then goes open necked when he needs it to carry home
trip's souvenirs. Check full, knotted *furoshiki* just like locked case.

LOCKERS in all railway and bus stns international-standard sizes apple box to golf
bag. Usually with 24-hour drop-lock. Rates per 24-hour period or part thereof, vary with
locker size, from ¥100 to ¥400 for golf bag size. Leave as long as you wish. Most stns
have checkrooms for larger pieces or in case lockers all taken (especially holidays): ask for
nimotsu azukari-sho (baggage checkroom). Checkroom hours same as stn functions, till
last train leaves. Hours posted, or ask *nan-ji madeh?* (what hour until?). Answer will be
in Japanese, supported by fingers or written in Arabic numbers, or spoken in English as
clear as your Japanese.

Can no longer check surplus luggage thru unaccompanied baggage while you make
various train stopovers en route. *See* EXPRESS PARCEL SERVICE under FREIGHT.

Charges to transport bicycle can easily exceed transporting yourself. Take folding bike
onto train as hand luggage, or regular bike with front wheel removed, strapped alongside;
surcharge sometimes levied. Be careful parking your bike, it is one thing that'll disappear!

If you stop in restaurant for lunch or in shop to make purchase, you can nearly always
leave unneeded hand baggage for few hours while you walk around town. Just say *'Chotto
nimotsu azukari kudasai?'* No tip expected or accepted. If traveling by bus in country,
shop which serves as rural bus stop, or that nearest bus stop, is understood to be *azukari-
sho*, leave your luggage there till bus time and take stroll.

CIGARETTES: *see* TOBACCO—for customs, availability and foreign brands.

CREDIT CARDS are common. Shops, hotels, restaurants display membership
plaques as at home. Plastic fit right in with old tradition: man of any repute frequents
wide circle (its width is mark of status) of shops, geisha tea houses, restaurants and what-
else, where he is known and need never carry anything but small change: even at that he

can take cab, or order cigarettes, charge it to restaurant or hotel to be charged to him. In Japan good credit rep is good as cash. Rarely any minimum, except at airport TaxFree. *Visa* and *American Express* were assured of success here, and succeeded, spawning host of local cards. *AmEx* is fast building solid base, with cashing facilities and widening acceptance; we find their cashing service, information, lost card replacement superior, but card less accepted due higher commission. *MasterCard* starts slowly. *Visa* ubiquitous. Unlike Hong Kong, rarely surcharge on card use except when getting big cash discount for cameras, electronics. Prior leaving home phone credit card info and ask latest details on check cashing, cash advance, where to do it in Japan, other destinations. Get their local English info phone, prefix 0120- means toll-free, find out what info available beyond puff on cards. Ask where to report lost card!

CUSTOMS OFFICERS US, UK, Japan are best psychic bloodhounds and judges of people on earth. Don't mess with them. They can also be money-saving friends.

ADVICE TO YOUNG PILGRIMS: Jesus said (and this is via one Zen Jewdhist) 'speak in language people understand'—or something. Body language, clothing lingo, included. Official can't understand 'hippy'. Jay flew Iran-Osaka to give lecture, after 35hr trek landed looking like he'd walked. Customs got rough—it dawned on him so he pointed to scruffy stubble, dirty shirt, explained—customs smiled, bowed apology, repacked bags. Garet, on good advice, has shirt-necktie for customs, officials, especially when applying for visa. Jay had in-law pre-cleared for student visa, who then showed up in NY Japan Consulate in tanktop, shorts, stubble beard—visa evaporated!

GOING HOME, reentering US choose older customs man, prefer WASPy looking. Gals & minorities, sorry, seem not self-confident enough to do job right: strip bags for no reason. Good customs officer psychic, doesn't waste energy on false searches.

DUTY PROBLEM–take up with officer, he'll help you do it painlessly. Jay did, officer said list high duty items first for $400 free allowance. Most souvenirs low or no duty, don't waste allowance by listing them first. In doubt, ask officer's advice entering Japan, or re-entering for residents. We repeat, don't fool with customs officers.

ARTWORKS signed, and anything over 100 years old, duty-free. Entering Japan may need written 'proof', signed statement on bill of sale might do. But if only few pieces, under-declare and say visiting gift or personal. If they block and hold for later clearance you are out few hundred dollars storage-handling fees. Entering US, wise officer asks value: if low may disbelieve you, so rate straight or even high. US, UK customs usually take word if you seem okay—not taxed anyway—but $5,000 may require expensive agent.

DOCTORS: We hope you won't need one. But you may at least want to take your shots if you suddenly decide to go on to SE Asia. International hotels, of course, have regular doc on call, usually fluent in English, often as not educated in Japan and US or Germany. *Japan Times* classified has professional notices column listing MDs. However, we personally recommend in Kobe, Dr Geoffery Barraclough OBE ☎241-2896.

DRIVER'S LICENSE: *see warnings*! also chapter GETTING AROUND, p.114.

DRUGSTORES: For you who persist in home brands, Tokyo has REXALL in Sangyo Keizai newspaper building, Sankei Kaikan (that's all you need tell cabby); **American Pharmacy** Tokyo ground floor Nikkatsu Building near Hibiya corner of Imperial Palace; Kobe first fl New Kobe Oriental Hotel. Prices steep: nontariff barriers.

Most general products you can get just as well on local market. Vitamins bring your own, tho local exported, prices prohibitive. All but very latest drugs are manufactured here under license with US, British, Swiss or Germans. For simple headache we prefer local powder, inconvenient to take but cheap and effective, called *Norshin*; tablet types also. For hangovers there are several powders to take direct and wash down with water. Ask druggist or hotel desk for *'futsuka-yoi kusuri'* (second day drunk medicine); many are *kanpo-yaku*, Chinese herbal. When traveling outside Japan, for possible tummy problems we carry little black beebees called *Sei Ro Gan*, easily available (ask hotel desk help)—brought Jay immediate relief from bad food cramp in Seychelles.

For short trip, bring enough toiletries and medicines as you may use. Women make sure have enough cosmetics, especially creams. International brands widely available, expensive; Shiseido well-known local, but local tones differ. Small bottle tax-free US or French cologne available in plane makes highly appreciated visiting gift.

Miracle moist towels now common, handed out in coffee shops and trains where damp towel *shibori* not available. Advise carry your own extras.

ELECTRICITY, APPLIANCES *see following* ODD THINGS WE CARRY.
FORWARDING LUGGAGE, *see following* FREIGHT, PRIVATE EXPRESS.

FREIGHT HOME: Shopping is one reason you came. International parcel post is expensive, max 10kg/22lbs, runs (sea/air) USA ¥7,150/16,500; to UK via USSR fast ¥9,500 +¥700 per extra kg to 20kg/44lb, via Suez ¥6,050+¥300 over, air ¥18,700+¥900; Australia ¥5,400+300/18,600+1,100. Hotel will handle, some will package for fair fee. **Air PP → USA** 10kg runs ¥16,500, almost = airline 30kg US overage abt ¥20,000. PO has air-sea mix SAL, 'surface airlifted', takes 2-3 weeks.

Best is (US only) take home as luggage; next best, parcel post; last resort for immense stuff is sea freight. High value or breakables, go airfreight or baggage. Freight involves stiff handling fees. Other than to US, mail home shopping wherever possible as seafreight is expensive for small loads, handling-forwarding charges both ends more than doubles total, suffers rougher customs procedures. Mark parcel *Unsolicited Gift*, for US limit each package to contents fair value $50. OK one daily to each addressee not yourself.

Flying back to USA baggage allowance is two check-ins up to 70lbs/30+kg per case, but in practice if you can heave it on to scale unassisted it passes. Then you have carry-on case to under seat size, (soft suit carrier often 'overlooked') which US airlines, when not crowded, often check in free: safer than cluttering cabin. If shop-crazy, pay for overweight at about $75 or so ($10 more E coast)—airline ¥-$ differs, so from here about ¥20,000, still good buy, per extra suitcase or carton up to size 155cm/62ins L-H-W (that is 5 cubic-foot box, if transhipping in USA by UPS use 10% smaller 4.5 cu-ft as that is UPS maximum). You can't send seamail this cheap: bless those airlines.

FOR EUROPE, check freight agent for air-sea combo, fairly fast, cheaper than air.

DOMESTIC parcel post within Japan now matches price-service of private express *(follows)*. If short of cash, shop can send it to your base hotel via *daikin hikikae*, *dai-biki* for short, COD, at no extra charge by PO. Internal parcel post 12 kilos/26 lbs, expanding services regularly to compete. Rates by distance.

PRIVATE EXPRESS *takkyu-bin* cheaper (about ¥1000 most up to mid-suitcase size, 20 kg, according to distance), faster (overnite, but over 20kg each 2-3 days) and can also be sent *chaku-barai*, COD purchase and express charges. Arriving Narita or Osaka *takkyu* services outside customs can forward bags to hotel base to allow you few days light travel. At hotel, porter handles: say *takkyu-bin* and he'll give you label/forms to fill out in clear printing, or do for you in Japanese, so get namecards from your base. Cheap.

HYGIENE: Just wash your hands as you do at home, forget Victorian bugaboos about travel in Asia. Water in Japan is safe, even in local noodle shop. What with Herpes and now AIDS, they worry about us! Thanks to local love of cleanliness (nôt necessarily neatness) and modern science intelligently applied, even local village is safe healthy place. You can even eat pork raw: no trichinosis, feed pigs marine waste—tho now import US pork. If offered bear sashimi in Hokkaido, pass—trichinosis. For sashimi, seafood is safe raw. Freshwater fish subject to dangerous fluke, which you hear much about, however, much as he may like raw fish, no one here is fool enough to eat most freshwater fish raw. Eat sushi without fear, it's deep sea. Eat raw oysters with little fear, they are *not fertilized with nite soil*. We lived in Hiroshima village where oysters are raised—oyster farmers laugh at this old wives tale. But, oysters will be oysters.

Vegetables served raw are safe: most farmers use only chemical fertilizers, as cheaper and more convenient. Worry is insecticides, as elsewhere. Public health authorities and housewives wage great educational campaign about reasons and methods for washing all vegetables carefully, preferably with detergents to remove chemical sprays. Farmers found nite soil gathering less economical as chemical fertilizers came available, changed over so completely that problem now is low-nutrition in greens, especially endemic calcium lack. Anyway, nite soil fertilizer was not major cause of disease, according to report by US Army MD: it was careless handling of foods after harvest, flies (now insecticides, preservatives worse). Common sense: choose where-what you eat as you would at home. Dysentery rare here, unlike endemic in New York. As for fruits, insecticides widely used, but with expensive loquats and peaches paper bags carefully wrapped around each fruit to protect from insect and spray, safe here to eat unpeeled, tho locals by custom always pare.

East Asians in general have always been conscientious about hygiene; primitive, perhaps, compared with our own modern standard, but one which, nevertheless, was far advanced over West until recent antiseptic decades. Thus, most Oriental food well cooked, Japanese use disposable chopsticks (separate ecological problem), train concessions serve foods, tea in throw-away plastic (pottery till 1960s) containers; no Oriental drank water until recent water systems made it safe: Confucius said 2,500 years ago there was more evil in single drop of water than in all governments in China. Tea (green or barley) served free wherever you go, first thing on arrival in hotel or restaurant or even business office.

You *are likely* to get runny tummy, but this will be due to *change* of water, *change* of food, *change* of climate and air and everything else your metabolism has been attuned to. Change weakens you and system is attacked by hordes of bacteria always present. Human mouth is filthy organ—bite by garbage-scrounging mongrel is safer than by girl from toothpaste ad, which goes to show how essentially unscientific all our aesthetics are. Thus, avoid trouble: avoid major change as much as possible if you are novice traveler. We don't mean avoid native cooking. We mean stick to basic type of diet with which you are familiar so that forays into adventures of local cuisine will find your body able to cope with temporary change. Rare few times in 35 years travel Jay or Sumi have gotten sick was never from pushcarts but from international hotel dining. If you are liable to react to change, or fear you might (fear is worst bug, there is no antibiotic for it), then have your family doctor prescribe preventive, take as instructed: ask yours.

Adventurous try *Kan-po-yaku* Chinese herbal medicine: (*see* DRUGSTORES) for tummy, little black beebees called *Sei-ro-gan*, available hotel druggist, inn desk will have some, harmless, often effective. Local home remedy for travel tummy is eat *ume-boshi*, sour plum, which Japanese tourists carry to USA, Europe. Near East cure we find works here, too, for both constipation or runs, raw yogurt, best brand *Bulgaria*, pure, natural nonsweetened.

LAUNDRY: Major Western-style hotels fast service: in by 10am, back eve. Rates posted, usual international, expensive; if you don't see, call room service. Resort inns tend to run even higher, beware if no prices posted. In budget Japanese inn common now to find washing machine available, slight charge or perhaps free. Old custom for Japanese to rinse their linen in *o-furo* in one of extra basins—not tub. Take back to room to dry; or do in room sink. You may, in less expensive inn, see some hanging to dry in dressing room next to bath. Rooms have small lacquer rack, similar shape to clothing rack, near dressing table meant for drying towel, or laundry.

Soaps & detergents, available brands include some US, but locals similar. However, cheap one-dose packets *shampoo* (strangely familiar Japanese for shampoo) universally available. Tooth paste in pencil stub-size tubes can be found in any souvenir shop, and towels with decoration portraying some local sightseeing marvel. All inns, most hotels provide all these, including disposable razor, free—influence of Love Hotels on international luxe hostelries. Jay also carries small pocket-mirror for shaving, old military metal type handiest, tho even cheapest room always has mirror. Business hotels, many inns, have coin machines for toiletries, drinks (including whiskey), cigs, prophylactics.

MONEY: *Yen*, written as '¥' (old *sen* of crossword fame vanished in 400-fold 1945-9 inflation) fluctuating 120-220 to U$dollar, 200-300 UK£, up from 1964 edition's ¥360=$1 or ¥1008=£1. Healthy many years, now too healthy for some, open exchange. Bring in yen freely, but may be asked to declare any you have: no problem.

You may change money only at licensed changers, which include cashiers of most hotels, better inns, JTB offices and many shops catering to foreigners (usually only US$ accepted), tho latter often accept traveler's cheques only. On leaving you may change any amount of yen back into your original currency, but usually only US$ available. (Going on to Hong Kong or SE Asia yen cash preferred). Check as details change slightly time to time; minor details lead to last minute problems. Japanese love rules, so take care.

Heady official impressed with his position can give you hard time over most trivial accidental infraction. If you run up against this type, smile, apologize profusely, ask him for his advice to get you out of this unfortunate predicament, offer to write note of apology to Japanese Government thru him. Then when his ego has been fed, he will slap his chop, personal signature stamp, on paper and you're clear. *Then* you can blow up, best way to write well-worded letter of complaint, copy to English press.

MONEY IN COINS & BILLS. Coins are one-yen aluminum, with big numeral '1' on one side, worth almost one-cent US; ¥5 brass, most with hole in middle, only coin with no roman numeral, =4¢ (at ¥125); ¥10 copper big numeral '10' one side, worth 8¢; ¥50 nickel, hole in middle detracts none from value varying from one quarter to 40¢, 25p; ornate ¥100 nickel worth 80¢, 50p, slightly smaller than ¥10; large ¥500 cartwheel worth $4, £2.50. (¥1,000 silver coin expected after 1964 never came about except for special collector coin).

PAPER MONEY slightly larger than US, less cumbersome than European. Heights all same, lengths differ slightly. Approximate value various denominations are ¥500 = $4.00, £2.50; ¥1,000 at $8, £5; ¥5,000 $40+ or £25+ and ¥10,000 worth about $80/£50. Old notes of 100, 50, 10, 5 and even *one yen* seen no more except at coin collector counters in department stores. We used to use paper *one yen* for Valentines, as value written on back in roman *1 yen* is visual pun for 'I yen (for you)'.

Banknote personalities: ¥10,000 is Prof FUKUZAWA Yukichi first nobel laureate; ¥5,000 is NITOBE Inazo (1862-1933) Christian educator, married American Quaker, authored *Bushido* apologia; ¥1,000 is NATSUME Soseki, novelist; ¥500 is IWAKURA Tomomi, head of phenomenal first overseas mission, 1860s.

Quick calculation for $ equivalent: take yen by 4/5s (80%), round off, decimalize; thus ¥1,000=$8: close enough with daily fluctuation. Keep closest ¥1,000 value in mind: if $ = ¥120 ¥1,000 = $8.33; @¥125 = $8.00; @¥130 = $7.70; @¥140 = $7.15; @¥167 = $6.00; @ old 1964 ¥360 = $2.77!—byebye cheap Japan, hi cheap America, flood of Japanese tourists.

Buy at least $100 in ¥ before departure! at exchange, bank, airport: you may need cash to get into town, tho airport limo or train Narita-Tokyo take plastic. No foreign cash accepted even in emergency except luxe hotel, airport limo counter. Unlike many countries – especially Hong Kong–if you change $ on arrival at airport you get honest bank rate.

Letter of credit or big cashier's check good, but only at branch or bank with correspondent agreement with issuer: avoid, unless settling in. Bigger shops catering to foreigners often accept personal check for merchandise they are to ship for you—if in doubt they can hold till check clears (month!). Most prefer plastic; check your card's cash draw links.

TRAVELERS CHECKS: Accepted at all top, mid and most budget hotels at day's quotation. TC rate usually ¥2 (1%) or so better than cash. Banks are pain: AmEx or Cooke's TC at Bank America pays heavy check cashing fee for each TC! Japanese banks worse, except those posted for TC exchange. Carry mix of TC, cash, plastic—proof of TC purchase in separate place. AmEx immediately replaces lost checks: not so BankAmerica. Credit cards will extend automatic machine sales of TCs against cards out this way, so ask before you leave. Postal Service Cash Card (built-in IC) allows to draw cash at dispensers anywhere in Japan, France, Holland, Norway, Spain, Switzerland, UK. Check your PO.

POSTAL ACCOUNT—*Yubin Chokin* best way student traveler to keep funds. *Any* PO no matter how small, open ¥en account over either signature or *hanko*-seal; get passbook and/or cash card. Take to any PO 9am-4:30pm (X-sat, sun, hol) & draw cash over signature or seal. If you lose seal you're lost: tho with seal & passbook proxy can encash for you. Also use cash-dispenser for magnetic PO Cash-Card (*see* preceding).

PASSPORT and passbook, a.k.a. Alien Registration Certificate: *see* **warnings!**

PHOTOGRAPHY:
Naturally everything you need is readily available, probably at higher price than home. Only top Japanese discounters can match such as New York's 47th Street Camera. 35mm, 120 films readily available; large format at top pro shops only. Kodak as cheap or cheaper here than US, cheaper than local Fuji or Sakura–both fine films. Better camera shops have professional films in coolers. Most colorprint processing overnite, many one-hour service, cheaper than US-Europe and better, use only top materials, immediately replace or refund inferior work. Transparencies 1-2 days. Black & white studio quality processing readily available, ask hotel desk or camera shops, reasonable.

Warning: photos forbidden in most temples, all museums (except our PERSIA HOUSE Kobe & ORIENT-KAN, Nara), public or private galleries. Art scholars need special permit even for snaps for file or personal lecture use. (Should our museums reciprocate and ban photos by Japan profs?) No other photo taboos. Young Japanese will ask to pose with you (say *'cheese-oo'*) for their camera clicked by chum. DomJuans (Dirty-Old-Men-Johns) might enjoy chance for innocent arm-around-shoulder cuddle. You are tourist sight.

POST SCRIPT ON POST OFFICES: Plentiful and efficient. Usually handle telegrams–overseas cables main POs only. Mailbox UK-style red cylinder, called *posto*. Rare blue for air or express, otherwise drop airmail in red post. Hotel/inn desk handles.

   MAIL RATES: Prestamped airletters ¥80 worldwide, ask for *koku-shokan* or *eya-rettah*. Airmail letter USA, Canada, Central America ¥100; Europe & S America ¥120; Australasia, SE Asia, India ¥80—per 10 grams (half-ounce); unsealed greeting cards with up to 5 written words, printed matter, bills, forwardings, Aus ¥70, US ¥80, UK ¥90 for 20g. Local letter 25g ¥62, cards ¥41, express *sokutatsu* +¥210. Hotels handle at service desk. Philatelic counter all large POs, but small POs happy to show stamps in stock.

   PICTURE POSTCARDS: 9x14cm min to max 10.5x14.8cm *airmail*- worldwide ¥70; *seamail* ¥60, except India-east ¥50; *local* ¥40; incl 3% tax.

   Warning Japan adheres strictly to size limits: surcharge for oversize letters; but under 9x14cm rejected as jam cancellation machines, but you can paste on paper extension.

   Parcel Post *see* also FREIGHT HOME, rates high: *see* MONEY for handy PO account.

TELEPHONE ☎:Real time trek, still **nickel/¥10** per call by time unit **anywhere!** Coin phones come in several delicious colors: red, yellow, blue, pink, green. All take ¥10 coins, several at time, some also take ¥100 (yellow, green, some reds), greens also for **telephone cards**, bought in advance from machines or at souvenir counters in denomi- nations of ¥500, ¥1,000, ¥3,000, ¥5,000—use for international calls from green phones, gold English label, common at stations—ask hotel, TIC for nearest—direct dial w/001, total rate same as from private phone. Calls charged by time-unit, same ¥10 gives 3mins (may shorten) local calls, shorter times outside area code: Tokyo-Kobe few seconds, but 2- 3 ¥10 coins enough to tell wife grabbing plane, be home X-o'clock, heat supper... Put in too many, phone returns excess on hang-up. For ¥100 boxes, start with ¥10s, confirm call add ¥100s. Bill changing & phone card machines usually nearby in heavy traffic areas.

   LOCAL COLLECT CALL, domestic dial 106, in Japanese—except Tourist Info, which English, say slowly, enunciating clearly, 'Tourist Information, Please'. Prefix 0120- indicates free-to-caller collect call like USA 1-800-number.

   INFORMATION, 104, Japanese; out of town is same 104, say city. **English** info in Tokyo ☎3201-1010, in Narita ☎28-1010, Yokohama ☎322-1010, Nagoya ☎541-1010, Osaka ☎313-1010; and from other out of town ☎(03)-3201-1010. ☎O'seas 0051.

   TOURIST INFO, Kyoto schedules taped 90secs toll calls, dial ☎(075)-361-2911. Agent answers your queries 9am-5pm: dial in Tokyo ☎3502-1461, in Kyoto ☎371-5649, insert ¥10. Free elsewhere dial ☎0120-, then 444-800 (to Kyoto), or 444-600 (to Tokyo).

   EMERGENCY, no coin: dial ☎110 police; fire or ambulance 119; if red button, just push. Talk slowly in simple English, don't panic, automatically traces call so no gags.

   TELEPHONE CARD handy, buy one ¥500 first chance. Light indicates units unused. Card-only phones trains, stations, hotels and increasing. Insert in green phone upper slot but observe arrow, usually parallels design. Pops out when finished, alarm sounds till you take it. Come in scenic designs which collectors here love; often given as PR gifts.

   ALTERNATIVE LINES since deregulation; look for 2-color pastel phones, cheaper.

   OVERSEAS calls go by time units of 6 seconds, stn to stn, prime time 8am-7pm, cheaper 7-11pm & 5-8am, cheapest 11pm-5am. From public phone use green/gold only.

   HOME COUNTRY OPERATOR for credit card or collect call ☎0039: USA-ATT ☎0039-111, Hawaii +111 or 181, MCI-☎0039-121; UK ☎0039-441, Australia +611, Hong Kong +852; access from private phones, or green phone with overseas gold plate.

   COLLECT O'SEAS dial 0051, use English, French, other language operators some- times available. **Info**/directory service 0051. Phone surcharge in hotel less than European or US piracy, but high—advise use green phone w/ prepaid card, pay per 6-second unit.

   TOKYO NUMBERS Jan 1-1991, Paris/London-like increased to 8 digits all nos.

TIPPING: Bless 'em all, compliment, smile, laugh, bow, wave, but **don't tip!!** Japanese friends tell us they feel happy to get home after trip overseas, no longer need worry about filthy custom. (Not quite true, Japanese must tip heavily in top ryokans—and in advance!) We'd all bless this but unfortunately, most places that cater to foreigners, and now many local 'better' concerns follow suit adding 10-15% 'service'. House gets this, simply way to up price. Imperial Hotel manager said 'service charge' ('64) paid 50% staff payroll–yet entering and leaving hotel we had to carry own bags! In W Japan especially

Hiroshima, *sahvisu* often 15%; as also at many ryokan. However, it's their only gimmick; there are no other table charges or special Paris-style taxes. Only national VAT of 3% basic or 6% over ¥5,000 (thus total of 13-16% over posted price). During international expos, Olympics etc, tax often waived for foreign passport holder; expect similar tourist reduction to ease high ¥en strain on tourist as show of national hospitality.

Jay left tip in small restaurant his first time in Kyoto and waitress chased him two blocks in rain to return money he had 'lost'. Priest-guides in temples or shrines insulted if offered money for hospitality rendered, which they won't show except to lower eyes, say nothing, and leave you standing there with your money hand mid air. If you wish, reward temple or shrine, hand money (Japanese handle gift money in white paper wrapper much as we hand over with concealing closed fist) or leave on table, or floor if seated on *tatami* mats, and say *'o-saisen'* which means offering money for sacred purposes. Shrine, temple has large *o-saisen* box into which you can drop some coins with loud clatter, or folded bills, bowing to your host in accompaniment. In hotels *don't* tip bellboy, porter, anyone.

In Japanese inns you may ask maid to do some extra things for you: we'd send out to buy milk or fruit for baby, do our laundry, play nursemaid or baby-sitter. (Laundry put on bill in hotels, irregular in *ryokan*, budget inns have coin washers.) In this case we leave *small* tip on departure, giving it to her in privacy of our room. They will really go all out for you in anything you ask, not for tip but out of love for extending hospitality on scale they couldn't possibly do in their tiny homes. Manager may give saccharine hail-fellow but nice one nonetheless. Working gals do it sincerely, breaks monotony of lives—and attitude here is that as long as one must do job, do it right and go all-out.

PORTER at airport, main station (*aka-bo,* literal translation of our 'red-cap') gets ¥200-250 each bag standard...whopping big bag, double it: he'll ask if not enough, it's fixed fee not tip—considered pay for service, not begging. Porter will pick up bag at taxi stand, make hand sign to see your ticket to know which track and car to take bags. (If you have no ticket, tell him city you want to go to he'll take you to window where clerk speaks some English.) He'll guide you to your car, see to it luggage is loaded and stow you away. If you lose him, don't worry, go to train car. If you arrive by train and are lucky to find porter, large stations *only*, just tell him *'taxi'* and follow him.

Warning: don't carry more baggage than you can handle, porters rare. Do not tip sleeping-car, green-car (1st class) attendants or anyone but red-caps—who get flat fee per piece, will change big bill.

TOBACCO: Allowed one carton (200) cigarettes per adult tax free, another 4 cartons taxable, no more under any circumstances. American cigs available, better hotels (more as trade pressures exerted), sometimes British, slightly high prices competitive with local—which good, smoker friends tell us. Come in packs of 10 and 20, varying prices depending upon ratio domestic to imported tobacco. Tobacco was until recently monopoly of government which once claimed their cigs proven to contain no carcenogenic elements!

Cigar smoker must bring stock; use your experienced judgment at customs declaration. Pipe smoker has one type to choose from here, *Momoyama.* Not bad for tyro or adventurer. To buy any type tobacco product: *tabako* means cigarettes *only,* tho *shi-gah-retto* is understood; pipe tobacco is *pipe-oo* and nothing else will work. Cigar, *hamaki* or *shi'gah*, locals, some imports including Cuban. *Ma'chee* gets you book or box of matches, free in all restaurants, coffee shops, bars, barbers, elsewhere whether you want them or not.

For street shop selling cigs, look for red British-style mailbox post; nearby small stall sells stamps, tobacco, chewing gum. Vending machines ubiquitous on streets, stations.

TOILETS are most readily available and cleanest in world. Public toilets in parks or subways safe even for kids—even when, as common, not segregated by gender. In dept stores at least every other floor, if not every, usually on stair landing between floors. Smallest noodlery or tea shop or bar has, ask for *toy-reh* (Japlish) or *tei-arai* (hand-wash) or slang *benjo*—so that unlike British, Japanese never had to develop stiff upper lip. Dept store ladies' rooms all have special counter for baby's diaper changing.

Native style is floor level and is to be squat over, hard on weak-kneed but ultimate in sanitation. Windshield-like arch is forward splash-shield, not to sit on—but if necessary reverse and back up onto it for support. Trains and small shops may have it on low platform (towel-rack-like wall bar to hang on to), step up and squat–or if squat is uncomfortable, dais enables you to back up, hold fanny in air and....

Where there are several booths one is usually W-style, so labeled, but no paper seat cover, make own paper ring of toilet paper. May see stick-figure cartoons showing how to, and how not to, use western throne, as unwesternized yokels tend to climb up on donut with shoes on and squat, thus seat may have footprints. In countryside potty may look like floor type till you get on and find it is gaping drop hole into open cesspool. Careful of wallet in back pocket!

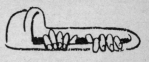

Paper now usually provided, but we strongly advise carry wallet of pocket kleenex, readily available, ask for *tissue*. Japanese invented it—French called first *tissue japonaise* —but Japanese now use our word, even *kureenex*. Paper towels rare.

VALUE: As handy reference to relative buying power, we wrote in 1964, treat ¥100 then worth actual 28 cents, as if it were one dollar. That was relative buying power to locals for food and basics *on their standard of living* tho it took them, on average, two and half times work to earn it, wages averaged only one tenth those of USA or quarter those of wealthier nations of Europe. After generation of both inflation and productivity advances it seems reversed. Prices now about equal ours, some more (especially those tourists see), some less. Japanese now have decent incomes—1986 per capita $17,600 vs USA $16,000 —with as much or more expendable, especially young working folk, mostly gals, who usually live at home and keep whole salary. Except for latter, living standard far lower than income warrants, tho 'quality of life' self-assessed as very high, anyway.

WARNINGS: DRIVER'S LICENSE: Only **International Driving Permit** issued by your US AAA or European or Australian equivalent is valid: using your US state or European permit is legally driving without license. (*See* GETTING AROUND.)

PASSPORT or **Passbook: Nowhere** is it posted at Japan consulate (it **is** in your local consulates which you have little reason to visit) nor in airline literature, nor upon entry, but local law requires all non-Japanese to carry on their persons at all times either valid passport or, residents, **Alien Registration Certificate** which South Afrikans call *Passbook* when foisting on blacks. If you stay over 3 months you must get this *Gaikoku-jin Torokusho*—simply done, at any city or ward office.

(You can get one sooner if you say you 'plan to stay'. Makes nice souvenir. Go to ward or city office, *kuyakusho*, where resident, or where friend lives, with passport and 2 photos from photo machine booth or photo shop polaroid. Report it 'lost' on leaving and keep it, no fines, just apologize. And then for additional souvenir you can go thru half day hassle to get local driver's license by showing original home license and taking simple 20 question written test in English and eyesight exam. Ask at police station, takes time to do, you or someone with simple power of attorney must pick up locally.)

You can be **arrested** and jailed on spot for not having one or other. And if at nite or weekend they may deny your legal right to call embassy or consul thinking no one around —there is always duty officer available by phone, tho possibly useless. US hi-school teacher left passport 'in safety' at Osaka base hotel (normal wise thing to do) when he went to Hiroshima, in which City of Peace hot-shot rooky cop stopped him on main street near Peace Monument for random arbitrary check—illegal in Anglo-Saxon democracies. Spent weekend in clink till US proxy-official was found who vouched for him. No apology for false arrest: cop was promoted for 'apprehending criminal red-handed'. Longtime resident out jogging in shorts was stopped by neighborhood cop, *who knew him well*, but had hard time talking way out of arrest!

Born-in-Japan of Korean or Chinese descent who know only Japanese, must carry, with fingerprint, even tho native need carry nothing except driver license if driving. This and matter of fingerprinting are sore point with human rights activists in Japan. If you are caught empty-pocketed, smile and lie: as you must send passport to consulates for on-going visas, such as Korea or People's Republic of China, say you sent it to consulate and smile, bow slightly, *dovven*, apologize '*sumi-masen'*. Resident who has *gaijin toroku* but forgets, say you lost it then within 14 days report it to your ward office and get new one with no hassle: but under no condition 'find it' again as then not *lost* but *mislaid* and that, as Jay found out, is criminal offense, worth long condescending lectures.

Japanese visitors overseas nowhere submitted to such indignities. Reciprocity, please.

ODD THINGS WE CARRY AT ODD TIMES

Journey of 2,000 leagues starts with but single step' or, we might add, single misstep. Go prepared to miss many accustomed conveniences especially in cheap *minshuku* inns.

Main sightseeing attractions are temples and shrines and, at least in case of former, treasures therein. Whether they were built to awe man by their unseeable mystery, or only be appreciated by unseen deity, they aren't lit like better modern museums. Lighting on great masterpieces of Buddhist sculpture is to put it mildly, inadequate. Old hand temple-crawler carries **flashlight** (*kaichu-denki*). But one that throws good light is cumbersome. We carry tiny pocket-size folding camera flash-bulb attachment, reflector folds like folding fan to stow into case, powered by penlights. In place of flash bulb insert test bulb; for more light single element motorcycle headlamp bulb. Power drain hard on cells (use goldtop) but used only intermittently, get few day-long trips out of battery set.

AIR PILLOW indispensable, inflate to use, deflate to pack. At dept store, camping or luggage section; say *kuuki-makura*. For snooze on train, pad and support small of back on long uncomfortable journeys. Airport shops sell marvelous donut-shaped collar-pillow for snoozing seated, no more cricks. Sleeping in cheaper inns: standard *ryokan* pillow fine for playing bean bag or touch football: Japanese tuck it under back of neck, we tuck it in closet. In pinch roll up *zabuton* seat cushion, cover with towel or pack under sheet.

ELECTRIC APPLIANCES: 100 volt AC, 50 hertz Tokyo, 60 hertz Nagoya, Kyoto-'down'. Plugs US type. US appliances work–except turntable in Tokyo as low cycle slows them. Local gear works either cycle. Iron not as hot due to low current: turn up.

European won't find alternate continental plugs or 240volt outlets, except *razors only*.

Use electric razor, iron or electric blanket? Wall outlets insufficient in small inn, only new hotels have any near bathroom mirror. Carry extension cord and maiden plug (std US). Small hotel bathroom US-European multi-plug usually low-amp for razor only, won't handle dryers etc, so carry extension. Get maiden and cord locally.

COFFEE 'FOR THE ROAD': Budgeteers carry instant coffee or tea bags, plastic spoon, sugar, powdered milk (*Creap* locally). Inn gladly provides hot water, *o-yu*. Most hotels, inns, minshuku now have hot thermos and green-tea bags standard, *free*, or many tourist & business hotels, inns, have water heater with powdered coffee, tea kits available in vending machine. Carry own thermos? Inn will with courtesy fill with hot water or green tea. Restaurants do same. Man with tea wagon on platform of main old JR stations also fills your thermos, as he does pots of his customers. ¥50 here if doesn't ask.

KEEPSAKE LOGBOOK: When Jay's kid sister left Japan some time back after long stay she took home the most interesting and original logbook, or travel diary, we've seen. None of us keeps diary, but like to recall where we've been. Here's how she solved this.

Most temples, shrines, scenic attractions, plain tourist traps, post offices in or near them, have desk with ink pad and large rubber stamps of stylized line sketch of some attraction (or in temples or shrines, significant or sacred calligraphy). Pilgrim on round of temples or shrines has white costume marked with these to record visits, or carries scroll of Shinto or Buddhist deity, which they similarly stamp, later hang in family shrine. Purely lay tourist buys small book, bound in Oriental accordion style, called *stampu-cho* or just *stampu-booku*, and has page imprinted by stamp-man in shrine or temple office, souvenir shop, usually ¥50-100 per whomp, sometimes free, at each place visited.

Kid sister got one of smallest, 3+ x 4+ inches, for pocket or purse. Had it stamped in time-honored way, jotted notes, sketches, impressions. For trips planned in advance, went to philately counter PO, got commemorative stamps of places on itinerary. One for page for that spot, 'canceled' by local *stampu*, others to post picture cards from there, stamped with special cancellation available free in post office serving scenic, tourist spot.

Stampu-cho come in various sizes. Sis regretted later she didn't get next larger size, postcard, so she could mount picture cards she felt worth keeping. She left place for small photos, and tipped in other mementos–temple or shrine charms, *o-fuda*, such sentimental garbage emotional travelers manage to collect: ticket stubs, chopstick wrappers, advertising stickers, pressed flowers, autographs, personal chops...

Stampu-cho available in stationer, souvenir shop, dept store, larger temples. Sizes vary from smallest about size of pocket diary, to about paperback size. Prices from ¥200 to ¥1,000 depending size and ornate covered binding. Paper approximates watercolor paper, bound accordion style opens into long single strip, frameable.

"Oh do let us get on, there's no one of any interest here".
So we drove on...familiar road making us feel quite as though
we were on our way to the festival.
—Sei Shonagon, *The Pillow Book,* 10th cent

PERSONAL DATEBOOK

JANUARY, month of Janus of 'Two Faces'. No country greets her with two more different faces than Japan. Yet no schizophrenia is involved—both, Picassoesque, overlap, blend, share common ear, common hairline. Japan's 15 days of New Year share much symbolism of ancient European pagan Yule: evergreens, lights, feasts, toasts, good cheer. Moving 'Happy Season' to overlap Christmas–New Year as in West has been easy. Most old customs remain alive: superficial changes kept abreast of changes of times, tho essence remains. New Year should be greeted in presence of Almighty, as elsewhere. Offerings made, Almighty (be it singular, plural or collective) invoked for favors. This basic rite governs holiday observance. Shinto shrines see steady flow of worshippers. Both shrines and Buddhist temples see numerous *Hajime-* First ceremonies, with first *bugaku* performance, first *kagura*, first *Ebisu* (merchant god) market; firemen in ancient costume offer their first parade; in Tokyo and elsewhere trucks are decorated gaily for first delivery (alas, less so each year); your first bath, first writing or painting. Everywhere, doorway pine and bamboo New Year decorations, exchange of gifts, and best decoration of all, people in gay kimono—tho also fewer each year.

First few days of year are spent visiting relatives and friends, receiving visitors, feasting and being feasted. Visiting gifts are taken, for children especially *O-toshi dama,* 'hon year's coin', now not coin but crisp new bills straight from one's bank in special gift envelope; 1989 kids reportedly raked in average ¥45,000, while adults averaged ¥30,000 in such outlays, testifying to ageing of population. If you're visiting Japan at this time you'll find it golden opportunity, for while Japanese are normally reticent about inviting outsiders to their homes, your arrival unannounced at New Year, even at doorstep of just passing acquaintance, will be greeted with warmest hospitality. Should you participate in season's customs, sipping *toso* sweet wine, eating red rice of joy and perhaps being discreet enough to bring small New Year gift (make it small, expensive one would embarrass recipient into even more lavish return gift) wrapped in season's festive paper and modestly offer this 'just little nothing', you'll find wall of restraint completely melted for rest of your time in Japan. In west Japan, visiting round may include visit to graves of ancestors.

To those you cannot pay *nenga* visit in person, mail *nenga-jo* (New Year's postcard) which, if use special semi-postal lottery cards sold at year end with special stamp on, or mail before **December 24,** will be delivered on New Year's morn—actually post office now holds anything marked so, or that looks like, New Year greetings for special service. Postal Ministry tells us Mr Average gets 260 such postcards, leading movie starlets several 1,000s; we get about 1,200, send as many. If you get card from someone you didn't send to, you have 2 weeks to make up.

January festivals would fill book, there are that many in this most festive month of year. When our New Year begins, some rural areas are observing lunar November harvest festivals with *kagura* folk-play performances until around 12th; others are asking for good season entertaining gods with all-nite *kagura* dances; and others are cleaning up old year with fire festivals, smoking out demons, bad luck.

January 1, 1873 was first day Japan used Western or Gregorian calendar in changeover from Chinese Lunar calendar, so December 1872 had only two days. Old style New Year (Zodiac p,197) is first new moon after first full moon after Winter Solstice, roughly mid-January to mid-February: (Feb-4, 1992; Jan-23,'93; F-10,'94; J-31,'95; F-19,'96; F-7,'97; J-28,'98; F-16,'99; F-5, 2000).

15th marks New Year for some as demons come out of Niigata mountains and invade farm towns. This day New Year officially ends with rites: burn decorations and build huge bonfires to forecast year's crop or catch. Pilgrims make *kan* (cold weather) pilgrimages to icy mountain streams; karate-*ka*, judoists and modern athletes take special outdoor drills and even geisha harden themselves by practicing their instruments till their fingers freeze. Farmers get ready for their lunar New Year and cycle begins again. It is not likely that many of you will care to come halfway round world to share their discomfort and we leave more detailed accounts for another book mentioning only few bigger affairs in each area DATEBOOK.

FEBRUARY: IN SPRING Japan's fancy lightly turns, so lightly one can hardly note start of turn or its completion in summer's fullness. In Occident, spring begins when days-nites balance at Vernal Equinox. In Japan, spring opens when last excuses for holding New Year parties have been exhausted, midway between Solstice long nite and even nite-day of Equinox, **February 3-4**. First Rite of Spring, *Setsubun*, winter and its demons of cold and pestilence are exorcised as beans, symbolic of impregnation of earth with seed of life, are cast about temples and shrines in sole remaining major Shinto-Buddhist combined rite, and into dark corners of one's home.

As in fabled Isles of Immortality ancient Chinese thought it to be, youths in rural Wakayama Prefecture welcome in light and warmth of spring **Feb 6** with wild torch race. Near Nara, neolithic God of Dance and Soil, Saruta-hiko, dances about great stone phallus of ASUKA SHRINE, with pumpkin-faced maiden Ame-no-Uzume and bullock sows first seed of spring. To teach earth what's to be done, he rapes consort and distributes souvenirs of cleaning up this fertility Rite of Spring to farmer audience.

MARCH sees things warming up. Stores full of Girl's Day **March 3**. Emperor, Empress dolls and their whole court; cost some ¥100,-300,000 per set, bought by doting parents for perhaps half 1987's crop of 650,000 baby girls–market worth one hundred billion yen. Most are made in Iwatsuki town, near Nikko. Plums (really apricots) pop out on mountainsides. First reports of cherry blossoms dent more serious front pages. Promise of spring has worked its way into city thru great torch-light, torch-dance ceremony of Nara's *Mizutori-sai* climax **March 12**. This date every 12th month pure water mysteriously flows in spring beneath NIGATSU-DO February Hall (by lunar calendar, month behind our solar) and at 2 am, hour when gods bathe, wild tantric rite in inner sanctum—where no photography nor women are allowed—ushers Spring onto mountains of Nara. More tantric, if more leisurely, Tibetans and Nepalese celebrate rite every 12th year at Temple of Eye in Katmandu. By **Ides of March**, Rites of Spring have made their way as far as Nagoya when non-too-subtle symbols of great male fertility shrine of TAGATA and nearby great female fertility OGATA SHRINE wed. And **last sunday** at Koshien stadium between Kobe-Osaka, Grandest Rite of Spring sees phallic wands popping balls across field for 10-day, 80-year-old *Senbatsu* High School baseball tournament.

Firewalking atop Miyajima's Mt. Misen

APRIL: Month of multi-color tourist brochure and picture postcard: month of cherry blossom and geisha. Single-petal variety blossoms first and falls quickly, followed immediately by hardier double-petal. Spring is really here. Symbolic rites are forgotten and spring is lived. *Sake* shops do rushing trade, picnic boxes are loaded with snacks and hors d'oeuvres, kids are packed off on tours and folks head for hilly parks now buried in low, rolling pink clouds of blossoming trees, and song-rocked air shakes blizzard of falling petals from heavily-laden branches. Bacchanalia reigns.

As Hebrews celebrate their Passing Over from historical winter of Egypt into their 40-year spring in desert which preceded fruition of summer of Israel, as Christian fetes rising from earthly death of Son of God, so Buddhist religious awareness is rekindled by miracle of spring and birthday of Lord Buddha is celebrated **April 8**–rebirthday really, for Buddha has been many. But about 2,550 years ago (arbitrary estimate admittedly) that Buddha of our era, Gautama, Prince of Shakya, was born in Lumbini, Nepal. Today temples blossom with toy shops, candy stands, flower and tree stalls as children pour sweet tea over statue portraying precocious infant Gautama standing and preaching at birth. Many celebrate **May 8**, approximating lunar calendar.

Tokyo lags behind Nagoya by almost whole month, as on **2nd sunday** in Kawasaki city (Tokyo's soapland suburb) at WAKAMIYA HACHIMANGU shrine Kanamaru festival, great metal phallus and other fertility falderal are paraded, 11am, some by raucously devout *gaijin*. While there see their newly expanded Fertility Museum. Previous eve, saturday 6-9pm, kagura dances amid cherry viewing. Similar Dec 7-9 nr Tokyo (*see*) in Chiba.

Sacred isle of Miyajima, near Hiroshima, covered with bank of pink floral mist, sees devotees of tantric Buddhism climb Mount Misen (devotees of comfort ride cable car) **April 15**, and just after lunch, exorcise ills of winter by fire walking (*above*). Now buttercup-yellow blossoms of rape fill field after field. As sap rises in vegetation, so does urge to vegetate rise in saps: it is season for annual strikes and you can count on railways being out for half to several days, usually JR and other on different days, at least. They always strike and as foregone conclusion, win–why this silly rite of spring?

Geisha quarters of Gion, Pontocho, Kitano in Kyoto and Shimbashi in Tokyo each put on grand Spring Dance shows thru much of **April-May**. One dance usually portrays spring clam digging parties, *shiohi-gari*, adventurous clam eaters try real thing along shell-rich shores off most of Japan. Dance tradition carries over into modern Japan as International Arts Festival regales Osaka for several days, and smaller spin-offs elsewhere.

Last week into May is **Golden Week**, consisting of late Emperor's birthday **29** followed by May Day (*not* official holiday), then Constitution Day **May 3** and Children's Day **5**. With Hirohito's death, his birthday will, we prophesy due to his great popularity and longest reign at such critical era, be retained but renamed–just as emperor Meiji's November 3 became Culture Day. Under no circumstances plan any intercity travel this week without confirmed reservations. Everything is packed as millions move.

MAY sees man and nature combine forces to make it truly colorful month. All over country huge red and black cloth or paper carps, often more than 30-feet long, flutter in breeze from long bamboo poles for **May 5**, 'Children's Day'. These are left up for month as many areas celebrate lunar date. Countryside gradually becomes colorful patchwork quilt. Beautiful, unjustly-ignored *renge-so* (clover), Mother Nature's robe of imperial purple grown to be plowed under for nitrogen-giving fertilizer, joins yellow rape in true Imperial Robe. Filling in with Nile-green wheat, which is harvested so rice shoots can be planted next month in same plot. Mint-green lotus leaves, sparkling with diamond dew add accent to scene. Little white plastic caps protect young plants in orderly rows while larger vinyl shelters glisten in sun. Hillsides burst out in delicate pinks of early wild azalea, then magenta, salmon colors, while man adds multi-hued garden azalea.

May 11 marks opening of cormorant fishing for *ayu* (similar to trout) and delicacy here, grilled. Nagara River in GIFU near Nagoya hosts most colorful spectacle. If bypass Gifu, experience it in other sections: Kyoto's ARASHIYAMA and nearby Uji River by graceful Fujiwara era BYODO-IN Phoenix Pavilion; in Hiroshima area at Iwakuni City under famed Kintai Bridge, or MIYOSHI out in mountains en route Izumo and Matsue.

May 15 Kyoto has its *Aoi Matsuri* where one can glimpse into magnificent Heian Period as costumed courtiers participate in imperial procession. Good season to shoot rapids on Hozu River in flat-bottomed boats and enjoy scenic mountains with beautiful cedars and pines. In contrast, over in NIKKO two days later (**17th**), at 1,000-man procession of armored samurai, robed priests and *chigo* children we see splendor of Tokugawa Shoguns unfold at their annual spring festival.

JUNE breaks out all over with music again. It's time to transplant young rice plants from their cramped but protected nursery beds to final, spacious, open paddy fields. Rice is no crop for solitary farmers. It's community crop, farmers must cooperate in planting, transplanting and harvest. It encourages communal spirit (hunger is alternative) thus, community socials, such as festivals. First festival of the rice cycle is transplanting dance.

Near Hiroshima, in rural mountains of Asa-gun and Yamagata-gun, transplanting is still done traditional way. In villages where it isn't great party, it's still done by womenfolk who lighten burden, speed pace with impromptu songs. In few places where ogre of westernization has gotten good bite, men bend over seedlings with women (formerly job for maidens only). **June 14** in Osaka's SUMIYOSHI SHRINE, rice is ritually transplanted and rustic dances are offered here to entertain workers and propitiate

Oriental Zodiac

Ne—Rat: 1900, '12, '24, '36, '48, '60, '72, '84, '96
Ushi—Bovine:1901, '13, '25, '37, '49, '61, '73, '85, '97
Tora—Tiger: 1902, '14,'26,'38,'50,'62,'74,'86,'98
U—Rabbit: 1903, '15, 27, '39, '51, '63, '75, '87, '99
Tatsu—Dragon: 1904,'16,'28,'40,'52,'64,'76,'88,2000
Mi—Snake: 1905, '17, '29, '41, '53, '65, '77, '89, 2001

Uma —Horse:1906,'18,'30,'42,'54,'66,'78,'90
Hitsuji—Sheep: 1907,'19,'31,'43,'55,'67,'79,'91
Saru—Monkey: 1908,'20,'32,'44,'56,'68,'80,'92
Tori—Cock: 1909, '21, '33, '45, '57, '69, '81, '93
Inu—Dog: 1910, '22, '34, '46, '58, '70, '82, '94
I—Boar. 1911, '23, '35, '47, '59, '71, '83, '95

Sexagenary Cycle (60-year) started 1984, with 12 signs modified by 5 elements (wood, fire, earth, metal [iron], water), 2 years each elder-younger, or +/– : 1992 = monkey water elder/+.

fortunes of crop; same festival is seen 2 days later at KYOTO's Fushimi Inari as also during following weeks in Ise.

Now fields sparkle with light jade rice saplings, and by lakesides waft graceful *shobu* (iris) which Korin and so many other artists immortalized ...why did they neglect rice seedlings?   Countryside is garden of rice, but for iris MEIJI GARDEN, KODAKA-EN, HORIKIRI-EN in Tokyo, HEIAN SHRINE in Kyoto best.   Descendant of dance to propitiate newly transplanted rice is torchlight *noh* offered in Kyoto's HEIAN SHRINE garden, **June 1, 2**.

Summer has its seasonal specialties which help keep one psychologically air-conditioned. Since electric air-conditioning, wind chimes are less common but still found. As we start feeling summer heat, Japanese take to ghost stories and gory tales to chill your spine. You'll see posters of *Yotsu-ya Kaidan*, revenge-ghost story, which makes new appearance every summer. Don't know if this is part of scheme, but in Kagoshima, Kyushu, sometime in June, at spider fight 100 pair of arachnid spar, many to death. Elsewhere children start hunting with long-stick nets various singing insects—if their raucous leg rubs can be called song. Cicadas rise out of pine glades after 7 years underground for several noisy days of above surface life, many to end up in cages.   Later it will be crickets, also sold at nite from sidewalk stalls, as are rhinoceros beetles and other fauna.   Creepy = cool.

JULY FIRST marks Opening of Mt Fuji to climbers. Summer has set in... on city streets you'll see vendors selling singing crickets, hermit crabs, goldfish, at nite firefly and circulating lantern sellers take over.   In various parks such as Tokyo's UENO PARK, nurserymen's markets are set up with potted plants, shrubs, trees galore.   In early July, *asagao* (morning glory) fairs are numerous.   These highly cultivated plants bloom all summer long and into fall, giving huge blossoms.   There's bustle around shrine compounds as gay summer festivals roll around and *mikoshi* (portable shrines) are hustled thru streets. Everyone flocks to rivers, lakes, sea or mountains. Even gods take to water as *mikoshi* get carried out to sea: some get dunked, others take to decorated boats.   Two most colorful of these boat festivals occur **June 17** according to lunar calendar (p.666)—Miyajima's *Kangensai* and Sendai-Matsushima's fete.   Many festivals are held according to this old Chinese reckoning, but where relevant we compute Western date for you, varying 3 to 6 weeks later, in local DATEBOOKs.

July 14-17 in Kyoto, *Gion Festival* reigns, with its fabulous parade of floats pulled by *happi*-clad youths while dancers ride atop accompanied by musicians clinking catchy *Gionbayashi* song. (Best: nites 14-16, AM 17). You can get costume and join in parade (*see* KYOTO DATEBOOK *Join-in*. p.514). It's hot during this season, if weather is too debilitating you should try *kabayaki* (barbecued eel) to perk you up. Kyoto is delightful place for this summer pick-up, especially at eel-places on platforms over Kamo River.

Fireworks are seen everywhere at local river banks or beaches. Biggest splash takes place in Osaka. evening of 25th at annual *Tenjin Matsuri*.

Hundreds of boats brightly lighted with paper lanterns ply rivers of Osaka, sometimes dubbed 'Venice' of Japan. Smaller version of same fete is held **sat-sun** following **July 24** in Kobe, with foreign participation and if you'd like to perform 10-15min gig on shrine offertory stage, see HANSHIN DATEBOOK p611 for details—we welcome you, we started festival in 1981 where we have internationalized bon-dancing to include disco-bon, samba-bon, and when we have fiddler-caller, barn-bon or square-bon.

Vacationing in Inland Sea area is wonderful. At Miyajima, you can rent sailboats; hire fishing boats by day (about ¥5,000 includes boatman, lines and bait; or go netting with them); enjoy clam digging and swimming. For hiking, mountains are right behind you. All this holds true in almost all seacoast areas of Japan–Zushi-Hayama area, Izu Peninsula, Ise and Wakayama area, just to mention few. Swim by moonlight in warm Inland Sea. Greater sport is to join villagers in evening, carrying carbide lamps or torches and short-handled nets. Idea is to catch leaping shrimps attracted to torch; or be consoled with scooping long slim young blue *sayori* swimming along surface. Join others spear-fishing or octopus-fishing by moonlight (check ubiquitous diving gear shops for details, gear rental).

AUGUST in ancient Sumeria was season of death when world died under blazing sun, to be reborn with cooling breezes and showers of late August or September. This was marked by feast of Ishtar, bacchanalia of renewed fertility, when most-reserved and proper males and most-secluded matrons were granted fullest license of action and moral. Sanskrit-speaking peoples called it feast of *Ullabon.* Japanese celebration is called '*Ura' Bon*, occurs during seventh month of lunar calendar, perpetuates Sumerian Bacchanalia.

It's not as wild and loose as it was in Sumer—- but it isn't as wild and loose now as it was 80 years ago, either, when it was great mating festival where young men and girls of village got acquainted, intimately, and often followed by having aunt or uncle arrange marriage. Dance is main thing now. Some areas, old dances have given way to American square dances. In Tokyo and Kobe it has become popular postwar, and for weeks on end people roam town in summer *yukata*, joining dancers some place in town every clear nite. In GUJO HACHIMAN area north of Nagoya, they dance almost nitely for 6 weeks, all nite long 4 days of lunar-*bon*, **August 13-16**.

In Sumeria, it was end of terror of summer. In Japan, it is end of plea-sure, leisure of summer. Time for children to return to school, for farmers to get ready for next great surge of communal work; harvest and communal, partying and drinking create spirit of camaraderie necessary for great com-munal labors to follow. Flutes and drums of *bon odori* fade off and lovely loneliness of autumn is hinted in coolness of evening and clearer tone of neighbor's bamboo flute now sounds in nite.

August 8 is official start of autumn–tho with little break in heat. Spring is season for our eyes, but in Japan this is season for our ears. Yet autumn in Japan is most colorful spectacular ever staged by Nature. To get even slight idea of how this can be, you'll have to feast your eyes on polychrome Japanese woodblock print then try to conjure up aural apparition of sym-phonic concert that could make you forget what you're looking at.

Listening to songs of insects was esthete's late-summer pastime in medi-eval era. You can enjoy it now in Tokyo at annual insect freeing festival **August 29-30** HYAKKA-EN, Garden of 100 Flowers—after poetic illusion which Maotse-tung distorted (Mukojima, E bank Sumida River, Terajima 2-chome). Most gardens close 4:30 pm. For more conventional sounds, autumn is in-ternational concert festival time: refer to newspapers or guide magazines.

SEPTEMBER boasts full moon of 8th lunar month, famed 'August Moon'. Poets get out writing sets and drinking equipment to feast mother of evening skies. If weather is clear, many people take evening outings, stroll parks or dine outside for last time–if typhoons haven't already put end to it. For us, it's lovely time to take advantage of numerous garden restaurants.

Autumnal equinox is, like spring's, important Buddhist holiday, graves again cleaned, services held during this *Higan* week **Sept 20-26**. National holiday **23**, Imperial Court holds rite for imperial ancestors, prewar important at state Shinto shrines. *Higan* today again predominantly Buddhist, especially at all Kannon shrines, as Tokyo's dramatic ASAKUSA KANNON.

As month draws to close, chrysanthemums open—and exhibitions of them. 'Mum is flower of autumn (we always associate flowers with spring), season Japanese love most. Needless to say chrysanthemum is national flower, and autumn truly national season. As many as 15,000 varieties are grown here. Showiest displays are *kiku-ningyo* (chrysanthemum dolls): larger-than-life arrays portraying literary figures or *kabuki* heroes, often in tableaux dramatizing entire play. Aside from heads, hands and accessories, entire garment is composed of live flowers, carefully chosen to bring out pattern in different colored blooms. Best known spots: TOKYO Tamagawa-en, OSAKA Hirakata Park and Ayame-ga-ike near NARA. Smaller displays evident everywhere and all town parks from TOKYO'S Shinjuku Gardens to village temple yards, have potted chrysanthemum displays.

OCTOBER is month known as that of no gods, for all local deities leave their home shrines on group tour to assemble in grand celestial convention at GRAND SHRINE OF IZUMO. Festivals are mostly harvest rites to get everyone in mood to work as well as to supplicate heaven for successful harvest, and later festivals of thanksgiving. Typhoons discourage festivals and harvest must be taken in at specified period regardless of which calendar is used. Therefore, with change-over of calendar it was not practical to change over dates of some festivals. Many are still held according to old Chinese or lunar calendar. Festivals now are heavy on theater. Costumed processions called *Daimyo Gyoretsu* are held at this time of year because during feudal era, with harvests safely in, it was time for local lords to go themselves, or in alternate years to send family member, to Edo-Tokyo as hostage.

Modern innovation is *undo-kai* (field-day) held in all schools thruout month. You can't miss them, their music and announcements from school p.a. systems blanket neighborhoods. Of odd events we have seen at these, what impressed most was obstacle race in which tiny participants rehearse white-collar futures by grabbing up, en route, items of clothing to dress while running, carrying brief case, lunch box and umbrella.

Full moon of autumn is most beautiful and if moon is full, your appetite healthy, then go maple viewing one afternoon. And stay over for supper to see modern Japan living poetry of antiquity. Most tours include scenic maple spots as they're everywhere. Nikko's gorgeous costumed procession **October 17** adds to autumn colors starting to turn, as do other local fetes.

NOVEMBER is best in Kansai. Best spot is probably NW KYOTO with MAKINO-O and TAKAO, nestled together at foot of Mt Atago, about **20th** on. Furthest north is TOGANO-O with KOZAN-JI temple, where four scrolls of comic animal caricatures by TOBA Sojo (1053-1140) are kept. Near town, ARASHIYAMA celebrates **Nov 10** with *Maple Festival* on Oi River with decorated boats. Nara Park turns riot of colors. Out towards OSAKA is TATSUTA-GAWA, long sung about for its glorious foliage. En route to see beauties at Takarazuka Theater is Mino-o Park. Near HIROSHIMA City,

Miyajima Isle's Momiji-dani is breathtaking, and on **15**th has both fire-walking at noon and ancient Bugaku dance out on floating stage at eventide. In Kyushu, see UNZEN and especially Yabakei Valley in OITA. In general, we have found that maple viewing around Tokyo is best late October; and west of Osaka, 1st-2nd week in November.

Culture Week, centered around 3rd, birthday of late Emperor Meiji (who modernized Japan after Perry) sees last great spate of public festivity. Marvelous time to be in Tokyo, endless theatrical offerings and art exhibits. Other cities also put on displays of stage and graphic arts, and theater buff could easily spend two weeks all but sleeping nites in theaters—and in mountains where all-nite harvest *kagura* is on boards, do even that.

Now, not June, is traditional wedding time as harvest is in, time is free and one wants to get ready for long, cold nites. Hotels are full of wedding parties, you can sit in lobby and wait for costumed bride to shuffle past in multi-layered kimono under her towel hiding her horns of jealousy, white to match mountain of white envelopes full of mint-crisp cash left at reception table by guests. Mr average middle age manager leaves ¥10,000 to ¥50,000 depending on relationship, totaling ¥160,000 per year on such, more than his ¥100,000 for funerals. Such gifts lighten financial load of such events on bride's family or deceased's survivors, tho both donors earn small commemorative return gift later. November picks up from October's offering of seasonal delicacies, and with hunting season starting game restaurants dust off special menus, wild boar is in season as *botan-yaki* porcine sukiyaki.

DECEMBER sees winter ski grounds getting ready for snow-mad hordes, hot spring baths distract one from chill, Christmas carols fill air. Christmas trees go up in shops, bars, nite clubs, and here and there some combine old and new to place wiggly pine at gate to serve both modern year-end fete and ancient Japanese New Year. We recall years ago riding trolley from our village in to Hiroshima, passing church steeple with foreign missionary clambering up ladder to hang wreath as elderly fellow passenger remarked, "Look, *Kurisumasu* is so popular now even foreigners celebrate it".

We expect from 1989 it will assume more attention now as new emperor Akihito's birthday Dec 23 is new holiday, perhaps kicking off year-end 'Golden Week' as dad Showa-Hirohito's April 29 did in spring. How about Dec 25 as International Brotherhood Day?

Each New Year we notice gradual passing of 'old Japan'. At *hatsu-gama* or 'first pot' of tea at Ura Senke tea center in Kyoto since mid '80s, Jay is almost sole male guest in kimono, among audience of numerous otherwise conservative elderly Japanese, all in dark three-piece suits.

Sketching here above highlights of each season as we experienced them, we pass on to you some flavor and color of various areas thru their local festivities. Details of these and numerous other events are in each area's PERSONAL DATEBOOK, with calendrical index after TABLE OF CONTENTS (p.xx). Refer to them when planning your trip, and note which fetes you'd like to include—some are worth building your itinerary around.

English newspapers and magazines carry more detailed festival and special event news: *Mainichi Daily News* feature page "Japan-o-file" runs lists of festivals Monday, as does *Japan Times*. But best, handiest are *Tokyo Journal* (*TJ*) for Tokyo, in Kyoto-Osaka-Kobe *Kansai Time Out* (*KTO*), as well as *Kinki* or Kyoto-only *Kyoto Visitors Guide*-(*KVG*). Government officially classifies (1991) 152 matsuri as Intangible Cultural Assets.

"It is not far between barriers, since 53 stages are all our country."
...You will find...much that is worthless in the book, which is more-
over overburdened...in fact there is a great variety of objects and
everything is as mixed as goods in the shop of a general dealer.
This much by way of preface. Now we will start on our journey.
— Jippensha Ikku (1822), *Hizakurigé*
or *By Shank's Mare Down Tokaido*

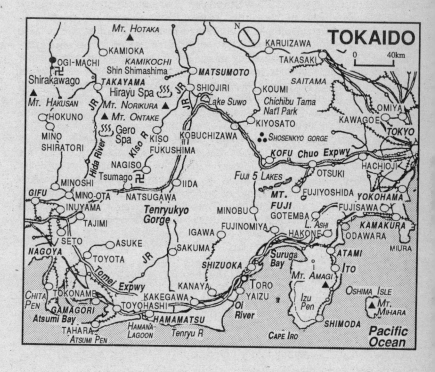

TOKAIDO 東海道
GREAT EASTERN SEA HIGHWAY

To-KAI-DO, Eastern-Sea-(-side)-Way, main pedestrian artery in feudal era, most important of GO-KAIDO—'5 highways'—fanning out from Tokyo Nihonbashi and controlled directly by shogunal central government thru armed barriers. TOKAIDO coast-road ran between shogunal and old Imperial capitals, Edo-Tokyo and Kyoto. En route to NAGOYA we might detour into mountains on KOSHUKAIDO which went from Edo thru central Japan along Southern Alps to join NAKASENDO alias KISOKAIDO at Shimo Suwa—as now JR Chuo-Line–Chuo-Expressway–Route 20 run parallel to obliterate most of old Koshukaido footpath. After Nagoya we again can detour into mountains on Nakasendo or Kisokaido, being developed for tourism as sole industry amenable to its isolation. Other two roads were NIKKOKAIDO and OSHUKAIDO north from Edo as one road then branching at Utsunomiya, former veering left to Nikko, shogunal cemetery and ancestral shrine, latter continuing on north.

Tho main arteries, what would be in Europe post roads or turnpikes, these were narrow, unpaved and without bridges except within cities. No carts used them, even slow bullock carts. Such were shogunal restrictions on possible movement of armaments. Horses were limited to special couriers and feudal lords. Rivers were crossed at fords, where several classes of toll-portage was available, from portered rafts carried well above water level to piggyback (tip well to keep your bottom dry) or for 'tourist class' just join hands in guided daisy chain. Road was usually elevated on dike when traversing rice paddy, and lined both sides with pine trees—to contain erosion and make sword-fights difficult. Each half-day walk, every ford, had its post station, totalling 53 on this road as illustrated in popular Ukiyoe woodblock print series *Tokaido, 53 Stages* by pioneer travel writer ANDO Hiroshige (1797-1858)—readily available today in inexpensive reproductions. There were inns for overnite, or roadside lunch or tea-break, with plenty of sake, girls and local souvenirs. Some tree-lined stretches and old architecture remain, which we guide you thru.

Road traffic was controlled by system of internal passports issued by your hometown lord, checked at numerous *sekisho*, barriers. Lack of one could mean immediate beheading, tho barrier chief used much discretionary power, tempering 'duty with humanity'–*giri-ninjo*. System hangs on in *gaijin-toroku*, passbook required of all foreigners here over 90 days—tho infraction is less serious, if similarly 'mindless'. Priests and pilgrims, told apart from others by their special costumes, seem to have had easier time of it. Then 19th century saw easing of feudal suppression, boom in travel reflected in boom in publishing travel books and color prints like Hokusai's. Ise Shrine alone received 1,000,000 visitors annually.

In modernizing, Japan invested in railroads not highways, and for century Tokaido was little changed, never widened. When we drove it on our honeymoon in 1955 most stretches thru towns were too narrow for two large US cars to pass (few Japanese cars then, just trucks). Meeting head-on in town meant one had to back to nearest wide space, usually entrance to shrine or even private doorway. Dirt roads when wet splattered housefronts in mud, when dry coated them in choking dust—so folks constantly wetted down roads as lesser evil. Road etiquette and cooperation were matters of mutual survival and made to work—whereas travel on trains was chaos little short of riot, little old ladies diving into trains thru open windows before any doors opened. This went on into '60s until series of tragic accidents saw school girls shoved off crowded platforms in front of trains causing then-JNR and press to mount national campaign creating today's order.

As in Europe, roads and pilgrimages generated their own literature. Most popular was that comic novel quoted above, *Hizakurige—By Shank's Mare Down Tokaido*, by JIPPENSHA Ikku (1822), subject of several movies and innumerable movie and TV episodes and emulations.

Tokaido is living history. We see it, treat it, as such. Our main itinerary carries us down to TORO, oldest settlement in Japan (reconstructed), on in chronological order to country's oldest shrines in NAGOYA-ISE area (with OFFBEAT 'time machine' detours) on to oldest Buddhist temples in NARA (6-8th centuries)—tho not on Tokaido itself, and these again in order of antiquity up toward today. Then on to younger capital (9th century) KYOTO, highway terminus, and again seen in its own chronological order.

Thus we travel parallel in both Space and Time.

Yokohama – Kamakura – Enoshima – Atami – Izu – Shimoda – Hakone – Miyanoshita – 5 Lakes – Mount Fuji – (Samurai Byroad) – Shizuoka – Toro – Hamamatsu – Gamagori – Nagoya – Seto – Toyota – Gifu – Inuyama.

I would ask of you whither is it that you head
little fishing boats floating, drifting aimlessly
on the waves of the sea . . .
—Nijo Yoshimoto *Mirror of Increase* (1370)

YOKOHAMA 横浜
OPEN PORT & GREAT CAVES

POOR FISHING HAMLET when 'opened' to outer world as port near
enough Tokyo to serve it, yet far enough away to spare capital from butter
smell of Occidentals. Commodore Perry's Black Ship fleet off nearby Uraga
brought enough pressure to force open Japan's isolation, and port officially
opened in 1858 with signing of *Commerce Treaty* between first American
ambassador Townsend Harris and Tokugawa officials. This 'Harris Treaty'
as Japanese refer to it, gave Edo time to steel itself while Nagasaki, Shimoda, Hakodate opened 1854 by Perry, bore foreign traffic. Formal
'opening' took place June 2, 1859. Harris moved consulate from Shimoda to
Hangaku-ji temple in Kanagawa (present Yokohama Station area), official
port. As main stop on Tokaido it offered every possibility for friction between brash *gaijin* and resentful Japanese. To avoid such trouble warehouses and wharves were built across harbor from Kanagawa in tiny village
of Yokohama, present Kannai, meaning 'within barrier'. Harris protested
this move to further isolate foreigners, to no avail. Tho off main Tokaido,
move to Yokohama only delayed trouble. Some foreigners and proWestern
officials were cut down early 1860s. Infamous *Nama-mugi Incident* saw
bodyguard of southernmost Choshu Clan daimyo slice two English remit-
tancemen, killing one to cause Royal Navy retaliatory shelling of Choshu
capital Kagoshima (*see*) 1863—thereby creating Japanese navy.

As gateway to Westernization, Yokohama boasts many firsts for Japan:
Racetrack 1866; Public Toilet 1868 (tho remains of medieval one found 1988 in Kyoto);
Telephone 1869; Moveable-type Newspaper, Movie House in 1870; Railroad to Shin-
bashi, Gaslights 1872. Lesser 'firsts' are: Laundry Service, Foreign-Trained Barber 1869;
Hotel & Indoor Plumbing 1873, to go with first beer also '73; Girls' School 1879; Ice
Cream.

There are few antique sights today. City long had flavor all its own, but
what little survived Great Kanto Earthquake of 1923 was buried in rubble of
World War II. Tokyo has since absorbed most of Yokohama's function
except for actual berthing of ships. All that remains of her past are few turn-
of-century W-style houses which, out of and above center, escaped wartime
bombing and rebuilding to near-3,000,000 population.

Shore leave town with honky-tonk bars, became 'clean and respectable'
in recent years. From 70s much money, effort spent to beautify city:
shopping malls cum-pedestrian paradises at main stations, face-lift for once-
faded Chinatown. More boom due till 2,000, great plans for old dock area,
including new 'foreign settlement' with housing and quality amenities to attract back once considerable foreign populace who worked in both Yokohama and Tokyo—as well as pioneer true, now only bandied about
'internationalization' for like-minded locals.

But for now, with little to see or do, Yokohama interests us mainly as
alternate to going into Tokyo if arriving too late to go to Kamakura,
Hakone or Atami-Izu, or as day-pause in this cultural halfway house. *Yoko-
Hama*, long+beach, often translated simply Long Beach, wrongly. It means
'along the beach'—which word order inverted from normal Japanese is
said to indicate Polynesian language origins (as also Yokosuka).

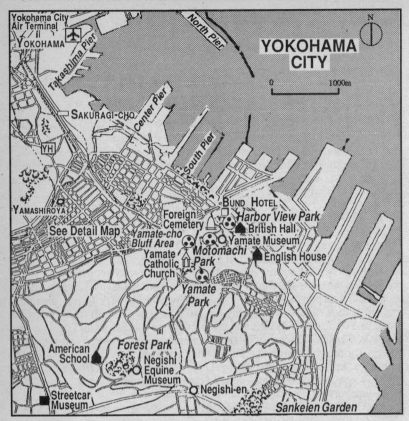

GETTING THERE: RAIL: JR **Narita Express** all rsvd seats (unsolds sold on spot, can usually get on next) 2cl ¥4,100, 'green'-1cl ¥6,720, 4-psgr room available. **Railpass** validate at JR counter before buy'g ticket. **Helicopter** Narita → Mirai nr Intercontinental hotel. Express BUS → YCAT Yokohama City Air Terminal 3hrs to within 5min walk of Yokohama JR stn E exit. 30 r.t. daily–12 Keihin Kyuko luxe *Sea Gull*, 18 on **Tokyo Air Transport**; *Gull* direct, stop **Haneda** Airport for local lines, *China Air* pick-up. First YCAT-bound bus dep Narita 7:00 (9:00 *Sea Gull*); last 23:00; Narita-bound 5:30, 19:40. Check-in YCAT or Narita; o.w. ¥3,100/1,550 tots. Haneda cheaper, frequent local buses from Sogo DS, ¥410 1hr. **Rent-a-car** Narita → Higashi Kanto Expway → Wangan *doro* (Tokyo Bay Hiway) → Yoko-hane Expwy **toll** roads.

From TOKYO → by Shinkansen 12mins but expensive (unless Rail Pass), inconvenient as requires additional 10min local shuttle. JR regular 3 lines ↔ Tokyo Stn by Tokaido main line 30min; Yokosuka Line 33min; Keihin Tohoku 40min. Private line Tokyu-Toyoko ↔ **Shibuya** stn 18min Ltd Express, 22min express, 38min local.

TILT: Do heart of city around **Yamashita Koen** park–Chinatown–kannai in pleasant half-day stroll; or full-day with long lunch Chinatown, shop or see exceptional Sankei-en garden. **Home visit** originated here, allows to experience firsthand eve with J-family; arrange **Municipal TIC** 1st fl **Silk Center** ☎(045)641-5824, ☎651-2668. Volunteer bilingual guides sat-sun for city or Kamakura: Mr NAKAGAWA Tatsuya, ☎(045)864-3380; also **student guides** hang out sun a.m. front Kamakura Stn.

Good place to pick up any special forgotten item: *warning*—stock up on hard-to-finds as contact lens cleaner, fluid at **Kokusai Contact Lens** 3 blks from Kannai stn, or any modern DS at Yokohama stn: especially **Sogo**, open '85 as Japan's biggest, each of 13 fl larger than Tokyo baseball stadium, expanding thru '94, Mitsukoshi, Takashimaya DS

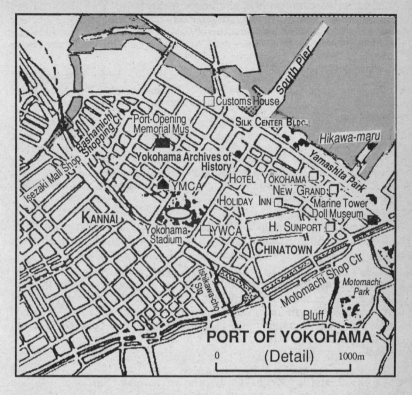

PORT OF YOKOHAMA
(Detail)

0   1000m

enlarging, Isetan a-building in metro Tokyo-Yokohama's 3rd largest retail market after
Ikebukuro, Shinjuku. CitiBank, more overseas banks to come, near Prefectural Museum.

WHERE TO STAY: International hotels mostly port area 5min **cab**
from JR Yokohama stn or YCAT, same price as Tokyo: used to be cheaper.
Best along waterfront Yamashita Park. Helicopter Narita↔Mirai waterfront.

LUXE RATE: ¥-L+%: Grand Inter-Continental, mirai Port of Future, great view all
restaurants, suites feature jacuzzi by picture window with port view; ☎(045)-223-2222.

STANDARD RATE: ¥-S+% (var lows): **New Grand**, mid park, grand but not so new,
convenient locale by port since 1873, best view of port from Startlight Grill 5th floor;
MacArthur stayed here after landing at nearby Atsugi Airbase. ☎(045)-681-1841.

Hotel Yokohama block W along park, ☎662-1321.

Holiday Inn N gate Chinatown few blocks Yamashita Pk. ☎681-3311.

Yokohama Tokyu ☎311-1682 R at Yokohama stn W Exit.

Prince, with newer annex, retains old beach resort hotel feeling, on Isogo Beach,
Yokohama's 'backside' 10min **cab** from stn. ☎753-2211, ¥-rebuilding, upgrading.

TOURIST RATE: ¥-T+%: Sunport ☎661-2211, at Chinatown E gate.

Bund, old, comfortable, small, SE end Yamashita Pk across Nakamura River, quieter
than rest, best buy. 1,1-chome ShinYamashita-cho ☎621-1101. ¥-S.

JAPANESE RYOKAN inns, all these are **tourist** (¥-T) which at ¥8,-15,000w/2 means
couple sleep-and-eat for no more than rm charge at major international:
Yamashiro-ya ☎231-1146 nr Yamashita Pk; **Echigoya** ☎641-5960 N Motomachi;
Negishi-en ☎321-2932, 500m W of Sankeien garden. Nr Takashima-cho subway, TIC
booked our friends into **Daikokuya**, nice helpful, ¥-B.

Cheaper ryokan, **budget** Business Hotels, mostly around stns. Book all thru **Station Information Center** or **Silk Center Info Office**. Also YMCA 7-1-chome Tokowa-cho W of Baseball Stadium (home of Taiyo Whales, owned by world's biggest whale-killer firm) 300m from Kannai stn. YWCA across ballpark, 225 Yamashita-cho. Youth Hostel 300m W of Sakuragi-cho stn; ☎241-6503.

SETTLING DOWN: City guide *Yokohama, My City* profuse maps and details, ¥2,500, ✍ or phone **City Hall** ☎(045)-671-2078; also monthly *Yokohama Echo*, what's on & fascinating trivia ☎671-7128. Big modern housing expansion under way.

GETTING AROUND: Convenient to begin at **Kannai stn**, 2 stops from Yokohama Bayside and port near stn now under reconstruction to *Minato Mirai*, Port of Future, with pier for **ferry** across port (¥450) to *Hikawa Maru* mooring, **Double-decker bus** runs Kannai → South Pier → Chinatown Gate → Motomachi → Harbor View Park, returns Yamashita Pier → South Pier → Kannai: daily 10am-6pm, 20min o.w., ¥200/100. Pleasant **walk** from stn front L 2 blks to Basha-michi 'Horse-cart Rd', city's oldest shopping street.

5min down which on L is...
Prefectural Museum, domed W-style building constructed as main office of Yokohama Shogin Bank (present Bank of Tokyo) 1870, prefecture bought 1964, converted into museum of local history & culture.

Head E on either perpendicular street here 5min (4 blks) then L (N) to...
Port-Opening Memorial Hall, *Kaiwan Kinen-kan* W-style neo-Renaissance structure completed 1918 to mark 50th anniversary (1910) of port opening. Few more buildings nearby survived war, like Miyo and Yazawa shipping supplies (both 1882) 3 blks towards stn. Continue N past old blue-domed **Customs House** to pier which has 2 brick warehouses, first in town.

Head E again one block to Nihon Oodori, L to...
Yokohama History Archives, *Yokohama Kaiwan Shiryokan*. Nihon Oodori was western boundary of old foreign settlement. Barely escaping 1866 fire which leveled much of town, foreigners decided to cut fire lane and this avenue is result. Recently opened Archives has several exhibit rooms on city's history and foreign relations. Older half is ex-UK Consulate site of signing of Perry's *Kanagawa Treaty*, with camphor tree in courtyard only remainder of reception hall. Plaza next to it has plaque commemorating signing. Daily 9:30-16:30, X-mon, day pre-holiday & last fri, ¥200.

Next to plaza is Japan's...
First Protestant Church, 1872, rebuilt 1933.

Facing plaza is 9-story...
Silk Center completed 1959 port centennial. On site of Yokohama's first 'addressed' building of British traders Jardine Matheson Co, then called *Ei Ichiban-kan*, English #1 House. Basement–1st fl shopping arcade, pref-city **TIC** 1st fl, **Silk Museum** 2nd-3rd fls, ¥200, 9:00-16:30 (X-12/28-1/3). Informative displays, models cover each phase entire silk process from care-feeding of worm to silk yarn dying, weaving, silk clothes of Japan, recreations of ancient costumes and antique originals of last few centuries; western, Japanese styles, traditional decorations and accessories.

Silk was prime early export (until US invented nylon–Now You Lousy Old Nip–in response to Japan rayon) readily available, easily produced in local countryside and in great demand overseas. Cottage silk industry provided initial capital for industrialization, and Japan still has major share of global silk market. Most of it, now as then, passes thru Yokohama, rest Kobe.

Trade Center Basement **restaurant arcade**, dozens serve good ¥-B-¥-T Japanese.

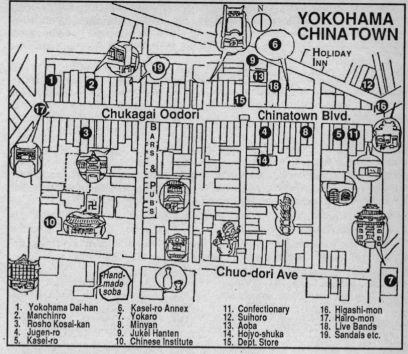

YOKOHAMA CHINATOWN

Chukagai Oodori

Chinatown Blvd.

BARS & PUBS

Handmade soba

Chuo-dori Ave

HOLIDAY INN

1. Yokohama Dai-han	6. Kasei-ro Annex	11. Confectionary	16. Higashi-mon
2. Manchinro	7. Yokaro	12. Suihoro	17. Hairo-mon
3. Rosho Kosai-kan	8. Minyan	13. Aoba	18. Live Bands
4. Jugen-ro	9. Jukei Hanten	14. Hojyo-shuka	19. Sandals etc.
5. Kasei-ro	10. Chinese Institute	15. Dept. Store	

Facing Yamashita Koen-Park is 5-storey glass-paneled...

Doll Museum, *Ningyo-no-Yakata* 3,000 dolls of world, 1,200 shown at one time; 2nd fl antique US-Japan goodwill exchange dolls, 3rd fl myriad Japanese dolls; occasional puppet show; 10-5 (-7pm July-Aug); X-mon, day after hol, Dec 29-Jan 1; ¥300/150 kids.

Few min walk down to:..

Yamashita Koen, built on landfill of rubble from '23 quake, to 106m tall **Marine Tower** commemorating centennial as world's tallest lighthouse (*Guinness Book of Records*). Elevator up, great view, takes full minute. Lounge 1st fl, shops 2nd, **Marine Science Museum** 3rd, Bayview Restaurant 4th fl, 5th aviary; ¥600 admits to **observation platform** topside 10-6 winter, 10-9 summer. *Facing tower* **SS Hikawa-maru** launched in Yokohama, since made 238 transPacific luxury, troop, repatriation and emigration crossings 1930-65, now moored permanently in old home port. Until recently Youth Hostel, now museum of sorts, restaurant. Next to it pier for *SS Sea Bass* cross-port ferry over to new **Minato Mirai,** 'Port of Future', 1991, port resort of exciting architecture with grand theater, galleries, boutiques, luxury balcony apartments at top rates—California-cum-Costa del Sol on Tokyo Bay.

Ferry ends nr Sogo DS, Kannai Stn, board there to here, stroll Yamashita Park reverse.

CHINATOWN 5min walk N of Silk Center or Marine Tower lead respectively to *Hairo-mon,* **Main Gate** or *Higashi-mon,* **East Gate** at either end of main *Chuka-gai Oodori,* China-Street Blvd. Most shops and restaurants located on Oodori. From original port opening 1859, there was large influx of Chinese, mostly merchants and laborers from Shanghai and Canton. In response, Tokugawa 'granted' Chinese settlement area, along present-day Oodori. By 1880, 2,400 Chinese (roughly 60% of Chinese in Japan) were here, and with city's rapid expansion it became nation's most prosperous Chinatown. 1887 saw start of area's 'architectural Sinification', becoming so characteristically Chinese that it was called 'Little Nanking', name for

Chinese man here was *Nanking-san*, 'Mr Nanking'. Another major boom followed first Sino-Japanese War (1894-5); then it re-emerged even larger after both obliterations of 1923 quake and WW II. Since our '64 edition has once again surpassed Nagasaki Chinatown as most prosperous in Japan.

CHOPSTICKS: Roughly 300x300mtrs, Chinatown's 3,000-odd residents run over 70 restaurants, 20 food suppliers, dozens of souvenir stores, bars, cabarets, and tea houses. Main styles of Chinese food—Peking, Szechuan, Canton, Shanghai—dominate, but also Taiwan, Nanking and Fukien styles served. Range from flashy first-class establishments (full courses per person ¥7-9,000+ with virtually no real top limit) to holes-in-wall with full-course at ¥1,500, or tiny noodle stalls serving full large bowls for ¥300. Hard to go wrong, prices clearly posted.

Best Taste...
Canton: L of Hairo-mon gate is moderate **Yokohama Dai-hanten** [1-on map] with daily special for two ¥6,000. Five doors down is slightly more expensive **Manchinro** [2] from ¥4,000/per, many rarities, ie: bear paws with natural honey-flavor.

Shanghai: Across from Manchinro is 1st class **Rosho Kosai-kan** [3]; 2nd shop on next blk same side is **Jugenro** [4].

Pekin: Most famous is grand **Kaseiro** [5] S-side Oodori one block before Higashi-mon [16]; new **Annex** [6] half-block W on other side. Often used for weddings, company parties, belly-bursting full course with Shark's Fin soup ¥4,500-15,000. Almost as good, cheaper: **Yokaro** [7] 150m down Minami-mon Dori, running Higashi-mon to Minami-mon/south Gate: Peking Duck ¥10,000, Shark Fin soup ¥1,000; full meals from ¥5,-15,000 but will create menu to suit your wallet. **Minyan** [8] (no, not kosher-Chinese) 6-course 'Service' ¥4,400/2person; opp Kaseiro annex.

Szechuan: Established since turn of century is classic **Jukei Hanten** [9], L up 3rd alley from Hairo-mon Gate [17] 30m on R; from ¥3,500, special lunches (12-2 X-sun) main dish with rice and soup ¥650. **Annex** block S of Hairo-mon, Ist-2nd floors **Yokohama Chinese Institute** [10]; also runs **Chinese confectionery** [11] two doors E of Kaseiro. Representative Szechuan cooking is somewhat mellowed at Jukei. For real Szechuan spices try **Suihoro** [12] 50m from Higashi-mon on NE corner; also serving Peking style, 3 or more people can fill up sampling several dishes, ¥3-4,000 total; open late nite, popular hangout for local musicians.

Taiwan: Only at **Aoba** [13] two shops down from Jukei main store. *Dim-sum* small snacks popular in US at bustling **Hojyo-shuka**[14] R down 3rd alley from Hairo-mon 20m on L. Top meal off with any kind Chinese or Japanese tea or coffee, R down alley before Kaseiro main shop at **Soshu Tea House**.

  Almost anything Chinese—folk arts and crafts, gifts, clothing, daily items—can be bought here; even record store of solely Chinese music old and modern. **Chinese department store** [14] and Chinese government-sponsored trading company.

Western Restaurants: Abound in Yokohama, but are not major concern of this book, except where outstanding, will rarely be detailed. Hotels often best, or as good as any, for standard western food. Budgeteers find it behind plastic sample windows in popular areas like Motomachi. Several good Indian.

PERSONAL DATEBOOK: While Yokohama Chinese community is active in all city fetes they have several of their own. Chinatown major festivals are Chinese Lunar New Year and Independence Day **Oct 1**; Taiwanese celebrate original **Oct 10=** double tenth. **Jul 25** fetes legendary Chinese Confucian hero Kuan Yü (?-AD219) at Jukei Hanten restaurant shrine dedicated to this 'guardian of warriors'. All festivals usual *lion and dragon dances*, accompanied by thousands of firecrackers to exorcise bad luck.

TRADING PORT-SHOPPING: Since Perry sat offshore waiting for permit to land, millions of foreigners have come ashore here: ships' crews, officers, passengers, longtime residents. Local shop owners long ago learned their wants. For its size Yokohama has biggest concentration of shops geared to western tastes of all sorts. Our longtime **favorite** round has been Motomachi and adjoining Chinatown for exotic local and Chinese curios, souvenirs and, we learned early, much export-only stock not available elsewhere (watch for your old chinaware patterns).

We exit Chinatown by S Gate, cross Horikawa River, now middle of 300m-long...
MOTOMACHI shopping street. Created to cater to early Foreign Settlement, it has always been leading area in international fashion from traditional suits and evening dresses to newest releases. Japan's fashion designers no longer mimic New York or Paris, their works rank with best. In addition to clothing, one can find excellent jewelry and accessories, art store and western restaurants. Prewar customers were 60% foreign; tho not that today, still popular among expats and visitors alike.

We start at W end of Motomachi, 3min walk from Ishikawa stn. Good landmark **Papa-san's** curio shop on R. Working our way E, some popular stores are: **Sumino** for Women's fashion (**Sumino for Men** block and half further), K.K. **Tazawa Shoken Brass** established 1923, and **Arai-ban Brass** since 1872; both have antique and new brass items, many accept special orders by foreigners; **H. Ono Pearls** where budgeteers can find beautiful little pieces priced just right; two curio shops called **Y. Hari Art Co.** with fine selection; **Takarada Shokai** western ceramics established 1882 carries fine imports from Europe, also excellent Noritake ceramics; **Arai** for ukiyoe block-prints. Restaurants for all tastes from Denny's and Kentucky Fried Chicken at W entrance, to German Deli, Italian House, **Baraetei**, assorted Japanese food; **Hakurai-ya** cafeteria; **Captain's** steaks; **Mutekiro** French cuisine. Place everyone suggests for dining-dancing, posh nite club **Cliffside** in hills above Motomachi overlooking the bay; Motomachi Daikan-zaka, ☎(045)-641-1244.

Up steep side alley just before E entrance, to...
Old Foreign Settlement at Yamate foothill. Few old houses left. Tho city exerts special effort restoring Victoriana, not as good as Kobe. Past **foreign cemetery** (*Gaijin Bochi* founded 1860s, now open to public) go L to **Yamate Museum**, *Yamate Shiryokan*, early Meiji building housing early foreign items, ukiyoe prints of life in foreign quarter, Yokohama old maps; open daily 11:00-16:00, ¥200. Next door is **Yamate #10 House**, *Yamate Juban-kan*, now serving steaks in outdoor beer garden. Next intersection is **Harbor View Park**, stone marker on corner commemorates city's first cleaning service. To park's L is site of **ex-French Embassy**; R one blk to red brick **Iwasaki Museum** built on site of Japan's 1st Western theater **Goethe Hall** in which Shakespeare play was first performed in Japan. Across from it is white-walled **Yamate English House**, home for British Garrison here, building shipped over, prefab, from England in 1867 to serve as Consul's residence. Now public hall for special affairs. Can only see outside but custodian will sometimes let you in for quick look if you go to his office. Western building beyond is **Osaragi Jiro Memorial Museum** dedicated to late internationally-famed author.

Short bus or cab to any of 4 stns of Yokohama, we go to Kannai for look at another shopping area ...
Isezaki Mall, thru double-helix 'Welcome Gate' extending 1.5km W from Kannai stn. First 4 sections lined with modern shops, last trio still retain older air. Many good restaurants, especially for Japanese food, mostly sections 3 to 7. Will find almost any hi-tech gadget at **LAOX** Yokohama, half-block in on R, branch of highly reputable store in Tokyo's Akihabara, 5 floors of stereos, watches, cameras, musical instruments, computers, furniture tended to by multilingual salesmen. Another good shop **Sanwa Trading** block and half S of Silk Center. UNDERGROUND MALL links Isezaki to Kannai.

2 blks N on other side of Kannai is BASHAMICHI (Horse Carriage) shopping street. Name because it was route often used by foreigners' horse carriages and traffic became so congested that street had to be widened in 1867.

*What we've seen so far of Yokohama is not necessarily what one comes to Japan for,
and saving best for last, we head out to...*

SANKEI-EN GARDEN 三溪園

GETTING THERE: 25min from Yokohama or Sakuragi-cho stns on #8 or
#106 **bus** for Honmoku Shimin Koen-mae, get off at Honmoku Sankei-en Mae. #106
goes to Kannai stn, Motomachi main entrance. #8 cuts down after Sakuragi-cho stopping
1 blk N of Prefectural Museum, 2 blks S of Silk Center, Chinatown East Gate, Bund
Hotel. Sankei-en is 2.5km E of Negishi stn 3 stops from KANNAI on Keihin-tohoku
Line which continues on to OFUNA, KAMAKURA. **Bus** #54, 58, 99 and 101 from
Negishi to Honmoku stop and 10 min walk, 300m S to Sankei-en bus stop 200m S to
main entrance. **Taxi** from Yamashita Park Motomachi area 10min, 2x-mtr. **Drivers**
follow road along Yamashita Park SE to Honmoku stop, sign marks turnoff to L, fair-
sized car park at entrance. ¥100 adm Outer Garden *Gai-en* (¥20 child), Inner Garden *Nai-en*
¥100/¥40. Sankei-en opens 9:00, Inner Garden X-16:00, Outer 16:30; X-only year-end.

Garden completed 1906 by local rags-to-riches millionaire HARA Tomitaro who made fortune in silk trade. Using pen-name *Sankei*–Three Valleys–Hara planned it as his main house. Garden open to public even when
he lived here. 1953 taken over by *Sankei-en Hoshokai*, private conservation
group, uses admissions to maintain garden. 47 acres, exquisite traditional
landscape garden contains 16 houses amid ponds and hills; most centuries
old relocated here, Important Cultural Assets (ICA).

Best take path between ponds to see **Inner Garden** first, circling
counter-clockwise. Passing thru early Edo gate, on R is **Haku-un-tei**
'White Cloud Mansion', Hara's residence. Built in 1920, he spent his later
years here, turning it into gathering place for artists.

Straight ahead is...
Rinshun-kaku (ICA) palace moved here 1917; built 1649 as Tokugawa
Yorinobu's residence, 1st Daimyo of Kishu (Wakayama) Province. Consisting of 3 attached buildings, first at far R is **Hikae-no-ma** Waiting
Rooms, 4 chambers for lord's guests. Middle **Sekken-no-ma** official
rooms where lord received guests; 3rd is **Okugata**, 5 'back' rooms used as
living quarters for lord's family.

Beyond Rinshun-kaku at far R is...
Gekka-den (ICA), guest house of 1st Tokugawa shogunate, Ieyasu—
Shogun of TV—built 1604 in Kyoto Fushimi Castle, moved here from
original site 1917. Behind is **Kinmo-kutsu** Tea House built 1918 by
Hara, so named because central *tokonoma*-alcove pillar was handrail from
Kinmo-kaku gate of Daitoku-ji temple, Kyoto. Nestled in far corner is
Tenju-in (ICA), lesser hall from Kamakura's Shinpei-ji temple, late
Muromachi (1500s).

Backtrack, cross two bridges to...
Choshu-kaku (ICA) 3rd Tokugawa Shogunate Iemitsu's residence at
Kyoto's Nijo Castle, 1623, to **Shunso-ro** Tea House (ICA) designed by
teamaster Oda Urakusai (1547-1621). Next is **Renge-in**, another Tea House
built by Hara in 1917, main column and lattice brought from Ho'odo-
Phoenix Hall of Kyoto's Byodo-in temple. Toward pond is **TENZUI-JI**
Juto Oido; built 1591 by Toyotomi Hideyoshi to house *juto* monument-
offering for his mother's spirit; originally in Daitoku-ji, Kyoto.

Exit Inner Garden, go R to circle...
Outer Garden counterclockwise. Pass another Tea House built by Hara,
take path uphill, take R at 'T' to **Shofu-kaku**, 1890 mansion dedicated by
first Prime Minister ITO Hirobumi. Original destroyed World War II,
reconstructed 1964. L at 'T' to hilltop **TOMYO-JI Sanju-no-to** 'Three-

tiered Pagoda' (ICA), 26m tall, built 1457 as part of Kyoto's Tomyo-ji temple, moved here and now Sankei-en symbol.

Wending downhill to...
Rindo-an Tea House built 1971, dedicated by YAMADA Sohen master of Sohen Tea School. R to **yokobue-an** flute hermitage; *at dead-end is...* ·
TOKEI-JI BUTSUDEN (ICA), Buddha Hall of Kamakura's Tokei-ji, nunnery for battered wives established 1285. Hall dates 1509, moved here 1907. Large farm house near Yokobue-an is **Yanohara House** (ICA) built 1650 by Iwase Sasuke, one of richest men in mountainous Hida Province, present-day Gifu; constructed by famed Hida carpenters, no nails nor metal. L half *Shoin-zukuri* palatial Momoyama style contains *genkan*, R half built in rural *Irimoya-zukuri* thatched-roof style is main house. Moved here 1960 when new dam flooded several farm communities (*see* Hida). Entry ¥50. Pass another Hara Tea House, shrine, to exit.

Leisurely 1hr30min to fully enjoy garden, which is must-see for this fantastic collection of buildings, not to mention exquisite garden itself.

Worthwhile detour from Sankei-en's South Gate to...
Honmoku Civic Park, *Honmoku Shimin Koen,* and **Hassei-den Museum,** *Hassei-den Kyodo Shiryo-kan.* Main attraction: statues of 8 sages of world; but more interesting is collection of traditional fishing, farming tools (Free, 9:30-16:00 (–12:00 Tue) X-wed, last of month, hols).

2 km W, bus #58 from Honmoku near Sankei-en and walk 200m, or bus #21,22,55 from downtown → **Negishi Equine Museum** fine historical exhibits and artistic shows on horses and various matters equestrian, which Yokohama long led country in.

PERSONAL DATEBOOK: Bulk of Yokohama festivals occur late spring-summer, centered around *Port Festival* commemorating June 2, 1859, opening of port. Due to several postponements because of rain main event moved to **May 3**–parade international costumes, US Navy marching band, Chinese dragons, all headed by 'Miss Yokohama'. Begins Yamashita Park, up Bashamichi street, Isezaki Mall ending Maita Park. Ceremonies on **Jun 2nd** (if good weather ?) mark actual date.

May 14-16 Ise-yama Jinja (affiliated with Ise Grand Shrine) *Shrine Festival* carrying festive mood to *Dontaku Matsuri* (Sunday Festival) **Jun 1st weekend.** Dontaku is Japanization of Dutch Zontag-sun: parade of J- and W-costumes of 1850s. Same time as Port Festival Commemorative Bazaar, local & international goods sales Yamashita and Oodori (Isezaki Mall) Parks. **1st sun Jun** has traditional *Jamokamo Festival*, 10m long straw snake carried thru town to 'absorb' evils which are then expelled by ritual burning of snake, ward off evil. *International Fireworks* Jul 20 is official end 2-and-half-months of Port Festival, best view from Hikawa Maru top-deck beer garden.

Rest of year taken up by traditional festivals. **End Jul** (dates vary) TAKIGI NOH outdoors at Yamashita Park if rain across street at Pref Citizens Hall *Kenmin Kaikan.* **1st or 2nd sun Aug,** *Ouma-nagashi*, Setting Afloat of Horses, several mtr-long straw horses set adrift in sea, carry away misfortune, illness. Small grass boats set adrift **Sept 1** *Shio Matsuri*, Ocean Current Festival as prayer for bountiful catch and fishermen safety at sea. *Osannomiya Autumn Festival* Sep 13 or 15, Iseyama Jinja (W of Sakuragi-cho stn) offers Noh, sacred kagura, and mikoshi carried around area. Not to be confused with *Yokohama Autumn Festival* **end Oct** at Yamashita Park, with somewhat more modern entertainment ranging from Chinese lion dances to disco. **Oct last weekend** is 150-year old *Kyokudaimoku* dance by children beating hand-drums to accompany chanted Buddhist scriptures. Then there is clump of New Year's festivals lasting thru Feb 2/3 Setsubun. *Apricot blossom viewing* Sankei-en gardens variously thru **Feb.** Bunraku puppet festival sat-sun about **Mar 21.** *See* also CHINATOWN DATEBOOK.

Establishment of Yokohama as international port spelled finish to dominance of that old Tokaido Highway of ancient woodblock prints. Leaving bustling, modern Yokohama then, our itinerary starts us on our trip back thru time...

WHERE NEXT: Yokohama 30min rail or bus → KAMAKURA, hour →
HAKONE. *See* end of OFUNA, following, for alternate WHERE NEXT tips.

GREAT CAVES & CAMERAS OF OFUNA

Taya-no-dokutsu of JOSEN-JI temple close to Ofuna are worth hour
detour especially in spring. Japanese who must liken everything local to
something foreign call them Japan's *Daito Caves* (China's Datung) after
fabulous complex SW of Beijing. No comparison—but they are interesting
for themselves and there is nothing else like them in this country.

Solid hill of flawless sandstone—soft enough to carve with coin. Legend
has it prehistoric men dwelt in natural caves here. Partly excavated in medieval times, used to store arms in Warring States era of 14th century; for
religious austerities after that. 1851 wealthy local peasant SATO Shichizaemon was inspired by dream to devote his life to extending caves, carving
Buddhist images, especially local goddess Benten—of whom more forthcoming in Kamakura. Sato continued until 1892 using local talent and his
own funds. Caves are three storeys high and you are led up and down stair-
cases past excellent light and air vents. Larger dome rooms seem to have
been carved by first cutting out low dome and then digging down.

Quaint English leaflet proclaims caves display "brilliant superiority of
Japanese in the field of formative arts". If this is your first look at Buddhist
sculpture rest assured this is not great Buddhist art. As folk art, it is fine
example of intensity of simple devotion.

GETTING THERE: JR **train** to Ofuna stn; 2x-mtr **cab** from Ofuna stn, cabbies know it as **Taya-no-dokutsu** rather than JOSEN-JI—one didn't even know that's
what temple is called. Also **bus** bound for Dreamland 5min to TAYA-NO-DOKUTSU stop,
then walk 5min N. Adm ¥300.

Tho several ancient shrines & temples are within walking distance of Ofuna stn, best
to **save energy till Kamakura**, avoid overdose. Trio of varied sites can be visited for
extra hour in Ofuna.

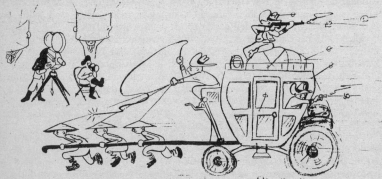

From stn cross, turn L to Tokai Bank, R to...

Shochiku Movie Studio, 'Hollywood' of Japan where most modern
movies made since 1936, still 15 annually including *Guinness* record series
Otoko-wa Tsuraiyo-"Being a Man is Tough" (*see* p.1188), plus 30 TV
dramas, hundred-odd CMs. Limited visitors, best if you're small group 3-10; ✍
ahead from home expected date: **Shochiku Ofuna Studio**, 6-1-1 Ofuna, Kamakura-shi
247; in Japan few days ahead have friend phone in Japanese ☎(0467)-46-7111, mon-fri,
'**Mori-san of Jigyo-bu**'. Photography limited. Good pamphlet ¥500.

Sword-play-Easterns, *chambara* (onomatopoetic sword clashing), made
in studio in Kyoto city: *Eiga Mura*—Movie Village—more open to tourism,
because far less active.

Ofuna Kannon modern but eye-catching 25m tall concrete bust visible from train's right side approaching town. Exit from W (main) gate, cross first bridge to small arcade and L uphill 5min. Construction was begun in 1939 but interrupted by war and not completed till 1960. You can enter statue which has several altars, figurines. Around statue is small park (¥100, 9:00-17:00).

Also contains...
JIKKO-JI temple and special memorial dedicated to those who perished in atomic bombings of Hiroshima and Nagasaki.

Castle Ramparts (1.5km/mile, 20min walk, NW of Ofuna Kannon) once heart of powerful Hojo clan. Starting as father-in-law of Yoritomo, becoming Regents to Kamakura shogunate in 1203 Hojo were de-facto rulers of Japan until demise 1333. Ensuing 270 years, Warring States era, Hojo regained power locally until defeated by Hideyoshi 1590. Hojo's main power base was nearby Odawara (*see*) but secondary castle built here 1512 to protect Kamakura, Miura estates. Ramparts only remain of what was one of grander castles, scale model in Yokohama **Prefectural Museum**.

5min on Fujisawa-bound bus to Okamoto at **Flower Center Park** and 5min walk E and N thru tunnel. If hiking from Ofuna stn, cross 2nd bridge.

500m N on bus road and 3rd L another 500m to bus road and R past tunnel is...
Ishii House, *Kyu-Ishii-ke*, 300-year-old **samurai house** in **RYUHO-JI** temple grounds. Only 3 rooms, in old farmhouse style; despite humble appearance Ishii family was of high status, advisors to Hojo. (To arrange free tour of house interior telephone ahead to temple ☎(0467)-46-2807). Ryuhoji built in 1575 by Tamanawa castle 3rd and last lord, HOJO Ujikatsu. Rebuilt 1688; all but main gate, bell tower burned 1951 rebuilt '60. Large complex is popular flower-viewing spot. Stone monument is to one of Tokugawa shogunate's top advisors, ARAI Hakuseki (1657-1725), scholar-pol who served 6th-7th Tokugawa shoguns Ienobu and Ietsugi as chief administrator over this Imperial fief under direct shogunal control. His writings on clan responsibilities and relations and on occident were major influences in Tokugawa policy-making. Grave of HOJO Tsunashige, 1st lord of Tamanawa castle, on hilltop behind.

WHERE NEXT: Roundabout way to Kamakura, can take **bus** via **Kamakura-ko lake** *for short hike on* → **HANSOBO GOBLIN** temple and *15min more* → **KENCHOJI**, *or direct hike latter in 15-20min then on* → former...

SIDE TREK: *15min bus Ofuna* → **Imaizumi Fudo** via old countryside dotted with thatched farmhouses, and central to above lake, shrine and temple. Few mins backtrack W along bus road from Imaizumi Fudo stop is **SHIROYAMA JINJA** built by MINAMOTO Yoritomo in 1191 to shelter Bishamonten image he 'acquired' from Kyoto's Kurama-dera temple.

5min E of bus stop is **SHOMYO-JI**, also known as Imaizumi Fudo: said to have been built by 9th century saint, Kobo Daishi, in early effort to unify native Shinto with imported Buddhism represented by *In-yo*, Yin-Yang Waterfall near main hall. **Fudo Hall**, Buddhist, atop stone steps beyond waterfall, its lovely thatch roof more resembling Shinto shrine.

HANSOBO is 30min hike from here.

Also see KAMAKURA-NORTH LEG, p.226, for HANSOBO etc link-up.

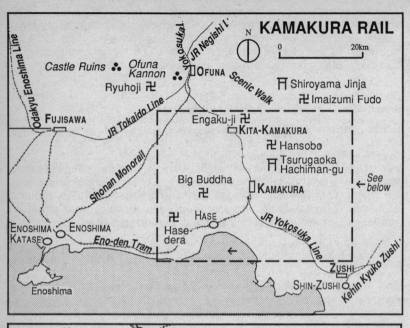

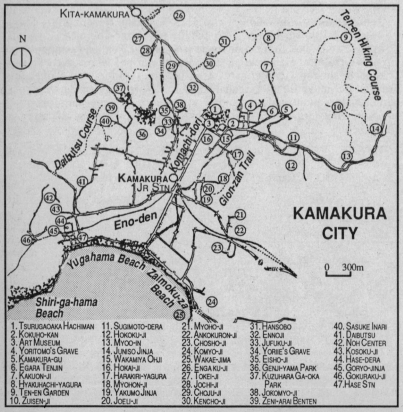

1. Tsurugaoaka Hachiman
2. Kokuho-kan
3. Art Museum
4. Yoritomo's Grave
5. Kamakura-gu
6. Egara Tenjin
7. Kakuon-ji
8. Hyakuhachi-yagura
9. Ten-en Garden
10. Zuisen-ji
11. Sugimoto-dera
12. Hokoku-ji
13. Myoo-in
14. Juniso Jinja
15. Wakamiya Ohji
16. Hokai-ji
17. Harakiri-yagura
18. Myohon-ji
19. Yakumo Jinja
20. Joei-ji
21. Myoho-ji
22. Ankokuron-ji
23. Chosho-ji
24. Komyo-ji
25. Wakae-jima
26. Enga ku-ji
27. Tokei-ji
28. Jochi-ji
29. Choju-ji
30. Kencho-ji
31. Hansobo
32. Ennoji
33. Jufuku-ji
34. Yoriie's Grave
35. Eisho-ji
36. Genji-yama Park
37. Kuzuhara Ga-oka Park
38. Jokomyo-ji
39. Zeni-arai Benten
40. Sasuke Inari
41. Daibutsu
42. Noh Center
43. Kosoku-ji
44. Hase-dera
45. Goryo-jinja
46. Gokuraku-ji
47. Hase Stn

But when the morning prayer is prayed
Think ere ye pass to strife and trade
Is God in human image made
No nearer than Kamakura...
—Rudyard Kipling

KAMAKURA 鎌倉
BRONZE BUDDHAS & BATHERS

"BEHEADING-SCYTHE STOREHOUSE" is what ideographs of name mean, which pretty well sums up its history. No single storehouse could have held all headsman's axes used here. City rose as power center of Minamoto clan of doughty warriors who contended with effete Taira, a.k.a. Heike, headquartered in Kyoto, Kobe and Seto Inland Sea. Taira/Heike world was that courtly exoticism of Lady Murasaki's *Tale of Genji*—of esoteric Buddhism, poetry parties and paradise gardens. Minamoto (a.k.a. Genji) world was of samurai, sword, puritan simplicity, Zen stoicism and stark stone gardens. They were two of 'four great families', with Fujiwara (Prime Ministers) and Tachibana (not much heard about)—all descended of early emperors. Long and bloody Genji-Heike cousin rivalry often called Japan's 'War of the Roses'—red for Heike and white Genji, with lotus in place of rose.

In 1192 after exterminating Heike in series of battles down Inland Sea, Minamoto leader Yoritomo converted old office of shogun from frontier marshal (full title Sei-i-Tai-Shogun translates: Great General for Subjugation of Barbarians on Eastern Marches—Ainu) to dictator of entire nation. Power of Imperial Puppet-master now passed along from Prime Minister (hereditary office of Fujiwara dynasty of Imperial Fathers-in-law) to shogun. After Yoritomo, shogun also fell to being puppet. We then had peculiarly Japanese situation of nation ruled by God-Emperor, himself controlled by Premier (FUJIWARA family) in turn controlled by shogun (MINAMOTO clan), only puppet of Regents of in-law HOJO dynasty. Minamoto dynasty died out in ambush in hotspring bath after less than century. Next shogunal dynasty, ASHIKAGA whom we shall meet again in Kyoto, wrote end to this political daisy chain and commanded direct from 1338 till 1573, virtually ignoring emperor and institutionalizing inter-Daimyo warfare, to set off century of Warring States.

Acme of power under Minamoto-Hojo 13th century, Kamakura's 'camp capital' -*bakufu* (*baku*, curtained area in camp to mark off 'court'+*fu*, capital) henceforth till 1867 synonym for shogunate. Population exceeded million (now 175,000). Rule restored to Kyoto by Ashikaga; Kamakura declined, suffered several sackings culminating in almost total destruction 1455. What survived was spared World War II when US unilaterally declared this, with Kyoto, Nara, Kanazawa, open cities. However, its beaches were to have seen main United Nations amphibious landing had there been invasion instead of A-bomb.

GETTING THERE: NOT on main Shinkansen line Tokyo–Kyoto, but on commuter trunk out of YOKOHAMA. Also direct **train** from Tokyo Stn by JR YOKOSUKA Line (to US Navy base town few stops beyond), branches off old main line at OFUNA: 85min, ¥1,000; from YOKOHAMA about half. See also available **bus tours** by JTB and Fujita out of Tokyo.

CAST OF CHARACTERS IN KAMAKURA ERA 1185-1335 ON KAMAKURA STAGE

OPENING SCENES

Minamoto Yoritomo 1147-1199, founded shogunate and Kamakura dynasty, built Big Buddha, supported Zen, died from 'fall off horse' going home from tryst.

Masako (neé Hojo) 1157-1225, strong-willed wife of Yoritomo, power after him.

Hojo Tokimasa 1138-1215, first Regent *Shikken* over Kamakura shogun 1203; overthrown by daughter Masako 1205 after having Yoriie killed; became monk.

Yoriie 1182-1204, son of Yoritomo-Masako, 2nd shogun, killed by grandpa Hojo Tokimasa (all kin loving as European royalty!), personality beautifully drawn in new kabuki play *Death of Yoritomo*.

Sanetomo 1192-1218, Yoriie's brother, 3rd shogun at age 11, poet, pawn of Hojo, ambushed by high priest Kugyo, Yoriie's son, at foot of giant tree in Tsurugaoka.

Yoshitsune 1159-1189, popular hero, misunderstood half-brother of Yoritomo (with 'faithful' Benkei); at 30 committed family suicide in Hiraizumi up N, but whom legends have living on in Hokkaido, as we shall see, or migrating to Mongolia to become Ghengis Khan.

Benkei ?-1189 giant hero of noh-kabuki-film *Kanjincho* (*see* Kiyomizu Kyoto).

Shizuka Gozen, Yoshitsune's mistress, forced by Yoritomo to dance before giant tree (above) in vain try to abort her child, whom Yoritomo later murdered anyway.

Oë Hiromoto, Yoritomo's most able advisor and brains behind government.

LATER SCENES

Hojo Tokimune 1251-84 #8 regent at Mongol Invasions 1274, '81, Zen patron.

Nichiren Shonin (St) 1222-82, founder nationalistic Lotus Sutra, or Nichiren 'new' Buddhism, predicted Mongol Invasions in street corner harangues, claimed savior-typhoon *kami-kaze*, God Wind, to be answer to his prayer.

Nichi-x various disciples of Nichiren, names all start with Nichi-.

Crown Prince Morinaga failed to oust shogunate to restore Imperial rule 1335.

Nitta Yoshisada co-destroyer of Kamakura city and of Hojo family 1333.

Ashikaga Takauji, 1305-1358 rebelled against Hojo, destroyed them 1333, overthrew and killed 'rebel' Prince Morinaga, set up new Shogunal Dynasty at Muromachi, Kyoto 1338 (till 1573, known as Ashikaga or Muromachi era).

GETTING AROUND: Long best by *jin-rikisha*, as in our '64 edition: long only afoot, bus or taxi or combinations. However, New Year '85 saw return of **riksha** with AOKI Noboru ☎(0467)-24-3739 who keeps in trim jogging, weight lifting, rather pull than sit at desk. Has been joined by YAMADA Yukio ☎22-8711. Both wait at Engaku-ji in AM, Tsurugaoka Hachiman in PM. Rates '89: ¥2000-pair, scenic run stn → Hachimangu (about 10min, 800m); can arrange tours for about taxi-rates, most romantic way to see. Best to reserve June-Aug.

Free guide: sat-sun, Kanagawa Student Guide Fed still exists and at present city planning similar service; guides also hang out in front of Kamakura JR Stn. Eminently walkable, **cabs** readily available at main sights. **City tours** from stn.

TILT: Minimal, JR from Tokyo early (not crowded, goes against rush), walk from stn to Tsurugaoka Hachiman, then bus, toonerville trolley or taxi to GREAT BUDDHA, same on to HASE-DERA Great Kannon; lunch nr Buddha or Hase; last leg to ENOSHIMA, see and dine nearby, thence to ODAWARA for Shinkansen continuation down to HAKONE for Kyoto etc or return Tokyo. To flesh out add from sites underlined in various legs. Worth overnite, in which case reservation advisable, add more **sites** from various legs.

Zen Meditation or *Zazen*: Master YAMADA Mumon (*see* OKAYAMA) stated "search for Oriental spirituality is of more interest to Westerner than to Japanese... America has over 20 meditation halls... shame but Japan does not have even one" (1972). Profoundly associated with Kamakura, *zazen* practice is still alive and several temples welcome sitters, novice or otherwise: **HOKOKU-JI, HOKAI-JI, ENGAKU-JI, SHOREI-IN** and others; (*see* each temple for details). *See also* KYOTO, NARA, KOYA (non-Zen). New book published during our proofs: *Zen Guide* lists more; **long term visitor** or **resident** needs *Exploring Kamakura* by Michael Cooper (both Weatherhill).

PERSONAL ORIENTATION: ZEN (*see* BUDDHISM, p.32).

WAKAMIYA OHJI (grand avenue) spanning 1.8km/mile+ from shrine to beach at Yuigahama, was modeled after Miyako Ohji, capital Kyoto's main boulevard. As offering for Masako's safe pregnancy with Yoriie, 1182 Yoritomo built elevated path (*dan-kazura*) down its entire length; only segment between 2nd and 3rd torii remains, rest flattened in early Meiji road construction. Early April it becomes tunnel of color under cherry blossoms. First torii near beach built by 4th Tokugawa shogun Ietsuna in 1668, collapsed during great Kanto quake, but rebuilt with same stones.

TSURUGAOKA HACHIMAN-GU [1]: Shrine to God of Scythe and Sword, tribal agricultural deity of some of pre-Buddhist immigrants from Korea whose worship first wed local ideas then later-import Buddhism to be subsequently proclaimed *dai-bosatsu* (great bodhisattva) in early Shinto-Buddhist syncretism. Later became Lord of Battles (scythe and plowshare into sword), then Minamoto Clan guardian. Buildings eclectic mix of Shinto and Buddhist styles, what is called *Ryobu-Shinto*-'combined Shinto'.

In 1063 Minamoto ancestor commemorated victory over related Taira by moving Iwashimizu Hachiman from Kyoto to his new frontier base here in Kamakura, renamed it Tsurugaoka, after new locale. Then, 1180, Yoritomo relocated it to present site at base of Daijin-yama hill; centrally located and more imposing. Shrine first renamed Wakamiya, but when more spectacular main Hongu built 1191, resumed Tsurugaoka name with new importance. Now Yoritomo made Hachiman his clan patron. Major center of *Shin-butsu konko* (Shinto-Buddhist amalgamation) for seven centuries, going thru '2nd wind' under 2nd Tokugawa shogun Hidetaka (1624-43). 1817 fire leveled all but old Wakamiya, rebuilt 10 years later when 11th Tokugawa shogun Ienari completed new Hongu. Meiji 1870s nationalism favored 'pure' Shinto, purged all traces of 'foreign' Buddhism. Handful of post-World War II stone markers note locations of old Buddhist structures.

One block E of Kamakura stn puts you at 2nd torii, up grand avenue now lined with interesting shops for curios and *kamakura-bori* (lacquered wood carving), budget eating places.

Walk on under 3rd torii...
Drum Bridge, *Taiko-Bashi*: Long life to whoever makes it across without using hands. Easy enough going up, it's coming down that shortens lives with broken necks. *Danger*: leather, composite soles, heels slide–rubber only.

Flanking bridge are Gempei-iké **ponds** dug 1182 by Yoritomo vassal Ohba Kageyoshi as receptacle for purifying water instead of usual small basin or trough. East (*Kanto*) is larger Genji-*iké* Minamoto pond, west (*Kansai*) is Heike-*iké* Taira-pond. At first each pond had four isles but as campaign against Heike exploded into full scale war, Masako as offering for Minamoto victory changed balance: one isle removed from Genji-iké (*san* in Japanese is homonym for 3 and birth); Heike-iké remained with 4 (*shi*, homonym for death). For yet better luck Masako covered Genji pond with white (purity) lotus, Heike pond with blood-red lotus for death.

Flower Datebook: new variety giant winter peonies late Jan into Feb.

Kanagawa Modern Art Museum on Heike-iké N bank is excellent, exhibiting all types of art, loan shows, old or new but from 'modern point of view.'

Main complex is straight ahead. Halfway path is bisected by...
Yabusamé-baba (mounted archery lane) spanning 300m between W and E toriis. Along it, Yoritomo's warriors honed their martial skills galloping full

speed controlling horse with their knees while shooting arrows in quick
succession at released running dogs—now more humanely at small
stationary wood targets.

Yabusamé begun by Yoritomo 1187 for ceremony here, soon became in-
tegral part of ceremonies. Serious display of skills, winners were well rewarded; great honor to participate. Energetic, colorful event twice yearly:
April as part of greater *Kamakura Matsuri*, and **Sept 16** *Yabusame
Matsuri*. Master archers of Ogasawara archery school dressed in Kamakura
period hunting dress vie for top honors. Must see if in town, but crowded!
If you miss it here Yabusame takes place all over Japan at different times
(*see* INDEX), as also nearby.

Turn R on Yabusame-michi 100m to...

Museum of National Treasures, *Kokuho-kan* [2], city's finest
antiquities. Concrete version of Nara's Shosoin, built 1928 after '23 quake
flattened much of Kamakura; annex 1983. Stone marker in front has carved
into it poem composed by Sanetomo. 9:00-16:00, ¥150, X-mon, hol.

Straight up from Kokuho-kan to...

SHIRAHATA JINJA, erected 1200 by Yoriie for his father's spirit. Sanetomo also enshrined here. Completely covered in black lacquer, special
roiro-nuri ; this exotic coating and rare *mitamaya-zukuri* architecture single
out this shrine. Meticulously rebuilt 1897. Shrine visited by Toyotomi
Hideyoshi 1590, after once more defeating powerful Hojo in Odawara
Campaign. Jubilant Hideyoshi strode to enshrined figure of Yoritomo,
patted its shoulder and exclaimed, "greatest heroes under the sun, just you
and me."

*L in front of Shirahata across gourd-shape HYOTAN-IKE POND, first building you
come to if straight from Taiko-bashi...*

Offertory Dance Stage, *Mai-den*, (pronounced as my-den) properly called
Shimo Haiden (lower sanctuary) where Shizuka Gozen, Yoshitsune's
mistress, was forced by Yoritomo to dance in unsuccessful attempt to abort
her child, later murdered anyway by Yoritomo's men. Present structure
postquake reconstruction. Shizuka dance relived yearly Kamakura Matsuri **2nd Sun
April**; rest of year have shrine maiden dance *mi-kagura* (maiden kagura) for ¥20,000,000!
(was ¥10,000)–no longer for tourist but for big Jpn corporate ceremonies.

Just beyond on R is...

Wakamiya, miraculously having survived every disaster, is unchanged
since Yoriyoshi brought it from Kyoto in 1063, part of it repaired 1626. To
L is 1,000-year old gingko tree behind which hid high priest Kugyo, waiting
to cut down his uncle Sanetomo. Up stone steps is vermillion HONDO, main
sanctuary, relatively new (1828) but nonetheless spectacular. Passing thru
ROMON GATE, roofed-over open hall surrounds inner sanctum. **West hall**,
museum of lesser treasures, ¥100– best are on display at Kokuho-kan and
Tokyo National Museum. Here 'lesser' means mere Important Cultural
Assets (ICA), one notch below National Treasure (NT).

Back down stairs, turn R before great gingko, up winding steps to...

MARUYAMA INARI shrine. Predating Tsurugaoka Hachiman, it was
area's primary shrine, dedicated to Inari fox god of rice. Originally occupying site of present Hondo, was moved here by Yoritomo to make way for
his shrine. Built sometime 9th century, it escaped fires, was repaired mid-
15th century. Untouched since, excellent example of Muromachi period architecture (ICA).

Down rear steps leads out to main road, old Kamakura Kaido, pedestrian
hiway, leading to KITA-KAMAKURA and our NORTHERN LEG.

PERSONAL DATEBOOK: Heart of City, Tsurugaoka Hachiman hosts numerous festivals thru year. Grandest is *Kamakura Matsuri* spring fete lasting week **2nd Sun–3rd Sun Apr**. Entire town is involved, with major events at Tsurugaoka. Highlight is parade from coast up Wakamiya Ohji to shrine, of several hundred dressed in Kamakura period costumes representing past notables like Yoritomo, Yoshitsune, Yasuko, Hojo regents, Nichiren and other priests. Shizuka's dance April **2nd Sun** 13:00; **3rd Sun** is Yabusame, 13:00. Outdoor tea ceremonies whole week. Various food and entertainment booths set up here and at Great Buddha. Also popular time to visit as most temples, shrines allow viewing of 'hidden' treasures.

Jan 1, sunrise: as popular is *Hatsu-mode* first visit **Jan 1-3**. Even more crowded is *Hatsu-hinode*-first sunrise, on beaches of Kamakura, mostly YUIGAHAMA. Friend went in 1985 said beach so full of people waiting all nite it was miserable; but Macdonalds had field day, setting up several 'emergency' burger booths to feed masses.

Jan 1-2-3 *Hatsu-mode*, first visit, also held at other shrines but again largest here when millions of worshippers come for new year blessings, from midnite set off series of New Year festivals. 4th is *Chona-hajime*, start of work for carpenters, who, all in traditional garb, commemorate Yoritomo's building of Tsurugaoka by hauling sacred wood from shore to shrine; offertory rites at Mai-den. Procession noon, rites at 13:00. 5th is *Joma-shinji* exorcising Evil Spirits by shooting arrows at large target; from 10:00 near MAI-DEN. 15th is *Sagicho*, ritual burning of old charms. Bamboo and straw hut set up near GEMPEI-IKE, old new year charms and decorations, last year's talismans placed inside, burned to chase away past evils and start clean. Burning starts 7:00am, lasts hour. From 10:00 is *Seijin-shiki* coming of age (20th year) ceremonies.

Early Feb all 3 INARI shrines celebrate *Shogo-sai*, marking **First Day of Ox** (dates vary over 12 days). Maruyama Inari, 14:00, ritual followed by *miko* (shrine maiden) dance offerings.

Aug 7-9 Tsurugaoka hosts Kamakura's main Summer Fete *Kaya-no-wa Kuguri*, 3:00am 7th, marks start of 2nd half of year; passing thru massive reed ring 3 times brings health for rest of year. At this time, prayers offered to erase first half-year's evils, gain health and protection from fires for second half. **7-9th** *Bonbori Matsuri*-Lantern Festival, 350 lanterns lit between Taiko-bashi and Mai-den along Yabusame-michi; outdoor tea ceremony at Wakamiya, 10-15:00 daily. 9th at 10:00 is *Sanetomo Matsuri*, Festival, Shirahata Jinja.

Sep 14-16 Tsurugaoka Hachiman *Autumn Fete*, highlight 15th *mikoshi*-portable shrine-procession, 16th Yabusame. 14th nite *zenya-sai*, nite-before celebration.

EAST LEG

Shirahata-daimyojin [4] → Kamakura-gu [5] → Egara Tenjin → **Kakuonji** [7] → Tenen trail → Hyakuya-yagura → **Zuisen-ji** → **Sugimotodera** → Summer manse → **Hokoku-ji** → **Myoo-in** → Juniso Shrine   (**bold** = Recommended)

GETTING THERE: Leaving **Tsurugaoka Hachiman** thru E torii to main E-bound bus road at Daigaku-mae bus stop. Called *Kanazawa Shio-kaido*, Salt Highway, was used to transport salt from Kanazawa.

Heading E, take third L 400m to stone marker on former site of Yoritomo's residence; just beyond on L is...

SHIRAHATA DAIMYOJIN [4] where his spirit is enshrined, built on site of *Hokke-do*, Lotus Pavilion, where he spent his last years. Up stone steps is *Yoritomo's* **grave**, simple stone 5-tiered pagoda, 2 meters tall and covered with moss– not what one would expect for one of Japan's greatest leaders. Nearby is rustic *Yoritomo-Chaya Tea House* looking out over his city below. **Apr 13** small rite honors Yoritomo.

Further up hill is **grave** of Oë Hiromoto, Yoritomo's most able advisor and brains behind government. This ultimate administrator, he was above political power plays and so indispensable that he remained in office under successive leaders until his death of natural causes in 1225. Tho pleasant wooded hills, this area is not worth detour unless you have time to spare, at that better spent on next section.

We now pass tennis court, site of what was once Kamakura's greatest temple cluster. Yoritomo modeled it after spectacular Motsu-ji and Chuson-ji complexes in Hiraizumi (*see* TOHOKU), which he flattened when 'retaliating' against Hiraizumi's Fujiwara Yasuhira for helping Yoshitsune. This NIKAIDO area gets name from main hall of now-destroyed Eifuku-ji temple. Yoritomo built it in 1192 to placate spirits of Yoshitsune, Yasuhira and countless casualties of his attack on Hiraizumi. Completely destroyed by fire in 1405, tennis courts cover Eifuku-ji, solitary stone marker what remains of its past.

GETTING THERE: 15min walk from Tsurugaoka Hachiman E torii, up L fork in road just beyond turn-off to Yoritomo's grave. **Bus** 5min, make sure you get one heading → **Daito-miya**, others take R fork in road. From stn get bus at pier #6.

Built on site of older Toko-ji temple, also razed 1405, is...
Most popular site in area, imperial **KAMAKURA-GU** shrine [5], built by order of emperor Meiji in 1869 to honor imperial prince Morinaga imprisoned here and executed in 1335. His death caused end of Hojo and Kamakura. In 1259 imperial primogeniture was broken and royal house split into two competing branches: *Jimyoin* (senior) and *Daitoku-ji* (junior) under precarious balance of alternate succession overseen by Hojo. 1331, emperor Go-Daigo (Daitoku-ji) set off *Kemmu Restoration* in attempt to secure his branch and restore imperial power. He was defeated, captured and exiled to Oki Island in N by Hojo. Escaping 1332, he found himself at head of full-scale uprising aided by powerful anti-Hojo clans (still unhappy with insufficient reimbursement for their part in repelling Mongols decades earlier) led by Ashikaga Takauji who captured Kyoto for Go-Daigo while his cohort Nitta Yoshisada razed Kamakura and slaughtered Hojos. Go-Daigo thanked his 'faithful warriors', proceeded to heap awards only on courtiers, giving them high military posts; his son, Prince Morinaga, became shogun in attempt to control both civil and military power. Expecting to become shogun himself, Takauji rebelled again in 1335, locked Morinaga into cave, again captured Kyoto following year setting up rival emperor Komyo (Jimyoin) who of course, in return, made Takauji shogun in 1338 establishing new shogunal dynasty, Ashikaga.

Takauji further increased shogunal power, taking over joint civil-military offices begun by Go-Daigo; confiscating imperial land holdings, his military land stewards doling out allowances to courtiers. What little political clout Court had left was eliminated as military leaders no longer required Court appointments. Shogun had royal carte-blanche enforced by same military now occupying and ruling from Kyoto.

Ashikaga attained Yoritomo's dream of efficient, totally centralized state. Elimination of cumbersome imperial system forced Ashikaga to rule with iron fist to maintain uneasy balance of power over other power hungry vassals. Further aggravated by Go-Daigo and followers holed up in Yoshino hills near NARA (*see*) still claiming sovereignty; rallying point for anti-Ashikaga clans until capitulating 1392. Weakened by constant warfare, Ashikaga lost all real power half-century later; competing daimyos threw nation into era of Warring States, eventually reunited late 1500s by Nobunaga, Hideyoshi and Tokugawa Ieyasu, whom we meet farther on down Tokaido.

L of main sanctuary are two small shrines dedicated to men who aided Morinaga. First honors Murakami Yoshiteru, who as Morinaga's double was killed in Yoshino hills. Next to it honors Minami-no-kata, who, sympathetic to Morinaga gave him food and water and tried to prevent his execution. Here path leads behind main sanctuary to cave where Morinaga was held for 9 months, heavy wood grill which kept him in now keeps you out.

Path continues thru small garden to...

Treasure Hall, *Homutsu-den*, contains Morinaga related items. ¥200 donation at office to see **cave** and **museum**, but suggest saving yen for KAKUON-JI as can't see into cave and museum has nothing spectacular. Morinaga's grave 10min walk E on other side of Nikaido-gawa River on grounds of RICHIKO-JI temple, also burned 1405. Richiko-ji's head priest secretly retrieved Morinaga's head, which headsman had unceremoniously tossed into bushes, and buried it in temple.

Sep 21, 22 torchlight *Takigi-Noh* performed outdoors on special stage from 17:30. Komparu, Kanze, Hosho schools act Noh dances, comic Kyogen by Yamamoto school. **Free** admission, but must reserve seats by sending request with self-addressed stamped envelope to: **Kamakura City Tourist Organization**, *Kamakura-shi Kanko Kyokai*, 1-10-5 Komachi, Kamakura-shi, Kanagawa-ken, *zip*-248. Only accept cards postmarked Sept 1-8, lucky few chosen by lottery; can't specify preferred date. Call ☎(0467)-23-3050 for details.

Interesting sites nearby, first R of Kamakura-gu W of Tenjin-mae bus stop is...

EGARA TENJIN [6] built 1104, red-lacquered building enshrines Japan's greatest calligrapher, Sugawara Michizane. Yoritomo made it "Protector of Northeast Approach" to his capital in 1192. Michizane-Tenjin is patron of education. Students flock here to offer prayers for good grades, school admission, inscribing hopes on *ema* offertory plaques which they hang all over shrine walls. 900-year-old sacred gingko grows nearby. Unusual stone dedicated to Shimizu Ran who drew his famous Kappa (water imp) cartoons centuries ago. On one side is brush-wielding kappa caricature of Michizane, on other is written *"Shimizu Ran's Kappa Rock"*, penned by Kawabata Yasunari, Nobel Prize-winning author who based many of his stories in Kamakura, such as *Thousand Cranes*, *Sound of the Mountain*.

Jan 15 memorial rite, *Fudé-kuyo* for old writing tools to bring New Year luck.

Heading N from Kamakura-gu, road heads uphill 10min to...

KAKUON-JI temple [7] with soaring thatched roof, most 'Kamakura' of all sites, buried in ancient trees. One of few remaining old temples, founded 1218 by 2nd regent Yoshitoki, enlarged 1296 by 9th. Later, official Shingon temple of emperor Go-Daigo and Ashikaga. One of Kamakura's 'hidden' temples, worth effort (**cabs** go to main gate); prefer to Kamakura-gu. Donate ¥200, see temple with priest for guide. To avoid 'Kyoto-izing' temple, head priest wants visitors to fully appreciate its beauty, only allows small groups (no bus tours), and only on good days—so you might call ☎22-1195 before heading up.

First, **AIZEN-DO** hall moved here 1905 from abandoned DAIRAKU-JI temple (stone marks spot 300m S); oldest structure here with several fine idols including: wood Aizen Myo-o, bronze Fudo Myo-o, wood Ashuku Nyorai. To its R are priests' quarters. Behind is small JIZO-DO hall full of jizo images, among them *kuro-jizo*-black jizo (ICA). According to legend this jizo takes on suffering of criminals burning in hell and is burned black in their place—no matter how many times polished to its natural brown it turns black overnite. At far back is rustic but spectacular thatched roof YAKUSHI-DO hall housing even finer Yakushi-medicinal Buddha Trinity; also sitting Amida and other statues from Richiko-ji temple. Tucked away in temple grounds is attractive, rare 17th century *minka* (folk house) restored 1981.

Aug 10 this temple comes alive for *Kuro-jizo Ennichi* temple fair.

TEN-EN (Heavenly Garden) [9] **hiking trail** begins 300m S (across from DAIRAKU-JI marker), one of several trails crossing hills of Kamakura:

20min up is...

Hyakuhachi-yagura, 108 graves of samurai and priests [8], small caves
carved into soft limestone; each has niches for cremated remains. Date 11th–
mid-15th centuries, found only this area, special historic asset. Each cave
has 5-tier stone pagoda modeled after mainland Buddhist stupa. Tiers represent **Basic Elements**: base-earth, body-water, roof-fire, lotus-air, jewel-
'ether' or heaven. Earliest, simplest of these *gorin-no-to* looks like roofed
egg, each tier marked by Sanskrit symbol. Late Ashikaga they become
gaudier, squared off. Zen priest graves marked by *mubo-no-to*, inverted
'egg' on lotus petal ('ether' tier largest). About 5,000 Yagura dot Kamakura
area, 200 are around here. (Not open to public, too much looting of stone heads.)

From here trail forks: L 30min stroll to HANSOBO, where previous roundabout route
from OFUNA (*see*) reaches Kamakura and KENCHO-JI, R 30min to *Ten-en* peak (has tea
house) and another 45min down to ZUISEN-JI.

10min walk E of Kamakura-gu is...

ZUISEN-JI temple [10], its Zen gardens. Just inside main gate is rock
garden and to L plum garden. But temple best known for 'natural' rock
garden behind main hall. Carved out of hill, it uses no arranged trees nor
rocks; just waterfall-fed lake with central island. Restored 1970, is only
such *zenrin-chikutei* style garden of Kamakura era remaining in city. Larger
cave R, was used for Zazen meditation. Templegarden constructed 1327 by
Zen Rinzai sect leader Muso Kokushi (1275-1351), spiritual advisor to
Ashikaga Takauji. Famous designer of Zen gardens, his work includes
gardens of Kyoto's Saiho-ji Moss Garden and Tenryu-ji temple, which he
also founded. Becoming Takauji's spiritual advisor sealed relationship between samurai and Zen; all Ashikaga shoguns also took Rinzai advisors.
Unlike earlier mingling of church and state, Zen kept to its policy of political
noninterference and served only as spiritual safety valve. ¥100 admits to
temple.

Near Zuisen-ji's lower gate several small **tea houses** serve snacks and full meals. If
feet bit tired by now, **cab** stand nearby; if no cabs use phone there to call Keihin Hire
☎22-0946 or 22-2185 and one will be by shortly, 1.5x-mtr to Kamakura stn. If you have
bit more time, follow our route heading further E on Kanazawa Shio-kaido. If direct from
Kamakura-gu by foot head W, L first intersection 300m to main road then E 200m.

If bus from stn, board at #5, 10min to Sugimoto Kannon-mae, to...

SUGIMOTO-DERA [11] Kamakura's beautifully rustic **oldest temple**
built 734 by Tendai priest Gyoki. On N side of street, old narrow stone
stairs lined with white banners pass under thatched-roof Nio-mon gate to
Kannon-do hall (also thatch). Favorite of Yoritomo who rebuilt it 1191 of
local cryptomeria (*sugi*) to give it present name. Big, white banners replace
usual offertory plaques, costlier, say 'Eleven-faced Sugimoto Kannon'—3
fine ones inside. **Secret Buddha** image shown **monthly 1st & 18th** 12:00-
14:00 only.

Hill behind temple, site of **Sugimoto Castle** of local Miura clan.
During Nanboku-cho civil wars (1331-1392) torched by rival Kitabatake
clan. Lord retreated to Sugimoto-dera where with surviving followers
committed harakiri. *Nanboku-cho*, Northern-Southern Dynasties, was era
with 2 separate imperial lines. Go-Daigo's 'renegade' Northern Dynasty
ruling out of Yoshino-Nara, and main Southern Dynasty out of Kyoto.
Short-lived Northern Dynasty ended when its 6th emperor, heirless Go-
Komatsu, gave up cause 'for sake of national unity'. Actually, he was offered throne in Kyoto after 99th main-line emperor as face-saving escape for
both sides, each aware Northern line was at its end with Go-Komatsu.

5min E of Sugimoto-dera on stream's opposite bank is...
Summer Manse, *shikan-tei* of imperial prince Ekan with lovely soaring
thatched roof built 1644, moved from Kyoto 1959. Not open to public.
Rsve group of 10, ¥3,000 ea incl tea in 300-year old tea house, ☎22-5557.

Another 5min down main road to...
HOKOKU-JI [12] RINZAI ZEN temple on R. Buildings themselves not
much to see, all rebuilt after Kanto quake; but fantastic Zen **bamboo
garden** in rear (enter thru ¥100 auto-turnstile L of main hall). Path winds thru
thick, cool bamboo forest interspersed with lanterns, stone buddhas, to 2 tea
houses at far back. Sip green tea, munch sweet cakes in cool to rejuvenate on
hot summer day. Upper tea house looks across to hill side with pair of
yagura –L for Ashikaga Yoshikane (temple founder), R Ashikaga Yoshihisa
who slit his belly in this temple after flubbing revolt against cousin shogun
Ashikaga Yoshimitsu. Tho pardoned, rebels (all Kamakura branch of
Ashikaga) followed suit with several hundred disembowelments that day.
   Zazen meditation open to public sun 7:30-11:00AM, then meal of *oka-yu* -rice
gruel, talk on zazen. No rsvtn or fee but 1st-timer should be there 7:30 for short intro.

   Few more rustic temples and shrines further E to hiking trail which ends at Asahina
bus stop, thence 25min back to Kamakura stn. But we turn around here, catching bus at
Jomyo-ji stop, 10min to Kamakura stn.
   For those with time, continuing E most notable sights are **MYOO-IN** temple, **JU-
NISO JINJA** shrine, both rustic wood, thatched roof buildings naturally blend with sur-
rounding nature; neither spectacular but possessing air of ancient Kamakura.

MYO-O-IN [13], also known as *Godai Myo-o*, 5 Great Guardian Kings,
25min walk from HOKOKU-JI (2 stops bus to Sensui); road crosses river, 150m beyond
sakura-lined lane cuts off L (back across river) to its solitary main hall. Ask to see 5
Myo-o figures inside, follow with *matcha* thick green tea. Built 1235 by 4th
Kamakura shogun Yoritsune, it at one time ranked 2nd to Tsurugaoka as
center for Ryobu-Shinto. View + tea, if not specified offer ¥500.

JUNISO SHRINE [14] is 30min walk further (3min bus, 3 stops). L at bus stop,
shrine sits on small rise overlooking rice paddies. R at bus stop, old Kanazawa Kaido
follows stream, becomes Asahina **hiking course** (40min to Asahina bus stop). Part of
trail is carved thru rocks to form easily defensible entrance to Kamakura. Called *kiri-toshi*
-carved passages, Yoritomo had 7 such made, some true tunnels, at otherwise impassable locations thru Kamakura's hills.

SOUTH LEG
   Hokai-ji → **Myohon-ji** [18] → Joei-ji → Myoho-ji → Ankokuron-ji → Chosho-ji
   → **Komyo-ji** [24] → Zaimoku-za Beach between **Tsurugaoka Hachiman** &
   coast is for you with extra half-day, or few hours just to see main sights of
   Myohonji, Komyoji.

Begin again E torii of Tsurugaoka, 200m S of Daigaku-mae bus stop to...
HOKAI-JI temple [16], on site of Hojo family manse, built 1335 by
Ashikaga Takuji to appease spirits of Hojo killed here. Didn't actually build
anew, just moved Hojo family temple of Tosho-ji (which we visit next) here.
Main hall has wood *Jizo-bosatsu*; temple treasures (which can see for small
offering) including several other late Kamakura era wood figures (all ICA).
HOKAI-JI holds **zazen meditation** open to all: call ☎22-5512 to get next zazen day's
schedule and reservation.

Block S, L across river 200m to...
Site of TOSHO-JI. Nothing remains of Hojo family temple built 1224 by 3rd Regent
Yasutoki, except buildings of HOKAI-JI. Just behind it is Hojo Takatoki **harakiri
yagura** [17], small cave graves of defeated Hojo. Surrounded by Nitta Yoshisada's army
over 1,000 men, women, children, last of Hojo led by their lord Takatoki, committed
mass harakiri, oops, pardon, *seppuku*, here.

From cave starts Gion-zan hiking course, 15min thru woods to...

MYOHON-JI [18] family temple of Hiki, Yoritomo's maternal line whom Hojo Tokimune wiped out in 1203. Daughter of Hiki Yoshikazu was Yoriie's mistress, bore his son, Ichiman, whom Yoshikazu felt should be 3rd shogun instead of Yoriie's brother, Sanetomo. Hojo Tokimune tried to set up dual shogunate of Sanetomo and infant Ichiman but father-in-law, Yoshikazu, wanted all (with himself regent), so Tokimune destroyed family to keep peace. Marking spot of Hiki manse, Myohon-ji was built in 1274 as Nichiren sect temple to appease his family spirits by surviving son Hiki Yoshimoto, who survived slaughter because being raised in temple. Most of this quiet temple is dedicated to Saint Nichiren; main hall in rear is soaring tile-roofed **Founder's Hall**, with wood statue of Nichiren; to R, graves of Hiki family. R of second gate is **stone monument** under which is buried kimono sleeve of Hiki eldest son Ichiman (6 years old), all that remained of once great family. Trapped middle of nite in burning mansion, any who tried to escape flames were shot by waiting Hojo archers.

MYOHON-JI 10min walk due E of stn, those on limited time skip other 2 and head straight here. From here, Gion-zan hiking course continues 15min to 900-year old **YAKUMO JINJA** [19] shrine, from where 100m S to main road (rte134) at Oomachi Yotsu-kaku bus stop; W to stn, 500m E to 2 more historically important Nichiren temples: MYOHO-JI, ANKOKURON-JI.

But first, block N of Yakumo is...

JOEI-JI temple [20]. Legend has it that on his way to his execution, Saint Nichiren was offered *onigiri*, rice balls by nun from Saji Convent at this spot. She dropped them. Nichiren picked up dirt-covered *onigiri*, ate them, saying they were *bota-mochi* (sesame-covered rice balls). Followers built temple here to honor nun, buried here next to small but colorful main hall.

Sep 12-13 *Botamochi Fete* ceremony offering *botamochi* to Nichiren statue.

MYOHO-JI [21], northern of pair, (not to be confused with MyohoNji) where Nichiren lived in grass hut when he first came to Kamakura in 1253. Temple built 1357 by his disciple Nichiei who is buried on grounds. Nowadays, temple famous for its superb mossy steps (also called *Kokédera* 'Moss Temple') cultivated over centuries by priests. Best seen on sunny day just after rain, especially in rainy season, Jun-Jul. Moss steps **off-limits** and we use spare flight parallel to L to reach upper buildings.

Few minutes walk S to...

ANKOKU-RON-JI [22] where Nichiren wrote militant nationalistic Rissho Ankoku-ron, *Essays on Proper National Salvation*, 1260.

5min further E on Route 134 is another Nichiren temple...

CHOSHO-JI temple [23] itself is uninteresting (newly rebuilt) but site of one of city's top winter events. **Feb 12** several dozen priests end special 100-day ascetic training, strip and douse selves with ice cold water reciting lotus sutra. Procession starts stn at 9:00, purification rites Chosho-ji 11:00; open to public. Chosho-ji is 10min bus from stn; take bus leaving platform #4.

Same bus to MYOHO-JI & ANKOKURON-JI; one stop earlier at NAETSU 5min out. Several more temples and site of original Tsurugaoka Hachiman—marked by small shrine S of here.

Most not especially worth time, but must-see is...

KOMYO-JI [24] Jodo sect temple, founded 1240 as HOKKE-JI (Shingon esoteric sect) temple by 4th regent Hojo Tsunetoki, buried here. Moved to present site 1243 and greatly enlarged, when changed name to Komyo-ji, and sect to Jodo (Pure Land) as head priest Nen'ari Yochu had just converted Tsunetoki to Jodo. One of top 4 Kamakura temples, continued to flourish under following Ashikaga era, survived Warring States era and in

1597 Tokugawa Ieyasu made it one of top 18 temples in Kanto—all major centers of Buddhist studies until early Meiji purge, 1860s; during Edo period was ancestral cemetery of powerful Uchiwara clan, local Daimyo. Imperial fief, Kamakura was under direct control of Tokugawa shogun, Uchiwara being their cousins. 1245 KOMYO-JI chosen to hold *Juya-e* ten-nite service memorial rites for Amida Buddha, ritual initiated in 1198 by emperor Go-Tsuchimikado.

Ceremony Oct 12 for 3 days-nites (reduced from original 10) Jodo followers from all Kanto gather, chant *nenbutsu* prayer *"Namu Amida Butsu"* Sacred Name Amida Buddha. Outside, festival stalls stretch to Zaimoku-za beach to entertain all sorts of pilgrims.

KOMYO-JI is 200m in from coast, 10min bus from stn (take any from platform #1). If coming from ANKOKURON-JI area, go 400m E of Chosho-ji to SUIDOSUJI bus stop and 4 stops (on any S-bound bus) to KOMYO-JI stop.

L of main gate is...
SENJU-IN, 1000-armed Kannon subtemple, main study center until 1887. Thousand-armed Kannon statue in Main Hall.

R of main gate is...
RENJU-IN, Shingon sect temple predating KOMYO-JI by century; later became part of greater KOMYO-JI complex and Jodo sect. In line with its main gate is **Hondo** main hall with Amida statue, R of which is statue of Benzai-ten goddess of music, wealth, eloquence—muse supreme. Legend has it Benzai-ten (enshrined nearby at Enoshima isle) became enchanted by Amida's teachings and refused to return to isle.

One of *Shichifuku-jin* or Seven Lucky Gods of Japan, Benzai-ten is only female of septet. She and her companions were pre-Buddhist deities—some possibly Hindu origin, some local tribal—later incorporated into Japanese Shinto-Buddhist pantheon as popular folk-deities to be found in shrines and temples thruout Japan. They are shown sailing to Japan from West in Chinese-style ship. All bring some sort of good fortune. You will meet them several times in Kamakura, most commonly Benzai-ten (Benten) and phallic Daikoku, of foreskin hat, standing erect upon his scrotal rice bales.

L of Amida is statue of Naito Tadaoki, Edo daimyo who made Komyo-ji his family temple. Outside on R, *Sanzon-Gosoraigo* (3-God 5-Saints) rock garden; white-pebble 'stream', shrub 'mountain' with 8 rocks which represent Jodo's 3 deities—Amida Buddha and attendant bodhisattvas Kannon & Seishi, and 5 saints–2 Chinese, 3 Japanese. Attached to Main Hall is Kaisan-do hall which now serves as guest rooms (*see* STAY). Behind 2 halls is another garden of lotus pond ringed by sakura and pine. Lotus are from 1,-2,000-year-old seeds discovered 1938 in Chiba pref; bloom late Jul-Aug.

Zaimoku-za Beach stretching for 1km is now popular swimming area. During Kamakura period it was called Wakae, main loading area for city's merchants. Its shallow waters made loading difficult and in 1232 Japan's 1st man-made island, WAKAE-JIMA [25] was built just off S end of beach to accommodate trading ships. All that remains of this Historic Relic breaks surface at low tide, rocks formed 40m-wide, 200m-long pier (2 football fields end-to-end). Next to stone marker is **Rokakku-no-sei,** one of Kamakura's ten fresh water wells.

2min inland from here is...
SHOGAKU-JI temple where Yochu lived before opening KOMYO-JI. In 1512 Sumiyoshi castle behind burned down in attack, flames spread, gutting temple. Rebuilt 1541 by 18th head priest of Komyo-ji, Amida statue put in main hall. Temple not much now, but beautiful view of bay below; idyllic **sunset** for those staying at Komyo-ji.

NORTH LEG

KITA-KAMAKURA: N of TSURUGAOKA HACHIMAN are several fine Rinzai Zen
temples worth several relaxing hours; best visited early am from **Engaku-ji** [26] →
Tokei-ji → Matsugaoka Library → Jyochi-ji → **Kencho-ji** [30] → Hansobo Goblin
Temple → Ten-en trail → ending at Tsuruoka — or late afternoon reverse course,
top off with *shojin-ryori*-Buddhist veg lunch or dinner, prior reservation in temples or
unreserved at 2 fine restaurants, nr Engaku-ji & Kencho-ji.

*Next to Kita-Kamakura stn, tracks cut thru lower temple grounds, 1 train stop or
15min bus (from platform #9) from Kamakura stn; 10min from Hachiman bus stop is...*
ENGAKU-JI with **Byakuro-chi** (White Heron) pond to its W, front gate
to East Pond's name reflects power of Zen in Kamakura. Legend says
when saint temple founder Mugaku Sogen entered Kamakura, spirit of
Tsurugaoka Hachiman took on form of white heron, its alighting on this
pond was then taken as 'blessing', or acquiescence from local Shinto *kami*
that it was OK for foreign faith to build here.

Built 1282 to accommodate overflow of disciples from Kencho-ji, it also
honors Japanese casualties of Mongol invasions of 1274,1281. Modeled
after China's top Rinzai (Chin: *Lin-chi*) temple, was Japan's first completely
Zen-structured temple; buildings laid out almost in straight line. Soon became one of main Zen centers (#2 Gozan), but several fires during Warring
States period eliminated most structures and clans were too busy fighting to
spend money rebuilding temples. Under Tokugawa regained past splendor,
only to be flattened in 1923 Kanto quake; most of what you see put back
together after that. At its peak there were over 40 halls; now 18 remain.
Still very much in use, you can roam entire compound but only 2 halls
(**Butsunichi-an** and **Obai-in**) can be entered other than on special
occasions. Compound open 8:00–17:30 (16:30 winter), ¥100.

L from first gate...
Enma-do has large statue of Enma (Yamma) king of underworld. Just
beyond massive main gate is central *Butsu-den* (Buddha hall) housing
temple treasures. Open to public only **Nov 2-4** (¥300). To its L is gently
sloping thatched roof *Senbutsu-jo Hall* (1699), main research-reading center
for trainees. L of main gate is **Shorei-in zazen center** for laymen. Once
dojo for Yagyu school of swordsmanship, was moved here in 1928 to serve
more Buddhistic purpose. Behind and to R of Butsu-den are priests' living
quarters and library.

Still major Zen center, ENGAKU-JI offers zazen daily for anyone: 1 hr sunrise zazen
from 5:30 Apr-Oct, 6:00 Nov-Mar. Special sun sessions followed by talks on Zen 2nd
and 4th sun monthly. Two-day (sat, sun) *sesshin* with overnite at temple on most
weekends. For real enthusiasts special 5-day summer course for students only; ¥5,000 full
sesshin—arrange well ahead of time for this one, for others just call at least one day
before; ☎(0467)-22-0478.

Past Myokochi pond on L is...
SHOZOKU-IN subcompound, training center for monks from all over
Japan. At its rear is spectacular thatched roof **Shariden** (National
Treasure) hall housing ashes of Mugaku Sogen; Japan's oldest example of
Tang architecture imported with Zen. Open to public only first 3 days of new year.

Up stone-paved path from Myokochi pond, on L you can enter...
BUTSUNICHI-AN to partake of *matcha* (green tea) in garden, ¥500. Served
as Hojo clan's meditation hall; small thatched roof hall in garden is
Mausoleum of regents, housing wooden figures of Hojo Tokimune and
Takatoki, first and last regents.

Beyond Butsunichi-an to...
OBAI-IN subcompound dedicated to saint Muso Soseki. On R of steps leading to Obai-in is *Hakuroku-do* cave, from where herd of white deer was said to have appeared upon temple's opening.

Back down near main gate, long flight of stone steps far R leads up to **bell tower**, Kamakura's largest temple bell (NT) representative of Kamakura style with 4 prayers engraved on it: "10,000 years (*banzai*) for Imperial family; 1,000 autumns for ministers; fair winds and rain; national prosperity, peace for people."

Take breather at tea house here, gaze across valley to...
TOKEI-JI [27]: Started 1285 by Kakuzan-ni (8th Hojo Tokimasa's wife) to take in wives wishing for divorce. In pre-Meiji Japan men needed only to submit 'request for divorce' and it was done; women had no right but to flee to convents designated marriage cutting temples, *Engiri-dera*, where 3 years ascetic training gained legal divorce. Greater admission 'donation', better treatment. At first any convent sufficed, but under Tokugawa became limited to here and one other, MANTOKU-JI in mountainous Gumma prefecture. In 1873 women gained equal divorce rights, Engiri-dera quietly fading out of existence, changed to priests' temples. Now simple rustic Rinzai Zen temple; pleasant, but nothing spectacular. Popular for abundant flowers, quiet compound is full more of young couples getting together than of older ones trying to separate.

200m S on other side of road from ENGAKU-JI, stone steps lead up to quaint little thatched roof **Sanmon gate** (little old lady takes your ¥50 donation). To L is empty **bell tower** (bell now at Izu's Honritsu-ji temple; main Butsu-den Buddha hall, now Yokohama Sankei-en–*see*). On R, several original halls (repaired 1983 with donations) house superb Kannon images. Mid **Taihei-den** built 1297 for standing Kannon brought from abandoned Taihei-ji temple, now in nearby Matsugaoka Treasure Hall (*below*), replaced by less valuable Shaka-nyorai.

Next door...
SUIGETSU-DO, 1285, shelters beautiful *Suigetsu Kannon* Jade-moon Goddess of Mercy, seated on rock.

At far end...
Matsugaoka Treasure Hall (¥300, 10:00-15:00, X-mon) contains temple treasures, including private possessions of foundress, other famed nuns like Go-Daigo's empress Yodo-ni, Hideyoshi's wife Tenshu-ni.

At far R is...
Matsugaoka Library started by SUZUKI T Daisetsu foremost modern scholar of Zen—numerous English works *Zen and Japanese Culture* etc. His ashes rest in cemetery here, also dozens of noted writers, scholars.

150m from Tokei-ji down first R is long moss-covered steps leading up to unusual...
Chinese-style **Sanmon gate** (2nd floor is bell tower) of JYOCHI-JI, #4 Gozan. Founded 1281 by 5th Hojo Tokiyori and headed by 2 prominent Sung Chinese Rinzai priests; had at its peak 18 main halls, only few remain. ¥100 donation lets you in to *Dongé-den hall* with Sansei-butsu trinity of Amida (L), Shaka (center), Miroku (R): Buddhas of past, present, future.

*At far back of compound is start of 1.8km (25min) trail to **Great Buddha** via Zeni-arai Benten Shrine. Another 500m down to quiet...*
CHOJU-JI [29] Rinzai-Zen temple popular for spring and summer blossoms. *Admission by request only.*

2min from Choju-ji to...
KENCHO-JI [30], #1 of Kamakura Gozan, 'Five Mountains' or great Zen temples and Japan's 1st center for Rinzai Zen studies. Open 8:45-16:30, ¥200.

Also built by 5th Hojo Tokiyori 1253 as commissioned by emperor Go-Fukakusa, founding priest Sung China's Ran-kei Do-ryu (Lan-hsi Tao-lung). Name comes from its completion in reign of Go-Fukakusa, Kencho era. Most other local Rinzai sect priests studied here before founding their own temples—like Engaku-ji's Mugaku Sogen, who with Rankei Doryu also buried here at top of stone steps compound far R. At its peak, Kencho-ji had over 40 training and study halls, most of which burned down during Warring States era. Most of what now exists dates to mid-17th century when Zen master Takuan, inventor of pickle of same name and sword teacher of Miyamoto Musashi, convinced Tokugawa shogun to rebuild deteriorating complex. Central structures mostly moved here from other cities over centuries. Like Engaku-ji, Kencho-ji is modeled after China's top Zen temple in linear ground plan, tho not as pure in style.

SO-MON **entrance gate** (1783) moved here in 1943 from Kyoto's imperial Hanshu Sanmai-in temple to replace original flattened in Kanto quake. Straight ahead semi-Chinese style **Sanmon main gate** rebuilt 1775 entirely from commoners' donations collected by head priest Bantetsu, has original name-plaque written by emperor Go-Fukakusa. To R, original (1647) bell tower houses 750-year-old bell (NT) inscribed by Rankei Doryu.

Buddha Hall, *Butsu-den*, behind Sanmon houses fine wooden figures, center 5m tall jizo-bosatsu—usually not central image in Zen temple this one has story behind it. Originally execution ground and small Shinhei-ji temple had jizo to meet their spiritual needs. Thus when Kencho-ji built on grounds, jizo was set here as main icon, in part as special pacification of souls of executed. Hall itself moved here 1647 from Edo's Zojo-ji temple front of Prince Hotel. **Dharma Hall**, *Hatto,* behind (rebuilt 1814 like original) is largest wood Buddhist structure in Kanto. All major rites held here. Junipers in front of Butsu-den were planted by Rankei, 1240s.

Sairai-an subcompound far R of Butsu-den is holiest of holies, *off-limits* to visitors. Spiritual center of temple (like Kencho-ji Shozoku-in) it includes *Zen-do* (meditation hall), *kaisan-do* (founder's hall), and thatched roof *sho-do* (hall of enlightenment)—temple's oldest structure, built 1458.

Behind and L of Sanmon, *Chinese-style Kara-mon* (Tang Gate) leads to priests' quarters. Largest, **Dragon King's Palace**, *Ryu-o-den*, once head priest's quarters, now used for services by Kencho-ji supporters. Can be entered, and rear walk-way looks over beautiful early Edo period garden (ICA) behind, pond-shaped like ideograph for *kokoro* (heart/spirit).

Here path heads past 2 tea shops 10min uphill to...also entry from OFUNA...
HANSOBO–GOBLIN TEMPLE [31] 1890, Kencho-ji's head priest moved it from Shizuoka prefecture temple. Dramatic walk in. Dedicated to demi-goblin Hansobo Dai-gongen (great Buddha avatar) for domestic safety and prosperity. Local Shinto deity before being incorporated into Buddhism, Hansobo also serves as Kencho-ji's tutelary guardian god. Perched among climbing rock garden behind are 10 bronze statues of *tengu* (long-nosed and crow-beaked goblin) in various poses and sizes. Near end of WWII Japanese Army seized these unique statues to melt down for shell-casings. Found unharmed, returned 1979. Spectacular views on it's hiking course.
Mar 17 Hansobo Reisai annual festival. New year prayers, exorcisms **1st week Jan**.
Ten-en hiking course starts here, 50min to KAKUON-JI, 90min to ZUISEN-JI.

200m S of Kencho-ji to...
ENNO-JI temple of *Enma Dai-o*, King of Hades, Stone steps leading to it (on other side of street from Kencho-ji) indicated by painting on wood of

Enma Dai-o. Not particularly attractive temple, there are some interesting statues in appropriately dim main hall of Enma Dai-o and his jury of 10 attendant kings. Everyone after death is judged by this royal jury, verdict passed on to Enma Dai-o who judges if you go to hell or heaven. Belief originated early Heian period, and with it came special Buddhist rites to favorably influence this jury—services held on 7th and 49th days after death. Nichiren *'Namu myo-ho renge-kyo'* and Jodo *'Namu Amida Butsu'*, instant-salvation prayers sought to bypass this judgment. Enma carving by Kamakura's first priest, Unkei, is supposed to be 'true' portrait of underworld king. According to legend, Unkei suddenly died while meditating and so met underworld king who sent him back to world to 'finish his duty'. Reviving, immediately carved whom he had seen.

Affiliated temple of Kencho-ji, Enno-ji was originally near coast in 1250 but moved here early 1600s after tidal wave destroyed its protective hall. In that tidal wave, several children were saved by clinging to statues. As result this grim figure has become guardian deity of children; many brought here to receive name-blessings. *Enma Ennichi festival* Jan 16.

10min walk rear gate 5min bus Kencho-ji → Kamakura stn.

WEST LEG

Hills W of TSURUGAOKA HACHIMAN have several historically interesting if visually uninspiring sights, thru wooded **Genji-yama Park,** offers pleasant strolls popular spring sakura and flower seasons, and 2 of 3 main sights in town. Jufuku-ji [33] → Tatsumi-jinja → Eisho-ji → Jokomyo-ji → **Zeniarai Benten** [39] → Sasuke Inari → Maruyama Inari → **Daibutsu** [41] → **Hase-dera** [44] → Goryo-jinja→ Gokuraku-ji. *Hikers* cross rolling hills to **Daibutsu** in slightly over hour; **bus, cab** or **tram** for others. 'Sleeper' well worth visiting en route.

GETTING THERE: **Zeniarai-Benten** is hardest to get to (no bus stops within several km), choice of **foot** or **cab**: 1.5km from Kamakura Stn, 2km from Tsurugaoka, **cab** 1x-mtr o.w., 3-4x-mtrs r.t.; only slight but worthwhile **detour** heading to Great Buddha & Hasé Kannon adds only about 2-3x-mtrs selfmade cab tour. Or 4-5x-mtrs o.w. **Kamakura–Zeniarai, Great Buddha.** On **foot** 45min (2 routes) from Tsurugaoka, 30min from stn– W on main road 750m → intersection (turn R), another 350m → 'T' and R 200m (L → Sasuke Inari shrine, Daibutsu Hiking Course).

Leave **Tsurugaoka** main gate, R on front main street, continue W down alley at corner, under tracks → first intersection where 2 choices → **Zeniarai Benten**.

Straight on to....

JUFUKU-JI temple [33], #3 Gozan. Oldest of five 'Greats'. Built year after Yoritomo's death (1200) by shrewish wife Masako on site of Yoritomo's father's mansion. Founded by pioneer Zen monk Eisai.

10min walk N of stn West Gate, passing on R small...

TATSUMI JINJA built 801 by first *Sei-i Tai-shogun* Sakano-ue Tamura-maro on his way to battle Ainu. Long paved-stone walkway to Jufuku-ji's gate, passing under natural tunnel of trees. At its peak 22 halls filled compound but several large fires reduced number and only half-dozen remain. Can only peer into compound, may be interesting for architects. Garden in front of main hall styled after Sung Chinese Zen temples.

Road L of gate heads into hills to cemetery; at far R back end being **graves** [34] of **Yoriie and Masako,** each has its own *yagura*-towers. **No entry.**

Nearby, rarely used trail heads 10min to **Genji-yama Park** [36].

5min further to...

Kuzuhara-ga-oka Park [37] on next hill top, whence 10min to ZENI-ARAI. Other way to ZENI-ARAI is to head N from crossroads in front of JUFUKU-JI 10min to 'T' in road, L 150m and another L 5min up wooded Kewai-zaka hill to Kuzuhara-ga-oka park.

20min from Jufuku-ji crossroads on L is...

EISHO-JI [35], Kamakura's sole remaining **nunnery**, Jodo sect, founded 1636 by Tokugawa Ieyasu's mistress; successive head nuns, women of powerful Mito family (Tokugawa branch) so became known as Mito Palace. All buildings original—tho not open to casual visitor, may enter compound by calling ahead ☎22-3534, possibly be shown around on short tour.

5min E of Eisho-ji. Cross tracks at Eisho-ji, R at 'T' to...

JOKOMYO-JI temple [38] built 1251, if interested in Buddhist statuary, several fine examples (to pre-arrange admission call ☎22-1359). Beautiful **Amida trinity** shows strong Chinese Sung influence; in addition several other notable statues and paintings. Main **Amida-do** hall moved here from Yoritomo's fabulous YOFUKU-JI temple complex in Nikaido area.

ZENIARAI BENTEN [39], money-washing goddess Benten, formally UGAFUKU JINJA shrine to *kami* of prosperity, is one of most interesting and popular places. Flanked on 3 sides by rock hills, thru front torii to tunnel carved in rock leads to compound inside. Dozens of red torii line this and rear entry, put up by important visitors indicating shrine's high status. Has somewhat mysterious air about it; never very warm, compound is almost completely canopied by trees, rustic shrines and tea houses scattered about, small waterfall suddenly springs from rocks, and incense smoke billows out of *Oku-no-in* **sacred cave** with natural spring, in which money washed returns tenfold to spender. Almost any time there are people washing their money and offering prayers for prosperity at altar, especially on days of snake (every 12th day). Incense-filled cave is surprisingly light, illuminated by hundreds of candles. From low ceiling hang countless chains of *senba-zuru*, each thousand small cranes painstakingly folded out of colorful paper as offerings for prosperity.

Shrine founded by Yoritomo, visited in dream by god Ugafuku who said if this sacred spring was found and properly cared for peace would reign. Needless to say one source of his power was newly rising merchant class. Yoritomo found spring on day, month and year of snake (symbol of prosperity), dedicated to Ugafuku (avatar of Benten/Benzaiten). Money washing here began in 1240s. 1st day of snake Jan *Zeni-arai Benten-sai festival* with *mikoshi*, money-blessing, purification rites; grand event snake years (1989, 2001).

Both **tea houses** in compound will serve snacks, drinks; by rear exit **Kokuni-chaya** will prepare *Shojin-ryori* from ¥5,000 if phone ahead ☎22-3452, special zen-vegetarian **boxed lunches** always ready from ¥2,500 (no need call).

From rear exit, road first L winds between walled houses to lane, off R, past shrine office, climbs passing under succession torii flanked by red banners; houses give way to woods.

10min there suddenly pops into view small gay decor shrine...

SASUKE INARI JINJA [40], built 1193 by Yoritomo, dedicated to fox/rice-god Inari who inspired him to fight Heike. Mini-torii offerings hung here can be bought at shrine office below, also carved wooden horse charms. *Hatsu-uma* festival on **Feb 1st day of Ox** has free tea ceremonies all day, kagura dance performed at lower sanctuary 12:30-13:00.

Just enough time to get to...

TSURUGAOKA MARUYAMA INARI to catch their lovely offertory dances.

Steps heading up past shrine rejoins **Daibutsu hiking course**, *45min on to...*

DAIBUTSU: GREAT BUDDHA OF KAMAKURA [41]. Located in Hasé.

GETTING THERE: 2km from Kamakura stn, **cab** basic-mtr o.w. (no need to keep, many here); or **bus** 10min from stn (any from piers #3 or #7) to **Daibutsu-mae** stop; **drivers** follow bus route, head W on Rte134 (passes just S of Kamakura stn) R at end. Other choice **Enoden tram terminal**, adjacent to JR Kamakura stn, one of most-fun rides in Japan, real-life Toonerville Trolley not to be missed; convenient, 5min (¥110) 3 stops to **Hasé** stn and 10min walk N on Rte 134.

Great Buddha at Nara was refurbished, even rebuilt, several times and Yoritomo at one such rededication conceived having similar object of worship at his capital. His dream came true only after his death. Six years in making, 15m-tall wood idol completed in 1238 by donations collected by priest Joko of Kotokuin, but lasted only 10 years before typhoon flattened. Joko set out again on begging pilgrimage, present big bronze was dedicated 1252. Large original covering building twice destroyed by tidal waves and not replaced since 1495. Image and roof were originally gilded, so Marco Polo wrote—secondhand—on Japanese lavish use of gold.

Colossus at Nara bigger—4x weight, half again taller—tho one confused Kamakura official recorded in *Azuma Kagami* that 8-*jyo* (24m – double) *Shaka* (whom you'll recall is historical or earthly Buddha of our age, whereas here is Amida, Shaka's celestial counterpart and these two are often hard to tell apart unless labeled) statue had been completed. Nara is 500 years older, but so often restored to point of esthetic obliteration with only base, legs and stomach original, rest dating to Edo period repairs. Where Kamakura was funded by donations, Nara was built by 'volunteers' drafted for emperor Shomu's show of national unity, nearly bankrupting new nation. Nara is Dainichi, *Roshana*, Timeless Universal Buddha of Boundless Light. Kamakura is Amida, *Amitabha*, our era's Buddha of Boundless Compassion. One is saved by Dainichi by studying and acting upon his esoteric way (*see* Mount Koya). One is saved by Amida thru belief alone and instilling faith in oneself by almost hypnotic technique of repeating Nichiren's chant, *Namu Myoho Renge-kyo* "I take refuge in Lotus Sutra"— or roughly-contemporary Shinran's (1173-1263) Jodo sect *Namu Amida Butsu*, "Holy Name Amida Buddha".

More MUNDANE FACTS OF BIG BUDDHA are: (for comparisons, *see* NARA).

Height with base	49ft 7ins	13.35meters
Image alone	37' 7"	11.45m
Circumference	97' 2"	29.20m
Face length	8' 5"	2.35m
Ear to ear	17' 9"	5.77m
Eye width	3' 11"	1.20m
Eyebrows	4' 2"	1.24m
Mouth width	3' 2"	.82m
Ear length	6' 6"	1.90m
Nose	3' 9"	1.15m
Knee to knee	35' 8"	9.10m
656 curls each hgt	9"	.20m
" " " dia.	10"	.24m
Topknot wisdom bump (dia)	2' 4"	.69m
Thumb (circumference)	3'	.83m

Total weight 121 tons. Eyes pure gold. Forehead boss of 80lbs or 36= kg pure silver.

Cast in sections, brazed together and finished. Despite 2 tidal waves, 8 centuries outdoors, has undergone no repairs. Survived 1923 quake, but 1962 several measures were taken in case of another: special shock-absorbent base supports body even if base crumbles, and hidden supports in neck prevent head from falling off.

Hollow interior has small shrine—for ¥20 enter world of Buddha's mindlessness.

Exemplifies Buddhist dictum that "spiritual peace comes of perfected knowledge and subjugation of all passion". As work of art it impresses with familiarity. Privately owned, reportedly offered for sale for scrap in 1870s, and again after World War II, when shrewd art-conscious US Army officer 'arrested' statue on suspicion of violating US Army Occupation law on separation of state and religion, held without bail until domestic monument protection law could be passed.

Juke-box joint once in courtyard has been removed, but as aesthetically criminal is new high wall built around to prevent viewing without payment of ¥150.

Daibutsu first part of KOTOKU-IN temple. Founded ca. 730 by saint Koki of Shingon sect, converted to Jodo sect, completely swept away in 1495 tidal wave leaving Buddha, temple abandoned till 1712 when revived as Jodo sect dedicated to, of course, Amida. (*See* **Daibutsu hiking course**)–photogenic rear view Buddha gazing out over bay.

Heading down main street towards Hasé stn first R (150m down) leads to...
Kamakura Noh-butai [42], modern (1971) 2-story Noh center. Noh, kyogen roughly once monthly, also other traditional performances. Schedules available calling ☎22-5557. All seats ¥4,000, groups of 10 or more ¥3,400 each.

Third R from Daibutsu to...
KOSOKU-JI [43] tucked back in vale, quiet temple known for **spring blossoms**. Once mansion of Yadoya Mitsunori; Kosoku is Chinese reading of ideographs for Mitsunori. Minister of Religion to 5th regent Hojo Tokiyori, he recognized militant, anti-government ring to Nichiren essay on national polity, convinced regent to exile him to Sado Isle. Led suppression of Nichiren Buddhism, imprisoned Nichiro (Nichiren's main disciple) in cave behind his manse. Touched by Nichiro's devotion to his master, Mitsunori became follower, converting mansion into Nichiren temple. Thru red-lacquered Sanmon gate is 3m tall stone with characters carved on it written by Nichiren. In rear is cave where Nichiro was imprisoned.

Next R off main street leads to...
HASE-DERA [44] 10min walk from Daibutsu (2min bus, 1 stop), 5min walk from Hasé stn, 6min bus from Kamakura stn. Fourth of 33 holy Kannon temples, built 736 by regent Fujiwara Fusasaki. **Main hall** KANNON-DO houses city's 2nd giant, HASE KANNON. Standing figure 9.18m tall of gilt camphor wood of 11-headed Goddess of Mercy. Carved in 721, 1 of 2 figures out of single tree: other, as large, was housed in Nara's Hasé-dera (*see*) but burned with temple in 16th century civil wars. To its L is lovely bronze Dainichi Buddha presented by Ashikaga Takauji after his clan had restored power to Kyoto. Flanking Kannon figure are 33 earthly forms of Kannon, mid-14th century. All 33 are rarely together now, several at time rotating in exhibits at Kamakura KOKUHO-KAN at Tsurugaoka Hachiman.

Just inside **Sanmon Gate** several stalls sell wealth-attracting charms; of **DAIKOKU-DO** temple, part of local 7-Luckies pilgrimage. Jolly, plump and always carrying fish over his back with *uchide-no-kozuchi*, mallet of luck similar to cornucopia, Daikoku-ten is god of wealth; one of 7 Lucky Gods. Nearby Benzai-ten hall ensures fame to go with Daikoku-wealth. Even if you think charms hocus-pocus, fun memento at stalls is small woodblock print of 7 Lucky Gods, *Shichi Fuku-jin*, a-sailing in boat of luck, ¥300. R of pond, cave where Benzai-ten said to have lived. Halfway up stairs **Jizo-do hall** enshrines guardian of children: 100s of small stone staff-bearing jizo statues fill landing, each dedicated to spirit of deceased child. Another short ascent leads to **Kannon-do hall**. Large **bell** hanging to R one of best in Kamakura and oldest, cast 1264.

R of Kannon-do is **AMIDA-DO** with Amida image. To its L is small **treasure hall** with valuable scrolls, 'Hanging Buddha'. Far L **temple library** houses 100s of ancient scrolls.

From Hasé-dera Enoden tram 18min→ Enoshima sacred isle, but first, short detour:
GORYO JINJA [45] for its collection of humorous ancient masks. Commonly called Gongoro Jinja, dedicated to Kamakura Gongoro Kagemasa who, age 16, in spite of one eye shot out, led Minamoto forces to victory against rebel Kiyohara clan in Gosannen-no-eki war of 1083-87. (Loser='Rebel'). Tale, slightly fictionalized, became outrageous Kabuki classic *Shibaraku*, with Kagemasa as superhuman hero. Thru torii, 2nd house R is subshrine to Fukuroku of local pilgrimage of 7 Lucky Gods, nice amulets. Main shrine also preserves ancient theater masks for *dengaku* (field-play) and *bugaku* (court dance), at one time were performed at Tsurugaoka Hachiman. Must ask at shrine office to see masks (donation expected); or see them in use during: **Sep 18** *Menkake Gyoretsu*, mask-wearing procession, shrine festival. Starting 13:00 offertory kagura dances, procession of masks begins around 15:00, pass thru town halfway to Gokuraku-ji temple and back. Leading procession of pre-Buddhist gods and demons is 'pregnant' fertility goddess Haramitto; prayers for bountiful crops. Parade also known as *Haramitto Gyoretsu*.

Goryo Jinja is 10min walk from Hasé Kannon: S on main street 50m, first R and 300m ahead. Half-way, street cuts L and forks, take R, whence street goes to coast road, first L after tracks takes you directly to Hasé stn. Just beyond is fair-sized road, R (W) 700m to GOKURAKU-JI temple. Part way there road passes thru *Gokurakuji-zaka kiritoshi* one of 7 passes into Kamakura. This carved thru hill by St Ninsho founder of Gokuraku-ji to connect temple to coast. When Nitta Yoshisada attacked Kamakura pass was site of one of bloodiest battles, all-consuming sea of flames.

2min walk from Enoden Gokuraku-ji stn to...
GOKURAKU-JI [48] built 1259, unknown until 1267 St Ninsho (1217-1303) took over—great humanitarian, devoted life and temple to helping poor, housing some, caring for masses during famines, epidemics in late 13th century. Acclaimed *bodhisattva*, living Buddha, by those he aided, and after death officially given such status. Buddhism, originally, basically charitable, but rarely so in Japan. His work with needy continued by disciples. Sponsored by Hojo regents, temple grew to 56 halls spreading over hill. Entire complex razed 1333 when Nitta armies burned city. Temple revived 1656 by followers of Ninsho's Shingon sect, but no longer served as haven to poor and sick. Present structures 17th century, except thatch-roof gateway rebuilt 1863.

As you enter, to L are priests' quarters, on R is **Taishi-do hall** and *Tenbo-rinden* **Treasure Hall** housing several fine statues of Shaka-nyorai (Historical Buddha of our epoch Sakyamuni, a.k.a. Gautama, or Siddartha) and 10 main disciples, among others. ¥300, 10:00-16:00 open only sat, sun, hol. **Main hall** straight on has special *Seiryo-ji* style sitting-Sakyamuni wood image, black-bead eyes and quartz in ears. Important Cultural Asset, can only be viewed **Apr 7-9** during Temple flower festival of **first half Apr** as crowds come to usually quiet temple to view sakura here. In compound is small **tea house** where *matcha, sencha* (thick or fine regular green tea) with cakes ¥300 served outside under wide red umbrellas. Also *chasoba* (tea-noodles) ¥450, *inaka-jiru* (country-soup) ¥350, coffee and cakes.

Return to **Enoden tram** to continue → **ENOSHIMA,** *15min farther...*

ENOSHIMA 江ノ島

SACRED ISLE dedicated to goddess Benzai-ten, or Benten, sole female of popular '7 Lucky Gods'. Ancient records mention shrine built here mid-6th century. Small shrine to this muse also in approach to Kamakura HACHIMAN, which represents her in pilgrimage of Kamakura 7 Gods, *see*. Since then, grown in popularity and is now combination of sacred shrines and gaudy amusement quarters. Benten-kozo (*kozo*='urchin'), anti-hero of kabuki classic *Shiranami Gonin-Otoko* made his living picking pockets here in 18th century. Major beach resort on mainland shore of Katase with several 'resort hotels' is called 'Miami of Asia'—rather more like Coney Island. If looking for resort areas we prefer any of our next stops along Tokaido.

GETTING THERE: 25min **tram** from KAMAKURA → ENOSHIMA, 10min beyond. Hase and 15min walk across causeway; **bus** from Kamakura stn (from #8) *Enoshima-yuki*, Enoshima-bound, takes you on to island, others let you off mainland side of causeway. Check baggage at rice store on N side of tram stn for ¥200–should do so as Enoshima shrines involve lot of stairs. To make pilgrimage easier, 4 outdoor covered escalators to island summit (¥230) were installed 1959.

In spite of touristy facade, sign that Benten indeed helped local merchants to prosper, shrine has some beautiful buildings and rare nude statue of Benten. Worth visit if you have extra time (don't sacrifice another sight to see this); allow hour which includes r.t. from stn, round of main shrine. Second hour to take in everything.

On isle 250-year-old bronze torii still marks entrance to shrine, but beautiful arched wooden bridges of Hiroshige's woodblock prints long since replaced by harsh concrete pedestrian and car bridges.

But thru torii and up narrow store-lined lane to...

HETSUNO-MIYA: Coast-side Shrine or **Main Shrine**, a.k.a. SHIMONO-MIYA, lower shrine. Shrines get holier as you ascend. Founded by priest Ryoshin of Tsurugaoka Hachiman, 1206, under 3rd shogun Sanetomo. Present building 1976 reconstruction reviving older pure *shinmei-zukuri* style shrine architecture to match upper shrine. Small octagonal hall L of main hall is *Hoan-den* **treasure hall** housing 2 rare statues of Benzai-ten: *Happi*-8-armed with weapon in each hand and milk-white *Hadaka*-nude, seated on cushion on rock playing lute. *Hadaka* Benten is unclothed because if colored cloth put on her, salt air will soon cause dye to stain white body. Underside, not publicly shown, of remarkable anatomic fidelity—protected by silk cushion. Old-time kabuki actors & musicians prayed here to nude muse-Benten for musical talent and eloquence. Samurai prayed to armed, 8-armed Benten.

Next to Hoan-den is...

YASAKA JINJA, enshrining practical-joker Susano-O, unwanted 1st son of Japan's founding *kami* Izanagi and Izanami, brother of Sun Goddess Amaterasu; deity of storms and violence enshrined at Izumo Grand Shrine (*see*). As worshipping ground for sea gods Enoshima predates even formal Shinto. Yasaka Shrine was built over yet earlier sacred ground, later incorporated into *Hetsuno-miya*. Tho best known as Benzai-ten shrine, Enoshima's most important festival is pacification of ocean gods.

Sept 14 *Kaijin-sai* Sea God Festival: mikoshi blessed at Yasaka Jinja carried into sea.

5min up winding path or paralleled by escalator to...

NAKATSUNO-MIYA, Midshore Shrine a.k.a. KAMINO-MIYA Upper Shrine of Enoshima Shrine. Built 853 by saint Jikaku-daishi to house 8-armed Benten (now in Treasure Hall) which he carved while undergoing ascetic exercises in cave backside of Enoshima. Present rebuilt 1689.

On past arboretum & horrendous steel-scaffold viewing-tower, 10min to far back...
OKUTSUNO-MIYA, **Inland Shrine**, built by Yoritomo. Halfway on L is
1 mtr-tall stone with carved 36 monkeys in lieu of live ones inhabiting most
sacred isles. Includes famous Speak-See-Hear No Evil trio. Late 17th cent.
Path branching off nearby heads straight down to Hetsuno-miya; more scenic.

Shrine built by Yoritomo is spring to autumn 'home' of *kami* enshrined
in caves below. Steep stone steps behind shrine lead down to rocky shore.
Part way down is **stone** with engraved poem by Basho, who visited on
way N, (*see* Tohoku). Cliff below famous for *shinju,* double love-suicide, of
Princess Shirakiku and priest Jikyu from Kencho-ji.

Just beyond rest house is...
Iwaya cave-hermitage of Jikaku-daishi, earliest preshinto sanctuary on
Enoshima. 13m-high entrance stretches back 145m to small Iwaya-Benten
figure molded out of ash from ritual fire of 8th century saint Kobo-daishi,
who later founded Shingon (*see* Koya), and also meditated here.

Boats mainland ↔ rest house area, 10min, ¥300. Good alternate return to mainland
to pier under Benten-bashi (first bridge N of Rte 134), no set schedules, frequent.

Whence 200m N of Enoshima tram stop is...
RYUKO-JI temple marks site of *Tatsu-no-kuchi,* famed Dragon's Mouth
execution grounds, and Nichiren's botched execution, 1271. Temple
got its start in 1337 when Nichiren's disciple Nichiho set up grass shack
with statue of Nichiren inside, now rather beautiful wooded complex boasts
Kamakura's sole pagoda. Just L of entrance is where Nichiren was to be
beheaded, but legend has it miraculous lightning bolt rode down raised
sword incinerating headsman. Hall behind it housed stone beheading dais,
now in Hondo. Behind Hondo is cave in which Nichiren was kept until
banishment to Sado. Bell which used to hang in now-empty bell-tower was
1st Kamakura object expropriated 1942 by imperial army for melting down
for arms. Unobtrusively rising above trees on hillside is century-old early
Meiji pagoda.

Another execution here in 1275 worked, as Mongol, Persian, Christian-
Uigur, Chinese and Korean emissaries' heads were sent back to Kublai
Khan in gift boxes, bringing Mongol 2nd invasion of 1281 down on Japan,
to be destroyed by *Kamikazé* 'God Wind' typhoon, for which effective
prayer Nichiren claimed credit. (*More* in FUKUOKA and KYUSHU isles).

Sept 11-13 services commemorate Nichiren's persecution and thwarted execution.

WHERE NEXT: Leaving ENOSHIMA, Enoden **tram** 12min → FUJISAWA on
JR Tokaido Main Line, hour further → HAKONE. Best: **monorail** from ENOSHIMA cuts
over hill → Ofuna JR in 15min. **Drivers** follow coast road down to OISO where join
Route #1 → ODAWARA and HAKONE.

Pilgrimages are lifeblood to temples and shrines. There are many,
from arduous 88 of Shikoku to miniature locals. Kamakura has several
sites which figure in Pilgrimage to 33 Kannons of Kanto Area. It also has
its own mini-*Pilgrimage to 7 Lucky Gods* encompassing mostly quiet,
rarely visited locales. All have good talismans, from small charm figurines
to *ema-e* painted plaques, make nice collection. Start at KITA KAMAKURA
stn, 10min walk to JOCHI-JI where in far rear beyond graves is small
shrine to *Hotei,* 'laughing Buddha'. For lonely romantic, approach is one
of most appealing in Kamakura, up thru decrepitly lovely woods-lined,
stone-staired path past Nectar Pond to entry gate of Modigliani-straight
stone torii capped by Buddhist gate roof. Then 25min to big **HACHIMAN**
(stopping other sites described in main text) where on small artificial islet is

shrine to Lady *Benten*, talismans sold nearby. (Alternately, if you miss this little spot, get your Benten charm at ENOSHIMA). Next stop another 10 min walk in quiet residential lane near ubiquitous inscribed obelisk *"May Peace Prevail..."*, is **MYORYU-JI** with shrine to *Jurojin*, god of longevity. 5+ min on is **HONGAKU-JI** with *Ebisu*, fisherman's deity, protector of businessmen, patron of Osaka. Another few minutes on is **ANYO-IN** to warrior *Bishamon-ten*, one of guardians of Buddha popular in Nara art. Then out at **HASE**, Enoshima-dentetsu coastal tram, or 30min walk (with many sites en route to lengthen trek), take in *Daikoku*, deity of kitchen and fecundity, his shrine just in gate, L. 5min walk **GORYO JINJA**, pass thru torii to 2nd building R for *Fukuroku-ju*, manifestation of Lao Tse of Taoism, ensurer of long life. Finish this pilgrimage and buy shovel when back home to handle all incoming luck.

Heading out of Kamakura by JR, or continuing W from Enoshima we come to **Odawara**, gateway to HAKONE, Fuji Five Lakes & IZU PENINSULA, next chapter. **Detour** for naval or modern history buff, half-day, pre leaving downtown Kamakura.

Or, from Hayama, take JR Yokosuka line SE to terminus, or Keihin Kyuko to...
YOKOSUKA, noteworthy only for more beaches and as home port for 2 great ships —*USS Midway* and older *HIJMS Mikasa*, flagship of Admiral Togo Heihachiro in Battle of Tsushima 1905, when fledgling Japan trounced aging Imperial Russia. Naval buffs will want to take in *Mikasa*, now set in concrete in **Mikasa Koen Park**, short walk from stns. 'Tween decks is museum of old navy, pix, uniforms and memorabilia of Togo and crew, his posh apartment and their cramped seagoing rabbit hutch, fine white Russian tablecloth used as surrender flag, etc. Statue of Togo aside ship. She was built at Vickers yards in Jay's mom's hometown of Newcastle-upon-Tyne, UK—wherein lies digressionary tale.

Grandpa was off to wars (Boer or Khartoum or somewhere) and grandma rented out spare rooms in big house. Mother was infant, so was 1900 to 1902. Front room was rented by 2 Japanese from shipyard. Jay asked grandma in 1958 if she remembered names. "Oh, yes, true gentlemen, too, and their names weren't those Wiki-waki-moto long Japan names, they were short...yes...Mitsui"—2 wars later Mitsui Nagasaki yard launched world's biggest battleships, 85,000-ton *Yamato* and *Musashi*. Few years later itchy-pants grandpa was off again. Master stone-mason, in army he was engineer/sapper. Japan, then building Kobe-Hiroshima Sanyo railroad, was having trouble digging tunnels, asked closest ally for tech help and Britain sent nearest available engineers from East Africa. Gramps worked on tunnels his daughter, grandson (Jay), granddaughter, and 2 great-grandsons Cellin and Garet later used often. Conversely, in 1985 UK-France recognized Japan's now top tech and contracted their help to dig Chunnel.

Back at *Mikasa*, in 1964 Jay took visiting Iranian friend to see it. 1904-5 Russia had occupied northern Iran including Tehran—then suddenly for no apparent reason Cossacks withdrew. To Iran it was miracle—but cause was here. Russia, licked in Far East, recalled all available troops to fight Japan. Port Arthur was higher priority than Tehran. Only Teddy Roosevelt and perhaps Meiji's closest advisors knew that tho Japan was winning all battles, at horrendous costs, Russia's unlimited resources would surely win protracted war. TR admired Japanese 'guts' as exemplified in kabuki play *Chushingura*, Vendetta of 47 Ronin. TR pushed treaty of Portsmouth to get Japan out alive (there were already street riots against taxes, shortages etc). Meiji 'reluctantly' agreed—ticking off more riots by ultra-nationalists for foregoing just spoils of war. US Admiral Nimitz also admired Togo, reputedly helped save ship when due for demilitarization-scrapping 1945, converting it to USN dance hall. Public subscription raised half-million dollars to restore for 56th anniversary of battle, May 27, 1961. Togo saved Tehran.

Recommend ferry for Sarushima-Isle in Bay for good seaman's view of battlewagon.

WHERE TO STAY: Because close to Tokyo, 1hr by train, Kamakura is popular day trip, and for such major tourist spot has few places to stay. So not always easy to find rooms, especially during school summer vacation (Jul-Aug) and sakura season (early Apr). In summer inns along coast almost always full, better chance Wakamiya Ohji area. If here for any of Kamakura's major festivals, book rooms several months ahead or stay in Yokohama. If determined you can wait around for possible cancellations. Rest of year should have little trouble finding room. Most along WAKAMIYA OHJI & KOMACHI-DORI (great nite life) & around HASÉ. Few outlying inns quiet areas of town. Main area code ☎(0467), Zushi (0468), Enoshima (0466).

ALONG WAKAMIYA OHJI

Hotel Tsurugaoka luxe modern J-style ¥-Sw/2; Komachi 2-12-27, ☎24-1111.

KOMACHI-DORI

Few **minshuku** tucked away in corners along street, good inn is **Iwata Bekkan** 2min → stn, ¥8,500w/2, Komachi 2-3-13, ☎22-0986. We stayed at **Ushio Ryokan** ¥-B-w/bkfst only. 4min from stn (take 2nd L), lge well decorated tatami rooms. Just far enough from main street to be pleasantly quiet, yet not far from main restaurants. Komachi 2-3-9, ☎22-7016. *Budgeteers* willing to sacrifice for price try **Akiyama** middle Komachi-dori. 3rd fl Akiyama Bldg, embroidery school by day, minshuku at nite. Check-in 19:00 checkout 9:00, ¥-P rm only: Komachi 2-8-9, ☎22-3499.

OUTLYING

Kofu-en at Ogigayatsu 3-10-21, ☎22-0114. Tucked away in hills W of Tsurugaoka at end of dead-end lane (15min walk from Kamakura or Kita-Kamakura), just few mins **cab**, basic meter. Stone tunnel-like gate leads to old wood Meiji era house, surrounded by magnificent garden, luxury at ¥-Sw/2. Walking head N along tracks R, 10min to Iwabune Jizo & L up Kamegayatsu-zaka hill, end of 2nd R.

Not as exquisite but also tucked away in hills minshuku **Suigetsu-an** (jade-moon cottage) base Kewai-zaka hill (women only). 17min walk from stn, ¥-lo-Bw/bkfst. Ogigayatsu 4-14-2, ☎24-7906.

NEAR KAMAKURA COAST

Two government-run inns 100m S of Rinkai Gakuen bus stop 5min from stn on any bus from #1, #2 are 150m from beach: **Kamakura-so** Zaimokuza 5-8-40, ☎22-2522; ¥-Bw/2; **Kaifu-so** Zaimoku-za 5-8-30, ☎22-0390; ¥-Bw/2.

EAST ALONG COAST

Towards Hasé is another Kamakura fine, old establishment **Kaihin-so** with spectacular garden of 1,000-tsubo, 36,000-sq ft. Yuiga-hama 4-8-14, ☎22-0960. Most rooms tatami but 'Western Annex' has antique-packed W-style rooms. All incl: ¥-Sw/2. 1-min walk S of Enoden Yuigahama stn (2 stops from Kamakura), or **cab** 5min Kamakura stn. Another classic, **Kamakura Hotel**, Meiji era structure with J- and W-style rooms. R near Yuiga-hama beach, dinners massive feasts of freshly caught seafood. 3min walk S of Hasé stn. ¥-lo-Sw/2; Hasé 2-22-29, ☎22-0029. Next door, oldest **Minshuku Ai** (Women only) ¥-Pw/bkfst. Hasé 2-22-31, ☎23-0711. **Taisen-kaku**, old fashioned inn near entrance to Hasé-dera ¥-Bw/bkfst, ¥5,000 room only (*sudomari*). Hasé 3-12- 9, ☎22-0616. **Hasé Ryokan** 50m N of stn room only ¥-P, Hase 2-17-23, ☎22-2916.
Komyo-ji (24) is sole temple lodging, ¥-lo-B-w/2; some rules–out of bed by 6:00, bkfst 7:00, lights out 22:00. Apply week in advance, 2 or more; ☎22-0603; or ✍ **Kamakura-shi**, Zaimoku-za 6-17-19. Combine with their *Shojin-ryori* meals (*below*).

DOWN COAST

Towards Enoshima is **Youth Hostel** Nihon Gakusei Kaikan, not worth nonmembers ¥-Bw/2, members ¥-P. Barely cheaper than minshuku but herded into bunk beds, early lights-out; convenient to nowhere; Saka-no-shita 27-9, ☎25-1234. 10min walk Hasé stn on coast road. **Kamakura Park Hotel** few 100m beyond, near city pool. ¥-S+w/2. Saka-no-shita 33-6, ☎25-5121.

ENOSHIMA AREA

Many lodgings, mostly gaudy resort-style hotels ¥-S. Several minshuku ¥-Bw/2. In pinch only: **Futami** 22-4066; **Rinkai-so** 25-1190; **Watanabe** 25-6400; **Asae** 23-

7705; **Ogawa-tei** 22-6782; **Jusuke** 23-1932. Bath connoisseurs will like **Iwamoto-ro** at Enoshima 2-2-7, ☎26-4121, cab 2x-mtr from Fujisawa stn; ¥-S-Lw/2. J-style upper class stopping place in antiquity, served as temple with fine Benten image in 'temple room'; bath outside entered thru row of red toriis to natural tunnel-cave, dramatically lit natural hot spa. Roman Bath built 1930 with stained glass from Italy for best of 2 worlds: Italian light and drama and Japanese hot spa, food.

ZUSHI

Great **find** offers treat in ryokan **Shindo-tei** near Zushi stn, 2-10-3 Zushi, ☎(0468)-71-2012, member Japanese Inn Group, friendly Mr-Mrs ZAMA Yoshikazu offer room-only at almost half-price to foreigners, ¥4,500 plus tax. Nov-Mar season hunter Zama-san serves wild boar; communal *iwaburo*-rock bath will be privatized if requested—but why spoil fun. Socialize.

CHOPSTICKS: Our '64 edition said "limited, but adequate"; now dining far less limited with good selection of menus/prices on each itinerary.

Shojin-ryori. No visit to Kamakura is complete without this Buddhist multi-course vegetarian meal. Only 2 **temples** now offer full treatment:

KOMYO-JI [24] 10-course feast, ¥3,300. Must reserve by phone at least 7 days ahead ☎(0467)-22-0603, min 2 people. X-tue, all July-Aug. You'll get 2 different soups, *goma-dofu* (fine sesame seed curd cakes with orchid relish), *dengaku* (fried beancurd cakes with *miso*), knotted seaweed crackle, vegetable tempura, various *aemono* (mountain herb tidbits), pickles, thick green *matcha* tea. Best combine with STAY (*see*).

CHOJU-JI [29] (near Kencho-ji) offers similar meal for ¥3,800. Reserve ☎22-2147, and usually won't accept groups under 5. Generally closed to public, temple grounds quiet, few old wooden halls surrounded by flowers.

If solo or just passing through you can still partake of *shojin-ryori* at several fine private establishments, mostly near main temples. Longest established are 2...

Hachi-no-Ki: rustic thatched main shop ☎22-8719, S of Kencho-ji; and Kita-Kamakura **branch** ☎23-3722 in 2-storey ferroconcrete by Tokei-ji temple. Both serve same meals but main better atmosphere, ll:00-19:00 X-mon; meals run ¥3,800-10,000 plus tax, service for 10-20 items. Specialty *matcha-gohan*, tea-flavored rice.

KITA-KAMAKURA: try **Monzen** just S of stn. Favored by Nobel-novelist Kawabata Yasunari; building traditional, rooms decorated with superb art. Open daily 11:00-19:30, call for reservations ☎25-1121, (same day OK); meals from ¥2,500. Also serve *kyo-ryori*, classic imperial Kyoto-style veggies and meats cooked on hot rocks. **Sa'ami** halfway on Komachi-dori on R from stn to Tsurugaoka Hachiman ☎25-0048 also *shojin-ryori* ¥1,500-3,000. ll:30-17:30, X-thur; only 'advertisement' is large black *noren* curtaining small doorway, with wood sign post (menu) next to it.

Other Kamakura favorites are *kaiseki-ryori* (traditional table) and *tofu-ryori*, multi-course meals with assorted types of *tofu* bean curd. Classy old family-run houses serve these and other Japanese meals in all price ranges. *Budgeteers* have no trouble finding cheap good joints all over town. If looking for non-Japanese food, you'll find many Asian and European national cuisines, and of course ever present Kentucky Fried Chicken, etc, and slew of local fast-food stalls around stn.

DOWNTOWN

Wakamiya Ohji and **Komachi-dori** shopping streets have greatest variety of food and prices. Several interesting restaurants serving assorted traditional foods (models and prices in display windows) down R from stn E Exit. Heading up Wakamiya Ohji on R of 2nd torii is *unagi* (eel) specialty **Asabane-ya** ☎22-1222. 11:00-20:00, X-thur. Tender fillets of grilled eel served with fresh mountain herbs, soup, for ¥1,500-up. 1st alley L of 2nd torii, then R to tempura specialty **Hiromi**. Further up on L, **Tsurugaoka Ryokan** has restaurant serving *kaiseki-ryori*, 11:00-20:00. Just beyond is Oike Bldg, on 2nd floor is **Ajanta** Indian food. Another, **Madras** 150m E of Drum Bridge.

JUST BEYOND STN-side entry to Komachi-dori on L is **Komachi**, best *tonkatsu* (pork cutlet) joint around. 11:30-20:00, X-tue, *teishoku*-table d'hote from ¥650. L down next side alley to **Dengaku-ya** specializing in *dengaku* fried bean cakes with different *miso* sauces, ¥100 per stick. Good day-time snacks but mainly night spot, sitting around open hearth sipping local sake while broiling *dengaku* over flames. Also serves *teishoku*-dinners. 16:00-21:00, X-tue.

BETWEEN KOMACHI AND DENGAKU-YA ALLEY on L is **Komachi Akagane Bldg** wide front stairs to 2nd floor crepes shop. Exquisite seafood restaurant **Uogashi-ya** 3rd floor serves various big combination dinners ¥1,800-6,500 of sashimi, tempura, fried fish, vegetables, soup, rice, pickles.

FOREIGN further up street is **Kaltikka** Indonesian food; across it is robata-yaki **Uzuki**. Continuing we pass **Lindenbaum** (Italian); **Matsuzaka-ya** steak house, on 2nd floor of meat store, **Roshia-tei** borscht and other Russian dishes.

NEAR JR STN, 5min walk **Shi-Getsu-An**, fine traditional cuisine specialty seafood and *sansai*-mountain vegetables, midst koto music, view of garden; moderate to luxe. Enter freely lunch 11-15:00, rsv after 18:00, ☎(0467)-23-3883—enlarged now so might try without prior call.

LITTLE OUT, short taxi **Kamakura-yama**, at Kamakura-yama 3-11-1, ☎31-5454, rsv, 12pm-2, 5-8; top roast beef (northland Yonezawa beef), rustic architecture, fine garden, view of city, full table d'hote lunch ¥5,000 worth every finger lick.

Other Suggestions. Each of our legs thru Kamakura have several restaurants from budget noodleries to full-course traditional Zen monk, to nobleman's meals.

KITA-KAMAKURA
Front of TOKEI-JI temple, traditional **Matsugaoka** with light lunches and dinners from ¥1,500; *matcha* & cake ¥500. **Hachi-no-Ki**, above.

Just north of KENCHO-JI, **Buan** exquisite Kyoto-style dishes served in converted folk house up side-alley, temple side of street. Popular *noasobi-bento* 'field-games' box lunch for ¥1,800 offers far more than name implies: filling 2 trays with clear soup, *kayaku-gohan* (rice steamed with herbs), assorted vegetables and herbs, fried fish and sashimi, topped off with *warabi-mochi* (rice cakes) and fresh fruit. Filling but easy on stomach. 11:00-14:30 X-mon; reservations only ☎(0467)-25-1952. Across from Kencho-ji entrance **Ooka-tei** is modeled after Edo era restaurants, red cloth covered benches in front. Photos and prices of main meals displayed in front. Suggest their *Ooka-bento* lunch: Main tray has 5 courses representing Kamakura's *Go-zan* or 5 great temples and dessert representing Tsurugaoka Hachiman, with rice and soup ¥2,000. Can also add tempura and sashimi. By ENGAKU-JI **Koko-tei** garden restaurant up narrow alleys taxi 3x-mtr; rsv ☎46-5467.

HASE-DAI BUTSU AREA
Also has several restaurants, best are 2 *tofu-ryori* and 2 Chinese between Great Buddha and Hasé Kannon. At entrance to Great Buddha is *tofu-ryori* **Chiori** noted for tofu, made fresh every dawn; grand 9-dish meals ¥4,500-8,500 (*matsu* course), seasonal specialties superbly served; also budget meals from ¥1,500; 11-21:00, X-thu, rsv for after 18:00 ☎(0467)-23-0400; other is **Hakuho** further down street next to Hasé post office; cheaper smaller meals, fine.

Kasei-ro our 1964-favorite Peking-style Chinese restaurant set in magnificent Japanese garden mansion, 20m down from Great Buddha gate. Light lunch. Dinners allowing full choice are ordered from English menu, or by 'table for so many...' average L-¥5-,6,000 per head. Call ahead for rsv ☎22-0280, open daily 11:00-20:00.

Horai-kaku Chinese restaurant across street more relaxed, cheaper, no rsv.

Kaikotei welcome addition making above 4-some into quintet; 5min from Hase-dera. Serves *kaiseki*, classical Kyoto fare of endless exquisite small portions, modernized with addition of meats. Building is relocated Hida-Takayama modified *gassho* farmhouse with high-peaked roof. Prices range: lunch Hida country special soba noodles ¥800 to *bento* box kaiseki ¥3,-5,000, with dinners ¥6,-10,000. Rooms sit J- or table W-style, all with lovely view of gardens. 11:00-21:00, X-thurs; advise rsv hols ☎25-4494.

BEACH-SIDE

Between Kamakura-Enoshima, old drive-in **O-Ebi** 'slightly deluxe' specialty W- and J-style shrimp dishes, most meals ¥2,-3,000 range, usually packed; nearby **Sea Castle**, cheaper. To reach from Hasé tram stn, S 150m to coast road and L 300m.

ENOSHIMA AREA

ENOSHIMA AREA, as all pilgrimage destination has many ¥-P places to eat. Shopping street from Enoshima tram stn to island mostly budget noodle, *okonomi-yaki*, at island-end of bridge flanked by large restaurants with veranda seating overlooking water serving typical sea food *teishoku*. Choose for prices (in window) and setting.

ZUSHI

One stop farther on JR, opposite stn is **Gin-no-To**, exotic *Kaiseki Francaise* or French cuisine served J-style, great variety in palatable small portions—origin of *nouvelle cuisine* anyway. Enjoy without pigging; 11-21:00, X-thur, ☎(0468)-71-5130.

Hikage-chaya, in nearby Hayama (beach) 6 bus stops from Zushi stn to Abuzuri Kaigan stop, at Horiuchi 16: lunch 12-2:30, then 5-9:30. Bento ¥3,500, table d'hote ¥4,500up+%, ☎75-0014; paired with...

La Maree, French restaurant next door, 3-storey blue building by sea, rsvtn advised, ☎75-6683. Both run by our old family friends Marti and Christine Noda.

SHOPPING: Still rather limited, but local specialty *Kamakura-bori* items of wood with carved designs and lacquered. Craft as old as Kamakura introduced by Chinese monk 1227. Originally used only for temple utensils, made available for general use 17th century. Commonly used are gingko & Judas tree, seasoned 5-10 years. Drying makes for easy carving, longer life. After carving, gets 8-14 coats lacquer, 1 each day. Kamakura-bori has always been bit expensive; popular are: hand mirrors (¥5,000+), trays (8.5 in/22cm ¥7,000+), jewelry or cigarette boxes (¥5,000). Prices vary with quality of wood, carving, number of layers of lacquer. To ensure quality city inspects all, gives special mark to real Kamakura-bori producers: mark prominently displayed on store-front, stickered on goods.

If further interested in Kamakura-bori, there is workshop and museum...
Workshop-*Kamakura Kaikan* just N of 2nd torii on main Wakamiya Ohji. View entire process, or make your own with professional instructors:¥2,000 registry fee, ¥3,000 2 sessions–most items take several. If you want to carve at home on your own, plain pre-shaped pieces, other basic materials sold at **Issui-do** N of stn on Komachi-dori shopping street. **Museum**, *Kamakura-bori Shiryo-kan* on Komachi Ohji street block E, parallel to Wakamiya Ohji 300m N of stn. 10:00-16:00, X-mon ¥150, exhibits masterpieces Kamakura era to present.

SAMURAI SWORDS & STEAK KNIVES

SAMURAI SWORDS & STEAK KNIVES: Short stroll starting from **Drum Bridge** front of Tsurugaoka Hachiman ending at stn. Just L of torii is **Hakko-do** oldest *Kamakura-bori* shop, 28th generation of carvers occupying same spot 700 years. Most Kamakura temples still commission work here. Top work, matching prices, little under ¥10,000.

Kamakura-bori shops 1st blk down Wakamiya Ohji, less famous but good, cheaper.

ANTIQUE BROWSING

ANTIQUE BROWSING: Several fine old shops. Near Drum Bridge on our R **Hachiman-do** large collection of swords; across Wakamiya from it **Horii Bijutsu-ten**. Continuing down street, find many interesting shops on R, good selection of budget eats on L. **Kikuya** antiques on R; next block down on L **Sagami-ya** swords; on R past Tsurugaoka Kaikan Hotel and Nagasawaya ryokan is **Imai** antique art, **Tsubo-ya** antiques; further down R **Shinobi**,or attractive purses, handbags, place mats & *noren*-curtains of popular Japanese *roketsu-zome*-batik. **Yutaka** *mingei*-folk art next door. Blk further, R, **Sakai** ukiyo-e block prints. *Also on R, large sign in English announces*...**Kurokawa Sword**–fun just to browse this miniature museum. Owner collected swords as hobby, ended up in business. *Upstairs* fine sword collection, samurai armor, accessories. *Street floor* watch artisans sharpening, refurbishing old swords.

Forging swords was major Kamakura craft, home of legendary Masamuné swordsmiths; only most affluent could afford their blades. Best 'damascene' blades begin with steel heated, folded, pounded, water-dowsed alternately several hundred times before finishing. With little market for fine swords, present 28th generation Masamuné sells more practical items from scissors and kitchen knives to flower shears and hunting knives all hand-forged with same care as his swords. His craftsmen recently branched out to handmade steel furniture. **Masamuné Kogei** 1 blk N of stn W exit: follow alley along tracks, L at 1st cross-street, 30m down L side.

Komachi-dori parallel to Wakamiya Ohji 1 blk W has interesting stores near Tsuru-gaoka end. Several mingei stores; **Yamato-ya** on R has interesting *mingei* from all over Japan, gathered by owner in his travels. Next blk also on R is **Shato** specialty handmade *washi* (Japanese 'rice' paper) from all over Japan. Exquisite sheets, envelopes from ¥100, hardy miniature boxes, purses from ¥300, *washi* dolls ¥150 and up. Just before Shato on L, bamboo crafts at **Takahashi**. Another good bamboo crafts store **Yamago** further down on R has everyday-use goods, but specializes in ikebana & tea-related articles. Next door **Yama-no-Be** has folk pottery from all over.

Fun memento is *e-maki* scroll map of Kamakura done in old style inked with *fudé* brush, ¥300; at **Donguri** coffee & mingei shop in front of Kamakura-gu shrine.

OUT OF WAY AND WELL WORTH EFFORT: Antiques & old crafts fill lovely 250-year-old **farmhouse** of Reiko & Yoshihiro **Takishita's House of Antiques** in W Kamakura's hills above Zeniarai-Benten. New Annex nearby, by appt only; ☎(0467)-43-1441 to make sure not away stock hunting—or entertaining others. Taxi knows 'Genji-yama-no Takishita'. Tansu chests, heaps of blue and white porcelains, baskets for ikebana addicts; **no** netsuke, swords or tea gear. And if you like this 1733 feudal manor in which you sit, have them dismantle similar antique farm house to ship anywhere in world and set up again to fit local zoning laws and all your modern needs: prices per square unit of *tsubo* (6x6 feet or two tatami mats side by side) run ¥120,–130,000 or some ¥60,000,000 ($450,000) average 2,500 sq.ft. house, with new traditional-appearing shingle in place of fire-trap, buggy thatch. Shipping and your local permits extra, regulations vary with state and city. His crew of traditional carpenters recently set one up in Buenos Aires for about $1,500,000, and one whole 3-house compound in Honolulu, suitably termite-proofed.

Kaikodo ☎(0467)-46-6630, *by appointment only*; museum and collector quality.

CHARMING FOLK ART CHARMS OF SHRINES & TEMPLES:

Kamakura-gu's *shishito* 'clapping' lion heads (good luck, prosperity) ¥700-2,000. **Sugimoto-dera** has red (averting danger) and white (good luck) carved cranes on hanging plaques, ¥450. Similar plaques at **Hokai-ji**, white crossed-*daikon* (horse radish) for health, red money bag for wealth. Decorative 10cm-tall carved wood sacred horses of **Sasuke Inari shrine** are good luck, as its mini-toriis. **Zeni-arai Benten** has fortune-bringing 1cm long turtles (*zeni-gamé*) carved of tortoise shell, ¥700, in individual pine boxes, priest will perform sacred Shinto fire-purification rite for each.

Another uniquely Kamakura *o-miyagé* gift is miniature *jizo dogu* (clay figure of Jizo) ¥400, only at **Kamakura Dogu-gama** just N of Omachi Yotsukakku bus stop (nr Yakumo Jinja, S end Gion-zan trail). Also small *no-butsu* (field buddha) figures, clay masks for under ¥1,000.

PERSONAL DATEBOOK:

Jan–1st Snake day, *Zenri-arai Benten-sai* fest, mikoshi (p230). **Feb–1st Ox day** *Hatsu-uma-sai* fest, kagura, tea ceremony (p230). **Aug 10** *Kurojizo ennichi* fair (p221). **Sept 14** *Kaijin-sai,* mikoshi carried down beach into sea, YASAKA JINJA (p234); **18** *Menkake Gyoretsu* Masked Parade, UGAFUKU JINJA (p230); **21-22** Torchlight noh, by Kamakura city (p221). **Oct 12** *Juya-e* 10 memorial rites, stalls, KOMYO-JI (p225).

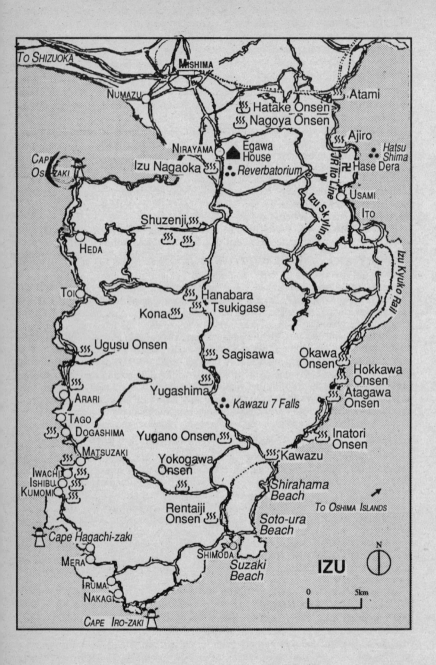

Hon Foreign Professor's arrival (in bath) *attracted everyone's attention.*
I could easily tell which of these gentlemen were familiar
with the eccentricities of the occidentals, knew how easily
they are often scandalized by a little nakedness.
—Thomas Raucat, The Honorable Picnic

IZU PENINSULA 伊豆半島
TOKYO'S INSULAR RIVIERA

ATAMI, MOST FAMOUS of Japanese hot spring spas—popularly called Riviera of Japan—is actually one big juke-box also known as Tokyo's 'Spare Bedroom'. Tone is set in very by-line of above quotation, author's name pronounced in its original French is Tomah-Rawkah, which means in Japanese, "Will you sleep with me?" You can relax in baths, but go for walk and you get wound up again in traffic, neons, pinball parlors–with no place to just sit down for leisurely cup of coffee or drink. With 360 hotels and ryokan, Atami beds 200,000 overnite, is still growing. Wild and gaudy, it attracts busloads of local tour groups and bosses dictating weekends to secretaries on their pads. Bachelor will not be lonely long. Students of photo anatomy will find nite courses, photo studios that never saw film box opened. 'International' stage shows abound in hotel niteries.

GETTING THERE: 53min Shinkansen from Tokyo; 1hr40min old Tokaido Main Line express, 2hrs local.

WHERE TO STAY: Atami is 'standard', (¥-S): at least ¥13,000 sgl-w/2 (plus 15% service plus tax). We suggest Atami itself be passed over for smaller spa. But if you insist, then one of our friend's parents have delightful little family-run **Yamaki Ryokan** ¥-S, ☎(0557)-81-2121. Several similar places nearby, like **Minaguchi-en** & **Tamanoi-Bunkan** (¥-S+w/2). We have booked friends into **Atami Fujiya** ☎81-7111 (loud but efficient; twin ¥-S-L) with huge cinerama bath; new wing (same rates) ☎81-0111 boasts sauna, huge outdoor bath, famed nite spot with nitely shows. Hotel **Uruko-ya** (¥-S+w/2) quieter, smaller, and bit older, out along western curve of bay. **Ono-ya** ☎82-1111 just S, with 'Roman bath' also fine (same rates).

If you want real traditional small, wood, gardens—best is **Kajika-so** ☎81-5223 Hida-style soaring roof, each room has its own *hinoki*-cypress tub and meals around communal *irori* hearth, ¥-Lw/2. Nearby **Minaguchi-en** ☎81-2208, bit larger, in 10,000-tsubo garden, meals in your room; ¥-hi-Lw/2. W foothills has **Arakado** ☎81-6185 quiet, with Kyoto-style *kaiseki-ryori* dinner, ¥-S-Lw/2. Central are 2 fine old-timers: **Tamanoi-Honkan** ☎81-3685 ¥-S–Lw/2; **Otsuki Hotel Wafu-kan** ☎81-6111 N end of bay, ¥-L-LL. Same phone reaches W-style **Otsuki Hotel** next door. Other splashy new places all with HOTEL appended, both W- or J- accommodations, ¥--hi-T+ include working W from stn: **Akao** (open-air pools), **Kaijo**, and **Kanichi** with its slowly revolving (1hr) penthouse dining rooms, **New Grand**, **New Asahi** (spacious bath halls have 'semi-nude' dance shows), cylindrical **Nishi-Atami** and **Konomi-ya**.

Warning: Only in Atami is this true: do not be introduced to inns by touts. Elsewhere they help; here they skin. If unsure, go to **Station Info Center**. Arriving late at nite use only official **Japan Ryokan Association** (*Nihon Ryokan Kumiai*) touts distinguished by their JRA badges.

Everything in Atami is geared to baths. Artificial geyser fronting stn imitates real one in town which was symbol of Atami until sealed by Great Kanto 'quake, 1923; but once again gushing thanx to artificial resuscitation. ¥400 r.t. ropeway up to Hilltop **Atami Castle** rebuilt 1959 has in addition to usual samurai exhibits (plus 130 ukiyo-e by Utamaro and other great Edo artists), radium bath, stage, game center and shops. Also hilltop pagoda housing Buddha relic presented by India Prime Minister Nehru. But with all this we much prefer smaller outlying spas.

Well worth half-day visit whether staying in Atami or passing thru is...
MOA Museum of Art perched on hill overlooks Sagami Bay. Atami stn → 10min
walk or free shuttle, or taxi, steep hill: 9:30-16:00 X-thur, worth steep ¥1,000 entry.

Truly Temple of Muses, house sacred to beauty. Enter to escalator hall
and become part of modern art creation 'Aurola' running 200mtrs in 4
stages, rising thru arched hallway with lights changing color, laser beam
show and synthesizer music that literally blows your mind clean and clear to
be able to approach in ritual purity those masterpieces of art which follow,
whether house collection or travelling show (NY Metropolitan's superb
Ancient Near East collection first shown all at once here while Met rooms
were being rebuilt and enlarged: new Met section, marvelous as it is, can't
compare).

One of largest private collections of ancient Oriental art: 3,500 pieces
include 2 National Treasures (great Ninsei wisteria painted-ceramic tea jar
and pair Ogąta Korin red-and-white plum blossom screens), 56 Important
Cultural Assets, 46 Important Art Objects. Founder Okada Mokichi (d.1955)
also headed *Sekai Kyusei-kyo* (now called MOA-Mokichi OKADA International Association, also stand for Museum Of Art) religious foundation
which believes, along with similar groups evolved of folk Shinto esthetic
(as opposed to Imperial or Shrine Shinto), that Art is Mother of Religion,
that sacred reality is reflected in beauty, which it is man's main mission to
create and preserve, that our path to enlightenment lay in practice and appreciation of art. These religions (Omoto outside Kyoto, P[erfect] L[iberty] of
Osaka, several others) support traditional fine and martial arts, noh, tea,
encourage international art.

They also promote natural foods, Omoto and MOA maintain major natural farms,
MOA with efficient sales distribution; mid-**Aug** Izu Ohito *Agricultural Festival* at Ohito
farm, visitors welcome, 30min drive from Museum (enquire here).

Within fabulous architecture, display is superb. Don't miss great
viewing windows which look out over one of those exquisite landscapes
which adorn posters but which one rarely sees, of pine-crested hill beyond
hill, tiny castle in foreground and not single cable or 20th century vestige to
spoil this grand landscape screen effect, wondrous still painting but for that
single moving speck, lone soaring hawk. Inner courtyards, Henry Moore's
King and Queen, others, illustrate how all great art fits together: is of one
heart.

Elsewhere, Hideyoshi's **golden tea room** repro: gold leaf definitely
not for Rikyu-style *wabi-cha*-humble tea. Original, long lost, was moved
into Kyoto Imperial Palace 1586 so Hideyoshi could present tea to emperor.
More wabi taste is **noh theater**, among most beautiful anywhere, modern
seating and presentation shows how relevant this ancient theater is today.
Also in garden **Korin Mansion** retreat built by OGATA Korin (he, 1658-
1716, of plum screens), its tea room, painted room, painstakingly and
beautifully restored.

Same art-crazy folks bring you **Hakone Museum of Art** with its Bamboo Garden,
its Chinese style architecture matches contents. Nearby is also their **Hakone Outdoor
Sculpture Garden** (*See* HAKONE, following).

PERSONAL DATEBOOK: *Atami Kogashi Matsuri* **Jul 15-16** Kinomiya
Shrine in town: men 42-up cart mikoshi, tengu-masked god *Sarutahiko-no-mikoto* tosses
barley, health to whom hit. Shikajima odori dance at shrine derived from hoary fertility-
agricultural rite, slow dance picks up speed as dancers become possessed. *Same days* new
Atami Tourist Festival pull 40 massive wheeled floats thru town. Fireworks spectacle end
Jul-early Aug; **Aug 3** similar at Izusan. **Oct 10-11** re-create Edo period procession
carting onsen water to Edo castle.

FAMILY TRAVEL: Advise **Fujimiland** several km W, S on Atami Driveway. **Fuji-View Hotel** (¥20,000+w/2), **-Hostel** (¥7,000+ self svce) or **-Annex** (¥16,000+ room-only), wkdays only. Lots for kids to do safely alone while parents enjoy view, golf, tour, etc. Info and rsve **Fujimiland Tokyo Office**, ☎(03)-3253-7777.

YUGAWARA, 10km (1 stop old-JR) before, N of Atami, stretches up vale 4km into mountains to OKU-YUGAWARA, on winding back road to HAKONE. Tho over 100 inns and hotels line river it is relatively quiet, steep wooded mountains come right down to river. Across river, smaller IZU-YUGAWARA ONSEN. Unlike Atami, which punches time-clock, most inns here keep their spa-baths open all day; many more are older, classy-classic inns.

WHERE TO STAY: All within 15min **bus**, 10min **cab** (3x-mtr) from stn. Prices ¥-S+w/2. Old-time traditionals: YUGAWARA (all ¥-Sw/2): **Ashikari** ☎(0465)-62-4151, **Nakanishi** ☎62-3355; **Rakusan-so** ☎62-8531; **Uenoya** ☎62-2155. IZU-YUGAWARA: **Furusato** ☎62-8585 ¥-Lw/2. OKU-YUGAWARA: **Kamata** ☎62-2151 ¥-hi-Lw/2 with view from bath.

Other fine ones ¥-S but lower hi-ends ('Hotels' also W-room w/2), YUGAWARA: **Fujiya** ☎62-3711; **Otaki Hotel** ☎62-7111 outdoor observatory/baths, big garden; **Kameya** ☎62-2145 outdoor rock bath. IZU-YUGAWARA: **Suimei-kan** ☎62-2511 outdoor bath; **Hotel To-Yoko** ☎62-4141 with large segregated indoor baths, mixed-bathing outdoor tubs. OKU-YUGAWARA: **Seiran-so** ☎63-3lll outdoor bath; last back **Yamaga-so** ☎62-3138 top floor bath-view. Can swim at beaches near Yugawara; **not** Atami. Can also drown in debt: top inn runs s¥530,000-w/2 per person...really.

Just E of Yugawara is...
MANAZURU PENINSULA, several quiet fishing hamlets along E coast, all with budget minshuku. Good time to come this way is **Jul 27-28** for boat festival at 1,100-year old Kifune Shrine, 10min bus from Manazuru stn. Recreating Gods' arrival here, 2 skiffs pulled by horse-head boat cross Manazuru harbor to shrine. After rites there, another boat brings mikoshi back across to be paraded thru town and returned to shrine at nite. Way is lit by hundreds of lanterns, fireworks later.

IZUSAN, (between Yugawara and Atami), lovely cove with cliff-hanger inns, nicest near Yugawara: Traditional ryokan best-known **Horai** ☎80-5151 ¥-L-LLw/2; slightly more moderate **Suimei-so**; **Kanun-tei** ☎81-3714 overlooks Atami 5min walk to MOA, ¥-hi-S-Lw/2. Nearer Atami, **Suiyo-tei** ☎81-7145, **Sagamiya**, **Kairaku-en** all ¥-Sw/2.

Isuzan was discovered in 717 by emperor Gensho, since which time it was reserved for successive emperors until 1868 when it became public and inns popped up. Hot spring water gushes out of unusual horizontal hole, falling into bay. It dried up in 1964 but started again 1970. Soon after its discovery shrine was built on hill above reached by 624 steps. Made equal rank to Hakone's Shrine by Yoritomo, at its peak had over 3,800 halls both Buddhist and Shinto. Decimated by fires and Meiji purge of Buddhist-Shinto mix, only main hall remains. Part way up on L is HANYA-IN, once affiliate temple of Izusan shrine. Housed here is small 12th-century wood figure of Izusan Gongen (Buddha Shinto-ized), once enshrined above.

AJIRO is lovely little fishing village with 'sort of flavor we've come halfway round world to see' as we wrote generation ago, but Garet notes now "'taint as quaint as in yore days, but still nice". Served as TV/novel *Shogun* location for Anjiro village, Blackthorne's (a.k.a. Will Adams, *see* ITO, below) local 'home'. 11km beyond Atami, 15min train, too quiet to deserve its alias of South Atami.

Just before it at...
IZU-TAGA, (10min train from Atami) where road runs high along cliff, perched below is gorgeous **Kangyo-so Shiraishi Ryokan** ☎(0557)-68-2323, noted for its seafood, ¥-Lw/2. Neighbor **Akane Ryokan** similar rates.

In AJIRO along town beach and with view of its active harbor, colorful boats, nets hung out to dry: are ¥-Sw/2 **Sanoya** at top end, **Seiyo-kaku** and its new wing best location, **Ajiro Onsen Hotel** and **Ichi-ryu-kan**, first and last perhaps best (slightly higher). Budgeteers have 20 minshuku at Taga, 10 in Ajiro (*See* RYOKAN INFO CENTER). If you want to fish, have inn phone to rent you boat and gear. Good beaches between Ajiro and Taga. **Aug 16** annual fireworks festival; **Apr 26-28** *Aji* (Mackerel) *fete*, free *Aji-no-tataki* (minced mackerel) to visitors.

10min walk S around point is ...

HASE-DERA, temple treasure Kannon image said to be from same tree as great Hase Kannons of Yamato and Kamakura: shown only once every 60 years: sorry, next not until 2032AD.

USAMI, 8km (1 stop JR) beyond Ajiro, with lovely long beach and dozens of budget minshuku, but most important if **driving**, this is turn-off point for taking Skyline Drive toll road back to HAKONE; or cut inland to central SHUZEN-JI.

ITO, 25km beyond Atami, has almost as many inns (250+), famed for its variety of ingenious outdoor onsen-pools and baths. We have never cared for it, advise continuing on further S unless here for some fun festivals: particularly *Anjin-sai* **Aug 6-10** commemorates 1st modern sailing vessel (80 ton) built 1607 by Will Adams for Tokugawa Ieyasu. Floating lanterns **8th** nite, taiko drum contests **9th**, parade of motorized floats, huge fireworks every nite from **6th**–, special ship-shaped display of fireworks on **10th**. Monument at mouth of river dedicated to MIURA Anjin, as Adams is called here.

PERSONAL ORIENTATION: WILLIAM ADAMS: Born 1564 in Gillingham, Kent, went to sea in search of fabled Northwest Passage. Spoke Dutch, Portuguese, Spanish, captained supply ship against Armada 1588. Left wife and 2 children behind 1598, sailed as pilot-general (chief navigator) to fleet of 5 Dutch ships for Japan. His *Liefde* alone made landfall in Bungo, Kyushu April, 1600, Adams senior of 24 survivors, of whom 6 soon died despite good care of Japanese. Portuguese missionaries insisted *Liefde* was pirate ship, called for their execution, but his straight answers and technical know-how impressed Ieyasu during intensive grilling thru Portuguese-speaking interpreter. Shogun kept him as technical advisor, gaining up-to-date knowledge of navigation, gunnery, shipbuilding. Sent to Ito, noted for shipwrights, he built 80-tonner, launched from beach digging pool around it to float it out on tide: traces of this unique shipyard remain. Next ship was 120 tons, large for its time. Other Dutch, English traders arrived, whom he advised: Dutch listened and prospered, blimpish-English went their own way and failed. English, unlike Catholic Spanish and Portuguese, weren't expelled from Japan, they quit in failure. Denied permit to go home, Adams wed local girl. Took family name *Miura* after peninsula in Izu where he was granted samurai estate by Ieyasu. His personal name became *Anjin*, 'pilot', and area where he had his lordly town-house is still known as Anjin-cho, near Mitsukoshi department store in Nihonbashi, Tokyo. Monuments to him there and Hirado, Kyushu where failed English trading post stood (he had advised it be set up nearer Edo), Ito where he is feted, and Hemmi near Yokosuka. Had son and daughter, whose offspring melded into populace without trace. Blackthorne in *Shogun* is of course based on him.

PERSONAL DATEBOOK: Walking upstream from his monument **1st Sun of Jul**, river is full of people racing downstream in 1-mtr-wide (39in) wood *tarai* tubs in annual *Matsukawa Tub Races*. **Oct early-mid**, all of area's shrines simultaneously hold their *Autumn* (post-harvest) *Festivals* together; **1st Sun Mar** is ritual burning of Mt Oshitsu behind Sengen Shrine (10km inland), remnants of neolithic agricultural society's pre-seeding field-clearing rites.

Ito is port for ferry to OSHIMA Isle (*see* TOKYO ISLES). Also fisherwomen islet of **HATSUSHIMA** (also reached from Atami), worth 30min boat ride for adventurous who wish to see some of famed diving girls in diving season **Apr-Oct** (easier seen near Ise; **best seen** on Japan Sea's Noto Point). Dozens of quiet minshuku all over; S shore invaded by massive resort hotel.

6km (bus, **cab** 3x-mtr) beyond Ito are fabulous Kawana golf courses, with comfortable **Kawana Hotel**, ☎(0557)-45-1111, ¥-Lw/2, expensive for boondocks.

A shower swept toward me from the foot of the mountain, touching
the cedar forests white, as the road began to wind up into the pass.
I was nineteen and travelling alone through...

IZU PENINSULA

...WROTE KAWABATA Yasunari in his eternal story 'Izu Dancer,' which opens as above. Perhaps most beautiful area within easy reach of Tokyo, especially popular with legion of Kawabata readers. Popular weekend retreat for residents, Izu offers much for tourist, is now under booming development adding still more luxury facilities and dozens of attractions (tropical-, aloe-, banana-, mikan-, alligator-centers, safari and amusement parks, countless aquariums) for busloads of Tokyo-ites escaping city. Area is so rugged and rural however that much of its hidden charm will survive and adventurer will find it rewarding always. Yet it is compact enough and transportation such that comfort-demanding traveler will find it pleasant 1- or 2-day addition—we even recommend it as **alternate to Hakone.**

Numerous lovely hideaway hot spring towns along E coast served by private Izu-kyuko Rail from Ito (direct connections Tokyo → Ito 2hrs; plus 1hr to Shimoda). Climate cooler summer, far warmer winter than Tokyo even in mid-peninsula Amagi Mts where several fine spa towns-N to S: HATAKE, KONA, NAGAOKA, SHUZEN-JI (numerous top inns) and YOSHINA at Yugashima Onsen cluster deep in middle. FUJIMILAND recommended for resident families. Hunting good in mountains in winter; **Nov 1-Mar 15** local delicacy is wild boar, makes finest sukiyaki, called *botan-yaki*—perhaps best at **Yoshina Hot Spring Hotel's** rustic samurai-style dining lodge.

GETTING AROUND: To **avoid** crowds of Atami and Ito, plunge right into Izu's quiet hot springs, better to start at MISHIMA and train down to SHUZEN-JI. From here, 12 **buses** daily make 90min run to E coast Kawazu, half continue on 30min to Shimoda. Easy-going tourists who seek comfort have **2 options: 1.** ATAMI → SHIMODA → up W coast cutting in to → SHUZEN-JI → MISHIMA. **2.** MISHIMA → SHUZEN-JI-bus → SHIMODA → up W coast → NUMAZU. Adventurers with time but low budget do better MISHIMA → SHUZEN-JI → SHIMODA, with stops at any of several backwoods onsen en route then take your time around S shore and up → W. Good way to do entire FUJI → HAKONE → IZU: HAKONE, around 5 Lakes to Fuji from where boat → TOI, around S coast → SHIMODA, exiting → via SHUZEN-JI. Or rail → NUMAZU (*if* W-coast first) or → MISHIMA (*if* Shuzen-ji first).
Paralleling rail ITO → SHIMODA are frequent buses along coastal Rte135; also up middle from KAWAZU → SHUZEN-JI on Rte414; in fact all around and across peninsula. Or hop up W coast in clunky **steamers**. Rail also connects Shuzen-ji to JR at Mishima. Good roads for **driver**; Rent-a-car agencies (Nippon, Nissan, Toyota) at Atami, Ito, Shimoda, Shuzen-ji, Mishima, Numazu for those who want to **drive**.

Izu is soaked in ancient history and legend, especially Shuzen-ji area, is long favorite locale for fiction. Yoritomo was exiled here as youth, returned for secret meetings with his mistress Yoegaki after becoming shogun: **Nov 10** *Shiri-tsumi Sai* (Fanny Pinching Fete) at Otonashi Jinja, Ito has all lights turned out around 10pm so crowd, in memory Yoritomo and commoner lover Yaegaki Himé, emulate their secret rendezvous in dark by searching each other out to present royal pinch; afternoon Parade, other entertainment. He in turn exiled most enemies here– Saint Nichiren spent 3 years in exile at Butsugen-ji temple in Ito.

Izu is particularly apt place to start tour, for here Japan first met modern world: Englishman William Adams (Blackthorne of *Shogun*) built Japan's first European-style ship 1607 at Ito. Unsuccessful Russian would-be Perry sailed in to open Japan but got shipwrecked at Heda Port on W coast in 1853 and with Japanese permission his crew with local carpenters built new ship, *Diane*, in which to return. Same Japanese carpenters later built 10 replicas, starting Yokosuka naval shipyards.

US Commodore Perry appeared off its coasts in 1853-4 and landed at...
SHIMODA: In town 700m S of stn is **RYOSEN-JI** temple where Perry signed Shimoda Treaty, May 25, 1854, allowing first US ambassador. Townsend Harris of New York in 1856 sat in his lonely converted temple **GYOKUSENJI** (*below*) amid giant spiders (still around) to wear down patience of shogun to sign 1st treaty opening Japan to world. Few artifacts at RYOSEN-JI now more noted for collection of Buddhist & folk erotica (¥200).

100m S is **CHORAKU-JI** where December same year, Tokugawa officials signed commerce treaties with U.S. and Russia. Catering to Harris' house-keeping needs was local geisha O-Kichi. Gossip-loving locals built legend on this, which drove O-Kichi to suicide years later and slanders Harris' name since. Japanese scholars today find no basis for it, despite having been perpetuated in movie and book, *Barbarian and the Geisha*. O-Kichi of legend, however, has many disciples in this area, bachelors will nowhere feel lonely—more speak enough English here than in other areas.

Between Ryosen-ji and stn is...
HOFUKU-JI temple where O-Kichi is buried, with exhibit (¥200) on O-Kichi, and knick-knacks of Harris's.

Before Hofuku-ji is...
TODEN-JI where shipwright Tsurumatsu, O-Kichi's intended spouse lies. **GYOKUSEN-JI**: here Harris lived, 2km E of town at entry to Suzaki Peninsula (3min bus from stn); now museum, on grounds is grave of one of Perry's men, another for Russian sailor from *Diana*.
Stone tower to 1st cow butchered in vegetarian Japan for Harris' table. Harris in his *Journal* (Sept 4,1856): "...I raise the First Consular Flag ever seen in this Empire...Grim reflections...Query–if for real good of Japan?"
Nearby, statue of YOSHIDA Shoin looks out over bay where Perry's Black Ships anchored—one of founding fathers of modern Japan, tried to sneak aboard Perry's ship to go west and learn modern military tactics, was turned over to shogunal officials. He escaped death penalty for violating Seclusion Law thanks to his teacher SAKUMA Shozan's influence, spent year in jail. He then plotted to kill Shogun's emissary en route to get imperial approval of US treaty. Caught again, was taken to Edo, beheaded in 1859. Monument near Benten-jima isle just offshore marks where he rowed from. Perry **bust** across harbor marks where US Commodore first set foot. He delivered President's letter to Emperor's legate, incidentally, by handing it to him via his black sergeants-at-arms.

Shimoda 'castle' reached by ropeway **should be avoided**— real rip-off joint, ¥600 for bad exhibits in new concrete monstrosity where no castle ever was.

GETTING AROUND: Can see all sites in 2 hours on **foot**; or half time by cab ¥4,000, 9-10x-mtr. Sightseeing **boat** (3x-daily) down to Point Iro, ¥1,000 40min o.w. lovely sail, some others make regular runs ending at Iro; or ¥600 for 20min cruise around Shimoda in Black Ship 'replica' or steamer. Also daily departure from pier near Perry bust to Izu's primitive isles (*see*) Shimoda-Kozujima-Shikine-Niijima-Shimoda, return alternating days; link with ships plying these isles and TOKYO-ISLANDS runs.

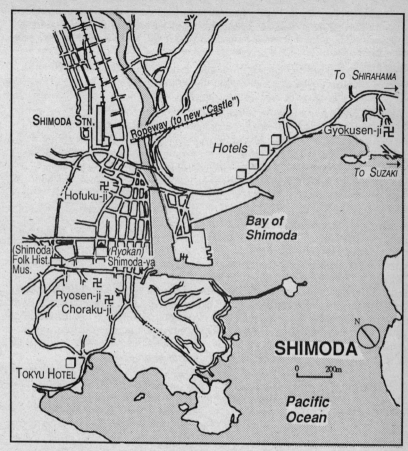

WHERE TO STAY: Shimoda has over 40 ryokans, ¥-B-L: best is **Shimoda Tokyu Hotel** ☎(05582)-2-2411 above sandy cove/beach S of town, ¥-T-Sw/2 -twin per 2 people. Nearby 200-year-old *gassho-zukuri* **farmhouse** moved from mountainous Hida looks very out-of-place in this clime, but serves food amid display of folk items: sign in front reads "Opening and closing time may change by feeling of Day and Season. To enter or not is not da? Just come right in!" How can you resist? -food's good. Just along shore here are **Shimoda Kaihin Hotel** ☎2-2065 ¥-Sw/2, and **O-ura-so** ☎ 2-2076, ¥-T-S. In town is ¥-T, traditional **Shimoda-ya** ☎2-0446; several more crammed along coast E end of town. We found on other side of river our **Ryusen-so** ☎2-1364—nothing fancy just clean, ¥-B+ cheap and quiet—thru stn info. No minshuku in town, but many at most beaches (*see* swimming).

Tho Shimoda inns all draw onsen water, you can go right to hot source at...
RENTAI-JI ONSEN 10min bus from Shimoda. Nearby river pool where O-Kichi drowned herself, is marked by small shrine. O-Kichi fans, mostly kimono-clad women, gather here from all over Japan **Mar 27** to pray for her soul. Rentai-ji also preserves several folk houses with *namako-kabe* white grid on black slate walls characteristic of southern Izu. Some yet remain in Shimoda, mostly in older section of town near harbor.

WHERE TO STAY: **Best inn** here is traditional, wooden **Seiryu-so** ☎(05582)-2-1361 with country's largest stone lantern, swimming pool, **outdoor baths**, ¥-S-Lw/2, superb meals (1st Japan member France's exclusive *Relais et Chateaux*,

President Carter ate here in Shimoda visit); will pick-up at stn. Another wood old-timer, **Yubata-kan** ☎2-2244 ¥-S+w/2. Next door is traditional ryokan **Rentai-ji-so** ☎2-3501 beautiful garden, interior, ¥-S+w/2. Some ¥-Tw/2, like **Aizu-in** ☎2-1648; avail thru stn Info Ctr.

At W end of onsen near Tenjin shrine is house where YOSHIDA Shoin hid before aborted stow-away; nearby public bath he used to go to is still in use.

If you want to 'get away' without too much trouble, head to...
YOKOGAWA ONSEN, *Ikken-yado,* one-inn town (must use public bath) only 20min bus from Shimoda. 35min bus on to W coast Matsuzaki.

Swimming 3km from Shimoda on E coast at...
SHIRAHAMA is one of better (but more crowded) beaches: 1km long, 3 resort hotels and 200 minshuku ensure full capacity in summer. To reach Shirahama, cut across Sugisa Peninsula, rugged but with good beaches at S tip Suzaki 15min bus, W base Sotoura halfway to Shirahama, 4min bus. 70 minshuku at SUZAKI, 60 at SOTOURA. Heading W from Shimoda are more beaches, with best ones up W coast.

But before heading out there, let's backtrack little up E coast...
For your average tourist we suggest by-pass E coast, but for adventurer with time, or traveling expatriate, there are some fun stops before Shimoda. 35min on JR from Ito is another resort-onsen, ATAGAWA, which we avoid, but just before it are 2 small onsen-both of which have outdoor sea-side bath:
OKAWA, 28min from Ito; **HOKKAWA**, 31min from Ito. Continuing 2 stns past Atagawa is **INATORI**: largest fishing port in Izu, inns sprouted up in 1956 when onsen water gushed out of ground. Bustling town, one boat daily to/from Oshima (*see* TOKYO ISLES); not much here to see or do unless passing thru **June 6-7** to catch *Dontsuku Festival* fertility rite, young men in long-nosed tengu masks run around batting women with *dontsuku* phallic poles.

Another 2 stops down...
KAWAZU, coastal gateway to Kawazu onsen cluster stretching upriver. Good beach here (with most minshuku) and hot springs are small, quiet. We pass Kawazu-hama and Yazu onsens (closest to stn) in favor of inland ones. Also pass Miné onsen, more popular with groups come mainly to see steam towers—open only sun 9:00.

15min bus from Kawazu stn,...
YUGANO ONSEN, quiet hamlet on steaming river; noted as setting for KAWABATA Yasunari's story *Izu Dancer* which made his reputation in 1926; now re-doing main street as in his time, gas lights and all. Building movie house to show regularly all 6 Japanese movie versions of story.
WHERE TO STAY: Four small ryokan here (¥Tw/2), half-dozen minshuku. Some fun inns: minshuku **Teppo** ☎(05583)-5-7501, was workshop for only gun (*teppo*) smith in Izu and now known for its great boar dinners. Another, **Kagoya** ☎5-7351, run by bamboo weaver who likes to teach guests how to weave bamboo baskets (says anyone can make good one in hour). **Family Ryokan Yamamoto** ☎4-0850, family spa-inn, ¥-B minshuku rate, especially welcomes foreigners; phone ahead in English for rsv, itinerary advice.

600m up road is...
JIGEN-IN temple, Harris spent nite en route Edo for commerce treaty; chopsticks he used now temple treasure. Now part of temple is Youth Hostel.

As nice as this is, would be better to head little further to...
Seven Waterfalls of Kawazu, *Kawazu Nana-daru* (25min bus from Kawazu, 55min from Shimoda). Waterfalls are nice to see, largest is 27m high, but baths are better. In spite of popularity of both, it is not built up—3 ryokan, dozen minshuku. **OTAKI ONSEN** by Otaki (big) waterfall has

large outdoor bath by river; near by are 'tunnel' baths, where hot water has partially filled old copper mines (all horizontal, you won't suddenly drop) making for some unusual baths in little caves lit by single light bulb. Both run by ryokan **Amagi-so** ☎(05583)-5-7711 (¥-Sw/2) but open to all. Path follows river along falls. Perhaps best time (tho crowded) to visit falls is **Nov 20-22** for *Nanadaru Festival*. To honor river deity, participants are given all cooked boar you can eat and sake to drink—just buy (¥300 each) commemorative cup and plate and fill 'em up as many times as you want.

70min bus to central Shuzen-ji, thru more backwoods hot springs. Back to coast...

SOUTHERN SHORE OF IZU

FOR ADVENTURERS, most pass by, going direct to Matsuzaki on W coast. Not much to do here except swim, stay in tiny fishing villages—all off main road. Following have dozen or so minshuku each, almost all run by families who decided to open up rooms.

TOJI, (15min bus from Shimoda), known for its huge sand dunes you can ski or sled down on rented boards.

2km coastal hike W to larger...
YUIGAHAMA, and one of longest sand beaches on Izu. In feudal days it used to be main stopping place for ships plying between Osaka and Edo. Point S of harbor has cave at its tip with buddha trinity carved on back wall. Best seen in morning with sun reflecting into cave; you can enter it at low tide but only by chartering local fisherman to take you in.

IROZAKI POINT, (40min bus or boat from Shimoda), is small but gets crowds visiting nearby **Jungle Park.**

Just beyond are 2 isolated villages of...
NAKAGI and **IRUMA**, (about 1hr bus from Shimoda). Both are tucked away in little coves walled in on 3 sides by mountains. In winter cold winds come tearing in, and homes are surrounded by rock walls; walls along back sides keep mountains from rolling in. French will be welcomed at Iruma—monument in **KAIZO-JI** temple marks 1873 shipwreck of Marseilles Postal Lines' ship *Neil* which drowned 83 sailors; villagers were able to bury 21 of them here. 4 survivors lived here till 1874.

Further on at...
MERA and **KO-URA** at either end of Mera Bay, for irregular boat services 30min up W coast to Cape Hakachi-zaki (1hr30min bus from Shimoda, 1km walk) with magnificent 260m ramparts, and...

Diving girls of isolated villages of **KUMOMI, ISHIBU, IWACHI**, each in its little cove, but accessible by bus. Girls work May-Oct to gather *tengusa* seaweed from which gelatine base is made. Half-dozen buses stop between Shimoda—Matsuzaki, many more make quick run from Matsuzaki and back. *Adventurer* need never fear getting stuck in such small towns at dark with no transportation out. All three are small onsens (Ishibu has outdoor seaside bath) with several dozen minshuku each. Iwachi fishing festival **May 3, free food** and drink.

Boat from Mera chugs on as far as... (also reached by 55min bus from Shimoda)...
MATSUZAKI, large in comparison to what you've just passed thru, few hundred meters any direction and you're out of town. Lot of old namako-wall houses remain, some are folk inns Ishida-ya, Sanko-so, Ita-ya.

NODA, 7min bus inland, has interesting combination local and western architecture at Iwanashi **Local History Museum** in ex-Iwanashi High

School built 1880; 9:00-17:00, X-tue, thur-pm, ¥200. From here **sightseeing ships** ply to Cape Hakachi or up coast to Dogashima and its weird sugarloaf islets and flowers which bloom all winter for Tokyo market. Continuing on, some boats stop at Ugusu, Toi, Heda, Ida, then gorgeous Cape Ose, end at Numazu on JR Tokaido Main Line. Heda, Ida best reached by boat: NUMAZU → IDA → HEDA → NUMAZU and reverse: 2 ships daily (summer only) make 2hr crossing to SHIMIZU, near Shizuoka city.

DOGASHIMA, superb white sand beach here, with great view of rugged isles just offshore and Mt Fuji in distance. Coastline stretches for several km either side of village, best southernmost...

OHAMA *kaisui-yoku-jo*-swimming beach (closer to Matsuzaki).

WHERE TO STAY: Minshuku villages abound: 27 at OHAMA, 10 at HAMA 500m N, 96 at SAWADA 1 km N where friends stayed at **Kaisui-so** ☎(05585)-2-0260. Dogashima itself is onsen village with dozen hotels and ryokan most above ¥-Sw/2. If you want to stay here, **best** is traditional old-timer **Hotel Sanshiro** ☎2-0346, fully Japanese style despite 'Hotel', with giant seaside outdoor bath facing isles and Fuji. ¥-Sw/2, dinners are seafood extravaganzas fresh from ocean. If full, try **Rinkai Hotel** ☎2-1234 or **New Onsen Hotel** ☎2-0275, both are little further up coast and ¥-S+w/2. **Ryokan Information Center** at Dogashima bus stop books you in to anything around.

Sightseeing boats from Dogashima take you around myriad isles here, and in to some caves carved out by waves. Most spectacular is *Tenso-do* Heavenly Window Cave with natural skylight illuminating inside. 20min cruise ¥600, leaves when full or captain feels like.

1km up coastal trail leads 2km to...
TAGO (bus also), visited by some boats running between Dogashima and Toi; further up is **ARARI** whose bowl-shaped port is used as trap for dolphins which are herded in and bottled up. MISHIMA Yukio spent time here writing *Runaway Horses*, and his room at old but fine inn **Horaiya** ☎(05585)-6-0015, is still kept as it was. Both villages full of minshuku, half of which draw hot water from volcanic hill behind. More ¥-B inns, beaches and **campsite** at UGUSU ONSEN with its view of Mt Fuji and special viewing platform.

Only 25km up from Dogashima. is...

NORTHWEST CORNER

TOI has long been known for hot springs and gold. Former appeared in 1577 when latter was dug for. Gold much depleted and mines closed, but hot water continues to gush. Mines are at S end of town and can be visited: larger one behind **Toi Marine Center**. Of original 100km tunnels 300m section is open to public (8:00-16:30, ¥300), dummies showing how it was mined in olden days. 300m S another, which was dug all by hand (8:00-18:00, ¥450).

Despite some new resort hotels, this is still small fishing village at heart. 50 ryokan and hotels, and 100 minshuku make it easy to find room here; you can fish off pier or from boats or swim. **Ryokan Info Center** by central bus stop.

E on main road, L at Town Hall to Seiun-ji temple whence short (50m) path to...
ANRAKU-JI temple you can bathe in area's original onsen bath, **Mabu-yu** (cave bath). Back in 1596, according to legend, head priest of Anraku-ji was instructed in dream to bathe in water from mines, and it cured his pains. So he set up bath in his temple to cure people. Ask at temple, and they'll take you to cave for bath.

In addition to boats up W coast, others run to TAGO-NO-URA harbor near Fuji city.

40min bus from Toi, 55min boat from Numazu...
HEDA is naturally enclosed harbor and base for deep-sea tuna fleets. Following Americans and British, Russia's emissary Admiral Putyatin signed commerce treaty at Shimoda. On his return voyage, earthquake-generated tidal wave almost capsized his ship *Diana*, and in trying to reach Heda to hide from French and British warships heading to Crimea, *Diana* sank. Heda shipwrights helped build new *Diana*, several months later came up with their own ship, 100-ton *Heda*, modeled after *Diana*.

5min S of bus stop is...
HOSEN-JI temple where *Diana*'s sailors stayed, with graves of those who drowned; Putyatin was in local chief's home.

20min walk from Heda bus stop to...
Shipbuilding Museum, Mihama Point; 9:00-16:30 (¥200), parts of original *Diana* and *Heda*, notes and blueprints used then. 2nd floor has various deep-sea creatures in Suruga Bay, which at points reaches 2,500m depth.

CHOPSTICKS: Unusual but delicious, *taka-ashi-gani*, world's largest 'spider crabs' whose legs get as long as 1.5m/5ft each. Largest ever caught (1974), measures 3.2m across, 20kg weight, displayed at Kokumin-shukusha People's Hostel **Izu-Heda-so**. Local delicacy (only other place is Kaomaishi in northern Iwate pref) available Sep thru May, average size 2m across feeds 4 for around ¥10,000. Larger inns will serve it for dinner, but must arrange and will cost more; and their regular meals will include all sort of other seafood–crabs, shrimp, lobster–all locally caught. **Isaba Hotel** ☎(0558)-94-3048, boasts best.

WHERE TO STAY: Other good inns are **Uoume Ryokan** ☎(0558)93-2014; traditional **Hotel Tokiwa-ya** ☎94-3333. All ¥-lo-Sw/2. Others little cheaper; 250 Budget minshuku arranged thru bus stop TOURIST CENTER, or just wander in.

3km up coast is...
IDA for those looking for quiet retreat. Mainly agricultural village, with no hot springs, hasn't grown and thus is referred to as 'Izu's Last Hideaway'. Only 10 minshuku, campsite on sandy beaches. Campers can buy fresh seafood at Heda's Fisherman's Co-op at budget prices; most items ¥100-200 per 100 gms.

Just before Ida are **Matsue Kofun**, cluster of 26 small tumuli millennium old. More outside Heda; artifacts from both at Heda Ship Museum.

3km up coast to wooded...
OSE-ZAKI POINT, good sandy beach inner side, budget inns, campsite (4 person bungalow ¥4,500, ¥600 if own tent), super view of Fuji ☎(0559)-42-2423. Near tip is old Ose Shrine, guardian deity of sailors. Behind is sacred lake, one of Izu's '7 Wonders'; only 50m from sea, fresh water full of carp. Best **Apr 4th** *Ship Festival* honoring deity. 100+ bannered boats from all W Izu fishing ports gather; on them men wearing women's red *juban* under-kimono dance to flutes and drums.

From here, coast-line cuts E to...
MITO, not much here unless planning to spend nite at floating hotel *Scandinavia*. Built in 1927, it used to be *Stella Polaris*, Swedish luxury cruiser of 5105 tons. ¥-S-L twins. Or visit it during day (¥500); or at nite for nite club lounge Hokkyoku-sei, 20:00 to midnite. For much less (¥-lo Sw/2), you can stay at traditional **Yasuda-ya** ☎(0559)-43-2121, and enjoy heaps of yellowtail, caught locally. Ships from Numazu go to Ose Point and Mito, with infrequent connections between 2.

NUMAZU has nothing to offer tourist; just gets you back on JR to continue down Tokaido. But let us first visit central IZU and SHUZEN-JI spa.

GETTING THERE: Buses cut inland from TOI and IDA via HEDA to Shuzen-ji –*or* if you avoided crowds of Atami and Ito, plunged right into Izu's quiet hot spas, you started at MISHIMA and trained down, as suggested, to...

SHUZEN-JI, long ranked with Ito and Atami, has been outstripped in recent developments and has only fraction of their inns. We prefer it to big coastal 'bedroom of Tokyo'. It is several clusters of spa villages, Shuzen-ji itself largest, set around Katsura River with volcanic Mount Daruma, sakura-covered Arashiyama-hill as backdrops—best early Apr, lanterns light blossoms at nite. Nearby **International Country Club** has 18-hole golf course. This (*not* golf course) was center of intrigue 8th-12th centuries when court nobles and warrior lords were exiled here, and saw downfall of Minamoto dynasty. Paranoid Yoritomo banished his brother Noriyori here in 1194, later ordering him to cut self in *seppuku*. Later, his widow Yasuko with her co-conspirator Hojo Regent Tokimune, banished son 2nd shogun Yoriie here, to be murdered in bath in 1204…Nice family.

That bath, **Tokko-no-yu,** sits on little rock outcropping in river. Enclosed by wood slat walls and roofed, still open to public, free. It is said to have been discovered by saint Kobo Daishi in 807 when he hit rocks with Buddhist altar ornament and hot water spouted forth–some dowser!

SHUZEN-JI temple, built by saint, 807. Apr 21 at 'Water Carrying Rite' priest, aided by 3 kimono-clad maidens, takes 2 buckets of bath's water as offering to Kobo Daishi's spirit.

Across bridge from Tokko-no-yu...
Treasure Hall (8:30-17:00, ¥100) contains mostly Minamoto-related objects. Most famous is 'death mask' of Yoriie. According to legend, Yoriie ordered it from famed carver Yashao, whose daughter Katsura fell in love with Yoriie. No matter what Yashao did, mask had deathly look. Yoriie finally demanded it. Soon after, assassins raided his home, Katsura donned mask to lure them, was sliced. They then cornered Yoriie at bath, did him in. Katsura staggered back to her father, who finished mask, modeling it after dead daughter's face. Tale basis for OKAMOTO Kido's novel/kabuki play *Tale of Shuzen-ji,* translated in Cellin Gluck's *You Mean to Say...*

S of Tokko-no-yu is...
Shigetsu-den Hall, built 1204 by Hojo Yasuko for her son Yoriie's spirit, his grave is behind hall, but his ashes are buried beneath Shigetsu-den. Untouched since its construction, it is oldest original wood structure in Izu; inside is rare Zen-style statue of *Shaka-nyorai* (Sakyamuni Buddha) holding lotus flower in right hand. Graves of Yoriie's 13 retainers are further uphill, uncle Noriyori's grave at W end of town.

WHERE TO STAY: has few large or medium sized hotels, no W style rooms. Best: HOTEL Miyuki ☎(0558)-72-2112, ¥-Sw/2. Like true onsen most are small wooden traditional ryokan, set in sculpted garden; dedicated to excellent food, baths, and service. BEST of these are Arai ☎72-2007, Kiku-ya ☎72-2000, and Asaba ☎72-0700 with outdoor bath, all ¥-S-Lw/2. ¥-T+w/2 are Kinokuniya ☎72-2223, Izuno ☎72-0304, Taisan-so ☎72-0331, Nakada-ya ☎72-2345, Asahi ☎72-0180, Keizan-so ☎72-2070, Isuzu-so ☎72-0510. BUDGET ¥-B+w/2: Tsuyuki ☎72-2100 Kajika ☎72-0357, in row at W end. RYOKAN INFO CENTER faces PO E end.

Shuzen-ji South:
AMAGI ONSEN CLUSTER for leisurely adventurer to/from Shimoda on Rte414. N to S: TSUKIGASE, SAGASAWA along Karino River parallel to road, YOSHINA 1km W in hills along Kona River. Above Tsukigase, main Rte136 cuts W to Toi; 3km down Rte136 is FUNABARA ONSEN; before which is HOZO-IN temple, its main gate details carved by left-handed Hidari Jingoro (*see* Nikko). These spas are small hamlets with 2 or 3 ¥-Tw/2 fine old inns; Funabara has 4; *best* YOSHINA with 3; many with outdoor public baths. Going on to TOI 2km trail crosses over to Funabara on Rte136–saves changing bus at Deguchi, where Rtes136-414 intersect.

10min bus on Rte414 is...

YUGASHIMA ONSEN: Larger, has several fine inns and long popular with Japanese novelists such as KAWABATA Yasunari who came here to write: which literary tradition is preserved in special 'sensei's' room available at handsome **Shirakabe-so** inn ☎(0558)-85-0100, folk-art decor and crockery, good indoor hot baths (men-women apart), cozy smaller one outside; riverside swimming pool summer. Local feature: tame-boar shows. From here, you cross Amagi Pass and another 7km to Nanadaru waterfalls (P250) and on to Shimoda. In case you're wondering why all those people get off and on bus at either end of tunnel, they walk thru abandoned 'Amagi First Tunnel' made popular in Kawabata's *Izu Dancer*, "...when I came to the tunnel I finally shook her off."

From here, 12 buses daily make 90min run to E coast Kawazu, half continue on 30min to Shimoda. Heading N from Shuzen-ji, go four rail stops to...

IZU-NAGAOKA which we especially like; boasts 10 historic spots, 2 not to be missed are **Reverbatorium** (1km E–bus 5min–of Izu-Nagaoka stn) where 100 cannons that Egawa Tarozaemon made for shogun 1857, under whose loaded but silent muzzles Perry sailed into Edo Bay. 'Reverborating' type foundry refers to heat flash-back system, not gun 'boom'. With 16m tall chimneys remains as it was, built from plans in Dutch book brought as part of annual tribute, now last such in world. Hedgerows on hill opp are tea, processed behind big waterwheel, served *free* in shop to R. *Also to R...*

Traditional Toy Museum, *Gangu Hakubutsukan* (¥500) fabulous collection Edo-to-prewar kites, clothespin-shape kokeshi dolls (owner boasts each worth price of new car or more), pinky-size miniature dolls with clothes woven or brocaded to microscopic scale–magnifying glass free on table.

Other 'must' is **Egawa House** (2km NE–bus 5+min–of stn) country's **oldest extant private house**–seven centuries. Tarozaemon 36th generation to live there. Note no tatami, just wood floors polished by daily wipe. *Behind is* town **History Museum** with Egawa's notes, models, local folk items. **Nirayama Castle** (1442) REMAINS are along stn-side of lake near Egawa's; near which young Yoritomo spent 20 years in exile.

WHERE TO STAY: Charming rustic inns: our find **Yamada-ya** all rms over big garden view Fuji, rotenburo, ☎(0559)-48-0715, ¥-loS; finest **Sanyo-so** baronial estate, fab garden ☎48-0123 ¥-L–¥100,000, used by imperial family; Sukiya-style **Nanzan-so** ☎48-0601, lge garden, separate cottages, ¥-hi-S; **Kona Hotel** ☎48-1225 ¥-hiS; **Tokiwa** ☎48-1555 ¥-S; Sukiya-'Hotel' **Izu-Nagaoka** features rotenburo women only, try indigo dyeing, ¥-hi-S, ☎48-0801. Minshuku **Taro** ☎47-2600. All +25% sat.

Halfway to Tokaido Main Line Mishima are two hidden hot spring spas...

HATAKE & NAGOYA ONSENS: on local road E of Rte136, reach only by bus from Mishima (28min → Hatake, 30min → Nagoya (not big city of same name). Road curves back to main road at Haraki (2 stops past Nagaoka), one can only taxi, hitch or walk 2km/30min Haraki → Nagoya, quiet 1-inn onsen 700m E of which riverside outdoor bath **Koma-no-yu** in beautiful vale. Hatake about 1km N, 10 inns all ¥-B–T.

MISHIMA: little for tourist besides **Sano collection**, noted ancient East Asian art: **Museum** 2km S of JR Mishima stn, **taxi** 1x-mtr; to/from Shuzen-ji pvt rail Mishima Tamachi, 2nd from Mishima, museum 100m E; 10:00-17:00, X-thu, ¥500.

MISHIMA TAISHA grand shrine SE of JR is grand structure best **Aug 16** for annual fete: parade of Yoritomo, attendants, massive floats, *yabusame* mounted archery.

Rakuju-en Park just S of JR was created early Meiji Era, 1860s, as villa for then-imperial prince Komatsu-miya Akihito, now run by town.

WHERE NEXT: Circling Izu Peninsula you end at MISHIMA, for Shinkansen stn to return TOKYO, **or** continue down coast; **or** go back to ODAWARA to join our next itinerary into HAKONE Mts and Mt Fuji. **Or** skip Hakone and train old JR line MISHIMA up to GOTEMBA at foot of sacred mountain and heart of Lake Country.

PERSONAL DATEBOOK: IZU PENINSULA

January

7 Ritual blessing of fields Mishima Grand Shrine.

15-Mar 15 Atami *Ume* (Apricot) *Festival*, Atami Apricot Garden, dances by Geisha, tea ceremony, assorted shows.

15 Mid-winter purification cold-water swim, Atami.

28 Chase evil, Izu-Nagaoka, evil dancing monkey/tiger/snake are all 'slain' at finale by our hero samurai.

February

10 *Onsen Festival* Atami, Yuzen shrine.

March

1st Sun, Ito, burn mt, (text p246).

27 Okichi memorial, outside Shimoda.

April

4 *Boat Festival*, Osé point (text p253).

21 Yukumi water blessing, Shuzenji (*see* text p254).

26-28 *Ajiro Horse Mackerel Fete*, horse mackerel free to guests (text p246).

May

3 *Iwachi Fishing fest*, Kumomi, free food, (text p251).

16-18 *Kurofune* (Black Ship) *Festival*, Shimoda fetes 'star' Perry, Harris, Okichi, treaty signing; US Marine band marches, unless withdrawn in disarmament.

June

Early Jun *Dontsuku Festival* at Inatori (*see text*).

1st Sat- Sun Toi Onsen fetes golden days, shipping of gold to Edo, boat-shaped floats with lanterns, musicians parade, fireworks.

July

Early All beaches Izu officially open.

1-2 *Genji-ayame Festival*, Izu-Nagaoka. Pray soul Yoritomo Yorimasa wife Ayame, geisha dance, parade mikoshi, samurai.

1st Sun Barrel-ride Matsukawa R, Ito, (text p246).

15 *Summer Fete*, Tenno shrine, Kawazu.

15-16 *Atami Kanko Matsuri*, (text p244).

17 Memorial Minamoto Yoriie, Shuzen-ji.

22-23 *Daimon-ji yaki*, burn massive character *dai* on water at Atagawa.

23-25 Dogashima Fireworks nitely, burn 'pirate ship' replica; started Kamakura era by local fishermen to scare real pirates.

31 *Toro Nagashi* at Shimoda.

August

1-3 *Bon Odori* nitely at Shuzen-ji.

2 *Summer Festival* at Shuzenji.

3 Izusan Grand Fireworks Festival.

5 Grand Fireworks at Atami.

6-10 *Anjin Festival* Ito City;

-8 nite lanterns float on Matsukawa river;

-9 *Taiko* drum contests; Anjin parade and fireworks, nightly climax **10**.

14-15 *Taiko* drum fete, Hachiman Shrine Shimoda local *taiko* teams show off skills.

15 *Bon Odori* at Mera village, W coast.

15-17 Mishima Grand Shrine summer fete.

16 Mishima City, feudal costume parade of Yoritomo and followers.

Mid- Fireworks at Kawazu, E coast.

21 Fireworks at Shuzenji.

September

Full moon lion dance Koina, Minamiizucho

Mid- Lobster season, fishing village—best Shimoda, Dogashima, budget prices.

October

All- Izu's **mikan groves** (mandarin orange) open to public, pick your fill for nominal fee. All shrines in Izu autumn festivals, any day at least 2 fetes in area—

7-15 Izu Yugawara; **9** Katase;

10-11 *Yukumi dochu* samurai parade Atami;

14-15 Kawazu;

14-16 Ito, 15 mikoshi carted on boats.

November

1-2 *Taiko* drums S Izu, best Iro Point.

2-3 *Sambaso* puppet dance, Sawa Shrine, Dogashima. From noh dances (old man, Okina) introduced late 16th cent by noh master Okubo Choan taken over by more popular puppet show: 3 men to puppet, head is 150-year-old Prefectural Treasure.

Same days, original human dance version, neighboring Matsuzaki Inashimo Shrine.

Same days, Hirose Shrine at Ohito in central Izu, main festival of year.

10 *Shiri-tsumi Fete* (fanny pinching), Otonashi Jinja, Ito, (text p247).

10 Atami, *feudal procession*, (text p244).

11 *Geta Burning Festival* at Izu Nagaoka; all inns burn old geta in ritual flame.

20-22 *Taki* (Waterfall) *Fete*, Kawazu Nanadaru, all boar & sake one can eat, drink: buy commemorative 'sacred' dish, cup each ¥300, fill both many times as like– p251

Mid-Nov: Best view maple, Shuzenji.

Mid-winter Festivities here few: except for traditional year-end, New Year events.

To see Mount Fuji...in a dream...what a blessing
No weariness of journey...no travelling expenses
— I-Taiyu Teiryu (1654-1734)

MT FUJI 富士山 & HAKONE 箱根
TOKYO'S MOUNTAIN RETREATS

JAPAN'S most popular resorts draw hordes of guests all year. Entire area dotted with countless hot springs ranging from back-country hamlets to modern resorts. HAKONE is 1st in line, from where you can circumambulate FUJI FIVE LAKES; and IZU PENINSULA side trip can be done before or after.

ODAWARA: Old castle-town, E gateway to area, uninteresting itself but it is turn-off for Hakone.

GETTING THERE: From TOKYO: 42min Shinkansen or 85min old JR Tokaido Main Line express; from KAMAKURA: JR 50min via Ofuna.

All that remains of its past glory is **Castle** HOJO Soun built here in 1495, destroyed century later by TOYOTOMI Hideyoshi. When Tokugawa came to power, chief advisor Ohkubo gained control, built new castle. At peak, castle grounds measured 3km E-W, 2.2km N-S. What remains has been repaired within past 20 years. Central keep has small **Museum of Local History,** usual samurai armor, weapons, top floor view. Also small **Folkcraft Museum** in castle park.

May 3-5 *Oshiro Matsuri*, castle festival highlights costume parade honoring Hojo. **Dec 6** 400-year-old secret fire ritual of *yamabushi* mountain ascetics at Ryokaku-in. Massive torches lit, prayers offered to ward off illness, 6pm fire walk; reached by bus heading to Hakone-Yumoto from Odawara stn 5min to Itabashi stop and 10min walk on.

Odawara is cheaper alternative to Hakone inns for budgeteers, with several Business Hotels near stn. But we suggest spend extra ¥1,000 or so for Hakone minshuku, and avoid staying here unless too late to head up to...

HAKONE

WEDGED BETWEEN Mt Fuji and Izu Peninsula this most popular year-round mountain resort of Tokyo-ites offers little but views of Fuji and lots of re-sort recreation. Few hours from Narita, ideal for that 1st relaxing night.

Formation of Hakone began around 400,000 years ago with eruption of Mt Hakone, similar in shape and size to Fuji. Center collapsed into caldera, subsequent eruptions creating small volcanos inside—Komagatake 1327m, Kamiyama 1438m. Water trapped in caldera formed Lake Ashi; main outlets Hayakawa, Sukumo Rivers carved their routes downhill to form beautiful rugged gorges which are main venues of transport. Hot spas popular since early Heian era. Hideyoshi built his personal outdoor bath near Miyanoshita and Hakone's water was carted to Edo castle for special occasions.

GETTING AROUND: Hakone hills is easy with Odakyu's extensive train, bus, mountain tram, cable car, ropeway and boat system. Four-day *Hakone Free Pass* good for multiple trips on all, abt¥4,000 from ODAWARA, abt¥5,000 from SHINJUKU. If continuing, pass gets you to GOTEMBA (for Mt Fuji), ATAMI & MISHIMA (for Izu).

Basic route (without pass) from Odawara by rail and cablecar, across lake and bus to ODAWARA is ¥5,720 (more if stopping en route). Pass discounts admissions to many sites in Hakone. Odakyu runs special ltd express *Romance Car* double-deck train with posh seats SHINJUKU-ODAWARA 70min (¥1,250) or HAKONE-YUMOTO 85min, ¥1,490. Extra ltd express fee required if using in conjunction with Free Pass. Dep Shinjuku every 30min 7:30-17:00; Hakone-Yumoto every 30min 9:12-18:42.

Hakone Tozan Tetsudo (funicular railway) connecting Odawara–Gohra has dubious distinction of being slowest train in Japan, and sole funicular. Begun Oct 1, 1935. 55min (¥520) covers 15km to GOHRA, 1/3 in tunnels, 3 switchbacks aid its steep 527m climb. Pass thru beautiful wooded slopes, over sheer ravines along Hayakawa River, special views announced on board only on climb up, 9min, ¥290 cable car every 15min from Gohra to SOUNZAN, here change to ropeway 35min ¥1,180 to TOGENDAI. Dep every min on 2nd longest ropeway in world. **Boats** cross lake Togendai to MOTO-HAKONE or HAKONE-MACHI in 40min, dep every 30min ¥800.

Numerous **tour buses** circle Hakone area, scenic views abound and only historic spot visited is **HAKONE barrier gate.** Only Hakone Tozan Tetsudo 'D' Course crosses Lake Ashi by boat, others circle it by road. Most operate btwn Odawara–Atami, few btwn Yugawara–Odawara. All pass thru Hakone's various spas; can get on or off anywhere en route, prices vary accordingly but arrange prior to departure. 2 main bus companies are **Hakone Tozan Tetsudo** ☎(0465)-24-2111, **Izu-Hakone Tetsudo** ☎(0559)-77-1200. **Hato Bus** ☎(03)-3201-2725, 1x-daily from Tokyo stn 8:30: Kowaki-en garden → Lake Ashi → Hakone Barrier Gate → Odawara castle return Tokyo stn 19:00, ¥9,980.

Cabs abound, personal tours can be easily arranged: half-day to take in all Hakone, full-day includes Atami's spectacular MOA museum or Lake Yamanaka, one of Fuji's 5 lakes. 3 or 4 people covering Hakone by cab cheaper than bus: basic rates for *chugata* mid-size (as of summer 1990) are ¥220/km, hire rates 7-8x-mtr/hr.

Drive thru Hakone hills is pleasant except sun/hols when traffic jams near base. Several fine scenic roads cut across mountains. From ODAWARA Rte1 follows rail to MIYANOSHITA then S to MOTO-HAKONE, on to MISHIMA gateway to Izu. Just before HAKONE-YUMOTO, Hakone Shindo toll road (13.8km, ¥200) follows Sukumo-gawa river valley to HAKONE-machi. Parallel to it (entrance closer Hakone-Yumoto) regular bus road follows old pedestrian *Hakone-kaido* hiway to MOTO-HAKONE. Hakone Turnpike (16km, ¥550) from YUGAWARA to DAIKAN-YAMA peak with drive-in and observatory offers fine **view** Lake Ashi-Mt Fuji. From Daikan-yama Yugawara Tsubaki (camellia) Line Hiway winds down 19km to Oku-Yugawara and YUGAWARA **hotsprings** near coast. Or continue 2km to intersection of local road to HAKONE-machi and Yugawara Parkway (5.7km, ¥400) to OKU-YUGAWARA. Ashinoko Skyline (11km, ¥450) skirts lake's E shore across Mikuni mountains from Hakone-machi to Togendai. Part way branch leads to Rte138 - GOTEMBA Interchange on *Tomei Expressway* (on to Kyoto, etc) Rte138 starts Miyanoshita to Sengokubara, continues past Gotemba becoming Rte139 **circling Mt Fuji** counterclockwise.

Half-dozen major and several small spa areas provide dozens of lodgings in all price ranges. All hotels offer both W- and J- facilities at international standard rates. Hakone's medicinal hot springs famous for over millennium, but onsen/ryokan clusters did not flourish until Tokugawa made Tokaido Hiway. *Shichi-yu* **7 Baths** of Hakone-Yumoto, Tonosawa, Kiga, Miyanoshita, Dogashima, Sokokura, Ashinoyu founded during Edo period; half-dozen more built up after 1868 for tourism. Seven all set along Hayakawa River, except for Ashinoyu in hills near Lake Ashi. Just before Miyanoshita are Hakone-Yumoto and Tonosawa with several fine traditional spa-inns. But having come this far we suggest go further into mountains to GOHRA or on to **Lake Ashi,** *Ashi-no-ko*, alias Lake Hakone for justly-famed view of inverted Fuji reflected on surface.

Tourist Information Center 100m W of Hakone-Yumoto stn helpful finding rooms at all price ranges. Also **Annai-jo** across from Kowaki-en Hotel.

HAKONE-YUMOTO, oldest established onsen here, now main shopping area crowded with modern stores and hotels near stn. Head few blocks from stn and enter quiet wooded areas where most best inns are. Two superb traditional ryokan here, small (only 8 rooms in each) with excellent service, food. Both have cozy guest cottages hidden in lovely gardens: rates equally grand ¥-LLw/2. **Kiyomizu** ☎(0460)-5-5385; **Gyokutei** ☎5-7501.

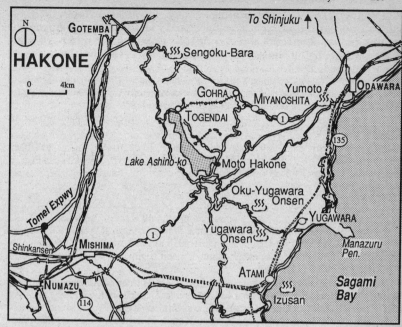

TONOSAWA, (next stn up), actually part of Yumoto more picturesque, quieter. Lodgings cheaper here, though not as fancy. Along Hayakawa River are 3 larger traditional ryokan (20 rooms), each ¥-B–Sw/2. **Fukuju-ro** ☎(0460)-5-5301; **Shin Tamanoyu** ☎5-5341; and **Kansui-ro** ☎5-5511 with its rock bath.

MIYANOSHITA, area including **Dogashima** and **Sokokura** spas, center of Hakone with finest W-style hotels and J-ryokan. Popular spa for upper class ever since Hideyoshi had outdoor rock-bath built here after siege of Odawara. 30min rail or bus from Odawara; **bus** is more convenient with stops in front of all main lodgings.

Our favorite of major hotels is...
Fujiya Hotel, rambling old world charm and gardens, one of oldest hotels in Japan, 1st in Hakone. Specializes in catering to Westerners, most of staff speak English; fine French cuisine, their own golf course. 150 rooms range ¥-T-LL-twin w/2; ☎(0460)-2-2211. Or equally fine Japanese annex **Kikka-so**, ex-imperial villa. Save money—forego room w/bath for **hot spring indoor & outdoor baths!**
Near Fujiya is fine traditional **Nara-ya Ryokan** 20-room, 3-storey wooden inn nestled in expansive garden, perched above Hayakawa River valley. ¥-hi-Lw/2, ☎2-2411.

Spectacular sculpted garden with miniature waterfall and shrine spread down slope to...
DOGASHIMA, quiet wooded onsen right along river. Two moderate ryokan here (¥-Sw/2), ferroconcrete **Taisei-kan** ☎2-2281, and traditional **Yamato-ya** ☎2-2261 with riverside rock bath. Only 1 narrow road descends to Dogashima, but Yamato-ya has **private ropeway** (top near Nara-ya), Taisei-kan **private cablecar** (top 200m N of Miyanoshita stn) to shuttle guests.

From here, path follows Hayakawa River 1km up to...
SOKOKURA, easier reached by Rte138 which branches from Rte1 near Fujiya. **Bus** heading to Togendai from Odawara or Hakone-Yumoto stops at TSUTAYA-MAE. On other buses get off at **Miyanoshita-annai** (one after Fujiya) and 3min walk. Tho only across bridge from Miyanoshita, Sokokura far more isolated air. Only one ryokan: **Tsutaya** ☎2-2241; ¥-Tw/2, displays all 10 scrolls *Shichiyu no shiori*, 250-year-old illustrated guide book to 7 Baths.

KOWAKI-DANI 'Little Boiling Valley' in Mt Soun foothills, most modern of Hakone's onsen developed in 1950s, gets its name from its sulphur fumes. Recreational center of Hakone with game rooms, bowling alley, banquet halls, pools, and of course assorted spacious baths. Fujita Group's sprawling **Hotel Kowakien** ☎(0460)-2-4111 with W- (¥-S) and J- (¥-T-S-L) rooms is one of finest; fabulous Yutopia (*yu* = hot water + Utopia) baths include 13 outside *rotenburo* (can wear bathing suit or not, use baths only ¥2,000+¥500 kids), coffee bath ('you're the cream in my coffee…') but lacks charm of older establishments. Summer dine in garden *Gehinkan* to shakuhachi, lute music; also *kaiseki-ryori* dinner in garden villa *Kihin-kan* ¥15,000.

Just down road is smaller, traditional **Mikawa-ya** ☎2-2231, ¥-S-L, *Horai-en* Japanese garden mind-blowing in **May**, one of finest azalea-apreads anywhere: open to public, no fee; small **tea house** inside serves light meals.

GOHRA is secluded, forested, Swiss-like resort with Oriental flavor boasting numerous fine inns and hotels, including **Gohra Hotel** ☎(0460)-2-3111, once reserved for US Forces now open to all, still serves fine steaks, ¥-S-Lw/2. But our personal recommendation is traditional family-style small ryokan **Kinokuniya** ☎2-2446 ¥-Sw/2. Most exquisite is traditional **Kansui-ro** ¥-lo-Lw/2, ☎2-3141 in 10,000 *tsubo* (360,000m^2) garden. Another good traditional wood-built ryokan is **Ishikura** ¥-S, ☎2-2471.

Between Gohra and Lake Ashi are few somewhat secluded spas. Along **ropeway** (also reached by **bus, cab**): **UBAKO** has several fine hotels, inns with views of Lake Ashi below and Mt Fuji. Long established **Shumei-kan** has exquisite meals and spacious rock bath; ☎4-8478. Lower down, **Hakone Kanko Hotel** boasts top view, top rates. Friends on honeymoon had high marks for **Kagetsu-en** great view of lake from spacious observatory/bath halls. ¥-Sw/2, ☎4-8621.

ASHI-NO-YU, (along Rte1 btwn Kowaki-dani–Moto-Hakone), is quiet wooded hill onsen once only for noblity. Few inns: top is traditional **Matsuzaka-ya** ¥-S ☎(0460)-3-6511.

If staying up at Lake Ashi, better at eastern end **MOTO-HAKONE**. Separate from main cluster is **Yamano Hotel**, former palatial manse of Baron Iwasaki, who liked to build grand with gardens to match; ¥-S-Lw/2, ☎3-6321. Further along N shore is wooded *Hakone-en* park and superb **Prince Hotel** complex, main building with separate cottages; traditional Japanese annex **Ryugu-den** 'Dragon Palace': W-bedrooms ¥-S-twin w/2; annex ¥-L ☎3-7111. Closer to pier **Matsuzaka-ya** ☎3-6315, **Hotel Ashinoko-en** ☎3-6341 both ¥-Sw/2. Several ryokan in ¥-B-T range but **budgeteer** does better at minshuku: 3-dozen scattered around Hakone, mostly at lake, Gohra, Sengokubara. Half draw water from hot springs, many near lake have fishing boats, gear for rent. Only one **Youth Hostel** Hakone Soun-zan at Gohra, ¥-P. 3-campgrounds around lake, open only summer with rental tents and cabins as well.

SIGHTSEEING: Most visitors to Hakone come mainly to bathe, some make short tour of lake area. But there is much more to see for those with extra day. Around Hakone-Yumoto are several fine temples.

500m S of stn…
SOUN-JI built 1521 as temple of Odawara's Hojo clan, has many treasures such as Tiger & Dragon painted on sliding doors.

5min W along old pedestrian Tokaido…
JOGAN-JI built 1181 to honor Soga brothers, tragic heroes whose attempts to avenge father's death is source of many kabuki, bunraku plays. In back, **Soga-do** hall contains statues of pair.

In foothills 30min walk N of Tonosawa stn is…
AMIDA-JI with beautiful soaring thatched roof. Many stone Buddhas line path leading to this secluded temple sitting amidst field of azaleas.

Closer to beaten trail are 2 museums:

Chokoku-no-mori Forest of Sculpture or **Hakone Open-Air Museum**, over 100 works of Western (Rodin, etc) and Japanese artists on permanent display. Finer ones are in special hall, outside are dozens of modern sculptures. 300+ paintings in another hall; at far back **Picasso Hall**, opened July '84, displays his works in various media. Complex open daily 9:00-17:00 (to 16:00 Nov-Feb), ¥1,000. 10min walk from **Gohra**, 2min by bus or train to **Chokoku-no-mori** stn.

10min walk uphill from Gohra stn (4min cablecar to Koen-kami) is...

Hakone Art Museum with over 100 excellent examples of Japanese pottery from earliest times thru 15th century. Opened 1952, its founder Okada Mokichi heads *Sekai Kyoseikai*, one of several modern Shintoist sects who believe human spirit is 'elevated thru direct contact with art and beauty.' Surrounding it is fabulous bamboo-moss garden, tucked away in corner is one-time residence of Mr. Okada. *See* also their fabulous MOA Museum in Atami, preceding, (p244): 9:30-16:00 X-thur, ¥500adult/¥ 200child.

Just below museum is...

Hakone Park, French-style garden opened 1914. On grounds are tropical birdhouse, arboretums for tropical and mountain plants—not really worth ¥800 admission, but worth seeing is its **Hakuun-do Tea Garden** tucked away in back, ¥200, with 3 classic tea houses representing recent Meiji, Taisho and Showa eras. Established 1922 by Hara Tomitaro founder of Yokohama's Sankei-en garden. Additional ¥300 gets you tea and sweet cakes.

Most popular sightseeing route: Ropeway from **GOHRA** → **Lake Ashi W** end, stop en route to see *Owaki-dani*, **Great Boiling Valley** most recent Hakone's many volcanic eruptions. Though landscape hellish, smoke volume has decreased over years as more hotels draw water from it. Nonetheless, short stroll from ropeway stn puts you in middle of enough hellish fumes. While those of Noboribetsu in Hokkaido or Beppu and Unzen in Kyushu are far more impressive, this is only hell in central Japan. Natural Science Museum of area near stn. Owaki-dani offers superb view of Mt Fuji.

Many **ferries** cross lake from northern **TOGENDAI** to **MOTO-HAKONE** and **HAKONE-MACHI**; some gaudy 'replicas' of galleons and paddle-wheel steamers. Smaller boats run from **KOJIRI** 500m S of Togendai stopping along N shore at **Jumoku-en** and **Hakone-en parks**, Moto-Hakone, Hakone-machi. Lake offers water sports; motor boats, skis, rowboats, sailboats for rent. It abounds in bass and trout, popular with anglers. Beaches poor, but good swimming off boats. Trail circles lake 20km, road also follows N shore Togendai to Hakone.

40min walk around lake's eastern end...

Fukara Yosui water tunnel passing under Hakone Mountains to Fukara village. Brain-child of Fukara village chief who convinced Shogunate that water from Lake Ashi would improve harvest for entire valley. Digging from both ends, this meter-wide 1,342m long tunnel was completed 4 years later. Project required 83,000 laborers at cash cost of 7,300 gold *ryo* — with approx value then of one *ryo* =15gms gold, gold equivalent 1989 = ¥300,000,000.

During Tokugawa era, Hakone was main *Seki-sho*-Barrier Gate on Tokaido to watch for *iri-teppo to de-onna*—guns going into Edo, women going out, both signs of possible rebellion. Unwanted and unneeded symbol of Edo feudalism, Hakone's *seki-sho* was razed soon after Meiji Restoration, but in 1965 part reconstructed as museum and historical asset: N of **Hakone-machi pier**, main structure *Goban-sho*—inspection room with kimono'd mannequins posing searches of suspects and other less pleasant events here. Nearby **head-washing well** for those caught trying to evade barrier– their bodies stayed behind at chopping block.

Hakone Exhibit Hall on site of original Barrier, displays early Edo era items ranging from farm implements to armor. Also old local maps and plan of Barrier. Daily 9:00-16:30, ¥150.

Next is...

Hakone Detached Palace Garden, 16,000m² promontory out into Lake Ashi for another great view of Fuji soaring above Hakone hills. Built 1887 as Imperial Household villa, opened to public 1946.

Parallel to Rte1 between Palace Garden and Moto-Hakone is famed photogenic...

Cryptomeria Avenue of trees planted 1618 by local lord MATSUDAIRA Tadatsuna to mark founding of Hakone-juku, officially sanctioned stop along Tokaido. Also served practical purpose—providing cool, shady path for travellers in summer, kept it free of snow in winter and made swordplay difficult. Many cut down early Meiji, but over 400 towering trees remain along 800m section, now National Treasures.

500m from Moto-Hakone on N shore lies...

HAKONE GONGEN SHRINE built 757 by Buddhist saint Mangan. Always popular with samurai Hakone Gongen became official shrine of samurai following Minamoto Yoritomo's visit, and prominent center of mixed Shinto-Buddhism. Both roles ended with Meiji Restoration when warrior class was abolished and nationalism forced clear-cut separation of Buddhism and Shinto. Purge of Buddhism led to removal of many shrine treasures. Those that survived housed in **Treasure Hall** (9:00-16:00, X-rainy days only, ¥200). Massive red torii newly erected on shore commemorates Japan-US peace and friendship.

Part of Tokaido, called Hakone-kaido, follows Sukumo-gawa River 9.6km...

YUMOTO–MOTO-HAKONE, 4hrs walk up, most people take easier downhill (2hr30min). Bus runs course in 55min stopping at all main sites mentioned; taxi Moto-Hakone → Yumoto via Hatajuku 6x-mtrs with stop at Yosegi Kaikan. 4 legs of trail are original Hakone-kaido footpath, paved with rocks (*ishi-datami*) facilitating climb.

Dotted with historical sights...

Amazake-chaya, (30min down), reconstructed Edo period wayside **tea-house** provides refreshment. Next to it is **Historical Museum** (9:00-16:00 daily, ¥50) introduces life & customs on old hiway.

Further down...

Hatajuku Hamlet still retains some Edo house facade, but better known for its *Hakone-zaiku,* combination of inlaid and mosaic marquetry. Highly skilled craft originated around Odawara in early Heian period, but main centers of production soon moved into hills for easier access to materials. Two main forms are *hiki-mono* (plates and bowls made on lathe) and *sashi-mono* (small boxes). Latter includes 'magic boxes' with hidden compartments. Sold throughout Hakone, entire process can be seen at **Hatajuku Yosegi Kaikan** daily 9:00-17:00.

Trail continues 1km, 15mins to **Sukumo-gawa** hamlet; last section (1hr by foot) is on bus road, ending at SOUN-JI temple.

Between MOTO-HAKONE and ASHINOYU more relics of pedestrian days. At foot of Futagoyama pass (now Rte1), cluster of rock-carved Buddhist images, stone pagodas, 1300-1312, to ensure safe crossing of pass. Nearby is cluster of 25 bodhisattvas; 2 massive stone monuments mark graves of tragic Soga brothers of kabuki fame.

Hiking Trails of all lengths abound in mountains. 20min above **Fujiya Hotel** to Fuji View Platform on Mt Asama. Most popular long trail, relatively easy, is *Yuzaka-michi trail* 4.5km Hakone-Yumoto to Mt Asama whence 3 trails down to Miyanoshita (1km), Kowaki-dani (1km), Ashinoyu (3km). Another crosses from Gohra to Owaki-dani or to Komagatake peak whence ropeway to Hakone-en or cablecar to Ashinoyu. Other circles most of lake, E 3rd is road. Any map of area shows trails, all well marked.

PERSONAL DATEBOOK: Autumn's colors reach their peak as all of Hakone prepares for one of Japan's top fetes, *Daimyo Gyorestu* Nov 3. 180 men and women in costumes of retainers accompany feudal lord in colorful re-enactment typical Edo era procession. Fireworks 10:00 start off 5hr parade; route Soun-ji Temple–Sarukawa Bridge–Nanpo Inn–Katakura-Yumoto and Homare Bridge on old Tokaido to Sanmiso Inn in front of stn, thru Shinmei-cho, back to Soun-ji Temple. Daimyo Gyoretsu dates back to time of 3rd Tokugawa Shogun Iemitsu (ruled 1623-32) who implemented policy of *sankin kotai*—alternate residence in which lord spent half each year in Edo, wife or children other half..Thinly disguised hostage system ensured peace in provinces as lord never home long enough to plot, and family held in Edo guaranteed compliance rest of time. Hakone Barrier checking women going out was to make sure no wife held in Edo sneaked back in disguise. Semi-annual trips to Edo were enormous drain on provincial coffers impoverishing any revolts, but boon to road-side economy. Three main foes of Tokugawa: Tosa, Choshu, Satsuma clans, had costliest trips coming from far S with large processions to flaunt their claimed-status. During 360 years of Tokugawa rule only one clan was exempt from this costly trip—Matsumae of southern Hokkaido. Festival, started 1935 by Yumoto's citizens, re-enacts march of Odawara's ruling Ohkubo family. **Jul 15** kicks off summer festivals with *Yudachi Shishi-mai* lion dances at Miyagino Suwa Shrine (2km W of Miyanoshita). Gives thanks for abundant hot springs and hot spa water sprinkled around with bamboo leaves ensures healthy year. **31** *Kosui Matsuri* Lake Festival at Lake Ashi is Hakone Shrine's main event. Special red rice and saké dedicated to Kuzuryu-myojin, 9-headed dragon enshrined at Kuzuryu Jinja S of Kojiri. 31st night Shrine head priest rows out to deliver offerings as spectacular fireworks burst overhead, thousands of lighted lanterns set afloat.

Aug 5 *Torii Matsuri* offering light to Dragon, highlighted by burning of two 5m tall wood torii built on water and floating of 1,000 lighted lanterns. **Aug 2-3** *Taiko Hyotan Matsuri*, Miyanoshita marks Hideyoshi Odawara attack. **Aug 16** another fire festival *Daimonji-yaki* nitemarks end of O-bon, send-off spirits. Takes after Kyoto's Daimonji-yaki, 110m x 162m character of *Dai* lit at 19:40 on side of 924m Mt Myojogadake accompanied by massive fireworks display visible from all onsen areas, **best viewed** from Gohra Park or Soun-zan. Dances and other folk entertainment around Gohra stn.

Warning: To stay during these festivals, book rooms at least 2 months in advance.

5km beyond Gohra...

SENGOKU-HARA boasts trio of golf courses which expose you to view sure to distract your putting. Unlike rest of mountainous Hakone, Sengoku-Hara is wide plateau in long extinct, filled-in crater lake. Warmed from below, 50,000m^2 of marsh wild flowers break out in colors May-July. In autumn acres of *susuki* pampas grass blossom white in sharp contrast to red and gold leaves creeping downhill.

WHERE TO STAY: Another cluster of fine inns and hotels scattered among 5 hot springs, mostly in central **SENGOKU ONSEN**. Finest of old traditional inns, ryokan **Hyoseki-kaku** in foothills; ¥-Sw/2, ☎(0460)-4-8531. J-style **Hakone Koshien** outdoor bath ¥-Sw/2, ☎(0460)-4-8561. Also several ¥-B ryokan, dozen minshuku.

Hakone has many relics of Japan's earlier cultures; several *Jomon* sites have been excavated around Miyanoshita while later *Yayoi* settled Sengoku-bara. One excavation on permanent display is **OHARA ISEKI.**

Car buffs will find 28 rare Porsches at **Porsche Museum** near Botanical Garden.

WHERE NEXT: This is also your **take-off-point** for circuit of Mt Fuji and Five Lakes. Approximate *chugata* **cab** rates from other Hakone areas to here are: MIYANOSHITA 7km 3x-basic mtr, GOHRA 5km 2x-mtr; KOWAKI-EN 10km 5-6x-mtr, MOTO-HAKONE 20km 10x-mtr On to Gotemba is 16km over magnificent Nagao 'Long Tail' Pass, taxi 7-8x-mtr, **bus** 1hr ¥840 (shave off 6km and much time via Otome Pass toll road).

From Sengoku-bara, additional 21km, bus 40min ¥730, taxi 22x-mtr to first of...

FIVE LAKES OF FUJI FUJI GO-KO

CIRCLING NORTH around Mt Fuji, 5 lakes (E-W) of *Yamanaka*, *Kawaguchi*, *Sai*, *Shoji*, *Motosu* offer year-round recreation–swimming, boating of all sorts, fishing, camping in summer; smelt-fishing all year breaking thru ice, ice skating in winter. Lakes formed by Fuji's eruptions of which 18 major ones recorded, greatest being 800AD, 864 and November 22, 1707–latter continuing intermittently until December 4, 1707 covering Edo-Tokyo in 6 inches of ash. Prehistoric eruption sealed off several rivers, forced up subterranean water to form 2 large lakes *Utsu-ko* (E) and *Seno-umi* (W). 800AD blast split *Utsu-ko* into present *Yamanaka* and *Oshino*, and *Motosu* separated from *Seno-umi; Kawaguchi* also appeared. 864 blast cut *Seno-umi* into *Shoji* and *Sai*– even now 3 lakes originally *Seno-umi* have same surface levels. Fuji is not extinct, only dormant. Plans to build new capital on Tokyo-side slope abandoned in 1963 out of fear of future blows. Many seem to expect blow soon; pointing to mystery rise of Lake Kawaguchi surface by over 2 meters 1982-83 said to be caused by increased volcanic activity-—2 years during which Kawaguchi did not freeze either. In World War II, USAF talked of bombing it into activity.

GETTING AROUND: Circle all lakes easily in few hours by cab (about 33-35x-mtr; ¥10,000 extra to go part way up Fuji), or full day bus (local and tour). Local cab companies have many hire-car tours from few hours to few days to cover all or part of region, as well as *Koshu-kaido* (*see*); or make your own itinerary, 7-8x-mtr per hr. With many young people driving, Garet had no trouble hitching; excellent roads make it easy to self-drive area. GOTEMBA-(16km)-YAMANAKA-(13km)-KAWAGUCHI-(15km)-SAI-(5km)-SHOJI-(4km)-MOTOSU-(30km)-FUJINOMIYA.

Warning to drivers: road circling lakes is Rte138 to E of Fuji-Yoshida, Rte139 to its W. FUJI-YOSHIDA has most car-rental agencies: Nippon, Toyota (best 2), Fujimi, and more. At 4 people per car, cab or rental cheaper than bus tours.

Bus Tours: *Fuji Kyuko* Company financed most of area's development, hotels to amusement parks, has virtual monopoly on local bus tours. *Fujita* runs out of Tokyo. Either can be arranged thru JTB, most Japanese travel agents, hotel desks or call direct Fujikyu Tokyo office ☎(03)-3374-2221. Fujikyu also has local booking offices at Gotemba, Fuji-Yoshida, Mishima, Fuji cities, Yamanaka and Kawaguchi lakes. Some *start/end* at MISHIMA heading clockwise via Gotemba or FUJI clockwise via Fujinomiya; sadly most overnighters spend night at gaudiest Kawaguchi. On our routing, best are those starting YAMANAKA—avoid stopping Fujikyu Highland amusement park, best seen solo if at all.

But having come this far, it would be shame not to spend night soaking in large bath with spectacular view of sun setting behind Mt Fuji. Some spas more built-up than others, but all have lodgings from ¥-L to minshuku. Tokyo-ites coming to lakes usually go direct to central FUJI-YOSHIDA (set between Yamanaka and Kawaguchi). But on our route down Tokaido from Hakone or Izu-Numazu we circle whole quintet in order, *starting from...*

GOTEMBA just beyond Hakone outer mountains. From NUMAZU 40min JR Gotemba Line express; from TOKYO 2hr bus or JR special direct express *Gotemba-go*; From Shinjuku 1hr45min by bus; or train on combi-JR/Odakyu Private Lines' special express *Asagiri-go*, 1991 new double-decker Bullet-like speedy trains extended Shinjuku–Gotemba–Numazu in 2hrs. Not much here to see, but one way to ascend Mt Fuji.

Some places to spend few extra hours: **Intestinal Cave** *Inno Otainai* 7km W (20min bus). Formed by lava flows from Fuji, U-shaped cave is entered thru 'small intestines' passing thru other 'organs' and out thru 'birth canal'. 155m tunnel has interesting rock formations, but bring **flashlight** as not lit. Adventurer ought buy good one in Gotemba since Fuji area abounds in caves, and need one to climb mountain. Park (8:30-17:00, ¥100) contains several more lava-carved caves among hundreds of high altitude trees from Fuji-Hakone area. Don't be too surprised to hear or see cannon fire in distance—Otainai Park is in middle of Self Defense Force Gotemba Training Ground, maneuvers and mock battles held occasionally.

One of largest and earliest caves discovered, **Komakado Fuketsu** extends several hundred meters into base of Fuji in two branches. Dark and cool (constant 13°C) it harbors several species of pale, eyeless creatures. Open daily 9:00-17:00, ¥200; 15min S of Gotemba stn on Mishima-bound **bus**, or 1km walk SW of JR FUJIOKA stn (2 stops S).

FOR AUTOMOBILE ADDICTS: Race fans will find world-class Fuji Speedway 7km N of Gotemba. National and international races from motorcycles to Formula-1 (most notably *Fuji Grand Prix* **May**), pro as well as amateur. Non-race days anybody may use 4.4km course; also have go-carts. 30min on Ueno-bound bus to track's subgate-**FUJI REI-EN**. Direct buses race days. Open 9:00-17:00 X-tues; ¥500 weekdays, ¥1,000 weekends, higher on race days.

Jul 27-29 Kakutori Jinja near FUJI REI-EN has *Wind Festival* in which sacred *shimé-nawa* ropes are trailed around rice paddies as prayer to stop harsh winds which occasionally blow, ruining new rice crop ripening August.

Sports Car Museum SW of Gotemba stn Rte138 (HAKONE-bound bus to NINO-OKA) has numerous rare sportcars from all over; same owner Sengoku-bara Porsche Museum, 9:00-18:00, ¥1,000. **Fuji Motor Museum** between stn and speedway has over 100 old and new racing motorbikes, 10:00-17:00, ¥1,000.

But rather than dawdle here midst what we have more of at home...*on to lakes.*

LAKE YAMANAKA-KO: Highest at 980m, air rarely gets hotter than 25°C/ 87F, and largest of 5—about same size as Lake Ashi but with fine sand beaches. This lake and Kawaguchi are southernmost habitat of *marimo*, rare spherical free-floating algae first discovered (and in greater numbers) in Hokkaido's Lake Akan. Discovered by Yamanaka Middle School's headmaster, Fuji-*marimo* are smaller than their more famous Hokkaido cousins and can only be seen coddled in some few private aquariums like one at **Asahigaoka Drive-in**.

ASAHIGA-OKA on S shore for most inns; **tour boats** around lake (30min, ¥700), rentals of row-, sail-, motor-boats, water-skis. In winter, NE 'hook' of lake near HIRANO hamlet is huge outdoor ice-skating rink. Some dozen campsites, most near Asahigaoka. Two minshuku 'villages' at E and W ends of lake with almost 100 **budget** inns between them ¥-Bw/2; W end (also called *Tennis Village*) most minshuku, hundreds of tennis courts. S are numerous *pensiones* ¥-Bw/2. **Hotel Mount Fuji** ☎(0555)-62-2111 one of oldest and finest hotels among 5 lakes atop 1102m Oshitsu peak NW shore of Yamanaka. As name boasts, *raison d'etre* is to offer grand view of famous mountain, and if you cannot get glimpse during your stay, room fees (except food) will be refunded: ¥-hi-S-Lw/2. Lodgings in all price ranges arranged through **Kanko-annai**, Asahigaoka.

En route Kawaguchi is main town Fuji-Yoshida and...
OSHINO ONSEN–alias Fuji Onsen, one of few hot springs around. 10min bus from Asahigaoka, 20min from Fuji-Yoshida, pleasant alternative to lakes. Main attraction is *Oshino Hakkai* 'Eight Seas', actually small lakes around which numerous rustic thatched-roof houses, barns and water-wheel sheds recall days when it was one of Fuji's prime farm communities. **Eight ponds**: *Choshi*-Sake Cup, *Deguchi*-Outlet, *Waku*-Boiling, *Shobu*-Iris, *Kagami*-Mirror, *Okama*-Pot, *Sokonuke*-Bottomless and *Nigori*-Muddy can be circled in hour (stops included), which devout pilgrims did as part of Mt Fuji pilgrimage. And this was but part of greater 'Eight Bodies of Water' pilgrimage, including this as one, plus Five Lakes and 2 smaller ones near Fuji-Yoshida. Tho hardly anyone does full pilgrimage anymore, numerous trails circle Five Lakes area; **Tokai Nature Trail** from Hirano passes thru Oshino taking inside course around lakes ending near Fujinomiya. Best sections to hike are Hirano to Oshino (10km); Sai to Shoji.

Oshino is just N off Rte138, some **buses** detour around Oshino area, others let off at
OSHINO IRIGUCHI stop for 10min walk to Oshino Onsen, 1.5km further to Oshino
Hakkai. Most lodgings are along Katsura-gawa River or around Eight Lakes. Only hotel,
Oshino Fujikyu, ¥-T-Sw/2, is at onsen, many traditional ryokan ¥-Tw/2 as well as
over 40 minshuku, mostly around ponds can be booked thru **Information Centers** at
FUJI-YOSHIDA stn or ASAHIGAOKA.

FUJI-YOSHIDA: Until buses (and taxis) began to climb to Mt Fuji 5th
Stn, this was 2nd largest base for trek up, teeming with white-clad pilgrims.
Now, most pass thru here on way around lakes or catch bus up Fuji; place to pick up last-
minute supplies for climb. Tokyo-ites stop here for big **Fujikyu Highland
amusement park** (9:00-17:00, X-tues, year-end; extended summer hrs, ¥1,200/adult
¥600/child hols, ¥1,000/500 weekdays.

Otherwise only place to see here is 15min walk SW of stn...
SENGEN JINJA shrine properly *Kitaguchi Hongu Fuji Asama Jinja*, Fuji
North Base Asama Main Shrine. Enshrined is *Konohana-sakuya-himé-no-
mikoto*, spirit of Mt Fuji. Sengen shrines located in almost every town and
village around Fuji are all *ge-gu*, outer sanctums (main at Fujinomiya) from
which begin trails up Fuji. *Nai-gu*, inner sanctum is on summit. This
Sengen shrine is oldest, built 788AD. Main event, *Fire Festival* **Aug 26-27**
originally was to appease mountain and prevent further eruptions by substituting sacred
fires for real thing. Now marks end official climbing season in one of Japan's most
spectacular summer-end festivals. Hordes gather from all over, and even with several
hundred lodgings around Five Lakes district, rooms can be hard to find so book ahead or
camp. Main event begins afternoon of 26th transporting 1.25 ton red lacquered Fuji-
shaped *mikoshi* from shrine thru town to special 'resting' spot. As sun sets, 3m-tall
torches lit thruout town, massive bonfires lit simultaneously all mountain huts giving
illusion Mt Fuji afire. Climax 18:00-22:00. **27th** mikoshi is carted back to shrine,
blessed and stored till next year.

LAKE KAWAGUCHI-KO: (6min train or 10min bus from Fuji-Yoshida),
most popular tourist spot around. Easiest to get to for Tokyo-ites, gateway for
drive up Fuji, Kawaguchi is all glitter. Scenic toll road bridges lake, teeming with all
sorts of craft filled to overflowing with vacationers. Do not suggest staying here; comfort
can be had at Yamanaka's **Hotel Mt Fuji**, and budget, peace and quiet at other lakes.

Of 5, this alone has island, *U-noshima*, **CORMORANT ISLE**, with fair
swimming and campsite. **Funatsu** at SE tip and **Ubugaya-saki** across bridge are
main centers cluttered with hotels and lights, but we circle around N shore to quiet
hamlets of **Hirose** and **Oishi**.

Kawaguchi's **SENGEN SHRINE** built 865AD after 2nd great eruption.
10min bus N from Kawaguchi-ko stn to Kawaguchi-kyoku mae and 10min walk N.
Drivers, up Rte137, R at Kawaguchi-kyoku bus stop, next L. Tho shrine is not special
(rebuilt 1605), but has rare offering of shrine dances by girls under 10 years old. *Chigo-
mai* **Apr 25** and **Jul 28** started same year as shrine to appease spirit of Fuji.
You may want to take quick stop at Funatsu for different sort of folk museum. **Fuji
Museum** along main lakeside hotel row is beautiful traditional mountain farmhouse; 1st
floor has over 10,000 folk items from area. Then upstairs (which those easily offended
should avoid; closed to under 18) is *Amano Collection of sexual folk items*— many quite
humorous. Daily 8:30-16:00, ¥50 +¥350 extra for Amano Collection.

LAKE SAI-KO: Clear, dark blue to 100m depth, least developed. Only 3
inns, minshuku villages S & W (Neba) shores, many secluded campsites amid dense
forests. En route Lake Shoji is *Jukai* or **Sea of Trees** in Aokigahara. 64km² dense
primeval forest teeming with wildlife, 2nd most completely natural area in Japan: even
most experienced avoid going too deep in for fear of never emerging— ever since heroine
of novel *Tower of Waves* wandered in to commit suicide at least 20 bodies are found every
year. Few well-marked trails thru; one Shoji → Fuji summit, another Sai → Shoji via
interesting caves.

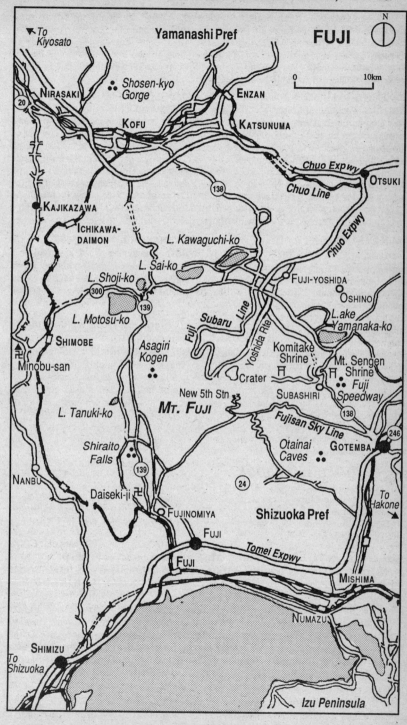

FUJI

N

To Kiyosato

Yamanashi Pref

0   10km

Shosen-kyo Gorge

NIRASAKI

ENZAN

20

KOFU

KATSUNUMA

Chuo Expwy

Chuo Line

OTSUKI

138

Chuo Expwy

KAJIKAZAWA

ICHIKAWA-DAIMON

L. Kawaguchi-ko

L. Sai-ko

FUJI-YOSHIDA

OSHINO

L. Shoji-ko

300

139

L. Motosu-ko

Subaru Line

Lake Yamanaka-ko

Fuji

Yoshida Rte

SHIMOBE

Minobu-san

Asagiri Kogen

Komitake Shrine

Mt. Sengen Shrine

Fuji Speedway

Crater

New 5th Stn

SUBASHIRI

138

MT. FUJI

L. Tanuki-ko

Fujisan Sky Line

Otainai Caves

GOTEMBA

246

Shiraito Falls

139

To Hakone

NANBU

24

Daiseki-ji

FUJINOMIYA

Shizuoka Pref

FUJI

FUJI

Tomei Expwy

MISHIMA

NUMAZU

SHIMIZU

To Shizuoka

Izu Peninsula

Just S of Lake Sai, 10min walk from minshuku village, is 386m-long *Komori-ana* **Bat Cave**—where fuzzy fliers are protected as national natural treasures. Another bat cave 2.5km SE at Narusawa just off Rte139. 1.5km E of Bat Cave#2 on Rte139 is **Narusawa Lava Cylinders**, formed by lava cooling around tree trunks which burned leaving hollow centers. Varying in size, these Special Natural Monuments can be found thruout Aokigahara area, tho in lesser numbers.

20min further S of bat cave #1 is **Dragon God's Cave** *Ryugu-dokutsu* with ancient shrine dedicated to Sai dragon god. Recent landslide closed it off—may reopen? Lake Sai's Dragon Festival **Aug 2** begins with offerings here for rain, followed by prayers and offerings from ancient dragon-boat on lake, then night fireworks. 15m S is **Ice Cave**, *Narusawa Hyoketsu* and nearby **Wind Cave**, *Fugaku Fuketsu* formed by lava in one of 9th century eruptions. Dark interior of both constantly near freezing with unusual columns of natural ice several feet tall of various thicknesses. During Edo period Ice Cave used to store ice-compacted snow from Fuji for Shogun's summer pleasure, rushed to Edo at his will. Far rear of Wind Cave (discovered 1909) is used by Yamanashi Prefecture as natural cold storage for tree seeds. Both charge ¥150 admission (8:00-17:00 X-Dec-Feb), and can be easily reached few min walk from respective bus stops on Rte139.

LAKE SHOJI-KO: U-shaped, ringed by mountains on 3 sides, Sea of Trees filling 4th– by far smallest, shallowest. Abundance of plankton makes it angler's paradise; top anglers vie for 1,000 spots in late April *Lake Opening* contest. Other times relatively quiet with only two dozen budget minshuku and few small ryo-tels of which **Shoji Lake Hotel** ¥6,000w/2 boasts 3rd floor bath-observatory. Coolest of 5 lakes, top 20°C.

LAKE MOTOSU-KO: Deepest lake, 138m, clearest water and no visible outlet would be as quiet as Lake Sai except for motorboat racers' training school on SW shore. Main center is E end just off Rte139, with few stores and only six minshuku here. Motosu village was major junction in old pedestrian Kaido highway (now Rte300), with its now-gone barrier. Many old *minka* folk houses remain, giving ancient air in spite of modern gift shops. These houses have unusual roofs with *chigi*-crossed beams usually found only on shrines, prehistoric Yayoi houses. More of village's historic past found in rustic **OYAMA JINJA** shrine near barrier-remains and **KOGAN-JI** temple, E. Several campsites along secluded N shore, **Koan-so** inn and all-year **campsite** lies in beautiful secluded cove on NW shore, promontory to its S cuts off sight and sound of boat racers.

PERSONAL DATEBOOK: **Aug 3** lake fete starts with usual blessing ritual then water-ski contest, fireworks. **May 17** Oyama Shrine relives 150-year-old *Daimyo Gyoretsu* feudal costume parade. Excellent short hike to 1,328m **Panorama hill** btwn Motosu & Shoji, 1hr from either, **grand view** of all 5 lakes, Mt Fuji, Kofu plateau to N, Japan Alps beyond. S from Lake Motosu over Ishiwari pass we enter Shizuoka prefecture, 10km to...

ASAGIRI KOGEN, 'Morning Mist' Plateau, with several prefectural parks, more caves and Jumbo Golf Course. In middle is Asia's largest trout farm *Ken-ei Fuji Yoson-jo* 100,000m² with over one million trout, one-fifth released or shipped out annually. Separated by size into 120 ponds, you can lunch on these well-fed trout catching them yourself along Shibakawa River meandering thru wooded park ¥1,000 per kg, or have them caught for you. Prepared to your taste sashimi, *shio-yaki* (broiled whole with salt), butter-yaki or deep-fried fillets. Any way, served in *Masu-no-Ie* **Trout House** restaurant, exquisite soaring thatch-roofed *Gassho-zukuri* mountain farm house. Grounds open 9:00-16:30, ¥200, Masu-no-Ie X-thur.

3km N at Asagiri Green Park...
Makigari Honjin restaurant serves Daimyo Course—trout, mutton grilled on iron plate ¥1,000-2,000—modeled loosely on Yoritomo's *makigari* hunt/feast outing. Inns and campsites here, but **campers** would do better at man-made TANUKI-KO lake 3km S of trout farm.

15min bus S of Tanuki (24km from Motosu) IS *Shiraito-no-taki* **White Thread Waterfall**, said to be 1000 streams falling 20 meters, across width of 200m. Few min walk E, thundering *Otodomé-no-taki* **Silent Waterfall** plummets 30m into deep pool. Area famous not only for falls but also as climax to Soga brothers' saga: waiting 18 years they caught father's murderer Kudo Suketsune here. Otodome falls said to have gone silent at moment of their revenge; nearby is cave where brothers hid waiting for Kudo.

15 km on... **FUJINOMIYA** site of **FUJI SENGEN HONGEN** main shrine 2hr40min from Tokyo by Tokaido JR express, change at Fuji stn for 20min on Minobu line. Mainly base to climb Fuji, town has little to see other than shrine 500m NW of stn. Accenting shrine's dominance, huge red lacquered **torii** stands outside stn, built 806 (rebuilt 1604 by Tokugawa Ieyasu), unusual form basis for *sengen-zukuri* style of shrine architecture. Tho located in mid town, large complex is quiet, with Wakutama lake from where early pilgrims took water for climb up Fuji. **May 4-6** *Yabusame* mounted archery contests held since 1193 when Yoritomo started it during *makigari*-hunting expedition around Fuji. Small but ancient **MURAYAMA SENGEN** shrine (25min bus NE of town to Murayama village) built 702, visited by Sakano-ue Tamura-maro on way to fight Ainu; interesting mix of Shinto and Buddhism shown in only 2 remaining structures– main **Sanctuary**, and **Dainichi-do** hall dedicated to Dainichi buddha of light.

Yoritomo had his *makigari*-feast near village of **KARIJUKU** between town and Lake Tanuki-ko, 40min bus to **SHIRAITO** via Kamijo. 1.2km downstream Shiraito falls; 800m walk W from Karijuku Iriguchi stop on Rte139, E of bus stop is **SOGA SHRINE**. Much of grand mansion built here for feast remains. Many visit in spring for blossom of 1,000-year-old pink-budded white-flowered sakura to which Yoritomo tethered his horse.

En route is...(via Shinkansen → Shin Fuji stn, then bus ¥900 or taxi 9x-mtr)... **DAISEKI-JI**: one of 5 Nichiren temples around Fuji, built 1290 by disciple of St Nichiren as main temple of *Nichiren Shoshu*-True Nichiren. Little remains of original but **gate**; its **Main Hall** built postwar by donations is reputed largest religious hall anywhere, fascinating modern architecture.

Fuji Museum of ancient art; superb collection J- and Chin, also top loan shows; nearby branch **International Folk Art Museum–**Art Museum 8:30-17:00, ¥650–(¥1,000 spec show), FolkArt ¥200, both ¥700; X-26th-2nd. In 1930 MAKIGUCHI Jojiro branched from mainline Nichiren Soshu to form new lay organization *Soka Gakkai*, Value Creating Society. Persecuted by state during World War II for pacifism, Makiguchi died in jail '44; SG has grown into largest single 'sect' in Japan with 8 million followers, 7% of populace. Propagate peace thru education, promotion of art & culture thru regional culture centers, universities Tokyo & LA, 'churches' in USA under S.G.I. (-International). In Japan also most expansion under SGI.

Taxi → Fuji 5th Stn o.w.1hr/17x-mtr, all year; advise in climb season only early am.

CLIMBING FUJI

PARTIAL ASCENT can be by taxi (from Fuji 17x-mtr o.w.), bus or horse. Kids, oldsters do it, meditation student recently did for *Guinness Book of Records* on pogo stick, tho how he hopped in gravel is to us beyond comprehension.

GETTING THERE: Other than by our main routing: TOKYO JR Chuo line Shinjuku → Kawaguchi-ko, whence connecting bus → 5th stn. Alternate, Fujikyu luxe reserved bus direct (daily from **Jul 8**) from TOKYO-HAMAMATSU-CHO terminal in World Trade Ctr (monorail stn) 08:15/¥2,340 via SHINJUKU (opp Keio DS), arr 5th stn 11:10. Other departures: SHINJUKU 07:45, 08:45 (above), 19:30/¥2,160; Return from 5th stn at 13, 14, 15:00 (☎3374-2221). **Bus tours**: JTB (☎3276-7777) Fuji-Hakone Full Day pickup major hotels, only visit 5th stn, lunch Lake Kawaguchiko, boat Lake Ashinoko → Odawara Shinkansen return: ¥18,540/14,110 child. **Fujita Travel** (☎3573-1011) **Fuji Country Tour** all bus→ 5th stn → Kawaguchiko lunch → Erinji temple ('old pond' into which Basho frog jumped) samurai exhibit → winery sampling → return hotel: ¥18,540/¥13,910 child. **Budgeteer** do 2 days under ¥5,000 all fares, fees, Tokyo return.

Our routing for hardy hiker: **Yoshida Rte** start Sengen Shrine 5hrs → 5th Stn, en route 1hr is left branch for longer picturesque hike via Takizawa Forest Road. Drive your own Jeep or off-road vehicle all way to Umagaeshi 1st Stn on Yoshida Rte possible, (horses formerly took one up this far, or further).

Since buses now take you to 5th Stn, on all routes except Yoshida Rte, unused lower hiking paths are becoming obliterated.

Alternative: bus from Lake Kawaguchi up → 5th Stn on Fuji Subaru Line (1hr), or taxi about 25x-mtr. Either route is crowded during climbing season **July 1–Aug 30.** *Don't* try climb out of season: acquaintances of ours years ago were blown off slopes and killed. Buses run 4/3-11/3.

Then, if you are glutton for punishment and believe old saw that there are 2 kinds of fools in our world: those who never climbed Fuji, those who've done it more than once...

CLIMB entails 10-15 miles of tough footwork, overnite on mountain (you could do it up and back in full 10hr day, 6 up-4 down, but prize of climb is sunrise view). 5 popular routes— Gotemba, Subashiri, Yoshida, Kawa-guchiko, Fujinomiya. Each is divided into 10 *go* (legs) of varying lengths, stn ends each. Bus to 5th Stn (taxi not advised in season–traffic jams), walk 2 or 3 stns to meet descending route.

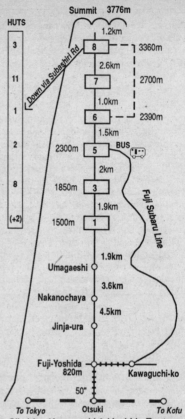

Climbing Kawaguchi & Yoshida Routes

Easiest: Yoshida, Kawaguchiko rtes which join at 6th Stn—recommended fun descent is *subashiri* sand-slide down 8th–5th stns; Gotemba rte also fun. Treeline ends 5th Stn. White 'poles' are trees killed by acid fog from Tokyo traffic. Sun scorches—backs of hands and neck need cover. *Subashiri* route up joins others at 8th Stn, from where it's steep 24° incline for kilometer.

Climb times: 5th → 6th Stn normally 30min; under 2hr to 8th Stn, then about same to summit at lofty low-oxygen 3,776meters/12,397ft. Climbers usually start early afternoon, reach 7th or 8th Stn before dark, sleep in *ishimuro* (stone huts) under ¥3,000 with 2 spartan meals. Then about 4am make dash up last leg to be on summit at sunrise.

Crater is 600m across at top, tapering to level bottom about 75m across. You can circuit crater in hour or so. Only simple shrine on top, but views make it worthwhile. Not flat rim, there are 8 minor peaks. Descent in is 230m (730ft), is more mountain climbing chore than outer climb, but it's possible. Crater is known as *Naiin* (sanctuary), supposedly regarded with special reverence. Japanese, however, joke it's becoming shallower every year—garbage bin for beer and juice cans, lunch wrappers carried up by 'nature lovers' who climb to admire pristine view. *Don't miss descent rtes.*

Few true pilgrims climb today, tho you see some, perhaps, in traditional white blouse, knickers and 'mushroom' hat, periodically reciting *rokkon shojo* (may 6 senses be purified). Average climber youth eager to escape stifling city, treat self to more challenge than balancing on daily rut.

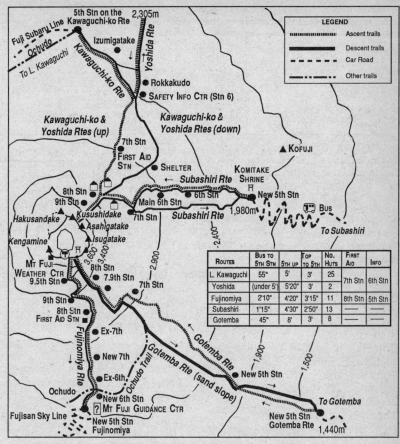

Climbing routes up Sacred Mount Fuji

ROUTES	BUS TO 5TH STN	5TH UP	TOP TO 5TH	NO. HUTS	FIRST AID	INFO
L. Kawaguchi	55"	5'	3'	25	7th Stn	6th Stn
Yoshida	(under 5')	5'20"	3'	2		
Fujinomiya	2'10"	4'20"	3'15"	11	8th Stn	5th Stn
Subashiri	1'15"	4'30"	2'50"	13	—	—
Gotemba	45"	8'	3'	8	—	—

One of our students on return wrote............... ah, me

    Gear must include *Kongo-zue*
(climbing staff), sold at bottom,
to brand for slight charge at each
stn, special brand at summit to
prove you did it. Wear high-top
shoes (which you'll probably toss away after scuffing from volcanic gravel)
which cover ankles. Sun glasses, and shade hat, kerchief to cover face,
back of neck, gloves or cloth to cover back of hands–all locally available.
Sun hot, little atmosphere to dilute it. Carry sweater, nite cold.

ah, me
sacred mt Fuji
from afar her slopes
glittering diamonds & stars
I climbed to gather this treasure
to find reflecting bottoms of beer cans

    Mount Fuji and hot springs since time immemorial objects of veneration,
which has changed in character from religious to mundane (if not profane),
but has not in any way diminished. Fuji is Ainu (some link it with Indo-
Aryan term for fire, as French *feu*). Ainu venerated mount. Supposedly rose
in single nite leaving cavity that formed Lake Biwa (Kyoto). In later ages
was so sacred that no woman could profane by setting foot on—first on
record to climb was Lady Parkes, wife of UK ambassador 1864. Even now
top is shrine. Its hot springs were also thought to embody deities and oldest
known were worshipped for restorative-medicinal qualities. Older public
spas still often have Shinto or folk-Buddhist shrines nearby.

ACCESS FROM TOKYO OR LOCAL

Climbing Route	Start	Via	Time to base	+ Bus to 6th Stn
Yoshida Rte	Shinjuku	JR Chuo L., Fuji Kyuko	2hrs	55min
Kawaguchiko Rte	"	JR Chuo L., Fuji Kyuko	2'30"	55"
	"	Bus	1'45"	55"
	"	Bus direct to 5th Stn		2'30"
Gotemba Rte	"	Odakyu "Asagiri" Express	1'45"	45"
	Tokyo Stn	JR Tokaido, Gotemba Line	2'30"	45"
Subashiri Rte	Gotemba	Bus to Subashiri Shrine	25"	50"
Mishima Rte	JR Mishima	Bus direct to 5th Stn		2'05"

WHERE NEXT: GO-KAIDO were 5 pedestrian main highways fanning out from Tokyo Nihonbashi and controlled directly by armed levies of shogunal central government at *sekisho*-barriers. TOKAIDO coast-road was of course main. Can detour here onto #2-NAKASENDO or KISO-KAIDO (p898). KOSHU-KAIDO, #3 (next, p271), went from Edo thru central Japan along southern Alps to join Nakasendo/Kiso-kaido at Shimo Suwa—today, JR Chuo-Line, Chuo-Expressway and Rte20 run parallel to obliterate most of antique footpath. (#4 NIKKO-KAIDO & #5 OSHU-KAIDO ran N from Edo as one, branching at Utsunomiya).

Most readers will continue Tokaido trek, *following*. Adventurer eager for bit of old Edo period pilgrimage should try **Samurai Byroad** up feudal Koshukaido pedestrian highway (*see* TOHOKU) as offbeat alternative from FUJI with links across Chubu inland to NAGOYA to rejoin historic Tokaido routing; **or** detour for more feudal hiway to TAKAYAMA; **or** MATSUMOTO where rail over mts to scenic reclusive TAKAYAMA to join another old Koshukaido segment back to NAGOYA, or on up JAPAN SEA COAST to KANAZAWA, either circling to TOKYO or continuing N to top of Honshu and HOKKAIDO. These choices of detours require anywhere from day-trips out of 5 Lakes stopover or Nagoya or treks of 2-3 days to weeks.

Well, we're up here, so what?

The people are generally courteous, affable and
full of compliments...feed not much upon varietie.
—Rev Arthur Hatch, 1625

SAMURAI BYROAD 甲州街道
FUJI & CHUBU KOSHU-KAIDO

SPECTACULAR Chubu Area is offbeat to Tokaido not just for adventurer-wanderer: anyone travelling Tokaido should take time to visit **at least part** especially if in Gifu-Inuyama. Usually visited by wanderers with time to spare travelling between Nagano–Tokyo, can see main sites in day-trips out of FIVE LAKES, or out of Nagoya or link with KISO-JI (p898) for continuous adventure thru olde Japan of samurai 2-sword Easterns. Several intelligent International Tours, designed for economy and variety now do part/s for fascinating firsthand view of 'real Japan'—which conservation of romantic antiquity made possible by another 'real Japan' of hard work and high tech.

KOSHU-KAIDO

PEDESTRIAN main artery in feudal days, one of GO-KAIDO, 5 highways fanning from Tokyo-Nihonbashi and controlled directly by shogunate thru armed men at *sekisho* barriers. TOKAIDO coast-road (p201) was main; later we detour on NAKASENDO or KISO-KAIDO/-JI (p898). KOSHU-KAIDO went from Edo thru central Japan along Southern Alps to join Nakasendo/ Kiso-ji at Shimo Suwa. Now JR Chuo Line, Chuo Expwy & Rte20 parallel to obliterate most of old KOSHU-KAIDO footpath. (Other 2 were NIKKO-KAIDO & OSHU-KAIDO running N from Edo as one road till forking at Utsunomiya).

TILT: Entering from top: Fuji-kyu Pvt Rail 1hr from Lake Kawaguchi → Otsuki (**driver** Rte139); or 90min **bus** Kawaguchi, Fuji-Yoshida (Rte137) or Shoji (Rte356) Lakes → KOFU; Lake Motosu → Minobu (Rte300). All 3 inter-connect by good roads, JR. Direct KOFU—SHINJUKU, JR express *Chuo Honsen*, Chuo main line, 2hrs.

Heading to TOKYO after 5 Lakes & Fuji, JR Minobu Line from Fujinomiya clockwise: 5 Lakes → KOFU → Yumura Onsen → Kiyosato → Otsuki → Sasago Onsen → Katsunuma wine country → Dai Bosatsu Toge pass → Isawa → ICHINOMIYA Sengen.

We'll be seeing quite bit of Takeda-clan-related sites, so some...
PERSONAL ORIENTATION: Known in feudal times as *Kai-no-kuni*, mountainous Yamanashi Pref N of Mt Fuji was home of once-contender for Shogunal honors, powerful Takeda clan branch of Minamoto exiled here to Kai by Taira, 12th cent. Off main stream of Japanese politics, Takeda were minor power until late 15th cent when 14th head Nobutora built Kofu castle, began to expand taking much of central Japan up to Nagano. Son Shingen (immortalized in KUROSAWA's 1983 film Shadow Warrior, *Kagemusha*) took over in 1541 to create most powerful army in Japan. Only Ieyasu and Nobunaga combined slowed Takeda juggernaut—they too would have failed had not Shingen died of illness, 1573. Knowing son Katsuyori was brave but tactically inept, his final order withdrew army home, hid death 3 years until grandson could rule. Foolish Katsuyori attacked Nobunaga. Victorious, he over-extended and 15,000 finest soldiers in Japan died to last man in Battle of Nagashino 1575—invincible Takeda blitz of cavalry-led foot soldiers mowed down by 3,000 farmer-musketeers of Nobunaga in sole major use of gun *vs* sword. Gun was banned as barbaric, un-samurai: machinegun of its day. General Oshigami commented 1913 that not much had improved since in butchery-tech. Katsuyori survived, but clan never regained power, was exterminated by Nobunaga in 1582, almost to last woman and child.

Main town is...
KOFU, with easy access from **5-Lakes**, or 2hr JR express train from
SHINJUKU. One day covering town and immediate vicinity will give you
good introduction to Shingen's realm. Massive statue of Shingen glares
down at you just outside stn S exit. Crystal Fountain nearby pays tribute to
Kofu's other attraction as Japan's top quartz producer.

Best time to visit is mid-April *Shingen Festival* marking his death, celebrated 3
days from 1st sat **before Apr 12**. Shingen no less popular now than 400 years ago.
Highlight is feudal costume parade of 1,300-man army headed by Shingen and his 24
generals ahorse; followed by Peace Parade of children's mikoshi. As in Shingen's time,
army grouped under 4 banners: Blue (Wind), Green (Forest), Red (Fire), Yellow (Mount).
Called *Fu-Rin-Ka-Zan*, they represented cavalry as swift as *wind*, spears as thick as *forest*,
unstoppable like *fire* and immovable like *mountain* (Shingen himself). Join in fun, join
festive army (for participation fee of ¥3,000, incl insurance); at least month ahead ✍
postcard with name, address, occupation, age and Japan contact address to **Yamanashi-
ken Shingen-ko Matsuri Koshu Gundan Shutsujin Iinkai**, Yamanashi-ken
Kanko-ka-nai, 1-6-1 Marunouchi Kofu-shi Yamanashi-ken 400, or phone ☎(0552)-35-
2722. You will be fully costumed and briefed to join locals.

Around same time (sun nearest **Apr 10**) *Tenzushino-mai*, ancient puppet dance; one
of few festivals preserved by government as National Folk-Cultural Treasure. Kose-cho
district of town, 9 costumed puppets dance to flute and drums herald spring.

Modern center of town is S of stn, around remains of...
Maizuru Castle, built by post-Takeda Asano clan (1596-1615) only to be
taken over by Tokugawa-ally Yanagisawa until 1868. Dismantled in early
Meiji, only double moat and stoneworks remain, grounds now municipal
park full of cherry trees. This area also has most lodgings and restaurants,
but all things to see are N of stn where Takeda was based.

10min walk N of stn...
Yamanashi Gemstone Museum, *Hoseki Hakubutsukan*, has 1st-floor
display of raw gem-stones from around the world, cut gems, mounted
jewels and outline of quartz refining process. 2nd-floor shop sells assorted
gems, raw and cut. Open daily (except end of year) 9:30-16:30, ¥200. Fine selection
of gems also sold at **Chikyu-do** downtown (next to Oriental Hotel); quartz at **Omori**
(next to Konaya Hotel); both at major department stores in town—of which **Seibu** best.

2km N of stn (10min bus to Takeda Jinja) at end of Takeda-dori Avenue is...
Remains of Takeda mansion built by Nobutora and clan headquarters until
death of Katsuyori when burnt down leaving only moat of outer wall, which
measured 284m x 193m. Shingen did not believe in fortified capital, saying
entire province of Kai was his castle. Red-lacquered bridge leads to Takeda
shrine built over main house in 1917. Wood W-style building nearby is
early Meiji elementary school (built 1875) moved here later, and now **Local
History Museum**. 9:00-16:00, free, X-mon, wed, fri.

E side of town is line of hills, among which lie several quiet temples and
final resting place of Takeda greats.

15min walk E of mansion is...
ENKO-IN near which stone pagoda marks spot where Shingen was secretly
buried for 3 years until his death was revealed: pagoda erected later.

1km S of it (20min walk from stn) is...
DAISEN-JI built 1521 by Nobutora as family temple, has graves of Nobutora, Shingen, Katsuyori. Burned several times, little original remains;
treasure hall has usual Takeda-related items.

15min walk E of stn is...
CHOZEN-JI and its pagoda, only major temple to escape torch, 1551.

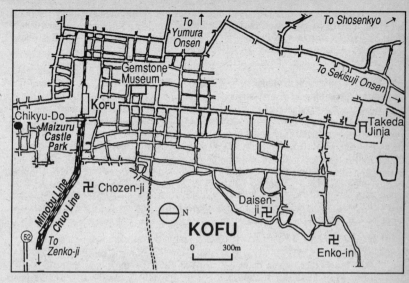

There are many more, but if you want just one temple, save it for...

ZENKO-JI (15min bus E to Zenko-ji stop, 20min walk N or cab 3x-mtr). Shingen had it built in 1565 to house treasures, scrolls brought from Nagano Zenko-ji. Was exact replica of Nagano's, but larger, and present main hall (rebuilt 1796) largest in Kanto: 37m wide-26m tall. Treasure Hall (9:30-16:30, ¥200) has pair of lacquered Amida figures mid-12th century, among others.

Little stretch of legs to rugged...

MITAKE SHOSEN-KYO GORGE; 30min bus to bottom **Tenjin-mori** 45min to central **Shosen-kyo**, 70min top **Taki-ue. Buses** branch-off 2km past Tenjin-mori on Shosen-kyo Green Line toll road to Shosen-kyo stop, or **horsecart** (30min up, 20min down, ¥1,000) along river from Tenjin-mori to same. No buses between Shosen-kyo–Taki-ue, which reached by back road via Kanazakura Shrine. Best way to see all is to start at top, 20min walk to Shosen-kyo, 25min further to Tenjin-mori. Passenger **cars** can only go up along river on weekdays, prohibited weekends, holidays.

Top of gorge...

Senga-daki waterfall drops 30m in 3 levels, continuing 4km to **Tenjin-mori** past spectacular cliffs on either side and strange rock-formations in river. 6min ropeway from Taki-ue to **Panorama platform** across river; every 15min 8:30-17:30, ¥450 o.w., ¥850 r.t., 1hr hike from platform to Tenjin-mori. On riverside road is small gemstone exhibit hall, abandoned

RAKKAN-JI temple across gorge, once major center for mountain ascetics.

For another beautiful riverside hike, Itabashi Keikoku 3km upstream from Taki-ue beyond small dammed-lake passes dozens of waterfalls thru wooded valley ending 1km at 40m drop Otaki falls. Area frequented by monkeys, which may give you surprise, but harmless unless provoked.

KANAZAKURA SHRINE, built 1,500 years ago was prayed at for national unity, visited by Emperor Juntoku, regularly by Takeda and Tokugawas. Much neglected since 1945, burned down 1955, replaced by present shrine.

Nearby...

MEOTOGI fertility shrine visited by women unable to give birth: prayers offered at sacred *Mé-oto-gi* (Husband-Wife Tree), hoary chestnut with large 'male' branch protruding into 'female' crack in tree trunk.

Stretch your legs in different direction to **Suntory Yamanashi winery** for those not going to wine center of Katsunuma; 25min bus from Kofu stn W to Tomi and 40min walk N; **cab** 5x-mtr from Kofu, or 1x-mtr from JR Shiozaki 2 stops W. Call ahead ☎(0551)-28-3232 to tour wine, brandy process, **Suntory Wine/Whisky Museum** followed by ¥1,800 mutton & wine lunch at outdoor eatery.

TILT: **Yamanashi Kotsu Bus** ☎(0552)-37-0131 with terminal at stn S-exit has sole **tour**. Kofu Meguri Course starts from Yumura onsen's ryokan Shosen-kaku 9:30 with Kofu stn bus terminal dep 10:10 → Takeda Shrine → Shosen-kyo Gorge (ropeway) → Suntory Yamanashi Winery → Prefectural Museum → Hayakawa-cn (pick grapes) *or* Gem Museum → Zenko-ji → end Kofu stn 16:30. Gift replaces museum visit on closed days. Run 4/1-11/30; ¥5,650/Adult, ¥3,090/child incl lunch. Same by **cab**, 30x-mtr.

Local **buses** also depart stn S-Exit, intra city (incl Yumura, Sekisui-ji onsen) W side of Yamanashi Dept, out-of-town from bus stn behind Dept Store: #1 → SHOSEN-KYO; #2 → KATSUNUMA → YAMANASHI CITY; #3 → NIRAZAKI; #4 → TAKI-UE → KAJIKAZAWA → ICHIKAWA → express → SHIZUOKA; #5→ KAJIKAZAWA → express MINOBU-SAN; #6→ KATSUNUMA → YAMANASHI CITY → ISAWA. Nippon **Rent-a-car** next to Tourist Info, S Exit.

WHERE TO STAY: In town or 2 nearby onsen. In town best are S of stn: **Kona-ya Hotel** ☎(0552)-35-1122, ¥-T; and J-annex **Kona-ya Bekkan**, ☎22-7111, ¥-lo-Sw/2. Most other ryokan range ¥-T; for ¥-B but good, try **Sansui-kan** ☎52-8541 1km NE, or **Manshu-kaku** ☎22-5513 S of stn. **Higashi-Yanagi-ya** ☎35-3731 is at SE corner from Shingen statue. Several Business Hotels S exit of stn with singles ¥-P. More to chose from at S Exit Info Booth.

Central downtown 500m S of stn has most hotels and inns among dozens of restaurants of all sorts—Japanese, Chinese, Korean, French, German, Italian, Indian. Area's distinctive dish is *Hoto*, thick udon in hot miso sauce with beef, potatoes, vegs, ¥500-800. Found all over, but more enjoyable at old style, folkcraft-filled stores: **Kosaku** N of stn past Hotel New Stn, better main branch S of stn L side of Kasuga-dori St 2 blocks past Dai-ei Dept; **Narata** also S on Heiwa-dori St, R on alley before Taiyo-Kobe Bank.

YUMURA ONSEN (10min bus NW of town or cab 2x-mtr) has large ryokan, most luxurious are **Tokiwa Hotel** ☎52-1301, **Shosen-kaku** ☎52-0361 both ¥-Tw/2; others start slightly higher. Arrange at stn **Info Center** or **Ryokan Kumiai** (Co-op) center of Yumura. Hire-**cab** stand across from Tokiwa for tours to Shosen-kyo Gorge or town. Yumura also boasts 2 *minka* folk-houses from outlying farms converted to restaurants. 100m E of Ryokan Kumiai is **Seburi**, 100-years serving local specialties; and 200-year-old **Inaka-ya**, robata-yaki grill in Tokiwa Hotel compound: ¥4,000 at either will fill you with their best dishes, with drinks.

ENTAKU-JI temple N end of onsen established here 808AD.

5min walk N to...
Kan'na-zuka Kofun, 1,300-year-old round tumulus: 39m across, 7.2m tall, horizontal entrance to 10.3m long x 1.5m wide x 2.6m high room. Two more tumuli (30min bus S of town to Shimo-sone) **Choshi-zuka** (keyhole shape 167m x 85m, vertical entrance) and **Maruyama-zuka** (circular 8m high); excavated items displayed at nearby **Prefectural Antiquities Museum**, *Kenritsu Koko Hakubutsu-kan*.

SEKISUI-JI ONSEN: 30min bus from stn (4x-mtr cab) 15min from Takeda Shrine in hills is far quieter with only 2 inns in small hamlet, ¥-Tw/2: **Koyubo** ☎52-3211, **Yogai Onsen** ☎53-2611. Also popular with day visitors, small fee for bath.

Nearby...
SEKISUI-JI temple, mid-8th century, Shingen born here Nov 1521, small shrine in complex dedicated to water in which he was first bathed. 30min up hill behind Sekisui-ji, earthwork & stone remains of **Yogai castle** built 1520 by Nobutora. For those with time, more along Koshu-kaido, E between Kofu & Otsuki; S between Kofu and Fujinomiya.

WHERE NEXT: Those heading to central Japan continue N on JR Chuo Main Line or **drive** Chuo Expwy, Rte20 to Lake Suwa, Nagano (*see* p941). En route is ancient Nirasaki with several 8th century structures (Ana-kannon, Ganjo-ji temple, Takeda Hachiman Shrine) and Sakai Iseki archaeological remains of Jomon, Yayoi sites: artifacts displayed at Mr Shimura's **Sakai Hozon-kan** call ☎(0551)-22-4270 to see, leave donation (in envelope). All 10min bus, cab from stn. Further on in **Japan Alps**, 50min JR to Kobuchizawa and 35min Koumi Line to Kiyosato; **drivers** branch-off Rte20 at Nirasaki to Rte144, from Expwy at Sutama IC, or local Yatsugatake road from Kobuchizawa town or I.C. on Expwy. Here we head W from Otsuki, S → Fujinomiya.

KIYOSATO KOGEN PLATEAU 清里高原

POPULAR RESORT of secluded pensiones and farms, early big US-style Christian-missionary experimental farm.

Good, if haphazard way to see entire area is Hakone → Yamanaka (Oshino) → Fuji Yoshida → Otsuki → Kofu → Minobu → Motosu → Fujinomiya, or from Kofu → Kawaguchi or Shoji → Fuji Yoshida. Garet did something similar to first but crammed into 2 1/2 days = Hakone → Yamanaka → Oshino (nite) → Yoshida → Otsuki → Kofu → Minobu(n) → Motosu → Shoji → Fujinomiya → and on to → Kyushu; also did Kofu → Otsuki 1983 driving → L Nojiri.

OTSUKI, southern gateway to area (where Fuji-Kyu Line branches off JR to Kawaguchi, as does branch of Chuo Expressway) was major stop on Koshu-kaido. Remaining homes of that time are among modern stores W of stn, notably, **Shimo-Hanasawa Honjin** (Important Cultural Asset) now occupied by Hoshino family. Built in 1852 to accommodate travelling Daimyo, 2-storey tiled structure has old records and room used by Emperor Meiji in June, 1880: tour house for small donation. **Monkey Bridge**, *Saru-hashi*, said built during Empress Suiko's reign (592-628AD actual) when Buddhist monk Shikimaro saw troop of monkeys cross here. When repaired (latest Aug 1984) care taken to adhere to original design with no central supports, projecting high beams support outer thirds. Long-famous site, appearing in Hiroshige woodblock prints and considered one of Japan's top 3 scenic bridges, with Iwakuni's *Kintai* **5-hump Arched-bridge**, Shikoku's *Iya-no-kazurabashi* **Vine-&-plank Suspension Bridge**, once common in premodern era. Is midpoint of E-W 48km maglev test line Sakaigawa-Akiyama (opens '96); try to imagine what Hiroshige would have done with this subject.

5km W of Otsuki, local road heading N off Rte20 runs thru two mineral baths...
Magi Kosen and **Hashikura Kosen** (15, 20min bus respectively), popular as day-time stops. But if **bus** to Kofu along Rte20 just before Sasago tunnel;

40min bus from Otsuki, or 14min JR to Sasago and 10min bus, you may find...
Sasago Kosen mineral baths more convenient, tho not as quiet. Famous for **puppet theater** during Koshu-kaido days and tho no longer performed, centuries-old puppets displayed at Amano farm house. Ancestors were puppeteers, similar to bunraku still seen in Osaka and Awaji Island. To see his 120 heads and dozen costumes call ahead ☎(05542)-5-2545.

Rather than tunnel thru to Kofu, can start at Sasago 3hr hike over Sasago Pass to...
HAJIKANO on little-used road built right on old Koshu-kaido, halfway is millennium old 27m-tall (9-10 storeys) cryptomeria, which got its name of 'Standing Arrow Tree' because Kai warriors used to pray here for victory by shooting arrows into tree: sometimes at vanquished foes tied to it.

2km before Hajikano is...
KOMAGAI-JUKU hamlet, other than paving of road passing thru, little changed since feudal-pedestrian days, ancient soaring thatched-roof farm houses lining either side. Several km N of Hajikano stn is were Katsuyori and clan were wiped out (only 3 family members spared) March 1582.

KEITOKU-IN temple nearby erected months later by TOKUGAWA Ieyasu in honor of Katsuyori since Takeda's ancestral temple was afraid to bury him there lest Nobunaga flatten them as well. Only main Sanmon gate remains, as do graves of Katsuyori and infant son.

Pleasant 2hr round-trip hike up scenic Ryumon-kyo Dragon's Gate Gorge to...
SEIUN-JI Zen temple built 1348 honoring Takeda soldiers, boasts fine Buddhist images and Takeda-related treasures. Spacious garden in rear also has numerous Buddha figures, all carved out of rocks. Facing temple is **Tenmokuzan Minshuku Village**, 6 budget inns (¥-Bw/2); 4 more at Keitoku-in.

History buffs can follow another part of old Koshu-kaido E of OTSUKI, part on back roads, part trails: start from UENOHARA (with longest escalator, 690', 8min, from stn to housing area) 3hr30min to TORISAWA. 4km further along crowded Rte20 is Saru-hashi bridge. Hamlets along way still have many old houses and inns, but best are clumped near Uenohara and Torisawa stns and can be seen easily without long trek.

If history not your game, then head to next stn...
KATSUNUMA for some fine wine. Tho major grape-producing center since 1186, it was not until after Meiji Restoration that farmers filled in rice paddies to plant entire area with grapes and peaches. Now over 80% of local economy is grape- and wine-oriented; still few sake distilleries W of new wineries. Aug thru Oct, vineyards offer pick-all-you-want; *Grape Festival* **end Sep-early Oct** has in addition to typical festival fare all grapes you can eat, all wine to drink, fireworks. **Gyokusui-en** vineyard, ☎(0553) 44-0147, wine & Genghis Khan BBQ lunch ¥1,300; **Kohaku-en** has regular BBQ with wine ¥1,500, must rsve ☎44-0128. Sapporo, Suntory, Manns, Mercien all have wineries in area with free tours, sampling. Call ahead (tho Mercien let us in on spot): **Mercien** ☎44-1011, **Manns** ☎44-1151, **Sapporo** ☎44-2345.

Town-run *Budo-no-oka* (**Hill of Grapes**) Center, rambling European style winery is perhaps best place to go, laid out for sole purpose of 'understanding' wine; with dining halls, rooms for rent (¥-P, bkfst ¥500 extra). Also small **museum** on history of grapes and wine in area and old artifacts from feudal days. Another **museum** is *Wine Shiryokan* near Mercien winery housed in Miyagi #2 brewery built 1893. Oldest extant winery, looks more like traditional sake brewery. Inside are diaries, notes of Takano and Tsuchiya, first to bring wine-making from France. Tools first used, bottles of Japan's oldest wines.

E of winery row is...
DAIZEN-JI temple (NT) est 717-723, first patronized by Imperial family, later by successive shogunal clans and Takeda. Only main hall left, unfortunately not representative of 8th century architecture. When 9th Hojo Regent rebuilt it in 1286, he used mixed Japanese-T'ang style then prevalent in Kamakura. Nonetheless beautiful, contains many treasured statues from early Heian to Edo eras: ¥300 admission for temple and garden. Two unique festivals held here. **May 8** *Fujikiri-matsuri* (Wisteria Cutting): cranes of wisteria attached to large 'snake' hung from sacred tree, cut down by sword-wielding youths. **Around beg Oct** (part of *Grape Fest*, above) *Torii-yaki* is prayer for bountiful grape harvest and elimination of crop-damaging insects, 90m tall 50m wide torii burned on hill side just W of Daizen-ji.

ENZAN takes its name from 554m tall 'Salt Mountain' in middle of town where salt was mined. Enzan Onsen, dozen old but clean ¥-B inns at its base, popular with hikers heading into Japan Alps, or following part of old OME-KAIDO pedestrian highway linking Edo (from Shinjuku) via Oku-tama to Kofu. If here for this hike, best section Yanagisawa Pass → Ichinose.
Bus 30min to **Daibosatsu Toge** on Rte411, then walk.
Town itself is interesting blend of old and new, former best seen in **Takano mansion** (3min walk N of Enzan stn). Impressive 3-storey structure built 1720, Takano produced licorice and other medicinal herbs for shogun. Various tools displayed inside; to *see*, ☎(0553)-33-2734 (*in Japanese only*), no fee.

5km (15min bus) NW of stn is...
ERIN-JI, Takeda clan temple built 1330 by MUSO Kokushi (*see* KAMAKURA) one of his most famous gardens in rear (¥300). Burned totally when Takeda clan destroyed, over 100 priests died in flames. Head priest Kaisen Kokushi, himself trapped on main gate, showered prayers of forgiveness down on attacking army. Complex later rebuilt by Tokugawa Ieyasu who held great respect for Shingen in spite of their differences. Takeda Shingen **Treasure Hall** opened here 1969, displaying hundreds Takeda treasures. Special exhibits spring, autumn (¥300, 9:00-17:00, X-thur in summer, winter).

Erin-ji is also where poet Basho wrote his epitomal haiku:

Furu-ike ya ... Kawazu tobikomu ... Mizu no oto
old pond, oh   frog jumps in   water sound

Offers *shojin-ryori*, table d'hote ¥2,500+, box lunch ¥800, noodles ¥450; reservation not needed; served rustic outdoor style. Visited on Fujita Travel Mt Fuji Day bus tour.

5min beyond is ancestral temple of their predecessors, Kai Minamoto...
HOKO-JI built 1184, stretched well into hillside until burned down at same time as Erin-ji. Also rebuilt by Ieyasu, now Shingon training center. Can enjoy meal of *shojin-ryori* here, too, but call at least day ahead ☎(0553)-32-3340.

30-40min beyond on Rte140 are some backwoods hot springs with few modern but inexpensive inns. Further on past Hirose Lake come to Nishizawa-keikoku gorge (hour bus from Enzan) with pleasant trail winding thru numerous waterfalls and pools.

Enzan's inns are cheap, minshuku rate in town, similar at hot spring, but it's only 25min train to Kofu, or 15min bus or rail to hot spring town of...
ISAWA: Kai province seat of government for 3 centuries until Nobutora moved to Kofu, lived on quietly as small farming community until 1961 when hot water suddenly gushed out of vineyards and most farmers cashed in their grapes for inns, of which there are over 150. Larger ryotels try to out-do each other in 'ultimate' bath: large bath halls, outdoor or top-floor observatory-baths. Usually run ¥-T+w/2; smaller outlying family-run ones cheaper tho not as grand baths. Any price bookings at stn info, *Ryokan Kumiai* at town center (600m S of stn on L). KASUGAI ONSEN 20min walk NE of stn (10min from prior stn Betsuden) is quieter, slightly cheaper but not as convenient to Isawa sights.

For one thing, Fuefuki River flowing just S of Isawa ryokan cluster is perfect for **Ugai cormorant fishing**, ancient art (best at Arashiyama-*see* Kyoto). Supposedly introduced here by Taira no Kiyomori's brother-in-law as livelihood, now mostly for tourists July-Aug on wed, sat, sun nites. Watch from shore, or better yet join one of many party boats and float among fishing boats. Ryokans will arrange for you, most offer to pack picnic dinners. ¥1,000/person, ¥10,000 for your own boat.

500m E of Ryokan Kumiai, 15min walk from stn is...
Yatta-ke, remains of Tokugawa official's mansion. Inside moated, walled compound is library for official documents, built 1601. Privately run, there is no charge but call ☎(0552)-62-5511 to let them know you're coming. Cluster of old storehouses, **Koshu Kura-Yashiki** (150m N of stn) has several small exhibits on Shingen and gems (with largest piece of quartz in Asia), restaurant of local cuisine. **Yamanashi Ancient Art Museum** (150m S of Yatta-ke), with over 20,000 pieces ancient folk arts from pottery and scrolls to dolls. Daily 8:00-18:00, ¥400. Also small town-run **Folk History Museum**, *Mingei-kan*, in old *minka*-folk house, central Kobayashi Park. Free, 13:00-16:00, X-tue, thur.

Monde Winery in town offers tours suns, hols: call ☎(0552)-62-3161 to arrange; their store sells everything—wine (720ml/qt ¥1,000+), brandy, and liqueurs.

PERSONAL DATEBOOK: *Peach Blossom Festival* **mid-Apr** during which time mock feudal battle, geisha mikoshi parade, and several Sengoku battle paintings displayed. *Onsen Festival* **Aug 19-21** has taiko drum contests, dancing, fireworks.

ICHINOMIYA SENGEN shrine, it and other nearby shrines and temples are pleasant, easier reached by bus from nearby Yamanashi-shi stn, but mainly for those interested in area for festivals. **Apr 15** Ichinomiya Sengen has *River Blessing* rite; **early Apr** ancient *Taitai Kagura* dance at Yamanashi-oka Shrine, 15min walk S of Yamanashi-shi stn, derived from agricultural fertility/harvest offering; original dances simpler; probably as old as shrine, which age no one is sure of. Records claim it built by Suinin, early semi-mythical chieftain/emperor #10, said to have ruled 97-30BC (actual c.300+?AD) Present structures mid-14th cent, built by master craftsmen from mountainous Hida (considered best), fine Muromachi era (16c) architecture.

KOFU TO FUJINOMIYA

NOT AS MUCH along this route but several secluded hot springs in hills flanking Fujigawa River, some ancient hamlets, dominated by mountain-top main temple of Nichiren-shu. JR Minobu Line and Rte50 meander thru fertile back-country in pleasant, if roundabout way to Fujinomiya. *See* preceding chapter for main entry as start of Mt Fuji climb. KOFU → Ichikawa Daimon → Kajikazawa → Shimobe → Minobu-san → Amehata Onsen → Nambu → FUJINOMIYA.

25min express, 35min local from Kofu is...
ICHIKAWA DAIMON, once capital of Kai-Genji, now famous for its fireworks and *washi* (so-called 'rice' paper) artisans. Washi making began here around 923-930 and now accounts for 35% of nation's production. Unfortunately, demand has forced most places to replace natural fibers with rayon. (One of best places still using natural *kozo*, mulberry, is KURODANI in N Hyogo). Only one store, **Tomikawa** (500m E of Honmachi stn), still does entire process by hand. While they usually don't allow you to see process, it's best place to buy. Express stops at main Ichikawa Honmachi stn, around which are dozens of washi shops.

Your time would be better spent wandering around, 2 stops beyond at ...
KAJIKAZAWA, planned town built 1596-1614 as terminus for Fuji Canal. Section of canal remains, along which are numerous old inns, restaurants and merchants, homes with massive clay storehouses. Most concentrated around Yamanashi bus center (5min bus, 10min walk from stn). Canal main mode of transport for rice from Kai-Yamanashi, salt and fish from Suruga-Shizuoka until JR Minobu Line early this century. One of best preserved houses belonged to head of Canal Ship Firm in early Meiji era.

GETTING THERE: From bus center, 30min (¥380) to JIKKOKU ONSEN in western hills; 3 ryokan (**Genji-so**, ☎(0556)-27-0224, ¥-Tw/2), 6 minshuku. 'Hidden Bath' seekers will find one of area's many *Ikken-juku* (one-inn) hot springs at **Akaishi mineral spring**. 30min bus to HIRABAYASHI and 40min walk, or call **Akaishi Onsen** inn ☎2-5188 for pick-up at Hirabayashi bus stop. ¥-Bw/2; Winter only.

SHIMOBE, more convenient hot spring (5min bus, 15min foot from Shimobe stn). Buses from Lake Motosu join rail 2 stops up at Ichinose, end here. Spend quiet night here, bus (30min, ¥390), cab 6x-mtr (inn pick-up OK), or train (12min+ 10min bus) to Minobu temple in morning. Just looking for good bath? Try town-run ONSEN KAIKAN, 5min walk from stn; 8:30-17:00 X-mon, ¥250 bath only, ¥450 extra to use pool (summer only). Inn rates match Minobu's, ¥-lo-T+ deluxe, ¥-B+ moderate, & minshuku. Conductor we met often comes here, suggests **Yumoto Hotel** ☎(0556)-36-0021, large, old but deluxe yet bit cheaper than newer tourist hotels; great food, large rock bath and 'sonic wave' bath, both open 24hrs. Back in hills on bend in Shimobe River, it's considered one of Shingen's 'hidden baths'. He came here after Kawanakajima battle to heal wounds; water here is said to help heal cuts, bruises, broken bones and rheumatism.

Clear and pure, drinking it also aids stomach ailments. Onsen honors Shingen **May 13-15**: when his reputed cane at **KUMANO SHRINE** is purified; *Taitai Kagura* dances held on shrine stage; samurai procession down main street; fireworks. Steps up to KUMANO SHRINE start behind Yumoto Hotel.

3km beyond onsen...
YUNO-OKU hamlet has 300-year-old *minka*, folk house, in excellent shape. Owned by Monzai family, village chiefs since 14th century they will gladly show it off to anyone trekking out that far (hour walk, 5x-mtr cab r.t. incl wait); anytime during day, no charge. Road ends here, 3hr hike on to summit of 1,945m Kenashi-yama 'Hairless mountain', so named for gold mines carved into it during 16-18th centuries. Equal distance down other side to Asagiri Kogen (on FIVE-LAKES circuit).

MINOBU-SAN, properly **MINOBU-SAN KAKUON-JI**, is foremost Nichiren sect temple. After his expulsion from Kamakura Nichiren wandered and preached, and converting local Nanbu lord, gained his patronage and settled here 1274 at age 53, making Kai region bastion of his sect. In 1474, sect head Nitcho built massive complex here for bicentennial. All yet existing rebuilt after major fire 1880 destroyed all but front Sanmon gate, 1km downhill. Minobu 57min ↔ Kofu express, 40min ↔ Fujinomiya; 1hr+bus ↔ Lake Motosu.

Old complex was said to be larger than present one with yet over 60 buildings covering hillside. Still very active, has hundreds of disciples here training and runs university, hospital and old folks' home as well. 20 priests' quarters take in guests ¥-Bw/2; arranged at **information booth** ☎(0556)-62-0502 at Sanmon main gate. Most of those staying are pilgrims from all over Japan come to pay their respects, and you get glimpse of temple life. Attend early morning rites, see temple at its most beautiful in early morning mist as white-clad pilgrims make their rounds, silently chanting "*Namu Myo-ho Renge-kyo*" (Blessed is Lotus Sutra) then get head start of several hours before first bus-load of regular tourists unloads. Main temple on central hill, priests' quarters W and E Valleys, by main gate.

WHERE TO STAY: You can bus within 200m of main gate and run gauntlet of usual souvenir shops, restaurants (ask price on way up, shop on way down), and inns. Tho suggest staying at temple or Shimobe Onsen, there are good inns here. Best closest to main gate: **Tama-ya** ☎(0556)-62-1001 on L and **Tanaka-ya** ☎62-1035 beyond on R, ¥-T-S+w/2. Closest **Ume-ya** ☎62-0660 on L, ¥-T+w/2, will serve breakfast from 6:00 for early starters. **Isago-ya** off main street, down alley leading to E Valley, old but classy, ¥-B+w/2. Gift-store items here no different than other major temple towns: from sacred (icons, rosaries, prayer-charms) to secular (porn saké sets) and usual assortment of local goods: here quartz sculptures, as expensive as they are beautiful.

Surrounded by centuries-old cryptomeria, Sanmon gate impresses; one of largest at 42m wide, 10.3m deep, 21.2m tall. Rebuilt 1907 dedicated by 79th head priest since Nichiren (present one is 88th in line). Emerging from its darkness you are faced with steep 105m climb of 287 steps. Cut by master stone masons from Sado mid-17th century, divided into 7 sections, one for each syllable of *Namu Myo-ho Renge-kyo*, devout pilgrims recite prayer 41 times, syllable each step. Two paths zig-zag uphill for those unable to make tough steep climb. Suddenly, main halls pop into view, as does well-placed sacred ablution font: used to purify oneself—most at this point purify from inside out, drinking then pouring over head. Front **Great Hall** DAI HON-DO finished 1982 for 7th centennial of Nichiren attaining nirvana, 1282: basement is Treasure Hall. To its R is equally large **Founder's Hall**, *Soshi-do*, 1881, contains statues of Nichiren surrounded by his parents (good farmer stock) and Six Disciples; plaque was penned by late emperor Showa (Hirohito). Next, and heart of temple, 8-sided *Goshinkotsu-do*, **True Bones Hall**, houses Nichiren's ashes. Far R past *Butsu-den*,

Buddha Hall, is head priest's quarters (*off-limits*) with early Edo period garden in rear which can see from hallway around main halls. Early Apr people from all over come to see rare *shidare-zakura* weeping cherry blossoms.

Path from L-rear of Great Hall goes down to W Valley, far end of which is enclosed site of Nichiren's grass hut where he spent final 9 years, and behind it his mausoleum. Also mausolea for his Six Disciples, as well as for all ninety-odd head priests. Part way down path is stn for 7min (¥950 r.t.) ropeway up to summit of **Mt Minobu**, also reached by 5.5km pilgrim path starting behind Founder's Hall, to **Oku-no-in** inner sanctuary, built 1284 by Nichiren's disciple Nichiro. Nichiren came here to pray for his parents, thus name *Shishin-kaku* (Parents' Memory Pavilion).

From here, real pilgrims (and hikers) continue on 5hr trail (well-marked) to...
KEISHIN-IN temple atop 1,982m Mt Shichimen-zan. En route you hit Akazawa hamlet whence narrow road 2km to **Shiraito Waterfall** and trail again to summit. White statue of woman pilgrim at falls is Oman-no-kata, lady-in-waiting-cum-mistress of Tokugawa Ieyasu, early feminist who, determined to complete her pilgrimage, broke ban against women climbing Shimen-zan; thousands have followed her since. Keishin-in was also built by Nichiro, dedicated to 7-faced Shichimen Dai-myojin who looks after followers of Lotus Sutra in Age of Decadence to come (now?). Keishin-in takes in guests ¥-P-w/2, but you might call before coming this far: ☎(0556)-45-2551. Famous early morning *goraiko* or viewing of sunrise from main gate, of Mt Fuji silhouetted. Going down, save hours by other trail which heads straight down N slope (hour+ down) to SUMISE, whence 55min bus (9x-daily)→Minobu stn: best to check bus scheds at stn before you start all this; bus stop at Sumise is Shichimen-zan Tozan-guchi.

For real wanderer continuing into hills on Minobu-Sumise road are some rural hot springs. W base Shichimen-zan...
AMEHATA ONSEN hamlet (1hr15min bus 2x-daily from Minobu) with 1 inn **Takimi-so** ☎(0556)-45-2270, ¥-Bw/2. Amehata famous among calligraphers for their *suzuri*-inkslabs, reputed to equal finest Chinese Tankei inkslabs. Using rocks from Amehata River, sole artisan Mr Mochizuki carves out each stone. Glad to show visitors his craft, his inkslabs cost anywhere between ¥6,-10,000. Fishing and boating on man-made Lake Amehata. 25min bus from Sumise's Hichimen-zan Tozan-guchi stop, 5km walk. Continuing past fork to Amehata, pass thru **Tamogawa Mineral Baths** 1hr40min **bus** (7/day) from Minobu to **NISHIYAMA ONSEN** and **NARATA ONSEN** 10min farther. All three along Hayakawa River, Narata has dammed lake, camping, fishing OK. NARATA 7 ryokan, NISHIYAMA 4 ryokan, all ¥-B+w/2. TAMOGAWA 1 ryokan, ¥-B+w/2; and 3 minshuku at KUSASHIO, 500m downstream. Book thru Hayakawa Town Hall Tourist Division ☎(0556)-45-2511.

There are also backwoods hot springs closer to main transportation between Minobu ↔Fujinomiya. Three centered around...
NAMBU, town served by Utsubuna stn 25min from Minobu. Few km W of town are **FUNAYAMA & JUMAI-SO ONSEN**. Former (20min bus from stn and 10min walk) has one inn **Funayama Onsen** ☎(0556)-64-2343, ¥-B+w/2, end of dead-end road in hills. JUMAI-SO, 20min bus, small farm community with one inn (¥-B+w/2), few minshuku. 20min walk E of stn UTSUBUNA ONSEN has two similar priced inns, hikers' base for 1031m Shishin-zan. Another *Ikken-yado*, SANOGAWA ONSEN further in hills boasts large outdoor riverside bath. 50min walk either Ide or Toshima stns.

WHERE NEXT: For real adventurer, head SW from Minobu into hills and end at UMEGASHIMA ONSEN, 2hr bus N of Shizuoka, our next stop down Tokaido, resume main historical route; or from Minobu, bus to last stop OSHIRO whence 4km to end road and trail over Yasui-toge Pass another 4km to UMEGASHIMA (*see* JAPAN SEA); or from Fujinomiya JR to MATSUMOTO; rail over mountains to scenic reclusive TAKAYAMA, where join another old Koshukaido segment (*see* Hokuriku-North) back down to NAGOYA. **Also** direct KOFU from/to TOKYO Shinjuku Stn by bus or JR.

*Well, we're not willow trees, to be planted by
the road side...Don't you think we might stop
here for the night?*
—Jippensha Ikku, *Hizakurige*, 1802

SHIZUOKA 静岡
STARTING HISTORICAL TREK

YOU NOW enter Tokai (Eastern Sea) Region, running Shizuoka–Nagoya.
Battlefield for final unification of nation, all great 16th century warriors
passed this way. And so did much of population if we are to accept tradition
of woodblock prints (Hiroshige, Hokusai) or paperback novels like comic
Hizakurige—its English version *By Shank's Mare Down Tokaido*, quoted
above. Tokugawa Ieyasu spent his youth in Shizuoka home province
Totomi just E of Lake Hamana. Great Takeda clan was destroyed in battles
of Nagashino (inland nr Hamana) and Takatenjin on coast. Ieyasu had final
victory over Toyotomi armies at Sekigahara, W of Nagoya. You cannot
pass thru area without running into 3 great unifiers of Japan (Oda Nobunaga
set himself up at Gifu), or Ieyasu's legacy such as great barrier gate at Arai
near Hamana.

Coming down from Fuji and across Shizuoka Plain, you wonder if those
mountainsides with their rows and rows of neatly trimmed hedges are part
of gigantic landscape garden setting off Mt Fuji. Especially in April–May
you realize that these are famed tea plantations. Women in indigo splash-
patterned *kasuri* kimono, wide-brimmed straw hats or cone-shaped sedge or
bamboo-skin hats, fill huge bags with newly clipped tea leaves. Shizuoka is
largest tea-producing area in Japan. Further along Tokaido you see similar
scenes between Nagoya and Lake Biwa as you near famed Uji tea area.

In winter, gold-flecked dark green wonderland with mandarin oranges
filling terraced hillsides. Farmers take advantage of heat reflected from
stone terracing to grow giant strawberries Dec–Jan. Early May lovely, air
fragrant with orange blossoms, kimono-clad women cutting first tea of year.
At Mishima, wiggly pines line old Tokaido planted 3 centuries ago, for
beauty's sake as much as for practicality.

Shizuoka is thriving prefecture as factories shoeing foot of Fuji indicate.
Shimizu Port is small but bustling and center of mandarin orange canneries.
It's also connected by steamer to MATSUZAKI on Izu W coast.

For some interesting factory tours, or more info on adventuring into winter wonder-
land of Japan Alps or great hydroelectric dams at Hatanagi, ☎ or visit **Prefectural
Tourist Association**, 44-1 Otemachi, Shizuoka City 500m N of stn main road R past
City Hall; or **Trade Promotion Association–JETRO**, 3 Aioi-cho, Shimizu City.
PREF TOURIST ASSOC displays local better known crafts as *take-kogei* bamboo wares,
Shizuhata-yaki pottery. Visit makers **Take-kogei Kyodo Kumiai**, Aratomi-cho,
Shizuoka City; call ☎(0542)-52-4924, tours 13:00-16:00 daily X-sun, hol. Shizuhata-
yaki is available only at home kiln of Mr **AOJIMA Akio** ☎71-2480, Yanai-cho, 15min
bus W of stn; accept visitors 9:00-4:00pm.

City itself is modern—small-town atmosphere yet all comforts of any metropolis.
Downtown district N of stn centers around **Sumpu Castle**, much as in days of Ieyasu.
He spent much of his childhood here as 'hostage' during treacherous last years of 15th
century, retired here after relinquishing title of Shogun to son Hidetada whom he coached
15 years to ensure family supremacy. Only stonework, moat remain, grounds now
municipal park. On Shizuhata hill NW of town 15min bus ride from stn is **RINZAI-JI**
temple where Ieyasu studied as youth, and 8min walk on beyond to **SENGEN SHRINE**
with its red-lacquered hall.

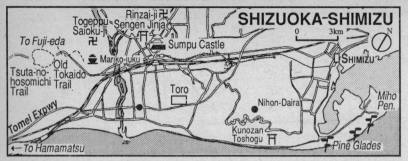

Good place to end day coming from Fuji or Izu, but little to see here other than...

TORO   BEGINNING OUR HISTORICAL TREK

STONE AGE **Yayoi Village**, reconstructed several houses and storage sheds complete with old-style rice fields. **Archaeological Museum**, *Kokogaku-kan* (¥150) houses artifacts from site, as well as other Jomon and Yayoi period objects.

Next to this is beautiful and well laid out...

Serizawa Keisuke Museum showing his own dyed works, as well as his personal collection of North and South American Indian folkarts, religious items from Europe, Ethiopia, Persia, Thailand, etc (¥400). Toro Museums, daily 9:00-16:30 X-mon, day after hol, last of month.

Stone Age Toro people occupied this spot first centuries A.D. They hunted and grew rice in wet paddies (originated in Southeast Asia) for which they built ornate irrigation system of wooden plank-lined canals, remains of which can still be seen, along with present reconstructions. Unlike their Jomon predecessors, they had domesticated horses and cattle. Their tools were mostly for farming, mostly of wood. Some hoes, tipped with iron, indicate ability to smelt iron and forge simple tools. They lived in round houses with lovely soaring thatched roofs similar to those still seen in countryside, except that roof reached ground, and floor of one-room house was 'sunken living room' about foot deep with open hearth. Donut-shape mounds indicate sites of other houses not yet reconstructed. Storehouse log cabins were set high on rat-shielded piles.

We know from pictures of this period that people often lived in these pile houses in summer. Ainu in Hokkaido still use them (*see* ASAHIGAWA) and we've seen similar but larger ones in northern Iran on Caspian. They make ideal storehouses and with higher technology which came from China 6th cent, developed into fabulous *azekura* storehouse exemplified in Shosoin Imperial Repository in Nara. Yayoi established Japanese architecture, particularly shrines of earliest *shinmei-zukuri* style exemplified in Ise Grand Shrine. "Type of construction used shows certain affinities to houses of Malaya and South Sea Islands, suggesting that originally it may have been derived from some common source in south of China, since settlement of South Sea Islands by Polynesians is of more recent date than the origin of this type of structure in Japan." (Munsterberg, *The Arts of Japan*)

Religion of these people included worship of earth or hearth goddess (replica idols for sale) borrowed from earlier matrilineal Jomon culture, and phallic worship as to be seen at Nagoya or near Nara. This patrilineal worship eventually won out over existing Jomon. Burial practices were more advanced than those of Jomon; Yayoi dead were buried in stone and earthenware jars in common grave site outside community; low mounds over graves presage practice of dolmen building which was dominant 3rd-6th centuries' Kofun (tumulus) period.

If unable to make this interesting stop, similar smaller Stone Age reconstructions at Hamamatsu SHIJIMI-ZUKA, Toyohashi URIGO, Gero Onsen MINE-ICHIGO.

Souvenir shop by entrance to site has replicas of *haniwa* (from later Kofun period, see Nara) ¥300 for small 10cm/4-inch singles or 'mini-sets'; ¥7-900 for medium, up to 30cm/foot; and ¥5,000 for large. Also Jomon period clay fertility figures (*dogu*) same price range; make wonderful gifts, and store will mail them for you.

GETTING THERE: TORO is 2km S of SHIZUOKA Stn (Shinkansen also stops), 20min #10 or #14 bus, (cab basic-mtr), and 1km N of Tomei Expwy. Many Tokaido bus tours stop here, as do city tours. Buses between Shizuoka stn ↔ Miho Peninsula also stop.

Seeing main sites of SHIZUOKA takes half-day or less: TORO 1hr; KUNOZAN 1hr; MIHO 2hrs. Advise come thru early in day, spend nite on down Tokaido at Lake Hamana; hurried travellers can cut out Miho and go direct to GIFU, 65min Shinkansen Shizuoka → Nagoya, where change for 25min further to Gifu on Tokaido Main Line. Wanderers may want to spend nite at one of mountain onsen or HAMANA/BENTEN-JIMA. *But if here late day or seeing it all...*

WHERE TO STAY: Excellent budget lodging in SHIZUOKA at **Tomita Business Hotel**: well-known house run by hospitable lady, many regulars include corporate heads from Tokyo who shun flashier hotels for good service in relaxed atmosphere at good prices; about 10min walk S of stn S exit. All cabbies know it; hotel reimburses ¥400 for cab even if you walk: down main street to 2nd large intersection (Kanebo-dori) turn R, cross 1st pedestrian overpass (front of shrine), then 2nd L. New 5-storey building, W-style rooms with bath and toilet (¥-B), older annex J-style rooms, toilet in hall (¥-P), room larger, but cheaper because building is old, tho immaculate. Bath downstairs main building. Meals extra, ¥1,200 dinner, ¥600 breakfast, sumptuous. Often full, call ahead ☎(0542)-83-6800. Budget lodgings clustered at stn. Almost 200 ryokan and hotels in Shizuoka, but if plan to spend time in area—looking for class...

NIHON-DAIRA: 10km SE of town, 35min **bus** from Shizuoka stn, **cab** 7x-mtr (¥500 less if avoid toll road). Plateau offers yet another spectacular view of Mt Fuji rising above tea fields. Boasts 18-hole golf course, zoo, several hiking trails; lots of space to lounge around. **Nihon-daira** best inn; W-style twin main building ¥-T, room only, or w/2. Several fine restaurants in hotel. Extra bed ¥2,000, baby crib ¥1,000. J- annex ¥-T double w/2. Luxury bath has **view of Mt Fuji**. ☎(0543)-35-1131. Nihon-daira Lodge **Youth Hostel** located behind hotel: ☎34-2738.

From Nihon-daira ropeway down to coast, ending at impressive...
KUNOZAN TOSHOGU shrine, dedicated to Shogun Ieyasu by his son. Shogunate effort to build cult of religious reverence around themselves, Ieyasu arranged before death for his own deification, re-oriented religion of Japan so that he would take premier position. He took posthumous title of Toshogu (Saint Nikko/sunlight). Kunozan is one of top 3 Toshogu shrines along with Takizan in Okazaki City and, most famous of all, his opulent mausoleum at Nikko. As Great Gongen, Shinto-Buddhist reincarnation, he was imposing deity and no town in Japan lacks its Toshogu. Successors took posthumous titles; all buried in one of mausoleums of Nikko, Shiba or Ueno. Kunozan's lacquered hall full of carvings and statues, **museum** (¥300, 8:30-17:00) houses Ieyasu's personal belongings, and more: 40min **bus** (#14 via Toro) from Shizuoka stn, hefty climb 1,159 stone steps from bus stop to shrine. **Strawberry fields** (gorge yourself ¥900) line road below shrine, stalls sell Jan-May.

10km E of Kunozan (30min bus) we come to...
MIHO-NO-MATSUBARA, Pine Glade of Miho, of folk tale-noh drama *Hagoromo* in which fisherman takes winged robe of descended angel while she bathes, makes her dance for its return. Pine tree off which he took robe *Hagoromo-no-matsu* is on coast, dying of polution, one of hundreds.

Halfway btwn Hagoromo tree and JR Miho stn (branch line from Shimizu) is ...
MIHO SHRINE, in which treasure hall is sash to angel's robe. At tip is
good beach, Miho Bunka (Culture) Land with miniatures of famous
structures from around world, **Natural History Museum** with 26 dinosaur skeletons, including 10m/33ft monster excavated China's Gobi Desert. Boats Miho ↔ Shimizu 15min, abt every 40min 9:20-16:30 suns-hols all year,
daily Jul–Aug.

Another interesting area near Shizuoka is...
MARIKO-JUKU hamlet, one of 53 stops on old Tokaido, now Rte1.
Several old buildings of this once-bustling hamlet remain, most notably
Choji-ya restaurant, famed centuries as serving best *tororo* (mountain
yam) along Tokaido. MATSUO Basho, 17th cent wandering poet ate here,
and stone marker in front has engraved on it haiku he wrote about Mariko's
tororo. Finely grated mountain yam mixed with white miso and soup
served on wheat costs ¥850, hefty price for what was once cheap gruel.
Restaurant still looks same as in one of Hiroshige's prints of Tokaido, copy
of which is on board in front. Convenient for those who **drive** down Tokaido; also
reach Mariko by **bus** Shizuoka → JR Fuji-Eda stn, get off at Shin-Mariko 20min. S (L)
down narrow side road and R at next road, actual pedestrian Tokaido, to Choji-ya past
many old folk houses. Few mins past Choji-ya, Rte1 at Togeppu-iriguchi bus stop.

On small road across Rte1 ...
TOGEPPU SAIOKU-JI temple famed for moon-viewing & tea parties,
both of which still occur: former full moon nites, latter daily. Saioku-ji area
has more pre-Meiji folk houses, one of which is folkcraft store **Waraku**.
Across from SAIOKU-JI, 1.1km path cuts thru tea fields, *mikan* orchards and
groves of cryptomeria, past remains of Mariko Castle, ending at SEIGAN-JI
temple whence few min walk to Niken-ya bus stop on Rte1. Shin-Mariko →
Niken-ya 2hr30min with stops.

For another pleasant hike, start at UTSUNOYA-IRIGUCHI bus stop (10min/3km, beyond Niken-ya) on Rte1. L (S) of stop, old wood bridge starts Tsuta-no-hoso-michi,
pedestrian highway of Heian era 9th century; R (N) 700-year-later 'old' Tokaido passes
thru **Utsunoya Shuraku** hamlet. Both rejoin Rte1 at Sakashita bus stop 1.3km down.
Much of Tsuta-no-hosomichi is still paved with rocks, placed there over 1,000 years ago
to make hill climb easier. Road to Utsunoya hamlet can be driven; hamlet has old house
Haori-ya, with haori outer kimono that belonged to Tycoon Hideyoshi, ¥200 to see.
Hiking do Hosomichi first (40min) and right before reaching Rte1, old Tokaido, still
path, branches off R to Utsunoya hamlet; part way is early Meiji brick tunnel, ending
back at Utsunoya-Iriguchi stop 90min later (stops incl).

We rejoin JR at Fuji-eda stn. Two stns down is...
KANAYA, from where Oigawa Tetsudo railway takes you inland and up
to Oi Dam from where roads lead into Oku-Oi Prefectural Park and Southern
Japan Alps. Old SL still runs in season.

Oi River was greatest barrier along pedestrian Tokaido. Almost 1.5km
wide here Tokugawa forbade building bridges or boat crossings to impede
crossing by any large force. Crossing also forbidden at nite, or if water level
rose above 4.5 *shaku* (feet). There are good bridges today so that traveller
need not be held up at Oi River at Shimada waiting for low enough water for
porters to carry him across: 1st-class palanquin or horseback, 2nd-class on
porter back, or 3rd-class led across in mob. 'Service charge', then called
'tea-money', has always been headache for, if as 1st- or 2nd-class passenger you didn't tip well enough, porter's legs would shorten just enough,
or horse hit spot just deep enough, to get your bottom soaked; cause for
many frequent brawls.

5km S of Kanaya is...

MAKI-NO-HARA Tea Plantation, largest single farm in Japan supplies close to 12% of all (green) tea leaves.

Maki-no-hara Park (adjacent) statue Saint Eisai first importer of tea from China. Every odd-numbered year *Tea Festival* **May 2-3**, purification, offertory rites and tea-pickers parade. Coast curves to fishhook Omae-zaki point, lined with fishing hamlets, beautiful white sand beaches, dozens minshuku; good fishing. Bus on coast Rte150.

Oigawa rail line is popular among Japanese, only one of two still covered by old 'iron horse' steam locomotives (other between Ogori-Masuda, southern Honshu). Makes one round-trip, 40km/25mi each way, fri thru mon (winter–sat, sun only), almost daily mid-July thru Aug (check at any JR stn or timetable), leaving KANAYA 11:45 for SENZU 13:01, ret 14:42 arr KANAYA 16:00. Peak summer, main hols 2nd SL 9:55am. Must reserve. SL, 4-passenger cars date to 1937-42 made for Hokkaido's Shibetsu Line. Rail Pass not valid.

Regular trains make several runs daily between Kanaya–Senzu, most start at Shizuoka or Hamamatsu. Last hour and half of rail from Senzu to Igawa is even smaller mountain train which chugs over spectacular gorges ending at LAKE IKAWA-KO (also reached by 2hr40min bus from Shizuoka). We are now officially in Japan Alps. 258m rickety suspension bridge (longest of type in Japan) crosses lake for thrilling but safe hike.

In these mountains are two backwoods hot springs...

UMEGASHIMA: 2hr bus N of Shizuoka, with 11 ¥-Tw/2 inns, one minshuku. Those who hiked over mountains from NANBU CITY end up here (*see* KOSHU-KAIDO). Smaller **KONYA ONSEN** is few km down road from Umegashima, has budget ryokan, several minshuku. Suggest **SUMATA-KYO ONSEN** along Oikawa rail line. Most direct way here is Oikawa rail from Kanaya 80min to Senzu and 1hr bus to Sumata Onsen. If coming from Lake Ikawa, take rail to Oku-izumi and 30min bus. Two dozen inns here, all small, more like mountain huts, ¥-B-Tw/2. Short or full-day hikes throughout area, or lounge in outdoor rock-bath by river. Out of way but well worth trek.

Those who continue down coast, pass miles of massive sand dunes on beach stretching from Omae-zaki Point 30km to Hamamatsu, site of famous *kite war* **May 3-5**. **AGARA-CHO** town on E side of Omae-zaki Point (due S of Fujieda) has 'red' and 'white' teams of kites (about 1m^2), each side trying to cut other's rope or force down. Same days at Hamamatsu City's **Nakata-jima sand dunes** much grander; each of city's blocks sponsors kite, at least 10x6 feet requiring 15 handlers, terrific designs. Can get smaller replicas of these kites in area; we found good selection at **Sumita-ya** folk-toy store in Hamamatsu, 4 blocks N of Seibu dept store.

Halfway between battling kite sites lies remains of **Takatenjin Castle** where Ieyasu won decisive battle over Takeda Katsuyori in 1581.

PERSONAL DATEBOOK: *Tea Festival*, **May 2-3** and *Tako Gassen Festival* (kite-fighting) **May 3-5** (*see* above). Other festivals in this area are:

Nohitsu-sai offertory rite: Lake Sakuraga-ike, Hamaoka-cho, near tip of Omae-zaki Point on windward side. Held on autumn equinox and following day (**Sep 21-22**), barrel of special red rice is sunk in lake, ancient ritual to great Dragon God. *Obi Matsuri* Sash Festival: Oi Jinja grand fete, **mid-Oct** every 3rd year (1989, '92, '95, '98...) 1km long parade of dancers, great wheeled floats, Daimyo; main event is O-yakko (grand attendant) parade of 25 men in flashy kimono with 2 swords 6ft long, off which hang colorful obi sash. Shrine is 500m W of Shimada stn JR Main Line. *Kakegawa Festival*: **Oct 10-12**, usually small, but especially grand every 3rd year (1991, '94, '97, 2000...) when massive parade of 40 wheeled floats, small & large *shishi-mai* lion dances, from singles to grandest shishi-mai with 250 people-legs.

HAMAMATSU

OUR EXPRESS pulls in and doors open as down-beat to operatic chorus of tea and *bento* (lunch) vendors, each of whom sounds his chord in harmony with others like some great organ. We were not surprised after several trips thru to learn that town is center of organ and piano manufacture, since Mr

YAMAHA Torakusu started making organs here 1880's. Hamamatsu now makes 90% of *all* musical instruments made in Japan.

Traditional craftsmanship, especially in lacquering which is outstanding in this area, has made grand piano Japanese export money maker. Goddess of Music is Benten (only woman in Seven Lucky Gods) and just at end of Hamamatsu proper huge Kawai Piano works faces **BENTENJIMA**, island with some nice beaches, lovely vistas, good inns, acting as stopper to lagoon of Hamana-ko where famed eels raised. For fine lunch or dinner, try *kabayaki* or *unagi teishoku* (broiled eel) dinner especially summer. In Hamamatsu, popular place is **Daikoku-ya**, 500m N of stn, full meals about ¥1,700.

Arrange to **visit factories** thru stn JTB or Kanko-annai; tho they advise apply 10 days in advance, you might be able to get in on tour at any of great factory groups— such as **Kawai** ☎(0534)-57-1211, or **Yamaha** ☎60-1111 (no English tour) which also makes motorcycles with usual unharmonious voice boxes. Honda bikes and sports cars are made here too, as are Suzuki bikes. Same arrangement to see factory– **Honda** ☎36-1111; **Suzuki** ☎47-1111.

Visit **Air Self Defense Force** (ASDF) base at Mikata-ga-hara plain, 25min **bus** (**cab** 2x-mtr) NE of town to *Minami Kichi,* South Base: ☎(0534)-72-1111; free 90min tour of S base radar facilities and noncombat aircraft (fighters N base, no tours), 3x-daily.

Popular local art: *Zazanza-ori* weaving using thicker threads, natural dyes. Visit main center **Akane-ya**, ☎61-1594, Hamamatsu City, Nakajima-cho; **bus** 5min to Shakai Hoken Byoin-hospital, 5min walk further. Call ahead, X-sun, mon, hols, no fee.

SHIJIMIZUKA, reconstructed Neolithic Jomon period village near Lake Sanaru-ko, 15min bus (**cab** 3x-mtr; keep if continuing to Kanzanji or Benten-jima Onsens) E of town. Not as extensive as TORO, nonetheless one of few Jomon period restorations. Excavated artifacts displayed in museum here. Jomon were hunter-gatherers. Evidence of their existence is found in shell mound 'trash heaps' which they left scattered about their huts. They lived in small communities of sunken hut-dwellings much simpler and smaller than that of Yayoi, used stone and bone tools (fishhooks and spear points), had developed laminated bow from which arose historical Japanese bow. They domesticated dogs, developed sophisticated pottery style marked by rope-like designs from which their name derives, *Jo-mon* ='cord pattern'. Clear differences (chronological and regional) in Jomon style indicate several distinct stages of development, possible immigration waves. Jomon people most closely related to forest dwellers of northeast Asia and even America, with claims of similar cultures in New Guinea and Peru. Were matrilineal society worshipping Earth Goddess represented by stumpy *dogu* female figurines. Dead were stuffed into burial jars and buried within their camps. Jomon flourished for several millennia until immigration of superior Yayoi in 3rd cent BC. Yayoi spread rapidly, reaching Kanto Plains by 1st century BC, but there were no violent confrontations as Yayoi melded with existing Jomon. That is, until Kanto Plains where Jomon remnants intermixed with Ainu, whom Jomon had forced out centuries earlier (called Emishi, or Ezo by Wa Japanese) created frontier not entirely conquered until 9th century by first shogun SAKANOUE Tamuramaro.

Near Shijimizuka is...
Saiga-gake ravine where Ieyasu, in order to protect Hamamatsu Castle from Takeda Shingen's superior forces chasing him from battle at Mikata-ga-hara (1572), mounted successful guerrilla raids. Familiar with area, they caused enough confusion among enemy to make Shingen question real size of defending army and retreat. Had he gone on, he would have vanquished

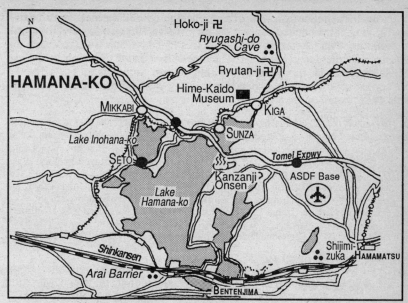

Ieyasu, but as fate would have it he didn't, never got another chance, as he died soon after (as we know from Kurosawa film *Kagemusha*). Nearby **SOEN-DO** temple dedicated to fallen on both sides. Castle, built by Ieyasu, is 15min walk towards town: postwar tourism replica.

SHIJIMIZUKA also easily reached from lakeside onsens KANZAN-JI & BENTENJIMA, following either of which preferred to staying in Hamamatsu City —which is industrial center with most of its lodgings plain hotels lacking usual Japanese spark we have come so far to experience.

LAKE HAMANA-KO: Linked to Pacific by narrow opening, fully enclosed until late 15th century tidal wave breached stretch of sand dunes; closes at low tide. 10th largest lake in Japan, shaped like open hand fed by dozen rivers.

On S shore is BENTENJIMA ONSEN, NE is KANZAN-JI ONSEN, several villages along its N shore, growing due to Tomei Expwy. S shore cluttered with eel fisheries Japan's top supplier (30% of annual 25,000-ton harvest) of these delicious fish; and *suppon* terrapin, delicacy available most inns but must reserve early.

Many places to stay on lake, but for most we suggest...
BENTENJIMA, lovely place for walks as bridges connect 10 little islets in lagoon. Picturesque from Oct to May as tiny boats weave in and out among stakes in bay for seaweed culture. Competing with them are all manner of craft (rented anywhere) from wind-surfing to water-skiing, or simple row boat and fishing pole for laid-back folks.

Motorboat race area in Arai-machi section of lake, 3km E of Bentenjima. One can enjoy several ways of fishing on lake, most popular is *takiya* ('*Taki*'-fire,'*ya*'-spear) nite fishing. Boat at nite, spear or net whatever is drawn towards light. All boats and pilots for these outings come from next village of YUTOH, right granted to them since they lack hot spring to lure customers. **Apr-Oct**: ¥21,000 for 3 plus pilot, ¥24,000 for 4. Starts after sundown, continues for 3hrs; reserve Hamana Gyogyo Kumiai ☎(05359)-2-1063. During day, at Bentenjima, go out bay at low tide to dig for clams, or rent boat with outboard motor to fish, ¥10,000 for 2 people, 2hr; prices vary with engine HP. Can also take part in *Hiki-bune* herding of fish into nets, ¥53,000 for 10, 4hr; reserve Yusen Kumiai ☎2-0933. All inns can arrange for any outing, all prices up by ¥500 sun and hol. Good beach at Bentenjima.

Novel experience is *to-ami* (casting weighted circular nets from boats), and having catch cooked as tempura on boat. In 1960 we found **Ami-sumi**, elderly man who, it turned out used to live in Tokyo and was leader among *to-ami* men there, and knew our Tokyo friend of original edition Ami-Yasu in Shinagawa. He has passed away, but his son continues tradition and tho no longer offering his experience to tourists, he has on occasion taken out guests of his inn (*see* below).

WHERE TO STAY: Numerous inns line narrow spit of land that is Bentenjima, and tho some have 'Hotel' appended to name, all are J-style rooms with large baths–often overlooking lake or ocean. Most transformed into large *ryotel* after hot spring water spouted out in 1960. Prices start ¥8,000w/2, ¥-T–S. Garet stayed at **Yusen-ya**, ☎(05359)-2-0204, across from stn, which completed new annex and overhaul in 1984. Immaculate rooms and excellent service, and cheapest of large inns. Others nearby are **Myoga-ya** ☎2-2525, **Hamana-ko Kanko** ☎2-2211, **Marubun** ☎2-1611. Also several minshuku here: **Inoue** ☎6-1166, **Asashio** ☎2-0761, **Iwamoto** ☎2-2466, dozen more, also budget ryokan **Amisumi** ☎2-0165 run by our net throwers. TOURIST INFORMATION OFFICE in round building at pier behind very helpful in finding places.

Hamanako Youth Hostel at...
ARAI-MACHI, site of one of 4 old main barrier checkpoint gates along Tokaido (*see* HAKONE), only one with original building still intact. Museum has old documents, artifacts. ¥200 gets you in both, X-mon, day after hol. 15min walk from Arai-machi stn, or 10min bus along Rte1 from Bentenjima. 3km W; also recent onsen with dozen inns (same price range but only few draw true onsen water) along white sand beaches separating Hamana-ko from sea.

KANZAN-JI ONSEN, on lovely spit of land further inland E on lagoon scenic spot longer than Bentenjima, more popular. Hot springs gushed out 1958 resulting in building boom to become family-oriented recreation center.

Now has amusement park, zoo and Flower Park, but still nice. Inns here run few thou more per nite, but 2 Kokumin-shukusha provide budget lodgings, book early for mid-summer or year-end: **Kanzan-ji-so** ☎(0534)-87-0257; **Okusa-so** ☎87-2111; both set atop OKUSA HILL, reached by 4min ropeway from main onsen cluster –on Tateyama hill with KANZAN-JI temple. Tateyama actually isle barely separated from shore, connected by 2 bridges. Shijimizuka 4km E of here. Little **tour boat** chugs Kanzan-ji to Seto across lake, ¥450/o.w., ¥800/r.t.

OKU-HAMANA or backside of Hamana, N shore still has some small villages where wanderer can find budget minshuku, quiet countryside in spite of nearby expressway (I.C. at Mikkabi).

E to W main towns are...
KIGA, SUNZA, MIKKABI all reached by bus from Hamamatsu in 50min, 1hr, 80min respectively. Also bus from Kanzan-ji. SETO, at mouth of Lake 'Wild boar-Nose' INOHANA-KO, is also reached by bus from Bentenjima. Futamata Line JR also passes thru, branching off Tokaido Main Line at Hamamatsu, rejoining at Toyokawa.

During Edo period this route was branch road of Tokaido, known as *Hime-kaido*, Princess Road, so called since it was most often used by women of nobility who wished to avoid embarrassing body searches at Arai barrier. **First weekend Apr** is feudal costumed re-creation, *princess' procession* down sakura-lined Miyakoda Riverbank in Kiga town. **History Museum**, *Hime-kaido*, thatch-roof ex-Hime-kaido teahouse N stn; 9:00-16:30 daily X-mon, hols, ¥150. 2km W of stn.

Old section of Hime-kaido starts at NINOMIYA SHRINE for 6km hike to MIKKABI; or head S on trail intersecting midway at INASA PASS, ending SUNZA or SAKUME, with good swimming. We suggest this route for those with much time, or wandering expatriate in search of something new.

Several spectacular temples tucked away in hills here: worth noting are...
RYUTAN-JI and **HOKO-JI** in NE mountains. Furthest back HOKO-JI
(1384) is still active Zen temple, with over 30 halls sprawling over hillside.
Also called OKUYAMA HANSOBO, dedicated to Hansobo goblin-saint,
guardian against fires. Complex had many copper *tengu* statues which were
moved to Kamakura's HANSOBO temple where they narrowly escaped being
melted down into bullets during World War II. As you approach, 500
Rakan, Buddha-disciple figures appear, carved into sheer rock face along
path, then many monks' living quarters come into view, perched high atop
stone walls.

WHERE TO STAY: Monks' quarters for ¥-lo-Bw/2 vegetarian meals, join daily
zazen sits. Arrange thru **Kiga Town Hall**, or go early and ask in person. They can
accommodate up to 330 people at once so it should be no problem unless you coincide
with occasional group sessions winter or midsummer *kan* 'extreme seasons' that
companies have their employees undergo. HOKO-JI is 25min **bus** from Kiga stn; 1hr
from Hamamatsu, to last stop OKUYAMA and 10min walk.

Having come this far, stop part way to see spectacular early Edo sculp-
tured garden by master KOBORI Enshu, carvings of famed 'lefty' Hidari
Jingoro at **RYUTAN-JI** temple, built 733. Same **bus** to HOKO-JI, 10min from
Kiga stn to temple; or 50min from Hamamatsu → Jingu-Mae bus stop, 15min walk S.

Midway between 2 temples...
Ryugashi-do Caves, excavated from Oct 1981, open to public 1983.
Depth 1km, parts have 30m ceilings, many underground streams, hilite large
subterranean waterfall far rear. 8:00-17:00, ¥500.

*Like pair of pincers, **Atsumi** and **Chita Peninsulas** reach into Pacific Ocean,
separating Mikawa Bay. 'Crotch' of two is...*
GAMAGORI port for hydrofoils and ordinary ferries to TOBA-ISE, points
in between. Boats from Mikawa area to Toba:

Hydrofoil: GAMAGORI (9:30) TOBA (10:50) via NISHIURA ONSEN → IRAGO.
GAMAGORI (11:00) → TOBA (12:45) via Nishiura → Himaga → Shino Isles → IRAGO.
IRAGO → TOBA direct in 35min at 10:20, 12:10, 14:55.
Passenger Ferry: 1hr direct IRAGO-TOBA: 08:00, 09:10, 10:25, 11:35, 12:45,
14:00, 15:15, 16:25, 17:40. Four extras on sun, 17 daily main hols: New Year (12/31-
1/5), Golden Week (5/3-5/5), Obon (8/13-8/16).

Near hydrofoil port is fine beach, scenic, and best of all with good range of
accommodations. Old world **Gamagori Hotel** ☎(0533)-68-1111 was long one of best in
Japan—of old, long ranked with Miyako and Nara hotels in charm and class—but alas it
closed. Best news of '87 was its reopening, fully refurbished as #56 of fine **Prince** hotel
chain; only 26 rooms, but 6 good restaurants. Near hydrofoil port is gigantic **Takeshima
Hotel** ☎69-1256, resort in itself—16 bowling lanes, game center, sushi bars, other
restaurants. Rooms ¥-lo-S+w/2. Huge baths to soak in, nitely live shows on their stage
of various local *taiko* drum & folk *kagura* combinations—flashy, touristy but well done.

*Nearby gaudy Takeshima **aquarium**, from near which 417m narrow bridge leads to...*
TAKESHIMA, sacred isle **YAOTOMI SHRINE** complex to dragon gods,
busloads of tourists invade isle in human waves ensure dragons never return.
Pleasant 30min stroll between hordes (eve or early morning quite nice).

MIYA ONSEN, picturesque fishing port of Gamagori City with hot
springs and good beach, scenic and, best of all, fine range of accoms.
Tokaido Main Line Miya stn is close but more convenient to **bus** from GAMAGORI
(10min) or TOYOHASHI (30min) stns where expresses stop. Rambling old luxury hotels of
early '60s have been replaced by new resort hotels, each with their spacious lobbies, shops,
and grand baths; you can also get **geisha** companions ¥15,000 for 90min, out of 100 licensed by city. Hotels directed towards large tour groups, except for sole remaining old-
edition **Fukinuki ryokan** ☎(0533)-69-1211 at ¥-Sw/2, W- and J-rms, no singles; facing

beach is unusual landscaped **mixed bathing** outdoor onsen bath, separate indoor baths. Meals here get grander with better rooms: even cheapest offers smorgasbord of fresh seafood. Charming festival **lunar Oct 9**, (half-moon Nov) rural dances & folk kagura, carrying mikoshi into sea. KINGO-JI temple on hill behind MIYA has 30m tall statue of Saint Kobo-daishi. Several ryokan ¥-Tw/2, arrange thru **Kanko-annai** Gamagori stn.

Several more coastal onsen W of Gamogori City, Rail Pass but suggest staying in area:
KATAHARA, just 5km W of Gamagori stn (20min bus, cab 4x-mtr) is only onsen in hills overlooking bay. Most inns here are smaller, more personal than at Miya. Average prices ¥-Tw/2; best is old-timer **Kimura-kan** ☎57-2121. Budget but good family-run **Kataoka** ☎57-2115 with rooms from ¥-Bw/2.

NISHIURA ONSEN on spit of land jutting into bay has hydrofoils to IRAGO (35min) and TOBA (95min). Just offshore, two small islets, 'Rabbit Isle' and 'Monkey Isle', each inhabited by animal named after: ferry visits these two in 2hr course (¥900), time on each included.

GETTING THERE: By 30min bus from GAMAGORI stn, or Meitetsu Private Line GAMAGORI → NISHIURA (10min) and 8min bus to Onsen. Atmosphere like Miya, with mostly large, modern inns (same price range), but affords great view as it is on hill. Here too, can arrange thru your inn for **geisha** (¥10,000/30min) or masseurs (¥3,500/40min). Nearby **INAMURA JINJA** dedicated to Nitta Yoshisada 'conqueror' of Kamakura (*see*).

History buffs may want to head further down coast on bus or Meitetsu rail to...
KIRA ONSEN, ancestral home of KIRA Kozukenosuke, arch-enemy of 47 ronin in *Chushingura*. One of 47 came from Himagashima isle in bay, which we visit next. In area is **KEZO-JI**, Kira ancestral temple where Kozukenosuke is buried; boasts fine painted fusuma doors by 18th century master Ike-no-Taiga, and sculptured garden by Kobori Enshu. Bit down coast, KIRA YOSHIDA whence ferries ply to SAKUSHIMA ISLAND. Other ferry terminal to Sakushima is MIKAWA ISSHIKI, 7km down. **SUWA JINJA** shrine near Isshiki stn, *Giant Lantern Festival* **Aug 26-27**. Best 26 nite as gaily painted lanterns 11m high and 6m across are illuminated and hung in shrine precincts.

SHOPPING: Try and. resist (we couldn't 1963 nor '88) exquisite Komatsubara white horse dolls (¥8,000 for 1 ft long—were ¥850 in '64, inflated less than hotels) sold at most large inns and gift stores around Gamagori.

Note If **driving**, *and by-passing Toro, short detour before Gamagori to...*
URIGO archaeological site, smaller but older than Toro. Coming down Rte1, cross river just past Toyohashi stn and 2km further, on L (S) of Rte1. If on Tomei Expwy, exit Toyokawa, down Rte151 → Rte1, then L (towards Toyohashi) 1km to Urigo.

10km W from TOYOHASHI on Rte1 or parallel Meitetsu Nagoya Main Line are 2 Edo era lodging hamlets on old Tokaido. Bypassed by Rte1 and rail line, are still mostly centuries-old folk houses in good condition, some old inns still have rings to tie horse's reins. Old Tokaido now paved parallels Rte1, S/sea side. 15min rail to GOYU JUKU whence 30min walk thru pine groves to AKASAKA JUKU. Were quite large towns in heyday allowing more freedom to let loose in than in castle-dominated Toyohashi. 15min rail further on similar hamlet of FUJIKAWA JUKU. *Juku* was midway place btwn post towns.

Toyohashi is also entrance to OKU-MIKAWA region; on JR Iida Line or Rte151.

TOYOKAWA, city is home of beautiful **TOYOKAWA INARI**, one of top 3 *Inari* (Fox god of rice) shrines. This one unusual in that most of complex is temple; one of few to survive Meiji forced separation of Shinto and Buddhism. Enter thru MYOGON-JI's temple gates; Inari Shrine is to L beyond pair of guardian foxes. Long hallway connects shrine main hall to temple BUDDHA HALL, still-functioning **Zen center** with over 90 halls and priests' quarters. You can **stay** here, call ☎(05338)-5-2030. Path leads thru woods to *Oku-no-in* sanctuary. Behind zazen hall is small pavilion dedicated to Daikoku, of 7 Lucky Gods, Shinto-Buddhist deity. 5min walk Toyokawa stn, 30min bus Toyohashi stn.

22km inland from Toyokawa to remains of...

Nagashino Castle where Nobunaga's musketeers wiped out Takeda sword- and pike-men, which slaughter brought on Japan's self-instigated withdrawal from age of guns. N of castle site is battlefield, nr which is IO-IN temple, Takeda Katsuyori's command center, now small Museum of Local Farm Tools. **History Museum**, *Rekishi-kan*, btwn Nagashino-jo stn and castle is dedicated to battle. From Hamamatsu, Rte257 cuts inland to Nagashino; occasional buses.

Further inland is 1,200-year-old...

HORAI-JI temple complex. We have not been here, it's reputed to be quite spectacular; especially for those who don't mind some backwoods hiking. 10min bus from HON-NAGASHINO (one beyond NAGASHINO-JO), 1hr50min from TOYOHASHI. Bus lets you off in small village (HORAI-JI bus stop), whence 1hr walk via **Ni-o-mon** gate is pleasant up 1,425 stone steps thru cool glade. At one time 36 main halls and dozens of living quarters covered hillside, now half-dozen main structures remain, including scaled-down replica of Nikko's Toshogu built by 4th Tokugawa Shogun Ietsuna. Main hall is 45min from gate, originally built 702, rebuilt many times, last in 1974 is concrete replica of older wood. 40min beyond to *Oku-no-in* sanctuary; hiking trails ring surrounding peaks past several more isolated halls tucked away in forest, with sheer rock cliffs for backdrops. May thru Aug wooded hillside of Horai-ji echoes at nite with 'faithful' owls cry of *'buppo-so'*, or 'priests of Buddha's Law'.

WHERE TO STAY: 4 rustic inns (¥-Bw/2) in village, such as *gassho-zukuri*-style folk house **Unryu-so** ☎(05363)-5-1181. Near Horai-ji Sancho bus stop opp Toshogu Shrine are **Shukubo priests' quarters**, ¥-lo-Bw/2. Late Mar-late Nov, bus continues on Horai-ji Parkway toll road to HORAI-JI SANCHO bus stop closer to main complex. Parkway begins at JR Yuya stn.

YUYA ONSEN on rail line has dozen inns, some modern ryotels, all ¥-Tw/2. 3km towards Nagashino smaller **AKAHIKI ONSEN** with one inn, same price. Between two onsen, nr JR Ohno stn is **OHNO JUKU**, lovely find of Edo era hamlet little changed since; few budget inns among old folk houses. From here, 4km trail to HORAI-JI.

Inland from here, rail and road continue on to IIDA, which we visit later on in Chubu chapter to ride along Tenryu river. Wanderers may want to head up into hills beyond to catch any one of several country folk festivals; OKU-MIKAWA is known as treasury of folk festivals (*see* DATEBOOK).

Back on bay, numerous hydrofoils and ferries ply between GAMAGORI–IRAGO–MOROZAKI and several islands in bay. Three largest islands of SAKUSHIMA, HIMA-GASHIMA, SHINOJIMA, located between pincer tips, have dozens of budget inns among them, excellent for loafing. Especially, hardest to get to SAKUSHIMA, is, well, most beautiful of trio and not yet caught up in recent development of other two. Shinojima and Himagashima isles reached from Gamagori, Nishiura, and either tip of pincer, also linked to each; Sakushima reached only from Kira-Yoshida or Isshiki, not linked to other two.

Wandering budgeteer may want to stop in Gamagori area long enough to take luxurious bath in one of large inns (nominal fee around ¥300-500), then go down either peninsula or out to isles, boat Morozaki or Irago to Toba.

ATSUMI PENINSULA: Flanking Mikawa Bay on E, IRAGO at tip is best for ferry to TOBA 40min hydrofoil ¥1,800, hour car ferry ¥1,030. IRAGO hour hydrofoil from GAMAGORI, 40min from NISHIURA, and 50min ferry from other tip MOROZAKI. By road, it is 50km from TOYOHASHI on Rte259; 80min express bus or 1hr35min local (¥200 less). From Toyohashi you can also take Toyotetsu Private Rail 35min to last stop TAHARA halfway down peninsula and 50min bus on. **Driving**, skip GAMAGORI, in which case overnite at HAMANA-BENTENJIMA, TAHARA or IRAGO.

Suggest Tahara Sep 15-16, combined festival of MYOJIN AND HACHIMAN SHRINES in which colorful *dashi* (festival floats) are pulled thru town—geishas perform dances atop platforms at nite while fireworks burst overhead.

WHERE TO STAY: Tahara's inns are mostly for traveling business people –
simple but with good service and cheap (¥-Bw/2). For ¥-Tw/2, there is one fancier inn at
TAHARA ONSEN at foot of MT ZAO 3km N of town. IRAGO has twice as many ryokan
(around ¥-Tw/2), 15 minshuku and **Kokumin Kyuka-mura** (Peoples' Rest Village)
with main hall, cottages, and campground, slight extra for cottage, but only few hundred
yen for campsite if own tent, otherwise small rental fee. No matter where you stay at
Irago, all serve heaps of fresh seafood, better at ryokans. Sand skiing at Kozuka; see draft
oxen hauling in fishing nets at AKABANE on S shore flower center (you can buy time on
net, ¥45,000, and keep all that it hauls in) and lovely scenery at point.

CHITA PENINSULA across bay is better if coming from Kansai, doing
our routing in reverse. JR Taketoyo Line and Meitetsu Private Rail run Chita's leeward side from Nagoya to midway Taketoyo where JR ends, Meitetsu splits, one line goes
on 10km to KOWA good beaches, boat terminal of Himagashima-Shinojima-Morozaki
circle; other line cuts across to windward to end at **UTSUMI ONSEN** with long stretch
of beach. Buses up both sides, and between. Before Utsumi on same side are **SAKAI** and
CHITAHAMA ONSEN, with few inns each; also several small villages, with beaches.

'Twixt' Utsumi and Sakai is...
NOMA DAIBO temple, built by Yoritomo to honor his father Yoshitomo,
murdered here by 'faithful' retainer. Yoshitomo's grave is marked by stone
sword: unarmed when cut down, his last words were: "Would that I had
even my wooden practice sword."

MOROZAKI at tip, 30min bus from KOWA or UTSUMI, is linked to TOBA by 90min
car ferry. Middle of peninsula is **U-no-yama** hill, on which is lake full of *U*-
cormorants that migrate here in winter; replaced by *Goi-sagi* nite herons in
spring. Save seeing cormorants for Gifu's or Kyoto's fishing birds.

Interesting festival **TOYOHAMA** village 5km from MOROZAKI, windward coast, **mid-
July** (varies, exact date available thru **Tourist Info offices** Gamagori, Nagoya,
Toyohashi; also poster ads at stns): timeless summer fete originated from Yayoi offertory
rites for better catch, giant fish 20m long and 5m high is paraded thru streets and floated in
sea, skeleton of wood and bamboo covered by hand-painted cotton skin. Meitetsu Private
Rail's Tokoname Line runs 40min from Nagoya to last stop...

TOKONAME Kiln town. Pottery-making began here early 12th cent,
mostly large urns until Meiji era when given freedom to make whatever they
pleased; now area famous for its persimmon-red pottery as well as larger
urns. Quiet little town with no mistaking its means of livelihood. Narrow
lanes lined with walls made of urns; elementary schools have walls of
glazed mosaic; kiln rejects clutter whole area dominated by dozens of brick
chimneys of nationally famous *tokoname-yaki* pottery kilns of which there
are over dozen. Few hours wandering thru streets is best and only way to
see town, many signs (in Japanese) posted to let you know where you are.
Some places to introduce you to *Tokoname-yaki* are:

City Pottery Hall, *Tojiki Kaikan*, for display, sale of everything made
(100m SE of stn to 1st intersection, L 400m). **Pottery Research Center**, *Togei
kenkyu-jo* (1.5km E of stn), old pots excavated from 12th cent *nobori-gama*
(climbing kiln); modern workshop. Next to it is **Folk History Museum**
Both 10min bus from stn to Kusaki-guchi stop. All three daily 9:00-17:00, X-mon, free.
2 main **clusters of kilns**: 1st is near **Tojiki Kaikan**, L at intersection;
2nd is in center of town near shrine; also remains of ancient *noborigama*.

If **on your own**, we suggest taking hydrofoil or ferry across to Toba.
JR Rail Passers heading to ISE must go to NAGOYA and change to Ise Line.
Drivers, Rte1 to just beyond Yokkaichi, where change to coastal Rte23.
If on bus tour, you will, for some unknown reason be dragged
into...(NAGOYA, next).

PERSONAL DATEBOOK: SHIZUOKA TO NAGOYA

FETES found only in Oku-Mikawa area are year-end *Hana-matsuri* 'Flower Festivals': nothing to do with flowers, just wild, energetic demon dances to scare out illness and misfortune for coming year. Starting **3rd sat Nov**, these dances (30-40 in row going all day and nite) occur in over 20 villages north of Horai-ji on different nites, ending with wildest on **lunar Jan 15** (full moon nite of February) at Shimo-tsugu. All are within 15km radius, most centered around Higashi Sakae-cho village. These dances declared National Intangible Cultural Assets (ICA) in 1976.

New Year is greeted in somewhat quieter manner, with each local shrine offering *dengaku* dances. Dengaku started out as marking first planting of rice, with village women planting in step to drum-flute music of village men. Stylized over centuries, now performed as prayer for prosperous, healthy year—*see* addt'l Datebook, p287.

January

3 *Horai-ji Dengaku* at hilltop Dengaku-do hall at 10:00, ends 6hrs and 27 dances later, (*text* p293), Aichi Pref.

6 *Kurosawa Dengaku* at Amida-do hall of Kurosawa village, 10km E of Yuya Onsen in middle of mountains. Starts noon with offertory dance to local kami, ends 7pm with 37th dance, driving out evil spirits.

8th nite to sunrise 9th at Kawana, 12km beyond Terano, mark New Year with *Fire Festivals* in which 2m long torches carried around, called *Hiyondori* in local dialect; and other villages other days.

February

11 *Damine Dengaku* at Damine Kannon, nite-long dances followed by *mura-shibai* village plays all day; Reach Tamine by bus from Nagashino, 20km N on Rte257. Next major series of festivals is *mid-summer O-bon*, with almost every village and hamlet celebrating.

April

1st weekend Feudal costumed recreation, *Princess' procession* down sakura-lined Miyakoda Riverbank in Kiga town, p290.

Early Ancient Taitai kagura, (*text*, p280).

First Sat before 12th *Shingenko-matsuri*, 1300-man feudal costume procession, 5-8pm, Kofu City (p274).

Sun nearest 10th *Tenzushi-no-mai*, old puppet dance, Kose-cho, Kofu City (p274).

May

8 *Fujikiri Matsuri* wisteria cutting festival, Daizen-ji, Katsunuma-cho, (p278).

13-15 *Shingen festival*, Taitai kagura, samurai procession, fireworks, Shimobe-cho, (p281).

July

Mid 20m-long fish, parade into sea at Morozaki Pt, (*text*, p294).

August

15 Best around Nagashino said to have begun end 16th century with local villages praying for souls of thousands lost at battle of Nagashino: *Shingen-bara Hiyondori Fire Fest* dedicated to Takeda soldiers, 60-70 massive torches 10ft long, 3ft around, lit 21:00, carried around town;

15 Mikawa Togo, 3km S of castle. Same nite at Norimoto, E across river from castle, dozens of massive lanterns carried around by chanting loincloth-clad youths in *Norimoto Mando Lantern Fest* Similar *Nabetsuru Mando Fest*, simul-taneously at Ichikawa, Shinshiro City 2km S.

14-15 *Hoka-ofori*, get-rid-of-worldly-attachments dances, led by drumming youths with massive fans tied to their backs at Shiose, Genji, Furi, Isshiki villages in Horai-cho, 12-15km N of Nagashino on Rte 257. Larger one, same days at Ohmi Sensho-ji temple near Nagashino castle.

26-27 Giant Lantern Festival, Kira Onsen [*see text* p292].

September

Sat-Sun nearest lunar Aug 10 *Hadaka-mairi* at Iwaki City, Shizuoka Prefecture. Young men after 3 days purifying selves in ocean run thru town from Mitsuke Tenjin Shrine, clad only in straw skirts, relaying flaming lanterns.

15-16 Atsumi Peninsula, p293.

End–early Oct Grape fest, *torii yaki*, burn 90x50m torii, Katsunuma-cho[p278]

October

9 Lunar Miya Onsen festival, [p.292].

November

3rd Sat *Sansoro Matsuri* Tsushima Shrine Shitara-cho Mitsuhashi on Rte 257 20km N of Nagashino. Villagers dressed as 7 Lucky Gods put on show & dialogue w/ audience, lasts well into nite.

December

6 *Fire walking*, Odawara (text p257).

15-16 *Fire walking*, Shimizu City, Akiba shrine, priests undergo cold water rites, 9pm.

...picture of Japan as a land of cherry blossoms and geisha has gained such a hold on the imagination of many Westerners that they find it hard to remember that Japan is a modern industrial nation.
— Donald Keene, *Living in Japan*

NAGOYA 名古屋
FOR BUSINESSMEN ONLY

JAPAN'S FOURTH LARGEST CITY, present population 2.1 million, was first war-leveled city to be rebuilt according to modern planning with wide straight streets—lovely by day but morgues at nite. Handsome city, but of little tourist interest except for art buffs at Tokugawa Museum or anthropologists March 15 at 'His & Her' fertility shrines TAGATA-OGATA. We do not advise putting LA's sister city on any itinerary, but you may well be in town on business: brief catalogue of its features will suffice. There are several craft towns nearby: SETO for porcelain, OHARA-MURA handmade *washi*-paper, ARIMATSU for dyed cloth, and pleasant rural village of ASUKE.

This working man's town was armaments prodcenter during war, now heavy industry. Imaginative Love Hotels line expressway as you approach city, itself full of budget eating and drinking spots. It lives up to its claim as *pachinko* (pinball) capital of world, boasting over 250 centers with over 6,000 machines, out of national 15,414 hall w/3,000,000 machines (proportionately more than Tokyo's 1100). Making these machines kept city alive while switching from wartime to peacetime industry, is still major product. National retail grosses double defense budget, ¥13,000,000,000,000 in '89 and rising, 2+% of GNP. With constant hi-tech improvements to pinball machines they must be replaced at least every three years, more in flashier parlors. Game makes major maker world's 8th ranking billionaire ('90).

GETTING THERE: Air Intn'l WEST COAST direct Delta, HAWAII America Air West, Continental → South Pacific via SAIPAN, GUAM, FIJI etc → HAWAII → WEST COAST; EUROPE Lufthansa; near future Hong Kong →, Shanghai →, Manila → Nagoya direct links. Domestic air hub for central Japan linking → TOKYO, OSAKA, JAPAN SEA; Shinkansen 2hrs from TOKYO, under 1hr → OSAKA–KYOTO; also long distance sea ferries up Pacific coast N as far as Hokkaido's TOMAKOMAI , or S to OKINAWA.

WHERE NEXT: Chuo old JR Main Line detours → Tokyo thru central Japan; Takayama Line cuts across → Japan Sea at TOYAMA passing thru backwoods Gero Onsen and soaring thatched roofs of SHIRAKAWA-GO, beautiful HIDA; Nagaragawa Line heads N → Mino. All 3 are inroads into OFFBEAT CHUBU we cover later. For ISE itinerary (p.311), better than JR is Kintetsu vista-dome trains → Ise, 2hrs and → OSAKA matches Shinkansen time straight into downtown at half-price; Mie Tokyu has 4hr express buses from Nagoya stn via ISE (follows) → KASHIKOJIMA; drivers go coastal Rte1 & Rte23 or Higashi-Meihan Expwy, to Ise Expwy at Kameyama. Higashi-Meihan also into NARA.

WHERE TO STAY: On pleasure stay out of town, as following pages—business good selection international hotels: **Hilton International** ¥-hi-S ☎(052)-212-1111, central at Sakae 1-chome, taxi-basic, full array health club, restaurants, etc. Former favorite **Nagoya Castle** ¥-S, ☎521-2121, pool, slightly inconvenient but scenic and nothing in Nagoya really out of way. Clustered around JR stn, var 1 to 5 min walk: **Dai-Ichi** ¥-S, ☎581-4411; **Terminal** ¥-T, ☎561-3751; **Meitetsu Grand** ¥-lo-S, ☎582-2211; **Miyako** ¥-lo-S ☎571-3211; **Castle Plaza** ¥-T-lo-S, ☎582-2121 w/gym, sauna, gym & indoor pool—best buy for young fitness-conscious businessman. HOME STAY: International Center ☎581-5678, Homestay Circle ☎451-6540, Tomodachi ☎751-2308. *Warning* hotels all booked year ahead for Oct Suzuka Auto Grand Prix!

GETTING AROUND: Good English Info, *Calendar*, scheds, available from **Nagoya International Center** ☎581-5678, or **City Tourist Info** in main stn. Also E-calendar mag *Eyes*, ☎761-5430. JR stns convenient for most sites in city. Adjacent JR Nagoya stn are main terminals for private Meitetsu and Kintetsu rail lines; former is most extensive and best for getting around greater Nagoya area and our next 2 stops INUYAMA and GIFU; latter rail onward for ISE-SHIMA area, best non-rail pass r.t. to/from OSAKA. In **town 4 subway** lines offer extensive coverage of metropolitan Nagoya, easier to use than equally extensive bus system. Main subway center is SAKAE, 2km (2 stns) E of Nagoya stn, in heart of downtown. Meitetsu Seto Line also starts Sakae. **Taxis** abound, rarely will you have to keep, pay for waiting—another will be along soon.

   Good **taxi tours** by **Tokyu Kanko Taxi**, ☎211-3456: 3hr tour town 27x-mtr, 4hr/ 36x-mtr, 5hr/45x-mtr or ¥3,910/9x-mtr per hr plus site admissions. **Out of town:** INUYAMA CASTLE & MEIJI MURA 5hrs/40x-mtr; then 6+hrs runs TAGATA-JINJA sex shrine, MEIJI-MURA and boat down Nihon Rhine, ¥25,000/48x-mtr. Good package is to KISO-JI SHUKUBA collections of old houses at MAGO-JUKU & TSUMAGO-JUKU up old pilgrim mountain hiway, 7+hrs/¥47,000per car. GERO ONSEN & lovely TAKAYAMA city ending there, 7+hrs/¥47,000. Fascinating Ise GRAND SHRINES (both) & wedded rocks at FUTAMI-GA-URA, end at TOBA, 7+hrs/¥49,000. Longer itineraries for pilgrimages, run 2-days/overnite ¥73,000+hotel up to 11days/10nites; real long distance deal, pilgrimage to 88 HOLY PLACES OF SHIKOKU Isle (*see*) at ¥390,-430,000—say ¥37,000 or 75x-mtr per day car w/driver, to give you ideas for computation. Own itinerary will be similar price.

   After months here '91 filming "Mr Baseball", Garet and big brother Cellin confirmed original opinion of town: great place to live, but no place to visit.

TILT: Our route begins center city, works S to spiral counter-clockwise E and N to possible overnite at INUYAMA or farther W at GIFU.

Nagoya Castle dominates town: built 1610-12, bombed out 1945 and for most part postwar reconstruction. Great finial dolphins atop roof (male and female) are gilded with 45kg/99lbs of 18-karat gold and have pure silver eyeballs, new. Three outer turrets, front gate and stone parapets remain of original structure. Central keep is **museum** with several thousand items from original castle, top fl **observatory**. 2,000 cherry trees, fete **early April**.

   Almost as photogenic are **municipal buildings**, tall Occidental structures with handsome pagoda roofs in 1930s 'lost empire' style.

6km E of Nagoya stn (15min bus, cab 4x-mtr), short walk S of Meitetsu Seto Line Morishita stn, or 10min SW of JR Ozone on Chuo Main Line is...

Tokugawa-en Park, once summer home of Tokugawa advisor's family. In SW corner **Hosa Library** houses major collection of medieval literature, started by Tokugawa Ieyasu 1617. Bought by Nagoya city 1959, now has over 80,000 volumes, including original *Tale of Genji*, parts of *Nihongi* anthology, other National Treasures. Open to public free, researchers and interested parties can see top documents for small fee. Daily 9:30-17:00, X-mon, hols, 3rd fri; when hol falls on sun, library open then X-mon and tues; exact information ☎(052) 935-2173.

In SE corner is...

Tokugawa Art Museum, superb Tokugawa family collection of feudal Edo era art, most fabulous are 'secret' and rarely shown, only once about every 5 years, but still main attraction of Nagoya for art buffs. Its most prosaic items marvelous. Many of these secret treasures showed to sell-out crowds in US and Europe in **Shogun Exhibition** 1983-84—if you saw that you've seen more than we in Japan. 10:00-16:00,¥300; X-mon, year-end, few days exhibit rotation.

Boston Art Museum Annex abuilding, semi-permanent home its fabulous screens.

2km SE of Tokugawa-en, or 10min walk N of subway KAKUO-ZAN stop...

NITTAI-JI Japan-Thai temple atop Kakuo-zan hill houses relic of Buddha, golden image presented by Thai king in 1904. Few hundred mtrs E of Nittai-ji are **Gohyaku-rakan**, images of 500 'enlightened' disciples of Historical Buddha.

1.5km SE of Nagoya stn (5min subway) halfway to Atsuta Shrine...
OSU KANNON District, similar to Tokyo's Asakusa district, major
entertainment center with several theaters, handful of antique stores, hundreds of tiny mom n' pop shops selling everything imaginable, and as many
cheap but good local eateries and drinking places frequented by students.
Tucked away amid this maze of shop-packed back-alleys are over 20
temples with many *ennichi* fairs between them adding even more color to
this area, especially around New Year.

Most famous of them is sprawling...
OSU KANNON, built elsewhere 1333 but moved here 1617 to escape Kiso
River's frequent floods. Did not survive WWII carpet bombing, present
main hall is concrete, but still impressive. Its scroll storage is one of top 3 in
Japan, housing over 15,000 ancient documents, including oldest existing
(1371) copy of *Kojiki* anthology (*see* by appointment). **Mid-Oct** *Osu Commoners'
Street Festival* same days as city-wide *Nagoya Festival*, but much more down-to-earth
folksy. Lots of **good eating** around, we gorged at **Baba-ten**, *Old Hags' Tempura* shop,
excellent budget joint run by pair of humorous old ladies; 1 block front of OSU KANNON.
We wound up nite with some students we somehow latched up with at cozy **Kadoya**
yakitori stand few blocks SE of Osu Kannon on corner of Honmachi-dori–Iwai-dori streets.

1km SE of Osu Kannon, or 3min walk NW of Higashi Betsu-in subway stop...
KIKOKU-JI temple: site of Senbon Matsubara prison where 258 Christians
were killed in 1664. Prison was moved to another spot after, and local lord
Tokugawa Mitsutomo erected temple to appease souls of victims. On 300th
anniversary of their execution, **Christian Artifacts Museum** was opened
in priests' quarters, exhibiting handful of *Kakure* (Hidden) *Kirishitan* related
items. Mound nearby covers mass burial, all peasants from central Hida (we
see more of same in Takayama). Museum *free*, 9:00-17:00, X-mon.

GETTING THERE: 6km from ATSUTA Shrine on road in from Gamagori bit
N of Rte 1, 25min from NAGOYA stn; if coming from other old Tokaido hamlets of
GOYU, AKASAKA, FUJIKAWA reached by Meitetsu Nagoya Main Line from Toyohashi.

*From Nagoya stn by JR to Atsuta, 5min, or Meitetsu to Jingu-mae, 8min, or subway
to Jingu-nishi, 14min, or cab 3x-mtr...*
ATSUTA SHRINE: Three sacred regalia of emperor are *magatama* jewel
(kept in Tokyo palace), mirror (at Ise) and sacred sword called *kusanagi-no
mitsurugi* (grass-cutting-honorable-blade) which Susano-O-no-Mikoto, local
Saint George, cut out of tail of femnivorous dragon we'll meet again in
Hiroshima. Sword (or ancient copy–original was lost) is kept here. New
building is not interesting in itself, you cannot see sword (tho teenager
almost ran away with it 20 years ago). One theory of origin of sacred swords
in Japan is that originally in Stone Age phallic stone wand was both weapon,
symbol of status.

PERSONAL DATEBOOK: At **ATSUTA SHRINE**, you can see full
bugaku program of 8 numbers on **Jan 11** (10:00-14:30), **May 1** (10:30-15:00)
and at 13:00 on sun btwn **Oct 10–20** when 4 dances are part of their autumn 3-day
festival. Most suns and hols there's some sort of noh program at Noh-gakudo (Noh
theater)–check NIC %581-5678. Their *Summer Festival* **June 5** rates imperial envoy,
with entertainment, portable shrines, harnessed horses and floats. At nite, huge boat with
straw torches and 365 paper lanterns lights up Atsuta Beach. Other festivals include: **Jan
7** 'divination' of year's clear days by measuring amount of water loss in sealed jar. **Jan 15**
rite for prosperous year, shooting arrows at shrine's ornamental cross-beams. **May 4** eve,
shrine priests gather front of kagura-den, have good laugh; said to show joy all felt with
return of Emperor Temmu in 686 AD. **May 5** mikoshi parade, 10am. **Jun**18 *Otaue-sai*,
ritual transplanting of rice, 10am. **More** dates:*Nagoya Avenues* free most hotels, or ¥200.

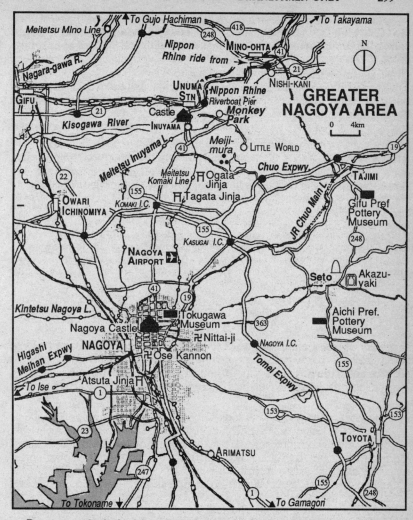

Bus tours take in 2 of 3 main sites of castle, Tokugawa Museum *or* ATSUTA. None do all—either castle + museum, or castle + shrine. We don't suggest either as they waste time at other uninteresting sites; do all 3 cheaper by **cab** if more than 2 passengers, almost as cheap for 2 considering time saved, freedom.

ARIMATSU, stretch of old Tokaido pedestrian highway, where famed *shibori* tie-dyeing is done. Here too, most buildings are Edo period, almost 1/2 of 130-odd houses stretching 800m from Matsunone Bridge W to Gion-ji temple are over century old, 1/4th over 200.

   Dyeing process can be seen at...
Arimatsu-shibori Workers' Co-op, S off main street; suggest call ahead ☎(052)-621-1747, but we got in without. Just past turn-off to Co-op is **Arimatsu Narumi Shibori Kaikan** where tools of trade shown, demonstrations, and store (9:00-16:00, X-wed, ¥300). Arimatsu dyeing began here in 1608 when local merchant Takeda Shokuro (his descendants still live and dye here) spotted tie-knot dyed towel used by samurai from Kyushu working on construction of Nagoya Castle, and imitated its style. With Co-op now,

artists rarely work at home, but many still sell their goods direct: next to Co-op **Yamamori**; behind Co-op **Nakahama**; **Yamaguchi** 2 doors before Shibori Kaikan. Midway on street, **Yamada** tailors will fit, make, send full *shibori* kimono or summer yukata of Arimatsu.

Before Shibori Kaikan on other side of street is...
Igeta-ya, 250-year-old home open to public (10:00-18:00 X-wed, ¥300). Free cold green tea in summer–hot matcha green tea in winter ¥100. Spring & autumn Takeda family displays over 5,000 samples of local dye. Every other year (1991, '93, etc.) **1st sun Oct** is *Arimatsu Festival*; 3 colorful floats bedecked with *Arimatsu-shibori* are carted thru town, starting at Hachiman Shrine.

Toyota Factory visit E of Nagoya is company-city renamed recently after main industry: car factory. Toyota City 1hr from Nagoya on Meitetsu Toyota Shinsen line to Toyota stn, taxi 3x-mtr to **Toyota Kaikan** Exhibition Hall; budgeteers bus from stn for Hirayama off at Toyota, walk, bus driver will point out. Hall 9-5; tours M-F 10:00 & 13:30 (Japanese) and 13:30 & 16:00 (English), see assembly and engine plants, takes 90min plus exhibit hall old cars, present models, prototypes, etc (X-mon, ¥1,000/¥600 student). ✍, or better tel ☎(0565)-29-3355 **Public Affairs Dept #3** staff, English, say slowly 'interested in tour'; must reserve at least 2 wks in advance if special factories desired. (NISSAN *see* TOKYO; MAZDA *see* HIROSHIMA). From GAMAGORI coming from Shizuoka, etc, **taxi** 15x-mtr, or Tokaido JR Main Line to Kariya, change to Meitetsu Mikawa Line.

TILT: Make all-day loop from Nagoya or Gamagori → Toyota, then KATO Tokuro then KATO Takuo by day taxi charter, end up in hot bath in Inuyama. This area leads in **porcelain** production, little to N, or...

*35min from Nagoya stn on Meitetsu Seto Line (change at 2nd stop SAKAE), 80min by JR Bus (free to Rail Passers) to last stop **Owari Seto**.*
SETO, main town is scattering of kilns, chimneys crawling up hills, even high school specializes in ceramics. Seto made earthenware since Nara era.

Middle of town is...
KAMAGAMI SHRINE made to look like *nobori-gama* climbing kiln, dedicated to KATO Tamikichi, 18-19th cent potter who studied Kyushu Arita-yaki ware and introduced porcelain ware to this area. So dominated market, *Seto-mono* in Japanese like 'china' in English means 'porcelain'. Potters offer pieces or other gifts here at shrine at New Year and before each firing. Fine china clay used locally is taken from behind shrine. Huge wholesaler's market where makers dump their *Seto-mono* goods during *Fall Festival*, **3rd weekend Sept.** Over 300 stalls line river, thousands from all Japan throng to benefit from cut-rate prices. Annual **Founder's Day Fest**, Apr 20 has mini-pottery sale near shrine.

Ceramics Center *Tojiki Sentah*, if here to look or shop, in *Shimin Kaikan* Peoples' Hall near PO has 1st floor gift store and 2nd store exhibit of old and new Seto ware, samples of present potters and tools and outline of ceramics history here. Better displays at **History Museum**, *Rekishi-kan*, 5min walk from Shin-Seto stn, 2 before last; City Hall-*Shiyaku-sho* if by bus. Half 7,000 pieces displayed are National Assets. 9:30-17:00, X-mon, ¥100.

5km E (20min bus) of Owari-Seto stn is...
Akazuki-yaki Museum, made since Heian period, display of historical and major artists' work as well as sale of modern *Akazuki-yaki* pottery. 25min bus S of Owari-Seto (only 2 daily) **Aichi Prefectural Museum**, has exhibit with pieces from Jomon to present and reconstructed Muromachi period kiln. 9:30-16:30, X-mon, ¥250.

KATO Tokuro was probably century's top potter—died recently in his late 80s, potting to his last breath. ITaught Picasso technique, worked with Miro, prolific writer, author top Japanese encyclopedia of ceramics (alas too much to translate), traveled widely including traditional kilns of Iran with us. Over dozen generations making pottery and porcelains since ancestors migrated from Korea to set up kilns in Seto, made his name in more individualistic Shino-, Oribe-wares. Sole Living National Treasure to have title recalled because 'expert' mistook one of his historical experiments for genuine antique (*Einen-no-tsubo*) despite fact Tokuro had marked it with calligraphic style of different era. Son Shigetaka continues kiln and greatness. Tokuro, avid scholar-collector, recreated many lost techniques thru his workshop-'archaeology'. Private **Memorial Museum** on grounds *Suisho-en Togei Kinenkan*, shows his work, usually one main type plus great examples from antiquity; 10:00-16:00 X-mon, ¥200. Nr Suishoen Stn, Meitetsu-Seto line, best by taxi; very near Chuo expwy Suishoen IC; phone to see if convenient ☎(052)-795-2110 to visit Shigetaka's gallery; can't ethically give much 'advantage' to buying direct, but greater selection for serious collector. No Tokuro work available, priceless when on market.

On Chuo JR mainline & Chuo Expressway; or from Tokuro's 10x-mtr taxi N...
TAJIMI, another ancient ceramic center in SE Gifu noted for tea-style Mino-ware. **KATO Takuo** (no relation except perhaps generations back, most old-line potters around Nagoya are 'Kato' and from Korea), another kiln-'archaeologist' who thru study of sherds and reading, re-created medieval Persian gold-like underglaze lusterware—made elsewhere only by scholar-potter Craiger-Smith in Aldermaston kiln, UK. (Soft overglaze luster easier, less beautiful). Much Takuo work is Persian-style, but in porcelain; after years of copying, recently developing fascinating style marrying two of world's great ceramic traditions, Persia and Japan. Fascinating private museum in moved-from-Takayama *gassho-zukuri* country manse: ☎793-1475.

OHARA-MURA, village known for its *washi*, handmade Japanese paper. Village-run center shows process of making *washi*; can also try your hand at it, ready to take home at end of day. Hour bus from Kinen-bashi stop, front of Seto Shimin Kaikan, must change halfway at Iino. **Driving**, take road to Akazuki-yaki Museum, 8km further to IINO, where N on Rte 419.

WHERE TO STAY: 3 inns at SETO, 3 more at **IWAYA-DO ONSEN** 3km NE (15min JR bus from Owari-Seto); ¥-Tw/2 range. 2 backwoods hotsprings **SASATO & KONAMI ONSEN** around Ohara-mura, have ¥-B lodgings.

ASUKE VILLAGE and **KORANKEI GORGE**: Garet stumbled onto this well-preserved medieval village while hitching, shown to us by our ride who took back roads to avoid Tomei traffic jam, ended up guiding us around. Korankei is sole major maple viewing spot along Tokaido, crowded late Oct-mid Nov. Asuke village was crossroads of busy Iida-kaido pedestrian highway & *Shio-no-michi* 'Salt Road', salt from Mikawa bay was packaged here and shipped inland to central Shinshu. Many white-walled salt storehouses still remain along timeless streets of century-old homes.

GETTING AROUND: Bus makes 4 stops in Asuke; so start at either end and walk 1km thru town. We suggest start top end Meitetsu Bus Terminal (where you can check departure schedule for return), crossing river on bridge upstream of Bus Terminal and walking thru old town, taking in gorge, topped off with meal there; catch bus out at Korankei stop near 1300-year-old **ASUKE HACHIMAN** shrine. You may want to depart from Bus Terminal, especially midsummer and maple-viewing season, to ensure seat.

WHERE TO STAY: Spending nite, stay in town at E end **Yamashiro-ya**, or W-end **Hasui-kan**, best is 300-year-old **Tamada-ya** in middle. Or along Korankei Gorge at **Momiji-kan**, **Koran-tei**, Asuke Onsen Nishiki-so with hot spring baths. Also **Hakuro-kan** sole inn at tiny HAKURO ONSEN few km downstream. All ¥-Tw/2. Or **Asuke-mura** cabins, ¥10,000 per cabin for 6. Rates-per increase slightly with fewer people per cabin: must reserve, ☎(0565)-62-1188.

Gorge stretches 1km upstream Tomoe River from its joining Asuke River; popular for fishing in summer. Thousands of maple lining river owe their existence to Sanei Zen-shi, 11th head priest of **KOJAKU-JI** temple midway along gorge, who began planting them over 350 years ago. Within temple grounds is massive maple which changes color 5 times in autumn.

Front of Kojaku-ji temple is...

SANSHU ASUKE YASHIKI Folkcrafts Village, cluster of old rural homes rebuilt here. Town elders spend day here, live day to day chores, do traditional crafts of rural village: weaving, basket-making, wood or bamboo crafts, *washi*-paper-making, lacquering, charcoal-making, blacksmithing. 9:00-6:30, X-thur, 1st & 3rd sats, ¥400. At far end of maples, across from Asuke-mura, is restaurant **Ichi-no-ya**, cluster of *gassho-zukuri* thatched roof farm houses serving full course meals of *ayu* (trout), *sansai-ryori* (mountain vegetables), and in autumn *shishi-nabe* (boar-sukiyaki). Nearby **Ochibe** serves smaller, cheaper meals. Beyond here, road cuts inland via Asuke jr high and grove of sakura, rejoining main road halfway to Bus Terminal cutting out 1km backtrack for those ending at terminal. It has retained old charm thanks to its remoteness, as only way here on public transport is 40min bus from Meitetsu Toyota-shi stn, or 70min from Meitetsu Higashi-Okazaki stn. Best done before Nagoya.

NORTH OF CITY

GETTING THERE & AROUND: Handful of **Bus tours** from Nagoya, Gifu & Inuyama take in any combination of RHINE RAPIDS, MEIJI-MURA, LITTLE WORLD. Most extensive is **Meitetsu Bus** ☎(0568)-62-4680. *Inuyama Culture Shu-yu Kanko* tour, leaving INUYAMA stn 9:40, 2hrs each at Meiji-mura, Little World, optional end at Inuyama Yu-en stn, or continue to Inuyama Castle, Uraku-en garden to end INUYAMA stn 16:00. Runs only sun and hol from 1st sun Apr thru Nov: ¥3,400 incl all admissions (meals on your own); ¥2,900 if end Inuyama Yu-en stn. Other packages on **Meitetsu** which you do solo, rely on its public rail system: best from NAGOYA or GIFU, buy at Meitetsu rail ticket windows, incl rail, bus to/from, entry to Little World, Meiji-mura, Nihon Monkey Center.

Gifu Bus ☎(0582)-66-1611 has separate runs Little World & Meiji-mura from GIFU which include shooting Nihon Rhine: leaves Nagara-gawa 8:30 with Meitetsu Shin-Gifu stn pick-up 8:10, heads to Rhine Center, you boat down and bus meets you at Inuyama, then to Meiji-mura, ending at Nagoya stn 16:00. Daily June thru Sept, ¥6,500/adult, ¥4,000/child covers all except meals.

Nagoya Yu-ran Bus ☎(052)-561-4036 has: *Meiji-mura Course* ¥4,980/adult, ¥3,080/child with adm, lunch incl, dep Nagoya Terminal Bldg (S of Nagoya stn plaza) 10:00 → TV Tower → Nagoya Castle → Tagata Shrine → Meiji-mura → Nagoya Terminal 16:45. Can include Nagoya Yu-ran tour into **JR Regional Passes** *Shuyu-ken* sold in Japan for reduced fare; run all year X-Jan 1.

Meitetsu Bus ☎581-4561 has: *Little World Course* ¥3,400/adult, ¥1,900/child, adm only incl, dep Inuyama stn (30min from Nagoya stn) 9:40 → Little World → Meiji-mura → Inuyama stn 16:05 (sun, hol only during Mar-Nov).

Cabs abound and no need to keep one waiting, easily catch one at end of rapids run, front of Little World & Meiji-mura. Budgeteer has frequent local **buses** to all places.

Drivers have adequate free parking at Little World, Meiji-mura; for those shooting rapids ¥1,500 per car has your's ferried, waiting for you at end. Road well marked, often signs in both Japanese & English, relatively direct, no side streets distract.

'HIS & HER' SHRINES: Sites of some of undoubtedly most anthropologically interesting fetes in all Japan (*see* DATEBOOK, Mar 15).

TAGATA, male, is more sensational; main festival is, beware, on Ides of **March (15)** when gigantic 10-foot long shrine-red 'sacred object' (enshrined in main hall with lesser 'sacred objects') is paraded 2 miles to marry its equally immense better-half straw donut enshrined at **OGATA** (20min walk from next rail stop Gakuden). Women desiring children buy talismans at Ogata;

men desiring children or usually just stamina and libido buy those at Tagata. People also scavenge in shrine's bacchanalian grove for strange 'pubic hair' moss which appears at about this season in crotches of numerous suggestively-shaped twin pines. Jay went years ago when nearby airport was US airbase. Crowd buying male talismans in little household shrines was disrupted by shouting of excited farmer who held up shrine box with larger-than-life ceramic phallus in shocking pink. Hard to savvy his accent, crowd took while to catch gist of problem, as did hawker-priest—then all roared. Most talismans are tan or light brown, some pink. Farmer was excited that should he put up pale-pink talisman on household altar his wife would have white babies, he wanted brown one for truly Japanese results. Priest assured him he'd swap, apologized for error explaining shrine also had Caucasian clients from airbase and all were equal under heaven.

Fete very photogenic; supposedly can't send shrine picture postcards by mail, but they usually reach other end. Lesser monthly fete every 3rd & 18th.

GETTING THERE: On bus or train rte NAGOYA or TAJIMI → INUYAMA (from which one shoots Nihon Rhine Rapids): Meitetsu Komaki Line starts Kami-Iida stn, 1.5km N of Tokugawa Museum; bus and rail let off in front at Tagata Jinja-mae stn 3km SW of Meiji-mura; from MEIJI-MURA-GUCHI stn on Meitetsu one stop to Ogata Gakuden stn, another one beyond to Tagata Jinja-mae stn. Drivers from MEIJI-MURA take local road to Meitetsu tracks heading S, Tagata is on this road, for Ogata take L (E) at Gakuden stn. From TAJIMI take Chuo Expwy W to next IC, then R(N) few km.

30min bus between MEIJI-MURA–LITTLE WORLD, both can be done together in full day. One stop from INUYAMA on Meitetsu Komaki Line to Meiji-mura-guchi stn, 10min bus. Direct from NAGOYA 9:40,10:40 (return 14:03,15:03,16:03), others change Inuyama. Also rail-bus-admission package for all. Daily 10:00-17:00 (16:00 11/1-2/28).

MEIJI-MURA (Meiji- or Victorian-era village) is over full sq km with 50 plus Meiji era buildings, ranging from traditional Japanese to contemporary Western, including grand entry to Frank Lloyd Wright's old **Imperial Hotel** (actually Taisho-era built 1916-22), and everything in between. All originals brought here from all over Japan and rebuilt; there is also old Japanese sugar-cane harvester's hut from Hawaii, and another from Brazil (both drew hordes of Japanese immigrants early 1900s) and church from Seattle. To help you and your feet get around 7 sections of park, they installed several modes of transportation. Japan's first steam locomotive, which came from England in 1874, used to chug between Yokohama–Tokyo, now covers half park making 'Nagoya → Tokyo' run in 5min. Other half of park is serviced by original from Japan's first tram line in Kyoto, in use *in situ* at time of 1964 original edition, complete with net 'cow/people-catcher' in front. Train and tram are ¥160/adult, ¥100/child per ride. What would early modern Japan be without rickshas? Was *jin-rikisha* (real full name 'man-powered-cart') service thru park, who knows when again available. English booklet at entrance, most buildings and displays labeled in English (adequate albeit poor).

CHOPSTICKS: There is only one place to eat in compound (tho you can bring your own box lunch, or pick up at diner across from entry) and it's in keeping with village image—unlike Disneyland. Ooi meat shop just to R as you go in, originally opened in Kobe in 1887, served customers there until moved here in 1968. It still functions as restaurant upstairs, serving suki-yaki (using Kobe beef) cooked over charcoal: regular meal ¥3,200, special ¥4,000. As popular now as when it first opened and you should reserve time when you first enter: hrs 10:30-16:00 (15:00 winter).

Uji Yamada Post Office, opened 1909 front of Ise's Outer Shrine, from where you can mail anything (commemorative postcards, stamps, postmark) during park hours. By man-made Lake Iruka excavated Meiji 10 (1877), 25min (¥400) cruises hourly 10:00-15:00 every 30min sun, hol; pier just S of compound.

LITTLE WORLD: World's only outdoor **Folk-Tribal Museum** (opened March 1983) is truly spectacular set-up, worthy of its name Museum of Humanity. Enter onto World Plaza, L of which is main exhibit hall, two storeys crammed, but tastefully and well displayed, with over 30,000 (and growing) authentic folk-tribal artifacts from around world. Enter via screen-room showing Japanese country girl talking about being only one of billions on world. Screen rises and enter first section which traces evolution and spread of humanity. Pass thru tunnel on which walls are projected famous cave drawings, to **Hall 2** of tribal tools for survival in extreme conditions. **Hall 3** devoted to language; **Hall 4** on life, tracing from birth to death, with videos of tribal rituals for birth, fertility, adulthood and death. **Hall 5** is 'inner spirit', man's interactions with heavens. Numerous high tech audio-visual displays all over to keep you occupied for several hours and well informed, in spite of lack of English labels. Special theme hall, rotating exhibits on 2nd floor of other building, which also has cafeteria and *bento* (box lunch) stalls from which you can eat while circling outside.

1.3 square km park with traditional **folk houses** from around world, and special regional exhibit halls. When we visited just after opening they had 15 such houses and 2 regional exhibits completed. Director is Japan's top international archaeologist, Dr EGAMI Namio. As of 1985 there were 24 dwellings, by '89 27, with plans for at least 60. All houses are originals, brought over and rebuilt, except for concrete replicas of Sahara dwellings: original packed mud would have dissolved in first summer downpour. Unfortunately, fear of sticky fingers has left interiors rather bare. Persia's nomadic Qashgai black goat-hair tent was smaller and lacked piles of colorful rugs we had grown accustomed to in Iran. English language illustrated guidebook and pamphlet for complex are available, ¥800, along with English labels inside.

GETTING THERE: From NAGOYA to INUYAMA by Meitetsu 20min ¥440 and short bus, ¥380. Coming from GIFU or NAGOYA, buy Meitetsu package ticket, incl rail both ways, bus, admission. Bus from Monkey Center also connects Little World. Open daily 9:30-18:00 (10:00-16:30 11/1-3/31), ¥1,000, count on good half-day to take in leisurely—takes 2hrs to walk 2.5km around park, see sites; can save time on electric cars circling, ¥500 full circle pass 20min, or get off at any site to look, hop next bus.

INUYAMA 犬山

CENTRAL to several fine places to visit, and with *ugai*-cormorant fishing, tho not as good as at GIFU. Ugai started early 17th cent, then obscure law made it illegal here and Inuyama's ugai boats headed down to Gifu. Was revived in 1899, now done Jun thru Sept, same rates as Gifu, on Kiso-gawa river over-looked by Inuyama Castle. Arrange thru your inn, board boats near Inuyama Bridge, same place where disembark from shooting rapids (*see* p306).

GETTING THERE: Only 20km E of GIFU on Meitetsu, 2 stns serve Inuyama: INUYAMA YU-EN S of river is convenient if just passing thru, is closest to city's sites; 2min beyond is main MEITETSU INUYAMA stn, 30min from Shin-Gifu, 40min Nagoya, 30min from Nagoya airport, with branch lines to Meiji-mura & Little World. Rail Pass users can take JR from Gifu 5 stops (30min) to UNUMA, 100m N of river.

WHERE TO STAY: Dozen ryokan in town, mostly ¥-Tw/2; 3 minshuku, 1 in town and 2 near MOMOTARO SHRINE 4km NE. Best is **Meitetsu Inuyama Hotel** ☎(0568)-61-2211, with J-style annex, next to castle hill; ¥-S-Lw/2—most helpful place to arrange area tours as Meitetsu owns everything. Cheaper inns most along Kiso river, try old time traditional **Kikusui-kan** ☎(0583)-84-1301 on N bank, picks up at stn; next door **Kigetsu** ☎84-1281. Several more along S bank: At pier for *ugai* and rapids' boats, **Tanaka-ya** ☎61-2251; **Inuyama-kan** ☎61-2309. Those listed here start ¥-lo-T+w/2, half-dozen cheaper ones along river where you can compare prices, or arrange any thru **Kanko-annai** Inuyama Yu-en stn. **Inuyama YH** 2km out nr Monkey Center.

Much to see and do around here, count on 2 full days especially if using Gifu as base. Main are shooting Nihon Rhine rapids, Meiji-mura, Little World & sites in town. Can cram rapids, Meiji-mura Little World into full if rushed day, but better to spread it.

Inuyama Castle dominating town since 1201 when ODA Nobunaga's ancestors built it. Avoided destruction in Sekigahara campaign as occupant wisely gave up when Gifu fell. In 1618 local Naruse family received charge of it, and it's still theirs: sole privately owned castle. Also oldest extant castle in Japan. Most of it was dismantled 1871 by new Meiji government (final step in dismantling feudal *han* system) but central keep left standing. Inside (¥200) is museum of Naruse family: usual samurai-alia.

E of castle (5min walk from Inuyama Yu-en), just behind Meitetsu Hotel, is...
Uraku-en landscaped tea garden. Created mid-16th century by brother of Nobunaga, Urakusai; original structures, *Jo-an tea house* (National Treasure one of 3 with this rank) built by Urakusai, and his hideaway in Kyoto's Kennin-ji temple (moved here lock, stock and barrel); recreated from blueprints is another tea house, and herb garden with over 300 different types of tea. Daily 9:00-17:00 (16:00 winter) ¥500. ¥300 for bowl of thick green *matcha* tea and sweets.

At S base of castle hill (5min walk from Uraku-en) is...
HARTSUNA SHRINE, itself uninteresting, but 340-year-old annual festival is rated as Prefectural Cultural Asset. **1st or 2nd sat-sun Apr**, peak of cherry blossoms, 13 massive 3-tier floats with moving puppets atop are pulled thru town and displayed. Return to storage next day. If you miss festival, scaled-down replicas of floats can be seen at Inuyama Historical Museum 1min S of shrine. Also on display are swords and other samurai items, ancient Inuyama pottery, folk items over 10,000 total. Open daily 10:00-17:00 (16:00 winter), ¥200.

3 streets S, 1 street E of museum (10min walk) is 380 year old...
Kojima Sake Brewery, operating out of its original *kura*-style vaults. Tours and sampling possible, especially when they hang large wood ball over entrance to announce 'new' sake is being bottled and served.

4 streets E, 1 N of brewery (5min N of Inuyama stn) is 150-year-old...
Okumura Mansion, owned by prominent cloth merchants in Edo era. Classic example of well-to-do late Edo urban home in prime location: street in front was old pedestrian Nakasendo Highway. In grounds is *Ginmei-sui* **well**, where Nobunaga celebrated on hearing of death of TAKEDA Katsuyori. Interesting are rebuilt **turret** and **granary** of Inuyama Castle. Former is History Museum, latter Folk Museum. 9:00-17:00 (16:00 winter) X-wed, ¥300. Yu-en stn → Inuyama stn, via all these sites in town takes about 2hrs.

5min monorail E of Gifu Yu-en stn is area taken up mostly by...
Nihon Monkey Park & Center. Former (open daily 9:30-17:00, ¥1,000) is amusement park and zoo, latter is home to over 1,000 simians representing 100-plus species. Also **museum** exhibits collection of TOMIZAWA Enjiro: 10,000 folk art pieces of monkeys from around world. Tribe of wild Japanese monkeys romp free at outdoor monkey park few km upstream. Visit them for ¥200, or glimpse them as river rapids ride nears its end.

Nearby...
MOMOTARO SHRINE, dedicated to Okamizu-no-mikoto, guardian deity of children, is now better known as dedicated to Momotaro (peach-boy), famed demon slayer with monkey side-kick of children's folklore. Claims to be site of his birth; in most versions he lived and battled demons on Shikoku Island. Anyway, it goes well with monkeys.

5min walk E of Yu-en stn is...
ZUISEN-JI temple, fine **treasure hall** (¥200) full of ancient art, including large bell with see-, hear-, speak-no-evil monkeys engraved; paintings by

KANO Tanyu early 17th century master of Kano school and official artist of TOKUGAWA Ieyasu (his best work is bold pine trees in Kyoto Nijo Castle); and *Chi-daruma* 'Blood Bodhidharma' scroll of Ashikaga clan. Story has it that when Ashikaga mansion was burning servant rushed in to save priceless scroll. Trapped by flames, he slit his belly and inserted scroll, saving it from fire, and thus endowng scroll its reddish tint.

SHOOTING NIHON RHINE RAPIDS: Meitetsu Hiromi Line → **Nihon Rhine Imawatari** 45min from Nagoya, 20min Inuyama; or JR 45min GIFU → MINO-OHTA. Both 5min car from starting point, 2 companies shooting rapids have free shuttle. Needn't have imported nickname, its real name is River Kiso. **Must**–well worth detour off Tokaido: nothing similar later. Board at Ohta Bridge for hair-raising 90min ride thru series of 7 rapids to Gifu Bridge. Bit upstream of Ohta is confluence of Hida and Kiso Rivers, both originate in soaring mountains of central Japan (we follow these rivers up to reach OFFBEAT CHUBU). Runs all year X–during severe rain or snow. **Mar 15-Nov 30** roughly every hour 9:00 to 17:00, with few extras midday during August peak. Rest of year 3-5x-daily. ¥2,670 each. For exact times or rsvtn (tho you can usually just show up and get on next or so), go to Stn annai-jo, or call **Meitetsu Nihon Rhine Center** ☎(05742)-6-2231; or 2 boat firms of Nihon **Rhine Yu-sen** ☎6-1201, or Horyu Yu-sen ☎5-2083. Call last 2 for stn pick-up if no cars there. Extra runs, discounts for groups can be pre-arranged.

N of Inuyama are 2 folk art towns...
SEKI, known for centuries for swords, today biggest maker of tableware, cutlery. **lst sun**, 3x-daily demo at NIHON-TOH TANRENJO; **2nd sat-sun Oct**, *Hamono Matsuri*, Shingyo Center, where swordsmiths hold blade-making demonstrations; exhibit fine swords. Goods at cut rate. If you miss fest, sword-making demos at Tosho-no-sato, resv req, ☎(0575)-23-2606. **Nov 8** *Fuigo Rite* for swordmakers, SENJU-IN temple. **May 11-Oct 15** *Ugai* small group 2km W at Ozu, arrange w/ Seki Yusen ☎(0575) 22-2506; JR 20min 4 stops, from Mino-Ota; Meitetsu rail 50min Gifu–Seki.

2 stops Meitetsu to end of line, or 1 stop JR to...
MINO, where famous *Mino-shi* paper is hand-made, and find everything from thermal paper for photocopy to fine old-fashioned Japan art papers and modern decorator papers with interred butterflies. Records in Shosoin dating to 720 mention this already famous paper town; main natural ingredients of *kozo* (mulberry) and wood abound in area, lots of water. Most places in town now make by machine; can see handmaking process at **Handmade Paper Conservation Society**, *Mino-shi hozon-kai*; first call ☎(05753)-4-0327.
    Head for hills: 2hr30min JR beyond is summer bon dance capital GUJO HACHIMAN which we visit at end of our circle thru fascinating rural CHUBU (*see* also DATEBOOK).

GIFU 岐阜   FISHING IS 'FOR THE BIRDS'

HOW THEY DO IT in Japan: tie leash to ring around neck of cormorant and let him go after trout, ring prevents his swallowing until leash-handler plucks it from him. We see it again later in Kyoto, where we think it is easier and cheaper to get to see, if on slightly smaller-scale. Yet both differ: Gifu has narrower, flowing river, Kyoto's is wide, deep, and slower. It is also done on smaller scale at Inuyama, just upstream from Gifu, which we visit next; and smaller scale yet at tiny Kozu, 15km upstream near Seki. But most famous of cormorant fishing (*ugai*) is on Nagara-gawa River in Gifu, from **May 11 thru Oct 15**, except at full moon or when water is muddy. Jul-Aug crowded, should book rooms and boat in advance.

    Foreigners' tours take it in, but you can do it yourself cheaper. *Ugai* usually runs from 19:00-21:30 but board anytime from 17:30, earlier better. Check exact time at your inn, since start any time after sunset. Rates for covered *yakata-bune* run ¥2,400 per person May, Sept, Oct; ¥2,600 June,

July, Aug. If all 70 *yakata-bune* full, uncovered boats run ¥2,100 per person all seasons. Group rate is 10x-person rate per boat. Dine on board, inn arranges, or agent or boatman if not staying-over.

Don't just rush out from Nagoya: best is to stay nite at Gifu in riverside inn, of which there are countless designed for every pocket, down to Youth Hostel. **If** you must rush out, **Nagoya Yuran Bus Co**, ☎(052)-561-4036, runs 5hr **tours** daily **Jul 1-Aug 31** X-sat; must rsve, leave Nagoya terminal 17:00; ¥4,570 incl boat & meal) Several budget inns in town, short bus (cab 2x-mtr) or tram to river. Inn will provide boxed 'picnic-meal' (as your inn supper), arrange boat reservation as well. Other boats with dancing geisha float around, as do *'Ugai taiko* drummers', and guide boats from which you can have detailed demonstration-explanation of this whole fish story: Possible origins in India, China, *ugai* in Japan is recorded from Yamato period, detailed in *Nihon-shoki* and *Kojiki* chronicles. Gifu's, about 1,200 years old, was patronized by 14th cent Ashikaga shoguns, Oda Nobunaga and Tokugawa Ieyasu. Each boat has up to 12 birds, is operated by 3 men: oarsman, bird-handler and fire-stoker. Huge torch or grill of burning wood is suspended at bow, sweetfish or trout attracted to light (full moon distracts, so X-) are gobbled by birds. Several times nitely, boats perform *so-garami* 'fish-herding': 6 boats form 'V' and race down-river, birds catching any fish in their way. Big fireworks **May 15**, and claimed biggest in Japan **1st sat Aug**—that means *big*.

    INFO: City *Kanko-ka* ☎(0582)-65-4141 xt303; Pref Int'l Relat'ns ☎72-1111 xt2195.

WHERE TO STAY: Best lodgings along **Nagara-gawa** river, bus or tram lets you off on either side of **Magara Bridge**, *ugai* boat pier is on S end. Many inns are large 'ryotels', multi-storey concrete monsters, but with personalized service of traditional ryokan. Prices are reasonable considering double attraction of Nagara-gawa's *ugai* and onsen; hot spring water is piped from nearby source. 15% increase in cost during *ugai* season; if here off-season, it may be better to stay in Inuyama (p. 304). Most inns on N bank and E of bridge where *ugai* concentrated. *Working E from bridge*: **Sugiyama** ☎(0582)-31-0161; **Nagaragawa Hotel** ☎32-4111; **Nagara-kan** ☎32- 7117; **Gifu Grand Hotel** ☎33-1111. **Grand** by far splashiest, but all are roughly same price, from ¥-lo-Sw/2 during *ugai* season, 10-15% less when no cormorant fishing. Sugiyama, Nagara-kan little cheaper. In 1985 Garet spent 2nd nite in town at **Ishikin** ☎31-8156 (N bank near bridge) traditional with new annex. From ¥-T (*ugai* season) in newer half (excellent rooms), little more old half, w/2 superb meals: dinner incl cormorant-caught trout (thankful to have done meal-on-board nite before or might have missed this). More *personally oriented* than larger hotels, service as good or better, relaxing bath followed by dinner with owner despite Garet's dishevelled backpacker appearance upon entering. **Ogawa ryokan**, S bank almost directly across from Ishikin, similar in style, rates. Next to it, **Seiran** ☎65-6528, is budget for its location at ¥-Tw/2. At boat pier is **Ukawa** ☎62-7188; and behind it, **Matsu-gen** ☎65-0220, both ¥-T. Cheaper inns downstream of bridge include N bank **Taga Ryokan** ☎31-0167. Cheaper still in town, but river best. Garet spent first nite **Shinano-ya ryokan** ☎62-0328 (¥-Tw/2). Small but good place, used to catering to foreigners; booked by stn *annai-jo* which was most helpful. ¥-T business hotels **Gifu Dai-ni Washington**, **Sun-route Gifu**, **Gifu Dai-ichi**, all near stn, ¥-B-T. None preferred, if you want budget try Youth Hostel, another of which is **Gifu YH** ☎63-6631, on hill near Gifu Planetarium (daily, ¥400).

Also in Gifu, cable car up to **hilltop castle**, used by Oda Nobunaga, and claimed indestructible until flattened by Ieyasu during Sekigahara campaign. Only original stonework remains, Keep is cement replica built 1956 and has usual samurai museum. Cable car starts just S of Nagara bridge.

Nearby...
SHOHO-JI temple of Lacquered Buddha: 13.6m-tall seated Ashoka Nyorai figure was built 1832; lacquer over wood and basket-weave bamboo frame,

from which it gets its other name of 'Basket Buddha'. Inside Buddha's gut is enshrined Yakushi Nyorai—Medicinal Buddha.

MIE-JI temple, treasure is mid-8th century lacquered 11-faced Kannon. 2km N of stn, annual fete Mar 1; huge floats are pulled thru town and good fortune to any who can catch or be hit by wooden ladles tossed from top of floats, without being trampled to death (your survival proves your luck).

CHOPSTICKS: Three fine restaurants in Gifu, all are at Nagara-gawa: Uo-tetsu, on R at N end of bridge, has been serving fish from river for century. Open 12:00-20:00 (X-2nd tue monthly): *shio-yaki*, lots of salt trout grilled over open hearth. Excellent steaks from beer-fed cows of Matsuzaka (*see*) can be had at Senryu, located between Nagara-kan main hall and annex, old traditional home with beautiful garden, serving ¥8,500 steaks, and ¥6,800 shabu-shabu or sukiyaki. Or try mountain dishes of Gujo-Hachiman (we visit in TAKAYAMA OFFBEAT) at Shichi-ryo San-bu restaurant on N bank, L of bridge, near Gifu Girl's College and Youth Hostel. Dishes from ¥2,000 include mountain herbs and vegetables, river fish and wild boar in season—all cooked in open hearth on hot rocks, or in kettle with broth, superb either way. To refresh self, advise Coffee Shop U, 2 alleys behind Sugiyama ryokan—owner, bird-handler on boats, keeps his 22 cormorants in courtyard, will show them.

S of Gifu stn...
KANO-CHO District, famous for its *wa-gasa* Japanese paper umbrellas, over 20,000 handmade monthly. Thickly waxed paper is spread over delicate but sturdy bamboo ribs; gets name from classic pattern *ja-no-me,* snake-eye, with center and rim dyed navy blue or scarlet to leave white band in middle. Nowdays, most prefer cheap western umbrellas for general use (easier on pocket when you forget it on train, as millions do annually), but traditional ones are popular items for interior decorating and now come in all sizes and patterns. Fun to walk around Kano-cho and visit smaller stores and watch them work; every open plot of land in area is full of just-finished umbrellas put out to dry, looking like village of colorful lilliputian teepees. If properly cared for, these paper ones will withstand any summer torrential downpour; just let it dry open after each use. They make inexpensive gifts: start from ¥1,000 for your basic ones, finest (paper light, lacquered) rarely go above ¥10,000. One of best shops is Sakaida Shoten between JR and Meitetsu tracks, 400m E of JR Gifu stn's S exit.

Just NE of Gifu is where are made those delicate summer lanterns seen in all department stores during hot season: known as *Gifu chochin* with delicate paintings on pale turquoise-colored silk. They are hung mid-summer *bon* season in honor of returning spirits of dead. Pure white ones are donated by friends and relatives to remember someone who died during past year and will be observing first *bon.* This too, has become popular as interior decor and you can get regular lamps of this style. One of Gifu's top shops for lanterns is Oseki Tsugishichi Shoten nr HIGASHI BETSU-IN temple: R at intersection before Daigaku Byoin-mae bus and tram stop.

Before resuming trek on down Tokaido, those with time may want to head out to...
YOKOKURA TEMPLE & Ibi-kyo Gorge, 20km NW of GIFU. One of main Tendai sect temples, has fantastic treasure hall (MINO SHOSOIN, to Japanese who like to compare places to more famous ones) full of National Treasures and slightly lesser buddhist art. Main hall has glass-encased, well-preserved mummified body of its founding priest, still sitting in same position, wearing same robes as when he finally 'attained nirvana' centuries ago.

Takes full day to do from Gifu as trains out that way are infrequent. Best to take 9:45 out of Shin-Gifu Meitetsu stn direct to TANIGUMI in 1hr, from where 3 buses daily out to temple (25min). Last train from TANIGUMI back to GIFU is 15:00. Cab from GIFU, 4hrs r.t., *chugata* ¥17,000/38x-mtrs, *kogata* 10+% less.

10min walk from Tanigumi stn is...
KEGON-JI temple, also Tendai sect and one of 33 Kannon pilgrimage spots of western Japan. Area has several ¥-B ryokan and minshuku. Also campground at Tanigumi, 2 more at MAGASE, and one out at **Ibi Gorge**.

If taking nondirect trains to TANIGUMI, must change at KURONO from Ibi Line to Tanigumi Line. For Ibi Gorge, stay on Ibi Line to last stop MOTO-IBI 50min from Shin-Gifu, 25min bus to gorge. It is popular hiking-camping area in spring and summer, with boats (motor- and row-) for rent on man-made lake.

Note: Meitetsu rail–bus system over entire NAGOYA-GIFU-MIKAWA zone is most convenient, and far cheaper than JR if paying cash. Main stn at Gifu is SHIN-GIFU, 200m NE of JR Gifu. One of few cities still to run ancient red street cars of Gifu—some of which become short trains out to MINO and GUJO HACHIMAN). Meitetsu is also area's prime developer with luxury hotels (best at Inuyama); runs fabulous complexes of MEIJI-MURA and LITTLE WORLD. All train times on Meitetsu are for expresses on longer runs such as btwn Toyohashi–Nagoya–Mikawa–Gifu–Inuyama.

30km W of GIFU, just N of JR Tokaido rail and Meishin Expwy is battlefield of...
SEKI-GA-HARA where on Oct 21, 1600, hordes of Tokugawa's Eastern Army and Toyotomi's Western Army met head on—over 200,000 soldiers. As junction of 3 major inland roads only 15km from Tokaido; control of it was essential. After Ieyasu's resounding victory he marched unobstructed to Osaka in 10 days (it took 4 months of bloody battles to get this far), eventually feeling secure enough to claim title of Shogun in 1603. Hiking course now meanders 4.5km thru battlefield, important spots marked (J-only) for historian or romantic.

Drivers can next head to ISE itinerary S on Rte365, 60km to Yokkaichi on Ise Bay where various choices for onward to Ise, Kansai etc.

WHERE NEXT: This spectacular Chubu Region is noted as possible offbeat to Tokaido not because it is mainly for adventurer-wanderer, but because anyone travelling down Tokaido should take time to visit at least part of it, especially if stopping in Gifu-Inuyama area. Several intelligent International Tours, designed for economy and variety now take in part/s of it for fascinating firsthand view of 'real Japan'—which conservation of romantic antiquity is made possible by that other 'real Japan' of hard work and high tech.

Two main routes run thru central Japan, both start in greater Nagoya: each offers completely different views of rural antiquity totally dissimilar in style, geography, weather and most anything else.

KISO-JI ROAD (p.899) (also called KISO-KAIDO and NAKASENDO), one of GO-KAIDO or '5-hiways' of Edo shogunate, 500km/315mi long w/ 67 post stations, ran from Nihonbashi Tokyo thru mountainous back country to Kusatsu near Kyoto, where it joined coastal grand trunk highway TOKAIDO. We can still go along old pedestrian highway, thru villages little changed since 17th cent, except that gift stores now sell modern souvenirs instead of old (they had tourists then).

INA-JI road curves back to Tokaido at TOYOHASHI from Kiso-ji apex SHIOJIRI City. Supplemental **HIDA-JI** and **MINO-JI** roads take you into beautiful, rugged mountains of Hida to villages and towns some few steps behind in time. *See* OFFBEAT CHUBU (p.897) for solo tips and bus tours.
Adventurer can make great circle on these romantic rustic routes taking all in at once; or do one now and other going up JAPAN SEACOAST heading back to Tokyo. Doing all count on at least 5-7 days, or hilites 2-3 nites.

PERSONAL DATEBOOK: NAGOYA AREA

(See also Personal Datebook for Atsuta Grand Shrine p.298)

January

('Lunar' = month later approx.)

Lunar 13 *Hadaka-matsuri* Naked Festival, Konomiya Shrine, Inazawa City, Aichi Pref. Primeval 'erotic' origin of 'romantic' Valentine's Day?

Lunar 15 (if weekday, next Sun), *Kowai Festival*, Myojin-sha Shrine, Nakamura-ku, Nagoya City. Masked dancers run around to scare away evil for NewYear.

Lunar 17 *Iwazuka Kinekosa Festival* at Shichisho-sha Shrine, Nakamura-ku. Farmer rite started 12th century w/ freshly pounded mochi offered to Shrine. About noon 12 male shrine attendants at Shonai River bank—one climbs bamboo pole, others shake it until it breaks. If pole and man fall E or S, coming year should be good, N/W bad. Then return to shrine.

March

15 10-foot long shrine-red 'sacred object' (m) enshrined in main hall Tagata Shrine with lesser 'sacred objects' is paraded 2mi/3+km to marry its equally immense better-half straw donut (f) enshrined at Ogata shrine; marvelous fertility talisman-fetishes are sold (*text* p.302).

1st or 2nd Sat & Sun *Cherry Festival*, Haritsuna Shrine, Inuyama, (*text* p.305).

April

Pottery Makers' fairs:
1st wknd, Mizunami City; **2nd wknd,** Tajimi City; **3rd wknd,** Seto. *See* Sept.

16-17 *Toshogu Shrine Fete*, Naka-ku.

May

7-8 *Benzai-ten Festival*, Togan-ji temple, Chigusa-ku; koto, shakuhachi, ikebana.

15-16 Floats make rounds, Hachiman Shrine, Naka-ku.

17-18 *Taiko* (Hideyoshi) *Festival* Toyokuni Jinja Shrine Nakamura-ku; music, dance.

June

5 *Grand Festival*, Atsuta Jinja, *see* p298.

4th Sun *Otaue-sai* rice-planting, 10am,at Atsuta Jingu, Hikami-aneko Shrine.

July

15-16 Summer *Shrine Festival* Nagoya Jinja, Naka-ku.

16 Tobe *Shrine Festival*, Minami-ku.

18 *Otaue-sai* rice-planting Atsuta Jingu shrine 10am.

20-21 *Minato-matsuri* Nagoya Harbor Fete main summer event, anniversary of port opening. General festivities, booths, parades harbor area; log-rolling contests. Climax 20th nite, streets fill with dancers as 8 massive lantern-covered floats pulled thru streets, fireworks, 7:30-9pm.

31 *Mimae-sha Festival*, Rei-no-mime-sha Shrine, Atsuta-ku. Participants jump thru sacred straw hoop to purify self of evil.

Late *Tanabata Festival*, Owari Ichino-miya City, commemorate being major weaving center since Heian times.

28-Aug 1 Osu Kannon *Summer Festival* yatai food, game stalls, sidewalk artists all over Osu district, Naka-ku.

September

3rd weekend Pottery wholesalers' cut-rate fair; Seto, one of largest in Japan.

October

1st Sun *Arimatsu-matsuri* Midori-ku, p299.

10 Grand *Autumn Festival*, Tobe Shrine, Minami-ku.

2nd Sat-Sun *Hamono-matsuri*, Swordsmith Festival, Seki, (p306).

Mid around 2nd weekend city-wide *Nagoya Festival* begun 1955 after city could afford break from postwar reconstruction to have some fun. Sat, feudal costume parade of Nobunaga, Hideyoshi, Ieyasu, each w/ full retinue. Repeat Sun larger parade massive cart floats, flower floats, marching bands. Also *Osu Commoner Street Festival*, p.298.

23 Kenchu-ji temple in Higashi-ku airs out its scroll treasury, displays to public.

Late Auto *Grand Prix*, Suzuka Circuit.

November

8 Memorial service for Oda Nobunaga Togan-ji temple, Chigusa-ku.

8 *Fuigo-BellowMatsuri*. Shinto priests parade sword-making gear, Kanayama Shrine

Mid, *Idea Olympic,* Toyota; wacky cars.

Cock Days *Tori-no-Ichi*, Susano-O Shrine, nite, buy luck rake; check dates at ☎482-5576.

—thru Jan, *HanaMatsurii* dances var sites.

December

16 *Fire Walk*, Akiwa Shrine in Entsu-ji complex, Atsuta-ku ☎671-6987 downtown Nagoya subway Tenma stn; pyre lit 10am, rites all day, walk 7pm.

*countless are mountains in Yamato
but perfect is heavenly hill of Kagu
when I climb it and survey my realm
beautiful land it is, this land of...*
— Emperor Jomei (593-641)

YAMATO 大和
HEARTLAND OF JAPAN

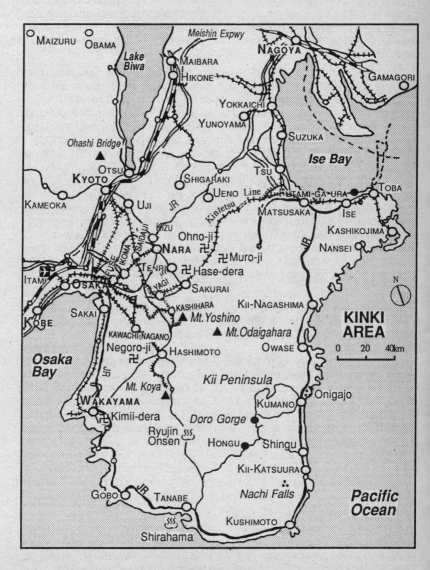

NOWHERE ELSE is there such concrete and living record of one nation's culture and history in such compact area as here on Yamato Plain between tourist centers of Kyoto, Osaka, Nara and Ise. This district is now properly called **Kinki** in Japanese, but rarely so internationally because of awareness of English homonym, and generally called by name of much larger area of which it is heart, **Kansai.**

Two-hour comfortable vista-dome electric train ride takes us across widest part of this plain. Yet within this tiny area lie several major great historic sites of Japan and two of its main modern industrial cities. Here thanks to Japan's cult of preservation, her modern citizens–and foreign guests–may see and experience this concrete evidence of their ancestry. Here is Japanese history in digest, cross section of Japanese culture in capsule.

Japanese purposely shut themselves off from world for centuries, inbreeding until they are perhaps sole nation today which might also call itself one race. Their language is related to no other spoken (tho it links distantly to Ainu, Korean, more distantly perhaps to Turkish, and attempts have been made to trace it to Sumerian, Gujerati or some Amerind tongues). Yet they did not just appear out of nowhere; tho isolated and inbred today, they are of greatly mixed origin. Perhaps even more mixed racially than we Americans. Their ancestors came from Siberia, Korea and China, Southeast Asia, South Pacific and as far afield even as Persia. Their ancient culture preserved and nurtured during centuries of isolation is best preserved on Yamato Plain due to wars, which ravaged other great cities but spared these ancient treasures. Here, too, great variety of primeval Japan is yet preserved. Several major migrations which peopled Japan came together here, lived long at peace if apart, and eventually confederated to found their empire. Here first capital of Asuka was built in 6th century AD, moved to Nara in 8th, and followed century later by Kyoto now just half hour away by train.

Our itinerary is composite of ones we followed ourselves as students under tutelage of Japanese professors, modified to suit peculiar demands of modern jet-age tourist. It is almost as if ancient gods created this chain of Japanese historical development with convenience of tourists of future in mind, for this panorama of past unfolds along convenient geographical line. We re-experience history from Stone Age remains and giant burial mounds of first emperors, some as large as all three great pyramids of Giza combined; thru Grand Shrine of Sun Goddess, ceremonially rebuilt every generation for at least 1,200 and perhaps 1,800 years; to oldest wooden buildings on earth, twelve-century-old Horyu-ji monastery; and great bronze Buddha's 'air-conditioned' log cabin museum storing imperial tribute from lands as far afield as Indonesia, Siberia, Persia and Rome; thru farming villages where strange Stone Age rituals are preserved, performed by farmers who use most modern farm machinery. And we take short detour to medieval castle town of Iga-Ueno, birthplace of famous early medieval wandering poet Matsuo Basho, and to see authentic *ninja* house.

Each area has its own peculiar characteristics. Some preserve primeval Japanese culture, some reflect their ancestral origins in China or Korea or lands unknown. Collectively they are living museum of Asia, of mankind. Together they illustrate this dynamic, composite culture which is Japan.

*The fact was...that around the 20th day of the third month,
youths in my neighborhood suddenly became restless...
as if they sensed an apocalypse. Within three or four days
almost the entire population of the city set out on
the Pilgrimage to Ise.* — Oliver Statler, *The Japanese Inn*

ISE DAIJINGU
HOME OF SUN GODDESS

HERE IN FOREST PRIMEVAL is Japan's birth bower. In first centuries of Christian era these islands witnessed progressive waves of foreign human and cultural invasions, which melded with original inhabitants and with each other, gradually creating this amalgam we know as Japan. Seal on this unification of groups as well as of wedding of continental organization with indigenous aesthetic, was establishment of JINGU, Grand Shrine of Ise, which stands today, unchanged for at least fifteen centuries.

This most sacred of Shinto centers is actually two principal shrines set apart by some 7 km/4 miles of virgin woods and 123 lesser shrines. Two main ones are referred to as *Naiku* (Inner Shrine) and *Geku* (Outer Shrine), 14 lesser ones being known as *Bekku* (attached shrines). *Naiku* houses spirit of Amaterasu, Sun Goddess ancestress of Imperial Line. *Geku* houses Toyo-uke-hime, Goddess of Grain, likely older indigenous Yayoi deity too powerful to be completely displaced by deity of Yamato invaders. Grain/Rice Goddess was moved here from Kyoto on command of emperor Yuryaku in 478AD, Sun Goddess had come 22 years earlier, perhaps originally from Kyushu via Kyoto. But prior to that, site had been sacred to Kuni-toko-tachi-no-mikoto, whose name Earthly-ever-standing-augustness indicates 'earthly' fertility deity of type we met in Nagoya, and whom we meet again at next main stop Kashihara at ASUKA-NIIMASU Shrine. In fact *chigi* (horn-like cross-boards extending above roof, front and rear) indicate, by point upwards, *Geku* intended for masculine inhabitant, tho it houses goddess, just as they show that *Naiku* is, of course, feminine.

But regardless of who lives here, these stately buildings and primeval grove compose one of most beautiful and soul-satisfying religious settings on earth. Ise has attracted millions of pilgrims over centuries. Tenth century novel describes rather romantic one; numerous medieval stories are set in pilgrimages by samurai or shopboys. Pilgrims today number in hundreds of thousands annually (including members of Imperial Family 'reporting' major events to their ancestor, or Prime Minister 'reporting' elections or overseas trips). For those who cannot make Ise Pilgrimage, six volunteer 'minstrels' wander around country on foot, performing dances in distant towns. Donations to them are received as if given to shrine. Sextet spend half year traveling, rest working odd jobs in Ise area. Local TV often feature them when they pass thru town.

Your 'pilgrimage', we suggest, will prove more satisfying in early morning or at dusk. Allow at least 30min for Geku, hour for Naiku.

These two shrines are similar except in scale, *Naiku* being slightly larger. We also prefer landscaping of *Naiku* and so describe it here in detail, noting points where *Geku* differs.

NAIKU is across crystal-clear sacred Isuzu River which we cross by **Uji Bridge [1]** entering and leaving it under two gigantic wooden torii. In feudal days, those with 'round heads' (i.e. shaved, Buddhist priests or nuns) were not allowed beyond bridge and offered their prayers from special platform along riverbank. Shrines have been preserved this long in form only, not actual substance. They are fully rebuilt every generation, about every 20 years, as we shall see. Great **torii** are made of main pillars of previous main shrine and upper parts of bridge are also made of this one-generation-old lumber. Supports are made of new zelkova, wood noted for its water resistant qualities. Under second torii, we turn right following pilgrim route **[2]** across great garden court and small second bridge beyond which is font where worshippers purify themselves by rinsing mouth with fresh water **[3]**. Just beyond is another torii **[4]**, to its immediate left hall for priests' ritual purification **[5]**, and that for emperor to purify himself and rest. Few yards beyond, right turn brings us to landing on river **[6]**, where more devout perform their water purification.

Few Japanese know proper way to **purify** oneself, just scoop up water, chug down mouthfuls. This water is only to purify, drink elsewhere (or sneak sip during rite, OK). Show them up by doing it right: hold scoop in R hand, rinse off L hand then vice-versa. Next, pour water from scoop into L hand and sip water into mouth, rinse and spit onto gravel. With last bit of water in scoop, raise scoop vertical so that water runs down handle to clean; make sure no water accidentally drops back into clean water in trough.

Also, proper way to **offer prayers** at shrine is, coats and hats off, bow deeply twice, followed by 2 claps and final bow. But any show of respect is appreciated.

Reverse course brings us to another torii **[7]**, beyond which is **stable [8]** for two sacred white horses, which are paraded, beautifully caparisoned, **monthly 1,11,21**. Structure ahead to left is **Hall of Ritual Dance [9]** where **maiden kagura** is performed (as also, and more usually, at *Geku*) for offerings or donation of ¥10,000 or more—'more' performance is more ornate. Dancers, called *miko* everywhere else, are referred to here as *bujo*, or *mai-hime* 'dancing princess'. These girls work here at longest two years, and tho most do it for religious merit, many recognize that being Ise shrine maiden is great plus for later *omiai* match-making. Following along right side of walled dance pavilion, pass **Pavilion of Sacred Rice Wine [10]** (where on three great festivals priests brew 'white' and 'black' sake-wine for Sun Goddess) and **Hall of Pure Fire [11]** where food offerings are prepared over ritually pure fire ignited using bow drill of virgin cypress.

Path bears right now, past stone embankment on left, turns left again and climbs. Trees here are even grander and more awe-inspiring than ever. Some are said to be over one thousand years old. Up flight of rough stone steps turns us left and at their top is shrine **[13/14]**. We can go only few feet beyond torii at last step and before us **curtained gate [15]** blocks our way. We have been lucky every visit: wind has risen to raise curtain and allow us impressive view head on. Only imperial personages go beyond—and at this point you are 'in church'; no photos or noise. But slightly angled view is permitted thru fence at either side of gate, of succession of four fences forming courts within courts from outer of 202 x 364 feet, to innermost, 150 x 144 feet (134 x 131 at Geku), and farthest back, holy of holies, with large building in its center flanked (rear Naiku, forward Geku) by pair of smaller identical structures.

This inability to examine buildings up close need not frustrate secular visitors: there are identical, if smaller, buildings all over glade, housing lesser deities. Architecture is believed to represent purest, most archaic Japanese style of era prior to Chinese cultural influence. This may be. Or, too, it may be even older Chinese style, perhaps lost wood architecture of

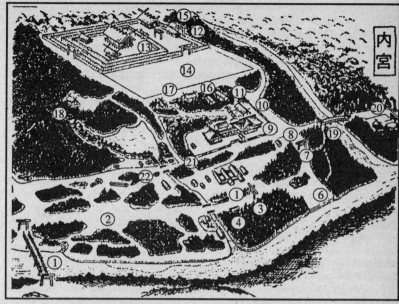

KOTAIJINGU OR NAIKU (Inner Shrine)

1. Isuzu River and Uji Bridge
2. Pilgrim Route
3. Place for Water-Purification
4. Torii (Gateway)
5. Saikan (Purification Hall)
6. Mitarashi (Water-Purification Place)
7. Torii (Gateway)
8. Miumaya (Stable)
9. Kagura-den (Hall of Ritual Dance)
10. Gojo-den
11. Imibiya-den (Sacred Kitchen)

12. Minie-Chosha (Cooking Ceremony Bldg.)
13. Inner Sanctuary
14. Kodenchi (Alternate Site of Shrine)
15. Minami-Gomon (Southern Gate)
16. Mishine-no-Mikura (Rice Storehouse)
17. Gehei-den (Treasure Hall)
18. Aramatsuri-no-Miya Affil Shrine
19. Kazahinomi-no-Miya Bridge
20. Kazahinomi-no-Miya Affil Shrine
21. Place of Water Purification
22. Miumaya (Stable)

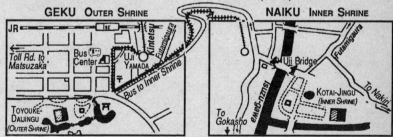

Hours: **May-Oct** 4:00-19:30, **Nov-Feb** 5:00-17:30, **Mar-Apr** 5:00-18:30.

GETTING AROUND: Taxi ISE Stn → NAIKU about 2x-mtr, 12min bus ¥280; same GEKU → NAIKU, former is short walk from stn. Walk GEKU → NAIKU pleasant, passes thru old part of town reminiscent of older era (FURUICHI, called 'pilgrimage breaker' consisting of dozens of brothels, now stately old houses), but not recommended except for those who can take 5km/3mi. But about 1km of this is in NAIKU itself. Those who can't walk even this should limit themselves to GEKU which has more modest glades.

earliest China, Shang Period. Whatever it is, it is superb craftsmanship and architecture. When buildings are new (present ones date from 1973) they shine in sunlight in golden hue purer than any metal. Compared to them, Kyoto's KINKAKU-JI Golden Pavilion is tinsel box. But even now that they are greying, only golden roof-ends glittering, they are magnificent.

Oldest palaces of Japan must have been built in this style. Chinese record of Han Dynasty writing of conditions in Wa-kuo (Wa-land, known to Romans, Arabs and Persians as Wakwak), or Japan, ca 190AD, states that Queen of Wa was "devoted to magic arts...few people see her face except one man who serves her meals and is medium of communication with her. She dwells in palace of lofty pavilions, surrounded by stockade".

This palace style reflects southern origins, for it faces south and opens on its long side under shade of eaves. (Izumo Shrine shows snowy northern origins with door at end under peak.) It also presages modern folk shinto sects founded by similar 'magical' women who built castle temples. Great *chigi* (horned roof beams) indicate to some archaeologists probable common origin with Indo-European styles in north central Asia. Thatched roofs are barbered to perfection. Yet as simple and 'purely Japanese' as they may be, they are paradox, more so as one studies them. And in this basic paradox they are, in truth, pure Japanese. As Kidder points out they are "most primitive structurally yet most advanced organizationally of all pre-Buddhistic types still in use today". Which is essence of their Japaneseness; they epitomize Japanese knack to adapt, absorb and to create new simplicity thru organization of complex.

Naiku houses spirit of Amaterasu personified in Sacred Mirror of Three Sacred Imperial Yamato Regalia (other two, magatama beads and sword were probably emblems of other absorbed peoples, sword certainly that of Izumo). Mirror was originally possessed by emperors, having been given to Ninigi-no-mikoto, great-grandfather of first emperor, Jimmu, by his grandmother, Sun, when he descended from heaven to conquer Japan. Tenth emperor, Sujin, ordered it enshrined in its own palace in 4?BC (traditional date, considered to have reigned about 300AD at earliest). After being moved to various sites it came to rest here in following reign. It supposedly had not been seen by mortal man since, for mirror itself is wrapped in brocade bag, which is never removed; and when this begins to disintegrate from age, new one is placed around it. Wrappings alone probably comprise world's most fabulous museum of brocade weaving. This is placed on wood stand, over all of which is wooden cage with gold ornaments, itself covered by coarse silk wrap. This only can be seen at special rites when door is opened.

It is not said what this physical embodiment of Cereal Goddess in Geku is, but mirror replica, whether same or different, is housed there. While recurrent fable has mirror back inscribed in Hebrew,*"I Am That I Am"*, HIH Prince Mikasa, brother of late emperor and Semitic scholar, notes absolutely no one, even imperial family, has seen back of mirror. Bronze mirrors were usually buried with nobles in burial mounds we will visit on our next stop. Their rare inscriptions are Chinese and on later ones only.

Feeding this Jewish link legend is set of 100+ stone lanterns bearing Star of David. On wide road between Geku-Naiku and leading to shrine university they line both side of avenue. Each atop stone pillar, is shaped like small peaked-roof shrine, with imperial 16-petal chrysanthemum at apex above light face, and directly below light is star. Chief priest knew nothing of it—local lore attributes it as salute to Jacob Schiff for raising loan 1904 and subsequent, which financed Russo-Japan war.

Grove around Naiku includes cryptomeria and camphor trees. Latter protected by railing as seamen like to peal camphor bark for charm to throw upon and calm stormy seas. Here we might note that gigantic mirror 5 feet across now housed in ASUKA-NIIMASU SHRINE was once kept at Ise. On its back is inscription for protection of seamen. In Macau, Mateo Ricci, late 16th century, reported main shrine to be of Goddess of Sea, Ama; Sea Goddess of Okinawa is Ma or *Ma-meko* (sea-princess?). Remember that first emperor Jimmu's mother was daughter of Sea Goddess. Amaterasu then would seem to be amalgam herself, originally no doubt goddess of people who invaded Japan by sea from south. Or perhaps she was set here by Sujin to absorb dangerously powerful sea goddess and rambunctious followers? History of shrine prior to 7th century is blank (tho legend takes us back earlier) when...

Sengu-no-gi, rite honoring custom of rebuilding entire shrine complex every generation was initiated in 689; 60th rite took place October, 1973; super 61st, start of new 60-generation grand cycle, will take place 1993 (*see* DATEBOOK); 59th rite took place 1953 which most sacred of Shinto rites we, with Jay's sister, Ruby, and French writer Alfred Smoular were first foreigners to witness. Some brief account is in order, as we reported in *Nippon* (now *Japan*) *Times*:

Two thousand people sat in almost total darkness and no sound was heard save for crickets. Ahead in darkness, 15-foot wall stood out in faint silhouette against glow of small bonfires burning beyond within its compound. Reflections of their flames danced on leaves of tall cryptomeria trees within and around walled enclosure. Directly ahead lay opening in wall, but baffle beyond it barred direct ingress. To L, wall continued off into darkness about 65 meters. Halfway down was slight break, beyond which wall appeared darker. It was adjoining old shrine (identical compound in place of which present shrine would be erected in 1973), in which flames suddenly glowed brighter, lighting trees above in weird, dancing light and showing in outline more structures within, odd structures with 'horns' continuing up from their steeply slanted roofs like monster Teutonic helmets.

Eerie cry, like that of child lost, rose from distant enclosure. I later learned it was chief priest, who had entered innermost sacred *Mizugaki* enclosure, struck his headgear three times with his fan then cried out like one of their sacred cocks, to open doors of main shrine and remove chest with sacred mirror. 2,000 silent onlookers started slow, spontaneous hand clapping; nothing like applause of onlookers at show, but that light, reverential clapping, in two's and three's that Japanese will do in front of temple or shrine. Despite number, claps were so muted that crickets could still be heard and baby-like cry rose in volume to become now recognizable as sound of *fue*-ancient Japanese flute. It took up slow rhythm of two see-sawing notes as low moaning chorus joined in, and dark, robed figures slowly emerged from now-glowing gateway of distant compound, moving in unison with sound of flute and chorus.

Torch-carrying figures with flames held close to ground provide dramatic stage-like illumination, move down straw mat-covered pathway; gravel beneath mats crunches in mounting, whispering accompaniment as they come closer to lighter section of wall enclosing new shrine. Two men move down path behind torch-bearers, each carrying long, mirror-like object that reflects light of torches just as they were to deflect arrows in their function as shields of Sun Goddess Amaterasu.

More bearers follow two giant-sized, sheathed swords; then two gigantic halberds bearing pennants of three swirling comma-like forms: two giant 'fans' on black lacquer stems so highly polished they shone in dim torchlight. Other objects pass, including tassled, dome-like object that hangs above altar of many large shrines and temples. Flutes sound louder as they too, come nearer and new sound can be heard, like rustling of fine bamboo in light wind: ancient koto (horizontal harp) carried by two men, one of whom strums it every 20 seconds or so in slow, never varying, wiping motion. Behind him, two men gently tap percussion sticks.

Torch bearers, leading somber procession, turned and entered gateway directly in front of our position and detoured around baffle within. Their torches illuminated gate as they entered and new, friction-polished wood of wall and gateway shone dull, yellow and metallic like pure gold.

Now it was dark, but robed figures still traversed path. Suddenly visible, attention brought upon it by odd crackling sound of its motion, was box-screen, its bearers silhouetted against its whiteness. One gradually came to see that it was stiff white silk and its box shape became evident as did heads of men who walked inside its small enclosure of about 20ft by 4ft, carrying 'soul of shrine', brand new replica of sacred mirror of Sun Goddess (original, actually ancient copy of even older copy, one of 3 'crown treasures' of Japan is in inner shrine 6km away).

Behind spirit-bearers, straw carpeting was being rolled up, remaining procession followed; their large, black, Dutch-like, wooden shoes crunch loudly on pure white river bed gravel path.

Chief priestess, oldest member of Imperial Family, literally floated down gravel way, ethereal in gorgeous silks of 8th century Heian style. Behind her marched Imperial Proxy and chief priest and only other woman in rite, chief attendant, dressed in coarse but pure white. In light of more torch bearers, first figure to break spell of timelessness of this ceremony appeared. But for Prince Takamatsu, Emperor's brother, dressed in morning clothes solemn rite could have been one of any of previous 58 observances of *Sengu-no-gi* (Transfer-of-Spirit Ceremony) that had taken place approximately every 20 years over past 1,200 years.

Last of procession disappeared within newly erected gateway and torches illuminating front and inside of distant, older shrine were extinguished.

Soon, grey 20-year-old shrine was to be dismantled and by 1973 this present new golden-wood edifice built in its place, identical to 59 structures before this. And then, when what is now new structure itself is old and grey, spirit will be transferred (next 1993, see schedule following) as endless process of regeneration continues and new generation of men comes upon this earth, dependent for life itself upon sun to which this shrine is dedicated.

Smaller version of this Transfer of Spirit Procession can be seen every year just at midnite **Dec 16-17** at WAKA-NO-MIYA SHRINE in Nara park. It is also basically similar to South Chinese funeral procession sometimes seen in Hong Kong or Macau.

When we first asked to be allowed to see rite, we were told it was "Impossible". "Why?" we pleaded. "Because no foreigner ever has!" "Has any foreigner ever asked?" "Come to think of it, no," was answer. "Then no foreigner has ever been refused". We have never had intelligent and sincere interest meet with rebuff in Japan—except by lesser clerks. But go to top man.

All lesser shrines [18, 20 etc] are also rebuilt. Lumber is from exclusive preserves in mountainous Kiso. (On walls of Minshuku **Yaoki**, where we stayed in Tsumago, are old Meiji era photos of sacred lumber being carted over mountain on special scaffold to avoid scratching wood.) Rebuilding every generation reflects original human nature of deity; in pre-Buddhist times capital was abandoned upon death of ruler—custom followed by commoners as well is said to account for Japanese reticence today to keep homes in good repair. Old lumber goes into bridge, torii (as above) or pilgrim talismans, family shrines—*kami-dana* 'god-shelves'.

Shrine vernacular book discusses 'why' of this rebuilding, why not make more sturdy structure, even this would last generations if rethatched and maintained. They say it is to renew spirit and body of traditional craftsmanship (implying form of godliness on earth), that 20 years, while 'limit one can count on one's fingers', was rather limit of productive professional life in shorter-lived eras and ideal time to rebuild with former ordinary carpenters now masters, with presence of previous work as model. Also some 2,500 decorative items–swords, bows and arrows, clothes, inscriptions, offeratory 'household goods' of dishes and cooking utensils for ritual meals etc–are all remade.

Before Meiji, last set would be kept and displayed as model to prove new were exact and of equal quality, older were ritually burned or buried, as what was god's should not be defiled by mundane use. Since Meiji, old are kept in Treasure House midway Naiku-Geku, and can be seen. They call it their 'Shosoin of craftsmanship and technology', for it preserves worksmanship of Shosoin era, best of Tang China. However, they admit to recent degeneration. Two special feathers for main sword no longer available as bird is extinct, thousands of eagle feathers for arrows now replaced by swan, fine textile-quality basketry for arrow cases simply can't be done anymore. Even plastics are edging their way in for lunch boxes and simple containers. Scholar YOSHIDA Mitsukuni notes how in mid-Edo era, samurai demand for special imported deer leather for small sword decorative wrapping caused extinction of variety of deer in Thailand. Problem is not new in our time.

Returning, you can follow wall and alternate site edge around to back. Midway along side are smaller buildings. One, in peculiar style on stilts, is sacred rice storehouse [16], reflecting buildings shown in earliest Japanese prehistoric pictures and seen at Toro, Shizuoka City, and at recently discovered Yoshinogari site, Kyushu. Rice stored here is for use in food offerings and is grown in shrine's own fields with unchanging ritual tradition (which you can see) marking various stages of planting, transplanting, harvesting.

All other food for offering is specially gathered by same families who were originally assigned catering honor millennium ago. Water from special well is drawn by man who undergoes all-night special purification before drawing it. Salt is drawn from sea and prepared by men who have inherited post thru centuries. All food comes from similar sources, abalone from diving-girl group which undergoes special annual purifications in January, wading nude into ice-cold sea. New earthenware is prepared for each offering by hereditary potters, with 50,–60,000 pieces used annually.

SARUTA-HIKO SHRINE is mile beyond *Naiku*, dedicated to fertility god with phallic nose, 'Monkey-field-prince', husband of goddess of ritual dance. (This is 'queer' shrine, too, with female *chigi*, oblique-cut end with flat edge up, for male tenant.) It may be as old as Ise, or may be where fertility god retreated after he was evicted from Geku by rice goddess. If you see tiny bags of sand for sale, they've been specially blessed for your home's ground-breaking ceremonies to sanctify plot.

PERSONAL DATEBOOK: *Minor rites* spring, annually **Apr 4** (7pm), **5** (2pm); **monthly 5**th 10am. **May 5** 12:15pm rites; 1:30 *Rice-planting ceremony*, in shrine field.

If you've time to kill, wander along river north of Uji Yamada stn in **Kawasaki-cho** district. Entire area is full of old houses, narrow shop-lined streets make for fun exploring. Bit over km east, above-mentioned **Furuichi** district has more old houses to wander around. Between two areas Kuratayama Park has **Museum of Jingu History**, *Jingu Choko-kan*, and **Farming Museum**, *Jingu Nogyo-kan*. Former in large Renaissance-style building with past shrine treasures and garments; latter, interesting early Meiji white wood Western-style building (¥300 both, X-mon).

DATEBOOK: 61st REDEDICATION 1985-1993 (62nd, 2005-2013)

1985 (Showa 60) **May 2, Repeat 2005.***Yama-guchi-sai*, Mountain entry rite, to move spirit of tree to sacred place to cut first pair of trees in Kiso, full altar set up before pair of trees at entry of preserves of Naiku & Geku, where trees were in early times actually felled; prayers for success of rebuilding. Axe used referred to by special ideograph, 'execution axe' as it kills sacred being, tree. Simultaneously, *Kyo-zen* invite chief builder & staff to feast after rite, all involved in white shrine robes, court caps. **Nite** *Ko-no-moto-sai* Tree base rite, enter dark woods near actual shrine precincts by torchlight to select 2 trees for Naiku & Geku main pillars, wrap sacred straw about each and place axe at base of each tree and pray for success of venture. Taboo talk about anything associated with trees for main pillars.

Jun 3 *Mi-yama-hajime-sai*, Hon Mountain Beginnings, ritual cutting tree for equipment such as, first tree—30 years old, 30 meters tall, 65cm (2'2") diameter—for inner altar-box to house main spirit; after cut, rejoin tip of tree to stump to house original tree spirit; held in Nagano Pref, Kiso Agematsu-cho. Cut in special manner, axed 3 places thru center, leaving tree standing on remnant tripod, one of which legs then cut to direct fall; after cutting, ceremony to transport logs to Ise, decorated with 5-color banners.

Jun 5 same at Gifu Pref, Ena-gun, Kashimo-mura, second preserve.

Jun - *Mihi-shiro-gi-ho-ei-shiki* Rite begin hauling cut wood 270km to Geku, 320 Naiku.

Sep *Mifune-shiro-sai*, similar rite to cut tree each shrine for box to house altar.

1986 (S 61) **Apr 12 (2006)** Naiku (Inner Shrine = IS), 13 Geku (Outer Shrine = OS) *Oki-hiki-dezome-shiki* Log hauling start, people who work in shrines perform *kiyari-ondo* dance and song, local youths chosen to pull logs.

Apr 21 prayers for well-being of cutting 13,000 trees needed.

Apr 26-Jun 1 *O-kihiki-gyoji* Hon Lumber-hauling Rite, part I, some 173,000 people gathered plus old shrine staff, repeated *Hoei-sai* both IS, OS.

Jul rite to move and honor tree spirit, start to cut wood for utensils; proceed cutting.

1987 (S 62) **Jun, (2007)** *O-kihiki-gyoji* Hon Lumber-hauling Rite, part II-delivery, most colorful preparatory fete. For IS haul floated lumber from Isuzu-gawa; OS has been hauled overland thru streets on carts accompanied by colorful dance troupes from all over.

1988 (S 63) **Apr, (2008)** *Chinchi-sai*, placate spirit of site of new shrine-to-be.

1989 (S 64-Heisei 1) **Nov** *Ujibashi-watari-hajime-shiki* rite to start crossing Uji River on new bridge (of old wood of previous shrine). Assemblage of lumber progresses.

1992 (H 3) **Mar, (2012)** *Ritchu-sai*, set main pillar of new main shrine; then *Gogyo-sai; Joto-sai* rite place 1st cross beams, main Inner (Nai-) & Outer (Ge-) Shrines progress **May** *Nokitsuke-sai*, start thatching of roofs of main shrines.

Jul *Iraga-sai*, thatching completed and metal decorations put in place to finish roofing.

1993 (H 5) **Aug (2013)** ceremony to lay white stones (Polynesian-style purification barrier?) around shrines, major event with representatives from entire nation participating.

Sep *Mi-to-sai*, Hon Door Rite, start final altar-box (of June '85 cutting) for main spirit, mirror. *Mi-funa-shiro-hono-shiki*, Hon Boat-house Offering, spirit placed in 'boat' which is to say its altar box, to 'float' from old shrine to new in main *Sengu-no-gi*. *Arai-kiyome* sacred washing of new shrine. *Shin-no-mihashira-hoken*, new main pillar mystery rite. *Ko-tsuki-sai*, building rite, harden base ground of new shrine main pillar.

Oct *Go-chin-sai*, Last Thanks to Site Spirit for watching over work, show gratitude. *O-shozoku-Shinpo-tokugo* examine 2,500 new shrine treasures. *Kawara-Ooharai*, Riverbed Big Purification, new treasures to riverside purification site to purify. *Okazari*, new decorations, furnishings ritually placed in new buildings. *Sen-gyo*, dates chosen by HIM as auspicious for real transfer of main spirits IS & OS. Eye-witness of #59, precedes.

O-omi-ke day after, first rites in new shrine; same day *Ho-o-hei* first day, messenger from Emperor with *hei*, paper money offering. *Mikagura-mike*, eve, 1st offering of maiden kagura dances, rites. Days later *Mikagura* maiden dance, imperial courier, others in main rites attend, *Kunaicho* Imperial Household musicians (12) offer 'secret music'.

Almost simultaneously, other major shrines Aramatsuri-no-miya and Takano-miya have own Sengu-no-gi rites, while 12 other shrines including Tsuki-yomi-no-miya follow, rebuilding in following year, initiated with similar small rituals.

PERSONAL DATEBOOK: JINGU & AREA

Food Offerings only at Geku **daily** 8:00,16:00 spring-summer, 9:00,15:00 autumn-winter.
Until 729AD offerings at both shrines: that year dinner to Sun Goddess carried past unclean object in road, emperor sickened. Diviners linked two incidents, since then Sun Goddess goes out to Rice Goddess' Geku to eat. For each: 4 cups water, 16 of rice, 4 of salt plus fish, fowl, fruit, seaweed, vegetables. Lesser deities get same, except half portion fruit. Shrine horses parade **monthly** 1,11,21. Rites in *kagura-den* all national hols.
Principal fetes held in both Inner Shrine (IS) and Outer Shrine (OS) unless noted.

GRAND SHRINE
January
1 New Year: OS 4am, IS 7am.
3 Court New Year: OS 4am, IS 7am.
February
11 National Day: IS 11am; OS 7am.
17 Prayer for Good Harvest: IS Sacred Food 11am, Imperial Offer 2pm; OS Sacred Food 4am, Imperial Offer 7am.
March
21 (usually) Equinox: Bless fields that supply all greens used at Ise Grand Shrine - Jingu Gyoen, Futami-cho Town, 10am.
April
5-6 Music & dance festivals 2-day Bugaku, Mi-Kagura, top rural troupes: folk kagura, puppets, mystic medieval religious plays, dances; IS. Must-see!
May
14 Pray for mild weather IS 9am; OS 5am.
Mid Gala affair followed by rice- cycle dances, 9am-on; O-Tsuchimi-oya detached shrine in Kusube Town.
June
15-17 Offerings: IS Sacred Meal, etc (16, 10pm), (17, 2am), Imperial Offerings (17, 12pm); OS Sacred Food (15, 10pm), (16, 2am), Imperial Offer (16, 12pm).
24 11am similar rice-planting rites to May last Sun at Kodai Jingu, Izo-gu (Izawa-no-miya) detached shrine, Isobe, (p328).
August
4 Pray for good Weather: IS 9am, OS 5am.
September
20-22 (equinox) Repeat Apr 5-6 IS.
October
14 Garment Offerings: IS 12pm.
15-17 Thanksgiving Sun God Amaterasu: IS Sacred Food (16, 10pm), (17, 2am), Imperial (17, 12pm); Mi-Kagura & music (17,6pm). OS Food (15,10pm), (16,2am), Impr'l (16, 12pm), dance (16, 6pm).
November
23 Divine Tasting New Rice Harvest: IS Sacred Food 11am, Imperial Offer 2pm; OS Sacred Food 4am, Imperial Offer 7am.
December
15-17 Solstice IS: Food (16,10pm) (17, 2am) Imperial Offer (17, 12pm); OS: Food (15,10pm, 16,2am), Imp'l (16,12pm)
23 Emperor's Birthday: OS 7am, IS 10am.

> **Note: Rites Feb 17, Oct 15-17, Nov 23, Dec 23 in IS at 10am; OS 7am.**

GREATER ISE-SHIMA AREA
January
1 *Geita* 'Fake Sun' *Festival* on Kamishima Isle, Toba (*text*).
1 Ritual Purification at Ijika Village, entire town wades nude into ocean (*text*).
1-3 *Hipporo Festival*, Ukuhi Jinja,Tategami Ago-cho nr Kashikojima welcome prosperous new year: Solo lion-dances **1st**; duet- lion dances **3rd**; fire dances at nite.
11 Arrow Fete, Koshika Shrine Shima T Sacred arrow shot into sea for good catch.
Lun-18 (Feb full moon+1) Boat F, Toba.
April
First weekend Norinaga Fete Matsuzaka.
May
5 Change *shimenawa* (sacred rope) binding two rocks at Futami-ga-ura.
5 Rites 12:15; 1:30pm, Rice transplanting in shrine field, dances, Sarutahiko Shrine.
June
6 Lobster Fete, Hamashima-cho, (p331).
July
11 *Shirongo Festival*, for ama-divers on Sugashima, Toba (*text*).
mid *Matsuzaka Gion Festival*, smaller version of Kyoto's Gion Festival.
3rd Sat-Sun Toba Port Festival, parade of boats around harbor, fireworks at nite.
August
14-16 Kanko-odori dances to *kanko* drum, each group different, ornate headdresses, dozens of places around Mie pref.
September
5 Change rope, Wedded Rocks.
- Day of Monkey: Waraji Straw Sandal Fete, Nakiri Shrine, Shima (*text*).
24-25 Bunraku puppet plays Anori Hachiman Shrine (*text*).
October
8-10 Fighting Monks Festival, Sangaku-ji Temple, Yunoyama Spa, geisha mikoshi parade; nite torch procession, fighting monks lead flame-decor mikoshi.
9-11 Tsu City Fete, samurai procession, wildly costumed dancers wind thru town.
Year end: Change *Shimenawa* sacred rope linking Wedded Rocks, Toba.

GETTING THERE

ALTERNATE ENTRY OR EXIT: OSAKA → ISE best by frequent, comfortable
Kintetsu expresses (2hrs) which end at KASHIKOJIMA; NARA → SAIDAIJI catch Kyoto
→ Ise exp (2hrs) by Kintetsu; KYOTO deluxe tokkyu 2hrs Kintetsu; JR expresses → ISE
in 3hrs, 3xfers. JR Kisei line runs from OSAKA around Kii Peninsula → ISE, about 8hrs
along beautiful coastline, but suggest several stops en route (*see* SOUTHERN KII p406).

Those on our main Tokaido itinerary end up in TOBA after ferrying from MIKAWA.
If coming from GIFU or INUYAMA, quickest way is rail (Kintetsu or JR) out of NAGOYA.
Drivers take Higashi-meihan Expwy to SEKI Interchange, change to Ise Expressway
which now ends before Matsuzaka but eventually will go past Ise to some unknown
destination. Avoid toll fees, take Rte1 → YOKKAICHI and Rte23 → ISE.

*to the sacred isle I cross on hearing
how they dive for abalone pearl
I'll wrap and bring some home*
— Yakamochi (749) *Manyoshu*

ISE-SHIMA 伊勢志摩
LAIR OF DIVING GIRLS

GODS LIVED in caves hereabouts; Sun Goddess Amaterasu is enshrined locally in Japan's most sacred and loveliest shrine-grove; Nereids still emerge from depths of these waters—diving *ama* daughters of Sea Goddess, Ama. This gateway to Japan of primeval mythologies is favorite setting for official tourist posters—yet it earns but scattered paragraphs in official guides. Despite this, you won't be lost behind any language barrier, epicures have treat in store, less adventurous whose knees bend poorly will find perhaps Japan's best-run Occidental-style hotel, and budgeteers are in for luxury ball.

Traveler tired from long journeying, perhaps ending trip thru Southeast Asia and flying into nearby Osaka International Airport, or long trek thru Japan, will find this is excellent place to stay over few days and rest up preparatory to 'bust' in Tokyo. Recommended would be superb W-style **Kashikojima Kanko Hotel** or our old 1964 'find' and still treasure, **Hirohama-so** at diving girl beach of **WAGU**. Golfers will like dozen inns at **KOU**, near golf course which itself competes with diving girls for use of beach. Few miles N is secluded isle of **WADAKANO** in bay with fine inns and ferry service; tho slowly becoming another Japanese 'weekend retreat', with oversized hotels and gaudy amusement center.

GETTING AROUND

TRANSPORTATION within peninsula excellent (detailed on map & in itinerary); distances are sufficiently short to make **taxi** travel practical. And you are in for some of loveliest boat rides in Japan, by ferry or hired diesel sampan. Numerous scenic roads now wind up coast and inland, making for easy, pleasant drives between Kashikojima, Toba and Ise.

Rent car at ISE, agencies in and near JR and Kintetsu stns, to which return it to avoid prohibitive drop-off fee; also available at TOBA or KASHIKOJIMA.

We circle peninsula clockwise starting at Ise, usual entry point–tho we recommend TOBA–ending again at Ise, saving its architecturally and atmospherically exciting Grand Shrine for last.

WHERE TO STAY

ENTICING beaches, isles, rustic scenery are just around corner, but if overnite here, we suggest favorite with friends **Hoshide Ryokan** w/ macrobiotic rest'nt 7min N of stn by Kawasaki bus stop, Eng spkn, ¥-B-w/2, ☎(0596)-28-2377. Highly recommended and unique at Furuichi midway btwn OS and IS in former gay quarters is lone remaining inn **Asakichi**, reminescent of olde Edo days, ¥-B-w/2, ☎22-4101. Most ryokan here are traditional-J. **Miyamae-kan** "front of shrine" is as name implies in front of Jingu Outer Shrine entry, truly trad, excellent view, ¥-S-w/2, ☎28-3617; R beyond NTT well-known ryori-ryokan **Kyuka-en**, ¥-hi-T-w/2, ☎28-3124. On OS approach is **Yamada-kan** on R, ¥-hi-T-w/2, ☎28-2532. R of stn beyond Tsukiyomi-no-miya Shrine is **Toda-ya Ryokan**, ¥-hi-S–L-w/2, some *hinoki*-cypress baths (annex at Toba, L of stn) and small friendly family-run **Okubun**, ¥-B-w/2, ☎28-2231. For budgeteers, **Town Hotel** Ise, E of stn, ☎23-4621; **Danke** is on Jingu Sando approach, ☎22-1849, both business hotels ¥-lo-T.

Before we start down peninsula, let's backtrack to **MATSUZAKA** *for...*

CONTENTED STEAKS FROM CONTENTED COWS: STEAK and beer is popular combination. Here at Matsuzaka is one place you can have it even if doctor ordered you off beer—they feed their cows on it. Matsuzaka beef is justly reputed to be finest in world. Home range is 10min out of Ise by electric, where until 14th century virgin priestess of Ise lived. We stayed at Futami-ga-ura, ran into Matsuzaka City **Wadakin** for dinner.

Go in bit early and see farm. Here they bring virgin cows of *Wa-Gyu* (Japan cow) strain only, and only those calved in Mikata Kinosaki-gun, Hyogo pref., tho they are finding some others from other locations work out as well (as do some in U.S.). They weigh about 1,500 pounds, are kept 3 months or more for special feeding, which runs over ¥30,000 per head. They get beer appetizer (all brands are used) followed by gallon of cooked fermented fodder three times daily, plus heated hay. In winter they wear padded coats; all year round sees them groomed and massaged daily to even out fat into good marbling. Barns are spotless. On each stall is Buddhist blessing paper from Dainichi-dera in town picturing Dai-Nichi-Nyorai (Great Sun Buddha) riding cow. Blessing or not, when normally yellow fat whitens and properly marbles, cow is led out, slugged at base of skull with mallet, throat slit almost simultaneously.

Unfortunately for steak connoisseurs, demand for this beef so great that it is on your table within days. Finest cuts stay at **Wadakin**, fascinating, rambling Japanese gardenmanse in Matsuzaka. Top cuts also go to three top Tokyo restaurants: **Yugiri**, **Hasejin** and **Okahan** where it gets properly aged before going on charcoal.

(Many places advertise 'Matsuzaka beef' but this can sometimes refer to any draught ox that was sent thru town on train.)

Because meat isn't aged, we do not recommend Wadakin steaks, but we do recommend highly their J-style beef offerings (all full-course, with rice, soup etc): *sukiyaki*, *ami-yaki* (charcoal broiled), *shio-yaki* (salted & charcoal broiled), *butter-yaki* (sauteed in butter), *oil-yaki* (cooked in oil), and *mizutaki* (cooked in water with vegetables). We prefer *ami-yaki*. 1989 prices for any of above ¥5,600, ☎(0598)-21-1188 most major credit cards OK. At butcher shop out front you can buy cuts to take home or as gifts for Japanese friends who highly prize this luscious luxury. Wadakin is **cab** basic-mtr from stn, or 10min walk down main road, 3rd R. X-4th tues monthly & Aug 16, 23.

If you have some time to kill, head to...

Castle Park, 10min walk from Wadakin (20min walk, cab basic-mtr from stn). Continue up main street from stn, take R at next main road, 400m past Wadakin turn-off. Another 400m where 20-odd **old houses** line street, built 1850s to house 20 samurai families and their retainers sent here to protect castle. Present residents are their descendants. Large red wood building at end is Japan's oldest technical high school. Castle grounds are now park. Veering L as you enter leads to **house of** MOTOORI **Norinaga**, 18th century writer whose analysis of *Kojiki* annals was major force in late Tokugawa proimperial, anti-foreign nationalism. Nearby **Memorial Hall** holds most of his works. In back, shrine dedicated to him and colleague HIRATA Atsutane.

Circle around back of castle grounds, 200m to river; downstream, R at bridge thru old section of town with interesting houses (Motoori's house originally here). L at end of block first R takes you back to **Wadakin**. Looking out from castle you notice another smaller castle in town: project of local merchant, his son now uses part as dentist office.

About 60km N of Matsuzaka is...

Suzuka race circuit for car, motorcycle, amusement park go-karts, assorted U-drives. 6km race course hosts numerous international events, but non-race days, inner 2.3km is giant go-kart track. Hotel, campsite, budget lodgings in compound. Open 9:00-17:30 (to 21:00 summer), ¥800 for adm and ¥3,000 all rides incl. Hourly bus from Kintetsu Shiroko stn.

TILT: Following itinerary high spots visited by 4hr **Mie Kotsu deluxe bus tour** deps Uji-Yamada 9:10 for Ise Shrines → Kongosho-ji Temple via Ise-Shima Skyline → Futami–skipping Toba and down coast → end Toba 13:00. ¥3,100, must reserve. Can do reverse; or get off Kashikojima (notify first). Mie Kotsu Bus Co has several other tours covering parts of area. Most start Kintetsu UJI YAMADA stn, ending TOBA, or reverse. There is also **'On-board BBQ' Boat Cruise** leaving TOBA 9:20 and 10:20 down coast for cruise thru oyster beds of Ago Bay and BBQ before returning to Toba 5hrs later; ¥6,300. Similar course leaving TOBA 9:50 includes lobster BBQ; ¥9,700. Arrange all tours at JTB offices in Japan or overseas, or on spot. Getting off or on part-way changes fare accordingly.

FUTAMI-GA-URA (just 15min bus or JR from ISE; cab 4x-mtr) is location of photogenic but uninteresting **'Wedded Rocks'**, two sugar-loaf formations offshore, one larger (poppa), one smaller (momma), joined in wedlock by straw *shimenawa* sacred straw rope. New Year sun rises between them. *Shimenawa* are changed in Shinto rite 3x-yearly: **May 5, Sept 5 & end Dec.** Futami-ga-ura is solely devoted to these rocks, resort consists of long stretch of inns and souvenir shops lining beach from stn to rocks and nothing else in way of village. Beach fine, good summer hideaway, crowded weekends.

Near rocks is small shrine with frog images all around it. Dedicated to patron kami of local fishermen, because frog in Japanese, *kaeru*, is homonym 'return' and wives prayed here for hubby's safe return. More recently, people pray here and buy little frog talismans to increase wealth since it is hoped money put out will promptly 'return'. Continuing beyond rocks and first R takes you to TAIKO-JI temple, early Kamakura period (12th cent) 1,000-handed Kannon statue.

About 1km along coast opposite direction from rocks is...
'Salt Palace' of MISHIO-DEN, where sacred salt used at Ise Grand Shrines is produced. Just beyond Futami Middle School, you can't miss two squat, thatched buildings. 4x-yearly, ocean water is 'harvested' at Mishio-hama beach further down, evaporated in one of sheds, taken to Grand Shrine for their special ceremonies. This process and site have been in use for about 2,000 years, at reasonable estimate. Special purification rites **Oct 5.**

Fact that there really is little here makes it ideal to stay, as bulk of visitors just pass thru for quick look at Wedded Rocks and rush on.

WHERE TO STAY: **Asahi-kan** ☎(05964)-3-2001, straight down from stn, flashiest, ¥-hi-T–Sw/2, boasts all rooms facing bay. Another classic is **Futami-kan** ☎3-2003, near Rinkai-ro, ¥-S–Lw/2. Between these are numerous more in all price ranges. Of mid-range (¥-Tw/2) fun old-fashioned ones are: **Iroha-kan** ☎3-2024; 2 doors down **Mano-kan** ☎3-2014; and next door **Ise-ya** ☎3-2008. ¥-B ryokan **Chitose-ya** ☎3-2179, and **Shima-ya** ☎3-2017 on L side of road from stn to beach. Few hundred yen cheaper for minshuku along same street or down side alleys from coast road. We found store owners helpful in finding inns of any range; boorish man at **Kanko-annai** on main highway told us no budget inns around, whereupon woman there excused herself, came out and apologized for his ill-mannered misinformation. Taiko-ji temple runs **YH**, ☎3-2283, ¥-lo-P.

TOBA of Mikimoto Pearl fame is port for hydrofoil NAGOYA → GAMAGORI; terminus for JR, start of TOBA → KASHIKOJIMA electric (17min bus, cab 4x-mtr from Futami-ga-ura; half hour bus, cab 8x-mtr from ISE). All sights and resort hotels are along shore; town itself is still small. We do **not** suggest staying here as it is so commercialized, but it does, however, have large nitelife area if you are looking for little diversion, in which case, **Visitors Center** can find rooms to fit almost any pocket.

With its natural bay protected by many islands Toba was favorite haunt of pirates during chaotic Warring States period (14-16th centuries). Notable was KUKI Yoshitaka whose ancestors had been granted area around Toba for past favor to 12th century Minamoto. He aided Toyotomi Hideyoshi in his campaigns, rewarded with more land, and in 1594 built spectacular castle here. But he sided with wrong army at Sekigahara battle and barely making it home, committed suicide on Toshijima Island in bay. Only parts of stonework remain of his castle, but it offers good view of bay and its islands.

Closest of which is...

MIKIMOTO PEARL ISLE which we escaped as soon as possible, both in 1962 and again in 1985. Place is farce: see it and have no taste for Mikimoto quality forever more. Most pearls sold there are trinkets no fine Mikimoto shop would handle. Such cheap souvenir counter appearance prevails that whatever few good buys may be here are lost in sea of mediocrity and no savings on anything you might suffer. As gifts for kids back home, okay, get framed sets (also available on mainland-side Pearl Bldg) showing pearl-oyster development, ¥6,000. You are gouged ¥500 just to get on isle to see regularly staged *ama* diving for oysters (real pearl-oysters are in protected cages), collection of gaudy objects made of pearls, and 'pearl museum'. Far better pearl museum near KASHIKOJIMA; real pearl rafts, but no demonstrations. Few diving girls work at pearling today —and these only out of feudal charity honoring old obligations, or as show girls for Mikimoto. Most gather shellfish or edible kelp.

What you learn at Mikimoto is that 50% of pearls are yellow and gold color, 25% silver, 5% blue and 10% pinks (roseate just means deep pink). Orientals preferred yellows. Occidentals demand pinks, few Caucasians can wear yellow—but auburn or jet-black-haired women can and should try them, as you get far better pearls for your money if you can wear this color.

Pearl, you will see in exhibits, is excrescence formed about foreign body in mantle of oyster. Mikimoto process of 'cultured' pearls involves artificial insertion of this 'dirt' then domesticating oysters, keeping them in controlled areas, safe from their enemies – especially starfish. It was found that best foreign body is ball of shell from Mississippi River clams, now from China. Kinki Nippon Railway has excellent English pamphlet on this whole process available usually at Kashikojima Kanko Hotel. **Visitors Center** near Mie Kotsu bus center, L of Pearl Bldg, occasionally has pamphlets; always has several English flyers and maps of area, and small English display on pearls and diving. One other point in passing: 'Mikimoto process' was invented by Prof Nishikawa and his assistants, Fujita brothers. Mikimoto was former noodle-hustler who hustled pearls. He wasn't inventor; he was crack promoter who made world 'pearl conscious'. Mikimoto pearls are no different from other cultured pearls. But if you don't know what you're buying, it's far safer to go to Mikimoto shops with their Yankee-style merchandising and guarantees.

Pearl Building (round one) and adjacent **Toba Ichiban-gai** have usual gift shops, upper floors are full of restaurants peddling assorted seafood and delicious eels of nearby ANAGAWA. All have samples in front with prices posted to make choosing easier. To R and behind these two buildings are piers for boats to islands and regular cruise boats. Large, permanently moored boat is *Brazil-maru*, former immigrant carrier of Japanese heading to Brazil at turn of century. Now museum showing what shipboard life was like, as well as exhibits on Brazil.

TOBA BAY ISLANDS: There are five main islands in bay.
Closest is...
IRUKAJIMA (Dolphin Isle), just offshore of Obama (10min by ferry): children's amusement center, best known for its Marineland. Nothing special out on other four islands, which as result are blissfully still quiet.

SAKATEJIMA (10min ferry) *avoid* as it is being built up into resort.

SUGASHIMA, gourd-shaped, only 4km at its longest is perhaps least visited; no roads cross this island, only paths. 7 boats daily (¥350) dock at sole village located far side of island. Dozen budget inns here, good swimming beach nearby. Over 100 ama divers here, all can be seen at N point on July 11 for *Shirongo* Festival, offering to local kami for good catch and safety at sea. At blowing of conch-shell horn, all race into water to be first to find certain type of abalone shell (best with red and black markings) and deliver it to nearby SHIROHIGE SHRINE. First to make offering becomes head ama for year. Hitch ride out to festival site on boat: it's only way out.

TOSHIJIMA, floating next to Sugashima, is largest, with MOMOTORI village on W end (nearer mainland) and WAGU and TOSHI villages at E end. 8 boats daily to each village: ¥290 to MOMOTORI, ¥360 other two, but only way from one end to other is hour walk. Numerous inns (mostly at E end) in 3 villages: ryokan slightly expensive (¥-Tw/2) but half-dozen minshuku. Several isolated swimming beaches on long S shore. Ama also work off this island, but main attraction is fishing, for which you can rent boats and tackle thru your inn. Apr-June, and Sept-Nov join fishermen on boats, help haul in *tai-ami* (sea bream nets). Supposed to arrange ahead of time costs ¥2,000 for which you get portion of catch which your inn prepares, but similar circumstances other places have found us out on boats at crack of dawn, invited on by fishermen.

KAMISHIMA: 'God's Island', furthest out, is closer to Irako Point on Atsumi Peninsula, but is reached only from Toba. 4 boats daily make 50min crossing (¥500) to this most isolated island. It is slightly better known, however, as setting for MISHIMA Yukio's novel *The Sound of Waves*. His island was called Uta-jima, but other than that, everything is same and life here now is little changed since story took place. Population has shrunk as young folk seek their fortune on mainland. Chances are any fellow visitor here will be some starry-eyed college girl carting around copy of book and searching out spots mentioned. Dozen inns here, all budget, minshuku rate; and rather large beach.

Above village, atop long flight of stone steps, is...
YATSUSHIRO SHRINE, dedicated to sea and wind gods. Here, in pre-dawn of New Year's Day, is held most unusual festival: fake 'sun' fashioned out of wood and paper in donut shape is beaten down to ground with long bamboo poles. Fake sun is then taken to shrine and offered. This ritual originated from ancient saying "As there are not two Suns in Heaven, so there shall not be two Emperors on Earth". It was prayer for peace, and warning that any usurper of sacred throne would be dealt with accordingly. Bold for such small place off beaten track. Perhaps they had ancestry of some noble lineage? Or is this true home of god-emperor idea?

BACK ON MAINLAND
IT'S 35MIN EXPRESS electric to KASHIKOJIMA, 80min bus via scenic Pearl Road. If you have time, meander down coast thru some beautiful rustic fishing villages. Entire coast is full of budget inns and campsites, any village you stop at will have place to stay. Fishing and swimming is also good all along coast, also in season, shrimp, abalone, oyster and lobster abound.

Note to campers: most sites are officially open summer only, often crowded. Having camped all over Japan we rarely use these sites; just pick semi-isolated spot late in day, no one will complain as long as you leave it clean. We've never been told not to camp in any place. Ignorance is bliss– but ignorance of guest-etiquette denies that bliss to those who follow.

Just S of Toba is...
ARASHIMA Peninsula. Side closest to Toba is crowded modern resort, but on far side, road dead-ends at Arashima Village (18min bus from Toba). To exit, must backtrack to Toba.

Or, head back 1km where side road connects with main coast road to...
IMA-URA Village, entrance to Pearl Road (toll), marked by arched bridge spanning Oura Bay, dotted with oyster beds which supply tables of local inns Sep–Mar.

Few kilometers beyond, we round point to windward side and lovely cliffside...
IJIKA Village. This is real *ama* village; lack of flat land has forced houses to literally climb up sides of craggy shore. You can see ama at work around Ijika. Here, at 3:00am New Year's Day, entire village strips down and takes purification plunge into ocean. Another ancient custom here is for each household to make *shimenawa* (sacred rope) every year as prayer for safety at sea.

4km down coast is...
KUZAKI where almost entire female population are ama divers. One of oldest ama communities here, Kuzaki was chosen centuries ago as supplier of abalone to Ise Grand Shrines. In June, October, December, ritually purified elders prepare specially dried and cut strips of abalone, called *noshi-awabi*, in special room at **AMA-KATSUGIME SHRINE**, dedicated to goddess Ama-goze.

Turning off Pearl Road at Kuzaki, local bus road continues to...
OSATSU with beautiful white sand beach and dozens of minshuku near mouth of long, narrow Matoya Bay.

Heading to inner tip of bay (or 30min bus or rail from Toba) reach...
ISOBE: nothing here except **Kawahachi** eel restaurant (below), but it's major bus center with lines plying coast we just came down; down mid of peninsula from Toba; to Kashikojima and Wagu and out to Gokasho.

1 stop rail or short bus on is...
ANAGAWA with neighboring ponds elevated above sea level by dam. Oysters are farmed in one, eels in other. Best place for scrumptious eels is **Kawahachi** restaurant, 10min walk N of ISOBE stn. Founded 1878, basic eel table d'hote begins ¥1,000, or splurge on full course feast of 12 variously prepared eel dishes ¥5,000. Open daily 8am to 8pm, it is also inn, ¥-T–Sw/2 (of course eel), ☎(05995)-5-0005. **Ise-Shima YH** is quite near Anagawa stn.

Few hundred meters N of Kawahachi is...
IZAWA-NO-MIYA, commonly known as IZO-GU affiliated Shrine of Ise, worth visiting **June 24** for *Ota-ue*, rice transplanting festival, one of top 3 in Japan. Starting around 10:30am, local fishermen roll massive bamboo mesh cylinder (and themselves) thru muddy paddy to 'prepare' it for young rice, seedlings transplanted by kimonoed women to beat of flutes and drums. You can have 5-man drum teams perform at your inn any time of year, ¥60,000 during day, ¥35,000 at night for 20min. Call ☎5-0230, may tell you where they're playing that night if not available.

From Anagawa there are almost hourly boats out to lovely isle of...
WATAKANO-JIMA; bay, if you can call it that, winds for several kilometers, yet is only few hundred meters wide until finally opening up. In its mouth lies Watakano, protected from open sea by 2 points virtually enclosing bay.

Boats used to go via two small harbors at mouth of bay, MATOYA on N and SANKASHO on S, now reached only by special charter. Boats run 70-80x-daily Wabe → Watakano, 5min, ¥100. All end up same spot on Watakano, along SE shore with over dozen inns (all sizes and prices), average start ¥-Sw/2, tho best two New Osaka-ya ☎(05995)-7-2811 and Asashio ☎7-2621 are half-again as much. Despite newer large inns and small amusement center, Watakano is pleasantly quiet with superb view of bay.

During feudal times Watakano was major port along coast, and many farmers' daughters came here as *hashiri-gane* pleasure women for sailors. (In 1857 census 175 of total 634 population here were such). Times have changed, but near pier you'll find many bars and clubs. Most people come here for pleasures of water, if just to watch it from hilltop or play in it. Wind-surfing, water-skiing, fishing in bay or out in ocean, and various chug-boat tours of entire area can be arranged thru your inn, whether Watakano or mainland. Area famous for its edible oysters, best raw with dash of lemon, in season October-March. July 17 *Tenno-sai* festival dedicated to mischievous Susa-no-O starts off with daytime fireworks, mikoshi parade and other events at local shrine; festivities continue into night with lanterns lining streets and more fireworks overhead.

GETTING AROUND: Ferry from Watakano 5min (no set scheds, arrange on spot ¥60 to ¥120) to WABE part way up Anori Point. May be able to arrange ride to tip of Anori Point; if not, few min walk from pier to main road and bus stop whence just under 2km to tip. Frequent buses. If not via Watakano catch bus at Ugata stn front which has rental cars (half day from ¥5,000) and bicycles (¥1,000/day).

Tip of point (10km, 20min bus from Ugata) boasts Japan's first lighthouse built by Englishman in 1873 (then wood, now concrete and metal) and molds used to make cannons with which Toba Clan planned to repel Perry's Black Ships in any attempted landing here; also tiny ANORI SHRINE with museum of bunraku puppets. Puppet plays on lunar Aug 15-16 (Sep 24-25) special performances by locals. Tradition dates back to 1593 when Toba's pirate-lord KUKI Yoshitaka came to offer thanks for victory in battle, made village plays into shrine offering. Performed annually since (except brief period 1924-48), performances begin both days at 18:00 and last until midnite, include one show by local school kids. Another interesting fete here is *Shime-kiri* sacred rope cutting on Jan 10 in which 2 thick shimenawa are twisted together and hacked with sword by village men; fewer cuts it takes to sever chord, better omen for year. 2 dozen inns (mostly ¥-lo-T+w/2), handful of minshuku clustered together near tip.

Windward shore has numerous ama working rocky shore and offshore from boats. They can also be seen farther down at Shirahama beach in KOU Town, except in summer when too many swimmers and surfers around. On beach is 18-hole, 5,500 yard Shima Country Club. Near beach are dozens of inns, mostly budget minshuku, but also some few ryokan catering to golfers.

Budget inns, bungalows and camp sites all down this lovely coast.

WHERE NEXT

FROM HERE, two routes to cover tip of peninsula and tasty Wagu ama beach: one via Kashikojima and ferrying across, or other continuing down coast. Kashikojima is 20min via Ugata, cab 8x-mtr. If by bus, coastal road continues down to DAIO-ZAKI Point but no bus for last 5km; backtrack to Ugata and take one for WAGU via Daio-zaki 40min, or 30min direct. Daio-zaki also known locally as Nakiri, name of fishing port there. Lighthouse here, many budget inns; ama also work off point. Village is photogenic, with wind barriers and winding stone steps. Lunar August day of Monkey (Sep 5) is *Waraji-biki* (Straw Sandal) festival at NAKIRI SHRINE in which sacred rice and sake are set adrift on tatami mat-sized sandal to ward off seafaring spirit of one-eyed *Dangara-hoshi*; several mikoshi parades in town. If to Wagu via Kashikojima, take 25min ferry (10x-daily), ¥500 thru pearl oyster rafts to Wagu and 10min bus or cab.

1km across narrow peninsula to...

WAGU and **diving girls of Hirohama-so** which looks like it is 'only' some little Japanese inn, but it really makes Wagu tourist gem, one of our favorite finds. Off by itself right on long white beach, which in June, July, and August swarms with over 400 honestly-working ama divers and more offshore in boats at Oshima and Koshima islets (you can also get here from Kashikojima by **cab**, about 13x-mtr, or ferry Kashikojima to Goza and bus down coast, or **cab** 3x-mtr). Here we got our personal orientation on ama, feasted on fabulous seafood which in itself makes coming all way from Tokyo worth-while. Then-manager, SAKAMOTO Jiro (now run by son), told us 1963 were some 7,000 (1987 3,000) ama in Ise area. Wagu still best place to see them— **Mar 19** onward.

They work part-time at this job, farm rest of year. Women do better than men as they can take cold better (they claim this work would kill men), have more fat under skin and, at least in Japan, control their breath better, hold it longer (even tho ama women didn't get to use phones very often). Peak diving season mid-July.

Ama are concentrated along coast among islands and bays from Toba S around peninsula to Ago Bay. Seasons vary according to supply and dictates of fishermen's cooperatives. In some areas, divers can put in at most 7 months March thru September, shortest being 2 months of July-August. They dive for such as *awabi* (abalone) their biggest money-earner, *sazae* (turbot), many varieties of kelp, *tengusa* (agar-agar), *namako* (sea cucumbers), and *kaki* (oysters)—latter used to be big source of income, as they were needed for implanting irritant in cultured pearls. Pearl farms now raise them completely from seed. However, to assist in local economy and at insistence of fisher-cooperatives, at least week to ten days is set aside when diving girls go out en mass for oysters, which pearlers buy to supplement their own.

There are two types of ama: more numerous *shore ama* who work from base on shore, and *boat ama* who work in deep water off boats, usually handled by hubby who is fisherman (probably with small plot of land to work alternate seasons). From oldest Japanese records we know that ama have been diving here since early Christian era at least. You can rent boat and be taken out among them for hour (about ¥10,000, inn will arrange). Many women work farms in early morning, head for sea in mid-morning leaving from this beach—stroll down and hitch ride, they're hospitable. If they are boating ama you might go out to watch these independent couples work, ask to be dropped off at Oshima to be in center of diving. Ama work right off inn's beach, too. Women come in at frequent intervals to warm up and rest by fires on beach. Fosco Maraini's excellent book *Meeting with Japan* deals with most traditional girls, found on Hekura Island off Noto Peninsula in Japan Sea (*see*). Ise area divers effect new clothing styles (many wear wet-suits but traditional white garb can be seen, especially around Matoya area), off Noto they stick closer to old-fashion birthday suits.

Chinese ideographs used to write ama are 'sea women', except in Noto where they were granted superior status of homonym 'sea samurai' by 17th century local lord and are on whole more traditional, submerging deeper, longer, and working in harsher conditions.

PERSONAL DATEBOOK: Fishermen & ama of Wagu hold joint festival **lunar June 1st** (new moon end June, early July). After offerings at Oshima's tiny shrine, all pile onto boats and douse each other with sea water, get too close and you too are 'blessed' for year.

WHERE TO STAY: Oyama-kan bekkan (annex) Hirohama-so is inn's
full name, as it's addition to Oyama-kan, few minutes away by taxi in main part of town.
Hirohama-so ☎(05998)-5-0502, rates are ¥-T-Sw/2; Oyama-kan, ¥-B-Tw/2.
Reservations necessary Apr-May, July-Aug. Dining-specialties with top rate are: in
Apr & May *Ise-ebi* (large clawless lobster); summer is sea bass and abalone done 'their
way'; and *Daruma Tai* (monster sea bream) served in 'fish net' of deftly sliced or sculpted
daikon Japanese radish. Regular meals are themselves feast of fresh seafood.

 ¥-B minshuku right around Hirohama-so are (looking out to sea): to its L, **Ama-no-
Sato** ☎5-1727; just inland from it, **Wagu** ☎5-0765. Further R is small cove where
fishing fleets moor, and good place to hitch your ride out to Oshima islet. Many more ¥-
B inns in village.

Continuing along peninsula next village **Koshika** also has ama working
off beach; few inexpensive inns just off coast. With its own small cove-
beach, it is relatively quiet as it lies between two main towns of Wagu and...

GOZA on leeward tip of peninsula. Known mostly for its beach, served by many
¥-B minshuku and campsite, it is also frequently-running ferry crossing to
KASHIKOJIMA, 25min (¥510); ferry crossing to HAMASHIMA 15min (¥250), 11x-daily,
site of **National Pearl Research Center**. Ama work its rocky shores.
Their main catch is Ise-ebi clawless lobster, and is marked by **June 6th** *Ise-
ebi Festival* on Kurosaki beach W of town: 4m-long wood and paper Ise-ebi
is carted out to sea by ama who send it off with thanks for its kindness in
keeping them working.

KASHIKOJIMA ends our rounding of coast, back on mainland; our
choice for overnite stay over any other stops, with exception of Wagu.
Terminus of Kintetsu rail lines, it has excellent transportation facilities as well as
accommodations. Superb W-style hotel **Shima Kanko** sometimes called Kashikojima
Kanko, ☎(05994)-3-1211. Rates, with private bath, run ¥-S for twin; meal costs low-
average for W-style hotels, but quality excellent, with seafood and Matsuzaka beef buys.
View from roof observatory is one of best anywhere. And little extras hotel offers make
it real vacation. Staff has plenty of helpful hints and information; movies at night include documentary on pearls and sights of Ise-Shima area. 9:30am year-round, hotel runs
1hr tour boat (¥1,440) thru islet-studded bay to see pearling industry in all its phases, not
posed. They will also get you boat to Wagu diving girls (above) or rent you fishing boat.
Under same management nearby is Kashikojima's **Wafu Bekkan** (J-style annex), ¥-T-
Lw/2, ☎3-1237. **Kashikojima-so**, original inn updated (26rms) in pure sukiya-style
architecture, ¥-Sw/2. **Daisan Kashikojima**, ☎3-3111 and **Shin Kashikojima-so**,
☎3-1221, both ¥-Sw/2. Avoid Wafu Bekkan (J-style) as it is for large tour groups.
Budgeteer who would like some luxury, recommend **Kashikojima Lodge**. Too good,
crowded in summer, **reserve** essential—as Shima Kanko, too. Several other luxury class
inns, roughly same rates, and handful of minshuku. All can be arranged thru stn front
Tourist Information.

 AGO BAY CRUISES can be arranged thru any inn or Tourist Info; 1hr ¥1,440 (child
half), or ¥3,-6,000 includes BBQ on board (reserve). **Ferries to Deguchi Pearl
Factory**, also reached by foot, 1km from stn at southernmost tip of Kashikojima. In
addition to above are regular hourly ferries to WAGU, GOZA and HAMASHIMA, you can
get nonscheds to cruise among isles and drop you off somewhere, just set time for pick-
up. There is also restaurant out on otherwise uninhabited **KANZAKI-JIMA isle**.

 From here, most common is rail or bus via TOBA → ISE but recommend bus or **taxi**
(8x-mtr plus ¥1,000 toll) over mountain on Ise-Shima Skyline, to Ise Grand Inner Shrine.
En route is...
KONGOSHO-JI temple, started 825 by Kobo-daishi (Saint Kukai),
converted into Zen temple 1392 and rebuilt in present form. Its importance
and proximity to Grand Shrine made two somehow connected in minds of
early pilgrims who claimed "pilgrimage to Ise was not complete unless one
also prayed at Kongosho-ji". Bus stops in front, worth having your cab

wait for quick look. Pleasant little compound, simple landscape garden with half-circle drum bridge over pond. Near treasure hall is what locals call (for obvious reasons, using our term) *penis-jizo*, prayed at for libido or wanting children. Easy 10min walk to top of **Mt Asakuma** for panoramic view of whole Ise-Shima area, Mt Fuji on clear day. On way you pass cluster of jizo statues wearing all manner of clothing (hats, ties, polo shirts) and accessories; local tradition dictates that jizo offered in memory of lost ones should be adorned with that person's favorite items. Virtual forest of long wood plaques lining road beyond are grave markers of those whose ashes are kept in OKU-NO-IN beyond.

Another way out is over mountains from...
ISOBE (12km) to **ISE INNER SHRINE** *Naiku* by bus or **cab** 7x-mtr. Adventurous types can, after crossing Goza to Hamashima, head W by bus 20min to TASO-URA or end of bus line SHUKU-URA at mouth of Gokasho Bay. Numerous campsites, budget inns and bungalow villages surround bay which boasts assorted water sports. Yet, its semi-remoteness makes it much less visited than rest of Shima area, even in peak of summer. You cannot go around bay by bus. From Taso-ura or Shuku-ura, ferry to innermost GOKASHO from where bus to ISOBE. Drivers can head to Inner Grand Shrine via Tsurugi-toge Pass, head inland at Gokasho bus/boat stop, taking R fork 1km up, then 22km to Shrine. Most of year, 3 buses daily follow same route, but check. Boats criss-cross Gokasho Bay. **June 24** *Rice planting*, Izo-gu, Isobe-cho (*see* p328), gaily costumed girls transplant new shoots, drums, flutes.

Adventurer who has already seen Ise heading for Southern Kii route, boat → Ogaura on W mouth of Gokasho Bay whence bus along really rugged coast on to Kumano, next lodge (*see* Southern Kii, p406). May also JR from Ise to Kumano, doing our Kii course and rejoining main Tokaido itinerary again around NARA, via KOYASAN, whence do HASE-DERA, MURO-JI, IGA UENO to pottery town of SHIGARAKI and circle to Kyoto.

Angling is notoriously fine in bays here. You only need hand line for *kisu* (sillago) or *kuro-dai* (black bream) from February thru year-end, with *kochi* (flatheads) starting March, *ika* (cuttlefish) April, *bora* (mullet) May and short run of *kodai* (small-bream) Aug-Oct. With rod you can take *saba* (mackerel) from June, and *aji* (horse-mackerel) July (both of which are superb charcoal-broiled), *mutsu* (mackerel) August around Toba and Matoya only, *haze* (goby) run Sept-Nov. With boat, easily available thru inn or hotel, up to five miles out, 8km, you can take *tai* (sea-bream) from April as well as *hirame* (flatfish) and *karei* (sole), with May bringing *suzuki* (sea-bass) and young *inada* (yellow-tail). July brings *sawara* (mackerel) and *katsuo* (bonito). Winter fishing, Dec thru Feb, is for *buri* (yellow-tail).

Your inn will prepare your catch for your dinner.

IGA UENO   CASTLE TOWN OF NINJA AND POET BASHO

ROMANTICS WITH TIME following our time machine routing are recommended to cut across from ISE to birthplace of Japan, YAMATO, alias Nara basin. Kintetsu electric has some of best trains in Japan serving Nagoya to Namba, downtown Osaka, nonstop at 190km in 110mins (Rail Pass not valid). Itinerary entails slight time warp skip in chronology on to early Buddhism. Between ISE ↔ NARA on old pilgrim back road are several worthwhile beauty spots, inconveniently located and thus generally overlooked except holidays during special flower seasons.

GETTING THERE: Kintetsu's superb electric, commuter-frequency, from ISE via UJI-YAMADA for all following points, or any one or combination. Local **taxis** available most stns. **Drivers** find it still breathtaking countryside with fine roads, as we did on honeymoon generation ago along then-dirt paths which cut thru folks' front yards.

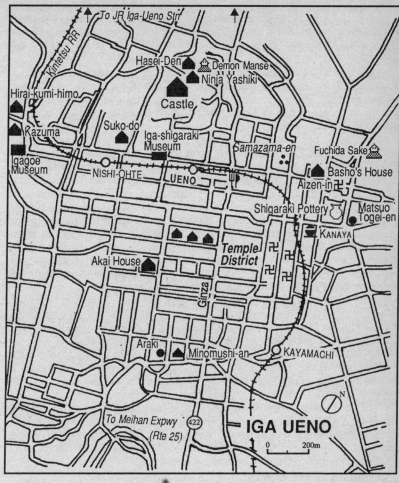

Leaving ISE-SHIMA area AM, you reach IGA UENO under 2hrs on Kintetsu, changing at Iga Kambe to UENO-SHI, passing thru beautiful rural towns. Rail Pass users take about same time JR, change to Kansai Main Line at Kameyama (some need not change, check) → IGA UENO whence 7min bus or Kintetsu rail → UENO-SHI. **Drivers**: Ise → Rte23 up coast → Takachaya 24km, L-inland Rte165 → Aoyama-cho abt 35km, R-N Rte422, parallel river and rail abt 15km → Iga Ueno.

Alternates: coming from Nara, combine with beauty spots HASE-DERA, MURO-JI (*next*). From Iga Ueno, can bus to pottery town of SHIGARAKI (drivers Rte422) whence Shigaraki-kogen Railway 23min (hourly 6:00-22:00) → Kibukawa then hour local on JR Line (45min rare express) → KYOTO or circle LAKE BIWA. Also few JR buses from SHIGARAKI → NARA (2hrs) daily, ¥2,000. **Drivers** can take Meihan Expwy to NARA and OSAKA; get on Higashi-guchi (E ramp), bottom of main road Ginza-dori.

You can 'do' Iga Ueno in 1hr or so, concentrating on Castle grounds with Basho Memorial Hall and Ninja House; or spend day leisurely taking in all pleasant town has to offer: almost everything walking distance of stn. Frequent buses go to main sites, Kintetsu rail winds thru town with 5 stops in 2.5km stretch. Small **Tourist Info booth** at stn exit near giant statue of Basho has good English brochure & map. Can also book you inn for any budget: about 20 regular inns (¥-Tw/2) around town, dozen *ryori-ryokan* 'dining-inns' specialize in sumptuous meals, mostly featuring delicious tender, local beef: about ¥1,000 extra each per nite. *Budgeteers* do best at business-style **Hotel Castle** but bit far from center of town, bottom of Ginza above concrete 'construction horse' bridging street (Ueno City **Symbol Arch**?) and near Mino-mushi-An hermitage. No personal recommendations, other than leave it up to Info Center. Best maybe to leave here in time to spend nite at Muro-ji or Hase-dera (*see*).

CASTLE (¥300) built 1585 by local lord TSUTSUI Sadatsugu on site of Heiraku-ji Temple, which Oda Nobunaga torched to punish its fighting monks. In 1608 TODO Takatora, ally of Ieyasu, was sent here by that new shogun to create massive castle, first line of defense against Toyotomi forces. Planned as one of largest ever, 5-storey donjon was flattened by typhoon just at completion. Soon after Toyotomi forces were subjugated, castle not needed. Fascinating story about original **donjon**—Takatori used several 'sacred trees' to ensure good luck. Local priest decried it as sacrilegious, claimed would be brought down by wrath of gods: sure enough, unprecedented off-season typhoon hit, down it came. Remained without donjon long after outer walls dismantled, until 1935 local tycoon KAWASAKI Koji built present one—unlike reconstructions of concrete this one built of wood in true Momoyama Era castle style. First 2 floors **museum** of usual samurai paraphernalia and local arts; 3rd floor **observatory** overlooks town Takatori also designed, surrounding plain (ideal for rice) and ring of mountains which made Ueno strategically important being near all major roads to Imperial Kyoto.

Just before crossing main street from stn to castle park: **Pottery-Hall**, *Iga Shigaraki Kotokan*, with 1st floor display and kiosk of present day Iga potters; 2nd fl small display of ancient Iga and Shigaraki wares (¥200 X-year-end). Good place to get idea of prices, but advise hold off on buying as we later visit kiln/shops of local potters.

Basho Memorial Hall (¥150) just as you enter castle park. Of interest to Basho poem fans, or those who read Japanese, or have read Basho in translation (Penguin paperback *Basho–the Narrow Road to the Deep North and Other Travel Sketches* translated superbly by Yuasa Nobuyuki.) Here we learn poet, 1653-1704, of poor samurai house, orphaned at 10 becomes companion of lord's son TODO Yoshitada for education. Todo led raising haiku from minor poem form. When he died young Basho wandered to popularize, enrich, demo-cratize as expression of daily life this simple 17-syllable 3-line stanza. Made it national literary form, now composed worldwide.

Otherwise, we head straight to...

Ninja Yashiki (¥300), innocent thatched-roof farmhouse. Once inside, you are guided thru incredible array of traps, secret passages and other means to befuddle any invader while allowing occupants plenty of time to escape. House, moved here from nearby Takayama hamlet, was home of TAKAYAMA Tarojiro, village head, master of *ninjutsu*, secret *ninja* arts. Tho there are several ninja houses locally, this one is easy to find and well done.

Spies were used as early as time of Prince Shotoku, but it was not till 11th century that ninja as specialists in death and deception appear. They began here in mountainous regions close to capital, relying on Sun Tzu's *Book of War* to develop guerrilla warfare to fine art. Two main schools of Iga and Koga styles (we visit Koga ninja house near Shigaraki) ran dozens of secret training centers in most inaccessible places of these mounts, offering services to various lords. Wanderer can visit home of MOMOCHI Sandayu, founder of Iga style ninjutsu, near Akame Waterfalls (next stop). He was *jonin* (upper ninja) who contacted clients. Under jonin were *chunin* intermediaries to contact *genin* (low ninja) who did actual dirty work. House belonged to genin, suspicious of all as potential enemies, thus its elaborate defenses. Cellar is museum of ninja weapons and tools.

Ninja is usually clothed in shadow-man black, sword across back to be drawn over shoulder in instantaneous down-slash. Common ready stance has toes pointed out, knees slightly bent, set for leap in any direction. Hands in front with right fingers clasped in left hand in mudra of invisibility, sympathetic magic and mind-set symbol. (Easy, comprehensive read, *Ninjutsu: The Art of Invisibility* by Donn Draeger, or less-romantically exaggerated chapter by Jay in *Zen Combat*.) Open daily 9:00-17:00, X-12/29-1/1.

¥300 *for Ninja House also admits you to...*
Demon's Mansion next door. Old castle granary preserves costumes and masks of annual *Demon Parade*, 400-year-old autumn spectacle of *Ueno Tenjin Festival*, **Oct 23-25**. Main parade is **25**th; predawn drums call participants to prepare at Sugawara Shrine, town center: Mikoshi procession starts 10:30 followed by 100-odd demons, 7 Lucky Gods, 9 colorful *danjiri* wheeled floats. Spring has *Ninja Festival* in which ninja, samurai, other feudal characters parade thru town to castle park, filled with food & fun stalls—**first sun Apr**; rain postpones to next sunday. **July 23**, Citywide festival.

Ninja

Odd looking two-storey domed-building nearby is **Haisei-den Hall**, built 1942 to honor Basho, symbolizes his traveling guise: upper cypress bark roof his sedge hat, first storey roof his straw raincoat, pillars his legs and cane. Best viewed head-on thru lovely, tall thatched-roof gate. Inside, Iga-yaki pottery figure of Basho, visible to public thru window, seen formerly only once yearly. *Basho Festival* marking death anniversary, **Oct 12**.

Back on main road btwn stn & castle, 2 blocks W (L from stn) next to...
Suko-do Middle School, classic Meiji era ex-clan school built by 10th lord of Iga Ueno, 1821. Much of original structure is intact, tho texts from its library (including several on secrets of ninjutsu) now kept at city library next door (9:00-17:00, X-12/28-1/4, mon, thur afternoon; no fee).

Continuing 700m W come to...
Kagiya Crossroads marked by giant **stone post** on which bold script *"Left to Nara-Right to Ise"* made famous by kabuki and bunraku play *Igagoe Dochu Sugoroku*, based on Nov 7, 1634 Igagoe Vendetta which took place here at Kazuma tea stall, faithfully rebuilt to serve tea & dumplings. That day master swordsman Araki Mataemon and brother-in-law Watanabe Kazuma cut down Kawai Matagoro, who'd killed Kazuma's brother.

Next to tea stall...
Igagoe Museum (¥100) shows duel-related items, behind it is pond where Kawai's head was washed after being cut off. Glorified in plays, act gets completely blown out of proportion in movie which has two avengers hack their way thru 36 foes. Official record of this officially sanctioned vendetta lists 11 foes, only 4 of whom died. Annual memorial service **Nov 7th**.

One block further W is...
Braiding Exhibit Hall, *Hirai Kumihimo* (free), where you can see these beautiful cords being made by hand—and good place to buy. Two distinct methods of braiding, *marudai* round base and *takadai* raised base. Marudai can be done by anyone on first try, is like hand-held chording toys in which colored threads are suspended thru hole, interwoven into desired pattern, finished product coming out middle and pulled to tighten weave. Takadai is

form which must be mastered, and resembles weaving on loom: set up horizontally, after each round of braids it is hit into place and tightened by bamboo spatula-like tool. This creates much finer, sturdier weave, and also leaves endless possibility to patterns. Silk most often used tho cheaper strands made of cotton or nylon, or on machine. Begun here 1902 by HIRASAWA Tokujiro who spent 8 years study in Tokyo; his grandson keeps tradition alive at **Hirasawa Kumihimo-ten**, 300m S of Nishi-Ohte stn. *Kumihimo* nets roughly 5 billion yen ($40,000,000+) annually to Iga Ueno. Roughly 90 shops do kumihimo by hand, employ 6,300, mostly women working at home. Average age 50, as youngsters don't like time-consuming hand work, prefer machines. Still, over 60% by hand, city accounts for over 90% of nation's kumihimo braiding. Beauty of it must be seen to be truly appreciated; uses are many—tho precipitous decline of kimono mid-80s bodes ill. Nice handmade one can cost as little as ¥400. Similar but larger setup at **Iga Kumihimo Center**, 2.5km (10min bus to Namimatsu stop) down main N-S shopping street Ginza-dori. Hirai Kumihimo open daily; Iga Kumihimo X-mon.

From here, head E of stn...
House of Basho's birth, *Basho Oseika*: 2km/1.2mi walk along main street, or five stops on bus from Kagiya crossroads to Akasaka (make sure it's not one ending at stn), around basic-mtr by **cab**, or short walk from Hirokoji stn, 500m from Ueno-shi stn. Typical 17th century house, well-preserved. Basho lived here until teens, then started his journeys, wrote first collection of poems here. Have your favorite Basho poem calligraphed by caretaker here. ¥150, X-mon, day after hols & thurs pm. Basho's ashes, brought home by disciple, enshrined at **AIZEN-IN** temple across street, block E.

One block W of Basho's House is...
Samazama-en, home of castle official student of Basho: its garden boasts magnificent sakura tree which inspired Basho to write poem from which came house's name. Open only to individuals or small groups; must phone ahead (stn TIC can do) ☎21-0193.

SHOPPING: R 1 block after Basho's (at Caltex gas stand) and little way down on R is good **Shigaraki pottery shop** marked by big *tanuki* (badger), symbol of Shigaraki, in front. Best place to pick up true Shigaraki ware for those who can't make it to kiln itself. Owner is young man who studied in Shigaraki, came home to set up shop, following Shigaraki style. Brown pieces only go thru first firing and are glazed. Green drip glaze is Shigaraki trademark. Blue comes from ash which mixes with glaze; light blue being rare. Prices reasonable: cups and bowls from ¥500, vases ¥2,000+, sake sets ¥2,000+, small dishes ¥300+, set 6 coffee cups ¥6,-10,000. Iga-yaki more expensive, higher-fired, harder.

Mita Kilns (2) Iga-yaki kiln outlets near parking lot castle E entry, out lower exit turn L almost to corner, L side unobtrusive converted house shows wares of Tanimoto Mitsuo and son. Lovely, dad's bit pricey but if pots draw you, ask for taxi to either kiln, 10 min N in hills where more showrooms, some bargain seconds. Fine ikebana *suiban*, ¥5,000+. End of street NE corner is **Matsuo Togei-en** one of *Iga-yaki* kilns in town. Iga ware is similar to Shigaraki in using mostly earth-tones, minimal glazes; there are, however, some who use brighter colors, painted designs, especially in decorative tiles.

Takimoto sake brewery faces Matsuo. Another local brewery **Fuchida** is up same street about 100m beyond Caltex stn. Head W from Matsuo Togei-en 3 blocks (just beyond RR tracks), brings you to top of Tera-machi, **old Temple District**. Nothing special here, but it is another interesting-to-stroll section of typical castle town.

Bagworm Hermitage, *Minomushi-an*, where top Basho disciple Hattori Doho lived: named from poem Basho sent at its completion. Nothing wormy here—minomushi also straw raincoat, shaggy like hermitage thatch —beautifully laid out in Japanese studied rusticity (¥150, X-mon, thur pm,

12/29-1/3). 1.8km/20min walk S of stn, or **cab** basic-mtr. **Araki**, town's largest curio shop, first street W to Nakanotachi-cho St, R, up half-block on L—fine arts, to 2 back rooms heaped with treasures to near-junk; no great bargains but immense selection. Convenient Hotel Castle-Inn. We suggest walk at least one way (back easier) to take you via old section of town with several Edo era houses, shops, ex-samurai homes. Centered along Ni-no-machi, San-no-machi streets running E-W–3,4 blocks S of stn–between Ginza-dori St on E and Nakanotachi-cho St W. Largest samurai home is **Akai House**, Nakanotachi-cho St block S of San-no-machi. Another on San-no-machi St, block E of Ginza. 2 blocks E puts you in above-mentioned Temple District.

CHOPSTICKS: Above-**Kazuma Tea** stall for good noodles–pay extra ¥100 for location, but nice. Light snack, **Kagiya**, at crossroads marker. Many places offer hard, square piece of *mochi*-rice-cake skewered fried, covered in sauce: called *kata-yaki* (hard-fried), minus drippy sauce but with dried veggies was basic staple of ninja: compact, energy-packed. Numerous tasty budget eateries along Ginza below park. 500m W of City Hall, **Wakaya** for charcoaled *dengaku* and Tofu in miso, ¥500, 11:00-19:00, ☎21-4068.

If time for full sit-down meal, suggest sukiyaki of fresh local vegetables, much-boasted Iga beef–quite good, tho no match to Matsuzaka. Best: 50-yr-old **Kanaya** cozy, private rooms, just E of Hirokoji stn on road below. Meat is properly aged, well-known enough to be sent to special Tokyo markets: ¥5,400 huge portion, about same *Butter-yaki* (butter-fried) or *ami-yaki* (char-broil) steaks. If this little steep, **Ito**, across from stn TIC. Atmosphere not as nice, but meat good (run meat shop nearby), *suki-yaki* abt ¥3,500; ¥1,500 for *gyu-teishoku* (beef table d'hote) of stir-fried beef, rice, soup, veggies, pickles.

BEAUTY OFFBEAT

Two stops from **Iga Kambe** *to* **Akame-guchi** (*also 2 from* **Muro-guchi-Ohno**) *& 10min bus into mountains, last stop* **AKAME-TAKI**, *which translates as...*

RED-EYE WATERFALLS, another hill beauty spot justly 'worshipped' but boasting no holy buildings. Natural paradise-garden in vale. Pleasant hiking course takes you thru roughly 4km valley with countless waterfalls of all sizes and shapes. Area gets its unusual name from legend that En-no-Gyoja, founder of ascetic mountain brotherhood, Yamabushi, meditated under waterfall here and was 'visited' by fiery god Fudo riding on giant red-eyed bull. Most beautiful in spring with sakura in bloom, or autumn with changing maple leaves, but fine all year and less crowded 'off-season'. About 9min walk to last falls, or continue on 2hrs to next vale KOCHI-DANI (hitting road at Ochiai) and another 2hrs, now thru rock formations, to **Kochi-bashi** bridge, whence 10min bus to NABARI stn. **A**vid hiker head S at Ochiai, towards Oku-Kochi-dani valley further in hills with even more spectacular rock walls. From there, **Tokai Nature Trail** cuts across mountains to MURO-JI, about 5km.

30min walk W from Akame-taki bus stop takes you to...

House of MOMOCHI **Sandayu**, 16th century founder of Iga style ninjutsu. Descendants still live here. Part of house now ninja museum, which alas had plans to incorporate with... Similar, but easier to get to, collection of ninja items at **Akame Folk Museum** (X-4pm) nr bus stop.

Nearby is...

Salamander Aquarium, area habitat of giant species, grow meter long. Aquarium has local monster, dozens other species from around Japan.

MURO-JI TEMPLE LADIES' KOYA, LADIES' RETREAT

GETTING THERE: Published **taxi** 'course' 1989: SAKURAI → HASE-DERA → OHNO-DERA → MURO-JI → stn 4 hr, ¥18,700 (about 20x-mtr). Following our route suggest reverse course from MURO-GUCHI stn → SAKURAI in middle of Yamato Plain; or discharge taxi at HASE for overnite, save 7km, 3.5x-mtr or so. Extra hours run 6-7x-mtr per. Train, bus and local cab convenient. From NARA, **Nara Kotsu bus tours** cover HASE-DERA and MURO-JI together; flexible **taxi course**, abt ¥25,000/50+mtr (*see* NARA GETTING AROUND, p373).

Two stops from AKAME, 2 before HASE-DERA from ISE on local (express change at Nabari for local *futsu*); or from HASE continue on 2 stops: MURO-GUCHI-OHNO. Across stn plaza **bike rental**, recommended only for pedal-philiacs, hills steep. 7 km stn to Sanmon-gate: **taxi** 3.5x-mtr; frequent **buses. Train** 90min from OSAKA, 2hr KYOTO, 3hr NAGOYA; same **drive** in light traffic.

FLOWER DATEBOOK: Sakura late **Mar–Apr** flabbergasting *shakunage* rhododendron & *botan* peonies, late **Apr-May**; *momiji* maples hills late **Oct–Nov**.

Setting breathtaking. Grounds officially open 8am-5pm (¥300) but arrivals early or late will find no barriers, only sculpture pavilions closed. Up some 77 stone steps to cedar-shingled *Kondo* main hall partway up, and 93 more to 5-tiered pagoda, 16.7 meters tall; both national treasures of 8th century architecture. Other fine buildings date from various periods, all gems.

Treasure house of sculpture, rank just below Horyu-ji, Kofuku-ji. Isolated from time amid primeval forested mountains, is even better to view icons in atmosphere for which originally meant. *Kondo* on first platform up 77 steps houses many sculptural treasures. Subtly lit by under-powered incandescent spots, slight rose tint simulates candle-tones. Exquisite 11-headed Kannon (NT), 2m, retains much original color as muted example carried over from brilliant T'ang China art, its earlyish Heian date indicated by face starting to puff (later = puffier). Contemplating rather flip guardians of Buddha, he, in front of main image next to 13-tier oil lamp for light offerings seemed to listen with us to songs of summer cicadas. Several national treasures (NT), important cultural assets (ICA) here, small bldg L.

DRAGON CAVE SHRINE, *Muro Ryuketsu,* famous Shrine to Rain God long pre advent of Buddhism. 1km upstream from Temple is dedicated to Dragon Rain God; 3 of his caves around Muro-ji. First temple here thanked for priests' prayers credited with recovery of emperor Konnin in 777AD. Early Buddhist compounds were laid out on geometric plan. Muro is early example of esoteric temple built to meld with natural setting. This aspect of Buddhism appealed to Japanese, soon nationalized. Chinese tiled roof here set aside for cypress shingle. When other temples in mucho-macho-middle ages forbade women, Muro-ji welcomed them; thus earning accolade as Ladies' Koya after great male-only Shangri-la we visit after Nara.

Literally, figuratively breath-taking hike up 390 steep winding stone steps beyond great pagoda is **OKUNO-IN** Inner Shrine. Halfway up on R, giant camphor tree invites us to sit back to it to energize. Along route lichens bedeck rocks like flowers on altars. Atop, *butai*-stage supports prayer hall, in grill doors of which pilgrims jam bus, train ticket stubs or excursion ticket packets in testimony. Tube-tiled building behind is **Mie-do**, Kamakura era 12th century (ICA). Small 7-storey stone pagoda crowns peak.

SHOPPING: **Ichiyado** (One-cut house) on bus road opposite temple entry, sculptor OKUMOTO Matsuo carves fine decorative masks ¥4,-10,000, Buddhist statuary reasonably priced for what they are: some worth close examination by serious art buyer: priced by quality, not size. He is working right there, his fierce lion-dog-poodle on guard.

CHOPSTICKS–STAY: Several simple restaurants advertise local mountain herb cookery, *san-sai-ryori*; outerside entry bridge **Hashimoto-ya** ¥-T-Sw/2. Lovely ryokan, lovely spot, some rooms face main gate across river. Full in flower seasons: ☎(07459)-3-2056, Osaka ☎(06)-954-5888. Lunch *sansai-ryori*; from ¥2,000. Minshuku up hill behind gas station up from bus stop, below-opp *san-mon*.

Above MURO-JI on main road 200m to police box, 300° hard R, up hill 200m to Matsuhira Bunka-kan private museum (¥300, X-thur), not much to see. Road in front continues 8.5km over scenic hills as local hiking-cycling course ending at Haibara stn, midway Muro-guchi-Ohno ↔ Hase-dera stns on Kintetsu.

Bus back to stn, to next to last stop; *or* on way up **taxi** and hold 10min, or bus #43, 44, 45, 46, one km, or walk 15mins (and check bus scheds onward at bus stop) at...

OHNO-DERA temple thru whose simple unguarded gate enter, drop some coins, go straight dozen meters to end: on L mossy-cedar-roofed wall-less altar thru which across vale primeval framed view of 14m/46ft *magai-butsu* or standing *Miroku*-Messiah-Buddha engraved in cut-out halo-outline cavity, reminiscent of Afghanistan's Bamyan, illustrating Nara's position as Eastern terminus for ancient Silk Road. Carved in 1207, decayed scroll was found some time ago in its chest. Setting is exquisite, rich shrubbery on vertical cliff-face makes whole into gigantic flower arrangement.

FLOWER DATEBOOOK: Drooping cherry, *shidare-zakura*, late Mar-mid Apr.

EN ROUTE: Contact or visit (with appointment only) John Toler, sole Caucasian head of Zen temple in Japan. In recently converted 200-year-old manor house (first Buddhist temples were in converted manors—thus little difference between secular and sacred architecture), 4 bldgs with 6th century tomb mound on 4,000 *tsubo* (1,200 m²). Can put up sincerely interested guests; we suggest you leave offering in envelope equal about what you normally pay, plus up early and sit, then—no free lunch—help sweep, rake that lovely gravel and learn why it always looks so clean and ever-fresh. SHOGEN-IN, Ouda-cho, Uda-gun Nara-ken 633-21, ☎(07458)-3-0384, (*see* p.90) taxi from Haibara stn, next from Nara-Yagi beyond Hase-dera on Kintetsu electric from Nara;.

OUDA Village, below temple, scenic, relatively untouched old houses. *See* **Morino** shop & herb garden, each of many plants on hillside fully labeled (pay entry in shop); make candy, starch, medicine of Kudzu-'weed' in USA; important, tasty food here.

HASE-DERA 長谷寺   LONG-VALLEY TEMPLE

GETTING THERE: Kintetsu line continuing from ISE, 2 stops from MURO-GUCHI-OHNO, or from NARA area 3rd local stop out of SAKURAI: HASE-DERA. Walk 1km up inn-lined road to San-mon Gate; **taxis**; **bus** infrequent. Vale leading up 1km to immense temple complex lined with pilgrim onsen-inns, moderate, but average price 1986 of ¥6,000w/2 did not include 15% service, bath fee of ¥200-500, then tax, totaling almost ¥8,000. Inn rooms mostly overlook street, baths on R (up) overlook valley stream. Dine only, ¥-T. Jay stayed '86 at **Yamatoya** ☎(07444)-7-7402, top R, short walk from parking, gate R. Previous year Garet stayed across street at **Shirozake-ya** ☎7-7855; first floor budget diner, upstairs rooms 'classic old inn'—arrive early if you want full dinner, otherwise pay room only, eat in diner. Garet pulled in late, they still dug something up. **Itani-ya** ☎7-7012 ¥-hi-T, big place but good food, big onsen bath. **Bus** Hase-Dera Gate ↔ Sakurai infrequent; Gate ↔ Muro-Ji special peony season. *See* NARA GETTING THERE, p372, for full day **bus** and **taxi** tours out of NARA.

After decade-plus by 1963 of temple crawling we admittedly had become rather jaded. But Hase, visited almost as afterthought at eventide, brought back long-forgotten early emotions of fun-of-discovery. We recommend it to lonely esthete or romantic couple: Can also go into temple *before* and *after* 'official hours' of 8:00-17:00, lamps lit till 10pm. Garet had inn-keeper wake him early AM to catch sunrise from platform. 8th of 33 pilgrim places of W Japan, is thankfully inconvenient and still comfortable even when relatively mobbed by flower viewers.

Capping 'Long Valley' temple's outer *nio-mon* fierce-guardian gate foots seemingly endless flight of stone stairs— steep flight of 63 outside gate, then 399 shallow ones under long canopy with its great brass lanterns lit till 9pm making climb in rain almost erotic experience. Beds for 7,000 peony step along either side on stone terraces. Crowning all is great *butai*-stage jutting out from mount on gigantic log piling. All is in style of 7th century hillside palaces, as also at Nigatsu-do in Nara or Kiyomizu in Kyoto, tho present buildings are 16-17th century rebuilding of originals razed in civil wars of 16th century.

View from stage is one of 'Lost Horizons', of magnificent mountain setting with this great temple compound spilling down hidden vale. Especially just after sunset as mist rises it becomes slowly-changing sumi-ink painting. Three distant power towers on mountain opposite-left almost evade notice, occasional fluorescent light in temple doorways substitute for candle of yore: otherwise view is as of twelve centuries ago. Return visits, always at dusk still bring flush of excitement. Autumn '85 Jay watched crosswinds sworl postsunset dark fuming clouds over hilltops like dragons mating.

Backdrop to great stage stone-paved, lantern-lined corridor fronts holy of holies in which by dramatic lantern light you can see full formal esoteric Buddhist altar. Beyond it is object of worship, 8+m/27ft high gilded-wood **Kannon** image, singular in carrying staff jizo-like and not standing on lotus. Sibling to similar 9+m giant in Kamakura (*see*), both carved out of single camphorwood tree in 721, this replacing one burned in 16th century.

Enter from R, facing stairway top, for small fee: if not dunned, donate ¥200-300.
Note conch trumpets of tantric Buddhism near entry, used in rites. To Kannon's back are two **fortune wheels**: tie your *omikuji* paper fortune to one and spin and if stops with paper at bottom (odds it should) wish will come true. Most temple treasures surviving numerous fires are now in NARA NATIONAL MUSEUM, far safer if less dramatic setting. Back wall of Kannon facing rear has **great mural** of Amida heaven, Kannon being spirit-link between celestial Amida-father and earthly-son Sakyamuni to complete trinity of our kalpa-era. Can be seen in part from outside thru small grill in back door on platform surrounding hall on which pilgrims circumambulate holy-of-holies 1,000 times keeping tally on those bamboo slats. Occasional special exhibits in ex-abbot's quarters (*next*). One which periodically repeats (Garet saw in '84) is 1538 scroll painting version of temple's 11-faced Kannon. As impressive as model, scroll is 16.5m x 6.2m, weighs 200kg. When shown (once every few years), portable copies (h.45cm x 15cm/ 18" x 6") scroll, and pocket-size folding *omamori*, talisman version, are on sale.

Down across temple vale are...
FUDO-DO and **JIZO-DO** pavilions as well as **SENJO-JIKI** (1,000-mat hall) formerly abbot's residence with, by count, only 150 tatami, but numerous sliding door panels painted by various artists of Kano dynasty.

FLOWER DATEBOOK: Apricot (alias plum) *ume*, late Feb-Mar; rhododendron *shakunage* mid Apr-early May; and especially peony *botan* time **late Apr-May** or hydrangea *ajisai* **Jun 23-Jul 14**; then maple turning **Oct** first chill (late) thru **Nov**... it's well worth crowds, which are still slight by big city standards anyway.

PERSONAL DATEBOOK: Hase-dera, early pm **Feb 14** no Valentines, but 3 masked demons attack priests on stage, fight with big torches—beaten by recitation of sutras and convert to loving humans heralding first day of Spring in local tradition. **May 5** Rice planting rites Sarutahiko Shrine, 12:15pm; 2 huge fans paraded to *shinden* sacred field, transplanting 1:30pm; procession back to shrine for dances, music, breaking fans, visitors vie for piece—good luck. **Jun 24** Rice planting all day, Izo-gu shrine, Isobe town, (*see* p328).

WHERE NEXT: Walk down to Kintetsu line stn, two stops → Sakurai; or **bus** from San-mon Gate → SAKURAI occasionally; **taxi** about 4x-mtr. SAKURAI center of Yamato Plain, birthplace of Japan, hub for our itineraries of **Great Tombs**, but it is only reference point, not suggested as stopover. Next overnite should probably be NARA, (p371), ¥-B-L, or even HORYU-JI, (p357). Leisurely budgeteers will find selection of minshukus, Youth Hostels, business hotels, etc thruout Yamato Basin.

And the King of Egypt said unto them...
"Get you unto your burdens"
—Exodus 5: 6

GREAT TOMB MOUNDS
BIGGER THAN EGYPT'S PYRAMIDS

At ISE we were introduced to mythical beginnings of Imperial Family, who trace selves back to Age of Gods and specifically to Sun Goddess Amaterasu enshrined there. As we move into Yamato Plain, our first stop is KASHIHARA JINGU, where Jimmu Tenno, Japan's first emperor is said to have set up court. This period is generally referred to as *kofun-jidai*, or Tumulus Period, dating about 300AD to 550AD when Buddhism's coming ended extensive tomb building (lingering past 700 in frontier Tokyo). Nara-Osaka has high concentration of tumuli, and we take this opportunity to cover some representative types. After circuit of mounds near Kashihara Jingu, we add for more specialist readers that complex of huge tombs located toward and convenient by cab or bus from Osaka.

GETTING THERE

Following our historical itinerary, we will be coming in from HASE on Kintetsu electric, or bus, to YAGI, whence transfer S to Unebi Goryo or Kashihara Jingu or Asuka, etc. stns (*see* GETTING AROUND). Alternatively, Rail Pass users can come slower roundabout way Ise to Nara on JR Kansai Honsen. And from:
OSAKA take Kintetsu train 34min Ltd Exp from Abenobashi → Kashihara Jingumae, or from Namba to Yagi and transfer S to Unebi or Kashihara Jingu or Asuka stns; or Rail Pass users on JR from Tenno-ji to Saidai-ji, where change for Unebi.
KYOTO, Kintetsu from southside Kyoto stn, 50mins; Rail Pass users JR → Nara then:
NARA JR down thru Sakurai where can transfer to Kintetsu, or continue on to JR-Unebi stn, bit off N of main areas. See also bus tours, below.
WAKAYAMA or KOYA-SAN on Kii Peninsula alternate, JR up to Takada, transfer to Unebi, locals only over 2hr from Wakayama but scenic. *But first, short historical...*

PERSONAL ORIENTATION GREAT TOMBS

KASHIHARA is where first emperor Jimmu was enthroned at 11am on February 11 (that year lunar New Year) 660BC, according to national fable. This date was set by Prince Shotoku when compiling his since lost *Tennoki Kokki*, 'Histories of Emperor and Nation' (possibly rediscovered recently in questionable *Kujiki*) about 620AD, as 'auspicious'—China's solar-lunar calendar had only been introduced few years before. But its antiquity must be based on some rationale. Perhaps given two facts: A: Wa emperor #1 was Jimmu of uncertain hoary date; B: China's first emperor according to calendar just introduced to Japan in 603, had reigned full large cycle (21 of 60-year zodiacal cycles) previous—therefore, as both were 'Firsts', A=B, they must have been contemporaries. It was rational for its time, based on inadequate data—certainly no excuse for observing it today as history. Only romantics, who celebrate yearly, take it seriously and no less authority than Emperor's professorial uncle, HIH Prince Mikasa, founder-director of prestigious Society for Middle Eastern Studies in Japan, publicly denounced it before it was restored in 1966 as National Foundation Day. Leading Kashihara government archaeologist states "Practically no scholar in this country swallows dosage of names assigned occupants of royal tombs handed down by Imperial Household". Shotoku also was first to use title 'Tenno' for emperor, replacing older 'Dai-O', great king—still used for non-Japanese like Egypt's Rameses the Great, or Alexander the Great, etc.

This in no way detracts from this being cradle of Imperial Japan; or that some immigrant progenitor of Imperial line set up housekeeping here, was more than likely buried in one of large tumuli about. And since names emperors are remembered by in records are granted posthumously, there is no reason why progenitor #1 can't be called Jimmu Tenno, who alive was called Kamu-Yamato-Iware Hiko-no-mikoto. However, he'd date back no further than 100AD, and more likely as late as 300AD.

If Jimmu Tenno returned now he'd probably come by train. We can only hope he would not get as confused trying to find his old home as some of us are—there are two Kashiharas only 20km apart: both important tomb areas. When we refer to Kashihara we mean YAGI-KASHIHARA or KASHIHARA JINGU where Jimmu was supposedly enthroned. On roman-lettered maps there is often spelled Kashiwara (but on road signs Kashihara) and sometimes Kashiwabara tho in fact both places can be read by these same variants. This second we refer to as Kashihara #2, to be safe. It is near Osaka.

Each is written with different but homonymic ideograph: #2 is *kashi* or *kashiwa*, juniper or oak *quercus dentata* plus *-hara*, plain; #1 = plain also preceded by *kashi*, but another type of oak, not clearly specified nor used otherwise today. Both then mean 'Oak Plain'—is this 'mighty oak' complex another hint of some distant common origin with Indo-Europeans? Iran's first emperor, memorialized in Persian name for Persepolis (which is Greek name) *Takht-e Jamshid*, 'Throne of Jamshid', is also known as Jam and sometimes Jim. Homeland of Aryans was Eran or Iran, 'paradise', on high plain of Central Asia, perhaps that High Plain of Heaven of Jimmu's grandfather?

Sun Goddess Amaterasu whom we visited at Ise, sent her grandson Ninigi-no-mikoto, down to earth from High Plain of Heaven—implying immigration. He landed in Kyushu, which archaeology shows us was important early hub of neolithic and bronze age cultures. Mound-tombs are found there, as we see in our archaeology side-trip out of Nagasaki. Oldest so far is early Yayoi, about 100-0BC, containing imported bronze swords. Indeed Yamatai, presumed predecessor-kingdom to Yamato, was probably around Fukuoka, perhaps Yoshinogari. Earlier type tombs are also found out of Izumo, as if coming across straits from Korea.

Jimmu was Ninigi's grandson. His mother was daughter of Ama, Sea Goddess, implying intermarriage between paternal Korean immigrant and maternal Pacific islander—Ama as Sea Goddess is still known in Ryukyu, Hong Kong, south. He led gang of adventurers up Inland Sea, presumably migration from Yamatai-Kyushu of some frustrated faction: our guess is that descendants of 'Ama' were southern half-breeds in this North-Asian immigrant-dominated society, treated like 'mixes' anywhere. Jimmu beats more advanced less dynamic cultures, till beaten back by tough Osakans, then lands on flank in Shingu, southern Wakayama-alias-Kii, below here, to fight way up overland. Plain was thriving rice-growing center—its high level of economy (producing rice surpluses), as well as its beauty (which earliest records show us impressed Japanese) made natural base for capital.

Jimmu's people called themselves Wa, written originally by Chinese with character meaning 'dwarf', pronounced *Wo-gwo*, dwarf-country, which name traveled west so Arabs and Romans knew of isles of Wakwak off China. When Jimmu's descendants took to writing ideographs they chose another less demeaning homonym meaning 'peace' or 'circle' (supposed ultimate origin of industrial QC, Quality Circle), and his kingdom became Great Wa written to mean Great Peace, but which when read together referring to Japan is, for no accountable reason, pronounced *Yamato*—classical, poetic name for Japan even today. (It seems in Kyushu *Yamatai* was main 'country' in that 'Wo-gwo' or Wa kingdom). But when used for businesses, like major bank, is pronounced 'logically' *Dai-wa*; or in case of some local villages, even *O-wa*—all quite arbitrary, in some alternate logic.

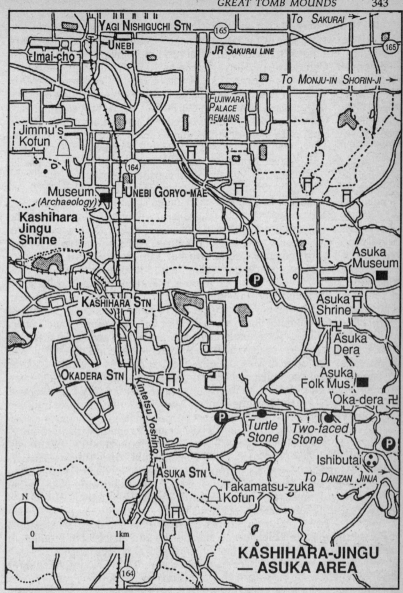

KASHIHARA-JINGU — ASUKA AREA

Traditional history of era comes down to us in *Kojiki*, 'old-time record' (translated early by Chamberlain) and *Nihon Shoki*, 'Nippon-record' (early tr. Aston, recent Phillippi) compiled respectively 712 & 720AD of recitations of tribal memorizers, probably under tutelage of Paekche-Korean scholars. Among first 15 emperors are several Methusalehs (Jimmu, crowned age 45, legendary reign 660-585 BC, died thus at 120), Ojin (born 37 years after dad's death, carried in mother's womb those years); two said 10 feet tall (converse of Tenri-kyo legends of lilliputian progenitors). Records passed down by memorizers are understandably confused as each would favor own employer. With familial rivalries, big spats between main centers Yamato and Kyushu (own internal strife) and Izumo (own contradictory record, *Izumo-fudoki*,

733AD), there was more than one line. Chinese annals confirm some of these rulers did exist, usually at far later dates than tradition—more 8th century naive science, fit known names into presumed time frame.

Example: 'Conqueror of Korea' Empress Jingo, trad reign 201-269AD between murdered spouse Emperor #14 Chuai and her late-born son Ojin #15, might be either of two invaders mentioned in Korean records of 249 or 346AD. Covell (*Korean Impact on Japanese Culture*) has her last royal princess of militant Puyo (Altai-Turks?), "most civilized of Eastern Barbarians" in Han records, driven out of Manchuria in 356 into Korea. Descended of Haeburu, King of Heaven, shaman-princess was of sacred lineage. Married to Chuai, King of Kaya, SE Korea, worked to unite Korean kingdoms for Paekche and cross sea to conquer Wa—in reverse of Japanese version.

However, Chinese history tells of nonagenerian shaman-queen Pimiko or Himeko, "clever in deluding people" who united strife-torn "many rulers" of, Wa (Kyushu?) about 200AD, sent her emissary to Wei China via Korean introduction, 239, receiving from emperor recognition as "Queen of Wa, friendly to Wei". Pimiko also might be Yamato-Hime-no-mikoto first High Priestess of Ise, or someone else in Kyushu. Pimiko was murdered in 250, interred under mound "100 *pu*-paces long" (est 25-30m) accompanied by "100 male and female servants"—which tomb is unknown. Nishitonozuka tomb in Tenri recently identified from 3rd century pottert sherds nearby as oldest, is possibly hers. Legend has early rulers accompanied in death by sacrificed courts of human retainers until patron deity of wrestlers, writers and potters suggested clay effigy substitutes (these *haniwa* figures, works of art, have been 'rediscovered' by modern artists). Archaeologists find no evidence of sacrifices, as was done in Mesopotamia, Central Asia, even China. By time this mound-raising complex reached Japan, effigies had replaced slaughter. Mongols revived bloody custom centuries later. Pimiko, say Chinese, was succeeded by 13-year-old shaman-queen Iyo—while Jingo in local tradition was followed by son Ojin. (Women not relegated to inferior status until macho-samurai, 12th century Kamakura). Gap 'twixt fact and legend now mere century.

Ojin (trad 270-310, historically ca400) is probably Homuda of Chinese annals' '5 kings of Wa' 420-479? Ruled when Hata/Yuzuki tribes (whom we meet in Kyoto-p.451) migrated en masse from Korea. He re?subdued Kyushu up to Kinai. His gigantic tomb in Habikino (p569), SE Osaka toward Nara, is 2nd largest at 415m length, reasonably identified from *Nihon Shoki*. His #4-son Nintoku's near Osaka (p.354) is easily visited on Osaka city tour.

As among both horse-riding tribes of North Asia and deep-water sailors of Polynesia, *uji* clan chiefs chose emperor by consensus from brothers or cousins of principal 'Sun Line' family, until #26 Keitai (trad reign 507-531AD) moved capital from Osaka to Yamato, was enthroned in Sakurai, fixed three imperial regalia and was first to choose his own successor.

Little is known of architecture of this period except that it probably resembled basic thatched-roof farmhouse of four rooms adjoining around central *honbashira* pillar, just as does Izumo Shrine on Japan Sea, north, perhaps nation's oldest. Tradition has palace style resembling that of Ise. To us, these represent respectively northern- and southern-origin immigrant styles. No art remains to speak of any greatness, but these tombs reveal that these were no primitive, unorganized people and thus explain how they were able to absorb and adapt so much Chinese and Buddhist culture so fast to build this new nation culture. Tombs also show how rich and varied is this heritage—not peculiar to Japan but part of tomb-building tradition back to Central Asia, Near East, even linked to East Europe. It is no coincidence that early giant 'keyhole' tumuli of Japan resemble great beehive tombs of

Greek Mycenae full millennium earlier. Gods of old Japan were supermen who lived in heavens much as those of our own ancestors—and unlike any but earliest, most Western-like of Chinese cultures, Shang of 1300-1122BC.

GETTING AROUND

AREA BY Kintetsu electric running W side of plain, stns near most major sites; **taxi**, bus or rent **bicycle** at stn plazas (¥1,030 per day, pick up at one stn, drop off most any other ¥210 extra except Kintetsu Asuka stn rental, which no drop off, so rent from private stand across plaza). **Bus pass** Nara–Yamato-ji (plain)-area ¥2,600 valid 2 days: Nara Kotsu ☎(0742)-22-5263, Tokyo info ☎(03)-3281-7737.
Bus tours mostly partly follow our history route, all depart from Nara JR or Kintetsu stns (*see* NARA) except Japanese language (**F**) *Asuka-Manyoshu meguri* ¥5,720 incl sites in Manyo poetry anthology, dep NARA stn 9:10 → TENRI stn → YAGI stn → Kashihara Archaeology Museum → Asuka-dera → Oka-dera → Ishibutai → Tachibana-dera → Tsubosaka-dera → KASHIHARA stn → YAGI stn → TENRI stn → NARA stn; 7hr30min.
　　Taxi for 4 or 5 people can match above prices in less time, add more sites.

　　TILT: Greater portion of this itinerary is of interest to archaeology buff with time—for general traveler with half-day stop at Kashihara stn for 1hr in **Archaeology Museum** and nearby **Kashihara Shrine**, tumulus of Jimmu, quick taxi or rental bike run with passing look at **Maruyama Kofun** tomb mound, to reconstruction of newly discovered **Takamatsu Kofun** tomb (P front), will suffice. Possibly continue cab or bike across to **Asuka Fertility** shrine, next door **Asuka Big Buddha**, dismiss taxi or bike back at Kashihara stn. Opp stn, **Kashihara Kanko Hotel** possible for W- or J-lunch. Pushing it, can do all by **taxi** in half-day, returning to Kashihara Jingu, or up to Sakurai Stn, or slightly more either to Tenri or Hase-dera for overnite, 30x-mtr.
　　Budgeteers find train and bus touches most sites, but are suggested to do as Sumi did as Gakushuin College student on school tour, walk part of it (or now bike), especially Museum → Takamatsu Tomb → Asuka Big Buddha → Asuka-za Fertility Shrine → Ishibutai. Southbound train one stop from Kashihara Jingu Stn → Oka-dera Stn (bike rental stn plaza), go E across road → **Maruyama Kofun** tomb mound, from which only 1.2km down → **Takamatsu Kofun** tomb, then 2mi/3km, 1hr hike, via **Asuka Daibutsu** and **Fertility Shrine** → **Ishi-butai** and **Oka-dera**.
　　Suggest arrive **Tenri** after lunch, afternoon around grounds, see *Sankokan* museums, sunset service 17:45 or later, 19:00 summer, (carry shoes with you for flexible exit) and on to Nara for dinner; taxi Tenri-Nara 8x-mtr (or, if in reverse, HASE-DERA, 4-5x-mtr). We often combine with morning to HORYU-JI (in which case lunch small restaurants front Horyu-ji) bus direct HORYU-JI–TENRI, frequent departures, 20mins. Rush round allows lunch at KASHIHARA or HORYU-JI after morning at tombs; or from NARA leave after early lunch, taxi HORYU-JI, 1hr, on to TENRI about 2-3pm to see art museum, evening service, stroll grounds at lantern lighting, return to NARA for dinner (*see* NARA).
　　One stop down from Yagi to Unebi Goryo stn and almost facing it E, or from Osaka-Abeno 34min Kintetsu to Kashihara Jingu stn and short taxi or walk due N. **Drivers** adequate parking. Using **taxi** advise see museum on foot, get new taxi after at nearby Unebi Goryo stn, then on to Jimmu Tumulus and onward S.

KASHIHARA ARCHAEOLOGY MUSEUM, *Kashihara Kokogaku-kenkyusho Fuzoku Hakubutsukan*, annex of prefectural archaeological research institute (9-5, X-mon, hols, ¥300, special exhibits ¥600).
　　Enter, L to follow historical order from...
Room 1 Old Stone Age of 30,000 years ago when Japan joined to Korea by land bridge and Nauman elephants, mammoths, bison and hairy horses roamed land—to first pottery, which in Japan appears to be as old as any in world, perhaps some 10,000 years ago.
Room 2 Late Stone Age, has cutaway model of house of time, tools and bronze dotaku 'bell?' (87% copper, 7% tin and 6% lead).
Room 3 is *kofun-jidai*, tomb era, perhaps finest selection of *haniwa* tomb figures anywhere, of men, horses, houses and animals. Horses wear

medallions on saddle belts like West Asian horses on Iranian rock reliefs. Haniwa found with more important remains (or frequently turned up by plow) have individual characteristics and may well be portraits of loved ones or friends, often shown in some attitude as performing on instrument or even telling joke. Note Korean style grey pottery, evidence of migrations. Tombs all found so far interred males (except? Fuji-no-ki tomb *see* Horyu-ji) usually armed or even armored where bodies found—most had been robbed. Armor is slatted iron shingle or plate type. Sword trappings and occasional rusted blade all continental type, as are mirrors. Imperial regalia are mirror, sword and *magatama* comma-shaped jewel, peculiar but not exclusive to Japan, all said to be common to local big tombs.

Room 4 continues with agriculture of Yamato showing high irrigation ditch technology, wood shovel looks modern Western, unlike traditional Oriental. Tools at least as interesting as weapons and plate-armor. House model on storey-high stilts looks more like Thai than Korean or Chinese.

Room 5 Asuka-Nara era, shows more advanced tomb structure of this era just before Buddhism banned them as ostentatious and wasteful. Earliest temple roof tiles are best ever made, technically and artistically. These few remaining clay Buddha images show early icon makers obviously were former *haniwa* molders. Such clay Buddhas are rarer than *haniwa* as were never 'safely buried' away from daily wear and tear. Early Nara horses look like early Greek or Persian with their tall flowing manes and trappings. Then comes small area covering miscellany of Heian (Kyoto) thru Edo (shogunal) eras. **Special Exhibit** sometimes in additional room. By exit on R is **video room**, dialogues all tapes only in Japanese but visually expressive, often beautiful, and easily followed.

Walking, 400m due W then **choice:** R 300+m with L at either first or 2nd road thru wooded park → **Jimmu Tenno Ryo** tomb; or L at **choice** 300m S, first R into wooded park and 300+m on curving path → **Kashihara Jingu Shrine.**

Jimmu Tumulus, *Jimmu Tenno Ryo.* Stone ballustrade holds mortals back on earth. When we first visited it, and again years later when taking friends, group of boys and girls marched in behind banners flying, executed miltary turn with normal Japanese school-kid snap, halted before inner torii and under leadership of wild-eyed one with towel band around his head, gave three arm-raising *banzais.* Wild-eyes harangued few minutes and they wheeled and marched off. This mix of naiveté and fanaticism is common to both these 'rightists' as to Zengakuren-student or union leftists—sole differences being banner colors and terminology, but hysteria of their screaming voices are same. Standards by which this tomb was 'identified' as Jimmu's do not satisfy modern scholarship, even locally. But it is symbol to great many people, to whole school of thought.

1km S, 15min walk, as above, is...
KASHIHARA JINGU: dedicated to first emperor Jimmu, was set here century ago in Shinto-Imperial Restoration over spot it was believed he had his capital. From parking plaza, pleasant few hundred meter walk in across wooden bridge (which, golden new when we first crossed it in 1963 emitted aura of lovely fresh cedar). Construction recent, style supposed to be 'pure Japanese' but is in fact rather modern creation of style in vogue after China's influences had been thoroughly absorbed, and which in turn was reaction against massive impersonalness of China. It is Japanese, nothing that Jimmu would recognize. And it is lovely—modern in its economy of line. It is palace style, and unlike any other shrine—in fact was made from

wood from former Kyoto Imperial Palace. In its inner courtyard stand two 'Court Minister' trees, Lord Tachibana (orange, L) and Lord Sakura (R), as in Kyoto Palace. If you wish to enter court, make offering of few hundred yen and get sacred sakaki branch and follow shrine maiden around corridor to present it at 'throne'. Donations maintain shrine which no longer receives state dole. Amulets of Jimmu Tenno's 3-legged black crow (Korean and Central Asian sun symbol) are for traffic safety.

Shrine still modern political problem: here is held main celebration for anniversary of Jimmu's enthronement **Feb 11** (DATEBOOK). Main prewar national holiday *Kigensetsu* (calendar origin day), purged by Occupation to most folks' relief, long post-Occupation agitation to revive it. Despite outspoken objection by Emperor's historian-uncle Prince Mikasa for its lack of historicity, revived in late 60s, if with slightly toned-down name *Kenkoku Kinenbi*, National Foundation Day. We still hold same reservations as we did in pre-revival first edition, but confess fears of looming black dragons have not been any way realized beyond slight rise in noise level of blackshirts' big black riot PR buses.

Walking, to Kashihara Jingu stn, take Kintetsu stop to Okadera stn whence short walk or bike W & N or walk down hiway 1.3km from Jingu exit.

Maruyama Kofun: Typical medium-size mound tomb atop small hillock in manner of earlier mounds. You can ascend part way to its small shrine. Not imperial, still unknown but high ranked as has stone ballustrade (1880s) surrounding part way up—imperial tombs encircled at base. (For gigantic imperials see BIGGER THAN EGYPT'S PYRAMIDS following). To see inside similar tomb, continue 1km E to SHOBU IKE KOFUN, easier seen after TAKAMATSU.

900mtrs S, on L, is moated...
Keyhole tomb of emperor Kinmei (d.571AD). View it, continue 150m, L, E 450m and first R then 7-800m winding hilly road to **Takamatsu Kofun;** or direct from Kinmei 800m fairly straight road to first L, on 600m to emperor Mommu (d.707) tumulus, hard L 150m to P-lot below Takamatsu. Bicycler/hiker signs on paths chaotic & misleading both E- & J-.

Drivers beware, seeming thru roads narrow to trails, no warnings. Hard to find as we and friends got lost several times within coin throw of it.

Takamatsu Kofun painted-chamber tomb mound, 1972 fascinating major postwar archaeological find. First-known Japanese tomb of so-called 'International Style' common on mainland, with figural murals. In 1983 another, KITORA tumulus was found 1km S when fiberscope inserted into it photographed directional animal mural, snake and tortoise, like that in Takamatsu. Mound itself is 5m/16ft4in tall x 18m/59ft diameter. Its finished stone-slab chamber measures l-w-h 2.6m x 1m x 1.1m (8ft8in x 3ft5in x 3ft8in). Animals of directions grace each wall: azure dragon E, white tiger W, snake-turtle N. Ceiling bears sun, moon and recognizable constellations with gold details. Long E & W walls each bear 4 groups of men and women; latter dressed in fingertip-length jackets over long pleated skirts of Chinese Sui type (ca600AD) but common in Korea, where national dress evolves from it (Japanese is from later T'ang style). Men are also in Chinese style trousers and long coats. Painting of deceased is on west wall with canopy held over him as mark of status (custom from ancient Near East). All this strengthens embarrassing (to some) thought that early royalty were mostly immigrants. May be tomb of Prince Takechi (654-96), son of 40th emperor Temmu. Long thought to be tomb of emperor Mommu until mound just S of here 'identified' as his. They found remains of male in his 40s in Takamatsu—Mommu is known to have been cremated.

Original tomb itself is sealed for conservation, too small to enter anyway, but neighboring hillock has been tunneled into and exact reproduction made with subterranean exhibit hall to create relevant mood (9-4:30. X-mon, ¥150).

Back up winding road to previous turn, now turn R 100m to first L and 100m to...
Shobu Ike Kofun (Iris Pond Tomb) on hilltop with small shrine by which is stone tomb chamber. Representative later (than Maruyama, above) being fully man-made mound built in field. Chamber is barred but open to view, of two 'Aryan house-shape' stone sarcophagi end to end, one with great lid slid back to show had been lacquered red inside and green outside. Occupant and date unknown, probably late tomb era.

Return S to main E-W road, turn L and almost immediately see on R...
Tortoise stone, *Kameishi*, carved 10-ton granite boulder, mysterious but probably pre-Buddhist, naive and humorous like most similar roadside monsters in Nara area, including one 2-faced demon?

400 m E on R at...
TACHIBANA TEMPLE, marking probable birthplace of Prince Shotoku, builder of Horyu-ji (*see*) and first modernizer of Japan. Statuary nice (ICA).

Return to main E-W road, turn R, at first fork R, 1km on winding road to...
Ishi-Butai (stone stage tomb), skeletal remains of full square mound, complete with dry moat and stone burial chamber which is not covered over with earth so that it can be clearly seen. Small compared to Imperial tombs nearer Osaka. Whether stones are bare by design, or because never finished, or eroded, is not clear. You can no longer enter, fenced off now, but can approach close enough to appreciate tremendous labor that went into putting immense stones into position. Statistics give idea of its size: corridor 11.5m/38ft long lined with stones average over 2m/6ft high, leads to huge chamber 7.6m/25ft long by 3.3m/11ft, and almost 5m/16ft at high point of roof made of two huge boulders over 100 tons each. Note obvious planned drainage for water—grooves on sloping roof, gutters in floor.

SOGA Umako, d.626, believed first buried here. Recent excavations revealed fragments of stone house-shape sarcophagus. So as first Buddhist, builder of first temples, adoption of which religion led to sudden abolition of ostentatious burials and simple cremation and interment in urn in temple, would make this last large tomb built in Kansai—Tokyo area continued to build mound tombs for some decades. Buddhist son returned from China and removed his remains to nearby Danzan Temple, now Shinto Shrine.

He also built first known landscape garden, paradise style lake and isle—was nicknamed after it 'Lord of Isle'. Remains found recently 200m NE of this, his reputed tomb. It had twisting elongated natural-shape T'ang-style pond 5x20m (never seen since, later all roundish), 2 streams to float poem leaves and sake cups down at flower viewing time, 85m² rustic hut, size of standard farm house—all pure T'ang, probably built by imported Chinese labor, but appealing to naturalistic spinal pole of Yayoi-Japan soul.

Across road is large mound of perfect shape, perhaps tomb, terraced to top for crops. Until Shinto revival of late 18th century led by Motoori, which after several decades led to overthrow of Shogun and revival of imperial power and State Shinto, all tomb mounds were farmed this way. Identification of imperial tombs, often highly iffy, then took place based on rather flimsy evidence, rarely accepted today by even official scholars.

300 years ago due to land shortage and to ferret out secret Christians cremation was made obligatory in towns. In poor rural areas with uncultivatable land available but fuel in short supply, burial continued in style common to Stone Age—corpse flexed in womb-like position and squeezed by village strongman into coffin of two large clay pots end to end, or sometimes wooden tub as seen in samurai movies. These old tombs, however, are typical mainland burials of fully clothed or armored person laid out full length in coffin or sarcophagus, accompanied by daily needs.

We have come some 5km from Kashihara Jingu stn, 3+km from Okadera stn.

Return back along road, after Ishibutai Parking main road turns R, (N), follow 600m to R turn into... P, stiff climb to top, only for those with full day...

OKA-DERA, Hilltop-temple, with largest clay image 5m/16ft Nyoirin Kannon Bosatsu (ask to see, donation). Statue itself is made of clay from China, Korea and Japan, reputedly by Kobo Daishi. But real reason for puffing up 500mtrs of slope and stairs is for this setting. (New road facilitates driving up if no pedestrian crowds). Street is fascinating and till recently smaller shrines and temples lining it were interspersed with traditional crafts industries working in old houses, which at least still stand...shops are gone but new tourism may revive.

Until '63 students could put up in cliffside pilgrim hostel. Sumi did on student history tour from Gakushuin College. Labor shortage put end to it. Sometimes still accept small to medium groups (facilities pilgrim level) if you ✍: Oka-dera, Asuka-mura, Takaichi-gun, Nara-ken. Noodle shop foot of steps, another eatery at shrine road entry.

Back to base of hill, go on 700m to fork, L 200m and on L is...

ASUKA-DERA Great Bronze Buddha, *Asuka Daibutsu,* of Asuka era in ruins of one of two oldest Buddhist temples in country. Nothing left but foundation stones for pillars and this now 2.8m/9ft (original 5m/16ft) cast-bronze image, some 150 years older (605) than Great Nara Buddha and like it, technological marvel of its age. Temple, founded 588, gave name to era from 552 (date Buddhism introduced) to 710 move of capital to Heijo-Nara.

King of Southern Korean state of Paekche (on which Yamato was long technologically dependent, tho even in its own records it admits being 'client state' subject to Yamato) sent Buddha image to patron Japanese emperor advising this new religion as worthwhile. Immediate dispute between supporters of traditional beliefs, shinto, and those favoring new faith erupted—which has never really ceased, again bursting forth violently in 1868. Soga nobles supported Buddhism and set up temple in their home at Naniwa, present Osaka. Pestilence erupted, blamed on this foreigner and image was tossed into Osaka canal. Obviously to no avail for more images came in, and knowledge with them. Short-lived emperor Yomei (586-7) "believed in Law of Buddha and reverenced Way of Gods" (*shin-to*) to establish prototype for most Japanese since in being both, as some today may even be Christian-Shinto, and one recent Shinto priest of ancient lineage converted to Judaism without renouncing.

On Yomei's death war of succession brought alliance of Soga and Prince Umayado (prince 'born-in-stable'), better known by posthumous Buddhist name of Shotoku Taishi. Each vowed that on victory he would build temple. Interestingly, each set his temple in other's power center. Shotoku founded his own Shitenno-ji in Osaka, 593 (destroyed 1614, rebuilt, bombed out 1945, rebuilt on newly excavated old foundation accurately reproducing original but in concrete), while Soga completed Asuka-dera, ordered its Great Buddha image cast in bronze. Asuka was built on ground plan never repeated in Japan and known only in Korea: Shitenno-ji is in popular Korean Paekche style. Work on image started 596, took 10 years. Now much damaged and repaired, retaining only head, (illust p24) and hands of original, which tho notable in their beauty, it is today of more historical than aesthetic interest.

Incidentally, chief priest of ASUKA-DERA is one of few musicians able to play ancient two-string *yagumo-koto*, zither-like plucked-string instrument.

Imperial court also moved into this area with predominance of Soga, tho imperial palace remained in southern Osaka (Naniwa), at times on elevated ground above rivers and marsh at site of present Osaka Castle, changing site with each ruler. Sinification progressed in both court and church as old clan systems were abolished to centralize power. But Chinese ways were adopted more in outward form, not essence—except in art where great, broad international stimulus was at work and development was prodigious. Just few years after immigrant-sculptor Tori cast Asuka Buddha, his atelier was producing wholesale what survive as art masterpieces. Japan's first city was built, Fujiwara, a.k.a. Asuka, well-planned Chinese checkerboard 1.3 x 2.4mi (2 x 4km) rectangle: its southern limit present Asukadera–Kashihara Shrine road, its northern Yagi–Ise Kintetsu rail. Completed 687, nothing today remains (as we see for we are standing on it) but low square earthen rise outlining mud platform and walls of palace enclosure. This city existed barely 20 years, two reigns, when old habit of abandoning house on death of tenant coupled with realization that site was too restricting to Japan's grand dreams. In display of social organization and capital-wealth that astounds even today, in 710 all buildings were disassembled and moved to contiguous new site of HEIJO, of which present-day Nara is but one corner, which has become since our first edition, grand archaeological site with decades of reconstruction and restoration ahead (*follows*).

Fertility Cultism has always been major aspect of agricultural Shinto and archaeology indicates it may be oldest form of continuing religion in Japan. As old as agriculture itself, it has extolled earthly fertility in rather earthy mammalian idiom, likening fertilization process of rice to that of man. Just across from Asuka Daibutsu is **ASUKA SHRINE**–written Asuka-za Jinja, pronounced **Asuka-ni-Imasu Jinja**–on hillock visible 10m in front, to R of Asuka-dera gate. Its phallic idols are not naturalistic man-made as at Nagoya; they are natural water-worn boulders, largest almost man-size.

DATEBOOK Fascinating rite **first sun Feb**, perhaps old form of our Valentine's Day. In this masque play farmers demonstrate for rice what is supposed to be done. Sarutahiko, earthy deity of Dance and Soil, waltzes with consort, Ame-no-Uzume, around huge stone phallus, then on stage (with comic interplay of bullock) ritually rapes her, his phallic nose mashing her rosey-cheeked pudenda-visage, thus sowing first seeds of spring. She then uses that marvelous Japanese invention, tissue, to clean up, then dispenses these unique souvenirs of their conjunction to mainly farmer-audience who receive them eagerly to take home to enshrine on household *kami-dana*, god shelf, to ensure good crops.

Talismans sold here are also unique, sometimes must be asked for due to off-on 'religious intolerance' of local police: phallic cigarette holders, sake cups of vulval-clam plus phallic mushroom, etc, of fine red pottery—at house of priest, just below main shrine level on aside, knock if closed. Also has good archaeological collection in foyer which you might ask to see. He may show you shrine scroll—pictures shrine festival as it was centuries ago —little different from today except for fashions.

Gigantic mirror in his home said to be largest bronze mirror, reputedly long kept at Ise, till Asuka managed to get back. And it was obviousy not theirs originally as for on its back is inscription to Ama asking safety for seamen (drop donation in box).

Afoot or on bike it is some 2.7km due W back to KASHIHARA JINGU stn. Continuing on by **car** or **taxi** to HASE-DERA, TENRI or NARA, follow R fork from ASUKA-ZA SHRINE to Sakurai City. If you can spare time, few stops of interest are listed below: bit difficult by public transportation, easy by bike or cab.

Two km before (below) Sakurai is...

MONJU-IN, Buddhist temple with fine 12th century sculptures, sole indication that this was once great monastery complex of 49 temples. Shinto shrine on grounds marks two prehistoric tombs, of which west tomb is fine example of stone cutting and fitting: corridor and chamber of finely finished granite can be entered, examined—which is exceptional.

Continue on into Sakurai and backtrack by parallel road 1.2km to...
SHORIN-JI, treasures finest example of Nara period dry-lacquer sculpture, 11-headed Kannon. Moved here 1868 after purged from nearby...

MIWA GRAND SHRINE, by immense torii at roadside, walk in (if driving go to innermost parking, past main P which is too far out, tho jammed) only if spare time, interesting mountainside Grand Shrine atop great flight of stairs.

Continue on 3.5km to...
DANZAN JINJA once great Chinese-style temple in bright red built to house ashes of Kamatari, founder of Fujiwara clan (which started around here as Hata-clan immigrants, took their name from nearby Fujiwara capital —we will meet them again in Kyoto where they moved and ruled). He was last to be buried in great mound, probably Ishi-butai, but when his Buddhist priest son came back from China he had him disinterred, cremated, reburied in this then-Buddhist temple. Compound romantically decrepit, some buildings faded red, another *azekura* style log-cabin treasure house. Unique wooden 13-storey pagoda built 679 (rebuilt 1532) imitates T'ang Chinese stone original in Xian and is often used on posters, especially framed in sakura. In 1868 Buddhist temple because it interred national hero Kamatari, was rededicated as Shinto shrine and its escapee from Shinto burial is Shinto again. It took whole millennium but they eventually got him back.

Driving: can't drive Danzan-Okadera, must circle around or hike/bike across 4km. Asuka Toll Rd from base Danzan to top ¥150, noted maples. YH before toll rd.

SAKURAI, fork where one chooses either Tenri-Horyu-ji-Nara following our historical itinerary, or 'BEAUTY OFFBEAT' if in reverse. This whole run is thru lovely country meant more for escape into its setting as sites themselves offer distraction only minutes more than it takes to read about them. Numerous small sites not mentioned here, more oddly-sculpted boulders and such. Old homes of Asuka Plain, as all about Nara, are singularly lovely, tho giving way to stucco shoeboxes, tho some state encouragement to preserve. Many roofs have what look to be tile penthouses of pidgeon coop size: chimneys for old open fireplaces, seen nowhere else. Tradition of tile roof on homes is older here than elsewhere. Entire Asuka bowl is dotted with soulfully decrepit shrines and temples of historic import; many mentioned in poems in hoary "anthology of myriad leaves", *Manyoshu*. Japanese poetry lovers will walk entire area, book in hand looking for places described to sit down and reread poem. It is small area, meant for leisurely, pointless travel, afoot as others have done here for centuries, on bike as so many do now.

N of Asuka, in Tenri, from Kintetsu-Tenri stn walk E 2km to large grove...
ISO-NO-KAMI JINGU, ☎(07436)-2-0900, is on Yamanobe-no-michi, oldest road in country. Reputedly oldest shrine with Izumo and Ise, was *ujigami*, patron shrine of once dominant Mononobe clan defeated by Shotoku and rise of Buddhism. Houses sword given by order of Sun Goddess to Jimmu to commemorate conquest of Japan—more important and real is seven-pronged iron sword bearing oldest inscription in Japan, "made by Crown Prince of Paekche for ruler of Wa, 369AD" in gold inlay, probable origin of above legend; or perhaps imported in 372 by 'Korea raider' Empress Jingu. Oratory, *haiden*, one of oldest in country (NT) and 2-storey gate, both 12c.

Adjoining *Gassho-no-ie* Museum, belongs Tenri, if you missed this 'hands in prayer' rural architecture in Takayama; 9-4pm, ☎(07436)-2-3406 in advance to see.

DATEBOOK: Nov 22 5-7pm Secret Kagura in dark.

*Therefore, one day He searched through the muddy waters
to see what materials He could find for the Creation-*

—Doctrine of Tenrikyo

TENRI 天理
NAVEL OF WORLD

HEAVEN IS MATRIARCHAL in Japanese tradition. Despite foreign cultural invasions of knight-emperors and Buddhist priests, of samurai and stag-parties, this undercurrent matriarchy has persisted in Japan, especially in religion. Shinto priests have traditionally been managers of ritual. But more ancient, more influential seeresses were prototype for Sun Goddess and Grain Goddess (as at Ise) and their priestesses. She is medium who may act as human vehicle for celestial power, or simply one who may locate lost articles, lost animals or lost people, and in trance commune with dead, as portrayed in film *Rashomon*. She may cast spells, usually good, sometimes evil. Many in modern rural, even urban, Japan. She may lay claim to higher levels of possession and several such women have founded major movements—most successful (3,000,000 followers today) founded barely over century ago by devout woman acclaimed as human abode of Universal God—folk Shinto has strong element of monotheism. Great-grandson is patriarch over her followers 10.5km N of Sakurai, 8km S of Nara at Tenri.

GETTING THERE
AFTER ASUKA area, Kintetsu **train** from main hub YAGI, or from SAKURAI 3 stops → YAGI and change, or from ASUKA, OKADERA or Kashihara Jingu, N-bound 3rd stop N → Yagi, then 2nd stop HIRAHATA, Xfer to short Tenri trunk. JR SAKURAI → TENRI. **Bus** Muroji-guchi-Ohno Kintetsu Stn via Hase-dera → Tenri; or HORYU-JI → TENRI.

GETTING AROUND
From TENRI **bus tour** of Nara Plain partly follows our historical rte, Nara Kotsu bus (G) *Yamanobe Tonomine Meguri* dep NARA stn 9:30 → TENRI stn 9:55 → Ishigami-jingu → Chogaku-ji → SAKURAI stn → Abemonju-in → Shorin-ji → Danzan-jinja → Sakurai stn → TENRI stn → end NARA stn; 7hr, ¥6,220. Same on your own using 1-day **bus pass** ¥700 (*see* NARA GETTING AROUND), 4 in **taxi** match tour price.

TILT: Suggested arrive Tenri after lunch, PM around grounds, see two museums, sunset service 5:45 or later, on → Nara for dinner (or in reverse, HASE-DERA). We often combine with AM → HORYU-JI (in which case lunch small restaurants front Horyu-ji); bus direct HORYU-JI → TENRI, frequent departures, about 20mins. Rush round allows lunch at KASHIHARA or HORYU-JI after morning at tombs; or from NARA leave after early lunch, taxi HORYU-JI, 1hr, on → TENRI 2-3pm to see art museum, evening service, stroll grounds at lantern lighting, return NARA for dinner (*see* NARA, p379).

Growing walled city built by volunteer labor is center of stable, steadily expanding Shinto-like religion, Tenri-kyo—'Shinto-like' because, while government-classified as sect of Shinto, many young Tenrikyoans object to term. Draws its stimulus, rite and dogma from folk tradition, folk-Shinto; main following in provincial towns and farming areas where traditions of communal service still valid and principle tenet seems to be regular practice of Good Deeds. Dance considered medium of communion in Japan, still major offering at Shinto shrines; *noh* and *kabuki* are of offertory origin, discipline of commercial dance schools and troupes resembles medieval monasticism. See dance-prayer of Tenrikyo at main temple daily at sunset when young worshippers, at 'Vatican' for religious training and voluntary labor, assemble for services accompanied by traditional instruments.

When this prayer ends follow great wooden corridors thru to inner temple where slightly higher service is held. *Advise* best to carry shoes to allow you alternate exit.

Tenrikyoans welcome visitors. Move about without qualms. They believe in faith healing, not as sole cure but as basis to any cure which surgery and medicine can only supplement, and maintain sanatoria, hospitals. *Ten-ri* means 'Heavenly Reason'—God manifest in reason. Simple farmers happily support good university originally college of languages for their foreign missionaries (now world-famed for Korean department) which welcomes all applicants regardless of religion, fine library (top English section in Japan, ex-Perkins Collection of Hearniana). Superb ethnology museum not to be missed for icollection of Ainu, Persian folk art (formerly ours), Chinese shop signs, gallery of Oriental arts— ancient Chinese, Japanese tomb, ritual art, Persian pre-Islamic pottery. Both are in new 'pentagon', signs in Japanese, English, Spanish.

To learn more ask guides posted about grounds for English-speaking guide who will gladly show you around (hospitality is also tenet of faith), answer questions, offer translations of their 'bible' and outline of faith's history and development. Tho not pushy, they actively engage in missionary work, with over 100 churches in Americas, others Korea, Nepal, Pacific Isles and Africa. On first visit in 1955 we asked roving guide for info on any nearby inn, were put up in guest house and dined with Patriarch, late dynamic Shozen Nakayama (whose personal collections became museum). This seems not to have been irregular. Tenri University accepts foreign students wishing to **study Japanese**, summer or regular session. But each seems individual case, with no set policy or set charges; ✍ **Tenri University,** Foreign Student Advisor, Tenri City, Nara Pref, Japan.

Empty space center of main room around which everyone prayer-dances is where first man was created (midget, each generation has grown in stature in all ways), where foundress NAKAYAMA Miki was born 1798. House she lived, died, in 1887 is preserved. As deity cannot die and she was, as vehicle, holy incarnation, tended to as if she lived, is served meals, bath is fired. Our favorite tale is of her state persecution. In drought she told followers to pray for rain: It rained. Government confirmed her deed by arresting her for tampering with water supply.

Educated Tenrikyoans troubled by her naive 'revelations' comprising their bible, undergoing interesting intellectual phase developing theology equating primeval midget theory with growth of man's soul-mind-reason rather than his legs. However, astounding growth of Japanese during two great periods of dietary change at end of feudalism 100 years ago and end of World War II seem to add credence to Up from Midget theory. None of this bothers rural rank and file who just go on doing good deeds.

New Year serve free *O-zoni* mochi rice cake in sweet soup–'85 used 40 tons of rice.

SHOPPING: Streets stn → shrine typical bazaar catering to residents, volunteers, pilgrims, mostly rural. Tenri uniform is denim happi-coat, ideograms dyed down lapel with group ideograms; gals wear *mompei* baggy ankle-length knickerbockers of traditional *kasuri* (yarn-alternately resist-dyed or left clear so when woven patterns appear, mostly floral) indigo. Lovelier ancient form of jeans; priced as jeans were once. Wear at home as pricey-looking harem pantaloons (midcalf OK if legs long) or in place of jeans.

Before tatami mat was invented Japanese sat on polished wood floor on circular-woven straw cushion, as seen in ancient 8-13th century scrolls. Tenrikyoans still use these in rites at home, widely available in general stores along street: hardy, handsome and cheap– excellent on veranda. Another ancient artifact in modern Tenrikyo use is *magatama* comma-shaped jewel similar to that in archaeological reconstructions worn by primeval Japanese and which is, with mirror and sword, 3 Imperial regalia. Every Tenri home has stone or glass necklace of these 'tiger teeth'. Handsome, in numerous small shops. Watch for wooden buckets, other attractive paraphernalia. Altho made for religious use, there is no hesitation, no sacrilege, in selling to outsiders for whatever use you might put.

BIGGER THAN EGYPT'S PYRAMIDS   MORE TOMBS

FLYING into Osaka your plane often circles giving unobstructed view of immense keyhole-shaped mounds covered with trees, surrounded by moat and outer arch of forest park–gigantic tombs of **KASHIWARA** (#2).

GETTING THERE: From KASHIHARA SHRINE take Kintetsu bus 20km → FURUICHI, or next → DOMYO-JI, btwn which is tomb area. Or Kintetsu rail from either SAKURAI or YAGI toward NAMBA → KOKUBU stn, then minimal taxi → DOMYO-JI.

Largest tomb (2nd largest in Japan) is that of emperor Ojin, son of empress Jingo who conquered Korea while carrying him in her womb 14 months after dad died. Ojin has since been deified as Shinto God of War, identifying with Hachiman, warrior deity of Korean artisan immigrants of perhaps same period as momma Jingo's invasion. Ojin's tomb is perfect keyhole shape–round mound with flange extending below, surrounded by moat. Father Chuai's tomb is of identical shape but 1/5th as long (1/125th volume). Area is peppered with no less than 29 tomb mounds, plus whole mountain of 39 small mounds just at **Tamateyama**, with cliffside dotted with open cave tombs—now mostly surrounded by housing developments which as they expand uncover more small tombs which now are mostly just surveyed, salvaged and built over, even tho hallowed ground.

SAKAI, southern Osaka, boasts largest tomb of all: that of Ojin's son 16th emperor Nintoku, trad reign 313-399, probably actual 395-427.

GETTING THERE: To **Sakai** and complex of 20 tombs, including several giants, from KASHIWARA take JR → end of line, TENNO-JI, change to JR Hanwa line → MOZU stn, walk 2min to big green hill–tumulus; by Kintetsu, from KASHIWARA → end of line ABENOBASHI, part of Tennno-ji stn complex where cross over to neighboring JR line as above. From downtown OSAKA Midosuji subway → TENNOJI, as above.

It is of greater mass than all 3 pyramids of Giza combined with Sphinx and all lesser ones thrown in. But where pyramids are geometry and finished stone, this is heaped earth. Still, no quicky construction job for 'primitives', easily matching in relative social scale new land fill-isle of nearby Osaka international airport. Diameter of outer of triple moats is 2,695ft, almost full kilometer. Round main mound heart is 243m/800ft, 2.5 football fields. Round and keyhole flange total 486m/1600ft, covering area of 80acres/32+ hectares. It is 40m/130ft height, or about double that allowed by Japanese construction code until revision of 1963.

'Keyhole' mound shape, common in Korea, first appears on mound of legendary emperor #10, Sujin (trad 97-30BC, ca350AD if actually existed) where it resembles round hairbrush with straight handle. With succeeding tombs this handle widens into wedge shape, eventually becoming wider at its base than diameter of main upper round mound.

At Nintoku's collossus in mid-19th century landslide in handle revealed great stone house-shape sarcophagus, and several treasured artifacts which were duly sketched and reinterred. One was glass bowl, probably from Syria or Persia. Smaller tomb of rival branch emperor #27, Ankan (trad 531-35, about right) also gave forth glass bowl, but of cut crystal, almost identical to one in Shosoin (732AD), of Persian origin. Over 20,000 haniwa ceramic cylinders encircle base of Nintoku tomb. Scholars now believe Great Pyramids, whatever their true purpose, were intended in part to redistribute labor during agricultural off-seasons as well as redistribute wealth, so perhaps these man-made mountains served similar socio-economic purpose.

Whatever, this monument to wasted labor was erected by Nintoku himself while he was alive, unlike usual local post-mortem tradition. He records it was out of consideration for others because he wished not to trouble anyone by his death. No emperor again ever held such power—tho in absolute terms dictators tycoon Hideyoshi and shogun Ieyasu exceeded it, and relative to percentage of GNP perhaps approached it in such as Nikko.

Continue JR Hanwa Line([from Osaka-Tennoji to Wakayama) to Shinodayama stn, 5th stn S from Sakai, then 7min walk.
Yayoi Culture Museum handsome new '91 building houses 1,000-odd artifacts and replicas of notable objects held elsewhere (Nara, Kyushu, etc), large scale models of architectural complexes (incl legendary towered-kraal of empress Himiko, probably in Kyushu, p710), to illustrate development of seminal era 3d cent BC–3d cent AD (*see* pp 5, 569). Refreshingly, stresses contact with Korea, etc; X-wed, ¥600, ☎(0725) 46-2164.

Another **tomb complex** NW of **Nara** between Dreamland and race track, is impressive from air but up close just wooded knolls. One of these is said to be sole known female's tomb and entomb Korea-invader Empress Jingo. Area has good posted cycling paths around Ground Self Defense Force ('non-army') garrison.

Large **Shima-no-yama Kofun**, 'Isle-mount Tomb' near **Tenri** is key-hole several hundred feet long in mid of man-made lake. Mostly terraced over by crops, it can be reached by long earthen dike after 2km walk from Yuizaki stn on Kintetsu Yagi-Saidaiji line; or from Hirahata stn same line whence bus to Koyanagi.

For more information on tumuli etc, inquire in Japanese at **Kashihara Archaeology Museum** or Tenri **Sankokan** Japan Archaeology section.

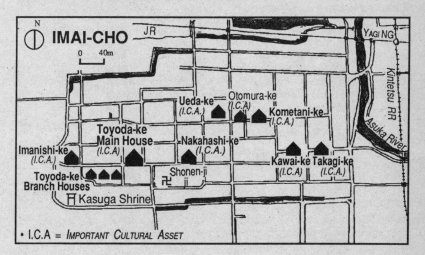

FEUDAL SIDETRACK

YAMATO AREA is also known for its characteristic folk houses, but most fine ones are randomly scattered thru area and hard to find.
IMAI-CHO area of **Kashihara City** is different–800-plus houses here, over 600 are Edo feudal era. Imai-cho has long been merchants' district, and you come across all sorts of old businesses while wandering its lanes. Area, strollable (E-W 600m, N-S 400m), was surrounded by wall and moat,

portions of latter remain. During Sengoku (warring states) period, 1467-1568, residents successfully repelled all attacks; during 350-year peace under Edo-Tokugawa, wall fell into disuse, was slowly dismantled.

GETTING THERE: Bordered by JR Sakurai Line N, on E by Kintetsu Kashihara Line. 10min walk from Kintetsu Yamato YAGI stn, Nishi-guchi (2 stops up from Kashihara Jingu-mae); just over basic-mtr **cab** KASHIHARA JINGU. 10min walk JR Unebi. Convenient, shame to miss.

Octet of houses, Important Cultural Assets, can be visited. All but one are private homes so suggest calling ahead to tell them you're coming. No gifts needed. All houses charge ¥100 fee. There are several large maps posted thru area; **info booths** at any of nearby stns (sometimes also at Nara stn) should have pocket maps.

We list these 8 houses and their phone numbers:

at E end...
Takagi-ke ☎(07442) 2-3380;

and next door...
Kawai-ke ☎2-2154;

in center are...
Kyu-Kometani-ke ☎3-8297 (bought by gov't, open 8:30-12:00, 13:00-16:00),
Otomura-ke ☎3-0039,
Ueda-ke ☎2-2915;

in line from W in are...
Imanishi-ke (open Oct 15–Nov 14 and Apr 15–May 14) ☎5-3388,
Toyoda-ke ☎5-0418 and
Nakahashi-ke ☎2-7288;

facing which is...
Shonen-ji temple, around which town grew.

In building the Great Sanctuary
That she may flourish long as last
Heaven and earth,
Awe and gladness fill my heart.
—Kose Natemaro, (750AD) *Manyoshu*

HORYU-JI 法隆寺
TEMPLE OF NOBLE LAW

HOARY & HUGE as it is, covering 25 acres, world's oldest wooden buildings of this thirteen century-old Temple of Noble Law are more justly famed, and for us, thus, more worthwhile, as exemplary large monastery complex housing fine collection of ancient sculpture: total 45 NT, 145 ICA. If you must limit yourself to seeing one temple intensively, Horyu-ji will be most rewarding. It lacks only garden to complete our expectation, but Nara, one grand garden park itself, generally lacks them. (If bus tour from Nara or taxi, which so instruct, later stop at garden-temple JIKO-IN for tea—Sekishu 'samurai' style, E-pamphlet.) Because it is out of way, somewhat inconvenient, Horyu-ji is not constantly full of tourists. Compound so immense it can absorb convoy of student tour buses at each end while you keep off to yourself, allowing one horde to stampede past to leave you in eye of storm.

Thus, with all it offers, Horyu-ji is ideal place for our PERSONAL ORIENTATION on Buddhism and its iconography, and we advise you browse, flashlight in hand, with this book open to INTRODUCTION chapter, pp23-31.

GETTING THERE

BY OTHER than our historical routing: from NARA most convenient taxi o.w. 7-8x-mtr; (*see* Nara Tours); bus #52,60,97,98 (to Oji) from Nara Kintetsu stn via Nara JR stn every 30min, 7am-8pm also stops Daibutsu, Yakushi-ji, Toshodai-ji temples between NARA stn ↔ HORYU-JI, ¥560. Horyu-ji bus stand on hiway has good bilingual bus map-sign of area. Train JR Kansai-*sen* (line) OSAKA Tennoji-Osaka stns ↔ NARA: 10min from Nara, 45min Osaka → Horyu-ji stn, whence 1.3km (15min) walk across tracks N toward hills to hiway, L past Oji bus stn (L) and Horyu-ji bus stand (R). Alternate cheap train from OSAKA-Kintetsu Uehonmachi stn → SAIDAI-JI, transfer to Kashihara line → KORIYAMA, bus #52,97,98 or continue by taxi → HORYU-JI. From KASHIHARA JR → OJI whence bus, or transfer JR Kansai-sen one stop → HORYU-JI.

WHERE NEXT: Bus #53 → Daibutsu-mae or Yakushi-ji – Toshodai-ji en route.

WHERE TO STAY: Alas our old restaurant-ryokan Shoun-kaku overlooking West Gate went out of business Jan '86. Below Toin-Yumedono, small family ryokan Dai-koku-ya ☎(07457)-5-2767. Minshuku Higashi-no Furusato ☎4-0917 L-above Yumedono only takes foreigners who speak some Japanese, or with Japanese, due to problems of Frenchman who got soap in bath. Walk 1km E of Horyu-ji on Rte25, new Horyu-ji Grand Hotel, ☎5-3311; fine, most rooms with view of pagoda, tourist rates (twin ¥-lo-S), dining; also tatami rooms; swimming pool. 600m beyond, for adventurous couples, two good new fashion hotels: England, and easy-to-spot simulated white L.A. clapboard-towered Santa Monica (*also see* NARA, following; TENRI, preceding).

TILT: We suggest arrive for overnite (above), spend leisurely AM Horyu-ji, lunch any of several restaurants by Nan-dai-mon Gate—soba noodles, up to ¥1,000 lunch set, or nabe like *kani* (crab)-sukiyaki etc to ¥3,000, add ¥700 for soup, salad etc 'set'—or Grand Hotel; afternoon to outlying Yakushi-ji–Toshodai-ji for lovely full day. Limited time, advise need minimum 1hr just to walk thru Horyu-ji; half day preferred: start at KONDO, veritable museum, see statuary, frescoes (bring flashlight) & KAMI-MIDO, walk thru TREASURY, then over to nunnery CHUGU-JI for famed 'Thinker' Miroku Bosatsu.

At gate plaza shops, watch fall-winter for *hoshi-gaki* dried persimmons.

With time, stroll scenic alleys W: 300m W of West Gate is small tumulus...

Fuji-no-ki Kofun (circa 550-590?, 40m across, 8m tall with chamber 16+m long), "awesome room, ranking in scale and beauty among best chambers... unearthed in Japan," from which late '85 excavated usual grey pottery, like Korean. Otherwise stripped by ancient tomb robbers, gilt bronze saddle (NT), arabesque, elephant in bronze saddle grillwork "indicate import from Korea...trace origin...ultimately [to] West Asia,...arts which encompassed several lands", indicates excitingly important denizen, horse-archer chief (of Kashiwade or Weguri clans?), possibly historical SOGA Iname—even emperor Sushun d.592? If so, luckiest accident in Japanese archaeology since last century's collapse of Nintoku tomb chamber Osaka (pp354, 570). Loose pieces moved to Kashihara Archaeology Institute "for study, possible later display"—'85 exhibit security man hinted never show again, tho shown since. Horse trappings similar to those in Korean Silla tombs, where murals show equestrian decor of Parthian Persian style. Sarcophagus is hollowed block of solid stone coated and sealed with vermilion lacquer (royal treatment in China) suggests imperial tomb, taboo to open. But after much public debate 2-ton lid lifted '88 revealing remains of couple: he tall (170+cm/5ft10in), Altai-Turk?, fully armored, imperial regalia–mirrors, beads, swords–age 20ish; she (buried earlier?) in remains of spangled silks, scraps preserved by 99% humidity in chamber, which fogged first film records.

MAKING ROUNDS

PINE-LINED *ave leads us across what in our '64 edition were rice fields, now parking lot, approach used by pilgrims for centuries so that it is for us bridge back across time to...*
NAN-DAI-MON (South Great Gate), rather ordinary, dating only to 1439. Stepping thru we enter world of ancient grandeur. Broad avenue beyond is lined either side by gates of priestly residences, tile-topped white walls with 5 horizontal lines indicate imperial patrons. Stone steps to Chumon is where on school excursion (Apr-May, mid-autumn) students line up for class photos. Gate open 6AM–6PM, enter free and wander; fee-charging buildings open 8AM–enter by 3:20PM; **admission** to entire Horyu-ji complex ¥700—CHUGU-JI add ¥300.

Here note that Horyu-ji is complex made up of several compounds. Directly before us is **SAI-IN** (West Pavilion), actually great corridor joining or acting as circumvallation to several buildings, grouped with other outbuildings included. Looking R from foot of stone steps, few hundred yards E is smaller **TO-IN** (East Pavilion), just E of which is nunnery **CHUGU-JI**. To L, on to wall, R up slope and stone steps to **SAI-EN-DO** (West Round Pavilion) actually octagon, here **Feb 3** *Setsubun* flaming demon quelling goes on in icy cold evening after 7pm. 1km N again is HOKKI-JI, slightly younger than Horyu-ji, but not included in it. 45min walk above Chugu-ji is MATSUO-DERA, p365.

100yds short broad flight of steps brings us onto temple platform, famed...
CHU-MON (Middle Gate): Gates in China or Japan usually have either one or three portals; this stands alone in having two for no known reason. It is said East is for living to enter, West for dead to exit to Paradise. This and five-storey pagoda within and to L are all that remain from original building of 670AD. Giant **guardian statues** in either side of gate are oldest in Japan of these *ni-o* or *Kongo-rikishi* (Diamond Power Lords). Almost always found guarding approach to Buddhist temples, one on L his mouth closed, inhales to build up tension: *yin*. Partner on R, mouth open, exhales in explosive release to attack: *yang*. Celestial karate-ists. Their costume and features hint Central Asian Turanian origin, just as entasis or tapered bulge of pillar, not found in later period structures, shows purported Greek influence in basic architecture.

Within gate, two buildings stand in courtyard. That to R is...
KONDO (Golden Hall, for main objects of worship), recent copy of original (enter R side, E—oh if only they'd put in some slight incandescent light—use flashlight, exit L facing Pagoda). Testimonial to tragedies of Horyu-ji, formerly housed its most important frescoes, which were beautiful as well, until 1949 fire caused by careless priest either smoking in bedding or using faulty electric heating pad. Still houses 2nd and 3rd oldest metal sculpture in Japan (Soga's Asuka Big Buddha oldest) and these commemorate tragic history of Horyu-ji's founder. When Yomei, first Buddhist emperor, fell ill 586AD after performing his first and only ritual tasting of first fruits, was decided to have Yakushi (Healing Buddha or Medicine King) cast in supplication for his cure, above. Died following year and in war of succession against Shintoist Mononobe clan, as we have seen, Prince Shotoku and ally Soga Umako each vowed to erect temples if victorious. Vow to build Horyu-ji predates that of Asuka-dera and Osaka's Shitenno-ji by year, tho actual work began later. (This most ancient temple trio represent 3 different basic architectural temple ground-plans.)

After Shotoku became regent for aunt Empress Suiko, Yomei's sister, plan for temple in honor of his father Yomei revived, completed 607 with unveiling **Yakushi-nyorai** (NT) in KONDO, where it stands now. Soga, as representing clan system, were set aside in favor of central state authority.

In 622 Prince Shotoku and his consort also fell ill and in supplication *Shaka-sanzon*, **trinity** (NT) centered on Shaka, historical Buddha, was ordered. Finished following year, in time also to be dedicated as post-humous memorial to Shotoku and set up here in Kondo as central piece. These two bronzes, terra-cottas in pagoda and Asuka Daibutsu were all executed by Tori *Busshi* (title=master-maker of images), Korean immigrant naturalized as Japanese. Yakushi, who usually offers bottle, has R hand raised in 'fear not' pose, L palm up, fore-, mid-fingers extended in variant of 'giving' usually found in Shaka Buddha—as center figure of adjoining triad, seem cast from almost same body mold but for heads. Such arbitrary mudra make attribution difficult. Shaka's attending bodhisattvas wear crown like those from Korean royal tombs but more notably typical of Persian Parthian coins ("When you see Parthian charger tethered outside synagogue, day of delivery is at hand": OT). Enigmatic smile, flat planality emulate Wei China stone, characterize this era's style. Yakushi R of Shaka Triad w/ later Bishamon-ten wooden statue of 1078 between. Balancing Yakushi L is **Amida Nyorai bronze** (ICA) in imitation Asuka period style but date 1231 as substitute for stolen piece. Figure to L is female **Kichijo-ten** (NT) paired with warrior **Bishamon-ten** (NT). On each of four corners stands one of **Shitenno** (NT) 4 guardian kings (650), popular in Korea, perhaps their earliest extant Japan examples, definitely oldest example of sculpture from single block of wood—older woods interlock like 3-D jig-saw puzzles.

Frescoes, destroyed, had been copied exactly few years before fire. May have been done originally by Korean, Tamjing (579-631), reported to have come from Koguryu in 610 as art instructor: tho claims are also made for Japanese and Indian artists and prototypes have been noted in Central Asian Buddhist cave murals showing even Persian elements: painting was major art form of Iranian Manichaeans who came at least as far east as southern Korea, were amalgamated into Buddhism. Color reproductions suitable for matt or frame are sold in temple.

Details of architecture peculiar to Horyu-ji are equally mysterious in origin—Greek entasis in pillars and recent finds also hint connections with West and Central Asia and Persia. Canopies over main altars in Kondo

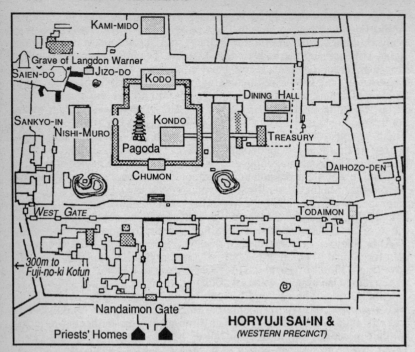

Map labels:
KAMI-MIDO
Grave of Langdon Warner
SAIEN-DO   JIZO-DO   KODO
DINING HALL
SANKYO-IN   KONDO
NISHI-MURO   TREASURY
Pagoda
DAIHOZO-DEN
CHUMON
WEST GATE   TODAIMON
← 300m to Fuji-no-ki Kofun
Nandaimon Gate
Priests' Homes
HORYUJI SAI-IN &
(WESTERN PRECINCT)

acknowledged by Japanese scholars to contain design elements from China, India, Persia and glass probably from China and Levant, angels derived of west Asian prototypes and phoenixes are like Indonesian Garuda and even older Achaemenid Persian Homa. Buddhist priests who came to Japan at this date included Indian, Afghan and Persian (pharmacist Li Mi I). Our two main bronzes further illustrate great interinfluences at this time: note squared-off base of each looks chiseled out of stone, flat planality of figures indicate limitations of sculpting hard stone rather than free-molding clay from which bronze is cast. In fact, these bronzes are based on style developed in China in Buddhist cave temple stone sculpture. There is no satisfactory stone available in Japan. This stony flatness is characteristic of much sculpture of Asuka era (522-710) midphase Hakuho. Motifs include *karakusa*, west Asian vine, or arabesque of Persian rugs. Facial features are anything but Japanese, tho dwarfish standing attendants may indicate attempt, however naive, to present figures in more Japanese proportion.

Five-storey Pagoda (NT) (34.1m, 110ft), *goju-no-to*, on L: its roofs less slanting, proportions squatter than usual for Japan, indicate its design by mainlander. (Japan prefers roofs, as in their thatch, that soar heavenward like cathedral spires). Pagoda ground floor (hope you have flashlight, even then, damned grills obscure view without protecting adequately) houses terra-cotta (dry or unbaked clay) **sculpture groups** (NT) attributed to Tori Busshi of Kuratsukuri family (storehouse makers?) first Buddhist sculptor in Japan, probably Korean (fl.605-623). On E facing Kondo, aged Vimalakirti lectures Manjusri on frailty of human body; west is portrayed depositing of mortal remains of Shakamuni or Sakyamuni, historical Buddha, and on N we see his entry into Nirvana, with magnificently realistic seated figures 45cm/18ins tall expressing grief as nowhere else in art—Busshi's style of enlarged heads and hands enhances expressiveness.

KODO (NT), large main building rear originally used as lecture hall, set here in 991 but older, having been dismantled and transferred from Kyoto to replace original destroyed in fire of 925. Images inside are again of Yakushi Triad and four guardian kings (NT), but these are all of wood, 10th century. Original *Kodo* sat closer to pagoda and *Kondo*, and not linked by corridor, but fires seem to have suggested dispersal.

COFFEE SHOP

CHUGUJI

E-DEN

SHIKYAKU-MON

YUMEDONO

TOIN
(EASTERN PRECINCT)

Table with **roof-tiles** piled up is selling them, not to take home as souvenir, but to leave as piece of posterity: buy one ¥1,000 flats (¥3,000 for end pieces), inscribe your name or that of loved one you wish remembered and tile will go into next roof restored.

Exiting Kodo, on our R is... **KYO-ZO** (sutra repository) (NT) and on L **SHORO** (belfry) (NT) with one of oldest, finest bells in Japan, 1.8m/6ft high x 1.2m/4ft across.

Various outbuildings ringing corridor are of little interest, listing clockwise:
SANKYO-IN NISHI-MURO (Three Sutra Pavilion West Hall) (NT) double hall used for lectures on Three Sutras and general accommodations, contains several 12th century sculptures and one 8th century seated Miroku; **SAI-EN-DO** (West Octagonal Hall) (NT) fits its name, sits atop small hill, housing great 8th century Nara Period dry lacquer Yakushi (NT) and 12 guardian gods (ICA) of later centuries. Just to its R is small **JIZO-DO** with 13th century Jizo; directly behind Kodo is **KAMI-MIDO** (Upper Hall), 13th century, housing another Shaka Triad (NT) and four guardians, 9th century.

Nara's **American Saint**: art professor Langdon Warner is memorialized in his 'second' grave just to L of Saiendo, few meters up narrow alley. Buddhist custom is to separate ashes and inter in more than one memorial, as we'll *see* in Koya Monastery, following. Warner, professor at Harvard, was one of cofounders of Jay's alma mater Asia Institute School for Asian Studies in New York whose founder-chancellor Arthur Upham Pope and wife Phyllis Ackerman are equally honored in national monument tomb in center of Isfahan, Iran (well cared for even by new Islamic regime)—this trio being perhaps sole occidentals so honored in all Asia.

Warner, credited with saving Nara, Kyoto, Kamakura, Kanazawa from USAF bombing in World War II, himself denied it. Probable credit should go to Harold Ickes, if perhaps at instigation of Warner. Jay studied aesthetics and Persian art before coming to Japan and as Japan introduction had only lectures by New York Public Library's genius John Mish on Psyche of Japan, and Warner for 5+ hour marathon of what proved later to be draft of his marvelous *The Enduring Art of Japan*. This guidebook owes him much, as also Mish, and especially Pope and wife Ackerman.

Directly E (R) of main compound, parallel to it are three long buildings. In first is group of memorial portraits, popular with pilgrims for centuries,

Shotoku Taishi seated with four attendants: his son, two brothers and his Korean teacher. Next building over just called WESTERN ROOM and last is sealed treasury (NT), log cabin like Shosoin and like it set upon mystic 40-pillars, most important of whose art treasures are in DAI-HOZO-DEN (Sacred Treasury), modern museum opposite, which we visit last, after Toin and Chugu-ji unless your taxi is waiting at Shikyaku-mon. Last 2 buildings R of log cabin, rear behind open pavilion is DINING HALL (NT).

TO-IN (Eastern Pavilion); to reach, pass front of Daihozo-den Treasury, descend platform turn R pass thru TODAIMON (East Great Gate) (NT) down boulevard lined again with white-walled compounds, cherry trees, souvenir stalls sell folkart papier maché masks not seen for years. *5 mins to...*

Coffee break: exiting alley from *Sai-in* before entering *Shikyaku-mon* gate to *To-in* take L hundred yards up alley past intersection to cedar-steepled building, pleasant tea shop Higashi-no-sato: for coffee, tea, *matcha* (thick tea) and good bento of rice or noodles, ¥700-1500, *zenzai* dessert, X-4:30; next door minshuku limited to those who don't soap in bath (smile and say: *O-furo wakarimasu*). Midway on L below is small pilgrim-rate noodle shop. R down alley, first L leads to small inn Dai-koku-ya, sole ryokan in area. If making one way stroll thru and meeting your taxi, it can wait at *Shikyaku-mon* taxi stand or coffee-shop Parking.

SHIKYAKU-MON (Four-Legged Gate), Toin East Compound sits on site of Shotoku Taishi's Palace, but most buildings have been replaced due to fires. Compound much smaller than Sai-in. Center, ringed by outer corridor is Yumedono (Hall of Dreams or Visions) (NT). Eight-sided pavilion set on octagonal stone pedestal was built 739 by adoring monk Gyoshin Sozu to sanctify site of Shotoku's home, destroyed after his and his wife's death by vengeful Soga who forced prince's entire family to commit mass suicide—popular reaction to which atrocity eventually unified tribes into nation.

Houses holiest statue in Horyu-ji, Guzé or Savior Kannon (197cm/6ft6in tall with halo) (NT) said to be life-size portrait of Shotoku as earthly manifestation of Kannon. This secret Buddha *hi-butsu*, was swathed in muslin for centuries and forgotten until American E.F.Fenollosa, Japanese government inspector of ancient art, in 1884 insisted this strange cloth mummy be explored. Enigma of smile matches Mona Lisa. R hand has strange mudra of palm out, thumb down. Critics point out hairlocks falling over shoulders strangely abstract, archaic—likely remains of shoulder-flame aura of Wei and earlier West Asian pre-Buddhist iconography. Shown to public 2x-yearly: Apr 11-May 5, Oct 22-Nov 3 plus NT portrait images of Abbots Gyoshin & Dosen.

E-DEN Hall of Painting (NT), above Yumedono. On its walls is pictured life of Prince Shotoku, 1784 copy of 1069 original now in Tokyo.

DEMPO-DO Instruction Hall (NT), impressive building N of E-den and belfry. Sole remaining residence of this era, having been home of Lady Tachibana (wife of editor of *Manyoshu* poem anthology), moved here 739. This type of architecture persisted for centuries until those elements evolved which are today considered so characteristically Japanese: namely *tatami* floor mats and *shoji* sliding panels. Dempo-do is floored in hardwood. You will note in older Horyu-ji buildings we did not remove our shoes for floors were stone in Chinese style. This residence shows how early was Japanese predilection for removing home from earth (halfway to heaven?) which becomes even stronger in following centuries' reaction against Sinification. We know from ancient scroll painting that people removed their shoes, sat around on circular straw cushions. Court (as today) probably used Chinese tables and chairs—but not at home. Dempo-do's outer walls are great horizontal half-shutters. It houses large collection of wood, lacquer-on-wood and dry-lacquer statues of 8-9th centuries. Gate and small compound N of *Dempo-do* are priests' living quarters from 15th century.

Turn R here, pass thru gate leaving Horyu-ji proper, pay another ¥300, which seems to keep away most local bus tours to leave us in peace, into...
CHUGU-JI nunnery of Middle Palace Temple, not antique to be important as building but extremely pleasant of atmosphere. Original site was 1.5km/mile E at Shotoku's mother's palace, built in her memory. Burned often. New pavilion since first edition is exquisite, concrete with copper roof all in ancient style and color, floating in garden pool and allows us to see its two treasures as they were meant to be seen.

Tenjukoku-Mandara, Mandala of Land of Heavenly Longevity (NT) about mtr/yard square fragment of Japan's oldest embroidery made by prince's widow Lady Tachibana Oiratsume (who soon followed him) and her court, picturing prince's rebirth in heaven: L rear of hall. Originally far larger and pair, suffered until 13th century nun restored temple and arranged fragments in their present form. Four tortoises remain of original 400, with 4 ideographs on backs of each spelling out history and purpose of tapestry, first one top has name of prince's mother, Empress Anahobe no Hashihito. Textile is described in detail in prince's contemporary biography.

Nunnery also show exquisite camphorwood statue of **Miroku Bosatsu** Messiah-Buddha (NT), now set in replica of ancient gilt canopied altar rather than plopped in corner as before. Its original gilt has worn away leaving base wood to age gloriously. There are two similar works, this and one we visit in Kyoto at Koryu-ji (*note* K), as well as probable original in Korea shown at Osaka-Expo 1970 Korean Pavilion. This Chugu-ji Miroku is characterized by its hairdo of two round topknots (atop which was real crown); Koryu-ji has unembellished simple wood crown. Both probably portray Shaka (Gautama) as boy, or before becoming Buddha was thus Buddha-to-be, Messiah. Pose of both similar to Rodin's *Thinker* but these are true art: one can make toilet jokes of Rodin's, not of these, of any great art. Both probably carved by Koreans in first years of Buddhism in Japan. Flanking Miroku, which nunnery calls Nyoirin Kannon Bosatsu, are attendants Ashuku (L), Yakushi (R) nyorai. Nunnery originates with mother of Shotoku and even today chief is Imperial princess, if only nominal nun.

FLOWER DATEBOOK: *Sazanka* **Dec-Feb**; Globe Flower *Yamabuki* **late Apr-May**.

(From here, **adventurer** might hike on to *Hokki-ji, Horin-ji, Matsuo-ji*, p364).

DAI-HOZO-DEN (Sacred Treasury), museum gallery wherein thousand-odd Horyu-ji top treasures are superbly displayed in comfortable setting which is peaceful, quiet and, even on hottest days, refreshingly cool. See this with us open to INTRODUCTION chapter (pp22–31) as guide to images.

Kudara Kannon (NT), Jay's favorite in small end room in corner in immense glass case, 2.1m/6ft10in, physically resembles Wendy Hiller of 1950 movie *I Know Where I'm Going*, and exemplifies that expression. Quite Greek in proportion, long waist, longer legs (head-navel-foot ratio 3:5), head barely eighth total height like caricature of fashion model, yet exquisite as no model is, even few if any Greek statues. Her body, slightly arched in shallow *S*, appears about to soar heavenward. How often on hot summer day has Jay sat on floor in corner admiring her, letting crowd surge thru, leaving timeless silence in their wake. With Goethe: "Merely glancing at an object does not enhance one's understanding of it. Only by looking again and again can one develop that degree of contemplation that leads to meditation and final involvement". Take time.

Six Kannon images in wood, beautiful child-faces suggest later Gothic statuary as well as older clays of Tun Huang, Central Asia. Drapes on arms are ancient Persian symbol once denoting kingship, here mark sacredness.

Hyaku-man-to case of bottle-size towers of turned wood, their 'antenna' removable like plugs to allow access to printed scrolls within, world's first printed books these 'million-towers'—indicating size of first edition.

Tama-mushi 'jewel-bug' shrine in last room, tabernacle to Buddhist altar some 2.3m/7ft8in small house upon pedestal with openwork bronze laid over thousands of wings of electric-blue jewel-beetles. Painting on face and ends of pedestal of bodhisattva's self-sacrifice are mix of late Han Chinese and earlier Parthian styles, flying angels on face like those in Iran.

This fabulous complex of masterpieces within masterpieces was built by migrant Koreans, who in Kongju across Korean Straits had just built complex quadruple size of this with 9-storey pagoda over double Horyu-ji's height—long since gone. Master artists among them were 'naturalized' and honored (in 9th century one-third or more of nobility claimed Chinese or Korean ancestry, if Imperial clan concealed theirs). But laborers upon completion were declared unclean, some even untouchable and never allowed in to worship: tho this may not have happened till Koreaphile Shotoku died and chauvinistic Soga came back. Oh, well, nothing changes!

FLOWER DATEBOOK: As at nearby Horin-ji, Hokki-ji, rape *na-no-hana*, **end Mar-early Apr**; *sakura*, **late Mar-mid Apr**; Chinese milk-vetch, *renge-so*, **Apr**.

Detail from lost Mural

1km N and E of Chugu-ji is...
HORIN-JI, founded 621 by Shotoku's ill-fated son, unanswered prayer for father's recovery. Lovely 3-storey pagoda in Horyu-ji-style ca621-650, rebuilt after lightning struck in 1944. Main buildings blown down 1645, rebuilt 1737. Long building rear houses fine statuary: shoes into rack, if L door closed, ring bell, await admittance to fireproof Kondo: 8am-5pm. Offer ¥200 at desk, needed for maintainance.

Central standing piece, **11-faced Kannon**. Note fat neck, double chins —typical of Heian period: 3.7m/12ft high of single block with gorgeous 14ft halo single plank; colors on halo and sarong still vivid, tho include Meiji era restoration. Flanking are two exquisite painted-wood Asuka period pieces: remaining color mostly century-old restoration. To L, seated figure appears to be Amida by pose with 'fear-not' and 'giving' hand signs, but is

Yakushi, Medicine Buddha; while on R looking like standard Medicine Buddha offering bottle of balm is Kannon, called here Kokuzo, 'national guardian', 7th century. All ICA and deserving of promotion.

HOKKI-JI (500m, 10-15min walk E of Horin-ji) was also originally nobleman's palace, converted to temple 638 as dying wish of Shotoku. National treasure 3-storey pagoda built 686, rebuilt 706, oldest remaining.

FLOWER DATEBOOK: Rape, *na-no-hana*, late Mar-early Apr.

MATSUO-DERA, 45min walk above Chugu-ji into hills; drive winding road as we did, to come to 'Parking Lot #3', immense but empty indicating seasonal tour traffic to temple to *Yaku-doshi* jinx-year purification. Most reckon 4 *yaku*-jinx years each for men–women, but this temple treats sexes alike with *dai-yaku* big jinx at ages 2,7,9,13,17,25,33,37,41-43,45,47,57,61,73,85 and *sho-yaku* little ones at 1,15,19,22,27,29,39,49,59,65. Temple has little of antique interest atop its 99 steps but for main object of worship, 11-headed, 1,000-arm, 1,000-eye **Kanzeon Bosatsu**, secret Buddha closed in on main altar behind Shinto mirror and shown once yearly Nov 3. Founded mid-9th century by En-no Gyoja noted ascetic, Shingon tantric sect retaining strong Shinto element. Numerous small stone Buddha images around red torii behind *kondo* and Kanzeon Bosatsu is referred to by staff as temple *kami*, Shinto for god. Cement-'log' bonfire pit is to burn old talismans. Big bell can be rung: drop coin in box, pull log rope back, thrust forward, jerk back on contact to keep note clear. Nice at cherry blossom time, when we went; otherwise not much but scenery and serenity and bell to ring.

JIKO-IN (4km/2.5mi from Horyu-ji toward Yamato-Koriyama, en route Yakushi-ji) is exquisite domestic-type temple in epitomal Edo tea style, 1663, more like fine mansion. Rare for Nara, fine garden, viewed from main rooms thru open shoji, trees block out low-rise detritus of 20th century so that lovely hills of Yamato are captured as extension of very private enclosed garden of moss and maples. Much as tea master KATAGIRI Sekishu designed it 4 centuries ago.

GETTING THERE: Direct from Kintetsu Koriyama stn, bus #23, 24; about hourly 9:00-15:00, 25min, ¥310. But most of us will walk back from Chugu-ji, perhaps even detouring bit as we've oft done thru eternally unchanging vehicle-free backstreets to Horyu-ji Treasury above. Bus to NARA frequent, from hiway below entry to Horyuji.

NARA WEST SIDE NISHI-NO-KYO

BETWEEN Horyu-ji and Nara, in what was then west side of capital, Nishi-no-kyo, are several lovely temples which also fall between them in time. Where rice fields intervened between them and downtown in 1964 is now excavation revealing immense ground plan of this ancient capital's center.

Recommended are YAKUSHI-JI and TOSHODAI-JI, pleasant 10min walk apart, each few minutes from Nishi-no-Kyo Stn on Kintetsu line. From Horyu-ji, it's 10km taxi (5-6x-mtr); or bus #52, 60, 97, 98 to either. From Nara-Kintetsu or JR stns, also bus #63, or 10min walk from Kintetsu Kashihara line, Nishino-kyo stn.

KORIYAMA (bus #52, 97, 98), worth short look for here is center of Japan's goldfish-raising industry, greatly reduced since 1964 but still some: thruout Japan in summer you'll see men in great umbrella-shaped sedge hats waddling along with strange gait (won't slosh fish out), shouldering horizontal pole with wooden tub at each end full of live goldfish which they sell door to door. Trans-Pacific jets now carry Koriyama goldfish live across world. Reached also by bus tour, taxi course from NARA (*see* GETTING AROUND).

Capital city of FUJIWARA (after which great PM dynasty later took its name, to pass it on in turn to period in Kyoto) was first built 688 some 25km/15mi away at Asuka, but found not suitable for Japanese dreams. In 708 existing buildings were moved to new location of Heijo, and guardian temples were set up on its flanks, **Sai-dai-ji** to *west* and **To**-dai-ji of Great Buddha to *east*, many others within this area. Great grid was laid out on Chinese pattern after Chang-an (modern Xian), in turn based on Sasan Persian paradise garden-palace plan. (Garden-palace of Narenjestan which we restored in Shiraz, Iran was this same plan in microcosm.)

YAKUSHI-JI

Temple of Healing Buddha is worth visit if only for pagodas—and lovely duplicate Yakushi Triads. Founded in Asuka, 680, by emperor Temmu supplicating recovery of empress. She recovered, he died, she ruled as Jito and dedicated temple 697. Moved here with establishment of new city of Heijo, not moving actual buildings, but rebuilding on grander scale.

Pagoda (NT) alone remains of original (40m/131ft) erected at time of founding of Nara, 720– but it may be older as one tradition has it transferred from previous site in Asuka, to this site which was then well within new city limit. Tho six roofs, it is three double-storeys. Formerly one of pair, other of which (W) only foundation platform remained until exquisite replica erected in 1981. Previous temples had single pagoda in straight N-S axis with *Kondo-Kodo* reflecting central role of Sakyamuni as human-personal focus of faith, and whose relic traditionally reposed in pagoda. Horyu-ji put *Kondo* and 5-storey pagoda side by side as equals, but Yakushi-ji gave rule to *Kondo* showing new popular dominance of enshrined Healing (or other) Buddha, now guarded by two pagodas, each demoted to 3-storeys. *Sorin* 'TV antenna' atop still has nine rings, but pinnacle orb is diminished and between orb and rings is great openwork bronze flame decorated with angel-musicians like those on Horyu-ji *kondo* canopies. Indeed, whole pagoda and enclave has been likened to musical composition, and fact that now true music enters from all over mainland, symphonic *gagaku* replacing cacaphonic vaudevilley *gigaku*, both imports.

KONDO, Golden Hall, (rebuilt 1976) is focus: on marble dais and bronze base is **Yakushi Triad**—Healing Buddha in center, Gekko-Moonlight Bosatsu on its L, Nikko-Sunlight Bosatsu on R, (NT). It's odd how with several representations of this pair of celestial light bodhisattvas, that of moonlight is always softer, more appealing. Demonic dwarfs peering out of portals in base are among most popular pieces of Japanese art, usually said to represent Tsuchigumo (Earth Spider People)–of whom we'll hear more in Hokkaido. In fact this motif of sacred-atop-monster is almost universal Asian art symbol, going back to Gilgamesh epic in Ur, representing not primitives, but primitive desire which one must quell. Reputed date 726.

KODO, Lecture Hall, for years closed to public except on special request but now thankfully open, has almost identical Triad of mysterious origin. May be unsuccessful earlier casting. It is said it was abandoned in nearby woods for several centuries as there are no records of it pre-1500, tho it is stylistically contemporary to Triad in *Kondo*. **Painting** of Kisshoten, (NT), shown here in confessional period **Jan 1-15**.

In **garden** interesting stone engraving of early 7th century represents **footprint of Buddha** (NT) popular south Asian Hinayana (smaller vehicle) 'relic'; 47cm, with *Horin* ovals of true teaching engraved on sole.

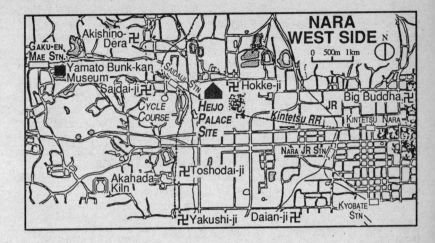

TOIN-DO, East Hall (NT), lovely 13th century (orig 721, rebuilt 1285) boasts lovely larger-than-life-size **Sho-Kannon** (NT) (188cm/6ft2in) carved about 700-710, with traces of Indian Gupta (4-7c) lithesomeness and roundness as translated thru Chinese intermediary, "divinity thought out in human form". Four guardian king images, painted wood, not especially well sculpted, but their color in superb condition (we have seen none other as good) shows us what much of brilliantly painted sculpture looked like in its own time–in this case, late 8th century. Much faded since our first edition of 1964 was written due to bleaching by movie lights in 60s. Also in *Toin-do* (shown only **Jan 1-15** in KONDO, here **Oct 22-Nov 3**), small 30x60cm (1x2ft) painting on hemp of Kichijo-ten, goddess of learning and peace, which with "woman under a tree" in Shosoin are only extant examples of Nara era paintings, which is to say painting of T'ang Chinese style. (Similar painting from central Asia now hangs in Hakone museum.) There is also 12th century portrait painting on silk, of Jion-daishi. Building now used as Zen meditation hall, oldest in country.

SHOPPING: At gate, Harry Shepherd sells cheap Buddhist curios sun, hol.

FLOWER DATEBOOK: Cherry *sakura*, late Mar–mid Apr.

CHOPSTICKS: Across temple parking lot, lovely building with collection of stone lanterns rear is **Van Kio**, excellent lunches from ¥1600, most around ¥3,500; for 3+ advise order 'family tables'. Noted for its hot stone steam cooking, viands like venison, boar etc, mixed Western-Japanese meals but all excellent. Owner Nishigami speaks flawless English; also sells and ships those stone lanterns; and art on walls including top antique and recentartists. Presents **Bugaku** free in garden some pleasant evenings: ☎(0742)-33-8942.

HACHIMAN SHRINE (50m beyond South Gate) with images of Hachiman, god of scythe and sword, as priest, another as 'Napoleoness'-Empress Jingo invader of Korea, and as Empress Nakatsuhime—all NT. 'War(rior) God' of Nara era mainland immigrants (ideographs for name also read as *Ya-hata* are equated by some with 'terrible swift sword' aspect of *Yahweh*-Jehovah); main Hachiman shrine is in Usa, Kyushu (p.770), and great shrine of Kamakura (p.217) is one. Building rebuilt 1603.

TOSHODAI-JI

T'ang dynasty China (618-935), its sole remaining building. Our visit takes us over 500 miles in 500 meters. Set in this museum of architecture of Nara, Japan: we have Chinese temple pavilion, Chinese palace, its fully natural-ized Japanese version, and superb *azekura* log cabin storehouse as known across Central Asia to Iran's Caspian Sea south shore, here similar tho smaller than famed Shosoin.

Built after peak of Nara period saw Todai-ji erected (this fifty years is whole epoch after Yakushi-ji), this late Nara masterpiece was built for blind T'ang (Jpn *To*) emigré monk Ganjin 759: thus name means T'ang monastery. Public health must have improved for Medicine Buddha is no longer center of worship. Now microcosm revolves around central Vairocana-Roshana (Jpn: *Dainichi*, Great Light) as with Great Buddha in TODAI-JI, ultimate and original Buddha, exemplifying rise of central authority with emperor, son of sons of sun, Dai Nichi's counterpart on earth in Nara.

Entering, KONDO is seen first, pure T'ang temple with fantastic soaring eaves overhanging. Original roof was half height of present (keep in mind how Japanese prefer soaring spires, imagine how subsequent repairs modi-fied it) and this overhang must have given original temple appearance of phoenix about to take off in flight. In China this upturn evolved till in Ming dynasty eave curled up like Persian harem shoe. Apparent motion is further accentuated by diminishing spans between 8 pillars from center out.

Statuary in great KONDO show continental grandeur, masculinity and perfection of technique far beyond contemporary (759) works elsewhere: indicates they were executed by Chinese craftsmen under sculptor Ssu-t'o (Jpn: Shitaku) in entourage of temple founder, Chinese archbishop Ganjin.

Central piece is...
Roshana Buddha of Light, 3.3m/ 11ft high seated on 2.4m/8ft pedestal, largest hollow dry-lacquer sculpture extant, as Great Buddha Roshana is largest bronze. Halo contains 1,000 Buddhist images and walls of hall retain slight traces of original paintings of 2,000 more, together representing Lotus (total) Universe over which Roshana is Lord.

To L is...
1,000 armed Kannon (with literal Chinese count of 42 large and 911 small arms, unlike Japanese 42 shorthand suggestion), 5.4m/18ft high, dry-lacquer on wood, phantasm. This largest 1,000-arm Kannon was supposedly created by heavenly messenger during ten-day fog. To R of Roshana is 3.6m/12ft, dry-lacquer on solid wood **Yakushi** of same period: strange in that its hand symbols are not those usual for Yakushi and so is believed to be in more ancient lost iconography. Other sculpture in KONDO and adjoining buildings are also typically T'ang Chinese. Shitaku introduced technique of carving large image from single block of wood, subsequently known as Toshodai-ji style and which soon became standard. All statuary NT.

In back is longer building...
KODO originally audience hall of Nara Palace, built in pure T'ang style, tho also simplified and slightly scaled down in process of repairs over centuries. R of these two truly Chinese buildings at R angles to them is...

Priests' residence, perfect example of what Japanese will do to formal Chinese building to give it homey Japanese touch, make it more livable: Kamakura era, as is also bell tower. Behind this, two large log cabins with shingled roofs, world's most beautiful air-conditioned storehouses, best example of which is Shosoin in Nara City of about same date, but not always viewable. Yes, air-conditioned for lay of logs allows for year-round air temperature stability of some few percent: logs of triangular cross section laid on edge swell in humidity to close space between them thus closing in dry air, then shrink in dry air allowing air exchange between logs.

Kaisando (Founder's Hall) behind-R KODO, long held portrait statue of temple founder Ganjin (Chin: Chien-chien). Now relocated to newer...

Mieido (Hon Shadow Hall) to rear. That this ethereal dry-lacquer portrait statue of Ganjin, to us finest portrait image anywhere (80cm/32ins), is no one-shot freak is borne out by contemporaries in HORYU-JI YUMEDONO. Invited to Japan because young country lacked great ranking bishop, banned from leaving China by emperor (as too valued), driven back at least five times by storms and shipwrecks which killed many of his entourage, his perseverance cost him his health and his eyes. One aide who arrived with him in 753 known only by his Chinese name Li Mi I, was Persian, doctor of natural pharmacopeia, perhaps originally Zoroastrian, original worshippers of 'Roshana' as Sun or Light. Statue dates to 763, year Ganjin died; can be seen only **June 5,6,7.**

FLOWER DATEBOOK: Camelia-*tsubaki*, **late Mar-early May**; lotus-*hasu* **July**; bush clover *hagi*, **late Aug-early Oct.**

Especial beauty of Toshodai-ji and Yakushi-ji is that they are often devoid of tourists, and even when moderately crowded seem not so as they were designed to absorb pilgrim mobs. Quoting Langdon Warner opening:

...instead of exercising one's fallible imagination in trying to bridge thirteen centuries and recreate Horyu-ji or Todai-ji or Yakushi-ji monastery where I sat, the more rewarding method was to abandon so doubtful a process and, quite simply, to exist in the ambient air for deep weeks at a time. Gradually it came to pass that there was no rupture in the eighth century thread when it came time to board the little steam train for its twenty-minute trip to my inn, nor need to dodge the troops of Japanese trippers who clustered there. The space within which I moved was that of those ancient times.... Twelve hundred years ago Shotoku Taishi himself had taken no longer to walk from his Golden Hall to the great statue in the Yumedono than I took along his very path, seeing the same things as I went.

AKAHADA KILN: At Furuse bus from Nishinokyo stn W and N → Akahada-yama bus stop, **taxi** basic-mtr; walk 20min. Kiln-shop-home of FURUSE GYOZO, 7th generation descendant of 16th century reviver of 7th century traditional local red-ware (*aka-hada*) pottery, found plentiful in excavations of nearby original capital site. Clay from near Toshodai-ji at Akahada-yama (mount). Revived by ancestor FURUSE Jihei 400 years ago by order of Lord Toyotomi of nearby Koriyama Castle, for tea ceremony use, so family still uses Toyotomi *mon* seal. Present popularity due mostly to master MASUDA Katsuya, who also helped get TACHIKUI (*see* after KOBE) now-popular kilns going again, postwar.

Here are 3 *nobori-gama* (climbing kilns) of different sizes, and which original site undoubtedly did not have, as introduced from Korea 15-16th century. Note roof, dome of round plug cone bricks. Visit workshops: wheel here electric now as almost everywhere. Need 10 men to run big kiln. Fire with red pine fuel to 1260-1300° for 2-3 days, cool off 2 days. Front chambers used for high-oxidizing firing, top chamber for low oxygen reduction firing. Note glazing on kiln chamber ceilings, natural from ash. Grey-white wares tomb-ware type, clay contains kaolin, frit and rice straw ash. Prices are reasonable, quality is top, nice folks—will pack to ship, handle takkyu-bin to your Japan base. ☎(0742)-43-6115.

DAIAN-JI temple: E on road Yakushi-ji ↔ Toshodai-ji 15min, cross tracks. Also bus from Nara JR stn 3.5km (or continue on way → Nara). Opp direction of Akahada kiln, not convenient to see both unless bus or drive Nara → Daian-ji → Yakushi-ji, etc.

Minor interest for temple hikers. Established 745; sculpture within much like older at Toshodai-ji, mostly carved from solid block of wood rather than joined or hollow dry lacquer. 4 Guardian Kings, worn away to point where it accentuates their power. Some believed to be enlargements of miniature sandalwood prototypes brought from China, perhaps by Ganjin. These miniatures are sole wooden images that were not brilliantly painted.

SAIDAI-JI temple, Great West (*sai-*) Guardian to capital, matching east (*to-*) side Todai-ji; built 769. 10min walk from Kintetsu Saidai-ji stn, now of little interest and hard to get to, mere shadow of former glory, but for some fine statuary. Ongoing archaeological excavation in courtyard revealing original ground plan and water ditches, foundations of former greatness.

Museum Yamato Bunkakan: 2km walk, or Kintetsu local from Saidai-ji 2 stops → Osaka-Namba-wards (4th from Nara) → Gakuen-mae stn, off, then short walk SE; **drivers** find adequate parking. 10am-5pm, ¥300; X-mon, 12/28-1/4, few days at exhibition changes; free films alternate suns 2pm. Built and owned by Kintetsu. Rarity in being devoted not to any special art or archaeology but simply to beauty, and its exhibitions, about 8 changes per year including 2 loan or traveling shows, while uneven are always worthwhile—above average, some exceptional. Architecture by YOSHIDA Isoya is classical Japanese sense in modern medium, square donut surrounds interior bamboo grove flooding interior with natural light, set in lovely old pine grove pond garden (pond sadly poisoned by runoff from neighboring fields?).

Hiking Course: Toshodai-ji → Yakushi-ji → Akahada Kiln → Saidai-ji = 5km/3mi. Horyu-ji → N is maze of well-marked courses thru **Yata Prefectural Park**, *Kenritsu Yata Koen*. Good map *Hiking Course-Ikaruga* free from Nara Kotsu Bus or Kintetsu Rail, in Japanese but easy to follow, tho best taken shared with fellow-student guide—consult Nara guide-info desk.

OUT OF WAY: Farther W towards Osaka, easily reached from OSAKA out of Namba or Tennoji stns on Kintetsu line for KASHIHARA (tomb area), or 4 stns W of latter. **Rail Pass users** from Osaka take JR from TENNOJI → OJI where change to train for SAKURAI, 4 stops to GOIDO, taxi 3x-mtr, or bus. For those encamped near HORYU-JI, JR → OJI, then as preceding, *for*...

TAIMA-DERA

Treasures here are woven picture of Amida's Paradise and sole pair of original 8th century 3-storey pagodas. Main Mandala Hall is 12c remodeling of basic 8c T'ang style (thus its 'bird-in-flight' eaves). Lecture Hall similar Kamakura (12c) is archaic-style reconstruction by Minamoto patrons. Fine Miroku image in clay, 4 guardians in dry lacquer. Anarchic layout of buildings first example of Japanese departure from Chinese ground plans. Pagodas off to side marked originally planned entry from S, which proved not practical due to hilly land, so plan was abandoned and construction was 'ad-libbed' to suit both irregular terrain and naturalistic bent of native Japanese, seemingly chaotic but pleasant aesthetic.

Tea room noted for its round doorway. Presently functioning room built by Sekishu, mid-17c, of Sekishu School of tea based nearby at JIKO-IN Temple (p365) which is popular tea-stop on bus and taxi tours.

PERSONAL DATEBOOK: *Nerikuyo matsuri* May 14, 4pm; Dramatic 8th cent gigaku-like procession of masked and brilliantly costumed celestials.

Perhaps never in all history were people so conscious of what they lacked, materially and spiritually, so avid to receive it, or so capable to make use of it, as were the Japanese in the middle of the 6th century... –Langdon Warner

NARA 奈良
CITY IMPERIAL

EVERYONE DOES NARA WRONG! Standard run is taxi, train or bus from Kyoto morning, return evening exhausted, out fortune in taxi fare, having seen next to nothing. Nara deserves better: it is tourism's big sleeper. If you see Nara at all—and we think you should—minimum is overnite sleep-in with full day of comfortable sightseeing, continuing on next eve or second morning by train or even taxi to KYOTO or train to MT KOYA Monastery. Better yet, use Nara with fine hotel or inn as base for further adventuring around Yamato Plain in reverse of preceding chapters.

No one can laze thru **Nara Park** without being affected by its almost erotic beauty. We discovered it one drizzly autumn afternoon and still think such seemingly unlikely time and weather best. We have walked in middle of summer and winter nites, alone but for ghosts of past conversing around us in what we later learned were eerie nite calls of park deer. Nara *is* Nara Park. This green space is larger than urban area, our present city is but corner of original 8th century metropolis, some 90% of which now lies underground leaving remaining temples islands in sea of rice paddy, new housing or immense new archaeological excavation. Drive or stroll thru maze of Nara Park has always been our favorite; spread out enough that vehicle is desirable (taxi advised, private cars banned in season) yet small enough for those strong of calf. Snaking thru park paths is adventure and you are more than likely to get lost and stumble on exciting byways you'd have passed over relying solely on any guide book.

Since Kyoto's big temple shut-out of 1985-6, Nara has been promoting itself as major tourist stop of area, and justly so. It has almost as much to see as Kyoto (more if Yamato environs included), greater variety and perhaps in better atmosphere as it has avoided self destruction of Kyoto which has seen art-historical sites destroyed by even Bank of Japan that USAF bombers and Army of Occupation forces made efforts to save—and worse, mass plastification of old neighborhoods in manner no other cultural preservation-conscious city would tolerate. Good luck lovely Nara.

On our historical-chronology routing, we arrive in Nara for supper after Tenri sundown services. Following 'conventional' tourist rut from Kyoto, we repeat, come in evening, at dusk taxi up to **Nigatsudo** platform, admire view, then stroll down to your hotel or inn—especially if romantic duo!

As for name, if Yamato with its odd ideographs is enigma, 'Nara' is pure puzzle. It has no meaning in itself, is named after nowhere or no one else, has no prototype in Korea or China, it just 'is'. First literary reference, according to our old teacher late PY Saeki, is 8th century poem mentioning "nara-no-kawa", "Nara-river". Saeki maintained that foreign words in old Japanese were usually used in pair with translated local equivalent, so this indicates 'nara' was foreign word meaning 'river'. Most Near Eastern languages, whether Aryan Persian or Urdu or Semitic Hebrew or old Syriac have word for river approximating this, sometimes with 'L', *nula*, some 'R', *nara*. Indicating again Near East immigrant factor in early Yamato.

GETTING THERE

AS ALTERNATES to historical route, access from nearby hubs: **TOKYO** → Shinkansen → Kyoto then as below; or join **JTB Tours: 2-day** ¥64,/67,/80,000 according to 2nd class or green car rail and hotel level, take in Nara half-day on 2nd day; various **3-day** ¥77,/83,600/97,000 same variants, see Nara 3rd day full-day as below. **NAGOYA** → 2hr30min direct JR express, 2hr20min Kintetsu scenic, quick change Yagi. **OSAKA** → best Kintetsu from Namba (subway) or JR-loop-Ueroku *tokkyu* exp 32min, 1x-hr, *kyuko* 40min, 3x-hr; **railpass** users JR from Tennoji on loop, exp 33min; **KYOTO** → Kintetsu from S-side Kyoto stn *tokkyu* 33min 2x-hr; JR local 58min.

We recommend, if traveling to/from KYOTO, alt break midway at **MAMPUKU-JI** temple for Buddhist lunch (*see* KYOTO p463, or following WHERE NEXT, details).

Bus Tours: JTB Sunrise tour: half-day KYOTO → Todai-ji → Deer Park → Kasuga return; dep after 1pm most major hotels, last pickup New Miyako (S of stn) 13:35, ¥5,670/kids4,640. Fujita **half-day** pm, ¥5,670/kids¥3,910; similar to Sunrise tour but uses Kintetsu train between Kyoto and Nara. MK **Taxi** from Kyoto 8hr 5psgr ¥34,610 (Lincoln ¥67,980)), E-spkg driver available.

Driving: ill-advised Nara proper, parking expensive, often full; hi-season Apr-May & Oct-Nov private cars **banned**, anti-'My Car' (*mai-kah*) signs abound. Leave at hotel and hoof Park; drive → Horyu-ji, Tenri, any outlying temples, where adequate parking.

WHERE TO STAY

QUICKY from Kyoto made sense once as few rooms except echoing old, to us magnificent **Nara Hotel** ☎(0742)-26-3300; classic now enlarged—still prefer high-ceiling old wing, rooms w/park view get traffic noise, am, inner rms no view, quiet. 1909 decadent elegance, ¥-lo-S-up (double least). New wing 'modern' comforts. Tea lounge, lovely view, X-6pm.

IN TOWN: Facing JR stn are **Nara International** and **New Iroha**; along Sanjo-dori shopping street are ¥-S chain hotels, well-run, convenient to Park & stns, no need taxi: **Miyako** ☎23-5544 at JR end of st; & **Fujita** ☎23-8111 midway (avail w/2); and btwn Sanjo-dori and Kintetsu stn **Kasuga H** ☎22-4031, Shosoin in concrete, attractive W. 1min W of Kintetsu stn on Hanakoji arcade, **People's Inn Hanakomichi** ☎23-8753, enter thru 100-year-old house to new multi-storey in rear; rm only ¥5,000 incl; popular w/gals. All w/W- & J-restaurants. Most 15-20% less Feb, some higher main school hols.

PARK: Around Sarusawa Pond fromW, all ryokans, most ¥-T-Sw/2: **Tempyo Hotel** ☎26-0200 (¥-T); **Uosa** ☎23-6035; **Yoshidaya H** ☎23-2225, bit cheaper annex **Yamatoji** ☎26-2225; **Ryokan Kosen** ☎23-3289; above pond on slope to Sanjo-dori **Daibutsu-kan** ☎23-5111; **Daimonji-ya** ☎26-2262; then **Kikusui** ☎23-2001, ¥-LL (¥35,000w/2+%)–w/fine W-restaurant for lunch-dinner, ¥-S, central opp torii; across Sanjo-dori st **Shikitei** ☎22-5531, ¥-Lw/2. **Petit Hotel** (pron *puchi*), small, above pond R in inn cluster, ¥5,000ea rm only, w/2+¥2,500 or ¥15,000w/2 all incl for couple; (has tearoom-rest'nt **Cotton 100%**). Nearby in park atop Sanjo-dori hill is **Edo-san** ☎26-2662, ¥-S, several cottages amidst park—deer pop in; dine only ¥7,000+%. Most serve seasonal dishes. block SE of pond Hotel **Sun Route** ☎22-5151, W, ¥-T rest'nts.

NARA-MACHI: Edo era houses below Sarusawa-no-Ike pond, our great find **Seikanso** ☎22-2670, ¥-B/¥3600 ea +¥700 bkfst, Economy J-Inn, English spoken, great inner garden like in samurai movies as it was bordello in olde days–take loop bus from stn to Kitakyobate, walk N up Mochidono-dori St 2min; or walk 15min from stns. Small inns like **Harishin** ☎22-2669, next street E, ¥6,500ea/incl-w/bkfst but only 6 rms (¥-T fine bento rest'nt 11-3pm). **Matsumae** ☎22-3686, S-side Sarusawa pond ¥-Tw/2. Other ¥-P-or-B inns nearby. Great neighborhood walks esp Aug weekend eves. Below pond **Nodaya Minshuku** Ima Mikado-cho, also good lunches, soba light pilgrim fare.

TEMPLE STAY: Gango-ji ☎23-1377, rsv, prefer return postcard, ¥-lo-Bw/bkfst.

¥-P/B: Opp Gango-ji E gate **Nitta Ryokan** ☎22-2714, most sgl, rm ¥3,800ea, +bkfst opt. City **International Seminar House**, J,W-bkfst opt, 7rms, ☎23-5821.

ABOVE SHOSOIN: Hotel Yamato Sanso ☎26-1011 ¥-Sw/2; romantic eve walk.

Book thru TIC Sanjo-cho (9-9pm), both Nara stns, or direct. If stuck, another cluster of new ¥-S hotels at Shin Omiya, 2nd stop from Kintetsu stn, taxi 2x-mtr from park.

HOME STAY enquire **Nara International Federation** ☎22-1101 ext 2742.

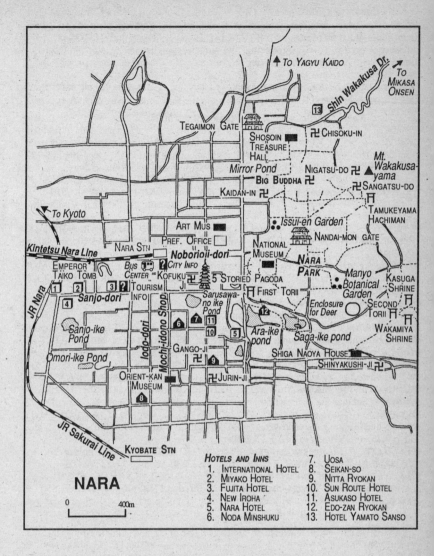

To Yagyu Kaido

Shin Wakakusa Dr.

To Mikasa Onsen

13

Tegaimon Gate

卍 Chisoku-in

Shosoin Treasure Hall

Mirror Pond

Nigatsu-do 卍

Mt. Wakakusa-yama

Big Buddha 卍

卍 Sangatsu-do

Kaidan-in 卍

To Kyoto

Tamukeyama Hachiman

Issui-en Garden

Nandai-mon Gate

Art Mus

Pref. Office

Nara Stn

Noborioji-dori

National Museum

Nara Park

Kintetsu Nara Line

Bus Center

City Info

Manyo Botanical Garden

Kasuga Shrine

Emperor Taiko Tomb

Kofuku-ji

5 Storied Pagoda

Tourism Info

First Torii

Second Torii

JR Nara

1   2   3   ?

Sarusawa-no ike Pond

Sanjo-dori

4

Enclosure for Deer

11   7

6

Wakamiya Shrine

Sanjo-ike Pond

Jodo-dori

10

5

Ara-ike pond

Saga-ike pond

Omori-ike Pond

Gango-ji 卍

12

9

Shiga Naoya House

Mochi-idono Shop

Shinyakushi-ji 卍

Orient-kan Museum

卍 Jurin-ji

8

JR Sakurai Line

Kyobate Stn

NARA

0   400m

HOTELS AND INNS	
1. INTERNATIONAL HOTEL	7. UOSA
2. MIYAKO HOTEL	8. SEIKAN-SO
3. FUJITA HOTEL	9. NITTA RYOKAN
4. NEW IROHA	10. SUN ROUTE HOTEL
5. NARA HOTEL	11. ASUKASO HOTEL
6. NODA MINSHUKU	12. EDO-ZAN RYOKAN
	13. HOTEL YAMATO SANSO

Tourist Info: Nara City TIC, Kintetsu Stn ☎24-4858; Nara JR Stn ☎22-9821; City Tourist Ctr in local exhibit hall Sanjo-dori mid shop area at SW corner Jodo-dori– 9am-9pm, some English till 3pm, ☎22-3900; also Sarusawa-no-Ike Pond ☎26-1991. All others open 9am-5pm daily.

GETTING AROUND

Best way to do park in '60s was by *ricksha*. Best for park if weak of calf is **taxi** to KASUGA SHRINE top of Park, walk down; or keep taxi. Show him map above, mark places you wish him to stop (*see* WALKING TOUR p374).

   Guides: *free* thru YMCA ☎(0742)-44-2207; or **Student Guide** HQ in TIC below park above Sarusawa-pond ☎26-4753. All ask call day ahead. No fee or tip, buy lunch, cover all cash outlays; take name–address of guide, send Xmas card, perhaps small gift from home. We use them often, vouch for these dedicated and professional caliber guides.

Bus Pass: Nara–Nishi-no-Kyo (W) → Ikaruga (Horyu-ji) area, ¥1,350 whole day; Asuka → Tsubosaka-dera Temple area ¥700day; entire Nara–Yamatoji-plain ¥2,600 2 days **Nara Kotsu** good **bus tours** ☎(0742)-22-1171, 26-5501; Tokyo info ☎03-3281-7737. Inter-city (Horyu-ji, Tenri), sightseeing, and intracity loop bus (#1, 2) stops in front JR, Kintetsu Stns, TIC in either can direct to relevant side of plaza and numbered stand.

Bus Tours: Nara Kotsu also runs thrifty J-language (you've got us) bus tours from Nara stn, 5min later stop Kintetsu stn; some tours use E-tapes, small discount for couple.

(A1) *Nara Koen Meisho meguri*, 3hr30min hilites of Nara Park → TODAI-JI Big Buddha → KASUGA SHRINE up Kasuga scenic drive → Wakakusa Yama → *ju-koku dai* view & rest → KOFUKU-JI → Nara Stn end, ¥2,980 (*avoid* A2-dreamland park option unless with small kids who on all tours about half price), dep every 30min 8:15-10:15, then 11:15, 12:00, 13:00, 14:00 (may vary), from JR & Kintetsu Stns.

(B) *Nara-Horyu-ji Nishi-no-kyo meguri*, STNS → TODAI-JI Big Buddha → KASUGA with Treasure House, lunch → HORYU-JI → JIKO-IN tea → YAKUSHI-JI → TOSHODAI-JI; dep JR & Kintetsu Stns 9:00, hi-season (3/20-11/23) 10:00; 7hr, ¥5,870.

(C) *Horyu-ji Nishi-no-kyo meguri*, STNS → HORYU-JI → CHUGU-JI → JIKO-IN tea → YAKUSHI-JI → TOSHODAI-JI, daily 9:10, 10:10 hi-season 11:10; 5hr20min ¥5,080.

(D) *Heijo meguri*, STNS → HOKKE-JI garden → Heijo palace site → tea at SAIDAI-JI → Akahada-yama kiln → Yamato Bunka-kan Museum (if X-, KOFUKU-JI TREASURY alt) → TAKAYAMA CHASEN → end, 6hr30min, dep 9:40 year-round, ¥5,460.

(E1) *Jyoruri-ji Ikkyu-ji meguri*, STNS → IKU-JI → IWAFUNE DERA → JYORURI-JI → end, 4hr40min, dep 10:20 year-round, ¥4,130.

(E2) only IWAFUNE-DERA → JORURI-JI, 2hr30min, dep 9:20, 14:20 year-round, ¥2,300.

(F) *Asuka-Manyoshu meguri*, → KASHIHARA ARCHAEOLOGY MUS → ASUKA-DERA → OKA-DERA → ISHI BUTAI → TACHIBANA-DERA → TSUBOSAKA-DERA → end, 7hr30min, dep 9:10, ¥6,370.

(G) *Yamanobe Tohnomine*, STNS → Tenri Stn 9:55 → ISHIGAMI-JINGU → CHOGAKU-JI → Sakurai Stn 12:25 → ABE MONJU-IN → SHORIN-JI → DANZAN-JINJA → Sakurai Stn → Tenri Stn → end, 7hr, dep 9:30 year-round, ¥6,220.

(H1) *Kasuga-Okuyama meguri*, STNS → Wakakusa-yama → Kasuga-Okuyama Stone buddhas → Takamado-yama → BYAKUGO-JI → SHIN YAKUSHI-JI → end, 4hr, dep 9:25, 13:25 run 3/20-11/23, ¥3,260.

(H2) *Heijo Nishi-no-kyo meguri*, STNS → HOKKE-JI → Heijo palace site → TOSHODAI-JI → YAKUSHI-JI → end, 3hr, dep 13:30 run 3/20-11/23, ¥2,650.

(H3) *Nara no Yuhi sunset view*, STNS → TODAI-JI → SHINYAKUSHI-JI → Wakakusa-yama → Kasuga-Okuyama → end, 3hr, dep 17:30 run 7/20-8/31, ¥2,850.

JTB bus tours from Kyoto with **English-speaking** guide pm half-day Nara Park area only ¥5,700 hotel pickup in Kyoto.

Taxi Tours: Nara Kintetsu ☎(0742)-23-1181 or 22-5501: approx route bus–

(1) above A, 2hr, ¥8,240 or 9x-mtr per carload of 4 (vs bus ¥2,980 ea–so for 2 same).

(2) above B + small sites, 4hr ¥14,830 30x-mtr, and both 5hr30min 37x-mtr ¥17,900.

(5) *Manyo-drive course* up scenic drives and stone buddhas, 2hr, ¥8,240 or 18x-mtr.

(6) *Asuka Mei-sho meguri*, Asuka famous spots: Asuka Ancient History Museum → OKA-DERA → ISHI-BUTAI → Takamatsu-tomb → ASUKA BIG BUDDHA, environs (ask for ASUKA sex shrine, *see*) → around in Nara, 5hr30min, ¥23,380/45x-mtr.

(7) takes in outlying, lovely HASE-DERA → MURO-JI → TENRI, 5hr30min, ¥29,250 about 50x-mtr–save 25-30% taking it one way, either way, from Hase or Muro-ji → in or Nara → out.

There are others but these seem best. With **taxi** make own itinerary, above rates as guide—speed up or take more time at meter rate—most match bus rate for 3-4 people.

Bicycle: Kintetsu Stn **Sunflower Rent-a-cycle** 3 min W Konishi-dori shop'g St & JR Stn pkg lot **Eki Rent-a-car:** ¥720/4hrs, ¥1,030/day—2days (K'tsu only) ¥1,750. Saidai-ji or other JR & Kintetsu Stns—bike rentals facing, outlying have drop-off deals.

WALKING TOUR WITH TAXI LEG ALTERNATES

Map at most shops: YAMADA Hiromi *Pictorial Map of Nara*, informative, fine souvenir. Best freebie: *Nara City* by Nara City Tourist Office, English, good bus-stop details.

Full Walking Course, suggest start at Nara Hotel → SHIN YAKUSHI-JI → up Lover's Lane to gigantic **First-(*ichi-no*)-torii** on our R which marks entry to KASUGA WAKAMIYA SHRINE (where winter solstice rites begin) → KASUGA GRAND SHRINE along foot of Mount Wakakusa (shops) → TAMUKEYAMA HACHIMAN-SHRINE → SANGATSU-DO → NIGATSU-DO (best view sunset head on, or eve) → GREAT BELL → circle SHOSOIN → DAIBUTSU → via Nandai-mon Gate → Nara National Museum → KOFUKU-JI → Sarusawa Pond* → Hotel or either Stn. Walk down is under 3km/2mi, 40-50min nonstop, so time to allow worthwhile dallying for elapsed time 2hr but 3 better. Local **buses** parallel rte. *Possible add: after Sarusawa Pond S 5min to GANGO-JI thru newly promoted old NARA-MACHI feudal era merchant neighborhood with fine old domestic architecture, some good shops, good lunches, new developments, incl our private museum **Orient-kan** displaying Persian influence in early Nara (*see* below).

TILT: All but exacting art buff can cover this in morning for lunch Nara Hotel or in park or Nara-machi area. To complete Nara area in one rushed day (other than by our historical route), after lunch **taxi** to HORYU-JI with short stops at TOSHODAI-JI & YAKUSHI-JI (**bus** tour **B, C**; or **taxi 2** with extra stops at smaller nearby sites 4hrs– ¥14,830 ('91) or about 30x-mtr 4-psgr car, add 10% for 5-psgr *chugata*) reach Tenri about sundown to see dance rites, with return to Nara for dinner or back to Kyoto. To slash taxi, discharge at Horyu-ji and take bus back from front of Temple to either Nara Stn or Park.

WALK thru ichi-no-torii 'first torii' to Shrine, 400m to R turn, on L is entry to...
Manyoshu Gardens, *Manyo-shokubutsu-en* (9:00-16:30, July-Aug 8:30–, ¥200), 900 plants of 300 varieties mentioned in Nara era *Manyoshu* poetry anthology. Flowers most of year. Gagaku on stage on pond May 5, Nov 3.

Continue on thru Ni-no-tori, 2nd Torii, to...
KASUGA TAISHA (Spring Day Grand Shrine) in middle ages ranked in trio of main shrines of State Shinto with ISE and IWASHIMIZU HACHIMAN, Kyoto. Ancestral shrine of Fujiwara clan, founded *ca* 709 while Nara being built. Fujiwara (family name from that of previous capital) engineered, financed second move to Kyoto 784, eventually coming to dominate government and art so that 10th and much of 11th centuries called Fujiwara Period. Even after decline from ultimate power, until late emperor Showa they retained monopoly to provide brides for emperors: empress Dowager Nagako first non-Fujiwara, paving way for new empress Michiko, first non-noble. Thus KASUGA nickname, 'Shrine of Imperial Fathers-in-law'.

KASUGA SHRINE and KOFUKU-JI TEMPLE are inseparable. Four deities enshrined in Kasuga are guardians of Kofuku-ji. Architecture of Kasuga, tho Shinto, is heavily Buddhist- and Chinese-influenced, once had two great pagodas (originally Buddhist reliquaries) of its own identical to Kofuku-ji's. Relationship survived divorce of Buddhism and Shintoism 1867 and even today they cooperate in festivals. At *Setsubun Rite* (Feb 3) priests of two unite to expel demons from Kofuku-ji, while Kasuga lights its thousands of lanterns this nite as it does for Buddhist *Feast of Dead* Aug 14-15. Shrine brilliant vermilion, white plaster paneling, soaring curved tiled roof in grand Chinese Buddhist tradition of Palaces of Paradise—yet purely Japanese in how it blends with natural setting, rock glade mid giant ancient cryptomeria.

PERSONAL DATEBOOK: *Bugaku* on white gravel forecourt Jan 15, 1pm; Feb 3, 8pm (2 dances); Feb 11 (music—*gagaku*—only); May 5, 1:30pm (children dance) Shokubutsu-en Botanic Garden; Nov 3 Shokubutsu-en; Dec 17, 12am (midnite of 16), 4–10pm WAKAMIYA JINJA in park. These 2,700 bronze and stone lanterns are lit Feb 3 & Aug 15; while April courtyard immersed in wisteria; at anytime, for donation of ¥5,000 or more, shrine maidens will perform kagura on wooden forestage.

Most of buildings date to 10th-12th centuries, but old records indicate shrine has changed little since 8th century, except for 12th century addition of covered corridor in which bronze lanterns have since been collected. SW outer gallery is **small shrine** dedicated to Saruta-hiko (Monkey-god of Soil) who, legend goes, occupied area previous to present shrine, as he formerly did Ise. He agreed to lease 3 feet of earth to god Kashima. Celestial ancestral Fujiwara showed skill for which his earthly descendants became famous and during nite staked off 3 square leagues of present Park, claiming 'three feet' in contract meant depth of soil. In consequence, it is claimed no tree in park today roots more than three feet below surface. Sounds like prototype for Ogden Nash poem *The Japanese*: "...So sorry, this my garden now".

One Fujiwara celestial supposedly arrived riding on **deer**, thus they have sanctuary here over centuries, appear on shrine *mandala* (holy pictures). **Special wafers** to feed moochers (ask for *shika-senbei*) are sold thruout park and at temples by li'l old ladies. Also buy some fun *Shika-no-fun*, 'deer droppings', tasty local cookies for people, sold in many local shops. *Beware* big antlered bucks show off by butting visitors, especially autumn mating season—when all that can be caught by lariats are dehorned in rite **mid-Oct**. *Shika-yose* deer calling by trumpet, winter **thru Mar 18** X-NY, dly 10am.

Mount Kasuga, above shrine, is sacred virgin wood with fine hiking paths. Coming out of shrine then turning R, and next hill over is bare **Mount Mikasa**, popularly called Wakakusa-yama, burned off **Jan 15**. Leaving shrine, down one flight, is shrine **treasure house**, small museum with especially fine collection of ancient *bugaku* dance masks.

Shops along foot of Mt Wakakusa are interesting, carry better selection of usual souvenirs, sometimes curios.

600m or so beyond Kasuga Shrine, downhill, pass...
TAMUKEYAMA HACHIMAN SHRINE (lovely at maple season), branch of central one at Usa in Kyushu, and tutelary Shinto guardian of...

TODAI-JI EAST GREAT TEMPLE (NT)

Boasts world's biggest bronze statue: **Big Buddha**, *Daibutsu*, at foot of our hillside in gigantic temple with two golden horns on roof, right ahead. Originally flanked by pair of seven-storey pagodas, long gone, buildings here are all part of immense monastery compound of Todai-ji, one of our favorite sites, including National Treasures:

SAN-GATSU-DO (High Mass of 3rd Month Hall, also called HOKKE-DO) looks like photographic double exposure: its two halves built in 733 and 1199, former oldest building left in TODAI-JI, in all Nara. Both house fine collection of sculpture (12 NT) taking up historically where Horyu-ji begins to taper off. Main image is imposing, immense dry lacquer *Fuku-ken-satsu Kannon* as old as older hall. Its barbaric splendor is in powerful contrast to two accompanying figures, simple, staid Sunray *Nikko Bosatsu* and ideal beauty Moonbeam, *Gekko*, which two clay statues are masterpieces of Nara art. Moonbeam appears to float upon her name, always softer of this common pairing. Numerous attendant guardians: across rear L-R are trio of Nara clays, *Kichijoten*, *Shitsu-Kongojin* (secret, enclosed) and *Benzaiten*; flanking dais are *Bonten-Brahma* (R), *Taishaku-Indra* (L), and before them *Jizo* (R), wood Kamakura, and fierce *Fudo* (R), Muromachi; while vajra-guards Kongo and Missha flank dais front; and at corners *Shi-tenno* -four kings to total 16 images, mostly dry lacquer, some wood as noted) give us idea of sculptural 'court' which once attended bronze Big Buddha, tho those were far larger, as remaining pieces testify. Secret image is in closed altar behind central altar: *kongo* door guardian, shown only **Aug 2** and occasionally in spring and autumn, which because of this protection from light and dust retains its original 8th century brilliant colors.

KAIDAN-IN (Ordination Hall) just below (L) *Daibutsu*-Big Buddha, also houses some fine sculpture of this period (*see* below, following Big Buddha).

Pass thru lovely 12th century gate (built in Kamakura Era reconstruction) to...
NI-GATSU-DO (Hall of Second Month Mass), named for great festival of *Shuni-e* or *Mizutori* (Water Drawing) annual since origin **Mar 1-14** (climax 7pm-midnite **Mar 12** which is in 2nd month, Feb, by old calendar), one of Japan's most fascinating rites with its fiery tartar exorcism. Great stone steps up to temple set on piles against hillside is lined with offering lanterns, stone stelae 'receipts' marking cash donations of supporters. Present building is 1669 replacement in similar–much simpler–style to original of 752, which had survived other great holocausts. View is superb; golden horns of Daibutsu atop rooftops, trees mesmerize. Your fortune cast here considered especially auspicious, we never miss shaking bamboo tallies from octagonal tumbler– turn tumbler upside-down and shake stick out for attendant to read number and give you matching fortune slip. Kannon image enshrined here is so secret that even priests have not seen it for three centuries and it is not known how much damage it suffered in great fire of 1667. End of corridor around other side, seclusion hall wherein 11 monks participating in *Mizu-tori* rite undergo their severe purifications and 6x-daily somewhat masochistic rites to stay awake 3 weeks, (*see* DATEBOOK) fasting noon till dawn.

Hut at foot of piles is *Akaiya* mystery **wellhouse** counterpart to Temple of Eye in Tibetan quarter of Khatmandu, where like rite held every 12 years.

Street down R (N) end is our favorite for atmosphere of old Nara. Homes lining it belong to priests and retainers to temples. Usual descent is straight down from stone steps, down others past **SHI-GATSU-DO** (Meditation Hall of 4th Month). Great 34-ton **bell** is one of Japan's oldest (cast at same time as Big Buddha), 2nd largest (Chion-in, Kyoto boasts bell 4 ft/1.2cm taller, but 4in/1.6cm less across, cast 1633) and could be rung by anyone until tourist boom threatened millennial wear annually. Bottom of stairs is corridor wall of Daibutsu-Big Buddha, to which we return after this **DETOUR** illustrating René Grousset's "Nara...eastern terminus of Silk Road":

Around R to its rear and across open space to bring us to...
SHOSOIN, treasure repository of **TODAI-JI**, one of world's most fabulous buildings, our visit to which is trip not thru museum but thru time. Aura of timelessness pervades even quiet garden in which this simple hewn-log cabin stands. You cannot speak—if you must, only whispers issue forth.

One's first view upon entering fully enclosed garden is disappointing for you meet building end on and it appears small. Moving around to front, elevated structure slowly assumes appearance of immensity, solid grandeur. (This is present far view thru cement railings, between entry to Okuyama Driveway and Daibutsu). You may no longer enter building during annual autumn 'airing', as we did several times pre-1961. We recall climbing temporary wooden stairs, on thru one of three doors into one of three separate two-storeyed vaults. We felt like HG Wells' time traveler hurtling thru dry coldness of timelessness, for inside this engineering masterpiece temperature and humidity remain as constant as in any modern scientifically designed humidor. But tourist boom has been its bane. Tour bus diesel exhaust from nearby main highway seeping in necessitated 1961 moving treasures to new concrete SHOSOIN with its filtered air. Foreign visitor may enter grounds and see building from outside by asking at gatehouse, tho similar *azekura* style buildings, smaller single-section sizes, may be seen at temples, shrines in outlying districts (TOSHODAI-JI, p368).

Selection of treasures is exhibited annually **Nara Museum** new wing, **Oct 21-Nov 8**, should not be missed: Jay has been some 20 times, different objects every year. What impresses most about these fine articles is, first of all, their simplicity, almost humility; secondly their 'un-Japaneseness'.

They fall into four types: (1) **souvenirs** of Eye-opening Ceremony of Big Buddha, including such as brush used by visiting Indian bishop to paint on eye, counterpart to our wine-christening, magnificent masks of *gigaku* dancers (extinct form not to be confused with *gagaku*) include humorous caricatures of Sasanian Persians; (2) **armaments**, mostly sword and halberd blades presented as offerings; (3) **drugs** from all over Asia, for early Buddhist monks were medics, (early popularly-worshipped *Yakushi-nyorai*, 'medicine buddha' images offered elixir of life) and Shosoin was free medical clinic in memory of emperor Shomu by his widow Komyo until practice of medicine died out with immigrant doctors; (4) **personal household effects** of Shomu himself stored here after his death.

You stop in front of hammered silver table-tray (cat no 606), 8th century, strung with beads, floral border pattern, in center hammered goat with single circular antler–Persian. All thru entire collection Persian element stands out–in paintings on screens, in forms of ewers. Our **Orient-kan** museum expands upon study of this theme for those interested in interrelations. Abstract tapestry design built up in layers and executed in imitation of Indian monk's rag-pieced cape, spots worn in outer layers reveal new and different colors underneath. Another tapestry has fabulous history: when Chosroe First, Sasan Emperor of Persia, conquered Syria from Byzantium early 6th century he had famed weavers of area weave great victory tapestry. Justinian reconquered area for Byzantium, repeated tapestry order. Chosroe II later reconquered area for Persia and ordered third tapestry. One of these got to China in ensuing century after Arab conquest of Persian Empire. Weave was copied in China and/or Japan, and at least one remnant of those copies (or original?) is in Horyu-ji having been brought back as personal standard of Kobo Daishi—2 monochrome versions of this, probably simplified adaptations, are in Shosoin. (*see* Tatsumura Silk shops in hotels for modern re-reproductions on handbags, neckties, etc).

This Sasanid-T'ang-Nara period saw artistic unity in borderless internationalism. Asia as generalization was in mood it approached again only in era of Genghis Khan when united, by brute force, under single head.

Before we came to Japan, Jay's Chinese art professor said, "I envy you your trip, for Japan is museum of China". Shosoin shows it to be as much museum of all Asia—how truly international Nara-Japan was.

Some 350m to R, best seen on way to Kyoto as road passes in front of it...
TEGAIMON (Gate of Tegai-rite), one of few original structures of TODAI-JI, and with Chumon (center) Gate of Horyu-ji, sole remaining Nara Era gates—this is largest. Note its oddness in that it is festooned with *shimenawa*, sacred Shinto straw rope, marking off ritually pure area. This tells that thru this gate enters temple's Shinto guardian deity.

Straight ahead from Shosoin we round...(coming in from rear-side we will not pass thru main NANDAIMON GATE till we exit. If you come in from front, skip on ahead to Nandaimon description, p380). Direct from either Stn, 10min **bus**.

DAIBUTSU-DEN (Hall of **Big Buddha**) (NT) formal KONDO or main pavilion (¥300) is but bare wraith of original 8th cent colossus. Even corridor now less than half original. Building housing statue was originally 11 spans wide, or 12 pillars thus 11 spaces between—but has been reduced thru rebuildings to present 7. Floor space today is less than half that 12 centuries ago, height of building much lower. Even so, it is imposing, grand even on Chinese standards. Statistics for image itself atop pedestal quoted in part from admission ticket, only suggest immensity of production:

	NARA		(comparison with KAMAKURA)	
Height of Body	48ft 11in	15.0mtrs	37ft 7in	11.45mtrs
Length of Face	10' 6"	3.2	8' 5"	2.6
Length of Eye	3' 4"	1.02	3' 11"	1.3
Length of Ear	8' 4"	2.54	6' 6"	2.0
Length of Nose	4' 7"	1.42	3' 9"	1.15
Ht of nose Bridge	1' 7"	0.5	—	—
Length of Thumb	5' 5"	1.67	—	—
Height of Lotus	10' 0"	3.05	—	—
Weight	c.500 tons	500,000kg (437 tons bronze)		121T/121,000kg
Pure gold	288lbs	131kg (also 165 lbs/75kg mercury, etc)		

Built as charm against smallpox which had swept nation in 735, was undertaking of entire nation led by devout 45th emperor Shomu. He built public pharmacies, some drugs of which are preserved in *Shosoin*. Buddha was begun 737 near Lake Biwa, but casting failed and operation was moved to present location, at which time every province of empire was ordered to cast Buddhist triad in bronze. Idea for colossus came from big stone Buddhas of China and Afghanistan, but never had such in bronze been attempted. Actual casting was done by Korean immigrants (main repairs in 12th century were to be done by Sung Chinese). Just before it was finished gold was discovered, gilding went on without importing ore. To clear image with older Shinto gods, oracle was consulted at Ise, at which time Sun Goddess appeared in emperor's dream proclaiming she and Roshana Buddha of Light were one–*avatars*. Emperor Shomu abdicated 748 after highly constructive reign which saw great advances in technology and government. Daughter succeeded (abdicated then resumed throne, but her misrule and carryings on with monk brought on end of women on throne, end of imperial power and rise of Shogun puppet-master system). In 749 his Big Buddha was gilded, its *Eyes Opened* by Indian monk in 752. Shomu shaved head to be ordained by famed Chinese immigrant-bishop Ganjin, died in 759 and his personal effects joined mementos of building of Buddha in Shosoin.

Image itself has been heavily damaged several times (1200, 1679 near total), head fell off three times and present one dates to 1700. 1200 redo sponsored by Kamakura shogun MINAMOTO Yoritomo, promoting power to Nara vs Kyoto, his presence here gave him idea to build Kamakura Great Buddha. Of original perhaps sole remains are knees, few lotus petals in pedestal. Present image may not be highly regarded artistically, but original must have been as magnificent as it was stupendous—remaining petals show how original adornment was truly fine art, each illustrates existence in various realms of form, formlessness, desire etc. Great **octagonal lantern** (NT) fronting building dates from this time, shows us what metal casters of era could do. Tho it is fair to note that Greek Colossus of Rhodes in Mediterranean Sea some 1500 years earlier was also cast-bronze, about twice its height and in technically far more difficult to build standing posture.

Buddha here is **Roshana** (that at Kamakura, Amida) alias Vairocana or DAI-NICHI whose ultimate manifestation is Light (*see* KOYA-SAN, p397, for chat with monk). Portrayed as dwelling upon lotus flower of 1,000 petals, each petal represents one universe (or galaxy?) in each of which there are myriad worlds. On each petal is Shaka, Roshana's earthly manifestation (that is, human or historical Buddha). In each of myriad worlds Shaka manifests himself. Thus Buddhism does not face that problem of universal validity as does Christian dogma with possible coming discovery of life on other worlds, "Did Christ die (or Buddha live) for them?"

"In this same way" according to Prof Serge Elisséeff, "emperor occupies in Japan the supreme rank, corresponding to Roshana Buddha; the imperial will is transmitted to the thousand officials...." etc, down chain of command with separation of social worlds within Japan just as arbitrary as selection of lotus petals, and as total as between actual worlds of our physical universe. You are in your fixed 'world' in Japan—school tie, ancestry, company, etc —and you keep to your own tight little orbit.

Big Buddha formerly was served by court of bodhisattvas, guardians, devas etc, as in other temples. Two flanking gilt **wooden figures** are *Nyoirin-Kannon* and *Kokuso-bosatsu*, date from 17th century restoration. Pair of gigantic (18ft/5.4m) standing figures to L rear are but few centuries old, perhaps only fine sculpture done in Edo era and are 2 of 4 guardian kings. *Komokuten,* on L, brush in hand, is popular with anyone writing anything (students taking tests, lovers writing love letters, writers doing book), outcome of which is foretold by one's chewing up wad of tissue paper to toss at goliath. If it sticks, result will be good: woe, if it falls.

Then too, there are good and better spots to have it stick. When we started this book in 1961 we tossed oracular cud and it missed dead-navel center by inch and stuck fast. Can't do much better. Custom died out in '70s, discouraged as form of pollution.

Behind Big Buddha **model of original compound** shows pair of pagodas since lost. These were each 100mtrs/328ft tall, that's 60% of Washington monument, quarter of Empire State building! Rear R corner is pillar with hole, thru which people squeeze to measure themselves for paradise—hole same size as image's nostril thru which one enters mind (or mindlessness) of Buddha. Kids get thru, so can adults: place one arm along your side with other over your head to pull self thru, angle your shoulders thru. Oh, yes, empty pockets—you can't take it with you.

Entering building, outside on R is large sculpted figure squatting in throne...
Binzuru, originally one of 16 rakan, sits outside having been expelled for violating vow of chastity in remarking on beauty of passing woman. But Buddha had conferred on him special healing powers so today as in old times people make pilgrimage to him to rub his corresponding ailing spot. It is said one typist pilgrim hobbled miles to him—only to cry out in frustration that, as he was seated, she couldn't rub her painful ailment.
Exiting ...
Above entry of main building is small door, opened only last nite of year and for special rites, gives view of Dai Nichi's face, or enables him to gaze out at this world. Faces due west—sunset, tomorrow, and Paradise.

Fronting building: in center of walkway, great **octagonal lantern** (NT) dates from origin: heavenly attendants–our angels–play musical instruments. Owes much stylistically to both India, Persia. Bronze mix is phenomenal, having resisted corrosion standing outdoors over twelve centuries! Reliefs on facets often found on scroll-mounted rubbings in antique shops.

NAN-DAI-MON (South Great Gate) (NT) is largest in Japan, main wooden pillars 21m tall, built during great 12th century reconstruction after Taira-Minamoto battles destroyed 8th century original; in what is called *tenjikuyo,* Indian style, architectural form developed in south (Sung) China. Actually, pillars and bracketing do resemble stone gates of India. Enormous plain bracketing, corbelled out in six stages, is special characteristic: 27m/89ft tall. Two gigantic **nio-guardians** (NT)—note yin and yang postures, mouths—at 4.2 and 4.8m largest in Japan and are by Unkei and Kaikei, last great sculptors. Most *nio* carved since imitate Unkei's realistic style here. Pair **guardian lions** in inner portals of gate are pure early Sung by Chinese sculptors: no yin-yang contrast. Older imported Chinese tradition of previous centuries was highly international eclectic T'ang style, while from 12th century thru 16th later, more 'Chinesey', Sung tradition had great influence (as we shall see in KYOTO, with Zen tradition culminating in flamboyant impressionism of 16th century Momoyama Period).

KAIDAN-IN (to R/W of gate, atop steep stone steps), main temple of Risshu sect introduced by sainted priest Ganjin of T'ang China (portrait in TOSHO-DAI-JI). Present building is Tokugawa rebuilding of thrice-burned Nara original. Superb sculpture, its life-size *shi-tenno* four guardian kings, illustrated in numerous art books and gracing countless posters, rank with Moonbeam-Sunbeam as finest clay statuary of Nara era. Tho representing ferocious aspects, they, like beam-twins, are noteworthy for their softness reflecting qualities of confidence and true power, great spiritual energy at high efficiency; 'reality in itself'. Three wear Central Asian topknot, fourth Chinese helmet. Upper L-R pair stare into distance (future?), nearer duo admonish something closer, perhaps ourselves. (All National Treasures).

KAISAN-DO, Founder's Hall, Kamakura era (NT) housing some fine pieces of interest to specialist. Heian period (1019) portrait of Abbot Roben holding his actual staff (NT) secret image shown only **Dec 16**, hiding preserved its brocaded colors. Exquisite portrait (NT) of octogenarian Abbot Chogen, 1206, who captained rebuilding of Todai-ji after 1180 fires; ranks with older portrait of Ganjin as top two masterpieces of portrait sculpture.

SLIGHT DETOURS CENTRAL

W side (L) of Gate to Todai-ji Daibutsu is...
Isui-en Garden strolling garden, original early Edo 17th cent with mostly Meiji era late 19th cent additions, taking advantage of 'captured landscape' of Mts Mikasa & Kasuga, designated National Scenic Spot, in grounds of which is:
Neiraku Museum, *Neiraku Bijutsukan*, Private collection Chinese bronzes and ceramics, Korean celadons and paintings (¥600).

300m W across bus road to Kyoto behind overbearing Prefectural Office is...
Nara Prefectural Museum, *Kenritsu Bijutsukan*, temporary exhibits, ¥-var.

National Museum, *Kokuritsu Bijutsukan*, just into park from entrance to Big Buddha. Collection is excellent, duplicating for most part sort of thing we have seen so far, *in situ*, in temples themselves—for this reason it is less interesting, tho we get clearer look at statuary. Main hall displays historical development, technique of Buddhist sculpture, as also gallery thru L-center wall, which circle and back out R to front of hall, R to circle clockwise outer halls for more history, crossing main hall again to farside galleries showing excavated Buddhist relics. Back into main hall at front which again cross to rear, thence underpass to new East Gallery for usual standing exhibit upstairs R of "World of Buddhist Images & Priests".

Periodically mount special integrated exhibits in new annex, such as SHOSOIN Exhibit, late Oct. Don't miss fine illustrated catalogs; 9-4:30, X-1st & 3rd mon.

More interesting because of original temple setting is superb collection in...
KOFUKU-JI, Hosso Sect HQ, twin temple to KASUGA SHRINE (often even called KASUGA-JI or Kasuga temple) set between Museum and Nara Hotel just to townward (big pagoda marks it). Founded in Kyoto in 669 by Fujiwara family and moved twice till present location set in 710, Shomu's empress added pagoda (rebuilt 1426). Decline of Fujiwara clan in 12th century marked decline of temple. Sacked in Genji-Heike wars, especially at first when

sided with Minamoto-Genji who at time were losing, then their victory brought Kofuku-ji renaissance and rebuilding of Nara—as many fine Kamakura era buildings, as well as sculptures of masters Kokei and Unkei, thruout city testify. Suffered further neglect with decline of Kamakura shogunate and subsequent power return to Kyoto with Ashikaga shogun and rise of Zen at expense of Nara's esoteric sects.

TREASURE HOUSE (¥400) is modern fireproof building in Kofuku-ji style. Great collection of superb sculpture of *hachibu-shu* (eight classes of celestial beings) arrayed basically along religious lines approximating original setting under exceptional lighting (all NT). Outstanding is three-faced, six-armed *Ashura*, 734AD, adopted Hindu demon, dry lacquer whose original ferocious aspect, beautifully pacified by gentle Buddhism of time, is no less threatening for it; her sarong is painted representation of brocade cloth of time. Several fine early Nara era portraits of priests in dry-lacquer, especially standing figures of *Ten Great Disciples of Buddha* (all NT) coloring is 12th cent Kamakura era restoration; numerous guardian quartets (two fine sets of *shi-tenno*, 4 guardians, plumper pair are of course typically Heian period, 200 years later) to twelves from early Nara Period. Several heftier, massive guards out in long TOKONDO are obviously 9th century Heian style; degeneration of sculpture can be seen in late Heian 12th century in 12 guardians, flat-relief on wood, pseudo-folk style. Oldest bronze image in Kofuku-ji is fragmentary giant head meter tall, remnant of delicate 2.5 meter colossus of Yakushi Nyorai (NT), cast 685, burned 1411; its delicate smile brightens our day. Museum's fine pamphlet invaluable here as no English labels; sculpture periodically rotated on loan to Museum itself.

Renaissance of Kamakura Era, late 12th century, when Nara was rebuilt by Yoritomo, perhaps best seen here in pair of *ni-o* (*Kongo-rikishi* Diamond-mace power-lords) life-sized, almost alive, stripped to waist in flowing sarongs, power surging thru their straining veins and muscles in veritable textbook of martial arts kata. (Also *Fukukenjaku Kannon*, 1189, 3.4m, seated gilt figure with 8 arms, out in NAN-ENDO, below) and seated sextet of patriarchs with piercing eyes said to be of obsidian, but similar others recently discovered to be blown glass. All show return to naturalism of Unkei and his school, which carries us on to idealism, as in standing 2m tall portraits (ca.1208–) of unbelievably gentle-visaged *Muchaku* and *Seshin* standing figures in HOKUENDO, historical founders of Hosso school ranked as bodhisattvas; which stripped down eventually to impressionism to result perhaps understandably, next century, in fall of sculptor's art, rise of pure impressionism of 'Zen-arts': bare gardens, black ink painting, noh-theater. While latter are not Nara, perhaps seeing their bared base early here we may better understand what came to pass in Kamakura and Ashikaga-era Kyoto.

Between Museum and Pagoda is...
TO-KONDO, East Golden Hall (NT) with fine array of statuary (most NT) and dramatic setting for flaming madhouse torchlite battle **Feb 3**. Five-storey **Pagoda** (rebuilt 1426 after Nara original) sometimes open to visitors when Kofuku-ji needs cash. We advise only limber try slithering up thru its intricate beams to lovely view platforms. (If topside guide tries to put bite on you, ignore.) At 55m, 2nd tallest in country. Flanking is lovelier, older but smaller 3-storey pagoda of early Kamakura rebuilding.

Next to it is...
HOKUENDO, North Octagonal Pavilion, 1208 (NT) with small pagoda two oldest standing buildings in complex. Houses magnificent seated, gilt **Miroku** messiah, carved wood by Unkei; 1208; 4 **Shi-Tenno** (NT).

There is 15th century (Muromachi era) bath-house just up from pagoda:
—but more important to us is 20th century W-style **toilet** opp pagoda,
townward.

Just below Kofuku-ji is...
NAN-ENDO, 'Circular-Pavilion,' octagonal garish 1741 rebuilding on
813 Nara era base, now busily functioning pilgrimage site of '33 of West
Japan' enshrining Fukukenjaku 8-armed Kannon (NT, *above*), pilgrims
circumambulate, light candles, bringing its uninspiring architecture
poignantly to life. Smaller temple to R within its enclosed court usually has
elderly pilgrims, chanting and chinking their sonorous silver hand-bells.

With more time—pleasant scenic driveways in hills behind city: **Ko-en, Kasuga**
(best) and **Shin-Wakakusa** mountain roads which may be taken singly, or all in line.
There is drive-in restaurant on Ko-en, some outdoor noodleries where Shin-Wakakusa and
Kasuga link. View is long, but we still prefer old pedestrian view from NI-GATSU-DO.
There are some interesting 7th to 12th century cave images, pure native Japanese in their
naive comicness, some carved much in style of stonework in Korea at Kongju (referred to
on Japanese TV as 'Tempyo era *furusato*,' or old home town) and some painted in living
rock up old pilgrim road parallel lovely Kasuga ascent which passes 'sleeper' Shin-
Yakushi-ji temple (*see* **Taxi** and **Bus H2** tours, above).

10min walk S/slightly W from Kasuga Shrine big ni-no-torii in residential area...
SHIN YAKUSHI-JI (¥400) preserving original setting amid lovely
narrow mud-walled alleys, retaining Tempyo-era mood, of which it is last
pure—and modest—architectural remnant. Founded 747 by empress
Komyo as offering for cure of eye illness of emperor Shomu, five
horizontal lines along walls announce imperial patronage. Within starkly
simple **Main Hall** bare beams reveal structure which Japanese savants, for
some reason these days of touting internationalism, insist derives of Greek,
but could be any simple bare beam roof construction. Superb array of
statuary set in original heavenly court, surround Yakushi-nyorai, healing
buddha (NT) carved of single block of hinoki wood ringed by 12 fierce
guardians (NT), one wood, others of painted clay (on skeletal wood) date
750. Their shibui aging belies fact that all were once brilliantly colored
(some traces remain, underparts) like similar painted terra-cotta figures in
West Chinese cave temples. Howling *Mekira Taisho* subject of ¥500
postage stamp. These human size surprises, their photos project immensity.
Fierce eyes glare out from old faces, long mysterious electric ever-living
quality only recently discovered to be blown glass. Pillar floral paintings are
medieval, Edo era. Large **painting of Nirvana** (heaven) full of angel
types makes pair with one in museum at Mt Koya Monastery, where far
more easily appreciated, better lit —are of following Fujiwara-Heian era.
Poorly lit, flashlight desirable—rented at entry ¥20, drop coppers in box, honor
system, in sheer gratitude we left more.
Bell tower is superb example of such Kamakura era (12c) structure. Bell
within original Nara period. S and E **Gates** also Kamakura period.

FLOWER DATEBOOK: Noted for *hagi*, bush clover, late summer-fall.

CHOPSTICKS: Small garden **restaurant**: cool weather *yudofu* ¥1,500, hot day
cold *hiyashi somen* noodles ¥500; rice, veggies, soup ¥1500; matcha ¥500, other. Foot of
hill **Momoya** 10:30-17:00 X-thur, ¥800 *chagayu* + 2 side dishes in 100-year-old house.

WHERE TO STAY: Took us 30+ years to stumble on this treasure: 10 temple
rooms hung with calligraphy in main bldg, most w/ garden view; ¥4,900 w/bkfst, +¥400
entry-fee, rove halls and gardens early am before public; *mongen*-lockout 8pm, call day
ahead ☎22-3736.

700m SE (go S → T-intersection, L → next T, R across stream 250m and L again...
BYAKUGŌ-JI: Pleasant isolated temple for addicted strollers (*see* YAGYU ROAD, next) thru antique streets untouched by modernity. Gate offers fine view of city. Oldest parts Hondo, Miedo are of Kamakura-era great reconstruction of city; temple founded 8th century, but nothing left of early era.

YAGYU ROAD, one of those romantic feudal era roads still relatively unspoiled, that were subject of old literature as they are of modern costume movies. Runs from central Nara to Yagyu village, once home of great Yagyu kendo-fencing school, and clan of master swordsmen.

GETTING THERE: Either walk Nara-Yagyu as we did years ago, or 50min bus → Yagyu from Nara Kintetsu Stn (1-2 per hr ¥700, Nara Kotsu Bus or TIC for more info) and walk back: 6-7hrs whole way or two legs of some 3-4hrs each with **ENSHO-JI** temple as midpoint. 3 minshuku in Yagyu so take late pm bus and hike from early, or end up in Yagyu and bus back next day, or leave road and grab bus almost anywhere on nearby parallel paved road; also campsites; rsvtns Nara TIC or **Yagyu Info Ctr** (J) ☎(0742)-94-0002. Road is posted in Japanese, tho poorly. From NARA, starts **BYAKUGŌ-JI** (*see* above) nr **SHIN YAKUSHI-JI,** while from YAGYU *KTO* advises from **Yagyu-kami** bus stop go R past JrHi on R, then 2nd R, to poorly posted start, then downhill along wall and keep alert for nondescript signs. Asking, names are *Tokai Shizen Hodo*-Tokai Nature Road or *Yagyu-michi*-Yagyu Road. 'Nature Road' is more descriptive as it is steep climb thru forest, from pine to bamboo to lovely glade of fruit trees. Intersections poorly posted, bear straight. 9km (10 from Nara) is village of **ENJO-JI** with ¥-B noodlery. Bus stop for those who've had enough, or who bus in to here to start. On thru tea gardens, over tar road thru forest to small teahouse (zenzai sweets, etc) where soon after original stone-pavement, flanked by old stone Buddhas. End at SHIN YAKUSHI-JI. If one leg only, advise ENJO-JI → NARA, from out-in, start with noodles, stop midway for tea and zenzai or manju-buns, as in old samurai flicks.

15min walk W from Shin Yakushi-ji past hiway, Nara Hotel (L), enter alleys of...

NARA-MACHI   OLD EDO-ERA TOWN

SINGLE STOREY, aged-brown wooden houses with slatted fronts line streets little more than alleys, some off to sides are barely paved-trails. Few houses redone in aluminum siding, but anodized bronze to simulate old wood even to identical slats and window bars—good taste which Kyoto should note. Cubist red-white cloth 'monkeys' hang in trains from eaves—*Migawari-saru Omamori*—Hon-monkey-charms—each has name inked for each inhabitant, as scapegoat for illness. Seen this neighborhood only.

Numerous photogenic small temples, gates open but usually barred–if not, enter freely and wander thru small courtyard or garden.

Flip coin into each temple's offering box, please, needed for maintenance.

GETTING THERE: Just at top of Sanjo-dori before steep up-slope, take R descending fork to **Sarusawa-no-Iké** pond—or if at Tourist Info just above, go out R to first R down grand flight stone steps, once entry to great Gango-ji; (from Nara Hotel out roadway R, first R straight W to near Sun Route Hotel). Thence thru old merchant residential section of Nara-machi, undergoing restoration-revival as walking course — praise City Hall, every intersection, corner, turn has old fashion highway post (metal instead of stone/wood) w/ arrows & names of sites in Japanese & English.

5min walk—from Sun Route block S to newly widened st, R, next L, enter...
GANGO-JI temple: originally at ASUKA-DERA, but when capital moved to Heijo-kyo in 710, reestablished in new location as SHIN-(new)-GANGO-JI, and Asuka-dera was left as minor temple. Grew to one of famed '7 temples of Nara', 2nd only to Todai-ji, encompassing with dependencies all modern Nara-machi from Sarusawa pond S to Korin-ji temple, E from Sun Route

Shops ○
1. Maru-maru, *mingei*
2. Yu, *linen & crafts*
3. Monju-an, *pottery*
4. Mu-a, *stone & ceramics*
5. Ittoh-bori, *wood carving*
6. Uzura Club, *craft shops*
7. Kikuoka Mingei, *crafts*
8. Esaki, *lanterns*
9. Kobai-en, *ink sticks*

Restaurants △
a. Mangyoku
b. Asuka-en, *tempura*
c. Harishin, *J- bentoh*
d. Soba
e. Ikkyu, *sake, J- meal*
   Tosaya, *J-meal (Shikoku)*

Museums □
A. Orient-kan
B. Clock Museum
C. Historical Museum

Hotels ⌂
Nara Hotel
Sun Route
Asuka-so

Budget Ryokan ⌂
Nitta Minshuku
Noda-ya Minshuku
Matsumae Ryokan

Hotel and Jurin-in Temple (SE), W to beyond Orient-kan. (Now-minor Daian-ji and Saidai-ji also held such glorious rank). Move of court to Kyoto decreased influence, fires took grandeur, last original part burned 1859, till today it is but minor temple. Only main and meditation hall—which Kamakura era rebuilding of Nara monks' dorm is, none-the-less, NT. **Yakushi Nyorai** is 9th cent wood; 5.5m/18ft pagoda model is 8th cent. Other statuary, also ICA, are later Heian to Kamakura, 9-12th cent. Two major mandalas, wood 13th cent and silk copy 15th cent, shown rarely.

Little here to arrest but specialist, tho walk here and briefly thru (¥300), and around main hall, pleasant. Hill of sculpted stones set up when graves moved early 17th cent, is 1,200 choice 15-16th cent gravestones set in pyramid.

PERSONAL DATEBOOK: **Feb 3** *Fire rite* led by 20+ Yamabushi, called fire walking but not really as logs first put down as bridge over pit of flaming brush, walk barefoot thru flames licking thru logs, rather than directly on hot coals—still fun, try it, we did, 1pm. **Aug 23-24** *Jizo Bon*, loveliest fete, myriad kimonoed kids, lanterns, highly photogenic.

Shojin ryori temple dinner min 10 people ¥2,500 ea incl entry-fee, rsvtn required, ☎23-1377; Temple Stay, ¥4,500w/bkfst only. (Also opp temple E gate: ¥-B **Nitta Ryokan** ☎22-2714).

SHOPPING: Walk out same gate as entered, L, block on, turn L several good shops with singular merchandise, local and imported handicrafts, Block N above **Orient-kan** is new bldg with ricksha parked in front, **Uzuraya-kurabu**: good selection local crafts, souvenirs. Continue down, L, to T at **Kikuoka**, fun shop for Asian handicrafts.

Then R, road-post, jag L-R, on L is...
Nara-machi Shiryokan, area 'historical storehouse' (free) shows many fine old *kanban* trade signs of sort toured US museums '87.

Opposite on N side of street is...
Clock museum, *Toki-no Shiryokan*. More of interest to locals, collection of world timepieces from ancient times (free).

Next L, go half block S, on R...
KOSHIN-DO tiny neighborhood shrine not much more than shopfront, home of local Migawari-saru O-mamori, scapegoat monkey talismans, *above* on sale here, various sizes. Main fete **2nd sun Mar & Nov 23**, street fair with residents prepare, serve konyaku & daikon-radish (free).

Narrow road was in Heian era main pilgrim hiway Kami-kaido. Few doors on, R...
Orient-kan our art museum in restored Edo Era 19th cent rice wholesaler's storehouse, unchanged but for installation of artifacts, with our Persian collection (*see* also Kobe, p.588) especially documenting ancient Persia-Japan interrelations. First storehouse shows dioramas of nomadic life, old-town bazaar stall showing folk art illustrated in our *Survey of Persian Handicraft* book ($95/¥12,000). Rear storehouse (center to corner R-rear) Persian items sharing decor with objects in Shosoin; 9:30-17:00 X-mon, NewYr, ¥300–show this book for reduction. Caravanserai-teashop: ¥300 glass *chai*-tea, free refills, sweets; Persian handicrafts, lesser antiques, coin & glass-bead reproductions, for sale.

Numerous other small sights, promise of others, developing this as new tourist stroll and locals firmly intent on preserving old feudal atmosphere of narrow streets and original houses. Hope Japan's galloping real estate inflation doesn't hit Nara too soon.

WHERE TO STAY: Cheaper ryokan: ¥-T **Harishin** ☎(0742)-22-2669, **Matsumae** ☎22-3686; ¥-B: **Seikanso** ☎22-2760, **Nodaya Minshuku** ☎22-3714, **Petit Hotel** ☎22-7171, **Nitta Ryokan** ☎22-2714; Temples: **Gango-ji** and not-far **Shin Yakushi-ji** (*see* WHERE TO STAY, *preceding*).

CHOPSTICKS: Several nice places good lunch, supper from barely above ¥-B thru ¥-L; new places opening as Nara-machi grows (*see* main CHOPSTICKS p.388).

NORTHWEST CORNER
OLD HEIJO CAPITAL Excavation Area: for archaeology-history buffs:

GETTING THERE: Best by **bus** from Kintetsu Stn, lets off in center at **Historic Relics Center**, exhibition hall; or **walk** 1km to NW corner from Yamato Saidai-ji Stn, transfer point when coming up by Kintetsu from Yagi-Kashihara tomb area, or from Nishinokyo Stn of Yakushi-ji etc. **Taxi** from Nara hotel, 8km/4x-mtr– reasonable with wait, but not necessary to hold as easy to get cab back or onward from gate. Hall open 9:00-17:00 but grounds not closed off after hours so good stop after full day West Nara just to stroll this 'dig'. Pass if little time.

This was center of Tempyo era city, heart of Nara Period 710-784. Guardian temples to town were TO-DAI-JI and SAI-DAI-JI, East and West Great Temples. Remaining city center moved eastward after transfer of capital, with most of its actual buildings, to Kyoto after 784. Todai-ji area developed and once-equal status Saidai-ji slumbered as small local temple, great capital foundations were covered with blown leaves turning to soil and farmers moved in. Private efforts to study, conserve area began in 1850s, accelerated after Meiji reform 1870s and were given over to national and prefectural governments in 1920s. Since our first edition, excavation has progressed remarkably with ground plan of capital center uncovered and laid out in novel, attractive manner—original buildings were constructed with wooden pillars set into ground, mostly without foundation stones of later Kyoto style. Tall shrubs have been set in these excavated post holes and kept trimmed to approximate pillars. Capitol sat on raised earthen platforms bit east of center line of walled palace-town.

This 'Palace Town' itself was surrounded by low wall enclosing 1km N-S x 1.3km E-W (1100x1400+ yds), in which were 7,000 homes (50,000+ people) around palace. Model on site (site shelter–junior museum in main entry near bus stop, free parking) shows layout, with brown roofs indicating wooden roofs and grey = tile. Whole city of Heijo, E-W between Todai-ji and Saidai-ji was almost 4.5km, and N-S about same—some 3x3 miles.

Paved bicycle paths lace area above Heijo site, which we advise as only way to see it except for bus tours taking in HOKKE-JI, or garden buffs interested in Nara's sole temple garden, (with Manyoshu garden next to only garden).

Just E of Heijo site is...

HOKKE-JI, sole major temple in Nara with formal garden; also called *Himuro Gosho*, Himuro Royal Palace which is what it was until Komyo, consort of Daibutsu-builder emperor Shomu in 747 converted it to nunnery. Restored by Tycoon Hideyoshi's widow, 1601. Main treasure is 9th century wooden 11-head Kannon, NT. Pond garden meant to be viewed in meditation from its building, rather than strolled, noted for iris and azalea. (*See* Nara Kotsu tours [D-1] & [L]).

Bike paths meander N to Self Defense Force camp (bus #13, to *Jiei-tai-mae*) foot of moated **tomb mounds** of Konabe (L) and Uwanabe (R), & behind them larger keyhole tomb of Princess Iwanohime-no-mikoto.

Cycling in search of more tombs: continue W 1 km, meandering thru fields and houses, to trio of tombs, two large in rear are (L) #13 emperor Seimu, late 4th cent, and (R) Princess Hibasuhime-no-mikoto, and small in front is fascinating Koken last reigning female 'emperor' (#46, r.749-758). As daughter of Shomu and his anointed successor, she dedicated his Big Buddha in 752. Abdicated in 758 to distant cousin, re-ascended throne as reigning empress Shotoku (#48, 764-770) and had reputed romance with her chief subordinate and power broker, monk Dokyo, planning to name him her successor taking throne out of family. On her death he was banished and no woman ever held power again—tho 2 reigned as titular female emperors in Edo era. Tho devout Buddhist she is buried in Shinto-style mound—which is one of many factors casting strong doubt on so-called identifications of mound-tenants by non-archaeologists in Imperial Court.

Continuing on our feminist cycle-tour take road along W-side these tombs 700m N to large mound of semi-legendary empress Jingo, never reigned as emperor but wielded power as Regent after death of husband Chuai, #14 early 5c. Gave birth to Ojin on return from Korea "after carrying him 3 years" but kept him from throne till her death. She completed subjugation of Kyushu and invaded Korea. She may be Shaman-queen Himiko or Pimiko of old Chinese records, or even Korean shaman-princess and invaded Japan.

Hikers can return S 400m to Kintetsu Heijo Stn, train back one stop to Saidai-ji (*see* HORYU-JI, p.370); bikers can return bike there or continue WEST SIDE tour.

NARA WEST SIDE NISHI-NO-KYO

BETWEEN Horyu-ji–Nara, what was W side of capital Nishi-no-kyo are several lovely temples which also fall between them in time. We visited them in chronological order as convenient to Horyu-ji (*see* preceding). They are also convenient hike from here: hike Saidai-ji → Akahada Kiln → Yakushi-ji → Toshodai-ji = 5km/3mi, plus 1.5km (1mi/20mins) on to entry to Heijo excavation area.

Good map *Hiking Course-Ikaruga* free from Nara Kotsu Bus or Kintetsu rail, in Japanese but easy to follow, tho best taken shared with Japanese-speaking or fellow-student guide. Consult Nara guide-info desk.

Where rice fields intervened between here and downtown in '64 is now excavation revealing immense ground plan of this ancient capital's center. **Recommended** are YAKUSHI-JI & TOSHODAI-JI (*see* p.366) pleasant 10min walk apart, each few min from NISHI-NO-KYO Stn on Kintetsu line. From HORYU-JI, it's 10km taxi (5-6x-mtr); or bus #52 to either. From Nara-Kintetsu or JR Stns, also bus #63. To/from → KORIYAMA bus #51, 52, worth short look for here is center of Japan's goldfish-raising industry. Reach also by **bus tour** or **taxi** out of NARA.

CHOPSTICKS: *Cha-gayu* local specialty: name means basic tea & rice-gruel, but is euphemism for full classical Japanese *kaiseki* meal. Most operate 11:00-or so-18:30-usual last entry time but dawdle till 21:00 as they don't expect you to rush thru epicurean seasonal-symphony at ¥6,000up all incl–some run extras higher; rsvtn advised, thru hotel desk or TIC, at:

Toh-no-chaya, Pagoda Tea house, ☎22-4348, E-W st opp Daimon-ji Hotel top Sanjo-dori, go N to first corner on L, up garden path. May-onward *chagayu-bento* seasonal lunch served in garden, ¥2,500, 11:00-16:00; dinner 18:30; X-tue.

Yanagi-chaya, Willow Tea House, ☎22-7560 continue N from Toh-no-chaya, take first R and it is on L side: ¥-L lunch (*shokado* ¥3,300) or early supper (¥7,000-all incl) 11:30, dinner at 17:00.

Hiraso ☎22-0866 in Nara-machi on Ima-Mikado St below Sarusawa pond NW-corner; full seasonal vegetarian *chagayu* ¥2,000, or *chagayu* snack plus side dish ¥800; also famed *kaki-no-ha sushi*, persimmon-leaf wrapped-sushi, & *ayu*-(trout)-*sushi*; X-mon.

Ninai-chaya ☎22-7788, in (run by) Kasuga Taisha shrine halfway up Omote-sando main path from First Torii: *okayu*+one ¥800, spring specialty *yomogi-dango* (mugwort-herb-dumpling), *matcha* ¥500; July-Aug special *Manyo-gayu* of matcha powdered tea sprinkled over cold *cha-gayu* with special mountain herbs.

Uma-no-Me, horse-eye (after antique ceramic design) R of First Torii on L toward Nara Hotel, interior all antiques, paintings; home cookery on antique crockery. Lunch 11:30-14:00, ¥3,500; dinner 17:00-20:00 rsve day ahead ☎23-7784, kaiseki ¥12,000+%.

Nara Hotel offers similar above, sun only. Also **Fujita** 11:00-16:00.

Kikusui on road → Nara Hotel nr Park SE corner; W-only ¥-S-L; light lunch a la carte.

Van Kio, S gate YAKUSHI-JI (*see* p367) fine restaurant, Japanese-Western, ¥-S–L.

Tosa, Shikoku-style food, *our favorite* run by Jay's ex-student, get by dinner ¥1,000 to Kaiseki ¥3,000up; nr Kintetsu Omiya stn opp Grand Hotel, taxi 2x-mtr, ☎27-0618.

SHINYAKUSHI-JI (*see* p.383) small restaurant in garden, seasonal specials ¥500-¥1500; matcha ¥500, other. Foot of approach hill 100-yr-old **Momoya**, X-thur, ¥800 *chagayu*. Most major temples have similar ¥-T snacks, ¥-B a la carte; will help you order.

NARA-MACHI: **Mangyoku-ro**, 1-block W of Sun Route hotel, below pond architecturally lovely ex-geisha house, light J-meals, a la carte, ¥-T, ☎22-2265. **Kappo-Eho** ☎22-1858, Minami-ichi-cho, tiny, in maze behind Hiraso; seasonal delicacies on beautiful dishes ¥-T. **Tempura Asuka** continuing down Ima Mikado St to next block called Shonan-In-cho, on L, *Yumedono-bento* 3-tiered lacquer boxes, tempura etc, ¥1,500; table d'hote ¥2,000+. **Harishin** ryokan ☎22-2669, lunch only *kamitsu-michi-bento* 'Nara-era highway-lunch' in J-parlor of 200-yr-old squire's home, gourmet bento-boxes, upper full of 7-8 portions fish, meat, herbs, vegetables, bottom large rice portion, plus soup; ¥2,500; cheaper a la carte abt ¥1,000. **Saiko-in** temple, on lower Taka-Mikado St, block above and W of Orient-kan, ☎26-2234, monthly 20th-only, 7:00-sutra recital, sermon, then serve *Mikado-gayu*, emperor's gruel, drop donation. **Aoi** up Taka-Mikado to Shimo-Mikado St, trad J-, 5pm–, ¥-B, kamameishi ¥800, a la carte.

MOCHI-IDO-NO-SENTAGAI (Lord Pounded-Rice St), between Sarusawa-no-Ike pond and Nara-machi, is first St W of & below pond in arcade: noted eatery lane 1200 years. Midblock W-side on R is open plaza, escalator to 2nd fl: facing is **Ikkyu**, drinks and tid-bits, ¥-B-T. Neighbors are dozens more, like **Nelson** ☎22-9445, 2nd alley L down Mochidono, and on L—morning set ¥300, good records. Before 3rd turn, on R, is **Raku** in old country house, serves imported mild Sri Lankan curries, ¥-B-good; 8:00-20:00, X-2nd, 4th thur. **Geppo** on St crossing Sentagai above Ikyu, go W next NW corner; interior, menu mixed J-W serve French & *yose-nabe* local bouillabaisse & *Ba-sashimi*, horse sashimi. Waterwheel on Ima Mikado St marks **Nodaya Minshuku**, also ¥-B lunches from soba, ¥-T teishoku full lunches.

Sanjo-dori shopping street has many ¥-B–T noodleries & W-style light meal houses, samples in window. One worth hunt is *tachi-nomiya* (stand-up drinkery) **Kichitaro Shoten** in maze opp Sumitomo bank: plenty to eat-drink under ¥2,000, serve *genmai* sake mash: look for curtain with painted Darumas next to antique-shop (daughter's) 10:00-19:30, X-tue. Also several others along L side of block before Daibutsu gate, in season often full of country-folk tours, in which case advise eating slightly off-hour. At bus road corner Daibutsu entry street is lovely classical restaurant, **Miyama** ¥-T, lunches ¥1200-

1900 and a la carte, tasty and beautifully presented. Exit R two doors below, **Yumeido** curio shop serves matcha tea and J-cakes, ¥800, good midday pick-me-up, also *sakura-cha* cherry blossom tea (salty) in season.

WESTERN ¥-S meals, advise eating at Hotels. **Kikusui** excellent ¥-S-L; **Nara Hotel** dining room fine, ¥-S-L, basement grill ¥-T-S, serves until 23:00. **Sun Route** basement restaurant good ¥-S, good American or Japanese bkfst ¥900; lobby coffee shop cheaper, lunch under ¥1,000. Other ¥-S hotels similar.

SHOPPING: Old capital rich in sight-seeing, leaves little time to shop except on run or eves. From JR go L to & R up main shop st Sanjo-dori → Nara Park; from Kintetsu Stn walk back away from wide st, one block to same Sanjo st, L for Park. Combine shopping–pm stroll on Sanjo-dori–shops open till at least 7pm, many–9pm.

LACQUER: Arai raden mother-of-pearl inlay in lacquer, local Akahada-yaki pottery.

CURIOS: H. Kimura for 30+ years has drawn us in, good prices, pair of shops either side Sanjo-dori just below Fujita Hotel. Other antique shops along road invite browsing.

Several good shops for *sumi*-india inksticks, brushes, various *shuji*-calligraphy and sumi-painting paraphernalia for which Nara famed for ages, makes 80% of nation's sumi.

CARVED DOLLS, *Ittoh-bori*: **Somekawa's** has fine selection exclusive local specialty, identified by single cut (thus name) forming planed cubist look, richly colored. Noh dancers favorite subject, catch their special aura admirably; from souvenir price to art.

ANTIQUES and cheaper curios in evening phone **Harry Shepherd**, ☎22-7808 (before 10am for eve appointment, or after 5pm). One stn down on JR at Kyo-baté, or short taxi ride to Kita-kyo-baté-cho 57-12; 15min walk from Sun Route Hotel or back door Nara Hotel: he or assistant will have to meet you to guide thru ancient oriental alley maze to old farmhouse-in-town with 17 rooms full of curios, antiques and both plain and fancy junk well-worth mining. Visited just after he'd shipped 400 small buddhas off to US dealer and he was down to only 100-odd, including fascinating lilliputian pencil-stub-sized masterpieces that samurai enshrined in their helmets. Good selection old porcelain priced near new wares. Occasional low-priced screens—but check how much repair may be needed—possibly remove picture(s) and reframe. Recently collecting old textiles large enough for wall hanging or bedspread. "I admit I don't know art"—few Japanese dealers do either, unless pricey—and he is happy if you can teach him something while you find good buys. Advisor to Buddhist altar maker, has fine selection of gilded carved detail work salvage of antique household altars, which are attractive framed, especially in black—and at prices that make for ideal gifts (*see* also NARA-MACHI walking tour, preceding).

STONE LANTERNS, Antique garden ornaments: Kawatake Gardener at restaurant Van Kio, S gate Yakushi-ji temple, combine sight-seeing–meal stop; handles shipping.

Save minor souveniring for temples, roadside stalls in park, or Horyu-ji to Chugu-ji.

First stop, unless religiously following our chronological itinerary, is usually...
Big Buddha where shop inside near exit has souvenirs, papier maché and compress authentic reproductions of 8th century gigaku religious play masks used at 'eye-opening' rites in 752 AD: clown, red-faced drunkard, dragon king etc all reasonably priced. Also available SHIN YAKUSHI-JI. Good shops outside SANGATSU-DO, top of stairs; with budget restaurants line path at foot of Mount Wakakusa. Park stalls sell tons of deer-horn carvings, whole antlers: cut off at annual de-horning done to protect sightseers and deer from rutting horny bucks. Some stalls gross half-million dollars yearly!

Out by HORYU-JI parking are tastier budget restaurants, shops with tasteful souvenirs including terra-cotta *haniwa*, tomb figure repros. Each shrine or temple has its special pilgrim talismans: most fascinating are erotic fertility items at ASUKA-NI-IMASU-JINJA.

National Museum has good selection of finely illustrated art guides and postcards. Outside opp old museum, **coffee shop** has good frameable art photos. Our long time favorite... **Asuka-en**, across bus road from museum, 59 Nobori-oji St, alas, phasing out sales to do photo books for publishers—tucked away in boxes are photos of sculptural treasures of East Asia taken by late father OGAWA Seijo over rich lifetime. Students will recognize his pix from most basic textbooks. Outside to R down few doors is good **antique** shop. Then tuckered from gazing at beauty step outside L up past shrine entry to **Yumeido** teashop for *matcha* thick green tea & cakes, fine pick-me-up: ¥800; & curios.

Perhaps the most moving experience of our visit to Japan was the illumination of the ancient stone lanterns around Kasuga Shrine. (see Feb 4 & Aug 15)
— Henry W. Taft, *Japan and America*, 1932

PERSONAL DATEBOOK

NARA has its share of great fetes, plus something special to theater buffs. Ancient forms of music and dance are seen at various times, especially *bugaku* (ancient court dances) presented often by well-organized Kasuga Shrine group. There is no opportunity like Wakamiya Shrine's December *On Matsuri*, 'Honorable' or 'Sound' Festival with all-but-forgotten instruments, dances, songs performed. Here also are principal rice-transplanting fetes of Ise Grand Shrine, tho already covered along with other events, in preceding Ise Personal Datebook.

* = 'Must See' or base itinerary around. *See* also pp.375, 385.

January

1-15 Deva King, goddess Kissho Tennyo on view, Joruri-ji, ¥300, 40min bus.

3 *Kagura Hajime,* 11am Kasuga Shrine. First offering maiden-*kagura* holy dance.

5 *Hatsu Ebisu,* Ebisu Shrine, Minami-ichi Nara, 7am, all day (also 10am Ebisu shrines Kohten, Ichinoi, Sumiyoshi in Nara). Stalls line streets Ebisu Shrine → Sarusawa Pond; parade some 10 or more palanquins with Minami-ichi geisha.

1-15 *Kisshoe Kechigan,* Yakushi-ji, Nara outskirts. Service Kondo, to Yakushi-Nyorai daily 1-15th, painting Goddess Kisshoten shown 1-14.

15 *Burning Grass, Wakakusa-yama, Nara, 6pm; var programs pm. Grass torched by firemen; fireworks. Farmers burned dead grass to kill insects, Todai-ji fearing fire damage, set aside annual day for it.

15 *Bugaku Hajime,* Kasuga Shrine, first offering of one *bugaku* dance, 1pm.

February

First Sun *Rice Planting* ritual rape of earthy goddess by masked monkey-god sympathetic magic shows nature what to do; sympathetic audience gets 'neolithic' fertility talismans, Asuka Shrine, *(text).*

3 or 4 **Setsubun Tsuina-shiki*, Kofuku-ji. Demon-chase 6pm opens Nara's most exciting dusk, as sutra read at Kondo before Yakushi-Nyorai, father & mother demon, son, others in magnificent masks and brocade rush out. Stopped by Bishamon-ten, violent torch battle ensues. As they try to escape, priest shouts "*oni wa soto*" (out demons). 1000s lanterns lit Kasuga Shrine, bugaku dances there-rush up from Kofuku-ji, just make it. Similar demon battle at Horyuji, after dark, not as wild, Zao-do of Mt Yoshino.

3 *Goma Fire Walk*, led by dozen *Yamabushi* walk slat-bridge over, not on, coal 1-2pm, Gango-ji's Gokuraku-bo, 2 blocks SE Nara Hotel, near our museum.

11 *Kigen-setsu* (Jimmu/Foundation Fete) Kashihara Shrine, Kashihara. Classic & folk dances, parade, oft darkly chauvinist, potentially militarist; best 11am-12:30.

11 *Sand-Throwing,* Hirose-jinja, Kawai-cho – Kintetsu RR Takada Stn, bus to Jyoko.

14 *Branding Festival*, Hase-dera, demon trio in huge (45cm) masks, carry torches, mix in crowd, best 2-4pm; dusk stamp parishioners' foreheads visas to heaven.

March

1-14 *Omizu-tori Sai* (Water-drawing Rite) Todai-ji Nigatsu-do. 'Mongol exorcism' Tibetan rite similar to one Katmandu, 7pm 11 huge torches lit and 11 priests swing around pyromaniacally in corridor (opp.). Followed by drawing sacred water about 1:30am, best nites are *12-13 & *13-14. *Warning* women segregated, can't see.

2nd Sun Eat lucky *furofuki daikon dengaku* (boiled radish in miso), free to first 2,000 11am-2pm Koshindo Temple Nara-machi by our Orient Kan Mus. 20min walk JR Nara.

13 *Saru* (Monkey) *Matsuri*, Kasuga shrine to prior celestial landlord monkey fertility god. 9am solemn 1st rite; 10 offer food, clothes, money, Yamato*mai, bugaku.*

21 *Higan* Equinox Buddhist rites temples, families clean graves, offer incense.

21-May 20 Images of blue-faced deva king, lucky goddess Kissho Tennyo on view Joruri-ji, ¥300.

22 *Memorial Rite*, Horyu-ji for Shotoku Taishi (d.620); oranges, kumquats, gingko nuts, dry persimmon offer at altar, ancient music 1pm. Stalls, plant mart all day.

O-mizu-tori Exorcism

30 *Hanae-Shiki* (Flower Rite) Yakushi-ji. Interesting 850-year-old rite, temple decor huge paper flowers: 3am, repeat 1pm, 7pm, each lasts 2 hrs; confession, thanks, prayers for future; thru April 5 (*see*).

April

1 *Spring Fete*, O-yamoto Shrine, Tenri. Portable shrine carried to Nakayama in city where displayed and returned at nite. Dragon dance, other ancient dances.

5 **Onioi-shiki*, Yakushi-ji, Nara. Closes *Hanae-shiki*, (above) 8:30pm demon chasing: red, green and black torch-bearing demons tussle as all lights are turned out.

5 *Chinka Festival*, Kasuga Mizutani Shrine Nara, ward off ills, offerings to Susano-O-mikoto as Shinto God of Medicine. 10am offering cherry blossoms; day of music and dance: *noh, kyogen, kagura, bugaku*.

8 *Shunie*, Shin-Yakushi-ji offer flowers, 7-9pm at main image & 12 guardians. 12 priests march with torches to main hall for *zange*-confessional.

11 **thru May 5**, Public showing of Guze Kannon at Horyu-ji *Yumedono*.

Mid-month *Cherry Blossom Festival*, costume parade thru city, Japanese dances at Nara Outdoor Music Stadium. Check Nara TIC for exact dates.

2nd Sat-Sun *Dai Cha Matsuri* Tea Party w/giant implements incl cup big enough to bathe in, Saidai-ji temple; join in.

17 *Hosyo-e* at Kofuku-ji, Nara. Since 578ad introduction of Buddhism prohibits killing, 30 kg of live fish offered at altar as sutras read release into Sarusawa Pond.

18 *Fire walk*, Shoryaku-ji, ☎62-9569; rites, bugaku 10am, pyre 1pm, walk 2pm; JR Sakurai line Tenri, bus to Kubonosho, temple bus awaits.

May

2 *Emperor Shomu Fete*, Todai-ji. AM, long sutra reading, flower arrange, tea rite before Big Buddha. PM chigo (kids in ancient Tempyo 8th cent, Muromachi 16th cent costumes) mile of itinerant priests in black robes, others var period costumes parade Jokyo-ji temple Sanjodori

to Mirror Pond front Daibutsu. Tea svce, flower show, sutras chanted main hall.

5 **Shobu* (Iris) *Fete*, Kasuga S, prayers for Children's Day; *bugaku* 10am main shrine, kids *bugaku* 1:30pm Shokubutsu-pond.

10 *Kencha Sai*, Heads 3 main Tea schools rotate gigantic tea offering Kasuga Jugetsu-kan teahouse; 100s ladies in best kimonos.

11-12 **Takigi-* (Bonfire) *Noh:* Kofuku-ji temple Nandaimon, 4-9pm (if rain, Nara Pref Hall); Kasuga, 11am.

14 *Nerikuyo Matsuri*, Taima-dera, masked celestials in gigaku-procession at 4pm.

15 *Juko-ki Dai-cha Kai* (Tea Way Fete), Shomyo-ji. Juko a.k.a. Murata Shuko (1422-1502) founder of tea way, enshrined. Formal Tea, exhibit utensils.

19 *Uchiwa* (Fan) *Fete*, Toshodai-ji, outskirts 4pm; fan away ills, 1,000s thrown off bell tower: 100s by top artists, authors; protect vss lightning, sickness; safe birth.

June

17 *Saikusa* (Lily) *Fete*, Isakawa S, Nara. Offer dark & light sake 10am, 1pm ancient costumed girls, children as chigo, parade new city from Isakawa Shrine (oldest shrine Nara, 3 blocks W Sarusawa Pond).

24 *Rice Planting Dance* Ise Shrine, smaller detached Izakawa Shrine, contest.

30 *Annual Fete* minor shrine Kasuga 10am

July

10-12 *Rock Quarrying Fete* Kuwana Shrine Mie Pref. Start 10 nite, 11 nite parade; 12 best, 8am offer stones; eve 30 huge floats.

End *Rice Transplant*, O-Tsuchi-mi-oya Shr Isobe-cho Ise. 9am plant by young men, women, 10 dancers, 10 musicians; dance in planted paddy by pair bearing huge fans painted with Daikoku, Ebisu. Parade to shrine, many dances of rice cycle. Priest breaks two fans, crowd grab bits as charms

August

Early- *Bon Odori*-dances, plaza, Nara Stn; Dances, Ayame-ike and Sarusawa Pond largest. Ayame-ike's is contest of various groups from Yamato Plain in 3 divisions traditional, modern, W-folk.

End- Winners dance Kashihara Shrine—sponsor Nara-*Nichi News*. Platform built mid Sarusawa pond, public dances around gaily lit pond all nite; all welcome to join.
7 *Tanabata Festival,* Kasuga Shrine, 10am. Maiden *kagura*, classical music, offerings.
14-15 *Illuminate 2,700 lanterns Kasuga Shrine and thru park approaches.
17 *Oyagyu Taiko Odori,* Oyagyu Yamaguchi Shrine, Nara. 7:30pm-about 2 hrs, rural atmosphere, many costumed dancers, musicians, drums: join *bon* dances. *sumo*.
23-24 *Jizo-Bon,* Kids in *yukata* visit Jizo temples, Gango-ji Gokuraku-bo photogenic.
Lunar July 17-18, August Full Moon+2 *Kanko Odori* Takatsuse-mura Sochi-cho, Suzuka-gun, Mie. Pray anti drought; both eves till 2am; 25 youths in Polynesian costumes dance around fire, drums, chant: 8/15-16/1992, 9/3-4/1993, 8/24-5/1994, 8/13-14/1995, 9/1-2/1996, 8/21-2/1997, 8/7-8/1998, 7/17-8/1999, 7/16-7/2000 etc.

September

Lunar August 15 = Full Moon Sept *Uneme Matsuri* at Uneme Shrine, Nara. Rite at 6pm **14** opens fete; **15** from 4:30, procession starts Sarusawa Pond. Kimono-clad boys carry 8-ft fan decorated autumn flowers, Princess Uneme on Imperial Cart, flutes, drums, retainers parade thru Nara to Uname Shrine 6pm too offer food, dances. If moon full fan put on *kangen* (woodwind & strings) boat end of rite, float fan on pond. Faithful dip feet in, anti frostbite.
15 *Konda Hachiman Festival,* Shrine, Habikino City, Osaka Pref. 9pm carry national treasure portable shrine accompanied by torches to Emperor Ojin mound.
25-week Gango-ji temple Fete, Nara-machi throbs in new fete to knit tourist site, incl our Orient-kan museum, numerous shops, rest'nts around one of oldest temples

October

Most-*ChrysanthemumDolls* Ayame-ike Park
1 *Autumn Festival* at Himuro Shrine, Nara. Rites, ancient form of *bugaku*, nite.
1-Nov 30 Deva King & Kissho Tennyo on view, Joruri-ji, ¥300.
5 *Autumn Fete,* Tamukeyama Hachiman Shrine, one of Nara oldest.
9 *Autumn Festivals* small shrines— Saoka Shrine & those Nara Heijo, Tsuseki areas.
9 *Incense Day,* 10am incense party by head of Shino School, 1pm, Kasuga.
12 *Death Anniversary Poet Basho* at Ueno birthplace; *haiku* reading am (*see* p332).
Mid-month *Dehorn Deer,* Nara Park; protect tourists in fall mating season, dehorn deer

'lucky' day in picturesque roundup using pole-lariat, daily 9:30am. Horn to souvenir
21-Nov 8 *Nara Museum displays treasure of *Shosoin Imperial Repository* 2 wks, after 4pm & final mon least crowd.
Year-round **Treasure Exhibit* Kasuga Treasury—slightly less antique treasures.
22 *Public Showing* Beauty Guze Kannon of Korea, Horyu-ji *Yumedono* -thru Nov 3.
23-25 *Ueno Tenjin Fete,* for Michizane.
23 nite, portable shrines lit, go thru town.
24, 25 masked demons, portable shrines parade. Best: 10am–noon; 25 Higashi-chodori, Ueno C, Mie Pref (*see* p332).
26 Tenrikyo *Annual Festival,* Youth club; ancient Bugaku to Country & Western.

November

1-20 *'Mum Show* opp park, Nara Pref Hall.
13 *Jion-e* Memorial for Jion Taishi founder Hoso Sect; Kofuku-ji, Yakushi-ji. Regal-clad priest prays, gets question to discuss from Jion spirt: vivid Q&A betw priests.
15. *Shichi-go-san* (7-5-3 Fete) nationwide. Boys age 3, 7, girls 5 in Sunday best visit shrines, be blessed; best at Kasuga Shrine.

December

16-18 *On Matsuri Hon. Sound Festival, **absolute must for theater buffs** Waka-miya Shrine, subsidiary of Kasuga. Open Dec 15, 5pm when display offerings from various people, followed by rite.
16 4pm Kasuga & Wakamiya. 1yr 268 pheasants, 36 rabbits, 43 *tanuki*-badger 100*tai*-sea bream,106 barrels *sake* offered.
17* Midnite (of 16), spirit of Wakamiya, Young Sun appears as light struck in total darkness, ancient *gagaku* instrumental *On*-music switches beat from chaos to geos; torch parade escort Light in tent thru dark park as deer mew, to temporary shrine N side of entry to shrine park; mini-version Ise Shrine vingitennial Sengu-no-gi rite.
1am spirit enshrined, offerings, music, sacred dances; 10am Wakamiya Shrine rite 1pm parade. *Noh*, *kyogen*, *dengaku* at *Nakano-monguchi* with drum, flute and *henboku* bones; costumed kids horseback, ancient jockeys, archers, fine horses, sword bearers, Yamato warriors; *daimyo* procession 100s samurai. Prayers for harvest followed by true living museum of ancient dance forms— *oni-kagura, Azuma-asobi,* shrine maiden *mikagura, dengaku, sei-no* dances, 12 *bugaku* 5pm, *Yamato-mai,* all by photogenic bonfire until late into nite.
18, 1am return spirit thru park to main shrine and end with ritual to douse light of visiting spirit of sun for another year.

although across plains of sea I came
passing through eighty islands
not once has this city of Nara
left my heart —Anon, *Manyoshu*

EN ROUTE KYOTO

NARA TO KYOTO follows moving of Imperial Capital in 794AD. But now there are buses from Kintetsu Station, which stop near museum to take road past Tegai-mon gate of Daibutsu, enjoyable 45min-1hr drive.

GETTING THERE: **Trains**: JR infrequent. Best: electric NARA Kintetsu stn → KYOTO → Kintetsu Kyoto stn (southside JR), all air-conditioned, with 1st-class cars. **Taxi** will run about ¥10,-14,000, 20-28x-mtr. Suggested is stop en route (for which see **Kyoto Murasaki #2 route**, p463) at **Byodoin Phoenix Pavilion**, and additional choice to enter Kyoto long way, via **Uji Rhine** boat and **Biwa Lake of Lute** (*see*, p496), or direct w/stop DAIGO-SAMBOIN. Good Buddhist lunch stop, min 4, rsve ☎(0774)-32-3900, ¥3,800-¥5,800ea; or *Fucha-ryori* opp gate in lovely thatched **Haku-un-An** any number, rsve, ¥4,400-¥7,500+% ☎31-8017; pilgrims ¥1,000 Zen kaiseki R of gate, door in left corner of wall **Icho-An**, rsve as arrive temple (eat later) as supply short; also matcha, dumplings, other refreshments 10-17:30; all 5min walk of OBAKU stns of JR or Keihan Uji line.

NARA → **KOYA** MONASTERY, hour train and funicular (*following*), our highly recommended sidetrack for overnite or longer, or even forever.

NARA → OSAKA best by Kintetsu rocket expresses, several hourly, 30min; or by bus over lovely Hanna-Ikoma mountain toll road (*see* OSAKA, p566).

MT YOSHINO 吉野山   SACRED REFUGE

GETTING THERE: 33min by Kintetsu express from KASHIWARA JINGU; or drive south on Rte169; or 95min bus from JR NARA stn, get off at 2nd to last stop YOSHINO JINGU; train or bus take bus last 4km via YOSHINO SHRINE, or skip shrine, take short ropeway from last rail stop.

THIS MOST FAMOUS of sakura-viewing spots in Japan with its 'three thousand' cherry trees, of several varieties, blanketing mountainside is for those with extra half-day, except during fabulous cherry-sakura season (starts **early Apr**, lasts over month, blooms start from hill base to peak) when it is worth battling even weekend crowds. There is nothing quite like seeing sakura on such grand scale. Plums are also lovely earlier and various fruit trees bloom later. Temples and shrines here nice, but not for those with no great interest in looking at more old temples and shrines.

If **limited in time**, 1-2hrs on lower part of mountain, or whichever is lower blooming of three levels *Shimo-no-Sembon* (lower-1,000 trees), *Naka-no-Sembon* (mid-1,000) or *Oku-no-Sembon* (rear-1,000) will suffice. Someone will invite you to join their group on their mats. Why not? Sometime you'll be asked to sing something, college song, etc. Warm up your school days impersonations or pantomime. Basis of traditional Japanese democracy that enabled folks to survive Tokugawa totalitarianism and 20th century militarism is that great art of gently making asses of oneselves in public together.

Wandering monk En-no-Gyoja started meditation hall here in 7th century, soon populated by retired emperors and other court nobles escaping tedious life at court. Its remoteness made it also ideal haven for marked men. YOSHIMIZU JINJA is where MINAMOTO Yoshitsune and wife Shizuka-gozen and Benkei hid out here for three years in 12th century to escape wrath of brother, Shogun MINAMOTO Yoritomo.

Every tree and rock in garden is tied to them "tree to which Yoshitsune tied his horse", "rock into which Benkei drove nails to prove strength," etc.

Two centuries later, renegade emperor Go-Daigo hid out here and created his Southern Court of emperors in response to being 'cheated' out of his turn on throne. From 1336-1392 his junior line claimed control of court but becoming ignored, rapidly losing what clout they held, one of his wiser descendants, emperor Go-Kameyama, chose to rejoin mainstream. So ended short-lived *Nanboku-cho* (North-South Era). Go-Daigo's room at Yoshino is still there, he's buried on hill opposite in NYOI-RIN-JI.

While this question of sovereignty was solved to satisfaction of most 600 years ago, Go-Daigo's heirs still make waves: during US Occupation, Nagoya shopkeeper KUMAZAWA Hirokichi sent letter to 'Shogun' MacArthur, with his detailed genealogy, family Imperial Chrysanthemum crest, other items, claiming to be rightful heir to Chrysanthemum throne. Claim still makes news on dull dog days.

Near mountain's base is YOSHINO JINGU shrine, built 1889 in honor of Go-Daigo for his early efforts to restore control of government to imperial line. (Go-Daigo got enough military backing to topple weakened Kamakura Shogun but he neglected to reward military supporters while rewarding his ineffective court pals, so army revolted and created Ashikaga Shogunate.)

Atop cable-car is one of Japan's three **'great' torii**, this one of bronze said left over from Great Buddha's construction, stands 25ft. Beyond on R is **Zao-do hall**, main pavilion of mount's original Kimbusen-ji temple. Present structure (NT) rebuilt (with gate) 1591 by Hideyoshi: impressive, at 34m tall ranks close behind Nara Daibutsu-den as world's 2nd largest wood structure. Approach up shop-lined lane differs little from Tycoon's time with pilgrims and Sunday-best spiffed farmers alongside us, one of most photogenic walks anywhere. Inside, Buddha triad, all of wood, central 8m tall, *Zao Gongen*, ferocious aspect of Buddha—unfortunately, 'secret Buddhas' *denpo-kanjo*, shown to public only once every 4 years (next 1990, '98). You can, however, see triad copy about half size. Building was undergoing 'great Showa facelift' finished Oct '85. Behind, remains of Yoshino Palace of Go-Daigo—buried further uphill near Nyoirin-ji Temple.

5min walk on to...
YOSHIMIZU SHRINE (on left) which boasts Japan's oldest unrestored-original *shoin* library hall (ICA), packed full of assorted treasures (¥300). Yoshitsune and faithful side-kick Benkei supposedly hid here from shogun brother.

Upon their parting Shizuka-gozen danced for Yoshitsune at...
KATTE SHRINE (5min beyond at fork in road) is interesting in that 3 main shrines connect by long thatched-bark roof. Small tea shop here serves light snacks, pleasant break in this wooded compound: Hideyoshi thought so too, giant kettle here was used for his extravagant cherry-viewing tea party.

Down side road in front of Katte's torii is...
DAINICHI-JI temple, not much in itself, but its main hall contains *Gochi Nyorai*, 5 Buddhas of Wisdom: Dainichi, Ashuku, Hosho, Shaka and Amida. Dating from Fujiwara era, it is unusual to have all 5 in one place, especially as single set. Our *Buddhist Dictionary* disagrees on last two names, lists Muryoju and Fukokuju, proof that popular tradition doesn't always agree with formal. *To see*, must phone ahead ☎(07463)-2-4354, easiest to have **Visitors' Center** near ZAO-DO call. ¥200 donation to see.

10min up to...
CHIKURIN-IN, with fabulous landscape garden in back (¥200); **stay** here ¥12,000+w/2. Most inns here match international hotel rates, better reserved in advance thru JTB or Kinki Nippon Tourist, and standards are high for emperor has stayed on hillside. Inns here hang along hillside, usually are entered from 3rd floor and amazingly, private rooms take advantage of views.

SAKURAMOTO-BO temple opposite has 1,200-year-old Shaka-nyorai. Just beyond is entrance to toll road to summit; nontoll just beyond. Suggest bus up as it's over hour walk, all on road. Continuing past bus turnoff, road hairpins back and up next branch-off is 25min climb to **NYOIRIN-JI** temple and Go-Daigo's mausoleum.
Bus to top lets off OKU-SENBON stop just beyond top toll booth.

25min walk to...
Saigyo's Hermitage, *Saigyo-an*, where he spent 3 years evading Kyoto problems (*see* his *Ten Foot Square Hut* and *Tales of The Heike*, tr. A.L. Sadler). Not much as architecture, but it sits so serenely in grove of ancient trees and hike is pleasant. En route is rustic old **KIMBU SHRINE**, tiny storage shed behind is another spot where Yoshitsune hid while attempting to flee from Yoshino.

From here, walk down non-toll road, halfway is...
YOSHINO MIKUMARI SHRINE, beautiful inner garden surrounded by several mellowed-with-age buildings. Shrine treasure is 13th century bronze statue of Tamayori-Hime-no-Mikoto, Sea-Goddess mother of emperor Jimmu: but not allowed to view it (maybe shows her as foreigner she was?) Few hundred meters below is viewing platform, and for hiker easy 40min riverside trail down to MIYATAKI 'shrine-waterfall' whence 15min bus to Yamato Kami-ichi stn on Kintetsu. Excavations near falls have come up with Jomon and Yayoi period artifacts, displayed to public at nearby **Nakasho Primary School**. From stone foundations and tiles excavated here, scholars conclude that this was also site of **Jimmu's Detached Palace** at Yoshino, mentioned in *Kojiki*.

30min bus from Yamato Kami-ichi stn via Miyataki falls...
Washi-no-Sato, tiny hamlet where Japanese *washi* paper is hand-made. Actual making of paper using hand-held, square sifters can be seen all year. But main ingredient, paper mulberry of *kozo*, *mitsumata*, *gampi* varieties, harvested late autumn and after stripping bark must be rinsed in cold water —so done in winter when visit worth shivering thru. **Dec thru Mar** best time to see entire true process of preparing materials.

Other crafts in Yoshino vale include woodworking of Yoshino sugi-cedar into fabulous buckets for Japanese bath and other specialized buckets you can never guess use of unless shown. Watching these craftsmen at work is like going to ballet, their movement beautiful in its impeccable efficiency, reflected in their final products. Chopsticks here made by hand by elderly crafts-couples famed–local cedar noted for its resiliency is easier on teeth and food doesn't slip. Not only foreigners have trouble using *hashi*.

Kaki-persimmon trees abound on mountain, especially around Shimo Ichi-cho and local delicacy weds leaves of tree with salted *saba*-mackerel, square-wrapping *saba* slice on sushi (vinegared rice) in leaf, then packing tightly into cedar tub, pressing overnite with rock: *yummy*. Appears **May**, but best **June**-on when all inns, tea shops and eateries in area tout it.

OMINE: 1,719m/5,638ft, main temple-mountain of Yamabushi ascetics, seen around country in special costume of baggy white robe, pants, powder-puff-embellished vest, animal skin back-apron and strapped-on small black cap resembling Jewish phalacteries. Remnants of pre-Buddhist mountain-cult who undergo shamanistic austerities like fire walking, cold-waterfall immersion, practise exorcism. Supposedly organized by 7th century 'magician' En-no-Gyoja, who by tradition established their main temples. Came into being as organized sect in 10-11th century, Shingon and Tendai branches with secret teachings, orally communicated. Mixed with Shinto, seen at shrines. Commune with deity in mountains, common to many shaman types. Other mountains associated with them, some of which we visit, are Kongo-zan in Nara, Kumano in south Wakayama, Daisen nr Tottori, Dewa Sanzen shrines in Tohoku, Mt Misen on Miyajima where they teach us to fire walk. Ascent by women banned till 1960 women-libbers assaulted it as last bastion of men-only faith; now accepts women as Yamabushi. Banned in Meiji era purification of Shinto, US Occupation-mandated freedoms revived them.

GETTING THERE: From Yoshino, above, whence for real adventurers ascent-return takes full day, many ups and downs, last sections require pulling oneself up chain ladders—which mark entry to holy of holies where devout pilgrims change to clean sandals so as not to defile. Temple atop has only prayer wheels we've seen in Japan, *a la* Tibet—tho Mt Koya has entire library building mounted on axis like Brodignabian prayer wheel. View one of most impressive in Japan—19th century writers reported being able to see Mt Fuji almost 300km away! No smog then. Ancient pilgrim trails lead on thru mountains W to Mt Koya Monastery town, S to Kumano or E to Ise, but really require Japanese ability or co-pilgrim. Many simple pilgrim huts, places to camp, beckon true adventurer.

*There is furthermore a place bearyng name Coia,
very famous for the multitude of Abbeyes the
Bonzii have therein....*
— Father Froes, *History of Travayle* 1577

KOYA-SAN 高野山
REAL LIFE SHANGRI-LA

TWELVE CENTURIES AGO Japanese saint Kukai (posthumously Kobo-daishi) decided he wanted someplace where he could get away from it all, far from Kyoto's earthy distractions. In 816 he hiked into these almost impassable high mountains just south of Osaka and Yamato Plain, then-center of infant Japanese empire, and after tossing his staff into sky (in what was obviously dowsing) followed it to this hidden high vale that suited his purpose. At 900 meters and ringed by eight peaks of another hundred-plus meters, he called it Koya-san, High Field Mount. Probably already holy to mountain ascetics, he built his secluded monastery. It soon grew into Shangri-La city of temples (complete, just as in James Hilton's paradise, with pleasure quarters) where today after dozen centuries one can yet escape everyday hubbub—yes, even Yankee tourists may ascend this mountain to eat lotus, and other Buddhist vegetarian fare. This comparison with Shangri-La is no mere journalistic gimmick, for Saint Kobo expounded tantric form of Buddhism similar to that of Tibet. Even literary Shangri-La's lost Christian link may have its parallel in that Saint Kobo studied several years in monastery near China's great Nestorian Christian Center in Changan (Jpn. Cho-An, modern Hsian or Xian).

Saint Kobo's sect is called **Shingon**, lit. True Teaching, and shares common Chinese origin with peculiar Tibetan form known as Lamaism (overlay of Chinese tantric buddhism on even more tantric older worship known as Bon, which came from farther west). Most easily recognizable difference between these two **tantric** (Sanskrit for 'loom', used now as 'magic') sects and others is visible demonic form of many so-called 'gods' and concern with such exotic rites as midwinter immersion in cold water or waterfalls, and fire walking (*see* Miyajima, Nara, Tokyo) etc.

Unlike Shangri-La, there have been changes in this vale. Holocausts have swept these great wooden pavilions five times from 994. One medieval noh play mentions '990 temples of Koya'. Prior to last great fire of 1887 there were still 680. Today there are only 117—most scant 3 centuries old, tho some few date back seven centuries. Of course altars, images and treasures they contain may date back to origin, whether native manufacture or import from mainland. Each temple or monastery no matter how small, has its own abbot as each is principal temple supported by many other temples in other towns and cities. Major function of these at Koya has long been as hostel to pilgrims from subsidiary supporting temples, 53 bigger ones take guests.

GETTING THERE: No longer act of penance as it was for over 11 centuries. **Nankai RR** runs frequent thru-expresses out of OSAKA Namba stn, just over hour to mountain base, thence funicular. KYOTO → : go to OSAKA then Midosuji line subway to 4th stop NAMBA up two flights for Nankai line, as above. NARA → : JR to YAMATO-TAKATA change for WAKAYAMA-*yuki* (bound), about 1hr, detrain HASHIMOTO, change to toonerville to GOKURAKUBASHI whence funicular; WAKAYAMA → : JR for NARA, midway 20min to HASHIMOTO, same as previous. **Taxi** OSAKA-¥14,000/30x-mtr.

From **HASHIMOTO** travelers from Nara or Wakayama or those from Osaka-Namba who took ordinary train, transfer to puffing two-car toonerville trolley which follows, as does thru-express, old pilgrim mountain trail, up thru primeval forests of cedar, cyprus and umbrella pine into almost vertical mountains. Views from train windows breathtaking: great forests, steep gorges, isolated hamlets perched on sides of mounts like hats dropped onto hat-rack; terraced fields form giants' stairways to and from nowhere. Soon mountains become so steep even intrepid railway builders gave up, we transfer to funicular (every 30min 5am-11pm) to rise almost like skyscraper lift to taxi and bus stand at top. Few minutes ride on to last pass between steep hills and DAIMON, Great Red Gate (900m alt), beyond which until 1872 women were barred entry to great cluster of monasteries beyond, now with 400-500 clerics in population of some 10,000.

Drive: up exciting series of hairpin-curved toll road from **Koya-guchi**, next town to Hashimoto Wakayama-ward; about 40-60min depending on traffic, heavy summers. Occasional closing by slides in summer rain or September typhoon, quickly repaired. Over 26km (16mi), latter 18km climbing over kilometer turning, twisting incessantly with no straightaway over 50m. Parking spots along road allow for restful views. We prefer old lumber road up from Hashimoto when not in hurry, or when toll road crowded: private trail owned by lumber interests who work forests—more often closed by slides. Most of way parallels trout-laden stream with several good natural swimming holes we have often bared ourselves to on sweltering summer days.

Taxi from Hashimoto about 22x-mtr. Tho train preferable, from Osaka or Nara (via Horyu-ji) some 50x-mtr; Wakayama slightly less. From Osaka, train far better, city roads jammed.

Bus runs up toll road from Koya-guchi JR stn, & irregularly up lumber road from Hashimoto. Alternate bus route up from Minoshima stn near Shirahama Spa, W coast below Wakayama city: 'goat trail' of '64 edition now well paved (*see* p405).

WHERE TO STAY: Koya even more popular retreat now that religion is on wane. There are no hotels in vale tho some 50 monasteries offer hostelry to all comers; no link to your religion, or lack of it. Student monks serve us in our roles as temporary 'guest monks'. Rooms vary from plain cells to treasure-muraled halls opening on antique gardens. Unrelated casual visitor should expect to pay ¥7,000-10,000 for futon and 2 good meals—lot more than 1964 edition's ¥1,000-1,800 but still for couple about room only at ¥-S hotel, and thus still bargain. Keep this ratio in mind, as readers of old '64 edition were showing up even 1985 at our favorite monastery and leaving ¥1,500 despite fact that taxi basic-mtr had risen from ¥70 seven-fold to ¥470! This old system of "no formal charge, on leaving just hand donation in white envelope" now simplifed, as best way to get room is thru information office **Kanko-annai**, variously at Namba Nankai stn, at top of funicular and in Koya town center: will reserve for you, collect fee in advance (average ¥8,000 1989) or give you chit with exact sum due written. Beer, sake or other extras should be paid for in cash on leaving, no plastic in paradise.

Do not expect special monastic architecture to quarters as there is but one general Japanese architecture whether palace, temple, home or ryokan. Most rooms for non-introduced visitors will be simple, but with access to gardens and altar rooms. Not all temples serve visitors full vegetarian, so specify if you prefer *shojin-ryori*, Buddhist vegetarian. On Koya this is haute cuisine, includes such local specialties as *koya-tofu*. Our favorite, **Shin-no-in**, is pure vegetarian, not even egg served. First visit 1955 stayed at **Sai-nan-in** rooms decorated with ages-old painted fusuma doors opening onto magnificent modern garden by late SHIGEMORI Mirei (local pronunciation of namesake painter Millet) of Kyoto, leading designer and garden historian. Son-successor SHIGEMORI Kanto has written much in English. Suzuki Daisetsu's writer-wife Beatrice wrote many of her essays on Buddhism here. Another favorite **Seki-sho-in** new detached wing cuddled in magnificent isolation in even more magnificent middle-Edo garden (early 1700s). But just go stumble on your own treasure. 1988 put up Paramount staffer at big **Fukuchi-in**, ¥8,-12,000, booked by Annai-sho, English spoken, Shigemori garden.

If student hoboing it, **Kanko-annai** might be able to help with cheaper digs, perhaps in simpler acolytes' quarters as they used to decade ago, sometimes without meals. Youth Hostel, even W-hotel—but why really 'leave this world' you've come so far to see?

Warning: Temples can hold 20,000 overnite guests and in summer around *O-bon* do, so don't go without reservations at that season. Only Shin-no-in refuses groups; may not even be on Kanko-annai roster; accepts only introductions, such as our readers. Its abbot Nakagawa was long-time head of Koya University and recently grand abbot of whole mountain: ☎(07365)-6-2227-Japanese only, English-speaking nun no longer incarnate. Offer money (¥7,-10,000 each) on arrival so he'll know you're not using '64 edition. We advise you ask be awakened before dawn to attend services.

Coming up from hot humid lowlands to cool heights may chill your belly and cause temporary discomfort; advise wrapping towel around midriff as *haramaki* before sleep.

Drivers park your car where temple assigns as police 'gather alms' by slipping summonses under windshields. And they diligently pursue collection before you leave.

PERSONAL ORIENTATION: Koya, wonder of nature, is also living history of Oriental architecture and art.

Dine from thousand-year-old lacquer plates, centuries-old ceramics (when they wear out they said they jog down to corner shop and buy new set, as they did originally) or tasteful modern ware, in gorgeous apartments whose treasured ancient murals slide aside to reveal paradise gardens. Hoary rafters echo chimes and bells and deep sing-song of some recluse at his matins in distant apartment.

For long no one knew what treasure was hidden here, definitive inventory has only been carried out since our last edition. Major art works are kept in **Treasure House**. Those in situ in your hostel can be seen freely, just explore—carefully slide doors open and altar room will be obvious by its size, often wooden floor, and fact that at far end dark will be pierced by flicker of oil lamps on altar and glitter of altar paraphernalia in its light. Show basic respect and all will be satisfied.

There are usually two services held daily: morning at or before dawn at 5-6am, evening some time after supper. These may consist of simple group chanting by monks and acolytes seated outside sanctum (as is usual if abbot is not present) or may be full service with incense offerings, even *goma* (fire offering), at low fire altar. It all depends upon occasion and, it would seem, upon mood of particular abbot.

Mood of particular abbot thru whom we became personally oriented is rather singular for he is last of true monks on mountain–Vy Rev Zenkyo NAKAGAWA of *Shin-no-in*, 'Parent King Pavilion'. Other monks are married or intend to. However as all perform priestly function (intermediary between worshipper and worshipped), Rev Nakagawa feels all can be properly referred to as priests: despite fact that lay scholars insist there are no priests in Buddhism.

"What is your concept of 'Ultimate'" we asked our host, qualifying that his response be oversimplified if necessary to keep it within limitations of this short book. Abbot replied there was no need to oversimplify as basis of True Teaching is simplicity itself: The One, referred to in Shingon as Dainichi (Great Sun or Light, in Sanskrit Roshana) Nyorai (Buddha), whose essence is Light, is that Truth inherent in all things in our universe. You and I are Dainichi and Dainichi is essentially ourselves. But human nature is burdened with impurities, so our goal is to rid body and soul of these vices. True Teaching is but discipline to attain this end. "Ultimate is not obliteration or nothingness." But here, he intimated, simple explanation was complete for any attempt to define Ultimate in words is futile or it would not have been subject of such universal disagreement throughout human history. Identity of Ultimate can be revealed to individual thru enlightenment, is thus indescribable.

Shingon priests in olden times were traditionally bachelors. We asked if sex were sin? He answered any vice was what may be called sin: tho he stressed all 'sin' can be atoned for, washed away. Sex in marriage is natural and so cannot be sinful. Even Shakyamuni, historical Buddha of our kalpa-era, married, had one son. No, Shingon celibate tradition was based on practical situation of marriage: husband-father must be selfish in that his first consideration must be for family. Thus priest with family is distracted from primary mission of ministering to needs of his public, of using that specialized education which is not practical for all to receive, applying his education to guiding all people towards salvation. Marriage tho not prohibited is discouraged. Buddhism not being dogmatic cannot mandate anything: spirit of law not letter of law is all important. Thus as temperament changed opinion toward view that not having wife can be more distraction to young priest than having one Shingon was able to tolerate both points of view. All decisions must be one's own.

Abbot rises at 5am. Lesser clerics arrayed behind him chanting sutras, he leads them himself performing *mudra*, hands dancing thru mystic exercises whose inner symbolic meaning is as abstract as any sacred music and which serves similar ends in aiding him to get in tune for day. After light breakfast he begins function as religious leader. Some days he teaches philosophy at Koya University, assists divinity students to read old scripture in *kanbun* hybrid form of written Chinese as used in ancient Japan. He also has priestly rites, particularly memorial service supplicated by his congregation. He sees individuals who bring personal problems, or advises lesser clerics on ritual. At 4pm he gathers subordinates for that service he refers to in English as "grace"—roughed it in America when young, picked up smattering of English. At 9pm he leads memorial rite for those who have passed on leaving no descendants to "honor thine father and mother". Full vegetarian, abstains from even eggs or staple Japanese broth made from dried bonito—as do you in this temple. However when traveling he will not inconvenience others for selfish sake of his own ritual purity and does with what comes. We bumped into him in Osaka one nite and dined together at Royal Hotel, ordering 'whatever is convenient'—(one sight of his robes and special vegetable platter appeared). He sleeps five hours nitely, observes no special periods of retreat or disciplinary rites of purification such as in other sects form center of some of Japan's most exotic rituals.

GETTING AROUND ON PILGRIMAGE: Koya is quite spread out but it invites walking. However, if you want to do it by **taxi**, will run about 20x-mtr for 3-4hr. End up at KONGOBU-JI temple then take this last central section on foot. No English guides; guide available Japanese-speaking (as is taxi) at **Kanko-annai** Tourist Info. If hoofing, June-on **horse-drawn** buses run between necropolis of OKUNO-IN and KONGOBU-JI, ¥300-350. They will also take you anywhere at about taxi rates.

Central sights are **Taishi Kyokai**, neighbor **Treasure Hall**, head temple **Kongobu-ji** . Latter is usually taken first: upon entering purchase postcard ticket ¥500.

KONGOBU-JI was built by Hideyoshi for his mother, but rebuilt since, for usual pyrotechnic reason. You are led past main altar room to room with *fusuma* panels by Kano Tanyu. Next very cool room has each wall decorated with mural illustrating one season. Main wall shows pine tree in snow that really chills viewer. Surprisingly, these paintings date from early Meiji Period, century ago ('surprising' because they are good, as little Meiji art is). Original room on this site is where Hideyoshi's son Hidetsugu committed suicide after disagreement with cantankerous father. Next room, in gold-foil, is for imperial visitors or their proxies, while next has paintings by UNKOKU Toeki, Sesshu IV. Down back hall is room *O-Chigo-no-Ma* with sliding panels by KANO Tansai concealing closets in which armed guards hid to protect high-ranking visitors, yet not apparently defiling quiet

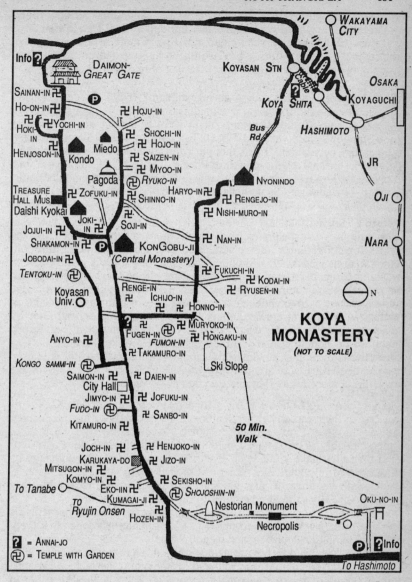

sanctity. Last place visited is immense **kitchen**, where you will note that
monks eat at table on benches, that open fireplace has chimney, 'peculiarity'
of Koya. You should visit kitchen of monastery in which you stay nite, if
possible while they are preparing meals. Each kitchen has large rice oven
with Buddhist shrine set over it. In this shrine fiery Fudo stands as avatar
of native kitchen god. (At Shin-no-in Fudo is surrealistic shadow picture
carved in wood, which closer inspection shows to be sample of Sanskrit
calligraphy adapted to Fudo's form).

Before leaving KONGOBU-JI you will be served tea and Koya pilgrim
sweet cakes and given small pilgrim picture of Saint Kobo, which religious
pilgrim takes home to paste up as talisman. Sort of thing you see in

KONGOBU-JI will be seen on smaller scale—and thus perhaps more enjoyable—in dozens of other monastery buildings. Feel free to visit any: regardless of hospitality shown, do not tip. Small offering dropped unobtrusively in any offering box would be appreciated and put to use maintaining buildings and gardens, sole source of restoration funds.

From Kongobu-ji, cross square to...

Taishi Kyokai. On this square during midsummer *bon* dances are held every Saturday—and rooms on weekends are at premium. Constant series of services held all day at grand Taishi Kyokai, should not be missed. When Shingon's closely related Tibetan Buddhism was first 'discovered' by 16th century occidentals it was thought from its ritual to be 'lost church,' perhaps Nestorian Catholic church of Prester John. When Catholic rite was first witnessed by Japanese at about same time they thought them to be some new form of Buddhism. So do not expect particularly exotic foreign ritual.

From *Taishi Kyokai* visit Treasure House, trio set on diagonal line, *Taishi Kyokai* center.

Treasure House is actually Museum of Koya, to which number of finest, oldest paintings and sculptures from various monasteries have been moved. This is for convenience of viewers; also because museum is fireproof. Some fabulous pieces here. Skylights and generous spacing make viewing pleasure. Coins in front of various pieces are placed there by pilgrims, as you are sure to see some do. If Catholicism-Buddhism confusion of past centuries seems hard to understand, then take note of Nepalese Mandala, or meditation picture, in corner gallery: composed around central 'Star of David': one might wonder what would have been written had, say, Rabbi Benjamin of Tudela reached Himalayas before Roman Fathers. Many Amida treasures in museum are held sacred to Nichiren adherents, as ancient group called Hijiri were ardent followers of Kukai tho Pure Land Amidaists. Hijiri absorbed into Shingon by shogunal order 1606.

GARDEN PILGRIMAGE: Monastery-temples of Mt Koya are proudest of their gardens. Excellent examples abound to illustrate history and development of Japanese garden over past five centuries. Understandably, gardens have better survived periodic holocausts (like 1888) than they have gardeners. Our first Koya visit was in company of SHIGEMORI Mirei, garden designer and pioneer historian. He did some 35 avant garde versions of 'dry' gardens, using only sand, rock and moss around pond. His gardens take little upkeep once moss has properly rooted: thus later generations of gardeners need not tinker with them and temples won't go broke paying for their upkeep. Ponds in 'dry' gardens not merely esthetic—temples need handy and plentiful supply of water for firefighting.

Shigemori showed us how to date gardens or elements in them (as also *byobu* folding screens). Muromachi and Momoyama (16th century) gardens, built in period of relative personal freedom, are more natural, broader in sweep (even if small) with graceful curves accentuated by mild pruning, they fade off into their natural wild background. Tokugawa Shogunate (1603-1867) set up absolute state with tight, arbitrary control in unnatural social order: reflected in gardens this becomes more obvious closer we come in time to Perry's 'opening' of Japan, as shrubs become unnaturally distorted rather than shaped, clipped down in size so that more can be crowded in to allow garden paths to devolve into hopeless mazes. Late Tokugawa garden paths are enough to drive white rat crazy. Meiji (1860-1912) gardens are hodgepodge but becoming relaxed, while our modern reflect exciting chaos and uncertainty, 'about to become' state. Shigemori pointed out similar keys for dating stone lanterns, architecture, sliding panel paintings: freedom and soaring hope degenerating into tight control and technological perfection, dream of infinity into long-range fineness, shear voloptuousness into tight bra. His gardens, he hoped, will similarly reflect his times (one in south Osaka is to be viewed from air). Several of his most bold have not taken; moss has not rooted, stone gardens still stand out like scarred earth against forest backdrop. It is yet too early to judge them—tho 30-odd years we have seen them bode well.

We pass on interesting info gleaned when garden master Shigemori Mirei guided us around many gardens he had created as well as restored. Among temples known for their gardens are: TENTOKU-IN, lovely Momoyama period by ENSHU Kobori, FUMON-IN's early Tokugawa period garden. Other Tokugawa gardens are found at HOKI-IN, KONGO SAMMI-IN (also hoary Kamakura period one), KONGOBU-JI, RYUKO-IN and YOCHI-IN. Best modern garden is that by Shigemori at Sainan-in; other Shigemori gardens can be seen at KONGO SAMMI-IN, FUDO-IN, FUKUCHI-IN, HONGAKU-IN, RYUSEN-IN, SAIZEN-IN and SHOCHI-IN. Garden addict might tour them carrying in hand anything by his devotee-friend Loraine Kuck, especially *The World of the Japanese Garden* (Weatherhill).

CITY OF DEAD: Great necropolis of Koya **Okuno-in**, covers some two square miles, 5km^2. Old custom is to bury portion of one's ashes here, part at one's home temple. (For old Issei it means international burials). Usually teeth, or cartilage 'jewel' from Adam's apple (*nodo-botoke*) which is sometimes found in ashes, come here—latter as sacred relic.

Necropolis is interesting, pleasant place. Numerous pilgrims sit along-side main paths begging alms, less for selves than to pass on to temples. (You'll feel better if you begin your walk with dozen small coins in pocket.) Some look so old one wonders if they have not come here to die—in old days, yes. Some giant trees have hollows in them, and you may see pair of straw sandals set outside indicating pilgrim rooming within. Piles of pebbles, broken idol-talismans, tiny paper or cloth pennants will be seen set in root crotches of many trees, again reminiscent of pilgrim paths of Tibetan Himalayas. One great monument marks common grave of 1,000s of Japanese dead of Korean invasions of Hideyoshi, four centuries ago.

Near entrance, to right of main gate about 100 yards in, is replica of **Nestorian monument of Hsian Fu** (Xian). Original set up by 'Prester John's Christians' in China 13 centuries ago. Their main monastery was not far from where Saint Kobo studied. Some try to make case for Kobo having been heavily influenced by Christianity, one such wealthy American matron subsidized tremendous job reproducing monument in stone and moving it here. Dr Paul Yoshiro Saeki, long-Japan's oldest Christian, noted scholar of such things, said this just so much wishful thinking. He wished case could be made out for Kobo's Christianity, but no support can be found in fact. Recognize monument by stone tortoise base. It's inscribed:

Commemorating propagation of Ta-ch'in (Luminous Religion) in Middle Kingdom (China) By Adam, Priest and Pope of Chinastan Behold! There is one who is true and firm, who, being Uncreated is Origin of Origins; who is ever Incomprehensible and Invisible yet ever mysteriously existing to last of lasts; who, holding Secret Source of Origin, created all things and who, surpassing all Holy Ones is sole unoriginated Lord of Universe—is not this our Aloha, the Triune, mysterious Person, unbegotten and true Lord?... Imperial Rescript of Autumn (638 AD) says; 'The Way had not, at all times and in all places, selfsame name; the Sage had not...selfsame body. Heaven caused suitable religions to be instituted for every region and clime...

—*Syriac and Chinese bilingual inscription, Saeki tr.*

Original is in 'stone forest' in Xian, China. Next to it here, is fascinating English-inscribed tomb of 'non-violent?' Buddhist insecticide millionaire.

At far end of necropolis Saint Kobo himself squats in his cavern vault– not dead, believers maintain, but meditating till Day of Judgment when he will reappear. Highest ranking abbot of Koya enters vault every Mar 21 to change Saint Kobo's clothes. Before vault is octagonal Hall of Bones where ashes of devout too poor to afford private burial may be deposited in slot. Hall of oil lamp offerings here burned down few years ago, since rebuilt. One lamp was lit by Kobo and has been kept burning since. It was saved from fire. Had it been lost, it could have been rekindled only from sacred wood fire kept burning atop Miyajima's Mount Misen, because Kobo lit it also. Stone bridge before this final complex is said to admit passage of no one who cannot enter Kobo's paradise. Hideyoshi visited Koya after his Korean slaughter and walked bridge alone at nite to test his eligibility. Bridge didn't collapse, he returned next morning to cross in state.

When Saint Kobo does reappear he expects to see things just about as he left them. Up on Koya, he won't be too disappointed.

SHOPPING: SHANGRI-LA: Fulfills its promise of priceless paintings and sculptures, beautiful gardens and lovely architecture. And for us shoppers, we found gem —unpretentious little place, looks like religious bookshop until you look carefully and notice some statuary in window. Enter, there are many small carvings in showcases; against back wall are some sarcophogi-like black lacquer cases, around nine feet tall: small altar-shrines containing images of various buddhas. YOSHIDA Sakutaro is name of shop, elderly proprietor 6th generation handling religious art goods for temple city. His prices are reasonable, if no great bargains. But he does have exciting collection of images of Buddhas, bodhisattvas, numerous other deities. Asked to see *Fudo-myo-o*, lariat- wielding demonic figure, he showed us few small ones for few thousand yen. Then from one of his back rooms he produced exquisitely carved masterpiece in sandalwood ... Fudo high astride rocks, two accompanying male and female aides in stream below; Ashikaga Period. Who knows what untold treasures lie in back rooms, for we can almost say that entire mountain top is his storehouse. On main thorofare leading from Treasure Hall and Kongobu-ji to Okuno-in, across from Koya Yakuba (town hall) and Saimon (West Gate).

Climb narrow curved street by *Saimon* entrance, you come to town's sole curio shop but which handles mostly tea ceremony equipment.

Pilgrim's mementos are big souvenir item: bells with eight-inch long wooden handles, scrolls showing Kobo-daishi seated on Chinese chair, really temple throne.

Another figure often seen is that of tiny boy acolyte Ishidomaru and his mother. Legend says lord of ancient Fukuoka, Kyushu, left home to renounce this world. Unknown to him, son was born. Little Ishidomaru and mom's search led them to Koya. He left his mother as no women were allowed on sacred precincts. He finally met his father, now monk, but who concealed his identity and led Ishidomaru to believe him dead. Ishidomaru returned to find his mother had died. He again returned to his monk 'friend', became his disciple. KARUKAYADO where two lived is now museum retelling this tale, situated in middle of main street. Fun collector-items for bibliophiles are well-produced religious comic books, in most shops.

Koya has given its name to one of Japan's earliest dehydrated foods. Ordinary *tofu* (bean curd) cakes dehydrated by freezing in natural icy atmosphere of Mt Koya. *Koya-dofu* origin is attributed to Kobo-daishi. Good visiting gift; good pilgrim traveling food.

NITE LIFE OF GODS: Well, there is some, beside prayers, bells, gongs and drums. Three bars on main street between bus stn (sole illuminated, citified intersection) and necropolis. First is about 40-50m down on right towards necropolis. Crowd here younger. 3 bartenders of summer were all bald despite their evident youth: all divinity students at Koya Seminary; *ah* tradition. Assured hostesses are not nuns: but they aren't temple dancers, either. Little way down also on right, is cozy bar Miki; crowd here bit older, thirties-up, more interesting, but erratic. Last bar, almost down at end of lights on left, isn't worth effort.

MISCELLANY: Skiing on small but cozy scale most of winter, bars have potbelly stoves. Mountain empty, air intoxicating, gals love to chat around stoves over hot drink. Plows keep tollroads open, trains rarely miss sched by much after heavy snow.

Lunch can be ordered at any temple, add 40% to your bill if staying, give fair notice, or about ¥2,000 if only lunching (arrange thru **Kanko-annai**). On shopping street are numerous budget lunchrooms, usual noodle-dishes-in-window type. Best is **Koya Shokudo** two doors beyond P.O. at town's only intersection; *yose-nabe* and full line of rice and noodle dishes, coffee and tea. Few doors toward Okuno-in and across street, is **Grill Mountain** (sign in English), similar menu.

WHERE NEXT: Back door out to South Kii coast, bus (2x-daily, 10:10 & 14:10 Apr 23-May 16, July 16-Aug 31 & sun-hol Apr 2-Nov 23; from back of Okuno-in via Ryujin-Koya Skyline → **Tanabe** in 4hr via fine hill spa midway at 47km/80min of Ryujin-Onsen (*see* SOUTHERN KII); ¥3,000 = to Ryujin, +¥1,960 Tanabe.

Then suggest going up → WAKAYAMA-OSAKA or down around KII → ISE-YAMATO – *Or* right to follow SOUTHERN KII coast back up → WAKAYAMA, and on → OSAKA; – *Or* back down way you came → HASHIMOTO whence bus down center of penninsula via OMINE (*see* HORYU-JI end, p365) → KUMANO SEA coast, thence left → ISE-YAMATO.

NEGORO-DERA, another great monastery complex, once far larger than Koya now mere romantic shadow at foot of mountain Wakayama-ward on JR Hashimoto to **Iwade** (coming other way, 25min from Wakayama), thence 10min bus, moderate taxi to... Branch of Koya dedicated to Fudo, once independent and so powerful as to challenge and hold off ODA Nobunaga until succumbing in 1585 to ferocious secular state-building of Hideyoshi. Tranquil remaining temples with lovely paths thru ruins now form park of cherry trees, reflective wandering for adventurer, but of little interest to more casual tourist. Oft burned, most recently early '60s just after we had seen numerous and marvelous fusuma-screens still there, which fire we venture was itself at least suggested to cover demands of voracious local art market. Oh, well.

Area on north side of river has interesting Chinese-style residential compounds of courtyard fully enclosed by four wooden connected buildings (in China usually brick), entry thru huge gate in one wall. Just meander...

PERSONAL DATEBOOK: KANKO ANNAI ☎(0736)-56-2616.

Mar 17 Changing of Saintly Robes at Mt Koya Hoki-in temple at Okuno-in as new robes are put on Saint Kobo Daishi's mummy each year.

21 *Kyusho-mie-ku*, death anniversary of St. Kobo, elaborate rituals, 8am Toro-do at Okuno-in; 12 noon, Mie-do.

Apr 21 *Mando-e*, hundreds of candles lit at Toro-do, Okuno-in, 9am.

25 *Go-Eika* (Sutra reading) by thousands attending annual services at main temple, Kongobu-ji temple. Held at Daishi Kyokai; followed by *Buyo Taikai* (dance contest) representative regional groups vie for honors.

May 3-7 *Kechien-kanjo*, 8am-5pm, Kondo. Toss flower upon mandala—where it falls decides which is to be your guardian Buddha.

Jun 15 *Aoba Matsuri* fetes birthday of St. Kobo. Procession, dances, chigo at Kongobu-ji.

Aug 13 Candles light entire pathway to Okuno-in, observance of bon rites.

13-15 *Urabon-e*, Rituals during Obon period at Kongobu-ji.

Sep 22-23 *Hoshizukushi Koya-san* is recently started annual event for Mt. Koya with takigi noh, concerts, etc.

"Now let's go to the whale spearing at Kumano...."
Her demands were endless. Surely if men yielded
to all such whims, these hussies would insist on
crossing the ocean. — Ejima Kiseki, *Wayward Wife* (1716)

KII PENINSULA 紀伊半島
RUGGED AND RUSTIC

BACK IN THIRD CENTURY BC, Chinese tour group led by scholarly
Ch'in Hsu Fu came ashore on southern Kii, liked what they saw and settled
down. China used passports then, Japanese (if any were around) hadn't
discovered visas or Alien Registration Passbooks, so Mister Ch'in entered
local lore as Shin-no-Jofuku. His 300 chosen 'perfect maidens and perfect
youths' began peopling south Wakayama.

Some centuries later adventurer with baggy pants and destiny led his
shipload of travelers from Kyushu thru scenic Inland Sea to this same
shore. He paused long enough to fight close battle with some tribe in hills
and with help of Chinese tourists' decendants, won. He continued on up
Wakayama coast to Osaka and in toward Nara where, at Kashihara in
Yamato, he was enthroned as first emperor, Jimmu Tenno.

Perhaps Kii's baths invigorated Jimmu and band. Ch'in had been sent by
Chinese emperor Shi Huang Ti (who built Great Wall and Xian great tomb
with thousands life-size clay warriors) to find Fountain of Youth, and
Chinese records claim he did just that. This area is famed for its hot spring
resorts even today. First recorded onsen in Japan is that of Yuzuki in
Shirahama, dating back at least 14 centuries as Fountain of Youth capable of
actual regeneration. Shirahama's scenery and beaches are justly famed; so
famed, in fact, that it has become major resort area with enough varied
attractions to keep you busy for days. If this is not your style, Kii has many
more onsen to offer, from coast on deep into rugged mountains. Other than
its baths, peninsula is known for KUMANO SANSHA, 3 Shrines of Kumano,
each worth visiting and each located conveniently near excellent hot springs.

GETTING THERE & AROUND: Itinerary we follow assumes entry via
our historical routing from ISE/NARA → (or nearby NAGOYA) doing peninsula
clockwise. This is route followed by rare US package tours to area, worthwhile. Other
common entry would be from OSAKA-KOBE or KYOTO, in which case follow
itinerary below counter-clockwise, or in reverse. Enter from afar, by air from TOKYO →,
or ferry from KOCHI Shikoku →. No more Inland Sea entry (as 1964) a la Jimmu.

Locally, SHIRAHAMA is main transportation hub, with **air** from TOKYO. 3x-daily
JAS from Tokyo-HANEDA (o.w. ¥18,350, r.t. ¥33,040) at 7:55, 9:10, 13:40 return
10:10, 13:00, 15:50, 90min flight. Prices as of '91. Plans to extend air service with
other cities...but when? Had more air access in 1964! *See* p431 for new '91 **helicopter**
service. Alternate entry mainly for leisurely adventurer is **Katsu-ura ferry** link TOKYO
(Nihon Kosoku Ferry depart TOKYO even-numbered days) 14hrs, ¥9,060 2nd class &
KOCHI on Shikoku Island (same company, leaves Kochi odd-numbered days) 7hr30min,
¥5,560 2nd.

From ISE/NAGOYA, JR Kisei Main **Rail** Line hugs coast; from TAKI halfway
between ISE-MATSUZAKA, (tho some Ltd Express trains begin NAGOYA) and cuts across
mountains to coastal NAGASHIMA; from OSAKA runs via WAKAYAMA; from NARA
quickest is via Osaka with slower alternate Wakayama Line from SAKURAI via YOSHINO
and HASHIMOTO (turn-off to KOYA-SAN) whence 4hr **bus** to TANABE on coast, or
30min further to SHIRAHAMA. Kisei Main Line runs 2 hourly ltd expresses & expresses
(hourly nites) both directions, many locals in between. Osaka entry more used, with at
least 9 *Kuroshio-go* Ltd Exp daily. NAGOYA entry only runs 3x-daily (*Nanki-go*).

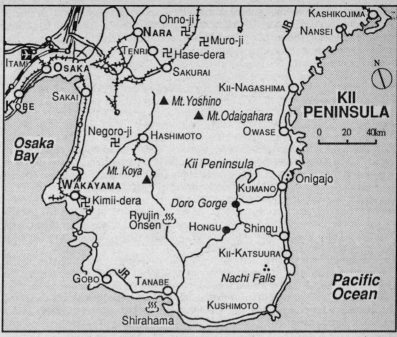

Note: No single train goes full circuit: trains from OSAKA end SHINGU (some Ltd Exp only to SHIRAHAMA), those from NAGOYA/ISE end KATSU-URA. Trains here can be adventure: July sudden rains, late summer-autumn typhoons, sometimes block rail and parallel bus road with mountain slides, tho rarely more than day delay while JR supplies alternate route. Terrain breathtaking, railroad engineering feat: single track with almost 200 tunnels and more bridges.

Frequent **bus**es also cross from YAMATO Plains: one line starts YAMATO KAMI-ICHI (base Mt Yoshino) → SHINGU 5hr via Doro-kyo river ravine (*see text*); other starts GOJO (E of Kami-ichi) → HONGU 4hr down center via Tozugawa Onsen; HONGU either 3hr W → TANABE or 1hr E → SHINGU. Many routes, frequent buses make exploring inner vales easy like backroad KOYA-RYUJIN SPA-TANABE we explored pre-1964 but could rarely use due to landslides until fine new road done.

TILT: Yet, with all this local transportation, Kii Peninsula is not really for short-termer, tho some well-received and intelligently-planned air tours out of US occasionally follow our basic routing. Shirahama is nice, but there are better onsen on well-beaten track. However, for patient adventurer it can be rewarding. With latter in mind, we continue our route from ISE-KASHIKOJIMA → SHINGU-NACHI-KATSUURA area. **Overland** ideal route would be **Ise → Kashikojima** thence along coast to join main rail or bus rtes → **Shingu**, which, as seen at end of Ise route, involves alternating between rare buses and ferry to get beyond Kashikojima: but it can be done with extra day, offers several quiet fishing villages at which to spend nite. From W shore of **Gokasho Bay**, it is 1hr bus to **Owase** where pick up JR, but suggest staying on bus (**if** it continues on). From **Kashikojima**, backtracking about 90min is required to Taki beyond Ise to join JR Kisei Main Line. Alternate routes onto (or from) this southern Kii route may bypass ISE-SHIMA area: above-mentioned **bus** routes from YAMATO area.

For *wanderer*, we suggest route via KOYA-SAN, covering main part of Kii Peninsula to KATSU-URA and taking ferry to KOCHI to wind around Shikoku, rejoining our itinerary at KOBE or other spots down Inland Sea. YOSHINO-KUMANO-SHINGU bus passes thru peninsula center's primevally beautiful Yoshino-Kumano Nat'l Park. **Back-packer** can exit/enter Southern Kii thru park, from/to either YOSHINO or ISE directions.

So, our first entry on Kii is for real adventurer, backpacking his/her way in...
ODAIGAHARA, heart of backpacking area, so we cover it first and
describe alternate routes in or out. Most common route to Odaigahara is 2hr
Nara Kotsu **bus** from YAMATO KAMI-ICHI. From YOSHINO, there is **3-4 day trek**
across mountains via Omine-zan, another ancient ascetic site which forbade women until
few years back when women's lib acted, with several budget temple lodgings and
campsites. If from ISE direction, 2hr Mie Kotsu **bus** from MATSUZAKA → OSUGI (dep
7:55, 16:45; Apr-Oct also 10:00, 12:20). It stops at several stns along JR, last before
turning into mountains is MISE-DANI. Bus lets you off at OSUGI DAM, where you can
catch **shuttle boat** to DAINICHI at start of trail. Boat dep OSUGI → DAINICHI 10:30,
ret 12:30 (end Apr-Nov 30, 11:00, 13:00); all match bus deps. It is 27km up gorgeous
Osugi River valley to Odaigahara. Most people do slightly easier reverse course, break
halfway at MOMONOKI KOYA hut or AWADANI KOYA hut (emergency shelter at
DOKURA KOYA). Several short trails meander thru Odaigahara area, whence can descend
8hrs to coastal Owase for start of our regular run around Kii. Odaigahara has 2 other ¥-B
lodgings, **Odai-sanso** ☎(07468)-2-0120, **Yamano-ie**; ¥5,500+w/2 or ¥-half room-
only. Operate only late Apr thru late Nov. As noted before, OSUGI → ODAIGAHARA is
main route (well marked); then descent to Owase, as only other way out is to bus down
Odaigahara Drive Way to Rte169 (or all way → YAMATO KAMI-ICHI) and catch bus
heading → Kumano.

Between ISE and SHINGU (coastal bus or rail) there is next to nothing for tourist.
30min before SHINGU is KUMANO with more strange rocks, Castle of Demons, at Oni-
ga-jo. 1.5km E of Kumano stn 5min bus, or 40min bus Owase → Oni-ga-jo Higashi-
guchi. Round point and back to stn or pick up bus and go on. Before Kumano are several
good beaches in coves, especially nice in summer when most people head to better known
beaches of Shirahama area.

25km stretch of beach Shichiri Mihama, (7-league beach) runs from Kumano to...
SHINGU on W bank of Kumano River, border of Mie and Wakayama
prefectures. Pleasant, friendly town full of little children with immense
round eyes looking more Near Eastern than Japanese.

One of three Kumano Shrines is here...
KUMANO HAYATAMA JINJA, alias Shingu, or New Shrine. It is
newest of trio, so-called because Great Spirit of Kumano tried out two spots
in this area before settling here. In NW corner of town, compound was
repainted classic vermilion in 1975 giving it new look, but structures themselves date to early 18th century. Site itself is much older, its origins lost in
mists of prehistory. This and its sister sites in mountains preserve rites
supposedly originating with mountain- and cave-worship of *tsuchi-gumo*
earth spider people who inhabited land before first emperor Jimmu. Its
location near sea and major river would make it more logical site for first of
three, but it is HONGU SHRINE, deep in mountains upstream which holds
senior slot, perhaps closer to gods. **Treasure House** (¥300) near entrance on
R, has 1,000 sacred shrine items, most National Treasures (NT) or Important
Cultural Assets (ICA).

PERSONAL DATEBOOK: Shrine's main fete, *Mifune* (boat) *Festival*, **Oct
16**, sees shrine's sacred objects placed on 300-year-old gilded *mikake-bune* 'gods' boat' and
pulled upstream (nowadays by power boat) to holiest-of-all-spots (perhaps earlier site of
worship) for rites, then returned. Later, 9 rafts with 10 rowers each race up river and back.

1.2km S of Hayatama thru temple district, bottom of 538 steep stone steps up to...
KAMIKURA SHRINE. Site #2 in Kumano Spirit's search; now dedicated
to Takakura-no-mikoto, who lead Jimmu to land. This event is commemorated **Feb 6** *Otou Matsuri* Torch Festival—100s white-clad men heft torches
in seemingly endless line down from shrine. Climb offers great view, but
hard work. Trail along hill top connects to Hayatama. 'Shrine' is massive
rock with torii in front.

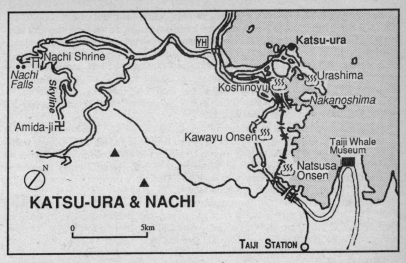

Number 1 site in Kumano Spirit's search is marked by...
ASUKA SHRINE (500m NE of stn; 15min walk straight E of Hayatama). Little shrine dedicated to all gods enshrined at Hayatama. Excavations here revealed 2,000-year-old pit dwelling community and Yayoi period artifacts: now on display in adjacent museum (¥200, X-mon and day after hols), reconstructed pit-dwelling in front.

Between two Shrines is remains of **Shingu Castle**: castle-like structure on hill is Tenri-kyo temple. Between Asuka Shrine ↔ stn, 8 small mounds; Ch'in is supposedly buried under one, rest hold his 7 closest followers.

400m NW of stn is...
'Forest on Floating Isle', *Ukijima-no-mori*. Tree-covered isle sits mid-small lake; methane gas from rotting humus gives it loose base so when water level rises it literally floats, good breeze can move isle around.

From Shingu choice of head upstream to HONGU (Main) shrine and several idyllic mountain onsen, or continue short way down coast to fabulous onsen at Katsu-ura. Latter ideal base to explore former in quick day tour (just Shingu-wards of Katsu-ura is road up to NACHI FALLS → one of trinity of KUMANO GRAND SHRINES).

So we head 15km (30min bus or train) to...
KATSU-URA: Ideal place for any overnite spent around Shingu-Nachi area. Old inns which were 'precariously' located during our 1960s visits have grown into large modern resort-inns, but sole taxis servicing them are still boats.

WHERE TO STAY: Of dozen or so inns here, top trio: **Urashima**, ☎(07355)-2-1011; **Koshinoyu**, ☎2-1414; **Nakanoshima**, ☎2-1111. Our favorite is Urashima (¥-T-S-Lw/2), on N end of peninsula, one of rare spa-inns which actually offers one of oddities seen on travel posters: bath is in great natural cave with view out over beach and gigantic tree growing inside. They actually have 2 natural cave baths here, and 3 indoor baths. It is largest, literally crawling up hillside, top floor of hilltop annex (connected to main by tunnel and elevator up middle of hill) offers 360° view. Strolling paths crisscross Urashima peninsula for more spectacular views (you can see Nachi Falls in distance). Top rated ryokan here is **Koshinoyu**, (¥-hi-Tw/2) at S end; boasts large and medium outdoor baths, larger indoor rock bath. **Nakanoshima** (same rates) sits on tiny isle in bay. It too, boasts giant outdoor bath (for those worried, baths are segregated by at least bamboo partition). All serve enormous meals of assorted fresh seafood; (**Urashima's** covered whole table, just for one person!) Urashima and Nakanoshima **shuttle boats** (every 5-10min) to mainland pier; you can walk to Koshinoyu.

Budget ryokan (¥7,000w/2), minshuku in town, and **Youth Hostel** *at...*
KAIO-JI Zen Temple 500m NE of stn; booking office by stn. Zazen meditation for non-Japanese for 5- to 7-day sessions during early part of even-numbered months (no set days), 2 sits daily 10:30 & 19:30; plus lessons in calligraphy, sumi painting, tea ceremony or yoga some midaft free time; stay w/2 ¥2,000 plus ¥1,000 sheet, *samui* zen work-clothes charge. Open sit monthly 2nd & 4th sat, sun, 7:30am, 5:30pm, ¥2,000 per nite w/2. Stay only ¥1,000, prefer limit to around sits as facilities slight. For long sessions, ✍ Rev TAKEUCHI Sosen, **Kaio-ji Zen Temple**, 642 Katsu-ura Onsen, Wakayama 649-53; ☎(07355)-2-0839. Fireworks 6pm, Aug 1.

Budgeteers need not lose out on incredible baths of big-3, all open to nonguests for fee (usually ¥1,000). Friends who stayed at minshuku here were fed all fresh *maguro* (tuna) sashimi they could eat, then headed over to **Urashima** to bathe. Minshuku around stn are: **Iwanami** ☎(07355)-2-1358, and **Kamenoi** ☎2-0642. Despite many big ryokan suggest call ahead, especially summer, weekends. Guarantee get room on spot Jan-Feb, June-July, Sept and Dec. Had no problem May, not close to full.

Katsu-ura is unlike other major onsen resorts in that town itself is not usual 'tinsel-town' catering to rich urbanites. It is in all aspects just small fishing village and all tourist entertainment (bars, shows, etc) are located within massive resort hotels. You can, however, wander narrow streets of town and find few local hangouts which (as we found) are far more receptive and friendly to foreigners than to 'outside' Japanese.

TOURS: Scenery at Katsu-ura is main attraction—strange rock formation in sea are as popular with modern oil-painters as Nachi Falls with traditional sumi painters, as also isles in bay which excursion launch visits:
A Course Katsu-ura pier → circles islands → Taiji Whale Park (free sched, hop any boat when done) → back to Katsu-ura. ¥1,340, 1hr on board.
C Course is 40min (¥920) cruise just around islands. Each course half-hourly departures from same pier as hotel shuttles, 8:00-17:00 (16:00 winter). Staying at **Urashima**, arrange tour at front desk, they have ship stop by and pick you up.

4km down (7min bus) from Katsu-ura is 'forgotten'...
YUKAWA ONSEN (don't confuse with Kawayu onsen in hills near Hongu) on shore of tiny lake. Several budget ryokan of which suggest quaint old **Yanagiya** ☎2-0317, or **Kaede** ☎2-0140. Minshuku also. Just upstream from Yanagiya is outdoor bath, another on opposite bank 200m on. **Boating** on lake.

15min walk to coast via tunnel thru hill to one-inn...
NATSUSA ONSEN with **Momiji-ya** ryokan on own cove. Only direct way is 20min cab (2.5x-mtr); isolation makes ideal escape even in summer boom. All can be booked at Katsu-ura. **Campsite** at beach near Yukawa stn 500m from onsen, lake.

Boat (preferred, unless choppy) or bus (20min) from Katsu-ura stn to...
TAIJI, whaling port since time immemorial, major center since 16th century. Till now, many of its young men signed up on Antarctic-bound whalers and tho most of action moved to Antarctic with voracious factory ships, sea mammals still run past here occasionally April-May to follow warm Kuroshio Current. If you are in luck (depends of course on your sentiments) local whalers will be in action. Town shows sensitivity to anti-whaling sentiments: after dolphin slaughters on Iki isles in early '80s locals refrained from catching dolphins to sell as feed to zoos, cooperated with California conservationists to release large herd accidentally trapped, saved stranded mother-calf. They had hoped for limited exemption as being traditional land-based small catchers. Last Antarctic fleet left November '86. In '60s heyday, deep-sea whalers harpooned over 20,000 whales annually, coastals another 3,000. By '76 catch was down to 9,000. Japanese publicly claim this due to cut back in fleet. Jay worked on whaling problem, was told by fisheries reduction due to lack of whales, industry was bankrupt, looking for way out that would preserve jobs. But when offered alternate possibility by same conservationists who eventually killed whaling,

companies and government seemed amenable but at last minute union 'refused to sit at same table with plutocrats', killed project. Japanese fisheries subsidize whaling by cheap labor non-IWC countries. Alas, whale meat is delicious.

Boat from Katsu-ura docks at **Whale-Beach Park**, *Kujira-hama*; ¥800 ticket bought at museum gets you into everything here. Museum covers history of local whaling, displays of old and new tools, info on whales in general. Ship sitting on land is 700ton Whaler #11 *Kyo-maru*, plied Antarctic until put permanently on display. Inside shows all workings of whaler. Aquarium next door: dolphin, seal shows regularly; cove behind holds few live captive whales and dolphins from area.

Those who would like to taste whale meat, best at Kokumin-shukusha **Hakugei** (White Whale). *Namban-zuke* (Southern Barbarian Food – us) is choice filet charcoal broiled to tender: juicy and like good steak. *Obake* (ghost) is blubber, thinly sliced, takes some getting used to. They also offer combination dish which gives you taste of every type of meat variously prepared.

TILT: Out of KATSU-URA: Kumano Kotsu offers several fine daily **bus tours** of for quick, easy access to surrounding areas. Best (and only one you must reserve for) is 7hr *Kumano Sansan Meguri* (Nachi 3 Shrines' Tour). Deps KATSU-URA stn 9:00, with pick-ups at KAWAYU ONSEN 10:29 and YUNOMINE ONSEN 10:36, then to Hongu Shrine → Hayatama Shrine → Nachi Falls → Nachi Shrine → end KATSU-URA stn 16:00: ¥9,450 from KATSU-URA, ¥7,900 from KAWAYU or YUNOMINE hot springs. **Short runs** → Nachi Falls & Shrine leave KATSU-URA stn 8:40, 12:55, 13:40, 14:40, on 2hr40min tour (¥3,750), but that only gives you hour at Falls and Shrine, so suggest this run solo (*see* below). 4hr10min ¥4,590 tour → Nachi Falls → Shrine → Taiji Whale Museum leaves KATSU-URA stn 12:55. Also taxi tours pre-set or U-make. KATSU-URA → NACHI 8km, KATSU-URA → SHINGU 13km, SHINGU → HONGU 38km. Part way to Hongu, from Shiko, are **jet-boat** cruises → up Doro Gorge, for which we suggest **Bus and Boat Tours** for convenience and price break. Also by **Kumano Kotsu**, arrange at their offices, JTB or hotels; or if solo go direct to SHIKO. Round-trip ↔ KATSU-URA ¥5,900; ¥5,400 if starting or ending SHINGU; r.t. from SHINGU ¥4,900; end at SHIKO (to continue on to Hongu), from KATSU-URA ¥4,500, from SHINGU ¥4,500.

NACHI FALLS AND GRAND SHRINE (28min bus, cab 8x-mtr from
KATSU-URA, 20min bus, **cab** 7x-mtr NACHI stn → falls): Popular pilgrim target, falls are narrow shaft of water (13m wide) plummeting 133m (400ft) straight down: outstripping famed Kegon Falls at Nikko by half again. Pilgrims often perform ascetic rites in lesser fall at main falls' foot. For adventurous, 2nd and 3rd falls above main are lovely. There are 48 in all, trail winding thru forest primeval. At base of falls is HIRO-O—**Flying Dragon Shrine**, waterfall is its enshrined spirit. One of smaller buildings near waterfall has fine *ema-e* (shrine votive picture plaques) for sale here. There's three-legged **black crow**, always associated with Kumano Shrines and noted also for having guided Jimmu Tenno to landfall (opposite of Noah's whitey). Then there are 12 beasts of zodiac (pick that for your year of birth) humorously and vividly painted. Leave money for it (marked, was ¥400) in offering tray there. If out of your year, wait till NACHI SHRINE for more of same. ¥100 to enter main grounds, dragon spewing water from falls as you enter; use new small saucers to drink, which you can keep for donation—¥100 or whatever you can afford. They make excellent (and *cheap*) gifts, 13-petal gold-emblazoned Imperial-like crest. Water claimed to promote longevity and jugs of it sold here. Photo-bug will find that falls stand in open but are in deep crypt-like shade of cryptomeria forest. Lively concessionaire will rent strobe flash, even take your picture with your own camera and his strobe, setting everything to fit his light: fee ¥200.

5min walk beyond falls, after you climb back up 100 slippery stone steps to bus stop, is entrance to **KUMANO NACHI GRAND SHRINE**. Don't stop at restaurants to eat till you see shrine and temple as climb will not help your digestion any: it's some 500 steps. Pathway is lined with shops selling **Japanese ink slabs** of customary black stone. This site was once noted for black stone, called *Nachi-guro* (not to be confused with dark, rock-hard candy balls sold here), but it has since been exhausted and craft reputation maintained by stone brought in across Yoshino mountains. **Bonseki fan** will find fine selection of miniature mountains and rocks for his or her tray landscape. There is also some beautiful free-form sculpture of various sizes in rich brick red: **petrified cedar** found in abundance in surrounding hills, right gift for modern flower-'deranger'. As all good temple/shrine shop areas, there are profane who cater to less sacred, with their share of **pornographic sake cups** and sets (we see same all over, most notably at holy Kompira-san on Shikoku). One particularly good one to liven up parties at home is set of 5 sake cups of different sizes, and with small holes on bottom. Roll accompanying die, drinking out of one with corresponding character, or sing (odd side out). Hole is to make sure all is downed in one shot, for to put cup down one must remove finger, anything left in cup is on your lap. Browse around and they bring items out of back which they can't display in front. Take it all in stride, Japanese don't have puritan taboos of most Americans. For gift shopping, pick out on way up, pick up on way down.

At fork: L → shrine, R → temple; both meet at top so we head L first to...
NACHI GRAND SHRINE: Present buildings built 1848, repainted 1983 in brilliant vermillion. Of three Kumano Shrines, this said to be closest architecturally, to original *Kumano-zukuri* style. But site is old, recorded to have been moved here from coast during reign of emperor Nintoku (4th c AD). To L is small treasure hall housing images of Fudo-Buddhist deity, and Buddha; in place of honor is En-no-Gyoja, originator of strange lay brotherhood of Yamabushi, men in white pantaloons and animal skin aprons often honking conch shells, seen at many of Japan's most exotic rites. Most are Shingon Buddhist, some Tendai Buddhist, but in practice still often as not Ryobu Shinto (combined Buddhist-Shinto). Behind Treasure House is building of shrine slightly separated from rest. In it is enshrined black crow of Kumano. Odd-shaped rock behind main hall said to be crow, who returned here and transformed into rock after guiding lost Jimmu thru wilds.

Donation ¥5,-10,000 gets you priest-guided tour into sacred inner sanctum for ritual purification, followed by **shrine-maiden dance** outside. Or wait around, chances are you'll see dance performed for some pilgrim group, Garet saw three in half-hour. In addition to usual *omamori* (charms), shrine sells unusual clay bells in shape of crow-faced tengu head; small pair ¥1,700, large single ¥2,000 (¥1,000 extra for red cushion it sits on). Large, sacred camphor tree on shrine side of gate has large hollow in trunk with small altar inside—crawl thru hole is said to bring good fortune.

Thru gate at R, by tree is...
SEIGANTO-JI temple. Present **main hall** was built 1587 by Hideyoshi, but site is centuries older. Legend has it that Ragyo, 6th century wandering Buddhist priest from India is credited with finding Kannon statue at Nachi Falls and enshrined it here in grass hut, origins of this temple which at prime had 7 temples and 37 training halls. Fact is, it dates to at least early Heian period when newly imported esoteric Buddhism led to this becoming major study/training center. With Heian merging of Shinto and Buddhism, main Kumano deities were declared *gongen* (avatars) and took on Buddhist properties.

Thus, HONGU's kami *Ketsumiko-no-kami* became Amida, SHINGU's *Hayatama-no-miko* became Yakushi, NACHI's *Fusumi-no-kami* became Kannon. NACHI already possessed temple compound; it surpassed HONGU as main pilgrimage spot in trio. SEIGANTO-JI is also #1 of 33 holy Kannon pilgrim temples of West Japan, which may have saved it from total annihilation in forced separation of Shinto and Buddhism after Meiji Imperial Restoration. Then, all other Buddhist structures and idols were purged from shrines or, mostly, destroyed. In 1972, temple's 3-tiered pagoda was rebuilt, but admire it from afar for up close it is disapointment: thick concrete with, would you believe, elevator leading to 3rd floor. Does have best view of Nachi Falls—but costs ¥100 and photo-bug will get more interesting shot from shrine viewing platform where you get falls and pagoda in same shot.

Shoes are kept on in this temple; but to go all way inside to see altar with Kannon and other image, shoes off and ¥300.

Outside is...
Temple Shop, where some lovely wooden Kannon images are for sale: about 10cm/4in high ¥8,000: 20cm/8in-¥10,000 and 30cm/foot-¥13,000: well done, as new folk Buddhist art rarely is. Material is cedar, carved *itto-bori* (single-cut style). Faces radiate peace and humor. In addition they offer quite beautiful unmounted painting in traditional Buddhist style of Kannon on silk, ¥10,000: white space is for pilgrims to 33 Kannon temples to get chop of that temple stamped in red. But standing alone painting is rare example of fine Buddhist painting being done today. Well worth price, both painting and image. 33 was chosen since that is how many different forms Kannon is able to assume as avatar, supernatural being who can help man by assuming some earthly form, be it human or animal. Small building behind Seiganto-ji is DAIKOKU-DO housing statue of Daikoku, one of Seven Lucky Gods, deity often found within temples dedicated to Kannon. Trail to second and third (and beyond) Nachi Falls starts out behind temple.

PERSONAL DATEBOOK: Nachi Shrine has spectacular *Ogi (Fan) Festival* **July 14** well worth scheduling for. From 10am there is series of ancient offeratory dances held on temporary *mai-den* (dance platform) which include Dengaku (farm dance), rice-planting dance, and dances by children. At 1pm, 12 giant mikoshi (one for each of kami enshrined here), each 7m tall and decorated with 32 gold fans with three red suns on each, and 8 sacred mirrors, is carried from shrine towards falls. Shortly thereafter, 12 massive torches (56kg, 1 meter around) are lighted at falls and carried towards shrine. Two groups meet on steps and intermingle. Festival originated sometime in 12th century to ensure that Buddhist-ized gongen spirits of Nachi do not lose their Shinto-ness. Purifying fire originates from purely Shinto spirit of Nachi Falls, while their mingling with 12 mikoshi representing 12 deities is to cleanse them, imbue them with essence of Shinto.

From shrine Nachizan Skyline toll road (¥700) climbs 6km to...
AMIDA-JI temple, founded 815 by Saint Kobo-daishi. Like MURO-JI temple took in women excluded from male-only monasteries of KOYA-SAN. Spectacular view of coast below. 20min hike to the OKU-NO-IN, whence backpacker can follow old pilgrim trail to HONGU, little over 20km, hitting either KAWAYU or YUNOMINE hot springs. AMIDA-JI is 15min (¥420) bus from NACHI SHRINE, but only 3x-daily. Round-trip cab is about 6x-mtr, plus ¥1,400 for toll road.

From Nachi Shrine, must return to coast (Nachi or Katsu-ura stns) for train or bus to SHINGU, from where up to HONGU area. If you have time, we recommend our route: nite at KATSU-URA, next day → NACHI → SHINGU → DORO GORGE → YUNOMINE ONSEN 2nd nite, next morn early → HONGU Shrine → out. Or spend 2nd nite in DORO GORGE → HONGU next day and out. Adventurer may visit Hongu late day 2, saving Doro Gorge for next morning and trek to TOZUGAWA ONSEN. Rail Pass users should check buses at Shingu, as JR has few runs to SHIKO and on to YUNOMINE. There is also an exciting logging raft ride worth looking into. You have three choices out of here, for which see following.

Jet Boats up Doro Gorge begin from SHIKO, 70min bus from KATSU-URA (cab 20x-mtr), 40min from SHINGU (cab 12x-mtr). Drive up Rte168 in itself lovely. Boats leave hourly between 8:00 to 15:00 for 2hr (¥3,280) round-trip up the spectacular gorge.

June-Sept you can cover upper-half of gorge on logging rafts from Otonari down to Komatsu or Doro-hatcho. Each raft is chain of 7 sections, each one made up of 6 or 7 logs (4m/13ft long, up to 30cm/1ft across) lashed together: hand-rails and you are given life jacket. It is for adventurous because tho safe (over 20 years of accident free record broken during June '86, no injuries) it is wet ride. 1hr bus (2x-daily) KUMANO → SHIMO-OI Ikada (raft) Center, then to OTONARI, to KOMATSU for shorter ride. OTONORI → KOMATSU is 70min, ¥5,000, 2 runs 10:40am, 13:00; OTONORI → DORO-HATCHO (top end of Jet Boat run) is 2hr30min with rests, ¥8,000, 1 run. These go every sun, hol May; sat, sun, hol Jun-Sep, 1 run; add fri thru mon Jul-Aug. KOMATSU → DORO-HATCHO 70min, ¥5,000, 1 run daily, 12:30 May-Sep. Fee includes insurance, only requirement is to be in good health and between 10-70 years age. Must arrange at least 10 days in advance by calling **Kitayama Village Tourist Bureau,** ☎(0735)-49-2331. If you haven't done so, it might be worth calling at least day or two ahead from Katsu-ura to see if you can get on any unfilled boat.

WHERE TO STAY: 3 budget ryokan and 3 minshuku at SHIMO-OI. At DORO-HATCHO are: top **Doro Hotel** ☎(07466)-9-0003 (¥-Tw/2) and minshuku **Yamabiko** (¥-Bw/2). Kitsuro camp grounds about 2.5km S of hotel, on horseshoe bend in river. Hotel spans three prefectures: main hall in Nara, annex in Wakayama and opposite bank is Mie. Doro is beautiful place to spend nite, you can catch boat back in morning, or continue on bus to **TOZUGAWA ONSEN** (1hr30min, 3x-daily), from where exit to Yamato Plains, *or 1hr bus to...*

HONGU, Main shrine of Kumano: 30min bus from SHIKO. Bus from SHIKO, SHINGU, KATSU-URA and Nara direction stops in front of shrine at Hongu Taisha-mae, but those from/to TANABE and SHIRAHAMA stop only at Hongu stop 700m down road.

This shrine is as old as other two, but site is relatively new, building having been moved here after 1889 flood which washed it all away (ultra-nationalists of time claimed it was divine act to cleanse it of Buddhist influence). Old site along river, between lower Hongu bus stop – shrine. Of 3, this looks most ancient as hasn't been painted, original wood has aged beautifully, its gold leaf ornaments shining brilliantly.

PERSONAL DATEBOOK: *Main Festival* here is **Apr 13-15**. 13th starts off with children's dances at YUNOMINE ONSEN, kimonoed kids are then carried to HONGU, going over Dainichi mountain, with more dances performed at hill top DAINICHI SHRINE, old Hongu shrine site, and back again at Hongu. Several dances held 14th; but main is 15th when giant procession accompanies mikoshi to old shrine site where sacred bonfire is set ablaze, followed by hours of ancient dances.

10min bus (JR or Nara Kotsu) from Hongu on Rte311, is...

YUNOMINE ONSEN: Our favorite of three onsens around Hongu. Tiny hamlet straddles steaming Yunotani River. Best out of numerous ryokan (all ¥-T-Sw/2) is **Azumaya** ☎(07354)-2-0012, midway on L if facing uphill. Ise-ya, ☎2-0128 across from it; **Yunomine-so,** ☎2-1111, at bottom of street boasts its own outdoor bath. Azumaya also runs minshuku just down road where Garet stayed in '84. There are another half-dozen minshuku at top end of street. Main attraction of Yunomine is its outdoor riverside bath **Tsuboyu**: holds 2-3 people, partially enclosed for privacy. Water is said to change color 7 times daily to various hues of blue and green; ¥100, pay at public bath just up side street. Steamy cauldron downstream from Tsuboyu used by residents to boil vegetables; not diluted with cold water like baths it seethes at 90 ° C.

Nearby is...

YAKUSHI TEMPLE with Yakushi image carved out of rock, hole in its chest used to spout hot spring water which gave onsen its original name: YU-MUNE (hot water chest), but once it stopped flowing, name gradually changed to YU-MINE (hot water peaks) after its location and surroundings.

2km down steam (branch off Rte311) is single-inn...

WATARASE ONSEN, with cabin **Watarase-sanso** ☎(2-0230), ¥-Tw/2; boasts outdoor bath, and area features fireflies in summer.

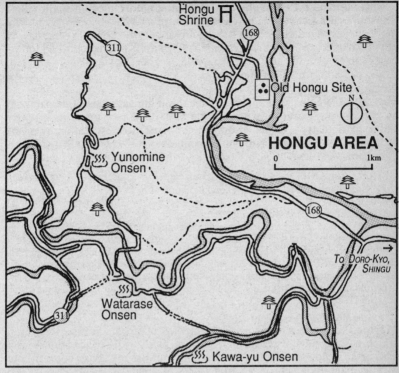

Pass thru tunnel and you are at...

KAWAYU 'river water' **ONSEN**. As its name implies, dig hole in pebble bank and it fills with hot water. Kawayu is crowded summer weekends, with many families coming to play in river which during day is full of swim-suited kids. But at night, it quiets down and you can enjoy nice relaxing bath outside; most places supply you with lantern, bamboo partition to shield you, and large umbrella (borrow for small fee if not staying). **Hotel Urashima** chain has recently completed all-rate luxury inn here **Sansui-kan** ¥20,000+w/2 ☎(07354)-2-1011, price same as their KATSU-URA inn; few thousand cheaper are **Kinokuni** ☎2-0353 and **Fujiya** ☎2-0007. Next to Fujiya is old time classic **Kameya** ☎2-0002, slightly cheaper still, ¥-T. Also 5 minshuku, one Youth Hostel, campsite here. Inns can arrange for fishing, and boar hunting in season. If all onsen areas full (unlikely except possibly summer weekends), there are 3 inns around HONGU Shrine. Shrine also runs inn **Suiho-den** ☎2-0361, minshuku prices, at bottom of main steps.

We exit via Shingu and Katsu-ura; to eliminate this backtrack seeker after scenery can get back up into Yamato Plain or Nara area from Yunomine next morning: 4hrs if driving, 5hrs if bus N thru primitive woodlands, broken only by small hamlets and dams, to GOJO back on Ancient Yamato Plain. From GOJO it is hour by train, mountain rail and funicular up to Shangri-La mountain temple city of KOYA; or in opposite direction, under hour to YOSHINO; or alternately 30min on to NARA.

Also from YUNOMINE, another picturesque ride is due W 3hrs JR bus to TANABE.

Backtracking to coastal Rte42 or Kisei rail line, your next stop up coast will be...

SHIONOMISAKI PENINSULA—OSHIMA ISLE Mainly for wanderer and famous for odd needle-like rock formations, *Hashigui-iwa*, Bridge-post rocks. Reaching out from shore towards Oshima, you get superb view of them from train or bus. So-so beach there is boosted in popularity with unusual backdrop of sea rocks.

Shionomisaki Peninsula is also southernmost spot on main island Honshu (which fact you can have commemorated for ¥200 on spot). Windward shore sheer rugged cliffs, fine fishing down below. 20min bus out to tip from KUSHIMOTO stn (40min rail, 1hr bus from KATSU-URA). Kushimoto drilled for hot water some years ago and connected; don't suggest staying here but there is public bath in town which draws from it.

Worthwhile stop is...
MURYO-JI temple (800m from stn). On exhibit here are many fine paintings by NAGASAWA Rosetsu, main disciple of 18th century great MARUYAMA Okyo, particularly spectacular dragon and tiger. Rosetsu did many pieces for numerous temples in Kii, but best collections are here, at SODO-JI near Shirahama, and JOJU-JI near KOZA, few km Katsu-ura-wards of here.

OSHIMA ISLAND can be reached by 10min car ferry; or longer to S shore (*another*) Shirahama (25min), or N shore Kashinozaki (30min). Car ferries leave from Kushimoto pier, near rail stn; others leave from yacht harbor 500m down. Kushimoto, Shionomisaki, and 3 villages on Oshima are full of budget minshuku. Bus shuttles back and forth along main road across Oshima, but one can walk its length in half day. Most interesting sites are at eastern tip: First is 3.5m tall memorial to Turkish warship which sank here in 1890, going down with all hands (581), including Turkish Ambassador; nearby pavilion displays salvaged items. Down ruggedly beautiful S shore 1.5km/mile to Japan-US Friendship Memorial Hall, comemorating American merchant ship's visit here in 1724. Event did not start anything major, but locals in 1974 erected this hall to outline history of Japan-US relations.

15min bus W of Kushimoto is...
Marine Park with aquarium and submerged platform (6m under water) from which unique view of coral covered ocean floor. ¥1,030 for both, ¥1,340 *kyotsu-ken*, combi-ticket, gets you 20min cruise on glass-bottom boat. Marine Park included on all **bus tours** of area: 2hr30min course (¥2,960) Kushimoto → Hashigui-iwa Rocks → Shionomisaki Point → Marine Park → Kushimoto. There are courses which start at KATSU-URA and end here, include visit to Taiji Whale Museum (4hr, ¥4,590 course) and also NACHI (7hr, ¥8,610). These can also be done reverse KUSHIMOTO → KATSU-URA; they do not include admission to Whale Museum or Marine Park. 5hr course deps KATSU-URA 10:00, 11:50, 12:55; 7hr course deps KATSU-URA 8:40, reverse deps KUSHIMOTO 11:15, 12:20, 13:10.

Just over 1hr JR express from Kushimoto, 1hr40min from Katsu-ura is...
SHIRAHAMA white sands, one of leading spas in Kansai area, as Atami is to Tokyo, ever-increasing number of honeymooners, package travelers and weekend tourists flock to area. Its reputed milder climate (not so), natural beauties with blue seas 'reflecting subtropical skies', plus efficient service offered by its many well-equiped and over-priced inns, have made Shirahama most popular playground in Kansai. Also boasts various recent attractions like Japan's first Safari Park, Marine Land, golf course and amusement centers. Widely known since 1919, Shirahama is so named because of its long beach with glistening white sands.

Actually, Shirahama is made up of 4 small hot springs:
YUZAKI ONSEN in Nishino-misaki (S end, W coast) boasts long history, and area's only outdoor seaside public bath;
HIGASHI SHIRAHAMA ONSEN in Tsunashirazu (E coast);
OURA ONSEN and
KOGA ONSEN, both on far quieter Kogaura Bay, with *hamachi* (yellowtail) breeding grounds, pearl oyster rafts. Shirara Beach just N of Yuzaki, is heart of Shirahama, greatest concentration of inns, all seem to run just little above national average: ¥-S-L.

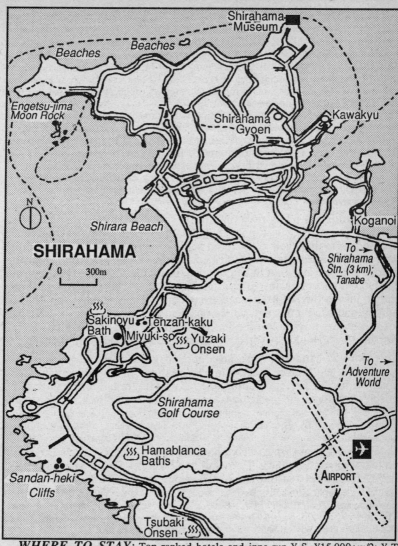

WHERE TO STAY: Top ranked hotels and inns run ¥-S, ¥15,000+w/2; ¥-T run ¥10,000+w/2. Well known hotel/ryokan are **Koganoi** ☎(0739)-42-2922 at Koga, perhaps largest in Shirahama; similarly 'isolated' **Kawakyu** ☎42-2661, and **Shirahama Gyoen** ☎42-3400, Higashi Shirahama; Yuzaki has **Miyuki-so** ☎42-2708 on rise, and all in row along shore are **Tenzan-kaku** ☎42-2500; **Yanagiya** ☎42-3360; **Yuzaki-kan** ☎42-3019; **Awajiya Choto-kaku** ☎42-4010, first and last ¥-T.

Very few budget ryokan, but 4 **Kokumin-shukusha** (Peoples' Inns): most desirable is Kokumin-shukusha **Shirara** ☎42-3655, right on beach; **Meiko Shirahama Lodge** ☎43-5003, is few hundred meters inland, halfway to opposite shore as well; **Hotel Shirahama** ☎42-3039, is 300m N; **Hotel Taiyo** ☎42-3328, is in Higashi Shirahama (all ¥-Bw/2, about same as minshuku).

There are about 27 **minshuku** equally divided between Yuzaki and Oura. **May**, **July-Aug**, **Oct-Nov** and **Year End** are most crowded; must have early reservation. Booking offices at JR stn, airport, and in town at bus center.

GETTING AROUND: Most scenic spots (not including parks) in and around Shirahama covered conveniently by local **sight-seeing bus**, ¥3,400 for 3hrs including **glass-bottom boat** with cruise at Rinkai and admission to Hamablanca. If you want to spend more time at some spot, just catch next bus. They leave central **Meiko Bus Terminal** every 30min 9:00-10:30, and hourly 11:30-14:30. Also 6 similar tours leave from JR Shirahama stn (10min bus to onsen area) 10:17-13:10, one from Meiko bus terminal 9:00. Regular buses also run all over, for which, check into Meiko Bus Co's 'free' ticket good for multiple use. **Tour cabs** run 7x-mtr/hr. Nanki Air runs various Cessna **airtours** of area ranging from 12min (¥4,000) to half-hour charters (¥26,400 for 3 people) and more; call NANKI KOKU, ☎43-5500. **Cruise** around Shirahama Peninsula on *Hayatori* #2, 200 ton luxury yacht capable of carting up to 100 people. 90min course (¥2,300) deps 10:00, 13:00, from Tanabe pier between Higashi Shirahama and Oura goes to SANDAN-HEKI cliffs and back. This and glass-bottom boat pass in front of Shirahama's symbol **Engetsu-to**, Full Moon Isle, rocky isle with circular hole thru it. 50m high cliffs of **Sandan-heki** '3-Tiered Wall' can be partially descended by elevator (¥300), to cave below.

Anthropological buffs may find oldest shrine in Shirahama of interest. Spa was first known for rejuvenating qualities, even today it's used much by execs bringing their own 'room service' or rejuvenation nurses from their office. Shrine is also dedicated to this. Kanki-Ganesha, elephant-headed god of wisdom in Indian original, is usually shown as two elephant-headed deities embracing to cast phallic shadow. This is old style Kanki shrine, just shadow of itself, magnificent member about two feet tall. Just to its L and back few steps, where obedient wife always stood, is Kanki's mate, natural tiny cave in excellent vaginal form into which devout worshippers now piously flip coins–shades of old Mexican border bars.

Shirahama Museum once ('64) appendage to little shrine has now engulfed it and houses Tibetan tankas, sculpture from Mohenjodaro and other Ganesha figures including one on way in 2m tall, other interesting miscellani. **Shop** in museum sells various *omamori*-good luck charms, in true museum-shop format of reproducing their more notable treasures, other fascinating folk art of Kinseyana. To get to shrine-museum, walk from Sanbashi, or elsewhere **bus** to Sakata-yama, NE corner of Shirahama. ¥400 admission includes both.

Westward from shrine, whole northern shore is sandy beach, extending around western tip (where it's rocky) to Rinkai-ura Beach near Full Moon Isle. Aforementioned Shirara Beach about 2km S. As for **baths**, there are several large public bath halls. Best is outdoor seaside **Saki-no-Yu** at YUZAKI which is town-run and *free* (10:00-17:00, -19:00 summer), segregated. Others all indoors: **Murono-yu, Hashiri-yu, Shirara-yu. Hamablanca** gaudy show/dining palace also boasts 3 giant tropical baths, ¥900, fun for kitch collectors.

RECREATION: Fishing fine all along coast; ¥13,000 for 3-person boat, add ¥2,500 to get to offshore isles. Fishing from off-shore rafts, ¥3,000, 6:00-16:00 **Shirahama Fishing Cooperative** ☎42-2997.

Golfers have two 18-hole courses to choose from: 5,550m **Shirahama Golf-jo** ☎42-2955 on grassy Heisogen Plateau; 5,955m **Shirahama Beach Golf-jo** ☎22-1300 at SE end of peninsula. Fees for visitors run about ¥15,000 wknd, ¥8,500 weekday. **Tennis** Club in 'town'; **Riding** Club near Adventure Land.

TSUBAKI ONSEN just before (below) Shirahama, is quiet alternative, only 30min bus from central SHIRAHAMA, some expresses on JR stop. It has half-dozen budget to moderate ryokan, Kokumin-shukusha **Hirami**, and 4 ¥-B minshuku. Also fishing on its rocky shore (small sandy beach at N end), but main attraction here are 250-plus monkeys inhabiting ISEGATANI VALLEY at S end of town. They often wander out to beach, and have become quite accustomed to people, which they often outnumber.

Alternate way out of Shirahama is to boat (from same pier as Hayatori #2) to...
TANABE: Quiet little town, with little to offer; pine tree-lined **Ogigahama Beach** and part of town between pier & stn lined with old samurai houses, but it is turnoff to Ryujin-Koya Sky Line, passing thru...

2hr bus up from Tanabe, ¥1,640, or same down back road from Koya-san, see...
RYUJIN ONSEN: Hot Spring of Dragon God is perched precariously along river-ravine, you could almost miss it if you blink at wrong time. Perfect place to break otherwise tedious, but beautiful ride (especially if driving); public bath here has 4 outdoor riverside pools, mixed & segregated.

50m above public bath is...
Ryujin Onsen Center which also has **outdoor baths** (¥300) and budget lodgings. Hot water bubbles out of rocks along Hidaka River, supplying many fine, rustic lodgings here. Best are: **Kami-Goten** ☎(0739)-79-0005, and **Shimo-Goten** ☎79-0007, 'Upper-and Lower-Palace', both built exclusively as 17-19th century retreats of Wakayama's Tokugawa lords (they are reconstructions as entire area destroyed in 1884 fire), exquisite architecture; between these two are **Arinoki-ya** ☎79-0013. Palaces are ¥-T-Sw/2, **Arinoki-ya** few thou' cheaper; 7 budget minshuku here; large Kokumin-shukusha **Ryujin Onsen Lodge** ☎79-0331 on opposite bank.

From Shimo-Goten, stone steps lead up to...
ONSEN-JI Hot Spring Temple, from where easy 30min round-trip walk to **Mandala Falls** in lovely ravine. Koya-Ryujin Skyline Drive passes thru lovely hills, rustic villages carving living out of steep mountains. Nankai Dentetsu buses, however, do not cover distance every day: only weekends and hols **Apr 1-Nov 23** and daily **Apr 29-May 5** and **July 20-Aug 27**. One way **cab** about 25x-mtr. Hitchhikers have constant stream of locals and friendly truckers on weekdays.

Back along coast is...
DOJO-JI's Original Dragon Lady: DOJO-JI temple, is setting for noh and kabuki play in which frustrated lover Kiyohime chases reluctant monk Anchin who was on pilgrimage to Kumano. His fellow monks hide him beneath great temple bell. But Kiyohime, literally spitting fire in her rage, transforms herself into dragon, wraps around bell and bakes refugee. This temple is midway between SHIRAHAMA-WAKAYAMA, 40min express from TANABE (10min more from SHIRAHAMA) to GOBO stn and 10min bus; or 5min walk from DOJO-JI stn but only occasional locals stop here. Temple is worth this detour; its treasure hall contains double scroll paintings (20m long) of Anchin-Kiyohime tale, and numerous Buddhist figures. Main treasure is 3.6m tall 1,000-handed Kannon figure, carved out of one solid piece of hinoki cypress; but it is shown only once every 33 years, last time was 1972. Another 1,000-hander, 2.4m tall, once temple's principal image carved in Nara era, was not seen for 4 centuries until recently discovered hidden inside 15th cent 3.3m Buddha. Mass for lover-boy Anchin **Apr 27**.

Other side of tracks, on coast, is...
America Mura, settled by returnees from U.S. and Canada. It is another of those places labeled in Japanese as *ekizochikku* (exotic). Strange houses are painted clapboard and have window boxes and other traces of Americanization in what amounts to inverted Chinatown. Even now, over 200 of 900 residents (mostly elderly) are returnees, speaking odd mix of English and Japanese. Many spent at least 20 years working in Canada and still receive old-age security pensions.

25min from Gobo stn on bus bound for...
Hinomisaki Park at tip of peninsula. Good beaches, with several campsites and budget lodgings line entire S shore of peninsula, past

America Mura to tip. On tip is bust of Danish captain Knudsen, who sank his own ship trying to save crew of burning *Takasago-maru* in 1957.

30min beyond Dojo-ji we enter famed...

KII *mikan* tangerine, mandarin orange, country. Trees cover entire mountainsides, terraced way up to tips for miles and miles along shore. Train ride May-early June worth it just to open windows for orange blossoms, one of few times and places in Japan that flowers have any smell, and they almost make up for all other odorless blooms of this land. Hillsides change their kimono design with seasons, from floral in spring, to refreshing green, to rich dark green polka-dotted with gold fruit. Even late winter has its patch-work pattern of beige and green as trees are tenderly wrapped up with straw mats against frost.

One stop beyond Gobo to **Kii Yura**, *10min walk from which is...*

KOKOKU-JI Zen Temple, also known as Shakuhachi-dera, where Oct 13 itinerant monks from all over Japan gather for shakuhachi (bamboo flute) contest.

Bit beyond is small fishing village spa of...

YUASA where they fish nites for *shirauo* (white-bait) by dipping huge nets; fishermen perched on wooden 'lifeguard' platforms lift them out of sea full of fish attracted to torches.

5km further, at Arita River is small-scale *ugai* (cormorant fishing) from **Jun 1** thru **Aug**. 6-person boat rents for ¥23,400; contact **Arita Tourist Bureau** ☎(07378)-3-1111, or have inn arrange. There are several at ARITA ONSEN few kilos downstream at mouth of river. 4 stops on, dozen kilometers from Wakayama, is old lacquer or *urushio*-producing center of KAINAN, of slight tourist interest (lacquer avail in any dept store) but for large villa, ONZAN-SO, lovely landscape garden nestled in tiny cove, open to public.

Two stops further (10min bus, or same on infrequent local JR) to...

KIMII-DERA, mentioned every spring in newspapers as spot where sakura bloom earliest in Kansai. It is another mountainside 'stage' temple with lovely air. Site dates to 770 AD, but all structures were rebuilt during mid-15th to early 16th centuries.

On coastal side of Kimii-dera stn is small rocky point with...

WAKANO-URA AND SHIN-WAKANO-URA; noted sights, but inns clutter up area. They base their claims to fame on poem in first anthology *Manyoshu* referring to difficulty cranes have at high tide of finding dry spot to land on among reeds. There's sea wall there now, reeds and cranes are gone. Tides still problem. 2km due W of Kimii-dera small isle connects to mainland by arched stone bridge, good view of temple. W one km to fine, red-laquered TOSHOGU shrine built in 1621 by Wakayama's Tokugawa Yorinobu in memory of father Shogun Ieyasu.

First is...

SHIN-WAKANO-URA, from where 40min chug-boat circles to end of point and back, many inns. However, pass thru WAKANO-URA and its inns (on road or coastal trail), on around small peninsula to next bus stop and fishing village of TANO-URA, gradually being submerged by more inns and on to SAIGA-SAKI, remote fishing village, hanging down mountainside where much of old '60s movie *Escapade in Japan* was filmed. Energetic inn-building post '64 has thankfully sputtered out and Saiga-saki is still pleasant. This tiny cove is filled with large fishing boats, all about same size and coloring: beautiful picture. At westernmost tip, small promontory juts out, once used as watch post for Perry's Black Ships, now Bansho-tei-en, pleasant expanse of lawn looking out on small isles beyond. Continuing to **Suiken beach**, and one of Tokugawa seaside villas, **Yosui-en**, was worth visit till locals converted into overly-touted tourist trap, charging ¥500.

Continuing on completes circle, 25min bus to...

WAKAYAMA   YANKEE DOORS

CADET TOWN for Tokugawa to train future leaders for Edo (Tokyo). City tactically important as it enabled Tokugawa to outflank traditionally upstart Osaka. Center of city out as far as our old faculty residence by economics campus of Wakayama University totally destroyed in World War II. Town boasts lovely **castle** built in 1849. *Murray's Guide* (1907) praises it as finest extant old-style Japanese castle, built just before collapse of feudalism. Present structure dates to 1958, rebuilt after old plans and prewar photos. Park it is set in is sad fossil of what once must have been lovely.

Across road from castle where, Murray wrote almost century ago, billets of samurai stood, shabby wooden barns looking, by their condition, to be remnants of feudal era are Wakayama national university liberal arts campus. Its pocked wooden floors, broken windows, leaky roofs stands in mute contrast to beautiful, new and fabulously expensive castle; mirror-twin monuments to folly of modern Japanese public economy: little wonder its student body was long one of politically most ill-tempered in Japan (contributing much to our doing 7 interesting years teaching here: most of this book's original was written at university, Garet and elder brother were born here). New campus at last, N of town near zoo.

City itself ugly midst gorgeous countryside. Textiles important economic role: flannel first produced here in Japan; cotton prints for export to Africa and Near East until cheaper labor producers did to Japan's industry what Japan did to US, what England did to India etc two centuries back: who's next? Lumber town, center for *shoji* sliding doors; many fancy lattice-doors exported. Deep water port for immense Sumitomo steel plant.

Lovely offbeat sidetrack out of Wakayama is to coastal suburb of...
KADA, nice beach, boating, scenery; ¥-B Kokumin Kyuka-mura (People's Hostel) and some superb inns (¥-T) specializing in freshly caught seafood.

25min boat out to...
Tomogashima Isle, halfway to (but not connected to) Awaji Island. Nankai Electric Rail, 25min WAKAYAMA → KADA.

WHERE NEXT: From WAKAYAMA continue on to OSAKA (JR → Tennoji, or Nankai pvt line → Namba), or take JR Wakayama Line → HASHIMOTO and (if you circled Kii out of Nara or Nagoya) transfer for KOYA, or on → NARA.
    Driving → NARA (or → KYOTO) do not take → OSAKA main road N but Rte24 E → HASHIMOTO → GOJO → KASHIWARA → NARA (thence → KYOTO): less traffic, better roads, far prettier. Also convenient aside to KOYA (*see*) if missed earlier.

Just outside Wakayama on this hiway **detour** to **NEGORO-JI** temple, which area on N side of river has lovely Chinese style residential compounds: courtyard completely enclosed by four buildings, entry thru gate in wall. NEGORO-JI 10min bus from IWADE stn JR 25min from WAKAYAMA (*see* preceding chapter, p405).

Shortcut into INLAND SEA ROUTE from here might bypass Osaka by **boat** direct → AWAJI ISLAND or TOKUSHIMA on eastern end of Shikoku: FUKE port, just up coast from KADA (35min Nankai Electric), ships → YURA on Awaji and → TOKUSHIMA. Also for 2hr crossing boats → KOMATSUSHIMA S of TOKUSHIMA, leave Wakayama harbor, 5min Nankai train from central stn. Departure schedules available thru stn TICs.

HELICOPTER: Kii Peninsula long had good amphibian air service, cancelled for years, then July '91 saw new 'copter service (dep 8:05) running OSAKA → WAKAYAMA → SHIRAHAMA → NACHI KATSUURA → SHINGU, overall time 90min, return same route; ¥10,000 one leg, ¥25,000 whole. **Hankyu Airlines** is expanding routes, and charters (¥300,000-600,000 per hour, by size, tops 8-psgr).

PERSONAL DATEBOOK: KII PENINSULA

Wakayama Tourist Info: ☎(0734) 32-4111 — Mie Tourist Info ☎(0592) 24-2391

January

15 Tengu Dance Kyokoku-ji (*Shaku-hachi-dera*) temple, Kii-Yura Town.

15 *Funa-danjiri* (Boat Float) *Fete*, Naga-shima Shrine, Kii-Nagashima. Happi-clad kids pull boat-float thru fishing town.

February

1-5 *Yaaya Festival*, Owase Shrine, Owase. Main: 4th *hadaka* (naked) *matsuri*, hundreds of loinclothed youths show off macho. 5th lion & other dances 10:00, costumed daimyo parade, floats thru town.

2 '*Flower-Cave*' *Fete* Hanano-iwaya Shrine, Kumano C. Sacred shimenawa rope hung from rock- cum-shrine. Repeat Oct 2.

6 *Torch procession*, exciting, worth cold, Kamikura Shrine, Shingu (p.408).

8 *Hari Kuyo* Rites for Broken Needles, Awashima Shrine, Kada, Wakayama City.

March

3 *Rites for old dolls*, Awashima S, Kada, Wakayama City. Old dolls put on 2 wood boats set afloat in Inland Sea.

Late – Begin *Cherry viewing* fetes thru...

April

— Kickoff at Kimii-dera temple.

8 Commemorate founding of Seiganto-ji, Nachi-Katsuura. After rites, their usually hidden-from-view Kannon image shown.

13-15 Kumano Hongu Shrine Fete (p414) Kimonoed children dance, 15th main procession, ancient dances. Hongu Town.

20 *Kakko Matsuri*, Yabuta S, Kuwana C. Flower-headed dancers, demon dancers.

27 *Memorial* for Anchin, Kiyohime; Dojo-ji, (p.419) 'dragon procession'. Kawabe T.

May

4-5 *Ageuma Shinji*--horseman climbs steep cliff, 1pm, Tado S, Tado-cho, Mie.

Early *Wakayama Fest*. Toshogu, Wakano-ura.halberd & lion dances, mikoshi.

2nd Sun Wakayama City enact splendor of important castle-town of Tokugawas.

20 *Ebi* (shrimp) *Fete*, Kasuga Shrine, Kada City. Prayers for good catch, giant mikoshi parade, lion dances.

June

1st *Onsen Fest* Shirahama, all public baths and most hotel baths *admit free at present*

1st thru Early Sep *Ugai* (Cormorant Fishing) Arida-gawa River (*text* p.420).

July

14 *Fan Fete*, Kumano Nachi Grand Shrine

(p.413); parade sacred fan-shape ornaments on 12 mikoshi, 12 massive torches.

18 *Wakamiya Festival*, Kenkoku Shrine Yuasa T. Youths cart mikoshi thru town.

24-25 *Tanabe Festival*, Tanabe City-wide. Cockfight, Tokei Shrine pits red (Mina-moto) vs white (Taira) bird: local pirate chose Minamoto at Battle of Dan-no-ura.

24-25, *Boat Festival* at Kochi S, Koza T, celebrates Minamoto Victory. Horse race re-enacts Paul Revere-like ride telling victory.

Last Weekend *Kokawa Festival*, Kokawa Town nr Wakayama, one of main Kii festivals. Various dances; procession Sun *chigo* (child dancers) on horseback, drums, lion dancers, floats.

Last Weekend Tado Jinja *Summer Fete*, lantern procession, Tado-cho, Mie.

31 Gion S, Kuwana C, dance & fireworks.

August

1st Weekend *Ishitori Matsuri*, Kuwana, Mie. 30 floats both days, sun eve best 7-9pm lantern procession, flutes, drums, dancers.

12-24 Traditional Dai-Ise *kagura* lion dance, Masuda Shrine, Kuwana C, 10am; makes round of towns nationwide.

15 *Toro-nagashi* (Floating Lanterns) down Ki-nokawa Riv, fireworks. Hashimoto C.

September

15 *Whale dance* Hachiman Shr, Shingu. Dancers form whale of ropes, etc.

October

2 *Repeat* of February 2.

4-5 *Gobo Festival*, Shino Hachiman Shrine, Gobo City. Wild dances earn fete nickname 'Fighting Festival'.

– *Gourd Festival*, Hachiman S, Gobo City, *nembutsu-odori*, religious dance w/gourds.

10 *Laughing Fete* Nyu Shrine Kawabe Town

10 *Kakko Odori* dances, Iga Jinja, Ayama-cho, Mie.

13 Shakuhachi contest; itinerant monks, Kyokoku-ji temple, Yura Town.

16th *Mifune Boat Festival* at Kumano Hayatama Grand Shrine, Shingu (p.408).

November

14-15 *Momiji* (maple) *Fete*, Nachi Shrine as hills draped in autumnal brocades.

I wonder what other joys wait for me in Kyoto,
the widow Royal City, where I will arrive tonight.
— Nikos Kazantzakis, *Japan and China*, 1935

KYOTO 京都
CITY OF CITIES

KYOTO's two ideographs mean "capital of capitals", "metropolis of metropolies". Emperor Kammu laid it out in then-wilderness in 794AD to be world's greatest city—and at several times in its history it has probably been just that. He called it *Heian-kyo*, City of Peace. But whether egotists or dreamers, its citizens have never called it other than by its present name and for full millennium lived up to it elegantly. Here bloomed one of those truly great original cultural epochs of world history, as vividly recorded in world literature's first novel *The Tale of Genji* by Court Lady Murasaki Shikibu. (*See* masterpiece translation of Sir Arthur Waley, or new by Edward Seidenstecker).

Characters in this novel, written ca 1000AD, were aware that Kyoto was past its peak, in decline. Two centuries later Zen boom brought Kyoto once more to life. Late 14th century Kyoto again became seat of power, as well as Imperial Court, entering its most flamboyant era of Gold and Silver Pavilions, Nijo Castle, Saint Francis Xavier, South Seas ventures followed by those quiet inward-turning reactions of Katsura Palace, tea arts, shibui, and sealing border. Artists and artisans gathered here from all Asia, as well as Japan, to cater to Imperial Court, Buddhist cathedrals and their courts, even more splendid courts of real power: Fujiwara Regents, Ashikaga Shoguns, Tycoon Hideyoshi. Tokugawa Shogun moved de facto capital to Edo 380 years ago, but Imperial Kyoto continued to set fashions, provide artwares, silks and artists to Edo. When emperor Meiji moved Imperial Court to Edo-Tokyo 1867, Kyoto froze in time in its traditional medieval culture.

Best of all, this established tradition of elegance, beauty and refinement, as preserved in this ancient city untouched by war, makes Kyoto for us one great sightseeing and shopping paradise. It is vermilion pavilions and multi-storeyed pagodas, wiggly trees and stone gardens, exotic shops and tea houses. Most of all it is still—however fewer each year—women and children in florid kimono, men in rich earth-hued robes.

Kyoto is no exotic freak, no tourist trap: this living city's exotic products find worldwide quality markets, its denizens combine deep attachment to antiquity and love for modernity. These cosmopolites were first to adopt then-new Korean-Chinese arts, architecture and technology millennium-plus ago, as they were more recently first to adopt such westernization as electric trams (oldest one uprooted only since our first edition). They welcomed Korean, Chinese and other immigrants and nomads of 1500 years ago as they welcome modern jet-age nomad-tourists. Kyoto hosts 38,000,000 Japanese tourists yearly (1/3rd of population), welcomes 700,000 foreign tourists (1989) into its gardens. And this welcome is sincere.

And will become warmer—if only out of gratitude—as 1987 saw serious drop in both foreign and domestic tourists due to Yen rise. Americans can less afford to come, while Japanese better afford to fly off to 'more exotic' foreign destinations like Hawaii or Australia. But 1988-89 saw rebounds.

To those of us who have long known Kyoto, its steady loss of its Kyoto-ness, its unique Japaneseness, is alarming, saddening. But writers have never failed to comment on this, even *Murray's Guide* at last century turn records similar plaints. Some recent horror stories include loss of Silk Mansion above Kyoto Hotel: its wonderful gardens survived and expanded in Edo times when it was sole house allowed to trade overseas (by barge down canal to Port of Sakai and SE Asia), then survived US Occupation receiving special dispensation relieving it from becoming sergeants' mess, to open as showroom for smaller weavers–only to be bulldozed and disfigured with ugly cement box of Bank of Japan 'repository of nation's wealth'. Yet shanties on two facing corners survive for years.

In Nishijin weavers' neighborhood where walking cadence may yet at times be marked by rhythmic clack of looms, low traditional architecture steadily gives way to higher rise in understandable need to make better use of explosively expensive real estate–but what happened to that age-old Kyoto aesthetic, to allow such boxy ugliness (and not at all functional). And their denizens still deal in beauty–kimono, obi, etc. 45-meter height limit matches pagoda of Toji, less its finial. Kyoto Tower's phallic 131m violated this to commemorate '64 Olympics. Now to desecrate city's 12th centennial in '94 they want to match this across street with new 131m station eggbox. And horrid 1992 plans for skyscraper Kyoto Hotel. Even commercial metropolis Berlin limits to 8 storeys. Opposition, thankfully, is fierce. As it is locally by temples resisting highrise 'mansions' whose elite slum-dwellers would use view as 'captured' front garden. Some temples ask donations to buy up enemy—drop coins.

Worst, and least understandable as it's had, continues to have immediate effect on perpetrators' cash income, is destruction of lovely antique-shop lanes Furumonzen, Shinmonzen—first by our otherwise-favorite modern art gallery which should have had better taste, certainly historic awareness of roots of so much Western modernism in Japan style. Then very association of those local merchants built plastic-front boxy eyesore-office in midstreet.

And so much more we read of constantly in newer writers on Kyoto.

Admittedly, having lived in it, traditional Kyoto architecture is uncomfortable in muggy summer and damp shivery winter—but our experience of these new stacks of boxes are little better, often worse.

Yet visiting friends whose taste we respect comment as how beautiful this city is, how quintessentially 'Japanese', how less-crowded it seems than other cities in Japan.

Some note its compensations. Department store-viewing is our favorite pastime in any city, tells more of any nation's life and culture than shelves of books. One guest commented that Kyoto's shortage of parks and public spaces is compensated in great part by these department stores.

One would hope to see some interesting functional new lay architecture, based on eternal local verities. Designs of objects and interiors are so well done here: why not exteriors? Container art, boxes and wrappings here are so beautiful and functional: why not better 'people boxes', buildings?

Will Kyoto's sense of beauty hold up against crush of future?

Pessimistically, in sharp contrast to quote opening next page, we quote our favorite author-photographer of Japan:

If you wish to enjoy unadulterated, glorious, refined ugliness come to Kyoto! This ancient capital used to be a beautiful place, but now it resembles more and more a monstrous version of Las Vegas...If you want to see something of Kyoto's fabled wonders be quick, tomorrow may be too late.
                                   —Fosco Maraini, in *Japan Times*, 1988

*I will go back... for the ancient town of Kyoto is,
with Paris, Rome and Pekin one of the few towns of
the world where the breath of the spirit can be felt....*
— Robert Guillain, 1960

IRASSHAI-MASSE
WELCOME TO KYOTO

GETTING THERE

FOLLOWING OUR original historical itinerary down Tokaido brought us thru ancient areas of Ise and Nara into Kyoto.

Or, at great risk of repeating ourselves, fly in direct via Osaka International Airport from Los Angeles, San Francisco, Honolulu or Hong Kong or even Europe. If limited in time, save money and aggravation: skip Tokyo. It is same elapsed time, or even less, San Francisco to your Kyoto hotel as it is SF to Tokyo Hotel, and 2-3 hours less from Hong Kong. If on long time tour, fly into Kyoto anyway, rest, base yourself down here, and treat Tokyo as side trip on Shinkansen bullet train. And who needs that hassle of Narita airport's fortress and hour-long super train into town or alternate hundred-odd-dollar taxi?

What you have come halfway round world to Japan to see is all in Nara and Kyoto. It's also cheaper down here at all budget levels, ¥-Pilgrim thru ¥-Luxe–most older top hotels charge ¥-S rate for 'L' facilities.

By our chronological routing we then arrive from NARA by Kintetsu train to Kyoto Station southside (next to Shinkansen exit of JR), or by JR old train northside, or from Nara via BYODOIN by same JR or Keihan line into midtown at Shijo or Sanjo St E-side of river. Others may arrive by Shinkansen from Tokyo or elsewhere, or Hankyu line from Kobe or Osaka into Shijo-dori W-side (or by alt JR). Most arrivals will hop taxi from station to hotel. For ¥-L & ¥-S hotels, have English-speaking-chauffeured 5psgr car or even Lincoln limousine waiting (for JR-Shinkansen it will be waiting at Shinkansen S-side Hachijo exit to left [E] end) phone ahead to **MK Tourist Taxi** ☎(075)-721-2237: Kyoto Stn to hotel ¥3,200 (¥7,600 for Lincoln or similar); will meet at Osaka International Itami airport ¥12,800 (¥22,800), or take at your Osaka hotel ¥14,400 (¥22,800), or Kobe ¥19,200 (¥26,600)–road-tolls extra, 1992 rising 10% to keep abreast Tokyo rise in '91.

Luxury (¥-L) and standard (¥-S) tourists will usually have reservations in advance. If visiting Kyoto mid-March thru October this is strongly advised. Handle thru your travel agent. If booking your airline direct, most of their computers are linked in to handle this as well as your air tickets. Major ryokan-inns especially must be reserved. Minor inns are rarely on any computer link-up and so have fewer advanced reservations anyway, can usually be booked on arrival direct–tho annual increase in youth traveling during school vacation may change this adversely. **TIC's** new (1991) **Welcome Inn Reservation Center** helps book room under ¥8000/person. Appear in person, *see* p138.

Caution: Ryokans, from better class to minshuku, are upset at high rate of no-shows among tourists who make their own advanced reservations. Many innkeepers don't like to commit themselves to such high risk, so use agent or use your guaranteed reservation and late show privilege of your credit card, if it has one. If you are going to be late, notify by phone–or risk losing any unguaranteed reservation. Or if there is sudden change en route, phone, and innkeeper will cooperate to best of his ability–often even to extending reservation date without penalty. But thankfully because of these no-shows, sudden arrival in town even at season peak has reasonably good chance of finding accommodation in most any price range. But it's some gamble.

Best idea is to get to travel agency before you leave previous point—in your hotel if ¥-L or ¥-S rate, for lower rates usually several in or near central stations one of which will be JTB, another is probably local RR, and JR is expanding into everything and efficiently. Minshuku and JIG cheap inns, members of similar associations, will usually help you book next stop thru association fellow, at cost of direct-dial long distance phone call at most, no hotel-style phone surcharge. 1991 initiated **Welcome Inn** plan thru **TIC**, which will book rooms under ¥10,000—but you must appear in person at TIC desk in Kyoto or Tokyo (*see* p.127).

If not, go to station JTB or agency on arrival; or opp JR Kyoto Stn at foot of tower visit Kyoto JNTO-**TIC** ☎(075)-371-0480 (9-5 no-X) or from out of town toll-free ☎(0120)-444-800 (9-5, –12 sat, X-sun, hol) which will help with bookings in this area, free.

Get map, for adventurer best is *Kyoto Transportation Guide* by City Transport Bureau and local Rotary, in English, *free* from TIC, some hotels– has good details of bus routes. *Tourist Map of Kyoto-Nara* by JNTO also good bus details, *free* at TIC—serious bus-rider (get **One Day Pass** ¥960) needs *City Bus Subway Route Map* in hardish-to-follow chart form but more detailed and bilingual with odd bus symbols in ideographs. Month's DATEBOOK update info in freebies *Kyoto Visitor's Guide* (*KVG*) and *Discover Kinki* (*Kinki*)—both have good maps, too–but better to put out ¥300 and buy *Kansai Time Out* for more dope (tho no city maps) info on neighboring cities, for greater accuracy regarding events, they seem to check closer.

DISCOUNT TRAVEL   Kotsu ko-sha/JTB shukuhaku plan...

Nice Inn: Discount coupon for hotel, allows 20% off train ticket for minimum 2 persons. Sat & day before holidays surcharge.
    Example: Hotel **Sun Route** (51 in Japan). Cheap plan, tax/svc incl....3 plans: w/bkfst; w/2; room only. Osaka w/bkfst ¥6,500ea; w/2 ¥9,000; room only tw¥-T.

Economy I-I Yado (economical-good inn) book thru JR for discount coupon for hotel, 20% off on train ticket (min 2 persons for train discount).
    In season: ¥6,000 ea. (2 in room), ¥7,500 ea. (3 in room); off season: ¥7,000 each for 2 in room, ¥8,500 ea at 3 in rm; sat & day before holiday surcharge ¥1,500 ea.
    See pp.106, 129 for general JR Rail-Hotel packages.

Shinkansen O-fuku Plan 'Shinkansen Round-trip Plan' offers various discounts of 18-27%: *Kodama yonin kippu* (Kodama ticket for 4) for those who use slightly slower (stops often) Kodama, free seating, between Tokyo & Shin-Osaka, 4 persons go for price of 3: one way valid over 2 days; round-trip 4 days (i.e. allows 3 o'nites). Similarly, small booklets of 4-6 or more identical tix usually available at discount, valid in either direction, use for group or same people repeating. Frequent changes in details, seasonal variations with specific region-wide transport package *shuyuken*, but essence remains.
    See p.107 for other similar.

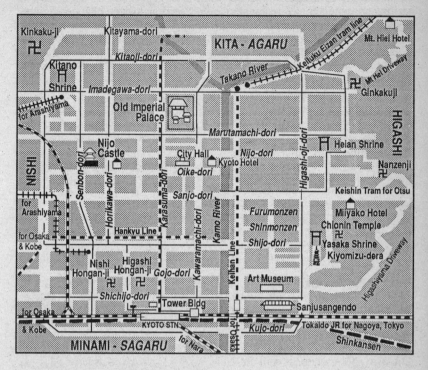

PERSONAL ORIENTATION

CITY WAS planned, checkerboard like Nara and earlier Naniwa-Osaka. But where Nara streets each bear names (usually only for each block, changing at cross-streets), Kyoto refers to name of intersection, or to two main cross streets, with smaller lanes and houses being so many -*agaru*, above (N), or -*sagaru*, below (S), and -*higashi* E (or toward nearer mountains), and -*nishi*, W. What you need to know then are main downtown streets and key Kyoto directions -*agaru*, -*sagaru*, -*higashi*, -*nishi* –and here we forego our usual redundancy of -*dori*-street, etc, and drop latter translation.

Suffix -*dori* describes main thoroughfare, whether wide vehicular or narrow pedestrian lane as in case of most of Sanjo-dori (E-W) or predominantly market street Teramachi-dori (N-S). Those including -*jo* in name—Nijo-dori, Sanjo-dori, Shijo-dori, Gojo-dori, Shichijo-dori, Kujo-dori (2nd Ave, 3rd, 4th, 5th, 7th, 9th) run E-W. Lesser streets may be suffixed -*koji*. But -*dori* or -*koji* are parts of their names and such as asking for *Ane*-street instead of *Ane-ga-koji* will usually get you nowhere, even with fluent bilinguals, Japanese or Occidental, tho *Shijo* or *Sanjo* seem to get by without -*dori*.

Kyoto is set in horseshoe of mountains open at south, thru which you enter. This circumvallation by shock reflectors earned it a nomination to become first A-Bomb target, plus fact that it was traditional ceramics center and in US and UK main parts for radar were made in such places (not here). From Kyoto JR Station facing town we look north, in local Kyoto parlance -*agaru* (up or *a*bove) (both start with 'a'). Behind us, direction in which midtown Kamo river flows is -*sagaru* (south), (both start 's'), down–true sociologically as well for this area, noteworthy by its lack of development until recent hotels S of Shinkansen stn, is traditional home of *Eta*, outcasts, or *burakumin*, ghetto-people. Economics equalize as efficiently as six-guns in Olde West and property values will accomplish what fiat failed to do, raise their status to 'human' as area—now junk yards and till recently skin tanneries—steadily opens to low-pollution high tech industries now returning to Kyoto (electronics, super ceramics, etc).

To our right is -*higashi* (east) always recognizable by ever-nearby Higashi-yama 'East-mountains'. Miyako Hotel and many of our top inns and most-interesting sights are at base of this long hill. Mountains on -*nishi* (west) are out beyond city limits at Arashiyama, oldest part of city well beyond KINKAKU-JI Golden Pavilion and RYOAN-JI Zen stone and sand garden. City was originally laid out with Kamo River running down E side, and W-side Ryoan-ji was in town. Center was then-Imperial Palace, where NIJO CASTLE is now. IMPERIAL PALACE was moved after 1600, saw populace shift with it, even spreading east across river, so that modern **downtown** is now mostly below palace,-*sagaru*, as well as around river. This is where it was when our predecessor BH Chamberlain wrote *Murray's Guide* some century ago. Subsequent growth of sleepy art-town to become once again great city left usurpatious Nijo Castle, former center, out on western edge.

Recent PR campaign led by local hi-tech industrialists calls for return of Imperial Household to old palace, and restoration of Kyoto as seat of Imperial functions. Romantic—good chance to get new ambassadors out of Tokyo at least once, good to help relieve Tokyo traffic. But if it comes to pass (unlikely, as 1990 Imperial Enthronement rites usurped Kyoto's traditional place, even snatched throne pavillions by Self Defense Force helicopter and airlifted pair of them over heads of would-be saboteur radicals), yes if it happens, God help Kyoto.

Rational, yet so un-Japanese is this geometry, that no other city emulated for millennium until Sapporo was built 19th century, then postwar central Nagoya and Hiroshima—but even there, in all for downtown areas only, while outer areas are traditional warrens. Kyoto's checkerboard was enhanced in world war II when some roads were greatly widened as firebreaks for bombings that never came. These are today picturesque but modern, efficient boulevards.

A city that was saved from American bombs is being destroyed by Japanese greed...put in anything trashy because everyone wants to cash in while the money is good. —Okada Mayumi, Kyoto Activist, in *Japan Times Weely*, 1990

Kyoto Journal, fine literary quarterly (not info-mag), published special issue 1991 of interviews with long-term residents both native and guest, concluded

"...we had convened a wake. Whether they were talking about art, business, street life, politics or food, the majority of the fifty-odd speakers are in mourning for the Kyoto they knew five, twenty or fifty years ago, alarmed at the triumph of alienation and dehumanization...
....What are we going to do about it?"

*Though your room has one thousand mats
you can only sleep on one mat...*
—Japanese proverb

WHERE TO STAY

WESTERN-STYLE HOTELS

ONCE SEVERELY limited, have multiplied –and in high seasons are still short of demand. Most cheaper (¥-S) than in usual big city with international trader clientele, as here they have few businessman-oriented expensive special services and extras, like money-saving 'convenience' stores.

But if anywhere, this is one town where stay at ryokan is in order: cost competitive, used to foreigners and usually more convenient for morning or evening sightseeing strolls (or if hesitant, first try J- room in most hotels). However you will want to limit your w/2 meals to one or 2 days, take some overnites w/bkfst-only to allow sampling of town's restaurants—especially at least one summer's nite dining out on *yuka* platform over midtown Kamo river, perhaps one summer supper out at Arashiyama at cormorant fishing. Most inns, from ¥-L to minshuku, offer room-only or w/bkfst as fair alternative. Many smaller inns do not offer dinner at all, usually simple bkfst. But, as we detail following, if you want geisha party then have it in your ryokan for economy. If budget-oriented, for 2 persons, good ¥-lo-T hotels end up cheaper than minshuku or same as inexpensive inns.

Hotels seem to cluster and we treat them in order, first, of our choices for two best, then clusters by convenience. First numeral is map designation.

Miyako Hotel [11,J-8] Sanjo Kéagé, ☎(075)-771-7111; mostly ¥-L but ¥-S from ¥14,000. Inconvenient as requires taxi to get almost anywhere, strollable range Nanzen-ji temple (E) and Heian Shrine (W). Still best, "even its proverbially slow service," as we wrote in '64, "is still Kyoto's best". For ¥-L would-be adventurer perhaps not enough-so to risk ryokan, try semi-detached J-style tatami-matted cottage, each off garden with direct access. J- or W-meal by room svce duplicate traditional ryokan. Airport limo.

Takaraga-iké Prince [12, J-2] Takaragaike Convention Center ☎712-1111, ¥-hi-L, top Seibu chain; at extreme N of city, most inconvenient unless here at convention. Have *matcha* green tea 'ceremony' in lovely garden tea house. Take early morning stroll 20min W to lovely dry-garden temple Entsu-ji [H-2].

DOWNTOWN [H/I-7/9] *convenient to popular restnts, nitelife, late strolls:*

Kyoto Hotel [13,H/I-7] Kawaramachi Oike ☎[211-5111] doyen of downtown hotels *closed* 1990– to rebuild as hotly-opposed 60fl violating city skyline. Hopefully to be modified but official taste what it is...

Kyoto Royal [14,H/I-8] Kawaramachi-Sanjo ☎223-1234, ¥-S, 2 blks S Kyoto H.

Hotel Alpha [15,H-8] Kawaramachi-Sanjo-agaru (opp above)☎241-2000 ¥-hi-T

Fujita [16,I-7] W end Nijo bridge riverside ☎222-1511, short walk N of center, ¥-S.

Gimmond [17,H-7] Oike-dori W of Takakura, ☎221-4111, ¥-lo-S.

Tokyo Dai-Ichi [17a,H-7] Higashinotoin Sanjo-S, Karasuma-E; ☎252-4411; ¥-S.

Pension Higashiyama Gion [18,I-8] Sanjo-S Shirakawasuji, ☎882-1181;¥-lo-T.

Higashiyama YH [19,I-8] Sanjo-dori Shirakawabashi ☎761-8135,great loc; ¥-P.

Traveler's Inn [20,J-7] Enshoji 91, Okazaki ☎771-0225/6 ¥-B; S of Heian Shrine.

Sun [21a,H-8] Kawaramachi mid-Sanjo-Shijo, ☎241-3351, ¥-T.

Central Inn [21,H-8] Shijo-Teramachi-E, ☎211-1666, ¥-hi-T.

Gion Hotel [21b,I-8] Gion Ishidan Shita ☎274-1818, ¥-lo-S; Shijo W of Higashioji

Karasuma Kyoto [22,G-9] Karasuma S of Shijo, ☎371-0111, ¥-lo-S.

Sun Route [23,H-9] Kawaramachi N of Gojo ☎371-3711 ¥-T; nr Gojo potter walk

Rich [24,H-9] Kawaramachi N of Gojo, ☎341-1131, ¥-T–S.

Econo-Inn [25,H-9] Kawaramachi S of Gojo, ☎343-6660, ¥-B.

Park [26,I-8] Sanjusangendo Mawaricho ☎525-3111, ¥-lo-S; nr National Museum.

IMPERIAL PALACE [GH-6/7] *less convenient than above, see palace early*:

Palace-side [27,G-6] Karasuma-dori, SW of Palace, ☎431-8171, ¥-T.

Kyoto Brighton [28,G-6] ☎441-4411, 1st Kyoto all-suite hotel ¥-S, dbl ¥15,000+. Shinmachi-Nakadachiuri, block W Imperial Palace middle, behind Pref Hall; var restnts

YWCA Hostel [44,G-6] Muromachi St N of Demizu, ☎431-0351, ¥-B; in by 10pm.

You-And-I [29,G-7] Karasuma-dori block N of Palace-side H, ☎441-9161, ¥-hi-T.

Garden [30,G-8] Oike-S, 2nd st W of Karasuma, ☎255-2000, ¥-hi-T.

NIJO CASTLE [G-7] *bit out of way but scenic, see castle before mob*; bus #9:

International Kokusai [31,G-7] ¥-S views Castle opp, ¥-T tiny back rms; J-style ¥-S; ☎222-1111, good restnts, tea ceremony lobby, spec maiko, garden-shows

Le Lion d'Or pension [G-7] 100m N of above, ☎256-1355, ¥-T, bkfst ¥800.

New Kyoto [33,G-7] above Castle, SW Horikawa-Marutamachi ☎801-2111, ¥-hi-T

ANA [32,G-7], Horikawa-dori opp Castle, ☎231-1155, ¥-S; good rest'nts, art-deco-japonais shops, interior. Airport limo stop.

City [34,G-5/6] Kita-Funabashi Horikawa-dori N of Imadegawa, ¥-T, ☎431-7161.

Puchi (Petite) Pension [G-5/6] Imadegawa-dori W-Horikawa, ¥-lo-T ☎431-5136

STATION AREA [G-11] *convenient only to trains, Hongan-ji, no nitelife*:

Grand [2,G-10] Horikawa-Shiokoji, ☎341-2311; ¥-T-S, W of stn, inconvenient but good restaurants including revolving 'Top of–', indoor pool, sauna. Airport limo stop.

New Miyako [3,G-11] S of and opp Shinkansen exit, ☎661-7111, ¥-hi-T-S, orphan li'l sister of grand old Miyako bears little resemblance in quality. Airport limo.

Keihan [4,G-11] opp SE corner Shinkansen Stn, ☎661-0321, ¥-S.

Kyoto Tower [1,G-10] N of main exit on Karasuma-dori corner, ☎361-3211, ¥-T; TIC on main fl; tall viewing tower itself is as uninteresting as it is ugly.

Hokke Club [5,G-10] bit W of Tower H, ☎361-1251, ¥-hi-T (+¥1,000 wkends).

New Hankyu [6,G-10] opp NW corner (bit W/L of tower) ☎343-5300,¥-S; J- ¥-L.

Kyoto Daini (#2) **Tower** [7,H-10] E of stn, adjoining above, ☎361-3261, ¥-T.

Century [8,H-10] E of stn, ☎351-0111, most pleasant of Station cluster, ¥-S; J-.

Tokyu [9,G-9] Horikawa below Gojo just above Nishi Hongan-ji ☎341-2411, ¥-S; above usual Tokyu lo level, free shuttle

Dai-san Tower [H-9] on Shinmachi across from Tower H, ☎343-3111, ¥-hi-T.

NORTH OF TOWN

Sunflower [35,K-7] Higashi-tenno-cho Okazaki, ☎761-9111, Marutamachi E of Heian Shrine, walkable, also Philosophers' Walk to NE; ¥-hi-T, J-style ¥-lo-S.

Holiday Inn [36,IJ-4] N up R fork river, ☎721-3131, ¥-T; inconvenient but free stn shuttles; good restnts, lots 'holiday' extras.

Prince [37,I-5] Matsubara-cho Shimo-gamo, ☎781-4141, ¥-lo-S, some J- ¥-S.

ApicalInn [38,A-2] Kitayama St W-bank ☎722-7711¥-T; Shugakuin 10min walk

Mt Hiei Hotel [off map NE] for those preferring lovely nite view to nitelife ☎701-1111 ¥-S.

HIGASHIYAMA EASTERN HILLS [IJ-8]–first 2 *Ladies Only*:

Kyoto Ladies' Hotel Yasaka Jinja minami-mon-mae, ☎561-3181, ¥-P bunks, ¥-B, J-style; geisha here in evening, dress you as maiko—*see* GEISHA, SHOPPING.

Maruyama-gyoen, Hotel Gion, Sakano-ue 9pm-10am ¥-B love hotels.

Choraku-kan in Maruyama-park, ladies only, ☎561-0001, ¥-T (*see* SHOPPING text) former baron's mansion Victorian posh, popular 'romantic' tea room.

U's Higashi-oji Ave S Yasaka shrine fancy love hotel 9pm-11am ¥-hi-B, nice rest'nt

WESTERN SUBURBS [AB-6/7] PURPLE PERIOD area (*see* MAP-WEST):

Pension Arashiyama [39,B-7] Miyano-motocho Saga,nice suburb ☎881-2294;¥-T

Pens'n Utano [40,C-6] Narutaki-honmachi Ukyo-ku, ☎463-1118, ¥-loT, bus #26.

Utano YH [41,B-5] Nakayamacho Uzumasa ☎462-2288,¥-P, best w/2, unltd macaroni; special programs—check; bus #10,26,59.

Arashiyama Ladies' Hotel [42,A-7], in Keifuku Arashiyama stn, opp Tenryuji tmpl, ☎882-0955, ¥-Bw/2 or w/out; cheap renta-bike ideal for exploring; rent kimono.

Kitayama YH [43,D-3], NW hills next to Koetsu-ji temple ☎492-5345 bus #6, 61.

EASTERN SUBURBS OTSU & BIWA *see* BIWA p.497; UJI *see* p.462.

OUR RANKING: 1992 EDITION			
Ryokan: per person			**Hotel**: twin/dbl room
¥50,000+	pricey-princely	'¥-LL'	¥35,000+%
¥25,000-50,000w/2	international luxe	'¥-L'	¥20,000-35,000+%
¥13,000-25,000w/2	standard	'¥-S'	¥12,000-20,000+%
¥7,000-13,000w/2	tourist/business	'¥-T'	¥7,000-12,000
¥4,400-7,000w/2	budget	'¥-B'	¥7,000-under
¥4,500-under	pilgrim	'¥-P'	

Under ¥5,001 per person (¥10,001 dbl) rm chge add 3% tax; ¥5,001-up 6%; rm w/ meals to ¥10,001 per person tax +3%, ¥10,001-up 6%, with any service chge incl in taxable base.

RYOKAN–JAPANESE INNS

KYOTO, as we recommend repeatedly elsewhere, is where you should experience your ryokan stay: not having been destroyed in WWII there are still traditional inns of wooden architecture with interior woodwork lovingly rubbed and polished for over hundred years. Accommodations offered at ryokan at same as minimal Western-style ¥-L rates (figured at ¥50,000 per couple with 2 meals) are generally of luxury style such as *House Beautiful* have led us to believe is Nippon's paradisical par. All Standard (¥-Sw/2) and Luxe are air-conditioned, have W-style toilets and best have bath tubs of *hinoki* white cedar (its fragrance and tactile warmth are sensation one does not forget), usually two-room semi-suites. Among these, English is usually spoken, variously from adequate by someone, to such as **Hiiragiya** where all maids manage some. As rule of thumb, middle of announced rate range is best buy, to which inn has geared their operation, and two per room is far better meal buy for same person-rate than single room. *Warning*: Most inns charge extra nite before Sun, hols.

Most better ryokan make their money on meals–are in fact mainly restaurants–and are best buy taken with two meals ('w/2'). Some refuse room only, but Kyoto's top ryokan have long catered to guests from overseas and know that many prefer to dine out some evenings, so they will gracefully oblige (usually 20% off w/2 rate).

Your looked-forward-to **geisha party** is best and most economically arranged for at and thru your inn–geisha rates are standard, but inn will guard you against any chance of being clipped, and extras and liquor charges will be kept legitimate, being on inn's bill direct. We suggest you request at time of reservation to have geisha attend you at dinner in your inn. Rates ('91) for one *maiko* (apprentice geisha) or *geiko* (trained geisha) ¥35,000 for *isseki* (one session), 6:15-8:00pm. Sometimes taxi fee home *kurumadai* of ¥1,000 will be requested, but that is all, no tipping, etc. *Geiko* preferable tho slightly less ornate, better trained in dances and games.

LUXE RYOKAN are listed separately with additional info, as are SHUKUBO stays at temples with national treasure fusuma sliding doors, large formal gardens, exquisite architecture. Main division is by area, each subdivided: ¥-S, ¥-T, ¥-B (incl Minshuku and Pensions), and ¥-P.

STANDARD: ¥-S w/2 rates offered by some basically ¥-L inns, as: **Sumiya** ¥-hi-S, ***Kaneiwaro Bekkan** ¥-lo-S, **Seikoro** ¥-hi-S, **Yachiyo** ¥-S, **Kikusui** ¥-hi-T. Special treat in summer (Jun 1 to Sep 15) are *ryori ryokan* with charming only-in-Kyoto experience of dining over Kamogawa River on special *yuka* platforms (marked * here); charges start ¥-lo-S –good buy as their full *kaiseki* dinners alone on *yuka* start at ¥8,000.

TOURIST: Some mainly Luxe inns even have some rooms at ¥-hi-T, especially if 3 or more to room. **Hiiragiya Bekkan** (above) is one such, **Kikusui** is another. Some ¥-lo-Sw/2 offer ¥-Tw/2, esp weekdays off-season. But sat nite and pre hol, surcharge.

BUDGET: means ¥4,500-7,000 with two meals, or room charge only at ¥7,000 couple. At ¥4,000 per person rm only in new larger Minshuku, often inexpensive inns like JIG ryokan (without meals or bkfst-only) are cheaper and innkeepers are just as warm and personal as small true-minshuku owners. Increasing in Kyoto is Guest House or Inn, where rooms with bath, tiny kitchen or communal kitchen, laundry and living room facilities are available at ¥-Budget rates.

Boon to ryokan owners and budget-minded is ryokan owner Hiraiwa of Kyoto who formed association JIG (Japanese Inn Group) whose member ryokan cater to non-Japanese guests with special attention to amenities to make them comfortable; make effort to speak English. Publish excellent guide in English, available TICs & JNTO overseas. Contact **Hiraiwa Ryokan**, 314 Hayao-cho, Kaminoguchi-agaru, Ninomiya-cho-dori, Shimogyo-ku, Kyoto 600, ☎351-6748. Having tried their inns, we can say "they care" (marked 'JIG' below). Rm chg +(optional) bkfst or dinner still makes ¥-Bw/2 if some barely. Most following inns belong to either JIG, or are recommended by TIC Kyoto and *Kyoto Visitor's Guide*, are acquainted with foreign tourists' whims. Most give room charge (RC) only or room+bkfst, and most fall in ¥-B group, at most ¥-lo-T.

MINSHUKU: *List of Minshuku in Kyoto* shows 40 in Kyoto alone, tho city usually not associated with them, ¥3,500-4,500 stay only, top ¥6,000w/2. Some offer *chado*, others pottery making, traditional music– whatever hobby owner-manager plays at. *Free*, **Kyoto Minshuku Rsvtn Ctr**, ON Bldg 7fl, Kyoto-eki-mae (Kyoto stn-facing), Shimogyo-ku Kyoto 600; ☎(075)-351-4547. To visit, it's near JNTO-TIC, which can direct you, but TIC can help book.

PENSIONS differ from term 'Pensione' in Europe, usually new buildings that simulate W-style homes, w/bed+bkfst. Generally room only ¥4,-5,000 (some ¥1,000 extra weekends), ¥500-800 bkfst; dinner ¥1,500-up; ¥6,500-7,000w/2.

LUXE RYOKAN: Clustered just off Oike blvd on Fuyacho-dori (2 blks W of ANA bldg) are trio of Kyoto's best, all well experienced with international guests, advance reservations essential:

Hiiragiya [A,H-8] 160 years old, originally catered to wealthy lords and samurai, has air of quiet opulence. Known for its warm reception. 33 rooms, each in its own individual taste. Starts ¥-lo-Lw/2, ☎221-1136. ¥-S Bekkan annex block and half N on Gokomachi-dori.

Across street is...

Tawaraya [B,H-8] run by 11th generation, only 19 rooms, many face onto own little garden, each room different yet ultimate in refinement and beauty. Catering to royalty, novelists, artists and elite, every detail is just right. Starts ¥-Lw/2, ☎211-5566.

Block and half down street is...

Sumiya [C,H-8] careful of aesthetic detail, changes tatami covers 2-3 times yearly for fragrant fresh greenish color; relatively new, started by noh, tea, painting connoisseur 75 yrs ago. Note details of sukiya-style rooms, all are quite different. ¥-hi-S–Lw/2, ☎221-2188.

Yoshikawa [D,H-8] blk W on Tominokoji betw Oike & Anekoji, known for its tempura, ¥-Lw/2, ☎221-5544; tempura course ¥6,-8,000 (run tempura restnt Hotel Fujita B-1).

Pleasantly located on Kamogawa River nr Gojo-dori...

*Kaneiwaro Bekkan [E,H-9] 60-yr-old, all rooms *sukiya-shoin* style face river. Jun1-Sept15 enjoy dinner on *yuka* platform built over river. ¥-lo-S-Lw/2, ☎351-5010.

Just across river south of Gojo-dori is...

Seikoro [F,H-9] 150-yr-old, rarely-seen lovely split bamboo *yarai* mud guards protect long outer wall. Intriguing bits of art nouveau incorporated into Meiji-era main bldg. Each room *sukiya-* or *shoin* style, overlooks small garden; ¥-hi-S–Lw/2; ☎561-0771.

Over by NANZEN-JI Temple are...

Yachiyo [G,J-8] formerly estate, ryokan postwar, highly rated, located E of zoo in Okazaki. Rm only ¥-S; ¥-S–hi-Lw/2. ☎771-4148.

Kikusui [H,J-8] *ryori ryokan*, huge classical garden, one wing beautifully rebuilt in traditional wooden cottages. Nanzenji Fukuchicho 31, ¥-hi-Tw/2+, ☎771-4101.

Awata Sanso [I,J-8] Kyoto Hotel's J-annex, N of Shorenin Temple, E of Jingu-Mae, below Sanjo Keihan tram line, large garden, ¥-hi-L–LLw/2, ☎561-4908.

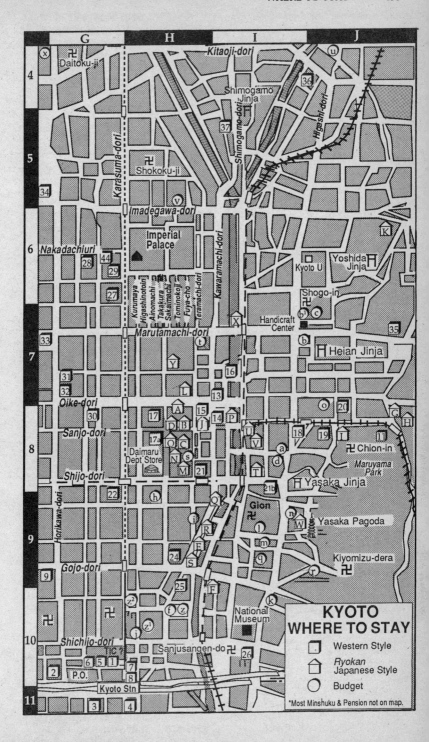

KYOTO
WHERE TO STAY

☐ Western Style

⌂ Ryokan
Japanese Style

◯ Budget

*Most Minshuku & Pension not on map.

Right downtown, on Sanjo-dori in few
doors W from Kawaramachi is...
Daimonji-ya [J,H-8] known for cuisine;
small, intimate, all interiors traditional
wooden bldg with tiny '6ft-sq' tsubo-niwa,
¥-Lw/2, ☎221-0603.

OUTLYING: KURAMA, KIBUNE:
Hiroya, across shrine, summer dining over
running river, ¥-lo-Lw/2, ☎741-2401.

BY KYOTO UNIVERSITY:
Yoshida Sanso [K,J-6] former home of
imperial prince, large wooded estate,
traditional wooden house, beautiful
interiors. Enter via Imadegawa, E of Kyoto
Univ, at Yoshidayama. Suggest lunch
(¥6,000+) to enjoy gardens. ¥-hi-Lw/2,
☎771-2028.

OTHER RYOKAN LISTING BY AREAS

DOWNTOWN (area within map ref H-7)

STANDARD:

See above Luxe inns that also offer ¥-Sw/2.
Hiiragiya Bekkan [L,H-7] see above–
cheap annex of our favorite ¥-L ☎231-0151
Convenient, comfortable, personal are
these 3 family-run inns in midtown [H-8]
Kinmata [M] on Gokomachi-dori N of
Shijo-dori just before famous Nishiki food
alley, charming small family-run traditional, meals top, E-spoken, ¥-lo-Sw/2,
☎221-1039.

Chikiriya [N] known for its tsubo niwa
tiny garden off each room, conveniently
located one block N of Nishiki food alley,
W of Tominokoji-Takoyakushi. ¥-lo-Sw/2
☎221-1281.

One block N is...
Nishitomiya [O] J-style arch,
Tominokoji S of Rokkaku, ¥-lo-Sw/2,
☎211-2411.

ALONG KAMOGAWA RIVER BANK [H-9]: With *yuka dining-on-
platform facilities, listing from Sanjo-dori to Gojo. Rooms facing river bit higher.

*****Yaehiro** [P] N of Sanjo, ¥-lo-Sw/2; just
tempura or kaiseki dinner alone ¥6,000+,
☎231-1093.

*****Shokaro** [Q] S of Shijo just S nxt bridge
¥-lo-Sw/2, meals only yuka ¥6,000+.

*****Tazuru** [R] N of Matsubara, ¥-mid-Sw/2,
☎341-3376.

*****Kaneiwaro-Bekkan**, ¥-L, but also ¥-
mid-Sw/2 (see under 'Luxe'), ☎351-5010.

*****Tsuruse** [S] Kiyamachi Gojo agaru on
corner, ☎351-8518, share yuka with annex
Tsuruki nxt door, ☎361-9261, w/ bath-
toilet ea rm, both ¥-lo-Sw/2.

GION & HIGASHIYAMA [I,J-8,9]

Shiraume ('white plum blossom') [T,I-8],
GION geisha area. Enter Nawate-dori curio
st N from Shijo-dori to Shirakawa canal,
R few doors to scenic bridge to lovely
ryori ryokan; formerly catered geisha
parties, so interior beautifully appointed;
noted for –tempura, kaiseki, nabe dishes,
¥-hi-Sw/2; rm only ¥-lo-S, ☎561-1459.
Continue N past Fuji doll shop on R to...
Yamana [U,I-8] another ryori ryokan, 100-
yrs as rstnt, 40 ryokan, warm atmosphere.
Chef trained at well-known Tsuruya Osaka.
River view ea room; ¥-lo-Sw/2, ☎561-1717

Inn Yoshiima [V,I-8] helpful illustrated
English brochure with useful information
on customs and sightseeing attests to
experience with foreign guests. Lovely tea
house. All J-rooms have pvt bath, also J-
bath available. ¥-hi-Sw/2, ☎561-2620.

Rikiya R [W,I/J-9] lovely classic inn
directly opp stone steps to Ryozen Kannon
en route Maruyama Park from Kiyomizu
Temple, ☎561-2814.

DOWNTOWN [H7]

Hiiragiya Bekkan (annex), above, ¥-hi-T
Yamato-ya [X,I-7] faces Kamogawa R, N
of Marutamachi. ¥-mid-Tw/2, ☎231-1930.
Hirota Guest House [Y,H-7] Nijo-dori
W of Tominokoji, remodelled kura storehouse in J-garden, 2-rm unit, furnished
kitchen, all self-svce. Owner's daughter
Hiromi is old friend of ours, fine English,
☎221-2474, advance rsve advised.

Iwanami [Z,I-8] Shinmonzen 2 shops E of
Yamada Art Gallery, w/small inner garden,
rooms w/ balconies over Shirakawa canal.
Traditional J-style. ✍ Higashi-oji nishi-
iru, Shinmonzen, Higashiyama-ku, Kyoto;
Serves bkfst only, ¥-lo-T, ☎561-7135.
Gion Fukuzumi [a,I-8] opp Chion-in
Temple on Shinbashi St, ¥-hi-Tw/2;
☎541-5181. Stucco exterior.

OKAZAKI AREA NEAR HEIAN SHRINE: [I/J-7/8]

Three Sisters Inn & Annex [b,J-7]
Charming English-speaking hostess and
home long catering to thrifty foreign
guests, Okazaki Kurodani-mae. ¥-T,
☎761-6336.

Shogo-in Goten-so [c,I/J-7] with large
garden, NE of Higashioji-Marutamachi
corner by Shogoin Temple ¥-hi-Tw/2,
☎771-4151.

Ryokan Kitanoya [d,I-8] lovely old, 1
block N of Sanjo Higashiyama stn next to
Manzoku Inari Shrine on E, ¥-lo-Tw/2,
☎771-1488. Just room only ¥Budget
class.

BUDGET:
(Guest Houses noted °)
Economical Japanese Inn Group JIG).

Yuhara R [f,H-10] small, kind, friendly
inn overlooking Takasegawa Canal, center
of Pontocho geisha area, E of Sanjo
Kawaramachi ☎371-9583.

Tomy Rich Inn Kyoto [g,H-10] brand
new building, Tominokoji N of Sanjo,
friendly owner Matsumoto offers by-road
tours, ☎255-0137.

Nakajima R [h,H-9] Takakura N of
Bukkoji-dori and block long Bukko-ji
Temple, ☎351-3886.

Hinomoto R [i,H-9] (JIG) Matsubara
agaru, 2 blocks from Shijo Kawaramachi,
☎351-4563.

°**Hirota Guest House** above, ¥-B rooms.

HIGASHIYAMA AREA—FOOT OF EAST MOUNTAINS: (I-9/10)

Mishima R [k,I-10] (Shukubo) (JIG) on
Shibutani St, S of Gojo, E of Higashioji
St. Can borrow shrine outfits for personal
photo. ¥-lo-B. ☎551-0033.
Masuya R [l,I-9] opposite Yasui Kompira
Shrine W of Higashioji Yasui bus stop
☎561-2253
Yukiyoshi [m,I-9] W of Kiyomizu-michi
bus stop, Higashioji. ☎561-7080.

MINSHUKU

Higashiyama Area many, most w/bkfst
only (or rm only) as good dining abounds.
Young Inn Kyoto [n,I-9] 1 block E of
Higashiyama-Yasui bus stop, Higashioji
St, ☎541-0349.
Kyoto Traveler's Inn [20,J-7] almost
hotel, both W- and J- rooms each w/bath;
popular foreigners. Nr bus stop Bijutsu-
kan-mae. 91 Enshoji-cho, ☎771-0225.
Koumekawa [o,I/J-8] 1 block N of Sanjo
Furukawa-cho E of Higashioji ☎761-4631
Ladies' Satomi [p,J-8] in Chion-in
Temple complex , run by ex-Takarazuka
star and husband, offers tea ceremony and
koto music, ☎561-8301.

Rokuhara-ya [q,I-9] W of Higashioji nr
Gojo-zaka on Rokuhara St, Takemura-cho
147, ☎531-2776.
Terada-ya [r,I/J-9] up Kiyomizu Temple
slope, go R opp Spice Shop, ☎561-3821.

PENSION

P.Higashiyama Gion [18,I/J-8] (JIG),
newly built inn, can dress up as *maiko* or
court lady in *junihitoe* costume. Shirakawa
-suji S of Sanjo . ¥-Bw/2, ☎882-1181.

PILGRIM

°**Tani House Annex** [s,H-8] (Lax 2-3F)
downtown, Gokomachi-Rokkaku SW
corner. ¥5,000 (for 2) w/bath, free use of
house kitchen.
°**Uno House** [t,H-7] Shinkarasuma S of
Marutamachi, ¥1,400 dorm, pvt ¥3,500,
☎231-7763.
°**Kyoto English Guest House** [m,J-4]
¥1,300/day, ¥8,000/wk; 1-19 Takano-
Izumi-cho Sakyo-ku; mon-fri 9:00-17:00
☎223-1059,17:00– & sat-sun ☎722-0495

ARASHIYAMA–NORTH OF TOWN:

STANDARD

Arashiyama in NW Kyoto [A-7]

Rankyo-kan [A-7] in cluster of buildings
along quiet river, natural spa. To get there
stop by Rankyo-kan Annex across Togetsu
bridge, then boat takes 8min to main inn.
¥-S–Lw/2, ☎871-0001.

Hotel Rantei both J- and W-style rms;
long famous as restaurant Rantei, facing
river, backing onto hills. In summer order
cormorant fishing boat for supper
¥6,000+tax & svce.

Takao, NW Kyoto (off map): 100-yr-old Momijiya, Umegahata-Takao in gorge by river, folk art, cherry blossoms, azalea, watch fireflies from dining platforms over brook, maple viewing. From ¥-lo-Sw/2, ☎871-1005. Recommend Bekkan annex.

Yase, NE Kyoto (off map): **Kikakutei**, tucked in foot of mount by Takano River, former villa wealthy hotelier-industrialist who built Keifuku line to Yase. Unique igloo-shape *kamaburo* steambath for guests, diners. ¥-Sw/2, ☎781-4001.

Kurama-Kibune, NE of Kyoto (off map) cool in summer: S of Kibune Shrine is 180-yr-old **Kibune Fujiya**, ¥-Sw/2, ☎741-2501, first to offer *yuka* meals; others emulating with *yuka* across from shrine and N in same rate ¥-lo-Sw/2, are... **Nakayoshi** ☎741-2081, **Ugenda** ☎741-2146, and **Beniya** ☎741-2041.

TOURIST
Arashiyama   [A-7] (By Tenryu-ji Temple, Keifuku RR Arashiyama Stn):
Pension Kokyo [A-7] 100-yr-old Meiji house with original art nouveau elements, N of temple entrance, ¥-lo-Tw/2, ☎882-1817. Also runs restaurant.
Saga-no-Sato [A-7] across from temple entrance, originally built, lived in by samurai actor KATSU Shintaro (Zatokichi series) & wife. Price depends on meal, but best still ¥-lo-Tw/2. ☎882-5160. Tea room next door serves tofu ice cream (uses soy milk).

BUDGET
Nashinoki R [v,H-5/6] Imadegawa opp R (NE) end of Imperial Palace, ☎241-1543.
Rakucho R [w,I-3] (JIG), 67 Higashi-hangi-cho, Shimogamo, on Shimogamo Hondori St, 8min N of Kitaoji, E of Kamogawa river, ☎721-2174.
Pension.Arashiyama [39,B-7] (JIG), S of Kurumazaki Shrine, newly built, wonderful location, 67 Miyanomoto-cho, Sagano, Ukyo-ku, ☎881-2294.

MINSHUKU
Horikawahan Umemura [G-6] nr Nijo Castle, Gosho, many foreign guests, S of bus stop Horikawa-Nakadachiuri, ☎441-8404. Rm only (¥-lo-T) ¥4,500.
Tangoya [G-6] S of Nakadachiuri on Senbon-dori in NW, 3-storeys w/coffee shop, all rooms w/bath, pleasant, considerate host, ☎441-7164. RC ¥-lo-T.

Moriyama [G/H-4] small, only 3 rms, warm reception, family atmosphere. 10min from Kitaoji subway, 71 Takanawa-cho, Shichiku, Kita-ku, ☎491-4858.

Ohara area, wonderful escape from busy cities, taste rural Japan, however many are unusually large, but still keep personal touch (off map NE).
Ohara Nodaya, very large minshuku at Todera entrance to Ohara has *hinoki* cypress construction, large landscape garden, ☎744-2534, and nearby smaller **Yoshiko** with comfortable new rooms, ☎744-2709, are both in Todera-cho, Ohara, Sakyo-ku, 601-12.
Ohara Sanso, "Big, friendly sunny" minshuku owner has kiln, make own pottery. Bus to Ohara, 13min walk bus stn. 17, Kusao-cho, Ohara , Sakyo-ku, 6501-12, ☎744-2227.
Ohara-no-sato, 41 Kusao-cho, ☎744-2917; **Tsuji**, 'large' near Jakko-in Temple, Kusao-cho-45, ☎744-2225; **Kusao-no-sato** "small family minshuku" 263 Kusao, ☎744-2601.

In Ueno-cho are
Uenae, veggies and rice homegrown, "charming personality of owner", bus to Nomura-wakare, 348 Ueno-cho, ☎744-2155; and...
Kitsune (Fox) annex is for guests, in Ohara Nodaya.
Kochihira (past Ohara) bus to Kochidani after change at Ohara, ☎744-2603.

Northwest [A-6] *favorite Sagano area– use Kyoto bus #28,91,92 for Daikaku-ji...*
Umejiro large old farmhouse converted. Food fresh from farm, 2min from Kobuchi-cho bus stop, ☎871-5874.
Nogiku newly-built farmhouse, home grown veggies, 2min from bus stop Kobuchi-cho. ☎872-5231. *Nearby is...*
Kawarabayashi with restaurant, same bus stop, good meals. ¥861-2414.
Daikakuji-Michi (ladies only) bkfst only 1min from same bus stop. ☎881-6555.
Tsujimura [A-7] near Tenryu-ji Temple, bus stop Nonomiya, ☎861-3207.
Iwasa (Yamada), next door to Seiryo-ji Temple, 3-storey J-style, 11 Kitachuin-cho, Nison-in-monzen, ☎871-5732.
Takino en route Nison-in Temple, small, garden, bus to Shakado-mae, ☎861-0417.
Obata Natsuko, largest almost professional serv. Bus to Kiyotaki, off at Daikakuji-michi. 2min walk. ☎871-6406.

PENSION

P.Arashiyama Sagano [B-6] (JIG) 67
Miyanomoto-machi, Sagano, Ukyo-ku,
606, ☎881-2294.

P.Utano [C-6] French, Spanish spoken,
110-5 Narutaki-honmachi, Ukyo-ku, 616,
☎463-1118.

P.Sagano [C-7] nr Uzumasa bus stop, 26-
4 Yamagoe higashi-machi, Ukyo 616,
☎881-2310.

P.Shimogamo [I-4] Kitaoji to E, 20
Kamikawaracho, Shimogamo, Sakyo-ku.
☎711-0180

PILGRIM

°**Takaya** [G-5/6] Muromachi St few doors
N of Ichijo St, ¥2,500, ¥4,000 for 2pers,
☎431-5213.

°**Green Peace** [J-2] 14-1 Shibamoto-cho
Matsugasaki, Sakyo-ku, ☎791-9890; ¥-P
¥1,400+ per-day, ¥8,400+-wk, ¥23,000+-
mo; share or pvt rm, kitchen, bike rentals.

°**Tani House** [x,F-4] 8 Daitoku-ji
Murasakino, ¥1,400 [¥-P] dorm, ¥-B pvt
room, share kitchen avail. Rsve-dep
required. ☎492-5489. AM join zazen next
door Daitokuji.

°**Guest House Kyoto** [y,F-5] 5-1
Higashi Hirakicho, N of Kitaoji on block
(Royal Host corner) W of Senbon St nr
Kinkaku-ji, pvt rms share kitchen; sgle¥-B
¥-P 2pers, ☎492-8855.

NEAR KYOTO STN, HONGAN-JI TEMPLES [H-10]

BUDGET

Ohtomo Bekkan [j] Akezu N of
Shichijo, 3min walk N of TIC. ¥-lo-B,
☎341-6344.

Hiraiwa R/Annex [z1] (JIG), S of Gojo,
block W of Kamogawa R on Ninomiya-
cho-dori, ☎351-6748.

Riverside Takase [z2] Kyoka annex (JIG)
NW of Hiraiwa on Takase R ☎351-7920

Kyoka Ryokan (JIG) in 2nd block E of
Higashi Hongan-ji Temple N side of
Shimojuzuyamachi St, ☎371-2709 and...

Murakamiya Ryokan (JIG) ☎371-1260
same block facing Kokuku-tei Garden.

Matsubaya Ryokan [z2] (JIG), W of
temple on Higashinotoin on Kamijuzu-
yamachi-dori, ☎351-4268.

Pension Station Kyoto [G-10] (JIG)
W of Higashi Hongan-ji on Shinmachi
above Shichijo.

MINSHUKU

Convenient, 7mins from station are these
Niwa ☎371-7246; **Takigawa** ☎351-7471
both opp Higashi Hongan-ji main gate.
Heianbo [G-10] ☎351-0650, between
Nishi- and Higashi Hongan-ji's.
Miwaya [G/H-10] ☎371-3483, old wood
bldg, closest, 5min walk to Kyoto stn.
Bit out W down by Toji Temple is
Rakunan [G-11] 2min from Toji stn,
☎681-3914.

PENSION

Guest Inn Kyoto (Tani Guest House),
Shichijo St, N of Omiya, bunks & J-
style, pvt bath ¥-lo-B/¥-P share bath. Stn
pickup, ☎341-1344.

P.Koto, 132 Kuzekawahara-cho, Minami-
ku; ☎934-5010.

SHUKUBO TEMPLE 寺 STAY

NUMEROUS TEMPLES accept overnite guests at *shukubo*, or guest houses. All require
prior notice—or phone 3-7 days ahead, state 'rm only' or '1 or 2 meals' (bkfst is J-style).
Some request deposit ¥1,000. Bring own toiletries; a.m. service not compulsory.
Usually 9:30pm curfew. Charge usually ¥3,500w/bkfst, ¥-B. Two more expensive ¥-T
examples lead off, followed by others equally pleasant but in new buildings, ¥-P-B-T.

Enryaku-ji (Tendai Sect) 1,200 yr-old
temple atop Mt Hieizan 'guarding' NE of
city, founders of major early sects all
trained here. Large shukubo for pilgrims.
Annual training seminar 7/25-27, ¥18,000
all incl, can participate in 32km mountain
pilgrimage from 2am. Notify in advance
7days; Sakamoto Honmachi, Otsu 520-01,
¥T-w/2. ☎(0775)-78-0047.

Chishaku-in, 900-yr-old temple, share
huge garden and great art works with
guests in **Chishaku Kaikan** shukubo
[I-10] Arise 5:30am, 6:00 must join sutra
reading, then view nat'l treasure fusuma,
gardens, short lecture, bkfst. Rsve 7 days,
earlier for flower-viewing April.
Higashiyama Shichijo, Higashiyama-ku,
605, ¥-Bw/2, ☎(075)-541-5363.

NORTH KYOTO (A/H-5/6) *see* map Northwest Kyoto on which all are marked 卍 temple.

Myoken-ji [G-5] (Nichiren) maples, bamboo glade, run by nuns in quiet Teranouchi area near Ura Senke Tea center. Shukubo is traditional building with *tsubo-niwa* garden of bamboo. ¥3,500 w/bkfst only. 7 days notice: Teranouchi-dori, Horikawa Higashi-iru, Kamikyo-ku, Kyoto 602; ☎431-6828. Many foreign guests stay here.

Myorenji [F/G-5] (Nichiren), rooms with seasonal scenes on fusuma sliding doors face outstanding stone-sand garden (rebuilt 1936). Highly recommended by TIC. Accustomed to foreign guests. Teranouchi Omiya Higashi-iru, ☎451-3527. ¥3,000 w/bkfst, rm only ¥2,500.

Zuishun-in [H-5] Shokoku-ji Temple. Known for fusuma door paintings of Wild Geese; small, 7 days notice, ¥1,000 deposit by mail. *Women only*, some knowledge of Japanese necessary, rm only ¥3,500, ☎431-3703

Hokyo-in [A-6] (Zen Rinzai) quiet 900-yr-old imperial origin. Shukubo (only 3 rms) is old shoin-style bldg with treasured fusuma paintings, etc. *Women only*. Notify & send ¥1000 by day before. ¥4,000 w/bkfst; Minami Naka-in-cho, Saga Shakado-mon-mae, Ukyo-ku Kyoto 616, ☎861-0610.

Rokuo-in [B-6] (Rinzai) graceful 600-yr-old Zen temple in Arashiyama accepts *women only*. 6:30am serv, zazen. ¥4,000 w/ bkfst only, 7 days notice. 24 Saga Kitahori-cho, Ukyo-ku 616, ☎861-1645.

Ninna-ji [C-5/6] (Shingon) founded 1,100 yrs ago, full of nat'l treasures. Shukubo new bldg. No spec rules, ¥6,500w/2. 60 days notice: 33 Omuro Ouchi, Ukyo-ku 616 ☎464-3664.

Myoshinji's (Rinzai) Shukubo **Daishin-in** [D-6] former large shoin. W/bkfst only ¥3,800. Can order a la carte or dinner day ahead. 57 Hanazono Myoshinji-cho Ukyo-ku 616, ☎461-5714. Also stay in old **Torin-in**; bring nitewear, ☎463-1334.

Jikko-in (Tendai) NE outskirt *women only* Attend dawn sutra recital; ¥3,500w/ bkfst (bring nitewear). ✍/☎ 10 days prior, Ohara Shorin-in-cho, Sakyo-ku, Kyoto 601-12, ☎744-2537. Recommended by TIC.

Jorenge-in (Tendai) rural Ohara, shukubo uses fine shoin rooms. Head priest enjoys talking to guests. ¥4,800w/2. Apply 407 Ohara Raigo-in-cho Sakyo-ku, ☎744-2408

Nanzenji-Higashiyama Area: [I/K-7/11]

Hiden-in [I-11] (Shingon) set up 1,400 yrs ago by Prince Shotoku as rest home for elderly, ill, orphans; ¥3,500w/bkfst, ¥3,100 rm only. Apply 1 day ahead, Sennyuji, Higashiyama-ku, 605, ☎561-8781. TIC recommendation.

Nanzen-ji [K-7/8] (Rinzai), one of Kyoto's top temples, our favorite for beautiful dry landscape garden, fine paintings. **Nanzen Kaikan**, Modern shukubo ¥5,800w/2. (**Chosho-in** sub-temple nearby famous yudofu restaurant). Rsve one week or more ahead, Nanzenji Fuku-ji-cho-86, Sakyo-ku, ☎771-2846.

Enman-in (Non-sectarian) of **Mii-dera** temple (K+-off map), one of 8 beauty spots of Lake Biwa (*see* p.498), gorgeous setting of temple and gardens, modern shukubo Sanmitsuden ¥7,800-9,000w/2. Can also visit only for Shojin-ryori in temple rooms ¥6,000 up. Rsve 3 days ahead. Miidera-san-nai Nio-mon-kita, Otsu 520, ☎(0775)-22-3690.

Being at one end of a great street, it is impossible to reach the other with the eye because of their extraordinary length, the dust and the multitude of people they are daily crowded with. — Kaempfer, 1690

PAGEANT OF AGES
PLANNING OUR TILT*
*Tour in Limited Time

THREE FAVORITE adjectives of Kyoto—true millennium ago and today—are *okashii* (elegant, gay), *imamekashii* (modern, 'now-ish') and hard to translate *natsukashii* (endeared, beloved...with some sense of nostalgia).

Kind of New Yorker Kyoto-ites dig was exemplified by late octogenarian archaeologist-explorer Arthur Upham Pope, Jay's teacher and our cupid. As when young, he still had *okashii* penchant for fast cars, stylish tweeds, with dilettante universal interest, lived in *natsukashii* Connecticut Valley colonial with red barn, furnished in antiques from everywhere, equipt with modern *imamekashii* plumbing, heating, kitchen. Went out for *okashii* good time in *imamekashii* Italian shoes, then back at home changed into *natsukashii* old house slippers.

Trying to balance natsukashii and imamekashii has kept Kyoto okashii. Eighth century Nara Era was one of overpowering imamekashii, when everything 'modern' foreign pushed out 'antiquated' native. Beginning with removal of capital to Heian or Kyoto in 794, era is known both as Heian (auspicious title) and Fujiwara (after dominant family). It was time of national reaction and renaissance, of rejection of much of formal Chinese style now felt unsuited to Japan, while adapting and absorbing what was deemed useable. Choice was not always clearcut, far from always wise—but it was made, and made to work in ways henceforth to be recognized as Japanese. This process was to be repeated in alternate epochs of foreign influence and chauvinistic reaction continuing thru today.

We can see this in relics remaining from this Heian Period and eras subsequent, conveniently grouped together so that we are able to fashion itineraries following historical lines. Center of city, RAKU-NAI, has 2 fine examples of earliest Heian palaces, HEIAN SHRINE and IMPERIAL PALACE, both reconstructions—former modern on reduced scale, latter because of frequent partial rebuilding, one complete relocation, restorations.

Next two routes emphasize ultra-refinement in taste along with extreme emotionalism that developed in Heian Period dominated by Fujiwara family: **Purple Period** (Western Outskirts) & **Uji, Murasaki's Tea and Phoenix** (Southern Outskirts). Authoress Murasaki Shikibu (literally 'Purple Lady') epitomizes era's elegance, grace and extreme sentimentalism, so we refer to this century as hers.

Third and fourth itineraries stretch over next 500 years until late 1500s. 'Decadent' Kyoto, overpowered by virile samurai headed by Minamoto clan ruling from their stronghold in Kamakura (*see*), from which era derives name (1192-1332), is reflected in **Decline, Fall & Renaissance**. In 1336 power is restored to Kyoto by Ashikaga clan, who find Kyoto ravaged by civil and feudal wars. Zen Buddhism leaves its mark at this time. Now trade resumes with China resulting in great Chinese influence as seen in sumi-ink paintings, ceramics, tea, etc to give us Muromachi Period (1336-1573) symbolized by great Zen gardens and temples, tea ceremony, flower arrangement, noh.

Thus, **Bells, Drums and Marrying Monks** reflects era of building of huge temples by now-popular Buddhist Shin sects.

This was overlapped by 'Christian Century' of ODA Nobunaga, TOYOTOMI Hideyoshi and TOKUGAWA Ieyasu during which there is both heavy cultural incursion from Korea in backwash of Japanese invasion, while European influences enter in wake of St Francis Xavier, 1549. Then aesthetic reactions against over-indulgences set in, and together compose age of magnificent castles and palaces and exquisite tea-drinking hermitages, extravagant gilt arts and reserved Korean-inspired hi-tech folk arts—Azuchi-Momoyama Era (1573-1613). During it, essence of tea ceremony is revived by SEN Rikyu. Simplicity and perfection in gardens by KOBORI Enshu culminate in perfect gem of Katsura Imperial Villa Garden, visited in **Tea Time—Great Reactions.** However, Kyoto now takes back seat as shogun TOKUGAWA Ieyasu moves capital to far-away Edo-Tokyo (1590). Kyoto population drops in few decades from million-plus to barely 300,000. In 1640 all foreigners in country are expelled except for handful at Nagasaki, and Japan enters 220-odd years of total isolation under rule of 15 Tokugawa shoguns till Perry's visit 1854 sparks Meiji Restoration in 1868. At this point we can no longer cover Kyoto historically, but geographically following eastern hills of Higashiyama in **Rambles Northeast.**

Historians note that Japan is singular in never having built walled cities, as nearly universal on Eurasian mainland from Korea to Britain. Wars here were not against citizenry, but against ruling powers alone who sat in walled fortresses within open cities. Sacking of conquered towns, declaring as part of surrender terms so many days of free plunder, pillage and rapine, seem unheard of here. Oldest *Kuni*, 'capital', excavated in Yoshinogari, Kyushu 1989 and thought to be original Yamatai-Yamato, was surrounded by earth and log stockade, in turn moated. But subsequent 'capitals' here in central Yamato are not fortified. Heijo-Nara, capital of nation of 6million (*vs* China's 20million, only triple, while today it is almost ten-fold), had low walls around administrative center, more symbol than defense.

Ninth century Heian Kyoto was ringed by similarly symbolic fencing. Hideyoshi after rebuilding Kyoto (with major extensions east of Kamogawa river into foothills) for its then population of half million, encircled it with *dobei*, earthen wall with outer moat, 25km/15mi long by at least 30ft/9m tall (in places perhaps double this) which he built typical Osaka style in frenetic 5 months in 1591. Probably less meant against attack from outside than for riot control against unruly inhabitants, especially cussedly independent Hongan-ji Buddhists. *Raku-nai* or city limits then were Kamo river, new across on E bank were *Raku-gai* (suburbs). JR tracks-south with extension including Toji; W side was about Nishi-oji ave including Kitano Shrine in NW corner and, oddly, N enclosed open fields above Kitao-ji ave which have been developed only since our '64 edition. Most of this city burned in 1708, but subsequent rebuildings have followed this Hideyoshi 'restoration' of original 9th century city.

TILT: To catch bit of this city's mood we recommend at least 3 days—but one can squeeze in highlights in 2 (average taxi-tour pace one site per hr —*see* p.443), manage shopping, enjoy Kyoto nitelife, cuisine. We sketch out crowded 2-day itinerary. We suggest to expand to 3 or 4 days so that you merely slow pace, or choose your own additions from text. With 5 days, you can follow leisurely all historical routings thru which we present whole of Kyoto. But one year would do fine. Folks come for one year and stay for life.

PREPARING FOR ARRIVAL: But however long you plan to stay, on first arrival there is some preparatory work to do. **Home visit** must be reserved one day, preferably two, in advance. And several famous sights require advance **permits**—from 20min to 2 days ahead—also obtainable by letter from home for pick up here.

Permits required for **Gosho & Sento Imperial Palaces, Katsura Imperial Villa, Shugakuin Detached Palace:** forms available at hotel or JTB, apply in person w/ passport to Imperial Household Agency ☎211-1211, in Gosho (Imperial Palace), enter by Gishu-mon gate–to save time, do all at once first day while taking in Gosho, Sento. Or advise apply by mail to: Gosho, Kyoto: send 2 copies of application (or simple letter in dupe) giving name, age, address (home, and hotel/inn in Kyoto if permits to be forwarded there), your occupation, date, choice of time, varies, *see* text —am, pm M-F, or am sat; gardens X-sat pm, sun, hol. **SAIHO-JI Moss Garden** also required, ✍ direct 3mos ahead, *see* text p458; ¥3,000.

Admission fees charged all temples, shrines except CHION-IN, most ¥300, some to ¥500, most 9am-5pm except KIYOMIZU temple till 6 or later, HEIAN SHRINE 5:30, TENRYU-JI 5:30; no-X; go in by 30min before close. Bus tour incl entry fees, as much as ¥2,000 per tour. Plan mooted '89

lump-sum tour pass or discount book: ask.

Home Visit: apply by mail ✍ or on arrival, one or two days ahead at TIC office.

Bicycle Rental: Rates ¥500+ half-day, ¥800-2,000 full, var w/type, longer period rentals available; also ask your inn.
  Ladies Hotel, Keifuku Arashiyama stn;
  Nippon Renta-, S-side JR Kyoto stn;
  Taki, Kaminokuchi st E of Kawaramachi;
  Yasumoto, Kawabata st N of Sanjo;
  Shin & Steve, ☎464-2028, delivers; w/basket no gear ¥1800, 10spd ¥2,000.

Seasonal specials *see* DATEBOOK: **April-May** cherry-viewing and geisha dances tickets for which thru hotels or major inns or direct at theaters. Jun-Sep dine over river in-town; evening cormorant fishing at Arashiyama. **Oct-Nov** geisha dances, maples. Oct-Nov special Temple Treasure House openings for traditional autumn airings of artworks, listed in *KTO, KVG* or from TIC. **Hikes** by environmental groups also so listed.

TOURS: Our old favorite has long been town character Joe Okada whose **J.O.Tours** have always been original. In our first edition, 1964, he was still JTB guide pioneering new ideas to keep visiting firemen happy, then went on own to be complimented by having everyone copy him. Alas, recently discontinued fixed tours, now by appointment.

J.O. Tours, presently sole offering is his highly personal and purely orginal *Samurai Nippon Show,* performed so far over 1700 times: book it for your main banquet, ¥200,000 for demonstrations of karate and Joe placing watermelon on reclining guest's midriff and halving it with slash of razor-sharp samurai sword, etc—and his samurai topknot hairdo is for real.

   Or charter him as MC for show, or have him put together special floor show for your group.

   He can **customize tours** for you with your or chartered transport and give you his highly inimitable guiding for ¥40,000 per day for him, plus any rental of car, minibus or bus as needed. Act as interpreter ¥10,000 per hour (going rate).

   Phone ahead [from overseas: o'seas access code + Japan country code 81, then 75 for Kyoto +] ☎241-3716, fax 241-3746 (home ☎0773-64-0033) and arrange advance deposit...you won't regret.

JTB Sunrise Tours, in English. *Morning Palace Tour,* 9-12:30, ¥5,000: Nijo Castle → Kinkaku-ji Gold Pav'n → Gosho-Imper'l Palace (sun-hol Higashi Hongan-ji) → Handicraft Ctr. *Afternoon Historical,* 13:30-17:30, ¥5,000: Heian Shrine → Sanjusangendo → Kiyomizu temple. *Full Day* both above, incl lunch ¥10,400. *No more Garden Tour* but check, should resume this once popular run. *Rapids Shoot,* Mon-Fri Apr-May & Jul-Oct, 13:40-18:00, ¥8,500: bus → JR stn, train → Kameoka, 90min flatboat down rapids → Arashiyama, train-bus → hotel.
Kintetsu Gray Line *Holiday Tours* offers similar: pickup major hotels 8-9am ¥4,800; pm ¥4,800; all day ¥10,000; Kyoto-Nara day ¥11,500. ☎691-0903.
JTB from OSAKA, half-day ¥6,500, full-day ¥10,700; dep Hilton 8:00, 12:30, Osaka stn 12:40, by JR. *All tours vary annually.*

BUDGET BUSES: Budgeteer or adventurer who wants to tour by bus, take those designed for locals. Guides speak Japanese only, but some arrangements are available to help in English, like summary of seasonal specials of **Teiki Kanko Bus** in *Kyoto Visitors Guide*, *KVG*, or with **Keihan Bus**. Most sights are covered in this book. Prices are lower, selections are far greater. More popular runs of **Keihan Bus** depart several times per day, and from 3 locations: JR Stn Shinkansen-side Hachijo entrance E-end of Plaza E of New Miyako Hotel, in front of Avanti Bldg; 2nd is N-side old stn Karasuma entrance in midst of plaza in front of Hankyu Hotel (block W of TIC); 3rd start is from Keihan Sanjo Stn, E side of Kamo river across Sanjo bridge E of stn and S 1 block.

Rsve bus ticket at any travel agent or at departure point–detailed pamphlet in Eng, order by code letter or just point. Popular tours start as early as 8am. We stress, start sightseeing early, get more in and beat that heat. Relax and you are sure to befriend someone who speaks some English–however hesitant, shy, ungrammatical.

Kyoto Teiki Kanko Bus, Dep stns; seasonal specialties, mostly all day, like: Jan-Mar Zen temples KOETSU-JI, RYOAN-JI, SAIO-IN plus museum, with lunch and *matcha* tea in temple; or midsummer highlights of rarely-visited sights, temple treasures opened, trad lunch in good restn't; autumn to special viewing of normally-sealed temple treasuress being aired in dry weather (or see *KTO* for open dates and take some in on your own); usually abt ¥7,000 w/lunch. Others; info TIC, JTB, agent, ☎672-2100.

Keihan Bus, J-speaking, but most sights covered in our book. Reserve at hotel or any agent or starting stn: JR Shinkansenside (most start), JR N-side, Keihan Sanjo S-side (E-side of Sanjo bridge); many departures: in-season extra tours 1/1-5, 3/20-5/31, 7/25-8/31, 10/1-11/23; kids 40-50%-off; buses '@' are double-deckers, top +¥500. A, AS, B, BS incl souvenir.

A Half Day Kiyomizu-dera, Kinkaku-ji, Heian Shrine, Chion-in, 4+hrs, ¥4,600.

AS 3 Great Temples: Kiyomizu, Kinkaku-ji, Ginkaku-ji 3+hrs am, pm, ¥3,800.

B One Day AS & Heian, Sanjusangendo, Arashiyama, 6+hrs, 9:00, 9:30am; ¥6,500.

BS Grand Panorama @ same as B but double decker. 8:35, 10:00, tops ¥7,020.

T Panorama @, Nijo Castle & Toei Movie Village, 9:30, 13:20, 3+hrs, topside ¥4,670.

C Nijo Castle, Nishijin Textile Ctr, Koryu-ji (*see* Murasaki), Arashiyama, Ninna-ji, 10:30 + in season, 6hrs ¥5,800.

D Fushimi much our UJI, TEA & PHOENIX run: Rakusuien-Jonangu (modern), Momoyama castle (new), Byodo-in, Manpuku-ji, Daigo-ji; 9:40am 7hrs, ¥7,300 incl *fucha ryori* Chinese-

style temple lunch.

F Gardens in West much of our DECLINE & RENAISSANCE NORTH-WEST: Taizoin (not incl herein), Daitoku-ji, Daisenin, Ryoan-ji, Tenryu-ji; 9:30 + season 10ish, 5+hrs w/*shojin ryori* priest lunch; ¥6,900.

J Gardens East see our STROLLS EAST: Konchi-in of Nanzen-ji, main Nanzen-ji, Hakusa-sonso 1920s modern dry, not herein, Shoren-in, Daigo-ji, Kanshu-ji; 10:00, 6hrs incl *kyo-bento* lunch, ¥7,400.

R Three Gardens: Ryoan-ji, Tenryu-ji, Zuiho-in modern dry garden by our teacher-friend late SHIGEMORI Millet; 14:00+9:00 sat-hols in season, ¥3,650.

U Gardens & Philosopher's Road Ryogen-in Murinan, Hakusa-sonso, Tetsugaku-no-michi Philosopher's Rd, Eikan-do; 10:50, 6+hrs incl *Kyo-bento* lunch, ¥6,600.

Q Gardens South Rakusuien, Ikkyu-ji, Shokado tea hall, Otokoyama cablecar, Iwashimizu Hachiman Shrine for fine view; sat-hols 10:10, 6hrs; incl *Sansai zushi* mountain-herbs and rice lunch; ¥7,250. *None above incl Moss Garden.

SH Saga Toei Movie Village, walk thru scenic Sagano alleys (*txt*); 9:40 3/20-5/31 and 10/1-11/30, 6hrs; ¥5,250 w/map.

H Modern Sights Umeko-ji Steam Loco Museum, Movie Village, Arashiyama War Museum, International Conference Hall; sat-hols but 3/20-4/7 & 8/1-31 daily; 6+hrs ¥5,950+ get your own lunch-may discontinue.

P Imperial Palace & Temples Imperial Palace, Kodai-ji, Toji, Chishaku-in, *Kaiseki Ryori* at Sakaguchi in Sanneizaka; 10-ish M-F X-days palace in use; ¥8,490 w/lunch.

K Royal Court Traditions Yuzen Culture Center see dyeing, Nishijin Textile Ctr, Shiogamo Shrine see dressing of 12-layer court lady kimono, court dance, Traditional Craft Museum demo, Kiyomizu-yaki Kyoto Porcelain making; 9:30 3/1-6/30 & 9/1-11/24 sat-hols, 5+hrs w/ lunch, ¥6,200.

E Mt Hiei & Lake Biwa bus, Hieizan driveway, Mt Hiei top for view, Oku Hiei drive, Enryaku-ji Konpon-chudo lanterns, Yokawa-chudo down farside of mountain, Biwa Lake Bridge, Biwako Hotel, Biwa freshwater aquarium; 9:30 +seasonals, 7hrs, incl tea; 3/20-11/24 ¥6,000.

Z Paddle-wheeler & Mt Hiei Cruise lake on Mississippi stern-wheeler *Michigan*, Hieiizan Hotel view, Summit Mt Hiei, Enryaku-ji Konpon-chudo; 9ish 3/20-11/23, 6+hrs; ¥8,850 w/ lunch.

OA Famous Otsu Temples Hiyoshi Taisha guardian Shinto shrine of Enryaku-ji Buddhist Temple, Mii-dera (of 8-views *see* BIWA), ENMAN-IN temple for vegetarian lunch → cruise on sternwheel *Michigan* → ISHIYAMA-DERA (of 8 views) room of Lady Murasaki; 9:40, 7hrs ¥8,450 w/lunch. 3/20-11/24.

BY NITE: JTB in English: *Special Night* Wed, Sat, 18:40-22:00, ¥9,500 w/Zen tempura dinner, *matcha* tea & stroll to 'gay quarter' alleys to end up in Gion Corner for show.

Maiko Special Night 5:30-8:30, 'exciting evening' of maiko dance and traditional *kaiseki* dinner unlt'd beer, sake, ¥58,000! –do it yourself in own ryokan same as each for 2 of you, or less each in party of 4.

Keihan Bus in Japanese: *WS Grand Panorama Lake Biwa Showboat* Nite drive dble decker bus, Dinner Biwako Hotel, cruise stern-wheeler *Michigan*, 4+hrs; ¥9,950 +@¥520, incl dinner.

N Kyoto Night, Gion Maiko to see Maiko train, Shimabara Tayu courtesan show, Heian dance for nobility in 12-layer court kimono 6:20pm, 3hrs, ¥4,570.

NS Kyo-ryori Gion & Shimabara Gion Maiko to see Maiko in training, Traditional *Ryori Ryokan* Shinsenen for *Kyo-ryori* dinner, Shimabara Tayu courtesan show; 5:20pm, +6:20pm during 3/1-11/23; 3hrs; ¥6,300 incl dinner.

G Golden Night Shozan Garden for *Kaiseki Ryori* dinner, Show at Gion Corner; 5pm, 4hrs; ¥6,850 incl dinner.

DH Panorama Night Drive U p Higashiyama Driveway to Summit for view, *Kyo-ryori* dinner at Shinsenen, nite drive dble decker; 6:10pm, abt 3hrs; ¥6,000+extra ¥520 @ seat on upper deck.

TAXI TOURING: Advised. As with most places, 2 couples sharing cab by hour match or beat bus tours, no time lost at picking up/ dropping off 50 fellow tourists.

First Day: 9:00am Gosho Imperial Palace, where apply for visit next day to **Katsura Imperial Villa** or **Shugakuin** (for Moss Garden apply direct, see p458) prefer 9am or 1:30 group; *see* GOSHO; SENTO inner apartments viewable only by permit 11am, 1:30pm, or *free* Nov. Exit W to Karasuma-dori Ave to catch taxi; or S to Marutamachi where just outside SE, far L corner Palace Park shop-see **Amita Damascene**, Uchida Woodblock Print-makers (limited time catch all together at Kyoto Crafts Center); hail taxi or short walk 15min. 10:00 HEIAN SHRINE; shop-see nearby Nishimura Lacquer. 11:30 NANZEN-JI Zen Temple gate, gardens, paintings. **Lunch**: cafeteria Kyoto Kaikan nr Heian or various Japanese ¥-T at **Minokichi**; or luxe-W- or ·J- at Miyako Hotel; or light temple *yu-dofu* meal at NANZEN-JI OKUTAN or same with more creature comfort GINMOND garden restaurant btwn Nanzen-ji and Heian great torii. 1:00pm taxi 3x-mtr NISHI HONGAN-JI cathedral Tycoon Palace (alt: Nijo Castle); stroll or drive thru old play quarter to SUMIYA courtesan mansion. Taxi S thru TOJI temple ground, E cross Kujo-dori... 2+pm SANJUSANGENDO hall of 1,000 buddhas (X-4pm); cross street to National Museum. Shop-stroll Gojo-zaka pottery lane up Kiyomizu Dera (X-7pm) discharge taxi to stroll; for one-stop shop'g TOJIKI KAIKAN; stroll down and resume pottery-lane stroll to YASAKA SHRINE & Maruyama Park in heart of town, to Gion Corner eve show 7:40, 8:40, ¥2,100.

Second Day with *permits:* 8:00am RYOAN-JI before crowds deluge, taxi KOETSU-JI or KINKAKU-JI Gold Pavl'n; 10:00am Katsura Imperial Villa (*permit*) by taxi which can wait or catch anew 11:00 taxi 10x-mtr Kameoka 25min or bus (*see* text), shoot Hozu River Rapids 90min, downstream; alt short drive Ochiai for once-daily noon boat short 35min rapids shoot to **1:30 lunch** Arashiyama Kiccho or Tairanbo or ¥-B temple lunch TENRYU-JI or 15min taxi or bus #11 to RYOAN-JI for same. **2:00** taxi via NINNA-JI to KOZAN-JI and back. **3:00** DAITOKU-JI or Movie Village–etc, *see* p458 **3:30** taxi E crosstown to GION SHRINE or shorter walk Yasaka Pagoda for shop-walk up to KIYOMIZU-DERA (X-6pm, shops later); or if did yesterday, taxi NANZEN-JI, stroll Philosopher's Walk.

Alternate: if Thurs am after KINKAKU-JI go to Ura Senke (*see* TEA p480) for tea ceremony having phoned Wed ☎451-8516 for appt bet 10:00-3:30, ¥1,000.

IF KATSURA appointment for **1:00**pm, in am go to Ura Senke, as above, KINKAKU-JI with temple lunch nearby, or Arashiyama; KATSURA **1** pm and/or SAIHO-JI Moss Gdn then shoot rapids, last boat Kameoka 4pm. Summer eve Arashiyama cormorant fishing, *funa asobi* and lantern floating, dine at Kiccho or Nishiki, or other obvious ¥-T & ¥-S restaurants along river.

IF KATSURA **permit** is for **2:00**pm: am to KINKAKU-JI, RYOAN-JI, as above, lunch at Arashiyama's Kiccho or Tairanbo; after lunch to Moss Garden or Saga stroll; **2:00**pm KATSURA (don't be late)—no time for Hozu Rapids so, if summer, see TENRYU-JI, perhaps stay eve in Arashiyama; otherwise return to town stopping at TENRYU-JI and/or KORYU-JI.

Third Day: Add places from text you'd like to see. We recommend far SE corner, lonely lovely SENNYU-JI; E-side walk KIYOMIZU–GION open to our **Rambles Northeast**-GION TO KIYOMIZU p491 & **SHOPPING** stroll same route can link to 'Philosopher's Walk' SHUGAKUIN (permit)—GINKAKU-JI p538; NE corner for exquisite ENTSU-JI or tram or bus on up to Ohara Village or Kurama.

Evenings: Home Visit 7 or 7:30, late dinner (8:30 or 9pm) after, having snacked by 7. If summer, definitely include dinner at Arashiyama, cormorant fishing and lantern floating; rent boat, invite friends for *funa asobi* (playing on boat) in ancient style. Also recommend composite traditional show **Gion Corner** 7:40, 8:40pm, ¥2,500 (3/1-11/ 29, X-Aug 16).

Half-Day Nara JTB or Kintetsu bus 9am or do y'rself–FUSHIMI INARI ask shrine maid dance. **10:00**–DAIGO SAMBO-IN

Lunch at temple rest'nt Haku-un-an *or* 1:00 BYODOIN Phoenix Pavilion Uji. 2:00 to Nara, see. If returning to Kyoto, dine Nara Hotel, or others listed, or wait return to Kyoto for late dinner, beat. Buses dep var hotels from 8-9am; ¥9,680.

MK Tourist Taxi ☎721-2237-English

(who regularly lead battle to block gov't attempts to hike local taxi rates), or **Kyoren** ☎221-1210. Both have tours with English-speaking drivers, or follow your itinerary: ¥4,800 first hr ¥1,600 per addt'l 30min ¥30,400 9hr day (1991 up 10%?), pay own temple entries yourself (¥300-500 ea). Thus half day tour for 4 costs ¥17,200 by bus, but 4hrs=¥14,400 by taxi (plus lunch) in which time see same plus extras. Taxis advise one sight per hr, suggest several itineraries of selection, or mainly gardens or crafts, range 3-8hrs. MK has US limo +25%; 9psgr mini-bus same rate as 5psgr sedan.

MK Taxi 8hr Nara: ¥27,200+¥1,600 per extra 30min; 2 couples beats bus tour.

We most *strongly recommend* that Nara include at least one overnite, but if schedule can't allow it, follow above.

City bus routes mentioned in text are those as of major change-over of late 1988. Each number bus of course runs different routing and may not pass bus stop where you are waiting, so take whichever number quoted in selection that comes by. For safety sake tell driver (at other door from rear entry) your destination–he will let you off at no charge if wrong bus or direction, let you know when arrived so sit up front. On boarding pick numbered zone stub, put in driver's box at end.

One Day Pass allows unlimited free use of almost all city commutation buses (no sightseeing buses) from Ohara in NE to Arashiyama W, Fushimi in S, running abt 6am-10:30pm, and city subway NS under Karasuma-dori (*not* EW Shijo-dori Hankyu line or other private intercity extensions), 5:30am-11:30pm; adult ¥1,050, child ¥530. Single ride: bus ¥180, subway ¥160-190.

Early Start: Beat crowds and heat by starting 8am with those few sights which open that early: **8am** Kiyomizu, Koestu-ji, Ryoan-ji, Sanjusangendo, Zuiho-in. **8:30am** Ginkaku-ji, Heian Shrine garden, Jonangu Garden, Konchi-in, Nanzen-ji, Sanzen-in, Tenryu-ji . All others open 9am.

PAGEANT OF AGES OCTOBER 22

FOR VISITOR here in autumn, understanding Kyoto's past and our itineraries is made easier by Pageant of Ages, *Jidai Matsuri*, costumed procession which illustrates history of Kyoto in reverse chronology 1868 back to 795AD. Oct 22 8:00am rite transfers spirits of 2 imperial deities enshrined in Heian Shrine. Palanquins carried thru town to old Imperial Palace and further rites held 11 to noon; grand procession, hour+ to pass any point, gets underway noon to return spirits to Heian Shrine 3:30. Stand *free* anywhere on route, or buy **reserved seat** prime spot thru hotel or TIC.

Bibliophiles and feminists will note that several great medieval authoresses and authors march, all of whom are available in English translation.

Fantastic procession of over 2,000 paraders. Costumes, authentic in design, color, represent all aspects of court life. Those taking main roles in procession undergo purification rites on 15th and receive court rank–albeit only tempoarily for duration–of minister, regent, prince, samurai, etc.

See it now with us as we unfold it so that you follow fascinating multiplicities of Kyoto history as graphically as possible. Best place is reserved-seat reviewing stand in **Imperial Palace** or **Oike-dori** nr Kyoto Hotel, or **Heian Shrine**; tix ¥2,000, rsve at TIC ☎371-0480, your hotel or at Playguides any Dept Store. Budgeteers just find open curb and stand or squat, *free*, as we usually do. *Do not t*ake numbered seat you don't have reserved ticket for.

First section represents Tokugawa-Edo Era. Uniforms of imperial army who successfully fought against shogun to restore imperial power in 1867, leading to end of Kyoto's history as capital. These are called Yamaguni, from village of that name near Kyoto, one of many groups who answered call to arms. Hodge-podge of Orient-Occident, Japanese costume with European rifle slung across back, marching in swingy European quick-step to fife and drum rendering jazzed-up versions of Japanese martial music, their banners flying, ancient halberd standards twirling.

Next group of this era to pass portrays entourage of deputy sent by Tokugawa shogun from Edo-Tokyo to pay proxy respects to his nominal superior, emperor Komei. Footmen carrying spears and lord's luggage, wheel in dancing march to toss their burdens to one another.

Third consists of half-dozen women of era noted for beauty and culture. Accompanied by their entourages, they begin with Princess Kazu, sister of Komei, last Kyoto emperor, who was married off at 16 to Tokyo shogun, Iyemochi, by desperate shogunal court in order to try to prolong fast-failing shogunate system. She is shown travelling to Tokyo in her wedding robes. Next come poetess-nun Rengetsu; mid-18th century fashion plate Madame NAKAMURA Kuranosuke, who consistently won all best-dressed contests over other exotically dressed merchant wives by just as consistently wearing same *jimi* (chic) costume of black kimono over white *habutai* underskirt; poetess Kaji with renowned granddaughter Gyokuran, painter-wife of painter Taiga (*see* TAIGA MUSEUM, W-Kyoto **B-10**). Representing women of ukiyoe prints is famed courtesan YOSHINO Taiyu, and last is Izumo-no-kuni whose dance shows on Kamo riverbed 350 years ago began kabuki.

Fourth historical period represented is flamboyant, international age of 'Christian Century', Azuchi-Momoyama Period (1573-1613). Here we first see fantastic cortege of country boy who unified Japan, Tycoon (*Tai-kun*, or Great Prince) TOYOTOMI Hideyoshi, as he travels in state to present his son to emperor for his coming of age. Ox-drawn carriage is accompanied by feudal lords in their typical dress. Next is ODA Nobunaga, Hideyoshi's ill-fated and mad-genius senior, here depicted at head of his army as they marched to capital in 1568 in response to call for help to quell civil war.

Fifth Ashikaga-Muromachi Era (1393-1572) saw triumphant but short-lived return of exiled emperor Go-Daigo escorted by his faithful generals, KUSUNOKI Masashige and Masasue. During this time Ashikaga shoguns had headquarters in Muromachi, Kyoto, thus name of period. Masashige had aided emperor Go-Daigo overthrow Kamakura shogunate in 1333, sack city.

Next Ladies of era again take stage, and some of these seem not so ancient for we can still see their descendants on streets of Kyoto, identically dressed: *Ohara-mé* (maids of Ohara village) with their firewood bundles balanced atop their heads and *Katsura-mé* with their fish and vegetables for sale. We see Momoyama Period reflected in luxurious dress of Yodogimi, wife of Hideyoshi. Altho wives as faithful as she are common in Japan today, none dress quite so fancifully as she who violated family code by remaining faithful to husband against the wishes of her own kin who had them married for selfish ends (*see* Himeji, following). Next come tragic authoress of *Izayoi Nikki*, 14th century travel book, Abutsuni, widow of FUJIWARA Tameie, with Lady Shizuka Gozen dressed as *shirabyoshi* (female dancer in male robes), mistress of great generalissimo MINAMOTO Yoshitsune (*see* Kamakura, Hokkaido, *et passim*), tragic hero of *Tale of Heike*.

Next Mounted archer knights lead off Kamakura Period (1185-1335). They, with help of *Kamikaze* God Wind (*see* FUKUOKA), repelled Mongol invasions of 1274 & 1281, now ride by in their great straw 'cowboy' hats. See such men at any performance of *yabusame* (archery ahorse).

Following are Shinto priests with offerings to spirits of Heian Shrine accompanied by Shinto ritual gagaku musicians and child dancers in *kocho* (butterfly) and *karyobinga* (mystic bird) costumes, their wings fluttering on their backs; escort two *Go-horen* (sacred imperial palanquins) which transport enshrined spirits of first and last Kyoto emperors, Kammu and Komei. (Court music played at Sakaimachi Gate and at Jingumichi.)

Lastly Fujiwara Era (983-1170), after immigrant family who monopolized all posts below emperor including that of empress and in-laws to emperors, is represented by Prince Fujiwara and his courtiers in summer dress, on way to make their daily reports to emperor. Women of this period are as famous in world literature as those of any nation. Wake-no-Hiromushi, foundress of Japan's first orphanage, passes by with poetess Ono-no-Komachi and and beauty Kino-Tsurayuki, daughter of another great poet. Certainly everyone knows authoresses Murasaki Shikibu and Sei Shonagon who wrote, great novel *Genji Monogatari* (Tale of Genji) and witty diary *The Pillow Book* respectively, about 1000AD. Faithful, if somewhat amazon, widow Lady Tokiwa, grand dame of Minamotos, along with frustrated romantic lady Yokobue, warrior-wife Tomoe Gozen end distaff procession. Behind these come warrior train of great hero Sakanoue Tamuramaro conqueror of Ainu and 'northern barbarians' (read as: tax-dodgers and outlaws) of late 8th century and subject of much of Japan's folk theater– sort of St. George of Japan.

Court nobles and archers of first emperor Kammu of Kyoto end parade.

ENDS in time to have supper and take tram from Demachi-yanagi terminal, NE part of city, ride little over 30min to **Kurama-dera** temple halfway up 1,800ft Mt Kurama. At nitefall is brilliant, exciting torchlight procession at headquarters of strange tantric Buddhists reputedly descended from great red-faced, long-nosed Tengu-goblins—Jay suspects originate in wandering dervish of West Asia. There's little to describe other than torchlight and torch swinging procession. But entire air of all fetes of this temple reeks of exotic and mysterious, those qualities which make travel exciting.

*To eighteenth century French philosopher-writer,
Jean Jacques Rousseau, the Chinese were
the quintessence of wisdom and moderation,
the incarnation of universal reason.*
— Henri Cartier-Bresson

RAKUCHU 洛中 OLD CITY
MIRROR OF ANCIENT CHINA

TWO LARGEST examples of original 8th century Kyoto stand apart for our first itinerary. Heian Shrine [J-7] fits into several routes; Gosho-Imperial Palace [H-6] requires special permit and better part of half-day so that it is itinerary all its own. Either is good place to see *Jidai Matsuri (preceding)*. Both are conveniently located in old city, *Rakuchu*, and luckily stand apart from next Murasaki itinerary, for neither is delicate fragment capable of projecting any suggestion of *Tale of Genji*.

HEIAN JINGU, palace and, coincidentally, shrine—its 2nd word means shrine or palace, also priest or prince. Built in 1895 to recreate part of original long-lost palace whose eleventh centennial was being marked. Original palace was located where Nijo Castle stands today. Basically Chinese, it already reflects nationalist reaction and return to older Japanese concepts. Earlier Imperial Palaces: Osaka Castle (683-), Fujiwara (690-710), Nara (710-784) and Nagaoka (784-794) probably were similar, tho with less Japanese element, Chinese model for all being Chang An, now called Xian, capital of Sui (pronounced not as hog-call, but as *sway*) Dynasty.

Nagaoka was just SW of SW corner of Kyoto. 300,000 men built it in 5 months in 784. Abandoned in 793 while city around it was still under development, what was finished was merely dismantled, transported and rebuilt in Heian, present Kyoto, just as much of it had already been transferred from earlier Heijo-Nara.

Capital was moved from Nara to Nagaoka thru backstage machinations. Emperor Kwammu succeeded several ruling empresses, seemingly susceptible to wiles of powerful Buddhist monks (illicit affair attributed to at least one). There was mass mercury poisoning in Nara from gilding of Great Buddha. Hard-headed, efficient Kwammu received support of wealthy immigrant tribes from whom much of taxes other than food crops were drawn: Hata and their relatives Fujiwara (who named themselves after old capital city of pre-710). He promoted them and they financed his moving out from under thumb of Nara monasteries. Subsequent sudden move from Nagaoka was due to combination palace intrigue, lack of water, but also bad omens and superior beauty of new site—any reader of *Tale of Genji* knows how superstitious they were at court, and how conscious of beauty.

Later removal of palace itself from what is now Nijo Castle site to present site was again result of more intrigue among puppet masters. Imperial line split in two at one time (1336-1394), at another was moved to Kobe (1185). During most of Kyoto era, 795-1867, emperor was pawn in these power plays. It would seem that only moves made by any emperor on his own were move to Kyoto by Kwammu and move from Kyoto to Edo-Tokyo by Meiji in 1868. Heian Shrine enshrines memory of Kwammu and Komei, father of Meiji (reigning when it was built): respectively, first and last Kyoto emperors. Nijo site in previous era was palace of immigrant Hata lords (from whom Fujiwara descended, and we meet next chapter in Arashiyama) —who presented this and entire city property to promote move.

Kyoto was laid out on symmetrical grid 794 in classical Chinese imperial style, in turn probably adapted from *paradisa* garden-city plan of Persia. It measured E-W 1,508 *jo* (abt 4.5km/3mi, and N-S 1,753 *jo* 5km/3mi)–about 400m longer than Nara-Heijo and 200m wider. There were 13 E-W *oji*–avenues and 13 NS, each of 10 *jo* width, 30m. Between *oji* were usually 3 *koji* streets half as wide. Central N-S approach was Suzaku-oji 28 *jo* or 84m wide boulevard (no trace now, W of Omiya St), flanking which were great guardian pagodas of long gone Sai-ji (W), and still lovely TO-JI (E).

Three great enemies of city have been fire, civil war and earthquake which periodically destroyed city. Add new fourth horseman: 'development' or 'modernization' which has ravaged city since our first edition, with no sense of aesthetic evident, nor even vestige of traditional Kyoto good taste.

Palace to all outward appearances looked Chinese. But classical Chinese interior was less comfortable. Ever-adaptable Japanese compromised: Chinese *imamekashii* modernist-grandeur outside, Japanese *natsukashii* 'old-shoe' comfort inside. Area for court administration stately-symmetrical Chinese except probably had wooden floors. Chinese stone-floor style can still be seen on Mt Hiei and in Toji temple S of town, and in older Nara.

Heian Shrine rather faithfully reproduces this from ancient scroll paintings and literary descriptions—tho approximately 65% scale. Roofs are tiled with upturned tips, woodwork is brilliant vermillion. There are stone walks and courts and entry is from center. Floor plan of reception hall was identical to Nara monasteries: God Emperor was enthroned here, Buddha in other. But in back, where emperor lived, monotonous Chinese symmetry was abandoned: placement of buildings seemingly random but casually convenient, shallow tile roofs give way to steep Japanese cedar shingle and steeper thatch; fixed walls of China to sliding panels of Japan, painted however in Chinese fashion but set in natural, unfinished woodwork. Present Imperial Palace–Gosho, tho often rebuilt, removed, preserves this residence style accurately, even wall paintings are new copies of destroyed copies of how-often destroyed copies.

Heian Shrine is to be strolled. Garden beyond main gate (enter L rear ¥500) faithful redo of original in style if not detail. **Seasonal features:** April crowds stroll 'neath cascades of weeping cherry blossoms, early June wonderful iris gardens *shobu-en*, impress more as resembling Degas rather than Korin, and midwinter not least being snowscape.

Romantically run-down remnant of original is **Shinsen-en garden [F/G-7/8]** S of Nijo Castle. Take this in only if garden buff or Murasaki romantic, with visit to Nijo, as also **Nijo-Jinya** daimyo's 'secret' town-castle, p479.

Traditional weddings held in Heian Shrine almost constantly, in autumn wedding season run on assembly line. To see one, contact shrine office ☎761-0221. Would be nice to bring small gift as you are guest, perhaps posed in group photo taken afterwards. Bride wears ceremonial bridal kimono, white head-towel concealing horns of jealousy, but groom usually Western morning. At home she changes to skirt, blouse for free movement, he perhaps to kimono to lounge. Shinto wedding, as institution, is only as old as Heian Shrine, nationalistic fad of 1890s. Prior to that, marriage sanctified by exchange of gifts and agreements between contracting families, transfer bride's name from her own to mate's family register. Christian church weddings denting Shrine business–not by Christian converts but westerly romantics–to benefit of church coffers.

Bordering Heian Shrine and Okazaki Park, in which it is set, is...
Municipal Art Museum which houses magnificent traveling exhibits; and nearby **Modern Art Museum**, architecturally interesting new public hall, also has programs; zoo & playland. Across canal W of public hall is **Nishimura Lacquer** (factory-showroom)–worth visit; *see* SHOPPING, MANSIONS route, *following*. **Sosui Canal** 100-yr-old thru-transport from Lake Biwa, used till recently for tourist flatboats—walk its bank especially in sakura blooming season. Tough hike all way to Lake Biwa.

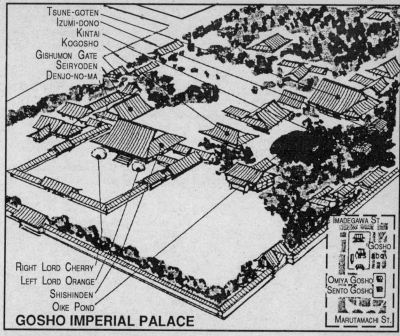

TSUNE-GOTEN
IZUMI-DONO
KINTAI
KOGOSHO
GISHUMON GATE
SEIRYODEN
DENJO-NO-MA

IMADEGAWA ST.
GOSHO
OMIYA GOSHO
SENTO GOSHO
MARUTAMACHI ST.

RIGHT LORD CHERRY
LEFT LORD ORANGE
SHISHINDEN
OIKE POND

GOSHO IMPERIAL PALACE

GOSHO Imperial Palace (prior-permit necessary, groups thru 2-3x-hourly, sometimes only 10am and 2pm). Chinese-red pavilions of 'Palace of *Hei-an*, Peace and Tranquility' were frequently further reddened by flame. During course of rebuilding court would move to some noble's mansion, which would then be declared *Sato Dairi* (Temporary Palace). After great fire of 13th century, old palace was never rebuilt and there were several Sato Dairi– further complicated by political situation, for in this period it was usual to have, in fact, several emperors, each with his own Sato Dairi. Reigning emperor was often helpless child who retired upon (and if) attaining manhood, to join his predecessor(s) as another 'cloistered emperor', monk in name but puppet-manipulator in fact. Many died in early childhood, perhaps by unintentional poisoning from breast-feeding court ladies who heavily powdered themselves in cosmetic white lead.

Present palace site was major Sato Dairi from late 14th century, before which it had been palace of FUJIWARA Tsuchi-Mikado or August Gate of Earth, that is, temporal ruler (with his feet on ground) as opposed to papal emperor who was Tenno-Mikado, August Gate of Heaven (with head in clouds). In 16th century original palace site was taken over by shogun for his Nijo Castle-Palace (which see). In 1781 Sato Dairi again burned and in 1789 nobleman MATSUDAIRA Sadanobu, shogun's son and himself high official in charge of putting off insistent pre-Perry Russian delegations, ordered new palace built here in exact reproduction of 10th century styles. Scholars searched their literary sources. Bidding on contract was awarded to highest bidder, on grounds that you only got what you paid for and nothing was too good for Son of Heaven. (Frustrated foreign would-be exporters keep this in mind, thus Benz sells better than Chevy or even VW). New palace was born when United States was. In 1854, few months after United States Navy task force under Perry demanded that Japan be opened, it burned down—many people took it for great omen, but no one could agree as to just what it augured.   Parts have burned since 1869 reconstruction and been rebuilt.

Palace grounds within moat and low stone wall, now pierced by dozen gates (formerly nine in accordance with Taoist numerology), reflects older palace parks of Nara and China. Today it is public park of 268,000 tsubo, 1,000,000sq yds. Eighth of it taken up by inner palace proper, upper half off center to west. Below this, SE quadrant is smaller enclosure containing **Sento Gosho** (to see, separate **permit**) small palace held in readiness should emperor retire & **Omiya Gosho**, used by Imperial Family when visiting Kyoto—or by state guests, as king and queen of Thailand, 1963. South side INNER PALACE best place to view *Jidai Matsuri* (12:00noon) **Oct 22** or *Aoi Matsuri* (10:30am) **May 15** (see DATEBOOK).

Inner palace is divided into 3 sections: *Shishin-den*, palace of audience and ceremony; *Seiryo-den*, official apartments; and *Tsune-go-ten*, ordinary palace and actual residence until 1869. *Shishin-den* is Japanized 10th century version of what started out in 8th like HEIAN SHRINE. Flanking guard towers of Chinese-style Heian Shrine become two flowering trees: *Sa-kon Sakura*, cherry of (emperor's) left, and *U-kon Tachibana*, mandarin orange of right. You will also see these in doll display March-April. There is no Shishin-den in Tokyo palace as certain rites may only be performed here, such as coronation, and here this late emperor Hirohito's was held, as was to be, until pre-empted by Tokyo for 'security reasons', Akihito's, reign name Heisei. Floors are polished wood, walls painted Chinese-style with portraits of Chinese sages. Center of main room has simple frame throne on dais, covered by canopy. Emperor does not in public sit on tatami, and never at floor level.

Pass thru *denjo-no-ma* hall where ministers once waited for audience. *Small fan-shaped window in wall was for court ladies to peek in on them, to....* *Seiryo-den*, formal apartments, Heian style. Two guardian trees here are bamboo. Along west side are highly decorated rooms for court ladies, where such as poetry parties mentioned in *Tale of Genji* were held. In *Asagarei-no-ma*, imperial breakfast nook, household utensils are displayed during public openings. East side was for emperor himself and his raised tatami are set in one broad wood-floored room. Ornately painted walls are modern restorations: those in jewel-like *Ko-gosho* (little palace) east of Seiryo-den done late 1950s. East is **Oike garden** remaining from Heian period original; **tea cottages** here all that remain from pre-1854.

North of garden is... *Tsune-Goten*, in which last Kyoto emperors actually lived. Architecture old *shinden* (palace-temple) style, but furnished tatami-floored medieval *shoin* (manorial) style of Edo Period, best seen in NIJO CASTLE. Covering tatami are wall to wall carpets, introduced into Japan 15th century; real Persian carpets decorate gigantic floats of *Gion Matsuri* (**July 17**).

With planned decentralization of government there is serious Kyoto-based move led by hi-tech Kyocera prexy INAMORI Kazuo to move Imperial Household back here. Main opposition seems to come from black-shirt "revere emperor..." (and "...expel barbarian?") nuts who threaten him.

Permit to see main palace necessary, separate one for Sento Gosho: apply thru hotel desk, or **Imperial Household Agency** at Gishu-mon gate of palace; ☎211-1211. Groups with able English guides enter on the hr at 9-11am, and 1-3pm mon-fri, sat morns; X-sun and hol; allow 30min each. *Public opening* 2nd week Nov. If pressed for time, choose either GOSHO or NIJO and latter is preferable, but NISHI HONGAN-JI best for real art, unreconstructed. At other extreme, real Murasaki addict could take in HEIAN at 8am garden open 8:30, GOSHO 10, then smaller palaces which we prefer, of....

....the old life still breathes in the corners of the city.
— Osaragi Jiro, *Kyoto*

PURPLE PERIOD
WESTERN OUTSKIRTS

"...JAPAN at end of our tenth century. Lady Murasaki in her *Tale of Genji* has left a picture of a life (lived, to be sure, 'above the clouds' as she herself says) of a subtlety, of a refinement, and at the same time of a genuineness of delicate human feeling, never surpassed in world literature," wrote Bernard Berenson. He also sagely notes, "Nothing in the graphic arts of Japan contemporary with Lady Murasaki or later (including many attempts to illustrate her masterpiece) so much as suggest a visual equivalent". Later Katsura Rikyu succeeds in expressing views and sentiments of her novel.

Heian's way of life was more to be felt, experienced, rather than seen. Even were Lady Murasaki's own manse and garden to have survived intact, it could not appear to one's eye as her verbal pictures do to one's mind's eye. Any Heian cityscape would cease to exist by very presence of rubber-necking tourists. Perhaps it is fortunate that those few remnants, fragmentary as they may be, are inconveniently located and not touristy popular. Heian way is frame of mind, attitude. It can perhaps be sampled by viewing remnants as painters of its period presented that same scene–contrary to BB –delicate fragments revealed as if by accident peeking from 'neath golden mist, any single part projecting on our mind holograph of its whole.

For these suggestive fragments our first routing is W-ward: first stop (entry ¥500) is... KORYU-JI temple [C-7] whose founders were ancestors of Fujiwara, top family of Heian period and palace. Also known as Uzumasa, perhaps oldest site in Kyoto and one of most mysterious. It was important center of culture and industry even before Nara was built. Also houses one of world's most beautiful statues. Site was center of immigrant clan called Hata or Yahada who were naturalized in 390AD. Some can be traced to origin near present Russo-Chinese border in Turkestan; introduced much mainland high culture, its governmental organization and technology– reputedly sericulture and silk weaving (recent archaeology casts doubt on this), for which Kyoto is noted ever since. Japanese still call loom, *hata*.

At rear of compound is small stone well, mentioned in *Manyoshu* poetry anthology of 8th century, called **Well of Isarai**. Some believe this to be corruption of 'Israel', as 'Uzumasa' is corruption of Syriac for Jesus-Messiah. (Syriac was 'Latin' of many Oriental Christians). Ideographs read in Chinese *Da-wi* or Chinese for David? (Jesus was of House of David). Many other linguistic, cultural similarities to our own heritage serve to complicate mystery further. Zealots claiming Hata to be Lost Tribes of Israel have only served to becloud mystery and there is now little serious effort to clear it up. Probable center of old tribal settlement was odd three-legged torii set in pure water spring at rear. Origin, date–unknown.

[Past Well of Isarai and 3 times around temple wended odd procession **Oct 10**, *Ushi Matsuri* (Cow Fete) of Uzumasa. Odd flat paper masks with attached noses in open front houses around well were worn by man in white who rode sacred bovine, a la Zoroastrian legend of First King, Jamshid or Jam (Jimu?). Singularity of now-discontinued rite, plus fact that no one has any idea of its meaning or origin, added to mystery of site].

Fujiwara family were Hata. They engineered move of capital from Nara to enhance their own power; financed it as well and for over thousand years thereafter had monopoly concession to provide empresses to imperial line.

(Nagako, Empress of late Hirohito/Showa, was first exception to this). Koryu-ji was founded 622 in memory of Prince Shotoku Taishi by HATA Kawakatsu, most famous leader of tribe...his name denotes strange origin: found as baby adrift in reed raft in river by royal princess. (As also Korean folk hero Hong Gil Dong who 'fled to found kingdom on volcanic isle').

Temple boasts fine collection of sculpture of Nara Period, including its greatest treasure, Buddha image in **Thinker** pose. To André Malraux it "symbolized eternal sublimity transcending race and religion". Oldest sculpture in Kyoto, oldest lacquer on wood (older lacquers are on hollow basket shells). Legend has it carved by Prince Shotoku as self-portrait, but it's certainly by some unknown Korean hand—identical if smaller gilt bronze shown at Korean Pavilion, Osaka Expo-'70. Its delicate upraised fingers were broken off by demented student, 1961, since restored. It is Miroku Bosatsu, Messiah who will become next Buddha. Some say it childhood portrait of historical Buddha, Gautama Shakamuni of 2,500 years ago—and of course before becoming Buddha at age 35, he'd have been then-Messiah.

L is smaller statue in similar posture, one of many forms of Kannon, this one called Nyoirin, also of Korean style. Other sculptures are of both Nara style and Heian. Note differences in period ideals of beauty. Nara are slender, more in Western bodily proportions: ideals of Sui-Wei Chinese teachers and imported artists. Heian images are Japanese work: models proportionately larger-headed, plumper of body, more squat with shorter legs, as *Kokuzo Bosatsu*, seated with lotus in left hand. Main building, **Lecture Hall**, housing 2.5m/8ft Amida, is oldest (9c) standing structure in Kyoto–historical interest only. Finer works in gallery building L rear.

GETTING THERE: Keifuku tram from SW corner Shijo Omiya [F/G-8/9] to Uzumasa stn opp temple. Or **bus** #11 at Shijo Kawaramachi or Shijo Omiya, or terminus Arashiyama.

CONTINUING ON: Take same train one stop W to Katabiranotsu-ji stn, transfer to train doubling back on Kitano line to Omuro Stn; walk straight (N) 2min to gate of **Ninna-ji** temple and its Omuro Imperial Palace [C-6]. *Alternative*, 30min walk N on road to E side of Koryu-ji, front of PO; pass below Toei Movie Village (*see now?*), cross JR tracks, R fork to **Myoshin-ji** Zen compound, at N gate main road, turn L, follow main road third of mile, half km—**or** from here bus #8, 10, 26 to...

NINNA-JI [C-6] built 886-8 by emperor Uda preparing to abdicate throne to infant relative and retire, giving much of Heian nickname: Era of Cloistered Emperors. Here in part-palace part-temple he could seek salvation while playing power politics against clan of imperial fathers-in-law, Fujiwara. Site, frequently rebuilt, still retains more of Heian residential atmosphere than Imperial Palace itself, as from Uda on chief abbots were from imperial family for 1,000 years until separation of religions in Meiji period. Thus it is classed as *Monzeki*, Imperial Palace-Temple, also called **Omura Gosho**.

Inseparable combination of garden and building is Chinese concept fully adopted, adapted and improved upon in Japan. Formal Chinese court, as in Heian Shrine and Imperial Palace, as well as Ninna-ji **main gate** (17c), pleasure apartments where banquets and such were held, all face south across gardens; gardens are set off in rear of palace office-compound. It was this later, minor aspect of court architecture which Heian Japanese made their hallmark, revealing "unique hedonism of their ideal of life". Temples also faced south across garden illustrating Western Paradise. Palace and temple came to differ little, are same basic architecture except for functional appointments.

A   B   C   D

5   Mausoleum of
emperor Saga

To Kozan-ji,
Takao Pkwy   162

Shuzan Kaido

Kinkaku-ji 卍

Ryoan-ji 卍

Saga Bamboo Craft

Daikaku-ji 卍

Osawano-ike   UKYO-KU

Hirosawa-ike
Pond   YH
12

Ninna-ji 卍

TAKAOGUCHI

6   ←ToTakao Pkwy

Seiryo-ji 卍
(Shaka-do)

卍 Rakushisha

SAGA

Shinmarutamachi-dori

OMURO

NARUTAKI

TOKIWA

MYOSHIN-JI

Myoshin-ji 卍

SAGA
SAGAIKIMAE   KURUMAZAKI

JR Sanin Main Line

HANAZONO

7   卍 Tenryu-ji
Kameyama
Park

卍 Rokuon-ji*
卍 Rinsen-ji
■ Arashiyama Mus.

ARISUGAWA

KEIFUKU Arashiyama Line

● Movie Village

UZUMASA

8   Arashiyama Park
Horin-ji 卍

Iwatayama Park

Nakanoshima Park
ARASHIYAMA

Umemiya
卍 Taisha

Shijo-dori

ARASHIYAMA

9   Matsuo
Taisha 卍
Shrine

HANKYU Arashiyama Line

MATSUO

Embroidery
Mus

Sports
Center

Nishigojo-dori

Yuzen
Cultural
Hall

NISHIKYOGUKU   Shichijo-dori

10   Kegon-ji 卍

Saiho-ji 卍
(Moss-garden)

Ikeno
Taiga
Mus

卍 Jizo-in

KAMIKATSURA

Hachijo-dori

WEST KYOTO

0   2km

To Kameoka

9

To Umeda

Katsura-rikyu

11   NISHIKYO-KU

Resultant style, *shinden-zukuri*, combines pomp of Chinese palace, intimacy of Japanese home and other-worldliness of Buddhist monastery. Framework monumental Chinese, but floors wooden for stockinged feet, rather than stone as in China; Chinese plaster walls become Japanese paper sliding panels with paintings, tile roof reverts to old Japanese cedar shingle or thatch, open veranda completes wedding of house and garden which (unlike 17th cent Tokugawa styles) was bridge between man and landscape view.

Pagoda, added in 17th century, adds Heian air, sigh of scenic beyondness making **garden view** from veranda one of Kyoto's most memorable. Green garden is Heian era (9th cent), but 15th century reconstruction inserted effective Zen gravel bed of present reality in foreground.

GETTING AROUND: Immense compound beyond small palace not worth exploring, except to stroll beneath cherries at blossom time. Below compound, get bus #28, 91 or 92 heading R, W, for **DAIKAKU-JI** temple [A/B-6]. Pass Utano YH [C-6]

R, park-like main **tree nursery** area of Kyoto must resemble great park gardens of ancient palaces. Great pond on R is **Hirosawa Pond [B-6]**: bus stops here so you might get off for refreshment at waterside tea stalls, continuing on next bus. Kyoto-ites consider this most "classical Heian" view with thatched roof cottage across pond, wooded mountain beyond mountain: rapidly being spoiled by shoddy new housing. Alas, where is Lady Purple's superb taste?

Alternative routing: while historically this chapter precedes Zen gardens, it is usually more convenient to combine with later KINKAKU-JI & RYOAN-JI—Ninna-ji → Ryoan-ji is one bus (#59) stop, or 10min walk NE, thence on by #59 or #12 → KINKAKU-JI–midway perhaps see Domoto Art Museum (to L of bus stop Kinugasa).

Or walk or bike from Tenryu-ji (rent bike nearby stn)–Saga area–Daikaku-ji → Ninna-ji → (Myoshin-ji ? nearby S, or detour 4km up dead-end N to Jingo-ji & Kozan-ji, return) → Ryoan-ji → Kinkaku-ji → (detour into hill 1.8km hike up road E-side of Kinkaku, or bus #6, 61 from next bus stop E, to Koetsu-ji) → return → Daitoku-ji → return Arashiyama stn via Koryu-ji . **Walking** about 6km incl Saga alleys, add 8km r.t.- Kozan-ji, 3.6km-Koetsu-ji detours. **Cycling** all abt 26km/16mi w/ bike return, nice day's pedal, or eliminate one hill detour.

Few minutes on at end of bus lines #28, 91, 92...
DAIKAKU-JI [AB-6] by smaller Ozawa Pond, equally noted, on which at April 14-16 *Ikebana Festival*, glides phoenix boat like that used by ancient emperor Go-Mizuno-o to view 'mums, which he later set in vases thus founding Saga Go-ryu (prefix Go- notes imperial origin) school of ikebana, and is today its headquarters. For 3 days ikebana arrangement by top instructors nationwide fill room after room. Enjoy *matcha* tea on boat,

Set in this ancient landscape garden is jewel of temple pavilion...
Reimei-den, very small and very new, far L rear of temple down numerous verandas across garden bridges. Tho rebuilt numerous times as temple, was originally imperial villa 9th century and became Palace of Abdication. This miniscule pavilion is bright red—not mere paint but pure gem-like urushi-lacquer. Even floors are black lacquer. This is how inner sanctums of ancient Chinese and Japanese palaces were.

Of importance and beauty are *fusuma* **painted panels**, main buildings. **Shin-den**, wall panels painted in Peonies, by KANO Sanraku (1561-1635), one of best examples of early Edo Era painting. Others by KANO Motonobu (1476-1559), -Eitoku (1543-90), -Tanyu (1602-74); also Korin (1658-1716). ¥500.

From Daikaku-ji [AB-6] bus 11 → Tenryu-ji [A-7], or leisurely 2.5km/1hr walk...

HEIAN TOUCH

ARASHIYAMA favorite beauty spot of Heian court, later retirement village for aesthetes, is worth whole day aimless ambling thru its back alleys, worth small book in itself. Buses #11, 28, 93 direct or take following hour **walk** with several minor stops, especially at **cherry** or **maple time**.

From Daikaku-ji gate 350m/yds, R at road end another 400m to gate on R of...
SEIRYO-JI or **SHAKA-DO** [A-6]. Little interest here except **Apr 1st or 2nd** wknds (dates vary) ancient masked folk dance, & **19** secret image, 5ft tall sandalwood Shaka from India, viewable. Good noodle shop opp gate bit E.

Beyond front of Shaka-do go R then first L about 200m along narrow streets which set Kyoto-ites to sighing in nostalgic *natsukashii*.

On R is pedestrian lane thru bamboo grove to private garden gate, enter, to exquisite...
Enrian tea garden [A-6], Rinzai Zen monastery. Here in this hidden jewel-setting FUJIWARA Teika made his great anthology of *Hyaku-nin-shu*, 'One Hundred Poems by One Hundred Poets', as seen on poetry cards played at New Year, subject of endless paintings.

Walk back down bamboo grove path, turn R, follow road R and L 300m to...
GIO-JI [A-6] where widow & daughter of TAIRA Kiyomori, successor to
Fujiwara, became nuns; lovely, lonely. Adjoining is TAKIGUCHI temple.
150m N up narrow trail is tomb mound of emperor Go-Kameyama d.1424. Return...

At first corner on L is Shoan-in, at which corner interesting short detour L to...
Doll Museum, *Sagano Ningyo-no Ie* fine private collection of antique J-
folk art dolls of paper, papier mache, clay, cloth etc; ¥1,000, high but worth
it just for exquisite house and garden; 9:30-5pm, X-tue; ☎882-1421.

Out of Enrian first L, 300m past temples, R, Nisson-in & Jojakko-ji, in L...
Rakushisha [A-6/7] which stands abandoned in **cherry blossom** time,
when most other orchards are swarming with people and garbage, its
blossoms especially natsukashii amid romantic dilapidated temples.
  Go E 200m from Rakushisha to main road (you can see SHAKA-DO on L) whence R
under 1km (12min) → TENRYU-JI [A-7]. Alternative route is S and W from
RAKUSHISHA past Ozawa Pond, over hill to Oi River along which to bridge and L. One
could easily spend day strolling or cycling (rent at Keifuku-Arashiyama stn) these alleys.

TENRYU-JI [A-7] directly opposite Arashiyama terminal of Keifuku electric line.
Buildings new (1900), paintings garish imitations of ancient styles. But
garden grand, southern Sung Chinese-style paradise garden of Heian, dates
from next era, Kamakura, about 1340 and is by one of great garden
designers Monk Muso Kokushi. Touch of Zen was later added in foreground sand and stone section. Note that this is one of only two major
kare-sansui (**dry gardens**) not chopped off by wall, as at Daitoku-ji,
Ryuan-ji, etc (–second is Entsu-ji). Walls were all added later in Edo era,
when country was shut off from world and myopia force-bred into national
psyche by Tokugawa shogun. Wall was to obstruct any long view,
dangerous mental activity in police state. Beyond sand garden (now, beyond
wall) is always older paradise garden. Sit in temple meditating on harsh
reality of Now as embodied in bare sand and rock, looking across to
promise of better times in paradise garden beyond—perhaps, if exiled noble
or emperor, to dream of nostalgic better times past again becoming future.
Such thoughts breed revolt, and Tokugawa avoided or suppressed revolt
with amazing efficiency for 250 years. Tenryu-ji and Entsu-ji leave no
room for walls. Here cliff serves as wall as well as indication of paradise
above-beyond. (ENTSU-JI, *see*, uses 'captured mountainscape' beyond as
paradise with again no place for wall). Opens early 8:30am, entry ¥500.

CHOPSTICKS: 50m below gate Izusen branch for Buddhist vegetarian
meal in lovely garden; rsve ☎881-1235. Opp gate R is Tea house.

ARASHIYAMA [A-7]: Heian courtiers came here blossom- and maple-
turning seasons for pleasure boating. Tradition lives on today in numerous
restaurants and tea houses (all good, mostly budget to tourist with few
secluded luxe) along water, and large flatbottom picnic boats. Actual Heian
Court picnic reenacted during lovely *Mifune Matsuri* **3rd Sun May** noon, again
at *Momiji Matsuri* in maple season on **2nd Sun Nov**, 10:30am. Ornately decorated
boats with costumed musicians, dancers poled about river pool, playing ancient melodies.

Heian sport-fishing—once really economical, is done with *ugai*
cormorants July-Aug eves. If choice, we prefer seeing here to other areas.
Men dressed in uniform of their trade, Heian period style of black tights and
grass apron, odd Frisian ceremonial cap from our own Biblical area and era
(like cap of Mlle La France), pole long boats with great torches and fire-
baskets held on davits. Pole man drums eerily against boat side while bird
handler manipulates half-dozen or more leashed fisher-birds. Noise and

light attract fish which long-billed cormorant dive at, capture in their gullet. But ring around bird's neck, to which lcash is attached, prevents fully swallowing fish. Handler reins in bird, retrieves fish and sets his living trap out again. Boat's weird approach as it swishes by within inches of one's picnic craft, sibilant rush of water at its prow, eerie drumming, soul piercing caw of black birds often invisible in dark but for their iridescent wakes, all coming out of dark nite and illuminated in hellish flicker of hanging torches, is unforgettable experience, scene from some other world–underworld.

Year-round ¥1,000 on public boats, ticket-boarding 100m up river from bridge. Group boats available: advise rsvtn or thru agent, tho on-spot possible.

Japanese evening bus tour often takes in boating. Or rent 3-psgr rowboat anytime ¥1,200 hr, or your own *Yakata-bune* boat abt ¥2,800 for 2 persons per 30mins.

Art (War) Museum at hiway overpass, exhibits paraphernalia ('art'?) of WWII. Alas, no campaign or battle paintings by field artists, some of whom led modern art revival postwar, include some top names today–potential for fine collection, somewhere.

OFFBEAT NORTH

LITTLE TEMPLES tucked away in glades which hot summer or blood-red autumn days when temple-crawling palls, offer quiet, privacy.

JINGO-JI [A-2] lovely old compound of 9th century, isolated here deep in NW mountains in typical Shingon seclusion, with some superb 9th century sculptures "more expressive of Japanese temperament", especially seated Kokuzo Bosatsu. Also rare Kamakura era secular screens like earlier at Toji, one of most famous Japanese portraits, that of MINAMOTO Yoritomo, patron, c.1200, by Takanobu in new style of painting for that new age. **Bus** #8.

SAIMYO-JI short distance up with its grand 12th century main hall...

KOZAN-JI just beyond with 13th cent Chinese style Buddha Hall, but best is treasured picture scrolls including comic 12th cent precursor of Pogo, *Animal scroll of Toba Sojo*, satire of frogs as Buddhist priests. Entry ¥400.

Bus #6, 61 from intersect 500m E of Kinkaku-ji, or W-bound front Daitoku-ji, to...
KOETSU-JI [E-2] for its tea houses, exquisite tea garden details, entry ¥200.

SHOOTING HOZU RAPIDS

THIS SIDETRIP ends at picturesque Togetsu Bridge in Arashiyama. Scenic and exciting pastime, especially in spring blossom or autumn maple season. JR 45min ¥380 local or 25min ¥1080 ltd exp from Kyoto stn, or **Romantic Train Sagano** along river from Saga stn 7.3km in 20min to Kameoka stn, ¥600 4x day X-wed Dec-Feb; or Kyoto Kyotsu **bus** from Kyoto Stn terminal #2, W-side stn plaza above PO, 50min; or at Arashiyama terminal Keihanshin line [B-8], that's across bridge away from town; or JR from Saga Stn [B-7], 'town' of Arashiyama; or **taxi** 30min/10x-mtr to...

KAMEOKA, old castle town. KONGO-JI temple has paintings by MARUYAMA Okyo. **Castle** built 1579, dismantled Meiji, site bought by **Oomoto-kyo Shinto** sect, whose great prophet-artist co-founder DEGUCHI Onisaburo after World War I prophesied destruction of Japan if militaristic policies continued. Co-foundress, his mother-in-law DEGUCHI Nao, illiterate wife of country carpenter, had begun in 1892 to have religious experiences and thru automatic writing 'illiterate' Nao issued immense corpus called *Ofudesaki*. Pacifist religion boomed. As opposed to Imperial-line State Shinto based on monotheistic-prophetic folk Shinto–with influences from Old Testament, felt-links to early Hebraism with soul-origins of prophetic line in 'Asalem', believed by some to be Jerusalem, by others to be Assalem on Caspian Seacoast NW Iran, where Abraham's prophetic forebear originated. Officially credited with 2,500,000 followers in 1930s, their own claims of 5,000,000 more likely, maintained one of country's largest, best daily papers. Leaders all arrested in 1921 for lese majeste, like Onisaburo riding white horse, etc; released, pressured. Onisaburo published 81 volumes of his own religious experiences *Reikei Monogatari*, started overseas missions, promoted Esperanto (still do), created major corpus of original artworks in pottery and painting. Built near-impregnable 'Paradise on Earth' on castle hill. 1935 army tanks destroyed Paradise, mowed down unarmed believers, all leaders re-arrested and held in dungeons till US Army released them 1945. Believe 'Art is mother of religion', important group of Shinto sects branched off and prosper today, include Osaka's PL, Atami Museum MOA, etc. Pacifism gave birth to nonaggressive martial art—aikido originator UESHIBA Morihei was follower. Present superb non-sectarian 'aesthetic boot camp' June-July (*see* LEARNING ABOUT JAPAN, p.92).

Not much to see, but artist might appreciate few hours there, call ☎(07712)-2-5561 International Division *Kokusai-bu*.

Then board flatbottom boat to resume shoot of...
Hozu Rapids from **Kameoka**: boats 9, 10, 11am, 12:30, 14:00, 15:30 weekdays Mar 10–Nov 30, suns-hols as soon as full; Dec 1–Mar 9, pm only and heated; X-new yr. Eat lunch—or better, buy box lunch for trip at Hozu Kanko (Tourist) Kaikan; *or* put up there at moderate rate, shoot rapids early morn. Spring or autumn flower/ maple seasons advise reserve Hozu-gawa Yusen ☎(07712)-2-5846—however, we've found that one or two can almost always get aboard and if group, boat will run for eleven fares. JTB may, as for us, insist you must reserve several days ahead. We wanted to go same day, JTB said impossible, so we bussed out to find boats hadn't had customer for days. Trip 20km/13mi down river takes almost 2hrs, ¥3,400/1,800kids (¥67,000 charter 16psgr boat) thru time-sculpted stony gorges, endless rapids and races like Hut Rapid, High Rapid, Lion's Maw. Lightly wetting, mildly exciting but scenic, no danger, no serious accident yet.

Terminating– 10min walk down river E of main bridge, beyond bus lot, on road L fork, first L down alley to red torii (if **driving** park car, free, inside torii to R).

...Or take Keifuku tram back to town via Kurumazaki stop to enter rear of...
KURUMAZAKI Shrine **[B-7]**. New Year week swarms with *mizu shobai* people: musicians from classics to pops, geisha, tea people, actors and grunt'n groaners etc. Fence posts inscribed with names of donors: first shrine on R, L stakes are Tea Master SEN Soshitsu and pro wrestlers—some combination, two styles of strength! Musicians discard damaged old samisen plectrums, dancers old fans, to be burned in ritual fire like sacred talismans or flags. As these objects of beauty will soon be destroyed, we have never considered it sacrilege to encourage friends to pick one up to take home and enjoy—use enobles art. Many circumambulate main shrine dropping counting sticks. Before it is large pile of flat, round pebbles reminiscent of stone coins: written on them are prayers, usually for show-biz success. Shrine office sells little yellow bags (drop few hundred yen in box) in which is sacred pebble. Take this home 'on loan', pray over it, match it with another from riverbed near home—if prayer is answered and you want to parlay it, return 2 to shrine next year. At least it works for shrine. *Ema-e*, small shrine board picture, lovely, unforgettable souvenir or gift. Aforementioned *Mifune Matsuri* **3rd Sun May** is shrine's main festival.

Cross river 10min walk in hills—**Monkey Park** wild monkeys come to play and be fed and photographed and where 'Hundredth Monkey Effect' was first observed. (Young monkey dropped food in dirt by water, then in water and noted it lost grittiness, did it regularly. Other young monks copied. When about 100 were doing it, monkeys nation-wide were observed to be washing food.)

Across picturesque bridge just beyond restaurants is...
HORIN-JI temple [A-8], also called after its main image, Kokuzo,
bodhisattva worshipped for great wisdom. March 13 procession of 13-year-
old boys pays homage here. Kyoto student of Jay's told how he was
brought here for 13th birthday in first adult kimono. Had to demonstrate his
literacy, knowledge of simple family Buddhist ritual, have service in his
honor and receive talisman. Then he was to walk back, cross bridge to
Arashiyama without looking back. If he obeyed, he would be wise; if he
looked back, he'd never succeed in work demanding diligence. In noble
families of old 13 was age of adulthood when youth received his second, or
long-, sword, wore adult hairdress, was eligible for marriage and responsibilities: Buddha-Mitzvah?

20min walk S, or short bus #28 or 69 ride from bridge or Keihanshin stn, is...
MATSUO Grand Shrine [AB-9], lovely spot, usually quite empty.
Festivals mid-Apr & early May according to variable calendar of 12 beasts (so check
contemporary festival lists at TIC or in *KTO* or *Kyoto Visitors Guide*), lovely ceremonial
transplanting of rice seedlings by temple maidens 3rd Sun Jul.

15min walk beyond Matsuo, or 10min bus #29, 69 from Arashiyama...
SAIHO-JI Moss Garden, Mass Paradise [AB-9]: must-see (if possible) in
singular development out of Heian paradise garden. Permit required—
complicated for foreign tourist as *must apply direct* to Saiho-ji, Matsuo, Nishigyo-ku,
Kyoto 615, 3 months ahead with return postcard, self-addressed to where you expect to be
in Kyoto, or well in advance at home. But try phone call in Japanese ☎391-3631, or
check TIC, as some places kept open for overseas tourists. Admission ¥3,000! ($20+).
Not on any tours.

Some places have special auras. Moss Garden is its own. Trouble with
this earthly paradise, friends tell, it was usually crowded—tho dozen times
in 30 years we visited we didn't find it so. Human body effusions damage
moss so permit was introduced. We've experienced trio of such auras:
Venetian-glass red dawn in California redwood glade, golden blossoming-
desert of autumn Iran, emerald presence of Saiho-ji—especially in light rain.

For centuries princes chose this natural glade for religious seclusion and
rite started here by Kobo-daishi 808 to earn merit by releasing captive wild
creatures. 1198 Fujiwara noble laid out pond section as vision of *Saiho-
Jodo*, Westerly Paradise. Era's painters liked to envelop isles of paradise in
mist. Garden here had natural conditions to create in fact this ideal
pictorialization in living Yamato-e (characteristically Japanese, long horizontal scroll
painting).

MUSO Kokushi, green-thumbed genius, remodeled this garden around
1340 when it became Zen temple. (Later did Tenryu-ji and Silver Pavilion).
But destroyed by flood and remodeled so often that no single artist can now
claim authorship. If anything, peculiar micrometeorology of glade is
responsible, makes natural mossy vale singular—gardeners merely shaped
and refined it, and have never done anything like it again.

Yet as natural and free as whole appears, influence of gardeners is subtly
evident. Large isles in main pond are parallel with lines of building. Islets
of upper pond form lines diagonal to building axis. Larger
islets divide pond up to form ideograph *kokoro* (heart) ➤
–including 'mind' and 'soul' in its concept. Smaller islets,
'nite mooring rocks', represent boats bound for Horai (paradise) sitting
at anchor. By side of path is flat-topped rock on which one squats cross-
legged to meditate upon this vision of heaven—flat slope eases sitting, as in
temple one is given seat-prop to angle you. Atmosphere hypnotizes...

suddenly seemingly from nowhere some ethereal cry, then answer from opposite side—deer calls. Deep *clok* noises you hear are water-powered seesaw **bamboo alarms** to scare deer from delicious moss.

Over 50 varieties of moss thrive in this red clay. Protected from wind, sunlight by hills. Always cool, damp. Claim evergreens block weed growth (gardeners take note). Several treasured **tea houses** dot grounds and as we exit, to R of gate, **garden of stone** and sand, *kare san-sui* (dry landscape) is oldest such in Japan—set like pungent dessert to this rich feast. Opposite **Dragon Well** has never gone dry even in worst droughts.

Ikeno Taiga museum [B-10] 10 min walk E from Saiho-ji. *Bunjinga*–literati painter (1723-'76) who nationalized Chinese dilettante tradition, prodigy at 6, influenced by Chinese art, Japanese masters, Western painting. He painted tall hanging scrolls, sliding panels in both sumi ink and colors, often with fingernails. 140 in collection, show 50 on monthly rotation. His works are also in Hondo attached to Ginkaku-ji . 10-4:30, X-wed, ¥450; ☎(075) 381-2832.

Katsura Rikyu Imperial Villa [C-11] (*see* TEA, p486) is 30min walk, poor bus connection by #33 or 69; S-E– or 15min walk to Kamikatsura stn Hankyu line (which starts at Arashiyama, stops Matsuo, continues on to Osaka-Kobe) thence one stop down to Katsura stn and 1km walk E; **permit** also needed from Gosho-Imperial Palace office—try for same day as Saiho-ji, you might get lucky, especially if you write from overseas. **Bus** from Katsura stn to **Kameoka** enables you to combine Hozu Rapids shoot as return from either these superb sights, ending day dining Arashiyama, summer see *ugai*, cormorant fishing.

On way back into town near Uzumasa stn or bus #11 *stop and walk 5-7min, is ...*
Movie Village [C-7] *Toei Uzumasa Eiga-mura*, last of several town-size movie set-ups that once made Kyoto Japan's film capital. Still turns out 4 feature films and some 300 TV shows annually–thus unlike Hollywood Universal, tourist can see actually production in progress, so *Quiet!* Studio for period pix, *chambara* swordplays thru early Meiji 'Victorians'. Modern soaps, cops'n robbers (as we saw) are shot at Ofuna outside Yokohama. Numerous outdoor sets from woodblock-print redlight area complete with girls at barred windows, to old bathhouse, feudal fire station and ancient Nihonbashi-bridge as it was when center of empire before overhead hiways turned it into tunnel. Also 19 indoor studios. Its new TV technology enables us visitors to make video in costume (Japanese video/TV system is same as US, but not Europe, UK) or be magically superimposed by computer onto ready-made clips–attracts 2.5 million fee-paying fans annually: ¥1,550, kids ¥700; Mar 15–Nov 15, 9–5, winter 9:30–4. Info ☎881-7716.

From town or Arashiyama: JR → Hanazono stn; or Keifuku tram → Uzumasa stn; or bus #11 from Arashiyama or #75 running btwn Myoshin-ji–Kyoto stn.

...as much in Japanese culture is colored with an ineradicable sadness –a nostalgia for a world, as if once known and lost where the solitary cricket or the lonely bird crying in the night is able to express more clearly than any voice of man the sum total of human understanding and disillusionment. — David Kidd, *The New Yorker*

UJI 宇治 *SOUTHEAST OUTSKIRTS*
MURASAKI'S TEA and PHOENIX

ISHIYAMA (Stone Mountain), our starting point for this second 10th century routing covering southern outskirts of Kyoto, noted for its temple, azaleas, giant fireflies, autumn moon. Lady Murasaki spent 8th full moon (September, Harvest Moon) 1007 here, which set her juices flowing to begin writing *Tale of Genji*. Her reputed room and writing brush are still in ISHIYAMA-DERA temple. String concert and classical dance commemorate this 'August Moon': **8th full moon**: Sept 11-12,'92; Sept 31-Oct 1,'93; Sept 20-21, '94; Oct 9-10,'95; Oct 17-18,'96; Sept 15-16,'97; Sept 3-4,'98; Sept 23-24'99; etc, free admission from 6pm, dances from 7pm, free *jiizake*-local sake; ☎(0775)-37-0013.

GETTING THERE: We start this Heian routing outside Kyoto working inward. You can work this in part on way in from NARA as alternate. *Or* from Kyoto en rte NARA in reverse. From **KYOTO**, Keihan electric from Sanjo Keihan (info booth has sched on Uji-Rhine **boats** for which train to Hama Ohtsu then 25min boat to temple); JR old main Tokaido line from Kyoto stn then bus to temple gate or cab; **taxi** Miyako Hotel-Ishiyama 10x-mtrs, +2-3x from downtown. Coming from (or going to) **NARA** you can join (or leave, after reversing) routing at BYODOIN PHOENIX HALL, bus upstream if you want to sail Uji-Rhine or see ISHIYAMA-DERA temple. *Or* link with BIWA LAKE OF LUTE route, which ends where this begins. **Drivers** from Tokyo-Nagoya use as alternate entry from Tokaido highway, sidetracking at SETA BRIDGE, Lake Biwa.

ISHIYAMA-DERA temple **[M-13]** founded 749 by Monk Roben for emperor Shomu in prayer for finding gold to gild Great Buddha—started nearby till casting failed, project moved to Nara. Preserves room with typical Heian bell-shaped window, where Lady Murasaki reputedly wrote several chapters of *Genji*–probable nearly contemporary reconstruction after fire of 1078–as well as such mementos as her inkslab. Elsewhere in temple deva kings in main gate by greatest of Japan's sculptors, Unkei (d.1223); *azekura* log-cabin storehouse is contemporary of Nara SHOSOIN, 1200-year-old naturally air-conditioned marvel (p.377); 4.8m/16-ft Kannon image, 1098 remake, itself but shrine housing within it chief object of worship of temple, 15cm/6-inch gilt-bronze Nyoirin-Kannon treasured by Shomu, and Roben's object of prayer, above—now shown only every 33rd year or upon enthronement of new emperor. Main hall has fine collection Buddhist sculpture. Fortunes cast here especially auspicious. *(See also p499)*.

Near temple humorous Otsu-e, polychrome satirical cartoon paintings, souvenirs sold to pilgrims to Hongan-ji temple formerly located here (now nr Kyoto JR Stn) are still reproduced by artists. ISHIBASHI Karaku has large shop **Karaku** directly in front of ISHIYAMA-DERA Temple. He imaginatively applies ancient illustrations to *noren* cotton curtain, towels, stationery, pottery, woodwork; revived *hyotan*-gourds for carrying water and wine, sells them, reasonable. Try your hand at painting on *raku-yaki* pottery for fun souvenir—fired and ready in 20min, most other kilns take o'nite.

Overnite stay, alternate stop is nearby spa of **NANGO**. Dine over water, see fishermen cast nets for your supper, enjoy bit of rapidly disappearing Japan of PR pix.

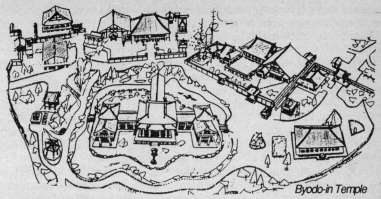

Byodo-in Temple

GETTING AROUND: From **NANGO** 20min **bus** along Uji riverbank, past TACHIKI-KANNON → SOTOHATA where resume **riverboat** service for 30min down-stream (40min up) between lovely cliffs, thru white water passages of Deer-Jump and Rice-Boiler Rocks, to **Uji Dam**. 30min on by bus is UJI, riverside resort once famed for firefly parties, still for its tea and **Phoenix Hall** (which is also stop on JTB full day Nara **bus tour**). Several inns, riverside restaurant, on-boat dining and summer cormorant fishing. Direct from **KYOTO** 15min by Keihan Uji line from Sanjo or Shijo to terminus Uji stn cross bridge → BYODOIN; or JR Nara line → Uji, in which case stop 2nd station earlier at Obaku stn either line for MAMPUKU-JI, *following*. Going on to NARA or coming from take only JR Uji-Nara line, 25min. **Bike rental** opp Keihan stn, many lovely sights around off hiway: tea plantations, pottery kiln in hills–get illustrated (J-) map at Tourist info. Midway stop on JTB Sunrise **Nara full day tour** out of Kyoto.

If entering from parking lot, go R and first L down alley to river, then L to enter front-on–parking lot entry comes in from unattractive backside...

PHOENIX-HALL [L-17], *Byodo-in*, reputedly built late 900s by Minamoto-no Toru, live prototype for Prince Genji of Murasaki's novel. 'The Lady of the Boat', seventh book of *Tale of Genji*, is set here. Area became favorite with nobles of Heian court 1,000 years ago, who built country villas here among earliest tea plantations. Converted to Buddhist temple by son of later owner Fujiwara Michinaga in 1053, other buildings were added over 2 decades. Main hall fully restored for 9th centennial, 1953. T'ang Chinese (7th-9th century) image of pavilions of Western Paradise takes its name, not from two rooftop phoenixes, but from appearance building gives of being itself in flight–of having been great bird in act of taking off when some strange power transformed it into garden pavilion. Perfect example of inseparability of garden and building.

Considered one of three masterpieces of Japanese architecture–but when Jay finally saw it after decade in Japan, was first entranced, then infuriated. As beautiful as it is, it is not architecture. It does not envelope space. Conversion to temple must have entailed rebuilding in present form for it is hard to believe anyone building villa for parties with two-foot tall ceilings. Unusable except for its central hall, now Buddha-image repository, graceful wings are stage props, one third scale of any usable rooms, barely two feet high inside. (Ladders of 30 years ago long removed). This doll's house exemplifies complete Japanization of foreign form–reduction to toy. Everything for appearance. Thus perhaps it is anti-architecture, subtle parody on emptiness of future promises (take cash, let credit go). It is not architecture, yet masterpiece it is—of sculpture. See it from across pond—'other shore', reflected in still waters. And, if possible, see at sunset for full *mono-no-aware*, mournful awareness of this period's poetry.

Within this outer sculptural shell is superb **Amida** Nyorai, principal image, sole known work of artist-priest Jocho, who perfected system of large carvings from multiple joined blocks, which when finished were coated in lacquer soaked hemp, then lacquered and gilded. Jocho also initiated Japanese style of sculpture, more feminine than Chinese. He sits on lotus of 64 petals–Taoist, not Buddhist numerology–each single plank mere 2cm at thickest, set one above other rather than in alternating 'fish scale' pattern. Above Amida's head are most delightful small sculptures found anywhere: **orchestra of apsaras** (angels) fluttering high on walls. They are also rare in being action figures–also originally brilliantly painted. Amida faces latticed doorway with round window to gaze on paradise. Auriole and ceiling canopy are finest examples of wood carving–canopy circle within square symbolizes heaven and earth, philosophical squared-circle which in west Asia evolves into Persian then Islamic dome. Door panels restorations (fading remains of original moved to treasury) of Japan's oldest *Yamato-e* – native style polychrome paintings as opposed to Chinese style.

Most old buildings are more beautiful now than they were when new, when they would have been gaudy–today's somber temples, like now-pristine Greek marble sculpture, were brightly painted in their heyday. But Byodoin must have been even more lovely with full makeup.

Elsewhere in garden, R/N near front gate, is...
Kannon Hall, pure bold Kamakura-era style, housing life-size, single-block Heian era 11-headed Kannon, flanked by Jizo and Fudo. L of Phoenix Hall is **belfry** with one of finest bells in Japan, 2m high, 3 tons, exquisite reliefs–copy...

Original in...
New **treasure house** above belfry, holds original roof phoenixes, door panels, bell etc; open twice yearly in spring and autumn (see KTO or TIC).

Flood wall now cuts pavilion off from river and former view. But Heian pleasures still pursued beyond wall and **Jun 15–end Aug** there is cormorant fishing and netting. Public boats charge ¥1,400 each, or you can get your own 10-passenger flat-bottom ¥17,000 or 40-man for pro-rata. Water muddied when dam opened rainy season, cancels fishing, safer after mid-July; better in Arashiyama. Agricultural chemicals have terminated firefly parties, but boat still plies to Asagawa Point, ¥10,000 for 10 person boat, 1hr. Net casting party with catch tempuraed on board, ¥30,000 for party of ten, after 3-4pm for abt 2hrs, May thru Oct. Tourist Info office outside Byodoin can arrange, or go direct to little house to R at river edge just before road ☎(0774)-21-2328, 23-3334.

CHOPSTICKS: BYODO-IN exit near river amid budget ryokan & restaurants is city-operated **Taiho-An** tea house serving formal **matcha tea & cakes**, for Uji is oldest center of tea cultivation in Japan and fields of tended 'hedges' you see are tea. At BYODOIN main gate **Koen Kikuya Bekkan**, good sukiyaki, chicken sukiyaki, ¥3,500-5,000; overnite ¥-T-stay only, ¥-hi-Tw/2. Upstream bit is concrete international-rank **Hanayashiki** on river edge ☎21-2126, ¥-Sw/2. **Seisanso** ☎21-2181 next to it has party platforms on river: dinner ¥6,000, overnite ¥-Tw/bkfst only, or ¥-B-Tw/2.
In shops nearby, lovely tea-picker **dolls** in folk costume. Don't pass up candy sour-balls made of green tea, naturally 'no sugar' sweet...with white streaks have sugar.

On river isle across red bridge near tourist info, is...
13 storey stone pagoda, 15m tall, built 1286 during great Kamakura era of Chinese (Mongol refugee) influx; collapsed in flood 1756, only dug out and reerected 1908.

For garden buffs, across river by bridge from isle to lovely thatch roof...
UJI **SHRINE** thence slightly on upstream (walkable or rental bike from Keihan Uji stn)...

KOSHO-JI temple with its Alice-in-Wonderland garden of geometric trimmed azalea bushes.

Walkable/bikeable 3km (**cab** under 2x-mtrs) or 2nd stn Keihan, or next on JR, from BYODOIN → OBAKU stns of Keihan Uji line or JR (18min Kyoto stn, 45 Nara), whence short walk → great Chinese Zen gate. Main reason for this offbeat stop is temple **garden restaurant**, mentioned in NARA–GOING ON (P.393) as delightful break en route Kyoto, best meal stop in area for Buddhist lunch, minimum 4, must rsv ☎(0774)-32-3900—or opp gate at **Haku-un-An** (White Cloud Retreat), any number guests, rsv not necessary except in blossom seasons, but advised, ☎31-8017; arrive, order meal, sightsee 20-60min—return for leisurely aesthete repast in lovely manse overlooking garden. Budgeteer can get by for ¥1,000 5-dish *shojin ryori* in garden of **Icho-An** to R of inner main gate, small door L corner of wall by red mat on bench; also various refreshments from milk, coffee to matcha & tea cakes; 10-5:30—advise rsve when you first arrive at temple, as settings limited, eat after seeing sights.

OBAKU MAMPUKU-JI [L-17] founded 1661 by Chinese priest Ingen as Ming Chinese style Zen temple–bit toned down, fewer curlicues on roofs than in China (for temple connoisseur, pure Ming style is branch Kofuku-ji, in Nagasaki). Entering never-shut great Sanmon gate **3** (¥300, get Japanese color map with *numbers*) straight on to **Ten-no-den 4** pavilion, enshrines main object of temple, **Hotei**, 'Laughing Buddha' of Lucky 7. Pennants outside list where other 6 enshrined in Kyoto area for pilgrimage of septet. Follow vestibule around to R, most main sights labeled in English, to **Daiyuhoden 8**, of imported Thai teakwood—with main image, along walls sitting in court are larger than life portrait statues of 18 Lohans, Ming style, obviously mostly Chinese, Central Asian and Indian. Note floors, no tatami, all Chinese black tiles. Whole more austere than usual, perhaps at first less attractive, different from what we've seen. Note priests' Chinese shoes, in deference to first several head abbots who were Chinese.

Zazen monthly first Sun 2-5pm; 'easy' sesshin first 5 days, all welcome, some English help available—if just sightseeing, observe silence when zazen in progress.

Fushimi Momoyama Castle skip, for tho site is ancient, buildings new, no value.

Train Keihan to Rokujizo stn, change to taxi 15min 2x-mtrs; or bus #21 30min (from Kyoto stn bus South-5, or from Shijo & Gojo Kawaramachi stns #8 or 9) to...
DAIGO SAMBOIN [L-14] boasts jewel of setting that has successfully inspired its builders—and rebuilders—since 874. DAIGO-JI great temple complex stretches few miles up mountainside; Samboin is one of its temples near bottom, thankfully, but in itself almost worth walking all way out here to see. In our historical itinerary it bridges Purple Period of Lady Murasaki and golden medieval. Enter down plain wide avenues lined by great white walls to superb, small, cypress-shingled gate with imperial 16-petal chrysanthemum crests. Up hill right of SAMBOIN is five-storey **pagoda**, national treasure, built 951, recently restored. Dimensions jewel-perfect, with interior T'ang Chinese paintings of Diamond Real Mandala and 8 patriarchs of Shingon sect.

Grounds of temple popular for **flower-viewing** parties in spring, maple and **moon-viewing** in autumn. Fame as partying place over centuries caused SAMBOIN itself to be erected here late 1700s. Tycoon Hideyoshi held one of his famous tea parties here–at which everyone who could make it was welcome and lords, warriors, merchants, farmers rubbed elbows, passed tea bowls; demonstrates essential democracy of Way of Tea. His most famous last cherry-viewing party is still reenacted by geisha **April**.

See DATEBOOK. **Spring & autumn** special opening of **Treasure house** with top collection paintings including panels from pagoda–manuscripts, decorative arts, sculpture in semi-annual revolving exhibits. See *KTO* or TIC for dates. Entry ¥500.

SAMBOIN itself built originally in 1115, mostly destroyed in Onin wars. Then Hideyoshi added main building and himself designed garden, one of most fascinating in Kyoto with little bit of everything, almost too much of some, yet maintaining moderation and balance. Difference in impressions from various angles is amazing: view from upper temple gives you elevation to look down on garden upon odd-shaped moss in foreground, angles of surrounding roofs and tremendous variation and mixture of texture–even in variegated roofs. Still HQ for Shugendo yamabushi mountain ascetics.

Painted **door panels** on way in startlingly 'modern' impressionistic, in textured golds. How gold could effect such muted, misty depths– technique of KANO Sanraku (d.1635) more than matches his medium. In **uppermost building**, temple proper, one room has elevated tatami for visits of imperial princes. Odd long window opening onto adjoining room on left is not to serve tea thru—bodyguards sat other side. With KANO Sanraku taste still in mind-mouth-toes, other paintings, modern ones by late DOMOTO Insho, look like wallpaper in comparison.

For adventurers, about 45min walk → Kami-Daigo, top, head temple for Yamabushi; lovely hiking route, posted, numerous small shrines, temples in hills: **GODAI-DO** one of best examples Momoyama architecture. **Hiking courses** cross over hills S → Uji 13 km, or N → Yotsuno-miya on Otsu-Kyoto electric. Few hundred mtr above Samboin pagoda is vale where refreshments are sold outdoors along creekside.

KANSHU-JI temple [L-13] Kyoto-wards of Daigo and first left, for garden buffs, has lovely, small 10th century garden.

Taxi–available DAIGO TEMPLE gate–straight W 6x-mtrs → Kyoto; 3x-mtrs or bus #7 roundabout; from town best is JR Nara line to 2nd stn Inari...

FUSHIMI INARI [I-12], grand shrine to 'fox god', Shinto deity of rice. Odd ethno-religious mixture–rice goddess is of south element in pre–historic Japanese culture, fox is north, Siberian element. Perhaps amalgam of two populations into Yayoi people, early Christian era. Fox is not god, but guard. Two lions guard most shrines and temples–here 2 foxes on job. Small Inari shrines common countrywide, easily identified by multiple red torii in front, so numerous as to form arbor. Here at Fushimi Inari, biggest shrine, are thousands, commonly pictured on tourist posters. Interesting fetes here so check DATEBOOK. Pilgrimage here especially popular with restaurateurs. You can have maiden kagura, for usual fee.

'Bar' fox holds in his mouth, is 'scroll of ultimate truth', *tora-maki*. *Tora* is ancient mystery word implying 'law', *maki* = scroll, thus tora[h]-scroll = ultimate law. Any idea?

From Fushimi 10min by Keihan electric → Sanjo or Shijo stns, or short taxi run.

On way into town is...(from town, JR or Keihan or buses #202, 207, 208)...

TOFUKU-JI [I-11], immense compound, Kyoto's first Zen temple (1236). Only passing interest, boasts no special architecture as early Zen had none. Zen gardens younger, but interesting, usually fairly free of crowds. **Reiun-in** sub-temple has miniature landscape garden–actually outdoor live *bonkei* (tray landscape) from Lady Murasaki era when such Chinoiserie was popular, set in large carved stone table resembling colonnade base. Fascinating room of wall paintings of Dante-esque aspects of hell. TOFUKU-JI also owns oldest Zen sumi (-ink) landscape by last of great Buddha painters CHO-densu (1352-1431) which with his 500 rakan, Buddhist enlightened ones, are shown only during annual summer airing. Big ceiling dragon modern, by DOMOTO Insho, perhaps only of his temple paintings worth surviving (see his museum near Ryoan-ji, p.470).

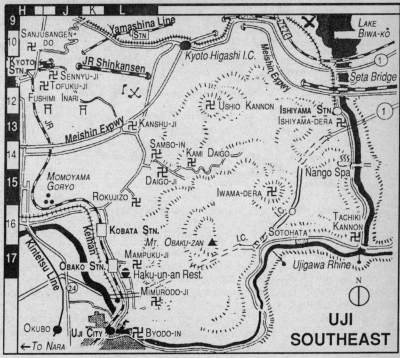

Great *Nehan-e* painting of Buddha Passing to Nirvana shown **March 15**, worth trip.
Behind TOFUKU-JI...we enlarge upon from old edition not as it has anything special
(beside exotic image) but for its air, once common to Kyoto temples but now, alas, so
rare in this era of mass tourism: Few visitors!...(500m from Keihan Tofukuji stn, or
buses #202, 207, 20).

Quiet stroll, thru many walled imperial tombs attached to...
SENNYU-JI [J-11] 'Temple of Bubbling Spring' reclusive Shingon
complex of 57 acres on site of former retreat of Kobo-daishi ca830AD. In
1218 complex built here as study for Shingon, Tendai, Jodo and Zen at
which time fresh water burst forth. In 1224 became place to offer Imperial
prayers and in 1242 emperor #87 Shijo was buried out back, then his father
Go-Horikawa and sometime later #108 Go-Mizuno-O thru #121 Komei,
plus many imperial relatives. (Imperial family until Shinto purge of 1867
was both Buddhist and Shinto). **Hall of Souls**, *Reimei-den*, houses 136
memorial tablets of emperors Tenchi (#38) thru Komei, last Kyoto resident.
Inner rooms are carpeted, with tables and chairs–Imperial family can not sit
on floor, even tatami. (Tokonoma originally raised dais for guest, double
height for royal).

Main art/adoration attraction is life-size image of Kannon *Yo-kihi-kannon*
Yang Guei-fei in *Yokihi-kannon-do* (bldg L foot of entry road nr [2nd] main
gate)–tragic princess of China T'ang dynasty, consort of emperor Hsuan-
tsung (846-859). As country girl in harem she soon caught his fancy, came to
dominate Court, appointing family to posts of power, ripping off treasury
until army rebelled, who spared emperor only on condition they execute her
(strangled with silk scarf). He commanded portrait statue of her as Kannon
be carved–odd person to memorialize as God(dess) of Mercy, but love
works odd effects even on emperors. Historically more Marie Antoinette

than Martyr. Statue was imported 1255 during great Sung retreat to Japan when so much else Chinese escaped from Mongol imperium. Perhaps Imelda Marcos will be thus remembered and someone import and enshrine her shoe closet. Entry ¥300.

We are now near SANJUSAN-GEN-DO (Hall of Thousand Buddhas) [I-10] at southern end of our RAMBLES NORTHEAST–GION–KIYOMIZU, *see* p488.

Or bus #202, 207, 208 due W (from Kyoto stn bus #17[N or S side] or S-side #71, 78; or from downtown #17, 18, 202, 207, 208) to...
TOJI [F-10] 'East Temple', with short lived West counterpart, Saiji, were guardians flanking gateway of capital main street on original city plan. As remnant it is grand for Kyoto, but modest on standards of Nara era when it was laid down, with only one pagoda which took century to build. Far more grand complexes were raised during Heian era–of 9-storey pagodas, halls as tall as Daibutsuden of Nara–but none survived wars. In 835 Toji was assigned to Kobo-daishi as his home monastery, and it stands today as relic of that era. Approach is unforgettable–to Jay, at least, who first saw it December 24, 1951 right after sunset, having been driven thru ruins of Osaka and over country road from port after 67 days on freighter at sea. It stood out in purple silhouette, smoke rising from open cooking fires of homes around, deep red traces fading from western horizon as night crept in. Driving into Kyoto today from Meishin hiway interchange past same corner always brings back sweet pang of nostalgia of that first Hiroshige-print sunset in Japan.

We are saddened at ugliness–to us–of Kyoto today, yet friends whose judgement we respect seem as much impressed by Kyoto at first view as were we then.

Pagoda is still grandest in Kyoto, standing in empty-feeling yard on wrong side of tracks midst industrial wasteland. Main hall stone-floored in Chinese style, anything but empty: statuary–Shingon tantric-demonic–notable, grand but lost in dull unlit interior. 5 *kokuzo* statues brought from China 847. Important paintings include large landscape screen of hermit visited by noble, rare early example of secular screen for Heian era imperial formal use; 12 Gods by SHOGA Takuma, 1191, earliest standing figure paintings as Shingon iconography now too physically complex to express in round sculpture–Goddess Gatten, doubly notable as in rare profile.

PERSONAL DATEBOOK: Monthly 21st grand flea market in honor of St Kobo, 1,000s of stalls, everything from potted plants to curios, second-hand kimonos, obis, *manto* capes. Go very early, especially summer to escape heat as well as to get good buys. Temple entry ¥400

What if my feeble legs move slow
like Paradise, the temple
is not far from here
— Zeami, 1363-1443

DECLINE, FALL & RENAISSANCE
1000-1500 AD (NORTHWEST)

LUXURIOUS DEGENERACY of which Lady Murasaki was already aware in 1000 eroded rapidly. There was fixation on paradise (as evidenced in gardens) and afterworld and, amazingly paralleling European frenzy, general expectation that 1052 AD (as in Europe, 1000) would be end of world –or at least of good material life, with fall into millennial Dark Age. This added to degeneration, general tenor of terror.

Great T'ang dynasty of China (once world power extending to borders of Persia and warring and trading directly with Arab Empire) was now in such decline that in 894 Japan saw no further gain in maintaining relations. Full Japanization of art and culture accelerated, foreign craftsmen no longer came over. Realism of China and Korea was humanized, then emotionalized. Soon latter element dominated, as we know from Murasaki.

In religion, Buddhism which had started by bringing such immediate, real benefits as salvation-now thru medicine and faith in one's own acts, became more metaphysical. Simple Buddhas were no more. Almost Tibetan-like pantheons of Shingon sect of Koya Monastery, of militant Tendai sect on Mount Hiei overlooking Kyoto, complicated belief and took it further from popular understanding.

Emotionalism dissolved into sentimentality. Science became superstition, medicine magic. Metaphysics became new unreality. Religious concepts were so complicated they could not be represented in sculpture and stress shifted to paintings, with sculptures appearing outside painting in support–as apsaras of Byodoin-Phoenix Hall. Belief involved costlier ritual afforded only by wealthy few, who became wealthier and fewer. Earthly paradise of Lady Murasaki was supported by slave economy, more and more concentrated in hands of Fujiwaras. There was great unrest and mass misery. For tax evasion, more land was transferred to gigantic religious foundations which soon became so powerful they challenged imperial authority. Buddhist time-cycle prophesied end of millennium of good, coming of darkness in 1052. And great monasteries obliged prophesy by warring with each other. Great temples were mutually sacked. Kyoto was periodically threatened.

Two great families rose to contend with Fujiwara for temporal power–Heiké aka Taira, and Genji alias Minamoto. Taira won out for while, from bases in Inland Sea where about 1150 they built their great vision of paradise on earth, MIYAJIMA, but soon succumbed to same genteel degeneracy. In 1185 power shifted to puritanical Minamoto warriors in their camp capital of Kamakura. They discarded religion which had become little more than incomprehensible mumbo-jumbo, turning inward to harsh self-analysis, self-discipline of Zen. Slave system collapsed and feudalism sprouted. Kyoto fell into decline as new establishment in Kamakura left it to wither on limb, paying token respect to papal emperor. Kyoto was like Byodo-in Phoenix Hall built at this time—grand central room of great beauty surrounded by exquisite structure that is but empty facade.

Mongols of Kublai Khan invaded in 1274 and 1281—as we shall see when we visit Kyushu. Japanese won pyrrhic victory which left them alone to enjoy ensuing peace of graveyard. Then when strength had been regained, various Kyoto and Kamakura factions resumed fighting. With two principal branches of imperial family contending for throne, branch families of Kamakura shoguns contending for puppet-mastery fought among each other and in alliance with various imperial factions.

One man emerged all-powerful: ASHIKAGA Takauji. Enters fray against one imperial claimant, emperor Go-Daigo, later switches sides to win throne for him and shogunate for himself. Then Go-Daigo showed inclination to rule and Ashikaga switched again forcing Go-Daigo to form court in exile. For 60 years, 1336-92, Japan had two imperial lines. Third Ashikaga, Yoshimitsu, finally brought peace by compromise in 1392, actually united nation along its present lines, then retired to his golden temple to make tea and meditate.

If all this sounds like sort of sport that went on in Europe in Renaissance (Crusades yet Notre Dame-Oxford, Inquisition yet Dante-Aquinas etc ad inf) you will be comforted to learn that Japan had, as fruit of all this political copulation and adultery, its own renaissance.

Ashikaga dynasty were shoguns for two and half centuries, returning power to Kyoto and creating glory of Ashikaga, alias Muromachi, epoch (1336-1573). This can still be seen today in Kinkaku-ji [E-4] (Golden Pavilion), Ginkaku-ji [K-6] (Silver Pavilion), great dry garden Zen temples of Ryoan-ji [D-5], Daitoku-ji [F/G-4] and others; and in architectural orgies that ended period, ushering in final forming of Japan in Momoyama (Peach Mount) interlude (1573-1613), Nishi Hongan-ji [G-10] temple-palace and Nijo Castle Palace [F/G-7].

It was era of both Spartan-simplicity and sumptuousness; of Zen ink paintings and multiroom murals on pure gold; stupendous monasteries, artist-sages rusticating in cottages; of now-forgotten ten-year war (that of Onin, 1467-77) ending as both sides in exhaustion and disgust just gave up, leaving Kyoto in ashes (note how our earlier period itineraries have been in suburbs), and of subsequent idealization of arts of peace which so impresses us today; of emulation and continuation of great Chinese traditions of Sung Dynasty (obliterated at home by Mongols, and subsequently considered 'Japanese'), and of birth of such native great arts as noh theater.

Just as 6th to 8th centuries had been period of importation, emulation and absorption followed by 9th thru 12th century flowering of native arts. So era of Kamakura power (13-14th centuries) saw import, Ashikaga-Muromachi was one of 'naturalization' of immigrant. Brilliant as this native flower is, it was again pollinated—perhaps grafted onto is better, for it had not withered and gone to seed as had Murasaki's Japan.

Century of new contact with Europe and simultaneous overseas adventures, invasions of Korea which brought back captive hordes of artists, especially potters, and of Okinawa which brought geisha and samisen, revived culture with dynamic immigrants.

Japan now becomes Japan we know from story book and picture book.

Alternative routing: while historically this chapter follows UJI, it is usually more convenient to combine KINKAKU-JI & RYOAN-JI with earlier chapter NINNA-JI p.452 etc —Ninna-ji to Ryoan-ji is one bus (#59) stop, or under 10min walk NE, thence on by #59 or #12 to KINKAKU-JI—midway perhaps see **Domoto Art Museum** (to L of bus stop Kinugasa).

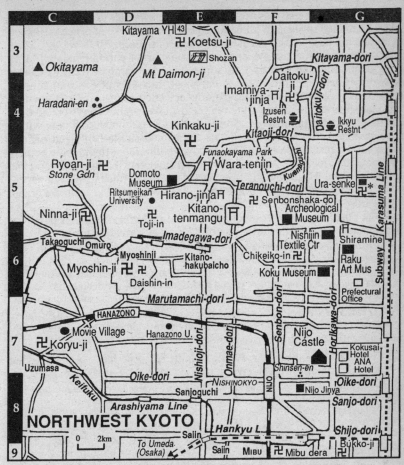

COTTAGE OF GOLD & GARDEN OF GRAVEL

ASHIKAGA shogun #3, Yoshimitsu, ended war (which Japanese also call *Namboku-cho*, or south-north war, suh) between two rival imperial courts by having factions take turns providing emperors—uncle to nephew or cousin rather than father to son—ended other regional fighting to bring peace to Japan for first time in at least century. Only 34, 2 years later, 1394, 'abdicated', gave shogunal baton to 10-year-old son, shaved his head and became monk.

Ritual of tea is both aesthetic worship, stimulating preliminary to meditation. Yoshimitsu built himself cozy little cottage in which to partake of beverage and arrange flowers, covered exterior with pure gold leaf.

Palatial temple it was attached to is no more but...(bus #12, 59, 204, 205), walk Kinkaku-ji → S-Domoto Art Museum → W-Ryoan-ji → SW-Ninna-ji temple—*or* from Arashiyama Keifuku rail to Omuro stn, N-Ninna-ji, reverse above. Walk 40min.

KINKAKU-JI [E-4] **Golden Pavilion** stands now in its quiet pond garden much as it did in his day. It was burned in 1950 (*see* novel *Golden Temple* by MISHIMA Yukio), recently rebuilt. Purists lament that shiny new place lacks great shibui charm of weathered original. But original wasn't least bit shibui in 1397, it was glittery, gaudy gold-leaf just as it is today—probably even more so as then it formed center piece of group of fabulous structures. Yoshimitsu was not one to battle fate and try to take it with him; he was satisfied to spend it all here. One technique to keep peace is to keep everyone too poor to fight. Yoshimitsu kept this peace.

Painting, religion, tax systems, tea-serving art of period emulated Ming China—painting so exactly that some Japanese painters went to China, where they were praised. Many 'Japanese' treasures of era are Chinese-made. Architecture was purely Japanese–eclectic perhaps, as Gold Pavilion with suggestively Chinese silhouette and Indian architectural bracketing: inside plain, of little interest. Something fascinating occurred now within bare, wooden floored room with its occasional single-bed sized padded straw *tatami* mat: these mats came to cover entire room floor, some corners sectioned off as alcove (*tokonoma*), all surrounded by hallway of wood and separated from it by sliding lattices pasted over with fine translucent paper–our traditional Japanese interior is born. Thus one sees that Japanese do not sit on floor, but walk on wall-to-wall bed. Lunar 7-7, *Tanabata-sai*, 1399, shogun Yoshimitsu held competition-exhibit by lords and monks of flower arrangements, which marked origin of *ikebana* as formal art form.

Tea served in Sekkatei teahouse atop hill beyond pond with seasonal yellow lilies. Japan sent half-scale reproduction Kinkaku-ji to 1910 San Francisco Exposition, designer of Palace of Legion of Honor Arthur Pope talked Japanese into presenting it to University of California which had no money to ship it to Berkeley, put it in storage and lost it for unpaid rent. Now reportedly Oriental restaurant Sho-fu-den near Delaware Water Gap.

CHOPSTICKS: just E of gate, Ungetsu for ¥15,000+ *kaiseki* light lunch. Kinkaku (written homonyms 'brocade crane') 100m S of gate, 11am–11pm, no-X, general J- ¥1,800 to top *kiji-nabe* pheasant dinner ¥4,000; ☎462-4949.

GINKAKU-JI [K-6] Silver Pavilion built 88 years later, is this era, but as on other side of town we cover it in CEREMONIAL SANDPILES, p489.

Midway between Ryoan-ji–Kinkaku-ji, 10min walk from either, or one bus stop from either just at Kinugasa bus stop, is interesting museum of contemporary art...
Domoto Art Museum [D-4] of works by traditionalist–modernist, late DOMOTO Insho (1891-1975). His Buddhist paintings grace pillars of main temple KOYA MONASTERY as we saw (tho have not aged well, as we predicted in '64 edition), Osaka's TENNO-JI as well as new Imperial Palace in Tokyo. (Jay hung small exhibit of his, first in USA, at Asia Institute, New York, in 1951). He was also pioneer modernist, designed this handsome functional building in 1964. Kept two separate studios for E-, W-styles. Son follows him, perhaps blending cultures more successfully, see his work in Guggenheim, NY.

RYOAN-JI *var*. Ryu-an-ji [D-5] Dragon-safe-temple (bus #12, 15, 26, 50, 51, 52, 55, 59) is home of that most enigmatic of gardens, totally–like dragon namesake–non-vegetarian 15 stones and trainload of white gravel. It's been likened to tennis court in size and proportion and to about everything else imaginable.

It is supreme Zen expression, being supreme enigma. Fifteen great black rocks are clustered so that from no angle may one ever see more than 14. It is said they represent tiger swimming with her cubs. We have never seen this, and we must both admit we have both seen strange things in staring at oil slicks, arabesque Persian carpets and beer foam.

Our elder son then four-years-old, however, was there with us once and chose photo postcard of garden and asked us to buy it for him.

"Why?" we asked.

"'Cause it's picture of tiger swimming with her babies".

Little child leads...Zen?

There are older *kare-san-sui* dry landscape gardens, oldest being in Moss Garden Temple. But they are rock in earth, in which moss or greenery grows. Ryu-an-ji is oldest purely non-organic garden and none after it match it. (It is often said, "You Occidentals may be puzzled by us Japanese calling plot of space in which nothing grows, garden" but as ones who have lived in those "Garden of Allah" deserts of Iran and American West, this is not at all puzzling). Rock garden impresses some, eliciting "oohs", "ahs". Others see it and leave. We are in latter group. But we must admit, other gardens we have seen and loved at first sight, yet later tired of. This one we could live with.

No one knows who made it–names are suggested but men behind these names are unknown. Plausible theory has it (Ernst von Harriga's, who died before his book on garden was finished) that it must have been made by Chinese from west China, where such gardens seem to have existed: that its conception is too implicitly grand to have been Japanese. Farside wall is later, Japanesely restrictive, addition–garden formerly bridged viewer and view of grand and ancient (Heian) pond-garden across road. Fosco Maraini in *Meeting with Japan* states that Japanese do not care for views or vistas. Admittedly they don't now, but they certainly did until such as RYOAN-JI and several DAITOKU-JI gardens were walled in during Tokugawa seclusion –symptom of general restrictions against broad viewpoints and flights of imagination.

'Gravel-pit' has been duplicated in Brooklyn Botanical Garden.

Tips: *Warning* garden after 10am contains more tourists than gravel so go early, open 8am. Monks wake up at dawn, if gate is locked bang hard, they just might open up for real garden bug, in which case bow. Don't miss miniscule moss garden at far end. Contrast of seeing Ryoan-ji & Kinkaku-ji (open 9am) one after other is ideal, in either order.

CHOPSTICKS: Zen temple light lunch of yudofu ¥1,700 or full feast of Shojin Ryori ¥3,000 in Seigenin annex of Ryoan-ji, ☎462-4742, below near main bus road.

Near Ryoan-ji is NINNA-JI (see PURPLE route preceeding, p452); also...
TOJI-IN (D-5–not to be confused with downtown TOJI, F-10) with its romantically decrepit Ashikagawa era garden, housing several portrait statues of Ashikaga shoguns, including those of Takauji (and his grave), Yoshimitsu builder of Gold Pavilion, and Yoshimasa of Silver Pavilion.

Bus #59 for Ryoan-ji from town (also #1, 9, 12, 61, 67) along Kitaoji street past Kinkaku-ji midway, runs (3km, 30-40min walk) in front of main S gate of...
DAITOKU-JI [F-4] Zen monastery complex, tho reconstructed at various eras, preserves original structure of 13th to 16th century buildings (Kamakura has better), themselves identical reproductions of Chinese originals by Chinese architects or by Japanese sent to south China to study. Gardens are post-Ryoan-ji and most of treasured paintings are 16th-17th century. **Hatto** is pure 12th century Sung-style Chinese worship hall in 17th century incarnation–stone floor and extreme inside height, raised pulpit. Black ink dragon in round ceiling is standard for such Zen monastic halls.

Numerous dry gardens–noted on Daitoku-ji plan–but of special note are:
DAISEN-IN, most famous of all, is considered by many "perfect piece of art", three dimensional 'painting' that is "finest piece of landscape gardening in Japan". Probably by painter Soami (d.1525) who did some of panel painting originals, of which these are copies only. Garden would fit in good-size living room and it is squeezed into what is certainly far too crowded space. To us, it is bit too perfect, too precious. It impresses better

than Ryoan-ji at first acquaintance, but where Ryoan-ji grows on one, Daisen-in palls. Then again, this feeling may be due to general mood of Daisen-in, which sickens us with its cheap huckstering–only lacks bald *bonze* barker out front chattering "come on in, enlightenment begins in 7 minutes, folks, only ¥500 per satori, two for ¥950, children half price...go away little boy ya bother me..." And we are annoyed at priest's insistence that panel paintings are originals, when they are quite obviously cheap substitutes for treasures long ago moved to museums–very cheap, as pine needles are all painted backwards, whereas painter's brush-stroke should flow to follow nature.

Matcha and cake available ¥250 in small room behind desk, *bento* can be ordered in advance for groups.

To see what real thing looks like, go–with some luck–next door to...
SHINJU-AN, not open to circus, but which one may visit on VIP official, non-commercial tour, or special publicised seasonal openings–and just maybe if you enter gate call politely and with humble sincerity say you wish to see treasured paintings...please.

After Daisen-in, Shinju-an is like coming out of dry of desert to cool mountain brook. Paintings on sliding fusuma panels are electrifying in their simplicity. We too, prefer simple garden here, its backdrop of imperial-style ornate gate with its eerie feeling of opening (it is closed) upon nowhere.

HOSHUN-IN has Chinese two-storey palace-style pavilion (enter and ascend) of unknown antiquity surrounded by 17th century garden of rich foliage. High-arched, roofed bridge across garden pond to pavilion is vision out of our childhood chinoiserie tales of Marco Polo.

KOHO-AN at far west has photogenic little tea garden off room with peculiar sliding shoji, top and bottom halves separate and bottom is usually opened, top left closed for viewing aspect of garden most conducive to introspection. Blending of room and garden are superb.

All these temples and their gardens are open to public upon payment of fixed donation, usually ¥300-500, **except** SHINJU-AN & KOHO-AN, which are closed except at discretion of whoever answers your call, if anyone deigrs answer at all. Often visit on special tours; for special **seasonal openings** enquire TIC, or see *KVG, KTO*.

Just stroll alleys of great complex without entering temples themselves, roof lines appearing over white walls like paradise palaces in mist of Yamato-e painting. Walls are low, peak over. And on path pass eager monks, their eyes intent slits, and even more eager American students of oriental philosophy, their intense eyes popping. If you see anyone with eyeballs dangling against his cheek-bones, lithp *"Auf Wiedersehen"*.

Zen Restaurant, Izu-sen in DAIJI-IN sub-temple, excellent. Choose mid-range table d'hote menu unless voracious appetite; portions not Zen frugal. *See* CHOPSTICKS.

Zen Meditation, most temples but by introduction only; for non-J-spkg beginners English instruction in RYOSEN-AN sub-temple, most latter part of week 7–8:30AM, arrive earlier, free but donation proper: sit, clean up, drink tea; rsv ☎491-0543.

...or same bus S/E, or 15min walk past Ninna-ji brings us near...#8, 10, 26, 91.
MYOSHIN-JI [D-6] another great Zen complex, not commercialized like Daitoku-ji, tho both are same Rinzai sect. Contains several fine gardens, perhaps not as spectacular as Daitoku-ji, some fine architecture and numerous masterpieces of painted wall panels, hanging scrolls. While not one of *Gosan*, five main temples of Zen, it is by far largest and most complete of principal Zen foundations. Tho most closed off to public (doesn't need tourism income as has several thousand dependent temples), monks have been and can be most receptive and generous to visitors.

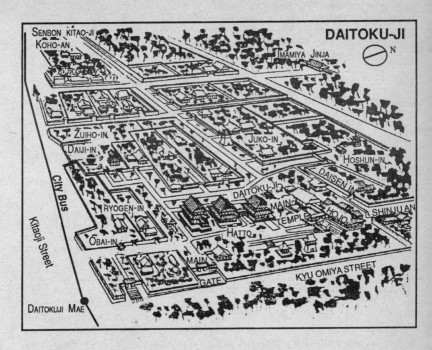

Recommended way thru maze is to present self at temple office (*jimu-sho*), preferably with interpreter tho they have English leaflet, and ask to be allowed to look around.

TAIZO-IN is one of few open temples, noted for its superb landscape-painting garden–garden modeled on painting modeled on garden– reputedly by painter KANO Motonobu (1476-1559) as part of rebuilding after destruction of Onin war. To be viewed from varying angles, but highlight of this dry garden of textured rockery and greenery, is dry waterfall of flatshale rocks feeding gravel pool, with natural rock bridges. Other rock formations signify mystical Isles of Horai-paradise, and crane islets.

Other gardens occasionally accessible include...

REIUN-IN, former emperor Go-Nara's hermitage (ca1544), its once-imperial status so marked by five horizontal white lines along length of clay wall backing dry garden.

GYOKUHO-IN built 1335 for emperor Hanazono to meditate, later pattern-raked gravel is pure mid-Edo 1720 geometry—tho seemingly as if swept by Modigliani.

SERMON HALL, *Hatto*, 1656, similar to that of Daitoku-ji, with ceiling dragon 10m/42ft across by KANO Tanyu; *Hojo*, **bishop's quarters** 1290, not used so now, with magnificent wall panels by Tanyu; *Kuri*, immense **kitchen** (ca1289) with 11m/45ft-high rafters, under which 500 monks can sit at one time at truly monastic wooden tables.

Old **Saturday** Zen group, formerly under tutelage of late-great Dr Hisamatsu, still meet here for lecture-sitting, overnite sat 5pm–sun am, or 2nd sun 2:00-3:30pm sit then 30min talk; abt 10-15th monthly sit 3 days; ☎463-3121, free; much of international activitylessness of yore has since moved out of tourist belt to **SOGEN-JI** in Okayama (*see* HANSHIN-WEST, p.628).

474

Lo! now the day of mingled life is come
The high cathedral chimes, the temple drum
The minster organ, the pagoda bells,
Unto each other shall no more be dumb.
  —Arthur Davidson Ficke, *The Earth Passion*, 1908

BELLS, DRUMS & MARRYING MONKS (SOUTH-CENTRAL)

ZEN WAS NOT sole religious movement of medieval era. It was restricted to warrior and court classes and, readily adaptable to ritual of artistic creation, attracted many artists to its discipline. It demanded too much to be popular–tho today sect claims more adherents than any other. Religion of Zen and cult of Zen technique must be differentiated.

Older Buddhist sects–Shingon (Mt Koya), Tendai (Mt Hiei), Hosso and others that have all but died out–complicated enough at first, become almost incomprehensible by 1200. Coming out of Tendai sect Saints **Honen** (1133-1212) and his chief disciple **Shinran** (1173-1262) adopt comprehensible promises of western garden paradise, Jo-do, which bears striking similarity to Judeo-Christian heaven. Path was neither that mystic mass of formulae of Shingon, nor highly select acts of some of earlier sects, nor harsh self-discipline to attain end of total nothing as in Zen. It is path of simple faith with all religious learning, ritual and formula rolled into memorization and recital of one simple formula, incessant repeating *"Namu Amida Butsu"*, holy name of Buddha of personal salvation (he of great statue at Kamakura). Honen established Jodo sect at CHION-IN (*see* RAMBLES NORTHEAST, following). Shinran started his Jodo shin-shu ('new sect') at HON-GAN-JI which was first built on road to Otsu and later moved downtown, then split into East- and West-. Stressed 'naturalness', abolished celibacy, allowed clergy to marry.

This stress on naturalness has had some interesting sidelights in history. Jodo-shinshu, also called 'Hongan-ji' or 'Shin', has fostered independent spirit. Its followers established renaissance-like city-state at Osaka in 15-16th Christian Century, run by cultured, enlightened merchants who traded with Southeast Asia and welcomed European ships. They successfully held warlords at bay, even Oda Nobunaga who conquered everyone else. Next dictator, Taiko Hideyoshi, bought them out and built his main castle on site of merchant fort. Osaka has been chief mercantile center since. To control Hongan-ji, it has since been rule to marry imperial princess to its 'pope', thus putting state in official position of nagging mother-in-law. Before World War II government declared sons of Dai-Nippon killed fighting in China for glory of emperor who were Shinto would immediately become *kami* (gods), while Buddhists would become Buddhas without having to be reborn or earn salvation otherwise. Most religious leaders acceded. Nishi Hongan-ji leader immediately announced that those killed in action could indeed become Buddhas—assuming they fulfilled all other prerequisites as well, that 'naturalness' which presupposed good living, kindness, and basic tenet of Buddhism, non-violence especially non-killing. Militarists purged him. Hardworking Japanese pioneer immigrants to USA were predominantly Jodo-shinshu, tho many America-born offspring have become Christian, more recently Zen or Nichiren. Most American Buddhist temples are Shin—thus Hongan-jis have good English guides.

Nichiren (1222-1282) was another reformer, but out of Shingon sect. We met him in Kamakura, his main sphere of action. Like Shinran he was national 'protestant', advocated salvation thru simple faith as in recitation of formula *"namu myo ho renge kyo"* (oh scripture of lotus of wonderful law) referring to ancient scripture not otherwise required for layman to learn. He built no great temples in Kyoto, is associated with Kamakura, Hommyo-ji at Ikegami between Tokyo–Yokohama (fantastic fall festival Oct 12), and Fukuoka in Kyushu where he claims credit for having summoned typhoon kamikaze which destroyed invading Mongol fleet. Was caustically critical of all other Buddhist 'mumbo-jumbo' to verging on intolerance. Modern offshoot of Nichiren-shu is 'true Nichiren', politically militant Soka Gakkai. Local Nichiren temples or pilgrims can easily be distinguished by ubiquitous tambourine-drum being struck to make syncopating rhythm of chant *namu myo ho renge kyo*, often accompanied by side-man on silver bell.

As Ashikaga shoguns succumbed to grand life in their gold and silver pavilions, daimyo ('great names' or warlords) resumed playing musical chairs with thrones of shogun and emperor. When 13th Ashikaga shogun died in 1565, number 14 and all heirs were assassinated down list until checkmarks stopped at agile young priest who ducked. He reached safety with young daimyo Oda Nobunaga who eliminated all opposition, including powerful Tendai monastery on Mount Hiei which he sacked and put to torch, sword in 1571. Then shogun Ashikaga Yoshiaki made same mistake that had put his family into shogunal dignity in first place (when emperor Go-Daigo thought Ashikaga Takauji getting too forward, p.468). He tried to eliminate Nobunaga, who then turned around and very graciously allowed Yoshiaki to reshave his head and return to his priestly meditations. Monk died in bed in 1598, outliving two successors Nobunaga and Hideyoshi. Nobunaga—who, not of Minamoto-imperial descent, could not be Shogun —now ruled by imperial fiat as Regent, *Kwampaku*.

Three key political leaders of this Christian Century were ODA Nobunaga (1534-82), minor noble, somewhat of medieval black-leather jacket type; and his two lieutenants: TOYOTOMI Hideyoshi (1536-98), warrior-farmer started out with stolen suit of armor made it to top on sheer ability; and TOKUGAWA Ieyasu (1542-1616), scion of great house descended of Minamoto Shoguns. Their personalities as those of epochs each dominated are shown in popular story which has on eve of battle each in his own tent, awaiting nightingale's evening serenade.

Concert is late. Impetuous Oda Nobunaga roars, "If nightingale does not sing, I will kill it...." Hideyoshi in his grand tent grits, "If nightingale does not sing, I will teach it....". While wily Tokugawa reflects, "If nightingale does not sing...I shall wait".

Nobunaga killed off most opposition, almost united Japan before he was murdered by trusted general 1582. First Europeans arrived off Kyushu 1542; Saint Francis Xavier landed 1549, came to Kyoto to see emperor and convert him, but Ashikaga in progress of collapse and no one was seeing anyone. Nagasaki (p.732), made international port in 1565 to handle expanded trade and contacts, flourishing by time Nobunaga gained control. He got along well with Christians (in this case, Nobunaga waited, Hideyoshi 'taught' and Tokugawa killed)—perhaps he favored their potential opposition to Buddhist temple armies, Buddhism in general; wanted technology they brought in, built first true castle in Japan (previous were just hilltop stockades) at Azuchi near Biwa 1573, using Jesuit design modified for local materials—no longer exists. In four decades some 2,000 more were built, greatest being

Osaka by Hideyoshi 1585, Edo by Tokugawa after 1600, and Himeji earlier than either. Only Himeji remains complete, original (*see* p618).

After Nobunaga's death and further musical chairs, 'peasant' Hideyoshi, succeeded to total power. Also not Minamoto descent, he took title *Tai-kun,* 'Great Prince'. Nobunaga had extravagant tastes in art. Hideyoshi gave his artists and builders even greater reign and Tokugawa brought all to technical perfection (as in Nijo Palace p479)–for several decades of most explosively flamboyant art Japan, if not Far East, had ever seen or was to see again.

HONGAN-JIs EAST AND WEST COUSINS

POLITICAL and family rifts split powerful Hongan-ji sect into two in 1602 so that today there are two great cathedrals of same name in Kyoto, as in most every town. Boulevard in front of Kyoto Stn leading to town passes on L great gates of junior (East) Hongan-ji. (**Bus #4, 5, 14, 26, 52, 73**).

HIGASHI–EAST HONGAN-JI [G-10]: present structures are recent (1895), originals burned in 1864 when rebel samurai from Choshu (now Yamaguchi W of Hiroshima) tried to kidnap emperor Komei, Meiji's father. Popular building subscription raised million yen when yen was silver dollar. More donated in kind included most timber by peasants and workers who could thus better give of selves, of own skills. Pillars and beams were raised by 29 gigantic hawsers of hair donated
by women, one of which is displayed. Continuing strength of Shin sect is reflected in quiet power, immensity of structures. Main hall ()L alone is just short of one New York City block, equivalent 13-storey height, contains 96 great pillars and 175,967 roof tiles. Mirror-bright wood floors get that way from several times per day polishing with wet cloth by devout volunteers, often seen.

Pleasant few-minute stroll. Friendly photogenic pigeons deserve fame of Venice Saint Mark's. Emerald-green summer lotus in moat challenges color film, dew drops like jewels. Great main porch is one of coolest spots in Kyoto in summer, kept hospital-shiny by woman volunteers. Five horizontal lines on outer walls, imperial 16-petal chrysanthemum boss on gates, proclaim patronage of imperial-in-law as head traditionally weds princess.

Garden buffs ask to see *Kikoku-tei* Fujiwara era **garden**, in east annex across plaza. Streets nearby make for pleasant strolling, lined with shops catering to pilgrims, selling religious articles, old & new. Many ¥-P ryokan.

NISHI–WEST HONGAN-JI [F-10]: block W behind Higashi Hongan-ji, smaller, but no less impressive scale than younger Higashi. Not visited by tours: buses unload at Higashi but only buzz Nishi (behind, dummy **spirit wall** of Chinese custom blocks view in from street). We passed it by ourselves for many years, and since discovering it consider it most rewarding sight in Kyoto. Built 1591 on land grant from Hideyoshi, burned 1617, present structure rebuilt 1657 with portions moved from Momoyama palace. In three parts. (**1**) Front *open to public* worship area similar to Higashi Hongan-ji. L is larger *Goei-do* **Founder's Hall**; R *Amida-do* **Hall of Amida**, its **nave** of plain *keyaki* (zelkova) wood, each side of chancel is great chamber with gilt pillars and walls on which hang centuries-old gold-on-blue invocations—ornateness speaks as much of power as of devotion.

(**2**) But for true view of power generated by that devotion, for picture of grandeur of Christian Century Japan that impressed Europe, go to left end of front buildings into office. Enter now only 6x monthly, much reduced by need to preserve paintings, all of which are real, none restorations: write from o'seas encl self-addressed envelope to home, or reserved-hotel/inn in Kyoto, or in Japan use double return postcard, address Nishi Honganji Sanpai Kyoku, Higashi Nakasuji Rokujo-sagaru, Shimo

ask for *Sanpai Kyoku* ☎371-5181, FAX 371-3080 to see when open and if room for you, (English guide sometimes available on prior request); or if in temple just head for office far left, hope for best, ask if any group entering today with room for you.

State Apartments are marvel of Momoyama era. Originally not temple buildings, but palace (tho one major guidebook calls them "superb example of Buddhist architecture... finest..."), transferred from stupendous palace-castles of great Tycoon Hideyoshi who led nation during flamboyant Momoyama Era. On Hideyoshi's death (as on Nobunaga's) his castles and palaces were dismantled. Palace, given to Nishi Hongan-ji, reassembled for priestly use is preserved today behind temple proper...

We enter thru *Daidokoro-mon* (kitchen gate), past *Imperial Messenger Gate* brought from Momoyama Castle and *Higurashi-mon* which name means that it would take full day to look at all detail in foyer paintings and carvings. Only daimyo who ruled fiefs worth 1,000,000 koku used this gate (*Koku* is measure of rice approximating one man's yearly ration, also land to grow it on). Carving, like much else in palace, was done by Hidari ('Lefty') Jingoro, famed for his sleeping cat and three monkeys at Nikko.

Then we enter...
Tsuru-no-ma (Stork Chamber), **throne room** of Momoyama Castle, now used for fortnitely sermons by chief abbot. Every bit of wall and ceiling space is painted. Audience of lords squatted in lower section which measures 162 mats (each mat, 90x180cm/3x6ft or equal to single bed which is what tatami mat was originally). Taiko Hideyoshi sat upon slightly raised dais, tokonoma behind him and to his left another raised dais in semi-partitioned room in which imperial proxy sat, as in gilded cage.

Walls are painted in Chinese Sung palace style, subjects from Chinese history–but low matted rooms are purely Japanese (Chinese would have had high ceilings and throne on tall pedestal), as is adaptation of paintings to architecture. Whole esthetic is Japanese, manner developed by Kano Eitoku (1543-90). Massive use of gold-foil background suggested as system of lighting, adding reflective surfaces to oil lamp illumination.

Far left wall has fantastic painting of gigantic pine tree, smaller maples, peonies, numerous birds spread over 2 sets of doors (one set being 6 doors, 90cm/3ft wide by 1.8m/6ft high)–common enough treatment, except it continues on above doors onto upper wall. Beyond these doors are three anterooms: *Suzume-no-ma* (Sparrow Chamber), *Gan-no-ma* (Wild Geese room) and *Kiku-no-ma* (Chrysanthemum) for lords of different rank, thus no one lord would see two rooms. **Ranma** (open woodwork transom between rooms) of wild geese align with moon painting in next Chrysanthemum Room so that from proper squatting position you see geese silhouetted against full moon. And rank of next room is as far from you as moon.

In other rooms painting continues around walls, broken here by window or shelf, jumping outcropping to continue on in tokonoma, or inside closets —then suddenly it will be broken as if by accident by series of small panel doors painted in completely different style and subject. Yet it does not clash or confuse. Tho tokonoma walls were painted with ornate scenery, one could and did hang another painting over part of mural. Final rooms not always shown, being inferior in style as originally meant only for formal reception by Hideyoshi of former enemies whose heads were brought him to verify deaths—not reconcilable with present use as Buddhist temple.

Of two **stages for noh** plays (Ashikaga development) in yards off palace rooms, rear one off Bamboo Room, is from Momoyama Castle, oldest and finest in Japan. (Special performances 1 pm, May 21.) Bamboo are painted with geometric perspective, under European influence, by

MARUYAMA Osui (late 18th century), son of Okyo. Room after room amazes, but what we remember best is outside Chamber of Wild Geese—wooden panel door of great flower cart. *Kokei-no-niwa*, Tiger-vale dry garden, was also transferred from Hideyoshi's Juraku Palace: its sago palms imported from southern climes by Momoyama era roving merchants show era's love for foreign and exotic. Many lords at this time wore Japanese Kimono of French brocade mixed with Chinese and Japanese materials, and great Flemish ruffle collars.

Next building over is...
Kuro-shoin, named for its use of polished *black* wood. It was built for private use in 1656, after Momoyama flair had fizzled. Its elegant simplicity contrasts with barbaric splendor of *white* **Shiro-shoin**. Its "high finish is so cunningly matched by naturalness that one has almost the sense of being in a different world, where nature of herself takes purer and clearer forms". Many painted panels are by KANO Eitoku.

(3) HI-UN-KAKU (Flying Cloud Pavilion), Hideyoshi's answer to Gold & Silver Pavilions: (**Special permit** necessary, infrequently granted, apply from o'seas) In style known as *sukiya*, literally 'artless', this three-storey rambling garden cottage is also from Juraku-dai, Hideyoshi's great Kyoto palace (Momoyama Castle was in Fushimi where now is plaster playland castle). Restraint of Hiun-kaku is product of discipline of tea, to which Hideyoshi was addicted. (He rebuilt Sambo-in, p463, for grand party, met with SEN Rikyu in tiny cottage for more personal party). Hiun-kaku originally sat in middle of lake, it is suggested for defense. In one upstairs room is gold-paper sketch called Fuji of Good Manners, its delicate outlines can barely be distinguished except from respectful kneeling position. Downstairs is lord's bathroom, not hot tub as today but older-form steam bath, like sauna.

Exit by one of 3 Momoyama style south gates; stroll old alleys to recapture past, interplay of planes of walls, finely carved gilt **kara-mon** (Chinese gate, NT); along moat, photogenic lonely **drum tower** by canal (NE corner). Alas, August moat no longer full of lotus with diamond dew-drops, we'd go at dawn to listen to blossoms pop open.

SHIMABARA is famous old red light district behind, west, of Nishi Hongan-ji. It served acolytes and pilgrims of HONGAN-JI, 'naturally'. Its *tayu* have long been famous for their fabulous brocade costumes—in recent years things have been up in air what with the anti-prostitution law and no one quite sure just where geisha ends and older profession begins and young gals preferring to become bar hostesses anyway. One grand old courtesan house stands amid shabbier recent bordellos and middle-aged middle-sized places. Quarter is still walled and approach is dramatic jog thru kara-mon on which US Army Medics' faded 'VD' warnings could long be seen, but no more. Aah, progress. **Apr 21**, *usually*, gala costume procession.

Sumi-ya is aged-red, once of near-Heian Shrine brilliancy. Pass thru courtyard to grand old inner building. Room at top of stairs shows sword marks in posts from fighting of imperial restoration, about 1867. **Brocade Room** is papered with imported Spanish brocades. Elsewhere, note Dutch glass. MARUYAMA Okyo did horsey room (which it seems every men's club has to have), where great tokonoma was for VIP guests to sit in. Long room is *kashi-no-ki*, **face showing room**, where girls in fabulous silks paraded before clients for selection–if she was popular enough she did selecting. Even now it's exclusive: dinner party ¥40,000 per person, geisha 50-60% extra, by introduction of known customer or 'member' only (or major agent). Even in run-down state Sumi-ya impresses, brings block prints to life. **Nite bus tours** N, NS 6-9pm, *see*, visit for tea ceremony or dinner, special oiran show *kashi-no-ki* line-up–but don't handle goods, boys, photos only. Geisha parties are still held here in great attached garden room (*see* above) which was long-ago photographed for *House Beautiful* (*see* How To GET YOUR GEISHA). Don't confuse with noted ryokan **Sumiya**.

Dec 25 rice-pounding ritual mid-morn, *taiyu* (now movie, stage celebs in costumes) entertain for charity. Down street from Sumi-ya, resume in old house after repairs, 1990.

If you didn't see TOJI en route up from Uji, it's 15min walk S (under tracks) or minimum taxi from here.

NIJO CASTLE [F-7] Ieyasu's answer to Juraku-dai and Momoyama Castle of Hideyoshi. After death of Hideyoshi and demise of his line, long-waiting Ieyasu gained control, finished uniting country and, being of true Minamoto descendant, took for himself and his line both job and title of Shogun. Then he moved to Edo, built Nijo as rest house for Kyoto visits over previous Imperial Palace foundation. Ieyasu's grandson, 3rd shogun, Iemitsu (who built Nikko as mausoleum for grandpa and sealed off nation), expanded Nijo into well-defended castle. Both builders modeled most of their ideas on Hideyoshi's fabulous palaces, transferring and reusing much of his actual palace of Juraku-dai. Nijo burned 1750 and 1788, lay in ruins until 1868 then suffered further ruin being used as municipal office with memos and calendars tacked to painted panels. Restored 1939, remaining pavilions of Juraku-dai Palace were transferred from Fushimi site to Nijo.

Cross moat at...

Great East Hand Gate, *Dai-Higashi-Ote-mon*, bridge into **castle court** and wind around this traditional defense entrance thru 'Chinese' *Kara-mon*, into grounds of **Outer Castle**, *Ni-no-maru*. This is larger version of state apartments of Nishi Hongan-ji, while more imposing from outside due to expansive garden setting, is far inferior within–in fact, obvious imitation. Special occasions, great palace rooms brought to life with excellent life-like dummies dressed in clothes of era (check TIC).

Inner Castle predominantly defensive, entered across inner moat, also boasts large **inner garden**. NIJO famous for **nightingale floorboards** which when walked on squeak like nightingale cry, said to be alarm system to foil assassins. Nishi Hongan-ji has, as do many temples–we have been told it's not special built-in feature but result of wood aging, is in fact fire hazard (friction on dry wood). Sumi's century-old ancestral simple farm house near Hiroshima had it–embarrassing to guests going to toilet middle of nite. We have tried to check out both stories–choose which you like.

Enter 8:30-4, ¥450, 35min suggested minimal. Refreshment stalls in garden.

SHINSEN-EN [F-7] Garden of Sacred Springs, built by first Kyoto emperor Kwamu 794 to S of his then palace. Little remains of grand 16,000m^2 Chinese park-garden 16X size of present, with large T'ang type pond in which dragon reputedly lived. HEIAN JINGU garden replicates it. For garden buffs. **Datebook** *Nembutsu-kyogen* (ICA) **May 1–4**.

NIJO-JINYA [F-7], S of Shinsen-en: NIJO, above was castle-palace of sho-gun, so this is fortified castle-hostel for daimyo visiting shogun 2 blocks N. 20-odd rooms in casual sukiya style, with both strict security arrangements and reserved-opulence and successfully fire-proofed with hi-tech of time.

Kasuga-no-ma room off garden decorated with mural of scenes of Kasuga area of Nara, and garden has Kasuga type lanterns. **Onoh-no-ma** is large tatami room in which mats can be raised to reveal hardwood floor for acoustically-true noh stage. Hidden ladderways in halls, **Kainyo-an** tea room has secret door. Ogawas still own it, rsvtn required ☎841-0972 or reply-prepaid postcard ✍ NIJO-JINYA, 137 Oike Sagaru Omiya-dori, Nakagyo-ku, Kyoto 604.

*To reduce material desires does not always
bring peace of mind. In order to live in peace
spiritual desires must also be reduced.*
— Akutagawa Ryunosuke, *Kappa*, 1927

TEA TIME お茶
REACTIONS (NORTH)

GRAND PALACES of Azuchi-Momoyama era (1573-1613) emulate China's grand manner of decor, its long-dead Sung (960-1280) Dynasty styles. Gold painting was Sung, as also high-vertical colored landscapes (called today *nan-ga*, southern paintings); but so were black ink sketches, *sumi-e*. Sung was florid: Sung was simple. So Momoyama Japan was both flamboyant shout and shibui whisper.

Country was fully united and peace reigned supreme. Great expenditure on fine homes, colorful clothes, graphic art and artistic practical goods expanded further in 17th century. Armies of craftsmen brought back as prisoners from Hideyoshi's ill-fated invasion of Korea (his supply fleets were wiped out by world's first iron-clads when Japanese Napoleon met his Korean Nelson in Admiral Yi–1589) and spawned great Japanese ceramic industry (KYUSHU–POTTERY RUN, p720). Peace, rising merchant class, new technology and skilled labor, redistribution of wealth by central government policy to keep daimyo-lords spending on consumer goods.

City Japan of 17th century was raucous. Society was getting little too light-headed and people were "forgetting their place". It got so you couldn't tell playboy of fine old family from lucky bellhop. So powers did what all such have dreamed of doing elsewhere—pass anti-sumptuary laws whereby silk was only for elite and cotton for commoners (so weavers developed rustic, tweedy silks); gay clothes were for some and not for others (so shibui colors were developed, with somber tweedy outer clothes lined with brilliant polychrome silks which were not seen except undressing); great outer gates were for some, subtly varying simplicity and plainness of wall and frontage for others (so Japanese homes and inns have dull sameness outside whether inside is cottage or secret palace with paradisiacal inner gardens)–"difference between lord's house and commoner's is incomparably less than in 18th century England". Schizophrenic Japan was born.

Too much of any good thing can be poisonous: but poisons rightly dosed make surest medicines. This itself is bromide, but its recognition could help cure alternating light-headedness/indigestion of so many writers on Japan.

KONNICHI-AN [G-5] (Today Pavilion): rambling cluster of exquisite Japanese cottage rooms of sort you see in slick magazines, travel posters, but rarely encounter on tours. Now only **open to public** in limited way, they welcome their 'members' or disciples and one should first make contact with branches in New York, San Francisco, Los Angeles, Honolulu or London (phone listing under *'Ura-'*) and visit to have tea in their transplanted tea rooms as ideal preconditioning to cultural tour of Japan. New York is in lovely old carriage house with Japanese cottage complex transplanted to old covered courtyard of Mark Rothsco's ex studio. Annual memberships, regular activities, includes sub to*Chanoyu*, fine quarterly on aesthetics.

Prospective student (scholarship available) contact Ms Mori, International Section **Ura Senke**, Ogawa-gashira, Kamikyo-ku Kyoto; ☎(075)-451-8516 ask for *Kokusai-bucho, Mori-san*. Good sampler every **Thurs** *participate* in tea demonstration 1:30-3pm, ¥1,000; and stay over at their Japanese-style rest house, rsve required ¥4,500—also call Mori-san; big Autumn lecture-party, end Oct, phone Mori-san for details, get there before

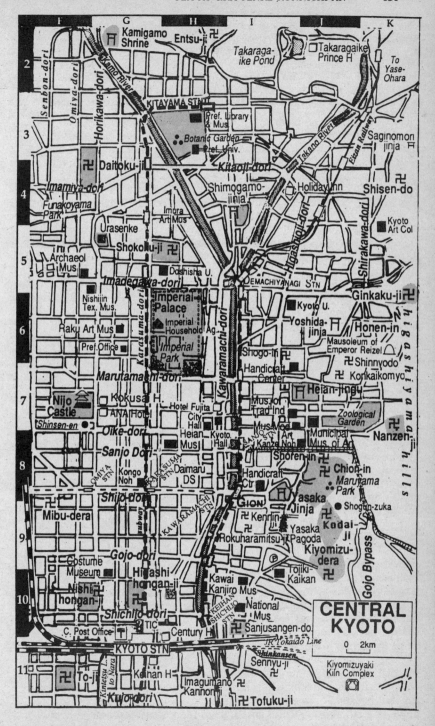

CENTRAL KYOTO

0   2km

1pm lecture, then tea and snack, *free*. **TOKYO**, Ura Senke International Sado (Tea-way) Dojo, 7 Niban-cho Chiyoda-ku 102, ☎(03)-3264-7801; also Ist & 3rd wed 10:30–noon, New Otani Hotel ☎3255-1111; Hounsai's sister SHIOZUKI Yaeko Sado Kyoshitsu, ☎3400-4491; or Imperial Hotel ☎3504-1111; Takanawa Prince ☎3445-5311. Also Omote Senke 6-Niban-cho, ☎3261-1352. In **KOBE**, Jim West, Dai Nippon Chado Gakkai ☎(078)-412-2820. **KYOTO** Ura's neighbor-cousin Omote Senke ☎432-2195. Most major hotels any city have garden tea houses, or basic tea service in lounge, ask for *matcha* any time; notably Kyoto Takaraga-ike Prince with lovely tea cottage, fair fee.

Most anywhere on earth, warmest welcome to stranger or friend is hot cup of tea (or coffee). Over its studied preparation host appraises guest–who, appetite whet by anticipation of refreshment, awhile refreshes himself with appreciation of his immediate surroundings. Simple hospitality. Often called man's basic art, in Japan as any art it has its teachers and masters. Konnichi-an has been home of dynasty of such masters for 15 generations. It is home of Sen Soshitsu Hounsai (Ho-oon-sai), Grand Master of Tea-Way.

Tea was introduced from China (where its first recorded use was 273AD) in 8th century as stimulant for monks and artists. First came in compressed bricks of fermented leaf, chipped off to use, as still preferred by Tibetans–travels well. Then came dried leaf. Powdered 'instant' entered 12th century with Zen, with which since intimately associated. As treasured beverage, served in treasured cups, ornate ritual developed out of tea party. SILVER and GOLD PAVILIONS among palatial parlors built for its rite. Hideyoshi rebuilt DAIGO SAMBO-IN for tea party to which invited everyone, lord to peasant, for most democratic affair Japan ever saw—could stand to see revived. About this time reaction against such extravagance set in. Leader of aesthetic revolution was SEN Rikyu, Hideyoshi's personal aesthete, true renaissance man, cosmopolitan background. Raised in international port town Sakai, south Osaka, his origins are unclear, but family believes him to have been Korean. Japan was then in its most intimate contact with Korea (conquered, looted of art and artists), China, Southeast Asia, as with Spain, Portugal and Holland. Rikyu organized this complex heritage into simple rite of aesthetic education centered on hospitable act of serving cup of tea.

This simple rite involves all peaceful arts so that devotee following thru by rote was subtly forced into contact with products of every art and craft: garden and stonework; architecture simple in outward appearance including many materials, assorted fine woods; interior decoration allowing no repetition of select representation of plain lacquer furniture, woodwork; painting (written pictures) or calligraphy (drawn words) chosen for mood of meet and personalities involved; simple natural arrangement of flowers in season; utensils of tea service, iron kettle, bamboo scoop, lacquer containers, plain or brocade silk serviettes, and incomparable simple bowls or handleless cups of every known ceramic.

It is communion preparatory to appreciating or 'doing' art. In brain-level terms, to Jay, its annoying need for rote memorization of actions is way of involving and thus tying up in distraction that reptilian level of our brain to release higher brain for creative act—all artists should experiment with it. As 'martial art', squatting on heels in *seiza* and whipping wrist to mix tea helps turn on *ki*, Chinese *chi*, that mysterious body force (Wilhelm Reich's *Orgone Power*, plain *juice* to Ernest Hemmingway) that is subject of all mystic quests—all karate-ka, aikidoists, etc, should try it. In terms of brain wave feedback, whisking tea is *alpha*-generating exercise. ABCs of Sado involve possible answers to many of our modern psychic quests. More down to earth, most graceful girls Jay has seen, sloe-eyed or blue-eyed, got so from practicing discipline of dance, or this way of tea.

There are several schools of this participatory art, descended of Rikyu. URA SENKE, 'Back-House Sen', best known, is least inaccessible to us.

GETTING THERE: Bus #9, 12, 61, 67 → Horikawa Teranouchi, on first N-S street to W; or taxi.

Come to exquisite rustic *Kabuto-mon*, **Helmet Gate**: see angled path between hedges, first morning glories in Japan were grown here brought from Korea by Rikyu. Hideyoshi came to see them, arriving late afternoon to find all cut down. Furious, he stormed into tea room, where he saw one perfect flower in simple vase: true essence, one representing all.

If rare invitee, beyond gate as you approach house, clack wooden fish gong. You will be led thru ancient tea rooms, really meditation cells, philosophers' studies, built by each generation of Sens each in essential taste of its time. House is built around well whose pure water makes for perfect tea. Within *Konnichian*, 'Today Pavilion' as it is called, you are led thru to shrine of Rikyu, tiny dark room with dark alcove in which portrait statue of great aesthetician stands—your guide may have flashlight to enable you to see face better. Whatever, it is family shrine, show respect as best you can: preferably kneel on mats and bow, or clasp hands in prayer and nod. Then you are off to tea-communion with art. Last room of series, you may be relieved to note, has chairs. Built by previous master while Jay was living there as guest in 1952, epitomizes contemporary Japanese taste—blend of West and East. It contrasts with general shabbiness of modern Japan, yet is modern Japan. And you wonder if all these paradise pavilions we have seen haven't stood in similar shabby settings–or shabbier for lovelier ones. All this, of course, only if you are lucky in having special invitation, such as consular or cultural officer at New Year, or overseas branch member.

Alas, *you will instead* be allowed to admire that superb gate, gaze down lane, then, as such wooden cottages can't bear much traffic, be led across to tea rooms in International Chado building; *see* thursday open house. L-hall don't miss fine **Gallery**, changing exhibits of tea-related art. Casual visitor to Gallery is invited to have cup of *matcha* thick green tea in adjoining hall, seated garden bench style–no cramping of legs.

Whether in ancient Konnichian, modern tea room or gallery hall, tea will be mixed for you, your host performing ritual of work that is, in essence, dance. Your imbibing is personal communion (secret Christians in fact used this as secret communion in 17-19th centuries, tea for wine, teacake for wafer)—so relax, be natural: if *seiza* squat on heels painful, sit as you wish—but, hopefully, with grace.

As you enter imagine you're playing 'break devil's dishes'–don't step on cracks, that is on door sill or on *heri* black edging to mats. Right foot enters room first, leaves it last. But most of all relax, you are honored guest.

TEA, How to Drink: You are served cake made of sweet bean, which start to eat at host's signal while he makes tea. Master suggests informal alternation of sweet cake and bitter tea may be more enjoyable, so you might wait and nibble and sip. (If cake doesn't suit your taste, or you want to save some for later, it's polite to wrap it up in paper napkin, put in pocket or purse–just don't leave any behind, anything at all). Lady should place purse behind you, as J-guest does fan.

Host will be squatting on host's mat in corner, or seated on stool, just as you are, fronted by steaming iron kettle set over charcoal brazier–whole set into floor in winter. He or she will pick up long-handled bamboo ladle, dip water and rinse out handleless cup, wipe. Then pick up small lacquer cylinder, wipe with silk serviette in hand-dance, open it and with curved bamboo spoon (which he probably made himself) scoop out mound of jade-green powder, tap into bowl with clack of bamboo against pottery lip. With ladle again, dip hot water from iron kettle into bowl, returning surplus 'noisily' to kettle. Now pick up what appears to be bamboo skeleton of shaving brush, place it in bowl now held firm on mat or table with left hand, clack it few times in bowl, grasp, whisk-mix tea and hot-water–*cha-no-yu*. We admire each article as it is used, how used, each efficient act.

"All there is to *chanoyu* is making cup of tea". That's all?

Each tea bowl, as work of art, has soul, its own personality. Thus it has front and back and is served front to you in honor. (You should have quietly slipped off any rings to avoid chipping valued bowls, any dangling necklace.) You pick it up with cupped right hand outside, thumb over lip, place it on left palm and return compliment by turning bowl clockwise twice or so to 180 degrees. Coddle it in cupped hands, feel its shape, reflect upon hands of potter who made it, as if holding his hands in communion, thus completing his creation. Nod slight bow to host, companions, and drink.

There will be three sips and one slurp in bowl. If more or less don't worry, just tip head back and slurp it dry. You will be tempted to examine bowl, turn it over–which is just what it is hoped you will do, as foot-ring is hallmark of master potter. Expert would identify ware and maker. Interested party will ask questions about it. (If you don't give dam, just return it and look bored as most have not honesty to do.) We use term 'communion' of tea freely. Rite as formulated by Rikyu was heavily influenced by church communion, as Catholic or Episcopalian tea-sipper may note. But it is non-sectarian–tho by repute, another 'zen' art.

'Tea Ceremony'–unfortunate English non-translation of Japanese *cha-do* or *sa-do*, 'tea-way', or *chanoyu*–is fascinating experience for some, drivel to others. It is essence of art: to too many it is utter hypocrisy. Nowhere else is dynamic schizophrenia of Japan better seen.

Bodhidharma, Daruma, introduced Zen into China 520AD, with it tea stimulant to prevent nodding in meditation. Tea drinking came to Japan with Buddhism, as fermented pressed brick tea, was elite priestly rite incorporating prized utensils. In Kyoto became popular aristocratic drink – non-sectarian tea drinking originates here. Local wild tea sometimes used as leaf. China tea first planted in Kyoto by Zen-returnee Eisai around 1200. Uji soon found best for growing it, as still today. Tea promoted by itinerant Zen priests for its medicinal properties—we find it great for shaking summer headaches. Chinese etiquette of drinking was expanded upon and ornate rite developed using costly artifacts, even gold bowls. Under Ashikaga shoguns were numerous -*awase*, 'comparison parties', where art works were displayed, floral arrangements as art (origins of ikebana) exhibited and critiqued in extemporaneous poetry. Tea tasting parties developed in this milieu and, as with flowers, became medium for showing off possessions, mostly costly Chinese imports.

This seems to have been helpless reaction to horrors of Onin wars, withdrawal from century of civil strife: one way to organize life and Japanese have always respected organization. Aesthetic organization is right-brain, analogous to left-brain activity of science. As science evolves to apparent simplicity thru organization of complex, Japanese art into their highest form in *wabi-cha*, rustic tea, evolved thru series of Ashikaga-sponsored monk-aesthetes: Ikkyu (his childhood is seen in ever-popular TV cartoon serial),

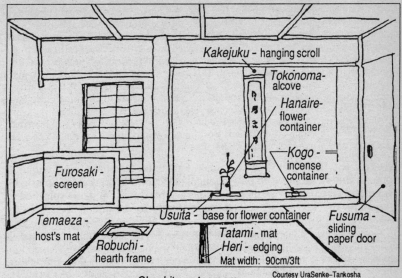

Chashitsu —tearoom
Courtesy UraSenke–Tankosha

MURATA Shuko (1422-1503) and TAKENO Jo-o (1504-1555). Latter was wealthy merchant of Sakai, nearly free city-state of internationalist merchants near to Osaka. His chief disciple SEN Rikyu (1522-1591, son of wealthy Korean immigrant fishmonger) reduced all to minimal, seminal, most significant, best: *wa-kei-sei-jaku*–harmony, respect, purity, tranquility. No value in material worth–out went golden bowls–all value is added by hand of artist or unknown artisan. No object used, no action, may detract or distract from anything or from atmosphere. All complement. Whole compose artistic hologram, each part in itself like dewdrop reflecting entirety.

Artists and artisans for four centuries have been challenged to produce their best for this little room of 10-foot square (*yo-jo-han*, $4^1/_2$ tatami mats) to be appreciated by people of highest aesthetic—aristocracy of merit for all in tea room are equal. Always male art, in early modern days degenerated into idle ladies' pastime. Revived postwar under present Ura Senke master's strong-willed feminist, egalitarian, mother Kayoko–'momma Sen' to us, as many. She taught war widows art to give them minimal financial independence as local teachers in towns and villages, developed concession-like pyramid of teachers promoting national self-respect thru return to basic cultural values. Ikebana, other arts, emulated her. Together they became basic rite of passage for young ladies, local groups formed under neighborhood teachers, clubs in high schools, colleges, company dorms. Elderly moguls returned to fold. When Japan regained independence in 1952 these arts listed dues-paying student rosters of millions per school. Grand masters of tea and flower are star-figures, arbiters of taste, listed prominently annually among top income taxpayers. Many have adherents overseas. Most are surprisingly approachable by clear-eyed fellow-aesthetes.

We three savor this drink. Powdered green tea originated as stimulant to keep meditator from dozing. Jay used it to beat afternoon slump working on this book. Garet introduced at college during exams replacing black coffee—which less effective, causes gas, plays havoc on stomach, which *matcha* does not. High in caffeine but also in vitamin C and other elements which override caffeine bad side effects. Major hotels offer 'tea ceremony' at reasonable rates; we note on our travels where they serve *matcha*, sometimes with honorific *O-*., also *o-usu* among initiated We recommend it as head-clearing pick-me-up.

NOTE on Tea: Variety of camelia, first used in China 273AD, to Japan 7th century. However 3,000-year-old ewers in our Persian pottery collection have strainer-spouts like modern teapots indicate infusions brewed then—probably medicinal herbs, as still today. Most common tea in West we call 'black' after color of leaf, Japanese call *ko*, 'red', for color of drink (*ko-cha* vs *O-cha*, hon green tea). World production 2million tons, 80% black, 15% green, 5% mid-range oolong. Difference: black-leaf kiln-dried, fermented for shelf life; green-leaf air-dried, short-life freshness. Japan produces 5.5% world tea, all green, mostly in Shizuoka and Uji; consumes 6.5% of which all black is imported. Since 1985 Chinese oolong tea craze, even canned cold from dispensers.

Matcha served in lobby or special room major hotels, best **Takaragaike Prince**; Geisha dances, evening tours feature; **Yoshiima Ryokan** invites all to tea, Zen gruel, view inner garden and family altar ¥2,200, Zen-meal ¥1,800, 3,600; rsve ☎561-2620.

KATSURA RIKYU [C-10], detached Palace on Katsura River, what can come of unlimited purse to buy practical perfection in contrast to splash. To pragmatic Occidental eye there is nothing superfluous, no frills splashed on simply for display, no space dispensed merely for grandeur. It is built for living use and for comfort—basic elements of functional beauty.

Permit necessary: simple form from JTB, hotel or TIC, take to Imperial Household office in Gosho palace for automatic OK: as long waiting list in season, ✍ ahead from home advising date you're in Kyoto, name of inn or hotel if known—posh **Hiiragiya** or pilgrim **Hinomoto** no difference, democratic. March '91 reopened after 14 years of full restoration work now free of barrierrs and construction gear. Choice of entry time: 10am, 2pm, sometimes 9, 11am, 1:30, 3pm. Arrive late you're out of luck; small groups. *Katsura Rikyu* English picture booklet at any book stand, not at Katsura.

GETTING THERE: Bus #33, 69; **train** Hankyu RR 3rd stn from Arashiyama, or downtown Shijo-dori stns, or Osaka-Kobe; **taxi** 6x-mtr o.w, min from Arashiyama – going back catch cab of next visitors. Combine with MURASAKI itinerary, *preceding*.

Superbly integrated whole, hard to single out parts for comment. Most memorable are broad verandas of natural wood which speak for choosing lovely natural material and not painting it. Interplay of house and garden, planes of roofs, verandas, garden paths (note stonework) and bridges, all viewed from within, like looking at world from inside cubist sculpture thru multiple frames of window-walls and down halls. This complex simplicity is its key to success—organization. Katsura Detached Palace, masterpiece of this development, has more to teach us than any other structure in Japan: not just for what it accomplished, but for what it forewarns.* Never has it been even nearly equaled. Built 1620-1645 in last spasm of creativeness that preceded seclusion and total dictatorship, but its perfection is its own death.

Alexander Soper points out other possible limitations and dangers:
...standard of taste involved is so peculiarly a Japanese creation that the Westerner should not expect to follow it in complete agreement. Japanese critics warmly praise some Katsura details that to Western eyes are likely to look like demonstrations of the ease with which charm can pass over into cuteness or simplicity into affectation.

Rational organization henceforth degenerates into mechanical control: arts of Edo Period (1613-1867) become too 'pretty-pretty', 'cute'–spark is gone. As ornateness of Momoyama and early Edo art, when later discovered by Europe, will contribute to development of *Art Nouveau*, so crisp and clean-cut notan-cubism of late Edo, especially its lacquerware, will spawn *Art Deco*–which degenerates almost immediately for very same reasons Edo art declined, loss of spirit due to dominance of form over substance.

Is present renaissance of Deco in 1980s (perhaps best here in Japan) indication of rediscovery of spirit, or does it foreshadow further decline.

Katsura, however, is perfect, flawless. Therein lay its fault—Oriental basic art tenet holds that there must be some imperfection: only Heaven/God can be perfect, man dare not so presume. Katsura's builder presumed.

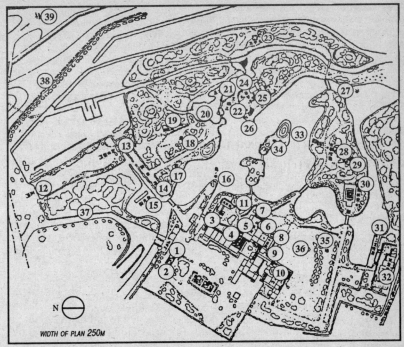

Official plan, Courtesy Katsura Rikyu

KATSURA RIKYU AND ITS PALACE GARDENS

1. Tsuyo Mon, side entry
2. Tsumesho, guardhouse
3. Chu Mon, middle gate
4. Shin-no Shikiishi
5. Mikoshi yose
6. Ko-sho-in original section 1620-25 by Toshihito
7. Tsukimi-dai, moon viewing porch
8. Chusho-in, phase II, by Toshitada, 1640s-'50s
9. Gakki-no Ma, musical instrument room
10. Shin-sho-in, ca1658
11. Geppa Ro, moon wavetower after Chinese poem
12. Sei Mon, front gate

13. Miyuki Mon, royal gate
14. Miyuki Michi, royal path
15. Ofunaya, boat house
16. Kame-no Ko, turtle-child rock islets
17. Momiji Yama, maple hill
18. Sotetsu Yama-hill
19. Omachiai, waiting room
20. Taki-guchi, waterfall
21. Michi-hama, road beach
22. Ama-no Hashidate *replica* famed Japan Sea beauty spot
23. Manji Tei, swastika (Buddhist sun symbol) hut
24. Shirakawa Bashi bridge
25. Shokin Tei, after typical *minka* farm house -1660

26. Hashi-dai-ato, remains of bridge post(s)
27. Hotaru dani, firefly vale
28. Mizu-hotaru-no Toro, firefly-over-water lantern
29. Shoka Tei, after typical roadside tea house
30. Enrin Do
31. Sanko-doro, lantern
32. Shoi Ken
33. Oike, pond
34. Naka-jima, middle islet
35. Shooting Place
36. Mariba, ball court
37. Hogaki, inner fence
38. Katsura-gaki, outer wall
39. Katsura River

SHUGAKU-IN RIKYU is another detached palace for which **permit** is required, see one or other — ardent architecture student should try for both. Text for SHUGAKUIN, *see* RAMBLES NORTHEAST, follows, next page.

Loop up to **Moss Garden–taxi** or **Hankyu** electric up one stop → Kamikatsura stn and 10min walk W–for which hopefully you got **permit**, and for following open time, then take in PURPLE PERIOD itinerary (or *see* preceding, and follow text reverse order). **Alternate** bus from front of Katsura, W 20min → KAMEOKA, shoot Hozu Rapids back down → nearby Arashiyama; summer *ugai* fishing, good place to dine ¥-L-B.

Page 488

> What is the value of the individual?
> It is something ephemeral, while a garden
> as every work of art, must have elements of eternity.
> — Nikos Kazantsakis, 1935

CEREMONIAL SANDPILES
RAMBLES NORTHEAST

SHUGAKU-IN RIKYU [K-3] is one of our last historical sights in this half-historical route. Another detached 'cottage' palace built 1665, decades after Katsura, it carries control of Katsura on to artificiality, but in manner comforting to most occidental visitors as it resembles English country manse in outline and landscaping. Begun as abdication palace 1655 by emperor Go-Mizuno-O when he realized power had irrevocably passed to Tokugawa shogun in Edo, that all that was left for him was Zen meditation and poetry. *Senshi-dai*, literally 'poem washing veranda', is where he sat for inspiration. He abdicated to 5-year-old daughter, Meisho, Kyoto's sole reigning (r.1629-43) empress.

Go visited Katsura 1663, then nearing completion. He completed upper and lower gardens and pavilions at Shugakuin. On his death 1680, 11th daughter Ake-no-miya finished mid-garden as nunnery. After her death uncared for, restored few times in Edo period, opened to public maintained by admissions 1870-83, then Kunai-sho, Imperial Household Office took over and restored. There are actually three *rikyu* or palaces: *Naka*- mid, ex-nunnery to south; *Kami*- upper to northeast; *Shimo*- lower to west, separated by leased-out rice fields and known collectively as *Ochaya*, 'teahouse'. Architecture noted for its simplicity, if not spartan sparseness. In *Kami's* lake is isle with thatched **Pavilion of Golden Waters**, *Kin-sui-ken*, original building of complex. Roof ridge bears huge tiles with Imperial crest. Name tablet inscribed by Go himself. House is one room, part raised higher, *Jo-dan*, of six special small tatami mats, while rest of room has 8 standard mats of 6 feet and pair nearly 8 feet.

One **bridge** is solid stone with wooden parapet and roof-ends shaped like palanquins with seats in west (with phoenix atop) for emperor, east for consort. Bridge was gift of imperial admirer, but shogun frowned on such gifts and donor paid for audacity of 'sticking out' (Jap saying: "Nail that sticks up invites hammer") by having to disembowel himself.

Naka-no-Rikyu or ex-nunnery, has original *Rakushi-kan* and *Goten* with fine panel paintings. One on cedar of Gion festival cart so realistic that to prevent its rolling out into lake, net was painted over it. Garden has famed pine tree trained into shape of giant umbrella-hat, called *kasa-no-matsu*, **umbrella pine**. Palatial style RINKYU-JI was moved from Imperial Palace by Go-Mizuno-O's empress. 3-storey **stone pagoda** came from Korea.

Gardens are most noteworthy aspect of estate, especially for *shakkei*, captured landscape background best seen on stroll thru and across bridges to isles set in ponds with waterfalls formed by stream diverted by Go. Whole garden has its own **eight views**, pointed out by guide. Approach thru rural thatched homes and garden-like farm fields, vistas, long views of great park gardens and natural backdrop will impress most and it is worth getting **permit** just for this: following usual ritual, Imperial Palace office, Gosho.

Visit 9, 10, 11am, 1:30, 3pm. Illustrated English book sold at gate. **Bus** #5, 31, 35, 65.

Warning: If sensitive to **insect bites**, apply bug repellent—especially bare-legged women–or cover yourself, wear slacks. Fields hereabouts full of *buto* (biting gnat) whose attentions can leave you looking like short-term Elephantiasis sufferer.

Nearby are several small temples, built also for recluses of more modest status. Less famous, thus rarely visited and perhaps more comfortable...
KONPUKU-JI [K-4], overgrown azaleas amidst which poet Basho lived...
MANSHU-IN [K-4], 1656, 8-windowed tea house ICA, with dry-sand garden with lush green isle by Kobori Enshu, who did KATSURA, entry ¥500...
SHISENDO [K-4] exquisite temple hermitage of bureaucrat-poet Josan (1583-1672), with panels painted by KANO Tanyu, portraits of 36 Chinese poets, bamboo-overhung lane to sand garden, sculpted azalea bushes; entry ¥400.

From Shugaku-in nearby Keifuku electric Eizan line stn it's short distance to Yaséyuen stn, or parallel bus Kita-6 (for Ohara), and cablecar-ropeway combination up Mount Hiei; or same bus past cable base to Jakko-In Temple, Sanzen-In and Ohara.

With this, we leave historical routings and ramble nearby.
GINKAKU-JI [K-6] Silver Pavilion–a.k.a JISHO-JI. Zen-ly touted for wrong reasons. Built in imitation of Gold Pavilion 1465-83 by ASHIKAGA Yoshimasa (r.1445-74, d.1490) 8th Ashikaga, as retirement hermitage. Never finished, so silver was never applied, thankfully. Monument worthy of Medici, for Yoshimasa pauperized all under his power to bask in reflected glory of being retired ruler. With his rule order ended and horrible Onin Civil Wars set in, to level most of Kyoto.

Fame of SILVER PAVILION is its strange sand garden consisting of what appear to many to be two heaps left behind by builders—which is just what one garden expert suggests they were until someone had good humor to sculpt them. They make no sense in daylight, hemmed in small space, despite hordes of students pausing before them to ponder their greatness and mystery. Their function is to reflect moon during viewing parties: and as you might expect, temple and gravel-heap 'garden' are closed evenings.

Right reasons to praise Ginkaku-ji are **green garden** by Soami, pond, and lovely **tea house** *Togu-do*, designed by Yoshimasa as first 4½-mat (10-foot square) tea room, prototype of all. Of dozen original buildings only this pair remains, along with rebuilt *Rosei-tei* for incense ceremonies. Bus #5, 32 direct to temple, #17, 203, 204 to nearby Ginkaku-ji-michi.

Philosopher's Walk [K-6/7], *Testsugaku-no-michi*, pleasant canal-side hour stroll (not counting stops) 2.5km Ginkaku-ji → Nanzen-ji, mostly on non-car bike-path at foot of mountain, lovely small sights distract en rte, good matcha tea-stop below Eikando, or lunch of *yu-dofu* at Nanzen-ji temple garden. *Note:* most popular maps don't show actual path, (*KVG* does), only canal along W (L) side of which is narrow pedestrian-cycle path. Whole area Ginkaku-ji–Yasaka beautifully covered in '3-D pictorial' map *Bird's Eye View of Kyoto #1* by ISHIHARA Tadashi, ¥1,000—practical yet even frameable.

HONEN-IN [K-6] just below Ginkaku-ji, retreat of Saint Honen, founder of Pure Land or Hongan-ji sect. He's buried here. Garden favored by crowd-avoiders, lovely and often empty—except when koto (horizontal harp) groups give concerts. Irregular schedules, but check Kyoto TIC.

EIKAN-DO [K-7/8] houses 'looking back Buddha' standing figure not like any other, looks back over one shoulder. Numerous tall tales attempt to account for its miraculously turning after having been sculpted straight.

Murin-an garden, exquisite tho recent, laid out Meiji era by OGAWA Jihei, *shakkei* style–captured landscape using scenery beyond. Tours visit, occasional concerts, events, check TIC.

NANZEN-JI [K-8] is favorite locale of ours. For years every trip down to Kyoto from Tokyo saw us head here for no reason other than that we like feel of place—so much so it was years before we actually got around to going into temple itself. We would cross little bridge, down alley to open space in middle of which, with no road leading to it or from it (only circling it), stands magnificent gate to nowhere, classic Zenist gateless gate: *Nikkwa-mon* moved from original old Imperial Palace. In it Japan's 'Robin Hood' Goemon hid for many years until he was captured and boiled in oil in great iron vat (1632?)—since which time household iron bathtubs, standard until recently, have been called *Goemon-buro* (bath).

Beyond, R is Roman-style **aqueduct**, built in last century when pseudo-Roman set style for waterworks next to Miyako Hotel. Pass under it and go L up slope, up steep flight of stairs past small shrine, over small bridge to wooden shed before narrow waterfall: hoary **hillside shrine** of Brilliant King, Celestial Howler, Fudo. Here penitent pilgrims in coldest weather of *Dai-kan*, mid-January, stand 'neath icy mountain waterfall chanting Buddhist sutras. (Jay described rite in book *Zen Combat*-Buddha in a Cold Shower.) All around in cliff face are small holes with offerings and candles set before them: snake holes, remnant of man's most primitive religion. From Miyako Hotel to Fudo, short walk runs gamut of Kyoto sights, of human history.

Nanzen-ji itself contains rich variety of gardens and decoration. Originally Imperial detached palace 1288-97 given over as Zen temple, sacked 1393 by Hiei-zan monks, burned often till rebuilt 1597-1611. **Dry gardens** (especially HOJO-1597 and sub-temple KONCHI-IN rank among best examples of such) here are as satisfying, if less famous, than most at DAITOKU-JI; while more conventional gardens in sub-temples enliven contrast. Paintings excel, are real: include magnificent tigers on gold by KANO Tanyu, other panels by others of Kano clan. Some rooms were moved from IMPERIAL PALACE. **Buses** from town to nearby #5, 27, 46.

CHOPSTICKS: TEMPLE RESTAURANTS around gate, are spice to feast, literally, specializing in *yu-dofu*, rather simple vegetarian *mizu-taki*. Sit in garden or on temple veranda preparing it yourself, drinking sake. Good light lunch, tasty. Three temples serve but take turns closing, so just round great Gate and look in on any open gateways. Best known is **Okutan**. Prices mid-range ¥1,700up; excellent hot tofu dishes in winter make sitting in open garden pavilions pleasure, if chilly at very outset.

Below **Miyako Hotel** is favorite shop-seeing stroll (*see* SHOPPING). Main sights are:

SHOREN-IN [J-8], a.k.a AWATA PALACE, empress' temporary residence 1788-1813, old site of retirement palace 9th century, burned 1893, rebuilt as miniature of imperial palace. Garden is palatial paradise style with contributions to it by both Soami, early 1500s, and KOBORI Enshu, d.1647, two of greatest of garden designers, popular because of its setting and acoustics as site of koto concerts. (One Japanese **nite tour** takes this in for music —if not on tour just show up about 8:30pm). In daytime, rooms are worthwhile for wide selection painted panels, especially sprightly paintings of Gion Festival carts by SUMIYOSHI Gukei, d.1705, others by greats of Tosa and Kano schools and rarely seen Chinese painter CHO-Shaku-Ran.

(**Yamanaka** curio shop-mansion is across street, old **Curtis** closed).

CHION-IN [J-8] is principal monastery of Jodo sect (*not* Jodo-shinshu) and rather resembles fortress with raised position against hill, and largest gate in Japan. All tours take it in, but it has not impressed us as much as others half its size, except for atmosphere its **San-mon gate** (built 1617 by second Tokugawa, ornate ceilings) gives area. Fine views of city however from various galleries as buildings climb hill. Great 74-ton hanging **bell** (1636) in Sho-ro **belfry** (1678) contends with millennium-older Nara TODAI-JI bell for heavyweight champion title, rung most of week starting **Apr 19**. **Tea house** stands near belfry. Structures *O-hojo* and *Ko-hojo* are palace type built 1633-40 by third Tokugawa Iemitsu (who erected Nikko Toshogu Shrine). Panels by various Kano artists: especially wooden door with popular cat, its eyes follow you wherever you walk, snow scenes in adjoining rooms cooling. But we must admit our feeling for place tainted by fact that friend checked shoes here going in, coming out found only dirty sandals.

GION SHRINE [J-8], properly YASAKA, is spiritual heart of Kyoto, shrine to patron deity Susano-o, storm god. Its mixed history is Kyoto's. Founded by Korean in 656. Gion, Buddhist temple formerly in grounds when two faiths were together, is Japanese name of monastic park in India where historic Buddha Sakyamuni received conversion of famed courtesan. Today is tutelary shrine of Gion geisha. *Gion Festival* centers here **July 17**. Most of time lovely lanes behind shrine which lead to Maruyama Park are lined with colorful stalls and it seems as if fairs are held here most summer evenings, officially monthly every First.

Maruyama Park between YASAKA and CHION-IN is one vast restaurant, with innumerable little places, lovely and budget (*see* CHOPSTICKS). Area south of it bordering our favorite walk from KIYOMIZU, (for which see SHOPPING) has over dozen Love Hotels and some lovely traditional restaurants. From Gion Shrine's gate west is main '**Gay Quarter**' of Kyoto, **Gion**, with higher class Gion-*koh sagaru* (down-side) to left of Shijo, and more profane Gion-*otsu agaru* (up-side), with more Love Hotels and some good restaurants.

GION TO KIYOMIZU

REAL SHOPPER'S paradise stroll details in SHOPPING, p540. Best route is to take it from KIYOMIZU 'up' into Gion, mostly downhill or North to South.

Main points of scenic interest, working uptown on parallel Higashi-oji Ave are..
SANJUSANGEN-DO [I-10] 'Temple of 33 Spans' included on all tours, built what is almost theater marquee entrance, undoubtedly most hideous entry to any temple in Japan, complete with turnstiles. Unfortunate, for temple is worthwhile for its imposing statuary: most famous 1,000 human-size gilded statues of 1,000-armed Kannon in formidable, imposing array around central gigantic Kannon of almost Tibetan power, melodious peacefulness reflecting 13th century sculptor Tankei's 82 years. Any monotony one might expect is broken by slight variations, no two having same disposition of hands.

If numbers impress, counting eleven heads on each (ten in crowns) and those in halos and in hands of some of larger: head total = 33,333. This dizzying array makes walk around back of altar even more rewarding, for here are superb, individualistic statues of 28 subordinates of Kannon, some of most appealingly human, best portrait sculpture anywhere. These, like 1,000 Kannons, are from vibrant Kamakura Period, 13th century. Many of both groups are by Unkei, others by almost as great contemporaries of his school. Flanking 28 are wittily fierce Wind God (bag of breezes on back) & Thunder God (in halo of drums holding in each hand thunderbolt like Norse Thor does). At far ends are 2 superb *nio* 'Turkish Wrestler' deva dervishes.

Block-and-half long front veranda scene of great archery display **Jan 15**. Originally was contest to see who could shoot most arrows length of building within 24 hours, limited by overhang blocking lob shots. Record 1686: 13,053 arrows fired, 8,133 going to end. **Buses** #202, 206, 207, 208.

(For more on Japanese archery, *see* Jay's paperback *Zen Combat*).

National Museum [H-10] (across from SANJUSANGEN-DO, Shichi-jo dori) great assortment of Japanese art and prehistoric artifacts, also special exhibitions. Many fine statues here, moved from temples for safe-keeping. Family favorite, if one can pick from this fabulous treasury, is psychedelic 12 cent portrait of priest Hoshi of China (d.514 at 97): standing figure, beatific face split vertically down center, another face emerges in Dali-esque surrealism illustrating legend that Chinese emperor ordered artist to paint Hoshi from life, during which subject tore skin from his face thus revealing bodhisattva within (loan from Saioji). But treasures galore, simply, spaciously displayed.

Behind (N of) museum several small temples, of little interest, include so-called...
GREAT BUDDHA OF KYOTO, HOKO-JI, built by Hideyoshi, originally (1589) bronze, 16m/59ft tall, bigger than Nara; twice destroyed, rebuilt, of wood of which only head, 1801, remains. East of museum, 660 steps up to **Hideyoshi's tomb** for good view; opp, **Mimi-zuka** (Mound of Ears) his trophies from invasion of Korea, worth mention only as historical fill. Many ears walked here still on heads settled here to found **Gojo potteries**.

CHISHAKU-IN, MYOHO-IN temples (E of museum across Higashi-oji Ave) have fine gardens. Both are Shingi-Shingon sect. Buildings given by Ieyasu 1615 from Hideyoshi temples, contain superb *fusuma* panel paintings by KANO Eitoku & Sanraku. **Kara-mon** Chinese Gate may be from Hideyoshi's Castle at Momoyama, which gave fabulous art era its name.

KAWAI Kanjiro house [H-8], collection and pottery workshop (*see* MUSEUMS); first street W of Higashi-oji Ave, 2nd block below Gojo ave, pioneer in crafts movement.

Alternate starting point, working in from Gojo-dori pottery shopping...
KIYOMIZU-DERA [J-9] atop shop-lined, fascinating Gojo-Zaka '5th Ave Hill', favorite with everyone. Saw it best one windy day as all shops were boarding up for typhoon so we were alone on its windswept flying stage. Worse is weather, lovelier is Kiyomizu. Hundreds of stairs but no vehicular shortcut. History of singularly beautiful temple to Eleven-headed 1,000-armed Kannon is mystery. Notably, main architecture books don't mention it except in passing. Present building with great swooping shingle roof reputedly dates from 1600. But style is older and original was said to have been palace at Nagaoka, short-lived predecessor of Kyoto (784-794) and dismantled with that city and moved here. 1600 rebuilding was grand repair job with modifications. Atmosphere is of most ancient Kyoto, great pilings remind one of Izumo Shrine before it was brought down to earth off its 100-foot pilings. Resembles exquisite Hase-dera outside Nara. At entry to main pavilion, great iron **pilgrim staffs** and iron sandals, said to have belonged to gentle giant Benkei, who met master-to-be Yoshitsune in battle below at Gojo bridge–try to raise staff straight up, now one-hand! In **waterfall** below, ascetics shower most of year-round in rock-carved shrine of Fudo. Garden across vale looks too good to be true–we looked at it from afar innumerable times over years before venturing across to roam thru and were not disappointed. **Bus** to hill base #1, 2, 3, 4, 5, 8, 202, 206. Temple till 6pm+.

Following shopping route, back down main shop-lined street to first fork, obvious spice shop, turn hard R down stone steps, refer to SHOPPING ROUTE, to...
Ryozen Kannon is gigantic postwar ferroconcrete image en route shopping run back to Gion. When new it was monstrosity; but we must admit, three decades' aging has improved it. Dedicated to all war dead of

World War II and associated idiocy. They welcome your telling them name of any loved one who perished so that they might record it within and pray for his peace of soul beyond. Sincere and non-sectarian, leave any names...
Which seems to bring us up to today and into tomorrow.

OFFBEAT KYOTO
NORTH, with little temples tucked away in glades which on hot summer days when temple-crawling palls, offer quiet, privacy and beauty to be savored; in autumn unforgettable maples.

JINGO-JI, SAIMYO-JI, KOZAN-JI [all A-2], KOETSU-JI [E-2] see PURPLE PERIOD.

2.5km E, 30-40min walk; or from town bus #37, 46, 54, 67 from JR stn up...
KAMIGAMO JINJA [G-2], shrine has two conical piles of sand as in Daitokuji-Daisen-in, like sitting in vortex of some gigantic Klein bottle. Also perhaps last shrine horse-in-residence in Kyoto, who stamps and scrapes his hoof for you to drop coin into vending machine to treat him to carrots and greens. Once all major shrines had them, white or palomino.

DATEBOOK: July 1, offering to paddy field, sacred Noh dances, 1pm, ¥2,500.

CHOPSTICKS: Several good eating places up here: facing Kamigamo Shrine entrance, kitty-corner to R, handsome building of dark wood **Ikadachi**, 11am-9pm X-tue. A la carte under ¥4000; recommend *Inaka-zen* ¥1,200; *Obento*, ¥1,700. ☎791-6793.

Ten, neat art deco setting black lacquered look with nouvelle cuisine. We ordered set dinner ¥3,800 and enjoyed series of 8 individual dishes served in succession. Kita-ku, Omiya, Higashi shonobori machi-l, ☎492-7799, open 6-12pm, X-mon.

Block or so to L is Chinese restaurant **One-One** run by young couple. Noodle dishes ¥600, most others under ¥500, course ¥530. Asakiriga-hara cho. ☎721-3450.

In opp direction (R) from shrine is famous pickle shop **Narita**. Good chance to see architectural composition of outer gate, stone walk to front gate, etc. This place and waterway along street have been designated important cultural sites. Entire area is famous for its pickles, and walking around this area you will see number of places where big barrels with long beams with large rocks attached, used to extract liquid from vegetables.

Nishimura Teien garden, end of block large compound, at one time belonged to head of Kamigamo Shrine, garden recently opened to public.

Bus #4 from subway N terminus, or #66, to Midorigaike, walk W 500m/10min...
ENTSU-JI [H/I-1/2] with its lonely airs, its dry garden with backdrop of Mount Hiei as its captured landscape; so offbeat that Tokugawa shoguns never got out to wall in garden as they did all others, so that we have here one of only 2 *kare-sansui* left in original innocence–**must** for garden buffs. Gate, apartments date to emperor Go-Mino-O, 1670s, whose retreat it was. Rinzai Zen. Nice morning stroll from Takaragaike Prince Hotel.

Ohara-bound bus Kita-6 from JR Kyoto stn, xfers from Keihan Sanjo or Shijo stns; or electric from Demachiyanagi Stn [I-6] Keifuku-Eizan line N to end, then bus #6...
OHARA VILLAGE, (far NE) home of maids who carry flowers and kindling atop heads around Kyoto to sell door-to-door. From May 15-July 19 come up and pose in traditional 10th century blue & white tie-dye costume with apron and bonnet amid 3,000 blooming hydrangeas at lovely SANZEN-IN. Apply 5/15-7/19 between 10–2pm X-sun to ☎(075)-53-7305.

SANZEN-IN temple [N-1+] garden (¥500); trees "suggest...remains of ancient Greek temple". Tendai sect, origins date to earliest Kyoto, but elsewhere as moved here after Onin Wars, 1477. Older main hall built trad 985, probably 1148, tho in typical early Heian or Fujiwara. Houses Amida, pair bodhisattvas and Kannon, used for meditations upon Amida for those desiring rebirth in Pure Land. Inverted boat-shaped ceiling singular. **Garden** *Ruri-kotei* noted for its lovely maple. Subtemples bear strolling: **Raigo-in** birthplace of Tendai chanting–which you may stumble into.

JAKKO-IN [N-1+] exquisite nunnery across vale. Reputedly dates to Prince Shotoku who founded Horyu-ji ca600, but real history begins with tragic Kenrei Monin, daughter of TAIRA-no Kiyomori (he built Miyajima near Hiroshima). Married emperor Takakura 1172, bore prince later child-emperor Antoku. When Taira lost naval battle off Dan-no-Ura westernmost Inland Sea 1185 to Minamoto, she dove into sea with boy and Imperial sword. Baby drowned, she survived, returned to Kyoto to become recluse here praying for souls of her father, husband, son and whole Taira clan. (*See* 13th century novel *Tale of Heike*). Object of worship now Jizo bodhisattva, guardian of travel, birth, death–and children. Entry ¥500.

KURAMA: Tram from Demachiyanagi [I-5]...en route get off train Iwakura stn for worthwhile long walk to really Shangri-La temple garden of **JISSO-IN**.

Kurama itself is lovely, its tantric **Oct 22** *Fire Festival*, **June 20** *Bamboo-cutting Rite* are worth trip. Home of legendary Kurama Tengu goblin, in vale lined with restaurants, bamboo-slat porches bridge creek to provide natural air-conditioning. Some are budget, almost pilgrim. Others announce by ornate lanterned gates prices approaching international hotel standard. Cool smell of pines invites using numerous small inns: **Kanki-in**, large luxury ¥-S inn, adds new look to area.

Hikers: tho KURAMA and YASE-OHARA are reached by diverging routes from NE Kyoto Demachi-Yanagi and Takaraga-ike stns, they're under 5-forested-km apart, walkable.

HIEI-SAN COLD MOUNT & WARRIOR MONKS

NORTHEAST is most unlucky of directions and to protect capital from its evil influences guardian monastery of Konpo Chudo was set up in 794 within...

ENRYAKU-JI [N-1] founded pre-788 by priest Saicho (a.k.a Dengyo Daishi) atop 848m/2,780ft 'chilly mount', like sacred sergeant-at-arms its shadow looms over imperial city. Already sacred, Hiei Shrine was already here: **EAST** Shrine legendary date 9IBC, **WEST** more likely 668 when Otsu was capital. Home shrine of 3,800 branch Sanno Shrines, including 21 big ones like Tokyo's near hotel hub Akasaka-mitsuke. Temple's 3,000-odd *sohei* monk-warriors often acted like obnoxious kibitzers over political mah-jong table, in 12th century raiding Kyoto by 'force of alms'. Yet in this turbulent period most founders of new sects were educated here in this great religious university: St Honen of Jodo, St Shinran of Shin, Eisai of Rinzai-zen, Dogen of Soto-zen, and even St Nichiren.

Not until 1572 were monks subdued by nation-builder Nobunaga, who destroyed monastery, to be rebuilt by Hideyoshi and Tokugawa on today's much smaller scale. Little survived successive destructions and constant fires (latest 1962), yet what there is, is still magnificent enough to compete with natural setting and view from either side of Kyoto and Lake Biwa.

Enryaku-ji **main hall**, *Konpo-Chudo*, rebuilt 1642, like something out of *Lost Horizon*–especially if you come upon it front on, viewing third-largest wood building in country from top of stone stairway, its vermillion pavilion set like great bird just alighting (NT). Inside you find self on balcony when you approach altar barrier, stone-floored chamber below, high elevated altar across chasm, its gold fixtures, polished bronzes glitter eerily in light of eternal oil lamps.

Nearby in enclosure...
Hall of Study *Daikodo* (1634) has numerous statues of Tendai sect patriarchs. Other buildings JODO-IN, KAIDAN-IN, AMIDA-DO.

Temple follows hillscape, in 3 walled sections: oldest **To-to** (E) of main hall and others above, younger **Sai-to** (W), and **Yokawa**. Sole structure to survive Nobunaga's attack is **Shaka-do**, center of SAITO group.

Stroll, explore freely. As head temple of esoteric Tendai sect surrounding mountain paths still locale for extreme ascetic rites of endurance and fore-bearance like winter cold-water immersion, 100 day-jog circumambulating mount, big fire festival. Never can tell whom you'll meet on wooded paths.

Pilgrims still walk up...try it from Yase, paralleling cable car, on L.

Living up to its name, 'chilly mount' is popular summer escape.

WHERE TO STAY: International **Mount Hiei Hotel** ☎(075)-701-1111, ¥-S; every room with view, giant double beds, outdoor terrace dinner-dancing. Temple stay **Enryaku-ji Kaikan** ¥-Tw/2 shojin-ryori; lunch or dinner only, ¥1,500–7,000; ☎(0775)-78-0047.

Amusement park beyond (thankfully not near temple), offers summer evening events, visited by bus tours with Enryaku-ji.

GETTING THERE: Taxi, bus or cable. **Taxi** up scenic drive from town 10x-mtr and worth it for views. Drive also has approach from Lake Biwa side. Hiei-san Driveway **Bus** #7, #51 from JR Kyoto Stn, #7 via Sanjo Bridge summer nites, service every few mins (*see* **bus tours** for this and daylight or nite view packages that take it in) otherwise infrequent. **Cable car**: bus #3, 17, 202, 203 to Demachi-yanagi **[I-5]** or Takaraga-ike Stns, xfer to tram to Yase stn, whence 9min cable thru virgin cedars then 3 min suspended ropeway; pilgrim trail winds up from Yase on road L side of cable stn, also from Biwa-Sakamoto. Also cable from Lake Biwa side Sakamoto stn, end of Keihan branch line from Hama Otsu; moderate **taxi** from **Biwa-ko Hotel** or **Otsu Prince**. Suggest take cable car or road up from Kyoto and return via Biwa cable or road, like Japanese bus tour; or reverse. Link with BIWA–LAKE OF LUTE itinerary, follows next.

On road up from Kyoto, before reaching toll road, is small, **budget hot spring** area. Jewel-like setting on R (restful stop, room to park), in garden against grotto wall, is shrine to longevity where oldsters come for blessing; famed for ancient monks, hermits who lived here in past, whose modern counterparts come **monthly 25**th for rites.

*...omits just as the eye omits in looking at a landscape,
and the spectator brings to the scene his own
image-making faculty that we all share, no two of us alike,
the exercise of which is the highest creative delight.*
— Langdon Warner

BIWA 琵琶
LAKE OF LUTE

TRADITION has it that Mount Fuji rose in single nite and in west land sank to form Lake Biwa, (Biwa-ko). Date given is fifth year of reign of emperor Korei, traditionally 286 BC, but probably closer to 300 AD. In size Biwa-ko is slightly larger than Lake Geneva, its surface sits at altitude of some 285 feet above sea level and its deepest point is not much below sea level. Its present name refers to its shape, that of pear-shaped lute, biwa. Formerly known as Omi, written with characters 'Near Lake', meaning near Kyoto, but now written with ideographs for 'Freshwater Sea'. Still referred to as Omi in art: *Omi Hakkei*, Eight Views of Omi, favorite subjects for painters and poets, all located along shores.

Miidera temple as bell sounds
Katada with wild geese alighting
Yabase with its fishing boats
Seta and sunset over Korean bridge

Karasaki in nite rain
Awazu, sun shining, breeze blowing
Mount Hira's snow-capped peak at twilite
Ishiyama by autumn moon.

TILT: To Kyoto residents Biwa-ko popular traditional retreat from heat 45min **tram** from Sanjo bridge or **bus** from town. For visitor, suggest Biwa cool headquarters for sallies down to Kyoto for morning sight-see, return Biwa for afternoon swim, sail or loll. Could be even more practical and pleasant, however unlikely, if old Biwa-Kyoto canal punts reinstated: for decades best way Biwa-town was down 10km (7 mile) canal, much of trip thru tunnels, part on land with boats towed around steep inclines on tramway. Still see unused rails and winches alongside road just beyond **Miyako Hotel**. Canal ends, as did boat ride, by NANZEN-JI temple opposite Miyako Hotel.

PERSONAL ORIENTATION: Otsu City is focal point of resort area –its JR stn few mins from lake. City-run **Tourist Office** (Kanko-annai) in front of stn has interesting collection of **Otsu products**: Otsu-e woodblock print repros, pottery, humorous scroll by cartoonist-priest TOBA Sojo whose KOZAN-JI temple [A-2] animal scroll is famous...but this one is of flatulence contest. Hama-Otsu on lakeshore is resort center. Frequent **bus** & Keihan electric **tram** link Osaka-Kyoto-Hama Otsu. For nearby **swimming**, Yanagasaki Beach by BIWA-KO HOTEL-OTSU PRINCE, and Gotenhama-beach at Zeze best. Rowboats, sailboats, fishing boats, motorboats can be rented or chartered; arrange thru your inn, hotel or concessionaire.

GETTING AROUND: 8 VIEWS OF OMI can be taken in on 2hr50min boat excursion around S portion of lake; dep Hama-Otsu 9:30am & 12:40pm daily Mar-Nov, sun/hols extras at 11:00, 14:00 Jul-Aug; ¥2,890. (New hydrofoil cuts time.) Mar-Nov, US Mississippi River paddle-wheeler *Michigan* cruises 90min dep 11:50, 1:40, 3:30, ¥2,000-4,000; steak dinner ¥6,000, also ala carte. **Other excursions** do far end of lake beyond Hikone Castle, Chikubushima Isle, 6hrs incl visits; dep Hama Otsu 10:30 daily Mar-Nov, 1st cl ¥6,200, 2d ¥3,200, kids 1/2. Alt: suggest JR train Kyoto → Omi Imazu dep 7:58, 8:58, 9:34, 10:58, 11:55-Exp, 11:58etc, ¥900 in 70min, express ¥2,000-33min; then Biwa-ko Kisen boat Imazu → Chikubu-shima Isle ¥1210 o.w.dep 10:10, 11:40, 13:10, 14:40 etc take 40min, spend hour, ferry ¥1630 on → Hikone 11:45, 12:45, 13:45, 15:20, 16:15 for sumptuous dinner, train back 2 per hr, take hr ¥1,060; or o'nite. Alt: Chikubu-shima tour boat dep Nagahama 10:45, 13:15 ¥1,420, and Hikone 12:00, 14:30 ¥1,580. Takeshima Tour dep Hikone 10:00, 11:40, 13:30, 15:10, Jul-Nov extra at noon, ¥1,660, allow 30min on isle enough to walk around 500m circum. Boat info ☎(0775)-24-5000.

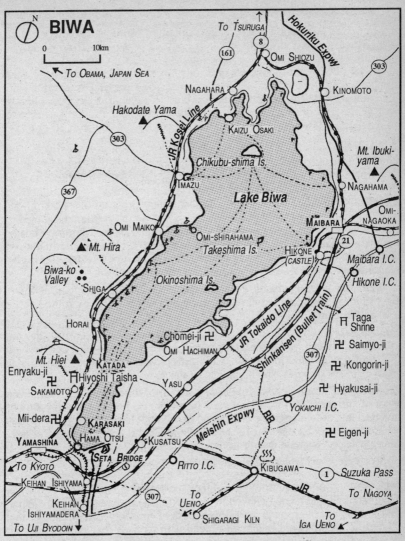

N

BIWA

0   10km

← To OBAMA, JAPAN SEA

To TSURUGA ↑

8

161

OMI SHIOZU

Hokuriku Expwy

303

NAGAHARA

KINOMOTO

Hakodate Yama ▲

JR Kosei Line

KAIZU OSAKI

303

Chikubu-shima Is.

Mt. Ibuki-
yama ▲

IMAZU

367

Lake Biwa

NAGAHAMA

OMI-
NAGAOKA

OMI MAIKO

OMI-SHIRAHAMA

Takeshima Is.

MAIBARA

▲ Mt. Hira

Okinoshima Is.

HIKONE
(CASTLE)

21

Maibara I.C.

Biwa-ko
Valley

SHIGA

Hikone I.C.

HORAI

JR Tokaido Line

Shinkansen (Bullet Train)

Taga
Shrine

卍 Saimyo-ji

Chōmei-ji 卍
OMI HACHIMAN

307

卍 Kongorin-ji

Mt. Hiei ▲

KATADA

Enryaku-ji 卍
SAKAMOTO

Hiyoshi Taisha

YASU

卍 Hyakusai-ji

YOKAICHI I.C.

Mii-dera 卍

KARASAKI

HAMA OTSU

KUSATSU

Meishin Expwy

BB

卍 Eigen-ji

YAMASHINA

SETA BRIDGE

RITTO I.C.

KIBUGAWA

♨

1 Suzuka Pass

←To KYOTO

KEIHAN ISHIYAMA

To NAGOYA

KEIHAN
ISHIYAMADERA

307

To
UENO

JR

To UJI BYODOIN ↓

SHIGARAGI KILN

To
IGA UENO ↙

(Old seaplane aerial sightseeing no more—but ask, who knows...?)
   Nite excursion boat (June-Aug) dep Hama-Otsu 6:15 for 3hr cruise, sunset Seta
Bridge; check hotel, TIC; also nite tours from Kyoto (see) do lake and Hiei-san.

   WHERE TO STAY: Mount Hiei ¥-hi-T-S **Hieizan Hotel** ☎(075)-701-2111
overlooks lake. Several inns along lake front at Hama-Otsu, from boat landing (**Kikuya,
Hakkei-kan**), across river to **Biwa-ko Hotel**, new **Otsu Prince**, below. All have
resort hotel swimming, boating and fishing. All offer lakeside dining. For overnite,
Kikuya ☎(0775)-23-0193 has lowest bottom rate at ¥8,000w/2, ¥-lo-T+; while
Hakkei-kan ☎23-1633 from ¥-hi-T; all top at ¥-S. Temple Stay at MII-DERA *shukubo*
Enman-in ¥-Tw/2; ☎22-3690 (see p.438).
   Biwa-ko Hotel, ☎(0775)-24-1255 ¥-S W-style w/ some J- from ¥-S built in
elephantine Victorian proportions (rather than more modern elfin closets) offers lazy
luxury at prices well below ¥-L. Also J-annex. **Otsu Prince** ☎21-1111, every room
faces lake; ¥-hi-S, W-style, J-family rm for 4 ¥33,000; 7/21-8/20 all +10%.
   Other accommodations in UJI, etc, listed in Eight Views (*following page*).

EIGHT VIEWS OF OMI

Mii-dera temple as bell sounds...just outside Otsu on hillside. View of lake is lovely and traditionally is accompanied by sound of famed bell at eventide: on hot evening, "cool gong". Mii-dera is ancient center of indigenous mountain-asceticism of Shugendo. One of 33 pilgrimage places to Kannon in west Japan. Edo era center for traveling minstrels who entertain educated populace with Buddhist tales; as did Otsu-e, coarsely drawn pictures of Buddhistic lore, from 1620s on popular souvenir of pilgrimage to Mii-dera. Good modern versions. Entering Biwa area via road over Mount Hiei brings one right past MII-DERA. Shop at **Takahashi Otsu-e** store.

Karasaki in nite rain...with its pine-clad point just up west coast from **Biwa-ko Hotel** is usually viewed today from nite excursion boat (June thru Aug) leaves Hama-Otsu 6:15 for 3hr cruise.

Katada with wild geese alighting...little further up coast boasts Ukimi-do, Heian style moon-viewing pavilion set on piles out over water and joined to land by graceful bridge. Ogoto Spa is at this point, some 22min by bus or train from Otsu City, boat from Hama-Otsu port. It's duck-hunter paradise. Famed fish weirs of Biwa are best seen here. Inns feature duck dinners in season: popular is KIKUNOYA ¥-Sw/2.

Awazu, sun shining and breeze blowing...located below Otsu, at Zeze. Best savored traditional style, dine on veranda over water by ruined castle **Ryokan Kimpa** (Golden Waves): dinner ¥2,500+, overnite from ¥-Tw/2.

Yabase with fishing boats...part-way up east coast—still plentiful, tho not as exotic as of old. Boat rental from your hotel or Hama-Otsu enables you to sail or row out and join view. Wind-surfing center. Just beyond Yabase is camp area for students known as Miami—not in old tradition.

Mount Hira's snow-capped peak at twilight...affords cooling view even most of summer. But we found view best from far end of lake, opp side of inverted lute at lovely castle compound of Hikone, leisurely reached by 10:30 steamer, stopping Chikubushima Isle hour, reach Hikone about 3pm in time to sightsee before sumptuous dinner at spot we nominate as gem of entire lake (below).

   Seta Bridge and **Ishiyama temple** are detour, *following*.

HIKONE CASTLE popular subject for travel posters—and justly so. Small enough that it can be taken in visually from close range; small enough that it does not overpower with sheer mass of masonry; small enough that landscape artists could manage to blend it in with its magnificent setting. Built by Ii family in 1603-1623 (tho actually older, as will be seen) and managed to escape wholesale destruction of castles in 1867. Ii Naosuke was assassinated at Tokyo's Sakurada-mon on March 3,1860 for his signing commerce treaty with US envoy Townsend Harris.

   Keep was moved from Otsu Castle; two-storey **Tenjin-Romon Gate** from Hideyoshi's Nagahama Castle. **Taiko-Romon Gate** remains from temple formerly occupying spot, reputedly dating 1080. Great stones formerly parts of Ando, Nagahama and Sawayama; themselves only few decades older than Hikone. Its beauty was recognized by emperor Meiji, who spent nite here when they were beginning to tear castle down. He ordered them to desist. It then became public park, since noted for its cherry trees. In grounds are two former palaces of retreat: **Raku-raku-en** of elder abdicated daimyo, neighboring **Genkyu-en**. You, too, can retreat to these to dine in quiet splendor, like color-photo sections of slicks.

CHOPSTICKS: **Raku-raku-en** (Garden of Pleasure upon Pleasure), 125-year-old retreat of tragic II Naosuke, presently loaned by city as restaurant managed by friendly descendants of councilor of Ii clan. Architectural masterpiece. *Most beautiful room* is Jodan-no-ma, decorated in gold foil for retired lord. Fascinating Jishin-no-ma (Earthquake Room), earthquake-proof on floating pillars joined by linen cables across ceiling. From Raku-raku room view across lotus field to Ohara Benten, Seiryo-ji temples. Dinner, lunch ¥7,-10,000; o'nite ¥-hi-Sw/2; must rsv sat, sun, cherry season **April**; ☎(0749)-22-4560.

Genkyu-en, also known as *Hakkei-tei* (Eight Views Arbor), is luxurious Sukiya-style manse, smaller than Rakuraku-en, 150 years older. Kaiseki (regular full course) lunch or dinner, ¥5,000 and reservations insisted upon with manager suggesting JTB or agent. Overnite runs ¥-lo-S+. Each room has own framed, private view of truly superb gardens, which recreate in their own medium Eight Views of Omi and Siao Siang. For those with less time and/or stamina, Eight Views are best digested here, in privacy.

Might return Otsu by **steamer**, leave about 11am, arr Otsu 5pm. Hour out by boat is **Chikubushima** (boats allow 50min stopover); also reach from Nagahama.

SHOPPING: Nearby Samegai (stop beyond Maibara on JR **train** or **bus** from Hikone Stn) has two attractions. Celebrated **trout farm** has 2,000,000 rainbow trout: you can fish here. Other, **Kami-Nyu**, charming village of woodcarvers, nestled at foot of Mount Unzen (15 mins **bus** from Samegai Stn) along Nyu River. About 200 houses make up this hamlet, three out of four do wood carving. Till last war, religious works comprised most of sculpture; but postwar Samegai **Woodcarvers Guild** set up workshops to make more popular items: badgers, owls, deer and frogs of cryptomeria incorporate grain in design. Frogs measure 5-45cm/2-12in long.

From Hikone follow Omi Tetsudo railway line or Tokaido Highway #8 south. At Echigawa, 3min walk southwest of station brings you to **Omi Art Embroidery**, who make lovely **hand-embroidered** pictures, intricate landscapes painstakingly stitched in natural colors, black and white or in monochrome with delicate shadings. Views of Mount Fuji by Hokusai and Hiroshige's Tokaido series, 8x11 inches, in original colors are lovely. Good place for large items like their 5 x 6ft four-panel screens; wall hangings in 3 x 4ft sizes. If you don't see what you want there, perhaps you can find it at next town of Gokaso, **Shiga Art Embroidery**, 682 Miyanoso; deal in similar work, but wall hangings with brocade borders go up to 1.2m/4ft x 1.8m/6ft size. Both accept special orders. OMI ART displays small selection at **Kyoto Handicraft**.

UJI-GAWA Rhine → Kyoto: best return via OTSU → KYOTO or → NARA for last of 8 views:

Seta and sunset over bridge...is still lovely, old Korean wooden bridge was rebuilt of steel and concrete in imitation of original—actually two bridges meeting at isle in middle of Seta River where lake feeds in to flow to Uji thru 'Uji Rhine'. **Driving** Tokaido-Meishin Hiway from Tokyo you might arrive around sunset, tired from drive, then you come upon Seta Bridge and all is right again long enough to get thru shanty scramble to Kyoto, or around to Biwa-ko Hotel.

Ishiyama in autumn moon...setting gives 'Temple of Stone Mount' fame. Name derives from large rock around which garden formed. #13 of 33 Holy Places of western Japan, attracts many pilgrims. Beauty of place still attracts many leisurely diners and as in Lady Murasaki's day, from here downstream are numerous natural rock formations. Site selected in dream by monk Roben, who founded it 749 to pray for search for gold to gild Nara Daibutsu. Success enabled Roben to build temple, with earlier image of Kannon embodied into newly-carved wooden Kannon, now sealed and viewed every 33 years. Recluse for nobility, Lady Murasaki ca1000 reputedly wrote several chapters of *Genji* here. **Murasaki's room** is preserved, tho original probably burned 1078 after she left, then rebuilt soon after. MINAMOTO Yoritomo late 12th century built two-storey **pagoda Taho-to**, oldest extant in Japan. Princess Yodogimi, Hideyoshi's mistress (we met her at Kyoto's Jidai Matsuri) endowed temple with many of its treasures (*see* p460).

GET THERE: From **Seta Bridge** by rental motorboat (¥3,000/hour) for
traditional water approach to this last of Omi Eight Views, 15min downstream, and onsen
spa of NANGO. Boats also depart Hama-Otsu every 30-60min on 40min cruise via Seta →
Ishiyama-dera Mon mae (Temple Gate). At river landing, inns face water, cater to
overniters and dinner parties; mostly ¥-T-S (*see* UJI, preceding, p460). Direct from
KYOTO, JR Tokaido line → Ishiyamadera stn thence bus to gate, ☎(0775)-37-0013.

En route to Ishiyama-dera, last of Omi Eight Views, sidetrack bit to...

SHIGARAKI: city of potters...and badgers. You see big ones, little ones
—all carry characteristic bottle of sake in one hand, chit-book in other—
in store windows, gardens, almost every home. Badgers relatively new to
this pottery center founded 1,200 years ago when emperor Shomu, who
built Shosoin Treasure Repository, had roof tiles made for his original
palace at Shigaraki. FUJIWARA Tetsuzo started badgers 80 years ago, his old
yard is full of them, 2m tall down to miniatures. Many kiln shops around
town, welcome to browse in workshops. Badgers are both hand-sculpted
and mass-molded. Late Emperor Showa visiting Shigaraki was greeted by
200 flag-bearing badgers—wonder if they put *fundoshi* (jockstraps) on?...
that's no cushion he's sitting on. Tens of 1,000s still sold each year.

Highly prized Ko-(old)-Shigaraki tea pieces of Muromachi-Momoyama
era are priceless in antique shops. New blue glaze developed late 1800s
long highly popular as hibachi-household charcoal braziers, still main
source of home heat in first edition '64. 90% of those in Japan made here.
Modern heating reduced sales from peak 900,000 in 1948 to 500,000 in '62
to 0 now, make great planters—cheap at flea markets until recent 'retro'-
craze for semi-antiques seized local yuppies. However, porcelain stools,
garden tables, decorative plant pots and interesting abstract shapes for
architectural use make up loss.

'Peppermint arches' block past Nakamura's (below) are kiln monument.

SHOPPING: We like **Nakamura Toki** (out from stn to hiway, R 5min walk),
bought big badger as gift and humorous 60cm/2ft seated kappa imp for our garden rock;
Konishi Pottery Export, **Omi Kagaku Toki** Mfg Co for good architectural pieces.

GET THERE: From Ishiyama Stn take scenic Konan **bus** → terminus Shigaraki,
or single track Shiga Kogen line from Kibugawa stn on JR Kusatsu line running between
Nagoya ↔ Kusatsu (on to Kyoto).

SIDE TRIP: from Shigaraki to *Ninja Yashiki* **Ninja¯Manse** in Konan
(next stn down from Kibugawa junction on Kusatsu line, then **taxi** 5min → Omi Seizai
Kaisha) where house is preserved. Here you see various escape traps, secret
tunnels, hidden doors, other trade tricks of masters of Koga-ryu school.
This area and Iga-Ueno City further S were centers of activity of Ninja
masters of *ninjutsu* concentrated here under orders of Tokugawa shogunate.
See IGA-UENO, p.334. (Read about these warrior-magicians in Jay's *Zen Combat*).

WHERE NEXT: GIFU, cormorant fishing and lanterns only 90min on
by JR Shiga Kogen–Kusatsu lines (p.362). 1hr N → Japan Sea, along whose
lovely coast local boats ply to numerous offbeat summer escapes: W →
IZUMO (p.821), or N → exile SADO ISLE (p.951). **Driving** → NARA (p.371),
L from stn, R at fork, L at Kyowa Golf Club (area full of 18ers), Rt307
over scenic hills, hour; out of town first L is Rt422 for IGA-UENO, *above*..

*...wonderful little people who have
renewed, for Europe and America,
the whole idea of Taste.*
—Henry James, 1893

ARCHITECTURE

Cedar Museum Kitayama, *Kitayama-sugi Shiryokan,* 101 Ono-Shimono-cho, Kita-ku, JR bus JR Kyoto stn to Greengarden-mae; ☎406-2241. 9:00-5:30. No-X.

Nijo Jinya, [F-8] Momoyama-style Daimyo (feudal lord) House, *Motorikyu Nijojo,* Nijojo-cho Nijo-dori Horikawanishi-iru, Naka-gyo-ku, city bus #50, 52, 9 from JR Kyoto stn to Nijojo-mae; ☎841-0972 rsve required. 10am-5pm, allow 50min, ¥700, X-NewYear. Combine w/Nijo Castle.

Ohkochi Villa, *Ohkochi-Sanso,* Saga-Ogurayama, Ukyo-ku, 15min walk from Keifuku Arashiyama stn or 10min walk from city bus stop Arashiyama stn or 10min walk from city bus stop Arashiyama; ☎872-2233, 9am-5pm.

Teradaya old-style Inn, *Shiseki Teradaya,* 263 Minamihama-cho, Fushimi-ku, 5min walk N from Keihan Chushojima ☎622-0243. 10am-4pm.

ART

Domoto Insho, Japanese Paintings, [E-5] *Domoto Bijutsukan,* 26-3 Hirano-Kamiyanagi-machi, Kita-ku, city bus from Keihan Sanjo/ JR Kyoto to Ritsumei-kanmae; ☎463-1348 10am-5pm, X-mon–open if nat'l hol. Traditionalist–modernist. Midway betw Ryoan-ji and Kinkaku-ji.

Fusuma Painted Sliding Doors Coll, *Yogen'in,* Sanjusangendo-Mawaricho, Higashiyama-ku, near city bus stop Sanjusangendo Hakubutsukan-mae or Higashiyama-Shichijo; Viewings 11am, 1pm, 2pm, 3pm, X-New Year & for Buddhist services. Call first ☎561-3887.

Ike-no Taiga Art Museum, [B-10] *Ike-no Taiga Bijutsukan,* 57 Matsuo-Mangoku-cho, Nishigyo-ku, 15min walk from Hankyu Kami-Katsura stn on Arashiyama line or Kyoto bus from JR Kyoto stn to Kokedera, ☎381-2832. 10am-5pm, X-mon -if hol, then X-tues.

MUSEUMS 美術館
"X-New Year"= about Dec 24-Jan 7

Imura Art Mus, [I-5] *Imura Bijutsukan,* 29 Shimogamo-Matsubara-cho, Sakyo-ku, 100m south city bus stop Tadasuno-mori ☎722-3300. 10am-5pm, X-wed.

Kitamura Art Museum, *Kitamura Bijutsukan,* Kawaramachi-dori Imadegawa-minami Hitosujime-higashi-iru, Kamigyo-ku, city bus #4, 14, 205 from JR Kyoto stn or Hankyu stn at Shijo-Kawaramachi to Kawaramachi-Imadegawa & 2min walk; ☎256-0637. Open mid-March–mid-June & mid-Sept–end Nov. 10am-4pm, X-mon & day following nat'l hol.

Konpira Ema Museum, *Konpira Emakan* offertory painted plaques of travellers, Yasui Konpira-gu, Higashishioji-Matsubara-agaru, Higashiyama-ku; ☎561-5127. 9:00-4:00, X-mon–open if nat'l hol.

Korean Art Museum, *Korai Bijutsukan* Shichiku Kami-jishi-cho 15 Kita-ku; superb collection of Japanese-Korean businessman Chung Jomun, open 1988, who purchased in Japan art treasures looted from Korea in Hideyoshi's day to Japanese 1904-45 occupation as well as brought in by trade, to eventually return to Korea if reunited. Grateful for loving care and appreciation shown treasures by Japanese, he wants Koreans in Japan to learn more heritage, Japanese to acknowledge cultural indebtedness. Superb art. ☎491-1192; ¥500, stdnt 400; 10-4:30, X-New Year.

Modern Art Museum, *Kahitsukan–Kyoto Gendai Bijutsukan,* 271 Gion-machi-kitagawa, Higashiyama-ku; ☎525-1311. 10:00-6:00, visiting and standing exhibits; X-mon & New Year.

Modern Art Mus, National, [K-7] *Kyoto Kokuritsu Kindai Bijutsukan,* Okazaki Park, Okazaki-Enshoji-cho, Sakyo-ku; ☎761-4111. 10am-5pm; X-mon, NY.

Movie Village, [C-7], *Toei Uzumasa Eiga Mura –Movie Museum,* *Eiga Bunka-kan –Celluloid Art Ctr,* *Eizo Bunka Center,* 10 Uzumasa Higashi-Hachigaoka-cho, Ukyo-ku, 5min walk from Keifuku Dentetsu Uzumasa stn or 13min JR Hanazono; ☎871-3820. 9am-5pm Mar 16-Nov 1; 9:30-4:00 Nov 16-Mar 15; X-Dec 21-Jan 1.

Municipal Art Museum, [K-6/7] *Kyoto-shi Bijutsukan*, Okazaki-Enshoji-cho, Sakyo-ku, ☎771-4107. 9am-5pm, X-mon (open if nat'l hol), and New Year.

National Museum, [J-9], *Kyoto Koku-ritsu Hakubutsu-kan*, 5-27 Chayamachi Higashi-ku; ☎541-1151. 9:30-4:30, X-mon. Top collection Buddhist sculpture from temples.

Noh Paintings Museum, *Noh Kaiga Bijutsukan*, Akimoto-cho, Yase, Sakyo-ku 1min walk from city bus #17, 18 Tozan-guchi stop; ☎712-4757 10am-4pm X-mon.

Nomura Art Mus, [K-6], *Nomura Bijutsukan*, 61 Nanzen-ji Shimo-Kawara-machi, Sakyo-ku, 7min walk from city bus stop Eikando-mae or 10min walk from Keihan Keage stn; ☎751-0153. Open March-mid-June, Sept-Nov 10am-4pm, X-mon, hols.

Paintings Japanese-style Hashi-moto Kansetsu Collection, *Hashimoto Kansetsu Kinenkan*, Hakusa-son-sho, 37 Jodoji-Ishibashi-cho, Sakyo-ku, city bus to Ginkaku-ji; ☎751-0446. 10am-5pm. ¥600/500/450 incl Japanese-style garden and gallery.

Raku Pottery Museum, [G-7], *Raku Bijutsukan*, Aburanokoji Nakadachiuri-agaru, Kamigyo-ku, city bus #50, 9 from JR Kyoto stn to Horikawa-Nakadachiuri; ☎414-0304. 10am-4pm; X-mon (open if nat'l hol), Aug 15-29.

Shibunkaku Art Museum, *Shibunkaku Bijutsukan*, 2-7 Tanaka-Sekiden-cho, Sakyo-ku, 50m W of Hyakumanben; ☎751-1777. 10am-5pm, open for special exhibitions, check *KTO*. ¥500.

Shotenkaku Art Museum, *Shotenkaku Bijutsukan*, 701 Shokokuji-Monzen-cho, Imadegawa-dori Karasuma-higashi-iru, Kamigyo-ku, subway to Imadegawa stn, then 5min walk NE; ☎241-0423. 10-4:30; special exhibits, loan temple treasures, etc.

Sumitomo Collection of Ancient Chinese Bronzeware & Oriental Art *Senoku Hakkokan*, 25 Shishigadani Shimo Miyanomae-cho, Sakyo-ku, 200m walk E from city bus stop Higashi-Tennoji-cho; ☎771-6411. 10-4:00, X-sun, hol, all of July-Aug, Dec-Feb.

Tea Ceremony Research Center, *Chado Shiryokan*, in Ura Senke Center, Horikawa-dori Teranouchi-agaru, Kamigyo-ku, city bus #9 from JR Kyoto stn or #12 Keihan Sanjo stn to Horikawa-Teranouchi; ☎431-3111. 9:30-4:30, X-mon, for exhibit changes, & New Year. Excellent book & video library upstairs, E & J.

ART-CRAFT

Arts and Crafts Gallery, *Sankan Gallery Kachikuan*, 69 Hanase-Bessho-cho, Sakyo-ku; ☎746-0312. Open only sun, nat'l hol, 10am-4pm.

Bamboo-ware Museum, [A-5] *Kyoto Rakusai Chikurin Koen-Take-no-Shiryokan* Ohe Kita Fukunishi-cho 2-chome, Nishikyo-ku, city bus Nishi-3 from Hankyu Katsura stn to Minami-Fukunishi-cho 5min walk; ☎331-3821. 9am-5pm; X-wed, NY; free.

Ceramics Center, *Kyoto Tojiki Kaikan*, Gojozaka, Higashiyama-ku, near city bus stop Gojo-zaka from JR Kyoto stn or Hankyu Shijo-Kawaramachi/ Keihan Sanjo ☎541-1102. 9:30-5:00, X-New Year; free.

Craft Center, 275 Gion-machi-kita-gawa, Higashiyama-ku, 10min walk E of Hankyu Kawaramachi stn; ☎561-9660. 10:00-6:00, X-wed; free.

Designers Association Museum, *Nichizu Design Hakubutsukan*, Dento Sangyo Kaikan 3fl, 9-2 Okazaki-Seishoji-cho, Sakyo-ku, nr city bus stop Kyoto Kaikan-mae; ☎761-5381. 10:am-4:00 (sat 12:00). Open special exhibits only.

Doll Museum, Hokyo-ji Temple, *Hokyoji-monzeki*, Teranouchi-dori Hori-kawa-higashi-iru, Kamigyo-ku; city bus #9 from JR Kyoto stn, or #12 from Hankyu Shijo-Kawaramachi or Keihan Sanjo to Horikawa-Teranouchi; ☎451-1550. Mar 1-Apr 3; Oct 15-Nov 10 10am-4pm.

Doll Museum, *Sagano Ningyo-no Ie* pvt coll old J-folk dolls of clay, paper, papier mache, cloth etc; ¥1,000, in lovely house and garden; 9:30-5, X-tue; ☎882-1421.

Fan Museum, *Ohgaido*, Higashi-Toin-dori, maker, 543 Matsubara-kudaru Shimogyo-ku. 10am-5pm, X-sun, hol, 2nd sat; free.

Flower Arranging Mus, see IKENOBO.

Folk Art Museum, *Kyoto Mingeikan*, Ichijoji-Hayama-cho, Sakyo-ku, city bus #5 for Iwakura from JR Kyoto stn to

Ichijoji-Sagarimatsu, then 5min walk; ☎791-2949. 9am-5pm; ¥500.

Ikenobo Ikebana-Flower Arranging Museum, *Ikenobo Shiryokan.* Exhibits historical documents, pictures of ikebana; also seasonal flower shows. Karasuma Sanjo-sagaru Nakagyo-ku, 3min walk from subway Oike stn; ☎221-2686. 9:00-4:30 (sat-11:30), X-sun & nat'l hol. Admit free, but reservation required.

Kawai Kanjiro House, [I-10], *Kawai Kanjiro Kinenkan.* Major pioneer (1874-1965) with HAMADA Shoji and Britain's Bernard Leach in Japanese & worldwide folkcraft movement 1930s; Exceptional Korean crafts, heart of 'movement'. 569 Gojozaka-kanei-cho Higashiyama-ku, first St W of Higashi-oji-dori, 2nd block S of Gojo Ave; or city bus #206 from JR Kyoto stn to Umamachi, walk W 2min; ☎561-3585. 10am-5pm, X-mon, mid Aug & New Year. Combine with visit nearby Gojo pottery market and Kyomizu temple, or walk N from National Mus to Gojo.

Kiyomizu Pottery, *Kotobuki Toshun,* 7-2 Kawata Kiyomizuyaki-danchi-cho, Yamashina-ku, city bus #1-5 for Daigo Shako from Shijo-Kawaramachi to Kawata ☎581-7195; 9am-5pm (Dec-Feb: X-sun, nat'l hol, New Year); free. Exhibit & sale, watch process.

Kiyomizu Pottery Art Museum, *Kiyomizuyaki-danchi Sogo Tenji-jo,* 10-2 Kawata Kiyomizuyaki-danchi-cho, Yamashina-ku, city bus #1, 5 for Daigo Shako from Shijo-Kawaramachi, get off Kawata. ☎581-6188. 10am-5pm, X-wed; free. Exhibition and sale.

Kyoto Museum, to mark 1200 years of city in 7-storey new bldg and historic 1906 converted Bank of Japan; life-size repro of old alleyway (fast disappearing since our first ed); model of long-gone-Rashomon Gate etc, dummies illustrate period costumes etc; 3rd fl 60 local artists of Kyoto tradition; library classic Kyoto movies shown on rotation; old bank vault now Meiji era cafe. Nr Karasuma subway Oike stn; 10-8:30; X-3rd wed.

Lamp Museum [C-11] *Kusa Lamp-kan,* 8-40 Yamada-Rokunotsubo-cho, Nishigyo-ku, city bus from Hankyu Katsura stn to Chiyohara-guchi then 1min walk; ☎381-9178. 9:30-4:30. Rsv required; free.

Pottery Workshop, *Kyoto Seiyo Kaikan* 20 Sennyuji Tourin-cho,

Higashiyama-ku; ☎531-5678. 10am-5pm, X-sun and New Year; free.

Traditional Industry Municipal Museum, [J-7] *Kyoto-shi Dento-Sangyo Kaikan* 9-2 Okazaki-Seisshoji-cho, Sakyo-ku; city bus #5/300 JR Kyoto stn to Bijutsukan-mae; ☎761-3421. 9am-5pm, X-mon, NewYear; free. Exhibition and sale of traditional art- and handi-crafts, demonstrations of techniques.

HISTORICAL

Archaeological, Mitsui Coll, [K-6] *Mitsui Kyoto Bunkazai Tenjishitsu,* Kyoto Mitsui Bldg, 2fl, 8 Naginata-hokomachi, Shijo-Karasuma-higashi-iru Shimogyo-ku, nr Hankyu Karasuma stn & subway Shijo ☎231-8438. July 11-16: 10:00-7:00; July 17: 10am-4pm (for Gion Festival); other: 10am-4pm, sat 10:00-2:00; free.

Archaeological Museum, [G-5] *Kyoto-Shi Koko Shiryokan,* 265-1 Imadegawa-dori Omiya-higashi-iru, Kamigyo-ku, take city bus from JR Kyoto stn or Hankyu Omiya stn to Imadegawa-Omiya Koko Shiryokan-mae; ☎432-3245. 9am-5pm X-mon (open if nat'l hol, then X-tue); free.

Cultural Museum of Kyoto, *Kyoto-fu Kyoto Bunka Hakubutsukan,* Takakura-dori Sanjo-nishigawa, Nakagyo-ku 2min walk E from subway Oike stn; ☎222-0888. 10:00-8:00, X-3rd wed, New Year. ¥500; 4th fl rotating exhibits.

History of City Museum, *Kyoto-shi Rekishi Shiryokan,* 138-1 Teramachi-dori, Marutamachi-agaru, Kamigyo-ku, city bus from Hankyu stn Shijo-Kawaramachi to Kawaramachi-Marutamachi, then 5min walk; ☎241-4312. 9am-5pm (sat 9-12:00) X-sun, nat'l hol, & New Year; free.

History of Japan Museum, *Nihon Rekishi Shiryokan,* 4 Narutaki-Ondoyama-cho, Ukyo-ku, city bus #26 from JR Kyoto stn or #59 from Sanjo Keihan to Utano; ☎461-0095, 9am-5pm, X-New Yr.

Literature Department Museum of Kyoto University, *Kyoto Daigaku Bungakubu Hakubutsukan,* Yoshida-hon-machi, Sakyo-ku; from subway Imadegawa stn city bus #201, 203 to Hyakumanben, then walk S 60m; ☎751-2111. Open abt 2 months in spring & autumn, 9:30-4:30 (sat -12:00), X-sun & nat'l hol.

Military Museum Arashiyama, [A-7] *Kyoto Arashiyama Bijutsukan,* 33-22 Saga-Tenryu-ji Tsukurimichi-cho Ukyo-ku—weaponry from samurai to WWII, pose photo in samurai armor. Keifuku Dentetsu from Hankyu Shijo-Omiya to Arashiyama stn and 5min walk, or 10min walk Hankyu Arashiyama stn, Arashiyama line; ☎882-1010. ¥700; 9:00-5:30.

Pref Archive Museum, *Kyoto Furitsu Sogo Shiryokan,* Shimogamo-Hangi-cho, Sakyo-ku; ☎781-9101; 9am-4:30pm, X-20th monthly & hols, free.

Ryozen Museum of History, *Ryozen Rekishi-kan,* 1 Seikanji-Ryozen-cho, Kyoto stn to Higashiyama-Yasui, 10min walk; ☎531-3773. 10-4:30, X-mon & New Year.

Traditional Artifacts Collection, [E-5] *Kozu Kobunka Kaikan,* 61 Tenjin michi-dori Imadegawa-minami-iru, Kami-gyo-ku, 5min walk from bus stop Kitano Tenjin-mae; ☎461-8700. Open for special exhibits in spring and autumn.

SCIENCE

Agricultural Tools Museum, *Kyo-no Inaka Mingu Shiryokan,* 2 Koyama-Ogawa-machi, Yamashina-ku; 5min walk S from city bus stop Koyama; ☎581-2302. 9:00-4:30, X-mon, New Year.

Electricity Museum, *Denki-tsushin-gijutsu Shiryokan,* Kawaramachi-Maruta-machi-higashi-iru Kamigyo-ku ☎256-4114 10am-4pm, X-sat, sun, & nat'l hol; free. Edison's first successful filament of carbonized bamboo was from Kyoto.

Science and Nature Museum, *Hieizan Shizen Kagakukan,* Hieizan Sancho, Sakyo-ku, Ropeway from Eizan Dentetsu Yase-Yuen stn or bus stops Yase Yuenchi to Sancho; ☎781-4089. Apr-Sept 9:00-6:00, July 16-Aug 31: 9:00-9:00 pm.

Shimazu Memorial Museum, *Shimazu Sogyo Kinen Shiryokan,* Kiyamachi Minami-iru, 3min walk from city bus stop, Kawaramachi-Niji; ☎255-0980. 9:30-12:00, 1:00-4:00, X-sat, sun, nat'l hol, and New Year; free, rsvn required.

Steam Locomotive Museum, *Umekoji Joki-kikanshakan,* Kankiji-cho, Shimogyo-ku, city bus #205 from JR Kyoto stn to Shichijo-mibu-dori, walk W; ☎314-2996. 9am-5pm, X-mon, New Year.

Weighing Scales Museum, *Hakari-nosho-rekishikan,* inside of Ishida Koki Seisaka-sho, 44 Shogoin-Sanno-cho,

Sakyo-ku, city bus from JR Kyoto stn to Kumano-jinja-mae, then 1min walk; ☎771-4141, 8:30-5:00, X-sun, nat'l hol, 2nd & 4th sat; free. Reservation required.

TEMPLE TREASURE HOUSES — HOMOTSU-KAN

Most only for dry season airing, Nov 1-10. ☎561-1795 for details of year's specials, *see KTO, KVG, Japano-file.*

BYODO-IN temple T.H., *Byodo-in Homotsukan,* 116 Uji-renge, Uji-shi, 6min walk from Keihan Uji stn or 13min JR Nara-line stn; ☎0774-21-2861. Open for 2 mos spring & 2 mos autumn. 9:00-4:00.

DAIGO-JI temple T.H., *Daigo-ji Reihokan & Sanboin,* 22 Daigo-Higashi-Oji-cho, Fushimi-ku; city bus at JR Yamashina stn or Keihan Rokujizo stn to Daigo-Sanboin-mae; ☎571-0002. Open only traditionally dry periods Apr 1–May 25, Oct 1–Nov 25, 9:00-4:00.

DAITOKU-JI, *Cha-shitsu,* tea rooms & gardens normally closed except Nov 1-10.

KITANO TENMANGU SHRINE T.H., *Kitano Tenmangu Homotsuden,* Bakuro-cho, Kamigyo-ku, city bus #8, 55 Hankyu Shijo-Omiya stn or #50 JR Kyoto stn to Kitano-Tenman-gu. ☎461-0005, open 25th monthly mart, 10am-4pm, X-if wet.

KORYU-JI temple T.H., [C-7] *Koryu-ji Reihoden,* 36 Uzumasa-Hachiga-oka-cho, Ukyo-ku, Arashiyama Randen-line from near Hankyu Shijo-Omiya stn to Uzumasa. ☎861-1461, 9-5:00, X-New Yr.

NIN'NA-JI temple T.H., [C-6] *Nin'naji Reihokan,* 33 Omuro-Ohuchi, Ukyo-ku, 100m walk Keifuku Dentetsu Arashiyama line or near city bus stop Omuro-Nin'naji; ☎461-1155. Open: Oct 1-15, 9:00-4:00.

NOGI SHRINE T.H. *Nogijinja Homotsu-kan* 32-2 Itakura-Suo, Momoyama-cho, Fushimi-ku, 10min walk E from JR Momoyama stn or 15min E Keihan Fushimi Momoyama stn; ☎601-5472. 8am-5pm.

Religious Treasure, *Kuramayama Haku butsukan* 1074 Kurama-hon-machi, Sakyo-ku, city bus at JR Kyoto or Hankyu Shijo-Kawaramachi to Demachi-Yanagi; ☎741-2368. 9:30-4:00, X-mon & mid-Dec to Feb.

SHOKOKUJI, *see* SHOTENKAKU ART MUS.

Shotenkaku Art Museum *Shotenkaku Bijutsukan,* Shokoku-ji Monzen-cho 701, Imadegawa-dori Karasuma-higashi-iru,

Kamigyo-ku, subway to Imadegawa, 5min walk NE; ☎241-0423. From 10:00-4:30; special loan exhibits temple treasures, etc.

TOJI temple T.H., *Toji Homotsukan*, 1 Kujo-machi Minami-ku, 7min walk W from Kintetsu Toji stn or bus JR Kyoto stn to Toji-higashimon; ☎691-3325. Open March-May, Sept-Nov, 9:00-4:30.

TOYOKUNI Shrine T.H., *Toyokuni Jinja Homotsukan*, 530 Yamato-oji Shomenchaya-cho, Higashiyama-ku, 150m N of city bus stop Sanjusangendo-mae; ☎561-3802. 9:00-4:30.

See also **National Museum**, [J-9], art treasures on loan from fire-prone temples for safe keeping.

Miroku in Koryu-ji Temple Treasure House

TEXTILE ARTS

Braid Museum, Adachi, *Adachi Kumihimokan*, 9 Kamigamo-Aoinomori-cho, Kita-ku, city bus from Keihan Sanjo stn to Kamigamo-jinja-mae; 9:00-5:30, X-sun, hols, 2nd-3rd sat; free. Rsve ☎722-0008.

Costume Museum, *Fuzoku Hakubutsukan* Horikawa-kado, Shinhanaya-cho, Shimo-gyo-ku, city bus #9 from JR stn to Nishi-Honganji; ☎361-8388. 9am-5pm, X-sun, early to mid-June, & New Year.

Dyeing and Weaving Museum, *Juraku Senshoku Shiryokan*, Teranouchidori Shinmachi-higashi-iru, 10min walk W from subway Kuramaguchi stn; ☎441-4141. 9:00-6:00 (Sat 9:00-1:00), X-sun, nat'l hols, 2nd and 3rd sat. Admission free.

Dyeing Gallery of Shozan, *Shozan Senshoku Gallery*, 47 Kagami-ishi-cho, Kinugasa, city bus #6 from Kyoto stn to Dotenjo-cho ☎491-5101; 9am-5pm X-NY.

Dyeing, *see* also YUZEN, TEXTILE.

Embroidery Museum, *Nihon Shishukan* 36 Nishi-kyogoku-Umatsuka-cho, Ukyo-ku, 20min walk N from Hankyu Nishi-kyogoku stn or city bus #32 from Hankyu Omiya Kawaramachi stn and get down at Nishi-kyogoku-Umatsuka-cho; ☎313-2151 hra 8:30-5:30, X-Aug 14/15, & yearend-New Year.

Kimono Mus, *Azekura Kimono Kogeimura*, 30 Kamigamo-Okamoto-cho Kita-ku city bus #4 JR Kyoto stn to Toyota-cho.

Kyoto Yuzen Dyeing Cultural Ctr [C-9] *Kyoto Yuzen Bunka Kaikan*, Nishikyogoku-Mameda-cho 6, Ukyo-ku; demonstrate art dyeing; from Hankyu Nishikyogoku stn walk E 2min; ☎311-0025. 9am-5pm, X-mon & New Yr; ¥300.

Necktie Museum, [I-7], *Hishiya Kinshoku Hakubutsukan*, Chiyoda-Seimei Bldg 4fl, 640 Nanakanobu-cho, Karasuma-dori Rokkaku-sagaru, Nakagyo-ku, 4min walk from Hankyu Shijo-Karasuma stn; ☎255-4841. 10am-5pm, X-sun, hol; free.

Orient Textile Coll, *Rakufurin Senshoku Shiryo-shitsu*, Iwakura Hataeda-cho 1130 Sakyo-ku, call ahead ☎721-3273, non-J antique, folk fine pvt coll of textile maker.

Textile Center of Nishijin, [GH-5] *Nishijin-ori Kaikan*, Horikawa-dori Imadegawa-minami-iru, Kamigyo-ku, city bus #9 from JR Kyoto stn to Horikawa-Imade; ☎451-9231. 9am-5pm; free.

Textile Culture Hall, *Kawashima Orimono Bunka-kan*, Shizuichi-Ichihara-cho, Sakyo-ku, near city bus stop Komachi-dera or Eizan Dentetsu Ichihara stn; ☎741-3111. 10-3pm, X-alt sat, sun & hols. Leading textile maker, research lab & ancient collections. Call before going.

Yuzen Dyeing & Kimono Museum, *Kodai Yuzen-en Yuzen Bijutsukan,* Takatsujidori Horikawa-nishi-iru, Shimogyo-ku, 5min walk from Hankyu Shijo-Omiya stn or city bus #9/28 at JR Kyoto stn to Horikawa-Matsubara; antique kimono gallery, see Yuzen hand-painting & resist-dying process, English video; sales room. ☎811-8101. 9am-5pm, X-New Year. See also KYOTO YUZEN.

MISCELLANEOUS

Kyoto-style Sweets Shop Private Collection, [J-4], *Kyo-gashi Shiryokan– Girudo House Kyo-gashi,* Karasuma-dori Kamidachiuri-agaru-Nishi-gawa, Kamigyo-ku, subway JR Kyoto stn to Imadegawa stn on Karasuma line, then 3min walk; ☎432-3101. 10am-5pm, X-wed and New Year. Admission free.

Musical Instruments, Traditional Imperial Court, [E-8], *Gagakki Hakubutsukan,* Nishikoji-dori Oike-agaru Futasujime-nishi-iru. Nakagyo-ku, city bus #75 for Narabiga-oka-Kurobashi from JR Kyoto stn to Nishi-koji-Oike, 1min walk; ☎802-2505. 10am-5pm. Rsve req.

Rice Museum, *Okome-No-rekishikan,* Shindo Shokuryo-ten 2fl, 366 Niomon-agaru-Kashirasho, Shinaino-machi, Sakyo-ku, 8min walk NE from Keihan Sanjo stn; ☎771-2987. 10am-4pm, X-sun, hol; free.

Special Exhibition Hall, *Rakuto Ihokan,* 472 Nishibashi-cho, Tonyamachi-dori Gojo-sagaru 3-chome, Higashiyama-ku; ☎561-1045. Open: April 1-May 5, Oct 1-Nov 3, 10am-4pm, X-mon.

Stationery Museum, *Bungu Shiryokan* Buntendo (famous shop, itself sightseeing worthy) 2fl, Teramachi-Sanjo-agaru, Nakagyo-ku; ☎223-1660. 9am-5pm, X-sun & nat'l hol.

Tin Toy Collection, *Antique mama Kyoto,* Shijo-dori Horikawa Higashi-iru, Minamigawa; ☎223-2416. Toy shop, but unique collection beloved 'Made in Japan' junk predecessors of today's hi-tech.

See Also in *KTO, Kyoto Visitors' Guide, Kinki* or daily newspaper for **Department Stores'** 1-2 week special loan exhibitions and art dept, *bijutsu-bu,* commercial shows.

Kyoto is in season all year round...
—late Mr Kawana, *Manager, Miyako Hotel*

PERSONAL DATEBOOK

WE AGREE. For this festive town in our master file are over 400 dates, besides 100-odd *ennichi* (feast day marts) of local shrines, temples. If in search of local color, but your days in town don't match this list, check TIC-Tourist Information Center, ground floor of tower, opp Kyoto Stn.

Check also *Kansai Time Out* or *Kyoto Visitors Guide, Kinki, Japan Times*, or *Mainichi Daily News* Monday 'Japanofile'. Worst weather is in January-February, but many fascinating fetes take place. July-August is hot, humid, but happily lively. May *Aoi Matsuri*, July *Gion Matsuri* and October *Jidai Matsuri* are outstanding and worth building your itinerary around. April-May and October-November see geisha dance extravaganzas.

Monthly Ennichi, temple **flea markets**, *see*, at Toji [F-1] 1st Sun (antiques only), 21st; Kitano [E-6] 25th—great buys, go early, carry spare film. **Not listed** monthly below. Great pottery fair Aug 7-10.

Rituals of New Year are still part of Kyoto way of life, with many fun events:-*hajime* and *hatsu-* rites are 'firsts' of year.

* indicates event worth building Itinerary around

Information: **T.I.C. ☎075-371-5649**, or 0120-444-800 (from out of town)

January

*1 Midnite, 108 bells have sounded, **hatsu-modé** first shrine visits, several days. Eat New Year noodles for long life. In dark climb nearby mountain to view year's first sunrise from peak.

2-4 Kakizome, First Calligraphies Rite: Kitano-tenman-gu, [I-8], 9am.

3 Kyogen theatrical Noh farces. Gion Yasaka Shrine [I-8], 9am; *Karta-tori* poem card contests by kimonoed gals, 2pm.

4 *Kemari-hajime* ancient court football: Shimogamo-jinja [H-6], 2pm.

8-12 *Hatsu Ebisu*, Ebisu Shrine fair, monetary offerings to Ebisu patron of business. Most shrines observe 9, 10, 11.

14 *Hadaka Odori* Naked Dance Hino Hokai-ji temple [L-16] 7pm, loin-clothed mob chant, rub against each other back, forth.

15 *Toshiya 'zen'* archery rite Sanjusangendo [I-10] 8am all day. (*See* text).

*21 *Hatsu Kobo* First St Kobo Day grand *ennichi* fair Toji [F-11] stalls cover great monastery grounds, sell novelties; special statuary treasures to public view this day only; lesser ennichi monthly 21st.

*25 *Hatsu Tenjin* First Tenjin *ennichi* Kitano Tenmangu [E-6], 1000s of stalls. Sugawara Michizane, patron of education & letters, enshrined; calligraphy-hajime, exhibit; monthly mart, antiques, kimono.

Late Winter Comedy (noh-kyogen) show, Shigeyama-kyogen, at Minamiza, for date check TIC, watch *KTO*, *KVG*.

February

Mid- thru mid-March added tours offered to normally closed temples and collections for winter dry-weather openings; individuals may go on own, entry-fee ¥200-600, also special theme tours such as 'special taste' taking in noted folk restaurant then to temples which offer special good-luck foods, little pickle shops etc; another *wabi* course takes in tea ceremony houses and gardens, some normally closed; another *miyabi* to temples, shrines relate to Imperial House; *uruwashi* course takes in temples & sites with reference to famous women. Two dozen to choose from, guides in Jpn but TIC can arrange for English PR. Starts abt 10:30 at Kyoto stn Karasuma side, abt 5-6hrs. ¥7,200+w/meals.

First Sun Monthly antique only fair-Toji.

*3 *Setsubun-Tsuina-shiki* Bean Tossing rite, sometimes **4th**: most shrines & temples, throw parched beans to get rid of demons. Most spectacular Yoshida Shrine [J-6] & Rosan-ji temple [H-6]. First nite, grand tsuina demon purification Yoshida 6pm, talisman mart, rituals, burn old talismans, then Grand Goblin confronts priests. 3pm (usually 3rd) fire fight that'd turn New York fire marshals white as 3 hideous demons invade Buddhist temple Rosan-ji [H-6] twirling torches to stop rite. Quelled by reciting of full sutra, become 'good guys', sit outside to bless children. To see more good fights: after Rosan-ji, eat and train over to Nara to catch either great nite rites: 7pm, Kofuku-ji (better) or Horyu-ji; then rush up to see Kasuga Shrine for bugaku dance 8pm, amid 3,000+ lanterns lit only twice in year—tonite being one, other Aug 15.

11 *Hoshi Matsuri* Fire Festival, 7am start daylong biggest mob event, 10s of 1,000s crowd new religion Agon-shu's stadium at Kitakazan E Kyoto hills, to burn millions of prayer-sticks to daylong drum beating.

11 *Kyogen* by Shigeyama clan, all day, Kanze Kaikan, free ☎771-6114.

21 Monthly fair, Toji temple.

25 *Baika-sai* Plum Blossom Fete, Kitano Tenmangu Shrine [E-6]; 10am rite for Sugawara Michizane, 9th century scholar-statesman for whom shrine is consecrated. Thick tea served in lovely garden, fee. — Monthly market, ditto Kitano Shrine.

*Late (date varies) Traditional Folk Entertainment Festival, rarely presented folk dances, theater rarely seen by locals, ancient rites ¥1,500, Kyoto Kaikan #1 Hall ☎771-6051.

March

1 Hokyo-ji Temple of Dolls [G-5] displays fabulous collection dolls till Apr 3.

13 *Ju-san Mairi* Horin-ji temple [A-8], Saga, pilgrimage of 13-year-olds.

*14–16 Memorial for Shaka (Historic) Buddha many temples observe Feb 15-16. Many show treasured Nehan-e pictures of 'death' or ascension of Shaka; especially Tofuku-ji [I-11] with 24 x 48ft picture; Sennyu-ji [J-11] slightly larger. Tofuku-ji unique as only one includes cat mourner.

15 3:30, 5:00, 6:30pm *Saga Dainenbutsu Kyogen*, religious comic pantomimes. *Taimatsu* Fire Festival Saga Shaka-do [A-6] 8pm. Burn trio 20-ft torches predict crop.

Mid–end Equinox brings people to clean, decorate family graves, rites all temples.

21, 25 Monthly flea markets.

April

Oh, to be in Kyoto now that April's here. Beauty reigns—cherry blossom parties & festivals; geisha dances, all 4 main troupes (all have extra showings Sun); top price includes special tea ceremony by geisha. Beginning and ending dates vary annually.

*1–30 *Miyako Odori*, Gion Geisha, Gion Kaburenjo Theater [I-9] noon-, 4x-day.

15-25 *Kitano Odori* of Kami-shichiken Geisha, at Kitano Kaikan [E-6].

First Sun–3rd Sun *Kyo Odori*, Geisha Miyagawa Kaburenjo [I-9] 1 & 3:30pm.

Cherry-viewing big attraction, rightfully so for Kyoto has numerous lovely areas. Our favorite is stroll up to picturesque Kiyomizu Temple [J-9], end Maruyama Park to dine. Down from Kiyomizu turn R just before buspark at spice shop, continue bear R, come out by big Ryozen Kannon (vegetarian meal across at Ikkyuan) and Kodai-ji [J-9] to Maruyama Park [I,J-8,9] lovely trees. Complete evening with dining full dinner here in park at Sa-ami Restaurant or Nakamura-ro by Yasaka Shrine [I-8]; or choice of picturesque restaurants lining N side driveway entering from Yasaka—recommend *sukiyaki* or *mizutaki*; or light meal at Hiranoya Imobo. Northwest lovely, we make circle route from Hirano Shrine [E-5] to Arashiyama [A-7,8]. From Hirano (10-*Cherry Festival*) visit Omuro's ancient palace-style Ninna-ji temple [C-5,6] drive thru rural area of Hirosawa-Ozawa Ponds to little-visited Rakushisha [A-6], end up at Arashiyama. Other spots: Yase-Ohara NE; Heian Shrine [J-7] has musical concerts and tea ceremonies in garden blossom time, fee; most elaborate affair lasts 3 weeks at...

1-21 *Cherry Blossom Fete* Daigo-ji [L-14] site of grand cherry-viewing parties by Hideyoshi; show many temple treasures.

2nd Sun 1pm gala historical parade of Hideyoshi, wife Yodo-gimi & court; Daigo-ji, big tea party, dances, *kyogen*.

15 1 pm, kyogen farces under blossoms at Seiryu-gu in Daigo-ji.

Entire month filled with festivities; temples, shrines and groups hold annual spring fetes and shows. There's even firewalking: for which *see* also Nara, Miyajima (How to).

First Sun *O-yumi* Archery Fete, Wara Tenjin a.m. bout with 8ft 'zen' longbows.

Beginning *Hana Matsuri* Flower Fete, (main day 8) Buddhist Easter, all temples; best Higashi Hongan-ji [F-10].

2nd Sun *Yasurai Matsuri* Demon Procession, Imamiya Shrine [F-4] huge cherry blossom and camellia-decorated parasols fend off demons. From morning, but best about 2pm shrine; splendid costumes, demon dances.

2nd Sun Gosho Imperial Palace [G-6] open free to public. Crowded. No set date, check.

14 Shiramine Shrine [G-6] gala Spring Fete, 11am kagura dances; *bugaku*; *kemari* Heian era court football played in elaborate brocade robes. Check for times.

14-16 *Ikebana Festival*, 9-5pm, Saga School, Daikaku-ji temple (*see* p.454).

16 *Spring Fete* Heian Shrine [J-7], procession of priests 10am; great tea rite 10am, dance & *gagaku* music pm.

18 *Spring Fete*, Yoshida Shrine [J-6], Yamato-mai pre-bugaku dance form 10:30am by Nara's Kasuga Shrine group.

19 *O-mi-nugui*, annual cleaning Buddha Image at Seiryo-ji [A-6], 2pm.

29 *Kyokusui-no-utage* Heian era poetry party, costumes. Jonan-gu, 2pm, free.

21-29 *Mibu-kyogen* (masked farces), old noh form, Mibudera temple [F-9] daily 1pm 5 plays, nite show added on 29th.

28-29 Iwaya-yama *Hiwatari* Fire walking, on Fudo's feast day; most unusual rite led by *yamabushi* (priests), as huge bonfire burns down to hot coals, follower men, women, children walk over hot embers: *Iwaya*-yama Shimyo-in [L-1], 1pm just past Yase (*see* Miyajima for how-to).

Sun after 20th *Spring Fete* Matsuo Shrine, patron shrine of brewers [B-9]: palanquin parade 11pm. Best as cross Katsura R, abt noon.

*Mid Week-long *Ikebana* Flower Arrangement Show sponsored jointly by 30 different Kyoto Ikebana Schools, Daimaru Dept Store [H-8].

May

Geisha dances continue into month (see April); but *Aoi Festival* 15th steals spotlight (often rained out) as spring festivals continue in full swing with . . .

1-24 Kamogawa Odori Pontocho Geisha, Pontocho Kaburenjo [I-8] 12:30pm, 3 shows. Perhaps best geisha dance of all.

1-4 *Dai-nembutsu Kyogen* religious mime at Shinsen-en [F-8], like Mibu-Kyogen, see April 21, 1-6pm. 3-4 till 10pm.

3 Fushimi Inari Shrine [I-12] huge priest procession 2-5:30.

3 *Fudo Bonfire Ceremony* Tanuki-dani, yamabushi mountain priests parade, noon.

*5 Ancient horse race, brilliant costumes, Kami-gamo Shrine [G-2] 1 pm.

5 Fujinomori Shrine Fete, [I-l4], 7:30 am.

5 *Purification Rite* for Aoi Festival queen in 12 layer kimono, her court, Kami-gamo [G-2] even-, or Shimo-gamo Shrine [I-5] odd-, years. No set date, check.

*15 *Aoi Matsuri* Hollyhock Festival, both Kami-gamo [G-2] and Shimo-gamo [I-5] Shrines. Colorful Heian Era parade, hollyhock-bedecked imperial ox-cart 10am from Imperial Palace [H-6] Contact TIC, playguides, for res'd seats in review stand. Down Oike past City Office [H-7] back to Kamo Shrine for bugaku.

Mid-Sat, Sun *Annual Fete* Kan Daijin Tenman-gu Shrine [G-19]: Sun 10am tea ceremony, Sat 1pm yamabushi parade; Sun main event portable shrine procession 2pm kyogen farces.

3rd Sun Ebisu Shrine [I-9], procession 9am mikoshi-floats.

18 Shimo Goryo Shrine [H-7] largest palanquin in Japan; short procession boys in Heian Era robes.

Mid (3 wks after Apr-sun-20th+ fete) *Spring Festival* Matsuo Shrine [B-9] 6 palanquins return from temporary quarters where taken previous month. Start 8am, gather Karahashi Bridge abt 12pm, wade river, proceed along Nishioji-Shichijo area, arrive Matsuo Bridge 5pm.

*3rd Sun *Mifune Boat* Festival Arashi-yama Park [A-8] 1pm. Gaily decorated boats for musicians and guests reenact imperial boat party of Heian era. Kuruma-zaki Shrine [A-8] sponsors can arrange place on boat, as Japan Fdtn often helps scholars board.

June

1-21 Dress up as Ohara-me flower girl in blue & white kimono, *see* Join In, below.

1 Kibune Shrine Fete,*mikoshi* float parade, 2-6pm; lovely outing in mountains; Kurama branch Keifuku Line NE Kyoto.

*1-2 *Takigi Noh*, Heian Shrine [J-7]: 5:30pm. Outstanding joint outdoor program by all *noh* schools, stage bonfire-lit.

7-9 Annual *yamabushi* mountain priests *Pilgrimage* to Holy Mt Omine Nara Pref. 7am; abt 1,000 picturesque yamabushi gather at Daigo-ji [L-14] then Hoo-in, Abenobashi, Osaka, proceed to stn on to Omine.

Around 6-8 Iris best at Heian Shrine Gardens [J-7], open free 1 day; usually fee.

10 *Otaue* Rice Planting Festival, Fushimi Inari [I-12] 1pm; 4 shrine maidens dance followed by actual rice planting in sacred paddy to traditional songs and dances.

15 Monthly festival Yasaka Shrine [I-8] 14 *kagura* dances 7pm.

20 *Takekiri* Bamboo Cutting *Ritual* Kurama -dera Temple (NE of Kyoto) 2pm. Old legend has 1000+ years ago, saint under-going ascetic practices attacked by huge serpents which he subdued by prayer; today 4 in warrior-priest outfits divide into two teams, vie to see who cuts thru 4 bamboo 'snakes' fastest. Taxi 6x-mtr, train Eizan line 30min from Demachi-Yanagi stn on hr & half-hr, ¥320 o.w.

21, 25 Montly flea market: Toji, Kitano.

July

Heat hangs low over bowl that is Kyoto; as *Gion Matsuri*, truly one spectacular of Japan takes up most of month with rites; July 1 *Cormorant Fishing* (opp) begins at Arashiyama Togetsu Bridge [A-7] till Aug 31, nitely 7:30-9; floating of lanterns. During first week on *Gion Miya-bi*, Gion geisha in matching *yukata* do pilgrimage from Yasaka Shrine [I-8] to Shijo-Tabisho [H-8] Kawaramachi. Rice-planting season over, many shrines, temples hold festivals to pray for hot summer, thus good crop.

1 *Business Prosperity Fete* Fushimi Inari [I-12] 8am-4pm; Ward off Insects Kamigamo Shrine [I-5] noh 1pm.

First Sun *Antique Market*, Toji Temple.

7 Shiramine Shrine [G-6] Kemari costumed Heian Court football 3pm, also Tanabata Star Festival here 2:30pm and at Kitano Tenman Shrine [E-6] 1pm.

7 Kibune Shrine (NE Kyoto) festival 10:30am tea ceremony & *Bugaku* dances.

10 *Gion Matsuri mikoshi*-washing rite, at Shijo Bridge [I-8] by participants who gather 5pm at Yasaka Shrine [I-8]; then at 7:30pm carry *mikoshi* to Bridge.

9-12 Senbon Shaka-do [F-5] thanksgiving by potters, 3-day pottery fair in temple.

*14-16 *Gion Festival* Eves, all floats gaily lit, displayed downtown, musicians sing; treasured Gobelin tapestries, paraphernalia displayed in nearby quarters. *Byobu* Folding Screen Fete: shops, homes N of Shijo in Muromachi area open home to show-off treasured screens, art to public -Lovely stroll, easy contact with everyday Kyoto-ites. May board many floats to examine.

14-16 6-10pm Gion, music & kagura dance

*17 *Gion Festival*: In 869 plague, emperor asked gods at Yasaka for relief; repeated 975AD, annual since 1124. Decorated floats more elaborate in Tokugawa Era as each area tried to outdo. 9 steeples with halberd top called *hoko*, 'spears', 25m tall carry bands, 17-20 century Persian carpets, (which we introduced to NY Met museum experts in 1961, '68—finally came to study '88,'90), 17 cent French & Korean tapestries; 23 flattops *yama* 'mountain', dolls & folks illustrate history. (Similar to India Juggernaut, also in Katmandu, Nepal). Start Shijo W of Karasuma 9am → Shijodori → Shijo Kawaramachi 9:35 → Kawaramachi-dori → Oike 10:25 → end Oike Shinmachi 11:20. 5pm carry

Yasaka *mikoshi* thru shrine area. Mobs, but special tourist seats, fee, TIC.

17 *Sagi-mai* Heron Dance, purification rite, 2.5m/8ft tall man-birds in loveliest dance offering anywhere, Yasaka Shrine inner court 4:30, riverbank Sanjo Bridge 5:30.

21, 25 Monthly flea market: Toji,Kitano.

23 *Rice-planting* MatsuoShrine [B-8] 10am

23-24 *Gion Matsuri* repeat of 17 but much smaller procession from Shinmachi Sanjo

24 *Hanagasa* Umbrella parade & Sagi-mai (repeat of 17th) Yasaka Shrine 11am.

25 *Kyogen* Yasaka Shrine [I-8] 11am.

*27 *Fire walking* Tanuki-dani Fudo-in [I-7] Ichijoji Sagarimatsu ☎781-5664; 5pm, chant sutras, build bonfire, 7pm faithful walk hot coals-*see* Miyajima.

28 Wash Yasaka*mikoshi* Kamo River 8pm return Shrine 8:30pm closes Gion Fete.

Doyo Day of Ox Traditionally hottest day of year, best to eat energy-giving broiled eel. Renge-ji [K-2] nr Omuro Stn Kitano Line, pray over cucumbers; *Mitarai* Fete Shimo-gamo Shrine [I-5] wade thru pond.

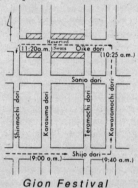

Gion Festival

August

Rokusai Nembutsu dances held this month various places. Gets name from Rokusai (Six Days of Fast 1, 8, 14, 23, 29 + last of month) when dances held, 7:30pm or later; *Nembutsu* means offering prayers. Started late Heian Era, however character changed till now it's folk dance. On fast days, 4 Deva Kings are said to rule, demons try to divert folk. Kissho-in Temple's five 30-man teams perform as drums, flutes, bells all accompany their catchy tricks. Dances mid-Aug bon season. Dates vary but recent list:

9,10,16 Mibu Dera temple [F-9];

22 Jozen-ji at Kuramaguchi-Teramachi; Kisshoin Tenman-gu Shrine [E-12] 8 pm;

27 or 28 and Sept 4 Umenomiya Shrine Ukyo-ku [B-8]; Check TIC, varies.

Hassaku, **First of Month**, elaborately groomed geisha & maiko make rounds to thank teachers, clients, etc, good time to see costumes on streets of Gion, 11am-on.

*7-10 *Rokudo Mairi* pilgrimage to Roku-do Chinko-ji temple, believed gateway to nether world; ring bell, many food and souvenir stalls 6am–midnite; bus # 202, 206, 207 to Kiyomizu-michi, walk 5min.

*7-10 *Toki Matsuri* Pottery Fair; all Gojo pottery area [I-9] huge mart, wholesalers, shopkeepers dump wares: bargains. Fun atmosphere, lovely stroll, good buys.

8-10 *Rokuhara Manto-e* 100's of oil lamps burning, Rokuhara Mitsu-ji temple 8pm; at Matsubara-Yamatooji sts.

14-16 *Manto-e*, Light Lanterns 6-9pm Otani Sobyo (Higashi Otani) cemetery [J-10], S of Maruyama Park.

*16 *Yuzen nagashi*, rinse long bolts yuzen-dyed fabric in Kamo river nr Sanjo Bridge 11:30, 12:30 pm; former summer long sight in river till anti-pollution drive—pure water of river became less so.

–5-9:30pm, *Bon dance*, *Yukata* contest, *yomise* nite stalls Okazaki Park [J-7] nr Heian.

– *Manto nagashi* 100s lighted lanterns float in river at Arashiyama bridge [A-8], in mem WWII dead, sunset-on. Cormorant fishing; & ideal view huge bonfires of...

9-16 *800 Lanterns lit* Mibu Temple 6pm.

– *Toro nagashi* lantern float Hirosawa Pond [B-6], 7pm.

16 *Daimon-ji Okuri-bi*, huge bonfire in shape of Chinese character *dai* (great): Nyoidake Mountain, Higashiyama. Last *bon* rite, lighting path back for souls after visiting loved ones. Huge bonfire lit 8pm: horizontal stroke 230 feet long, downward L-stroke 510ft, R 410ft. Simultaneously, bonfires form ideograph *Myoho* N on Mt Matsugasaki [I-3]; Japanese boat on Mt Funayama [E-2] –lit. 'ShipMount'; another dai on mt behind Kinkaku-ji [E-5]; great torii lit Mt Saga.

21, 25 Monthly flea market: Toji, also Kitano which features children's art thru 29

23-24 *Jizo-bon* festivities all neighborhood Jizo shrines (5,000 in Kyoto) kids worship Jizo, guardian of kids & travelers.

24 *Hanagasa Odori*, flowered-hat dance, Shikobuchi Shrine, rural NE Kyoto.

September

1 Open Sacred Mountain: yamabushi, banners flying, dep Shogo-in [I-7] Temple 8am annual pilgrimage → Mt Omine.

First Sun *Hassaku Sai*, Matsuo Shrine [B-9], 10am, harvest prayer to patron deity

of agriculture, offerings include sumo, Rokusai Nembutsu dances.

— Monthly antique fair, Toji temple.

9 *Karasu* Crow Sumo at Kami Gamo Shrine [G-2] 10am. Children's *sumo*. Early Kamo inhabitants were Karasu Clan.

15 or wknd near full moon, 3-9pm, tea ceremony on boat or riverside, view moon Nakanoshima isle, Uji. See *KTO,TIC*.

– *Iwashimizu Festival*, Iwashimizu Hachiman Shrine parade of Gohoren *mikoshi* 3am, return 5pm in torchlight procession.

21, 25 Monthly flea market: Toji, Kitano.

21 *Festival* of Shiramine Shrine [G-5,6], 10am rite, noon *bugaku*, other dances.

Nite pre-Autumnal Equinox *Nagoshino Shinji*, loin-clothed men shoot purifying arrows into pond, Shimogamo Shrine, 7pm

23 *Autumnal Equinox*, national holiday as entire families visit graves 23rd.

Full Moon-viewing at Daikaku-ji temple, enjoy tea ceremony on boat or garden with koto music; 6-9pm; see TIC.

20–Nov 23 Homotsukan Treasure Hall of Toji Temple open to public, daily 9-4:30, ¥400, check TIC for exact dates.

October

Tho Gods, all 80,000-but-one, supposedly left for meeting at Izumo Grand Shrine Shimane Pref, month has local shrine fetes, rural harvest fetes and biggest event of year, *Jidai Matsuri*, Pageant of Ages. Nature starts coloring mountainsides and Kyoto's geisha add color to local scene with semi-annual dances.

First Sun *Tea Festival*, Uji City's Uji Bridge [L-20] 9am. Uji is famous for tea; its river water liked by Hideyoshi for tea.

3rd Sun Nasu Shrine [H-6] 9am rites; 1pm parade 0–mikoshi, big floats, 25 Buddha, *chigo* & *yamabushi*.

1-5 *Zuiki Matsuri* Kitano Tenmangu [E-6]. 4th noon parade *mikoshi* of fresh *zuiki*-rhubarb, vegetables.

15-Nov 7 *Kamogawa Odori* geisha dances at Pontocho Kaburenjo [I-8] 3x-daily: 12:30, 2:20, 4:10pm.

9 *Fall Festival*, Imamiya Shrine [F-4], 10am. *Azuma-asobi* bugaku dances.

9 *Fall Festival*, Shimo-gamo Shrine [I-5], 1pm ceremonies, dance offerings.

1-10 *Hanagasa Matsuri*, Goko-no-miya Jinja [H-15], 1 & 9 eve kimono'd youths carry huge *hana-gasa* flowered parasols.

10-11 Fushimi Grand Shrine's largest festival, SE of city, 1pm music, dances.

10 *Shamenchi Odori*, Yase Akimoto Shrine [L-1]. Rites 10am; 8pm unusual primitive dance by men dressed as women with huge paper cut-out lanterns on heads.

10 *Ushi* Bull Festival, Koryu-ji [C-7]. Sad, but cancelled 5 years ago: revive?

12-14 *Fall Festival* Yoshida Shrine [J-6]. Colorful mikoshi procession thru parish, hundreds chigo, samurai, **14th** 11:30am.

3rd Sun *Bosatsu Parade* Sennyu-ji temple [I-11] 1pm. Portray descent to earth from paradise by 25 children garbed in bosatsu robes, Kannon masks proceed down raised way from Hondo-paradise to Jizo-do-earth.

15-Nov 7 *Kamogawa Odori* Ponto-cho geisha full dance program. Only 2 geisha dances in fall. ☎221-2025.

16 *Festival*, Ima-Hie Shrine [I-10] opp Myoho-in; rites 10am, *Kagura* dance.

17 *Fall Festival*, Hyuga Dai-jingu [K-8], **16-17**, 2pm, *mi-kagura* and other dances.

19 *Funaoka Festival* Kenkun Shrine [F-5] where Oda Nobunaga enshrined, 1-5pm.

19 *Memorial Service* Heian Shrine [J-7], brief rite in memory of emperor Komei, last Kyoto emperor, 10am.

19-21 *Hatsuka* (20th) *Ebisu Fair*, Ebisu Shrine [I-9], businessmen make pilgrimage to shrine colorful. Most Ebisu Shrines do 10th-day fairs, but this special.

21, 25 Monthly flea market: Toji, Kitano.

22 *Jidai Matsuri* Pageant of Ages, p.439 reserved seats Imperial Palace, Oike-dori, Heian Shrine, *fee*. Spectacular 4km/2.5mi long costume parade of varied ranks since founding of Heian Kyoto in 794 till Meiji era, 1867 when capital moved to Tokyo. Starts Imperial Palace noon, passes along Karasuma St, Shijo-Kawaramachi, Sanjo, arriving Heian Shrine abt 4 pm. *See* text.

22 *Kurama Fire Festival*, Kurama-dera, p.446. For **Getting There** *see* June 20.

23 Festival of sub-shrine of Yoshida Shrine [J-6], 1-5 pm, small procession.

25 *Harvest Offering* Fushimi Inari Fox God Shrine [I-12]. Sacred paddy rice cut, offered to Shrine 11am; dances follow.

30 *Founder's Day* Tenryu-ji [A-7] for artist-priest Muso Kokushi; 10am.

November

Mountains around Kyoto riot of color early November as maples turn to brilliant reds, oranges & yellows. Best seen Takao [A-2] in NW, Arashiyama [A-8,9] Yase and Ohara NE. In city, entire Higashiyama range, Kiyomizu Temple [J-9], Shugaku-in Detached Palace [K-3], Shinsendo [K-4], Ho-nen-in [K-6], Maruyama Park [J-8].

Chrysanthemums also best Nijo Castle [F-7] **Maruyama** Park [J-8], Zoo [J-7],

Daikaku-ji [A-6]. Annual Flower Arrangement show mid-Nov by Ikenobo School at Rokkaku-do [G-8]. *See* daily papers & *KTO* or *KVG* for 'mum doll shows.

1-10 *Treasure Airing* varied temples annually, *see KTO, KVG, Japano-file*.

7 *Kamogawa Odori* cont'd (*see* Sep 15).

1-10 *Gion Odori* dances by Gion geisha at Gion Kaikan [J-8] 2x-daily.

Oct 15-Nov 5 Doll Temple Hokyo-ji [G-5] shows dolls all month.

Fall harvest, many O-*hitaki* fire rituals as 'first fruits' offered and prayer sticks burn in bonfire, various shrines, temples.

First Hare Day of Month (varies 1-12) Matsuo Shrine [B-9] Festival gathers sake, liquor makers from entire nation.

1 *Fall Festival* Kibune Shrine NE Kyoto lovely maples; simple rites 10am.

1 *Kenka Sai* Flower Festival, Fushimi Inari Shrine [I-12] flower offering 9am.

3 *Fall Fete* Tanuki-dani Fudo-in [K-4]; 1pm parade yamabushi, *chigo*, priests 2pm large service.

3 *Poetry Party* Jonan-gu Shrine [G-12] garden, 2pm; after dance 7 poets in 8th cent garb jot 31 syllable tanka poems before sake cups float by; free, including *sencha* tea service. Kintetsu RR to Takeda stn, bus 1, 2 or 3 to Shrine stn, walk 200m. ☎611-0575.

8 *O-hitaki* (Harvest festival) at Fushimi Inari Shrine [I-12] new rice straw offered God of Fire in fire rite, with prayer for prosperity and warding off evil; 1pm main shrine; 2pm and 6pm at shrine garden: *kagura nincho* dance by bonfire.

2nd Sun *O-hitaki* Kazan Shrine 2:30pm; as fire burns down oranges tossed in, people scramble for them as talismans against colds, evil, bad luck etc.

2nd Sun *Momiji Matsuri* Arashiyama Maple Festival [A-8], 10am, colorfully decked boats of *noh, bugaku, Rokusai-nembutsu* dances; *koto* playing, outdoor tea ceremony, art exhibition.

2nd Sun *Memorial*, Kuyado, Gokuraku-in [G-8] for St Kuya 1pm Rokusai-nembutsu.

11 *Memorial service* Myoshin-ji temple [D-6] for emperor Hanazono, 10am service; 9-4 pm tea party, famed gardens.

13 *Lacquer Fete* Horin-ji temple [A-2] 11am, area of Hata immigrants who brought skills. Lacquer deity enshrined here, all involved in lacquer attend.

14 *O-hitaki*, at Ima-Hie Shrine [J-10] 3pm ceremony, *kagura* folk plays, bonfire of wooden prayer sticks.

Cormorant fishing, Summer pleasure

15 *Shichi-go-san* Mairi or 7-5-3 Pilgrimage, nationwide as kimonoed children 7, 5, 3 years old visit shrines to thank for health.

***15** Migawari Fudo* Hoju-ji Temple [I-10] *Bugaku* noon. Large fire festival 2pm by *yamabushi* w/ full ritual, parade thru city.

21, 25 Monthly flea marts: Toji, Kitano.

21-28 *Ho-onko Memorial Service* at Higashi Hongwan-ji [G-10] for St Shinran continuous daily 7am-4pm.

22 *O-hitaki* at Koryu-ji T [C-7] home of lovely Miroku Bosatsu, early Asuka era: rites to Prince Shotoku 1pm; secret statue shown yearly only this day from 9-4.

23 *Fude Kuyo* Memorial for writing brushes, pencils Tofukuji [I-11] Shokaku-an. 1pm. At Shokaku-an thousands of old writing brushes burned in rite, *chigo* & *yamabushi* [mountain priests] parade; writers, painters, school children attend.

23 *O-hitaki* Shiramine Shrine [G-5,6] 7pm.

26 *Ochatsubo Hoken Sai* at Kitano Tenman-gu Shrine [E-5] offering teas of various growing areas by tea masters; parade from city hall thru city to Shrine.

December

Nov 30-Dec 25 *Kaomise*, Minami-za [I-8] 'face-showing' rite announced actor hired for next season, this month top actors Tokyo-Osaka-Kyoto present year's outstanding kabuki. One of rare shows of classical *kabuki* in Kyoto. *Naga-uta, Tokiwazu, Kiyomoto* singing accompany.

1 *Ken-cha Sai* tea offering Kitano Tenman-gu Shrine [E-5]; tea brought Nov 26 by growers served at gigantic tea parties at various tea houses around shrine grounds, and Kami-shichiken kaburenjo; Tycoon Hideyoshi 1587 held huge party here.

1-8 *Ro-hatsue* (8 Days December) all Zen temple priests practice week-long *zazen* sitting, as Buddha is said to have to attain enlightenment Dec 8 under Bodhi tree in Bodh Gaya, Benares, India.

8 *Hari-Kuyo* Memorial to broken sewing needles Horin-ji temple [A-8] thousands of old needles collected from nation; 1pm, dances and music.

8 *Daikon-taki* Senbon Shaka-do [F-5] 9-4; China radish cooking of secret recipe from St Kobo Daishi, parishioners eat to ward off arthritis, strokes.

14 *Memorial Serivce* Oishi-jinja Shrine for leader Oishi Kuranosuke and 47 ronin or masterless samurai of *Chushingura* fame, who avenged their master on this day.

***21** Shimai Kobo*, Toji Temple [F-ll] year's last big temple fair and flea market.

– *Rice-cake pounding*, [G-10] Shimabara geisha, ¥2,500. TIC for date and time.

25 Last flea mart, New Year supplies, Kitano.

***31** O-kera Mairi* Yasaka Shrine [I-8], 5am **28**, start new fire with fire-drill. Pilgrims to Yasaka receive fresh fire, bring home on wick-*kera* to cook New Year meal, all nite **31**. Feverish activity as all clean house, pay bills before city of temples resounds to 108 strokes each temple bell – as last one strikes, New Year comes in.

MONTHLY MARTS

Toji shrine, First Sun [F-1] antiques-only (junk to treasure) flea market, recent supplement to monthly fair 21st (*below*).

Chion-ji temple, 15th [J-6]. Handmade goods, crafts. N of Kyoto University at Hyakumanben crossing.

Toji 21st [F-1] well known to tourists, bigger 'inside' stalls more expensive pros; we advise head for North Gate, *kita-mon*, 'outside' smaller dealers with lower prices.

Kitano Tenjin 25th [E-6], fewer stalls, more for locals, cheaper; sellers not such pros, some just bring leftovers from Toji, late pm eager to unload, will haggle.

See **Free Handout** *Kansai Fleamarkets.*

JOIN IN

May: Dress up as *Ohara-Mé*, maid of Ohara, lovely ikat-dotted denim short peasant kimono of 10th century, headscarf, leggings, carry bundle of flowers on your head? And enter free lovely Sanzen-in and Jakko-in temples. Apply by letter w/s.a.envelope, to your home if time, or planned hotel (mark 'hold', arr date) to Ohara Kanko Hoshokai, Raiko-in-cho 81-2, Ohara Sakyo-ku, Kyoto 601-12; in Japan phone ☎(075) 744-2148.

July 17: Dress in antique costume, drag *hoko*, immense float, in Kyoto's greatest (hottest) festival *Gion Matsuri*. ✍ or phone by May 10 to: Mr Takada-san at **Utano Youth Hostel**, Uzumasa, Kyoto, ☎(075) 462-2288; must rehearse end June, Yasaka Shrine. Check for other special events, great ¥-B festival tours.

ON STAGE

Kyoto offers neither quality nor variety of Tokyo theater—perhaps as city itself has such theatrical qualities. What it does offer however is of exotic and antique and more likely to be of interest to tourist as well as theater buff. Best sources for Info—*Kansai Time Out* (KTO) & KVG monthlies.

Bugaku: Gion Corner nitely traditional theater whiff, alternates bugaku court dance & bunraku puppets, Mar 1-Nov 29. Ichihime Shrine practice sessions Sat, 5pm. Heian Shrine: April 16; *Bugaku Day* April. Check TIC for date & time.

Bunraku 3-man puppets: Alternate with bugaku, above, Gion Corner. Occasional full program at Minami-za, see *KTO, KVG.*

Burlesque, exotic and also antique—was performed before sacred cave by Goddess of Ritual Dance to lure petulant Sun Goddess back out. Recently bumped out of downtown, now at Fushimi Myujikku (Music Hall) at Kintetsu Fushimi stn, ☎641-1732; Sen Naka Music Hall, Senbon Nakadachuri [F-6] ☎451-1545; & Toji DX (DeluX) on E side of Toji Temple [F-11].

Dance: Main offering geisha dances Apr-May, Oct, *see* Datebook. Girls' Review Takarazuka, hr by rail or taxi (35x-mtr)

Folk Dance: *Rokusai Nembutsu* end July-Aug several temples, see above. *Mibu Kyogen* Apr 21-29. Also Gion Corner every nite, Mar 1-Nov 29.

Kabuki: Minami-za theater about every other month, usually sharing mixed program with new melodrama or modern kabuki; notable exception Dec 1-25 grand annual *kaomise* (face showing) award title promotions, best show in Japan of year. English summaries usually available. About Dec 27/8, whacky amateur kabuki, noted locals, occasionally including foreigners in misfit roles, much fun.

Noh: When public performances not on boards, semi-private shows usual as nohmen must dance daily to keep in shape. Check *KTO, KVG* for full listings, or TIC, or have hotel check theaters direct:

Kanze Kaikan [J-8] Okazaki Ensho-ji, nr; incl int'l, avant garde; bus #5, 27, 32, 46;. ☎771-6114.

Kawamura Noh Butai [G-5] Heian Shrine stage 100+days annually, own or other groups; ☎761-0221.

Kawamura; ☎ 451-4513.

Kongo Nohgaku-Do [G-8] Muromachi Shijo (nr Karasuma) ☎221-3049.

Oé Nohgaku-do [H-7] Yanagi-no-bamba Oshiko-ji; ☎231-7625.

Oné Nohgaku-do nr Oike subway ☎561-0622. English summariy usually sold. Tix ¥1,500/student, regular ¥3,200.

For **avant garde**, etc, check *KTO, KVG*. New 'spaces' opening regularly—some temporary, others fun architecture.

Study 3wks Aug intensive 'boot camp', **International Noh Inst** ☎722-3668.

Concerts: vaudeville, drama, amateurs etc at Minami-za, alternates with kabuki;

ALTI Art & Life Theater Int'l [H-6] best acoustics ☎441-1414;

Kyoto Int'l Community House [J-8] small hall ☎752-3010;

Kyoto Kaikan [J-7] Okazaki Park ☎771-6051;

Maruyama Outdoor Music Hall [J-9] Maruyama Park; several good small halls show experimental dance, avant garde, fusion theater—*see KTO.*

Movies: most on Kawaramachi btwn Shijo-Sanjo, and on parallel (W one block) roofed promenade Shinkyo-goku. No Art-film or Oldies–if you want *Rashomon* join Japan Society at home. More US movies than local fare, all subtitled, none dubbed except Disneys. Last show abt 6pm!

*Traveling is like wine; you drink
and you can't imagine what visions
will come to your mind.*
    —Nikos Kazantsakis, *Japan and China*

CHOPSTICKS

KYOTO IS ONE PLACE where going out on town to eat is essential! Kyoto-ites more than anyone else believe atmosphere to be part of cuisine. There are tiny shops in garden settings for dining for pittances, luxurious restaurant inns in grander surroundings, charming miniscule places with matching mini gardens. Kyoto's seasonal specialties are enhanced further by summer dining over Kamo River, winter savoring *nabé* cook-yourself in rustic open-hearth kitchens. Except for few exclusive garden-dining inns and geisha houses and spots specifically catering to foreigners, restaurants in Kyoto are moderate. Even these exceptions are reasonable for what is offered. And if willing to pay top hotel-dining rates, brings epicurean delights. Our special garden-inns are meant to be savored slowly and experienced to fullest. Several of our expensive inns run about same as first-class hotel's top dinner—but for full evening of sumptuous dining, reasonable drinking and moon- or flower-viewing. It should be considered not as meal alone but as evening out—way one would take in good dinner and show or nite club. Reckoned in this way, it is moderate in price.

As eating in Kyoto is one of more enjoyable aspects of local sightseeing, we give it rather full coverage, take you to those places you came to Kyoto to experience. Kyoto-taste is stylish with Tokyo executives and Tokyo's Ginza area (as we show you) abounds in fine small Kyoto-style houses, but more expensive than here, starting about ¥16,000, averaging ¥22,-25,000 per person. For Kyoto, keep in mind that by carefully balancing one's budget even pilgrims can save on some meals—without scrimping quality, quantity or atmosphere—to revel in luxury at least one nite.

LUXURY JAPANESE dining, you will go (by reservation) at about 6pm to your garden-inn restaurant, be met ceremonially and treated to ritual and show of local hospitality you have seen in color magazines back home—perhaps take bath and change into cotton yukata (lounging kimono)–and then take 2-3 hours about your meal and minimal light drinking. You can-and really should–arrange to have geisha come for entertaining-serving, as we suggest, *see* GEISHA chapter, following.

We always recommend that at least one nite be spent in luxury at one of top restaurants, and another nite *hashigo* (pub-and-eatery-crawl) such as outlined in 'Stroll Alleys of Pontocho' in GEISHA chapter following. Eating out is pleasant experience, for most Japanese restaurants are more like private homes where you dine in private room with waitress all to yourself, or in smaller houses across counter from personally-catering host-chef—all quite different atmosphere from hotel sukiyaki and tempura halls.

Chef will be concerned whether you eat J-foods. If anything goes with you (as it should) assure "*Nan demo tabemasu*"—I eat anything. Or sign '3-0' with your raised fingers and smilingly say "Okay". If there is something you don't like, if in *itamae* lean over counter top to peak, point at what you don't like and simply say (smiling, keep your humor and thus his cooperation—he doesn't need your problems), "No". Chef will usually pull out other delicacies and hold them up to you, questioningly.

PERSONAL ORIENTATION KYOTO RESTAURANTS

THEIR CUISINE is referred to as *kaiseki-ryori*, and *itamae-ryori*—ryori meaning 'cookery'.

Kaiseki originally applied to formal tea ceremony meal, but is now often used for most fancy table d'hote, even modern style E-W mix in nouvelle cuisine. It is often expensive and we advise that best way, in terms of most pleasant and most economical, to experience it is to stay at good ryori-ryokan and eat in–for as we have said before inns are basically restaurants and their rate for room w/2 meals is about same as this dinner alone plus room at far inferior inn or hotel. Then you can do whole feudal lord bit of leisurely bath, lolling dinner–even have inn arrange for geisha at fixed fee.

Kyo-ryori refers to houses that fix Kyoto cuisine according to rules set up by number of centuries'-old schools of cookery still thriving, characterized by lighter taste, somewhat bland even to Tokyo-ites, less soy sauce.

Itamae-ryori, popular form of above, is done at small place with owner-chef doing all a la carte cooking, while chatting with his guests over counter. Back and upstairs may be rooms for kaiseki guests, but such as these are difficult places for uninitiated since season's specialties come from far and near, some of which may be very expensive. You can overcome this worry by setting your price range first.

Because Kyoto doesn't have ocean front it is, unlike Tokyo or Osaka, not known for special sashimis or deep-sea fish cookery. Old Kyoto specialties are such as *kawa-zakana* (fresh-water fish) at **Hiranoya** and **Heihachi chaya**, *suppon-ryori* (terrapin) at **Daiichi**, *takenoko* (bamboo shoots) and *kamo* (duck). With refrigeration and new live-fish transport perfected, there is little you cannot get in Kyoto, whereas in '64 even good sushi was rare as too far from sea. Now all sorts of flesh is prepared in traditional local ways to fit this delicate Kyoto palate, but less and less subtle, or less bland to some. We once asked Doi madame if she had problems with foreigners not appreciating Kyo-ryori subtlety. She replied that at least they tried it as served, unlike many uncouth Tokyoites who douse it in soy sauce—like dumping ketchup over French cuisine.

Bento (luncheon, 'box' lunch) is one of most popular moderately-priced meals, complete lunch served in novel ways—on beautiful odd-shaped lacquered tray shaped like *han-getsu* (half-moon), or sometimes in drawers in lacquered boxes, moderate to top restaurants offer bento with romantic names as their economy specials served only until 2:00 or 3:00pm—economical way to try top garden restaurant at 1/3 menu fare.

Tofu (bean curd) meals are popular here. *Yudofu* is tofu cooked in broth and served with cooked vegetables, soup, tempura and rice as yudofu meal. Best at NANZEN-JI temple's **Okutan**, or neighboring **Koan** or out in **Seigen-in** annex to RYOAN-JI or **Sagano** way out by TENRYU-JI in Sagano.

Vegetarian restaurants of traditional type (we list modern ones separately right after) serve amazing assortment to make up 6- and 8-course dinners. We list these under TEMPLE RESTAURANTS. Best at **Ikkyu** in front of DAITOKU-JI monastery complex, or **Izusen Daiji-in** inside DAITOKU-JI.

We've selected what we feel are restaurants offering something special: unusual decor, picturesque setting, seasonal delicacies, and, of course, good food, worked over by Kyoto chefs using recipes treasured over centuries. All good chefs treat cooking as art, Kyoto chefs go one step beyond; not only is cooking art, but art must also be presented in proper frame.

RESERVATIONS usually required, best made thru bilingual clerk at your hotel or agent. Most rates quoted are plus 10-15% svce and tax runs double at 6% on higher tabs.

SEATING at *itamae* is on stools or chairs, most temples and inns are on tatami, others are mostly tatami but often have chairs or *kotatsu* drop-well for legs available.

TOP GARDEN RESTAURANTS All require reservations:

HIGASHIYAMA HILL 'Eastern Hills' area (corresponds to our Pottery and mansions shopping routes) favored for garden restaurants and nestled on gentle slopes are **Hyotei, Tsuruya, Doi, Kyo-Yamato**—best in Kyoto. One should telephone for reservations, especially flower seasons.

Huge villas dominate this area, many converted postwar to *ryori-ryokan* restaurant-inns (overnite w/2 meals—*see* WHERE TO STAY): such as **Kikusui** (¥-hi-T), **Yachiyo** (¥-S+w/2), **Awata Sanso** (¥-LLw/2). Trick is to go early, either for long leisurely 2-3hr lunch having bento (usually under ¥5,000) or early dinner (start 3pm) to appreciate garden by daylight, stroll it while waiting for meal; most nestle Higashiyama hills noted for blossoms. Can they survive real estate inflation of double digit annually since '81?

NANZEN-JI TEMPLE (working south)

Hyotei [J-8] next door to **Murin-an** garden, W of NANZEN-JI temple gate at Kusagawa-cho 35, ☎771-4116; is ranked first by locals, but little experience handling foreigners. Lovely garden, expensively exquisite *Kyo-ryori*. Separate little huts set in quiet compound. 'Pilgrims' can enjoy lovely setting with special *asa-gayu* ('morning porridge') set 8-11am in *bekkan*-annex ¥3,600, lunch noon-5pm *shokado-bento* ¥3,965, reminder of 350 years ago when wayside rest stop for monks and pilgrims going to Nanzen-ji, then largest Zen temple. Full *Kaiseki* in main bldg lunch ¥15,000, dinner ¥20,000+, 11:30-19:00 last order.

Tsuruya [J-8] bit N faces So-sui-canal and Zoo; ☎761-0171. Large restaurant, mostly parties, many formal dinners for foreign VIPs, probably best way for you to go; expensive, *shokado* lunch ¥13,500 (t/s incl), dinner ¥42,000. Internationalist, ran restaurant at Brussels Expo '58, where Jay lunched.

Yachiyo [G,J-8] W of NANZEN-JI. Separate dining room w/ chairs but no garden view, lunch *Ugetsu bento* ¥3,000 (gets name from *Ugetsu Monogatari* whose author UEDA Akinari retired nr here 1793) in pvt room w/view btwn 11am-2pm, *kaiseki* ¥10,000; must rsve ☎771-4148. STAY ¥-S+w/2.

Kikusui, best all-around—exquisite garden, kind service, lower prices; [H, J-8] Nanzen-ji, ☎771-4101; features superb *Kyo-no-aji*, specialty 'Kyoto-taste' bento luncheon abt ¥5,000incl; or *kaiseki* lunch from 11am ¥6,-10,000, dinner 3-7:30pm at ¥10,000+. STAY ¥-S+w/2.

Nanzen-ji Gimmond [J-7/8] exquisite garden opp Sosui canal and Zoo, block E of Heian shrine big torii, main Museums, run by Gimmond hotel so E-spoken. Lunch Nanzen-ji *yudofu* ¥3,000 and trenchermen's Nanzen-ji- and Gimmond-Zen ¥5,-6,000; dinner *kaiseki* ¥10,-12,-15,000, sukiyaki or shabu-shabu ¥6,000+; ☎751-1320, no rsve necessary except for beef dinners; –10pm but last order 8pm.

GION

Awata Sanso, lovely architecture, huge garden; [I, J-8] annex to Kyoto Hotel, E-spoken; Awata-guchi Sanjobocho 2-15, ☎561-4908; lunch *bento* ¥7,000, *kaiseki* ¥10,-15,000; dinner ¥15,-35,000. Can STAY ¥-LLw/2.

Sa-ami [J-8] Maruyama Park, ☎561-2200; *kaiseki* lunch ¥6,000, dinner ¥10,000; shabu-shabu, sukiyaki (rsve), lunch or dinner ¥6,000; call in geisha w/ samisen ¥30,000, maiko w/ musician to dance ¥70,000incl, 2hrs.

Nakamura-ro [I-8] Yasaka-Jinja Torii-nai, just inside Yasaka shrine torii on E; from ancient times one of roadside *niken-chaya* (two tea houses) every pilgrim stopped at for refreshment. Over 100 years ago this became lavish restaurant as feudal lords congregated here to plot restoration of power to emperor Meiji. Dine in luxurious setting. Early diners view garden, profusion of flowers entire year; *kaiseki* starts at ¥10,000 mid-day, evening from ¥15,000; 11:00-19:30, X-last thur, ☎561-0016.

KIYOMIZU TEMPLE AREA

Kyo-Yamato [J-9] directly N of DOI, another similar restaurant inn on spacious grounds, Higashiyama Kodai-ji ☎541-1126 Lunch ¥15,000+, dinner ¥30,000; cheaper branch below, **Kodai-ji Yamato** ☎541-9111, lunch ¥3,500+, dinner ¥6,000.

Doi [J-9] Higashiyama Kodai-ji, ☎561-0309, our personal favorite, cozier scale, yet large garden. Lovely ryori-ryokan featured in *House Beautiful* classic issue on Japan generation ago that initiated ryokan consciousness in US (alas, no longer takes roomers, only diners). Buildings on knoll, lovely pond and carefully tended gardens rise up slope with tea houses above. No matter what season, garden is superb. Refined elegance, hint of different incense lingers in each room. Best if with someone who can handle some Japanese; rsve well ahead; *kaiseki* only, lunch ¥20,000+%up, dinner ¥25,000+%.

Kyoto Sakaguchi [J-9] on our Sannenzaka walk, with Kobori Enshu-style stroll garden w/pond and spring, huge waterwheel. Sun, hols & flower, maple season drop in just for matcha green tea ¥800 in garden; July-Aug visit 'beer' garden, *tenshin* meal with 2 jugs of draft beer ¥5,000; bento ¥5,000; *kaiseki* lunch from ¥8,000, dinner ¥20,000.

OUTLYING

Higashiyama Villa [J-8/9] on mountainous Higashiyama driveway midway btwn its Sanjo-dori (Miyako Hotel) and Gojo-dori terminals, offers pleasant mix of day-long antique shopping and folk art bar in old mansion (9am-10:30pm) and evening dining (5-10pm) of Kobe beef *shabu-shabu*, or 'one pot' chicken *mizutake* ¥7,-8,000. Allow time before or after dinner to browse co-owner Amy Takeda's **antique shop**. E-spoken, sit tatami or chairs. ☎581-3510; (Miyako Hotel taxi 2x-mtr, downtown 3x-mtr).

Nishiki [A-7] Arashiyama, S (far) end of woodblock-print Togetsu bridge, ☎871-8888; famous 7-course *oshuku-zen* bento in drawers of lacquered workman's box, ¥3,500 in dining rm, ¥5,000 in pvt cottage rm; 11-7pm, X-tue.

Rankyo-kan [A-7] Arashiyama, Hozugawa hata, rustic riverside setting, at S end of Togetsu Bridge, go by their boat from its Bekkan Annex to main inn or stroll 15min mountain path. Lunch *Ranzan* ¥3,500; any time *kaiseki* ¥8,000; *Rankyo-nabe* (wild boar, seafood) ¥8,000 Dec-Mar; ☎871-0001.

Okoji-sanso [A-7] villa known for its beautiful mountaintop garden, stroll garden ¥800, includes matcha tea; mini-kaiseki ¥3,000 11:00-5pm; kaiseki runs ¥10,-¥35,000. 10min walk from Keifuku Arashiyama Stn, behind Tenryu-ji. Ogurayama Tabukuchi Yama-cho ☎872-2233.

Kitcho [A-7] Saga Tenryu-ji, ☎881-1101, is place to be taken as guest as *kaiseki* only from ¥45,000, branch in **Grand Hotel** basement (G-10) with same menu, price for bento from ¥4,500, *kaiseki* ¥12,000, shabu-shabu etc ¥8,000; X-2nd, 4th wed.

*Momijiya-bekkan [A-2] Takao, 120 yr-old house in mountain setting, *yuka* summer over small river; *Kitayama teishoku* ¥4,000; *kaiseki* ¥6,000; *botan nabe* ¥7,000; Umegahata-Takao, ☎871-1005.

Furusato in Yase [L-1-off map NE] Kyoto bus JR stn for Ohara, off at Furusato-mae, or Eizan tram from Demachi-yanagi stn to end Yase and bus 10min, or call and they'll pick you up; in ancient Shirakawa-style farmhouse moved here from mountains of Gifu when dam was built; has KAMABURO ONSEN featuring replica of 7 or 8 old Persian-like *kamaburo* steam baths, long famous here for bathing before dinner; ☎791-4126; o'nite ¥15,-20,000w/2; lunch only ¥2,500 *bento*, to ¥6,000 *kaiseki*; dinner only *kaiseki* ¥6,000+, autumn leaves season rsve must.

SMALL KAISEKI HOUSES

*Chimoto [H-8] Shijo Ohashi Saiseki, ☎351-1846, mini-*kaiseki* ¥7,000.

Minoko [I-9] Kioi-cho 480, Gion Shimogawara-dori, S of YASAKA SHRINE behind hoary gate & noren-curtain 11:30-23:00, X-2nd, 4th wed, ☎561-0328; well-known smaller restaurant; fine chef, complete dinners hotel rates ¥10,000; beautiful tea ceremony utensils cleverly adapted for Sumi's favorite *cha-bako bento* (tea-box lunch) make for interesting light lunch specialty ¥3,500.

Ten Kitamura [F-3] Kita-ku, Omiya, Higashi-shonobori machi-l, ☎492-7799; neat art deco setting black lacquered look with nouvelle cuisine '*kaiseki*'. We ordered set dinner ¥3,800 enjoying succession of 8 dishes; 6-12pm, X-mon.

ITAMAE RESTAURANTS

Order *o-makase* ('leave it to chef') course at counter:

Hama-saku [I-9] Gion Tominaga-cho S of YASAKA SHRINE stone torii opp Kyoto Ladies' Inn, ☎541-1061; noted for *fugu*, 5pm–till run out of sashimi; prefer rsve.

Kawashige [I-8] Sanjo down Kawaramachi to theater and in alley E; ☎221-5031, lunch ¥13,000, dinner ¥20,000, any time *bento* ¥5-11,000; 4-9pm X-mon, 4th tue.

Kawashige annex [I-8] in Pontocho from Sanjo Kiyamachi go S 150m, pass flower shop turn in alley L/E, it's on L; ☎241-3672; *bento* ¥5,500, full meal ¥13,000+ anytime 4-9, X-mon, last tue.

Tankuma [I-8] Kawaramachi Shijo-agaru (N) 3rd alley in E/R, ☎221-5490 *Itamae o-makase* abt ¥15,000+%; originator of now-'orthodox' black lacquered 4-partition box *shokado-bento* ¥5,000, mini-*kaiseki* ¥8,000.

MODERATE RESTAURANTS

Shinsen-en Heian-den [F-7] great buy, S opp Nijo Castle, fantastic garden once part of castle grounds, branch of Heihachi below; set up for groups, economy-conscious, less individualized; *Heihachi-bento* ¥3,000, *tempura* or *sashimi teishoku* ¥3,400, *sukiyaki* ¥4,300; 11-9pm, no-X, free access to garden.

Minokichi [K-8] Okazaki Hiromichi Sanjo-agaru, ☎771-4185; Popular, efficient and nice folk art decor, lovely garden. E-menu; also a la carte ¥1,500+, *Awata-gozen* tray-meal ¥3,500 to *shabu-shabu* ¥4,500+ and *shun-kaiseki*, season's best ¥5,500+; order by 8pm, *kaiseki* by 7:30; chairs, but tatami room +5%.

Tamahan Chamise [J-7] Okazaki in front of Heian shrine; ☎751-8285; *tempura teishoku* ¥2,000; 11-7, X-mon.

Grill Kaiyotei [I-8] on romantic Kiyamachi-dori W of Pontocho (geisha) alley; W-presented a la J-, lunch ¥1,500+, stew ¥2,100, steak dinner ¥7,000; noon-9:30pm.

Yagenbori [I-8] Kiyamachi 4th alley N of Shijo, W/L across small bridge; also 2 branches E of river; J-food, Hida-Takayama decor, 11:30-2:30/4-10:30; ☎2121-5903.

Umenoi [I-8] Nawate-Shijo-agaru (N) ☎561-1004; donburi ¥800+, tempura-*tendon* or eel *unadon* ¥1,500; dinner *tempura-*, *unagi-teishoku* ¥2,500; 11-9, X-wed.

Rokusei [I-7] Okazaki Nishi Tempo-cho, W of Heian shrine; *tei-oke bento* in wooden bucket best of season ¥2,500, deluxe course ¥5,500; 11:30-9pm, X-mon.

Tagoto [H-8] Shijo Teramachi-higashi next to Central Inn Hotel in alley in *sukiya*-style bldg; famed lunch *Koetsu mizusashi bento* ¥2,500; 11-8:30, ☎221-1811.

BUDGET RESTAURANTS

RESTAURANTS ABOUND, most have plastic or photo menu-display outside; or old-style J-noodleries etc just signs with prices. Some W- & J-:

Miyako hotel-run beanery in Kyoto Station tower for train departures and arrivals, amid several better J-style eatery inexpensive branches.

Takashimaya Department Store [H-8] corner of Shijo-Kawaramachi, 7fl restaurant 10:30-7pm, no-X; inexpensive branches of such top local houses as **Tankuma**, **Tagoto** etc with *teishoku* from ¥900, separate elevator by main DS (corner) entrance. Annex 2 doors W separate entry, from ¥-B+, till 9pm X-wed.

Hankyu Department Store [H-8] corner of Shijo-Kawaramachi, 7-8fl loaded with economy branches of Kyoto's best kitchens, W-, J-, Indian, Chinese, novelty, etc.

Daimaru Department Store [H-8] subway arcade, Shijo midway Kawaramachi and Karasuma main N-S streets, many good ¥-B annexes of upbeat major W- & J-houses.

O-Edo [H-8] on Shijo opp DAIMARU, noted for *tonkatsu*-pork cutlets, also various *teishokus* ¥1,600-2,500; till 9pm, X-wed; ☎221-7301.

Tensei [H-8] tempura, owner blends sesame and veg oil for special flavor. Donburi large bowls topped with vegetables ¥530, veg, shrimp, fish, squid, ¥850, other dishes; Shinkyogoku above Nishiki, 10:30-8:50.

Murase [H-8] E-spk; known for Omi-beef, -cutlet ¥950, -stew ¥1,100, set ¥1,400; 11-8:45, X-tue; Teramachi & Shinkyogoku above Nishiki.

Coronna [I-8] S of Shijo on Kiyamachi-dori W of Takasegawa canal; W- presented a la J-, pork cutlet ¥700, beef ¥1,300; 5-10pm, X-tue; ☎351-0567.

Kawakyu [I-8] Takasegawa canal S of Oike, opp rear of Royal Hotel; *Itamae* W- & J-, beef stew or roast duck ¥1,800, menu 40-50 items; 4-9:30pm, X-mon.

Fujiya Sanjo [I-8] on SW corner Kawaramachi, also **Shijo** [I-8] Kiyamachi-dori NE corner, nationwide chain, good, cheap cafeteria-grade W- and soda fountain specialties.

Min-min [I-8] on Hanamikoji 1st N of Shijo; fantastically cheap national chain of 'greasy-chopstick' Chinese, beloved of students; gyoza dish of 7 dumplings for ¥200, Chingis Khan lamb ¥450, luxe shark fin soup ¥700; 6pm-3am, X-sun; ☎525-2855.

Min-min-Shijo [I-8] on Shijo-Nishi Kiyamachi, S of Shijo on alley W side of canal; similar menu, famed for *gyoza*; 11:30am-1:30am, no-X; ☎351-1960.

Heihachi [F-7] Shijo-dori block E of kabuki theater, 4 storeys, open 10am and all nite till 6am; a la carte, *teishoku* ¥1,500-¥3,000, *sukiyaki* ¥2,500-3,500, *oil-yaki* ¥3,500; branch Shinsen-en Heian-den opp Nijo Castle, preceding.

Un [K-6] mingei decor, popular chain several outlets; main at Shirakawa-dori N of Imadegawa on Ginkakuji-dori catty-corner to Kani Doraku crabs, ☎701-0340; our favorite is *nattoo gyoza*, Chinese dumpling filled with fermented soybeans 5 for ¥400. Simple family-style dishes of oden ¥100ea, ochazuke, vegetables, as well as sashimi, sushi, tempura *teishoku* ¥600; 5pm-2am, no-X.

Yatai open stalls & pushcarts along streets; delicious, safe, well-cooked; our favorite is *sazae*, small spiral-shell conch which we spiral out with toothpick. *See* also NOODLES.

SPECIALTIES

BAMBOO

Kinsui-tei [W off map] Nagaoka Tenjin stn of Hankyu line taxi 1x-mtr, or JR 3rd stn Kotari, by Tenjin shrine and pond Hachijo-ga-ike; ☎951-5151; *bento* ¥3,000, *kaiseki* ¥10,000+; 11:30-7pm last order, no-X.

Izu-toyo [nr above] ☎951-4327; *bento* ¥3,500, bamboo set ¥7,000; hrs same.

BEEFSTEAK, SUKIYAKI and SHABU-SHABU

Sa-ami, *above* GARDEN INNS.

Ashiya Steakhouse [J-7/8] Higashiyama Kiyomizu-4, up Higashiyama-dori st N of Gojo to firehouse on L, opp side up alley E then R to house w/ ricksha; ☎541-7961;

established just after our original edition so we missed pleasure of writing up this singular international kitchen started by inimitable Bob Strickland, American stand-up comic of Japanese stage; steak *teppan-yaki* pan-broiled in front of you, uses Omi beef. Bob asks "Would you trust a drunken cow in your kitchen?"; E-menu, complete dinner: fillet 150g ¥11,000, sirloin 180g ¥12,500; 5:30-10 last order; X-mon; 2nd fl **gallery** has expat art, pottery Doug Lawry, etchings Sarah Brayer, paintings Brian Williams, prints Clif Karhu, whose prints hang in J- restaurants worldwide.

Gion Suehiro [I-9] Gion Minami-gawa, behind Gion Kaburenjo theater (Gion Corner) ☎541-1337, originated shabu-shabu in 1950s, their dip-sauce made of 25 spices; Matsuzaka beef shabu-shabu ¥7,000+, sukiyaki ¥6,000; 12-11pm.

Junidan-ya [I-9] **Main** Gion Hanami-koji, 50m from Shijo off in alley on L, ☎551-2352, enter 12-2pm, 5-6pm, pvt rooms rsve, mainly shabu shabu ¥8,10,12,000, steak & sukiyaki by advance order. **Annex** on Hanami-koji, 50m from Shijo on L, ☎561-0213, open restaurant, steaks and J-beef, ¥5,000.

Mishima-tei [H-8] old landmark Teramachi-Sanjo SE corner, ground fl meat shop upstairs restn't; 11:30-10pm no-X, ☎221-0003; ¥7,300-8,500.

Morita-ya [G-7] raises own beef, meat shop since Meiji, 1869, serves beef sashimi ¥2,500; sukiyaki set ¥3,000, shabu-shabu ¥3,800, roast beef rare (*tataki*) ¥1,500; 12-10pm, no X, S of Shijo on Inokuma-dori (2nd st W of Horikawa), ☎842-0298.

Tivoli [I-7] in Okazaki Park opp HEIAN shrine, ☎771-0075; advertise that for dinner their car will pick you up; E-menu steak from ¥4,500+, *sukiyaki* ¥4,-6,000, *yudofu* ¥1,900, *mizutaki* ¥2,800; main fl chairs moderate W- & J- a la carte, 2nd fl tatami dinners; 11:30-10, no-X.

BOAR

Botan-nabe–boar sukiyaki (oddly, meat never burns tongue), in season October-March, off-season some may serve domesticated boar.

Kinsuitei [B-4] on Shuzan Kaido en route KOZAN-JI temple & Takao Driveway, serves mountain cookery: boar *botan-nabe* with vegs, tofu, mushrooms ¥6,000; chicken sukiyaki ¥2,500; 10am-9pm, X-var; Takao-Tonohata-cho, ☎861-0216.

Also served at **Rankyo-kan**, **Momijiya** (above), as well as **Heihachiro-Chaya**, **Hiranoya** and **Fujiya** (below).

CHICKEN

Sankaku ('triangle', also chicken's rear) [I-9] Kiyamachi by canal S of Shijo at triangle, one of our favorites, seats 7 slim eaters at tiny counter, chicken parts BBQ'd, with his chicken broth and fried rice; 6 items ¥1,200, ¥3,000 is full filling meal, or order chicken bits ¥200+: don't miss chicken sashimi, caviar-quality raw liver–cock and hen differ; walk in 5–10pm; ☎351-0606.

CHICKEN MIZUTAKI *yuka platforms in summer

*Shinmiura [I-8] Kiyamachi-Oike ☎231-1297; *mizutaki* ¥4,100, *yakitori* other a la carte ¥800+; 5-10pm, no-X; yuka platform over river in summer.

*Tori-iwaro [I-9] Shijo bridge few doors S of tall Chinese restn't, backs on river; ☎351-6001; tatami and chairs; lunch *tesage-bento* ¥2,300, free-range chicken *mizutaki* ¥5,300, beef shabu-shabu ¥5,300; 12-10pm. X-wed.

*Toriyosa [I-9] Kiyamachi Shijo-sagaru, below Iwaro beyond next small bridge, ☎351-0555; *mizutaki* ¥6,500, *kaiseki* ¥8,000+; 12:00-8 entry, X-2nd, 4th wed.

Toriyasu [K-7] E of Zoo in lovely old estate, great gate; ☎771-0081; rms face lovely garden; *aka bento*, *yudofu* set ¥2,500, *mizutaki* ¥6,-7,000, free-range chickens specially raised in Nara; 12-9:30pm, X-tue.

CRAB (Not local specialty–served only since '64 edition)

Kani Doraku chain, 2 on Teramachi-dori, first at NW corner Sanjo, [H-8] ☎211-0671 2nd block S at NW corner Rokaku-dori, [H-8] ☎223-0822; 3rd nr GINKAKU-JI N of it and Imadegawa intersection on Shirakawa-dori [K-6] ☎721-3900; meal from teishoku 3 dishes ¥3,000, 7 dishes-up 'course' ¥6,000+; 11:30-11pm, no-X.

DUCK

Hokusai [I-9] Nawate-dori Shimbashi, above canal mid Shijo-Sanjo, ☎561-7121; *goryo-nabe*, hunter's meal, beef, duck, chicken braised on spade-shaped pan ¥3,700.

EEL **yuka* platforms in summer

*Kandagawa [I-8] along Kamogawa River S of Shijo-dori, excellent to overcome summer weariness dining on yuka over River at no extra charge. 100-yr-old restaurant's wonderful *kabayaki donburi* ¥3,000; teishoku bit more expensive at ¥4,500-6,800, but well worth difference; ☎351-1832.

Matsuno [I-8] (sign in English 'Mrs. Matsuno's Kitchen), across Shijo Bridge next to Minamiza kabuki theater, E-menu. Charcoal-broiled unagi also called *kabayaki*, or tempura teishoku set for lunch is ¥2,500; 11:30-20:30, X-tues; ☎561-2786.

FRESH-WATER FISH

Heihachi-chaya [off map, E] in foothills of Mt Hiei-zan at end of cablecar from Yase, perched on bank of Takano River, famous for river fish served by maids in picturesque *Ohara-me* costumes, lovely mountain view. *Chashitsu bento* ¥3,000, fish *kaiseki* lunch ¥5,000, dinner ¥6,000, boar *botan-nabe*, ¥6,000; ☎781-5008.

Hiranoya [B-4] Sagano nr Adeshino Nembutsu-ji temple in old thatched house, 400-yr-old pilgrim stop for those going to Atago-dera. Well-known for its fish cookery *aiyu*-trout (sweetfish) ¥12,000+, as well as Spring herbs and game, *botan-nabe* ¥8,000, *yudofu* Sept-Mar ¥3,500; 11am-9pm no-X; ☎861-0359.

Fujiya, up N at Kibune, located in front of KIBUNE SHRINE torii, long-time favorite retreat for Kyoto-ites. Dining on *yuka* platforms over shady mountain stream 6/15-9/15; lunch 11-2 *haika-zen* ¥3,-4,000, 11-7:30 *kaiseki* ¥8,000+, winter *botan nabe* ¥7,000. Since typhoon, main building rebuilt in modern style, but annex charming *sukiya*-style, ☎741-2501.

Hiroya, further up on R, Kurama-jingu-mae, equally lovely setting, *yuka* over bubbling stream, tasty but unusual food; lunch *yama-gazen* ¥3,500, *kaiseki* ¥5,- 8,-10,000 all day 11-7:30, ☎741-2401.

KUSHI-KATSU (tidbit 'cutlets' broiled on bamboo kushi-sticks)

Kushi Yasu [I-8] Kiyamachi-Takoyakushi corner by parking lot; ☎241-0026; ¥130- 150 per stick, 26 var fish to meats, vegs etc, stuff self, drink ¥2,000; 5-12pm, no-X.

NOODLES

Azekura [H-2], immense grounds with 'architecture park' of 300-yr-old *kura* storehouse from Nara and great *gasho-zukuri* farmhouse from Gifu, fine teahouse, set in large historic garden; former is main restaurant, latter houses working weavers, can watch, also occasional exhibits. 9am for noodle bkfst till 5pm only, X-mon; ¥600+; ☎701-0164; nr Kamigamo stop of bus #37, 46, 54, 67 and walk E past Ota shrine 10min.

Challenge Ramen Kyoka [H-8] Shinkyogoku-Takoyakushi NW corner, ☎221- 5883; 11am-11pm, no-X; only *ramen*-chop suey noodles in soup, ¥450 for 50% over normal portion, eat more free but if you leave any you pay double.

Daikokuya [I-8] Kiyamachi Takoyakushi, ☎221-2818, handsome wooden grill, big red lantern front just off canal bridge, E-menu (¥430-1,030); till 10pm, X-tue.

Kawamichiya (aka **Misoka-an**) [H-8] favorite since '52. S of Oike-dori on Anegako-ji, same street S of inns Hiiragiya, Tawaraya, Sumiya in Fuya-cho Sanjo-agaru ☎221-2525; walk thru 3 fine interior gardens; handmade soba; *Hokoro-nabe* Korean charcoal-fired pot of udon, duck, greens etc for 2, ¥6,000, E-menu; 11am-8pm, X-thur.

Matsuba [I-8] Shijo Kawabata at bridge, L of Kabuki theater, ☎561-1451; from ¥660, famed as originator of *nisshin soba* (smoked herring on soba, broth) ¥880, *tempura teishoku* ¥1,600; till 11pm.

Omen [K-6], basically noodle shop (which is what really non-occult name means), but one with imagination in fabulous rustic decor and especially appetizing dishes using mostly natural foods, budget (¥750-set) and bit up. Main shop near, E of, GINKAKU-JI

Silver Pavilion, S of City parking lot; 11am-11pm, X-thur; ☎771-8994. Branches midtown at **Shijo**-dori W of Kawaramachi nr Fuji-Daimaru DS, ☎255-2125, –10pm, X-thur; **Sanjo**-dori inside Bunka Hakubutsukan museum, 2min walk E from subway Oike stn; ☎255-2161, –8:30pm; X-thur, 3rd wed. And one in New York's Soho.
See Kyoto Visitors Guide for longer alternative list.

ROBATA-YAKI

Kappa [I-9] upper Nawate-dori, first traffic street E of Shijo bridge and N just before canal, 2 shops either side of street; choose your own from display of seafood, meats, vegetables to be cooked in front of you, *ippin* 'one dish' from ¥300; 6pm–2am; ☎551-2775. Fun place, guests banter with cooks.

TEPPIN FONDU *yuka* platforms in summer

*Yamatomi [I-8] Pontocho N of Shijo; menu lists 200 varieties–chicken, shrimp, etc kushi-katsu–but novel is *teppin-agé*, form of ozashiki tempura (cooked at private room table), but we might call it fondu as you cook your own 15 or so varieties of seafood and vegetables in iron *teppin* kettle ¥2,700; bento is ¥3,800; dine out on yuka in summer; 12:00-23:30, ☎221-3268.

TERRAPIN

Daiichi [F-6] run by 12th generation family in 300-year-old rural home, staircase has interesting built-in drawers as in ancient homes; ultimate in taste, white meat of *suppon*, terrapin, cooked quickly in pottery nabe pot at high temperature keeps flesh tender, broth used for finale of *zosui*-rice gruel; course ¥18,000; 12:30-19:30, X-tue; Shimochojamachi-dori, Senbon Nishi iru, 5th st above Marutamachi to L/W; ☎461-1775

WESTERN

IN KYOTO main hotels, unlike Tokyo, are mediocre and expensive. Tasty W-, convenient, was best buy **Kyoto Hotel Grill** [HI-7] Hotel X for reconstruction but Kyoto is for dining out—especially if staying W-hotel.

Morita [G-7] W of Horikawa below Marutamachi on Dote-machi; owner-chef 7 yrs Europe, E-name on door also "Eng., Fr., German, Italian and Spanish spoken". Fujiko & Hajime Morita owners are Tibetan Snow Lion Friendship Soc, helping Tibetan refugees in India. ☎256-0859; lunch ¥1,500-3,500, dinner ¥3,500-8,000; 11:30-2, 5-10pm, X-mon.

Suehiro [J-7] Okazaki E of Heian Shrine, E-side of Sunflower Hotel, brick bldg, ☎751-1529; steak lunch ¥2,300+, dinner a la carte filet 150g ¥4,700, teishoku ¥6,100.

Tsubosaka [I-8] in Gion on bordello alley parallel to and one N/above Shijo, just in off Hanamikoji; ☎541-1065. Pure Kansai cozy family milieu, good example of cultural blend–menu 'Western' but fully Kyoto-ized, prices match big hotels (a la carte ¥1,400 +), but quality excels; X-wed.

Paul [I-8] 2nd corner Hanamikoji N of Shijo; once town's sole late nite eatery, homey, *tataki* roast beef ¥3,500, steak or dinner set ¥7,000; till 11pm, X-wed; ☎561-2556.

With You [H-8] on Teramachi-dori just above Nishiki-dori (food-lined E-W street just N of Shijo) in bldg of same name, ground floor 'market floor' with bakery etc, counters where you can sit for self-designed sandwiches in selection great breads, salads, coffee etc–simple good and cheap, ¥3-400, eat at counter or take-out +¥100 surcharge; 2nd fl restaurant close to natural foods; 11am-10pm; generous lunches like specialty black pasta dyed with cuttlefish ink, ¥900-2,000; dinner ¥3,-5,000 and a la carte; E-menu.

Knuckles [F-4] nr Daitoku-ji S of W-end, 2 blocks E of Senbon-dori on Kita-oji S-side at Funaoka bus; ☎441-5849; E-menu, owner Chas Rosche; sandwiches, lasagne ¥750, best cheesecake in Kansai, lunch ¥650, stuff self ¥1,500; 12-10pm X-mon.

Izutsu [I-8] Nawate-dori S of Sanjo-dori few doors below Furumonzen antique street; "Japanese spirit in Western dishes", noon-11pm; ☎541-2121;

ITY's in basement of above **Izutsu** bldg, budget sandwiches.

TEMPLE RESTAURANTS TIME-SAVER as we savor lunch in temple.

DAITOKU-JI TEMPLE

Ikkyu [F-4] outside opp front gate ☎493-0019, over 500 yrs old, top-class pure vegetarian *shojin-ryori* meal; rsve, holidays full; 12-6pm, no-X; lunch *bento* ¥3,400incl, *kaiseki* ¥6,-8,-10,000.

Daisen-in temple [F-4] in DAITOKU-JI: *matcha* and cake ¥250.

Izusen chain of charming houses serve 7-13 course vegetarian fare, each empty bowl nestles in next; 11:00am-5:00pm last order; 7 choices ¥2,500-5,600, generous portions advise choose mid-range or small; Oct-Nov sublime *dobin-mushi* mushroom chowder:
Izusen DAIJI-IN [F-4] N of main gate, in DAITOKU-JI complex; ☎491-6665.
Izusen DAIKAKU-JI opp gate, ☎881-6505.
Izusen ADASHINO NEMBUTSU-JI in Sagano, on R before temple, ☎881-7016.
Izusen in front of KYOTO stn, Surugaya Bldg 2F, just N of TIC, ☎243-4111.

NANZEN-JI TEMPLE

[K-8]: area is known for *yudofu* (soybean curd-cake cookery); lovely light lunch in any of several temple garden restaurants around Nandaimon gate– goes well with hot sake on cold days; luxury experience at tourist rates even for real trencherman:

Okutan was one of three restaurants set up for their thousands of monks, '64 was sole remaining, now others reopened. Lovely setting under big trees, big pond. Hard to spot, but to L of big gate and go R at corner. Just walk in, no rsve. Soup, vegetables, tempura and tofu, rice ¥2,-6,000, sake extra.

Koan is beyond nr corner on way to Nomura museum behind magnificent gate; *yudofu* ¥2,000. ☎771-2781, 11am-4pm, X-wed.

Seigen-in [D-5] annex to RYOAN-JI Stone Garden: *yudofu* in small house facing big pond in front of temple, R out of temple and follow garden path; ¥1,700 yudofu meal, ¥3,300 complete *shojin-ryori* meal; ☎462-4742.

Tenryu-ji temple [A-7] serves vegetarian tempura, ¥2,-4,000 plus ¥600 entry fee to see temple; 9-5pm, phone ahead, ☎882-9725.

Sagano Yudofu [A-7] Susuki-no-baba-cho 45, just S of Tenryu-ji; lovely *sukiya*-style bldg in bamboo grove viewed thru full windows; ¥3,000 set veg tempura & abt 8 dishes, on fine blue-&-white porcelains; 11am-6pm last order, X-New Yr; ☎861-0277.

Ikkyu-an [J-9], *fucha-ryori* Chinese temple-type tho not pure vegetarian, not temple linked, on SHOPPING-WALK Kiyomizu–Gion, on W btwn Ryozen Kannon & Higashi-oji St, ☎561-1901, lunch 12-2pm ¥3,900incl, dinner enter 3-6pm ¥5,-7,000+%.

Kanga-an temple [H-5], head priest is woman, on Kurama-guchi-dori 200m E of Karasuma-dori, 4 people min *Takezen* 'Chinese temple style' (=family style); 12-2pm, 5-8pm, X-New Year; ☎256-2480, rsve 3 days ahead.

OUTLYING

Kaiho-ji temple *fucha ryori* Chinese temple semi-vegetarian meal in temple grounds southern outskirts of Kyoto on way to Nara at Momoyama Saijo-81, Fushimi; 11-5pm, X-thur; ☎611-1672, ; ¥4,200-5,400. Rsve.

Obaku Manpuku-ji temple garden restaurant [L-17] (*preceding*, p.460) also betw Kyoto-Nara, in temple mentioned as delightful meal break en rte Kyoto, for Buddhist lunch (only), min 4 rsve ☎(0774)-32-3900—or opp gate at...

Haku-un-An (White Cloud Retreat), any number guests, rsve unnecessary except in blossom seasons, but advised ☎(0774)-31-8017; arrive, order meal, sightsee 20-60min, then return for leisurely aesthete lunch (only) in lovely manse overlooking garden.

Icho-An budgeteer gets by for ¥1,000 for 5-dish *shojin ryori* in garden to R of inner main gate, small door L corner of wall by red mat on bench; also various refreshments from milk, coffee to *matcha* & tea cakes; 10-5:30pm—as settings are limited, advise rsve when first arrive at temple, then sightsee, return to eat.

NATURAL FOOD RESTAURANTS

WE ARE RELUCTANT to list this group as we have found in Japan that many have closed down almost as fast as they opened; main thing that sets them off from *shojin ryori* temple eating is that they serve brown, unpolished rice, so rarely seen here—macrobiotics may have been born here, but it took up residence and citizenship in USA.

Bio-tei (pron B.O.) SW corner of Sanjo-dori st and Higashinotoin (first N-S street E of Karasuma st) on 2fl; 11am-2:30pm, 5-8:30, X-tue, sun, hol; noted for bean croquets.

Cosmos up in Kita-ku at Kamigamo Takanawate-cho 39, noon-9pm, ☎781-4806; rsve 2 days ahead for their all-organic *genmai* brown-rice temple-type *shojin kaiseki*, ¥3,000; cherry trees in garden gorgeous.

Mandara [HI-3] Kamigamo Aoita-cho 1-7; Indian vegetarian operated by Iris & Tsugio EMI. Curries, chapatti, dal soup, gluten-tempura, and German sour-dough bread and cakes based on Iris' native German recipes so reasonable most dishes w/ chapatti or dal under ¥6-700; 11-8pm, X-wed, hols, ☎722-1435.

MAIN AREAS

AFTER THIS APPETIZER of culinary delights to be found in Kyoto, so you can coordinate sightseeing, shopping, strolling and dining, we offer here dining by main areas.

NANZEN-JI TEMPLE

[K-8]: area is known for *yudofu;* oldest is **Okutan**; another **Koan** (*see* facing). Other specialty houses are **Yamasaki**, featuring mountain dishes of Akita in northern Alps, and **Minokichi**, general menu.

South of Nanzen-ji area are...
MARUYAMA PARK and **KIYOMIZU TEMPLE** areas, where many of top garden restaurants located. (See map, page 541).

Entering MARUYAMA PARK from Shijo-dori, you'll notice lovely little budget restaurants bordering on drive (complete meal): **Izumoya** eel, next to archery range and photo shop, then comes branch of **Tori-iwa-ro** with thatched gate (chicken mizutaki). Directly opposite latter is **Hiranoya Imobo** taro-potato, and block up by CHION-IN TEMPLE gate is their main shop for lunch in tiny tea houses. East exit of Park up hill from old gate is **Sa-ami** converted from lovely old temple (tempura, sukiyaki). Before south gate of YASAKA SHRINE is **Nakamura-ro** (dinners, *see* p518) at Yasaka Jinja Torii-nai (by torii), while annex with *noren* retains name of **Niken-chaya** from days when it was one of two roadside stops catering to pilgrims with pilgrim *dengaku*, pilgrim price, Gion-tofu.

In front of huge outdoor Ryozen-Kannon statue is...
Ikkyu-an, vegetarian restaurant, based on temple menu, ¥-S; up mountainside is **Kyo-Yamato** ¥-L, **Kodai-ji Yamato** (cheaper), and **Kyorinsen** (budget), then deluxe **Doi**, above.

For dining spots in adjacent area, *see* Kiyomizu Temple SHOPPING p539.

GION GEISHA AREA

[I-9/10] (btwn Kamo River—Higashi-oji, our CURIO MAP p537): From Kiyomizu area, crossing Higashioji ave toward town, we enter area known as Gion with its geisha and restaurants, main street of Hanamikoji (Flower-viewing Alley) and two curio shopping areas. Near Gion Geisha **Kaburenjo Theater** (site of Gion Corner) are restaurants frequented by foreigners: **Gion Suehiro** in large old home serves *shabu-shabu* (paper-thin slices of beef cooked in broth in Korean-style braziered metal pot). **Toriimoto** for *shippoku* Japanized-Chinese on individual elegant lacquer tables with dishes and service in drawers for each guest. **Shinmiura** chicken mizutaki, branches. **Junidan-ya** sukiyaki, shabu-shabu in lovely folk art atmosphere, folk pottery–**annex** opp tops for steak.

This brings us out to Shijo-dori by dull red walls of famed kabuki-locale...
Ichiriki Chaya, but few doors before on Hanamikoji is cluster of former *chaya* now turned geisha-run restaurants many with menus posted outside, with bento and kaiseki meals about standard.

Among these is...
Yuranosuke 3 doors before Ichiriki Chaya, who had charming place with waterwheel outside on Nawate, now used no more at this new location, worth its ¥-S price.

Go out to Shijo-dori and block up Shijo are two attractive refreshment places...
Kagi-zen, 200-year-old sweet shop, traditional store front, summer treat is ancient health food *kudzu* gelatin with honey (¥700 upstairs). Few doors up **Ohara-me**, matcha green tea and special *kamaburo* sweets; with modern torii-like entrance, similar fare, upstairs.

Continue on Hanamikoji from Shijo with budget ...
Min-Min Chinese a la carte ¥-B, **Tsubosaka** W-family grill, 4 sushi shops, tempura and on corner is old-time friend **Paul's** (1st fl Yokota Bldg). L here for fun place **Kappa** (robata-yaki), but back on Hanamikoji is **Senmonten**, excellent bite-size gyoza dumplings 10/¥350, then more sushi, tempura places, but fare thins out as Shinmonzen-Furumonzen antique area approaches. So here take L thru architectural preservation area saving charming old Kyoto-style homes in triangle formed by Shimbashi-dori, Shirakawa-minami-dori and Nawate-dori with charming **Shiraume** ryori-ryokan. Going S towards Shijo brings Steak House **Mikaku** few doors down first R turn. Back on Nawate by robata-yaki **Kappa** are **Umenoi** (tempura, unagi), budget branch of **Minokichi** called **Tabecco**, **Nomikko** good place for drinks (sake ¥400, beer ¥550) to go with tasty dishes ¥400-900, 5-11pm, X-sun. On 6F is Russian food at **Kiev**, borscht ¥800, Kiev set ¥3,000; 2F is Kiev's bar.

Retracing our steps back to Nawate and canal, there's...
Torishin chicken house, **Tomihisa** for *fugu* (blowfish). On L is novel **Hokusai**, specialty sliced duck braised on iron pan in shape of farmer's hoe, old hunters' meal, condiments in miniature farm house; charming setting. In next block on R take note of—**Nexus** building with exterior that seems to have been here for years and yet when you enter, you find that interior has smart modern look; · downstairs is **Chinoiseries** (Chinese). Next **Jubei sushi** main shop, inexpensive and good. On L is **Izutsu** bldg with W-meals, budget at **ITY** in basement, or Japanese table d'hote next door at old **Izutsu**.

ALONG KAMO RIVER
[I-8/9] Narrow, short Pontocho Geisha Alley btwn Sanjo–Shijo streets and Saiseki Gourmet Alley S: 'must' for Kyoto summer eves for luxury and budget alike is to dine out on *yuka* platform built over river. WHERE TO STAY lists most ryori-ryokan with *yuka* (* notes *yuka*). We used to shy away from going into shops on this alley because we were told they were mostly *chaya* where well-heeled visited geisha-run bars and restaurants. When we did our first edition there was change taking place with tea shop and pizza shop just opened. Now, we can go without fear as many *chaya* have been converted to such as **Robata-yaki Suishin** opp Kaburenjo, or **Kappa Sushi** with sushi ¥-B, under ¥100.

Just above Oike on Kiyamachi-dori is...
*Shinmiura [I-7] chicken mizutaki from ¥4,100, 5-10pm, X-sun, *yuka* summer.

S of Sanjo-dori starting from...
Pontocho Kaburenjo geisha theater, working S: on R are small bars and budget snacks *yakitori*, *oden*, *kama-meshi* and **Robata-yaki Suishin**, ¥250 for most while nabe ¥1,400+. You might want to try *karaoke* singing at **The Carotte**, salads, fried chicken ¥-B, next door to Kaburenjo. Opp parking lot is ***Matsutomo**, *kaiseki* ¥10,000, *yuka* summer; **Izeki** small old standby has lunch *Kyozen* ¥1,800-3,500, seasonal *omakase* course ¥4,500, nabe ¥1,700, ☎221-2964, 5-8pm, X-wed; **Kappa Sushi** on L best and cheapest, excellent fresh sushi each sardine ¥30, maguro ¥60, set ¥600, counter & table, 5-12pm, no-X; and **Siori**, coffee shop with big picture windows. Near Shijo end is moderate ***Izumoya** eel, plastic window menu, where we send many friends to dine on *yuka*; eel ¥-T, 12-9:30pm, X-2nd, 4th thur.

S across Shijo-dori in tiny...
SAISEKI ALLEY, excellent sample of Kyoto best. All L have summer *yuka* platform. Next to big Chinese restaurant **Toka-en** on Shijo is ***Chimoto** top *kaiseki-ryori*; ***Tori-iwa-ro** chicken *mizutaki* chain; ***Kanda-gawa** fine eel; ***Ginsui** various nabe ¥-L, kaiseki ¥-T; ***Jin-no-hana** of retired sumo wrestler *chanko-nabe* ¥4,500, 5-10pm, X-2nd, 4th sun ***Kanoko** for oil-yaki, sukiyaki ¥-T, 2-10pm. Past Donguri-bashi bridge about 3rd house is 175-year-old ***Tori-yosa** behind intriguing black wall; delicious moderate chicken-mizutaki. Opposite KANOKO on tiny triangle is TORI-YOSA's offspring **Sankaku**, our favorite chicken bits, exquisite, ¥-B.

MAIN STREET

[H-8] (Kawaramachi and Shijo, Shijo to Sanjo: most shops on main streets close by 9pm, but on side streets from 10pm-12midnite). On first alley R is charming tiny **Shiruko** famous for Japanese *miso shiru* soup, ¥500, Rikyu *bento* delicious; and at end of block is 6-storey **Pleasure Dome Imagium** of discotheques, bars and clubs, mostly 5pm-midnite or 5am. Out on Kawaramachi, landmark **Suehiro** beefsteak has closed (branch in Nanzen-ji remains); 3rd alley R **Tankuma** top Kyoto *Itamae* cuisine, ¥-L and **Hyomasa**, off-shoot of top HYOTEI of Nanzen-ji. On Kawaramachi is **Koraku**, private rooms, neat, family style W-. Down next alley (LIPTON TEA on corner) is **Pub Beatles** and **Daikokuya** best known of buckwheat soba shops downtown, E-menu, budget, then **Kushi-yasu** from ¥-B per *kushi-katsu* stick. Coming back down other side of Kawaramachi, corner of Rokkaku is **Maizaka** *unagi* eel, open till wee hrs; has branches nearby. Then tiny Kyoto-style budget **Mikuni** set back from street, tempura teishoku ¥-T.

Shijo to DAIMARU DEPT STORE [H-8]: Shijo W to Teramachi-dori: next door to Central Inn is pretty **Tagoto**, down long narrow entryway, quick service, simple moderate lunch ¥2,500. For moderate and budget this area is top with department stores: **Daimaru, Takashimaya & Hankyu** each with fine selection of Kyoto's favorite dining spots (*see* p520), then 3 colorful streets **Ura-Teramachi-dori, Shinkyogoku, Teramachi-dori** with popularly-priced restaurants which we cover in SHOPPING walks of area.

OUTLYING AREAS are covered in preceding listing, and main area text.

528

*When it comes to women, have you heard
of any place better than the capital?
For one thing...*   — Ihara Saikaku, d. 1694

HOW TO GET YOUR GEISHA

W ISHING to be innocently entertained by 'art-ladies', we originally consulted at some length with man who was undoubtedly *the* expert on geisha, late P.D. Perkins of Perkins Oriental Books in Kyoto. PD was sole Caucasian associate of geisha union, being himself acknowledged dance drummer. He wrote *Geisha of Pontocho*, sole book on subject until recent PhD researcher, Liza Dalby's excellent *Geisha* (made into movie). He agreed, you should not go to geisha entertainment alone...too expensive–about $250+ basic for Pontocho–and you won't enjoy yourself. Go in or with group. For best results, fellahs, take your wives along. You're not going to get anywhere with these girls so you might as well enjoy yourselves as much as possible. Geisha see all they care to of men, all of whom are same to them and you even less so as you and she have no common medium of communication. Geisha really go all out in female company.

When doing business in Tokyo we had recourse to Japanese custom and used geisha restaurant in Shibuya. Jay always took Sumi–as interpreter first time, as life of party after that.

Years ago Jay squired American tourist party, consisting mostly of elderly ladies, around Kyoto on JTB-arranged package tour. Highlight was geisha supper at Sa-ami–after wall of ice had been broken. Our geisha tried her best to warm things up, but she had no idea of what blue-eyed ones wanted. JTB interpreter, nice fellow, was hopelessly out of his milieu and helpless. Blue-eyes sat around cooing at geisha as they would any exotic doll, very lovely and all that but with really no place in their accepted ideas of room decor, and while apparently enjoying themselves they were all obviously looking forward to dessert.

Then Jay recognized one young geisha. She was one of those listed as 'English speaking' ("Hello", "Good nite", "No please" and such). Our artist-friend, 'Tom', had lived in Kyoto for about year, his wife had taught English to Gion geisha group. Tom's son, then 12, was not considered old enough to be charged for geisha's time by union so gals used to take him out on their own time. One of smilingly-bored American women asked Jay to ask geisha, Kimihatsu, if she had any patron or boy friend. Kimihatsu, of course, answered, "No"–'of course' because she was far too independent and strong-willed to appeal to old expense-account fogeys who patronize geisha quarters. (Younger men don't care for geisha as they are, often as not, in love with their wives—and can't afford them anyway.) Jay added in loud, simple, slow English that she really did have boy friend, then went on to recount tales of rendezvous with this mysterious foreigner. Kimihatsu was appalled and tried to deny it, but her English failed. She sputtered in fury, Jay was libeling her.

Then she realized it was Tom's son who was being described and recognized Jay as having taken some photos for her with him and she burst into relieved laughter. She leapt to her feet and shouted, "Let's fun".

And boy, did we. She lined up ladies and taught them dances such as *Tanko-bushi* coal miner's dance, *bon* dance, naughty wading dance, dressed them up in idiotic combinations, went thru her whole antic repertoire and capped it all with lessons in hilarious *Yakyu-ken* or *Basuboru Dansu* (Baseball Dance). It was one very tired, happy and reluctant-to-leave party that finally broke up after union's third call to Kimihatsu to come home for her next date.

Perkins suggested some other geisha party gimmicks which we have tried and enthusiastically second. If *maiko* is present, and one usually will be because these apprentice geisha are twice as picturesque at same cost, ask to see her combs (*kushi*) and accessories. She will gladly take them out to pass around for examination, explaining herself or thru interpreter what each is made of or what they mean. She may even have you try them on.

If there are no prudes in crowd, ask to see geisha's personal amulet. You'll need good interpreter for this. Even Perkins didn't know its real name, but in Japanese *"Jibun-no o-mamori misete kudasai"* (Your own talisman show us, please) should do it. It may be carved *netsuke* (ivory ornament) or shrine charm or picture, almost anything—but odds are that it will be erotic.

Then ask to have her dance—only if full *geiko*, *maiko* don't yet dance. Ask for *Kyo-odori* or *Gion-kouta* dance. (Asking for specific dances will put her at her ease and she will suggest others.) If you want to learn, start with Baseball Dance. Good to take back with you to liven up parties at home, it's fancy scissor-paper-rock game done to music involving silly dance any clod can master in one try. There is *Yakyu-ken* record put out by King, often out-of-stock. From here you might try other dances she may suggest, usually folk dances.

Geisha's main job is to serve wine, dance, play samisen and generally entertain. So, she'll start by offering you drink. Pick up your tiny *sake* cup and hold it out. She'll fill it. *Sake* is mild, if you take it easy. Try thimble or two. You also make her feel more at home and it's easier for her to find ways of entertaining you. If you don't go for *sake*, Japanese beer is tops. If you don't intend to at least take few sociable sips of something (at least have someone in group drink) then either stay home or go in expectation of drab time. She can also pour some Coke. If she fills your cup you may offer her your emptied cup (finger-bowl-like dish of water is usually set out for dipping cup for rinse) and exchange roles and fill it for her. If *maiko*, she may refuse or take just token tippling into cup and raise it to signify enough—don't force her. Serving and exchanging cups are part of her artistic repertoire and not drinking cuts you out of best part of show, that personalized attention Japanese old fools go into hock for—and ours would if they could.

Geisha now number some 15,000 nationwide, mostly mid- (semi-pro) and lower-class (amateur at best) in onsen towns. Peak was 1920s when some 80,000. Kyoto 1989 has 300 incl full *geiko* and *maiko*, and Pontocho and Gion are so short-handed that for their semi-annual *Odori* performances must recruit extras for chorus line from student dancers.

PRIVATE GEISHA PARTY

ARRANGE at most any J-style restaurant, including your own inn. Ask your restaurant or ryokan where you are staying to make arrangements, because they already have proper contacts. If at hotel in J-room, ask desk or JTB to arrange. If type who likes to go direct you could contact *cha-ya* direct, or geisha *kumiai* (guild), but without proper introduction that's more hassle than it's worth. As we discuss in WHERE TO STAY, most better ryokan make their money on meals—are in fact essentially restaurants. Your looked forward-to geisha party is best and most economically arranged for at and thru your inn. Geisha rates are fixed, but inn will guard you against any possible clip or misunderstanding, and extras and liquor charges will be kept legit as they go on your tab as part of inn service. We suggest you request at time of reservation, whether weeks or days ahead, to have geisha attend you at dinner in your inn. Rates ('90) for one *maiko* (apprentice geisha) or *geiko* (trained geisha) are ¥35,000 for *isseki* (one session) 6:15-8:00pm. Sometimes might request taxi fee home, *kurumadai*, of ¥1,000, but that is all, no tipping, etc. Geiko is preferable, tho slightly less ornate, as better trained in dances and games, probably plays banjo-like samisen. If you are large group, live it up and get one of each. Whatever, talk it over frankly with your inn manager.

'Proper' way is to have someone introduce you to *cha-ya* and if you're introduced by regulars, then you don't discuss such mundane things as price...just pay bill when sent out to you, perhaps not till weeks later. However, most of us are out of that class. Times are changing and *cha-ya* are sending out circulars in English (such as **Minoya** in Gion—didn't work out but they welcome you if you have someone who is bilingual). *Cha-ya* can arrange two different types of parties: dinner party with geisha attending 2hrs (*see* above) or full time—very expensive—or shorter after dinner meeting with geisha entertainment, drinks and *tsukidashi* (hors d'oeuvres).

Another way if staying at hotel or lesser ryokan is to arrange for dinner at select Japanese restaurant-inn. Elegant atmosphere with lingering scent of incense, beautiful garden, quiet setting: finest in Japanese cuisine topped with geisha chit-chat can be experienced at beautiful **Doi** at Kodaiji, **Kyo-Yamato** nearby, or **Sa-ami** with gorgeous view in Maruyama Park, **Tsuruya** in Okazaki, **Nakamura-ro** by Gion Yasaka Shrine, **Minokichi** Awataguchi, or **Kiccho** out west in Arashiyama. Dinners at above run high (*see* CHOPSTICKS immediately preceding) and charges for geisha run standard geisha-union rate.

Sumiya, exotic ancient *oiran* (courtesan) house, over in old Shimabara geisha quarters used to arrange to serve dinner and have their *ukiyo-e* woodblock surroundings come to life, and after present major restoration is complete may resume–check your hotel or JTB; expensive, but unforgettable splash for gang of you. Often on geisha party nite tour (*see*).

WHERE TO SEE GEISHA

BUT IF YOU just want to see some geisha and grab few snapshots, there's no need to go to much, or even any, expense. Stroll thru geisha quarters of Pontocho along alley parallel to river on west between Sanjo-Shijo, and Gion centered on famous Ichiriki-chaya, that dark red wall up Shijo-dori on S side between river and Yasaka-Gion shrine at end of Shijo (*see* KYOTO MAP), between 3 and 5 in afternoon when geisha are on their way to or from bath, hairdresser or music teacher. Little before 8pm, carefully made-up and elegantly gowned, they walk to their nearby late appointment (first dinner stage, remember, was 6ish to 8pm).

JTB has **Maiko Special Night Tour** 5:30-8:30pm, 'exciting evening' with English guide, of maiko dance, dinner, unlimited beer or sake, for ¥58,000 each–$450! –if 2 couples you do better throwing your own party.

Thru hotel or JTB ☎341-1413. More affordable is, also in English: *Special Night* Tues, Thurs, Sat, 6:40-10:00, ¥9,500 w/Zen-style tempura dinner, *matcha* tea & stroll to 'gay quarter' alleys to end up in Gion Corner for show. At other extreme is go on your own for glimpse of Maiko at **Gion Corner** eves 7:40 and 8:40, various theatrical arts shown, *matcha* tea served, etc, ¥2,100 per person, and get there by pleasant stroll there past Ichiriki-chaya thru main Gion restaurant-geisha district to **Gion Kaburenjo** theater.

Keihan bus tours offer four different J-speaking nite courses: make rounds of Gion to watch *maiko* dances, visits infamous **Sumiya** geisha, watch *oiran* (courtesan) procession, end up in temple garden for *koto* music and ceremonial green tea. Another drives around Arashiyama and then Gion Corner show of geisha, puppets, *koto* music, flower and tea ceremony, followed by drive along Higashiyama Driveway (¥5,000 w/out dinner, up to ¥6,000 with, all start 5-6-ish, take 2-4hrs; *see* BUS TOURS, earlier).

Yosaku Miyagawa-ten offered *Maiko-no Yuuseki* 'Dine with Geisha' July 1–Aug 31, 1hr 5-6pm or 8:30-9:30pm ¥9,800 each, min 2 people up to group of 30, or 2+hr 6-8:30pm ¥16,800 each; both include *Yosaku Kyo-gozen* dinner of tempura, sashimi, duck with one bottle each beer or sake, present of *shikishi* artboard signed by maiko and you can take picture with her; at Matsubara-dori Miyagawa-suji higashi-iru, ☎561-3259—*discontinued* late '89, may resume if demand, check TIC or phone direct in J-.

Fast rising geisha group are Kitano, who also hold excellent spring and autumn dances at their own Kaburenjo theater, along with Pontocho and Gion at their's. They specialized mainly in more earthy, older arts of entertainment. You can sometimes visit them on Keihan Bus Nite Tour when Shimabara not taken in. But to find their quarter for eve stroll: from var stops in town take bus #10, 50, 51, 55 or 203, get off at Kitano Tenmangu-mae, walk along R(W) of Kitano Shrine [E/F-5/6] on Onmae-dori st, and you'll find **Kitano Kamishichi-ken Kaburenjo** theater, beer garden July 1–Aug 31, 6-10pm, ☎461-0148; buy ¥700 beer ticket, good for one medium *chokki* stein of draught beer, additional eats ¥700+. Geisha in diaphanous summer yukata sitting around fanning themselves, will pose for photo with you gratis.

Other chances to see geisha (usually maiko) are at...
International Kokusai Hotel [31, G-7] ☎222-1111, tea ceremony in lobby, special *maiko* shows, daily 5:30-6:30 in front lobby.
Pension Higashiyama Gion [18, I/J-8] (JIG), S of Sanjo on Shirakawa-suji ☎882-1181 or **Pension Arashiyama Sagano** or **Pension Station Kyoto**, new inn, guests can dress up at **Gion** as *maiko* or at **Station** as *maiko* or Lady Murasaki-era court lady in *junihitoe* 12-layer costume; owner says can accommodate non-guest foreigners at **Station** as courtesy, ¥2,200, incl full ornate whiteface makeup, 7:30pm, rsve ☎882-6200.

STROLLING ALLEYS GION AND PONTOCHO

BY NITE—especially touring on budget. Tree-lined streets paralleling river on W or town side, alleys on either side of tiny Takase-gawa canal are lined with bars and restaurants. Those overlooking river with entrances along Pontocho Alley (between river and canal) are most pleasant, having *yuka*-balconies over river in summer and one eats, dines and is entertained in open air (horrors—rumor city may do away with them, cultural suicide). They are intermixed, both for ¥-T to ¥-S moderate diners and some ¥-L, even ¥-LL *itamae* or *kaiseki* restaurants by appointment. At **Dai-Ichi**, traditional old cha-ya where we played one eve, geisha acting finger puppets while *komuso* (Zen pilgrim) in his great mask-helmet like some inverted wastepaper basket, strolled beneath our *yuka*-porch along riverbed playing his *shakuhachi* bamboo flute, as could happen to you when eating outside in *yuka*-restaurants (*see* CHOPSTICKS, preceding).

Pontocho Kaburenjo Theater is at N end of our favorite Kyoto alley. We'll always recall it as we saw it one nite during our honeymoon, with CBS Symphony of the Air gang, geisha lanterns with abstract Pontocho symbol of *chidori*-sandpiper bird silhouette at each door reflecting in rain slick. We propped our camera on balustrade and let it go for time exposure in color—successfully.

Along these streets—Pontocho Alley, above, by river, Kiyamachi facing canal and across it, and starting just above Sanjo and running to Gojo, unnamed alley of bars—are many little eating and drinking places which are pleasant adventure. Sake runs fairly standard restaurant ¥500 per tiny porcelain *go* bottle for top grade *tokkyu*, less for 2nd grade *nikyu*. (remember this is less grading for quality than alcoholic content) but sometimes more where special services rendered, or just plain posh, or more and more where special *ji-zake* 'home town' natural sake served. Beer is ¥500 to 700 'quart' (633cc) bottle or stein of draft.

Yakitori, or barbecue meat on stick, runs ¥130–180 yen per stick, is safe and delicious—first time order *mori-awase,* tray of assorteds. Little oden stalls, where various delicacies can be chosen from shallow-pan stew at ¥60 to 120 per piece. These dishes have evolved as accompaniment to.alcohol. And don't bypass push-carts, especially oden-stew carts and specialists selling fabulous broiled conch in spiral shell, *sazae-no-tsuboyaki,* abt ¥300 —choose middle size for best taste, work out with toothpick in corkscrew action like Englishmen screw out winkles. All pushcart food, as we often stress, is well-cooked—no uncooked food may be sold out-doors, by fanatically-enforced health department regulations. Mike Royko will be relieved to know you can not sell sushi to Japanese yuppies at baseball games here, even if they would eat it—would you eat caviar or even raw oysters in your baseball stadium bleachers?

Osome's Nite Club, long run by Gion Geisha Osome, one of most beautiful women in Japan, is *alas no more.* Back in '51 when Jay first fell for--uh--met her, she had tiny bar on willow-lined canal which held bartender (George Nonoguchi-san, spoke fine English, was addicted to crosswords), Osome, four or five girls, perhaps as many customers. All Gion and Pontocho were off-limits to occupation troops, but not to such as student Jay who had no official standing. It was hangout for government ministers, ex-ministers, local communist boss and sole GI who could ignore off-limits signs—US Army Intelligence chief in Kyoto. It was homey, especially on rainy nites when, if nature called, Osome herself would hold oil-paper and bamboo umbrella and guide your wobbly steps across street to edge of canal. Osome retired to Tokyo. Kyoto plumbing, sigh, has been modernized.

As you stroll alleys, little men or old ladies will pop out of shadows or parade down street in some goofy get-up handing out handbills, which you will have to reach for as they are intended for Japanese. Some advertise, quite obviously, budget cabarets and their present stage shows (usually nude dances). Ad is in Japanese, but either he will show you way or get yourself cab and hand driver ad.

Then other much smaller leaflets of about memo pad size advertise Escort Services, by whatever name now going—switch every few years after periodic token anti-prostitution crack-downs. Sometimes hand-written with phone number predominant—and price, which is girl's rate per two hours. Unfortunately, we have tested dozen of these numbers and found none who speak English, but this did not seem to dampen enjoyment of visiting firemen friends for whom we called to help. Gals know town, do not here steer you into clips, but guard you. They go home only when you pay them off and their union does not observe labor regulations against nite work or long hours. Regular police clamp-downs clean away ads for short time, but they return.

One ad we especially liked is of socio-linguistic interest. Altho written in Japanese syllabary, almost all nouns and adjectives were of English-origin (*italics*): "This is *Instant Age*, we have had *instant milk* and *instant coffee* and *instant foods*, now we offer you *instant romance*, *instant kiss*, *instant love*, *instant sex—our girls like* to go for *drives*, go to *movies*, to *tea shops* or *dining*, take 'kyukei' (rest) *with you some place*, or what else, etc... ¥-x per two hours, ¥-x each additional hour (season rates negotiable?), phone xxx-xxxx." And believe us, those girls have telephone personalities. They are usually dishes and are shown 'on approval'. No service charge or tax no matter how taxing service. (Probably no VAT, either, as small mom'n-pop business with gross sales under ¥35,000,000 not VATaxed)

Kyoto by nite is as interesting as Kyoto by day, altho its exact opposite. After all, you haven't come halfway round world to see imitation of what you've got at home. Paris is nearer and cheaper, anyway.

Until anti-prostitution law went into effect you could still walk thru woodblock print scene down among fleshpots of Shichijo Shinchi. Here two long streets, branching off like two legs of V, were lined with gaudy bawdy houses catering to all tastes. There was no question of what you'd find inside, for wares were on display in front. Girls in kimono lounged on *tatami*-matted platforms, often behind barred windows as in antique block prints of long-gone Yoshiwara. Girls who worked in western dress lounged in evening gowns on stately thrones, colored spotlights playing upon them.

Jay walked thru one nite, down one street, along willow-lined canal and back up other. On return leg word of his coming preceded him. Luscious wares were spread out for his minute examination. Still he passed them up. As he neared end of street solicitors were getting more puzzled, desperate. As he swung past last display two mobile samples swished in front, waggling hips and throwing every enticement his way. Then followed tightly-slacked gays. Still no taker...much puzzlement. It just happens he was out for cool stroll, some research perhaps. Besides, "I was broke".

When law went into effect, Shichijo died. Papers played up fact that houses were being converted to student dorms. Actually, Shichijo was dying anyway. Other areas more lively when law hit have reformed (take that to mean what you will). Shimabara, known for its procession of *oiran* (star courtesans) April 21—when law hit, they canceled festival for couple of years (since resumed) and prepared to disband, or something. They 'or-something-ed'. Picturesque alleys of Shimabara with ancient Oriental gates and wall enclose quarter and fine Muromachi- and Tokugawa-era buildings inside, as restaurants and bars replaced old bawdy houses. And big Turkish bath, plumbing ran into old 'cells'. Then came second and serious clean-up, as bathhouses and such hanky-panky moved out to Steven Speilberg-like setting on shores of Lake Biwa at **Ogoto**, 45min/10x-mtr taxi from

Kyoto. Approach from afar looks like Star Wars special effects, with more light outside than inside.

Shimabara is just behind—W of—great HONGAN-JI temple complex, opposite great Buddhist cathedral's back gate. Quarter was set up in ancient times to cater to pilgrims and student priests. Business was good. We prophesy it will be again after restoration completed 1990.

And should you have money to splash on Gion or Pontocho and want to splash more and later and your playmate insists on following time-honored 'code of conduct' for geisha, or at least first class geisha—well, you'll find this appetite can be catered to, too. In Gion these specialists are not termed geisha but *joyu*-easy to remember, like 'joy-you'. In Pontocho they are *yatona*. But again this will little concern you as arrangements for their services must be made according to time-honored, traditional, old-fashioned ways by appointment thru *machiai*, which is called in English, tea house (not to be confused with those little garden cottages where they really serve tea), but more accurately translates directly as 'waiting place' or place of assignation. Law or no law, *joyu* and *yatona* and others will ply their trade unmolested until Japan gets strong female prime minister. And *oiran* and whatever you want to call others will not be too much inconvenienced either. For better or worse, that's Japan.

OSAKA has novel Geisha restaurant we wish Kyoto would emulate: **Club Maiko**, branches in *Kita* (N) entertainment district in VO bldg basement, Sonezaki-kita-shinchi 1ch-6-10, ☎344-2913, and *Minami* (S) district in Minami-VO bldg 2fl, Sennen-cho 38, ☎253-0581; either one ¥6,000 all incl for 3 real drinks, hors d'oeuvres, souvenir color photo with gals, gourd sake hip-flask; full meals avail moderate extra *see*. They join you at table, pour and serve, give 20min dance show hourly 7:40, 8:40. 9:40, 10:30. Also one in Tokyo Ginza in Aster Plaza Bldg 4fl, Ginza 7ch-7-6, ☎574-7745 (¥8,000-set)

But as we said before, if we "go on describing ladies' manners...."

There is scarce a house in this large capital where there is not
something made or sold...in short there is nothing that
can be thought of but what may be found at Miyako
— Kaempfer, 1690

SHOPPERS' PARADISE

ALL KYOTO is one big Oriental marketplace where traditional arts and crafts are still mainstay of local economy. Kyoto ceramic traditions continue in old forms, while simultaneously evolving into hi-tech silicons. So it is with other crafts. Kyoto-ites and sophisticates of similar tastes nationwide maintain steady demand for these products. Kyoto taste has been fighting better rear guard action in its crafts than in its architecture and city planning (what there is of it). Time your visit to catch great monthly open-air markets: 21st at **Toji Temple** and 25th at **Kitano Shrine**. Blocks of stall after stall sell ceramics, antique furniture, curios, old kimono, trivia and all kinds of junk, plants, foodstuffs. August 7-10 **Gojo-dori** wholesale area has 4-day grand pottery clearance sale, with other areas now emulating.

Make your shopping tour educational. Some shops maintain veritable museums of their craft in private collection rooms. Or visit those few which still demonstrate their age-old processes—made easier now by grouping of several together in **Kyoto Handicrafts Center** [J-7] and **Museum of Traditional Industry** [K-7] as well as shops and museums. A complete listing is given on pp.555-556.

English is understood widely—at all shops on Curio St, and well at some specialty shops mentioned, to reasonable degree at most.

Several shopping strolls are detailed following. Some lead into one another and determined hiker in good shoes could make full day of it, eating en rte at restaurants mentioned in passing as well as some inns and hotels. Shops will personally deliver reasonably-sized purchase to your hotel arrange at cost for same—or next-day delivery by *takkyu-bin* or faster in-city delivery by *aka-bo*. In brief, our routes:

I. CURIO STREET [MAP p.537] within 15min walk of center hotels near Kyoto Hotel or taxi basic-mtr. For determined shopper not to be combined with other sightseeing unless limiting street to half day.

II. WHOLESALE CERAMICS, POTTERY LANE & CRAFT WALK continues on into **Yasaka Shrine** & **Maruyama Park** [MAP p. 541].

III. MANSION AREA [MAP p.545] for gluttons and should be taken with spare finger in RAMBLES NORTHEAST (p.488) for its sights in latter part Nanzen-ji to Kiyomizu, in reverse order.

IV. MAIN STREETS: **Shijo-dori–Teramachi-dori–Kawaramachi-dori** [MAP p.547] are each separate but again linked, include our center hotels, and as are open till late make for enjoyable pre-dinner strolling, or short after dinner walk.

CURIO STREET [I-8, MAP p.537]

THIS AREA favored by foreigners is filled with shops that have long dealt with foreigners, most every shop has someone who speaks English. Bordering on Kamo River it was set up to export goods overseas. It covers NAWATE-DORI St running parallel to river, with SHINMONZEN and FURUMONZEN Streets running E-W off it. Most open daily, some X-mon. In 25 years since our first edition some shops have gone, mostly death of aged proprietor, but many more new ones have opened up.

Area's character has changed, with Nawate dealers now catering to Japanese as well as their former main foreign and museum collectors. Former touristy-cluttered windows now feature few exquisite antiques. For someone with genuine interest in certain arts, they will be pleased to bring out objects from storerooms in back. If you espy hanging scrolls hung bunched together, tagged usually from ¥7,000+, it shows they cater to casual shoppers. We suggest you start on **Nawate-dori** from Sanjo-dori Street by Keihan Line's (from Osaka and Nara) Sanjo terminal and stroll up as far as canal, then return part way back to and R up **Furumonzen St** (English sign) to end of first block, turn R to Shinmonzen St and L to **Nawate**, backtrack up **Shinmonzen**, continue across **Shirakawa canal** and on along popular tourist-oriented antique street.

We retrace this route entering Nawate at Sanjo terminal, on L is...
Kawakatsu antiques; then **T. Nakamura** (☎561-4726, no-X) noted for ancient textiles for collectors, especially fine pre-Meiji (Edo) kimonos, noh costumes; **S. Kataoka**, ivory, has collection of old netsuke and runs own workshop (Japan now joins total ban on ivory trade); and **Yamazoe** hanging scrolls. Across street is new **Yoshioka Kogei** for hand-dyed textiles, crafts and books, run by Sachio, son of late YOSHIOKA Tsuneo, top expert in ancient dyes and dyed textiles. Few doors on is **Tessai-do** (moved from other side of street when founder-father died and now one of four shops in this area run by family) with quality selection of inexpensive scrolls—exciting finds in boxes of old sketches and paintings salvaged from worn-out scrolls and books (¥2,000up). Next are **Mizutani Shukodo**, **Yoshida**, fine arts; **Konjaku Nishimura** antique textiles made into ties, bags and old garments (sister of Nishimura on Shinmonzen). **Sekisen-Ishinosuke Mizutani**, unique in having albums filled with photographs of all their hanging scrolls—over 9,000. Opposite side of street are several antique shops including **Yanagi Takashi** screens and scrolls, one of four Yanagi-family antique shops in here; **Nakagawa Senshoku** dyes happi coats, banners, towels to your own design (¥7,000+, 1 month). Across on R is **Yokoyama** with bit of everything for hurried shopper (screens old and new, ceramics, baskets, prints, kimonos); **Yamana**, small classical ryori-ryokan is few doors on; **Fujii** antique dolls; and **Shiga Pref Products** shop with dried gourd bottles, Otsu-e paintings, pottery badgers (1m/39in tall ¥27,500). Then we reach **Shirakawa canal.**

CHOPSTICKS: We are happy to see favorite of our first edition again, looking L up canal we see small private bridge straddling canal, leading to **Shiraume**, lovely ryori ryokan, formerly restaurant that catered geisha parties so rooms all well appointed—enjoy tempura, kaiseki, and any of numerous nabé dishes, ¥-hi-Tw/2; restaurant open 16:00-21:00, ☎561-1459. Good eating places up to here from Sanjo-dori: **Izutsu** Japanese budget table d'hote, **Izutsu** bldg with W-meals next door, budget at **ITY**'s basement, **Jubei sushi** (☎791-2131, X-mon), **Toh-en** Chinese, while further on by Shirakawa canal are **Hokusai** (☎561-7121, no-X) novel *goryo-nabe*, hunter's meal with beef, duck, chicken grilled on spade-shaped pan ¥3,700, **Tomihisa** for *fugu* blowfish and chicken mizutaki **Torishin** (☎561-1362, no-X).

Beyond canal are **Umenoi** (☎561-1004, X-wed) tempura; budget *izakaya* and *robata-yaki* **Kappa** (☎531-4048) on L corner and branch across street. Here in front of counter, rows of day's menu uncooked: fish, vegetables, meat is spread out—just point to item, watch it being cooked. Look on menu in English (they're used to foreign guests) for salads, soups, other dishes prepared aside. It's fun place. No one comes to take your order, just catch eye of colorfully garbed cook in front of you, order portions individually or in batches.

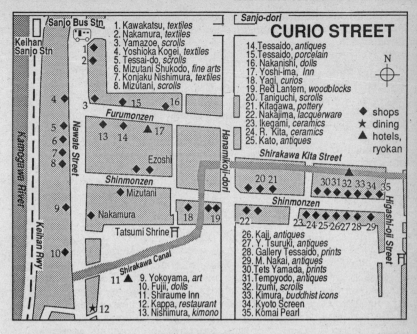

Curio Street

Continuing on to **Shijo-dori St** there's...

Tsujikura lantern and parasol shop they can have name painted on them by next day as they have workers there (relative of Kawaramachi shop); **Hirata** shop for bamboo blind.

Double back to Furumonzen Street off Nawate-dori St to find our old Koshida Satsuma-ware and Yamamoto handbags have moved to Kyoto Handicraft Center, but **Nishimura** with many old kimono, obi is still there. New on L is inviting small shop **Tessaido** with lots of porcelains, dishes, plates, bowls in all sizes, colors and prices, with big drawers of beautiful combs and hairpieces from few thousand yen up–owner is sister of Tessai-do on Nawate. Across street is her husband KIDO Akira's **Tessai-do** (in Japanese one is written in kanji, others in different syllabary) with paintings, especially in *sumi* ink of Edo period. Then follow antique shops on both sides of street, of which **Nakanishi** almost last on L specializes only in old Japanese dolls, and has largest collection in Kyoto. For historical look at dolls, visit **Sagano Ningyo-no-ie** (Sagano Museum of Dolls) part of HEIAN TOUCH stroll, (p.454); ☎882-1421.

In middle of block is **Yoshi-ima,** inn experienced with foreign guests as can be judged from amenities such as illustrated English brochure with useful information on customs and sightseeing. Lovely tea house, serves ceremonial tea, small fee. Tatami rooms with bath, ¥-hi-Sw/2, ☎561-2620.

Turning R from **Furumonzen** St...

Past curio shop **Obata** on L, take R turn onto Shinmonzen, where until relatively recently there were no shops, we go down R side. Antiques of **Yanagi Kunio; Ishinaka** then **Ezoshi** owner YAMAO Go dealing exclusively in old woodblock prints–prices extremely reasonable—claims he and Nishiharu (corner Sanjo-Teramachi) are only ones dealing exclusively in woodblock prints. Continue on to 5 more fine antique shops including

Kanzando Mizutani (next door and across street) antique dolls, unusual old-fashion farmer's 3-layer quilted cotton kimono from days before wool was introduced to Japan.

Turn back up Shinmonzen...after jog in street is...
Yagi Art Shop chock full of curios among which we found nicely carved wooden noh masks (¥50,000+). Cross Shirakawa canal to old **Red Lantern** (☎751-0180) which now sells only modern artists' woodblocks since original owner died. We cross Hanamikoji St to find shop after shop of curios and antiques: on L **Kotera** has Chinese art; **Taniguchi** huge stock of fine hanging scrolls; **Kitagawa** lots of lovely affordable old Imari, fell in love with rectangular old tea pots (¥7,000). Haven for collectors is **Chishoken Imai** founder K. IMAI died years ago, but son carries on in modest shop which houses old Nabeshima, Imari and netsuke carefully stored in back rooms and shown only to discriminating buyers upon request or who show intelligent interest.

At this point we go back to Hanamikoji for shops on opposite side of street.
Nakajima and **Ikegami** featuring lacquerware and ceramics come first, then few doors on are **R. Kita** large selection of ceramics especially *aka* (red)-Kutani ware; **Kato** general antiques, some inexpensive netsuke; and 2 large shops **Kaji's Antiques** and **Y.Tsuruki** filled with antique screens, scrolls, lacquer, etc. New **Gallery Tessaido** bldg (antiques at Nawate shop) only modern prints and paintings—we hate to see ambience of area being destroyed by shining metal and glass buildings. Across street is **Tets Yamada**, modern print shop, artist himself, handling modern artists and some old prints and inexpensive new editions. **Tempyodo**, Korean chests, ceramics; **Izumi**, rare scrolls, paintings; **Kimura** Buddhist paintings, sculpture; **Kyoto Screen** has changed emphasis onto old screens, with some recent ones, not too gaudy for ¥50,-¥120,000 for 3x6ft 4-panel screen, also fairly priced woodblocks. End of block is **Komai** pearl, formerly exclusive Mikimoto, but now many brands.

Cross Higashi-oji Street, walk few blocks N for some junk shops, or thru Shinmon Temple gate towards Miyako Hotel; or S toward Yasaka Shrine and beyond to...

WHOLESALE CERAMICS, POTTERY LANE & CRAFT WALK (Map p.541)

IN THIS SEGMENT we have three distinct areas: **GOJO-DORI**, many wholesale ceramic shops, but sell to individuals, too; the main road up is Kiyomizu-zaka long known as **TEAPOT LANE** for souvenirs, parallel to former back street now newly built up and called **TEACUP LANE (Chawan-zaka)** also leading to Kiyomizu Temple; and charming **SANNENZAKA & NINENZAKA** branching off N from Kiyomizu-zaka with all kinds of crafts way out to **Maruyama Park** at top of Shijo-dori. Old shops and homes that line latter two areas give picture of old Japan with shop front, making things in back and living upstairs or in back. Again we mention sights, dining spots, inns or hotels in passing for convenience.

GOJO-DORI

Gojo-dori has ceramics made today, from utilitarian to fine art pieces. Start along **Gojo-dori** just E of Kamo River and work up towards **Higashi-oji**. This used to be manufacturing-wholesale area with pottery kilns dotting this entire Kiyomizu area, but since pollution ban on firing kilns in city, most makers moved kilns to Kiyomizu Danchi in Yamashina, about 15min away by taxi. However, lining L side are huge shops and wholesale stores where it is possible to go in and buy individual pieces. First among these is old-time popular **Manjudo**, exquisite and expensive ware. Satsuma ware is found at **Okada,** and by pedestrian bridge are **Maruko** and **Azuma-Bankodo,** both wholesalers with almost any type of ceramic vessels you'd want. At **Rakushien**, tea ceremony bowls and utensils made by well-known ceramic artists at connoisseur prices, as well as large selection of nice works at lesser prices. Along this street we spotted new hand-painted blue and whites that look like antiques, but find prices quite steep for new (¥23,000 for five 5" plates).

Number of small shops follow with goods overflowing—have porcelain teapots, cups, soba bowls, coffee and tea cups and saucers, at budget prices not to be matched elsewhere. However, many of those colorful bigger bowls and platters here are from Kyushu and not hand-painted but are new photo processed ware copying old Arita colored ware and priced fairly. Remember this is wholesale area. At Higashi-oji end huge **Fujihira** made name specializing in art vases, modern, novel shapes as well as standard in varying textures–exquisite new technique Shibagaki vase with raised pattern using gold and other metallics in delicate floral motif, many sizes to 3ft tall ¥3,000,000.

Incidentally, across Gojo Blvd is showplace-home of late well-known Kawai **Kanjiro**, leading potter of folkcraft movement. Home-workshop made into museum since his death. Rare example of many-chambered climbing kiln. Open 9-5; X-mon. Nearby, too, was kiln of late national treasure Kiyomizu **Rokubei VI**, and their sales shop faces Gojo.

Corner is landmark **Sawakichi Stone Mason** whose stone lanterns grace gardens worldwide. Years of experience shipping, their English pamphlets with photographs, and fine workmanship make it easy to shop here. For example, *yukimi* (snow view) stone lantern with wide octagonal 'roof', 60cm tall is ¥150,000, 75cm ¥330,000; freight approx ¥130,000 including insurance to closest port or large city, 2 months by sea. Catalog: ✍ 551 Gojozaka, Higashiyama-ku, Kyoto, ☎561-2802.

Before going up Gojozaka hill, long known as TEAPOT LANE or POTTERY HILL note couple of shops N on Higashi-oji. Across alley from Sawakichi is tiny new **Seikado** (brother's antique shop on Shinmonzen) with semi-antique dishes and lacquer, textiles.

PERSONAL DATEBOOK: Visit this area during **Aug 7-10** to revel in ceramic bargains as streets are lined with stalls selling leftover stock as well as rejects.

WHERE TO STAY: Next alley is **Minshuku Rokuharaya** ☎531-2776; and down next alley is **Minshuku Yutaka** with ¥-B restaurant. Beyond Higashiyama-Yasui intersection is **Hayama Ryokan**, minshuku rates, E-spoken.

POTTERY (TEAPOT) LANE

First part is Kiyomizu-zaka up to two modern buildings on R–first **Bijutsu Kogei Gallery** now run by city as rental gallery (ex-Kyoto Craft Center, moved to Shijo-dori). **Kyoto Tojiki Kaikan** has fine porcelains and they will ship anywhere; upstairs often has artists' exhibits. Few doors up is **Higashiyama-so**, inn for JR employees, but if vacancy exists anyone may stay; ¥-Bw/2, ☎561-0468 (no English). Used to be only few places to eat, but now there are many: across street coffee shop **Kyoryori**, and further up street just after Y-split in road on L are 3 more—udon, table d'hote, and soba, and coffee shop.

Y-split R takes you up...

CHAWAN-ZAKA (TEACUP LANE)

With numerous new shops on what was formerly just back street. Back on L main split you soon reach parking lot for buses and taxis on L. On R is narrow alley with **Yamamoto Ryokan** on corner and down alley is ¥-lo-Bw/bkfst **Ryokan Teradaya**. ☎561-3821. On lane **Minshuku Yoshikawa** with tea shop.

Rest of climb to lovely...

KIYOMIZU TEMPLE is lined both sides with souvenir shops with interesting dolls, masks, miniature masks, well-known local sweets, pickles, textile products. Almost at temple on R is **Asahi-do** with fine assortment of ceramics and pottery-making demonstrations (call in advance), can do *rakuyaki* painting on teacups, to be fired and delivered to you in Japan (¥1,500, postage extra). Cross over to Chawan Lane for another *rakuyaki* shop where is also located Asahi-do's annex **Tohgoroh**.

After seeing Kiyomizu Temple come down same hill, halfway at fork go R at...
300-yr-old **Kiyomizu Shichimi-ya** ('7-spices') shop for our favorite walk for crafts, altho some of its charm is disappearing with so many new ceramic shops and eateries opening up. *Shichimi* is mixture of slightly hot spices, served in bamboo shaker at all noodle shops. Sold in small bamboo cannister or in tiny lidded ceramic pot. Get their preserved cherry blossoms (*sakura no shio zuke*) for tea—rinse off salt, place in teacup, add hot water or tea and watch blossoms open before you.

Turn R and down steps to start stroll Sanneizaka, popularly called...

SANNENZAKA

On R is **Akebono-tei**, large new restaurant, followed by old bamboo shop **Kaede Ippo-do**. On L woodblock & pottery shop, and **Hyotan-ya** with hundreds of dried gourds hanging inside for use as canteens for sake or water, made in age-old process of drying gourds there on premises. There's pottery shop, followed by shop making handmade rice wafers. These four shops are old-timers here.

CHOPSTICKS: Next block on R is old-time high-class restaurant-inn **Kyoto Sakaguchi** ryotei: sun, hol & flower/maple season drop in just for *matcha* green tea ¥800 in garden; July-Aug visit 'beer' garden, *tenshin* meal with 2 jugs of draft beer ¥5,000; *bento* ¥5,000; *kaiseki* lunch from ¥8,000. Local soba shop, next old estate tastefully converted into **Bougatei** sandwich and sweets shop with adjoining unique gift shop. Across alley is branch of **Okutan** well-known *yudofu* restaurant by Nanzen-ji.

Back on L are shops with cloisonne and pottery, and original home of **Yatsuhashi** wafers; **Maruyama** doll shop with fine collection of rolly-polly *gosho ningyo,* inexpensive with exquisite features. In fact, there are two more doll shops further on, but most gift shops have their own little line of paper, clay, ceramic dolls. Shop next door worth making special trip for **Matsuda**, singular in having large selection of reasonably priced semi-antique ceramics—his post- and late-Meiji blue & whites are our find. Exquisitely hand-painted in top coloring, set of covered rice bowls ¥6,000 each; many fine less expensive pieces. Phone as he is often out, ☎541-4008.

Diagonally across street: **Yamamoto Rakuzendo** and **Roku-rokudo** antiques, especially *sencha* equipment; and **Koishi** new Kiyomizu ware.

Go down stone stairway, enter...

NINENZAKA

Actually called **NINEIZAKA** and on L is what shops on this old lane looked like until quite recently. It is **Kasagiya**, famous for its Japanese sweets, especially *o-hagi*, glutinous rice and rice lightly pounded, covered

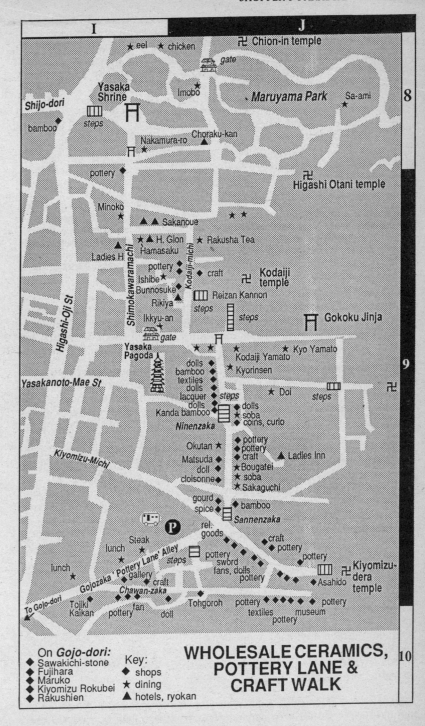

I   J

8

★ eel   ★ chicken

卍 Chion-in temple

🏯 gate

Yasaka Shrine

Shijo-dori

Imobo ★

Maruyama Park   Sa-ami ★

◆ bamboo

⊞ steps

🈁

Nakamura-ro ★

Choraku-kan ▲

卍 Higashi Otani temple

◆ pottery

Minoko ★

▲ ▲ Sakanoue

★ ★

★ ▲ H. Gion
Hamasaku

★ Rakusha Tea

▲ Ladies H.

pottery ◆

◆ craft

卍 **Kodaiji temple**

Shimokawaramachi

Kodaiji-michi

Ishibe ★

Bunnosuke ◆

Rikiya ▲

⊞ Reizan Kannon

Higashi-Oji St

Ikkyu-an ◆

⊞ steps

🏯 gate

🈁

steps ▦

🈁 **Gokoku Jinja**

9

Yasaka Pagoda 🏯

★ ★

★

★ Kyo Yamato

★ Kodaiji Yamato

dolls ◆
bamboo
textiles
dolls ◆
lacquer
dolls ◆

★ Kyorinsen

Yasakanoto-Mae St

★ Dol

⊞ steps

Kanda bamboo

steps ▦

◆ dolls

◆ soba

◆ coins, curio

Ninenzaka

◆ pottery

◆ pottery

▲ Ladies Inn

Kiyomizu-Michi

Okutan ★

Matsuda ◆

doll ◆

cloisonne ◆

◆ craft

★ Bougatei

★ soba

★ Sakaguchi

gourd ◆
spice

◆ bamboo

rel.
goods

Ⓟ

Sannenzaka

🅿 Steak

★

lunch ★

◆ craft
◆ pottery

★ *Pottery Lane' Alley*

⊞ steps

lunch ★

pottery ◆
sword
fans, dolls

◆ pottery

◆ pottery

Gojozaka

gallery ◆

◆ craft

⊞

卍 **Kiyomizu-dera temple**

Chawan-zaka

◆ Asahido

To Gojo-dori

Tojiki
Kaikan ◆

pottery ◆

fan ◆

doll ◆

Tohgoroh ★

pottery ◆ ◆ ◆ ◆ ◆ pottery

textiles
museum

pottery

10

WHOLESALE CERAMICS, POTTERY LANE & CRAFT WALK

with azuki bean paste or toasted soy bean powder. Have it with green *matcha* tea. Charming old-Japan interior, such becoming rarer and rarer. More pottery-shops, sweet shops, gift shops with distinctive selections of dolls, fans, textiles and paper articles, especially things in mini sizes. After first alley there's antique & curio shop **Kyobido** on R where 35 years ago we bought our first old coins which were made into cuff-links. Owner died but widow keeps things going (prices in *kanji*). In next block on L is **Kanda Bamboo**, only place where you can see baskets being made—from wonderful dark tea ceremony flower baskets ¥12,-19,000 to chopstick holder ¥100—recently remodeled, we miss old lived-in look of boat-shaped baskets and ladles hanging from ceiling, baskets piled in corner. Then doll shop, fine lacquer ware, another doll shop, and across on R pottery, tasteful crafts, and then tea and snacks, followed by...

CHOPSTICKS: Cluster of 3 restaurants one above other on hill, new restaurant **Kyorinsen** branch of **Kodaiji Yamato** restaurant just up hill, part of famous *ryotei* **Kyo Yamato**, ☎541-9111; lunch ¥15,000up, dinner ¥30,000. Kyorinsen lowest down of trio, has inexpensive meals basically catering to passing tourist, serving Japanese foods plus tea, coffee, desserts, its hinoki cypress wood glows gold, but soon will become restfully shibui. Kodaiji Yamato in middle now serves lunches from ¥3,500, kaiseki from ¥6,000, a la carte from ¥1,500.

Opp Kyorinsen is...
Kamanza stylish wear in indigo dyed cloth textile shop and bamboo shop **Kameyama** and dolls by unique *ittohbori* single-stroke method, **Matsumoto**. This stroll, combining sightseeing and shopping which we pioneered in early '50s, is one we like to have all our foreign visitors take.

If time permits continue on, turn L onto wide street with stone torii gates and lovely old wooden front gate to KODAI-JI temple, where **Ikkyu-an** has been serving *fucha-ryori* Chinese temple vegetarian fare (tho modified for taste in using dried bonito fish-broth as base). Lunch ¥3,900, 12 to 2pm; dinners ¥5,-7,000+t/s, 3 to 6:30pm, rsve required ☎561-1901. Turn R onto Kodaiji-michi, street in front of huge concrete Kannon statue, which we suggest you pass up. Take this path leading to Maruyama Park and Yasaka Shrine. Hardly any shops here, but first L turn is charming old narrow cobblestone pathway known as 'Ishibe-koji' lined on both sides with walls of exclusive little inns. This alley is setting for many films and TV ads. There is tea shop **Ishibe** run by ex-Pontocho geisha, coffee ¥300 in lovely garden. Back on Kodaiji-michi and almost 2 blocks further on is banner bedecked gate of **Bunnosuke Chaya** which we had recommended for orchid blossom tea, but sad that it has not been available for years—but garden is charming for Japanese sweets, *amazake* (sweet rice wine) and we hope their *rakuyaki* shop will reopen, where you paint your own biscuit-fired cups or plates which will be glazed, fired and either sent to you or you can pick up later. Across is well-known trademark large red parasol on R of **Higashiyama Kogei** still here and thriving with novel gifts—Otsu-e pilgrim sketches on textiles and wood. Next, watch for small garden visible on R full of huge gold and multicolored carp over 90cm/3ft long at 10-yr-old **Rakusho** tea and coffee house. Alcove has dozens of trophies carp have won—and on hot day what's nicer than sipping shaved ice topped with green uji tea watching carp cavort.

WHERE TO STAY: In this lovely area convenient to center of town we find inns for women. Greatly advertised as place you can meet *maiko* (young apprentice geisha) is **Kyoto Ladies Hotel** ¥-T (¥-B bunk bed), rsve required ☎561-3181. Turn L down street from Rakusho tea shop. Maiko appear almost every other nite at 8:30 to 9 pm to pose with you; another attraction is to be dressed in maiko outfit complete with makeup for ¥6,000, 2 photos, service basically for hotel guests, but manager said that for foreigners, he can make special dispensation but rsve required. Few doors towards Yasaka is quiet retreat, **Minoko** kaiseki restaurant, always included among Kyoto's best, with excellent *chabako bento* lunch—such subtle difference in flavoring, ¥3,500, ☎561-0328. Rsve for full kaiseki dinner from ¥10,000.

Recently fancy Love or Fashion hotels have opened here: L for **Maruyama Gyoen**, **Hotel Gion** and brand new **Sakanoue**, ¥4,500 double room after 9pm–10am. Block W on Higashioji-dori is **Hotel U'S Yasaka**, unusual with restaurant facing Higashioji, bar in basement, ☎551-2225, 9pm-11am, twin ¥6,800 (¥7,000 deposit).

YASAKA SHRINE and MARUYAMA PARK

This entire Higashiyama hill area was exclusively villas of Kyoto's wealthy. As years went on and fortunes changed, especially after WW II, they were converted into tea houses and exclusive restaurants, and now we see many of them changing into shops or restaurants catering to tourists.

CHOPSTICKS: Continuing north from Minoko or Rakusho and its carps brings you to walls of **Nakamura-ro** on outskirts of Yasaka; was from ancient times one of roadside *niken-chaya* (two tea houses) every pilgrim stopped at for refreshment. Sit down, enjoy *dengaku*, skewers of bite-sized tofu topped with miso, and *dengaku* lunch ¥2,800 at its *chamise*, original tea house; *amazake* sweet sake mash ¥400, mini-kaiseki ¥4,000; in main section *kaiseki* starts at ¥10,000 mid-day, evening ¥15,000. 11:00-19:30, X-last thur, ☎561-0016.

Next door up is entry to **Choraku-kan**, former villa of Meiji tobacco king, converted to hotel for ladies, is example of Meiji architecture. Around corner is entrance to its 'lavish' tea shop/restaurant entrance. Across street on corner is **Maruyama** restaurant overlooking garden and pond, tempura or *shiki bento* ¥1,800. Up hill leads to kaiseki/sukiyaki restaurant **Sa-ami**, good view of Maruyama Park and city; kaiseki lunch ¥6,000, dinner ¥10,000; shabu-shabu, sukiyaki ¥6,000 anytime; ☎561-2200.

Daytime, stroll down Maruyama Park to and thru huge old wooden gate, continue past Chion-in Temple over to Yamanaka & Co and our former...

MANSION AREA (Map p.545)

STONE LIONS still guard entry to **Yamanaka**, but inside, that aura of pre-war grandeur when it had branches in NY, Boston and Chicago has faded. They still have good, but small selection of antiques, furniture, scrolls and screens, many woodblock prints. They have started exclusive line of modern artists' creations: exquisite baskets by NOGUCHI Ushu, ceramics by YASUDA Michio and prints. Next door **Robert E. Curtis**, furniture and antiques, finally closed its doors 1989, long after original owner's murder.

Continue on to Sanjo-dori, turn L abt block on L to...
Inaba Cloisonne factory. Showroom is full of vases, plates, miniature screens, watches, cigarette and jewelry boxes, and jewelry. With big shift in dollar exchange, Inaba has full line of goods at Handicraft Center, while here their wares have been geared to Japanese customers. New *shibui* motifs are replacing colorful floral patterns of past. This new technique presents feeling of lovely paintings, some modernistic. Transparent crystalized cloisonne costs 60-100% more than general opaque ware; red most expensive. Handy gifts are cuff links, earrings and other small items, under ¥1,500. Demonstration of this painstaking process regularly.

We continue E on Sanjo and turn onto Jingu-michi with huge vermillion torii gate of Heian Shrine in view.

But sidetracking for bit...
Continue E on Sanjo beyond Jingu-michi to 250-yr-old ever-popular **Minokichi Restaurant**, with huge red parasol out in front. Spacious with charming folk art decor, lovely garden visible from all rooms, good food and not expensive: *bento* ¥2,500 (lunch); *teishoku* from ¥3,-4,500 for tempura, shabu-shabu and *kaiseki*, ¥5,000 (mini-), ¥9,-20,000. 11:30-21:00, no-X, ☎771-4185. It now has branches at Karasuma-Shijo ☎255-0621; Daimaru and Hankyu D.S.'s; Shin Hankyu and Keihan Kyoto Hotels.

Back on Sanjo-dori St on R side is...
Heian Art, good selection of antiques: chests, especially proud of folding screen collection. Continue on past Miyako Hotel and taxi up Kujo-yama hill, to gorgeous mansion (featured in book *Japanese Style*, NY Times press) full of FINE ANTIQUES of Japan, China, Tibet, for serious collectors —**David Kidd**, only by appointment: phone *never* before noon for late appointment even for after dinner, ☎751-8552. Heian Art has another shop **Heiando** on Jingu-michi leading to Heian Shrine and that's where we'll head. It's nice to find shop that carries new pottery that looks like old Imari ware: rectangular teapot ¥7,000; old scrolling *karakusa* patterned bowls, 5 for ¥2,500; 30cm *tako karakusa* plate ¥3,800. At end of block is **Tivoli**, restaurant, basically for steak. Two museums **National Museum of Modern Art** and **Kyoto Municipal Museum of Art** are here (*see* MIRROR OF OLD CHINA, p.447).

Turn L on Nijo, at end of block by canal is...
Museum of Traditional Industry where guilds and trade associations of various arts have showcases of their prize works with many for sale and daily at least five out of more than 20 crafts alternate in showing work process involved. Especially useful booth is **Kimono Reform**, where spots are removed, and if not removable, or hole, they will either embroider or yuzen dye matching patterns.

Across street is KYOTO CITY TOURIST SECTION in Kyoto Kaikan Hall.

Now cross canal, turn R and up canal to...
Nishimura Zohiko showroom. Before they built this modern showroom, we could see artisans at work at time-consuming repeated cycles of lacquering drying and polishing and we marvel that pieces can be sold as reasonably as they are. Here only natural wood-based lacquer (a.k.a. *urushi*, urushiol, japanning) is offered...no plastic or compressed woodshavings. They also miss foreign tourists and now gear their products for local clientele. Being one of oldest houses, their Zoojirushi (elephant symbol) is trademark of quality. Upstairs, is museum of their private collection: gold lacquer box for noh mask belonging to Yodogimi, Tycoon Hideyoshi's mistress; lavish picnic sets for Tokugawa shoguns. Drop in, for there are exquisite trays, bowls, boxes of all sizes and shapes, some in elegant simplicity, others elaborately ornate, many we can afford and anyway, it is feast for your eyes.

Tourists may ask what happened to that mansion of lovely silks, Tatsumura Silk Mansion with its garden of beautiful carp—alas, also gone.

We'll now cross canal and turn L toward Handicraft Center...
En route is fascinating martial arts outfitter **Budo Enri**, you can't miss it with its display of wooden swords, *kendo* fencing masks. Even if you're not into martial arts, from among outfits for judo, kendo, *i-ai*, archery are loose-fitting white jackets with black geometric stitching (¥3,-7,500) or vice versa with either black or white trousers, or exotic long navy, black or striped *hakama* (floor-length culotte) pleated 'skirts' (¥4,-8,000).

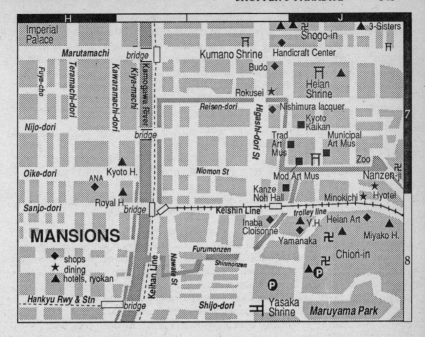

Imperial Palace

Marutamachi   bridge   Kumano Shrine   Handicraft Center   Shogo-in   3-Sisters

Fuya-cho   Teramachi-dori   Kawaramachi-dori   Kiya-machi   Kamogawa River   Budo   Heian Shrine

Nijo-dori   Reisen-dori   Rokusei   Nishimura lacquer

Higashi-dori St   Kyoto Kaikan

bridge   Niomon St   Trad Art Mus   Municipal Art Mus

Oike-dori   Kyoto H.   Mod Art Mus   Zoo   Nanzen-ji

ANA   Kanze Noh Hall   Minokichi   Hyotei

Sanjo-dori   Royal H.   bridge   Keishin Line   trolley line

Inaba Cloisonne   Y.H.   Heian Art

MANSIONS   Keihan Line   Nawate St   Yamanaka   Miyako H.

Furumonzen   Chion-in

◆ shops   Shinmonzen

★ dining

▲ hotels, ryokan

Hankyu Rwy & Stn   bridge   Shijo-dori   Yasaka Shrine   Maruyama Park

'Mansions'

Across **Marutamachi-dori** is...

Handicraft Center, enigma, people tend to lump it all together as cheap souvenirs. Well, it has that, but besides that it is outlet for quality merchandise from some top line stores, for example Amita Damascene (who run it and have name to maintain). You'll find painted scrolls & screens, woodblock prints, paper crafts, pearls, jewelry, ceramics, kimonos both new and old, dolls, and just about anything you might want in their 7 floors, and they have a new annex with restaurant and shops.

MAIN STREETS ALONG SHIJO-DORI (Map p.547)

YASAKA SHRINE is starting point for this area, patronized by geisha with their extremely *shareta* (chic) good taste. Our last coverage takes us down **Shijo-dori** St to heart of downtown **Kawaramachi-Shijo intersection** where, continue on Shijo to Daimaru Dept Store or turn R up **Kawaramachi** St, 'main street', taking you back to Kyoto Hotel.

Almost all shops on this street are open till 9:00pm. YASAKA SHRINE across to L on wide Higashi-oji St is red-faced store front of **Nishikawa Bamboo** shop with novel modern adaptations, fine place-mats of thin bamboo, exquisite gold-lacquered bamboo decanter and wine cups ¥70,000; ask for pamphlet on *misu* blinds or sliding doors for summer, you'll be amazed at range in price according to different materials.

Back on Shijo-dori we'll go down R/N side to Hanamikoji and back up L/S side. First, we visit **Hayashi Senrakuda,** father ran coin shop, now still have some for collectors, but mainly original accessories. They will mount stones in rings, etc., repair and make jewelry. Next door is 'one of a kind' **Kazura-Sei**, where owner-carver SHIMOFURI Cho-on designs, carves and lacquers all those lovely hairpieces and combs found there. Son collects and sells European antiques in rear half of shop.

Have your name painted on long paper lantern. **Kasagen**, parasol and lantern maker, can write it for you in day if ready-made one is available, otherwise 2 weeks to make one. They can make to any size and color. Romantic huge red parasol used in tea ceremony, diameter 1.8m/6ft, ¥55,000.

Miura Shomei has also been here for generations and makes Japanese lighting fixtures from wood, bamboo, metal. Hanging lampshades beautifully shaped, and modernistic floor lamp type reminiscent of *andon* both cylindrical and rectangular. We find skewered meat, sushi shops along our way.

Then **K. Kondo** antiques, and well-known old incense shop. Next is shiny building with **Kyoto Craft Center** which used to be on Kiyomizu Gojo-zaka. Interior spacious, carries new, novel paper, ceramic, textile and in distinctive designs. Next, we find **Kyoto Museum of Contemporary Art**, ☎525-1311, X-mon.

Nearby is **Tsubosaka**, old favorite W-restaurant listed in our first edition, turn R at Hanamikoji and R again at first street. Still just as tasty, a la carte ¥1,400+.

Having reached Hanamikoji, cross street, work up S side...
On corner is imposing red wall enclosing **Ichiriki-tei**, Kyoto's elite geisha house, remembered by all kabuki fans as place Yuranosuke, leader of tragic *47 Ronin* masqueraded as drunken samurai, biding time to avenge his lord's death. Here, one needs introduction, or book thru major agent or hotel.

Turning down Hanamikoji (S) takes us into main Gion geisha district past several fine restaurants (*see* main CHOPSTICKS), those dimly lit, grilled old house fronts are *machiai*, 'waiting houses' from which your geisha is dispatched her to you.

Back to our main trek up Shijo-dori...
Further up street is **Monju**, just 11 yrs old, with large array of fine lacquerware, not plastic based. Some less expensive ones are made of compressed wood shavings and so marked on price tag. Bowls, covered and uncovered; boxes for stationary, chopsticks for one or 2 pairs, music boxes ¥5,-7,000; and noh masks, ¥15,000. (*Warning*: good lacquerware must be treated carefully, wash only in lukewarm water, and make certain it is dried immediately, preferably with silk cloth. Rectangular objects with seams are most vulnerable to cracking or separating. Plastic-based ones stand up under wear, can be machine washed. ☎525-1617, X-thur.

Gion Hotel next corner, convenient, adequate, ¥-S (¥-B if 3 to rm), suite ¥25,000, royal suite of 2 rms ¥33,000, ☎274-1818.

Gion Ishi attractive stone shop next: 1st Fl stone lanterns, semi-precious gems, stone sculpture. Inviting are *Warabe-jizo* with child-like faces, rough-carved stone (¥25,000+). 2fl tearoom; 3fl steak broiled on stone.

Back to Hanamikoji. Work W on R/N side of Shijo-dori from newly opened...
Mitsukoshi branch store. **Kagizen Yoshifusa**, traditional Japanese sweet shop with picturesque store front has retained its antique look. Any Japanese family would appreciate box of sweets from them and would wonder how you knew. Upstairs, enjoy some of their sweets with *matcha* tea. Decor, utensils and furnishings are exquisitely chosen, befitting this elegant shop. Next door is **Konchiku-do** with beautiful hair accessories of boxwood, inexpensive, large selection of old-fashioned *kiseru* tobacco pipes ¥650-6,000. In next block is old curio and antique shop with doors almost ready to fall off, but inside are interesting objects piled here and there. Next, sweet shop, **Ohara-me**, sells *Kama-buro* cooking-pot shaped Japanese sweet, has well-appointed restaurant tea and meals; then, **Okuda**, antiques, and then comes Keihan Shijo Stn.

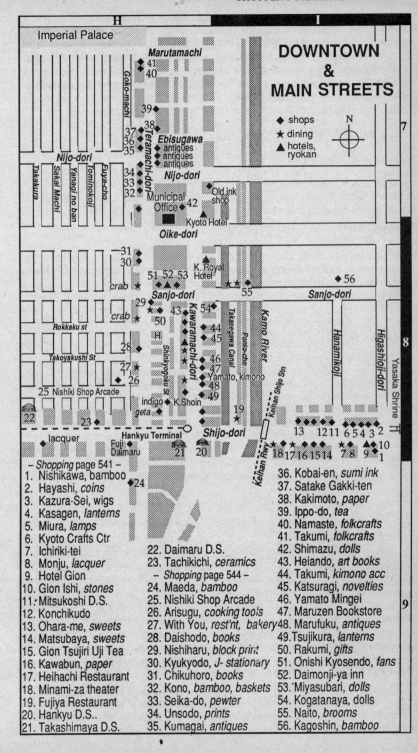

DOWNTOWN & MAIN STREETS

Imperial Palace

Marutamachi

◆ shops
★ dining
▲ hotels, ryokan

Goko-machi
Teramachi-dori

Ebisugawa
antiques
antiques
antiques

Nijo-dori

Nijo-dori

Takakura
Sakai Machi
Yanagi no ban
Tominokoji
Fuya-cho

Old ink shop

Municipal Office
Kyoto Hotel

Oike-dori

crab

K. Royal Hotel

◆ 56

Sanjo-dori

Sanjo-dori

crab

Rokkaku st

Kawaramachi-dori
Takasegawa Canal
Kamo River
Ponto-cho
Hanamikoji
Higashioji-dori
Yasaka Shrine

Takoyakushi St

Shinkyogoku st

Yamato, kimono

25 Nishiki Shop Arcade

indigo   K. Shoin

geta

Keihan Shijo Stn

Shijo-dori

13   12 11 6 5 4 3 2

lacquer   Hankyu Terminal

Fuji   Daimaru

18 17 16 15 14   7 8 9 1
10

Keihan Rwy

– Shopping page 541 –
1. Nishikawa, bamboo
2. Hayashi, coins
3. Kazura-Sei, wigs
4. Kasagen, lanterns
5. Miura, lamps
6. Kyoto Crafts Ctr
7. Ichiriki-tei
8. Monju, lacquer
9. Hotel Gion
10. Gion Ishi, stones
11. Mitsukoshi D.S.
12. Konchikudo
13. Ohara-me, sweets
14. Matsubaya, sweets
15. Gion Tsujiri Uji Tea
16. Kawabun, paper
17. Heihachi Restaurant
18. Minami-za theater
19. Fujiya Restaurant
20. Hankyu D.S..
21. Takashimaya D.S.

22. Daimaru D.S.
23. Tachikichi, ceramics
– Shopping page 544 –
24. Maeda, bamboo
25. Nishiki Shop Arcade
26. Arisugu, cooking tools
27. With You, rest'nt, bakery
28. Daishodo, books
29. Nishiharu, block print
30. Kyukyodo, J- stationary
31. Chikuhoro, books
32. Kono, bamboo, baskets
33. Seika-do, pewter
34. Unsodo, prints
35. Kumagai, antiques

36. Kobai-en, sumi ink
37. Satake Gakki-ten
38. Kakimoto, paper
39. Ippo-do, tea
40. Namaste, folkcrafts
41. Takumi, folkcrafts
42. Shimazu, dolls
43. Heiando, art books
44. Takumi, kimono acc
45. Katsuragi, novelties
46. Yamato Mingei
47. Maruzen Bookstore
48. Marufuku, antiques
49. Tsujikura, lanterns
50. Rakumi, gifts
51. Onishi Kyosendo, fans
52. Daimonji-ya inn
53. Miyasubari, dolls
54. Kogatanaya, dolls
55. Naito, brooms
56. Kagoshin, bamboo

*Going back to **Hanamikoji**, we go down L side of **Shijo-dori**...*
Matsubaya Japanese sweets, with beautiful pressed, cut out and molded sweets, beautifully packaged. **Gion Tsujiri Uji Tea Shop** has tea from Uji where tea was first cultivated, having been brought from China in early 12th century. Tea by weight or teabags. Powdered green ceremonial *matcha* tea, sugar added so use with ice cream mix or as cooling iced drink. Also makes tea-flavored hard candy.

In case, you'd like **sauna,** here's one next door, ladies on 3Fl, men 7Fl (¥1,700, 11:00-17:00; ¥2,000, 17:00-02:00). In same building is **Maharaja**, unique disco with lavish Indian decor, popular with foreigners; entry fee male ¥3,500, female ¥3,000 incl ¥2,000 worth of food & drinks; E-menu; 18:00-all nite; ☎541-5421, no-X.

Kawabun, shop with old world charm selling unique pieces made by Kyoto's craftsmen using paper, not ordinary but all hand-dyed papers, made up into dolls, little boxes of all sizes and shapes, chests, and pads. In long drawers in back of shop are fancy handmade papers embedded with maple, bamboo leaves. Some rare antiques. 11:00-21:00, X-wed, ☎561-0277.

CHOPSTICKS: Then one is shocked by sign '*Open 10:00 to 6:00am next morning*' on 6-storey **Heihachi Restaurant**, a la carte, *teishoku* ¥1,500-¥2,000; branch of Heihachi at huge estate opp Nijo Castle. Simple homemade soba noodle lunch at **Yagumo**; sweetshop, then **Nishiri** pickles (some packaged will keep fresh all week, best refrigerated, but others will keep for month without loosing freshness). Famous for *senmai-zuke*, pickled thin slices of turnip.

At end of block is **Izawaya**, specializing in accessories made of brocades, yuzen silks and everything best-dressed kimono person will need. Main shop is diagonally across by Shijo Keihan Stn building.

We come to block with **Minami-za theater** with broiled eel, sushi and soba shops, all 3 catering to theater-goers. They'll take box-lunches to your seats in theater. **Matsuno**, broiled eel *unagi* shop with sign in English '*Mrs. Matsuno's Kitchen*'. If you like *teriyaki* sauce, you'll like this. *Unaju* is served in lacquered box; 'Unagi *donburi*' is rice in large bowl topped with broiled eel (¥1,500) or try full course teishoku. 11:30-21:00, X-tue. **Matsuba's** *nisshin-soba* smoked herring cooked in light sauce, having been invented by founder is Kyoto specialty. They also have usual *soba* menu plus teishoku. When upstairs full, basement often has room, 10:30-22:00, X-thur.

*This ends our **Shijo-dori** east, now cross Kamogawa River to continue...*

DOWNTOWN MAINSTREETS SHIJO-DORI CONT'D

AFTER BIG bridge SHIJO-OHASHI, we enter Pontocho geisha area. First alley (Saiseki) after bridge to R and L is full of fine eating places, many run by former geisha. Most put out *yuka* wooden platforms for summer dining over Kamogawa (*see* CHOPSTICKS). This intersection of Kiyamachi-dori, Takasegawa canal at Shijo-dori with **Fujiya** (¥-T W-food) at center is corner with smart, elegant ware. Across from Fujiya is tiny **Tawara-ya**, handcrafted kimono fabrics made into bags. N of Fujiya is chic Japanese accessory shop **Sumiya**, clever well-designed accessories, novel handbags from Japanese fabrics; *samu-e* Buddhist priest's indigo-dyed work outfit (¥21,000); 2-piece *kasuri* woman's kimono (¥11,000). Few doors up is small family-run inn, **Tomoe-ya**, ¥-B rm only, ☎211-3534, where we often send friends. Designer **Kenzo's** shop here heralds change.

Cross canal, first turn R up along canal and then back to Shijo to continue on...
You'd expect some charming shops facing canal, but here found only **Meikyoku Muse**, classical music *kissa*-tea shop with tea, coffee. Incidentally, behind it across alley is public bathhouse, open 14:30-03:00am, X-sun.

Back on Shijo, few doors on is famous...

Nijusan-ya *tsuge* boxwood comb shop. Present fifth generation master religiously observes painstaking traditional methods–each tooth sawed, polished by hand. Combs improve with use, will last lifetime (Jay's in use over 20 years). **Ito-chu** footwear, lovely *zori*, but see gorgeous, yet shibui *zori* ¥65,000 matching bag ¥380,000 in handwoven *Saga nishiki* brocade.

For **DEPT STORE SHOPPING**, this area is perfect (10:00-18:00, 19:00 sun, hols). **Hankyu** and **Takashimaya** dept stores dominate Shijo-Kawaramachi intersection, heart of downtown Kyoto and terminal for Hankyu trains (from Kobe-Osaka). Fujii-Daimaru and Daimaru are to E. **Takashimaya** Kyoto branch of one of oldest DS has 7 fls of smart quality innovative goods as well as traditional. Basement grocery, delicatessen, fish and vegetable section excellent with large organic foods section. Newly expanded, it looks same from front, but it takes up space behind small shops on Shijo, up to restaurant annex entrance further E; rooftop children's playland, X-wed. **Hankyu**, recent addition to scene is basically 5 floors for young men and women, dominated by boutiques, plus seven to eight good spots for dining with two floors of restaurants (branches of Kyoto's best) and coffee, tea rooms, 11:00-22:00 (separate elevator after DS hours). Best to miss rush hour, X-thur. **Fujii-Daimaru**, much smaller DS (no relation to Daimaru, below) is few blocks W of Takashimaya, basically for Japanese yuppies. **Daimaru**, one of Japan's main DS was founded by Kyoto entrepreneur and still caters to old families. It has all amenities of first-rate DS, English-speaking personnel at information desk. Recent remodelling gives it smart up-to-date look. Children's clothes worth dropping in to see with fashions by top adult haute couturiers. X-thur.

Sad to see once-smart Shijo-dori W beyond Daimaru being killed by banks and investment houses taking up huge frontage, pulling down opaque shutters at 3pm. But from Kawaramachi-dori to Daimaru on R, there are few top traditional shops. Start with **Erizen,** ultimate in fine kimono, obi materials and accessories; **Karafuneya** coffee, snacks, (open 24 hours); tasty **Tagoto**, traditional restaurant down narrow passageway (tables and tatami), lunches ¥2,500up; and hotel **Central Inn**, business hotel, ¥-hi-T, ☎211-1666; then elegant lacquer shop **Ryusendo**, and then shallow but wide-fronted **Jusanya,** selling beautiful combs, accessories for your hair.

SHINKYOGOKU (running N to Sanjo-dori St) gaily lit movie street with air of old (read 'pre-sleeze') 42nd Street in New York with its souvenir shops and fun eating and drinking places, and next street is Teramachi-dori (temple street) with Ready-in-Hr color print shop, ¥25 each. Continuing E traditional Japanese cutlery (ikebana scissors, knives for any/everything imaginable, even swords; sharpen knives in 1hr). At Tominokoji inter-section is **Tachikichi** ideal shop for budget-minded with ceramic gifts, lovely sets of Japanese bowls, plates, tea cups many sets under ¥5,000. Don't miss their huge periodic clearance sales, often held in nearby halls. This holds for their branches nationwide too. **Junku**, book store, has books in English. Next block is **Daimaru DS** mentioned above.

We cross street here, as nothing but banks, etc, all way to Karasuma St. Novel for us is window of **Matsuya** with elaborate gold, silver, red and white cords woven into beautiful storks, tortoises, pines, all symbols of happiness, long life, faithfulness, etc. Essential to J-ritual of exchanging betrothal gifts. Not just one, they form set. Next is **Asobe** lacquer shop, with usual good assortment. Now continue W to Teramachi-dori past two of Japan's top sweetshop chains **Tsuruya** and **Toraya** to Fuji-Daimaru.

TERAMACHI-DORI

Going S from Shijo is newly developing electronics section, imitating Osaka's Nihonbashi area. Two old favorites **Shimizu Sue** old signboards and **Satake**, classical instruments, have moved to Teramachi N, but holding out here is **Maeda Heihachi-Ten**, with exotic wide *misu* (extra slim bamboo blinds), bordered and trimmed with wide brocade bands; 6x6ft with colorful tassels and hooks, ¥45,000. NY's Metropolitan Museum has 12x12ft from here. They have normal range of *sudare* (coarser bamboo or reed blinds) at varying prices. Some curio and book shops still survive, but no more old prints or old block printed calligraphic books with which we used to paper fusuma doors. **Sanmitsudo** across street has fine old woodblock printed noh libretto, *noh kyoku no mokuhan-zuri*, for ¥200-300. On R corner is **Nishimura** with brushes, mainly circular bottle brushes, some with brush head measuring 30cm long. Also has long feather dusters with which every chauffeur is seen pattering car as he waits for his master.

And this being Teramachi-dori (temple street) there are many temple goods shops with brass and bronze articles, candlestick holders of all sizes, beautifully carved wooden statues. Some shops specialize in reproductions of ancient Chinese bronze vases with patina-like finish. Down past Takatsuji-dori is **Heian Shumi-no-mise** with old coins, stamps, curios. Shop may be in disarray, but he reassuringly says "I'll get out whatever coin or stamp you ask for, because everything is in order," as he works meticulously on his stamps, his love for over 60 years.

We'll go back to Shijo-dori...
TERAMACHI-DORI at Shijo becomes pedestrians-only arcade; most shops open until 8:30pm or later. Being next to colorful Shinkyogoku street it has taken on some of its glitter at this point, especially first block. If you missed picking up inexpensive souvenirs or sweets try **Kyogoku Ichibangai** on L side. Few doors on exuding old world charm is **Horai-do**, Uji tea shop. Not only does it have all varieties, qualities of tea, it also has all utensils needed to make and serve: tea cannisters, whisks, cloths, papers, tea cups, tea pots. Here since 1803, are said to have invented fragrant *genmai-cha* which combines toasted popped rice Price-list in English.

Sidetrack L at next narrow red, yellow and green striped awning-covered cross street...
NISHIKI-KOJI-DORI, literally 'Brocade St', so named not for picturesque colorful merchandise but to defer attnetion in old times from its then-pungent odors; famed for shops lining both sides with unusual hard-to-get delicacies, fresh fish, clams, lobsters, meats, vegetables, fruits. Restaurateurs go mid-morning, housewives later and many of us from Osaka or Kobe drop in for special treats after full day in Kyoto. They even have sushi and cooked foods to go. And here's one shop you shouldn't miss on R one block **Aritsugu** supplier of traditional cooking utensils, knives and gadgets. All are works of art—their hammered copper or aluminum pots, pans, scoops; wooden tubs, lids, candy and such molds; stainless steel vegetable cut-outs (butterflies, leaves, fans) which could double for cookie cutters, larger cut-outs for pretty-shaped sushi. Who can resist them! Same holds true for myriad of little specialty shops that fill this alley about 6 blocks long. Most close about 7pm.

At Takakura turn L and you'll come out to Daimaru D.S. at Shijo-dori or just turn back to continue on Teramachi-dori...
As we proceed, on L is neat-looking restaurant and bakery **With You.** Street floor has bakery, delicatessen; pick up food and sit at tables informally placed throughout area. Upstairs has light spacious dining room,

lovely decor, inexpensive (E-menu), 11:00-22:00. Bit beyond on same side on corner is old book shop **Daishodo**. Large collection of relatively inexpensive woodblock prints, old and new, as well as old books on art. 11:00-20:30, X-1st, 2nd thur. Some E-spoken. Few doors on sign in English *Incense burners* marks **Nagamatsu**, temple accessories. Across from Daishodo is 90-yr-old sushi shop **Izumo**, delicious, inexpensive, 15:00-22:30. Few doors up is tiny booth-like **Kawakami Naimu-ya**, machine-embroidering names on whatever you need.

Not much in coming block unless you want to note two large *izakaya* serving Kyoto's best sake, might be fun later on when they open at 17:00. We reach Rokkaku-dori, and big crab restaurant **Kanidoraku**, Rokkaku branch. Next block on R is public bath **Sakura-yu**. As we approach Sanjo-dori, we see another **Kanidoraku**, crab restaurant with huge crab mtrs above store front on L. Dinners from ¥3,000. 11:30-23:00, no-X.

But before crossing Sanjo-dori on left is...
Mishima-tei, old sukiyaki restaurant in nice wooden building with meat store on street floor. **Nishiharu** (Nishimura) next door in old original wooden building is Kyoto's oldest antique woodblocks-only print shop. All are originals, Meiji (1900) or older. His shop may look forbidding with no stacks of prints visible, but dropping in you'll be rewarded by finding just what you want, as present owner Sekigawa-san speaks English. Prints are carefully put away in old lacquer boxes in cupboards, every one carefully researched and identified, even to such details as what play at what theater, and labeled in both English and Japanese. Tho *yago* or shop name is Nishiharu, everyone calls it Nishimura as it was known when original owner Nishimura-san was alive. Sekigawa-san's son Hitoshi is also interested in old ceramics, which now grace window.

Beyond Sanjo-dori, on R is...
Tori-ichi J- pickles, where in spring shop front overflows with bamboo, in autumn *matsu-take* mushroom. Ship any place in Japan. Neighboring **Daiyoshi**, same business, in good weather workers can be seen preparing pickles into big vats. Next, **Buntekido** stationer for 85 yrs, now modern building, has traditional Japanese papers, etc, and museum of stationery and office equipment. Few doors on **Tamaru** carves your name in wood, advertises 10min for name cards. Then two picture framers, **Yamamoto** on R, is maker, and **Yamashita** on L. Also on L is **Kichudo**, Buddhist book shop, small selection in Eng.

At Anekoji-dori street is...
Kyukyodo with elegant Japanese stationery, paper, ceramics, lacquerware. Any gift from here will be appreciated. From times past they have handled fine incense for Imperial court. (Tokyo branch on Ginza 4-chome). Further up on L is old book store **Chikuhoro** which still has stand in front with discounted books. Ask for books with paintings by hand or woodblocks. They have become rare but one never knows what he might have in store. Then there's **Ayumi** with imported ethnic folk art items; two antique shops and lovely sweet shop end this block and we reach Oike-dori, and as traffic becomes thin, most shops close around 18:00-19:00.

Crossing over we have city office taking up R side of whole block. It is from here on that we can still see bit of what old Teramachi-dori looked like and here's where we find curio and antique shop, resembling New York's old Third Avenue. Many still maintain old buildings. Ideal tidbits with tea or beer are rice crackers at **Eiseido**, made by hand and still toasted over special charcoal from Wakayama. Boutique **Vessel** has hand-painted and dyed ready-to-wear in modern designs; challenge, but successful. This block ends with **Koyama-do** handling only new tea ceremony supplies and equipment of Omote Senke school of tea.

Next block we start on L with antique shops **Fukuda Genei-do** with bit of everything. **Kono Take-kogei-ten** makes and sells bamboo baskets of superb workmanship, used for tea flowers and ikebana. We're happy to see 150-yr-old pewter shop **Seika-do** still here. E-speaking owner Yamanaka-san will gladly tell you about various pieces and how best to care for them. He not only makes them, but has pieces by other artists. Today, he carries objects of all kinds of other metals. **Unsodo**, art printers, is only company in Japan that makes books by woodblock process. It always has great array of inexpensive block-printed *shikishi*, cards and note papers.   In window of artistic sign maker **Shimizu Sue Shoten**, you can see owner Shimizu-san carving ideographs on boards new or old. Among old are those from waterwheel (¥150,000, takes 1 month), old ships, enhanced with beautiful calligraphy, either engraved or raised, latter much more expensive.

At end of this block is tiny **Daikichi**, ex-*itamae* restaurant run by Sugimoto-san, avid potter, many of dishes he used to use were made by himself. Being *itamae* each day menu was different, for he served best of each season. He loved his dishes so much that when he got too ill a few years back for strenuous for work, he closed down and reopened as more leisurely antique porcelain shop. Good wares at good prices for he loves to buy and sell and gab with fellow connoisseurs.

Above NIJO-DORI is where most antique shops are, and first on R is fun shop, old **Kumagai Dogu-ten** still full of affordable old ceramics, some not so old, lacquerware, nick-knacks you never know what you'll find. Across is **Aoi-ya**, little more expensive, but good. Then come two *sumi* ink stick and brush shops. **Ryushi-do** has good line of calligraphic supplies. Upstairs, they have periodic exhibitions of artists' works.

Kobai-en has everything that calligrapher or *sumi-e* painter would need, huge brushes as well as fine pointed ones and special papers for *sumi* work. This shop is branch of inkstick makers Kobai-en in Nara. *Next door–*

Satake Gakki-ten (classical bugaku and gagaku instruments) which with Shimizu Sué sign boards was below Shijo-dori until electronics shops took over. Both old Mr Satake and his son have passed away since our original book, but Mrs Satake carries on. Order any instruments and she will have them or get them for you in bamboo or bakelite, one tenth in cost, take less care and fine for non-expert use or decoration. Fine *tsuzumi* drum of wood and leather ¥100,000; while complete hanging drum set for gagaku is about ¥800,000. Still has fine, hand- carved wood noh masks for use for practice at ¥70,-¥100,000.

Across street is large glass window of **Kakimoto** paper shop with one whole wall covered with slots holding different kinds of hand-made papers of many colors. Asking for what might be what Rembrandt used and ordered from Japan as Japanese vellum, he brought off shelves from other wall heavy firm paper *Fukui-shi*, ¥700 per sheet, 55x70cm. Of course, he has paper imbedded with leaves, one variety ¥900, 3 different leaves of 3 different colors, ¥1,500. They've interesting articles made from paper. When asked how long they'd been here and why we might have missed them when on my rounds for original issue of JIO, they laughed and said they had small shop with dark slatted windows and from outside we probably couldn't tell what they sold.

Then next is tea shop with store front covered with dark noren curtains each with **Ippo-do**, 4 characters in white on them. Fine tea of various types available here, and they'll make cup of whichever you might want to buy. Open until 19:00, X-sun, hols, but even then, attendant on call until 18:00. From here on to Marutamachi and Imperial Palace, among loads of shops are number of antique shops on both sides. On L in last street before Marutamachi-dori is **Suzuya** uniform shop which has *samu-e* temple acolyte work outfit, which usually comes in indigo blue, light and dark, but they also have blue and brown (¥12,000, 3 sizes). At end of street are two folkcraft shops. First, **Namaste** whose owner goes himself to buy what he likes in SE Asia countries and as far west as Turkey; inexpensive, colorful garments, textiles, beads, nick-knacks. Then **Takumi**, has many Indian textiles, garments, bags, etc. En route there are **Uchida Woodblock** print maker and **Amita Damascene**, whose products are found in many hotels, Handicraft Center.

From here we'll cross over E three short blocks to...

KAWARAMACHI-DORI

As we go down to Kyoto Hotel, on R art reproductions of noted museum objects in Cimastone made by **Shimazu Scientific Specimen Co**, across from Kyoto Hotel. S of Oike are no unusual shops, but on L/E is well-run Kyoto Royal Hotel, ¥-S, ☎223-1234; on R/W, small Hotel Alpha, ¥-T, ☎241-2000. On Sanjo corner on R is sushi shop, sign in E- "Take Out Sushi"... all sushi shops pack take-out box if you say *"mochi-kaeri desu"* (I'm taking it home). **Fujiya Restaurant** is on corner of Sanjo-dori. Continuing down R side, **Daigakudo** bookstore used to have good used Eng books, and at alley past Scala-za and Takarazuka theaters is good eel restaurant **Maizaka** and **Heiando** secondhand book store with good art books. Conveniently located is Sun Hotel, ¥-T, ☎241-3351. Rest of block on this side, not much except for doll shop **Kabuki**, and **Kyoto Shoin** book store near Shijo, has always had fine art and crafts books, many published by them.

Let's go back to Sanjo and come down L side of Kawaramachi, at corner is ...
Daiyasu large pickle-shop (products found nationwide). In winter their vinegared *senmai-zuke* (thinly sliced turnips, lightly vinegared) in demand. Two blocks down is **Takumi**, kimono accessories, exquisite long silk yuzen-dyed shawls with bits of silver and gold painted into pattern, fully silk-lined; silk *furoshiki* squares that will double for scarf, blouse-dickey for favorite suit, or get 2 and make blouse. Myriad uses for exotic silk *obi-age* (25x100cm) for long scarves, embroidered *eri* collar pieces.

Attractive plaza with fountain is Aji Bldg with loads of ¥-B–T restaurants.
Fascinating 120-yr-old folkcraft shop **Katsuragi** with novelties such as huge wide-brimmed reed samurai hats, ¥7,000; tin sushi cut-outs and presses (use for cookies) in floral, fan shapes; wooden tubs, papier mache masks ¥1,400 up; graters for garlic, lemon rind, of shark skin; lovely charcoal and alcohol braziers covered with calligraphy ¥850-2,000. Past **Shakey's Pizza** another block down is old favorite **Yamato Mingei**, sophisticated folkcrafts articles: ceramics, glass, paper and paper products, with textiles upstairs hand-dyed hand-woven textiles, especially indigo-dyed. Next is **Maruzen** bookstore and stationery, biggest line of books on Japan in English, foreign magazines, books. Yamato has gallery on next alley to L with artists' exhibitions. Two blocks down is **Marufuku Shokai**, antiques, fine quality items.

Beyond next block is **Tsujikura**, favorite bamboo lantern and umbrella shop. *Kasa* umbrellas are of many kinds: *Ban-gasa* are large, oil-treated paper still used at inns with their names printed on them; *Janome-gasa* finer, smaller with more ribs, with delicate patterns and colors, sometimes covered with silk; *Odori-gasa* for Japanese dance, with fold-up handle; *Hi-gasa* are parasols of paper or silk with paintings. Our favorite is large red tea ceremony one, measuring 60cm (2ft) radius, opens out to 120cm, ¥38,000 in oiled paper; (2.5ft, ¥48,000; 3ft, ¥58,000) & 3.5ft/105cm one is cloth covered, more durable, ¥80,000. Handles collapsible. Their lantern selection is getting smaller, but they do have ready-made ones such as red *yakitori* and festival lantern. Beefsteak Suehiro was one of first steak houses in Kyoto, closed here, with branch in Nanzen-ji open, reasonable steak. Almost at end of block is Eiraku, top gourmet shop. Besides famous sweet cakes, we always pick up their packaged goodies: pickles, especially *rakkyo* small white onions wrapped in red *shiso* beefsteak leaves, rape flowers in season; *tatami* (small white fish about 2cm long dried together in sheets, excellent when toasted lightly), *ikura* red salmon caviar. This brings us to Shijo.

2nd alley R/W of Shijo-Kawaramachi intersection, sidetrack R up to gaily lit...
SHIN-KYOGOKU covered arcade—basically this caters to movie crowd, mostly for eating, amusement and casual shopping. However, at end of first block on left is *geta* shop Ofuku, with *geta* wooden clogs of light *kiri* paulownia with thongs and *zori* (thonged sandals of cork sole covered with sedge or plastic). He has 28cm (US size 10.5) *geta* (¥7,800); *zori* ¥23,000, or cheaper at ¥4,000. Ask to have thongs put on *very* loosely ("*hana-o wo sugoku yuruku shite-kudasai*"). That way your foot slides forward and fits better, as well as not hurting. Kentucky Fried Chicken is in next block, on R side is Central fitness club, well-equipped gym with swimming pool. Quite reasonable, we joined morning session in Ashiya, monthly cost about ¥7,000, 6:30-9:00, X-sun. Next corner is Takoyakushi street with Izumo-ya Eel restaurant. Next corner becomes like plaza with large souvenir shop Bentendo on R & L (main shop) sides of street: found well-done decorative noh masks here, wood from ¥4,800, ceramic ¥10,000. In next block opposite Shochikuza theater is wonderful gift shop Lakumi where family speaks English, French. They have taken care to get sizes, styles and designs favored by foreign guests: silk kimono yuzen-dyed from ¥15,000; with embroidery ¥28,000–are especially proud of their original T-shirts of exceptionally fine cotton, ¥1,600 (L-size). Shin-kyogoku street ends with Sakurai shop full of cute little things that appeal to high school girls at Sanjo Cupola arcade.

Turn R onto covered arcade...
SANJO CUPOLA: Onishi Kyosendo, making of folding fans since 1830. We learn large *buyo* dance and noh dance fans come in 2 qualities, *keiko-yo* for practice and performance fans, ¥2,500 and ¥6,000up. Noh dance fans are bit larger from ¥5,000 to ¥20,000, ☎221-0334, 10:00-21:00, X-thur—branch in Tokyo's Marunouchi, ☎03-3216-3888. Daimonji-ya Ryori-Ryokan (¥-L) hidden down narrow alley on R is aesthetic surprise. We first found its discreet sign—'Kaiseki lunch 11:30-14:00 ¥5,-7,000', served in tatami room looking out over garden; dinner, 17:00-20:00, ¥10,000up, served in private room with tiny garden; rsve ☎221-0603/5; overnite w/bkfst ¥-S. However, they ask that someone speak some Japanese. Just after Daimonji-ya is Miyasubari, with lovely noh dolls (¥13,000) and wooden masks (¥7,500) and catty-corner is Tanaka, gifts in good taste, noh masks (¥12,000). R onto Kawaramachi for Akao old books, some in English; across street is another secondhand book store.

Crossing Kawaramachi-dori, two shops beckon to us on Sanjo. First on R (across from JTB) Kogatanaya Chubei, doll shop since 1656. Great dolls, especially theatrical, kabuki (¥9,-11,000 and up). Noh masks, so beautifully executed that it was almost unbelievable that they were made of ceramic by famous carver of masks who works with ceramic artist (¥12,000). Across street past canal and just before River is **Naito**, old-fashioned broom shop with all kinds of brushes and brooms hanging in shop—worth visiting for image of old shop. All handmade, these goods are more and more difficult to find. Mrs Naito, widow, has been handling shop since her husband died. Brushes for all needs in Japanese house such as brown soft-bristled *shuro* brushes for tatami, and green-yellow *kibi* brooms for floors last much longer than machine-mades. You'll find many new uses, and anyway they are so decorative. Popularly-priced **Ganko sushi** is next door with *robata-yaki* in basement.

At **SANJO KEIHAN**, we find station and trains moved underground as new subway line joins it to Demachi-Yanagi opened in October (one stop en route at Marutamachi). Wonder what will take its ground space along river—a wider street? And popular **Pig and Whistle** U.K. pub where local repats from London and expat Brits gather, is just beyond Keihan Sanjo Stn, 2F, Shobi Bldg, 17:00-24:00, ☎761-6022. If addicted to Korean bbq, on 3F is **Karube-tei**, reasonable.

Up on L beyond 1st stop sign is **Kagoshin**, present master is 5th generation bamboo artist, whose family has impressive background of imperial awards and patronage. Today, Kagoshin baskets and works grace many tea aficionados' tokonomas and gardens. Every tiny detail beautifully executed in baskets ranging from ¥3,500-20,000. Especially interesting are *kikko-dake* (knotty hexagonal-shaped) natural patterns used for containers as well as bamboo spread flat like board, then bent up for hanging container (¥20,000). This is another artist who treasures old shop his ancestors used.

And this just about ends our leisurely shopping routes. Following are some special topics that need covering.

TEMPLE FAIRS (*See also* p.513)

TWO MAJOR are *Toji Temple Fair* [F-11], Omiya-dori and Kujo-dori on **21st** of every month: Huge two-by-four block area filled with vendors of plants, daily foods and necessities, household goods, etc, but for most of us foreigners it is used kimono, curios and antiques. We find best antiques outside north gate, cheap and lots of fun going from stall to stall, most of them with wares spread out on ground along narrow streets. Real shoppers go early by 7am, others go near about 4pm as closing approaches. Now, on **1st sun of month** fair of only antiques, curios.

Kitano Temple Fair [E-5/6], Imadegawa-dori and Onmae-dori on **25th** of each month has equally exciting assortment of vendors in equally, if not larger space around and in temple grounds. If you find antique chests, large Imari platters, or so much you can't carry all, most vendors will arrange to send to hotel by Takkyu-bin or Benri-ya movers or help carry goods to taxi.

DEMONSTRATION OF ARTS

LISTED HERE are interesting spots where you can watch demonstrations of various arts as well shop. Be sure to phone and check as demonstrations may not be available daily. Detailed info under MUSEUMS, *see* p.505.

MULTI-DEMOs AT ONE PLACE

Kyoto Handicraft Center, [J-7] 'demo' daily of Amita Damascene inlay of pure gold, silver into metal; woodblock printing from carving block for each color, inking and printing; difficult tapestry weaving; and painting on delicate Satsuma ceramic; only during May-Dec doll making, potter at wheel, and brush painting, ☎761-5080.

Traditional Industry Municipal Museum, *Kyoto-shi Dento-Sangyo Kaikan* [K-7] 'demo' of brocade weaving, difficult ikat splash pattern weaving, *norioki* first step of resist paste application of yuzen dyeing, kimono making, dressing Kyoto dolls, damascene inlay, folding fan, noh mask carving, cutting yuzen-dyeing stencil patterns, kumihimo braiding, wire net work, but many only on certain days, ☎761-3421 to check. X-mon.

ART

Uchida Woodblock shop in Handicraft Center, can see Woodblock complete process simplified.

Gallery Gado [E-5] on Kitsuji-dori btwn Golden Pavilion and Stone Garden Ryoan-ji. Offers free try at printing postcard; also 'demo' on 1st & 3rd Wed each month btwn 1:30-4:30pm, fee ¥1,000 incl. materials, 10-6pm, X-bon, New Year.

JEWELRY

Inaba Cloisonne [I-8], cloisonne work demo at main store at Sanjo dori, has staff there where visitors may watch intricate work of inlaying silver bands and then filling with color for exquisite pieces, ☎761-1161, X-sun, hol.

Amita Damascene's work inlaying of gold and silver on metal for accessories seen at **Amity Plaza**, new annex to Handicraft Center [J-7], ☎761-0551, X-New Year.

POTTERY

Not that easy to see workshop but some shops have tea cups and bowls ready for painting your design in process called *rakuyaki*, usually cost of cup under ¥1,000 plus delivery charge. They glaze and fire it and mail to you. Others have demonstrations of how pottery is made, painted and these are labelled 'demo'.

Kyoto Seiyo Kaikan [J-11] pottery workshop, *rakuyaki* on porcelain, ☎531-5678, X-sun, rsve day before;

Traditional Industry Municipal Museum, *Kyoto-shi Dento-Sangyo Kaikan* [K-7] 'demo' ☎761-3421, X-mon; **Asahi-do** [J-9] 'demo', ☎531-2181, X-sun; **Handicraft Center** [J-7] 'demo' May-Dec only; also...

Kiyomizu-yaki Pottery Village, Kotobuki Toshun [K-11], *rakuyaki* on porcelain, ¥400, ☎581-7195, X-sun Dec-Feb. **Get There:** Taxi 3x-mtr; bus from Kawaramachi S of Shijo Hankyu DS # 1, 2, 3, 4 or 5, ¥180.

TEXTILE ARTS

Most places have demonstrations and fine collection of ancient pieces displayed in gallery. Clustered in south are:
Embroidery Museum, Yuzen Cultural Hall, Kodai Yuzen-en Gall'y and **Costume Museum; Nishijin Textile Center** is up N in Nishijin weaving area; **Shozan Gallery** is further out; **Azekura** in NE.

KUMIHIMO BRAIDING: Adachi Braid Museum, ☎722-0008.

DYEING & WEAVING: *Juraku Senshoku Shiryokan* [G-5] ☎441-4141; **Azekura Kimono Kogei-mura** 'demo' ☎701-0161; **Dyeing Gallery of Shozan,** *Shozan Senshoku Gallery* [G-9] 'demo' ☎491-5101, ¥460; **Nishijin Textile Center,** *Nishijin-ori Kaikan* [GH-5] 'demo', kimono show; **Yuzen Dyeing & Kimono Museum,** *Kodai Yuzen-en Yuzen Bijutsukan* [G-9] 'demo' ☎811-8101, ¥500; **Kyoto Yuzen Dyeing Cultural Center,** *Kyoto Yuzen Bunka Kaikan* [D-9] demo ☎313-2151, ¥310.

EMBROIDERY: Embroidery Museum, *Nihon Shishukan* [map C-9] ☎313-2151, ¥310.

For full listing of **Textile Arts** *see* MUSEUMS, p.505.

FOR THE HURRIED SHOPPER

LARGE DEPARTMENT STORES are excellent, hotel arcades are good but Kyoto Handicraft center has much larger selection with products geared to overseas visitors. For truly last minute shopping Kyoto Stn's 2nd fl arcade is good, especially being open until late. Good underground mall that takes you to **Tower Hotel** filled with souvenir type shops. This directory lists our favorite shop first, otherwise in alphabetical order.

ART, ANTIQUES AND MODERN

We list Shopping Map page designation. Hurried shopper's one stop might be **Handicraft Center** [see p.545], cloisonne, woodblock prints, pearls, modern crafts, kimonos old and new, etc. ☎761-5080; if it's antique porcelains go to Shinmonzen-Furumonzen-Nawate area with just shop after shop (try **R.Kita, Kaji's Antiques** and **Y.Tsuruki** on Shimonzen). **Tessaido** [see p.537] Nawate-dori, inexpensive hanging scrolls and paintings ☎531-5403; **Sekisen-Ishinosuke Mizutani** [see p.537] fine and museum quality scrolls, screens, ☎525-0113. Don't miss Temple Fairs, see p.555.

FINE ANTIQUES

David Kidd, of Japan, China, Tibet, only for serious collectors–phone for private appointment: phone *never* before noon for late appointment—even for after dinner, ☎751-8552; see p.544.

Yokoyama [p.536] bit of everything, notably ceramics, textiles, prints, screens, ☎541-1321, X-New Year.

Art Kura Ashiya's Hirozawa Noboru has fun place, old storehouse, filled with affordable antiques. 31 Nakakoji-cho, Oyake Yamashina-ku, ☎581-7703, open 3days/month, check by phone, E-spkn.

Nishimura, Konjaku [p.537], antique textile bags, ties; Nawate-dori ☎561-2572, X-sun.

Nakamura, T [p.537] antique textiles pre-Meiji, Nawate-dori, ☎561-4726, no-X.

Tessaido [p.537] Shinmonzen, great collection of antique ceramics, ☎531-2829, X-every 9th.

Kyoto Screen [p.537] Furumonzen, good old screens, ☎531-2829, X-sun.

Taniguchi [p.537] Furumonzen, huge stock of fine old scrolls, ☎461-9121, no-X.

BAMBOO

Kasagen [see p.547] beautiful handmade baskets for ikebana, etc, sodegaki fences right out of painting. No-X, ☎561-2832.

Kono Take-kogei-ten [see p.547] on Teramachi-dori above Oike Blvd.

Nishikawa Soetsu [I-8, see pp.541, 547] W of Yasaka-Shijo-dori, baskets, blinds, antique and art pieces, X-wed, ☎561-1269.

Maeda Heihachi-ten [p.547] on Teramachi-dori, mostly screen and blinds, special order luxurious temple-type wide blinds 'misu', ☎351-2749, X-sun, hol.

Yamanaka [see p.549] baskets by artist NOGUCHI Ushu, just N of Chion-in, X-mon, ☎561-0931.

CERAMICS

Antique:

Chishoken Imai [p.537], exquisite old Imari, Nabeshima and netsuke, supplies museums overseas ☎561-0586, X-random, no set day.

Tessaido above; **Matsuda** [p.541] toward end of Sannenzaka after Kiyomizu Temple. Fairest prices and good selection of old blue and white Arita and Imari-wares. ☎541-4009, X-no set day.

New:

Tachikichi [p.547] Shijo-dori Tominokoji corner, exquisite inexpensive sets all sizes and shapes, cups & saucers, everyday fine porcelain Kyoto ware; also exclusive pieces; will pack safely and ship overseas. ☎211-3143, X-wed.

Asahi-do [p.541] up by Kiyomizu Temple large supply of top quality ceramics for mostly useful everyday pieces and gift pieces. ☎531-2181, No-X.

Fujihira [I-10, p.541] maker of modern pieces, corner Gojo-dori & Higashi-Oji, exceptional ikebana flower vases, other. ☎561-5110, no-X.

Kyoto Tojiki (Ceramic) Kaikan [p.541] near beginning of Teapot Lane (Kiyomizu-saka) has grand selection of Kyoto makers as well as some from other areas like Kyushu, some by well-known artists. ☎541-1102, X-New Year.

Koshida Satsumaya in Handicraft Center [see p.549] has delicate Satsuma ware, some eggshell thin, painting with gold and silver, ☎761-5780, X-wed.

Maruko [I-10, see p.541] wholesale, retail good daily-use tableware, Gojo-dori. ☎561-2035, no-X.

Okada-ya [I-10, p.541] Crackled Satsuma ware pottery, painting w/gold, silver on Gojo-dori, ☎561-4372, no-X.

Rakushien [I-10, see p.541] Fine quality artist's pieces, many signed; Gojo-dori. ☎541-1161, X-wed.

DEPARTMENT STORES

There are four major department stores, of these Takashimaya seems to have best all-around selection, Daimaru ranks next.

Takashimaya [see p.547] Shijo Kawara-machi, 10am-7pm, ☎221-8811, X- wed.

Daimaru [see p.547] Shijo Takakura, 10am-7pm, ☎211-8111, X-wed.

Hankyu [see p.547] Shijo Kawaramachi, 10am-7pm, ☎223-2288, X-thur.

Kintetsu block N of JR Kyoto Stn on L, 10am-7pm, ☎361-1111, X-thur.

DOLLS

Antique:

Fujii [p.537], Noted collector of dolls, Shimbashi Nawate, X-tues, ☎561-7863.

Nakanishi [p.537] Furumonzen, largest coll of antique dolls, ☎551-0262, no-X.

Mizutani [p.537] Furumonzen, has some dolls, also old silk textiles ☎561-5711, X-tues.

New: Kyoto dolls in traditional kimonos show subtle refinement over Tokyo dolls; roly-poly Gosho-ningyo are Kyoto's own. Refined elegant dolls, works of art, made by such as Tanaka-ya, Kabukiya, are all quite expensive but beautiful.

Kogatanaya Chubei [p.547] on Sanjo E of Kawaramachi, 330 years-old, excellent theatrical dolls, masks, inexpensive; ☎221-6349, no-X.

Tanaka-ya [p.547] Shijo Yanaginobanba has exquisite dolls and price is also high.

Kabuki-ya [p.547] Kawaramachi Tako-yakushi, all quite expensive but worth it; ☎221-1959, X-wed.

Maruyama Dolls inexpensive [p.541] on Sannenzaka at Kiyomizu Temple, charming Gosho-ningyo, 2 more doll shops. Many shops carry dolls, esp minis.

Nakayama Dolls. [p.545] in Handicraft Center, moderate, ☎761-5680, no-X.

HANDBAGS AND PURSES

Focus on Japanese cloth bags, which also make ideal W-style evening bags.

Izawaya [p.547] for well-dressed Kyoto madams, 2 shops across from each other at Shijo E of Minamiza kabuki theater.

Sumiya [p.547] X-wed, ☎221-6654 and...

Tawaraya X-wed, ☎221-2789 at Shijo and Kiyamachi-dori.

JEWELRY AND ACCESSORIES

Pearls, cloisonne, damascene are mainstays in all hotel and JR stn arcades and Kyoto Handicraft Center.

Amita Damascene runs Handicraft Center [p.545], open daily ☎761-0141.

Inaba Cloisonne [p.545] large Meiji era mansion Sanjo Shirakawabashi. X-sun, hol, ☎761-1161.

Komai Pearls [p.537] at end Shinmonzen near Higashioji St. No-X, ☎541-8171

Yamakatsu Pearls, our favorite, passage by Mitsui bank NE corner Shijo-dori & Karasuma, X-wed, ☎211-8981.

KIMONOS

Secondhand kimonos, wedding robes—in recent years these have become popular especially with top Japanese dress designers using them. You'll find great selections at Temple fairs; at Toji some vendors will have piles just marked "¥500 (or ¥1,000) each", ¥3,-5,000 buys good stain-free garment or *obi* sash. Shops along Nawate-dori, Shimonzen Curio Shopping Walk (p.535, map p.537): **Nishimura** only kimonos, while others including **Yokoyama** 'also carry...'; as does inimitable **Handicraft Center** with.2 or 3 stallss with new and old kimono.

Takashimaya DS [p,588] holds periodic sales early Jan, mid-May, Aug, Oct of used rental kimono, obi, uchikake robes; ¥3,000-up; ☎221-8811.

Eiraku, has good stock but also has W-style garments made up from old kimono. Bit out of way, south of Kyoto Stn, 30-5 Shimogawara-cho, Fukakusa Fushimi-ku. ☎641-6644, X-sun, hols.

Bon Kyoto, Shirakawa-dori bet Kita-oji & Imadegawa sts; large stock, also W-garments made from old kimono. Bettoh-cho, Kitashirakawa, ☎711-7095.

Kikuya, [H-9] N of Gojo at Manju & Yanaginobamba sts, wedding '*uchikake*' robes, 9-7pm, ☎351-0033, X-sun, hols.

Tomo Design Ctr, successful designer using kimono materials, Senbon-dori and Sanjo, E-spkn, prices match temple fairs, has ready-mades. Appointm't ☎812-4822.

LACQUERWARE

Warning: good lacquer must be washed only in lukewarm water, and dried immediately, preferably with soft silk cloth. Rectangular pieces with seams most vulnerable to cracking. Don't keep in warm dry room. Cheaper wares for everyday use are plastic-base, safe to machine wash.

Nishimura (Zohiko) [p.545] in huge building near Heian Shrine, their Zojirushi trademark is guarantee of finest quality, from budget to luxe items, ☎752-7777, X-sun, hol.

Monju [p.547] on Shijo-dori, E of Hanamikoji, grand array of fine lacquer. Plastic-based lacquerware not carried, wood compress is all clearly marked. X-thur, ☎525-1617.

LANTERNS & UMBRELLAS

Many shops did their own work in back of store, still make, but painting personalized ideographs sent out. Usually made paper umbrellas, too; colorful huge red tea ceremony umbrellas. Better known shops are:

Tsujikura [p.547] Kawaramachi nr Shijo, ☎221-4396, another Tsujikura [p.537] on Nawate-dori just in from Shijo-dori, ☎561-4544, X-tues.

Kasagen [p.547] Shijo-dori S of Yasaka Shrine and Higashioji-dori. ☎561-2832, no-X.

PAPER

Lucky to have two great shops who, tho really wholesalers, also sell retail. If interested in handmade paper process, 2hr30min bus ride N is Kurodani, traditional paper-making village, not far from Ayabe city, with museum, and can also try your own hand at-making real *washi*.

Morita Wagami [p.547] on Takoyakushi-dori W of Takakura with huge store filled with Japanese handmade papers of all kinds. Owner wrote *Encyclopedia of Hand-made Japanese Paper*, visiting all makers. Annex shop has papers and papers products, and even has lessons upstairs for art of '*chigiri-e*' art of tearing paper and pasting on as color. ☎341-0121, X-sun, hol & 1st of month.

Kakimoto [p.547], lovely shop on Teramachi-dori—we missed it in our first edition though it has been in same place, because it had ordinary house front, but now easy to find front window. Inside are walls lined with shelves for papers of all kinds. Also paper products. ☎211-3481, X-sun, hol.

PAPER PRODUCTS & STATIONERY

Kawabun [p.547], Shijo-dori nr Hanami-koji. Unique papers done into dolls, boxes chests, fancy papers; ☎561-0277, X-wed.

Kyukyodo [p.547] art supplies, incense, stationery, papers; Teramachi-dori corner of Anekoji. ☎231-0510, X-sun, hol.

Morita Wagami & Kakimoto [*above*], as well as Kawabun, have good supplies.

Rakushi Kan in Museum of Kyoto 1F, Sanjo & Takakura sts, fine assortment of papers & products. X-3d wed, ☎251-0078.

STAMPS:

Heian Shumi-no-mise [p.547], Teramachi-dori nr Takatsuji St, old coins & stamps all neatly filed, curios; tiny, chock full of anything, ☎351-5367, X-sun, hol.

WOODBLOCK PRINTS

Classic old prints

Nishiharu [*see* p.547], aka Nishimura Woodblock prints, corner Sanjo-dori & Teramachi, deals only in antique prints, ☎211-2849, no-X. E- spoken.

Ezoshi [*see* p.537], Furumonzen, also only traditional antique prints, relatively young shop; ☎551-9137, no-X.

New woodblocks:

Clifton Karhu *Playboy* calendar fame, still better cubist cityscapes; ☎415-0606, appt.

Red Lantern [*see* p.537] Shinmonzen St, modern prints only; ☎541-0931, X-mon.

Yamada Gallery [*see* p.537] artist-owner Tets Yamada, Shinmonzen; moderns, old prints, new editions; ☎561-5382, X-mon.

Yamanaka [*see* p.545] opp Shorenin N of Chion-in, graphics, ☎561-0931, X-mon.

NOVELTY

Artistic signs:

Shimizu Sué Shoten [p.547], carves artistic signs on old boards, Teramachi-dori N of Oike-dori. ☎231-4838, X-sun, hol.

Carved Seals:

Tamaru on Teramachi-dori nr Anekoji-dori carves names on wooden seals, 2 kanji ¥3,500, ready in 6 hrs; ☎221-2496.

Kyoto Inban Shinmichi N of Shijo, better quality ¥15,000-up; ☎221-4967.

Dyed to order:

Nakagawa Senshoku [p.537] makes happi coats, towels, etc. to your personal design. ☎561-0065, X-thurs.

Cooking utensils:

Aritsugu [p.547] Teramachi-dori at Nishiki-koji-dori, maker-supplier of traditional cook utensils of wood, hammered copper, sushi-molds, etc. ☎221-1091, X-sun, hol.

STONE

They now have compressed stone chips or cement look-alike made up into stone lanterns, non-specialists pass off as "stone". They're lighter and cheaper but weather poorly—and there's nothing like real stone.

Sawakichi Stone Mason [p.541] with stone lanterns of every imaginable shape and size. Illustrated catalog available, ☎561-2802, no-X.

Gion Ishi [p.547] Shijo-dori & Higashioji Sts below Yasaka Shrine. Fun 'warabe-jizo' image, ☎561-2485, X-sun, hol. Main shop & branch at Avanti, Kyoto Stn.

WESTERN ARTISTS

Many have been attracted to, and live in, Kyoto. Some have works in top museums overseas: British Museum, Museum of Modern Art NY, etc.

Girma Belachew, traditional Ethiopian painting, prints of Solomon & Sheba; J-painting, J-*yuzen* silk dyeing; ☎882-4535.

Sarah Brayer, watercolors, etchings, and now papermaking montages; studio ☎493-6012, (h) ☎491-5208.

Dan Kelly, versatile stained-glassworker, fine watercolors, etchings, oils; combines oriental mood in mixed mediums; studio ☎701-0194, (h) ☎722-2044.

Robert Milgrim, pottery with traditional J-tea taste; studied at Urasenke; lovely studio 1 hr drive N, ☎07717-3-0320.

Brian Williams, watercolors, oils, etchings; detailed landscapes of J- & China; lives in lovely ancient farmhouse out by Lake Biwa; ☎0775-98-2590.

Clifton Karhu, *see above* WOODBLOCKS.

*When foreign merchants first landed in Kobe January 1st, 1868
it was a village of small houses, many with roofs of thatch, straggling
along a mean narrow road that was later (thrice) to be widened into
Motomachi of today... The population of Kobe was less than 1,000.*
— Harold S Williams, *Tales of the Foreign Settlements*

HANSHIN 阪神
MEGALOPOLIS OSAKA-KOBE

TAKE IDEOGRAPHS for O-saka and Ko-be and make new composite name in traditional fashion by using one ideograph from each, in this case *-saka* of *Osaka* and *ko-* of *Kobe*. We pair these together to make new name, which, by peculiar logic of this language, we pronounce *not* as *saka-ko* but rather as *han-shin*. (You recall from our Introduction that almost every ideograph has at least two ways to pronounce it, Wa-Japanese and 'naturalized' Chinese: much as numeral '1' in English is pronounced under most circumstances 'one' and under some as 'fir[st]', even 'prime'.)

If this is confusing, it is only because it mirrors physical circumstances of this great twin-city metropolis. Kobe and Osaka have no green area left between, one drives from one to other passing thru intermediate towns en route never leaving city traffic. Their excellent intercity transport is in fact one vast metropolitan intracity network, connecting to smaller networks of neighboring cities ad-inf. Problems of each city interlink. Talking for over generation of amalgamation into one great megalopolis of over 7 million—expected to surpass 12 million at millennium. Each barely 30min apart, there is no reason for tourist to consider them apart. We deal with them here as one single leg. Two principal close tourist suburbs—Mt Koya, Japan's Shangri La, & South Kii Peninsula—were dealt with earlier, historically—as too, tourist meccas Nara & Kyoto. See access to other ESCAPES (p566).

Osaka elicited from British Buddhist writer John Blofeld in 1960, "precisely what I fled Birmingham to get away from". Generation later, local disc jockey Jim Doyle was ecstatic most of his years here (working in Osaka, living in Kobe as do most *gai-jin*) and mourned his departure. In fact almost no native powers who run Osaka live in that workplace-playground city, 30% more crowded than Tokyo. Osaka has, no doubt, improved since our first '64 edition. And Kobe has rebuilt from near total destruction to most liveable, greenest city in Orient. Nonetheless, tourist should not allow anyone to put either in your itinerary unless you are music lover visiting in April or May for *Osaka International Music Festival*, or *International Trade Fair*–May in even-number years. We would not cover either city here except that many people must visit this industrial-market hub of Japan on business—businessmen, after all, are pioneers of tourism: Marco Polo was no travel agent or Fulbright exchange prof, he was in import-export.

This is not to knock Osaka. As residents we find it great place to eat, play and shop and Osakans are great folk who greet you with '*Mo kari makka-* making any money?' And just as old cloak-'n-suiters from lower Manhattan punctuate conversation with mellifluous rising intonation, 'Nuu^u?'—so too Osakan textile merchants, in falling intonation sigh nasally, 'Na$_a$oh'.

But is this what you have come halfway round world for?

Businessmen ought keep in mind that Kyoto and Nara in terms of sight-seeing accessibility for half- and full-day tours, are suburbs of Osaka-Kobe. From Kobe at one end (W) of Hanshin zone, to far opposite Kyoto (NE) is one hour by fast suburban electric, or Nara (SE) only minutes more. Himeji, W of Kobe, is equally convenient to Osaka over in E Hanshin, as are several other points in our Inland Sea itineraries (*follows*).

We do not (as we repeat in our Osaka and Kobe chapters) recommend either city to casual tourism. But for those many who must go there for other reasons, glance at any map or transportation plan of greater Hanshin—including Kobe-Osaka-Kyoto-Nara-Koya-Wakayama together called Kinki —will show clearly how accessible you are to places of greater tourist interest, even if you must overnite in either Kobe or Osaka.

For most Osaka-Kobe will be short business trip to Japan's manufacturing heart, others two-three year stay expanding that business. Traditionally for century since laying of Osaka-Kobe rail initiated Asia's (if not world's) first commuter community, foreign traders work in Osaka but live in Kobe. Osaka vivacity is stimulus to work and play and appetite, while Kobe, air filtered, noise muffled by over thirteen million (count 'em) new in-city trees, (more planted regularly in new parks and along streets lined by almost 200 modern sculptures) provides snug nest in which to recharge for tomorrow.

GETTING THERE

Itami Airport domestic & international in adjoining terminals. Local lines serving airport are **ANA** ☎(06)-534-8800 (Int'l 372-1212), **JAL** ☎201-1231 (Int'l 203-1212), **Japan Asia** ☎223-2222 and **JAS** (ex-TOA) ☎856-6851. 'Rimojeen' **bus** from front of domestic bldg, 100m/yds walk L of Int'l: 80min → KYOTO, 40min → KOBE-Sannomiya, 30min → OSAKA nr Hilton, or OBP nr Otani, or Namba nr Holiday Inn, Tower, Nikko; taxis, minivans plentiful. **Kansai International Airport** will float in Bay in '93 (more likely '95+?) with mile-long terminal for 100,000 daily.

Several international lines now serve ITAMI. We again emphasize that travelers to or from Southeast Asia save time and money using ITAMI. Internationally served by *Cathay Pacific, Korean, Thai, Singapore, Air France, British, JAL, United, NW Orient*, and more in offing with *ANA* International tied up for US internal with *American*, itself now serving Japan and hungry for expansion, as is *Delta* into Nagoya.

We stress that with direct flights NY, SF, LA or Hawaii → ITAMI, or painless quick change at Narita with customs at Itami, tourists from USA do well to consider Itami your main port of entry/exit: most of what you have come this far to see is here! It takes less time from touch down at transfer-Narita to check in to Kyoto hotel than to go NARITA → TOKYO hotel! Two-week tour couldn't possibly exhaust possibilities of this area. Top tour of Japan can be made up skipping Tokyo completely, or taking it in reverse of usual by Shinkansen quicky up and back. This has added and considerable bonus of avoiding what must be world's most inconvenient, generally worst-run landing field, Narita, where everyone excepting ace customs officers seem infected with chronic grumpitosis—little wonder, world's worst daily commute thru heavily fortified Oriental Maginot line, its understandably tight and efficient security frequently picketed by masked zombies.

TOKYO → OSAKA by **Shinkansen** 2:30hrs. Following our historical itinerary from TOKYO down Tokaido from ISE or NARA short cut → OSAKA on JR Rail Pass, or paying cash use cheaper local lines, or from KYOTO in 30min, continue our westward itinerary.

GETTING AROUND   OSAKA, KOBE, KYOTO have subways with maps readily available in tourist handouts. Tel **English info** ☎(06)-313-1010.

Goodwill Guides volunteers in all cities. OSAKA sometimes arranged thru Systematic goodwill guides at Osaka **TIC** ☎(06)-345-2189 or ✍ ahead to '**Tak**' **Watanabe**, Nina 3-chome 9-11, Minoo City, Osaka 562; KOBE ☎(078)-821-5456 Ms IMURA Chijiko, advise ✍ ahead, postcard OK, **Ms Imura Chijiko** Nakago-cho 2ch-3-4 Nada-ku Kobe 657. Doesn't like to impinge on work of pro-fessionals, so only handles individuals, no tour groups—prefers visiting relatives of residents (*see* NARA, KYOTO).

Aerial sightseeing takes off from Yao (SE Osaka) airport: small planes make runs over KYOTO, NARA or OSAKA: 3-psgr Cessna ¥60,000 per hr, 8-psgr ¥150,000: Hankyu Koku, ☎(06)-373-1661. Singles ¥6,000per 15min: Daichi Koku ☎(0729)-91-2961 or Showa Koku ☎(0729)-23-0026. Airport 15min walk, basic taxi, E of Tanimachi subway line Yao Minami stn, taxi 4x-mtr main hotels. Spectacular sightseeing: helicopter 3-psgr ¥220,000, 4-psgr ¥280,000 per hr, short runs ¥1,000 per psgr-min: Naka Nihon Koku ☎(06)-541-5818, Hankyu ☎373-1661, Kobe ☎(078)-302-7071; from heliports Osaka Asahi bldg nr Osaka stn, Kobe Port Island. Heli-shuttle for new airport '93.

Taxi: OSAKA and KOBE full rate city taxis, KYOTO and NARA 10+% less. 1990=¥540 per 2km, total=?-x-mtrs for future reference. Sightsee by cab hourly *chugata* ('90) ¥4,000/7.5x-mtr, ¥25,000up full day. ITAMI International Airport → KYOTO ¥11,500/22x+1,400 tolls; → TAKARAZUKA ¥6,200/12x-mtr; → KOBE ¥6,600/13x-mtr; → OSAKA CENTRAL ¥3,000/6x-mtr; → HORYUJI ¥9,000/18x-mtr; → NARA ¥14,400/27x-mtr; → KOYA MONASTERY ¥17,000/33x-mtr+¥1,050 tolls.

Osaka center → Kobe ¥6,700/13x-mtr; → Mount Ikoma up, continue on across to Nara Hotel ¥9,000/18x-mtr, or direct hiway 15x-mtr, or along crest to Shigi 15x-mtr back to Osaka 30x-mtr; → Kyoto ¥10,-12,000/20-22x-mtr: Osaka jams monthly 5,15,25.

In all cases smaller 4-psgr *kogata* =10% less. Add 10% 1991, same 'x-mtr'.

WHERE TO STAY

COMING TO this area with its efficient convenient transportation, choose your city according to your main purpose.

If business stay near business associate in Kobe, Osaka, tho if wife along remember that main hotels KYOTO or NARA are under hour door-to-door downtown Osaka offices. On business in KOBE, anything from two of Japan's best Portopia, and Okura to business hotels; and OSAKA has fine old Royal, convenient station-plaza Hilton, midtown Nikko (JAL), and 'resort downtown' New Otani, numerous ¥-T hotels.

If tourism, KYOTO traditionally, but it would be wise to give careful consideration to tourist sleeper, sleepy NARA, or even head out of town with us, as detailed below.

OSAKA: Hotel fare now fleshing out to what metropolis this size needs. High international rates mostly N near Osaka-Umeda stn (old train and commuter hub) down to Nakanoshima, and further down center near Daimaru-Sogo DSs. Shinkansen bullet trains stop at Shin-Osaka stn, which has small business hotels, convenient to nothing, avoid— take subway to Umeda stn for Terminal, Hilton, Dai Ichi, Hanshin, Shin Hankyu Hotels. Next past Umeda is Yodoybashi stn where upstairs to free, infrequent, riverbus to New Otani. Or on to Shinsaibashi stn farther down S on Mido-suji line into basement of Nikko Hotel, or one stop to Holiday Inn, Nankai South Tower.

TIC ☎(06)-305-3311 will make same day reservation as will JTB ☎344-0830 in Japanese. Osaka International Airport has hotel reservation.

TOP OF LINE: New Otani [City Map: D-7—subway map p571 #44] ☎(06)-941-1111, next to Osaka Castle, captive view from half its windows, sole worthwhile view in town from topside Aurora room especially sakura time—not deficiency other hotels, Osaka simply has no views. 'Resort downtown' midst of 21st century center-to-be OBP, Osaka Business Park. ¥-L hotel, restaurants galore. Especially if bringing wife along on trip, leave her here while you biz. Exotic approach: take hotel riverbus (free, if erratic, to hotel guests) on Osaka's 'grand canal' from Yodoyabashi [D-3] easy taxi from any stn and even reached by Midosuji line subway. Direct bus Itami → Osaka Business Park.

Hilton International [Map: B-1/2–#42] ☎347-7111, most convenient of all, ¥-L but slightly lower bottom rate. Superb art deco decor in best of international designers' and craftsmen's work, most excitingly designed W-hotel in Japan...tourist sight in itself. Loaded w/ restaurants. Opp Osaka stn complex of old JR, commuter Hankyu and Hanshin stns, subways, all interconnected by underground shop-filled labyrinth—modern Japan's bazaar—& to several dep't stores on plaza, its own high-rise emporium next door. Convenient transport direct → Kobe, Takarazuka, Kyoto; one transfer within Osaka → Nara, Mt Koya Monastery; one stop JR to Shin Osaka stn for Shinkansen bullets up to Tokyo, down to Hiroshima, etc.

OUR RANKING: 1992 EDITION

Ryokan: per person			**Hotels:** twin/dbl
¥50,000+	pricey-princely	'LL'	¥35,000+%
¥25,000-50,000w/2	international luxe	'L'	¥20,000-35,000+%
¥13,000-25,000w/2	standard	'S'	¥12,000-20,000+%
¥7,000-13,000w/2	business/tourist	'T'	¥7,000-12,000
¥4,400-7,000w/2	budget	'B'	¥7,000-under
¥4,500-under	pilgrim	'P'	

Under ¥5,001 per person (¥10,001 dbl) rm chge +3% tax; ¥5,001-up +6%; rm
w/ meal/s to ¥10,001 per person tax +3%, ¥10,001-up +6%, with any service
chge incl in taxable base.
Abbreviated in text as: ¥-LL, ¥-L, ¥-S, ¥-T, ¥-B, ¥-P; "+" = higher end; ¥-S-L =
basic overlap main price range, tho most inns & hotels also range higher.
Minshuku all = ¥-B; w/2 indicates 2 meals included; ¥-lo-hi-T = lo to hi end.

Many hostelries-notable exception of Int'l Luxe and Standard hotels, some ryokan-
now quote you set price already including both, ('incl') but if not sure ask if generally
quote *komi*, as do business hotels. Love hotels quote total. Minshuku always quote
full rate, no service charge.
  Note that 20% or so they deduct from inn rate if you go room-only is not enough
to get nearly comparable meal outside, so take w/2 unless special room-only rate.

Terminal Hotel [AB-1/2–subway map p571 #5] ☎344-1235, towers over stn ¥-lo-S.
(ACTY-Daimaru DS lower floors, whole upper floor variety good ¥-B & ¥-T restaurants).
Royal [D-1-#7] ☎448-1121, ¥-L, out bit W of stn, long-time top, taxi only, as also-
Plaza [#26] ☎453-1111, ¥-L, probably best run of older hotels, favored, but
inconvenient, taxi basic-mtr from stn, need taxi to go anywhere.

ANA-Sheraton [C-2-#35] ☎347-1112, ¥-L few blocks S of stn along river.
Nikko-JAL [H/I-2-#22] ☎244-1111, ¥-L, mid-Midosuji opp Daimaru & Sogo DS's.
Nankai South Tower [J-3-#23x]☎646-1111, ¥-L, over Namba stn rail to Koya, Nara.

STANDARD RATES (¥-S) nearby (most others on *Hotel & Subway* map, *see* OSAKA):
Dai-Ichi [A-3-#4] ☎341-4411, ¥-S, in *maru-biru*—round building next to Hilton.
Hanshin [A-1-#11] ☎344-1661, ¥-lo-S, just above next to Osaka stn E, &...
New Hankyu [A-2-#8] ☎372-5101, ¥-lo-S, atop Hankyu Umeda stn W-end Osaka stn.
Grand [CD-2-#2] ☎202-1212, across river, oldest timer, ¥-S.
Holiday Inn [J-3-#23] ☎213-8281, ¥-lo-S, fun locale S end Midosuji in restaurant-lined
Minami-'south' Namba stn-subway, nr top sauna NEW JAPAN (lady's section). Bus→Itami

TOURIST RATE (¥-T), not low enough to compensate for out-of-way inconvenience:
International [F-5-#14] ☎941-2661; **Tennoji Miyako** [N-5-#19] at stn ☎779-1501;
Echo ☎633-1141 ¥-lo-T; and unhandsome but convenient **Toyo** [H-4-#25] ☎372-8181,
newly jazzed up. Try new business hotels proliferating block or two parallel either side
Midosuji Blvd by Daimaru-Sogo/Shinsaibashi subway stn. Ask TIC main JR stns.
Hokke Club [A-3-#12] 'Hotel that cares' chain, ☎313-3171, 10min walk E across
Shin-Midosuji Ave, next R (S) 2nd block R; sgl/twn ¥-lo-T no bath, use common spa.
Global ☎357-8882, block N Kyobashi stn JR,Keihan; w/Pakistan rstnt; *show this book*

  Plenty of other business and ¥-T hotels, especially in Kita ('North' area around Umeda)
& Minami ('South' around Namba stn), but we stress Osaka is only for those who have to
be here on business—not for general tourist; *see* p571.

  For variety there are some flashy modern *ryokan*:
Shin Toyo at Hagoromo, taxi 12x-mtr of Namba stn, 14x- of Osaka stn, *onsen* baths,
private spas, indoor golf, bowling, in season shellfish hunt, swim, firefly fetes; ¥-Tw/2.

PILGRIM RATES (¥-P): **Pine House**, ☎(06)-581-6338 ask for Keith; at Esaka,
Midosuji subway N from Umeda; ¥1,500 daily, ¥45,000 month. For more of similar,
check TIC. **Rinkai Hotel Dejimaten** [#53], ☎(0722)-41-3045 despite area code it's
in Osaka at Minato (port) stn, 12min Nankai line S from Namba stn, all w/TV, kitchen.

OSAKA HOTELS
Left-hand number refers to subway map locations.
(*See* OSAKA — Hotel & Subway *map* p.571)

1	Umeshin E	364-1151	19	Tennoji Miyako	779-1501	37	MoriguchiTerminal	993-1111
2	Grand	202-1212	20	Ark	252-5111	38	Shin Osaka Stn	325-0011
3	Shanpia	312-5151	21	Do Sports Plaza	245-3311	39	NCB	443-2255
4	Daiichi	341-4411	22	Nikko JAL	244-1111	40	Esaka Tokyu Inn	338-0109
5	Terminal	344-1235	23	Holiday Inn	213-8281	41	Tokyu	373-2411
6	Tokyu Inn	315-0109	24	Nankai	649-1521	42	Hilton Int'l	347-7111
7	Royal	448-1121	25	Toyo	372-8181	43	Koho	213-3441
8	New Hankyu	372-5101	26	Plaza	453-1111	44	New Otani	941-1111
9	Toko	363-1201	27	Shin Osaka Seni City	394-3331	45	Gaen	541-0438
10	World	361-1100	28	Corona	323-3151	46	Plaza	303-1000
11	Hanshin	344-1661	29	Sunny Stone	385-1281	47	Korakuen	252-2111
12	HokkeClub	313-3171	30	Oaks	302-5141	48	Veneto	354-1111
13	Castle	942-1401	31	Chisan Shin Osaka	02-5571	49	Nakanoshima Inn	447-1122
14	International	941-2661	32	New Naniwa	213-1241	50	Dojima	348-0111
15	Lutheran	942-2281	33	Osaka Miyako	773-1111	51	Sport Suminoe	82-1101
16	Yamato	245-1851	34	Kitahachi	361-2078	52	Lion's	201-1511
17	Green	532-1091	35	ANA Sheraton	347-1112	53	Rinkai	(0722)-47-1111
18	New Oriental	538-7141	36	New Osaka	305-2345	54	Chisan Shinsaibashi	263-1511

KOBE: Hotels, till recently not what City tourist office wants you to think, are fast improving, with some of country's best ¥-S and ¥-L. Tho with lower land prices, little reason to visit—all business but fashion moved to Osaka—there is little excuse for ¥-L rates at new L-hostels. Staying in town is for business itinerary, or one nite stand waiting for ferry. Many good business hotels around old Kobe stn, 2 stops W on JR, under 2x-mtr taxi, inconvenient for tourist. We limit to **downtown–Port** up thru **Sannomiya** to old foreign quarter **Kitano-cho** above, adjoining **Shin-Kobe** Shinkansen stn: *map* p.589.

Kobe, unlike Osaka, has *views* which make ascent to hotel Sky Lounges worthwhile.

New Kobe Oriental [1] ☎(078)-291-1121, ¥-L skyscraper at Shin Kobe Shinkansen stn linked by walkway; immense party rooms, small bedrooms; restaurants ¥-T (in OPA) to topside ¥-L, grand shopping arcade, movie, live theaters in OPA– 'Oriental Park Ave' on first 5 floors below lobby—'24-hour city-in-city' planned with never-closing shops and restaurants—but we wonder if establishment will let it be, not find some 'inconvenience' to close with last train. Owner Nakauchi brothers Yankee-Oriental dreamer-entrepreneurs.

Portopia Hotel [12] ☎302-1111, on new man-made isle taxi 2+x-mtr of Sannomiya or ¥180 Buck Rogers computerized crewless monorail from JR stn, one of best in Japan, luxe at ¥-S rate, every room breathtaking view of either sea or hills (specify); excellent reasonable buffet breakfast topside, well worth even budgeteer binge, especially Sunday. Also top bar, expensive, music surcharge 6pm. Good rest'nts, cafeteria to Luxe (atop).

-**Annex** ¥-L–truly luxury, every room outside veranda, art deco 'in style of' Osaka-Hilton.

Gaufres (*go-fré*) **Ritz** [13] ☎303-5555, next door in FASHION TOWN small 120rm ¥-L w/¥-S sgle, 'Barcelona style' after original Ritz; big bed, J-bath, topside restaurant. First of small European type to restore old Kobe image, more coming.

PORT
Okura [7] ☎333-0111, ¥-L, convenient to Meriken Pier in main port area; best bedrooms, best of everything as to be expected of this name; if starved for reasonably-priced full W-meal, their main-floor coffee-shop restaurant is tops..

Towerside [6] ☎351-2151,¥-T,at Meriken pier (port-tower), to await morning ferries. [11] was **New Port**—from '91 **Fuji Museum**-Soka Gakkai International Ikeda Culture Center.

New Otani Inn, ¥-T?, due late '92 opp Okura. Probably more 'inns' will follow.

SANNOMIYA
Oriental [8] ☎331-8111, ¥-S, staff old, jaded rather than experienced, but roomy rooms & most convenient location make it good buy. Just bought by people who run Portopia & New Oriental, in blitz of Nakauchi brothers (Daiei chain) to dominate hotels, buying up old & building new —great hope for Kobe future.

Terminal Hotel [10] ☎291-0001, ¥-lo-S over JR stn; +¥1,300 bkfst. Good ¥-T–S public restaurants on 11th fl—Chinese, Japanese, European—all with good views.

Tokyu Inn [7] ☎291-0109, ¥-T adjoins Sannomiya stn on SE.

Washington [5] ☎331-6111¥-T; 2 blocks NW of Sannomiya stn is buy for adequate dbl, top location, basement has one of our favorite eateries, folk artsy chain **I-ro-ha-ni-ho-he-to** serving a la carte everything imaginable in J- pop cuisine: prices ¥-B obvious by youthful crowd – till 2am!

Kataoka ☎332-2221 ¥-T, 5min walk NW, L, of Sannomiya stn: friend of our festival runss friendly, simple place.

ABOVE SANNOMIYA

Kobe Union [4] ☎222-6500¥-T business, min-taxi/5min walk up Flower Rd R above bridged-intersection Kameyacho.

Green Hill #1 [3] ☎222-1221, 2+ blocks up on W(L)-side, ¥-T+...

-2 annex [2] alley W, ☎222-0909, ¥-T+.

Zentan, 43 Shimoyamate-dori-4, ☎391-3838, W of Tor Road nr Pref Hall or Kitano-cho w/ good ¥-T crab restaurant, top-floor fine Hyogo **Ceramic Museum**.

Kitano Hotel [15] ☎271-3711, ¥-LL; small 30rm, 'British Manor House B&B' classic hostelry full of Persian carpets (wear better) top of famed old foreign shopping street, mid of Kitano-cho, 10min walk W/N from Sannomiya stn, or from Shinkansen stn city loop bus to door.

Tor Road [14] ☎391-6691, ¥-lo-S, mid-size 81rm; nr above, also loop bus to door.

Gajoen (W off map) at Shimo-Yamate-Dori 8ch 4-23 ☎341-0301, old romantic restored Victorian era survivor, dbl ¥-T.

Hotel Kobe, Kumochi-cho 5ch-2-31, ☎221-5431, ¥-T.

Kobe is one place where **Romance Hotels** seem to have discovered that there is as much money in legit trade, converting to Business or Family Hotels, regular hours. **KITANO-CHO**, 'young' tourist area along Yamamoto-dori above Mosque & Sacred Heart Church, has successful convert in **Arçon** (nonsense name, sonorously Frenchy) ¥-B ☎231-1538–bkfst after 10am; top Kitano-zaka St, L 1 block below our American House 'roaring 20s' restoration, convenient to Kansai's sole synagogue. Area still has several 'Romance' short-timers. Young tourists like to visit *Ijinkan* "foreigners' houses", imagine being abroad, pop in for romantic interlude—now accustomed to conventional trade.

Possible **ALTERNATES** to staying in Osaka or Kobe:

KOBE BAY Sheraton, ☎857-7000, ¥-L, Rokko Isle betw Osaka-Kobe; from either go JR to Sumiyoshi stn, or Hanshin to Uozaki stn, xfer to Rokko Liner crewless overhead rail to new land-fill "international isle", 21st century version of Nagasaki's Dejima ghetto; homes for foreign residents, good school, etc, but inconvenient tourists.

HILLTOP: Mt Rokko [14] ¥-T ☎891-0301; **Rokko Oriental** [15] ¥-S ☎891-0333.

SUMA JR or Sanyo line 15 min W from Sannomiya, beach, taxi 9x-mtr.¥-B-S hotels **Maiko Hotel** ☎782-1155, weekends *dai-an* days full of kimono-clad weddings ¥-S; Ryokan **Enmei-Kan** ☎731-4051; and **Sumad Kotobuki-Ro** ☎731-4351; all ¥-S **Shiritsu Kokumin shukuhaku**, City citizens' Lodge at Suma beach ☎731-6815 ¥-Bw/2.

NISHINOMIYA: midway Kobe-Osaka (taxi 10x-mtr from either) has **Harihan**, once Japan's most beautiful, certainly most exclusive, ryokan, now in decline but still fine, Sukarno trysted here; ¥-Lw/2 and worth it for garden alone. Introduction only or thru JTB; as also fine traditional *bento*

lunch ¥12,000, or ¥22,000 *kaiseki* lunch or dinner only. ☎(0798)-73-1800.

TAKARAZUKA: served from Osaka and Kobe by Hankyu RR who own entertainments: 40min express from Osaka-Umeda, same from Kobe-Sannomiya change at Nishinomiya. Excellent old-fashion ¥-S **Takarazuka Hotel** ☎(0797)-87-1151, many *ryokan* w/onsen, top golf links; **Takarazuka Girl's Opera** of *Sayonara* infamy, not so much feminist revolt against all-male kabuki as throwback to pre-kabuki era when girl troupes played in riverbed at Kyoto (from which kabuki evolved); PLAYLAND for tots, fun, photogenic.

ARIMA ONSEN-SPA: From OSAKA bus rear Hankyu stn behind Kinokuniya bookstore (E books), 8:40–17:40 better than hourly, 55-65min, ¥1,180, stops Shin Osaka stn. From KOBE S side Sannomiya stn, ¥580; slow but scenic cablecar alternatives (*see* p.597) Taxi ITAMI 14x-mtr, OSAKA 16x-mtr, KOBE 9x-mtr.

MINO-O PARK: relocated folk architecture (*see* p.581); cleaner, cooler air summer.

ESCAPE ROUTE

From **OSAKA**: UMEDA, Osaka Station Plaza complex of 4 stns, all linked thru subterranean shopping plaza: JR-old main lines, Hankyu and Hanshin under their respective neighboring terminal department stores, 3 city subway lines. JR takes you almost anywhere in country. Hankyu interurban private line serves Kyoto-Osaka-Kobe along foothills; Hanshin similar but Osaka-Kobe only along bay-shore. KOBE-bound reader can go from Umeda by JR, expresses every 20min, Hankyu or Hanshin take 30min, cheaper. Hankyu line perhaps best. All let you off at **Sannomiya**, main downtown stn for Kobe. TAKARAZUKA Girl's Opera 40min direct by Hankyu; which stn far R-end is track to...

KYOTO best by Hankyu express every 15min → Shijo-Kawaramachi terminal in 40min. Branch off this line also serves KATSURA RIKYU and ARASHIYAMA. JR will get you into Kyoto stn in 30min, plus 2x-mtr taxi or subway to city center and is inconvenient to everything except JNTO Information Office (TIC), Honganji Temples.

NARA: **Bus** → over scenic Mt Ikoma driveway leaves from Osaka stn Plaza. Bus lines → other suburbs also from here. Meishin Expwy buses → Nagoya → Tokyo, or down Chugoku mountain expwy → Hiroshima, *see* (transfer en route) and → tip of Honshu.

SHIN OSAKA: stn is Shinkansen terminal for Osaka, frequent bullet trains NE → Tokyo (3hrs); & W/S → Okayama (hr), → Hiroshima (2hrs), → Hakata-Fukuoka (3+hrs). Also ¥-B hiway **bus** down central mountains → HIROSHIMA backwoods (*see*).

YODOYABASHI STN, next subway stop down from Umeda, or 5min walk beyond great Eki-Mae office complex is subway terminal of Keihan line → Kyoto's Shijo and Sanjo stns along Kamo River, expresses two or more hourly, take 45min. Transfer at Sanjo terminus for Lake Biwa.

UEHONMACHI stn [J-6] Kinki Nippon (Kintetsu) line, direct rocket express → Nara in half-hour every half-hour. Locals stop at Mt Ikoma, Ayameike Park, Yamato Bunka-kan museum en route. Another branch from this station serves Mt Shigi (cable car up one side, down other, on to Horyuji, *see*). Still another track sends out luxurious vista-dome express for Ise 2hrs away, and Nagoya at near-Shinkansen speed but half-price.

TENNOJI JR stn [N-5] economically important, but of almost no interest to tourist. Across tracks is Osaka Miyako Hotel and...

ABENO-BASHI stn [N-5] of Kintetsu line at Tennoji reached by subway or taxi, serves → Mount Yoshino hour out, with lovely Taima-dera Temple en route.

NAMBA [J-2] of Nankai line, S end of Midosuji Blvd has frequent thru expresses → MOUNT KOYA (1hr), and better than hourly express → Hashimoto from which Koya is short transfer. Wakayama line: 65min → Wakayama City where this first edition was for most part written and Garet was born; Osaka resorts of Shin Waka-no-Ura & Saigasaki. Continue → South Kii Peninsula JR only. Kintetsu starts here via Uehonmachi, *above*.

MINATO-MACHI stn [J-2] is JR Kansai line, going via Nara to join Tokaido old main line and Shinkansen at Nagoya.

TEMPO-ZAN HARBOR: Inland Sea cruises start from Osaka—but don't schedule yourself into Osaka just to be handy to port, as all stop next at Kobe, more pleasurable stopover by far (*see* following); also hydrofoils and car-ferries → Shikoku and Kyushu at several ports bet Osaka-Kobe, reached via Hanshin line, Umeda-Osaka stn (underground).

From **KOBE**: SANNOMIYA is main entry-exit. Above-noted JR-Hankyu-Hanshin rails link to Osaka about 30min; all stop Nishinomiya en route. JR on → almost anywhere. Hankyu → central Kyoto in 1hr+ via change midway at JUSO. W from Hankyu Sannomiya stn → Suma → Himeji Castle, W-bound Sanyo Dentetsu line cheaper but only JR continues on down Sanyo/Sunny Route (*see* following).

Taxi basic-mtr stn → Meriken Hatoba (American pier) Inland Sea main ferry port, Okura and Tower hotels.

SHIN-KOBE for Shinkansen bullet, minimum taxi or one stop on subway (¥140) above Sannomiya stn, next door to Shin Oriental Hotel and OPA shopping-entertainment complex. 15min → Kyoto but expensive tho Rail Pass valid; up 3+hrs → Tokyo; 45+min → Okayama, 1hr45min → Hiroshima, etc → end Hakata, Kyushu.

HOT WEATHER ESCAPES

Nearest OSAKA is **Mount Shigi**, fascinating Coney Island-cum-Shangri-La 440m/1440ft altitude lovely mountaintop town of temples of Koya sect Shingon tantric Buddhism—highly commercialized yet attractive for it all, with air much cooler, fresher. Our favorite English sign in Japan is on Shigi:

The home of reorganizing for fleshly and spiritual Mt. Shigisan Fasting Sanatoriums. Originator Mr Osamu Yoshida Instruct of Fasting and rightful ailment Therapy or moral culture.   —This Way Tel Oji 507

CHOGO SONSHIJI, or SHIGISAN-JI, main temple founded by Kobo-daishi, destroyed by Nobunaga 1577, rebuilt by Osakan Hideyoshi 1602. Noted for 3 superb horizontal scrolls *Shigisan engi emaki*, 1156-80, of 3 miracles of monk Myoren of Shigi—oldest narratives, highly individual caricatures set in landscape, folklore rather than court romance, 31cm/1ft high by 8.7 to 14+m long. NT art, as well as devotional object of pilgrimage.

WHERE TO STAY: San Raku-So ☎(07437)-3-2245; ¥-S hotel-inn lovely, oldish, rambling, commanding superb view. Near funicular which takes you down in few minutes to sea level Kintetsu line Shigisan-guchi stn for transfer to Namba; or taxi 7-8x-mtr → Osaka center in under 30min. **TEMPLE STAYS: Jyofuku-in** ☎(0745)-72-2581 from ¥7,000w/2; **Gyokuzo-in** ☎72-2881 from ¥6,000w/2; **Senju-in** ☎72-4481 from 6,000w/2. Roam lanes and temples and with half-day to spare take opp (2km) E-side cable car down → OJI, and 3x-mtr taxi → marvelous Horyuji temple (preceding) or 7x-mtr → Nara, or JR direct → Nara, or Kintetsu line → Kashihara tomb area S of Nara.

Mount Ikoma (betw Osaka-Nara) pleasant bus, or taxi up 10x-mtr; cross mountain crest to Shigi. **Drive** across → Nara on Hanna tollroad via Ikoma; bus; or **hiking course** from Ikoma 3.2km/2mi down stone-paved old pack-oxen road lined with 100s of red-bibbed idols past dozens of small temples, shrines including several cavern waterfalls where yamabushi-mendicants stand and chant in active meditation even midwinter—parts unchanged of pilgrims' Ise-kaido from old Japan, bottom end at Kintetsu Ishikiri stn and fascinating complex of shrines, temples, street-side great bronze Buddha, lovely homes with gardens visible over nose-high walls. Bottom is great...

ISHIKIRI-JINJA Shinto shrine to ancestor of Mononobe clan (p.351), alive with believers and no tourists; roof top upright 'stone-cutting' sword and arrows hint of Iron Age migration?, gate guardians seated Yamato era pig-tailed warriors, but still Yin-Yang. Within, numerous small shrines and temples, buy candle (honor system 3 for ¥100 into box), light and ring gong. Talismans for air travel, inscribe wooden stick w/ name, illness to burn 8th. **Torii** near upper and lower stns, main one midway, 'suit-hanger' variant on Ryobu-Shinto, odd as rectangular in section.

DATEBOOK: **Aug 3** carry mikoshi up mountain; monthly **8** burn old talismans.
CHOPSTICKS: Outside main gate and torii, soba shop on corner delicious, cheap.
Rejoin Kintetsu rail for Nara at mountain base, or below big shrine at Shin-Ishikiri stn.
GET THERE from Osaka Loop JR Namba or Tennoji stn Xfer to Kintetsu Nara line

TAIMA-DERA, 15x-mtr taxi+¥750 toll from Osaka, or Kintetsu rail from Tennoji stn to overlooked 'offbeat' temple; like KOYA (p397) can stay in temple; *see* (p370).

From KOBE same as above, or head W via itineraries in following TACHIKUI & SASAYAMA—Alt Hill Rte→ Himeji, or main SANYO 'SUNNY ROUTE' (all p.575) → Himeji, Bizen kilns, Okayama, Kurashiki folk art town; or INLAND SEA ferry routes.

KYOTO TIPS: From KOBE/OSAKE go Shinkansen to – only if have Rail Pass

otherwise prohibitive; 33min, from Shin-Kobe stn. From Sannomiya stn regular JR 1hr, next door Hankyu bit longer, change at Juso, but straight into Kyoto center, half-price; *or* MK Taxi of KYOTO will pick you up, going or coming ☎(075)-721-2237; *see* p.425.

Emperor Nintoku was on his tower (in Naniwa, Osaka),
looking far and wide, saw smoke arising plentifully....
"When smoke fills the land, people freely
attain to wealth".
                                        — Nihongi, 729 AD

OSAKA 大阪
SMOKY CITY

OSAKA LIKES to call itself 'Venice of Japan' because of several rivers flowing thru downtown area, some little more than open sewers (thankfully at last being covered or cleaned) which were once barge canals-cum-moats to Osaka Castle. Waterways and businessmen once made it in spirit very much like Venice. These rivers and gingko tree-lined main boulevard, Midosuji (Osaka-Umeda Station to Namba Station), are almost sole conventional physical attractions of this tradesman's city.

Osaka may yet come to live up to its nickname, for it has been sinking and bridges are so low that *Tenjin Festival* barges (**July 24-25**) and world's lowest-slung river ferries can barely pass under them. First impression is less of Venice, more of Chicago: opinion enhanced by acquaintance as there is little culture and even less distraction in this Oriental typhoony city.

Town has undergone 3 rebuildings postwar. Arriving in Osaka port by freighter December 24, 1951, Jay was driven 40 minutes thru rubble to city center, then rebuilding from horrendous bombings of war's final week. Second phase rebuilding was for Expo '70, following model of Tokyo Olympic '64 building frenzy, and like it included elevated expressway system, general widening of streets, new subway lines. Third is still far grander recently started Osaka-21st Century Plan which has been reviving some of city's original Venice-like verve and internationalism. Modern architecture as art has yet to be introduced to Osaka, as it has to Tokyo and even next door Kobe. But Osaka 21-Center is making modest attempt, at least of scale if not necessarily originality. And new Hilton International Hotel may set role model.

That Osaka was long well-organized (old Osaka trait) and populous is evident from passing mention in ancient records that Jimmu on his march up Japan in legendary 661BC (probably about 300AD) was beaten back from here and had to reroute his migration up Wakayama-Kii peninsula into Yamato Plain. Records do not denigrate Naniwans with epithets as spider-people, pit-dwellers or other synonyms for savages, which implies respect as equals. Recent dig in south of town turned up Jomon textile swatch some 3,000 years old, identical to hemp cloth known in poor north country till this century. Numerous archaeological sites of Yayoi era (300BC-300AD) have recently been, or are being, excavated, supporting local arrival of migration from south about 200BC. With rich alluvial plain once florid with wild edibles, its streams full of fish as was nearby bay, there is little wonder that regional deity, now incorporated into national Seven Lucky Gods, is Ebisu of that smiling face, his fishing line hauling in plump *tai*-sea bream. These fisheries are still rich, and major expense of new afloat-in-bay Osaka International Airport is compensation to fishers (many sail across from Kobe) for loss of livelihood.

Largest of imperial tombs are in Osaka at Habikino SE towards Yamato, and at S of town near Sakai. Habikino has tombs of early 5th century *tennos* Chuai #14 and son Ojin #15, whose warrior wife and mother, Jingu, invaded Korea and carried Ojin in her womb 32 months to be born back in Japan well after dad Chuai's death. During Ojin's reign mass migration of skilled Hata-Yuzuki and Aya tribes came over from Korea to introduce high-tech of their time, giving host chieftains economic-technologic power base to set up imperial system—thus Koreans claim Jingu was Korean invader. Priest Wani came from Paekche-Korea to tutor Ojin's son, brought Confucianism and basic text *1,000 Character Classic* to introduce literacy to Wa. Ojin's tomb is 415m/1,260ft long, second largest in Japan, five times size of his father's indicating sudden increase in national wealth coinciding with mom's invasion of Korea and new immigration. Nearby in Sakai off bay, short taxi from hotels, is another field of great tombs dominated by 486m/1,595ft-long, 32.3hectare/80acre mausoleum attributed to Nintoku (pyramid of Cheops in Egypt covers only 13acres), #16 mid-5th century, p354.

Identification of tombs by Imperial Household is not accepted by archaeologists. Ojin and Nintoku are probably of 'Five Kings of Wa' of Chinese Liu-Song Dynasty annals (420-479) who sent 9 embassies between 413-478 claiming suzerainty over most of southern Korea. Chinese-noted Kings San, Mi or Chin, Sei, Ko and Bu, who link thru variants in pronouncing characters in different languages as likely being Ojin #15, Nintoku #16, Ingyo #19, Anko #20, Yuryaku #21. Both records note succession usually not father-son but thru brothers, as was also custom of west Asian horsemen. These records help redate Chuai and Ojin, traditional dates 192-200 & 270-310 with 70 year hiatus, to acceptable early-mid-400s.

We thus have good date for beginnings of Osaka power in early 400s when Ojin reconquered Kyushu whence his ancestors had migrated, just as his mother Jingu had reconquered origins of her tumulus-building, horse-riding forebears in Korea—and obviously begat him while on road. So, was Ojin Korean? Or Central Asian thru Korea? If they'd open these tombs!

Economic importance is shown by fact that first Buddhist temple Shitennoji was founded here 593. Earliest urban planning, formal imperial palaces are reported in Naniwa, notably those of twice-empress Kogyoku (#35, reign 642-45, & as Saimei #37, r655-661) and Temmu (#40, r672-686) thru Mommu (#42, r697-707) until just before building of Heijo-Nara in 710. In 679 Emperor Temmu built official complex, laid out grid for capital city 4x3 km/2.5x2mi, with 16 by 12 boulevards, covering area between present castle and Osaka Station, larger than later Nara. Successors expanded small actual built-up area until Shomu (#45, r724-749) built new palace Naniwa-kyo 732. Sole remnant of this early square grid is street layout in NW center below Hilton Hotel. Shomu also experimented with palace and big buddha at Shiga near Lake Biwa, but casting failed. He then moved full seat of government to center of culture, Nara, in 745 where casting Great Buddha succeeded. New Nara seems to have combined competing power bases from Asuka-Nara and Naniwa-Osaka into one great metropolis.

'Naniwa' uses various ideographs, and there being no agreement on this today it is written commonly in hiragana syllabary. Name may mean: difficult waves, rapid-waves, wave-spray, or even garden of fish.

With shift of religio-political power to Yamato, then Nara, later Kyoto, Osaka quietly went about its favorite pastime of minding its own business— which has always been simply business: make goods and make good. As port of trade with mainland and port of entry to inland capitals Nara and Kyoto, by Middle Ages it was business hub of Japan. In 1500s it was center of powerful religio-secular group of Honganji (later split into E and West, as in temples by Kyoto Station or those two giants on Osaka's central Midosuji-blvd) merchant-knights whose temple-bastion sat atop Osaka Castle mount, with their flourishing trading port of Sakai closest Japan ever

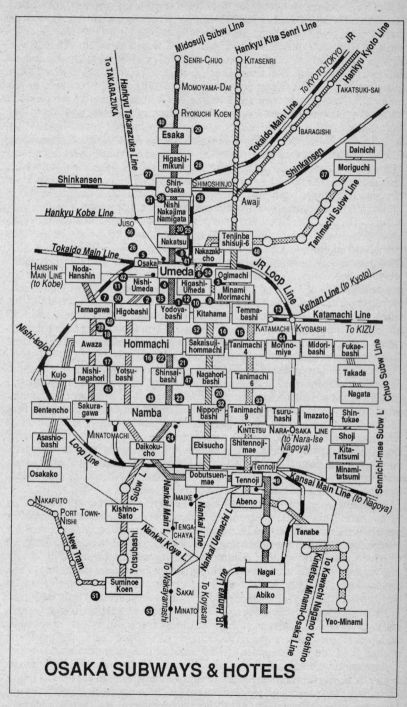

OSAKA SUBWAYS & HOTELS

Numbers indicate Hotels—see preceding Hanshin p565 for key

got to Venice-like city-republic. Hideyoshi broke temple power, got traders to cease carrying swords in 1560s (which then became exclusive symbol of samurai class), emasculating independent Osaka.

Osaka again profited from influx from Korea when craftsmen and intellectuals like family of aesthetician SEN Rikyu immigrated, bringing in Sung Chinese arts, Korean 'folksy' aesthetic. Rikyu codified *cha-do* (English misnomer 'tea-ceremony'), Tea-Way. As art advisor to Hideyoshi, peasant-warrior risen to *Tai-kun,* Great Prince, he set path for national aesthetics from then on. It is interesting to speculate how much Sen may have had to do with selecting craftsmen brought back from 1589 invasion of Korea which gave birth to all modern ceramic industries. Christians were active early in Sakai, influencing Rikyu who borrowed many elements of tea rite from Catholic mass (tea for wine, cake for wafer, special handling cloths), was suspected of being one, which may have contributed to his execution—tho other charges are suggested, from denying Hideyoshi his daughter, lese majesty, and even antique faking.

With Hideyoshi *kampaku* (regent or aide to emperor) Osaka was de facto capital. He was in fact *shogun* but could not aspire to title as he was not descended of emperors—nor was nobleman Nobunaga. This period, called Momoyama (after his south Kyoto castle site) was history's richest; brilliant renaissance of Sung China as well as all that was Japanese. Its art is characterized by power and freedom: it was as free politically as anything in Europe, especially in lively Osaka. It was as open to rise by ability as Europe's Renaissance—and just as racy, treacherous, violent. 1583-86 Hideyoshi built impregnable Osaka castle, 1.5x2mi/2.4x3.3km, in better time than he'd make today. Workers were brought from all over nation. Most stones are from nearby isle of Awaji, fit together in masterpiece of masonry. His son Hideyori was overthrown by 'trusted' Tokugawa Ieyasu who founded last great shogunal dynasty (he was descended of emperors) and moved power to Edo-Tokyo. Castle was impregnable. But Tokugawa never stormed it. He conned (great Osaka business skill) naive Hideyori into filling in outer moats as token of trust, then double-crossed him, stormed keep, overrunning thick walls (interstices filled with years' siege supply of everlasting dried tofu cakes, early K-rations). Hideyori, mother Yodogimi committed *seppuku* (a.k.a. hara-kiri). Rebellion 1637 at Shimabara (which we visit in Kyushu) included not only Christians but *ronin*, masterless samurai, survivors of this destruction of Toyotomi clan.

Osaka now became Tokugawa base to control impetuous, rich Osakans, flanked to south by cadet bastion of Wakayama castle. Osakans let politics go to Edo and went about minding their business, becoming center for textiles, limited overseas trade to southeast Asia, various manufacturing. All of which put them in ready position to grab up western technology in 1860s and lead nation into industrial revolution and international trade. Sept 1868 Osaka became open port and foreigners moved in to extraterritorial settlement in Kawaguchi S of W end of Nakanoshima. When railroad linked Kobe, they moved there to fever-free clime. Only Kawaguchi Christ Church remains. Area still center of textiles, electronics, machinery and many basic and hi-tech home and export industries, as can be seen on industrial tours. To see goods go to Tokyo—but to buy from source, come to Osaka.

Osakans are shrewd, literal-minded. Popular l7th century novel recounts how official inspectors enforced minimum standards in textiles. Towels classified by *momme*-weight were periodically weighed in 'surprise' raids. One merchant got usual day-ahead tip, laid out towels on tile roof overnite: they absorbed just enough dew to pass minimum weight. Osakan greeting is special: no formal singsong inquiries after one's health, but smiling nod and informally abrupt, '*Mo kari makka*— making any money?'

That's Osaka. And they make it quietly. **Osaka Stock Exchange**, *Shoken Torihikijo*, was founded 1878 at Kitahama in city center on site of early 18th century money exchanger. To our surprise, it is world's third largest. Market capitalization of ¥250,000,000,000,000 (1.9 trillion dollars) is bigger than London. 82 seats held by member security houses with exclusive rights to trade. 1987 listed 793 stocks in first section, 268 in 2nd, compared to Tokyo's 1096–432. That it doesn't attract much international attention like Tokyo, might well be major Euro-American oversight. It is old-fashioned floor trading with few machines evident, no glass insulates visitors' gallery from trading floor area, and more like old Wall Street movie set than Tokyo's computer showroom-exchange, Kabuto-cho.

GETTING THERE & AWAY: *See* preceding HANSHIN, p566. Under 1hr train are: KOBE (*follows*), TAKARAZUKA, and preceding NARA, KOYA MONASTERY, KYOTO; 2hrs Kintetsu vista-dome ISE GRAND SHRINE, Kashikojima. Port for Inland Sea cruises, hydrofoil to SHIKOKU, etc—ferries from ports along coast, schedules, p612.

GETTING AROUND   Day pass for subway, bus, new tram ¥800, kid ¥400.

OSAKA divides conveniently into two areas, **north** and **south**, linked like great dumbbell by its main boulevard, attractive gingko-lined **Midosuji.**

North-*Kita* (map p.579) is area around Umeda (apricot field), old main Osaka Station Plaza with its several stations (*see* ESCAPES, p566), Hankyu and Hanshin DSs, their mid-rank hotels, plus Hilton International, Terminal and Dai-Ichi Hotels in maze of theater-, bar- and little eatery-lined alleys, down to Nakanoshima (middle isle) on which are New Osaka, Osaka Grand, and ANA-Sheraton hotels; International Trade Center, Festival Hall, Nakanoshima Park and across river E, Stock Exchange and Mitsukoshi DS. This is Osaka as laid out 1300 years ago. To its NW are Plaza Hotel with near-acousticly-perfect The Symphony Hall. Just to SE outside main area looms immense Osaka Castle and new castle of business, Matsushita 21st century complex with its own detached-palace Hotel New Otani; its exquisite concert hall Izumi. Whole composing exciting new ever-growing Osaka-'Manhattan'–worth exploring.

Midosuji Boulevard runs due south from Osaka Station (Umeda) lined with great office buildings, gigantic department stores (3 each in north and south districts) in center are two immense modern temples. Boulevard reflects that power that has been Osaka's for centuries as center of factoring and manufacturing. Taxi down Mido-, Umeda stn to Namba, 3x-mtr. With time stroll its northern area and alleys either side of Nakanoshima central isle, or S between Daimaru DS–Namba stn, or at center N and S Mido-temples and surrounding wholesale alleys. First ferro-concrete building in Japan is in this area, local temple, 1914.

South-*Minami* (map p.575) is area around Namba Station of Nankai rail line which links Osaka with Wakayama and Southern Kii Peninsula (*see*) and Mt Koya Monastery. Encompasses complex of Nama Station with Namba City-mall and Takashimaya Department Store on its south; and Takashimaya Art Annex 1km to its E with large electric goods wholesale section between; vehicle-free covered shopping street paralleling Midosuji called Shinsai-bashi-suji, with kabuki theater on boulevard and maze of movies, saunas and eateries branching out around 'theater street' Dotonbori, cabaret METRO last of immense blimp-hangar dance halls, and satellite galaxy of bars, good

¥-B–T eateries; and north to its upper limits at Shinsaibashi bridge above
Daimaru and Sogo Department Stores. Alley to **Hozenji** temple romantic
below, parallel to Dotonbori. Note guys in slick hair, leather, their sandals
always 3 sizes too small even on small feet—fashionably 'cool'.

Good stay is ¥-S **Holiday Inn** on boulevard just N of river, midst pure Osaka hustle.

Beyond these two areas are three other hubs...
SHIN-OSAKA STN for TOKYO-OSAKA-KYUSHU shinkansen, is north of
Umeda-Osaka stn linked to it by direct subway or one stop on main line JR;
Osaka Castle, with new high-rise 'Manhattan' complex mentioned above;
KYOBASHI nearby, minor hub but terminal for new subway using Japan's
first linear motor car, only 5 stns to Flower Expo '90 site on old city dump
(in tradition of NY World's Fair '39), being developed; TENNOJI area with
its two stations (JR & Kintetsu), Miyako Hotel, park, museum, zoo, 103m
Tsutenkaku 'touch-heaven-tower' built 1912 with first elevator, now
Bowery of Osaka; rebuilt Shitennoji temple—all SW of Namba, linked to it
by JR train and Midosuji-line subway or short taxi.

TRAVEL AIDS

TIC at wicket New Osaka Stn 8-8pm ☎305-3311, or Osaka Stn 8-7pm ☎345-2189,
6020 at far E-end (R-facing) in last storefront before pedestrian bridge to Hankyu Stn.
Guides: Systematized Goodwill Guides, SGG, (*see* p562) or thru TIC ☎305-3311.

Maps: Good free maps available front desk or bell desk most hotels. Our favorite: good
maps *Discover Kinki* colorful monthly tourist tabloid. Also pocketable *Meet Osaka* (Q).

Home Visit thru TIC, above, free, no interpreter needed as families cooperating have at
least one English-speaking member. Nice, but not required, to bring visiting gift—if
possible something hometown or personal, low price, as personal remembrance.

Industrial Tours: special Osaka offering, take you to everything from
fabulous electronics makers to local brewery, with extra volunteer guide;
¥3,000 regular, occasional special ¥4,000, incl lunch. Arrange thru your hotel desk,
JTB office, or Osaka Municipal Tourist Information Office, TIC Osaka Stn, Eng –7pm
☎345-2189/6020 or New Osaka Stn–8pm ☎305-3311. Held only tourist seasons, check
by phone; Advise phone rsve as soon as possible as often fully booked, but one day ahead
will usually get you in.

1989 includes: Snow dairy, Coca Cola, Bureau of Mint, Asahi Press, Vinegar, Glico
Confections, Hakutsuru Sake (Kobe), Lion Dentifrice, Kansai Electric, Meiji Seika
Cookies, Sapporo Beer, Kirin Beer, Osaka Gas, showroom Panasonic Square, Tekijuku
ancient med school, NHK broadcasting, Port of Osaka sightsee by boat; daily, take in var
2 of above, in season only; meet abt 9am at Osaka Stn TIC, tour one company, lunch
(prepay ¥500 or brown-bag it), tour 2nd company, end abt 4pm at TIC or at last site.

Kirin Brewery, Amagasaki, most popular beer with 70% of market, world's 4th
largest brand. Eng guide, rsve req ☎(06)-499-3521, 90min tour mon-fri, some sats, *free*.

SIGHTSEEING

IN THIS after-dark town negligible. PM 3-4hr bus tours ¥2,010-3,540 from Osaka
Stn plaza, but we do not recommend them. Possible are evening offerings irregularly,
Shin-Osaka (new Osaka) **Course**, 6pm, 3hrs with cabaret stops; **Flower Course**,
5pm, 4hr30min, for Tsutenkaku 'downtown', **Bunraku-za** theater (hopefully, *Bunraku*
puppets on boards) and tea parlor; ¥ varies. **River Cruise** *see* AQUABUS, next.

Aquabus, world's lowest-profile passenger boat only 6ft above waterline, plies city
waterways, ducking under bridges, as most dramatic taxi to New Otani free to registered
guests from pier at **Yodoya-bashi** bridge in center Nakanoshima by Midosuji Blvd, to
Castle Park nr New Otani. Additional pier at **Temmabashi** nr Tenjin Shrine.
Regular year-round cruise (unless noted–¥1,600, kids half) 10am-6pm every 30-60min
from Castle, Temmabashi +10min, Yodoyabashi +20min, board any, get off any, cruise
rivers. Mar 1-Nov 30 last boat 4pm, Apr 1-Sept 30 weekends, hols last 6pm, **evening**

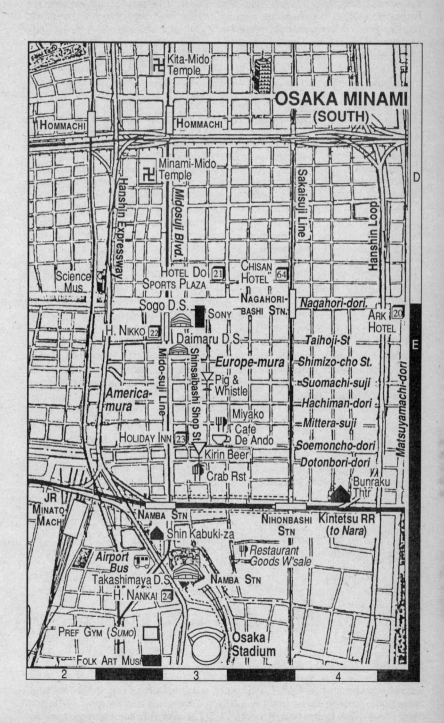

OSAKA MINAMI (SOUTH)

Kita-Mido Temple

HOMMACHI

HOMMACHI

Minami-Mido Temple

Midosuji Blvd.

Hanshin Expressway

Sakaisuji Line

Hanshin Loop

D

Science Mus.

HOTEL DO SPORTS PLAZA 21

CHISAN HOTEL 64

NAGAHORI-BASHI STN.

Nagahori-dori.

ARK HOTEL 20

Sogo D.S.

SONY

E

H. NIKKO 22

Daimaru D.S.

Taihoji-St

Shimizo-cho St.

Matsuyamachi-dori

Europe-mura

Suomachi-suji

Shinsaibashi Shop St.

Pig & Whistle

Hachiman-dori

Mido-suji Line

Mittera-suji

America-mura

Miyako

Cafe De Ando

Soemoncho-dori

HOLIDAY INN 23

Dotonbori-dori

Kirin Beer

Crab Rst

Bunraku Thtr

JR

MINATO-MACHI

NAMBA STN

NIHONBASHI STN

Kintetsu RR (*to Nara*)

Shin Kabuki-za

Restaurant Goods W'sale

Airport Bus

Takashimaya D.S.

NAMBA STN

H. NANKAI 24

PREF GYM (*SUMO*)

Osaka Stadium

FOLK ART MUS.

2   3   4

tours from 5, 6, 7pm, Jul-Aug 8pm—also **Twilite Cruise** w/2 jugs tap-beer and snacks, Sept 15-30 *Tsukimi* **Moon-viewing Cruise** with *matcha*-tea and koto music, all extra feature tours ¥2,000. *Cherry Viewing* early April 10–4pm. Rsve ☎444-5000.

Summer Walking Tours by editors of *Discover Kinki*, Aug all day sat, may expand if demand ¥1,000/kids-500 + admissions. **Calvin Yamada** ☎763-4926 (Eng).

KYOTO-NARA full day tour **Fujita** ¥11,000 w/lunch ☎(075)-222-0121 or hotel desk.

We suggest **taxi** from hotel and make half-day round on your own. Hire-cars available thru hotels for 4hr half-day trip in and around Osaka, ¥20,000 1990. Taxi on your own, while more trouble and slightly smaller, run ¥3-4,000 (negotiable with driver, no fixed rate) per hr for 5-psgr *chugata* mid-size, 10% less for smaller 4-psgr *kogata*, or 7-9x-mtr.

Sample o.w. escape rates '91: center → TAKARAZUKA ¥5,000/11x-mtr; → KOBE-Sannomiya 13x-mtr; → HORYU-JI 25x-mtr; → NARA 20x-mtr; → KOYA 50x-mtr; → KYOTO 30x-mtr; plus addit expressway tolls ranging KOBE ¥800 to KYOTO ¥2,300.

Warning: traffic '80s into early '90s getting worse, especially **monthly 5, 15, 25** & last day when small-medium business cashiers race around making personal collection calls coagulating traffic so that arterial roads get sclerosis. Check on traffic at desk.

From Kita area...

Hilton International, Dai Ichi, Terminal, Hankyu, New Osaka or **Grand Hotels**, we suggest **taxi** to station plaza, drive down **Midosuji Blvd** (no down blvd) between lines of gingko trees which gild autumn air, past **NORTH** and **SOUTH MIDO TEMPLES** R (respectively E & West Honganji *see* KYOTO) and L great **Sogo** and **Daimaru** Department Stores. Pass **Holiday Inn** L and cross Ebisu-bashi Bridge and pause to look L along Dotonbori and its many popular theaters, fun to come back to later when afoot at nite to see lights and fountains in river, neons galore and one block E on corner **Kirin Beer Hall**, its space age architecture so fascinated Michael Douglas in his movie Black Rain. Continue past, R, theatrically dramatic **Kabuki Theater** (new shows monthly but mostly melodrama, Kabuki only few times yearly, no *tachimiseki*, see KTO). Next block is Namba Stn, with **Takashimaya DS** atop and new ['90] **Nankai South Tower Hotel** and **Namba City** mall behind, acting as stopper to Midosuji.

Exquisite...

SUMIYOSHI SHRINE (Alt #29 NAMBA dock opp Takashima-ya DS, on street L/W of Midosuji Blvd) prime example of Shinto architecture, vermillion Shangri-La escape in busy city, blending with nature; originally bayside, now 5km inland. **June 14** exotic rice-transplanting rites here—all work done by women, which might be secret of Osaka's success.

Then loop past (taxi only, no bus), pause at, emperor Nintoku 5th century moated **burial mound**, almost 2.5 times volume of pyramid of Cheops, perhaps largest man-made tomb-mound in world, tho far less treasure laden (we presume, tho Sasan-Persian glass came out) than China's Xian. City hopes to make more attractive, accessible. Budgeteer alternate is SUMIYOSHI → TENNOJI by #48 thence JR Hanwa Line local 19min → 10th stn MOZU (written '100-tongue-bird') walk 5min to base of keyhole tomb; circle halfway either way, to MIKUNI-GA-OKA stn same line or same name stn Koya line if going/coming Koya → Namba; or return same way.

Back to **Tennoji Park**, with **Botanical Garden** (pass), **Keitaku-en** Japanese garden-**Municipal Art Museum**—its main **Kurayashiki gate** feudal era remnant (fine Buddhist art collection, loan shows–LACMA Japan Collection previewed here years before LA bldg started: *see KTO* or *Kinki*), and 1912 Osaka version of Eiffel Tower **Tsutenkaku** in 'Bowery' once Shin-Sekai 'future city' and now full of lost, drifting old men. N to **SHITENNOJI** temple, handsome, first in Japan tho now all 'archaeological restoration' in concrete of oft-war-ravaged wooden original. This and Asuka, Horyuji temples

(Nara), were first three Buddhist temples in country; each represents one of three basic temple ground plans (various placements of buildings, orientation, etc). Its archaic silhouette, unlike other surviving temples in Japan, reminds of Himalayan monasteries. **Apr 10, 22**, stately 8th cent **Bugaku** court dances in fabulous brocade, Tibetan masks: rarely seen tourist poster stuff. **21st**, monthly flea market.

GETTING THERE: *Alternate* subway Tanimachi Line to Shitennoji-mae stn, Midosuji Line and JR Loop Line to Tennoji stn, walk 10min.

Osaka Castle Japan's largest—reconstruction except some out buildings, gate and gigantic stone foundations original or 17th century Ieyasu rebuilding of smaller keep he totally leveled 100m NW of present. Now center of handsome sport complex. Forego entering Castle itself, unless glutton for samurai memorabilia found in all castle-museums, or with time to sit it out at **New Otani Hotel** (good lunch break, ¥-L restaurants/¥-T coffee shop). Site successively of neolithic Yayoi village, 7th century palace, medieval Buddhist Honganji temple-fort & Hideyoshi's castle, of which remain only Otemon-main gate, Inui, Sengan & Tanon turrets; rest leveled by victorious new Shogun TOKUGAWA Ieyasu after betraying Hideyori and Yodogimi. Tokugawa Castle was destroyed in civil war of Imperial forces vs Tokugawa shogun in 1860s. Keep rebuilt 1930 of concrete, US Army Wolfhounds HQ in US Occupation. Drive into castle grounds, circle inner moat and out again. Top floor of great castle donjon commands unobstructed view. However high views of Japanese cities generally unrewarding, and that of besmogged, shabby Osaka is particularly so (anyway, better–only good one in town as good view of castle–from next door Hotel New Otani, or from 2nd highest pinnacle, Hilton's Top-of- restaurant). Castle was built by Tai-kun, Great Prince, Hideyoshi late 16th century on European model. Tales of his opulence gave us term 'tycoon'. Facing this are **Twin Towers & Panasonic Square** (elctronic 'wonderland' showplace), of his late 20th century counterpart tycoon MATSUSHITA Konnosuke, self-made lord of Matsushita companies–National, Panasonic, Victor, etc, etc. Osaka of old and new, but ever Osaka the Grand. This area fast developing further as future city center.

GETTING THERE: N under 3km 1.5x-mtr, or JR loop Tennoji stn 5 stns → Morinomiya, walk 10min, or #1 → Castle-front terminus; then taxi or afoot circle... *Otherwise* subway Tanimachi line → Tanimachi-4-ch or Chuo-line → same.

Continue on W then N across first bridge to Nakanoshima, thru park, cross 2nd bridge, turn L (10min walk) to...
TENMANGU SHRINE, *Osaka Tenjin* which **July 25** is center of great Osaka *Tenjin Boat Festival*, **24th** grand boat procession, fireworks **24th nite**. Worth stroll thru any time, very Osaka. From here suggest walk last km, 10-15min, back down toward river, but R at fork then L (*alt*, catch river bus at 10min past hr for hr river tour).

Cross bridge to...
Nakanoshima 'Middle Isle' continuing on across 50m's of isle, cross next bridge and down block takes us to **Osaka Stock Exchange**, 3rd largest in world. On Isle, turn R, walk paths toward stone buildings.

New one on S (L) is...
Museum of Oriental Ceramics, former Ataka Collection (Korean, Chinese, Japanese), not to be missed by ceramic buffs, one of best in world, rotates its plentiful treasures (*see* below). ¥400, X-mon.

Direct access Midosuji subway to Yodoyabashi stn or Sakaisuji line to Kitahama, or riverboat from Otani hotel; 15min walk (R) hotels Hilton, Dai Ichi, Terminal etc.

Yodoyabashi stn, exit rear R to Kitahama underground 300m to exit #17, upstairs in front, L, on Uchi-Kitahama-dori, next W to big Nissho Iwai bldg is...

School of 'Dutch Studies', *Teki-jyuku,* of interest to MDs and educators: oldest wooden merchant's house in Osaka, 1843, locale of first school of *Ran-gaku*—written with ideograph for orchid, *ran,* being short for *Oranda,* 'Holland', plus 'studies' and meaning 'Western Science'. Established by OGATA Koan (1810-1863) after his own private studies in Osaka, Nagasaki, Edo. Returned to Osaka 1838 to set up medical practice, moved to this site in 1843. In 1858 cholera epidemic, despite conservative opposition introduced vaccination with vaccine from calves. Many graduates became Meiji Restoration leaders: FUKUZAWA Yukichi great educator-founder of Keio U, SANO Tsunetami founder Japan Red Cross, OGATA Koreyoshi (his son) founder Osaka U Medical School (one of two fountainhead med schools), others. After his death in Edo, where he was shogun's personal physician, building was used as hospital. Named ICA 1969, restored 1978. At Chuo-ku Kitahama 3-30, ☎231-1970; 10-4 X-sun, mon; ¥200.

Sometimes visited on **Industrial Tour**, above.

2nd stop Midosuji subway S, or 20min walk down boulevard back (L-S), to...

Sony Bldg modern tower, and block E of it stone bridge elevated to cross avenue—old Shinsaibashi bridge raised as pedestrian crossing after canal it bridged was made underground parking. Bridge was remarkable in that original, replacing country's first steel bridge (German) used no mortar, no two stones same size, all held together by pressures of arch—sacrificed in reconstruction as road portion minus supporting arch sits on steel frame.

Idemitsu Museum of Arts (2nd corner E, on N-side Nagahori Blvd) major international traveling shows and loans from main collection in Tokyo, of Chinese, Middle Eastern, Japanese or other major fine art; 10-5, X-mon, ¥-var.

This Sony Bldg corner begins...

Shinsaibashi-suji, interesting half-mile or so shop-stroll of small good shops down from **Sogo** and **Daimaru** Dept Stores to **Takashimaya** and **Printemps** DS. Alleys facing Takashimaya to R (E & S)—especially block E to N-S street *Dohgu-ya-suji* (Tool-St)—are wholesale district: open-front restaurant suppliers best places to buy various quality utensils, some quite decorative, and those vinyl food replicas used in eatery windows as menus (restaurateurs bring color prints of your own specialties to have reproduced, not cheap, but how original). Best probably Kimura Display 2nd block down Dohguya-St on R (W). Many places sell *aka-chochin* red lanterns, other decor.

Road R from Takashimaya winds 15min stroll to electronic wholesale area of **Nihonbashi** a.k.a. **Den-den Town**, as good as Tokyo's Akihabara but not so publicized. Always haggle, even tho first quote may be under list.

SPORTS

Sumo, one of six national tournaments Mar, 15 consecutive days sunday nearest 10th thru sun: ask at hotel desk, or Sumo office ☎641-0770. Box for 4, ¥30,-75,000 w/bento-lunch most fun, sgle ¥4,-5,500 in pairs; on sale mid-Feb 2 days only and usually sell out; but Visa has some seats for card holders, sell out 6-8 wks ahead, ¥14,000 chair, ¥65,000 box, ☎(06)-64-6301; budgeteer check playguides dept stores or main stns or go on day 9am, try luck at 400 non-rsve upper bleachers ¥500, mid level ¥1200, 1 per person, get ticket and return. Taxi *Furitsu Taiku-kan* Pref Gym or Midosuji subway front car to Namba stn exit 5, few min SW (down-R).

Horse racing, track hour from town, nr Kyoto at YODO (taxi 10-13x-mtr).
Hotel desk has seasonal schedule for major tracks, free by Japan Racing Association.
Bicycle racing, Nishinomiya, by Hankyu line towards Kobe, midway.
Baseball-crazy Osaka-Kobe have 2 teams (of national 12) both RR-owned: '85 champs Hanshin Tigers in Nishinomiya (midway Osaka-Kobe, taxi 7-10x-mtr from hotels, Hanshin train to Hanshin Koshien, from Umeda plaza terminal). Kintetsu

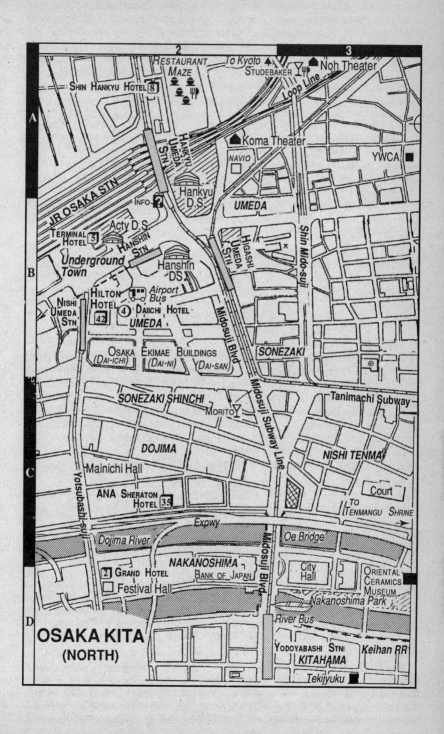

SHIN HANKYU HOTEL 8
RESTAURANT MAZE
To Kyoto
STUDEBAKER
Noh Theater
Loop Line

A

Koma Theater
NAVIO
YWCA

JR OSAKA STN
INFO 2
Hankyu D.S
UMEDA

HANKYU UMEDA STN

TERMINAL HOTEL 5
Acty D.S
HANSHIN STN
Underground Town
Hanshin D.S
HIGASHI UMEDA STN

B

NISHI UMEDA STN
HILTON HOTEL
Airport Bus
DAIICHI HOTEL
4
42
UMEDA
Midosuji Blvd
SONEZAKI

Shin Mido-suji

OSAKA EKIMAE BUILDINGS
(DAI-ICHI) (DAI-NI) (DAI-SAN)

SONEZAKI SHINCHI
MORITO
Tanimachi Subway

DOJIMA

NISHI TENMA

C

Mainichi Hall
Yotsubashi-suji
Midosuji Subway Line
Court

ANA SHERATON HOTEL 35
TO TENMANGU SHRINE

Expwy
Dojima River
Oe Bridge
City Hall
ORIENTAL CERAMICS MUSEUM

NAKANOSHIMA
2 GRAND HOTEL
BANK OF JAPAN
Midosuji Blvd
Festival Hall
Nakanoshima Park

River Bus

D

OSAKA KITA
(NORTH)
YODOYABASHI STN
KITAHAMA
Keihan RR
Tekijyuku

Buffaloes E of town toward Nara at Fujiidera on Kintetsu RR, from Kintetsu DS at its terminal Abenobashi stn (Tennoji). At least 2 games on TV daily, one on TV Osaka UHF, most are niters. Braves and Hawks moved franchises.

For total baseball nuts, country stops functioning for 10 days each of spring (late Mar) & summer (end Aug) High School Baseball Tournaments at Koshien stadium (above), emotionally wilder than all US Bowls combined, usually sold out. Watch on NHK-TV. Boosters good Anthropology PhD.

We have seen Japan in capsule, and we haven't even left Osaka yet.

Aquarium *Kaiyukan*: stupendous, tank 4 storeys, view var depth/life-form levels. Sea life around Pacific "Rim of Fire": local Inland Sea to Tasmania, Chile.... Documentary film areas but no E signs. Heart of newly developing port area with great future potential, but more for resident than int'l tourist. Fab view sunset betwn lighthouses Nov 22-Jan 22 from rear plaza. ☎576-5500 Adm steep ¥1,950 worth it; open–8pm, Jul-Aug–9pm, even weekend crowd nil after 5pm. GET THERE: subway Bentencho → Osaka-ko-port. Next door shops, ¥-T fish eateries.

EXHIBITIONS

SEVERAL FINE private art galleries, superb DS galleries (especially **Takashimaya** and 2 **Daimarus**) and rotating sections of excellent **Tennoji National Museum**, covered in *Mainichi Daily News*, *KTO* & *Kinki*. Small museums in outskirts, also in papers. Museums listed from N Osaka to S.

Navio Gallery, top traveling shows, many international, in Navio Hankyu bldg 3rd fl, E-side Hankyu Stn-DS, 11-7:30PM (entry); X-varies, ¥-varies.

Museum of Oriental Ceramics, *Toyo Togei-kan* on Nakanoshima Isle houses superb Ataka Collection of 1,000+(rotated) Far Eastern ceramics presented to city as testimony to devotion of collector-aesthete, in fine building exquisitely mounted and lit; 9-4:30, X-mon, ¥400; (*see* p577).

Idemitsu Museum of Arts (*see* p578).

N across river, 5min walk from JR Katamachi Stn...
Fujita Art Museum Castle, top classic Japanese shows, (10-4 Mar-Jun & Sep-Nov only, ¥-var, X-mon); combine stroll thru **Taiko-en Garden** across street, *free*, 10am-9pm, firefly viewing summer, restn'ts.

Natural History Museum in Osaka Castle, not very worthwhile, may improve.

Below Namba to R (W)...
Folk Art Museum, *Mingei-kan*, by Folk Art Society, has good shows, mostly Japan, occasional imports, good shop (another in **Museum Park**).

(**Gutai Pinacotheca**, that real far out modern art gallery is, alas, gone.)

Osaka Municipal Art Museum (in Tennoji Park) one section visiting shows ¥500-up, varies; separate House exhibit Japanese and East Asian fine art includes superb collection Chinese stone Buddhas, ¥200; 9:30-4.

Museum of Liberty, *Jinken Rekishi Shiryokan*, a.k.a. Museum of Discrimination, originally devoted to plight of Eta or Burakumin (ghetto-folk) in Osaka, added other ignored victims of prejudice: handicappped, Minamata mercury victims, collections to Ann Frank as well as toys & trivia insulting to Blacks. 10-5, X-mon,hol; ☎561-5891. **Get There:** JR loop-el Ashiharabashi stn, 8min walk S on wide st to R curve, on R.

Mondo-Yakujin, collection of our favorite artist: early 20th century Zen painter-cartoonist TOMIOKA Tessai (1837-1924), marvelous religious parodist and discovery of NY Met curator. Fascinating temple complex, scenic pilgrim shopping lane leads from station. **Get There:** Hankyu to Nishinomiya, midway Osaka-Kobe, change at rt angle track to N-bound Takarazuka line, to first stop.

MUSEUM PARK at *Banpaku* expo '70 site: subway main Midosuji line to Senri-chuo, Expoland bus or monorail to Nihon-tei-en mae, short walk (time = last entry) **Japan Folkcraft Museum**, Banpaku-complex, X-wed, great academic collection, but not nearly as interesting setting as KURASHIKI, p628; 10-4:30, ¥500, ☎877-1971.

National Ethnology Museum, *Minpaku*, for hi-tech plus hands-on displays (you may fondle some exhibits, thump drums, etc) of world traditions. Growing fast and procuring wisely if still inadequately-financed; computerized video disc libr has great selection of documentaries, many in Eng, but exhibit labels only J. 9:00-4:30, X-wed, day after hol; ¥360, ☎876-2151.

National Museum of International Art also Expo '70 Park, mostly imported Occidental traveling shows; X-wed, 10-4:30 entry, ¥1,100, ☎876-2487.

Nihon tei-en, classic Japanese Landscape Garden, seasonal flowers rotate, 9-4, ¥210.

Yayoi era Culture & Archaeology Mus, JR from Tennnoji: *see* p355.

OPEN AIR MUSEUM of Antique J- Farm Houses, in Mino: dozen-odd typical regional antique (2-300 yrs old) homes in landscaped setting. Many we will see, or have seen, in situ if travelling byroads, but for those with little time for off-mainline touring yet interested in lovely domestic architecture, this is your only opportunity to see such. Archaeological reconstructions (like TORO, Shizuoka) often have old style log granaries on stilts with rat blocker-rings, similar to those engraved on ancient bronzes of 2,000 years ago, as still seen in Ainu villages in Hokkaido or here. Japanese theater was highly developed even in villages, as we see in our travels, or here in this Kabuki theater from Shodo-shima isle off Kobe, itself reached by ferry.

Local wooden architecture is in essence prefab modular, as units of fixed measurements precut, moved to final construction site, with roof raised first on main posts then house—or temple or palace—assembled under it by mortice and tenon linkages, or in older cases by lashing. This allows for disassembling and moving, as we see was done often in early succession of capitals in Nara and Kyoto. Lately with dams filling great mountain valleys in Hida area, those marvelous *gassho-zukuri*, 'praying hands' construction 'extended-family tenements' of up to 5 storeys and holding perhaps 3 dozen relatives and supporters, were moved to towns and cities and rebuilt as *Furusato* chain restaurants, or as pottery museums (KATO Takuo, Nagoya, p301) or folk art museums, etc. (To buy one and have it erected with modernizations anywhere o'seas, *see* KAMAKURA–SHOPPING p241). We can stay in gassho-zukuri minshuku in Hida, or just visit one here. *Magari-ya* or 'bent house' is L-shape combination barn-home of northerly horse breeders, where again we can visit them in situ as minshuku, restaurants or museums, or here as they were in their original unadorned, unadapted simplicity.

Best assemblage of folk houses in country, each superb: 4 National Treasures (NT), 5 Osaka Prefectural treasures. Alas, meant to be thoroughly refurbished each generation, costly labor now prohibits unless subsidized (so far not), which also accounts for steady demise in smaller towns. So enjoy here while you can; ¥400, X-mon, New Year.

GETTING THERE: Midosuji subway up to Hattori Ryokuchi Park Stn then 500m/7min walk W past *Saboten-Koen*, **Cactus Park** Amusement Ctr with good reasonable restaurant, tropical cocktails; 10min walk on thru park, past ponds, is **YH** stay, ☎(06)-862-0600, and if summer take dip in Cactus Park swimming pool.

SHOPPING

KYOTO OR KOBE, 30min away offer more of interest to tourist, in comparison shopping in Osaka is limited despite its seeming plenitude. We like to stroll Shinsaibashi covered shopping street where better variety shops are: start **Daimaru** & **Sogo** DS, end **Takashimaya** & **Printemps** DS Namba stn. Hachiman-dori, first traffic signal below Daimaru, has several interesting art & curio shops both sides; highish, some English. Novel ikat weave folk cotton denim like cloth in **Kurume-Kasuri** shop SW corner of Suomachi intersection.

On down, **Fujiya Restaurant** ¥-B place for good W-lunch.

Little further on, there's ivory shop and then snake shop, actually *Kanpo-yaku*, Chinese traditional medicines (powdered snake for your ills). E of this area, L, toward Nihonbashi 3-chome Takashimaya DS Art Annex (of no interest) is **wholesale electrical goods** section, great discounts. Then *Setomono-cho* **chinaware street**, Nishi Yokobori, wholesale-retail shops have all 3rd week in July for pottery fair at bargain prices. Look for shops selling plastic model food for show-window menus, great souvenir.

Best shopping is at huge department stores, of which Osaka can rightly be proud. Our favorites are **Takashimaya** at Namba Stn with **Daimaru** and **Sogo** 10min walk N, and **Hankyu** facing Osaka Station and new **Daimaru Acty** rising above it into **Terminal Hotel**. Fun shop-stroll is from basement of **Hanshin** DS (facing Osaka Stn), especially for those staying in **Hilton** with direct access to underground city, thru subway arcade under Umeda-Osaka Stn plaza. Here you find entire subterranean streets of shops, one alley 2nd R from Hilton exit is just of shops each selling folkcrafts and special products of different regions. Whole area is honeycombed with 2 storeys of subterranean shops, good ¥-B-T restaurants (most quite good, show-window 'menus') amid plazas and fountains. Most dept stores have folkcraft *mingei* section: long best is **Takashimaya.**

*Block SE of Takashimaya...***Mingei** city's sole folkart-only shop; 1st fl pottery, glass, basketry. 2d fl furniture, textiles. 10-6, X-wed, ☎633-3836.

We found only maker in Osaka of hand-painted Boys' Day cloth flying carp streamers which color countryside around May 5. Makes them from 2 to 30 feet in length year round in his family-shop. Lovely souvenirs. Knowing maker is helpful as they're hard to get out-of-season. You can get them from stock at his home or choose special for made-to-order: **Takagi Shoten**, Sakai City, ☎(0722)-63-2205, Nankai Line from Namba, Haguromo stn.

Such products as cameras are, if not cheapest in Japan, as cheap in Osaka, where prices are well below list depending upon brand name and whether bought for cash or plastic. Motomachi in Kobe also as good. But check your prices back home before planning major shopping.

30min by fast electric gets you to...
KYOTO, as it will to even older **NARA,** also shopping adventure.Bit further afield, still convenient to full-day's expedition, would be shopping in Kyoto, ancient seat of culture and center of arts manufacturers.

For exotic shopping one of top curio-antique furniture dealers is in Kyoto (p.544) in ancient mansion of *New Yorker* author—art expert **David Kidd** ☎(075)-751-8552, never before noon, for appt, prefer evening to round out day in Kyoto. Serious collectors only.

However, anything made in Japan today—electronics to folk baskets—can be found within minutes of main hotels. Japanese make shopping adventure yet leisurely pleasure. No one will hustle you to buy. Display is art. In Dept Stores counters are interspersed with fascinating eating. Budgeteer or addicted nosher should go downstairs to usually two basements of food counters, where endless tasty nibbles, samples of local exotica are set out in trays on counters for you to pick at—stand of toothpicks evident to avoid greasy fingers. And when you do purchase something, watch it being wrapped—great art Japanese excel in whether wrapping fish in bamboo leaf, or *How to Wrap 5 Oranges* (title of exquisite coffee table book on this art) or art works (mostly in specially made fine-wood fire-retarding boxes) to sado-masochistic nude trussing and bondage knot-tying. Best of all—in marketplace, back alley or subway station labyrinth, as ancient travelers all recount one sees local folks at their most natural, 'native' behavior.

ON STAGE

ALSO THIN, with few good stages more often dark. Home of *Bunraku* puppets at new **Bunraku-za Theater** [E-4] (Nihonbashi E of Sakai-suji, N-side of elevated hiway) ☎212-1122/1081, more often stages human modern mellerdrammer, trio-handled dolls on stage only about 13 weeks in year–Jan, Apr, July, Nov–alternating to Tokyo; with experimental rock-bunraku; 2 different shows 10–2:30 abt, & 4–8, both ¥4,200, one ¥3,500, 15% student discount.

Kabuki at Shin-Kabuki-za theater [J-2] on Midosuji few blocks above Namba stn (Midosuji subway), opp Holiday Inn. Plays less flamboyant than Tokyo but more use of stage gimmicks; some months mixed program with soap opera-ish modern plays. To be sure it's *kabuki,* check program-scheds in *KTO* or *Mainichi*. Alas, no more *tachimi-seki* peanut gallery tix for single plays.

Bugaku at **SHITENNO-JI** temple [M-5] April 10, 22.

Noh, Osaka Nohgaku Kaikan [A-3] ☎373-1727, tel or check *KTO*, *Mainichi*.

DOTONBORI [I-3] is local theater-row once noted for several kabuki stages and, until recently Asahi-za Bunraku theater, now lined with movie houses showing both Japanese films and imports, several with stage shows, family music halls, burlesques. (Just off this street where it crosses Midosuji Blvd is **Shin Kabuki-za** Theater [J-2]). Fun stroll especially at nite, theaters are inexpensive enough to invite your dropping in casually for brief sampling. During spring and autumn, when all cities burst forth with stage shows and special exhibitions many of these theaters stage galas.

Takarazuka Girls' Review, Takarazuka City, p.566, 40 min out by Hankyu RR (who developed theater to build iness for its train) from its Umeda Stn: taxi 11x-mtr; weekdays 1pm, sat, sun, hol 11am & 3pm, X-wed; program in *Mainichi, KTO* which also check for any special offerings of folk dances or such at either of main concert halls: **Festival Hall** and **Mainichi Hall**, both few min walk from Kita main hotels; or DS theaters. These, also superb **The Symphony Hall** of Asahi TV, and newest acoustic wonder **Izumi Hall** next to New Otani, show top local artists and imported stars. Especially springtime during Asahi and Mainichi Cultural (theater) Festivals.

Modern theater becoming more active on numerous small stages, tho nothing like frenzy of hall-building of Tokyo. Watch *KTO, KINKI, Mainichi*.

CHOPSTICKS

FOOD IS something Osakans talk much of, and do much about. There are some good restaurants at reasonable prices, but they cater almost exclusively to limited clientele and are hard to get to, harder at times to get in. Hotel restaurants were long below Tokyo standards, over-priced, unimaginative, until Hilton and Otani stormed in in '86, raised levels along with prices. But you get what you pay for, and if at one or other on iness stay, selection of restaurants is daunting, Western thru Japanese and Chinese (Otani's excellent menus are detailed explanatory textbooks on each cuisine), all top quality ¥-L.

North (*Kita*) has 2 of 3 best *classical* Japanese restaurants: **Kitcho** at Koraibashi-3-chome, ☎231-1937, 4th block below Midosuji-Yodoyabashi and 3 E; and **Tsuruya** of Worlds' Fairs fame since Brussels '58, Imabashi-5-ch, ☎231-0456. Expensive and worth it; advise hotel or local iness associate call ahead to rsve and set menu; expensive, but no more than ¥-L hotel restaurant.

Club Maiko for moderate-price affordable Geisha & *kaiseki* ¥6,000 geisha svce, 20min show, (*see* details SOUTH); VO bldg, B1fl, Sonezaki-kita-shinchi 1ch, 6-10, ☎344-2913.

KOBE STEAK: excellent **OX-1** lunch ¥3,-5,000, but dinner rustler price ¥10,-15,000, till 11pm, at Fukushima JR stn, nxt W from Osaka stn, min taxi ☎458-0901. *Tops* is... **Morita** small posh expense acct bar of type that scares us off, but barten-owner 'Johnny' spks E-, welcomes foreigner: hotel prices, 3-4 liesurely drinks w/nibbles, gab ¥4,-5,000ea ...And his steaks best anywhere: just choose weight of fillet, tell how rare and he disappears behind bar. Lady is his wife, young gal daughter, your fellows mostly execs. Nr Hilton, SE to Mido & Ume-shin, corner Toei movie, down Mido- first R, nxt corner on L, [**C-2**], ☎344-9387. Cash only, no plastic, regulars never see bill sent to company.

Basement of Hilton's neighbor Hilton Plaza, is **Victoria Station** for affordable US beef, salad bar, bar. Out from Plaza basement into vast underground Station Plaza, full of cubby-hole drinking spots and nibbleries for salarymen—cheap, good, hospitable.

Other good restaurant and nite life alleys for common worker are from E of Hankyu Umeda stn cross movie lined street and go behind Navio ship-shaped theater bldg head E, almost any attractive-to-you restaurant, window model menus, coffee houses galore, safe cheap bars like Suntory chain; cross under overhead hiway where several stages advertise good *real* live Dixie, Banana Hall offers avant garde theater, modern dance irreg (see KTO).

Another, perhaps even cheaper, runs perpendicular to this one block in E from Midosuji blvd, back of 'Greek Temple' facade diamond store on Mido- where it angles into blvd—mix of cheap food and peep shows. All safe and worth at least stroll just for their street shills and touts, to see how common 'salaryman' enjoys himself in Osaka.

For those who insist on modern spic'n'span this rabbit warren tradition continues in modern buildings with in-house cubist fountains and surrealist landscapes such as **Kappa Yokocho**, water-imp lane, behind Hankyu stn N of **Kosho-no-machi** (rare old book town good for ukiyoe. prints, picture-books etc till 7-8pm) with numerous eateries, window models, from trad J, robatayaki, noodles to Korean, Chinese and W-; all ¥-B-T.

Natural Food: **Sugi-no-ko**, *teishoku* ¥1,000, Nishitenma, near Umeda JR, next to Kansai TV, 11:30-2:30, 4:30-9pm, X-sun, hols; ☎363-3456. **Gen-gen**, *genmai teishoku* ¥750, Sonezaki-shinchi, N of Mainichi News Bldg, 11-6pm, X-sun, hols, ☎348-0115. **Country-life Restaurant**, ¥800, 11-2:30pm, 5-8pm, 3min from Tenmabashi stn on Tosabori-dori, 7th Day Adventist's, 11:15-8pm, X-sat, ☎943-9597.

South (*Minami*) has one of best classical Japanese restaurants: **Yamatoya**

on Soemon-cho, ☎211-0058; Geisha on call for ransom, advise hotel or local iness friend call ahead to rsve, arrange menu. But at other architectural extreme is our favorite...

邑 ミ
　 ヤ
　 コ

Miyako

Miyako on Mittera-suji st, that's 2nd neon street above river parallel to Dotonbori, 3rd cross st E in from Midosuji on S (R), 3rd door W, before corner is lovely small polished wood traditional grill front, white electric sign; [**E-3**], ☎211-9482, till 12 X-sun, hol. Advise going with Jpn friend, but you can swing it on your own with humor. Part curtain and enter world of *ko-ryori*, 'small cooking'. Master his wife (full staff) seat you at one of dozen chairs at bar (preferred) or single on-tatami table. If crowded ask when to come back. Start with nibbles chosen from bowls atop counter—don't miss *yokowa*, teenage 'virgin' tuna (under 2m) too delicate for sushi, eat only as sashimi, unforgetable taste sensation. Sake, beer. Entreé or two, he shows you fish on counter, choose, tempura advised if none to your taste. Total abt ¥7,000 ea, worth double. Friendly chatty clientele, sake experts.

For *sushi* out on Midosuji Blvd W-side below Dotonbori 3rd small shop, **Maruhachi** choose a la carte, or order *Tokujo* course abt ¥2,000; excellent.

Alaskan King Crab: corner Shinsaibashi arcade–Dotonbori **Kani Doraku** under giant crab robot scaling building, lavish window model menus a la carte to sumptuous feast, ¥T+, excellent. Few doors E excellent *Unagi* eel **Izumoya**, window menu—both offer seating view over river, as do most on L/N side of Dotonbori; all are good, safe, ¥-T.

Geisha: **Club Maiko**, Minami VO bldg 2fl, Sennen-cho 38, ☎253-0581; ¥13,000 incl for drinks, hors d'oeuvres; full meals ¥-T extra ¥3,000+, *kaiseki* ¥-S. *Maiko*, novice geisha more ornately dressed, and *geiko*, young geisha, join you at table, welcomes with your national flag which she flutters with dancing fan, pours, serves, all give 20min dance show 7:40, 8:40, 9:40, 10:30. Also in Tokyo *Ginza*, Aster Plaza Bldg 4fl, Ginza 7ch-7-6, ☎574-7745 (¥12,000 base).

Tomoyoshi 'folksy' *mingei-ryori*, down Shinsaibashi-suji from Daimaru, L/E to 1st R/S, on nxt corner L; ☎211-6517, 5pm-11pm, X-sun, hols. Prop KOBAYASHI Chieko spent time in US.

More reasonable are numerous inexpensive restaurants along Shinsaibashi-suji shopping arcade and on many streets branching off. W-style, 2 **Fujiyas**, better one midway at Shinsaibashi-suji one st above Mittera-suji alley, 3rd above river; several other similar places along this same street; **Wien**, 2nd alley up from Namba between Midosuji and Shinsaibashi-suji; cheaper J-style nibbles off to either side on cross streets.

SOEMONCHO started in Edo era, long before Dotonbori, as theater and dining street and with numerous teahouse hangouts for artists and conversationalists. Tradition hangs on today in some of its coffee shops, like our favorite **Gallery-Café de Ando** [sic]. In from **Kirin Beer Hall** block, on N side (L), look for E-sign with drawing of facing peacocks, long tails hanging down (after original 5th century mosaics inside); till late, ☎213-8775. Ando couple run it: she of beauteous noh-mask smile, 'Egg-chan', ex-classical dancer-turned-painter and flower arranger; he of shaggy mop, 'Chuggy', speaks good English with much to say of art, as architect-turned-flower arranger, right hand to Teshigahara, master of Sogetsu-ryu. With them 'flowers' are avant garde sculpture, arrangements can run scores of meters long. Sip coffee while viewing exhibition-sale, and catch Chuggy for chat.

Interesting food shops in underground plazas at both Namba and Osaka Stations, for Japanese nibbling. If prowling, try alleys behind Mainichi and Asahi newspaper buildings for both small bars and restaurants: epicureanism of press is international. Fun beer halls atop roofs of highest buildings, especially around Osaka Stn Plaza, obvious on summer eves. Town is early-closing. Many restaurants stop serving by 8:30, clubs at 11 and by midnite and last subway or commuter trains streets are clearing and taxi rush is on, almost impossible to hail. Late traffic around all-nite coffee shops (by whatever name changing laws cause them to call themselves) and discos.

However, for late snack, or even different dinner, we prefer foregoing restaurants to make counter-hopping pilgrimage around little specialty counter-stalls which stay open late enough to catch cabaret trade going home. There is heavy concentration of these at both main nite villages—*kita*, north below Umeda-Osaka and *minami*, south Hotel Nikko to Namba Stn. We used to prefer latter, but now living in Kobe *kita* is more convenient, has developed more, with several new discos and American '50s-style live-music restaurants. Just stroll, look at window displays and order food by pointing, or peer into smaller, displayless 3-4 guest stalls and see what's on counter and duck in and try it. You will be hard put to spend hotel dessert money at this nomadic oriental smorgasbord. Food, we stress, is good and as safe as it is tasty—all cooked as no raw food may be served outside. You will not be clipped even so much as 10% service charge. Every place serves beer, most also sake, for this type of meal developed as nibble to accompany social drinking–thus tends to be protectively oily. Japanese in general, Osakans in particular are more openly friendly in such places. Strangers are always welcome. Person you meet in stand-up stall may be laborer trying his TV-lesson English, or company president: DJ pal who worked in and loved Osaka ended one pushcart dinner in limo going to penthouse of restaurant-chain mogul for nite cap.

OSAKA BY NITE

EVIDENCES FACT that city was built by hard-trading shopkeepers who got up earlier than Kyoto or Tokyo merchants. Offerings far more plebeian than Tokyo's. Rare bigger places have solid iness philosophy of mass production and good and regular turnover. As result they are far larger, or far less sophisticated, but far safer than Tokyo's traps, morning-after easier.

Most bars have hostesses, but not discos, and floor shows. 'Biggest cabaret in world' is **Metro**. Popular entertainment district is at Osaka Station end of Midosuji to its E, where numerous alleys of *Kita Shinchi* are lined with eateries, bars and coffee shops. In here you'll find discos, mostly reflecting 'retro boom' of US '50s, like flashy **Studebaker** where waiter/resses stage shows from 7pm; (¥1,000) ☎372-1950, 2nd street E of Hankyu DS/stn, L/N of JR track in Umeda Center bldg with fun **Little Carnival** eatery, others; **Maharaja** in Daichi Hotel 2nd fl, (¥4,000) ☎345-3050.

South (*Minami*) has at its northernmost in 2nd basement of Nikko Hotel, opp Daimaru, **Samba Club** ¥2,000, ☎244-1433. Farther S is **Desse Jenny**, holds 1,000 at ¥4,000 buffet & drink, ☎643-0245, 5min E of Namba stn basement of Yoshimoto Kaikan. **Pig & Whistle** is block E 2nd fl Dunhill, opp side of Suo-machi St in 'European Village' ('American Village' is behind Nikko Hotel) as Brit-type darts'n **real** fish'n chips ('n meaty bangers 'n stout) ¥-T pub, till 1am; ☎213-6911. Quiet types might also check geisha service/show at **Clubs Maiko** in both *Kita* and *Minaami*.

When these close by midnite you've time for *sauna* nr Namba at **New Japan** (ladies' section also). If still not sleepy **Boston Club** 'futuristic city space' rocks till 5am; ☎244-1433 (¥4,000 incl food, drink) go E btwn Sogo–Daimaru to street beyond Shinsaibashi arcade; as does **Namba Ichiban** (¥1,500) ☎231-7392 on Shinsaibashi Arcade 2nd crossing below Daimaru.

North (*Kita*) has **Umeda Kentos** (¥1,500) ☎375-9090 block above Hankyu Hotel. These all close 11 or midnite, have minimal dress codes—no shaggy jeans or armpits, no sneakers, min age mostly 20 but we've never heard of foreigner being carded. ¥-prices quoted are for males, gals usually ¥500 less, includes drink, and if over ¥3,000 food, but ¥500 surcharge usual fri-sat nites and before hol. Sometimes stag parties discouraged, but not hens.

To **dance** close with your own wife or date, stick to 'Top-of...' lounge of your (major) hotel, where at least you can see where you are. Luckily these are usually lovely spaces, especially Hilton's art-deco mirror-and-cut-glass, so you are little tempted to look at view, which of Osaka is dismal—except from New Otani overlooking flood-lit Osaka Castle.

You've come halfway around world to see Japan of its travel literature. Well, it's almost all within half-day or full-day easy tours of central Osaka, first Japanese city of 21st century. All these out of town famous sights can be reached by tours arranged in hotel, or with help of good guide book and some tips from front desk, can be done on your own.

And if you do want to see Tokyo, and peer at Mount Fuji en route out of L side windows of train (in case you missed it flying down to Osaka), then hop cab for 10min ride (from Kita hotels, 15 from others) to Shinkansen Shin-Osaka station and zap up in under 3hrs.

Of course you may have come on business. Fine. Then compliment your Japanese counterpart that you know Japan: come to Osaka, where his home office and factory probably are anyway. Tokyo is for showrooms and government liaison: Osaka is where work is done, where most goods are.

Bring your wife—while you are at conference or hosting business lunch in your hotel's exclusive Luncheon Club, let her roam on scenic tour to Kyoto or Nara, or go shopping in Osaka, this old traditional storehouse of Japan where at Osaka Station (Kita) you have Daimaru-Acty above station, and facing Hankyu and Hanshin department stores and hi-rise Hilton Plaza full of boutiques—all linked by shop-lined underground passageway city.

Osaka is where 'I can get it for you wholesale' always tops local hit parade, sales are perpetual, no one remembers list prices.

*And I feel no remorse in this busy city of Kobe, because
seeing and hearing while I ramble about the earth
is my passion.* ———Nikos Kazantzakis

...half return to Western life... ———Lafcadio Hearn, *letter*

KOBE 神戸
BIT OF SAN FRANCISCO

KOBE IS PERHAPS rather Oakland in miniature squeezed between hills, shipyards and docks, almost showing pretensions, but not energy, to play San Francisco and climb its mountains. Not much to visit, but lovely city to live—as you can see on Home Visit tour, or if lucky enough to be assigned here to work. No old city, it is product of opening of Japan century-plus ago, steadily drawn eastward by magnet of Osaka power into strip 30km long until now virtually western extension (negotiating amalgamation as long as we can recall). Original open port Hyogo, west of present center.

Port history goes back to era of earliest mainland link, under different names and slightly different locales on storm-swept bay—Muko, where Korean emissaries settled, and Ogawa where Sung Chinese traders came. Finally to Fukuhara to which Taira no-Kiyomori was attracted to develop port, and in 1180 briefly moved capital of puppet emperor Antoku from Kyoto. This move sparked terrible Genji-Heike war. After Kiyomori's great breakwater, port never developed further and re-named Hyogo, it remained but sleepy coastal-trade port. Chosen open port 1868 by Western captains not because of its history as port, unknown to them and not obvious by its then-sad state, but because their sounding surveys revealed it to be good deep water with fair access to shore. Life returns to area with new high-rise Harborland development, New Otani Hotel, etc, thru 1994.

Otherwise useless tidal flats sparsely populated but for several hoary shrines which gave it its name, *Kan-be* or *Ko-be*, 'God's Door'. Border of original foreign *kyoryu-chi*-settlement, ran along E side from present Trade Building (first stn *Portliner*) inland to rail tracks at Sannomiya from where it extended west almost to Motomachi Stn (its NW corner being Daimaru DS, where plaque opp entry to modern Motomachi shopping arcade then-main hiway thru old town), with Inland Sea lapping at modern Kaigan Dori— 'Shore Road'. Hearn wrote above letter on moving to Kobe in 1894 after few years teaching in Matsue, which he loved and where he married Miss Koizumi, whose name he took to assume Japanese citizenship (name change mandatory till recently). In this nation of ancient towns, Kobe, incorporated only five years earlier in 1889, was spanking new. As Priest Sato of Kitano Tenjin shrine says, "All Kobe people are boat people".

Kobe-Osaka railroad in 1874 drew more international business away from other foreign settlement in crowded old Sakai in south Osaka. Local *to-jin*-'red men', alias *i-jin*-'strange men', a.k.a. today's *gai-jin*-'outside men' or foreigners (*ke-to,* 'hair-red' is old uncomplimentary term) prospered along with their Japanese associates newly relocated from older towns. Hearn arrived 1894 to edit *Kobe Chronicle*, city population was 150,000, one tenth today's crowded in 1/24th present area. Prosperity pushed to 'north-field' of *Kita-no* in foothills of heavily wooded mountains that confine Kobe to strip along shore. Mountain and sea make Kobe warmer winter, cooler summer than Osaka or Kyoto, less damp—thus more healthy—than other great treaty port, Yokohama, where miasma brought fatal fever-chill.

GETTING THERE & AWAY

JR stn on old main line called Kobe is W of old Hyogo (now Motomachi stn) original foreign 'open port', and also W of present city-center. Do not disembark here, but rather earlier at **San-no-miya**, 'Third Shrine' at which all expresses stop (indeed some even skip Kobe Stn itself). This is terminus of JR Tokaido train line, main **JR** continuing here on down as Sanyo line. Here suburban **Hankyu** private line from Kyoto-Osaka-Takarazuka terminates—linking with W-bound Sanyo Dentetsu line to HIMEJI, as does parallel coastal HANSHIN pvt line from OSAKA, also with W-bound link. **Portliner** starts by JR platform for Port Island circular rt. Underground all link with Kobe Municipal **Subway**. From Kobe **International Ocean terminal**, where cruise liners dock, to Sannomiya is short 2x-mtr taxi. Port is jump-off for Inland Sea itineraries (which *see* following) and 5hr old train to HIROSHIMA via castle town of HIMEJI, folk art town KURASHIKI, etc, or under 2hrs by bullet train skipping most of our intermediary sights. OSAKA-Umeda → KOBE-Sannomiya stns 25min by any of above 3 express trains, or taxi 13x-mtr. Kobe port adds 2x-mtr to any taxi rates: KOBE → TAKARAZUKA with numerous fine onsen inns, **Takarazuka Hotel**, of course **All Girl Review** of *Sayonara* fame, taxi 12x-mtr—which drive is slightly higher but more than worth it for breathtaking vistas and views of Kobe-Osaka via Futatabi or Rokko toll road over mountain thru national park. Takarazuka 10km from *Itami* airport, taxi 5x-mtr.

Maps: Plenty of good free maps available front desk most hotels. Best Kobe alone *Map of Kobe* by Kobe International Association. Good maps *Discover Kinki* tabloid.

WHERE TO STAY: *See* HANSHIN p.565-6. Don't be without local mag *KTO*.

KITANO-CHO   NORTH FIELD, 'THE VILLAGE'

GETTING THERE: 1.5km N of Sannomiya stn, min taxi (instruct 'Kitano-cho Sanbonmatsu'); 800m W of Shin Kobe stn, 10min walk W from New Oriental Hotel. **City Loop** 'Antique trolley'-bus circles both JR stations, Kitano and Port; in one hr every 15-20min, ¥200 each ride, ¥500 day pass, 9:58-19:40. *Only* if interested in early Western—mostly poor New England—architecture in Japan. Our suggested route is from Sannomiya: walk up first street L of broad Flower Rd, angling L from Hankyu stn, Kitano-zaka (Kobe uphill streets called -*zaka*, 'hill'). Pleasant window-shop in boutiques, bars and international restaurants appealing to 2,500,000 visitors annually, mostly young.

Discussed in historical order, not visiting order. *TILT* follows, p593.

1890, year after city incorporated, UK architect Alexander Nelson Hansell arrived. In 30-year stay he built for prosperous traders and missionaries 40 stately pleasure domes of Xanadus of their own imaginations, befitting expatriate quality of their lives, on verdant virgin pine-hillside at foot of...

KITANO TENMANGU shrine, 'Tenjin-san', built in *Kan-be* 1080AD. Oldest structure, stage, dated 1742 on carpenter's inscription found during restoration after first International Matsuri. Gave name later to village, still later absorbed into Kobe. Atop steep flight stone steps R of Kobe landmark Kazami-dori house, above narrow lane hugging mountain-base, then grand trunk pedestrian highway. Now locale of Japan's first International Matsuri —join us, (*see* DATEBOOK, p.611) **Jul last sat-sun**. Small flea mart most suns.

Architecture of Hansell's manses was as eclectic as clientele for whom he built. Earlier occidental buildings downtown, like extant 'House 15' (on Sakai-machi between Mainichi newspaper building and Chinatown) built in 1881, were southern colonial style, as found across India and southeast Asia to lesser Pacific isles, but on smaller scale and in case of #15 in stone. Similar **Bischof House** on Tor Road, now **Totenkaku** Chinese Restaurant was built year Hearn arrived (1894) by British engineer, Gulliver.

Persia House museum of our personal collection (with **Orient-kan** Nara, p.386) above upper road, also dates from this time if not slightly earlier, 1890-95(?). This is sole building with decorated pediment and its design of

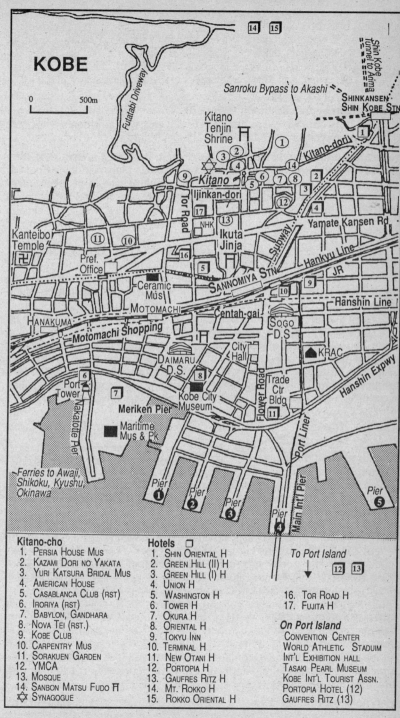

KOBE

0 ___ 500m

Futatabi Driveway

Sanroku Bypass to Akashi

Shin Kobe Tunnel to Arima

SHINKANSEN
SHIN KOBE STN

Kitano
Tenjin
Shrine

Kitano-dori

Kitano

Ijinkan-dori

Kanteibo
Temple

Pref.
Office

Tor Road

NHK

Ikuta
Jinja

Yamate Kansen Rd

Subway

Hankyu Line

JR

Ceramic
Mus

MOTOMACHI

SANNOMIYA STN

Hanshin Line

HANAKUMA

Motomachi Shopping

Centah-gai

SOGO
D.S

KRAC

City
Hall

Hanshin Expwy

DAIMARU
D.S.

Flower Road

Trade
Ctr
Bldg

Port
Tower

Meriken Pier

Kobe City
Museum

Nakatotte Pier

Maritime
Mus & Pk

Ferries to Awaji,
Shikoku, Kyushu,
Okinawa

Port Liner

Main Int'l Pier

Pier
1

Pier
2

Pier
3

Pier
4

Pier
5

Kitano-cho
1. PERSIA HOUSE MUS
2. KAZAMI DORI NO YAKATA
3. YURI KATSURA BRIDAL MUS
4. AMERICAN HOUSE
5. CASABLANCA CLUB (RST)
6. IRORIYA (RST)
7. BABYLON, GANDHARA
8. NOVA TEI (RST.)
9. KOBE CLUB
10. CARPENTRY MUS
11. SORAKUEN GARDEN
12. YMCA
13. MOSQUE
14. SANBON MATSU FUDO
✡ SYNAGOGUE

Hotels
1. SHIN ORIENTAL H
2. GREEN HILL (II) H
3. GREEN HILL (I) H
4. UNION H
5. WASHINGTON H
6. TOWER H
7. OKURA H
8. ORIENTAL H
9. TOKYU INN
10. TERMINAL H
11. NEW OTANI H
12. PORTOPIA H
13. GAUFRES RITZ H
14. MT. ROKKO H
15. ROKKO ORIENTAL H

To Port Island
↓

16. TOR ROAD H
17. FUJITA H

On Port Island
CONVENTION CENTER
WORLD ATHLETIC STADUIM
INT'L EXHIBITION HALL
TASAKI PEARL MUSEUM
KOBE INT'L TOURIST ASSN.
PORTOPIA HOTEL (12)
GAUFRES RITZ (13)

palmetto and arabesque is, quite by coincidence, traditional Persian. This pediment is usually carved and painted wood or plaster: here it is plastered-over modeled wattle and daub. Was residence of Iranian (Persian) Consul in 1930s. (Exhibits: main fl, folk arts & handicrafts of recent Iran, mostly illustrated in our book *A Survey of Persian Handicraft*, on sale ($95/¥12,000); 2nd fl Persian Pottery 4000BC–17th century; both are major collections, no-X, 10-5pm, summer till 6, ¥300.

Best-built and preserved of colonial style...
Hunter House moved to Oji Zoo (2 stns toward Osaka on Hankyu line, open rarely) of imported SE Asian hardwood indicates was built later when foreigners more prosperous; others of local pine, highly susceptible to rot.

Hansell set new style for these *Ijin-kan*, 'strange-man-houses', befitting their sobriquet. With his oldest extant home, 1895 Georgian-style built for Dithlefsen, he paid tribute to his host country with post-and-beam architecture (externally Occidental, internal structure of houses traditional Japanese) and grey ceramic roof tile, which he further Orientalized with green Persian shutters and rooftop 'orcs', architectural term meaning sea-monsters or indefinable fishy doodads, to set so-called Moorish mood. Generally, southern exposures have bay windows in long 'Moorish' or Persian-style *talars* (columned porches now glassed in to form sun rooms) relieving otherwise dark and heavy timbered Victorian interiors. Exteriors were North American clapboard. Architecturally classifiable as Orientalized (south or garden-side) Queen Anne (north–street facade), which despite name is American style developed for US Centennial of 1876 when British names had US sales appeal. Now preserved on Ijin-kan Dori west, green and white house with name **MonChoko**. Best example now open to public, and still lived in, is home he built for himself next door, 1896, now **Choueke House** (9-5, ¥300)—with worthwhile private collection of 19th century Ukiyoe woodblock prints of foreigners, and lots of homey overstuffed ornateness much as other such houses used in fact.

Another Hansell of this type is...
Hassam House (not always open) moved to **Sorakuen garden** W of Kitano-cho above Prefectural Office *(Kencho)*.

With passing of 19th century and Victorian era (end 1901), local fashion evolved out of American pseudo-English to pure Yankee in such as **Dr Hager House**—now **Minato Ijinkan** (relocated to Port Isle North Park next to red bridge), and **Moegi-no-Yakata** *Green House* (former 'White House', named after its postwar color till recent restorers found it was originally green, renamed it and reassigned WH name to gallery for Kobe artists) built by Hansell for US Consul Hunter Sharp, 1903, privately, in age when consul offices were bought and lucky entrepreneur got to keep all fees tax free. Many smaller-country consulates today still run on this system of official graft. Moegi-no Yakata is block W of Kazami-dori and open to public. If intelligently furnished to period it could make fine monument to long Kobe history of Japan-American interrelations.

Adjoining it S-side is...
American House, 1929, built by Japanese in contemporary California small-house style for rental to Americans. Restored by us in 1929 middle-class style, all furnishings from US date 1927-32 (except 1918 player piano)—1929 for Buck Rogers-like art-deco mantelpiece lamps, intervening dates for stuffed furniture, lamps, radios, morning glory record player '27. Toy lead soldiers upstairs in kids' rooms are Jay's from 1937. Color scheme from contemporary magazines. All ijinkan 'restored' by Japanese have white walls, heritage of US Occupation period and space heaters—originally all were open fireplace-heated thus all had colored or papered

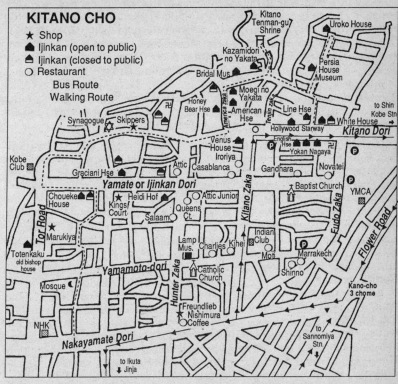

KITANO CHO
★ Shop
▲ Ijinkan (open to public)
△ Ijinkan (closed to public)
○ Restaurant
 Bus Route
 Walking Route

walls so as not to show smoke residue. Sole house on hill restored to true period and class. Jewish mezuzah on most doors—all tenants Jewish, when US Jews left during war, Italian Jews moved in. No-X, 9-17:00/-18, ¥300, reduced combo tix w/PersiaHouse, others; prohibition-era home bar decorated with posters of 3 top trumpeter pals of '29: L-R Satchmo, Bix, grandpa Gluck. Baby pix upstairs Jay.

Later Hansell houses sprouted polygonal domes of grey traditional tile. Successors such as German architect who built Kitano-cho's two now most famous houses, tho youngest, switched to shingle, flexibility of which enabled them to curve domes into true minaret cupolas as in *Kazami-dori* **Weathercock House** built for Gottfried Thomas 1915, part well-restored with some original furniture presented by daughter who lived there as child. (City-owned, free); and **Fishscale House**, *Uroko-yakata* 1922 (¥500—see from outside unless ready for coffee break in old bldg main fl, and great view from top fl, new 'museum' clone, L, usually exhibits Chinese art reproductions).

Thus Kobe would seem more like home to next wave of foreigners: White- and Jewish-Russians, and Turks, who would add to Kitano-cho skyline **Orthodox Church**, (other churches; Gothic-in-Concrete Catholic, New England clapboard-steeple Baptist), **Jewish Center,** (one of two synagogues in country, mostly Sephardics, regular services fri sunset & sat 8:30am, present ferroconcrete structure is recent) & finally Turkish-style **Mosque** 1935-37—service noon fri, open to visitors daily 1-4pm. Just one Turkish family remains of original colony, and their children are in USA, with dad retiring soon, leaving mostly new Pakistani-Bangladesh community. Most recent Middle East edifice (1986) is **Jain Temple**, wholly of exquisite imported sculpted white Indian marble (open to public afternoons, 'except ladies pregnant or in period').

Early in World War II 15,000 Estonian Jews evaded 'final solution' thru transit visas for Japan (consul Sugihara who issued them against not-too specific orders, was drummed out of service and not rehabilitated till 1991, is enshrined in Israel among Noble Men). They crossed USSR to Kobe. Questioned by irritated Japanese naval officers, "Why is our ally Germany so hostile towards you?" Their old *reb*, rabbi, stroked his long beard, looked them straight on, "Because as is said in *Mein Kampf*, we are, like you, Orientals". Tea was instantly served and there were no more problems. Relocated to Shanghai, most migrated postwar to Israel and US (as told in *Fugu Plan, see* p39). Kobe – Riga now sister cities.

To us, coming back in 1970 after some years in Iran, Kobe was 'half return' to Japanese life. Access from Kobe to older parts of Japan we love —Hiroshima, Kyoto-Nara—is convenient. Kansai cuisine is our preference. Both local fish and Kobe beef are justly famed. Kobe is full of good, reasonable restaurants of every flag, and gentle Kansai palate has lightened heavier European fare, even *wa-fu* J-style steak is more delicate. Cluster of such good restaurants corner Hunter-zaka at Ijinkan Dori (*see* CHOPSTICKS).

We moved into all Japanese neighborhood out of town in nearby Ashiya, into large house of early 1930s, half-Japanese, half post-Frank Lloyd Wright (his last extant local building nearby, *see* ASHIYA, p.596). Garet and big brother attended international school housed in pseudo-Tudor.

Kobe's foreign community had come full circle since Hearn's time. From trying to teach Orient about cultural superiority of our naval cannon, imperialism and Sunday brunch, foreigners were now trying to learn secret of superiority of Japanese electronics and QC management and sushi bars. As part of this revolution foreign schools now finally, after half-century of dillying, deigned to teach Japanese as second language! (And we wonder why we can't sell overseas). Results were amazing. In May 1971 Canadian Academy students actually performed kabuki play in original classical Japanese. Blue-eyed *gai-jin* kids, painted and kimonoed, yodelled pentatonic plaints of dying samurai and jilted geisha. They amazed Japanese by identifying with their reputedly inscrutable culture, as much as Ijin-kans amused them with their peculiar brand of orcish occidental inscrutability. Our sons appeared in fourth thru tenth seasons and we never could decide which was more incongruous: seeing kids of dozen nationalities in rehearsal straining their jeans in painful heel-squat while ululating their deep-throated libretto, or slouching typical teen style in brilliant kimono and surrealistic face makeup slugging Coke. That's Kobe.

Japanese came to see them first as exotic novelty, but most became devoted fans. Professional actors and artists poured accolades upon them. **Canadian Academy Kabuki**, or CAbuki, outgrew school auditorium, appeared annually in professional Kobe Bunka Hall. Each year kids essayed more ornate and difficult plays to professional standards. For Grand Tenth Performance some graduate stars of past years came back to repeat old triumphs. In all some 45 young people representing dozen-plus lands, danced on and off stage by way of that *hanamichi* kabuki 'flower bridge' that bridged East–West, linking God's Door with rest of our world. Alas, CAbuki died out, not due lack of audience or even of funds, but indifference on part of American 'educators' sent out to teach our kids to be mediocre so as to continue our slide to 2nd-class provincialism. Visiting late summer or autumn watch *KTO* for dates—**Japaneseque Kabuki** resurrected by ex-CAbuki director Mitsuko Unno privately. *See* their translation book of 7 kabuki plays, *You Mean To Say You Still Don't Know Who We Are?* ed Cellin Gluck.

VIEW: long-famed for from upper floors of hillside houses, now best from *Kobe Dream Balloon*, 1,470m/0.9mile suspension car from behind Shin Kobe stn to hilltop in 10min for ¥1,000 r.t. (!); till 10pm or later.

GET THERE: street escalator front New Oriental Hotel, L across bridge, follow sign

TILT: Top of Kitano-zaka turn R, 50m ahead E cluster of old houses. L up steep steps is **Hollywood Starways**, collection of US movie memorabilia, old US movie posters in Japanese. R is **English House**, built 1908 but refurnished in anything Brit imaginable, first 'commercial ijinkan' on hill, started it all. Next door **'French? House'**, built 1910 as *nagaya* or paired-tenement to house lesser foreign clerks, now 'restored' in luxury furnishings that barely fit thru doors; combo ticket with English H, skip. Next is still smaller **Ben's House** in which it is imagined great hunter 'Ben' lived thus tiny rooms cluttered with stuffed trophy heads. All ¥300 ea & var combo tix. N side is *free* White House till recently US consular residence, now **Art Gallery**, changing exhibs.

If taxi from town to SANBONMATSU, you are 50m E of here at small intersection.

Facing on mountainside up stairs is **Rine House** (named in popular contest, means 'line' house for its 'nice lines'–usually thought to mean 'Rhine', either OK) city-owned, *free*, not furnished, occasional gallery shows upstairs; real German lunch and coffee house main floor. Continue narrow lane, top stairs jag L-R uphill to **Persia House** 1890-95 on L. At peak is **Uroko-Fishscale House**, 1922, ¥500, see from outside, return **Persia House** for our art collection, ¥300 or combo w/ American H, Hollywood Star, Bridal Museum, Honey Bear Wonderland, all for ¥1,500 (incl drink). Exit back gate, down, to R on 100m to stone steps of **KITANO SHRINE**, try jog up 64 steps. (City's new plaza boasts luxury restrooms.) Next door **Kazami-dori** 1915, important cultural bldg, *free*, X-wed. Then **Katsura Yumi Bridal Museum**, on L ex-*Shiroi Ijinkan* renamed **Moegi-no-yakata** 1903 (US consul built from his 'fees'), *free*. Turn L down hill, if on combo ticket w/ Persia House drop in **American House**, sit down awhile to think about how Japanese see us after your tour of 'reverse Chinatown'. Opp American House is **Honey Bear Wonderland** (for kids), L-downhill to corner Arçon Hotel, R 100m on Kitano-dori St to **Jain Temple**: if gate open OK enter *free*, shoes off. On 100m to **Jewish Center** on R, not public. Continue W, road curves L past entry to **Kobe Club** foreigners' private club, to intersection. Down 50m on R is **Totenkaku** Chinese restaurant, dinner NG, lunch OK. Or at light turn L, E on Yamamoto-dori a.k.a. Ijinkan St, to **Choueke House**, 1896, ¥300, still lived in, fine collection Ukiyoe foreigner prints. Cut R down any alley, snake thru Kitano-cho of old, no cars just room for pedestrians, to next cross vehicular st, near **Mosque**, only one in Japan, Tokyo to rebuild; welcome to enter 1-4 if anyone there—little to see but simple and stately, no furnishings, balcony for women. If enter, shoes off. Next R, downhill from mosque to wide avenue, then Shrine or...

OTHER SIGHTS WITHIN WALK OF KITANO-CHO

Carpentry Museum, *Daiku-hakubutsukan*, walk down to main E-W ave Naka-Yamate-dori, turn R (W) to 4th small street past Tor Road, R again, see traditional white building (but ferroconcrete); X-mon, ¥300. Fine collection tools, illustrated techniques of world's greatest house carpenters, mostly from Hida, which we visited. Carpenters, architects, lovers of good tools–don't miss. Read *Way of the Carpenter*, WH Coaldrake.

Ceramic Museum of Hyogo Pref, *Hyogo Kenritsu Togei-kan*, 4th fl Zentan Hotel, NakaYamate-dori 2 blocks W of Tor Rd, near Kencho, subway stn (good inexpensive crab restaurant 2nd fl); fabulous collection of one man, late Zentan bus company president Tanaka, given to public, one of best museum displays in Japan. All wares, from muddy stonewares to enamel rainbows, were made in Hyogo prefecture, tho all kilns except TACHIKUI now extinct. Celadon kiln at SANDA recently making comeback (good restaurant there, too, **Sandaya** same compound, Rolls Royce parked in front, dinner dancing, celadon on sale, all inconvenient except car or long cab—alas, chain branches around Kansai only so-so).

IKUTA JINJA shrine, handsome vermilion postwar rebuilding of ancient shrine that gave Kobe its name, literally 'Gods' Door', few min walk N &

W above Sannomiya stn amid restaurant-bar district, which adds great zest to its annual festivals, especially midnite New Year's Eve. Shrine preserves several ancient dances and rituals and sends troupe overseas occasionally— for special performance for group, ☎(078)-321-3851 in J few days ahead (donation varies ¥30-40,000+, with special consideration often shown for student groups); but for simple *Miko-mai* shrine maiden dance, early same day or day ahead okay, donation ¥10,000.

KANTEI-BYO Chinese Temple, sub- of temple in Nagasaki. Garish compared to local temples, 'joss sticks' or incense quite different in odor; steady stream of petitioners light joss, bow in prayer—mostly Kobe-born of Chinese descent, still 'foreigners' after any number of generations.

Kobe Municipal Museum, *Shi-ritsu Hakubutsukan*: block S of old Oriental Hotel in preserved converted bank: noted *Namban* (southern barbarians, oldest term, from Chinese, for foreigners) art collection on main floor, formerly in old museum of its own which we preferred—more clutter then but more shown—for good view Victorian Kobe era of Hearn. Upstairs video room dial yourself well-done English videotapes on local history, archaeology etc. ¥200 unless special show when up to ¥800, 10-4:30-enter, X-mon.

Fuji Art Museum foot of Flower Road opp port; annex of beautiful Sokka Gakkai museum on Mt Fuji, great special shows, regular rotations.

Hyogo Modern Art Museum, *Ken-ritsu Kindai Bijutsukan*, fine visiting shows but not much of interest to tourists except early-spring annual overview 'Art Now' show of recent works, and standing exhibit of local painters—fair, but no match for Okayama, (*follows*). 5min walk SW of Oji stn, 2nd → Osaka-ward on Hankyu line, or from Sannomiya taxi 2x-mtr.

PORT ISLAND: From upstairs JR Sannomiya stn S-side, Portliner (computer-controlled-no-crew Toonerville Trolley monorail) ¥220, 10min. City is biggest real estate developer in country, runs chronic budget surplus, moves rear range of mountains thru tunnels to dump in bay, sells flattened mts for houses and new isles for new city. Go to view modern architecture **Portopia Hotel** (¥-S) & '88 Annex (¥-L) see lobbies and ride glass elevator up for ¥-L meal, drink or coffee, top-buy Sunday brunch Top-Of- for views, out thru back boutiques to stroll **fashion street** and **Exotic Town**, numerous ¥-T youth-oriented cafes, restaurants, fine architecture of sports complex where swim and ice skate, S.F.'s own Fog City Diner, Exotic Town restaurant w/ live entertainment nitely, UCC Coffee Museum.

Tasaki Pearl Bldg has **Pearl Museum** with fine displays, videos in English on 'culture' process—Kobe is also called Pearl City, center of pearl market, fair but not best place to buy. We buy ours in Tokyo, (which *see*). Beyond hotels filling in 2nd island for **Adventureland** Theme Park, 1996; 3rd isle beyond will be 2,000AD Kobe Municipal Airport—missed to get Kansai Int'l here.

MIKAGE area museum group: Taxi from Sannomiya 3x-mtr any following; or Hankyu line 4 stops → Mikage (2 from Oji), walk or min taxi.

Ohara Art Gallery, personal archaeological-ethnological art collection of flower arrangement master OHARA Houn, head of one of 3 major (100s of minor) schools of *ikebana*-'living flowers' (as giving life to cut flowers); & adjoining is his school studio **Ikebana Kaikan** where he holds teacher classes and special seminars. (Kaikan-bldg itself interesting to walk up inside-outside spiral stairs around Gaudi-esque mosaic-tile center tower, leads out not onto roof but onto lawn, like Alice out of rabbit-hole, with superb sea view over low parapet). Art collection strong on pre-Columbian, especially textiles–best outside Peru? Also ancient Persian pottery. Not open to public; 'Specialists' ☎ Ms Suzuki in J- (078)-811-2871. Hankyu or JR Mikage stn, walk uphill 10min or taxi *Ohara Sankokan* (museum); taxi Sannomiya to Ohara 3x-mtrs.

Can combine with nearby ...
Hakutsuru Art Museum, *Hakutsuru Bijutsukan* only exhibits 2-3x year
of sake brewery's own collection Chinese bronzes, fine T'ang silvers... (for
openings check *KTO*). Alt from Sannomiya, JR → 3rd stn Sumiyoshi, bus up river →
Chinese green-tile roofed building L of river, or from Hankyu Mikage stn min taxi; from
Ohara Museum, min taxi, or walk E 15 min to river, L upstream, extraordinary
chinoiserie roof visible.

Can combine with nearby ...
Kosetsu Museum fine Tea- (chado-) related arts, collection of ex-prexy
of *Asahi Shinbun* when it was world's biggest daily; nr Hankyu Mikage Stn,
down to wide Yamate Kansen, L 100m in narrow lanes; 9:00-17:00, X-mon, ¥300.

SAKE MUSEUMS: All Free. Walking map from TIC E exit Hankyu
Sannomiya stn, 2nd fl. For studious biber, here best mineral spring gushes
forth *miya-mizu* sacred waters, thus make best Sake. Water available
commercially delivered by tank car to special coffee shops in Kobe. Well-
preserved wooden buildings exhibit tools of this fine Nada rice 'wine',
actually beer. S of above taxi basic-mtr or bus from Hakutsuru Museum S to Hanshin
Sumiyoshi-mae stn (from Sannomiya, Hanshin train to this stn).

Change to monorail Rokko Liner to Minami Uozaki, 3rd stop by...
Kiku Masamune Sake Museum in old wooden *sakagura* sake storehouse amid many similar buildings of once great Sake center, now replaced
by mechanical process and mostly chemically induced 'fermentation'. Daily
9-4pm, X-tues, rsve ☎851-2275.

Nearby 5 min walk W along Expressway is similar...
Hakutsuru Sake Museum source of wealth that built art museum above.

15 min walk further W thru similar buildings is...
Sawanotsuru Shiryokan (sake museum), Nada 1-29-1 Oishi-Minami-machi
(☎882-6333—phone ahead and free guide will greet 10-4, X-wed). Old *sakagura*
brewery of **Sawanotsuru** (est 1717), courtyard lined with wooden sake vats;
note great cedar-shingle ball, hung out over door to signify new brew ready.
Displays illustrate historic processes, video shows modern process with
reference to old; English sound-track available, ask for it if not shown, *free*.

Whence 10 min walk N across and under double-decker highway to Hanshin line Oishi
stn to return to Sannomiya in 5+ mins.
American watercolorist resident in Kyoto area, **Brian Williams**, painted stunning
series of these buildings. See some in Ashiya at **Sam's Restaurant** first street N of JR
Ashiya stn and to E (R) of new hotel-boutique complex (*follows*).

Bit farther E, between Kobe and Osaka is...
Kirin Brewery, Amagasaki, country's largest beer-brewer with over 70%
of local suds market, world's fourth largest brand. English guide, rsve required
☎06-499-3521 for 90min tour mon-fri, some sats, *free*.

SIDETRIPS FROM KOBE
ASHIYA, from Sannomiya Hankyu 6th stn, or 2nd from Mikage → Hankyu
Ashiyagawa. Also express stop on JR, Ashiya, less convenient for following sights but
Rail Passers use, and take taxi, basic-mtr, or walk NW extra 10min...

Taxi, basic-mtr, or walk back across river NW 12min...
Tekisui Museum several month+ exhibits annually, 9:00-17:00 X-mon, ¥500.
Japanese ceramics or tea-related arts. Also has good practical arts instruction
especially ceramics in on-site kilns, recommended; ☎0797-22-2228 (*see*
LEARNING ABOUT JAPAN) Min taxi or 12min walk up L side river, last bridge L, 3rd R
300m to sign, R.

Facing Ashiyagawa stn (4 blocks N) is...
Frank Lloyd Wright House—a.k.a. YAMAMURA House. Oya-stone on ferroconcrete, miniature of Old Imperial Hotel (1922), built for local steel baron Yamamura, '25, whose Yodogawa Steel company still owns it, use it on TV to advertise tin storage shscks. Similar in its unstable hillside site, construction style and material, size to Ennis House, Los Angeles, where Oya-stone replaced by Wright-made concrete-stone, as also contemporary LA Hollyhock House. Oya-stone worse than concrete for use in damp clime; inside walls rain for days after rain ceases outside—but faults aside, house is fun place for parties. Recently restored, furnished (at our advice) with Wright furniture copies. On knoll R-side upriver from Hankyu Ashiya-gawa stn —open to public: 10:00-16:00 sat, sun, hol—other times possible (esp wed) by appt, ☎(06)-245-1111, Osaka **Yodogawa Steel** international liaison office.

Tanizaki Junichiro House, Nobel author 1886-1965, genius recognized with college publication of short story *Tattoo Artist*, much anthologised modern classic. Moved often due to champagne taste and beer pocketbook, 1923-postwar lived several houses here and in neighboring villages now part of Kobe city; *Makioka Sisters* ['48, brilliantly translated by Seidenstecker] set in Ashiya in setting like this memorial, which is intended to reproduce mood of *Sisters*. From Hanshin line Ashiya stn walk down river E-side 4th R to mid 5th block L, or from JR/Hankyu line stns by Hankyu bus to Midori-cho. 10:00-17:00, ¥500 (¥200 coll student) X-tue ☎23-5852.

CHOPSTICKS: ASHIYA (*See* KOBE CHOPSTICKS, p.603).

DRIVEWAYS vein mountains backing city...
Futatabi-drive starts from just W of Kobe Club, winds up mountain past old **foreign cemetery** *gaijin-bochi* with Catholic, Orthodox, Protestant, Jewish, Muslim sections, joining skyline drive to Mt Rokko, rounding 108 curves (each numbered), about 10x-mtr taxi; or 4-hr circle, sidetrack to Maya and return down **Rokko Driveway**, lined with flowers in seasonal rotation; ¥14,000 or 30x-mtr at 1989-¥3,500/7.5x-mtr hr.

Bus serves route from Sannomiya stn, SE-corner; also go up Rokko Driveway from Hankyu Rokko Stn (between Kobe → Osaka 3rd stn).

Royu Drive from Ashiya to Arima, **bus** from Ashiya JR and Ashiyagawa Hankyu stns, runs past Wright House and up over mountain.

Cable-cars: taxi 3x-mtr, or **bus** to **Maya Cable**-sh'ta, base of Mt Maya, cablecar every 20min, ¥350, 5min up Mt to its lovely pilgrim temple to Maya, mother of historic Buddha Gautama (Jpn Shaka-sama), then **ropeway**, ¥380, 5min, across vale to Mt Oku-Maya whence connecting-**bus** or taxi (2x-mtr) to Rokko Hotel area. Walk back down parallel to cable takes only 30min. Another way up is taxi 4x-mtr to **Rokko Cable**-sh'ta (or Hankyu train to Rokko, then bus to cable), cable and taxi/bus to summit observatory or **hotels** (*next*). Rokko cable top stn adjoins stn for onward aerial **Rokko-Arima Ropeway** (9-20:40, every 20min, ¥700/12min to midway platform, ¥1,300/35min all the way to ARIMA to within walk or cab basic-mtr all hotels).

MOUNT ROKKO, cool and above smog, offers beautiful view of city, combined at nite with starscape for which Kobe itself was, until recent smog years, widely famed. Main W-style hotels, **Rokko-san** ☎891-0301 ¥-T and **Rokko-Oriental** ☎891-0333, ¥-S, offer fair dining. Former has sky room and rooftop beer garden, latter lovely outdoor terrace. Both serve Genghis Khan BBQ, ¥-T. For ¥-B, opp Rokko-san Hotel, cliffside eatery also serves Genghis Khan BBQ.

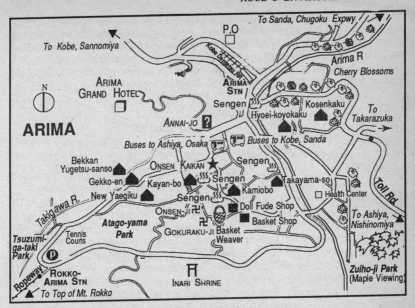

ARIMA, sole Kansai onsen. Highly touted as nation's oldest hot spring, founded as healing **ONSEN-JI** temple by wandering priest Gyoki (*see* DATEBOOK); mentioned in annals of *Nihon Shoki*, 720; popular with Osaka Tycoon Hideyoshi 16th century, Osaka business tycoons ever since.

GETTING THERE: Most scenic way up is ¥1,300 **cablecar-ropeway** combo, p596. **Bus**: from S-side JR Sannomiya Stn 6:50–18:45 at least hourly, ¥550. From ASHIYA JR, Hankyu stns hourly on 30min, ¥680 over high snaking drive. From OSAKA under Umeda Hankyu stn rear of Kinokuniya, hourly+, ¥1,180. Taxi OSAKA 16-20x-mtr, Airport 14x-mtr, KOBE 8-11x-mtr, ASHIYA 7x-mtr, Tachikui kiln 11x-mtr, SANDA 6x-mtr. **Train** KOBE Hankyu → SHINKAICHI stn then Kobe Dentetsu 40min → ARIMAGUCHI ¥510 **Walk** like pilgrim of yore, incl Hideyoshi, several emperors, many foreign residents: from bottom stn of Rokko Cable, marked path under 4hrs; or from Ashiya Hankyu stn up L/W-side Ashiya river to curve, follow up then R up 15min to Koza-no-Taki falls, up climbing route to Rock Garden, onward well marked, 4–5hrs, highly scenic. Then bathe, cable/train/bus home.

Clear 'silver' saline waters full of various minerals—said good for liver intestinal, stomach plaints. Some pools rusty 'gold' from another spring of *kinsen*-water with iron oxide and radium salts (for that happy glow?) reputedly good for sore muscles and sciatica, but advised against for heart problems. So dip and soak, then splash off rusty film with water from adjoining clear-water pool, then soak in that. You keep red-stained inn towel, red washes out and does not stay in or stain hair.

WHERE TO STAY: 25 inns ¥-T-L **Kanko-annai** ☎(078)-904-0708, 9-19:00 in front of bus terminal, some E.
Arima Grand H ☎904-0181; with bowling, game center, inferior cabaret—all things we don't want (most big spas so) but great bath lovely view; ¥-S.
Geko-en ☎904-0366, ¥-S-LL suites, old wing and new annex, advise specify old; linked by covered bridge enclosed by shoji panels, popular movie location; we especially like its *rotenburo* outside 'golden' baths (separate but marvelous) along river edge.
Koyokaku ☎904-0501, also monster 'self-contained resort', even greater baths, ¥-S.
Kosenkaku ☎904-0731, our long-time preference, ¥-Sw/2, traditional, farthest from stn, min taxi, but nearest Royu driveway from Ashiya, 10min stroll to 'town'. Go for

shojin-ryori Buddhist vegetarian lunch in garden thatch-roof house can have 11:00–19:00, ¥-B soba set ¥1,500 or full ¥4,500–9,000 incl, w/either take leisurely bath while waiting +¥700—phone rsve, especially flower seasons. (Their famed, lovely Hida-Takayama giant farmhouse-restaurant burned and new fire regulations forbid rebuilding in wood).

Takayama-so ☎904-0744, ¥-Tw/2 special for foreigners, Japanese pay ¥-S; tiny right in town, English spoken, Mrs Tsurukawa was airline stewardess.

Kami-obo ☎904-0531 in town; & **New Yaegiku** ☎904-0635, higher up; both ¥-T, mgr offers 'will match price to your budget'.

BATH only: Kosenkaku above, most ryokans w/meal pkge; or *sento* public bath at **Arima Onsen Kaikan** ¥380, 8-22:00, not mixed, bring own soap, towel or buy here. Most locals collect at bath, hikers from Ashiya, etc, end their day here 4pm.

SHOPPING: Stroll narrow alleys in hotel yukata, pleasure now rare in onsen-towns, here thankfully lacking neon-affectations of other big-name spas like Atami. Oldest shop street straight up opp **Kanko-annai**—and **bus terminal** for Kobe, Osaka, Ashiya—on up thru 'new town', loads of shops and ¥-B,-T eateries to **Onsen Kaikan** then start circle, snake up L side up alley; on L is **Daikoku-konbu** and *tsukudani* (condiments) and red mail post landmark; on R shop **Nishida** doll-brushes. On up to 2nd R, just on L is outlet for baskets **Arima Kago** and halfway up block on R his workshop, Kᴜᴛsᴜᴡᴀ Shochikusai. Turn R, continue on curve to next L past Nᴇɴʙᴜᴛsᴜ-ᴅᴇʀᴀ temple, immediate R front of temple past Oɴsᴇɴ-ᴅᴇʀᴀ on R, down steep stone steps, 2nd R back past senbei shops to **Onsen Kaikan**. Up few alleys along this route, several neighborhood shrines and temples, including original Oɴsᴇɴ-ᴊɪ temple behind public bath, invite casual inspection and coins, little shops and thatched roof farmhouses equally photogenic. Comfortable tiny coffee shops. Keep eye open for any of 18 *sengen*, spring heads gushing near-boiling water for inn baths—which it reaches much cooled, to be reheated.

Traditional art-craft long woven, *bamboo baskets* for tea ceremony and flower arranging. Kᴜᴛsᴜᴡᴀ Shochikusai sole craftsman, works in own shop, has older baskets of others and from Kyushu Beppu where craft moved years ago. His best start ¥6,000, seem to have no top—worth it especially for ikebana. Misc less. 4th lane behind Onsen Kaikan, on 50m, 9-6.

Hyotan fudé, ordinary writing brushes minutely entwined in silk thread in elaborate patterns, some with pop-up doll's head, *ningyo fude*. See being made up alley from public bath, available hotel sales counters.

Every spa has its edible *meibutsu* 'name goods' souvenir—here it is *tansan sembe*, sweetish cracker with carbonic acid-*tansan* from spa; also *matsutake konbu*, mushroom and kelp. Good gifts when visiting Japanese.

WESTWARD SHORE: Sᴜᴍᴀ-Uʀᴀ Pᴀʀᴋ (JR W out of Sannomiya stn to Suma stn & W 1200m or min taxi; or W on Sanyo Dentetsu next stn Suma-ura) has cable car up Mt Hachibuse from which superb view of Kobe coast; also overlooking shore short walk W from Suma-Ura stn is **Atsumori-zuka**, a.k.a. Goshiki-zuka or Five-color stone tumulus, immense restored *kofun* tomb mound, only one in country restored-refaced with stones etc, way most probably were—as late emperor Showa-(Hirohito)'s built Jan '89 at Hachioji near Tokyo, is—plus stairs to enable climb, small showroom of limited aechaeological excavation. (Good model in Kobe Museum).

Sᴜᴍᴀ ᴀɴᴅ Mᴀɪᴋᴏ beaches are 30min W of Kobe; taxi 9x-mtr. Good swimming, boating, wind-surfing, with **Maiko Hotel** ☎(078)-782-1155, ¥-S hotel with garden dining, popular for classical weddings so good place to see traditional bridal kimonos wafting thru halls, especially on weekends and *dai-an* lucky days. On seaside is **Rokkaku-do** six-sided towered old Victorian house where Sun Yat Sen stayed while in Kobe—now exhibits his works illustrating his life. China-history student will find similar exhibits in similar Victorian houses in various cities of China. Alternatively, bus from Sannomiya or JR train or Sanyo Dentetsu from Hankyu-Sannomiya stn, to MAIKO.

Next JR stn out, Akashi (taxi Sannomiya → 20x-mtr) is one of several ports for ferry to Awaji Isle (*see* INLAND SEA).

KOBE CHOPSTICKS

PLEASANT AND international, tho not adequately reflecting exotic mixture of nationalities one sees on city streets, except perhaps in welcome continentally lower prices–especially considering generally high quality.

Kobe pioneered with its underground shopping plaza **Santika Town** under Sannomiya adjacent to basement of Sogo DS, with fashion section of smart boutiques and budget outlets of top restaurants—all of which have showcase menus. Out from Sogo DS basement towards Hanshin trains is **Shumi-gai** 'Tasteful alley', Santika's original restaurant section where fantastic noodle maker starting with lump of dough, keeps stretching and flipping it into yards of continuous udon noodles; then there's crab, sushi, eel, yakitori, spaghetti, chanko-nabe for Sumo-type appetites, etc. This underground market stretches into **Sun Plaza**, then **Center Plaza** under Center-gai shop arcade, where it's basically restaurant world, budget meals complete ¥600-1,000; good J-*kaiseki*-type restaurant **Kitahama** with 3 shops— excellent *nabe* dishes under ¥3,000. Take your pick from gamut of *soba* noodle, *tonkatsu*-pork cutlets, salads only, spaghetti, sweet shops, ad inf.

Out on street...

Escargot, tops in our '64 edition, still is, we recommend it for those who can't make up minds. W-menu amazes us for variety, reasonableness. L-¥1,800; D-¥3,500 11:30-8pm no-X, ☎331-5034. Hard to find but worth hunt—on alley parallel to and below Center-gai, btwn Seidensha back door, same side, & Flower Rd in well posted basement.

Cosmopolitan in first main arcade crossing Center-gai from Flower Rd, towards sea, for luncheon milk shakes, sandwiches, soda fountain menus and owner Morozoff's own borscht soup. They are Kobe's own original chocolate maker, marketing as Cosmopolitan chocolates, superb black unsweet, other.

Musashi at Daimaru end of Center-gai, Kansai style kitchen with spotless blond cypress counter and tables, specialty *tonkatsu* (pork cutlet), full *teishoku* ¥1,600. 11-7:30pm, X-wed, ☎331-3771. Branch in Sun Plaza B-l.

Osteria del Ghiotto first st W of Tor rd 2nd block above el tracks, E side red brick front; by martial-artist Fausto, moustachioed caricature of Italian restaurateur and best Ital food in Japan; –10pm, X-thu, ¥-S. Fabulous veal, Ital cheese cake; ☎333-7427.

Chinese: Once-famed China Town now but backstreet name *Nanking-machi*, tho internationalization kick from '87-on brought recognition of ethnic minorities and Kobe city built Chinese Plaza with lovely red gate. Only few—much improved since '64—top Chinese restaurants in town: several good, tho not in CT. (But best *Indian* restaurant **Raja** 2 blks gate-W, cellar Sanotatsu Bldg, L-¥900, D-¥2,500, till-9pm, X-wed, ☎332-5253).

Bekkan Botan-en, just N of Nanking-machi, *Cantonese*, old-time favorite of locals; ¥-T-S, noodles handmade. 11-9pm, ☎331-5790. Our favorites two small, delicious budget, by Hankyu Sannomiya W exit on Kitanagasa-dori beyond Tor Rd: first, **Shinai-en**, *Shanghai*, few doors N, family-type, mama-san will help you choose. Best reserve table, ☎331-0924. Return to Kitanagasa-dori, one block W, original **Gunai**, *Cantonese*, ☎331-2740.

Gunai , newer and spacious, top end of Koikawa-suji, 12-8:30pm, X-thur, ☎321-1972. Advise reserve. Half-block W is **Wesley's**, tiny family-run by Eng-speaking Wesley, ☎331-1132, 11:30-10pm. E of Tor Rd on Ikuta Shinmichi is **Gaen Shuga** *Cantonese*, tasty, inexpensive, 11:30-9:30pm, no-X, ☎331-8828. Few doors to 4-storey **Shinsenkaku** *Peking*, good in large group at ¥4,-5,000 per head, rsve. ☎331-1263;

Gaen Shuga branch way E of Shin-Kobe stn, ideal for family ☎222-5329, no-X, 11:30-9:30pm. *Szechuan* **Mandarin Palace**, spicy, reasonable, rich decor, diagonal from Tokyu Hands S of Ikuta Shrine; 12-8pm, no-X, ☎321-2882.

Hai-Whan, deluxe, known for its fresh seafood, new location, 11F Port Island Bldg at Naka Koen stop; course ¥3,500-10,000 ea, 11:30-10pm, no-X, ☎242-0008. Nearby Portopia Hotel has **Shukei-en** ¥-L, lovely view; as also New Kobe Oriental skyroom **Keirin** (*Chin* Guilin).

Kobe Beef is justly world-famed.

In 1961 epicure Maurice Dreiser was in Japan and after sampling 'new' beer-fed beef in Tokyo, flew here to its home, mouth watering. Didn't find decent steak in all Kansai, flew right back to Tokyo's France-ya. He never got to best steak house...

Aragawa, whose owner-chefs believe in restful atmosphere, leisurely attitude, totally aloof to whim of customers—you order your cut and how rare you want it, which style spuds, and then shut up, don't bother masters –but shocking prices: couple=¥40,000. Filet, sirloin, of course charcoal broil (200gr) ¥12,000, dinner invites bankruptcy at ¥-LL ¥20,-30,000 hors-d'oeuvre, soup, salad, dessert, coffee or tea. Decent assortment of imported wines, starting ¥4,000 per bottle. They recommend Chassagne Montrachet from Burgonne at ¥15,000; all+%. Small and always crowded with leisurely regulars – 10 PM, so best phone ☎221-8547—show up two minutes late and they don't even look at you, you vegetarian. Nakayamate-dori 9-2.

A-One is excellent for cheaper steak, teppan broil w/salad ¥4,400; w/soup, rice, wine ¥5,600. 4-1am, X-wed ☎331-8932. Small, one long wooden counter so crowded with regulars that they won't deign suggest upstairs tables might be open—expect you to know to walk to back, upstairs and see for yourself. Ikuta Shrine Rd above tracks on R.

Misono, Shimoyamate-dori Ikuta Shrine Rd corner, fashionably overpriced *teppan-yaki* ¥8,000 for 200gr/half-pound (¥-L), w/salad–up; 11-30-2, 5-10pm, no-X; ☎331-2890.

Teppan-yaki next door, upstairs over quaint but inviting English sign *teppan-yaki*, thick steak chunks and vegetables broiled in front of you Kansai Kitchen-style. Oxtail soup–misnamed perhaps–shouldn't be missed.

Steak House Kobe, also *teppan-yaki*, 3F Nikaku-sushi facing N-side of Sannomiya stn. Small, neat shop. L-¥2,500; D-¥7,000 (¥-S), 6pm-3am, X-sun ☎332-6694.

For atmosphere and taste **Goji** is experience not to be missed–set in 2-storey Takayama farmhouse enhanced w/ antiques, music, kasuri-kimono'd maids–meat charcoal-broiled, served on hot grill. Kobe beef L-¥2,500; D-¥4,300-8,800 *Goji-fu* which is served on hot pebbles, eaten dipped in special sauce. From mid-Motomachi Shop Arcade, 3-chome, turn N (R) by Natural House. 11-11pm, X-wed; ☎332-3201.

Out to Tower Rd then cross Motomachi arcade–few houses down is...

Rokudan, all charcoal broiled steaks, L-course ¥1,700+; D-¥4,800+, *shabu-shabu* ¥4,800; recom. ¥5,600. ☎331-2108, 11:45-9pm, X-1&3-wed;

Ito Grill, old shop, reasonable, take family, L-¥1,600, D-¥3,000-7,000; charcoal broiled. From Daimaru-end of Motomachi arcade take 3rd alley to L, few houses in on L. 11:30-3, 5-8pm, X-wed, ☎331-2818.

Miyasu for over 30 years serving charcoal broiled steaks ¥-10,000, ¥-L, but a la carte hamburger, curry rice available; SW corner of Ikuta Shin-dori and Tor Rd, inexpensive, delicious, noon-10pm, no-X, ☎391-3088.

Iroriya near N end of Kitano-zaka on L. Service and attention of top Japanese restaurant. Steak & *sukiyaki*, L-*teishoku* ¥3,000, D-(200g) ¥4,500, *shabu-shabu*. ¥4,100, 12-10pm, no-X, ☎231-6777. Downtown branch **Tokei-ya**, same menu, opp N-side JR Sannomiya behind Kobe Taiyo Ginko Bank.

Komon, mingei decor, no steak but good *shabu-shabu*, *sukiyaki* ¥5,000, New Gate 4F, 50m N up Higashi-mon-dori at foot of Ikuta Shrine, 12-9pm, ☎331-0673. Also branch at Motomachi 3-chome, on Tower Rd which runs above Port Tower.

Kobe Beef was already famous by time of our '64 edition, but almost exclusive to foreigners' restaurants. Generation later Japanese had turned carnivores but not many could afford their beery-beef (we've seen some in butcher shops rivaling Beluga caviar in price), so Daiei entrepreneur Nakauchi brought in Victoria Station chain of restaurants for far cheaper Kansas beef. Also 'family restaurants' of several names offer good USA and Australian beef menus ¥-T (¥1,200-up), best of which are several **Royal Hosts**, open late. Off in side streets and not-much-advertised are numerous **Mos-Burger** for teriyaki-burgers on rice-flour bread—justifiably fastest growing burger chain in country.

Korean: *Yakiniku* BBQ, open late, great mixed grill at table for 2 or more: **Ox** across from JR Motomachi S exit, basement of Plaza-biru, ¥-T, 'kind owner, says be full at ¥2,000, burst ¥4,000.' Table over cut-out floor to dangle legs. X-sun. ☎392-2929. We frequent **Kalbiland** in ASHIYA (*see*). For true taste main **Imakita no Koraihan-ten** in AMAGASAKI is tops ☎06-416-0328, but in KOBE either **Dairakuen**, noon-1:30am, no-X, ☎321-1439, up Tor Rd at Yamaguchi Ginko (bank) intersection, L, about 15m from corner. Or **Nandai-mon**, noon-2am, from Hankyu W exit, up alley btwn Kotobukiya and Aoyama tea shop, to end of block on L. **Wakamatsu** is interesting & good, bit W at Ninomiya 3-12, ☎242-222.

KITANO-CHO, developing area has cluster of good ¥-S international restaurants at top Hunter-zaka at E-W Ijinkan-dori St: Starting from W-end, there's Ijinkan Club building where on 4F Yankee-baseballer Marty Kuehnert-run sawdust-and-peanutshell-floored **Attic**, good suppers, their hamburger plate makes you wonder why folk eat steak, ¥3,000 big dinner; **Tor Road Delicatessen** branch is in basement. Marty has larger **Attic Jr** sportsman's world—billiard table in one room, free, photos and posters of baseball greats, wonderful 'antiques?' hanging from rafters as in Attic-1. Diagonally across intersection 2 doors E, English sign, basement (underground attic?). Burger dinner ¥3,000, fine US steak dinner ¥4,000; hols ¥500 cover to non-member.

Few doors S down Hunterzaka on E side is moderate Edwardian-style luxury salon...
Queen's Court, nouvel cuisine (J-taste French), host Rudi Miura pioneered commercial restoration of area. Open thru midnite usually, for table advise rsve ☎242-2469, or eat at bar, ¥-T-S. As we go to print, temporarily closed for redecoration.

Back up at corner on Ijinkan-dori is Swiss-run, tasty, **Swiss Chalet**. Continuing E past supper-club CASABLANCA (*see below*), then good quick sandwich at Belgian-run **Jardin de France** on corner; mid-next block beneath golden mask of King Tut atop modern building, original **Gandhara** Indian (tiny, ¥-B-T), softest of palette of Kobe's several good true Indian eateries.

Few houses further E is true find...
Nova-tei, delicious inexpensive pleasant Japanese place. Overwhelming is L-¥1,500 with tempura, sashimi, soup, rice, W-wine and coffee; *kaiseki* from ¥4,500. ☎291-0661. Continue to end of this street and turn up hill. At top turn R and nxt L up steep slope is **Kitano Club**, 64 Kitano-cho l, posh dinner with view that rivals San Francisco's Mark. D in main room beats ¥-L hotel in quality, below in cost, L-¥3,000, D-steak ¥6,500, full course ¥10,000; 11am-2:30pm, 5-10:30pm.

Another great view, bit W, taxi basic-mtr up Futatabi Driveway in Park at Tenbodai observatory. **Tour d'Or**, good French, ¥-S D ¥5,-8,000+, –10pm, no-X, ☎241-0168.

Casablanca, supper-club, half-block E of Ijinkan Corner intersection, amazing for its low prices–high quality and imported live music, small dance floor where you may legally dance with your own wife or date—no hostesses. Private club, but as owner-couple are our associates in our Persia House Museum (*see*) *showing this book entitles you to guest member privileges* while in Kobe, visitor surcharge waived. Jamaican singer-manager Winston gives 'Bogey' air to place, expect police raid by Claude Rains any moment. Set menu has 'member's dinner' ¥2,000 ('90), no % extras, or ¥3,000 vegetarian, Indian, Middle East and near-best W-meal we've had is their higher special, ask Maitre de Winston what's on. till midnite, ☎241-0200, later if enough clients dally.

Middle Eastern: Village has trio of Japan's only M.E. restaurants. Oldest **Salaam**, is run by Israeli, Hunter-zaka below Ijinkan corner, W-side red brick bldg 2nd fl, til 9pm. Next is **Marrakech**, E-W street down, E 2 blocks to end of straight run, on R (downside) owner-chef Simon brings dishes seasoned with spices and herbs from Morocco, charcoal broiled brochette ¥1,200; popular cous-cous ¥2,000; dinner from ¥3,000; 5-11pm, ☎241-3440, X-mon. (Casablanca formerly had Simon and still offers good simple ME course on good international menu). **Bukhara** said to be Central Asian, but Japanese-run, we taste modified Indian—however many foreign friends adore it—reasonably ¥-T, spicy, cozy and 'ethnic': street above Daimaru, mid-block, small English sign upstairs, till 10pm, ☎331-1734.

Back on street with Mosque to E: **Grand Micaela-i-Dago**, small, run by Chilean Meririan Dago and wife, both always helping with charity for South American causes. Songs by Dago on his guitar, 5-11pm, X-tue, ☎242-0043; and **Tijuana**, one of first ethnic restaurants in town, seasoning tempered to Japanese taste, also live music, 6pm-2am, ☎242-0043; latest on scene is **Chico & Charlie's**, hotter dishes, 11am-12am, 4F Corner House, Yamamotodori 1-7-11.

Japanese: Best in little places up alleys, of which Kobe has plenty. Meat dishes listed above in Western (as is Korean) show there really isn't all that difference between E–W. Remember that *soba, udon, sushi* shops have variety of *teishoku*, table d'hote meals, and lunchtime have *o-bento* specials in lovely ceramics, lacquer, baskets, var ¥-B-T, rare ¥-S.

TEMPURA: **Okagawa**, lovely setting, wonderful view, up next door to Kitano Club, *teishoku* ¥4,000 and full course ¥8,000; *shokado* lunch, ¥3,500. **Tengayu**, charming elegant, uses lovely ceramics and lacquerware. Chef prepares in front of you, fresh seasonal seafood & vegetables, fresh shrimp from tank. L-¥1,000; D-¥4,500-8,000. On Kitano-zaka St, 1 blk from Sannomiya, 4 doors beyond Fugetsudo teashop, in rear; 11:30-2, 4-10pm, ☎392-0895. Branch in Ashiya city nr JR stn ☎0797-34-1788.

Tenfuji's refined air reflects owner. Small, counter only. Set ¥3,000, dinner ¥5,000. Across from Ikuta Shrine west gate, 11-2pm, 5-9pm, X-sun, ☎392-3630.

SUSHI: **Gin-zushi**, real inexpensive, but super, gets plaudits from all. Just opp police box R of entry to Ikuta Shrine, ☎321-1392.

Maruman typical ¥-B family style *sushi, soba* and *udon* house. *Teishoku sushi* or *udon* ¥500, 11-9pm, X-tue. From Nishimura Coffee Shop on Nakayamate-dori 1-chome, up Hunter-zaka slope few doors past **Freundlieb Bakery**—which incidentally has best pumpernickel in West Japan, good visiting gift.

Sakae zushi, basically sushi bar, tray of mixed *jo-nigiri* ¥1,500, bento ¥2,300; tempura *teishoku*, lovely ceramic and lacquer dishes used. 11:30-9pm, X-wed, ☎331-0069. Cross street W-end of Center-gai, R at Sano Sports—next door on alley side.

Otsuki famed for low price, up Tor Rd from el tracks, first R, then L, on L; ☎331-7831

UNAGI a.k.a. *kabayaki* (broiled eels); nutritious delicacy, summer especially **Chikuyo-tei**, eel tops, also J-*teishoku, sashimi, shabu-shabu*, in charming mingei decor museum of ceramics of national treasure potter HAMADA Shoji, KAWAI Kanjiro, Bernard Leach, woodblock artist MUNAKATA Shiko, btwn W&E exits Hankyu Stn under el tracks N-side. L-¥2,000; D-full ¥8,000+, but cheaper a la carte.

Aoba excellent, small, counter, teishoku ¥-T, *kimo-no kushiyaki* (barbecued livers) so good for you, Motomachi 3-chome-8, ☎331-2845.

Fukue, inexpensive, lunch ¥650; *kabayaki teishoku* ¥2,500, other dishes. 3-floors, X-sun, 1 block S (to sea) of Motomachi 4-chome, ☎341-2118.

Kitahama in Center Plaza basement, and Santica underground town.

SOBA: Shops are in every arcade, but *easy to find and bit special are...*

Masaya with waterwheel outside, N of Sannomiya Hankyu stn foot of Kitano-zaka, just above Ikuta-shinmichi st.

Akoya-tei with mingei decor serves only handmade udon noodles: 2F Aoyama Coffee Shop across from Hankyu Sannomiya Stn W exit. 11-1am, no-X, ☎233-3003; larger shop in striking new Tasaki Pearl bldg S of ShinKobe Stn, across from and E of Kitagawa Koen park ☎232-2400.

Doga makes own noodles from stone-ground Nagano Pref soba. 11:30-2; 5-8pm, X-mon. ☎392-1043. W of Kano-cho 3-chome pedestrian bridge intersection, next door to Kyodo gas stand. Try their *sanshoku* (3 colors) soba; and Kisoji.

YAKITORI: Bite-sized meats & vegs on bamboo skewer, barbecued.

Sanukiya, tiny unobtrusive, superb. Connoisseurs claim it is Kansai's best and VIPs come from afar. Inexpensive, 4-8pm, X-sat, sun, mon. Strongly advise phone ☎221-5286, or go early before regulars come.

Toyokuni, old well-known, small; 11:30-2, 4:30-8pm (sat & sun no break). Sannomiya 2-35, off Tor Rd E 2nd alley from Center-gai, turn at Paulista. ☎331-4538.
Doi, popular, reasonable. Course ¥3,000. One block S of Center-gai nr Flower Rd. 11:30-10pm, ☎391-4401.

KUSHI-KATSU: Skewered deep fried breaded bite-sized chicken, shrimp, meat, etc. (when pork it's *ton-katsu*), mostly plebeian inexpensive:
Kushinoya, opp W exit of Hankyu Sta., 3F above Aoyama Coffee shop. Eng, Ger spoken. 12-1:30pm, 5-9:30pm. (Sun. 12-9:30pm), no-X, ☎391-4194.

TON-KATSU: Pork cutlets, usually in bite size, on rice, best in Kansai at **Musashi** plain wood front shop W-end (Daimaru) of Center-gai, Mt-side; moderate.

FUGU: (blow fish): Small family run **Stand Hama**, carefully prepared by owner HAMAJI Kazuo; ☎331-4492. Off Tor Rd, in N-S alley W of Tor Road in narrow block N across from Daimaru DS.
Naha is for real *ero/exotic*, 'Okinawan restaurant' in same alley as *fugu* place above, and next door to Itohei eel house. Decor is 'new stone age', that is, all souvenirs and talismans from sex shrines. Menu is collector's item; best order table d'hote sampler *teishoku* for portions you barbecue yourself, of goat, duck, pork, etc. Specials, a la carte, include *mamushi* (viper), cobra, *hai* (viper that bit Cleopatra), *hoden* (testicles) and guess what you get when you ask for *penisu, wagina, uterusu* or *mamma*.

CRAB: **Nishimura-ya**, with small red lanterns hanging from eaves; mingei interior, suggest order *teishoku*. Block E of Sogo parking lot; ☎232-3663. Next door tasteful sister shop **Tajima-ji** ☎291-0246 serves Japanese dishes ¥-B.
　　Also at **Zentan** Bus Company's restaurant on 2nd F of Hyogo Kenritsu Togei Kan (Prefectural Ceramic Museum-*see*) nr *Kencho,* Prefectural HQ.

NATURAL FOOD: **Sun Tomato** in **Natural House**, excellent & inexpensive. Salad bar ¥500, tofu dish set w/ brown rice, soup, salad ¥700; selection soya white sauce gratin sets, vegetable protein dish sets all ¥650-900. Motomachi Shopping St. 2-chome, in basement next to Yamaha music store. Sun Tomato 11-8pm, no-X, ☎392-3661.
Shinno, newly opened, serves innovative dishes of fish, organically-grown vegetables. Set with main dish of soybean hamburger, tempura or fish plus brown rice, miso soup, boiled greens, *hijiki* seaweed, *tsukemono* only ¥600-700. English menu. 11-11pm. From Nakayamate-dori and Kitano-zaka intersection, go W to o.w. street leading to police box then L, same bldg as Marrakech. ☎261-0208, X-3rd sun.
Rokudan, *sansai ryori* (mountain greens). Owner YAMADA Yukio collects some of mountain materials himself, makes own aperitif from wild berries, fruits. Exhibit of outstanding artists' works hangs on dining room walls. *Sansai Gozen* L ¥2,500, tempura ¥3,000; tenshin ¥3,500; D-course ¥4,500, a la carte. Opp N exit Sannomiya JR block N of Nishimura Coffee House, 4F Sankin Bldg ☎231-0406.

ASHIYA: Many foreign residents-to-be make first short stay in this lovely hillside town while apartment hunting, often staying at **Takezono Hotel** (N-side JR stn across pedestrian bridge from stn 2nd fl), new, ¥-T, ☎(0797)-31-2341, hangout for pro-baseball teams in season. JR stn itself 5fl houses Mont-et-mer (mount and sea) complex of restauarants including first **Victoria Station** ¥-T US roast beef (owner Nakauchi lives near, brings guests); Chinese **Totenkaku** far better than mediocre main in ijinkan in Kitano-cho Kobe; also several good J-style with window models, all good, ¥-T mostly.
Bellini, one of best W restaurants in Kobe area, ☎32-1777, W-side Ashiya river 2min walk S from Hankyu Ashiyagawa stn to old pine tree jutting into road; or 5min W from JR where cross river tree is to R; brick bldg, menu outside on stand, Park, E-spkn; Kosher, L, D–9pm. New Cuisine Italo-Japan, ala carte, but advise table d'hote D: meat ¥5,000, fish ¥3,000, both ¥7,000. Good choice import wines reasonable for Japan.
Kalbi-land, our favorite Korean, bit blander than others for J-pallet: Go down-river from Hankyu stn across main ave at 2nd bridge, R from gas stn; ¥-T, till 2am.
Sam's Place, good reasonable steaks, top steak tartar, Sam speaks Yankee, he and wife golf nuts. Behind hotel, R first block, R, E-sign; –9pm. Cheapest best steak tartar in Jpn to ¥-B dinners, decor old diner of '50s; plus walls full work of local foreign painters.

NITE LIFE

TAME, despite long history as international port. Many bars are for Japanese only—'no here' they'll say. But in Kobe it's purely language problem and if you or friend speak Japanese, barrier dissolves. Japan is notorious for its gyp joint bars—we list inexpensive good places where you're safe. Jazz premiered in Japan in Kobe in '20s—Jay has found his dad's ancient '20s discs in local collections—never lost popularity even in WW II. There are numerous small clubs, 'live houses', where our local English-speaking friends sing or play. Solid proportion of black musicians —American, Jamaican, local—add pizazz to local jazz scene. (See *KTO* for October *Jazz Street*, occasional public- or stn-plaza concerts).

KITANO-CHO: On Kitano-zaka just below Ijinkan-dori, **Cross**, live soft music, basement of Namban-tei, 5pm-4am, ☎222-2423. Opp Catholic Church, **Charlies**, owner-guitarist Charlie runs small comfortable snack-bar where guitarist Sho been coming every sat-sun to duet for years. 7-3am, ☎222-6909. Next door is **Dips**, pianist and tiny dance floor, 6-12am, ☎221-5335. Down street W nr Mosque, **Grand Micaela-i-Dago**, Chilean food, owner Merilian entertains with guitar, 5pm-1am, ☎241-0367.

Further E...
Tijuana, Mexican food, live entertainment, 6pm-2am, ☎242-0043. **Compass**, (pop music) across wide Nakayamate-dori in Palais Kitano-zaka Bldg, 9F. (Sho & Diane play after 12am) 7pm-3am. Small music charge. Next block, is 'adult' disco **Shekinah**, records, 7pm-3am, ladies ¥2,000, men ¥2,500, and all drinks free. ☎332-0666.

DISCOS come and go, check KTO or ask hotel front for timely recommendation, but ¥-L hotels have good ones, geat decor and reasonably priced.
Kentos, on Tor Road is disco, live music of '60s, space to dance. Opp Highway Rest, near Ikuta-Shinmichi crossing, 5pm-1am, no-X, ☎392-2118. **Garage Paradise** where enjoy live 'imported' music nitely, play pool or dance in small back room to live DJ. Drinks bit high, but nice decor and good mix of natives and foreigners; Nakayamate-dori, B1, 6:30pm-4:00am, ☎391-6640. **Polo Dog,** small but lively place for hotdog and beer. Check dates of live Country & Western band. 2-5-12 Sannomiya-cho, 11am-10pm ☎391-1460.

PORT ISLAND Exotic Town, has foreign entertainers providing live music on 1st floor, possible to dance. Basically young crowd. 12:30-3:30am, no-X. Portliner to Minami Koen Stn, walk straight into Exotic Town; late return taxi only.

Most of above frequented by younger crowd. For more adult crowd...
Tom Chianti in Washington Hotel, IF, piano bar; **Wine Bar** on street N-side Sannomiya-Hankyu Stn, in middle block, sign in neon jungle if you look carefully, elevator up; successful rip-off of US original but unrelated except bar-sinister: reasonable, good noshes and often imported entertainment, usually gal guitar-singer soloist.

When Kaz Nakagawa of Doctor Jazz died in 1990 we lost a favorite hang-out. We fill in with **MM Join** well-known to old-timers. Makoto Ozone with trio to quintet entertain nightly from 8:30. Good relaxing sweet jazz. Son Makoto made name for himself in US...now has couple of albums; hangs out in dad's joint when on one of his extended visits home. 2 F of Fuji Sangyo bldg, just above **Satin Doll** another popular club, on Kitano-zaka, ☎222-5313.

For dinner with dancing, cheek or jitter, no loud rock...
Casablanca Restaurant in Kitano-cho (see CHOPSTICKS) where always imported talent. **Portopia Hotel** 'Top-of-' dine or wine, pianist and dance floor, as **V&V** next door atop slightly taller World Fashion skyscraper; both have dinner dancing; ¥-L.**New Oriental Hotel City** expected to outdo all others, innovate, at international ¥-L hotel rates; OPA–Oriental Park Avenue in adjoining non-hotel multi-storey arcade of hundreds of shops and restaurants including cobble-stone Old Edo Street (4th fl) chock full of good restaurants mostly ¥-T, while atop hotel are ¥-L Chinese, Western & Japanese. Great **theater** 4th fl, top original and import plays, classic to avant garde, run as loss leader to create trade for hotel and OPA restaurants, most open till late.

SLUMMING

FUN IN MAZE of alleys between Ikuta Shrine and el tracks where little bars and clubs run solidly E to Sannomiya stn, and around Washington Hotel (¥-T), midst of which on broad taxi-clogged E-W street (2nd above tracks) is fairly good **Kobe Sauna**, no hanky-panky just good bath, sauna and straight-massage. Note sign at entry barring people 'with large tattoos or wearing clogs'—yakuza uniform, and Kobe is their town.

Bars catering to foreigners declining with rise of small-crew container ships. Stroll Nanking-machi–**China Town** (area seaside of Motomachi arcade) for these, names in English. Beware only their touts, who invite you to bar with promises which mean only that their high commission must be added to your bill—tho now disappearing since demise of ship-crews. If interested, take his handout, lose him, go alone later.

Bar strip along W-end...

Shinkaichi (subway to Minatogawa or Kamisawa stn walk S 5min, or from Sannomiya stn W-bound extensions of Hanshin or Hankyu RR to Shinkaichi underground stn; or taxi 2x-mtr), where used to be strip acts on stage behind bar—alas, no more. Mostly frequented by yakuza, who when on town in Kobe are charming chaps despite gang wars recently popping out in Kobe with real guns. You can tell them by flat-top haircut and suit (sleeves rolled back) in imitation of George Raft of 1930s movies. Don't laugh, they're real, but don't bother anyone but their own. That's not to say there's no danger—but from occasional nuts who start out babbling anti-foreign nonsense, usually high on something (speed)—politely evade and call waiter for bill. And this not just Shinkaichi, but Kitano, too, anywhere.

HOME VISIT PLAN

BRINGS YOU INTO Japanese home few hours in evening. Arrange thru hotel desk, or **Kobe International Tourist Association** ☎303-1010, but requires trip to Port Island office–not worth it unless going out to see Pearl Museum or other–and probably more than day in advance. As elsewhere, cost is only for student interpreter (if needed tho most families now have at least one English-speaker) plus your taxi fare (bus if budget). Small visiting gift is in order according to Japanese fashion, should be under ¥2,000, budgeteers token only is fine, we suggest candy or pastry from **Cosmopolitan, Juccheim, Freundlieb** or such quality delicacies in W- taste, which are most appreciated; or souvenir from home, if available, is best by far.

Goodwill Guides volunteers in **Kobe** ☎078-821-5456 Ms IMURA Chijiko, advise ✍ in advance, postcard OK, tell date etc, **Ms Imura**, Nakago-cho 2ch-7-3, Nada-ku Kobe 657. Doesn't like to impinge on work of pros, so handles individuals especially visiting relatives of residents. (*See* also Nara, Kyoto, most cities).

SHOPPING

KOBE HAS LARGE resident foreign population and constant stream of ships' crews (greatly reduced since advent of large automated container ships with small crews) and passengers. Shops cater to foreign tourists and residents. Good way to orient oneself is to choose as landmark **Daimaru DS**— excellent line of general J-goods especially kimono, arts, china, furniture.

Take as starting point and face mountains, go to street on right and head for hills: this is **TOR ROAD** (named after early English engineer, renamed by xenophobes during war as *Toa*, 'East Asia', and again postwar to Tor) which used to be bustling street with many foreign shops leading to original Oriental Hotel, now expatriates' Kobe Club. Today, there are still some foreign shops like Tor Road Delicatessen and some Chinese tailors, number of silver and jewelry stores on this street, two ANTIQUE shops (*see* below).

Back at Daimaru, going L (W) is...

MOTOMACHI covered shopping arcade (original post-town of Hyogo before foreign settlement, which covered area from Daimaru corner to sea and E to Sannomiya-Flower Road, then river), long street of 340 shops, first few blocks typically modern starting with Maruzen Book- (best selection of English books) followed by camera-, fabric-shops, Kobe beef butcher with marbled meat at ¥4,000 per 100g–$140 per lb! Western half is a bit classical Japan, shops for fine kimonos, art goods, fans, traditional sweet shops, accessories, and in passing, several fair curio shops. Nice stroll. Few blocks up from Daimaru running parallel to sea and hills, is popular Sannomiya shopping arcade.

Better known as...

CENTER-GAI, Center street, has all kinds of utilitarian shops. Starting at Tor Road going E, there's nicely stocked kiddies' shop **Familia** (pricey but local kiddie styles are without peer, quality to match British of 1930s). Continue, and as you near Sannomiya on R-seaside, department store noted for electronics, **Seidensha** for complete line of hi-fi equipment; info counter where you can inquire in English. Tax-free products of nearly all hi-fi makers in Japan, veritable hi-fi supermarket. Then **Gotoh** old books.

Just across street is...

Inahara typewriter and office equipment store, for Japanese typewriters, now called *wah-p'ro* (word processor) into which you type either form of kana or roman-alphabet and get kanji output. (Doesn't work for Chinese, different input system and mostly different version of 'kanji' and while Chinese sets are made here, all are presently exported). Opp small curio shop **Yamaichi** chock full of fine old things, coins to antiques; expensive.

This brings you out by Sannomiya Stn and right by...

Kobe International House arcade with usual pearl, damascene, optical, fur and silk shops. **Kanebo** here has best silk selection in Kansai. Pearls in general are always good buys and Kobe, 'Pearl City' center of international wholesale trade, is head office of **Tasaki Pearl** (specialist in large South Sea pearls, see their **Pearl Museum** on Port Island); **Yamakatsu Pearl** (retail in Santika Town); **Mori Pearl** (Port Island), and numerous small companies. Highly recommended by foreign residents is old-timer jeweler **WF Schultz**, show- and sale-room N opp Daimaru.

ANTIQUES: 20 years ago Kobe great market, but no longer–but where is? Some good shops remain, especially for home decoration quality. On Tor Road top on R, just below and opp Kobe Club, standby for residents is **Marukiya**, fair prices; down street just above el-tracks on opp (W-) side is **Namba**, Kobe branch of immense shop in OKAYAMA city we like.

LESSER ANTIQUES and *mingei* folk art, two shop-homes on small scale, especially for *tansu*-chests, late 19th century usable porcelains:

Ancrum House Arts, wily Scot Orientalist Alistair Seton hauls his sporrin and station wagon around to country auctions to stock residents less-mobile or lesser linguists in *tansu*-chests, 19th century china tableware. Occasional special show at his modern home, welcomes visitors other times if stock in hand, esp weekends or eves. Has English prints for J clients. For instructions & appt: ☎851-6654, taxi 4x-mtr from Sannomiya, great view en route.

Art Kura also monthly exhibition-sales 'at home' but available by appt if in stock or if not away buying. Seawards from Ashiya Hanshin stn; or taxi 5x-mtr from Sannomiya. ☎(0797)-32-6219; if no answer try Kyoto ☎(075)-581-7703.

ASHIYA also has two small curio shops worthwhile for avid shopper or resident. From Ashiya River (down from Hankyu Ashiyagawa stn, or up from Art Kura) on main road, rte2, W to Kobe first block N- (R- or Mt-) side **Keibi-do** misc ceramics reasonable; farther W toward Kobe 3 blocks on R is tiny **Banri**, gals who run it lived in California few years, spk-E, good for old textiles, misc usable ceramics, inexpensive. Both open fairly late, Banri X-25 when at temple fair.

Fine curios & Oriental art, **David Kidd** was long recommended in Ashiya, starred in our first edition. Alas for Kobe, he's moved to Kyoto (*see* p.544): ☎(075)-751-8552, by appt, pm & eve only.

HARBOR CRUISES
SPRING THRU end-Nov from Nakatotte (*Meriken Hatoba*) pier, base of Port Tower, walk or taxi basic-mtr down from Motomachi stn (slightly over mtr from Sannomiya). Cruise thru Akashi Straits outer harbor 11:40 for 3hrs, ¥2,570. Osaka Bay A tour 3:30 for 2hr20min, ¥2,570; **Night tour** B 6:50 2hr20min, ¥2,570. **Luminous Kanko Co** ☎333-8480. Similar offerings, plus 11am Awaji Isle circle in 4hrs-¥7,800, nite tour 90min-¥2,500 but irregular as also available for charter (160 psgrs), many rooms and lounges, ¥500,–800,000 2-4hrs + catering); **Awaji Ferry**, ☎735-0888.

Hydrofoils dep Kansai Kisen pier once or twice daily for SHODO-SHIMA → TAKAMATSU run. Plan service Kobe to Naruto Strait to see giant whirlpools, 75min each way, departures vary with tide.

HELICOPTER TOUR
FIXED, FREE or commute, 5 psgr min but Wed sgl OK –Akashi Straits course covers W-area, Osaka Intl Airport course E-area, 25min ¥28,000 each psgr, other courses average ¥1,000 per minute; **Hankyu Kuko Osaka** ☎(06)-373-1661, or Kobe flight control ☎(078)-302-7071. 'Copter services proliferating, check major hotel desk or TIC.

KYOTO is 1 hour by JR express via Osaka direct, 3-4 trains every hour to Kyoto JR stn; half-price but 10-20min more by Hankyu electric with change at JUSO (tracks labeled in English and where one also changes for TAKARAZUKA coming from Osaka) into midtown Kyoto at Shijo-Kawaramachi terminus. **Full-day taxi** r.t. from KOBE thru KYOTO and NARA with sightseeing will run about ¥25,000+¥4–5,000 tolls ('89) according to our local owner-driver Mr Kitamura, ☎(0797)-22-6112—he'll pick you up early morn at hotel and return you after dinner, understands just enough English for clearly stated instructions but cannot guide–that's what we are for. If taxiing one way (almost same as r.t.), spend little more and make half-day trip of it via Takarazuka and combining view of Kobe from...(*see* DRIVEWAYS, above).

MK Taxi from Kyoto will pick you up, or deliver you here from, in 5-psgr large Toyota from Kobe ¥18,130 (or Cadillac ¥37,080), includes one way empty but all road tolls extra. English speaking driver sometimes available; can also arrange Kyoto city tours (*see* KYOTO) to their set- or your selected-itineraries: ☎(075)-721-2237.

SEA-GOING FERRIES TO CHINA
FERRIES lv OSAKA-KOBE head S under Shikoku, Kyushu on to Okinawa, SHANGHAI: Kobe Port Terminal or Osaka Nanko Kamome, tues 12:00 **Nitchu Kokusai Ferry** ☎078-392-1021; –TIENTSIN, Port Terminal, fri 18:00pm, **China Express** ☎321-5791.

FERRY ROUTES INTO INLAND SEA
US, UK 'FERRY' means any passenger boat from one port to another. In Japan it means ship carrying cars & trucks as well as passengers. Passenger only ship is *kyaku-sen*, or *renraku-sen* for ship meeting scheduled trains.

Ferries from most mainland cities go to Shikoku, Kyushu; some stop en route at large isles like Awajishima or Shodoshima this end of Inland Sea. Until recent bridges linked isles, ship sole mode of transport so hundreds of small lines link myriad isles to each other with *kaijo-bus,* water bus. Convenient as small isles often have only one or two ships stop daily.

TYPE: Regulars **ships** *kyaku-sen, ferry* while **hydrofoil** *suichu-yokusen* and **hovercraft** *kosokutei* cut time almost in half; and newer **jet foil** *jetto hoiru* moving faster. Must usually reserve for latter three, as well as for special accommodations on regular, and best to reserve for cars.

So choose itinerary, inform your travel agent as most overseas don't know local lines, book you on main and best known 13-16hr KANSAI – BEPPU of Kansai Kisen, which run length of Inland Sea, 3x-daily from OSAKA–KOBE: Get *KTO* June issue, which carries complete schedules, which vary some annually, incl → Okinawa, China, Korea, Taiwan.

1) Lv OSAKA (Benten Port) 15:00 → lv KOBE (Naka Pier) 16:20; via SAKATE (on Shodoshima) and TAKAMATSU; → arr BEPPU 7:00am; 16hrs. No cars.
2) Lv OSAKA (Nanko) 19:00 → KOBE 20:30 → arr BEPPU 08:00; 13hr. Psgrs, cars.
3) Lv OSAKA 21:00 → Kobe 22:30 via IMABARI–MATSUYAMA → arr BEPPU 11:55am. *Skip*—as all above pass lovely Okayama isles at nite, except return from BEPPU 21:00.

Kansai Kisen OSAKA ☎(06)-572-5181, KOBE ☎(078)-391-6601, BEPPU ☎(0977)-22-1311. KOBE has several piers: downtown Naka-totte pier, E are Rokko Isle Ferry quay-*futo*, Uozaki (Higashi Kobe Ferry *futo*), and Ohgi *futo*. W is Suma Port & Akashi.

FARES (lo-hi only): OSAKA → BEPPU: 2nd cl ¥5,870, 1st ¥11,740, spec ¥18,850; car ¥11,840 (3m), ¥23,690 (6m). Can arrange to get off by paying for separate legs.

We suggest go OSAKA → BEPPU overland to Kyushu, return from BEPPU → KOBE by 21:00 boat. Or boat OSAKA → get off at IMABARI as few isles Imabari–Matsuyama.

Best **daylite** sched lv KOBE (Ohgi) 9:00, X-sat (also 22:40-NG) **Ehime Hanshin Ferry.** KOBE → IMABARI (7-8hrs) → MATSUYAMA (10-11hrs). Fares (1991): Imabari ¥3,090–¥7,210, VIP ¥20,500; car ¥9,270+; Matsuyama ¥4,430–¥8,860. ☎(078)-451-1068, ☎(0898)-23-3110.

Continue from IMABARI → HIROSHIMA or KYUSHU. Many possibilities depending on your time: fastest is **Jet Foil**, 1hr45min (reg 4+hrs) to OSAKA-KOBE-TAKAMATSU; via SAKATE, ret via TONOSHO, **Kansai Kisen** ☎ above; **Kato Kisen** ☎(06)-572-3031, ☎(078)-331-8532, ☎(0878)-51-5211; ¥5,990.

OTHER SCHEDS: OSAKA → KOBE → **TAKAMATSU: Leave** from Osaka (Benten Port) 10:30 → Kobe (Naka) 12:00 → Tonosho 16:10 → Takamatsu 17:14. **Return**: Takamatsu 22:00 → Tososho 23:20 → Kobe 4:10 → Osaka 5:40, run by **Kato Kisen** ☎ above; ¥2,780–¥9,890.

Via SAKATE: lv Osaka (Benten) 8:30 ferry, 15:00 psgr; Kobe (Naka) 9:30, 16:20; Arr Sakate 12:50, 19:30; Takamatsu 14:00, 20:50. Ret Takamatsu 7:55 psgr, 14:30 ferry; Sakate 9:15, 15:40; Kobe 12:25, 18:40; Arr Osaka 13:45, 20:00; ¥2,370–¥5,970; cars ¥6, 590–¥8,240. **Kansai Kisen** ☎ above.

Via KOBE: direct 15x-daily summer, other 10x-; 4hr, **Kansai Kisen, Kato Kisen** ☎ above. Lv KOBE (Ohgi) → Takamatsu about every 90min 1:10am thru 23:50; ¥2,060–¥4,630, cars ¥7,620–¥9,470. To SHODOSHIMA: (*see* p.685) ONNOMICHI → IMABARI (*see* p.700).

→ **MATSUYAMA:** 8+ hrs, good if saving on hotel, but not for sightseeing as by nite; Lv Kobe (Rokko Isle) 20:00, 22:30; lv Matsuyama 20:35, 22:40; **Diamond Ferry** ☎(078)-391-6361, Matsuyama ☎(0899)-51-2266; ¥3,500–¥8,760; car ¥10,–¥12,870 (5m-long). OSAKA (Benten) → Kobe (Naka) 21:00, 7hrs Imabari → Matsuyama; 1x-daily. Ret leave Matsuyama 21:05; Imabari 23:00; **Kansai Kisen.**

→ **TOKUSHIMA:** from Kobe (Naka), Hydrofoil 1hr45min, 5x-daily, *see* p678.

→ **SHIMOTSUI:** (from Uno-Marugame) 45min via Honjima-Yojima; UNO → TAKAMATSU 1hr, 24hr-svce, every 30min, ¥380) **Udo Kokudo** Ferry ☎(0878)-51-5001, Shikoku Ferry ☎51-0131; cars w/psgr only, ¥4,060, **Unno** ☎(0863)-21-5351.

thus let us drink and be merry
even grass and tree thrive in spring
only to fade and fall with autumn
— Lady Otomo, 759, *Manyoshu*

PERSONAL DATEBOOK

(K=KOBE, O=OSAKA)

(* ='Must See' or base itinerary around)

January

2 *Ritual First Bath* at Arima onsen (p.596) Mikoshi & geisha parade from Onsen-ji 10am to Arima elementary school, bronze statues 2 patron saints ceremoniously bathed by ornately-dressed geisha. Kobe.

7 *Tsuina Shiki* (Demon-Chasing rite) at Oyama-Dera temple in Kobe City.

8-12* *Ebisu Matsuri* familiarly called *Tohka Ebisu*, observed at many shrines countrywide. Imamiya Jinja in Osaka best known in Kansai. Every year makes headlines with staggering total monetary offerings that require days to count. Osaka merchants take Ebisu, their God of Wealth seriously. Imamiya Jinja include rice-pounding rite on 8th 10am, 11am cakes passed to all. *Bugaku* 2 pm. **10th:** 10:30am 12 geisha carried on gaily festooned sedan chairs leave Yamato-ya, Soemon-cho, arrive noon at shrine, 1pm geisha dance offering.

9-10 *Tohka Ebisu* at Ebisu Jinja shrine Nishinomiya city w/ *kagura* on 10th.

14* *Doya-doya Festival* Shitenno-ji temple Osaka, horde of near-naked youths parade, return temple 2pm, encircle central pillar and rub against each other in midwinter rite also seen elsewhere.

Lunar 1-3* *Chinese New Year* Feb 4, 1992, Jan 23, '93; Feb 10, '94; Jan 31, '95; Feb 19, '96; F-7, '97; J-28, '98; J-16, '99 (J-'old' new year). Newly-revived, imported 40m-long male dragon, 20m female, with dozens of kungfu-suited human legs, dance several times daily 3 days from noon, Chinatown nr Motomachi, Kobe.

February

4* *Setsubun* nationwide, most colorful rites in area at Nagata Jinja, Kobe; 3pm. Demon-chasing rite, 7 masked demons guarding 7 temple gates dance with flaming torches, said to prevent illness from entering area. Kobe Kosoku line extension of Hanshin & Hankyu lines to Kosoku Nagata, or subway to Nagata stn; 10 min N. Kyoto, Nara better (*see* p.390).

March

3 *Children's Day*, Emperor-Empress dolla with ornate court, shows-sales all DS, doll shops. *Nagashibina*–setting afloat of paper *hina* dolls on paper boats, by little girls casting off evil for good health, at Nakanoshima Park, central Osaka.

18-24 *O-higan* (SpringEquinox) observed nationwide. Shitenno-ji temple festival, Osaka, fair, 100s of stalls out to sell to throngs at memorial services and making pilgrimages to their family graves as is custom for this period.

April

9 *Hana Matsuri* nationwide; birthday Shakyamuni, historical Buddha born in Lumbini Garden, Nepal. Temples hold rites, sacred bower decorated in cut flowers. In it stands infant Buddha over which faithful pour sweet tea. *Chigo*, children dressed in heavenly garments, usually parade in neighborhoods.

10 *Spring Festival* Shitenno-ji temple, Osaka, *bugaku* ancient masked dance.

13* *Hanatsumi Matsuri* (Flower Picking Fete) Otori Shrine, one of largest in Osaka area, Sakai City, S of Osaka. *Mikoshi*, flower girls, *chigo* parade, 1-6pm shrine to Hamadera Park on beach.

14-16* *Ikuta Matsuri* at Ikuta Jinja, Kobe; fest highlighted by parade of *mikoshi* with local children colorfully dressed as celestial *chigo*.

Mid 10 days, *Sakura viewing*, best at Osaka Mint, illuminated till 9pm; top view from riverboat Suijo-bus, 40min; view from upstairs New Otani hotel.

22* *O-Shorai* (Prince Shotoku Memorial) Shitenno-ji temple, Osaka, observes death of founder-Prince Shotoku of 6th century Nara. Full program of *bugaku* dance offerings on outdoor stage built over large pond in shrine garden.

29 Birthday late emperor Showa (Hirohito), national holiday, now *Greenery Day*.

Late–early May, Osaka Music Festival, fine concerts galore, imports & native .

May

1-10 *Nozaki Kannon fete* observed by lunar calendar at Jingan-ji temple at Nozaki in Daito City, SE of Osaka City. Reader of playwright Chikamatsu Monzaemon, 'Shakespeare of Japan', will recall *Nozaki-mairi* pilgrimage to Nozaki in his many love suicide plays.

2-4* (approx) *Azalea viewing* at Mt Asaka Water Filtration plant, Sakai S of Osaka *free*, 10min walk from Asaka Station on JR Hanwa Line, which starts out of Namba; ☎ (0722)-33-7548.

5 *Kodomo-no-hi*, Children's Day, 'double-5' former Boys' Day observance with carp streamers decorating entire country-side. Ends festive 'Golden Week' with most offices closed all or part of week.

8 *Hana Matsuri*, of Jingan-ji, above.

12 *Nerikuyo* (Kannon Procession) at Taisan-ji temple, Nishi-ku in Kobe City finds number of persons wearing *kannon* masks and robes in solemn procession enacting descent from paradise to earth.

Mid – *Kamigata Hanabutai*, Osaka's geisha give program for few days, Bunraku-za theater, Osaka, ☎212-2531.

June

14* *Otaue* (Rice Planting) Sumiyoshi Jinja, Osaka. Shrine prays for rich harvest with day of festivities, planting of rice shoots in sacred shrine paddy. Originally planting performed solely by virgins, but today dance and song offerings as well as rice planting are by Shinmachi geisha. Rites start about noon at main hall with dance offerings and ceremonial rice transplanting from 2 pm.

30-Jul 2 *Aizen Matsuri* Shoman-in temple Osaka. Aizen-do pavilion built by Prince Shotoku for mother. Being one of first summer fetes, it is also known as *Yukata Matsuri* as people blossom out in *yukata*. . . .

30 Main day, with geisha from various quarters arriving carried in their decorated sedan chairs, leave Imasato (10:00) Ueroku (13:00), Shitennoji (15:00) arrive at Aizendo (17:00).

July

12-13 *Natsu Matsuri* with *danjiri* portable shrine wheeled floatss, Hirano S Osaka.

15 *Sentoh Sai* (Thousand Candle Fete) at Ikuta Jinja, Kobe.

Mid – school vacation season starts.

22-26 *Toki-ichi* Pottery Fair, Zama Jinja, Osaka. Wholesalers discount their wares as many shops set up outdoor stalls along street. Lovely way to spend eve, scenic journey getting there.

24-25 *Daigaku* spectacular lanterns hang on huge poles. Procession, Ikune Shrine, Mishimari-ku, Osaka.

24-25* *Tenjin Matsuri*, Tenmangu shrine to Heian era scholar Sugawara Michizane enshrined all Tenjin Shrines, observed on grand scale in Osaka. During. . . .

25 pm, 3km- long procession of 300: huge *mikoshi* each carried by 100 boys, many dance groups. At nite, land procession boards boats, make their way from Nakanoshima to area by Osaka Castle. One of largest firework displays over procession. Most hotels have reserved seat area at riverside: but go early, crowds unbelievable. Origin dates back to days when this shrine gave parishioners paper dolls which they rubbed against themselves, then sent from boats down river as we watch them float out to sea. Dolls carry away illness.

Last* Sat-Sun, *Kitano Kokusai Matsuri*, Japan's sole truly **International Festival** (illustrated facing) small but fun, in Kitano Shrine, Kobe, atop Kitano-cho old foreigners residential district. Begun by us with friends of dozen nationalities and *"Goofy-Guji"*, priest Sato of this local shrine to patron saint of education (historical figure SUGAWARA Michizane). 2 days of entertainment on 810+-year-old shrine stage by non-Japanese: American modern dance, Korean fan dance, Spanish guitar, English pub-style honky tonk piano, Chinese dragon dance, singers, Yankee clog dancers, mime, whatever you can do, plus food stalls by many nationalities; and Sumi and her pals run odds-'n-ends sale of thrift-shop salvage to raise $,-10,000 or so for small charities, especially Thai and Philippine rural schools, orphanages. — *Join us* — drop postcard to Sato-guji (priest), Kitano Kokusai Festival, Kitano Jinja, Kitano-cho 3-chome-12-1, Chuo-ku, Kobe 650; or show up and hope for open slot (we'll work you in) as offering for charity. Secular fete, no religious rites. Your kids can join in carrying miniature mikoshi in costume (wear own or we lend *happi*) parade Sun 1pm. Both days, 6-8pm bon dancing a la modern—alternating real bon dance (instructors), disco-'bon', samba, sometimes American square-. Then help clean up 8:30, party w/crew (*see* p.588).

Kobe's Kitano International Festival—from life

Jul 31-Aug 1 *Sumiyoshi Matsuri* of Sumiyoshi Jinja **O** is one of last summer fetes. 31st at 3pm shrine attendants and parishioners walk thru big hoop of *ashi* reed to purify selves of summer ills, then geisha, *chigo* parade around pond. Since 1962, *mikoshi* is carted around on truck, and no more colorful spectacle of *mikoshi* of Sakai & Sumiyoshi battling in Yamato River, but smaller neighborhoods do.

31 *Yo-Ichi*, nite auction of fish, Sakai City. Was essential complement since 12th century of *Sumiyoshi Matsuri* for fishermen come to Sumiyoshi Shrine to offer fish, what was left was auctioned on beach at nite. See loads of octopus as this was also part of *Sumiyoshi Fete*. Along with fish auction 5-9pm, Zaviel Park.

Last Sat or 1st Sun Aug* *Fireworks show* on sea off Port Island, Kobe, best seen from Portopia hotel, or along shoreside from New Otani hotel mainland — if resident, don't drive, traffic jam hours to return across bridge; use portliner.

August

1-2 *Danjiri Kenka Sai* (Palanquin Fight) at Kibune Jinja, Amagasaki City betw **O–K**. Fishing boat captains, workers at Central Fish mart carrying huge palanquins in procession start to push each other down.

3-6 *Natsu Matsuri*, Ikuta Jinja **K**, scads of fun nite stalls.

8-9 *Yo-mairi Shiman-roku-sen Nichi* (Nite Service of 46,000 Day Rites) at Tenno-ji temple on Mt Maya, **K**. Pilgrimage on...

9 said to be worth attending 46,000 times. (observed at temples throughout nation) 1pm, 50 *yamabushi* in fire ritual. Thus, many climb up to observe rites at 12 midnite of 8th.

9 *Yamanaka Kannon Hoshi-Kudari*, also 46,000 Day ritual of guardian descends to escort Shaka to heaven; Yamanaka-Dera, Takarazuka. *Chigo* parade, offerings.

11-12* *Takigi Noh*, Torchlight Noh, Ikutama Jinja Shrine, Osaka, subway stn Tanimachi-9-chome, 5-9pm; ¥2,000.

11-12* *Takigi Noh*, similar, Osaka Castle.

September

14-15* *Danjiri Matsuri* of Kishiwada City, (S of Osaka) spectacular nite procession on 14th. 6-10pm; 15th from 10am; 20 floats (each 2.75 tons) are pushed around city decorated with paper lanterns forming huge sail-like racks. Kishi-shiro & Sugawara shrines.

October

2nd Sun *Osaka Autumn Festival* monster Parade down 3.3km Midosuji from Nakano Shima to Namba, all afternoon, 12.000 paraders in 100+ groups of bands, ethnic folk dancers of residents and sister city imports, gigantic floats modern and traditional, classic cars, you name it.

12 *Kaijotogyo-Shiki* (Sea God Fete) Watatsumi Shrine, Kobe; *mikoshi* blessed, carried out along Maiko Beach **W** to Suma; pray for safety at sea.

3rd Sat-Sun *Tamba Pottery Fair* at kilns, shops, Tachikui, N of Kobe.
Late–into Nov, *Chrysanthemum shows* Sorakuen Park, Kobe; and 'mum-dolls in Hirakata Park, outside Osaka.

November

1–4* *Dai-chakai* grand tea party at Arima Onsen Zuiho-ji Park to thank Hideyoshi (who loved big tea parties, had some here with Sen Rikyu) for popularizing spa. Ura & Omote Senke take turns annually.
3 *Wasso-* Welcome Festival, Shitennoji T, new 1990 but all ancient elements, fetes importance Osaka internationalizing early Japan by visits of Koreans and Chinese. Parade 2pm on Tanimachi-suji blvd to temple of 1000s of 6th cent J-, K- and C-; ancient music, plays; will expand.
3-4 *Kanamono Matsuri* (Hardware Fete), Kanamono Jinja Miki City, observed by dealers in hardware. Offering of art exhibits; hardware exhibits, N of Kobe.
14-15 *Momi-ji* (maple) *Matsuri*, Nachi, South Kii; but Gingko trees lining Osaka's Midosuji Blvd are gorgeous, too.
22-23 *Shinno-san*, Sukuna Hikona Jinja, Dosho-machi, Osaka. Shrine to god of medicine. Cholera epidemic struck 1822, medicine men mixed pill of ground tiger skull. On this date Dosho-machi area home of pharmaceuticals decorated w/ huge streamers reminiscent of Sendai *Tanabata*.

December

31 Midnite at various shrines, all cities, start of *hatsu-mode* first visit, buy new talismans, dispose of old ones in bonfire. Kobe all ships in port sound horns.
Best places
Kobe: Gomo Jinja (Rokko); Ikuta Shrine & Kitano Tenman-gu (Kitano-cho); Nagata Jinja & Hirano Jinja (W Kobe); Ebisu Jinja & Kannon-ji (Nishinomiya).
Osaka: Shitennoji Temple & Ikutama Shrine; Imamiya Jinja Shrine.

FLEA MARKETS

1st Fri Ohatsu Tenjin, nr Osaka central stn Umeda, all rail, subway lines.
1st Sun Kobe-west, Sannomiya Sanyo line to Sumadera temple; rain, next week.
1st-3d Sun Ferry Terminal, Osaka
21 Osaka Tanimachi subway to Shitennoji Temple; *see* also Kyoto datebook.
4th Sun Kobe bus #2 from either end Sannomiya or Hankyu Rokko to Gokoku Jinja. ☎(078) 871-4484.
25 *See* Kyoto Datebook, p.507.

As **Nara** and **Kyoto** are so close to both Kobe and Osaka and are noted for their fabulous festivals, and **Kii** and **Koya** so near Osaka, readers are referred to their respective Personal Datebooks.

FLOWER CALENDAR

Feb-Mar: Plum blossoms: Nakayama Kannon Bairin near Takarazuka; Kitano Tenman-gu, Kobe; Osaka Castle Park.

Early April: Cherry blossoms: along banks of Shukugawa and Ashiyagawa rivers at Hankyu stns midway **O-K**; Osaka Castle Park, Osaka Mint.
May 1-Jul 26: iris, Takatsuki Hana Shobuen garden ☎(726)-88-9133; 9-5pm, –9pm Jun 15-30.
May: Azalea, Asaka Water plant, Sakai; hillside W-side Shin Kobe Stn and Shin Oriental Hotel—take suspension car.
June: Iris (*shobu*) Sakai Otori Taisha, 20,000 plants (40 species) ☎(0722)-62-0040), JR Hanwa Line, Otori stn.
End May-End Jun: Kada Awashima Hana Shobu-en, Wakayama ☎(0734)59-1111, 3 million plants.
Early Jun-Early Jul: Hana Shobu-en nr Sanda ☎(07956)-6-0935), 3 million (600 species); 8am-9pm.
All-Jun: Banshu Yamasaki Hana Shobu-en ☎ (07906)-2-7727, 9-6pm; one million.
All-Jun: Amagasaki Nogyo Koen Park. ☎(06)-489-6542. 25,000 plants. Open 24hrs, near Hankyu Sonoda Stn.
Late Sep-Early Dec: Chrysanthemum: Life-size 'mum' dolls, Hirakata Park, Osaka ☎(0720)-44-3475; fine exhibit, Sorakuen Garden-Koen, Kobe.
Sep 15-25 Bush clover *Hagi Matsuri*, Toko-in temple, ☎(06)-852-3002, Sone Stn, Hankyu Takarazuka line.
Oct–Nov: Maple Viewing: Arima's Zuihoji temple; Minoo hills near Osaka.
Nov-Dec: hills behind Kobe become gorgeous brocade backdrop to city spires.

BEST THEATER SELECTION
(see above list for details)
Apr 7 Okagura (Ninjo mai)
" **10 & 22** Bugaku, Shitennoji.
May (late) Kamigata Hanabutai, geisha.
Aug 8 Torchlite bugaku, Shitennoji.
" **11-12** Takigi Noh, Ikutama Shrine.
" **11-12** Takigi Noh, Osaka Castle.

CHECK National Bunraku Theater for Joruri puppets, Japan's top: ☎(06)-212-2531.

*I yearn for a tranquil moment to be out upon
the Sea of Harmony in that enchanted boat
Oh boatman, do you know my heart?*
—Sarashina Diary, 1037AD

SETO INLAND SEA 瀬戸内海
PARADISE REGAINED

KOBE IS HEAD of Inland Sea and to journey in these waters is to journey into Japan's heart. Your ferry steams between peaks of mounts that rise from floor of sea to form myriad isles, glistening in perpetual dew thru almost invisible but perspective-destroying haze. This is what our world must have looked like to Noah when Flood waters began to recede and Ark settled on Ararat. This is **Seto Naikai**—Inland Sea of Japan.

No matter how highly touted, this Inland Sea never fails to impress. To many even more beautiful than Grecian Isles or Elba, with concentrated beauty of Scottish Loch Country—lacking but its poets. Widely advertised for generations, it is only accessible to tourists on limited time since advent of hydrofoil, *suichu-tosen*—much-touted Osaka–Beppu steamer passed thru only by nite until 1960, as most still do, so check scheds before booking.

Now, we laze thru seascape one prince seven centuries ago deemed so beautiful that he declared whole sea his palace garden. Or you can zoom thru its heart on excellent STS hydrofoil out of Miyajima. Japanese of eight to nine centuries ago appreciated its beauty, but those who did were exterminated by those somber samurai of Kamakura. First foreigners in here after Perry rediscovered this grand natural garden and called it Inland Sea. There was formerly no Japanese name, but it now has one translated from English: SETO-NAIKAI. Rather, each of its basins had its own name: working west from Kobe these are Izumi-nada, now called Osaka Bay, and seven *nadas* (seas) of Harima, Bingo, Hiuchi, Mishima, Aki, Iyo, Suwo. Each has its own characteristics. It is middle seas of Bingo, Hiuchi, especially Mishima (between Okayama–Hiroshima) which attract us.

TAIRA Kiyomori went as governor from Kyoto over western Inland Sea in 11th century. In Kyoto nobles built grand paradise gardens with large ponds on which they floated mock boats filled with musicians supplicating gods with music. Kiyomori's garden was scaled in line with his aspirations. He chose entire Sea of Mishima, proceeding to re-landscape it more to his taste—and military needs. As family shrine and moon-viewing arbor he built GRAND SHRINE OF MIYAJIMA, floated fleets of real ships laden with entire orchestras to entertain at his grand picnics. He deepened channels moved mountains and dug canal which changed currents of 'his' seas.

Taira clan in next decades rose to power as puppet-masters over helpless emperors. Barely century after Kiyomori, they were in decline, forced to retreat from Kyoto, defeated in battle first at Suma near Kobe, then again at Yashima, one of scenic gems of Inland Sea scenery near Takamatsu, finally forced to very end of Inland Sea, very tip of main island, where they were virtually exterminated at Shimonoseki. Great ladies of Taira clan plunged to their suicides in sea, carrying their puppet infant emperor with them. Surviving women were forced to work at 'Gay Trades' to survive, modern geisha of area claim descent from these noble ladies, honoring them in colorful festival in Shimonoseki **April 23-25**—best 24, 1-3pm in shrine. Japanese literature was enriched by tales of these garden-lovers—*Tale of*

Heike and its modern rendition *New Tales of Heike* (both available in English) tell their rise; poignant incident in battle of Kobe-Suma is recalled in marvelous noh play *Atsumori*; romanticized in Kabuki play *Ichino-tani Futaba Gunki*; Lafcadio Hearn recounts eerie tale of ghosts of dead of Shimonoseki. At Yashima-Takamatsu on Shikoku Island, spidery Heike crabs bear likenesses of massacred warriors on their shell-armor.

With Heike power broken, island people reverted to their original piracy, terrorized shores of China and Korea, sailed to Siam. Today most have shifted to more profitable piracy of running tour ships, inter-island ferries. Still others are nautical nomads as we see at Onomichi near Hiroshima, live on isles terraced and planted to very steep crest—mostly with sweet potatoes. Some isles are fabulously fertile; some must have water trucked to them by small boat, vividly portrayed in award-winning silent movie *Island*.

There are pine-covered isles: lumber preserves. Others have mandarin orange orchards (ripening Nov-Dec) rising on stone terraces above sea walls, tended by farmers who commute from nearby residential isles thru countless intricate channels, working from their diesel sampans like farmers from their tractors. And scene and smell in May orange blossom time! Innoshima Isle seemed snow white, covered with white buds which were used to make mosquito repellent spiral incense—alas, production small. Other isles are olive groves. And everywhere fishing boats, diesels of all sizes, shapes.

Ferries serve all inhabited isles with frequent service, like rural buses (and like rural buses in so much of Asia your fellow passenger is more likely to be pig than fellow tourist). There are stretches of water like giant mirrors. There are channels of 'white water' where our boat must step down or climb up, thru varying sea levels as ocean tides drain or fill land-locked basins thru narrow, shallow channels. It is no place for amateur skippers, and ferry captains are usually wizened old sea dogs.

Inns, which abound on every inhabited isle, are simple and budget (but you can expect sea food dinner that wouldn't be budget in big city). Inland Sea fish with no hard currents or harsh temperatures to battle, are luscious. Many inns are quite good, and at least one, set in perhaps most lovely of all picture-book locales in **Tomo**, is international luxury standard.

Scenic area ends at Hiroshima, with its fine hotels. 30min beyond, giant red torii stands in water, tourist poster symbol of Japan, marking Miyajima itself, Taira's grand garden pavillion, Paradise in miniature.

At lunar June 17, which is full moon of July or early August (exact dates, *see* MIYAJIMA) hundreds of fishing boats assemble from all over Inland Sea. Gay banners and laundry bedeck them as families aboard come to greet high moon tide in Orient's grandest and most exciting festival: *Kan-gen-sai*, wind-string-fete, or festival of sacred orchestra.

As they have since great lord Taira built first ones, orchestra boats set off in setting sun leading parade of fisher-boats, all aboard singing, feasting like their jolly pirate ancestors. Full moon rises behind mountains of mainland. They cross to mainland and hold solemn ceremony ashore, repeated at other shrines long into nite, ending again beneath gigantic torii, flutes accompany sibilant lapping of ebb tide between bandboat and torii.

We describe KOBE-HIROSHIMA legs in detail so that you can decide just which places you'll want to see. We follow Sanyo railroad: KOBE-HIMEJI-BIZEN-OKAYAMA-KURASHIKI-ONOMICHI-HIROSHIMA; treat AWAJI and SHIKOKU as asides. Rustic detours are included at several points for those with more time. Our favorite Inland Sea portion, ONOMICHI-HIROSHIMA, is found at end. You can combine individual sections to follow your own personal itinerary, as we have done in our *TILT*, which follows.

Anyone coming to Japan on a long-term business assignment should take the time to travel and get a firsthand feeling for the country and the people before settling into the routine of living and working here. — Carl Pascarella, Mgr VISA Asia-Pacific

SANYO 山陽
'SUNNY' ROUTE

KOBE → TACHIKUI kiln → HIMEJI Castle → BIZEN kilns & swords →
OKAYAMA garden → Offbeat mountain trail → KURASHIKI folk arts →
TOMO fish → ONOMICHI ferry detour

OUR TRAIN pulls out of Sannomiya station, past Kobe and Hyogo stations of older town and in few minutes is at Suma, squeezed into narrow hundred-yard strip between mountain and sea. Here Heike suffered their first great defeat which sent them retreating across Inland Sea thru successive defeats to their final destruction at Dan-no-ura, Shimonoseki, on tip of Honshu. On Suma beach was fought one of tragic duels of Heike wars which has so enriched literature: victorious Genji champion Kumagai caught fleeing Heike youth, noble Atsumori. Thinking of his own son, Kumagai wanted to let him go. But demanding to be recognized as adult, Atsumori demanded battle, was slain. Beautiful noh play Atsumori is in paperback *Treasury of Asian Literature*. Kabuki version has classically kabuki-esque plots and counter-plots so Kumagai ends up saving, hiding and delivering Atsumori to safekeeping while sacrificing his own son in Atsumori's place, to fool prying eyes, fill audience eyes.

But where once resounded clashing of swords one strains to hear more romantic hints in tinkle of glasses and clatter of fine silver of occidentals and Westernized Japanese who have built their houses here, e.g. celebrated James Estate and Shioya Country Club. Onward to Akashi where early migrations from Korea landed 15 or more centuries ago to raise immense GOSHIKI KOFUN, a.k.a. Atsumori-zuka, sole externally-restored tumulus, near Shioya, short walk W of Suma-ura stn Sanyo Dentetsu RR (*see* Kobe).

Within 30min out of Sannomiya on Shinkansen we are on wide plain, out of sight of sea, walled on right by line of mountains, blue of which is suddenly broken by some ancient, stately great white bird perched over ugly city, like sentry at edge of unknown world lying beyond mysterious hills.

But first, this alternate day-long detour for pottery buffs, day-trip for Kobe-ites...

TACHIKUI & SASAYAMA ALTERNATE RTE → HIMEJI

TACHIKUI: Somewhat out of our way, this scenic detour is to kilns of *Tamba-yaki* pottery, once made at several towns hereabouts and one of famed **'six ancient kilns'**: with ECHIZEN (not far away), TOKONAME near Ise (with local museum), SETO outside Nagoya which gave Japanese their name *setomono* for Chinaware and now immense industrial ceramic area as well as having fine artists, SHIGARAKI active kiln east of Kyoto, IGA near it, and BIZEN which we visit later this leg. Tho dubbed 'ancient kilns' dated 12th century or earlier, these are not oldest kilns in Japan: this designation was put on by master tea-men in 17th century to note pottery (not porcelain) kilns with tradition of common wares producing work acceptable to tea use. Each kiln has its own characteristics, Tamba especially noted for its deep black matt glaze in which thick green tea sets like some shimmering gemstone. Other glazes abound at Tamba and young potters migrating from outside are greatly expanding vocabulary of kiln.

GETTING THERE: JR KOBE → OSAKA change to Fukuchiyama line hour → AINO, thence bus → KAMI-TACHIKUI where hill side of road is lined with 61 family kiln-shops, up from handful of dozen years ago.

Facing bus stop on triangle corner is small grocer (cold drinks), lane runs up from there to thatch-roof home–kiln shed of ...
SHIMIZU **Toshihiko** ☎(079597)-2647 disciple of late Ikuta whom we visited in early '60s when one of few new potters migrating into old kiln town to revive it. Shimizu has 4-chamber *nobori-gama*, climbing linked-chambers kiln up side of hill, introduced from Korea 17th century; also *ana-gama* older form of kiln tunnelled into side of hill. He fires roomy *nobori-gama* 3-4 times annually. Fine decorative pieces, but better yet superb practical wares like plates, cups and teapots. 60-neighbors also worth stroll thru. Buildings across valley are tour bus park: first **cafeteria**; 2nd **shop** with big selection wares of all 61; 3rd, pair of galleries, R moderns, L ancient—Sasayama museum better. **Reading**: *Tamba Pottery: Timeless art of a Japanese Village*, by Daniel Rhodes, (KI).

SASAYAMA: Pleasant town with slightly worn remnants of its feudal heyday. It is mostly for leisurely, or second-time visitor, also good as day-trip out of Kobe. Wanderer can continue on JR to HIMEJI to rejoin our mainline SUNNY ROUTE, or head up to Japan Seacoast, *or* take Chugoku Expressway bus to join our OKAYAMA OFFBEAT route.

GETTING THERE: From TACHIKUI **cab** 7-8x-mtr, or **bus** back to JR stn for short ride → AINO, as following: **from KOBE** most direct is 2hr express bus (3-4x-daily) from Kobe's SANNOMIYA stn; or 1hr35min (6x-daily) JR bus via OSAKA → SASAYAMA-GUCHI stn to change to any of numerous buses from stn into town, 20min (some are JR buses for Rail Pass users). If by JR rail, 30min SANNOMIYA → OSAKA & 80min express Fukuchiyama Line to SASAYAMA-GUCHI. **From OSAKA** as above Fukuchiyama line. **Cab** stn to town is under 3x-mtr.

Small farming community until late 1500's when HATANO Hideharu built castle here. Too close to Kyoto or Osaka for comfort, TOYOTOMI Hideyoshi had it destroyed and Sasayama went back to farming. Not ten years later, after Battle of Sekigahara, TOKUGAWA Ieyasu rebuilt castle as base to attack Osaka. It grew to major town, until Meiji Restoration did away with castles and it has once again become quiet town.

Castle's soaring hoary **stoneworks** dominate, its moat-surrounded compound now occupied by Sasayama elementary and middle school. At day's end, waves of kids come charging out like some defending army sallying forth to battle. Most buses circle it clockwise, so we start at **Sasayama Historic Museum**, *Rekishi Bijutsu-kan*, 3rd bus stop as you enter town. It is in ex-**Tamba Regional Court house** built 1888. Worth ¥300 just to see giant painting of fountain of eternal life, with dozens of fiery red-haired old women, men and children merrily drinking out of obviously alchoholic fount with giant sake cups. There are few more painted panels, room full of Tamba pottery, small collection of *kofun* (tomb) era artifacts excavated from nearby tumuli. All X-mon, otherwise all open 9:00-17:00.

Backtrack W on bus road to first alley, N to...
KASUGA JINJA, uninteresting shrine but site of good Noh dances: midnite **Dec 31-Jan 1**; also **mid-Apr** & **mid-Sep** (both usually 2nd weekend, but best check) for full-day performances; **Oct 17** several comic Kyogen pieces.

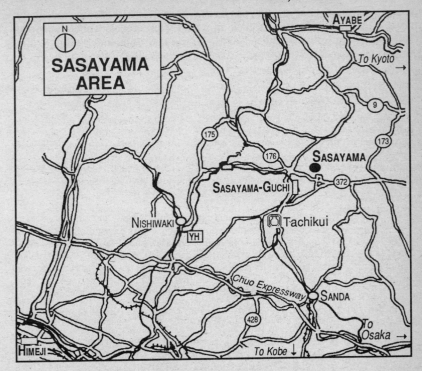

*2 blocks S of museum to castle **moat** which we follow W to 2nd street which follow S (L) to cluster of thatched-roof houses on either side of street...*

Old houses of lower ranking samurai: were more here even ten years ago, but without outside financial help, their occupants (mostly descended from original samurai) can't afford maintenance. While city ponders what can be done, some have been torn down, others have their thatch covered with tin. Thatch are beautiful to look at but uncomfortable to live in: keeping them insect- and rot-free requires keeping smoky fire year-round.

Continue on street 500m to small power plant, L back to moat to its SW corner...

Samurai House, particularly well-kept long, thatch roof. Huge black gate just south is all that remains of feudal era school. Small chunk of land outside main moat surrounded by its own little moat is where stables were. Another small moat on northeast corner.

Now, E along moat, cross stream 700m to...

Old Merchant section of town its sturdy white-walled houses in better condition than those of samurai. Merchant section is still quite active, fun to browse thru. Intersection at start of merchant section is JR bus terminal, where those from KOBE-Sannomiya come in; also **bicycle** rentals there.

Short way down on L side is enormous gate leading to . . .

Tamba Pottery Museum, *Koto-kan* (¥300), long courtyard surrounded by great, Edo era storehouses and lined with gigantic vats; personal collection of NAKANISHI Koichi ranging thru history of old Tamba wares, 12th-19th cent; English labels, good English pamphlet (ask) covers basics of Tamba ware. Only made now at village of TACHIKUI 15km SW (*above*). Note that some older storage pots have inscriptions engraved: name of potter to identify works fired in common in immense old communal multi-chamber kiln of up to 9 chambers and 50 meters long.

Two doors down is...

Noh Museum, *Nohgaku Shiryo-kan* (¥250), superb collection assorted Noh masks from 8th thru 18th centuries, several costumes, and stage replica in which you can see huge earthenware jars placed under dance platform as echo chambers to amplify foot stamping.

SHOPPING: Mainly for Tamba (Tachikui) pottery, its characteristic matt-black glaze especially appeals, for which several shops in merchant district, another 100m E of Historic Museum. Also along merchant district are several antique shops: all fair. Kiln-shop of SHIBATA Masaaki also Tachikui disciple of Ikuta, worth visit for pottery buffs: hard to find but taxi only basic mtr, easy walk back or call for one.

WHERE TO STAY: If you must, suggest for pottery buff Kokumin-shukusha Sasayama-so ☎(07955)-2-1127, on small hill behind merchant district. Quiet—whereas most other inns are along top shopping street, which has heavy traffic.

CHOPSTICKS: Mountains around here are full of boar, and Nov thru Mar is boar season, with all inns and most restaurants serving it. It's easy to tell if already or still **boar** season, streets are lined with banners bearing boar. Best place to enjoy it (usually *botan-nabé*, sukiyaki style with lots of vegetables) is restaurant-inn **Kakitei**, on NE corner of moat. They have their own boar farm outside town and serve boar meat dishes all year, instead of usual limited Nov-Mar season. For quick, cheap, good **noodles** there is **Kakugen**, 300m W of Historic Museum. Not much else in town, except half-dozen coffee shops along top shopping street front of Historic Museum; L of castle N-entry, two coffee shops have view over outer moat from back windows.

If full-day pot-hunting trip from Kobe, return via Fukuchiyama line, or drive →
SANDA to dine at great restaurant **Sandaya** ☎(0795)-64-4195, taxi basic-mtr from stn, excellent food, classical combo; kiln-shop of **Sanda Celadon** on premises, very reasonable. Now within 4-5x-mtr taxi of ARIMA ONSEN for overnite (*see* KOBE preceding) or 10x-mtr KOBE.

WHERE NEXT: SASAYAMA → HIMEJI bit over 2hrs rail, depending connections. Must change from JR Fukuchiyama Line to JR Kakogawa Line at TANIGAWA 3 stops N; from there → HIMEJI can involve none or up to 2 changes. Part way is TAKINO, old soy-sauce producing town; 3min bus from its stn → Chuo Expressway bus stop whence 2hr *Chuo-Kosoku-doro* bus to TSUYAMA to join our OKAYAMA OFFBEAT, (*see*). Or...

Take 2hr40min JR rail W to...

HIMEJI 姫路   WHITE HERON CASTLE

FINEST EXTANT CASTLE of feudal Japan in that it is complete, with its original buildings standing. There are lovelier ones—but much smaller (Inuyama near Nagoya) thus 'incomplete'. There are larger: Edo (now Tokyo Imperial Palace) Nagoya and Osaka (*see*). But these are either, as with Edo, partially old or as with other two, modern rebuildings of ferroconcrete (Osaka 1930, Nagoya 1960). Sole comparable original is Matsuyama, Shikoku, and it is missing major portions—its palace section being erected at Hawaii U. Himeji underwent ambitious restoration (1964), rickety old wooden-frame castle dismantled, repaired, parts replaced and set up again with steel beams taking load off old wood skeleton which was reinstalled.

Let's look then at Himeji as most typical of Japanese castles.

GETTING THERE: Rail Pass users take Shinkansen from KOBE-Sannomiya near-commuter-frequency departures, 20mins, first class available; **budgeteer** sans pass from Sannomiya Hankyu Stn take SANYO DENTETSU commuter electric, hour-¥710. *Alternate* backwoods route from Kobe (or day trip out of Kobe), *above*.

Himeji's fortifications date to 1332. Castle as such however, is European introduction dating only to Christian Century of Japan, late 16th century. First true castle was probably that of Lord Oda Nobunaga, Azuchi Castle, 1576-1579, built on shore of Lake Biwa, now destroyed. Full castle plan, as at Himeji, consists of central keep or *hon-maru* (base *maru*-'circle', but really top honorific) with its immediately surrounding inner walled fort, or *ni-no-maru* (2d-maru) and outer fortifications, *san-no-maru* (3rd-maru). Each maru has its own walls and moat, as in Europe, entry across moat by drawbridge with portculis into heavily fortified gate foyer. But in Japanese castle, gate leads thru intricate maze rather than simpler walled inner courts of European forts. J- builders do better job than Europeans in allowing for probability of having gates breached. High-walled mazes, wrong turn led to cul-de-sac, made it easier to defend, break up large attacking forces.

Term *maru* is applied to castles, supposedly means 'round' (ideograph with which it is expressed has this meaning) because original castle shape is supposed to have been round. Ship is also called -*maru* (so ship names 'X-Maru') supposedly so that it will complete round trip—not so. Swords were also called *maru* (nothing round there) as were certain other highly valued objects, all of which have one thing in common in that they possess personality, concept brought in from Central Asia in early Iron Age. Names of early heroes often also suffixed-*maro*. Both probably derive from Syriac 'Mar', here Eastern Christians will recognize prenom for Saint, '*Mar* -'.

All castles have patron deity, genus locii, or spirit of place. In Himeji 'she' is Osakabe-Myojin, Shinto-Buddhist combination, enshrined on topmost floor of *tenshu*, central keep.

Bungaku-kan, outside L-rear castle, exciting architecture, surprisingly by Ando, whose international high rep was, to us, undeserved until this.

Entering Himeji Castle (¥300, 9:00-16:00 daily), we pass into...
Outer Castle, *San-no-maru* now public park. Great multi-storied **gate** between this and *Ni-no-maru* is *Hishi-no-mon* named after now-extinct river Hishi which once flowed nearby. After this are six *mizu-no-mon* or water–gates: so called because attack is 'fire': in old alchemic concepts of universal five elements—fire destroyed wood basic construction material, but was itself conquered by water, thus gates so designated in sympathetic magic.

After 6 magical water gates we enter keep, or hon-maru with...
Tenshu, 'heavenly guard' five-storey central **keep tower**atop 15m/50ft high stone base some 28x20m/92x67ft. **Main hall** said to be 1,000 mats area, but by measure is actually 330 (660yds^2). From this base rise two great main cedar pillars each 3m/10ft around and 26m/84' high, on thru 5th fl. Stockade-fort built here 1346, not yet true castle. Hideyoshi built 3-storey *tenshu* 1581. Present tower erected by successor to castle IKEDA Terumasa, 1608. Bottom two feet of west pillar was patched in 1687. Topmost floor, 6th, is 70 mats size (115m^2/140yd^2) surrounded by veranda commanding magnificent view. This was siege-residence of lord and his last line of defense.

Suicide-tower, *Seppuku-maru*, is 5.5x15.5m/18x60ft turret at *tenshu* exit. Here were performed executions by self-destruction (*seppuku*, a.k.a. *hara-kiri* or belly-cutting). In this ritual victim sat in ceremonial white under-kimono on straw mat he brought himself (to save his host trouble of cleaning up). Surrounded by witnesses, officials and friends, he would take short sword blade set in simple wooden haft, jab it horizontally under his lower left rib cutting edge in, and pull it across his abdomen to his right rib, then twist it up to cut out liver or slash into heart. Friend stood behind with drawn long sword to decapitate him as coup de grace—in actual practice coup usually delivered as soon as he inserted blade, even sometimes reaching forward to pick it up off ceremonial white-wood offering tray. Cutting thru reflexively tightened abdominal muscle was chore, even with finest blade, and coup was meant to quickly end lingering and painful death—often as not, by passing out and bleeding to death. There is detailed eye-witness description in classic *Tales of Old Japan*, by Lord Redesdale of seppuku execution of Bizen samurai who cut down English sailor in front of Kobe's Sannomiya Shrine on January 11, 1868. MISHIMA Yukio committed classical *seppuku* at Self Defense Force barracks in Tokyo when his comic opera coup failed, and his second, after beheading him, followed, also beheaded.

Down stone path, right of Seppuku-maru is...

Lady Chrysanthemum Well, *Okiku-ido*, named after ghost haunting it, wife of faithful retainer of late 16th century lord, who was strangled by her husband and tossed into well for breaking precious family heirloom of lord. Kabuki theater took hold of tale, resited to Edo, added samurai-commoner love story, and play *Bancho Sarayashiki* is still summer favorite.

West-castle, *Nishi-no-maru*, lies to west of tenshu. Added about 1617, defensively as flanking position to tenshu, but also to serve as residential palace. Its most famous tenant was Sen-hime, Princess Sen, after she had, on feudal period standards, 'eloped' with handsome ranking samurai on way to Edo to see her mother after her first husband, Hideyoshi's son Hideyori, was beseiged in Osaka Castle and killed by her own father, second Tokugawa shogun Hidetada. She was widowed here again in 1626, at age 30, after some eight years of uxorious luxury.

SMALL DETAILS: End **tiles** of roofs bear crests of various lords who built that section, or who in later occupancies repaired it. Between 1332 and date of its seizure by imperial forces in 1868, 44 lords of 13 clans held hill. Firing ports of two types: wide inside with narrow outer slit for bowmen; narrow inside, fanning wide outside for musketeers. Also of several shapes: round, triangle, square and tall rectangle—first trio said to be for musketry and 4th for archers, but musket wasn't that much used after 'gentleman's agreement' to ban weapon that made peasant foot soldier equal of samurai— if not superior. Cannon not much used, so that castles remained in use until very end of feudal age when modern gunnery introduced after Perry made castles obsolete (as would have earlier but for samurai-gentleman's agreement not to use guns). Osaka Castle died under such modern guns, as did many others at end of feudal age when they opposed imperial forces. Himeji is noted for its cherry blossoms.

WHERE TO STAY: ¥T hotels around stations. Enkyoji temple, rsv week ahead, ☎0792-66-3240. High over city among tall cedars, ropeway open 8:30am to 6:00pm, winter -5:00pm; ¥5,000 w/2.

WHERE NEXT: From HIMEJI, JR Ako Branch Line paralleled for drivers by Rte25. For pottery buffs, ghastly modern city of HIMEJI ends suddenly as hills close on rail lines. Temples and shrines and graves cover hills in profusion like blaze of flowers in short violent spring; small shrines in hillock crannies and roadside Jizos dot landscape like first spring blooms. In spring actual blossoms are profuse. In autumn, haystacks punctuate open fields we are now entering. We notice two kinds: larger like Zulu huts; smaller ones set in groups teetering in all directions, like squads of little coolies wobbling in wind under great straw hats. Much of this still beautiful countryside is lost to rushed traveller zooming thru on Shinkansen which only comes out of tunnels long enough to load or unload. If you have time, regular Sanyo Main Line (only locals beyond Himeji) may take longer, but is more pleasing to eye.

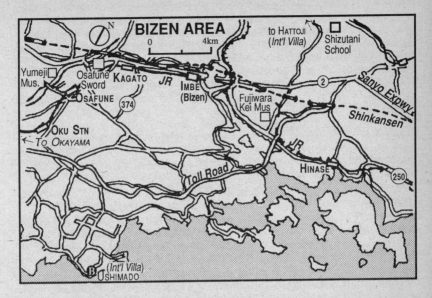

JR rail soon (at AIOI) cuts off coastwards, passing—Kabuki buffs stop off ...
BANSHU AKO, home-town of loyal 47 samurai in *Chushingura*. Only portion of leader Oishi Yuranosuke's mansion & garden, not much here for tourist except **Dec 14** festival honoring 47 martyrs. Lord Asano's castle is now public park, small museum of material which made him rich—salt.

Continuing on: tall thin chimneys standing like burned-out tree trunks among homes indicate that we are amid famous pottery cottage-industries of...

IMBE BIZEN-CHO 備前町 POTTERY TOWN
KILNS of coarse ware of great earthy beauty, bit (but not too) hard to get to on HIMEJI-AIOI-AKO-OKAYAMA branch off JR Sanyo Main Line, 70min from HIMEJI, 45min from OKAYAMA → IMBE. Main highway Rte2 curves down to it, **driver** saves time (if not yen) on new Sanyo Jidosha-do Exp'way from HIMEJI to just before IMBE. From OKAYAMA, 29.5km do by **cab** 16x-mtr; or from HIMEJI about 65km, 35x-mtr.

Bizen ware is one of few types of pottery that retains ancient primitive qualities of earthenware of prehistory and hard Sue stoneware which followed. Legend has it when Susano-O-no-Mikoto slew eight-headed dragon he carried flask of Bizen ware: full of sake, not water. Bizen ware flourished nationally from Kamakura era, reaching peak late 16th century when it was sought after by such esthetes as Hideyoshi, early tea master Sen-no-Rikyu. During Edo era, thin-walled white-glazed pieces with gold trim were produced to compete with popular new Kyushu porcelain, but six families—Kimura, Mori, Kaneshige, Terami, Oai, Tongu—subsidized by Tokugawa shogunate, stuck to traditional style as one of Six Ancient Kilns (*see* TAMBA). Bizen specialties include storage vessels, vases, sake and tea sets and tea bowls, but more practical items such as pipes, bricks and tiles were mass produced in early Meiji and, during World War II, even hand grenades. In 1950s, old JNR (now JR) stn kiosk disposable teapots and noodle bowls in this area were low-quality bizen.

Early Bizen ware was made from coarse, gray, mountain sand-clay—but from late 1500's dark, smooth, rice-paddy clay was mixed in, and eventually

was used predominantly in response to tea masters' wishes. Today they dig
in old paddies to depth of 5m then take clay to 80cm which is best, which is
further stored in dark 3-5 years, then repeatedly sift and add mountain sand
for hardness. Best known for lovely burnt-sienna colored *yakishimé*, as this
type of unglazed hard pottery technique is known, Bizen formed its own
characteristics. There is *ao*-Bizen, grey-green ware, and *hidasuki*, pumpkin-
colored or burnt-orange streaking obtained by wrapping straw around vessel
then firing. Finished design is difficult to predict as potters say streaking
comes about 'accidentally'—partly due to natural glaze from salt in firing.
Same with *sangiri* which refers to cloud effects of blackish purple whorls
brought out by reaction of charcoal ash to heat, more difficult process to
control. Most potters use small version *nobori-gama* (multi-chamber
climbing-kiln), in which firing takes 10 days, followed by 10 day cooling.
Some fire monthly!

During Tokugawa period, these *nobori-gama* got as long as 55m/180ft and
5m/15ft wide, with firings taking 30 to 50 days. There are around 200
potters here now, two men of past generation were recognized as Living
National Treasures: FUJIWARA Kei and KANESHIGE Toyo, both now dead but
equally skilled (if not yet recognized) descendants carry on. You'll find
predominance of potters called Kaneshige and Kimura, two main families of
six originally subsidized by Tokugawa shogunate.

Among various ornamental techniques which are all subtle and subdued,
there is use of gold and silver. Some Bizen ware is slightly hand-glazed (as
opposed to ash glaze occurring naturally in firing). Imbe is another name
for Bizen pottery, tho often used to refer to slightly glazed, thin, lighter
ware. *Hidasuki* plates are cheaper than *sangiri* as former, protected by
straw wrappings, can be stacked in kiln.

Old pottery town itself, formerly known as IMBE and now part of larger
BIZEN township, is centered across Rte2 from JR Imbe stn, on side road
off at right angle. Can leave bags at stn (¥200 until 18:00).

To R of stn (E) before we cross Rte2 is...

Togei Kaikan (¥300, X-mon) museum of representative wares of major
local potters, 2nd floor collection ancient Bizen ware. **If no time**, from here
cross Rte2 into old town, shops along entry road are mostly higher priced,
slicker, with less representative selection—tho at **Togei Club** (R side about
20m from Rte2) are works of masters such as late-Living Intangible Cultural
Asset KANESHIGE Toyo at not so intangible prices; facing it on L side is annex
with more modest wares in ¥5,-7,000 class up of various workshops.

With more time for background on ware, go in 50m to 'T'-intersection, ancient
Sanyo pedestrian hiway, L at T 1.5km—or to avoid backtracking, **cab** basic-mtr from stn.

Walk back into town, after...

Bizen Togei (Ceramic) **Center**, ex *Togei Shikenjo* test labs, which
besides exhibits has sample kiln and workshop where watch or partake in all
phases of pottery.

Short 10min walk toward town from Ceramics Center, on L, is...

Ancient Ceramics Museum, *Bizen Kotoh Bijutsukan*, with over 200
superb pieces arranged chronologically from Heian period on; ¥300.

Take L fork in road at tracks, passing several kiln-shops on L...

Many potters will let you watch their work, and depending on mood, *may*
show you around their workshop and kiln. Short walk on from Museum,
other smaller shops in between, on L (mountainside) KANESHIGE Toko's
kiln Rito-en with shop, neighbor MORI Tozan and seaward across lane
ISEZAKI Mitsuru, all old line top potters. Few doors on to late treasure

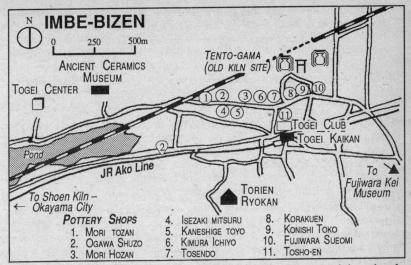

POTTERY SHOPS
1. MORI TOZAN
2. OGAWA SHUZO
3. MORI HOZAN
4. ISEZAKI MITSURU
5. KANESHIGE TOYO
6. KIMURA ICHIYO
7. TOSENDO
8. KORAKUEN
9. KONISHI TOKO
10. FUJIWARA SUEOMI
11. TOSHO-EN

KANESHIGE Toyo now run by son **Michiaki** with exquisite simple window showing one piece—no entry, their work goes to major galleries; have hosted numerous western disciples, who came adequately prepared. Facing Kaneshige are newer (1973) **OGAWA Shuzo**, interesting and reasonable; also carries unusual calligraphic bamboo pens and brushes (hairs are frayed bamboo) of friend **HOSEKI** Yoshinobu. Next is **Kibido** and small workshop of **MORI Hozan** and son Yasushi: not much in this small front, which was last holdout against gentrification—always shows flair, with special rack loaded with simpler pieces. Next door atop T corner is **KIMURA Ichiyo** with artier wares. Seaward just before T is **Mori Gofuk-ten**, everyday kimono and accessories and one wall of odd pots, tagged, but final prices depend on what he thinks of you—loves to use his limited but adequate E-.

At T intersection on right corner (from stn) is...
Tosho-en, large selection of fine, expensive wares, but also small 'bargain corner' (¥5,000) in store for less affluent. Facing Tosho-en is our favorite, SHIBAOKA Kozan's big shop **Tosendo** with larger more representative selection in wider price range. Few doors on, atop R wing is vegetable shop with lane separating from **Koraku-en** potters, lovely—take this narrow lane up to ancient preserved nobori-gama chamber-kiln called **Tento-gama** on hillside.

Back at vegetable shop & Koraku-en, continue L few doors (facing parking lot) is...
Konishi Toko run by 3rd generation KONISHI Tozo, from first edition, own works, exquisite, also affordable.

Next door is newer...
Fujiwara Sueomi, outlet for several of Fujiwara clan, mostly priced to fit maker's rank, not ware's apparent quality. Opp side of street about 10ft on shop specializing in old Bizen, mostly (to us) over-priced, but some moderate so browse, might find real buy to your eye.

At end are two small local shrines...
AMATSU JINJA and remnant **IMBE JINJA**.

There are other shops up and down street. Seen everywhere in 1970's, less so now, were 4-5 inch reclining cows (¥400), which are offered **Jan 5** to *ushi-gami* (protector of oxen) at nearby **TAKURA JINJA** (btwn Mitsushi stn & Yoshinaga).

Worthwhile 30min side trip is to FUJIWARA Kei *Kinen-kan* **Memorial Hall**, 20min walk or 10min bus or cab basic-mtr-plus, E of Imbe stn on Rte250.

HIROSHIMA-wards past stn on Rte2, 2x-mtr **cab**, or **bus** to KAGATO-HIGASHI, or **train** to next stn KAGATO, walk back 5min, turn hillward at Kohtoh village intersection-

15min to Shinkansen and beyond tracks on L is big compound of...
Sho-en, 4-chamber nobori-gama fires 4,500 pieces monthly. Genial BUYO Ikkan set up in 1971 on return from Brazil, 2 years at Indiana U (speaks fine English), will pick up small group at any stn, or advise—☎(0869)-66-9138. Says if up this way, see lovely 3-tiered **pagoda** (NT) at OTAKI-SAN temple above old hiway on way to Bizen—30min walk up beautiful vale—he'll take you, drop you at **Kotoh Bijutsukan**, loves chance to chat with fellow art-nuts. Fires monthly, takes month, phone ahead for exciting *kama-biraki*, kiln opening early in month; or help chuck in kindling. Shop has interesting selection, away from heavily traveled center, less expensive.

Shizutani School, Japan's first public school est 1670 by lord IKEDA Mitsumasa. Unique as for children of commoners. Compound in near-new condition (roof tiles Bizen of course, triple overlaid on lacquer boards); now Prefectural Education Ctr, open ¥300; in Shizutani-'Quiet Vale'. E-pamphlet, *free*.

GETTING THERE: 8km NE of IMBE, 10min **cab** 5x-mtr; or **bus** IMBE stn 4km Rte2 E to IRI-NAKA Xing walk N. 3 buses dly to YOSHINAGA stn 3km NW on Sanyo JR.

6km W of IMBE on Rte2 cab 3x-mtr, or few mins bus bound for Okayama, or short walk from Kagato stn next stop down on JR...
Osafune Sword Museum, *Nihon-to Hakubutsu-kan*. Bizen also famed for master Osafune smiths. Excellent damascene steel J-swords forged since 8th-9th centuries, process becoming fine hi-tech art by early 11th century. Peerless cutting edge and strength attained by hundreds of alternate folding-hammerings of steel to meld various contents into uniformity give J- blade its unique quality, *jihada* (texture)—like grain in wood. What is to be cutting edge is where steel is folded, creating much more stable, arch-like structure.

To produce tough, yet nonbrittle steel smith uses special charcoal from certain woods, instead of coal as in Europe, to cut down trace impurities like sulphur, phosphorus. After repeated hammering, blade is ready to temper. Coated by thin layer of muddy mix of water, clay, polishing-stone powder, fusible salts in secret formula passed from master to apprentice, blade heated to temperature judged in dark forge by red of its glow, plunged tip down edge first into water. This creates protective super-hard edge, mixture of iron carbide compound (cementite, Fe_3C) and near-pure metallic iron. Final polish done by specialist polisher rather than by smith. Using old skills developed thru centuries, he grinds down rough surface with progressively finer stones and copious water as lubricant. Despite their strength J- swords are delicate. Body oils dull cutting edge, so never handle edge, thus blades were immediately (or first possible chance) wiped off with paper after cutting anyone. Even slight breath rusts, so in examining you hold paper napkin in mouth bent up to nose to deflect nasal exhale, and never touch blade with bare skin.

If you own good sword, return it to Japan to be cleaned and certified, necessary for evaluation. Procedure complex (weapons control by police at customs): check Japanese consul; or consult **Japan Sword Co** in Tokyo ☎(03)-3434-4321; **Osaka Museum** also certifies, bring in thru Itami. In Osafune, consult direct—but **consult first, or risk!**

Osafune one of best of 200 sword making schools, blades engraved with name of smith, place forged, date. Sometimes faked, connoisseur can tell which school, or master made particular sword by moiré pattern on blade or wave-motif of cutting edge or overall shape. Demonstration of forging, traditional down to smith-as-shaman in ritually-pure white kimono, at **Osafune Museum**: 1st & 3rd sunday, 11:00-12:00, 13:00-14:00, *free*; ¥300 to see collection.

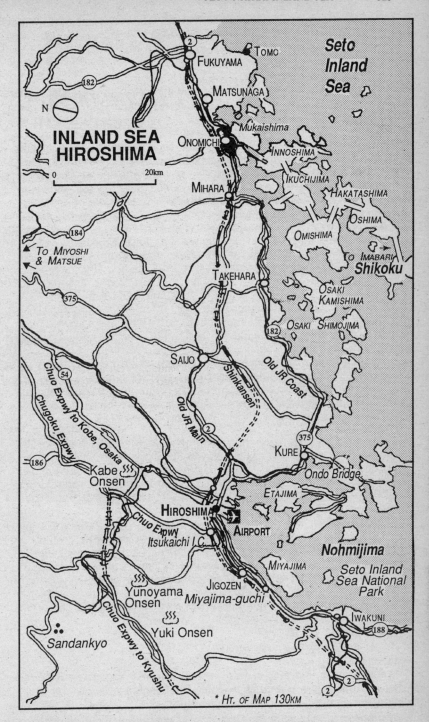

INLAND SEA
HIROSHIMA

0   20km

N

Seto
Inland
Sea

182

2

FUKUYAMA

TOMO

MATSUNAGA

Mukaishima

ONOMICHI

INNOSHIMA

IKUCHIJIMA

HAKATASHIMA

MIHARA

184

To MIYOSHI
& MATSUE

375

TAKEHARA

OMISHIMA

OSHIMA

To IMABARI

Shikoku

*OSAKI
KAMISHIMA*

OSAKI SHIMOJIMA

182

SAIJO

54

Chuo Expwy to Kobe, Osaka

Chugoku Expwy

Shinkansen

Old JR Main

Old JR Coast

375

KURE

186

Kabe
Onsen

Ondo Bridge

ETAJIMA

HIROSHIMA

Chuo Expwy
Itsukaichi I.C.

AIRPORT

Nohmijima

Yunoyama
Onsen

Miyajima-guchi

JIGOZEN

MIYAJIMA

*Seto Inland
Sea National
Park*

Yuki Onsen

Chuo Expwy to Kyushu

Sandankyo

IWAKUNI

188

* HT. OF MAP 130KM

2   2

WHERE NEXT: continue on → OKAYAMA 45min **bus** or JR **rail**...

> *If the repetition of a machine is the death of all art,
> manual repetition by a craftsman is the very mother
> of skill and skill is mother of beauty.*
> — Soetsu Yanagi

OKAYAMA 岡山
FOLK ART HEART

TRANSPORTATION, industry hub of Sanyo region, new airport promises direct air links with all major Japanese cities from N-SAPPORO to KAGOSHIMA, S-tip of Kyushu and now some international. SETO OHASHI (Great Bridge), first of several to span Inland Sea, opened with gala festivities on both ends. N-S Trans-Chugoku Expressway will (1998) make access into Okayama Prefecture beautiful back country easier; coastal Sanyo Expressway (now ends Bizen) will link Hiroshima–on. Several rail lines snake N thru mountains eventually reaching Japan Seacoast. We take small circle via some of them for adventurer seeking old rural town (*see* OKAYAMA OFFBEAT, *following*). Short JR Uno Line heads to UNO port (34min ltd exp, 50min exp, 1hr local) where 150 dly **ferries** cross over to TAKAMATSU on Shikoku—no JR for Rail Pass users. Hovercraft and steamers alternate, former cross in 20min, but cramped, and don't offer lovely view of cheaper hour steamer. Old JR stn is favorite with us, fairly long stop where on platform in summer they sell ice-cold peaches, in fall delicious chilled muscat grapes, both unrivalled in Japan.

If we sound like we're preparing you for hasty exit from Okayama City, you are correct—there is little here for tourist except some fine museums, five clustered with castle and famed garden 10min walk of each other in clockwise trek: various *kyotsu-ken* combi-tickets for var 2 or 3 (except Pref Art Mus) save 20%, valid 2-days; all but Orient open till 6pm spring–autumn.

Okayama must see is...
Koraku-en Gardens sprawling symbol of local feudal lord Ikeda's wealth. Created about 1700 as their playground, took 14 years to complete. Ranks in top three daimyo gardens in Japan—with Kairoku-en in Mito and Kenroku-en in Kanazawa. On E bank of Asahi River, man-made stream along E side makes garden into exclusive island. 15min **bus** from stn (#9 stall), **cab** basic-mtr.

Water from river was diverted to create maze of streams, waterfalls and ponds in garden. Created to make you forget outer world while strolling, it is beautiful all year—groves of plum and cherry in spring, myriad colorful flowers in summer, maple leaves in autumn—except winter, unless snow. ¥200, 8:00-18:00, best seen early or late in day, count on at least 45min.

If making full museum circle, start northernmost...
Yumeji Art Museum N of Horaibashi Bridge and Garden, paintings of YUMEJI Takeshita.

Direct S to Garden...
Prefectural Museum history of area, ¥150.

S of garden en route...
Crow's Castle, *Karasu-no Jo,* across **Moon Viewing Bridge**, *Tsukimi-bashi* is just as well appreciated from garden: ¥200 enter for usual samurai museum and view of unattractive cityscape.

Beyond moat is...
Hayashibara Museum (¥200), fine display of feudal art.

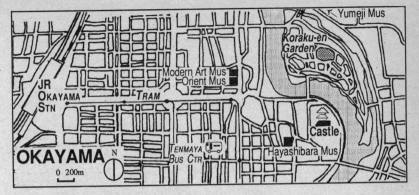

200m NW to major intersect to catch bus or tram back to stn 1.5km W, 20min walk.

Or at intersect head N (R) half-block to....

Ancient Orient Museum, *Kodai Orient Hakubutsukan,* ancient Middle Eastern art, mostly pottery, glass; frequent traveling shows; (¥200 X-mon). Local entrpreneur-collector donated to city who built locally designed attractive museum.

Prefectural Art Museum, *Kenritsu Bijutsukan,* two doors up from Orient, (¥3-700, X-mon) 'local artists' sound like small town C of C deal till you hear SESSHU (1420-1506), nations' greatest sumi painter; Niten, better known by his real name MIYAMOTO Musashi (1584-1645) master swordsman, two-sword victor in 60+ duels, subject of YOSHIKAWA Eiji's translated bio-novel *Musashi* and on his deathbed author of *The Book of Five Rings*; exemplar of dictum 'Zen-ken-shu—Zen=sword=brush', perhaps sole painter probably impossible to fake as one would have to master swordplay to match his brush slash. Moderns include HARA Busho (1866-1912), SAKATA Kazuo (1889-1956). Several top paintings by each owned, others shown on loan. To be #2 to masters like these is praise eno', Okayama has dozens of seconds. Display superb, building beautiful. Main hall hangs (on rotation) great Turkish 17th century Ushaq carpet, Japan's top rug—contemporary to Niten, but here because it was only art available powerful enough to fill that superb space against exquisite native stone surface.

SE of city on hill stands **pagoda** and near it 3 white beehive domes atop white box – Mongol style dagoba. It invites, excites—we hiked up lantern-lined path to find modern, uninteresting ferroconcrete mortuary. Commands long but uninteresting view of city.

SHOPPING: Several small antique, curio shops by big intersect nr Orient Museum; good one with 3 floors of reasonable treasures, **Namba Doguten** ☎22-0981, 2 blocks Orient-wards from main stn on R. Stationwards from intersection, in L, is giant **Tenmaya Dept Store** with 2nd major bus terminal in front, good folk art shop inside —pottery, sedge mats, textiles. Many good small restaurants line shopping streets W of Tenmaya, especially at Sakae-machi recommend folk-artsy ¥-B **Ichi-raku**. In stn, as visiting gift to Japanese or just to munch on while travelling, get any of several varieties of local sweet-rice marshmellowy candy *Kibi-dango*, boxed.

WHERE TO STAY: ¥-S & ¥-T Business hotels like **Washington** etc at stn; for museum-round advise **Lexton Inn** or **Chisan**, both ¥-T, opp Orient Museum, views of castle, garden; but advise out of town at KURASHIKI (*follows*) or at WASHUZAN by Seto Ohashi Bridge or lovely rural villas for foreign guests in folk villages designated and preserved as nostalgic *Furusato-mura*.

Okayama Prefecture has been pioneering in what others must emulate: **International Villas**, small inns in traditional architecture with modern conveniences, some futon some beds; for 'members' (non-Japanese join at check-in) ¥2,500 rm only per person 2 to

rm, further discount to student, Japanese accompanying may stay. 1991 in **FUKIYA**
(p637, W of Takahashi), **KOSHIHATA**, N of Tsuyama (only here exclusive occupancy
¥15,000), **TAKEBE** (near airport), **USHI MADO** (on Inland Sea), **HATTO-JI** nr
Shizutani School; **SHIRAISHIJIMA** (off coast); others in progress. (*See* OKAYAMA
OFFBEAT, *follows*). ☎ in English: **Okayama Pref Int'l Exchange Section**
☎(0862)-24-2111 ext 2805; ✍ 2-4-6 Uchi-Yamashita Okayama 700.

SOGENJI: Large Zen monastery, worth visit if you have not seen other,
undergoing extensive restoration courtesy president local Ryobi Bus Co in
gratitude to late (d.'88) superior YAMADA Mumon of MYOSHIN-JI Kyoto,
(*see*)—leading Rinzai Zen master with international following. Now main
dojo to train non-Japanese, who don't need sadism usual to Japanese Zen.
All welcome to join zazen sitting every sun year-round, 8-9am, advise arr by 7:30am.
Several-day sesshin often, consult in English resident abbot Hojo, or asst Priscilla or
monk George if interested on going further: ☎(0862)-77-8226. Accept even total
greenhorn if they think you have right stuff, or may refer you elsewhere to fit your needs.
   GETTING THERE: Bus at Tenmaya or JR Stn (far R end tunnel under hotel
to back) bound for SAIDAI-JI, tell driver destination, he'll let you off in about 20mins.

SAIDAI-JI temple by riverside, site of fabulous winter fete **Feb, 3rd sat
midnite** *Hadaka Matsuri* Naked Festival, hundreds of youths clad only in loin cloths
tussle in temple outer hall in Dante-esque vision of writhing, steaming bodies, climbing
rafters and leaping into human maelstrom to catch phallic baton talisman tossed by priest.

   For wanderer looking to sample Inland Sea, there is...
HINASE: Small fishing village with budget lodgings. Backtracking Himeji-
wards 3 stops by rail or 20min bus along Rte250. Good restaurant **Hinase**, with tanks
of live fish; specialty is immense platter of sashimi of many types for 5 people only
¥5,000; teishoku reasonable and large—we had to doggy-bag half of our ¥3,300-for-2
lunch; another time ('88) gorged 3 of us on choice dishes for ¥5,000.
   More interesting are 2 tiny islets just offshore (10-40min boat) each with
budget minshuku. One, **Kakui-jima** isle, was used as offshore prison by
local Ako clan, now full of wild deer. Another, **Tsuru-shima**, was used
only to banish Christians. Mostly covered with orange or olive trees, while
on mainland are region's famed peaches and grapes. Especially in winter,
narrow waters between isles are packed with floating oyster-growing rafts.
   Also boats across to **Shodo-shima** Isle, whence on to SHIKOKU,
(*follows*), or rejoin our Sanyo route at any of several places beyond.
   Drivers from BIZEN can take scenic, coastal Blue Highway (toll) to OKAYAMA.
   Wanderer suggest OKAYAMA OFFBEAT (p632) route to ancient castle
towns and backwoods hot springs, JR rail circling conveniently inland
down to KURASHIKI. Semi-adventurous types with less spare time take our
slight detour to KURASHIKI via fantastic **KIBITSU SHRINE**. In OKAYAMA
long enough to rush out to Koraku-en, it is only 15min JR to KURASHIKI,
quicker, easier than bus or cab: **note:** Kurashiki has Shinkansen stn, but inconveniently out in nowhere 3x-mtr **cab** to center and only some Kodamas stop, which means
if coming thru you must change at Okayama and by time you backtrack 2 old-rail stops to
town, you've lost any gained time—take old JR from Okayama.

KURASHIKI 倉敷   FOLK ART TOWN

OUTSIDE its hotel-flanked stn is shabby modern industrial town, home of
Kurashiki Textiles. In feudal period this was transportation hub for rice tax
or tribute coming overland from Japan Sea areas, west Japan, and by ship
from Kyushu and Shikoku. Here it was all collected, recorded, stored until
assigned to specific places. City of *kura* (stone storehouses) grew up,
served by heavy-barge canals. Main historical section clusters around end of

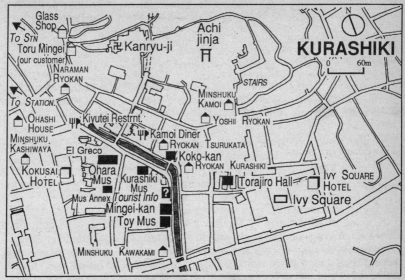

sole remaining canal and **Maegami-bashi** bridge—its lovely arch accommodated full barges—marks former fishing port of Maegami-ko which 350
years ago was island port in Inland Sea. Local lord filled intervening sea
making Kurashiki mainland port. Since then shoreline was extended several
miles, rich rice basket with irrigation lakes is today below actual sea level.

Modern textile company prexy Ohara, heir of feudal era rice tycoon, set
these few blocks of his lovely home town aside as monument to nation,
preserved many old buildings. Still others have been salvaged lately and
restored. Modern European art collector, Ohara gave city his collection.
(Properly Oh-hara, 'big-field'; don't confuse with ikebana master O-hara, 'small-field',
whose museum we visited in Kobe, p.594).

Ohara Bijutsukan housed in pseudo-Greek concrete barn. To Japanese
tourists, this collection is main draw. Long characteristic of third rate work
by name European artists bought up by Japanese, who even in their own art
worship signature rather than art itself. 'Expert' ordered them from menu
by name. But spurred on by Ohara tradition, recently expanded and display
greatly improved till now almost as good as intended. Great view from
gallery of superb **traditional garden**. ¥500 (X-mon) entry to its many halls.
Others built neighboring Folkcraft, Archaeological and other museums.

Race thru Honkan main hall to fine...
Ceramics Museum, *Toki-kan*, filled by pottery of UK's Bernard Leach,
his contemporaries TOMIMOTO Kenkichi (Nara) & KAWAI Kanjiro (Kyoto), two
foremost then-living potters, and pieces of equally, justly-famed Leach pal,
inimitable late HAMADA Shoji (*see* Mashiko kilns, p.1040).

Behind it, thru garden, is...
Ohara *Bun-kan* **Annex**. It used to contain mostly Egyptian and Near
Eastern art (with fine Persian medieval ceramics)—but all that has been
moved to Ivy Square to make room for more European art and hideous
modern Japanese works that resulted from imitating inferior European
imports—yet Hiroshima City has built superb collection (*see*) by being
selective, rejecting garbage. Perhaps low level of modern Japanese rather
reflects low level of selection than art itself.

Beyond Ceramic Museum is...
Woodblock Museum *Hanga-kan*, with masters like MUNAKATA Shiko.

Next to it is...
Dyeing-Weaving Museum, works of world-renowned SERIZAWA Keisuke (whose works, personal collection are at his Memorial Museum in Shizuoka). Forming fourth wall of courtyard is **East Asia Museum**, *Toyo-kan* with fine Chinese art from pre-history thru T'ang era. Across canal from Ohara Mus complex are residences of Ohara clan, exquisite splotched yellow- and green-tile roofed one is understandably nicknamed **Green Palace**, *no entry.*

From Ohara's museum R 20 yards, around canal bend, is village belle...
Japanese Folk Art Museum, *Mingei-kan* (¥400, 9:00-17:00, X-mon) main reason for our visiting this town, houses jewel-like personal collection of TONOMURA Kichinosuke. May spot attractive elderly man in black home-spun kimono, Tonomura, who in excellent English will probably proceed to guide you thru his museum, show looms on which he is expert. (Has also Museum of International Folk Art, Kyushu between Aso and Kumamoto–*see*). Museum is in beautiful *kura* complex, windows offer views as fine as its contents. He set original standard of quality for town, alas not widely emulated lately.

Entry desk has small selection fine art-crafts turned out by his students at his year-long weaving course run in feudal apprentice style; also good-English beautifully illustrated catalogue-books of collection. Serious weavers ask to see school. Only one foreign grad.

Several other museums, buildings being themselves restored feudal era storehouses.
At canal inner bend is...
Kurashiki Museum, *Bijutsukan*, (¥300, X-mon), closed for repairs all recent visits; can just as well bypass. Collection of ancient Egyptian, Greek, Roman, Etruscan, Persian (latter we vouch for as most formerly our collection), plus bilious 19th century European falderal Japanese love—but then see junk Dutch ordered special-made here in Kyushu, 17-19th centuries.

W-style wood structure on corner used to be City Hall dorm, now **public rest house** with upstairs display of local crafts.

Across bridge is...
Oriental Archaeology Museum, *Koko-kan* (¥300, 9:00-17:00, X-mon) prehistoric J- and early Chin, some Inca, sprinkling of early Indian and misc old Persian. J-artifacts all local, Okayama area until 6th cent was powerful kingdom (Kibi-no-Okoku), major culture center along with Yamato & north Kyushu. Countless kofun dot area, comparable in size to largest in Nara.

Little beyond Tonomura's Mingei-kan, is...
International Folk Toy Museum, *Kyodo Gangu-kan* (¥300, 8:00-17:00). First *kura* is international, other 3 stuffed with toys from all over Japan. Front is toy shop, handmade folk toys and gifts.

Timing—30-60min each museum; as much as museums, old town itself worth stroll. Best stretch to wander after canal zone is street immediately behind it, passing side of green-roofed Ohara home to 2nd street back.

Up narrow steps by tunnel to...
KANRYU-JI temple for fine view of town below. Main entry along shopping street puts you at two excellent stores (*see* SHOPPING). L at intersection leads back to stn thru shop street, R thru old town, narrow street lined either side with antique stores.

Few minutes onward, long, flight of narrow stone steps lead up to...
ACHI SHRINE on hill top; beautiful in May, covered with wisteria.

Block beyond shrine turnoff we cut R, to massive outer wall of...
IVY SQUARE: Old English brick textile factory nicely converted to **hotel**. Good, tw w/bath ¥-T; ¥-B no bath but use fine great sento with lovely big W- size towel; ☎(0864)-22-0011; plaza with restaurants, several stores selling junk, some exhibit halls.

Worth visiting only is...

Torajiro Memorial Hall (first on R) Near Eastern art once housed in Ohara Museum; in one room old factory workshop atmosphere is preserved as monument to sweat-equity that built city and much of Japan.

SHOPPING: When our first edition came out two shops had opened selling local crafts. During next decade, many flourished. But now, many sell cutesy mass-produced junk favored by *burikko*—'modern' rich, spoiled, bratty yuppy gals for whom everything 'worthwhile' is modified by adjective *kawai-i*, cute. Hawkers set up rug-on-road shops along canal, which could add to town's charm if they didn't all sell same mindless trinkets.

You can still find good folkcrafts hidden among this junk. Fine but small selection sold at Tonomura's **Mingei-kan**; and above-mentioned **Toy Museum**'s kiosk. Antique shops in center of town have become grossly over-priced, but still some good buys on back streets. Kurashiki hand-blown glass is fine and well-priced. Unusual local specialty is toy popular in 19th century, glass 'trumpet', looks like wine glass with base missing, come in all sizes: blow in small end and thin glass membrane across wide end emits popping sound. Good shop specializing in Kurashiki glass on Ebisu-dori shopping street at main entrance to KANRYU-JI temple. Another at entry-end of canal same side as Green Palace. Fine cups, bowls, coffee cups with saucers start from ¥1,000. Glass not well-tempered, so (especially in cold) must warm up cups before putting in hot liquids.

Next door is **Kibi-do**, with good selection of Bizen pottery, ¥500 and up for cups and sake bottles, sake sets from ¥2,500. Other local specialties are decorative woven sedge mats, equally beautiful visually or olfactorily. All around Okayama-Kurashiki area are fields of reed thru which wend narrow channels. Planting takes place in January, cutting July-August, followed by drying, dyeing and weaving. Farmers in mushroom hats pole small boats thru oceans of reed. Reed-shortage and labor costs are making these more expensive, limiting use. In 1986 Japan sent Peace Corps-like technicians to Africa to teach weaving, and now imports papyrus mats to make up shortage.

L from Ohara Museum: **El Greco Coffee Shop**, homey, good sandwiches, snacks, interesting local specialties in tiny boutique inside— just as likely to find Tonomura here, or snorting fine coffee across at **Kohikan** cafe in small *kura* next to Ryokan Kurashiki, if not at museum. Most Japanese head to 'elegant' dining in **Ivy Square**—unless you crave mediocre W- food (which get for half that price at number of places along Ebisu-dori Shopping Street)—avoid. Enough places along canal to suit most tastes and budgets:

Expensive but elegant, steak house **Kiyu-tei** in stately Japanese manse top end canal. L of Archaeology museum (if facing) is **Kamo-i**, with *teishoku* (table d'hote) sashimi or tempura moderate, also sandwiches and curry. Several noodleries across canal from Toy Museum; and *okonomi-yaki* (pancake-like with vegetables and/or assorted meat mixed in, fried on hot plate before you), good, cheap meal at **Tanakaya**, bottom end of canal area. Picnickers can get good local sake at **Mori sake** store across from Toy Museum: odd bottles they come in make ideal gifts, whether you or recipient empties.

WHERE TO STAY: For stopover, which we advise if at all possible, next door to Koko-kan Museum is **Ryokan Kurashiki**, restored storehouse on site of former custom house, converted into gorgeous inn, ☎(0864)-22-0730; ¥-S. Specify you do NOT want private bath, their special room for foreigners is nice but in back next to kitchen and bkfst clatter starts 4am! Hair cheaper is **Ryokan Tsurukata**, in refurbished 230-year-old merchant's home just other side of Koko-kan, ¥-S, ☎24-1635. On back street to Achi Shrine is **Yoshii Ryokan** old merchant house newly fixed up, ¥-S, ☎22-0118. **Naragu Ryokan** on narrow back alleys near entry to Ebisu-dori shopping street is also old home, but cheaper, ¥-T, because of location and no major fix-up, ☎22-0143.

Budgeteers have dozen minshuku to choose from. Suggest **Kamo-i** ☎22-4898, run by same family as canal-side restaurant, in rambling house, base of stairs to Achi Shrine. **Kawakami** at bottom end of canal area (next *okonomi-yaki*) doubles as folkcraft store. **Kashiwa-ya** ☎25-2507, nr main street to/from stn. **Ivy Square H** W-style w/bath & toilet, ¥-T, ¥3,000 less w/out bath, use big communal; room spartan, ¥ not incl meals. **Kurashiki Kokusai Hotel** back of Ohara Mus about same, room little larger. Advise phone ahead for good ryokans during holidays; can book thru stn **Tourist Info**, or at TIC in **Kurashiki-kan Rest House**. Several ¥-B-T lodgings around JR stn.

OKAYAMA OFFBEAT - I   RURAL TOWNS DAY TRIP

FOR YOU with extra day or so in Okayama area we've 2 offbeat courses:
1st—*Kibi-ji,* **Kibi Road,** short historical run; **2nd** to feudal castle-town
and rural village thru heart of ancient Kibi kingdom—one of 4 main centers
of Japanese civilization (other Izumo, N. Kyushu, Yamato) until absorbed by
Yamato. Kibi chiefs also built great *kofun* tumili. Later shrines deify area's
Great Unifier Kibitsuhiko-no-Miya *Shido Shogun* (Subjugator of 4
Districts) in reign of emperor Sujin. Many sites sit in straight 'ley' line.

GETTING THERE & AROUND: Short run, 23km OKAYAMA City →
SOJA City, whence 12km rail → KURASHIKI. **Cab,** basic 7x-mtr per hr; count on little
under 3hrs, + 30min for worthwhile detour to ASHIMORI **samurai home.** Do same in
5hrs by bus/train: rail 15min to KIBITSU where buses follow main sites ending SOJA stn,
15min train to KURASHIKI. Or catch **cab** at KIBITSU and do run ending at SOJA, about
9x-mtr + 4x-mtr to incl Ashimori. Many Japanese rent **bicycle** at **Bizen-Ichinomiya**
(stop before Kibitsu) or SOJA stns, or near KIBI-KOKUBUN-JI temple midway and drop
off at any of 3 rental places; ¥800 full-day *nori-suté* (ride'n'leave). All flat ground, renters
give you fairly accurate map, and just in case, they've painted white arrows all along road
to make sure you don't get lost. Much of it on special car-free bike path. En route first
stop, *below*, are: KIBITSU (HIKO) JINJA shrine, earlier dedication to Great Unifier of first
stop; and HANAGURI-ZUKA, memorial mound for cows slaughtered in Japan, buried here
are nose-rings, *hanaguri*, of six million cattle. Prefecture intelligently developing lovely
new 'Villas' for international travellers at Fukiya, Koshihata, Ushimado, etc. E-Info,
rsvtn call **Pref International Exchange Section,** ☎(0862)-24-2111 xt 2805.

10min walk S of Kibitsu stn is...
KIBITSU SHRINE, also reached 30min **bus** from OKAYAMA stn or TENMAYA. If
by **bike,** ICHINOMIYA → shrine, 2.5km. Dedicated to Kibitsuhiko-no-Miya, said
buried in hilltop *kofun.* Semi-mythical hero took area from demons (as all
non- or pre-'our guys' types always called), basis for later children's tale
Momotaro-Peach Boy, who with monkey, dog & pheasant defeated demons
(pirates) of Inland Sea. Shrine's actual origin unknown. Legend has it 1st
cent BC; 8th cent record mentions shrine here. Either way, present structure
is 1425 rebuilding. Upstairs thru great red gate to inner sanctuary of shrine,
which enter after checking with priests there. Inside gorgeous red pillars
with 'rainbow' arches; pairs of wood *koma-inu* dogs protect two entrances
to innermost hall, one of each pair covered in gold leaf other silver. Main
hall best seen from side, sleek roof with double gable is ultramodern look.
R top stairs takes you thru covered walkway—at 300m, longest in Japan—to garden.

Part way, branch-off to lovely garden and...
EN-MUSUBI SHRINE, amulets for luck or constancy in love. Behind is
Cauldron Hall, *Kama-dono, naru-kama* **cauldron divination** done by
shrine maidens and priests: water boiled in cauldron if sounds like mooing
of cow all OK, but watch out if no sound—¥3,000 gets your future divined
on love, business, health: apply by 4pm. Back door to shrine are former
priests' quarters in great Edo era white-walled houses. Start of long hall is
happy looking horse surrounded by sake bottle offerings. On table L of
main hall front *omamori* amulets (¥200) with various plants: *susuki* (pampas
grass) for strength, *sugi* (cryptomeria) for wealth, *icho* (gingko) long life.

Walk down hall, see across street...
UGA JINJA sub-shrine with lovely garden.

Heading W 5km to next major stop...
KOKUBUN-JI temple, with soaring 5-tiered pagoda. KOKUBUN-JI temples
and convents were built in pairs all over Japan in 7th century by edict of
emperor Jomei; 2 here covered large area. Present temple early 17th century
reconstruction; only convent's foundations remain on small rise 500m east.

Kura-storehouse walls of Kurashiki

Between two...

Museum of Local Artifacts, *Kibi-ji Kyodo-kan,* items dug from *kofun* —more at **Ancient Art Museum,** *Kibi Koko-kan* 1.4km W of KOKUBUN-JI bus stop; and at Kurashiki's **Koko-kan.** Kibi museums 9:00-16:00, ¥100 each, X-mon.

S of it is...

Komori-zuka *kofun,* one of two here which you can look into (has stone sarcophagus), could go in but recently barred as Japanese tourists snatch rocks and anything small for memento. Said to have been grave of princess Kuro-hime lover of emperor Nintoku—he of grandest tomb near Osaka— but no one is sure, and occupants of other tumuli here are also unknown.

1.3km northeast...

#1 Tsukuriyama *kofun,* keyhole shape, largest locally (#4 in Japan): measures 350m long and 30m at highest point. Just S of it is smaller, also key-hole shaped, **Chiashi** *kofun.* Sworl decoration on sarcophagus room walls rare on main isle, but found in several *kofun* of North Kyushu area.

500m N of Kibi Koko-kan is...

#2 Tsukuriyama *kofun* also keyhole, 9th largest at 300m. Write these 2 homonymous *kofun* with different ideographs, both mean 'created-mount'.

At KOKUBUN-JI bus stop is another small *kofun*; over dozen more small to medium ones in area—chances are good that almost any 'hill' you see was man-made.

If on bike or foot, path meanders thru fields from KIBITSU SHRINE.

Just across river (back on bus road) is...

KOI-KUI JINJA, Carp-eating shrine: site of last battle between demons and Kibitsuhiko-no-Miya. Legend says demon leader Ura transformed self into carp, jumped into river, so Kibitsuhiko turned into cormorant and ate him. Great rock formations said to be **demons' lair,** KINO-JO 12km NW of here.

From Kibi Koko-kan, it is about 3km to SOJA stn; **drivers** or **taxi-ers** can backtrack to KOKUBUN-JI to head down branch-Rte429 to KURASHIKI stn about 10km. Otherwise, from SOJA, train or bus to KURASHIKI alongside lovely Takahashi River.

On bus road to Soja, you see on L...
Yayoi era storehouse, elevated thatch 'house'—not shrine (reconstruction) elevated to protect grain from rodents. Up road is **Mukashi-koen**, park with reconstructed Yayoi **pit houses**.

5min walk E of Soja stn...
SOJA-GU shrine, gathering spot for all deities enshrined in 324 *jinja* of Okayama area. Main hall recently reconstructed after 1977 fire, but old covered hall circling complex was saved; as was beautiful garden in back.

ASHIMORI: Small but interesting town 15min frequent bus from Ashimori stn, halfway KIBITSU—SOJA. **Bikers**, walkers follow river at KOI-KUI JINJA upstream (on E bank), past main bus road (Rte180) and railroad tracks, about 4.5km. On Rte180, take road up W bank of river. Some buses direct from SOJA or KIBITSU, also direct 45min from OKAYAMA stn via Kibitsu; **cab** r.t. from KIBITSU or SOJA 8x-mtr.

Just up side street by parking lot near Naka-no-machi bus stop....
Samurai House, unusually well-preserved, 400 yrs old, first resident was SUGIWARA Iesada, younger brother of Nene, wife of TOYOTOMI Hideyoshi, came here March 27, 1601 to rule over Ashimori province. Last resident SUGIWARA Yoji, direct descendant #18 who donated house and land to Okayama City 1973. Can't enter rooms, but all can be seen from outside. Small structure in back has *goemon-buro* iron-vat bath, outhouses.

Just up street is...
Omizu-en garden, with **Ginpu-kaku** pavilion. In garden small house shows Sugiwara family treasures, feudal odds'n ends—free, like everthing else to see here (all X-mon), but no custodian so call ahead ☎95-0981 to see. If you have some time till bus, wander around back streets near bus stn.

PERSONAL DATEBOOK OKAYAMA CITY & *ENVIRONS

23rd Hikiri jizo day, monthly outdoor stalls at Daiun-ji, Okayama, noon till evening.

FEBRUARY 3rd sat *Saidaiji Naked Fest*, midnite in Kannon-in pavilion *see* p628. **lst day** of Horse: *Inari-no-hatsuuma* at Saijo Inari shrine 5:30am-4:00pm.

APRIL 1st sun *Munetada-jinja Goshinko* parade Munetada shrine—Korakuen, 8-4pm.

MAY 2nd sun *Kibitsu no shichiju-gozen-sai* offer food, mainly bamboo shoots and rice, prayers for good crop, 10:30am-12:30pm, Kibitsu Shrine. (repeat **Oct 3rd sun**). **Mid-month** *Okayama Momotaro Matsuri* with parade, stalls. **3rd sun** *Chatsumi matsuri* pick new tea in old costumes, dances, Korakuen, l0:30-2pm.

JULY Last sat *Bitchu Kagura* Nariwa-cho, folk theater, huge dragon killed by hero, 7:00pm-all night with fireworks. Excellent opportunity, repeat 3rd sat, October. Other towns hold similar nights. *Fireworks Festival* at Asahi River, 7:30pm. **Last sat-sun**. *Summer Festival*, all day bon dances and stalls, streets of Kurashiki. **31** *Miyauchi-bon-odori* at Kibitsu-jinja, city; ☎0862-87-4111, 7:30-9:30pm.

AUGUST 1st sat & sun, *Natsu matsuri* summer festival throughout city. **2-3** *Otaue matsuri* at Kibitsuhiko-jinja ☎0862-84-0031; on 2nd 6-11pm, 3rd 4-5pm. **14-16** *Shiraishi bon dance*, console souls of dead of Minamoto and Taira clans in 1183. Costumed dancers nightly 14,15,16 from 7-9pm; Shiraishi Isle, Kasaoka City. **14-16** *Bon Festival* largest in Pref at old castle town Takahashi, dance nitely 7-midnite. **Lunar 15** (full moon of Sept) *Meigetsu*, 9pm, Korakuen Garden, matcha, koto music.

OCTOBER Mid-month *U-jo matsuri* Ujo castle festival, Bizen drums, floats. **3rd sat**. *All nite Bitchu Kagura* folk dramatized legends, exciting costumes, slay 20m serpent, drums, Nariwa-cho. **3rd sat-sun** *Autumn Festival*, Achi-jinja, Kurashiki. **3rd sun** *Kamo Festival* 8 ornate floats carried around at Soja Shrine, Kamogawa-cho, Mitsu-gun, 7am-3:30pm. All-day traditional fun: lion, stick dances, swordsmanship. **3rd sun** *Tsuyama Fall Fete* pull ornate neighborhood floats thru Tsuyama C, l2-4pm.

DECEMBER l5-16 *Ohitaki matsuri* Fire Festival Saijo-inari shrine, 5:30am-4:30pm.

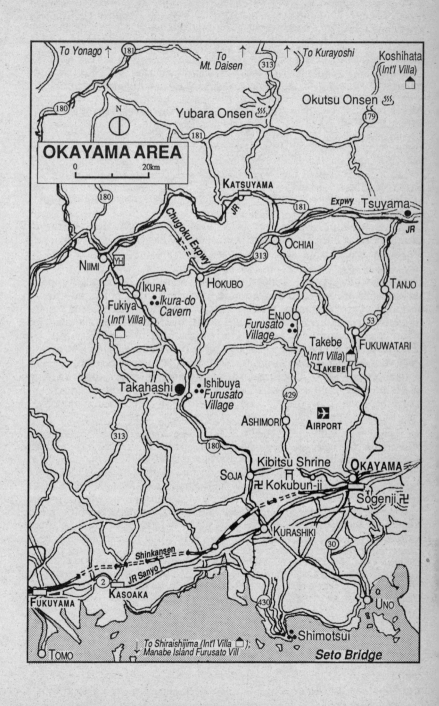

To Yonago ↑ (181)
To ↑
Mt. Daisen (313) ↑ To Kurayoshi
Koshihata (Int'l Villa)

Okutsu Onsen ♨

(180)
N
Yubara Onsen ♨
(181)
(179)

OKAYAMA AREA
0   20km

(180)
KATSUYAMA
JR
(181) Expwy Tsuyama
JR

OCHIAI
(313)

NIIMI YH
IKURA
Ikura-do Cavern
Fukiya (Int'l Villa)
HOKUBO
Chugoku Expwy
ENJO
Furusato Village
TANJO
(53)
Takebe (Int'l Villa)
FUKUWATARI
TAKEBE

Takahashi
Ishibuya Furusato Village
(429)
(313)
(180)
ASHIMORI
AIRPORT
SOJA
Kibitsu Shrine
OKAYAMA
卍 Kokubun-ji
Sogenji 卍
(30)
KURASHIKI
Shinkansen
JR Sanyo
(2)
KASOAKA
(430)
UNO

FUKUYAMA
TOMO
To Shiraishijima (Int'l Villa) ;
Manabe Island Furusato Vill
Shimotsui
Seto Bridge

OKAYAMA OFFBEAT - II TWO-DAY RURAL SIDETRIP

TAKAHASHI: 25km N of SOJA on Rte180, 25min JR on Obi Line. From
OKAYAMA via KURASHIKI it is hr (40min Ltd expr Yakumo), hourly Ltd expresses stop
KURASHIKI & SOJA. Best to see town on foot, for which 2-3hrs good—add trek up to
castle and back, another hour plus. Can hit main sites by **cab**, but town small, don't
advise except for castle, which case combine trip out to FUKIYA. Arrange at taxi stand
across from stn exit prior to departure; rate per hour runs about 7x-mtr (¥3,100 in Jan
1989). While Kibi-ji area truly for those with time, we feel TAKAHASHI-FUKIYA is
worth extra day w/ overnite: **cab** 10x-mtr, 35min; bus 3x-daily.

Stretching N–S along Takahashi River, also ideal town to spend nite for
early start to **Fukiya Folk Village** next day, or vice-versa if staying at
International Villa (*below*). Classic castle town, thriving merchant
district of Edo era buildings and well-preserved section of samurai homes,
one of which is open to public.

Behind stn are...
SHOREN-JI and YAKUSHI-IN temples built on high stone platforms.
From here road heads N thru temple district to...
RAIKYU-JI temple, fine garden made 1609 by local lord KOBORI Enshu,
later to become one of Japan's greatest landscape designers.

*Another route to Raikyu-ji: R (N) on street front of stn, few blocks on is old W-
style building on R, flanked by ugly modern concrete blocks is...*
Local History Museum (9:00-16:00, ¥200) hundreds of interesting odds
and ends from old farm implements to early Meiji clocks and radios.
Beyond just as you come to small river is quaint little Christian church 1889
Upstream here, L just across tracks is **RAIKYU-JI,** beyond which is Ishibiya-cho
district, where **samurai houses** are concentrated. All still occupied by
their descendants except one near far end on R which city opened to public
(daily, but Dec-Feb only wknd, hol, 9:00-16:00; ¥200). Best preserved stretch, tho
several streets either side of tracks have old samurai houses, lower ranking
closer to river. Streets closest to river make up merchants' district, with
many beautiful old homes. Old samurai houses end at another river,
upstream to castle.

Road winds up 2.5km; trail branching off L at first curve is shortcut under 1km.
From end of road at castle's parking lot, it is another 500m (ascending 100m) to...
Castle itself, built 1683, sits 420m above sea level, highest extant castle in
Japan. There is no caretaker here mon and thurs so you cannot enter
buildings. View is superb, especially in early morning mist, but much more
celebrated is view of this castle from surrounding hills. Morning mist
obscures all but hilltops, making it seem like island-studded, foaming ocean
with castle rising out of deep. By **cab**, r.t. stn ↔ castle is about 3x-mtr. Part way
up on trail is branch-off which leads to **Monkey Park**.

CHOPSTICKS: Quick, cheap, big meals at diner just N of taxi office. Local
special *ayu* (sweetfish) caught in river here, served in several places in town. Light snack
or coffee at folkcraft cafe **Nishimura**, large *kura*-style house W end of first small river.

WHERE TO STAY: All convenient, with ¥-P-T; even high-class **Ryokan
Aburaya** (across from Nishimura coffee shop) ☎(0866)-22-3072 only ¥-Tw/2. Dozen
others ¥-B-T. Most are concentrated S end of covered shopping street just W of stn and
you can choose one to your liking or arrange thru **Kanko-annai** at stn. Garet stayed at
pleasant **Midori-ya** ☎22-2537 in that clump. **JORIN-JI** temple ☎22-3443 runs
women-only minshuku; KOFUKU-JI temple runs Youth Hostel, ☎22-3149. Other ¥-B
choices **Business Hotel Takahashi** ☎22-6766, also at start of shopping street; also
(*see* FUKIYA, below). Only time town gets crowded is **Aug 14-16** for colorful, wild
Bon-odori festival, rest of year should be assured room sans prior call.

TILT: Unless you catch first bus out to FUKIYA, we suggest see TAKAHASHI first day and FUKIYA next. You may also want to spend second nite here if heading further up into mountains to KATSUYAMA and outdoor river baths of YUBARA ONSEN, otherwise, you can head down to KURASHIKI in under hour by rail.

SHOPPING: Special here mostly *kagura* masks: 2 good shops in covered mall just beyond inns: **Matsusaka** on left, and just beyond on right **Yoshikiku**. Full-size masks ¥6,500-8,000, small (15cm) mounted masks ¥1,500-2,000. Clay masks at **Tanabe Hakusan-do** along same shopping street beyond covered section, from ¥3,300.

FUKIYA: INTERNATIONAL FOLK VILLAGE.

Fukiya is one of six such *Furusato-mura* folk villages preserved with help of Okayama prefecture. Others are: **ISHIBIYA-CHO** in Takahashi; **ENJO** 25km N of Ashimori or 20km E of Takahashi; **KOSHIHATA** (also International Villa ☎0868-54-2111) hr bus N of Tsuyama City; **HATTOJI**, 30min bus N of Yoshinaga stn (N of Imbe Bizen kilntown); **MANABE ISLE** off Kasaoka City.

GETTING THERE: Fukiya is hr bus (¥850) W of Takahashi, which as of '89 left 10:35, 13:50, 17:45; returns dep Fukiya 6:50, 12:45, 15:50.

WHERE TO STAY: There is only one ¥-B inn, **Fukiya Sanso** ☎(0866)-29-2727, open only mid-Feb thru Nov. **Ryokan Mizuno** ☎29-2804, is nearby but it too not open all year. **Fukiya Inn** is lovely pref-run **International Villa**, new bldg in traditional architecture with beds, ¥-B; rsve in E **Pref International Exchange Office** ☎(0862)-24-2111 ext 2805 (Okayama City), or direct J– ☎(0866)-29-2222. So unless you've called ahead, don't miss last bus out. During summer months, campsite just outside village. In worst case, **UJI** town 6km from Fukiya has several inns, many buses to/from Takahashi; last UJI → TAKAHASHI 17:40. Hired **cab** r.t. from Takahashi, including mine, bengara factory and Hirose house about 17-20x-mtr, set course and price before departure; extra 3x-mtr or so to include **Takahashi Castle**. Small *kogata* (4 psgr) and mid-sized *chugata* (5 psgr), latter 25% more per hr; rates here cheaper than in major cities. Villa has free bikes.

Until turn of century, Fukiya was prospering industrial merchant town, producing *bengara* red dye, and boasting largest gold, silver, copper mine in Chugoku region. Of Japan's present top 3 zaibatsu-business monopolies, two exploited area before moving on to better grounds. First was Sumitomo back in days when it was called Izumi-ya, but they found better gold mines easier reached in Kyushu. At turn of century Mitsubishi tried its hand here, but after 5 years decided mines were pretty well depleted. Then *bengara* production ceased, as more scientific, economic and safer means of getting dye were developed. Old method started out by burning iron sulfide rock to get rid of sulphur. Left over green rock was burned again and came out red porous material which was ground down. This process released poisonous sulphur gases, which, combined with massive amounts of wood needed for fires denuded surrounding mountains and last batch was made in 1965. Huge orders for *bengara* came from all over country, essential component for red lacquer, glazes and cloth dyes. Many stately old merchant homes still line main street, many over 100 years old.

Best is...
Kyodo-kan Museum (¥200, if no one there, ask at pharmacist 2 doors down), where pharmacist caretaker (minimal English) shows you around. **Fukiya Elementary School** on side road branching from middle of main street, is worth look—stately wood stucture 1887. Campsite just beyond.

CHOPSTICKS: Two restaurants, both top end of main street: nr FUKIYA SANSO inn at end of street is regular noodle shop; diner **Irori** on corner has wider food assortment–their *okonomi-yaki* is cheap and huge, more relaxing atmosphere where you can also sit & have coffee.

Side street next to noodle shop leads to...
YAMA SHRINE, shiny new wood torii promises more than little building atop steps. Next to it, another **small museum** with few odds and ends; no caretaker, let yourself in. This is everything in town, hour or so will suffice, but suggest first bus in, last bus out gives enough time to see Mine, *Bengara* factory, Hirokane House, all few km, hour total, walk.

At bottom end of village, road cuts off R and down, leading to all three.

About 1km further, dirt road branches off R leads to...
Bengara Factory, recently fixed up as museum. Road continues as shortcut to Hirokane House. About 500m beyond fork to Bengara factory on main road is **Fujiya Dozan Mine** with large section restored and open to public (9:00-16:00, ¥300). **Hirokane House** about 3.5km from village by main road, cut off about 600m on shortcut via bengara factory. Impressive, castle-like structure sitting on high stone foundation, and belonged to owner of bengara factory, (9:00-16:00, ¥200). Usually caretaker there, but if not, call ☎29-3188 from phone there, someone will show up momentarily. Tea house nearby, light snacks.

Back at fork below village, buses take round-about main road down, but small lane cuts straight down 1km to **SHIMOTANI HAMLET**, another cluster of old houses. Can catch bus back to TAKAHASHI here.

If **driving** or **cab**, there is slightly longer, but fun route to **TAKAHASHI**. At midway UJI town, take road → NARIWA town via Wayama Ravine and road is quite exciting. At ravine huge rock overhangs road, having been carved out to make enough head room for cars. Turn corner and next is long tunnel hewn out of bedrock, too narrow for two-way traffic. Just when you think it can't possibly get worse, you find yourself plunging into huge natural hole in massive boulder, and you know why buses don't come this way. If you can tear your eyes off road, you'll notice that river ravine along troad is worth look.

20km N of Takahashi on Rte180 (50min rail) is...
Ikura-do Cavern, short walk from IKURA stn: spectacular, stretching 1.5km with gorgeous stalactite formations, pools, waterfalls and natural bridges. Largest of over 50 caverns in area. Daily 8:00-16:30, ¥500. Nearby is **Ikura Ravine**, along Takahashi River.

From Ikura, 20min rail to Niimi City, where change to Himeshin Line and 1hr to...
CHUGOKU KATSUYAMA, gateway to YUBARA ONSEN. Katsuyama City is pleasant and if you have time between bus and train, stroll along old part of town, stretching 1km north of stn, along river. At top is **Gonzenshu** sake brewery, one of top brands. Cross bridge to bus stop where bus to YUBARA ONSEN, 20km N of Katsuyama; also 35min direct bus from Katsuyama; also 3hr express bus from OKAYAMA few times daily easiest, most direct route here.

YUBARA ONSEN, claim to fame is its riverside outdoor pools of hot water just below dam there. Most people wash up in inn's bath, have dinner and then head out to riverside bath, borrowing inn's yukata and geta clogs: at most 15min walk from inns. Closest **Kokusai Hotel**, ☎(0867)-62-2111 boasts own outdoor bath—it and other top class inns are minimum ¥-Tw/2 no singles. There are almost 2 dozen 'economy inns', ranging ¥-B-Tw/2; and fine Kokumin-shukusha **Tori-so** ☎62-2021, ¥-Bw/2. Choose dinner to fit your budget, can get cheaper one-dish meals as well, dropping up to ¥1,200 from price. If room only (¥3,000), you can get noodles in 'town'. Can arrange all lodgings thru **Kanko-annai** in middle of 'town', but suggest calling ahead for Kokumin-shukusha.

Those coming from Sasayama hit rail at TSUYAMA hour rail E of Katsuyama: not too interesting, but if you have time to kill here, check out old merchant district 1km E of stn on town side of river. Town tourist office boasts of samurai houses W of castle remains, but all are run down, not worth effort.

Go thru merchant section 30min walk or cab basic-mtr is...
Museum of Western Studies, *Rangaku Shiryokan*, in 100 year-old W-style bank building. It contains works of several local *Rangaku* 'Dutch Studies' scholars, odd assortment Meiji era goods.

In mountains near Tsuyama is...
OKUYU ONSEN, small hot spring worth visit if headed that way to Japan Seacoast. Its attraction is unusual way locals do laundry—stomping on it in circular pool of hot water along river developed centuries ago when fear of all too often bear or wolf attacks made people decide that usual method of crouching head down over one's laundry was asking for trouble. No bears or wolves attack women now, but it is nonetheless performed every morning along river for benefit of tourists.

TSUYAMA is 1hr30min local or 1hr10min express direct ↔ OKAYAMA.

SHIKOKU ALTERNATE

Seto Ohashi Great Bridge, completed March 20, 1988, links Honshu's WASHUZAN POINT to Shikoku at SAKAIDE btwn Marugame–Takamatsu (start of our Shikoku itineraries p678). Carries trains across 31 km span to link to isle's grand total 30km of electrified rail to Takamatsu; cars to 40km of expressway, none yet linked with span. JR car ferry used to average ¥4,000, bridge toll is ¥5,000. 150 private ferries chug to TAKAMATSU, many island-hopping. JR from Okayama stn (not Kurashiki stn) crosses bridge saving 2-3hrs, stopping...

KOJIMA, jump off for ¥1,200,000,000,000 ($9 billion) graceful marvel of engineering which took 20 years to stretch across gorgeous islet-studded Inland Sea narrows. Worth few hours here if detouring to join Shikoku itineraries (*follow*). JR train from Okayama, or Shimoden bus 1hr from Kurashiki stn. Excursion tix from other areas, like Kobe ↔ Okayama, often include bridge r.t. add-on free.

From Kojima Stn old fun narrow gauge 'Toonerville trolley' replaced by **bus** to **Shimotsui Port,** whence boat (¥1,500, hourly 9-15:00 just after hr) among nearby jewel-like isles back to port on other side of Kojima stn, by 9m tall light house built 1863 by Nozaki salt maker to guide salt boats.

Alternate boat from main Kojima stn-port loops out among isles, hourly, ¥1,500.

Block N of this little stn is...
Old Merchant's House, *Kyu Nozaki-tei* of NOZAKI Buzaemon, 'king of salt fields', once major industry here. One of loveliest preserved residential compounds in country, home set in domestic-style garden with exquisite tea house, several fine kuras, covering 3,000 tsubo, 2.2 acres, houses cover third of this, built 1851. Enter **long gate**, *nagaya-mon*, past 5 kuras called *shonin-no-shiro* or merchant's castle. Kuras differ according to original use, from business documents to bedding, art etc—now large one museum of furnishings of house and process of salt making, explanatory VTR. Then mid gate to rare domestic **dry garden**, *karé sansui* and *omote-shoin* main house for entertaining, along interesting rock path to thatch-roof tea house. Daily 10-16:00 X-mon, ¥500, parking ¥200. Outside, **obelisque** near bus stop erected by public subscription to memorialize popular salt king.

Take coast bus to 3rd stn for seaside boat races, hilltop entertainment park and **Setouchi Kojima Hotel,** ¥-S, and cab or hike up hill for tea in lounge overlooking bridge and crown of islets. Odd place for hotel?—main trade is weddings, secondarily bridge gawkers. Some buses from Kurashiki stop here before going in to Kojima, so get off for tea or lunch, continue on coast bus, see NOZAKI-TE last.

Rejoin bus back to Kojima stn, or on to Shimotsui-terminal for connecting boat tour thru nearby isles back to Kojima Stn, whence cross **Seto Bridge** to Shikoku, or budgeteers take one of 150 daily isle-hopper chug boats. Drivers find car ferry cheaper.

SHIKOKU → ON: Our next big stop is HIROSHIMA. But between are slew of fun small towns—back on JR local chug down Sanyo Main Line 6 stops (25min) to...

KASAOKA: Pirate captain Murakami made this his base during 15th century; Tokugawa converted it into major port, dismantled his fortress and hill is now covered with sakura trees. After Meiji Restoration it became seat of government for newly created Oda pref, later incorporated into Okayama. Town is much like KURASHIKI, full of white plaster *kura* and **old houses** but much smaller and not touristized. Hour detour will allow you to meander thru its streets, old prefectural office 500m inland from stn. Kasaoka coast is set aside as nature preserve for native giant horseshoe-crabs which breed in this area of Inland Sea, includes government-run **crab breeding** center.

GETTING AROUND: 6 hi-speed **hydros** & 3 steamers daily dep KASAOKA, stopping at several isles, to end at TADOTSU on Shikoku. First stop KOUNOSHIMA, 35min boat, can also be reached by 20min bus. Flat land between island and town was filled in by Tokugawa. 10min boat to Takashima, where Jimmu is said to have landed on his way to conquer Yamato Plains. Next, SHIRAISHIJIMA, International Villa, hour from Kasaoka (25min hi-speed) has beautiful rugged rock spine site of special *Bon dances* on beach **Aug 14-16.** Many colorfully kimonoed groups perform here, started as offering to Heike and Genji dead washed up on shore after Yajima naval battle. 30min steamer, 15min hi-speed on to KITAGIJIMA, largest of chain and famous for its granite which went to build Osaka Castle in 16th century, and more recently as foundation stones for Tokyo Olympic stadium. On **lunar Mar 3** *Girls' Day* here, paper *hina* dolls are set afloat on straw boats as prayers for health and safety for island's women. 25min hi-speed, 50min slow steamer from Shiraishi is MANABEJIMA winter flower paradise (**Oct-Mar**) and known for its excellent seafood inns; designated *Furusato-mura*, no Int'l Villa yet. SANAGIJIMA last of chain picks up floral baton to break out in colorful bloom **Apr-Jun.** Twice daily hi-speeds betw mainland FUKUYAMA and Shikoku's KAMEYAMA stop at Shiraishi; 25min SHIRAISHI ↔ FUKUYAMA. ¥-B inns in Kasaoka and on all isles.

KASAOKA → FUKUYAMA DETOUR: Igasa RR **Museum** (15min bus) in NIIYAMA stn on now defunct Igasa rail line has German-made early Taisho-era steam locomotive and cars.

15min bus further to...
Denchu Museum, near which is *Kojo-kan*, another Edo period **school** for commoners. Whence 35min bus to FUKUYAMA, part way there can rejoin rail at KANNABE town, which boasts some mid-18th century **samurai houses** in excellent condition.

At FUKUYAMA (15min from KASAOKA) we are in HIROSHIMA prefecture. **Castle** looming behind stn is part postwar reconstruction, with outer turrets moved here from Fushimi Castle near Kyoto, fine in its completeness; now **Museum of Local History.** Shinkansen Kodama stops here, which is ideal, for after its 90min from KOBE, another 25min bus from terminal #11 (taxi 8x-mtr) takes us to picturesque fishing inlet-islet combination of...

TOMO: Still, as it was in '50-'60s, ideal spot for quiet retreat for luxury and middle-range travelers; pilgrims must camp or stay at slightly inconvenient Youth Hostel as no minshuku in town. Former still have sumptuous **New Kinsui Kokusai Hotel,** J-style located offshore overlooking sea, reach by jitney boat. Superb inn boasting lovely view of islet-studded Inland Sea (meditate on sunset from their observatory bath); ¥-Sw/2, ☎(0849)-82-2111 or about room only at International rate hotels—and all are 2-room suites; top rate includes fabulous 11-course dinner & 7-course bkfst, also local specialty 'Life-Preserving Wine' *Homeishu.* Dinners at all inns here massive feasts of assorted seafood delicacies. This is one spot where we suggest putting out extra yen (save some by getting room w/dinner only as most bkfsts are only average). Campers are also on island, can sometimes get in to Kinsui's baths for few hundred yen.

Island popular swimming spot summer. On mainland, Kinsui's annex **Seaside Hotel** ☎83-5111, ¥-Tw/2, where Garet stayed 1983; in January '86 he stayed at **Keisho-kan** ☎82-2121, ¥-Tw/2, with magnificent rooms and better view. Cheapest **Taisan-kan** ☎83-5045, ¥-B-Tw/2, on tip of point by boat pier to island.

It is best off-season when quiet and empty, but exciting time to visit is **May 1-31** (reservation essential) when colorfully bedecked fleets leave TOMO to net *tai* (sea bream) on Inland Sea. Inns run own boats, abt ¥2,300 adult, ¥1,150 child to join in netting. Sun and hol 2 excursions out: 10:30-12:30 and 13:30-15:30; weekdays only a.m runs. Charter small boats ¥19,000 for 5 people (¥1,900 for each additional), or ¥29,000 to include your catch of fish cooked on board.

You can rent sightseeing boats around island and its neighbors; and/or to...
Abuto Point, past lovely clifftop shrine's Abuto Kannon, fisherman's goddess of mercy at which ancient Korean embassies worshipped.

YH is out this way, 20min bus or hitch ride on boat and be dropped off. In summer, 25min steamer from TOMO main port → HASHIRIJIMA isle swim, ¥300, 7 r.t. daily. Inland Sea SST **hydrofoil cruise** has early morning departure out of Tomo, ending western terminus Hiroshima or Miyajima; after that one sailing, ONOMICHI down coast becomes starting point. Last E-bound of day from same ends TOMO.

Town itself is interesting to stroll, particularly area near main pier with large cluster of old homes. Town tourist map (free at bus stop **Info Booth** or at inns) conveniently outlines in color best route to walk. You can circle whole course in hour; good way to build up appetite for evening feast.

SHINSHOJI temple, 4-5 km NW up coast in Numakuma-cho, has **International Zen Center** ☎(0849)-88-1200, established 1988 by its resident roshi NORITAKE Kotoku of Hanazono Zen University, for anyone of any gender or language who wishes to experience for one day or one life zen monastic life (sans its sadism, as also only at SOGENJI, preceding, p628). Can help visa if serious. 'Guests' usually mix of *gaijin* and native—who have as much difficulty trying to find place to accept them and start them on Way. Several W- & J-style rooms, ¥3,000, supper ¥800.

15min rail on from FUKUYAMA, or 30min bus from TOMO (check as they have only 3 daily, in '91 was 7:50, 11:15, 17:30; ¥670), at...
MATSUNAGA, 'Norman watch towers' or fat chimneys of light wood 'bricks' dot town—blocks for *geta*-wood clogs, stacked to season: town is center of their manufacture; fine **Museum of Japanese Footwear**, *Hakimono Hakubutsukan*—which has our Persian nomad's shoes.

We become wedged now between mountains and island-jeweled sea. Fishing boats nuzzle docked to sea wall, separated from rail line by narrow strip of paved highway. Suddenly hills, rising straight out of sea, explode in wild circus of temples, great swooping tiled roofs, pagodas and dagobas; and nearest isle is only few score meters across water. From here to IMABARI on Shikoku, isles are stepping stones separated by channels barely as wide as city streets; dozen bridges are done or in progress to span these islands with road to Shikoku. Nearest isle is modern shipyard; others terraced tangerine (Xmas orange) orchards.

We are in...
ONOMICHI 'Tail Road' is still town of narrow lanes. Only since 1960 has main trunk hiway running length of long narrow town been widened to more than alley barely two midget passenger cars wide (bus coming other way made you back into shop door)—and, as *Murray's Guide* of 80 years ago describes it, "...of fine, tho decaying temples: two best are **Senko-ji** and Saikoku-ji. Flights of steps that seem endless lead up to former, which stands near top of very steep hill. Huge granite blocks jut out quaintly from

soil, helping to form picture at once weird and beautiful **Saikoku-ji** branch of great monastery of Koya-san, very stately with its big stone walls". Modern cable car goes up to SENKO-JI and one of Japan's loveliest views. **Castle** hanging precariously off hillside (as everything in town) behind stn is modern addition, built by local castle maniac. Inside is **museum of castles**, detailing how made: models, photos of Japan's great castles.

This is town of temples, with over thirty in narrow stretch of land under 2km long. **TENNEI-JI** is one at base of Senko-ji's steps; halfway up hill is its 3-tiered **pagoda** originally built in 13th century as 5-tiered. Furthest east across town from stn is **JODO-JI**, reputedly founded by Prince Shotoku in 616AD: present structures date to early 17th century. Nice, with yet another pagoda; winding path up 178m high hill behind.

WHERE TO STAY: Tho different in nature, Onomichi is budgeteer's alternative to TOMO, many minshuku (most on nearest MUKAIJIMA-isle, to which you can bus across). Youth Hostel on hill. Ryokan in town almost all budget, not much more than minshuku. And food is as good. For lunch, pick any of several seafood joints clumped together in midtown (where rail curves inland slightly): **Yura, Uroko, Higashiyama**, or **Aoyanagi**.

Bus station near train, whence 20min bus into hills for fine YORO ONSEN.

At west end of mid-sea scenic bottleneck Hiroshima Prefecture is well on way to completing series of bridges island-hopping Onomichi–Imabari on Shikoku, with 5 bridges ready '90 and 2 to go. Or **boat station** is block down from train stn. From here you can:

1) Zip thru Inland Sea on SST express hydrofoil. TOMO (1st run, or terminus for last run only) → Onomichi→ Setoda (3hr30min stop for Nikko-West) → Omishima (1hr30min stop for shrine museum) → Ondo-no-Seto → Ujina Port of Hiroshima → MIYAJIMA (or *come back* this way).

2) More adventurous can hike or bike across bridges (have buses) Onomichi → Mukaijima → Innoshima → (bridge opens 1991) Ikuchijima (Nikko-West) → (bridge planned by 1999) Omishima → Hakatashima → Oshima then switch to ferry for Ujina, or continue ferry (bridge opens 1999) → Imabari on Shikoku, which explore or switch to steamer heading back to Hiroshima. Fastest is hydrofoil **Imabari Kohsokusen** ☎(082)-254-7555, (2hrs, ¥4,220, 5x-daily). However, take any of many ships out, changing lines en route. Many are hydrofoil, which is like traveling in eggshell, missing beauty of area while you try to peer thru encrusted windows at high speed. Ferries are cheaper, have open decks. Bridges have walkways, charge tolls for motorbikes—as do ferries.

3) Reach garish 'Nikko of West' at Setoda on Ikuchijima isle by boat in 90min, or combination bridge-ferry.

MIHARA, one stop JR down has more of same for steamers, hydrofoil— but no SST.

INNOSHIMA: Hydrofoil zips into HABU port (30min), steamer chugs into HABU (1hr) or OMOI (40min), or numerous buses to Habu on suspension bridge via MUKAIJIMA. From HABU 20min steamer to any of three small isles with nothing in particular. Innoshima was main base of 15th century pirate skipper Murakami, and in middle of island is **KONREN-JI**, his family temple, where on Aug 16th are wild *Bon dances* said started by him. **Museum** nearby has Murakami family treasures, remains of his **fort** on nearby hill. Murakamis were immense Inland Sea pirate clan.

IKUCHIJIMA, just across narrow strait, which steamers cross (buses circle island, anticipating soon-to-come bridge); but most land at SETODA port on other side, first stop of SST. Infamous for **KOSAN-JI** temple monstrosity pompously called 'Nikko of West' built by eccentric old Osaka

millionaire for his dead mother. In its compound are 20-plus replicas of
famous ancient religious structures which he spent decades building. You
have to admire his devotion. You might take it in for kicks if you have time,
for strolling Setoda isle is pleasant, views exquisite, especially with sun
setting over entrance to tiny port. Art buffs will find ancient art treasures
housed in Kosan-ji's **treasure hall**. On overlooking hill **KOJO-JI** temple
has lovely 550-year-old 3-tiered pagoda, much nicer atmosphere than
imitation complex below. Nakano village short bus ride down coast is full
of well-preserved **old houses**, lovely atmosphere, highly photogenic.

Other side of isle slightly inland, is...
NAMOTSU village. *Kagura* performances at shrine there **1st sun Apr** to
commemorate miraculous end to devastating plague 250 years ago. Other events on
island include: special mothers' day fete at KOSAN-JI; *Obon Festival* **Aug 14** at
NAMOTSU in which dozens of lanterns hung from bamboo clusters are carried thru town;
Setoda Summer Festival **Aug 14.**

OMISHIMA: 25min steamer on to INOGUCHI port on its east coast (SST and some
steamers into west coast MIYA-URA), whence 15min bus (5min from MIYA-URA) to
OYAMA-ZUMI JINJA, main shrine of *suigun* (pirates), and powerful
mainland lords came here to pray, hopefully be granted strength and
cunning of these aquatic samurai. It enshrines gods of war and ocean. As
offerings, visiting warriors left behind prized weapons or armor, and as
result shrine **treasure halls** (¥800 for all 3 halls) are filled with perhaps
greatest collection of feudal weaponry, almost all National Treasures (about
80% of all NT weapons and armor are here). Among them is rare suit of armor
made for woman, longest sword in Japan (180cm-6ft!)—never used, made
specially as offering. Two main **festivals** of Omishima take place **lunar May 5**
and **lunar Sept 9** (abt month later than our date). First marks start of crop planting,
2nd is in thanks for good harvest or better luck next time. At both you see unusual *hitori-
zumo* (one man sumo) in which local champ goes against shrine deity. Needless to say
who always wins 2 out of 3.

Between Omishima and mainland is small isle...
OKUNOSHIMA: Now gigantic government-run rest area with beaches,
hostels. As primary production site for chemical weaponry in World War II
was so secret that erased from maps till 1945. Many islanders suffer keloids
and aftereffects as horrid as A-bomb victims from mustard, other gasses
made here. **3 ferries** daily INOGUCHI ↔ OKUNOSHIMA; 9 **car-ferries** and 6
passenger **steamers** daily OKUNOSHIMA ↔ TADANO-UMI on mainland.

From OMISHIMA, SST, hydrofoils and most steamers head to HIROSHIMA-UJINA
port, but wanderer has several isles still to pass thru. All are pleasantly devoid of
anything but beaches and budget inns. **Osaki Kamishima** and **Shimojima**, next big
two from Omishima, used to be center of islands' red light district and tho practice no
longer continues, some of rambling old houses used remain. Other options from
Omishima (Miya-ura) is to head over to IMABARI on Shikoku, or to TAKEHARA on
mainland; 3 ships r.t. daily each way.

Along shoreline for miles west of Onomichi, right where shoulder of
road should be, fishing boats by hundreds snuggle up to shore. This fleet
nuzzling against mountainous coast reminds of Hong Kong. These are
floating homes of modern remnant of People of Sea—nautical nomads, sea
gypsies. Rapidly dwindling, they have their base here, follow harvests and
seasonal fish-runs around isles and shores of Inland Sea to work as
farmers, fishermen, fish packers, oyster shuckers or packers, local
freighters. Many work in shipyards on isles and Kure. Many live aboard
ship; others have cottages on shore where they may leave old folks and
school-age children while on migration.

They were often considered to be near-pariah, for they rarely have family registers (having no land) and so statistically did not exist. This has caused trouble with taxes and school district allocation. This is further complicated by fact that they don't move as single unit (schoolboat once considered was thus useless) but, like desert nomads or Plains Indians of last century USA, break up into smaller bands on move. Arrangements are now made to board children of nonlandholders while schools in session. Many send offspring to live with landlubber relatives or friends. Building of factories pollutes Inland Sea waters and changes fish runs, changing nomadic patterns. More now work oystering or on farms at harvest. By end of this generation, they will almost all have moved to land. Great 'Flower Fleets' were once operated by these people—armadas of gaily bedecked floating tea-houses, gambling dens, wine shops and bordellos. These nautical red light districts plied their perfumed piracy as far as Kobe, were written about by early European residents. Pity modern Marco Polo that these wilted Flower Fleets have not reseeded.

But then they say, 'Kobe people are all boat people'.

OVERLAND **ONOMICHI → HIROSHIMA:** Railroad branches at MIHARA, where car ferry connects with IMABARI. Sanyo Main Line continues over mountains, 75min to HIROSHIMA; Kure Line follows shore 2hr20min to Hiroshima. Along coast now great rafts appear in such profusion they seem to put floor over sea: oyster farms. Hiroshima is justly famed for its oyster cooking and fast becoming famous for pearls, tho not available retail. At Kure amid oyster rafts, shipyards build world's largest oil tankers.

Third of way to Kure is...

TAKEHARA with several steamers to/from isles; hydrofoil to IMABARI. Pleasant town of white-walled feudal era houses owes its existence to great salt fields started here in first years of Tokugawa, using skills learned from Banshu Ako near Bizen. Nice town to stroll thru before getting on old JR train (hourly either direction). Follow canal up from port, past rail tracks puts you in best part of town with 200-300-year-old manses of town 'fathers', *kura* sake brewery and *kura shoyu* (soy sauce) maker—both still at it. Also some lovely rustic temples, all date first decade 17th century; most obvious is **SAIHO-JI**, up hill on stilt-supported platform.

On overland main line to Hiroshima, halfway was...

SAIJO recently renamed **HIGASHI HIROSHIMA CITY** as center of Hiroshima's new **University City**, including one of country's several new Technopolies, hi-tech research centers. It seems only appropriate to put area's intellectual cream in one of largest sake brewing towns around—more than 10 **breweries** in town, all around stn. Many are in their original *kura* factories; most offer tours and samplings.

Beyond SAIJO/HIGASHI HIROSHIMA there are many two-storied houses, upper storey blank. Some within are single storey with external fake upper on facade for prestige. Even those with true top floors are windowless because of feudal prohibition against commoners looking down upon passersby of higher status. At **SENO** wall terracing is astonishing, like gigantic old forts. Each terrace from 1 to over 2m high. In many places there are as many as 40 storeys of terracing. To us this indicates trace of early rice-agriculture migration from SE Asia-Philippines, which latter also boasts similar hillside skyscrapers, but much older by perhaps millennium.

Suddenly we drop out of mountain passes, into midst of breweries and auto factories –its unattractive facade masking lovely interior–into...

$E=mc^2$ — Albert Einstein

I am become Death, shatterer of Worlds
— Robert Oppenheimer quoting Hindu Epic, July 16, 1945

Enemy has begun to employ a new and most cruel bomb...
— Emperor Hirohito, Rescript on Surrender, Aug. 15, 1945

HIROSHIMA 広島
FIRST CITY OF ATOMIC ERA

MANY TRAVELERS AVOID HIROSHIMA. Rather it is must-see on any intelligent tour of Japan: pleasant, modern city, comfortable hotels, good food and hospitable people whose reputation for tight-fistedness and quality-consciousness results in best buys in hotels and restaurants in country. Here and in surrounding villages large concentration of locals who have relatives in America assures that more English is spoken here than any place else in Japan. Test-market for cigarettes, liquor, chain-store consumer goods and fashions—to flop in Hiroshima is fatal. As First City of Atomic Age it takes optimistic view of our future, yet cherishes past, makes most modern rotary-engine autos, yet preserves functioning *chin-chin densha* ting-a-ling trolley-car system, moving museum of trams phased out from other cities. Lovely Ota River, never very dirty, is being restored so one may again swim right in town. Imagine having river front town house with pleasure boat at our back porch.

All approaches to city poignantly illustrate how geography has shaped its history. Our Inland Sea liner or hovercraft from Kure winds thru narrow channels between sugar-loaf mountains to emerge suddenly onto a small open bay facing a flat delta plain cradled in hills. Above this last channel, thru which our boat seems barely able to pass, soars graceful suspension bridge seemingly set upon great coil spring—spiral approach ramps to alleviate lack of flat land at either end. This is Ondo Strait, excavated mid-12th century by Taira Kiyomori, who ordered sun to stand still so his men could finish by deadline. Our plane from Tokyo or Kagoshima skims mountain tops to come suddenly upon city and, using one peak as pylon, turns into open end of horse-shoe of hills. Our Bullet Train emerges from its long subway ride and in 2min stops behind old station downtown. Budget bus snakes thru mountains to Bus Center, block from hypocenter.

GETTING THERE

Fly from Hong Kong '92 presages international links. ANA into Hiroshima 7x daily from TOKYO, 80min; 2x KAGOSHIMA Kyushu in 1hr, OITA-BEPPU & MATSUYAMA, Shikoku. Deregulation will see more flights: JAL, JAS now fly in. Deplane practically in town, only 4x-mtr taxi run to hotels, or under 10x-mtr to MIYAJIMA (*follows*). **Shinkansen** hourly or better from TOKYO-4hr35min, OSAKA-1hr40min, OKAYAMA-46min; up from Kyushu same frequency, 1hr. Scenic route in by Inland Sea (*preceding*) arr Ujina port, taxi 4x-mtr, or tram direct to center. **Budget** land route by old **train** stopping as suggested preceding pages at BIZEN, OKAYAMA, KURASHIKI; or **bus** from OSAKA down scenic Chugoku Central Highway spine of Japan about two-third Shinkansen fare (1991: ¥6,700 vs ¥9,770); dep SHIN-OSAKA Stn/Bus Terminal 8:30*, 10:45, 14:30*, 17:00 via Senri New Town, Takarazuka I.C., Tojo, Taishaku, Shobara, Wachi, (4hr30min) MIYOSHI terminal, whence check area events; 8:30* and 14:30* continue on 40min → Chiyoda, kagura town (*see* DEMONS). Connecing bus → City Bus Center + ¥570, hourly, 1hr. **Overnite buses:** Lv JR Tokyo 20:00, ¥11,840; Osaka (Namba) 23:30, ¥6,700. **Trams** from Bus Center or Stn direct → ferry port of MIYAJIMA-GUCHI; JR **train**; or **hovercraft** from UJINA direct → MIYAJIMA isle.

TIP: Budgeteer arriving w/out reservations, first stop at *Kanko Sentah* **Tourist Center** upstairs main floor Bus Center: not excellent Hiroden Service of old, but hopefully they can help get room in your budget. ANA and Grand Hotels have fine **Hiroden Info-booking** desks with English speakers, business hours only. ANA top hotel, moderate, numerous others of different budgets nearby. If Bus Center no help, try:

Rest House-Info Center parkside of Motoyasu bridge below Dome and Hypocenter (map) where esprit good and they try harder. Arrange **Home Visit** day ahead, free; sightseeing films. 2nd-best **English map** in Japan from City Tourist Office is free here, most hotels. (Best is larger one only with *Living in Hiroshima* info kit free to those planning stay: ✍ **Mayor's International Relations Section, City Hall**, 6-34 Kokutaiji-machi 1-chome, Naka-ku, Hiroshima 730-91). City tours, *see* GETTING AROUND. **International Lounge** ☎(082)-248-9329; hostess should speak English. Their excellent map of Park we gratefully reproduce with their numerical keying.

English information, Hiroshima TIC ☎(082)-247-6738 & 261-1877.

WHERE TO STAY: (Capital letter prefix indicates location on maps).

[A]-ANA (Zen Nikku) Hotel ☎241-1111 newest, best; choice locale near Noguchi's Peace Bridge on Peace Blvd; rates ¥-lo-S, some ¥-T. Good late hours penthouse-bars: one with live piano, one quiet; reasonable drinks, food.

[B]-Hiroshima Grand ☎227-1313, grand (390-room) town oldy since Tange's New Hiroshima in Peace Park demo'ed; ¥-T-S; loc nr Castle, Museums, Shukkei-en Garden.

BY AREA: Others charge ¥-T-S, but for relatively better digs than other towns:

NEAR ANA E & behind is **[C]-Hokke Club** ☎248-3371 ¥-T; across blvd.

[D]-Tokyu Inn ☎244-0109, 10+% below Tokyu norm, ¥-T+; & w/2 oyster dinner.

BELOW AIOI BRIDGE nr A-Dome: **[E]-Aioi Ryotel** ☎247-9331 looks like hotel but tatami rooms ¥-Tw/2; **[F]-Green Hotel** ☎248-3939 Aioi end Hondori, ¥-T.

HATCHOBORI: **[G]-Silk Plaza** ¥-T ☎227-8111; **[H]-Kokusai** ¥-T ☎248-2323.

STATION-SHUKKEI-EN: **[J]-Stn** ¥-T ☎262-3201; **[K]-NewHiroden** ¥-T ☎263-3456 cross river to **[L]-Riverside** ¥-T ☎228-1251. Down from stn, 10min walk to garden **[M]-Hiroshima City** ¥-T ☎263-5111; Inari-cho by Cathedral **[N]-Hiroshima Central** ¥-T ☎243-2222.

SOUTH & PILGRIM: **World Friendship Center** run by *hibakusha* bomb survivors managed by resident foreign volunteer, non-sectarian, for those whom visit is pilgrimage. Minami-machi 3-3-16, Minami-ku; ☎251-5529; ¥2,400 per, reduction longer stay.

YOUTH HOSTEL, ¥-B, inconvenient and childishly early lock-out ☎221-5343, pass

RYOKAN have not fared well, several old favorites have folded, others converted to ryotei traditional restaurants for sukiyaki, *kaiseki*-formal dinners, *nabemono*-stewed before you like bouillabaisse, etc. Those still operating are mainly ryotei with few rooms, usually dozen or so, ¥-S-L, ¥30,-70,000 dble incl 2 gourmet meals, E- rarely spoken, but used to foreigners. Most prices all inclusive. Check City Info or JTB. Rsve by phone or see agent ahead. Hotels better located for walking. For ryokan, stay out at Miyajima.

But in Hiroshima we advise:

Mitaki-so Mitaki-machi Nishi-ku, NW nr Mitaki temple, taxi 3x-mtr; ☎237-1402, 8 J- style, 1 W- rms, sgl to suite, all face garden; ¥-S. Mainly dining [x-hotel map].

[O]-Family Inn Ikedaya cross river W from Peace Park on Heiwa-dori one block, R & L to 6-36 Dobashi-cho, ☎231-3329; from Stn tram 2 or 6 to Dobashi or red bus 24; from port tram 3; ¥-B rm only, bkfst ¥500. Helpful with useful English material.

TILT: Best way around is **trolley** (*chin-chin densha*, ting-a-ling electrics), surplus from other towns, refurbished, includes restored burn-outs from Bomb. Watch for historical relic of 1910s #101. Day pass ¥600. **Bus tours** from N Shinkansen gate Hiroshima Stn; 2hr30min ¥1,500; *City and Miyajima Isle* 3hr30min ¥2,530; 7hrs, ¥3,330; etc: **Hiroshima Bus Co** ☎(082)-261-7104. Theme tours in season, especially summer, use buses, trams; info desk for 'Sun-Sun Hiroshima Event' sched in Japanese.

Taxi: tight-fisted Hiroshimans pay 10+% less. With English taperecorded explanation 3hr tour of city from depot at stn Shinkansen side 'approximately' ¥12,500 (25x-mtr),

vary with your timing; save some ¥2,000, use smaller *kogata*-cab: **Taxi Association** ☎255-3344. Even better rates available from hotel special tourist taxis, inquire of **Hiroden desk** lobby ANA or Grand Hotels: 2-3hrs at ¥3,400 (7x-meter) per hr.
Cruises: Inland Sea and harbor, *see* end of this chapter. **River Cruise** on glass--domed boats, from landing near foot of A-Dome [7]; abt 1 hour, ¥1,000; worthwhile.

HIROSHIMA'S FAME derives from that great tragedy of August 6, 1945. (We discuss earlier history at Castle Museum). But Hiroshima's attitude to it is best seen on anniversary of that event. Morning commuters were swarming to work when 'flash brighter than a thousand suns' destroyed their city. (1985 warhead total punch = 1,250,000 times this bomb).

Various groups have tried to make political or ideological capital of annual commemoration, but people of Hiroshima will have none of it. To them it is special Bon memorial to honor souls, memories, of those who died in, and as result of, the atomic holocaust. August is when spirits of dead return home, lanterns lit to guide them, offerings of food set out and shared with gusto. This is Bon, gayest, most important Buddhist fete of year: Christmas in midsummer. Celebrated commonly in Kanto area **July 13-15**, whole week nationwide holiday; in most locales **Aug 13-15**, by traditionalists 7th full moon from lunar New Year, that of August, for steady procession of Bon lanterns and dances all summer long.

Bon as ancient rite is as old as man's awareness of death. But it owes its most modern manifestation to the atomic era: may even be called the first festival of the Atomic Age.

Services are held in...
Peace Park morning of **Aug 6** before CENOTAPH [25] which enshrines names of all known dead, and FLAME OF PEACE. Thousands assemble from just after dawn. At 8:15 moment the bomb flashed, great flock of white doves of peace is released. Speeches by honored guests follow, then memorial services by reverends of various Buddhist, Shinto and other native sects, Roman Catholic and Protestant.

Mourners crowd Peace Park this whole day offering prayers before various memorials, filling air with clouds of pungent incense smoke thru nitefall when piles of incense become so hot they no longer smolder but burst into open flame. That great monument to what must be man's last major war, that skeleton known as the ATOMIC DOME [7] is outlined in eerie glow from arc lights of baseball stadium across park where holiday nite game for home team Hiroshima Carps is usually in progress.

Park is full of stalls vending refreshments, children's games, as well as incense, *sakaki* sprigs and flowers for grave offerings. It is solemn yet gay for our dead's spirits have come home and one is never sad welcoming loved ones. Japan's most magnificent display of fireworks, of dandelion and weeping-willow rockets, illumines scene periodically in brilliant colored flashes. On this and next nite, tens of thousands of brightly colored lantern-floats are set adrift in rivers surrounding island park to be carried out into Seto Inland Sea by ebbing tides in guiding visiting spirits back to their heavenly home across celestial sea.

If you are Malaysian you might offer lanterns in memory of at least two students who perished. British might offer them to score or so POWs who evaporated. Names recently came to light of at least two American airmen shot down over Japan who were here: 'Ens Tony X' and 'John A Long' and 5 of 9 crewmen of downed flying fortress *Lonesome Lady*, and some of early GIs into city later died 'suspiciously'. 1986 Japanese estimates for US, UK and Dutch POW dead here and Nagasaki now as high as 1,740 plus over 1,000 US issei-nisei returnees. Hospitable Buddhist tradition encourages strangers to offer incense or light in memory of unknowns who passed on leaving no kin to honor their names. Lantern floats sold wherever people are seen placing them on river: cheap. Vendor, often priest, will inscribe in formal calligraphy name to be memorialized or some general dedication. Elsewhere, incense offerings are received—which Catholic priests we know simply offer according to their own fashion.

Lovely time to visit. There is no bitterness. People consider themselves martyr to universal stupidity of man, as much victim of their own human faults as of weapon of foe.

Traditional Bon in surrounding villages equally scenic, usually observed **August 13-15.** Gay *toro* lanterns of multicolored paper, dangle at end of five-foot bamboo poles over graves, lit by candles nites so that cemeteries— usually on hillsides to conserve scarce farmland—appear from afar as festive lilliputian cities. White paper toro indicate who passed on since previous Bon.

'Professional Martyrs' label was pasted on Hiroshima by some critics, notably *Time*. We say, "Nuts!!" Since 1955's big tenth anniversary when communists tried to turn it into propaganda fete (negated to great extent by hilarious clandestine activities of USIS American Center Japanese staff on their own time) city has banned political activities, physically blocked or ejected left and right extremists and discouraged 'Peace Groups' who play politics. Then Nagasaki welcomed these big Peace Rallies, which ended up in Tokyo when even Nagasaki had its fill. Finally, both cities now work together. In 1955 local edition of vernacular national daily *Mainichi* asked Jay to draw cartoons lampooning city's famous sites. After much soul-searching, consulting friends, did series of ten. In one, Sumi and Jay huddle under Peace Dome ruins on rainy day looking up in surprise and commenting, 'This roof leaks'. Friends we have taken around Hiroshima rarely fail to comment how Hiroshimans laugh, not grin, more than other Japanese, seem gayer and more outwardly friendly. This healthy city is full of healthy people with healthy faith in our future. We honeymooned in nearby village two years—we're nuts about town.

Peace Park center of this delta city was bullseye. City zero-milestone, map[O] is few steps SW of hypocenter. Three-ended bridge **Aioi-bashi** [1], at its apex, was sighting target—from air, river forks here to form great silver arrow pointed at city's heart. Parachuting bomb strayed in light wind few hundred yards to '*pika-donn*' (Japanese onomatopoeia for this explosion) almost over **Atomic Dome**, hypocenter monument stands next door in front of **Shima Clinic**.

N across avenue, Hiroshima Carps Baseball...
Stadium, seating 32,920, now stands on former parade ground for Hiroshima garrison, used to drill troops for whom this was port of embarkation. Our old friend of generation ago, son of missionaries once stationed here, recalled his 'stirring childhood memories' of Russo-Japan war troops drilling, then later of wounded being mustered out by platoons. Home stadium of Hiroshima Carps, baseball team named after old Castle, was built here in 1956 to obliterate all militarist memories. Carps sole privately-owned team in Japan: all others belong RRs, companies.

Forest in park is far thicker than originally designed by TANGE Kenzo because of gifts of trees and shrubs from all over world. Especially lovely at cherry time. Monuments thicker, too—there are some 50 around Park or along its border.

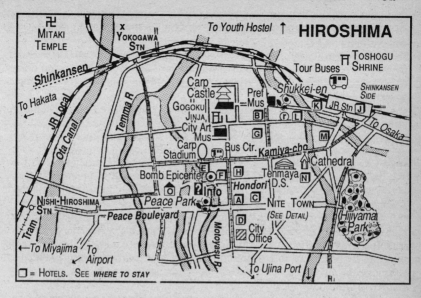

Easiest place to start is excellent...

Rest House-Info Center parkside of Motoyasu bridge just below Dome and Hypocenter. Arrange Home Visit **International Lounge** above.

Peace Memorial Museum [39] in Peace Park is sometimes referred to as chamber of horrors. Don't miss it...but preferably before lunch. Intelligent and unemotional display of what this Model-T A-Bomb did: also paean to what atomic power, intelligently used, has potential to do for mankind. These latter aspects would be better presented except for bureaucratic apathy of US State Department. Eisenhower 1956 *Atoms for Peace Exhibit* came to Hiroshima: museum was emptied of horrors for free use. Attendance tripled expectation: whole schools chartered fleets of buses, some driving hours. Hiroshima offered itself as permanent home for Atoms for Peace, but despite heroic efforts by then-USIS chief Abol Fazl Fotouhi, his devoted Japanese staff, local people both native and American, including ourselves, those pusullani-mice of Foggy Bottom prevailed.

Permanent exhibits detail events of that day. The Bomb arrived Tinian July 26 aboard cruiser USS Indianapolis—Japanese sub sank her 4 days later off Guam, and in modern Greek tragedy most of crew were eaten by sharks. Loaded in B29 superfortress *Enola Gay* for 2740 km (1710 mi) flight of 6hr30min. In Hiroshima, at 25min past midnite red alert sounded, all-clear 2:10; at 7:09 yellow alert, all-clear 7:31; at 8:13 warning flashed 'Three enemy superforts proceeding W over Saijo, strict precautions...' but alarm never tolled. At 8:15, 4-ton *Skinny Boy* with U-235 (all subsequent bombs Plutonium) of 20-ton TNT 'bang'-equivalent, exploded under parachute at 580m altitude, melting ceramic rooftiles for 600m and granite for one kilometer. *Skinny Boy* didn't fully work: loaded with 10 to 30 kg of Uranium, fission occurred only in one kg, equivalent to 13 tons TNT.

Seen from 9 km (6mi) away, fireball at 300,000 degrees temperature was variously reported as 'bluish-white' or 'pinkish-white', at ten times brightness of sun, could have been visible from Mars. Enormous pillar of smoke soared at 320kph/200mph to stratosphere edge to spread into that great mushroom cloud. Hypocenter ground temperature was 3,000-4,000°

celsius, (melting point of iron 1536°). Within half-kilometer over 90%, within 1600m/1 mile 20%, died instantly. Then came fires and fire-storm. After-effects raised these totals to 98.4% and 45.5%.

Casualty estimates vary. Prewar civilian population of 420,000 in this, Japan's seventh city shrunk due to emigration of elderly, children and non-workers to countryside. City Hall August 1946 accounted for 320,081 present (excluding military) as 118,661 dead, 3,677 missing, 30,524 seriously- 48,606 slightly- and 118,613 nonwounded. Previous December police HQ had accounted for 306,535 as: 78,150 dead, 13,983 missing, 9,428 & 27,997 wounded, 176,977 'general sufferers'. There is still no agreement, but with after-effects since, total dead estimated over 200,000, including 10,000–40,000 Korean slave-laborers no one will count.

Sort of trivia Greeks wrote plays about: Code name for Almagordo first bomb was 'Trinity'—heavily Protestant Hiroshima and historically Catholic Nagasaki were country's main Christian cities. Largest single warhead now = 450 Fat Men, or triple *all* WWII firepower. One single Trident sub now packs enough warheads to destroy all cities in north hemisphere.

"How well we meant" said I.I. Rabi, project scientist. Einstein summed up best: "If I'd known they would do this, I'd have become a shoemaker." Hours 9:00 to 5:00, but no entry after **4:00**. Token fee.

E (exiting L) of Peace Museum is...
Peace Memorial Hall exhibits show city life in wartime, present activities. Highlight is large painting Atomic Holocaust by Mr and Mrs IRI Maruki, whose paintings of horrors of war, all sides, are justly famed and fill their museum outside Tokyo (book *The Hiroshima Murals*, Kodansha). You can see 2 short English videos, *Hiroshima—Document of Atomic Bombing*, 29min, from 9:30, 11:15, 13:00, 14:45; and *Hiroshima and Nagasaki - Harvest of Nuclear War*, 46min from 10:00, 11:45, 13:30, 15:15, and May-November both again at 16:20, 16:50. Also changing exhibits of art and permanent exhibits of gifts from sister cities, drawings and art by survivors. Budget restaurant, terrace teashop, lavatories.

Balancing W is...
International Convention Center (Kokusai Kaigi-jo) [31] on site of former New Hiroshima Hotel, completed July '89 for HIRO, Hiroshima International Relations Organization, generously endowed by public subscription to push citizens'-level exchange. (Inquire: c/o City Hall International Relations Section). These buildings and overall Park were designed by then-novice, now world-renowned architect TANGE Kenzo.

S of Memorial Hall, what looks to be decapitated watermelons at each end is...
Peace Bridge [50] by Japanese-American artist NOGUCHI Isamu, long side rails curve up-out, terminate in half-globes. Opinions differ. Our dear friend, great painter INOKUMA Genichiro considers it masterpiece. Jay's cartoon in local daily had him looking at half-balls with Japanese, noting, 'Musta been handsome bridge before bomb hit it.' It is said half-globes portray lotus-pods, symbol of rebirth.

Just N is...
Cenotaph [25] housing black stone case containing names of dead (score or so added annually) and inscribed in Japanese:

— REST IN PEACE: THAT THIS EVIL (ERROR?) NOT BE REPEATED —

Dedicated during first postwar memorial 1952, rebuilt 1985 (postwar concrete didn't hold up). Resembling American 'covered wagon', in fact modeled after ancient thatch-roofed Hiroshima houses as found in earthenware effigies dug out of great burial mounds north of town.

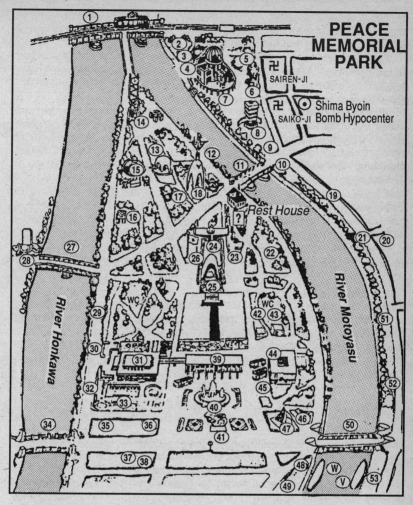

PEACE MEMORIAL PARK

SAIREN-JI

Shima Byoin
SAIKO-JI Bomb Hypocenter

Rest House

River Honkawa

River Motoyasu

⊙ A-Bomb Hypocenter
X Rowboat rental
1 Aioi-bashi bridge, Bomb target
2 Monument to author Suzuki Mekichi
3 to former Aioi-bashi bridge
4 to local home ministry officials
5 to lumber control workers
6 to poet Hara Tamiki
7 Atomic Dome
8 to mobilized students
9 City zero-milestone
10 to postal workers
11 Motoyasu-bashi bridge
12 Stone Man of Peace
13 Peace bell
14 Clock tower
15 Mound to Unknown Dead
16 Merciful Goddess of Peace
17 Fountain of Peace
18 Children of the Bomb
-?- Rest house & info ctr

19 General Memorial
20 to coal workers
21 to gas workers
22 to Tenjin-cho area
23 Statue of 'Prayer'
24 Flame of Peace
25 Main cenotaph
26 Madonna and Child
27 Honkawa-bashi bridge
28 to Korean conscript labor
WC Public toilet
29 to Volunteer army corps
30 to Students 2nd middle schl
31 Convention hall
32 to Students of city school
33 Flower Clock
34 West peace bridge
35 to teachers & pupils
36 Verdure statue
37 Peace grove
38 to friendship

39 Peace memorial museum
40 Fountain of Prayer
41 Mother & Child in tempest
42 to Lumber office workers
WC Public toilet
43 to poet Toge Sankichi
-R- Rest place, public phone
44 Memorial hall, Pope John
    peace appeal
45 to Insurance unionists
46 to Dr Marcel Junod
47 Tower of Peace
48 to girls of city Hi School
49 to S Tenjin-cho area
50 Peace Bridge by Noguchi
51 to agricultural assoc workers
52 air monument
53 Buddhist Affectionate Mother-Goddess
    of Mercy for Mobilized Students
v Oyster barge Kanawa
w Oyster barge Kakiune Hiroshima

Sighting thru Cenotaph to L is just such ancient-style tumulus, as...
Mound to Unknown Dead [15], modern but in style of ancient burial mounds, symbolic tomb for those without resting place.

Facing is...
Peace Bell [13] in small echoing dome, you may strike in traditional Japanese manner by pulling horizontally suspended log. 1985 duplicates (made in Tokyo) presented to sister cities Honolulu (where with similar criminality began what ended here), Russian Volvograd (ex-Stalingrad) and German Hannover (what symbolism here?). Relations with Polish Auschwitz were declined (!?) which is sort of link one would expect along with such as Rotterdam ('punitively' bombed after surrender), Coventry (first blitz)—perhaps Nanking (Japanese deny 'anything' happened), and ally Dresden (worst 'conventional' bombing).

Next to which is...
Monument to Children of the Bomb [18]—51,000 dead under age 9—bronze bell cast from coins contributed by children worldwide. Always festooned with chains of *senzuru,* thousand folded-paper cranes, favorite soul-offering of Japanese children now adopted worldwide.

Madonna Statue of Mother and Child [26] as Prayer for Peace.

Photogenic view thru Cenotaph is of...
Flame of Peace [24] often miscalled 'Eternal Flame', hopefully not so as to be ceremonially extinguished when all atomic weapons abolished, cradled in abstract sculpted outstretched hands rising in supplication from reflecting pool.

Beyond which vision across Motoyasu River lies reality of...
A-Bomb Hypocenter [O] small engraved marker in front of Shima Clinic adjoining Sairen-ji temple.

Facing...
Cenotaph for Mobilized Students [8], tiered pagoda standing just below A-Dome—

And looming behind it...
Atomic Dome [7], steel skeleton of prewar Industrial Exhibit Hall which, at 6 towering storeys, then-pride of Hiroshima modern architecture as tall as any building in Japan, sat almost at bomb hypocenter. This and Fukuya Department Store are about all downtown that survived (if dome can be said to have 'survived') both the bomb and the clean-up. Dome was more interesting when we lived near town in 1955-6—giant sunflowers blooming and three signs in English in shabby little plaza. First was:

THE ATOMIC CASUALTY SHOP
Bomb Victim #I K.(iyoshi) Kikkawa

I am introduced in the LIFE, TIME and other magazines as Atom Bomb Victim #1. Over half my body was burned by the Atomic Bomb on August 6, 1945. I was taken to the Hiroshima Red Cross Hospital, stayed there for 6 years and during that period I had 16 operations. Miraculously I was saved and now I want to support myself. Thank you for your kind attention.
—Bomb Souvenir Materials

In his stall you could buy those usual scenic picture postcards and tourist brochures. But his specialty was twisted beer bottles, light-bleached roofing tiles and heat-discolored bricks from blast rubble. (Curie's century-old notebooks auctioned in Paris 1984 were found still radioactive—what about Kikkawa items bought by GI tourists now innocently sitting on mantle-pieces?) Later he added souvenir dolls.

Across path was another shack housing remains of...
SAIREN-JI Buddhist Temple, before which stood another sign:

"FORGIVE AND FORGET"
Forgive my own debts as we forgive our debtors. And to forgive is, humanly speaking, to forgive wrongs done us by others in order that we have only good will to all, bearing malice toward any. This picture presents young Seishimaru. He saved his father from the deadly enemy who attempted at his life in the Spring of 1141 A.D. It was this time just before he breathed his last that he kindly told Seishimaru not to take revenge upon the enemy but also to requite hatred with virtue as taught by the old philosopher of the East. The boy did as he was told to do. And many years afterward the boy became the founder of (Pure Land) JODO sect of Japanese Buddhism and is well known by the name of Honen Shonin.

Locals didn't like Kikkawa's commercialism. Anonymous students erected third tin sheet sign near his in broken, thus perhaps more poignant, English to announce that other victims did not parade their wounds and that if any visitors felt remorse in their wallets they might contribute to one of many small, reputable outlying sanatoria helping silent sufferers. This tin sheet often vanished, to return days later battered, bent, but patched and carefully retouched.

We recall when first we saw these three signs in 1955, Kikkawa's rusty old hand-crank victrola was squeekily serenading prospects with Old Black Joe. By 1960 only 'Forgive and Forget' remained. By 1963 that too was gone. (Kikkawa spent rest of life helping *hibakusha* groups protest nuclear arms. Died in '86 at 74 of stroke.)

SAIREN-JI, Western Lotus Temple (Jodo Shinshu) is still there, white pillbox building E of Dome backed up by small graveyard and parking lot —which today is main source of income of many shrines and temples. **Temple bell** hanging outside to L of altar grill has interesting tale. Temple was used as air-raid station, bell was to bong in warning of approaching planes. In blast, temple evaporated. Bell subsequently seems to have fallen prey to pitiful Japanese troops sent in to scavenge for scrap metal, finally ending up in Berkeley, Cal as souvenir of Navy Captain Nealey, who had salvaged it from army scrap. Years later he had its inscription translated by Buddhist scholar SUZUKI Daisetzu to reveal name of original home. On September 22, 1969 Captain and Japanese wife landed in Hiroshima Port aboard USS Wyoming with bell of Sairen-ji, home after quarter century. Tale could make modern Noh-drama.

SAIKO-JI is simple traditional-architecture temple across alley.

Around fringe of park across Motoyasu River E, or Honkawa River W, are numerous lesser monuments (*see* map) like aforementioned Cenotaph for Mobilized Students [8] at 2 o'clock position. Most are monuments to government offices or workers or neighborhoods as:
At 2 o'clock, to **Postal Workers** [10];
about 3 o'clock, **Coal** [20]; and next to it
Gas Workers [21]; **Agricultural Association Workers** [51]; then
Hair Monument [52] since much hair survived where bodies did not.

At 5 o'clock...
Buddhist Affectionate Mother-Goddess of Mercy to **Mobilized Students** [53] accents tragedy of high school-age students who were drafted but, being too young for military, were sent to work in local factories, suffered heavy losses.

At 9 o'clock across midpark Honkawa Bridge...
Cenotaph to Korean Conscript Labor [28], small Korean turtle-stone marker long not mentioned in any vernacular guide except Resthouse Map (which we reproduce here), located out of way across river 'outside' at foot of bridge—desecrated May '90, but to mark Emperor's apology for 1910-45 occupation city promised to move into park during year ('91 not yet done). In all fairness, fault is not with Japanese alone: haggling between resident Korean factions linked with governments of North (*'Chosen-'* in Japanese) and South (*'Kankoku-'*) cause delays. More Japan-born Koreans are North-linked due not to deliberate self choice but to Japanese government ploy in early '50s when registration of foreigners started and all Koreans who refused to recognize Seoul government of Syngman Rhee were listed as 'North'—most opposed both totalitarian governments, but opposition to North was not recognized by Tokyo unless accompanied by statement of allegiance to Rhee. Children born in Japan of foreign parentage inherit only citizenship of father—birthpace does not count, nor with mixed marriage offspring until recently did citizenship of mother. Numerous third generation born-in-Japan kids still are Korean (and Chinese). Korean dead have been studiously ignored (totally so at Nagasaki) by Japanese officials and individuals—just as American POWs (never mind Japanese-American) dead are overlooked by Washington, Dutch by Hague and British by London.

Numerous memorials around park to literary victims: (see key to map.)

Rent Rowboat across river from Rest House, foot of Motoyasu Bridge, or at base of A-Dome, for pleasant hour or so paddle around park. Several stone steps where you can land and stroll, returning to boat. From A-Dome 100m E is Kamiyacho main-intersection, municipal center and **Bus Center** for entire countryside.

Few doors below Kamiya-cho crossing is **Sumitomo Bank** on which granite face for many years stood blast-etched shadow of unknown man who, sitting there at 8:15, dissolved. Now moved to A-Bomb Museum.

Lovely, wide but short boulevard running N, lined with fine examples of local modern architecture, well-built, -maintained—Hiroshimans notoriously thrifty—leads to...
Castle of Carp vaporized that morning, present replica built in 1958. Black, singular in looks from other Japanese castles and also unlike most rebuilt castles in being intelligently designed **museum** of local geology, biology, archaeology and history with, miracle of miracles, glaring evidence of Hiroshima's link with America's most educated minority—explanations in proper English. Let's review history of Hiroshima here thru these 6,300 exhibits, better to understand this city.

Hiroshima straddles six branches of Ota River delta, growth of which silting into Hiroshima Bay over past thousand years is illustrated in Castle Museum. Only area suitable for large town on mountainous main isle W of Okayama. Stone age peoples inhabited foothills at edge of town where many tumuli were raised early centuries AD by 'horse-archer' invaders who came over ring of hills from Izumo, Korea, points west. Other immigrants, Malaysian in type or Filipino-like, came via south seas to become Inland Sea pirates whom TAIRA Kiyomori was sent down from central Yamato to control eight centuries ago (bringing Five Sagos clan, Sumi's ancestors). 'Pirates' only disappeared in recent decades, apparently absorbed into local water transport and tourist industries. Descendants still live in boats, sea-gypsies sailing with seasonal jobs port to port. Meet them at their annual market fete, full moon July or August, MIYAJIMA, next chapter.

First Japanese records about 400AD tell us warrior-empress Jingo replenished her fleet here at Aki to invade Korea. Probably used Aki ships, as around 600AD formal China relations opened and in 200-odd years some 24 embassies in 3- or 4-ship convoys (usually 100-150 men each, about half students) sailed in ships of Aki— preferred over those of Kobe, Kyoto or Okayama. By late 14th century five small hamlets on various delta isles were collectively called *Gokason,* 'Five Villages'.

Another invasion of Korea in 1592 by Hideyoshi brings area into history —staff headquarters was nearby on Miyajima. Lord MORI Terumoto built Castle of Carp in 1589 and name Hiroshima, 'broad isle' is first used. During Shogun Age under lords Asano from 1619 for 250 years was westernmost stronghold of Edo-based Tokugawa Shoguns, west of which were only nominally-client lords of Satsuma (now Kagoshima) and Choshu (Yamaguchi), whose Sa-Cho alliance eventually toppled shogunal dynasty in 1867 restoring Emperor Meiji to power. Bad crops late 19th century sent many local farmers as indentured laborers or adventurers to USA, hoping to make enough to buy back lost farms. Most, like Sumi's father, stayed on. But Hiroshima was always essentially military. Incorporated city 1889; 1894 Sanyo railroad reached it; becoming virtual capital of Japan when Emperor Meiji moved personal China-War headquarters here. Main staging base for seizures of Okinawa, Formosa, Korea and defeat of Russia. Nearby Kure became major naval base more populous than Hiroshima. Etajima, today favorite resort beach of Hiroshima, was pre-'45 Japan's Annapolis. Neighboring Iwakuni major Kamikaze airbase, still US Marine airbase. Prewar civilian industry limited to bathtub factories and motor-cycles of Toyo Kogyo (Mazda), which during war produced Zero fighter planes, now Japan's #3 car manufacturer, well up in world's top 10, rising.

Hiroshimans had no doubt their city was prime target. But, by time bomb fell, few troops and little supplies were left for few ships afloat.

Sumi's relatives say US planes dropped leaflets warning of coming total destruction (originally scheduled August 4th to impress Yalta conferees, but weather-delayed). News of saturation bombing of other cities supported this fear in yet-unscathed Hiroshima. Local military poohpooed American threat, forbade picking up leaflets. When bomb did drop, emigration to nearby villages had reduced population of some 420,000 considerably. Hiroshimans genuinely feel they 'provoked' major bombing. Thus double entendre on CENOTAPH that...

...THIS ERROR NOT BE REPEATED

Problem remains however of the nature and medium of this bombing.

Brief digression, but certainly not out of place. We often hear it argued that sample bomb should have been dropped on some uninhabited isle. 'Impractical'? It has recently come to light that such was consensus among top planners—Nobel laureates Ernest O Lawrence, Arthur Compton and Enrico Fermi. Records show Fermi argued that last nite of planning until 5AM. Then 67 senior scientists at University of Chicago atomic HQ sent petition to Truman for demonstration shot. Neither HST nor Secretary of War Stimpson ever heard of either dissent. Director J Robert Oppenheimer dismissed fears of radiation, claiming it would just make 'very big bang.' (Test blast at Almagordo heard 200 miles; Gen Leslie Groves 'We must keep this whole thing quiet'). Oppie stifled opposition, asked all trust that military knew what to do. Estimated 15% energy generated was radiation *vs* 35% heat, 50% 'bang'. After 40 years, 170-bed A-Bomb Hospital yet has patients dying of Oppie's 'non-existent' radiation. Only 2 bombs then existed, but plans called for 8 ready by late September, then dozen monthly, with perhaps 50 to be used.

Tokyo Rose broadcast that radiation was causing widespread death and injury to survivors—Japanese scientists, some working on their own bomb, realized immediately what had hit them. (Due to their distaste for military they worked with 'deliberate slowness'). US scientists at field HQ, Tinian were 'surprised'; General Leslie Groves, military leader of bomb project, dismissed Rose report as hoax. Japanese troops sent into city immediately after tragedy—not to help survivors, but to scavenge for metal scrap for war effort! Many soon died in agony—but army dead barely 6,000. US GIs were sent into city soon after arriving, some reportedly suffered since.

Hiroshima constructively dedicates itself as monument to two choices before mankind: atomic destruction or intelligent construction. Hiroshima is one of few intelligently designed modern cities in Asia, in many ways most attractive—tho hasn't fulfilled our '64 wishful prophesy: 'by 1970 it may well be...most beautiful'.

Castle Museum, *above*: open 9:00-17:30 Apr-Sept, winter only till 16:00; X-only Dec 29-Jan 2; admission ¥300 (kids ¥150).

City Art Museum, *Hiroshima Bijutsukan*, in central parkway which leads to Castle, on L. Superb architecture housing superior collection 19-20th century, especially impressionists–nothing to come halfway round world for perhaps, but of interest to see what impresses Japan. Parallel collection of native painting of past century, mostly *yo-ga,* Western style, superior to more 'famous' collections we've seen. Revelation how Japan's artists succeeded in creating beauty in imported aesthetic to make it their own, as they had also done millennium earlier. Sculpture in inner garden between central circular, surrounding square galleries–truly temple of art. Debt of thanks to Hiroshima Bank who funded, Nikkin Seike architects, designers–most especially Director ITO WAO whose sophisticated eye made selection. Adm ¥500/300/150, entry by 16:30, X-mon & Dec 28-31.

Cinema & Audio-Visual Library, special showings of classic films, special documentaries including full collection films on Hiroshima, children's films, record concerts, exhibits. Free loan audio-visual equipment to 'community, social' groups. 169-seat theater, small preview room, Videotape library viewing facilities etc. Tue-sat 10:00-20:00, sun till 17:00, X-mon, national hol, Aug 6, Dec 28-Jan 4.

Science & Culture Museum for Children NW of stadium w/ major planetarium, many child-operable mechanical and robotic displays. Adm. ¥400/200; X-mon, Dec 28-Jan 4, day after holiday and Aug 6.

Hiroshima Prefectural Museum, *Ken-ritsu Bijutsu-kan*, E of Castle, adjoins Shukkei-en, handsome native-stone building, fair house collection, frequent fine international travelling exhibitions. X-wed; ¥200/100.

Shukkei-en Park alias *Sentei-en,* built 1620 by lord ASANO Naga-akira as riverside villa, 9.9 acre miniature (seems much larger, cut off from city) after justly-famed city-size T'ang 'West Lake' garden in Hangchou, China, which figures heavily in Chinese literature. Noted for *ume* apricot mid-February, early and regular *sakura* cherry April, azalea end April, late-azalea May. Like most gardens, best seen early morning: gatekeeper says if not yet open bang loudly, will gladly open for garden buffs. Endless strollways, but don't try crossing ancient stone moon bridge unless wearing nonslip heels—go around. Formal garden teashop—*matcha* & cake—L inside gate. Open daily 9:00-17:00 Oct-Mar, till 18:00 Apr-Sept; ¥200/100.

5min, 400m walk E from castle, or Tram to Shukkei-en stop, short walk S & E...

Memorial Cathedral: Roman Catholic. Fascinating modern architecture unfortunately in cluttered surroundings. Carillons gifts of many lands, some cast from weapons. Tabernacle from Bonn, Germany, pictures Atomic Dome and three crosses of Gesthemane, from each of which rises an imploring hand. Special mass Aug 6, and first sunday after, spiritual adventures. Organist was long our old village neighbor Father De Changy, S.J., naturalized as Father Nagai, working with juvenile delinquents.

5min walk S of garden, also 5min to or from...
Hatchobori commercial-entertainment center of city with...

SHOPPING: Conveniently centered here in department stores: **Fukuya** building survived blast and **Tenmaya** still best, tho big Tokyo stores invaded this major market. Tenmaya has good folkarts (*mingei*) corner. **Hondori** behind Fukuya is roofed car-free shop mall continuing past Fukuya-rear almost to Peace Park. Local *fudé*-writing brushes account for 90% national total product (ink mostly made in Nara). Also carved dolls of ancient bugaku dancers of Miyajima, kagura demon dancers, local *Kakiuchi Musumé* doll, popular souvenirs.

Great Find: we wrote about it 1955, lost it, 1986 found it again; shrine and temple supply shop sells fabulous kagura masks (*see* DEMONS, *following*), works of art in lacquered carved wood, ¥10,-50,000; behind Hatchobori Tenmaya 2nd road down 3rd block in (Horikawa cho 2-18), opp Wine Bar/Zakuro [dining map 'p'] are two big shrine supply shops side by side, inner/easternmost is **Yokota-Anraku-do**. Also small shrines, o-mikoshi, images, porcelain fox-pairs (male fetches 'Scroll of Ultimate Law': which in Japanese is, s'help us, '*Tora*-scroll'), etc.

From Hatchobori take tram to Hijiyama-shita (Hijiyama-base), or taxi up...
Hijiyama Park, called by favorite-son poet-historian RAI San'yo (1781-1832): Mt Gako, 'reclining tiger.' Favorite spot April for cherry-viewing. Developing as art park: open-air **library**; sculpture-lined path up hill leads to new international **Contemporary Art Museum** (mostly postwar—Henry Moore et al, Japanese) permanent & alternating loan galleries, fine 'black box' **theater**, 10:00-17:00, -19:00 summer, ¥900/700 student; then new municipal museum built '90. Good **coffee house** overlooks city view.

Radiation Effects Research Organization, *Hoshano Eikyo Kenkyujo* –ABCC Atomic Bomb Casualty Commission of yore, doing unenviable but necessary job since 1945—studying effects of blast. Not treatment center tho its researches are useful. **Tour** facility any time normal business hours: phone ahead in English ☎261-3131. If taxi up, don't keep–when ready to go another will be along soon. Walk down recommended—best views in town.

Hiroshima City Museum, *Kyodo Shiryokan*, illuminates old economic history in lovely 1911 brick building built as army cannery, survived blast, restored. Exhibit on rotation 300+ objects from collection of 4,000 incl 17th century mat-sail boat of which 1,000 plied rivers in 1689, with all tools used to make and run it; demonstrations of weaving, silk spinning, basketry etc; old photos and panoramas. Ujina tram to Ujina 2-chome. Return by Kamiya-cho-bound tram or bus back to Peace Park area.

Peace Boulevard, *Heiwa O-dori*, or popularly *Hyaku-metoru-dori*, 'hundred-meter-wide road'. Planned to reach Hijiyama from downtown—however, between this hill and river separating it from town lay Eta *buraku*, untouchable ghetto, so rather than raise property values, some local interests seemed to prefer to forget where boulevard was to go and never built adequate bridge linking boulevard-Hijiyama. Pre-'60 boulevard often called Hyaku-metoru Doro, '100-meter mud-path'—wasn't paved. Since been developed into beautiful center city park with lunchtime exercise facilities, lounging areas, now threatened by need for parking!

OTHER SIGHTSEEING

In, around Hiroshima might include **Mazda** (ex-Toyo Kogyo) Japan's third largest **automobile factory** ☎(082)-286-5700—phone call will set up) at SE edge of town. How does Japanese car get named 'Mazda?' Motorcycle maker's founder Mr Matsuda in 1932 wanted auspicious foreign name sounding like his. (Just as diesel genius Yamaoka chose Yanmar, Buddhist Underworld judge, as his brand homonym). Rugged 3-wheel motorcycle truck was transportation miracle that rebuilt Japan—later copied bolt for bolt in China. 1963 Mazda built Japan's first true People's Car (Jay test-drove '64 in Iranian desert). Expanded exponentially thru imaginative, not always fiscally-shrewd, leadership. Brought out 'unworkable' Wankel Rotary, now world's only working rotary auto. Workers' near-mystical affection for company because it lay behind 212m Mount Ohgon, Yellow Gold, (view of Inland Sea from top worth 20min bus, 40min hike up) shielded them from blast at shift change—2/3 staff commuting in its safe shadow.

Only two structures of antiquity—

Out on edge of town of course, are:

FUDO-IN temple to N, E of first fork of Ota River, built mid-14th century by Shogun ASHIKAGA Takauji. Exquisite gullwing-roofed main hall national treasure, seated Yakushi Nyorai (Medicine Buddha) sculpture (ICA). Moderate taxi, or Blue bus from Center, or JR-red bus from stn, to Fudo-in-mae, short walk; also few minute walk N from Youth Hostel.

MITAKI-JI temple, also early Muromachi era (15th cent) noted for setting in lovely 'three-falls' (thus name) and mossy maple glade, cradled in hills. Branch of Mount Koya Shingon tantric Buddhism. Wooden sculpture Amitabha, national important object; treasure hall prefectural treasure worth trek for art buffs. Red bus to NW terminus Mitaki-kannon, walk 15min (**Mitaki-so** *ryori-ryokan*-restaurant-inn nearby, ☎337-1402).

10min walk N of stn...

TOSHO-GU Shrine classical Shinto memorial to Tokugawa shoguns, handsome, new. Lovely **Peace Pagoda** (really dagoba) behind it on hilltop overlooking city.

ETAJIMA, enjoyable summer playground pleasant short ferry ride from Ujina, **Japanese Naval History Museum** in old brick Academy of former Nippon Annapolis. Founded 1936 to instill esprit de corps in recruits, now open to public limitedly. Illustrates 80-odd year history of fleet from founding 1860s (*see* KAGOSHIMA) to sinking, August 1945. 2-man suicide subs were based at neighbor isle of Kurahashi. One of five released against Pearl Harbor from mother-ship 13km out was captured and recently returned, on show outside museum, while inside heroic panels eulogize senseless death of 9 good men in fruitless suicide attack. Panel in English (could use more elsewhere, odd chauvinism) reads:

> Nine heroes. On 8 December 1941 (7 December Hawaii) ten men aboard five special small submarines penetrated Pearl Harbor, Hawaii and attacked ships of the US Pacific fleet. Nine men died in this attack and are honored in these portraits.

They fail to mention tenth was captured, thus 'shamed', lived out war became Christian clergyman-pacifist. Badly-built subs, after discharging torpedoes became unbalanced, upended, converting to two-place coffins and sank. Opposite granite wall records names, units and places of death of thousands of fine young sacrifices to idiocy; showcases contain their last letters, etc. 'Romantic' as it seems, many whom we know (who didn't make last trip thanks to A-bomb) were not such gallant volunteers, were virtually drafted–tho that madness was essentially democratic as many were from elite families who elsewhere might have bought exemptions.

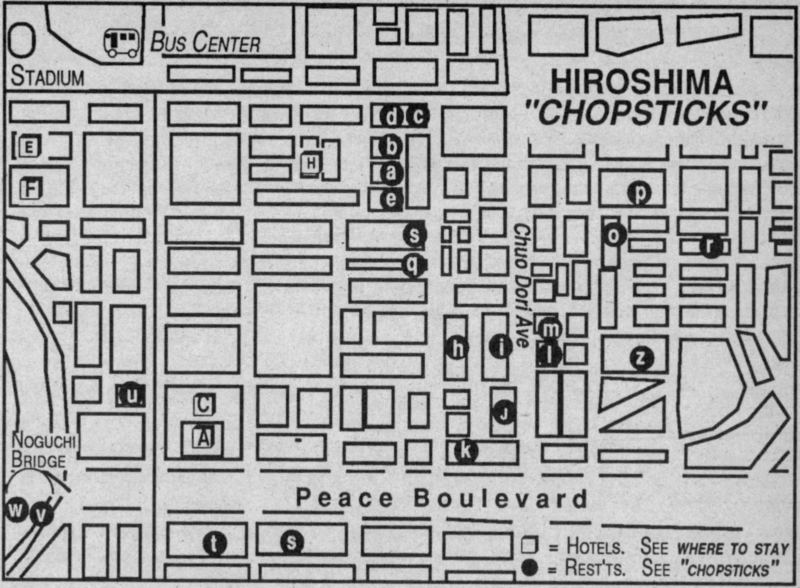

Elsewhere in building, atop main stairs, is room for enshrining 3 Fleet Admirals' Hair: locks from TOGO Heihachiro who (with newest British naval rifles and ships and gunnery observers), 1905, sank decrepit, leaky Russian fleet off Tsushima Isle (*see*), and Harvard-grad YAMAMOTO Isoroku, commander-planner of Pearl Harbor attack, and far from least four-foot-ten one-eyed patron deity of all this world's navies, SeaLord Horatio Nelson.

Free, but limited to **free tour** (Japanese spkg) of Maritime Self Defence Force First Service School at 10:30, 1pm, 3 Mon-Fri, and 10am, 11, 1pm, 3 Sat, Sun, hol.

RECREATION

Golf: Check at ANA or Grand Hotel Hiroden info desks for special local links guest deals, prices vary with season, as also whether weekday, weekend or holiday.

Races: motorboats at Miyajima-guchi, bicycles at Ujina; weekends and holidays, with pari-mutuel betting facilities: (*see* INTRODUCTION–SPORTS) for how to bet.

CHOPSTICKS (§=Still cooking from our 1964 first edition)

HOTEL FOOD in Hiroshima is above average for Japan. Like Osakans, Hiroshimans like having their cake and eating it too—demand good food at low price and generally get it! Local prehistoric shell heaps show Japanese eating oysters for millennia, but oyster farming started locally 17th century, followed 100 years later by *nori*, seaweed, farms. Local dishes favor these. Local restaurant fronts usually handsome old-fashioned, even when multi-storey buildings, interiors also—Hiroshimans are traditionalists.

Sake is famed local product. Not as old industry as Kobe Nada or Kyoto Fushimi. No feudal era breweries remain, all date from late Meiji (1903) when local brews were revolutionized. Local taste dry, more delicate than Nada. Ask for *gen-shu*, that's local-brew (called *ji-zake* when bought outside of its home area). We prefer **Suishin** especially with eating 'poisonous' blowfish or raw oysters at their restaurant: available tax-free airports. This is *ni-kyu* or 2nd class, referring not to quality but to alcohol content—and price, which tight-fisted Hiroshimans prefer low.

§ **Suishin [a]** girls in blue folk cotton prints, chefs in *happi*-coats and head towels a la old woodblock prints. Counter and tables, former fun at lunch to watch cooks' capers. Food luxurious, prices ¥-B-T. Spread from original shop to neighbor bldgs, then towns and even Tokyo. Main stairway main shop climbs face of immense ceramic-tile wall by Japan's top ceramist—probably 20th century's top potter anywhere—late KATO Tokuro, whose museum we visited near Nagoya (*see*). Tokyo went hometown one better as entire several-storey building face is Tokuro ceramic. Special *kamameshi*- (kettle-steamed rice; choice of *yasai*-veggies, *tai*-sea bream, *kashiwa*-chicken, *ebi*- shrimp, *kuri*-chestnut (wow) *kaki*-oyster. Also *sugaki*-raw oysters, succulent and safe. Caviar-rank seasonal delicacy (Sept-Mar) *fugu*-blowfish, affordable: as ethereal sashimi or *fugu-chiri*-chowder. *Supon*-terrapin soup and much else. Order justly-famed house saké. Will pack *bento*-box to go, from pilgrim price to special-order ransom. English menu, crowded lunchtime; dinner till 9:30. If main black-front shut (X-wed), next door shop open.

Suehiro [d] steak house (Tate-machi 1-21) chain pioneered serving Matsuzaka beef, cow that gets drunk. Steaks ¥3,600-6,500, dinners ¥3,800 to ¥8,000. Also *sukiyaki, shabu-shabu* and *teppan-yaki*. Last order 8:30 (no-X). ☎247-7175.

Morishita [g] straight down from Suishin, across Hondori-mall, top steakhouse run by mother of superb ballerina MORISHITA Yoko—maybe where Yoko got her power. ¥1,300 small to ¥8,000 for one pounder. In by 8:30, ☎247-0455.

§ **Kanzashi [j]** fine tempura; name means 'hairpin'—needed to squeeze into old place. Now enlarged by adopted son to seat 15 at counter 2nd fl. ¥-S: lunch from ¥2,500; 9-course dinner ¥5,000 (by 8:30pm); sake local Sen-puku (1000 luck) ¥600 per tokkuri.

§ **Yagumo [m/o]**, 2 shops, lovely folk art decor including *kasuri*-clad girls. Makes up loss of old Zakuro nearby. Specialty *susugi-nabe*, beef, walnuts in secret 10-spice sauce, ¥4,500; also *Seto-nai nabe* Inland Sea small fish and vegetables simmered in earthenware-*nabe*, ¥6,500; *fugu* sashimi platter ¥3,500. Long noted for budget tempura lunch ¥1,500, and *donburis* till 4pm; dinner till 10:30pm, never closes.

§ **Sendan [u]** folk art decor, classical music. Basement Parkside Hotel, N of NHK. ¥-B, X-sun, hol.

§ **Kanawa [v]** novel boat restaurant still anchored on Moto-yasu-kawa river by Noguchi bridge. Top *kaki*-oyster-house, serve raw year-round (summer frozen). *Kaki-chiri* stew, and *kaki*-fry noted for volume for price. Special *kara-yaki* baked in shell. Summer *unagi*-eel, various local fresh fish year-round. *Ozashiki* style (tatami svce) Lunch from ¥4,000+%, dinner ¥6,000+%; X-sun. ☎241-7416. Branches JR stn 4fl, bus ctr 7fl.

§ **Kakibune Hiroshima [w]** opp on W-side river, like above, but more reasonable, dinner only, 5-10pm; X-sun. *Ippin-ryori* (a la carte) available: tempura ¥1,000, *kaki*-fry ¥800, O-rice ¥1,500, etc. ☎243-0754.

RYOTEI, classical restaurants, includes our 'Three top inns' of 1964 original edition:
§ **Amagi [r]** Nobori-machi 10-10, below Shukkei Garden nr Riverside Hotel [hotel map]; ☎221-2375; tastefully *shibui* modern J- decor in pleasant atmosphere that's survived plasticization of most traditional inns. In by 8:30; (X-sun). Some rooms ¥-S.

§ **Itaya [q]** Hashimoto-cho 10-15, E of Hatchobori before bridge, N-side, ☎242-1011; attractive lantern and bamboo-lined entry, classical ryotei upstairs, *kaiseki, nabemono* ¥4,500-8,000; rustic *sukiya*-style tea house for traditional; last serve 9:30 (X-sun).

§ **Mitaki-so [x-hotel map]** Mitaki-machi, nr Mitaki Temple [hotel map]; ☎337-1402; old residential inn burned, rebuilt mainly as ryotei, quality classical dinners, ¥-S.

§ **Hada Besso [y-hotel map]** Funa-iri nakamachi, taxi basic-mtr+ from ANA, ☎231-2018 for delightful evening meals, moon-viewing mound in ancient nobleman's garden where waterfall feeds home of Japan's biggest frog. From ¥20,000, X-sun, hol.

BUDGET EATING abounds here. One of our Wakayama College students of generation ago who helped our original edition as DATEBOOK researcher, Kurosumi, now runs:

Elm [t] salaryman's tasty budget beanery across Peace Boulevard facing ANA Hotel in Toto bldg basement: set lunch about ¥580. Jay's old Wakayama College student hasn't forgotten his English. Experienced budget hoofer in SE Asia, go late lunch time–1 pm–after officeworker rush, stay on to chat. ☎244-3992. 7:30am-6pm, X-sun.

Hanaoka [c] *shabu-shabu,* main drag just W of Fukuya. Sister **Restaurant Hanaoka [s]** Heiwa dori block E of Elm, opp ANA Hotel, nr Tokyu; similar, 11am–7:30pm X-sun, ☎241-0502.

§ **Zakuro [p]** folksy garden-cottage is gone but on ex site on once quiet street now neon-brighter than Ginza is 5-storey tower with **Zakuro**, 5th fl, mixed J-, W-, Chin dishes.

Yagura-chaya 2nd floor, where check shoes in locker and enjoy Takayama-style country decor and food. Flagship of new chain now owned by **Wine Bar** (3rd floor and nation-wide) noted for good buys. Basement houses **Sushi-Fuku**, sushiya.

Gonbei [r] most hillbilly name in Japanese, serve low-down delicacy *oden* best to push sake down with; ¥100-500 portion. Gorge till last 11:00pm; X-sun/hol.

§ **Horuko [b]** N of Suishin with excellent *tonkatsu, shumai, teishoku.* ¥700-¥1,500 fulfills owner's wish for "joy of dining out" for family. 11am-9pm, No-X.

§ **Shubo [e]** opp SUISHIN, block from end of Hondori mall, was our favorite coffee shop, also served 'best tenderloin'–now popular spot justly proud of tasty-generous daily special ¥3,000; *hito-kuchi-ryori* one-bite-dinner of 2 trays of 6 & 9 dishes, French cuisine a la japonaise, ¥3,000. Lunch 11am-2pm, *yoshoku-bento* (western picnic) ¥800.

§ **Kirin Beer Forum [f]** (*ah*, these classicists) E end of Hondori shopping mall corner below Suishin; beer 'n'pickins.

Lake [i] written with ideograph *ko*, 'lake' and part of new cheap-trad chain by Lake loan sharks. Better deal than their loans, *ippin-ryori*, Japanese smorgasbord, ¥200-600 per plate. Last order 10:15pm. Down from Hatchobori, 2nd block past movies.

Den-sukeh [k] –love this name. Noted for cheap good sake ¥350 and 'stamina' oxtail at ¥1,000, other meats cheaper. Little hard to find, street above 100m Blvd, block W of Chuo-dori, 4th floor Shimoi Bldg. In by 9:30, X- sun.

Okonomi-mura [h] 'as you like it-village' building where all pushcarts were moved from Shintenchi Square, now W side of Square, behind movies. Little less romantic summer eves, but warmer winters and just as much fun. Lower level office workers eat here, as well as some nostalgic execs. Safe, cheap, delicious, friendly. Note Hiroshima way to eat *okonomi-yaki* omelet is with cooking spatula as spoon, not chopsticks.

Naka-chan [xx] great all-nite *yatai,* alley behind Yayoi-cho police box. ☎243-6067.

'LICENSED QUARTER'–NITE TOWN: Nagarekawa and Yagenbori areas on both sides Chuo-dori-Ave, modern neon-flowered concrete-jungle version of what old woodblock artists dealt with century ago, includes most of above plus hundreds more stacked several storeys tall. Many w/ prices or plastic models posted outside indicate young worker's price range. All safe, good to superb. Town thankfully lacks clip-joints, even among bars in Namekuji-yokocho (slug alley). Discos and clubs come and go but...

§ Cabaret **Casablanca [Z]** old favorite of ours, still there, not tried lately.

CRUISING

RIVERS IN TOWN: from boat landing near foot of A-Dome, up and down city"s rivers in glass-domed cruisers like those on Paris' Seine River or Osaka's Yodogawa; about one hour, ¥1,000.

INLAND SEA: Seto-nai-kai Kisen (Inland Sea Steamer lines) ☎255-3344 info-reservations, in '84 added deluxe 1,000-ton short-range liners. Promoting Seto Sea as 'Japan's Aegean,' even gave top-tub pseudo-hellenic name SS *Cruising Ginga (Cafenion)* complete with figurehead of Cupid (alas, where be proud Dragon-prow Boats of yore?), deluxe restaurant serving mostly French cuisine—in heart of fresh-fish land this is almost obscene. SS *Ginga* (*Cafenion*, ancient Greek for place where people gather to eat and chat) schedules regular 2hr cruises daily 11:45 (¥2,090), and 18:40 which involves mandatory dinner (¥10, -30,000).

Day Cruises, to Miyajima: deps Hiroshima 11:45am, leisurely 70min am, lunch on board before quick turnaround; 14:10 return, ¥1,120 o.w.; scheds vary seasonal.

Sunset Cruise leaves 18:45 for 2hr+ cruise for dinner enjoying exquisite sunset, theatrical performances on board as well. Book thru hotel here or tour agent at home. Pick-up buses from major hotels. SS Southern Cross is available for group charter only.

Hydrofoil Cruise Akinada Line, daily Mar-Nov r.t. ¥10,300 incl lunch, o.w. ¥6,380. Dep MIYAJIMA (8:50) → HIROSHIMA (9:00) → OMISHIMA (12:50) → Setoda 14:45 where you can ferry to Mihara or Onomichi on mainland to join Sanyo RR, JR or ferry to IMABARI on Shikoku, or same hydrofoil back from SETODA (15:00) → KURE (16:50) → HIROSHIMA (17:15) → MIYAJIMA (17:36). Same ship runs as regular scheduled course year-round. Mar–Nov is dubbed cruise.

UJINA, terminal Ujina tram or taxi 4x-mtr from stn, embarkation for myriad of possible nautical itineraries on regular ferries, putt-putts to liners (*see* INLAND SEA, various).

HIROSHIMA → BEPPU (dep 21:30, arr 6:00), various classes ¥3,600-10,710 ☎253-0909). To MIYAJIMA, near hrly 8:25-16:45, 22min; last boat ret 17:15: 17km, ¥1,250. We recommend this for boat lover over alternate ride by bus, tram ,train or taxi since charm of coastline ruined by landfill.

BOOKSHELF

READING SHOULD include John Hersey's classic *Hiroshima*. Then translations *Hiroshima Diary* by Dr HACHIYA Michihiko, survivor-medic worked on spot. Fiction is rare: novel *Devil's Heritage* by AGAWA Hiroyuki deals with attitudes in city eight years after blast; *Black Rain* by IBUSE Masuji (KI); *The Crazy Iris and Other Stories of Atomic Aftermath* ed. by OE Kenzaburo (Grove) and *After Apocalypse, Four Plays* (Columbia Univ). *Ukiyo*, translation anthology by Jay has touching diary by victim SETO Nanako; for more of which *Hibakusha–Survivors of Hiroshima and Nagasaki*, 25 essays by, (Kosei).

Most moving are two autobiographical comic book translations *Barefoot Gen* 1 & 2 by NAKAZAWA Keiji (New Society Pub, Philadelphia) which belong in every English-language school library. Equally naively heart-rending is *Unforgettable Fire–pictures drawn by atomic survivors*. And there are any number of scholarly-journalistic after-studies, of which by far best *The Day Man Lost* by Pacific War Research Committee (KI) and follow-up *Legacy of Hiroshima* by SHOHNO Naomi. Museum and file photos collected in *Days to Remember–An Account of the Bombings of Hiroshima & Nagasaki* (Hiroshima-Nagasaki Pub ¥400). Some of these available in Hiroshima **Rest House**.

If simply pushing a button can produce massive destruction and loss of life, how can passive resistance prevail...love and reason pursuade an enemy?
— Max Kampelman, *Entering New Worlds*

Sank you very much for dropping bomb. People in Hiroshima and Nagasaki didn't have to decide which old buildings to keep. We really appreciate it. But don't do it again.
— OTSUKI Tamayo, Japanese comedienne
JapanTimes Weekly

WHERE NEXT

Hydrofoils, *sui-jo-ki* (reservations ☎253-8231,1212) via Kure to IMABARI on Shikoku dep UJINA every 2hrs between 7:10-17:10, takes 2hrs. MATSUYAMA and Dogo Onsen, Shikoku, hrly or better 7:20-18:00, takes 1hr, ¥4,950, extras Spring thru Autumn 17:10, 19:00. **Ferryboats** to MATSUYAMA, more leisurely, far cheaper: take 3hrs, dep almost hourly 6:45-20:05, ¥3,700 1st cl, ¥1,850 2nd.

Bus Center, *Bus Sentah*, bus terminal for westernmost Japan. Major tourism development drive underway since 1985 to develop hinterland of this beautiful prefecture, so check here (or **Rest House**) for special offerings. Frequent comfortable buses, most air-conditioned, leave for mountain area N (MIYOSHI Platform 3 or JR train, CHIYODA platform 11) where ancient rice-planting dance-rites and *kagura*-dances on stage Jun thru Nov (*see* DEMONS p672) and on to MATSUE-IZUMO (platform 10) and Japan Sea (TOYAMA platform 9, Arifuku Hot Spring 11). Buses down to KYUSHU; or back to OSAKA via Miyoshi transfer.

TAISHAKU GORGE JR train NW 3hrs → 16km-long **SANDANKYO GORGE** for cool summer retreat or autumn maples, exquisite scenery, like exquisite Kuroguchi falls, cascading over jet black rock cliff; and dining, nice inn, **Sandankyo Hotel**; return via bus → **Yuki Spa** where **Kajika-so** ryokan with radium baths; (dep for Yuki in reverse via platform 2, in 90min). Area noted for 'mountain cooking', as they had no fish in old days such delicacies as *fugu sashimi* (raw blowfish) imitated in vegetable *konyaku* (konjak) etc; *botan-yaki* wild boar sukiyaki in season (Nov-Mar); sometimes farm-bred boar 'off-season'.

For more rural, millennium-old...

YUNOYAMA SPA for *Kami-no-Yu* 'God's Water' warm (18°C/65F) waterfall good for warm water-massage in great *rotenburo*-outdoor bath; walk from YUKI, or bus center Hiroden bus → MINO-CHI.

GO WEST: Bus platform 1, tram from stn or Hatchobori → MIYAJIMA (*follows*); bus or JR onward to five-humped 'Bridge of Brocade Sash' IWAKUNI for summer *ugai*-cormorant fishing; thence antique town of HAGI and natural wonder SHUHODO GROTTO. Alternate IWAKUNI → OSHIMA → MATSUYAMA (Shikoku) by hydrofoil 2hrs30min.

AIR: → TOKYO 7 flights daily, 7:45-19:45 in 80min; → KAGOSHIMA 8:30 and 14:00, takes 70min; → MATSUYAMA (Shikoku) 9:45, 12:20, 17:15 in 20min; → OITA 9:15, 11:50, 16:45 in 30min; → OKINAWA 11:00 abt 2hrs.

AIRVIEWS: Oh, sad progress—no more low-flying prop planes link Hiroshima on main runs, but new feeder lines to Beppu and Matsuyama, etc stay low, in nice weather afford aerial view of beautiful seascape. Also **Helicopter** rentable: 4-psgr, by hour ¥268,800; **Naka Nihon Koku**, ☎(082)-295-0903.

TRAINS: Shinkansen W/S to HAKATA-FUKUOKA Kyushu, 70mins, hrly+; NE to OKAYAMA 1hr, TOKYO 4'30"-5hrs, hourly—old regular trains take 17 hrs but far cheaper, many stops, as KURASHIKI (old stn near museums) in 2hr15min. Old JR Kure Line offers lovely sea/landscape.

Memo: US Military Far East Network radio Iwakuni can be heard in hotels, or on portables; all-English programs, DJs, news etc AM 1575 kHz. TV bilingual news & programs require special adapter stereo TV, generally not available local hotels. Ask at check-in about CNN English cable TV, some hotels, in more and more rooms.

PERSONAL DATEBOOK HIROSHIMA, MIYAJIMA & HILLS

*See Miyajima or Demons text for details
Kanko annai-jo: HIROSHIMA ☎(082)-263-6833 —MIYAJIMA ☎(082)-944-2011

January

1 at 5am New Year *bugaku dance* (1), Miyajima Shrine red stage.

2 11am 1 *noh*, 1pm 2 *bugaku* dances Miyajima Shrine red stage.

3 1pm 5 *bugakus*, Miyajima red stage.

5 5:30am 5 *bugaku* dances; 11am *sennin* (holy man) songs Miyajima red stage.

1st Tiger Day lunar, *Fire-walk*, Daisho-ji in Kaita-cho ☎0828-23-3248; 1pm.

March

Week of 20, *Kiyomori-sai* Miyajima, dances on red stage and rear noh stage.

April

Early *Gokoku-jinja Shrine Festival*, next Castle, west-side (L, facing), Hiroshima.

15* *Fire-walking* noon, Daisho-in temple, Miyajima (*see* p.669); 6pm big show of 10 bugaku dances by torchlight on main shrine stage.

16-18* *All day Noh*, Miyajima Noh stage, to right rear of main shrine.

28-29 Minato (Port) festival, Hiroshima.

May

3-5 *Flower Fete*, Peace Park flowery in giant arrangements. Parade, concerts, events all aft; Hiroshima.

18 10am 5 bugaku dances, Miyajima.

Last Sat, Sun, like Kyoto's Aug 16, but electric lights replace flame to form great ideograph *dai* 'big' on Mt Takamatsu shrn, Kabe-cho, Asa-kita-ku, Hiroshima.

June

1st or 2nd Sun*, *Hanagasa-taué*, rice transplanting dances, Chiyoda-cho.

1st Sun* *Dengaku*, field dance contest, Kake town. (*See* Demons p.672).

8-10 *Toka-san*, start wearing yukata, summer cotton kimono. Eve crowds mill outdoor mart Enryu-ji temple, Chuo-dori Ave 1st big crossing E of ANA Hotel. Don hotel yukata, stroll like denizen out of woodblock prints, Hiroshima.

July

7 *Tanabata Fete* local areas.

Lunar Jun 5 (*see text* to extrapolate, 12 days earlier) 10am, 5 bugaku, Miyajima.

Lunar Jun 14-15 (for W- dates *see* p.666) *Sumiyoshi Boat Fete*, deity of Sumiyoshi Shrine nr 2nd bridge below Noguchi Peace Bridge sail sacred boat, escorts up Moto-yasu R past Peace Park to Sorazaya Sh nr first bridge above Aioi Bridge, spend nite. Returns next nite down Honkawa R W of Peace Park. Mini-version of 3 days later.

Lunar Jun 17*, *Kangensai*, Miyajima (for W- dates *see* p.666).

Lunar Jul 18*, *as about*, day of midday hi-tide, *Tama-tori-sai ritual* 'water polo' in bay before shrine at Miyajima.

End Jul *Port Fest*, Hiroshima port area; brass band parades, painting contest, you can tour patrol boats even take short rides, fireworks eve.

August

6-7* Peace Memorial Rites at Peace Park, lantern floating, Hiroshima (*see* p.647).

6 Sun after 6, special Mass, Cathedral.

10 *City Summer Festival* along Ota River, select annual Miss Hiroshima, enjoy pop music, fireworks.

September

14 All nite kagura (*see* p.673).

October

1st Sat* All-nite kagura 4pm-3am, Chiyoda-cho shrine; check Hiroden bus tours, or any numerous other dances in neighbor towns all month. (*See* p.673).

9, 19, 29* variously, main kagura demon dances in villages btwn Hiroshima & Japan Sea Izumo Shrine. (*See* p.673).

15 Chrysanthemum offering Miyajima Shrine, 10 bugaku dances from 6pm.

2nd Sun (varies), Miyajima kimono-clad maidens in huge *sado*-tea party.

23 10am *bugaku*, Miyajima red stage.

22-23 *Gokoku-jinja* Festival, Carp Castle, Hiroshima.

Late: *Chrysanthemum Fest* with 1,000+ pots of fancy mums shown in Central Park, westside of Carp Castle, Hiroshima.

November

thru Nov *Inoko Fete*, Hiroshima wide, happi-coated kids parade big stone by spider-like radial straw ropes, yank, rock leaps, pounds. Pound *mochi* rice-cakes.

15* *Fire-walking* atop Mt Misen, Miyajima, noon (*see* p.669); best time maples.

18-20 *Ebisu Market*, Businessmen's Ebisu Shrine, Ebisucho nr Hatchobori. Decorate w/bamboo rake talisman to 'rake in' prosperity: big year-end bargain sale helps; loads of outdoor stalls, Hiroshima.

December

23 10am 4 *bugaku* in honor emperor's birthday, Miyajima shrine red stage.

31 *Torch fete*, Miyajima 6pm, run street with scary giant torches, purify year end.

*We love nature partly because she
does not show us any hate or anger...*
— AKUTAGAWA Ryunosuke, *Kappa*

MIYAJIMA 宮島
FLOATING RED GATE

HALF-HOUR and about 10x-mtr by taxi from Hiroshima, picture postcard
'floating red gate' *torii* marks sacred isle of Miyajima, one of Japan's three
great scenic beauties. Little did we dream when we first moved in to Sumi's
empty ancestral home near Miyajima that here we would sail with colorful
fleet of fisherfolk, drink tea with mountain witch or walk over red hot coals
after Buddhist 'dervishes' in ancient fire walking rites.

'Shrine Isle' is thickly wooded with pines, cypress and cedar to its peak,
Mt Misen, ancient home of mountain god and five founding fairy princesses
and, till recently, home of late-old Witch of Mountain. Except for tiny
community nestled in and around little cove where ITSUKUSHIMA SHRINE
sits over lapping tide, this virgin-forest island is barely inhabited. Our dear
late old witch repopulated isle with wild deer since our '64 edition (old herd
had been eaten during war) and wild monkey gangs now roam mountain top
snatching tourists' lunches. Alas, typhoon Sept '91 badly damaged all.

GETTING THERE

LIES OPPOSITE small port-station of MIYAJIMA-GUCHI on JR Sanyo RR, trunk line
express stop, no Shinkansen; stationmaster speaks English.

From HIROSHIMA Stn via town center & Koi/West Hiroshima, local commuter
electric Hiroden ends at Miyajima-guchi; also frequent **buses**. At MIYAJIMA-GUCHI, 3
boat lines offer 11min crossing to Miyajima, literally Shrine Isle. Romantic glass-
bottom dragon-prowed ship no more, just monster ferries w/ more car capacity than isle
itself. By **Sea** hydrofoil direct from HIROSHIMA (*see*).

WHERE TO STAY

FEW W-style beds on isle (Grand Hotel and Royal), but 23 inns are good to fine. Here all
prices per person, inclusive tax-svce. Best still **Iwaso** ☎(0829)-44-2233; run down for
years, now beautifully revived, new tall annex. Location can't be beat, coziest spot in
Maple Valley, buried in maple in autumn, cherry in spring. New annex ¥-lo-Sw/2 each,
12course dinner good but not exciting, lovely separate cottage ¥-Lw/2, pvt baths but great
segregated public tubs; their free car meets ferry if advised. 'Downtown' inns mid 80s
seemed to get 10% more expensive every year, budgeteers are in trouble, ¥-T
uncomfortable—but all often crowded, popular place. **Kamefuku,** ☎44-2111 is biggest,
¥-S+w/2. Most along shopping street similar rates; ¥-T+w/2, may rise 10-15% in
season. Only rooms facing sea are: **Kin-sui kan,** ☎44-2131, with 2nd fl private
terrace rooms, middle of next block. **Grand Hotel,** ☎44-2411, just beyond on hillside,
some bedrooms, ¥-Sw/2, higher in season; *wa-yo* suite bedroom, tatami area adjoining,
¥-Lw/2. **Royal,** ☎44-2670, new annex of Kinsui, L of pier, mostly tatami rooms but 7
beds, 1 *wa-yo* suite, ¥-S+w/2. Sole ¥-B is **Lodge,** ☎44-0430, nice inn-style, beyond
shrine, ¥-B+; or **tent** in camp area, Hiroshima end of isle.

Book all thru **JTB** or **Hiroden**. Arriving without reservation, enquire at Tourist Info
(8:30am-8pm), Ferry bldg; good English pamphlets, some E- spoken, conscientious.
MAINLAND at Miyajima-guchi, forget it—**Issa-en**, lovely gardens and view of isle,
now only restaurant. New **Coral Hotel** looks uninteresting, except for rooftop view.

Bit away, take train, or taxi 4x-mtr, from Miyajima-guchi to **MIYA-HAMA ONSEN**
where lovely view of Inland Sea and end of isle, *rotenburo* in garden, fine foods: ¥-S.

Plan long mooted since first edition to erect luxury hotel on pilings in mid-channel—
still nothing definite yet, and hopefully never.

GETTING AROUND

EMINENTLY walkable; for Iwaso Inn beyond shrine, their car picks you up free ☎44-2233; free bus to ropeway stops along way, labeled in English; bicycles for rent ¥300–2hrs, ¥100 add 1hr, ¥1,000 day 8am-6pm, arrange **Kanko-annai** in ferry building (R). Ask of frequent cheap nature walk groups—guide in J-, but someone will speak English.

Cyclist, motorcyclist or hiker might circle isle. There is now car ferry, but only mini cars can negotiate island's back roads—even they should be banned. Side towards Hiroshima has huts for summer camping, swimming beaches, yacht basin where snipes and dinghies can be rented. You could circle island on hired diesel sampan in 2hrs; or 1hr cruise of surrounding isles, which stopped in 1980, but resumption planned ☎(0829)-56-0124, Yanase Marine. Or arrange thru Hiroden, your hotel, or thru interpreter, at Miyajima boat landing **Tourist Office**.

MIYAJIMA impresses different people different ways. We lived across channel (3km Hiroshima-wards, JIGOZEN, fishing-farming village), resisted going for sometime. 'Famous' scenic spots don't impress us, but Miyajima did – we must confess to long-term running love affair with this fascinating isle.

Shrine to sea goddess has been here for at least 15 centuries. Perhaps oldest extant shrine on island is obscure, and locked, phallic shrine at foot of stairs down from great running 85-foot-long **'Dragon's Whiskers'** pine tree of pagoda hill. Island was center of sea peoples and Taira clan chose it as their garden center, main shrine and market place.

Great shrine remains today much as it was built about 1070AD by Taira. Being of wood it has, of course, been frequently repaired with numerous minor changes. These can be safely assumed to have been quite minor, for change is proscribed on Miyajima. So much so that, until recently, even death and birth were forbidden–dying had to be ferried across to mainland, as did pregnant in late stages. There are no butchers. Virgin forests may not be cut (it took special dispensatory sacred services to allow trees to be cut to pass ropeways). Farming, disturbing soil, is banned, tho this ban is ignored on small scale out beyond yacht basin facing Hiroshima. Isle's woodworking craft—sole industry besides tourism—have always depended on imported lumber, or salvage from shrine repairs. (Last time great *torii* was rebuilt, old one was cut up for giant table tops.) Whole shrine was built so as to appear to float just above high tide. At low tide you can walk out beyond great *torii*; at high tide rowboats are available for rowing thru.

Woodwind & String Festival, *Kan-gen-sai,* is best time for your visit: **lunar-Jun 17**, end of sixth full moon according to Chinese lunar calendar, which falls on **Jul 16**, 1992; **Aug 4**, 1993; **Jul 25**, 1994; **Jul 14**, 1995; 8/1/'96, 7/20/'97; 7/8/'98; 7/28/'99; 7/17/2000; etc. Then great *Kan-gen-sai* is held, except for interference of some motor boats and of course shutterbugs, much as it was in days of Taira nobles.

In Kyoto court nobles built ponds with mock boats in which musicians supplicated goddesses and gods with music. Kiyomori of Taira clan chose whole Seto Inland Sea for his grand garden and had boatloads of musicians solemnly offer music to main shrine of Miyajima and outer shrine across bay at Jigozen, highlighting three-week long market, bringing together exotic wares from China and Korean coast–alas, now no such imports–but high-yen-encouraged offshore manufacturing might change that.

Kangensai is not just another festival held for tourists; it's still living fete of Inland Sea fisherfolk. If you come by Inland Sea steamer week prior to festival you will see fishing boats making their way from various islands, gayly decked out with runners and flags and packed with families on their way to Miyajima. Huge flags flying and kids howling, they gather with

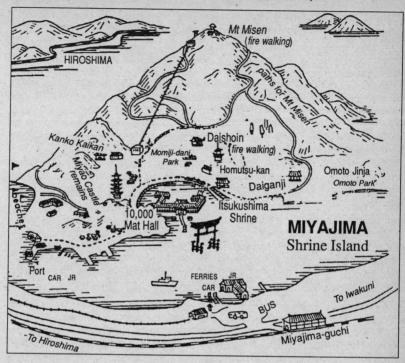

Mt Misen
(fire walking)

HIROSHIMA

paths for Mt Misen

Kanko Kaikan

Miyao Castle remains

Momiji-dani Park

Daishoin
(fire walking)

Homutsu-kan

Daiganji

Omoto Jinja

Omoto Park

beaches

10,000
Mat Hall

Itsukushima
Shrine

MIYAJIMA
Shrine Island

Port   CAR JR

FERRIES JR
CAR

To Iwakuni

BUS

To Hiroshima

Miyajima-guchi

rising tide before, and enter with it thru, red *torii*, traditional entry to shrine basin. When this area is packed solid with fishing boats and interisland freighters, overflow swarm against wharves three and four deep, becoming city of boats linked by gangplanks. There's great activity few days before fete as these fisherfolk enjoy their holiday at shrine, sleeping and eating on boats. Women and children dig clams; *hibachi* (braziers) appear and there's cooking even on long corridors of shrine, tho less every year.

Old market is no longer main reason for fair, but gypsy vendors of traditional wares, tools, dishes, toys, pornography, gimmicks and common factory rejects pack paths around great shrine. Minor ceremonies and rites are held on several occasions during 40 days (Noah's flood interval?) preceding, including 14th day before, wonderful *bugaku* court dance.

Two days before *Kangensai* at midday, richly decorated oxen prepare beach in ceremonial clearing and deepening of tidal shelf, *sun-hori*, at Jigozen across bay, where shrine boat lands. About same time on island proper, shrine boat is readied. Three new boats are built each year (sold after festival to local fishermen) and tied together to carry musicians and high priests. This trimaran is tested and rehearsal is held next nite. Starting early on morning of festival, officials row to each vessel and bless. At about five o'clock in afternoon, solemn ceremony is held and white-robed attendants carry portable shrine out into sea to shrine boat off shore.

At six o'clock just as sun sets, oarsmen in large boats pick up their stroke and start towing shrine boat, circling before shrine three times. Then rush is on! Drums beat, rowers pick up speed, seeming to keep time with pitching of waves which marks rhythm for their lovely work song, *Tawaramomi*. Hundreds of boats jostle into position and join procession. Color, mass movement and excitement of moment create such picture that one might imagine he's in midst of one of Hideyoshi's armadas during his Korean invasion. Halfway to Jigozen, entourage stops and makes preparations— lighting of 365 lanterns, readying offerings—waiting for full tide at full moon, about 8:30 or 9pm, to touch beach at Jigozen, signal for mainland villagers to dance at Jigozen shrine. Lanterned sea procession reaches Jigozen and 4 musical offerings are made and spirit of Itsukushima Himé, Princess of Shrine Isle, boards sacred palanquin boat to be escorted back to Miyajima, where fleet makes several stops—offering *kangen* music at Nagahama Beach and at OMORI SHRINE; *saibara*, seldom heard form of ancient folk song. By this time, it's midnite. Special ferry boats and trolleys to Hiroshima operate till late.

See from boat: no longer allowed to charter fishing boat; but ferries join in fleet for 80min cruises, dep ferry bldg 4:30pm & 5:40, later better, ¥2,000, must reserve one week ahead, ☎(0829) 44-2011, verbal reservation o.k., ask for 'Miyajima Kangensai funé'—or thru agent.

ON STAGE

Mar 20 approx; week-long festivities commemorate Taira-no-Kiyomori: special events, dances, mountain *kagura*. Shrine over waters is perfect setting for dances: vermillion *bugaku* stage fronts main shrine and national treasure *noh* stage is little further on. Both *bugaku* and *noh* dances are offered to shrine gods thruout year. April and October particularly good months for these. **Apr 15** is exciting date for at noon there is *fire walking* at Daisho-in temple, outside exit of shrine, (was atop Mt. Misen); evening from 6pm is full program of richly costumed *bugaku* ancient court dances. **Apr 16, 17, 18** all-day *noh* programs, where unlike sophisticated crowds at city programs, you'll notice simple farmers and fishermen intently following libretto. In old days, all island youths participated in these *noh* programs, but today professionals and leading artists from Hiroshima area perform, as well as diligent local amateurs. **Nov 15** noon *fire walk* atop flaming-red-mapled Mt Misen reached by ropeway and 15min walk along main path.

Bugaku, most famous dance *Ran-ryo-O*, dragon king, can be seen for donation of ¥30,000; ✍ week ahead or more, giving date; but not after 3pm, alas, nor during Jul-Aug as it is too hot under costume. If **full moon**, might just try to ask for dances after dinner by torchlight, tide lapping rhythmical accompaniment beneath stage—would certainly cost more, we'd offer ¥50,000 and cross fingers, well worth it. For reservation ✍ to Ven. Nozaka, High Priest, **Itsukushima Shrine**, Miyajima, Hiroshima-ken; or phone Shrine Office, *Shamu-sho* ☎(0829)-44-2020; or ask Hiroden or JTB, Hiroshima branch. Regularly scheduled *bugaku* offerings are: **Jan 1**, 5am, 1 dance; **Jan 2**, 11am one Noh, 1pm two dances. **Jan 3**, rites at 9am, then at 1pm are 5 dances; **Jan 5**, 5:30am, 5 dances also at 11am, *sennin* songs. **April 15** 6pm, 10 dances. **(Apr 16,17,18** *noh*); **May 18**, 10am, 5 dances; **Lunar June 5** (12 days before Kangensai), 10am, 5 dances; **Oct 15**, 6pm, 9 dances; **Oct 23**, 10am, 5 dances for harvest festival; **Dec 23**, 11am, 4 dances for Emperor's Birthday, (Nat'l Hol).

Shrine Treasures Exhibitions: Feb first Sun, full month; May 21-month; mid-Sept for month; mid-Nov 3 weeks; each show has different theme, every exhibit different pieces shown, at **Ho-mutsu Shu-zo-ko** shrine treasury, behind central shrine.

SIGHTSEEING

SHRINE is better less talked about, more experienced. Enter, pay offering— we used to put straw farmers' sandals on over shoes, but now cost of replacing sandals is greater than repairing wooden floors, so just walk in. To L (across road) before entry is small stable where generations of shrine horses (usually white but last two were palomino) were kept until recently when their care became just too much. Alas, main passageway now blocked off nites except when bugaku—used to be romantic after-dark stroll among ghosts of history.

Torii in bay, and lovely **pagoda** on hill behind, are floodlit at nite. Great pavilion near pagoda is **Thousand-mat Hall**, so named because supposed to measure 1,000 Japanese 3x6-ft floor mats—not quite. This was Hideyoshi's staff headquarters during 1588 invasion of Korea—he supposedly built it from single gigantic camphor tree. Here, too, wounded from Sino-Japanese War of 1894 were returned home. They started custom of leaving rice ladles, name of which, *shamoji*, is typical GI pun objecting to his plight. Folks still deposit ladles following custom, pacifist meaning of which totally escapes them. New custom is for romantic couple to buy big one and inscribe together.

Despite many writers, there were no wild deer remaining on island till recently—eaten during war. Late-Old Lady of Mountain brought few over from mainland early 60s from which present horde of pretty pests descends.

10min walk to...
Vale of Maples, *Momiji-dani*, (taxi, unfortunately, now available, also free minibus)—maples at their flaming best first two weeks of November; cherry blossoms here gorgeous mid-April, if you don't mind mountains of picnic garbage from operatic horizontal viewers.

From Momiji-dani, you are carried to top of...
Mount Misen by succession of two ropeways to wild monkey park (watch your purse), then you've still 15min walk across till you see row of red *torii* marking Shinto shrine of Yama-no-obaa-san, Old Lady of Mountain. This Mammy Yokum-like old witch was in fact fabulous lay-psychiatrist, prescribing seeming-voodoo gimmickry which carefully analyzed was seen to contain gems of sound folk-psychology. Alas she left us in late 60s, her shrine reverting to ruination like fable dream fading.

Hundred yards back and further up peak is...
SHINGON Buddhist temple, outbuilding with smoky fire under **great tea kettle** which has been kept burning for 1,200 years–this and one at Mount Koya–since lit by Saint Kobo on his return from China. Plaza before this building every Nov 15, shortly after noon, sees...

Fire walking rites, described in detail by Jay in book *Zen Combat*. In very brief outline, gigantic **bon-fire**, or *Dai-Gomma* (Great Burned Offering, as opposed to Smaller Burned Offering made on small fire altar, many temples) is lit in plaza from sacred eternal fire under tea-vat. *Yamabushi*, members of lay mendicant sect we have seen often, dance about fire exorcising evil spirits. Faithful bring old talismans to be disposed of in sacred fire, or toss in prayer sticks with name of supplicant and his wish inscribed upon them–you can buy one yourself for few yen. Rosaries or underwear of bedridden are blessed in smoke. Devout chant sutras, their voices rising in pitch and intensity as fire builds up. When whole has been reduced to glowing ashes, chief yamabushi performs *mudra*, with his fingers dancing thru various mystical cabalistic hand signs. Then he steps out and walks across coals in his bare feet, other yamabushi following, then visiting witches and all audience. We have each walked dozen times or more, often in position of honor behind *yamabushi* and before witches. It is hot, but you won't get burned if you step out confidently—not too fast, slow and steady (as in business here), roll feet evenly and don't think about it. We've shown dozens of friends how to walk. Your doing so greatly pleases participants. Some get burned, as you shall see—they are nervous (i.e. 'unfaithful'); confident (i.e. 'faithful') have no worry. If you see prayers on lips of others, do like Sumi did when she pioneered, clasp hands in supplication, step out and chant 'I hope I don't get burned, I hope I don't get burned....'

Up stone steps is...
Temple of Long Nosed Goblin where you can buy peculiar goblin red head bell bank, found only here. Higher up is peak itself with refreshment stalls, stone idol cave and telescopes. Hiking addicts are advised to walk back down to MOMIJI-DANI.

Or better yet walk up old pilgrim route from...
DAISHOIN temple, past **Cave of 1,000 Buddhas** where **deposit pebble** to release soul of some child from purgatory, pass thru great **Nio Gate** to witch's ex-shrine, going to ruin; *return* go back down other steeper route direct to Momiji-dani, which starts at stone steps by eternal fire pavilion and leads thru some magnificently eerie stoney pine forests. Paths are steep, ascent good calf-straining hour, but budget tourist will appreciate saving fare on ropeway, as much as adventure.

Other points on island are...
DAIGAN-JI temple at rear exit from main shrine, with fine Buddhist sculpture formerly housed in Grand Shrine until 1867 when divorce of Ryobu Shinto, combined Buddhism-Shinto, brought on 'purging' of idols from predominantly Shinto shrines. Also facing this is **Treasure Hall**, quarterly special exhibits, fine sutra scroll collection of interest only to religious art history buffs.

SHOPPING

Local pottery *Miyajima-yaki*, variant of *Hagi-yaki*, two kilns near train station of Miyajima-guchi; one is block to W, other few doors from ferry landing, **Kawahara Miyajima-yaki kama-no-moto** (main-kiln). Not outstanding—tho fairly good, practical—if you have few minutes to spare, peek into workshops.

Over on island, from ferry boat landing all along way to shrine, both sides of street are flanked with souvenir shops that look like those anywhere, but careful glance shows unusual wood carvings for which Miyajima is famous. Best buys are wooden trays and bowls. In these, check grain of wood, make sure that it has been cut from long grain, showing *moire* pattern—those cut out of cross section will show even, concentric circles, are apt to crack or warp. *Tochi* (horse chestnut) is soft and cheapest, *sakura* (cherry) and *kuri* (chestnut) higher. Interesting salad bowls of crepe myrtle, purposely cut on cross grain to use bark as decorative trim. Bowls run from 8 to 11 inches, 20-30cm, in diameter, matching individual bowls.

Only one curio shop, **Kimura-ya**, on L, block before stone torii; once very good and not gleaned for years, owner now in her 80s and as she says, she's just selling what she has in stock, so you might skip curio shopping unless you see something special that appeals. Shop selling tea near police station sells *Hagi-yaki*, pottery from Hagi (*follows*) on N coast of neighboring Yamaguchi Prefecture.

Our favorite shop is **Hirano**'s on corner just before Iwaso Inn en route ropeway. Specialty used to be large *keaki* (zelkova) tables made to order, but they seem to have become overshadowed by their neighbor. SENSHO Sasaki, carver, has converted old family workshop across alley into huge new shop, **Sasaki Yaeko-no-mise**, next door to grand old Iwaso Inn. Array of Buddhist statuary overwhelms (we learned his main job is supplying statues to temples thruout Japan). Superb seated camphor wood Yakushi-nyorai (goddess of medical mercy), about 3ft/90cm including lotus base and halo, plus two separate attendants, is ¥1,800,000. Most of his carvers are of Hiroshima area, with OKITA Toshiki, best, 46, at prime of carving life. Of course, many smaller works at more affordable prices. In his old store across alley, exciting array of reproductions—beautifully carved and antique gilded—lower prices. For example, kannon about 2ft/60cm tall, gilded, is ¥250,000, as are many others, finished to appear antique. Reason they are cheaper is that lacquering and gilding makes it possible to use wood that is not top quality, might have flaws, knots, can even be pieced, and carving need not be as painstakingly detailed.

Irregular zelkova tables with natural edge now cost about ¥100,000 for small ones, those from 3 to 5 feet cost up to ¥180,000. Finer, with legs part of body, whole like some abstract sculpture, run to over ¥1,000,000, and worth it. Popular new large-sized *naga-hibachi* cost ¥400,-1,000,000 for those up to 5 feet long.

Most attractive were carved *hinoki* (cypress) kagura folk masks, measuring about 20cm long at ¥4,900 to ¥8,000. No limit to variety, sizes and prices of carved trays, bowls, boxes—final price dictated by wood, and workmanship.

Mr Hirano, *noh* enthusiast-art connoisseur, lamented loss of aged carvers and lack of new ones, in our old edition. But ex-carver Sasaki seems to have gotten over that former lack. Hirano may still have few beautiful Kannon statues carved by late outstanding carver. Prices on carved boxes, bowls and chests differ according to workmanship involved. He had large stock of camphor wood from which he made beautiful storage chests with huge peonies and other overall designs. It's best to ask about them, for no telling when he'll spot another wood supply.

Unusual shops are found off beaten track and there are couple on little lane up from red drum bridge to Daisho-in temple past Sesshu Garden in Gion Oshimo. One is carver's and other exporter of bowls, trays and novelties. Keep eyes open for papier-mache *kagura* masks, unavailable outside Hiroshima area (even rare here); inexpensive for their dramatic impact. These are real ones used in mountain dances.

MISCELLANY

EARLY BIRDS, turn L few yards from dock for coffee shop which opens to greet the first ship: eggs, coffee, toast available. If you have to wait for ferry back, lobby of **Kamefuku Inn**, few doors on, has bar and tea or coffee service till 10pm; kick off shoes and enter. In Momiji-dani at foot of red bridge and dragon font, **Iwaso Inn** has tea shop, light snacks, English-speaking attendant; lunch at inn restaurant **Momiji**, reasonable. Top of ropeway has teashop-restaurant, budget. Atop mountain, bottled drinks only. Pilgrim path up has several Japanese tea stalls with bottled drinks, benches with exquisite views—hike up takes 1hr at easy pace—at least hike down. ¥-B-T restaurants abound on shopping street. Local delicacy tasty conch-shell cookery, get nr stone *torii* at end of first shopping street. Coffee and light snacks at mainland end of ferry, shop run by old returnee from Hawaii, speaks English.

WHERE NEXT

Taxi basic-mtr 15% under big city standard (¥470 '91) → Miya-hama 4x-mtr; → Yuki Onsen 18x-; → Iwakuni Kintai-Brocade Bridge 13x-; → Hiroshima stn 13x-; → airport 10-11x-; → Atomic Dome/downtown hotels 10x-mtr.

...and while lamplight still gittered on the first frost,
lively shouts of 'the show is about to start'
drew eager customers young and old into the theater.
— Chikamatsu Monzaemon, *The Mirror of Craftsmen*, 1706

RURAL HIROSHIMA
KAGURA DEMON DANCES

WE MUST ADMIT our suspicions were first aroused when he entered our garden smoking—with no cigarette in evidence (claimed later he'd thrown it away outside our gate). But no doubt about it his way of slithering into our room and enveloping proffered teacup: Mr Nakaoka was one real dragon.

Barely over five feet tall in his human form—at which time he poses as farmer in Yae town in mountains of Hiroshima prefecture—his working size runs 20m/66ft fully uncoiled. Nor is he singular phenomenon, with several disciple dragons under wing continuing his 400-year family tree, and elsewhere another hundred or more. Any may be seen at various thanksgiving festivals between Izumo and Hiroshima when ancient pre-*noh* and ancestral *kabuki* called *o-kagura* are performed and legend of Susano-o slaying femnivorous dragon of Yawata goes on stage of local Hachiman Shrine.

Kagura is purely folk theater performed by amateurs, found over most of Japan but most notably in dependent areas of IZUMO GRAND SHRINE and almost always in local shrines to Hachiman, god of sword and scythe, patron diety of Hata 'nationalized tribes' who came from North and Central Asia 15-17 centuries ago. Performing is limited to men, and not to be confused with *mi-kagura*, or maiden *kagura*, performed only by vestal virgins at almost any type of Shinto shrine. Male *kagura* is wild and gaudy and vibrant dance-drama using masks and ornate costumes: *mi-kagura* is dainty, feminine, slow, with no story and costume always red skirt with white top uniform of shrine maidens.

This is living theater. It does not preserve ancient forms rigidly, tho ancient scripts are followed religiously. Conglomerate itself, sets and pieces of stories and plays and dances have been picked up over centuries, as have tales of gods and heroes, demons and hayseeds.

Confucious' Book of Odes *Shih Ching*, mentions thanksgiving offerings of tenth lunar month of two and half-millennia ago: ceremonial masquerade, weapon dance to spirits of mountain and river, dance of tufted wands to spirit of earth and cereals. These are all here. Chinese annals mention Central Asian and Persian dances and our *kagura* hero battles albino ape as Rustam of Iran battled White Div of Caspian. Japanese Saint George saves beautiful maid and slays femnivor Dragon of Yamato. Brer Fox is there with his tricks, as is that caricature of foreigners and foreignism, red-faced big-nosed Tengu—all linked by undercurrent of irreverent satire resurgent since WWII. NAKAOKA Mitsuru's troupe in Arita town, Yamagata-gun, Hiroshima prefecture, dates back over 400 years, many nearby are postwar. Yamagata county alone has over 100 troupes, neighboring Takata county another score and dozens scattered about suburbs of Hiroshima. There is notable difference in aesthetic between mountain troupes and those along sea, with latter seemingly softened and tropicalized by South Seas influence.

Kagura gave birth to classical noh and kabuki, but it has in turn been influenced in technique by advances made in these derivative forms. Their repertoire of 45 or 46 plays mostly portray legends from Shinto annals or medieval hero tales. Comic interludes or at least comic strain interweave, from which noh kyogen (comedy tradition) is probably derived.

General public interest outside of rural home areas has risen in *kagura*. Several troupes' performances of various pieces (such as *Yawata-no-Orochi* mentioned above, their *Ama-no-Iwato* rendition of luring of sun goddess from her cave, and *Kami Oroshi* calling down of gods) are designated as Intangible Cultural Treasures by government. NHK television often runs folk art festivals on nation-wide network, as do regional TV companies.

As autumn Thanksgiving nears—usually 9th, 19th and 29th of October, varying with villages—troupe breaks into frenzy of activity common to theater world over. Village shrine, usually hillside or streamside Hachimangu, is cleaned and decorated with colored paper cutouts. Dancers go into purifying seclusion. There may be other festivities such as sumo and *gyoretsu* costume procession, but big event is all-nite marathon performance of entire *kagura* repertoire which starts about nine in evening before festival with *Sambaso*, twirling, stomping dance of purification and dedication by male virgin—or at least young fellow of not too bad reputation.

For more adventurous, trip up to dragons' (they actually use two on stage) lair is more than worthwhile. USNSA first Japan Study Tour, summer 1961, stopped at Yae. Our American students called it one of highlights of their summer in Japan. (Yae also has small **Folkcraft Museum**, random collection of interesting old farm paraphernalia, and **Historical Museum**). Theirs was special performance, which can be arranged for abt ¥50,000; not fee, but contribution toward wear and tear, (at newly-built **Chiyoda Park Hotel**, ¥8000w/2). Dragon skins, made of special Izumo paper on wire coil, last about dozen performances and used to cost ¥8,000—run ¥150,000. Masks wear out, and these papier-mache and laquered wood folk art masterpieces cost from few thousand yen up to fortune for dragon and grand demons (complete with sulphur smoke bombs built into tongue). Costumes of hero Minamoto-no-Raiko and real sneering bad guys in flamboyant play *Oe-yama* run price of haute couture.

Troupe will travel, for cost, which involves say for trip to Hiroshima about ¥200,000 plus food for basic 10 actors and five stage hands. They make some 40 such appearances annually, and if they handled all requests they would have to turn pro and give up farming. Why don't they? Nakaoka said doing it for living wouldn't be any fun.

PERSONAL DATEBOOK: Chiyoda (formerly Yae) *Thanksgiving Festival* used to be held lunar Sep 28, but new rice calendar changed this. **First sat of Oct** Chiyoda town hosts *grand contest* of ten best troupes, not including their own which performs non-competitively. Boards rattle and demons scream all nite from 4pm until after 2-3am at Kaihatsu Center, set up with stage. Admission ¥1,800, and from our experience at these affairs, hospitality is overwhelming. Ryokan at present Chiyoda where we stayed in 1961 was **Kyoya**, now ¥5,000 w/2 meals, ☎(08)-2672-2250. There are about 10 buses daily from Hiroshima bus center to Chiyoda, about 1hr30min ride. Taxi split 4 or 5 ways would barely run cost of good theater ticket.

Sep 14 Toyohira-cho (Yamagata-gun), as do 18 local troupes, hold their kagura performances in their own area. **Hiroden Bus** keeps track of many of them; runs special tours up to mountain villages such as Arita in Chiyoda-cho, on **first sun Jun** to see *hanagasa-taue* (ceremonial rice-planting dance) and special un-seasonal performance of dragon drama. Also **first sun Jun**, Kake town holds grand *Dengaku-Taikai*, dance costumed women in chorus lines do back-breaking rice planting, helped along by gaudier-costumed menfolk beating out work rhythm on huge drums and fifes and *sake* bottles. Another way to track down *kagura* fetes is thru HTV Hiroshima TV which often sends video team up into hills.

Villages along shore of Inland Sea near Hiroshima also have *kagura* on smaller scale: Hatsukaichi, just before Miyajima, **2nd sat/sun Oct** at Hatsukaichi-shi (with *samurai gyoretsu* procession **sun** noon); on Western outskirts, Itsukaichi Hachiman shrine, Saiki-ku, Hiroshima-shi holds festival on **2nd sat/sun Oct** (*mikoshi* parade in afternoon). Many towns in summer fetes, around grand *Kangensai festival* **mid-Jul**. Itsukaichi's other shrine, SHIOYA JINJA, invites mountain kagura on Sunday nite; Miyajima stages guest troup during Kiyomori-sai, **end Mar**; street behind shrine. Kagura performances annually in Tokyo during Culture Week, week of **Nov 3**, usually at **Seinen Kaikan** (Young Men's Assoc Hall) in Meiji Park.

Spring Festival at Mibu, Chiyoda-cho **June, first Sun**, Grand *rice planting festival* w/ hundreds of costumed in kasuri ikat-kimono & sedge, bulls dressed up and chance to see women with huge flower-decked *hanagasa*, large parasol-like headgear. Schedule: 9am children's dance, 9:30am Kagura plays from 5 troupes, ¥1,000. 1:00pm procession of bulls at Mibu Jinja; 1:40 parade of Dengaku troupes and at 2pm *Hanagasa-odori* thru town. Rice planting with chanting & songs, huge drums dress in farmers' clothes tossing fancy streamered batons.

SHOPPING: For kagura masks at shrine supply shops, Hiroshima, (*see* SHOPPING, p657); and shops on Miyajima, especially those nearest ferry dock.

WHERE NEXT: From Hiroshima overland → MATSUE (for which latter *see* JAPAN SEA, P821), morning and overnite diesel expresses, about 5hrs (Hiroshima about noon & midnite; arrive Matsue 5pm & 6am) thru mountainscapes which never fail to elicit raves from friends we send. Also numerous bus routes for more adventurous. **Drivers** will find roads quite good, with negligible truck traffic and many friendly drivers. Mountains too steep for bicycles, but lightest **motor bikes** were built for such roads, even 50cc putt-putts. In 1961 we went Hiroshima-Mount Sambe (near Japan Sea west of Izumo)-Izumo-Matsue-Mionoseki (at east end of Matsue peninsula)-Tamatsukuri-Yae-Hiroshima taking 5 days, 4 overnites by rented **Hiroden** light bus ☎(082)-295-1095 (20-passenger, two-man crew) for charter rate of about ¥21,000 including all charges for crew. Excellent vehicle, ideal for small groups, but now would cost ¥530,000.

CHOPSTICKS: **Suiko-en** in Kabe town (taxi 13x-mtr) for *ayu* (river trout); after which return to Hiroshima by boat down Ota river. Eat here on way up to evening of demon dancing, or on way back from afternoon festivals in area. Hiroden taxis all know place.

IWAKUNI, (20km down coast from Miyajima, 40km from Hiroshima) main castle-town of Kikkawa domain.

GETTING THERE: Shinkansen drops you at Shin-Iwakuni 8km W, regular JR gets you to heart of Iwakuni, dominated by US military base. Town is btwn two.

20min JR or City-bus from Iwakuni or Shin-Iwakuni to...
Bridge of Brocade Sash, *Kintai-kyo*, lovely wood 5-arched bridge on piled stone foundations spanning 200m wide Nishiki (brocade) river. Kintai-kyo is Iwakuni's claim to fame, one of Japan's top three classic bridges, along with Saru-hashi of Kai, and Shin-kyo of Nikko. Built 1673, survived centuries intact until washed away in 1950 typhoon. 1953 exact replica of original right out of Hiroshige woodblock print; no nails, all metal is purely ornamental.

¥100 to cross over to west bank to...
Kikko Park and old samurai district of narrow walled lanes. We first come to remaining portion of Kikkawa **lords' house**.

Cross moat to...
History Museum, *Choko-kan* (9:00-17:00, free), with books, art, odds-and-ends of feudal era. Left across another moat to **KIKKO JINJA** shrine, dedicated to Kikkawa clan, with several lovely old buildings (Kin-un-kaku pavilion, Kikko library, Noh stage) rebuilt in its grounds. Another left back

across 1st moat to ropeway stn, near which is **Nishimura Hakubutsu-kan**, museum (8:00-18:00,¥500), superb collection of samurai armor and weaponry spanning 11 centuries, Heian thru Edo eras. South of cablecar is well-preserved **Mekata Manse**.

Cablecar 3min (¥520 r.t.) to 1962 replica of...
Iwakuni Castle main tower. Built 1608, dismantled only 7 years later under new Tokugawa 'One nation–One castle' policy. W of cablecar stn is *Momiji-dani*, **Maple Leaf Vale** spectacular late October. On small pond near Dosen-ji temple is red, 6-sided **Azumaya Rokkaku-tei Pavilion**, brought over from Korea end of 16th century; Kikkawas aided Hideyoshi's Korea campaign, area was staging ground.

Between Iwakuni stn and castle area is...
HAKUJA-DO, shrine dedicated to red-eyed *Shiro-hebi* White-snakes. Albino form of common, large but harmless Ao-daisho snake, whites have for centuries been symbol of good fortune for merchants—as coincidentally are to Persian nomads.

Old Iwakuni is nice, but not really worth stopping if rushed: Leave MIYAJIMA morning 20min frequent JR → IWAKUNI, 2-3hrs to see town and hop bullet to be in HAKATA-FUKUOKA mid-afternoon. It is cheaper alternative to more expensive inns on Miyajima; 6:41am JR IWAKUNI → MIYAJIMA-GUCHI 7:00, in time for first ferry across to Miyajima while still quiet and cool. Most convenient if taking ferry to/from MATSUYAMA on SHIKOKU.

WHERE TO STAY: Mostly ¥-Bw/2. Around Iwakuni stn are several Business Hotels, single room only, ¥-B. To stay around old part of town, try: **Matsuoka** ☎43-1155, **Mihara-ya** ☎41-0073, **Yamane**; ¥-B Kokumin-shukusha **Hangetsu-an** ☎41-0021; members-only Youth Hostel. Book thru **Kanko-annai** at either stn.

To further enhance stay: spring boat rides down Nishiki River and summer ukai cormorant fishing. Former daily March thru May, start Misho-bashi bridge west of town (15min walk from Shin-Iwakuni), downstream in wood skiffs 7km to Kintai-kyo Bridge. Usually rent entire boat for ¥28,800, but call ahead ☎(0827)-41-0470 to see if space available on someone's boat, usually ¥2,980 each. Ukai nitely June 1-August 31 except full moon or murky water. Smaller scale than Gifu or Kyoto, Iwakuni's is highlighted by Kintai Bridge with backdrop castle illuminated on hilltop. Take box dinner (some inns provide) or snacks.

From Iwakuni, JR Iwatoku Line, bullet, and Rte2 all cut inland across to Tokuyama, but Sanyo Main Line takes scenic coastal route, on which is lovely...
YANAI, town with much of its old architecture intact; worth hour or so for shutter-bug. All rail rejoins at Tokuyama, offshore of which is **Otsushima** Isle, once base of *kaiten* kamikaze-manned torpedoes used by Imperial Navy end of Pacific War. Drivers from Tokuyama Rte315 → Rte9 and to Tsuwano.

30min rail down coast (1hr30min from Iwakuni) to...
HOFU: Ancient town, 'capital' of prehistoric pre-Yamato Suho-no-kuni kingdom, centuries later main town of Mori domain until divided and administrative center moved to Hagi—Hofu remained Choshu naval base.

5min bus (2km) N of stn is...
HOFU TENMAN-GU, first of these nationwide shrines dedicated to scholar SUGAWARA Michizane who, exiled from Kyoto to Dazaifu in Kyushu (*see*), spent time here with old friend and local lord HAJI Nobusada. Hearing of Michizane's death, Nobusada had this shrine completed following year, 904; before completion of head shrine in Dazaifu. Present structure rebuilt 1963. *Rekishi-kan*, **History Museum** (9:00-18:30, ¥200) at entrance contains shrine treasures offered over centuries. West along front street to some fine **old houses**.

10min walk E to...
SUHO KOKUBUN-JI, one of countless Kokubun-ji temples built all over
by order of Emperor Shomu, mid-8th century: this dates 741AD, rare as
almost complete. Numerous images dating Heian, Kamakura eras (¥500).

Another 10min walk W is...
Hofu Mansion, *Mori-hontei*, of Mori ex-lords post-Meiji Restoration built
1916 of finest wood from central Kiso area. Part of main house is museum
of Mori clan art treasures (9:00-16:30, ¥500), as is part of its superb garden
(9:00-17:00, ¥200). Also fine garden at 2nd mansion of Mori lords during
feudal times; Tsuki-no-Katsura-tei **rock garden** (9:00-17:00 X-mon, ¥300)

HOFU 20min JR → OGORI to catch bullet → KYUSHU, or change to Yamaguchi Line
cut across to JAPAN SEA COAST via YAMAGUCHI (25min) and TSUWANO (2hr).

Or JR bus (or drive) 20km (35min) up Rte262 to Rte9 at...
YAMAGUCHI, once so splendid it was called Miyako (Kyoto) of West.
Founder, mid-14th century OUCHI Hiroyo, borrowed ground plan, names of
Kyoto. Official Protectors of Western Provinces since Heian times, long-
lasting Ouchi clan (Hiroyo 24th generaton) had wealth, power for such under-
taking. Free from power-struggles of Kyoto, Yamaguchi flourished as
center of culture, learning. Also main link with mainland. Even St Francis
Xavier found tolerance here—1551 converted 500 in half-year. Xavier left
for China none too soon—following year, coup against 34th Ouchi destroyed clan and most of city, pit lesser lords against each other, from which
Mori clan emerged victorious to rule over all of Honshu west of Hiroshima.
Then defeated half-century later at Seki-ga-hara, their once massive domain
was divided. During those years Yamaguchi went unrepaired, when Mori
moved base to Hagi city fell to quiet anonimity till end Tokugawa era when
became capital of post-Restoration Yamaguchi Pref. Several temples and
shrines remain; easy half-day tour, tho not really worth special detour for
short-timer. Yamaguchi is optional nite, especially if next day bus to
Akiyoshi-do Cave and Nagato area, from where quick bus or rail to Hagi;
reverse course to Hagi via Tsuwano (often on nostalgic steam locomotive).

WHERE TO STAY: Many Yamaguchi inns are ¥-T rate, clustered around stn,
tho several homey ¥-Bw/2 especially—**Fuku-ya** ☎(0839)-22-0531, 5min walk N of stn.
Owner Ms. Fukuda Chikako speaks fine English, full of helpful info on entire area.

Most visitors stay at W fringe of town at...
YUDA ONSEN: Used to be outdoor riverside bath, few inns along now covered
Nishiki river. Still one large **public bath** house, **Sennin-yu**, midtown. Yuda one of
most popular hot spas in south Honshu; modern, with 60-plus inns for all budgets. Top
of line is 300-year-old **Matsuda-ya**, used by many early Meiji leaders ☎(0839)-22-0125,
¥-S-Lw/2, old & new wing. Similar old timer **Sansui-en** ☎22-0560, w/garden
restaurant, same rates. *Recommended* ¥-Sw/2: **Nishimura-ya** ☎22-0250; **Mizuno**
☎22-0044; **Midori-ya** ☎22-0051; **Nohara** ☎22-0018; **Kame-fuku Bekkan** ☎22-
2090. *Also* (¥-T-Sw/2): **Kame-fuku** main ☎22-7000; or better **Kotobuki** ☎22-3800.
Budget (¥-Bw/2): **Furukado** ☎22-0776; **Miyako-so** ☎22-2525; **Ohashi-ya** ☎22-
3523; **Hisago** ☎22-0761. 4 minshuku ¥-Bw/2, Kokumin-shukusha **Oteru** ☎22-3240.

YUDA ONSEN is 10min bus from Yamaguchi stn N of Yuda Onsen local JR stop
Yamaguchi to Akiyoshi-do Cavern buses all stop here; some from/to Hagi start/end here;
as do all buses from/to Tsuwano. Rte9 passes thru Yuda.

TILT: 3hrs walk main sites: Stn → **Xavier Church** → **Yamaguchi Dai-
jingu** → **Doshun-ji** → **Ruriko-ji** → Stn, extra 90min for **Joei-ji**. Rent bike stn,
¥300 2hrs, ¥800/day. **Taxi tour**, 2hrs 10x-mtr; or cab → **Ruriko-ji** (1.5x-mtr), walk
back to church, and r.t. cab → **Joei-ji** (5x-mtr incl wait). **Bus tours**: dep Yuda Onsen
8:40, 13:40 → Yamaguchi stn → **Ruriko-ji** → **Satellite Transmission Ctr** →
Niho Pass → **Joei-ji** → **Xavier Church**-stn → Yuda 12:10, 17:10. ¥1,650, Mar
thru Nov, 8:40 am, also only on sun, hol, during 12/1-25.

Xavier Memorial Church, *Kinen Shu-do*, (Mid town, 1km 20min walk stn) built 1952 for 400th anniversary Saint's arrival in Japan (actually year he left Japan for China). Built on wooded Kameyama hill, site of DAIDO-JI temple which lord Ouchi Yoshitaka gave to Xavier for first church. Lovely stained-glass panels imported from Spain relate his life. Next door is **Xavier Memorial Hall**, *Shiryo-kan*, (9:00-17:00, ¥200), with odds and ends on Saint and Catholicism in Japan.

Continuing another 600m N to major intersection, we come to...

Moat surrounded Mori clan administrative center, moved from Hagi end of Tokugawa era. Only lovely **rear gate** remains—Prefectural Office in place of old center. Now historic monument, modern Office takes care business. L to **YAMAGUCHI DAI-JINGU** Grand Shrine, 1518 as affiliate of Ise Jingu by special permit to lord Ouchi Yoshioki. Also has *naiku & geku*, inner & outer shrines, rebuilt each 21 years, next 2002. Trail beyond Taga Shrine thru several torii to Iwata Shrine, hilltop Takamine **castle remains**.

R at old Pref Office, along moat then cut N to...

DOSHUN-JI temple, built mid-16th century by, dedicated to, first Mori lord to rule, Mori Motonari. Kannon-do hall at far back left predates by over 120 years, was moved here from nearby Kannon-ji temple in 1929.

RURIKO-JI temple complex just beyond, 31m-tall 5-tiered **pagoda** (NT). Built mid-14th century by first OUCHI Hiroyo; pagoda 1404 by OUCHI Morimi young brother of 3rd OUCHI Yoshihiro to whose spirit dedicated.

Left of sanmon main gate, is Ruriko-ji...

Treasure Hall (¥200, 9:00-17:00). Sandwiched betw Doshun-ji and Ruriko-ji is **Kozan-en**, burial grounds of last Mori lord Motonori and his family who moved here from Hagi. Now museum to Motonori, w/ 2 old buildings from original site nr Pref Office: Rosan-do **tea-house** Motonori plotted with Shishi, anti-Tokugawa rebels of Satsuma & Choshu, 'Sat-cho'. Next **Chinryu-tei**, annex to Mori mansion, where secret alliance of Sat-cho set March 1866, uniting 2 major anti-Tokugawa clans—until then, fighting.

2km (cab basic-mtr) NE of stn...

JOEI-JI temple, best known for fabulous landscape **garden** by zen monk Sesshu for lord Ouchi Masahiro. Sesshu (1420-1506) patronized by Ouchi lords, sent to study painting in Ming China 1467-69. Returning became one of Japan's top painters in new *suiboku* (water & ink) monochrome style. After return was commissioned to do garden, took ideas from his paintings. Centered around pond in shape of *kokoro*, character for spirit-heart; rock 'mountains' represent great peaks of W Japan, bounded 3 sides by sculptured tree 'clouds'. Daily 8:00-17:00, ¥300, matcha green **tea** & cakes ¥250. Two more gardens by Sesshu at Japan Sea coast town of Masuda, where buried.

SHOPPING: Yamaguchi's special **lacquer**, *Ouchi-nuri*, 'imported' here centuries ago by Ouchi lords; at gift stores thruout town, bowls, small trays from ¥4,000. Can see being made in any of 12 stores: best is **Hokuno**, near Ise-Ohji bus stop 400m E of Prefectural Office; **Kuwahara**, N of stn. Latter also makes popular *Ouchi-ningyo* wood dolls, egg-shaped, lacquered with gold flakes.

PERSONAL DATEBOOK

Feb 15 *Fire walk*: Hanaya-ji, Hirao-cho Yanai city; rites 11am, walk noon.

Sat closest Apr 5, *Yuda Onsen Fete* feudal costume parade, white-fox dances.

Early April *cherry* viewing best along Ichi-no-saka River, Furukuma Jinja.

Late May to mid-June, *fireflies* along Ichi-no-saka River.

Jul 20-27 *Yamaguchi Gion Festival* kicks off with fabulous Sagi-mai Heron-dance 20th, 18:00 Yasaka Jinja shrine (W of Pref Office), 21:00 nr stn; var events thru wk.

Aug 6-7 *Lantern Fete*, over 100,000 red lanterns strung up along station-front.

Nov 22-23 *Tenjin Fete*, Furukuma Jinja shrine, 5min walk W of stn, across river.

*This is where one begins ...worshippers stream by ...
light their candles and their sticks of incense ...
singly, in families, in tour groups ...*
— Oliver Statler, *Japanese Pilgrimage*

SHIKOKU ISLAND 四国
QUIET, RUSTIC END RUN

ALMOST 12 CENTURIES AGO priest Kukai, better known as Kobo-
daishi, Saint Kobo, returned from years of study in China as anointed
master and set about wandering over Japan teaching. He was remarkable
engineer, built great reservoirs still in use. His Buddhism was another step
from first personalized worship of human Shaka, to abstract healer Yakushi
then to statist-of-heaven Dainichi. With Dainichi's heavenly organization
now duly reflected on earth in Imperial Court, Kobo preached new idea of
personally-earned salvation that may account for Japan's several notable
historic spurts of creativity and productivity: that each and every person has
within him that same seed of Buddha which with hard effort he can nurture
and thus attain enlightenment. Pilgrimage, as act of faith thru deed rather
than blind faith in formulae or recitation of abstractions, was one way. His
best known 'tour', *henro* (which means both pilgrimage and pilgrim), was
around his home island of Shikoku—there are several smaller regional ones.
   Shikoku offers much more–from rugged mountainous interior to equally
rugged shores. Our original edition called Shikoku 'beautiful but primitive
...many areas will not admit four-wheeled vehicles up narrow pilgrim
paths'. Well it is still mostly for adventurer with time, but while narrow
trails still abound, scenic new roads invite. Garet and friend pedalled
around most of it; hitched and railed next time thru–much easier on
surrealistically mountainous isle. There are spots where even trains seem
barely to make it up (one particularly hot summer, diesel local gave out near
top of hill and had to coast down backwards to stn to rehitch to another).
Now even adventurer can circle in comfort on fairly frequent trains and

plentiful buses. Driving is pleasure in sparsely-travelled interior, fantastic new roads bridge vales on slender sky-ribbons–but you need sense of humor when lost up unposted dead end and find you have to back out.

GETTING THERE & OUT: Long limited to air or ship, Seto Ohashi-Great Bridge (p.639) from Kurashiki and string of island-hopper bridges from Onomichi now in progress. **Trains**: thru express TOKYO-TAKAMATSU; OKAYAMA-SHIKOKU 28 daily to start, but save less than hour over ferries, which still run at greatly reduced frequencies, cheaper for autos. Transport Ministry in all its wisdom showed rail bridge plans with top tier for cars and lower for rail from KOBE via AWAJI ISLAND–only there is not one inch of rail on Awaji to get from one bridge to other (Awaji-Shikoku done). Ah well, it'll keep ferries working. Rail 'wide' *Shuyuken*-excursion tix: free use all JR trains, buses, ferries, plus 20% off on going and return. Usually valid 7 days, inquire JR, JTB etc.

Ferries from KOBE-OSAKA go into TAKAMATSU, IMABARI; to TOKUSHIMA from KOBE-Ohgi, 3+hr 5x, ¥1,970, Kansai & Kyodo Kisen, Suehiro pier; from KOBE-Naka, Hydrofoil 105min, 5x, Hankyu Kisen ☎(078)-331-5007, ¥4,530. OSAKA–TOKUSHIMA Kansai & Kyosei Kisen ☎(06)-612-0768; Kyosei Kisen. MATSUYAMA links mostly with HIROSHIMA, IWAKUNI and KYUSHU ports; but carferries o'nite, 8+hrs from Rokko, **Diamond Ferry** (078)-391-6361. Ferries from TOKYO land TOKUSHIMA as do those from WAKAYAMA, TOSA; also links to KATSU-URA on Kii Peninsula and OSAKA. HACHIMAN-HAMA near UWAJIMA and SUKUMO further S run occasionals to KYUSHU. Info on particular runs thru **Travel Centers** at major JR stns, JTB, JNTO, or bilingual TIC (Tokyo Ginza or Kyoto); accessable by collect call 106 *Travel Phone*.

By **air**: TOKUSHIMA: NAS from Osaka, Tokyo; TAKAMATSU: ANK from Osaka, Tokyo (also ANA) and Kyushu's Fukuoka; KOCHI: from Tokyo (ANA), Nagoya (ANK, ANK, JAS), Osaka (ANA, NAS), Fukuoka (JAS), Miyazaki on Kyushu (ANA); MATSUYAMA: ANA, JAL from Tokyo; ANA from Nagoya, Osaka; JAS from Fukuoka, Miyazaki, Kagoshima, Asahi from Hiroshima, Oita-Beppu. If from TOKYO, not many directs, change at Osaka. If seeing Shikoku after Hiroshima, best is air out of Matsuyama to any of 4 points on Kyushu–to Fukuoka and rail down to Kagoshima if exiting Japan thru that port, or reverse if heading up Japan Sea coast back to Tokyo.

TILT: Short on time, almost everything is on Inland Sea coast and can be done in 2 or 3 days; extra day for either Pacific coast cities of TOSA or UWAJIMA— and you have just done whole island. Good **bus tours** for each of sections, listed as we come to them, so here we mention **88 Pilgrimage Tours** for any interested. All run from mid-Mar to mid-Apr, 11nites/12days ¥163,000 for everything but by different companies: *Kotosan Bus* ☎(0878)-51-5103 starts from Takamatsu's **Hotel Gekko-en** 6:00; *Iyo Tetsudo* ☎(0899)-48-3174, starts from **Matsuyama main office** 8:30; *Seto-uchi Unyu* ☎(0898)-23-3711 starts from **Imabari** port 8:00. Sep thru mid-Nov, same companies have 3nite/4day tours covering one (of 4) prefecture, ¥51,500. Book thru major agent or JTB. Rail circles most of island except two southernmost points, cuts across middle to Pacific coast. Luxury JR bus links MATSUYAMA ↔ KOCHI, 3hr20min regular or 20min quicker non-stop express; departs either end every hour on hour 7:00 to 19:00, extra express departures 9:00 and 14:00. Where no rail along coast, plenty of connecting buses.

Drivers find good roads, particularly along Inland Seaside (tho' crowded, ugly road-sides), well labeled, and constantly being widened and added to. Main cities have several **rental** agencies, but again beware drop-off fees. New trans-Shikoku N-S expressway is breathtaking where completed, growing fast. If not doing full circle, best is start TAKAMATSU or MATSUYAMA, drop off at other. Main distances: TOKUSHIMA (85km)→ TAKAMATSU (164km) → MATSUYAMA (96km) → UWAJIMA. TAKAMATSU → KOCHI (123km); UWAJIMA → KOCHI by coast 270km, hills 108km. KOCHI → TOKUSHIMA via Cape Muroto about 220km. **Hitchhikers** will have little trouble except around Cape Muroto and Cape Ashizuri—which cut across base on Rte56.

PERSONAL ORIENTATION; HENRO: To this day white-clad pilgrims make pilgrimage to Kobo's appointed 88 Sacred Temples, its egalitarian nature testified to by numerous women who make it, as by simplicity of uniform of plain white cotton, unadorned but for red ink stamps. These officially prove pilgrim's personal presentation at each temple office and almost redden costume on completed pilgrimage as walking certification wearer has done it. Very few do it now all on foot, or at one shot, many whip thru on chartered bus tours (*see* TILT), others do section by section spread out over several visits in any convenient order. We do not suggest this pilgrimage for casual visitor—even bus tour takes 11 days. But for purists seeking joys of yore, we suggest superb book *Japanese Pilgrimage* by Oliver Statler, and check Japan Society if they'll repeat his fabulous pilgrim tour of 1985.

Pilgrimage traditionally starts above Tokushima, inland from old crossing from Awaji and Kii Peninsula, whence many *henro* came after first visiting sacred Mount Koya. Around Tokushima, before heading south to circle isle clockwise, are 22 numbered pilgrim spots—plus 7 *bangai*—unnumbered stops but just as traditional as numbered 88. There are some 52 *bangai* and true pilgrim hits them, too; these include two Shinto shrines—oddly not Kompira/Kotohira, founded by St Kobo, tho many pilgrims obviously combine 88 with pilgrimage to Kompira. Then comes arid stretch along SE coast with one numbered and 2 *bangai* before Cape Muroto's #24, 25, 26 and cluster of dozen around Kochi, sparse stretch to Cape Ashizuri, up W coast to small cluster at Ehime then cluster on road into Matsuyama and around NW peninsula thru Imabari to literal traffic jam of #66-88 around NE hump into and out of Takamatsu, old Sanuki.

Foreign *henro* with compunctions about crossing religious lines might keep in mind that this pilgrimage is general act of faith, not rite of any specific church. First bona-fide pilgrim we met back in 50s was Nara bus president. This millionaire walked it budgeting ¥130 per day (then 35¢) which he begged along way, leaving any surplus at nite with temple. Met him at Zen sit, which puzzled us till he said many sects make pilgrimage, not just Shingon. In fact handful of temples on route are Zen, Jodo, and even non-Buddhist Shinto—and in ancient days before 1868 religious purge, Shinto must have played even larger role. In 1960 Paul Yoshiro Saeki, D.LITT, OBE, Japan's then-senior Christian at 95 noted 'When we rightfully recognize Kobo as true Christian Saint he is, Christianity will have rooted in Japan...till then we are just one foreign exotic religion.'

SHOPPING & OUTFITTING: Main pilgrimage temples have shops inside or by entry selling authorized gear, from narrow band of purple cloth indicating starting at temple #1, RYOZENJI, above Tokushima (this is really all there is to official Buddhist priest's wardrobe thus many now wear it over business suit when preaching), white hiplength overshirt and pantaloons (Statler advises usual slacks okay) of simplest pure cotton (some synthetics, but cottons usually cheaper as well as better) and sandals (not required, shoes advised), sedge umbrella hats (good idea as sunshade and with usual vinyl cover, rainproof) and walking stick (very good idea and required of true *henro* as symbolizes leaning on Saint Kobo) and rugged plain shoulder bag which can always be used anywhere later as overniter or camera bag. Other accessories like rosary and brass bell (hung from hip) or silvery handled-bell (for very devout) are for more sectarian, or perhaps curiously orthodox foreigner, too. There is no sacrilege if you buy all or some (shoulder satchels are great) and get imprint of few temples you do visit on satchel, shirt or in accordion *stampu-chò* booklet, excellent memento, used as official pilgrimage proof. In turn, you carry stack of 'visiting cards' papers imprinted with calligraphed name of pilgrimage and likeness of Kobo, with space to write your name, age, home address date of visit to leave at each temple in return for vermilion stamp and certifying *sumi*-ink signature of priest (often quite beautiful). Temple shops have other souvenirs: talisman of temple, often singularly attractive, and religious artifacts which make handsome decorations.

Coast between Tadotsu port and Matsuyama is uninteresting, so our itinerary is lazy 'S' via TAKAMATSU across → KOCHI, up → UWAJIMA, and exiting from MATSUYAMA.

You're as crazy if you dance as if you don't

TOKUSHIMA: Traditional entry for pilgrims and town still as handsome as when Moraes, Portuguese teacher-author, ex-Consul to Kobe-Osaka and contemporary of Lafcadio Hearn, lived at turn of century and wrote, "This place...gives us an authentic Japanese spectacle...great merit". He and Japanese wife Koharu are buried in local **CHO'ON-JI** temple, **Memorial Museum** containing his works, some possessions is on hill-top Bizan Park. Scenic cable car to top, ¥600 r.t.. Dagoba at top dedicated to war dead of Burma, many from this area; contains small exhibit of Burmese art. Moraes' house was at bottom of hill but burned down with most of city in wartime bombings.

One spot which survived is 380-year-old...
ZUIGAN-JI temple, (5min walk S of ropeway bottom), has beautiful tea garden. But these are all usual sights, with little else for tourist here except for Awa puppets, or famed Awa Odori...

PERSONAL DATEBOOK: *Awa-odori*, Crazy Dance, held every **Aug 12-15** —was lunar July. For four wild days and nites entire town and over million visitors turn out in groups to watch or perform simple group folk dance—70,000 dancers 1990— down decorated main street, pausing for special performances in front of judges' platforms. Good groups are awarded prizes and pennants. Inns often field groups of mixed employees and guests, or neighborhood association to which your small inn belongs may field one. Just borrow your inn yukata, get fan and join in. Foreign group, or group with some blue-eyes mixed in, is sure to win some prize. Dance step is ridiculously simple. Even if you don't join in, stroll in yukata and get in mood. As they say here *Odoru aho ni miru aho, onaji aho nara odoreh!* or 'Dancing is foolish—watching is foolish. You can't win, so dance'. *Kansai Time Out* magazine usually takes group down. Inns which book thru JTB or other agencies are usually booked up well in advance. But there are many independent middle class and budget inns, and we have found it easy to get room in one of these without reservations— just go walk around center of town trying inns. If worse comes to worst, parks, beaches and river bank are only stone's throw away.

Awa Giant Puppets, even larger than bunraku dolls of Osaka are here at Tokushima, which with Awaji Island itself now supports most active of folk puppet groups, accompanied by shamisen-players and chanters who recite tale and sing various parts, were only means of recreation for local populace. They always gave performances at shrine and temple festivals. 80 years ago Tokushama alone had over 30 puppet houses, but with passage of time and coming of movies and TV, only one place has regular shows:

Awa-no-Jurobei Yashiki has one 30min performance sat 15:00, sun & hol 10:30, 15:00. Performances can be arranged for ¥13,000 by calling ahead ☎(0886)-

52-8777. Also day-long series of performances at City **Culture Hall**, *Bunka-kaikan*, 300m W of stn, during **mid-Apr** *Tokushima Matsuri*, and early **Aug** *Joruri-taikai* puppet contest: ☎52-9671 for exact dates, reservations or special showing. Theater at Jurobei Yashiki is next to main house: small-scale replica of samurai-style house belonging to Jurobei, actual person who, as scapegoat for illicit sales of government rice, was banished. Kabuki and puppet theater picked up his story, romanticized it and this hometown boy's story (*Keisei Awa no Naruto*) has become most widely performed piece in area. ¥300 to see house, inside local odds-ends—North of stn, across Yoshino River; 20min bus (#7), **cab** 2x-mtr.

Tokushima is known for *aizome* deep blue indigo-dyed cloth; see how, and try your hand at it ¥500 to dye whatever you have on hand: *Kosho Somé-kojo*, **Dyeing Studio**, 3km W of stn along Rte 192, 5min bus to Sako Shichiban-cho, **cab** 1.5x-mtr. Area also noted for its *washi* or so-called 'rice paper', with occasional seminar in making held in English; ✍ **'Tesuki Washi Kenshukai'**, c/o Awa washi dento-kaikan, 141 Azakawa Higashi, Yamakawa-cho Oe-gun, Tokushima-ken, or phone Mr Fujimori ☎(0886)-52-2772. One held Aug '91 (tho main season winter) included accoms 5 nites, all meals, lessons, total only ¥90,000.

NARUTO, famed gigantic maelstrom caused by rush of tide in, or out— first hour of every 6hr25min—of Inland Sea thru this narrow and peculiarly shaped passage. It is one of three major whirlpools of world. At other places in Inland Sea other passages form natural locks at tide change and you will find your ship suddenly ascending or descending watery flight of stairs, moving from one sea-level to next thru what appear to be rapids. Whirlpools at their traditionally fiercest on 3rd day of 3rd moon, late March or early April, and at full moon monthly. It was first feared that construction of bridge now spanning Naruto and Awaji (finished March 1985) would change current enough to destroy whirlpools, but no effects, as you can see. Naruto Point is actually three islets barely separated from mainland.

To see, observation tower in...
Naruto Park atop *Tsutsuji-ga-oka*, **Azalea Hill** (20min bus from Naruto stn; 40min rail or hour bus from Tokushima). Perfect spot to see whirlpools is from observation post here; also see entire panorama of Naruto Straits. Best time at high tide, twice daily, best when falling midday. You can also boat among 60-foot wide pools (¥1,300, 30min), from Naruto kanko port behind park (30min walk, 7min bus from park). Departures every 40min 9:00-16:20. Similar out of FUKURA on Awaji 9:30, 10:40, 11:50, 13:00, 14:20; 15:40; which have 1st and 2nd class (¥1,300). Tours run daily. Those coming across from AWAJI, or on evening ferry from KOBE will find host of ¥-B minshuku at tip of Naruto near pier, or around stn. If early morning, beaches are perfect for wake-up dip.

TILT: **Tokushima Bus Co** ☎(0886)-22-1811 has tour departing Tokushima Stn 9:50, pick-up Naruto stn 10:30 → Tokushima Bizan Park, Jurobei Yashiki for puppet show, → Naruto for boat to whirlpools, end Tokushima stn 15:50. ¥4,200, weekends and holidays Apr–Nov, but daily end Apr–early May and Jul 20-Aug 31.

AWAJI ISLAND: Has little for tourist except fine beaches, and what it has is conveniently close. Awaji Ningyo puppet troupe is at FUKURA port, just as you get off boat. Performances daily 10:10, 11:10, 13:10, 15:10, ¥800. Large groups should call ahead day before, ☎(07995)-2-0260. Good English pamphlet with synopsis and script of chanters. Examine extra heads and costumes between shows. Narrow triangular monument on clifftop as you come in by boat is Memorial to Student Casualties of World War II. Coming from Kobe by boat, or up island by bus, you can't miss isle's other peace memorial, unhandsome 101m/300ft tall concrete Kannon statue.

Back on Shikoku where you can see puppets being made at little workshop of 4th generation master puppet-maker Oe Minosuke. Actually he carves only heads and hands and fits controls; body is stuffed elsewhere and costumed. He made most of heads for troupe which played Seattle World's Fair in 1962, as he makes heads for greatest of Osaka bunraku masters. En route back to Tokushima, or on to Takamatsu, cab from Otani Stn to **Minosuke's workshop**, 5km down main road from Naruto. By rail, get off at Otani and short walk Naruto direction. Otani is 200-year-old pottery town, known mostly for its sturdy, monster sized storage jars.

Few km Takamatsu-direction is Meiji style...
German House, built 1972 to commemorate Japan-German friendship. Site of house was temporary home for 953 German POWs 1917-1920. Japan sided with allies mainly to get German controlled areas of China and Pacific Islands—but army-biased government much preferred crisp, military Prussians over Brits or Yanks (Navy was pro-British). Still wishing to keep door open for good relations after war, prisoners were shipped over in class, treated more like visiting dignitaries, with all comforts of home, plus. Arched stone bridge and other things around here were built by Germans who struck up great relation with locals (similar hospitality shown Russians 1904-5). Plans in works for surrounding 'German Village'.

First 23 of 88 Pilgrimage Temples are in Tokushima pref; Kobo-daishi started out near Naruto and headed inland up Yoshino River. Readers cutting out TOSA area can follow his trail by rail or bus (Rte 192) to IKEDA junction and nearby **Oboke Gorge** for river run and Japan's only remaining vine suspension bridge (*see* TILT). Kobo turned back before Ikeda and headed back to coast, meandering down to Muroto Point (temple #24) and up to Kochi. This leg is for adventurer with time, rail ends 2hr20min beyond at Kaifu, from where regular buses. Not much other than swimming, fishing and rugged scenery. Tip of Gamouda Peninsula 50km S of Tokushima is best place to see 100-150kg *umi-game,* **giant sea turtles** wade ashore to lay their hundred-odd eggs at nite, mid-May thru mid-Aug. They also come ashore further S at Kiki and Hiwasa; Kokumin-shukusha **Umigame-so** at latter leads silent excursions to view behemoths come in with tide between sunset-sunrise. Jul 21, *Umigame Festival,* Hiwasa, commemorates Urashima Taro (who visited undersea Dragon King's Palace on turtle) and king's daughter Kotohime by toasting sake with turtles and guiding them back out to sea.

Between Tokushima—Takamatsu are several popular bathing beaches:
Tsuda Beach Kinrin Park (about 20km E of Takamatsu), is lined with luxuriant growth of hoary pine trees whose gnarled roots stand out above white sand. 15km further E at SHIRATORI, coastal cliffs are white granite striped with great bands of black mica. Just E of this about 30km out of Tokushima, at HIKETA is Japan's only salt water fish farm, **Adoiké Pond.** Along this route you notice odd conical hills inland: look out to sea where identically shaped islets poke their coneheads out of water, particularly as seen from Goshiki-dai hill just past Takamatsu.

NARUTO → TAKAMATSU must change to Takatoku Main Line at IKEYA, from where 75min exp, 1hr50min local. 1hr35min exp from TOKUSHIMA.

TAKAMATSU: Two main attractions **Yashima Plateau** and **Ritsurin Gardens** with possible 3rd-4th: bonsai village of **Kinashi** or E at **Mure NOGUCHI Isamu Sculpture Garden.** From pier or stn, follow wide blvd to end (2km; cab basic-mtr, 10min bus or tram). Takamatsu is main transfer point on several Inland Sea iti neraries: airline, hydrofoil, express (Beppu run) and local steamers from Kobe-Osaka; various ferries, steamers and hydrofoils from Okayama-Kurashiki area; and JR boat line. It is most common place to start round of Shikoku; short-timer coming in here morning can shoot out to Awaji to catch afternoon showings of puppets, see whirlpools and be back for dinner (preferably at KOTOHIRA).

JR local from Tokushima to Ritsurin stn, garden enthusiasts find...
Ritsurin Park garden laid out on grand scale—6 ponds, 13 hills, countless bridges, islets, everything Japanese garden should have. Advise follow garden paths counter clock- wise, keeping ponds on your L. By this rule common to gardens of Edo era, you're at best vantage point no matter where you stop. Opens early, 5:30-18:30 Apr-Sep, 6:30-17:00 Nov-Mar, ¥310; ¥310 extra for **Kikuzuki-tei** pavilion incl *matcha* green tea & cake; **Sanuki Folkart Museum** 8:30-16:00, X-year-end, New Year; houseful of J-pottery, dye works; other full of local goods. As all gardens, best seen early or late to avoid crowd or heat—worth overnite.

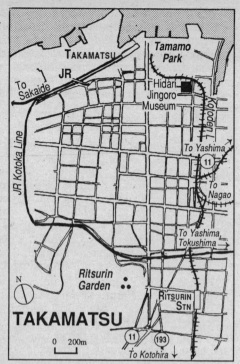

Bus and tram (Takamatsu-Kotohira Dentetsu) continue on to Kotohira.

True garden enthusiast can take in pleasant...
Tamamo Garden in Takamatsu Castle grounds, right at pier and rail stn (¥100, 7:00-18:00). Just outside its south wall is **Hidari Jingoro Museum** (¥500, 9:00-17:00), with some of his works, those of his descendants—also carvers—and local artists. This left-handed (*hidari*) artist is best known for see-, hear-, speak-no-evil monkeys at Nikko; later commissioned to work on Takamatsu Castle by local Matsudaira lord—most of his finer works burned during World War II bombing. He is buried at nearby JIZO-DERA temple. 10th generation descendant runs museum.

7km away cab 4x-mtr, 15min JR; 20min by more frequent, cheaper electric...
Yashima Plateau (Ropeway ¥510 o.w.; ¥1,010 r.t.) worth it for view. From up here you can see narrow spit of land where retreating Taira clan awaited attacking Minamoto on February 19, 1185, only to have attackers land troops behind them while empty ships made feint where awaited. Flanking blitzkreig by mere 200 horsemen forced superior Taira to flee into sea where slaughtered by pirates siding with Minamoto. Taira retreated further down Inland Sea. Yashima-ji temple's small **treasure hall** has battle related items; souvenirs here are sonorous natural stone bells and gongs.

Just E of Yashima-ji is...
MINOYAMA DAIMYOJIN shrine, home of badger priest Yashima Tanuki (whom we meet all over Shikoku), deity of marriage and good luck, popular with ladies of 'gay' trades. Trail leads down to site of massacre...

Catch bus back to ropeway base for...
Folk Village, *Shikoku-Mura* (¥500, 8:30-17:00), with many classic old houses, representative of all isle's four prefectures—old feudal domains of Awa on E (now Tokushima prefecture), Sanuki on north (Kagawa), Iyo on

west (Ehime) and Tosa (Kochi) on south. Many folks, particularly older generation, still use these feudal names, rather than new ones.

Elevated house at entrance is from Sukumo area far SE point, was used to house teen-age younger sons of villagers—keep rowdies together—also acted as watchtower. Cross imitation vine bridge into 'rural Shikoku'. Large W-style house is sole 'outsider', built 1905 for English family, Downs, in Kobe's Kitano-cho foreign residents' district and moved here.

SHOPPING: *Kimma* lacquerware with designs carved into black lacquer, then filled in with cinnabar-colored lacquer; bamboo trays with designs of bamboo strips in complicated basketweave, gaily decorated parasols in all sizes. Convenient spot for folkcraft articles and souvenirs is kiosk at Sanuki Mingeikan in Ritsurin Park. **Bonsai** of Kinashi, 8km (2 JRstops) W of town, is known all over Japan, grown in Takamatsu.

To take bonsai overseas requires special shipping-quarantine procedures, handled only by specialists at top shops; best check with your travel agent, carrier or Nippon Express before buying. Not all that complicated or extra-expense when done by licensed expert.

Taxi 4x-mtrs E to...
MURE—NOGUCHI Isamu Sculpture Garden (1991) where great US-Jpn artist (1904-84) lived final years, to be close to source of his stone.

WHERE TO STAY: W-style hotels include best **Grand** ☎(0878)-51-5757, near Tamamo Park, ¥-T; **Station Hotel**; **Washington** halfway to Ritsurin, and few more along road to Ritsurin: range ¥-B-T for singles, room only, Washington cheaper. J-style inns best **Kawaroku** ☎21-5666, ¥-hi-Tw/2; **Idoya** ☎51-0558, and **Orizuru** ☎51-8888, both ¥-lo-Tw/2. Few budget inns; arrange thru stn **Kanko-annai**. Several moderate-priced inns atop Yashima, Youth Hostel at base. Nr peninsula tip by Yashima is **Aji Onsen**, one ¥-T inn, 30min bus from Takamatsu, 5min bus from Yashima.

ONIGASHIMA, Demon's Isle, just 20min steamer every other hour; hourly summer, from Takamatsu, popular for camping and swimming. Here, children's hero Momotaro, Peach Boy, with his 3 helpers, dog, monkey and pheasant, conquered demon pirates at local cave. 18 ¥-Bw/2 inns here. Homes surrounded by high stone walls to ward off wind; much more spectacular ones at SOTODOMARI near Uwajima.

1hr ferry (35min hydrofoil) from Takamatsu...
SHODO-SHIMA: Quarry and olive grove isle (*best* late Apr, May, also azalea), circle by bus in under 5hrs, Good beaches N at **Silver Beach**, S along **Naikai Bay**, smaller beaches all around. Island is lovely in itself, in spite of gaudy new tourist attractions like hideous Olive Palace—feeble 'replica' of Hellenistic temple. Cable car up **Kanka-kei Ravine** for Seki-mon-do natural stone arch worth effort, then bus or hike along Blue Line scenic road to **Mt Hoshigajo**. Island also known for its white *kujaku* peacocks–can be seen among few 1,000 peacocks at **Kujaku-en Park**, 3km E of Tonosho. Simian fans can romp with over 1,000 'wild' monkeys at **Choshi-kei** ravine. Rocky isle supplied most stone for Osaka Castle.

Main sights covered by **Shodoshima Bus Company Tours** ☎(0879)-62-1200: **A Course** 6hr30min, ¥4,980; B- 4hr30min, ¥3,080; C- 5hr30min, ¥3,850 several times 7:40am-10:40 plus more Bs; 12:40am, 13:40, from TONOSHO pier; but if planning to wander, buy 2-day 'Free-Pass' ¥2,000, good for multiple trips.

Shodo has its own smaller version of Shikoku-88 Pilgrimage, started in imitation of it in 1686. Whole route some 150km/100miles, on foot takes week with well-mapped, detailed English guide book in hand: KAWAHARA Akihira *Eighty Eight Pilgrimage Sites on Shodo Island* ¥2,500, or postpaid ¥3,000 Japan, $30 foreign from author: 566 Yasuda, Uchinomi-cho Shozo-gun, Kagawa Pref 76-44 (☎0879-82-1368). Advise first contacting this pilgrimage's Service Organization HQ in Tonosho, near port for ferries from Kobe-Osaka, to help with supplies, reserve or introduce inns, etc. Shodoshima Bus (above) has monthly tour.

Village Kabuki was popular here prewar, but, like puppets declined. Can still be seen twice yearly: **May 3rd** RIKYU HACHIMAN JINJA shrine at Hitozan, Tonosho; **Oct 3**, nearby KASUGA JINJA shrine, Nakayama.

GETTING THERE: Ships from Takamatsu, Okayama, Kobe, Osaka pull in to main town, westernmost TONOSHO. Others less often to SE SAKATE; occasionals from Himeji into E coast FUKUDA; and into north shore OBE from Hinase near Imbe Bizen. From Himeji: Kansai Kyuko Ferry ☎0792-34-7100; from Okayama, Ryobi Unyu ☎0862-74-1222, Shikoku Ferry; from Takamatsu Kankyu Marine ☎0878-51-8171, Naikai Ferry ☎0879-82-1080, Kokusai Ferry ☎0879-75-0405.

WHERE TO STAY: Lodgings range from several fine W-style hotels such as sprawling **Shodo-shima Kokusai** near Tonosho down to scattered all over island 100-odd budget minshuku, even cheaper inns for pilgrims like **Ajikan Ashram** near stone arch; many campsites. Spring & autumn special **boat tours** (r.t.) out of KOBE Meriken pier to view cherries, red maples are worthwhile.

W of Takamatsu road, rail follow lovely coast of many fine beaches, 20km...
SAKAIDE, center of salt production, watch for ancient and modern salt processes: former look like square tidal pools, latter like bamboo hedges. Traditional systems supplemented modern plants until recently and some are still kept around for nostagia: health food shops claim no sea salt made in Japan now but has market, so may have some future. Town is Shikoku landing for Great Seto Bridge from Okayama-Washuzan (p.639). Landing plaza has fine rock composition by NOGUCHI Isamu, worth trip.

MARUGAME, 300-year-old castle, fine garden, *and opp JR stn, docks is...*
Marugame INOKUMA **Museum of Contemporary Art** (MIMOCA), INOKUMA Guen[ichiro], b.1902, our favorite modernist, student of Matisse and married one of his famed J- models, postwar several years New York, still winters Hawaii. 1,000 paintings done over 75 yrs, illustrate evolution of J- 20th century art, rotate. Museum by Taniguchi, 1991, excellent.

You may see myriads of *uchiwa* non-folding, drum-shape fans drying on racks, filling every open plot around castle. Accounts for 80% of national production of these popular hand-made coolers, over 160 mom'n-pop shops in area employ 1,000+ makers to crank out 51 million annually.

2-3x-mtr cab from stn and ferry docks...
Nakatsu Bansho-en garden, fabulous stand of immense antique pines (sadly being decimated by pollution-induced pine worms) ring feudal lord's garden of 1688, exquiste tea house, bridges, etc, setting for fine small pvt museums of ancient Persian ceramics, Barbizon paintings. ¥770.

STAY: **Okura Hotel** W-luxury at ¥-T rate, ☎(0877)-23-2222. Others nr Castle, stn.

Shiwaku Isles seen to N of city were infamous for centuries as pirate lairs which archaeological excavation indicates was old center of civilization. It was just E of here, between Shodo and Awaji Isles that creator god Izanagi reputedly thrust his spear into primeval mire to create islands of Japan, drawing out these very islets first and working outwards.

Many Inland Sea island-hopper ferries land at MARUGAME, or 5km W at TADOTSU.

20km beyond Tadotsu on coast is...
KANNON-JI temple, #68-69 of Sacred 88. Next to it, in **Kotobiki Park** is giant sand sculpture on beach made to look like coin and created overnite 350 years ago by peasants to welcome new lord to district. Looking down from Kotobiki hill it appears circular, but this 2m tall *zeni-gata* (coin-shape) sand sculpture of 345m circumference, is actually oval, measuring 122m up-down (E-W) by 90m across (N-S) to compensate for viewers' paralax. And they say Japan didn't get perspective until European painting was copied?

Park, Temple 20min JR or Kotohira bus from KANNON-JI stn.

Buses on 50min to...

ZENTSU-JI where Kobo-daishi was born 774 on spot now so sacred no one may step on it: so temple has been raised over it, tunnel for pilgrims under it. Temple here then; his family were priests (family name Saeki tells they were originally of Sahaka or Saheki clan of Nara, aborigines who allied with immigrating Wa, became Guardians of Nara sacred deer until caught unBuddhistically eating them and banished to outer areas all now known as Saeki-*gun*, counties, in Hiroshima, Kyushu and here) so this became #75. Tunnel runs under it into which blackness pilgrims enter, as you will, led by priest who pauses and prays then guides you directly under sacred spot to tiny grotto, in which candle and incense burn and before which he squats and chants. This is just site of family home—he was actually delivered at mother's home, as is still custom, 10km north at Beach Temple. Left-side walls of pitch black tunnel said to have been painted (by Kobo-daishi) with deities of 88 pilgrim places. If no guide, do 100m tunnel by running L hand along wall (no light allowed) which is same as visiting all 88 pilgrim spots on foot. Tho priest may guide you thru all temple apartments do not offer money to him, drop donation in alms box. Full services daily 5-7am.

ZENTSU-JI, one of three main Shingon pilgrimage temples with Kobo-daishi's own temple Kyoto's TOJI, and KOYA MONASTERY, where he 'died', or rather entered suspended animation awaiting judgment day. **Treasure Hall** (¥300), some fine sumi paintings, upstairs sculpture said by Saint Kobo. On special days (**Jan 21, Mar 21, Jun 15**, all lunar calender—about month lag) has display of Saint Kobo's staff brought back from China, other personal items. Lovely 5-tiered pagoda dominates town, easy to spot. Outside in temple grounds and just within gate, usually fishing gear being sold, which speaks for its parishioners. Zentsu-ji City is fun town to spend short while walking around. Escaped wartime bombing in spite of fact that it was large army base since 1889. Ground Self Defense Forces now here.

From here, one stop JR, or 15min bus; or also reached by 1hr direct JR from Takamatsu via Tadotsu; or same Kotoden Electric Rail Line which cuts inland.

KOMPIRA 金毘羅 MOUNTAINTOP SHRINE TO SEA GOD

KOTOHIRA: Cimb up to **KOMPIRA SHRINE** is hard but fun. You can take palanquin up part way to main gate, ¥4,000—don't gripe if it increases, was ¥850 in 1964 whereas taxis up seven-fold! On way up are numerous stores selling masks; excellent wood carvings, from few hundred yen to small fortune; baskets; up to 40cm/15inch replicas of Bumbuku Chagama, magic badger-pot; and watch for pornographic sake cups. To break ascent, is small but worthwhile **museum**, *Homutsu-kan* (¥200, daily 8:00-16:00, from 9:00 winter), midway up on R; *Farting Contest* scroll by 12th century priest-cartoonist TOBA Sojo must not be missed (you can buy copy of it for few hundred yen at Otsu tourist office just outside Kyoto).

Just beyond museum is...

Shamusho temple office and *Sho-in*, former residence of Buddhist priests, boasts *fusuma* panels painted by MARUYAMA Okyo (1733-95) of wisemen, storks, tigers (never having seen real one, he used house cat as model) and others by KISHI Gantai and Jakushu (1716-1800) In one landscape of Kyoto, waterfall painted in *tokonoma* 'feeds' pool out in real garden, which was laid out by KOBORI Enshu. Same hours as museum, also ¥200. From this building to shrine is still 572 stone steps, bit beyond which *kago*-bearers may give up and help you walk, hefting your baggage and cameras. Last 100 steps are special: devout pilgrims will run up and down 100 times—stone tortoise with wooden sticks is tally for them to keep score.

View from top is worth climb: notably dome of lovely...
Sanuki Fuji Hill. Shrine at top may surprise you in looking like Buddhist temple, which it was: founded by Kobo-daishi in ninth century from older Sea Goddess holy place with probable earlier Indian connections (Kompira is Japanization of Kumbhara, crocodile god of Ganges). After *Ryobu* (combined) Shinto divorce, Shintoists seized it 1872, purged it of 'idols' and burned most of buildings, 'excommunicating' Shinto-Buddhist avatar Kompira Daigongen to enshrine Omononushi-no-Kami, Shinto deity mentioned in *Kojiki* as having 'come from beyond, lighting up seas'. However, when they rebuilt they retained imitation Buddhist style—official cleansing aside it's still popularly known as Kompira-sama (polite form of *san*, title and in homonym designation of Buddhist cathedral). Shrine is sacred to travelers, its *fuda* (talismans) are sold for sea travelers and fishermen. Those over ¥5,000 are blessed in full ceremony, at your convenience, in holy of holies into which you are invited, shoes off (photos OK, but not from center directly in line with inner sanctum). Dances by shrine maidens will be performed in inner shrine for donation of ¥50,000up. Available cheaper on outer stage erratically, ask.
Ema-do, pavilion of votive pictures, is interesting. Modern votives include racing boats, steamboats, look for gigantic print of Brooklyn Bridge presented by ocean-going sea captain. Tokyo circus gave bronze elephant. Hardy devout can continue farther up mountain 30min to OKU-SHA (rear shrine). Part way is sub-shrine to Emperor Sutoku (1119-64).

WHERE TO STAY: Suggest overnite here rather than Takamatsu: Many good inns: famed is hoary **Toraya** at foot of shrine stairs (¥-Tw/2) and **Annex**, facing. Further down street is lovely **Bizen-ya** (¥-Tw/2) of 300 years experience; facing it **Shikishima-ya** (¥-Tw/2); several more in same range line this street, cheaper ones on perpendicular street, bottom end. Budgeteers have few minshuku ¥-Bw/2, or Youth Hostel. Walk around and choose, or arrange thru stn **Kanko-annai**.

PERSONAL DATEBOOK: Great festival is Oct 9-11 with its main procession 10th in which mikoshi leaves main hall 9:00 winding thru town to reach offering spot 3hrs later. Small festival monthly 10th. Ancient ritual sheepskin-football *kemari* by staff of shrine in flowing brocade robes on **May 5** 10am-noon; **Jul 7** 10am-noon; **end-Dec** (date indefinite). Other annual events scheduled are *Kompira Festival* from Cherry Festival **Apr 10** thru *Rice-planting Festival* **Apr 15** with kabuki at Kanamaru-za (below); *Maple Festival* **Nov 10**. In all these, long procession makes offering of 3 plants at shrine; and for rice-planting there is ritual planting in nearby fields.

Since early Edo era, pilgrimage to Kompira has ranked close behind that to Ise Grand Shrine in popularity, and even now 4 million visit every year. Those unable to make pilgrimage get together and fill *taru* wood barrel with offerings for shrine, attach banner to it and set it afloat in Inland Sea. Any fisherman who comes across one brings it on his next visit, thus increasing his own celestial credit, as well as that of barrel offerers. In similar vein, Ise Grand Shrine has band of roving lion dancer-musicians who circle entire country by foot performing in rural towns, villages for those unable to go to Ise in person, whose offerings pay for performers' living expenses on road.

Coming down from shrine, take R at bottom of flight of stone steps, 300m to...
Kanamaru-za, Japan's oldest extant theater, built 1835. All great Kabuki actors thru 1920s performed here. Restored 1986 as museum, kabuki performed by top visiting actors during *Kompira Festival* **late April**, afficionados check JTB. ¥300 to see inside, old revolving stage (invented same time—or before?—Europe) was and is operated by 20 men.

Down footpath here 300m to river puts you right at...
Saya-bashi Bridge: lovely arched, covered as used only **Oct 10** when mikoshi procession passes over it.

L at bottom of shrine steps leads to annex of...
Homotsu-kan Museum, *Gakugei Sankokan* (¥300), assortment of old
folk toys, votive *ema*-pictures, and those sea-faring offertory barrels. Two-
storey wood tower near stn last rebuilt 1865; served as guiding light for nite
travelers, and even now flame is lit nitely.

   TILT: **Kotohira Sangu Dentetsu** ☎(0877)-22-2151; and **Kotoden Bus**
☎(0878)-51-3320—these 2 bus companies all run identical tours all year: Dep
TAKAMATSU harbor/stn 8:45 & 9:20, → Yashima → Chikurin Gdn → Marugame
Castle → Zentsu-ji Temple → Kotohira return → TAKAMATSU at 17:30 and 18:05:
¥4,660, can also disembark KOTOHIRA in which case ¥4,060. 9:20 bus doesn't run Nov-
Feb. Must reserve by calling, or at travel agents like JTB or stn Travel Center. Suggest
complete day bus trips, night at KOTOHIRA and do OBOKE solo or on **Shikoku
Kotsu's** Oboke-Iya Valley bonnet-bus tour: AWA IKEDA stn 10:55 → boat down Oboke
Gorge → see Ivy Bridge → Heike Museum → Iya Onsen → back to IKEDA 15:30; all
¥4,500 operates weekends and holidays Apr-Nov, except during June (rainy season) and
Sep (typhoons). Reserve thru ☎(0883)-72-1231; day before from Kotohira OK, have inn
make call.

   From KOTOHIRA, local diesel train chugs up 70min (35min express) → IKEDA,
passing tiny lumber hamlets precariously poised on great log foundations. Ikeda is main
bus terminal, whence hour → Iya-kei Gorge, 20min farther → vine bridge Kazura-bashi.
Note: To go to Kazura-bashi you must use Shikoku Kotsu Bus. If by bus, Ikeda-Kazura-
bashi ¥1200 o.w. Tour Ikeda → Oboke → Kazura-bashi (museum) → Ikeda, ¥4,500.
Buses infrequent, run only sat-sun 10:55am, catch bus back at 3:30pm. Midway between
two is cliffside IYA ONSEN with outdoor pool of hot water at base of mountain trolley
along river into which one plunges, bareback of course; nearby **Iya Onsen Hotel**
☎(0883)-75-2311, ¥-Tw/2. Crossing vine bridge (only one left in Japan in situ, tho steel-
cable-reenforced) is quite thrilling, but to cut down on wear, ¥410 is charged. Bridge is
also reached by 50min bus from OBOKE stn, 5 stops (35min) beyond Ikeda. Expresses
(but not Ltd express) stop at Oboke. 15min walk backtrack from Oboke stn is boarding
spot for wooden skiffs thru Oboke Gorge, 30min ride, ¥620 round-trip. Koboke Gorge
narrow, water too swift for boats. 30min walk along riverside trail N of stn exciting.
Oboke is more spectacular of two, **boats** run end to end 9:00-17:00. If looking for
budget lodgings in area, 700-year-old JISHO-IN temple, ☎84-1934 30min walk E of
Oboke (down side road near boat terminal) runs minshuku.

   *From Oboke, rail and road winds thru seemingly endless (especially on bicycle)
mountains, finally begins long downhill run to...*

KOCHI 高知

MAIN CITY of Southern Shikoku, all of which is favored by warm weather,
helped by Kuroshio, warm Japanese gulf stream, and can harvest rice
successfully twice yearly. People usually still refer to this area as Tosa, by
which it was known in feudal period. It is still relatively untraveled,
especially by foreign travelers. (Fairly extensive air service (*see* above) makes
it somewhat convenient to major mainland cities, but express trains from
northern Shikoku take 3hrs from Takamatsu; just over hour from Oboke).

   Tosa is battered by typhoons during autumn, taking brunt of their fury,
weakening 'great winds' before they hit mainland. Harshness of elements,
and Tosa's relative isolation led to fiercely independent group of people,
never quite part of mainstream Japan. During Edo period Tosa was never
really subjugated by Tokugawa, just hemmed in by loyal Tokugawa allies.
And during turbulent 19th century, Tosa was one of three strongest anti-
Tokugawa forces, screaming for immediate annihilation of Perry's Black
Ships and imperial restoration. Tosa supplied many early revolutionaries
(notably Sakamoto Ryoma), and first leaders of Meiji Japan after concluding
that Westerners where here to stay.

People here are still independent and wild, but extremely hospitable and fun-loving. All of which best seen at grand summer street-dancing festival **Aug 9-11** (*see* DATEBOOK p692) Garet's short stay here stretched out into two crazy days, as every nite, locals insisted that he stay for 'just one more drink'. Jay found driving up center in 1985 one of freest experiences ever in 35 years in Japan.

Kochi is also main port, with natural harbor, surrounded on three, almost four sides by mountains. Long distance **ferries** from OSAKA, KATSU-URA (Kii Peninsula) and TOKYO dock here. Buses thru town are extensive, but easier to use are *chin-chin densha* **trams**, running N-S KOCHI stn ↔ port, and E-W btwn INO ↔ GOMEN stns, JR. Restored 1987 and running oldest functioning trolley in country, maroon colored #7 of 1904. Other extreme, watch for cartoon-covered trams that outdo New York graffitti-car—ads.

Two E–W + N–S lines cross at midtown...
Harimaya-bashi, red-posted bridge, famed as rendezvous for 17th century love affair between acolyte of Chikurin Temple & local merchant's daughter. There used to be river until filled in and built on in postwar boom.

GETTING AROUND: SE corner of this intersection **Seibu Bus Terminal** for **Tosa Dentetsu buses** → Cape Muroto, Ryuga-do Cavern, Godaisan Park; W of intersection (past JTB) is terminal for **Kochi-ken Kotsu Bus**, to MUROTO, and most points W like NAKAMURA and CAPE ASHIZURI. Airport is 33min on Tosa-den bus. Both companies run identical **tours** every day starting and ending at Kochi stn. **Best** are: 'A' Course dep 9:25 → Kochi Castle → Ryuga-do Cavern → Katsurahama (Shell Museum →*To-ken* Center) → Harimaya Bridge → end stn 16:15: ¥4,710. 'B' Course also 9:25 → Kochi Castle → Godaisan (Makino Garden) → Katsurahama (same as above) → Harimaya Bridge → stn 13:50: ¥2,740. We suggest shorter 'B', do RYUGA-DO solo, with stop off at **Nagao Bird Center**, good idea as includes admission to dog fight and botanical garden. Only front gate of castle (3min stop), includes group photo. Arrange at either bus company's main terminal or at stn terminals. JR long distance buses to Matsuyama leave from stn front. **Taxis** abound; arrange own tour at stn, going rate about 7x-mtr per hour. Full-course tour will run about 4hrs, cut out Ryuga-do for 3hrs. 3 people by cab about same as bus tours, 4-5 people save enough on cab to pay for sumptuous meal. Energetic types rent **bicycles** from JR bus area at stn, ¥200/hour, ¥800/day.

Aside from usual castle & temples are some from Ripley Believe It or Not...
Long-tailed cock, *Onaga-dori*, some with tails measured at 13mtr/44ft long (and which grow meter each year) and body feathers about 1.2m/4ft long. They have been developed over centuries from wild fowl with chicken and pheasant. They can be seen not far from airport at **Nagao-dori Center** (daily 9:00-17:00, ¥300); 15min walk S from Shinohara tram or bus stop (catch either at Harimaya Bridge, head E), 25min walk S from JR Gomen stn or **cab** mtr basic; 7km from downtown Kochi, **cab** 3x-mtr. Here, birds are raised by KUBOTA Masao, their long tails kept intact by never exercising—they never leave their cages except for show and spend rather limited life. Many shrines and temples in area keep one or two of these birds for good luck, tho their tails are usually not as long as Kubota's.

Giant water lily petals so big that tots can ride on them. Many unusual tropical plants at **Makino Botanical Garden** (9:00-17:00, ¥350), in memory famed botanist MAKINO Tomitaro, **Godaisan Park**, 20min bus from Harimaya.

CHIKURIN-JI temple, (atop Godaisan Patk) number #31 of Shikoku pilgrimage stops; also excellent view of Kochi and lovely Kyuko Bay below on west. Temple dates to 724 AD, but present structures were rebuilt 13th century, at which time was added beautiful landscaped garden done by Muso Kokushi, whose gardens dot Kamakura. ¥200 to see garden also gets you into **Treasure Hall** with several fine Buddhist statues.

And if you notice lots of fierce dogs down in Kochi, they're no doubt aspirants for sumo *ozeki* title, for here is home of famed Tosa *to-ken* **fighting dogs**. There are two divisions: according to height and weight. Over 66cm, 48kg, and 65cm under, 47kg. There are five sumo ranks: Yokozuna (grand champ), Ozeki (champ), Sekiwake, Komusubi and Maegashira as in sumo. Bouts are held in **mid Mar–mid-May, end Jul–end Aug, end Sep–end Nov** (dates indefinite, but usually around 2nd weekend) to establish ranks from more than 90 entries. Rest of year, head to **To-ken Center** down on Katsurahama Point, 35min bus from Harimaya, about **cab** 3x-mtr from town or Godaisan Park. Open 9:00-16:00 daily, but bouts only at 12:55, 15:10 (¥1,000), unless over 30 people, or ¥30,000, in which case set own time. Occasionally, dog owners hang out in front of Kochi Castle with their dogs fully decked out, and you can take your picture with them for token fee. Well-trained, they're not always as fierce as they look. Some *Onaga-dori* birds are kept at castle, also *Shamo fighting cocks*; can arrange cock fight.

Gnarled pine trees stand out in extreme contrast to white sand beach of point, with statue of Sakamoto Ryoma glaring E over Pacific Ocean.

Nearby is...

Aquarium (¥950) showing some of odder fish found in Pacific.

Shell Museum (¥500) with thousands of shells.

Ryuga-do Cavern: 22km E of town, 1hr bus from downtown HARIMAYA or 25min JR bus from TOSA YAMADA stn which is 20min rail from KOCHI. Several kilometers of this cavern have been excavated, yielding Yayoi period settlement and over 100 species of subterranean life forms—all small and harmless. Some rocks are exciting surrealist sculpture and lighting accents nicely. About 1km is open to public and makes up one of top three stalactite caverns in Japan. ¥850 (8:00-17:00, winter 8:00-16:30) includes museum at entry, which displays artifacts excavated inside and panels on cavern's animal life; also nearby **Chincho** (rare bird) **Center.** Tosa-ites seem to have knack for breeding odd birds, for on display here are some more of *Onaga-dori* and fighting *Shamo* and host of other wierd fowl including tailless *Uzura-chabo* and *Toten-kon* whose cry lasts as long as 30 seconds.

If combining RYUGA-DO with above Kubota Masao bird center, do birds on return getting off at Gomen. More ways back *from* Gomen than there are ways *to* cavern.

SHOPPING & CHOPSTICKS: What town is noted for. Castle offers great view. Town boasts several weekly outdoor markets where local farmers and fishermen sell their goods at low prices. Also, local potters bring their wares, and many others sell antiques, curios, old kimono, or just odds and ends. Largest is *Sunday Market* with hundreds of stalls lining street from stn to castle, has most non-food shops, lasts from 8am to sundown. You should be able to find lots of large porcelain platters—blue and whites or brocaded Imari. Area is known for its buffet specialties served for any gathering of clan—weddings, funerals, get-togethers—heaped on these huge platters so guests can help themselves. Curio dealers from Kansai make special treks out to buy these. Street heading S from castle is site of *Thursday Mart* and 600m W of it and running parallel but 1 street S of tram line is *Tuesday* and *Saturday Market*; while few blocks W of stn along tracks is *Friday Market*.

Coral gathered at Cape Ashizuri sold here; best **Kiyo-oka** and **Yonezawa Coral** stores just N of Harimaya Bridge. Full assortment of local crafts is found at Harimaya-bashi **Meisan Center**, nearby **Tosa Folkcraft Center**. Tosa area is also noted for handmade paper goods, found almost anywhere in town. One small factory where making of it can be seen is 25km SW of town, at USA town near Shoryu-ji temple.

PERSONAL DATEBOOK: Aug is month for festivals. Entire Kochi goes all out for 3 days, **9-11**, when dance teams sponsored by clubs, companies and groups dance all day thru city. Not as spectacular as Tokushima, but more original and getting daffier yearly: groups design wild uniforms from yukata to gym-suits or punk-samurai, trucks carry rock and jazz bands, combos of great taiko drum, synthesizer, you name it. Fireworks on **9** in suburbs. Just before this, on **first fri–sun Aug** is *Susaki Festival*, Susaki-shi 20km W of Kochi. Colorful parade sunday of *dashi*-floats and feudal costumes, fireworks at nite shot off from rafts floating in ocean for spectacular effects. **14** sees ancient folk dances, supposedly started by vanquished Heike who hid out in hills, and over 4,000 lighted lanterns set afloat in *Toro-nagashi* dedicated to Heike dead; at *Kosui Festival*, Oku-Monobe Lake, Monobe-mura 50min bus NE of Kochi. Then, **24-25**, Tosa Shrine in Kochi's Ikku district holds summer festival with procession of palanquins, accompanied by lighted torches. Virility of Tosa men has been praised in song since ancient times.

Nov 3 at Kagami-mura Shrine, two groups of young men—one red team, other white —after tissue cutting test of blade and purification rites, leap out armed with genuine swords and duel each other in ritual sword-dance (*tachi odori*) as part of village festival; lasts only 15-20min. 40min bus from Asahi stn (2nd W of Kochi). Chances are you will see sword dance at several other festivals, especially those held at shrines. If not, you can arrange performance by calling any of following three places: Tosa City, Mr. Nishiyama ☎(0888)-52-2563; Kagami-mura, Mr. Tsutsui ☎(0888)-96-2818. Afternoon special charter performance ¥50,000, eve ¥27,000. **Early Apr** (usually 1st wknd) *Doronko mud festival* near KATSURA-HAMA, young women of village rub mud from sacred rice paddy into faces of men in neolithic women's-lib.

WHERE TO STAY: Lodgings abundant, most better places along main Kagami River, or smaller Enoguchi River closer to stn. Best is **Kadan**, ☎(0888)-45-2100, personal, but slightly over-priced at ¥-hi-S+w/2. With 180 years experience, recently enlarged **Hotel Sansui-en** ☎22-0131 by Kagami River due S of castle almost as fine, ¥-T-w/2. Another long-established inn W of castle is **Josei-kan** ☎75-0111, ¥-T. Others along Kagami River same price range; slightly cheaper along Enoguchi River.

Most minshuku (about 20) and Kokumin-shukusha at KATSURA-HAMA. Few moderate to budget ryokan in town, but most budgeteers stay at Business Hotels by stn or **Ekimae** (Stn front) Youth Hostel. Usual **Kanko-annai** at stn books rooms.

UP W COAST N TO UWAJIMA

FROM KOCHI, JR Nakamura Main Line runs 2hr30min → end of line NAKAMURA, from where bus → UWAJIMA: roundabout way is via CAPE ASHIZURI, or straight across → SUKUMO and up → UWAJIMA. 40min rail before Nakamura, at KUBOKAWA, can switch to Yodo Line and train → UWAJIMA, 2hr30min local (6-8 daily) or just under 2hrs on express (1-2 daily). **Buses** are much more frequent, 1-2 every hour if directly across; almost hourly if via Cape Ashizuri. Either route, must change at Sukumo for last 2hrs to Uwajima.

Sukumo is 40min direct from Nakamura, 4hrs via...
CAPE ASHIZURI-MISAKI, beautiful but only for wanderer with time. Southernmost tip of Shikoku, just rugged point jutting out into Pacific; but its beauty has encouraged inns. Detour off main coastal highway Rte 321.

Continuing on Rte321 20min beyond Ashizuri turnoff (80min from Nakamura) is...
TATSUKUSHI where most of coral sold on Kyushu is gathered. Here is **Coral Museum**, glass-bottom boat **cruise** thru coral reefs, and aquarium where look out into open sea from underwater observatory, ¥300.

Glass-bottom boats go out to...
Minokoshi Rock Formations (¥600 r.t.) where you can get off, take pleasant stroll (about hour) for some spectacular sights. Boat 3-4x hr.

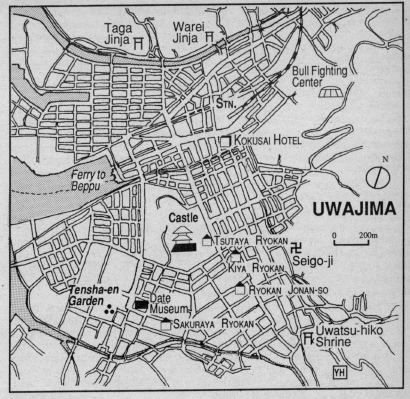

Taga Jinja
Warei Jinja
Bull Fighting Center
STN.
KOKUSAI HOTEL
Ferry to Beppu
N
UWAJIMA
Castle
0   200m
TSUTAYA RYOKAN
Seigo-ji
KIYA RYOKAN
Tensha-en Garden
RYOKAN JONAN-SO
Date Museum
SAKURAYA RYOKAN
Uwatsu-hiko Shrine
YH

SUKUMO where above two bus routes converge; must change here, 1hr45min to Uwajima. If you have time between buses, 15min walk W of Bus Center is **Sukumo Shell Mound,** one of largest Jomon era excavations on Shikoku, yielding pottery, stone tools, idols and bones—both human and animal.

35min bus N of Sukumo, with many of both **Sukumo** ↔ **Johen** ↔ **Uwajima** *and Johen* ↔ *Nishiumi buses, change bus at Johen and head 35min out to...*

NISHIUMI PENINSULA: We come out here to see fortress-like houses of SOTO-DOMARI village, each one surrounded by solid rock walls to protect from typhoons. You can also get good look at it from ocean: village is 2.5km, 15min bus along north shore from boat terminal; or from which 10min chug-boat from boat terminal to Naka-domari and 5min walk.

Boat chugs out 10min to...

Kashima Isle, full of deer and monkeys, from where you can boat around next point and end up at NAGASAKI village to catch bus to UWAJIMA; or Jul-Aug 2hr boat ride KAJIMA ISLE ↔ UWAJIMA. Nishiumi area is perhaps best place to break journey from Kochi, with numerous minshuku in each of these several villages—Soto-domari itself has 7, all in these lovely fortress-like homes. Conveniently close to Uwajima, frequent buses and summer boat 2x-daily.

UWAJIMA is one of island's larger towns, but pulling into stn, you really feel like you're at road's end. Yet it draws many spectators for **bullfights,** bloodless variety *tohgyu* or *ushi-zumo* (bull sumo). Tho records date it to 1801, according to local legend it was started in Kamakura Era, 12th century, by farmers. Actually it is found over much of SE Asia—especially places inhabited by Malays—from South India thru Sri Lanka and Burma, Thailand and isles of Indonesia and north to Philippines, Okinawa and on Japan Seacoast's Oki Isles. Fighting champion earns his master higher stud fees, and value of sport lay in improving breed; all bulls used are farm work animals. He is relieved of chores about one month before tournament and put into fighting shape by practicing technique (there are certain neck-holds used) and by rest and diet— including two dozen raw eggs daily (interesting version of steak'n eggs), meat of poisonous mamushi snake and lightly fermented garlic. He is dressed in ceremonial costume much as human sumo wrestler (and work bulls in Hiroshima rice-planting festivals), some of which are works of art worth thousands of dollars. Fight is not completely bloodless (tho' very little and that infrequently) and unlike human sumo match may last hour or more until one animal gives way, is forced out of ring or down on its knees or moos. Bulls average about 800 kilos, 1,760 pounds.

Matches used to be hard to see, but are now held at city-run **Tohgyu Center** on Maruyama Hill near stn. Regular bouts are: New Year match **Jan 2nd**; Spring tournament **3rd sun May**. Summer tournament **Jul 24, Aug 14**; Autumn tournament **3rd sun Nov.** Each tournament starts at 12:00 and lasts at least 2 hours; ¥2,500 per person. Can also arrange offseason matches by calling **City Tourist Office** ☎(0895)-22-3934, or **Tohgyu Center** ☎25-3511. Cost from ¥45,000 per match, depending rank of fighters you wish to see, ¥85,000 for two bouts, prices negotiable.

PERSONAL DATEBOOK: Main festival here is **Jul 23-24** Warei Shrine *Grand Festival* when giant dinosaur demon cows are paraded with fireworks and hundreds of flag-bedecked fishing boats jam scenic harbor. *Tohgyu* on **24** is offering for good catch at sea; 24th nite main event *Hashiri-komi*, with several mikoshi unloaded from boats in harbor are carried by young men who race up waist-deep Suka River to see who reaches Warei Shrine first. **Oct 29** is Uwatsu-hiko Shrine *Autumn Festival* Yatsu-shika (8-deer) dance. Wearing great ornamental deer heads, 7 antlered-males and 1 female, dance to beat of giant drum. Started in 1615 when DATE Hidemune was made lord of Uwajima, brought dance from his home in Sendai where similar dances still done. Demon-cows also appear this day. Other autumn festivals feature mikoshi parade, competing drum squads, and lion dances: **Oct 14** Mishima Shrine, **Oct 16** Hachiman Shrine, **Oct 19** Tenman Shrine. Oct bullfight sometimes rescheduled to coincide with Hachiman Fest.

200m N of stn across Suga River is **Warei Shrine,** *W along river 5min to...*
TAGA SHRINE alias *Deko-boko-ji*, with truly outstanding erotica collection from all over Japan; much of it humorous 'folk art' and open minds should be amused, not shocked. Gigantic wooden penis in shrine main hall is sign of what to expect. Museum occupies three floors of modern building, 1st and 2nd are mostly old Japanese, 3rd international. Oddest exhibit is collection of pubic hair taken from literally hundreds of women, labeled by name, age, and where from. Why can only be guessed at. (Jay saw collection being made before Garet was born, was even asked to pick up contributions for it— Tsukumo of **Nara Folk Museum**, *Ayame-ga-Ike* with local elderly doctor friends accumulated it; always wondered where it went?). Talismans sold at shrine are obviously phallic or vaginal. Minors, drunks not allowed in. Daily 8:00-17:00, ¥600.

Uwajima Castle on hill in middle of town is 1602 original.

200m W of castle is lovely...
Tensha-en Garden (¥200, 8:00-17:00) built 1866 by 7th Daté lord Munetada; nearby is **Daté Museum** (¥200, X-mon), small collection of Date family treasures.

In middle of temple district is...
SEIGO-JI, temple nestled at mountain's foot 400m E of castle hill, has lovely 360-year-old garden where one can relax and forget one's troubles or

heat. Temple is dedicated to Enma Dai-o, king of underworld, and colorful festival here in his honor **lunar Jan 16.**

10min walk S is...

UWATSU-HIKO, shrine from where you get great view of temple district, surrounded by tiled roofs of old town.

Uwajima Jidosha Bus from JOHEN in 70min stops **Bus Center**, base of Castle hill. Also at stn; continues on to MATSUYAMA via → Ozu → Uchiko → Iyo (*following*).

CHOPSTICKS: Home country for famed Sanuki *udon* noodles. Along shop street *Ginten-gai*, many restaurants, few blocks W of stn running S to castle hill.

SHOPPING: **Miyamoto Pearl** shop along *Ginten-gai* is outlet for local pearlers. Choose pearls in your budget (set in trays by price), have them strung on spot. Discounts often given, reliable. Daughter who also works here, speaks English, helpful.

WHERE TO STAY: There are over 100 inns crammed into town, and you can find room even during summer festival. Garet stayed at **Kiya Ryokan**, ☎(0895)-22-0101, on quiet street 2 blocks SE of castle in pleasant old, wood building with fine service—they've been at it for 100 years, ¥-T. Claimed best in town is **Kokusai Hotel** ☎25-0111 near stn, ¥-T+w/2. Other good, moderate rate inns are **Jonan-so** ☎22-4888, and slightly cheaper **Sakura-ya Ryokan** ☎22-7511, both 4 blocks S of castle. We suggest using stn **Kanko-annai** to find budget ryokan and minshuku, rather than using Business Hotels which run about ¥5,000 room only. Youth Hostel on Atago-yama hill, just behind Uwatsu-hiko Shrine, 800m SE of castle.

NAMETOKO GORGE: (90min bus, 6x- daily from Uwajima stn): series of waterfalls and cool pools along Meguro River. 5 budget inns, Youth Hostel, Gov't-run Youth Village, campsite near bus stop, and another campsite halfway up river (40min hike). Campers must watch out for 100-odd monkeys here, which tho harmless, have been known to make off with anything that catches their fancy. It is about 2hr hike upstream to top of mountain, from where about 90min down to UWAJIMA, coming out behind UWATSU-HIKO SHRINE. Bus takes long as it does 270-degree circle around mountain. On same bus, 25min out of Uwajima to Narukawa bus stop, from where it's short hike up to NARUKAWA GORGE: not quite as spectacular as Nametoko, it does however have small one-inn hot spring 45min hike up from bus stop. Also campsite. If JR Yodo Line from Kochi can get off at MATSUMARU and 45min bus to Nametoko.

All over Shikoku we have seen pilgrims making rounds of 88 holy places. For lazy but well-intended, there is 88-birds-with-one-stone pilgrimage site just north of Uwajima atop **Jishi-koku-yama**, 88 stone images of Kobo-daishi himself, touching reverently each of which is considered equivalent to visit on foot to all 88. (Other short cuts to salvation in popular Buddhism include reciting prayer composed of initials of main holy books, equal to reciting all books; turning great bookcase mounted on axle, as atop Mt Koya, equivalent to reading and turning all pages of holy scriptures therein—but all somehow less hypocritical than our own custom of avoiding chore of doing good deeds by speaking much of our intentions.)

Ferry to BEPPU, hot spring spa on Kyushu in just over 3hrs, ¥1,900, one daily. There are also 6 daily ferries from SUKUMO ↔ SAEKI, down Kyushu coast from Beppu. In either case, suggest taking scenic JR express bus KOCHI → MATSUYAMA working way down coast to UWAJIMA or SUKUMO. Then to sea.

Taking local diesel TAKAMATSU → UWAJIMA in one of hottest summers in recent history, train could not quite make it over last hill and we coasted back down to YOSHIDA to wait for new locomotive; took this as sign to get off and visit two temples here we had heard about. DAIRAKU-JI and DAIJO-JI are both zen temples, diametrically opposite in appearance, but each one's head priest attains to same ultimate goal of inner peace.

DAIRAKU-JI (3km NW of stn) is run by worldly 15th generation priest ASANO Gyokon who lives modern life. His 'museum' is jumbled collection of several generations of collecting odds and ends; odd assortment of gadgets he has created over years. He guides you thru temple to beautifully manicured garden, like temple, also carved out of mountainside. One of his gadgets, solar powered motor, maintains artificial sea in his garden, keeping proper mineral balance to allow assorted salt water life to thrive—gigantic outdoor aquarium. Another of Asano's hobbies is bamboo, and he proudly shows off his bamboo which do things supposedly not possible, in all shapes and twists. Temple is also called *Musasabi-dera*, for nocturnal flying squirrels, *musasabi*, which inhabit grounds. Has even managed to breed some in semicaptivity, allowed to come and go as they please. Pleasant two hours here on otherwise sweltering day, and borrowing phone to call cab (some pilgrim) to head to...

DAIJO-JI, (2km NE of stn). Epitomal zen temple run by quiet saffron-robed priest who goes only by his title of *Roshi*. Opened as zen center 1980, for anyone interested—whether hour meditation, overnite, weeklong stay or to enter as full *deshi* (disciple) living frugal life of monk in training. Roshi with deshi spend hours together meditating, deshi must undergo rite of begging for their food and what is eaten here is all true *shojin ryori* vegetarian priests' fare.

Thanks to ancient locomotive we spent pleasant afternoon here in Yoshida, truly experiencing temples of Shikoku in way that very few modern pilgrims rounding Sacred 88 by tour bus would.

YOSHIDA only 15min rail from UWAJIMA, expresses stop but not limited expresses.

En route Matsuyama from Uwajima, stop off at...
OZU, (2hr local, 1hr20min express, 1hr ltd exp). Here, you can ride down river in wooden boats 6/1-9/20, ¥8,000 (10 persons) for 2hrs. Cormorant fishing here on small scale early Jun-Sep 20, ¥2,500 per person. Must arrange former thru City Tourist Bureau ☎(0893)-24-2664, as you rent whole boat (7 persons), but may be able to get on with other's small group if lucky. Covered *yakata-bune* boats for cormorant fishing leave from Kokumin-shukusha Garyu-en at 18:30.

PERSONAL DATEBOOK: Aug 25–mid-Oct *imo-taki* several spots along river bank near cormorant fishing: that is, local specialty of finely chopped sweet potato, quail meat and vegetables cooked in giant cauldron, ¥1,500 per person.

WHERE TO STAY: Kokumin-shukusha Garyu-en, ¥5,150w/2 best, but call ahead ☎24-3133. Few ¥-B-T inns: Shoraku ☎24-4143 in heart of town, Tarui ☎24-4585 nr stn. Youth Hostel behind castle.

200m downstream from Kokumin-shukusha is namesake...
Garyu-fuchi pool, near which is **Garyu Sanso mansion**, built early Meiji by local trader KOCHI Torajiro. He used Detached Kyoto Palaces of Katsura-rikyu and Shugakuin-rikyu as models and had best carpenters spend several years building it: wander thru, ¥200. Nearby section of town has *kura* storehouse-like houses.

Across river (which Apr-Oct has boat crossing from Garyu Mansion) is...
Tomisu Hill, with dolmen, stone age archaeological remains.

From Ozu, JR branch line heads inland 30min to last stop; also reached direct since spring '86 on newest, last-built JR Matsuyama Ozu mountain line stopping...
UCHIKO, pleasant feudal era merchant town with many old buildings and fine atmosphere. Two hours or so in this highly photogenic town (Hatsuka-ichi district, 10min walk from stn, near river) will do; but leave time to see Mr Ohmori, sole remaining maker of Uchiko's *wa-rosoku* (Japanese candles)

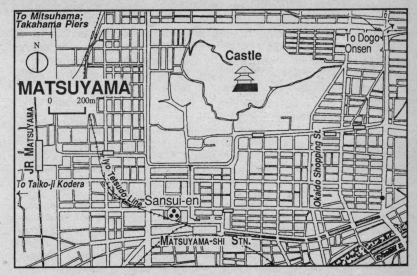

which made town prosper during late Edo & Meiji eras. This 5th generation candlemaker works out of little shop top end of town. Many old houses here belonged to Haga Family, long movers of town. *Kami* (upper) **Haga house** is small candle-making museum (¥200), coffee shop upstairs.

Few budget inns in town, try **Matsunoya Ryokan** ☎(08934)-4-2161. Rail and JR buses out of OZU only twice daily, but now frequent out of UCHIKO. Talk off and on past decade to halt red-ink Uchiko rail line and replace it with bus negated by new rail across mountains. Local Iyo-tetsu Bus has several daily out of Ozu stn; Uwajima Jidosha Bus Co, working its way up coast, passes thru Ozu hourly, stopping at center of town Honmachi bus stop, & stn. This bus continues beyond Uchiko, hour to...

MATSUYAMA 松山　*DOGO* 道後

MATSUYAMA, major port town, still has atmosphere of small town. Little for tourist to see besides castle and *kasuri* weaving museum, but fun city to visit or live in, and known mostly for its outlying hot spring ...

DOGO ONSEN, only 15min bus or tram from MATSUYAMA stn; most long distance buses to Matsuyama end at DOGO, rather than stn. All inns are at Dogo, whence short excursion into town, (buy day pass for inner-city trans, ¥400), return Dogo for relaxing bath at one of Japan's most famous baths, probably its oldest. E-info **Matsuyama International Assoc** ☎(0899)-48-6242

It is not typical hot spring resort in some rural setting. Main attraction is 100-year-old public **Honkan** bathhouse, set off from surrounding ugly concrete-box inns by its lovely antique Muromachi-style curvaceous helmet entry portico. Clumsy urbanite teacher, hero of novel *Botchan* by SOSEKI Natsume (he of ¥1,000 note)—loosely based on own teaching experience—had his misadventures teaching here, caught swimming in big bath by his unruly students: tho Soseki himself used 3rd floor private bath. Dogo onsen said to be over 3,000 years old, 'discovered' by stork which dipped injured leg into spring here. Has always been popular with nobility, and court from Kyoto used to make special bathing expeditions here for bath's healing. Prince Shotoku ventured here from Nara in 596AD.

Present structure was built in 1894, bringing end to outdoor baths and professional 'back-scrubbers': woeful 'modernizing' effects of prudish

Western thought in early Meiji era. Even if not to bathe, building should be
seen. It is marvelous, doesn't seem so large from outside, but it's
incredibly spacious once inside. It is in excellent condition for its age and
heavy traffic; let us hope that when it finally has to be fixed up (in another
century or so), common sense prevails and some modern monstrosity is not
put in its place. If that should happen, there will be absolutely no reason to
come here.

Bath is open daily 6:30-23:00. Drum in rooftop tower thunders out at 6:30 letting
you know bath time has started. Has four 'ranks': cheapest is bath only ¥250; ¥620
also gets you into large public sitting room, *yukata* to lounge around in, *matcha*-tea
and cakes. These two ranks use large *kami-no-yu* (god's water) baths on first floor.
Then there are smaller, 'personal' *tama-no-yu* (jewel water) baths on 2nd floor:
where ¥980 gets you sitting room, *yukata*, tea and cakes. Royal rank, ¥1,240 gets
you beautiful private sitting rooms on 3rd floor with *yukata*, tea & cakes, and use of
tama-no-yu. First 3 ranks have hour time limit, top gives you 80min, but these
limits usually not enforced except for top rooms when crowded. Chances better to
get top floor room in morning, but big rooms are fun. Garet found top rooms taken
(put name on list and come back) at nite, so had enjoyable time for ¥620 and came
back early next morning to see what ¥1,240 is like. Both fine, one lets you mingle
with locals, who line up outside from dawn to rush into lower ranks at opening
drum, many for daily dip; other is quiet and relaxing. Jay & Sumi returned '85 with
overseas visitors, and after almost 30 years found it as enjoyable as generation ago.

Slippery feeling of water is due to its high alkali content, good for complexion; everyone just lies around on stone floors, but unless empty, swimming
will get you same treatment as Botchan. ¥210 for short guided tour of truly
imperially adorned **Yushin-den** annex, specially built in 1899 for Imperial
Family, including lacquered drop-toilet (never used, which is why stiff-
upper-lip universal with royalty). **Botchan-no-ma**, 3rd fl sitting room not
used any more, where Soseki did some of his writing. Colored dumplings
on stick which come with your tea (¥50 each for extras) were his favorite and
are called *Botchan-dango*.

At other end of shopping arcade and opposite spectrum of public bath
aesthetic is superb, modern **Tsubaki-no-yu**. This superb example of
sento-public bath tradition grafted onto modern taste shows Japanese
artfulness is not dead. But it seems to be having little influence on hideous
cement pillboxes sprouting up all over like concrete toadstools.

WHERE TO STAY: There are some 100 officially registered inns and hotels
here, most are ¥-hi-T-Sw/2; best of which recent **Katsuragi** ☎(0899)-31-5141, right near
bathhouse, some English spoken; New **Takara-so** ☎41-7151 on hill next to bathhouse;
and **Dogo International** ☎41-1137, next to Katsuragi. All three have W-style rooms
as well; resort class **International** has completely J-style annex, **Yamato-ya Besso**
☎21-7771 on hill overlooking Dogo, and has just opened **Yamato-ya** ☎41-1171 near
by. Of moderate range inns, we stayed at **Midori-so** ☎21-3807, fine family-run place
down side alley 2min walk from bathhouse; booked thru **Ryokan-annai** at Matsuyama
stn. Coming from stn, thru covered shopping street (worth strolling thru, in your inn
yukata) and first R, **Midori-so** is on L. Alley may be bit shoddy, but it is no reflection
of inside. They even did our laundry while we slept. Youth Hostel **Matsuyama**, ☎33-
6366 conveniently few minutes from bathhouse, up behind ISANIWA SHRINE. Wherever
you stay, be within short walk of **Big Bath** as that's why you came here, hotel and inn
baths are nothing in themselves yet Japanese tourists come for them and bypass fun of old
bathhouse!?! Better idea would be to stay elsewhere distant and schedule Dogo as midday
bath stop then go on.

SHOPPING: Covered shopping street from tram stn, recently restored to Meiji-
Victorian quaintness (ignore taxi-touts, you want to be down near bathhouse) takes sharp
R halfway and continues R to front of bathhouse. From stn about 100 feet on R is

interesting bamboo goods store, **Takeya**. Near it, also on R is **Piccolo Mondo**, a *Tobe-yaki* store: local porcelain made in hills outside of Matsuyama-Dogo at Baizan-kama kiln (where you can see potters work), at town of IYO-TOBE. It was started here between 1596-1615 by Korean artists brought over after Hideyoshi's Korean campaign. Easiest way there is on JR express bus to Tosa, 30m into TOBE. Also frequent buses from Iyotetsu Matsuyama-shi stn. Further down street, also on R is **Akitsuki-do**, specializes in wood masks (¥4,000-15,000). Turn corner and on R is **Koizumi,** reasonably priced gift shop with mostly local crafts. Further down on same side is interesting shop called **Tanuki Noren**, with all sorts of bric-a-brac, mostly having to do with tanuki (badger). Facing is coral specialty store, branch of Shikoku's main coral dealer, reasonable.

There are numerous temples and shrines in Dogo area, making for pleasant day of wandering, particularly in April when cherry blossoms are in full bloom. Dogo has put out orienteering course covering all 28 points of interest in area; you might pick up accordion-like stamp book (*stamp-cho*) to record your visit, ¥200 at almost any store or inn.

Worth seeing for casual visitor are some sites right around spa...
ISHITE-JI temple (#51 of 88). 15min walk SW, up hill from Dogo center, lovely pagoda in quiet compound, gate 1318AD, draped in pilgrims' sandals. Also has wood workshop, tea shop and view of Kobe Daishi Monument.

ISANIWA, beautiful red & white Shrine built 1667 by then-lord of Matsuyama in thanks for victory at *yabusame* mounted archery contest (prizes were often priceless art objects or large parcels of land). Many swords, armor and other samurai weaponry in its treasure hall; covered hall surrounding complex decorated with many *ema*, votive shrine pictures.

Of historic, but little visual interest is...
RAIKO-JI temple about 1.5km W of Dogo. On its grounds are graves of several dozen Russian soldiers captured during 1904-5 Russo-Japanese War. Injured were cared for at this temple. In that war Japan earned international renown for toughness of her soldiers and graciousness of her jailers (officers brought over wives, etc).

Around it are several of 28 sights of Dogo...
TENTOKU-JI temple up street is prime for viewing sakura. One particular tree in complex is called '16th-day sakura', from local story immortalized by Lafcadio Hearn. Son of temple's ailing priest heard that one should not die without seeing sakura, and prayed feverishly for his father to make it thru to spring. Instead, legend says this tree miraculously blossomed 16th day of new year, so dad died happy.

From here, it is little under 1km, 15 min walk or 5min tram from Dogo; take any tram *but* #6 to O-KAIDO. S from tram stop is main shopping street, with many fine budget eating places. We head N 300m to ropeway and parallel chairlift, (¥160 o.w., ¥310 r.t.) up to castle; ¥570 r.t. and castle admission, latter only is ¥260.

Matsuyama Castle: Mostly original, completed in 1627 after 24 years construction, for KATO Yoshiaki. After his death it was granted to Matsudaira, sub-clan of Tokugawa. Built to withstand any size attack from unruly Tosa clan to south, its hilltop location saved it from wartime bombs which leveled city below.

Street from tram stop to ropeway has some good stores: about 15m/50ft in on L is **Mingei-kan**, packed with local folkcrafts. Slightly farther up, just after road angles R, also on L, is small antique shop **Furukawa**, English sign almost as big as shop itself. Owner Mr Furukawa speaks English, and carries lots of pre-Meiji and early Meiji goods; old *Tobe-yaki* and Kutani wares; and mountain of old scrolls—many fine ones if you have patience to dig thru. Tell him roughly what you want and he usually comes up with it.

1km W of JR stn...
TAIHO-JI temple, graceful sloping 1200-year-old roof.

Opposite is...
Kodera Museum, hundreds of artifacts excavated from Kodera (500m W), Yayoi period village discovered 1972. Museum free, X- mon, hols.

It is 10min bus from here back into town at...
MATSUYAMA-SHI stn, main terminal of Iyo-tetsu Electric Rail, 500m S of castle (some trams end here). One stop north of Matsuyama-shi is OHTE-MACHI stop, in front of JR MATSUYAMA stn. Iyo-tetsu Bus Center is just across from Matsuyama-shi stn.

From here, 10min bus (cab just over basic-mtr) to...
SHINONOME SHRINE better known as *Noh-men Jinja* (Noh mask Shrine). Housed here are several hundred Noh masks and costumes dating from mid-12th thru 19th centuries. Also large collection of samurai weaponry offered here by various lords of Matsuyama.

Matsuyama is famous for its folksy, indigo blue-dyed textile *Iyo-kasuri—Iyo* is this area and *kasuri* indigo ikat weave. Started here 250 years ago, it ranks among Japan's top weaves. Sold all over town (slightly over-priced in Dogo), but best place is **Iyo-kasuri Kaikan** Hall, (2km N of JR stn; daily 8:10-16:55, ¥50): see weaving being done on looms, dyeing, with good, large exhibit on making and history of *Iyo-kasuri*. Prices at store here are competitive with best deals in town, starting from ¥10,000 for one *tan* (roll 12+mtr/yds long) depending on pattern. Museum is on way to Mitsuhama harbor, convenient by bus or Iyo-tetsu rail. 15min by bus and 2min walk, or 10min electric to KOROMO-YAMA, 3rd from Matsuyama-shi, and 5min walk.

3 stops from Koromo-yama (15min from town) is...
MITSUHAMA HARBOR, from where ferries for IWAKUNI and YANAI, some to HIROSHIMA. Most leave from MATSUYAMA KANKO (tour) Harbor, 2km beyond, electric's last stop.

TAKAHAMA: Boats from here head to KOKURA and BEPPU (4hrs) on Kyushu, ONOMICHI (1hr25min hydrofoil), MIHARA (same), KURE, HIROSHIMA (2hr40min ferry, hour hydro) on our Sanyo route. 9hr to KOBE. Most runs frequent, especially to Hiroshima; get exact schedule at JR stn **Kanko-annai**.

GOGOSHIMA ISLE, just 2km offshore from two harbors; 2 hils, great view from Takadosan platform. Interesting festival **Oct 6**: makeshift stage set up on 2 boats to recreate battles of Iyo pirates in dance-drama. Villagers watch from shore. You can get fishing boat to cart you over for festival.

If in Matsuyama **mid-Aug** you will see thousands of people dancing in streets. Not celebrations for winning summer national play-offs of high school baseball; it's part of Matsuyama *Summer Festival* parades and honors one of founding fathers of baseball in Japan— SHIDO Masaoka: author and friend of Soseki (two lived in same boarding house for some years) and also teacher of English in Matsuyama. Baseball was first seen in Japan around 1873; 15 years later, Shido began to teach students at Matsuyama Junior High how to play and it spread. But it is as writer that Shido is best remembered, **Memorial Museum**, *Shido Masaoka Kinenkan* in his honor near Matsuyama-shi stn.

PORT OF IMABARI, 40min express or hour local JR up coast, ferries to BEPPU, ONOMICHI, HIROSHIMA, MIHARA, TAKAMATSU, KOBE, OSAKA, and island-hoppers. ONOMICHI–via Habu–Yuge–Iwagi–Kinoura (90min 9x ¥3,280 Imabari Kosoku-sen ☎0898-32-6890; via Setoda–Ohmijima (85min, 6x) Setonaikai Kisen ☎0848-22-4178.

*people tractable, civile, wyttye, courteous, without deceyt.
in vertue and honest conversation exceeding all other nations
lately discovered...* — Father Froes, *History of Travayle*, 1577

KYUSHU 九州
NINE STATES

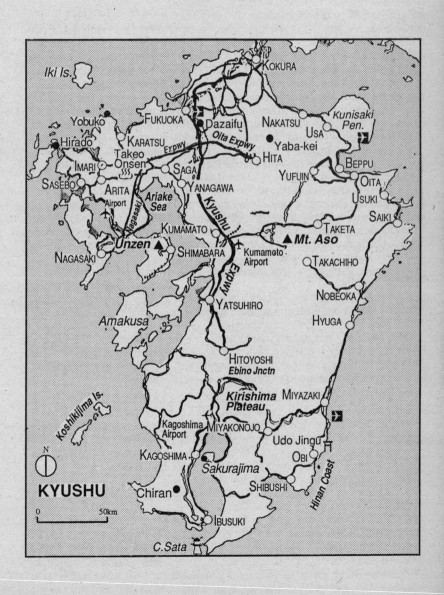

SOUTHERNMOST main island, its name means 'Nine States', referring to its former feudal subdivisions. Most of Kyushu was never thoroughly under repressive thought control state of Tokugawa shoguns in Edo-Tokyo. Kyushuite to this day stands out among other Japanese for his individuality and independent ways, his directness which other Japanese consider coarse but which Occidentals long in Japan find refreshing (if at first somewhat shocking). Yet he is conservative, clings to old ways central areas of Japan have long given up: and to many which other parts of Japan never knew. It was southern Kyushu's powerful Satsuma clan, along with Shikoku's Tosa and Honshu tip's Choshu, who brought about downfall of Tokugawa shogunate and return of Emperor as head of state. They are isolated, not because they reject our world but rather because they chose isolation from other Japanese and thus cut themselves off from much of foreign contact and influence which filter down thru bottleneck of Japan's main gateways to outside world – Tokyo and Kobe-Osaka. This has not always been so; and surging 'internationalism' in southernmost Kagoshima should soon make that pleasant city another major gateway to Japan.

It was here that Ninigi-no-mikoto, grandson on mother's side of God of Creation Takamimusubi-no-mikoto, and on father's side of Sun Goddess Amaterasu-no-mikoto, which two primary deities sent him 'to pacify and rule over isles of Japan'. He landed at Mt Takachihonomine in S Kyushu. His divine spouse, whom he married against wishes of his parents, is Goddess of Mt Fuji, indicating intermarriage between invader and native. Their great grandson continued this pilgrimage of conquest across Inland Sea to Yamato to become first earthly Emperor, Jimmu Tenno. Kyushu saw Empress Jingo in 2d or 3d century AD and Hideyoshi in late 16th century set forth on their conquests of Korea. Here, too, Mongols made their attempts to conquer Japan in late 13th century, near modern port of Hakata-Fukuoka –for millennium gateway to China and Korea. Five centuries ago Japan's first contact with West brought Roman Catholicism, which made great inroads hereabout. Century ago it was this area which first welcomed Western civilizational technology – armaments – fittingly enough, to use to preserve their own isolation against more Western incursion, sifting that which they wanted and rejecting balance.

Tho isolated, inhabitants were not ignorant of outside world. Many migrants to Hawaii, mainland US and South America came from here, as did bulk of pioneers in Japan's own westward imperialist movement into Korea, Manchuria and north China earlier in this century.

Our Kyushuite, then, is no provincial bumpkin. 'I'm from Missouri' in Japan can be rendered as 'I'm from Kyushu'. He retains enough of both naivete of man of soil and practicality so necessary to survival. He respects old ways that work (or which comfort or at least don't do harm) and doubts new until proven. He has been close enough to mainstream of history but not afloat upon it, rather on its banks where he had good view of all that went on and could often see both sides better.

Kyushuites of 16th century examined Christianity. Many accepted it, and stuck to it thru persecution and in secrecy during 300 years of proscription. Missionaries 'returning' to Japan in early Meiji era were amazed at number of Christians who, still furtively, came up to them to be blessed. In early days of Japan's modernization century ago some of most profound Western and Christian influence came into Japanese culture thru such as Kumamoto Band, group of young pragmatic idealists. It was these people who overnite adopted Western skills to 'expel barbarians' and thus avoid multinational occupation and annexation of Japan, as had happened to China only decades earlier. Kumamoto men and other Kyushuites quickly mastered Western techniques and concepts of imperialism and led Japan's expansion over her 'Asian Brothers'. Presence of major coalfields forced upon Kyushu confrontation with worst aspects of industrialization, begetting some of toughest and 'sincerest' Marxists in modern Japan. Large industrial complex of Kita-Kyushu, Japan's Ruhr, is here; greatest industrial slum lies nearby. Between two lies low mountain range, vales preserving picture-book Orientalism.

Thus Kyushu as 9 states might well refer to as many states of mind.

GETTING THERE & AROUND: Meandering down thru Honshu, best is by **rail**: Bullet train now ends at Hakata (Fukuoka), from TOKYO 6hr30min, OSAKA 2hr40min, HIROSHIMA 90min; where connect to any of several lines. Ltd Express from HAKATA → SASEBO 2hr20min, NAGASAKI 2hr40min, KUMAMOTO 1hr45min, KAGOSHIMA 4hr45min. Train will get you almost anywhere, trunk lines have many runs every hour, even smallest branch lines run at least hourly. **Buses** as frequent, much more extensive. **Steamers** to outlying islands at least daily, usually more. **Air** links from all over Japan → FUKUOKA, NAGASAKI, KUMAMOTO, KAGOSHIMA, MIYAZAKI, OITA (Beppu); from our last main stop HIROSHIMA → southernmost KAGOSHIMA allows you to head up west coast to Nagasaki and out via HAKATA-FUKUOKA, covering best spots of Kyushu. East coast Kyushu is for *wanderer* with time.

Numerous **international air** routes → rest of Asia, just JAL now, but others expected. FUKUOKA connects → Hong Kong, Manila, Seoul, Pusan; KUMAMOTO → Seoul; KAGOSHIMA → Hong Kong; and NAGASAKI → Shanghai and on to Beijing. Others serve with still more in offing. **Ferry** 8+hrs FUKUOKA → Pusan, or 3hrs hydrofoil. Unfortunately, most domestic long distance **ships** are limited to Kokura and several ports around Beppu area, tho there is 20hr run from OSAKA → KAGOSHIMA.

TILT: Kyushu has so much to offer, you can spend anywhere from 2 days to 2 weeks wandering around. For *wanderer*, start from HAKATA-FUKUOKA → NAGASAKI and on → UNZEN, SHIMABARA, KUMAMOTO, down → KAGOSHIMA and up east coast → Beppu and ship out, or rail back → FUKUOKA via HITA or → KOKURA along coast.

If *short of time*, limit yourself to NW corner between FUKUOKA, NAGASAKI and KUMAMOTO as this area has most; add quick overnite jaunt down → KAGOSHIMA. For us, bright light of island is NAGASAKI. Those with little time need not see anything else in Kyushu; **fly** into new 'floating' Omura airport (completed 1983, first of its type in Japan) from most anywhere in Japan; **trains** are frequent, overnite sleepers (all classes) from Tokyo, Shin-Osaka, Hiroshima and points in between, pull into Nagasaki before noon.

With little more time, and linking with Inland Sea itinerary, one could take in hell-spa of BEPPU, taking day overland via government-proclaimed **International Tourist Route**: runs NAGASAKI → BEPPU in 12hrs on public transport, including side trip → top of ASO; NAGASAKI across UNZEN → SHIMABARA by bus or taxi, ferry, then car or bus-train combinations thru KUMAMOTO → across MT ASO; overnite ASO or force on → BEPPU. This can be done in various runs on comfortable **luxury buses** of **Kyushu Kokusai Kanko Bus**, some of *best runs* are: NAGASAKI abt 9:00 → UNZEN HELLS → AMAKUSA → around KUMAMOTO City, ASO abt 18:15, ¥10,210, overnite Aso and next morning on any of numerous from ASO crater → BEPPU 2hr bus (3hr rail); or nite at UNZEN, leave next morning 8:20 → KUMAMOTO → ASO Crater → BEPPU abt 18:14, ¥10,290. Continue on **International Tourist Route** by overnite boat to KOBE-OSAKA; or 2nd nite in BEPPU and day flight out to OSAKA or HIROSHIMA.

In reverse, day boat from KOBE-OSAKA arrives at nite, giving you 2 nites in BEPPU with early morning start to make NAGASAKI by nitefall; or one nite at Beppu, 2nd ASO. If Beppu is inconvenient to your itinerary, UNZEN is under 2hrs lovely drive from Nagasaki. Tho popular, we do not suggest making special trip to Beppu as it's gone downhill over years, worn out from too many visitors, instead **Ibusuki Jungle Spa** is much more exciting.

TOURS are available most seasons from Tokyo, Kyoto, Osaka etc, rail or fly; best JAL **Yu-Yu Tours** by Nishitetsu rail and JAL, no English spoken but you have us; examples: 4day 3nite out of TOKYO from ¥86,800, → Sujiyu → Mt Aso → Takamori for *dengaku* 'field lunch' → Takachiho Gorge → Iwato Shrine → Usuki stone buddhas → Beppu-Kunisaki. JAL's Creative and Domestic Tours have good seasonal offerings. More and cheaper planned from '91, to compete with cheaper Hawaii tour packages.

Rather, we suggest our own ending to International Tourist Route: from SHIMABARA, boat across → OMUTA and short rail → YANAGAWA, lovely feudal town of canals for pleasant nite, whence head down → southernmost KAGOSHIMA, which offers more ways out than Beppu. Comfortable, long-distance ferries to Osaka, frequent air links to all major cities on Honshu and to various Southeast Asian destinations. Globetrotting island-hopper can meander down beautiful Amami Oshima and Okinawan Islands by small boats to Taiwan. Kagoshima city is pleasant, with more for *wanderer*, in spite of volcanic Mt Sakurajima in bay constantly spouting smoke and ash.

For pottery and porcelain buff enamored of such hallowed marks as IMARI, ARITA, IRO-NABESHIMA, we have outlined fascinating tour we pioneered ourselves, to still-thriving, centuries-old home kiln-towns of these famous wares (*see* following). You can route this in long day by JR from NAGASAKI, ending up at seaside resort outside KARATSU near Fukuoka. Add extra day to this and take ship from SASEBO thru lovely 99-Isles to HIRADO, overnite in W- or J-style comfort, early start on our **Pottery Tour**. Trains are comfortable, but if you insist, our kiln tour by **cab** HIRADO → KARATSU runs around 40x-mtr; from NAGASAKI 50x-mtr: should be arranged prior to departure thru cab company, and set your rates. For leisurely doing it in two days, choice of lodgings at ARITA or nearby mountain hot springs, Takeo or Ureshino. Or skip Karatsu for feudal town of YANAGAWA, meander thru town canals on boats; or as slight detour on International Tourist Route from SHIMABARA. Budgeteers stay outside FUKUOKA toward DAZAIFU (Futsukaichi good), or overnite at YANAGAWA, or push on to FUKUOKA if early morning departure, 90min JR or Nishitetsu, latter via DAZAIFU.

What impressed us most traveling in late '80s as much as '60s thru Kyushu was incredible hospitality and friendliness of local folks. Here we must still agree with Father Froes, quoted top of our Kyushu title page—in fact this is still in agreement with first Chinese travellers of early centuries of our era who met Yamatai court of Kyushu. Some things don't change, thankfully. Many of our great 'finds' are due to advice from locals—*wanderer* will find incompetent Kanko-annai attendant, so common on Honshu, here rare exception if at all. Our two favorite big cities of Nagasaki and Kagoshima are no exception. In 1964 we wrote that Nagasaki had far and away best JTB nationwide: today, if their excellent station Kanko-annai can't be of help to you, there should be full-staff of local volunteers at Peace Park. Kagoshima has highly motivated, bilingual youths staffing city's International Tourist office. Burgeoning **Goodwill Guides** carry on Kyushu tradition of friendliness, and Arita here is especially outstanding. We suggest going to **Kanko-annai** to find inn–not out of desperation, but because we were shown to good places every time, which friends following us confirm in late '80s just as back in '60s.

Here for under ¥1,000/day—100 foreigners young & old invited to Saga and Nagasaki prefs annually for 14 days, end July-early Aug, fee ¥12,500.

Home Stay program of Terra People Assn in 33 cities: headed by Mr KOGA Takeo ☎(0952)-24-3334, who says their aim is 'not international, but interpeople exchange'.

far off hills multiply
in the jewel eye
of the dragon fly
—Issa (1763-1828)

HAKATA 博多 FUKUOKA 福岡
GATEWAY TO NINE STATES

Fukuoka – Dazaifu – Yanagawa – Hita – Yabakei Gorge –
Mongol Invasion Iki-Tsushima Isles – Fukuoka – Pottery Tour

COMING DOWN Honshu, regular rail and bullet pass under narrow
Shimonoseki Straits to emerge again in heart of hideous Kokura, alias Kita-
Kyushu industrial armpit. Your train quickly departs and 70km later pulls
into Hakata stn. We refer to city as Hakata-Fukuoka or one half of name or
other—both are same place. In feudal days, section east of main river was
merchant district called Hakata; west of river was where samurai lived,
Fukuoka. In 1889, city council met to choose name. Vote split evenly but
upper-class came out ahead—city was named **Fukuoka**. As compromise,
new rail station is called **Hakata**. However, area's arts and festivals are
better known as Hakata such-and-such, as from yore were merchant-town
affairs. City itself offers little for tourist, but is good base for short trips to
interesting sites in general area. Those who have wandered down Honshu
may find hopping nitelife here welcome change.

City of parks: old castle site west of downtown now public sports park;
just west of it watery **O-hori Park**, (10min subway from Hakata stn, 3min from
downtown Tenjin). Enormous man-made lake with isles and bridges bisecting,
once part of castle moat. SE corner is **City Museum** (¥150), with fine
garden outside, superb Buddhist and feudal era art inside (skip 2nd floor
modern art). US Consulate NW corner.

15min bus (#10 or #15) E of stn is...
Higashi Park, with great NICHIREN temple opposite monument to Saint
Nichiren—object of pilgrimage to followers of his sect. Around its base are
pictured in bronze high relief episodes from his life: miraculous lightning-
bolt which slew his would-be executioner in Kamakura, his mountain exile,
praying against Mongols and subsequent destruction of armada for which he
takes credit. Man in group with head polished by adoring strokes of
believers is St Nichiren. Behind is **Mongol Memorial Museum**,
Higashi Koen Genko Kinenkan (9:00-17:00, ¥200), fine collection of relics of
invasions. In our first edition all dumped in heaps and needed flashlight to
see, but now properly displayed, tho no telling how much still sits in some
dark corner. See famous helmet of Christian general of Christian forces,
Nestorian cross on one temple, Sacred Heart on other.

Smaller collection 500m E at...
HAKOZAKI SHRINE, however some of Mongol gear here are much later
souvenirs. One of Japan's top Hachiman shrines, dedicated to god of war
did not save it from flames of Mongols who landed at Higashi Park area
(among others) which used to be pine-lined shore. Wall remains at Imazu,
Iki-no-Matsubara, Nishijin, Takatori-kiln.

Other main site in town is...
City History Museum (free) in downtown Tenjin district, next to New
Tokyu Hotel. Building itself gem, great, red brick, copper-roofed W-style
dating 1909 when built as Kyushu branch office of Nihon Seimei Insurance

Co. Outlines Kyushu's long history of contact with continent, using mostly artifacts excavated from north Kyushu. (*See also* Mongol invasion site after following IKI-TSUSHIMA section).

WHERE TO STAY: Hundreds of places fit any budget, but we suggest stay out of town at KARATSU (**pottery course**) or YANAGAWA (handy to almost any route).

But if you find yourself here on business, late in day, or need to stay for early ship out to Iki or Tsushima Isles, in which case **Kanko-annai**, one each JR exit, large one mid-stn, helpful finding budget (say price, J- or W-style, area), sometimes some English can get you into any place. Top hotels, all W-style, ¥-S near-Tokyo rates (no Hiroshima-type 'buys') start ¥-S+%, sgl, room only: **New Otani** ☎(092)-714-1111; **Zennikku** ☎471-7111; **Nishi-tetsu Grand** ☎771-7171; **Tokyo Dai-ichi** ☎281-3311.

Top notch traditional Japanese inn **Kanaya ryokan** ☎761-2518, equally convenient to downtown or stn, but along river and with fine garden runs as much w/2 as ¥-S W-style hotel room alone (¥-Sw/2).

¥-T-range W-style hotels numerous: such as **Hotel Rich** ☎451-7811; **Personal Hotel Ryu** ☎711-9111; **Lions' Hotel** ☎451-7711; **Hokke Club**, ☎271-3171 (stayed in ¥-B wing after late nite arrival from Tsushima, small, spartan but clean rooms).

¥-B Business Hotels abound, some include breakfast, usually continental: cheapest are **Green Hotel** ☎451-4111; **Riverside Hotel** ☎291-1053.

GETTING AROUND: **Airport** is 10min cab (2x-mtr) from town, 20min **bus**, most top hotels have shuttle 10-15min. **Port** is 1km from downtown, same distance as Hakata stn, 15min bus stn to port. **Subway** starts Hakata stn and Higashi Park, converges middle of town heading W under main downtown district, to Meinohama where it merges with JR out to KARATSU. Nishi-tetsu Electric **rail** starts downtown Tenjin district, across from which stn is main bus terminal for out-of-town runs.

BUS TOURS: We suggest for those here on business but with time: **Yanagawa Course**: take Nishitetsu from FUKUOKA. At YANAGAWA canal cruise visits main sites, ret to Yanagawa Stn 15:50; ¥4,400. **Aso Course**: changes often, but typical for summer is: dep Tenjinbashi Bus Center 8:10 via stn (8:50) to Aso volcano, Kikuchi Keikoku Gorge, ret 19:00; ¥6,700. Both tours daily (from Mar-Nov weekends & holidays only). Nishi-tetsu rail is quicker, more convenient than JR for trips to DAZAIFU, YANAGAWA, KURUME and AKITSUKI (combine with bus). However, Rail Pass users can do all on JR.

NITELIFE: Friends who grew up here rightfully call Fukuoka drinker's paradise. Hundreds, or rather thousands of establishments in town range from local *yaki-tori* or *sushi* joints barely large enough for 8-10 (both in buildings or some of 250 *yatai* push-carts, Japan's biggest concentration) to great student drinking halls. Restaurants equally divergent in type and style. Most everything concentrated around two main downtown districts: **Nakasu** is small isle in middle of river, long since overflowed on to W bank, merging with second district **Tenjin**.

Street Life more active and colorful than elsewhere, more fun even if you are vegetarian nondrinker just observing. On pedestrian bridge to Nakasu is usually some street theater, from small bands to one-man kabuki, obviously long tradition nonbugged by prudish police as they have portable electric generators for lights and ornate sets: fun, watch, photograph freely and *drop some money, please*, and smile your thanks. We leave you to choose drinking/eating place to fit your fancy, move on to...

CHOPSTICKS: Hakata is home of *tori-no-mizutaki*, chunks of chicken in rich broth, stewed with seasonal vegetables and eaten with grated radish and citron-juice, best in winter. Well-known shops are old-timer **Shin-miura**, 800m E of port tower on Ishido River bank, has easier to reach, but not as classy branch in basement of Tenjin Bldg near Nishi-tetsu stn; and **Nabe-han** in Nakasu 4-chome has full course meals from ¥5,000. Other unusual treats: *fugu* (blowfish) as *sashimi* (raw fillets) or *chiri* (chowder). At **Tori-ichi** at mouth of Muromi River W of town, tiny transparent *shirauo* (whitefish) are kept alive, scooped out on plate and eaten with vinegar sauce; easier to reach branch store at Nakasu 4-chome, on Nakasu isle W side. Called *'odori-kui'*, dance-eat, after sen-

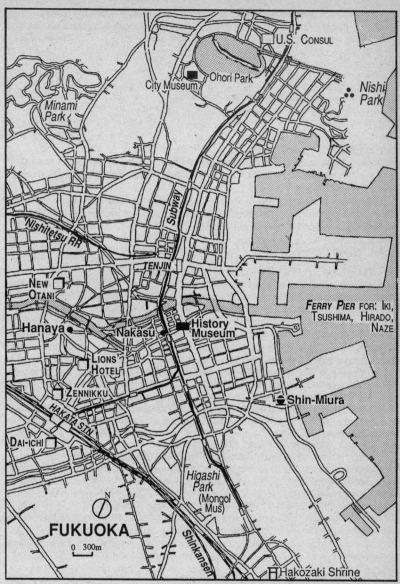

sation of miniature fish dancing their way down your throat. Guaranteed to have it in season (Feb-Mar), but not necessarily other times, at **Kawataro**, main store Nakasu 5-chome, branch at Nakasu 1-chome, and **Iwashiya** at Nakasu 2-chome. All equally known for their other (cooked) seafood dishes. Those longing for good old home town meat 'n taters will find USDA choice imported spare-ribs and international beer at **Cotton Boll**, E on main road thru downtown, L (inland) after Nishi-tetsu Grand Hotel, 2 blks.

SHOPPING: **HAKOZAKI HACHIMAN** shrine art-deco clay pigeon pots (actually white doves, messengers of Hachiman, god of sword and scythe), used for bean-popping. Opp and to L of entry is good old mingei, folk art, and curio shop. Downtown, several shops where famous *Hakata-ningyo* dolls are sold. Beautiful women are complimented on having skin as smooth as Hakata doll...of baked clay, portray common folk at traditional everyday affairs in bath, eating, playing games; prices range from few thousand to hundreds of thousands of yen—not meant to play house with. Series of small tots in mischievous attitudes are delightful, inexpensive. Classic shops **Hakata-ya**, front of **Tamaya** Dept store middle of Nakasu Isle E side; **Hakusen**, Shintenchi district between Nishi-tetsu stn—Grand Hotel.

Hakata-ori is special weave of silk, firm like grosgrain ribbon, famous for kimono obi sashes; made up into handsome men's ties and other such trappings. Good selection at **Nakanishi** where it is made, 4 blocks E of **Tamaya** Dept store; **Matsui**, on 4th floor of Matsui Dai-ichi Bldg, next door to Hakata dolls' Hakata-ya; see it being made at **Hakata-ori Kaikan**, 5min walk S of stn along tracks, from JR 'back', E exit. *Hakata-ningyo* and *Hakata-ori*, along with folkcrafts from all over Kyushu, sold in JR stn at Datos' **Omoide-no-machi**. Hakata is also known for beauty and superb cutting edge of its scissors, *Hakata-basami*, now made only at **Takayama Shoten**, down main street from stn and L at first street past Gion subway stop. Can be bought in several department stores and stn Datos.

If you can't make our **Pottery Run**, *(follows)*, fine Karatsu-ware at **Imaemon** and Arita at **Fukagawa** porcelain. Both stores are on small shopping street, 2 alleys harborward of Nakanishi Hakata-ori store and 1 block S.

PERSONAL DATEBOOK: *Tamasaseri*, sacred football melee at Hakozaki, **Jan 3**; 1-3pm. *Toka Ebisu*, **Jan 8-11** Ebisu Shrine procession of geisha in palanquins. **May 3** *Dontaku* combined with port festival, sees assorted colorful processions and dance groups put out by local neighborhoods, companies, anyone that gets it together. **July 11-15** *Gion Matsuri*, is Hakata's main summer fete, during which time, every section of town puts out huge floats (16m tall), each gaily decorated and adorned with lanterns. 12th and 13th afternoons is parade of floats, as all gather at Kushita Shrine. 15th, 5am, all floats start out at 5min intervals from shrine, race thru town to Susaki pier. Almost 5km run with 28 young men carrying 750kg (1700lb) floats. Fete dates to Kamakura era when plague was on city, local priest said purifying city with mikoshi and smoke would cure it; apparently did, as festival still happens. **Sept 12-18** *Hojo-e Festival*, Hakozaki Shrine, 100s of stalls around shrine. *Hakata Okunchi* **Oct 23** and closest fri-sat, autumn festival of Kushita Shrine, guardian spirit of Hakata. Sat procession starts with sacred mikoshi pulled on ox cart, children's procession, feudal parade, modern items like brass band, etc.

For more spectacular summer festivals, head up to Kokura (otherwise avoid). Bit hectic, but using Fukuoka as base and shuttling you can catch main days of Fukuoka's and Kokura's *Gion festivals*: **Jul 10-12** Kokura *Gion Drum Festival* each district in town fields *taiko* festival drum squad, colorful floats. Climax **11** Kokura Castle as all drum squads compete for prize and 100-odd floats gather. **13-15** *Toba Gion* with daily processions of giant floats, at nite each district puts out 10m tall floats, each covered with 309 lanterns and weighing 2.5 tons. **14** nite, all gather at Aso Hachiman Shrine and race. **Jul 18-23** *Kurosaki Gion* procession (usually 23) 9 floats accompanied by drums, flutes. **Jul 21st** nite is *Takato-yama torch procession*, as 2,000 torch-bearers ascend hill across narrow inlet from Toba, suburb of Kokura 5km W; Kurosaki same distance beyond Toba.

Nov sunday nearest 10th, Sumo Grand Tournament (*see* p.62), 15 days ends sun. Rest of month rikishi travel thru countryside for demonstration matches.

DAZAIFU: Main Kitano Tenjin shrine to SUGAWARA Michizane, alias Tenjin-sama, Shinto apotheosis of scholarship. Exiled from Imperial Kyoto 901 AD and made governor of southern approaches, where he was chief customs and immigration inspector. Posthumously exonerated and promoted, later 'deified', more accurately beatified, and by popular acclaim rose to his present popularity. At Dazaifu are his shrine and nearby archaeological remains of capital—only foundation stones for wooden pillars of buildings remain. City began 6th century as center for contact with mainland; for emperor Tenchi's military excursions into Korea (660AD) developed into major military, economic, government center and by mid-Heian era was one-third size of immense Kyoto. After Michizane's death, son tried to avenge father, city was razed, never to regain former splendor.

Shrine is noteworthy for hundreds of thousands of students who make pilgrimage to it every year in supplication for success in high school or college entrance examination or graduation employment test. They leave little *ema-e*, house-shaped wooden plaques on which is drawing: usually self portrait of supplicant, often pictured performing that act he is asking help for. You will see them hanging in hundreds on shrine grills. Shrine sells, as talismans, writing brushes, ink sticks (Michizane was noted calligrapher), and such traditional scholars' paraphernalia, at school child prices, as well as modern W-style schoolbags, pencil boxes and such. These, of course, are considered especially auspicious. But in case this is not enough there are *Gakko Gyo-no Omamori* (miraculous medallions to assure scholastic success), from ¥500, much cheaper than tutor or crib-sheet. Small **museum** (¥200) in shrine compound has Michizane memorabilia. Facing shrine is **KOMYO-JI** Zen temple, was part of shrine complex until Meiji split Shinto-Buddhism. Has wonderful moss and white sand landscaped garden. 10min walk E of it is Fukuoka Pref **Kyushu History Museum** (9:30-16:30, free, X-mon), with artifacts unearthed here and at other excavations; set chronologically.

Few km down road from Dazaifu palace site is...
KANZEON-JI temple, lovely ancient compound in which beautiful temple treasures include 20 fine Buddha images and one of most beautiful masks for bugaku (court dance) we have seen, all reset in new **museum** building (¥300). Further down road are old capital's stone foundations.

GETTING THERE: Can be reached from FUKUOKA by **cab** in under 30min (10x-mtr), cabs available for return; 40min **bus** or Nishi-tetsu electric (some change at Futsukaichi for last 2.5km); JR 20min to FUTSUKAICHI and bus or 3.5km walk. On way one passes thru ancient 7th century great earth wall of city. For driver or cyclist there are excellent English and Japanese direction signs and historical markers which with fine roads make this whole area pleasure for exploring.

GETTING AROUND: Full tour of DAZAIFU and environs about 3.5km circular walk from Nishi-tetsu stn, and if not in luxury of **cab**, can rent **bicycles** at stn Kanko-annai, ¥400/2hrs. Pleasant walk tho, especially late March when over 8,000 plum trees around shrine burst into blossom. **Alternate lodgings** for Fukuoka, nearby FUTSUKAICHI is hot spring spa, with dozen inns (most ¥-Tw/2). Weary budget-travelers find public onsen bath, **Gozen-yu**, in Futsukaichi; ¥50 to bathe, ¥400 for all day in upstairs lounging area, towel and soap supplied. Budgeteers have Youth Hostel 600m behind above shrine, up side road at 'L'-bow in main road before shrine. Bit beyond YH is *Kokyo-no-Yado*, Public Inn, **Nenkin Center**, ¥-Bw/2. Particularly during spring plum and cherry, and autumn maple viewing, 'unofficial' inns open up, worth checking at **Kanko-Annai**. Numerous good coffee shops around. Great children's schooling pilgrim trade has resulted in amusement park being erected next door and you are likely, as we did, to walk up hallowed shrine path to accompaniment of March of Wooden Soldiers.

PERSONAL DATEBOOK: *Ennichi Shrine Fair* **24-25th** most every month, plus Jan 1, 4, 7, (when demons are smoked out & original Liar Birds marketed), Jan 15; Feb 11; lunar new year, Mar 15; Apr 3, 10, 29; May 3, 5; June 30; Aug 31; Nov 3, 15, 20; Dec 15, 31.

Much of North Kyushu is for *adventurer*, its scenery is adventure. Plains are scarred by miniature 'Mount Fujis', black and unbeautiful: slag from old, often abandoned, coal mines, which were also mines for some of modern Japan's major economic, social, political ills, & Marxist stronghold. Poverty of this area sent many of its people migrating to Manchuria, which conditions were further aggravated by their replacement by Korean slaves, crowded by subsequent forced repatriation from Manchuria at war's end. New industrial complexes since first edition are alleviating economic woes.

. *Long-time Fukuoka resident friend of ours introduced us—if in Dazaifu area with time to spare, see pleasant old feudal town of...*

AKITSUKI, 'Autumn Moon', which is nearby. Was main outpost castle town of Fukuoka's Kuroda clan, and many old *buke-yashiki*-samurai houses and merchant sections remain, albeit weathered.

Midtown is...
History Museum (¥200) in one buke-yashiki; across from it is old school for sons of samurai.

Up behind Info booth is Akitsuki...
Pottery Kiln & **KOSHIN-JI** temple, ancestral cemetery of Kuroda, fine rock garden. Two each of budget ryokan and minshuku here, of former: **Akitsuki-so** is noted for its cooking, could be pleasant nite in countryside for those looking for peace and quiet. Those with less time can, as we did, head on to YANAGAWA, *next page.*

GETTING THERE: Easiest for **driver**, 25min (**cab** 7x-mtr): 10km W from FUTSUKAICHI on Rte386 → AMAGI, where N 5km on Rte322. **Bus:** 25min to AMAGI from FUTSUKAICHI (80min from Fukuoka), change, 15min → AKITSUKI. Express bus FUKUOKA → HITA (another feudal town, *see* p.713) stops AMAGI. **Rail:** Nishi-tetsu 35min → KURUME, change, 40min → AMAGI; JR 2 stops (12min) to KIYAMA, change, 15min → AMAGI, only 7x- daily.

12km E of Akitsuki on local road...
KOISHIBARA, pottery town created 1667 solely to supply Kuroda lords of Akitsuki. Still 40+ kilns in village. *Pottery fair* **May 5, Oct 10.**

Go on: 2hr30min express bus to Fukuoka, Rte 211.

KURUME, home town of ISHIBASHI Shojiro, founder of Bridgestone Tire Co. It has little to see, but is home of *Kurume-kasuri*, best type ikat hand-woven cloth, basic fabric of farmer's *mompei* pants. Much of it is done by machine, but there are still some artists who do entire dyeing-weaving process old way. See, **Kurume-kasuri Cooperative**, ☎(0942)-34-1951.

Some 15km N & W are archeologically exciting...
YOSHINOGARI RUINS, probably most important postwar archaeological dig in country: may be legendary 'Kingdom (or Queendom) of Yamatai' of 3rd century Wei Chinese annals, ruled by Shaman-Queen Himiko, earlier home of Yamato people before Jimmu's migration up Inland Sea to Nara. Nation's sole known walled habitation on continental-universal model— Japan, unlike China, Mid East, Africa, Europe, Americas, seems not to have walled its towns, only its central fortresses or castles. (Kyoto, late 1500s was another exception—but that was to wall people in, as also red-light districts of 17th century Edo).

Settlement sat atop low hill ringed by 2.5km (1.6mi) moat and log stock-ade. Evidence for warehouses on stilts, tall watchtowers and homes has been built on for excellent restoration. Excavation of cemetery produced, so far, 2,000 funerary urns of large two-piece clay jars joined mouth to mouth to contain corpse in fetal position. Two large burial mounds are 'royal', one excavated revealed large pair of urns; goods accompanying were large bronze sword with long singular crossbar-butt and green-blue cylindrical glass beads, all ancient symbols of royalty. Dig continues. Museum on site; open 9-5pm, Apr-Sep-6pm.

GETTING THERE: Fukuoka → Nagasaki JR main line on → Mitagawa stn. **Bus** from Kurume 40min Nishitetsu bus → Tade bus stop Rte 34; from Fukuoka get Nagasaki-*yuki Kosoku Bus* → Kosoku-Kanzaki, taxi under 2x-mtr to site; budgeteer hike 30min. **Drive** Fukuoka-Nagasaki expwy to Higashi-Sefuri IC, on abt 3km.

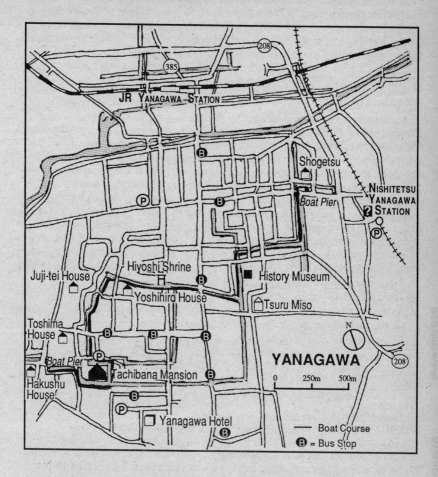

Pass up stopping at Kurume continue instead on Nishitetsu Line, tokkyu 17min to...
YANAGAWA, beautiful town along endless canals which we boat on—
especially lovely in light rain.

GETTING THERE: 50min express Nishi-tetsu rail from FUKUOKA (40min
from Futsukaichi); for **Rail Passer** JR slower, suggest spend ¥400 for Nishi-tetsu from
DAZAIFU, but if you insist: catch any train out of FUTSUKAICHI, they head either →
NAGASAKI or KAGOSHIMA. If Nagasaki-bound, get off at SAGA (all stop), change to
Saga line, 30min. On Kagoshima-bound, get off at SETAKA (some ltd expresses don't
stop). Stnmaster at Futsukaichi can help choose quickest route (depends on connections),
takes at least 90min. Better place to spend nite after seeing Dazaifu, and from here can
shoot back to Fukuoka for Pottery Run → NAGASAKI, boat → TSUSHIMA; or →
NAGASAKI via Shimabara Unzen, doing our **International Tourist Route**-Part I in
reverse. Central to almost any route across Kyushu, great place to ponder 'where next?'

Meander thru town in zigzag to SW corner **Tachibana Mansion** (below)
or reverse. Our man (college student working part-time) poled off when he
saw cluster of squealing young *burikko* (present slang for 'stylish' cuties)
girls approach (there were 3 of us on board), told us you can negotiate own
boat if you wish for not much extra, to do full course which can take you

back to stn by different course. These canals were made by 16th century Tachibana family (lord of Yanagawa area) to create maze of moats around castle. Castle long gone, burned 1872, schools occupy site. Canals' source, Okinohata River empties into Ariake Sea and canal W of Tachibana Mansion full of tiny fishing boats. Boat ride started Meiji era by ex-lord for guests.

3min walk from Nishitetsu stn (first R then L) are 3 spots to board canal cruising skiff (JR stn 1.6km NW). Dep whenever full (12 max, usually 6-8) or oarsman decides to. Run all year, from 9am to sunset; in winter have *kotatsu* (foot-warmer, table with quilt over). Basic course 1hr+ (¥1,200, child ¥600), own boat for up to 5, ¥6,500.

Starting out, we pass long stretch of ancient *weeping willows* gracefully drooping down to water (whence town name, Willow-river), turning R at old sluice to control moat level. Brick buildings on L are *ramuné* factory, where they make bubbly soda in odd-shaped green bottles with marble-stoppers in them. After next L turn, giant red brick storehouses in row among old houses part of Tsuru *miso* (bean paste) company. Across from it hangs *kumote-nawa* (spider-net) used to scoop fish and eel; several more around town on side canals. R turn here down one of best stretches. Steps down to canal was only means of getting fresh water for cooking, washing until advent of modern plumbing.

Just past 2nd bridge, on L, is...
HIYOSHI SHRINE with unusual Memorial to Eels. Our boat heads to Juji-tei, old samurai residence, turns L.

Little zigzag, full frontal view of...
Tachibana Mansion, also called *O-hana* (flower), built 1697 as lord's guest house, Victorian W-fronted building hiding Japanese rear section (architectural statement of Meiji Japan) was added 1870s, expanded 1909. Garden of 280 pines in rear modelled after pine-covered isles of Matsushima Bay in northern Sendai, one of Top Three Scenic Spots of Japan; home every winter to 500 wild ducks: ¥420 to see mansion, inside museum of Tachibana family treasures—they own and manage hotel. Or can stay here in newer '85 annex O-hana Hotel ¥-T+w/2 (*below*). Boasts superb restaurant, *unagi* (eel)-seafood combo or *kamo-ryori* duck & veggies Nov 15–Mar 31, ¥8,000 each in special rooms; much less a la carte in main dining. Must reserve ☎(0944)-73-2189, same to reserve rooms.

At bend is...
OKINOHATA SUITEN-GU shrine, dedicated to *kami*-spirit of water who looks over children. Locals bring newly born here to be blessed, and 'introduce' it to *kami*, which will then protect it from mishaps like falling into canals. Colorful *Children's Day* fete here May 3-5.

Few minutes north of shrine and Kitahara house is ...
Toshima House, built 1801 by clan administrator YOSHIDA Toneri. Appropriated by clan and used as tea house. U-shaped thatch house was classic style of Kyushu rural farm house: not many left, but you can still see several from train window between Saga and Arita. Wander in (free) and enjoy *matcha* green tea and cakes in superb garden; waterways subtley tiered so water flows in from sub-canal, and out another.

R at intersection, and next R leads back to O-hato stn where can have cab called for your restaurant or...
O-hana Hotel: 2x-mtr if you pick one up, 3x-mtr if comes for you. Walk back is about 3.5km, hour, and worth it if you have time.

White house with diagonal grid-patterned wall was home of prolific Meiji period poet KITAHARA Hakushu, who, writing even after going blind, left over 200 volumes of poetry to his credit. Former sake brewery, went out of business 1909, city restored it 1967 and filled it with his works; ¥300. Stone markers stand out all over town, each inscribed with one of his poems.

WHERE TO STAY: O-hana Hotel: (previous page), ¥-Tw/2, ☎73-2189. Dozen other ryokan in town, mostly small, traditional, and with superb seafood from Ariake Sea and eel raised here. At stn-end boat dock is Shogetsu ☎72-4141, and nearby Wakariki ☎72-2009, both ¥-Tw/2. Looking for cheaper, little ways behind, near lovely Mihashira Shrine (gala *Autumn Festival* Oct 9-11) is fine little Hakuryu-so ☎73-1188, ¥-Tw/2, where Garet stayed. Tiny Akune ☎72-2483, near Nishi-tetsu stn, ¥-Sw/2. Some mid-range (¥-Tw/2) inns, and Hotel Yanagawa (rm only ¥8,000 for 2) in corner of town near O-hana. *Budgeteers* try Saifuya ryokan, old 8 rooms, ¥-Bw/2, *Kokyo-no-yado* Public Inn Yanagawa Hoken Center. Kanko-annai at Nishi-tetsu stn helpful finding rooms.

CHOPSTICKS: For spur of moment meals, many equally delicious restaurants around O-hana and Nishi-tetsu stn. Town famed for unagi eels (just try them and you'll see why), each house has its own recipe for flavoring and broiling. Just as you get off boat at O-hana is unagi specialists (for 200 years) Wakamatsu-ya; also good next door 'folk teahouse' Mutsuki. Corner closest O-hana is branch store of old-timer Motoyoshi, main store is 3 blocks W of stn-end dock. Shogetsu Ryokan at dock is also one of finer unagi restaurants. If ¥1,500-up too much for big lunch, head away from O-hana (W) along canal from dock past bend, restaurant Momoya with varied dishes. Odd tidal fish, not so odd shellfish of Ariake Sea can be had in seafood potpourri at Fukuyama, next to Mutsuki; or at Hama-no-Ie beyond Momoyama.

HITA (about halfway between Kurume and Beppu), should see if going Beppu → Fukuoka—but we put it here since our route exits Kyushu via Beppu. Another well-preserved feudal town–in sections, mostly along river and along road to castle grounds sans castle; has added attraction of *ugai* (cormorant fishing) late May thru Oct along Mikuma River. Onsen town, but with many ¥-B and ¥-T priced inns, nonetheless. Ideal base for adventurer wishing to explore ruggedly beautiful hinterland of North Kyushu dotted with rustic, backwoods onsen.

If avoiding Beppu, you can 'do' Hita after Yanagawa, then bus → volcanic Mt Aso and circle back → Kumamoto, Yanagawa, then do Shimabara → Unzen → Nagasaki. From Kurume → Hita is 75min local (50min by infrequent expresses) on JR Kyudai Main Line, which links Kurume to Oita.

90min bus N of Hita on Rte 212, thru some of Japan's most beautiful scenery to...
YABAKEI GORGE: All beautiful, but most beautiful part is at village of AO, popular overnite, near which RAKAN-JI temple hangs out of great cave, with 3,770 stone images. Ao-no-domon Tunnel (setting for marvelous novella by AKUTAGAWA Ryunosuke) which highway passes thru, was dug by killer-samurai turned repentant priest.

30min bus from Yabakei down to Nakatsu on N coast, where rejoin JR to Kokura.

If in Nakatsu, stop off at...
Fukuzawa Mansion, childhood home of FUKUZAWA Yukichi (1835-1901), whose father was minor Nakatsu clan official stationed Osaka. He was *Rangaku* Dutch (read: 'Western') studies scholar, foremost pre-Meiji proponent of Westernization-cum-modernization for Japan, head of first official fact-finding delegation to US, founder of Keio University, etc, ad inf–portrait on ¥10,000 banknote. It is not really mansion, but unassuming, beautiful thatched-roof house inside which are displayed samples of his writings (¥200 entry).

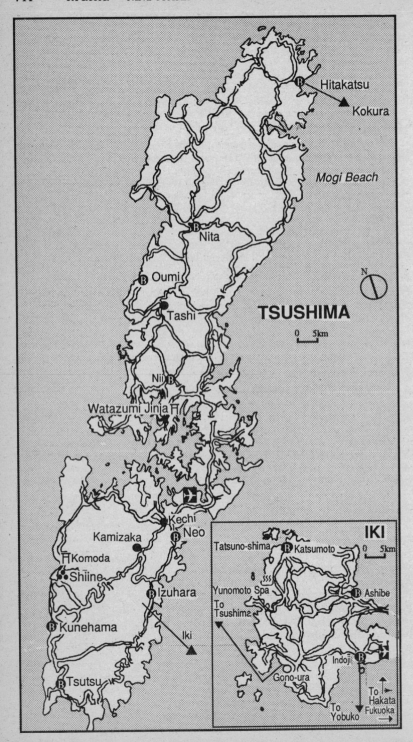

Hitakatsu

Kokura

Mogi Beach

Nita

Oumi

Tashi

TSUSHIMA

0   5km

Nii

Watazumi Jinja

N

Kechi

Kamizaka   Neo

Komoda

Shiine

Izuhara

Kunehama

Iki

Tsutsu

IKI

Tatsuno-shima   Katsumoto

0   5km

Yunomoto Spa   Ashibe

To
Tsushima

Indoji

Gono-ura

To
Yobuko

To
Hakata
Fukuoka

*From distant China across the sea
bridged by a myriad ships galloped
a hundred myriads of Mongols...*
— Japanese annals

IKI 壱岐 & TSUSHIMA 対馬
IN WAKE OF KUBLAI KHAN

OFF COAST of Fukuoka and towards Korean Peninsula are IKI and TSUSHIMA, great hideaway island paradises. If going out to these isles, we suggest further-out Tsushima, much more beautiful.

GETTING THERE: Until recently, ferry was only way out to either, but NKAir has 8 turbo prop **flights**: 3x-daily FUKUOKA → IKI, 4x-daily NAGASAKI → IKI, 7x-daily FUKUOKA → TSUSHIMA, 2x-daily NAGASAKI → TSUSHIMA. IKI is 30min from either FUKUOKA or NAGASAKI; TSUSHIMA 40min. Air departures change seasonally, check. **Ferries:** 2x-daily FUKUOKA → TSUSHIMA: 9:50 is via IKI's main port GONO-URA (arr 12:25, dep 12:40), landing TSUSHIMA's main port of IZUHARA 14:55; ret 15:45 via GONO-URA (arr 17:55, dep 18:10) → FUKUOKA 20:40; and 18:40 out of FUKUOKA direct IZUHARA 23:00 which deps next am 8:30 → FUKUOKA 12:40. 1x-daily from KOKURA 22:40 → TSUSHIMA's N end port of HIDAKATSU arrives 4:35, dep 13:30 back to KOKURA 19:20. FUKUOKA–IKI ferries land at main GONO-URA, or E end ASHIBE: FUKUOKA 13:10 → ASHIBE 15:30, with 20min wait before return → FUKUOKA 18:10. 21:05 to GONO-URA, turns around next morning 6:40 → FUKUOKA 9:10.

Also passenger-only Sea-Ace **Hydrofoil**: FUKUOKA (8:40) → ASHIBE (10:00) with 10min wait before returning HAKATA (11:30). FUKUOKA (15:50) → GONO-URA (17:20) with 25min wait and back → FUKUOKA (19:15). There is extra FUKUOKA → GONO-URA → FUKUOKA hydrofoil at 11:55 only weekends and holidays 3/15-11/5, 8/21-10/31 but daily 7/20-8/20. Tiny port of YOBUKO, near pottery town of KARATSU has 65min ferries to INDOJI port on Iki's S end: dep YOBUKO 9:00, 10:40, 12:30*, 14:10, 15:50, 18:00; returns dep INDOJI 8:10, 10:50, 12:30*, 13:50, 15:50, 19:30. FUKUOKA → IKI fares ¥1,890 (2nd cl), ¥2,670 (2nd cl rsv), ¥3,800 (1st cl), ¥4,740 (special 1st cl); FUKUOKA → IZUHARA ¥3,520 (low 2nd), ¥5,140 (2nd rsv), ¥7,030 (1st), ¥8,790 (spec 1st); IKI → IZUHARA ¥1,830, ¥2,610, ¥3,650, ¥4,570; KOKURA → HIDAKATSU ¥4,190, ¥5,810, ¥8,390. YOBUKO–INDOJI has only regular 2nd, ¥1,290. Hydrofoils FUKUOKA → IKI ¥4,020. Times have not changed for over 10 years, but you can confirm both at **Fukuoka JR Travel Service Center** which has scheds of all runs out to islands; or call **Kyushu Mail Steamship** (Kyushu Yusen) locally at ☎(092)-281-0831, or in Tokyo ☎(03)-3453-8422.

IKI

IKI IS FINE, but Tsushima is better. Buses circle isle in both directions. For those (like Garet) coming from Yobuko, shortly after ferry arrival is...

Bus to GONO-URA, where port is short walk from in-town bus center; **cabs** also come out to meet all ferry arrivals at any of Iki's ports, and to airport. Small, circular isle about 50km around; many fine beaches (best near airport, on SE corner, 2.5km from INDOJI and YUNOMOTO ONSEN on W coast 10km N of Gono-ura. Several ¥-B and ¥-T ryokan at all main towns here, almost 100 minshuku dot isle, and fine Kokumin-shukusha Ikishima-so ☎(09204)-3-0124, at YUNOMOTO ONSEN—best place to stay, quiet, close enough to catch noon ferry to TSUSHIMA; next best INDOJI area for beaches, northernmost KATSUMOTO, or ASHIBE. Anywhere you stay offers feast of freshest seafood, or meat lovers can head to **Pensione Iki Bokujo** ☎4-5818 for steaks from their own *wagyu* Japanese cows. Pensione, also serves steak lunch to nonguests (call ahead), is on Tsuzuki-hama beach, N of airport. This excellent white sand beach stretches all way around to Indoji.

Wander about isle, see 'floating' **stone jizo** on Hachiman Point SE of Ashibe or rows of humorous stone '**monkey men**' made as offerings centuries ago by some lord, at ONTAKE SHRINE N of Ashibe. We took first boat out of Yobuko, quick dip at beach, headed counter-clockwise around island and ending in Yunomoto for nite. Just off Katsumoto, **Tatsunoshima Isle** with 150-foot cliffs, is Iki's only 'scenic spot', tho whole island is national park, and much of it beautiful. July-Aug has regular chug boats out, hitch ride rest of year. Hot bath at YUNOMOTO ONSEN, followed by gorgeous sunset and superb meal in not so bad room, we rested for boat to...

TSUSHIMA 対馬

ACTUALLY TWO ISLES like exclamation mark; smaller southern one is KAMI (Upper, or closer to mainland), northern one pointing like finger at Korea is SHIMO (Lower). Originally just one, in 1896 Navy blasted passage for its ships at narrowest point, now spanned by 80m long arched Manzeki bridge. W side of this canal is lovely islet-studded bay, where Admiral Togo's fleet laid in wait for exausted, leaking obsolete Imperial Russian Navy 1904— considering this lopsided sure-thing-win as great accomplishment instead of PR bonanza, set nation on suicidal road to Pearl Harbor. Main town of IZUHARA is small—pleasant 15 min walk from port to town bus center (next to bus company-owned **Tsushima Kotsu Hotel**, W-style rooms). When you get off boat, don't be surprised if pleasant local police chief comes down to welcome you, and make sure you are 'properly registered' visitor and not one trying to sneak out of country. Korea may only be 60km away, but it's long swim, no fisherman will give you lift out. Crossing Rhee Line, 3hrs out by boat, will land them and you in Korean jail. Behind bus center on small hill is **Visitors' Center**, run by well-informed and helpful Miss KOJIMA Kyoko; can arrange rooms for you. Nearby **museums** on local flora and fauna (free), historical artifacts (¥150). At former, you will find that beautiful mountains of Tsushima (which make up 90% of this National Park island) are full of unusual beasts like elusive wild cat, no bigger than house cat but as fierce as equally rare martens here.

Izuhara was headquarters of local So clan, sent here by Kamakura tent government early 13th century. Heading W up river from Visitors' Center are remains of **So Clan Castle**, built 1560s. Little further on road ends at lovely wooded compound of **BANSHO-IN**, ancestral temple built 1620 by 20th lord So, full of graves of each lord wife, and noted warriors of Mongol invasions centuries earlier. Follow main river thru town, curves just beyond police station you come to first cluster of old **samurai houses**, *buke-yashiki*, surrounded by thick stone walls. Better cluster is further upstream, part of which you pass on buses heading north.

Tsushima makes for great wandering if you have time; *interesting is...*
KOMODA, on W coast of Kamishima, 45min bus from Izuhara. October 1274, Mongol invasion fleet of several hundred ships landed. Opposing them were 100-odd samurai led by SO Sukekuni who, in valiant but hopeless defense, were forced to retreat. Top of first hill out of Izuhara has monument of two wooden posts by roadside, commanding view worth stopping for. Here defeated Japanese commander and few remaining men committed harakiri. His family, trapped in little wooden castle, also committed mass suicide. Judging from Mongol tactics on Asian mainland, they would all have been decapitated anyway. Small shrine at Komoda enshrines Sukekuni; later *ema-e*, shrine offering picture, portrays mounted Sukekuni in action against Mongols. Beach where they landed is fine for swimming.

Just down coast (5min bus) is village of...

SHIINE, where you can still see dozen or so stone-roofed houses which once dominated area. There are also few left at Komoda. Roofs are flat stones laid out like today's *kawara* tiles as only way to keep roof from being literally blown off during autumn storms. Last afternoon bus back gets you to Izuhara in time to catch last one up coast to our special inn. Just outside Izuhara, near memorial markers to Sukekuni, is **Kami-zaka** hill, for grand view of islet-studded Aso bay below.

Southern tip of island is...

TSUTSU, isolated fishing village with ¥-B inns, campsite, beach. 10km down coast from Shiine, no buses, only one covers half-distance Tsutsu → Kunehama.

Wandering northern isle is for those with time, either start out early morning and/or spend nite at one of towns there. **WATAZUMI JINJA** is few kilos S of NII town, ancient shrine dedicated to gods of sea, has 'floating' stone torii in small bay in front. In 1871, Watazumi became secondary sea shrine, as **KISAKA KAIJIN JINJA** further up W coast was made into one of main National Shrines as guardian of this frontier of Japan. Twice daily boats from nearby NII-HAMA pier cross to southern isle. Mostly for school kids, AM run heads S, afternoon runs back N. During summer extra tourist runs added. Branch bus line from TASHI to shrine; and at top of hill there. Over next hill is hamlet of OUMI-NO-SATO, climbing up hillside from ocean and where bus ends, whence can take it back, or hike coastal trail 5km to catch separate branch line to NITA.

HITAKATSU, at tip, is few kilometers closer to Korea than to Izuhara. This port town has nothing for tourist, tho there is good beach at **MOGI,** (20min bus down E coast) with some ¥-B inns and campsite. There is small Self-Defense Force radar stn near Hitakatsu. At village of **MINATO** on W end of Sasuna Bay they use **flat log boats** for harvesting kelp. This type of boat (*mogari-bune*) was introduced from Korea, and probably made it to mainland Japan via Tsushima. Ancient records tell of its use in both Japan and Korea, but today they remain in use only here. Forming stepping stones to Asian mainland, Iki and Tsushima figured prominently in usually peaceful bilateral contacts, but also bloody as first stop for Mongols, and pregnantly so as this was also major staging area for Hideyoshi's 16th century invasion of Korea.

Don't take nite boat in as you'll be too late for any good inns, and if coming out here we highly recommend **staying** at our find Minshuku **Ueno-so** in **NEO**, small fishing village conveniently located 15min bus from **IZUHARA**, 20min from **airport** (**cab** 2x-mtr from either). NEO is home of *Ishiyaki-ryori* (stone-cookery) for which Tsushima is famous. All types of seafood and vegetables are cooked on large super-heated rock, same way our Persian nomad friends make their fabulous Qashgai *nun*-breads. At Ueno-so fish is caught that day by hubby, vegetables are freshly plucked from backyard garden, where they also grow their own tea. Even sake which comes with dinner is brewed locally. ¥5,000w/2, and dinner, which they keep bringing out until you can't even move, would cost double elsewhere if you could find it. Mr UENO can arrange fishing excursions for you or have him wake you up at crack of dawn to accompany him and rest of village for morning harvest of nets. Once back on land they split catch, and you get your share, which Mrs fixes up for breakfast. They have many rooms, but if here midsummer, call from mainland to make sure room available **Kanko-annai** ☎(09205)-4-3030 or direct ☎4-2975/4-2660. From Neo bus stop, walk down side street to village, continue along road curving R past harbor, and Ueno-so is at end on L-hand side, about 5min from bus stop at Mitsushima-cho. By bus, just tell driver NEO, and he'll make right stop.

WHERE TO STAY: Plenty of **inns** all over both islands, most in main towns of IZUHARA, TSUTSU, NII, KECHI and HITAKATSU. Kokumin-shukusha **Tsushima** ☎(09205)-4-2391, Takahama beach few km N of Neo, also serves *Ishiyaki-ryori*.

***GETTING AROUND*:** Buses extensive, but infrequent, with most lines only 5-6 round-trips daily; except central section from IZUHARA up to KECHI town and airport at northern tip of KAMISHIMA. Main trunk road (Rte382) continues past KECHI and airport, crosses N isle, 2hr30min up W coast to HITAKATSU at tip. Many branch lines rest of Kamishima, and both coasts of N isle, but you'll need 2-3 days to see most of Tsushima. If **bus**, pick up timetable, *jikoku-hyo*, at bus center. Its all in Japanese, but driver there will usually help you figure out which lines if you know where you want to go. People here all hospitable; it was bus driver who suggested our 'find' **Ueno-so** to us, as 'best inn on Tsushima'.

Bus fares for 2 people wandering isle will about pay for day's...
Car rental if heading up to Hitakatsu, which also makes getting around far more convenient and roads are fine. 50 **rental cars** here: **Yoshinaga Rent-a-car** has Izuhara office ☎(09205)-2-0505, Kechi (airport) office ☎4-4111, **Jingu** also rents in Kechi, ☎2-2406. Rates under standard, from ¥10,000 for 24hrs; if mid-summer call from mainland to reserve and if none available (doubtful), can rent at Fukuoka. **Taxi tours** from town which handles part of N isle, 4hrs ¥12,360 if ending airport, ¥14,420 if ending Izuhara. Can set own course and be dropped off at your inn; arrange at taxi stand near Izuhara bus center. **Bus tours** take in main sites: IZUHARA 10:20 to airport 11:00, up to Manseki bridge for view of bay, KECHI town and back to IZUHARA 12:20 for tour of town (Mansho-in, museums), leaving again at 14:00 to Kamimi-zaka hill for view, KOMODA area, and back to IZUHARA 16:45. ¥3,900 for full run, (you can do town on your own and catch 14:00 dep for half-fare); daily 7/23-9/30, wknd and hols 3/20-7/22.

***PERSONAL DATEBOOK*:** Festivals numerous, scattered thru year, majors are: **Apr 8** *Bansho-in Festival* in IZUHARA; **Jul 24** *Jizo-bon* also IZUHARA; **First sat-sun Aug** is largest, *Minato Matsuri Port Festivals* at IZUHARA (best), KECHI and HITAKATSU with various local entertainment, several folk dance troupes from Korea: Kechi written with characters 'chicken' and 'know' indicates probable old Korean religious site. **Lunar Aug 1** *Watazumi Shrine Grand Fete;* **lunar Aug 5** at Kizaka-Kaijin Shrine; **lunar Aug 15** at Izuhara Hachiman Shrine. **Nov 12** at Komoda-hama shrine gigantic Mongol drums are played.

Back at **FUKUOKA**, our ship approaches mainland and hopelessness of great Mongol invasion becomes obvious. Mountains rise straight out of sea, usually with no beach; those few beaches are shallow and completely walled in. Only great lagoon in which twin city seaport of Fukuoka-Hakata has grown up offers possible landing. Between islands are numerous rocks and reefs. Entering lagoon, it's 45min across to port by fast modern ship. Opposite side of lagoon is contrasting end of long flat spit of land where heaviest fighting of 1281 took place, one great smooth mountain. Mainland presents fantastically-shaped mountains, steep terracing making them appear even more weird. To right are long white beaches backed by pine rows, where main Mongol attack came ashore. We landed at port and drove out along scenic beach; it is lovely for summer swimming and picnicking. Several miles out are remains of great stone walls erected between 1274 and 1281, in readiness for expected second Mongol invasion.

Kublai Khan had sent small commando raid of about 30,000 men against Fukuoka in 1274, to scout out and scare Japanese. Commander had option of converting raid to full invasion if he thought it feasible. Totally victorious Mongols sent waves of well-trained and disciplined troops against massed mob of Japanese samurai, lined up behind beach like spectators at baseball game. Individual Japanese champions strode forth toward Mongol horde, each to announce his pedigree and call for individual combat: few got beyond grandpa's name before going down under volley of armor-piercing arrows and world's first guns (bamboo tubes) and bombs. Mongols were victorious, but before commander could decide whether or not to push on, he was killed by Japanese sniper archer, teenager who put long shot thru his eye. Mongol army automatically followed Plan A and went home.

Several years later, as Marco Polo reports, Kublai sent 5 ambassadors to Japan to negotiate recognizing him as Emperor of World. Warrior 'tent government' in Kamakura chopped off 5 heads, sent them home in boxes (one of 5 was Nestorian Christian and second may also have been— followers of so-called Prester John's lost Christian nation). Their graves are in Kamakura, as we saw. Kublai, infuriated, ordered invasion. Only troops immediately available were about 100,000 'Prester John' Nestorians, who had been raised for conquest of Palestine and Europe. These were bolstered by 2,000 Persian engineers and siege experts who had served with Marco Polo at Hanchow, plus about 300,000 convicts who would act as army of occupation. They set out, as Japanese report says, "hundred myriad of men crossing from China across bridge of myriad ships".

Meanwhile Japanese had built stone wall hidden from view behind dunes. They built walls behind city in mountain passes and at Mizuki on road to Dazaifu, then regional capital, and rebuilt great 7th century earthen wall from earlier invasion threat. (See this great wall on R side of main road out to Dazaifu, where 1 km of it remains, about 12+m/40ft high, now looking like natural hill, cut into and farmed in places). When you see that forest belt of pines behind beachside-wall and dunes you can imagine impossible task Mongols had of trying to land in force on a beach too shallow to admit many men and horses, (latter disgorged from LST-like boats) with advance blocked by stone wall backed up by invisible and impenetrable defense of archers hidden among stand of wiggly pines. (Antique-headed militarists of 1945 expected Americans to land here, too, which we realized and planned feint here).

Mongols hit June 1281, but Japanese put up well-organized, fanatical resistance. After about six weeks of fighting mostly from ships chained together like floating fortresses, catapults hurling bombs and Greek fire, and landing ships disgorging men and horses in greatest amphibious attack prior to World War II, or at least Gallipoli, Japanese defense began to collapse, even tho Mongols were decimated by disease. Then, as entire nation prayed at shrines and temples, black clouds arose on horizon, typhoon several weeks before regular typhoon season. (Some experts now call it just abnormal preseason storm). Most Mongol ships were destroyed; those manned by conscript Korean sailors had fled after Mongol command ignored their warnings of giant storm. Out at Hakozaki Shrine (in Fukuoka) Mongol commanders fell. Japan was saved and in thanks they named this typhoon *Kamikaze* (Divine Wind). Near end of lagoon on mainland is great mound reputed to have been mass grave of 'ten thousand Mongol dead'. Kyushu University archaeologists sank test pits some years ago, found it is just natural hillock. In 1961 Jay suggested to archaeologists possibility of scuba archaeological search for sunken fleet, but idea was dismissed: "Currents too powerful, would have torn apart, scattered and buried any remains long ago..." *National Geographic* readers now know otherwise. Some folks are always too many steps ahead.

See also preceding (p.705) Mongol Memorial Museum (9:00-17:00, ¥200) in Fukuoka **Higashi Park**, and Saint Nichiren Memorial.

Such a judge of blue and white and other kinds of pottery
From early Oriental down to modern Terra-cotta-ry.
— Gilbert & Sullivan, *Patience*, 1881

WILLOWY WARES OF IMARI
OUR POTTERY TOUR

THIS AREA holds for us one of most exciting sidelights in Japan, to experience actual history of ceramics by visiting hoary kilns which turn out such magic names as **Imari, Arita, Kakiemon, Iro-Nabeshima**. All are between NAGASAKI and FUKUOKA surrounded by beautiful **Genkai National Park**.

We start our trip from KARATSU up north, working south in order to trace local ceramic development chronologically. Starting NAGASAKI, you'll trace development of ceramics backwards in time. Either order is feasible.

1) ancient hard-baked, unglazed KARATSU pottery;
2) exquisite traditional **Iro-Nabeshima** porcelains & celadons produced in time of Tokugawa shoguns, in 17th century hide-away mountain village;
3) modern & traditional at ARITA, where entire town makes **Arita, Imari, Kakiemon** wares;
4) modern utilitarian ware of MIKAWACHI and modern 'folk pottery' at IENAGA.

TILT: One-day luxury trip by **taxi** takes you to important points and is affordable for 4-5 people. ¥36,000 (80x-mtr) covers entire distance NAGASAKI → FUKUOKA, 162km with stopovers. Starting from either of these cities makes for hard one-day trip. We recommend leaving NAGASAKI previous nite for SASEBO or URESHINO ONSEN, or from HIRADO, and start off in morning from any of three; or at northern end from FUKUOKA, start at KARATSU, which if subway-rail to, allows for lingering en route, reduces cab 1/3rd for total taxi fare ¥24,-28,000 (from Hirado) or 54-60x-mtr. This trip is easily made by trains and buses as roads excellent and service good, except for out-of-way MIKAWACHI and IENAGA. Starting from KARATSU in morning, budgeteer can, by rail, include ARITA and IMARI, ending late afternoon in NAGASAKI, or HIRADO whence cruise thru 99-Isles next day to SASEBO and continue on by land to NAGASAKI.

Devoted pottery lover will need 2 days, for which we suggest overnite stop either URESHINO or TAKEO ONSENS, where fine inns are available, going on to HIRADO, NAGASAKI or UNZEN 2nd afternoon. This also gives you chance to double back in morning to finish any visiting. If pushing thru from NAGASAKI, stop overnite KARATSU rather than strain to Fukuoka, 90min-55km away.

PERSONAL DATEBOOK: Incidentally, good time to visit is when *pottery fairs* see their surplus and seconds going at give-away prices. KARATSU holds their's fri-sun of 2nd or 3rd weekend of **Sept** (whichever closest to middle of month); ARITA is **Apr 29-May 5**; MIKAWACHI dates vary 3 days **early May–mid Oct**; and IMARI **Apr 1-5** held over for pottery, and **Nov 1-5**. Arita's coincides with Golden Week national holidays, and is largest such fair in Japan; JR runs special extras to move mobs, which usually run well over one million.

Ceramic terms can be confusing so we clarify our use here. We refer to soft clay baked at low temperatures as *pottery* (its softest variety usually made of earth only is also called *earthenware*, not found on this leg) and porcelain-based white translucent ware as *porcelain*. If it isn't translucent, it falls into catchall of *stoneware*, which means different things to different people. *Ceramic* includes both (technically it includes even glass, or anything fire-hardened). Ceramic made in certain place takes place name with addition of word *-yaki,* signifying '-ware'.

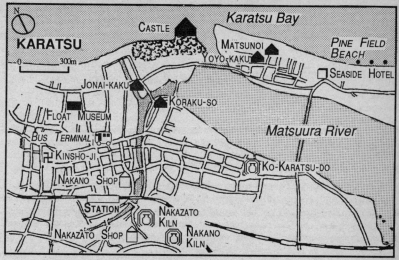

Starting Pottery Tour from N, first stop, and alternate lodging for Fukuoka City, is...

KARATSU: Already in prehistoric period, unglazed Sue-type pottery for home use and huge burial jars had developed from Korean originals. With further introduction of Korean techniques and kilns, simple colored glazes and monochrome brown paintings on pottery (*e-Karatsu*) were developed by 15th century. *Mishima* designs (incised in clay) and *hakemé* designs (created by brush marks) were two techniques highly developed by Karatsu potters. By 1595 TOYOTOMI Hideyoshi and his generals had brought back Korean potters whose techniques spread thru Kyushu as generals set up kilns worked by these Koreans to supply tea ceremony utensils.

Today in Karatsu are two quality potters, NAKANO and NAKAZATO, both of whom have their kilns just S of station, across river. Alas, but neither allow visitors into their work areas, but some junior artists do. Most convenient is **Ko-karatsu-do**, E end of town, take second road R from stn, cross river and pass thru interesting old section of town to kiln. NAKAZATO has lovely museum and sales room on stilts, across from kiln, combines traditional elements of bare ceilings with huge beams in modern, living building. His works reflect this combination of old and new with pleasant results, as seen in his gorgeous white dishes with simple light brown drawings. NAKANO has store just before bridge en route old town. Other kiln outlets also in town, most few blocks N of stn. Town-run **Exhibit Hall** next to bus center, samples of all artists for sale.

GETTING THERE: 1hr40min express bus from FUKUOKA Bus Center; or 80min rail, start on westbound subway from HAKATA stn, connect with JR at MEINO-HAMA stn halfway. Several trains go whole way to Karatsu, must change on others. Karatsu bus center is 5min walk N of stn on main Rte204; all buses stop here rather than stn for runs to Yobuko, Imari and Arita. Latter quicker by bus as rail is roundabout and requires one change of train.

Hoji Kiln store, by exhibition hall should be seen just for building and its garden, white-walled 'mansion'. Kabuki-bunraku aficionados find **grave** of Chikamatsu Monzaemon at **KINSHO-JI** temple, between stn and Hikiyama Exhibit Hall, W on main road. Spectacular main gate used to be that of nearby Nagoya Castle's; in one corner of garden is 'Christian' stone lantern, adorned with subtle crosses.

Castle 1966 reconstruction with good **museum** of usual samurai goods and local crafts. Stretching E from it is lovely pine tree-lined Niji-no-Matsubara, Rainbow Pine-Field, with fine sandy beach, most of best inns.

WHERE TO STAY: **Jonai-kaku** ☎(0955)-72-4151 (¥-Tw/2), beautiful setting in old palace grounds in fork in river near castle. Equally lovely surroundings is: **Koraku-so** ☎2-2136 (¥-Tw/2), across from Jonai-kaku; and **Wataya** ☎72-4181 (¥-T-Sw/2), known for its fabulous dinners. Just beyond, at W end of long **Niji-no-Matsubara** (Rainbow Pine-fields) are equally fine **Matsunoi Ryokan** ☎72-8131; and **Yoyo-kaku** ☎72-7181 (¥-T-Sw/2 at either). Further down **Seaside Hotel**, W-beds, tatami-roomed annex; neither worth their price. Next to it is budget Kokumin-shukusha **Niji-no-Matsubara** ☎72-5181 (¥-Bw/2) and **YH** ☎72-4526, at far end. Suggest either of these over in-town **Business Hotel**, ¥4,000 w/bkfst. Stn **Kanko Annai** is helpful in finding for any budget (80-odd inns here), can also book rooms at YOBUKO *(below)*.

CHOPSTICKS: There's not much choice for dining, unless leisurely at inns which feature specialties like *iki-zukuri* (sea bream sashimi) at **Yakko** in Chiyoda-cho and **Jonai-kaku**; but best at nearby port of YOBUKO. **Takeya** Honmachi (one block S, then one E of bus center) noted for eel dinner, also serves lunch. Around Takeya are several budget diners, ranging from regular Japanese, to curry.

PERSONAL DATEBOOK: **Sept** *Pottery fair* (see p. 720). **Nov 2-4** wild *Karatsu Kunchi Festival*, when 14 colorful floats parade thru town, led by giant, red lion head. Rest of year, floats are seen at **HIKIYAMA TENJI-BA** (9:00-17:00, ¥200), 10min walk N of stn.

35min bus N on Rte 204 35min bus N on Rte 204...

YOBUKO, small fishing village on narrow bay, which, with nearby Nagoya bay, was staging area for Hideyoshi's Korean invasion. Stonework of his castle at Nagoya remain. Built 1591, hills around castle held over 300,000 men prepared for invasion. Much of castle was dismantled and used to build Karatsu's, then after Shimabara Christian Uprising in 1637 (*see* following) what remained was flattened in fear of repeat revolt. **MADARASHIMA ISLE** in bay was major Christian stronghold.

WHERE TO STAY: Yobuko has over dozen ryokan lining either side, all ¥-hi-T-lo-Sw/2 range; two at NAGOYA, 2km beyond. Suggested at Yobuko are: **Kanamaru** ☎(0955)-82-3921 ¥-T-Sw/2; and slightly cheaper **Hiuraya** ☎82-2011, and **Matsudaya** ☎82-3734. Here in 1984, Garet asked for cheapest, and got it at **Izumo Ryokan** ☎82-3706 ¥-Bw/2, food was fine, rooms so-so. Several budget minshuku out on two small isles just stone's throw away—**KABUSHIMA & KOKAWAJIMA**. Frequent **steamers** to these isles start just up from bus stop (for Kabushima) and front of Izumo Ryokan (for Kokawajima). Yobuko is ideal for adventurer heading out to Iki and Tsushima. Bus stop is at S end of town, pier for boats to Iki at N end. Budgeteers would do best at Kokumin-shukusha **Yobuko Lodge** ☎82-3006, just around the point from Iki-bound pier; only few hundred yen more than minshuku.

CHOPSTICKS: Fukuoka's superb seafood restaurant **Kawataro** branch here, across from ferry pier. Out at Nagoya is floating seafood restaurant **Manbo**, full-course meals from ¥2,500, dishes from ¥1,000.

PERSONAL DATEBOOK: Giant tug-o'war **first wknd Jun**, pits *Hama-gumi* (bay-team, fishermen) against *Oka-gumi* (hill-team, farmers). Everyone from area participates, tug on 500m/1600ft, half-foot thick rope; with blessing of gods going to either good harvest or good catch at sea. **Lunar Jun 15th**, *Children's Gion Festival*, 50+ kids tote 15m long, 3 ton mikoshi. Summer fetes local shrines **Jul 28-30**.

If heading to TSUSHIMA from here, only **first 2 boats** to Iki will give you enough time to make connection for Tsushima ferry: 9:00 out of YOBUKO allows for bus time, 10:45 gives you 25min at other end to get from INDOJI to GONO-URA port for which must **cab**.

Continuing on our **Pottery Tour**, check if **buses** still run to Imari from Yobuko continuing past Nagoya along beautiful islet-studded Imari Bay. **Drivers** go Rte204. Otherwise, backtrack to KARATSU, from where 45min bus or slightly longer rail, change at 2nd stop YAMAMOTO.

Until discovery of porcelain stone at Izumi-yama, mid-1660s only earthenware and some stoneware was produced in Japan. Arita area now became porcelain center. These early porcelains are blue and white patterned after those of Korean Yi dynasty, later overshadowed by Ming blue and white styles. Porcelain was molded, fired at high temperature; decoration was painted on this baked biscuit with *gosu* (cobalt oxide) then transparent glaze was put on and it was again fired in muffled kiln. This method is called *sometsuke*. Although imported Korean potters knew art of enameled porcelains, it was Sakaida Kakiemon (1596-1666) who mid-17th century perfected applicâtion of color over first glaze: **Kakiemon-ware** characterized by milk-white porcelain with refined delicate designs in few simple colors. It was immediately exported by Dutch to greatly influence European workshops of Germany's Meissen, as well as Chelsea, Bow, St. Cloud of England. Today, in Arita, 13th generation Kakiemon faithfully reproduces his family ware. Others elaborated on these coloring techniques to develop intricate vari-colored brocade-like *nishiki* (brocade) one of finest of which was **Iro** (colored) **Nabeshima** (fief name). Arita itself had at one time developed neighborhood of pottery colorers, painting *aka-e* (red) brocade designs. In modern Japan this ware is generally referred to as Arita, after its center. But as it was all shipped thru one port, it is known world-wide by port name of...

IMARI: Goodwill Guides, TIC, opp stn, ☎(0955)-22-6820 notoriously fine; pottery buffs might be as lucky as our friends, draw local ceramic salesman 'Steve' Ikeda ☎22-4338 who took them to see potter-friends, or equally devoted Miss WATANABE Masako.

There's little in city itself which gave its name to porcelain, also called arita-ware, but fascinating ancient kilns of **Okachi-yama** are only 15min out by bus (¥190) to SE (cab 5x-mtr). Written *Okawa-uchi* but pronounced *Okachi-yama*, it is kiln town set against sugar-loaf mountain towers, seemingly at world's end, mountain setting from some old Chinese scroll. You climb up thru narrow dirt alleys paved with sherds. (Archaeologist could reconstruct chronology of local ware from test bore in any street.) Shop-kilns line alleys, smoke hovers below chimneys like mist below peaks, each shop little higher as each shared in ancient long sloping *nobori-gamạ* kiln up mountainside gully forming natural flue. Lord Nabeshima set up his private kilns in 1675, samurai guarded entries so only those with passes could enter or leave. This is home of Iro-Nabeshima ware designed for lord's exclusive use. Only limited number of best were kept, all others from same firing were smashed. When Nabeshima's personal demands were fulfilled, lower quality load then made for export to other areas, even Europe. Buy ceramic copy of pass at Sogo tenjijo for 10% disc all buys.

We visited SHIBATA **Gakuzan**, who works independently, mostly in biggish vases. He is one of few remaining one-man operations, throwing, painting and firing. Most Nabeshima-yaki has three colors, basically cobalt blue plus touches of nishiki brocade coloration. His painting is delicately executed, but strong and individualistic in stopping short of that deadly perfection that makes every piece look alike. (For generation many readers dropped in on him and we received messages from him via many countries, then Garet enjoyed meeting). Then we dropped in on OGASAWARA **Choshun**; rather arty items, but his celadons were lighter than usual Japanese and colors 'true'. Unusual was his 'pigeon blood' celadon, long-lost secret recently re-perfected. He uses clay from Amagusa for body and makes his own celadon mixture. Going down slope, opposite Gakuzan, KAWAFUKU Seizan's large modern place has interesting dinnerware. Our last stop was Hataman located down below bus stop: hand-painted and hand-thrown Japanese dinnerware, some with mountain landscape in blue & white. New museum (9:00-17:00, free, X-mon) fine display of Old Imari, Iro-Nabeshima.

Up on this fairyland mountain setting you see finest quality of traditional Japanese porcelains. All will fill orders and best to have them pack and ship (or freight to your final hotel, remember you've immense air baggage allowance to USA). Communal pottery market (Yogyo-danchi) can be passed up, below pottery village, which is as far as most Japanese shoppers get: fine selection of every artist's work, but you miss out on fun of seeing them at work.

PERSONAL DATEBOOK: **Apr 1-5** *Pottery Fair*. **Oct 22-24** *Ton-ten-ton* - one of Japan's top 3 'fighting' festivals. **24th**, several *mikoshi*-palanquins and wheeled *danjiri* floats pair up, get dumped into Imari River and all race to be first pair onto land– rough and tumble, no-holds-barred, yet (amazingly) no injuries. Wins special blessings. **Nov 1-5** *Pottery Fair*. **Nov end** *International Balloon Fiesta* ☎(0952)29-5247.

Warning: You will end up in Imari around lunch time, and there are no places to eat at Okachiyama, and only few budget mediocre lunch spots in town, near bus center or stn. It is not much better at Arita, though choices are greater.

ARITA is town where one could easily spend whole day.

GETTING THERE: Get off ARITA, *not* next stop Kami-Arita, which expresses between Nagasaki → Fukuoka pass. Locals from IMARI (20min) stop Arita first. Also 40min bus from Imari → Arita, runs between train times. IMARI has ace TIC opp stn ☎(0955)-22-6820, **Goodwill Guides** who can guide this far out for kilns. Can leave bags at stn, ¥200.

From station, we suggest taxi out to...

Kakiemon. There used to be two Kakiemons until about 5 years ago, but now only main line family exists: **taxi** to original **Sakaida-Kakiemon** 1.7km W (basic-mtr, but keep cab); occasional **bus** 3 stops to entrance of road to his kiln, 400m S down side street; 20min walk from stn. Got name Kakiemon from Lord Nabeshima for his lovely *kaki* (persimmon color) and his success in applying enamel color overglaze on porcelains around 1650. Ware is characterized by cloudy, milk-white foundation known as *nigoshide*, overglazed with small refined designs of flowers, fruits in delicate colors. For this *nigoshide* technique, 13th-generation Kakiemon was designated 'Important Intangible Cultural Property'. Present 14th-generation Kakiemon lives in extremely English-looking, long, thatched house with dark wooden beams across front. Produces for connoisseur and limited dept store sale: 6 morning coffee cups-saucers ¥150,000 (15x old 1964 price while hotels are 10x+); 18-inch vase with 53 stages of Tokaido, ¥3,000,000 (12x '64). Gorgeous, but bit 'too perfect' for us.

Visit museum attached with rare specimens of early Kakiemon and down thru years and early European copies of his ware. Visit separate sales and show room with more affordable pieces.

Back N towards Imari in Maruo district is Genemon's kiln and museum of early blue and white. His dinner ware is sold in Tiffany's New York.

From Arita stn, down main st, cross pedestrian overpass, follow path few mins to...

Kyushu Ceramics Museum, modern facility run by Kyushu University, excellent exhibits of all Kyushu ceramics, from earliest to present. Set up by region, mostly from Imari, Arita, Karatsu; and European imitations of fine Imari. All pieces labelled in English, also guide-cassette available at front desk (*free*). Daily 9:00-16:30, X-mon, ¥200; *do not miss*!

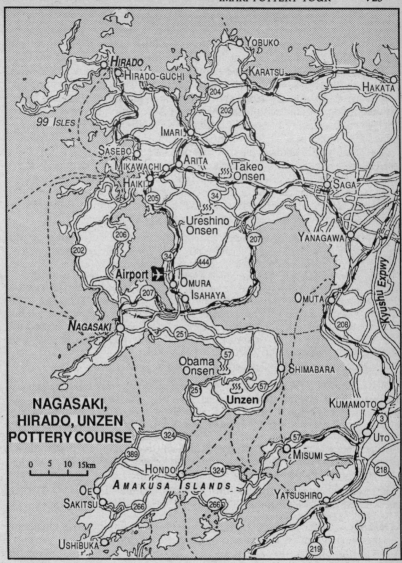

Main ceramics shopping area is 1.5km E on main road. Suggest **cab** or infrequent **bus** to E end Arita *Toji Bijutsukan* (Arita Ceramic Art Museum), walk thru town and bus or **cab** (many passing by) back. Museum (9:00-16:00, X-mon, ¥100) is in refurbished 200-year-old stone house, exhibits early preporcelain Kakiemon, early celadons ordered by Dutch (who had exclusive foreign distribution contract with Lord Nabeshima), European imitations of Japanese export ware (late 17th to mid-18th centuries) by Royal Saxon, Meissen, Delft, Chelsea (seems Meissen made best copies, even outright counterfeits – 'Oh, those Jap copycats...'). House was built as storage for export wares; was only building to survive 1828 fire which gutted rest of town. Upstairs are early Korean prototype pieces, early export ware, excavated Japanese pottery from old Kyushu kilns, half-scale reconstruction of part of Arita's first communal *nobori-gama*, climbing kiln.

L at first signal from museum is small street crossing tracks to...
TOZAN JINJA, Ceramics Shrine, dedicated to kiln-deity. Torii made by
Koransha, and guardian dogs and lanterns by Imaemon, are of ancient and
beautiful blue and white, but much repaired. Shrine was going to pot until
1970s when professional shrine-managers (originally from Arita, were
working at Nagoya's Atsuta Shrine) took it over. They are raising income
to fix shrine up, mostly from selling 'Japan's only' porcelain *omamori*
(amulets), copyrighted with National Shrine Association to prevent copies.
One for traffic safety is porcelain plaque with sticker on back; comma-
shaped *magatama* beads on string are for health.

R at same signal takes you past some odd W-style houses, *Ijin-kans* built
early Meiji as summer homes of Nagasaki British. 500m beyond, **Tengu-
dani** kiln, site of first noborigama built 1617 by Korean potter Lee San-pei,
buried nearby, marker above shrine was put up 1917 as tricentennial
commemoration of his building kiln. He also discovered Izumi-yama
quarry, 1km E, which still supplies kaolin to local artists.

SHOPPING: Back on main road, just beyond intersection is **Koransha**, for best
selection in finer more decorative Japanese sets; have lovely museum pieces upstairs.
About 100 yards towards stn **Yamachu** has inexpensive traditional platters blue & white.
Kinshodo few doors down was even better, where we discovered proprietor's uncle does
painting; will make any size, any pattern on order in month. Nearby are two well-known
shops, **Imaemon** known for Iro-Nabeshima ware and **Yoshijima Seito-sha**. Two
interesting shops are between two bridges beyond PO: **Seigado**, very small, but
distinctive with artistic selection; beyond next bridge is tumble-down looking second-hand
shop **Tani-ei Toki-ten**, whose owner does lot of excavating and is familiar with
various old kiln sites and history. His shop has old plates.

Reminder: **Apr 29-May 5** *Pottery fair,* largest in Japan.

WHERE TO STAY: Many ¥-B & ¥-T inns here: interesting looking traditional
inns near station (narrow alley L of main street) are **Matsuya, Yanagi-ya**, and
'business' ryokan **Chikushi**; new **Arita Kanko Hotel**, with W-beds, on Rte35 across
from Kyushu Ceramics Museum. But suggest **TAKEO** or **URESHINO ONSENS**:
former is 4 stops (20min) E of Arita; latter is 35min bus from Takeo, occasional bus link
to Arita. Unfortunately these once-quiet ('64 edition) Onsens have been developed into
hopping resorts, especially Ureshino; but many start ¥-Tw/2, some ¥-B. Takeo also has
3 *Kokyo-no-Juku*, **Public Inns**, ¥-Bw/2.

If interested in rural architecture **TAKEO** area and E to **YAMAGUCHI**
has squared-off, U-shaped thatched houses characteristic of Kyushu.

KOIHARA, IENAGA and **MIKAWACHI**, three tiny hamlets clustered
together just off main highway outside Arita en route Haiki or Sasebo.
These are bit difficult to visit, time-wise; best, MIKAWACHI is stop on JR
Sasebo-line, 8min from Arita. Ureshino-Sasebo buses bypass.

IENAGA, *Gagyu* kilns of YOKOISHI Shoun produce modern folk
pottery, which brings us back full circle to simplicity of early Karatsu.
Attractive line of subtle brownish-red marble glaze with *susuki-e* (Japanese
pampas grass) design, highly suitable for western dinnerware.

MIKAWACHI offers charming visit to potter HIRADO Gasho. Finding
him wasn't easy, for it seems that every other potter is Hirado and there are
22 potters here, descended from original kiln set up by Lord Matsuura on
Isle of Hirado up Genkai Coast, where they worked in clay and porcelain
stone imported from Korea. Upon discovery of porcelain raw material in
Arita, Hirado potters were moved here. We found Gasho (family name
Nakazato Tokio) almost last potter on narrow lane at foot of Shrine. He

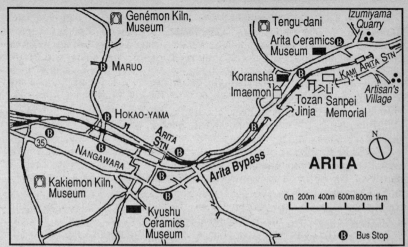

works as do most potters there, in blue and white porcelains. However, he only does *Karako-e* design of romping Chinese children. Watching this friendly roly-poly man in his early seventies, we see why his roly-poly Chinese tots have won for him recognition as 'living cultural asset'. Unlike his neighbors, his family has clung to slow painstaking hand-painting. He says its easy to spot stamped pictures, for it's impossible to print fine lines such as pine needle clusters to converge to point.

Reminder: *Pottery fairs* **May 1-5** & **Oct 6-10** (dates vary call Tourist Office ☎(0956)-24-9393).

This puts us at end of full day at...
SASEBO, pleasant town but little to see. It has, since Meiji times, been major Naval base: Japanese fleet mustered here Sino-Japan War (1894-95), Admiral Togo based here for Russo-Japanese War (1904-05) and sailed out to defeat Imperial Russian Fleet off Tsushima, sinking antiquated tubs with latest English gunnery and Tyneside ships bought with US Jewish loan (p316). After World War II US took over naval facilities, rebuilding into one of largest Asian bases. Most of it has been returned to Japanese, who filled void with own Maritime Self Defense Force. To help create local 'understanding' and support for supposedly nonmilitary force, they set up...

Museum of Naval History, across from entrance to US base. Nearby is exhibit hall on nuclear-powered ships, with sections on various types of energy and ships (both 9:00-17:00, free, X-sat-pm & sun). Bus to Kashimae passes US and M.S.D.F. bases, museums—just beyond which is massive SSK shipyards. On small hill E of town is Japan's only Naval Cemetery.

Between bases and stn is pier for ferries out to...
GOTO ISLE (*see* Hirado); nearby is site of daily *asa-ichi*, morning mart, dawn to 9am-ish, where local farmers, fishermen unload their goods at cut-rates.

WHERE TO STAY: Its fine selection of inns all budgets, for which phone ahead from Arita area, or arrange now thru stn **Kanko-annai**. Most grand are: **Yumihari Kanko Hotel** ☎(0956)-23-9221, on hill overlooking town and boasting 'Best view in Asia', road down from it leads to 99-Isles' pier; **Matsukura** ☎23-5271 conveniently across from stn, next to bus center. Both ¥-hi-T–lo-Sw/2. For slight economy, suggest stay out at **KASHIMAE**, convenient for 99-Isles boats to Hirado: **Kujuku-shima Hotel** ☎28-2111; **Kashimae Kaihin Hotel** ☎28-5151, both ¥-hi-T to–lo-Sw/2. *Budgeteers* have fine Kokumin-shukusha **Kujuku-shima-so** ☎28-5108, ¥-hi-B+-w/2, about same as business hotels in town which give no meals.

PERSONAL DATEBOOK: **Feb 24-26,** *Atago Matsuri* with plant sale. **Sun closest to end Jul or begin Aug,** *Saikai Fire Fete* at Kashimae, torch procession and dances, *taiko* drum troupes, Sunset Cruise. **Aug 1st-sat, sun,** *America Matsuri* at Nimitz Park, festivities US-Japanese servicemen. **May on day with 7, 8, 9** (ex 17, 18, 19 etc), *Haiki cha-ichi,* food, veg, goods. **Aug 8-11** *Fukuishi Kannon Temple Festival.* **Aug 20** Sarayama *Ningyo Joruri,* bunraku-style puppet plays, all day from 10am at Daijingu shrine, Watasami-cho town 15km W of Sasebo, at crossroads between Ureshino, Arita and Mikawachi. **Nov 1-3** *Sasebo Kunchi* Festival, Hachiman Shrine; regional folk dance groups perform all day at *Matsuri Hiroba,* festival plaza; parade of floats on 3rd.

NITELIFE: Bustling here, arose to keep, first, prewar Japanese navy boys, then postwar US gobs, busy and happy. Tho latter crowd has diminished, shopping streets in front of stn offer many from hole-in-wall bars (and better) to local *izakaya,* ¥-B eateries.

GETTING AROUND: **Kujuku-Shima Cruises:** Kashimae pier 4km E of town (15min **bus,** or 8min **cab** 2x-mtr). **Cobalt Line** to Hirado runs comfortable enclosed-cabin high-speed hydrofoils; ¥2,890, 70min. Times are: SASEBO → HIRADO: 9:30, 12:20, 13:35, 15:45, 8:10, 9:00, 11:00, 13:10, 14:20. HIRADO → SASEBO: 8:10, 9:00, 11:00, 13:10, 14:20.

Cobalt Line passes thru N **99-Isles** (actually over 170) to HIRADO, some with small communities which farm oyster rafts floating among them. Largest isle, closest to Sasebo, called Kuro-shima (black isle), not for its color but because as stronghold of Christians it came to be called *Kurosu-shima* (Cross Isle), which eventually became Kuro-shima. Traces of hidden Christian communities remain, and many catholic churches dot area. As you approach Hirado barely visible on R is large Setoyama church built in 1882. Combine with pottery run in 2 days and end back at Nagasaki afternoon—but if not enough time for that, some 45min circular cruises around S 99-Isles out of **KASHIMAE.** Schedules change seasonally, check at inn.

HIRADO, enjoyed boom during Christian Century (1543-1637), not so much from Europe discovering Japan but from reaction of Japan discovering Europe. Portuguese traders came shortly after 1542, initiating open trading by selling guns in southern Kyushu. Lord of Tanegashima, who overpaid for first few, proceeded to have his swordsmiths forge perfect replicas which were being mass produced within year (thus Japanese name of first muskets Tanegashima). Portuguese found other things to sell, notably Christianity (local tourist office claim that Xavier was captured by local pirates and landed here is false; he did visit in 1550, however). Spanish ship arrived in 1580, Dutch in 1597 and British in 1613. In 1600, 160-ton Dutch ship *Liefde* (Charity) arrived off Kyushu, survivor of fleet of five, and with only five able-bodied men and 13 litter cases left of 110-man crew. Its English navigator William Adams (*see* IZU), was to introduce Western naval technology and become advisor to first Tokugawa shogun, real-life model for TV film *Shogun.*

GETTING THERE: Little out of way but can be done in full one-day trip from NAGASAKI or easier one-day out of SASEBO and nite at NAGASAKI. If from canal town YANAGAWA, you will have done our **pottery run** Arita to Imari; at IMARI JR Matsuura Line follows coast 1hr to HIRADO-GUCHI (90min from Sasebo), whence 15min bus across new Hirado O-hashi bridge to HIRADO town. Walk 5min from Hirado-guchi stn to ferry pier and catch 15min boat across—old steel steamers replaced in 1984 by red **Chinese style boat** which had been on display in Hirado bay, but not drawing enough customers, so town decided to make it functional. Can also **taxi** from stn, but regular fare (2x-mtr) is quadrupled with addition of ¥1,400 to pay for bridge toll, r.t. as cabbies claim it's hard to get return fare. Cobalt Line boats dock in heart of Hirado.

Hirado became trading port for Dutch and British. Dutch also had factory, as trading posts were then called, in Nagasaki. Japanese suspected Spanish and Portuguese because of political nature of their missionary activities. Will Adams (known in Japanese as Miura-Anjin, 'pilot' of Miura, where he was assigned estate), veteran of defeat of Spanish Armada, advised shogun of Spanish imperial policy whereby priest and merchant were infiltrator-vanguard of military conquest and suggested Dutch and/or British be cut in on Japan trade. Drunken Spanish navy officer boastfully confirmed this theory to his smiling Japanese hosts, who soon banned Spaniards, and eventually Portuguese and then began to clamp down on Christianity. British had poorer administrators than Dutch, and despite Adam's advice eventually went bankrupt, themselves withdrawing before closing of Japan. As Protestant, nonmissionizing people, they might have been allowed to stay on, too, with Dutch who were certainly not missionaries as some were Jews—subject which bears study.

In Hirado, there are still many mementos of this era; Tourist Information Booth in boat terminal has good English brochure with map outlining major sites: top end of harbor is site of old Dutch factory which flourished here for 33 years from 1609 until forced to move to Dejima in Nagasaki. Only well, some of stone pavement and wharf with small guiding lamp, mini lighthouse, remain, and 30m stretch of 2m high wall which used to surround complex.

Nearby is small...
Imoto Collection Museum (daily 8:30-18:00, ¥300), with that era's trade items, 17th century European art and Japanese Ukiyoe prints. Tiny Kurokojima, floating just outside harbor, is covered with palm trees planted by Dutch in 1597.

Following Dutch Wall, we come to...
Tourist Museum, *Hirado Kanko Shiryokan,* daily 8:30-16:30, ¥200, on L.
In it are various Hidden Christian items. Hirado natives are predominantly
Roman Catholic, but of fascinating variety which bears little similarity to
original, having survived over three centuries of persecution 'underground',
cut off from Rome. In Himosashi village in center of isle live 217 families,
descended from these secret Christians. Two other families, descended of
old shogun anti-Christian inquisitors, are respected today because their
ancestors had secretly protected Christian neighbors by feigning ignorance
of their activities. As long as public peace was not violated, these Christians
worshipped such icons as crucifix with Buddha in center, by ignoring
decorative figure and adoring cross only, used Buddhist style rosary and
enshrined Christ in home in Japan-Shintoesque style as *Onando-Kamisama*.
Other secret Christians adapted tea ceremony as secret mass, tea for wine
with some change necessary in type of wafer used, or in humility of rite:
indeed tea rite adopted much form from mass. Their prayers and chants are
mixture of Latin, Portuguese and local patois. Still rather secretive, they
perform baptism on newborn child at home, local 'padre' touches forehead
with fingers formed cross, dipped in holy water.

HIMOSASHI (45min bus from Hirado) now boasts fine church; 10min bus
beyond to other side Nejishi is **Hirado Christian Museum** (8:30-18:00, ¥200,
X-wed), superb collection includes *Onando-sama* and *Maria-kannon* images,
fumi-e (stomping pix) and Buddha-crosses. There are also more of these
hidden Christian communities on nearby OSHIMA and IKITSUKI-SHIMA isles
(30min boat from Hirado to either) and out on GOTO ISLANDS. They all set up
on windward side of isles to get as far away as possible. In early time of
Dutch residence in Hirado there were many international romances. With
banning of Christianity and extermination of Western influence, mixed-
offspring and wives of these romances were exiled to Jakarta, Java. Here
are preserved some of heart-rending *Jakatara-fumi* letters from these exiles,
martyrs to near-universal bigotry.

Continuing up hill we come to...
Sakikata Park, with monument erected in 1949 for 400th anniversary of
landing of Saint Francis Xavier. Nearby is grave of Will Adams, who
locals claim died here in 1620. But Yokosuka, former site of Japan's main
naval station and present US Pacific Fleet base, has better claim to his
grave. Adams held his shogun-granted estates there, some 100 farms, and
actually died at Yokosuka. However, it is custom in Japan to 'bury'
honored person in more than one place, sometimes actually dividing ashes,
sometimes only erecting monument as his 'spiritual grave'. Area in Tokyo
where he had Edo home is also named after him. Girl in Kimono nearby is
memorial to *Jakatara-musume*, brides of foreigners, banished to Jakarta.
Adams' family not banished, but 'naturalized' and absorbed.

Few hundred meters W of park is...
Lord Matsuura's mansion, now historical library, museum (daily 8:30-
17:00, ¥250). Models of foreign ships of time as well as actual artifacts
including carved ship's prow and other relics; family treasures and bric-a-
brac from Matsuura clan. Continuing along this road, we see **Xavier
Memorial Church,** spires and cross rise up above surrounding Buddhist
temples (camera bugs: excellent shot of church spire rising over Jodo sect
KOMYO-JI temple). Built 1931. Heading back down to harbor brings us to
arched **Saikai Bridge,** or Dutch Bridge, leading to old British section,
now occupied by City Hall. Monument marks general location where

British kept money-losing factory 1613-23. **Castle** behind is 1962 reconstruction as **museum** (8:30-18:00, ¥300) of samurai goods, local crafts, finds from nearby excavations of stone age sites. Prominently displayed sword is said to belong to Matsuura lord who accompanied Empress Jingo's 2nd or 3rd century invasion of Korea. Original castle was built here 1599 by Lord MATSUURA Shizunobu (who began Hirado pottery center of Mikawauchi with Korean artisans), but he burned castle down, with self in it, grieving over death of son. Rebuilt in 1707 by 30th Matsuura lord, only to be dismantled 8 generations or 173 years later, following Meiji Restoration.

WHERE TO STAY: Resort-class hotels, both W- and J-style rooms: top ranked is sprawling International Tourist Hotel **Kisho-tei** ☎(0950)-22-3191, ¥-Sw/2, near Sakikata Park. Others in ¥-hi-T–lo-S range are **Ranfu** ☎23-2111, below Kisho-tei; **Kaijo Hotel** ☎22-3800, N of Ranfu; and **Kyokawa** ☎23-2488, on hill S of castle and known for its seafood extravaganzas. There are many smaller, more personal Japanese inns, ¥-B-T like **Kawamura Ryokan** ☎22-2712 along waterfront near boat pier and Tourist Info: which gets rooms for all pockets. *Budgeteers* have several minshuku good one is **Michishio** ☎22-3301, between Tourist Info and Dutch Wall. *Onsen-seekers* find tiny **TA-NO-URA ONSEN** N tip of isle, 30min bus from town some moderate inns. *Swimmers* fine beach **Nejishi**, near Christian Museum, minshuku.

PERSONAL DATEBOOK: Setsubun, Feb 3-4, *Crying Sumo*, Saikyo-ji temple children about year old are brought in contest to see who is first to cry: memorial service to child-priest Eitetsu. **Lunar Jul 16-17** hundreds of lighted lanterns set afloat in bay from Kurokojima, in **late Jul** *Benzaiten Festival*, topped off with kagura dances. **Last weekend Jul** is *Hirado Port Festival*, gaily decorated boats, dancing in streets. **Aug 18** entire city celebrates with folk dance in streets: features unique *Jangara* dance, dancers wear large bell-covered headdresses, beating drums in offering for good harvest, done on smaller scale. **Jun 8** *Tei-seiko Festival* honors 17th century Chinese merchant. **Oct 25-27** *Hirado Okunchi*, Autumn Festival: 25th samurai procession thru town; 26th parade of floats, lion & dragon dances, full program 24 kagura dances at Kameoka Shrine on castle hill; 27th *yabusame*, archery from horseback at Kameoka grounds. **Dec 1** kids go thru town selling *mochi* (rice cakes filled with red bean paste), which if you buy, is said to protect you from accidents in water.

OFFBEAT ISLAND HOPPING TO NAGASAKI

THIS COURSE is for real wanderer who has few days to spend doing nothing but cruise down chain of rustic isles. Christian historian will find rich, thriving secret Christian legacies here, especially around main town of FUKUE (several daily flights NKA → FUKUOKA, NAGASAKI and KAMI-GOTO, few isles up). For shorter trip, boat from SASEBO 2hr40min → ARIKAWA, 400-year-old whaling village on central Nakadori-jima.

GETTING AROUND: 2hr40min boat HIRADO → northernmost UKUJIMA (same from Sasebo) from where begin isle hopping over 100km down to southernmost FUKUE-JIMA, whence 3hrs30min to NAGASAKI. Numerous but infrequent **steamers** and **ferries** ply between half-dozen isles; infrequent **buses** meander thru four largest ('infrequent'=3-5 daily). Can also hire **ocean-taxis** for getting around at your own pace. Numerous budget inns dot isles, many fine beaches.

Bus or boat down to S tip Narao and 80min to...

FUKUE, which **Castle**, built 1863 to defend against possible foreign attack is last one built in Japan, more like fort. Dismantled 1870, walls, main gate, and Goto (local daimyo) family house with garden remain in compound. Nearby is ancestral temple **DAIEN-JI**, with many spectacular grave stones, except that of 19th lord GOTO Sumikata who, as devout Christian, ignored Buddhism. Walled **samurai residences**, *buke-yashiki* line several streets behind it.

My Christ ... does not necessarily gaze at the lake of Galilee.
Nagasaki Bay can also be viewed framed beneath a persimmon tree
bearing red-ripened fruit. — AKUTAGAWA Ryunosuke, d.1927, *Western Man*

NAGASAKI 長崎
CHOP SUEY & MME BUTTERFLY

EIGHT CENTURIES AGO area called Fukae-no-ura was assigned as fief by Yoritomo to one NAGASAKI Kotaro. About all that changed in following four sleepy centuries was its name. Port of Nagasaki was insignificant. Contacts between Japan and China continued to be thru traditional gateway of Fukuoka and nearby provincial capital of Dazaifu. In 1542, 3 Portuguese armed with arquebuses were shipwrecked in South Kyushu—trade began.

Then, on August 15, 1549, Jesuit father Francis Xavier (now Saint -) landed in Kagoshima, southernmost Kyushu. Failing to reach emperor in Kyoto (capital had been devastated by war, HIM was in seclusion), Xavier returned to Kyushu and southern Honshu, preaching, establishing centers. Calling Japanese 'best people so far discovered', but realizing they took their cultural cues from China, he left in 1551 in hopes to enter and convert Flowery Kingdom. Died in Macao 1552 waiting out entry permit visas!

His successors in Japan were, after decade of futility, meeting with success. In 1563 several lords of Kyushu converted; notably Lord Francis Otomo of Oita (Beppu) and Lord Bartholomew Omura of Omura, both of whom were hosts to lucrative Portuguese trade. Omura became fanatic in suppressing 'paganism' and causing anti-Christian revolt, from which he was saved by intervention of brother, Lord of Arima. Portuguese port of Yokose-ura and capital of Omura sacked by rebels, Yokose-ura church burned and for two years no foreign missionary dared set foot in Omura domains. Yokose-ura was abandoned. In 1565 more easily defended port of Fukae, or Nagasaki, chosen as Omura's entrepot for Portugal trade. In 1568 first church, All Saints, set up there in converted Buddhist temple. 1571 first Macao ship arrived and by 1579 it was most flourishing port in Kyushu. Lord Omura presented port to church domain in 1580 and it flourished as 'Little Rome' for several years, thus Nagasaki became center for Western culture in Japan.

Persecution of Japanese Christians began 1587 by Tycoon Hideyoshi; 1588 confiscated city, returning it to Japanese control. But its character as entrepot for Western culture had been set. Nagasaki remained major Portuguese market port. Later Spaniards came then Dutch and British. Population further increased during 8 years as native Christians migrated there in great numbers, massing around Oura and Urakami, which only in recent decades has been absorbed by city's growth. Chinese were attracted as China traffic shifted from Fukuoka to Nagasaki.

Hideyoshi's persecution of Christians increased, and after brief period of toleration by new Tokugawa Shogunate, anti-Christian edict was passed in 1612. Full-scale persecution began against these 'disturbers of national unity', foreigner and Japanese alike. After expulsion, first of Spaniards 1624, and then Portuguese in 1638 (British pulled out on their own about 1623), only Dutch remained. Unlike Spaniards and Portuguese, Dutch did not mix religion and politics with trade. They were permitted to operate from 1641 on, but only out of then-island of Dejima in harbor now part of downtown. Trade was now organized, government-supervised affair, no longer monopoly of random pirates. China trade was important; Chinese came in large numbers to handle it. From 1641 until 1854 only Chinese and Dutch were allowed into Japan, (British had forfeited by incompetence) and only in Nagasaki. (In 1792, however, due to shortage of Dutch ships American ship *Eliza* made annual run on contract to Dutch factory). In 1810 when Napoleon seized Holland and English annexed Holland's colonies, Dutch flag disappeared from flagstaffs of world, except Dejima here in Nagasaki.

Nagasaki became center for Occidental studies: *Ran-gaku*, literally Dutch learning. (Japanese pronounce Holland as Oranda, which abbreviates to Ran, written with homonymous ideograph for orchid). Interpreters trained here; doctors taught some of new European technical advances in technique. Part of annual Dutch tribute or business tax was stock of newest books for translation into Japanese by officials of secret Bureau of Dutch Learning. Only Dutch was studied, but after British man-o'-war sailed into port and terrified everyone and no English-speaking Japanese or Dutch-speaking Englishmen were around, Ran-gaku men were ordered to set up department of English taught thru Dutch books, which stood by unutilized except for occasional grilling of shipwrecked whalers. After 1868, this became Tokyo University.

Despite Dutch books and English buccaneers, flavor of Nagasaki after end of Christian Century was Chinese. True, Japanese culture had come from China: most Japanese architecture is from Chinese prototypes, but has been naturalized, Japanized in rest of nation. In Nagasaki it remains Chinese more so perhaps because it is in Ming dynasty (1368-1644) styles, that most 'Chinesey' of Chinese styles. And at that it is in tastes of most 'Chinesey' of Chinese, Fukienese people: lovers of bright colors, curlicues, varieties of wines and well-seasoned foods.

Only here can Japanese see *Bon Feast of Lanterns* in Chinese style (*Feast of Hungry Ghosts*); only here is there Chinese temple with Chinese priest, full Chinese-style interior, meant for Chinese use, tho Japanese welcome; and only in Nagasaki did Japanese Chinatown survive Second World War: famed Kobe and Yokohama Chinatowns have only in last decades grown again, Yokohama more so, but both lack real, lived-in feeling found here.

Nagasaki has given Japan one of its most popular exotic dishes: *champon*. What we would call in English chop suey: Chinese noodle dish changed to fit local taste but retaining enough of its original exoticism. Nagasaki serves best champon in Japan. Character of Nagasaki today is modern chop suey-champon (both words take on meaning of mixed foreign-native combinations): great Japanese city with Chinese savoring and sip of Dutch beer on side. Fun town, still very *inaka* (hick) in many ways.

GETTING THERE: Alt- OSAKA-UMEDA stn **bus** 9pm, arr NAGASAKI stn 8am, ¥10,800.

GETTING AROUND: Easiest by 3hr **taxi tour**, ¥9,000 (20x-mtr) for 5-psgr *chugata*, 20% less for 4-psgr *kogata*, +¥600 **English-guide** when available. Arrange on spot at stn taxi-stand, or Tourist Office also at stn. May take time to get guide so arrange ahead thru hotel or inn if you can, pick up anywhere at order. *Budgeteers* can do same by foot-and-tram in full easy day with lots of time to eat. **Tram** ¥100 per ride, or get **all-day pass** (¥500) at stn Tourist Office. **Avoid** tour bus which rushes you and misses some better spots. Simple outline of tram system: #1 starts **North end of city** → passes **Peace Park** → thru town to base of **Sofuku-ji** (last stop); #3 also starts **North end** → cuts across at **Nagasaki stn** → past **Suwa Shrine** → ends **Hotaru-chaya**; #4 runs Hotaru-chaya → Sofuku-ji; #5 runs Hotaru-chaya → Ishibashi hitting **Hollander Hill, ChinaTown & Glover Park** last stop. Xfer from 1,3,4 onto 5 at Tsugi-cho stop (single journey ask for *nori-kae*, xfer ticket). No #2 line.

We start from Nagasaki stn to **Peace Park** (tram 8 stops to Matsuyama-cho), marked by green tower atop 500-ft hill. 10m/33ft high bronze statue attempts to express mankind's plight: high right hand pointing up to frightening aspects of the bomb, left extended in peace. Right forefinger is lightning rod; base houses memorial tablets for dead. Sculptured by KITAMURA Seibo, guide always announced its price: ¥30 million, or about $84,000 when built 1955 for 10th anniversary. Used to be jail here, old wall of which now supports rest-house and souvenir shops, opposite, where one has nice view of city. Go by **Nyoko-do** (park's N side), house of Dr Takashi Paulo NAGAI, famous Catholic radiation scientist, writer on A-bomb who died 1951 after years of suffering from radiation effects—mostly from experiments. His *Bells of Nagasaki* is scientific-humanitarian classic from which this mosaic quote:

It was August 9, 1945. As usual the sun rose quietly from behind Mount Kompira; and beautiful Urakami welcomed its last morning....'How is the war really going?' asked a young student....'Whether we live or die, we don't want to be the laughing stock of the world'....And then came the flash...in the sky above Urakami rose a white cloud, and it got bigger and bigger and bigger...like a huge lantern wrapped in cotton...outside was white, but inside a red fire seemed to be blazing and something like beautiful electric lights flashed incessantly...colors within this lantern were now red, now yellow, and now purple, all kinds of beautiful colors....Then it gradually became cold, as at the end of autumn, and a strange and silent emptiness ensued. Clearly this was no ordinary event...."It's the end of the world," said Choro with res-ignation. —translated by William Johnston, published by Kodansha International

Past old facade of **Urakami Cathedral**, rebuilt 1959 but retaining battered statues in front and remnants of original destroyed by the bomb. It was, until August 9th, 1945, finest church in Japan, painstakingly built over 43 years (1880-1923) by small group of devoted Christians.

Taxi, disembark for...
International Hall of Culture, *Kokusai Bunka Kaikan* (9:00-17:00, ¥50) 2, 3, 4th floors museum of bomb material; 5th floor museum of art, which has perhaps only fine painting to result from this great torment. Painted by couple, Maruki and Akamatsu, black ink on silver two-panel screen: disfigured mother and children beseech statue of Christ who has turned his face away. Composition is parody of usual crucifixion. Nearby is case of burned Catholic rosaries, sculpture and decoration from old church, sumi painting by Paulo Nagai. Small array of old Christian items; more at **26 Martyrs**. Nagasaki bomb was meant for shipyard at other end of town: missed by several miles landing smack where over third of Japan's Catholics lived. (Hiroshima main Protestant center.) Also on 5th floor is **Language Resource Center**, started 1984 by Valerie Wilkinson, teacher at Nagasaki J.C. Will eventually have English-speaking staff at all times; already has much printed matter on bombings, info on worldwide anti-nuclear movements.

Large **black stone pyramid** in front of *Bunka Kaikan* points straight up to where bomb exploded 500m above at 11:02. It killed over 75,000 people, not including later radiation-caused deaths. Small **Pearl Museum** and **Antique Bekko** (tortoise-shell) **Museum** front of *Bunka Kaikan*.

Back by taxi past hospital, past one-legged...
Half torii (split neatly in half vertically) of HIE JINJA shrine of *ujigami* (genus locii or neighborhood spirit of Urakami) which survived blast and stands now as monument. **Sakamoto-cho International Cemetery** of post-Perry period is next. Dr Nagai and Thomas Glover are among local

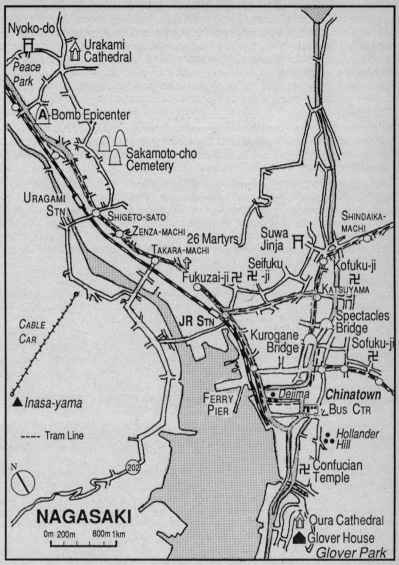

Nyoko-do

Urakami
Cathedral

Peace
Park

A-Bomb Epicenter

Sakamoto-cho
Cemetery

URAGAMI
STN

SHIGETO-SATO

ZENZA-MACHI   26 Martyrs   Suwa
                               Jinja

TAKARA-MACHI

SHINDAIKA-
MACHI

Seifuku
-ji

Fukuzai-ji卍 卍 -ji

Kofuku-ji卍

KATSUYAMA

JR STN   Spectacles
                                Bridge

CABLE
CAR   Kurogane
                Bridge   Sofuku-ji卍

▲ Inasa-yama

---- Tram Line

FERRY
PIER   • Dejima   Chinatown

                          ꞁBUS CTR

N

Hollander
Hill

卍 Confucian
Temple

NAGASAKI

0m 200m   800m 1km

Oura Cathedral
▲ Glover House
Glover Park

notables buried here. Can catch tram straight down from one-legged torii,
back to Nagasaki stn. Just before stn, L, is small hill where '26' were
martyred: 4 Spaniards, 1 Indian, 1 Mexican, all Franciscans, 1 Japanese
Jesuit, and 19 Japanese lay converts were arrested in Kyoto and Osaka on
Hideyoshi's orders and force-marched to Nagasaki where crucified here on
Nishizaka hill February 5, 1597. In next three decades they were to be
joined by some 4,000 more martyrs, plus 40,000 victims of Shimabara
Revolt of 1637: 15% of total Catholic population, pre-1940s world record
for Christians. 26 were canonized 1862 by Pope Pius IX, and for centennial
commemoration, memorial with 26 molded out of bronze (designed by
FUNAKOSHI Yasutake) and **museum** were built: houses extensive collection
of Christian objects and early maps of Japan. There is old Christian bell and

several *fumi-e* (step-on picture plaques) of Catholic holy subjects on which suspected Christians were made to tread (*fumi*) to prove their 'innocence' or face crucifixion. Behind museum is Gaudi-esque **26 Martyrs Memorial Chapel**, also completed for 1962 centennial: grotesque twin towers are covered in ceramics-sherd mosaic, collected off road between Osaka and Nagasaki to mark path of 26. One tower signifies man's prayers for peace (going up), while other signifies God's grace (coming down).

Short detour to 2 of Nagasaki's four...

CHINESE TEMPLES: Down side street from 26 Martyrs towards giant silver Kannon statue at FUKUZAI-JI, Ming style, was National Treasure, but flattened by bomb which left only main gate; now 'restored' in concrete but still showing unusual lion and elephant heads. Kannon statue built by citizens. Skip this temple, proceed 200m to SEIFUKU-JI, another of Chinese quartet: quiet temple, going up steps, in middle of gate one is confronted by fat, contented reclining Chinese god of fortune. Main hall, bell tower still remain, elegant sloped roof and lion-head tiles. Just back of hall to L is remaining segment of original compound wall, made of assorted tiles and clay faces of lions, other beasts, swimming fish and more. Eclipsed by other two famous Chinese temples, we prefer this one as still quiet, off main track in sleepy corner of town.

If walking, from here R at road-end past...

Prefectural Art Museum rotating exhibit on Spanish and old Nagasaki objects, on grounds of old Saint Mary's Church. First L after museum, down 50m to small **Apollo Gallery** specializing in original ukiyoe prints: sign claims 'AAA First Class Guarantee'. 100m beyond is SUWA SHRINE, site of colorful Nagasaki *Kunchi Festival* (see replicas of floats at Glover Park); at foot of shrine are several antique shops. Cut across street at Suwa Shrine, follow stream and up to KOFUKU-JI temple. Along stream is remains of KOEI-JI temple, burned 1585 as was used by Christians for services. Further down, stream is spanned by several old stone bridges, most famous is **double-arched** *megane-bashi*, spectacles-bridge.

From SUWA SHRINE can catch #4 tram to SOFUKU-JI temple, or #5 to Glover Park area. Back on main **taxi** course, we pass station again on our R: note roof, modeled after old atom-bombed church. First L after crossing river to site of old Dutch concession of DEJIMA (there is Dejima tram stop): man-made isle completed 1636 to accommodate Portuguese, effectively limiting contact with Japanese. After their expulsion, Dutch were moved onto then vacant lot 1689. Same year, Chinese were also clustered into small section, remnants of which still stand uphill of present Chinatown. Couple of old storehouses and part of retaining wall still stand, now small park showing 1/15th scale model of what Dejima used to look like. Rickety building across alley is **Dejima Museum** (9:00-17:00, X-mon, free): odds and ends on Nagasaki, Dutch, Chinese, Spaniards and trade. Area was residential quarters of Dejima. Green building next to it was built 1875 as church, converted to First Nagasaki High School in 1877, now it just sets.

Continue S main road 500m, L at New Hotel Tanda (tram stop hospital front) to...

Hollander Hill, *Oranda-zaka*, up which stone-paving is **Kassui Gakuen**, first mission school in Japan. Near campus gate is House #12 (all foreign houses were called by number, in order of construction) built 1879 for US Methodist missionary Elizabeth Russell who started all-girls' school above. One house here was **Russian Consulate**; **British Consulate**, in great red brick building near New Tanda Hotel, it is now **Science Museum**, next door was US Consul. Across from them, tremendous 'temporary' wooden building concealed from blue eyes construction of 70,000 ton super-dreadnought *Musashi*; this was **bomb target**. Hollander Hill curves just below House #12 thru old town and down to CONFUCIAN TEMPLE, *Koshi-byo*. Built 1893, recently restored and enlarged. Side hall shops sell trinkets from China, but main hall has some interesting stuff. In back is 1984-opened **Chinese History Museum**, with good collection ancient art on loan from Peoples' Republic.

Across river you can see...
Glover Park and **Oura Cathedral**, latter National Treasure as oldest standing Christian church in Japan, built 1865. Some madman disfigured interior in 1960, closing it to public for some years, but it again accepts visitors. Now used for tourism (8:00-18:00, ¥200), new church below has services. Adjacent to old church is Japan's first seminary built 1875; nearby is original bishop's house. Small showroom of Kirishitan items near entrance to old church. Church also known as site of discovery of secret-Christians—few months after dedication ceremony 14 local farmers came and asked Father Petitjean where statue of Holy Mother was. Upon being shown it, they knelt in prayer and told bewildered Father "We have same faith as you".

Glover Park (8:00-18:00, ¥600) on hill behind Oura Church is Nagasaki's **Meiji Village**, with half-dozen old foreign residences, all original here, and as many more other W-style Meiji buildings moved here—cost city 70 million yen. Central is namesake **Glover House**, 1863, supposed setting for *Madame Butterfly*, tho she had nothing to do with Glover. Oldest W-style house in Japan, parts of which were shipped out from England; ground plan in shape of four-leaf clover. Thomas Glover, British merchant-trader married Japanese girl; supporter of Choshu, anti-shogun faction, smuggled first Japanese students out to study in England (they griped about ship accommodations). One room has paintings recording his achievements, English and Japanese explanations. Only son, phoneticized to KURABA, married Westernized-Japanese, no children, worked to better Japan-UK relations but was treated as pariah, suspected of disloyalty on racial grounds, forced to sell house to Mitsubishi shipbuilding which it overlooked, committed suicide week after war ended.

·Up moving-sidewalk, top of which is 1878 Western restaurant **Jiyu-tei**. Next moving walk passes **Nagasaki Courthouse** (1883) and **Walker House** built 1877 for Englishman Robert Walker, captain of Japan's first mail ship *Takachiho-maru*, then in 1898 set up his own company making Japan's first soft drinks, *Banzai Cider* and *Banzai Lemonade*. Very top is **#2 Mitsubishi Dock-house** (1883).

Working our way down, first is rear gate to...
Nagasaki Industrial High School (1905). Below it is **Ringer House**, built 1864 for Frederick Ringer, partner of Glover. Behind it is **Alt House** (1865) for English tea trader, later occupied by Ringer Jr; houses Ringer and Glover related items.

In front of Alt is...
Steele Memorial Academy (1887). From here, you can look down on two massive buildings; they are main and annex of **Yuzuriha Hospital**, built around 1890.

Long building at bottom is...
Nagasaki Traditional Performing Arts Museum, dedicated solely to Suwa Shrine Festival, better known as *Nagasaki Kunchi* (*see* DATEBOOK); miniatures of floats and short video of most recent festival.

Down from it...

#16 House, built 1879 to house staff at US Consulate; now Glover & Hidden-Christian exhibition. 'Japanese are cheap imitators?'...well, see willow-ware and other **European imitations** of Kyushu-ware. Cozy tea corner, tables for two, bottled drinks, and lovely view of harbor. Next room furnished as it was in Glover's time: fireplace with mirror in torii frame. Fine collection Maria Kannons (Mary icons J-style) and picture of Japanese lady martyr Gratia Hosokawa. Below it and attached, is ¥-T rate inn. This house is not part of park, ¥400. Great W-style building down by bus stop and parking lot was built 1907 for Bank of Hong Kong and Shanghai; now **Nagasaki History Museum** (9:00-17:00, X-mon, free) with mix of things, Kunchi Festival's real floats, and boats used in *Peiron Festival*.

SOFUKU-JI temple trade mark of Nagasaki. Chinese temple, properly called **Chun Fu**, belongs to Huan Pi sect of Fuchow, Fukien Province, China. Chinese, only foreigners besides Dutch allowed in Nagasaki 1641-1854, were mostly from Fuchow. Suspected by Japanese of being Christian, in 1629 invited priest Chao Jan-tei to build temple to prove their Buddhism. Style late Ming. Present priest, 37th generation, demonstrated self control to OYAMA Masatatsu (*see* Jay's *Zen Combat*), karate champion, by plunging his oiled fist into kettle of boiling water. Main gate is beautiful example of Ming Chinese temple gates of gleaming white arch topped with pagoda-like roof with eaves curling heavenwards. There are some Japanese examples of this gate type, but their roofs have been Japanized, de-curled. Climbing up stone steps past numerous Chinese monuments, you enter second gate, example of late Ming architecture, prefabricated in China, brought over and set up in 1685. Even in China wooden structures this old are not too well preserved, having fallen victim to wars, fires and cultural revolution. In famine of 1680, priest Sengai, selling his personal belongings, boiled rice gruel for populace in great six-foot high pot, treasure to this day, displayed in building R of this gate.

You'll immediately notice difference in decor from other Japan temples: brilliant color combinations, different type offerings before images, main temple *Daiyuho-den* has stone floor in Chinese-style rather than raised wooden Japanese floor. Here are enshrined Amida, with two disciples and surrounded by 18 rakan. Just outside next structure is gate connecting main hall with priests' quarters, where hangs huge wooden **fish-shaped gong** which was rung at meal and bath hours for monks. Directly in front of this gate up few steps is most interesting building here: **Maso-do** or Bosa-do (Hall of Bodhisattva) which houses goddess of sea, Ama and possible southern prototype of Ama-terasu, very important to Chinese merchants as protection crossing sea. Statue itself is female and fully costumed. Here two fierce guardians boast eyes with thousand-mile vision and favorable wind ears. Chinese temples of Nagasaki, of which only SOFUKU-JI and nearby KOFUKU-JI remain complete, were unique in having this sub-temple to sea goddess. Each Chinese temple here was built by people of different region, Sofuku-ji is most 'Chinesey' of them all.

KOFUKU-JI temple, (not included on **taxi tour** unless requested), 1 km down street of 8 Japanese temples built 350 years back by Tokugawa shogun to encourage Buddhism against Christianity, strategically located on higher ground. Kofuku-ji was first of Chinese temples, built 1620 by Chinese priest Shin-en (Jpn pron) from Fouliang, Kiangsi Province. Quite different from Sofuku-ji, spacious grounds. Here, too, Amida Trinity, 18 rakan, sea goddess with two attendants (slightly newer, better condition), fish gongs.

Taxi turns halfway to Kofuku-ji to visit Nagasaki's important local product at...
Yezaki Bekko, oldest **tortoise-shell shop**, established 1709. Here we are shown how to differentiate between real tortoise shell (now protected as endangered species) and cheaper substitute of thin sheet heat-fused onto cow horn, which sells for one-third—turn it over and you can see. Most of inexpensive 'tortoise-shell' found in junk shops is plastic process introduced from Germany 1910. Yezaki is black *kura*-style shop with sign in Japanese, English, Russian (Nagasaki was hopping port of call until Russo-Japan War). *Warning* tortoise endangered species, US bans import and in '90 Japan at last showing signs of joining world in enforcing bans on such endangered species misuse (be careful of ivory purchases, too).

Head N one block from double-arched spectacles-bridge, L towards tram line 3min. Taxi lets you off anywhere in town; return coupon to driver. Elapsed time, 3 hrs.

CHOPSTICKS: Kajiya-machi street one S of temple street near Sofuku-ji, **Ginrei Grill** and next door bar **Bon Soir** (same owner), longfamed as coziest spots in town and certainly our favorites, *closed down Jun '90* due to structural delapidation. 5-storey block will rise in place, may reopen in modern-modified form; check. Walker taking our long course thru town will end up here around lunchtime, fill up and on to Glover Park. Known for decor as excellent museum of Nagasakiana, which makes for additional sighteeing loss.

CHINA NITE IN NAGASAKI

DON'T MISS *Shinchi*, or **Chinatown**. Practically next to busy Hamamachi where most Japanese restaurants are. Coming from Kanko-dori stop on #1 streetcar, head S, walk about 200 yards to bridge, after crossing which, first 3 alleys on R constitute Chinatown. At third alley intersection is small plaza with police box. Turning L here, pass numerous Chinese restaurants towards old Chinese settlement set up by shogun 1689. Present Chinatown is where all warehouses for goods from China were located. Best concentration of restaurants is in Shinchi center in middle alley to R.

Standing here you have your choice of several restaurants of all sizes, from culinary castles to real cheap pilgrim places, all with plastic samples and prices in window. Best for any Chinese dinner, of course, is to go as group, and possible choice is to join one of **nite tours** (see below) of Nagasaki which include dinner in Chinatown. Most here are Fukien style—recommended: **Horai-ken, Kosan-ro, Shinwa-ro, Chuka-ten**. All will set table for as little as ¥1,000 (of course, cheaper single dishes) even solo or double. Larger groups, especially if reserving ahead (which gets you better, more food, same price) get private rooms; top food anywhere from ¥2,000 per to ¥10,000 for house exceptional delicacies.

Champon is Chinese Nagasaki's special dish for individuals; for groups it is *shippoku*, multi-course round-table meal said to originate from Chinese priestly fare. Not strictly vegetarian, incl assorted meat dishes, soup topped off by plum-flower tea. Must rsv, at least 4 people. Can arrange for dinner at most good inns or hotels. In town, best is **Kagetsu**, ☎22-0191, in Maruyama-cho, 200m S of Shian-bashi tram stop: abt ¥8,000 per head here; you pay for atmosphere, Kagetsu has been around 180 years, was popular hangout for early revolutionaries SAKAMOTO Ryoma and company. Eat it in town for around ¥3,000 each, **Hamakatsu Bekkan**, 100m N of Shian-bashi stop; **Sakamoto** on Kanko-dori street; and **Restaurant Oura** in Tokyu Hotel.

For Japanese food, **Yotsu-so** just off Kanko-dori (one street N of Hamaichi Arcade, turn R) specializes in *chawan-mushi* (hot egg custard with veggies, meat) and *mushi-zushi* (steamed rice mixed with veggies, meat), plus usual run of Japanese food. House special combo-sets of chawan-mushi and mushi-zushi, ¥900. Can't miss it, large J-style facade with monster red lantern out front. Whole slew of budget, mid-range places around Shian-bashi tram stop: Shian-bashi Alley runs parallel to tracks, one short block S; Ramen (Chinese noodle) Alley on N side of tracks. This is also main shopping, entertainment, nite life area of Nagasaki.

ADDITIONAL IDEAS

DINE AT hilltop **Hotel Yataro** for view: **taxi** under 2x-mtr, **bus** or walk up for pilgrims who have cool cafeteria on roof of adjacent YATARO Kokumin-shukusha.

Ride up Nagasaki **ropeway** to Inasayama hill opp side of port for 'million dollar nite view', **taxi** (basic-mtr) or 10min bus from stn. Ropeway runs every few mins 9:00-21:00 (17:00 midwinter), ¥800 r.t. Suggest you get up in time for sunset over sea, look down on peninsula villages. Turn around, see in full contrast, Nagasaki lit up in all its glory. Inasayama Kanko Hotel halfway up at end of bus run.

Nite Tour by bus ideal for summer: **Course 1**: starts Stn 18:00 → Peace Park → Yezaki Bekko, Chinatown (dinner) → Inasayama →Stn 21:20; ¥4,260, daily 3/15-10/15. **Course 2**: Stn 19:00 → Yezaki Bekko → Inasayama → Peace Park → Hotel Yataro (nite-view) → Stn 21:40; ¥2,230, daily 3/15-11/15.

Cruise around Nagasaki Port by boat, 1 hour, Ohata pier daily 10:15, 11:40, 15:15, ¥770. Also Jun thru Sep special evening cruises, which check.

WHERE TO STAY

EVERYTHING FROM W-style ¥-L hotels and superb ryokan down to Business Hotels and four Youth Hostels, with plenty of everything in between. In stn, near exit, is *Nikkanren*, **Japan Hotel Assoc.** booth between taxi tour booth and city Info: can fit any budget; also at main **City Tourist Office** just outside stn, to L, next to police box. Over 240 lodgings, mostly concentrated near stn and heart of town. W-style hotels' top are: **Holiday Inn** ☎(0958)-28-1234, ¥-hi-S; **Tokyu** ☎(0958)-25-1501, ¥-S, below Glover Park; **New Tanda** ☎27-6121, ¥-lo-S, in beautiful brick bldg near Hollander Hill.

Cheaper are: **Parkside Hotel** ☎45-3191 in Peace Park; and **Washington Hotel** ☎28-1211 in heart of nite-life section 200m from Chinatown near which more ¥-B-T places. For view, J-style good buy hilltop **Yataro** ☎22-8166, ¥-T-Sw/2; adjacent Kokumin-shukusha **Yataro Inn** ☎28-1111 ¥-Bw/2; or **Inaseyama Kanko Hotel** ☎61-4151, ¥-hi-T-S. Classic *ryokan* is **Sakamoto-ya** ☎26-8211 ¥-hi-T-Sw/2, center of town 400m S of stn, its budget annex, **Sakamoto-ya Bekkan** ¥-hi-Bw/2.

Dozens of **Business Hotels**, range from ¥-B for single; several minshuku. Budgeteers have well-placed, clean, **Oranda-zaka** (Hollander Hill) YH ☎22-2730, on hill; **Kenritsu** (Prefectural) YH ☎23-5032, behind museum part way up to Yataro; better view from **Nanpo-en** YH ☎23-5526, on hill behind 26 Martyrs; inconvenient **Urakami-ga-oka** YH ☎47-8473, beyond Peace Park. Only time booking ahead is necessary during *Kunchi*, *Peiron festivals*, but even then, something is always open.

WHERE NEXT Two basic routes to get out of Nagasaki:

(1) **International Tourist Route** (p742) UNZEN → KUMAMOTO → ASO → BEPPU; (2) **Island hop** (p746) via HIRADO → FUKUOKA (combine Pottery Run–p720). If former, don't take boat or plane from BEPPU, suggest bus ASO → OGUNI where rejoin rail back to FUKUOKA via HITA.

UNZEN-bound **bus**, 2-3x/hr, takes about 2hr30min, ¥1,700, from opposite JR railroad stn. Most are local, but also about 4 direct express buses daily which cut off 30min but cost bit more. **Buses** start 7:10, last 19:00, buy tickets at terminal, or pay as you get off. **Taxi**: 90min, about 30x-mtr. Rail Pass users save half of bus fare taking JR → main rail junction ISAHAYA. Shimabara Tetsudo Electric rail out of Isahaya circles most of peninsula via Shimabara, but alas not Obama. If time to kill in Isahaya waiting for bus, 15min walk S of stn is **Isahaya Park**, with local history museum (X-mon, free) of local feudal Isahaya clan items. Double-arched *Megane-bashi* (**spectacles bridge**) built 1839, modeled after that in Nagasaki.

Take road over mountains which wall city, down to Mogi summer playground with pools, beach, aquarium and kiddies' park. 20min out is **BONSAI VILLAGE** raising dwarf trees, home of Koga pottery dolls, nursery fair in May. Beyond, road is tropically palm-lined; 55min out pass thru **South Pacific-like village** with reed-walled barns. Then atop ridge at midpoint of ride, stop **Aino Restaurant**, grand view off either side.

OBAMA 80min out is seaside spa (*see* next); from here road climbs over 2,000 feet past succession of lovely view to UNZEN (*see* p742).

ISLAND COURSES: Kujuku-shima, 99 Isles of Sasebo, another of Japan's exotic seascapes. NAGASAKI → SASEBO can be covered by boat out of Nagasaki-**Ohato pier**, up outer coast of peninsula to SASEBO; but more common and frequent is direct bus 2hrs → SASEBO up inside of peninsula, or JR-rail → SASEBO for which must change at Isahaya and/or Haiki. Another 25min bus (15min **cab**, 2.5x-mtr) to KASHIMAE pier for 90min **ferry** (50min hydrofoil) thru some of most lovely of 99 isles, which actually number 160. From HIRADO do our **Pottery Run** by rail: HIRADO-GUCHI → IMARI → ARITA → backtrack→ KARATSU or on → Yanagawa canal town. Either puts you at HAKATA-FUKUOKA whence out to beautiful IKI ISLE or better TSUSHIMA ISLE (from which one can some days see Korea), returning to main island via pleasant fishing village of Yobiko, on → KARATSU.

PERSONAL DATEBOOK
* These outside of city

February
5 Memorial for 26 Martyrs, at Memorial.

April
Every Sun Apr-May *Kite-flying* contests; kite-handlers try to force down opponents, or cut their tether (all have glass woven into rope).

27-29 *Port Festival* marks post-Perry 'opening' of port to foreign trade.

May
5 Childrens' Day, first Peiron boat races, school kids in 11m boats, thence . . .

June
Every Sun June-Aug *Peiron Boat Races* all over area but largest **4th Sun July** (may vary) as all compete in bay. Started 1655 by local Chinese, as offering to sea goddess after storm sank Chinese ship off shore; origin SE Asia as double-5, Lunar May 5, sometime in June as in Hong Kong

30 *Jumping thru Straw Ring*, Suwa Shrine start summer, to get rid of all evils.

July
*20 *Sea Festival* with all boats gaily decorated, huge fireworks, Iojima-cho.

23-28 Yasaka Shrine *Gion Festival* street mart

Late July thru Aug, various nations' attractions, Holland Village.

August
9 *A-bomb memorial*, Catholic torch parade.

13-15 *O-bon* (cemeteries on surrounding hills lit with colored bonbori lanterns); 15th nite's *Feast of Lanterns* event not to be forgotten: 25-ft long straw boats gaily decorated with huge lanterns are carried to Ohato pier by happi-clad youths, loaded on boats, set afire & guided out of harbor.

*13-16 *Peiron Boat Races*, tip of Nomozaki Peninsula, S of Nagasaki; dates and times vary, but daily at either Wakimisaki or Nomo in Nomozaki-cho.

Lunar July 26-28 (late Aug, early Sept) *Chinese Bon*, Japan's sole Chinese fete, colorful spectacle at Sofuku-ji temple with bonfire and firecrackers.

October
7-9 *Nagasaki Kunchi* (Kunchi is local dialect for festival), best time Oct 7th & 9th morn at Suwa Shrine, dances offered. City is divided into many groups which take turns different years for entertaining. Wild festival, each block trying to outdo others; most famous is *ja-odori*, dragon dance (annual): 7am groups perform at shrine and parade huge floats thru city. PM, *mikoshi* sacred palanquins of Suwa, Sumiyoshi and Morizaki Shrines are all blessed here, raced down to Ohato pier. **2nd day**, each performs in own ward. **3rd day** repeat of first: AM performances, PM 3 mikoshi returned to end festival. Special seating tix available for first and 3rd days, but should be obtained ahead of time thru travel agent, JTB, or direct thru **Nagasaki Tourist Bureau**, 2-13 Edocho, Nagasaki City, ☎(0958)-26-9407. Regular seats are free, always crowded; some people even show up day before and stake out spot—if you don't, then try to arrive early.

14-15 *Takengei Festival*, Waka-no-miya Inari Jinja, up side streets near Kofuku-ji. Acrobats dress as Inari, fox god of rice, perform feats on tall bamboo poles.

17 *Yagami Kunchi*, in Yagami-cho district of town; lion dances and kyogen comic noh performances.

*28 *Kinekari Festival*, comical harvest fertility dances, Emukae-cho.

29 *Shikimi Kunchi*, features women's sumo, Otome-jinja.

At heaven's edge a little dot appears ... through streets on all sides
the cry breaks forth; "The red-haired Westerners are coming!"
...the barbarian heart is hard to fathom.
— Rai Sanyo, *Dutch Ships* 1818

INTERNATIONAL TOURIST ROUTE
NAGASAKI 長崎　　ASO 阿蘇　　BEPPU 別府

PREWAR cruise ships brought tourists seeking refuge from heat and humidity of Shanghai to NAGASAKI, where they entrained southward to UNZEN thence KUMAMOTO and eastward for cooler Hells of ASO and BEPPU. This is still good overland route worthy of its old name.

Newest is...
OBAMA, good summer hideaway noted for its salt-water hot springs. Inns here average little under Unzen prices, from ¥-T; Kokumin-shukusha Boyo-so ¥-Bw/2 ☎(0957)-74-3141; minshuku Fukuyoshi across from it; both S end of town. All inns are on coast, S of bus terminal (which has Kanko-annai for booking). Two cheap public baths: Hama-no-yu ¥70, Otasshan-no-yu ¥40 per dip. Beach N of town, beyond which is rustic fishing village of TOZU (1km from Obama), in small cove with high cliffs behind. Budget minshuku Tozu-so ☎74-4563. Just before last hill to Obama is resort beach area of Chijiwa–particularly beautiful at sunset. *Onsen Festival* Apri 1-2, with feudal costume parade, mikoshi and fireworks at nite.

Bus climbs hill from Obama unfolding lovely view of harbor village with fabulous terracing to mountain tops for sweet spuds. On one of last bends before Unzen is old Edo era Rest House, *Rokubei-chaya*, for last view of sea and Obama. In addition to usual snacks and drinks of all sorts, specialty of shop is assorted potato dish using famed local sweet spuds.

UNZEN, noted for its hells, if less dramatic than Beppu far more comfortable in summer, winter has fabulous exotic frost, 'silver thaw', and doesn't have gross over-commercialized-rundown seediness of Beppu. Unzen residents try to keep natural beauty of area intact and have done good job. Most notably, they refuse garish entertainment centers which so often mar otherwise fine spa. Fame as spa, especially as summer resort, due to prewar China hands who developed it as escape from Shanghai heat, built Japan's first public golf course. Earlier history also linked to foreigners, where suspect Christians were made to tread on *fumi-e* or be tossed into bubbling sulphur hells. First 16 tossed in in 1627 by order of professional Christian-baiter lord Matsukura of Shimabara. Dozens more followed in next 5 years, but not one renounced faith. Cross on hill in middle of small hell is where *fumi-e* test was held. Those who would not walk were taken to big hell beyond and thrown in. Photographer telling this to Japanese was ashamed to tell foreigners "...to think that we Japanese did such things". He takes your picture with polaroid camera, or better with conventional film; which you can also have transferred onto souvenir plate. Hell used to be bubblier than now, but is still hot enough to boil eggs, which are sold at roadside. Dec 19, 1991 Yomiuri TV camera caught 'domed-disc' UFO hovering over spewing crater; estimated 5-10 mtr diameter—looked convincing

GETTING THERE: 25min bus from town to top of Nita Pass, whence short ropeway (¥700 r.t.) takes you up another 300m. Driver has scenic tollroad to ropeway, ¥600. Japan's first public golf course, 1913, at base of Nita Pass; 3,202 yards, 9 holes, par 36, total fees/club rental runs around ¥5,000. Trails either end of ropeway 1hr to next peak, 1359m Bugen-dake: 2 caves have pillars of *mannen-setsu*, 10,000-year old ice.

WHERE TO STAY: Excellent choice of hot spring inns for luxury and budget and anywhere in-between. Many got their start catering to early foreigner visitors (from China, not martyrs) and here is one place where W-style is comparable to J- in flashiness. Old hotel is **Yumoto** ☎(0957)-73-3255, ¥-T-Sw/2, close to bus terminal. Best is **Kyushu Hotel** ☎73-3234, only place right in hell, which is its landscape 'garden'. English-speaking clerk, rooms with view of hell ¥-S-hi-L for double suite of W-beds in palatial J-rooms with two meals, private bath. But huge communal bath should at least be seen, even if too bashful to sample (wall between sexes). Most fascinating hotel architecture anywhere: great 30-foot dome with skylite, immense mobiles floating above bathers. Log cabin-like **Unzen Kanko Hotel** ☎73-3263, with all W-rooms, facilities, best known to foreign travelers, very nice, but no view of hells (same rates as Kyushu). **Miyazaki ryokan** ☎73-3331, ¥-T-Lw/2; and **Fukiya** (own hell in back) ☎73-3211, ¥-lo-T+w/2 (has annex across road, ¥B-Tw/2) rank with Kyushu Hotel for views as they surround hells, both all J-style. Several other ryokan in annex's ¥-T range: **Yamadaya** ☎74-2174, E-spkn; **Yorozu-ya**, **Kaseya**, **Unryu**, **Unzen** & **Unzen Family** Hotels.

For budgeteers best bet is Kokumin-shukusha **Yurin-so** ☎73-3355, good baths and private rooms ¥-B+w/2; excellent location. If full, 2 other similar Kokumin-shukusha **Sengo-so** ☎73-3513, at far N end of town, and **Seiun-so** ☎73-3273. Last one has attached **Youth Hostel**, and is located;

10min walk down small road past Hotel New Unzen....
Small Hell, *Ko-jigoku*. Less-used path thru woods from behind Kanko Hotel ends above small hell. Youth Hostel and Kokumin-shukusha share prime location, built with back to scenery, however its large hot spring bath has magnificent view of valley. Between them and small hell are several budget inns which look like hell, but prices are ¥-P. Behind small hell is small Shinto shrine, forlorn and abandoned: smell was too much for its god, tho four stone Buddhas have stuck it out.

Big gray barn below is...
Public Hot Spring, ¥50. Two more in town, one opp Miyazaki Hotel, other on back street behind Kaseya Ryokan, both ¥100, 9:00–21:00. 5min trek down path from Youth Hostel is waterfall under which Saint Gyogi sat meditating. For those who want to do so (excellent massage), free robes in shed; just wring out and hang up after use. **Information Center** ☎73-3434 below Unzen Hotel, across from Police Station above Kokumin-shukusha **Yurin-so** can book you rooms, has English pamphlets, maps of hiking trails. 500m S of road to small hell is **Haku-un Pond**, with campsite in summer. Campers looking for something classier than public baths can use those of big inns: **Fukiya ryokan** charges ¥500.

In center of town...
DAIJO-IN MANMYO-JI temple was founded 701AD by Saint Gyogi. He named area *Onsen-yama* (Hot spring mountain), which thru local dialect became Unzen-yama with double meaning of hot spring and mountain of enlightenment (*unzen*=enlightenment). At its peak during 10-12th centuries, temple covered whole area where inns now are, had over 1,000 monks. What was left by 1637 was burned down by irate Christian-farmer rebels of Shimabara Uprising. Present structures built 1914. Trail from YH to waterfall continues back up to bus road, en route, L at fork in trail leads thru hole in rock wall to site of acolyte training center during temple heyday. Only small shack-temple there now, wonderful view.

Next to temple is old no longer active hell; behind is **marsh**, *gensei-numa* pleasant stroll. Underground heat keeps marsh colorful with blossoms even in winter. At back side of marsh steps lead up to small fertility shrine, with superb male and female 'gods' carved out of rock, called 'Unzen Yin and Yang Rocks'. Amusing *ema-e* (votive plaques) which hang there, of shrine's goddess of trees and flowers cradling giant phallus, sold at shop below. Shrine is for peace in home, safe childbirth. Surprising that it is not more popular, what with hordes of honeymooners here spring and autumn (for which times, should call ahead for rooms in better inns). Catholic church down road in memory of boiled Christians; now popular place to marry. Church has on long-term lease from Portugal, 18th century white horse-drawn carriage to cart newly-weds around.

PERSONAL DATEBOOK: **Dec 15** Unzen's *Hot Spring Festival*; colorful rites at shrine and temple in town, drum group performances to 'quiet' souls of martyrs.

Overnite at Unzen is relaxing change to energy and many things to see and do in Nagasaki. Refreshed with good bath next morning...

We head down other side of mountain, 40min bus, or cab (15x-mtr) to...
SHIMABARA, where Christianity was effectively destroyed during failed Shimabara Rebellion of 1637-8 when Christians, farmers and remnants of anti-Tokugawa followers of destroyed Toyotomi clan revolted against religious persecution, economic policies and traditional foe. It is pleasant town, well worth half-day stop on way to central Kyushu via Shimabara ferry. This entire area had been haven for Christians under Christian Daimyo Arima until he was replaced in 1616 by anti-Christian Matsukura of **Unzen Hells** infamy (*see* UNZEN). Mt Unzen erupting most of 1991 buried whole area in ash to cripple tourism, wreak havoc on several villages S-side so some had to be abandoned. Killed famed French vulcanologist pair.

October 1637 saw small Christian 'demonstration' at Kuchinotsu at end of peninsula; but handled badly by Matsukura it spread to Shimabara and Amakusa Isle, where it acquired leader in 14-year old firebrand AMAKUSA Shiro. Castle in Shimabara erroneously noted by most writers to be where 37,000-odd, of predominantly Christian peasant army and non-Christian dissident fellow farmers died in their last stand against far superior forces of professional samurai. Tragedy did not occur here (Shimabara itself makes no such claim) which makes Shimabara more interesting for tourist for while Christians occupied already ruined castle of Hara, Shimabara was main government garrison: today boasts sole remaining **feudal samurai garrison** architecture. Castle was government forces' HQ, no fighting occurred here. Rebels holed up at Hara (*see* p746) December 1637 and repelled first attacks by general ITAKURA Shigemasa who died in battle; replaced by shogun's own MATSUDAIRA Nobutsuna who with 12,500 surrounded Hara. Peasant army still held out 88 days. With no food or water left, were overrun February 28. Shimabara Castle, restored 1964, eruption rescue HQ '91, houses fine collection Christian mementos.

From castle walk away from sea, up main street to...
Military Quarters, *Buké Yashiki* recognizable from ancient town model in castle by stone walls lining street. Third street up still has old-style brook bringing drinking water down center, typical houses 300 years old in which ordinary samurai (those with under 70 koku of land) lived. Public rest house at N (R end, next to it **Yamamoto House**, restored, may enter).

Kilometer/10mins beyond is...
HONKO-JI temple, interesting for lovely assortment of stone images in stone veranda circling court; family temple of local Matsudaira lords where they are buried. Across from temple, behind Shimabara Agricultural high school are remains of Matsudaira clan **medicinal herb garden**.

Circling R (kilo N of temple, Buke Yashiki), is...
Grave of Magdalene *Madereina-no-haka* burial of some local Christians. Same distance S of castle is site of **Imamura Prison**, where Italian father

Navarre and Japanese followers were kept before being burned at stake on nearby hill. Numerous lumpy mounds around town, including one you will pass on way back to ferry and which almost reaches sea, were made by great eruption of nearby volcano in 1792: which at same time formed KUJUKU-SHIMA, '99-Isles', in bay—used to be 67, but many have submerged over centuries, leaving only 16 now. S of castle, on main non-coastal road are several temples, most with Christians' graves.

Furthest S, mountain-side, is...
GOKOKU-DERA temple, wood sculptures of **30 Guardian Spirits** commissioned 1738, each one by different master carver from Kyoto. Lined up in Banjin-do Hall, each sits in own gilded, lacquered case. Hidden behind and under them are some 70,000 scrolls of lotus sutra. Ocean-side of street is ETO-JI temple, with giant reclining Buddha (new); and grave of ITAKURA Shigemasa, who failed to take Hara Castle. Oceanwards two streets and back towards castle thru section of town is canal-stream with houses along one side, 1,000s of carp swim in it.

Mar 1-10 *Ten-day market*, reminder of former importance of Shimabara. Merchants set up stalls at Ota Hiroba square near castle. There may be nothing of special interest, but we find this good opportunity to pick up true rural folkcraft items and experience aspect of rural life which is fast disappearing: marketplaces and side shows, true country fair. Downtown shopping area puts on big sales to compete for trade of country folks coming in from outlying isles.

WHERE TO STAY: Hot spring waters were tapped in 1967 and all inns here now boast onsen baths. Several lovely seaside inns have up-to-date facilities, best two are: **Nanpuro** ☎(0957)-62-5111, ¥-Sw/2, with superb garden, in Benten-cho midway between ferry harbor and castle; and **Tsukumo** ☎62-3111 on small rise overlooking Ariake Sea, 500m S of ferry harbor, ¥-Sw/2. Both have new wings; seafood, especially crabs and shrimp are plentiful here. Numerous budget ryokan around ferry harbor, in town around City Hall; few minshuku; **Minshuku Nogiku** ☎63-1672 in Kita Senbonmachi features *sansai ryori* at usual ¥-Bw/2. Youth Hostel just behind harbor stn Shimabara Tetsudo electric. **Kanko-annai** in ferry terminal.

GETTING AROUND: **Buses** from Unzen are frequent, with two bus companies making run: Prefectural-run **Ken-ei Bus Co** with terminal at top end of Unzen near Kotobuki Kokusai Hotel; and **Shimatetsu Bus Co** with terminal across from Fukiya Ryokan. Both follow same route to Shimabara stn via ferry harbor (where some end). What we did was get off at ferry, leave luggage in coin locker, then bus 5km to castle. This also enables you to check ferry departure times, depending on which course you plan to take out of here. Can also go by taxi tour: Harbor → Castle → Military Quarters → Honkoji → Gokokudera → Etoji → Harbor 2hrs, ¥5,360 (12x-mtr). Can rent **bicycles** at castle, ¥150/hr; or if staying in town, most inns have few to lend for free.

CHOPSTICKS: Ofukuro, Mongolian-style garden restaurant was one of most delightful dining finds in Kyushu, between Castle and Buke Yashiki in private home of long Manchurian resident, Mrs Imazato. English-speaking daughter Seiko, runs cooking school, advises she may succumb to gourmet-boom and reopen, so check ☎(0957)-62-5005. (From castle ramp turn L, take first R then at dead end, L about 60m to stone wall on L, 2nd gate, white glass sign on door, hit gong on L.) We dined in house or in garden with lovely view of castle. Our '64 edition brought them boom till mom died—hopefully your calls will encourage her to resume fine institution.

Alternative, **Himematsu-ya**, top end of street closest to castle, with canal and carp – serves local specialities: cool weather *guso-ni*, assorted seafood in broth cooked in clay pot, ¥700; summer *nagashi-somen*, noodles chilled in natural spring water.

WHERE NEXT: 3 ferry routes: On-season March thru May, Oct, Nov; off-season Jan, Feb, Jun thru Sep, Dec: Most frequent is 1hr crossing to MISUMI on excellent **Shimabara Kokudo Ferry**, 13x-daily (12 off-season) with first out of

SHIMABARA 7:25, last 18:10; reverse first 7:25, last 18:40. 1st class ¥1,670, 2nd cl ¥830. From MISUMI, 50min JR rail to KUMAMOTO, where continue **International Tourist Route**; 3hr ltd express down → KAGOSHIMA; or 1hr45min → HAKATA-FUKUOKA with optional detour → YANAGAWA. Also **buses** MISUMI → HONDO on Amakusa, (*see* HIDDEN CHRISTIAN ROUTE below).

2nd ferry is Amakusa Pearl Line, SHIMABARA → MATSUSHIMA, halfway between Misumi and Hondo: 90min crossing, 3x-daily at 8:30, 11:30, 14:20, return 10:10, 13:10, 16:10 (off-season only 8:40, ret 16:30); 1st class ¥1,890, 2nd class ¥930. Similar from SHIMA.

3rd ferry (passenger only) is 50min (¥1,730), 6x-daily SHIMABARA → OMUTA, N of Kumamoto. Omuta is southern terminus of Nishi-tetsu private electric which connects to HAKATA-FUKUOKA via YANAGAWA; express 15min to Yanagawa, 50min on to Fukuoka. JR little longer. If continuing on to KAGOSHIMA, suggest taking electric back to OMUTA, where all Kagoshima-bound trains (local to ltd express) stop.

Drivers: Convenient to is Ariake Ferry link TAIRA (15km up coast from Shimabara) to NAGASU (btwn Omuta-Kumamoto), 26x-daily (22 off-season) convenient to Trans-Kyushu Expwy. Non-car wanderer heading to YANAGAWA: 20min bus or Shimabara electric → TAIRA; JR Nagasu → OMUTA 14min (2 stns) not quite hourly, or bus.

Ariake (Shining) **Sea**, thru which most of these ferries run, has one of world's largest tidal ranges (up to 7m) where in early times peculiar fishing techniques were developed and are still in use. In one, which you will see, stone wall of round boulders is built out in area several hundred meters offshore. Fish swim into these at high tide, to be left high and dry as waters recede. Bus or train from Misumi ferry port to Kumamoto passes along several miles of shore near Sumiyoshi, where at low tide you will see great fences standing on tidal flats, stretching in places few miles out. Entire fleets of trucks will be out there, thousands of workers tending edible seaweed crop on high fences, trucks scrambling shoreward as tide turns, carrying seawaters right up to our highway and submerging towering sea-weed frames. Seen all year, best and largest harvesting occurs November. In season (Mar-June), booths along highway sell secondary crops from tides —crabs, shrimps, oysters and other shellfish—at budget prices. At this time you may also see fishermen skimming over muddy ocean floor on ski-like boards herding local delicacy *mutsugoro*, odd-looking mud-dwelling fish, into nets.

PERSONAL DATEBOOK: Mysterious *flares of dragon king* light up open waters in 2 different areas. These *shiranui*, or lights of unknown origin, never fail to glow on nites of full moon: long strips of fluorescence stretch for miles. Who knows why or how. One spot embraces seas between Omuta City and Kinpo-zan near Kumamoto City. Best seen **lunar Jan16** (full moon Feb), also **lunar Aug 16** (full moon Sept) nites. Another area can be seen from Obama hot spring, along whole coast to Hara, as it lights up S side of Nomo peninsula (S of Nagasaki), **lunar Jan 15** and **lunar Jul 15** nites.

HIDDEN CHRISTIAN RTE   LONG WAY TO AMAKUSA

Hara Castle ruins at Minami-Arima, 28km/45min bus or rail from Shimabara. Ruins back on high cliff over sea, off which defeated surrendering Christians were marched to their deaths (*see* p744). One each of budget minshuku, ryokan, Kokumin-shukusha here; also small **salt-water Onsen Center**, ¥150 dip. Few kilos back up road to Shimabara is Sukawa **ferry** pier with 4x-daily (2 off-season), 1hr to MATSUSHIMA, 1st class ¥1,750, 2nd class ¥870.

Continue on half-hour to next town...
KUCHINOTSU: 3km down coast at **KATSUSA** village was site of first church school, 1590. Area has numerous communal graves of Christians

killed at Hara; all have crosses etched quite inconspicuously onto them.
Odds-and-ends **Folk History Museum** near pier, in old wood Western
building, ex-Customs house.

*From here, 17 ferries at 45min intervals make half- hour trips (¥300) run to Oni-ike
on N tip on western isle of...*

AMAKUSA. Two isles, *Kami-no-shima* (upper) and *Shimo-no-shima*
(lower), actually E & W. Secret Catholic colonies have survived here since
tragedy of Shimabara until this day. Many believers moved to most isolated
corners to avoid persecution. Still rather secretive about their worship; they
are called *Kakure-Kirishitan*, Hidden Christians.

GETTING AROUND: Buses on western Shimonoshima start at HONDO and
go down W shore, or down middle to southern tip USHIBUKA, whence frequent, short
ferries to Nagashima peninsula, back door to KAGOSHIMA and to MINAMATA on main
JR line to KAGOSHIMA. For intensive travel, work W or counter-clockwise if coming
from-, or clockwise if going to NAGASAKI. Many pleasant fishing villages with not
much in particular but good beaches and one rural hot spring; budgeteers may want to
head straight to Hondo and pick up **4-day bus pass** (¥4,000, possibly sold now at ONI-
IKE bus terminal) on main **Kyushu Sanko Bus Co**; also good for discounts at some
inns. Regular fares cost ¥1,350 just for HONDO-USHIBUKA run, even more if down W
shore; bus pass includes one-way to/from KUMAMOTO (¥2,700 reg). Just W of Oni-ike
is **ferry**-port TOMIOKA with several daily connections to MOGI, NAGASAKI. Halfway
down scenic W shore is SHIMODA ONSEN (1hr bus from Hondo); at western tip are two
villages, OO-E and SAKITSU, main hideaway for Christians. Both have fine churches
built 1932 & 1934, each boasted own priest imported from Europe. Oo-e's church was
first, funded personally by French missionary Garnier.

Half-hour bus E of Oni-ike is...
HONDO, pleasant little main port town bounded by fine, white sandy
beaches characteristic of Amakusa. Has its reminders of Christian struggle.
W end of town, on small rise (site of 16th century castle) is *Sen-nin-zuka*,
burial mound of thousand Christians killed at Shimabara. Nearby is small
Christian cemetery, bread loaf-shaped grave markers adorned with small
crosses. Building behind with giant cross is **Christian Museum** (8:30-
18:00, ¥300) with collection of *Fumi-e, Maria Kannons* and other secret
symbols, banner created by AMAKUSA Shiro for Shimabara Uprising—two
angels kneeling before Holy Grail. As Amakusa was Christian stronghold,
shogunate in 1647, after Shimabara, ordered building of temples and
shrines to break power of church. Among first built is **MYOTOKU-JI**,
behind and N of museum, with unusual 'foreign' jizo, Maria Kannons, and
crosses carved into steps meant to act like *Fumi-e* as anyone entering temple
was forced to tread on them. Between park and town is small Catholic
church, little cave here emulates Lourdes: **4th sun Oct** many make pilgrimages, candlelight procession memorializes start of Shimabara Uprising.

During persecution under Hideyoshi, first movable-type printing press
(printing in Japan far predates Europe, but on woodblocks) which had been
brought in by missionaries and set up at seminary in Katsuna, had to be
moved to Hondo 1592-1597, then to Nagasaki 1597-1611, and eventually
to Macao around 1614. Site of seminary where press was kept is kilo N.

Just N of Myotoku-ji, down one street is...
Amakusa Folk Museum (¥300) collection of Christian items, and several
hundred samples of local pottery, made since 16th century in 4 kilns around
town. Three closest kilns are: **Mizuno-taira kiln** just beyond folk
museum; **Maruo kiln** 500m W at intersection front of Myotoku-ji; &
Sueyoshi kiln, kilo N of Maruo kiln on main road Rte324.

WHERE TO STAY: Dozens of inns at Hondo, **Kokusai hotel** ☎(0969)-22-3161 and **Bai-rin** ☎22-5261, top list, both ¥-Tw/2. Most inns run ¥-hi-B–Tw/2, like **Chawan-ya** ☎22-2108. *Budgeteers* have several ¥-Bw/2 range; or Kokumin-shukusha **Amakusa Seaside Hotel** ☎22-5147, ¥-B+w/2; one minshuku, and Amakusa **YH**. **Kanko-annai** at portside bus terminal can also help you find rooms in rest of isle.

SHIMODA SPA has several moderate and budget inns; best is **Boyo-kaku** ☎(0969)-42-3111, ¥-Tw/2. Kokumin-shukusha **Amakusa-so** ☎42-3131, ¥-Tw/2; and few budget minshuku. USHIBUKA has numerous inns in all ranges.

GETTING AROUND: 4 ferries daily → Minamata on mainland, 2hrs. Hop on bus and head up 1hr to MATSUSHIMA at northern tip of KAMINOSHIMA—E shore of Kaminoshima has many little villages and fine beaches, irregular **fishing boat ferries** hopping up coast; also **bus**. Five bridges now span various Amakusa isles connecting them to mainland. Matsushima also has many lodgings, but not much to do or see; however, many boats from/to SHIMABARA. Also 4x-daily MATSUSHIMA → YASHIRO on mainland (JR exp stop), 50min. But rather than cross here, head to KUMAMOTO via MISUMI: 35min bus to Misumi, or meander thru isles, passing under great bridges on 40min **tour boat**, 3x-daily, out of MATSUSHIMA 10:00, 11:20, 13:00; reverse 14:00, 15:30; ¥800. Make sure you don't get on more frequent circular tours which end up back in Matsushima 40min later. This schedule has remained unchanged for years, and we were assured there is no reason to bother changing them, but you might confirm just in case, at Hondo Kanko-annai, and sched corresponding bus. HONDO → MATSUSHIMA → MISUMI **buses** frequent: locals hourly, many more expresses at ¥100 extra cut off 10min each leg. **Taxi** HONDO → MISUMI about 18x-mtr; about half that for HONDO → MATSUSHIMA.

KUMAMOTO, crossroad on NAGASAKI → BEPPU and NAGASAKI → FUKUOKA southern routes which offers our alternate S to KAGOSHIMA. Little for tourists; castle is 1960 reconstruction in concrete; only gingko tree at gate is old, planted by local hero KATO Kiyomasa 1607, conqueror of Korea. Museum of his relics in new donjon, as also KATO SHRINE nearby, HOMMYO-JI Nichiren temple. Area around castle offers good antique shops, not-bad prices. Main Kumamoto bus center is just S-side of castle (reached by tram or bus from stn); 500m E of either is small house where KOIZUMI Yakumo, **Lafcadio Hearn**, lived short time. Hanaokayama hill **pagoda** new, 1954, to souls of war dead, has relic of Gautama Buddha donated by PM Nehru. **International Folk Art Museum**, *Kokusai Mingeikan*, taxi 2x-mtr, offshoot *Kurashiki Mingeikan* of TONOMURA Kichinosuke. **Artpolis** city-wide modernization encouraging fun new architecture—stadia to pissoires—directed by ISOZAKI

CHOPSTICKS: Best sashimi and sushi in town, epicurean but ¥-S, **Mutsugoro** in basement of Green Hotel.

Taped info on LINK (Local Information Network of Kumamoto) specializes monthur on daily living needs for foreign residents, fri-sun on cultural & tourist matters: 3min, ☎(096)-383-9000. City planning drive to encourage **Home Visits** and budget-saving **Home Stays**: for info ☎381-4906 & -0782, LINK's prefectural office sponsor.

Reason for getting off train at Kumamoto is to take bus from stn via bus center, or ...
Steam Locomotive (SL): KUMAMOTO (10:29)–SUIZENJI–MUSASHIZUKA–SANRIGI–HIGOOTSU–SETA–TATENO–AKAMIZU–ASO (12:39)–IKIOI-NO-MURA–MIYAJI. Return dep ASO 15:22, arr KUMAMOTO SL STN 17:15.

MOUNT ASO (1hr40min past airport, 40min out) pronounced AH-so, quickly, and that is just about what you will sigh when you hear about it. Volcano, just over mile high—not much even in Japan, but biggest hole (i.e. caldera) in world and from top impressive because crater rim rises 700m. Legend is outer crater was once lake, but one day god of mountain kicked open only break (thru which rail, bus pass) emptying water, leaving plain fit for cultivation. Within great outer crater are smaller crater-mounts *Naka-dake* or Middle Mount, still active, *Kijima-dake*, *Eboshi-dake*, *Taka-dake*, highest at 1592m, and *Neko-dake*. Within egg-shaped outer crater of 128km circumference live some 100,000 people in three towns and dozen

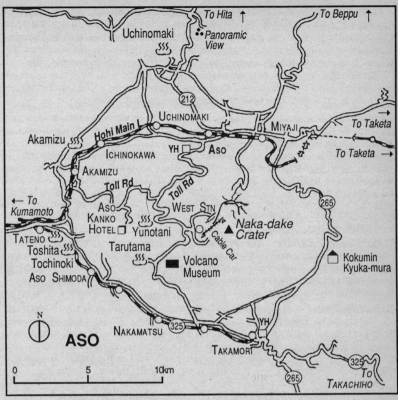

villages. Eruptions which have made life uncomfortable at times, are yet
frequent: 90 major since 796AD. Aso lava covers two-thirds of entire isle
of Kyushu. Volcano also provides for numerous small hot springs.

Ascent of Aso, actually **Naka-dake**, sole smoking one, is 30min bus
from either Akamizu or Aso stns on JR; or direct from Kumamoto. Fine,
scenic toll roads meander up to Aso Shrine, from where 4min ropeway
takes you across to volcano's rim, constantly and impressively fuming from
its 100m deep crater. Fame of mountain brings much income from tourists
to area, but it also brings much expense as popular pastime is to toss one's
disappointed miserable self in. If anyone comes up and politely asks you to
hold his coat, either do so and wish him bon voyage, or grab him and call
one of anti-suicide patrolmen. Despite depth and heat and gases, suicide
usually fails, ledges break fall and hold him till rescue squad can get down.
Hiker can circle crater and head E 2.5km (4km if via Taka-dake) to end of road SENSUI-
KYO **viewing platform** with nearby campground, whence 15min bus to Miyaji stn; or
head N 6.5km down to Aso stn. Or back W beyond ropeway to dead-end Tarutama Onsen.

Stay at **Aso YMCA**, ¥-Pw/2; 'camp'-style, separate male/female cabins, tatami
bunk beds. Cold rooms, friendly atmosphere.

Several hot spas on plain not particularly convenient to sole live crater.

Usually preferred by both foreign and Japanese at any rate is...
YUNOTANI, 820m above sea level, in foothills of Eboshi-dake. 20min bus
from Akamizu stn (also bus link to ropeway) offers fine view of Aso area and out
to Ariake Sea and Unzen. Various facilities here, from **Aso Kanko** W-style hotel
and J-style annex ☎(0967)-67-0311, ¥-T-Lw/2, to budget inns, pensiones and campsite.
Avoid sparkling, giant UCHINOMAKI hot spring 5km N of Aso stn on Rte 212.

Other spa villages worthwhile for more leisurely: single-inn...
TOSHITA, and nearby TOCHINOKI with waterfalls, both short bus from
Tateno stn in outer rim gap; Tarutama and nearby JIGOKU (hell), both
20min bus from Shimoda stn; boast *outdoor baths*, popular with hikers.
Tateno, Shimoda stns on dead-end Takamori Line, split from main Kumamoto-Beppu line
before outer rim. Buses circle from/to main Aso stn, Kanko-annai can book anywhere.
Halfway btwn Aso and Beppu along Yamanami highway is lovely YUFU-IN (p768).

International Tourist Route concludes at Beppu after detours. Scenic
Yamanami toll-road cuts across from Aso to Beppu, taken by most buses. Driver finds
cluster of tiny hot springs on Yamanami Highway beyond Aso outer ring: YUFU-IN.
Unless driving, you've no choice but to head to BEPPU, Kyushu terminal of old
International Tourist Route which continued by Seto-Inland Sea ship to KOBE; or
backtrack to KUMAMOTO and down → KAGOSHIMA (follows); or for wanderer. 80min
bus from end of line TAKAMORI stn to spectacular Takachiho Ravine (follows).

HITOYOSHI, if heading down to Kagoshima offers similar backtracking
detour but this time for one of Japan's top white-water river rapids:
18km down Kuma River.

GETTING THERE: Several expresses KUMAMOTO → HITOYOSHI (90min);
others change at YATSUSHIRO for hourly local departures, 80min. Direct bus 2hr30min
from KUMAMOTO via YATSUSHIRO. Rail, bus via coast to YATSUSHIRO pass UDO,
where those from MISUMI after SHIMABARA rejoin main trunk. Boats dep SHIMABARA
via MATSUSHIMA → YATSUSHIRO. Check re occasional SLs out of KUMAMOTO.

Shallow wooden skiff down river regularly Mar thru Nov: 4x-daily weekdays; 11 sat-
sun, hol; Oct-Nov several extras daily for maple viewing: ¥2,780/adult, ¥1,440/child;
¥41,700 to charter boat (fits 15) which is only way Dec-Mar. Boat ends 2hr30min later at
2km long Stalactite Cavern, *Kyusen-do* (¥700) across river. Osakama stn on same
side as boat pier, 1hr local down to Yatsushiro, 20min back to Hitoyoshi. Arrange river
rides thru stn Kanko-annai, your inn, or at departure pier 15min walk W of stn.

Hitoyoshi town is also pleasant place to wander around. Sagara clan was here 700
years, but little remains of its feudal glory but some run-down ex-samurai houses near
castle's remaining stoneworks. Behind stn are 20-odd 'caves' with faded animals etched
on walls: 1,200-year-old graves of local chieftains. Short walk from stn (block W of bus
center) is lovely AOI ASO SHRINE, which site dates to same period as burial caves.
Great thatched roof gate and present compound dates to 1610 rebuilding by Lord SAGARA
Yorifusa closely following architectural style of its Kamakura period (12th century)
predecessor, which probably bore little resemblance to 9th century original.

DATEBOOK: *Autumn Fete* Nov 9-11, dancing drummers in antlered helmets.

WHERE TO STAY: Hitoyoshi is also hot spring town, piped to all inns and
one public bath in section of town with samurai houses. Dozens of inns all ¥-B-T, best
along river. Suggest Grand Hotel ☎(0966)-22-2171 and classy Nabeya Honkan
☎22-3131, both near boat landing, ¥-T+w/2. As usual, check Kanko-annai.

If coming up from Kagoshima 2hr30min train (change Yoshimatsu). En route is...
KIRISHIMA ONSEN CLUSTER, S entrance to Ebino Kogen Plateau,
field of extinct volcanic caldera lakes and still smoking craters (total 23
volcanos here—rumbling late ;91), crisscrossed by hiking trails and scenic
toll roads. Onsen cluster is group of 7 hot spring areas within 5km^2 area,
each with its own bus stop; all but two are tiny, with one or two budget inns. Shinyu
onsen's one inn boasts outdoor bath. Of many trails, most direct one (among others)
to central Ebino Plateau, 6km N, starts Shinyu. Ebino has few budget and moderate
lodgings; and just up recently-built toll road is steaming river, pools forming excellent
natural baths at ideal 40° C. Also town-run outdoor bath little closer to inns; charges
¥100 per dip, also has room only for ¥600 night. Campsites all over, on and off beaten
path. Excellent maps, information, available in Kagoshima.

BEPPU: terminus of INTERNATIONAL ROUTE, *see* p767.

*As they filed over the side, someone
near me struck up the old sea chanty,
"Seafaring may we lay our bodies deep..."*
—Admiral YOKOI Toshiyuki, in *Ukiyo*

KAGOSHIMA 鹿児島
SOUTHERN GATEWAY TO KYUSHU

YOU CAN TELL you're nearing Kagoshima by great billows of smoke
rising above hills. Our train tunnels thru hills to large bay, and we see its
source — volcanic Sakurajima Isle just beyond city. Giant eruption 1914
buried all fields and villages on isle and created bridge to other side. During
our recent visit it was particularly active, covering city in layer of fine ash.
Didn't seem really to bother Kagoshimans who take this for everyday fact of
life, shrug, say 'it's usually not this bad'. Summer winds blow ash over
city; winter blows to other side. Called 'Naples of Orient', naturally has
sister-city relation with vulcan Italian namesake.

This beautiful prefecture of same name rightfully claims itself **southern
gateway to Japan**, boosted with increased international travel connections. Was primary point of departure for official envoys to T'ang China
much of 8th century. Trade with West began 1549 with landing of Portuguese ship on nearby Tanegashima Island, which introduced first guns,
called *tanegashima* by Japanese who mass-produced them from few originals bought. St Francis Xavier first landed here, bringing Christianity to
Japan. During Tokugawa ban on foreign contact, Satsuma (as Kagoshima
was called), long-time Tokugawa enemy, basically ignored ban and had
constant 'illegal' trade, using isolated ports such as Bonotsu or Amami
Oshima Isles. These isles make Kagoshima longest prefecture, 600km N-S,
provide tropical paradise escapes for modern Japanese who feel Hawaii is
just too 'foreign'. After Perry's opening to world, Satsuma rebelled against
Tokugawa, represented self as independent kingdom *Royaume de Satsuma*
at Paris International Exposition, where two 'Japans' exhibited. Continuing
S links us to Ryukyu Islands (Okinawa) which were also administered by
Satsuma, regaining semi-independence only to be conquered again by
Tokugawa Shoguns and century later become US territory 1945-72, then
returned to Japan as separate province.

Satsuma's anti-Tokugawa attitude made it perfect spawning ground for
makers of modern Japan. Sword-wielding hot-heads of 1850s sliced down
Tokugawa officials who tried to negotiate with West, and Westerners alike.
Having their beloved city pounded into rubble by British fleet, these men
did about face, recognized need to deal with West (can't lick 'em, join 'em),
and became 'Elder Statesmen' who pushed their country into modern era.
(Fact that British, French, Dutch and American ships soon after flattened
Shimonoseki, port of their chief allies Choshu clan, for firing on Western
ships, helped to convince Choshu die-hards.)

Anti-Tokugawa attitude also led to local lord developing secret language
among people so that Tokugawa spies would reveal themselves. This remained as peculiar Kagoshima dialect. During World War II army used this
as secret communication language, like US used Cherokee and Navajo native Americans as voice radio operators instead of codes, or British used
Welsh. It proved tougher than 'Magic' code to crack till one US Army nisei
of Kagoshima descent walked in on US signal corps' monitoring 'secret
Japanese code' and recognized his parents' home-dialect.

GETTING THERE: From NAGASAKI, FUKUOKA, KUMAMOTO direction, most trains end at main NISHI (West) KAGOSHIMA stn; Kagoshima stn only 2km on is not used much. Our references to *stn* means Nishi Kagoshima, unless otherwise specified. 6hrs **train** from NAGASAKI, 5hrs from FUKUOKA; **fly** either in 40min. Airtime: KAGOSHIMA → OSAKA 70min; → TOKYO 1hr45min. **International links** make this attractive alternate entry from SE Asia, preferable to Narita and roundtrip S: JAL connects Hong Kong, Bangkok, Singapore; Nauru Air to Nauru via Guam whence Continental southsea island hops to US. Check with your agent for new possibilities. By **sea**, Nippon Kosoku Ferry Co links OSAKA daily: dep Osaka 18:00 to land next day 14:40 Taniyama Pier 10km S of downtown, reverse dep 16:00 to Osaka-Nanko Pier 13:15 Kagoshima's internationally-minded government goes all-out to make city international, succeeding in getting many major luxury liners (such as QE II) to stop here.

Airport is 1hr bus N of city, and recommended course is to spend first nite (or last if flying out) at KIRISHIMA hot springs, direct airport bus, and then into town (or to airport). With extra day, head down to hot sand-baths of **Ibusuki Beach** to explore that area, most notably beautiful samurai houses and gardens of CHIRAN.

GETTING AROUND: Native Kagoshimans are friendly lot, intent on creating 'international tourist city' and doing good job at it. KAGOSHIMA 'i', Prefectural Tourist Center, with highly competent, bilingual staff of energetic young adults ready with up-to-date information, all sorts of assistance for city, entire prefecture: hours 8:30-15:00 weekdays, and till noon saturday; ☎(0992)-23-5771, or stop by 4th floor Sangyo Kaikan Bldg, 9-1 Meizan-cho; 2 blocks coastwards of Asahi-dori tram stop. Their **yellow brochure**, directions in English & Japanese available at stn, airport and ferry terminals. There is also information center at rail stn and tour information center in front. There are **bilingual Goodwill Guides**, noted by their badge proclaiming such, with dove sitting atop globe. You can arrange to have guide accompany you on **taxi tours**, bus or solo. Arrange thru Kagoshima 'i'; if no fee, get them small gift or take them out for dinner. Kagoshima also has one of most active **Home Visit** programs in Japan. To spend few hours with local family, arrange day before thru Kagoshima 'i', or **City Hall Tourist Bureau**, ☎24-1111.

Several **bus tours** but none worth suggesting. **Taxi tours** best bet for limited time and convenience: hourly rate, cheaper than most cities, as is basic meter: around 7x-mtr (¥2,680) *kogata* (4-psgr) and 8.5x-mtr (¥3,400) *chugata* (5-psgr), which is not much more than one person's bus tour costs. Set itinerary and price before starting, at stn front or hotel pick-up. Basic tour takes you to N end Iso Garden → back to town → Shiroyama Hill and S → Amami Silk Center to total 3-4 hrs; extra hour will ferry you across to SAKURAJIMA up to observation area, and back.

Most interesting, cheapest is to mix bus/tram (¥500 **all day tram pass** incl buses within city limits) with walking, for full day to see town; Sakurajima next morning. Three tram lines: #1 runs Kagoshima stn → Taniyama (near Oshima Silk center); #2 starts at Korimoto on #1 line, passes front of Nishi Kagoshima stn → Shimizu-cho, part way to Iso Garden; (#3 we don't use, betw Kagoshima stn → Ishiki-cho). All 3 pass thru downtown. Speed this up with occasional cabs, found all over city (listed rates are one-way from stn). Ascent of Shiroyama is mainly for view of Sakurajima, which you can cut out and get same view later: instead, save time and money for jaunt out to Sakurajima, or view at Reimei-kan Museum at base of Shiroyama. Several **car rental** agencies in town and at airport—we do not suggest one just to see city, but do if planning to travel around area. Roads here are good, well-marked (usually with alphabet), and not very crowded.

We start at **station**; people-covered **monument** in front is dedicated to young Satsuma men 'secretly' sent overseas by local Shimazu lord to become first leaders of modern Japan.

First stop (25min bus, cab 2x-mtr) is...
Iso Garden, beautiful landscaped, surrounding ex-villa of Shimazu lords. One could easily spend few hours exploring beautiful nooks and crannies of this monument to luxury. View of smoking Sakurajima makes it appear to rise out of pond here; another corner has series of narrow waterways:

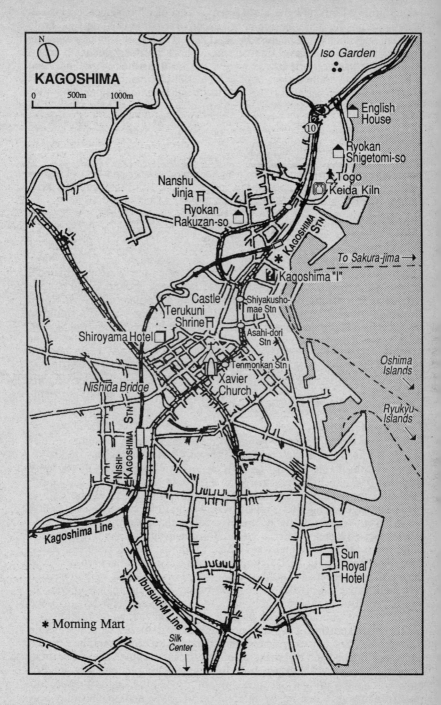

N

KAGOSHIMA

0   500m   1000m

Iso Garden

English House

Ryokan Shigetomi-so

Togo
Keida Kiln

Nanshu Jinja

Ryokan Rakuzan-so

KAGOSHIMA STN

To Sakura-jima →

Kagoshima "I"

Castle
Terukuni Shrine

Shiyakusho-mae Stn

Shiroyama Hotel

Asahi-dori Stn

Oshima Islands →

Nishida Bridge

Tenmonkan Stn

Xavier Church

Ryukyu Islands →

NISHI-KAGOSHIMA STN

Kagoshima Line

Sun Royal Hotel

Ibusuki-M Line

* Morning Mart

Silk Center
↓

here Shimazu lords and guests sat in emulation of Chinese peach-blossom party, composing haiku before next cup of sake came floating by. Truly relaxing spot should not be missed, especially if at end of long day in hustle and bustle of overactive Kagoshima. Short ropeway leads to small amusement park on hill for best view of **Sakurajima**. Stone building near entrance to complex was built 1852 by 28th Shimazu lord Nariakira as reverberating and smelting furnace to produce cannon, later ceramics, glassware. Inside is interesting **museum** of what was made here plus Shimazu family goods spanning 700 years (¥500 museum & garden). Mechanical looms imported 1867 as part of Nariakira's westernizing campaign and he also brought in English technicians who were housed in stately white W-style building down road. Drive back to town along coast road (some buses, 2km walk to Shimizu-cho tram stop), past good beach and old walls from atop which Shimazu artillery made fair but futile account of itself against British bombardment of 1863: pop-guns *vs* new naval rifles.

Sharp turn uphill to...
Grave of Admiral Togo Heihachiro, British-trained naval samurai who led Japanese fleet to victory over Chinese at Pung Island, blockade of Russian Port Arthur and destruction of Imperial Russian fleet off Tsushima May, 1905. Shimazu and his fellow 'revolutionaries' were pragmatists. Britain shelled Kagoshima in reprisal for failing to apologize and pay indemnities for cutting down some ill-mannered English tourist in Kobe. Humbled Kagoshimans welcomed British landing party to smoking Kagoshima and purchased part of attacking fleet, made lasting friends with Britain who then trained what, when Emperor Meiji restored imperial power in 1868, became Imperial Japanese Navy. Togo was born 1847, went to England for education in 1871, had British ships and gunnery instructors at Battle of Tsushima. He died at 88 in 1934, is buried here overlooking his beloved sea. US Admiral Nimitz was fan of his, whose photo is prominently displayed in Togo Memorial, Tokyo.

At foot of Togo hill is...
Keida, also called *Tanoura-gama*, kiln where best true Satsuma-ware is made. If this is end of your tour and if buying and planning to spend much time here, discharge taxi, or take quick look and onwards. Buses more frequent to Togo hill from town, or have kiln call cab after shopping. Catholics may want to visit **Xavier Memorial** marker, unimpressive, better one in town, but this is on site where saint first landed.

Satsuma-ware introduced by 80-odd captured Koreans 1598, made from imported Korean material until 1700 when suitable clay found locally. Higher class white Satsuma was limited to Shimazu nobles use only, until Nariakira lifted ban in 1850's. 'Popular' black Satsuma reflects commoners' tastes: most often made into beautiful sake bottles which look more like flattened teapots. Singular white ware baked 10hrs in small kiln, glazed, and baked 30-40hrs more in middle kilns to obtain its characteristic glaze and crystalline double-crackle. Then drawings and enamel decorations are put on and baked 3hrs at low temperature. About 1914 was great worldwide demand for Satsuma-ware, shortage of painters so after crackling, pieces were sent to Kobe and Kyoto for painting and final simple bake. Then more common *Kansai-satsuma* was born by counterfeiting base ceramics. But once you have seen real Satsuma, imitation looks flat, pale. Secret is in **multiple crackle** caused by interaction of glaze and special clay and cannot be imitated elsewhere. Finer crackle, higher price. Keida is last of old true Satsuma kilns in town; other three are postwar.

Back on tour, pilgrims continue along coast road 500m to rejoin main road, pick up #2 tram at Kasuga-cho stop; soon branches off R 2 stops to Tate-baba near which...
NANSHU SHRINE, dedicated to, and burial site of Saigo Takamori, who was also called (poetically) SAIGO Nanshu. One of top trio of leaders of early Meiji who led anti-Tokugawa coup, he and other ex-samurai (made commoners by Meiji) became disenchanted with course of events, lack of military adventures overseas (against Korea) to employ ex-samurai, and led coup attempt against new government. Saigo mobilized 10,000-odd students of his four-year-old military academy (remains nearby). Rebels at first easily victorious in home turf Kyushu, and southern Honshu home of equally rebellious Choshu men. Government mobilized new, all volunteer peasant army—which Saigo had helped start. Saigo's forces lost battle after battle (at Hagi on mainland, Akitsuki near Fukuoka and Kumamoto) and 8 months after their 'glorious start' ragtag remnants were holed up here around Shiroyama hill. On September 24, 1876 massed muskets of well-trained national army conquered last of sword-wielding samurai (much like Ieyasu's victory over Hideyoshi 380 years earlier at Sekigahara, or modernist Saigo's own successes against feudal Tokugawa), and as rebel soldiers fell in battle their leaders committed suicide. Just uphill is cave Saigo used as his battlefield command. He committed suicide just below cave; shot several times on his way to battle, he is said to have proclaimed, 'this is enough' and slit his belly while friend stood behind and dealt coup de grace, decapitation.

At this end of Shiroyama hill, remains of...
Tsurumaru Castle, Shimazu stronghold, flattened in Saigo's last stand. In its place is **Reimeikan Museum** (9:00-17:00, ¥200, X-mon), for which, stay on tram 4 short stops. Built 1968 for Meiji centennial, fine exhibits outline history of S Kyushu, from prehistory to Meiji leaders; folklore and folkcrafts. Much of it very visual, but unfortunately, no alphabetic labels. In back are reconstructed samples of rural Kyushu architecture.

Continuing now on foot along base of Shiroyama, pass giant....
Statue of Saigo Takamori, across from which is **City Art Museum** with fine collection of Satsuma-ware, and mostly cubist modern art, and small but pleasant garden. Another quiet corner is TERUKUNI (Illuminating-nation) SHRINE, dedicated to modern-minded lord Shimazu Nariakira, up wide street beyond Art Museum. Hoary Western building on corner built 1883 by Frenchman, now houses **Prefectural Museum**, best appreciated from outside. Heading away from shrine, take R at end of wide section of road, two blocks to **Xavier Church and Memorial**: in park across from church, was original church built early Meiji, but burned during World War II bombing so new church built 1959, 400th anniversary of his landing. Xavier spent 10 months here, mostly at loggerheads with local Buddhists, before heading up to Hirado.

Few minutes on same street puts you at river at spectacular 5-arched stone...
Nishida Bridge, one of 5 such bridges built across Kotsuki River in 1839 by local stone-mason IWANAGA Mitsugoro. This one is grandest, for Shimazu lords passed over it on their biennial visit to Edo-Tokyo. Heading downstream along riverside park, just before tram line is large **statue** of bearded Japanese in very Western clothes, OKUBO Toshimichi, who along with Saigo and KIDO Koin (of Choshu) made up Elder Statesmen trio of Meiji Japan. Okubo was cut down in Tokyo in 1878 by revenge-seeking followers of his one-time friend and ally, Saigo Takamori. Saigo's split from government was due to his insistence on need to invade and subjugate

Korea while Okubo advocated noninterference. Tho Okubo's policy out-
lasted him, it was Saigo's followers who eventually won, gaining control of
Korea after Sino-Japanese war in 1894-5, setting Japan on road to destruction and reconstruction. Stone monuments mark birthplaces of both
men, 100m apart, just down river.

Cross river at Nishida Bridge, 5min walk to stn. This whole leg is mostly for
follower of **history** of early modern Japan; and for **casual visitor**, we suggest hop
cab at Reimei kan, or walk down 200m to main road, catch #1 **tram** at Shiyakusho-mae
stop (next is Asahi-dori, for Kagoshima 'i') *for...*

Silk Center, *Oshima Tsumugi-no-sato:* **cab** 4x-mtr (5x- from Shiroyama) or
25min **tram** to end of #1 line. Die-hard Rail Passer take JR 2 stops S to Taniyama, but
time it right as only 1 or 2 hourly. Oshima silk is unique ikat woven in Amami
Oshima Isles from process learned centuries ago thru Chinese traders.
Watch entire process, from weaving to intricate dyeng, 100 alternate dye-
mud dippings at this center: beautiful complex created to 'give feel of
Amami Oshima', with Oshima-style rock garden and much of work done in
traditional thatched houses of islanders, all tropically-wooded surroundings.
It is worthwhile detour, for either scenery or silk.

While here, head to almost adjacent Honbo **Shochu Brewery** for
smooth but potent local potato brew. Shochu long considered 'poor man's
drink', mainly because its cheap ingredients made it popular with day laborers, especially depth-charged into stein of beer. In past few years it has
become 'in' drink with oh-so-fashionable youth of big cities, and now
you're nobody if you don't drink shochu. Most popular is *chu-hai*, mixed
with lemon or lime soda. You can make shochu out of almost anything that
will ferment (agent is rice, as in sake) and in addition to traditional *imo-*
(potato), *mugi-*(barley) shochu, they have corn, turnip, banana and more. It
is also recent, but popular, import item on special order, with France and
Canada supplying most. These import brands can cost you more than bottle
of best sake; good local *imo-shochu* on other hand is fraction of cost. Here
they make only true *imo-shochu.*

There are also two **Satsuma-ware** kilns out here: **Chotaro Kama**,
between Silk Center and JR stn; **Kinko Togei**, 500m S, near Taniyama
Harbor (whence boats for Osaka). Both places let you watch throwing,
firing and painting.

SAKURAJIMA, 15min ferry (¥100) across bay; only way up to YUNOHIRA
viewing platform is cab (6x-mtr r.t.). Couple of **tour buses** daily ferry across from
mainland, take you up (some also circle island); 4 daily Sakurajima's harbor → top →
back. Drive up thru lava moonscape beats view from platform, which is only 1/3 way up
but enough for panoramic view. Circle volcano by **bus.**

Interesting site is far side...
KUROGAMI SHRINE torii, of which top 4 feet poke above lava from
1914 big bang. That one was largest, disgorging three billion tons of lava in
about one month, burying entire isle in several feet, spewing ash up 8,000
meters, visible from as far as Kamchatka on Russian mainland N of
Hokkaido. Also created 400m wide bridge in 72m deep channel to farside
Osumi Peninsula; increased isle circumference from 40km to 52km. It has 3
peaks: 1117m *Kita-dake* (north peak), 1060m *Naka-dake* (mid), and presently
active 1040m *Minami-dake* (south). Sakurajima has extremely fertile soil,
produces great quantities of oranges, loquats, pears and radishes—which
are largest in world, 30cm/foot across, averaging 40 kg. Its oranges, on other
hand, are smallest in world at about 3 cm/1+in across, but sweet and juicy. Both are
harvested Dec-Jan by kimonoed women. Sakurajima has one hot spring spa,
FURUSATO, S shore, with ¥-B and ¥-T inns, and seaside bath in lava holes.

SHOPPING: Best place for quick overview of local arts and crafts is 1st floor of Sangyo Kaikan Bldg (same as Kagoshima 'i'), particularly for pottery, pewter, and Ryukyu lacquer—notable for its snake-blood Chinese red coloring.

Pottery: Besides *Satsuma-ware, Chotaro*-ware is dull with mocha colors like woodwork in old English inns, in folk styles; *Ryumonji*-ware is shiny brown outside, yellow in; *Naeshiro*-ware, similar to Karatsu or primitive Satsuma, also interesting. Pottery fan can visit original Satsuma-ware village of **NAESHIRO-GAWA**, 22km W of town on opposite coast. 30min on Nagasaki-bound trains to 3rd stop Ishu-in or 4th stop Higashi Ichiki and 5min bus (10min from former) to Miyama; or 1hr bus from town, leaves from HAYASHIDA BUS CO's main stop next to Takashimaya Dept Store on main street downtown. **MIYAMA** has 13 family-run kilns in pleasant, ancient village, all descended from originally 'imported' potters. Prices at Sangyo Kaikan are average for town; various types of pottery can be bought in major department stores and folk arts stores.

Pewter has been made here for over 100 years since English pewter was introduced and simultaneous Japanese discovery of tin here. However, there isn't much demand for it, other than as novel gift, and only one of old stores is left, **Otsuji Asahi-do**, at 56 Higashi Sengoku-cho. Okinawa Ryukyu **lacquer** industry was introduced here from isles which were colony of Satsuma. Also interesting folk toys, snake-skin leather products, and Okinawan *habu*- (snake) *shochu*—best, like mezcal, has snake floating in it. All sold in Takashimaya, Maruzen, Yamakata, Tenmonkan department stores as well.

Silk from Amami Oshima is made into gorgeous but fantastically expensive kimono; or more affordable blouses, neckties, bags and other everyday items for men & women. Good selection out at **Silk Center**, also department stores. Of department stores, main are **Takashimaya** and nearby **Maruya** along main trolley tracks thru town, little further down towards Sangyo Kaikan is **Yamakataya**. Perpendicular to main road, running along side of Mitsukoshi is **Tenmonkan Shopping Street**, main one in town, paralleled and intersected by Naya-dori and Izuro Shopping Streets. Crossing main street on Tenmonkan takes you to some more back shopping sections. Tenmonkan Street also has most movie theaters in town.

CHOPSTICKS: Kagoshima specialty, *Satsuma-ryori*, at first looks like any full-course Japanese meal, but notice more use of spices here and lots of deep-fried foods. Tho subtly Japanized over centuries, there was heavy Chinese (particularly Canton and Shanghai) and Southeast Asian kitchen influence here. Some of more common *Satsuma-ryori* dishes you can expect to get here: *Tonkatsu*, pork spare-ribs (with bone) stir-fried, flavored lightly with local miso and black sugar; not to be mistaken with regular Japanese breaded pork, *tonkatsu*. *Satsuma-age*, filets of locally caught white-meat fish, lightly spiced and deep-fried. *Satsuma-jiru*, miso-like soup with pork or chicken and local vegetables. *Saka-zushi*, is somewhat like regular Japanese *chirashi-zushi*, but rather than using vinegared rice, whole concoction is soaked overnite in local sake; served in Okinawan Ryukyu lacquer stacked three high with fresh seafood. *Kibinago*, small fish (8cm long) caught around southern Kyushu, is served in soup, salted and grilled, or tempura, but best as sashimi raw filets in strong vinegar and miso sauce. Strong flavor of most of these dishes make them ideal snacks with local shochu.

Except for *Saka-zushi*, all these, and many more interesting dishes can be had at most local restaurants and *izakaya* (local drinking joints) and cost from few hundred to about 1,000 yen per order. Best restaurants, which also serve full combination courses, are all concentrated in heart of town: take Tenmonkan Arcade N, 4 blocks after crossing main street front of Takashimaya. Go L and you see **Kumasotei** and **Satsumaji** restaurants; across from them **Warakuji**; one street earlier is **Shiru-an**. Similar fare at rustic **Satsuma-chaya** teahouse part way up Shiroyama hill, opposite Saigo's cave.

Main **nite-life** area is just behind Takashimaya Department Store, with mostly budget local hangouts where foreigner is often more welcome than out-of-town Japanese. Across street from Takashimaya is **Hayashida Hotel** (also main terminal of Hayashida Bus Co) with 3rd floor food plaza, featuring various Japanese, Western and Chinese establishments. It is also pleasant place for cup of coffee or drink to break day; they took out next floor, making it into indoor garden of sorts.

WHERE TO STAY: With volcanic Sakurajima and dozens of back-woods hot springs around, it should come as no surprise that Kagoshima is also noted for hot spring baths. Yet, there is no typically gaudy Onsen Center here, for water spouts forth from dozens of spots around town. Some inns and hotels will boast onsen water, while another next door does not. Kagoshima is popular with newlyweds (there is even **Newlyweds' Park** where young couple can plant tree together, already covered by thousands of trees) as well as with those making it thru second honeymoon, therefore has many luxury hotels with both W- and J-style rooms, with or without private bath. Here too, Kagoshima 'i' can be of great help, or stn **Kanko-annai**, which we relied on. Top of line all have bars, restaurants, saunas, etc, can get room only or with meals, at close to Tokyo rates: **Shiroyama Kanko Hotel** ☎(0992)-24-2211, atop Shiroyama hill with fine view of city and Sakurajima; **Sun Royal Hotel** ☎53-2020, near beach at Yajiro-ga-hama, 10min cab S of town; **Hayashida** ☎24-4111 conveniently located, W-style rooms only; but Japanese rooms **Rakuzan-so** ☎47-2115, foot of Shiroyama hill; or **Shigetomi-so** ☎47-3155, in old Shimazu family mansion, near base of Togo hill. Equally diverse choice of ¥-T and ¥-B lodgings in town, from ¥-Tw/2. Real *budgeteers* have several Business Hotel types from 15% less.

SOUTH KAGOSHIMA   HOT SAND, GIANT EELS

KAGOSHIMA BAY twists gently, almost all 20km wide, stretching N-S for 80km. Western pincer, Satsuma Peninsula, offers more for tourist and is convenient to Kagoshima City. Main town is IBUSUKI hot spring spa. East Osumi Peninsula boasts scenery at **Sata-misaki** point, national rocket launch pad.

TILT: Yet you can take it all in, or just part of it, on any of several fine **bus tours**, starting from KAGOSHIMA and IBUSUKI, ending same or other. Have Kagoshima 'i' arrange, or do yourself at stn-front tour bus office. Best is **A-5 Course**: NISHI KAGOSHIMA stn (10:10) → Chiran → Tokko Kannon → Bonotsu → Lake Ikeda → Mt Kaimon-dake → Nagasaki-bana Park → Ibusuki Jungle Bath (17:35) for 90min pause to take dip, and → Ibusuki stn (19:15); ¥3,590. Next day, take **B-1 Course**: IBUSUKI stn (9:20) with pick-up at Ibusuki Kanko Hotel (9:25), ferry across → Sata-misaki, drive up → 'back door' to SAKURAJIMA and boat across → Nishi Kagoshima stn (17:05); ¥4,020. You can get off at Kanoya stn (15:30) just above Sata-misaki; which makes it **B-2 Course**, ¥2,940. A-5 and B-2 Courses earn discount if combined with JR *Shuyu-ken* **Regional Pass** or **Rail Pass**. **Driver** can easily parallel this circuit on fine roads but will have little choice but to return to Kagoshima City, and save on drop-off fees.

IBUSUKI: 90min rail or bus, 46km down coast from KAGOSHIMA. In spite of its many large hotels and inns, it is clean, facing ocean, backed by beautiful greenery. Fame comes not only from 120,000 tons of hot water which flows daily (not spectacular in volcanic Japan), but from natural steam flowing in sand beaches, in which you are buried up to your neck, following with dip in ocean. Average temperature year-round 18°C, lows Dec-Feb 8-9° C (48-50°F). Swimming season starts 'officially' in Apr 3 months ahead of Honshu.

Sand 'baths' are town-run, ¥500 gets yukata-like covering, attendants to bury you, adjust sun-shade. Starts 8:30 every morning, till 21:00 Apr-Oct, 20:00 Nov-Mar. Over 70 inns and hotels serve visitors to hot sands, all take advantage of thousands of tons of hot water gushing out. Small minshuku and ryokan have nice, simple baths; larger place, larger baths, until you get to luxury hotels with spacious bath halls. None can compete with **Ibusuki Kanko Hotel** and its Health Center, i.e. **Jungle Bath**: over 60 baths of various sizes and content, all in somewhat tacky but fun 'jungle' setting (¥600 admission for non-guests), their own private hot sand bath (extra ¥600). Also bowling, game centers, dining and other diversions (7:00-22:00).

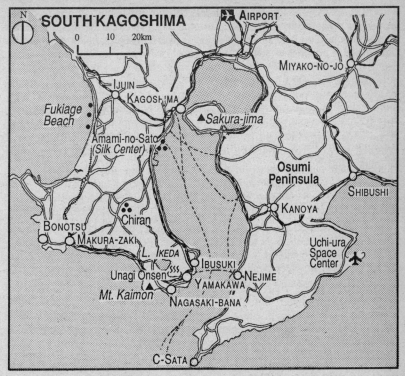

SOUTH KAGOSHIMA

0   10   20km

WHERE TO STAY: Most ¥-L & ¥-S hotels have both W- & J-style rooms (top rooms are W-beds with separate J-style sitting room), ¥-hi-T-lo-Lw/2. **Kanko Hotel** ☎(0993)-22-2131, is flashiest, at S end of Ibusuki. Nearby is mostly J-rooms **Kaijo Hotel** ☎22-2221. Town-run sand baths, **Suna-mushi**, is half-kilo N, same distance S of stn. Around it are smaller, but equally fine lodgings: **Kairaku-en** ☎22-3121 (2 W-rooms), ¥-Tw/2; superb, traditional J-style **Ginsho** ☎22-3231, ¥-Tw/2; and more. Also many budget and moderate inns around town, found thru stn **Kanko-annai** ☎22-4114, English spoken also ☎22-3252 Of dozen family-run minshuku, best located are **Hamami-so** ☎22-2722 (Eng), and **Katsumi**, both on beach 200m N of town-run sand bath, next to main source of hot spring water, which has large **public bath** (¥200). Two Youth Hostels also conveniently located: **Tamaya YH** ☎22-3553, is next to town-run sand bath; **Ibusuki YH** ☎22-2758, is on beach 500m N of Tamaya, W of stn. If Youth Hostel full, or you don't like their segregated arrangements, ask at **Kanko-annai** for **Toji-yado**, ¥1,200-or-so room only.

Those who find Ibusuki too resort-oriented try...

UNAGI ONSEN at *Unagi-iké* (**eel-lake**). Lake Unagi is in extinct volcanic caldera, but subterranean activity warms water, and lake is home to tasty eels that grow to 1.5m (5ft) long. Friends stayed at one of few budget minshuku here (nothing else) and lovely public bath. Beautiful hideaway spot, hiker can trek 5km W to even larger Lake Ikeda (largest lake in Kyushu, 19km around), where giant eels grow to around 2m (over 6 ft) long and half-meter around. Local lore claims lake has monster Nessie-like denizen lurking in 265m depths.

GETTING THERE: 30min bus from IBUSUKI, but only two round-trips daily so check in Kagoshima. Buses which circle southern tip Satsuma Peninsula all stop at UNAGI-IRIGUCHI, at entrance to turn-off to Unagi-ike, whence 3km to onsen. Or you can **cab** from Ibusuki (taxi 7x-mtr) or from one stop S Yamakawa stn (3.5x-mtr).

YAMAKAWA also has its own small coastal hot spring, and is terminal for ferries crossing mouth of Kagoshima Bay to Osumi Peninsula. At taxi stand, arrange **taxi tours** of area, saving slightly over Ibusuki departures. Buses around southern part of peninsula all stop here as well.

Our next stop is...
NAGASAKI-BANA point, 25min JR bus (hourly) from Yamakawa, 35min occasional bus from Ibusuki. Beautiful spit of land jutting out into ocean, with fine view of Mt Kaimon-dake. Unfairly called Satsuma Fuji, after great Mt Fuji, it is much smaller and only slightly resembles it in shape. One portion of point is **Nagasaki-bana Parking Garden** (¥800), with several thatched houses from southern isles; flamingos, pelicans and other small animals wandering around.

5km W along coast is tiny...
KAWAJIRI ONSEN (also 15min bus from JR Kaimon stn), secluded hot spring, excellent starting place for climb up 922m high Kaimon-dake.

From NAGASAKI-BANA, by bus, you can head back inland short way to HIGASHI OYAMA then W to **TOSEN-KYO** gorge, or follow coast towards Kaimon-dake then inland to Tosen-kyo (which tour buses do). Gorge has spring of ice cold water gushing out, where partake of *somen-nagashi*, thin noodles rinsed in cold water and dipped in soy sauce-like dip. Some buses go to Lake Ikeda for view and back to IBUSUKI or KAGOSHIMA CITY on Skyline toll road.

We continue along coast to end of JR at Makurazaki and 25min bus further to...
BONOTSU, rustic fishing village so tiny now it is hard to believe that it ranked with Hakata as major port for contact with Asian mainland. Home of Korean Buddhist priest Nichira (Jpn reading), who founded ICHIJO-IN temple here 583 AD. Ichijo-in hosted many more illustrious Buddhist priests thru Kamakura period, only to collapse in 1869 as Meiji Japan turned back to Shinto. Site now occupied by elementary school, near which stand two weather-worn giant stone Ni-o guardian figures and small graves of last 20 head priests.

Edo-period Bonotsu was major 'secret trading post', with many Satsuma ships heading to Southeast Asia and China, and Portuguese and Chinese ships coming in. Walking along narrow cobbled streets in town, you are often hemmed in by tall stone walls which used to surround secret trade houses. Few remain, best of which is budget minshuku **Kurahama-so** ☎(0993)-67-0073; non-guests pay ¥500 to see inside. Near Kurahama-so is pier for 30min **cruise** around lovely old style harbor.

Coming by **bus**, there are 3 stops in town. First is *Kaminobo*, 400m W of which is KURAHAMA-SO. Next stop half-kilo beyond is *Nakanobo*, near ICHIJO-IN remains. Last is same distance beyond, in front of Town Hall and small **History Museum** (¥200) with some interesting odds and ends from Temple and secret trade. Short hike out to peninsula hill, where locals used to watch for incoming ships.

WHERE NEXT: From Bonotsu, unless driving, must backtrack to MAKURAZAKI, from where you can take bus or private electric rail up W coast to IJU-IN and rejoin JR, 25min to KAGOSHIMA or up to KUMAMOTO direction. 50km of coastline up is **Fukiage Beach**, single giant stretch of sand dune, excellent swimming with budget lodgings, campsites. In middle is Fukiage town, small hot spring nearby.

Great detour for adventurers, but doing so suggest slight backtrack inland towards Kagoshima to...

CHIRAN, 40min bus from MAKURAZAKI, 1hr from BONOTSU on some buses to KAGOSHIMA. Check to make sure your bus goes via CHIRAN, as some go via KAWANABE on parallel road which misses Chiran completely. Can grab cab at MAKURAZAKI → BONOTSU with time to see, and back, 15x-mtr, and → CHIRAN another 15x-mtr, 20x-mtr more → either KAGOSHIMA or IBUSUKI. Try to negotiate set fee for full course, usual around 8x-mtr per hour. *Adventurer* heading up Fukiage coastline can, after Chiran, bus 20min W to KASEDA, S end of dunes, catch bus or train up coast.

With all these options you may wonder what is so great about Chiran. It was one of 120 *fumoto-machi*, or garrisoned samurai settlements established by Kagoshima Lords 300 years ago. Shogun's one-province one-castle policy forbade building more castles, led to tearing down most smaller ones, so Shimazus countered by creating high-walled, winding-street fortified settlements. Many houses remain in quite good condition, six in particular have fine gardens. Residents have opened their gardens to visitors, and ¥200 joint ticket gets you into all six (so far): sold at booths on corner of main street and each stonewalled side street, and at tourist bureau of Town Hall. For convenience we suggest start at **Town Hall**, *Cho-yakuba*, town W-end. If **driving** or **cab**, there is **parking** lot (most roads closed to cars during day); if **bus**, get off at *Nakagori* stop, front of Tomiya ryokan. From Makurazaki or Kaseda, you hit it first; from Kagoshima pass thru town first. Special express buses stop here only.

Behind (N) Town Hall is...
Chiran History Museum, with outline of area's history and some feudal era art and samurai weaponry. At Town Hall intersection, head S one block and L at stone-walled street, near which is ticket-booth. Street stretches for almost kilo, all open houses are along it. First on L is **Saigo Mansion**, just beyond on R **HIRAYAMA Soyo**, next corner also on R is cousin **HIRAYAMA Ryoichi**. Quite ways down on R, is **SATA Tamiko**, beyond which is **SATA Tada**; at far end is **MORI Shigemitsu**, only one with classic lake where you're given refreshing cup of Chiran's own tea, cultivation of which started nearby in 1872; known all over now for its mild sweet taste.

It will have taken slightly over hour to get this far, and if you have some extra time, continue beyond Mori house: walls end, road curves L, and 50m beyond narrow lane branches back on R thru bamboo grove (R at next, slightly larger road) to rejoin another walled street paralleling that with all gardens. Take it back E, on corner of second street branching R (N) are few more old samurai mansions; taking this one R takes you back to first street at Hirayama houses. Pleasant stroll, only adds extra 10min to return walk. If bushed or in rush, can have your taxi meet you at parking lot on main bus road, 100m due N of Mori house. 200m upstream from this parking lot is old stone **arched bridge**; in summer area is full of fireflies at nite.

CHOPSTICKS: Problem here, but at least food is available. We ate at budget diner **Eikyu**, btwn Nakagori bus stop and Town Hall. Also restaurant **Tsukimi** (Moon-Viewing) down side street behind Tomiya ryokan; we didn't get there, but claims to serve W-food, probably spaghetti, curry, burgers, sandwiches. Also budget ramen shop across from Post Office.

WHERE TO STAY: 7 ¥-B–T inns, mostly Nakagori & Town Hall area; book thru latter.

During World War II, Chiran was major training base for Imperial Air Force, churning out many of aces who fought in South Pacific. As tide turned against Japan, Chiran became launch pad for suicide kamikaze pilots in their futile one-way trips against American armada off Okinawa. From April 1945 to end of war on August 15, 1,026 *tokko-tai*, or special attack force pilots took off from Chiran in rickety old trainers, laden down with thousands of pounds of explosives, Talismans and prayer to even make it as far as Okinawa. **Giant Peace Kannon**, statue of pilot, now stands near old base, with 'Peace for Ever' inscribed on it. **Memorial Building** houses spiritual remains of 1,026, many boys in their teens. There is also display— drawers full—of uniforms, flying gear, photos of each squadron, their last letters home, etc. Many photos catch stupidity of it all; children being told to do impossible—in one, boy-pilot is given small puppy by his friends, final attempt to cheer him before his mission. Guide here is sole survivor of his unit, due to engine failure, but still seems to retain his old attitudes in Japanese explanations, which he would like to have translated 'for peace on earth for all men'—still naively unaware that in our culture, any but his own culture and period, his misguided principles make little sense, even offend. Powerful message of these exhibits need little explanation: war is asinine. Every **May 5**, *Boys' Day*, families of those lost, and survivors (thanks to lack of planes or mechanical failure) gather here in ceremony to appease souls of dead and pray for peace. **Peace Kannon** and exhibit is 2km S of old town, 5min **cab** from Nakagori bus stop. Similar statue near BONOTSU (above) dedicated to Navy *tokko-tai* who rode astride giant torpedoes, or 2-man midget subs, into US fleet. Italians, British used similar toys, but designed to allow pilot escape—were equally ineffective except against sleeping stationary target at anchor.

OSUMI PENINSULA is beautiful but only for *wanderer* with time, unless passing thru on **bus tour**. We ferry across from YAMAKAWA, landing at **Nejime** or **Onejime** ports. 1hr35min bus S from either to Cape Satamisaki, southernmost point of main Japanese islands, at 31° N latitude.

45min bus N of either port is...
KANOYA where you can rejoin JR back to Kagoshima, or on to Miyazaki via Shibushi City. Kanoya was also kamikaze base.

Or bus from either port 1hr45min to E shore Osumi Peninsula...
UCHI-NO-URA, Tokyo University Rocket Center, fine white beaches. **Space center** (10min bus from Uchi-no-ura Town) operation since 1962; '70 sent up Japan's first satellite. Unless testing, **free tour** of base by checking in at front gate; call ahead ☎(09946)-7-2211 and they may be able to arrange English guide. Also **Space Science Museum** (9:00-16:00, X-thurs, free) at front.

WHERE NEXT: From Uchi-no-ura short bus to OSUMI-KOYAMA whence 35min **train** or 80min **bus** both infrequent, to SHIBUSHI, also reached by hour express bus or train from SHINOYA. Shibushi is optional exit from Kyushu for *wanderer*, daily ferry service links it with OSAKA, 16hrs away.

PERSONAL DATEBOOK: **KAGOSHIMA AREA: Sun closest Lunar Jan 18** (Feb full moon) Kagoshima Shrine, Hayato Town, *Hatsu-uma* (First Horse Day), gaily festooned horses bear rice bales, mini drums parade. **May 5** *Shakyamuni* (Buddha) *Festival*, Homan-ji temple, Shibushi City. **May 5** memorial services for kamikaze *tokko-tai*, Chiran. **Jun, first sun** Yahata Shrine, Hiyoshi-cho, fun *Seppetobe fete* for abundant crops; local farmers sing, dance in muddy paddy-fields, no concern if spectator gets splattered. **Sun closest to Jun 10** *Spider Battles* at Kajiki Town Peoples' Hall. **Lunar May 28** *Sogadon Umbrella Burning Fete*, Kotsugi River bank Kagoshima: 100s of paper umbrellas tossed into bonfire, memorial service to 11th century Soga brothers who avenged their father's murder in famous vendetta; umbrella was their symbol.

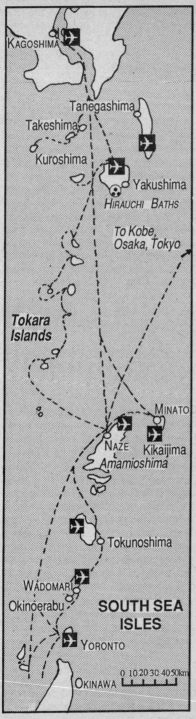

Nitely thru Jul 100s of paper lanterns
hung in every shrine, temple to guide spirits
of deceased ancestors. **Aug 3-5** Ibusuki *Hot
Spring Festival*. **First sun Aug** one of
largest *Tanabata Festivals* at Osato, Ichiki
Town. **Lunar Sep 14** (mid-Oct) *Myoenji
Festival* commemorates 17th century lord
Shimazu. Fierce-looking samurai march 20-
odd km Kagoshima City to his home village
of Ijuin. **Nov 3-5** *Ohara Festival* is
Kagoshima City's main autumn event, with
200 dance groups winding thru city streets,
best 3rd. Also **same days** *Yagorodon
Festival* at Hachiman Shrine sees 20ft tall
'doll' paraded thru town—represents chieftains
of Hayato, 6-8th century local 'kingdom'.

SOUTH SEA ISLES

ISLES OF KAGOSHIMA prefecture
stretch for several hundred kilometers,
divide East China Sea from Pacific
Ocean. In spite of few main towns
'touristized' for lazy younger Japanese
travelers, most still lovely, provide
great diversions for nomad. Numerous
air links connect KAGOSHIMA to main isle
AMAMI OSHIMA, and both to most of
smaller isles. Cheapest way to isles is by
ferry.

Kagoshima City is main port
heading S, with connections to:
closest OSUMI ISLANDS, with main
Tanegashima and Yakushima; which
via or by-pass to half-dozen tiny
TOKARA ISLANDS; which isle-hop or
also bypass for most popular AMAMI
ISLANDS; beyond which is RYUKYU,
or Okinawa, Isle Chain. Once-weekly
ferries continue to Taiwan. You can
spend several weeks getting to know
all these isles, and we have only been
to fraction of them, and that was few
years ago. Since then, they have
become 'in' with young Japanese and
as result many have been spoiled by
giant resort hotels for today's spoiled
youth. Yet, these kids stick to main
towns with discos and party joints, so
venture to far corners and find much
that has remained basically unchanged
for centuries. Local language
(unintelligible to Japanese), now with
official encouragement, still survives
despite linguistic repression since
conquest by Satsuma in 1609.

With so many islands and islets, we will just list them, pointing out special places. If coming down this way, advise getting up-to-date info, especially for ships, whetherr before coming to Japan, in Tokyo or as last resort at Kagoshima 'i'. All isles are full of budget inns—minshuku, Kokumin-shukusha, ryokan—and campsites; and larger towns even have luxury hotels.

OSUMI ISLANDS 大隅半島

TANEGASHIMA is singularly uninteresting except for **rocket launch** pad (open to public, good museum, non-military) at southern tip, 'monument' to its being ancient original home of gunpowder-propelled missiles in Japan. Also **Gun Museum**—first Portuguese sailor washed ashore 1543 introduced flintlock gun which local bell-casters immediatley stripped down and copied. Local lore omitted from most history books says first guns looked fine (museum has Portuguese original and first edition copy) but bore and firelock trigger gave problems. Next Portuguese who floundered ashore at Cape Kadokura knew more and was offered beautiful daughter Wakasa of smith YAITA Kimbei if he would show how to make trigger work. He complied, she was compliant and left with boat. Yaita improved on Portuguese model, added artistic decoration, technological innovations including double and triple barrels, shoulder-sling portable cannon, etc. Horrors of slaughter at early gunnery-battles lead to self denial of hi-tech weaponry and return to 'manly' sword. Guns were too democratically dangerous, anyway. Our friends spent happy week just bumming around this island, swimming.

CHOPSTICKS: Near rocket range in Minamitane-cho, **Kusakiri** where Mr Nagoe specializes in genuine local cookery, more like Samoan South Pacific than Japanese or Chinese.

If sticking to closest Osumi Islands, recommend...
YAKUSHIMA, called 'Alps of Sea' as 100km-around circular isle is dominated by 1935m tall Miyanoura peak and dozen other high mountains, snow capped in winter. Elevation averages 1000m above sea-level, and numerous trails cross deep (*yakusugi*) cypress forests which cover 90% of island—some of last virgin forest in country with trees mostly millennium old and including oldest tree, **Jomon Sugi**, cedar over 3,000 years old thus dating back to Jomon stone-age. Swarming with deer and monkeys, teetering vine suspension bridges cross white water streams. You can even take short rapids ride down two rivers here so full Arab tankers hope to freight water back. Weather highly variable, Nov–Mar especially, when '3 days see 4 seasons'. Best time is May for rhododendra and wild pheasant, and then monkeys frisky. Since so un-'tropical' not as popular with Japanese youth and is thus ideal for wanderer in search of isolation in nature. Lumbering & furniture making are main industries of 15,000 people. Most coastline is fine sandy beaches with campsites, nesting ground for giant sea turtles (protected). Swaying palm trees and pineapples grow in abundance on S shore which also has **natural outdoor seaside hot spring baths**.

Ferries dock on N shore, Kamiyaku, 2hr **bus** to S shore; **airport** is halfway down island.

TOKARA ISLES 吐噶喇列島

Half-dozen tall bumps on ocean floor with nothing at all on them except endless clear-water beaches and some tiny but hospitable fishing villages. *For real adventurer only.*

AMAMI ISLANDS 奄美大島

These half-dozen are most popular with Japanese, as *ekizochikku* (exotic) without having to go overseas. Main isle **AMAMI OSHIMA** 11hr30min boat or 80min air from KAGOSHIMA; 5-6 boats monthly from each of KOBE, OSAKA (30hrs) and TOKYO (39hrs). Recommend passing up Amami Oshima, as well as island of Tokunoshima, for last two of larger isles: **OKINO-ERABU** and **YORON-TO**.

But if passing thru, you will land at Amami Oshima's main town...
NAZE, near which are main centers of weaving and dyeing **Oshima Tsumugi Silk** pongee, and *habu* (poisonous) **Snake Center**. Tsumugi is dying art (no pun intended) for dyers seem to fall prey to more than their share of cancer. And there is no substitute income. But unintended help seems to be coming from Korea, which can produce imitation much cheaper thus cutting them from market.

50min bus down coast from Naze...
YAMATO VILLAGE preserves several local thatched storage houses, elevated to keep crops above rats. Hills around here are home to species of small black rabbit found only here and nearby Tokunoshima Isle. Further on **HEDA** is village of coral houses, strong enough to withstand any typhoon. Pocketed S shore of Oshima is perfect for raising pearl oysters, of which you'll see much down there. Boat between S shore's Kojiya port and Naze.

TOKUNOSHIMA is much smaller, but has all sights of Oshima, 4hrs boat. Best beaches are N section of E shore. You see many bulls around and they pit bull against bull in bloodless bullfight at **HANATOKU VILLAGE**. South of Hanatoku is **BOMA**, town which also produces Oshima silk.

OKINO-ERABU Isle managed to avoid tide of tourist kids who flock here each summer, but there are some hotels going up in main town **WADOMARI**. Besides sun and sand there are 2 large caverns, **Suiren-do** and **Shoryu-do**, at bulbous W end of this tear-drop isle. Each has 40min guided tour, every 90min, ¥1,000. In middle of island is grave of Yo-no-nushi, 15th century lord sent from Ryukyu Kingdom. His grave is of classic Okinawan style, with rock (in this case coral) wall with door dug out: it is northernmost example of such, tho it resembles coral houses of Amami Oshima.

GETTING THERE: 536km S of Kagoshima, daily isle-hopper ferry takes 18hrs30min; daily NAS flies in 1hr40min; isle-hopping Japan Economy Air from Amami Oshima in 40min.

YORON-TO is one of our favorites, Only 22km around, ringed by fine beaches all with campsites, beautiful coral reefs ideal for skin diving in crystal-clear waters. Ferry port & air strip 2km SW of main town **Chabana**, which we avoid, camping out or staying at any of 80-odd budget minshuku scattered all over island. **Glass-bottom tour** boat departs Chabana, circles isle clockwise to SE corner Akazaki, **folk house village** and small **stalactite cave**. Up E coast few km is long stretch of beach. From this 'Pearl of East China Sea', it is only short overnite hop on ferry to OKINAWA, which follows, p.773.

GETTING THERE: To Yoron-to 2lhr daily ferry from KAGOSHIMA, 39hrs from KOBE (5-6x monthly); 1hr45min NAS turbo-prop from KAGOSHIMA, 50min from AMAMI OSHIMA.

Beppu...built upon the roof of the infernal regions.
Stamp too hard and your foot may go through the thin
crust and come out parboiled.
—Willard Price, *Journey by Junk*

EAST COAST 東海岸
NICHINAN COAST TO BEPPU

THIS STRETCH up E coast has little you have not already seen in
Kyushu. But if more time on your hands, there is much in way of scenery
and beaches along this Nichinan, or called locally Hinan, Coast, with its
occasional ancient town.

From Shibushi, rail 30min up to Kushima and 40min bus to...
TOI-MISAKI, lovely grassy point juts out into emerald blue Pacific. Our
bus suddenly comes to high fence running width of point, passes thru gate:
to keep 100-odd horses which roam free from roaming too far. In 1697, local
lords began to raise stumpy sturdy *Nihon-uma*, Japanese pony. Out near
lighthouse troop of monkeys hangs out in woods. Numerous ¥-B inns, 2 hotels
located along coast; express bus #23, 3hrs → MIYAZAKI.

Continuing leisurely up coast, bus passes thru banana plantation. 40min from Toi is
small village of ISHIWATARI, several traditional S Kyushu homes reconstructed into
minshuku village, budget lodgings, diners. Bypass Marine Park, 20min on come to
Nango stn on JR infrequent-runs Nichinan Line, 90min to MIYAZAKI.

OBI is old feudal era town with much of original facade remaining, pleasant
place to while away few hours wandering around on foot, or rent bike at
stn. And it is quiet, most Japanese travelers stay out at coastal Aburatsu or
Nichinan; inns here are not for discriminating epicure, but budget, clean,
and available rooms. Obi is 30min rail from NANGO (slightly longer on bus, get
one to MIYAKONOJO, as one to MIYAZAKI misses Obi); just over 1hr to MIYAZAKI.

Obi has its share of samurai houses, *buke yashiki,* but unlike
garrison-town CHIRAN, was castle-town complete with thriving merchant
district. Only 40-foot tall main gate, *Ohte-mon* of castle remains; rebuilt
1978 after 1587 original, made of wood and no nails, only joinery. On castle
grounds History Museum has items relating to Itoh clan who ruled area
1587-1868. Slightly run-down gate L of castle gate leads to 120-year-old
mansion of clan, built in last years of feudal era. Fine garden, visit by
prior arrangement thru Nichinan Town Hall, ☎(0987)-23-1111.

Just behind train stn is hill-top park, best early spring cherry blossom
time. From stn, L on main road (Rte222) and across river to town. Rte222 used to be
main road thru town, and you see along it many interesting merchant
stores, some traditionally Edo period, while others have Western influences found in Meiji, Taisho and early Showa architecture. On L as you hit
town is Katsumoku Garden, open. Before it on either side of street are
two budget inns, few budget eateries along road; main bus stop is at far (W)
end. Just beyond bus stop small Merchants' Museum (¥100) displays
Edo era odds and ends. Cross river beyond Museum to small park: site of
HO-ON-JI temple and clan cemetery, only latter remains. Road from Rte222 to
castle has few old *buke yashiki* along it; take first R (E) as you head towards castle
from Rte222 and one house has many carp in canal in front. At castle gate,
road turns R, to more *buke yashiki.* L (N) next intersection to *Shintoku-do*,
School for Samurai Kids, 1831.

CHOPSTICKS: Local specialty *Obi-ten*, white-meat fish and tofu mixed and
deep-fried. Served at tea house in front of castle, and several other places in town.

PERSONAL DATEBOOK: **3rd sat-sun Oct**, *Castle Festival*. Main event both days, dance by groups of youths dressed as samurai; also in cherry viewing, **Apr**.

If you stayed on bus to Nango and continued up coast, (35min on express bus) is...
UDO JINJA, (10min walk from bus stop), interesting shrine in cave by sea. Coast road, rail from Obi rejoin 10km beyond continuing to **AOSHIMA**, recommended by everyone else except us for 'beautiful tropical' Aoshima—teeny, weedy, seedy, palm- and garbage-filled islet connected by short bridge to mainland, now just as generation ago!

MIYAZAKI: Possible exit from Kyushu: **air** N to TOKYO, NAGOYA, OSAKA, KOCHI, MATSUMOTO, S to OKINAWA. Lodgings for all budgets, best along Oyodo River, many ¥-B-T along river, one **Hotel Sun-Route**, popular with young folks.

Two interesting parks N end of town. First is wooded precinct of...
Miyazaki Jingu Shrine Park, with **Folk House Village** set up in N end. Shrine here since at least 8th century, present structure rebuilt 1907. Folk house village has fine examples (more planned) of old, rural homes brought from Miyazaki's hinterlands and reconstructed here.

Second is...
Heiwa-dai Park, 1km N, with its many lakes and Haniwa Park. Several hundred **giant replicas of clay Haniwa** figures found in and around giant burial mounds of 5-7th centuries AD, placed all around park. There is cluster of these *kofun*-mounds at Saito-baru Plain, 30km N of Miyazaki, where Haniwa exhibit hall displays real tomb figures.

GETTING AROUND: **Cab**, Jingu Park 1.5x-mtr from stn or downtown; HEIWA-DAI 2x-mtr. **Bus**, catch on main N-S road, 5min walk W from stn.

1hr express rail N of Miyazaki...
HYUGA has occasional Nihon Car Ferry to KOBE, OSAKA, or KAWASAKI near Tokyo. On way to Hyuga, you may notice something go shooting by on (or inches above) parallel tracks: testing of JR's '21st Century Vehicle', **magnetic levitation train**, *maglev*, capable of over 500kph/300mph. **Viewing platform** at Higashi Tsuno stn for quick glimpse as it shoots by on 7km long test track. Problems are tremendous electricity consumption, possible health risk of magnetism; call Test Center ☎(09825)-8-1303, for schedule.

25min rail beyond is Nobeoka, uninteresting town, but turn off for...
TAKACHIHO GORGE: **6 trains** daily make round-trip in 1hr35min; same by almost hourly **bus**. It is said that gods first set foot on earth at this spot after creating Japan by stirring primeval ocean muck. **Amano-iwado Cave** nearby said to be where sun goddess Amaterasu hid from her joker-brother Susano-o, to be coaxed out by goddess Amano-uzume dancing hoochi-kooch parody of her own sacred dance which 'made assembled gods laugh till high plain of heaven shook'. Here probably original, tho several grottos thru West Japan make same claim, one above Kyoto.

Ancient *kagura* folk dances performed in this area recount episode; held at various villages and shrines within radius of 15mi from MITAI in central mountain region, somewhere every sat nite and some weekdays by 29 different troupes: **Nov thru mid-Feb**. At each hamlet one house is chosen as stage, preparations begin midday, roughly 20 hour performances (first 33 kagura dances) begin around 6 or 7pm and continue all nite until finished. Call Tackachiho ☎(0982)-72-3181 in Japanese for schedule There is 1hr program **every nite** all year for tourists, at **TAKACHIHO SHRINE** from 20:00, ¥300; lacks ambience of real shows, but always available.

Gorge is equally famous for its spectacular **arch bridges**, two tallest in Asia for road (137m and 110m), and tallest in Asia for rail (105m above river). Train ride up is best: as you near end, you enter tunnel and coming out of it find yourself suspended 35 storeys above river for view that will take your breath away, no matter how ready you are. After AMANO-IWADO stn, two more tunnels, no ravines and 3.5km to end TAKACHIHO.

Dozens of budget lodgings (incl YH at each stn) and several moderate inns between Takachiho stn and river. **STAY** at **Ryokan Yamatoya** ☎72-3838, from ¥-P choice of w/2, nice J-style rms, reputation for cheap with great food, call ahead for rsve. Can rent **row boats** to meander thru river flanked by 50-100m high cliffs. Trail also, which winds down to campsite along feeder stream (1.5km S of stn). **AMANO-IWADO SHRINE** is 20min bus E; Youth Hostel also there. From TAKACHIHO can catch occasional **bus** 90min to TAKAMORI at Mt Aso. Giant waterfall, cool pools, at UNOKONO-TAKI, 30min bus W from Takachiho on Rte218, and 30min hike.

Back on coast **rail** runs slightly inland; nothing in particular, **driver** choice of coast or parallel roads. Rail hits coast again at SAIKI, where **ferries** to SUKUMO, Shikoku.

USUKI, up coast also has few daily **ferries** to Shikoku's YATSUHATA-HAMA. Town settled by Christian daimyo Otomo Sorin, 1563. He spent last years of his life in small temple-turned-church at Tsukumi between Usuki and Saiki. His Christian grave, defaced in 17th century, re-erected only 1977.

20min bus SW of stn to...
Giant Stone Buddhas, *Usuki Seki-butsu,* carved out of cliffs; reminiscent of older, greater Buddha caves along China's Silk Road. Images here date around 1000 AD, late Heian–early Kamakura eras, contemporary with some in China which inspired these. While China's impress us more, these far better preserved: no Japanese army looters. Four main groups clustered together here, and nearby **MANGETSU-JI** temple has some stone figures including giant Ni-o guardian, same dates. Whole area is single park, ¥300, can be walked in hour or so. If interested, there are similar but smaller clusters of these *seki-butsu* stone buddhas in neighborhood; best if **driving** or **cab** (few buses from Usuki cluster to next at SUGAO, and once there, trains infrequent): 15km W is **Sugao Seki-butsu**, 1km N of Sugao stn on JR line Oita-Aso; 5km N of it is **Inukai Seki-butsu**, 15min bus S of Inukai stn; follow Rte10 along rail tracks to outskirts of Oita City, to **Takase Seki-butsu**; and closer to Oita, **Motomachi Seki-butsu**.

9km W from Usuki Seki-butsu, village of...
NOTSU has small museum of **Hidden Christian Artifacts**; 50min bus from here to OITA, via Inukai and Rte10.

On Oita-Aso Line, 90min from Oita, hour from Inukai is...
TAKETA, feudal era town where still more Christian artifacts in **History Museum**. **Cave** behind HIROSE SHRINE was used by town's Lord Oka and fellow Christians as **church**. They even had European priest who lived hidden in cave. Hirose Shrine was built 1935 in honor of Lieutenant Hirose and 1,447 other locals who perished in Russo-Japanese War storming Port Arthur in famed 'human torpedo' charge. Taketa has fair amount of feudal architecture, *buke yashiki* L, most notably **Taketa Manse** rebuilt 1818.

From Taketa, 1hr rail to Aso. En route is **Sujiyu**, hideaway hot-spa with famed *utase-yu* falling baths, voluminous boiling brine flowing through overhead pipes to pour down on bathers backs. Suggest **Sujiyu Kanko Hotel** for its baths, or pilgrims seeking baths only **utase-yu** public bath in town center.

Halfway between Aso and Beppu along scenic Yamanami highway is lovely...
YUFU-IN. Serene, majestic town nestled at base of mts, reminiscent of Swiss alps. Townsfolk work together to preserve original beauty of area in delightful mixture of old and new; no shopping arcades or construction as in Beppu. Stroll N along canal past many thatched roofed houses, rice fields and traditional scenery. Visit Mingei **Folk Art Museum** (¥500) demos of glass blowing (traditional local craft), weaving and *washi* handmade paper. Walk N to small fishing lake, dip in tiny mixed *rotenburo* perched on edge; or if shy, 1 min walk to Pension **Kinrinko Toyonkuni** ☎84-3011, where bathe in enclosed outdoor onsen overlooking lake (¥300). Across small foot-bridge sip

coffee or hot chocolate upstairs in famous **Tenjosajiki,** old J-style building, folkcraft shop on first floor. For change of style, short walk to *Sueda Bijitsukan*, **Museum of Modern Art** (¥500).

Not too much for ¥-B traveler, but many European style Pension, from ¥-lo-T. Pension **Yufugoiki** ☎84-3766, swiss-style house w/ wood burning stove, J- or W-style rms, ¥-lo-T. For real treat, stay at magnificent old Ryokan **Tanamoyu** ☎84-2158, ¥-L. If can't stay, worth at least peek: garden, crafts shop or restaurant. If can't afford, or no time to stay, stop en route Aso or Beppu for half-day or day trip (bus #36 from Beppu stn). As few tourists, perfect town to escape crowds and roam leisurely; nice antique and craft shops, art galleries. Around bus stn, good ¥-B noodle shops.

On coast again, it is 70min rail from Usuki to Oita City, 20min further to...
BEPPU: One well-touted place we *downgrade* since last edition. Baths still great, rooms above average, but food...President of Beppu College '85 took us out to eat apologizing for 'no place worthwhile'. Hotels all cater meals to tour groups by *viking*, that is buffet. Japanese food does not 'vike' well—where there is choice, opt Western. If you dunked in good hot springs in UNZEN or around ASO *bypass* Beppu. But if you need rest after hard trekking, or had no good baths, make stopover before taking train for Moji transfer to Shinkansen or boat to Hiroshima, Kobe-Osaka or Shikoku.

At JR stn, Kanko-annai open till 7pm, enough English spoken.

Number of hot springs here phenomenal: 1,877 in 1964 now 3,000! Daily boiling water flow of 68,000 liters per minute in 8 adjoining areas is close 2nd to Yellowstone's gush but in half total area. Japan has 2,237 onsens to US's 1,003 or steamy Iceland's 516. Source is 200 meters deep. City not attractive despite handsome setting up slope of Tsutsumi Mounts. Hills cut off encroaching factories, shield city of *jigoku* or fiery-hells as fumaroles are called, from urban pollution hell. Most impressive hells in Japan, due to great variety: bubbling mud, spouting geyser, gurgly-bubbling brine, intense colors from blood-red thru yellow to green, cobalt-blue and milky white. Cotton textiles dyed in some pools. All have picturesque names.

Play Dante 2-3hrs, tour 8 main hells by **taxi** or **bus**. 2 are walking distance of Kamegawa stn near beach, others 5 min cab ride up hill, clustered within short walk.
Water-spout Hell, *Tatsumaki Jigoku*, just above Kamegawa stn. This small 20m geyser about every 25min; *Short walk is...*
Blood-lake Hell, *Chino-ike Jigoku,* claimed oldest natural *jigoku* in country.

5min taxi, or slightly more by bus, up hill to...
Golden-dragon Hell, *Kinryu Jigoku*, largest; **White-pond Hell,** *Shira-ike Jigoku*, blue-white; **Demon-mount Hell,** *Oniyama Jigoku*, crocodiles, alligators bred; **Cooking-pot Hell,** *Kamado Jigoku*; **Mountain Hell,** *Yama Jigoku*, mountain of mud, hippos; **Sea Hell,** *Umi Jigoku*, deep-sea cobalt-blue. Nearby, *Believe It or Not, Ripley*-famed giant lily pads on which kids can float as on boats.

Start **tour** at either end: *Umi*, or *Chino-ike*. Admission incl r.t. bus to all 8 is ¥1,500 adult, reductions for children, groups of 30-up. Taxi best arranged at your hotel. Hells open 8:00-17:00 daily (no nite sinning?) Drivers have free parking. Info, **Beppu Jigoku Assn** ☎(0977)-66-1577; info on 75 public bath houses at nominal fees.

If enough of boiling water, near pier at **Kitahama Beach** slip into yukata, or stroll over in hotel robe for **sand bath** buried to neck in hot volcanic beach sand. ¥600 at TAKEGAWA ONSEN 6:30-21:00; SHONIGAHAMA 9:00-17:00; sand and other baths in **Kannawa** at HYOTAN ONSEN 8:00-21:00 ¥500 onsen incl mud baths. HOYOLAND, few min walk from 'hells' (across from arched stone bridge). Onsen complex, separate indoor; variety of mixed (male/female) outdoors, bathe by moonlight in mud, gravel, shallow, cold you name it, ¥1,030. Not for inhibited, advise BYO towel.

WHERE TO STAY: Tops run about Tokyo ¥-S: ¥22,000 twin, but which here gets you suite and all you can eat plus all you can dunk in baths, as in: **Suginoi**, ☎(0977)-24-1141 atop hill and long best, all rooms front are suite of large W-twin plus large raised tatami area, private mineral bath. Hot competition keeps all hotels, ryotels same level and price. Bus up and take **bath only** at Suginoi, ¥1,800 includes admission to good pops **stage show** which go to in your yukata, Japanese version of Catskills-cum-Vegas, fun watching family audience; also game center, but museum extra even for hotel guests, not worth it, no more erotic art....where has that wild old collection gone Jay cited in *Encyclopedia of Sexual Knowledge*.

If you must stay in Beppu, there is still at least one old fashioned, quality, wooden Japanese-style ryokan, with its own private *rotenburo* and its own bubbling hell, and located convenient to Hells walking tour: **Kannawa-en** ☎(0977)-66-2111, (¥-S+w/2), owner Akiki spks English; lovely setting with private cottages but as they have no food competition in this tasteless town, seem to have lost old touch—but still best in town. Just for bath and dinner ¥8,000. Also spk E- at **Shoha-so Ryokan** ☎66-0013, ¥-T, bus #26 10min to Shoha-en stop; also at Minshuku **Kokage** ☎23-1753, 2min walk from JR stn, has own onsen. **Beppu YH** ☎23-4116, ¥-P choice of w/2, 9pm curfew.

Fifteen minutes down coast towards Oita is...
Mount Takasaki Park with its wild monkeys. You can tell Dirty Old Monkey by way they take after ladies. Also 'boasts' (?) larger-than-Kamakura **Great Buddha** made of mud and cremated people's ashes. Pass, thank you.

Adventurer interested in Buddhism or sculpture can circle...
KUNISAKI PENINSULA, (just N of Beppu, and on which SE shore is airport). Has several fine temples, more Buddha rock carvings, hiking trails (tho also good bus service), beaches, campsites and budget inns.

KITSUKI town, 50min bus from Beppu (20min bus from Kitsuki JR stn which 30min local rail from Beppu), is alternative to Beppu; no hot springs, but no crowds either, and dozen small budget and moderate inns. Another old town with remnants of feudal days, 30min bus, cab 10x-mtr to airport. Bus lets you off top end of town, head R (E) and road 'S'-curves gently for few hundred meters then takes sharp R heading out of town but thru some old **common folks' homes** where at sharp R corner, take small road straight. Ancient gate and wall on L once enclosed samurai kids school, spot now occupied by grade school. More remnants of once great **samurai houses** nearby and around Temple District, W. Few hundred meters E is **Kitsuki Castle**, 1970 replica.

Kunisaki Peninsula has for over millennium been closely associated with USA GRAND SHRINE (*see below*) and its many affiliated shrines & temples established in peninsula's hills. Until Meiji split of Buddhism and Shinto, Kunisaki was one of main areas of *Shin-butsu Konko*, mixed studies of Shinto & Buddhism. Even now you see occasional white-robed Yamabushi mountain ascetics. At peak there were 65 temple-shrines here; still 26 temples, in varied states of use or disuse.

GETTING AROUND: Best by car; cab KITSUKI → main Futago-ji → Fuki-ji → Maki Daido → Kumano Magai-butsu → USA about 80km, 40x-mtr. Same course reverse from USA ending at airport, about 50x-mtr; 35x-mtr if skipping Usa. Usually cheaper to arrange price and course before departure. If you have time, and solo or pair, **bus** inexpensive, tho infrequent. From KITSUKI, continue down coast 25min to AKI and change to one heading inland to Futago-ji (50min). If spending nite at, and getting morning start from E coast KUNISAKI town, only 45min direct to Futago-ji. From Futago-ji, get bus heading N to (Bungo-)TAKADA, 20min to AMAGI (from Takada 45min bus) and 4km walk W to Fuki-ji.

15min bus W, or 5km walk to...
MAKI DAIDO, fine large wood images (especially fiery Fudo riding bull), late Heian era. Between Fuki-ji and Maki Daido, two clusters of giant stone carvings: **Motomiya Magai-butsu** and **Nabeyama Magai-butsu**. From Maki Daido, head down towards JR Tateishi stn, where just beyond tunnel local road branches off L to **Kumano Magai-butsu**, largest Buddha cliff carving.

Several **tour buses** cover area on various courses, starting OITA, BEPPU and via
airport before heading in. Many run only wknds, hols; can be checked at Beppu's Tourist
Office, in large building between bus and rail stns. *Wanderer* will find campsites and ¥-B
lodgings along coast and in most villages. Some temples take in overnite guests, or have
nearby inns, may not always get dinner if showing up late and unannounced, but will get
a room, call ahead ensures food: Near Maki Daido, try **Gokuraku-ji** temple ☎(0978)-
26-2015; near Fuki-ji is **Fuki-ji Chaya inn** ☎26-2137; from Amagi village is short
trail across to TENNEN-JI temple, below is MATAMA ONSEN with ¥-Pw/2 inn (or rm
only) **Matama So** ☎(0978)-53-4390. Last few good bases for short trek up 721m
Futago-yama peak, on which is another small onsen, AKANE; and **temple lodging**
2km away at **Monjusen-ji** ☎(0978)-74-0820.

USA SHRINE, 40min express train from BEPPU, 8min bus stn to shrine; or 75min
bus from Beppu's Kitahama bus terminal on buses bound for NAKATSU. During great
anti-Japanese economic drive of 1930s ('buy American'), origin marks were
required on imports, some Japanese toys and cheap dishes were shipped
stamped *'made in USA'*. Many people thought Japan had renamed town
just for this, but Usa is one of oldest shrines in Japan dating back to at least
7th century. Probably of Continental origin as it is main Hachiman Shrine
(according to gov't 1985 yearbook, of 80,000 Shinto shrines over 25,000 are subsidiary
Hachiman shrines, 2nd only to 32,000 Inaris). Hachiman god of sword and scythe
came over with early Hata from Korea, before whom there probably were
no metal blades. In 738 AD MIROKU-JI temple was built here, Usa became
center of *Shin-butsu Konko*, mixed Shinto-Buddhism, and thus many sub-
precincts in Kunisaki. All traces of temple were effaced in early Meiji
purge. Usa also may have been capital of early Yamatai kingdom (one of
several candidates) ruled by mysterious queen Pimiko. Much that came in
from mainland in Japan's pre- and early history matured in N Kyushu, and
when ready, their progeny moved up main isles in various peaceful or
conquering waves, as in Jimmu's journey to Yamato Plain.

*Past tour bus park and gift shops, cross river and enter Usa's lovely wooded grounds.
Long walk up main Omote Sando, on R is...*
Hatsuzawa Pond, shrine offices beyond. On L, we come to **Offertory
Hall**, *Ema-den* for shrine pictures, looking out over larger Hishigata Lake.
Islet-hop by bridge to first large one with **noh stage**, from where can
recross to land and up long steps to **KAMEYAMA** and **WAKAMIYA
SHRINES**. We did this in reverse on way back down. Continuing on
Omote Sando beyond Ema-den, at crossroads on L is where sacred **white
shrine horse** is kept (when not roaming nearby pasture), on R **YASAKA
SHRINE** (many such sub-shrines dot complex). Beyond we come to more
long stairs leading up to Kameyama and Wakamiya. We took path to R of
torii, to **Lower shrines**, *Shimo-no-miya* whence path curves up to meet
other two sets of stairs and Wakamiya. We are now in front of main shrine,
entering compound thru **Great West Gate**, *Saidai-mon*: recently
repainted, bright vermillion wood stands out photogenically against white
walls. In three identical, adjoining main shrines are enshrined, L to R,
Emperor Ojin, *god Hiuri Omikami*, and *Empress Jingo* (invader of Korea
Ojin's mother, bore him after return few years after death of his emperor-
'father'). Nearby **Treasure Hall**, *Homutsu-den* (¥150) contains only
smattering of treasures left as offerings by great lords, warriors thruout
ages; who knows what else is hidden in other storehouses.

From USA, 20min rail to NAKATSU City, 45min express (1hr local) beyond to
KOKURA to catch Shinkansen or regular JR across to SHIMONOSEKI, where *San-yo*
(mountain-lite) main line continues up Seto Inland Sea coast, or for our circle-Japan route
San-in (mountain-shade) Main Line heads up northside Japan Sea coast.

772

No need to be so formal!
Living on the same ship
and eating food cooked in the same pot
makes us all like one family.
—Chikamatsu Monzaemon, *Love at Sea* (1719)

LEAVING KYUSHU
WHERE NEXT

LEAVING KYUSHU offers wide choice of routings. From BEPPU, airport is hour-plus away **taxi** or **bus**, light traveler can **hydrofoil** to it in 30min (some take 45min via nearby Oita). **Fly** on to OSAKA or TOKYO, or commuter plane 45min to HIROSHIMA or MATSUYAMA, or other routes which will open. Unless flying, advise local JR **train** link to Shinkansen at Fukuoka or Kokura and on to HIROSHIMA or OSAKA, or **boat** direct to HIROSHIMA or KOBE, best seascapes, dep late pm.

Return via Hiroshima for those who missed that lovely town on way down: **boat** direct to HIROSHIMA (or KOBE *see* p612), which boat no longer stops over en route at MIYAJIMA. Or train, as above.

Several alternates for those with time who missed minor sights described above, take cross-Kyushu train OITA to KURUME and on to FUKUOKA, which route takes you via rural YUFUIN ONSEN and HITA; or main coastal rail line via USA SHRINE and NAKATSU City, on to KOKURA, thence across to SHIMONOSEKI on Honshu where choice, as above, of *Sanin* rail up Japan Sea coast (follows after Ryukyu) for our circle-Japan route, or *Sanyo* rail line up Inland Sea coast to Hiroshima, etc (reverse of preceding).

Sanin-Japan Sea route which follows, again offers several alternates:

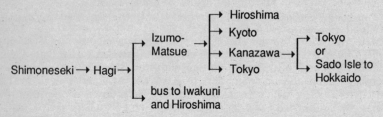

Ferry from Beppu via nearby Oita to Shikoku ports of Matsuyama (Takahama), or to Uwajima bull fight capital. Then leisurely across Shikoku isle of 88 pilgrimage sites.

Another alternative is to train to FUKUOKA, as above, thence boat or plane to OKINAWA, which follows immediately.

International departures may be made from FUKUOKA airport for Guam and South Pacific Islands (including leisurely route to Hawaii), Korea, Taiwan and Hong Kong, with certainly expansion of services on to SE Asia. Kumamoto will also develop as International airport. Fly on to NAHA for further international flights to Southeast Asia.

Boat departures are also possible from Moji for Pusan, Korea, including car ferries with taking of Japan-registered vehicles to Korea relatively simple —check JTB for latest requirements. Also from Naha, Okinawa catch few-monthly ferry to KEELUNG (northern Taiwan), some of which boats also stop en route at Ishigaki, southernmost Ryukyu. But first make sure you have *valid visa*.

We have honor to be subjugated by Chinese ... English ...
Japanese ... American. Okinawa very fortunate.
Culture brought to us, not have to leave home for it.
— Sakini, in *Tea House of August Moon*

RYUKYU 琉球
LAIR OF DRAGON KING

"IN SOUTHERN SEAS lie islands of Loochoo Kingdom, known widely for their scenic beauty...," is inscribed on Shuri Castle's ancient bell—using name for isles in local language. Once out of California gold rush and cowboy movie cattle-drive towns around main US bases, outer isles are still beautiful, natural setting for this potpourri also known as **OKINAWA.**

GETTING THERE: Main island of Okinawa, from TOKYO: by **air** JAL, ANA 10x-daily, 2hr30min, ¥34,900; by **passenger boat** from OSAKA-KOBE *below*. From NAGOYA by air ANA 3 daily, 2hr10min, ¥32,750. From OSAKA by air JAL, ANA, 6 daily, 2hrs, ¥29,100; by non-stop **Arimura Sangyo Ferry** 33hr40min, 2 weekly; **Kansai Kisen Ferry** via KAGOSHIMA, 41hrs, every 2-3 days; **Ryukyu Kaiun** passenger ship via Kagoshima or Fukuoka, 39hrs, every 2-3 days—all three leave from Nanko Pier, ¥15,450 2nd class. From KOBE by sea, **Oshima Unyu** Line (every tue, via Naze in Amami Oshima, Kametoku, Wadomari, Yoron) 25hr; or Ryukyu Kaiun Line (every 5-6 days) 50hrs, ¥19,670 2nd class; and **Kansai Kisen Ferry**, times and price (2nd class) same as Osaka, dep every 4-5 days. From FUKUOKA, 1hr35min JAL or ANA 6 daily, ¥23,100; **Ryukyu Kaiun Ferry** every 4-5 days, 29hrs, ¥12,970. From each NAGASAKI, KUMAMOTO, MIYAZAKI, daily ANA 90min, roughly same prices as from Fukuoka. From KAGOSHIMA 2 daily ANA 80min ¥21,050; daily ferries Oshima Unyu or Terukuni Yusen, 25hrs ¥11,840, or 21hrs Ryukyu Kaiun every 4-5 days. All boat prices 2nd class steerage, private room 1st class about double; some special 2nd private rooms priced midway. 10% off round-trips. Air should come down in price.

Globe-trotter heading on to Southeast Asia may spend nite or two in Okinawa limited to main isle; but if here longer, we recommend getting off main isle for any of smaller isles. Luckily, most ferries to Okinawa land in morning, and ferries to outlying isles leave afternoon-evening. If pressed for time but wanting to get off main isle, Southwest Airlines (SWAL) serves most isles. Two main groups of outer isles: 90min to 3hr30min boat W of Okinawa is KERAMA, KUMI; 12-13 hrs (overnite) S to MIYAKO, ISHIGAKI, IRIOMOTE group. Main isle has much to offer tourist, but coming down this far you are probably wandering type searching for sun and sand with peace and quiet, all better found on outlying isles. Main island referred to as Okinawa; other isles are referred to by name.

PERSONAL ORIENTATION: History of Okinawa shows archipelago as stepping stone between China and Japan. Original inhabitants were south seas mixture similar to those who moved up into Japan and South Korea in centuries around time of Christ. Jimmu Tenno's mother came from 'Sea Plain' thought to be Ryukyu. There seems also to have been movement down from Japan with perhaps Ainu migrants reaching islands. Women tattooed selves, as Ainu did, as Chinese writers tell us early Wa-Japanese did. China's first trade with what is now Japan was with Loochoo, and cowrie shells have been found associated with early Chinese knife-money late BC. Mother-lode for cowries (earliest Chinese money, ideograph for which is still basic to all 'money' and 'buy' terms) was Miyako-jima.

In 1135 great Japanese archer MINAMOTO Tametomo was exiled to Izu isles, later escaped to Ryukyu where he married noble's daughter. 25th king of local Tenson dynasty was murdered, then Tametomo's son overthrew murderer, founding new Sho dynasty. In 15th century Ming China claimed archipelago and Sho kings sent tribute regularly. After Tokugawa closure of Japan (1641) Satsuma daimyo invaded and also claimed tribute. Okinawa paid both conquerers until 1879. Satsuma never annexed Ryukyu outright, using island kingdom as puppet to play in forbidden China trade. (When Ming ships docked in Naha, Satsuma fleet hid in Machinato just off Suicide Cliff—no need to annoy Chinese).

In 1879 Japanese kidnapped last Sho king, annexed isles as prefecture of Japan. Since that time mutually unintelligible Luchuan cognate language of Japanese has been replaced by Japanese and isles have been culturally mostly absorbed into Japan, tho not accepted as *Jun-nihonjin* (true-Japanese); ranking between Korean migrants and Eta-untouchables on one hand and full-blooded mainlander 'humanity' on other. Reciprocally, Okinawans have little love for *Wa*-Japanese.

Three thousand Satsuma invaders stormed ashore April 1, 1609.

United States Army and Marines attacked April 1, 1945: 12,250 Yanks died, with 110,000 Japanese military and 150,000 Okinawans (one-third of then populace), who could not serve in army with 'genuine Japanese' but served as labor troops, armed only with bamboo spears. Many died at hands of own Japanese mainlander troops for capital crime of being heard speaking Okinawan near military emplacements. Mass suicides were instigated by Japanese. Nothing but few shattered stone walls survived 1945 holocaust and almost everything but ancient cliffside tombs dates postwar. Islands studded with war monuments to dead US and Japanese soldiers, Okinawan civilians and one American civilian – Ernie Pyle. Until April 1972, Japan held 'residual sovereignty' over archipelago while US held actual control to such degree that local currency was US greenback and US passport holders needed no visas for short stays. All this changed overnite as Okinawan archipelago was handed back to Japan: drivers were given few days grace period to learn to drive on left side of road, buses were rebuilt or replaced.

In spite of all their complaints while virtual US colony, many locals (particularly older ones) dislike Japanese even more. They remember days under cruel thumb of Meiji to wartime Japan when Okinawans were treated worse than dogs by their Japanese 'masters'–History Museum, Taketomi Isle. More and more even younger locals are coming to voice preference to be rid of both Americans and Japanese, but nothing will ever come of this except possibly more enlightened Tokyo policies. Most popular TV program since '87 is serial historical swordplay in Luchu language with Japanese subtitles, don't miss it—and watch fellow-viewer reactions.

TILT: Highlights of Okinawa can be seen on **bus tours** from main bus terminal downtown Naha. Four competing companies Ryukyu, Okinawa, Naha Kotsu (alias Kin Bus) and Toyo help keep prices down by running almost identical courses, same prices. Naha Kotsu and Toyo depart 30min earlier for major hotel pick-ups, Naha Kotsu at **Miyako, Grand Castle**, Toyo at **Tokyu** and **Harbor View**. All fares include admission fees and lunch. NANBU (S area) tours run ¥3,500, 6hrs, all lines dep 10:00 and 13:00 (except hotel pick-up runs), basic course: ex-Imperial Navy Headquarters, Himeyuri Tower → Peace Park → Gyokusen-do Cave. Only Naha Kotsu's A course visits Shurei-mon Gate. HOKUBU (N area) tours rush you thru too many man-made 'nature' parks too quickly to enjoy any of them. Some runs are good tho, especially for easy driving up length of Okinawa. Okinawa Bus: C Course leaves 9:00 to Manzamo → Nago → Hedo-misaki Point, returns 18:30; D Course dep 9:00, down Kokusai-dori → Shurei-mon Gate → Ryukyu-mura Folk Village → Marine Park → Tropical Garden ret 18:30. Both ¥4,100; stop at Okinawa City (Koza) Plaza House shopping center on return leg. Used to be **tours for foreigners**, check hotels or airlines, **taxi** for 3-4 same price as bus tour.

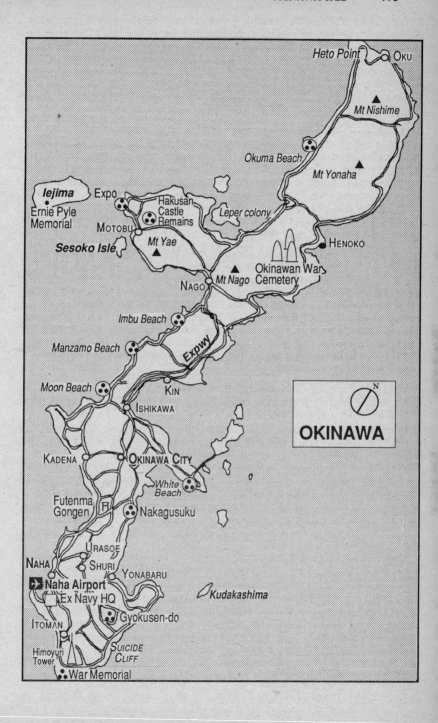

GETTING AROUND: **Public buses** extensive and frequent on most lines. **Taxis** abound, 3/4 price of cabs on main Japan: 3-5 tourists can parallel bus tours for same or less per person, with added luxury of additions and own pace. *Kogata* (4-person) tour of NANBU (S) district, 4hrs ¥9,600 (30x-mtr) to 6hrs ¥14,400; 10hr tour CHUBU (mid) & HOKUBU (N) districts ¥24,000 (78x-mtr); basic hourly rate just under 8x-mtr. **Hitch-hiking** easy, but stick to main roads. Six **rent-a-car** agencies scattered around Naha city. Airport with internal and international terminals (military planes on runway are Japan Air Self Defense Force) is 3.5km S of Naha; **cab** 2x-mtr or 10min **bus**.

AIR TOURS around Naha (15min, ¥15,300 for 3) or 2/3 up isle (1hr, ¥65,400 for 3) by **Nihon Flying Service**, ☎(0988)-57-4658. Can also arrange for any of 6 set courses of varying lengths and prices thru private airfield, ☎57-8443, which boast lower prices, 10min aerial tour of Naha area, ¥4,950 per person, 1hr40min tour of whole isle ¥33,000 per person. We have not tried it, recommend calling, comparing—hotel arranges.

There are three **boat piers**, which is no problem coming in, but should double-check which one you are leaving from for heading to outer isles. Naha Port Terminal (*Naha-ko*) is between airport and town, on townside of river/lake; ships to/from Kyushu's Kagoshima, and outer isles of Yoron, Miyako, Ishigaki. 2km up coast is Tomari Port Terminal (*Tomari-ko*) for outer isles of Kerama, Kumi, Aguni; but beware there are two terminal buildings 200m apart, and ships to various isles that make up Kerama leave from either. Naha New Port Terminal (*Naha Shin-ko*) is another 2km N; boats to/from Tokyo, Osaka-Kobe, Fukuoka, Kagoshima, and outer isles of Yoron, Miyako, Ishigaki. Of course, there is no guarantee that these will not change, so check still. All have **Kanko-annai** to help find rooms any budget, and friends have had good luck with touts. We did not: if anyone offers cheap rooms at Ichi-doru (One-Dollar) House, run other way—flea-infested surplus cots and blankets they probably got from junkyard, and only lodging in Japan where we (or anyone else we know of) were *robbed while asleep*. (*See* WHERE TO STAY), for more orthodox lodgings. Tourism Hall, *Okinawa Kanko-kaikan* 5min walk E of Naha Port up-to-date info on all isles; tho most written material is in Japanese; English speaking personnel there.

NAHA, main city of Okinawa, has developed rather well into modern city from postwar shanty-town look which lasted well into 1970s. First section to rise up from ashes of war was mile-long main street lined then mostly with blackmarketeers, now Kokusai-dori, International Ave. Tho old sight dwindling slowly, you can catch taste of what it must have been like by heading down side streets, particularly around Heiwa-dori area which has open-air marts, 'tent' markets and narrow winding alleys in which hide tiny stores selling almost anything from fresh fruits, vegetables and Chinese folk medicines to over-priced US Army surplus goods which find their way to these and other shops from local bases. Kokusai-dori itself with its new department stores and shopping plazas, is excellent for picking up Oki-nawan gifts and nightlife continues late here.

Left, right, up, down directions off **Kokusai-dori** are based on heading 'up' = inland from Naha Port on this street; thus, main bus terminal, near port, is 'down' at bottom.

SOGEN-JI temple, or what remains of it, was mausoleum of Shuri kings. Okinawan architecture unlike Japanese, being heavily of stone, section of old wall with three arched portals made it thru pre-invasion shelling. In reverence for kings buried here it was formerly custom for passers-by on bikes to dismount 100 yards from gates and continue past on foot. It is 4min walk, L from top end of Kokusai-dori.

One km W of Kokusai-dori, on coast, is...

NAMI-NO-UE-GU (Over-Waves Shrine), point with lovely view (shrine is new). Here visiting Chinese dignitaries were greeted. Below are some of Naha's finest dining places: **Matsuno-shita** is supposed to be model for *Teahouse of the August Moon*; *Juri-Uma Fete* brings teahouse dancers out in force, Feb (*see* DATEBOOK, *follows*).

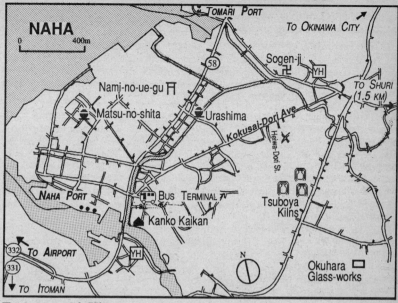

NAHA

0   400m

TOMARI PORT

TO OKINAWA CITY

Sogen-ji

YH

TO SHURI (1.5 KM)

Nami-no-ue-gu

Matsu-no-shita

Urashima

Kokusai-Dori Ave

Heiwa-Dori St.

NAHA PORT

BUS TERMINAL

Kanko Kaikan

Tsuboya Kilns

TO AIRPORT 332

331

TO ITOMAN

YH

N

Okuhara Glass-works

Tsuboya-yaki Kilns are 5min walk from Kokusai-dori, R at Mitsukoshi DS, on winding narrow street to next big road Himeyuri-dori; or from Naha Port 20min bus #17.

You come to group of traditional **red-tiled** Okinawan houses, some of which look as if they barely survived war. Tradition dates back to earliest unglazed wares like those of Annam and Thai for common use. Court imported Chinese porcelains, especially celadon. Satsuma conquest of 1609 saw subsequent profits of Okinawa-China tribute trade expropriated by Japanese. King Nei 1617 brought in three Korean potters from Satsuma, where they had been forcibly relocated by Hideyoshi's invasion of Korea in 1589. They introduced high fire and glazing techniques then left. One, Cho Kenko Ichiroku (Japanese reading of his ideographs) fell in love with local married woman, so King had her divorce and marry him to keep him on, as immortalized in poem and drama *Karaya Bushi*. He fathered Okinawan ceramic industry. King Sho Tei 1671 sent HIRATA Tentsu to China to learn *aka-e*, red overglaze technique. He tiled all thatch palace and temple roofs, developed ingenious white glaze and brought art to full flower.

In 1682 Court gathered potters from Takara-guchi (Shuri), Wakuta (Naha), and Chibana (Koza) and put them all together more convenient to steady supply of good clays, fuelwood, and new port to develop export industry. 'Discovered' by folk art movement in 1930s kilns prospered till war, during which produced electric insulators and at peace was first section of local economy to revive. Today kilns produce two types of ware. One kiln produces *arayachi*, red and grey clay mix fired at 900°C for 40-50 hrs so its iron content effects glaze-like sheen without glaze. Most kilns make *joyaki*, white, red and pink clay mix high-fired at 1200°C and glazed shell-gray outside and for additonal leak-proofing glazed inside greenish brown-black. Over this polychrome glazes are applied then topped with *tsuyaguauri*, shining glaze made of ground coral and white clay. After three centuries 19 families still make colorful Okinawan pottery, from muddy-green blotched *seiji* to sort of wild purple dragon wiggly stuff featured in old Fu Manchu movies. Kingdom early developed own approach to way of tea, called here 'tea celebration' which tamed and heightened esthetic of pottery. Thus, it is surprisingly lovely, carrying its gaudiness well. Colors may be as wild as some shapes: popular one being standing doughnut teapot plastered with French-pastry decor of purple dragons encircling hole.

Prices amazingly moderate, folkware folks can afford: small pots and vases from ¥500. Among various kilns (which you can visit to see potters and painters at work) is **Pottery Co-operative**, with samples from each kiln neatly displayed and on sale. Pottery buffs *see* booklet by Elizabeth Stockton, *Traditions of Tsuboya*.

SHURI, now merely part of sprawling modern Naha, was separate town as capital of old Kingdom. 20min bus #13 from Makishi stop near Mitsukoshi on Kokusai-dori, or 15min **bus** #17 from Tsuboya (often quicker walk back to Kokusai-dori and catch #13 or #17alternate); **cab** 1.5x-mtr from either. For our **walking tour** of Shuri (about 4hrs with all stops, actual foot-work under 4km), get off bus Yamakawa and work counter-clockwise, or get off Ikehata and go clockwise. Catch bus back to Naha at one you didn't get off at, and cut out half-kilo walk. **Taxi tour**, can do it in half-time.

Short backtrack (W) from Yamakawa stop to three-way intersection towards Grand Castle Hotel. There, 4...
Bingata workshops cluster together, where you are welcome to watch artists at work, but some don't allow photos so ask first. Bingata is Okinawa's classic stencil-dyed cloth, as colorful and gaudy as best pottery, and as beautiful. Patterns (often scenery, stylized animals) traced on cloth from paper stencils, color painstakingly added by brush, then 'set' or rinsed over and over in cold water to make permanent. Art some 400 years old said to have originated by combining aspects of Japanese yuzen dyeing with sarasa printed cottons from South Asia. Colors are of great range, from near garish to subdued, and like none other. Highly decorative wall hangings, go as well in Japanese tokonoma as on Yankee wall. Women's accessories, even men's ties are far more successful, cheaper than Japanese attempts at modernizing folk weaves. There are, of course, kimono bolts, but expensive. Table mats, small wall-hangings, ties from ¥2,000.

Taste of all Okinawan folk arts at...
Ryu-sen, S on small alley at intersection. Traditional Japanese-style building looks oddly out-of-place but inside (9:00-18:00, free) is Okinawan. 1st, 2nd floors display all sorts of cloth (bingata, kasuri weaving), pottery, folk tools; 3rd floor has workshops.

Few minutes walk E from Ryu-sen is...
Gyoku-ryo (8:30-18:00, ¥200), ancestral tomb of Sho royal family. Walled complex (original blasted in war, faithfully rebuilt 1978) was built 1501 by second Sho king of Second Sho Dynasty for his father's spirit (and body), kept in central tomb. Since then, bones of all succeeding kings and queens were placed in L (facing) tomb, those of princes and princesses in R.

Another short walk E to...
Shurei-mon, Gate of Courtesy, trade mark of Okinawa, is postwar copy of original which architecturally combines Shinto torii base and supports with ornate Chinese gate roof. Posts are 7m/22ft-long logs of some 3/4 ton each. Tour buses visit here only long enough to snap few quick photos. (Women in beautiful Okinawan kimono nearby are there to liven up your photo of gate, around ¥300 to have them pose with you.) Within castle were great pavilions and gardens, including Chinese-style mansion to receive Chinese embassies who came to collect tribute, and Japanese hall for Japanese collectors. Destroyed 1945, Okinawa University sprouted out of ruins, but moved out to larger campus few miles S, leaving empty buildings, sports field and park. Nearby **Sono-Hyan-Utaki** stone gate (restored 1957), all that remains of guardian shrine of ancient kings. Beyond it is **Kankai-mon** (also rebuilt), once main gate to Shuri castle; long section of old retaining wall also redone.

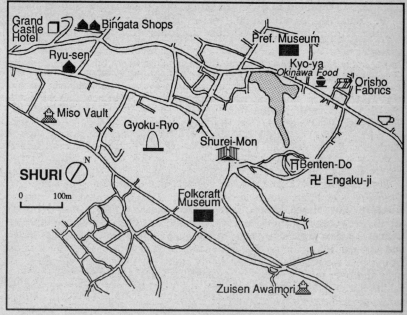

We follow road as it curves around park, but before passing thru Gate of Courtesy may we suggest 5min walk S to...

Okinawa Folkcraft Museum, *Nihon Mingei-kan, Okinawa Bun-kan*; (10:00-17:00, X-tue, ¥100). Building itself is traditional Okinawan house belonging to local lord (under Satsuma) Miyara-donchi; lovely **garden**. Short walk W of Folk Museum is another Bingata workshop; between two, on other side of street, is 500-year-old **cobblestone street** which used to lead to Sho kings' annexes. Only 238m of cobbles remain, take you nowhere, but pleasant stroll thru old neighborhood which escaped war damage.

5min walk E of museum is...

Awamori Distillery, where they make powerful local hooch, like shochu, made from rice or sweet potatoes. Tours and free samples anytime.

Continuing beyond castle gates, tiny...

Enkan Pond on our L, bridge to islet **Benten-do** Pavilion, built 1502 to house Buddhist sutras presented by king of Korea. Chinese style *kaen-hoju*, 'fire-retarding jewel' atop roof did not save it from flames of war.

On our R is remains of...

ENGAKU-JI temple dates to 1492, present stone bridge, gate, walls rebuilt 1968. From Benten-do, cut across Ryutan Park, in which lake Sho kings floated boats full of musicians, food, drink to entertain Chinese (but not Japanese) visitors. Okinawa had mutual and older relations with China, whose artists came and specialists in arts and sciences aided court, locals studied in China. Japan just came in, took over and dominated.

8min walk from Benten-do, N end of Ryutan Park is...

Prefectural Museum, *Kenritsu Hakubutsukan*, (9:00-16:00, X-mon, hols, ¥100); fine exhibits on Okinawan pottery, lacquer, cloth, other folkcrafts and arts; miniature replica of Shuri castle original; special Perry Memorial Annex devoted to American contacts with Okinawa, which preceded those with Japan proper.

2min walk W to Ikehata bus stop...
Soloing, full morning in Shuri for quick tour, main points **Shurei-mon**, **Pref Museum** & afternoon two choices: **southern Nanbu war memorial** tour; or **central Chubu** (combine with **north Hokubu** for full 2nd day).

ITOMAN, 15km S of Naha, 40-50min bus (#32-35), site of largest boat races held lunar **May 4** (*see* DATEBOOK), which *Festival to Dragon King* ends rainy season. Itoman is change-over spot for buses to Peace Park area. Itoman boat race festivals are held at **HAKUGIN-DO** shrine, 5min walk N of central rotary bus stop. Enshrined here is Itoman's *uji-gami*, indigenous guardian spirit who looks out for sailors and bountiful catch. Wives also pray here for male offspring. 5min E of rotary, 300-year-old stone **house-like tombs** (one large, 4 smaller) of Kochi family, largest non-royal tomb on isle. Smaller tombs receive bodies and after 3 years bones are transferred to large tomb.

Coming down this way, take roundabout bus #33, 20min from Naha to...
Ex-Imperial Navy Headquarters, *Kyu-Kaigun Shirei-bu*, series of winding man-made tunnels from where defense of Okinawa was conducted. ¥300 to tour maze (daily, 9:00-17:00), at entrance is museum of defenders' material remnants.

10min walk from Tomi-gusuku Koen bus stop, near which is remains of...
Tomi-gusuku Castle: On June 13, 1945, General Ota and 4,000-plus men committed mass suicide in these caves. 'Operation Iceberg', code-name for first invasion of Japanese home territory, proved to be bloodiest fighting in Pacific. Name proved prophetic, for there was much more to defense than met US eye. Days of constant shelling from American fleet offshore did not reach much of underground maze of tunnels and caves (some of which held airplanes), and Japanese military and civilians put up fanatical do-or-die defense. Monuments to fallen on both sides abound, most here in southern portion where final Japanese resistance was over-come: **Buckner Memorial**, where US commandant General Buckner fell is mile S of Itoman; to its E is **Yamagata-no-to**, where platoon from Yamagata area met their end. Near it is **Shira-ume-no-to** (White Plum) obelisk, marking cave where 74 high school girls and 11 teacher-volunteer nurses, committed suicide rather than surrender (propaganda of 'white devils' eating Japanese girls for lunch seems to have worked—and social pressure exerted by mainlander officials left them little choice).

This trio off main road, on way to...
Okinawa War Memorial National Park: If driving, 8km S of Itoman to **Chian-misaki Point**, southernmost spot of Okinawa. Ruggedly beautiful, these 200-foot cliffs are better known as **Suicide Cliff** where civilians jumped lemming-like—but mostly at bayonet-urging of mainlander Japanese troops, into rock-studded sea below. *Himeyuri-no-to* (Princess Lily Tower or **Cave of Virgins**) marks tragic spot where 187 girl students and 14 teachers hid, refusing to surrender—more, it has come to light, out of fear of own police than of fierce marines—and mistaken for hidden troops, were blasted out by flame throwers, June 19, 1945.

1.5km walk S to coast is...
Kompaku Mound, dedicated to 35,000-plus soldiers and civilians who died here in last ditch defense: simple mound erected by local villagers just after war when there was not yet money to squander on stone. It now has large stone on top; around it monuments to troops from Tokyo, Nara, Shimane, Hiroshima, Wakayama and Hokkaido. —None for locals?

Himeyuri-no-to is 15min bus #82 E from Itoman. Nearby is small restaurant serving local food: bowl of Okinawa noodles for few hundred yen, and 8-dish *Ryukyu-ryori* course for around ¥2,000.

5min/2km beyond on same bus to Kenji-no-to bus stop, entrance to...
Mabuni-no-Oka Monument: June 23, with no hope for promised, (never-delivered as non-existant), reinforcements, General Ushijima sent men on last futile banzai charge, then committed suicide in nearby cave after writing prophetic death poem:

"Autumn (i.e.end) of these isles will still herald New Spring for Empire"

Was it new spring of die-hard militarist clutching to hope of divine inter-vention on behalf of Japanese victory, or that of rational person who real-ized that what would remain of Japan after hopeless war would be totally unlike military state he knew. Here last Japanese resistance was annihilated. Boulder-like monument **Reimei-no-to** near cliff marks event. More tragic is **Kenji-no-to** monument with three youths—dedicated to headmaster, 17 teachers and 289 students of Okinawa Shihan-gakko (Teacher Training School) who were formed into glorious sounding Imperial Shield Brigade. Their mission was less glorious; each with land-mine strapped on his back was ordered to invasion beaches to dive in front of American tanks (many mines were duds, those that worked often at most blew tread). Most of Mabuni-no-oka is taken up by memorials representing 35 of Japan's prefectures, one put up by NHK, and one each for Bougainville and Davao, Pacific Isles which also saw heavy fighting. Ghastly memories, but many are fine art. Far end is **Peace Museum**, *Kinen Shiryokan* (9:00-16:00 X-mon, ¥100), with battlefield remains, photos, models of Okinawa campaign. Giant control tower-structure on height is **Peace Memorial**, *Heiwa Kinen-do* (¥500), enshrined inside is 12m tall Buddha, hands clasped in prayer. Work of Yamadas, Okinawan artist husband-wife team, coated with 3.5 tons of Okinawan lacquer. Behind hall is another museum:...

1hr here should do (many tours take lunch at nearby restaurant or drive-in), if doing it on your own by bus, check return schedules as runs infrequent.

1.5km W of Himeyuri-no-to is...
Ryukyu Glass Village, in lovely traditional white-walled red-tile houses of **FUKUCHI Village**. Visit glass-blowing center; also show-room shop. Mostly reminiscent of old, cheap American, but some fine pieces among them. Several such glass producing villages on Okinawa, try your hand at glass blowing near Moon Beach, N part of Okinawa.

5min bus #82 beyond (E) Peace Park (Heiwa-koen) is...
Okinawa Coral Museum, *Sango Bijutsu-kan* (9:00-18:00, ¥200), in Coral Park, bus stop Sango-en. Just beyond is **Himeyuri Park**; which we suggest passing up at ¥700, unless interested in cacti, of which they have hundreds.

Gyokusen-do Cavern, second largest stalactite cave in Japan, its form-ations are reputed to be best in Asia. Over 5km long, almost 1km is open to public; 30min to see, ¥700. ¥500 for adjacent **Habu-en** (¥1,100 for joint admission, *kyotsu-ken*) with room full of Habu and giant snakes from around world, and staged (4 times daily, more weekends, holidays) fight between mongoose and cobra. Habu is local viper distingushed by triangular head, grows up to 2m in length and inhabits most of Okinawan isles. Other isles have huge poisonous water snakes. Even with thousands of clumsy mainland Japan tourists, very few people get bit, deaths very rare as anti-venom can be obtained all over. Snakes are found only in deep jungle, are nocturnal and try to avoid man. If hiking just don't stick your hand into some dark nook

and you should have no problem. Local 'potion' for stamina and libido is
Habu-shochu, vodka-like drink with baby habu pickled inside bottle.

GETTING THERE: Gyokusen-do is 50min bus from Naha: #54 is little
quicker and stops in front, but only 4 daily, #50 runs every 30min, stops nearby Ara-
gusuku whence 10min walk. From Peace Park few go direct (which check); quickest may
be to take #82 to last stop Horikawa-bashi (25min) and 2km walk up (inland) either road
flanking river.

SE corner of Okinawa has little, but optional lodging for budgeteer. Few minshuku
each at O-o-jima isle (connected by bridge), Niibaru Beach, Hyakuna Beach, easternmost
Chinen Beach; beaches have campsites.

Up E coast to Yonabaru, where change to bus for...

OKINAWA CITY which many locals still refer to by old names of Koza
or Misato, two villages incorporated into Okinawa City on April 1, 1974.
From NAHA it is hour bus; #25 goes via SHURI. No. 2 gate to US military base at
Kadena is here, and many Japanese tourists come for its American flavor
(one such 'attraction' is giant **A&W**), wander thru American community at
Awase. They can even arrange tour of base. Kadena is one of largest US
overseas bases, its 4km long runways can accommodate any size aircraft, it
is emergency landing for space shuttle; B-52s taking off from here during
massive bombings of North Vietnam were major bone of contention for
Japanese who saw use of their land for attacks against fellow Asians as
breach of their 'Peace Constitution'. And highly probable storage of nuclear
weapons (not confirmed by US or Japanese govts) also went against 3 Non-
nuclear Principles of non-use, -storage or -production on Japanese territory.
Bases are legally part of America, tho non-nuclear principles vaguely agreed
to by honor system, probably loosely interpreted.

Okinawa City has many fine gift shops catering to large foreign popula-
tion; well-priced traditional Okinawan (and other Asian) folk items. Shops
and restaurants of all sorts along main avenue Nakanomachi O-dori
(Rte330) and intersecting Kuko-dori (Air-base road) to Gate 2, and Chuo
(Central) Park Ave. **Nitelife** concentrated 600m S around intersection of
Grand and Nakanomachi avenues.

W on Grand, past sports ground, is...

Kanko Togyu-jo, where you can see Okinawan **bullfights**. Similar to
what we find in Uwajima, Shikoku, probably introduced by Satsuma
clansmen since it is said that Okinawan farmers first pit bull against bull for
entertainment in mid-17th century. It benefits farmer, for stronger bull is
more valuable as breeding stock. Now, bulls are bred and raised only for
fighting (no menial labor for them, unless real losers), and undergo training
and get special diets one month before main tournaments. Ranked like
human sumo, Okinawa City annually hosts two national championships and
four inter-isle championships. As its name implies, Kanko Togyu-jo
(Tourism Arena) has biweekly fights for visitors (tues, fri from 7pm, ¥300).
Schedules for main tournaments in newspapers; can get thru **Okinawa City Tourist
Bureau**, ☎(09893)-2-8735, on SW corner of Grand and Nakanomachi Avenues.

5min walk S of Tourist Bureau, go R(W) across from Central Market 100m to...

Moromi Folkcraft Museum, *Mingei-kan*. 3-storey architecturally
appropriate mix of Chinese, Japanese, Okinawan; one wall imbedded with
sherds of pottery. Inside packed full of equally varied folkcraft items of
pottery, weaving, dyed cloth, farming & fishing tools. Good bilingual
catalogue profusely illustrated (Daily 10:00-19:00, ¥200).

Another 500m S is **Plaza House**, mall-like shopping center most N-bound tour
buses stop at so Japanese can buy imported goods; large selection Okinawan gifts.

Downhill NE from Plaza House (400m E of bus stop, 1hr bus #55 from Naha) is...
Koza-yaki Kiln, where you can watch, buy, or make your own pottery.

Childrens' Land, *Okinawa Kodomo-no-kuni* (¥500), 20min walk E (cab mtr basic) of Koza bus terminal, is zoo-aquarium-amusement center park. Tuesday, thursday and weekends can see rare Iriomote mountain cat, primitive wildcat found only on Iriomote Isle. This is one of few places where they've been raised successfully in captivity.

Okinawa City's **Koza bus terminal** is main one, with lines up either coast to Nago E to Yokachi Peninsula, tip of which is military port, now shared with Japan SDF; named with typical military originality, White Beach (also Blue Beach N of Okinawa City, same use). Swimming beach reserved for military personnel. Off tip, chain of isles perhaps only place in world where one can go island hopping by car: at lowest monthly tide you can drive out to each. But no need to wait for tide anymore, as scenic causeway connects all. First two are now almost one with landfill to create area for giant oil refinery storage depot. Beyond, on furthest out Ikei Isle is excellent white sand beach, but there are easier to reach ones on main isle.

En route Naha → Okinawa City are some stops of historic interest, easy if car or cab; slightly time-consuming by bus...
URASOE, 4km N of SHURI (40min bus #55 NAHA → AHACHA), was capital of Eiso and Satto dynasties until Sho kings moved to Shuri. Iso castle was built mid-12th century by king Shunten, razed by invading Satsuma and completely flattened by invading Americans, leaving only part of coral reef wall. Now hosts stone **Wako** (Light of Peace) **Jizo** monument above cove holding bones of local war dead. From its small rise, you can see Shuri. Cliffs just E have walled fronts with doorways excavated—these are **Yudori Royal Tombs** of King Eiso (facing, R) of some 720 years ago, and 500-year-old tomb of King Sho-nei (to L). After war, stone sarcophagi were found containing bones of Eiso and his queen, and sculpture. World War II name for this hill was Hacksaw Ridge, scene of vicious fight.

7km NE is...
FUTENMA: 45min bus from Naha, many as main stop for several lines. Near bus stop is **FUTENMA GONGEN**, 530-year-old shrine, of 8 main shrines of Okinawa. Famous for its *stalactite grotto* in rear of which *phallic Kannon* enshrined. Entering cave itself, what with its obvious peculiar shape and characteristics, realistically emulates re-entry to womb to be re-born again. Finest example of fertility shrine anywhere.

Nagasuku Castle remains mark another of numerous stone castles which sprang up on Okinawa in middle decades of 16th century, when castle architecture was introduced from Occident into Japan. This one is more European in style: several tiers of winding, thick stone walls, some with huge arched entrances until you are finally at top. Museum (¥500) at entrance has early imports from Europe, ancient local art. Near castle is tomb of its builder, tragic Gosa-maru, resembling giant stone turtle shell and first of this type of peculiarly Okinawan tomb. Tho it dates from 1458, most others on isle date late 1800's when copying it became fad. They are stylistically of Taoist origin (rather than Buddhist as influenced by Japanese burial custom), Chinese faith which had little direct effect in Japan proper.

10min walk N of Nagasuku Castle (back towards Futenma) is...
Nakamura House, *Nakamura-ke*, mid-18th century classic Okinawan rural mansion, open to public (9:00-18:00 daily, ¥200). Futenma-Nakagusuku buses not too frequent, so check schedule and see Futenma Gongen Shrine accordingly. **Cab to**

Nakagusuku is 10min, (2x-mtr). Futenma to Okinawa City is 20min bus; or few mins bus to Isa on W coast to catch frequent #20 (Nago W line, every 12min) bus up Rte58 to Moon Beach and Nago City. Less frequent (2-4 hourly) Nago E line leaves Naha, via Koza, Ishikawa town, Kin, to Nago.

Houses tiled and painted in mixed Oriental-Western style of gaudiest – tho some attractive ones can be seen. Beyond Koza into Ishikawa old styles begin to reassert themselves (tho more abundant further up) – shabby Okinawan thatch that looks like Japanese farmhouse badly in need of barber; peculiar tile with more Chinese sweep than Japanese and guardian figures, usually lion-dog, set on slope like house cat sunning itself or chasing birds.

Amid this potpourri, squeezed between neon garishness of Koza and golf-course green is village of **Shimabuku**—easily recognizable by church and near-paradisical orderliness. Village lives by Bible, perhaps purest Christian community on earth, started by 2 old men who early in this century after chance meeting with missionary decided they would live like Jesus and their village followed suit. Their determination survived Japanese military, war and occupation. Now, rapidly becoming part of greater Okinawa City will it survive modernization and new material prosperity?

KIN, 23km (45min bus) from Koza, boasts temple to Kannon and deep **sacred grotto** which no spelunkers have yet explored fully. Inside grotto is miniature temple housing thousand-armed Kannon. 22 passages branch out, one cuts 700 ft thru to emerge behind public hall; another off to R has been followed in only 1.6km/1mile, with no end in view, subterranean stream full of eels and lobsters. Legend says dog once went on from here and was later found on Kudaka Isle. About 300m open to public, ¥300. Nearby is Kin Okawa (Grand river) actually natural spring which spouts astonishing 1,200 tons of water every day.

10min bus up coast is...
Kanna Beach and campsite.

Several km beyond Kin at Henoko, bus cuts across to NAGO; **drivers** can cut across on local road from KIN which puts you in middle of most popular W coast beaches. Continuing N on E coast is for driver or adventurer with time. Bus ends part way up, rest is winding road, part on coast, part in hills, to meet bus again at northernmost **Hedo Point**. In spots were road cuts inland, dirt lane follows coast to some isolated villages which remain as Okinawan of last century.

UP WEST COAST

ON FREQUENT buses running Rte58, we pass Futenma and Kadena air bases (section of road between two lined with highly Americanized shops), hour N of Naha to **Ryukyu-mura Folk Village** (8:30-17:30, ¥500). Dozen traditional houses—both thatched and tiled—raised storage huts, local shrine and *nobori-gama* (climbing kiln) from all over Okinawan Isles have been reconstructed here; several have traditional arts such as pottery, bingata, hana-ori weaving—speciality of this YOMITAN area. Try your hand at any of these crafts for ¥3,000. Then there is ever-present habu center with mongoose *vs* habu fights 3x-daily (extra ¥300). One house converted into teahouse serves Okinawan snacks, tea. There is also 100-year-old water buffalo-powered sugar mill.

From here, we hit **Onna-kaigan Coast,** dotted with numerous fine beaches which bode well for Okinawa's development as major resort of Japan, especially with its subtropical winter months averaging 15°C/60F. This 30km stretch is where most Japanese tourists spend their time, whether on day trips from Naha hotels or staying at many luxury hotels of **Moon,**

Tiger, Manza or **Laulau Beaches**. Manza, and to lesser degree Moon, offer all sorts of **water sports**, such as: windsurfing 1hr ¥2,000 (instructor 2hrs ¥5,000); catamaran 1hr ¥3,500; water-skiing 25min ¥5,000; sailboat 2hrs ¥7,000; scuba-diving with instructor 2hrs 30min ¥10,000; or paddle around on your own, renting mask, snorkel and fins.

With their resort hotels (Moon's **Reef Hotel** covers almost as much space as beach), they are crowded in summer, spring breaks. Beaches with luxury hotels charge few hundred yen fee unless staying there. Some of hotel-less beaches in between are far more pleasant: **Green, Tanchamei,** bridge-linked isle **Seragaki, Inbu,** wooded **Kise** (town-run, ¥500). Most have budget inns, campsites nearby; if not, they are convenient 90min from Naha, or quick jaunt out of...

NAGO CITY, with Orion Beer (70% of local beer market) brewery tours and tasting. Nago also boasts first annual cherry blossoms in Japan, blooming usually last weekend of January at Nago Castle site. Other than hoary 400-year-old tree growing in middle of main street, town has little else but shopping and drinking.

Hour N of Nago is...
Okuma Beach with seaside cottage-style resort hotel, or campsite little inland near waterfall (one of few on Okinawa, there is also 100ft drop Todoroki-no-taki falls S of Nago). Giant antenna there is transmitter for Voice of America. 20min further is northernmost tip Hedo-misaki.

Bashofu-ori **weaving** is another Okinawan specialty using banana fibers, done by Mr Taira, in Kijoka, 50min bus N of Nago. You can visit his workshop, but should call ahead and let him know you're coming, ☎(0980)-44-3202. As for other crafts, try hand at blowing glass at **Okinawa Kyoei Glass,** just N of Moon Beach. Few kilos beyond that is similar setup at Ryukyu Kogei-mura at Tanchamei Beach.

MOTOBU PENINSULA pokes W into China Sea, with Nago City as its gateway. E end is covered with giant pineapple plantations, where you can pick in summer. 1hr bus #70 from NAGO (2hr30min direct #93 weekends only from Naha) at western tip is **site of Expo '75** with many pavilions, amusement park still here, and fine beaches. Entrance to park is free, but most pavilions charge small fee; floating city **Aquapolis** (¥500), **Okinawa Folk Village** free. You can spend full day wandering thru exhibits with their many short films; we just spent day lazing on white sand beaches there.

If you have time, drive or bus clockwise around peninsula, far side has beautiful islet-studded bay, almost completely cut off from sea by one giant isle at its mouth.

4km before Expo site is...
MOTOBU TOWN, from where 2-4 boats make daily round-trip out to tiny coral reef isle **MINNA-JIMA** (20min o.w.). Said to have fine beaches surrounding lush isle; also grows watermelons. No problem if you miss last boat back, there are two budget minshuku there.

IEJIMA is isle off-shore of Expo site, with **Hokon-no-to** monument to 2,000 Japanese soldiers and 1,500 civilians; and another for US civilian battlefield correspondent **Ernie Pyle**. W third of isle is off-limits: target of US military gunnery practice. Craggy N shore is reputedly good scuba diving; only beach is on E tip, with campsite. On- and off-shore fishing all around. **'1,000-man Cave'** on S shore served as natural air raid shelter for those locals who thereby did not earn listing on memorial monument. 40min ferry (4-5x-daily) from Motobu Port; we *recommend skipping it for...*

IZENA-JIMA and **IHEYA-JIMA** Isles, 90min (¥1,400), 1hr50min (¥1,900) N, respectively, on once-daily ferry from Motobu Port (10min bus E of Motobu town; 40min from Nago). Must go to one or other, but can charter boats or hitch for 4.5km crossing between two. Halfway is miniscule GUSHIKAWA ISLE with one village. Each has family-run ¥-P-B inns (from ¥3,000w/2): Izena 12, Iheya 6, and several campsites on each, with rental tents available thru Iheya Town Hall. Contacts are: **Iheya Town Hall** ☎(0980)-45-2001; **Izena Town Hall** ☎46-2001.

Southern of pair, smaller, circular (2-3km across) **Izena** has as many, if not more, cows and goats than people. Best beaches are all along N shore, it's almost completely flat, with narrow strip of white sand holding back lush green vegetation from multi-hued ocean. Microbuses cruise isle, and more likely than not innkeepers will give you lift out if they have car. There are even some places to see if looking for break from beaches: Sho-en first king of Second Sho Dynasty was born here, and at SE corner on small hill is remaining coral walls of his first castle and palace. 20min walk W, near Izena Beach, is 300-year-old folk house, serving as local museum. **Iheya** is in contrast, long (about 14km), narrow (1-2km), and hilly but as lush. Less good beaches, and thus less popular (tho both are well off beaten track anyway), unless avoiding people is your goal.

SHOPPING: Surprisingly good in Okinawa. Kokusai-dori in Naha has anything made anywhere in Okinawan Isles in its specialty stores to massive department store-like arcades with everything under one roof. Downtown Okinawa City is almost as good. In both, suggest window shopping first as prices usually similar but there are occasional bargain quality 'finds'.

In addition to already-mentioned *bingata* (dyed cotton) of Shuri, and pottery of Tsuboya in Naha, other local products worthwhile are coral, snakeskin accessories and various cotton weaves. Of **weaving**, most acclaimed is *bashofu*, found near Okuma Beach—subtle, unlike most Okinawan bingata, most commonly light tan or off-white base with mellow red or brown thin line patterns in reverse of white-on-blue kasuri of Kyushu and Shikoku. Moderately priced bolts make up into ideal summer yukata and shirts; also fashioned into fine women's handbags, purses, men's ties. Similar is Haebaru Town's *Ryukyu-ori* (near Naha, visit workshop **Oshiro Orimono Kojo**, good buys), Yomitan's *Hana-ori* 'flower-weave' (seen at Ryukyu-mura Folk Village S of Moon Beach).

Famed Ryukyu **lacquer** is not really that interesting and better examples especially of its striking snake-blood red are made by descendants of exiled lacquer-workers in Kagoshima, Kyushu. You can watch artisans making this lacquer ware at **Benbo** in downtown Naha, branch on Moromi Street in Okinawa City; **Kakuman** on Kokusai-dori, for which should call day before, ☎67-1591; and several other stores.

Snake-skin leather is good, comparatively cheap, much appreciated as *meibutsu* (local product) gift to take back to Japan, where it is imitated in many areas, less successfully and at much higher prices. There is no shortage of snakes in Okinawa; snake-farms supplement abundant wild ones: Yonachi-jima isle, off Yakachi Peninsula is so full of habu that villagers had to abandon it in recent years. Look out for metal fixtures, tho most are good, some are as bad as on Japanese mainland copies.

You see small bottles or bags of sand selling for few hundred yen. Look closely and they're star-shaped. Called *hoshi-zuna* (literally **star-sand**), it can be found on beaches of several isles, most notably southern Taketomi. No one took much notice of this unusual sand until early 1970s when, after first oil shock, Japanese prospectors discovered that star-sand was often found above oil deposits. Drilling was abandoned as too expensive and risky, not to mention intense local opposition. In cooperation with China, numerous American, European and Japanese test bores on China side of sea have yet to come up with anything other than false deposits yield from which would not even cover cost of recovery. Star-sand makes great cheap souvenirs, but if heading down to Taketomi, do as we did and fill up your socks with it there, free.

Also some interesting *washi* (hand-made 'rice paper') goods from **Motobu Washi Kogei-mura,** paper art village near Expo. Paper is done into life-like replicas of local fish, then hand painted. You can see them made there; sold also in town as relatively inexpensive but beautiful gifts.

Awamori, local liquor, sometimes referred to as potato-brandy but also made of rice and which at 40 proof is much more powerful than Japanese sake which runs 22-30 proof. Strongest is **Hana-zake** from Yonaguni Isle at 60! More you age awamori, better it becomes with mellower taste. Most is sold in beautiful Okinawan pottery bottles which look more like over-sized hip-flasks, make fine gifts in themselves when empty.

Okinawan **cigarettes** are 'stocking-fillers' of gifts taken back to Japan. Not good, but cheap. Many local brands: Violet, Hi-Tone, Uruma, Urizun.

CHOPSTICKS: Situation improving with growth of Japanese tourism after 1972. Till then US military had such cheap food on base and at clubs that restaurants could not compete. Okinawa City, particularly, now has many places catering to US military, with large American-sized portions of steak & seafood at prices cheap for Japan. Among them, suggested is **Sam's by Sea** at Awase Yacht Harbor 3km E of town, boasts filet mignon and lobster from ¥3,500; or **New York** Restaurant in town, for just steak. Cows abound in Okinawa, and tho not as tasty as beer-fed Matsuzaka or Kobe steaks, you get lots for your money. In Naha, try **Steak House 88** in Tsuji-cho, near Nami-no-Ue-Gu Shrine; nearby are 2 well-known steakeries **Parisienne** and **Jackie's.**

Okinawan restaurants with local entertainment, traditional cooking, we recommend Naha. ('Okinawan' cookery in places like Kobe is caricature of exotica, stressing rocky mountain oysters, penis, *uwajaina*, etc, using name like US ethnic Oki joke—good food itself but tain't Okinawan). Many require reservations; inquire for show times. Best old-timers located in *Tsuji-cho*, **old red light district** now all restaurants. Geisha of Japan are import from Okinawa of 16th century. Samisen originated here, known locally as *jamisen*, *'jami'* referring to its snakeskin belly which gives it more barbaric twang than catskin of Japanese instrument ('*sami*' has nothing to do with cat, just means 3-strings). Jamisen in turn originated in similar Chinese instrument, and can be traced back to Arab basic 'Ud' (*al-'Ud'* from which our 'lute'). Local dance has more verve, snappier rhythm than Japanese, seems more akin to spicy Korean, with hand motions more like Siamese. Music and dance of Tokyo Bay's Oshima Isle is akin, as most of population there came from Okinawa.

Most famous dine-dance restaurant is **Matsu-no-shita** (model for Teahouse of August Moon), ☎68-2945, 18:00-23:00, (X-2nd & 4th suns), full course meals and show ¥5,-10,000 per. 3 blocks towards Kokusai-dori similar **Naha** ☎68-5577, 18:00-22:00. Food is little cheaper (from ¥3,500 per) at newer **Urashima** ☎61-1769, 400m W (across river) from Yamagataya Dept Store in middle of Kokusai-dori; open 17:00-22:00, there are two 30min dance sets at 19:00 and 20:00. **Sky Tours** 2hr, ¥7,000 takes you to old restaurant for food, dance; rsv by 18:00 day before thru hotel, or direct ☎63-0491.

Dinner alone at such as **Mie**, ☎67-1376, lunch & eves 18:00-21:30 X-sun. In lovely Okinawan-Japanese house in Kumoji, serving 'Okinawan Royal Cuisine' based on pork, entree simmered-tender *rafutei*, other fish dishes. Private tatami rooms, dinner ¥6,500, awamori ¥1,000 bottle. Best traditional Okinawan.

Food served at these places are multi-course affairs of excellent fish, meat (pork), vegetables finely arranged like best Japanese meals. Native Okinawan cooking was mainly sweet spuds and pork, which along with other local and Japanese dishes can be had at budget restaurants. Like Japanese *izakaya* (sake and food joints) these serve good, cheap food to be washed down with local Orion Beer or awamori. Fine old folk house-like Ayajo restaurant, near Urashima restaurant, is classier of such places but still inexpensive. Urizun, E down side street just S of road to Shuri and Himeyuri-dori Street has every type of awamori made in Okinawa.

WHERE TO STAY: Naha has no **traditional ryokan**, tho some ¥-B-T J- style rooms available. Most lodgings are hotel style, except for dozen plus minshuku and some Youth Hostels. Book thru **Kanko-annai** at Naha's three ports, and City Tourist Office bottom end of Kokusai-dori. Best of these hotels (most with J- style wing), which run ¥-T+ for twin room only, are: new giant **Grand Castle** ☎(0988)-86-5454, near Shuri, private bath every room; also in Shuri is **Miyako** ☎87-1111; largest, **Harbor View Hotel** ☎53-2111, off S end of Kokusai-dori; **Tokyu** ☎68-2151, little far from downtown near Naha New Port. Outskirts of Okinawa City is **Hilton Int'l** ☎(09803)-5-4321, similar rates. City also has numerous ¥-B, ¥-T hotels, 2 minshuku.

PERSONAL DATEBOOK: Many Okinawan festivals follow Lunar Calendar, need confirm. **Jan** (date varies) *Cherry Blossoms*, largest is at Nago Castle site. **Early Feb**, *Lunar New Year*. Fantastic fete that has faded so entirely from Okinawan psyche since 1964 that almost no one has heard of it, is *Dolphin Calling*. Once held in fishing villages at unspecified times, especially **Feb-Mar** when Dolphin herds run close in-shore, whole village would go to beach, wade in and mentally call dolphins, who in time would swim in herds up into shallows, then calmly beach themselves for slaughter. Sometime **Feb-Mar**, porpoises for no known reason, assemble close in shore at Nago and fisherboats herd them to shore for slaughter.

Lunar Mar 3 (early Apr), *Girls' Day*, young women head down to seaside, 'purifying' themselves by walking barefoot on sand. **Apr** sees Okinawan families cleaning their tombs and picnicking on them with ancestors. **Apr-May**, Okinawa's 'state' flower, *deigo*, blossoms; main ingredient for red 'dragon blood' lacquer.

Dragon Boat Races 'Hale' at Itoman, Tomari, Nago and Minatogawa, lunar May 4th **(June)**. Biggest is in Naha, regular **May 3-5**. **June 23** marks end of World War II battle for Okinawa, official holiday, *Peace March* covers 24km from Naha to Mabuni-no-Oka. **Early Jul** (usually first weekend), *Iejima Festival*. **Last wknd Jul** *Motobu Festival*, parade of local dancers, folk groups, giant fireworks show at Expo site, windsurfing contest, Naha-Motobu yacht race. **Early Jul**, *Kadena Carnival*, only day when US base is open to general public, locals take part in yankee-style festivities. **Lunar Jun 26**, giant *Tug-o-war* at Yonabaru, again on **lunar Aug 15** at Itoman. **Lunar Jul 14-16** (August full moon), *bon dances* all over isles. Vary village to village, but in general men dance while beating drums.

First sun Sep, groups from all isles gather at Okinawa City for *grand dance contest*. **Oct 9-10**, *Naha Festival*; first day costume parade down Kokusai-dori, next day giant tug-o-war. **First wknd Nov**, *Okinawa City Festival*, folk dances, parades, fireworks, highlight parade recreates Okinawan kings' processions for visits to Edo.

Once every 12 years, **year of horse** (1990, 2001), women of Kudaka Isle off S shore Okinawa, have secret ritual, to which you may be invited if female and they like you.

Attaboy, dad...just like American cowboy

OKINAWA'S OUTER ISLES

DAITO Isles lie in Pacific Ocean, 360km E of Okinawa. Two main isles, Minami (South) Daito, and Kita (North) Daito. Isles (particularly Minami) are one giant sugar cane plantation. SWAL, 90min, 1-2 daily to Minami Daito (¥17,210), 5 weekly to Kita Daito (¥18,390); 18hr ferry 4-monthly, ¥4,120 to Minami, whence short local ferry to Kita.

While we hopped around southern isle, friends of ours spent 5 enjoyable days on...
KERAMA Isles, cluster of 20-odd mostly uninhabited isles lying 40km W of Naha. Only Tokashiki, Zamami, Aka, Geruma are inhabited, but you can get boats to take you out to other isles for some isolated swimming, diving, fishing, or just lounging around. Largest Tokashiki (10km x 1-2km) has couple of micro-buses, otherwise you walk.

GETTING THERE: Most commonly by **boat** from Naha's Tomari-ko Port: 1-2x-daily to TOKASHIKI (80min, ¥1,100) and ZAMAMI (90min, ¥1,500) on different boats. Bit more expensive, but worth view is 15min, ¥3,770 CESSNA; 4x-daily from Naha airport to airstrip on uninhabited FUKACHIJIMA ISLE. Naha contact ☎57-8443. Shuttle boats meet each flight and take you to whichever isle you are staying at.
Our friends stayed on ZAMAMI ISLE, 5km long with many inlets excellent diving; fine beaches (of which no shortage on these isles), with N shore having star-sand. There are 28 minshuku, ¥-Pw/3; two ryokan same prices. Arrange thru **Village Office**, ☎(098987)-2112, near pier. Tokashiki has 20 minshuku, AKA 13. All have campsites.

Because of 'primitiveness' of Kerama Isles, young Japanese prefer...
KUME-JIMA Isle 100km SW of Naha. MADOMARI used to be main trading port during Ryukyu Kingdom days; stone walls and gate of storehouses remain. Now resort type hotels, buses, cabs, rental cars and scooters. Main beach is E shore **Iifu Beach**, 20min bus from Nakadomari, with resort class **Eif Hotel**. Between Iifu and Une, long bridge connects to **Ou Isle**, which has unusual rock formations of 5- & 6-sided flat rocks that form turtle-shell pattern on beach, visible low tide.

GETTING THERE: SWAL flies from NAHA in 35min, 5-6xdaily, ¥5,620; 7min cab or bus, airport (on W end) to main town, S shore NAKADOMARI. Buses circle isle in just over 1hr, can get on or off other than at bus stops. KANEGUSUKU Port is 15min walk from Nakadomari, 3hr30min, ¥1,900 ferry odd-days, daily in summer. Even-days ferries dock at NE MADOMARI Port near Une town; these go via tiny TONAKI-JIMA Isle halfway from Naha.

Most things to see are along bus (5min) road N from Nakadomari...
250-year-old **Uezu-ke House** (¥200), residence of local Satsuma clan administrator. 5min further is **CHINBEI-DONCHI** shrine where in May and June *Inaho Festivals*, head shaman 'mother-goddess' speaks to gods. 1km walk W to *Yajiya-gama* **stalactite cavern**.

20min bus beyond shrine is...
'**Sun Stone**', *Teida-ishi* mini **Stonehenge**-like set-up used to time crops, fishing. Nearby are some spectacular cliffs. Isle has fine ¥-S **Kumejima Kanko Hotel**, several more ¥-T ones. 2 dozen minshuku (cheaper than on mainland) dot isle, several campsites. 15min E along coast puts us at UNE.

Kumejima-tsumugi, local woven silk, has been produced here for over 400 years, and was major trade commodity. You can see it being made at numerous homes in Maja hamlet, W end of Une town. You can buy direct from them, or for similar prices at **Folkcraft Center** near Iifu Beach Hotel.

Adventurer can try...
AGUNI-JIMA Isle, 60km W of Naha, and about 10km N of Kerama Isles. 9 ferries monthly make 2hr30min trip to this small isle. Not noted for much of anything, but provides escape from summer hordes. 3 ¥-B minshuku, and campsites.

300-400km SW of Okinawa lie...
SAKISHIMA Isles, as further sub-divided into MIYAKO-JIMA and YAEYAMA groups.

Main isle of former is...
MIYAKO-JIMA 45min-1hr by air (¥10,950), 10hr30min passenger ship (Naha-ko Port, 3-4 monthly, ¥3,810), 12hr ferry (Naha Shin-ko Port, 1-2 weekly, ¥3,810) from Naha. Boats dock at main port Hirara. We have not been to Miyako-jima or its nearby isles, nor have we heard much particularly striking or unusual about them – which doesn't mean they aren't worth exploring. This isle in ancient times was source for cowrie shells which Chinese used for money (thus ideograph for coin is 'shell') and attracted Chinese trading boats BC, before any contact between China and main Japan.

Rather, we stay on boats extra 5hr30min (¥5,100 from Naha, some are direct) to...
ISHIGAKI-JIMA, also hour air from Naha, 30min from Miyako-jima. Once this far we recommend going out to any of several other isles around Ishigaki, but we've had some good visits here—artist OKAMOTO Taro's book on Yaeyama Isles calls them 'forgotten Japan', primordial Japan before Sinification. Ishigaki makes great base for exploring all (no inter-isle boats, only from Ishigaki)—so brief intro to isle...

It is shaped like giant club, with 20km long, narrow 'handle' pointing NE; main Ishigaki City on S tip of bulbous end. Our boat from Naha passes down W shore (526m peak is tallest mountain in Ryukyu Isles) and passes tiny Taketomi Isle. Ishigaki City, sprawling town, but still very rural. In news last few years as government wants to raise tourism and move US Naval air landing strip here and build jet-port on fill which would bury world's last living stand of rare blue coral. Conservationists world-wide as well as many locals oppose this.

WHERE TO STAY: Mostly concentrated around port, all budgets. **Top** is all
W-style **Hotel Miyahara** ☎(09808)-2-6111, at rates comparable to Tokyo's best, ¥-lo-
S for twin or w/2. Bit cheaper are **Yaeyama Kanko** ☎2-3188; and **Grand** ☎2-6161,
¥-Tw/2 (W- and J-rooms in both). There are about 2 dozen other ¥-B-T rate hotels and
ryokan in town. *Budgeteers* have about as many minshuku (we stayed at OWADA near
port), all conveniently located; many have own tours of nearby uninhabited isles. Also 2
Youth Hostels **Trek Ishigaki** ☎6-8257, and **Yaesu Ryokan** ☎2-3157. For staying
bit out of town, there are 3 all W-style, same rates as Miyahara: **Sun Coast** ☎2-6171,
E near airport; **Sunshine** ☎2-8611, 3km W; further W at Fusaki Beach is **Villa
Fusaki Resort** ☎3-3040, with 38 cottage-style rooms (bath, toilet in each). There are
about 2 dozen minshuku around rest of isle, most around nearby Miyara town, and far side
Kapira Beach; sometimes operating around FUNAKUWA halfway up 'handle' (top half is
mostly cattle farms).

Peninsula at...
FUNAKUWA, is not even 400m wide, and its name, 'Boat Crossing',
comes from fact that fishermen used to carry their dugouts across land, from
Pacific Ocean to East China Sea, or reverse, which was lot quicker than
having to paddle all way around. One 'official' campsite at Yonehara Beach
and one more few kilos inland from Ishigaki City; one of our visits we just
pitched camp on good looking strip of beach – but didn't quite realize how
far tide can come in on shallow coral reefs surrounding isle and had to move
our tent about 50m up beach in middle of night to avoid floating away.
Another Youth Hostel 1/3rd way up E shore at Hoshino.

GETTING AROUND: Mostly by bus circling main part in both directions, with few buses out to northernmost tip, which is said to be excellent for diving. There is actually one **tour bus** (10:00 daily) which circles main part
of isle in 4hr30min, ¥3,700 including lunch. Skip tour and see what there is to see in
town in hour and spend rest of day at beach. There are **cabs**, mainly around port and
airport. **Rent cars** from several places in town (¥4,800–12hrs); or 50cc scooters at
Ishigaki Jitensha Shokai bike store ☎2-3255, ¥3,000 per day.

Several places to see, most within easy walking distance from port: get
town map at any of several tour offices at pier. 10min walk E brings us to
Yaeyama Museum, *Hakubutsu-kan* (9:00-16:30, X-mon, ¥100), with
various folkcrafts, tools, and other essentials of daily life, also excavated
items from Iriomote Isle's prehistoric Nakama shell-mounds. About 1km
further E (5min cab basic-mtr from port) is **Traditional Folkcraft Hall**, *Dento
Kogei-kan*; (9:00-17:00, X-sun, hols) with workshops and displays of various
local crafts; notably *Yaeyama-jofu*, woven grass-cloth. 10min walk N of pier is
Miyara-donchi Mansion (9:00-18:00, ¥100), rebuilt 1819 for Satsuma clan
administrator, and best such preserved house complete with traditional
Japanese-style landscape garden but local flora. Inside displays items used
here 17-19th centuries.

2 blocks seaward is...
Southern Isles' Folk Museum, *Nanto Minzoku Shiryo-kan* (10:00-
18:00, ¥300), items from all Yaeyama Isles, including costumes and simple
pottery of Panali Isles. Not made any more, they used to mix finely ground
shells with clay, and bake in open flame.

5min walk W to...
TORIN-JI temple, built 1614; two fine wooden *kongo* guardian figures
flank main gate, carved 1737, stand almost 2m tall, these are two of few
(and best) such figures on isles. Next to it is **Gongen-do Pavilion**, built
same time, to house Buddhist-Shinto spirit of Kumano Grand Shrines (*see*
Kii Peninsula). Not welcomed by local kami, was swept away in 1771 tidal

wave which left temple untouched; rebuilt 1786, oldest extant wood structure in Isles.

Another 5min walk further W is
Ishigaki family mansion landscape garden, 1819 (now Youth Hostel).

*From here, turn back to town, or catch **cab** at Mitsu-boshi (3-star) Cab Co just W of
Torin-ji temple, and head 10min (2x-mtr) out to...*
Kannon-zaki Point, S end of Fuzaki Beach, with **FUZAKI KANNON-
DO** temple, built 1742 to house local ocean deity. Nearby Chinese style
structure with green roof entwined with dragons is **Chinaman's Grave**,
Tojin-baka remains of 128 Chinese coolies killed during aborted revolt on
English ship mutineers ran aground here 1852. Monument-grave was built
only recently, in 1971.

Kapira Bay, 40min bus (clockwise run) from town, is one of those places so
often featured on promotion posters. Beautiful shallow bay with white sand
beaches and clear water, with several lush islets in bay. Black pearls are
cultured in warm waters of bay. Glass-bottom boats cruise around it, or
you might paddle around with mask and snorkel. We spent lovely afternoon here, in spite of threatening rain which never came.

Quicker to get to are some superb beaches on nearby isles; most popular is...
TAKETOMI 6km SW of and only 20min **steamer** (¥370, 3x weekly), or 10min
hydrofoil (7x-daily) from Ishigaki, thence easy 15min stroll pier to town, shuttle micro-
buses for those in rush. Japanese rush tourists charter these buses to take them out to far
corners, but we prefer walking as its only 2km from village to farthest S end.
Compromise by getting rides out on water buffalo-drawn carriages (which arrange thru
minshuku **Arata** or **Maruhachi**), or rent bicycles ¥200 per hour, ¥1,000 per day—
inadvisable.

Can see this 9km-circumference flat isle from town. Right in middle of
isle is lovely village, each house surrounded by high coral wall to break
force of typhoons August-September. One visit here, we tried bikes; except
for meandering thru village streets, forget it, roads rough, and found
ourselves being chased by much quicker buffalo with no choice but to dive
in bushes to get out of way. Strike out in any direction and you will come
to fine sandy beach; star-sand found W and S shores. Surrounding reefs
excellent snorkeling or diving, tho we were warned to stay within reefs.

In just 4 years between our first and second visits there was noticeable
change as more people ventured down this way. But it is (or was, how
now?) still lovely and unblemished despite blossoming of inevitable tacky
shops which seem to plague most tourist spots in Japan. Islanders flirted
briefly with rental scooters but abandoned noisy things after first year; let's
hope they stay away. Most people here reckon directions from main intersection in heart of village, where post office is; R (N) is toward pier. Short
walk L is isle's highest point from where panoramic view of it all – mere
40m high hillock which used to be old watch-tower. 3min walk W to *Nishito-
Utaki*, **tomb** of and shrine to local scholar-official Nishito, who served in
Shuri court. He is known for building Sono-Hiyan-Utaki Shrine at Shuri,
and several more on various isles. Taketomi was one of most religious
islands in Okinawa, 12 shrines dedicated to various indigenous deities of
land, sea and sky. Religion similar to primitive Japanese Jomon and Yayoi,
is maternalistic. Even now there is semi-divine 'mother goddess' lady-
shaman here (succession by divination) who presides over numerous local
festivals, rites. Largest is *Tane-doru-sai* Festival, for 5 days in **Nov**,
various offertory dances and rituals.

Just beyond is...
Folkcraft Hall, *Taketomi Mingei-kan* demonstrating local *Minsa-ori* weaving. 5min walk further to **Local History Museum,** *Kiho-inshu Shukan* (¥300). At far W end of road is **Visitors' Center** with info on isle, large collection of seashells.

WHERE TO STAY: There are about 20 budget minshuku here, one Youth Hostel, in which you can get **rooms** by wandering in, or thru **Yaeyama-cho Kanko-kyokai** (Tourism Bureau) 5min walk SW of Ishigaki port, ☎(09808)-2-2809. There are now also 2 tiny coffee shops, noodle restaurant for quick cheap snacks; otherwise bring own lunch from Ishigaki.

KOHAMAJIMA, 70min ¥610 **steamer,** daily (more summer), or 25min **hover-craft** ¥1,340 daily from Ishigaki, even smaller isle, almost doubles in size at low tide. Surrounded by fine beaches, lodgings choice of over-priced luxury cottage style **Haimuru-bushi Hotel** or 1 budget minshuku.

Other isles in area are...
KUROSHIMA (30min 3/day hovercraft ¥1,000; or 1hr 3/week steamer ¥690), **HATOMAJIMA** (2hr steamer 10 every month ¥1,130), and to pair of **ARA-GUSUKU** Isles (30min charter) better known by local name of Panali Isles. In northern Panali used to make simple open-fire pottery, southern is known for its *Ningyo Jinja*, or **MERMAID SHRINE**, dedicated to these myths of sea. 3hr, thrice weekly ferry to **HATERUMA-JIMA** Isle, lovely beaches said to be quite empty even during peak summer. Hateruma is southernmost in-habited island of Japan, same latitude as central Taiwan; actual southernmost point of Japan is Okinotori Isle of Ogasawara Isles, but it is uninhabited and under joint control of US military & Japanese SDF. E of Ogasawara is **CHIJIMA** isle off which President Bush was shot down March '44.

WHERE TO STAY: All of these isles have some budget minshukus on them, arranged there or thru **Yaeyama-cho Kanko-kyokai** in Ishigaki; Kuroshima also nice but over-priced cottages in **Kuroshima Marine Village.**

IRIOMOTE Isle (about 20km W of Ishigaki), second largest Okinawan Isle, but only has population of around 1,600. Over 90% of it is special **National Park** reserve, under direct central governmental control. It is also most beautiful of isles. Home to abundant unusual wildlife, notably *Iriomote yamaneko* (mountain cat) discovered in 1965. Most primitive species of cat, it has been compared to fossil remains of prehistoric felines and believed to have existed here for 7 million years.

You'd be incredibly lucky to see these deep-mountain nocturnal crea-tures, even if you hike trails cutting E-W across isle. Easier **tour** of Iri-omote hinterland is by **boat** up two wide Amazon-like rivers gently winding thru lush mangrove jungle. Shorter **Nakama River ride** only 6km (90min r.t, ¥1,000), starting 15min walk W of Ohara pier. Longer (20km) more spectacular **Urauchi River** winds almost entire width of isle to empty on W shore; 3hr r.t. ¥1,400. Boat just goes halfway upstream, you can get off at top end of either ride and hike to opposite shore; half-hour hike from Urauchi ride top end are some spectacular **waterfalls**, Kanpira and Miryudo—another 3hrs to reach E shore near Komi bus stop. Halfway between falls and E shore, 4km trail branches off S to top end of Nakama River ride. Full day jungle safari on blazed trail is Ohara (SE) via Funa-ura to Shirohama (NW). Great for birdwatchers, numerous rare varieties and SE Asian visitors. Beaches offer fine snorkeling even by Okinawa's high standards.

GETTING THERE: Most people 'do' Iriomote in day trip from Ishigaki (as we did). Optional **tours**, do either river run in day trip out of ISHIGAKI; 4 choices from ¥9,800, arrange thru **Iriomote Travel** near Ishigaki pier, ☎(09808)-2-9836, or **Ishigaki Tour Boat Co-operative**, *Kanko-sen Kyodo Kumiai* ☎2-7555. Main port of Ohara on Iriomote SE shore is reached by twice daily **hovercraft** (50min, ¥2,060), 2x-day **hydrofoil**, one via Kuroshima (70min, ¥1,370), 3x-week **ferry** (90min, ¥930). North shore Funaura port is 1hr **hydrofoil**, 1-3x-daily; every three days, **ferry** via Hatomajima to W shore Shirahama port.

GETTING AROUND: Cheapest by infrequent Iriomote Kotsu bus: 2 r.t. daily OHARA ↔ SHIRAHAMA, 1hr20min o.w.(¥310 to Funa-ura, ¥860 to end); 2-3 r.t. daily FUNAURA ↔ SHIRAHAMA. 20min bus FUNAURA → URAUCHI-BASHI near which dock for river rides up Urauchi River. Boat and bus runs increased summer. **Rent-a-car** (¥3,500 for 3hrs) at Ohara, Funaura; —**scooter** at Ohara, Funa-ura, and Uehara just beyond Funa-ura; —**bicycles** at each also.

Swimming is good all around, best is **Haimita-no-hama** beach, 2km stretch of white sand along S shore, closest part of which is 30min walk from Ohara. Often empty as most people like to head up to N shore beaches convenient to Funa-ura. Of those, windward side beach is full of star-sand, leeward is beautiful Tsuki-ga-hama bay. On tip is also private beach *Taiyo-no-mura*, **Sun Village**, exclusively for those on Optional Tour 'E'. Coral reefs surrounding Iriomote makes for excellent snorkeling or scuba – for which can rent equipment, get quick intro and guide at few shops, like **Mister Sakana** (Mr Fish) at Uehara.

WHERE TO STAY: Many places, all small, ¥-B: three ryokan in Ohara: **Wakanatsu** ☎(09808)-5-5151, and **Takemori** ☎5-5357 (with one W-style room), both ¥4,500w/2. Few more around Funa-ura, like **Iriomote Island Hotel**, ☎5-6225 (8 W-rooms, 4 J-rooms), **Hotel Iriomote** ☎5-6505, and **Miharashi** ☎5-6537, all ¥4,500-6,000w/2. 8 minshuku around Ohara, 22 around Funa-ura, all ¥-Pw/2, which arrange on spot or thru **Yaeyama-cho Kanko-kyokai** in Ishigaki City. There are also 2 Youth Hostels, one each at Funa-ura and Uehara.

YONAGUNI-JIMA, 6hr30min ferry every third day or so from Ishigaki, is westernmost point of Japanese archipelago, only 100km from Taiwan.

The days of heroic travel are gone,
our very curiosities have changed
growing more subtle amongst
the vanishing mysteries of the earth...
— Joseph Conrad, *Youth*

Chugoku Shimbun, Hiroshima

JAPAN SEA 日本海

OFFBEAT 'UPSIDE' SHADY LANDS

NIHON-KAI, Japan Sea, rugged 'back' side of Japan, is mainly for lone adventurer looking for new paths to beat out of remaining wilderness in this tourist-trodden land. Western-style oases in this tourist wilderness, easily reached from main cities by express train or direct air, and with comfortable hotels, are HAGI (p805), IZUMO-MATSUE (p.821), KANAZAWA (p.857). Other than these, traveller who is not willing to rough it some and who cannot speak Japanese or latch on to traveling partner who does, is advised to look upon next several chapters as bedside reading or to pass time on train, plane or boat, (then perhaps be enticed to try area after all?). But for adventurer (with local traveling companion?) offbeat shady sea coast offers experiences in scenery, festivals and views so often seen only in travel posters.

Japan Sea Coast divides into three major regions: SAN-IN (mountain-shade) from south Honshu's Shimonoseki thru Hagi, Izumo, Matsue, Tottori, ending due north of Kyoto; HOKURIKU (north land), middle portion, continues thru feudal Kanazawa and rugged Noto Peninsula; while northern/eastern portion of coast is lumped into TOHOKU (northeast) to include everything on Honshu from slightly north of Tokyo, way up.

Our Tokyo-last itinerary up from Kyushu (from which can cross over to Kyoto or Tokyo at any of several points, or alternatively on north to Hokkaido, with return to Tokyo via Sendai, Aizu Wakamatsu and Nikko) can cover main 'oases' in few days, or spend indefinite time wandering thru this back-country. If leaving Japan out of Kyushu or Okinawa, can cut overland (several routes) from Hiroshima area to Matsue-Izumo and down to Kyushu via Hagi. This, however, misses lovely Kanazawa—for which remedy, on Tokaido at Nagoya do central Hida area and go on to Kanazawa and use back entrance to Kyoto.

Whatever route you choose, adventurer will find countless rural or modern hot springs (inns, budget to luxe) to relax tired body and mind; spectacular rocky coastline suddenly broken by giant sand dunes of Tottori; fishing villages and mountain hamlets within shouting distance of each other; sacred mountains to climb; and Oki Islands, long used as exile for unwanted emperors, court nobles and samurai lords.

SAN-IN OFFBEAT SHADY LANDS

FROM KYUSHU we cross straits back to main Island Honshu at Shimonoseki to follow San-In (renamed Hoku-yo 20 years ago, but still called San-in by all including railroad people) 'Mountain Shady Side' route up Japan Sea toward Izumo-Matsue. ('Mountain' is Chugoku Range length of Honshu from Kyoto to Shimonoseki; Inland Sea Coast is called *San-Yo*, 'Mountain Sunny Side'—*In-Yo*, Jpn for Yin & Yang, dark-light, – +, etc.)

GETTING THERE: Chief transport is coast-hugging JR San-In Main Line cutting inland to KYOTO with frequent locals and expresses (including sleepers Hakata-Shimonoseki-Osaka-Tokyo), and buses for points inland; air & sea to IKI ISLES. **Drivers** find good roads: Rte191 SHIMONOSEKI → MASUDA, where join Rte9 (up Inland Sea coast with Rte2 to Ogori then inland paralleling JR Yamaguchi Line via Yamaguchi, Tsuwano to Masuda) parallels rail to Kyoto. **Hitchers** have little trouble on coast, many long-distance trucks.

Several ways to **HAGI**: quickest San-In Main Line, optional stop Nagato for Yumoto hot springs and Senzaki Omijima Island. Roundabout bus Yumoto → Hagi via Akiyoshi-do Cavern, also by 2hr bus from Shimonoseki City. From Hagi, lovely bus ride over mountains to Tsuwano, then rail to Masuda and continue up Japan Sea Coast.

TILT: 1st nite SENZAKI with boat around **Omijima**, 2nd/3rd nites HAGI, bus → AKIYOSHI-DO then → YAMAGUCHI and rail → (or direct to) TSUWANO. Kogata (4-psgr) **cab** HAGI → AKIYOSHI-DO → HAGI about 30x-mtr, if ending TSUWANO about 50x-mtr. **U-drive** same run for less on econo-rentals, but must return to Hagi or end Yamaguchi with drop-off fee (still no more than cab); or keep for drive up to **Matsue-Izumo** and fly out. Slow way up is along Inland Sea from SHIMONOSEKI to ASA or OGORI, then cutting across rugged Chugoku mountains. JR Mine Line links Inland and Japan Sea coasts; from Asa (25km E of Shimonoseki) on former coast and Nagato-shi latter: (locals only, hourly) passes thru Yumoto; Akiyoshi-do 40min bus from Mine stn.

Steam Locomotive buffs (steam-locos?) ride antique SL on JR Yamaguchi Line between Ogori (on Sanyo main & bullet lines)—Tsuwano. On operating days makes one r.t., dep OGORI 10:00 to TSUWANO 12:10, return dep 15:19 to OGORI 16:55. Several vantage points along rail often have train fans waiting to get photo of old 'iron horse' rounding bend, appearing over wooded rise, or coming out of tunnel. Even more people pay extra ¥500 reserved seat fee (Rail Pass doesn't cover) to ride popular SL. Tickets on sale 1 mth advance, arrange thru any JR *Midori-no-madoguchi*, 'Green Window' reservation office, or major travel agency. (We not-so-fondly remember when all main lines were SL; express OSAKA-HIROSHIMA took 7-8hrs, rounding bends so slow you could drop off open platform and walk alongside; summer cooling was open window which let in ash so train ride aftermath required long soak in tub to get soot out of pores—ah, nostalgia, nuts!) Last regular SL run discontinued Mar 1976; enthusiastic crowds welcomed its return Aug 1979 (similar run up Oigawa River valley near Shizuoka) and has seen almost 100% capacity since. Run at least every weekend Mar thru Nov, all national holidays, and almost daily July thru Aug; exact schedules thru JR or travel agents, ask about *SL Yamaguchi-go*.

TSUWANO → HAGI (or reverse), recommend direct bus (1hr50min, ¥1,800); rail travel time same, but often long transfer wait at Masuda. Buses main transport thru Chugoku mountains with backwoods hot springs and caverns for adventurer. Rail Passers save on JR buses: Tsuwano–Iwakuni bullet stn, Hagi–Ogori, Hagi–Yamaguchi. Local San-den and Ho-cho buses have virtual monopoly on runs to caverns and baths, tho JR runs from Mine and Ogori to Akiyoshi-do and Taisho-do. Hagi–Ogori run takes 2hrs (1hr less than rail) and got us out over mountains when summer storms washed out coastal rail lines.

With all these options, we meander up to Hagi, starting from...

SHIMONOSEKI, at W end of Honshu has interesting sites, but most folks pass over it—which we also recommend unless time to spare—mostly modern city, with heavy industry and shipping. If you have saved Iki and Tsushima Isles on our Kyushu run for end, you can ferry into Kokura (Kita Kyushu) from

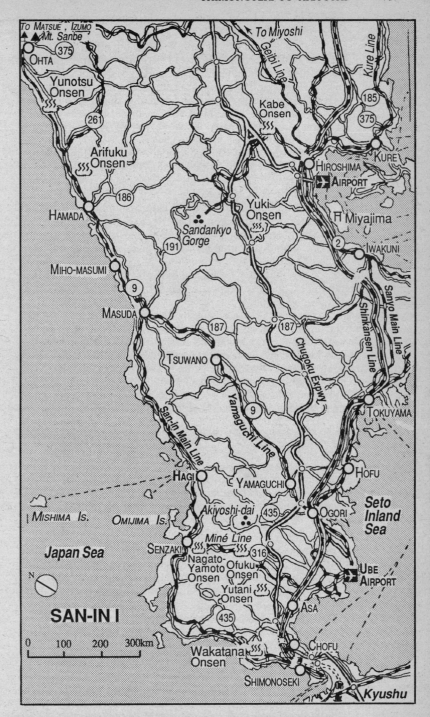

To Matsue, Izumo
Mt. Sanbe
375
OHTA
Yunotsu
Onsen
261
Arifuku
Onsen
186
HAMADA
Sandankyo
Gorge
191
MIHO-MASUMI
9
MASUDA
187
TSUWANO
San-in Main Line
Yamaguchi Line
9
HAGI
MISHIMA Is.
OMIJIMA Is.
Japan Sea
Akiyoshi-dai
435
Miné Line
SENZAKI
Nagato-
Yamoto
Onsen
Ofuku
Onsen
316
N
Yutani
Onsen
SAN-IN I
435
0   100   200   300km
Wakatana
Onsen
SHIMONOSEKI

To Miyoshi
Geibi Line
Kure Line
Kabe
Onsen
185
375
HIROSHIMA
AIRPORT
KURE
Miyajima
Yuki
Onsen
2
IWAKUNI
187
Shinkansen Line
Sanyo Main Line
Chugoku Expwy
TOKUYAMA
YAMAGUCHI
HOFU
OGORI
Seto
Inland
Sea
ASA
UBE
AIRPORT
CHOFU
Kyushu

San-in District, extreme west end of Honshu

Tsushima and 15min JR or 7x-mtr cab to Shimonoseki. Globe-trotter can take side-trip to Korea with ferries linking Shimonoseki to Pusan.

Shimonoseki has seen several events with far-reaching effects on history of Japan. First was end of Gempei War (1180-1185) where Minamoto warriors of Kamakura delivered coup de grace to Heike of Kyoto. **Dan-no-ura** beach (10min bus from stn, E of town) is where Heike remnants plunged into sea with infant heir emperor Antoku and imperial sword, one of three sacred regalia. Near battlefield **AKAMA JINGU** enshrines emperor Antoku and Heike. Also image of Mimi-nashi 'Earless' Koichi, who sang ballads of Gempei Wars to his lute (tale trans into English by Lafcadio Hearn).

Few km up coast are remains of Choshu artillery which tried to stem tide of foreigners in early 1860s. Allied with Kyushu Satsuma clan, followed policy of *Sonno Jo-i*, 'Revere Emperor, Expel Barbarian'. 1862, Choshu samurai cut down foreigners in Yokohama, burned down British legation '63. Later that year this cannon fired on Western ships and closed off Straits of Shimonoseki; in retaliation, allied fleet of British, American, French and Dutch bombarded guns and city for four days, followed by landing 300 soldiers, who dismantled remaining guns. Few months later, British fleet leveled Kagoshima for cutting down ill-mannered Englishman. These events forced xenophobic Choshu and Satsuma men to do about-face in their foreign policies, and few years later their British-trained and -armed forces defeated Tokugawa.

Three decades later, Japan flexed its own expansionist muscles on Asian mainland and declared war on China 1894. Her rapid victories alarmed Europeans and war was cut short by Triple Intervention (Germany, France, Russia) of 1895 which denied Japanese claims to Liaotung Peninsula—coveted by European powers. Tho Japan gained other major concessions in subsequent Treaty of Shimonoseki, her leaders never forgot this diplomatic slap-in-face and regained all losses by defeating Russia ten years later. Treaty was signed at posh restaurant **Shunpan-ro**; now high-class ryokan, its **Treaty Memorial Hall**, *Kinen-kan*, (open daily, free) displays table around which Japanese and Chinese delegations led by ITOH Hirobumi and LI Hung-Chang, respectively, signed, and other memorabilia.

Few hundred meters down coast road towards stn is...
2-storey red brick ex-**British Consulate**, built 1906, free, 9-17:00, X-Mon. Museum of ancient artifacts (*Yasuoka Shiryo-kan*, free, 9:00-16:00, X-hol), mostly from Ayaragi archaeological site, 3min walk from JR Yasuoka stn on Japan Sea coast side.

Just offshore of town is tiny...
Ganryu-jima Isle, where famed swordsman MIYAMOTO Musashi (author of *Book of Five Rings*) cut down foe SASAKI Kojiro. Kojiro issued challenge to duel at sunrise and, hoping to get advantage over Musashi, arrived early to position sun to his back. Suspicious, Musashi came hours later, waiting until sun was on his side.
Tour boats, 50min r.t. thru Straits of Shimonoseki Mar-Nov, one daily 13:00 sunhol. Summer also evening cruises. Dep pier in front of ex-British Consulate.

CHOFU, town 10min bus past Dan-no-Ura beach (20min from Shimonoseki stn) has several blocks of old samurai residences. Get off at Matsubara bus stop, take L fork off coastal Rte9, first L, then 2nd R past walls of low-ranking ex-samurai houses, to river (swarms of fireflies in summer), which take upstream to...

KOZAN-JI temple, W end of which is local **History Museum**, *Chofu Hakubutsu-kan* (¥200, 9:00-16:00, X-mon, day after hol). Temple founded 1327,

Butsu-den **Buddha Hall** (NT) replicates Kamakura's Engaku-ji Buddha Hall. Strong Chinese influence in architecture, double-layer roofs curling back up at corners. Late 16th century lord Ouchi Yoshinaga slit belly here after defeat by rival Mori clan, who ruled area until 1868. Temple also had much to do with elevating Mori clan to leaders of new Meiji gov't in 1868.

Young foreigner-slicing revolutionaries, *shishi*, (most from Choshu, this area's name; Satsuma, S Kyushu; Tosa, S Shikoku), were busy trying to create emperor-led government to get rid of Tokugawa and foreigners. One such home-boy was TAKASUGI Shinsaku, who burned British legation and instigated Yokohama killings. In December, 1864, he and band of 80 men grouped at Kozan-ji, pulled coup ousting pro-Tokugawa Mori daimyo and reinstating pro-imperial one. Six months prior, abortive loyalist coup attempt in Kyoto had killed most *shishi* radicals and remaining few realized foreigners were here to stay, but their help could be used to get rid of Tokugawa. Choshu, led by Takasugi and KIDO Koin, was first to find British sympathetic to their cause; as British diplomat said after defeating them, "We had come to like and respect them, while feeling of dislike began to arise in our minds for Tycoon." Joining forces with other 'loyalists' (all armed and trained by British) in 1866 repelled French-trained and -armed Tokugawa punitive expedition, signaling military end of Edo. Napoleon II offered troops to shogun, whose council was on verge of accepting when one asked, "if we invite French troops to get rid of rebels, who do we ask later to get rid of French?" To his credit, Tokugawa refused aid, accepting defeat. Temple has statue of Takasugi ahorse leading his forces—he died of sudden illness on April 14, 1867 in Shimonoseki, 29 years old—half-year before end of Tokugawa feudalism.

Several blocks N of Kozan-ji pass...
Ex-**Mori manse** on L, few more blocks and R E to **NOGI JINJA** dedicated to another local boy made good: NOGI Maresuke who as general of Third Army laid seige to Port Arthur in Russo-Japan War. Tho he succeeded, it was long and costly seige (Nogi lost own sons) and when Emperor Meiji died in 1912, General Nogi committed *seppuku* 'to follow his lord in death' and, many feel, to finally atone for his 'mistake' at Port Arthur. Within shrine compound are bronze statues of Nogi and wife (who also commited suicide in samurai fashion), their humble 2-room house, small **museum** (donate what you feel right) of his things.

Just E of Nogi Shrine is ancient...
IMINOMIYA JINJA dedicated to emperors Chuai, Ojin and empress Jingu. Few blocks E puts you at Torii-mae bus stop, from where 20min back to Shimonoseki stn, or 2hrs bus to Akiyoshi-do cave via...

Togyo-an Hermitage, built after Takasugi's death by his compatriots for his wife. Togyo was his pen name; wife became nun to spend rest of life here. Small **museum** of his personal items and writings, opened here on centennial of his death. 55min bus from Shimonoseki, some direct, others to Togyo-an Iriguchi stop from where short walk. **Drivers** Rte9 along Sanyo coast 10km to just beyond Ozuki and inland on Rte376. If heading only to caves, can take Chugoku Expwy to Miné exit.

CHOPSTICKS: In Shimonoseki and Chofu excellent: *uni* (sea-urchin) and *fuku*—local dialect for fugu (blowfish). Latter is most often eaten as sashimi which must be prepared by officially registered chefs who can handle raw filets without cutting liver and dousing meat with its poison. Best place for fugu is **Nakao**, few blocks N of ex-British Consul, where multi-course extravaganzas can run ¥13,000 per head, or their platter of sashimi for few thousand yen. Prices and stores vary down to ¥1,000 per sashimi platter, at cheaper but equally safe **Torafugu**, W of Shimonoseki stn. In Chofu, try **Rakuraku-an** S of river in old samurai district, which specializes in both uni and fugu, as well as other fresh fish; lunches at top-class inn **Kogushi-ya**, of uni, fugu, or their *Shokadobento* box lunch (¥2,500) of assorted sashimi. Fugu season is Oct-Mar, when most inns can arrange for fugu meal at extra cost, pre-arranged. Dried blowfish make interesting gifts, whether plain, or made into lantern; puffed skin almost translucent. These fugu-chochin are said to bring good fortune (fuku= homonym good fortune). Also huge paper blowfish kites and clay blowfish flutes.

WHERE TO STAY: Ryokan **Shunpan-ro**, where treaty signed, is best, classic old-timer still known for its superb service and food. But rooms run ¥-hi-S-Lw/2; ☎(0832)-23-7181. Almost as fine (but half-price) is **Okazaki** ☎22-4734 in town. Many more in all price ranges, including business hotels. W-style rooms at stn-side **Tokyu Inn** ☎33-0109, ¥5,900 for singles, bkfst ¥900; or cheaper **Grand Hotel** ☎31-5000, ¥4,500-5,500 singles (also doubles and J-rooms), bkfst ¥1,000. Budget (¥-B) Kokumin-shukusha **Kaikan-so** ☎23-0108), public lodge **Gempei-so** ☎32-5900, and **YH Hinoyama** ☎22-3753, all on wooded 268m high Hinoyama hill, 15min bus and 5min ropeway (9:00-18:00, to 22:00 summer) from Shimonoseki stn.

In CHOFU, best **Kogushi-ya** ☎45-0051, est 1871, from ¥-Lw/2 superb meals. Other inns (¥-Bw/2) are: **Kame-no-ko** ☎45- 0476, **Taguchi** ☎46-3472, **Haku-un-so** ☎45-1064, and ¥-T **Chofu Ryokan** ☎45-0404.

PERSONAL DATEBOOK: Lunar **Jan 1st**, *Mekari-shinji* offeratory rites for bountiful catch, Sumiyoshi Shrine, Shimonoseki. **Apr 23-25**, *Sentei-sai* Festival, Akama Jingu Shrine, Shimonoseki; spring rite is largest regional fest, dedicated in part to the fallen Heike. Main event Joro ('bed' Geisha) Parade winds thru town to shrine, reaching around noon. Women in colorful ukiyoe print get-ups pay respect to their ancestors of this ancient 'trade'—defeated Heike women were forced to turn to prostitution to survive. **Apr 29**, *Memorial Rites for fugu*, blowfish are released into Straits taking with them prayers to 'console' those which ended up on cutter's board, and for continued supplies of fugu. Similar ancient rites in which spirits of hunted animals are appeased for continued food supply are found thruout world; can still be seen in Pirika deer dances of Hokkaido's Ainu. **May 5** at foot of Honshu-Kyushu bridge, new '86, reenact Genji-Heike naval battle, fun. **3rd sun May**, *Ota-ue* rice planting Festival, Sumiyoshi Shrine, ritual dance planting of first rice paddy. **Aug 7-13**, *Suhotei-sai* Festival, Iminomiya Shrine, Chofu, dances every night thru town, men cart 10m tall banners while women carry kiriko baskets. **Oct 1**, *Memorial Rites for uni*, with sea-urchins in place of April's fugu.

HOT SPRINGS: Abound, some large and popular, others hidden away in mountains. We have been to several and list some you may come across wandering thru: Beyond Toko-an hermitage is **YUTANI ONSEN**, not off beaten path but still small (6 inns) and quiet. On JR Miné Line are small **YUNOTO** and **OFUKU ONSENS** (each with own stn). Local mountain roads parallel to, and sandwiched in by, Miné and San-in JR Lines have several:

About 15km N of Ozuki is hidden...
KAZAN ONSEN, and even more isolated one-inn **OKA-EDA ONSEN** between it and **YUTANI ONSEN**. Just beyond **KAZAN**, west to **ARARAGI ONSEN** with nearby **ICHINOHO ONSEN**.

Easier to reach along coast are...
KAWATANA ONSEN, (40min rail up Japan Sea coast from Shimonoseki and 5min bus inland), has dozen inns ¥-B–¥-T (start ¥10,000+w/2), excellent seafood meals (fresh meaty *hamachi* yellowtail or *tai* sea-bream from nearby hatchery). Stroll up 616m high Kurusan-yama hill; fine beaches on coast. **Apr 5-6** *Onsen Festival*, with mochi-pounding and other rites 5th nite. 2 stops up coast 20min walk inland from Yutama stn is 'hidden' **OKAWACHI ONSEN**, 3 ¥-B inns.

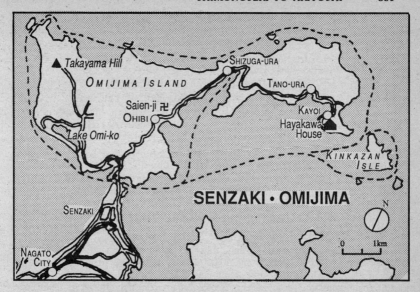

SENZAKI 仙崎湾 *& OMIJIMA ISLANDS* 近江島

HOUR RAIL beyond Kawatana onsen, train pulls into uninteresting Nagato city, change to Mine Line one stop (3min) to end; cab 1.5x-mtr, 5min bus, or walk 3km to SENZAKI, busy fishing port still retains old charm, ideal 1st nite on Japan Sea coast; worthwhile 90min **sightseeing boat** around Senzaki Isle to view wind-blown-craggy-rocks-and-gnarled-pines characteristic of coast; 4-8x-daily all year, ¥1,500.

TILT: Only 27km/16mi from Hagi, can see in half-day side trip (70min bus) from Hagi; long full day combines with Akiyoshi-cave trip, 1hr20min bus from Senzaki stn to cavern (all start from Omijima Bridge via pier to stn, some start from Yumoto Onsen).

Oblong ...
OMIJIMA, 3rd largest isle in Japan Sea, after Sado and Oki; population only 4,000. Boat circles clockwise, passing under Omijima Bridge to *Nami-no-Hashi-date*, 'Bridge over Waves', 1.3km long, narrow spit of pine-covered land separating fresh water Lake Omi-ko from sea. Round north point to 16km stretch of rugged cliffs of countless wave-carved caves, 'floating' rock formations—many with natural arches (one which boat passes thru) and tunnels. Rounding eastern tip between Omijima and rocky Kinkazan Isle, across calm Senzaki Bay (sloping shores here in sharp contrast) and back to pier. From same pier, 25min boats cross to Funaetsu camp grounds (space for 130 tents, running water, cooking pits, and rental tents and blankets; July-Aug only) at Shizuga-ura on narrow neck of Omijima. From pier closest to stn, 30min crossing to Kayoi at Omijima's eastern tip.

Wanderer dallying here can **bus** along leeward coast (roughly hourly); or you can **rent bicycles** at Nagato stn, ¥300/2hr, ¥800/day (8:30-18:00). Lake Omi-ko, its pine-covered land bridge, 10min walk W of bridge for pleasant strolls; 2hr r.t. trail to tallest 320m Takayama hill for fine view of island, sea and coast. 2km N of bridge (15min bus from Senzaki, 8min from pier) at Ohibi hamlet is lovely...

SAIEN-JI temple, with far corner pond in which rare blue-flowered lotus bloom mid-Jul-Aug. Just to its W is **Hosen-an** hermitage, Buddhist convent started by 8th head priest of Saien-ji. Its architecture more secular than Saien-ji, structured after mid-Edo period (1700's) rural folk house; still home to 20-odd nuns who live by strict commandments. 2km (5min bus) further at Shizuga-ura is 2km **Nature Trail** (*Shizen Kenkyu-ro*) across to N shore (island only about 200m wide here) and along portion of cliffs. 3.5km to next hamlet Tano-ura with another trail 1km across to N shore.

2km to last stop, 25min bus from bridge....
KAYOI, now rustic fishing village, was major whaling village during Edo era and thru early part of this century. When migratory school was spotted, fleet would set out to herd whales towards nets spread across bay and harvest their catch. Two species of small whales (*zatou-kujira, semi-kujira*) were main catch. South end of village is 200-year-old **Hayakawa-ke** family house, ancestral heads of whaling fleet. **KOGAN-JI** temple contains village's whaling past—3 volumes recording number, species, size and posthumous Buddhist names given to whales caught. Front of Shogetsu-an hall 2.2m tall granite **memorial** dedicated to unborn fetuses of captured female whales. Erected 1692 by Kogan-ji priest Sansei; around 70 fetuses honored here.

Memorial service for whales here **last week of Apr** (dates vary).

CHOPSTICKS: As can be expected, Senzaki abounds in superb seafood which inns serve in copious amounts. Gigantic **hatchery** at Shizuga-ura cove raises 600,000 tai (sea-bream), 100,000 hamachi and 50,000 buri (yellowtail) among others. Nearby floating restaurant *Shitsu-ura* serves multi-course *teishoku* (table d'hote) of these, from ¥1,400. Numerous small restaurants in Senzaki, many of which also serve fugu. Fugu are carefully skinned, which is saved to make fugu-chochin lanterns. See them being made, hung to dry at **Nagayasu Shoten**, just S of Senzaki pier; from ¥500 for one.

WHERE TO STAY: Senzaki has 10 ¥-T ryokan and 4 ¥-B minshuku; at OMI-JIMA hamlet near Lake Omi-ko is island's sole ryokan, summer-only Omijima Onsen **Seaside Hotel** ☎(08372)-6-1310, ¥-lo-T+w/2, and tapping hot spring water. Also 2 ¥-B ryokan out at KAYOI, and Youth Hostel just island-side of bridge. If full in summer (doubtful) NAGATO city has about 20 inns.

But rather than stay in that nondescript town, head into hills to...
NAGATO YUMOTO ONSEN, 10min rail inland on Mine Line from Nagato city and 10min walk; 7km, cab 4x-mtr from Senzaki, or 15min bus up Rte316. At fork in Otozure River, 2 dozen inns here, but wooded, quiet and pleasant. Discovered over 1,000 years ago, frequented by local fishermen and farmers, eventually to have 2 public baths, Onto and Reito, still operating early morning to late night, ¥130 dip—perfect for visitors to Senzaki who wish refreshing plunge in pure (no odors) hot water. Most inns sprang up past few decades, making Yumoto popular stop along San-In. Many provide fugu sashimi dinner in winter, extra cost (prearrange). Rates range from ¥-lo-T-lo-Lw/2, of which sprawling splashiest are: **Otani Sanso** ☎(08372)-5-3221; **Kokusai Kanko** ☎5-3111, far W end, up Daineiji stream; **Chinsui** ☎5-3211. Smaller, more traditional, slightly cheaper is **Harada** ☎5-3521. ¥-Tw/2 try: Otani's nearby annex **Bekkan Otani-ya** ☎5-3721; or we prefer classic 110-year-old **Shiroki-ya Ryokan** ☎5-3411, who to accommodate growing number of visitors, built splashy 7-storey annex Shiroki-ya **Grand Hotel** ☎5-3311, ¥-S+w/2 extravagant meals which include fugu in winter at no extra, other delicacies rest of year. **Budgeteers** find 2 minshuku near stn. Find rooms by wandering around, or book thru **Ryokan Co-operative** (Kumi-ai) 300m S of stn, in river fork.

PERSONAL DATEBOOK: 1st and 2nd sats of **Jun**, Genji-hotaru *Firefly Festival* at Lake Toyota, 5km further inland on Rte316; seen early summer around Yumoto, but best 500m up Yunoshiro-gawa stream flowing into middle of town from E. **Sept 10**, ancient Nanjo-odori and Gaku-odori *folk dances* performed in town; smaller versions also offered at Akazaki Jinja shrine 10min drive from onsen. Both dances used to be done solely at shrine on their special 390-year-old outdoor stage; stage still there but large performances stopped about 10 years ago.

Otozure River fork W along path front of Kokusai Kanko Hotel 10min walk to...
TAINEI-JI temple built 1410 by Ouchi lords, became major center of
learning in W Japan. Mid-1500's lord Ouchi Yoshitaka's chief retainer Sué
Harukata led successful coup, Yoshitaka family retreated to Tainei-ji, which
was burned down about them. All committed suicide, mass grave behind.

1km, 10min walk S of onsen (take 1st R (W), up Sou-no-se River) to...
Fukawa kilns of local *Hagi-yaki* pottery. Late 16th century Korean
founder of Hagi pottery, Ri-shaku-ko (Li Shau-gwang, Chin.), came here, left
behind disciples, of which Sakakura family has been here 15 generations.
Also 3 later families: Tahara, Shindo, Sakata. All will show you around.

TAWARAYAMA ONSEN, 10km, 25min bus (hourly) SW of Yumoto on
Tainei-ji road, is another backwoods hot spring centered around **public
baths**. Only here it is unmodernized and 4 large public baths are served by
40-odd small, ¥-B–¥S inns, few of which have their own onsen baths.
Local lore has it that bath was discovered by white monkey, Yakushi
(Medicinal) Buddha in one of his earthly disguises. If mountains and baths
are your choice, rustic Tawarayama is ideal, only 1hr45min from Shimonoseki
stn (10min less from bullet stn) on buses to Senzaki. 4 baths **Machi-no-yu, Kawa-
no-yu, Shin Kawa-no-yu**, and **Masa-yu**. First 3 regular bath halls, ¥170; latter
'family style' private baths, ¥1,000/hr for 2, ¥200 each extra person. All operate 6:00-
22:00, tickets sold at inns and each bath. Never full, or even close, but to be safe book
room thru Nagato stn **Kanko-annai** (or call ☎2-1444). Or walk around and choose your
own. Best is classic **Yamaguchi-ya** ¥-Tw/2–boar, fugu in winter; ☎(08372)-9-0050.
Some of cheapest (¥-P) also have room only for about ¥2,-3,000 with facilities to cook
own food.

15min walk N of onsen is...
Mara (tantric temptress of Shakyamuni, *not* Christian Maria) **Kannon**
phallic-shaped image. When Ouchi family was wiped out at Tainei-ji, son
was instructed to escape to avenge family honor. So he set out disguised as
woman, but was caught here and castrated. Local man heard tale, took pity
and carved statue.

PERSONAL DATEBOOK: Twice yearly, **Apr** at Kumano Jinja shrine and
Sept at Hachiman-gu shrine (dates vary, check Nagato city Kanko-annai) in Tawarayama,
country-style *all-girl kabuki* with village women performing mostly *juhachi-ban* 18
Classic plays as shrine offering.

For seaside hot springs, try...
KIWADO ONSEN, 7km W of Nagato city, with good beach, fine
seafood, and several budget to moderate inns. Coast west of Nagato mostly
fine beaches, especially along Yuya Bay (18km W of Kiwado), shielded
from Japan Sea by Mukatsuku Peninsula.

AKIYOSHI-DO CAVERNS, usually done as side trip from Hagi (90min bus),
is 80min (¥1,150) from Nagato city; from Yumoto, 25min rail or 35min bus to Miné stn
where 35min (¥500) bus. If seeing Akiyoshi-do after Hagi, bus 55min to Yamaguchi city
and rail 85min on to Tsuwano.

This is just one attraction, albeit main one, in 130sq/km rock-studded
Akiyoshi-Dai plateau **National Park**. 5min easy walk from bus center is
gaping entrance to cave; over 10km long, 1km open to public, 8:30-16:30,
¥1,000. Well-lit course takes you past spectacular sites, most famous of
which is '100 Plates'—dozens of shallow pits of water in multi-stepped
layers. 2/3rds-way thru cave, elevator takes us up 80m to ground level
whence short trek to hilltop Akiyoshi-dai **observatory**, or exit end

Kurotani tunnel. **Natural Science Museum** (*free*) at viewing platform has explanatory exhibits on formation of caverns, and animal and plant life in, Akiyoshi-dai area.

WHERE TO STAY: Dozen inns here ¥-lo-T-lo-Sw/2, 2 Kokumin-shukusha (¥-Bw/2), 3 minshuku and Youth Hostel. Concentrated around cave, book Akiyoshi Tourist Bureau, ☎(08376)-2-0115.

GETTING AROUND: Buses from/to Hagi or Nagato-Senzaki travel Akiyoshi-dai **scenic toll road** thru heart of plateau. Heading to Hagi from caves, few km up toll road is Chosha-ga-mori, small oasis of trees, all that remains of great prehistoric forest which once covered area. 3.4km Wakatakeyama **Nature Trail** parallels road from Akiyoshi-do to Chosha-ga-mori; or 15min **horsecart** ride (¥400 r.t.) part way; horses also rentable.

Other trails from Chosha-ga-mori fan out across plateau, one curves up to N end of toll road to...
Taisho-do Cavern, 25min bus (Hocho-, Sanden-, JR lines) from Akiyoshi-do. Several small caves dot Akiyoshi-dai, which one can explore on one's own, but Taisho-do is one of larger and charges ¥930 (8:30-16:30). 1km of it open to public; unusual vertical cave, each of 5 layers named various levels of heaven and hell. Visit both, 2nd cavern 1/2 price. Visit Safari Land first, get free ticket for 1 cavern.

5min bus or 2km walk NE of Taisho-do→1.5km long, low-ceilinged...
Kagekiyo-do Cave (8:30-16:30, ¥930), so named since Taira warrior Kagekiyo hid out here from Genji forces after Dan-no-Ura battle. First 800m are lit; **amateur spelunker course** covers last 700m; bring own flashlight, boots, etc.

Nearby...
Safari Land (9:00-17:00 ¥2,300) tour in own car or their bus (50min,¥300).

PERSONAL DATEBOOK: **3rd sun of Feb**, Akiyoshi-dai *Fire Festival*, controlled burning of plateau's vegetation, from 9:00am.

*...like a grub that takes refuge in solitude at the mercy of
the mysterious itch of nascent wings I vanished into Japan*
— Nikos Kazantzakis, *The Rock Garden*

HAGI 萩
SAMURAI TOWN

FIRST MUST-SEE stop along San-In, old cultural capital of west end of
Honshu, likened to being 'little Kyoto' as center of cultural revolution that
catapulted Japan into modern era century-plus ago. Abounds in beautifully
preserved architecture from old homes to temples, richly endowed in natural
beauty. Better yet for travelers, its people have reputation for being tight-
fisted, don't like to pay too much for good food and those good things of
life essential to travel—so we don't have to, either.

Hagi's main stn *Higashi* (E) *Hagi* is 30min JR express from Nagato,
2hrs from Shimonoseki; by **bus** 1hr30min from Yamaguchi, 2hrs from
Ogori, 1hr25min from Akiyoshi-do. Quick exit from Hagi by JR bus to
Ogori and Shinkansen is 4hrs to Osaka, 7+hrs to Tokyo. Long distance
buses stop Higashi Hagi stn and in-town Bus Center. Other stns are HAGI
(S of town), and TAMAE (W); in text 'stn' refers to HIGASHI HAGI, any
other is specified by name.

GETTING AROUND: Narrow streets of Hagi most enjoyable on foot
in full day or two easy days—with time at beach. **Save time** with low cost
rental **bikes** ¥150/hr, ¥1,000/day; over 20 rental places in town with total 2,000+ bikes,
most around stn. Some inns have own bikes, use free. **Hire cabs** ¥4,225/hr (9x-mtr)
for mid-size *chugata* (up to 5 psgr), 25% less for small *kogata* (4 psgr); set tours, or make
own. Arrange at stn taxi stand, or have inn call for pick-up. If set tour, recommend '2-A'
which covers main sites in 2hr30min; longer tours include *Hansha-to* 'reverbatorium' and
Kasayama Peninsula-scenic side-trip; **cab tours** leave only time for quick glimpse and
not worth extra ¥2,500. **Tour buses** can't make it down most streets so miss old
section of town.

But **best solo** with time to wander—for **walkers** regular *junkan* (rotary) buses leave
Bus Center every 25min, 8:20-17:05, stn 8:25–17:10; minimal fare (¥180) per ride. Stop
main sites counterclockwise from Bus Center: stn → Maebara house → SHOIN JINJA →
Tokoji–Kumaya Museum → Sufu house → Castle Park N entrance → Hagi Kiln →
Castle S entry → Kuchiha house → Tamae stn → Murata house → Joka-machi →
Meirin-kan → Bus Center. Runs end stn for easy rail departure; last bus to Tsuwano
leaves stn 17:08, Bus Center 17:16. Junkan buses run daily 4/1-11/15. Bike rentals, stn
and Bus Center **Kanko-annai** have good maps of town, which we use.

Archaeology indicates Hagi area first inhabited in Yayoi period, but remained small fishing village until 1604 when Yamaguchi's Mo(h)ri Terumoto set up castle here. Mori ruled from Hiroshima, domain covering
Honshu from Hiroshima to Shimonoseki. Sided with Toyotomi at
Sekigahara so winning Ieyasu halved their domain with Tokugawa allies
ruling over Hiroshima area, Mori domain reduced to western third—
Yamaguchi, Shimonoseki and Hagi—known as Choshu until 1868. For
two and half centuries, Choshu and Edo had uneasy truce; when
Commodore Perry's Black Ships shook foundations of Tokugawa
supremacy, Choshu was first to lock horns with their old enemy, soon
joined by Satsuma and Tosa. Supplying many of *shishi*, anti-Tokugawa
rebels and later founding fathers of Meiji Japan, Hagi-ites take great pride in
their role of pushing Japan into modern era. Most of what we see here is
related to these early leaders. Brief PERSONAL ORIENTATION on these men:

YOSHIDA Torajiro (a.k.a. Shoin 1830-1859) commoner adopted into low-ranking samurai family, was prime mover of modern Japan. 1854 he tried to stow away on Perry's ship, was caught, narrowly avoided execution thanks to intervention by his teacher SAKUMA Shozan. Imprisoned in Hagi, he was allowed to continue teaching, and expounded doctrine of revolution based on premise that Japan's rulers had forfeited right to rule thru inability to deal with foreign threats (especially directed at shogun whose title meant 'Barbarian-Subduing Generalissimo'). He believed Japan's only chance lay in hands of those samurai close to soil, untainted by wealth. He died following his belief, executed in Edo for attempted murder of Manabe, Tokugawa emissary to emperor. Followers from fervently pro-imperial · Mito retaliated by killing Ii Naosuke, only man capable of restoring Tokugawa political supremacy. Most of his Hagi students later became top leaders such as:

ITO Hirobumi (1841-1909) framer of Meiji Constitution. Another local low-ranking samurai son, defied Tokugawa seclusion edict and travelled to England in 1862 as deckhand on British ship. 1872-3 virtual head of historic Iwakura (portrait on ¥500 note) Mission to US and Europe to revise earlier unequal treaties and gain Western knowledge. Another trip in 1881 by imperial edict to study Western governments led to establishment of Diet (parliament) modeled on Bismarck's new Germany, whereas Imperial Court was, unfortunately, modeled on Tsarist. Ito's strong pro-Western stance and anti-militarism eventually got him killed by fanatics when he was Viceroy of newly conquered colony of Korea.

YAMAGATA Aritomo (1838-1922), father of modern Japanese army, one of Big Three Oligarchs along with Ito and Okuma of Satsuma. Seeing his forces decimated at Shimonoseki, he created conscript army based on Prussian system; defeated shogunal forces, and later, Saigo Takamori's Satsuma rebels. Tho he rose from army minister to chief of staff then field marshall, unlike militarists of 1920's-30's he was brilliant statesman, favoring diplomacy over use of arms. Home minister twice, premier twice (adopted Tsarist court protocol, cause of much 'sacred-emperor' problems) three-time president of Privy Council and prince of new aristocracy, he became chief elder statesman and advisor to throne, responsible for 'error' of adopting falderal of Tsarist court, and only one of Big Three to escape assassination. (Revision of this book done in great-granddaughter's house).

KIDO Takayoshi (a.k.a. Koin 1833-1877), chief representative of Choshu. Tho himself samurai, pushed for abolition of feudalism and privilege of samurai rank.

Hagi's isolation enabled these men to flourish, saved it from ravages of World War II. Much of its feudal atmosphere has been preserved.

MO(H)RI Terumoto chose Hagi as site of his new castle mainly for its natural defenses. Built town on island in Abu river fork, with Hashimoto River on W and Matsumoto River on E. He cut several canals across isle for additional defense and built castle on small hill at NW corner, separating it from main section of town by another canal-moat. Most sites in town are on this main isle, but we roughly follow junkan bus route and first take short side trip to...

EAST HAGI, E of stn, home of Yoshida Shoin and Ito Hirobumi. Perfect for PM arrivals for hour or two to fill out day, or as short visit in am before heading up coast—Hagi to Tsuwano buses stop Shoin Jinja bus stop. First L (S) from stn, L again after crossing narrow Tsukimi River 350m to bus stop, 15min walk (5min bus) from stn. (See below optional stn-Shoin route via Maebara House.)

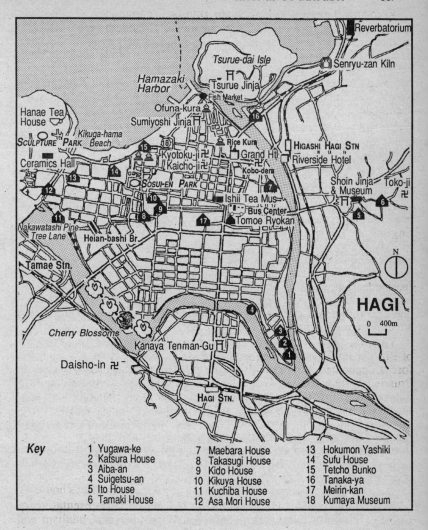

Reverbatorium

Tsurue-dai Isle

Senryu-zan Kiln

Hamazaki
Harbor

Tsurue Jinja

Fish Market

Ofuna-kura

Hanae Tea
House

Sumiyoshi Jinja

Kiguga-hama
Beach

SCULPTURE PARK

Rice Kura

HIGASHI HAGI STN

Ceramics Hall

Kyotoku-ji

Grand Hl

Riverside Hotel

Kaicho-ji

Kobo-dera

SOSUI-EN PARK

Shoin Jinja
& Museum

Toko-ji

Ishii Tea Mus

Nakawatashi Pine
Tree Lane

Bus Center

Tomoe Ryokan

Heian-bashi Br.

Tamae Stn.

N

HAGI

0   400m

Cherry Blossoms

Kanaya Tenman-Gu

Daisho-in

HAGI STN.

Key

1	Yugawa-ke	7	Maebara House	13	Hokumon Yashiki
2	Katsura House	8	Takasugi House	14	Sufu House
3	Aiba-an	9	Kido House	15	Tetcho Bunko
4	Suigetsu-an	10	Kikuya House	16	Tanaka-ya
5	Ito House	11	Kuchiba House	17	Meirin-kan
6	Tamaki House	12	Asa Mori House	18	Kumaya Museum

SHOIN JINJA shrine built 1891 to honor him, new main sanctuary 1955.
At entrance is Shoin **History Museum** (9:00-17:00, ¥390) with life-size wax
figures outlining major points in his life. Large folk house in compound
was home of SUGI Yurinosuke, Yoshida's real father, and where, in small
3.5-mat room at E end, Yoshida spent 2¹/₂ years under house arrest after
abortive attempt to stow away on Perry Black Ship—violating Edo ban on
foreign travel, usual punishment death. Yoshida spent 2¹/₂ years before
house arrest in Hagi jail. His release from prison was made possible by
guarantee of uncle TAMAKI Bunnoshin, well-placed official in Hagi
government who lived nearby. Bunnoshin started school for commoners
1842, where Yoshida studied and later taught. During house arrest was
allowed to continue teaching, which he did out of Sugi's coal shed—
converted into school, *Shoka-son-juku*, mainly for those of insufficient
status or education to enter clan school Meirin-kan. Many early Meiji reformists studied here, notably KIDO Koin, ITO Hirobumi, TAKASUGI Shinsaku

and YAMAGATA Aritomo. House & school partly open, can't enter all rooms. Nearby Shoin **Memorial Museum**, *Iboku Tenji-kan* (8:30-17:00, ¥100) has his writings and personal belongings. Lovely old tea ceremony house in compound belonged to Hagi's ruling Mori family.

Short walk S of shrine complex is house where...
ITO Hirobumi spent 13 years of his youth, from age 14 when his samurai father was sent here. He spent first 3 years as disciple at Ensei-ji temple in town, then studied under Yoshida. Quaint thatched-roof house with walled compound —which you can enter but not rooms—is excellent example of life of low-ranking samurai who was usually no better off than farmer next door. Ceramic bust of Hirobumi in front of house.

Next door is **Yamane store**, specializing in handmade bamboo goods.

10min walk E, on L as road climbs, is...
Ex-home of Yoshida's uncle Tamaki Bunnoshin, another superb example of **period house.** Bunnoshin was also related to General Nogi of Port Arthur (1904-5) fame, who in his youth lived with and studied under Bunnoshin before advancing to clan school.

Taking branch road at 'T' in front of Tamaki house we curve around to...
TOKO-JI temple, one of two family temple-mausoleums of Mori clan. Built 1691 by 3rd Mori, Yoshinari, final resting place for 5th, 7th, 9th, 11th Mori lords and their families—total of 44 graves (1st, 2nd and even generations thru 12th buried at Daisho-in). Surrounded by ancient pine, maple and oak, path leading to graves lined with rows of 500 stone lanterns erected by retainers. At its height, Toko-ji had 40 halls and 80 full-time priests; all that remain now are front and main gates, main hall, bell tower, Daiho Josho-in library and few sub-halls. Approach is awesome view, with *somon* front gate, *sanmon* main gate, Daiyu-hoden hall (all ICA) in line. Somon was designed after Chinese gate, unusual shape and red bengara color giving foreign air. Just inside, booth for ¥100 admission (8:30-17:30). Sanmon built 121 years later, 1812 by Mori Narihiro. Main hall given complete facelift 1966; path to R leads past library to Mori cemetery. First cluster of gravestones dedicated to Choshu men of failed coup in Kyoto, 1864. Chief Mori retainers Masuda, Kunishi, Fukuhara and followers were forced to commit seppuku by Edo, posthumously honored here 1897. Mori lords' graves on other side of pond.

On our rear approach to Toko-ji, halfway, lane cuts S to small rise, site of Yoshida Shoin's birthplace and grave; graves of his real and adoptive fathers, uncle and other reformists like Takasugi Shinsaku. Marked by statue of Shoin and disciple Kaneko looking out at Perry's Black Ships anchored off Shimoda.

This rear approach puts us at TOKO-JI Main hall; leaving temple by front (also reached direct from Tamaki house) we take bike/pedestrian-only road along Tsukimi River to Shoin Jinja bus stop, from where 10min junkan bus (30min walk) to **Kumaya Museum.** If on foot, our course takes us past **Maebara Issei House.** Walkers from stn planning to bus to museum can do this portion in reverse; 10min walk from stn down first alley on L, just before big road after crossing bridge to house.

From Shoin bus stop W across Matsumoto River and 1st alley R to Ogawa Family house's *nagaya-mon*, **gate** flanked by servants' living quarters. Several similar structures around town, best at Mori house near castle. This area, known as Hijiwara, was neighborhood of middle-ranking samurai and remnants of some houses and (mostly) surrounding walls remain.

*Continuing 200m N, L at fork and next R 150m to **house** of...*
MAEBARA Issei (1834-1876), student of Yoshida Shoin and top councillor of early Meiji government. He, along with Satsuma's Saigo Takamori disagreed with Tokyo's diplomatic dealings with Korea, favoring armed inter-

vention. Both left government, and in October 1876 Saigo found self leading rebellion against Tokyo. In November, Maebara Issei led 500 men in similar revolt which took over Meirin-kan school and used it as base to attack Prefectural Office. Tokyo sent contingent of marines to retake Hagi—well-disciplined gun-toting, but inadequately-drilled soldiers first proved to be no match for sword-wielding ex-samurai, tho they put up fight which destroyed large sections of Hagi. (French Emperor Louis Napoleon III offered French marines to put down revolt; Council of Elders met to vote; on verge of accepting heard one junior ask, "And when French get rid of rebels, who gets rid of French?"—offer was declined.) After revolt fizzled (*see* also Kagoshima) Maebara Issei was executed. House is excellent example of middle-ranking **samurai home**.

Backtracking from Maebara house to first alley, up 250m to main street to stn.

Across intersection is...
KOBO-DERA temple, with grave of Maebara Issei. Note here 'Christian' stone lanterns with crosses etched on. Other remnants of Hagi's Hidden Christians scattered around town; most similar lanterns on lone graves: to point out some if interested, they are blue numbers on brown fold-out map from Kanko-annai. W along main road, towards Kumaya Museum; 500m on, next big intersection, to fringes of Tera-machi, temple district.

200m S at intersect is...
JONEN-JI temple with photogenic 450-year-old **gate**, given to Mori Terumoto by Toyotomi Hideyoshi. N of intersect is giant kura **storehouse**, one of several emergency granaries set up around Hagi; 1709. W of intersect 2 stone markers on L, site of feudal Hagi's prisons: one, *Iwakura-goku*, was for samurai (like Yoshida) and rich merchants, other *Noyama-goku*, for common rabble.

Third street W of intersect, R (N), takes us thru...
Hamazaki-cho **fishermen district** of quaint, slightly shabby, ancient houses, reminds of days when Hagi was one of main Japan Sea coast fishing centers. 600m up this street, on R behind small playground is **giant storehouse** with triangular roof, thick stone walls, and massive door covering entire side—*ofuna-kura,* boat storage of Mori clan. Were 4 such kura, each 9m tall and 218sq/m floor space, all along river—subsequent silt-up separated it from river by 100m. Built early 1600's, when Mori Terumoto decided to keep part of his fleet here, tho main naval base was Hofu on Inland Sea.

If you have time, recommend strolling around this area, especially along Matsumoto River banks in early spring with dozens of tiny fishing boats dipping huge square nets in and out of river. They are fishing for *shiro-uo,* tiny white fish which you eat still alive in bowl of sauce, dish appropriately called *odori*, or dance (as we saw down in Fukuoka). Ryokan **Tanaka-ya** across river known for its various *shiro-uo* dishes. At N tip is **Hagi Fish Market**, surrounded by several grand old houses of fishing fleet leaders. Just beyond is **Hamazaki Harbor** where one can **ferry** out to nearby islands.

Save for later, instead, keep with mood and be poled across river mouth in skiff to...
TSURUE-DAI ISLE, with its narrow streets and old houses. Once mainland, 13th lord Mori Takachika dug Ubakura Canal connecting Hamazaki to larger Obata harbor.

200m W of Ofuna-kura is...
SUMIYŌSHI JINJA shrine, site of gala summer fest (*see* DATEBOOK, p814). From shrine, S 400m towards main street near Kumaya Museum.

300m E of museum is...
KYOTOKU-JI temple; lovely phoenixes, peacocks carved into doors, and 2.4m (7ft 10in) tall wood Bodhidharma statue.

Across street on S to...
KAICHO-JI temple which main hall is old Confucian temple of clan school Meirin-kan, brought here after 1874 fire which destroyed first main hall. We are now in heart of Tera-machi, with dozen-odd temples within 300m of these two.

Kumaya Museum is set up in Kumaya family storehouses, complex built 1764 by Kumaya Gorozaemon first official financier of Mori clan. Inside are finest examples of Hagi-yaki pottery, tea ceremony utensils, old books and maps, and Japan's first piano, given to Kumaya family by Englishman Siebold of Nagasaki, among 3,000 items. Pity you cannot enter main house (maybe soon?). (8:30-17:30, ¥500)

200m W of museum, up first lane on R to...
Tetcho Bunko Library, museum housing personal collection of local historian KADOYA Tetcho (alias YOSHITANI Koichi). Specialty was Meiji Restoration, among goods are rare photos of early leaders. ¥300, 8:00-17:00.

This also puts us in middle of...
Kiku-ga-hama, mile stretch of white sandy beach backed by scraggly pine trees. At its E end is 50m section of fortifications put up 1863 in anticipation of foreign invasion. 3m high and 12m wide, it was covered with pine trees for additional defense, built by Hagi's women. Beach has rest houses, shops, camp ground, rental boats in summer. At nite, **lights of squid boats** float on horizon.

Continuing W along main street, cross stream (outer castle moat) into...
Hori-uchi high-ranking **samurai quarters**, bounded on S by another stream moat, and on W by canal-moat. It is pleasant district to wander thru, narrow lanes flanked by ancient walls—behind some of which are stately mansions, behind others summer *mikan* (tangerine) groves. Before 1868, 98 wealthy families lived here, all ruling Mori family or chief advisors and samurai with stipend of over 1,000 koku. Entire area has been declared 'Important Traditional Architectural Area', special effort by city and citizens to preserve old look. Several modern homes were built, but new are now built in traditional style; during our 1984 visit, many new put up old style walls to blend with surroundings. En route castle, we pass thru N portion of area (along first street S of main) saving S for later.

Some sites here are...
Masuda Mansion (10min walk 4min bike from museum) Hagi residence of Lord Masuda family. Still remaining on its outer wall is watchtower, one of several used to guard entrances. 100m W to large *nagaya-mon*-'tenement' **gate** of **Hanazawa manse**; further on R to even larger nagaya-mon of **Sufu**, 21m long and 4m wide (69ft x 13ft).

Cross W end canal, 2min bus from museum, we enter...
Shizuki Park, grounds of Hagi (Shizuki) Castle, built 1604 by MO(H)RI Teramoto. Occupied by 13 generations until 1863 when center of government moved to Hofu on Inland Sea. Dismantled 1874 by new Meiji government then at height of anti-feudal zeal. Only stone fortifications and inner moat remain. Wander around outer section, **Sculpture Park** at W fringe built around massive stone monuments carved by 24 artists from 8 nations. Dose of modern, somehow at harmony with this ancient town. Or cross moat to inner section with several lovely buildings:

Hananoe tea house, moved here 1889 from Hananoe-*goten* palace, residence of 13th Mori lord Takachika. He held secret meetings here with *shishi* in guise of tea ceremony to elude Edo spies. (Matcha green tea and cakes ¥300). Nearby **Nashiba tea house**, also brought from elsewhere. SHIZUKI-YAMA JINJA shrine built 1879 to enshrine souls of 13 Mori daimyo, their crest emblazoned on curtains around shrine. Base of steps to shrine is library-house of Fukuhara family, chief councillors to Mori lords since mid-16th century. Now shrine office, shown inside are assorted samurai items and shrine treasures.

Continue 20min walk up to top of 143m Shizuki-yama hill, famed for fine view...
Stone remains of Tsume-maru watchtower and part of its protective wall also served as last defense for lord and family.

¥200 to enter inner castle (8:00-18:30), hold on to ticket as it also admits you to...
Hagi Mansion of Asa region Mori clan. Mansion covered area 69m N-S by 150m E-W. Dismantled early Meiji, only nagaya-mon **gate** remains. This dwarfs Sufu one; it is 51m long, and many of its rooms have displays.

Across from Asamori house is Hagi ..
History Hall, *Shiryo-kan*, (9:00-17:00 daily, ¥300) showing Mori clan valuables, works of Yoshida Shoin and his students, folkcrafts, and Hagi-yaki pottery.

Hagi-yaki Kilns: *Hagi-jo Kamamoto* and *Shogetsu-kama* in park, *Shiroyama Kamamoto* W of Shiryo-kan, across from Hagi-yaki **Ceramics Hall** *Jyozan-kama*. 1st fl shop (various artists' wares), 2nd fl exhibit (free) of masters' works (some on sale). Make your own pottery at 1st fl workshop. Just S is *Toryu-an kamamoto* kiln. Also store on 1st fl of Hananoe restaurant near Asamori house; 2nd fl is so-so diner.

Hop junkan bus at **Asamori house** (¥200), which takes you via **Kuchiba house**, Tamae stn (area is fishing village) and **Murata house**, to next main stop Joka-machi. Our foot course takes us again thru Horiuchi samurai district. E from **Asamori house** back across moat 250m to rear gate of **Mori house**, on L. Just before it on R is **Hokumon-yashiki** ryokan, lovely inn which uses old **castle gate** for entrance. Next intersection, R, along wall surrounding 2nd ex-**Masuda kyu-taku** manse to next corner and 2-storey wood W-building built 1887 as teachers' office **Hagi High School**. Pressed for time or feet tired, keep going E at either intersections direct to **Joka-machi** area for lunch, coffee or green tea. Can't enter most above, some following. On our meandering course, R (W), still following 130m long wall, past Fukuhara gate, next L two streets to...

Kuchiba-ke mansion main house and massive **gate**—largest in Hagi. Gate belonged at Mori mansion in Edo, but given to their trusty advisor and moved here. It sits in middle of lovely part of town to meander thru. Just W of it, along river to **Hananoe-goten** mansion, home of 13th lord Takachika. Can't enter (now), just look. E from Kuchiba manse along narrow wall-lined zig-zag alley (made so for defense), first L, then R to **Nashiba library**; next intersection R takes you across Heian-bashi **bridge** for 7km side trip thru S Hagi, which we save below for those with time and on bike.

A quick L at intersection and first L (N) 350m to...
Sosui-en Park, with statue of Tanaka Giichi, soldier-statesman and one-time prime minister. Stone marks where he was born, 200m SE. From park, few min walk E puts us in best-preserved section of town; three parallel alleys *Kikuya-yokocho*, *Iseya-yokocho* and *Edoya-yokocho*, NE of Joka-machi bus stop.

Kikuya-yokocho gets its name from top merchant Kikuya's **house** at N end. Kikuya were official brokers of Mori clan. Inside house and storehouses are exhibits of pottery, utensils, scrolls, etc (9:00-17:00, ¥370). Some places to grab bite here: **Waraji** for noodles, **Ocha-sho** for matcha green tea and cakes, fish at **Nakamura** on Edoya alley, coffee-shop **Iraka**. Middle of Kikuya-yokocho is house where Takasugi Shinsaku (who led Shimonoseki revolt) was born and spent much of his life, studying at Meirin-kan clan school and with Yoshida. Just S was home of SHIGA Takeo one of Japan Communist Party's founding fathers. Cut thru backyard to middle ISEYA-YOKOCHO *which we head up, then start our way down third...*

Edoya-yokocho: N end is **home** of KIDO Koin. Next to it is **home** of AOKI Shusuke, mid-19th century scholar of Western learning and medicine.

L at S end, cross bridge and R, then L to site of...
Meirin-kan school set up by Mori clan in 1719. In its place is lovely 100-year-old Western style building of Meirin elementary school. To R is Yubi-kan **martial arts hall** of old Meirin-kan, and behind it is large 1.5m deep stone-lined **pool** in which samurai kids were taught to swim.

This marks end of short tour around Hagi; southern portion is fine but much of same (see below). *There is one other stop en route to stn, near Bus Center...*
Tea-bowl Museum, *Ishii Chawan Bijutsukan,* (¥350, 9:00-17:00) spectacular collection of teabowls by various top potters thruout centuries just NW of bus center at E end of Tamachi Shopping Street stretching almost to Joka-machi.

SOUTH TILT: Should be done on **bike**, or have **cab** swing by Aiba River area after **Meirin-kan**. On our foot/bike course, after **Kuchiba House** area, cross **Heian-bashi Bridge** into Hiyako & Emukae districts for middle- and low-ranking samurai. First R follows river around bend thru lovely Naka-watashi **pine tree lane** along river. We soon enter another wall-lined lane zig-zagging thru old neighborhood. Just beyond are dozens of **cherry trees** along river, worth detour early April. Opposite bank lined with city's namesake, *hagi* (bush-clover), which blossom tiny purple, white flowers Sep-Oct.

Then 1km E to...
AIBA-GAWA, area known for its quiet atmosphere and quaint neighborhood of old houses along stone-banked river full of colored carp. When castle was built, river (rather, stream) served to feed moat and rice-paddy irrigation. Town grew and houses were built around mid-17th century. Near tip is particularly fine thatched-roof YUGAWA-KE family **samurai house**. Nearby is **home** of KATSURA Taro, turn-of-century Prime Minister who oversaw signing of first Anglo-Japanese Alliance (1902), declaration of war on Russia (1904). Next to Katsura house is beautiful tea-shop **Aiba-an** serving green tea, plum tea, and *natsu-mikan* juice made from tangy grapefruit-like tangerines. At base of tip along river is fine restaurant **Suigetsu-an** serving various fish dishes in old house; should reserve seats for lunch, ☎(08382)-2-0654.

E of Suigetsu-an, cross S on Hashimoto bridge, past ancient red-laquered...
KANAYA TENMAN-GU shrine (grand autumn festival, see DATEBOOK, p814), 700m to Hagi stn. Front of shrine used to be armed barrier gate to Hagi where all incomers were searched.

600m W of stn to...
DAISHO-IN temple, first of Mori clan ancestral temple/mausoleums. Built 1652-55 by 2nd lord Tsunahiro, it has graves of 1st and all even numbered lords and families. Dozen ancient wisteria scattered around quiet complex (few people come out here). Like Toko-ji, **602 stone lanterns** line front, lit for **Aug 13th** festival. At W gate is **Daisho-in kiln**. Started 1970, potter Ishimaru uses traditional *nobori-gama* climbing kiln to fire his *Hagi-yaki*.

KASAYAMA PENINSULA, largest of four jutting into Japan Sea, few km N of Hagi. 20min bus from stn or Bus Center on easy to **bike** (30min pedal from stn) coastal Rte191; ideal lazy half-day outing. En route is *Hagi Hansha-ro* **'reverbatorium'** where, from 1858, Mori lords forged cannons and guns for anticipated invasion, then for revolution. Pair of 11.5m tall brick chimneys remain; one of two such remaining structures, other at Nirayama in Izu, Shizuoka Pref. You get quick glimpse of this out train window if leaving Hagi by rail. Townside of reverbatorium is **Senryuzan kiln**, shop.

JO-GA-HAMA village straddles 200m-wide land-bridge to Kasayama. Several inns take advantage of pleasant fishing village atmosphere, flanked either side by ideal harbors. One is called *Yome-naki-ko*, Crying-bride-harbor, since women had to trek into hills for closest fresh water, problem solved 1868 when Yoshida Shoin's brother commissioned local potters to make 2,480 ceramic pipes with which he created aqueduct, used until modern system put in 1945.

W of village **Myojin-ike** salt-water lake, natural aquarium in which live ocean fish, put there as offerings by locals to **ITSUKUSHIMA JINJA** shrine (affiliated to Miyajima) on W shore, built 1652 by fishermen for kami of fish. Behind shrine is *Kaza-ana* **'Wind Hole'** in rocks, which blasts out ice-cold air continuously. **Tea House** Kaza-ana serves seafood snacks like *sazae no tsuboyaki* (top shell cooked in own shell), *yaki-ika* (broiled squid) and their famed *wakame-musubi* (rice-balls with kelp) with soup, all for few hundred yen. Scenic driveway up 112m high **Kasayama**, Japan's smallest volcano (extinct) with 30m across by 30m deep crater. Splendid view of coastline and Rokuto Islands. Climb it on **Kasayama nature trail**, continue to Toraga-misaki Point and back along N shore.

ROKUTO, 'Six Isles' scattered 5-10km offshore of Hagi with regular boat service (2x-daily) to largest isles Oshima and Aishima for adventurer. Can also **boat** to tiny Mishima Island, 45km offshore. Population about 2,000, Mishima was prison isle until 1868. Half-dozen ¥-T inns (¥8,000+w/2) in main village Honmura, campsite at smaller Utsu village, 2km walk N or 15min boat.

SHOPPING: For *Hagi-yaki* pottery, long valued by tea masters who ranked '1st Raku, 2nd Hagi, 3rd Karatsu' for best bowls. Kilns here since Heian times, but not until Mori Terumoto moved here in late 16th century did it become famous. Terumoto took part in Hideyoshi's Korean campaign and brought back two master potters, brothers Lee. They were given kiln at Matsumoto Naka-no-kura, E of Shoin shrine. Later, elder brother moved to Nagato Fukagawa thus creating two styles *Hagi Matsumoto-yaki* and *Nagato Fukagawa-yaki*. Both became 'official' kilns of Choshu lords, working exclusively to their demands.

Dozens of kilns, competitively priced stores scattered over Hagi; some sell just one artist's works, others mix. Name-pieces, best at **Hagi-yaki Kaikan** near castle with works by top masters. Oldest are Saka and Miwa families who were among first students of Lees and still out at Naka-no-kura. Miwa is more acclaimed, with two Living National Treasures in recent past.

Delicacy of Hagi are bitter-sweet dried and sugared skins of *natsu-mikan* summer tangerines, which also makes excellent marmalade. Sold in stores thruout town.

WHERE TO STAY: Hagi has more than enough lodgings to suit any budget. Best rated are large modern structures but with J-style rooms and excellent service. Best one is lovely 200-year-old **Tomoe Ryokan** ☎2-0150, ¥-T-Lw/2, 5min E of JR Higashi Hagi, used by emperor Meiji, re-opened July 1989 retaining much splendor in much of Estate. Convenient is new **Royal Hotel** ☎(08382)-5-9595, from ¥-Tw/2, in Rainbow Building adjacent Higashi Hagi stn with 1st and 2nd floor shops, TOURIST INFO and RYOKAN INFO on 1st. **Riverside Ogawa** ☎2-1195, is cheaper, ¥-lo-Tw/2. ¥-B with mostly small W-style rooms are **Orange** ☎5-5880; **Travel Inn** ☎5-2640; both across bridge from stn. **Grand Hotel** ☎5-1211, mostly W-style rooms, sgl from ¥10,000, or ¥12,-20,000w/2, next intersection W, 5min walk from stn or Bus Center; choice of

Western or Japanese dinner. Superb little inn, across bridge from stn is **Hifumi** ☎2-0123, ¥-T–Sw/2; *shiro-uo* in March, *fugu* in winter for ¥ extra. N of stn on same side of river is very hospitable riverside **Tanaka-ya** ☎2-7538, where Garet stayed. ¥-Tw/2 (shiro-uo in March), or room only; and nearby **Fujita**.

NEAR BUS CENTER is New **Takadai** ☎2-0065, ¥-Tw/2, in business for 100 years. In Horiuchi district is fine **Hokumon Yashiki** ☎2-6164, ¥-S-hi-Lw/2, *fugu* in winter, *shiro-uo* in March for extra. *Along beach*: **Kikuga-hama Kanko** ☎2-1022, ¥-Tw/2, **Hama-so** ☎2-0229, castle-like **Senshun-raku** ☎2-0326, all ¥-T–Sw/2. Another is lovely old **Tomita-ya Ryokan** ☎2-0025, ¥-Tw/2, *near Aiba River* area, on N side of Hashimoto Bridge. Near it is **Shige-eda** ☎2-0531, slightly cheaper, or ¥-B room only.

Near **JO-GA-HAMA** is resort-style **Rakutenchi** ☎5-0121, ¥-T–lo-Lw/2, with rock baths looking out over bay and pool. On **KASAYAMA** opp Hagi, ¥-T–Sw/2: **Hagi Kanko** ☎5-0211; **Kasayama Kanko** ☎5-0311.

HAMAZAKI AREA is ¥-B ryokan **Fuku-no-Ie** ☎2-0351. 400m NW of Bus Center *in center of town* are: **Yoshiyama** ☎2-0960, **Oda** ☎2-0511, and **Kotobuki-so**.

MINSHUKU 40+ ¥-B all over Hagi *near stn*: **Higashi Hagi, Arase, Suzume-no-Oyado**; *across bridge*: **Hagi-no-Ie, Senju-an**; in old *Horiuchi district*: **Itoh**, W of Tanaka Giichi statue, **Hagi-no-Sato** 3 streets N of Kikuya alley; *along beachfront road*: **Jotai-jo, Tachibana, Tsurukame, Shiroyama**; dozens around Bus Center. Several out at Jo-ga-hama, notably **Yome-naki-so** ☎5-0840.

KOKUMIN-SHUKUSHA: Jo-en, Castle Park ☎2-3939, has 21 J-rooms, 8 W-rooms, all w/toilet; ¥-Bw/2, more for better meals. **Hagi-ura-so** ☎2-2511, 400m S of stn; all J-rooms, same rates. **Hagi YH** ☎2-0733, also in Castle Park; 100 bunks in segregated rooms; 3,250w/2 Two town temples take lodgers: **SHINKAKU-JI** ☎2-5815, 300m N of Shoin Shrine bus stop; women only, ¥-P-w/bkfst. **CHOJU-JI** ☎2-2580, in Tera-machi district 300m SW of Kumaya Museum; anyone, ¥-Bw/2. **Campers**: Kiku-ga-hama beach campsite summer, or find secluded spot at Kasayama. All rooms can be booked at **Ryokan-annai** at stn or bus center.

PERSONAL DATEBOOK: Early **Mar, 2nd Sun** *Shiro-uo Fest* Hamazaki & along Matsumoto River. **May 25**, Shoin Jinja Spring Festival. **June, 1st Sun**, Oshikura-go *boat races* offered Itsukushima Shrine, Tamae. **Jul–mid-Aug**, official *swim* season Kiku-ga-hama **Jul 30-Aug 3**, Sumiyoshi Jinja Grand Festival-*Hagi Summer Festival* colorful parade 3rd nite with boat-shaped floats carted thru town, food and entertainment stalls around town all days, nites. **Aug 13** *Lighting of stone lanterns*, Daisho-in (19:30-21:00), **15th** Toko-ji (19:30-22:00), marks start of bon festival. **Mid-Aug** Kita-ura bon-odori contest. **Oct 27**, Shoin Jinja *Autumn Festival*. **2nd wknd Nov**, *Kanaya Tenman-gu Shrine Fest*, procession of feudal era costumed entourage.

WHERE NEXT: Can zip to next major stop IZUMO-MATSUE on JR rail, 3hr ltd express, 15min longer express, or 5hr50min local. Recommend checking schedule first thing in town, as not too many daily. But if you can spare half-day, recommend leaving Hagi morning and getting to Izumo area mid/late afternoon which leaves time for short detour 1hr40min bus (2hr10min rail via Masuda) from Hagi.

TSUWANO 津和野

PLEASANT TOWN nestled in Tsuwano River valley, with stn N end of town. Perhaps best known for thousands of colorful carp which swim in river and canals weaving thru town. Population of around 8,000 people, carp outnumber 50 to 1. Carp put in canals by lord Sakazaki Dewa-no-kami turn of 17th century to keep waterways clean. Major town since 1295 when Yoshimi clan built fortress, ruled 300 years till replaced by Dewa-no-kami. He aided Ieyasu at Seki-ga-hara and thus gained this fief, but was betrayed by Ieyasu and executed to make way for Kamei clan who ruled till 1868. Like Hagi, Tsuwano retains much of its old atmosphere—great white walls surrounding ex-samurai mansions bounded by carp-filled canals—yet more compact and even easier to get around.

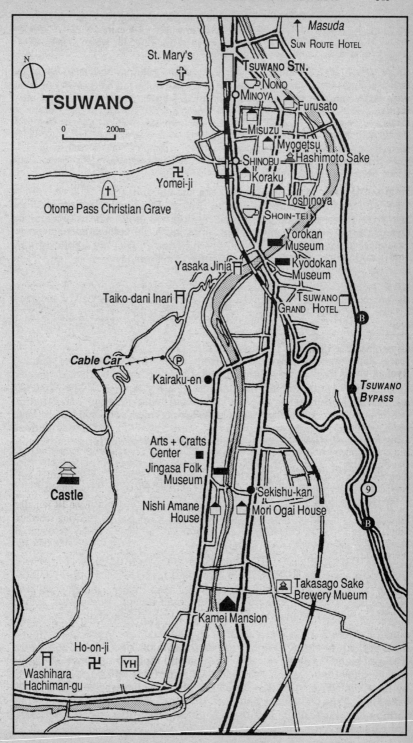

TSUWANO

N

0   200m

St. Mary's

↑ *Masuda*
SUN ROUTE HOTEL

TSUWANO STN.
NONO
MINOYA
Furusato
Misuzu
Myogetsu
SHINOBU
Hashimoto Sake
Koraku
Yoshinoya
SHOIN-TEI

Yomei-ji

Otome Pass Christian Grave

Yorokan Museum

Yasaka Jinja
Kyodokan Museum

Taiko-dani Inari

TSUWANO GRAND HOTEL

B

Cable Car
P

Kairaku-en

TSUWANO BYPASS

Arts + Crafts Center
Jingasa Folk Museum

9

Castle

Sekishu-kan

Nishi Amane House
Mori Ogai House

B

Takasago Sake Brewery Mueum

Kamei Mansion

Ho-on-ji
YH

Washihara Hachiman-gu

GETTING AROUND: Count on full 8hr day to see all on foot, cut to 5hrs by skipping castle site and Washibara Hachiman-gu shrine—easy hike over hills for those with extra time. 3-4hrs on rental **bicycles**, ¥400/2hrs, ¥800/day. **Taxi tours** ¥4,220/hr, or about 9x-mtr, for small *kogata* (4 psgrs).

WHERE TO STAY: Quiet place to spend nite, below average rates, but not too many inns and crowded spring and summer peaks. All within few minutes walk from stn: Best **Meigetsu** ☎(08567)-2-0685, in old mansion, ¥-Sw/2. Almost as nice, same rates: **Yoshinoya** ☎2-0531; **Misuzu** ☎2-0747; **Koraku** ☎2-0501. Dozen other inns in ¥-B-lo-Tw/2 range. Then there is castle-like **Kanko Hotel Shin-kan** new wing ☎2-0333, ¥-Sw/2. W-style at **Hotel Sunroute** ☎2-3232, sgl from ¥-Tw/2. Minshuku usual ¥-B, 2 dozen scattered around heart of town. **Tsuwano** Youth Hostel ☎2-0373, in **Ho-on-ji** temple S of town. Book room thru stn Kanko-annai, or Minshuku Center 150m S.

Main section of town is between stn and curve in river. 4 streets run N to S, all meeting 400m S at Tsuwano Bridge. Fun to wander, lots of shops and restaurants. 3rd from stn Honmachi-dori was (still is) heart of merchant district; midway along rows of old shops are 3 old-style **sake breweries**, recommend saving for last if tasting. 4th street from stn lined both sides by **carp-filled canals**, stately walls, marked boundary of samurai residences.

S corner stn front is...
Museum of Local Crafts, *Sangyo Shiryokan* (8:30-17:00, ¥150), show how sake, tea, soy sauce, paper, etc. were made in old days. Rest area has videos of Tsuwano festivals, main sites.

N of Tsuwano bridge on Honmachi-dori is...
Yoro Kan, ex-**clan school** where from 1786–1868, children of samurai and 1868–1916 all children, were taught literature, math, medicine, *rangaku* (Dutch or 'Foreign' studies) martial arts, military strategy. Now **Museum of Local Folk History** (8:30-17:30, ¥200) with sections on samurai, merchants, farmers, artists. Hefty **gate** across from Yoro-kan was to Tago family mansion, chief councillors of Kamei lords. Tiny Catholic **church** next door built 1890 in memory of Tsuwano's Christians during early Meiji purge when...

135 Christians from Nagasaki's Urakami district were imprisoned here from 1868 until 1872, when freedom of religion was declared. Under torture 59 recanted their Christianity, but 36 chose martyrdom, were imprisoned in abandoned Korin-ji temple in foothills of Otome Pass, 15min walk W of stn. In 1946 tiny **Church of St Mary** built on temple site.

Circling around 400m S to next vale and...
YOMEI-JI temple built 1420, and at one time covering most of area with sub-halls. Soaring thatched-roof main hall mid-18th century; ¥300 (8:30-17:00) enter main hall, treasury, garden. **Grave** of early Meiji writer MORI **Ogai** L of front gate; grave of Dewa-no-kami behind. 10min walk behind temple is large cross marking mass burial of Otome Pass 36 martyrs.

Back in town, S of Tsuwano bridge is newly enlarged...
History Museum, *Kyodo-kan*, behind giant samurai manse gate (9:00-17:30, ¥350; ¥600 *kyotsu-ken* combo ticket for here, **Yoro-kan, Sangyo Shiryokan** sold at any of trio). Old building has mostly works of city's 7 nationally famous writers, whose busts line steps up to 2nd floor, with castle-related historical items including small scale replica of castle,j; new hall has more Yoro-kan related items and fine art pieces from area. Also some local Christian items.

Continuing 1km S (15min walk, 5min bike) to...

House MORI Ogai (1862-1922) lived as child. Father was doctor, house set up as clinic. Ogai excelled in literature, medicine at Yoro-kan, underwent further studies after move to Kyoto with father at age 12. Army doctor, Ogai sent to Germany to study; much of what he brought back was tested in field during Russo-Japan War. While in Germany, Ogai sharpened writing skills and started literary magazine upon returning. Best known as writer.

Next door...

Sekishu Washi Kaikan demonstrates entire process for handmade *washi* paper (8:00-18:00). 2nd floor is sale and exhibit of washi from all over Japan. Try your hand at final 'sifting' into sheets, but should call ahead for this, ☎2-1563.

5min walk beyond to...

Ex-mansion of Kamei lords, actually built for Sakazaki Dewa-no-kami, then taken over by Kamei. House and **garden** open to public, also exhibit room (8:00-17:30, ¥500) and tea house.

Backtrack N to first L, cross river to W bank, go N past several sites back to town. (Option to come down W side, crossing for Ogai and Kamei houses, then 10min bus back to stn; or on to Washihara for hike back via castle.)

S after cross to W side, 1km (15min walk from Kamei) to...

WASHIHARA HACHIMAN-GU shrine (Ho-on-ji temple YH past 1st curve in road). Built 1295 to protect new castle, lord YOSHIMI Yoriyuki received official permit to make it detached part of Kamakura's Tsurugaoka Hachiman. Not as grand, it is still pleasant, quiet place to be, especially **mid-Apr** when mass of cherry trees bloom; same time hold *Yabusame* **mounted archery** contests, shrine Spring Fest. In 1567, 270m stretch cleared for event in which samurai race under cherry trees on horseback, shooting at 3 dish-sized targets.

Trail heads up, then along ridge 1km to stone wall remains of once-sprawling...

Tsuwano Castle completed 1295 after 30 years work, razed 1874. Covers 8,000sq/m (3 football fields) on hilltop, perfect defence during tumultuous Warring States period.

25min paths down to...

TAIKO-DANI INARI shrine, or **Jingasa Folkcraft Museum**; or 5min chairlift (¥310/o.w., ¥410/r.t.). Near chairlift are remains of 2nd fort built by Dewa-no-kami.

Up W bank from Kamei house (5min walk) to...

House of **Nishi Amane**, early Meiji Dutch scholar, sent to Holland by Tokugawa founder of Tokyo Normal College. Small walled thatched-roof farmhouse in middle of rice paddies, open to visitors.

5min further to modern...

Folkcraft Museum, *Mingeikan Jingasa* (8:30-17:30, X-wed, ¥250). Jingasa are feudal war helmets, and this place has over 150 in all shapes and sizes; samurai weapons, folkcrafts, and life-sized dolls clad in beautiful costumes of Gion Festival Sagi-mai Heron Dance (*see* DATEBOOK).

Across street is...

Traditional Arts & Crafts Center, *Dento Kogei-sha* where can see entire process of hand-making Sekishu washi paper, (8:00-17:30, free)

2min walk N, across from Tsuwano High School is...

Kairaku-en, garden of Auspicious Pleasures, in which Kamei lords' house was set. House is no more; white-walled **tower**, *Monomi-yagura*, in garden from which lord and family watched festivals. Side of high school is red-roofed stable *Babasaki-yagura* of Kamei lords. Both restored 1970s.

Castle chairlift starts road behind garden. 10min on (5min from lift) to bottom of...
TAIKO-DANI INARI shrine on hillside visible from almost anywhere.
Built 1773 by 7th Kamei lord Norisada to protect castle NE 'Demon Gate',
and prosperity for his subjects—Inari being fox god of rice. 'Borrowing'
spirit of Kyoto's Fushimi Inari shrine, Norisada built grand shrine, making
it one of top Inari in Japan. Still draws over million visitors annually.
Climb up winding path thru tunnel of 2,000 red torii to spacious vermillion
main hall. Tea house there for snacks and lovely view of town below.

At bottom of approach to Inari shrine is...
YASAKA JINJA shrine, which enshrined spirit also 'borrowed' from
Kyoto's Yasaka. Built late 13th century as first guardian of castle's Demon
Gate—NE approach believed to be most unlucky and having two shrines
protect it was even better.

This puts us back in main part of town near Tsuwano Bridge.

CHOPSTICKS: In main section of town is enough variety to satisfy most
palates, and if not, numerous coffee shops serve usual sandwiches and mild curry. Specialties are river fish; *sansai-ryori* (mountain herbs, often with pheasant); *tsuwabuki-gohan*, rice cooked with fragrant *fuki* plant, served with soup and sansai-ryori. Table d'hote-
teishoku (¥800-¥2,000); many places serve with coffee. For some reason Tsuwano and
Yamaguchi have many coffee shops, unusual even for Japan. Tea houses will most likely
serve local specialty *genji-maki*, bean paste wrapped in thin mochi sheet. *Yama*
(mountain)-*fugu* 'sashimi' dipped in wasabi and soy sauce looks, some say tastes, like real
fugu sashimi, but finely sliced *konyaku* (konjak root—more vitamin B than beef). Win-
ter-only specialty *sakakura-nabe*, steaming pot full of vegetables, meats, and *kasu* sake-
lees (sediment from brewing). Some restaurants, coffee shops have great atmosphere:

Along first N-S street from stn: **Minoya** noodlery in thatch-roof mini farmhouse,
50m down on R; 150m more to **Shinobu** for *sansai-ryori* (¥1,500up); first R before
Shinobu (along canal) to **Taberu**, which claims *shizen-shoku* 'natural food'. Along
street diagonal from stn are several eateries on L, and on R is interesting coffee-shop
Nono, with *tsuwabuki-gohan* set w/coffee (¥1,300), matcha green tea with cakes (¥450).
1st R, 150m down to **Fuki-no-chaya** for best *tsuwabuki-gohan*. Block before coffee-
house, **Koi** (Carp) has dozens of carp. 2nd R (Honmachi-dori) post office intersection,
ryokan **Furusato** for *sansai-ryori* and **Yuki** further on R, for same. Across from
Catholic church is lovely corner coffee shop **Sara-no-ki**. Next door, thru small red-tiled
gate with large lantern on L, traditional tea house **Shoin-tei** rightly boasts finest private
garden in town; matcha with *genji-maki* (¥500), *sansai-ryori* lunch (¥1,500). Week-
ends/holidays can get crowded, for which reserve by calling (in Japanese) ☎2-1661.
Otome-chaya tea house, en route St Mary's Church, serves various cheap local dishes:
yama-fuku, *yude-kuri* (boiled chestnuts), *zenzai* (sweet soup of red beans and mochi).
Train fans ('SL-maniacs' in Japanese) head to stn front coffee shop **SL-kan Miura**, full
of train memorabilia. Other specialty coffee houses (also along stn front street: **Takasegawa** displaying works of local potters; and just beyond Shinobu is brick **Ko-no-mi**
decorated with antiques.

PERSONAL DATEBOOK: Feb, 1st horse day, *Hatsu-uma Fest*, Taiko-dani
Inari shrine. **Apr 2nd Sun**, Washihara Hachiman *Shrine Festival*; on closest **Sun**,
yabusame archery contests 10:00 and 14:00. **May 3**, *Otome-toge Festival*, St Mary's
Church, *memorial service* for 36 martyrs, thousands of Catholics from all over Japan.
May 15, Taiko-dani Inari shrine *Spring Festival*. **Jul 20-27**, Yasaka Jinja shrine
Grand Festival: *Sagi-mai Heron-Dance* offered on 20th when mikoshi taken out, and 27th
when spirit returned to shrine (both days 3pm). Dance originated at Kyoto's Gion
Festival, where rarely done, adopted here 1542, and in Yamaguchi about then also: 2 men
with heron head crown and feather-cape dance to slow rhythm of drum and flute; from
1958, *kosagi odori*, children's heron dance added; both days around 15:00. **Aug 10-15**,
Obon, 340-year-old Tsuwano-odori *folk dances* (join in) nitely; main are **10th** *Kannon
Festival*, Kosho-ji temple, Honsei-ji temple *toro-nagashi* floating lanterns, **15th** bon
dance contest in town.

WHERE NEXT: From Tsuwano rail up JAPAN SEACOAST to next stop IZUMO-MATSUE. Only *Oki-go* ltd exp (3-6 daily according to season) goes all way with no transfer; others hourly locals end en route only 31km (40min) on at coastal...

MASUDA 益田

HAS TWO lovely Sesshu-landscaped **gardens** which can be seen leisurely under 2hrs between trains. ¥200 for each, anytime during daylight. Sesshu spent his last years at Taiki-an hermitage in hills 1km NE of stn; his grave lies in back. His two gardens are 10min bus E of stn; drivers from Hagi on Rte191 pass by both, Rte9 from Tsuwano joins Rte191 near stn and near...

IKO-JI temple, built 1363, Sesshu added garden century later.

8min walk back towards stn, via...

lovely 700-year-old AMA-NO-IWAKATSU shrine, to...

MANPUKU-JI temple, built 1374. In addition to Sesshu garden, also has fine Homutsu-kan **treasure house**, which ask to be shown. 2km walk or 10min bus to stn. Masuda was also home of KAKINOMOTO Hitomaro, one of major poets who compiled 8th century *Manyo-shu* 'Myriad Leaves' collection of poetry. KAKINOMOTO JINJA shrine, built 1681 in his honor is 5min bus (1.5km) SW of stn.

MASUDA–IZUMO is 2hr10min ltd exp, 3hr exp.

4 stops up from Masuda is...

MIHO MISUMI, main center of Sekishu washi handmade paper. Seventeen artists still do entire process traditional way.

Coastline from Masuda is lovely; beyond Miho Misumi is HAMADA not much for tourist, but end of line for buses from Hiroshima's back-country onsens YUNOYAMA, YUKI and SANDAN-KYO GORGE (*see* HIROSHIMA). Onsens dot mountains and coast of San-In; we have one each for wanderer seeking rustic hide-away:

ARIFUKU ONSEN, (Mt) 35min bus inland from Hamada: dozen mostly small and budget to moderate rate inns tucked along river valley, and four old-time public baths (¥150). Mountainous Iwami district of San-In lies strongly under magic of Izumo's Grand Shrine, fetes autumn thanksgiving (thru Oct) with wild, folk Kagura dances. Arifuku has several troupes in area; arrange thru inn for special kagura performance any time of year, about ¥30,000. 40min bus Arifuku to GOTSU.

10min before, at Waki bus stop, is...

Ogawa House with **garden** by Sesshu. Ogawa banished here late 12th century by emperor Go-Toba, himself later exiled to Oki isles by Minamoto. Open to visitors, garden part of still lived-in house, ask resident's permission to admit you (¥500).

YUNOTSU ONSEN, (coast) stn (all trains stop) is 30min from Gotsu, 6min bus (¥80, timed to meet trains) to hot spring. Can walk it in not much more, as bus inches down winding streets barely wide enough for it: 200m down to harbor from stn, follow to next st and you are at entrance to onsen. Well-known spa for over 1,000 years, is in early Izumo shrine records, which discovery is credited to fisherman who spied old badger washing its wounds. Medicinal value for healing external wounds still lives on, popular with workers at nearby Iwami Ginzan silver mines. From early 13th century until mines' closing in 1923, silver was carted down to Yunotsu's natural bottle-neck harbor to ship up coast and on to Kyoto, and later Edo.

Mid-town Yunotsu...
Tenryo-kan Museum (10:00-22:00, free) artifacts from mines, folk items.
In spite of fame, two dozen inns are all small, ¥-B—¥-T (starting ¥5,-8,000w/2); all line
narrow street.   Recommended are: **Kiun-so** ☎(08556)-5-2008, **Koraku** ☎5-2023,
Koyo-kan ☎5-2711. 2 public baths.

Shores of **Yunotsu Harbor** fine strolls; at tip (20min walk) is
Kushijima Park, 15min chug-boat (¥200/rt) from pier in summer. As
roads are improving, chug-boats may be discontinued. **Fishing** off shore;
or rent boat—¥22,000 for half-day up to 4 people, includes gear, bait,
captain.

Yunotsu is also known for its pottery, with three **kilns** short walk uphill. Characteristic are beautiful thin-walled spherical pots of local reddish
unglazed clay, also called *maru-mono,* or round-things.

30min rail to ODA, from where 30min bus S to...
Iwami Ginzan Mines, which had 200,000 people until closing of mines
1923. Some of old town remains, diminished greatly as 700-year silver rush
ended, great fire 1890s destroyed. When Tokugawa came to power, mine
was confiscated from Mori clan and put under direct control of Edo. Once-
grand *Daikan-yashiki,* Magistrate's residence, now **History Museum.**

40min bus S of Oda is...
SANBE ONSEN, main base for climbing 1126m Sanbe-san mountain and its
four smaller peaks.

Spread between Ginzan and Sanbe-san are 3 tiny backwoods hot springs:
IKEDA RADIUM ONSEN 25min bus from Oda (en route to Sanbe Onsen) and
20min walk down side road, is one inn **Hosen-kaku** ☎(08548)-3-3306, hidden in valley.

KOYAHARA ONSEN, another one-inn hotspring **Kumaya Ryokan,** ☎3-2101,
15min bus beyond Ikeda Onsen and 5min walk.

YUGAKAE ONSEN, 12km S.of Oda (40min bus, 10 daily, 9 are JR) is 'large' with
4 inns (**Nakamura Ryokan** ☎(08557)-5-1250) but just as isolated. Also reached by
10min bus from Kazubuchi on JR Mie Line running Gotsu → Hiroshima; but don't
recommend unless coming this way to/for Hiroshima as trains slow and infrequent.
Occasional bus (4-5x-daily) between Kazubuchi and Sanbe Onsen.

35min rail from Oda to **IZUMO,** 45min beyond to more popular lodging **MATSUE.**

There is strange wild beauty in Japanese landscapes, a beauty not easily defined in words. The secret of it it must be sought in the extraordinary lines of the mountains...every one having a fantasticality of its own.
— Lafcadio Hearn, *Glimpses of Unfamiliar Japan*, 1894

IZUMO 出雲 & MATSUE 松江
LAND OF EIGHT CLOUDS

IZUMO TAISHA, Grand Shrine, second oldest shrine in Japan—oldest being Yaegaki 4km south of Matsue station, probably ancestral to Izumo. Izumo was shrine-palace of one of 3 'kingdoms' eventually united to form core of imperial Japan. These were in Kyushu, Yamato and Izumo, whose mythologies have been inseparably united, with Izumo's Susano-o known as prankster younger storm god brother of Yamato's Amaterasu, sun goddess. It was practical joke played by Susano-o on his sister—flaying sacred piebald horse backward and defiling weaving cottage of Sun Maidens—that caused Amaterasu to hide in cave, instigating lesser gods to invent comedy to lure her out (*see* Demon Dancers of Hiroshima, p.672). Susano-o gave Imperial family of Japan one of its 3 sacred treasures when he emulated England's Saint George and Persia's Rustam and slew dragon which had been eating local maidens—in its tail was sacred sword, now purportedly enshrined (or replicated duplicate, one sank at medieval Genji-Heike battle of Dan-no-Ura when infant emperor drowned) in Nagoya's ATSUTA SHRINE, p.298.

IZUMO ROMANTIC STORM GOD
DAUGHTER of Susano-o by rescued maid Kushi-nada-hime, was Suserihime, who married last of 80 brothers, Okuni-nushi-no-mikoto, or King of Great Land, Izumo, after he defeated 79 brothers to unify kingdom. Probable deified leader of invaders from mainland, as folk deity was Daikoku-ten (means great country, same as O-kuni, but written with odd ideographs 'Great Black') of 7 lucky gods—local fishermen equated him with fisher-god Ebisu. Culturally advanced Izumo was main rival to Yamato thus myth of Japan's creation takes special note of its subjugation. Onamuji was pursuaded 'by heaven' to abdicate in favor of Mikado's line, which he did on condition he keep religion concession. (Thru Nara era, every new governor of Izumo had to go to imperial court to perform special rite of obeisance, repeating pledge Okuni-nushi presumably made to Amaterasu.) Site was political center, for myth has Susano-o order Okuni-nushi to...
"dwell at foot of Mount Uka making stout your *shinden* (elevated temple or palace) pillars on nethermost rock-bottom, and raising high cross beams to plain of high heaven itself ...you rogue"—accolade earned as he had swiped pa-in-law's sword.

It must have been quite some sight; archaeologists believe oldest in land temple/shrine-palace of Izumo—unlike Ise Grand Shrine (*see* p.313)—has been considerably modified since first built 5th? century. Spit of land may have been island when shrine first built; shoreline definitely reached shrine, courtyard of water-worn pebbles reflects this original setting. Tho building style was basically same as today, except for curlicues added since, whole originally stood below highest tide mark on pilings literally set on 'nethermost rock bottom' some 30-50m high, putting original shrine floor far higher than present rooftop. It really looked as if they had raised its 'cross-beams to plain of high heaven'. Whole stood at least double present 24m, may have been 100m high (330ft). Foundation of 4th century 48mtr shinden recently excavated at Tottori dunes, p.844, near tomb of 'queen'.

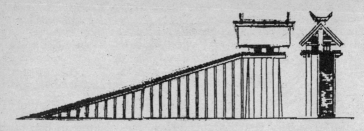

Izumo as scholars believe it was millennium ago.

...as reconstructed in recent centuries...

Prior to 1744 believed to have been larger, tho same scale. When pilings were shortened is not known. Izumo architectural style, *Taisha-zukuri*, or *Tenchi-kongen-zukuri* (earth-base heaven-roof) is square, 9 main supports, entrance off-center of building front (gable) as in snow-country style. Other main type Ise *Shinmei-zukuri* Sun Goddess-style, oblong, 12 main supports and entrance center side as in south climate. As said, Yaegaki believed older shrine site; 1km SE of which is Kamosu shrine, younger than either, smaller than Izumo but nearer in style to original Izumo architecture.

But shrunken, modified or curlicued, Izumo impresses with majesty of supplicant's approach thru successive torii, and final stretch thru soaring ancient cryptomeria and pines which separate all from outside world, and with its immensity. Even prepared for it, its majestic presence yet harmony with surrounding nature is breathtaking, no matter how many shrines you've seen. Imagine this larger, two to four times its present height, and you can suppose how humbled any visitor in past centuries must have felt.

We were taken into inner compound (only head priest enters innermost) for rite, which request at shrine office for donation of ¥3,000 up. Girl kagura in your honor for similar contribution. Larger offerings 'ensure' that Izumo's kami looks favorably on your wish—or try pauper's approach from back of shrine small door. Knock & pray; kami doesn't expect anyone from behind and his attention is all on you as he looks back to see what knocking was.

PERSONAL DATEBOOK: Main fete **May 14-16** gets special Imperial Envoy:·*Yabusame* mounted archery 14th, **15-16** *Ota-ue-sai* ritual planting of first rice, *shishi-mai* lion-dances, Izumo Jindai-kagura. **Jan 1** *Omike-sai*, offer ritually pure food. **Feb 17**, *Kikoku-sai*, offer sacred grain. **Jun 1** *Ryoden-sai*, air sanctuary. 2nd big festival **lunar Oct 11-17**, *Oimi-matsuri*, all Shinto gods in Japan from local river god to Amaterasu (except one ornery cuss in Kyushu) gather here—why those many little shrines surround. **Lunar Oct** is known in Japan as *Kami-nashi-zuki*, month without gods—except in Izumo where it is *Kami-ari-zuki*, month with all gods. Garet and friend visited this time, arriving at dawn as fine mist hovered just above ground making shrine look as if above clouds, with faint whisps wafting away as if to hide gods as they retired for day to heaven.

What do 8,000,000 celestials do when they gather? For one, arrange all marriages for coming year. Izumo Taisha Talismans are Japan's valentines and are exceptionally attractive, especially *ema-e* picture plaques, bronze mini bow and phallic arrow (cupid's?), 'replicas' of Susano-o's 'bow and arrow of life'. **SHRINE OF TOGETHERNESS** offers husband-wife chopstick sets. Also center of largest Shinto sect, *Oyashiro-kyo*, organized 1880 by TAKATOMI Senge whose ancestors established shrine and who thus

 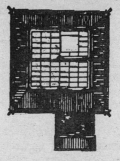 

claims oldest lineage in Japan second only to that of emperor (in that his ultimate ancestor is kid brother of sun goddess, imperial progenitor). Sect missionizes, has *kyokai* (churches) in L.A., Hawaii.

Shrine attracts several million pilgrims annually. Marriages performed here are believed especially blessed, ceremony imitates marriage of creator gods Izanagi-Izanami with 'chase' around sacred pillar. Shrine marriage rite however only dates back to 1889—before which were drunken parties taking place at groom's home upon delivery of female goods.

GETTING THERE: Quickest direct from: HAGI, 3hr Ltd Exp **Isokaze**, 3hr25min express (both infrequent runs); from TSUWANO, 2hr45min Ltd Exp **Oki** (3-6x-daily, starts Ogori on Inland Sea coast, via MASUDA for local connections from Hagi); Ltd Exp **Yakumo** (10 daily) cuts across from OKAYAMA, via Matsue, 3hr15min; and several long-distance expresses from TOKYO, OSAKA, KYOTO. All stop Izumo-shi stn, 8.5km SE of shrine, from where 11min JR on Taisha sub-Line (one per hour 5:37-21:01) to Taisha stn and 1km walk, or 5min bus to shrine. Ichibata Private Rail runs between MATSUE and TAISHA-MAE (between JR stn and shrine) in 1hr; no transfer and cheaper than JR, is better of two.

By **air**: JAS (former (TDA) 4 daily (90min) from TOKYO'S Haneda; 5 daily (1hr) from OSAKA; 1 daily (70min) from FUKUOKA. **Izumo airport** 10km E of Izumo-shi, 25min bus. Buses to airport from Ichibata Rail Izumo-shi stn leave 70min before flight time; from Matsue Onsen Ichibata stn leave 1hr30min prior. **Yonago airport** gets same number of flights from same cities; 15km E of MATSUE CITY, Izumo airport more convenient all around.

By **car**, up coast Rte9 to Taisha turn-off, 5km before Izumo-shi City (if miss turn-off, another follows JR tracks from Izumo-shi to Taisha-cho, as area around shrine is called). If **renting car** at Matsue (Eki-mae, Toyota, etc) to cover area–which we recommend–can take Rte9 along Lake Shinji S shore to Izumo-shi, or Rte431 along lake's N to Taisha (see below for sites along each). Driving around Izumo-Matsue area you see many houses flanked by walls of intertwined pine trees neatly trimmed into flat-tops. Called *tsuiji-matsu*, protect houses in open plains from bitter winter winds from Siberia.

Bus from stn lets you off **2nd torii** (main terminal 300m further W), 700m down cryptomeria & pine tree-lined avenue to great **copper torii**, erected 1666 by Hagi's lord Mori Tsunahiro, to main compound. Straight ahead is **offeratory hall**, *haiden*, where marriages and kagura performed. Rebuilt 1959, its massive shimenawa sacred rope is largest in Japan, 8m long, 3m thick, 1500kg, tied in suggestive knot Italian will recognize resembles finger symbol called 'fig' indicative of shrine's old fertility function. Behind is **8-legged gate**, *Yatsuashi-mon*, closest most people get. For extra offering, priest purifies you here, then tour inside.

Tower to R of Yatsuashi-mon is where Izumo's priest-governors watched festivals from. Flanking inside Yatsuashi-mon are 'Gate-guardian

Shrines' of uji-gami, indigenous protector kami. Inner gate flanked by 'dining halls' of gods; they and inner fence mark bounds of inner sanctum. Back outside, far L and R, long 'hallways' standing on their own, partially hidden by trees. These are *Nishi-Juku-sha* and *Higashi-Juku-sha*, West and East Shrines, 'dormitories' of gods (those of West Japan-Kansai, in west-*nishi*, and East Japan-Kanto in east-*higashi*) during lunar Oct gathering. Hall at the back end of East Hall is *Kama-no-Yashiro* 'Cooking Pot Shrine', where food and sake offered. This offers one of best views of main shrine. Continuing counter-clockwise, back R corner is old library. Straight back on high ground *Soga-no-Yashiro*, 1748, enshrines Susano-o. Back L house, *Shoko-kan* **treasury** with old scrolls, etc...but valuable goods moved to new *Shinko-den*, concrete building, front left compound; 1st floor rest area, 2nd **museum** (8:30-16:30, ¥150 for both).

SIDE TRIPS FROM TAISHA
IZUMO-SHI: Worth hour or so wandering around photogenic old section along narrow weeping willow-lined Takase River (5min walk N of stn) especially winter when local deep-blue *aizome* dyed cloth is being rinsed in icy river. 2 old workshops still do all by hand: larger **Nagata Some-kojo** and **Ito-ya**, at Jonari-bashi Bridge, 10min NE from stn. More on interesting Honmachi shopping street, including old fashioned sake breweries **Imaoka** and **Moriyama.**

En route (500m W of Taisha Bus Center) is...
Grave of Izumo-no-Okuni, shrine maiden who 'founded' Kabuki dance theatre (originally all women, now all men) on banks of Kyoto's Kamo River around 1600. Daughter of NAKAMURA Mizaemon, later Kabuki family and troupe took her name, still performing under Nakamura aegis, one of Kabuki's star families. Nearby Hono-zan hill (20min climb) has **memorial** to Okuni, erected by donations from Kabuki actors—some of whom make pilgrimage to offer their prayers.

20min bus W (1 stop JR San-In Line) of stn to...
CHII-MIYA, for *Izumo Mingei-kan*, **Folkcraft Museum** (8:30-17:00, X-mon, ¥500). In granary, wood 'shed', Nagaya-mon gate, servants' quarters of 300-year-old wealthy Yamamoto family farmhouse. Displays folk arts (mostly Izumo area) such as dyeing, weaving, carving, pottery, lacquerware, silver-work. Weekends, matcha & cakes served in tea house.

30min S of town, upstream Kambe River is...
Tachikue-kyo Gorge, 1km of fantastic rock scenery, lovely boating.

HI-NO-MISAKI, with lovely ancient shrine, one of Japan's first modern-style lighthouses, highest above sea level (British built 1903, ascend for ¥80), fine beach and coastline with glass-bottom boats, 35min bus from Taisha.

PERSONAL DATEBOOK: **Apr 14**, pm, *Hiwatari* Fire walking fest. **Bus** 30min S of Izumo-shi on Rte 54, Mineji temple, Mitoya-town, ☎(0854) 45-2111.

WHERE TO STAY: Most stay at MATSUE ONSEN and do shrine as side-trip. If planning to reach Izumo-Matsue late day, stay around TAISHA to avoid backtrack and to catch shrine at best time evening or early morning when less people. Of course, with time you can explore Izumo area for day, then Matsue area for another, staying at one of its hot spring areas. Some around TAISHA boast hot spring baths drawn from spring in middle of town. Most Taisha's 30-odd inns line main street (cheaper ones, ¥-Bw/2, in back streets); choose by walking along, or thru **Kanko-annai** at 2nd torii. Recommended ¥-T+w/2 range: **Takeno-ya** ☎(0853)-53-3131; **Inaba-ya** ☎53-3180; lovely old **Toraya** ☎53-2022. Step down in price (¥-lo-Tw/2): **Kato** ☎53-2214; **Hinode** ☎53-3311. One minshuku (¥-lo-Bw/2) in town, 3 out at Inasa-no-hama beach,

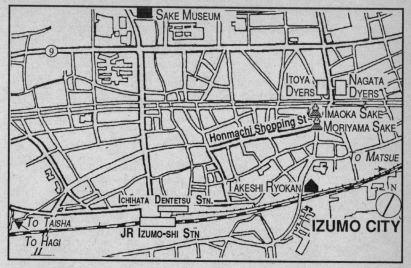

10min bus W; **Ebisu-ya YH** ☎53-2157 in town. **IZUMO-SHI** has about as many ryokan, mostly cheaper price; and 6 ¥-lo-B minshuku. 2 lovely oldies (¥-Tw/2) are: **Kami-ya** ☎21-3361; **Takeshi-sanso** ☎21-0316. **TACHIKUE-KYO** has several budget inns, Youth Hostel and summer campsite. **HI-NO-MISAKI** has dozens of ¥-B minshuku and one equally budget Kokumin-shukusha **Choran-so** ☎54-5111; **Kanko-annai** by bus stop. Tiny **YU-NO-KAWA ONSEN** at Shobara, 2 stops E of Izumo-shi;

But for isolation, and superb experience try...
Yakumo Honjin, 250-year-old mansion of Kowata family, regional Tokugawa official; used as inn by Mori, Matsue and other San-In daimyo traveling to/from Edo on annual *sankin-kotai* 'alternate residency' in Edo. *See* daily 10:00-16:00, ¥300; 3 stops JR E from Izumo-shi to Shinji and 5min walk W. Near Lake Shinji, part of it is lovely restaurant-ryokan **Yakumo Honjin** ☎(0852) 66-0136, ¥-T–Sw/2; special dishes like lake-fish & duck prepared on brazier in your room.

2 stops beyond Shinji is **TAMAZUKURI ONSEN** (*follows*) 30min from Izumo-shi; 2 stops 12min beyond to **MATSUE** (*follows*).

But rather than this route to Matsue, we follow Shinji-ko N shore to...
ICHIBATA YAKUSHI, popular name for Iozan ICHIBATA-DERA temple, 30min private rail from Taisha and Izumo-shi stns, or 25min from Matsue Onsen, to Ichibataguchi stn and 15min bus. **Drivers** Rte431 then branch N at Ichibata-guchi; total 27km from Taisha. **Bus** now direct to hilltop temple, until 1960s one climbed 1,600 steps from Sakashita bus stop; both stops on different lines, stn–temple shuttle 7x-daily, 5x-daily to Sakashita (30min walk).

First cluster of buildings are priests' living quarters and study hall, connected to main hall by long winding corridor, front of which is pot of burning incense, smoke from which is fanned towards eyes to cure. Temple founded 894AD, houses Yakushi (medicinal) Buddha pulled out of sea by fisherman, whose blind mother was cured soon after. Temple has been known ever since to be particularly good for eyes—as can be expected in bespectacled Japan, temple sees steady stream of visitors all year. Many more come for festival days. Nearby is Kokumin-shukusha **Ichibata-dera Kaikan** ☎(0853)-63-3111, **Nakamura Ryokan** ☎67-0029, both ¥-B.

PERSONAL DATEBOOK: **Apr 29-May 8**, Infants' Blessing, Ichibata Yakushi famed for it, best if tot brought here in first two years. **Mid-Aug** (dates flexible), Ennichi temple fair. **Sep 6-8**, special services.

MATSUE STORMY ROMANTIC 松江

LAFCADIO HEARN's great romance with Japan can be attributed to his early period in Matsue, and tho century has passed and much of Japan's beauty desecrated by shabby industrialization, Matsue has lost little of its charm. It is no quaint relic: it is thriving, modern prefectural capital. But it has managed to modernize gracefully and exemplifies what Japan could be if more Japanese practiced those traits they are so generously credited with. Matsue's setting is idyllic, located on what geologists call 'Shinji Horst and Graben'—elevated block of land (horst), adjoining depression (graben)—fault in earth's crust where one side has slipped down and other up. Natural beauty spot results.

City itself is on spit of land in Japan Sea which was, perhaps 2,000 years ago, island. Two lake-like lagoons remain of island-forming waters, with Matsue at narrow point between, shielded from sea by horst looming up behind to form perfect natural port. Lake Shinji-ko, at which E end Matsue lies, is 6th largest in Japan (surface area, 80km/sq) but only 6m at its deepest. Tourist posters of Matsue often show fiery sunset framed between pine trees of Yome-ga-shima Islet just offshore from Matsue. Ohashi River flows from Shinji-ko into Lake Naka-umi (Inner-Sea), almost as large but with two islands, separated from Japan Sea by narrow spit of land.

Volcanic action which formed fault has also given area some good spas: in-town MATSUE ONSEN; TAMATSUKURI on mainland 10km W; KAIKE also on mainland but at mouth of outer lagoon, reached by **train** or **bus** along mainland side, or bus on island-hopping cross-lagoon bridge to Sakai, whence bus, train, taxi to Kaike. Horst itself is beautiful and at far E end of it rises Miho-no-seki, justly famed for its natural beauty.

GETTING AROUND: Sites in and around Matsue are conveniently bunched in two areas: around castle with Shiomi-nawate **samurai houses** and **Lafcadio Hearn's home**, and Fudoki-no-oka area S of town. Direct buses to each, then some footwork. Schedule below is 1991; use as guide.

TOUR CAB ¥3,710 or 7x-mtr per hour.

BUS TOUR: basic tour of town is 3hr30min **Shinai Course**:
A (daily all year; ¥3,685) starts Tamatsukuri Onsen (8:40), pick up JR Matsue stn (9:00) and Matsue Onsen (9:10), Kyodo-kan museum → Castle → Samurai house → Hearn's home → Gessho-ji → end JR Matsue stn (12:35).
B (Jan 1-Nov 30, ¥3,325) starts JR Matsue (10:50) → similar to A → end JR Matsue (14:25).
C (daily, ¥3,685) starts JR Matsue (13:45) similar to A → Tamatsukuri Onsen (17:50).
D (Jan 1-Nov 30, ¥3,325) starts JR Matsue (14:38), similar to A → end JR Matsue (18:14).

FULL-DAY TOURS, incl lunch:
O-Yashiro (Grand Shrine) **Course** (daily all year, ¥6,140) starts Tamatsukuri Onsen (9:00) Izumo-shi stn (10:12) → Taisha → Hi-no-misaki → Ichibata Yakushi → Tamatsukuri Onsen (16:48) via Tamatsukuri stn.
Magatama Course (daily Jan thru Nov, ¥8,455) starts Matsue Onsen (8:30) → JR stn (8:40) → Hi-no-misaki → Taisha → Izumo-shi stn → Matsue stn where continue Shinai route: Kyodo-kan → Castle → Samurai House → Hearn's Home → Gessho-ji → Matsue Onsen (18:00) end JR Matsue (18:14).

All tours can be started and/or ended at any stn or onsen; arrange at each starting point's Ichibata bus office or prior thru JTB or major travel agent. Good brochure and map (English, Japanese) at stn Kanko-annai.

Toyota and Eki-mae **car rentals** front of flashy new JR stn; and **bike rentals** far L of stn-front plaza. Far R, stops for local, long-distance, and tour buses.

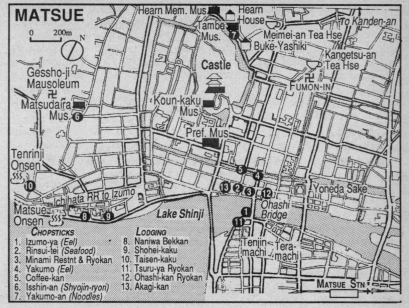

MATSUE

0 200m N

CHOPSTICKS
1. Izumo-ya *(Eel)*
2. Rinsui-tei *(Seafood)*
3. Minami Restnt & Ryokan
4. Yakumo *(Eel)*
5. Coffee-kan
6. Isshin-an *(Shyojin-ryori)*
7. Yakumo-an *(Noodles)*

LODGING
8. Naniwa Bekkan
9. Shohei-kaku
10. Taisen-kaku
11. Tsuru-ya Ryokan
12. Ohashi-kan Ryokan
13. Akagi-kan

Matsue Castle (2.2km NW of stn; 10min bus to Kencho-mae; just over cab basic mtr) is real, built 1607 by Horio clan. 1634, shogun Tokugawa Ieyasu's grandson MATSUDAIRA Naomasa became lord of Matsue as part of Tokugawa *go*-game policy of encircling old foes (this case, Choshu) with loyal allies. 234 years or 10 generations later, in 1868, Matsudairas dismantled all but main keep and made castle grounds into public park, building prefectural offices S outside moat.

100m S of bus stop is...
Prefectural Museum, *Kenritsu Hakubutsukan* (9:00-17:00, X-mon, ¥120) Buddhist art, old scrolls and pottery. Enter castle grounds thru SE main gate (parking lot for drivers); swing down to S end *Matsue Kyodokan*, **Museum** (8:30-17:00, ¥155) in 2-storey W-style building **Ko-un Kaku** Pavilion, built 1903 in honor of emperor Meiji projected visit. He never stayed over, but emperor Taisho did during his princely days. Inside are items on Matsue from prehistory to present, mostly post-1868. Between it and castle, **MATSUE JINJA** enshrines Tokugawa Ieyasu, 1st and 7th Matsudaira lords. Main keep is one of few in such fine original shape; inside (free) is museum of samurai goods, top floor magnificent view.

Exit park thru back (N) gate, follow moat clockwise to...
SHIOMI-NAWATE DISTRICT of high-ranking samurai residences. First is *Koizumi Yakumo Kinenkan,* **Lafcadio Hearn Memorial Museum** (8:30-17:00, ¥205). Used to be in hideous colonial style–built 1933 and modeled after Goethe Memorial Museum in Weimar Germany; but soon after our 1983 visit, taken down and rebuilt to better match surroundings. Next door house was **home of Hearn** and his new bride, KOIZUMI Setsu. Hearn arrived in Matsue 1890 as correspondent for *Harpers,* took on post of English teacher at Matsue high school from May to Nov 1891. Took wife's ex-samurai family name, 'borrowed' first name Yakumo (8-clouds), old name for this area where he had his fondest memories. He then taught 5 years at Kumamoto in Kyushu, spent time here again en route Tokyo. House typifies style of high-ranking samurai residence, now preserved in-

tact and untampered with; it is described in detail in his *In a Japanese Garden*. Many of Hearn's stories deal with Matsue, and extant bridges, rustic temples and corners of city may be familiar to readers of his books (most available in Tuttle paperbacks including masterpiece *Japan: An Attempt at Interpretation*). To us, he is still best writer on Japan, tho outside this country vastly underrated as literature. To Henry Miller, "My passion for Japan began with Hearn".

You are guided thru house by Negishi family member, who have owned this house since Hearn's time and opened it to public, 9:00-17:00, X-wed, ¥150.

Tanabe Art Museum, *Bijutsu-kan*, (9:00-17:00 X-mon, ¥500), next door thru giant gate, exhibits tea ceremony-related items—bowls, utensils, scrolls.

Next three houses are private, then to lovely noodle shop **Yakumo-an**, which we favor over almost as delicious tea shops in castle park. Izumo area renowned for **noodles** and Yakumo-an serves finest handmade *te-uchi* soba (*see* CHOPSTICKS). After lunch we head next door to dessert on sweet cakes and matcha green tea (¥300) in ex-miso mill of...

Buke Yashiki, 300-year-old manse of Shiomi family, top Matsudaira advisor, one of best such preserved residences we have seen. Completely intact, rooms loaded with authentic furnishings and everyday items, right down to fully stocked kitchen and ready to fire bath.

Continuing along moat, first L 200m to stone steps up to...
Meimei-an tea house, built 1779 for advisor ARISAWA Kazuyoshi. Moved here from Arisawa manse 1966, commands fine view of castle—see inside Meimei-an (9:00-17:00, ¥200) but tea & cakes served at nearby **Hyakuso-tei** tea house (¥350). Down at moat, catch bus back to stn from front of Yakumo Kinen-kan, or 5min walk back to castle front gate, total elapsed time slightly over 2hrs.

Another Matsudaira Harusato tea house on **FUMON-IN** temple grounds, 400m E: en route Shiomi-nawate to front of castle, L after crossing moat. For its huge window it is called *Kangetsu-An*, 'Moon-viewing Hermitage'.

Real tea fans can visit tea house **Kanden-an**, built 1790 by Harusato and his brother. Nearby is another tea house and waiting room; all part of Arisawa manse (9:30-16:00 X-Wed, ¥700). 20min bus from stn; from Fumon-in continue E 200m to big road where catch bus to Kanden-an Iri-guchi or walk 1.5km, and 15min walk up side street from bus stop.

GESSHO-JI temple (1km W of castle, 20min bus from stn on Matsue Onsen-bound, 10min from castle on same, to riverside Koyu-bashi stop and 10min walk NW). Built 1664 by 1st Matsudaira for his mother's burial, became mausoleum for all Matsudaira lords. As you enter (¥300), on L is 1st, on R is 7th; clockwise around rest are 5th, 3rd (stone tower between is for 1st's mother), 9th, 2nd, 8th, 4th, 6th (Korean-style pillar-on-turtle here appears in Hearn story; reputed to walk nites, to discourage which samurai decapitated it—can see where head was rejoined to body). In one corner is tea house **Sho-in** (matcha & cake ¥350). Out in front by ticket-sale booth is *Homotsu-kan*, **Treasure House** (adm incl w/temple) with Matsudaira family treasures. Nearby is **Isshin-an** tea house/restaurant which also serves *shojin-ryori* vegetarian priests' fare.

Wide Ohashi River, flowing out of Lake Shinji, between JR stn and castle divides city into N and S. On N side of Ohashi Bridge is **KYO-MISE** district, lots of fine restaurants, shops, and old inns; S side is **TENJIN-MACHI** shopping area and **TERA-MACHI** temple district. Tenjin-machi is street leading to Ohashi bridge, with many folkcraft stores selling pottery, *Yakumo-nuri* lacquer, handmade *washi* paper (see below), kasuri weaving from three nearby towns, and *menou* (agate) beads of Tamatsukuri onsen, among others. Kyo-mise offers much more of same, particularly along 'L'-shaped Kyo-mise shopping arcade, heart of old merchant district.

CHOPSTICKS: Common light lunch area specialty is *Izumo-soba* buckwheat noodles, served in stacks of 3-5 small lacquered bowls; which we had at **Yakumo-an** in Shiomi-nawate samurai district. *Bote-bote-cha* is special tea gruel served at **Yushu-an** in castle park. Developed as emergency food during poor harvest, now 'fashionable'—dried tea leaves whipped into bancha tea, mixed with salt, tofu, mushrooms, chestnuts, seasonal mountain herbs. In addition to various fish, delicious eel raised in Lake Shinji make for energizing summer meals; served at many places such as **Yakumo** along Kyobashi canal (parallel to Ohashi River, N of Kyo-mise), and **Izumo-ya** next to inn Tsuruya Ryokan facing Lake Shinji. Interesting coffee shop on Kyobashi canal, **Kohi-kan** just W of Kyobashi bridge. **Minami Ryokan** has lovely seafood restaurant along Ohashi River facing lake, specialty of *tai-meshi* minced sea bream and rice. Next door similar **Rinsui-tei**; both with seasonal specialties, teishoku table-d'hote ¥2,-3,000. *Shojin-ryori* vegetarian priest fare at **Isshin-an** near Gessho-ji.

PERSONAL DATEBOOK: **Apr 1-15**, *Castle Festival*, 2 days of folk dances by troupes from all over Shimane Pref. **Aug 1st Sat/Sun**, *Lake Festival*, fireworks over Shinji-ko, dances thru town. **Nov 3**, Matsue *Grand Festival* features Do-gyoretsu procession of giant drum thru town; said to have been started by townspeople in 18th century to celebrate marriage of their lord Matsudaira Nobuzumi.

SHINWA-NO-SATO 'Home of Mythology', also called *Yakumo-tatsu Fudoki-no-Oka*, 5km S, once political heart of Izumo region.

Abundance of *kofun* burial mounds indicate major center of power as early as 4th-6th century AD, tho none of tumuli come close in size to giants of Yamato. People inhabited area even earlier, as we see thru some reconstructed Yayoi period dwellings and hints of earlier Jomon culture. This area is also site of YAEGAKI and KAMOSU SHRINES. No bus tours cover area; r.t. **cab** from Matsue about 2hrs, 16x-mtr. By local Ichibata or Shigyo (city-run) bus, 20min to Yaegaki Jinja or Fudoki-no-Oka (separate lines). 40min bike from JR stn.

Our first stop is...
YAEGAKI JINJA shrine, 5 daily bus 20min direct, or more frequent to Yaegaki-danchi and 5min walk. Enshrined are Susano-o and bride Kushinada-hime whom this Japanese 'St George' saved from great dragon Yamata-no-Orochi—which he killed in nearby hills. Legend probably originates Central Asia, whence Izumo people came (?) as in Armenian version with George=Gewagis. Site predates Taisha, but numerous rebuildings have altered its original Taisha-zukuri style. Yaegaki Jinja is shrine of love. L of main is shrine to god of mountains, with wood penis enshrined. Cross stream in back to Oku-no-In sanctuary and paired husband-and-wife cryptomeria, *Fufu-sugi*. Mirror-Lake of *Kagami-no-ike* there is test: buy *kami-gata* paper (¥10) at shrine office, place coin on it and float on lake; quicker it sinks, quicker to find life-long happiness. **Treasure Hall** (9:00-18:00, ¥200) L of main gate has late 12th century paintings on wood of 7 deities.

From here, 20min walk across fields, past two groups of yoko-ana *burial pits dug horizontally into hills, SE to...*
KAMOSU JINJA shrine, last rebuilt 1346; is oldest, purest example of Taisha-zukuri style, tho shrine is younger than Izumo or Yaegaki. Enshrined here is Izanami-no-mikoto, female of first pair of gods to populate Japan. Its chigi crossbeams indicate female, while Izumo's is male. Sakura-lined approach to small shrine, perpetually shaded by ancient soaring cryptomeria trees. N of shrine, past **SHORIN-JI** temple are stone tablets marking remains of Senge and Kitajima family palaces—both were caretakers of Izumo Taisha.

10min walk E to...
Fudoki-no-oka Center, (also reached frequent 20min from Matsue stn on Yakumo-bound Bus). Modern rendition of kofun housing *Shiryo-kan*,

Museum (9:00-17:00, ¥130), artifacts unearthed from area—Jomon, Yayoi pottery, including rare Yayoi clay flute; Kofun era haniwa clay burial figures; artifacts from 8th century Kokubun-ji temple and Koku-cho governor's residence. Near museum is reconstructed **Yayoi dwelling**; and behind it, keyhole-shaped **Okadayama kofun**. Near parking lot was foundation remains of 9th-10th century mansion complex recently reconstructed. Amateur archaeologist can roam around for few hours:

From Fudoki-no-Oka bus stop 25min walk E to remains of Izumo Koku-cho governor's residence near Rokusho Jinja shrine; S of which across river to several kofun. 15min N to foundation remains of Izumo **KOKUBUN-JI** temple; E past remains of tile kiln and **KOKUBUN NI-JI** nunnery (this and temple built 741 by emperor Shomu's edict to create such all over country), to Takeuchi Jinja bus stop whence 15min bus back to Matsue.

For others, catch outward-bound bus from Fudoki-no-Oka stop to either of 2 places...
KUMANO TAISHA shrine, 20min from Fudoki-no-Oka on Suya-bound buses (9x-daily). Built in Taisha-zukuri style (redone 1983), roughly contemporary to Izumo, Taisha sometimes claimed to be site where Susano-o wed Kushi-nada-hime (tho Yaegaki more commonly believed to be so). Enshrined here is Kushimikenu-no-Mikoto, god of fire, whom some scholars equate to Susano-o. Kushimikenu is credited with first introducing fire to Man, when he showed his son Okuni-nushi-no-Mikoto, first ruler of Izumo, how to make fire.

PERSONAL DATEBOOK: This ritual transfer of fire is recreated annually at Oct 15th *Sanka-sai Fire Festival* in which ritually pure fire made by rubbing together virgin wood. Head priest of Izumo Taisha comes here with offerings of food, receives fire in return, which is used to cook sacred food for Izumo's October gathering of Gods. After receiving flame, group from Izumo performs dance marking end of ceremony. More famous Kumano Grand Shrines of Kii Peninsula in Wakayama are said to have been started by tribe of displaced Izumo-ites.

2nd stop is...
WASHI-NO-SATO, 12min from Fudoki-no-Oka to end of line Yakumo Bessho stop; drivers (or cab) can do this first, then to Kumano Shrine whence 10km back route to Tamatsukuri Onsen. 9km from Matsue (cab 12x-mtr r.t., incl wait); perhaps most worthwhile stop in this inland day tour. Washi-no-Sato, 'Home-of-Hand-made-Paper', where ABE Eishiro had his handmade paper factory in his home compound. Abe passed away in 1982, has since been made into **Museum of Special Papers**, his personal collection of old paper cloth (including fireproof firemen's coats), washi from all over, outline of process using his tools. In 1968 after our first visit he was declared Living National Treasure. Several houses nearby still make washi all by hand, continuing tradition which made Izumo-washi known thruout Japan since early Nara Period. Pleasant little village of stocky thatched-roof houses (once seen all over Izumo-Matsue area, but now rare), each surrounded by sheets of washi spread out to dry. Buy paper here for much less than in city. Rembrandt imported similar paper via Nagasaki Dutch traders for his sketches. We have found its smell and feel never fail to enchant.

Information sheet on handmade paper is presented to visitors to Abe's museum-house, giving basics about papers, which we loosely quote...

Materials for Japanese handmade paper are bark of *kozo* (Broussonetia kujinoki Siebold), *mitsumata* (Edgeworthia papyrifera Sieb. et Zuce) and *gampi* (Wikstroemia sikokiana Franchet et Savatier). Kozo plant belongs to Moraceae which grows everywhere in Japan. Mitsumata belongs to Daphnaceae. Gampi is also of Daphnaceae species, but since very difficult to raise it is necessary to depend upon uncultivated trees. What is more, wild gampi trees are rare, naturally making material expensive. Paper made of gampi resembles sheepskin and calfskin...tough, lustrous and smooth surface. It is naturally proof against both moisture and paper worms. In Europe artists (Rembrandt etc) treasured it as Japan vellum.

Paper made of *mitsumata* has fine texture and is lustrous. Perhaps it can be said that beauty of this paper is rather feminine. Paper made from *kozo* is typical Japanese paper, produced in largest quantities. Altho not so fine in texture as gampi and mitsumata, it is certainly more tough, more waterproof. That is why this paper is generally used for sliding-doors, umbrellas and woodblock prints.

Japanese handmade paper can be extremely varied in character; we can have almost all varieties by mixing like magicians, three materials, *kozo*, *mitsumata*, and *gampi*. It can be soft, hard, fine, rough, thick, thin or anything desired.

Japanese handmade paper is still produced in many provinces in Japan. For instance, Matsue has been long famous for making paper. Paper made in this particular village is famous among connoisseurs both in and out of country as most typical Japanese paper for export. About 40 years ago Mr Eishiro Abe, member of Japan Mingei (Folk Arts) Society, excellent paper manufacturer, began his school by making good use of traditional methods handed down in this village, adding to it his own ideas of size and color tone. There are about 50 varieties.

Since Bernard Leach, English potter who visited us in 1930s, introduced this Iwasaka handmade paper to his native land, it has been exported to various Occidental countries and appreciated by many as notable typical Japanese handmade product.

This paper is highly esteemed for its many wonderful uses; for instance, books (particularly book covers), wallpapers and other interior decoration, letter papers, and many others. (Regular size handmade sheet: 1m x 0.62m, or 39" x 24").

As stated before, this is one stop worth short detour by **cab** (buses take too long, one every other hour). *Abe Eishiro Kinen-kan*, **Memorial Museum** (8:00-17:00, X–mon, ¥500). Museum part of house, still lived in, recommend call ahead to make sure someone home to let you in: ☎(08525)-4-1745 or 4-0303.

Drivers can continue beyond Washi-no-Sato, 7km to town of **HIROSE** (no bus this stretch) for look at *handmade kasuri* weaving. Hirose is one of main kasuri centers on San-In; others also happen to be in generally same area: at Izumo-shi, Yumi-ga-hama on coast between Matsue and Yonago, and Kurayoshi farther up-coast. Best place to see is at **Amano Kon-ya** in middle of town (tiny town, can't miss it). Buses to Hirose from coastal Yasugi and Yonago pass thru lovely **SAGI-NO-YU ONSEN**, hidden backwoods hot spring with only 3 budget inns (*see* next page).

15min bus from Yasugi boasts...
Adachi Museum, (9:00-5:00, ¥1,500) started 1970 by local collector of modern art, surrounded by not-so-modern landscape garden, lovely match.

WHERE TO STAY: Most Japanese prefer large inns of Matsue Onsen, but nondescript place and we recommend older inns in town, or TAMATSUKURI ONSEN.

IN TOWN: Best is lovely 200-year-old **Minami-kan** ☎(0852)-21-5131, spectacular garden; in Kyo-mise district just W of Ohashi bridge, ¥-Sw/2; first in group of old houses along river. Two doors down is similarly old, but cheaper **Akagi-kan** ☎21-4631, ¥-lo-Tw/2. E of Ohashi Bridge is 150-year-old **Ohashi-kan** ☎21-5168, where Hearn stayed; ¥-Sw/2, cheaper rooms in adjacent 'new' wing. Several more ¥-T inns along river here, traditional **Naniwa** ☎21-2835. Along S bank at Lake Shinji is moderate **Tsuru-ya** ☎21-3378; behind which is ¥-B **Young Inn Matsue** ☎22-2000, room only or w/2.

MATSUE ONSEN (on N shore of Lake Shinji), is main hub of local transport with terminus for Ichibata Rail and tour bus stop. Pleasant setting, but unfortunately transformed into 'modern leisure center' of mostly large unsightly ryo-tels which sprang up with onsen water in 1971. But what they lack in structural aesthetics made up for with superb service and giant baths. Best here is **Ichibata Hotel** ☎22-0188; W-style (room only) singles ¥6,000+, doubles and twins from ¥-T, luxurious J-style rooms ¥-Sw/2 up. Worth mentioning are: lovely old **Shohei-kaku** ☎23-8000, ¥-Tw/2; **Naniwa Bekkan** ☎21-4132. Slightly inland on hill is **TENRIN-JI ONSEN** for grand nite view of city below. Fine moderate inn **Taisen-kaku** ☎21-7750, ¥-lo-T+w/2.

If hot baths are your thing, we much prefer pleasant...
TAMATSUKURI ONSEN, 5 stops (30min) JR E of Izumo-shi, 2 stops (12min) from Matsue, one of major hot springs in area. Atmosphere much more pleasant here, 30 inns along quiet sakura-lined Tamayu River in hills 2km S of Lake Shinji. Convenient for excursions around area, many tour buses stop here, local **taxi** office, hourly 10min bus shuttle to JR Tamatsukuri stn, frequent Ichibata local buses to JR Matsue stn (30min) and Matsue Onsen stn (50min) 6:30-20:30. Top ranked is recently modernized old-timer **Choraku-en** ☎(0852)-62-0111, ¥-S-Lw/2, boasts 'largest in Japan' outdoor bath of 150m circumference set in landscape garden, with fresh seafood feasts. Then there is traditional wooden **Seifu-so** ☎62-0031, ¥-S-L, which greets all guests with matcha green tea; all rooms face their garden. Generally same prices are: **Hosei-kan** ☎62-0011; **Minami Bekkan** ☎62-0331, annex to one in Matsue; **Shiraishi-ya** ☎62-0521. Cheapest at ¥-T+ are **Yuraku** ☎62-0211; and old-style **Choshin-tei** ☎62-0221. Budgeteers must head to **SHIN** *(new)*-**TAMATSUKURI ONSEN**, down at Lake Shinji, for Tamatsukuri Kokumin-shukusha **Reiun-so** ☎62-0431, ¥-Bw/2.

Enjoy spacious **outdoor bath** of Choraku-en if not guest **end July** during *Onsen-matsuri* Festival when all inns open their baths free to public.

TAMATSUKURI, known for centuries as hot spring, was famous much earlier as source of one of Three Imperial Regalia—*magatama* Jewel. In legend, it was here that Susano-o received magatama jewel from Ha-akaru-tama, god who dwelt here, which he took up to heaven and presented to his sister Amaterasu as peace offering for earlier mischief.

S end main street is...
TAMATSUKURI JINJA shrine, dedicated to Ha-akaru-tama; Shu-soko **treasure house**, modeled on Yayoi dwelling, in shrine compound has fine collection of magatama and other glass beads excavated from area's tumuli. Phone ahead ☎2-0006 (in Japanese), to be let in; small donation. From Kofun period (250-550AD) to early Heian period, special class of artists called Tama-tsukuri-be, making only magatama, stationed here to supply various nobles with sacred jewels. Archaeological remains of Tamatsukuri-be community lie just E of onsen marked by reconstructed Yayoi period dwelling. Nearby *Izumo Tamatsukuri Shiryo-kan*, **Museum** (9:00-17:00, X-mon and day after hol, ¥200) has magatama and other Kofun period excavated artifacts, tools used to make these jewels. People here still make magatama and other bits of glass or stone jewelry, but for tourists.

Those looking for small 'hidden' baths should head to above mentioned...
SAGI-NO-YU ONSEN with ¥-T inns **Yasugi-en** ☎(08542)-8-6262; **Saginoyu-So** ☎8-6211; and **Chikuyo** ☎8-6231. Further inland is **USHIO ONSEN** 1hr bus (20km S) from Matsue, with 4 ¥-T-S inns; it is also 10min bus from Izumo Daito stn on JR Kisuki Line (30min inland from San-In Main Line Shinji stn). Ushio is one of few places where entire cycle of Izumo-*kagura dances* are performed, **Sep 27-28** at nearby **Suga Jinja** shrine. There is one-inn **IZUMO YUMURA ONSEN**, 30min bus from Kisuki stn (45min from Shinji).

If in this area and driving, circuitous 10km SW of Yumura is...
Sugaya-no-Tatara 'furnace', 16km/sq plot which sand was used to forge steel from early Heian times...sole such remaining site in Japan, no longer used. Best swordsmiths of Japan used this sand for their swords. Edo period furnace-house is preserved here.

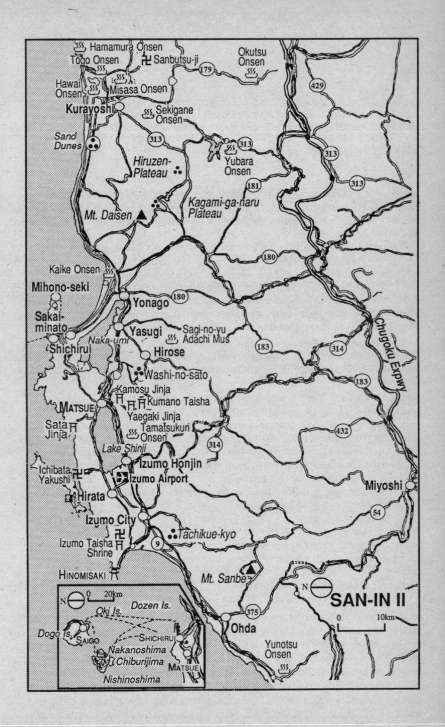

Hamamura Onsen
Togo Onsen
Sanbutsu-ji
Okutsu Onsen
179
429
Hawai Onsen
Misasa Onsen
Kurayoshi
Sekigane Onsen
Sand Dunes
313
313
313
Hiruzen-Plateau
Yubara Onsen
313
181
Kagami-ga-naru Plateau
Mt. Daisen
180
Kaike Onsen
Mihono-seki
Yonago
180
Sakai-minato
Yasugi
Sagi-no-yu
Adachi Mus
183
314
Naka-umi
Shichirui
Hirose
183
Washi-no-sato
Kamosu Jinja
Kumano Taisha
MATSUE
Yaegaki Jinja
Tamatsukuri Onsen
432
Sata Jinja
Lake Shinji
314
Ichibata Yakushi
Izumo Honjin
Izumo Airport
Miyoshi
Hirata
Izumo City
Tachikue-kyo
54
Izumo Taisha Shrine
9
HINOMISAKI
Mt. Sanbe
N
SAN-IN II
N
20km
Dozen Is.
Oki Is.
0   10km
Dogo Is.
SAIGO
SHICHIRUI
Ohda
Nakanoshima
Chiburijima
MATSUE
Yunotsu Onsen
Nishinoshima

Chugoku Expwy
375

MIHO-NO-SEKI 美保の関   DETOUR

TAKEN IN by most people as short tour bus side trip if at all, tho if coming this way is well worth stop.

GETTING THERE: 1hr25min **bus** direct from MATSUE, 20min bus from SAKAI—some direct, others from Ui bus stop across narrow channel, linked by 5min **shuttle boat** from harbor next to stn. **Rail Pass** users with time to spare can JR to YONAGO (45min) and Sakai Branch Line to end (40min; hourly); then 25min bus SAKAI to MIHO-NO-SEKI; (quickest 1hr20min direct bus from JR Matsue stn.) By **car**, leave MATSUE E on Rte431 along N shore of Naka-no-Umi lagoon; or island-hop across it on bridge to SAKAI-MINATO harbor—terminus for ferries to OKI ISLES—whence bridge across to MIHO-NO-SEKI, alias Shimane Peninsula.

We drove circuitous back roads via...
SADA JINJA shrine (7km NW, 30min bus from Matsue): used to be ranked just below Izumo Taisha. Gods also gather here for Oct *Kamiari-zuki,* Month of Gods. *Jinzai-sai Festival,* **Nov 20-25**, features ancient Izumo-kagura dances. Rebuilt 1807, duplicating earlier models, shrine is unusual triple set of *taisha-zukuri* structures.

Drivers go straight N from Sada shrine to dead-end at coast is **Shimane Nuclear Reactor** with PR pavilion open to public.

From Sada Shrine we headed NE, up to N shore (also infrequent buses) to...
MITSU, lovely little fishing village few km beyond which is **Kaga-no Kukedo** seaside caves (55min bus Matsue to Chikuko Iriguchi). **Sightseeing boats** cruise into them daily (unscheduled; leave when people show up) May-Oct, 40min tour. Good beach at Kukedo Point.

4km further along coast at ...
YANAMI is *Rekishi Minzoku Shiryo-kan*, **Folk History Museum** (10:00-17:00, X-sun, hol, ¥100), items cover aspects of fishing village life on land and sea.

Here road cuts N 2km to dead-end lovely rustic fishing village of...
OKIDOMARI at tip of Tago Point; ideal hideaway for romantics, with 4 ¥-B minshuku. Only 3-5 buses daily to here from Matsue; some follow our coastal route (minus Sada shrine), others follow leeward side of Shimane Peninsula, cut across at Tesumi to Kita-ura then backtrack. Check at Okidomari for continuing bus to Miho-no-Seki; some direct, most change at Kita-ura or next stop Nakayama.

Beyond Yanami, coastline cuts S to NOI harbor, whence another nonscheduled **sightseeing boat** (May-Oct) up coast to **7 Caves** of *Taga-no Nanatsu-Ana.*

As coastline levels E again, we come to...
KITA-URA village, with fine sandy beaches and excellent fishing; 30-odd budget minshuku. 9km further on coast SHICHIRUI harbor (1hr bus from Matsue, inland rte) where more ferries to OKI ISLES. Matsue → Shichirui direct about 30km; our rte about 50km—not much distance, but crammed with lots for adventurer with time.

Drivers from Shichirui follow bus road S to Sakai, then to Miho-no-Seki; or continue on local roads along rugged N shore and cut S to few km before...

MIHO-NO-SEKI: 'Just another' fishing village, but we found it relaxing and worth trip out. Narrow cobblestone lanes wind thru houses to mirror-smooth Miho harbor, once major port for official business during Edo period. It even had barrier gate here to inspect all incoming and outgoing vessels—old records indicate average daily turnover of 100 non-fishing boats. And 200-plus 'flower-women' accommodated sailors. Miho was also casting-off point for exiles to Oki Islands which were chosen as suitably isolated in 724AD. Some notables who stayed over at nearby Bukkoku-ji temple for boat out were emperors Go-Toba and Go-Daigo.

MIHO JINJA shrine was another reason for village's fame in days of yore. Sacred spot before advent of formal Shinto, enshrined kami no less venerable than Okuni-nushi, founder of area, and princess Mihotsu-hime, who brought down first rice seeds from heaven. As at Ise, later paternal conquering god not strong enough to displace already entrenched maternal earth goddess, but here both given equal status. Miho's architecture (*Miho-zukuri*) is unique form of taisha-zukuri with paired main halls—L is Okuni-nushi, R is Mihotsu-hime—distinguished by male (pointed) and female (flat) chigi roof cross-beams. Farmers favored Mihotsu-hime, fishermen prayed to Okuni-nushi equating him with Ebisu, one of Buddhist-Shinto 7 lucky gods. God of fortune, Ebisu is shown with giant fish slung over his shoulder—which according to legend, he caught from Chino-gozen Isle just off-shore nearby. He is patron of sea-faring folks. Shrine dates to 1813 remake. *Homutsu-kan,* Museum (¥50, ask to be shown) is veritable treasure trove of rare, ancient instruments offered here over centuries to shrine's music-loving gods. Also in nearby boat storage are collection of various ancient fishing boats, including two sacred *morote-bune* festival boats.

Sacred festival boats once used in...
BUKKOKU-JI temple, (2min walk E of shrine), 5 unusual, simplistic Buddha images in its Dainichi-do hall. Said to be all carved from one tree by 8th century Buddhist Saint Gyoki, to appease spirits of those banished to Oki and who died there.

From temple, half-hour walk thru woods out to...
Jizo-zaki Point and Miho Lighthouse, German-built, 1898. We drove short, scenic Shiokaze (sea-breeze) Line toll road (¥450 r.t.) out to lighthouse, snacked at small coffee shop nearby, housed in equally old W-style stone structure.

· WHERE TO STAY: In MIHO are ¥-B-Tw/2, minshuku ¥-lo-B even newer ones. May and Oct crowded, tho told no problem getting rooms even then, reserve by calling Town Hall, *Machi-yakuba,* ☎(08527)-2-2111. 8 ryokan & 3 minshuku, small, personal, serving superb seafood extravaganzas. You may find yourself invited along on crack-of-dawn fishing excursion with inn owners who all are part of fleet. Or have boat, bait and guide arranged for personal outings; thru inn or Town Hall fishing co-op. Fish caught will be prepared for your meal. Several small but superb restaurants near harbor if you want to try Miho's cuisine without trouble of staying over and waking up early.

BACKTRACKING FROM MIHO
SAKAI gala *Port Festival* (sat, sun closest Jul 20) and down Yumi-ga-hama Peninsula on Rte431 (1hr bus).

Or 35min rail to...
YONAGO, and up Japan Sea Coast. Midway is *Hama Kasuri Mingeikan,* Tie-dye Cloth Museum (9:30-17:00 X-wed, ¥300) grand old building in pine tree grove 10min walk from Wada-misaki Jinja bus stop. Hama-kasuri dyed weave has been made for centuries, museum covers process, samples and kiosk; also collection of old *tansu* chests. Further down curving Yumi-ga-hama beach – 20km stretch of sand and scattered pine trees.

At base of peninsula is...
KAIKE ONSEN, coastal hot springs with fine beach. Relatively new onsen, hot water spring discovered by fisherman in 1900; 20min frequent bus from Yonago stn. 40 inns clustered together, top-ranked of which (¥-Sw/2) are Toko-en ☎(0859)-34-111; Koraku-en ☎22-2236; Kaike Grand ☎33-3531, with several baths including outdoor; Seifu-so ☎22-4141, many large baths; Tsuru-ya ☎22-6181, with top floor observatory-bath; small, old-style inns, top are Hisago-ya Ichibata Hotel ☎22-2248; and Kaicho-en ☎22-2263. Few small inns ¥-Tw/2+; ¥-B at *Kokyo-no-yado* public inns: Kaike Onsen Kaikan ☎33-3671, and Yumi-ga-hama-so ☎22-7476.

Public bath located in Onsen Koen Park with pools, playground, etc, in middle of town, one block E of main bus stop.

Yonago, uninteresting city, but main JR terminal for lines cutting across from Kyoto, Hiroshima, Okayama. **Driving**, 2km E of city is **Fukada tei-en**, oldest garden in San-In area built early 14th cent by Fukada Masanobu as send-off gift to emperor Go-Daigo exiled to Oki Isles.

PERSONAL DATEBOOK: **Apr 14-15**, Katsuda Jinja *Shrine Festival*, kids' mikoshi parade framed by cherry blossoms at their height; adults sit under them to view, helped by much sake and food. Foreigners passing by always invited—not as oddity but as honored guest to share goodies with and entertain. **1st weekend Aug**, gala *summer fete* with regional folk dances and fireworks.

YASUGI, (8km W of Yonago), is passed thru if coming direct from Matsue on Rte9. **Driving**, just before stn, on Rte9, is *Wako Kinen-kan,* **Museum** (9:00-16:00, free), with tools and explanations of *tatara*, ancient method of getting iron from sand. Thru Meiji era, Izumo's back-country was one of main iron-producing centers and Yasugi was prosperous port shipping iron out. Town is still known for its fine cutlery. Sign of its former prosperity can be seen in lovely red brick W-style library on next corner, built 1905 as Yasugi branch of San-In Bank. Some turn-of-century homes of rich merchants remain in area near bank. Yasugi's humorous *Yasugi-bushi* dance, depicting people scooping up slippery eels of Naka-no-Umi lagoon, was mostly unheard of outside this area until early Meiji when local farmer's daughter, O-kei, made it more slapstick and took show on road to Tokyo's Asakusa entertainment district, making it overnite sensation. Performed here **Aug 14-17** for *Tsuki-no-wa festival*.

Yasugi is terminal for buses to backwoods Sagi-no-yu Onsen, and...
KIYOMIZU-DERA temple, 20min bus from stn (also 20min from Yonago stn), in hills SE of Yasugi. Built 597 AD to house 11-faced Kannon statue, it was grandest temple in San-In until burned down by soldiers in 13th century. Rebuilt later to present complex of 20-odd halls hidden in woods. *Homutsu-kan*, **treasure house** (¥300) at entrance has numerous 7th-13th century statues saved from flames. **Honbo-shoin** head priests' quarters and library is fine early Edo period example. Nearby **Renjo-in** pavilion, superb garden with tea house; ¥500 to see Honbo-shoin, Renjo-in, and have tea in garden. Giant *Nehan-do* **main hall** dates early 15th century; way behind which is 250-year-old 3-tiered pagoda (¥100 to ascend).

WHERE TO STAY: Five small inns, ¥-B+w/2, all serve authentic *shojin-ryori* vegetarian priests' meals—also served at tea shop restaurant in temple complex, from ¥1,500 for simple meal. Park around temple offers fine view from hilltop observatory of Naka-no-Umi lagoon, Yumi-ga-hama to Miho Peninsula, and soaring...

MT DAISEN (written *O-yama*, great mountain, pronounce arbitrarily) tallest peak in San-In at 1738m (6,050 ft) literally swarms with climbers, campers in summer, skiiers in winter. Best route up is from Yonago to monastery complex of **DAISEN-JI** temple, 55min (10 daily r.t.) bus. Extinct volcano, partially exploded crater rim forms lesser peaks around main, beautiful mix of smooth curves and ragged peaks. Entire mountain was held sacred—off-limits to women—inner sanctum of **OGAMI-YAMA** (Great God Mt) **JINJA** shrine near Yonago. Temple built 717-723AD as main sanctuary of Tendai sect. Its monks were as powerful fighting as force as were religiously strong, and Daisen complex grew in size to rival Kyoto's Hiei-zan monasteries. Army of 300 fighting monks descended on Kyoto late 11th century to ensure favorable court action, were also major contribution to emperor Go-Daigo's return to power after fleeing Oki exile—which led to fall of Minamoto-Hojo military dynasty, Kamakura. Tokugawa Ieyasu finally got rid of fighting monks by bribing them with 3,000 koku of land in return for laying down weapons. Daisen continued to flourish by cornering area's horse and cattle trade, but several fires over centuries reduced its size to present 10 halls (1/4th size of its heyday). Mountain ascetics of Daisen followed mix of Shinto and Buddhism, but Meiji forced split of two religions also led to decay of temple. 10min walk up behind temple is shrine's **Oku-no-In** (inner sanctuary), built 1605 as protector of temple complex. 25min walk to R of temple is **Amida-do** pavilion, oldest structure here dating to 12th century.

Daisen is now typical Japanese tourist attraction, with countless gift shops, inns, restaurants clustered at entry—but more pleasant than most, especially for hiker.

WHERE TO STAY: Lodgings cheap, many *Shukubo*, **temple inns**, where serve authentic *shojin-ryori*; regular inns boast Ghengis Khan Mongolian barbecue. Lunch at either shukubo or ryokan; shojin-ryori at former (from ¥3,000), Ghengis Khan at latter (from ¥1,500). Shukubo top buy ¥-Bw/2; ryokan range ¥-Tw/2; Kokuminshukusha ¥-Bw/2. Arrange thru **Kanko-annai**, 150m L from bus stop. Some numbers: Shukubo: **Domyo-in** ☎(0859)-52-2038; **Rikan-in** ☎52-2050; **Renjo-in** ☎52-2506; **Seiko-an** ☎52-2303. Ryokan: top ranked **Hotel Daisen** ☎52-2111, **Hakuun-so** ☎52-2331; cheaper **Toyama** ☎52-2431; **Miura-ya** ☎52-2031; **Setsuka-so** ☎52-2411 and others. Dozen minshuku, and budget Youth Hostel near **Kanko-annai**.

Interesting **gifts** are clay *karasu-tengu* goblin-crow bells (¥500+) mythical creature often associated with fighting monks.

Hikers get good maps at **Kanko-annai**; all trails well posted. Official climbing season starts 1st sat June; nite before 5,000 youths with torches parade up from temple via shrine to summit and back, in prayer for safety on this mountain. Numerous short **hikes** around Daisen area; most popular easy route from Ogamiyama to top along crater rim and back via Amida-do takes 4hrs. From summit 2hr trail down SE face to **Kagami-ga-naru Plateau** whence two 2hr hiking routes or infrequent bus to **Hiruzen Plateau**, another popular hiking area with numerous ¥-B inns, campsites. Several ski-grounds both Daisen and Hiruzen, better at Daisen: Nakanohara & Daisen Kokusai, 20 lifts between two.

Drivers can circle counter-clockwise around Mt Daisen, 3km to join **Daisen Kogen Line scenic toll** road (10km), then cut N to Kagami-ganaru (5km) and Hiruzen Daisen Skyline toll road (8km) to Hiruzen. From Hiruzen, E about 12km to Domegi hamlet at junction Rte313.

S on Rte313 leads to...
YUBARA ONSEN, lovely riverside giant outdoor baths (*see* BACKWOODS OKAYAMA, p636) and down to Okayama-Kurashiki on Inland Sea coast; or Chugoku Expressway for rush drive to Himeji, Kobe, Kyoto. 2-3 express buses daily Okayama → Yubara → Hiruzen.

We head N on Rte313 which puts us back on Japan Sea coast at...
KURAYOSHI, *shukuba* or lodging-post town during Edo period, fair-sized section of old merchant district remains. Frequent 10min bus from San-In Main Line Kurayoshi stn; town has own stn but branch line to it from Kurayoshi was discontinued 1984. Also 3 daily JTB express bus links with Osaka's Benten-cho (6hrs). Bus lets off in town, just off Rte313, which cross S to photogenic **old town** lined with hoary old storehouses along Tamagawa river, many of which are still-working sake and soy sauce breweries. Wooded Utsubuki Park hill was site of 14th cent fortress; popular for spring sakura and autumn maple viewing.

At its base is...
Kurayoshi Hakubutsu-kan, **Museum** (9:00-17:00 X-mon, day after hol, ¥100) with items excavated from area's sites, and old art; farm tools, kasuri weaving looms and other folkcraft tools in nearby modern white **Folk Museum** (same ticket to enter). 15min walk to hilltop HASE-DERA temple, built high on stilts like famous Nara counterpart, with fine collection of *ema-e* votive horse painting plaques (you see these commonly in most shrine outbuildings nationwide) from early Heian period on.

Kurayoshi is another of San-In's production centers of **kasuri** indigo-dyed ikat-weave; characteristic designs of *ka-cho san-sui* 'flower-bird, mountain-water' motifs. Best to buy is **Kurayoshi-Kasuri Tenji-sokubai-sho**, outlet for local artists. Items range from coin purses and address books (¥800) to placemats (¥2,000), *noren* door curtains (¥4,000); full-length bolts run from minimum ¥40,000 way up.

Kurayoshi offers pleasant lodgings in old section of town, range ¥-Tw/2 but we chose to stay at one of numerous hot springs in area...
TOGO ONSEN and **HAWAI ONSEN** on shores of lovely little Lake Togo-ko 3km up-coast from Kurayoshi; Togo Onsen is at next stop Matsuzaki stn, Hawai is 20min (hourly) bus from Kurayoshi, or 10min cross-lake boat (hourly) from Togo. Direct rail from Yonago 1hr express, from Matsue 1hr25min.

Freshwater lake full of fish, deliciously plump eels, served at inn dinners Apr-Nov. All around lake are little huts on stilts, with huge square net suspended just under water level used to scoop up fish. **Cruise** around lake on boats (2-daily, 30min, ¥400), or rent any time of year (¥5,000 up to 10 people). Inns at two hot springs are along lakeshore; most at Hawai hang over lake so you can fish right from your inn. Hawai has 20-odd inns, older Togo 12—including fine old-fashioned **Eisei-kan** with outdoor bath ☎(0858)-32-0111. Most are ¥-Sw/2, some ¥-Tw/2. Kokumin-shukusha **Suimei-so** ☎32-0411, near Matsuzaki stn ¥-B+w/2, eel dinner bit extra; Youth Hostel **Konpo-ji temple.**

Hawai is 2km from **Sand dune** *beaches which stretch few km; lovely old village...*
HASHITSU (Rte9 passes thru) is something out of old Japan, with thatched-roof houses and feudal era storehouses. **July 20,** *crazy dance* at Hawai, said to originate 400 years ago, when Hawai Castle burned down by attackers and few defenders left alive went crazy and danced out of flames.

We decided to head back inland for overnite, to...
SEKIGANE ONSEN, radium bath in quiet mountain vale with 10 small inns. 20min frequent bus (8km) from Kurayoshi (same bus from JR stn) back towards Hiruzen Plateau on Rte313, our choice after checking others out. We stayed at superb **Onsei-ro** ☎(0858)-45-3311, outdoor bath, ¥-Tw/2; also with outdoor bath **Torikai** ☎45-2121. Less expensive inns ¥-Bw/2; Kokumin-shukusha **Higashi-Daisen-so** ☎45-2211. Campground at Seishonen Ryoko-mura (Youth Village). Sekigane was once major shukuba town on Sakashu-kaido pedestrian hiway.

Oct 7th *Autumn Festival,* procession, palanquin with lord, attendants and samurai.

MISASA ONSEN 7km SE of Kurayoshi town, frequent 20min bus from JR Kurayoshi; 3 daily JR buses link with central Tsuyama via Okutsu Onsen (*see* OKAYAMA BACKWOODS). Perhaps best known radium hot spring in Japan, celebrate element's discoverer **Aug 3-4** *Curie Festival* presided by French Consul, dances, folk theater, fireworks both days at **Curie Park**, where statue of Madame. *Hana-yu Festival* **May 5-8** climaxes 8th nite with giant tug-o-war using 80m long rope; winning side gets good luck for year. Misasa in mountain river valley, but more crowded (40 inns all price ranges) with people come to cure nerves or arthritis; even have onsen hospital for therapy. What attracted us to drive thru in morning was its **riverside bath,** which must be nice at nite, but during day people enter, untypically, with bathing suits as it is right alongside road.

15min bus onward from Misasa, 25min from Kurayoshi stn, is Mt. Mitoku...

SANBUTSU-JI temple, its numerous halls snaking up rugged mountainside. Founded 7th century by Enno-gyoja, founder of yamabushi mountain
ascetics, as training and meditation center. 2 centuries later saint Jigaku
built temple to house images of Amida, Shaka, Dainichi Buddhas, thus its
name Sanbutsu-ji 'Three-Buddha Temple'. 300m up steps to *Hondo* **main
hall**, rough trail from behind to top of mountain past several precariously
built halls to **Oku-no-In** sanctuary built on stilts under rock overhang.
Fantastic scenery, but only for healthy, steep 2hrs round-trip.

Drivers continue past Sanbutsu-ji temple, rejoin coast at...

HAMAMURA ONSEN, (15km, 3 stops JR, from Matsuzaki). Tiny hot spring
epitomizes this part San-In coast as short walk from rolling sand dunes of
Hakuto kaigan beach. **Aug 6**, ancient dance *kaigara-bushi* depicts back-
breaking work of wives digging clams. In summer, *ama* women dive just
off Nagao-misaki Point to E. Only 10 inns here, half are ¥-Tw/2 while best ¥-lo-S.
Of latter, recommended are: modern **Hama-no-Ie** ☎(0857)-82-0321, with outdoor bath,
indoor heated onsen pool; or for more traditional atmosphere, **Tabako-ya** ☎82-0211,
outdoor & panorama baths.

TILT: Our madcap drive thru Izumo-Matsue covered all, but took only two+ days
(helped having fast car): early AM Izumo Taisha → Ichibata Yakushi→ Matsue for lunch
(sightseeing around castle) and Fudoki-no-Oka, → nite at Tamatsukuri. **Day 2**: Back
roads along Shimane Peninsula → lunch at Miho-no-Seki, → down Yumi-ga-hama →
up Daisen, around on toll roads (1hr) → Kurayoshi and nite at Sekigane onsen. **Day 3**:
quick stop Sanbutsu-ji, were thru Tottori (only 17km from Hamamura) by noon.

But before continuing up coast, let us take short jaunt out to...

OKI ISLANDS 隠岐の島

PROPERLY OKI-NO-KUNI, 'Oki-nation', four main islands and over 180
mostly uninhabited islets for total surface area of 350km² set 40-80km
offshore in Japan Sea. Furthest out to sea is largest **Dogo** (Back Island)
which with 20,000 people makes up almost 2/3rds total area and population.
Other main isles clump together 10km SW—Nakanoshima, Nishinoshima
and Chiburishima, collectively called **Do-zen** (Front Island). Beautiful
scenery and little else—for those with much time or passing thru San-In 2nd
or 3rd time, and who speak at least enough Japanese to get around, or with
Japanese traveling companion. Dogo much more popular, slowly suffering
fate of too many other new frontiers of Japanese tourism—all comforts of
Tokyo to ensure pleasant stay in primitive Japan. Still,...nice. But if out this
far, recommend smaller islands of Do-zen—especially Chiburi.

Excavations indicate Jomon man lived here from around 4,000BC, advancing into Yayoi almost at same time as mainland Japan. By time of
Yamato kingdom, Oki was its own kingdom only nominally ruled by Yamato court—not because strong, but because so far out. In 724, court decided
it great place to ship undesireables and Oki became home to many over-
ambitious nobles. Until Edo period, reserved solely for nobles or others of
high rank, and life here was not too harsh, albeit dull. During those 9 centuries over 4,000 noblemen, mostly from Kyoto, were exiled here. Local
dialect still uses many archaic medieval words of pre-Tokugawa Kyoto. At
beginning of anti-Tokugawa rebellion in 1867, declared independence based
on policy of *Sonno-joi*, 'revere emperor, expel barbarians'—actual nation
51 days till Shogunal contingent arrived to crush revolt, wrecked all 58
temples and decapitated stone jizos and other images, rubble still much in
evidence in temple yards.

GETTING THERE: Several flights daily to Dogo originate OSAKA: one direct (1hr), another via MATSUE & 3rd via IZUMO, both 2hrs; 1x-daily via Izumo, ¥15,370. 25min bus from Oki airstrip to main town of Saigo. Travel by **ferry** more pleasant and not much longer when taking into account ground time. And much cheaper: Special 1st class, about ¥6,000, or about 1/3rd airfare; with prices ranging ¥4,800 1st class, ¥3,200 special 2nd, down to ¥2,500 for all-in-big-hall 2nd. **Boats** between DOGO–DO-ZEN cost half that of mainland-islands runs. Ferry crossings 2hr30min to 3hrs direct to Dogo or Do-zen, 4-5hrs to Dogo via Do-zen. Mainland ports are SAKAI at tip of Yumi-ga-hama, and SHICHIRUI on windward side of Shimane Peninsula. Ports on islands are SAIGO (Dogo), KURUI (Chiburijima), URAGO and BEPPU (Nishinoshima), AMA and HISHIURA (Nakanoshima). Ferries run 2x-daily between Shichirui and islands, one between Sakai and islands. 3 different ferry boats run. Use schedule below as guide only, check:

Spring & Autumn (3/13-7/16, 8/18-10/31): **A.** Saigo (8:00) → Beppu (dep 9:30) → Ama (dep 9:55) → Kurui (dep 10:30) → Sakai (arr 13:05, dep 13:55) → Beppu (arr 16:45) → Ama (arr 17:10) → Saigo (arr 18:20). **B.** Shichirui (9:00) → Saigo (arr 11:30, dep 12:00) → Beppu → Ama → Urago → Shichirui (arr 18:30). **C.** Shichirui (9:30) → Kurui (arr 11:40) → Urago (arr 12:15) → Ama (arr 13:10) → Saigo (arr 14:30, dep 15:30) → Shichirui (arr 18:05). Times may vary with tides.

Summer (7/17-8/17): **A.** Sakai (7:10) → Kurui → Beppu → Saigo (arr 13:35, ret dep 14:05) → Beppu → Sakai (arr 20:00). **B.** Shichirui (8:50) → Saigo (arr 13:50, dep 14:10) Shichirui (arr 19:30). **C.** Shichirui (9:15) → Urago → Ama → Saigo (arr 13:50 ret dep 14:10) → Ama → Urago → Kurui → Shichirui (arr 19:00).

Winter (11/1-3/12): Similar to Spring-Autumn, but unpredictable weather, so check. Safer to check all scheds for changes or weather; can have Matsue stn Kanko-annai or Travel Center check, or call (in Jap) Oki Kisen Lines ☎(08512)-2-1122.

New high-speed passenger-only **hydrofoil** or **hovercraft** from Sakai to most Oki ports; 1-2x-daily, ¥4,910 mainland-islands, ¥2,230 inter-island: Sakai-minato (16:40) → Saigo (18:32) → Hishiura (19:19) → Beppu (19:70).

GETTING AROUND: In addition to above boat runs, two local lines ply between four main isles 1-2x-daily all year w/ extra runs summer. On islands infrequent **buses** on Dogo, Nakanoshima and Nishinoshima. **Tour bus** takes in main sites in few hours: **Basic course** Saigo → Tamawakasu Jinja → Mizuwakasu Jinja → Nakamura → Saigo; variations incl **sightseeing boats** Nakamura to Shirashima Isles just off N Point and return Nakamura, or all way to Saigo via Jodo-ga-Ura Point (basic bus-only tours via N Point observatory views Shirashima from atop sheer cliffs of Shirashima Pt). Prices average ¥5,000; 3-5x-daily. Various **boat tours** around Do-zen Isles; 7-10x-daily, only 4/1-10/31. All tours thru **Kanko-annai** at Saigo or Urago piers. Rushed or missed your bus for ferry? No problem, each town or village has small taxi stand (10-15% cheaper than mainland). More to island pace is to **rent bike** (¥1,200/2hrs, ¥3,200/day) or **scooter** at Saigo (tho most Dogo is hilly, distances far), Nakanoshima, Nishinoshima; do smallest Chiburi afoot or hitch on sporadic local traffic.

WHERE TO STAY: Most popular (comfortable) with Japanese tourists is well-equipped Saigo town with modern 9-storey W-style **Oki Plaza Hotel** ☎(08512)-2-0111, twin or double only, ¥-S+w/2. Dozens ryokan range in style from full W- to full J- and price ¥-B+w/2. Other villages on DOGO: Tsumamura (SW coast), Gokamura (NW), Fusemura (NE), much smaller and more pleasant, each have 1-3 small, budget but excellent family-run inns. Even cheaper minshuku scattered all over island; campsites at every swimming beach. Most of Fusemura's inns concentrated at Nakamura, with fine beach, pier for boats to N shore and to Saigo. Nakanoshima and Nishinoshima islands' main towns have several mostly ¥-B-¥-T rate ryokans and dozens of minshuku, with campsites at more isolated beaches. Top of 140m-tall Kinkoji-zan hill Nakanoshima is ¥-B mountain hut. Chiburishima main village of Chiburi-mura (near Kurui port) has 3 budget ryokan, Garet stayed at **Hino-de Ryokan** ☎(08514)-8-2350, ¥-Tw/2; 2 dozen budget minshuku, mostly at Chiburi-mura but 1 or 2 at each of other 5 small hamlets around island. Campsite at base of 325m-high Mt Akahage.

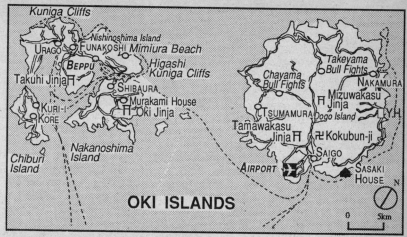

OKI ISLANDS

Some sites you will come across are...

DOGO: TAMAWAKASU JINJA shrine, 3km (10min bus) W of Saigo, oldest and main shrine of Oki. Giant 2,000-year-old cryptomeria tree there said planted by shrine's first priest. His descendants all Oki family head priests ever since. Site sacred 2,000 years ago (mid-Yayoi), but doubtful if actual shrine was there until at least Kofun period (250-550AD) centuries later. No one sure when present structure first built, but scholars place it sometime soon after 8th century for architecture (called *Oki-zukuri*) incorporates mix of Izumo *Taisha-zukuri* and Nara *Kasuga-zukuri* styles. Latter probably introduced after isles used for exiles in early 8th century. Nearby was site of Yamato period center of government, and several small kofun.

KOKUBUN-JI temple 20min bus N of Saigo, first built early 8th century; present hall within past 100 years, only stone foundation of original remains in back. Emperor Go-Daigo settled after exiled here 1332, until escape year later to topple Kamakura military government. You may notice there are no old temples left on any Oki Islands; all rebuilt in past century because of 1868 Oki Rebellion. Edo officials here, supported by 3,000-plus locals created own short-lived republic, antiforeign and antimodern in nature, embraced Shinto as law, persecuted nonrecanting Buddhists, destroying almost all trace of Buddhism from Islands. Movement was crushed two months later by contingent of samurai from Matsue.

MIZUWAKASU JINJA shrine, (30min bus beyond Kokubun-ji), similar in age and style to Tamawakasu Jinja.

Near it is...
Folk History Museum, *Oki Kyodo-kan* (9:00-17:00, ¥200) in 2-storey W-style building built 1889 as Town Office. Displays range from Jomon, Yayoi, Kofun period artifacts, old maps, records, to fishing and farming tools and fine display of costumes used in Islands' festival dances.

6km NE of Saigo, 30min bus up coast towards Nakamura beach is...
Sasaki Family House (9:00-17:00, 8:00-18:00 summer, ¥200). Oldest private house on Oki, built 1792 for Sasaki, village headman. Doubling as regional 'office', three gates used according to visitor's rank; one for Edo officials, one for other village heads, third for villagers. Inside is museum of life in pre-Meiji days, complete with tools, records and everyday household items.

DO-ZEN NISHINOSHIMA Isle is best known for spectacular cliffs towering over sea, best along N shore. 260m-high cliffs stretch 7km along W half KUNIGA Kaigan coast; E half, **Higashi Kuniga Kaigan**, is 15km of lesser cliffs. Midway along Higashi Kuniga at gap in cliffs is **Mimi-ura beach** and campsite; another similarly located Kuniga.

3rd between them at...
Funakoshi, narrowest point on isle where fishing boats were portered across to avoid long journey around isle. 1915, 335m-long canal dug here; 1964 expanded from original 3.5m to 12m width. Kuniga and Funakoshi reached by bus, Mimi-ura 10min cab from Beppu port or 3km hike. S end of Nishinoshima is 452m-tall Mt Takuhi-zan with 1,000-year-old TAKUHI JINJA shrine at summit built under giant rock overhang. Beautiful shrine is guardian of seafarers, long covered halls winding up to main hall. Local lore has it emperor Go-Toba en route to exile was lost at sea, mysterious light emanating from shrine drew his boat to port; thus its name *Takuhi-zan* 'Burning Mountain'. 45min hike from Hashi hamlet which 15min boat from Urago port. Highest mountain of Do-zen islands, superb view of all. SE base of Takuhi-zan has **seaside cave** where Buddhist Saint Mongaku did his time on Oki, banished here by Minamoto Wataru in 1205. Pardoned by Minamoto Yoritomo, Minamoto Yoriie later exiled Mongaku to Sado Island. He made it back to Kyoto, only to be sent back to Oki by emperor Go-Toba. Few years later, Go-Toba joined him here, exiled by Minamoto. Cave has torii in front; only way here is to **rent boat** from Urago.

NAKANOSHIMA Island is where Go-Toba spent his exile—1221 till his death in 1239.

He lived at ...
GENPUKU-JI temple which burned in anti-Buddhist blitz of 1868. Go-Toba's cremated ashes kept nearby in walled compound with torii in front. 5min walk to OKI JINJA shrine (10min bus from Hishiura port), built 1939 to commemorate 700th year of Go-Toba's death.

Nearby...
Rekishi Minzoku Shiryo-kan, Museum (9:00-17:00, Apr-Oct, ¥250) has some of his personal belongings.

5min other direction from shrine is...
House of Murakami Sukekuro, local headman who took care of Go-Toba. Every first son has since then taken name Sukekuro, still take care of emperor's burial place. They have small **museum** (8:00-17:00, ¥200) with some more of Go-Toba's belongings, gifts from him; also few items left by other notables they took under their wing.

15min bus further from shrine is...
Akiya Kaigan coast with small cliffs, at break in which is fine sandy beach with clear water, campsite.

CHIBURISHIMA, tiny (only 1,075 people), is our favorite hideaway here, literally nothing to see but nature. Kurui port across narrow neck of land from main village Kori. 325m-tall grassy Mt Akahage (with campsite) 2hr hike from Kori at W end of isle; one of few places left on Oki where they do traditional rotation of crops, once common site in less fertile soil of Oki. Now, most available land used to graze cattle and horses, including shaggy local breed. W shore is **Chibu Aka-kabe**, Red Cliffs of Chibu, soaring cliffs here stretch for over 1km ranging 50-200m high. Of various striking colors (vivid as struck by setting sun); best seen from **rented boat**, but grand view from coastal trail up Mt Akahage.

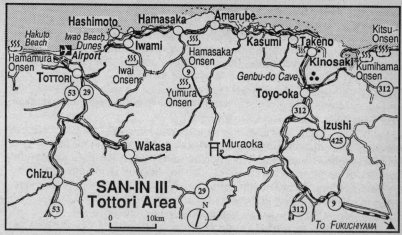

SAN-IN III
Tottori Area

0   10km
N

To Fukuchiyama

PERSONAL DATEBOOK: Oki known for bloodless bull-fighting, or bull-sumo, similar to what we saw at Shikoku's Uwajima and on Okinawa. Started over 750 years ago by emperor Go-Toba; here, it was mostly spectator sport to amuse wealthy court exiles, unlike most other places where to rank healthy bulls (*see* UWAJIMA). *Spring Tournament* **May 5** (sometimes **Apr 29**), *Summer Tournament* **Aug 15**, championship rounds **Sep 1** and **Oct 13**. All held on Dogo: **Sept** at Chayama Ushitsuki-jo, **Oct** Takeyama Ushitsuki-jo, others at Nijiyama Togyu-jo near Kokubun-ji temple. Finals free, others ¥2,500 for 4hr tournament. Daily shows for summer tourists at Kanko Ushitsuki-jo near Mizuwaka Shrine, **Jul 1 to Aug 31**, ¥500 for 1 or 2 matches which tour buses visit. **Apr 21** *Renge E-no-mai*, courtly dances of Nara Period performed at Kokubun-ji temple, Dogo, following special Buddhist memorial rites. **Jun 5** *Uma-ire Shinji Fete* ritual offering of horse to shrine, Tamawakasu Jinja, Dogo. **Jul 28-9** odd years only (1991, '93, '95 etc) Yurahime Shrine *Grand Festival*, Yura hamlet, Nishinoshima Island, sole boat festival on isles. At nite (19:00-21:00) sacred boat bears spirit of shrine, circles bay, followed by other boats with revellers on them; lucky few get to go on shrine boat. **Jul 1 thru Oct 31**, *Sazae-gari* top-shell gathering, along Kuniga Kaigan coast. Take it in as part of special **boat tour** (¥1,500, rsve) and spend over hour on beach eating all sazae you can. **Sep 15**, odd years only, Muromachi Period *Dengaku rice planting dances* on Nishinoshima. Dances and plantings alternate bet Mita Hachiman-gu Shrine (1989, '93, '97) and Hiyoshi Jinja Shrine (1991, '95, '99).

Oki is also treasure trove of *minyo*, folk dance-and-song. Minyo also done **sat**, **sun**, **hols** May thru Oct, and **daily Jul-Aug**, at Oki Kanko Meisan Tourist Center at Saigo (from 20:30, ¥300).

ADVENTURING UP-COAST
Continuing up Japan Sea coast from Kurayoshi area baths and Hama-mura, you pass thru great orchards of *nashi*, apple-like Japanese pear. This area of Japan Sea Coast is nashi capital, and these delicious fruit are in season late summer thru fall. Best are *niju-seiki* '20th-century' nashi which can get to grapefruit-size. Crunchy like apples, but more liquid than juiciest pears—best thirst-quenchers during hot summer. Unfortunately for summer travelers, prices are high until second-half of September.

TOTTORI CITY (137km or 85 miles E of Matsue, 113km from Yonago), offers little to interest general traveler except lovely countryside seen from train or car window. Beyond Tottori coastline is fascinating even for Japan. Tottori is famous for its nearby giant sand dunes.

Driving up coastal Rte9, we recommend Rte9 bypass of city and Rte178 which straight to dunes. By **rail** you must come to town and bus out, in which case:

5min walk N of stn to Tottori...

Folkcraft Art Museum, *Mingei Bijutsukan*, (10:00:17:00 X-wed, ¥310) in classic old storehouse. Superb collection of mostly old folkcrafts from Tottori area, tho also some newer items, and crafts from rest of Japan, China, Korea and West. Six-sided building L front of museum is **Jizo-do**, housing 147 jizo figures dedicated to souls of lost children. To museum R in similar building, is **Takumi Kogei-ten** Folk-arts store where local artists make and sell their crafts; also **restaurant** of local dishes such as belly-busting *kanisuki* (crab sukiyaki) of meaty *matsuba-gani* crabs, and *unagi* (eel).

With bit more time to blow, head to N end of town, 2km (5min bus, cab basic mtr) to castle remains and **Jinpu-kaku Museum** (9:00-17:00 X-mon, ¥150) in lovely 2-storey wood W-style building, 1907, are all sorts of items from feudal days, some from Meiji, Taisho. In back is lovely landscaped strolling garden. Near it is modern **Pref Museum**, *Kenritsu Hakubutsu*, (9:00-17:00 X-mon, ¥150) with more feudal era and ancient artifacts.

From here, 1hr city-recommended walking tour winds SE to...

OUCHIDANI JINJA shrine, built 1650 as Toshogu, enshrining shogun Tokugawa Ieyasu; **KANNON-IN** temple, built same year, with superb Kobori Enshu-style **garden** with lake (8:00-18:00, ¥500 incl matcha green tea); then W back to stn.

PERSONAL DATEBOOK: **Lunar Mar 3**, *Nagashi-bina* 'floating hina doll' Festival, washi paper dolls of man and woman are placed in straw circular boat, float downstream to sea, carrying with them ills meant for people. Set loose in Koromo River between 10:00-12:00, from Wakasa bridge E of stn; also from Mochigase village 20km upstream. **Aug 15-16**, *Shanshan Matsuri* feudal era parade thru town.

TOTTORI SAND DUNES, (20min frequent bus from stn), is 'Sahara' of Japan where one can walk on desert sand, pay ¥500 to sit astride camel to have instant photo snapped, or slightly less to freeze for birdie under papier-maché palm trees, head poked thru peek-hole in cardboard-silhouette Arab. **Camel rides** ¥2,000, or **horsecart** ¥1,500. There is nearby *Kodomo-no-kuni*, **Children's Land** (¥410) with field athletics obstacle course, **planetarium** and **sand dune pavilion** which explains formation of dunes. All of this, along with inns and restaurants lining rear of dunes...

What most Japanese miss are actual dunes they came to see, which stretch 16km from Hamamura Onsen's **Hakuto Kaigan** beach, 1-2km wide, sheer sand walls rising up 92m from ocean below. Running jump and roll to bottom takes minutes but tiring trek back up, worthwhile for ex-cellent *uncrowded* beach at bottom. Summer occasional sand-skiiers fly down slopes. Japanese also miss mile-walk beyond along unsoiled coast to beaches of **Iwato Kaigan** E end of dunes, where in spring and summer fishermen doing *tai-ami* fishing ride out in pairs of boats linked by great drag net, ride surf back to beach boats and have entire village join in whole-day task hauling in great crescent-shaped fish trap—we often lend hand.

From nearby Iwato or Hosokawa bus stops it is 25min back to Tottori stn, or if you do stay, rather than inns at dunes, keep going along San-In Kaigan coast to any of lovely little fishing villages, all with fine beaches, budget inns.

Warning drivers: just beyond Hosokawa Rte178 cuts off L to curve downhill from Rte9...

Which then heads inland to Kyoto, via...

YUMURA ONSEN mountain hot springs, (25min bus from up-coast Hamasaka). One of more popular spas this side of Tottori (next to up-coast Kinosaki), it is nonetheless quiet in spite of 2 dozen mostly large inns (few rooms despite size). Some old inns have rebuilt bigger, boasting **outdoor baths** and several indoor ones, such as New **Tomiya** ☎(07969)-2-0001, and New **Nishima** ☎2-1101. Then there are still small traditional inns like **Miyoshiya** ☎2-1211, **Izu-moya** ☎2-1126, and **Tomiya** ☎2-0275. Most ¥-T-Sw/2; others ¥-Bw/2. Some few ¥-B minshuku.

Middle of town original spring still spouts out 470 liters per minute; locals use it to boil vegetables and do their laundry, both common site early morning.

PERSONAL DATEBOOK: **Jun 1** *Onsen Festival* pays tribute to hot spring founder Saint Jigaku, followed by giant tug-o-war between two halves of townspeople.

Back along coast, our favorite, where Garet and friends went annually is...
IWAMI sometimes called Uradome. Center of **Uradome Kaigan** 2km stretch of fine beach with Makidani campsite E end in scraggly pine tree grove, and over 150 minshuku around. W end of beach is tiny Uradome village with 2 fine ¥-B ryokan **Seifu-kan** and **Kancho-ro**. Uradome is more convenient for **bus**, on frequent Tottori → dunes → Iwami stn, and hourly Iwami → Uradome → Tajiri routes. Makidani campsite area is harder to bus to (occasional Iwami to Hamasaka stn run) but better beach. Nite horizon lit up by lights of squid boats. To its E is Haneo-misaki Point at which tip is **Ryujin-do Dragon Gods' Cave**, 150m deep is largest seaside cave this part of San-In. 20min walk on path just before tunnel E of campsite; some energetic friends swam 2km along point to it. Half our stays were in minshuku **Morikawa** ☎(08577)-2-0667 at Iwami-cho Makidani 530 near Makidani-*kaigan* beach; other half at campsite officially open summer only, but OK rest of year—basic food (bread, eggs, milk) at nearby store up big street perpendicular to beachfront Rte178 near campsite, first L along stream at bottom of hill and few min walk to store on L. For bigger selection of food, we continue (usually hitch) 2km down big street to Iwami village and stn-area shops.

Just beyond village is Rte9 which we hitched down 3km to...
IWAI ONSEN, with large public bath (¥120 dip) or inn baths when possible–some let you use off-season for small fee. 10min bus from Iwami stn continuation some Tottori → dunes buses; miss last return bus can call cabs at Iwami stn. With only half-dozen small ryokan, Iwai quieter and inns fraction cheaper than Yumura. Top inns, each with outdoor bath, ¥-Tw/2: **Akashi-ya** ☎(0857)-72-1515 & **Iwai-ya** ☎72-1525. Others ¥1,-2,000 less.

Iwai Onsen—Uradome beach is combination we always find relaxing even in summer (tho July-Aug bit crowded on beach). Good for adventurers with some Japanese under their belt looking for few quiet days of camping or budget inns in rural Japan; but can get by with almost no Japanese and much gestures as people here used to foreigners (popular Kobe-Osaka-Kyoto expatriates' escape). Other than loitering at beach, going to dunes (bus from Uradome Kaigan Iriguchi S end of Uradome village, or hitch), or exploring other good beaches at Higashi-hama (other side of Haneo-misaki), you can...

View wild coast on 50min r.t. **sightseeing boat** (9x-daily Mar-Nov, ¥920) from **IWAMOTO**, 2km W of Uradome on Rte178 (1 stop dune/Tottori-bound bus). Tiny boat chugs down Urase River 1km to **AJIRO** harbor then E along craggy coast with arches and grottoes. 1km pier to Ajiro (2min bus), known for co-op fish market, from where scenic seaside trail 3km to **TAJIRI**, 1km on to Uradome.

Many more sailings from...
HAMASAKA, 15km E of Iwami 15min hourly **rail** or 30min hourly **bus** along winding, up-and-down seaside Rte178. Some talk of reinstating Iwamoto-Hamasaka **boat** (2hr) in 'near future'—not yet. Hamasaka's pier 10min walk from stn, 5 **tours** up E, or down coast range 40min ¥600 to 90min ¥1,500, all year from 9:00–16:00 dep when 5 or more passengers collect.

Or 1x-daily 90min ¥1,500 voyage E along fantastic craggy shore to...
KASUMI, with more similarly priced and scheduled cruises. HAMASAKA → KASUMI run deps 9:55, or when more than 10 psgrs. Driving from Hamamura, Rte178 misses coast, but as you rejoin it, you pass under **Amarube Bridge**, Japan's first tressle

rail bridge (1909-1911, 309m long and 41m high, one end in tunnel), greatest engineering feat in constructing San-In rail line. Passes over Amarube hamlet, said to have been established by vanquished, fugitive Heike late 12th century. From Kasumi road mostly hugs coast; then 10km on, scenic **Tajima Skyline toll** road (¥400) zips 18.8km to Hiyoriyama. Sometimes 1hr boat from Kasumi to **HIYORIYAMA**, from where 5km (10min infrequent bus) to...

Or Takano whence 10min rail to...

KINOSAKI, onsen-town since 593AD at which **express** stops on San-In rail line to KYOTO, 3hrs, or to OSAKA 3hr30min. Zentan bus runs 2 express buses daily from each KOBE and OSAKA, 3hr50min. Rte178 cuts inland from W end Tajima Skyline to Toyo-oka city, from where Rte312, 10km downstream to Kinosaki.

WHERE TO STAY: Quiet, rural atmosphere in spite of its popularity. Over 100 small inns on narrow tree-lined river; starting rates ¥-T+ most riverside inns, few (mostly in back streets) start ¥-Bw/2. **Hotel Blue Kinosaki** and **Nishimuraya Grand** have few W-rooms. All serve belly-busting portions of crab sukiyaki autumn thru spring. Walk around and choose inn, or book thru stn-front **Ryokan Kumi-ai** (Co-op)—just tell them price. Closest ¥-B lodging is **Genbu-do Kokumin-shukusha**, 5km (5min rail, 10min bus) towards Toyo-oka. Poled across river in wood skiff from bus and rail stn to basaltic **Genbu-do Cavern**, 35m high 70m wide entry (only goes back 10m) in giant rock wall. Just S is smaller **Seiryu-do cave**.

We drove thru Kinosaki too early to bed down but still got great hot bath to relax muscles from driving. 7 public baths here, working upstream from stn: **Jizo-yu**, behind it smallest **Sato-no-yu, Yanagi-yu**, largest **Ichi-no-yu, Gosho-no-yu**, only one on other side of river is **Mandala-yu**. Furthest up and loveliest **Ko-no-yu** is also oldest. All baths ¥200 for passer-by, guest free with tickets from your inn. Jizo, Ichi, and Gosho bath hours 6:30-23:00 (from 7:00 winter), Sato and Madala baths 16:00-24:00, Yanagi and Ko baths 15:00-23:30 (popular Ko-no-yu from 7:00 sunday). Behind Mandala-yu, 600-year-old **GOKURAKU-JI** temple with fine garden. Near Ko-no-yu is **ropeway** up to Taishi-zan peak; halfway up (3min ropeway, or 20min trek up steep stone steps) is **ONSEN-JI** temple, built 8th century by emperor Shomu (built Nara Great Buddha), with numerous buddha images, paintings in **museum** (¥150). From summit, trail circles down to mid of onsen strip.

PERSONAL DATEBOOK: *Danjiri Festival*, **Oct 14-15**, start front of Ichi-no-yu bath; two teams race up either side of river pulling danjiri festival floats.

DETOUR: From Kinosaki, San-In rail line cuts inland to KYOTO via **TOYO-OKA** (Miyazu branch line follows coast), **FUKUCHIYAMA** (whence Fukuchiyama rail line branches off to OSAKA via Sasayama-guchi for feudal town **SASAYAMA,** *see* p615), IZUSHI, 15km S of Toyo-oka (30min frequent bus) lovely rural town and worthy detour stop if driving down to Kyoto. **AYABE** whence Ayabe rail cuts back to seacoast via **KURODANI** paper-making village—(30min bus from Ayabe or 10min from 2-down Umezako stn), to **KAMEOKA**; latter with Ayabe main centers of Oomoto-kyo religion. Between them, on rail line SONOBE, few daily buses from/to Sasayama. From Kameoka (p456) do last 15km to Kyoto's **ARASHIYAMA** shooting 2hrs down **Hozu river rapids** on shallow boats (¥3,000): 6x-daily summer, 1-3 other (water level permitting); call ☎(07712)-2-5846; to finish with evening of cormorant fishing (*see* p454).

Oomoto's annual month-long **Summer Seminar of Traditional Japanese Arts** grand experience, study under top teachers, live in Oomoto castle grounds; trips to Ayabe, Kurodani, Japan Sea, Kyoto (*see* LEARNING ABOUT JAPAN p88).

Continuing up seacoast, rail 2 stops to TOYO-OKA where change to Miyazu line, 10km on hit sea again at **KUMIHAMA** bay—almost lake, linked to ocean by narrow channel. Sand-bar separating bay from sea called *Ko-Ama-no-Hashi*, **Small Bridge-to-Heaven**, smaller version unfairly compared to Ama-no-Hashidate just up-coast. At opening is small village of many budget lodgings, good beaches on windward side, 20min walk from local Tango-Kanno stn. Tango-Kanno and one before Kumihama have several budget inns, summer-only boat service across to Ko-Ama-no-Hashi. 1.2km E of Tango-

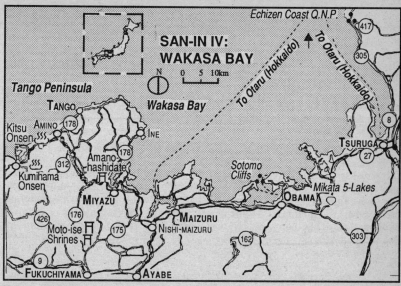

Kanno, cab basic meter, is rustic one-inn **KUMIHAMA ONSEN** with huge rock outdoor bath at **Yumoto-kan** ☎(07728)-3-1071, ¥-Tw/2. 4km up-coast is **KITSU ONSEN**, few small inns in fields; nearby sand dunes covered with flowers of local tulip farm.

Beyond Kitsu, rail and road cuts across base of...
TANGO PENINSULA around which coast runs Rte178. Scenic coastline dotted with tiny villages with budget inns, excellent beaches and campsites; 8-10x-daily buses circle it, running between Amino and Miyazu.

Tip is great fishing village of...
INE, (1hr 40min bus 48km from Amino, 50min 30km from Miyazu) natural harbor around which gaily decorated festival float-boats run **Jul 27-28** *Yasaka Festival*—perfect place to hide out, or visit if just to see old 2-storey waterside houses with boats docking 1st floor, people living 2nd. Water crystal clear, food delicious, several ¥-B inns; summer cruises along coast.

From here, we head down to Miyazu, site of..
AMA-NO-HASHIDATE 天の橋立   HEAVEN BRIDGE
FAMED as one of *San-kei* 'Three Great Sights' (with Miyajima & Matsushima), said to have been named in allusion to Ama-no-Uki-Hashi (Floating Bridge of Heaven) on which creator-pair, Izanagi and Izanami, stood when they stirred primeval brine with jeweled spear, dribbles from which formed isles of Japan. 'Bridge' is narrow sand spit ranging 15 to 150m width, some 3km long enclosing lagoon over 5km long. Grove of pine trees extends length of bridge, E shore is swimming beach. S end near Ama-no-Hashidate stn (10min bus from Miyazu) is **chairlift** to **Monju** viewing spot, from which it is screwy custom to turn one's back to scene, bend over and view it upside down between your legs, (no mooning). *It impresses us not,* but has left pleasant memories for some friends; worth it if passing thru (Miyazu is fun) but *not worth special detour*. Similar viewing spot (but higher up) at N end **Kasamatsu Ichinomiya**, 1hr walk across bridge; buses from Ine stop. Calm, mirror-like Iwatake lagoon lies on W, wind-flecked Miyazu Bay contrasts E, Bridge of Heaven dividing two like delicate green thread. Every 30min (14-17x-daily), **sightseeing boat** makes 15min crossing from Ama-no-Hashidate's Monju to Kasayama Ichinomiya.

3-6 runs am & pm start from...

MIYAZU, lovely old town with some sights to spend 1-2hrs meandering.

Across river from stn is...

Saint John's Cathederal, 1897, some fine stained-glass. Many old **merchant houses** remain, such as Imamura cloth dealers (300m W), and Fukuroya soy sauce brewers.

PERSONAL DATEBOOK: **Aug 16** is one of top 3 *Toro-nagashi* lantern-floating festivals, tens of thousands of lighted paper lanterns set out to sea at nite, fireworks bursting above.

*Local road from Miyazu heads S inland to join Rte175 to **Fukuchiyama**, just before which junction is...*

MOTO-ISE JINGU Grand Shrine. Like Ise, this has *naiku* and *geku*, inner and outer shrines, but here not regularly rebuilt so have much more ancient air about them. As at Ise, *Naiku* enshrines Yamato kingdom's Amaterasu sun goddess; *Geku* (4km S) enshrines Toyo-uke-hime goddess of grain— earlier indigenous deity too powerful to be fully replaced by chief deity of Yamato or Wa invaders. Some claim this is original site from which Ise moved 1500-ish years ago?

Road from Fukuchiyama follows San-In rail line to Ayabe to become Rte27, joining Rte9 (to Kyoto) before Kameoka.

Rte27 N from Ayabe (parallels Maizuru rail) rejoins seacoast at bustling port town...

NISHIMAIZURU, often visited by Russian ships, site of Hitachi shipyards and long distance **ferries** to Hokkaido's Otaru. Usual way out of Ama-no-Hashidate is rail via MAIZURU, down along lovely Yuragawa River to Ayabe San-In line.

Those with time to spare, continue up-coast 80km via: OBAMA → TSURUGA (also has ferry to **Otaru**), rail to N tip of Lake Biwa and steamer to Otsu or other points on Lake Biwa (*see* KYOTO, p.496).

Another alternative, and main reason for our continuing up Japan Sea coast after IZUMO-MATSUE, is 160km beyond from Obama on Hokuriku Main Line to centuries-old Dutch-designed city of **KANAZAWA**, (*follows*). Leaving our Iwami beach inn early AM bath stop Kinosaki, and driving along coast with stop at Ama-no-Hashidate, we made it up to Kanazawa late afternoon; save much driving time up relatively uninteresting stretch of coast by taking Hokuriku Expressway from TSURUGA (can go S to Kyoto via Maibara where join Meishin Expwy) to KANAZAWA.

Some stops worthy for time-insensible adventurer between Nishi-Maizuru and Tsuruga follow, as we venture into another historic stronghold on Japan's backside.

*...wonderful little people
who have renewed,
for Europe and America,
the whole idea of Taste.*
        —Henry James, 1893

HOKURIKU 北陸
NORTHERN LANDS

DOZEN kilometers east of Maizuru, we cross out of Kyoto Prefecture to
enter Fukui Prefecture and thus, officially, into 'northern land' made up of
Fukui, Ishikawa and Toyama prefectures. Our main interest here is
Ishikawa Pref, with lovely feudal KANAZAWA city and rugged NOTO Peninsula. Latter juts into Japan Sea at its warm Tsugaru Current, from which
Noto benefits in less biting cold (rarely below freezing) despite much snow.
Tho only 10km from coast, Kanazawa, conversely, lies at base of Central
Japan Alps and its winters compare to that of Tohoku Snow Country cities
further up-coast like Niigata. Popular saying of Kanazawa, which applies
equally to all Hokuriku is *bento wasuretemo kasa wasureruna* "even if you
forget your lunch, don't forget your umbrella". With long snowy winter,
rainy summer and sometimes drizzly spring and autumn, umbrella is invaluable. Most popular time to visit is July-August when rooms, especially
at good inns, need be pre-booked; but we prefer April-May or September-
October for cool weather and nature's vivid colors.

Adventurer can easily spend week getting to really see Hokuriku (even just Ishikawa),
but few first-time visitors have such time to spare, especially with more to see in central
Japan's Takayama (*follows*), or continuing up to Tohoku and Hokkaido. 4-5 days are
enough with local rail and bus for quick full coverage; we did it 3 days by car. Some
stops en route, from Ama-no-Hashidate, are: Obama and MIKATA-GOKO on Wakasa Bay;
leisurely drive up Echizen Kaigan coastline to MIKUNI; or direct Hokuriku Expwy to
KANAZAWA. There are craft centers around Takefu town; inland of Fukui City is grand
temple complex EIHEI-JI, from where alternate back entry to Kanazawa on public
transport (rail and bus) or drive, via Katsuyama to SHIRAMINE VILLAGE (*see* Hakusan,
below). Japanese tourists flying into Kanazawa's Komatsu airport often spend 1st nite at
one of KAGA ONSEN cluster's hot springs, but we find them little too built up, and rather
recommend drive, bus or cab from airport to rural TSURUGI ONSEN between Shiramine
and Kanazawa.

OBAMA, another pleasant fishing town (which are abundant along Japan
Sea coast) best known for its many traditional arts and *Kokuho-meguri* National Treasure-circuit of ancient temples nearby. 20min walk from stn at W end
of town is Sancho-machi ex-red light district; many of its beautiful old houses
now traditional restaurants. We passed thru just after light rain, sun breaking thru clouds to glisten off wet *bengara* 'thousand-slat' fronts of old
houses (which early Westerners called 'cages' to display women within).
Walking down empty streets, someone suddenly began to pluck shamisen;
we looked up to see stately old kimono-clad woman sitting at her second
floor window leaning out over wood railing, and we felt as if walking thru
century-old scene until small child joined in with her modern recorder,
which brought hearty laugh from woman when she saw us watching her.
Short exchange—fine day it was turning out, when mini-truck zooming
around corner brought us out of our reverie.

Sotomo, scenic cliffs of Uchitomi Peninsula 1hr r.t. **sightseeing boat** (hourly 9:00-16:00 Apr-Oct; hourly 10:00-15:00 Mar & Nov; 13:00 Jan, Feb, Dec; ¥2,000) from Obama harbor, 1km N of stn.

Kokuho-meguri National Treasure Circuit thru ancient temples & shrines spread among hills and vales of Higashi (East) Obama. Not for everyone, those into old Buddhist art will find treasure trove. Temples built during 8th century (each rebuilt once 13-16th cent), art dates to at latest 12th cent. Area, Wakasa, was long haven for religions, just far enough away from politics of Nara and Kyoto. Obama folk go to great pains to keep temples (¥200 each to see) in atmosphere free of usual commercial tourism.

GETTING AROUND: Local bus service inconvenient; adventurous can spend full day on **rental bikes** from Higashi Obama stn Cycle Center. Choice of 3 JR-run **tour buses** to take in all or part (free with some JR shuyu-ken regional passes, Rail Pass; 10% off on others): B-Course: OBAMA stn (9:00) → HAGAJI → ENSHOJI → MYORAKUJI → TADAJI → OBAMA stn (11:30). C-Course: OBAMA stn (12:45) → JINGUJI → MANTOKUJI → KOKUBUNJI → MYOTSUJI → Menoukojo workshop → Obama stn (16:20). A-Course: combo of B and C, 9:00-15:25. All run daily 3/22-11/30 and sun thru Nov; B is ¥820, C ¥760, A ¥1,580, none include adm fees to temples, ¥800 extra for B or C, ¥1,600 for A. **Cab tours** run about ¥8,800 (18x-mtr) for 2hrs; allows you to also see WAKASA-HIKO JINJA and WAKASA-HIME JINJA shrines; and pause long enough for shutterbugs to snap lovely old thatched-roof houses around here.

Obama's best known craft tradition *Wakasa-nuri* lacquerware, started late 16th cent, made and sold at over 100 mom'n pop shops in town, popular and cheap are lacquered chopsticks. *Wakasa-menou* polished and carved agates have been made here for over 250 years; colorful stones used to come right from beach here, but depleted this century, now imported from Brazil; sold in town. Bus tours A and C visit Menou workshop in Higashi Obama. *Wakasa-washi* handmade paper items also popular, especially *wa-gasa*, traditional Japanese oiled-paper umbrellas; best at **Kasada Wagasa-ten** —down leftmost street from stn 270m to 1st L and down 80m on L.

MIKATA-GOKO, Mikata Five Lakes, between Obama and Tsuruga (15km either way as crow flies), less famous than Ama-no-Hashidate, but we feel much lovelier. Five Lakes together make up one squigly mass of water, each barely separated from other, connecting channels between equally squigly strips of land; whole thing can be considered lagoon, as smallest Lake Hiruga-ko (only 900m^2) is mere 100m from sea with small opening to it. Hiruga is in turn linked to adjacent largest Lake Suigetsu-ko (4.1km^2); also connected to Suigetsu by narrow canal is long narrow Lake Kugushi-ko, 3rd in size. Hanging off east side of Suigetsu is 2nd smallest Suga-ko, raise eels; spit of land almost dividing two has longer arm cutting both off from furthest back Mikata-ko, with narrow channel. Mikata is fresh water, Hiruga salt, others mixed, from saltiest: Kugushi, Suigetsu, Suga.

Best vantage point is 400m high...
Mt. Baijo-dake, at NE corner of lakes; looking down, Hiruga on L with Kugushi behind, Suigetsu and Suga straight ahead, Mikata far R. In distance beyond Hiruga is purple suggestion of sacred Mt Hakusan, even further beyond and stretching off R to horizon are Central Japan Alps on clear day. Looking L, Sea of Japan fades over horizon, with Kanazawa and Noto Peninsula hiding behind Gozen Point; R is Sotomo Cliffs. Entire stretch of rocky coast from Tottori to Gozen Point is called Wakasa Kaigan coast, inside giant Wakasa Bay. Behind, Tsunegami Peninsula juts into Wakasa Bay; each of its isolated E coast coves is sandy beach, **glass-bottom sightseeing boats** (1hr, ¥750, late May-early Oct) at tip Tsunegami (3-4 buses daily 3/21-11/15 from

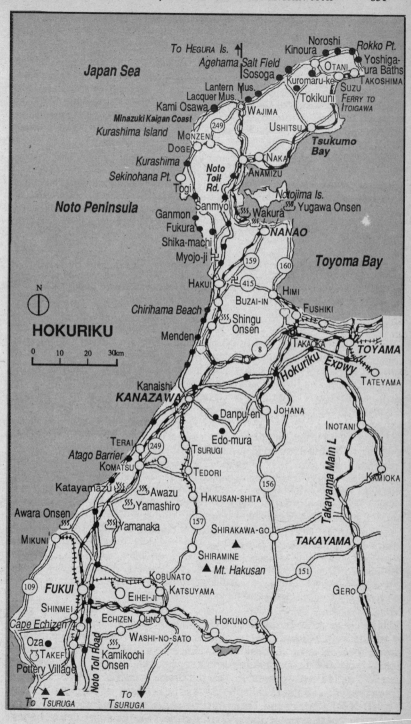

Mikata stn). Buses to Baijo-dake from Mikata stn (35min) and next Mihama stn (25min); buses to Tsunegami stop at Kaisan where snaking 2km trail up Baijo-dake; and scenic 11km Rainbow Line toll road (¥900), which from Kaisan winds to Baijo-dake with alternating grand views of lakes and sea, down other side for similar views, passing between Suigetsu and Hiruga, Hiruga and Kugushi, to end near **Lake Center** for sightseeing jet-boat around lakes, 35min (Mar-Nov every 30min 9:00-16:00; Dec-Feb hourly 10:00-14:00, ¥970). Shuttleboats Mikata-Sanbashi (10min)-Lake Center (20min): dep L.C. 9:30, 15:00; Mikata 10:10, 15:40. Take in Baijo-dake view and lake cruise on compacted **bus tours**: Tsuruga stn (12:00) → cruise lakes → Baijodake → Obama → Myotsuji → Jingu-ji → Lacquerware workshop → Tsuruga stn (17:50), ¥3,870 All run daily 3/21-11/23.

WHERE TO STAY: Lodgings around lakes concentrated around Lake Center, Mikata and Mihama stns; recommend avoid Lake Center as sometimes too crowded to enjoy serene lake, but location is ideal, with beaches nearby. Best located, and budget, is isolated Kokumin-shukusha **Baijo Lodge**, ☎(0770)-47-1234, at lakeside base of Baijo-dake, near Kaisan. Another prime one is old-style **Kogakujima-so** ☎45-0255, small wooden inn along canal between Suigetsu and Kugushi lakes, ¥-Tw/2. Good inns near Lake Center (if not crowded): **Hirose Ryokan** ☎32-1123, and **Kaiko-en** ☎32-0430, both from ¥-Tw/2.

EN ROUTE KANAZAWA

FROM TSURUGA it is 130km to Kanazawa: 90min ltd exp rail, about same on Hokuriku Expwy, twice as long on local roads Rte8 or Rte365.

Halfway up is...
FUKUI, uninteresting city, but base for side-trip to spectacular...

EIHEI-JI Monastery Complex: 30min exp Kyofuku Private Rail from stn adjacent to JR Fukui. If interested in temples or Japanese architecture, Eihei-ji is **must**, at least for day visit if not 2-requisite overnites. Built 1244 by priest Dogen of Zen Soto sect as meditation center, after tradition of Chinese ch'an master T'ienT'ung to set monastery in mountains away from secular concerns—escape Kyoto politics of anti-Zen Mt Hiei monks. In 1372 emperor Go-Enyu of renegade Northern Dynasty declared Eihei-ji #1 Soto temple, then it burned and declined until late 1500s from which time it has continued to grow as main Zen meditation center in Japan, presently with over 15,000 sub-temples nationwide (Tokyo branch *Betsu-in* holds zazen mon 9-12 also 5-6 daily by permit, nr Roppongi subway at 2-21-14 Nishi Azabu, Minato-ku 106; ☎(03)-3400-5232). 330,000m^2 wooded complex full of spectacular pavilions (over 70) linked by vast network of covered hallways. Over 300 priests here full time, dozens of acolytes in training or meditation all times—probably Japan's most stringent. Within ancient complex is fully self-sufficient generator, even elevator in one hall.

Anyone **welcome** to participate in **zazen**, from absolute minimum two overnites (if rising at 3:30 is 'overnite') to 1 week— ✍ in Japanese 10 days prior: **Sanzenkai Eiheiji**, Eiheiji-cho Yoshida-gun, Fukui-ken 910-12; or ☎(0776)-63-3102; longer by subsequent arrangement. Participants eat *shojin-ryori*; ¥-Bw/2.

21km S of Fukui...
TAKEFU, center of fertile Takefu Basin, designated area capital in 645 to be political and economic center of Echizen. Under Tokugawa rule, power moved to Kanazawa and Takefu became minor town. Now agricultural center of 60,000, also famed for its cutlery for past 700 years, loaded with ancient temples, but we come to visit **handicraft centers** outside of town:

20min bus E to Okamoto...
WASHI-NO-SATO, center of production of *washi* (handmade so-called 'rice' paper) since earliest times. Local lore says early 6th century emperor Keitai was shown how to 'sift' paper by local goddess here. During Edo era

Okamoto papermakers got patronage of local daimyo and prospered. Even now, over 600 families make paper old way here, everything from letter paper to fusuma paper doors. Wander freely among houses here, or visit... **Washi-no-Sato Kaikan** (9:00-16:00, ¥150) to see it done and explained.

30min bus W of town in Miyazaki village is...
ECHIZEN TOGEI-MURA, Pottery Village, home of Echizen-yaki pottery developed during 10th century. Here too, you can wander among scattered family workshops or visit central **Fukui-ken Togei-kan** (pref. pottery hall), 10min walk from Togei-mura Iriguchi stop. Modern workshop-museum displays samples from earliest times to present. Call ahead ☎(0778)-32-2174 to take part in twice daily (9:00 & 13:00) workshop to make your own, and at same time, reserve for **tea ceremony** in special teahouse.

2km SE is grand...
Aiki-ke house, built early 18th century; call ahead ☎32-2215 to arrange entry. N 2km is hot spring village of **ODA**, with **TSURUGI JINJA** shrine in which is enshrined copy of Susano-o's sword. Unifier ODA Nobunaga was born in this village, and prayed here for strength, as did Tokugawa Ieyasu.

KOWADA, suburbs of Sabae town, (1 stop JR, 4km N of Takefu), center of *Echizen-shikki* lacquerware. See various artists carving wood or painting on lacquer. Upstream from Kowada, 14km; 35min bus from Nishi-Sabae stn, is rustic one-inn **KAMI-KOCHI ONSEN**. Nishi-Sabae stn (of Kyofuku Private Rail) is 5min walk from JR Sabae stn; this line runs between Takefu and Fukui.

2 stops from Nishi-Sabae is Shinmei stn, 3min walk from which is...
SHINMEI JINJA shrine which has in its grounds **Uryu-ke** house, oldest folk house in Fukui prefecture.

Back route to Kanazawa from Eihei-ji is via...
KATSUYAMA, quaint rural town at last stop of Kyofuku Private Rail Echizen Main Line (change at Higashi Furuichi if from Eihei-ji). 2-3 buses daily (May-Nov) from Katsuyama to Shiramine Village.

4km E of town (25min bus) is...
HAKUSAN JINJA shrine built as Heisen-ji temple in 720 by St Taicho, founder of Hakusan shinto sect. Main Fukui area trailhead for pilgrims climbing Mt Hakusan (old trail is now Rte157 to Shiramine Village and Kanazawa), was once grand complex of 48 shrines and 36 temple halls with 6,000 priests. Burned 1574 by Ikko-shu forces, rebuilt in its present condition in 1583. In Meiji split of Shinto and Buddhism, all Buddhist traces were eradicated and made shrine.

Nearby sprawling...
Landscape garden at **GENJO-IN** temple, once part of Hakusan shrine.

Two rail stops before Katsuyama is...
KOBUNATO KAMABURO ONSEN with large vat-like baths, good view, cheap lodgings along Kuzuryu River.

PERSONAL DATEBOOK: Last weekend **Feb** (or 24-25), *Katsuyama Sagicho Festival*, whole town decorated with painted lanterns and dozen tall drum towers for drummers and musicians fielded by each section of town. Best 2nd nite 6-10pm; drummers on Chuo-dori street and burning of decorations with huge bonfires from 10pm along Kuzuryu River.

WHERE NEXT: From EIHEI-JI: frequent 55min buses to AWARA ONSEN near coast; if direct to Kanazawa best rail back to Fukui and JR up. **Drivers** on Hokuriku Expwy exit Kita-Fukui I.C. E 5km to Rte364 where S 8km to Eihei-ji. Leaving temple stay on Rte364 which curves NW to Maruoka I.C.; can stay on Rte364 to Awara Onsen and 3km S on coast Rte305 to **MIKUNI**, lovely rustic village worth stop if avoiding Hokuriku Expwy to drive Rte305 along beautiful Echizen coastline.

5-20km SW of Komatsu...

KAGA ONSEN CLUSTER 加賀温泉

FOUR MAIN HOT SPRINGS cater to luxury travelers, plus several small backwoods hot springs. Big 4 onsen of Awazu, Katayamazu, Yamashiro and Yamanaka were once quiet back-country spas until advent of large modern hotels in last decade. Much of their old-town air remains, but new high-rise hotels distract, as do crowds lured to them (Aug-Nov crowded, Apr-July so-so, Dec-Mar nice and quiet). Also expensive nowadays, inns ¥-hi-T-Sw/2, while best run luxury rates ¥-L-LLw/2. No ¥-B accomodations of any sort, tho hitchhikers or campers will find cheap, excellent **public baths** at all 4. We much prefer hot springs around Kanazawa and Hakusan, but you may want to judge yourself. All are easily reached on frequent buses on various lines (2-4x hourly each):

GETTING THERE: Komatsu stn → (takes 20min to) Awazu stn → (10min) Awazu Onsen → (5min) Nata-dera temple → (10min) Yamashiro Onsen; Kaga Onsen stn → (10min) Yamashiro Onsen → (15min) Yamanaka Onsen; Kaga Onsen stn → (10min) Katayamazu Onsen; Yamashiro Onsen → (12min) Iburibashi stn → (10min) Katayamazu Onsen; Daijoji stn → (20min) Yamanaka Onsen; Daijoji stn → (20min) Yamashiro Onsen; hourly are Kaga Onsen stn → (10min) Yamashiro Onsen; few daily between each and Kanazawa; 2-3x-daily link all to down-coast Awara Onsen.

8km S of Komatsu, is...
AWAZU ONSEN, oldest (found by St Taicho 718AD) and most pleasant of all; mountains flank 3 sides of this quiet farm area. Dozen ¥-S inns centered around **So-no-Yu public bath** (8:00-21:00 X-8th, 18th, 28th monthly, ¥200); best is **Hoshi** ☎ (0761)-65-1111, owner Hoshi Zengoro is 46th-generation innkeeper.

Nearby...
NATA-DERA temple (Important Cultural Asset) founded 717AD by St Taicho who carved 1000-handed Kannon into rock here, now kept in 500-year-old main hall built on stilts. Rustic pagoda, bell-tower, and priests' living quarters and kitchen with fine **moss garden** behind. Open daily 8:30-16:30, ¥300; ¥200 extra for garden, priests' quarters and **Tsumon-kaku**, grand merchant's house moved here from Hakusan area and now serving as temple's treasure hall.

KATAYAMAZU ONSEN sole spa seaside of rail line, discovered 1653 by Maeda Toshiaki while falcon hunting. 1877, became commoners' hot spring on shores of Shibayama-gata lagoon. Recently, it has become 'leisure center' and over 30 inns (most ¥-S but large) crowd lagoon where fishermen try to compete for space with all sorts of recreational craft. Castle-like **public bath** here is open 6:00-22:00 daily, ¥250.

YAMASHIRO ONSEN is also pleasant rural town with most large new inns on outer fringe of town. Most grand old inns (some have new annexes) are around **Yo-dono public bath** house, section of town that is particularly handsome with old, slat-front houses. Best are: **Shiragane-ya** ☎(07617)-7-0025, and **Ara-ya** ☎7-0010, both not quite luxury rates. Family oriented **swimming** and bathing complex opened outside town, ¥500 weekdays, double weekends.

About 2km N of town is...
Kitsune Yama Kofun, 5th century burial mound, which you can enter by calling ahead to Kaga City Education Bureau, ☎7-1111. Identity of occupant not known, but it escaped looting and provided treasure trove of jewels, mirrors and weaponry.

3km E of town is...
Ho-o-zan Yoko-ana Kofun, cluster of 7th century hillside horizontal burial pits. Since first one discovered in 1922, over 70 excavated; whole hill now park with trails leading to graves, some with small exhibit rooms of unearthed items.

YAMANAKA ONSEN, (6km S of Yamashiro), is another quiet mountain-ringed town (almost all rebuilt from scratch after 1931 fire), with 40 mostly small inns along Daijoji River's Kakusen-kei Gorge. S end of gorge is beautiful wood Korigi Bridge, with trail up E bank. Center of town is lovely **Kiku-no-Yu public bath** house. Site of original Kutani-ware kilns and known for its many post-Meiji Kutani potters, but now better known for its *Yamanaka-shikki* lacquerware, made by several hundred family workshops around town. Co-operative workshop, **Yamanaka-shikki Kogei-danchi**, halfway between Yamanaka and Yamashiro. Recently, imitations of plastic or synthetic 'lacquer' flooding market, but easily distinguished from real works by their cheaper prices; set of 4-5 real bowls with lids start from at least ¥5,000.

Some smaller, alternate hot springs for adventurer...
KAGA HACHIMAN ONSEN, 15min bus (bound for Ogoya), 4km E of Komatsu, has few budget inns. **AKAHO-DANI ONSEN**, 20min bus (to Nakada-shima), 7km SE of Komatsu, is isolated one-inn hot spring along secondary road en route to Mt Hakusan's Tedori (see below). **KIBA ONSEN**, between Komatsu and Awazu Onsen, is one-inn onsen at Kibagata lagoon; 20min bus to Kiba Danchi from Komatsu stn. **AKASE ONSEN**, 40min bus S of Komatsu to Osugi near Akase Dam, has some quiet old inns; nearby soaring thatch-roof gassho-zukuri farm house is *Hokkoku Minzoku-kan*, **Folk Museum**, packed with over 50,000 items from this area.

PERSONAL DATEBOOK: **May 13-16**, *Otabi Matsuri*, joint festival of Uhashi Jinja and Hiyoshi Jinja shrines, Komatsu city, one of Hokuriku's top three fetes. From 13th afternoon to 16th evening children's troupe of actors enact **kabuki** plays upon huge floats. Two of these theaters on wheels roll thruout city. Best 15th from 17:00-21:00: mikoshi procession with about 50 child groups of gaily costumed lion dancers; 30 floats. **Jun 4-5**, *Shobu-yu* (Iris bath) Festival, Yamashiro Onsen, celebrates Boy's Day (by modified calendar) with traditional iris leaves put into baths this day. Huge mikoshi piled high with iris leaves circulates and people pull these off. Huge outdoor stage—many drummers, dancing geisha. Town decked out with red lanterns, red bunting. **Jul 20-22** *Yu-no-matsuri*, Katayamazu Onsen, daimyo procession, shishi-mai lion dances and geisha dances day time with grand fireworks over lagoon at nite. **Aug 3rd sat** *Awazu Onsen Festival* features Osshobe-odori dance to heady beat of huge drums. **Sep 22-23**, *Koikoi-matsuri*, yukata-clad dancers wend thru town followed by mikoshi of three rice bales, 22nd evening to past midnite; both days, regular and slightly defective lacquerware sold thruout town at cut-rate.

TILT: Like Hagi for San-In, Kanazawa is gem of Hokuriku, also with much else nearby to see. We recommend at least full day for KANAZAWA; *second* for sidetrips to coastal KANAISHI and inland YUWAKU ONSEN (good overnite) with EDO-MURA DANPU-RO cultural villages. *Third* day quick circle of Noto Peninsula; but it is area to spend time in, for which: day 2, cut out KANAISHI; morning at EDO-MURA and DANPU-RO and out to Noto's tip WAJIMA (rail, bus); or better yet, SOSOGI 45min bus from Wajima or Ushitsu. Several fine 1-2 day bus tours make Noto easy to do, and overniters can choose finest inns, for comfort suiting even most selective travelers.

Long-time favorite of Japanese tourists, Hokuriku has only recently been put on itineraries of foreign tourists who want more than classic KAMAKURA-KYOTO-NARA tour. It is off beaten track, but not difficult to get to or around. Two main gateways to Hokuriku are: uninteresting, modern industrial TOYAMA, and its diametric opposite...

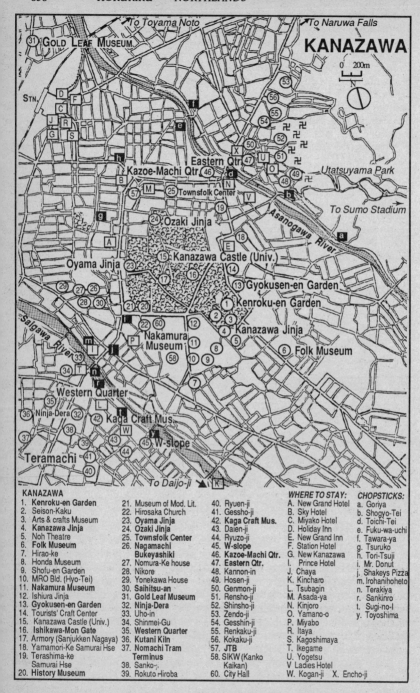

KANAZAWA

*Were works of art placed in a directly human context
in popular esteem, they would have much wider appeal
than they can have when pigeon-hole theories of art
win general acceptance.* —John Dewey, *Art as Experience*

KANAZAWA 金沢
MARSHES OF GOLD

CITY IDEAL for strolling (with its maze-like narrow streets, drivers should abandon wheels at inn or central Kenroku-en and castle area parking lots). Untouched by war, it retains flavor of antiquity in physical isolation which contributes to recreating aura of times past. Mecca of culture and education since early 1600s, Kanazawa is one of those rare places where modernity complements, rather than engulfs, antiquity.

Rich agrarian Kaga (feudal Ishikawa Pref included Kaga, Noto fiefs) was ruled by rich farmer-lords with private armies, one of whom, Togashi clan, gained power and was made governor by Kamakura shogun. Lords over richest rice lands, Togashi were benevolent rulers for feudal Japan. But 150 years' fighting depleted coffers, cannon-feed peasants got disgruntled with now-weak Togashis. Last Togashi, Yoshichika, also faced intra-clan strife and rising religious fervor among peasants who eagerly embraced militant *Ikko-shu* 'Single-mind Sect' of True Pure Land Jodo Shinshu as preached by radical priest Rennyo Shonin of Kyoto's Hongan-ji temple. Earlier esoteric Buddhism was too ritualistic-intellectual, Zen too restrictive for farmers, who could now gain salvation thru simple faith called for in Jodo Shinshu. And its monks could marry and have children—all of which made it popular with commoners. Rennyo and his Ikko-shu monks were not only out to save souls, but to enrich selves financially and politically, keep all taxes, armies, and recognize no authority other than Hongan-ji temple— none of which was looked on favorably by bulk of samurai lords.

Rennyo began converting area in 1471. Ten years later he was strong enough to topple Ishiguro clan south of Kaga. Backed by well-trained warrior monks and inspired peasants (their helmet-liners blessed, inscribed: "He who advances is sure of Heaven; but he who retreats, of eternal damnation". Ikko-shu defeated Togashi 1488, destroyed Takao castle, set up own fortified temple Kanazawa (Oyama) Gobo on hill in town. Noto taken in 1490, Echizen 1506; other Ikko-shu domains arose on 'front' side of Japan closer to political centers, at Ise Nagashima, Ishiyama near Osaka, Tomita in Owari (Gifu), all major trade centers, and several in Mikawa, political hotbed and later home-base of 'Three Great Unifiers'—ODA Nobunaga, TOYOTOMI Hideyoshi and TOKUGAWA Ieyasu. Ikko-shu grew so powerful that in 1529 plotted to place Shonyo Shoin, Head Abbot of Hongan-ji on imperial throne with his army chief as shogun. Their defeat was first major military success of shogun-to-be Ieyasu, then fighting for Nobunaga who later eradicated all militant Jodo factions. Ikko survivors were demoted en-masse to social untouchability, subject pregnant with PhD potential.

Rennyo's peasant kingdom had no such lofty or foolhardy aspirations (they already possessed richest land) and for full century was island of tranquility in war-torn Japan. Rennyo's disciples kept peasants happy with low taxes, and controlled politically by placing each village under temple linked to Kanazawa Gobo and so, directly to Hongan-ji. With Pacific coast Ikko-shu strongholds finally out of way (Osaka held for 7 years), Oda Nobunaga sent SAKUMA Morimasa to rid Kaga of Ikko-shu, which he did in 1580 with help of several local lords. Then conquerors wiped each other out in successive battles to control Kaga, and in 1583 Oda's most trusted vassal MAEDA Toshiie was directed to take over Kaga to rule jointly with his Noto domain—thus began *Kaga-no-Hyakuman-goku*, 'Kaga of million koku' (1 *koku* =5 bushels rice, about 1 man/year ration), richest fief in Japan. Toshiie's political skills matched his military—wisely sided with Tokugawa, marrying son Toshinaga to daugher of Ieyasu, all later Maeda lords married into shogun family. Toshinaga backed Ieyasu at Sekigahara.

Maedas were at first resented as 'outsiders' and had to deal with 100 years of Jodo influence, so they built their castle on site of old Kanazawa Gobo and used same political structure with Maeda men in place of village temples. While first two Maeda lords were busy consolidating hold on Kaga, 3rd, Mitsutaka, ruling in peaceful era of Tokugawa Shogunate, redirected Kaga's wealth from war to culture. Kanazawa grew to wealthy castle-town, master artists came from Kyoto, Edo to work under generous Maeda patronage, notably for 5th Tsunanori. Here, nobility hobbies of tea ceremony and Noh filtered down to large portion of townspeople, are still popular today. By end of Tokugawa era, 1867, Kanazawa was thriving city, 4th largest in Japan with 140,000 people.

Change from feudal to constitutional monarchy 1868 toppled top-heavy samurai bureaucracy ($^1/_3$ of population), and as unskilled jobless samurai moved to start new lives in northern frontiers as farmers, city shrank to 90,000. Tho powerful, Kaga played no part in Meiji Restoration other than dubious honor of being home of SHIMADA Ichiro, assassin of great Meiji modernizer Count OKUBO Toshimichi. Mostly merchant-artist populace was equally unprepared for leap into modernization, but silk cottage industries pulled Kanazawa thru early Meiji years, and other traditional arts developed as main exports. Great feudal schools of Western learning converted into modern institutions of higher learning, Kanazawa now boasts one national and several private colleges with thousands of students, who student-tourist can thank for cheap lodgings and eateries. As result, rural Kanazawa was treated as open city by USAF with Nara, Kyoto, Kamakura avoiding World War II bombings—while neighbor Toyama and Fukui cities went industrial, were virtually wiped out. Like most such 'old' cities, there is constant conflict on what to preserve *vs* what to modernize; both co-exist so far in peace, and tho we noticed many changes in visits especially over last 8 years Kanazawa's atmosphere is still soothingly antiquarian.

GETTING THERE: Our San-In route MATSUE-on by rail is full day, 2-3 xfers: **A)**. San-In Main Line → KYOTO (5hr30min) or **B)**. OSAKA (Fukuchiyama Branch Line, 6hr30min) where change → Hokuriku Main Line 3hr on special 'L' ltd express 'Raicho' 1-2x/hr, OSAKA-KYOTO → up W shore Lake Biwa (all other Hokuriku Main Line trains up E shore of Biwa). Adding 1-2hr xfer time, grueling day on too-small seat, for which we suggest break in Kyoto. **C)**. **Alternate** up coastline on our meandering course via Kinosaki, Ama-no-Hashidate, Mikata-goko; nonstop recommended only for budget traveler ready to take late-nite runs with several xfers to pull wearily into Kanazawa next morning; but pleasant if one or two overnite stops. Bus from KYOTO 9x-daily, ¥3,900. **From Tokyo** by rail 3 choices: **quickest** is Tokaido Shinkansen → MAIBARA (2hr30min) then Hokuriku Main Line 2hr → KANAZAWA; **picturesque** is Hida route across from NAGOYA via TAKAYAMA (for which itinerary *see*); or 9hr Meitetsu express bus from Nagoya via Gifu with lovely Shirakawa-go village ideal break, catching Takayama return on rail.

For double reserved seat express rail fee, ANA flies 5x-daily between Tokyo's Haneda and Komatsu (1hr), 45min bus to KANAZAWA; 1x-daily 70min from Kyushu's Fukuoka;

if coming from N, 1x-daily from Sendai & Hokkaido's Sapporo (1hr35min each).
Driver's parallel rail itineraries for best roads. Hokuriku Expwy 2 exits (IC) for
Kanazawa: Nishi (W), Higashi (E); Nishi direct entry to town.

GETTING AROUND: As said before, Kanazawa is for strolling;
farthest site from stn is across-town DAIJO-JI only 1hr hoof, 25min bus.
Count on 3-4hrs for central castle and Kenroku-en with stops; another 1-3hrs adds Tera-
machi temple district; 1-2hrs more for HIGASHIYAMA. City Tourist Bureau has easy to
follow **walking guide map**.

Bicycles ideal, tho somewhat hilly in town; 8km bicycle path along Saigawa River
to sea; 14km slightly uphill to EDO-MURA; ¥610/4hr, ¥1030/10hr. Half fun of seeing
Kanazawa is to meander back streets—but maze-like and narrow to confuse attackers, can
equally befuddle unwary tourist, tho locals help out. Buses for cross-town jaunts can also
confuse, but know destination and someone will steer you to right bus. Inner-city one-day
bus pass (*Josha-ken*, ¥800 *vs* fee 1 ride ¥180) sold at Hoku-tetsu bus offices at stn-front
across from Miyako Hotel and downtown Meitetsu Marukoshi Dept store.

Cabs easy to find (cheaper than in big cities) great for cross-town jaunts, most basic-
mtr; only 8x-mtr out to EDO-MURA. Cab **tours** run about ¥5,000, 11x-mtr/hour;
2hr30min for main sites in town, extra 2hr Edo-mura addition, even full day (8hr) NOTO
tours. For select out-of-town destinations, Hokuriku Dentetsu's rickety old electric trams,
fast and frequent: Asanogawa Line from JR stn to seaside UCHINADA, 17min; Ishikawa
Line from Nomachi stn (near Tera-machi) to TSURUGI 35min, TEDORI ONSEN (50min)
and end HAKUSAN-SHITA (70min) whence bus to backwoods hotsprings, **Mt Hakusan**
back entry to TAKAYAMA (follows) via Shirakawa-go.

TRAVEL AIDS: Kanazawa is one of few cities with active foreigners' aid groups
like JNTO-sponsored volunteer **Student Goodwill Guides** (SGG)—English, German,
French, Chinese. Arrange thru non-profit Society to Introduce Kanazawa to the World
(SIKW), located 4th floor of Shakyo (Social Education) Center, near International Cultural
Center (ICC), Nakamura and Honda Museums; ☎(0762)-31-3291, ext 205. They should
also be able to supply English brochures and maps of area, which we got at stn **Kanko-
annai**. Both helpful in local arrangements, but Kanko-annai rarely has English speaker,
for which try SIKW or main JTB office in Musashi district in Toyokuni Seimei Bldg
across from Marukoshi Dept store, which has English speakers on staff. This is good
place to book local rooms (mostly moderate to standard rates), as well as arrange for
ongoing travel.

English books, current mags and papers at Maruzen, Hokkoku Shorin bookstores
along main street W of castle; even catch English language movies at theaters here, list of .
current showings posted at ICC. Some hotels have English-speaking staff (see below).

Then there are 'independent' **volunteer guides**, usually students just looking to try
their English while making you feel at home in their town; they do not usually expect or
accept pay, but lunch gladly accepted (after much protesting). Also strong **Home Visit**
program gets foreign visitors to spend few hours with Japanese host family (take simple
gift); arrange by day before your visit date, thru English-speaking Mr Kunisawa at City
Hall General Affairs Section, ☎22-2075, or SIKW.

Last but not least is informative cover-all guidebook *Kanazawa: The Other Side of
Japan*, by 6-year resident Ruth Stevens, put out by Kanazawa Chamber of Commerce's
Tourist Bureau—250 pages packed with all you need to know about Kanazawa, right down
to corner eateries.

WHERE TO STAY: Top class (¥-hi-T–S) W-style rooms: best **New Grand**
☎(0762)-33-1311, with top floor (great view) cocktail lounge, bkfst spot, French cuisine
on fine Kutani-ware; notch below, **Sky Hotel** ☎33-2233, top 10 fls of Meitetsu Marukoshi dept store and plaza, with equally fine view. Both New Grand and Sky near castle,
English-speaking staff at both; similar **Miyako Hotel** ☎31-2202, **Holiday Inn** (larger
beds) ☎23-1111, across from stn. Business Hotels (¥-T), good, clean: **New Grand Inn**
☎22-1211, other side castle from big brother Grand, convenient Kenroku-en; **Station
Hotel** ☎23-2600, **New Kanazawa** ☎23-2255, several more cheaper, around stn:
Prince ☎23-2131; more by castle.

TRADITIONAL RYOKAN, many of which double as superb high-class restaurants, offer classic Japanese hospitality and atmosphere, which pay dearly for:

LUXE (¥-Lw/2) (dinner is royal feast) runs ¥35,000+: **Kincha-ryo** ☎43-2121, in Tera-machi, hosted many Japanese and foreign dignitaries like US ambassador-prof Reischauer; superb **Asada-ya** ☎31-2228, will make different meals for each person by prior arrange, in Jukken-machi, castle N corner near Owari-cho market streets; 100-year-old **Kinjo-ro** ☎21-8188, in Hashiba-cho between Kenroku-en–Higashiyama; **Yama-no-O** ☎52-5171, in old Higashi pleasure quarters now 7 charming sukiya-style O-hanare cottages.

STANDARD (¥-Sw/2): **Araya** ☎31-4188, near Kenroku-en; **Miyabo** ☎31-4228, former tea house of Kanazawa's 1st Meiji era civilian mayor boasts spectacular garden.

TOURIST (¥-Tw/2): Garet stayed centrally located near City Hall **Yamatoku** ☎31-4171 with great *kani-suki*-crab sukiyaki, or ¥-B-room only; **Itaya** ☎63-5451, **Kajima-ya** ☎21-0187, nr stn; **Hakusui** ☎41-2106, nr Tsubajin. Many *Budget* (¥-B) ryokan, dozen minshuku (¥-Bw2), some fine ones are: **Ike-gamé** ☎41-0306, in 100-year-old ex-restaurant on Tera-machi side of Saigawa Ohashi bridge 5min walk from castle area; **Yogetsu** ☎52-0497, lovely century-old former geisha house in Higashiyama, run by hospitable Mrs Ishitate. Similarly priced temple lodgings at Tera-machi riverside **Kogan-ji** ☎41-2280, **Encho-ji** ☎52-9081.

YOUTH HOSTELS: (¥-B): **Matsui** ☎21-0275, convenient in midtown Katamachi area but often full (member ¥2,100, non-member ¥2,800 room only); **Kanazawa YH** ☎52-3414, ¥2,100 room, on Utatsuyama hill, 30min walk from Kenroku-en or 25min bus from stn, last leaves 20:30 to arr just in time for 21:00 curfew. **Book rooms** direct or thru stn **Kanko-annai,** E- help thru JTB main office, SIKW, or ICC.

CHOPSTICKS: Ranges from all-nite Mr Donuts, coffee shops, J-style fast-food joints to assorted W- & Asian to classic local Kaga dishes served at finest restaurant-inns. Latter, called *Kaga-ryori*, developed over centuries to satisfy palates of Maeda lords using seasonal seafood delights from Japan Sea (winter *ama-ebi* sweet-shrimp, crab), vegetables, herbs and fowl from mountains, freshwater fish from rivers. J- tourists flock to Kanazawa for its food as much as for view of famed Kenroku-en garden. Favorite year-round dishes (tho best in season) are: spring *gori* (tiny river fish served sashimi, tempura, or in white miso sauce), winter *jibu* (vegetable-meat stew, varies with seasonal vegetables and meats, duck in winter), winter *kabura-zushi* (*buri* yellowtail and turnips sandwiched in rice lightly pickled), summer *dojo-no-kabayaki* (eel-like river fish dojo grilled in soy and sake sauce). Other local specialties: *oshi-zushi* (pressed cubes of rice with fish), *kobu-jime* (white fish wrapped in kelp),*tsugumi* (ouzel, local wild bird enjoyed grilled whole as yakitori)—banned in 1947 as bird became endangered species, but some places import from China and Spain. Winter best for seafood; various crab, ama-ebi, and *tara* tender white-meat codfish.

Top establishments are above mentioned restaurant-inns, reservations advised: **Kincha-ryo,** lunch ¥10,000, dinner ¥13,000; have slightly cheaper branch in New Grand's basement (not as nice atmosphere). **Tsuba-jin,** lunch and dinner ¥15,000+ from 11am. **Yama-no-O's** basic lunch starts ¥8,000. Hearty bento box lunches at **Asada-ya** (must reserve ☎31-2228) ¥5,000; **Kinjo-ro** ☎21-8188, ¥10,000.

Less exclusive restaurants are:

HIGASHIYAMA DISTRICT: Gori-ya ☎52-2288, along Asano River near Tokiwa bridge specializes in gori and other river fish, lunch, dinner ¥10,000+. Similar fare but cheaper (¥1,300 for lunch special sashimi or tempura) at **Shogyo-tei** near Tenjin bridge (next one N); steak lunch (¥1,400) and dinners (¥4,000) at **Rokkaku-do** across from it. 2 bridges downstream on W bank Asano River are **Toichi-tei** ☎61-6165, for sukiyaki, and **Taro** ☎31-5152, for exquisite *nabe-ryori* cook-it-yourself kettle cooking. 2 down to Kobayashi Bridge near which is lovely make-your-own udon noodle shop **Fuku-wa-Uchi,** where we lunched. ¥1,000 may seem high for udon, but you get matcha green tea and cakes while you choose from plain, beef, tempura, fowl, fish or mushroom udon—comes with pickles and rice,which mix with leftover soup to make rice gruel. Next door is newly-opened similar soba-ya **Oni-wa-soto**. Across Kobashi bridge to E bank and up 1st L to lovely old candy store **Tawara-ya**, 160-year-old building popular with shutterbugs. Their sticky candy of rice and barley, uses no sugar, sweetness from barley.

MUSASHI DISTRICT: Kyoto-style kaiseki-ryori at **Tsuruko** rsve ☎64-2375, few blocks S of Sky Plaza, ¥6,000+ dinner, lunch ¥3,500+. Cross N of Sky Plaza to budget *kushi-yaki* (cooked-on-skewer) **Toritsuji**, where we snacked late-nite, open evenings to 23:00 (X-thurs); choices laid out in baskets in front. Many student-oriented budget eateries in Katamachi district, like nation-wide chain of **Irohanihoheto** robata-yaki grill joints.

TERA-MACHI DISTRICT: Cross river at Saigawa Ohashi bridge and on L corner is fine fish restaurant **Teraki-ya**, above and behind fish shop. Hearty teishoku (table d'hote) around ¥1,500—if can't read menu go downstairs to point out fish to be cooked or served sashimi. L here and up Hamaguri-zaka Clam Slope is cheap okonomi-yaki joint **Sai-an**; across from which is excellent century-old Kyoto-style restaurant **Sankin-ro** with various sumptuous set lunches from ¥5,000 (dinners ¥1,-2,000 more). L down main street to **Tsuba-jin**, and cheaper (1/2 price) branch **Jinbei** in Century Plaza Hotel one street river-ward. Down riverside street, before Sakura-bashi bridge is nabe-ryori specialist **Sugi-no-i** (¥4,000 per head); just past bridge is **Toyoshima** with great tempura teishoku lunches for ¥500.

Restaurants and tea houses in **Kenroku-en Garden** (*see*). Superb *shojin-ryori* vegetarian priests fare served on finest lacquer at 100-year-old merchant house **Kotobuki-ya** E of Sky Plaza on Owari-cho street and up 3rd L, ¥6,000, must rsv ☎31-6245, 11:00-18:00. These listed here (and we have more listed in passing) do not even make up fraction of thousands of restaurants and diners here; Kanazawa boasts highest per capita of eateries, and number of budget local joints is probably close to that of Japan's greatest drinking center—Fukuoka.

TILT: Half-day; early start Kenroku-en & Seison-kaku → Honda → Nakamura → History Museums → Nagamachi samurai houses → Oyama Shrine. Lunch → Tera-machi and Higashiyama (quickest, cab across town, only 1.5x-mtr). Bicycles can really speed your progress without sacrificing seeing back streets, and you can get in all of central sites, Tera-machi and Higashiyama in full day.

MAIN AREAS IN TOWN

CENTRAL IS old **castle** grounds and **Kenroku-en Garden** 1.5km SE of stn, with Asanogawa River on N, across which is **Higashiyama** with *Higashi-no-kuruwa*, old **Eastern Pleasure Quarters** and Utatsu-yama Hill; on S is Saigawa River across which **Tera-machi Temple District**. NW corner of castle is major intersection (Musashi district) marked by giant **Sky Plaza** made up of Meitetsu **Marukoshi** Dept store and Sky Hotel—grand view from top floor coffee shop. N of Plaza is narrow **Yoko-Yasue-cho** shopping street, more shops along Owari-cho street which is main street heading E to **Hashiba-cho** with more shops and restaurants. Main road S from Plaza passes W side of castle to **Katamachi** and **Tatemachi** shopping-dining districts, both great for strolling, full of old shops, budget eateries, beyond which is **Saigawa Ohashi** bridge to **Tera-machi**. SW corner of castle has several good **museums**, with more at SE corner near Kenroku-en.

Main attraction of Kanazawa is...
KENROKU-EN, Six-Fold Garden (that is, six-fold excellence of size, running water, appearance, air of antiquity, view and love-labor bestowed upon it and to this day maintained) of Maeda lords. One of Three Great Gardens of Japan, with **Koraku-en** in Okayama and **Kairaku-en** in Mito. Began as simple garden to Maeda's outside-of-castle guest house; more

work added 1673-81 (then simpler, smaller) by 5th Maeda lord Tsunanori, when time name *Kenroku-en* (after Chinese garden in Lo-Yang) bestowed by lord Matsudaira (grandson of Tokugawa Ieyasu) who ruled nearby mountainous Shirakawa province. 1832 12th lord Narinaga built Takezawa-goten detached palace in garden, and most trees planted, waterways enlarged, so by his death in 1837 it was almost in present condition. Year later, 13th lord Nariyasu dismantled Takezawa-goten (under order of shogun who felt it too ostentatious) and put Kasumi-ga-Ike lake in its place. On lake shore is city symbol, two-legged *kotoji-toro*, koto-fret lantern (replicated in small stn-front rock garden). Opened to public 1874.

In 1975, city closed most gates and started ¥100 fee; meant to cut wear and tear of countless tourists (attendance suddenly grew after) and money for upkeep. But average 1,000 people daily barely covers third of upkeep, what with pruning each tree biannually, 100,000m² garden to clean at ¥166 million yearly. Entry now ¥300, daily 6:30-18:00 (10/15-3/14 is 8:00-16:30). Unenjoyably crowded 11am-1pm, best early morning or late day. Garden fans can join *Hayaoki-kai* 'Early Bird Club' of old folks who gather daily at Kanazawa Jinja 4am summer and 7am winter for dawn view of Kenroku-en, for which S gate (between Kanazawa Jinja and Seison-kaku) opens early. Special free entrance days, inevitably crowded, are 3 days of New Year and spring flower-viewing.

Aficionados who know history of every rock and tree claim 8hrs needed to see garden, return in all four seasons. We rushed it in 2hrs (bus tours allow you 30min) with break. Beautiful any season; most flowers spring-summer, autumn has wild colored leaves, and winter plum blossoms and famous *yuki-tsuri* 'snow-suspensions' put up early November before first big snow —branches of large trees supported by teepee of ropes so as not to break under heavy, wet snow. Friend thought they distracted, abomination of nature, but treat them as *kurogo* 'shadowmen' of kabuki theatre, invisible aids which make perfect tree in mind's eye. Beauty of Japanese gardens lie in their unnatural control and shaping of nature (which nature in '91 typhoon toppled over 50 century-old trees). Some worthy sites to look for:

Superb 220-year-old *Yugao-tei*, **Morning Glory tea house** in Kobori Enshu-style on W corner Hisago (Gourd) pond with view of small waterfall. In pond is *Kaiseki-to*, **Korean lantern**, brought back from Korean campaign by Hideyoshi and presented to Maeda Toshiie; **pond** lined with *shidare-zakura*, **weeping cherry**. Near Yugao-tei lovely restaurant **Miyoshi-an** specializes in Kaga cooking with **view of waterfall** thru wisteria curtain—expensive and reservation (thru SIKW or Kanko-annai) necessary, cheaper (no reservations) at branch behind Yugao-tei; lunch ¥1,500+, full course Kaiseki-ryori ¥6,000+, they also serve matcha and cakes ¥500 and sell souvenirs, like most other tea shops here. More little snack places nearby *Sazae-yama* **Shellfish Hill** so named for its circular path winding to top for highest vantage point. At base near Kasumi-ga-ike, Misty Lake, is old tea house **Uchihashi-tei** out over lake, no longer open to public since too old; next-door tea and noodle shop has almost as fine view. Behind Sazae-yama is another branch of Miyoshi-an, front are two **Christian-toro** lanterns with crosses etched on, reputedly brought by Christian daimyo TAKAYAMA Ukon who fled here to put himself under Maeda protection after Hideyoshi's anti-Christian edict.

For fine **view** from eastern corner **Yamazaki Hill**: follow branch of Tatsumi canal which fed river water into castle moat, entering Kenroku-en thru tunnel under hill, snaking to pour into now-covered castle moat separating Kenroku-en. Himuro Pond behind hill used to be natural ice-house for Maeda's, packed snow in deep brush-covered hole supplied ice for hot summer days, and for annual gift of ice to shogun on July 1, when huge straw-wrapped blocks were courier-raced to Edo in 5 days.

Seison-kaku Villa, S entrance to Kenroku-en, built 1863 by 13th lord Nariyasu for mother's retirement. White & black *namako* walls picturesque; ¥500 to see inside (8:30-16:00 daily, X-wed) is worth rare view of daimyo residence built solely to female taste. Display various scrolls, Maeda family treasures. Squeaky nightingale halls supposedly warn of approaching friend or foe. Tea house open only Jun 15 public ceremony.

Neighboring Castle and Garden are...
Traditional Arts & Crafts Museum, *Dento Sangyo Kogei-kan* (9:00-16:30 daily X-thurs and Nat'l hol, ¥250) is in nearby modern building; shown are various crafts of Ishikawa prefecture, including Wajima lacquerware, Kutani pottery, Yuzen silks.

KANAZAWA JINJA nearby, built by 11th lord Harunaga enshrines Sugawara Michizane (Tenjin-san) patron deity of scholars whom Maeda's claim as ancestor, and white snake spirit of safety at home (which we saw in Iwakuni). Modeled after main Dazaifu Tenman-gu, it even had ume plum transplanted from there. Sees steady stream of students coming to pray for good grades on entrance exams and hundreds of votive plaques (¥500 & ¥700) carry inked-in poignant wishes for such. **Phoenix hill** in front used to be shaped like mythical bird until battered by typhoons. Said to be site of magical well in which farmer Imohori Togoro washed his potatoes—which peels turned into gold, thus name of Kanazawa as Gold Marsh (traces of gold have been found in rivers here). Legend has it that Togoro did such to show his courtly wife (sent to be his bride by prophetic dream) that gold was nothing unusual here.

For wanderer with time, S across road from shrine to modern Prefectural...
Noh Theater, *Noh-gaku Bunka Kaikan*; stage moved here from drafty old hall in 1972 allows audience to now view traditional esthetic in splendid comfort. Hosho style Noh was one of most heavily patronized arts of Maeda lords and is another main aspect of modern Kanazawa—as seen by giant statue of Noh dancer front of stn. Full Noh and Kyogen performances 1st sun every month and several other times thru year, tickets ¥2,000; but also amateur performances almost every weekend of Noh, Japanese dance, music, and such, free.

Lovely Taisho 20s-era buildings next to Noh Theatre were ex-Military HQ and Officers' Club, now **municipal offices**.

Behind them is...
GOKOKU JINJA shrine to war dead, where out back at archery range you can watch students practicing kyudo.

Worthy detour 400m S of Kenroku-en on main road near Trad Arts Crafts Mus is...
City Folk Museum, *Minzoku Bunkazai Tenjikan*, (way down you pass long stretch of old wood wall on L, this belonged to Okumura manse now site of hospital). Building itself is rather remarkable Meiji W-style structure built 1899 as Kanazawa #2 Middle School, and free to enter and see fine exhibits. Displays of tools and laid-out self-explanatory process on every imaginable craft from geta and tabi makers to gold leaf and lacquer. (9:00-16:00 X-tue, day after hol).

On way back, L at church (150m from mus) thru quiet back streets about 500m to...
Hirao-ke, 130-year-old mansion of Hirao advisors to Maedas, *(no entry)*.

At nearby big road, L is to Tera-machi via Sakura bridge and 'W'-slope, R takes us back towards Kenroku-en, via...
Nakamura Memorial Museum, *Kinen Bijutsu-kan* (9:00-16:00 X-tue, day after hol, ¥300), grand old 2-storey home of rich sake maker Nakamura Eishun (1908-1978), tea ceremony devotee whose superb collection of tea utensils, old Kutani (and other, incl Sung Chinese) bowls, lacquerware,

gold and scrolls is on display—rotated seasonally. He moved his house here, donated it and collection to city. Gate fee includes *matcha* and cakes served in tea house looking out on garden, both of which he designed.

250m to E corner of Kenroku-en is...
ISHIURA JINJA, oldest shrine in Kanazawa (ca 9th cent AD), and one of most popular during festival time.

Alt rte to Nakamura Museum–return Noh Theatre corner after Folk Museum, past...
Honda Museum, *Karo Honda Zohin-kan,* (9:00-17:00, X-thurs Nov-Mar, ¥500) is bit expensive, but inside is superb collection of Honda family items, perhaps best known of which is 50,000-koku tea bowl. Chief Advisor to Maeda Toshinaga was Honda Masashige (whose father was top advisor to shogun Ieyasu), who when offered 50,000 koku of land and vast property near castle for his services, refused former and in its stead asked for this bowl. Treasures include dowries of Maeda daughters married to Hondas, gifts from shogunate, armor, lots of lacquerware and porcelain, and uniforms of Honda's private firefighters. Museum and nearby red-brick buildings were part of Arts College (*Bidai*) which occupied part of old Honda residence (this entire area called Honda-machi, housed attendants to Hondas), which spilled over to Kenroku-en, included Nakamura Museum grounds, and S to present Honda Park which includes...

Shofu-en, remaining 1/3rd of Honda main mansion's garden with pond, tea house and pavilion. Can only enter garden by special permission (try SIKW), but good view from restaurant Hyo-tei attached to MRO Hokuriku Broadcast Bldg, 2 down from Nakamura Museum.

From here, can take above mentioned route to Tera-machi, pass N thru it to Saigawa Ohashi bridge and up Katamachi shopping street to more sites along W side of castle.

Or Hyakken-bori St btwn Kenroku-en & castle, past great Ishikawa-mon gate to...
Gyokusen-en, much smaller, less-visited garden NE of Kenroku-en at E gate. Nishida family's intimate private garden uses Kenroku-en greenery as back-drop. ¥350 (9:00-16:00, X-mid-Dec to mid-Mar) to enter, extra ¥300 gets you *matcha* and cakes served in tea house overlooking pleasant terraced garden. Down street are two moderate-priced Kaga restaurants: Kenken-Ochin at S corner, Tozan next to Gyokusen-en.

Up near Kenroku-en NE gate is...
Tourists' Craft Center, *Kanko Bussan,* (9:00-17:00) with display and sales of regional arts and crafts, and coffee shop and diner with set Kaga-ryori meals (¥1,500-4,000). 50m N along Kenroku-en boundary is another Kaga restaurant Tanaka.

This puts us at N gate of Kenroku-en and...
Ishikawa-mon Gate, one of few remaining structures of Kanazawa Castle. One of largest castles in feudal Japan, 1881 fire razed most of its buildings except for gate and *sanjukken-nagaya,* 30-room armory in grounds. First symbol of powerful Jodo Buddhists, then of Maedas, it now is symbol of Kanzawa as major educational center. Military barracks occupied it until war's end, then after short stint as base of US Occupation forces, National University put here 1950. Signs say *No Tourists* but you can meander thru grounds; buildings made to blend into castle grounds, great idea but which limited growth so University moved to new campus.

From Ishikawa-mon, can head E to Higashiyama, which takes us past 2 old samurai houses: Yamamori-ke (150m E of New Grand Inn), excellent condition, can't enter.

But 5min walk from Ishikawa-mon just off road to Asano Ohashi bridge is...
Terashima-ke (9:00-17:00 X-thur, ¥300). Middle-ranking samurai Tera-shimas came to Kanazawa during reign of 4th Maeda lord, present owner is

16th generation, house last rebuilt 1871. Mr. Terashima shows you around house and explains (great English pamphlet): His great-great-grand-dad TERASHIMA Oyo was outspoken intellectual critical of clan's strictness during famine, and of its anti-foreign stance (20-odd years before Perry), so died in exile. Posthumously reinstated early Meiji by 15th Maeda. ¥300 gets you relaxing *matcha* and cakes in 160-year-old **tea house** viewing **garden**.

Road to Asano Ohashi bridge has many interesting old stores, including famed...
Ohi-yaki Kama-moto kiln of master potter Ohi Chozaemon, worth look at samples in display room but outrageously priced. Shop is old house next to Kinjo-ro Inn, with tile-roofed gate and noren 'curtain' in front. Ohi-yaki is characteristically light weight with subtle brownish *ame-yu* 'candy' glaze. This effect was first created by first Ohi Chozaemon early 1600's (present Chozaemon 10th generation) for grand tea master of Ura-Senke school. Since then Ohi were sole suppliers of tea utensils to Ura-Senke masters in Kaga, allowed to make only this one style. With Meiji Restoration came end to such artistic restrictions and some local potters took up Ohi-yaki. Tho they lack tradition, they are reasonably priced and quite good. One such newcomer is **Ohi Choami** just down street over on other side, another is **Ohi Choraku** across from New Grand Hotel.

Museum of Modern Literature, *Kindai Bungaku-kan* (9:30-16:30 X-mon, 12/26-1/5, ¥400). City boasts many nationally famous authors—poet Muro Saisei, novelists Tokuda Shusei and Izumi Kyoka all with works translated to English—among whom is one of our family favorites, the late (died Mar 1991) Inoue Yasushi (in English: *The Hunting Gun, Lou-lan, Tun-huang*) grad of Shiko. English versions sometimes available to rent here (often available in bookstore English sections); displays of authors' works, memorabilia. Stodgy W-style building R of museum is...

   Prefectural Office, built 1924 in Taisho-era style suited to cavernous bureaucracy, worth walk thru; some nice **art deco** touches.

History Museum, *Rekishi Hakubutsu-kan* (9:00-16:30 X-12/29-1/3, ¥250), Moved to old Meiji building just S of Kenroku-en Park. Houses assorted items from ancient pottery, Occupation-era English papers, and relics of the colorful Kaga clan. Grand red brick building built 1891 as 4th National High School, *Shiko* based on superb Maeda clan school; its many distinguished graduates include internationally renowned zen scholar D.T. Suzuki. Public **Central Park** around museum was Shiko's campus.

Other side of Hirosaka-dori, alley branches S to...
Hirosaka Catholic Church, next to City Hall, small but good collection Hidden Christian items including Maria-Kannon (Mary in guise of Kannon), Fumi-e stomping plaques for testing suspected Christians.

OYAMA JINJA shrine, N of Central Park is must, if just to see ornate foreign 3-storey **gate**. Designed 1875 by Holtmann, Dutch teacher at local medical school, thick arched (decidedly Western) stone base supports more Oriental 2nd and 3rd floors; 3rd has stained-glass windows, light inside served as colorful beacon to ships in Japan Sea until taller buildings blocked it out. Also boasts lovely **garden**, once part of Maeda mansion Kanaya-goten which occupied this spot—shrine moved here 1873; parts of Kanaya-goten used in its construction.

L of garden is...
Higashi-mon, **East Gate** of castle, which escaped fire to be moved here. Dragons carved under roof put there as dragons believed to supply water against fire, these were just strong enough to protect themselves but not castle.

400m further N...

OZAKI JINJA shrine, once-grand Toshogu Shrine dedicated to Ieyasu's Buddhist-Shinto spirit, but Meiji split of two religions made it into State Shinto Ozaki shrine and moved from original site of castle's N gate to here. As lords of richest domain in feudal Japan, Maedas were suspect as possible threat to Tokugawa supremacy and went to great lengths to assure Edo of loyalty. Marriages and grand gifts (like annual ice run) helped, but 4th Maeda lord Mitsutake in 1640 decided grand shrine to Ieyasu would be best. So he got master craftsmen from Edo and built replica of Nikko's Toshogu. He placed it at N Gate for two-fold reason: it was position of honor, but also weakest point in castle defense and placing Ieyasu's spirit there provided formidable psychological barrier against possible Tokugawa attack. Now sadly run down (gets most of its income from double role of parking lot) and not worth special trip, but it is enroute Higashiyama district. To E is **Ohte-bori**, sole remaining section of castle moat.

300m N is main Owari-cho shopping street and...

Townfolks' Culture Center, *Chomin Bunka-kan* (9:00-16:00 X-thur, free) with displays (rotate seasonally) on Edo period merchant life and permanent collection of *shishi-to* festival lion heads. Classic old building built 1908 as bank. Owari-cho was heart of Edo merchant district and many lovely old stores remain, most between Bunka-kan and Asanogawa Ohashi bridge.

Nagamachi Buke-yashiki, Samurai Residences, best known of Kanazawa's old samurai neighborhoods, pleasant to stroll thru; tho as in Hagi, most can't be entered, but seemingly endless hoary walls which lends ancient air to area. One to be entered is **Nomura-ke** (8:00-17:30 daily, ¥400), grand old house (moved here from another part of town) which wander thru, and fine Kobori Enshu style **garden** viewed while sipping *matcha* and eating cakes in tea house (¥250).

Or pass on tea and head several blocks N of Nomura-ke, W across canal to...

Nikore, old samurai house converted into rest house serving various teas and coffee (daily 8:30-18:00). Stevens' book notes: "Private home of Mr Yonekawa Hiroshi at Nagamachi 3-1-47, who will if home (best bet sunday), show you around his house and treasures. His family sent to Kaga 400 years ago as Imperial retainers. As well as being virtually unretouched architectural wonder, it is full of ancient lacquer and other museum-pieces".

Another known-to-all spot is...

Saihitsu-an Kaga-Yuzen Dyed Silk Center (9:00-16:30 X-thur, lunch noon–1pm, ¥500 incl tea and cake after tour), E of Nomura-ke. Set up as workshop for Kaga Yuzen silk painters where visitors can see all 18 steps done right there by skilled artists, and explained (excellent English pamphlet).

Yuzen method of silk painting originated by early 17th century master craftsman MIYAZAKI Yuzen-sai in Kyoto (where *see* Yuzen museum); Maedas got Yuzen-sai to come to Kanazawa to teach local dyers. Painstaking process hand-painting intricate motifs is done in numerous steps color by color; thin strip of water soluble glue is applied to keep colors from running, then rinsed in ice-cold flowing water to get rid of glue (leaving thin white lines between colors) and make dye stick. Classic Kanazawa tourist poster shows booted men rinsing long flowing bolts of yuzen in river, but you rarely see such now—considered river pollution. Most of final dyeing and rinse is now done at large Kaga Yuzen-danchi co-operative down by coast, which we visit later. Sold thruout town, it is expensive item. Hankies start from ¥1,000, small hangings ¥3,-5,000 and sky's limit for kimono—but still cheap if considered as large wall hanging or painting.

This ends our minimal tour of central Kanzawa; by foot, easily worth hard full day or easy 2 w/side trips to Tera-machi & Higashiyama, *follows...*

Place worth visiting, R behind stn (facing stn front, R, under tracks, backtrack)...
Gold Leaf Museum, *Yasue Kinpaku Kogeikan* (9:30-16:30 X-tue, thur ¥300) run by 85-year-old Mr Yasue who has been pounding gold leaf since age 7. He shows you how it is done, then to his fantastic collection of gold leaf objects and screens, followed by tea (with gold leaf flakes) with Mrs Yasue. Kinpaku gold leaf was one of feudal Kanazawa's main exports, and even now Kanazawa produces 90% of Japan's gold leaf and 100% of its silver leaf. Fine gold dust is also used in *Kaga Maki-e* 'sprinkle painting' gold on Kaga's famed lacquerware.

TERA-MACHI Temple District is one of two areas (Higashiyama is other) where all new non-Ikko-shu temples were set up by Maeda decree. They were kept out of town so not to offend or agitate Kanazawans still under heavy Ikko-shu influence. Putting temples outside town also was defense: attackers had to breach psychological barrier of sacred ground (which many peasant foot-soldiers would avoid) and if that failed there was still river and maze-like alleys before gaining castle's impressive moat and walls. Over 70 temples here, even most devout are overcome by temple overdose; most uninteresting.

Some worth visiting–most popular is...
MYORYU-JI, better known as **NINJA-DERA** for its countless hidden doors, passageways, stairs and traps. Myoryu-ji was never used by secret ninja tho it uses many gimmicks we saw at real ninja house in Iga-Ueno city. Intricate defenses built into temple by 3rd Maeda Toshitsune, who had Myoryu-ji built as official Nichiren sect temple (some unimaginative scholars claim lack of space led to this intricate layout). It boasts 29 sets of stairs linking 23 rooms on 7 staggered floors; courtyard well tunnels to Saigawa river (pulleys allowed water to be drawn up to 2nd floor tea room, which rope doubled as quick escape down), which romantics suggest was used by Maeda lords for discreet passage from/to nearby Western pleasure quarters; topmost room was watchtower, last resort for trapped lord who could slit belly here. Well worth ¥400 20min guided tour (every 1/2hr; some guides speak little English), but is extremely popular so time your visit. Supposed to call ahead ☎41-2877 to rsve space on tour, but 1-3 people usually can latch on to group. *Avoid* sun & hol, and around noon any day, when hordes distract; we went 3-ish, not too bad. Late PM, early AM best; 9:00-17:00 (-16:30 winter); X▪1st, 13th every month. It is in middle of Tera-machi, 3min walk S of Hiro-koji bus stop (15min bus from stn).

MYORYU-JI is few min **cab** (basic-mtr) from Kenroku-en & History Museum area. On **foot** or **bike**, S thru Kata-machi shopping street (lots of cheap eats) to Saigawa Ohashi bridge whence 5min walk direct to Ninja-dera: next main intersection Hiro-koji bus stop, L 100m and 1st R 150m, temple on R; another way is 1st L after crossing bridge up Hamaguri-zaka 'Clam Slope' (so called since area burned down twice but road opened again after each, like clam over fire) to temple.

Coffee shop **Jugemu** across street run by local potter who displays his pots in shop. We lunched corner restaurant **Teraki-ya**, upstairs behind fish shop.

On our winding course thru Tera-machi: 1st R after bridge...
UHO-IN temple is not particularly attractive or unusual but J- fans of poet MURO Saisei visit, he spent 20 years of his youth adopted by temple (many of his poems and stories deal with Saigawa River, and monument to Saisei on opposite bank further E). See some of his works kept here (*free*). Written on stone gatepost: "Bring lost children here, ask about them here". Put up 1827 during famine as many kids left on their own for lack of food.

L (S) takes us past superb minshuku Ike-gami in 80-year-old townhouse; on past...
SHINMEI-GU shrine known for giant 900-year-old *keyaki* zelkova tree to...

Ex-Western Pleasure Quarter, *Kyu-Higashi-no-Kuruwa* (if holy ground didn't stop invaders, this would).

Red light districts clustered out of town to monitor more easily, and to keep temptation away from samurai who went anyway. Most now exclusive restaurants where real geisha entertain with dance and music. Nice area to stroll thru, many lovely old houses, at nite lanterns along street are lighted, read *Nishi*, West. Sleazy real red light district is further W across canal.

Kutani-yaki Kosen-gama is only Kutani-ware kiln in town and anyone is free to wander in (8:00-17:00 daily X-mon, lunch break 12-1pm) to watch entire process from preparing clay to final painting and firing. At **gift shop** we were shown around by 84-year-old Mr Toshioka Kosen—great sense of humor, greater love of pottery. It is S between Nishi-no-Kuruwa and Nomachi rail terminus.

Everyone agrees that Kutani-ware was first made in Kaga Daijo-ji region (near Yamanaka Onsen) in mid-17th century, but no one is sure where it came from or why kilns totally destroyed soon after. Local lore claims Maeda overseer of Daijo-ji area sent vassal Goto Saijiro to Kyushu's famed pottery center of Arita to learn their ways which he brought back in 1655 to teach local potters. To further confuse, excavation of old kilns in early 1970's revealed only few dull sherds unlike colorful *ko-Kutani* (old Kutani), which led skeptics to believe ko-Kutani was grand hoax by Maedas. But to pull one of such grand scale and remain undetected in Tokugawa police state would be hard, and just as likely kilns were smashed by Tokugawa orders to prevent further fattening of Maeda coffers—Tokugawas already patronized Arita. Whatever its origins Kutani ware once again appeared during end of Edo period (Bunka years,1850s) in last ditch effort to bring in money. This new Kutani nowhere near quality of old; tho' good pieces made by local individual potters, most made in factories like **Kosen-gama.** NINJA-DERA is 5min walk E.

Kita Family House, *Kita Kinen-kan,* (8:30-17:00 daily, ¥700) is 180-year-old well-to-do merchant's home and brewery, moved here from Kanazawa's Zaimoku-cho area in 1850s. Kita family brewed soy sauce in Kanazawa, then changed to sake with relocation. In superb condition (lived in until donated to city in 1972), displays are explained in good English brochure. Brewing still goes on, excellent Fuku-masamune brand *jizake* (local 'pure' sake) sold in Kutani-ware jugs. High-ceiling front room with sturdy crossbeams and hearth reminds of fabulous Yoshijima house in Hida Takayama. Kita house is in Nono-ichi Town, 3km SW of Tera-machi: **bus** #46 (which stops Hiro-koji) 13min to Nishi-Nono-ichi; short walk W of Nono-ichi **tram** stop, 4th from Nomachi; or **cab** 2x-mtr from Ninja-dera. If going to Tsurugi or Tedori hot springs or Mt Hakuzan can take it in enroute on tram line.

Back in Tera-machi, short detour S from Ninja-dera: 100m to neglected...
SANKO-JI temple, infamous base of militant right-wing Sankoji faction; leader SHIMADA Ichiro cut down Meiji leader OKUBO Toshimichi in 1878.

200m to...
Rokuto-no-hiromi communal gathering spot, plaza, built as firebreak — now has many fine old stores around.

500m to...
RYUEN-JI, one of few temples to keep spacious Zen garden intact, viewed from terrace **tea** served during rainy season (when best).

Just before it is...
GESSHO-JI temple full of stone jizo statues saved from modern road construction. You may note many assorted jizo statues around Tera-machi —area was execution site before Maeda rule, many jizo put here to pray for souls of dead. Besides usual jizo dedicated to lost children such as those at Senju-in, others include jizo of *mizuko* aborted babies at Kaizen-ji, wood and human bone jizo at Daien-ji, pointedly unmentioned **syphilis-curing jizo** of Ninja-dera, and long-life jizo of Kio-in. N from Gessho-ji on nearby big street leads back to Saigawa River near 'W'-slope.

Passing up Ryuen-ji's garden, N from Ninja-dera to big street R, past Tsuba-jin inn...
Kaga Folkcrafts Museum, *Minzoku Bunka-zai Shiryo-kan* (8:30-17:00, free), assorted Edo period odds and ends pertaining mostly to items used by farmers and merchants. No English pamphlet, but things here fun to look at.

Facing museum, on its R is...
SHOGETSU-JI temple, famed for 300-year-old cherry tree partially poking out wall.

To L is...
FUSHIMI-DERA temple, reputedly built early Nara period by potato-digger Imohori Togoro, moved here early 17th century. Short tour (¥300, 8:00-18:00) with priest allows you to see 1,200-year-old gold and copper 21cm high figurine of seated Amida-nyorai Buddha, said to have been made by Togoro from his potato-peel gold. Rusted sword and tool remains found in Togoro's grave are also shown; and 12 Buddha figures with different zodiac animals on each hat. Sword would indicate higher-than-farmer status of Togoro, thus more likely local warlord strong enough to ally self with court thru marriage.

100m down road on same side is white-walled...
DAIEN-JI temple, with 300-year-old 4m tall jizo statue partially made of human bones (in face, neck, chest and limbs). They came from people who didn't receive proper Buddhist burials, and prayers to jizo puts their souls at ease.

Two temples down is...
RYUZO-JI, with Christian Lantern (*Kirishtan Toro*) in inner garden, mate to 2 in Kenroku-en, also brought here by Christian Daimyo TAKAYAMA Ukon.

Next L towards river, leads to...
'W'-Slope, steep zig-zagging staircase down to Saigawa River at Sakura-bashi bridge. Name coined by Shiko school students who came here with poet-teacher MURO Saisei; avoided during exam time since W in Japanese comes out as 'double', also means retaking failed exam. Mystery-seekers should come here **2nd of every month** (1-2am best) when ghost of kimono-clad woman appears. Police checked old Edo period records for murder here; none found, people still claim to see her. Street from Sakura-bashi bridge goes past Hirao-ke house, Nakamura Museum to Kenroku-en.

DAIJO-JI temple, beautiful complex at base of Noda-yama hill worth trek (we drove). Out of way, most visitors to Kanazawa avoid, so quiet, monks here hospitable will show you **zazen-do** meditation hall and giant **kitchen**. Also active zen center branch of Fukui's Eihei-ji temple; if here around sunrise, can join zazen sessions. 3km S of Ryuzo- ji, stay on big street 2.3km to Noda bus stop (5min bus from Tera-machi 3-chome stop near Ryuzo-ji or Hiro-koji stop) and 2nd R (W) road to S of Toun-ji. Daijo-ji built 1261 by governor Togashi Iehisa near old fortress at Nono-ichi, prospered for 2 centuries until Ikko-shu came to power and temple abandoned for almost century. End of Ikko-shu rule, Honda lords resurrected Daijo-ji, moved it to present site 1697. Spreading uphill is Nodayama cemetery, with first MAEDA Toshiie at top, surrounded by descendants and family; below them Maeda retainers placed according to rank, generation; townspeople buried at hill's base.

En route Daijo-ji, 1km S from Ryuzo-ji at Tera-machi 1-chome bus stop...
HOSHU-JI temple has one of Kanazawa's '3 Great Buddhas'. Small version of Kamakura's Daibutsu, dedicated to prosperity of Minamoto Yoritomo; built late 12th century by Togashi installed here by Yoritomo. Only copper head is original (body burned) and now sits on 17th century wood body. Housed in **Rokkaku-do** (6-sided) Pavilion, which actually has 8 sides; see this Buddha anytime during day.

Other two giant Buddhas kept at temples in...
HIGASHIYAMA 'Eastern Hill' District, Tera-machi's crosstown counter-part also reserved for temples, pleasure quarters and still thriving merchant districts—which, like Tera-machi, make for great strolling. Slightly shorter Utatsuyama hill (145m) closer to Higashiyama than Nodayama is to Tera-machi. We start at Asano Ohashi bridge, downstream of which on W bank is **Kazoe-machi**, lovely old remnants of once-thriving pleasure quarters.

Its 'big sister' across river...
Eastern Pleasure Quarter, *Higashi-no Kuruwa*, 3rd R after crossing Asano bridge 100m to Encho-ji temple and L then R to main street. Established 1820 as grandest pleasure quarter outside Kyoto's Gion or Edo's Yoshiwara. Like Tera-machi's Nishi, now mostly private homes and high-class restaurants entered only by special invitation. Walking around in evening, see gaily dressed geisha going to appointments, hear samisen of those already entertaining; *andon* paper lanterns here marked with character for *Higashi*. **Shima-ya** 5th on L as you enter main street is only one open to public (¥200, 9:00-17:00 X-mon and 12/15 thru Feb); worthy, rare chance to see inside of ex-geisha house. Dine or stay at expensive ex-geisha house **Yama-no-O**, E end of street; or budget lodgings at minshuku **Yogetsu**, another ex-geisha house at W end, before Shima-ya.

2nd R from Asano bridge takes us down...
Kannon-machi-dori (from where can turn up to Higashi), interesting old merchant district lined with stores, which thrived as gateway to **KANNON-IN** temple, now closed (except annual Aug *Corn Fest see* DATEBOOK) but once one of grandest temples in Kanazawa boasting giant pagoda (burned down by bum's campfire early this century) and outdoor Noh stage where annual Hosho-style dances done for 250 years till 1869. Fine view of city below: quiet streets of Higashi, shining black tile roofs of old houses flanking Asano River backed by green castle-hill and modern skyline.

Near base of steps is...
JUKYO-JI temple, front of which is small shed housing *Nana-ine* 'Seven Rice-ear' Jizo statues dedicated to 7 ringleaders of 1858 rice riots, beheaded after Maedas quelled masses who looted granaries in response to high taxes during famine.

If here 1994 or 33rd year thereafter, stop by HOSEN-JI above and behind Jukyo-ji. Temple treasure (shown only once every 33 yrs) is 6cm high, gold statue of Buddhist War God *Marishi-ten* (Tibetan Marici, goddess of dawn also shown as many-headed terror) which reputedly bestowed great fighting skills on owner. Given to Maeda Toshiie by previous owner (long-time Maeda vassal), it was kept in Kanazawa castle and adorned Toshiie's helmet in battle. In peacetime, Toshinaga built this temple for it, where it became jack-of-all-trades-talisman and people from all over came to pray: samurai for martial arts, merchants for profit, artists for talent, farmers and fishermen for better harvest and catch, commoners for all-around luck, and some postwar politicians venture here for campaign victory. Also known for its Gohon-matsu **pine tree** with 5 trunks growing out of single base.

Higashiyama temples are mostly clustered NE of Higashi-no-Kuruwa; 5min walk to...
GENMON-JI temple, courtyard full of children (financed by running nursery school) seems unlikely home to one of Three Great Buddhas. This is 500-year-old, 4.8m tall gilt-wood Amida brightly painted.

200m E is...
RENSHO-JI temple housing 3rd Buddha, 5m tall, camphor wood Kannon statue carved 1759 in memory of victims of devastating 1738 fire. Kept in L hall, partial view thru glass door or ask to enter for full view (small donation).

SHINSHO-JI temple (5min walk N) dedicated to Kishimo-jin, Buddhist goddess of children (Tibetan Hariti), child-devouring demon converted by Buddha who hid one of her 500 children to show her sorrow of losing child. In Japan, she is special guardian of children and women in childbirth, temple frequented by mothers wishing for child, or leaving gift in thanks for one. Thus many children's items inside, mostly dolls, from which temple gets alias of *Ningyo-dera*, **DOLL TEMPLE**. *Ningyo-kuyo* memorial rites for old dolls **Apr 29**. Note many see- hear- speak-no-evil monkeys around temple grounds, which is full of pomegranate trees (fruit often held by Kishimo-jin, its many seeds suggest fecundity). Among trees are graves of first Nakamura Utaemon of Kabuki, and Igarashi Doho founder of Kaga *maki-e* (gold-flecked lacquer). Shinsho-ji is marked by steep stone steps leading to it.

Under nearby torii up more steps thru trees 1min to...
RYOKOKU-JI, where Miyazaki Yuzen-sai (founder of Kaga-yuzen) is buried. His small grave was found only recently, yuzen artists made up for past negligence by building superb tea house where tea ceremony and Buddhist rites held **May 17th** anniversary of death, tea only **17th monthly**; all welcome. Nearby is hemorrhoid-curing SANBO-JI temple.

Other cultural notables buried in nearby temples:

200m NW of Shinsho-ji at...
ZENDO-JI is grave of 15th generation Hosho Noh master who founded Kaga-Hosho Noh, marked by huge **red gate** (alias *Akamon-ji* 'Red Gate Temple') and giant straw sandals hanging.

Halfway here is...
GESSHIN-JI, with grave of grand tea master Sen-no-Senso Soshitsu (5th of Sen family, 1st of Ura-Senke branch) who came from Kyoto to introduce tea to Kanazawa (Ura-Senke school still most popular here); memorial tea ceremonies **23rd every month**, open to all, fee of ¥3,000 (high price = small audience). Also grave of first potter OHI Chozaemon who accompanied Senso and made all of his tea bowls (descendant 10th generation Chozaemon has shop near Terashima samurai house).

100m N is...
RENKAKU-JI with lovely Enshu-style landscape **garden** and known for its temple treasure, 600-year-old painting of Amida Trinity now kept in Nara's National Museum.

KOKAKU-JI (behind Shinren-ji) temple has another Enshu **garden**.

N beyond temple area is...

Naruwa-no-taki waterfall, site of second half of classic Kabuki Kanjin-cho, in which shogun Yoritomo's brother Yoshitsune and faithful sidekick Benkei rest after Benkei foils barrier gate guard Togashi. Here, Togashi catches up and offers food and drink, and Benkei performs drunken dance to allow his master to escape. Small shrine now marks picnic spot near cool waterfall, festival every Oct 4-6. First half of play takes place at Ataka Barrier Gate which is down-coast near Komatsu.

Utatsuyama hill is beginning to suffer from encroaching city below, but pleasant to wander around, especially spring sakura and autumn maple viewing. Monuments to writers and other Kanazawa notables abound, another dedicated to 500-odd Christians from Nagasaki's Urakami imprisoned here 1869 when Shinto made state religion, until 1873 when religious freedom granted.

N to...

Shiunsan-en, natural landscape garden-park almost always empty. Then there is Kanazawa **Sunny-Land** (8:00-21:00, ¥2,000) leisure center with giant bath, pool, shows, rides, zoo, aquarium. Further back is **Sumo stadium** used June National High School Championship. Overlooking it is memorial to sole WWII civilian casualties of Kanazawa, 52 school girls killed in bombing of Aichi shipyards on August 7, 1945, just one week before war's end.

Far back is...

Peoples' Park, *Kenmin Koen*, ex-golf course (thus grassy expanses) converted 1970 as site of Kanazawa-Ghent (Belgian sister city) gala fest. Many trees here from Ghent. 9:00-19:00 (free), 40min bus from stn, no bus winter.

Visible white dome is Southeast Asian **Buddhist stupa** housing relics of Gautama Buddha, given city by Indian Premier Jawaharlal Nehru, 1954.

SHOPPING: In addition to above-mentioned Kaga Yuzen, *kinpaku* gold and silver leaf, Kutani and Ohi ceramics, there is also *Kaga urushi*, or **lacquerware**, most popular and expensive of which is 'gold speckle' *maki-e* developed by IGARASHI Doho early 17th century. Unlike other crafts, there are no main workshops one can visit (most work is done in small family workshop-stores around town, protected from visitors' breath or breeze from movement), tho examples of fabulous old maki-e items displayed in museums. Regular demonstrations of basic lacquer process are done at **Kanko Bussan** near Kenroku-en, where you will learn that much of prepatory work—woodcutting, applying base coats of urushi—is done in rural centers of Noto's Wajima and Yamanaka Onsen area. Wajima urushi-lacquerware is reputedly best, but now very expensive, while Yamanaka's is fine in its own way yet more reasonably priced.

Other crafts are: *Kaga zogan* **damascene**, which uses base of steel, copper or bronze with inlay of gold or silver. In Edo period many lords owned prized helmets of Kaga zogan as well as assorted household items. *Kiri-kogei* **paulownia-carving** is another local specialty. Light-weight, strong kiri best known for use in making geta clogs and chests, but here, is also fashioned into various items such as plates, bowls and vases. Finished items slowly roasted over low fire until it becomes rich dark brown—which color improves with age and use. Unique to Kanazawa, some also have raised motifs which are lacquered. Much cheaper than lacquerware, it is also much easier to take care of, for lacquerware (or its wood base) tends to crack or warp when exposed to adverse temperature, humidity.

Toys also make great inexpensive gifts, such as smaller *shishi-to* carved lion heads. Local lore has it that lord MAEDA Toshiie was so taken by lion dances which welcomed him into Kanazawa 1583, he encouraged populace to take up dancing and making of shishi-to. Sold all over town, they range in size from palm-sized for few hundred yen to giants with prices to match. There is also carved rice-eating mice; Hachiman Oki-*agari* dolls which resemble rolly-polly daruma dolls of other cities which right themselves up after knocked over. And don't forget health-food candy of **Tawara-ya** candy shop.

Kanko Bussan is best place to get quick overview of local arts and crafts, items competitively priced. But if you have time to wander around Kanazawa's back streets you will find greater selections at specialty shops, some of them makers or direct outlets, where items will be slightly cheaper.

AROUND KANAZAWA

SOME PLACES just outside Kanazawa worth quick jaunts to: EDO-MURA, coastal KANAIWA and down-coast to KOMATSU airport, and back-country MT HAKUSAN. EDO-MURA & DANPU-EN worth half-day, o'nite YUWAKU ONSEN **Hakuun-ro** hotel.

In order of preference, we start with...
EDO-MURA is village of Edo era houses of merchants, farmers, low- and high-class samurai; full of items used by ex-residents. Brainchild of Mr Sakurai, owner of Hakuun-ro hotel who collected them from around Kaga to make main attraction of Yuwaku Onsen–don't confuse with Nikko's Edo. Enter compound's **gate** (copy of ones which marked boundaries of villages and towns where guards checked to make sure no undesireables passed) to **farmer's house** (now office/ticket booth). Standing alone is old gate of Kamakura's **KENCHO-JI** temple. L to splendid 3-storey **pawn shop**-house with attached storehouse, owned by rich Yamakawa family of Kanazawa. Tho merchants were 'non-productive' bottom rung of 4-step feudal society (top samurai over provider-farmer, artist, merchant; only untouchable caste of eta below merchants), money made life comfortable. Compare to lesser samurai homes and easy to see why latter resented former. Next door **squat house** with wood slat and rock roof is that of lesser merchants, Saigo family seed-dealers—its outside looks like single-storey but once inside note 'hidden' 2nd floor. This, because located near castle S gate on main *Kitaguni-kaido* 'North-country' pedestrian hiway, commoners were forbidden to look down on passing daimyo.

Cross yard to **small house** of low-ranking samurai Takamine–generations of them were doctors of Chinese, and Western medicine learned from Dutch in Nagasaki. Last occupant was biochemist TAKAMINE Jokichi, internationally renowned for having synthesized digestive enzyme taka-diastase. Next door is **sprawling manse** of upper-ranking samurai Yokoyama, advisor to Maeda lords—his stipend was 32,000-koku, Takamine's 100-koku. Yokoyama house also *ka-den* hall of Koraku-ji temple; with section of temple wall extending to this unusual house-like **bell tower**. Next, segment of Kanazawa castle's *namako* wall with cutaway, glassed section for view of inner bamboo and wood supports. Another chunk of wall with gate to samurai manse; but entering, you come to rural Nagai house, behind which is **back gate** of Ekan manse, doctor to Maeda lords. Cross to 3...**farmhouses**: 1st is 18th cent Enda house from Futamata village—as most Futamata folks, he moonlighted as papermaker, house laid out as such.

Next large house is Nomoto family's, village head of Noto's Yanagida village. Theirs much nicer (note tatami rooms) than papermaker's or nearby Kawamura house (poor farmers) since Nomotos had to entertain visiting officials. Display here is *aenokoto*, traditional year-end farmer's ritual.

Last is giant Ishigura house which served as **inn** along old Kitagunikaido. Best rooms reserved for samurai-merchants, commoners had own rooms, porters and horse-handlers were put on top floor.

GETTING THERE: Edo-mura is 45min bus #12 from KANAZAWA stn (stops Hashiba-cho, Kenroku-en, City Folk Mus) to last stop whence 5min **walk**; **cab** 5-6x-mtr o.w. or about 15x-mtr r.t. with wait (more if lunch Hakuun-ro); can get return cab at gate.

Free shuttle bus from Edo-mura every 20min to sister village...
DANPU-EN, Traditional Arts and Crafts Village, included with ticket to Edo-mura, most tourists skip it, so wooded complex is quiet. Built on site of 13th century fortress, Danpu-en has numerous farmhouses of Kaga and Noto areas, **museum** of various arts and crafts, as well as ancient shrines, monuments, hoary gates of samurai mansions, temples.

PERSONAL DATEBOOK: Early **May,** *Ta-ue* demonstration of traditional first rice planting ceremony at Edo-mura paddies; dates vary annually, confirm thru Edomura tourist office or call ☎(0762)-35-1721. Dec **5,** *Aenokoto Festival* of Noto recalls when gods were invited into farm homes for dinner, bath and stay in thanks for good harvest; late AM.

EDO-MURA and DANPU-EN open daily 8:00-18:00 (17:00 winter), ¥1,100. Do not confuse with NIKKO EDO-MURA which is fun Disneylandish take-off, p1038.

YUWAKU ONSEN with its quiet mountain airs and fine inns on upper reaches of Asano River makes for great nite outside Kanazawa, easily reached with attraction of Danpu-en and Edo-mura, nearby Mt Iozan for easy hikes. **Hakuun-ro Hotel,** ☎(0762)-35-1111, which we 'found' 20-odd years ago, is itself sight to see, architectural mix of Orient and Occident. Host to slew of Japanese and foreign dignitaries from Prime Ministers to emperors, and briefly quartered US Occupation. ¥-L to-LL rates with J- and W-rooms and suites, dining rooms, grill, snack bar and cabaret with regular floor shows. Olympic-size pool is ice rink winter, then there are numerous hot spring pools, including one 'expurgated' mixed-bathing pool where 8-inch-high board divide sexes. Sprawling grounds hold tennis courts, lake with row boats and bubbling stream stocked with trout (angling gear at desk). Dressing room and private lounge-bar with view of lake, permits drinking raw hootch in equal raw. Call ahead (Mrs. Aoki speaks English) for lunch and use of baths. Specialty is *kuwa-yaki* 'hoe-grill' meat and vegetables grilled on steel plate and eaten with sauce. Originally farmers cooked meals in fields on back of hoe. (Popular sukiyaki has similar origins: meat and veggies boiled in broth in shovel.) Full meal about ¥13,000.

Atarashi-ya ☎35-1011 ¥-Sw/2, small (20 rooms) personal J-style. Half-dozen other inns along road, varying rates, from ¥-Tw/2. Also fine public bathhouse here.

Found our last visit is superb Japanese restaurant-inn **Zeni-gami,** ☎35-1426, run by old farmer couple who pick their own mountain herbs, vegetables and catch fish every day. Meals only (lunch and dinner, should call ahead) start ¥6,000; spend nite from ¥-hi-Tw/2. Their lovely 160-year-old farmhouse is loaded with turn-of-century items and you get guided tour with your meal. Little out of way, but well worth experience as rarely visited by tourists. **Cab** 8x-mtr from Kanazawa; on **bus** to Yuwaku Onsen, get off at Shibahara (just after Danpu-en) and 30min walk down branch road to L.

Drivers keep on main road SE beyond Danpu-en and Zeni-gami about 8km to Kenri Dam where SE on local road snaking thru hills, over Bunao-toge Pass 25km to Rte156 where 20km N to lovely village of Shirakawa-go, p907. Less adventurous driver, get to Shirakawa-go on Super-Rindo scenic driveway from Mt Hakusan (*see* below); or skip Kenri Dam turn-off for good road NE to Fukumitsu where SE on Rte304 to Rte156. For alternate return to Kanazawa, try Iozan River road to 969m **Mt Iozan** base village where many budget lodgings.

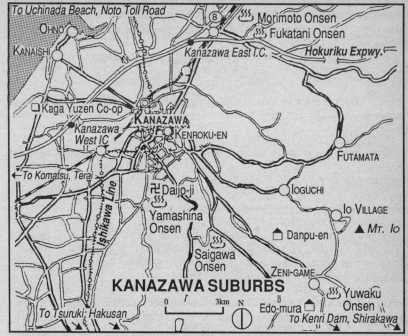

To Uchinada Beach, Noto Toll Road
OHNO
KANAISHI
Morimoto Onsen
Fukatani Onsen
Kanazawa East I.C.
Hokuriku Expwy.
Kaga Yuzen Co-op
KANAZAWA
Kanazawa West IC
KENROKU-EN
FUTAMATA
←To Komatsu, Terai
Daijo-ji
Yamashina Onsen
IOGUCHI
Io VILLAGE
Danpu-en
▲ MT. Io
Saigawa Onsen
Ishikawa Line
ZENI-GAME
KANAZAWA SUBURBS
0   3km   N
Edo-mura
Yuwaku Onsen
To Tsuruki; Hakusan
To Kenri Dam, Shirakawa

Side road from Io-guchi bus stop 5km NE to...

Futamata Paper-making Village about 10km SE of Kanazawa (40min JR bus), has been making paper from kozo (mulberry) for over 500 years, but now only handful of artists remain. Such as Mr Saito, whose workshop is across from post office. Also here is 550-year-old **HONSEN-JI** temple, once main base of radical priest Rennyo.

Only 6km from Kanazawa...

KANAIWA, was latter's main port during Maeda days, and Zeniya family, especially under 7th-generation ZENIYA Gohei (1773-1852), were richest merchants here. Gohei created own trading fleet which, in addition to usual routes of all western Japan, sailed to upper reaches of Honshu and Hokkaido. Many suspect he also did 'illegal' trade with Western ships, China and as far as SE Asia (he presented Maeda lords rare petrified bamboo from Siam). With Kaga in economic doldrums, Maedas created own official fleet of traders under control of Gohei. While enriching Maeda coffers, Gohei created as many enemies as allies, and merchant with such wealth and power was anathema to Tokugawa societal structure, especially if he enriched non-Tokugawa lords—in 1851 Gohei was tossed into jail. His troubles began with plan to fill Kahokugata lagoon (opposed by many), and he was stuck with trumped up charges of poisoning lagoon water to kill off fish. Unproven even to this day as Maedas (perhaps under Tokugawa directive) destroyed all records, he died in jail year later, denying it. Eldest son committed suicide, 3rd son was crucified, family fortune confiscated by Maedas.

Zenigo Ihin-kan (9:00-17:00 X-tue, ¥250) 30min from Kanazawa across from Kanaiwa bus stop; museum of Gohei-related items. Interesting, should be combined with pleasant stroll thru lovely, now sleepy little town. Gohei's grave is in HONRYU-JI temple down road, past which at main intersection is his grand house now lived in by another family; his tea house at SENCHO-JI temple is short way beachwards.

Continue up-coast at intersect, past large statue of Gohei (this one postwar, original melted down for bullets) for short walk to...

OHNO, (also 30min bus #60 or 61 from Kanazawa's Musashi bus stop) village famed for its soy sauce—which odor quite strong.

Beautiful...

OHNO MINATO JINJA shrine ringed by grand greenery and ancient moat is worth visit especially for...

PERSONAL DATEBOOK: May 14-15 *Shinji Noh*, annual outdoor Noh program since 1615 as Maeda tribute to Tokugawa victory at Battle of Sekigahara. Jul 24-25 *Ohno Summer Festival*, 3 villagers dressed as 'mountain demons' visit every home to exorcise evil spirits with dances to drum and flute. Aug 1-3, *Ohno Minato Jinja Festival* highlights colorful wooden floats while shrine's kami spends 2 nites at sea.

Lagoon which Gohei tried to land-fill is several km up-coast; he failed, but is now 2/3rds original size as rest reclaimed for farm land this century. Spit of land between lagoon and ocean, Uchinada sakyu sand dunes, popular summer swimming spot, stretches 20km. 15min tram from Kanazawa to Uchinada, 20min walk to dunes. Drivers might as well come this way as Uchinada is start of Noto toll road, scenic highway heading up Noto Peninsula.

KAGA YUZEN, *Senshoku Danchi* (Co-operative) 25min bus from Kanazawa stn #25 bound for Utsugi and get off Hama Senko-ji. Here you see 2nd major phase of yuzen dyeing. First phase hand-painting best seen at Saihitsu-an in Nagamachi samurai district; cloth then brought here, taken to various workshops for final phase tailoring into kimono or what have you. Important part of dyeing is rinsing cloth in cold, clean water which was done in Asano and Saigawa rivers. But early 1970's pollution and drop in water level due to upstream dams, made rivers virtually useless so dyers dug wells here and set up workshops where rinsing done in long troughs. Anyone welcome to view dyers during regular work hours (9:00-17:00, X-sun and hol); call ahead to arrange for English speaking guide, ☎67-3291. Buses run only once per hr, o.w. cab 2-3x-mtr.

25km (5 stops JR) down-coast of Kanazawa is...

TERAI, main center of Kutani pottery, accounting for over 70% of output. Terai off rail line, but only 5km N of KOMATSU; frequent buses from Komatsu, few from Kanazawa. See Kutani ware being made at Kutani-yaki Kaikan co-operative, in town on Rte8; other potters who let you watch are Yamada Toryu-do, Tokosha and Shinei-do. May 3-5 *Kutani Teacup Festival* sees numerous stalls set up with great bargains. Village of KUTANI itself is today only name, isolated in mountains: from Kaga Onsen stn 26km S of Komatsu, bus 11km to mountain-ringed Yamanaka Onsen (30min) and change to Kutani-bound bus 40min. Original Kutani kilns of 1655 discovered in 1970, *nobori-gama* (climbing kilns) have been repaired, but not in use.

Komatsu Airport 4km SW of town, frequent buses link to Komatsu, 2-3 hourly to Kanazawa. 3km W is Ataka Barrier, site of Benkei-Togashi confrontation of famed Noh and Kabuki play *Kanjin-cho*. Stones mark original site, museum has odds'n-ends reputed to belong to giant Benkei, guard Togashi, lord Yoshitsune. Pair of statues freezes scene from play.

This leg takes us to more backwoods hot springs S of Kanazawa toward sacred Mt Hakusan, with alternate back-country roads to central HIDA area for driver.

Before heading inland to Mt Hakusan, we visit some quiet, alternate overnites at...

KANAZAWA'S 'HIDDEN' ONSENS:
FUKATANI ONSEN (5km NE of Kanazawa), has 3 superb inns nestled in wooded hills; reached by infrequent (3-4x-daily) JR bus from Kanazawa stn (30min) which via two stops up-coast JR Morimoto stn (10min), or cab 3-4x-mtr. All 3 inns somewhat isolated from each other, best **Motoyu Ishiya Ryokan**, ☎(0762)-58-2133, ¥-Tw/2, samurai mansion-like inn which boasts grand garden and Noh stage. Slightly cheaper: **Kuchinoyu Izumi-kan** ☎58-2227 and **Nakanoyu Kiyomizu Ryokan** ☎58-2224. Buses stop in front of Ishiya and Izumi-kan; Kiyomizu is between and slightly behind. Fukatani Onsen is just off of Rte8, convenient to Kanazawa Higashi (E) IC of Hokuriku Expwy and several roads up Noto, like Rte8 branch-off Rte159 or head straight to coast to join Noto toll road. Between it and Morimoto stn is even smaller **Morimoto Onsen**.

SAIGAWA ONSEN is 4km upstream of town on Saigawa River, 20min bus or cab 2-3x-mtr. It too, has one lovely inn, **Taki-tei** ☎29-1122, ¥-hi-Tw/2.

TSURUGI, pleasant mountain town with modern comforts but old rural atmosphere (lots of family-run **sake brewers** and **cutlery makers**), is 14km S of Kanazawa. Best way is 30min on Hokuriku Tetsudo Rail's Ishikawa Line from Nomachi stn. Rickety trains were originally planned to wind thru mountains, across Honshu to Gifu and Nagoya to become part of latter's superb Meitetsu Rail system (thus Meitetsu Store in Kanazawa), but interest waned as costs of crossing formidable mountains grew. (Even JR with massive govt funding abandoned such plans and to this day, mere 15km gap separates Nagaragawa Rail Line (Mino-Ota–Hokuno) and Etsuminoku Line (Fukui–Kuzuryu). Runs hourly every day; half turn back at Tsurugi or next stop Kaga Ichinomiya, rest go to last stop Hakusan-shita, 1hr from Kanazawa.

Drivers: parallel Rte157 which cuts S from main road (from Kanazawa's Tera-machi) near splendid Kita Kinen-kan house. Road and rail follows Tedori River, especially beautiful on 7km stretch of Tedori-kyokoku Gorge beyond Tsurugi to Hakusan-shita where it flows between rail and road. Occasional **bus** from Komatsu stn via TATSU-NO-KUCHI ONSEN. Buses also leave Kenroku-en shita bus stop, roughly every other hour starting 6:45 to 19:35, 50min to Kaga Ichinomiya stn;

all but last continue 20min further to one-inn...

TEDORI ONSEN along Tedori River and popular base for hiking along river gorge.

SHIRAYAMA-HIME JINJA shrine has been Tsurugi's claim to fame for almost 1,200 years when founded as main shrine of Hakusan mountain worshippers. In addition to 6 other main Hakusan sub-shrines around mount, is head of 2,710 Hakusan shrines nationwide, putting this mountain not far behind Mt Fuji in sacredness. Enshrining creator gods of Japan Izanagi and Izanami, buildings of this beautiful shrine were last rebuilt over 500 years ago, but still in excellent condition thanks to care of immense popularity. Jinja is few minutes' walk SE of Kaga Ichinomiya stn; Tsurugi stn is 1.5km N.

1km NE of Tsurugi stn is...

KINKEN JINJA shrine, one of 6 main sub-shrines of Shirayama-hime Jinja. It predates Shirayama, reputedly built by 10th emperor Sujin (legend-1st century BC), becoming affiliated with Shirayama in mid-8th century AD.

Stroll from Kaga Ichinomiya to Tsurugi is pleasant, and you may want to fortify yourself with local specialty bear sashimi (also cooked, which is better, raw unsafe) served at **Wataya**, folksy restaurant-inn in Shirayama shrine compound. They also serve pheasant, badger, and more commonly, river fish, all accompanied with fresh mountain herbs and vegetables. All is washed down with excellent local sake, best of which is *Manzai-raku*, sold in regular glass bottles or the more attractive Kutani jugs.

Funaoka-yama, *Kodai jukyo-ato* (prehistoric site) is just N of Shirayama shrine. In 1949, 4 Jomon period fire pits were discovered here, and 2 of them have been recreated into Jomon pit-dwellings. Judging from remains excavated, this group was 'trading post' between mountaineers and coastal dwellers. Pits spaced about 5m apart, each sunken into earth 20cm, and 4m around ringed with stones. Nearby, chairlifts and ropeway leads to SHISHIKU KOGEN plateau for fine view; summer go-kart track, field athletics obstacle course, campsite, winter skiing.

PERSONAL DATEBOOK: Perhaps dating back to ritual of Tsurugi's Jomon inhabitants, Shirayama jinja main festival (**1st sun Jun**) has nothing to do with mountain, but is prayer for bountiful catch at sea. All sorts of seafood, both animal and plant, is offered to shrine, followed by unusual *tairyo-kagura* (great fishing kagura) dance done by miko shrine maidens.

IKKAN-IN temple, 1km N beyond KINKEN JINJA, was built to protect 7.5m high 1,300-year-old hillside carving of Fudo Myo-o done by priest Taicho after return from China. Severely faded by elements (before structure housing it went up), it is less spectacular than those of China which perhaps Taicho emulated, but it is nonetheless impressive with its red flames and giant sword, and popular as cure for bad eyes. Reputedly largest Fudo carving in all Asia, tho even in Japan, larger sculptures of other icons can be found in Yamato plains, Kunisaki Peninsula near Beppu and Oita on Kyushu.

WHERE TO STAY: Tsurugi has several low ¥-lo-Tw/2 ryokan of which, as of 1987, 2 draw hot spring water: **Sawada Ryokan** ☎(07619)-2-0180, and **Kagetsu-so** ☎2-1331. Above-mentioned restaurant-inn **Wadaya** ☎2-0570, runs ¥-Sw/2, dinners feasts of their delicacies. Handful of other moderate rate inns makes Tsurugi popular base for exploring...

MT HAKUSAN, for hikers who will find numerous mountain hot springs as trailheads for climb up mountain, accessible only from late April's spring thaw to October's first heavy snows. Many trails criss-cross Hakusan starting and ending at these backwoods baths, for which, get maps at Kanazawa's bookstores or various tourist organizations. Common way to climb is to reach main 2702m **Gozen-mine** peak late day or nite staying to catch *goraiko* sunrise reflected off clouds. We have not done Hakusan, but similar climbs we often start in cool of nite, to spend few hours watching grand show of dark becoming day, then reaching base onsens for relaxing morning dip. Stone hut was first erected at Murodo, south face of Gozen-mine at 2,440m level, in 1789 for mountain ascetics' training near Oku-no-in inner-most sanctuary of Shirayama Shrine. It is now much larger with less-spartan lodgings, and in summer (**July 1-Aug 31**) has medical center, post office and telephones. All trails converge here; about 30min to Gozen-mine's summit. Campsite nearby.

Arrange all Murodo lodgings thru **Shiramine Village Office** before heading up, or call ☎(06198)-2011 to make sure if sitting out cold in cold doesn't strike your fancy.

10 trails from 8 trailheads climb Mt Hakusan from E, N and S. Most popular and shortest trail up is from **Betto-shugo** from where two parallel trails 6km (4hr30min) to **Murodo**. Betto-shugo is 50min bus from Hakusan-shita rail stn; infrequent runs early May thru Oct.

On return trip you might take dip at one-inn...
HAKUSAN ONSEN (Ichinose bus stop) 2km down the road, or hop bus direct to Shiramine village (*see* below), halfway to Hakusan-shita. Longer trail from **Ichinose** due E to 2399m Bessan peak from where N across narrow ridge to Murodo; about 8hrs. North face trails are much longer.

Most popular is from...
CHUGU ONSEN, lovely 'hidden' mountain hamlet with 4 old inns (all ¥-lo-Tw/2):
Nishiyama ☎(07619)-6-7219; Kido ☎6-7953; Miyamura ☎6-7124; Yamada ☎6-
7131. 40min bus (3 daily) from Hakusan-shita stn, May-Oct; snow gets so deep in winter
that whole place evacuates Nov to Apr. Trail from here is circuitous 18km (full day) to
Gozen-mine, just before which is Midori-ga-ike lake, largest of several volcanic
caldera lakes. Chugu Onsen is also western end of Hakusan Super-rindo 'Forest Road'
(toll) which cuts across on scenic winding 33.3km course to fabulous Ogi-machi hamlet
of Gifu Prefecture's Shirakawa-go Village, famed for houses with steep thatched 'hands-
in-prayer' roofs (*see* KISO-KAIDO in OFFBEAT CHUBU area, p.898).

4km E of Chugu on this road is tiny...
SHINYA-NO-YU ONSEN; easy trail connects two, and trail from Shinya-no-yu
meets Chugu's trail to summit. Chugu, 'Middle-shrine', gets name from one of 6 main
sub-shrines of Shirayama-hime Jinja, now gone.

15min bus before Chugu is...
ICHIRINO ONSEN, much larger popular base for skiing, with small hotel, 3 ryokan,
Kokumin-shukusha and half-dozen minshuku. We recommend Chugu over Ichirino.

But for those who want even smaller hot springs, try:

SHIN IWAMA ONSEN, *ikken-yado* (one-inn-spa) about 3km up branch road from
Ichirino. 1hr30min walk from Ichirino, or call ahead to inn Yamazaki Ryokan
☎(07619)-6-7950, ¥-Tw/2, and they pick you up at Ichirino. It also closes in winter.

4km beyond Shin Iwama is...
IWAMA ONSEN, outdoor bath (*rotenburo*) in forest with unmanned shack. Road ends
here in 10km trail up to Gozen-mine. Iwama is 2.5km E of Chugu, trail linking two
which passes cluster of mini geysers along Nakanogawa River. You hear rumbling from
distance, and largest ones shoot steam over 10m into air, just one of wonders you will
find hiking Hakusan National Park.

Mt Hakusan is neatly bisected by border of Ishikawa and Gifu prefectures, E face trails
start from Gifu's HIRASE ONSEN on Rte156 near Miboro Dam. In summer, infrequent bus from onsen 1hr up to Oshirakawa Dam from where 5km to Gozen-mine,
otherwise, its 8km walk on road to dam with campsite near spectacular waterfall.
Adventurous hiker should start at one hot spring and end at another, best would be starting
southern Hakusan Onsen, camp at or near summit to end Chugu from where hitch ride on
Super-Rindo Forest Road to Shirakawa-go.

SHIRAMINE VILLAGE is for people seeking someplace more backwoods than Tsurugi but not quite as tiny or hard to get to as smaller mountainside hot springs.

GETTING THERE: Only 2 buses daily (30min) from HAKUSAN-SHITA; 3
buses daily (90min) from KANAZAWA stn; or 2 daily (50min) from Kyofuku Dentetsu
Private Rail's KATSUYAMA stn (1hr from Fukui, 40min from EIHEI-JI temple).
SHIRAMINE is also hot spring with half-dozen moderate rate inns such as Oda Ryokan
☎(07619)-8-2033, and dozen budget minshuku. All can be booked thru Village
Tourist Bureau ☎8-2011, or thru Kanazawa's main JTB office (English spoken)
which can also arrange for other mountain hot springs.

To deal with long snowy winters Shiramine's traditional homes look
more like *kura* storehouses—thick dirt walls and tiny windows, and most
often, thatch roof. They are in sharp contrast to stately wood and thick
thatched-roof homes of Shirakawa-go village but both areas have suffered
similar fate as need to modernize overpowered mountain villages. Hydro-
electic dam built on Tedori River in late '60s flooded entire valley, submerging several hamlets. Few houses saved and moved to Danpu-en.
Miboro Dam flooded much larger area of Shirakawa-go and received much
more publicity due to more unique homes, dozens of which were saved

thanks to public outcry. Tedori Dam damage's largest recognition came from American Japanologue Morton Huber who wrote and illustrated slim book *Tedori River Gorge: The Final Curtain Descends*, now out of print.

10min walk N of Shiramine bus stop...

Folk Museum, *Minzoku Shiryo-kan*, lets you see inside these houses as 3 of them, Kokura, Hida and Sugihara family houses, were donated to show region's life style. Many items are from *de-zukuri*, mountain shack where farmers lived during farming season to be near their fields.

RINSAI-JI temple (near Shiramine bus stop) has been associated to Hakusan shrines since founded 717AD by Taicho who started Hakusan religion. First to climb Mt Hakusan, he was met by mountain's kami, riding splendid white horse, and granted *satori* (enlightenment). Satori usually associated with Buddhism; many early priests followed blend of Buddhism-Shinto, both religions living in harmony with exception of early Meiji forced split lasting thru jingoist military government of wartime Japan. These bi-religious mountain ascetics still can be seen—albeit less often as modern youth shun them, are reciprocated—trekking mountains of Japan. Collectively called *yama-bushi*, they were particularly populous in rugged Hokuriku and Tohoku mountains (in play *Kanjincho* Yoshitsune and his followers disguised themselves as yamabushi while passing up Japan Sea coast to their goal in Tohoku's Hiraizumi). Anyway, Taicho converted shrines and temples in Hokuriku to Hakusan sect and mountain was home of **OKU-NO-IN** shrine and several Buddhist statues. In Meiji split of 1860s, statues were brought down from their high seats and placed here in Rinsai-ji temple 'divorced' from Shinto. This 'coming down' from mountain says much about Hakusan religion's power, for in most cases anything Buddhist was just destroyed. On Gifu side of Hakusan lesser Buddhist statues were saved from destruction by quick-thinking villagers who beat officials by hiding statues in secret building (*see* MINO-SHIRATORI). 11-faced Kannon sat atop highest Gozen-mine, while #2 Oonanji peak had Amida and #3 Bessan peak had Kannon-Bosatsu. All 3 icons, with 6 others, are kept in Rinsai-ji, shown to public only **Jan 1-3 & Jul 17, 18** tho you might be shown them if guided to see other statues kept here (leave small donation).

Artists' Studio, *Hakusan Kobo* (9:00-16:00 X-thurs, winter X-sun, ¥300) demonstrations of local silk weaving & museum of tools used; **kiosk** sells product; 10min walk S of Kuwashima bus stop (1 stop/1.5km walk N of Shiramine.

Another Hakusan specialty is joruri puppet play *Deku-mawashi*, developed here by villagers to entertain in long winters. Performed around lunar New Year, best show is at **Oguchi** hamlet's new **Community Center** nitely 8:30pm, **2nd & 3rd wknd Feb**. Take Shiramine-bound bus at Higashi-Futakuchi stop (2 before Shiramine), near Tedori Dam. Can stay at Shiramine inns, or call Oguchi-mura village, **Kyoiku-iinkai** ☎(07619)-6-7120 to arrange for nite with local family. Irregular performances also done at **Fukaze Shin-machi** (between Sodani and Shijima stns, Kanazawa-side of Tsurugi), which settled by dam-displaced villagers of Shiramine area. Get exact dates thru JTB or call **Fukaze Shin-machi town office** ☎(07619)-3-1791.

PERSONAL DATEBOOK:

1st Sun every month, noh-kyogen (*see* p.863).

January

1-3 Kenroku-en open (*free*).

6 *Kaga tobi dezome-shiki*, firemen's acrobatics on high ladders along Saigawa river bank. One of Kanazawa's top 2 festivals with over 1,400 men (all firefighters) clad in traditional happi perform stunts. Originated by Maeda's private army of firefighters stationed at their Edo mansion, reputed to be best firemen in old Edo.

Jan 6-Feb 3 *Kan-shugyo* (Winter ascetic training) sees priests of Daijo-ji temple going around town in straw sandals collecting food and other gifts, following 4:30am zazen session, all welcome to join.

25 10:00am Tanshin-sai celebrates Lord Toshiie's birthday at Oyama Jinja shrine.

February

3 *Setsubun* marks last day of winter at shrines all around town. Best at Kobashi Sugawara Jinja where Kaga manzai comic dances are done at nite.

March

1-3 Annual airing of Kosai-ji temple treasures including many saved from Ikkoshu's Kanazawa (Oyama) Gobo HQ.

April

15 Yasue Hachiman Jinja shrine festival.

Mid to late – , cherry blossom season Kenroku-en open (*free*); other popular viewing sites on Utatsuyama hill and Saigawa river banks.

19-20 Gokoku Jinja shrine's *Spring Festival* with special mi-kagura dances.

29 *Ningyo-kuyo* memorial rites for old dolls, Shinjyo-ji temple.

May

3-5 Kutani *pottery fair*, Teral (*text*, p.876).

14-15 *Shinji* outdoor noh (*text*, p.876).

17 *Miyazaki Yuzen-sai* memorial, Ryukoku-ji temple, special tea ceremony, geisha dances.

June

Early, National High School Sumo Tournament, Utatsuyama sumo stadium.

13-15 Kaga *Hyakuman-goku Festival*, Kanazawa's largest, sees all sorts of exhibitions and demonstrations around town, Kenroku-en open (*free*).

13-14 Highlight of above.

14 Feudal costume parade at castle area.

July

Mid Early *o-bon*, nitely dancing at temples, shrines with 100s of lanterns lit.

15-16 At Gokoku Jinja shrine where special *kiriko* wood lanterns lit in honor of war dead; another major at Daijo temple.

17-18 *Kanko-odori* dance fetes Taicho's descent from Mt Hakusan, when welcomed back by joyous villagers dancing to drums. Performed in Shiramine-Kouchi area for official mountain-opening rite, Shiraminemura. Confirm thru JTB or village office.

16,31 *Grand O-bon* dances Toyokuni shrine

August

1st week sees temples airing treasured scrolls, paintings, cloths and sutras to prevent mildew and bugs. About same time (1st or 2nd weekend) *Ishikawa Summer Festival* with booths of food, games, entertainment, fab **fireworks**.

Mid – Real O-bon season in countryside (July urban). Kanazawa best now: shrines, temples full of people and lanterns, more notable events are *Yuzen toro-nagashi* city's Yuzen craftsmen in thanks to river float colorful hand-painted lanterns down Asano river at dusk, you can get rare glimpse of wandering shakuhachi-playing priests; *Shiman-rokusen-nichi*, Kannon-in temple, only time to see special Kannon image and make rounds of 33 holy spots; 800-year-old Iyasaka-odori dances at outlying Futamata town celebrate local Genji-Heike battle (former won); prayer for peace at Gokoku Jinja shrine on . . .

15 Notes end of World War II; colorful Sakata-odori dance nearby Hatta village; famed local *Jongara-odori bon* dance Nonoichi school, dates to Heian era. *Daibutsu* (Great Buddha) *Festival* Rensho-ji notes 1736 fire, lanterns lit before giant Buddha.

September

15 *Autumn Festival*, Ueno Hachiman Jinja shrine, colorful mochi-pounding dance.

October

thruout *Autumn Festivals* such as:

2-4 at Oyama Jinja shrine and;

19-20 at Gokoku Jinja shrine with repeat of special maiden *kagura* dances.

November

Early sees *yuki-tsuri* tree suspensions going up at Kenroku-en.

December

30-31 Kenroku-en open (*free*).

882

*The reader should be carried forward...,
not by a restless desire to arrive..., but by
the pleasurable activity of the journey itself.*
—Samuel Coleridge

NOTO 能登 & HEGURA 舳倉
LONELY COASTS

THIS IS *INAKA*, real boondocks. Lifestyle here has changed little over ages. Most villages still operate small fishing fleets while women haul in and dry kelp on shore. At one place fishermen sit for hours on tripod stilts waiting for mullet to swim into suspended nets, while others still dry sea water into natural salt, and farmers in steeply terraced hillside paddies harvest rice by hand. Barren Hegura Isle far off north shore has seasonal *ama* women divers whose ancestors started centuries ago, abandoning it in winter. Things will remain unchanged as long as people remain in these villages, for rugged Noto has little else to offer; only modern industry that can survive here is nuclear energy, one plant is already set up. But like most rural communities, youth are mostly drawn to city life and Noto's timeless villages may not survive this century. While towns become more modern, villages are photog's dream come true, little different in appearance since feudal times with many superb houses kept intact by opening up to tourists. Much of Noto is for time-insensitive adventurer willing to rough it (budget minshuku and campsites abound), but even most discriminating travelers will find grand rural inns reached relatively easily in time and comfort from Kanazawa for memorable overnight outing.

Here Garet tasted that 'real Japan' Sumi and Jay loved decades ago.

NOTO PENINSULA
...HOOKS OUT INTO Japan Sea NE of Kanazawa; Kanazawa may be 'back' side of Japan, but Noto is even more rural as backside of Kanazawa. Its windward shore (W and N) is called *Soto-ura*, or outer-back side, while its leeward shore enclosing Toyama Bay is called *Uchi-ura*, inner-back side. All Noto is divided into 3 major regions: *Kuchi-Noto* 'Mouth of Noto' is everything S of valley linking W shore Hakui to E shore Nanao, generally flat fertile land and sandy beaches; *Naka-Noto* 'Middle Noto', N of Hakui-Nanao line to Monzen (W) and Mizuana (E), is rather similar; *Oku-Noto* 'Back Noto' is hook's end curving NE and is rugged in contrast—most interesting section of Peninsula; those short on time should concentrate here.

Noto may be out of way, but not too difficult, with many choices, for...

GETTING AROUND: JR's frequent-run Nanao Line fast Raicho (3hr39min 3x daily from start OSAKA → WAKURA Onsen), runs many expresses out of KANAZAWA branches off Hokuriku Main Line 3 stops, 11.6km up-coast TSUBATA, follows W shore → HAKUI (41.3km) where cut across NE → NANAO (66km); N along Nanao Bay → ANAMIZU (99.1km) then back across peninsula → N shore terminus WAJIMA (119.5km). At ANAMIZU Noto Line branches off to follow inside hook of Noto to NE tip Takojima (61.1km from Anamizu, Kanazawa 160.2km); many end 2 stops, 3.7km earlier at main SUZU-IIDA town. Half of trains from KANAZAWA go direct to WAJIMA, rest to SUZU. All express and most local arrivals at ANAMIZU allow just enough time (2–10min) to get connection to either WAJIMA or SUZU-TAKOJIMA. From Noto's eastern 'root' TAKAOKA City, short Himi Line goes up E shore hourly → HIMI town, 16.5km; reverse is optional exit from Noto for adventurers. Check seasonal JR excursions from Osaka by bus or luxury Raicho express compartment: JR West ☎06-375-8945.

Local **bus** service around Noto (most private Hoku-tetsu, some JR) extensive, but quicker rail much easier for nonadventurous non-Japanese-speakers who should **cab** to out-of-town sites. Buses involve many changes if trying to go direct (for which JR), but excellent (if somewhat expensive, tho no more so than local rail fee) way to see Noto's back side; little to attract native tourist (so no hordes even midsummer) but lovely villages, beaches with campsites and craggy coastline. Basic local **bus** route is: hourly (8:40-18:40) from KANAZAWA stn → HAKUI (1hr; same as rail) on Rte249, whence these, and many more starting from Hakui, up-coast → TOGI (2hr30min); some change at SANMYO. Some from KANAZAWA end 40min beyond at MONZEN; otherwise take local TOGI → MONZEN via SEKINO on coast-hugging secondary road, 1hr10min. From MONZEN, roughly hourly departures to WAJIMA, in 45min. For buses beyond Wajima, see below. Easy is Hokutetsu's Oku-Noto Tokkyu (express) bus from Kanazawa stn, 2-3 daily, direct 2hrs → WAJIMA. Beats rail time by 30min at roughly same cost; now takes Noto toll road missing shorter, rustic W shore Rte249 from Hakui, which rail also misses. Suggest change to Kyuko HAKUI → MONZEN (Rte 249), then local → WAJIMA, 40min. 4 express buses also between TAKAOKA and NANAO (and WAKURA Onsen).

TOUR BUSES: Two main choices: 1) *Noto Kanko* courses on Hokutetsu, set tours on luxury buses and 2) *Oku-Noto* courses on Hoku-tetsu and JR which are basically regular buses with tour guide. Oku-Noto limits to Wakura Onsen and beyond, has added option of getting off and on as many times on each route to spend more time at sites. Get transfer slip if connecting with following bus or spending nite somewhere en route; but beware midsummer buses often full and hard to get on at partway small stops. Oku-Noto mostly operates Wakura Onsen and Ushitsu (both on Uchi-Ura) to Wajima (on Soto-Ura), and return. Noto Kanko tours offer dozen variations mostly between Kanazawa to Wajima, best of which is combination of Noto Kanko #3 with #2 for 2-day full coverage of Noto: Dep KANAZAWA (#3 9:10) up Soto-Ura coast to Kita-ke house → Chirihama → Keta Jinja → Myojo-ji → Ganmon rocks → Kanko Center (lunch) → Sekino → Soji-ji → Wajima Lacquer Center → Wajima stn (opt end) → Tokikuni houses → Sosogi → Maura Onsen (#3 18:15). Nite at Sosogi or Maura (your choice) & next day Noto #2 dep Sosogi 7:40 and Maura 7:50 to visit Noroshi (NE tip) → Kibei-don house (Suzu) → Tsukumo Bay → Anamizu → Chirihama back to KANAZAWA (15:57). ¥11,750 for round-trip and lunch, #2 daily all year, # 3 daily 3/10-11/30. Best to arrange any bus tours at Kanazawa main JTB office (where some English is spoken), who will also help on itinerary for solo travelers by arranging schedule and lodgings. JTB branch company JTB-Ace also has various bus tours and hire-cab tours, latter made to suit your personal itinerary.

RENT-A-CAR is most pleasant way to see Noto. Best round-trip (avoid exorbitant drop-off fee) out of Kanazawa which has several rental agencies. 3-4 people for as many days will spend about as much on rental as on local transport but coverage much more extensive. Local eki (stn) rentals; Nissan, Toyota and NRS at Nanao, Wakura Onsen, Wajima and Takaoka for total of 15 offices. For less driving, advised is out of Wajima for easy half-day (60km r.t.) coverage of 'Lacquer Road' (see below), with option of night at Suzu to end Wajima or Wakura Onsen; watch out for drop off fee and make sure your rental company has office in Wakura or Hakui. *Noto Yuryo-doro* toll road starts at Uchinada near Kanazawa to roughly parallel rail, ending (as of 1990) at Anamizu, to be eventually completed to Wajima. It is fast, but you miss just about everything worth seeing. Rte159 hugs rail line whole way to Wajima; Rte249, which branches off Rte159 about 10km S of Hakui, circles peninsula coast to rejoin Rte159 at Anamizu. Rte160 links Nanao to Takaoka. Tho many local roads crisscross mountainous interior, most sites are on main roads and you almost have to try to get lost and enough road signs have English to be of help. **Chirihama**, strip of beach between Imahama N to Hakui has sand so hard-packed that it is natural Nagisa Driveway for cars.

HITCHHIKERS should count on some long waits and short rides unless lucky enough to get long-distance truckers on main Rtes 159 and 249. Anyone **bicycling** will find bike-only road along Noto toll road from Uchinada to Hakui where it branches off to run coast-side of Rte249 15km to Shiga town then roughly parallels Rte249 to Monzen.

HI-SPEED BOATS run regularly along E coast, main: Nanao → Wakura Onsen → Ushitsu → Ogi → Iida (Suzu). From Iida some slow boats cross Toyama Bay → Itoigawa, way upcoast on mainland near Naoetsu. SIGHTSEEING BOATS cruise several scenic areas on E coast; also old steamer links Wajima and isolated HEGURA ISLE of ama divers.

TILT: Soto-Ura side of Kuchi-Noto has some interesting temples (MYOJO-JI and SOJI-JI) and shrines (KETA-JINJA), but short-timer using rail can pass these up to spend more time in Wajima area. Leave early AM Kanazawa: express Noto-ji #1 dep 8:00 gets to Wajima 10:19 with no changes; Noto-ji #3 dep 9:56 becoming local from Nanao arriving Wajima 12:44 change at Anamizu. NOTO-JI #1 best as gives you time to see sites in Wajima, then bus, cab or rent-a-car around 'Lacquer Road' area, to spend nite in Wajima or Maura Onsen. Return direct to Kanazawa next AM, or for full day return trip take bus to Suzu (via part of Lacquer Road) where late afternoon train back (16:54 local becomes express beyond Ushitsu to end Kanazawa 21:03).

Cab to Suzu from Wajima 46km (25x-mtr), from Maura Onsen 28km (14x-mtr) lets you see Lacquer Road area without waiting for buses, to catch 12:22 express Noto-ji #10 from Wajima to Kanazawa 15:29. If exiting Noto by midafternoon, you might stop by Kita-ke house, for which change to local at Hakui and 4 stops S to Menden and 20min walk or basic-mtr cab. Extra nite on Noto lets you mix rail/bus to see main temples, reaching Wajima late day, for leisurely day 2 around Oku-Noto to spend 2nd nite Suzu or Ushitsu and boat down to Nanao to rejoin rail; or stay Wajima area (lots to do) and boat out for relaxing day on Hegura Isle. On most recent visit, Garet and friend drove all over Noto in 2 days; Wajima is only 88km from Kanazawa, and that is taking coastal Rte249. Including several stops en route, got to Wajima early afternoon, did Lacquer Road full circle, back to Wajima and nite at Maura Onsen. Day 2 was out to tip then down Uchiura to Takaoka (200km from Maura), to zip thru Toyama and head inland, making it to lovely Hida Takayama late that day. 5 years earlier, he hitched around loop in 3 days.

Our itinerary takes us clockwise around Noto; leaving Kanazawa, first stop is...

Kita-ke House (8:00-17:00 daily, ¥300), 15min walk from Menden stn (10th from Kanazawa, 40min) or 5min walk from Kita-Kawajiri bus stop (1hr from Kanazawa) on Rte159; drivers save some time on Noto toll road from Uchinada to Takamatsu I.C. Kita family (not related to Kita sake and soy sauce brewers of Nonoichi) were wealthy farmers acting as *to-mura-yaku* 'ten-village chief' in local governmental system unique to Kaga. In 1608 lord Maeda grouped villages into larger units of 10 over which to-mura-yaku were responsible. Grand thatched-roof gatehouse leads to spacious compound with storehouse and main house with four separate entrances, one each for Maeda officials, samurai, village heads and Kita family members—extreme example of culture of gates whereby status marked by relativity of gate, from emperor (*mikado* literally 'illustrious gate') down. Beautiful interior further enhanced by displays of farmer and samurai items including splendid gifts from various Maeda lords.

Okabe-ke House (9:00-18:00 daily, ¥300), 6km N, another to-mura-yaku house rebuilt 1736 with simple but beautiful strolling garden. Okabe family became to-mura-yaku in 1697, and claim noble ancestry: ancestor Tadazumi was general of Minamoto Yoshitsune in Genpei War.

1km NE of Shikinami stn (2 N); from Kita-kawajiri bus stop, can catch Nanao-bound buses (Kanazawa Kenroku-en-shita stop hourly on hour) direct dep Oginoshima (10min).

At Shikinami, Rte159 branches off towards Nanao while Rte249 continues N to...

HAKUI, bustling but rustic town with little for tourist, was one of earliest settlements on Noto attested to by many old temples and shrines nearby. Area said to have been settled by prince Iwatsukiwake, son of 11th emperor Suinin (trad 29BC-70AD), after prince got rid of poisonous monster crow terrorizing villagers. Prince reputedly buried in giant mound (63m x 100m) in grounds of in-town HAKUI JINJA shrine. **Folk History Museum**, *Rekishi Shiryo Minzoku-kan* (¥100), 5min walk E of stn, has archaeological miscellania from Noto digs. 15min walk S of stn is 2,000-year-old Karatoyama **Sumo-jo**, oldest Sumo ring in Japan which still has offertory sumo matches in Sept (*see* DATEBOOK, p.896).

WHERE TO STAY: Late departees from Kanazawa will find lodgings to suit all budgets and tastes in and around Hakui: In town are 2 dozen budget to moderate inns; boasting anti-rheumatic hot spring baths and seaside golf course is luxurious **Noto Royal Hotel** ☎(07673)-2-3111 (¥-T–Sw/2), 20min cab N of Hakui stn. Closer to town (5min cab) **Hakui Kanko Hotel** ☎(07672)-2-1236 (¥-Tw/2) boasts radium bath with grand view, at Ichinomiya near Keta Shrine. Budgeteers have 2 dozen minshuku spread between **Chirihama Beach** (where summer sees held-for-tourists hauling in of giant fishing nets) and Ichinomiya; over 40 more spread along white-sand **Shibagaki Beach** N of town, stretching 10km from Keta jinja shrine to Takahama (also called Shika) town, also with 3 campsites. **Youth Hostel** ☎27-1241, at rustic HONJO-JI temple at middle of Shibagaki beach.

Beaches get rather crowded midsummer for which, escape to cool mountainous...
SHINGU ONSEN, 30min bus SE of Hakui to last stop; along small river feeding down from wooded 637m high Mt. Hodatsu-yama. There is one old inn at Shingu hamlet, further up is budget Kokumin-shukusha **Shinguso** ☎(076729)-3141.

5min bus before Shingu is...
Kanaya Kofun 6th-century tumulus; stone sarcophagus with chigi crossbeams now displayed outside. **Drivers** from Okabe House continue up Rte159 to next main intersection where R to Shingu.

BUZAI-IN temple, (3.5km E of Hakui stn near Iiyama bus stop (19min) on rte159), first zen dojo of Noto, built ca.1310 by zen master Keizan, who later founded grand Soji-ji complex (see below). BUZAI-IN not very large, but its treasures make visit worthwhile, among which three Kannon statues carved out of single hinoki cypress tree, 600 scrolls of Dai-Hanya Sutra of Great Wisdom which written in blood took 60 years to complete, and blood painting of Amida-nyorai (8:00-17:00 daily, ¥200).

KETA JINJA shrine (10min bus N from Hakui stn to Ichinomiya, 5min walk) foremost shrine of Noto. Much of compound was rebuilt 14th-16th century but site much older. Like many great shrines, has strong Buddhist part to it which was 'exorcised' in Meiji and Keta became one of top National State Shrines in Taisho era. Just W is Buddhist half JOGAKU-IN temple, which treasure hall is loaded with Buddhist statues and other treasures salvaged from Keta Jinja. Both open 8:30-16:30 (¥100). Near shrine is **Isomi Seito-en kiln** of Taisha-yaki pottery. Its trademark is tree leaves burned into glaze; also sold at next stop Myojo-ji temple's gift shop. Visit workshop and display room (8:00-17:00 X-sun and hol). Radium-rich clay used is said to be good for health.

Side road from Keta and Jogaku-in shortcuts curvy Rte240, 3km N (or 20min bus from Hakui to Takiya-guchi, 15min walk) to...
MYOJO-JI temple built 1293 as main Nichiren sect temple of Hokuriku. Its complex, largest in Noto, grew to such size thanks to 70 years of patronage of 3rd to 5th Maeda lords of Kanazawa. Every building is Important Cultural Asset; includes stately 34m 5-tier pagoda best seen rising above landscaped garden of Shoin head-priest's quarters (8:00-17:00, ¥300).

20min bus beyond, in fishing village of Shika-machi is...
Taira-ke Tei-en, two grand landscaped gardens dating to mid-Muromachi era (early 15th century). House and garden belonged to descendants of Taira-no-Shibutayu (general of Kiyomori) who fled here after defeat by Heike at battle of Kurikara Pass (1182) 90km S of here; (7:00-18:00, ¥500).

Almost within spitting distance of hotel is...
Noto Nuclear Power Center, *Genshiryoku,* which Publicity Center (9:30-16:30, free) has displays on uses of nuclear energy, video library and other displays. Good view from rooftop observatory.

From Shika-machi, buses take slightly inland Rte249 20min to Miyoshi from where can continue 15min to TOGI; or change buses and 15min to coastal...

Ganmon rock formations, one section of scenic NOTO KONGO coastline, where **sightseeing boats** do 25min cruise among rocks daily Apr 1 to Nov 15; depart when 10 people show. Bus hits coast at FUKU-URA village, which got its start in 8th-9th century as official trade port to Korean kingdom of Paekche; continued to flourish during Edo period as stop along shipping route to Tohoku and Hokkaido, town's 60-plus 'flower ladies' were supposedly so skilled that well-known sailor's song of times says "once again today, they stopped our ships from leaving." Now its just sleepy fishing village. **Wooden lighthouse** in harbor (built in 1876) is oldest such in Japan; guide-fires burned on this spot for over 9 centuries prior.

Small ¥-B **Hotel Ganmon**, ladies-only inn, 3 minshuku at Ganmon; plus 40-odd ¥-B ryokan and minshuku spread between Fuku-ura and Togi, and more beyond.

Drivers take coastal secondary road from Shika-machi to Ganmon; pass **Fukiage-no-taki** 40m waterfalls (nearby campsite on beach) and one-inn **Kongo Onsen** near Unagami bus stop (Rte249 and secondary coast road rejoin here, can take any bus).

6km from Ganmon is...
TOGI, bustling fishing town with budget lodgings; most of 30 minshuku located along MASUHO-NO-URA, curving, pine tree-backed beach stretching 3km from Togi River to Sakami River (where Youth Hostel and Kokumin-shukusha), popular swimming spot known for its shells. Most up-west-shore buses from Kanazawa or Hakui end here, tho some go 26km further up-coast, or change here to local bus detouring along coastline via SEKINO-HANA point to...

MONZEN along narrow Yatsuga River valley.

Just before turning inland upstream, at Kurashima village is...
JIGEI-EN, home of *Noshu-tsumugi* pongee. Run by Mr and Mrs UESHIMA Yozan who came from Kyoto in 1965, blending colorful style of Kyoto's Nishijin weaving with simplicity of Noto's, and creating their own natural dyes. They teach you to weave on their loom in one-day crash course. Lesson fee ¥1,250 and cost of silk (about ¥1,000) will make you necktie or tablemat; you can also stay there at budget rates. Call ahead ☎(0768)-43-1524 to arrange. Or just stop by to watch them at work and perhaps buy some of their lovely work. It is 10min bus (or cab 2x-mtr) before Monzen which is 20km from Wajima; cab 10x-mtr or 45min hourly bus, or 15km from Anamizu (45min bus, some JR, cab 8x-mtr). Kuroshima village also has some interesting houses, one of which is splendid manse of Edo period shipping merchants.

SOJI-JI SO-IN temple is main attraction of Monzen, and should be your choice if only stopping at one temple along Soto-Ura coast. Founded 1321 by zen priest Keizan and ranked only 2nd to Eihei-ji as largest Soto zen meditation center. By Edo period, complex counted over 70 halls, 16,391 sub-temples all over Japan. 1898 fire destroyed much of complex, after which Yokohama's Soji-ji became head temple and Monzen's became secondary So-in 'founder's temple'. Still functioning zen center with 17 (some pre-fire 16-17th cent) halls remaining, it is one of most relaxing places we visited. Long covered hallways link main halls in large square, with carefully manicured garden inside of square. Enjoy true shojin-ryori vegetarian priests' fare (¥2,000 up) and/or spend nite (¥-lo-Bw/2) to partake in early **morning zazen** meditation: ✍ sending self-addressed return post card 10 days prior in Japanese to: Ishikawa-ken, Fugeshi-gun, Monzen-cho, Soji-ji So-in Jimusho, ZIP 6-69; or try calling few days ahead ☎(07684)-2-0005 or 2-1515, in Japanese. Monzen area has dozen ¥-B ryokan such as **Kameyama-so** ☎2-0131; and 2 dozen minshuku in town and all along coast from Kuroshima up along...

Minazuki Kaigan, 16km stretch of isolated coastline with alternating country roads (no bus) and seaside trails; ideal for full- or half-day escapes from people. Nothing but idyllic scenery along it, so pack some food. From Doge bus stop (halfway between Kuroshima and Monzen), 20min N on local road to start of Saruyama Shizen Sando (**Nature Trail**) at EIFUKU-JI temple; 3.4km (90min) on trail to Saruyama Lighthouse where rough-cut steps down to sea-level base of 200m cliff. 10min further, road resumes, 7km via fishing hamlets to midway MINAZUKI village, also reached by six-daily 35min deadend bus from Monzen. Minazuki is fishing village of some 200 houses, 3 ¥-B ryokan (**Kasuda-ya** ☎(07684)-6-2311, can reserve thru JTB), 7 minshuku and Youth Village with budget lodge and campsite. Start here for short hike on 5km (2hr) Ariso Shizen Sando trail to Kami-Osawa (also called Kamezo) where 50min bus to Wajima.

All along coast here, 3-4m high bamboo and reed stockades encircle houses, sometimes entire hamlets. They serve as wind-breakers against freezing Siberian winds in winter, as sunshades in summer. Like African kraals in old Tarzan movies, villagers issue forth from enclosures by dawn to fish, tend small tracts of rice paddies and pick mountain herbs.

We drove Monzen → Minazumi (12km) for scenery, then back towards Monzen about 4km road cuts L, 2km L again to Kami-Osawa and 15km to...

WAJIMA 輪島 MORNING MARTS & URUSHI-LACQUER

MAIN CENTER of Oku-Noto, Wajima is only tourist town on peninsula, most populous at 35,000 (other big towns Suzu and Hakui around 30,000). Yet, it has rural atmosphere with hordes of old *monpe*-clad farm-wives heading to and from outdoor morning (*asa-ichi*) and evening (*yu-ichi*) markets where you find wide array of fresh vegetables and fish, folkcrafts, herbal medicines and odd gifts. With more tourists going to popular asa-ichi (in Aug they almost outnumber locals buying food), balance is tipping in favor of gift stalls where almost all items handmade by country folk in spare time. Simpler, less-visited yu-ichi opens afternoon, W down street from asa-ichi. Women prepare stalls (about 200) from 6am, open 7am-ish, peak 9:00-10:30, close noon. Neither rain, sleet or snow stops them from setting up shop every day of year except first 3 days of New Year and 10th and 25th monthly; best days 4, 9, 14, 19, 24, 29th. Yu-ichi starts around 3-6pm (X-10th, 25th monthly) at Sumiyoshi Jinja shrine grounds. All seafood here supplied by Wajima's fishing fleet; 800 small (3-5 tons) ships operate out of port accounting for bulk of town's income.

Much of rest, full 35%, of Wajima's income comes from...

Wajima Urushi Lacquerware: Depending on which way wind is blowing, you are overcome by thick ocean air or pungent aroma of lacquer. Over 300 workshops of *kigi-shi* (wood-carvers) and *to-shi* (lacquerers) concentrated in Kawai-cho (N of stn) and Hoshi-cho (across river) districts, their wares sold in 50-60 stores on streets of this small town, generating income from endless trickle of tourists, as well as by shipping wares all over Japan. Items range from usual chopsticks, bowls, trays, and tea utensils to elaborate New Year's sake sets, chests, cabinets and tables. Most stores demonstrate wood-carving or lacquering in front. In stn is 2m high by 4m wide lacquer panel with gold inlay which took local artist KADONO Iwajiro 3 months to complete; 2nd huge panel 'The Crane' on 3rd floor of City Hall done by MAE Taiho, local man and Living National Treasure. There is... **lacquered house** near Sumiyoshi Jinja. People from all over Japan study at Wajima's Lacquer Research Center. But let's call it by its proper, 19th century English name, *urushiol* or *urushi*. As raw material is sumac tree sap, differs from occidental lacquer, even stronger. Excavated items from Chinese tombs show urushi can last colorfast 2,500 years.

Many claim urushi introduced mid-14th century by monk from Kishu's (present Wakayama) NEGORO-JI temple, but earlier bowls and trays discovered around town place first local urushiware around 10th century. Abundant base woods (keyaki, mountain sakura) and urushi base, sumac, along with high humidity made Wajima ideal urushi production center. Wajima urushi is perhaps strongest in Japan, best for exports as most likely to hold up under adverse climate conditions; extra durability attributed to *jinoko* silicate (steamed into paste) mixed in with base lac coats, weak spots reinforced with lac-coated cloth. Over 20 steps are involved from preparation and carving of wood thru 3 major phases of coating with urushi. Most have 70 layers of lac painted on, while finest have 124 layers. Takes 3-6 months to complete and year or more if embellished with *chinkin* (gold inlay), *maki-e* (gold sprinkle), *roshoku* (painted motifs), raised patterns and such. There are no mechanized workshops here, or cheap plastic or synthetic urushi imitiations; most artists sell direct cutting out middleman costs. *Wajima urushiware* is recognized as among finest in Japan—Wajima carvers also supply most of raw wood pieces for Kanazawa urushiware. Visit several woodcarvers and urushi artists to see all phases of production.

Or, visit 2nd floor of...
Lacquer Hall, *Wajima Shikki Kaikan* (8:30-17:00, ¥170), 700m NW of stn along Wajima River and Rte249. In addition to seeing all phases in one spot, there is fine collection of old urushiware and display of tools; sales kiosk competitively priced. Hundred-plus works of contemporary artists displayed at **Urushi Kogei Sakuhin Kaikan** (9:00-17:00, ¥300), 600m NE along coast road.

1km further E along Rte249 is...
Lacquer Museum, *Wajima Shitsu-gei Bijutsukan* (9:00-15:00, ¥300), with more of older works; it is just E of Tsukada bus stop, 5min (1.5km) from stn. Closer to bus stop is *Inachu Shikki Kaikan* one of larger **workshops** which has guided tour and small museum; in-town branch few blocks E of Shikki Kaikan. Inachu has large shop in Tokyo, which see.

Next to it is...
Wajima Komingu Tenjikan (9:00-17:00 X-1st mon monthly, ¥200), old folk tools (*ko-mingu*), displays lifestyle of Wajima farmers and fishermen.

Sandwiched between Shitsu-gei Bijutsu-kan and Inachu is...
Lantern Museum, *Kiriko Kaikan* (daily 8:00-17:00, summer 18:00, ¥350). Noto known for many festivals featuring giant floats and *kiriko* – rectangular wood and paper offertory 'lanterns' which get up to 15m high, 2m wide and 1m thick, taking dozens of men to carry. They precede sacred mikoshi in 18 major festivals mid-July to mid-Sept which have kiriko. There are about 700 of these giant lanterns in Noto, some dating to early 19th century when first begun. Most have written on one side in huge flowing characters, prayers for good harvest or catch at sea, and elaborate paintings on reverse. Kiriko Kaikan shows 17 kiriko, including largest in Noto (over 1 ton); also 3 elaborate mikoshi on 1st floor, and in back are *tomobata* banners which adorn festival boats. 2nd floor displays other Noto festivals such as *amamehagi, aenokoto* & *gojinjo-daiko* demon drummers. Videos of fetes.

Noto tourist posters show 3-5 men wearing demon masks, long straggly hair wind-whipped as they beat drums on rocky shore with thundering waves exploding behind. Local lore claims these peasant demons routed war-lord Uesugi Genshin's army when latter entered Noto in early 1570's. Outclassed militarily, farmers hid in rocky mountain passes waiting for Uesugi to pitch camp. Then with mud-caked faces, seaweed plastered hair and ripped clothes, bands of howling drummers broke out in manic beats, randomly appearing or disappearing as torches lighted or extinguished. Aided by foul weather, farmers sufficiently unnerved Uesugi's peasant army forcing general to retreat.

As well as performing at various festivals (*see* DATEBOOK, p895), done-for-tourist *gojinjo-daiko* seen **Mar 15** thru **Sep 15** nitely at Kasuga Jinja shrine at Sosogi, ¥250; sometimes at Sosogi larger inns; free nitely performance from 20:30 (fri/sat May-Oct, nitely summer) at Wajimaya Honten Urushi Center S across road opp Shikki Kaikan.

Festival Palace, *Omatsuri-Yakata* (9:00-18:00, ¥200), in white-walled rice storehouses of Sumiyoshi Jinja, has more *kiriko, mikoshi, danjiri* (wheeled floats), some of which coated with Wajima urushi. Hundreds of items relate to other festivals.

Few km W of stn 15min bus on Nishiho coastline to Miyaguchi bus stop...
Folkcraft Village, *Nishiho Kogei Mura* (9:00-18:00 X-wed), demonstrates various folkcrafts. Most popular is Wajima *ryusho-yaki* pottery with workshop to make your own.

CHOPSTICKS: In Wajima, without question, it means **seafood**; fresh-caught from Japan Sea direct from boat to table; variously cooked, tempura, or quivering fresh sashimi and succulent sushi. Inns fill you with whatever seasonal best; adventurous types able to speak some Japanese, or telegraph good sign language, can explore tiny backstreet local hangouts, most often frequented by those who catch this fish, downing food with strong local sake. Many fine tourist-oriented (in service but not in inflated prices) restaurants around town, mostly on main Honmachi-dori street (site of asa-ichi) and one street N on seaside Hama-dori: best for local cooking in folksy atmosphere is **Madara-kan** (middle of Hama-dori) where meals served around *irori* (sunken hearth) range from few hundred yen a la cartes to assorted *teishoku* (table d'hotes) around ¥2,000. 200m W is similar (less selection but cheaper) **Ikari. Yamaji,** across from post office 1 block E of main intersect on Rte249, specializes in shellfish. Excellent sushi at **Fumi-zushi** (middle of Honmachi-dori). Two doors W is **Warasho tonkatsu** (pork cutlet) shop for those full of fish. ¥1,000 tempura teishoku, ¥1,500 sashimi teishoku and full selection of local sake at **Meigetsu** 2 blocks E and 1 S of Shikki Kaikan.

In springtime, one sees people scooping huge nets into water from small platforms at mouth of Wajima River. They are fishing for tiny *isaza*, similar to *shirauo* whitefish of Hagi and Fukuoka. Delicacy served as *isaza-no-odori-kui*, eaten still squirming in various sauces; served at Madara-kan, Ikari, Meigetsu, and others. Popular winter fare is steaming pots of *yubeshi* stew. Main ingredient *yuzu* (citron) was once abundant around Wajima, but now most imported from Shikoku.

Jizake (local sake) is mostly smooth *kara-kuchi* (dry), strong enough to keep you fortified in cold winters. Eight family-run shops in town brew sake old-fashioned way, like 150-year-old **Kiyomizu Shuzo** (middle Honmachi-dori) which brews famed *Noto-homare* sold in collectible jugs. Best sake ready early Jan, from which time Kiyomizu and 5 other breweries rotate one week at time, opening their vaults to pass out fresh sake.

WHERE TO STAY: 30+ ryokan in town range from small family-run joints to giant hotel-class inns. W-style rooms in **Station Hotel** (¥-T). Top ryo-tels (all J-style): **Hosen-kaku** ☎(0768)-22-2200, ¥-S-Lw/2, S of stn; near stn is **Azuma-ya** ☎22-2063, ¥-T-Sw/2; **Hotel Yashio** ☎22-0600, ¥-Tw/2, somewhat secluded near curving Sode-ga-hama Beach 1.8km NW of stn with wooded park behind; just W of Tsukada bus stop is luxurious seaside Oku-Noto **Grand Hotel Koshu-en** ☎22-0461, ¥-L–LLw/2, grand meals, giant baths and all rooms facing sea; similar rates and service at **Yonehisa** ☎22-4488, few hundred meters W along coast. Best of traditional inns is seaside **Choto-kaku** ☎22-0482, 15min walk from stn near river mouth; cheap at ¥-Tw/2 and start in 1952 as restaurant accounts for excellent meals. Other fine inns (tho not as classy) at trifle less include **Hamachu** ☎22-0025; **Shinbashi** ☎22-0236; and **Ebisu-ya** ☎22-0296. Budgeteers have 70+ minshuku to choose from, many doubling as budget eateries ranging from seafood joints to noodleries and curry shops. Stn-side **Mangetsu** ☎22-4487, is well-known; we came across **Shintani** ☎22-0807, classy old house (lots of urushi work) worthy of being on sightseeing circuit, located diagonally across

Shinbashi Bridge from Shikki Kaikan. W of it is CHORAKU-JI temple, running **Youth Hostel** ☎22-0663. Kokumin-shukusha **Wajima-so** ☎22-2357, has best view of Wajima and sea, located part way up hill S of Horai-zan Park near...

Sode-ga-hama 'Kimono Sleeve Beach', 1.8km sandy stretch with campsite. N tip Kamo-ga-ura Point (path around it) where sometimes see ama women diving for shellfish, and diving for or gathering kelp. Late emperor Showa sat here 1958 watching them at work.

But to really see ama, head out to...

HEGURA-JIMA 舳倉島 ISLAND OF DIVING WOMEN

IN LATE MAY, almost entire Ama-cho district of Wajima gets on their boats, chugs out 48km N to tiny Hegura-jima isle to live until late Oct, abandoning in harsh winter. Hegura is considered part of Ama-cho thus part of Wajima city. Here, they spend whole day diving from boats into cold sea; May-Jun, almost every rock on Hegura covered with kelp laid out to dry. Tho some now wear wetsuits, you often see traditional white cotton garb, tho rarely their original real traditional G-string. Average dives range 10-30m in depth; they enter water 3 times a day, each time staying in for about 50 dives (2hrs) each easily over minute long. Wearing face masks and weighted belt, their tools are steel claw for prying loose awabi (abalone) from rocks, and wood tub linked to them by lifeline, to keep catch in, and to hang onto for short rests. Skill and endurance of Hegura's ama gained them special status by Maeda lords placing the women on equal level as samurai. Elsewhere in Japan, characters for ama read 'sea-women', but here they use homonymous characters 'sea-samurai'...were featured in great humanist-photographer Fosco Maraini's classic study, *Fisherwomen of Japan*, sending tidal wave of photographers here and divers quickly learned to ask for model fees, like any well-undressed lady.

Centuries-old tradition of semi-nomadism notwithstanding, some ama are setting up permanent residence here thanks to better ships to cross choppy sea in. Every day at 8:30, passenger boat leaves Wajima Harbor for 1hr50min crossing; halfway point marked by **Nanatsu-jima** cluster of 'Seven-Isles' frequented by ama. Return trip leaves Hegura 13:00, allowing enough time to wander around tiny isle, tho those with no time constraints might want to spend nite here at one of 2 ama-run minshuku (one stays open all year): **Tsukasa**, and **Tsuki**, both ¥-Bw/2 sumptuous feasts caught by owners; ¥1,500 extra for equally massive lunch. Book thru Wajima stn **Kanko-annai** (which also handles all Wajima lodgings). Modern technology has made life here easier, they even have paved main street, school, some mini trucks and comforts electricity brings. But Hegura's essence is still little changed in its mostly gravel lanes, sturdy homes with rocks weighing down roofs and families still drawing water from communal well; and it is idyllic escape in rural Japan. Friends hitchhiking around Noto camped here, buying food to cook from locals; few budget eateries around village.

Hegura is only 6km around (2km long, 1km wide), its highest point is mere 12m above sea-level, spot dominated by powerful lighthouse. Rent fishing gear and boat thru minshuku, swim almost anywhere (SE and NW corners popular), or hike around to various shrines linked by paths. Hegura has 8 shrines, one temple, no less than 33 stone jizo and kannon figures. S tip OKUTSU-HIME JINJA shrine of isle's *uji-gami* (local deity); N tip EBISU JINJA, dedicated to Ebisu of 7 lucky gods, always shown carrying huge fish-catch, is where prayers for good catch are offered, and site of annual early-spring offertory rites for safety and abundance are performed after most ama have come from mainland. Rocky W coast, especially around

YASAKA and KOTOHIRA shrines has water-worn caves; nearby **Ryujin-ga-Ike** 'Dragon-king's Pond', home of isle's guardian spirit.

Lacquer Road can be fit in after Wajima's in-town sites are done on foot in easy half-day. This recently coined name outlines popular tourist course of Sosogi, Tokikuni-ke and Nakatani Houses, Yanagida hamlet and Ushitsu. Best by **car** (Eki-Rental and Toyota in Wajima), **cab**, or local **bus** (hourly dep Wajima → Sosogi → Tokikuni-ke → Yanagida, ending Ushitsu). Best bus is dep Wajima 12:05 or 13:10 → Sosogi-guchi which gives few hours to stroll around, and return on 15:15, 16:30 or 17:10 bus to return to inn for dinner. R.t. cab Wajima → Sosogi → Tokikuni Houses → Nakatani House → Wajima, about 60km for 30x-mtr; Ushitsu adds 20km (10x-mtr).

Do reverse to end...
SOSOGI and MAURA ONSEN:
Sosogi village, 18.5km (40min bus) E of Wajima (of which it's part) is main junction on following bus lines: Wajima → Ushitsu; Kanazawa → Wajima → Maura express; Sosogi-guchi → Kino-ura where change to JR buses around peninsula tip to Suzu (several cut inland at Otani before Kino-ura and across to Suzu); and Oku-Noto tour buses. W end of rugged 2km long Sosogi Kaigan coastline, E end of which is Maura Onsen. Narrow pedestrian tunnel next to main road tunnels carved out of rock by 16th century priest Zuirin of nearby KAIZO-JI temple—took 12 years—after he felt sorry for having people plunge into ocean below failing to traverse treacherous sheer path. But back at Sosogi coastline is rolling sand dunes.

Rent bikes to explore area, Sosogi-guchi bus terminal & nearby Ueda Denki electric goods store.

Midway Wajima to Sosogi at Shira-yone (25min bus) are...
Senmai-da '1,000-sheet fields'. Ages ago part of mountain slid into sea but space-starved farmers carved paddy fields out of resultant slope—2,146 paddies in 2.5 acres stepping down to sea. Beautiful to look at, but harvesting takes 3 times as much effort as flat paddies.

Next hamlet...
NAFUNE has *Gojinjo-daiko Kaikan* (drum hall); **HAKUSAN JINJA** shrine site of summer fest featuring demon drummers.

When Taira were chased out of Kyoto by Minamoto in 1185 lord Taira-no-Tokisada fled to Noto, hiding out in Otani area. His son Tokikuni moved to this area to settle, and by time his son took over, they ruled over 300-koku village of Tokikuni-mura. Under Tokugawa they became responsible directly to Edo and ruled from **Kami-tokikuni-ke**, Upper Tokikuni Manse (8:00-17:00, ¥310), 15min walk S of Sosogi-guchi stop. Palatial house with huge thatch roof and garden to match was built 1808. Between it and bus stop is 'Lower' **Shimo-tokikuni-ke** (same hours, ¥310), built for branch line which separated at time of 13th-generation Tokihiro; present heads of both houses are 24th generation. Easy **trails** up 357m Iwakurayama hill start near Kami-Tokikuni-ke, Sosogi-guchi and from near Sosogi tunnel part way up is *Sen-tai Jizo*, **1,000 jizo rock** formation, eroded so by wind to look like rows of jizo statues.

Between two Tokikuni houses is...
Folk Museum, *Minzoku Shiryo-kan* (9:00-18:00, ¥150), in old school building displays farmers' and fishermen's tools and those used for various crafts. Well-built folk house in front seems much bigger once inside. 1km W across river is *Shuko-kan Nanso* (8:00-17:00, ¥400) **museum** of treasures of Minami family. Landlords of this area for 300 years, Minamis also ran trading ships out of Sosogi. Art pieces in converted storehouses; after seeing, have tea and cakes around cozy old-fashioned main house hearth.

YANAGIDA hamlet, 10km S of Sosogi, was once large urushi producing center predating Wajima, but no artists remain anymore.

6km W is...
Nakatani-ke, house open to public (9:00-17:00, ¥500). Nakatani were rich farmer landowners and Edo-appointed village heads. Visit to their moated manse enhanced by their all-urushi storehouse. 6 daily buses from Yanagida to Kurokawa (15min), and 10min walk to Nakatani-ke. Yanagida (12km from Ushitsu) is only landlocked village on Noto, but makes up for it by having hot spring; ¥-B Kokumin-shukusha Noto **Yanagida-so** ☎(07687)-6-1550. Kurokawa hamlet also boasts onsen, served by even cheaper minshuku **Kurokawa Onsen** ☎6-1771.

9km E on road from near Tokikuni houses cutting to Suzu, is...
Kuromaru-ke, house and complex of Kuromaru family, once *to-mura-yaku* (10-village heads) of this area; not fully open to tourists, but you can look at what is open.

WHERE TO STAY: Actual center of Sosogi town is 3min bus (10min walk) E of Sosogi-guchi and has most lodgings: **Sosogi-kan** ☎(0768)-32-1160, ¥-S; **Daikan-so** ☎32-1148, ¥-S; **Madoiwa Hotel** ☎32-1100, ¥-T; half-dozen more ryokan. 30-odd minshuku scattered between Sosogi-guchi and Sosogi Tunnel, and Sosogi Kajiyama YH; budget rooms at **Iwakura-ji temple** part way up trail to Iwakura-yama. Stayed fine **Kairaku-so** ☎32-1078, *tunnel E end near...*

Tarumi-no-taki waterfall; early Nov start of winter, ice-cold Siberian winds freeze spray of waves pounding coast creating *nami-no-hana* **wave-flowers** of frozen droplets floating thru air. Minshuku, beach campsites nearby.

At Tarumi-no-taki is ex-village headman's house converted into restaurant, **Shoya-no-yashiki.** Some folk prefer, and will spring extra few thousand on rooms to be at...

MA-URA ('Way-Back') **ONSEN** just down coast. Luxe lodgings at ¥-S rate **Hotel New Ma-ura** ☎32-1150, which has nightly performances of Gojinjo-daiko drummers; their bus picks up customers from other inns for the show. Many buses end here at **Ma-ura Center** which also has **Kanko-annai** for booking.

Nie kaigan coastline beyond next tunnel, also has few isolated minshuku such as **Age-Hama Enden,** ☎87-2857, 2km from Ma-ura. Nearby Mr Kakuhana and son are probably only people in Japan who still regularly make **natural salt** old-fashioned way from sea (Futami-ga-ura near Ise Grand Shrine still does, but only for shrine ritual use). Twice daily, sunny days May thru Nov Kakuhana comes out to his special 'salt-field', sprays buckets of sea water on fine sand. After hours of drying in sun, salt-caked top layer scraped off and rinsed in sea water vats to separate salt from sand. Concentrated salt water is then slowly boiled to evaporate water, leaving only handfulls of pure salt after 12hrs of back-breaking work. Their 'all-natural' salt sold in small jars. Kakuhanas are last of three-century-old tradition. Until turn of century whole area was covered with salt-fields worked by entire villages. Set up by 3rd Maeda lord Toshitsune who decided it would bring in more money. Noto salt used to be shipped all over central Japan. Kakuhana jr does this mostly for tourists, hoping to keep this traditional alive, but it looks like this art will end with him. 10min bus from Sosogi to Nie stop.

About 5km beyond, at Otani (14km from Sosogi), Rte249 cuts across to Suzu, but we drove on to E tip **ROKKO-MISAKI** Point, 30km from Sosogi, marked by squat, English-built (1883) lighthouse and many budget inns. Takes quite some time by **bus**, 7 daily 35min from Sosogi, 25min from Nie, to midway KINO-URA where change to JR bus for last 15min to Noroshi. Scenic seaside 10km trail starts from TAKAYA hamlet 1km W of Kino-ura (some buses end here), passing rocky shores with scattered pines, sandy beaches with campsites and isolated fishing hamlets, ending 3hrs later at tip.

One place worth staying out at tip is one-inn...

Yoshi-ga-ura Kosen mineral baths, 15min walk E of Yoshi-ga-ura bus stop (2.5km S of Noroshi) down country lane thru tobbacco fields. Facing sea, with rocks behind, is small *Ranpu-no-yado,* **'Lamp-inn'** for tho they have own generator, light by oil lamps. Popular with city kids who come for 'exotic' quiet and heaping portions of fresh seafood. ¥-lo-Tw/2, call ☎(07688)-6-2136.

JR bus around Noto tip 20km to Takojima end of JR Noto Line; 4km beyond is...

SUZU-IIDA, center of Suzu City and end of Lacquer Road. Town has hot spring which all inns draw from. Of dozen ryokan, recommended is... **Morishita,** ☎(0768)-82-0001, and **Aoki** ☎82-0016, both ¥-hi-T–lo-Sw/2; several ¥-B ryokan and 8 minshuku. About 5km S, at **NOTO-UKAI** (2 stops rail), is another small hot spring with dozen ryokan (try Mitsuke-so, 4-1212), more minshuku, and 2 Kokumin-shukusha. Good beach here facing battleship-shaped isle, so-named Gunkan-jima. Suzu-Iida also has asa-ichi **morning market** 6:00-12:00 on 2, 7, 12, 17, 22, 27th monthly; not as large as Wajima's but getting close. 1 daily boat makes r.t. to Itou-gawa beyond Toyama; several boats daily hop down Uchi-Ura coast to end Nanao.

Before leaving town, let us visit main attraction here...

Kihei-don, mid-19th century manse of rich farmer Sakurai family. In Edo era got rich making salt and lacquer. Main house, with gently angled tile roof, shows folk items 3 storehouse annexes; Hoshoku-kan has Sakurai family treasures, locally excavated items; Shisso-kan urushi-related; Shioji-kan tools used in *age-hama enden* salt making we saw near Sosogi. 10min walk S of Suzu-Iida stn, or few blocks W of Bus Center (8:00-17:45, ¥300).

TSUKUMO-WAN '99-Bay', is lovely multi-inlet bay which would be ideal for raising pearl oysters if water weren't so cold. **sightseeing boat** 40min cruises around bay, leaving from pier just E of JR Noto-Ogi stn. Deluxe ryokan **Hyaku-raku-so** only ¥-lo-Sw/2 ☎(0768)-74-1115 located on tip of small peninsula furthest inside bay boasts 'best view in Noto' and superb meals. Slightly cheaper ¥-Tw/2 inns with almost as fine view are **Grand Hotel** ☎74-1133, & **Kaga-ya.** Many minshuku around tour boat pier, and some at bustling fishing village of **OGI**, SW section of bay. Campsite either shore at mouth of bay, one Youth Hostel Ogi is stop on Suzu ↔ Nanao boat run; harbor is full of large (up to 300 ton) long-distance fishing vessels which scour seas, return home for winter.

Coast-hopping boats also stop at...

USHITSU, 10km (14min rail) W, most small stns between Suzu–Ushitsu are mere gaps in series of tunnels. Ushitsu is known for its *Ohshiki-ami-okoshi* giant-net-pull in which boatloads of fishermen haul in enormous net spanning harbor mouth. Done early morning and evening Sep thru Jun; smaller tourist version done in summer from 5am, which join by calling *ami-moto* (net-master) Uo Yoshitada at ☎(0768)-62-0841 (can have inn do). If you stay at any of many fishermen-run small inns, chances are you'll be invited along on regular hauls. Or head down to *uo-ichiba* fish market to see and hear sonorous early morning transactions between fishermen and buyers.

Tojima-yama Park, at E point on mouth of Ushitsu harbor was once site of Tanaki castle, where Maeda forces annihilated Uesugi's army. Now wooded park with 3.5km winding scenic path, *Kyodo-kan* and *Minzoku-kan,* **museums** and 2 other exhibit halls of folk arts, tools (8:00-17:00, ¥200 for all). Kyodo-kan is large thatched-roof farm house, moved here from hills; Minzoku-kan was home of Ushitsu's *ami-moto* chief fisherman. Worth visiting just to see these houses. Return to stn, pass thru old section of town with many grand houses, this was once hopping red-light district.

WHERE TO STAY: Ushitsu's best are minshuku run by fishermen. We found
2 great ones near fish market: **Muroya** ☎(0768)-62-0200, W of coast-hopping boat pier,
sturdy old ex-net master's house with spacious inner garden, beautiful rooms (note lavish
lacquer); **Fuwa** ☎62-1300, S along shore, similarly 100+years old with lovely interior,
docked behind is master's fishing boat—complete with radar and FAX (receive charts, etc).
We usually avoid W-style pensiones, but behind Ushitsu stn is restored farmhouse and
white-walled storage-*kura* housing superb **Oku-Noto Pension**, ☎62-3270.

32.5km from Ushitsu, junction of JR Nanao Line to Wajima & Noto Line to Suzu...
ANAMIZU with little to offer tourist. Shutterbugs might head to scenic
Nakai Hakkei Bay, 4km E of town (betw Nakai and Hira stns) to snap ever-so-
patient fishermen perched atop tripod stilt-platforms, waiting for *bora*-mullet
to swim over their suspended nets. Used to be found all over area but
dwindling as young folk don't keep up odd old tradition: spring to autumn.
Anamizu is alternate route → Wakura Onsen and Nanao.

Instead of taking rail down coast, hop on 30min boat, across Nanao Bay to...
NOTO-JIMA ISLE, land at N shore Marine Park. Dozens of budget inns
around isle—last chance for adventurer to spend quiet nite in rural village;
sandy beaches with campsites cover NE/E shores. *Tezukuri-Kogei mura*,
Handmade Crafts Village, new '91, part of 'Outdoor High Leisure'
complex including **Glass Museum** (rotates modern J, Chinese Ch'ing era
works, 9-5, X-tue, ¥700, ☎[0767] 84-1175), glass workshop, Kakashiyama
pottery kiln, such else as golf course ☎85-2311. 30min bus from JR WAKURA stn.

Isle was more secluded, but 1982 saw 1,500m (1 mi)-long bridge link Noto-jima to...
WAKURA ONSEN, most popular stop on Noto, for which reason avoid.
Prime location and view but packed with 50+ over-priced inns-cum-hideous
ferro-concrete boxes lining shore. Must have been quite beautiful before
late-1960s boom, but once-rustic charm is nowhere to be found. Geared for
luxury-seeking J-tourists ready to put out ¥15,-50,000w/2, high-class inns boast
grand baths and shows of drummers; cheapest inns run ¥-T+. Direct luxe Raicho exp →
Osaka. Weary budgeteer can relax in giant **public bath** *Sagi-no-yu* 100m N of central
bus stn, or at **Onsen Center** betw two, then head out of Noto, or find cheaper inns at...
NANAO, just another bustling fishing town 5km SE of Wakura Onsen.

ONSEN ALTERNATIVES: For adventurers: between Wakura and
Nanao on inland side of rail line is AKAURA ONSEN on Akaura-gata lake
with budget ryokan; 5min bus from Wakura or Nanao → Akaura, 10min walk inland.
Two more budget (¥-B) single-inn onsen on Nanao Peninsula NE of town: 5km to coastal
AKAZAKI ONSEN 3km further to inland riverside **YUGAGA ONSEN**.

WHERE NEXT: As far as we are concerned, our tour of Noto ends at
Anamizu or even Ushitsu where we advise hopping JR to hightail back to
Kanazawa and express train to central HIDA TAKAYAMA, which can follow
from here in reverse of itinerary described in earlier chapter.

Drivers can, at Nanao, head down eastern shore of Noto to HIMI, start of JR Himi
Line to TAKAOKA where Rte8 to TOYAMA and Rte41 inland to HIDA (gets little confusing in town; but if on Hokuriku Expwy Toyama IC lets out right on Rte41).

TAKAYAMA ROUTE → NAGOYA area is best return to Pacific side and up →
Tokyo whence leave Japan, or venture up thru Tohoku hinterlands → Hokkaido.
Adventurer following Japan Sea coast → Tohoku–Hokkaido has several choices:
Takayama area is must-see from where can return → Toyama thru many back-country hot
springs (*see* TOYAMA), or go Takayama → Hirayu Onsen on Rte158 end at Matsumoto
(*follows*), from where JR Shinetsu Line N to JOETSU on coast for boat → SADO ISLE; or
slightly inland Iiyama Line → Echigo Kawaguchi, choice of Joetsu Line → NIIGATA or
back inland on Futami Line → feudal-mentality castle town of AIZU WAKAMATSU.

PERSONAL DATEBOOK

Travel around Noto is highlighted by its many grand festivals. Most picturesque and often wild are summer to early autumn *kiriko* festivals, but winter and spring have their full share of unusual, dramatic folk fetes.

January

2,6 *Amame-hagi*, Monzen-cho district: (2) Igisu, (6) Minazuki. Similar to famed Nama-hage of Tohoku (Akita), demon masked men visit homes to scare out evil spirits in little children; best nite of 6th.

February

3 Repeat *Amame-hagi*, rural Uchiura-machi area setsubun.

6 *Zonbera Fest*, Kiya Jinja, Monzen-cho.

9 *Aeno-koto*, 'thank field god', once done all over Noto, now mostly limited to rural villages of Oku-Noto (Yanagida). Marks end of 'idle season', head farmers don best kimono, go to fields to invite kami home for bath, meal and bed for nite. Similar rite marks start of 'idle season' Dec 5. Staged at Edo-mura outside Kanazawa; for real, stay at Yanagida area inn and ask.

11 *Kishu* boat fest, Noto-cho, 100 gaily decorated fishing boats cruise harbor, sacred sasaki branches, offer sake (celebrants partake) to sea.

March

18-23 *Heikoku-sai* (a.k.a. Oide-matsuri) main fete of Keta Jinja Shrine, Haku-shi; sacred horse leads mikoshi parade from Keta Jinja across Noto via small shrines to Nanao City Kunitamahiko shrine where spends 2 nites, heads back. Opens spring.

April

2 *Saka-daru-gaeshi*, Sake barrel battles, Fujinami district of Noto-machi; fisher-youths from 2 villages, clad in fundoshi, gather either side of Yakushigawa River, scramble for sake barrel blessed at shrine. Top team blessed for great catch that year.

5-6 *Dashi* (Float) *Festival*, Wajima City, features big wheeled floats coated in Wajima-nuri urushi-lacquer.

8 *Genzo Festival* Mimanahiko Jinja, Anamizu all brides who came to town in past year visit shrine in wedding garb with go-between, official status as local person.

17-18 *Tomobata-sai*, Ogi harbor, marks landing of mythical founder Okuninushi-no-mikoto; boats fly giant banners, color streamers sail around Ogi, Tsukumo bays.

May

thru July, *Yonade* 'abalone picking', Noto-jima Isle, go to beaches at nite, your torch (avail at inns) illuminates abalone tossed on shore by waves, best east shore.

May-Jul *Bora-machi-yagura* (mullet-waiting-stilts) seen off Anamizu.

May-Aug, *Ika-tsuri-bune* squid-fishing boats dep Fuku-ura harbor, Togi-machi around 11pm stay out till 4am, scoop in squid attracted to bright lites on board; can join fishermen for full outing, or arrange shorter excursions (July-Aug) thru inn or Noto Kongo Center, ¥3,–5,000 person.

1st *Yama Matsuri* of Takaoka City, finds 7 gorgeously carved and decorated yama (mountain-size) floats from city famous for its gold lacquer artisans. Even wheels are all of black lacquer trimmed with elaborate gold designs; musicians ride on floats. Best just before noon at shrine, or along Katahara-machi-dori street.

3-5 *Seihaku-sai*, Nanao City, features 3 gant-wheeled floats (15m tall) with small stage on top where puppets do kabuki plays, accompanied by flutes and drums. Best 15th from 2pm.

June

Lunar 15 Full moon Jul or early-Aug *Hoto Festival*, Ishizaki-cho, Nanao City, sees six 12m tall kiriko carted all day thru town to lively drums, flutes and bells, to end late nite at Hachiman Jinja. Grandest kiriko fete, each takes 100 men to carry.

July

7-8 *Abare-matsuri* Rowdy Fest Yasaka Jinja Noto-cho. 7th nite, bonfires around town and harbor lit, 40 kiriko race around them; 8th day, rowdiness continues with mikoshi-carriers battling in river and sea.

Mid – All-Japan University Sumo Championship, Atago-yama Sumo Ring, Nanao City, Komaru-yama park.

15 *Matsunami Kiriko Festival*, Matsunami Village, Uchiura-cho.

17 *Roppo noryo-sai*, at Nakajima-cho Hiyoshi Jinja.

17 *Fire Festival* at Koi-ji, Uchiura-cho in honor of double love suicide here.

19-20 Nanao Harbor Festival.

20-21 *Dashi Matsuri*, Suzu-shi 8 wheeled floats thru town both day until late nite.

3rd Sat-Sun *Hasebe Shrine Festival*, Anamizu-machi, commemorates 12th century Lord Hasebe Shinren: samurai parade (12th century garb unlike usual parades) marching bands 22nd day, fire-works, toro-nagashi floating lanterns both nites in Anamizu bay for which can rent roofed wooden yakata-bune boats.

25-26 *Kaikai-matsuri*, Wakura Onsen features 'rain-making drummers' to call up all-important mid-summer harvest rains. Little drums recreate sound of rain, big ones that of thunder. Best seen for this festival but has been made into Wakura Onsen's tourist attraction and can have it done anytime by arranging thru inn, ¥9,000 for 10min, ¥25,000 w/ masks.

30-31 *Kiriko Festival* as part of Wajima's *Minazuki* Waterless month Festival.

31 nite, Koda *Hi-matsuri* (fire festival), Iyahime Jinja shrine Koda, Noto-jima Isle cart 7 kiriko & mikoshi shrine to plaza, where toss 200+ torches onto 30m high bonfire to create inferno; celebrates annual reunion of Iyahime's goddess with god of far-away Niigata's Yahiko Jinja S.

31-Aug 1 *Nafune-sai*, Okutsuhime Jinja, Nafune, Wajima-shi, has Gojin-daiko demon drummers 31 nite. Also done for tourists nightly March 15-Nov 15 (except July 31) at Sosogi's Kasuga Jinja.

August

6-8 *Suzu Matsuri*, citywide fete features various folk dances. Celebrate 6th at Suzu-Iida, 7 at Mitsuke (Ukai) with kiriko, and 8 at Matsunagi Kaigan Coast (near Otani) has *sunatori-bushi* 'sand-scooping' folk dances which imitate *agehama enden* salt-from-ocean process.

10-11 *San-O-sai Festival*, Hiyoshi Jinja, Minazuki, Monzen-cho, has procession of mikoshi, sacred horse, and giant drums both days, with 10th nite lighting of 365 lanterns on giant wheeled boat-shape float with yellow, red, blue streamers.

14 *Shingo noryo-sai* with kiriko at Naka-jima-cho's Fujitsuhiko Jinja.

14-15 *Sanya-odori* (3 nites' bon dance), Wajima City along river bank.

15-16 *Obon dances*, Minazuki hamlet, Monzen-cho features mugiya-bushi dances by women, now popular in mountainous Gokayama area of Hida.

17-18 *Tairyo*, Great fishing Fete Anamizu; kiriko carried from Ebisu shrine around town then charge into ocean with them.

17-18 *Tenryo Matsuri* Wakamiya Hachi-man Jinja shrine, in Kuroshima, Monzen-cho, giant floats, samurai puppets aboard are pulled thru town.

17-18 *Kiriko* at Wajima Kanko Matsuri held at Sosogi.

23-26 *Wajima Grand* Fest, *Kiriko-mikoshi* parades daily from 'X'-shrine to harbor–

23-24 Juzo Jinja, Okutsuhie Jinja–

24-25 Sumiyoshi Jinja–

25-26 Wajima-zaki Jinja–

24-25 *Niwaka Matsuri*, Umise shrine–, Ukawa River, Noto-cho; 10 giant kiriko (5mx9m) carted around town both nites.

25 More kiriko: *Togi-cho Sakami Summer Festival*.

31-Sep 1 *Hatsusaku-sai Festival*, Hachi-man Jinja and Sumiyoshi Jinja shrines, Togi; procession of 13 mikoshi and 80 kiriko of all sizes starts 31st 8pm from Hachiman Jinja, recreates wedding of two shrines' kami with carting Hachiman's kami and giant 'male member' 2km to Sumiyoshi to meet bride, returning early morning 1st. Popularly called *Kujiri-* (Pinching) *matsuri* as local bachelors used to use festival as excuse for going after unwed girls.

September

thru Oct *Tako-damakashi* Octopus hunt Noto-jima isle, get poles with red cloth on tip, poke around rocks until octopus latches on—rent gear from inns, ¥1,000, best early am or evening.

10-11 *Autumn Festival*, Takojima's Takakura Jinja (JR Noto Line last stn) has kiriko parade during days, nitetime comic performances called *hayabune-kyogen* done by young men of village, Suzu-shi.

12 *Kiriko* at Otani Autumn Festival; again–

14-15 Suzu-shi *Shoin Autumn Festival*.

16-17 *Kiriko Matsuri* at Yanagida village Hakusan Jinja shrine sees 6 kiriko 12m tall, gently carried around bonfires.

20 *Okuma-kabuto Festival*, Kumakabuto-arakashihiko Jinja, Nakajima-cho north of Nanao; features much music, dancing and banner waving as mikoshi of 19 villages gather here for grand festival trying to out-do each other.

25 *No-zumo* (Field Sumo) 2,000-year-old contest held at Karato-yama outdoor sumo ring, Hakui, as 80 amateurs from Noto, Kaga, Echizen are split into two teams and wrestle 15:00 to 21:00.

November

1-7 *Idori Matsuri*, Notomachi's Sugawara Jinja shrine; folks swear at giant mochi rice cakes offered at shrine to be rid of evil spirits.

December

5 Start of farmers' 'idle season' marked by *Aeno-koto* (see Feb 9th).

16 *Ukai* Festival, Hakui City.

*...these mountains ...they look so permanent
and peaceful, but they're changing all the time
and the changes aren't always peaceful.*
—Zen and the Art of Motorcycle Maintenance

OFFBEAT CHUBU 中部
CENTRAL MOUNTAIN RETREATS

WE INCLUDE SPECTACULAR Chubu Region here as offbeat not only
because it is mainly for adventurer-wanderer, but because anyone should
take time to visit **at least part** of it. Several International Tours now take
in part/s of it for fascinating firsthand view of 'real Japan'.

Two main routes thru central Japan, both start in greater Nagoya (*see*
p273): each offers completely different views of rural antiquity totally
dissimilar in style, geography, weather and most anything else.

KISO-JI Road (also called KISO-KAIDO and NAKASENDO), one of *Go-Kaido*
or '5-hiways' controlled direct by Tokugawa shogunate, was 500km/315mi
long with 67 post stns, and ran from Nihonbashi Tokyo thru mountainous
back country to Kusatsu near Kyoto where it joined coastal grand trunk
highway TOKAIDO. It still takes you along old pedestrian highway, thru
17th century villages little changed since those days, except gift stores now
sell modern junk instead of 17th century junk (yes they had tourists then).

INA-JI road near Kiso-ji's apex SHIOJIRI City, curves back to Tokaido at
TOYOHASHI. Supplemental **HIDA-JI** and **MINO-JI** roads take you into
beautiful, rugged mountains of Hida to villages and towns some few steps
behind in time.

GETTING THERE: JTB Sunrise **Bus Tour** 5days/4nites (incl 4bkfst, 2dnr)
¥185,400, kids ¥133,900. Dep tues, only April, Oct: TOKYO → MATSUMOTO N →
KISO-HIRASAWA → NEZAME-NO-TOKO → TSUMAGO → TAKAYAMA N →
OGIMACHI → KANAZAWA N → AWARA ONSEN spa (ryokan) N → EIHEIJI →
terminate KYOTO. Do Budget leisurely following our itinerary, or comfortable train in 2-
3 days hitting only highlights like TAKAYAMA staying at comfortable ¥-S or ¥-L inns.
Cheaper, **Bikkuri Tours** July-Aug peak season, 2nites in spas, ¥26,-28,000; daily from
Shinjuku in Japanese, ☎(03)-3253-6131, Kinki-tourist.

Adventurer can make great circle on these romantic rustic routes taking all in at
once; or do one now, other going up JAPAN SEA COAST when heading back to Tokyo. If
doing all count on at least 5-7 days for full coverage, or hilites as above 2-3 nites.

As off-beat trek from Tokaido, best is to do easternmost KISO-JI from top (NARAI)
→ TSUMAGO-MAGOME, bus across → GERO and up → TAKAYAMA, across →
SHIRAKAWA-GO and down → GIFU. You can avoid Nagoya altogether by going inland
on INA-JI from TOYOHASHI → SHIOJIRI and then start from NARAI.

Those with less time can do same in half-time: INUYAMA → MAGOME → TSUMAGO
N → via GERO → TAKAYAMA N → SHIRAKAWA-GO (optional N) → end GIFU.

Buses thru entire area extensive; **trains** fast but must return to Gifu or Nagoya to
take each line out. If really limited in time, do TSUMAGO-MAGOME (as representative of
whole Kiso-ji) in day trip out of INUYAMA; it's must for anyone interested in old Japan.

So let's start — (boldface denotes main towns, preferred overnites). Via KISO road→
Shiojiri → Niekawa → Hirasawa → **Narai** → Torii Toge pass → Yabuhara →
Kiso Fukushima → Komagane → **Tsumago** → Magome Toge pass → Magome
(alternate here bus across to Gero for HIDA-JI road, *follows*) → Iida → Tenryu rapids →
(via Nakasendo-rd) → Iwamura (alt exit) → **Ena** → Mitake → rail **Inuyama** →
Takayama for continuation on HIDA-JI samurai road, as *follows*, p.907.

KISO-JI 木曾路
OLD SAMURAI ROAD

Remaining SECTION of old pedestrian Nakasendo hiway (literally, Middle Mountains Road), alias KISO-KAIDO, 2nd of GO-KAIDO, 5 hiways (coastal TOKAIDO was #1). It also ran Edo–Kyoto but thru center of Japan above Mt Fuji via Lake Suwa where joined by KOSHU-KAIDO (*see* FUJI 5 LAKES, p273), crossing under Mt Fuji to form loop with upper part KISO-KAIDO. Still major route post-Tokugawa era, now forms base for JR Chuo, Central, Main Line, Chuo Expressway, Rte20 (Shinjuku–Shiojiri) and Rte19 (Shiojiri–Nagoya). Present preserved Kiso-ji is latter leg; we cover it here passing thru 11 (of original 67) *shukuba* or post stations. Of 11, 3 still retain most Edo era flavor: 2 'original', 3rd fully rebuilt after 1895 fire. Jay and Sumi on honeymoon drove Nagoya–Tokyo via upper loop 1955, found it literally breathtaking, but even unsuitable for non-4-wheel drive tourism (ripped out hand brake cables, muffler of high-riding Chevy shook out engine anchor bolts). 1970's prosperity led to leisure time local tourism from which income towns can maintain old buildings.

Kiso-ji follows Kiso River valley winding MATSUMOTO ↔ GIFU twixt Nomugi-Ontake mountains on W, Komagane-Central Alps E, both areas popular hiking, skiing.

Hurried traveller should limit to southernmost Tsumago and Magome towns; extra day allows northernmost Narai and lacquer town of Hirasawa for which: from NAGOYA or GIFU take *Shinano* Ltd Express to Shiojiri and backtrack 5 stops to Narai, or get off at Kiso-Fukushima and 4 stops N. From NARAI, direct to Tsumago-Magome (if *Shinano* to Nagiso and bus or cab to Tsumago). There are 10 Ltd Express *Shinano* trains daily (odd-numbers *kudari* from Nagoya; even-numbers *nobori* to Nagoya) stop Nagoya, Tajimi, Nakatsukawa, Nagiso, Kiso-Fukushima, Shiojiri on to Matsumoto, Nagano, pleasant town, junction to routes along Japan Sea (*see* p939, SAN-IN, for Matsumoto) or cross country road (buses) via Kamikochi to exquisite HIDA TAKAYAMA (follows, p912).

Whole stretch can be walked in 3-4 days, or mixed with rail or bus to do it in 2. Most of old NAKASENDO is Rte19, but mountain passes at either end still have old foot paths, and long sections between can be hiked on new *Shinshu Shizen Sando* (Nature Trail). They will be detailed for walker in text.

SHIOJIRI, major JR junction, 4hr express via KOFU to/from Tokyo's Shinjuku, 2hrs-Nagoya; Iida Line follows Tenryu River (we visit later to punt down) to Toyohashi on Tokaido. Still, it is small town known primarily for its vineyards, 5 wineries. In vineyards is **Hiraide Iseki** archaeological **stone age site**: where 2 small museums display artifacts excavated (¥100 each).

25min walk or 10min bus S of stn; bus continues down Rte19 to...
NIEKAWA: First of 11 official stops along Kiso-ji. Of interest here is Niekawa Sekisho **Barrier Gate** reconstructed 1975 using old plan found in 1960. Built 1334 as main northern boundary of Kiso territory for 535 years: basement museum of Stone Age artifacts excavated in area. *Osuyama-no-taki* waterfall, visible from stn and Barrier Gate, is popular autumn maple-viewing spot. Driving from Shiojiri, pass thru **MOTOYAMA-JUKU** hamlet halfway to Niekawa; pleasant town with many antique buildings. Not part of Kiso-ji, quieter, lacks tourism of similar towns. Between Motoyamajuku-Niekawa large stone marker notes entry to KISO road.

HIRASAWA (One JR stop beyond) is sole remaining center of Kiso lacquer —art begun over 800 years ago in Kiso Fukushima and soon spread, but it was not until 17th century when Hirasawa monopolized trade to make up for its lack of rice or other means of income. Also, special clay, *sabi-zuchi*, mixed with lacquer is most abundant around Hirasawa. Everyone in town

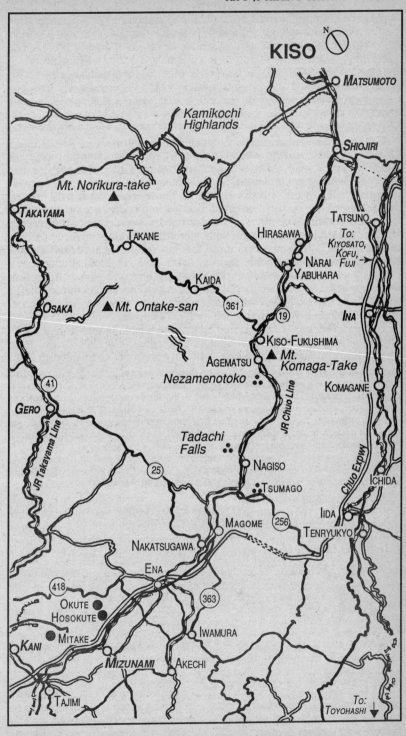

KISO

Kamikochi Highlands

○ MATSUMOTO

SHIOJIRI

Mt. Norikura-take ▲

TAKAYAMA

TAKANE

HIRASAWA

TATSUNO

To: KIYOSATO, KOFU, FUJI →

NARAI
YABUHARA

KAIDA

(361)

OSAKA

▲ *Mt. Ontake-san*

(19)

INA

KISO-FUKUSHIMA

AGEMATSU

▲ *Mt. Komaga-Take*

Nezamenotoko ⋮

KOMAGANE

(41)

GERO

JR Chuo Line

JR Takayama Line

Tadachi Falls ⋮

(25)

NAGISO

⋮TSUMAGO

Chuo Expwy

ICHIDA

IIDA

MAGOME (256)

TENRYUKYO

NAKATSUGAWA

ENA

(418)

OKUTE ●
HOSOKUTE

(363)

MITAKE ●

IWAMURA

KANI

MIZUNAMI

AKECHI

TAJIMI

To: TOYOHASHI ↓

seems to be involved in some or all phases of lacquering (39 separate phases from carving wood to coating) and with annual sales of well over 8 billion yen (1990), it should come as no surprise to get off train and see over 50 shops lining road. At far N end of town is **Kiso Lacquer Museum** (¥150, 9:00-16:30, X-mon) where all 39 steps of lacquering are displayed, along with works of art by past and present masters. Most shop owners will show you around their workshop and let you watch them work: many X-mon. Superb antique lacquerware private collection at TEZUKA Manzaemon's store **Chikiri-ya** open to all: annex fronts stn, collection is in main store 50m up, across from ¥-B inn **Matsuno-ya**.

Rather than stay here, suggest Hirasawa as easy 30min walk (5min cab or rail) from...
NARAI, pleasant village which could easily pass for samurai movie set except for paved road. May 1978 it became nation's 10th National Cultural Asset folk house-area, protected, partially funded by government to keep its ancient facade. Stn is village's N end, all houses flank road; with narrow fronts they stretch far back, result of Tokugawa property tax system which set levels by width of entrance. Homes of rich or inns reserved for travelling daimyo boasted their status with wide entrances. Overabundance of stores here is not wholly due to recent tourism (most still retain ancestral occupation with exception of some farmers who now run inns), but to early Tokugawa era decree which forbade cutting any of 5 types of cypress abundant here. It was enforced by cutting off head for tree, arm for branch. Sole ban exception was lumber for regular rebuilding of Ise Grand Shrine. Despite being in fertile valley Kiso's farmers could not clear land for rice paddies, and villages relied on travellers passing thru to buy goods which in turn paid for rice bought in Ina valley. *Gombei-kaido* 'Rice porters' Road' mountain trail Narai ↔ Ina city is paralleled by new Rte361.

You can see most homes here, browsing thru many stores selling lacquer and fine combs which we see made at next village of Yabuhara. Or take break at coffee shop **Tsuchiya**, beautiful folk house which used to be tea house; or lunch on excellent freshly-made noodles at **Echigo-ya** or **Ise-ya**. Next to Tsuchi-ya is **Hirano-ya** sake brewery; permanent decoration is its wood ball hung over doorway which used to be put out with each new batch of sake, travellers could tell when sake was made by looking at color of wood which starts out fresh green, to dry brown by end of season.

Some houses have been opened to public as museums: **Kamidon-ya** was local magistrate's residence, used by all officials passing thru, including emperor Meiji during his tour of area. Inside are fine art pieces and screens (¥200, 9:00-17:00, X-Jan-Feb).

Across street about 10 doors N is...
Tokuri-ya now **Museum of Local Arts**, similar but used by noble ladies passing thru; (free, 9:00-17:00, X-tue, Jan-Feb). While these 2 show how rich lived, S, past S-curve, same side as Kamidon-ya, classic example of commoners home is **Nakamura House** (¥150, 9:00-16:30, X-mon).

WHERE TO STAY: Of course, you can spend nite in one of these lovely **ancient homes** choosing from 16 minshuku in 'commoner homes' or 2 ryokan in large *hatago-ya* houses once reserved for nobility. Centrally located **Echigo-ya** (not to be mistaken for nearby noodlery of same name), ☎(0264)-34-3011 (¥-Tw/2), ranks in top 20 country inns of Japan; rsve well in advance since they only use 5 rooms: in business for over 200 years, present owner 8th generation innkeeper. **Abura-ya** ☎34-3016 (¥-Bw/2) nr stn, fairly new, and tho nice, suggest one of older minshuku at ¥-lo-Bw/2. We chose **Shimada** as first interesting looking place to duck into out of rain. Shimadas are great hosts, but judging from what they had to say about their neighbors, expect same friendly service at any you choose. Tho they speak no English, they like to have foreign guests and there is always someone in town who speaks at least some English. Minshuku **Iseya** ☎34-3051, unlike rest was old *hatago-ya* upper class inn. Also 2 temple hostels, **Chosen-ji** ☎34-3019, and **Seiryu-ji** ☎34-2360, both W down side streets S of Echigo-ya; same rate as minshuku.

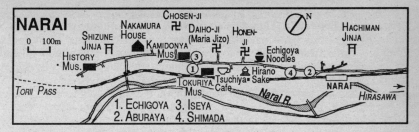

Fun time to visit here is for *Shukuba Festival*, **1st weekend June**. Starting fri, locals open their houses and have feudal era costume parades. Less formal than other such fetes, visitors can borrow kimono and take part. As food and sake flows, all break up into small groups which continue partying at inns or almost any open house. For change of pace, during same days Hirasawa has *Lacquer Fair*, bit more subdued festivities and wares sold cut-rate. For this weekend you should book room well in advance, call VILLAGE OFFICE ☎(026434)-2001; will also tell you exact dates of festival.

Other sites in town are...
HACHIMAN SHRINE near stn, 200 Jizo statues protect northern approach to town against bad luck.

W down side alley near Tokuri-ya is...
DAIHO-JI temple with landscaped garden and, more interesting, headless Maria-kannon statue cradling infant Christ who in turn holds flowers shaped as cross: face smashed during Tokugawa purge of Christians.

At S end of town is...
Local History Museum with some interesting items but can easily be skipped to save ¥150.

Nearby...
SHIZUME SHRINE was prayed at by travellers for safe crossing over...

Torii-toge Pass: pleasant hiking path and one of two remaining stretches of pedestrian KISO-JI, later roads and rail opting to tunnel thru pass, complete with original *ishi-datami*, paved stones, to make hills easier. Tea house part way up Narai side has drinks in summer, another shares peak with shrine and stone torii (from which pass gets its name) put there by 16th cent lord of Kiso after repelling 3 attacks on his domain.

Easy hour and half (6km) hike across pass to...
YABUHARA (also reached 10min rail or 15min bus from Narai). Handful of picturesque houses here, notably 370-year-old inn **Kome-ya**, but town famous for its **fine wood combs** (*Oroku-kushi*) with 90 teeth in 8cm. These originated in Tsumago, where they were made by carver's daughter, Oroku, as offering to spirit of Mt Ontake. Special wood needed came from *minebari* tree which grew in abundance around Torii Pass, but skill was handed down to select few in Tsumago; Yabuhara's craftsmen could not duplicate fine work until one succeeded in secretly viewing process, since then Yabuhara dominated market. *Ah*, industrial espionage! Most combs you see are mass-produced in large workshops (S end of town, nearest stn) where most of process is now automated. Only few men still do all by hand; 2 with stores are **USHIMARU Yoshio**, S end of town, and **KAWAGUCHI Sukeichi** N end of town near YABUHARA SHRINE (you pass it if coming over pass). Can visit automated workshops as well as see these two men work at home; everyone takes sunday off, but you may be lucky and catch occasional demonstration at **Village Folk Museum** below stn (¥150, daily 9:00-16:00). Mass-produced combs start from ¥600, hand-made combs from ¥1,000.

From Yabuhara we suggest train...; for walker it is 3hr30min mostly on Rte19 to...

KISO FUKUSHIMA: Largest town on KISO-JI, which isn't saying much; its sites can be done in 2hrs by foot. We list them in counter-clockwise order from stn: Downhill from stn is center of town, with sole old structures remaining after 1926 fire. Staying on E side of Kiso River, 15min walk to site of Fukushima's *sekisho* **Barrier Gate**, main check point on Nakasendo and one of top 4 in feudal Japan. Part of it is reconstructed as small museum (¥50, 8:30-17:00 daily). Next door is 240-year-old **Takase House**, used by head Barrier official.

Cross river here and continue up 10min to...

KOZEN-JI temple, fine rock garden and landscape garden (¥50 donation).

Back along river 10min to...

Yamamura Magistrate's Residence (¥150, 8:30-17:00). Continue down this side of river, cross next bridge for view of old homes built precariously atop high stone embankment. Back to stn 20min. **Rent bike** at stn, ¥300/hr.

If doing KISO-JI by rail you may want to pass up Fukushima to save time—except for *Mikoshi-rolling Festival* **Jul 22-23**, 400kg *mikoshi* is rocked end-over-end thru town until it falls apart, starts *Kiso-odori folk dancing* nitely thru **Aug 16**.

WHERE TO STAY: Numerous inns, from big riverside **Tsutaya Grand Hotel** ☎(0264)-22-2010 and its stn-front J-style annex **Tsutaya Bekkan** ☎2-2145 both from ¥-Tw/2. Budget inns (¥-B-Tw/2 range) at bottom of stn hill, suggest **Takei** ☎22-2068; **Murachiya** ☎22-3186; or **Minoya** ☎22-2336, where we stayed, behind Tsutaya Bekkan. Also have stn **Kanko-annai** find rooms—may be hard to get **Jul-Aug** as mobs flock here to climb Mt Ontake to W.

Mt. Ontake There are 4 trails; least used is 7hr (10km) up S face from NIGORI-KAWA ONSEN, 30min walk from Takietsu **bus** stop. Easier to reach trail-heads are **Naka-no-yu** (4hr hike to top) and **Ta-no-hara** (3hr to top), 1hr20min and 1hr40min bus from Fukushima stn, respectively. **Drivers** should use these two as they have good roads (one to Ta-no-hara is toll ¥800). Another long trail goes up N face (6hrs), from **Kaida Kogen Plateau**, 1hr10min **bus** from Fukushima. All bases have numerous budget lodgings, as well as several huts near top, and small onsens tucked into foothills. Good maps and current bus schedules at Fukushima stn **Kanko-annai**, which can also find you rooms on mountain, advise hiking conditions. You can descend W face to NIGORIGO ONSEN on our HIDA section. As sacred mountain, Ontake is close behind Mt Fuji and white clad pilgrims with straw sandals share trails with booted backpackers. Two outer shrines located at base of Ta-no-hara and Naka-no-yu roads, inner shrine on summit. 2 campsites at Kaida Kogen, 1 at Ontake Kogen ski ground halfway to Ta-no-hara. Kaida Kogen also has large horse farm where they raise miniature but hardy *Kiso-uma* horses which average 1.3m/52ins in height.

KISO KOMAGATAKE peak E of FUKUSHIMA rises 2956m. Ascent this side takes 7hrs from next stop Agematsu, and is on more difficult side but can be done without special equipment. Easier way up is from other side, with cablecar to 2600m point:

KOMAGANE stn (50min from Iida) on Iida Line, 50min **bus** to Shirabi-taira where 8min **ropeway** (¥950 o.w. ¥1,800 r.t.) to **Senjo-jiki Karu** '1,000-mat circle plateau of flowers': carpeted in colors late spring thru summer, ropeway has made this area accessible to all. Takes about hour around plateau; many hiking courses (intermediate and harder) going up surrounding peaks (including Kiso Komagatake). **Skiing** on some slopes until June. If planning to **climb**, can stay at **Lodge** (¥-lo-Tw/2) or its **cottages** (¥-Bw/2) near ropeway terminal. Former boasts 'observatory bath' top floor. There are also several mountain huts and campsite up peaks. If descending to AGEMATSU (5-6 hrs), another campsite near base. If descending by ropeway, check schedules as they stop around sunset. Would **avoid weekends** Jul-Aug as you could spend much of day just waiting for space on buses and ropeway, tho once you get up, higher peaks will be relatively empty, masses content to meander thru flower fields. Call ☎(0265)-83-5201 to check on rooms in Lodge, Cottages, or mountain Huts.

KISO
FUKUSHIMA

0   200m

1. Tsutaya Grand   4. Murachiya
2. Tsutaya Bekkan   5. Mifuku
3. Takei   6. Minoya

To Narai →

After FUKUSHIMA those short on time continue on for nite at TSUMAGO by JR to NAGISO (40min local, 20min Ltd Exp; beware not all stop), +10min **bus or cab.**

Walkers may want to overnite at **AGEMATSU** 1 stop down, instead of Fukushima. Walk takes about 1hr30min, most of it on footpath near main road. Halfway along is **KAKEHASHI ONSEN** with just one quiet inn by same name. Agematsu itself is of little interest, other than as major lumber center of Kiso, tho there is stretch of old houses few hundred meters N of stn: walker will come across them just after crossing river into Agematsu, take L off Rte19 at river. 30min walk S, beautiful gorge formed by Kiso river.

Nezame-no toko 'Waking-up Spot' should be seen in early mist. 1.5km stretch of massive rock formations—cubes which look like they had been hewn by giant, and flat tables. Largest and best are at top end closest to Agematsu (get fleeting glimpse of these out train window). Heading downstream, tourists thin out as rocks get smaller, until you are only person around.

15min walk down Rte19 is **Ono-o-taki** waterfall, made famous in woodblock prints series *69 Stops Of Nakasendo.* 3km to next town of **KURAMOTO**, but all on Rte19; if walking, take **Shinshu Nature Trail**: At Nezame-no-toko bus stop, head E on local road, after several hundred meters trail cuts off R (S) thru hills to KURAMOTO. En route are **YOSHINO** and **TONO**, 2 ancient hamlets along what was once main pedestrian highway of 9th-13th centuries. Shinshu Nature Trail and KISO-JI meet just past Kuramoto; latter continues along Rte19, former parallels on other side of river. 6.1km (1hr30min walk) to **SUHARA** where they rejoin; take back street 1hr (5km) to OKUWA via 600-year-old JOSHO-JI and IWAIDE KANNON temples. Just before Okuwa you pass near TENSHO-IN temple; among its many stone Jizo figures is *Maria-jizo,* holding child with crosses etched on its clothing. Hour from OKUWA mostly off main road to **NOJIRI,** where MYOKAKU-JI temple has stone *Thousand-handed Maria Kannon* figure holding cross in one left hand. From here, 2hr30min walk to NAGISO on Nakasen-do, but all on Rte19, so again suggest taking little longer Shinshu Nature Trail branching off just S of Nojiri stn to meander thru hills on opposite bank.

15min N of NAGISO stn to **TOKAKU-JI** temple, with dozen Enku-butsu statues; ¥100 donation, see anytime. If time limit allows you only short walk, we recommend this next section 1hr (3.5km) to...

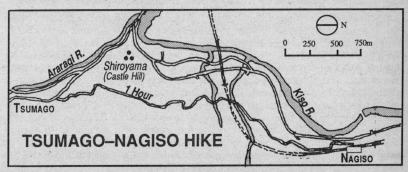

TSUMAGO—NAGISO HIKE

TSUMAGO: Easy walk, pleasant stroll thru fields, woods. Occasional house boasting beautiful landscaped garden uses rocks cleared from fields.

GETTING THERE: Bus (13 daily, more July-Aug) or **cab** from NAGISO stn takes busy Rte19. Bus doesn't enter town but stops just outside along bypass Rte256, no cabs allowed in town center. Coming from GIFU-NAGOYA area, quicker, cheaper **bus** or **cab** from NAGISO (some Shinano Ltd Expresses stop or change at NAKATSUKAWA to local) another option is to get off NAKATSUKAWA (1hr express from Nagoya, all stop) and 30min bus → MAGOME, change to 30min bus → TSUMAGO.

Walking from NAGISO, to TSUMAGO, there is waterwheel; giant signpost facing it was used Edo period to post new laws, criminals-wanted posters and announce executions. Behind it, **Sofutei**, cheap refreshments.

Town literally falling apart at seams late 1960s when townsfolk decided to fix up for Nagano pref's centennial. Now, 70% of pre-Meiji originals fixed, most others made over. Before fixing ('65) only 7,000 people visited; after, in ('72) 600,000 came; now over million pass thru annually. Citizens go to great lengths to keep old *shukuba* (lodging town) atmosphere: no coffee shops or snack bars, only old-style tea houses; to control commercialization one can only run one business. Fire hydrants covered with wood sheds to hide from view yet be easy to access; and even post office, mail box, phone booth are disguised to fit old look. When secondary back road is completed, they start next phase: tear up paved road thru town to further Edo era air. All agree to 3-point decree not to sell or rent their property. Justly proud of being in top trio **Cultural Asset Preserved Towns** (visited ASUKE, p301 & ARIMATSU, p299) aim to be best soon. Preserved Town reps meet here annually.

WHERE TO STAY: Mostly budget inns all small, personal, and relaxing. Best, ranks with Narai's Echigo-ya, is centrally located 200-year-old *hatagoya* style **Ikoma-ya** ☎(0264)-57-3013, ¥-T-Sw/2. Almost as good is nearby **Matsushiro-ya** ☎57-3022, 3rd is **Fujioto** ☎57-3009, N end of town near bus terminal, both ¥-hi-B-lo-Tw/2. Minshukus abound; we had excellent time at **Yaoki** ☎57-3114, run by Mr and Mrs Kumagai Yutaka —almost last house S end of town, it is quiet and tho they speak little English, but they have accommodated more than usual share of foreign guests. As usual, midsummer and major holidays can get bit crowded so best to book ahead. If Yaoki is full, leave it up to **Kanko-annai** in middle of town, call ahead, ☎(0264)-57-3123. There are 22 minshuku in town, dozen more scattered in quiet little hamlets just down road towards Magome, and half-dozen part way to Nagiso near remains of Tsumago castle; all are antique houses.

Sole fee-charging sight here is well worth its ¥200: **Okuya Kyodo-kan** (8:30-17:00 daily) used to be *honjin*, lodging for daimyo passing thru. Building was actually only *waki-honjin*, or secondary inn used only when main house was full. Main house (2x larger!) burned down and site now public park just S and across street. Present *waki-honjin* was completely rebuilt with almost all cypress. After ban on cutting cypress was lifted, it became status symbol to use it; thanks to ban area was full of gigantic trees used in this rather remarkable house. 3 years after completion it was used by emperor Meiji as rest stop. Tho here for only 20 min, every eventuality was prepared for down to lacquered toilet (which to this day sits there, never having been used—all royalty keep stiff upper lip) and make-shift high table for his tea (Japan Imperial family does not sit on tatami 'floor').

Start at rear...
Storehouse Museum before guided tour around house. Main gate remains closed since emperor Meiji used it.

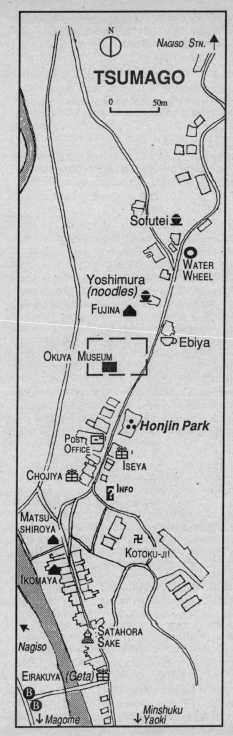

TSUMAGO

N

NAGISO STN.

0   50m

Sofutei

WATER WHEEL

Yoshimura (noodles)

FUJINA

Ebiya

OKUYA MUSEUM

Honjin Park

POST OFFICE

ISEYA

CHOJIYA

INFO

MATSU-SHIROYA

KOTOKU-JI

IKOMAYA

SATAHORA SAKE

Nagiso

EIRAKUYA (Geta)

B

B

↓ Magome

Minshuku ↓ Yaoki

Magome-toge Pass: Pleasant hike, mostly original Nakasendo footpath most people take slightly easier way, **bus** to Magome to start, then cross bus route bridge then branch R on local lane to Tsumago with many interesting homes where you can see old folks weaving straw horses and baskets: large house just before crossing river is workshop of *rokuro-kogei*, wood turned on lathe. Road soon becomes footpath, 2hr to summit, halfway, just beyond Kudari-tani hamlet, is pair of waterfalls.

From top, it's 50min down bus road thru more tiny hamlets, ending...
MAGOME: 3rd of Edo period villages, mostly rebuilt after 1895 fire but still interesting. Known primarily as birthplace and home of Meiji era writer SHIMAZAKI Toson, 4 museums here are dedicated to him and his works. Most interesting architecturally is **Toson Memorial Hall** (on R coming over pass) with large gate and fence. Equally photogenic **Daikoku-ya** gift shop next door, massive hanging saké ball in front. MAGOME can be used as optional lodging in unlikely event that Tsumago is full. Over 20 minshuku here, also 2 ryokan, most famous **Yomogi-ya** run by grandson of Toson.

Alternate Link to HIDA-JI Samurai Road From here 30min bus → NAKATSUKAWA rejoins rail; 10min (2 stops) N to SAKASHITA also 2 stops down from NAGISO, from where 5 buses daily cut across to GERO for HIDA-JI road walk, and TAKAYAMA, *follows*, one daily from MAGOME spring thru autumn.

SIDETRIPS: Before heading out of area, some **side trips** for hiker, or those who want to spend few relaxing days in TSUMAGO:

Tadachi-no-taki waterfalls: 2hr hike from TADACHI stn (1 stop S of NAGISO) to base of series of spectacular waterfalls, most beautiful in autumn when hillsides covered with fiery maple leaves. Large campsite, some budget minshuku at base of falls. Trail follows upstream 6.3km(3hr); at top heavily wooded park.

Continue down other side 5km (2hr) to JUNI-KANE stn (1 N of Nagiso) via Kakizore river valley with more waterfalls and cool, deep pools. Last km to Juni-kane is on road. Before crossing Kiso River to stn, **Shinshu Nature Trail** heads S 5km to Nagiso.

Urushi-bata 'lacquer fields': (35min bus E of TSUMAGO on Rte256) is small village of woodcutters of lacquered bowls and plates seen in TSUMAGO; several workshops turn utensils on lathe and lacquer them. To draw more customers to their area (much cheaper to buy here), locals have made summer recreation center of budget minshuku, bungalows, campsites and tennis courts. Also several short trails thru dense cypress forests.

Halfway is small hamlet of...
ARARAGI where conical cypress bark hats and bark boxes are made by older folks. Closer to Tsumago, river provides for refreshing fun in summer; heading downstream from town are some isolated spots with small pools which we found ideal for picnic and dip. Pick up *bento* box-lunch in town and, if you like, small bottle local sake, best of which is *Nana-warai* 'Seven Laughs'.

With one day to spare, try to fit in riding...
Tenryu River Rapids at ĪIDA. There are 2 separate runs; *Tenryu Funa Kudari* and *Tenryu Rhine Kudari*. Former starts Ichida (8km, 5 stops JR N of Iida), stopping at Benten (10min bus from Iida) and Tokimata (7 stops S of Iida) ending S of Tenryukyo stn after passing thru Tenryu-kyo Gorge. *Tenryu Rhine Kudari* starts at N entrance to gorge from either Shibukiso Inn or Miyako Grand Hotel, one on either side of river. Boat passes thru gorge to end Karakasa (3 stops S on JR). Benten → Tenryu 1hr ¥3,000; Tokimata → Tenryu 30min ¥2,000. Suggest either more convenient Benten departure or longer Ichida run. Also should call at least day before to make sure boats are running: ☎(0265)-24-3345. *Tenryu Rhine* takes 1hr, ¥2,570 and should also check. If more than 10 people, must reserve: ☎(0265)-27-2247, get own boat. Dec thru Feb must pre-arrange and rent entire boat ¥60,000 unless lucky to squeeze in with group. Touch of antiquity as oarsman do *to-ami* net casting in river with catch prepared and eaten on board.

GETTING THERE: Meitetsu express **bus** (from NAGOYA) dep MAGOME bus terminal (20min walk from Magome town on Chuo Expressway) first bus 7:06 with 2 buses hourly until 19:06: 40min to IIDA stn. Return bus from Iida stn to Magome dep every hour on 6:34-18:34. IIDA → MAGOME or TSUMAGO **cab** about 20x-mtr including Chuo Expwy toll.

PERSONAL DATEBOOK: TSUMAGO AREA: worth scheduling for its *Cultural Parade*, **Nov 23**. Locals dress in varied Edo period costumes, trek Nakasendo from Nagiso area to Otsumago. Other festivals are: **Apr 3**: *Kurashina Shrine Festival*, Kudari-tani prayer for healthy silkworms by offerings and dances. In 1585 Kurashina Shichizaemon on his way to deliver silk to Toyotomi Hideyoshi was murdered on this spot by bandits. Few days later landslide leveled Kudari-tani hamlet; villagers fearing it was his spirit erected this shrine in his honor and have since prayed here for good silk. **Jul** Early: Harvest dances, songs by children, Okuwa Daimyojin Shrine Kakizore. **16-17**: Higashiyama Shrine *Festival*, Midono Vill, Nagiso; mikoshi, Kiso dances **23-24**: Wachino Shrine *Festival*, Tsumago, mikoshi parade and dances thru town. **Aug 13-16**: Bon dances. (Same days at Nojiri, Noth Nagano local version Kyoto *Daimonji* fire festival; children with torches set fire, make different character each nite. **24**: *Fire festival* marks 16th cent Kiso lord's victory over invaders. Torch procession Atago-yama hill (N of Nagiso) and Shiroyama to castle remains where bonfire lit to dance around. **Oct 3**: *Flower-Horse Festival* at Itsu-miya Shrine, Tadachi. 3 small hardy Kiso-uma horses bedecked with flower-covered poles, parade thru town. At shrine folks take one pole each and offer to spirit there to pray for harvest. **2-3**: *Harvest festival* at Araragi, Hirose hamlets, Nagiso-cho. **18**: *Kagura dances*, 30min, PM, at Hakusan Shrine, Nagiso.

You can continue down old NAKASENDO beyond MAGOME thru several more old towns, ending up at MINO OHTA, to head up to TAKAYAMA. Start this leg from ENA City 2 stops S of NAKATSUKAWA; it is all on rural back roads and *Tokai Shizen Sando* (Nature Path)–no buses–involves several hour walk or hitch.

Interesting town not on actual Nakasendo, but on subsidiary pedestrian highway...
IWAMURA (30min rail on Akechi Line (12x-daily), or 50min bus (every 2hrs) from
ENA), most of little town old but well kept. Came into being mid-12th
century with building of castle, prospered during Edo period when occupied
by Matsudaira clan, related to shogun. Called **Fog Castle** for obvious
reasons, remaining stoneworks attest to its once massive size.

Before climbing castle hill, there are 2 small...
Local History Museums; other long, white-walled, tiled building was
part of Edo era school started by Matsudaira. Walking thru town notice that
old houses nearer stn are smaller than those near castle hill: large for
samurai, small for townspeople. In center of town are 2 exceptionally large
houses: one **Kimura house** built by same carpenter who did Takayama's
Kusakabe House. Just SW of stn is stone room holding 1,000 Amida
scrolls, 1,000 gilt Buddha images as offering for peace and prosperity by
Matsudaira Noriyoshi. Alas, open to public few days during golden week–
beginning May.

WHERE TO STAY: This town is to walk around and enjoy, couple hours
should suffice but if looking for lodgings there are 3 inns. **Mizuhan Bekkan** ☎(0573)-
43-2168 nr Iwamura Shrine is classic with landscape garden, ¥-Tw/2. Half-price (¥-B) are:
Maruko ☎43-2505, 200m S of stn; and **Yamato-ya** ☎43-2512, 400m E.

Walker can cut across hills to ENA in just over 4hrs, following *Daimyo-kaido* road,
now footpath. Hits Rte19 4km W of Ena at MAKIGANE bus stop where it joins up with
old NAKASENDO for our last leg. If starting out at ENA stn, head W (R) at 1st stop light
and just after joining Rte19 you come to SHINMEI SHRINE where take back road
branching off R; it becomes path just above MAKIGANE bus stop. You can condense 1st
hour of walking into 10min bus ride if lucky enough to catch one of 4 buses daily leaving
ENA stn down Rte19.

OKUTE-JUKU, 1st hamlet, over 4hrs from ENA, 3hrs from MAKIGANE bus stop.

From here, it is another 2hrs to next hamlet of...
HOSOKUTE-JUKU: Both were bustling lodging towns on Nakasendo
and tho they've mellowed with age, most old buildings are left. Has several
budget inns as well as 1 or 2 high-class inns which were *honjin* special houses reserved
for passing Daimyo. Tho there are no buses doing full run, there are infrequent buses
from MIZUNAMI stn: 2 daily to OKUTE (45min), 6 daily to HOSOKUTE (40min).
MIZUNAMI (3 stops S of ENA) is pottery kiln town, worth visiting especially **1st wknd
Apr** *pottery fair*; **2nd sun Apr** for 300-year-old *Hanbara Bunraku* puppet play at
Hiyoshi Shrine.

Walker may want to stay at Hosokute or Okute (or pitch tent en route), as it is over
3hrs to Mitake where catch Meitetsu Rail to **Inuyama** (or change to JR to use *Rail Pass*
part way at Kani stn whence 2 stops to Mino Ohta).

HIDA-JI 飛騨路
OLD SAMURAI ROAD

WHAT WE WANT most to see is medieval town of TAKAYAMA, and
SHIRAKAWA-GO village. If no time for both, *see* Shirakawa-go's *gassho-
zukuri* houses set up at well-done **Hida Folk Village**, Takayama.

Gero (join here bus from Magome) → Norimaki → **Gassho Mura** → Zensho-ji →
Hida Osaka → Shitajima Onsen → Nomugi-Toge → **Takayama** (join here from
Inuyama) → Hida-no-sato → Hirayu → Oku Hida onsen cluster → Kamioka →
Furukawa → Kokufu → Kawai → **Shirakawa-go** → Oak Village → Shokawa → Ogi
→ Shirakawa Gassho Minka → Nishi Akao → Kaminashi → Mino Shirotori → **Gujo
Hachiman** → Takahata Onsen → (Seki - Gifu).

TAKAYAMA is on JR Takayama-Hida Main Line, for SHIRAKAWA-GO must bus from Takayama, or from Hokuno stn end of Nagaragawa Rail Line; which splits off at Mino-Ohta, where also join Chuo Main Line from Kiso-ji. Old pedestrian hiway Hida-ji → Takayama is now Rte41; Mino-ji → Shirakawa-go now Rte156. Our course is circular from Gifu, up Hida-ji and down Mino-ji with sidetrips suggested for our adventurer.

TILT: Early morning out of GIFU 2hr, or INUYAMA (JR Mino-Ohta stn) 1hr30min to TAKAYAMA (nite), next afternoon 2hr30min bus to SHIRAKAWA-GO (nite) and back to GIFU via Gujo-Hachiman. With extra day, spend 1st nite at HIRAYU ONSEN (hour bus E of Takayama), finishing off TAKAYAMA day 2 with 2nd nite in town or at SHIRAKAWA-GO. Bit quicker is to return to TAKAYAMA to catch express train to INUYAMA or NAGOYA; SHIRAKAWA-GO → GIFU bus takes 6hrs, rail HOKUNO → GIFU saves some time *if* your bus catches rail, and ensures quick passage thru Gifu outskirts where you can lose hour on bus due to traffic (Shirakawa-go Kanko-annai has **English schedule** of bus, rail). If leaving Gifu-Inuyama area late day, can break at Gero onsen before Takayama, but avoid if possible. All bus tours concentrate on Takayama city (*see* city TILT); best long **tour, JTB-Ace Bus** Co (runs reverse of our course), 2-day out of Takayama; board at TAKAYAMA stn, take in major sites in town → GERO (o'nite) → MINO-OHTA shoot Nihon Rhine → Inuyama Castle → NAGOYA stn.

JR Rail Passers need only pay for bus between Takayama → Makido where change to JR bus running Rte156 between Hokuno stn end of Nagaragawa → Ogi stn near Shirakawa-go. Buses in this area infrequent, may want to **drive**: Nagoya has all major, minor rental agencies; Nippon Rent-a-car and 2 more at Gifu; Toyota, Nippon, and Eki (Stn) Rent-a-car in Takayama. Best to rent at Takayama round-trip to Shirakawa-go, 24hrs ¥8,000+. If renting in Gifu keep for full circuit to avoid astronomical **drop-off fee**. Eki-mae Rental usually cheaper, no mileage limit, but cash only. **Hitchhikers** will have little problem to Takayama as Rte41 is major link to Toyama on Japan Seacoast used by many trucks; Rte156 will involve some waits; most difficult between Takayama → Shirakawa-go. Main link between them is Rte158 to Makido, used by bus. Alternate: Rte360, narrow winding mountain road with sheer drops to valley below, hair-raising but beautiful way to enter Shirakawa-go, passing thru several isolated villages precariously set on mountainside. We drove this in late autumn after first snowfall, mountains covered by fiery autumn trees dusted with white more than made up for scary drive.

JR Note: Ltd Exp *Hida*, 4x-daily (extras peak season) Nagoya → Gifu → Mino Ohta → Gero → (*Hida* #1 stops Hida-Osaka) → Takayama. Some continue → Toyama on Japan Sea coast, others end Takayama or Furukawa connect to Ltd Exp *Kita Alps*. Reg Exp *Norikura* and *Takayama* make more stops, most notably Hida Osaka for mountain hotsprings. Note, odd numbers (ie. *Hida #1, Norikura #3*) go *kudari* ('down' away from Tokyo, towards Toyama); even numbers are *nobori* 'up' to Nagoya, Tokyo). Nagaragawa Rail Line between Hokuno and Mino Ohta only locals (2hrs). If not busing across from Tsumago-Magome → Gero, return Nagoya to catch Ltd or Reg Exp to Takayama.

Hida area is excellent in any season: Spring opens in burst of colors, plums bloom 1st week Apr, cherries week later coincide with returning swallows. Cool crisp days, mostly sunny, with 3 or 4 days of light snow. Light rains begin once or twice weekly end of March, crest June thru mid-July when often cloudy; light intermittent again thru Oct. Summer days are hot but less humid; nites cool. Wild flowers bloom May thru Oct when hills begin to turn fiery hues of red, gold, yellow, best late Oct. First snowfall usually mid-Dec (our early Nov snow was earliest in 15 years), sunny 18-22 days in month Nov thru March, but at same time at least 20cm snow on ground for 40-60 of those days. Winters are beautiful (especially seen from outdoor onsen-pool) but cold. Like rest of Japan, it is crowded New Year, Spring break, Golden Week, Obon. Takayama is inhumanly crowded for its spring and autumn festivals, but with 485 shrines thruout Hida, you have infinite choice of colorful, local fetes. Better known ones listed in text.

We start at...
GERO ONSEN: 2hr rail from Gifu, 30min less from Mino-Ohta; last 30km of rail and road thru rugged Nakayama-Shichiri gorge. Known onsen for over 1,000 years, local lore claims spring was shown to villagers by injured heron come to treat its wound (such romantic origins for onsen abound in Japan, best known is Shikoku's Dogo Onsen myth). ONSEN-JI hot spring temple in town has small Yakushi Nyorai (Medicinal Buddha) statue supposedly left behind by our heron. Early Edo scholar HASHI Rasan labeled Gero one of Japan's top 3 onsen (others Arima, Kusatsu) and it has prospered since. Now with over 70 inns, many large luxury ryotels, has lost much of its rustic charm and we suggest passing it up except for **puppet theater** year-round, and seasonal village **Kabuki**.

Geisha: Gero has over 100 registered, whom you can have entertain at set fee, arrange thru your inn. ¥15,000 (incl 10% svce) 90min, ¥5,000 addt'l 30min.

WHERE TO STAY: Ryotels (all J-rooms) run ¥-hi-T-L+w/2, boast spectacular baths, indoor and out. Best is one of few remaining traditional inns, **Yunoshima-kan** ☎(05762)-5-3131, furthest from river (only 300m) but on hill overlooking town. Others are **Ogawa-ya** ☎5-3121, across river from stn; **Sansui** ☎5-3288, N end. Several ¥-Tw/2 range, best are (descending price order): **Okuda-ya** ☎5-2838; **Hotel Yoshino** ☎5-3200; **Minori-so** ☎5-3038. Budgeteers have few minshuku, 3 Kokyo-no-juku public inns (¥-Bw/2). Too late for good room in Takayama we stayed at minshuku **Sho-en** ☎5-2110, stn side of main bridge. Book thru stn W exit Annai-jo, across from bus center; just tell them price range. Ryokan touts in front won't rip you off, but are usually from larger inns. Budgeteer need not forsake large baths, use baths at larger inns for nominal fee (around ¥400), except peak seasons; 3 old-time public baths in town: **Shirasagi-no-yu, Yakushi-yu, Ko-no-yu,** open noon till 10pm, ¥250; outdoor river-side bath, open 6:00-21:00, ¥600/2hr, best early am, late nite.

For little more quiet, try...
NORIMASA ONSEN 20min bus E of Gero in hills. 2 ¥-B ryokan: **Norimasa-kan** ☎6-2054; **Komeno** ☎6-2654. Usually room X-**Apr 14-15** *Spring Festival.*

5min walk from town (5min bus from stn) across Rte41 is...
Gassho Mura village, 7 reconstructed folk houses from Shirakawa-go. Each house has special display: one **Hida Folk Museum**, another about local adventurer TAKEGAWA Kubei who helped in 'opening' Ezo-Hokkaido, 3 are workshops for local folk arts which you can do: handmade *washi* Japanese 'rice' paper, bamboo weaving, painting ceramics (¥1,000 to do one, mailed to you in 2 weeks after firing). Most interesting is **Takehara Bunraku** (ICA), operated by single man, HORAOKU Ichiro, who does all movement, voice, sound, set changes. After graduating local elementary school, he studied puppet-making in Kyoto, returned here to create his own. Repertoire of 35 full plays includes classics like Chushingura, Rashomon; largest play has 100 puppets on stage at once. Performs twice daily 10:00 and 15:30 (15:00 Nov-mid-Dec), no show wed, 29-31 monthly, and mid-Dec to mid-Mar. Special performances **Jan 2-4** usually entire Chushingura cycle. Village open daily 8:30-17:00 (-16:30 winter), no offdays, ¥750/adult ¥350/child; admission includes puppet play and adjacent reptile park. If in Gero only for Horaoku's puppets, should call ahead ☎5-2239 to make sure he is not off or out of town.

Moved here from Mine Ichigo site is...
Hida kiln, make your own *Mashita-yaki* pottery, ¥1,000 fee + ¥50 clay + ¥300up to fire in kiln, depending on size.

5min walk S of Gassho Mura...
Mine Ichigo archaeological site, several reconstructed Jomon and Yayoi dwellings; artifacts from here and other sites in Hida in museum. ¥200/adult, ¥100/child, to site and museum (hours same as Gassho Mura).

ENTERTAINMENT: Gero abounds in local folk entertainment. **Minyo Kaikan Obako** in town center has nitely performances of folk songs and dance. Far better, and worth scheduling for, are outlying village Kabuki plays *(mura-shibai)* at 2 villages outside Gero, performed since mid-17th century. Local farmers trade in their hoes for prop swords, and have as much fun as audience. Each set runs over 6hrs (around 15:00-22:00) so bring food and sake (also sold on spot) to get into full spirit of things. Both plays popular, arrange ahead thru **Gifu Prefectural Tourist Office**, 1-11 Kanda-cho Gifu-city, ☎(0582)-63-7291; or Gifu offices in Tokyo or Osaka; or JTB. **Ho-o-za Phoenix Stage** 10km SE of Gero on Rte257 (links Nakatsugawa on JR Chuo Line to Gero), 20min bus to Mimayano, or cab 6x-mtr. Performed **May 3-4** (even yrs); seats 800 around ancient stage, complete with *hana-michi* center-runway. **Haku-un-za White Cloud Stage**, 15km S of Gero on local road off Rte257, 35min bus → **Kadowasa**, cab 7x-mtr. Staged annually **Nov 2-3**, mostly 18 Classics (*Kabuki Juhachi-ban*) of Ichikawa Family of actors.

PERSONAL DATEBOOK: Here equally unusual and energetic: *Ryujin Himatsuri Dragon God Fire Festival* **Aug 1-3**, is Gero's principal summer fete. 30ft fire breathing dragons controlled by 6 men race thru town in intricate dances, chasing bowl-shaped mikoshi. Derived from folktale in which dragon king seeks bowls lent to farmer but not returned. *Ta-no-kami Matsuri* **Feb 7-14** (National Intangible Cultural Asset) at Mori Hachiman Shrine in town starts off Hida's spring festivals. Dedicated to god of harvest, rice fields are tilled by chanting farmers while others sing and dance. Main event 14th is Hanagasa-odori dance, men wearing flower covered hats *(hanagasa)*.

CHOPSTICKS: Two old-time noodleries for quick light lunches while walking around: On road to Gassho Mura, before Rte41 on L is 2-storey **Hisago** for soba and udon, cheap; best is their *tororo-zaru*, soba dipped in finely grated *tororo* mountain yam. Another summertime favorite is *hiyashi-somen*, best at **Nakaya**, long squat flimsy-looking store with large blue-on-white rooftop billboard at entrance to Gassho Mura. Thin wheat-flour noodles served in long bamboo trough, kept cool by running water thru, thus store specialty *nagashi-somen* (rinsed somen). ¥500 per person, open March thru Oct. Also front of Gassho Mura is **Sugata-an** *sansai-ryori*, mountain of in-season vegetables sashimi, rice, noodles. Filling, yet light on stomach.

Tour Gero by cab, ¥10,920 (20x-mtr) for up to 5 people: Arrange thru inn, or cab stand at stn for 2hr circle of Gassho Mura, Mine Ichigo, and...

Upstream toward Takayama 1 rail stop or 15min bus to...
ZENSHO-JI, one of Japan's top Rinzai Zen temples. Landscape garden by KANAMORI Sowa, 17th century local lord of Takayama. Temple front restaurant **Ryusho-an** serves *shojin-ryori* vegetarian priests' fare, as well as local *sanso-ryori* herb-dishes with trout. Nearby is mysterious stone circle, left behind by some primitive culture; most likely Stonehenge-type sun/star dial; found thruout Japan from Hokkaido (*see* OTARU) to Kobe.

25min rail (4 stops) or 30min bus on to...
HIDA-OSAKA, gateway to trio of backwoods onsen and hiking trails up 3,063m Mt Ontake. All 3 have budget lodgings, ryokan from ¥-B+w/2, minshuku-usual w/2.

20min bus E, is rare...
YUYA ONSEN, 'Soda spa' (bubbly carbonic bath water). Not surprisingly, water is good for stomach problems. 2 minshuku and 7 ryokan, some are **Okuda-ya**, ☎(057662)-3006; **Sengaku-kan** ☎3010; **Momohara-kan** ☎3001.

Nearby...
Museum of Local History was formerly Kiyohara family mansion, massive 19th century silkworm raising house made of *hinoki*-cypress & *katsura*-judas tree—both high class materials. Open daily 9:00-17:00; ¥300.

Down local side road before Yuya is...
SHITAJIMA ONSEN, (15min bus to Ochiai and 15 min walk). Unusual in that 3 different types of hot spring are tapped: carbonic acid 'soda', alkali and radon 'radiation' baths. 2 ryokan: **Asamutsu-so** ☎(057)-662-3021, and **Senyu-kan** ☎3005; and 3 minshuku here. 1st of 8 levels up Mt Ontake, can start climb here, follow river 20min upstream to Gandate rock formation, 300m stretch of sheer cliffs soaring 110m, best seen autumn, capped with flaming red maple. This route is full day to summit, but mostly along spectacular river valley.

Most hikers however, start at...
NIGORIGO ONSEN mud baths at mountain's 6th level (1800m), highest onsen in Japan, 1hr40min from HIDA-OSAKA. Popular in summer Hida-side trailhead up Ontake, has 9 small ryokan **Yumoto-kan** ☎(057662)-3110; **Ontake** ☎2124; **Prince Lodge** ☎3167; **Asahi-so** ☎3528; **Kakumei-so** ☎3037; and one public inn, **Nigorigo Hoken Center** ☎3156 run by Nagoya City, must reserve. **Outdoor riverside baths,** 2 open to nonguests run by Ontake ryokan ¥400, Kakumei-so ¥150. From here, 4-5hr hike to summit. Ontake is active volcano, last blew its top 1973 closing off many trails linking various peaks, all open now. Most common route first to northernmost 2,959m Hida-sanjo, along ridge to Ontake past several mountain lakes. Best to climb late day or nite to catch *go-raiko* (sunrise reflected off clouds). Grand view of Japan Alps to N and on clear day Fuji in distance. 2 mountain huts open Apr-Oct ¥4,500w/2: **Gono-ike** and **Ontake-koya,** arrange at Nigorigo. Main peak Ontake volcanic group, it is sacred to mountain ascetics of Ontake-kyo religion, small shrine at summit. Mountain straddles Gifu-Nagano prefectures, down other side Kiso Fukushima.

4km E of Hida-Osaka stn, rock-lined river at **Josetsu** Canoe-jo. Quickest way here is cab (2x-mtr), tho bus stop nearby. One of few permanent **kayaking** places in Japan, summer sees many pros shooting roughest runs, **late July** is Central Japan Kayak Slalom Contest; used to have rental, but no more.

Driver with time may want to detour to take in unusual folk houses of...
KUGUNO: 15km, 2 stops JR; along Rte361 E toward Nomugi Pass, which we did ending up *eventually* in Nagano pref's Matsumoto City; Rte361 runs straight to Kiso Fukushima while Rte158 links Takayama-Matsumoto straight via lovely Kamikochi in Chubu-Sangaku Nat'l Park. Takayama and Matsumoto are both actually closer to Japan Sea coast SAN-IN (*see*) than to Tokaido. Houses have wood shingle-like roofs, rows of stones weigh them down in winter wind. TILT travellers can see these houses at Takayama's Hida Folk Village. Driving back from Nomugi Pass, short-cut to Takayama branches off Rte361, cuts 20km backtrack: halfway to Kuguno, 8km beyond Asahi dam, local road cuts R (N) across river, L at fork 3km, 5km on L at intersection and another 5km to Takayama.

NOMUGI-TOGE Pass: (2hr bus from Kuguno stn, change halfway Kami-ga-do on some or end up in Kiso Fukushima; others direct). 1,672m pass was major link between Takayama and Kiso River valley in feudal days, now popular hike. Buses from Kami-ga-do infrequent, sometimes 4hr walk quicker to Nomugi hamlet with its stone-roof houses. 3hr hike from hamlet thru pass to Kawaura on other side from where bus to MATSUMOTO. Campsite, 2 stone-roof budget inns, and lots of cows at pass. Avid hiker can trek 8km N up Mt Norikura and down other side 1hr to Tatami-daira and back entry to Takayama. Similar trail starts at Nomugi Hamlet joining near summit.

6km (20min bus from Kami-ga-do) toward Kiso Fukushima,...
HIWADA was once main horse-raising area for Kiso's daimyo, with annual gala horse fairs until 1930s (Japan took horsemanship gold at 1932 LA Olympics). Fair gone, but horses still graze.

Road links Ontake's Nigorigo to Rte361 at Asahi dam; en route is single-inn **AKIGAMI ONSEN,** ¥-Tw/2.

1hr bus from Kuguno or Hida-Osaka. Back on Rte41 (1 stop JR) to...
HIDA ICHINOMIYA with 2 sites worth seeing on special days:
DAITO-JI temple behind stn popular for cherry blossoms, some over
thousand years old and 20m tall. Temple treasure is Enku statue (more on
Enku later). MIZU-NASHI JINJA is Hida's highest ranked, and first-built
shrine—for fair weather, good harvest, and healthy silkworms.

PERSONAL DATEBOOK: *Iki-bina* (Living Hina) *Matsuri* Apr 3, sees 9
young women chosen from all Hida area dressed in multi-layered kimono of Hina Matsuri
dolls giving offerings. May 1-2 festival is National Intangible Cultural Asset, ICA,
full day of ancient offertory dances and rites.

HIDA TAKAYAMA 飛騨高山

THIS LIVING MUSEUM in heart of central Japan is one of our great favorites.
Despite millions who flock here annually, it has managed to preserve its old
charm. It is rich in history: prehistoric man lived here millennia before Wa
Japanese. *Nihongi* tells of 4th century emperor-chieftain sending punitive
expedition against 'hairy demons' (Emishi?) of Hida. Clusters of little villages were soon established, many started by remnants of Heike (N Hida),
and foes Genji (S Hida). Hida's master carpenters (see their handiwork everywhere, in Kobe at Carpentry Museum) built palaces, temples and shrines of Nara,
Kyoto, Kamakura, and later, Edo. Famed 17th century carver Hidari-
'Lefty'-Jingoro who worked on Nikko (3 monkeys), was Hida native.
Highly skilled carpenters of Hida, collectively called *Hida-no-takumi* after
their 1st great master, were in such demand that imperial edict of Nara era
required every 50 homes in Hida to supply 10 artisans to work 330-350
days annually in capital.

Takayama rose to political prominence when local lord Kanamori built
castle here in 1504. Chosen as his stronghold for its large basin-vale, ideal
for rice, he put town on narrow spot along Miyagawa River for easy defense. His clan was ousted 1692 to Dewa in Tohoku and area came under
direct Tokugawa control, ruled from Takayama *bugyo*-magistrate's office.
Shogun wanted direct control of area as it was major source of lead to make
bullets. Despite remoteness, town quickly grew to become major cultural
center, junction of several major roads. Its fame led to prosperous merchant
class. We come here to see perhaps largest remaining group of these Edo
period buildings, taking up entire 'Little Kyoto' section of town.

Takayama preserves its traditional art skills from Spring 1988 thru new
2-year arts-crafts college, campuses in Takayama and Gujo Hachiman —
depts of art/design, wood crafts/architecture, ceramics, fabric/dyeing, & foreign languages
(English, Chinese, German): ✍ Hida Global Institute of Human Arts,
Hanakawa-machi 80-2, Takayama-shi, Japan, ☎(0577)-34-8821.

GETTING THERE & AROUND: 3hr express from NAGOYA, 5+hr from
TOKYO, 5+hr from OSAKA, using Shinkansen. Several ways to see town. *Avoid* bus
tour, better take taxi: *kogata* (4 psgrs) ¥8,860 (17x-mtrs)/2hrs, add 50% each extra hour;
chugata (5 psgrs) 10% more. Book thru Tourist Info or taxi stand at stn. Nohi bus
(☎32-0045) has several routes reach main sites: A: start JR Takayama (11:05, 13:00,
14:20) → Hida-no-sato → San-no-machi → Jin-ya → Yatai-kaikan → Shishi-kaikan →
end stn (14:20, 16:00, 17:20), ¥3,070. B: JR Takayama (8:50) → Asa-ichi →
Kusakabe-ke → Yatai-kaikan → Senko-ji (Enku-butsu) → end stn (12:10), ¥3,070.

But best to take it easy and see it all on foot; or in man-power rickshas, ¥6,000/1hr
per person (fits 2) with running Japanese commentary on sights. Arrange thru Fujita
☎33-1223, or catch in old part of town. Speed up with bicycle rental ¥300 1st hour
+¥200/additional, ¥1,300/day; trio rental places R side stn plaza E (main) exit,

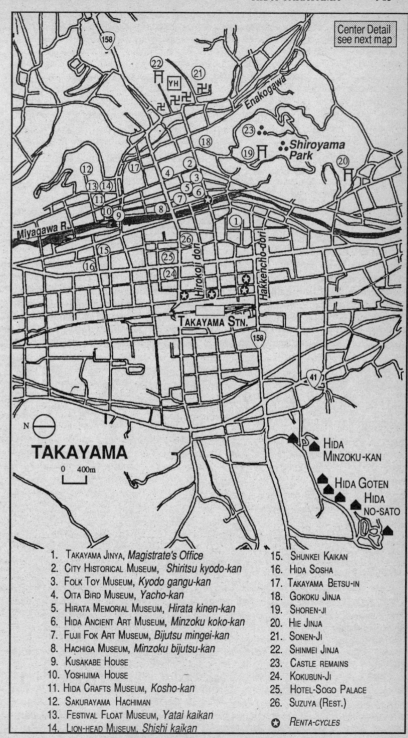

TAKAYAMA

0   400m

1. TAKAYAMA JINYA, *Magistrate's Office*
2. CITY HISTORICAL MUSEUM, *Shiritsu kyodo-kan*
3. FOLK TOY MUSEUM, *Kyodo gangu-kan*
4. OITA BIRD MUSEUM, *Yacho-kan*
5. HIRATA MEMORIAL MUSEUM, *Hirata kinen-kan*
6. HIDA ANCIENT ART MUSEUM, *Minzoku koko-kan*
7. FUJII FOK ART MUSEUM, *Bijutsu mingei-kan*
8. HACHIGA MUSEUM, *Minzoku bijutsu-kan*
9. KUSAKABE HOUSE
10. YOSHIJIMA HOUSE
11. HIDA CRAFTS MUSEUM, *Kosho-kan*
12. SAKURAYAMA HACHIMAN
13. FESTIVAL FLOAT MUSEUM, *Yatai kaikan*
14. LION-HEAD MUSEUM, *Shishi kaikan*

15. SHUNKEI KAIKAN
16. HIDA SOSHA
17. TAKAYAMA BETSU-IN
18. GOKOKU JINJA
19. SHOREN-JI
20. HIE JINJA
21. SONEN-JI
22. SHINMEI JINJA
23. CASTLE REMAINS
24. KOKUBUN-JI
25. HOTEL-SOGO PALACE
26. SUZUYA (REST.)

✪ RENTA-CYCLES

one more 2 blocks S, another 2 blocks N. Can arrange to keep overnite; leave extra bags in coin locker and pedal to inn, see town, next day pedal back to stn to catch bus to mountain hot springs or SHIRAKAWA-GO. Long distance buses to HIRAYU ONSEN stop front of HIDA BETSU-IN; for SHIRAKAWA-GO stop at entrance to HIDA-NO-SATO. Stn **Rent-a-car** R of stn exit, Nippon Rent-a-car 300m from stn back side; if using, don't bother picking up until ready to leave town, as you just end up parking while here and spaces are rare and expensive.

Coming out of stn, Takayama is like any rural city, but 10min walk E across Miya River is old town, little changed in appearance since feudal days but for paved roads and electricity (invisible: wonder of wonders utility lines underground). All roads E from stn hit old town, main trio *Hirokoji-dori* from stn front, *Hakkencho-dori* to S, *Kokubunji-dori* to N. Latter passes 1,250-year-old KOKUBUNJI temple and its pagoda (good shopping nearby). We take *Hakkencho-dori* street; near Miya river newer homes give way to cluster of ancient, but sturdy houses: JIYAKU-NIN YASHIKI, homes of descendants of local officials of...

TAKAYAMA JINYA MAGISTRATE'S OFFICE [1], end of *Hakkencho-dori.* Built 1586 as Kanamori residence, became Tokugawa administration headquarters after they dismantled castle. Added small garrison and prison in back, dismantled 1869. Mansion survived as it was only place large enough to hold new Meiji officials. Sole original magistrate's office existing (several fine replicas elsewhere), others dismantled by Meiji, or more often, by irate locals to eradicate traces of feudalism. Hida's farmers had much to be irate about; Jin-ya was site of severe repression of peasant revolts 1771-1789, (collectively called Ohara Rebellion after leader) over increased rice taxes during drought years. Over 19 years of unrest, marked by 3 major uprisings, 38 farmers were executed, 97 sent to island prisons (same as death), hundreds imprisoned, beaten, or fined. Finally abandoned early this century, local government spent 3 years restoring to mark 1974 centennial of Gifu. Living quarters not rebuilt; what now exists was administrative quarters. Walking thru (shoes off), first are series of small rooms which served as separate entrances and waiting areas for town leaders, religious officials and government officials (none could mingle with other); to **kitchen** and around main audience halls (posts in garden list size and location of sections not rebuilt). Last place before the granaries is **confession** room where criminals were beaten while suspended, pebble floor made for easier washing away blood. Granary now museum of feudal era and Jin-ya related items. Daily 8:45-17:00 (16:30 winter) ¥300.

From here we cross into old town on...
Naka-bashi Bridge. Hard to imagine pulling massive floats across its red lacquer for spring and autumn festivals. Citizens' group keeps Miya River clean; its banks lined with hundreds of colorfully decorated bamboo poles for *Tanabata 7/7 Festival*, celebrated here month later on **Aug 6-7**. Week later hundreds of paper lanterns floated down river for end of Bon, *Toro-nagashi.*

Now for some geographical orientation prior to GETTING AROUND:
Shiroyama Castle Hill is S of you; 4 streets fan out N to pass thru old town. First is *riverside street*, next *San-no-machi suji* (3rd street), next *Ni-no-machi suji* (2nd st) & *Ichi-no-machi suji* (1st); each passes thru corresponding *San-no-machi, Ni-no-machi, Ichi-no-machi* district. Intersecting (from S to N) are *Sanmachi-dori* (extension of *Hirokoji-dori*), *Yanagi-bashi street, Yasukawa-dori* (extension *Kokubunji-dori*, also Rte158 to Hirayu). Everything S of Yasukawa-dori called *Kami-...+machi* (upper, ie. closer to castle, +town), area from Yasukawa-dori N to Enako River *Shimo-*(lower)-*machi. Kami-* district is business, *Shimo-* residential. Areas are called by their street name preceded by location; so, *Kami-San-no-machi* or *Shimo-San-no-machi;* which are best preserved. N of Enako River is *Hachiman-cho* district, E is *Higashiyama Tera-machi* temple district, S to *Shiroyama* district; each of which we visit in turn.

There is too much in town to describe it all. Many old stores have been at same trade for centuries. See them making *miso, tofu, sake* (wood 'beehive' ball above entry means new batch ready to drink, you don't age sake); craftsmen (wood-carvers, potters, painters, *washi* paper fullers, lacquerers); stores with old and new folk art, antiques stores galore; restaurants, inns; old-time tea stalls serve imported coffee and western cakes, along with thick green tea and sweet bean cakes. Nite volunteer fire-watchers still make their rounds, hitting wood clappers along with their age-old warning cries of *'hino-yojin'*, fire-beware; competing on winter nites with newer, but still nostalgic wail of noodle pushcarts' *charumera* flute and that high whistle of *ishi-yaki-imo* baked sweet potato peddlars. Folk nocturne worth taping.

Numerous museums dot town, mostly in Kami section; working N up each street starting Ichi-no-machi to San-no-machi are (numbers correspond to map):

Takayama City Historical Museum, *Shiritsu Kyodo-kan* [2]: in 6 kura storehouses of Nagata mansion built 1868, contain over 10,000 items. Entering, on R, is part of main house, displaying local arts, folk items, belongings of Kanamori clan. Straight ahead to storehouses, containing sake distilling tools, historic items, items on Takayama's festivals, and paraphernalia of 10 local fire-fighting squads. Giant 'pompoms' on sticks held by squad leader who stood over hottest part of fire to direct where to throw water. Dozen buddhist statues by prolific peripatetic 17th cent carver-priest Enku, who made over 10,000 figures in his lifetime: *Enku-butsu*, unique in their rough-cut appearance and bold features. Roaming Japan, Saint Enku ended his travels in his home Hida area, many of his statues found thruout area. 8:30-17:00, X-thur in Nov-June, year end, ¥200 (child 1/2).

Folk Toy Museum, *Kyodo Gangu-kan* [3]: across street has 2,000+ toys from around Japan, which owner collected over past 20 years. Some sold at kiosk. 8:30-17:00, X-tues, last day each month, Jan 1, ¥200 (¥100/child).

Oita Bird Museum, *Yacho-kan* [4]: Owner of Oita sake distillery spent 60 years collecting and stuffing over 250 birds native to Hida and Japan Alps, with few foreign feathers tossed in. Tapes of birdcalls accompany. 9:00-17:00, X-wed (except Aug), Dec 26-Jan 5, ¥150 (¥100/child).

Hirata Memorial Museum, *Hirata Kinen-kan* [5]: 220-year-old home of candlemaker (owner now 10th generation); good example of mid-Edo merchant-artisan house, with small courtyard gardens and 3 storehouses displaying family treasures, tools of trade, various lamps and lanterns, other odds and ends. 9:00-17:00, no holidays, ¥200 (¥100/child).

Hida Ancient Museum, *Minzoku Koko-kan* [6]: former home of lord Kanamori's personal physician. To protect lord on visits, house had several hidden rooms and escape routes (tunnel leads to river bank). One room also has 'trap-roof' which comes crashing down when rope is cut (see its mechanism by peering thru hole in wall at top of staircase). Displays usual samurai goods, folk tools, and archaeological Jomon and Yayoi artifacts (mostly fertility 'staffs') from Hida area, ancient scrolls, documents, pottery. 7:00-19:00, no holidays, ¥300 (¥150/child).

Fujii Folk Art Museum, *Bijutsu Mingei-kan* [7]: Dr. Fujii's storehouse home (his dentist clinic next door now run by son) is his personal collection picked up in 60 years of house calls to rural villages. Can't miss ostentatious gate, was one of castle's sub-gates which he moved here. Among items displayed are rare Edo children's dolls, superb collection ornamental combs. 9:00-17:00, X-year-end, ¥300 (¥150/child).

Hachiga Museum, *Minzoku Bijutsu-kan* [8]: collection of 7 generations of Hachiga family. Most interesting are various religious items, Buddhist and Shinto statuary, and Hidden Christian (*kakure Kirishitan*) goods: figures of Maria Kannon (Mary as Kannon, Goddess of Mercy) holding infant Christ; what appears to be Buddhist figure is crucifix when seen from behind; *fumi-e* (stomping pictures) of crucifixions and saints which those suspected of being Christian were forced to trod, or face death. Christian Hachiga family fled here to escape Tokugawa persecution. 8:00-18:00, X-wed just in Jan-Feb; ¥200, (¥100/child).

Just across Enako River are 2 of *finest folk houses* in Hida, built for Edo period merchants by best carpenters using top material. Both burned down 1875, but Hida's finest rebuilt both almost exactly as they were, passing up Rokumeikan style western architecture sweeping Japan then. Tho completely different in appearance, both are characteristic Hida architecture; named Important Cultural Assets 1966, now protected and funded by gov't.

Closer to river...
Kusakabe House [9], which also has displays of local folk arts.

Next door...
Yoshijima House [10]. Kusakabe made fortune as money changers, Yoshijima as sake merchants. Both are must-sees and are included in any bus, taxi or ricksha tour. ¥300/¥100 child each (incl tea), daily (X-year end) 9:00-17:00; Dec–Feb Kusakabe X-fri, Yoshijima X-tue.

Hida Crafts Museum, *Kosho-kan* [11]: is another classic Hida folk house, belonging to Fukuda family. Outlet for local artists since 1868, inside are live demonstrations on carving, Shunkei lacquering and weaving, as well as collection of local folk art. Back storehouse full of odd-shaped tree trunks and roots. Goods sold here are guaranteed top workmanship, competitively priced. Fun item, sold also at other wood shops, is small traveller's amulet, ¥500, shaped like *inro* medicine box with strings, it opens to reveal pair of dice (to keep you occupied on road) and good luck plaque blessed at local shrine. About 2x1 inch, ask for *dochu omamori*. 8:30-17:00, X-year end and thur Dec thru Feb, ¥200 (¥100/ child).

Just beyond is gift store-lined approach to...
SAKURAYAMA HACHIMAN JINJA shrine [12], built 1623 by 2nd Kanayama lord to protect city. L of *torii* as you enter 3-tiered compound is EMA-DEN offertory hall, offered paintings cover walls. Purification rites **last day of June, Dec** in which you jump thru reed ring to rid body of impurities. 2nd tier has lesser shrines, L–R are: KOTOHIRA, for health; INARI, for wealth, good harvest; TERUSAKI, for healthy teeth; far R up long narrow steps is AKIBA, patron deity firemen. Top tier is main sanctuary, dedicated to 3rd cent 'Emperor' Ojin. Rebuilt roughly every 100 years, last time 1976, close replica of original. Shrine's autumn gala festival is one of 2 times to see Takayama's famous floats, some of which you can see at...

Takayama Festival Float Museum, *Yatai Kaikan* [13] located R of shrine entrance. *Miko* shrine maiden guides thru imitation azekura-'log cabin'-style hall. 4 floats displayed at one time, rotated twice yearly after each festival. Other 17 stored in special *kura*, tall narrow white-walled storehouses which you see all over town. Also displayed is massive *mikoshi* made for festivals, but never used since too heavy for originally planned 16 carriers, added frame to be carried by 36 men made it too large for city streets; largest in Japan. Took 4 years to build from 1888, cost around ¥2,500 (¥ = $ silver then) skilled carpenters and lacquerers got 15sen (0.15yen) daily. Regular showing every 20min of puppets from some floats. 8:30-17:00 daily, ¥460 (¥200/child).

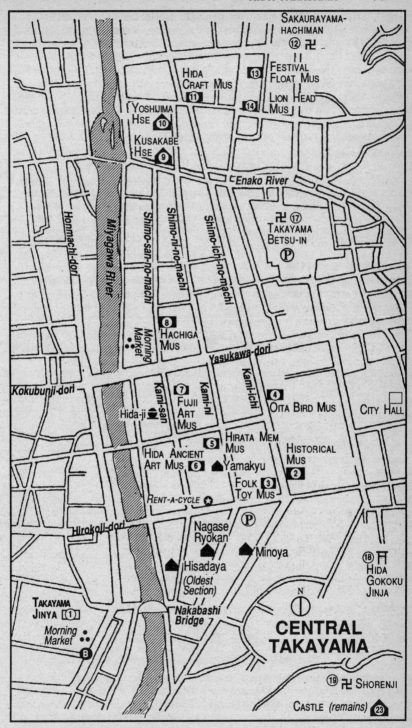

SAKAURAYAMA-HACHIMAN
⑫ 卐

FESTIVAL FLOAT MUS
⑬

HIDA CRAFT MUS
⑪

LION HEAD MUS
⑭

YOSHIJIMA HSE
⑩

KUSAKABE HSE
⑨

Enako River

卐 ⑰
TAKAYAMA BETSU-IN
Ⓟ

Honmachi-dori

Miyagawa River

Shimo-san-no-machi

Shimo-ni-no-machi

Shimo-ichi-no-machi

Morning Market
⑧ HACHIGA MUS

Yasukawa-dori

Kokubunji-dori

Kami-san

⑦ FUJII ART MUS

Kami-ni

Kami-ichi

④ OITA BIRD MUS

CITY HALL

Hida-ji 卍

⑤ HIRATA MEM MUS

HIDA ANCIENT ART MUS ⑥

▲ Yamakyu

HISTORICAL MUS ②

FOLK TOY MUS ③

Rent-a-cycle ★

Hirokoji-dori

Ⓟ

Nagase Ryokan
▲

▲ Minoya

⑱ 卉
HIDA GOKOKU JINJA

▲ Hisadaya
(Oldest Section)

Nakabashi Bridge

TAKAYAMA JINYA ①

Morning Market
Ⓑ

N
⊕

CENTRAL TAKAYAMA

⑲ 卐 SHORENJI

CASTLE *(remains)* ㉓

Floats appear twice yearly, for Hachiman Shrine *Autumn Festival* and
Hie Shrine *Spring Festival*. Spring fete since 1652, has 12 floats, autumn
fete (1718) has 11; only 2 appear at both. Began during Takayama's
heyday as main cultural center close behind Kyoto and Edo. Floats fantastic
works of art, financed by local merchants and built by Hida's craftsmen.
Over 6m/20ft tall, all originals. Variety of floats: some with puppets on top
tier, another has giant drum, all carry people, pulled by dozens of men.
Kept immaculate by regular cleaning done by Takayama's citizens, each
float takes team of 10 two days to do and shiny black lacquered cypress
with copious gold leaf ornaments always look brand new.

Spring Festival coincides with full bloom of sakura in **Apr**. On **14**th at 10:00,
12 floats gather S end Shinmei-cho below HIE SHRINE, procession starts noon, thru
streets S of shrine, arriving front of JIN-YA where on 2 floats puppets perform. Crosses
NAKABASHI, thru old section to end Yasukawa-dori street. Nite festival from 18:00, over
100 lanterns lit on each float. 20:00 start back across town to be kept front of JIN-YA.
15th is main day, pulled thru town again 9:30-17:00. Spring procession stays S of Yasukawa street, also called Kami-machi (upper-town) festival.

Autumn Festival Oct 9-10 stays N of Yasukawa street, called *Shita-machi*
(lower-town) fete 9:00 on 9th, 11 floats gather Hachiman Shrine to start procession thru
town N of shrine. Lanterns lit 17:00, 18:00 procession old town. **10** main fete 8:40
procession again from Hachiman Shrine, covers area N of shrine, again thru old town.

Ranked with Kyoto's Gion festival, fame has changed Takayama's fete.
Man we met remembers as child with mostly local viewers, returned home
after 10 years to find streets jammed with out-of-towners, so crowded he
fears for accident as shutterbugs run in front to get shots. He used to sit on
top and play instruments with other children, now music is taped in Tokyo's
NHK studio. Tho best time to see town, it's crowded, 2.5 million 1990.

Behind float museum is...
Lion-head Museum, *Shishi Kaikan* **[14]**: over 800 heads used in *shishi-
mai* festival lion dances. Gathered from all over Japan, spanning 400 years,
they offer rare chance to see so many variations at once. Videos of local
shishi-mai; downstairs dining hall/stage regular performances, not as much
fun as real thing, but you probably won't get chance for that and you've already paid ¥430 (¥200/child), 8:30-17:00, no-X.

Back S to sakura-lined Enako River, upstream on N bank around
Teramachi 'Temple-Town' district.

But first, short detour to ...
Shunkei Kaikan, **[15]** for information on *Shunkei-nuri* lacquerware.
Newly completed center has 1,000-piece display of *Shunkei-nuri* from early
Edo to present; outline of entire process using panels and live demos.
Kiosk shows largest selection, guaranteed genuine; standard prices, but
compare since some can be gotten for slightly less in old section's gift stores
(*see* SHOPPING). Open 8:00-17:30, X-only Dec 31, ¥200 ¥100/child.

150m NW is...
HIDA SOSHA [16], shrine built 931, rebuilt 1820. Dedicated to *kami*
creator of Hida, gathering place for all Hida's *kami* for their October venture
to IZUMO GRAND SHRINE (*see*) for *Kanna-zuki*, 'kami(god)-less month'.
May 4-5 *Shrine Festival* has colorful procession of priests, *miko*, mikoshi, one float.

Higashi Terayama Teramachi, or Temple District, is just that. Start at...
TAKAYAMA BETSU-IN [17], foremost local temple. First lord Kanamori
in 1588 transferred all Shirakawa-go SHOREN-JI temple priests here and
built this complex for them, surrounding it with 11 sub-temples. Plagued
by repeated fires, present main hall is concrete, 1961. Originally Pure Land

Jodo sect, affiliated to Kyoto's Higashi Hongan-ji in 1703. Priests' quarters complete contrast to concrete main hall, beautiful wood structure was house of wealthy farmer moved here 1948. Most of temple's rites held within; *annual airing of temple treasures* July 24 only time to see all.

S thru Teramachi, we pass row of 9 temples (all within 800m) with 3 shrines behind. None particularly special, but those of you with time will find it pleasant walk thru quiet, wooded precincts.

N → S:

KYOSHO-JI and EIKYO-IN both sub-precincts of UNRYU-JI; behind, KOMPĪRA JINJA and 1200-year-old HAKUSAN JINJA shrines; DAIO-JI, beautiful garden, sub-temple DOUIN-IN; SOGEN-JI [21]; TENSHO-JI behind it SHINMEI JINJA shrine [22]; HOKKE-JI; ZENNO-JI; last SOYU-JI. Some have gorgeous gates and halls which were part of old castle: most notably Shinmei shrine's **ema-den** offertory hall, former castle *Tsukimi-den* **moon viewing pavilion.** 3 Shrines' *Spring Festival* May 4-5. ENNO-JI temple has hour (extend if you want) **zazen** from 6:00, daily Apr thru Oct, open to all. Arrange day before ☎32-4516; eat AM gruel (¥500) or stay for ¥-Pw/2.

Few more small shrines and temples beyond, S to...
HIDA GOKOKU JINJA shrine [18] to local war dead esp 6,000 WW II. Shiroyama District offers view of old town below, other than that:
This puts you at...
SHOREN-JI [19] original Takayama Betsu-in, Jodo sect, moved here in 1959 to escape Miboro Dam flooding. Built 1504, oldest untouched Jodo-sect structure; beautiful soaring gull-winged roof, garden behind fits in so well with wooded hillside, was hill created for garden. **Treasure hall** fine. ¥200 entry to temple also for **Fukurai Memorial Hall,** front of temple. Native-son Prof FUKURAI Tomokichi of Tokyo U worked with telepaths 1920-30s; see 'spirit photos' he imprinted mentally onto film, including one of not-normally-visible moon's backside, uncanny resemblance to first real satellite photo half-century later.

HIE JINJA shrine [20], host to Takayama's *Spring Festival*; on N side of hill, is little far, but pleasant wooded complex.

CHOPSTICKS: Within complex is *Shojin ryori* restaurant **Kanenbo**, full-course vegetarian priests' fare of 15-20 dishes, ¥5,-10,000; must reserve ☎32-2052 except off-season (Nov-Mar) when 2-3 people OK without prior call.

Now you see why we suggest minimum full day here, even skipping Teramachi and Shiroyama.

After restful nite in ancient inn, you are ready for few hours out at...
HIDA MINZOKU-MURA folk village 10min bus SW of stn (cab 1x-mtr; 2x-from old town) to *minzoku-mura iriguchi*: daily 8:30-17:00, X-Dec 30-Jan 2, ¥500 (¥250/child) for both Minzoku-kan & Hida-no-sato, two areas combined contain over 30 Hida area rural folk houses, covering every type from stone roof to *gassho-zukuri* thatch of all types and sizes.

Minzoku-kan section is laid out as small hamlet, only few houses, one is restaurant **Furusato.** Largest is **Wakayama-ke** at 5 storeys, 13m to top, 240 years old, inside is museum of folk art and silkworm-related items. Across street from it is **Toyama-ke annex** (now gift store) where Toyama family elders retired while next generation remained in main house which we visit at Hirase. Behind this at **Shimotori-ke**, you can see 1,200-year-old *paper making* process—only in winter. Behind this is Hida's oldest (370 years) folk house, **Hokubi-ke.** Further 10min walk S to Tokugawa Ieyasu's memorial TOSHOGU SHRINE, 1619.

From Minzoku-kan area 10min walk up to...
HIDA-NO-SATO; Buses from Takayama → Hida-no-sato → Minzoku-kan → Hida-no-sato → Takayama every :15, :45. Halfway down road is **Hida Goten**, 30m-tall wood house built early Meiji; originally located in Kurobe City. Hida-no-sato is entire village, larger than Minzoku-kan, complete with village stage (moved from Tateho Shrine in N Kawai village) with occasional folk dance programs; also mill waterwheel, variety of storage sheds, firemen's watchtower and rice paddies. Circular paddy (*kuruma-da*) is planted by working around from center post, ancient method found only in Hida and Sado Island: see how it's done last sun May. First harvest is offered at Ise Grand Shrine. Also TAKUMI shrine, dedicated to Hida's greatest carpenter Hida-no-Takumi. Five houses form separate 'cottage industry hamlet', live-in artists demo dyeing, carving, lacquer, silk production.

SHOPPING: *Shunkei-nuri* is classic product of Takayama, started here early 17th cent. It soon became so popular that it spread throughout Japan; however, it now survives only in Takayama and Noshiro in Akita Prefecture. Red and brown lacquers, but most popular is clear amber; good pieces reflect almost perfect mirror image; more layers=higher quality. Wood most often used is *hinoki* cypress, with cherry for curved pieces. New pieces tend to secrete oily drops which safely remove with soft cloth and benzene. Recent imitations have come out, hard to tell from real thing but chemical coating in place of lacquer. No real tips when shopping, besides choosing trusty looking salesperson, and too cheap is suspect. These are quality objects; small trays (up to 30cm across) start ¥8,000, rice bowls and small plates from ¥2,000. If interested, suggest going to **Shunkei Kaikan** to get feel of what to look for; prices there standard. Good stores in town are: **Fukuda-ya**, corner of Kami-San-no-machi and Yasukawa streets; **Fukuzen**, 20m S of Shishi Kaikan; **Matsuzawa**, continue S of Fukuzen to river, one block E; **Yamada**, on main st to Hachiman Shrine; **Kokei-do**, southernmost block of Kami-San-no-machi st, specializes in Shunkei-nuri tea ceremony utensils; **Keicho-do**, just W of Yanai-bashi bridge (3rd from S). Shunkei-nuri geta wood clogs at **Mishima**, 75m E of Kokubun-ji temple, just past large intersection; and at **Maeda**, S-end Kami-Ichi-no-machi.

As classically Hida as *Shunkei-nuri* is form of *ichi-i itto-bori*, literally 'one spot-one cut' carving. Not of local origin, *netsuke* carver MATSUDA Sukenaga imported technique from Nara mid-18th cent, using new style in his works. Best carver here is 5th generation carver MURAYAMA Gunpo at his shop **Murayama** in Hida-no-sato: five dragons adorning festival dragon float are his works. Right next door is **Genda**. **Hida-no-takumi**, main approach to Hachiman Shrine; **Suzuki**, at gate to Kokubun-ji temple; **Chotaku-bo**, on Kami-san-no-machi near Yasukawa street, specializes in Kannon statues (¥1,000 up) and Darumas. Sold all over town, small pieces start ¥500, masks ¥2,500, to tens of thousands for large pieces. Many types of wood used, chosen to fit subject to be carved. Taken from part of tree with closest annual rings to get layered look. Originally bright colors mellow with age.

Saint Enku's carvings are one style of *ichi-i itto-bori;* can't buy any of his originals, but Mr Miwa Toshiro, called *Enku of Showa Era*, has been carving fine replicas for 50 years (his are antique-lacquered black). Workshop-store **Enku-do** across from Kokubun-ji's entrance; from ¥1,000.

Takayama has 3 local **kilns: *Shibukusa-yaki*,** porcelain, ***Koito-yaki*** and ***Yamada-yaki*,** pottery. Shibukusa is by far most popular, intricate designs hand painted on white porcelain. Shibukusa pottery began here early 17th cent, but it was not until 1845 when 20th kiln master, TOYOTA Fujinosuke, returned after 6 years studying Seto porcelain (in turn imported from Kyushu's Arita), began making porcelain locally. Most big gift stores carry; best buys at 2 official kiln outlets: **Hokoku-sha**, on Kami-ni-no-machi 100m S of Yasukawa street. Locals say coming here is 'New Year feast' for one's eyes, full of beautiful pieces, but expensive: small cups, bowls start ¥1,000; ¥5,000 for set of 4 coffee cups and saucers. Second outlet **Shunso-do** 100m E of Kokubun-ji temple. Visit kiln to see them make it, but can't buy: kiln in Kami-Okamoto-cho, 1km N of Hida-no-sato; 300m W of CHOSHA-GUCHI bus stop on Rte41. If cab (basic-mtr), keep for return. *Koito-yaki* is more popular of pottery, kiln/store **Hamamoto** between Hida-no-sato and Minzoku-kan. Glaze mostly rich dark shades of green, red, black, or dull white; personal favorites natural rust color, done by wrapping in straw before firing. Tea mugs ¥500, sake bottles ¥1,000, ¥1,500 for sets. *Yamada-yaki* has subtler glazes, kiln/shop **Kobayashi Tosha** in Yamada-cho, 1km W of Shibukusa kiln S of Yamayuri GAKUEN-GUCHI bus stop; but easier bought at pottery stores in town.

Countless other local crafts abound: *bamboo* weaving, folk toys all over; Hida-sashiko embroidery at Kami-San-no-machi's mingei store **Sanmachi**; *wa-rosoku*, Japanese candles (we see them made up road in Furukawa city); furniture stores sell traditional, sturdy wood cabinets and chests; expensive but fun to browse.

Takayama is treasure trove of antique stores where you can buy anything from ancient art pieces to folk art and tools. Some of largest, oldest and most fun to browse thru are: **Shiramasa** E end Sanmachi-dori; **Emacha**, N of City Museum; **Kurahei**, S end Kami-Ichi-no-machi; **Gogura**, on road between Hida-no-Sato and Minzoku-kan. *Garakuta-ichi* open-air antique fair **7th monthly** (10:00-16:00) May thru Oct on Sanmachi-dori street between Kami-ichi-no-machi and river. *Niju-yokka-ichi*, Jan 24th, open air market of folk tools, utensils along Yasukawa and Honmachi-dori streets, parallel to Miyagawa river on E bank.

WOODBLOCK PRINTS at **Hanga-do** on southernmost block of Kami-San-no-machi; **Matsuoka**, 50m N; **Ikoku-ya**, 80m W of Kokubun-ji temple. Handmade *washi* (Japanese paper) products best at **Shin-Kogei** 100m W of Jin-ya; we visit village of Kawai on rural Rte360 to Shirakawa-go, center of *washi* making. Washi dolls at **Mozumi-ya**, front of Tensho-ji temple made by Mozumi Eiko whose work is nationally known, classes upstairs for locals who want to learn. Much more graceful and artistic than typical paper dolls, small ones start ¥1,000, large ones in cases reach ¥50,000.

Next to her store is **Matsukura Kannon-do**, one of 3 sites for **August 9-10** *Ema-ichi market*, sale of offertory horse prints. Other 2 are YAMAZAKURA SHRINE, W bank of Miya River, and **Ikemoto-ya** on Hakken-cho-dori street. Original wood blocks kept at Ikemoto-ya. Horses carry either sacks of money or bales of rice, put them up in foyer at home to bring in good fortune. Have your name inscribed when you buy, then blessed and stamped with official red seal at Matsukura Kannon-do or Yamazakura Shrine. Some stores sell pre-stamped prints all year.

Known for **outdoor markets**, last but not least *asa-ichi* morning market, dozens of temporary stalls set up front of JIN-YA, and along Miya River E bank. Farmers from surrounding countryside gather 7:00 to noon; sell mostly fresh produce, but can find many gifts, odds and ends made by farmers. Good place to pick up light snacks, for real meals...

CHOPSTICKS: Hida is noted for its mountain herb cooking *sansai-ryori*, most refined form is *shojin-ryori*, vegetarian priests' fare, best at **Kanenbo** (*see* SHOREN-JI temple); or **Hakusho**, 1 street E of Kami-Ichi-no-Machi near City Hall. Latter classier, only 2x-daily (11:30 and 13:30), for which must reserve (must be 2 or more), ☎32-0174; ¥8,000 per person full-course, 15-20 dishes.

Sansai ryori with meat or fish dishes included at: top of line **Susaki**, just E of Nakabashi Bridge; lunch from 11:30-, dinner from 17:00-; must reserve (2 or more), call ☎32-0023; ¥10,500, service included. 2nd floor (no rsv) **Tsuji-chaya**, management same, serves smaller courses, sansai slightly more budget oriented, try **Suzuya**, off Kokubunji. If from old town, take Kokubunji-dori towards stn, L on 4th street after crossing Miya River. In rustic old house, we found it worth short walk; enough satisfy, yet, not bloat, and well priced, full meal from ¥1,300, single courses ¥500+, serves macrobiotic on request. Next door is **Bandai** *shojin-ryori* (reserve, ☎32-0130) set course ¥8,000. Across from Suzuya is **Bandai Kadoya** annex, no rsv, regular *sansai-ryori* with meat from ¥3,000. Over dozen other less-known ones in town: worth mentioning is **Hida-ji** on Kami-San-no-machi, average price, good food, convenient.

Traditional Hida specialty is *Hoba miso*, miso bean paste with scallions and grated ginger cooked on large leaf over portable clay hibachi. Simple, but delicious and packed with energy. Served as part of breakfast at every inn thruout Hida, get it as part of *sansai-ryori* meal, or itself for ¥300 in town. Suzuya [26] has *Hoba-miso teishoku*. Can make at home, grapefruit-sized hibachis sold as sets at gift stores, ¥500; miso paste found at Japanese food stores almost anywhere in world, health food stores carry; buy bundles of leaves at asa-ichi for ¥100 or use any large leaf, just put on sesame oil (salad oil OK) before cooking.

Locals claim town has 3 specialties. First is *tofu-ryori*, multi-course meals centered around assorted *tofu* dishes: plain, in soup, cooked, deep-fried. Best **Hoguchi-ya** on Kami-San-no-machi; also **Tofu Jin-ya**. 2nd, Hida beef (Holstein cattle ranches thruout Hida) as juicy steak at **Kitchen Hida** just N of Jin-ya on side-alley before Honmachi-dori, as spicy BBQ *yaki-niku* at **Tengu** few doors N. *Shabu-shabu* Hida beef at **Suzuya**. 3rd,*chirashi zushi*, heaps of assorted meats, fish, vegetables on flavored rice: from ¥800 at **Michiya Sushi**, L off Kokubunji-dori on second street W of Miya River. Thankfully, Takayama has yet to be invaded by Macs, and has no need since local fastfoods abound. Many good soba shops serve Hida buckwheat noodles; ramen stands, roadside stalls sell *mitarashi-dango*, sauce-dipped dumplings on spit, ¥100 per skewer.

To go with all this excellent food is Hida's famed **sake** made at 8 local breweries. With its abundant top-grade rice and pure mountain water, Takayama has long been known for its sake (excellent for keeping warm in winter here); late 17th cent, town boasted 56 breweries, putting it close 2nd behind Nada, Kobe. Most sake here is dry *kara-kuchi*, best of any brewery runs ¥1,600-2,500 per 720ml (quart); driest of which is appropriately labled *Oni-goroshi*, but pronounced *Kira*, meaning 'demon killer' (strong but smooth, best cold) at Oita brewery, ¥1,850. There are 10 different sizes of bottles (by volume) in all shapes and sizes, fit for any pocket (we picked up mix of small ones for outdoor baths of Hirayu). All breweries are in old town, open to public and happy to let you sample their finest. Near Kami-Ichi-no-machi S end is **Hirase**, top label Kusu-dama; on Kami-Ichi-no-machi, **Oita**, tops Kira (can cost ¥10,000 in Tokyo), Hida-jiman; on Kami-Ni-no-machi is **Kawajiri**, top Hida-masamune; **Hiki** with top Tamano-i; and **Hirata**, top Yama-no-ko; on Kami-San-no-machi is **Unazaka**, for Miyama-giku; **Harada** for Sansha; and further down San-no-machi is **Tanabe** with its best Toyotoshi. Over 700 establishments in town serve local sake; most niteries concentrated in Asahi-cho and Hiromatsu-cho areas between Kokubun-ji temple and Miya River. W-style bars abound, but we prefer local hangouts, of which there are many; for full choice try **Jizake-ya** with every type of sake from all over Hida: R (N) on 4th street W of river; or **Happa**, half-block E.

Before embarking on nite rounds, hope you have decided on...

WHERE TO STAY: Town has over 200 ryokan/inns to fit any purse. Sole resort-class, **Green Hotel** ☎(0577)-33-5500, nr Hida Folk Village, ¥-T-Sw/2. But we suggest one of old-timers in old town (S to N): in Kami-San-no-machi: **Saito** ☎32-1970 (¥-Bw/2); **Sakaguchi-ya** ☎32-0244 (¥-B+w/2); **Godo** ☎33-0870 (¥-B+w/2). On Kami-Ni-no-machi is one of best **Nagase Ryokan** ☎32-0068 (¥-lo-Sw/2). On Kami-Ichi-no-machi is **Mino-ya** ☎34-0340 (¥-Tw/2). Along Miyagawa River E bank **Sumiyoshi**, which friends loved,☎32-0228 (¥-Bw/2). 3 minshuku along Ni-no-machi: **Ueno-ya** ☎32-3919, **Sankyu** ☎32-0397 and **Hatago-ya** ☎33-5226. **Hayashi-ya** ☎32-3868; and **Bunsuke** ☎33-0315 near Betsu-in temple; **Hachiman** ☎33-9661, near Hachiman Shrine. Other friends stayed at 'excellent' classic minshuku **Yamakyu** ☎32-3756, front of Hokke-ji temple, heard monks chanting in AM. Late arrival last chance is **Sosuke**, opp Green Hotel, ¥-Bw/2, late arrival ¥2,000 no food, or negotiate for local bkfst. All minshuku ¥-usual; many more inns, minshuku rate up, around old town, Temple district and castle hill.

Another cluster of inns around KOKUBUN-JI temple, of which we suggest to its W traditional **Iiyama Gyoen** ☎34-2272 (¥-T-Sw/2). **Kinki-kan** ☎32-3131 few blocks E is 100-year-old house serving top notch *kaiseki-ryori* meals, ¥-S. For quiet, head out to

Hida Folk Village area, with several moderate inns. Best is *gassho-zukuri* style **Hishu-ya** ☎33-4001, ¥-T-Sw/2. Also in area **Gassho-en Shosen-kaku** ☎33-1388, 380-year-old *gassho-zukuri* home ¥-T-Sw/2. Also **Hida Gassho-en** ☎33-4531, ¥-Bw/2. Dozen budget minshuku, but if budgeteer heading out to Shirakawa-go, save staying in *gassho-zukuri* homes 'till then where cheaper.

If hoping to stay in **temple**, sole **Youth Hostel** in town is part of **TENSHO-JI** temple ☎32-6345, ¥-Pw/2. Or try **ZENNO-JI** in Temple District, ☎32-4516, ¥-Pw/2 and morning *zazen*; **ZENKO-JI** 200m up Hakkencho-dori from stn ☎32-3804, ¥-Pw/2, ¥2,800 room only (*sudomari*); **RIKKYOKU-JI** near nitelife center 150m E of KOKUBUN-JI, ☎32-0519, ¥2,500 room only.

Arrange any above at stn **Kanko-annai**; or **Minshuku Center** N of stn; or **Ryokan Cooperative** 2 blocks E of stn. Most better inns arranged thru JTB.

WHERE NEXT: Alternates: can continue from Takayama on JR to Japan Sea coast town of Toyama (some trains require change here) and on to Kanazawa, which see and continue on to Kyoto, seeing our Yamato area historical routing as side trip out of Kyoto.

Or return to Nagoya to resume our historical routing to ISE, ending NARA–KYOTO.

Or for those with extra day, direct JR, Meitetsu or Nohi Bus 1hr25min (or Nohi day bus tour) to SHIRAKAWA-GO.

Or, with still more time, we suggest you do as we did and spend nite out on...

OKU-HIDA ONSEN AREA 奥飛驒温泉

EASTWARD 30km of Takayama to mountain boundary of Gifu-Nagano prefectures, is dotted with backwoods hot springs; ideal for summer hiking, winter skiing in Northern Japan Alps. We stayed in heart of Oku-Hida at...

HIRAYU ONSEN, main of several hot springs. Oku-Hida has probably largest number of *rotenburo*, outdoor baths, in all of Japan with literally hundreds. Almost every inn boasts one: larger inn has larger bath. Area inns published *Guide to 88 Baths of Oku-Hida* and tho many were left out, it lists inns at every onsen with large or unique outdoor baths. Booklet (available any inn or **Kanko-annai**) works as pass, get it stamped at your inn and most others will let you in their bath free, or at most ¥100-200. Countless *au naturel* spas in hills, along rivers.

Buses relatively frequent; less so in winter. All leave from #1 stand TAKAYAMA stn but check which you board: one ends Hida Dai-shonyu-do Cave, 2nd Mt Norikura, 3rd SHIN-HOTAKA (this for HIRAYU); one links HIRAYU ↔ NORIKURA. **Nohi Bus Co** runs all buses, their Tour covers area: Leave TAKAYAMA stn 8:30 → NORIKURA → HIRAYU → Hida Cavern → return TAKAYAMA 14:30. Runs daily 7/21–8/26; sat, sun, hol in Oct and Sep 23-24; ¥6,320/adult, ¥3,380/child covers all costs and lunch. But to spend time relaxing in hot springs, take local bus or drive, and spend nite.

En route Hirayu...
NYUKAWA village has some stops for wanderer; if interested in Enku carvings we suggest SENKO-JI 15min bus Takayama → Machikata stop and 50min walk, or 20min **cab** from Takayama. If **driving**, L (N) up sidestreet at bus stop, L at 'T' either street OK at next fork, whichever one head R (N) next intersection straight to gate.

Once here, it's steep 900m climb to...
SENKO-JI temple: hill legendary home of Hida's *hairy demons* whose leader, 2-faced 4-legged Ryomen-Sukuna, was vanquished here and so temple erected. By 9th cent, one of Hida's largest with 19 main halls here, 25 affiliate temples thruout Hida. Burned down 1564 by Takeda forces, re-built 1588 by Takayama's lord Kanamori.

Next to it...

Enku-butsu Museum has over 50 Saint Enku carvings, largest single collection after Nagoya's ARAKO KANNON-JI (260 pcs). Foremost is his rendition of Ryomen-Sukuna. (Daily 9:00-17:00, ¥400). Hundreds more Enkus around Hida, some in tiny local shrines and temples, many have smooth heads from centuries-old belief that rubbing Enku-butsu and touching ailing part of own body effects cure. Saint Enku died in Seki city, aged 86, at MIROKU-JI temple—where over 600 of his works were all lost in 1920 fire. Neighbor **SHIMMEI JINJA** shrine has his self-portrait.

According to George Komarovskii of USSR embassy, collections of Enku are at: NAGOYA: Arako Kannon-ji temple, Nakagawa-ku, most (260); Natayakushi-do (several); Ryusen-ji (several); AICHI PREF Shogaku-ji, Fuso-cho in Niwa-gun (12+); Ongaku-ji, Konan City (several). GIFU PREF Takayama Kyodo Hakubutsu-kan museum (many from local temples for safekeeping); Senko-ji *(above)*; Seiho-ji *(follows)*; Ho-on-ji, Ogaki City (interesting); Kannon-do, Hashima City (early pces); Yakushi-ji, Hashima C ('very interesting'). SAITAMA (nr Tokyo): Yakuo-ji, Omiya City, (30+) and Shobo-in, Omiya (late pces). NIKKO: Kiyotaki-dera, 'most interesting of his Fudos', etc.

On Rte158, 1.7km to next bus stop is...

JOGAN-JI temple which ornate bell tower built solely by donations from Yoshiwara's gay quarters. In 1684, temple priest sent to Edo to collect donations fell in love with courtesan in Yoshiwara and they committed double-suicide. Yoshiwara's ladies collected enough gold and silver ornaments to cast bell. Melted down in WW II, less-valuable replica hangs in tower adorned with Hidari Jingoro's 3 monkeys. *Gassho-zukuri* farm house nearby is drive-in restaurant, with good local dishes in place of usual drive-in grub.

Last stop in Nyukawa village (perhaps most spectacular) is...

Hida Cave, *Dai-Shonyu-do*, also on tour bus itinerary. Direct bus from Takayama 43min; buses for beyond take 30min, but stop on Rte158 whence 20min walk to... 800m long stalactite cavern discovered 1965. Judging from marine fossils, was under sea level 3 billion years ago. *Gassho* house in front has rock collection of cave discoverer Ohashi Nobuyoshi; includes odd-shaped rocks, rocks from Mt Everest's summit, S pole. Admission to cave and rock museum ¥800, daily 8:00-17:00. Get package ticket before boarding if direct bus from Takayama: o.w. ¥1,510, r.t. ¥2,240, both include admission.

HIRAYU ONSEN, 65min bus (¥1,350), 40km from Takayama is major backwoods bus center; 35min to Shin-Hotaka, 50min to Mt Norikura; 80min direct Takayama to Kamioka, others start at Hirayu. Despite its popularity, still quite rustic, no glaring lights or ferroconcrete atrocities. Well-stocked **cab** stand at bus stop. Across street **Kanko-annai** will book you any place, most have *rotenburo*. 8 minshuku, we stayed at excellent old-timer **Imada-ya**, another nite at next door **Aiho-kan**; two dozen ryokan, top 3 boast superb baths clustered together in middle: **Funazu-ya** ☎(0578)-9-2306, ¥-Sw/2; **Hirayu-kan** ☎9-3111; **Nakamura-kan** ☎9-2321, both ¥-Sw/2; rest similar prices. During our latest mid-winter visit, minshuku were closed and we wandered over to **Okada ryokan**, ¥-Tw/2: rooms so-so, but sumptuous feast and excellent baths.

After soaking in several baths around town, we headed out to...

Kami-no-yu, outdoor bath, 20min walk E from town. You'll need flashlight at nite, we borrowed one from our inn and got directions (head down side road near Yumoto-kan inn). Along river at Hirayu Fudo-san temple (leave small donation) are 3 pools of varying temperatures, with candles for nite visitors. It snowed later that nite and we returned in morning for classic experience of bathing surrounded by snow, what rural Japan is supposed to be.

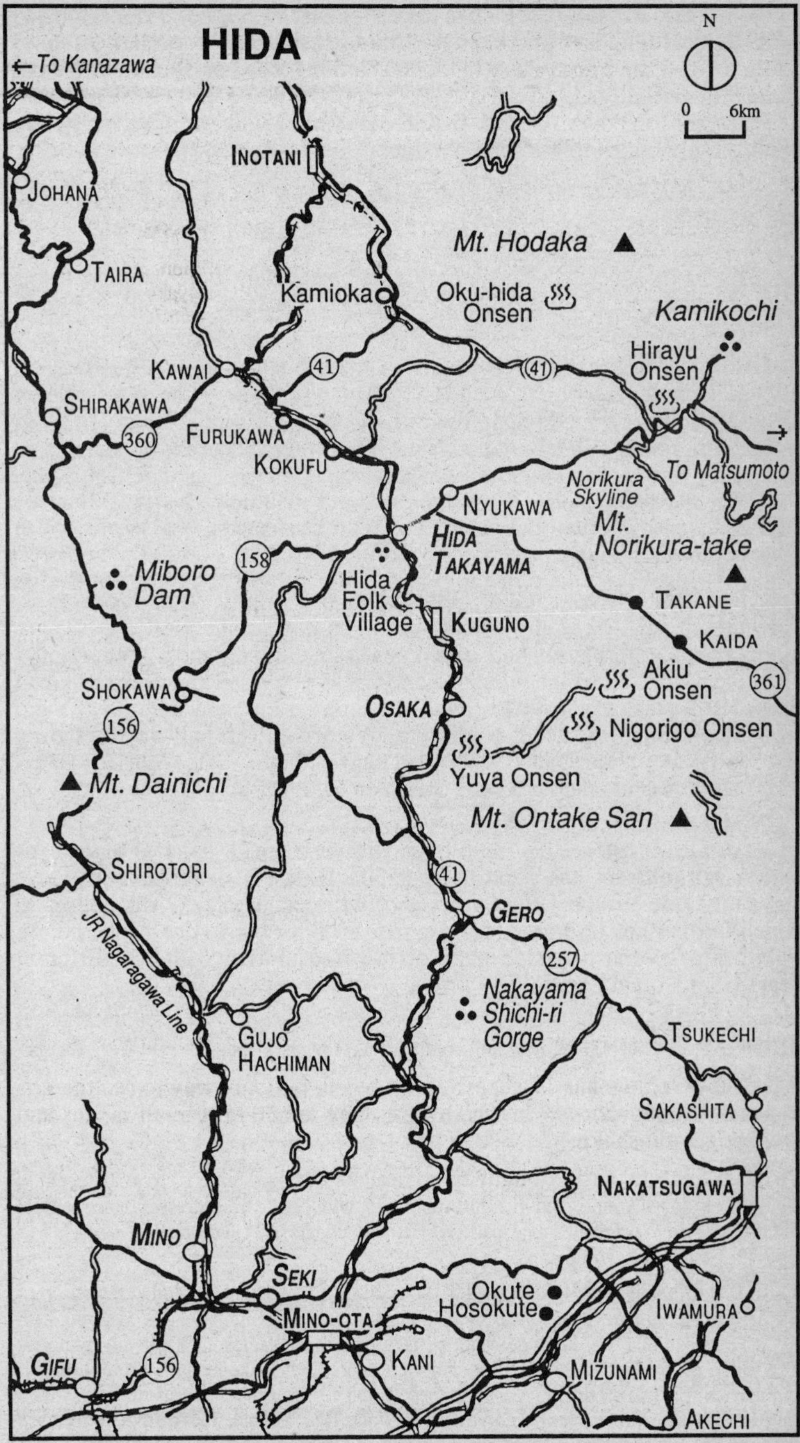
HIDA
← To Kanazawa
N
0 6km
INOTANI
JOHANA
TAIRA
Mt. Hodaka ▲
Kamioka
Oku-hida Onsen
Kamikochi
Hirayu Onsen
KAWAI
41
41
SHIRAKAWA
360
FURUKAWA
KOKUFU
→
To Matsumoto
Norikura Skyline
NYUKAWA
Mt. Norikura-take ▲
HIDA TAKAYAMA
158
Miboro Dam
Hida Folk Village
KUGUNO
TAKANE
KAIDA
361
SHOKAWA
Akiu Onsen
OSAKA
Nigorigo Onsen
156
Yuya Onsen
▲ Mt. Dainichi
Mt. Ontake San ▲
SHIROTORI
JR Nagaragawa Line
41
GERO
257
Nakayama Shichi-ri Gorge
GUJO HACHIMAN
TSUKECHI
SAKASHITA
NAKATSUGAWA
MINO
SEKI
Okute
Hosokute
MINO-OTA
IWAMURA
KANI
GIFU
156
MIZUNAMI
AKECHI

Hirayu Folk Museum, *Minzoku-kan* is cluster of 3 *gassho* houses filled with items found in rural homes, Enku-butsu, and costumed setup of Torigei folk dance festival, which we see down road at Tochio. Adjacent YAKUSHI-DO hall built over Hirayu's spring. Daily May–Nov 7:00-18:00, ¥200.

Eggs sold in town cooked 'inside-out'—hard yolk, soft white, get so when slowly boiled in hot spring waters.

Hirayu Nogyojo campsite S of town in white birch forest; ¥300 with own tent, rent ¥2,000; 8-man cabin ¥6,000, or ¥600per, communal 30-man cabins; Jul-Aug.

Up side trail between camp and town to...
Hirayu O-taki waterfall, thundering impressively, 9m/30ft wide drops 60m, 20 storeys, fed by melting snows of Mt Norikura. 6hr trail up mountain from waterfall, most people come for...

Hiking: Mt. Norikura, bus 50min to TATAMI-DAIRA for easy 3hr r.t. hike to 3026m summit. But don't take it too lightly, weather up there can suddenly turn ugly so be prepared. State-run Solar Corona Research Center (1 of 9 in world) and center to study radio waves from outer space, are on summit. 3 inns (¥-lo-Tw/2) at **Tatami-daira,** 2 mountain huts (¥-Bw/2, Jun thru Sep) at top. Buses run May thru Oct only, ¥1,500 from Hirayu, ¥2,350 from Takayama. Norikura Skyline Toll road OK May 15 thru Oct, ¥1,500 per car; closed several hours nitely to give nite wildlife chance to roam free.

OKU-HIDA ONSEN CLUSTER runs N of Hirayu into Japan Alps. Adventurer can choose any number of hot springs as alternative to Hirayu; hikers meander thru area, half-dozen peaks to climb around 3,000m/2mi— and hot springs all over, ending at Kamioka to rejoin rail and down to Japan Sea coast Kanazawa city or toward Takayama for Furukawa, Shirakawa-go. If short on time head back at Hirayu. We drove it in half-day including short stops at outdoor baths. Only 55km Hirayu – Furukawa via Kamioka; add 9km Shin-Hotaka side trip. Many buses run; enough car traffic to make fair game for hitchers.

We take them in order from Hirayu:
FUKUJI ONSEN, 15min bus (8km) from Hirayu is small, handful of inns, of which **Magokuro,** has good bath, ¥250. Hida **Nature Museum** here, and **Folk Tale Village** (*Furusato-mura*) with reconstructed folk houses in which locals show traditional rural crafts. ¥500 for both. Along river before Fukuji are several riverside baths; **Hida Bear Farm** with 150 different bears from around world.

Just down road to...
SHIN-HIRAYU ONSEN, new and cramped, we suggest passing except for 2 things:

ZENTSU-JI temple has 17 superb Enku-butsu, but only way to see them is to attend 5:30am *zazen*. In which case there are 30 inns in all ranges and few budget minshuku.

SHINMEI JINJA shrine ought be visited **Sep 30** for shrine festival *Torigeuchi dance.* Few dozen youths clad in colorful kimono, with ornate head-dresses dance to flute and drums, said to originate from scattered Heike remnants in 11th century.

It is repeated May 10 down road at...
TOCHIO ONSEN at MURAKAMI JINJA shrine: its festival has added attraction of *Henbe-dori shishi-mai*, snake-catching lion dance. Legend has Emperor Murakami at bath 1,000 years ago heard of huge poisonous snake hassling villagers. He lulled it by music then killed it. Derived from tale: lion dances around cloth snake to flute, drum, jumps it and carries it off in teeth. If you miss these 2 dances, see them staged nitely **1st half Aug** at Shinmei Shrine; *Henbe-dori* nitely at Folk Tale Village, **Jul–mid-Aug.** Onsen is miniscule, 1 ryokan and 2 dozen budget minshuku share giant communal riverside bath.

Road forks at Tochio, L (W) to Kamioka, R to...

SHIN-HOTAKA ONSEN, furthest E and largest of 7 hot springs along Gamata River (HOTAKA itself farther E in next valley, *see* Toyama on Japan Sea rtes). Short detour, ideal for bather-hikers, base for many trails and dozens of outdoor baths at inns or in woods. 10 years ago Shin-Hotaka was rustic hamlet for hard-core hikers, but ropeway made mountains accessible to almost anybody and large inns began to sprout up. Now over 40 inns from ¥-L to ¥-B minshuku and pensiones; campsite July-Aug, ¥300 per person, 5-person tents ¥1,500. 3.2km ropeway (2nd longest in world) to 2156m summit of Nishi-Hotaka. 1st leg (5min, ¥300 o.w.) to Nabe-daira plateau, 2nd leg (10min, ¥800 o.w.) to summit restaurant. Other onsens this stretch are, from Tochio: **GAMADA, KARUKAYA, TAKARA**, up side stream **NAKAO, YARIMI, SHIN-HOTAKA, KAMI TAKARA** nearest (8km) Kamioka, with exceptional ¥-S-L rate ryokan **Hotaka Hotel** ☎(0578)-9-2200 with fine baths, all season outdoor included. They abound in riverside and hidden mountain baths; free maps and pamphlets of baths available TIC, most inns.

Hiking: N Japan Alps is probably most popular hiking area in Japan. Dozens of trails from easy day-hikes to expert rock climbing; or spend few days hiking-camping (several mountain huts scattered about as well) in area.

NAKAYU ONSEN is tiny trailhead to 2455m Yaki-dake peak;

SHIN-HOTAKA ONSEN is main trailhead to Hotaka mountain chain with many peaks over 3000m. Top of ropeway **Hikers' Info Center**, also reached by trail, for weather info, good maps. 6km trail connects Yaki-dake and Shin-Hotaka ropeway; both connected by easy trail to beautiful Kamikochi Plateau Nagano pref's gateway to area. Winter heavy snowfall makes these peaks excellent for...

Skiing: Ropeway, 5 lifts for all levels of skiing (4km run from summit) Dec thru Mar at **Shin-hotaka**. Smaller one nr **Harukaya; Hirayu** 3 lifts, short but varied runs thru Apr. Summer skiing at **Tatami-daira, Horikura-dake** thru July, into Aug in years with lots of snow. Few more small ski grounds in area. All have many budget skiers' inns, as well as large luxe inns; jammed hols & weekends, when book well ahead.

Good stateside travel agent will have ski tour info, as will any overseas JTB office. In Japan, any travel agent can arrange full package of transportation and lodgings. Packages by ANA, JAL and JR.

25km from Tochio Onsen (1hr bus), we exit Oku-Hida at...

KAMIOKA (to rejoin JR or Rte41). Main stn in center of town is **Funatsu**, 1 stop (2.5km) from terminus Kamioka. Little to offer: 25min walk E of Funatsu are reconstructed castle of 1564 original, 2 museums; **Mine Museum**, *Kozan Hakubutsukan*, has tools and ores from 17-18th century mines; **History Museum**, *Rekishi-kan* with usual odds and ends. Looking across town from castle you see *Daruma* statue, made of bronze in 1970 it stands 8.9m tall weighing 8 tons. 25 more Enku-butsu hidden away at **ENKO-JI** temple, 15min cab NE of Funatsu. To see, call ☎(0578)-2-2036 before heading out, small donation. Kamioka has 3 major festivals, **Apr 24-25** *Spring Festival*, **Jul 24** *Taishi Dance* and **Aug 13-16** *Castle Festival* (*see* DATEBOOK).

FURUKAWA: 2 JR stops N of TAKAYAMA, 16km on Rte41; from KAMIOKA 50min bus (22km) or 70min roundabout JR via INOTANI. Pleasant town with interesting sites (old canal-side Edo storehouses make for great photos) and festivals; smaller scale than Takayama, still, we had fun here. Streets of Furukawa are quiet; those with extra time will find it pleasant change to walk thru equally photogenic town. If here on cold, wet day like us, warm your bones at public bath *Tanbo-no-yu*, **'paddy-water bath'**, at Kita-no-yu Inn, few minutes walk N of stn. It's not exactly paddy water, its deep red color is due to high iron content. ¥500 dip, also ¥-B Stay.

Small town, walk it in 2hrs, or **rent bikes** at stn ¥400/4hr. 300m W of stn is narrow stream along which runs street appropriately called 'White-walled Storehouse Alley'. Lane barely wide enough for 2 abreast follows stream and storehouses for few hundred meters, lined by ancient weeping willows and lanterns lit at nite. Carp swim in clear stream, boxes by each bridge have bags of crumbs (¥20). Block W to *Ichi-no-machi* street, center of town with old houses. S end: **Mishima-ya** has been candle-makers for over 220 years. Present master, 6th generation Mishima Takeo works with his son dipping paper and cotton wicks into melted wax, creating their beautiful candles. Some have pictures painted on them, classic is hourglass-shaped white or red (¥500 for 25cm/10in). Their candles used in city's festivals and temples, most notably **Jan 15** *San-dera Mairi*, 3 Temple pilgrimage to **Honko-ji**, **Shinshu-ji** and **Enko-ji** temples. Began 200 years ago as memorial service for local saint, became popular for good luck in love and marriage, now young women dressed in finest New Year kimono make rounds.

Enku-an (next to Mishima-ya) is workshop/store of NAKAMURA Masahiro who carves Enku-butsu replicas. Up street to **Gama** and **Watanabe** Sake Brewers, distinguished by now common wood balls in front. At N end is **Shirai** lantern makers, where 8th generation SHIRAI Kyujiro handmakes sole Furukawa-*chochin* paper lanterns in town—using only bamboo from Toyama city and Sado island, covered with handmade Sanchu paper from nearby Kawai village. His work best seen **Apr 19-20** *Furukawa Festival*. As popular as Takayama's festivals, also called *Okoshi-taiko drum festival*. 19th sunset, all homes put paper lantern out front. At 9:30pm drum procession starts at Kitawakamiya Shrine and proceeds thru town. Each block puts out 1 or 2 teams of drummers following main float of 6-10 men and giant drum, 2 straddling atop. Energetic festival with over 1,500 participants, teams charging each other, be careful not to get caught in between. 20th day, 9 impressive floats comparable to Takayama's are taken out of their storehouses and pulled thru town. Best seen from 2nd floor, locals are friendly and invite you up. If on street level, sake stalls hand out free cups full to anybody passing by.

Fukuzenji-chaya tea house in plaza across from Shirai has photos and videos of festival.

10min walk W across Miyagawa River near Rte41...
Okoshi-Taiko Kaikan displays drums, mikoshi used, with more pics, videos. 2nd floor collection of shrine guardian dogs from all over Japan; building is old cocoon house of local silk producer. Daily 9:00-17:00, ¥300 (¥150/child).

RINSHO-JI temple (10min walk S of stn); in small room next to main gate are 400-year-old stone statues of Emma Dai-o King of Hades, and attendants. Equally old murals behind them depict horrors of Hell, graphic warning to those who stray from Buddha's path.

WHERE TO STAY: Furukawa is good alternative for inns during Takayama festivals, close enough to train (15min), bus (35min) or **cab** (8x-mtr) for festivals and still get room on short notice. Best is **Busui-tei** ☎(05777)-3-2531, which began as restaurant 1869, started to take in overnite guests 1950, ¥-T-Sw/2; as to be expected, meals are superb. Located on E edge of town on Miya riverbank, 5min walk from stn. Mid-Aug to mid-Oct section of Miya River across from inn is fenced off fishing area open to all; your catch broiled on spot. Restaurant/inns ¥-T-Sw/2 range are: **Kiyokawa bekkan**, ☎3-2248, next to BUSUI; and **Yatsusan**, ☎3-2121, 300m E along smaller Araki River. Dozen budget inns around town, arrange thru stn front **Kanko-annai**.

Between Furukawa and Takayama is...
KOKUFU with some interesting temples and shrines, all along Araki River (1km N of Kokufu stn); seeing town by bicycle, include in added 2hrs.

W → E:

SEIHO-JI temple, (20min walk from stn) has 3 largest extant Enku-butsu carvings: 11-faced, 1,000-arm Kannon, 2 more Kannon figures. 10min E is ADAYUTA SHRINE.

3km E (15min bus from stn to HAKKAICHI, and 10min walk) is...
ANKOKU-JI, 650-year-old temple, built by 1st Ashikaga shogun Takauji; unique 8-sided revolving scroll case (NT) contains 2,208 scrolls brought from China in 1358. Rotates by pushing any of 8 levers. In temple compound is **History Museum**, with Enku-butsu, ancient *shishi-mai* lion heads, pottery; and **Folk Museum**, *Mingei-kan* with local farm tools from Stone Age to Edo. ¥100 each, 8:30-17:00.

15min E to...
ARAKI **Shrine** known for its autumn *shishi-mai* lion dance. Shrine's 600-year-old lion heads kept at History Museum. Kokufu has several unique *shishi-mai* dances thruout year (see PERSONAL DATEBOOK): *Kagura-jishi* Apr 28; *Kinzo-jishi* May 4, Sep 15; *Sugo-jishi* Sep 5; *Kane-uchi Shishi-mai* Sep 8.

KAWAI VILLAGE (12km N of FURUKAWA), is where carpenter HIDA-no-Takumi was born, better known now for hand-made *Sanchu-shi* **paper**. See process Dec thru Mar (papermaking winter work, needs cold water to set) at several houses in TSUNOGAWA, 15min (3 stops) rail from Furukawa.

Drivers branch off Rte41 just past HOSOE town. TSUNOGAWA is where you join Rte360 for beautiful drive to SHIRAKAWA-GO via Amo Pass. 1.5km from Tsunogawa on Rte360 is side road, 3km up which is ancient 2-storey thatched roof structure. During final feudal Edo era it served as checkpoint along Hida-Etchu border.

SHIRAKAWA-GO 白川郷

A NAME GIVEN cluster of hamlets over 800 years old; mostly started by vanquished Heike, 12th cent. Known for its majestic *gassho-zukuri* architecture of farm house with high pitched roof like 'hands joined in prayer', area came into limelight 1959 when new Miboro Dam threatened to submerge 6 hamlets with 350 of these houses; over half rebuilt in Folk Art Villages in area; others became well-known restaurants bearing same name FURUSATO (Old Home), serving country-style cookery in Tokyo's Dogen-zaka (sans fire-hazard roof), Arima Onsen near Kobe (since burned) Kyoto, etc. and Takishita's antique shop-cum-home in Kamakura. If short on time best head straight to OGI-MACHI hamlet, with largest cluster of *gassho-zukuri* houses; more along Rte156 for wanderer.

GETTING THERE: From TAKAYAMA 1hr25min (¥1,700) Nohi Bus on Rte158 → MAKIDO on Rte156. JR Buses run on Rte156, most start MINO SHIROTORI stn to Hagi-cho's northernmost HATOGAYA, tho some start/end NAGOYA stn, via GIFU. It is 4hr from OGI-MACHI to Gifu by bus, faster to get train at MINO-SHIROTORI, but beware: while buses ending at MINO SHIROTORI arrive around train departure time, long distance buses to GIFU-NAGOYA run during lull in rail schedule thus quicker than to wait for train. Nohi runs 4 round-trips daily; JR and Meitetsu run 8-10 r.t.'s combined daily, but beware as they do not share bus stops at most places other than at MAKIDO, and there each has separate departure rooms—go out back door Nohi building to JR building. Buses run year-round unless too much snow, tho which gets cleared off within first day.

Nohi Bus runs one-day **tours** out of Takayama, stop most places on our itinerary. ¥6,000/adult, ¥3,870/child, incl lunch. Run weekends & holidays Oct; daily mid-July thru Aug. Round-trip **cab**, 168km, about ¥40,000 (60+mtrs). If bus, **Tourist Info** TAKAYAMA stn has seasonal schedule in English (their prices may be last year's, but posted times are accurate) of Nohi and JR connections. For return Ogi-machi Tourist Info **English** sched also lists runs to GIFU-NAGOYA.

Unusual stop W of Takayama on Rte158...

OAK VILLAGE: Group of young adults, some with families, came here 1971, built their own village, supporting themselves by making oak furniture. Instrumental in starting new Takayama **Human Arts Institute**, teach there. They now also hire out to build wood houses. Use only wood from trees over 100 years old, guarantee any furniture or homes made will last at least couple centuries. Their work isn't cheap—

Dining room set of table and 5 chairs runs ¥200,000, single chairs from ¥40,000. Mid-July thru Aug, workshops here for anyone interested: 5 days, 4 nites/3 meals daily, materials and instruction ¥60,000 (making chairs) or ¥67,000 (making tables). Also **courses** in wood staining, weaving, rattan or bamboo weaving, ¥48,000 for full 4days/3nites, meals and materials, instruction. Must arrange in advance for any of above. ✍: Oak Village, Kiyomi-mura Makigado, Ohno-gun, Gifu-ken, ☎(05776)-8-2244. 30min from TAKAYAMA to RYUTOKU-JI bus stop then 20min walk.

SHOKAWA, (at junction of Rtes156 and 158) is small folk village set-up at *Shokawa-no-sato*, one stop before Makido. Called *Shokawa-zukuri*, these houses are older in style, differ slightly from more common *gassho-zukuri* of SHIRAKAWA-GO. Sections of side roofs extend out for more sun, makes space for work outdoors; surrounded with bamboo curtain during rain, also, roof comes down front and back, with small protruding window which folds down to become flush with roof thatch. Complex of 5 houses open daily 8:30-16:30, X-thur, and Dec thru Mar.

From here, 20min walk to Makido bus stop, via Shokawa Shrine, with which now are 3 shrines moved from hamlets flooded by....

Miboro Dam, 20km N of Shokawa but reservoir starts just beyond. At 120m, it is world's tallest rock-fill dam, half-kilometer wide at base. Autumn and winter when water level is lowest, you can sometimes see submerged hamlet from Iwase Bridge, closest to Shokawa.

2km beyond dam at Miboro bus stop is...

Kyu-Toyama-ke, ex-Toyama House one of largest *gassho* houses at 21m wide front, 12m sides, and 15m tall or equal 5 storeys. Built 1827, it held up to 50 people comfortably, now small museum, ¥210 open daily 9:00-17:00.

3km to tiny...

HIRASE ONSEN, dozen ¥-B inns (some *gassho* houses), large public bath, where we relaxed hour on drive to Takayama. Also base for climbing 2702m Mt Hakusan, easy but long trails, 7hrs to summit past **Shiramizu-no-taki** waterfall dropping 72m, numerous volcanic caldera lakes. Late July thru Aug, sporadic buses to **Oshirakawa Dam**, near falls, cut out 10km walk on road; round-trip hike Dam → summit just over 6hrs. Without bus 4-5hrs down, or descend other side to several dead-end hot spas whence hitch via Super Rin-do 'Forest Road' to...

OGI-MACHI, *Gassho Village*, 1hr (¥1,200) bus from Makido. Shirakawa-go has 200-odd *gassho* houses, 110 are here. *Gassho-zukuri* 'Hands-in Prayer' style is unique to Hida; sturdy base 1st floor with soaring A-frame supported thatch roof—at least meter thick and 9m tall. Under roof are 2-4 storeys (mostly for silkworm cocoons). Carpenters make 1st floor and roof frame, rest is entire village effort: roofs need anywhere from 8,000-15,000 bundles of straw 20cm across; takes full day to dismantle old roof, at least one day to finish one side of new roof. Straw and other materials are collected all year and stored in communal shed until needed. Tho houses last for centuries, roofs must be replaced every 40-50 years; all National Cultural Assets, cannot tamper with unless government approved, in which case repairs subsidized. Tho locals appreciate government desire to preserve their homes, it poses problem when even replacing door without OK means fines if done wrong. Roofs are usually 60° angle; rule-of-thumb to tell age of house: wider base older, narrower base (steeper sides) newer.

WHERE TO STAY: 26 of these houses are minshuku, ¥-Bw/2; others budget eateries, gift stores. Kanko-annai suggested we stay at **Furusato**, ☎(05769)-6-1033, one of oldest houses, near MYOZEN-JI temple. Doors in our room were lacquered with *Shunkei-nuri* and in present-day prices, each of 4 then cost $5,000.

Buses stop at S end HACHIMAN JINJA MAE, front of shrine, central Kominkan Mae, near which is **Kanko-annai** for booking rooms; and 500m further N at Ogi-machi stop at junction of Rtes 156 and 360.

400m up Rte360 is...
Masu-en Bunsuke Trout Farm run by hospitable Mr Noda, whose family has lived here for over 300 years farming land. We ate here after coming over pass on Rte360, and suggest same for anyone who follows. You get to experience fully what living in these fabulous houses is like, after which you can turn corner to be overwhelmed by sheer number of *gassho* houses in town. Fish for or net your own lunch or leave it up to Noda-san; sashimi ¥500, *shio-yaki* salt fried on spit ¥250, or table d'hote ¥500. Squat around open hearth; each house has several, thick smoke preserves house, curing wood, killing bugs which would otherwise eat thru roofs. He shows you around house while food cooking, knows everything about area. Father started trout farm, now over 60,000 rainbow trout, charr, to supply town inns (which serve his trout every meal). Noda-san went to Takayama for high school (all kids still do since none closer, staying with relatives or friends), spent years at good job in Tokyo. Tired of urban rat race, returned to quiet country to continue family business, now doesn't fear that all village kids will abandon their homes as home now can pay. Many like him tire of crowds and noise, prefer simple life; tourism also made living here pay.

Best view of Ogi-machi from **Shiro-yama Castle Hill**, few minutes walk up path from Ogi-machi stop. Only castle foundations remain, now occupied by restaurant.

10min down to village, L fork at bottom to 230-year-old...
MYOZEN-JI temple, with beautiful thatched roof hall and bell tower, *gassho-zukuri* priests' quarters, 2nd floor small Folkcraft Museum, ¥200/¥100 child. Rejoining Rte156 near Shirakawa Hachiman shrine, known as one of 5 local Hachiman Shrines to host...

Doburoku Festival, celebrating rice harvest everyone drinks *doburoku* fermented rice mash made from new crop. Procession of colorful banners, giant drum and flutes wind thru hamlets to each Hachiman Shrine where after several local folk and *shishi-mai* dances, sacred sake is passed around. Each shrine allotted 7 kilo-liters to distribute, enough for all to have good time. **Oct 14-15th** *here*; **16-17th** Hatogaya Hachiman, 1km N; **18-19th** at IIJIMA HACHIMAN, 1km beyond Hatogaya.

500m S from Shrine on Rte156 to...
Livelihood Museum, *Seikatsu Shiryokan* with hands-on displays of local crafts, looms and such, ¥200.

From central Kominkan bus stop, W 200m to rickety bridge across river thru long, narrow tunnel for pleasant 10min stroll to...
SHIRAKAWA FOLK VILLAGE, *Gassho minka mura.* In 1967 this corner of Ogi-machi was abandoned for lack of residents; rather than watch 2 dozen houses rot, they were fixed up into **Museum-Village**. One is tea house; some display folk tools; some craft demos: 8:30-17:00, ¥500, ¥250/child.

From suspension bridge riverside path to bridge N of Rte360 junction; 1km more on Rte156 to HATOGAYA hamlet with half-dozen budget inns. You can almost always get rooms in OGI-MACHI without prior notice, but Mr Noda (who also will find you inn, he booked us into minshuku FURUSATO near shrine) warns it gets crowded during *Golden Week*, mid-summer, and *Doburoku Festival*. Its rare that all rooms are taken, but should at least call before leaving Takayama to reserve, especially for room in *gassho-zukuri* inns: **Ogi-machi Kanko-kyokai**, Tourist Co-operative ☎(05769)-6-1013, or 6-1751; 8:30-17:00, open daily. Good times to pass thru are March to mid-April when with luck you'll see roof repair or renewal being done. It is also bear hunting season which cooked meat served most inns; Sakura bloom **mid-Apr-May**; Bon-dance Aug **14-17; late Oct** hills covered with spectacular fiery colors of autumn leaves.

37km N on Rte156 to...

GOKAYAMA VILLAGE, string of hamlets along road and river. Tho not full of gassho houses like Ogi-machi, Gokayama has its share, its own quiet charm. Everything spaced out, best seen by **car**, bus infrequent: suggest as optional route to Japan Sea coast's Kanazawa 2hr 40min bus NW, **drivers** take branch-off Rte304 to Kanazawa, via JOHANA, then follow alongside JR to Toyama.

30min bus from Ogi-machi...

NISHI AKAO to see giant **Iwase House** built 280 years ago for local gunpowder maker of region's Kaga clan, was also local official's residence and has several hidden rooms in which armed attendants waited during meetings; tools to make gunpowder shown. ¥200.

GYOTOKU-JI temple next to it is, of course, *gassho-zukuri* style.

SUGANUMA hamlet, (4km beyond) has small cluster of 12 *gassho* houses, 3 of which are minshuku, another is museum of local goods. YOUTH VILLAGE S of hamlet has campsite, 7 gassho houses are inns Apr-Oct, ¥5,500w/2, groups only. *Gassho* style **Etchu Gokayama YH**, 1km W.

KAMINASHI, (40min from Ogi-machi) has added attraction of being sole onsen around. Town-run public bath by bus stop, daily 16:00-21:00, ¥250. Near it is **Murakami House**, almost as big as Iwase's, displaying similar goods, ¥300. Miniature *gassho* house 2.8x3.6m x 3m tall across river was jail, now kimono-clad dummy inside.

Several budget inns (2 gassho) here but better at...

AINOKURA *Gassho* Hamlet with 20-odd houses, set as National Cultural Assets in 1970. 10min **bus** from Kaminashi, it's short way down Rte304, branching off from Rte156 at Shimonashi. **Drivers** can avoid few kilo's back-track on local side road just beyond tunnel. Centrally located **Matsu-ya Shokudo** budget eatery doubles as minshuku-**Minshuku Annai** to book you into other inns, 8 of which are *gassho zukuri*. Besides usual folk museum is *washi* **Handmade Paper Co-op** at junction Rtes 304 + 156 to see entire process, try your hand at making some yourself, 3 sheets ¥100. Washi dolls from ¥400 at gift stores in area. Just over 2hr bus on to KANAZAWA.

On main itinerary turn back at Ogi-machi to Takayama, or 1hr bus past Makido to...

MINO SHIROTORI: 60km from Ogi-machi, midway-75km either TAKAYAMA or GIFU. Nagaragawa Rail Line from Mino Ohta ends HOKUNO, 2 stops before Shirotori coming from Ogi-machi.

If time in Hokuno waiting for train, 15min walk S of stn to...

HAKUSAN NAGATAKI JINJA, main shrine of Hakusan mountain ascetics built 717. Grew over centuries into sprawling Buddhist-Shinto complex, only to be fragmented by Meiji separation of two. RYUHO-DEN Treasure Hall has ancient art from its days of glory; open to public only on festival days, can see by prior arrangement (¥300 donation) thru nearby **Wakamiya Shukokan**, home of Wakamiya family, head priests of shrine for centuries. Part of house has been turned into museum of family and shrine treasures: daily 9:00-17:00 X-Jan and heavy snow. Shrine's inner sanctum is on summit of sacred Mt Hakusan, ascended from Hirase onsen.

HAKUSAN NAGATAKI branch shrine (midway, 15km NW of Hokuno), was probably sacred ground in Stone Age, predates by several centuries above NAGATAKI SHRINE.

25min walk S of shrine is...
TAISHI-DO temple. In its halls are numerous fine Buddhist statues and items from CHUKYO SHRINE. Facing destruction in Meiji religious purge, locals were one step ahead, took all Buddhist things from shrine, hid them here. To see, call ahead to caretaker Mr Uemura ☎(05758)-6-3143; small donation. Infrequent JR buses run 1hr from Hokuno to Itoshiro for YAKUSHIDO, 5min beyond to last stop Kami-zaisho for shrine.

Mt Hakusan is close to Mt Fuji in sanctity, and as you may have noticed, dozens of Hakusan shrines dot Hida area, like Sengen shrines ring Mt Fuji.

GUJO HACHIMAN: Famed as **Bon dance** capital, usually quiet town jumps to life with almost nitely dancing early July thru August, best during **Aug 13-16** when nitely to 100,000 people fill streets dancing sunset to sunrise. We found rhythmical dance easy to join not just watch. Coffee-snack shops open all nite, to sit. 2hrs from MAKIDO on direct Meitetsu bus, 82km from Ogimachi, 53km Gifu. From GIFU-INUYAMA, trains infrequent, more runs on Gifu Bus from Meitetsu Shin-Gifu stn. Also 2nd campus new Takayama **Human Arts Institute** here.

When quiet, it is pleasant little town tucked around confluence of Kodara, Yoshida Rivers; stn 15min walk from town dominated by **Hachiman Castle**. First built 1559, dismantled 1873, rebuilt 1933 as **Feudal Era Museum**. 100m before 1st bridge in town from stn is *Omodaka-ya*, **Folkcraft Museum** in Mizuno family house, which was herbal medicine shop **Omodaka-ya** since mid-17th century. Present owner's father's collection of folk items displayed in back 3 storehouses, main house folkcrafts gift store.

Cross bridge straight ahead to section of town with old town houses, far end...
Samurai Residences, *Buke-yashiki*. Similarly photogenic corners of town makes for pleasant strolls, during which you come across several springs bubbling forth clear, cold, pure water. Each has small shrine built around it. *Suntory* comes here and bottles it as their mineral water.

WHERE TO STAY: **Kanko-annai** books you any of dozens from top inn— best 3 oldies began as restaurants still noted for superb fare **Mifuku** ☎(05756)-5-2145; **Bizen-ya** ☎5-2068; **Yoshida-ya** ☎5-2178; all ¥-T-Sw/2—to **Dosen-ji** Temple Youth Hostel.

Several recently excavated caves around Gujo Hachiman, foremost unusual vertical 6 tunnel levels stretch 100+m in all directions, to 80m deep. En route **Sunland Park** recreation area, 30min bus and 20min walk E of town, is **Otaki Shonyu-do Cave** 1+km, full of little waterfalls, 30m falls far end; daily 8:00-18:00, ¥500, 40min guided tour. 300m W smaller **Jomon Cave** where remains of Stone Age culture excavated. Cab tour all 3 stalactite caves, 12x-mtr.

45min bus E of town...
What is Demon's Skull kept at NENKO-JI temple? Obvious human head with pair of short horns on forehead. Legend has it was on man-eating demon in nearby hills until prematurely detached by FUJIWARA Takamitsu ca 950—descendant presented it here in 17th cent.

Those who can't bear to leave without one last outdoor onsen hot spa bath, we heard of single-inn TAKAHATA ONSEN, 15km W of town in lovely secluded vale along Nabi River. Cab 6x-mtr; 30min bus from stn, 10min walk N from bus stop. Most visitors come long enough to hop in bath and enjoy view; but to stay have Gujo Hachiman Kanko-annai call for room, or just head out on own.

PERSONAL DATEBOOK

*denotes dance or event classified as National or Prefectural Cultural Asset.
Prefectural Tourist Office (Kanko-ka) ☎(0582)-72-2222

Here are but few of 100s of fetes in Hida. *Note*: Many national festivals (Tanabata, Shogo-sai) celebrate one month later here, by old lunar calendar.

January

1 *Hatsu-mode*, first sunrise, all temples, shrines, most popular at Mizunashi Jinja, Hida Ichinomiya.

1 Harukoma 'Horse Dances', Shirakawa-go.

6 *Hanabai* (Flower Snatching) *Festival** Hakusan Nagataki Shrine, Mino Shiratori town: alias *muika-sai* (6th day fete), flower hats hung off main hall rafter as youths form human ladders to get. Folk dances.

14 *Kudagayu-sai Festival*, Itakiso Jinja, Nyukawa-mura, ancient fertility/harvest dance Okameodori, long-nosed tengu male goblin 'sows seeds' on female figure.

14 Norimasa Onsen (Gero) Festival features *shishi-mai* dances.

15 *Dharuma Festival* at Kamioka.

Mid Fishing season starts on Miya River, celebrated at Kawai Village & Furukawa.

24-25 *Kamioka Spring Festival*. Ranks with Takayama and Furukawa spring fetes, combine fetes Otsu, Asaura Hachiman Shrine, Hakusan Shrines; burst of public energy to thank *kami* for making it thru another long, cold winter. **25th** main fete begins 1,000-man feudal procession; dusk sees 100 torches at entry Otsu Shrine light up *Shishi-mai*, *Tokei-raku* dances and mikoshi palanquins paraded by torchlight.

Thru Mid-Feb Best time to make handmade *washi* 'rice-paper' process Kawai-mura Village; made year-round.

February

7-14 *Ta-no-kami Matsuri* (ICA) Mori Hachiman Shrine, Gero; start Hida spring.

March

3rd Sun *Hagiwara Spring Festival*, Suwa Jinja Shrine, Hagiwara-cho.

April

3 *Iki-bina* (Living Hina) *Matsuri*, 9 young women from all Hida dress in multi-layer kimono of Hina Matsuri dolls, offering.

14-15 *Spring Festival*, Norimasa nr Gero.

14-15 *Spring Festival*, Hie Shrine, Takayama, 10am parade big floats w/automata, 6pm lantern parade; sakura bloom.

3rd Sat-Sun Day-long *Grand Kagura show** at Kihitsurugi Jinja Shrine, Hachiman-cho in Gujo Hachiman.

19-20 *Furukawa Big Drum Festival*, Kitawakamiya Shrine, lantern procession 9:30pm, great drum contest; Furukawa.

24-25 *Spring Festival*, Kamioka.

28 *Kagura Jishi*, Kokufu.

28 *Kagura-jishi Lion Dance** Takada Jinja Shrine, Furukawa. Oddly slow tempo lion dance features male female lions 'mating'.

May

1 Hiking season starts Nomugi-toge Pass, Takane-mura.

1-2 *Mizunashi Shrine Festival**, Hida Ichinomiya: *Tokei-raku*, *Shishi-mai*, other ancient dances, *doburoku* sacred sake free.

Early – *Waterfall Festival*, food & sake at Utsue Shiju-hattaki Waterfall, Kokufu.

2-3 Shiratori town *Spring Festival*.

3 Shojaku-jishi *Lion Dance**, Fuji Jinja Shrine, Kawai Village.

3-4 Even yrs, Ho-oza Vill Kabuki, Gero.

4 Funayama Hachiman Shrine Fete, Kuguno.

4 *Kinzo Jishi* Tengu-masked male *kami* rescues Otafuku-lady *kami* from rampant lion; Hirose, Watarase Shrines, with added performance.

5 Fuji Jinja shrine, *Kokufu-cho Festival*, Kokufu.

5 *Dededen Matsuri Festival*, Nagataki Hakusan Jinja Shrine, Mino Shirotori.

4-5 *Hida Sosha Festival*, Takayama (p.918)

4-5 *Higashiyama San-ja Matsuri*, combine festivals of Higashiyama Tera-machi 3 Shrines, Takayama.

10-11 *Torigeuchi Dance**, Murakami Shrine, Shinhirayu Onsen, Kamitakura-mura (*see* p.926).

12 *Isurugi Jinja Fete* Fiukuchi Onsen.

15 Norikura-dake climbing season opens.

3rd Sun Hakusan Chukyo Jinja, Mino Shirotori.

Last Sun: Kuruma-da, circular-field rice transplanting, Hida-no-sato, Takayama.

June

15 Ontake mountain climbing season on.

30 Purification rite Sakurayama Hachiman Shrine, Takayama; jump thru straw hoop to rid body of ills.

HIDA TAKAYAMA 935

July

Jul thru Aug Gujo Hachiman Bon, (p.933).
20 Hakusan mountain climb season starts.
24 Annual airing of Takayama Betsu-in temple treasures.
24 *Taishi Odori** dances dedicated to Prince Shotoku-taishi; starts sunset Joren-ji temple Kamioka. Statue of Shotoku-taishi kept here.
26 2pm, special rite Hokkeji temple, Takayama.
End Central Japan Kayak Slalom Contest, Hida-Osaka. Competitors from all Japan.
End Hakusan Chukyo Shrine commemorative festival, Mino Shiratori.
End *Waterfall Festival*, Yokotani-kyo Kanayama-cho.
End–Aug Mino Shirotori *Bon Dance.*

August

Early *Iwabune Taki-Matsuri Waterfall Festival*, Nyukawa Village.
1-3 *Ryujin Himatsuri Fire Dragon F*,Gero.
6-7 *Tanabata 7/7 Festival* along Miya River bank, Takayama.
8 Norikura Summer Festival, Norikura Hongu shrine, Nyukawa Village.
9-10 *Matsukura Kannon Emaichi,* market of good-luck horseprints, Takayama.
12-13 *Hiwada Hachiman Shrine Festival,* Hiwada, Takane Village.
Mid- Takayama *Bon Dance*, Toro-nagashi floating paper lanterns; **16th** Shiogama Shrine Fete upstream; Miyagawa Village.
13-16 *Kamioka Castle Festival* nitely Bon dance, **fireworks**; main event Hida *Shishi-mai* contest—
–15th feudal procession 14:30, over 20 *Shishi-mai* groups from all over Hida, all then perform at Town Hall plaza 16:00.
14-17 *Bon dance*, Shirakawa-go Village.
15-16 Light 1,000 lanterns, Kuguno town.
20 Sogi-sui purification ceremony, Gujo Hachiman.
Last Sun *Children's Fete*, Hida-no-sato Folk Village, Takayama.

September

1-4 *Hakusan Shrine Festival* all 4 Hakusan Shrines in Shokawa Village.
3-23 Local festivals at shrines and temples thruout Nyukawa Village.

5 *Sugo-jishi Lion Dances**, 3 groups lion dancers, joined by fox, monkey, tengu goblin, harvest dances some 1,300 years old, in 2 sets: am/pm alternate at Matsuo Hakusan Jinja and Hakusan Jinja Shrines at Sugo Village, Furukawa.
8 *Kane-uchi Shishi-mai**, 11th century lion dances using equally old lion heads preserved at shrine; in addition to usual flute and drums, dance's namesake kane-uchi (hitting bells) comes from fact bells used. Araki Jinja Shrine, Kokufu. Same time *Kinzo-jishi*, Fuji Jinja, Kokufu.
8-9 *Kake-odori** ritual purification dance Kansui Hakusan Jinja, Myogata-mura Vill (30min bus from Gujo Hachiman).
15 *Kinzo-jishi**, Suwa Jinja & Kamo Jinja Shrines, Kokufu.
15 *Masujima Tenman-gu festival*, Tenman-gu in Masujima Castle nr Furukawa stn.
First Sat Kajika Jinja shrine festival, every 3 yrs '93, '96, '99, 2002.
17-19 *Autumn Festival* celebrated all Mino Shirotori town; folk dances, entertainments, food.
30 *Torigeuchi Dance**, Shinmei Jinja, Shin-Hirayu Onsen (*see* p.926).
Date varies *Kaki-odori** dance, Mino Shirotori.

October

9-10 *Autumn Festival*, Takayama City.
14-19 *Doburoku* Fest, Shirakawa-go (*see* p.931).
3rd Sun: Soshino Hachiman Jinja annual fete, *mikoshi parade*, offertory rite, dances, Kaneyama-cho.
24 Morishige Jinja shrine Festival, features *shishi-mai* lion dance, Kamioka-cho.

November

2-3 Haku-un-za village Kabuki (*see* p909).
12 *O-Myo-ko Festival*, Hokke-ji temple, Takayama. Devotees bring, drape Buddha image in cottons, believe more cloths brought means more snow for year.

December

Most shrines, temples Hida area, prayers & rites for prosperous year to come.

.....You can carry on your life without cousins,
but not without your neighbors...
— Japanese proverb

TOYAMA 富山
BACKWOODS HOT SPRINGS

TOYAMA CITY, industrial hub on Japan Sea with nothing for tourist but junction of rail and parallel highways: JR Takayama Main Line/Rte41 S via mountainous Hida District to Nagoya on Pacific coast; Hokuriku Main Line/Rte8 up Japan Sea; and Toyama Jitetsu private lines meander into Chubu Sangaku Mtns (alias North Japan Alps) for great back-country detours by rickety trains to hidden spas and spectacular mountains to hike: Tateyama Line for odd but comfortable way to cross Japan Alps on Alpine Route to Shinano's Ohmachi town; Kurobe Line cuts up Kurobe River where hardy hikers have choice of 20km trek to join Alpine Route or 25-30km treks to Shinano Ohmachi, Hakuba towns. These Chugoku Sangaku Mtns include sacred Mt Ontake, continue S to Pacific coast, end at Mt Fuji.

W of these mtns is narrow Hida River Valley, E is Nagano basin also called Shinano (also Shinshu) district, our next stop. Many Japanese tourists pass quickly thru this area on Alpine Route or rush up Kurobe River Gorge, best enjoyed by hiker with several days to spend. Transport to trailheads good, enough budget lodgings ensures relaxing rooms either end of few nites camping (also trailhead campsites for true hiker-budgeteer). Cross mountains sans tent by booking rooms in pilgrim-rate mountain huts. We give basic outline of area, but avid hikers should pick up detailed maps (locally in Japanese, or perhaps stateside mountaineering clubs have English info —they should if they don't, they are 'coming' mountaineering routes) or go with Japanese companion.

PERSONAL DATEBOOK: **Apr 2nd sat-sun**, National *Chindon-ya* Contest, finals sun of this fascinating indigenous 'jazz-like' street advertising band, fading from horn-cacaphonous lanes. **Aug 1-5,** *Toyama Festival.*

Tateyama Alpine Route: 1hr out of Toyama, Tateyama Line ends 34km/¥1,010 later at Tateyama, where → 7min cable car 1.3km (¥620) to Bijo-daira → 55min bus 23km (¥1,630), half on scenic Tateyama Kogen Park Line toll road to dead-end Murodo → 10min tunnel-bus 3.6km (¥2,060) to Daikan-bo → 7min ropeway 1.7km (¥1,240) to Kurobe-daira → 5min subway cablecar down 800m (¥820) to Lake Kurobe → 30min walk to bus stop → 16min tunnel-bus 6km (¥1,240) to Ogisawa → 30min bus 18km (¥1,230) to JR Shinano Ohmachi. Total travel time 4hrs covers 82km (about ¥10,000), but with time between transfers and some sightseeing (including boat around dammed Lake Kurobe) recommend spend nite at midway Murodo. Time-insensitive budgeteers hike most of it, but should probably spend ¥1,000 for 35min bus from Bijo-daira to Mida-ga-hara trailhead at start of Park Line toll road as 15km walk is all road and hitching not easy as private cars not allowed beyond Mida-ga-hara. If **driving**, special delivery service picks up your car at one end to deliver at other: **Mida-ga-hara** on Toyama side, contact ☎(0764)-22-4715; **Ogisawa** on Shinshu side contact info office ☎(0261)-22-3220; ¥25,000 per car includes insurance. Talk of creating joint ticket for full run (each leg now run by different Co.) at reduced rate has not materialized since popular despite cost. Rail users from main cities save some on JR 'Route Shuyuken' regional-tickets which include Alpine Route.

TILT: JTB affiliate Ace Co has 2-day hire **cab**, 3-day **tour bus** courses thru area. Cabs incl driver's expenses, room w/2 meals, ranging ¥30,-53,900 per person (child 15% less). Other Ace Co Bus Tours start/end Tokyo; book at least 11 days prior, such as:

Alpine Route & Kurobe Kyokoku (Tateyama): Dep Shinjuku 8:00 JR express via Matsumoto → Shinano Ohmachi stn for bus, cablecar, etc → Murodo for nite, **day 2** via Tateyama → Unazuki Onsen (nite), **day 3** tram → coastal Uozu and JR → Nagaoka where Joetsu Shinkansen → TOKYO'S Ueno stn 18:43. July 1-Aug 29 from ¥80,000 adult, ¥50,000 child includes all except lunch.

Okuhida Onsen & Kiso-ji Takayama: Dep Shinjuku 9:00 via Matsumoto → Kamikochi→ Shinhodaka Onsen (nite), **day 2** ends Hida Takayama city with free time that afternoon → Gero Onsen (nite), **day 3** Tsumago → Magome-shuku with free time Enakyo → Nagoya in time for 16:53 Shinkansen ending TOKYO 19:00. Tour dates irregular: leave 7x-June, 9x-Aug,.8x-Sep; from ¥120,000.

This unusual mountain crossing didn't start as tourism, but was developed by Kansai Electric, who spent 7 years and 51.3 billion yen on massive Kurobe Dam. They decided to get some money back by turning it into attraction, outfitting roads, tunnels and trams used in dam construction for regular passengers. 20km tunnel from Kurobe Dam to Keyaki-daira (near Unazuki) not open to tourists, but if ever is will make ideal link from dam to Unazuki. For now, private Toyama Jitetsu rail runs 2x-daily (Apr 25-Nov 10 only) special expresses Tateyama 90min → Unazuki Onsen; from Unazuki Onsen abt 8:00 & 9:00, Tateyama returns 14:30, 15:30. Otherwise, rail back to Toyama and change to Kurobe Kyokoku Line, total travel time 2hrs.

Tateyama Center *Fudoki-no-Oka* (10min bus from Chigaki stn, 3 before Tateyama), is near paired–ASHIKURA-JI temple and OYAMA JINJA shrine (linked until Meiji era split and once centers of Tateyama mountain ascetics), has several reconstructed local houses as well as Yayoi bronze-age dwellings. Museum displays relate to Tateyama ascetics, local folkcrafts (¥100, X–mon). Tateyama has several inns from ¥-B stnside Youth Hostel **Sugita** and 3 minshuku at nearby **Senjuga-hara Onsen**, up to ¥-lo-T+w/2 classy riverside inn **Seiryu-so**, few more. Top of short cablecar ¥-S is **Bijo-daira Hotel.**

TATEYAMA-SENJUGA-HARA ONSEN popular with hikers who bus (20min, ¥540 hourly or better, 6:40-17:00) to trailhead near spectacular **Shomyo-taki** falls plummeting 350m (almost height of Empire State bldg) flanked by 500m high cliffs. Spring, parallel, thinner waterfall appears, caused by spring-thaw. **Mida-ga-hara Hotel**, and Kokumin-shukusha **Tateyama-so** at MIDA-GA-HARA plateau.

But most prefer to stay at...
MURODO's excellent W-style **Hotel Tateyama** ☎(0764)-65-3333, ¥-S-L. Mid-Jun–Mid-Oct hotel runs *Go-raiko* (sunrise) bus to Daikan peak. Budgeteers choice of half-dozen *yamagoya* (mountain-hut) inns scattered around beautiful Murodo-daira plateau, all short walk from Tateyama Hotel and Murodo bus terminal. Some of these draw onsen water from nearby bubbling **Hell-valley**, *Jigoku-dani*, area around which is scalded bare, stained white and yellow from sulphur fumes. At closest and largest Lake Mikuriga-ike, **Mikuriga Onsen Ryokan** boasts large baths, open to nonguests ¥500. Great way to end day of hiking; 1km away is campsite along River. At 2,300m above sea-level, Mikuriga Onsen is highest onsen in Japan, tho Hakuba's Yari Onsen (2,100m) is better known as such. Murodo-daira crisscrossed by several easy hiking paths, fine for short jaunts, but hard-core hiker-climber should head further out.

Hiking Japanese call places like Murodo-daira *hikes*, while anything more is *tozan* or *mountain-climbing*; we call them all hikes, split into *easy* (anyone with good shoes can do), *medium* (climbing on easy trails) and *hard* (lots of huffing but okay for any healthy backpacker with no need for ropes or dangerous dangly ascents). These North Japan Alps are hikers' mecca and may seem crowded for those used to trail-blazing in Western USA where you can go for days without seeing anyone else.

From **Shomyo-taki** falls medium trail: 2hr to Dainichi-daira plateau (with hut) 2hr30min → Dainichi-dake peak (2498m, hut just below summit) → 1hr along ridge to 2606m Okudainichi-dake 90min → **Murodo-norikoshi** where 45min down → Murodo-daira or 90min further along ridge → **Bessan-norikoshi** (has hut) for choice of 1hr down → Murodo or 20+km (2 days) → Keyaki-daira for mountain tram → Unazuki—make sure to *avoid* L fork past Tsurugisawa hut which leads up 2998m

Tsurugi-dake, down to middle-nowhere Babashima hamlet—preferred R fork heads down valley to meander mountains to Keyaki-daira.

6km easy path **Midaga-hara** → **Murodo-daira** continues past Murodo-daira 4.5km to Daikan-bo ropeway for quick ride down → **Lake Kurobe** (or hike down). From dam end of lake, medium riverside trail all way → Keyaki-daira. 3hr hike S along W bank of lake → Hirano for **shuttle boat** across lake (huts both sides for latecomers) and then hard 3hr hike up → 2821m Harinoki-dake peak (hut) and down 2hr → Ogisawa bus stop.

KUROBE KYOKOKU RIVER VALLEY 黒部峡谷

UNAZUKI ONSEN (1hr private Toyama Tetsudo rail from Toyama, 90min rare express from Tateyama) is ideal mountain escape for discriminating traveler; easy to get to, yet beautiful. Two dozen inns line scenic Kurobe River Gorge, some large and modern but not clashing with rural atmosphere of town. Friends of ours own ryokan—Iwata family, **Chosen-kaku** Unazuki Onsen 5531-5, ☎(0765)-62-1001; here, budgeteers have five minshuku to choose from.

Unazuki Park is covered with flowering trees adding color most of year, while nearby slopes become small ski resort in winter. Summers, most people use as base to explore Kurobe Kyokoku Gorge, whether half-day jaunt, overnite, or long treks.

GETTING AROUND: Toyama Tetsudo Rail ends at Unazuki Onsen, where short walk to Kurobe Kyokoku Tetsudo Rail stn to board Disneyland-like small orange diesel or electric trolley. Rail was laid down early this century by Kansai Electric Co to haul supplies and men to construct power plants on Kurobe River, and later Kurobe Dam. First-half rail (to Nekomata) completed 1916, last-half (to Keyaki-daira) finished 1937. Until adding for-tourist runs 1953 visitors rode on regular mini freight trains, ticket backs stamped "We are not responsible for your life". Conditions have improved since, but no way luxurious, being exposed to elements except for small roof overhead. Trains run May 1 to Nov 30; about 16 round-trips between 7:37-16:01 so reserve on this popular ride, especially weekends, summer. Rail line is engineering feat, winding 20.1km in 95min over 23 bridges and thru 42 tunnels. From Keyaki-daira terminus tracks continue another 20km thru single long tunnel to end near Kurobe Dam, limited to Kansai Electric use only. Kurobe was 4th tallest dam in world at its completion in 1963. Several stops en route are hidden backwoods baths, each with one or two ¥-B inns, all of which boast meals of fresh mountain herbs and *iwana* bull trout. Inns operate only while trains run: book direct or thru **Unazuki Onsen Tourist Bureau**. Even summer deep gorge is cool and may want windbreaker; sweater spring, autumn.

First stop is 3 stns and 22min from Unazuki at...
KURONAGI thru narrow tunnel and 15min walk up side stream to one-inn **Kuronagi Onsen** ☎(0765)-62-1802 outdoor riverside bath facing 60m-drop Yugiri-no-taki **Steaming Fog Falls**.

4 stops further...
KANETSURI ONSEN has inns **Miyama-so** ☎62-1634, **Kanetsuri Onsen** ☎65-0023. Down by Kurobe River many outdoor baths make use of hot water gushing from rocky walls. Kanetsuri is popular with families who stay down at Unazuki but bring their kids up here during day to play in hot pools.

End of line is...
KEYAKI-DAIRA: Unazuki-based tourists spend few hrs wandering, take bath and lunch, or spend nite at one of 3 quiet inns, and where hiker can choose from several trails. **Sarutobi-sanso** inn ☎(0765)-62-1026, near stn but if this far, better walk 15min to **MEIKEN ONSEN**, inn by same name, ☎(0765)-52-1355, outdoor riverside bath. After dip, can get bowl of cheap but good noodles at inn. 20min walk on, thru tunnel is **BABADANI ONSEN**, also with one inn ☎62-1026.

Hiking from Babadani Onsen, 8hrs to summit of 2933m **Mt Hakuba**-dake NE of here. Choices from Mt Hakuba: E–down to Shinano's **HAKUBA** town (which avoid, teeny-bopperville) on several routes (one via Yari Onsen, another Hakuba Glacier); N few more hrs along mountain ridge to dead-end **RENGE ONSEN** and 2hr bus to JR Hiraiwa stn; hook back NW for full-day trek to dead-end **OGAWA ONSEN MOTO-YU** from where 6x-daily 25min bus to Japan Sea coast JR Tomari stn. Ogawa Onsen has ¥-B inn, baths here are in tunnels and hidden rock baths. From Babatani and Keyaki-daira stn, trail cuts S along Kurobe River, eventually to split with one ending at Kurobe Dam and other crossing peak to peak to end at Murodo.

Before split is...
AZOHARA ONSEN natural riverside baths, 8km from Keyaki-daira stn.

SHINSHU 信州

OR SHINANO, as better known, both old names for modern Nagano prefecture. For our wanderer, with little of special interest for casual tourist, but lots of pleasant rural towns to pass time in. Main cities are Matsumoto to S and Nagano to N.

Of these, we start out at more pleasant...
MATSUMOTO, which lives up to nickname 'City of Mountains', sitting along major river flanked by soaring peaks. Despite almost 200,000 people it is rural in atmosphere yet with most comforts of large city.

GETTING THERE: Also on several JR lines with parallel hiways: From NAGOYA (some start Osaka-Kyoto) Chuo Main Line (Rte19) passes thru our Kiso-ji Route (*see*), from which northern stop of Narai, Matsumoto is only 50min local; Chuo Main Line from TOKYO's Shinjuku goes thru our Off-beat Koshu-kaido leg (Rte20) to snake around Lake Suwa, where Iida Line (Rt 153) joins, having started Pacific coast Toyohashi city. N from MATSUMOTO, main Shinonoi Line (Rte19) thru Nagano City to end Japan Sea coast's Naoetsu; Oito Line (Rte148) takes western course via Shinano Ohmachi and Hakuba to Itoigawa. Shinano Ohmachi, end of Alpine Route, is only 50min local from Matsumoto, so perhaps after our Kiso-ji or Koshu-kaido routes and relaxing nite in Matsumoto or nearby Asama Onsen, you can do Alpine Route to end up in Kanazawa and on to Hida Takayama or down Japan Sea coast. Private Matsumoto Dentetsu rail heads W into Kamikochi Plateau, buses on parallel Rte158 go all the way to Hida Takayama (some legs seasonal) via Oku-Hida Onsen cluster (see). So even if Matsumoto may not be worth special trip to see, chances are back-country travellers will find themselves here in which case good spot to stop for nite between legs.

Matsumoto Castle (a.k.a. Crow's Castle for its black walls) has dominated town since lord ISHIKAWA Kazumasa built it in 1590. One of few original castles (outer fortifications dismantled by Meiji), classed NT. Illuminated at nite, adds much to town's charm. Inside is usual museum of feudal armor, weapons, but with simple artifacts showing everyday life; **panoramic view** from top floor worth ¥400 admission, especially on clear day. Castle grounds is public park, fun to visit during cherry blossom season (and last wknd Jul, *see* DATEBOOK). Entry fee for castle also good for **Folk Museum**, *Minzoku Shiryo-kan*, in park outside moat. It has little bit of everything from Jomon and Yayoi pottery to farm tools, old clocks, and some on early mountaineering in Japan. Castle, museum daily 8:30-16:30, X-year-end.

Kaichi Gakko elementary school is short walk N of castle, behind present modern school. Built 1876 in blend of Japanese and Western architecture. Inside is full of education-related items from early Meiji period; open daily end Apr to early Nov, rest of year X-sun, hol, year-end, ¥200.

These are two main sites in Matsumoto as far as most Japanese tourists are concerned, but there are several more fine small museums—new ones being added as private collections in lovely private compounds go public—which can easily be taken in on local transport, or self-made cab tour. Lots of cabs in town and you will have little trouble getting one.

Under new Meiji government, Matsumoto decided to pursue education—which city has done to this day, as seen in many schools of all levels here, up to university —and many fine schools established. Tho Kaichi Gakko most famous, there are other old ones in town: **Kyusei Matsumoto Koto Gakko** school (15min walk E of stn), was built shortly after Kaichi Gakko in similar style. From end WW II to few years ago, was dorm for Shinshu U.

Yamanobe Gakko, now **Folk History Museum,** *Rekishi Minzoku Shiryo-kan,* was built about same time but in totally Japanese style. 15min bus E of stn; folk items, daily X-mon, hol, year-end; ¥100.

15min bus from stn towards Utsukushi-ga-hara Onsen to Mingeikan-guchi stop is...
Folkcraft Museum, *Matsumoto Mingei-kan,* (daily X-mon, year-end, ¥200). Old kura museum displays personal collection of local artisan MARUYAMA Taro; over 5,000 items of crafts—carpentry, pottery, glass blowing, etc.

8min Matsumoto Dentetsu rail to 3rd stop Oniwa, 15min walk or cab 3x-mtr...
Woodblock Print Museum, JUM, *Nihon Ukiyoe Hakubutsukan* (X-mon, year-end, ¥500). Modern, cubic glass and concrete structure housing fabulous, perhaps largest collection of ukiyoe prints—some 100,000—of which 2-300 display any given time; series of slides show carving process.

Judicial Museum, *Shiho Hakubutsu-kan* (X-mon, year-end, ¥500), nearby in rebuilt feudal courthouse display law-related items of Edo, Meiji, Taisho eras–modern 1867–now.

Matsumoto is known for its old thick dirt-walled kura storehouse-style houses, made so to insulate against harsh winter. Strolling around town, especially along river between stn and castle, is good way to see these and other old houses and to find lunch spot.

CHOPSTICKS: Many eateries make use of attractive kura-style houses, menus range from usual coffeeshops—such as **Marumo** which also is good ¥-T inn, to tempura at **Kura** or Indian curry at **Delhi.** Natural Food: **Naja** uses only organic foods, *genmai* lunch ¥550, 15min walk from JR Matsumoto stn, 12:00-21:00, X-sun, ☎36-9096. Local specialty found at many places is *ba-sashi,* horse meat sashimi. **Taiman** French, with international textile collection, in amazingly Tudorish minka-style building.

WHERE TO STAY: Town has over 100 inns in various ranges of price and comfort. W-style rooms at numerous ¥-T or business hotels by stn. For J-style inn, **Marumo** ☎(0263)-32-0115, old-timer in kura-style house along river, ¥-T. Many hikers head to **Shinshu Kaikan** ☎33-0165, ¥-Bw/2, sexes separated, herded to communal dorms. For less, get own room at business-class hotel or ryokan;

Or own room at minshuku for few hundred yen more at...
ASAMA ONSEN, 20min frequent bus or cab 2x-mtr from JR stn. There are 9 budget minshuku here; **Asama Onsen YH** 500m S of main cluster around *Showa-no-yu* **public bath** (daily X-mon, ¥100). Asama is pleasant suburb of Matsumoto just N of town with many old houses. Garet and friend stayed at fine ¥-T **Kouran-so** ☎46-1014. Many other ¥-T–S inns incl ¥-T W-style Hotel **Asama-en** ☎46-1730, twins. Book inns here and in town thru stn **Kanko-annai.**

Matsumoto's other main spa...
UTSUKUSHI-GA-HARA ONSEN, 15min bus E of stn, was as nice until recent addition of many luxury hotels, we recommend Asama over it.

Adventurer, further E along Usugawa River into foothills of Utsukushi-ga-hara mts.
30min bus to...
IRIYAMANOBE ONSEN in quiet wooded valley with sole inn **Kasumi-sanso** ☎31-2101, ¥-T, is Meiji era beauty.

15min bus further up stream is...
TOBIRA ONSEN, equally hidden with two ¥-T inns.

Tobira Onsen is trailhead into...
Utsukushi-ga-hara Kogen, several peaks (all about 2,000m high) also called 'Japan Alps anyone can climb' for its many easy trails, most of which can be done from end to end in 2-3hrs. Also many regular and scenic toll roads for drivers, but most of high ground reserved for hikers. Bus serving trailheads other than Tobira Onsen run only during hiking season, late Apr to early Nov.

N of these mountains are two popular but rural hot spa clusters—only one reached from Matsumoto by bus tho both by car; both also reached from stops on JR Shinetsu Line. We have not been to either, but here is what we know from reputation and friends' visits:

MARIKO ONSEN-KYO made up of 3 baths of **Kakeyu, Oshio, Reisenji** all on Rte254. **Kakeyu** is largest with two dozen ¥-B–S inns; 50min bus, 5x-daily from Matsumoto; on Shinetsu Line bus starts Ueda stn (75min) via Ohya stn (50min). **Oshio,** 5min bus closer to Ohya stn, has 5 inns; **Reisenji,** with 6 inns, is 20min walk down dead-end side street from Miyazawa bus stop 40min from Ohya.

Out of town...
HOTAKA, var Hodaka for few day R&R, recommend **Hotaka Yojoen,** Mr Fukuda's plain new holistic retreat, holds 25+, ☎(0263)-83-5260: therapy—germanium baths ¥1500, shiatsu, acupuncture, yoga, herbal onsen; ¥-Bw/2 bland macrobio meals.

OGIHARA Rokuzan (1879-1910) **museum,** first Japanese disciple of Rodin and other early W-style sculptors incl Takamura; fine collection.

BESSHO ONSEN, just 4km N other side of hills from Maruko Onsens but unless driving, you must take rickety private rail from Ueda, 30min to last stop. Bessho is quiet little town full of temples and shrines (some rather famous) which add to its charm. Inns mostly small family-run ones ranging ¥-B–hi-T but superb in service. Dozen-plus clustered around two large baths, **Ishiyu** and **Taishiyu** at far end of town (10min walk from stn), some around **Ohyu** bath closer to stn. Jul 15, *Take-no-nobori* Bamboo banner fest here is rain-calling rite in which people carry long bamboo poles festooned with colorful cloth.

Shinetsu Main Line (parallel Rte18) eventually ends at Tokyo's Ueno; 30min express Tokyo-wards of Ueda is resort center and Tokyoites' escape of...
KARUIZAWA. Despite all noise over it, we still recommend skipping, even more than we did in '64 edition, since in recent years become just another extension of Tokyo, overpriced stores cater to rich youth. If you live in Japan and can't leave your ghetto even for vacation, or want to do sociological study of cross-cultural play, OK.

Btwn Karuizawa and Ueda at Komoro town, JR Kokai Line (drive Rte141) branches S to summer escape of...
KIYOSATO, site of successful early-postwar experimental W-style farm KEEP, developed whole society here amid rolling green farmlands. Dotted with countless small inns, new W-style *pensiones* which attract youth like *ryokan* attract us, where city-folk can come to relax away from it all.

.Stay at **Seisenryo,** ¥-T, +family cottages; fine W-dining. Horses, bike paths.
Kokai Line joins Chuo Main Line (Rte20, Chuo Expwy) at Kobuchizawa, 30min express from Kofu City (*see* p274). Ueda → Nagano City 40min local or 25min express.

LAKE SUWA-KO (about 30km SE of Matsumoto and easy to get to as it's on Chuo Main Line, Expwy and Rte20), circular, 16km around, is largest body of water in central Japan; source of Tenryu River which eventually empties out into Pacific. Summer has sightseeing and row boats, in winter freezes over to become giant skating arena. Particularly cold winters, (Jan-Feb) expanding ice explode into cracks accompanied by loud bang to create *omi-watari* 'crossing of gods'. Number and intensity of these upheavals taken as omens for year to come. S shore open farmland and hills, but N shore lined by civilization—E to W, Okaya City, Shimo-Suwa (Lower Suwa), and Kami-Suwa (Upper Suwa), which at some time soon may meld into one mass.

OKAYA, long center of silkworm raising. **Silk Museum,** *Sanshi Hakubutsu-kan* (1km N of stn), has items related to silkworms and silk, grounds have silkworms' favorite food, mulberry trees. Upstairs is local **ancient art museum.**

SHIMO-SUWA is our favorite of these 3 towns for it retains much of its rural atmosphere. Many people still live by farming nearby fields and fishing on lake. Old fishing tools and such seen at **Town Museum,** *Choritsu Hakubutsu-kan* (daily, X-mon, ¥100). Shimo-Suwa thrived during Edo period as junction of Nakasendo and Koshu-kaido pedestrian hiways. N of stn, 2 of 4 main **SUWA TAISHA** Grand Shrines *Shimosha* (Lower Shrine) *Harumiya* (Spring Palace), & *Akimiya* (Autumn Palace). Other two, *Kamisha* (Upper Shrine) *Honmiya* (Main Palace) and *Maemiya* (Front Palace), are at SE shore of Lake Suwa 20min bus from Kami-Suwa (nearby Suwa I.C. of Chuo Expwy). Suwa Taisha dates to at least 8th century as shrine for good harvest, healthy silkworms; later became popular with warriors seeking military prowess. Finest is *Honmiya*, with covered halls thru thick ancient cryptomeria, but harder to reach so most pilgrims settle for *Akimiya* near which is **SHIMO-SUWA ONSEN** with most lodgings in pleasant old section of town. Great inn is **Kameya** ☎(0266)-27-8023, former *honjin* (inn for daimyo-lords), ¥-Tw/2. Notch below are folksy **Urakameya** ☎27-7121, and **Minatoya** ☎27-8144; ¥-Sw/2. Top ranked **Bogetsu-ro** ☎28-2111, ¥-S, has grand view of lake. More by lakeshore. **Suwako YH** ☎27-7075 in fine old folk house midway Shimo-Suwa and Kami-Suwa, near Higashi Takaki bus stop; but usual infantile regulations.

KAMI-SUWA, 'busier' of pair, reaches out to grab tourism. Also onsen and so much hot water gushes forth that most every building in town taps it. Dozens of inns in all styles, sizes, prices from ¥-Bw/2 minshuku **Suwa-ko** ☎58-4821, to top class inns running ¥-T–Sw/2. Most clustered between stn and lakeshore, in their midst is **Katakura-kan**, old Western building with giant *sennin-buro* **'1,000-person bath'**, small private *kazoku-buro* 'family baths'. Built prewar by silk tycoon for workers. ¥260 bath only, ¥520 bath, use of rest area (10:00-17:00 daily, X-tue). Next door Katakura storehouse now **City Museum** of mostly W-style art, but also artifacts excavated from Jomon and Yayoi sites in area. **Takashima Castle** S of town built 1598, dismantled 1875, put back up 1970. Inside is usual local museum, good view from top.

PERSONAL DATEBOOK: In SUWA Spring *Onbashira-sai* Sacred Pillar Festival, main fete of Suwa Taisha occurs only 5-7 years on Monkey & Tiger years— 1993, 1998, 2005, 2010. 16 giant logs (13-17m tall, 3m around) dragged down from Mt Yatsu-ga-take by hundreds of men in lively wild race; each of 4 shrines has pillar set up at 4 corners, **early Apr** Honmiya and Maemiya, **mid-Apr** Harumiya and Akimiya; **early May** taken down and paraded thru Kami-Suwa and Shimo-Suwa in gala affair. Perhaps stylized fertility rite where mountain god joins agriculture goddess? Annual shrine festivals are: **Apr 15**, *Onkashira-sai*, kami of Honmiya and Maemiya meet; **Aug 1**, *Ofuna-matsuri* Boat-fete, where kami of Harumiya is placed on boat-shaped float and carried to Akimiya. **3rd sun Apr**, Suwa Lake Fest. **3rd sun May**, Takashima Castle Festival. **Aug 15**, massive fireworks over lake marks high point of O-bon, 100s paper lanterns floated in lake, down Tenryu River.

Drivers looking for new trails, N from Shimo-Suwa on Rte142 follow old **Nakasen-do** foot hiway. Along it are few hamlets which retain feudal era airs in varying degrees. S to N: Kamiwada-juku, Nagakubo-juku, Ashida-juku, Mochizuki-juku, Shionada-juku. **Ashida- and Mochizuki-juku** reputedly best (latter has been made into museum); between them, Motai has **Sake Brewing Museum,** Osawa Shuzo. Shionada not bad. Walkers do best portion in 4-5hrs: 90min bus Shimo-Suwa to Nagakubo → walk side road E over Kasatori Pass, thru pine trees, 2hrs-plus to Ashida → 2hrs to Mochizuki → 30min bus to either Komoro, Iwamurada stns. From Chino (near Suwa), scenic hiway Venus Line snakes NE, then cuts back NW across mountain ridge to end Utsukushi-ga-hara, total 65km; about 25km branch scenic road ends S of Mochizuki.

KAMIKOCHI HIGHLANDS (30km W of Matsumoto), is popular base to explore one section of North Japan Alps, and spot where English missionary Walter Weston made people aware of mountains as places for enjoying sports rather than only as religious homes of mountain gods. First person to actually settle down in Kamikochi was Kamijo Kamonji in 1880, but by 1884 it had developed into small cattle-raising community which survived until 1934. Weston climbed around here 1891, with Kamonji as guide, returned twice more to Japan to climb many more peaks. It wasn't long until crazy Western fad of clambering around mountains for fun took hold, and Japanese hikers still pay tribute to Weston every year on **1st sun June**, when hikers gather front of Weston's relief carved on hillside for festival opening hiking season. Mountain officially 'opens' **Apr .27** *Kaisan Matsuri* with blessing by Shinto priest, folk- and shishi-mai lion dances, opening giant sake barrels which contents passed among inn owners, guides and anyone else around. **July 1st** is memorial service for those who died in mountains—mishaps do happen, most often off-season climbing. **Oct 8**, mountains gods are thanked for safe year, in Autumn *Akiba-sai* of Hotaka Jinja Shrine at Lake Myojin-ike. Two colorfully painted phoenix-headed boats carrying shrine priests in finest garb circle around lake, chosen because god Hodakami-no-mikoto of these mountains is son of Sea Goddess.

Most-used route here is private Matsumoto Dentetsu rail 30min to Shin-Shimashima end and 70min frequent bus to Kamikochi. Rte158 continues W thru to Hirayu Onsen (*see* Hida-offbeat) from where 5-6 daily buses also to Kamikochi. Midway Shin-Shimashima and Hirayu, at Nakanoyu Onsen is side road to Kamikochi. Most popular and seasonally pleasant time to hike (as well as most crowded) is **early July** (end of rainy season) thru Aug, but official climbing season starts spring Golden Week to mid-Nov, weather permitting. Inns and buses shut down winter; should reserve seats and inn during summer and weekends. If no rooms, check bus terminal info booth for cancellations. Most inns began as mountain huts and cram as many people as possible, so expect packed rooms in season. For Golden Week, all July-Aug, weekends Sept-Nov, Oct leaf viewing, no cars beyond Nakanoyu Onsen, only buses, cabs. **Hikers** can start Shimashima-juku, 4km, 8min bus from Shin-Shimashima stn; up dirt road for few km, then trails. 6hr ascent to Tokumoto Pass, down 90min to Myojin-ike; reverse takes about 6hr30min.

WHERE TO STAY: Kamikochi has ¥-L at European style **Teikoku (Imperial) Hotel** ☎(0263)-95-2001. Next in line **Gosenshaku Hotel** ☎95-2111. **Nishiitoya Sanso** ☎95-2206, J-rooms ¥-Tw/2; half dozen more ¥-Bw/2 range like **Shimizuya** ☎95-2121, and **Shirakaba-so** ☎95-2131. Hoarding hot spring water is **Kamikochi Onsen Hotel** ☎95-2311. Downstream 2km at lake, **Taisho-ike Hotel** ☎95-2301, ¥-Tw/2. Upstream at Myojin-ike Lake are some ¥-B inns: **Myojin-kan** ☎95-2036, **Yoshikiya** ☎95-2216, **Kamonji-koya** ☎95-2418, **Yama-no-hidaya** ☎95-2211. Further upstream at Tokusawa are ¥-B **Tokusawa-en** ☎95-2508, and **Tokusawa Lodge** ☎95-2526. All three areas also have campgrounds with rental cabins and you really shouldn't pitch tents elsewhere. Further up in mountains are more campsites, manned and unmanned huts, even 3 fair-sized lodges. **Hotaka Yojo-en**, center for health training with microbiotic meals. Restful mountain retreat with bird watching, mountain climbing and walks. 10min taxi from Hotaka or Ariake stn, ¥6,000w/2, ☎83-5260.

GETTING AROUND: Kamikochi is actually narrow but relatively level Azusa River valley, at elevation of around 1,500m (1 mile). Many people are satisfied with just **hiking** along river on 3-8hr round-trips, but **climbers** have entire range of peaks to trek (most around 3,000m). 4hrs W to Nishi-Hotaka-guchi peak, whence long ropeway to **SHIN HOTAKA ONSEN** (*see* Oku-Hida); many trails head into Hotaka mts with top peaks **Nishi-Hotaka** (2908m), **Mae-Hotaka**, (3090m), **Oku-Hotaka** (3190m, 3rd highest in Japan but rock pile on top makes it 2nd highest, after Fuji), **Kita-Hotaka** (3106m); way N is needle-like **Yari-ga-take** (3180m), SW is charred smoking volcanic **Yaki-dake** 'Burned Peak' (2455m). Other trails head down W to Shin Hotaka Onsen. To N, and on E side of river are more peaks, **Cho-ga-dake** (2664m), and

Jonen-dake (2857m), from tops head down E to Toyoshina or Hotaka stns JR Oito Line–long trek with much of last bit on road. Better long trek out is via 2,922m **Daitenni-dake** (6hrs from Yari-ga-take, 3hrs from Jonen-dake).

From Daitenni-dake, 5hrs down to tiny...
NAKABUSA ONSEN with onsen pools, outdoor baths, ¥-B inn **Nakabusa Onsen** ☎(0263)-35-9704, Kokumin-shukusha **Ariake-so** ☎35-9701; 60min bus from JR Hotaka stn.

Or N downhill from Yari-ga-take 4hrs to...
YUMATA ONSEN (few huts) whence several hrs downstream to **Tsuzura Onsen** & 40min bus to Shinano Ohmachi stn.

WHERE NEXT: Two choices N from Matsumoto—#1 is JR Oito Line, on which are towns of **Toyoshina, Hotaka, Ariake & Shinano Ohmachi** (var Omachi) used by hikers. Train chugs thru scenic countryside of fields of *wasabi*, hot green horse-radish. After Ohmachi are some large lakes then ski mecca of **Hakuba** which also has great hiking in non-ski season—but avoid ski season, especially end Golden Week when teenybopper heaven. About 20km on, we come to cluster of several hot springs. Of those along rail line and river HIMEKAWA ONSEN nr Hiraiwa stn has outdoor baths run by big inns but open to all. 2hr bus W into hills from Hiraiwa is RENGE ONSEN, N trailhead to Hakuba mts. Adventurer might head to eastern foothills for hidden baths: 1-inn HONO ONSEN 7km up branch road from Nakatsuchi stn; 3-inn OTARI ONSEN 30min bus from Nakatsuchi stn; just before Otari is 1-inn ATSUYU ONSEN. Last two are old style mountain spas with little besides once-grand, now-bit-run-down inns: but good escapes. Not long after these hot springs our train pulls into Itoigawa on Japan Sea coast.

#2 If not hiker, might as well head up Japan Sea coast on quicker trains via Nagano City to Naoetsu, where catch boat out to SADO ISLAND: *but en route...*

NAGANO CITY capital of prefecture called 'Roof of Japan', not bombed but little for tourist except **1998 Winter Olympics**, preserves old, (arrival station in modern Buddhist temple style) grew around...

ZENKO-JI, major pilgrimage temple, est 670—no bldg remains pre-15th c. From stn → gate: 2.5km 30min walk, or bus 10min, or subway 3rd stn walk 2 blocks W (5:00-16:00, ¥300). Like Osaka-Tennoji laid out in Korean style. Noted Amida Triad images object of pilgrimage, oldest in Japan, legend says Sakyamuni made himself of gold of Mt Shumi, center of Universe. Transferred for millennium thru India (tho not accepted today as Indian), China, Korea, coming 552 as gift from Korean king to introduce Buddhism to Japan. Icon burned, sunk in river, etc in efforts to eradicate faith. Rescued and brought here 602 by HONDA Zenko (thus temple name), borrowed often by major leaders wanting its blessings; returned 1599. 61 local temples of same name many with triad copies, indicate cult popularity, send 4 million pilgrims.

JTB opp stn, ☎(0262)-28-5663; excellent Nagano Int'l Friendship Club, ☎32-6644.

SE of city is another cluster of sites for those with time...
Hachima-hara plain, 1553-64, was site of forays between TAKEDA Shingen of Kai-Yamanashi to S, and UESUGI Kenjin of Echigo-Niigata to N later romanticized by Takeda historians into crucial clashes of great chivalry.

MATSUSHIRO TOWN (12km SE of Nagano) is center of this history, with **Bunbu Gakko** school, est 1855 to teach martial arts, gunnery, literature to local lord's retainers; now historical monument. CHOKOKU-JI Zen temple (500m from stn), headed by noted savant, but no trainees. **Manse of Lady Sadako** 1863, beautiful gardens and house.

Birthplace of Electric Industry in region of many electric factories. Fascinating character among modernisers of Japan was SAKUMA Zozan

(1811-64). Xenophobic pragmatic Confucianist of "Can't beat 'em so join 'em" school of patriots, studied W knowledge, and thru Dutch translation of French encyclopedia made glass in 1844, cast bronze cannon, raised hogs here and grew potatoes. Taught many history-making hot-heads, said only "studying West thru books is like scratching itchy foot thru one's shoe", encouraged YOSHIDA Shoin to stow away overseas for which he later spent years under house arrest. Better at phrases than deeds, originated fiction of 'Eastern spiri tuality with Western technology'. Reputedly in 1849 experimented with electric telegraph—5 years before Perry brought one and only 14 years after first Morse machine, 6 after Baltimore-Washington telegram "What hath God wrought?" Restored to honor 1864 only to be killed by Emperor-worshipping extreme xenophobes in Kyoto.

8km E of Nagano City is...
JIGOKU-DANI ONSEN 'Hell Valley Baths': natural outdoor pools famed thruout Japan for 'amphibian' monkeys who hang out here in winter, keeping warm in water starring on endless TV specials. Baths around here for adventurer with lots of time to 'research' just baths.

S end of Shiga Kogen one of best known onsen clusters is...
OBUSE TOWN branch-train 4km, 20min E en route Shiga Kogen, taxi 3x-mtr.

Must for real art buff...
Hokusai-kan Museum (9-5, no-X, ¥400), ☎(0262)-47-5206. Hokusai spent summers of final years 1833-49 here under patronage of local rich squire-artist, TAKAI Kouzan. Museum just 2 rooms but exquisite, 25 paintings and 2 painted *danjiri* festival carts testify to simple fact Hokusai is one of world's great artists, his *manga* cartoons certainly rank with sketches of Rembrandt, adding marvelous humor. Fine bilingual brochure.

Next door...
Museum to painter patron Takai, bigger, 3-4 kuras, but missable (¥200).

Light Museum, *Nippon Akari Hakubutsukan*, oil lamps-*andons*, candle-flashlights, every sort of light instrument; whole fascinating history of light in Japan (X-wed, ¥300). Chikufu-do local shop with chestnut specialties from sweets to chestnut-rice lunch ¥900; also *free* display ancient local earthenware dolls and pottery.

Under 20km N, 30 NE of Nagano C, bit off main line N is...
NOJIRI-KO lake resort popular with resident foreigners since *Murray's Guide* wrote about it in 1890s; then missionaries swarmed in to build cabins. Noted for easy climbs to spectacular views. Little interest to transients, but base for day trips for residents with access to cabin here.

Just few km N is...
AKAKURA ONSEN in hills, popular ski resort for Tokyo-ites, with ¥-B pensiones, small inns ¥-T+ to Akakura Kanko resort hotel, ¥-S. Back in '53 Jay and Sumi spent idyllic week at nearby inn, ¥500w/3.

About 30km E of Nagano City is...
SHIGA KOGEN heights, popular ski area dotted with dozens of backwoods hot spas.

From Nagano take Nagano Tetsudo rail hour to end...
YUDANAKA (hot spring), whence various buses to each hot spring. Here is KUSATSU ONSEN, (E in Gumma Pref) reached by bus from central Shiga Kogen, or from Nakanohara stn JR Azuma branch line; direct from Tokyo's Ueno in 2hr30min, or 75min from Takasaki on Shinetsu Main Line. Also some buses from Karuizawa.

Continue up seacoast...

ECHIGO 越後

FEUDAL and still used name of present-day Niigata prefecture, convenient boundary between Hokuriku and Tohoku regions. Historically it's UESUGI Kenshin country. Mountainous Niigata is one of poorest prefectures in Japan with little for tourist but glimpses of old rural Japan, hard surface on which tough machine of industrial Japan was forged, little changed in past decades. Even onsen here don't rate high according to Japanese standards, which means great for pilgrims seeking backwoods hide-aways at low prices. **Niigata** City has some sites worth seeing if there to ferry from/to Sado Island, main draw of Niigata pref. Niigata airport 30min bus from town, flights to Haneda, Osaka, Fukuoka, Sapporo; JAL off-and-on uses as jump off for Vladivostok area. Niigata also has long-distance ferry to Hokkaido's Otaru.

For those following our route up Japan Sea coast or thru Shinshu, two JR lines cut inland to next-door Fukushima pref for scenic back entry to Aizu-Wakamatsu, our 1st stop in Tohoku (ideal, as avoids passing thru Tokyo): *Tadami Line* starts Koide (on Shinetsu Main Line), thru Tadami National Park to end AIZU-WAKAMATSU 4hr40min later, 4-6x-daily; *Banetsu Nishi Line* from Niigata (7-9x-daily) to Aizu-Wakamatsu in 2hr30min, not quite as scenic but gives option of stop-off at kura-town of Kitakata just before Wakamatsu. Tadami Line can also be paralled by infrequent bus, recommended for adventurer seeking rural onsen baths and pleasant scenery.

NIIGATA CITY: We don't recommend special visit here unless heading out to Sado Isle, or passing thru en route to Tohoku and Hokkaido, but there are some interesting sites to see in quick half-day round of town. Heart of town is on island, separated from mainland by wide Shinano River. Much of seashore is vast stretch of sand dunes. Niigata was one of five ports opened to foreigners end of Tokugawa rule (1850's), and Meiji Restoration saw great building boom resulting in fancy Occi-Oriental structures. Most flattened during war and subsequent reconstruction, but few remain.

Our tour of Niigata begins at finest...

Prefectural Memorial Hall, *Kensei Kinen-kan*, built 1884 as assembly hall, served as such until 1932. Fine building with terraces outside, inside (9:00-16:30, X-mon, free) restored as it was originally, with some historical displays added.

It is at edge of...

Hakusan Koen Park, 1st in Japan made for commoners, designed by Dutch in 1873. In park is **HAKUSAN JINJA** shrine with its 400-year-old soaring gate and main hall, popular for *en-musubi* ('fate-tying' marriage). Park is 8min bus from stn (use **bus** #5, 6, or 7; #14 to Sado Kisen pier), or **cab** basic-mtr; short walk from Hakusan stn (1 from Niigata) on JR coastal Echigo Line.

1.5km NE of Hakusan Park, 10min bus from stn...

Cultural Museum, *Kanai Bunkazai-kan*, classy 2-storey W-style wooden house built 1871 as Kanai photo studio. All sorts of items ranging from samurai armor to old cameras, scattered about randomly, but lots of fun to browse. Present owner's grandfather KANAI Yaichi studied photography under early Meiji great SHIMOOKA Renjo before opening own studio.

Nearby is Niigata branch of...

North Country Culture Museum, *Hoppo Bunka Hakubutsukan* (9:00-16:00, X-mon, ¥200), with more odds and ends; in branch house of Itoh family, with lovely garden. Main *Hoppo Bunka* museum (in main Itoh home) outside town; see below.

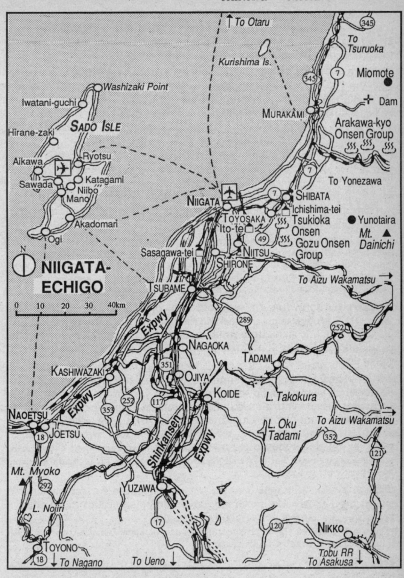

Few blocks W are twin spires of 80-year-old...
Niigata Catholic Church.

Local History Museum, *Kyodo Shiryokan* (9:00-16:00 X-mon, ¥40), in interesting ex-Customs House built 1869. Predominantly Japanese, kura style checkerboard *namako* pattern, but some unique W touches like arched entrance, not to mention *yagura* watchtower poking out of red-tiled roof.

20min walk S of Hakusan Park, 15min bus from stn...
Nihon-kai Tower, built to commemorate 60th anniversary of modern water system, has 63m high revolving (15min/round) platform for panoramic view of city, surrounding countryside and mountains, and on clear day far-off Sado Island in Japan Sea (daily 9:00-17:00, ¥200).

5min walk towards ocean is small...

Stone house, reputedly where poet Basho spent nite on return trip from writing his poetic guidebook to Tohoku, *Oku-no Hosomichi*, 'Narrow Roads to the Far North'. Beaches only 5min walk away.

WHERE TO STAY: Niigata has plenty of lodgings in all ranges which can be arranged thru stn **Kanko-annai**. Dining is no problem here, Furu-machi is giant food district with hundreds of assorted eateries along 3 parallel streets–Furumachi-dori, Nishibori-dori, Higashibori-dori stretching km W of Hakusan Park.

Rural Houses of Niigata: Some of finest preserved feudal era houses of Echigo (all national or prefectural ICA) are within easy reach of Niigata. Adventurer can spend leisurely full day using public transport to see all listed below (*in same order*) to end at **ARAKAWA-KYO ONSEN** for soothing bath. Then again, can leave Niigata anytime to start this course since almost every stop is conveniently close to backwoods hot springs, giving bath-lovers seemingly endless choice from outdoor baths in mountains to by-the-sea surf-sprayed pools.

Bus: Niigata Kotsu Bus runs 6hr tour of best houses Echigo Go-no-**Meguri Course** (sat-sun, hol April-Nov, daily Jul-Aug, ¥6,270/adult, ¥4,220/kid incl lunch, adm) dep Bus Center 9:20, stn 9:30 → Ashigaru Nagaya and Shimizu-en → Ichishima-tei → Saito-tei → Itoh-tei → stn 15:15 → Bus Center 15:20.

Cab 3-4 people can do same for less money, *and include visit to...*

Sasagawa-tei, sprawling 160-year-old mansion of wealthy merchant (daily 9:00-17:00, ¥250), few min walk from Mikata stn on Niigata Kotsu private rail line. This rural tram line starts from front of park to end about 30km down-coast at Tsubame; Mikata is 40min from Niigata. One of finest such houses in Niigata pref.

Itoh-tei, Northern Area Museum, *Hoppo Bunka Hakubutsu-kan* (8:00-17:00, ¥400) 95-year-old main house of Itoh family, 65-room manse & 6 kura storehouses packed with all sorts of things related to rural Niigata, Japanese art and some from China. Grand landscaped strolling garden surrounds; **garden tea house**, *Ido-koya*, uses mineral water from own well to make drinks; ex-miso storehouse is now restaurant **Miso-kura** where enjoy *Inaka-teishoku* 'Country-feast', but must call ahead ☎(025385)-2001. It is 50min bus from Niigata bus Center to Kamisoumi stop.

Ichishima-tei (12min walk from JR Tsukioka stn) made for merchant who made it big in early Meiji. Grand garden complex nestles **main manse** (with 108-mat room) and several other structures.

Nearby **TSUKIOKA ONSEN** has recently become bit commercialized, but few km S are budget baths of **GOZU ONSEN** cluster.

SHIBATA CITY (30min rail or cab 15x-mtr, 29.5km E of Niigata) offers us two variant views of samurai living conditions: **Ashigaru Nagaya** (X-mon) was home to 8 low-ranking samurai who lived in separate but adjacent apartments in this mid-18th century long-house—not much different setup than present-day rabbit-hutch apartments of Tokyo.

Nearby...

Shimizu-en garden surrounds 2nd house of ex-feudal lord Mizoguchi family. Early Edo landscape strolling garden centers around ponds in form of Chinese ideograph for water, placed around it are house and 5 teahouses, and **Museum of Samurai Memorabilia** (9:00-17:00, X-Dec 25 thru Feb, ¥350). Fee good for here and Ashigaru Nagaya; they are 8min walk W of stn. **Shibata Castle** (25min walk N is), only hoary rear gate and one watchtower remain. Numerous ¥-B & ¥-T inns around town, many near site of *asa-ichi* morning market.

Near Echigo Shimoseki stn (25min from Shibata to Sakamachi, change to Yonesaka line and 15min)...

ARAKAWA-KYO Onsen cluster has: **Watanabe-tei** (9:00-16:00 X-tue, 8/14-16, 9/15, ¥250), sprawling home of ex-shipping merchant sake maker; main house, various storehouses, grand garden (5min walk from stn). Two doors down is **Sato-ke** house with graceful roof, not open to public.

Nearby baths: across river, (7min bus), is YUSAWA ONSEN (4 inns); 2min bus further is largest TAKASE ONSEN (15 inns); 5min bus upstream on stn side KIRA ONSEN (3 inns); nearby KIRA JINJA enshrined object is giant wood penis plus smaller ones; 10min bus upstream to TAKANOSU ONSEN, (3 inns) ¥-B–T; riverside path links Takanosu–Takase onsens, campsite both ends of path. Similar situations elswhere, we camped and asked inn for use of bath (often small fee). Arakawa Onsen recommended place to stay on this rural farmhouse tour, especially if taking JR Yonesaka Line to central Yonezawa City

MURAKAMI TOWN (40min rail N of Shibata) is ex-castle town retaining much of its feudal airs. Best is 200-year-old middle-ranking samurai house **Wakabayashi-tei** (9:00-16:00, X-tue, year-end, free). Gorgeous thatched-roof, simple wood fence enclosing fair-sized garden.

Nearby...

Local History Museum, *Kyodo Shiryo-kan* (X–mon pm, tue, ¥200), displays feudal odds and ends, and 4 of giant floats used in gala July Murakami Festival. Both 10min walk E of Aramachi bus stop (7min bus or 20min walk from stn).

8min NE of stn is...

KANNON-JI temple, with mummy of Saint Bukkai-shonin, who in 1903 became last man to "attain Nirvana-in-body" thru meditation & fasting to physical death. 10min walk E of stn is 200-year-old **Yamaguchi-tei**, folk house. 8 ¥-B inns in town, or 2 dozen ¥-hi-T–S inns at nearby seaside SENAMI ONSEN where inn **Daikan-so** has seaside outdoor baths.

BACKCOUNTRY TREKS: For real adventurer which we have researched, sent friends out on succesfully—adding their feedback, but not yet done ourselves:

MIOMOTE hamlet was isolated, 'primitive' cluster of old farm houses, about 30km inland from Murakami, now destroyed to make dam. Infrequent bus 50min from village office Asahimura. Two isles in lake are campsites; extra boat runs May-Oct.

YUNOTAIRA ONSEN is for adventurer with time; series of outdoor baths part way up Mt Dainichi-dake trail. Only inn is **Yunotaira Sanso** (no ☎, for info, call Shibata Kanko-annai ☎(0254)-26-5558), open only during climbing season Jul thru Nov. From Shibata, take JR Akatani Line 40min to last stop Higashi-akatani, then 5hr walk up into hills.

Bullfighting: J-style, pitting bull against bull as we saw on Shikoku, Oki, Okinawa, has also been part of rural Echigo's festivities since at least early Edo era (17c). Here too, began as mix of sport and way to select best bulls. Matches still held **May thru Nov**, concentrated around Yamakoshi village near Ojiya town and Hirokami village on Tadami Line. Matches spread between several rings, check: **Yamakoshi Togyu-kai** ☎(025859)-2375, **Hirokami Togyu-kai** ☎(025799)-2867 Yamakoshi rings all 7-15km from Ojiya stn, cab or bus (few special buses run from Nagaoka city on match days): **Koguriyama Togyu-jo**, 18min bus Ojiya to Jotaki and 15min walk; **Mushikame Togyu-jo**, 50min bus from Nagaoka or cab from Ojiya; **Yamakoshi Togyu-jo**, 35min bus from Ojiya to Katsuraya and 10min walk. Hirokami village ring **Imogawa Togyu-jo** is 15min drive from JR Tadami Line's Hirokami stn. Regular seats about ¥1,000, front 'box' seats about ¥2,000; not much difference between two.

PERSONAL DATEBOOK
NIIGATA KANKO-KA ☎(025)-258-5511 — NAGANO ☎(0261)-321-0111

January
2nd Sat-Sun, *Ame-ichi,* Candy Fair, Matsumoto City, Nagano.

14 *Kento-sai* lanterns Sanjo City, Niigata.

February
All Ice-sailing Matsubara-ko lake, Nagano.

3 Honjo-ji temple *Setsubun,* Sanjo City, dance of five demons, Nagano.

10-11 *Muika-machi* snow festival Niigata

3rd Fri Big snow fete, Tokamachi temple snow sculptures, carnival, fireworks.

3rd Sat *Donzuki Matsuri,* Shibata City, *fundoshi*-clad youths fight in river, purify.

22 Memorial to geta clogs, Tsukioka Onsen 3,000+geta in giant bonfire, Niigata.

March
3 *Hadaka Oshiai Taisai* naked fete Fuko-ji T Urasa, Yamato-cho, *fundoshi*-clad, Niigata.

Early Oritate Onsen fete, 108 sandals fire exorcise sins, Okutadami-cho, Niigata.

17 *Hoha-sai,* Hotaka Shrine, Hotaka Town, arrows shot at bull's eye for luck; Nagano.

April
3 *Oyazawa Sanba-so* puppet Noh, Oyazawa Suwa Myojin shrine, Koumi-cho JR Koumi bet Kiyosato & Komoro, Nagano.

2nd Sat-Sun, National *Chindon-ya* Contest Toyama: fabulous fun! (*see* p.936).

Mid *Oiran-dochu* 100+ geisha parade, wear 35kg, peak blossom, Bunsui-machi N of Teradomari. Camera must, Niigata.

24 *Doburoku* copious sacred sake, Gozaishi Jinja, Chino-shi, SE Kami-Suwa Nagano.

29 *Fire walk* Yamato-machi Niigata, Mt Hakkai, 10am, info ☎(0257)-77-3111.

May
15 Hachiman Spring Fete Sanjo city, Niigata, immense samurai procession.

June
1st Wknd kite war Igarashi R Sanjo Niigata

14-16 *Enma-ichi* outdoor mart 500+ stalls, Kashiwazaki city; 8am-10pm, Niigata.

25-30 *Chinowa Matsuri,* Yahiko Jinja, go thru *chinowa* straw ring, rids ills, Niigata.

30th-Jul 3 Kanbara Jinja shrine fete, Niigata city, hundreds of outdoor stalls.

July
1 *Fire-walking* Hakkai-san shrine, 10am, at Muika-machi trailhead; ☎0257-73-6672.

6-7 Murakami C, 14 sacred horses, Niigata.

15 *Yabusame* mounted archery, Kinpu Jinja shrine, Nagaoka city, Niigata.

24-26 Kashiwazaki City *Gion Fest,* 1000s dance thru town, fireworks, Niigata.

25 Yahiko Vill Lantern Fest, 25 men lug 10 giants; hilite 9 day (**18-26**) fete Niigata.

First Sat Matsumoto gala *Bonbon* festi, dance nitely, fireworks, laser show, stalls.

Even year Japan Design seminar, worth look: inq Osaka ☎(06)-346-2611, Nagano.

End Muika-machi town festival, Niigata.

August
1st Sat eve, *Binzuru Festival,* Nagano C, Chuodori St to Zenkoji, all dance till 9pm.

1st Sun Horse races, Taka-botchi Kogen Plateau btwn Suwa-Shiojiri, farm horses in old-fashion day at races; check details at City Office ☎(0263)-52-0280, Nagano.

3 Nagaoka city fete 1st nite 1,000 dancers, food, game booths, fireworks, Niigata.

1-5 Toyama Festival, Toyama City.

4-5 Sanjo Summer Fete usual fun, Niigata.

7-9 Niigata City Festival, citywide fetes, fireworks, floating lanterns, etc.

8 *Fire walk* at Makihata Satomiya shrine, Shiozawa; ☎(0257)-82-0250, town off.

1-18 *Hasu* (Lotus) *Festival,* Joetsu city castle moat, Niigata.

14-15 *Fune-matsuri* Ship fete, Izumo-zaki -cho, colorful fishing fleet sails harbor; on land mikoshi, giant floats, Niigata.

16-17 Samurai parade, Joetsu city Niigata.

18 Arakawa-kyo Onsen fete, join bon odori folk dance troupes, fireworks, Niigata.

20 Tsukioka Onsen summer fest, Niigata.

27-29 Shibata City Fest, floats, Niigata.

September
Mid *Tanabata-sai* legend stars Vega-Altair weaver and cowherd, nationwide; here month late, week-long decor townwide.

14-15 Hachiman-gu Fete, Yamakita- town Niigata; amateur sumo tourney.

15 Kurohime shrine fest Kashiwazaki Niigata.

22-23 *Sanada Fest* Matsushiro, pm; kendo, demon dances, drum contest 'mum show.

Kikoriko Matsuri, wood cutters' fete, Taira-mura, N of Gokayama V, Toyama.

26-27 *Ofuna-matsuri* Boat Fete, Hotaka Shrine, Hotaka; maiden dances; boat fete at Kamikochi, but here cart shrine spirit around town in grand boat-float, Nagano.

October
20 *Fire walk,* Osaki-guchi trailhead to Mt Hakkai, Yamato-machi, Niigata spec bus Shinkansen Urasa stn; ☎(0257)-77-3111.

November
1-7 Nagaoka City Autumn Festival, hi-light show 'mums, potted & doll, Niigata.

1-24 Chrys'mum Fete, Yahiko T, Niigata.

3-8 Plant fair Sanjo Betsu-in T, Niigata.

5 *Ojin-sai,* prayers offered to salmon of Shinano River, Kinpu Jinja, Nagaoka.

*The enemies of the esthetic are neither the practical
nor the intellectual. They are the humdrum.*
— John Dewey, *Art as Experience*

SADO 佐渡
ISLAND OF EXILE

SHAPED LIKE flattened 'S', with top line Dai-Sado Sanmyaku (Great Sado Mtns), bottom Ko-Sado Kyuryo (Lesser Sado Hills)—linking both is flat Kuninaka Heiya (Mid-country Plain). Main city Ryotsu sits at bay east end of Kuninaka Plain; 18km away, at west end of plain is better harbor at Sawada town in more fertile area with rivers, more comfortable place to live as attested to by lofty denizens of Sado, exiles like 13th cent emperor Juntoku or Saint Nichiren from Kamakura. Tho Sawada is better suited to large town, Ryotsu got honors as nearer Niigata city, no prison-camp aura. With court struggles mostly over by 16th century, Sado lost status and became prison for common criminals during Edo era, kept around Aikawa near gold mines where they slaved until their time was up or they (most often) dropped dead. Seems fate chose Sado and Oki Islands (*see*) as sites of exile, since when creator-kami Izanagi drew his spear from primordial soup to create Japan from drippings, Sado and Oki were 'born' twins. Most visitors spend their limited time at Sawada, seeing Ryotsu or Ogi on arrival/departure. North and south coasts, on far sides of moutains, are dotted with fishing villages where wanderers can spend days in peaceful pursuit of nothingness.

GETTING THERE: By **boat** most popular is NIIGATA → RYOTSU, 2hr30min, 6-7x-daily all year (2nd class, ¥1,780) NAOETSU → OGI, 2hr30min, 4-5x-daily 4/1-11/20, 2x-daily 11/21-30, 1x-daily 12/1-3/31 (¥1,960); TERADOMARI → AKADOMARI, 2hr, 3x-daily 8/1-20, 2x-daily 4/15-7/31, 8/21- 9/30, 1x-daily 1/1-4/14, 10/1-12/31, (¥1,220). **Jet-foil** passenger-only runs NIIGATA → RYOTSU, 1hr, 6-10x-daily 4/1-11/5, 3-5x-daily 11/6-3/31, (¥5,460 o.w., r.t. ¥10,590); NAOETSU → OGI, 1hr5min, 2x-daily 4/-11/20, X-11/21-3/31, same fare. Weather strongly affects scheds—**Sado Kisen Co**, Niigata ☎(025)-245-5111, Naoetsu ☎(0244)-43-3791, Ryotsu ☎(02592)-7-5111.

For 30-45% over jet-foil rate, get **aerial view** of Japan Alps and Sado on local **airline**. Fly Niigata → Ryotsu 30min: **Shin-chuo Koku** 9-psgr planes 6x-daily Apr-Nov, 3x-daily winter, X-New Year, 4x-daily (¥7,210); no set scheds, Niigata ☎275-4352, Sado ☎27-3061. With Niigata airport 30min bus from town waiting time, air no quicker than jet-boats, but scenic, and good if flying into Niigata from other points, transfer can skip city. We prefer leisurely (and cheap) ferry crossing.

GETTING AROUND: Is mostly by **bus**. Trunk line RYOTSU → (35min) SAWADA → (20min) → AIKAWA 2-3x hourly 5:08-20:32 on central Rte350; as many runs on parallel route across S edge of Kuninaka Plain RYOTSU → NIIHO → HATANO → SAWADA in 1hr, few more daily this route but must transfer en route. We recommend this **southern route** as it has places to see. SAWADA → (75min) OGI on coastal Rte350 run 10x-daily; 2x-daily OGI → (2hr) SAWADA via southern port AKADOMARI (40min from Ogi). 3x-daily continue on S shore to OHDA where change to OHDA → RYOTSU run, 2x-daily. On N shore, RYOTSU → (70min) NE tip WASHIZAKI POINT, 7x-daily; AIKAWA → (80min) IWATANI-GUCHI 7-9x-daily, of which 2 end 20min from AIKAWA at SENKAKU-WAN; 20km span WASHIZAKI → IWATANI-GUCHI has only infrequent daily runs June-Oct. Other short lines help you get around if you can read *jikoku-hyo* bus sched picked up at bus stops. **Tour buses** exist, but take in mostly scenery in limited time, and we feel Sado deserves more leisurely pace.

Drive over on ferries, or **rent cars** locally thru Sado Kisen offices in Niigata (other firms also), Naoetsu, Ogi, Ryotsu, Aikawa. They also rent **bikes** (¥1,000/day), great for Sawada area, tho people have pedaled around Sado (210km along coast); tell them if keeping over one day.

We began in Ogi, meandering up-coast to Aikawa, then Sawada-Mano and across to exit from Ryotsu. But most people take more frequent Niigata-Ryotsu crossing by sea or air, so we cover island from...

RYOTSU: City got its name 'Double-port' in 1885 when former fishing villages of Ebisu and Minato (on either side of narrow opening linking Lake Kamo-ko to sea) merged and ferry service from Niigata began. Lake to ocean canal is relatively new, dug in early Meiji to create safe harbor. Until then Kamo-ko was freshwater, often spilling into ocean at canal site when water level rose. Boats have moved back outside lake and it is now saltwater breeding grounds for oysters which inns and diners serve Nov-March; most popular cooked in shell or raw (with lemon either way), but deep-fried and other ways. Ryotsu pleasant bustling town, boats dock S pier in Minato district, where main **bus** center, **car** & **bike** rentals tourist info center.

Streets around pier lined with mostly budget diners, more across canal Ebisu with fine inexpensive sushi joints like **Uoshin**, **Uoharu**, **Ishihara**. Thrice monthly streets come alive with bustling booths of **morning markets**, *asa-ichi*, from 9:00. **2nd** and **23rd** at Ebisu along Shinmeicho-dori street (1 W of main road); **13th** along Minato's Honmachi-dori street (1 E of main road), S of pier.

N of Ebisu asa-ichi site is...
Ryotsu Catholic Church, white chapel built by early Meiji French missionary. Ryotsu isn't overly Christian, but here church bells, rather than temple gongs, ring every morning and evening.

Famed *Sado-okesa* big-hat **dancers** and *Ondeko* and *Kodo* **demon drummers** perform almost every festive occasion, but those who miss fetes here can see staged demos nitely Apr 1-Nov 10 at **Okesa Kaikan**. ¥500 for 40min show from 20:30, inns in town have discount coupons which get you in for ¥300. Show includes Sado-okesa, Ondeko, shishi-mai lion dances and other local performance arts.

Sado's **Ondeko** drummers are better-dressed version of Noto's Onidaiko, but seem to have appeared here only recently, maybe imported from Noto where they began as psychological warfare against 16th century invader Uesugi Kenshin. Foreigners have joined, but it's like monastic version of marine boot camp with 5-mile runs every dawn, cold water baths, strict exercises to develop strength and timing necessary to make those great booms look so easy. If interested, need basic Japanese, good health, humility and persistence—and luck. **Kodo** is branch-off troupe, more international, appearing with Bantu colleagues and jazzmen; invite visitors but first: ✍ **Kodo Schoolhouse**, 526 Daisho, Mano, Sado Island 925-04, 2 months ahead, bit of self introduction, why want to visit, when, and await answer; ☎(0259)-55-2417. Building **Kodo Village** with hostel, etc, but won't be ready for few years; need donations. Subscribe to their fun quarterly newsletter *The KODO Beat*, make check out to Atsushi Sugano for $7 or £5.

WHERE TO STAY: 2 dozen mostly ¥-B-T inns dot Ebisu area; ¥-T-S inns along Lake Kamo, oldtimers began prewar as top restaurants are **Kagetsu** ☎27-3131, **Yoshidaya** ☎(0259)-27-2151, **Horai** ☎27-2141; new **Sado Grand Hotel** ☎27-3281, 1km W of town on promontory serves special dinner on yakata-bune boats on lake. Nearby classy old-timer **Shiiya** ☎27-2127, 80-year-old ex-merchant house, for spectacular seafood feasts off-season.

Alternatives within easy reach of town are 2 hot springs:

SUMIYOSHI ONSEN 10min bus S of town facing bay on beach, inns family style moderate **Yumoto Ryokan** ☎27-7511 to resort **Sado Seaside Hotel** ☎27-7211.

SHIIZAKI ONSEN is as far from town but on lake, half dozen inns. On W shore of lake is campsite, little hard to get to but quiet as no rental tents, swimming in lake. *Budgeteers* can usually get cheap room in town, or head 30min bus S down-coast to Higashi-kaigan area's **OKAWA** or **SUIZU** hamlets which have many minshuku and campsites. **Kawachi-so** at Suizu is lovely old ex-shipping merchant home. Best time to come this way is **Mid Oct–Mid Dec** when area celebrates *Ebi-kani Matsuri*, shrimp and crab festival, for which minshuku offer belly-bursting meals of shrimp and crab; ¥5,500w/2 or ¥3,000 for just food (served lunch to dinner). Book all above lodgings and shrimp-crab fest thru Ryotsu City **tourist info**, *which also books for...*

KATAGAMI ONSEN 15min from Ryotsu on southern bus across Kuninaka Plain to Tenno-shita stop and 10min walk S (or cab 3x-mtr) modern resort **Hotel Washington**, ☎22-2000. Sites around here: near bus stop **USHIO JINJA** shrine which main hall all over ornate carved woodwork, and old Noh stage where performances done for summer fete. Better stage is **Honma-ke Noh Butai** (10min walk from bus stop), in complex of Hosho school head teacher. Can just see stage, or call ahead to arrange for performance, ☎(0259)-27-7259. Nearby is *Hanashi-ke*, centuries-old **farmhouse** complex open to public. 5min walk from Hanashi-ke to Warekata Kannon-do bus stop, 1 towards Ryotsu.

10min bus W puts us in...

NIIBO where *Noroma-ningyo* **puppet** plays used to be done regularly at many sites, but now only at **Uryu-ya** where three men still perform each **Aug 14** at Nokyo (Farmers Co-op) Hall, or arrange for private performance at ¥45,000. Or stay at minshuku **Ohana** ☎22-3028, run by puppeteer Mr Ishii who shows his dolls and, if feeling up to it, performs. Puppeteer Mr Tsuruma lives just down street, his living room becomes theatre for private shows. Noroma-ningyo begun here 17th century by locals to entertain themselves, stories often ribald and humorous. Dolls are simple wood figures (usually clothed). Another form of puppet theatre here is *Bunya-ningyo*, using more detailed head-only puppets similar to Bunraku. Harder-to-do Bunya-ningyo died out, but revived early Meiji. 2-4hr show now done by Mr Honda & family at their minshuku **Kunimi-so** ☎22-2316 in fixed-up farmhouse at edge of town.

In town is...

KONPON-JI temple where exiled St Nichiren spent time. **SEISUI-JI** temple (30min walk S of town into foothills) is small version of Kyoto's famed, stilted Kiyomizu-dera to which affiliated. Kiyomizu-dera and Seisui-ji written same characters: former Japanese reading, latter Chinese. Nearby **HASE-DERA** temple is reputedly modeled after Yamato's grand Hase-dera; Kannon image here only shown once every 33 years. 40min walk S of bus stop at next town Hatano, or 10min bus which continues on to S shore **OHDA**.

SOUTHERN ROUTE: Bus hits western Mano Bay at **MANO**, 15min bus N of which is **SAWADA**. Both are popular places to stay, Mano has 7 ryokan and 8 minshuku, Sawada has 20 and 5; long stretch of **beach** spans two towns, most swimming done at either end (close to towns), with campsites. Book rooms thru **Town Hall Tourism Offices** (Kanko-ka), saves trudging to find one in right price range. **Sado Sports House**, ☎(0259)-55-2566, 15min walk from Mano bus stop has tennis courts, pool, track, gymnasium, go-karts; ¥-P at ¥1,300/room, ¥500/bkfst, ¥1,400/dinner. For ¥-S (from ¥10,000w/2) we recommend **Yahata-kan** ☎57-2141, sole inn at **YAHATA ONSEN**, midway Sawada and Mano; 40min bus from Ryotsu. On pine-covered rise, traditional inn with fine rooms and grand meals has large baths with glass walls facing out to private garden. Off-season, non-guests can use their bath, ¥600.

Museum, *Sado Hakubutsukan* (8:00-17:00, ¥300), nearby has assorted collection on Sado relating to history, life styles and pre-Yamato inhabitants; fine rock garden surrounds reconstructed farmhouses.

About 1km up-coast of Sawada bus stn is...
SAWADA ONSEN ¥-T Iriumi ☎52-3521, also runs adjacent minshuku.

WALKING COURSE: See Mano's sites (2hr30min) starting Takada-bashi bus stop (5min from central Shin-machi stop) on main S route: S down side road which takes you past Daizen Jinja shrine with 200-year-old noh stage, some small temples, to...

MYOSEN-JI Nichiren temple with garden and only pagoda on Sado, built 13th century by emperor Juntoku's attendant converted by Saint Nichiren.

Footpath shortcuts road, 600m W to...
KOKUBUN-JI temple where Juntoku spent his time. Present structure mid-17th cent, original 9th century foundations lie nearby.

Road 2km to Mano T, pass thru to next stream, road up past Mano-Gu shrine to...
Toki-no Sato Park grand landscape garden surrounding museum of Juntoku and Nichiren memorabilia, items from old gold mines, and section on local artist and ex-Living National Treasure SASAKI Shodo who cast figures by lost-wax style. Adjacent **restaurant** serves voluminous *Toki-no-teishoku* lunches (¥1,500), smaller seasonal teishoku (¥1,000), and various single dishes for few hundred yen. Toki-no-Sato is only 5-10min walk from town if cutting out earlier temple section.

10min walk beyond Toki-no-sato is...
Mano Goryo, burial site of retired emperor Juntoku who at age 24, forced to abdicate after 11 years on throne, was exiled here by Kamakura shogunal government. He spent 24 years on Sado— finally took his own life, but not before leaving behind several offspring.

SITES AROUND SAWADA: MYOJO-JI temple (20min walk N of Kaminagaki-shita bus stop, 2nd from Sawada Honmachi), is where Nichiren spent two years. Main hall with gracefully curving thatched roof built by Nichiren disciple Nissei; **'Founder's Hall'**, *Soshi-do* sits on site of Nichiren's grass hut.

600m path from temple leads to...
NIKUU JINJA shrine, with grave of Juntoku's 2nd wife. Between Road and Myosho-ji are two other Nichiren temples, HOKKE-JI and JISSO-JI with giant statue of Nichiren. **Reifu-kan** small tea house-like building up-coast from Sawada, built 1808 as school for children of samurai; fixed 1953. Short walk from Ikarijo-no-shita stop, 8min from Sawada on Aikawa-bound bus. Or **hike** over hill to Aikawa, path starts Sawane-shiraba stop 11min from Sawada; 1km walk from Reifu-kan past several **folkcraft shops.**

PERSONAL DATEBOOK: SAWADA has Kawarada-ichi *outdoor market* every 11th & 27th. About 250 tent-stalls set up by 9:00, stay open until sunset, sell everything from fresh fish and vegetables to clothing, geta, and folkcraft items.

AIKAWA has fun lanes to wander, often come across remnant Edo era facade. Unimportant fishing village until gold discovered in 1601, ensuing government-dominated gold rush turned it into rowdy frontier town. Most miners were convicts, few low-wage conscripts; nonlocal civilians mostly officials and guards, and 'entertainment'. Two brothel districts now in various states of disrepair. Magistrate's Office fared even worse, only few foundation stones remain in high school grounds.

About 200m N of high school is...
Museum, *Kyodo Hakubutsu-kan,* of mine-related items and other odds and ends. Brick W-style building built 1889 for new owner, imperial official. 200m SE of high school is long brick wall and bell tower of another old official building.

Few hundred more meters E, uphill, to...
Daiku-machi-dori, Carpenters' street, where some old buildings remain.

15min walk further uphill from Daiku-machi...
Gold Mines, *Sado Kinzan* has section of old tunnel open, with dummies of Edo period miners at work, **museum** nearby. Just beyond is hill with cleft middle, where gold was discovered in 1601. Soon after they found silver and copper and within years dozens of tunnels were burrowed into hills here. Mines prospered thru early Meiji when Mitsubishi (one of top 3 business cartels) set up here for while, but pulled out as profits shrank.

WHERE TO STAY: 2 dozen inns ¥-T–S. Better ones: old-timer **Sashu Hotel** ☎(0259)-74-3355, in classy old building; **Seishin-tei** ☎74-2019, ex-manse of mine's chief exec; **Musashiya** ☎74-3281 started as restaurant; deluxe **Royal Hotel Bancho** ☎74-3221, **Yamaki Hotel** ☎74-3366. Book at **kanko-annai,** main bus stop.

S of Aikawa on scenic Nana-ura Kaigan coast, lots of minshuku at Nagate-misaki village. Going N, up-coast of Aikawa are several quiet villages with many minshuku and campsites. **Hirane-zaki** even has hot spring water tapped from underwater fissure. Scenery is lovely, way up-coast at end of bus line **Iwatani-guchi** with dark sand beach and lush green paddies terracing down to ocean; minshuku **Genpei** ☎(0259)-78-2710 used to belong to shipping merchant, was used as inn for feudal officials of old *bugyo-sho* (circuit magistrate) from Aikawa.

OGI is fun port to pull into. Chances are you'll see kimono-clad women rowing out to meet your boat in tub-like *tarai-bune* 'barrel-boats'. Once common means of getting around rocky coast to search for abalone, seaweed, now solely for tourists. Lots of inns all rates. Landed here late afternoon found pleasant li'l budget **Kamome-so** ☎(0259)-86-2064 sole inn seaside **OGI ONSEN,** 20min walk from pier. Suggested by **Kanko-annai** at ferry terminal. Most minshuku at Yajima Point 1km W of town. *Sado-okesa* folk dancing nitely **mid-Apr-Oct** from 20:30, 2nd floor of Niigata Kotsu Building near pier. Island tip W of Ogi has sheer cliffs and craggy rocks, good view from 40min sightseeing boats from Ogi April 1-Nov 25; 12x- daily 7/21-8/31, 2-7x-daily rest of time.

On return get off at...
SHUKUNEGI rustic shipwrights' town (15min bus from Ogi). With only three minshuku, rooms may be hard to get during Sado's peak seasons of Apr-May, July-Aug, have Ogi Kanko-annai check before coming. Old elementary school converted into **Museum,** *Minzoku Hakubutsu-kan,* of local boat-building, odds and ends.

Short walk from bus stop is...
Shukunegi *Makai-butsu,* **cave** with 8 Buddha figures carved in walls reputedly by Saint Kobo-daishi, but probably by some other artist several centuries later.

AKADOMARI is smallest of Sado's ports, tho at one time most of Sado's gold passed thru here. Note house with small watch-tower on roof, built for early Meiji period merchant TANABE Kurobei who made Akadomari into 'modern' crabbing village. Handful of budget inns here helpful, as 3 of 4 ships arriving here do so late afternoon. Half-dozen more minshuku few kilos up-coast at Mushiroba beach.

PERSONAL DATEBOOK

January

3 *Ta-asobi shinji* Field-romping rites for good harvest, Hakusan Jinja S, Hatano.

February

6 Similar Otaue Shinji Rice Planting rites, Gosho Jinja, Akadomari.

April

– Month-long *Shima Matsuri* festival as spring hits isle, with music, dance, Jisake exhibits: main one listed below.

11 *Okura Matsuri*, Aikawa, sees yabusame mounted archery.

14 *Sanno Matsuri*, Hiyoshi Jinja shrine, Niibo, mikoshi parade, Ondeko drums.

15 *Akadomari Festival*, mikoshi and float parade, Ondeko demon drums.

– *Oda Festival*, Aikawa, shishi-mai, sword dance, barley-sowing dance.

– *Shinbo Festival*, Kanai-cho, yabusame, Ondeko drums, Bunya & Noroma puppets.

18 *Akadomari Festival* repeat of 15th.

– Hase Kannon Festival, Hase-dera temple, Hatano; gaily dressed and masked spirit on stick horse waves in spring, chasing out winter in Harikomi ritual, then Ondeko drummers, and offerings for good harvest.

19-22 *Sakura Matsuri*, Mano-cho.

21-22 Ryotsu Fishing Fleet Festival, parade of fleet around harbor while on land Ondeko, Harikoma, Okesa and such.

23 *Ichinomiya Matsuri*, Hamochi village Ichinomiya shrine; Tsuburosashi, stylized fertility dance, and Yabusame.

24-25 *Tarai-bune Festival*, Ogi; floating parade barrel-boats, Okesa, lion dances, Tsuburosashi.

25-26 *Okesa Festival*, Aikawa; many more local folk dances.

27 *Sawada Festival*, Okesa, feudal costume parade, giant lanterns and wheeled floats.

28-29 *Geino-matsuri* Art Festival, Mano; marks end of Sado's festive month with every type of performing art on Sado; only way to see all unless spend month here, but crowded.

Late in month for last day of rice planting, Kurumada gyoji 'wheel paddy ritual' when 3 women accompanied by flute plant rice in circular pattern in forgotten rite; at Kitau-mura village near NE point.

Apr-May *Shira-uo* whitefish season Mano.

May

5 Ryotsu Harbor Festival.

June

Sun first half June flowers at peak, Ohnogame promontory (near NE pt) is outdoor stage for Ondeko drums, Bunya puppets.

Mid Ushio Jinja's (near Katagami Onsen) grand fest offers Takigi Noh, outdoor torchlight Noh performances.

15 *Hamochi Festival*, troops of demon dancers with phallic wands from Sugahara Jinja & Kusakari Jinja (old Noh stage) shrines dance thru village, pass out sake.

15-16 Ryotsu Festival dances all main st.

July

25-27 *Kozan Matsuri* (Mine Fest), Aikawa. Among top 3 Sado's fetes, commemorates one day in year (25th) when mine workers could come to town; float parade, samurai procession, fireworks, and Sado-Okesa.

20th to August 20, nitely Sado-okesa for O-bon, Ryotsu port plaza.

Last Sat-Sun, special Noh performances, Honma Family stage nr Katagami Onsen.

August

1 Akadomari Harbor Fest, hilite is marine sumo, contestants wrestle on floating ring —if they can stay up long enough.

6-8 Tanabata Star Festival, (often celebrated 7/7 but by lunar calendar here) grand summer fete at Ryotsu; giant floats pulled thru town and left out for duration, fireworks at nite, 1000s lanterns fill bay.

14 Noroma-ningyo puppets (free), Niibo.

15 *Furusato-matsuri* Hometown-fest, Hamochi village (btwn Mano and Ogi) nitely bon dances, flea market 15th.

25 *Inakujira Festival*, Kitano Jinja shrine, Inakujira village S tip Nana-ura Kaigan.

28-30 Ogi Harbor Fest, *shishi-mai* lion dances, Ondeko drums, *tarai-bune* races. Fertility/harvest rite, long-nose demon w/ pepper-covered eggplant chases women.

September

15 Shimokuji Hachiman shrine, fest, *Hanagasa-odori* (flower hat dance), Ryotsu, 11–13-year-old boys don colorfully decked hats in offertory dance.

October

Mid-Oct–Mid-Dec, Shrimp and Crab Festival, Higashi Kaigan (*see* p.953).

15-16 *Mano Festival* features odd jizo-odori dance in which participants cart around stone jizo statues on their backs, many get up to 50-60kg, one is 120kg.

19 *Aikawa Festival*; Ondeko demon drums all day, Nat'l Okesa Contest from 1pm, torchlite mikoshi parade at nite thru town, ending Utou Jinja shrine to shoot divining arrow.

The train came out of the long tunnel into the snow country.
The earth lay white... — Yasunari Kawabata, *Snow Country*

TOHOKU 東北
SNOW COUNTRY

"IN WINTER cold winds blow down from Siberia, pick up moisture over the Japan Sea, and drop it as snow when they hit the mountains of Japan. The west coast of the main island of Japan is probably for its latitude (roughly Cape Hatteras to New York [*see* map p.1], or Spanish Morocco to Barcelona [*see* p.2]) the snowiest region in the world. From December to April or May only the railroads are open, and snow in the mountains is sometimes as much as fifteen feet deep."

So opens Seidensticker's fine introduction to *Snow Country*, and so we.

This region, which name translates East-North, is Japan's last great tourist frontier, even to most Japanese. To many, Tohoku (particularly bulk of it north of Sendai) is just to pass thru en route to/from Hokkaido. Those who do visit Tohoku fall into 2 categories: skiiers and bus-tourists passing thru natural spectaculars. Both spend but short time in Tohoku. Not many laze thru Tohoku, which makes it all that nicer for those of us who have entered back country to experience old rural Japan—so often seen in posters but elusive in real life. Whether in Tohoku for weekend skiing, or driving thru its natural wonders, or just meandering, everyone ends day soaking in hot onsen—one thing Tohoku doesn't lack. Almost any place you stop will be one, or have one nearby, and contrary to what most people say, there are numerous interesting places in Tohoku to stop in and visit.

Tohoku is made up of 6 prefectures: Yamagata and Akita up Japan Sea coast, southern Fukushima, Miyagi and Iwate up Pacific coast, Aomori at northern tip. Respective capitals Yamagata, Akita, Fukushima, Sendai, Morioka and Aomori provide comfortable modern centers for exploring back country, and slow pace of development has allowed these cities to grow into well planned metropolies with wide tree-lined avenues. Space and low cost, coupled with better transportation lures many high-tech industries to pump more life into area. Tohoku makes up 15% of Japan, almost 1/3rd (28.9%) of Honshu, but accounts for only 8% of national and 10% of Honshu population. Long, wet winters and 3 main mountain chains running parallel thru, it's easy to see why so it's empty. Yet, Tohoku supplies over 25% of Japan's rice, host of fruit & vegetable crops including 80% of apples.

There is no shortage of nature in Tohoku, with large National and Quasi-National Parks. Former are Bandai-Asahi NP in Fukushima, Iwate's coastal Rikuchu Kaigan NP, and Towada-Hachimantai NP spread across top 3 prefectures. Of 8 QNP, most popular is ski mecca Zao, others encompass choice tracts of coast and mountains with abundant hot spas. Bandai-Asahi, Zao and Towada-Hachimantai offer great hiking, but lose in height to soaring central Japan Alps, in spacious grandeur to Hokkaido's Daisetsuzan range. But then again, peaks of Tohoku are not as crowded.

Tohoku is blessed with hundreds of hot springs ranging from luxury resorts to one-inn spas you have to hike to. There are so many onsen clusters that if you miss one, don't worry, there'll be more just along way.

With hot springs come *kokeshi,* limbless carved dolls found nationwide, but most popular in Tohoku. Kokeshi make great gifts, can be found anywhere in Tohoku. There are also several kokeshi festivals, and exhibits thru-out Tohoku to help you get better idea of various styles. Varied in size, shape and color, there are 10 basic types, or guilds of *kijishi,* name given to kokeshi carvers but also applies to any worker of wood. These 10 are: Tsuchiyu Onsen guild near Fukushima, Yajiro guild at Kamasaki Onsen near Shiroishi, Zao Togatta Onsen guild, Zao guild at Zao spa, Sakunami Onsen guild west of Sendai, most famous Narugo guild to its north, Hijiori Onsen guild SW of Shinjo City, Nambu guild Hanamaki, Kijiyama guild mid Akita pref, Nuruyu Onsen guild near Hirosaki City.

GETTING AROUND

Main route up Tohoku links FUKUSHIMA, SENDAI, MORIOKA and AOMORI cities, following central Kitakami River with JR Tohoku Main Line, Tohoku **Shinkansen** (so far to Morioka, soon to Aomori), national hiway Rte4, and Tohoku Expwy. N of Morioka, Rte4 and JR Main Line veer E, via coastal Hachinohe; Tohoku **Expwy**, which begins OHMIYA (N of Tokyo), follows lesser JR Hanawa Line via OHDATE and HIROSAKI or use parallel Rte282. Planned branch of Expwy will follow main rail line via Hachinohe. Pacific coast from Sendai to Hachinohe is ruggedly beautiful Rikuchu Kaigan Coast—adventurer's course with little to offer of tourist interest, with so-so Rte45 for road users, rail users alternate between stretches of JR and local Sanriku Tetsudo lines. Second transportation trunk route links FUKUSHIMA to Japan Sea Coast's AKITA on JR Ou Main Line and Rte13, where they join Uetsu Main Line and Rte7 (both coming up-coast from Niigata) for rest of way to AOMORI via above mentioned Ohdate and Hirosaki. Spaced out roughly every 40-60km all way up TOHOKU and linking trunk routes are JR branch lines and parallel hiways winding thru narrow valleys, tunnelling thru mountains.

Trains, while extensive, are infrequent once off Tohoku and Ou Main Lines, tho most will have at least 5-8 round-trips daily and usually dozen. **Buses** pick up where rail leaves off, and while they, too, are infrequent, most match rail scheds. Zip thru main sites of Tohoku in comfort, but back country traveller must be leisurely, more by necessity than by choice. **Airports** near Sendai, Yamagata, Akita, Hanamaki, Misawa and Aomori, all with several daily flights from/to TOKYO's Haneda, OSAKA; AKITA Also links with Sapporo, while Sendai links to most cities in Japan.

Hitchhikers have best luck on Rte4 or 7, both of which have heavy truck traffic. Hokkaido-bound best on Rte4 with alternate **ferry** choice of NOHEJI which some truckers prefer to busy Aomori. Rte13 also sees much truck traffic. Other roads are hit-or-miss for trucks, but enough local traffic to keep you going. Other ferry links to Hokkaido: SENDAI → (13hrs) TOMAKOMAI, HACHINOHE → (9hrs) TOMAKOMAI or MURORAN.

Driving in Tohoku is pleasurable, with good uncrowded roads and miles of scenic toll roads thru park lands. While trains are extensive, car gives freedom of schedule and easy access to offbeat hot springs, great views. Signs abound, but outside of Expwy and around main cities, English is rarity. Good Japanese **road maps** abound, of which among top are **Japan Auto Federation** (JAF) books, but no one has good English and Japanese map. Best for non-Japanese readers is fold-out Handy Map of Tohoku by **Japan Guide Map Co, Ltd,** which shows and numbers all main roads, shows most lesser roads (no numbers), rail lines, cities also in Japanese, and city maps of all 6 capitals. **Nippon Kokuseisha Co's** Road Map of Japan has section on Tohoku, but roads not numbered. Both can be bought at English language bookstores in Japan, or thru Kinokuniya Bookstores in US (see book intro on Driving for ordering). JNTO color fold-out brochures on Tohoku and ones for each prefecture have good English maps as well. These will get you on right track, and once off main roads, little bit of character matching on signs and asking for directions will get you everywhere.

If Tohoku is first leg of Japan trip, **rent car** at Narita for whole trip (keep for Hokkaido if headed that far); first check drop-off fees if planning to leave it en route. Sendai is also good starting place for drivers, especially if you only want to drive part of Tohoku, for which we recommend: SENDAI → YAMAGATA → AIZU WAKAMATSU →

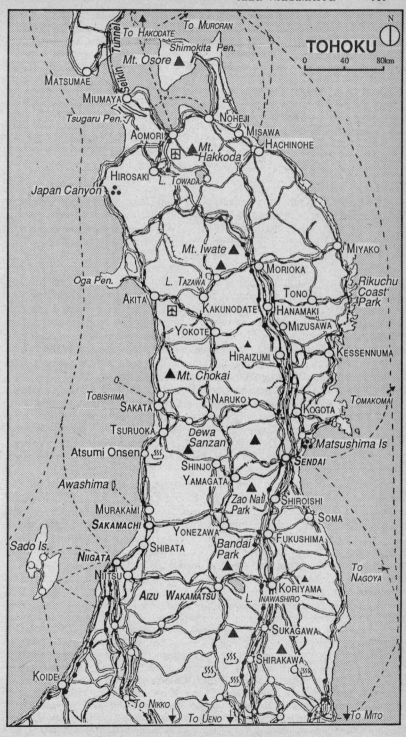

TOHOKU

0   40   80km

To MURORAN
To HAKODATE
Shimokita Pen.
Mt. Osore
MATSUMAE
MIUMAYA
Tsugaru Pen.
NOHEJI
MISAWA
AOMORI
HACHINOHE
Mt. Hakkoda
HIROSAKI
L. TOWADA
Japan Canyon
Mt. Iwate
MIYAKO
MORIOKA
Rikuchu Coast Park
Oga Pen.
L. TAZAWA
TONO
AKITA
KAKUNODATE
HANAMAKI
YOKOTE
MIZUSAWA
HIRAIZUMI
KESSENNUMA
Mt. Chokai
TOMAKOMAI
TOBISHIMA
NARUKO
SAKATA
KOGOTA
TSURUOKA
Dewa Sanzan
Matsushima Is
Atsumi Onsen
SENDAI
SHINJO
Awashima
YAMAGATA
MURAKAMI
Zao Nat'l Park
SHIROISHI
SAKAMACHI
SOMA
YONEZAWA
Sado Is.
Bandai Park
FUKUSHIMA
NIIGATA
SHIBATA
To NAGOYA
NIITSU
AIZU WAKAMATSU
KORIYAMA
L. INAWASHIRO
SUKAGAWA
SHIRAKAWA
KOIDE
To NIKKO
To UENO
To MITO

FUKUSHIMA → SENDAI circle includes **Zao QNP & Bandai-Asahi NP** and countless hot springs, optional detours of Shichi-ga-juku villages, Yamadera Mountain Temple, westward extension to Dewa Sanzan sacred peaks and Japan Sea coast towns Sakata and Tsuruoka. SENDAI → AIZU WAKAMATSU 140-180km depending on route, coast-to-coast SENDAI → TSURUOKA via Yamagata 125km. Train SENDAI → MORIOKA with stop-off HIRAIZUMI. Rent again at Morioka for lakes and mountains of **Towada-Hachimantai NP**, or breathe in salt air of **Rikuchu Kaigan NP** on following course: MORIOKA E Rte106 → MIYAKO village and **Jodo-ga-hama Beach** and rock formations (detour via Ryusendo cavern at Iwaizumi puts you on coast at Komoto 30km N), Rte45 down-coast to KAMAISHI iron town, Rte283 W to HANAMAKI ONSEN via rural TONO of folklore fame and back to MORIOKA, total 161km. Alternately, continue 76km past **Kamaishi** to thriving KESSENNUMA harbor then inland 48km to HIRAIZUMI via **Geibi-kei Gorge** (ride skiff thru) and **Yugen-do Cavern**.

WHEN TO GO

Unless you ski, avoid Tohoku early Nov to late Apr. Spring explodes with grand cherry-viewing fetes early May, but real draw to Tohoku are its grandiose summer festivals from late July with wild samurai horsemen galloping across fields at Soma, thru August's myriad lantern fetes. 'Top Four' (*see* DATEBOOK) all occur first week Aug. Summer festival season is best time to visit, but also most crowded and should book rooms if in towns at festival time. While most festival towns will have some rooms left for spot booking, chances are almost nil for 'Top Four' tho footwork, asking around and sheer luck will usually result in some room somewhere for persistent but nondiscriminating visitor. Autumn in Tohoku is beautiful, one of our favorite times to visit. Crisp mountain air rejuvenates especially at isolated hot springs; summer crowds have gone home, leaving behind great tracts of peace and quiet. Grand festivals still happen in fall, but first time visitors really should battle their way to summer greats.

In 3 centuries since wandering poet Basho passed thru jotting his poetry travel diary (translated), there has been relatively little written on this land. Even now we run across many literary romantics with copy of Basho in hand gazing at whatever scene had inspired that great poet. You can do same with Dorothy Britton's fine translation *A Haiku Journey: Basho's Narrow Road to a Far Province*, or our favorite, YUASA Nobuo's—tho more often than not, virgin trails which Basho trod are now busy hiways. For more practical info to really explore back country in greater depth than we do, resident Tohoku-ite Jan Brown's *Exploring Tohoku: A Guide to Japan's Back Country*. For budget-travellers, it picks up and continues beyond many of our off-beat runs in details only local could discover. Sendai draws many foreigners, and if planning to settle for some time there is English language guidebook compiled by locals, *In and Around Sendai*. JNTO has colorful fold-out brochures on all Tohoku, as well as one for each of 6 provinces, also some of their yellow 6-8 page brochures detail main sites of Tohoku; all available TICs.

Our jaunt up Japan Sea Hokuriku ended at Niigata, from where you can boat or fly to Hokkaido, in which case 'do' Tohoku top to bottom as follows: AOMORI → HIROSAKI → via Lake Tazawa and/or Towada-Hachimantai NP to KAKUNODATE → MORIOKA → HIRAIZUMI → SENDAI → Zao QNP → Yamagata Bandai Asahi NP → AIZU WAKA-MATSU from where you can now rail direct to Kinugawa Onsen and grand, gaudy NIKKO.

If **rail** up rugged Japan Sea coast (8hrs express direct NIIGATA → AOMORI), tourist interest are feudal towns SAKATA & TSURUOKA, nearby sacred peaks **Dewa Sanzan**, boat ride down **Mogami River Gorge**. Coast N of Sakata mostly for wanderers in search of nothing in particular—little fishing villages, sea. Cut inland at SAKATA on Rte47 or JR Rikuu Saisen Line to SHINJO on Ou Main Line, go up OU rte to AOMORI & HOKKAIDO or down Tohoku Main rte, leaving Tohoku by AIZU WAKAMATSU.

If coming up Pacific coast from Narita, we recommend via MITO, with **Kairaku-en Garden**, among top 3 in Japan, and 200-year-old **Kodokan school**, from where Rte6 and JR Joban Line hug coast to SENDAI, with alternate branch-off at TAIRA CITY on Banetsu Tosen Line and Rte49 cuts across inland to KORIYAMA, entrance to **Bandai-Asahi NP** and AIZU WAKAMATSU. Direct from TOKYO can take bullet to KORIYAMA 70min. Further up-coast beyond Taira is SOMA where each July sees wild horse festival.

TILT: Recommend leaving KANAZAWA morning express (8:10 or 9:16) 3.5hrs → NIIGATA or nearby NIITSU (10min earlier) for 13:44 train out of NIITSU → AIZU WAKAMATSU 16:28 in time for bath and dinner. Late leavers call Aizu inn or break at Niigata. Day and next nite in Aizu, bus or cab across Bandai-Asahi → FUKUSHIMA, bullet train 65min → Ichi-no-seki for HIRAIZUMI, 2 nites 1 day. Or 2nd nite MORIOKA (30min bullet) from where day-trip → Kakunodate and Lake Tazàwa, and/or rail MORIOKA → HIROSAKI (4hrs), then rail → HAKODATE or SAPPORO on Hokkaido. Return from Hokkaido can be **rail** (direct or down Rikuchu Kaigan Coast), **air** or **ferry** → SENDAI, then Shinkansen to, either UTSUNOMIYA for local JR run → NIKKO—or SENDAI-KORIYAMA where transfer → Northbound Banetsu-West line for AIZU WAKAMATSU (below) and on → KAWAJI hot spring and back entry → NIKKO and its surrounding hot springs for last 'taste of Japan' before bustling TOKYO, which we ease into by basing in old Shitamachi downtown, conveniently at UENO and JR Shinkansen, terminus of Tobu line from Nikko, or Shinkansen right into Tokyo Stn.

Our meandering route picks back up at NIIGATA where we board clunky old wood-floored diesel for 3hr ride thru wooded nothingness of Oku-Tadami wilderness (early riders can get off en route for few hours in Kitakata, see) for castle-town Aizu Wakamatsu.

KORIYAMA, 70min bullet or 2hr45min regular JR express from Ueno, is transfer point for Banetsu Saisen Line to Aizu Wakamatsu. **Kaisei-kan** lovely semi-Western style building, built as town hall 1874, now museum of local artifacts (9:00-15:00 X-Mon, ¥30); 15min bus W of stn.

Nearby...
Kaisei Koen Park is known for its 1,500 cherry trees which blossom sometime during **Apr 10-30** *Sakura Matsuri* festival. Rather than spend time here, we advise few hour detour to Miharu and/or Takashiba.

Locals say spring is most colorful at nearby town of...
MIHARU, which name 'Three Springs' comes from claim that plum, peach and cherry all blossom at same time here, covering castle hill park in clouds of white, pink and red. Most famous is 1,000+-year-old *shidare-zakura* weeping cherry tree—trunk 10m around, 13m tall. Miharu also known for its *miharu-koma* blockishly carved, colorfully painted wooden horses, *miharu-ningyo* papier-maché dolls, and masks. Walk around town center with many interesting old buildings, many of which serve as work-shop-stores selling Miharu folk arts. 15min rail (2 stops) E of Koriyama on Banetsu Tosen Line (from/to coastal Taira), 7min bus or 20min walk from stn to central Chuo Ohmachi bus stop. Chuo Ohmachi is also 30min bus from Koriyama stn-front. Another bus line via Hiwada; Hiwada-mawari, Miharu yuki, takes 40min...

But takes us via...
TAKASHIBA Village, cluster of 19 lovely old thatched-roof farmhouses, of which some are generations-old makers of folk art papier-maché dolls and masks, as well as carvings. Takashiba is living museum of old, rural Japan, and people here glad to show off their work to you. Area is called locally Takashiba Deko-yashiki, or Deko-houses, *deko* being local dialect for doll. 30min **bus** from Koriyama, 10min from Miharu; get off at Ohira stop and 15min walk. **Cab** one-way Koriyama from/to Miharu via Takashiba about 7x-mtr. **Drive** easiest Rte49 (parallel to rail) about 15km where Rte388 turns off to L to Miharu town. Then local road to Takashiba and back to Koriyama.

*...orgy of self-destruction was the salient characteristic
of Japanese behavior when confronted with defeat
and the prospect of capture.*
— Ratti & Westbrook, *Secrets of the Samurai*

AIZU WAKAMATSU 会津若松
WEST-SIDE STORY A LA SAMURAI

ONCE CAPITAL of 230,000-koku Matsudaira clan, established as castle town 1384 when Ashina clan set up here, losing out to Gamo clan 160 years later. Powerful Uesugi clan ruled briefly, but opposed Tokugawa at Seki-ga-hara and were displaced to smaller, nearby Yonezawa (which we visit next). Gamo was reinstated, but 3rd shogun Iemitsu wanted trusted ally near Uesugi, so sent half-brother MATSUDAIRA Masanobu to rule Aizu. Town thrived under Matsudaira, became bustling metropolis, many modern citizens proudly trace roots back 300 years. Shogunal ties strong; 9th and last lord Tadanobu was son of 14th shogun adopted into heirless Matsudaira clan. At 18, lord gained undying loyalty of adoptive clan when he led successful rescue of Kyoto to displace anti-Tokugawa advisors to imperial court in last years of shogunate. But Aizu was soon to pay for this affront to eventually-victorious Imperial forces. In brief Boshin Civil War following Meiji Restoration, Aizu men retreated home after April 1868 capitulation of Edo to Imperial forces and held out against superior forces for several months in climax of war. After fall of Wakamatsu, most of Tohoku rebels gave up, Shogunal navy fled to short-lived Republic on Hokkaido.

Most Wakamatsu historical sites relate to Boshin War and stubborn Aizu defense by some 1,500 local samurai plus as many renegade supporters from already-defeated clans, all sharing 500 muskets supplied by shogunate and 780 purchased from Dutch, plus home guard of boys, girls and old men. Facing them was new *Seigun* Western Army, over 10,000 of finest cannon-supported, gun-toting, European-drilled samurai from over 30 provinces. Having to defend 12 passes, defense finally gave in at Inawa-shiro Pass, August 23. Last line of defense there—*Byakko-tai* White Tiger Brigade of teenagers, trained in *bushido* but battlefield greenhorns—were mowed down by musketeers. 20 survivors fled thru drainage ditch to Iimori-yama hill from where they saw castle shrouded in smoke. Fearing it had fallen, all cut their own throats. 19 died, one found before bleeding to death spent rest of life in self-imposed shame trying to hide scar on neck, caring for graves of 19 comrades. Senseless sacrifice turned out even more pathetic: smoke was from houses below castle which, unharmed, withstood month of bombardment only to fall finally to lack of food.

In addition to graves of *Byakko-tai*, scattered around town are memorial stones to various other groups like *Joshi-gun* Women's Army, *Seiryu-tai* Blue Dragon Brigade of 36 to 49-year-olds and over-50 *Genbu-tai*; cemetery for *Seigun* dead; graves of countless men on both sides. City's grand autumn fete hi-lites parade of various brigades created for defense of Aizu. Locals still pride themselves in their hell-bent-for-leather attitude, call themselves 'people of Aizu' rather than 'of Fukushima', modern name, and like Wakamatsu, many places prefix name with Aizu-. Nowadays, their energy is directed at keeping Wakamatsu 'city without chimneys' and keeping up feudal heritage. City got boom in tourism: major TV network made 1987 year-long mini-series on battle for Wakamatsu centered on *Byakko-tai* and most of it was shot here on location.

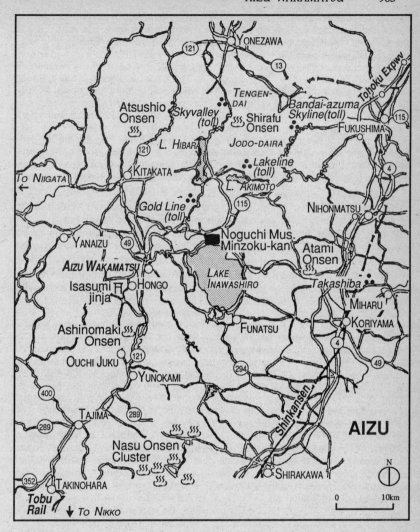

YONEZAWA

TENGEN-DAI

Atsushio Onsen
Skyvalley (toll)
Shirafu Onsen
Bandai-azuma Skyline(toll)
FUKUSHIMA

L. HIBARA
JODO-DAIRA

To NIIGATA
KITAKATA
Lakeline (toll)
L. AKIMOTO
NIHONMATSU

Gold Line (toll)

YANAIZU
Noguchi Mus. Minzoku-kan
Atami Onsen

AIZU WAKAMATSU
HONGO
LAKE INAWASHIRO
Takashiba

Isasumi jinja
MIHARU
KORIYAMA

Ashinomaki Onsen
FUNATSU

OUCHI JUKU
YUNOKAMI

TAJIMA

Nasu Onsen Cluster
Shinkansen
AIZU

N

TAKINOHARA
SHIRAKAWA
0   10km

Tobu Rail   ↓ To NIKKO

GETTING THERE: We approach WAKAMATSU from JAPAN SEA. Newly completed Tobu rail links end of JR Aizu Line to NIKKO and Tokyo's ASAKUSA, most popular route is to shoot up Tohoku trunk route to KORIYAMA (bullet stop), inland on JR Banetsu Saisen Line or Rte49. Rickety locals (80min) meander thru scenic countryside stop at toy-size stns give various views of volcanic **Mt Bandai** and **Lake Inawashiro**. After one set of switchbacks, train pulls off main rail to allow express to pass. Here, middle of nowhere, conductor calls out 10min break, at which time platform fills up with camera-toting train buffs who snap prewar wood trains with Bandai in back. En route is **Bandai Atami Onsen**, reputedly one of better hot springs around, but faded facades of 1960s concrete inns turned us off, and recommend you, too, pass for better baths to come.

GETTING AROUND: Bus and foot gets you to all sites in town in easy day, easier to deal with and fun way to see town is **bicycle** at ¥1,000/day rented thru stn-front **Urushiya Kogei** gift store by bus terminal or **Takahashi Shokai** 250m SE of stn. **City buses** round center of town clockwise and counter-clockwise, another does greater circle stn → Iimori-yama → Buke-yashiki → Castle → stn, also frequent runs via castle to

Higashiyama Onsen. Get *ichi-nichi josha-ken* **1-Day Pass** (¥770) at stn-front bus stop good for unlimited use in town. Tour buses are good, but for Japanese, and we do same in cab for same cost if 3 people, considerable savings if 4-5. **Half-day tour** starting pick-up at Higashiyama Onsen inn → Buke-yashiki → Oyaku-en Garden → Iimori-yama area → Yamada Lacquer Ctr → Castle is about 20x-mtr. Release cab at castle, continue on foot to nearby Sake Museum and short walk → **Takino** for traditional lunch, followed by stroll thru old merchant section of town and bus or cab basic-mtr back to inn. Or keep cab and follow lunch with trip out to nearby pottery town of HONGO (extra 5x-mtr); or kura town KITAKATA or time-forgotten OUCHI-JUKU village (add 20x-mtr for either). **Eki-mae** and **Nippon Car Rentals** (both stn-front) offer inexpensive half-day rates which allow you to cover same as cab for about half cost. Perhaps keep for 2nd day early drive to **Lake Inawashiro** and **Bandai Asahi NP**; better to return here, but check drop-off fees if return at Yonezawa or Sendai. Rail users tip: expresses stop only main stn, however, locals stop at two other in-town stns Nanukamachi and Nishi Wakamatsu.

20min bus from stn or cab 2x-mtr...
HIGASHIYAMA ONSEN is most popular place to stay in Wakamatsu. Quiet (except during week-long Aug bon dancing) river valley hot spring is just outside town. Spa's discovery is credited to 8th cent wandering priest Gyoki as named Teinenji Onsen in 1336, taking name of then-new nearby temple. Short walk upstream are several waterfalls, ropeway to top of 866m Mt Seaburi gives grand view of Bandai, Azuma peaks and Lake Inawashiro. Campsite up top. Look for grave to O-kei, first woman to immigrate to US, inscribed in English, died in Sacramento CA area 1869 at age 19.

WHERE TO STAY: 3 dozen inns range from smaller family-run (¥-Tw/2) ryokan to ¥-S 'hotels', which, despite modern fronts are fully traditional Japanese once inside. Furthest upstream **Higashiyama Grand Hotel** ☎(0242)-27-3500 has some W-style rooms. While larger inns mean larger baths, we prefer some fine old ryokan serving visitors for past century: 1st choice is lovely 2-storey wood ryokan **Mukai-daki** ☎27-7501 started 1873, rooms look out over grand garden with carp-filled pond; beautifully arranged dinner is Aizu's famed *sansai-ryori* 'mountain herb cooking' with carp or fowl. Just upstream and also on better side of river is similar, oldest **Shintaki** ☎26-0001. Can book any inn thru **kanko-annai** at rail stn or by bus stop in Higashiyama. Lunch on *sansai-ryori*, snack on local specialties with Aizu's famed sake, at **Tsurui-zutsu** restaurant, over 100-year-old house of village chief rebuilt nr ropeway by gaudy Tengame Hotel. Upstairs, hotel's kinky Kanki-butsu collection of Hindu religious erotica (¥200).

Penny-pincher staying in town, has usual run of Business Hotels, ryokan, minshuku; try minshuku **Higashiyama-an** ☎26-6014 at SE corner of town en route spa. Introduced to us by helpful stn kanko-annai, rooms were simple, bath miniscule, service minimal, but food was superb and lots of it. Inn also runs restaurant, where you have dinner and breakfast, and comparing what we were served to prices on menu items, our dinner of sashimi and tempura would have cost almost as much as our ¥-B charge for room w/2. Breakfast was equally sumptuous. You could always walk up about 20min to spa and use giant baths of hotels there. More service oriented and costing ¥-T old-timer **Tagoto Ryokan** ☎24-9182 in heart of old town near Nanukamachi stn, known for its cooking; friendly atmosphere, lovely interior with meals served around giant *irori* hearth—where you can also stop by just for lunch. About 40% less are nearby **Ryojin-kan** in old merchant manse and its women-only annex in stately old kura warehouse **Shukujo-kan**, both ☎28-4000.

We start our tour of town with early visit to...
Samurai Manse, *Aizu Buke-yashiki* (8:30-17:30, ¥600), reconstructed portion of chief advisor SAIGO Tanomo's residence, destroyed in Boshin War. We strongly recommend coming here early as it's popular with bus tours which file thru almost endlessly 10:00–16:00. Saigo family were chief advisors to almost every lord of Aizu since 14th century. Original house sat at castle's N gate; only living quarters, along with several other Edo era structures, rebuilt here 1978. Samurai drummer 'announces' visitors to

lord's mansion—central structure with rooms furnished as were. One room depicts tragic end of Saigo family and other high-rank ladies, who all chose suicide to capture. Clockwise around compound: water-powered **rice mill** brought here from nearby Shirakawa castle; two **museums** in kura warehouses; 150-year-old Nakahata Magistrate's Office brought from across town; Matsudaira family **tea house**; 15-year-old silkworm-raising farm house brought from Fukushima city which houses Jomon **museum** of 2,000+ excavated items; last 2 modern structures are **lacquerware shop** and Buddhist ritual items. Wakamatsu supplies 50% of nation's Buddhist items for bulk of city income, with much of rest from Aizu lacquer & sake. Good traditional restaurant **Kuyo-tei** here, but we suggest lunch in town, tho may want to try two interesting shops outside for snacks.

Buke-yashiki 10min walk downhill of Higashiyama Onsen or 8min from minshuku Higashiyama-an. Bus from stn to Higashiyama lets off in front, or some around-town buses stop at Yaro-ga-mae intersect in front of Higashiyama-an. Next main stop Iimori-yama few km N on route which few buses do direct—most via stn, or wait at Yaro-ga-mae for N-bound. Can usually catch cab front of Buke-yashiki.

In hills E of Buke-yashiki...
Mausoleum, *Matsudaira Go-byo*; TENEI-JI temple to N. Two snack stops en route to Yaro-ga-mae bus stop: first on R is **Ohide-chaya** tea house in tiny old folk house where guests sit around irori hearth snacking on skewers of *dengaku* (miso-coated tofu), *atsu-age tofu, nishin* (herring) or *sato-imo* potatoes, ¥120 per stick, ¥600 for set of 6. Further down near bus stop is **Yaro-ga-mae Chaya** tea shop.

Yaro-ga-mae intersect R branch (N) leads to Iimori-yama 2km, L branch (W) is 1.8km to castle.

We go 800m down middle branch (veer L next intersect) to...
Oyaku-en garden (8:00-17:00, ¥300), landscaped 1670 by 2nd Matsudaira who created medicinal herb garden in part of it. Lovely tea house overlooks pond in shape of character for *kokoro*, heart/soul.

SW of Oyaku-en is....
Hanaharu Sake Distillery, nationally known. As spring-time reaches Wakamatsu, age-old tradition of outdoor tea ceremonies is relived in Oyaku-en. Wakamatsu has long been center of tea, ever since city offered refuge to son of first Tea master Sen-no-Rikyu after Rikyu put to death by Hideyoshi.

Iimori-yama hill is where Byakko-tai slit bellies, now marked by their graves. Early pilgrims climbed long flight of steps to top, modern visitors take parallel moving sidewalk (¥200). Notice 2 monuments nearby, from Japan's wartime allies. One inscribed "To Aizu's young samurai from one German" gift of German military attache; Fascist Italy's spread-wing eagle atop marble column from Pompei, reads "To express our respect to those courageous young Byakko-tai men, the city of the birthplace of civilization sends this Fascist Party symbol with 1,000-year-old stone column, symbol of eternal greatness, to honor the Byakko-tai"; hidden from US Occupation, 're-discovered' late '50s. 6-sided 60m tall Sazae-do Conch-shell Pavilion is part of ENTSU-JI temple (ca 1750), now memorial museum to Byakko-tai.
Datebook: *Byakko-tai Sword Dance* **Apr 24**, and ends Aizu Festival **Sept 22-24**.

Takizawa Honjin (just N of Iimori-yama) was built 1668 as inn for travelling daimyo. MATSUDAIRA Katamori used it as front-line headquarters in Boshin War, and you can still see scars from bullets and swords in woodwork. Lovely old thatched-roof house (repaired 1979) is now small museum (9:00-17:00, ¥300). NW of Honjin is MYOKOKU-JI temple where Byakko-tai were cremated before buried on Iimori-yama.

Lining road to Iimori-yama are some interesting shops: 200m S is...
Morikawa Mingei-sha folkcraft store specializing in *aka-bekko* red bobbing-head lions, handmade in next-door workshop. Sold here, and at shops around town, are red-faced kites painted with fangs and huge tongue —called *Tojin-dako* or Foreigner-kites, were flown out of castle in Boshin War to show men in field that castle had not fallen. **Hondo Kokeshi-kan** (further S) is museum-shop of Tohoku's *kokeshi* dolls (*see* NARUGO, p991).

Crane Castle, *Tsuru-ga-jo*, still dominates town, but as 1965 concrete replica of original—which survived endless cannon barrage of Boshin War only to be torn down 1874 in government bid to erase relics of feudalism. Outer walls measured 2km x 1.5km (1.25mi x 0.9mi), ringed by 11 linked turrets—but everything beyond presently remaining inner moat became part of town leaving about 1/4 of original grounds. Enter compound thru N gate; en route is ex-samurai manse moved here when keep rebuilt. Inside keep is **museum** (8:30-17:00, ¥300) of Matsudaira clan items, Boshin War relics, excavated items from nearby Ozukayama Kofun tumulus; top floor panoramic view of city. 1,000+ sakura trees bloom **mid-Apr**. Fancy new Prefectural Historic Museum NE part castle grounds.

Sake History Museum, *Shuzo Rekishi-kan* (8:30-17:00, ¥300), is short walk N of Tsuru-ga-jo, with hard-to-miss white-walled kura building dating turn-of-century. Old fashioned way of sake-making is shown thru mannequins, but visit during Nov peak of sake making season and see it live—much same system except newer tools. This is sake vault of top class *Miyaizumi* brand, can taste all their various brews then wander upstairs to museum of sake paraphernalia. Clean mountain water and great rice, Aizu long famed for its *ji-zake* local brew. In Edo days, Wakamatsu supported 50 sake vaults, of which 23 still operate, most still man-mixing mash. If lunch time, continue N short way to Takino for *wappa-meshi* (*see* below). Shuzo Kaishu-ichi distillery in Yayoi-cho district 1km N of Takino has newly opened **Museum of Tea Ceremony Wares**, *Zohin-kan*.

Learn (or taste) more about sake at...
Aizu Sake Museum, *Shuzo Hakubutsu-kan* (9:00-17:00, ¥300), is in 400-year-old distillery of Kano family known for its *Konohana* brand. Part of museum dedicated to tools of various Edo period craftsmen and merchants (located 1.7km W, or NW of Nishi Wakamatsu stn).

300m to E (just E of tracks) is...
Honke Nagatoya, traditional sweets shop established 1848. Inside photogenic shop, workers still make all by hand, which you can watch.

1.2km N of Aizu Sake Museum, or just S of Nanukamachi stn...
AMIDA-JI temple is site of odd 3-storey **Osankai Pavilion** which used to sit in garden of Tsuru-ga-jo Castle, private meeting place for Matsudaira lords and advisors; moved here when castle dismantled. Buried here are 1281 Aizu casualties of Boshin War . Area used to be old pleasure quarters and still has some old houses intact.

Rte49 running E-W front of Temple is called Nanukamachi-dori Ave and has many interesting shops along it (*see* below).

600m N of main stn is...
Yamada Lacquerware Center, *Yamada Shikki Kaikan* (8:30-17:00). Massive lacquerware workshop here allows visitors to see all processes at same time, with artists at work all time. Store here also carries widest selection at competitive market prices; all labeled (in Japanese) as to what type of wood (or plastic cheap ones) used as base. While educational, we prefer family-run shops in town for shopping.

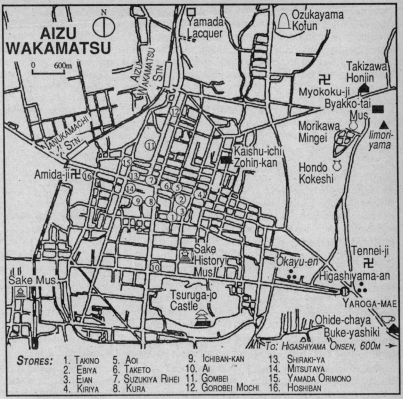

AIZU
WAKAMATSU

N

0   600m

AIZU WAKAMATSU STN

NANUKAMACHI STN

Yamada
Lacquer

Ozukayama
Kotun

卍 Takizawa
Honjin

Myokoku-ji
Byakko-tai
Mus.

Morikawa
Mingei

Iimori-
yama

Kaishu-ichi
Zohin-kan

Hondo
Kokeshi

Amida-ji 卍

Sake
History
Mus.

Okayu-en

Tennei-ji 卍

Sake Mus.

Higashiyama-an

YAROGA-MAE

Tsuruga-jo
Castle

Ohide-chaya
Buke-yashiki

To: HIGASHIYAMA ONSEN, 600M →

STORES:

1. TAKINO	5. AOI	9. ICHIBAN-KAN	13. SHIRAKI-YA
2. EBIYA	6. TAKETO	10. AI	14. MITSUTAYA
3. EIAN	7. SUZUKIYA RIHEI	11. GOMBEI	15. YAMADA ORIMONO
4. KIRIYA	8. KURA	12. GOROBEI MOCHI	16. HOSHIBAN

CHOPSTICKS: **Takino** is lovely old ex-daimyo rest house brought here from countryside. Guests sit around *irori* hearth eating *wappa-meshi*, dish name derived from *wappa* wood box which is filled with *meshi* rice cooked with various fresh herbs. Toppings are *zenmai* (fern shoots), *kinoko* (mushrooms), *tori* (seasonal fowl), *gyu* (beef) or *ayu* (river trout), served with miso soup and pickles, all for ¥1,000-1,500. At 5-31 Sakae-machi, known to all. If from castle, keep going N and 3rd L past Sake Museum, next R and its on R one block up. Just N of Takino is smokey old grilled eel shop **Ebiya**, serving satisfied customers for 4 generations. Two good noodle joints: antique **Eian**, btwn Takino and Ebiya; and **Kiriya** on Nanukamachi-dori.

SHOPPING: Most fun along Nanukamachi-dori Ave—listed below are some of better known stores, many in original centuries-old buildings. At NW corner of Nanukamachi-dori intersect (N of Ebiya) is **Aizu Aoi** traditional sweets shop in sturdy kura building. Heading W, next is 160-year-old **Taketo bamboo** goods in old wood shop. Next is **Suzukiya Rihei** folkcrafts, its lacquered wood front marks it one of oldest lacquer workshops in town, tho now sells other items as well. Their private **museum** (¥100) has fine collection of lacquerware spanning many centuries, as well as from Southeast Asia. Off Nanukamachi-dori, 1 block S of Suzukiya Rihei on main Shinmei-dori street is cluster of coffee shops, of which interesting are **Kura** and **Aizu Ichiban-kan**, both in refurbished kura warehouses. Ichiban-kan belonged to family of world-famed bacteriologist Noguchi Hideo, whom we meet again at Lake Inawashiro. **Kura**, R on Shinmei-dori, is loaded with antiques and folkcrafts; run similar sister store, **Ai**, on down Shinmei-dori near castle.

Back on Nanukamachi-dori, next street heading N (between Morikawa ryokan and Osakaya Hotel) is Ohmachi-dori leading to stn. About 300m up it is **Gombei**, sake shop featuring all *ji-zake* local brands, with assorted folkcrafts displayed; next door is **Oshima Hanbei** lacquer store. 500m beyond are more fun shops like **Maruichi Saito Shoten** folkcrafts and **Gorobei-mochi** sweets shop. Back on Nanukamachi-dori, past Osakaya Hotel is another lacquerware store, 300-year-old **Shirakiya** which also has private collection (free to see). Next intersect, on L is hoary 150-year-old **Mitsutaya** miso shop where you can nibble on *miso-dengaku* miso-tofu cooked on skewers over open *irori* hearth, or grilled trout, among various choices. R at this intersect 2 short blocks is **Yamada Orimoto** for Aizu *momen*, indigo-dyed cotton fabric, now fashioned into everything from coin-purses, neckties to placemats and shirts. It's about 500m W from Mitsutaya to above-mentioned Amida-ji temple, before reaching which is old fashioned painted-candlemaker **Hoshiban**—doubles as, more obvious as, cosmetics store. Between it and temple are classy moderate inns **Shukujo-kan** & **Ryojin-kan**.

WHERE NEXT: Tour local area with many interesting towns (below), or if en route down from Hokkaido advise continue on Banetsu West JR to its new link with Tobu line and on thru mountains into Nikko—stopping perhaps at Kawaji or Kinugawa Onsens for nite before Nikko, or on into Nikko for good digs there or above at Lake Chuzenji.

3 stops (14min) JR from Wakamatsu on Tadami Line; or 35min bus from Wakamatsu stn-front (bus, rail staggered); or about cab 4x-mtr one-way is...

HONGO, 400-year-old pottery town got its start in 1593 when GAMO Ujisato rebuilt Tsuru-ga-jo castle and 'volunteered' Hongo villagers to make roof tiles, since suitable clay was found nearby. Conscripted again in 1643 when Matsudaira Masanobu enlarged castle; but this time skilled potters from Nagoya's Seto village were brought here to teach local potters skills other than tile-making. Today, sleepy town has 12 families still operating own kilns where you can watch or make own pots.

Ceramics Museum, *Tojiki Kaikan*, displays works of all potters; sells their wares. First sun Aug is Seto-ichi open air market with wares sold cut rate.

4km SW of Hongo (or 25min walk or 8min bus from next JR stop Aizu Takada) is...

ISASUMI JINJA shrine, 1,300-year-old, 2nd-ranked shrine in all Tohoku. New **Treasure House** displays treasures offered here over centuries. July 12 *Otaue-sai* Rice Planting Festival is one of most colorful in Japan.

OUCHI-JUKU (20km S of Wakamatsu) is well-preserved feudal era lodging hamlet; on old pedestrian hiway Aizu Nishi-kaido, to Edo via Nikko, route used by Aizu and Yonezawa lords on annual compulsory visit to Edo castle. During Edo period Ouchi-juku had over 60 houses (half of which were inns) and thriving pack-horse business of 200 animals for rent to supplement busy trade route. 1884 new road (now Rte121) completed along Ohkawa River, marking decline of Ouchi-juku. Later completion of rail further isolated hamlet left behind in last century. Now 40-odd houses still remain (dozen are **budget inns**), flanking narrow dirt road. Old Honjin inn for daimyo in center of hamlet has been fixed up as Local **History Museum**, *Machinami Tenji-kan* (¥200). One of best such preserved villages, historic interest in Ouchi-juku has warded off modernization, allow visitors to experience unspoiled beauty of rural Japan.

GETTING THERE: Still hard to reach: 75min walk or 15min cab (3x-mtr) W of JR Yunokami stn, 6 stops (55min) on JR Aizu Line, or 1hr bus. Driving or by cab can easily fit into half-day tour; full day by rail or bus, or spend nite at excellent ¥-B minshuku: just show up and ask around for room; or call ahead to nearby Town Office ☎(0241)-67-2111 to arrange; or call direct.

WHERE TO STAY: Choices are **Matsukawaya** ☎68-2918, **Matsumotoya** ☎68-2919, **Daikokuya** ☎68-2003. Advise call ahead during slack season to ensure meals. Only time all rooms may be full is for Ouchi-juku's grand summer fete, *Bange Matsuri* July 7-8: begins morning with lion dances, float procession and daimyo-gyoretsu recreates lord's travelling procession. From 1pm, offertory procession to Takakura-gu Shrine to console spirits of fallen Heike of 10th century civil war. Ouchi-juku established by remnants of defeated Heike, as were other settlements in back country of Japan. Centuries later during Nanboku (North-South) War of imperial succession, son of renegade emperor Go-Shirakawa reputedly hid at Takakura-gu Shrine en route to allies in Niigata.

Alternative is to stay at...
YUNOKAMI ONSEN, 10min walk from stn. 6 ¥-lo-T ryokan and as many ¥-B minshuku draw hot water from riverside springs. Fishing is said to be good here, or just soak in outdoor baths by river.

Ouchi-juku and Yunokami good overnite for slow traveller headed down to Nikko. Aizu Line continues another 15km to Aizu Takinohara where joins Tobu Rail to Nikko. Halfway to Takinohara is Aizu Tajima town, bus center for trips out to Oku-Tadami wilderness, ideal for campers.

While waiting for back country bus, visit...
Local History Museum, *Rekishi Minzoku-kan* housed in 2-storey W-style District Office, 1885, displays everyday tools of residents.

1hr45min SW of Tajima is...
HINOEMATA village, another rural hideaway much of year, 30-odd ¥-B inns rarely even close to full. That is, other than 2 days in year when amateur **village Kabuki** on boards. Tradition dates back to late 18th cent and repertoire is all from that period; **May 12** performance at ATAGO JINJA shrine, **August 18** is at SHIZUMORI JINJA shrine. While there is always room for rare foreign visitors can assure seat and room for night by calling ahead to village tourist office ☎(024175)-2432. 4 daily buses TAJIMA → HINOEMATA; drivers take Rte121 to Tajima, W on Rte289 to local road S to Rte352, or Rte121 to TAKINOHARA and branch to Rte352, either way about 3hrs from WAKAMATSU. Optional return is Rte352 and local road to Rte289 which veers NW to TADAMI town and Rte252 to WAKAMATSU. There are several rural hot springs around Tadami.

20km NW of Wakamatsu (35min on JR Banetsu Saisen Line)...
KITAKATA, interesting town of 2,000+ buildings of sturdy *kura* style. Most are variations on traditional thick mud walls with plaster coating, but later ones of brick look distinctly 'foreign'. Located in fertile basin with many rivers, Kitakata became natural place to gather and store rice and other crops before being shipped to Edo, and so, kura, which are fireproof and yet remain cool, were built here. Numbers increased as kura proved to be excellent for production and storing of miso and sake, as well as for thriving lacquer trade supplied by woodsmen of nearby mountains. It soon became fad as everyone started building everything in kura style, from outhouses to temples. After early Meiji conflagration when kura proved to be indeed fireproof, kura production exploded. About that time Kitakata began mass production of bricks, needed for construction of rail tunnels and bridge supports, and wasn't long before home-builders got wind of this inexpensive yet exotic material. Kitakata can be done in half-day from Wakamatsu, but once here (and especially if using your camera) you can easily spend whole day, especially if taking in suburbs.

Kura are all over town, but best stretch is along Chuo-dori street parallel to, and to R (E) of stn-front road. There is another clump of kura in Higashimachi district just E across river, which has **Aizu Lacquerware Art Museum**, *Urushi Bijutsu Hakubutsu-kan*. Also on river's E side but further N are suburban kura hamlets of **Mitsuya** with many brick ones, **Sugiyama** with its kura farmhouses. Take Hirasawa-bound bus from stn (roughly every 90min), 15min to Mitsuya Iriguchi and 5min walk to reach Mitsuya; Sugiyama is few minutes bus beyond to Naosato and 10min walk; drivers NE on Rte121.

GETTING AROUND: Most enjoyable to get map at stn **kanko-annai** and walk around town; take **horse-drawn cart** across to Nishimachi area N end of town and walk back or do full circular route, carts depart few times daily from stn-front gift shop Kai Shoten, ¥1,300 for 1hr30min r.t.; or rent **bicycles** at ¥250-hour from stn-front Sato. Only recently exposed to tourist boom, more kura shops are opening up to visitors and creating small **museums**. There are **Nakano Echigoya**, and **Shimashin Shoten** on Chuo-dori next to Green Hotel, **Yamatogawa Shuzo** sake distillery in center of town with its brick chimney, and Nishimachi's **Kai Honten** (¥260) grand kura house with 'Western' room doubling as coffee shop. **Kura-no-Bijitsukan** at ANSHO-JI temple N of stn on is kura style, and just before it is kura **Shingin Bank**.

WHERE TO STAY: Kitakata has dozen ¥-B–T inns which you can book thru **kanko-annai**, most popular of which is old kura style **Sasaya Ryokan** ☎(0241)-22-0008 on Chuo-dori. Nonguests can come for tea and look around. Alternate lodgings are nearby mountain hot spas deadend **ATSUSHIO ONSEN** or **OSHIO URA-BANDAI ONSEN** both 30min bus N and each with half dozen ¥-T inns each. Drivers can continue 8km E of Oshio Ura-bandai Onsen to **Hosono** village at Lake Hibara.

30min rail or hour bus E of Aizu Wakamatsu...
LAKE INAWASHIRO offers all sorts of recreation: swimming, sailing, row- or motor-boating, sightseeing cruises, so-so skiing in nearby hills in winter when swans migrate here. 150-plus ¥-B minshuku and several campsites scattered around lake, tho most everything concentrated along N shore near main town **Inawashiro** (around stn) and **Nagahama** village (on lake), with good **camping** at **Tenjin-hama** (15min bus E of Inawashiro stn). Or you can stay at any of half-dozen small onsen which draw hot water from volcanic Mt Bandai, such as **OTTATE ONSEN** which has Kokumin-shukusha **Sagi-no-yu** ☎(0242)-65-2515, ryokan and minshuku.

NAGAHAMA was summer retreat for imperial prince Arisukawa-no-miya, and his grand W-style villa **Tenkyo-kaku** built 1904 still stands, open (9:00-17:00 X-Mon, ¥300). Nearby similarly imperial **Geihin-kan**—not yet open to public. Nagahama is 20min bus from Inawashiro stn-front, or 40min from Wakamatsu stn-front.

5min bus E, towards Inawashiro stn is...
Memorial Museum, *Noguchi Kinen-kan* (8:30-17:00, ¥300), dedicated to Dr NOGUCHI Hideyo (born Noguchi Seisaku), bacteriologist who first isolated causative agent of syphilis and worked on various other diseases, including vaccine and serum for yellow fever, which he died of in Accra (now Ghana) Africa on May 21, 1928. Dr Noguchi was born here Nov 24, 1876 into poor farming family, and with help of local teachers who recognized his abilities he graduated from medical school in Tokyo, then went to University of Pennsylvania in 1900, Rockefeller Institute for Medical Research in New York in 1904, which sponsored his work until his death. Enter museum thru modern Memorial hall which contains his tools, writings and personal belongings; in back is his preserved house where he was born. Note large *irori* hearth where he severely burned left hand as child, leaving it virtually useless.

Folk Museum, *Aizu Minzoku-kan* (8:00-17:00, ¥500), is adjacent complex of several old folk houses from countryside. Characteristically L-shaped homes called *Magari-ya*, bent-houses, were so built to protect valuable horses. Humans lived in longer segment, horses in short leg. Houses are full of folk arts and crafts, essentials of farmers, other displays. Many tours ignore phallic rock garden on grounds—fun to see, gives good idea of importance of fertility rites in rural society.

Next to Minzoku-kan is **Seisaku Chaya** restaurant in classic old farmhouse, serves traditional Aizu sansai-ryori of fresh mountain herbs and various meats.

BANDAI KOGEN PLATEAU, in mountains behind Lake Inawashiro, is heart of **Bandai-Asahi National Park** and worthy detour thru beautiful vistas. Smoking 1819m high volcanic Mt Bandai, rising above Lake Inawashiro, last erupted July 15, 1888 in series of 10 violent blasts within 15 minutes which wiped out dozens of hamlets and killed 477 people. Tho no lava flowed, debris blocked off rivers creating over 300 ponds and lakes. **Mt Azuma** (2035m) bounds plateau on N. Three largest lakes, W to E are: **Hibara-ko** (12.3km^2), **Onogawa-ko** (2.95km^2) and **Akimoto-ko** (4.16km^2). Myriad tree-covered islets clustered at inner points of lakes makes rowboating pleasure. Between Hibara and Onogawa are countless ponds scattered among woods and fields, numerous hiking paths winding among them. Spread between S ends of all 3 is area of numerous ponds called **Goshiki-numa**, 5-Color-Swamp, with easy 4km (1hr) scenic hiking trail winding thru.

N of Akimoto is...
Nakatsugawa Keikoku Ravine, best seen in autumn; dirt road parallels it for easy 8km hike to top of peak behind. We prefer this area over much-touted pine isles of Matsushima Bay near Sendai (p988) which we feel overrated. Spend extra time here instead.

Folk Art Museum, *Ura-Bandai Mingei-kan* (8:00-17:00, ¥400), compound with 3 reconstructed farmhouses full of various folk arts and folkcrafts. 3min walk from Ken-ga-mine bus stop, which is 2min bus or 10min walk N of terminal.

GETTING THERE: Bus from AIZU WAKAMATSU: 6-9x-daily from Wakamatsu stn-front via Nagahama, Noguchi and Minzoku Museums → Inawashiro stn (total 3-4 hourly from here) → then up local road via Kawakami Onsen, Goshiki-numa, Onogawa → Bandai Kogen-eki ending at Peoples' Rest Village. About 30min/¥780 from Inawashiro → Bandai Kogen-eki. 4-5 express buses go E → Fukushima City on JR Tohoku main & bullet lines, taking scenic route via 20km Bandai Azuma Lake Line toll road (¥920 for cars) and Bandai-Azuma Sky Line (¥1,540). We take local road between Hibara–Onogawa → Wasezawa hamlet at N end of Hibara, where 18km long Nishi-Azuma Sky Valley toll road (¥920) winds over Shirafu-toge Pass → Yonezawa City; 1 bus daily take this route, 2hrs Bandai Kogen → Yonezawa. Note: all buses to and thru Bandai Kogen operate only between Apr 23 to first half Nov.
    Other than local buses, use **cabs** to get around; cab stands at Bandai Kogen-eki, Onogawa and Goshiki-so inn near Goshiki-numa Info Office. Cab about 12x-mtr direct from Wakamatsu via Gold Line (+toll); or 17x-mtr via Inawashiro. Peoples' Rest Village has 100 rental **bicycles**, most minshuku have some, and places set up bike rental places at Bandai Kogen-eki and Onogawa; about ¥1,200/day. good 50km paved road encircles **Lake Hibara**, popular for drives and bike rides.

WHERE TO STAY: Small town of **Onogawa** is central, with school, post office and main **Kanko-annai** which has brochures on area and will book rooms; about 2km W is Bandai Kogen-eki, main bus terminal which also has Kanko-annai and also has pier for sightseeing cruises around Hibara. Lodgings concentrated around this middle section of park: ¥-S-L **Ura-Bandai Kogen Hotel** ☎(0241)-32-2211 near bus terminal is best choice with some W-style rooms. Best ryokan is **Banso** ☎32-2111 where all rooms are private cottages, each with own bath, between Goshiki-numa and Akimoto, has its own bus stop Banso-mae. There are many other less expensive ryokan around, and dozens of ¥-B minshuku and pensiones, Kokumin-shukusha **Ura-Bandai** ☎32-2923, **Ura-Bandai YH** ☎32-2811, and dozens of campsites. Ura-Bandai *Kokumin Kyuka-mura* **Peoples' Rest Village** ☎32-2421 has 2 main lodges, bungalows, campsite with various recreational facilities. Some small hot springs here, of which most interesting sounding is single-inn **Naka-no-yu** Onsen up at 1280m level of Mt Bandai; 20min walk W of Nekoma Happo-dai bus stop on Bandai Gold Line bus route, just 8min ride from Bandai Kogen-eki.

JODO-DAIRA PLATEAU, midway on Bandai-Azuma Sky Line toll road, gets 40min stop on local non-tour buses which is enough time to just look, or rush up and around **volcanic crater** of Mt Azuma-Kofuji (10min up, 30min around). Or allow for several hours here to hike around whole of area (7 buses daily allow much leeway): Bus Center → presently dormant **Mt Issai-kyo** → **Kamanuma crater lake** → **Uba-ga-hara fields** → **Okenuma crater lake** → Bus Center is 4-5hr easy hike. Jodo-daira 80min bus from Bandai Kogen-eki; 70min from Fukushima stn-front bus terminal.

Bustling...
TSUCHIYU ONSEN of *kokeshi* doll fame is on Rte115 running between Bandai Kogen and Fukushima.

FUKUSHIMA City, while prefectural capital, does not rate special stop, but if passing thru with time to kill between bus-rail transfers; interesting **Iwaya Kannon** (3km; 15min bus NE of stn) has 60-odd giant figures of Kannon carved into cliffside. Nothing special, but interesting to see example of folk Buddhist art showing intensity of simple devotion; date to late 1600s when local merchant commissioned them in thanks for prosperous business. Or lunch on delicious noodles at 150-year-old **Kitaya**, 1 block E of stn on main road.

25min by frequent local electric rail NW of Fukushima is...
IIZAKA ONSEN, popular but overcrowded hot spring spa (over 100 inns). *Sabako-no-yu* **public bath** is grand old bathing hall where one can still bathe for mere ¥50. If **staying** (we did not), highly recommended is hoary old-timer **Nakamura-ya** ☎(0245)-42-4050, 100-year-old sturdy kura style building, ¥-T.

PERSONAL DATEBOOK: **July 23-25** head to coast on Rte115 to **SOMA** for annual *Wild Horse Chase*. Originated as round-up for mounted samurai of Soma clan who raised wild horses in plains of Soma. By early 1600s with peace in Japan it had become more of celebration, took present form after Meiji Restoration. Actual festival takes place at **Hara-no-machi** town, 20km down-coast. By July 23, mounted samurai in armor gather from all over Japan into opposing camps, parade thru town 24th-main event Hibarigahara race track as teams compete in various equestrian events.
Get there Hara-no-machi on JR Joban Line, 2hr20 from Mito, 1hr from Sendai.

SHIRAFU ONSEN, backwoods hot spring at 1350m level on Mt Nishi-Azuma; popular, yet retaining its rural atmosphere. Main 3 inns have been around for several generations; honkan main buildings of each are traditional rambling thatched roof houses; all also have new bekkan annexes. They are oldest **Higashiya** ☎(0238)-55-2011 which was favored by Yonezawa lords, **Nakaya** ☎55-2111, **Nishiya** ☎55-2211; fine service at ¥-T (¥8,000-12,000w/2). Budgeteers have **Shirafu Kokumin-shukusha** ☎55-2207, sole minshuku **Shirafuya**, and **Azuma Sanso** 5min ropeway ride (¥450) to Tengen-dai Plateau, which has **Tengendai Hotel** ☎55-2231 with W-style rooms, runs annex **Tengendai Lodge** for budgeteers.

Tengen-dai Ski Resort boasts good powder snow for downhill thru eery snow-scapes December thru May. Light travellers can leave Wakamatsu in morning, spend day at Inawashiro and Bandai Kogen, to catch bus 14:30 to reach Shirafu 15:40. It's only 45min bus to Yonezawa.

Hikers can cross over Mt Azuma chain on well-marked trails from Bandai Kogen (continue on Nakatsugawa Keikoku trail), or Jodo-daira; either route about 6hrs.

"You will soon become accustomed to the Japanese way of life", said Tiger.
"It's their way of death that's got me a little puzzled", said Bond amiably.
—Ian Fleming, *You Only Die Twice*

YONEZAWA 米沢 & SENDAI 仙台
MUMMIES AND SHAMANS

YONEZAWA, EDO ERA capital of once-powerful Uesugi clan. Ironically, it took defeat of clan to make it into town of importance. In mid-1500s, as warring factions in Japan were beginning to form powerful alliances, lord of Echigo, Kagetora, managed to have himself appointed Guardian of Kanto, took over Aizu Wakamatsu, much of Noto and Kaga creating fief of 1.2 million-koku—land enough to grow rice to feed 1.2 million people. Kagetora changed his name to Uesugi Kenshin, and tho distantly related to Tokugawa Ieyasu, sided with Toyotomi Hideyoshi, his son Kagekatsu was on Hideyoshi's Council of 5—thus on losing side at Battle of Sekigahara, and Uesugi clan lost all Japan Sea coast holdings, were kicked out of Aizu, left with only 300,000-koku Yonezawa domain. Suddenly impoverished and with no wars to fight, lesser samurai became sword-wielding farmers to supplement income while wives took up weaving. Textiles were, still are, main source of income for Yonezawa. Locals are proud of their association with Uesugi clan, and their main spring festival (*see* DATEBOOK) is 5-day gala event honoring Uesugi, capped by fully and authentically armed recreation of famous Battle of Kawanakajima where Kenshin dealt severe blow to forces of Takeda Shingen, another prime contender for shogun, (*see* p293).

GETTING AROUND: Town is small enough to walk, full **tour** is 6km (2hr walking time), long half-day including sightseeing and lunch: Stn → **Joshin-an** temple → **Weaving History Museum** → **Sake Museum** → **Yamagata Univ** → **Matsugasaki Park** → **Uesugi Mausoleum** → 15min **bus** back to stn. Same can be done by **cab** for 5-8x-mtr including waiting time. Rental **bicycles** at stn-front Kanko-annai, ¥200/hr; particularly useful in exploring old lower class samurai neighborhoods Hosen-machi and Kayo-machi districts at SE fringe of town, which still have many old grand farmhouses of Edo era.

WHERE TO STAY: We spent half-day here, leaving in time to have dinner at our inn at **KAMI-NO-YAMA ONSEN** (25min local or 50min JR express), or at lovely **Goto Matabei** inn at **YAMAGATA** City (12-20min rail further). Yonezawa has many inns, but unless lots of time to spare, we recommend either of above choices. However, if staying, might try **ONOGAWA ONSEN**, 8km (30min bus) W of town. We have not been, but reputation is of quiet relaxation, dozen-plus ¥-Tw/2 ryokan. Book any room thru Yonezawa stn's **Kanko-annai**. Two nice budget public baths **Taki-no-yu** and **Ama-no-yu** give you chance to stretch out in big baths.

Buses to Onogawa Spa stop at N gate to...
Matsu-ga-saki Koen park (2km, 10min bus W of stn) occupies site of Yonezawa **Castle**—only moat and ramparts remain. Palatial manse now occupying grounds was built 1925 by UESUGI Motonori, 14th generation descendant of Kenshin. Now open to public as *Uesugi Kinen-kan* (9:00-17:00, ¥100), **Museum of Local History**, its garden one of top in town; enjoy traditional **dining** fit for lords, served in private rooms overlooking garden—perfect spot for lunch.

UESUGI JINJA shrine, enshrining Kenshin, occupies main area of park; nearby *Keisho-den* pavilion is **museum** of Uesugi clan memorabilia (¥300); **City Museum**, *Shiritsu Uesugi Hakubutsu-kan* (¥50), has rotating exhibits.

Just N across moat is...

Local Crafts Hall, *Kanko Bussan-kan,* where you get overview of local arts and crafts. Kiosk sells good quality, reasonable rates. Classic local toys are *sasano issai-bori,* simple but beautiful carvings of falcons; *sagara tsuchi-ningyo* clay dolls.

5min walk E of Matsu-ga-saki Park going out its E gate is best place for Yonezawa's main product...

Weaving History Museum, *Orimono Rekishi Shiryo-kan* (9:00-17:00, ¥200). Displayed are different types of looms, tools, dying processes used over centuries of silk weaving; many fine examples of *Yonezawa-ori* weave. Orijin gift shop 1st floor has great selection of various types of weave, fashioned into anything from coin purses to neckties to tablemats to wall hangings.

Next door...

Dewa-no-Oriza Sanko-kan museum (¥300) Simpler looking but more expensive cloth is made by primitive method 'imported' from clan's original home of Echigo. These are well represented here. Popular choice is red-dyed *Benibana-zome* weave, which dye comes from benibana safflower.

Drivers heading up Rte13 to Yamagata will pass...

Kanko Center *Yone-ori* tourist-oriented workshop and gift shop. It can also be reached 10min bus from stn to Fukuzawa and 10min walk, or 15min walk from JR Nukanome stn (2 stops N).

Block S of Weaving Museum, half-block E is...

Sake Museum, *Shuzo Shiryo-kan* (9:00-16:30, ¥300), better known as *Toko-no-Saka-kura.* Main brewery of Kojima family, official sake suppliers to Uesugi lords since 1597. See how sake was made in old way, and kitchen, main guest room and parts of living quarters have also been turned into well laid out displays. They still operate old style brewery Kojima Honten (about 500m due S at end of road) making select batches of top brand *Toko* which used to be reserved for lords.

Few minutes' walk W of Kojima Honten is...

Yamagata University Engineering Campus, in grand old Meiji era semi-Western buildings. Just beyond is **RINSEN-JI** temple known for its landscape garden (¥100). It's about 10min walk back N to Matsu-ga-saki Park.

1.3km W, 5min bus from park's N gate is...

Mausoleum, *Uesugi-ke Gobyo-sho.* Mostly of historic interest, lined up in row among towering *sugi* cryptomeria trees are ornate graves of all 12 Uesugi lords to rule during Edo era. Odd-number generations line up on L, evens on R, Kenshin is largest in middle of odds.

Short walk W of stn...

JOSHIN-AN temple dates to 12th century. Not outstanding in itself, enshrined here is mummy of founding priestess Baishin-ni who meditated herself into Nirvana.

LUNCH: Be served lord's meals at *Uesugi Kinen-kan,* **museum,** in private rooms overlooking garden. Traditional *kenzen-ryori* meal of fresh seasonal herbs, vegetables and fish with rice and soup runs ¥2,000-3,000; ¥4,000 meal adds sizzling platter Yonezawa steak, or thinly sliced beef sashimi. Yonezawa known for quality beef since American industrial instructor Henry Dallas took some back to Yokohama after lecturing here. Many places in town serve it sukiyaki, shabu-shabu or steak. Beef sashimi (tartar) popular, as is *miso-zuke* thin slices coated in miso sauce. Basic prices around ¥2,000-2,500 for sukiyaki, shabu-shabu, ¥2,500-3,000 steaks. Best **Takino,** 1km N of Matsugasaki Park, **Ougi** between park & stn, and **Ogawara** just W of stn. Yonezawa is also known for its noodles—oodles of noodle shops for filling, inexpensive lunches.

Amateur archaeologists can detour to reconstructed Jomon era **neolithic village** at *Jomon-mura* for several reconstructed Stone Age Jomon dwellings and primitive cemetery; nearby **museum** displays excavated items. 15min bus from Nagai stn-front bus terminal. Infrequent runs 1hr on JR Nagai Line from Akayu which is 15-20min rail N of Yonezawa; or take Yonesaka Line from Yonezawa to Imaizumi (35min) where join Nagai Line (30min). **Driver** take Rte287 from Yonezawa, about 35km to Nagai; about 13km beyond at Arato take Rte348 which curves NE to Yamagata City, about 20km.

Shichi-ga-juku Kaido '7-Station' pedestrian hiway once linked Sendai to Yonezawa, its name coming from fact that there used to be 7 official lodging towns en route. It is now Rte113 which has infrequent bus service for those adventurers who try this route to Sendai.

KAMI-TOZAWA best preserved village, little off beaten path. OK driving but time-consuming if by bus from Yonezawa: 50min to Takahata, change and 20min to Nii-juku and change again for bus to Shiroishi which you stay on 90min to Shimo-Tozawa then 5km walk down local road to Kami-Tozawa. Kami-Tozawa is easier reached from E end of Shichi-ga-juku Kaido; *50min bus from...*

SHIROISHI, on JR Tohoku Main and bullet (Shiroishi-Zao stn) lines, is also main eastern terminus of buses thru Zao Quasi-National Park.

25min bus NW of Shiroishi is quiet little...

KAMASAKI ONSEN, with four ¥-lo-T ryokan; best **Kimuraya** ☎(02242)-6-2161 which also runs adjacent Youth Hostel 3min bus or 10min walk up the road is hamlet of **Yajiro**, one of top *kokeshi* making areas in Tohoku.

Drivers can continue beyond Yajiro on local road which winds over mountains to...

TOGATTA ONSEN, another kokeshi making spa, on our run thru Zao QNP. Shiroishi is also known for its quality *washi* traditional handmade paper, and its annual *Kokeshi Festival* **May 3-7**.

KAMI-NO-YAMA ONSEN, discovered 1450s by Buddhist monk Gesshu has copious amounts of hot water pouring out of 6 separate springs: oldest and central Tsuruhaki-no-yu (also called Yu-machi), Tohka-machi, Shin-yu, Kawasaki, Akiyama and Takamatsu. Popular with commoners since early Edo period, now one of back country's top onsen—yet, despite many ryokan expanding into multi-storey 'hotels', manages to retain much of its old rural airs. Central is **Tsukioka Castle**, built here mid-16th century, this is 1982 replica, inside of which is local **Museum of Natural History**. Park around castle is known for its cherry blossoms, but fun time to visit is **Sept 8-16** for All-Japan *Scarecrow Contest* featuring traditional & modern scarecrows. Area around castle retains old castle-town atmosphere, and few streets N of castle are some old *buke-yashiki* **samurai residences**—bit run-down, but talk of fixing into tourist attractions.

One house open to public is...

Harusame-an hermitage and tea house, both built by local lord TOKI Yoriyuki in 1629 for Zen priest Takuan (sword-master and pickle inventor-namesake), exiled here by Shogun. Takuan was so taken by this hermitage that he dismantled it and took it home with him when pardoned and had it set up at Tokai-ji temple in Edo's Koishikawa area. It survived wartime bombings and was returned here in 1955 and restored: 5min walk E of castle, ¥100 admission, ¥250 extra gets you matcha green tea and cakes served in tea house.

5min walk S of stn on other (E) side of tracks...

Kaisen-do Museum, *Hakubutsu-kan* (9:00-16:00 X-Tue, ¥350), has private collection of Japanese swords, Chinese Ming and Ching (Qing) lacquer.

WHERE TO STAY: Generally speaking, Yu-machi areas N and E of castle are older, quieter; Shin-yu W of castle has more new big inns; Akiba, Kawasaki, Takamatsu are about 1km SW, with most inns at Akiba. Among best is ¥-S (¥18,000+w/2) **Murao Ryokan** ☎(0236)-72-2111 in Shin-yu, with spacious garden and five separate traditional cottages set around pond. Meals superb, featuring local specialties as well as Yonezawa beef. Same rate is much acclaimed **Koyo** ☎72-5454 in Akiba which started out as small homey ryokan in 1951 then expanded into modern giant, but still known for service. **Yumoto Gosuke** ryokan ☎72-2311 in Yu-machi is slightly less expensive but as good; opened doors in 1703, present owner likes modern art, has tasteful exhibits set up in his traditional inn. There are three dozen other ryokan in all price ranges (book thru stn kanko-annai) but no budget lodgings. There are, however, 7 budget *bath-houses* scattered among all spring areas—token ¥10 per dip, and open 'til late.

Kami-no-yama Onsen is one starting place for Zao QNP, other is...

YAMAGATA City (15min rail or 25min bus from Kami-no-yama Onsen, or 45min rail from Yonezawa) is town of temples and grand summer *Hanagasa-odori dance festival* (Aug 6-8) which began as thanks for good safflower harvest, area's main crop. As prefectural capital, is bustling metropolis serving as transport, economic and educational hub. Interesting stop, but one which should be skipped if short on time. Rather than spend nite here, suggest leaving Yonezawa or Kami-no-Yama Onsen early so you can 'do' two main attractions here, then side trip out to mountain temple Yama-dera before heading up to Zao; leave luggage at stn coin locker until bus to Zao. Going by meter distance, cab **Kami-no-Yama** → **Yamagata** → **Yama-dera** → **Zao** is 35x-mtr; about 70x-mtr if ending Sendai.

WHERE TO STAY: Yamagata does have W-style hotels ranging from ¥-lo-S **Grand** ☎(0236)-41-2611 and **Onuma** ☎23-4143 to semi-business hotels at ¥-hi-T rate: **Tokyu, Castle** and **Washington** ☎24-1515. Or stay in traditional splendor at ¥-T-S **Goto Matabei** ☎22-0357, grand old-timer; good ¥-T inn is **Shibataya Denshichi** ☎22-4433; both short walk E of Gajo Park.

Note: Buses to out-of-town destinations like Zao, Yama-dera, Shido and airport stop off at stn-front, but most start at Bus Terminal 300m E of stn on R side of big road. Assure seats by boarding here.

In-town sites are...

City History Museum, *Shiritsu Kyodo-kan* (9:00-17:00, X-Mon, ¥100), in Kajo Koen Park 20min walk N of stn and on other (W) side of tracks. Interesting Meiji era building which was Saisei-kan Hospital. Built 1878, 16-sided structure circles atrium and has towered entrance with large 8-sided 2nd floor and 4-sided 3rd. Moved to this site 1968 when new hospital was built, displays inside document entire reconstruction process; also old medical equipment, texts and photos. Most techniques used were introduced by Austrian physician Albrecht Von Loretz who came here 1880. Kajo Park site of old castle, city sports facilities now occupy much of grounds.

Prefectural Museum, *Kenritsu Hakubutsu-kan* (¥200), in nearby modern structure, small but good section displaying feudal era importance of Mogami River's safflower and rice trade, as well as other aspects of every-day life. Outside park is **Prefectural Art Museum**, *Kenritsu Bijutsu-kan* (¥300), with fountains in front, displays mostly modern art, but has some old scrolls, ceramics and folk art.

Can get cab at hospital at park entrance for cab 2x-mtr or 20min bus from stn to...

Hirashimizu pottery village, 4km SE of town. Potters introduced here in early 1800s and there are still 5 families carrying on tradition. **Seiryu-gama** kiln's pottery is best known, winning grand prize at 1958 Brussels World Expo. Others, such as Nanaemon, may be less prized but are affordable and hospitable.

Yamagata Airport is about 25km N of town, 50min on buses which depart 90min before scheduled flight; or short cab ride from Shinmachi stn, 7 stops N.

Between airport and town is...

SHINDO ONSEN, non-descript hot spring better known as shogi capital of Japan—Japanese version of chess, *shogi-goma* are pentagonal playing pieces. Tendo's craftsmen carve 95% of all shogi-goma sold in Japan, and everywhere you look is shogi related. *Spring Festival*, **last wknd Apr** when sakura in full bloom, features tournaments of *ningen-shogi* human shogi games where people represent pieces on giant playing board. 25min rail from Yamagata, frequent buses link Shindo to Yamagata (40min) and Yama-dera (30min).

HIGASHINE ONSEN (just N of airport) is another quiet backwoods spa, but 20min bus (Harajuku-bound) E of town is **RYUSEN-JI** temple with image of Maria-Kannon worshipped by secret Christians.

YAMA-DERA, which name reads Mountain-Temple, is just that. Sprawling complex (officially called *Hoju-san Risshaku-ji*) climbs up side of wooded Mt Hoju, with chains and ladders only way to reach some of smaller clifftop training areas. Tendai sect Yama-dera was founded 860 by Saint Jikaku and ranks in sect 2nd only to headquarters of Kyoto's Mt Hiei.

Main Hall, *Konponchu-do*, is to far R (facing); near it is modern building **Secret Treasure Hall**, *Mitsuho-kan*, where many hitherto hidden temple treasures displayed (¥200). Pilgrimage route from bottom San-mon **gate** up to Oku-no-In **sanctuary** is climb up some 1,100 steps. Suggested is 2hrs to see Yama-dera, hour more if branching off to lesser buildings and vistas, of which there are many. Yama-dera is 45min ride from Yamagata Bus Terminal; also stn on JR Senzan Line linking Yamagata to Sendai: 25-40min from Yamagata, 50-60min to Sendai.

Midway to Sendai is...

SAKUNAMI ONSEN, also known as major *kokeshi* peg-doll center. 7 ¥-T–S ryokan and hotels, and one ¥-B minshuku line busy Rte48; good location on main road and rail, and proximity to Sendai, has caused Sakunami's inns to expand into modern hi-rises, but a few retain their original traditional buildings which cost bit more for rooms but worth it. Best is 180-year-old, ¥-S Iwamatsu Ryokan ☎(02239)-5-2211, which has long flight of covered stairs leading from old thatched-roof main building down to 4 private mixed-bathing outdoor riverside baths. You can enjoy this great experience even if not staying here; few hundred yen gets you ticket to baths. Sakunami Onsen is 5min bus (2km) from Sakunami stn.

About same distance other direction from stn on Rte48 (20min walk from spa) is...
European style compound of **Nikka Whiskey Sendai Distillery**. Call ahead to ☎5-2111 for 1hr guided tour (between 9:00-11:00, 13:00-15:30), followed by sampling.

ZAO QUASI-NATIONAL PARK 蔵王国定公園

MOST POPULAR route to Sendai from inland Tohoku. Scenic Zao Echo Line offers spectacular views year-round; mountains offer some of best skiing in Japan, and great hiking in summer; and numerous hot springs provide comfortable bases for skiing or hiking. Those passing up central Tohoku and just going up Pacific Coast can take in Zao in easy day trip from Sendai, where we recommend renting car: 25min on Tohoku Expwy to Shiroishi I.C. (bullet train does same in 16min) and 1hr up to peak Katta Chusha-jo. **Car** allows for alternate returns via backwoods hot springs for optional nite; some in Zao (see below), others closer to Sendai like Akiu or Futakuchi.

GETTING THERE: Buses up to Zao not too frequent, but not overcrowded (except summer peak) since most Japanese drive, and many more pass thru briefly on tour buses. Western Yamagata-side starting points are YAMAGATA City and KAMI-NO-YAMA, from where **Yamagata Kotsu Bus Co** runs; eastern Miyagi-side points are SHIROISHI and SENDAI, served by **Miyagi Kotsu Bus**. No direct buses link Yamagata-side cities to Miyagi ones; transfer from one company to other at midway Katta Chusha-jo terminal, from where advise detour up lifts to peak of Mt Katta. Buses from YAMAGATA all via largest Zao Onsen, 45min to spa (dep half-hourly 6:30-9:00, hourly 9:50-20:50), 2-4 buses daily (9:30, 11:30; 4/29-11/3 only), extra runs 8/1-31 continue on Zao Onsen to Katta Chusha-jo in 50min. Buses from SHIROISHI (3x-daily) and SENDAI (1x-daily) go via Togatta Onsen where some branch off to nearby Aone Onsen (also reached direct bus over back roads from Sendai). From TOGATTA ONSEN buses to Katta Chusha-jo detour to top of Katta-dake Peak before ending Katta Chusha-jo where it turns around, skipping peak on return so those coming from Yamagata side must use lift to top. It is about 1km trail between top lift terminal and top bus stop.

Driving is pleasant, former 26km Echo Line and 6.5km Zao Line linking Zao Onsen to Echo Line are now toll free thru Park; while midway, 2km (¥500) High Line winds up to Katta-dake Peak.

ZAO ONSEN is heart of park, with 50 ryokan and hotels, 40 minshuku, and as many pensiones able to accommodate around 12,000 people at once tho rarely full, even in peak ski season weekends. **Kanko-annai** at bus terminal can book rooms anywhere and has good maps of area for hikers. Word of *warning*—avoid weekends, New Year week, national holidays and lunar New Years Day. Going skiing used to be expedition with rigamarole of advance reservations, standing in line and long tedious ride. However improved air travel and recently speeded-up Tohoku Shinkansen and special ski season expresses on regular JR lines makes Zao within easy access of Tokyo. Since early 70s, ski facilities thru-out Japan improved astronomically and now compare to US or European resorts. At last count 4 ropeways and 32 chairlifts lead up to miles of various ski runs Dec to Apr. Popular course is thru fields of Juhyo 'Snow Monsters' of Zao—snow-covered trees are molded into grotesque frozen lumps by wind. You can also cut across peaks and down other side of mountain (guide recommended) to...

Bodaira, much smaller resort with handful of lodgings, is at western entrance to Echo Line road.

KATTA-DAKE PEAK, at 1758m is tallest around, was worshipped as home of local gods. So sacred that women were not allowed up until 18th century. Near summit, **KATTA-MINE JINJA** shrine, *oku-no-miya* **sanctuary**; main shrine is at Togatta Onsen. Whether you've come up by bus or chairlift, view is same: looking down on blue water of Okama crater lake. Popular trail to hike is under 2hr from Okama N along Uma-no-se Horseback Ridge then W to Mt Jizo from where hike or ropeway down to Zao Onsen. Large **jizo figure** sitting atop Mt Jizo is dedicated to all those early pilgrims who died on mountain. Harder but nicer hike takes you counter-clockwise around Okama's crater, 3-4hrs to rural one-inn (¥-T) **GAGA ONSEN** with lovely outdoor riverside bath. Easier way to reach Gaga Onsen is Miyagi Kotsu bus to Ura-tozan-guchi stop (at start of Echo Line road) and 30min walk up side road. Or call ahead from Togatta Onsen to ryokan ☎(02248)-7-2021 and they will get you by car. Tho quiet and isolated, it is popular with hikers and you should call ahead July-Aug. Midway on one trail to Gaga Onsen is outdoor baths of Kamoshika Onsen.

45min bus from Shiroishi, 2hrs from Sendai, 1hr from Katta Peak...
TOGATTA ONSEN, is main Miyagi side base for Zao. Many ryokan rent rooms for day visitors just here for bath; there are also some ¥-B room-only ryokan and large public bath. Little more than cluster of dozen mostly small inns, some shops and shrine make up 'town'. You will see carvers making famed *Togatta-kokeshi* dolls, but real **village of craftsmen** is 10min walk across bridge—*Shinchi Kokeshi-shuraku*, where 2 dozen carvers carry on family tradition.

En route...

Kokeshi Museum, *Miyagi-Zao Kokeshi-kan* (9:00-17:00, ¥300), displays few thousand of kokeshi dolls from all over Japan.

AONE ONSEN (15min bus beyond Togatta) was favorite spot of Sendai's powerful Date lords who came up for grand view of their realm: Sendai Plain below, and on clear day, to Pacific Ocean, with Kinkazan Peninsula out beyond Matsushima Bay. Aone is even smaller than Togatta, popular escape for Sendai people in-know who choose from 9 quaint ¥-T-S ryokan. Best ryokan is **Yumoto Fubo-kaku** ☎7-2011 with reconstructed pavilion used by Date lords. Also 2 old public bath houses in 'town'. 2 buses daily direct from Shiroishi, 1x-daily to Katta Peak, and 4x-daily make 2hr trip from/to Sendai.

Planning to spend nite in Zao, we personally prefer quiet country air of Togatta, Aone, or Gaga over busy Zao Onsen, and these three are more convenient to next stop Sendai.

But before Sendai, we backtrack and take off-beat tour to...

SHONAI DISTRICT 庄内地方

YAMAGATA PREFECTURE'S coastal area, includes sacred peaks of Dewa Sanzan, scenic rides down Mogami River, coastal towns of Sakata and Tsuruoka. Thru area quick...

TILT: Dep YONEZAWA, see **Kami-no-Yama, Yamagata** morning and rail → SHINJO (1hr-1hr45min from Yamagata) where change to Rikuu Saisen Line and 70min → SAKATA (some start from Yonezawa or Yamagata with no need to change). Then to TSURUOKA (Nite): 2nd day → DEWA SANZAN (optional 2nd Nite) and back → YAMAGATA. 1st nite should be in Sakata if riding river; if you had to choose rather than short time in both towns, suggest skip Sakata to concentrate on Tsuruoka. Catch rural Noh in summer, **Aug 6, 15**, and 20 at **Yuza town**, 12km N of Sakata on rail line.

While we recommend nonskiiers and less-hearty people in general avoid Tohoku in winter, here is exception. In coldest **Feb** you can see two fine examples of village theater, passed down for generations: **Kurokawa Noh** and **Kuromori Kabuki**. Spaced 2 weeks apart (*see* p983), you've lots of time to explore other parts of N in between. But it also gives you good excuse to spend few days based in Tsuruoka or nearby hot springs; Mogami River boats operate still, and during **Nov-Mar** over 1,400 Siberian Swans winter around mouth of Mogami River to bask in 'milder winter of Tohoku.

Mogami River Rapids can be ridden on two different stretches. One actually back near Yamagata airport, shooting thru *Mogami-gawa San-nan-sho* '3 Dangers of Mogami River', stretch which was most hazardous for rice- or safflower-laden boats of Edo period. 1hr (12km) ride starts from Goten (basic-mtr cab ride from Tateoka stn) and ends near Oishida stn.

More popular course runs between Furukuchi and Takaya stns on Rikuu Saisen rail line; called Mogami-gawa Funa-kudari, or popularly...

Mogami-kyo Basho-Rhine after wandering poet (Japanese tend to call all river rides something-Rhine). 7 boats daily (roughly hourly 9:20-16:30) leave Furukuchi's dock (5min walk from stn) for 1hr (¥1,550) ride thru 4 sets of rapids to Kusanagi Onsen (5min bus or 30min walk to Takaya stn). Bus from Kusanagi to Tsuruoka in 55min. 1st boat only starts out 1hr upstream only in May (extra ¥400) at tiny Shinjo Onsen (3 budget inns) which is 30min bus from Shinjo stn, 10min from Furukuchi, either way to Sakashita stop and 10min walk. Ride is on large shallow barges run by two oarsmen; each seats at least 30 so seats should always be available (groups larger than 10 required to reserve), but it wouldn't hurt to have someone call ahead to assure seats: **Mogami-kyo Kanko** ☎(0233)-72-2001. From Kusanagi, there are 55min r.t. cruises on completely enclosed Jet-Boat, run when enough passengers show up—irregular, (¥1,550); contact **Mogami-gawa Jet Tour** ☎(0234)-57-2148. Barges and jet-boats operate in winter for 'snow-viewing'. In zippy world of Japanese bus tours, convenient jet-boats are preferred, but we stick to languid float down in open barge taking in sounds of surrounding woods or silence of snow, broken only by occasional squeaks of oar rubbing wood.

Infrequent buses (3x-daily) from Kusanagi Onsen via 2-stops-down Karikawa stn go to Mt Haguro in 40min, from where you can bus 40min down to Tsuruoka City. Use Tsuruoka as base to see Sakata, following, and bus back to Yamagata via Mt Gassan.

Were you medieval hitchhiker thumbing your way on old safflower and rice barges,
you would have helped (no free o-bento)unload at...
SAKATA, at mouth of Mogami River, was main collection point for rice, safflower, barley and other crops from fertile valleys of central Yamagata—which claims best rice in Japan, and many of whose large-scale farmers would like to chuck government protectionism and compete with US rice. Ever since several dozen renegade samurai families escaped here from 12th century shogun Yoritomo's destruction of Hiraizumi (follows), Sakata has thrived on trade; first with other provinces, and now as busy international port taking in lumber and other resources from Soviet Union. Oct 1976 fire razed large part of town, now 'progressing' into modern metropolis like any other, but there are many remnants of Sakata's unique feudal past.

By time Tokugawa shogunate had enforced strict social hierarchy with samurai at top and merchants at far bottom, Homma family had accumulated great wealth as coastal traders, with which profits they bought up huge tracts of farmland to become largest nonsamurai landlord in Japan. 2nd generation head of family also had golden touch and family business accounted for majority of Sakata's income. Much money was donated to shrines, temples, put back into improving overall lot of farmers, and loans were made to lords of Sakata (who ruled out of neighboring Tsuruoka) and even to neighboring clans. By early 1700s Homma were so powerful that it was decided to elevate them to samurai status with title of *hata-moto* standard-bearer, which of course came with more land. Now, at least, samurai did not have to borrow from merchants. Homma's prospered, and when US Occupation land reforms did away with old tenant-landlord system after war, Homma lost most of their land to 3,000-odd families who had been working it. But still prosper as traders, and also own much of Sakata's warehouses.

TILT: Stn coin-lockers come in handy, as in few hours we can cover main sites: cab or bus → **Homma House**, then walk → **warehouses**, *Bussan-kan*, then walk or cab → **Homma Museum**—can add short detour → **Hiyori-yama Park**. This should give enough time for lunch before or after starting tour, and still make it to **Tsuruoka** late afternoon. Sakata has many ryokan, hotels and minshuku; many are ¥-T catering to business-traveler. Tsuruoka area has better places to stay. Drivers will find Sakata pleasant, with grid layout and parking lots at all main attractions.

Main House *Homma-ke Hontei*, built 1768 by 3rd Homma head Mitsuoka for Sakata lords to use to entertain visiting Tokugawa inspectors. It was as much act of status-building as it was thanks in return for receiving rank of hata-moto. Great example of rich merchant life. 9:30-16:00, X-Mon, ¥200.

300m W at next big intersect is...
Local Products Hall, *Kanko Bussan-kan*, with samples of crafts made in and around Sakata; good selection at fair prices. Marker on corner near City Hall is dedicated to 36 founding fathers of Sakata who settled here.

Half-block before intersect, on R is...
Abumiya hoary 150-year-old shop of rice merchant; in fine shape, ask to look around inside.

Intersect good place to get cab; 1km (15min walk) N is...
Homma Museum, same distance W is **Hiyoriyama Park**; 300m S of Homma-ke on other side of Niida River is **Sankyo-soko** row of 11 sturdy kura-style granaries built 1890. At one time, dozens more lined riverbanks. One at far end is museum outlining history and importance of Shonai rice. Cross bridge at far end and 200m to Bussan-kan.

10min walk N of stn is...
Homma Museum, *Bijutsu-kan* (9:00-17:00, X-Mon, ¥450). Built 1813 as modest second home, overlooks beautiful landscape strolling garden. Hommas donated to city in 1948 as museum, and you can walk thru house, each room decorated with excellent art pieces. Have matcha green tea served to you while viewing garden from first floor. More valuable family treasures are displayed in modern, sloping-roofed annex built 1968.

Hiyoriyama Park is small rise on western fringe of town; good view of harbor, river, sea and mountains. Old white wooden lighthouse in park is among several claiming to be 'oldest in Japan'; **KAIKO-JI** temple at base of hill has mummified bodies of saints Chukai and Emmyokai who meditated to death—process of attaining corporeal nirvana involves 100s of days meditating while gradually reducing food intake until you no longer rely on anything, and mind is freed from self-preserved body.

Look up-coast, solitary conical mountain rising 2,237m from coast is **Mt Chokai** (understandably called Dewa's Mt Fuji) straddling border of Akita and Yamagata prefectures. Mountain alone makes up **Chokai Quasi-National Park**. Last erupted 1974 after 150 years dormancy. Rte7 and rail line to Akita City squeeze between sea and mountain; scenic rocky coast—dotted with sandy beaches, groves of pine trees and tiny fishing hamlets between Fukura and Kisakata towns—is called *Juroku Rakan*, **16 Disciples**, as clifftop rock formations resemble heads. Tho battered by waves, you can still make out 3 Buddhas and 16 disciples which were carved into these giant rocks by zen priest in mid-1800s—to protect villages from violent winter sea. 35km Chokai Blue Line toll road (¥1,640), scenic detour between Fukura–Kisakata loops up to around 1,100m level Hokotate, from where hikers climb 4hrs to summit; *alternate* trail down S face to dead-end **YU-NO-TAIRA ONSEN** (infrequent 40min bus → Sakata). On to Matsushima: coast beyond Blue Line is officially Rikuchu Kaigan National Park; several bays with beaches and ¥-B lodgings: **Nagatsura, Shizugawa, Motoyoshi, Oya**, then port town of **Kessen-numa** (*see*).

If you have time and car it's only 120km (3-4hr) to drive up along coast to Kisakata then back via toll road. On clear days with calm seas, you are supposed to see inverted reflection of Mt Chokai on Japan Sea below.

Look further out to sea, catch glimpse of...
Tobishima Island (floating 40km NW of town) for adventurer seeking nothing but swimming and fishing. Daily boat (2hr crossing, ¥1,750) goes out to community of 1,100 people; 10 ¥-B ryokan, 15 minshuku accommodate mostly summertime visitors (when 2nd boat added). Inns arrange for all your fishing needs, or have them drop you off at tiny **Oshaku-jima Isle** 1.5km off-shore for day of lounging. Can explore all Tobishima in few hours, only 12km around. **OGAMI JINJA** seaside cave shrine has been holy spot for countless centuries, perhaps since Jomon times, and women were allowed in only recently. While it doesn't bother locals that visiting women enter, traditions are hard to break and most older women of Tobishima still avoid it.

TSURUOKA (20-25min express or 40min local on JR Uetsu Main Line); few expresses daily direct from Yamagata in 2hr20min, or express bus 2hr40min from Yamagata on Rte112 via Mt Gassan. It, too, retains some of its castle-town charm, but you'd never guess it coming out of train stn. Area around stn is new with hi-rise hotels and department stores; old section of town is further S, closer to site of castle. Walking around old section of town, thru which winds Uchikawa River, reveals many hidden treasures in form of old shops, quiet neighborhoods and such. Stnwards of Sanno Hotel is 350-year-old candle-maker **Togashi Rosoku-ten** where you can watch painstaking hand-dipping process and painting on of elaborate designs. Whereas Sakata was commercial center of Sakata domain, Tsuruoka was administrative center and site of clan's castle—of which only moats remain, rest dismantled in 1875 and replaced by **SHONAI JINJA** shrine dedicated to Sakai lords. Head 2.5km SW of stn, 30min walk or 10min ride on Yu-no-hama, Yutagawa or Atsumi Onsen-bound buses—to site of ex-castle in center of town, now wooded **Tsuruoka Park**, for look at some old architecture. Within park grounds is white and red W-style **Daiho-kan** built 1916 as Town Hall to commemorate new emperor Taisho, now City Library. 200m E is small **Catholic Church** built 1893, with very J-style gate (land was house of samurai) leading to Gothic church, now Important Cultural Asset; just beyond SE corner of park is J-style **Chido-kan** built 1805 as school for children of samurai (9:30-16:30, X-Mon, free), only part of once sprawling campus remains; but best collection of Meiji era buildings have been moved from other parts of town to be preserved at...

Chido Museum, *Hakubutsu-kan* (9:00-16:30, ¥520), just W of park in what used to be retirement house of Sakai lords, where they could go to be left alone. Whole compound donated to city 1950 by citizen Sakai, grandson of last lord. Old manse, *Goin-den*, and its landscape garden remain, with Sakai family treasures displayed in Goin-den and adjacent museum building. Big white building with clock tower, facing Goin-den, was built 1880 as Nishitagawa County Office, now displays local history, Meiji era items. Other Western-style building built 1884 as Tsuruoka Police HQ now displays folkcrafts and tools used by Tobishima fishermen. Kura storehouse behind has more of same. Graceful thatched-roof farmhouse is 180-year-old **Shibuya Family House** moved here 1965 from tiny hamlet Tamugimata, which we visit with Mt Gassan. Handful more of these houses remain at Tamugimata. Far back corner is **Treasure House**, loaded with more folk-crafts, sturdy wood & metal *funa-dansu* shipboard safes, other furnishings At entrance is lovely little **Sanmai-an** which serves fresh, natural handmade noodles; regular soba and *mugikiri* local version of udon.

Popular gifts from Tsuruoka are *gotenmari* balls of colorful silk thread wound up into intricate multi-hued patterns; said to have been started by local weavers who wound up extra thread into colorful toys for their kids. Also *izumeko-ningyo* dolls of colorfully embroidered infants in bamboo baskets—stem from age-old Tohoku tradition of bundling up infants while folks worked fields; heavy quilting kept them warm, as well as immobilized, to prevent any self-inflicted harm.

WHERE TO STAY: Most visitors to Tsuruoka stay out at hot springs, so city itself has few tourist-oriented lodgings. W-style rooms at business class (¥-T) but comfortable **Sanno Plaza Hotel** ☎(0235)-22-6501; or enjoy traditional Japanese hospitality at **Tsuruoka Hotel** ☎22-1135, actually ryokan using reconstructed inn used by travelling feudal-era daimyo; conveniently located in old part of town, ¥-T–S.

Frequent **bus** service to each of following hot springs leaves from stn-front, all stop front of Chido Museum. YUTAKAWA ONSEN is 30min bus SW of town, in middle of quiet countryside; 16 ¥-T-S ryokan, mostly quaint old wooden buildings, and 2 large public bath houses. Relaxing, oriented towards families. YU-NO-HAMA ONSEN is 40min bus NW of town on Japan Sea coast; 20+ ryokan, and swimming beaches, it is favored by tour groups, so we suggest seaside onsen seekers head few km down-coast to tiny **YURA ONSEN** with 6 ¥-B–T ryokan and Kokumin-shukusha open all year, and over 60 minshuku open during swim season.

Yura is 35min from town on buses bound for...

ATSUMI ONSEN, 70min from town, down coast and slightly inland in hills. Railpassers can save about ¥650 bus fare by taking JR 6 stops (20-25min) to Atsumi stn and 5min bus to spa. Most of dozen-and-half ryokan lining Atsumi River are small, traditional inns, ¥-T–S. Two of best are on opposite bank: **Bankokuya** ☎(0235)-43-3333 here since early Meiji era, and traditional **Tachibanaya** ☎43-3111. **Kameya** ☎43-3017 on bus stop side of river, has been around since 1693, present master is 16th generation. Two public baths in town. Rooms for all onsen can be booked thru Tsuruoka stn kankoannai, also easy to get rooms by just showing up.

ON STAGE: *Kurokawa Noh* is unique **peasant noh** arising from primitive style introduced here 14th century. Performed all nite long both nites **Feb 1-2** at Kasuga Jinja shrine, Kurokawa village, Kushibiki-cho town; 30min bus SE of Tsuruoka.

Kuromori Kabuki is 350-year-old tradition performed **Feb 15 & 17**, at Hie Jinja stage, Kuromori hamlet, 30min bus S of Sakata; **cab** 10x-mtr from Tsuruoka. Shows start around 11:00, continue to 16:00. Seating on thick straw mats laid out on snow; no overhead cover so pray for clear day. Stalls sell food, drinks and games right outside 'theater' and everyone has food and sake while watching their friends and neighbors perform. It becomes real party as audience calls out to favored actors and kids.

Real experience in getting to know rapidly disappearing rural Japanese life, already hospitable villagers really appreciate foreigner coming to visit this little corner of world.

DEWA SANZAN, Three Sacred Peaks of Dewa home to yamabushi, (wandering monks of Buddhist-Shinto faith) are Mt Haguro-san, Mt Gassan, and Mt Yudono-san.

Until recently, pilgrims did all 3 by foot, now most visit just one by auto. Hikers still use trails of Dewa Sanzan, on which you may just meet modern day yamabushi—numbers are few, but there are still those who follow ascetic life of wandering, now open to women too. Hikers will find trailheads from picturesque hamlets where most houses offer budget rooms; temple lodgings; and huts and hot springs up on mountains. During **Jul–Aug**, 'healthy men and women with strong hearts' can undergo 3 days and 2 nites of training under yamabushi, which includes trek in mountains, meditation under thundering waterfalls, stay at Yudono-san Jinja shrine. Fee of ¥15,000 covers all; call in J-, ahead of time: Yudono-san Sanro-jo ☎(02355)-4-6131.

Haguro-san has always been most popular with regular pilgrims since it is closest, and at mere 419m tall could be climbed all year. Shrine at top is home to kami of all 3 peaks so visiting here is as good as rounding all. **Buses** from Tsuruoka (14x-daily 6:00-16:45; 50min) and Mogami River ride terminus Kusanagi Onsen (3x-daily 11:45,14:20,13:40; 55min, runs end Apr–end Oct) take you to Haguro Sancho stop up top near shrine; **drivers** pay ¥400 for toll road covering last stretch to shrine—meant to discourage too many cars from going up.

But coming this way is cheating, pilgrims save ¥300 bus fare and go to hamlet of...

TOGÉ (15min earlier, bus stop Haguro Center) from where you ascend 2,446 stone steps winding up 1.7km thru cool dense woods. There is one small tea stall 2/3rds up where little old lady serves you tea and specialty dumplings *chikara*-(strength)-*mochi*. Beautiful climb really gets you in mood for shrine, some of your climbing companions will be white-robed pilgrims. You're almost at Togé when bus passes thru 20m-tall torii gate. Togé has long been main lodging area for Haguro pilgrims and at peak Edo period there were 360 shukubo lodgings; 32 remain, and you can stay in fine old thatched-roof farmhouse for minshuku rate, ¥-Bw/2. Also one minshuku, plus 4 rustic ¥-B ryokan for those who want bit more service. Get rooms by asking around, or try at bus terminal.

Before heading up, backtrack 10min down bus road to...

SHOZEN-IN KOGANE-DO temple built 750 years ago by shogun Yoritomo to commemorate destruction of Hiraizumi's Fujiwara clan for sheltering brother Yoshitsune. Our climb starts thru another torii at top end of
village, beyond which is temple-style **gate**, *Zuishin-mon*, built 1688.
Shinkyo, **Gods' Bridge**, crosses Harai-gawa River of Purification, and to
R is waterfall, *Suga-no-taki*, outlet for subterranean stream. On L is
ancient **pagoda** (NT) built 934AD by general Taira-no-Masakado. Part way
up, detour to R leads to two small ponds which used to be part of garden
surrounding Betsu-in priest's quarters. Only stone foundations remain,
stone pillar commemorating one of poet Basho's haiku which he wrote
while here. Just before last torii at top, on L is **Saikan Pavilion**, 300-
year-old sole remaining Buddhist structure on Haguro, rest having suffered
during Meiji split of Shinto and Buddhism. Saikan serves **meals** of *shojin-ryori*
multi-course vegetarian priests' fare. ¥1,000-3,500; must call ahead ☎(023562)-2357 to
let them know how many and about when. If you forgot to call from town, try from Toge
and tell them about 2hrs, which gives time for climb and look before meal. You can also
spend nite here.

SANSHIN-GOSAI-DEN shrine, name literally means 3-Gods-Together-
Worship-Palace, dominates, and as its name indicates, enshrines spirits of
all 3 Dewa Sanzan peaks. Last rebuilt 1818, is among largest single shrine
buildings at 28m tall, 24m wide and 17m deep. In front is **Mirror-pond**,
Kagami-ike, so named since old tradition involved tossing mirror into pond
while offering prayers. Over 500 such mirrors have been dredged up, of
which 190 from Heian period are displayed in new **History Museum**
(4/20-11/23 only, ¥200) near bus parking area, along with other treasures. 370-
year-old **bell tower** shelters 19-ton giant, largest in Tohoku and 3rd
largest bell in Japan.

GASSAN:July 1 thru Oct 10, buses 3x-daily leave Haguro-sancho stop (9:50, 12:50;
13:40, extra run 7/15-8/18 at 11:30) crossing 24km of mountains (50min) to Gassan
Hachigo-me stop at 1,450m high **Mida-ga-hara marsh**, awash in colorful
flowers June-July. Resthouse and small lodging hut here; hikers trek S 2hrs
to summit of volcanic 1980m Mt Gassan. From here, 2hr hike W then S
down to Ubasawa village known for good spring skiing Apr to July. You
can get dropped by **helicopter** at top of Gassan and ski back. Dozen ¥-B
lodges at Ubasawa, dozen more at Shizu village few kilos down road. Bus to Shizu and
Ubasawa infrequent, summer only.

*Most common route to/from Gassan is 2hr W to Yudono-san from where 20min bus
or 3hr trail down to...*

TAMUGIMATA Village (1hr bus from Tsuruoka stn-front). Here are more of
those soaring farmhouses we saw at Tsuruoka's Chido Museum, some of
which still have budget rooms for pilgrims and hikers. Tamugimata was one
of main trailheads up sacred Mt Yudono and other Dewa Sanzan peaks, and
villagers had lively business supplying pack-horses, and go-riki musclemen
to help pilgrims up. Houses here were built big, 3-4 storeys, to accommodate constant stream of pilgrims. But Meiji era separation of Buddhism-
Shinto put heavy dent in pilgrimages to mixed Shinto-Buddhist Dewa
Sanzan, and business fell off. To make up for lost income, villagers turned
to making charcoal and raising silkworms, for which spacious top floors
were perfect with little windows to let in some sunlight. First put in to give
pilgrims air, these windows thru thatch are unique to Tamugimata area.

OHNAWA (6km Tsuruoka-wards of Tamugimata).rundown hamlet, also old
trailhead for Yudono-san, but when Rte112 bypassed it, business fell.

15min walk from Ohnawa bus stop is...

DAINICHI-BO temple; as far as women were allowed to climb, they offered prayers to temple's Dainichi Buddha. You will also be shown shrivelled mummy of Saint Shinnyo-kai who began his meditations at age 20 and finally attained nirvana at age 96. CHUREN-JI temple, 30min walk from bus stop in other direction, has mummy of Saint Tetsumon-kai. Both temples offer ¥-B lodgings. In case you're wondering about this profusion of mummified saints around here, 6 out of 24 thus 'enlightened' saints in Japan are located in this Shonai District.

WHERE NEXT: From Yudono-san you can bus back to YAMAGATA to cut across → SENDAI–MATSUSHIMA. While Sendai is pleasant town, we feel that Matsushima has been far over-rated as one of Japan's Top Three scenic spots. It's nice, but not worth detouring to, so back-country adventurer has optional route: JR Ou Saisen → SHINJO then Ou Tosen → FURUKAWA or KOGOTA from where up → HIRAIZUMI. FURUKAWA is on Shinkansen 15min → ICHI-NO-SEKI; KOGOTA is on Tohoku Main Line, 50min → ICHI-NO-SEKI or 1hr → HIRAIZUMI (some expresses skip). Ou Tosen has some choice hot springs along it.

But there are those of you for whom Sendai and Matsushima are on itinerary, so let us cut across to Pacific (E) Coast...

SENDAI 仙台

MAIN CITY in Tohoku of about 700,000 and growing; pleasant blend of modern urban and traditional rural lifestyles. Those who have been trekking countryside with us will find Sendai pleasant change, and those coming here direct from Aizu Wakamatsu will find Sendai comfortable base to explore Miyagi prefecture. With large resident foreign population, you won't stand out as much. YAMA-DERA temple, YAMAGATA City and ZAO QNP are only day-trip away, as is historic HIRAIZUMI; pine-clad isles of Matsushima Bay mere few hours round-trip. You can stay in comfortable W-style hotels, traditional ryokan or budget Youth Hostels in town; or choose from hot springs outside town—rustic AKIU ONSEN and FUTAKUCHI ONSEN, and above-mentioned SAKUNAMI ONSEN where you can enjoy great outdoor bath of Iwamatsu Ryokan.

First thing you will notice about Sendai is its wide streets and abundant trees. Rational layout of Sendai wasn't due so much to good city planning as it was to wartime saturation bombing. Unfortunately, much of city's rich historic past was also destroyed, but there is enough left to give good idea. Heading W from stn is tree-lined main Aoba-dori Ave to castle park. Avenue and others intersecting are site of one of Tohoku's top summer fetes *Tanabata-sai* on Aug 6-8, when about 2,000,000 tourists visit Sendai to see colorful decorations set up along streets.

Sendai got its start 1600 when one-eyed DATE Masamune set up his new Aoba-jo Castle here on Aoba-yama 'Green Leaf' hill (15min bus, 2km W of stn). 13 Date lords ruled out of Aoba-jo until Meiji, when castle was mostly dismantled 1871. What was left burned during war and sole remaining tower is postwar reconstruction. Now, GOKOKU JINJA shrine takes up much of old castle site; worth climbing just for view; statue of mounted warrior is of Masamune, one of greatest leaders of 16-17th century— imposing figure with his outlandish Crescent Moon helmet and eyepatch over right eye lost during near fatal bout of small pox as child. W part of castle grounds is Tohoku University Botanical Garden (¥150), beyond which is Tatsu-no-kuchi Kyokoku Ravine. There is also small Aoba-jo History Museum, on 2nd floor of gift shop near Date's statue, which has scale model of castle and Date (pron Da-teh) memorabilia. Much better collection of Date family treasures and such at **City Museum**, *Sendai-shi Hakubutsu-kan* (9:00-17:00, X-Mon, ¥400), at base of Aoba-yama 10min bus from stn. We've not been back since enlarged museum reopened January 1986, planned to be much better than already good older museum. Over 30,000 pieces allows for changes of displays during year and you may find yourself looking at pair of ornate crystal candlesticks which were present from Pope Paul V to Masamune. 1613, Masamune sent mission to Rome led by HASEKURA Tsunenaga and Franciscan monk Father Soleto, who saw it as chance to be appointed Archbishop of Japan and suggested it to Masamune, who saw it as chance to establish trade with New Spain across Pacific. Ever so shrewd TOKUGAWA Ieyasu, counselled by Englishman Will Adams and Dutch traders from Nagasaki, realized Vatican would reject Soleto, thus eradicating chances of Christian intervention (he had already stifled any chance of direct Spanish intervention, and spurned Jesuits had informed Vatican on anti-Christian nature of Japanese), and figured any trade Masamune could muster would fatten Tokugawa coffers with no effort on their part. Hasekura's mission of 140 Japanese and 40 'Southern Barbarians' on Japanese-built galleon (by shipwrights trained by Adams) landed at Acapulco, made their way to Mexico City where 87 Japanese were baptized, then set sail from San Juan De Ulloa via Havana to Spain and eventually to Madrid where Hasekura and other top Japanese were baptized.

After travelling around Spain for 8 months, they eventually made it to Rome were they were met with much ceremony but nothing concrete was established. When they got home in 1621, Christianity was on its way to being squeezed out of Japan and outlawed for next 250 years and trade had been restricted to Nagasaki. Hasekura died 2 years later, is buried at KOMYO-JI temple N of castle. Next to his grave is memorial to Father Soleto. Other items displayed include letters from Pope Paul V to Masamune and Ieyasu, maps and other items related to Hasekura's journey (Ieyasu and Masamune's letters to Pope are copies). Nearby is statue of Hasekura, copy of which was given to sister-city Acapulco on Hasekura's 400th birthday to commemorate Mexican leg of his trip. On other (stn-) side of Hirose River is **monument** donated by Portugal and dedicated to Christians who suffered under Ieyasu's later purge of Christianity. Central is Portuguese priest Carvalho, who was slowly drowned here at Ohashi Bridge; flanking him are farmer and samurai, representing many Japanese converts who were crucified, burned, decapitated, or otherwise 'martyred'.

20min walk from City Museum or 10min bus from stn to Otamaya Bridge and walk...
Mausoleum of Date Masamune, *Zuiho-den* (9:00-16:00, ¥515). Ornate Momoyama style building is 1977 reconstruction of original structure (was National Treasure) burned 1945. Exhibit room had photo display of Masamune's tomb uncovered during reconstruction and now in special underground vault. New, reconstruction of two other nearby mausoleums: *Kansen-den* of 2nd Date Tadamune and *Zenno-den* of 3rd Date Tsunamune #515—in which case ¥500 kyotsu-ken ticket to enter all.

15min from stn on Sakunami Onsen-bound bus, or cab basic-mtr from around City Museum area, in NE corner of town is...
OSAKI HACHIMAN SHRINE (NT) which survived flames of war. Built 1607 by Masamune who christened it as guardian spirit of Sendai. Every year on nite of **Jan 14** *Donto-sai Festival*, Sendai folk come up here to toss their old New Year's decorations, charms into huge bonfire.

15min walk NE of Osaki Hachiman is cluster of temples and shrines around Kita-Sendai stn on JR Senzan Line, among which is...
KOMYO-JI temple grave of Hasekura. Garden enthusiasts may want to

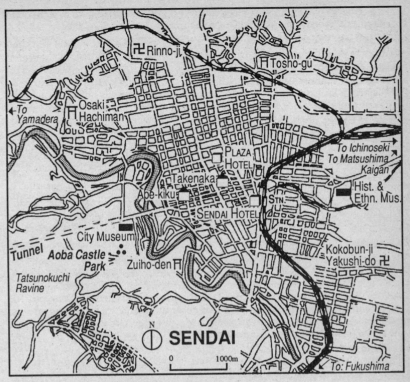

visit **RINNO-JI** temple's landscape garden (20min bus from stn; ¥200) best during **May** iris season and **SHUFUKU-JI** temple's rock garden. 360-year-old **TOSHOGU** shrine dedicated to Tokugawa Ieyasu is 15min bus N of stn.

10min bus or 15min walk E of stn is...
MUTSU KOKUBUN-JI temple, built 741AD by order of emperor Shomu who built Kokubun-jis nationwide. Excavations mid-1950s discovered that this was grand complex built along lines of Nara's Todai-ji complex. Now standing in its place is **YAKUSHI-DO** temple built 1607 by Masamune.

1km E of stn in Tsutsuji-ga-oka Koen Azalea-Hill Park...
History and Ethnology Museum, *Rekishi Minzoku Shiryo-kan* (9:00-17:00 X-mon, ¥200), is lovely old Meiji era building. Both floors are full of folk arts and crafts, old farm tools and some military memorabilia. Built 1874 as part of defunct Imperial Army 4th Infantry Regiment HQ. US Occupation Forces used it until 1952, when it became police academy, restored to original condition as museum in 1974. 5min walk S is Tsutsuji-ga-oka stn on JR Senseki Line out to Matsushima Bay.

Also on Senseki Line are remains of...
Taga-jo Castle, grand Chinese-style fortress with massive walls built 724AD as final frontier against Ezo (Ainu) tribes. Proverbial 'hell-hole' for Japanese 8th cent soldiers to be stationed out in middle of nowhere, cat-&-mouse guerrilla warfare against fierce Ainu, not finally subdued in this area until 795 by General Saka-no-ue Tamuramaro further N near Hiraizumi. Partially excavated, only markers show where old structures were, but small **Tohoku History Museum**, *Rekishi Shiryo-kan*, outlines Taga-jo's history, shows excavated items. You can stop by after visiting Matsushima,

Taga-jo is midway—15min walk from either Tagajo stn on Senscki Line, or Rikuzen Sanno stn on Tohoku Main Line, both of which link Matsushima and Sendai.

WHERE TO STAY: Over 2 dozen hotels, 130 ryokan in town, but almost all booked months in advance for Aug *Tanabata Festival*. W-style incl highly recommended **Sendai Hotel** ☎(022)-225-5171 near stn, **Koyo Grand** ☎267-5lll ¥-hi-T with fab art & antique-lined foyer, halls; **Tokyu** ☎262-2411, **Plaza** ☎262-7111 all ¥-S. Best, ¥-S– to fabulous ¥-LL **Zuiho** in Akiu onsen, *next*. Half that numerous business hotels like **Washington** ☎222-2111, **Sun Route** ☎262-2323. J-style ¥-B–T start ¥5,-9,000w/2. Recommend **Abe-kiku** ☎263-1811, **Takenaka** ☎225-6771, **Nakamura** ☎223-3161, **Iwamatsu** ☎221-1511. Budgeteers ryokan and business hotels ¥-B; or 4 YH around town. Book thru stn **Kanko-annai**, few doors to L as you exit ticket-takers on 2nd fl; sometimes E-spkrs. **Travel Center** (where can validate Rail Pass) to R of ticket booths. Either books hot springs outside town: above-Sakunami Onsen or Akiu Onsen below.

CHOPSTICKS: **Diet Restaurant Plateau** organic food, genmai lunch ¥700, gluten replaces meat for burger; 3min from Kosai Hospital bus stop, 11:30-2 lunch only, ☎265-8353. **Green Peas** organic grocer, corner for genmai lunch, ¥600; tea, desserts. Nr YMCA opp Nishi-koen, Hirose Bldg 1F. 10:00-19:00, X-mon, ☎265-7868.

AKIU ONSEN, 7x-mtr taxi (8x from airport), 50min frequent bus from stn, or from Sendai-minami Interchange Tohoku Expwy 7km W take local Rte286 for first half then branch off. Dozen ¥-T–Sw/2 ryokan, some large 'resort hotels', line Natori River along rocky Rairai-kyo Gorge. Here, too, are some *kokeshi* carvers. **Zuiho** ☎(022)-397-1111 ¥-LLw/2, lower rates weekday, W/J, ask Daimler pick-up stn or airport; splashy mix-W-J resort, gigantic lobby garden w/ carp stream; great baths, pool (non-guest use pm w/dinner ¥5,-7,-10,000); *taiko* drum shows nitely, also nite club; var rstnts; lady guests served in rom by young man in formal kimono.

10min walk downstream...
Tenshukaku Shizen-koen Natural Park is relatively new tourist attraction of gardens, large outdoor onsen bath.

KANGANE ONSEN and **KONOSU ONSEN** nearby, 2 old hot springs.

But adventurers should keep going 55min bus to...
FUTAKUCHI ONSEN mountain spa about 18km upstream of Akiu with single ryokan **Banji-sanso** ¥-T ☎(022)-399-2816.

10min bus (4km) before Futakuchi is...
Akiu Oh-taki Waterfall, one of better known in Japan; 55m (170ft) high by 5m wide. Base has tiny **FUDO-DO** temple first put here by Saint Jikaku-daishi when he founded Yama-dera temple, boasts 3.3m (10ft) tall bronze fiery Fudo. 15km (5hr) trail starting from end of road beyond Futakuchi climbs hills to end near Yama-dera. Road ends 600m beyond at Banji-Iwa rock formations of soaring pillar-like cliffs. Campsite and bungalows near Banji-Iwa, campsite outside Futakuchi.

MATSUSHIMA 松島

23KM UP-COAST NE of Sendai (25min Tohoku Main Line, 40min Senseki Line, 1hr bus) is in our opinion much overrated as one of Japan's Top Scenic Trio. But is still worth visiting, especially if you time yourself to avoid bus tours by going early morning or late afternoon. Other times, it's usually too noisy, crowded to enjoy what must have been truly beautiful in Basho's days (was still in first edition time). Nice in winter, when choppy seas and steely sky give it new face, with fewer visitors. Unfortunately Matsushima is over-commercialized for tourist trade, with even aquarium with regular seal shows. Some interesting historic buildings as well as viewing 128-odd pine-clad named isles, plus perhaps 300-400 more not 'officially tallied' (doing so 1991) filling bay; and among crowded waterfront are piers for all sorts of craft from rental rowboats to gaudy dragon-shape sightseeing boats.

GETTING THERE: Tohoku Main Line Matsushima stn is quicker to get to from Sendai, but is 3km (5min bus) from bay; Senseki Line lets you off right near bay at Matsushima Kaigan stn. **Drivers** take coastal Rte45 from Sendai, as you near Matsushima, Panorama Line toll road (¥300) veers off L and uphill for several strategic views of bay below, lets you out on local road behind Matsushima Kaigan stn; driving time 25min from town. One-way cab from Sendai runs about 13x-mtr; have him take Panorama Line (you pay toll) and let you off on waterfront. 2-3hrs sightseeing then take boat to Shiogama harbor from where 25min rail back to Sendai. Round-trip **cab** about 25x-mtr including reasonable waiting time.

ZUIGAN-JI **temple** (5min walk N of Matsushima Kaigan st) established 823AD by Saint Jikaku-daishi; present structures built 1609 by Masamune. Within temple grounds are few small caves carved into rock, small Buddha figures inside, were used for meditation by zen monks training here. One portion of temple you can't enter is adjacent *Intoku-in*, still used by trainees. But for ¥500 (8:00-17:00, -15:30 winter) you can enter most of Zuigan-ji's main buildings (most are NT), graced with old painted doors, scrolls and other treasures. In back is small museum of Date clan memorabilia, sometimes displaying Papal candlesticks brought back by Hasekura. In garden are two plum trees (one white, other pink) brought back from Korea by Masamune as memento of Toyotomi Hideyoshi's abortive campaign there.

ENTSU-IN temple, nearby, garden said to be made by famed KOBORI Enshu—unusual in being full of roses. *Donjiki-chaya* **tea shop** in front of Entsu-in is old folk house brought here from countryside; matcha tea and cakes, and inexpensive handmade soba noodles served.

Moon Viewing Pavilion, *Kanran-tei*, of Date clan overlooks Bay from what used to be private beach of Date lords. Built by Toyotomi Hideyoshi in 1592 it sat in Fushimi Momoyama Castle near Kyoto until Hideyoshi gave it to Masamune who had it moved here. ¥200 admission also gets you in to nearby **Museum** with more Date memorabilia, display of local fauna and flora.

Godai-do Pavilion (200m up-coast on red-bridged isle) houses figure of guardian Deva Godai-myo-o, shown only every 33 years. Said to have been first built by Saka-no-ue Tamura-maro on his way to fight Ainu, present hall rebuilt 1604 by Masamune. This is most photographed site at Matsushima, as you will see in most tourism posters. Ojima Isle, with arched **Moon Bridge** just S of Kanran-tei offers good view of latter; reputedly better from larger Fukura Isle, but cost ¥100 to cross 250m bridge so we let our imagination suffice.

Boats: Most have separate top-deck 1st class section. 5 daily runs around bay (more summer), 1hr; every 30min, 1hr runs MATSUSHIMA ↔ SHIOGAMA harbor (1st class ¥2,800, 2nd ¥1,400; fewer winter); last weekend Apr thru Oct 2x-daily (9:00, 12:00 return after 5min wait) make hour-long winding cruise thru isles to OHTAKAMORI where you can climb 106m hill for view of bay, ¥1,200. Best is 2hr cruise thru isles from SHIOGAMA, around OHTAKAMORI to its rocky far side, to Matsushima, but only 1x-daily (11:10) end Apr thru Oct (1st ¥4,200; 2nd ¥2,900).

SHIOGAMA, bustling fishing town where early visitors can see hectic fish market; auctions begin 5am, most wholesale stalls open 10:30am. 2km from main Hon-Shiogama stn; or 5min walk from next Higashi Shiogama stn. Pier is short walk from Hon-Shiogama stn.

8min walk behind stn and up 200 stone steps is...
SHIOGAMA JINJA shrine, home to all-purpose maritime gods since ages past. Present structures rebuilt 1704 by 3rd and 4th Date lords. Small **museum** displays shrine treasures, old fishing tools and giant mikoshi used in main festivals. Shiogama's mikoshi parades are known for their roughness, particularly **Mar 10** *Hote Matsuri*; **4th sun Apr** is *Hana Matsuri* Flower Festival; **1st wknd Aug** *Minato Matsuri* Port Festival has two mikoshi carted down to pier

where loaded onto two gaudy phoenix ships which lead parade of gaily decorated fishing boats around Matsushima Bay 13:00-18:00, join party boats for small fee.

Shiogama got its name 'Salt Vat' since this area was major salt producer. Near Shiogama Jinja is smaller **OKAMA JINJA**, 'Vat Shrine', where four old evaporation vats are enshrined.

Most people allow 3hrs to visit Zuigan-ji, Kanran-tei, Godai-do and other 2 isles. Early starters from Sendai (which we recommend) can get back before lunch and see city, or rail up to Hiraizumi by early afternoon; or direct to Hiraizumi from Matsushima stn. There are several restaurants along waterfront; some of few dozen ryokan and hotels here have dining rooms open to nonguests. Budgeteers will find lots of minshuku all around Matsushima, including out on largest isles; few dozen more out at 3 villages of Ohama, Murohama, and Tsukigahama (each with own beach) on far side of Ohtakamori Isle, which is linked by 7 daily buses to Nobiru stn on Senseki Line (6 stops-15min from Matsushima Kaigan). Nobiru itself has several dozen minshuku along its own long stretch of beach. Those who want more coastline can rail or bus further up to Ishinomaki and cut in on JR Ishinomaki Line to Ogota on Tohoku Main Line.

OSHIKA PENINSULA jutting into Pacific Ocean near Ishinomaki, 2 stops beyond which is Watanoha where drivers take branch road over narrow inlet & 30km drive along beautiful coast dotted with fishing villages to **Ayukawa** whaling village near point. **Whaling Museum** near pier outlines history of whaling here. Lots of minshuku in town, campsite and beach nearby; fishing boats take you out to two isles just off coast **Tashiro-jima** and **Aji-shima**, both with minshuku. Halfway up coast to Ayukawa is **Tsuki-no-Ura** village, whence Hasekura set sail for Europe.

You can drive 30km Cobalt Line toll road (¥800) from Onagawa (8km beyond Watanoha; end of rail line) to Ayukawa which follows ridge along middle of peninsula for grand views of both shores.

Floating 1km off point is small...
Kinka-zan Isle, one of most sacred spots in Tohoku along with Dewa Sanzan and northernmost Mt Osore. Was known as Kinka-zan Daikin-ji temple of ryobu Shinto mixed Buddhist-Shinto until 1867 split made it shrine only. **KOGANEYAMA JINJA** shrine still remains, its *oku-no-in* sanctuary atop 445m high peak. Quite popular despite its out-of-way locale; it is said that visiting here 3 years in row will ensure life-long prosperity. Kinka-zan known since mid-8th century as having veins of gold ore. Dirt road partially circles isle, numerous trails crisscross. 40min from shrine to summit.

30min down other side to...
Senjo-jiki '1,000-mat' flat white granite formation sloping into sea and nearby **Sennin-zawa** cliffs rising 70-80m from sea. Numerous minshuku here, all can get you fishing gear to use. You'll notice hundreds of deer, animals which are believed to be messengers of gods; always seem to be troops of monkeys with deer in Japan and Kinka-zan is no exception. **1st, 2nd sundays in Oct** see ritual cutting of deer horns. 3-10 r.t. boats daily from Ayukawa in 25min (¥780), of which one starts Ishinomaki at 9:50 to reach Ayukawa 1hr40min later and on to Kinka-zan (¥1,850). Also 2-4 r.t.'s daily from Onagawa in 30min (¥1,600).

GETTING THERE: From ISHINOMAKI, JR Ishinomaki Line heads W → KOGOTA where it changes, in name only, to Rikuu Tosen Line → SHINJO and our tour thru SHONAI DISTRICT (p979); or Tohoku Main Line from KOGOTA → HIRAIZUMI. Drivers take Rte108 from ISHINOMAKI → Rte4 of Tohoku Expwy. If driving around OSHIKA PENINSULA, rather than backtracking to Ishinomaki, continue past ONAGAWA on coastal Rte398 also called Rias Blue Line (no toll) 20km → OGATSU town where continue straight inland. About 6km on is Kitakami River which follow upstream (L turn) to Rte45 which goes up → KESEN-NUMA, or backtrack about 6km to Rte108 → KOGOTA. If going up to Kesen-numa for alternate entry to HIRAIZUMI, Rte45 quicker but coastal Rte398 more scenic.

EN ROUTE TO SHONAI

NARUGO 40-60min from Shinkansen at Furukawa & 15min more from Kogota; also reached by 4-5x-daily 2hr bus from Sendai; some express trains direct from Sendai with no transfers. Despite built-up facade, is prime location along Narugo-kyo Gorge, best stretch of which starts 15min walk upstream, makes it pleasant. Several *kokeshi* carvers in town, midway along road following Narugo-kyo is *Nihon Kokeshi-kan*, **museum** (8:30-17:00, X-12/16-3/31, ¥200) with 5,000-piece collection representing kokeshi from all over Japan; next to it is **KOKESHI JINJA** shrine. **ONSEN JINJA** shrine, dedicated to area hot springs, is ancient building on small rise overlooking town; hosts annual *Kokeshi Festival* **first sat/sun Sept.**

2 inexpensive public bath houses in town open all day: **Waseda-yu** in middle of town, & **Taki-no-yu Waterfall-baths** near Onsen Jinja, near original spring which burst forth around 837AD. Latter, lovely old building, wood pipes carry cascades of hot water into baths. Narugo has over 50 ¥-T-S ryokan & hotels, budgeteers have Kokumin-shukusha **Takishima Ryokan** 5min downstream of stn. **Kanko-annai** can get you rooms in any place. Or try out any of several old, farther back-in-woods hot springs along river, each with own stop on rail line, bus stop on Rte47: **KAWATABI ONSEN** and **HIGASHI NARUGO ONSEN** downstream, **YAMANAKA-DAIRA ONSEN** at upstream end of Narugo-kyo gorge.

2 stops along Rikuu Tosen rail line offer short interesting detours to Edo buildings...
IWADEYAMA, midway Narugo–Kogota looks like just any country town but for brief moment it was shining star of Miyagi area as HQ of Date clan for 11 years before move to Sendai. In 1663 castle burned, replaced by 'temporary' *Yubi-kan,* still there (15min walk from stn NW along tracks). Later became school for samurai kids, until Meiji Restoration. It is now **museum** (¥200) surrounded by lovely landscape garden. Footpath (5min) connects to castle site, now park with statue of DATE Masamune. Worthwhile hour wander around town reveals many old houses, shops reminiscent of bygone days. **2nd sat/sun Aug** *Masamune Festival*, samurai parade enacts his departure on Korean invasion.

SAKAIDA, (2 stops rail W of Narugo Onsen) site of 2nd building **House of Barrier Guard**, *Hojin-no-Ie* (15min walk from stn). Old barrier gate between Date–Mogami domains was 2km beyond, site marked by stone monument. Striking example of early Edo architecture, also famous for being only still surviving building in which poet Basho stayed during his Tohoku travels.

Backpackers or anyone searching for easy-to-reach backwoods spas should head to...
ONIKOBE ONSEN CLUSTER 10km N of Narugo, and entrance to Kurikoma QNP (which we visit next chapter). 6 buses daily (2 extra sun, hol) take Rte108 from Narugo Onsen to Kokumin-shukusha **Onikobe Lodge** ☎(0229)-86-2331. Dozen small ryokan are spread between Todoroki, Fukiage and Miyazawa springs, all within 10-15min walk of Onikobe Lodge, tho **Todoroki** has own bus stop by river before turn-off to Onikobe. **Houn-kaku Ryokan** ☎86-2243 at Fukiage has private outdoor rock bath (tho nonguest can use it for small fee), formed in pool below waterfall; nearby giant outdoor bath with **Kanketsu-so** *rest house* where you can relax in rooms after bath. Nearby is geyser, *Kanketsu-sen*, which shoots 10m high column of steam every 30min. One-inn **MITAKI ONSEN** is 2km E, up riverside trail from Mikami bus stop (5min before Todoroki). 3km (1hr) hike beyond Mikami is **Katayama Jigoku Hell**, with hellish sulphur landscape with boiling pools, smoking ground and constant rumbling underfoot. It can also be reached by 4km trail from Onikobe Lodge. On either approach to Katayama Jigoku, you will see geothermal power plants in operation.

From ONIKOBE about 15km hike N to regular Kurikoma trailheads of ARAYU, NURUYU or YUHAMA ONSEN. Choice of trails minimal, but may have trouble making parts out. If planning to trek from here, suggest good map or latch on with others more familiar. Good trail books sold in Japanese bookstores, but all in Japanese, but fine maps comprehensible to good map reader.

HIRAIZUMI 平泉

LAVISH JEWEL BOX

LOOKING AROUND this rustic town surrounded with rice fields, one finds it hard to believe it was once greatest city in Tohoku, ranking close behind imperial capital in opulence, reputed as "Mirror of Kyoto". 10-12th century Japan saw much juggling for power in court between Taira, Minamoto and Fujiwara clans, with various factions within each siding with factions of other clans so that there was no single dominant clan—tho Fujiwara held most important posts since Taika imperial coup of 645AD. When MINAMOTO Yoshiie defeated Taira in late 11th century, ally FUJIWARA Kiyohara was given northern frontier areas of Dewa and Mutsu. Financed by nearby gold mines and influenced by Buddhist priest, Kiyohara decided to create literal heaven on earth, far detached in distance and spirit from political mess of Kyoto. Son Motohira and grandson Hidehira followed his lead to further expand cultural center, but 4th FUJIWARA Yasuhira involved himself in politics bringing about downfall of Fujiwara 'Dream Century'.

During all this, down in Kyoto infighting weakened various court factions and TAIRA Kiyomori maneuvered to become by 1156 single most powerful figure. By 1160 he executed most Minamoto opposition, filling influential posts with trusted family members; in 1180 he placed infant grandson on throne as emperor Antoku. But that year saw rebellion led by MINAMOTO Yoritomo under imperial banner of Prince Michihito, and with Kiyomori's death in 1181, Taira were on defensive, defeated 4 years later down in Shimonoseki (follow this Gempei War on our trip down Inland Sea). Military genius of Minamoto victories was Yoritomo's brother Yoshitsune, who had spent youth in Hiraizumi. Ever-paranoid Yoritomo wanting no possible competition, ordered Yoshitsune's death, as he had done to other brother Noriyori and relative Yoshinaka.

Yoshitsune's flight to Hiraizumi is popularly documented in noh, kabuki and bunraku plays—best known is *Kanjin-cho*, his confrontation with guard Togashi at Ataka Barrier Gate (*see* KANAZAWA) while disguised as *yamabushi* en route to sacred Dewa Sanzan. Removed from politics, Hiraizumi's 3rd FUJIWARA Hidehira had vast wealth and power, rebuffed Yoritomo's demands to hand over Yoshitsune for punishment. On his deathbed, Hidehira advised son Yasuhira to ignore Yoritomo's promises of wealth in return for death of Yoshitsune, for only noninvolvement would save Hiraizumi. But Yasuhira, seduced by ever-increasing reward and frightened by prospect of attack by Yoritomo, turned on his childhood friend Yoshitsune and had him killed in 1189. Then Yoritomo, using "murder of my dear brother" as excuse, annihilated Fujiwaras, razed their Capital of Peace. But heroes are hard to kill: legends have Yoshitsune escaping to Hokkaido (where we meet him again with Ainu princess) then Mongolia, supposedly to reappear as Genghis Khan.

Little remains of Hiraizumi's grand past, for Yoritomo so thoroughly destroyed it that it has remained nondescript town ever since. But what does remain, combined with other nearby sites, is worth two-day stop in this pleasant and historical rural town.

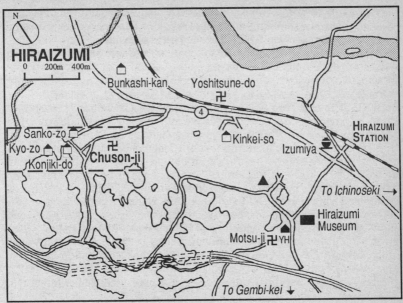

Nearest main city is **Ichi-no-seki**, stop for all trains JR Tohoku line, Shinkansen; 70min–100min regular rail from Sendai, 28min by bullet; sleepers out of Ueno arrive 4-7am. **Hiraizumi** is 7km from Ichi-no-seki; 10min rail Tohoku Main Line, 20min frequent direct bus, or cab 4x-mtr. *But rather than direct to Hiraizumi we recommend...*

TILT: Bus or cab (8-9x-mtr), **Ichi-no-seki** → **Gembi-kei Gorge** →**Takkoku-no-Iwaya** → **Motsu-Ji** → **Chuson-Ji** (nite) to enjoy evening and AM before tour bus crowds, then trip out to **Geibi-kei Gorge** for boat ride and **Yugen-do Cavern**, leaving you much of day 2 to reach next stop be it continuing on to coastal villages or backtracking to mountain spas for wanderers, or **Hanamaki Onsen** or **Morioka City** for less adventurous. **Note:** buses Ichi-no-seki to Gembi-kei frequent but Gembi-kei to Hiraizumi only 3x-daily (6:57, 9:30, 17:18); 2 cab stands Gembi-kei, 10km (5x-mtr) ride.

Mountain spa visitors should take in Geibi-kei 1st day, leave Takkoku Temple & Gembi-kei for 2nd day as buses up to mountain spas stop at...
GEMBI-KEI Gorge (20min bus or cab 4x-mtr, drivers Rte342, from Ichi-no-seki), beautiful if not breathtakingly so like Geibi-kei (follows +2pp). It is 400m of shallow gorge cut by Iwai River, most enjoyable in spring when lined with sakura and many other flowers. Alternate lodging for those who want quiet: 5 ¥-T–S ryokan, of which best is **Itsukushi-en** ☎(0191)-29-2101 at far end, lovely old inn with spacious garden stretching right to river. Midway on N bank is **Gakkoya** tea shop where you can get dish of 3 dango skewered dumplings and tea for ¥300; if on S bank go to their unmanned branch **Azumaya**, put money in basket, hit wooden gong and basket is pulled across on cable and returned with your order.

CAVE TEMPLE of *Takkoku-no-Iwaya* is halfway to town. Temple built on stilts into great cave is 1961 replica of earlier burned down version which in turn was 13th century replica of original built 795 by 'Conquerer of Northern Barbarians', Saka-no-ue Tamuramaro. He dedicated it to Bishamon-ten, warrior of 7 Lucky Gods, to honor fallen soldiers on both sides of his decisive battle against Ainu. While Tamuramaro broke back of organized military threat to northward spread of *Wa* Japanese, he in no way defeated Ainu, who still controlled rest of Tohoku. Tho in next 7 centuries they were assimilated into Japanese culture, Hokkaido remained theirs until this century. Ainu legacy is rich in local place names; adventurers wandering

back-country of north Tohoku will notice many decidedly un-Japanese-sounding places resembling those in Hokkaido. Tho not proven, romantic historians claim cave was fortified headquarters of Akuro, Ainu leader.
Above and to L of temple you can see weathered face and outline of 27m tall relief of Dainichi Buddha of Light carved into cliff; ordered by Minamoto Yoritomo to honor casualties of Hiraizumi raid.

Our bus or cab drives past some grand old farmhouses to let us off in front of...
MOTSU-JI temple (also 10min walk or 3min bus from Hiraizumi stn; ¥500) built 850AD by Saint Jikaku-daishi, didn't amount to much till expanded mid-12th century by Fujiwara Hidehira. Convert to new *Jodo Shinshu* Pure Land Buddhist sect, Hidehira planned to realize Jodo concept of heaven on earth, and came pretty close with grandiose complex of 40 buildings and 500 monks. Only foundation stones survived ensuing centuries since Yoritomo's sack, Hidehira's landscape garden has been restored, best exemplar Heian period *Jodo*-style paradise garden. Present temple built 1909; nearby small museum shows some temple treasures. Looking at panel showing how grounds appeared at peak, see that we are standing where great *Nandai-mon* Gate stood, bridges arched over isle in *Oizumi-ga-ike* Lake to main *Kondo* Golden Pavilion. By pond foundation stones of *Muryoku-In*, Hall of Limitless Light, resembling Byodo-in Phoenix Hall at Uji, but on grander scale, perhaps full-scale human architecture rather than doll house

Far R is...
Jogyo-do Pavilion, rebuilt 1732 by lord DATE Yoshimura. Dedicated to Matarajin, deity of dance and music, Heian period ritual *Ennen-no-mai* Dance of Longevity (Intangible Cultural Treasure) is done **Jan 20** from 9pm to early next AM. Can also see it at spring and autumn *Fujiwara Festival*. Late **June to mid-July** spectacular as 30,000 *ayame* iris bloom. Also temple-run Youth Hostel.
What is now bus road was wide avenue separating Motsu-ji from similar but smaller KANJIZAI-O-IN temple, under reconstruction.

Block stn-wards of bus stop is town-run...
Hiraizumi Museum, *Hakubutsu-kan* (¥300), exhibits assorted antiques, scrolls, swords and Buddhist figures.

20min walk or 6min bus via stn is...
CHUSON-JI temple, also first built 850 by Jikaku-daishi, FUJIWARA Kiyohira spent 21 years to transform into glittering complex of 60 pavilions by 1126. Buildings which survived Yoritomo's torch fell prey to fires over ages, most now remaining date to later centuries. Two buildings remain from Kiyohira's time, **Golden-Hue Pavilion** and **Sutra Storehouse**, both far back of compound; both NT.

Getting off bus or cab at temple entrance you may want to first visit...
Hiraizumi Cultural History Hall, *Bunkashi-kan* (¥300), across road, but pass if short on time or money. 1st floor has panorama display outlining Hiraizumi history, with some artifacts; 2nd has scale model of entire city at its peak under Fujiwara lords. Entrance to temple is Toko-bo Temple **Info Center** where you can get ¥500 ticket needed to see **Konjiki-do, Kyozo, Ohi-do** and **Sanko-zo Museum** (8:00-17:00; 8:30-16:30 Nov-Mar).

Cobblestoned *Tsukimi-zaka*, **Moon Viewing Slope** runs up ridge of densely wooded hill for pleasant walk, about 4min to **Benkei-do**, small wood hall on L, built 1826 to honor warrior Benkei, full of Benkei and Yoshitsune memorabilia. From viewing platform just beyond on R, look down to where Koromo river flows into Kitakami River, point where giant Benkei finally fell, pierced by dozens of arrows while protecting his lord. Further up on R is **Main Hall**, *Hon-do*, behind which is **Tabashine-so** temple inn for budget lodgings, *shojin-ryori* vegetarian priest fare (call ahead), visitors can join in zazen meditation. Tea shop nearby serves *matcha* green tea & *ama-zake* sweet sake.

Next, on L is...
Treasure House, *Sanko-zo*, concrete model of Nara era structure, museum of over 3,000 artifacts (mostly NT or ICA) including ornate coffins, jewelry, fabric and other treasures retrieved from 1955 examination of Konjiki-do vaults, delicate bronze (mix of gold and copper) *kenman* ornaments which hung from Konjiki-do, and some of Kyozo's scrolls. (Replicas of ornaments sold at gift shops, also indigo fans with sutras in gold ink). Numerous invaluable Buddhist icons include sole Heian period image of Ichiji Kinrin Buddha, exquisite white-painted, naturalistic Dainichi 'Sun' Buddha in intricate tall filigree crown, 3 crystal eyes, whom we know, by its hand mudra of right fist grasping upraised left forefinger, is Light containing all other deities and forms of being and cognition (76cm/30in).

Sometimes housed in adjacent...
Onnaisho-ja Pavilion (new) where you can be ritually exorcised, ¥3,000. On far side of Sanko-zo is small theater showing short film on treasures of 4 generations of Fujiwara, ¥50. Opposite side of path are several small pavilions dedicated to Yakushi, Dainichi & Amida Buddhas, one to muse Benzai-ten of Seven Lucky Gods.

On same side as Sanko-zo is...
Golden-Hue Pavilion, *Konjiki-do*, mausoleum of Fujiwara lords, epitome of Hiraizumi grandeur, small but spectacular pavilion coated in black lacquer, gold leaf and mother-of-pearl inlay, 'lavish as a jewel box'. Main figure is Amida-nyori Buddha, projecting monumentality yet under 60cm/2ft tall, flanked by Kannon and Fugen, guarded by 6 Jizos customary at funerary shrines. Each set in triplicate, for vault under altars holds mummified remains of first 3 Fujiwaras, and only head of 4th which was taken to Kamakura to be shown to Yoritomo. Konjiki-do decor hints how Uji Byodoin once looked, well preserved thanks to inaccessability and enlightened Kamakura official who in 1288 lamented its weathered state, ordered facelift and built protective building **Ohi-do** over it. Konjiki-do now sits in new protective structure put up 1962 when last restored; Ohi-do now is just beyond Konjiki-do, and is itself Important Cultural Asset.

Between them is...
Sutra Storehouse, *Kyozo*, built 1108 to house one of then-most spectacular sutra collections in Japan–30,000 scrolls of special indigo paper with gold writing, stored in ornate lacquer boxes with gold and mother-of-pearl inlay. It was 2-storey, top floor lost to fire 1337. Bulk of collection carted off to Kamakura by Yoritomo; some of remaining 3,000 scrolls can be seen in museum, & modern **archive** *Kaiko-kan*, across from Kyozo.

Path branching off between Benzaiten's pavilion and Kaiko-kan leads on up to...
Thatched-roof **Noh stage** in precincts of tiny Hakusan Jinja shrine. Special performances during spring & autumn *Fujiwara Festivals, takigi* (torchlite)-noh from 5pm **Aug 14.** Nearby viewing platform is best place to look across river to Mt Tabashine on which side is burned *giant dai-mon-ji* (character *dai*, great) two nites later. Also nearby is small **museum** (free) of old noh costumes, masks, maps and trivia. Main path continues beyond Konjiki-do to wind over hill to Motsu-ji.

Walk from Chuson-ji to Hiraizumi stn is 15min (4min bus; or 25min bus to Ichi-no-seki stn) thru quiet town.

Just after crossing tracks and river take road branching off L thru clump of woods to...
Yoshitsune-do Pavilion (also called *Gikei-do*) on small rise overlooking river, built 1683 to honor Yoshitsune, of whom there is 300-year-old painted wood figure inside. Site of his mansion, where he was cornered by Yasuhira's treachery, then committed suicide with wife and child.

WHERE TO STAY: Of dozen ryokan in town, best ranked is **Kinkei-so**
☎(0191)-46-2241 on wooded hill between Chuson-ji and stn, ¥-S+. ¥-T inns are
Hiraya, ☎46-2883, and **Benkei-so**, ☎46-2806. Motsu-ji temple offers rooms at
Shuku-in ☎46-2331 which also runs **Youth Hostel**. Kokumin-shukusha
Koromogawa-so ☎(0197)-52-3311 is about 2km upstream of Chuson-ji; near it is
Cycling Terminal ☎52-3520 with pilgrim digs (mostly bunks), sports facilities and
few hundred bicycles for rent at ¥300/4hrs—can leave bikes at stn branch. They have map
of area with bike routes to Gembi-kei and such worthwhile local sights.

CHOPSTICKS: In town sparse, mostly ordinary places. Stn-front main
intersection has 2 noodle shops for good quick lunch. 100-year-old **Izumiya** specializes
in homemade soba, not only in noodle form, but as sushi, tea, sake, pastries and such:
¥1,300 *soba-teishoku* special lets you taste little of everything, add few more yen and get
tempura and more. Across street from it is **Basho-an**, Tohoku specialty *wanko-soba* (*see*
Morioka), all-you-can-eat noodles for ¥1,600.

SHOPPING: Special craft of Hiraizumi is *Hidehira-nuri* lacquerware, started by
artisans introduced by 3rd Fujiwara Hidehira. Very ornate, not inexpensive; ¥25,000 for
set of 5 covered bowls, tho can get single items for ¥1,000-2,000. Best shop is **Ouchi-
ya**, on Rte4 between stn and Chuson-ji.

Head E to Pacific Ocean & Karakura Peninsula...
GEIBI-KEI Gorge (East) is much more spectacular than Gembi-kei
(Wesr); 2km stretch of Satetsu River lined with 30-100m (100-300ft) high
sheer cliffs & rock formations, late May sees cascades of wisteria hanging
over cliffs, autumn frames it in fiery colors. In contrast, river itself is
shallow and calm. You can ride shallow-bottomed wood **boats** up thru
gorge to rocky beach at best stretch of cliffs and back in 90min, or take
picnic and catch later boat back. Relaxing as boatman poles you upstream,
quietly singing old folk songs; at one spot he veers towards cliffs so you
can help pull boat up small rapid by using ropes set in rock wall.

Boats leave on frequent schedule from dock 3min walk from bus stop, fewer in winter
when you go on covered *yakata-bune* boats. Geibi-kei is 10min bus (cab basic-mtr+)
from Rikuchu Matsukawa stn on JR Ofunato Line, 30min from Ichi-no-seki thru scenic
countryside with rustic farmhouses clustered in isolated valleys. Frequent buses from Ichi-
no-seki 45min; **cab** one-way will run 8x-mtr, from Hiraizumi 7x-mtr. Boat ride ¥800.

1.5km NW of bus stop is...
Yugen-do Cavern discovered 1980 (¥1,000).

You can continue on rail past Geibi-kei 45min to bustling fishing fleet center...
KESEN-NUMA, bottom end Rikuchu Kaigan National Park. 15min bus
from stn takes you to harbor, where many midget ferries daily out to villages along...
Karakuwa Peninsula and on to **Ohshima Island**. JR ends 43km up-coast
at Ofunato City's Sakari stn, from where private Sanriku Tetsudo electric trains take you
Kamaishi to rejoin JR. But we recommend saving coast for later, and either head up to
Morioka;

Or detour E to backwoods hot springs of...
KURIKOMA QUASI-NATIONAL PARK: Encompasses volcanic Mt
Kurikoma and surrounding hills. Mt Kurikoma is not such hard climb at
only 1628m, abundant hot springs make it popular. Around base of Mt
Kurikoma are 9 tiny onsen, all with 1-3 budget inns, many with outdoor
baths. Kurikoma straddles 3 prefectures of Miyagi, Iwate and Akita,
accessible from all, but easiest from Iwate's Ichi-no-seki.
2 different public transport routes:

Regular bus from Ichi-no-seki via Gembi-kei Gorge W & spa 1hr 45min to...
SUKAWA ONSEN with one inn **Sukawa Kogen Onsen** ☎(0191)-23-3948 with
giant bath; also offers room-only where you cook own food. Campsite nearby. Just under
2hrs hike to summit. Sukawa has unusual natural sauna, *Fukashi-yu* steam

bath (5min walk up from inn). Stone floor of wood shack has holes thru which hot steam rises; you lie on reed mats over holes, bundle up and sweat.

Road continues beyond Sukawa, to...
OH-YU and KOYASU ONSEN, 75min bus from Yuzawa stn on Ou Main Line.

Other route is on private Kurihara Dentetsu electric trains from JR Ishikoshi stn, 20min S of Ichi-no-seki.

First and more popular choice is to get off after 30min at...
KURIKOMA, from where 1hr bus to KOMA-NO-YU ONSEN deep in wooded gorge with Koma-no-yu ryokan ☎(0228)-46-2110, campsite and Peoples' Rest Village Ikoi-no-mura Kurikoma ☎46-2011 with assorted sports facilities, 30min walk uphill.

30min beyond Ikoi-no-mura is...
SHIN-YU natural outdoor rock bath used by hikers. Late Apr thru Oct, buses continue 25min beyond Koma-no-yu Onsen to end of road at Iwakagami-daira where under 2hrs to summit.

2nd choice this route is Kurihara Dentetsu to last stop...
HOSOKURA (15min) and bus 1hr to NURUYU ONSEN, with Satoh ☎(0228)-56-2251 and Nuruyu Sanso ☎56-2040. There is remaining gate and guardhouse (now museum) of *Hanayama Go-bansho* Edo era barrier gate where Date clan guards kept watch over who entered domain. Those who want even more isolated hot springs continue on foot from Nuruyu Onsen to two single-inn onsen with no electricity, called *Ranpu-no-Yado* Lamplight Inns. YU-NO-KURA ONSEN is 90min walk (☎2872), again as far on is YUBAMA ONSEN which has no phone. Can drive this far, but road is rough. Trails from all three onsen 5-6hrs to summit. Except for Ikoi-no-mura Kurikoma and Nuruyu Onsen's inns, all others close Nov-Apr.

Another separate peak (about 30km N of Mt Kurikoma) is also part of Kurikoma QNP. It, too, has small GETO ONSEN trailhead operating early May to mid-Nov, catering mostly to hikers who trek around 1548m Mt Yaki-dake and 3 sister peaks. Two ¥-B ryokan, each with ¥-P room-only (*ji-sui*, self-cook) sections, and kokumin-shukusha Geto Sanso. Charm of this place is not only due to being hidden in mountains, but also abundance of natural hot springs which have resulted in dozen hot natural pools along freezing stream. One sort of steam bath–pool is in natural cave. Geto Onsen is also known for its high radium content, said to cure multitude of problems, especially stress and fatigue. Coming back from good hike and having outdoor bath to plop into is great, but to have this many to choose from is dream-come-true. Of course, if bathing during day, time your streaks to avoid occasional groups passing thru. Back in Meiji era hot spring connoisseurs created *sumo*-style ranking of onsen divided between East and West; Geto earned top of East list. Reached by 3x-daily bus (May-Nov only) 1hr from JR Kitakami stn, 30min from Hiraizumi or 18min bullet from Ichi-no-seki.

KITAKAMI is unassuming rural town, pleasant but with little to draw tourists tho you can pass time waiting for bus at Tenshochi Park (12min bus E of town). Late Apr, 10,000 cherry trees bloom along Kitakami River and centered around park. In park is lovely Taisho era building housing local history museum with usual display of rural folk items; nearby is stately 270-year-old farmhouse. See Kitakami's *oni-ken-bu* demon sword dancers and 10,000 floating lanterns during gala summer fest Aug 7-9 (*see* DATEBOOK).

Those not up to long bus rides and cross-country treks just for bath can still experience quiet mountain spas, not far from main Tohoku transport route at...

HANAMAKI, itself just another country town but has handful of small onsen within 30min or so by frequent bus, and which collectively make up **Hanamaki Onsen-kyo Prefectural Park**. Hanamaki is 40-50min rail on Tohoku Main Line from Hiraizumi; 28min bullet but Shin-Hanamaki stn to town is 20min bus or 2 stops JR on infrequent Kamaishi Line. Hanamaki Airport is 15min frequent bus N of town.

Many Japanese come here as 'pilgrimage' to honor MIYAZAWA Kenji, prolific writer of children's stories and nursery rhymes, something of legend in his work at improving rough life of Iwate's farmers, among poorest in Japan. He is internationally remembered for children's story *Ginga-tetsudo no Yoru* 'Night on the Milky Way Express', made into award-winning feature length animation in 1986. Born here 1896 (part of house remains in town), graduated from agricultural school in Tokyo, returned to Hanamaki 1922 to teach at his old high school where he created special program to teach modern farming techniques. He died of illness September 21, 1932. Memorial stone with his poetic words of advice "We can beat even rain..." to farm youths etched on is in town; every **Sept 21**, fans gather for memorial rite whre his works are recited and traditional *shika-odori* deer dance performed.

You can visit...
Community Center, *Rasu-chijin Kyokai*, he built and lived in, lovely old building preserved much as it was; scribbled on blackboard by front door are his immortal words "I'm down in the fields" where he was always experimenting with new farming methods. **Memorial Museum**, *Kinen-kan*, opened to commemorate 50th anniversay of his death (20min bus E of stn, near bullet line Shin-Hanamaki stn).

Followers of early modern Japanese sculptor TAKAMURA Kotaro also come to Hanamaki **May 15** to honor artist, born here 1883, son of traditional sculptor. Studied and worked in Tokyo until studio burned down in wartime bombing, then moved back here and stayed with Miyazawa Kenji's father. But Hanamaki was also bombed so he set up shop in rustic mountain house outside town...
Takamura-sanso (40min bus W of town) nearby **Memorial Museum**, *Kinen-kan*, shows some of his papers, sketches and works. Takamura moved back to Tokyo when commissioned to create Two Virgins sculpture on Lake Towada's shore; he died there 1956.

HANAMAKI ONSEN (25min bus NW), beautifully planned resort for farmers as envisioned by Miyazawa Kenji, has now become oriented towards more affluent, but not over-priced. There is also giant rose garden with flower clock, both created by Miyazawa. Half-dozen ryokan here run by farmers' co-op boast excellent service and rooms; book all thru ☎(0198)-27-2111. Grandest is **Kasho-en** tucked away from others recently rebuilt in sprawling classical sukiya-zukuri style; 40 rooms with private bath and toilet, spread out along long hallways, inner and outer gardens, 2 giant baths; worth its ¥-Sw/2. **Shoun-kaku** (¥-T+w/2) is lovely old Meiji era building with 13 spacious rooms overlooking garden. 20% cheaper than Kasho-en are two modern hotels (all J-style rooms) **Koyo-kan** and **Hanamaki** (new annex), all rooms with bath, toilet; former boasts huge baths with view of garden, latter has steamy bath halls with saunas. Facing is **Senshu-kaku**, less expensive version of Kasho-en at under half-price w/2. Cheaper still is **Aoba-kan**. Last have *kazoku-buro* private 'family baths' as well as large communal vats.

All of Hanamaki Onsen's hot water is drawn by pipes from...
DAI ONSEN (5min bus beyond), more casual, yet busy, with two dozen mostly small ¥-T ryokan, best of which is hoary **Nakajima** ☎27-2021, 4-storey wood construction, what all commoner onsen inns once looked like.

Other onsen located W of town along Toyosawa River...

MATSUKURA ONSEN with one inn Suisho-en ☎25-2323 is 25min bus; 2min beyond is family-oriented 'leisure ground' with onsen pool *sennin-buro* '1,000-person bath' and small animal zoo Shido-daira Onsen with 3 ¥-T ryokan, ¥-lo-S hotel; pilgrims can get ¥-B *su-domari* room-only.

5min further to...

OHZAWA ONSEN with ¥-T ryokan Sansui-kaku ☎25-2080 which has room-only in older building, and also runs budget annex ryokan Kikusui-kan. Each has own indoor baths (there are 11 all together), but lure here is large outdoor nonsegregated bath by wooded river shared by all. Five and eight minutes further are two one-inn hot springs, respectively: YAMA-NO-KAMI ONSEN, ☎25-2015, minshuku rate; TAKAKURA-YAMA ONSEN ☎25-2026, ¥-P room-only, Hanamaki YH. nearby.

2min to...

NAMARI ONSEN with old, ¥-T Fuji-san Ryokan ☎25-2311, hoary 3-storey inn with giant co-ed indoor rock bath. Also many ¥-B room-onlies.

WHERE NEXT: From HANAMAKI it is 1hr regular rail or 13min bullet direct to MORIOKA City, but we take coastal detour thru rural TONO to rocky Pacific coastline's Rikuchu Kaigan NP and back inland to MORIOKA. Rail line is one giant loop, but called Kamaishi Line from HANAMAKI to coast where it changes in name only to Yamada Line up then inland to MORIOKA. Trains every other hour 7:00-18:00 leave HANAMAKI for full 250km loop to MORIOKA, handful more thruout day cover lesser stretches of rail; same schedule reverse runs. Those using Morioka as base and visiting Tono can take occasional expresses which start Morioka for no-transfer 1hr-1hr40min ride. Those driving from Morioka can zip down expressway to Hanamaki I.C. and E on Rte283 (88km), or scenic mountain drive Rte396 (62km), to...

TONO (pron. Toh-no), folktale capital of Japan, side-trip into beautiful rural Japan. One of those communities which has preserved much of its rural past while taking advantage of modern goods, and it is this chance to experience *furusato* 'old country home' spirit many modern Japanese miss that draws people here. Tohoku abounds in such rural towns, but what made Tono so famous is its legends and folktales, over 100 of which were compiled into book *Tono Monogatari* by Waseda University professor YANAGIDA Kunio (tr. 1975 R. Morse *Legends of Tono*) after interviewing local storyteller SASAKI Kizen. Colorful intro to rural Tohoku makes for great reading on long train—English version is hardback (8x10in) but thin and easy to carry. Get map from kanko-annai, hop on bike, cab or bus and explore countryside. Kanko-annai usually has some English versions of *Legends*.

GETTING AROUND: Best on bikes, stn-front rental ¥500/day, they suggest 4hrs, we add more assuming you get lost—easy to do unintentionally but something you might do intentionally to see more. Maps, as usual, out of scale, hard to follow, but have 3 courses marked red, green, blue. While Green Route loops thru great countryside, sites are not that interesting, can be skipped, except for FUKUSEN-JI which we take in with blue route. Cabs keep you from getting lost; tour of main sites about 18x-mtr, tho you might arrange set fee before starting. Buses head out to main destinations: end of Red Route Chiba House (not too frequent) and near end of Blue Route to Fukusenji-guchi stop (about 20 daily, few go beyond to Yamaguchi hamlet or Mt Hayachine). Buses are always easier to get returning to town rather than finding one for right destination, so cab out, walk around then bus back, which we do.

First out to...

Chiba-ke Family House (9:00-17:00, ¥300), beautiful rambling farmhouse high on stone base is said to be oldest *magari-ya* house in Tono, built over 250 years ago. In great shape, chosen by Tokyo University as among 10 best *minka* (traditional folk houses) in Japan and fixed up as museum. Chibas were wealthy farmers, complex housed not only their family but handful of servants and 20-odd horses. These L-shaped houses—humans lived in longer portion, animals in short—were unique to Nambu domain, later spread thru Tohoku down as far as Aizu where we see few at hidden kabuki village of Hinoemata (*see* p 969). Several in museums around Tohoku, but Tono is easy to reach and best place to see them in natural surroundings and Chiba-ke is undoubtedly best: 25min bus, cab 5x-mtr, or 11km pedal from Tono stn on Rte396 for Morioka; or 25min walk from JR Futsuka-machi stn.

Strange rock formation of *tsuzuki-ishi* (500m before Chiba House) is monolithic rock poised above two support stones like some primitive dolmen. Some people feel it is natural formation; others attribute tilted state to passage of time since used in some primitive ritual; still others claim it was stacked by mighty Benkei who escaped from Hiraizumi with Yoshitsune and left his mark here.

On return trip some stops are: detour up local road branching N off of Rte396 at Ayaori stn to reach cluster of ramshackle *magari-ya* still in use, much smaller, more rustic than Chiba House.

Just before reaching town, across from Tono Bus Center (8min from stn) are tiny...
UNEDORI JINJA and ATAGO JINJA shrines, former dedicated to god of marriage, latter to god of fire prevention. Short walk behind shrines, wooded hillside has **500 disciples of Buddha**, *Gohyaku-rakan*, etched into moss-covered rocks scattered about. Good place just to sit and watch world go by. Carved 1765 by priest for souls of famine victims. At fringe of town we pass thru Motomachi district with few faded samurai mansions, *buke-yashiki*; Sunaba-cho merchant district has some old *kura*-style houses. Castle used to overlook town from hill S of town, dismantled early Meiji and is now Nabeoka Park; short walk E of Motomachi, S of stn. Nearby is modern red brick **museum** (9:00-17:00 X-Mon, end of month, ¥300) with puppets and animated films reliving some of Tono's legends.

Best part of Tono, where short-time visitors should concentrate, is 6-8km NE of town; area which figures prominently in *Legends of Tono*. We go whole way to **Yamaguchi Shuraku Hamlet** where story-teller Sasaki lived (24min bus or cab 4x-mtr). You can't enter house, but area around it is idyllic; photogenic tiny mill with water-wheel, field of flowers blooming in May. 1km earlier, near **Wano** stop (where Rte340 veers off) is **Kitakawa-ke** family's *magari-ya*, preserved as it was, family lives in modern house in front. Unlike Chiba House, this one feels lived in, more homey and simple. Granny Kitakawa shows you around her house, while telling stories and explaining things in her thick Iwate dialect, hospitality which is extended to all visitors to her house whether they understand or not. She will show you her pair of *oshira-sama* sacred stick figures.

Legend tells of marriage between girl and her horse, latter which was hanged from *kuwa* mulberry tree when her father found out. As crying girl hung onto horse, father cut off its head and both head and girl flew up to heaven. Thus, *oshira-sama* always are pair, one with horse head and other girl's head, each carved of mulberry, covered in bright red cloth which is changed with great ceremony **mid Jan** (date varies). *Oshira-sama* were used by *itako* blind women shaman (*see* Osore-zan, p.1021) while chanting in trance to call forth spirits. Later became good luck charms, found in every house.

15min bus from stn, near main stop Fukusenji-guchi is...
JOKEN-JI temple. Main image here is Obinzuru-sama, cheery faced rubbing god; rub him where you hurt then rub own body and pain is supposed to go away. His smooth complexion attests to much use. In back of temple is stream with small *Kappa-fuchi* **pool**, said to be home to many mischievous mythical saucer-headed *kappa* water imps. *Legends* tell of

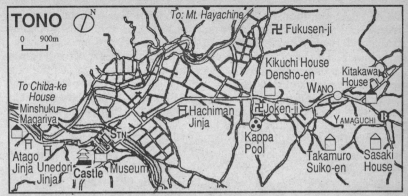

many evil deeds by kappa who like to pull children and horses into their pool; but there is one of kappa who was instead dragged out by horse and swore to bring fish everyday if he was allowed to return. They're kind if coerced, but they're also polite so if one tries to drag you in, bow to it. It will bow back thus displacing water in its head-plate and will have to jump back in to replenish it or die. One of two *koma-inu* stone temple dogs of Joken-ji has indented head and said to be part *kappa*. Across Rte340 from pathway to Joken-ji is weathered, broken ancient torii which once marked start of trail up holy Mt Hayachine. Near it is **Densho-en** compound (9:00-17:00, ¥200) with fixed up *magari-ya* **Kikuchi-ke** house, modern museum to legends of Tono, and folkcraft workshop. Here, you can buy your own set of *oshira-sama*, as well as other Tono specialties.

Short way townwards of Joken-ji local bus road cuts off N to Mt Hayachine.

Head up about 3km (5min bus) to...

FUKUSEN-JI temple, home to largest wooden Kannon statue in Japan, carved free-standing 17m tall. 4.5km back to stn from Joken-ji; halfway is **HACHIMAN JINJA** shrine, site of **Sept 14-15** Folk Arts Festival (*see* DATEBOOK).

WHERE TO STAY: Tono is great place for o'nite, and if you can do so, choose minshuku **Magariya**☎(01986)-2-4564 which as name suggests is converted *magari-ya* farmhouse. Large amounts of delicious local cooking featuring *sansai* mountain herbs and river fish; sit around *irori* sunken hearth after dinner and relax with family, or just wander around pleasant countryside. That is, just as long as some of Tono's spookier legends haven't gotten to you. Located by Tono Bus Center. **Takamuro Suiko-en** ☎2-2839 is town-run inn with magari-ya annex; within compound is small museum and their own solar generator which heats their bath and more. 10min walk S down side road between Joken-ji temple and Kitakawa House. In unlikely event both are full, there are over dozen more ¥-B accommodations in and around town, but none as unique.

Adventurers continuing towards Pacific Coast may want to stop en route at...

KAMI-ARISU stn (5 stops, 35min, from Tono).

3min walk from stn is...

Rokan-do Cave, narrow winding tunnel of glimmering marble sides for about 1km then you suddenly come to whispy subterranean waterfall cascading 30m down. ¥800 includes helmet, boots and flashlight.

We reach coast 1hr from Tono at **KAMAISHI**, bustling fishing center, known for its giant 49m tall Kannon statue looking out to sea. Completed 1970 as stylized pagoda to house relic of Buddha, also kept inside is ancient wooden Kannon image–climb to chest level observation platform inside.

KAMABURO ONSEN (20min bus S) where **Kamaishi Marine Hotel** ☎(0193)-26-5111 has giant clay oven-like natural sauna; ¥2,000 for sumptuous seafood lunch and use of baths; o'nite ¥-hi-T/w2. Here road and rail follow central portion of Rikuchu Kaigan NP 55km to **Miyako**, spend nite in town or out at *Jodo-ga-hama* Beach with spectacular rock formations.

En route, there may be some people snapping pictures of **Kirikiri stn** (4 stops from Kamaishi), setting for novelist IGAMI Hisashi's humorous fictional tale of rural community which seceded from nation to create own kingdom of Kirikiri-koku. One of things which made his story so popular was that he wrote it all in Tohoku dialect, labeling it national language of his kingdom. Tohoku dialect, called *zuzu-ben* slurred-speech, is so different that most Japanese find it hard to follow—almost impossible if locals really start going off in *zuzu-ben*. So if you think you've forgotten all your hard learned Japanese, don't feel bad. No one can understand them.

Jodo-ga-hama has several budget minshuku, small stretch of beach with small inlet is almost walled off from ocean by tall rock formations. Rent rowboats to paddle around. Path goes down to foot of cliffs along N shore, along beach to *rosoku-iwa* candlestick-rock and on to *shiofuki-ana* blowhole thru which geysers of sea water shoot 40m high, near which are ¥-B inns.

Continue up-coast on bus or private Sanriku Tetsudo electric trains 95min to...
Kuji where rejoin JR 2hrs up-coast to **Hachinohe City** (*see*). Around Kuji are villages where women *ama* divers go after shellfish, kelp; farthest N you will find.

We turn inland 4 stops (32min) up at Omoto and catch bus (they start 45min earlier from Miyako) 50min to...
Ryusen-do Cavern (8:30-17:00, ¥800) ranked among top three caves in Japan, is long network of subterranean ponds at points 120m deep connected by river which flows out of cave's mouth and into surface river. About half of 5km tunnel with 35 branch caves has been explored, most of that open to public, with network of bridges over water. Clearest water in world, visibility from surface is to 41-45m depth. Cave and *usagi-komori* rabbit-bats are natural monuments. Across from entrance, newly discovered cave is now natural museum. Ryusen-do is also 13min walk from Iwaizumi stn, end of JR Iwaizumi Line which is 1hr from Yamada Line turn-off point Moichi. Must change at Moichi if to/from Morioka; trains to Iwaizumi start from Miyako, 6-10x-daily.

There are also few express buses daily which link Ryusendo with...

MORIOKA' CITY 盛岡市
CAPITAL OF Iwate prefecture, ranks with Sendai as one of most pleasant cities in Tohoku. Modern, yet neighborhoods of narrow maze-streets retain much of old castle-town atmosphere when Nambu lords ruled. Conveniences of metropolis and pleasures of country. Comfortable base for day trips to **Tono, Kakunodate** and **Lake Tazawa**, and **Hachiman-tai** mountains. Many lodgings range from top class hilltop **Grand** and **Royal Hotels** thru full range of less costly hotels (stn-front **Terminal Hotel** is good) and as many inns from superb **Morikyu Ryokan** or rustic **Itoh-sen Ryokan** in old Zaimoku-cho neighborhood, to budget. Capable staff of stn **Kanko-annai** can book. Or head out to TSUNAGI ONSEN (35min bus W of town). Despite rapid modernization Morioka is clean city, you see people fishing in crystal clear Kitakami and Nakatsu Rivers flowing thru town. Providing backdrop to city is volcanic Mt Iwate rising NE of town, its cone earns its alias of Iwate Fuji.

There are several interesting **museums** to supplement walking around town; most are at outskirts of town and if going by bus you must return either to stn or downtown bus terminal for each leg. Yet distances are not that great so 4 people can tour by **cab** for same cost as city bus tour. Many cabs on roads here so you can usually find one quickly; tho if out at new Pref Museum, recommend keeping as didn't seem to have many out.

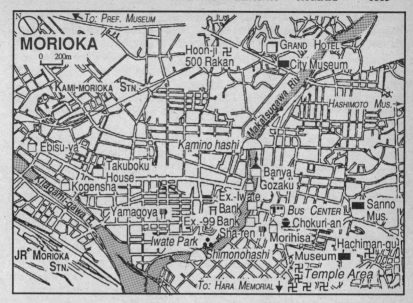

If you spend time in Morioka you should walk around some of its older neighborhoods, so we start with some quick walking tours around town:

Short walk W of stn then L after crossing Kitakami River 200m to next road beyond which is good section of...

ZAIMOKU-CHO. Convenient enough for short stroll between trains. As name indicates, this was lumber (*zaimoku*) yard; now modern shops blend in with generations-old neighborhood places, and entire street becomes outdoor produce market in summer. Near L corner is **Yamazen** traditional sweets store; **Kogensha** (beyond, also on L) is best folkcraft shop in town—lovely turn-of-century building worth seeing, as are other buildings within complex (including fine coffee shop). Across from it is **Itoyu** for *Nambu-tsumugi* silk. Go to end of street and on other side of intersecting road is cotton-dyer ONO Saburo's store/workshop **Ebisuya**. Here, Mr Ono will show you how to hand-dye his lovely patterns using same method his family has used for 350 years: special rice-powder and lime paste is put on cloth except where stencil covers pattern, so when dyed (natural) only pattern comes out. Ask to see family museum upstairs. You'll find some old samurai residence neighborhoods N of main Chuo-dori Avenue bounding Zaimoku-cho's N side. One popular house still in good condition is **Takuboku Shinkon-no-Ie**, or Honeymoon House of ISHIKAWA Takuboku, noted turn-of-century author. This was home of middle-class samurai, remnants of high-class samurai residences are scattered about further N and E.

Iwate Koen (5min bus or 20min walk E of stn).park occupies site of Nambu clan Kozukata Castle, was destroyed in Meiji Restoration's Boshin War leaving only stone foundations. No real reason to come here, other than we pass thru it to reach other side of Nakatsu River flowing behind castle park.

If **late Apr** *sakura* season get off bus at *Kencho-mae* which lets you off at Pref Hall and Court, in front of which is *ishi-wari-zakura,* giant stone-splitting-cherry tree, 350 years-old, growing out of huge boulder. Otherwise, next stop *Uchimaru* closer to Iwate Park, or stay on another 3min till you reach main city Bus Center. Crossing any of bridges behind park we enter another old neighborhood, best stretch of which is N of

Middle Bridge, *Naka-no-hashi*, at NW corner of park. There are two other bridges flanking Naka-no-hashi: 600m upstream **Upper Bridge**, *Kami-no-hashi*, built 1609 by first Nambu lord to commemorate completion of new castle. Tho rebuilt often since, its *giboshi* metal post covers are original and have become symbol of Morioka City, along with local Nambu-tetsubin iron goods (*see* SHOPPING). 600m downstream of Middle Bridge is **Lower Bridge**, *Shimo-no-hashi*, built few years after Upper. Stone marker near Lower Bridge marks birthplace of writer NITOBE Inazo, whose portrait graces present ¥5,000 bill.

KONYA-CHO district retains much of its castle-town atmosphere, tho first building we come to is grand Meiji era red brick Iwate Bank ex-Head Office. N up side street is Konya-cho; on R is stodgy Taisho era **Morioka Shinyo Bank**. Just beyond bend in road is **Kamasada-kobo** outlet for *Nambu-tetsubin*; here you see more modern items as well as usual traditional stuff. Next on L is oft photographed **Gozaku** old-fashioned kitchenware shop. Beyond on R **Soshi-do** for more *Nambu-tsumugi* silk; then old-fashioned rice cracker shop **Shirasawa Sembei** where interested people will be shown how it's made. End of this block on far L corner is Taisho era wood building **Konya-cho Banya**, which was local police HQ. To its L is **Wanko-ya**, one of best *wanko-soba* places in town. Next block of Konya-cho, to Kami-no-hashi, also retains much of old castle-town airs, this time merchant residential.

Head S from Iwate Bank building one block then L (E) and block-and-half on R is...
Coffee shop **Sha-ren** in fine old *kura*-style building. **Morihisa Tetsubin-ten** (next block on L) is run by Suzuki family who made items especially for Nambu lords. L at next big intersect back to main Naka-no-hashi-dori Avenue on which SE corner is **Chokuri-an**, another well-known *wanko-soba* shop.

But we keep going straight E another 700m to...
HACHIMAN-GU shrine, site of gala autumn fete featuring ancient float parade and yabusame mounted archery. If you miss it, you can still see some floats kept on show at small museum within shrine compound. Hachiman Shrine is also terminus of colorful *Chagu-chagu Horse Festival* **Jun 15** (*see* DATEBOOK). 5min walk N of Hachiman-gu, **Museum**, *Sanno Bijutsu-kan* (9:00-17:00, X-Mon, ¥300), mostly work of local artists, part is dedicated to many art objects of Nambu lords.

Back on W side on Nakatsu River, about 1km N of Iwate Park is old...
TERA-MACHI TEMPLE DISTRICT. HO-ON-JI temple is worth visiting to see its *Go-hyaku Rakan* 500 Disciples of Buddha, whose humorous positions were carved out of wood and lacquered. Took monk Hokyo Soshi and seven disciples four years from 1731 to carve them all, dedicating them to victims of great famine. One seems to have disappeared sometime, and it is said that among remaining 499 are figures of Marco Polo and Kublai Khan. Short walk from Honmachi-dori 1-chome stop, 8min bus fron stn.

It's not really out of your way since 4min bus further (or 10min walk) is...
Morioka City Museum, *Kyodo Shiryo-kan* (9:30-21:00 -17:00 sun, X-Mon, ¥150), built on grounds of old Nambu lords' summer house at base of Atago-yama Hill. Nambu mansion is long gone, but its landscape garden remains. **Nakamura-ke**, 18th century merchant house was brought here, also some other restored buildings. Modern old-fashioned museum displays Nambu clan treasures as well as basic commoners' items from Edo period, and good display on local festivals. Your cabbie may know it better as *Chuo Komin-kan* Central Citizens' Hall; bus stop is *Komin-kan-mae*.

Pref Museum, *Kenritsu Hakubutsu-kan* (9:30-16:30, X-Mon and 9/1-10, ¥200), is further N, near Matsuzono New Town housing complex; 30min bus from stn to *Nishi Matsuzono 2-chome*; some buses continuing beyond Kyodo Shiryo-kan Museum go to *Higashi Matsuzono 2-chome* 15min walk; adds about 6x-mtr there & back on taxi tour. Ultra-modern museum differs little from other prefectural museums in format—history and folkcraft sections interesting, with sections on local fauna and flora, etc. It does boast hands-on room where you can try on old costumes and handle various tools and such. All-glass 2nd-floor wall beautifully frames Mt Iwate. With lots of land to spare, they have created botanical garden, and relocated two old *minka* folk houses: *magari-ya* L-shaped **Sasaki-ke** house and regular **Fujiya-ke** house. Ideal if you don't have time to see real ones still in use in Iwate's countryside.

Hashimoto Museum, *Bijutsu-kan* (10:00-17:00, ¥500), is one of most interesting museums, styled after *magari-ya* house but much larger and using contemporary materials; haphazard setup can be attributed to fact that was built with no blueprint, done as-you-go. Architect was HASHIMOTO Yaoji, whose art (mostly dark paintings of people at work), and those of other local artists, is displayed inside. Mixed in are mediocre works by European bane artists, appealing to Japanese in name rather than quality. There is also Hashimoto's personal collection of traditional local crafts—lacquerware, weaving, pottery and ironworks. Best of all is reconstructed *magari-ya* farmhouse atop museum roof, full of items relating to daily farm life. Hashimoto saved 7 such homes from being submerged by dam. 20min bus from stn, or 10min from downtown Bus Center; 2km E of Kyodo Shiryo-kan Museum. Sits partway up wooded Iwayama Hill, where various winter and summer sports facilities and offers view of city which bus tours take in but you can do without.

One last place to visit is...
Hara Takeshi Memorial, *Kinen-kan*, (9:00-16:30, X-mon, ¥100), SW outskirts of town; 20min bus from stn, 10min from Bus Center. Dedicated to HARA Takeshi, first commoner Prime Minister 1918-21. Long-time politician, leader of liberals during formative years of Japan's foreign policy, cut down at Tokyo stn by militants who opposed his pacifism towards Asia. Displays mostly memorabilia like his bloodstained jacket, and poems; but his house and garden are nice example of traditional rural life.

CHOPSTICKS: Not all noodles and traditional cooking. Those who have had enough Japanese will find slew of non-Japanese restaurants including KFCs, other fast foods. But Morioka is famed for its *wanko-soba* eating contests, and hearty appetites may want to join in, but don't count on little Japanese having little appetites—champions easily down 100 helpings, and they figure 7 helpings equals average 1-person order of noodles. *Wanko-soba* comes in tiny bowls with mouthful or two which you eat with various toppings. As you down one load, waitresses pass by with more, ad infinitum until you quit. Going rate is ¥1,600-1,800 per person, but if not contest time most places add on once you go beyond certain point of 30-40 dishes. Among best are downtown's **Chokuri-ya**, Konya-cho's **Wanko-ya; Nambu Hatsukoma** on 2nd floor of Bus Center is also quite good. Good local cooking can be had at rustic sister-stores **Yama-goya** and **Suisha-goya** one atop other, at Sai-en 2-chome near Royal Hotel just W of Iwate Park. 1st floor **Yama-goya** Mountain Hut is *robata-yaki* grill with fresh mountain game, vegetables, herbs, seafood; 2nd floor **Suisha-goya** Waterwheel Hut specializes in *sansai-ryori*, mountain herbs and bird, and *nabe-ryori* (potluck dish) called *Nambu-hatto*, has various vegetables and chicken boiled in soup. Up side street, block W of these two, folksy **Rokuro** specializes in charcoal broiled river fish. At other side of town is country-style **Nambu Robata** grill between Hachiman-gu shrine and Morihisa Iron goods shop. Many coffee shops for rest during your walks around town; in addition to above mentioned **Sha-mon**, there is another converted *kura* shop **Bateren-chaya**, block and half NW of Nambu Robata, occasionally featuring jazz bands.

Natural Foods: Konsai-tei, uses organically grown local materials, genmai lunch ¥600, 'setto' of 7-8 dishes ¥1,200. Kami-no-hashi-cho 2-28, 11:30-21:30, X-sun, ☎52-0899. Soba shop **Kisaragi**, home-made local soba, ¥500-800, across from terminal Hotel. Park lot by JR stn. 10:00-21:00, no-X, ☎24-0273.

SHOPPING: Mostly for *Nambu-tetsubin* iron goods. Craft was introduced early 17th century when Nambu lord commissioned Kyoto craftsman to forge special tea kettles for tea ceremony. With abundant raw minerals nearby, ironworks became major industry of Morioka. Now, all sorts of things from pleasant wind-bells to pendants are forged, but tea kettle is still city's symbol—in case you didn't notice giant iron kettle sitting on Tohoku Main Line platform. While beautiful black kettles with various designs on them make great gifts, they weigh, so you might settle for lighter wind-bells. You might also pick up bolt of *Nambu-tsumugi* silk, or Mr Ono's cotton fabric; both materials have also been made into attractive accessories. If you don't have time to go to each store, stn gift shops carry everything, and 1st floor of **San-biru** Dept Store (at NW corner of Iwate Park) has good local crafts section. And don't forget **Kogen-sha** folkcraft store.

WHERE NEXT: From MORIOKA, we again have choices which boil down to 3 basic routes: up to Pacific Coast's HACHINOHE City, either meandering up **Rikuchu Kaigan** coast from MIYAKO, or straight up Tohoku Main Line; back across to Japan Sea Coast's AKITA City and up that side; *or* right up middle thru **Hachiman-tai** mountains. Hachinohe has some worthy sites if passing thru, its also good place to catch ferries to Hokkaido. Akita's coastline is beautiful, which we come down after Hokkaido–you can also end your tour of Tohoku at AKITA, fly back to TOKYO. Should you choose to take either of last two routes, you can still take in mountain hot spas of **Hachiman-tai**, castle-town KAKUNODATE and nearby **Lake Tazawa** as sidetrip from Morioka. We blaze up mid course thru sprawling **Towada-Hachimantai National Park** and cities of **Kakunodate** and **Hirosaki**.

HACHINOHE is 2nd largest city in Aomori prefecture, industrial base where once-fishing-only harbor now caters to tankers and cargo craft from around world. Most of town is postwar, and old neighborhoods of town have that faded air of some Occupation era town. Downtown is slowly becoming built up to look like any modern Japanese city, but with no major attractions to speak of other than its festivals, tourist trade is new here and most lodgings business oriented—tho some new hotels OK and there are some good old ryokan. Hachinohe festivals are good reason to visit, most notable of which are mid-summer *Sanja Taisai* gala fest of 3 shrines, and midwinter *Emburi*, one of Tohoku's many throw-backs to pre-*Wa* Japanese rites. So if in town to catch festival or boat, here's what you can do:

First of all, don't panic if Hachinohe stn seems bit too rural—downtown is centered around Hon-Hachinohe stn (5km E). Ferry Terminal whence 3x-daily to Tomakomai and 2x-daily to Muroran both on Hokkaido is 3.5km from Hon-Hachinohe stn. Your destination will either be downtown or area around Samé; former reached by 10min train or bus, or cab 2x-mtr+, latter by 30min bus or rail. To take in 2 main sites near town, we suggest using cab to save bus hassles. Start from **Hachinohe stn** and first stop **KUSHIBIKI JINJA** shrine is 2km SW, then another 2km to **Folk History Museum**. You can let cab go and catch 15min bus ride to main Mikka-machi intersect downtown.

KUSHIBIKI JINJA was ancestral shrine of powerful Nanbu clan's Hachinohe branch since 12th century. Soaring cryptomeria trees lining main path to shrine were planted about then; shrine itself is 1648 reconstruction of original. Main reason for coming here is to look at some ancient samurai armor hidden away in shrine's treasure hall; one with red embroidery, another white, both date to early 14th century, presented to successive

Nambu lords for military aid by successive emperors Go-Murakami and Chokei. These ornate masterpieces weigh about 30kg each including helmet; reinforced lacquer coating intertwined with thick cloth weave and covered with elaborate metalwork. If closed, get someone to open it, included in entry fee.

Folk History Museum, *Rekishi Minzoku Shiryo-kan* or *Koko-kan* (9:00-16:00, X-mon, ¥300), has one of Japan's foremost collections of Jomon period artifacts, all of which were excavated here on farm of Izumiyama brothers. They privately financed entire excavation, then donated property and its treasures to Hachinohe City which built this excellent museum in 1963. Excavations yielded remains of 3 late Jomon period mini-communities in one general area now collectively called *Korekawa-iseki* site. Over 6,000 pieces were found, including rare wood utensils which show some sort of primitive lacquer-like coating, and plain wood swords. These and countless superb pieces of pottery owe their preservation to high content of muddy volcanic ash in soil here. Late Jomon pottery is intriguing, characteristic whorly patterns become so exaggerated as to become almost grotesque. Era gave rise to those curious bug-eyed monster *dogu* clay figurines which many Japanese and Westerners from amateur UFOologists to reputed historians feel where modeled after visiting aliens. 2 Jomon pit-dwellings have been reconstructed on museum grounds. Get full overview of Hachinohe's history from Jomon thru Tokugawa periods at **Municipal Museum**, *Shiritsu Hakubutsu-kan*, on way back to town.

Samé is far E section of city, on S side of Hachinohe harbor. Getting off here puts you right in middle of city's busiest fish market; loud, fast-paced and slippery, but colorful part of old Hachinohe is in pleasant contrast to this modern industrial city. Armada of small family-owned fishing boats fills harbor here like Hong Kong scene, oblivious to giant tankers nearby.

10min walk E of Samé stn is...
Kabushima Isle with its hoary shrine dedicated to sea gods and muse Benten, linked to land by natural bridge. You'll want hat or umbrella to visit shrine from Mar thru Aug when Kabushima becomes summer home to thousands of *umi-neko* sea-cats, protected species of gull so called for their meow-like cry. Continuing along, coast curves S and down to **Tanesashi Kaigan** coast with rocky shores, beaches, expanses of grass with campsites and many minshuku make it popular in summer.

Being industrial city it is, Hachinohe offers many industry tours which can be done without prior arrangement. List in Japanese of 2 dozen tours available thru **Kanko-annai** or City Hall. They include **Yukijirushi** and **Meiji Milk**, **Tohoku Electric**, **Mitsubishi** and other metalworks. You can also visit **Ground Self Defense Force** base, and **airbase** used by air wing of Maritime SDF; both are N of city. Air SDF base is up at Misawa City (below).

Looking at good English map of Tohoku you notice that stretching up Tohoku to W of Hachinohe is whole string of similar sounding towns of *X-nohe* along Rte4; in fact, 7 more including tiny #9 Kunohe S of #8 Hachinohe. These are #1 Ichinohe, #2 Ninohe, #3 Sannohe, #5 Gonohe, #6 Rokunohe and #7 Shichinohe. Some say these numbers represent advancing camps of northward bound *Wa* Japanese, with Hachinohe due E of Gonohe, marking 40km loss of territory from northernmost Shichinohe. These towns actually came into being some few centuries after northern barbarian *Yezo* and Emishi tribes had been subdued, and marked centers of nine official horse-raising ranches of Kamakura government. There used to be #4 Shinohe but it has faded in time, probably due to fact that 4 is hononym for death and superstition kept it from growing after horse-keepers left. Some you pass thru on Rte4 are pleasant rural towns with hiway right thru heart of town, lots of interesting old architecture. Unless you've lots of time to enjoy these towns slowly, you will probably have just one memory of them—one which we always experienced hitch-hiking to Hokkaido—being frustrating bottlenecks as traffic inches thru town. Ichinohe is worst, and we always seemed to pass thru at morning rush.

MISAWA City (20min rail N) is site of giant US air base and suddenly you just become another *gaijin* on streets instead of some walking tourist attraction. In addition to all types of Americans and international (southeast Asian) hired help which seems to come with any US base, there's full assortment of Japanese from all over, making Misawa interesting, if small, metropolis in boonies. Misawans have long been exposed to foreigners, for well before US base was created (at height of Vietnam war, over 10,000 Americans were stationed here) world swooped down on this fishing village which just happened to be closest spot on Japan to US west coast. **Memorial** on stretch of packed sand **Sabishiro Beach** NE of town commemorates take-off point for first successful nonstop trans-Pacific flight to Wenatchee, Washington. Americans Hugh Herndon and Clyde Pangborn in modified monoplane Miss Veedol left Oct 4, 1931, landing 41hrs13min later. This threw then-small village into international slipstream, with merits like getting first phones to accommodate hordes of press, trials of sending down to Tokyo for W-style toilet fixtures, trying to come up with W-food —wonder why country inns get so flustered when foreigners show up.

Main reason for you to come to town now is right next to train stn at...
KOMAKI ONSEN complex, privately owned resort *cum* folk museum of lumber king self-made millionaire SUGIMOTO Yukio who began this pet project of his in 1961. Komaki's bath hall boasts largest rock bath in Tohoku, but is actually whole set of baths, waterfalls and artificial 'natural' surroundings said to represent Lake Towada's beautiful Oirase River area. Wall of plastic flowers separates men's section from higher-up women's, but men get their chance to peek as women have to pass behind large waterfall to reach more pools. We usually steer clear of such monster bathing pavilions, but Komaki is really experience worth catching, and there's culture nearby too. While baths are large enough to hold 100s, try to go in when no tour bus around. Sugimoto's first **Komaki Hotel** ☎(0176)-53-3131 is most traditional, at ¥-T–S. If full try newer **Komaki Grand** ☎53-5151 and newest annex, each more western and expensive than earlier one.

Rest of Komaki is taken up by one of best Tohoku folkcraft museums, several reconstructed *minka* folk houses, noh stage, replica of Izumo Shrine wedding hall, replicas of famed temples, ponds, landscaped gardens and rock gardens, and for pleasure seekers olympic-size pool and bowling alley with distractingly huge roof-top pin. One poor farmer's *minka* is museum of Jomon period artifacts unearthed at Lake **Ogawara-ko** N of town; another *minka* in different part of onsen comes from same village but belonged to wealthiest farmer. Newest addition **Saigyodo Koen** park has more old minka, temples, tea houses, museums around man-made Kappa-fuchi lake (small museum of kappa-related items). In addition to bath time you'll need few hours just to see sites of Komaki Onsen, each house is museum in itself, tunnel-like passageways lined with all sorts of displays, and who knows what else will be added. One museum is dedicated to SHIBUSAWA Keizo, pen-name was Saigyo, Minister of Finance during 1920s and mentor to Sugimoto. Admission to Komaki's older half and Saigyodo Park ¥500 each or both ¥800 *kyotsu-ken*; bath included. Guests at Komaki hotels *free*.

Sugimoto has been prime mover behind increasing Tohoku's tourist trade. In addition to Komaki, he has created smaller-scale but similar set-up at Noheji's **MAKADO ONSEN**, and his **Towada Kanko Tetsudo Tour Co** has built hotels at Shimokita Peninsula's **YAGEN ONSEN**, ryokan and hotel up at Lake Towada and operates tour buses to and boats around Lake Towada, as well as namesake Towada Testsudo electric rail line which has frequent runs 25min from Misawa to Towada City on Rte4. **Hitch-hikers** will find few hundred yen ride is worth hassle-free trip to Rte4, which often takes much time, tho well-travelled road thru Misawa joins Rte4 S of Noheji. Company also runs 3-4 nontour buses to Towada from Misawa (2hrs) via Towada City, whence 3-4 more daily start/end; all via beautiful Oirase River.

Komaki worthwhile stop, but keep in mind it's not all idyllic parks, baths—tacky in many ways and can get crowded, but it's unique. Gives short-time traveller chance to see many great minka, take onsen bath without having to leave main trunk route. Misawa only 2hr express, 3hr local from MORIOKA City, 1-2hrs AOMORI means morning departure from Komaki will get you across to Hakodate with lots of time to settle in, or 10hrs total to Sapporo. Drivers will find giant parking lot. There are cheaper inns in town but not by too much, so by the time you pay admission fees, savings are minimal, and food at Komaki is superb. Staying here also lets you bathe as many times as you want.

If rushing up by **car** towards Aomori on Rte4 bypassing coastal Haichinohe and Misawa, it is worth few hundred yen fee for cross-country Michinoku Toll Road, bypassing coastal fishing villages which really slow up traffic on Rte4. They're one reason we use **Noheji** for ferries across to Hokkaido when hitch-hiking. Noheji is right before these villages, where coastal Rte338 from Misawa rejoins Rte4. Ferry terminal for runs to Hakodate is 10min bus from stn or short walk from Rte4 for hitch-hikers. 5-6 crossings daily are spread out over 24hrs, so you can spend extra hours down at good beach nearby, or bus 10min past ferry to **MAKADO ONSEN**, another project of Misawa's Mr Sugimoto. This is smaller scale, with one ryokan as well as some reconstructed folk houses. You'll want to visit town during its colorful summer festival **Aug 18-20**.

Continuing N of Misawa and Noheji is mysterious **Shimokita Peninsula** (*see* Aomori). Now we backtrack to outline our main course up thru middle of Tohoku.

KAKUNODATE 角館   CENTER OF TOHOKU

ONE OF RARE castle towns to retain much of its feudal appearance architecturally as well as in feeling; in many ways similar to southern Honshu's Hagi city, yet different in many ways. Other places we have visited like Aizu Wakamatsu, Matsue and Kanazawa represent more metropolitan cities, while mountainous Hida Takayama and Kiso River Valley towns represent more rural settings. Kakunodate was always small country town since chosen for site of minor castle of Satake clan in 1620, and here we get to see and enter examples of various classes of samurai residences as well as old merchant homes and shops. Tho many neighborhoods are dominated by 20th century structures, they somehow retain airs of days past, and wandering among great walls of Uchi-machi's samurai mansions gives you good idea of what Kakunodate must have been like.

Best time to visit is **late Apr-early May** when cherry blossoms in full bloom. Lining streets of samurai district are hundreds of 360-year-old weeping *shidare-sakura* trees brought from Kyoto as saplings; merchant district has as many later additions; and 2km stretch of *sakura* along Hinokinai River were planted 1935 to mask harsh new concrete banks built to protect against floods and commemorate birth of crown prince. As Kakunodate is one of more popular cherry-viewing places in Tohoku you'll want to book rooms early, especially weekends (don't if you can avoid); same goes for visits during gala *Autumn festival* Sept 7-9. *Maple-viewing* in Oct is good, less crowded time to visit.

Short detour out to...

Daki-gaeri Keikoku ravine (15min cab NE of town). We came here in autumn, in many ways more beautiful than crowded *sakura* season, multicolored leaves covering trees and streets really add to aura of antiquity.

WHERE TO STAY: We spent relaxing nite at minshuku **Hyakusui-en**
☎(0187)-55-5715 in merchant part of town, lovely old house which belonged to clan's
doctor at end of Edo period. Profession of doctoring wasn't passed down and present owner
SAWADA Takesuke, great-grandson of doctor, prides his cooking skills and hospitality,
both of which were superb. Can arrange for lunch here, after which visit their *kura*
storehouse museum of family heirlooms. Balancing Hyakusui-en's homey atmosphere
with high-class service is 8-generation-old nearby ryokan **Ishikawa** ☎54-2030, ¥-T–S.
Half-dozen more each of ryokan and minshuku in town; ryokan **Natsuse Onsen**
☎(0187)-44-2220 10km NE of town (past Daki-gaeri Ravine). Arrange all thru helpful
Kanko-annai in modeled-after-samurai-mansion stn building; at Kanko-annai get their
illustrated maps of town; Japanese ones easy enough to use even if you can't read, 'soon-
to-come' are English brochures. Rail stn is 7min walk S of Bus Center.

Kakunodate is laid out N–S, with *Furushiro-yama* hill site of ex-castle
N of town. Spreading S from it is **Inner Town**, *Uchi-machi*, which once
contained 80 samurai houses; top-ranked nearest castle. Bisecting town E–
W is 25m-wide belt of green known as *Hiyoke* fire-break dividing Uchi-
machi from commoners' **Outer Town**, *Soto-machi*. Spread along it is
Public Hall, Town Hall and Library with small but good display of odds
and ends on Kakunodate. Town is small enough that 3-4hrs walk (or 2hr
bike) allows you to see all and lunch at one of several fine old restaurants.
It's only 1.5km (1-mile) from one end of town to other, but there are three
cab companies: one near stn, one near **TENNEI-JI** temple (with its Big
Buddha) W of Bus Terminal, one at far S end of town, and another near
Plaza Hotel at *hiyoke* green belt.

When we visited, **5 samurai houses**, *buke-yashiki*, were open to
public, as was garden of another. We walk to N end Uchi-machi to see
Aoyagi-ke and **Ishiguro-ke** houses, two of finest examples of top-class
samurai residences. Aoyagi were top councilors to Satake lords and their
house (last rebuilt 1860—Jay feels odd projecting such awe of antiquity on century-old
buildings when NY brownstone he was raised in dates to 1869) is best preserved in
town. Enter thru main gate which used to open only for Satake lords or
other official guests, all others used small door on L. Slatted *nozoki-mado*
peeping-windows protrude on outer wall from where guards could survey
visitors and shoot at attackers. *Kura* is museum of family heirlooms and
odd assortment of late Tokugawa and early Meiji Western antiques (¥300);
tea house in grounds serve *matcha*. Next door **Ishiguro** were few rungs
down in status from **Aoyagi**; their house one of oldest in town dating to
1809. You'll notice lots of giant trees in these grounds which in addition to
aesthetics served utilitarian purpose of blocking out harsh winter winds and
snow, shading in summer and natural firebreak to repel or contain flames.

At N end of this street is home of ex-daimyo Satake family (no plans to
open to public, except perhaps their *kura* as museum of samurai weaponry,
etc.); behind is castle park, 20min walk to top. Mid-rank **Iwahashi-ke** house
is block S, freely enter unoccupied home (dates 1852, minor facelift 1975).
Half-block S are two more mid-rank homes **Kawarada-ke** (sometimes open)
and next-door **Odano-ke** (garden only open). One street W of these three is
neighborhood of low-rank samurai, of which we can visit unoccupied
Matsumoto-ke dating to around 1850. There is another stretch of mid-
and low-rank *buke-yashiki* along far E side of Soto-machi merchant district.
Can't enter any (yet), but pleasant area to stroll especially *sakura* season.
Collectively called Tamachi Buke-yashiki, they housed late-comers to
Kakunodate who had no more space up in Uchi-machi.

After passing thru Tamachi, we hook clockwise around end of block.
Large piece of land on R belonged to wealthy merchant-landlord **Ohta-ke**

family—it is notably grander than homes of low-rank samurai who were richer status-wise than Ohta but poorer financially. Across from gate to Ohta house is early Meiji era red brick miso and soy sauce factory of **Ando-ke** family, which you should peek in. There are many interesting Edo, Meiji, Taisho and early Showa period shops all over town like *kura*-style **Sakamoto-yakkyoku** pharmacist, stone **Io-shoten** dry goods near Hyakusui-en, or old **Itsutsui-ke** family-run sake-shop which is part of their grand old house on corner near Plaza Hotel. Many are workshops and/or outlets for local craft *kaba-zaiku* cherry bark-covered woodwork.

Laborious woodwork process can be seen at ...
Densho-kan Museum (9:00-17:00, X-thu during Nov-Mar, ¥300) across from and S of Aoyagi-ke manse, modern W-style brick complex thankfully hidden from surrounding old neighborhood by walls. But worth visiting to see co-op-run workshop of *kaba-kaizu* craftsmen. This craft, originally done by country folk further N for cherry-bark tobacco pouches, was introduced to Kakunodate late 18th century when much of Japan's lower samurai were financially impoverished and searching for ways to supplement income. Shinjo's samurai turned to carving *shogi-goma* chess pieces, Yonezawa's turned to silk, and Kakunodate's turned to covering all sorts of woodcraft with strips of cherry bark. Lustrous ruddy bark keeps out moisture, and best *chazutsu* air-tight containers for powdered tea is coated inside and out with *kaba-zaiku*. You can buy trays, cigarette cases, boxes, and ornamets of *kaba-zaiku*, but it is not cheap: prices at Densho-kan's gift shop competitive to town shops, but better chance to get discount at private shops, more fun. Museum area shows many fine *kaba-zaiku* goods along with other local crafts, and array of feudal memorabilia.

Another local craft displayed here is *itaya-zaiku*—branches of young *kaede* maple woven into baskets and other useful farm objects. More popular are toys—carved up into packs of foxes, horses and other animals, which as set can be put back together to create original branch shape. If interested in *itaya-zaiku*, visit Mr KANBARA Shoji, recognized as best at craft. To get to his workshop-home, cross Hinokinai River on Uchigawa Bridge at S end of town, keep going to first alley past police HQ where L for short ways. You should call ahead in Japanese to ☎3-2609. It's just beyond old shop which has for generations been making one of Kakunodate's edible exports—pungent love-'em-or-hate-'em *natto* beans.

Third local craft worth mentioning is *shiraiwa-yaki*, simple utilitarian style of pottery introduced here, actually to nearby Shiraiwa hamlet, 1771. Six families had kilns producing everyday items in their characteristic earthy-brown and creamy glazes until 1897 earthquake-generated slide wiped out by-then economically faltering kilns. Densho-kan has good collection of wares ranging from simple vases and bowls to giant pickling vats; you may also run across some neglected pieces while browsing thru antique shops in this and other Tohoku towns. In 1974 some locals got together and re-introduced similar type of pottery and ceramics calling it *shiraiwa-seto*. Can visit these new kilns at **Shiraiwa** (20min bus E of town).

Two places to visit while out here, one is...
Shiraiwa-yaki Togei-kan Museum displaying items from oldest up to present, other is UNGAN-JI temple which is loaded with ancient *shiraiwa-yaki* items (including *sentai-butsu* 1,000 figures of Buddha) and other lkcrafts.

Town Museum, *Cho-ritsu Bijutsu-kan* (9:00-17:00, X-mon and weekend afternoons, ¥200), on W bank of Hinokinai River near Middle School, exhibits on various crafts of Kakunodate which rotate every 2 months.

CHOPSTICKS: Other than handful of noodle shops and budget diners is mostly local specialty of *sansai-ryori* mountain-cooking with assorted vegetables and some river fish, all artistically arranged on array of small dishes. Best in town is *ryo-tei* **Shoji** where it may be bit pricey for lunch (¥1,500 and up for better, more) but well worth it. Shoji is 150m W of Tennei-ji temple and as far S of *hiyoke* green belt. If closed or full, get much same for slightly less at nearby **Murasaki**. Carp and trout dishes served at **Ohgiri**, on W side of river across from Police HQ. We ended up spending almost as much on assortment of single orders for few hundred yen each at **Kakunodate Kurabu** (Club), dingy name not at all fitting for this lovely old building where you are served around old-fashion *irori* sunken hearths. It is on E-W street running between roads to stn and Bus Center.

GETTING THERE: Tho Kakunodate when seen on map seems to be out in mid-nowhere, it is convenient to almost any route up or down Tohoku. Hourly JR departures from MORIOKA City ride Tazawa-ko Line 1hr 50min local or 1hr express (alternating each hour). Expresses continue to Japan Sea Coast AKITA City (55min), local to OMAGARI City (location for flowery All-Japan *Fireworks Makers' Contest* **4th sat Aug**) where change for Akita-bound trains on Ou Main Line, which you can also take S towards YOKOTE City (site of **3rd wknd Feb** *Kamakura igloo* and Bonten lantern fetes), and on further to Yamagata and Yonezawa. **Drivers** take Rte46, 60km from Morioka or 50km from Akita. Pleasant 2-3-day driving.

TILT: Leave MORIOKA morning, 2hr → KAKUNODATE (nite); day 2 visit **Lake Tazawa**, up Rte341 → Aspete Line toll road across **Hachiman-tai** mountains (optional 2nd nite any onsen there; *see*) for total return distance to MORIOKA 170km. Or cut out much time and distance by-passing Hachiman-tai and still take in onsen at hidden baths above Lake Tazawa. Incidentally, drivers will find good parking lots around town; one right in heart of Uchi-machi. If using Akita airport to enter or leave Tohoku, Kakunodate is ideal first or last nite in Tohoku; airport is almost midway between Akita and Kakunodate, about cab 15x-mtr to Kakunodate. 90min buses from Akita City (not via Airport) make infrequent trips to Kakunodate, with some ending...

Lake Tazawa-ko deepest in Japan, near-sheer sides plummet 424m.

50min bus from Kakunodate to main town...
SHIRAHAMA on E shore (called Tazawa Kohan by bus Co) if via JR **TAZAWAKO** stn, 70min if via western **KATAJIRI** and clockwise around lake. Also, on main route from Tazawako stn: almost hourly departures for Nyuto Onsen Group stop at Tazawa Kohan, as do equally frequent buses which round Tazawa in both directions. In fact, just about any bus from stn will get you to Kohan, tho less runs Dec-Mar. **Drivers** may take scenic back way from KAKUNODATE: N on Rte105 to end of parallel JR Kakunodate Line's Matsuba town and E on local road 3km to **Goza-no-ishi** on lake N-shore. (Rte105 continues past Matsuba to hit Rte7 midway Ohdate and Noshiro Cities; rail yet to span 25km of mountains to Hitachinai stn, present terminus of short Aniai Line.) You can circle TAZAWA by bus in 40min, drivers must pay for Tazawa-ko Toll Road which circles 2/3rds of lake, clockwise SHIRAHAMA to GOZA-NO-ISHI, which has relatively few places to stop and look; or 4-6 sightseeing boats daily circle lake counterclockwise (40min) stopping all three spots, or just Shirahama-Katajiri (25min); or rent bikes at Shirahama for 2hr pedal around Tazawa.

Shirahama has most lodgings: posh **Sunrise Hotel**, 6 ryokan, 10 minshuku, Kokumin-shukusha, Youth Hostel and campsite; Katajiri ranks close behind tho bit more quiet; but Gozaishi has just one quiet ¥-B inn for those who want to experience the lake in relative peace and quiet. There is also pleasant little **GOZA-NO-ISHI JINJA** shrine, with its red *torii* on lakefront. Everything around here gets bit crowded July-Aug, and weekends May & Oct.

If you visit in winter and notice that Tazawa isn't frozen over, you can take scientific explanation that natural spring water pouring up from bottom of lake causes turbulence which prevents freezing, or go for local explanation that turbulence is caused by passionate love-making of Tazawa's resident dragon spirit Takko-hime and her visiting dragon mate Hachiro. Hachiro was once peasant boy who ate fish and become so thirsty that he drank from stream for 33 days, suddenly transformed into dragon then blocked up some rivers to create his new home of Lake Towada. Shortly later he was driven from his home by sorcerer who took over Towada, so Hachiro moved into shallow lake on Akita coast, now called Hachirogata. During all this, particularly beautiful girl Takko-hime decided she didn't want to get old and ugly so she began 100 days of prayer on mountaintop. On last day voice told her to drink from nearby stream, which she did and became another dragon, at which time thunderclouds exploded above to fill valley with water—which became lake Tazawa. Both Hachiro and Tazawa wanted Takko-hime, and this time Hachiro won. So every winter when Hachirogata freezes over, he comes up to Tazawa to be with Takko-hime and so ... isn't it obvious that two dragons mating generate a lot more heat and turbulence than some spring? But one wonders how happy locals will be to have them roiling up waters all year after Hachiro dragon becomes live-in mate. Landfill of Hachirogata begun prewar to create more farmlands now covers over 4/5ths of original lake surface. **4th wknd July** *lake festival* has two dragon floats paraded around. In 1968 large bronze figure of human Takko-hime was put up at Katajiri to honor this most famous of Akita-*bijin* beauties.

From stn via lake frequent buses 1hr to...
NYUTO ONSEN-KYO cluster of 6 mountain spas, each with one ¥-T inn and some sort of outdoor bath. Something we like to do at places with good lake, hot springs and mountain is to sit in outdoor bath before climbing at night to catch sunrise, back down to baths for early morning dip then lazy day of lounging around and in lake. Tho here, multitude of hot springs and cool river can easily substitute for lake. Good clear nite, moon and stars bright enough to climb by; topped off with spectacular sight of black but starry night sky being gradually pushed W by pastels of rising sun, as down below, lake begins to shimmer in new day's rising light. 3-4hrs to top of 1478m **Mt Nyuto**; backpackers can continue 2 days to **Hachiman-tai**, or 1-day loop along mountaintops to TAZAWA-KO KOGEN ONSEN (below).

WHERE TO STAY: Central ¥-B Peoples' Rest Village **Kokumin Kyuka Mura** ☎(0187)-46-2244 with lodge and campground, and one-lift ski area. If you're not here to trek up mountain just for view, you can plop your roots down here as base to explore Nyuto's baths, all nearby, and have inn with pilgrim *ji-sui* room-only section and ¥-Tw/2 *ryokan* section: Oldest **Tsuru-no-yu** ☎46-2814 (closed Nov-Apr) humble inn began as special lodging for Kakunodate's Satake lords who came for curative powers of its four outdoor baths. Barest essentials of electricity home-generated so can use lamps. 40min walk up side road (car OK, 10min) across river from *Tsuru-no-yu Iri-guchi* stop, 5min on bus before *Kokumin Kyuka Mura*. Past Rest Village is tiny **Tae-no-yu** ☎46-2740 with riverside bath; next is **Ohkama** ☎46-2438 with huge outdoor bath; similar **Kaniba** ☎46-2021 is 200m beyond last bus stop. Almost forgotten as it's only one you can't drive to is **Magoroku** ☎46-2224 15min walk from Kaniba. Three little wooden huts sit near riverside hot springs which have been formed into baths. Trail up **Mt Nyuto** starts nearby; another path cuts over 10min walk to **Kuroyu** ☎46-2214 similar cluster of 6 riverside hut-with-outdoor-baths, and *yu-no-taki* hot-water-falls which pour out of exposed pipes to give natural massage. Kuroyu is 20min walk down side road from Rest Village, 5min if you catch inn's shuttle van which meets incoming buses.

In winter more people stay down at TAZAWAKO KOGEN ONSEN (20min before Nyuto cluster), with its good skiing. Just down road is MIZUSAWA ONSEN, also with several ski lifts going up to 8th level of Mt Komagatake. Both places have lots of lodgings. June thru October climbing season 4 buses daily go from Tazawako stn via Kogen and Mizusawa Onsens to 8th level of Mt Komagatake. It's easy 1hr to 1637m summit from either 8th level bus stop or end of chairlifts which run most of summer.

*One of the pleasant things about life
in Japan are the unexpected complications. . .*
—John Fujii, in *Ukiyo*

AOMORI 青森 AKITA 秋田
HONSHU NORTHERN TIP

TOWADA-HACHIMANTAI NATIONAL PARK: One of largest parks in Japan—actually three distinct sections spreading 200km up Honshu from Morioka to Aomori City. S to N: **Hachiman-tai Mts** straddling Iwate–Akita prefectures, natural wonderland for skiier and hiker with countless backwoods onsen scattered about to make either sport more fun. Then wide gap to S fringe of Aomori pref and main draw volcanic **Lake Towada** (don't confuse with small Lake Tazawa down by Kakunodate). N of Lake Towada is last part of park, **Mt Hakkoda** with more hiking and hotsprings. Hardly anyone does whole park in one shot, but rather, treat it as three separate parts with breaks at cities and towns at fringes of park. However, you can 'do' all three sections in one trip: after visiting castle-town **Kakunodate** and **Lake Tazawa** bus across Hachiman-tai to summit onsen for nite. Hikers take various routes to trek up. Next day bus down 1hr40min to Hanawa town on rail line, from where 1hr20min bus to **Lake Towada** (some direct from Hachiman-tai); or 1hr20min-2hrs train to **Hirosaki** City (Nite) from where bus to Towada. From Towada 2hr10min to great backwoods **Suga-yu Onsen**, from where 1hr40min bus to **Aomori**, or hike across Hakkoda Mountains to Hakkoda Onsen and 1hr25min bus to Aomori. This is not really what one has come all this way to Japan for, but this is truly wonderful park whether just driving or hiking thru. And both types of visitors will appreciate it, with many scenic roads for former, long trails with many hot spas for latter.

HACHIMAN-TAI MOUNTAINS: Looking NW from Morioka City most noticeable is Iwate Fuji, but behind it are several 1,500-2,000m peaks crisscrossed with trails from dead-end onsen. These mountains give excellent skiing, with almost as many ski resorts as hot springs. Those on S-side like **Shizuku-ishi**, **Amihari** & **Tazawa** more popular as relatively easy to reach from Morioka. Except special ski buses, most buses quit during heavy snows Nov–Apr. 4 main entry points, 2 on S-side and 2 N.

GETTING AROUND: You can rail 25min from Morioka on JR Tazawa-ko Line to **Shizuku-ishi** town from where 45min bus up to **AMIHARI ONSEN** with several ¥-B inns and **Peoples' Rest Village**. 5hr climb up to top of **Mt Iwate Fuji**; backtrack bit down N slope of hills 3hrs to **MATSUKAWA ONSEN**. Or curve around SW via **TAKI-NO-KAMI ONSEN** from where about 6hrs trek to **NYUTO ONSEN Cluster**. Taki-no-kami also reached walking 2hrs up dirt road branch-off from main bus road halfway to **Amihari** at **GENBU ONSEN**. One stop before Shizuku-ishi is largest private farm in Japan **Koiwai** *Bokujo*, popular summer escape for Japanese tourists where they can romp on farm being 'mid-Western' and stay in **SL Hotel**, old steam locomotive-drawn train converted to hotel. From Koiwai, scenic toll road meanders to Amihari. Many buses from **Morioka** go to Shizuku-ishi in 35min, some continue up to Amihari; others go via Koiwai Bokujo and toll road to Amihari and end at Shizuku-ishi.

Above is more hiker's route, others try alternative bus from JR Tazawa-ko stn (40min from Shizukuishi) via **Lake Tazawa** (4-6x-daily Jun-Oct) up Rte341 thru more spas to **TOROKO ONSEN** W end of 27km **Aspete Line** toll road (¥800) midpoint of which is summit of Mt Hachiman and more spas. Backpacker's course from **NYUTO ONSEN Cluster** NE of Lake Tazawa takes 6-8hrs to **Matsukawa Onsen** from where again as far to **Hachiman-tai summit**; another is 2-day direct to Hachiman-tai. Hikers coming from S get here in 1-2 days depending where you start; it's about 15km from Matsukawa Onsen. Less hardcore hikers have several short hikes around Hachiman-tai summit.

Most popular entry way is from NE corner of park **Ohbuke** stn on JR Hanawa Line, 35min from Morioka. Hourly buses (which start Morioka 50min earlier) from Ohbuke take Aspete Line to Hachiman's summit. Midway up at **Kotsu Center**, some buses branch off for 30min trip to MATSUKAWA ONSEN, handful of ¥-B inns. Nearby is Japan's first and largest geothermal power plant; free tours.

Hachiman-tai's 1614m summit, boundary between Akita & Iwate prefectures, is actually just short walk up from bus stop, but 300m elevation difference from bus stop doesn't make much difference. Occasional buses take side-road S from summit stop 8min to **TOSHICHI ONSEN**, unassuming little spa of 2 ¥-T inns deep in woods where you can often ski on nearby slopes until early May. More small spas (some with big hotels) along Aspete Line.

25min bus E of summit is...
GOZAISHO ONSEN with large ¥-S hotel and YH. Popular ski resort borrowed Mt Zaos snow-monster ski tour, come up with their own cross-country trip across Hachiman-tai; equally popular easy 2hr trek in snowless months.

20min bus W of summit, on S side of Aspete Line is backwoods...
OHBUKE ONSEN with ¥-B rooms.

To its N...
FUKE-NO-YU used to be quiet one-inn steam bath which recently grew into one-hotel spa with area's largest, **Fuke-no-yu Hotel**. You can experience what it used to be like at one-inn (¥-B room w/2 or ¥-P room-only) **GOSHOKAKE ONSEN** just beyond, where men and women still bathe in same steamy bath halls with giant baths, sauna-like steam baths where you sit in box with only head poking out, massaging streams of hot water pour out of high pipes. Old ryokan section and pilgrim room-only buildings sit right in heart of steamy springs, newer more comfortable 'hotel' section is nearby. All rooms thru ☎(0186)-31-2311, **Sansui-so**. Pleasant path (2km, 40min) meanders thru surrounding area where you pass mini-volcanos, bubbling mud pots, some steaming fissures and spouts, and Ohyu-numa pond which sits in extinct volcanic crater.

20min further W is resort...
OHNUMA ONSEN with several choices from YH to hotel. Easy path links all of these onsen to summit. Few more small onsen spread between Ohnuma and Toroko Onsen at end of Aspete Line.

If looking for short trek with few people, 3hr intermediate trail from Goshokake cuts SW across peaks to **TAMAGAWA ONSEN** ☎(0187)-49-2352 on Rte341 from/to Kakunodate and Lake Tazawa. This quiet spa is surrounded by wooded hills in small valley filled with steam from one of most voluminous springs in Japan spouting 9,000 liters per minute. ¥-T ryokan and ¥-P room-only sections flank giant bath hall, and huge outdoor bath is few minutes walk S; water is high in acidity so prolonged soaks should be avoided or at least broken up by dousing with plain water.

We use fourth route to exit **Hachiman-tai**, from summit, bus W again to **TOROKO ONSEN** and Rte341 which takes us to Hanawa stn, from where one way to **Lake Towada**.

En route Towada near Ohyu Onsen is one of Tohoku's many mysteries....
Ohyu Stone Circle, *Kanjo-resseki*, man-made stone formations dating back about 4,000 years by some estimates. On either side of road are two pairs of concentric stone circles about 40m diameter, and between two is what appears to be sun-dial with oblong horizontal stones radiating out from upright central stone pillar. Compare this to another stone circle we see later up near Otaru on Hokkaido.

LAKE TOWADA-KO, major attraction in Tohoku is caldera lake formed eons ago as giant volcano blew in on itself. 4th largest lake in Japan, surface 400m above sea level, at deepest 327m; almost circular 44km shoreline interrupted on S shore by two small spits of land around which are main settlements of **Yasumiya** and **Utarube**. Sightseeing boats cruise lake, lodgings from ¥-L to campsites cater to all types; but beautiful as it is it is just another lake when compared to some volcanic lakes on Hokkaido. If 'progress' has continued at pace locals expected during last visit, Towada's S shore will have been much built up to accommodate more visitors, but it's large enough that one seeking isolation follows shore trail to N side **Taki-no-sawa campground**, 1km walk from Taki-no-sawa viewing platform, on route for 2hr buses from **Hirosaki** on Ou Main Line (*see*) to E shore **Nenokuchi** village.

But before deciding to skip Towada altogether, reconsider if autumn—best time to visit **Oirase Keiryu** stream, gorgeous 14km stretch of water flowing out of Lake Towada at Nenokuchi village to Towada Onsen. It continues on, eventually to become Oirase River pouring into Pacific N of Hachinohe City. Fiery hued leaves cover stream, with strategically placed benches at viewing spots; dozens of small waterfalls pour into stream, with itself some lovely falls. Lush greens and colorful flowers of early spring are preferred by some; cool stroll in summer's thick foliage; while others prefer almost barren snowscapes of winter. Area closer to lake nicer, path follows entire length to **TOWADA ONSEN** (5hrs), or rent bikes at either end to do in 2hrs, tho road is crowded at times with cars. Buses also run on road so you don't have to walk all. Towada Onsen is collection of many inns, and tho near to Oirase River, rather than stay here, we suggest small onsen beyond. 8-14 buses daily Tozawa-Aomori r.t. Apr 15 to Nov 10. Incidentally, about half of these buses are run by JR so Rail Pass works. There are also some buses which take this route to coastal Misawa and Hachinohe.

Some of those take us near another mystery site...
Grave of Jesus Christ, at Shingo village, marks spot where he died after leaving Middle East and making way across Asia to end-of-road Japan. Next to his is grave of brother who got himself nailed up in Christ's place—tho no one explains how he got here. To counter skeptics, locals come up with proof of Jesus' life here (apparently came here around age 21 to study from mountain mystics): old name for this village, now of nearest town, is Herai which they claim is from *Heburai*, Japanese for Hebrew; women of Shingo used to wear black veils to cover their face Middle East style (tho neither Jewish nor Christiam habit); on doors of grave caretaker Sawaguchi family's house are Star of David design which they claim was handed down for countless generations; name of local *bon* dance, *Naniyadoyara*, is gibberish in Japanese but supposed to sound like Hebrew song "we praise your exalted name.."; and they claim clincher is local Shinto rite for newborn kids which involves making sign of cross on infant's head. This last ritual we have seen down in isolated villages of Kyushu, stronghold of 'Hidden Christians' in 17-19th centuries. Whether you believe it or not, it's worth look if passing thru. May 3 they hold memorial rites for Jesus here.

From Towada Onsen, if you take Rte394 towards Aomori, you enter...
HAKKODA MOUNTAINS portion of Towada-Hachimantai NP has tragic place in Japanese history: with war against Tzarist Russia impending, Imperial Army decided to train for possible fighting in Siberia, so several regiments were sent to frigid Tohoku. On January 23, 210 men of 5th Infantry Regiment left Aomori to trek across Hakkoda to rendezvous with other troops starting from Hirosaki. On first day out, fierce unexpected blizzard hit and by day 2, 70 men had died or disappeared. By day 3, only

30 remained, at which point corporal Goto set out solo to find help. Rescuers found Goto, almost frozen solid but amazingly alive, and he led them to others. Recent movie on episode is monument to bureaucratic stupidity. By end only Goto and 10 others were alive with most losing limbs to frostbite. Bronze statue of Goto stands near spot where he was found, on N side of Hakkoda, and your destination if hiking over. If only they had come little farther to any of natural hot springs here.

Now, road to Hakkoda from Aomori is open by Feb when expert skiiers flock to ropeway to peak of Mt Tamoyachi for 4-6km group runs. If Ski Patrol feels you lack ability, you are sent back down by ropeway. Runs all year; just as popular once entire road opens early spring for trips to Lake Towada. As long as you avoid winter, Hakkoda offers great hikes; 1500m peaks only take 6hrs to cross S to N or reverse. Easy trails wind thru lush marshlands with seasonal flowers and many ponds, and of course, various hot springs at either end.

TSUTA ONSEN, Single-inn ☎(0176)-74-2311, (15min bus on Rte394 for Aomori) is best to stay at if you want to taste what real mountain onsen is about. Turn-of-century ryokan 'discovered' by Meiji era writer OMACHI Keigetsu, who decided this was his heaven on earth and spent much of his life here. Bronze bust of Omachi stands near inn and his ashes are buried across road. *Tsuta* is variety of hardy ivy which grows into tree-sized trunks, which you see lots of, along with much other fabulous woodwork, inside this grand ryokan and its annex. Its two huge wood baths—men and women separate—have naturally clear hot spring water seeping thru slat bottoms. We were lucky enough to get room, but you may want to call ahead in season to ensure nite in one of Tsuta's spacious rooms wich come with feasts of fresh mountain herbs and river fish and more. We find this much more enjoyable than cluttered tourist-trap that is Lake Towada.

Unless camping on Towada's far side we advise just quick look at lake, walk, drive or pedal thru Oirase River's first half and leave an hour or so to see Tsuta's own little treasure **7 Ponds of Tsuta**, *Tsuta-no-nana-numa*. Easy trail from onsen gradually climbs up and thru seven gem-like ponds hidden in lush green forest. For little extra (at times 'service'), have ryokan pack *bento* picnic lunch to enjoy back in woods. We stumbled across it almost by accident, but you should make effort to stay here if it sounds like your kind of place. At ¥-lo-T, steal for what you get. If you can't stay at Tsuta, there are two more isolated one-inn onsen down road, 15min and 20min bus respectively:

YAJI ONSEN ☎(0176)-72-2100 and SARUKURA ONSEN ☎23-7500, both ¥-B-T. We've seen neither, but don't seem to stack up to Tsuta by reputation.

Catch morning buses to reach Aomori in 2hrs, which you can skip if not festival time and still see giant paper floats at festival museum en route to city. Tunnel-train from Aomori gets you to Hokkaido's gateway at Hakodate; or adventurers can trailblaze up W Tsugaru Peninsula to Minmaya and ferry to Hokkaido's only castle-town of Matsumae, or up E Mutsu Peninsula to see shamans at sacred Osore-zan (p1021) then ferry across to Hakodate.

We get off bus 35min from Tsuta at...
SUKA-YU ONSEN where you can experience rare old-fashioned spa—giant 1,000-person-bath, *sennin-buro*, in rambling old wood building. Buy your ticket, go to separate dressing rooms, then come out to cavernous mixed-bathing hall with various tubs. Proper way to enjoy baths here is to sit first in hottest, then lukewarm, then quick douse in cold vat and stand under hot water 'falls' and back into hottest vat. 'Modest' westernized Japanese shun these places so most of your bathing partners will be just

friendly old country folk here to cure some illness. Shy folks can use separate baths in main part of **Suka-yu** inn ☎(0177)-38-6400 which has regular ryokan section (¥-lo-T) and *jisui* room-only at below budget minshuku rate.

Short walk down riverside path near campsite leads to...
Shack with outdoor sauna *Manju-fukashi* bun-steamer. Japanese 'bun' here also has double entendre of English. What you steam are not edible buns but ones you sit on. Long covered bench with holes sits above steaming spring, and you sit on bench. Watch it, gets bit hot if don't have something to sit on. Said to cure assortment of female problems and hemorrhoids.

Back at main road cross it and short walk to steaming...
Hell Pond, *Jigoku-numa*. Many people just pass thru for this bath, which is what we did then hiked over half-day to Hakkoda Onsen group for 90min bus to Aomori City next morning. You can take bus 20min further to bottom ropeway terminal for 10min ride up to Mt Tamoyachi for 2hr walk around plateau there, or shortcut hike down to **Hakkoda Onsen**, which at this point will be 'just another' one-inn hot spring. Hikers who want to keep this backwoods atmosphere for one last nite should walk 3km to moderate rate *Rampu-no-juku* Lamplite-inn **Tashiro Motoyu** Onsen with outdoor bath and several indoor ones.

AOMORI 青森

CITY WAS PASSED thru by almost everyone travelling up Tohoku—tho often seen just fleetingly while rushing for JR-link ferry to Hakodate. All major rail lines and roads ended in Aomori BT-'Before Tunnel'. Despite strategic location Aomori was always just small fishing town not worthy of even second-rate castle. Which is main reason new Meiji government made it capital of new prefecture—to get fresh start with no feudal connections. What little remained of Aomori's historic past was effectively wiped out in 1945 when well over 80% of town was reduced to rubble by USAF. What has risen is typical of postwar modern, barely distinguishable from other Japanese cities, little to draw tourists, particularly Westerners, to. There are, however, some museums in and around town to spend short hours.

PERSONAL DATEBOOK: You'll want to spend at least one nite here during **first week in Aug** for *Nebuta Festival* which ranks among Tohoku Top Three. Beginning with *zenya-sai* 'nite-before-fest' on 1st, top attraction parade of 20-odd *nebuta* floats down Shinmachi-dori Avenue begins **7pm on 2nd**, repeated nitely until **6th**; from 1pm on **7th**, fireworks from 7pm at which time is floating parade of *nebuta* taken around bay on boats. *Nebuta* are huge wheeled floats of paper-with-wood-frame shaped into fierce warriors, dragons, giant fish and more, colorfully painted and illuminated from inside. Separating each float are groups of gaily dressed dancers—which visitors encouraged (often on like-it-or-not basis) to join. Proper attire is not necessary, but you can buy full head-to-toe festival costume for around ¥10,000 at department stores; or rent them from coffee shop to L of stn-front plaza—but theirs go quickly. Parade is only part of this noisy festival which is just an excuse to eat, drink (lots) and be merry for week before returning to grind of farmwork. Word of warning to those strictly there to watch: don't stand in front rows or you'll find yourself part of dancing group. Personally, we think it best way to enjoy festivals, especially if you like lots of good sake—which is generously handed out to all.

Romanticized, most unlikely origin of *nebuta* dates back to 8th century Ainu-conqueror Sakanoue Tamura-maro who used similar contraptions to scare off surrounding Ainu guerrillas; floating ones were to convince that Japanese had retreated by boat and so ambush Ainu who then wandered off-guard into town. First of all, it's doubtful Tamura-maro ever made it this far N; it's also hard to believe skilled hunters who had resisted Japanese for so long would fall for such ploy—not to mention that there was then no town here. But it sounds good. More likely origin is credited to late 16th century lord of Tsugaru who entered colorful paper float in Kyoto's *O-bon* festivities which created such stir that it was repeated back home, rapidly growing in number and popularity.

Nebuta time is also incredibly crowded as 2 million visitors converge on Aomori during that week making rooms scarce. Most people book rooms year in advance, tho they say you can get room as late as May. If you don't care where you end up, you can usually get some place to stay by checking in at stn Ryokan Info by noon of that day. Several special such info booths set up around stn for Nebuta week. Many people stay nearby towns, such as convenient ASAMUSHI ONSEN 20min rail or 30min bus E of city.

Another choice is to take past-midnite ferries (JR or regular) for 4hr sleep to Hakodate—or 7hrs to Muroran on some regulars. If you time it right, gives great view of floating parade on 7th. Rest of year no problem getting rooms in Aomori, tho we don't advise it. En route Hokkaido, you'll find Hakodate much more interesting port town; from Hokkaido keep going past Aomori to Mt Hakkoda or Lake Towada, or to Hirosaki City (*below*).

40min bus S of city (en route Hakkoda)...
Nebuta-no-Sato has been set up for those who miss festival. Central is Nebuta Pavilion displaying dozen of best *nebuta*, lighted up and hooked up to move to background festival music flowing thru darkened hall. Also in park is field athletics obstacle course and some other outdoor recreation facilities which are included in ¥600 admission (9:00-17:30, X-Nov thru Mar).

Nebuta-no-Sato is en route to Hakkoda and Towada, and while out this way stop by 20min out of town at ...
Keiko-kan Museum (9:30-16:30, X-thu and all Jan-Feb, ¥300) of folk arts and crafts, as well as other items relating to life in northern Tohoku, like entire first-floor full of old phonographs. 2nd floor has more traditional items like sturdy *tansu* chests, pottery, and Tsugaru-*nuri* lacquerware characterized by its countless decorative concentric circles which gives it second name of *baka-nuri*, or idiot-lacquer—which is what you become from staring too hard at circles. Also good display of Ainu clothing and artifacts. 3rd floor of modern glass and concrete museum mostly dedicated to Aomori artists like modern woodblock masters MUNAKATA Shiko (has own museum in town) and SEKINO Junichiro, and writer DAZAI Osamu. You can buy Tsugaru-*nuri* in town, or visit nearby workshop/outlet of **Murata Tsugaru-nuri Kogei Kojo**, to which you can get directions and cab at Keiko-kan. Museum is easy to spot, across street from even easier to spot modern shopping mall dominated by red-logoed Jusco Dept store.

Aomori's sites can occupy idle hours before continuing across; but that doesn't include 3-4hrs it to visit above two sites and return to town. Save them for trip from/to Lake Towada. First stop in town is just outside rail stn —famed **fish market** where vendors line streets from 5am and hawk their catch until early eve. In season, nearby streets are lined with myriad little stalls selling Aomori's most famous export, juicy red apples. Markets are to R of main Shinmachi-dori Avenue, passing E from stn thru downtown. (Rte4 is few blocks S; bay is to N).

Continuing several mins walk down Shinmachi-dori and we come to canal; take 2nd or 3rd L after crossing canal and 2 blocks put us to either side of...
Prefectural Cultural History Museum, *Kyodo-kan* (9:30-16:30, X-mon, ¥200) in modern white structure built to commemorate Meiji Restoration centennial. From Jomon artifacts found at numerous sites around Aomori, displays go up to turn-of-century items. Kyodo-kan 6min from stn on some buses.

All buses go to our next stop...7min from Kyodo-kan or direct 11min from stn to...
Munakata Shiko Memorial Museum, *–Kinenkan* (9:30-16:30, X-mon,
¥200), which displays 30-40 of his marvelous 'mad' woodblock prints at any
one time.

If walking from rail stn to non-JR ferry terminal, en route is Meiji era building now...
Forest Museum, *Shinrin Hakubutsu-kan,* with displays on Aomori's
lumber trade. Short way beyond ferry terminal at suburb of Aburakawa is
Taisho era building now called **Italian House,** *Itaria-kan.* Built 1928 by
Guiseppe Fabri as home, adjacent to his new fish cannery—first in Japan.

If it's hot summer day, you can always head to...
Gappo Koen park (15min bus E of stn) which has sandy beach. Or if you
want to spend your time before boat in more hedonistic pleasures try
Yonise-dori alley beyond Kokusai Hotel. There are more cheap late-nite
eating and drinking spots between Utou Jinja and fishing boat harbor.

As you can see there really is not that much to Aomori City. Wanderers
with time can explore two peninsulas flanking Aomori's Mutsu Bay—
Shimokita Hanto on E and **Tsugaru Hanto** on W—of which more
interesting is Shimokita with its 'Mt Dread', OSORE-ZAN, and hot springs.

Shimokita-bound **buses** leave from bus terminal next to Matsukiya Dept store,
15min walk E of stn. Towns at tips of both peninsulas have **ferry** runs to Hokkaido
(will probably survive tunnel) providing alternate routes, good excuse to explore these
ignored corners of Tohoku. Heading back down Tohoku from Aomori we take you to
castle-town **Hirosaki,** p1024.

Out to Akita's rugged Japan Sea coast...
SHIMOKITA HANTO peninsula forms eastern side of Mutsu Bay,
beyond which is Tsugaru Straits and Hokkaido. 15km wide peninsula is
topped off with hatchet-head point, middle of which is ho ly OSORE-ZAN
(Mt Dread) far isolated in time but not far in distance from...

MUTSU, modern city home of Japan's first civilian nuclear-powered
tanker which set out on maiden voyage with much fanfare 1969 but soon
developed minor leak, then spent months wandering around Japan in search
of port which would accept it for repairs. Fearing radiation leak Aomori
fishermen created barricade of boats across entire bay; similar feats were
repeated around Japan, some instigated by radicals claiming *Mutsu* was first
step in creating nuclear-powered Navy.

Many Aizu Wakamatsu samurai families led by their young lord relocated
to Mutsu as farmers after Boshin War. Actually, there is no town of Mutsu;
incorporated city made up of 2 towns: coastal **OHMINATO,** inland
TANABU. Whichever route you choose to reach or leave Osore-zan you'll
pass thru lovely countryside and public transport choices of bus, rail or boat
allows for different views; strategically placed car ferries make it joy for
drivers, and main roads aren't that bad. Many bus and boat lines don't
operate Nov thru Mar, others cut down runs drastically. Also, smaller ships
will wait out strong seas, so check during stormy seas.

GETTING AROUND: Unless driving, Mutsu will be transportation hub
where you have to return for buses to other destinations on Shimokita. There are some
roads cutting across central mountains but most are winding narrow gravel logging roads
which were not paved our last time thru in 1980 and probably won't see tarmac for years.

Infrequent JR Ohminato Line from Noheji follows inside curve of Shimokita 70min
to OHMINATO town with giant MSDF base; one stop earlier at SHIMOKITA stn private
electric Shimokita Kotsu rail branches off 55min to OHATA town, N shore. Mutsu City's
TANABU stn is 15min from OHATA. Hourly buses from AOMORI and as many starting
from Noheji stn parallel rail line on Rte279 via MUTSU to OHATA; 3hr20min from

former, 2hr35min from latter. Buses from AOMORI bypass NOHEJI stn but stop at in-town bus terminal as do those starting Noheji stn. Less frequent buses from MISAWA follow Pacific Coast Rte338 to ODANOSAWA where road and bus cut inland to Mutsu then circles point clockwise. Rtes279 and 338 meet at northernmost point OHMA from where infrequent (2-5x-daily) 2hr car ferries to HAKODATE. From MUTSU good local road cuts NE 20km to rolling green pasturelands of SHIRIYA-SAKI Point. Between SHIRIYA-SAKI and ODANOSAWA is 20km stretch of **Shimokita** *Sakyu* Sand Dunes; buses most convenient to Odanosawa (40min), drivers can parallel dunes on local road. Check if planning to walk around southern half as it is sometimes used by SDF as firing range.

OSORE-ZAN, revered by Ainu as home of spirits. Japanese approximation of Ainu name was *Usori* which later became *Osore*, Japanese for 'dread'. Name actually applies to BODAI-JI temple complex begun here by 9th century Saint Jikaku-daishi (last met way down at Yamadera Temple) who tried to supplant local beliefs with Buddhism. It worked as well as it would have at any other place in Japan, which meant only useful (or at least harmless) aspects of Buddhism were melded into existing beliefs. Isolated sanctuary surrounded by hellish landscape is considered one of three sacred spots in Japan where spirit-beings enter our world to interact with living. Here, they are helped by trained *itako* blind shaman women who communicate with spirits of dead. 20-30 *itako* gather here twice yearly for special sessions during **July 20-24** *Grand Festival* and **Oct 9-10** *Autumn Prayers*, during which time countless people from all over Japan come here to hear messages from departed loved ones. Anyone can partake in sessions which run ¥1,000-2,000 per 15min, but you'll have to be able to understand thick Tohoku dialect of these old women. Even if you miss *itako* season, Osore-zan is worth visit to experience other-worldly atmosphere—just might meet *itako* or two. Osore-zan is not really morbid place, but it is eerie.

40min out of Mutsu, bus which has been travelling thru thickly forested mountains, suddenly bursts upon desolation of Osore-zan dominated by unmoving dark waters of **Lake Usori** in dormant volcanic crater. Whisps of rotten-egg-odor of sulphur gases pour out of numerous fissures and colorful bubbling pools around crater—one particularly red one is called *Chi-no-ike*, **Lake of Blood**, which figures prominently in Buddhist depictions of Hell. Other such spots include Buddhist River Styx, *Sanzu-no-Kawa* , (which you cross over on exquisite red-pillared bridge) and *Sai-no-Kawara* river which divides Heaven from Hell. There are pyramids of stacked stones either side of this river which represent make-shift stupas put up *by* dead who need more brownie-points to make it into Heaven. These banks are patrolled by Bodhisattva Jizo-*bosatsu* who helps unfortunates with their stupas and keeps demons from knocking them over. Many people leave offerings of straw sandals for Jizo's long walks over rocky banks. Main pavilion here is dedicated to Jizo. Multitude of smaller Jizo figures scattered around area are dedicated to souls of lost children.

There is *shukubo* temple-run lodgings here with room ¥-Bw/2, tho it fills up with pilgrims during July and Sept seance seasons. Whether staying here or not, pilgrims and tourists alike are welcome to soak in any of temple's 4 bath houses which draw hot spring water. They are pretty much lined along main approach to main Jizo-do Pavilion.

Most visitors stay back at Mutsu, or next most popular stop...

YAGEN ONSEN, 25min bus from Ohata or 40min from Tanabu (Mutsu); drivers can take winding gravel road from Osore-zan (begins as paved road branching off near Rest House along Sanzu-no-Kawa River). Despite bumps, it's only 10km and takes less than half time to backtrack to Mutsu and then take easier road following Ohata river which becomes rapids cutting thru beautiful valley, with spring to autumn colors comparable to that

of Towada's Oirase River. Yet, despite remoteness Yagen offers luxurious comfort at
¥-T–S in large but inconspicuous **New Yagen Hotel** ☎(0175)-34-3311, run by
Misawa's Mr Sugimoto. 4 other ¥-B–T ryokan and campsite.

Scenic path follows best part of river 2km upstream to...
OKU-YAGEN ONSEN with one inn and large riverside bath (also relatively
road-side so modest folk might wait till nite tho traffic is lite). Unlike Osore-
zan's sulphur onsen, Yagen and Oku-Yagen are naturally clear.

*Drivers can go past Oku-Yagen Onsen on road along Ohata River. After about 10km
road splits: R fork goes to W coast...*
SAI village which is 100min bus from Ohata town on Rte279.

L fork veers S to backwoods...
YUNOKAWA ONSEN with 5 rustic inns perched along Yunokawa River.
Water at Yunokawa is also naturally clear. Both Sai and Yunokawa are about
20km from Oku-Yagen. Good road (no buses) connects Yunokawa and Sai; only public
transport to Yunokawa is 3x-daily 30min bus ride from KAWAUCHI-MACHI town on S
coast Rte338. Kawauchi-machi is 55min frequent bus from Tanabu, some buses continue
another 35min to WAKINOSAWA on SW tip. These buses are JR-run so use Rail Pass.

Halfway to Sai on N shore is...
SHIMO-FURO ONSEN coastal spa; dozen inexpensive ryokan, as many minshuku
and one Kokumin-shukusha here draw from lightly sulphuric springs. Some inns only
have small baths, but there are two large public bath halls in town. Inns all boast heaping
dinners of *iso-yaki* assorted seafood cooked on hot rocks, and you know its all freshly
caught. On summer nights you will see endless chain of lights bobbing on horizon: squid
fishing fleets from Shimokita and southern Hokkaido just across Tsugaru Straits. On clear
days you can see mountains of Hokkaido, and if you had super vision might see people in
outdoor seaside baths of Mizunashi Onsen outside of Hakodate.

Road linking Sai to Wakinosawa follows sheer western coastline, but no
buses. Midway is 2km stretch of soaring rock-scapes of **Hotoke-ga-ura**.
Sightseeing boats (leave when ready) out of Sai make 2hr r.t. which includes
30min stop at best part of Hotoke-ga-ura. There's 1 daily passenger-only steamer between
Sai and Aomori (4hr40min) which stops briefly at Hotoke-ga-ura and Wakinosawa.

*Apr 15 thru Nov 10, 3 daily car ferries make 70min journey across mouth of Mutsu
Bay to Kanita town halfway up E shore of...*
TSUGARU HANTO peninsula: Forms W side Mutsu Bay, primarily
for wandering adventurer or travelling expatriate. Drivers will have best time
here for buses are few and most of Tsugaru's scenery is off beaten path.
There is little here for first-time short-term visitor to Japan, tho you may
find yourself going thru here by JR in new **Seikan Tunnel** from N tip
Tappi-misaki point to Hokkaido's Matsumae. Completed January 1988,
after 20 years work (double estimate) and cost of ¥700 billion, way over
estimate probably beyond pay-back. Projected to carry annual 13.5million
psgrs, 8.5million tons cargo, but now looks like 2.1- and 3.4-millions.

At 23km it is longest in world followed by 19km Alps tunnel linking
Italy–Switzerland. Construction of tunnel brought workers from all over
Japan who lived in modern concrete apartment complexes overlooking rustic
fishing village of **TAPPI**. We have met these workers on ferries across to
Hokkaido returning home for vacations, and have had great times with them
as we drank our way across. Working 300m/1,000ft under sea with
explosives is certainly good enough reason to let loose when you can.

Until tunnel opened, anyone wandering up this way ferried across in
2hrs from **MIMMAYA** at end of JR Tsugaru Line, 100min from Aomori.
Buses parallel on Rte280; rail cuts across land from **KANITA** town midway
up E coast (where ferries from Shimokita's Wakinosawa dock), but buses
follow coast all way to Mimmaya.

On their periodic visits to Edo, lords of Hokkaido's Matsumae clan also made 20km crossing to/from Mimmaya. They were only clan exempt from annual trips for required half-year residence in Edo since each trip could take several months. They would sometimes spend weeks in Mimmaya waiting for favorable winds and you can see inn where they stayed while waiting. It is now **Yamada Shoten** general store in front of Town Hall.

TAPPI is 40min bus from Mimmaya—road goes on but buses end Tappi. **Drivers** find Rte280 at Mimmaya becomes Rte339 which continues along coast to Tappi, down part of rugged W coast (buses pick back up at Kodomari village 25km S of Tappi) and curve inland at Lake Jusan-ko to eventually join main Rte7 down by Hirosaki (*see* below). Unless driving or at least hitching stretch between Tappi and Kodomari, you cannot yet make it all way around Tsugaru Peninsula on public transport, tho buses may at some point close that gap.

If not crossing over to Hokkaido, you might take second way in to peninsula: parallel to Rte339 up from **GOSHOGAWARA** is Tsugaru Tetsudo electric—at least hourly lilliputian one-car peach and orange trains (rather, glorified streetcars) cover 12 stns, of which 5 are just unmanned platforms. Goshogawara is on JR Gono Line which branches off from Ou Main Line at Kawabe town; Goshogawara is 1hr from Hirosaki (no transfer) 1hr25min from Aomori (transfer).

Halfway up Tsugaru Tetsudo line is...
KANAGI town, birthplace of DAZAI Osamu, highly popular and radically nonconformist writer who at age 39 killed himself in Tokyo, 1948. There are monuments all over Tsugaru dedicated to Dazai, and Kanagi is popular stop for school trips. Many of his works are translated into English, but if you come here read *Shayo* (The Setting Sun), story of Japanese aristocracy trying to deal with their new status as regular citizens following Occupation reforms. It is in many ways story of his parents who were once wealthy aristocrats here in Kanagi. Visit their grand house, odd mix of traditional and Western architecture build 1907 in middle of town—now ¥-T ryokan **Shayo-kan** ☎(0173)-53-2020, almost exactly as it was when Dazai lived here (owner not related to Dazai, whose real family name was Tsushima). Understandably popular place to stay, during Jul-Aug vacation recommend reservation 3 months in advance. If can't get room or just pass thru, you can see some of house; they have put coffee shop in one room to satisfy non-staying visitors. There are three other inexpensive ryokan and one minshuku in town. Dazai fans make it point to visit **UNSHO-JI** temple nearby—he wrote fondly of visits here with his nanny.

Other than Kanagi, attractions here NW along Japan Sea:

80min from Goshogawara is...
Lake Jusan-ko (if from Kanagi take bus for Kodomari village, get off after 50min at Sonai and walk S 5km). It's just giant shallow lake which fills up with migrating swans in winter.

1hr bus from Goshogawara...
Shichiri Nagahama 7-League-Long Beach, 28km of sand dunes, stretches S of Jusan-ko.

Bottom half of beach is most interesting, with lots of lakes and...
Kame-ga-oka Iseki archaeological site of Jomon community. Some of excavated items are now on show at Aomori City's **Folk History Museum**, but most of best pieces are shown right here at **Jomon Kinen-kan** museum. 2km N of Jomon Museum is monument (dedicated 1971 by US ambassador) to sailors of US merchant ship *Cheeseborough* which sank in stormy seas off-shore here 1889. 19 drowned but fishermen from nearby Shariki village were able to get 4 out alive and eventually get them back stateside.

Kanagi may seem out of way, especially if coming from Aomori, but it's easy half-day trip from Hirosaki. If you've come this way from Hirosaki rather than backtrack, stay on Gono Line which loops counter-clockwise along Aomori's Japan Sea side to Noshiro City. Drivers parallel on Rte101. You pass thru long chain of tiny fishing villages once road and rail hit coast.

After 15km or so is flat...
Thousand-mat Rock, *Senjo-jiki*, stretching into sea; **drivers** might stop but rail users probably won't want to since trains infrequent.

Beyond Senjo-jiki beautiful coast has good sand beaches, and near town of Fukaura is seaside campsite—tho we just picked good isolated beach and set up camp.

It's not much further to...
JUNI-KO '12 Lakes', cluster of actually 30-plus lakes in wooded hills 2km inland of Juniko stn on JR Gono Line. Juniko stn operational only in peak tourist seasons; rest of time visitors to lakes take 30min bus from quiet **Iwasaki** town, few stops S of **Fukaura**. Lakes closest to bus stop have been built up to accommodate tourists with big parking areas and gift shops, but short walk beyond to other lakes and you'd never know there was bus load of tourists nearby. There are 4 inexpensive ryokan among lakes, one campsite.

Near entrance to lakes area you will see white rock cliffs of...
Nihon Canyon, unfairly compared to Arizona's Grand Canyon— obviously by someone who never saw latter. **Juni-ko** → **Noshiro** bit over 1hr train.

HIROSAKI got its start 1611 when shogun allowed second Tsugaru lord Tamehira to build clan's main castle here (he married Ieyasu's daughter, in political alliance to keep eye on Nambu clan). His father OURA Tamenobu had Tsugaru name and province bestowed upon him by Hideyoshi after he wrested control of western half of northern Honshu from rival Nambu. Hirosaki remained northern Tohoku's center until Meiji Restoration split up clans to create Aomori prefecture out of northern halves of Nambu and Tsugaru domains, with port city Aomori as capital. But Hirosaki still remains cultural and educational center of modern Aomori prefecture. Kakunodate is more pleasing to eye as rural castle-town—metropolitan Hirosaki retains old-time atmosphere, many old neighborhoods blending with new. This mixture was allowed to develop slowly over time as town spared fresh but rude start given to other Tohoku cities by wartime air-raids. Despite modern downtown, Hirosaki has remnants of feudal past—around Hirosaki Park far side of downtown. It's no one place in particular, but mix of everything which makes Hirosaki this fun stop.

GETTING THERE: 35min express rail from AOMORI on JR Ou Main Line; close enough that you should spend nite here rather than Aomori City after coming over from Hokkaido. Or if you choose to visit Lake Towada after Aomori, can exit to HIROSAKI via **KUROISHI ONSEN group**. If on your way up TOHOKU, it is 3hr30min on JR Hanawa Line from Morioka City via Ohdate where it meets Ou Line. Before Ohdate is Rikuchu Hanawa stn where buses from Hachiman-tai stop. Long distance buses from/to Aomori, Ohdate, Towada and Morioka stop at stn-front but main bus terminal is 3min walk W near Itoyo Dept store.

Local **buses** have good coverage, but once at main sightseeing area around Park, walking is best. **Cabs** abound for short in-city jaunts or rent **bikes** at stn **Kanko-annai** which also has good English guide book on Hirosaki and walking maps. There are also few dozen 'You are Here' sign-maps around town. Walking, it's 2km/15-20min or more from stn depending on route.

Facing out from stn, one road shoots out to your R–shortest route to Park via...

Hirosaki Kyokai-do Church, Meiji era gothic cathederal. 3 blocks N and 2 blocks E of it is **Catholic Church**, also Meiji era. There must have been many Hidden Christians around Aomori, for Hirosaki became center of Christianity right at start of Meiji era before religious freedom was granted. From Kyokai-do Church head S 200m and we come to ex-Head Office of **Aomori Bank**, graceful W-style building, 1879; now **museum**.

Back at stn, another road shoots off to L which we follow for 6-8min to next major Oshu-kaido Ave. Turning L takes us to section of old shops with *komise* covered front walks which protect customers from rain and snow. R takes us down main street with interesting old shops: short way down on R is odd clock shop **Ichinohe**, across from which and one street E of main road is another old church **Shoten Kyokai**.

If interested in more old Western architecture, visit...

Hirosaki Gakuin University which has imposing early Meiji structure which was used by early foreign missionaries. Campus is short walk from Nishi-Hirosaki stn, 2 stops on private rail line which starts near Shoten Kyokai Church.

Short way beyond rail line terminus is...

SAISHO-IN temple with lovely 5-tiered pagoda, built 1667 and only one in Tohoku. Took skilled carpenters from central Hida province 10 years to complete, dedicated to Tsugaru soldiers who fell in battle against Nambu clan. Back on main road, cross river and few minutes to Aomori Bank. From Bank, few minutes walk W to **Main Gate**, *Ohte-mon*, of castle.

Hirosaki Koen park was once exclusive property of Tsugaru lords; ex-castle grounds is now lovely park with 5,000 cherry trees brought from Kyoto 1715 which bloom late Apr-early May. Come in Oct and as many fiery maple trees compete with thousands of chrysanthemums and *kiku-ningyo* dolls made out of 'mums'. Even in dead of winter people flock here for early Feb snow lantern festival featuring giant snow and ice sculptures also. During all this spotlights illuminate castle at nite. Original *tenshu-kaku* central keep burned down 1810, replaced by secondary keep which now occupies spot. Numerous lesser towers and gates still stand adding to charm of park. It's easy to spend hour or so just wandering around; more if you visit **History Museum** (9:00-17:00, X-Nov-Mar, ¥200) of Tsugaru clan memorabilia in present *tenshu-kaku*. **City Museum** with all sorts of displays on old Hirosaki is also in park, at S end.

200m W of castle is...

SEIGAN-JI temple's unique 17th century 3-part *San-mon* gate, worth short detour for anyone interested in temple architecture. Only gate remains, rest of temple burned down.

NAKA-CHO district (N side of Hirosaki Park) has several middle-rank samurai houses, 2 of which so far have been fixed up and opened to public. Both are on street one N of Park's grand *Kamenoko-mon*, **North Gate**, **Itoh-ke** house is at W end, **Iwata-ke** is 2 blocks E. Across from Kamenoko-mon is **Ishiba-ke**, 350-year-old merchant's house which features *komise* front.

Short walk from Kamenoko Gate at NE corner of park is...

Nebuta-no-Yakata Museum dedicated to giant floats of Hirosaki summer Nebuta Festival (local pron "Neputa"). Similar to Aomori's Nebuta, only these are fan-shaped with painted pictures on them. Aug 1-7 festival is as wild as Aomori's, and museum has been set up for those who can't make it then. ¥300 admission also gets you into adjacent **Kokeshi Museum** and Tsugaru **Kite Museum**, and don't forget to look at landscape garden. R (S) at next intersect beyond these museums leads back down to Aomori Bank.

5min walk SE of this intersect is simple...
TOSHOGU shrine dedicated to Tokugawa Ieyasu.

About as far NE of intersect is...
HACHIMAN-GU shrine, protector of castle's spiritually vulnerable NE 'Demon Gate' approach.

But rather than visit these two, we head back down to Park's southern Ohte-mon Gate and on 5min walk SW to...
TERA-MACHI Temple-town District with branches of all 33 Zen temples in northern Tohoku which were gathered here by lord Tamehira.

Passing down road lined on both sides with temples, at far W end is main...
CHOSHO-JI, ancestral temple of Tsugaru lords. First built 1528 at their old base Ajikazawa and moved here in 1608. There is carved figure of clan founder TSUGARU Tamenobu in **Mikage-do** main hall here said to be exact likeness. Visiting **late Apr/early May** you will also be shown mummified body of 10th lord Tsugaru Tsugutomi. **Shin-Tera-machi** New Temple District is roughly parallel street about 400m S, stretches W from pagoda'd Saisho-in Temple.

WHERE TO STAY: About 100 mostly small ryokan and handful of hotels in town. Best is 300-year-old **Ishiba Ryokan** ☎(0172)-32-9118 (¥-T–S) near Hirosaki Park and next to Kyokai-do Church. Across street is best **Hotel New Castle** ☎36-1211 (¥-S). Block S of Aomori Bank is another old ryokan **Kobori** ☎32-5111. Budgeteers might try minshuku-style rooms offered at Shin-Tera-machi's **Hensho-ji temple** ☎32-8714 where you can join in evening and morning meditation sessions. YH ☎33-7066 is few blocks S of castle's main Ohte-mon Gate.

Only 15min JR (or 30min local Hirosaki Dentetsu rail) S of Hirosaki...
OHWANI ONSEN is popular spot, especially in winter when nearby ski slopes open. There are 2 dozen ryokan and 10 room-only inns, and several large public baths here, but we prefer and recommend bath seekers to...

KUROISHI ONSEN GROUP: Follows Asaseishi River valley almost all way to Lake Towada, making up Kuroishi Onsen-kyo Pref Park. Visitors to Towada from Aomori should exit park via Kuroishi. About dozen little spas here of which 5 (all but one on Rte102) have lodgings; one is ranked among top kokeshi centers in Tohoku.

You'll want to spend hour or so wandering streets of rural...
KUROISHI one-time castle-town of Kuroishi clan (sub-branch of Tsugarus). Nothing singularly special here, but photogenic old-fashioned shopping street **Nakamachi-dori** is fun to walk along for its many old buildings. Here, too, you will find *komise* awnings which protect customers from rain and snow. It is one street E of somewhat modernized main street near stn. Near stn, next to Izumiya ryokan, is folkcraft shop **Nebuta-ya** which specializes in Nebuta related items. Owner makes all of Nebuta floats used in Kuroishi's scaled-down Nebuta Festival **Aug 1-7**. After week's rest town comes back to life for **mid-Aug** O-bon with nitely dances, best **18-19** when few thousand people fill streets. Kuroishi is 30min E of Hirosaki on frequent private Konan Electric which departs from adjacent to JR stn. (If exiting Kuroishi to Hirosaki, check your train as Konan Electric has 2 stns in Kuroishi; one line going to Hirosaki and other to Kawabe town, 10min JR N of Hirosaki).

Worthy detour of hour or so before reaching Kuroishi is...
Seibi-en Garden one of best Meiji era traditional landscape gardens, took 9 years (from 1903) to complete, financed by land baron MORIYOSHI Seito. More interesting is Saito family bizzare East-meet-West house of traditional Japanese style first floor topped by English style 2nd floor and turreted roof. Built during peak of Japan's love affair with West when Western

things seen as better, status. Don't forget to see their **treasure house** with its opulent Kamakura era altar, small but almost as ornate as Hiraizumi's Konjiki-do Golden Pavilion. On Konan Electric, 3 stops (6min) before Kuroishi → Tsugaru Onoe stn, 15min walk. **Drivers** from Hirosaki take Rte102 → Kuroishi turn-off to Seibi-en is 1.5km before reaching Inakadate stn but not marked in English, (¥200, X-winter). It's only 4km backtrack from Kuroishi on local road roughly parallel to tracks to Onoe.

Buses from Kuroishi → various onsens leave every other hour; spring thru autumn buses starting from Hirosaki go via Kuroishi and its onsen to Lake Towada. Heading E from Kuroishi, just before passing Tohoku Expwy is giant **apple orchard** and site of Pref Apple Inspection Center where they are always coming up with ways to improve Aomori's apple business.

First hot spring we come to is...
NURUYU ONSEN (25min from Kuroishi) known for its *kokeshi* dolls. Nuruyu looks more like small quiet farming community than onsen; 2 inexpensive ryokan, 1 minshuku and half-dozen pilgrim rate room-only inns surround giant old-fashioned bath hall.

About 1km upstream is paired spas of...
OCHIAI ONSEN & ITADOME ONSEN. Ochiai is 'largest' spa along Asaseishi River, but it too, is quiet little cluster of inns around large bath hall; Ochiai also has Kokumin-shukusha with top-floor mixed-bathing hall, Itadome has Youth Hostel. There used to be few more tiny onsen villages just upstream but they became submerged with 1977 completion of dam.

AONI ONSEN is most backwoods of them all, with just one inexpensive ryokan ☎(0172)-54-8588 far off beaten path. We didn't make it out that way but Aoni sounds like ideal spot to get away from it all. First draw is its large natural outdoor rock bath, and simple little inn has no electricity (uses oil lamps) or phone number above, **Konan Kanko** (Tour) **Co** in Kuroishi who will pick you up at Kuroishi stn in private van for 45min ride to Aoni (¥800 for r.t.). You can also take regular buses to Aoni Onsen Iriguchi stop (5min past Itadome) and either take winding 5km long dirt road or scenic trail which follows Aoni River and its many small waterfalls to onsen—little over 1hr either way. It is closed mid-Nov thru Mar, and they recommend calling ahead to ensure rooms especially Apr-May.

Last spa back on Rte102 is...
NURUKAWA ONSEN with 2 ¥-B ryokan and Kokumin-shukusha; 70min bus from Kuroishi, 50min bus from Nenokuchi village on E shore of Lake Towada.

AKITA COAST 秋田

Continuing S from Hirosaki, JR Ou Main Line and Rte7 take you to...
OHDATE, overgrown lumber center for Akita's majestic *sugi* cryptomeria. It is also recognized as home of Akita-*ken* dogs (statues of which grace stn-front plaza) and 12,000 blossoming *sakura* in spring. At Ohdate branch-off JR Hanawa Line and Rte103 (becomes Rte282) take you back to MORIOKA City,

Or stay on Ou Line and Rte7 which take you to Japan Sea coast at...
NOSHIRO, modern pleasant port where lumber floated down Yoneshiro River from Ohdate is shipped out. Lacquer buffs find Noshiro-*shunkei*, colorful but painstaking process of lacquering once wide-spread but now exists only here and in central Hida Takayama. Only one shop here in Noshiro still makes it: **Ishioka Shunkei-ten**. If you visit Noshiro keep in mind that bulk of town is centered around Noshiro stn which is one stop up on JR Gono Line from Higashi-Noshiro stn on Ou Main Line. Come here **Aug 6-7** for colorful *Nebunagashi*

Festival, similar to Aomori's *Nebuta Festival* but not quite as wild in partying and has— in place of Aomori's people floats—giant paper castles which are then floated down river to sea on last nite.

20min bus N of town is tiny seaside...
NOSHIRO ONSEN, discovered 25 years ago in drilling for possible oil. Quiet, and close to good sandy beach.

OGA-HANTO peninsula is known for Namahagé demons who come out to scare some sense into little children and motivation into sluggards on New Year's Eve. According to legend 5 demons came over from China to serve their master who had somehow ended up here. Once yearly, demons were allowed to have some free time and on that day they would plunder Oga's villages for food, wine and women. Later, villagers of Monzen and Namahagé reached agreement that demons would be given women every year, but only if they could lay down 1,000 stone steps leading up to GOSHA-DO temple on hill above MONZEN town. It didn't take demons long to do job but as last stone was almost put in place one villager imitated sound of cock and thinking dawn had come, demons left defeated. Things have quieted down since, but Namahagé (5 has increased to about 200) still show up at every house on Oga every Jan 31 to make sure there are no lazy folk sitting around. If you're not walking streets of Oga or staying at someones house on Dec 31, you can see these blue- or red-faced demons clad in straw coats and wielding giant butcher knives dance during Feb 13-15 *Sedo-matsuri* Festival at hilltop SHINZAN JINJA shrine on western shore. Monzen is at southern tip.

Peninsula itself offers some fantastic scenery spring thru autumn. Jutting 20km out into Japan Sea, Oga's western shore is chain of green hills, in sharp contrast to base of peninsula which is sprawling flat farmlands of **Hichiro-gata** experimental farm. Once second largest lake in Japan, was chosen as site of postwar experiments in large-scale American style farming with lake filled in to become huge land tracts worked by massive machines.

Unless driving, visitors to Oga must take bus or short JR Oga Line from...
AKITA City, fast-paced industrial capital offers little for tourist. If you are looking for place to spend night around here, we recommend any of above rural places, or continue few hours down-coast to Sakata or Tsuruoka cities. Akita is ancient town tho, first being 9th century massive fortified frontier against marauding Ainu. As frontier became pacified Akita faded back to quiet anonymity until becoming base of powerful Akita clan. Site of original 9th century fort now small park in N of town; feudal castle site is to its S.

WHERE NEXT: From here, continue down coast on road or rail, passing Fuji-like **Mt Chokai** to re-enter Yamagata Prefecture. Those who skipped this on way up Tohoku can see SAKATA and TSURUOKA, then bus thru sacred peaks of DEWA SANZAN, do Yamagata route in reverse to end at AIZU WAKAMATSU. From Aizu take combination of JR–private Tobu rail to NIKKO.

Personal Datebook follows with some of country's most flamboyant festivals, for which special tours often arranged out of Tokyo. One such visits trio of wild ones: *Sanja* in Morioka, *Nebuta* in Aomori and *Kanto* in Akita, dep 7am Aug 2, 3nites, in Japanese, about ¥30,000 incl bus, inns, main meals. Dep Central Marunouchi Exit JR Tokyo Stn, rsve **Bikkuri Tours** (Surprise T) ☎(03)-770-7777 (weekends Tourist Svce ☎984-6655). This is Tour #6047; others in high season to great events or great scenery, most 5day/4nite average ¥15,000 per nite incl bus, all %, some with many meals, thus ¥-T.

...composed of such a different kind of fabric,
that it seems as if they originated on other stars
in other millennia, or as if they were hallucinations.
— Herman Hesse, *The Journey to the East*

NIKKO 日光
GAUDY SUBSTITUTE FOR WAR

NIKKO MUST BE seen to be believed: most 'unJapanese' place in Japan
—wherein lies its Japaneseness. Most highly touted structure in Japan, but
few Japanese take plaudits rained upon it seriously. As long in building as
Egypt's pyramids, it took almost as many skilled artisans as they took laborers, used more gold, more fine lacquer, more of everything than any
structure in Japanese history. Yet it is mainly noted for its 'hear-no-evil,
speak-no-evil, see-no-evil' monkeys, small wooden relief carved on insignificant building by left-handed artist (*Hidari*, or 'Lefty' Jingoro). It
must be seen to appreciate what mad genius, totally absolute ruler with
fiendish sense of humor, can do. TOKUGAWA Iemitsu, third of all-powerful
Tokugawa Shoguns of Edo-Tokyo, ordered it built by his lords in tribute to
his grandfather whose mausoleum it is. But more important, perhaps, was
to keep ambitious lords too busy, too poor to rebel—as economic if not
'moral substitute for war'.

TOKUGAWA Ieyasu, our TV *Shogun* whom we have met often on our
travels, died in 1616 and was temporarily interred in his Shizuoka hometown amid tea plants and orange trees. In recreating spirit of unification that
had characterized Japan millennium earlier when high culture and Buddhism
were introduced from China, he united conflicting strains in this national
culture. First, as we have seen, he united warring dukedoms militarily,
politically and gradually economically. Main enemies of central authority
were conflicting religious interests, so once again Buddhism and Shinto
were brought into rapport as unified religious system. Christianity, as we
have seen, didn't fit into this and was eliminated. Despite forced breakup of
unified Shinto-Buddhism, *ryobu-shinto*, in revival of emperor system in
1870s when shrines were purged of Buddhist images and elements,
Toshogu is still to this day both Temple and Shrine and Buddhist images sit
here among Shinto symbols. This time, bonding element was Confucianism: that ancient Chinese systematization of family and social relationships
which had long been basis of both social and political organization in China.

Upon his death Ieyasu was deified as Gongen-sama, Buddhist avatar or
incarnation of Shinto or national deity—in his case named *Tosho Dai-
Gongen*: or 'Eastern Illuminating Great Incarnation'. Mausoleum-shrine-
temple to this national god was called TOSHOGU, 'Eastern Illuminating
Shrine'. It was to be to shogunal state what Ise was to imperial line, and
being northeast of Edo-Tokyo de-facto capital, stood as celestial guardian to
it as Hiei Monastery is to Kyoto, de-jure capital. Indeed, being in northeast
corner of empire center it would stand as guardian of entire nation. Over
100 smaller Toshogu shrines were built in local regions, subsidiary to great
Toshogu of Nikko. Old name Futa'ara, or Futara, is still used for local
shrine but new name NIKKO itself was now chosen, meaning Sun Ray implying it to be spiritual light of nation, source of all life. Modesty was never
claimed to be trait of any Tokugawa.

Ise is rebuilt every generation, symbolic of eternal rebirth and renewal. Nikko was not to be rebuilt, but to be maintained in perpetual non-motion, unchanged-unchanging in constant and continuous newness. Feudal lords were shouldered with staggering burden of maintaining at far-off Nikko armies of highly-paid artisans with full equipment and finest raw materials. (Total restoration of 1950s saw ancient permanent maintenance reinstituted). Lords were also goaded into overfulfilling their quotas by encouraging them to compete for establishment of 'face' by outdoing what was expected. It was all brilliant plan of third-generation Tokugawa shogun to stabilize nation and perpetuate dynasty, to overcome traditional whammy in Far East that great houses die out in three generations. Whole plan obviously worked, for Tokugawa line ruled not for three generations but for fifteen (tho only first four were father-to-son, other times abler cousins inherited), almost three centuries.

Japanese say "Never say *kekko* till you have seen Nikko". *Kekko* means marvelous, but also homonymously 'enough' and used commonly to mean 'That's all brother'. It is easy to be flip about Nikko: it is gaudy (some say hideous, some say bright). It is in royal-red grandiose tradition of China as first seen in Kyoto's Heian Shrine, revived on-the-cheap recently in love hotels, but probably always latent in Japan except suppressed by anti-sumptuary laws. But somehow that certain charm (soppy word, really not quite adequate here) inherent in Japanese arts and crafts shows thru despite it all. It is overdone: yet it's all smaller in fact than it appears in photos and this diminution lends much to jewel-like character. This overpolished jewel enjoys natural setting with few peers anywhere.

True, few care to see it twice. Truer, fewer should fail to see it once.

GETTING THERE: On our circle itinerary coming down from HOKKAIDO— flying down: with stopover SENDAI-MATSUSHIMA, Shinkansen on to UTSUNOMIYA, transfer to local for NIKKO or KINUGAWA ONSEN as below. Coming down from Aizu-Bandaisan National Park area adventurers will enter area thru KINUGAWA; stop here or at earlier Kawaji Onsen or even earlier. Cormorant fishing in river summer mid-season.

For most, Nikko is **side trip** from **TOKYO**: best is Tobu line from ASAKUSA stn just 101 minutes by 'Spacia' featuring its 'juke box saloon car'; or pm train under 2 hrs ASAKUSA → KINUGAWA ONSEN, possible but not especially recommended overnite. *Warning*: Spacias reserved only and booked solid at festivals, when far preferable is JR from nearby Ueno when take Tohoku Shinkansen (Rail Pass) 45min, frequent → Utsunomiya where quick-change platform for 30min connection → Nikko in 42min. For 1-day turn around, dep JR Shinkansen or Asakusa Tobu Spacia before 9am.

PACKAGE TOURS are run by **JTB & JAM** (Japan Amenity Travel, formerly Fujita), one- & two-day; all good, incl lunches, pick up/drop off at your Tokyo hotel.
JAM 1-day Nikko country **bus** tour: TOKYO hotels, dep by 8:00, ret 19:00; runs daily 4/1-11/30; sat-sun-hol ¥16,200adult, ¥12,100child, weekday ¥18,500/13,800.
JTB 1-day by **train**: dep ASAKUSA 9:00, ret 18:45; all year, ¥18,500 /¥13,800 child.
2-day: dep ASAKUSA 9:00 Spacia → NIKKO → TOSHOGU → KANAYA HOTEL (lunch) → IROHAZAKA d'way → FUTARA SHRINE → LAKE CHUZENJI → KEGON FALLS → NIKKO (nite), 2d day free. Return NIKKO → ASAKUSA 18:45; ¥28,000 /¥23,300 child.

Tours are convenient, but can **do same yourself**: Tobu express dep ASAKUSA frequently 7:20-20:10, 101min, ¥2,280 o.w. (hourly local ¥1,140); arrive NIKKO join Tobu Bus Town Tour A or B, or bus ¥270 from across street L corner, to Nishi Sando and Shrine; or we recommend walk 15mins or taxi (basic+) to great shrine complex, see it on our own, lunch ¥1,500 or less Kanaya Hotel, or many budget eateries by shrine entry. *Alternate* bus (¥980) from stn up Irohazaka drive → view platform foot of Kegon Falls → lunch **Chuzen-ji Boathouse**, boat → TOCHIKI 1,000-arm Kannon Temple to stretch day; ret shrine PM to see afoot, no need for tour; ret TOKYO Tobu luxe trains several btwn 17:00-18:00 ¥2,280, half-price slow trains hrly, saves ¥1,000 o.w., but...

Budgeteer going beyond Nikko: Asakusa Tobu stn buy Nikko-Kinugawa **free pass** ¥5,100 valid 4 days ASAKUSA → NIKKO train, onward unltd use bus → Chuzen-ji → Yumoto Onsen or Kirifuri Plateau, and → Kinugawa train with onward bus → Kawa-ji & Lake Ikari; but doesn't incl Ltd Express, ¥1,140 each way surcharge. Add up Tobu train 2x ¥2,000, Tokyo taxis hotel-Asakusa-hotel ¥2,-3,000 (subway ¥500), lunch ¥1,500 totals under ¥10,000; or pair or more do it using taxi (hour 9x-mtr) Nikko → Chuzen-ji in place of tour bus for about same each, or half advertised group tour. Overnite KINUGAWA (¥-Tw/2) brings 2-day total to equal quicky 1-day package.

Rent-a-car 2-3 days not worth traffic hassle unless planning longer trip onwards N.

For overnite at KINUGAWA ONSEN, Tobu deluxe dep ASAKUSA 8x-daily between 1:30-17:00 arr 2 hrs later KINUGAWA (if going into NIKKO on evening train must change at Shimo-ima-ichi); overnite at Onsen-spa hotel, reserved in advance, prepaid by all-inclusive coupon, anyplace ¥-T+; morning bus (Tour D, 9:00 from Kinugawa stn); or taxi down Cryptomeria Avenue into Nikko (specify Cryptomeria Ave, not bypass), disembark at shrine and see on foot, lunch, afternoon or eve return to Tokyo as above.

To reach TOBU-ASAKUSA stn from Tokyo hotels, **taxi** 2-5x-mtr allow 1/2 hour; or **subway** Toei Asakusa line to Asakusa (note, *not* earlier stop Asakusa-bashi), or Ginza yellow-line to Asakusa; Tobu-Asakusa stn same bldg as Matsuya Department Store.

May 18, Oct 17 major *Festivals* special JTB tour, advise book from home, crowded.

GETTING AROUND: LOCAL TAXI TOURS: all 5 psgr *chugata*, midsize
air-conditioned cabs; figure in ( ) is 9 psgr minibus.

A course 5 hrs anytime, ¥21,630 (¥29,360)—Pick up at NIKKO stn or hotel → up Iroha driveway → Akechi-daira → Lk Chuzen-ji etc with lunch advised on your time at Boathouse (Kanaya Hotel restaurant) → Tachiki Kanon temple → other falls → back down to Toshogu and associated temples—where taxi waits meter ticking so we suggest take **by hour** ¥4,400 (may rise bit) and leave it at Toshogu to go on foot at own pace.

C same as above but pickup at your Kinugawa hotel, ¥25,960 (¥38,160); from Kawa-ji Onsen ¥26,300 (¥40,300)—specify drive Cryptomeria Ave → Iroha → Nikko sites, same advice. Can do in reverse from Nikko, ending evening at your inn Kinugawa or Kawa-ji.

Your agent or hotel desk in Tokyo or previous stop can arrange to have you met at Nikko JR or Tobu stns to start tour, phone **Nikko Kotsu Taxi** ☎(0288)-54-1188.

LOCAL BUS TOURS (Japanese language guides–but you have us).

A Nikko Sights: ¥4,520 (inc. entry fees), daily from JR stn 9:55, Tobu stn 10:00 (12/1-3/10, 10:30), end 15:40—Tachiki Kannon → Futara Shrine → Toshogu → Rinno-ji → Roaring Dragon (Toshogu) → Iroha Drive → Daigo-in → Kegon Falls → Lake Chuzen-ji.

B Nikko Sights: ¥5,060, daily 3/11-11/30; JR 10:25, Tobu 10:30; ret 17:10—Iroha Drive → Kegon Falls → Lake Chuzen-ji → ex-Nikko Imperial Palace (museum) → Nikko Museum.

C Panorama NIKKO → KINUGAWA: ¥5,130 (incl lunch) daily 4/29-11/2; TOBU stn 10:20 ret KINUGAWA 17:20 — Ryuzu Falls → Lake Chuzen-ji → Kegon Falls → Iroha Drive (Lunch Nikko Lakeside Hotel) → Kirifuri Plateau → Roppozawa Bridge → Osasa Pastures → Kawa-ji Dam, (suns & hols Oct. cancelled because of crowded roads).

D Nikko Sights from KINUGAWA: ¥5,450, daily 4/20-10/31; Dep KINUGAWA ONSEN 9:00, end NIKKO Tobu Sta 16:10—Tachiki Kannon-do → Chugu-ji-Toshogu-Rinno-ji-Futara Shrine (Lunch Restn't Yumoto) → Lake Chuzen-ji → Senjo-gahara → Yu Falls → Ryuzu Falls → Kegon Falls → Iroha drive. (Tour cancelled suns & hols Oct due to crowds).

E Nikko Sights: ¥4,990 (incl. fees), daily, dep KINUGAWA ONSEN stn 9:20, ret JR NIKKO 16:00—Tachiki Kannon-do → Chugu-ji (Miko maidens dance) → Toshogu → Rinno-ji → Roaring Dragon Toshogu → Futara → Akechi Daira → Kegon-no-taki → Lake Chuzen-ji → Iroha Dr.

F Panorama Kinugawa → Nikko: ¥5,130 (incl lunch); daily 4/29-11/2 KINUGAWA ONSEN stn 9:30, ret TOBU/JR NIKKO 15:30– C in reverse. No tour sun-hols, Oct.

F-1 Edo-Mura ¥5,440, 4/29-11/3. Dep KINUGAWA STN 9:40 ret NIKKO 16:00: Edo-Mura Ryuo Gorge (lunch) → Kawa-ji Dam → Osasa Pasture → Roppozawa Bridge. For those of you with **kids.**

WHERE TO STAY: W-style hotels, some with J-rms also; J-style w/2. All incl tax-service unless noted '+%': (Season rates) = Aug, Nov, some hols.

NIKKO nr shrine: **Kanaya** ☎(0288)-53-2487, first ryokan in coumtry to speicificaly cater to foreign tourists (1873), tourist twins no bath ¥-B-Tw/2 thru 8 rates to ¥-L-LL), or ¥-Sw/2+, W-style, +%. Budget lodgings abound, 20min walk from stn in Tokorono are two minshuku **Rindo-no Ie** ☎53-0131 and **Narusawa Lodge** ☎54-1630 and Pensions **Humpty Dumpty** ☎53-2837, pick up from stn.

CHUZEN-JI ONSEN, Lakeside Hotel ☎55-0321 ¥-S-L. **Prince** ☎55-0661 ¥-S-L +%. Shobu-ga-hama trout hatchery 20min bus N of CHUZEN-JI is **Chuzen-ji Kanaya Hotel** ☎55-0356 ¥-T-S (+¥1,000 season) +%; with **Boat-house** Restaurant. **Chuzen-ji Hotel** ☎55-0333, ¥-T+w/2, J-style. Several ryokan in same range, check stn or ask taxi. All have hot spring baths, as do...

YUMOTO ONSEN, 30min past CHUZEN-JI **Nanma Hotel** ☎62-2111, ¥-T-Sw/2, J-style. If full, many similar inns here, book thru agent or hotel.

OKU-NIKKO ONSEN: Oku-nikko Onsen Hotel ☎62-2441 ¥-T-Sw/2, J-style.

CHOPSTICKS: For most tourists to Nikko lunch is at tour-selected restaurant, which we agree with, so if on own at Lake Chuzen-ji we recommend **Boathouse** or if near shrine **Kanaya Hotel**. For adventurer or natural-food fan, **Ebisuya** Shimohachi-ichi-machi 955, ☎54-0113, for novel soy-derived *yuba*, made from skim of soy milk and in infinite consistencies, tasty but bland, basis for *shojin-ryori* monks' food. Menu of day, no choice, 7 courses of different forms of yuba ¥4,180. 11:00am-2pm, 4pm-6pm only.

Budgeteers loads of usual plastic-model-in-window restaurants between stn–shrine.

Warning: Admission fees ('donation', 'offering') are complicated here: to see whole Toshogu incl Taiyu-in, not including Rinno-ji temple and Futara Shrine, but including all special sights in Toshogu (Crying Dragon, Sleeping Cat), ticket is ¥1030, then Rinno-ji takes additional ¥710, Futara ¥300, to total ¥2,040. To see Rinno-ji+Futara+Toshogu+ Taiyu-in *excluding* Sleeping Cat, admission is ¥730 for *kyotsu-ken*, with admission to pussy extra ¥430, total ¥1,160, saving ¥880. Toshogu Treasure House and Rinno-ji Treasure House each ¥300 extra. So entering Toshogu (ticket offices near bus park, or at pedestrian entry in from Sacred Bridge and before pagoda) or Rinno-ji, whichever first, **best buy** is *kyotsu-ken* for ¥730, buy Cat same time, or later at its entrance if you want to see, ¥430.

TOSHOGU is so publicized on travel posters it is hard to say anything new about it. Enough to say, again, its artistic poverty amid unrivaled technical perfection characterize essential sterility of Tokugawa era.

First temple was set in general area atop nearby mountain in 766, where first shogun Tamura-maro prayed on way N to 'subdue barbarian Ainu'. Site dates to 848, oldest extant building is 1617—neighbor Futara Shrine.

Bus tours enter W Entry for closer approach to central area. Pedestrians enter from E Entry facing...
Sacred Bridge, *Shinkyo*, picture-postcard-red lacquer 28m/91ft long, closed to traffic except for semi-annual festival parade. Set here to contrast with nature, it still contrasts with bus traffic at its foot.

Enter opposite bridge past...
RINNO-JI; Sanbutsu-do (¥320) original temple on site, first built 848 by Jikaku-daishi at Imperial order to extend influence of Kyoto government into wilderness thru pacific but statist Tendai Buddhism, often rebuilt. Houses trio of immense gilt buddhas, central Amida flanked by Horsehead Kannon (R) and 1,000-armed Kannon (L).

To temple R by pond is...
Gohoten-do with sweeping Kamakura era low roof built 1240 to house popular deities Daikoku, Bishamon and female Benzaiten, all of 'Lucky 7'.

Treasure House (¥300) contains mostly minor objects and sutras; Garden dates to founding, of interest to garden buffs, pass otherwise.

Toshogu Shrine

Pass on now to plaza in front of main Toshogu shrine, and at its foot...
5-Storey Pagoda, 1819 rebuilding of burned 1650 original. Note various storey's different hues of lacquer—that on 2,3,4 is 'merely' top quality architectural urushi, while usually more closely examined first and 5th, rich dark color is finest quality usually reserved only for art objects.

Urushi-lacquer used in Nikko is best available. Rich vermillion best, costs raw per *kan* (4kg, 8.4lbs) now ¥600,000. Best is Japanese, but in short supply, so of 400 tons used nationwide per year only 20% is domestic —rest from China and Vietnam. Chinese best runs ¥150,000. Even more expensive is blue detailing on sculptures, in descending order of blueness from lapis at ¥500,000 per square meter, down. Lapis as sacred or royal color is universal tradition descending from dynastic Egypt. In Treasure House is wall display of application of urushi, showing raw carved wood treated 7 times before linen layer applied, then processes 8-26 alternate coats and polishings and 27-31 final black or vermillion with gold, if any, 32. Even without material cost, expense is understandable from labor.

Up steps thru big torii, jag R as such indirect approach deflects evil, to enter past 2...
Log storehouses, in Shosoin azekura-style tradition, usually closed but open some days prior to main fetes to take out paraphernalia stored therein.

Ahead to L...
Stable, small building which bears that world-famed triad of monkeys, *hear-no-evil*, *speak-no-evil*, *see-no-evil* surprisingly small but no less effective. Part of long series of encircling door-top story-frieze.

Double-gabled roof tops **revolving library** wherein behind usually-closed doors, large shrine set on 'lazy susan' contains full set of Buddhist sutras. To push poles sticking out from shrine and revolve it equals benefit of reading all contents. Similar setup can be seen and pushed in Mt Koya.

Most popular to Japanese of whole decoration is barely life-sized relief of *sleeping cat* on minor gate, said so lifelike it keeps mice out of temple— upstairs R, requires extra cheese (¥300) to pussyfoot in to see, if you only have ¥530 tix.

To L is great revolving **bronze lantern** made on order in 'Oriental' style by Dutch craftsmen, who got hollyhock top decoration upside down, presented 1643 by Nagasaki Dutch as tribute. Opposite, snaky **candelabra** is from Korea, probably in thanks for being left alone—good relations then.

Upstairs is white...
Yomeimon, literally **'sun blaze gate'** NT explosion of light & opulence: illuminated at nite, giving new inference to nickname 'twilight gate' which meant one could study its detail from dawn till twilight, now into nite. Built 1634-6, took est 55,970 man-days of top skilled craftsmen.

Thru gate turn R below lovely...
Kara-Mon Chinese Gate NT matching Yomeimon and to far R of which enter and doff shoes to enter main **mausoleum** of shogun Tokugawa Ieyasu, star of movies and TV. Inner ceilings all *Ho-O* phoenixes by Kano school artists, each panel different. Lion wall doors are by KANO Tanyu, best and unretouched in room to R (if open, sometimes special groups admitted)—was resting room for visiting shoguns and finely phoenix-carved walls are of wood hard enough to stop musket shot.

Outside below Yomeimon to your R is largest building in whole compound...
HONJI-DO temple of Medicine Buddha. Ceiling of **roaring dragon** painting looks like done by Disney staff artist, feeble compared to Kano Tanyu lions. Dragon 'roars' when you stand below it and clap. In altar is Yakushi Medicine Buddha, 'Physician of Souls' in these later abstract times, but in ancient Nara actually represented introduction of medicine from China and Persia. Flanking central doors are moonlight–sunlight images and polychrome 12 guardians—it's hard to imagine, but quiet sculptures of Nara and Kyoto were probably just as garish when new.

Stroll down and leave Toshogu central compound going R past...
FUTARA SHRINE, oldest actual structure in area, yet only 1617, as well bypassed, or at best strolled thru without entering unless in group to see shrine maidens do Mi-kagura dance. If you hear music, run to front of main building and watch. For *private performance*, ¥300 per spectator, ¥2,000 min, almost always available on call—best deal nationwide. **Hiking trail** for enthusiasts, ancient, begins here up 2,484m/8,080ft Mount Nantai, takes all day.

Exit torii R...700m W close to W Entry approach of bus tours (enter, go L) is...
TAIYUIN, (¥300, 8am-5pm, till 4pm Nov 1-Mar 31) inters 3rd Tokugawa Iemitsu, grandson of Ieyasu and builder of Nikko. He died in 1651 and this great compound was rushed to completion by 1653. Enter thru **Nio-Mon** guardian gate, relacquered late 1987. Usually called 'smaller and simpler', in many ways Taiyuin surpasses Toshogu in quality of work, its ornateness is better controlled, and as far less popular it is refreshing after mobs of Toshugu. Fine large stone lanterns fill lower area, all beyond are bronze.

Up stone steps...
Niten-Mon, two heavenly guardians gate, named after flanking images not normal gate nio-guardians. Rear side of gate also holds images, of green-skinned Wind God (L) and red-skinned Thunder God (R) ringed in halo of thunder drums and grasping thunder bolts. Fronting this gate are several superb bronze lanterns, and from here on all lanterns are bronze.

Another gate, we've climbed 114 steps now, we're almost there, 10 more steps...
Kara-Mon Chinese Gate, smallest we've seen yet, but in worksmanship, tho not grandeur, perhaps finer than Yomeimon, like brocade.

Usually entered from R side, sometimes right thru Kara-Mon, is...
Mausoleum of Iemitsu, 3rd Tokugawa shogun and builder of Nikko. Built in Buddhist temple style vs Toshogu's mixed Buddhist-Shinto: note

fore-building's panels open out in horizontal halves in old Nara era style, rather than typical vertical sliding panels. Behind, linked by gilded corridor, AI-NO-MA, is narrower, taller building with tabernacle of Buddhist-style memorial name tablet, funerary portrait image of Iemitsu. Inside sanctuary of gold are fine crafts gifts by leading lords, including hanging lantern from Dutch king. Lion-dog panels again by Tanyu (models must have been fierce Pekinese pups). Rear building exterior almost as superb in detail as interior.

Crowning whole, just beyond and L...
Koka-Mon Gate in Ming Chinese-style, white plaster first storey with ornate roof, again brocade-fine detailing. Flanking gate are two most ornate lanterns in country, bronze with gilded and polychrome enameled detail.

Beyond, off limits to visitors, is heart of complex, almost unadorned...
Plain stone enclosure with lightly colored cast copper gate closing off roofed bell-shaped 4m tall bronze containing another mortuary tablet and image of Sakyamuni Buddha, topping crypt containing ashes of Iemitsu.

Down below between Taiyuin and Toshugu is...
Treasure House, *Homotsu-kan,* ¥300, main treasures of shrine always on view, vary with seasons from 6,000 stored. Main room has three great *Omikoshi* palanquins, from door in: Ieyasu's, predecessor Hideyoshi's (both capped w/ phoenixes), 12th century Minamoto Yoritomo's (sacred orb cap), to which trio of great unifiers shrine has been triply dedicated since 1873—but no one really considers it in anyone's memory but Ieyasu's.

Nikko Museum former Imperial Villa, interesting building, if time, houses local flora and fauna and crafts. Out of way, bus to Tamosawa stop.

Everything looks spanking new, latest restoration of whole area cost ¥4,200,000,000: US (@125) $33,600,000. Japanese prefer Nikko viewed in snow; hot spring heights above-beyond Lake Chuzenji are popular ski area.

KEGON FALLS bus up **Iroha Driveway**–refers to first 3 letters of Japanese cursive *hiragana* syllabary, *i-ro-ha*, written top to bottom remind of drunken worm's path–winds up mountainside on Iroha #2 (older #1 down traffic). Enlarging access with #2 brought total curves to 47-same number as full set of hiragana. Bus slows or stops at top to view Kegon Falls (note if flow good); or on city bus get off **Akechi-daira** Iroha (only #1) for 3min aerial cable-car to platform for view of Falls & Mt Nantai.

Bus stops next at...
CHUZEN-JI ONSEN, pleasant mountain lake is less for tourist, more for resident escaping city heat. Good place to stay outside Nikko (*see*), all hotels have hot springs. 5min walk to top of **Kegon Falls** and elevator (¥400) down 100m, further 100 steps down tunnel to viewing platform, top stage best–don't bother if water flow low, spectacular if flowing–falls 99m tall. **Ryuzu-no Taki** Dragon-head falls, gorgeous falls only 10m high but falling in steps over length of 200m+ into Lake Chuzen-ji; campsite nr foot.

20min walk from main bus stop or pleasant cruiseboat ride is...
CHUZEN-JI temple with its **Tachiki Kannon**, 1,000-arm Kannon. From Onsen bus stop, nearby aerial cable-car 6min ride up to **Chanokidaira** panoramic view and botanical garden of marshlands.

WHEN TO GO: Maple-turning season **mid Oct-early Nov** or lantern floating on lake **July 31-Aug 1**; or midnites **Jul 31–Aug 7** as fascinating flashlight pilgrimage of white-robed men wends up Mount Nantai. **Lake cruises:** 20min crossing Ojiri Pier (Chuzen-ji Onsen bus stop) to Shobugahama, ¥410, to 1hr-r.t. Ojiri-Shuzen-ji temple, ¥750. Motorboat from Boathouse—5psgr, 10min course ¥5,000, to full circle 30min ¥12,500. No boats Dec-Mar due to freeze. Bus Nikko → Chuzen-ji 50min, ¥980.

TO TOKYO: cyclists may be pleased to learn, bicycle columnists report it all downhill.

KINUGAWA ONSEN 鬼怒川温泉

GETTING THERE: From TOKYO late afternoon trains out of ASAKUSA direct to KINUGAWA ONSEN rather than NIKKO, follow our suggestion to overnite first at spa. Two stns, lower KINUGAWA ONSEN, upper Kinugawa Koen, with spa spread between. Train continues on to KAWA-JI ONSEN, 10min where *rotenburo* or *iwaburo* outdoor rock baths, or on to YUNISHIGAWA ONSEN, more rustic, if bit run down.

From NIKKO taxi ¥5,000 (11x-mtr), or 5hr Nikko taxi tour A plus ferry to here ¥23,480; Panorama bus tour C dep TOBU NIKKO stn 10:20, arr KINUGAWA 17:20, ¥5,130, ret am E course to temples, dep KINUGAWA 9:20, arr JR NIKKO 16:00, ¥4,990.

WHERE TO STAY: Enter your inn, walk thru to find you are on high storey of building clinging to side of deep gorge like swallow's nest. Paving both walls of great canyon are numerous inns—mostly calling themselves 'Hotel'—but all tatami rooms with 2 Japanese meals included, as are tax-svce. Each time we have just tried different ones 'blind'. Can't say we like giant Hotel-cum-Inns as we did old wooden inns—too big, cater to groups, being self-contained. Usually include 9pm imported shows (SE Asian mostly, plus busty Yankee grind-'n-bump, small extra fee), and halls of TV games. No one goes out so old-time stroll in inn-kimono to local bar or pachinko hall is thing of past. Recent trip, inns all full, but streets like ghost town and even pachinko parlor was empty, first we've seen in 36 years.

Each has some feature in its great bath: red arch bridge across giant pool, odd landscaping, live hot-waterfalls or some such, overlooking river. Your room views picture-windowed baths opposite, if advance booking specify riverside room. Rates range from ¥-Tw/2 (usually room in back, ask how much riverside minimum), thru princely ¥-Lw/2, healthy mid predominates. Food plentiful, good, but not exciting except at luxe level. Advise rsve, no hassle.

But most presentable (especially viewed from river): (Area code also 0288)...
On *rail side* down from Kinugawa Koen stn near suspension bridge is **Ichiryu-kan**, **Dai-Ichi**, **Keiraku-so**, soon **Kinugawa Kanko Hotel** (all ¥-hi-T+) West/Nishi-kan (*avoid* their East/Higashi-kan annex), **Hotel Fukumatsu** ☎77-3311 (¥-lo-T+) nearer K-Onsen stn, and after several more ordinaries at foot of stn above Rhine-Kudari boat pier is **Kanaya** ☎76-0001 (each room looks out over river and is 40 mats, run ¥-S-L, dinner served on fine Imari, main bath has view of ravine). Coming down *far side* Green Palace (¥-S+), and string of giants from multi-structure **Asaya** ☎77-1111 (¥-S+), each with nice baths over river (its luxe **Hachi-ban-kan** is concrete shell but all traditional fine woods inside; only 40 rms with some Sukiya-style, ¥-S-L; then huge but top-appointed **Kinugawa Onsen Hotel** ☎77-0025 (¥-S+ then Kuro-gane Bridge and **Ishin-kan** (¥-T) and nicer **Plaza Hotel** ☎77-1031 (¥-T+) jutting out over ravine.

BUDGET: across from Kinugawa Koen stn, **Kinugawa-kan Dai-ni Bekkan** ☎77-1023; ¥-Bw/2 and *rotenburo* outdoor bath along riverside. **Hotel New Kinugawa** ☎77-0546, along river 3mins from Kinugawa Onsen stn; and **Hotel Sarashina** ☎77-0366, ¥-T, 5min bus from Kinugawa Onsen stn on river. Minshuku Senju-so is just next to Kanaya at boat landing, near Kinugawa Onsen stn; ¥-Bw/2, ☎77-0120.

Boat cruise down river ravine, book Rhine-kudari at hotel/inn desk, almost hourly, ¥2,060, kids half, Apr 10–Nov 9, 40-50mins, from nr Kinugawa Onsen stn, foot of Kanaya and Okabe Hotels, for 6km to Otoro whence shuttle bus (¥250) back to stn, or bus to Nikko 50min, or taxi short run to Nikko-Edo Mura, or bus back to Kinugawa for its free shuttle.

Next morning early, bus or taxi (9-10x-mtr) from Kinugawa → Nikko...
Specify you want road thru impressive **giant cryptomeria** tree avenue, *sugi-nami ki*: 39km/23mi of 19,000 trees over 350 years old, planted as of-fering to shrine by Lord Matsudaira. Largest 51m (166ft) hi, 2m (6ft6in) across, barely stands out from slightly smaller mates. Some years ago city announced plan to cut down trees to widen road for buses: near riot ensued, stopped! In May at festival time rice paddies are filled with umbrella-hatted

**AROUND
LAKE CHUZEN-JI**

☐ Hotels
1. Kanaya Hotel   4. Lakeside Hotel
2. Nikko Youth Hostel   5. Kanaya Hotel
3. Daiyagawa Youth Hostel 6. Prince Hotel

women transplanting seedlings, and at autumn festival time harvesting–to us two of major sights of Nikko, which most tours overlook.

KAWA-JI ONSEN, next spa, 10min train above KINUGAWA, again two stns, Kawa-ji Onsen and Kinugawa Yumoto; or taxi from Kinugawa stn 5x-mtr. Our favorite years ago for its small inns, but all burned down in late '70s—thus new inns are all concrete, ugly maybe but fire-proof. Still more charm than Kinugawa, it boasts three smaller inns with *rotenburo* outdoor baths.

WHERE TO STAY: Kawa-ji Onsen Hotel ☎(0288)-78-0011, ¥-S+; one rotenburo only so gals exclusive 19:30-21:00, otherwise mixed bathing, 24 hrs. **Tozan Kaku** ☎78-1126, 5min walk from Kinugawa Onsen stn, ¥-hi-T+, separate outdoor baths 24 hrs. **Chosei Kaku** ☎78-0119, 5min walk Kinugawa Yumoto stn ¥-hi-T+, separate rotenburo, 3pm-midnite. OFFBEAT at Yunishikawa Onsen, 30min, taxi 6x-mtr, **Kanko Hotel Kameya** ☎98-0031, separate rotenburo, dining specialty *jingasa-ryori*, sit around open hearth *irori* and eat venison; ¥-T+.

From here on up is for adventurers, gorgeous mountain areas with numerous camp facilities, pilgrim priced mountain spas and plentiful old style comfortable country spas, many with rotenburo, most with exotic dining specialties, lots of game meat—some advertise *kuma sashimi*, raw bear meat, unaware it is dangerous (trichinosis) and now illegal. Some, as **OKU KINU SPA**, can be reached only on foot in 3 hours from already rather isolated Kawamata spa.

Get Tobu Railways excuraion **4-day Free Pass;** not free, but for one fee travel freely, unlimited use on Tobu trains and buses from Nikko → Shimoichi → Kinugawa Onsen and beyond past Ryuokyo gorge, Kawaji Onsen → Lake Ikari and backtrack as you like.

Back in lowlands we have...

NIKKO-EDO MURA (feudal village) Disneyland-history, valid in its own way as it helps place standing monuments in historical perspective. But it starts out with some unhistorical assumptions. **Entertainments** include *Edo-yugi-jo* game center with old time games, *Shibai-goya* theater for magic shows and comedies, Ninja House for ninja demonstrations, ghost temple, carni-throws using old fashioned ninja and samurai *shuri-ken* star daggers, 'zen' longbows, matchlocks, etc. Shopkeepers in costume, models stroll street to pose with you. **Free** festivals, dances in square, shops sell sort of old paper Japonica elders will recall from prewar before Canon, Honda and ilk changed image of 'made in Japan' from quaint junk to hi-tec. Mainly for kids, not as legit as Kanazawa Edo Mura (p.873), don't confuse with.

Entry ¥2,000/adult, ¥1,000/child. Entertainments are on ticket system costing ¥100 per 100 *ryo* coupon, old currency which in early Edo 1600s was worth 15gr gold or ¥45,000 at present market, tho had dropped in 1868 Meiji changeover to equal Yen, then silver dollar-Mex, like US$, now coin worth several paper dollars. Most run 100ryo (¥4,500,000?) to 300, or ¥1-300 less 10% for buying 100ryo tickets in 11-pack at ¥1,000. Info or group rsvs ☎(0288)-77-1777. Daily 9-17:00, Dec 1–Mar 31 till 16:00.

GETTING THERE: Near KINUGAWA ONSEN, best from stn by shuttle bus; or river boat trip to bus back to shuttle, or taxi 3x-mtr. From NIKKO taxi 6x-mtr, or train to KINUGAWA stn, take bus. From TOKYO, Tobu Kinugawa rail to KINUGAWA ONSEN, then EDO MURA **shuttle** (*see* Kinugawa); or Tobu Nikko from ASAKUSA to IMAICHI, whence taxi. **Drive** Tohoku expressway to Utsunomiya interchange, onto Nikko-Utsunomiya hiway—often packed so locals advise old road which takes you thru or alongside great Cryptomeria Avenue, exit Imaichi to Rte121 for KINUGAWA ONSEN, then follow signs.

PERSONAL DATEBOOK: Nikko best **May 18** and **Oct 17** for gigantic *Sennin Gyoretsu* 1,000-man feudal procession. For years our favorite character was photo-crazy old man with scraggly white beard dressed as *yamabushi*, honking conch—liked to have his photo taken with you (no handouts, just smile and thank you). We have rarely seen such tourist attraction where everyone is so cooperative for photobugs. Samurai may even plunk helmet on your head and lend you halberd to arrest him with. For either date, advise overnite preceding to leave you fresh on festival day. In chillier spots azaleas still out at May fete; autumn sees maples turning if early chill. **Apr 2**, *Rice Eating Rite*, 11am, 2pm; Monks at Rinno-ji temple gorge on mounds of rice. **16-17** *Yayoi Festival* at Futara Shrine, procession of 15 azalea floats. **May 17** *Yabusame* Archery on horseback at Toshogu Main Nikko Shrine, 1pm nr 5-storey pagoda; also longevity dance from T'ang China (8th cent) at Rinno-ji T. Make it 2-day stay. **July 22-23** *Ryuo-O Festival*, dragon king dance from Bugaku, and dragon drums in Kinugawa and Kawa-ji Onsens dedicated to dragon-protector of hot springs. **July 31 thru Aug 7** Mount Nantai *nite processions* at Chuzen-ji Futara Shrine (Chugushi), (*see*) lantern float first 3 nites, dances, parade best **Aug 1**; **Aug 4** archers shoot fans. **1st sat or sun Aug** *Waraku Dance* was one of Japan's biggest Bon Dance; at Kiyotaki Refinery between Nikko and Chuzen-ji, short bus or cab ride. Many lanterns lit, as are many of participant-spectators. **May thru Oct** *Fishing* in mountain lakes and rivers nearby. **Nov 25** *Rice Gorging Fete*, sees young priests cram prodigious quantities of rice down from heaped-high individual serving bowls size of wash basins. Anciently, rite humbled great priests and religious lords; now just pulls tourists to Rinno-ji. *Hunting* from **Dec**, but in recent years has been overkilling and except for wild boar is restricted ('88). *Skiing* in area **Jan–mid Mar**, back country packed weekends. See MASHIKO, next, for pottery fairs.

SHOPPING: *Mashiko-yaki* pottery made nearby, available here. Lovely farmers' sedge hats in some local general stores on back streets and nearby villages; blue-and-white *ai-zome* textiles they dress in, in bolts or readymade *mompe* (ladies' pantaloons) which make nice 'harem' house casuals: cheap, infinitely hardy. Petrified wood carvings, once popular local specialty, now available only farther north. At Kinugawa Onsen huge 30cm dried gourds make lovely baskets containers for flowers, etc., ¥2,500+.

Nikko

MASHIKO   FOR POTTERY FANS

TOWN OF SOME 350 independent kilns making everything from chopstick rests, teacups and dishes thru major art pieces. Kiln town, originally of great antiquity with sherds of natural-glaze gray ware from tomb period and early Heian, 9th century. Then falls off, perhaps ceases for millennium, until 1853 when OHTSUKA Keisaburo starts making glazed kitchenware, with own style, local lord supports, attracting other potters to produce for Edo market, sent by Kinugawa River barge.

Production fell off mid-1950s with changeover to modern kitchen, rise of plastic. Town saved only by producing marvelous disposable pottery for rice, noodles and tea sold on train stns (we saw exhibited New York Museum of Modern Art, 1951).

Meanwhile, HAMADA Shoji had returned from England imbued with its handicraft movement revolt against nonfunctional frills, to join others like YANAGI Soetsu in launching *Mingei*, folk art movement and set up his kiln here in 1924. He travelled widely, lectured and taught abroad in excellent English, donated work generously to European and US museums, attracted foreign disciples greatly influencing international ceramics. His fine work, generous personality and able PR drew other young potters to town, especially after 1950s. Senior artists now are his ex-student SHIMAOKA Tatsuzo, and Hamada's own son.

Characteristic glazes are black and rust, Hamada revived polychrome—especially characteristic off-red. Recently reviving cobalt, both pure deep blue and 'mis-mix' lighter blues. Noted for teapots, cups, saucers and tableware. Master potters make decorative works, vases, great bowls and platters. But all characterized by casual and natural brushwork and forms derived from function. Ware is hardy, lightweight for its bulk.

GETTING THERE: Coming down from N, Shinkansen from SENDAI to UTSUNOMIYA whence taxi 17x-mtr, or Tono bus from Tobu DS or JR stn 50min to here. From TOKYO on 2-day Nikko tour; or on own Shinkansen to Utsunomiya, then as above, 2hrs. From NIKKO 58km, taxi 30x-mtr; or bus or train to UTSUNOMIYA, then as above. From Gerd Knapper at Daigo (follows) 60km taxi 30x-mtr.

WHERE TO STAY: Small economy luxe-like 10rm **Mashiko Onsen Hotel** best ☎(0285)-72-7011; nr Nana-i stn, taxi basic, next above Mashiko (taxi 2x-mtr) but will pick up free either stn; wkday ¥-lo-Tw/2, ¥-T weekend, hols. Private & big baths.

All others are minshuku rate: **Okada-ya** ☎72-2016 on main street 1km from JR at snake in road, oldest inn, not much but convenient, clean, budget. Several lovely minshuku: **Toki** ☎72–3393, bit out of way S of town, but will pick you up. **Furusato** ☎72-3156 (potting available, *see*, nice people), and **Yama-ji** ☎72-2525 near each other between Tsukamoto/Hamada intersect and Kyohan Ctr. Others abound, can book from Kyohan, or late arrivals ask stnmaster.

GETTING AROUND: **Rent bike** 2hr ¥300, day ¥800, at Kyohan Ctr office, big bldg rear, R-end. Otherwise call **taxi** from inn, 9x-mtr per hr, or walk.

Throw pottery, several spots offer half-day course 8:30-noon, or 13-16:30, from ¥800, full-day 8:30-16:30 ¥1,-2,000, includes clay, use of tools and equipment etc, instructor; firing and glazing charge extra, from tea cups ¥300 to flower pots ¥700, medium vases ¥3,000, shipping chge extra average almost as much as firing, send to your final Japan stop. *Raku-yaki* painting only on pre-thrown biscuit-fired bowls, cups etc; cup from ¥2-300, with saucer ¥700, plates 6-10in (15-25cm) ¥350–900 etc, ready in few days, domestic shipping chges add another ¥500 each average. Fees vary, some run flat charges bit higher, balance with including more. We think best is **Tsukamoto** main kiln and shop, ¥500 for 2hrs up to full day ¥2,000. **Furusato** minshuku has *togei-kyoshitsu*, pottery intruction, with their own kiln on grounds, ¥1,500 per day or part, and if you haven't finished foot etc, host will finish and glaze as you instruct; firing ¥500 each or so, plus shipping. Stay there and work early or late. **Togei Mura** nice setup, bit away but near Hamada Sankokan Museum. **Kyohan Center** has full facilitities but not as attractive, angled more for bus tours.

PERSONAL DATEBOOK: **End Apr-early May** and **early Nov** *Toki-matsuri*, sometimes **Aug 13-17** at O-bon *Dai Toki-ichi*, great pottery fair—big discount sales Kyohan Center central lot. **Jul 23-25** *Gion Matsuri*, floats, sake-drinking contest.

Hamada's House and Kiln, major sight, ¥500, (X-mon, X-all Feb) far end of town from stn, basic taxi or 30min walk—not allowing for distractions of shops. Deeded by this late Living National Treasure (1894-1978) as **Museum** *Mashiko Sankokan*, compound of classical folk homes, storehouses moved by Hamada from elsewhere in area for preservation. Great gatehouse and century-old main house are thatch, storehouses of local Ohya stone, used by Frank Lloyd Wright for old Imperial Hotel. First stone storehouse shows typical Hamada pieces and, facing, those of lifelong friend Bernard Leach —who is probably better known in Japan than in his native UK. Elsewhere, works by him, furniture and other wares collected by him—we are proud that most of his several Persian pottery and glass pieces, both antique and contemporary, are from our collection. Out rear is his 8-chamber *nobori gama* climbing kiln (1943); two square ones are salt glaze kiln (large) and small red glaze kiln, both 1954. In large work shed are 7 small foot-kick potter's wheels and one single large hand-spun wheel.

Second house to L, on alley corner, is...
SHIMAOKA Tatsuzo top living Mashiko potter, ex-student of Hamada. Holds annual show in Germany; has works in Dusseldorf Hetjens and Munich Deutsches Museums, also V&A, Toronto, Fogg and New York's Brooklyn and Metropolitan Museums. Among younger artists he likes SETO-

Hiroshi, YOSHIKAWA, FURUKAWA and SUZUKI Jinnai. His own former-student, German potter Gerd Knapper, is in Daigo, hour away (*next page*).

SHOPPING: Shimaoka's works sell in **Tsukamoto** big center on corner, at their main kiln-shop **Kogeikan**, as well as in **Kyohan Center** #2 gallery. Serious collector might visit his kiln, where small gallery adjoins his house: phone first, in Japanese, ☎(0285)-72-2225.

Below Hamada Sankokan and Shimaoka, on main intersection...
Tsukamoto first to introduce Mashiko-ware to Tokyo thru their shop in Roppongi. 'Small' shop, **Togei-Hiroba** (Pottery Plaza) on corner below Hamada Sankokan; upstairs gallery has monthly one-man shows. Art works by leading potters and mass-produced works of their own kiln and other potters fill tasteful roomy shop, smaller adjoining shop has other folk art items. Coffee shop and cafe (good lunch under ¥1,000) in outer building. Further out are their workshops and kilns, which can be toured, where main showroom (15-20min walk past other interesting shops) and their... **Kogeikan** Crafts Gallery have works by Hamada, Shimaoka, etc. for exhibition and sale. For one-stop shopping, and especially try at potting, we recommend here.

From Tsukamoto corner to main shop, 15-20 min walk R, away from town. 3min from intersection along highway are two shops on L, second is...
Sudo where we found pale blue off-cobalt coffee cups we now treasure. Racks of seconds greatly reduced, few hundred yen for cups—look same to us but they have high standards. Spot them from large workshop in rear, which you can visit.

Few doors on...
Kotokan museum of old Mashiko-ware, ¥300, X-mon; private collection run by same folks as interesting antique and pottery shop in front. Road continues to **Togei Mura**, another kiln-shop complex of younger potters, few mins down on R—also has museum, workshop. On L facing entry is **Irori Chaya** which serves duck and wild boar in season. Or take first R back 135° 100m or so, then L on to **Tsukamoto** main complex.

Alternate, from Tsukamoto corner walk L back to town past another intersection, with minshukus Furusatao and Yama-ji on knolls on L. On R past small bridge is new 2-storey building, good antique shop **Kyobijutsu** with good tansu-chests at below city prices, good selection of much from junk up, worth stop in.

Few mins on to corner, R turn at tall old-style multi-storey peaked roof on R...
Kyohan Center with several large shops and galleries ringing bus-lot, where flea marts held few times yearly (see DATEBOOK). Good shops, not as tastefully done as Tsukamoto, but good for lower-budget shopping addict... Also can throw pottery or paint ready-mades (*see*).

15-20min walk past Tsukamoto Kogeikan or taxi from center town is...
SAIMYO-JI temple, out of way, but for architecture buffs rare in that **Sakura-mon** gate 1492 (NT), with Chinese T'ang-style gate guardians, and most buildings thatch-roofed, not tile customary in Nara-Kyoto etc. Atop knoll up 140 stone steps lovely 3-tiered **pagoda**, 1538 (NT), and **Hondo** central building, 1394, repainted 1701 with fine dragon ceiling and *ranma* panels above inner door-jambs of well aged carvings painted in flamboyant early Edo style. Pilgrim stickers everywhere give it folksy air, show to be living pilgrim temple, #20 of 33-Kannon pilgrimage of NE Tokyo area (Asakusa Kannon is #13). On L is old form of **bell tower**. Building R **Ema-do** 1714, has front peep hole thru which if you have flashlight you can see large statues of red laughing *Ema*, king of Hades, *zen-doji* and *aku-doji*, good and bad sons, and Jizo. Immense Koya-maki **tree**, R rear, was planted in 1209.

Japanese literature lists as 'must-see' OKURA JINJA, with adjoining JIZO-IN temple (Ryobu-Shinto combination before 1870s religious purges). We advise you skip them unless taking long hiking course with Japanese friends. Might take in with Saimyo-ji and interim views in hour by taxi, about ¥4,000, nice drive but Saimyo-ji alone enough.

DAIGO 醍醐   GERMAN 'JAPANESE' POTTER

IN 1971 Mainichi Newspapers initiated their prestigious annual ceramics concours, entrants identified only by numbers for fairness. Most made avant garde 'objets' in style of America and Europe of decade earlier. Largest was traditional Japanese section with 900 entries, dominated by Education Minister Prize-winner who turned out to be German student of Shimaoka (above) —**Gerd Knapper**, ex-house painter, stone restorer, traveler, jack-of-all-trades and master of several. He left Mashiko when he found immense thatch-roof house in Daigo, moved in to restore it and set up own kiln. Exhibits regularly in main cities of Japan, travels frequently to US and Germany for museum and gallery shows and to give workshops.

Serious collectors might phone him ☎(02957)-2-2011 (✍ from home in English or German: **Gerd Knapper**, O-Aza Hanawa 1222, Daigo-cho, Kuji-gun, Ibaragi-ken, 319-36, Japan) to see if can visit his exquisite home-workshop— largest thatch roof in Japan, with European dormer windows added when he rethatched in early '80s with 80 truckloads of *kaya* reed. Pottery style is highly original synthesis of German brass and Japanese silk, using old proven traditions from both with highest tec in ceramic art. See bridge he metal sculpted in town.

GETTING THERE: Not easy: 30km from MASHIKO, 15x-mtr taxi (opp direction from Nikko). From TOKYO start Ueno stn, take Joban line to MITO, change to Suigin line toward KORIYAMA. Coming down from SENDAI or FUKUSHIMA, Tohoku JR main line or Shinkansen to KORIYAMA, then Suigin local down MITO-wards.

OTHER SIGHTS: Fukuroda-no-taki waterfalls,

falling 120mtrs in 4 steps, but unlike better-known greats KEGON (only 99m) and NACHI (133m) no mere sliver of water, but 73mtr wide roaring 'Niagara'. Unlike these others, not in grand setting allowing long view, but jammed in narrow ravine and more dramatic for it. Beautiful any season, in winter becomes wall of ice on which alpinists practice. Enter at nite, thru pedestrian toll tunnel, see white water whiter yet in dark, exquisite at full moon. Stay **Fukuroda Onsen Hotel** ☎2-3111, ¥-hi-T, near falls, **taxi** 2x-mtr+ from above.

GETTING THERE: Tohoku Shinkansen to Nasu Shiobara stn then **taxi** 30min (5x-mtr); or JR Nishi Nasuno stn → Tono bus 35 mins; **drive** Tohoku expressway → Yaita IC, exit → 15km to OTAHARA → 10km KUROBANE.

DAIO-JI ZEN temple en route taxi Nikko–Daigo, Kurobane-machi ☎(02875)-4-0332. Built Muromachi era, 1448, rare as was never burned, just periodically rethatched. Roshi Kurasawa (runs it with son) found it in ruins and started its restoration. Whole compound thatched in *kaya* reed, indicative of poorer economy in olden days; architecture bare, interiors showing pillar tops, roof beams. Buy bundle of reed for roof and participate in restoration, ¥1,000.

Hondo main object sitting Shaka-nyorai, late Kamakura, 13th cent. High on walls are entertaining paintings of 16 rakan, disciples of Buddha. Side room has mysterious painted scroll of female ghost, said haunted so that anyone sleeping in room with it tosses and turns to face other direction. **Kyo-zo** sutra storehouse has superb standing Sho-Kannon (ask to see, leave small offering) guarding library of complete Tripitaka of 4,500 Ming-Ching Chinese sutras. **Zendo** far L bldg, exquisite Kamakura era seated Shaka-nyorai rare in having tall crown like Kannon, for which one might well mistake it.

Zazen 2nd, 4th sun 7:30. **Jul–Aug** (dates vary) local primary school student groups etc live in, daily practice and chores; ¥4,000 per day all incl. Accept overnite stays other times for groups of 4 or more, negotiable, amenable to discussing long term if speak Japanese or have own good interpreter; *shojin-ryori* groups of 10-up only, if less will try to put you in with others as and if available, rsve week in advance, *shi-un*, ¥3,300 ea.

PERSONAL DATEBOOK

I: FUKUSHIMA, YAMAGATA, MIYAGI

January

New Year heralded at Dewa Sanzan with ancient fire rite by *yamabushi* all nite, sunset **Dec 31** to **sunrise 1st**; main rite 23:00 blowing of conch shell to call all. Legend has 7th century Prince Hachiko founder of yamabushi sect, heard divine oracle tell him to use fire against plague of crop-devouring insects. Of course, it worked and been carried on since.

7 (nite), *Hadaka-mairi* (Naked Fest), Aizu, Fukushima; hordes of loincloth-clad youths vie to be first to reach sacred board climbing rope to rafters. One of countless *hadaka-mairi* thruout Tohoku early Jan.

10 *Tohka-ichi* (10th day fair), booths sell lacquerware, other crafts, line main Shinmei-dori Ave, Aizu Wakamatsu.

- *Hatsu-ichi* First Market of year, Yamagata City; 100s stalls over town.

12 *Daruma-ichi* Fair, Miharu town, Fukushima; stalls set up all over town sell red rolly-polly dharma dolls.

14 *Dondo-sai* festival, citizens of Sendai visit Osaki Hachiman Shrine, toss used New Year decorations, last year's charms into bonfire, smoke raising this year's wishes. Nite is *hadaka-mairi* naked fest of loincloth-clad men jostling for talisman.

17 Fire-walking 1pm Yama-dera temple Yamagata; onlookers welcome to walk after priests pass; *(See* Miyajima) how to.

- *Sasano Kannon-do Fete*, Yonezawa C, stalls sell *sasano-issai-bori* carved falcons.

February

1-2 Kurokawa Noh rural theater, Kurokawa Ville, near Tsuruoka C Yamagata.

1st Sun, *Kaki* (Oyster) *Festival*, Matsushima Bay; generous helpings oyster and local sake sold for budget.

11 *Kase-dori*, Kami-no-yama Onsen, Yamagata; folk in tradition straw rain-gear go house-to-house remind be careful fires.

- *Yuki-to-Hi Matsuri* (Snow-and-Fire Fete) Aizu Mishima-cho, Fukushima; bitter cold warded off with huge sacred bonfires.

2nd Weekend, *Uesugi Yuki-doro* (Snow-Lantern Festival), Yonezawa C.

15 Rural Kabuki at Kuromori Village near Sakata, Yamagata; shows 11am to 4pm. Repeated on 17th *(see* pp.979, 983).

25-26 *Waraji Matsuri*, Haguri Jinja S, Monobu-san Park, Fukushima City; cart giant *waraji* straw sandle thru shrine symbolizes pilgrimage to Daiwa Sanzan.

March

10 *Takote Festival*, Shiogama City, Miyagi; wild mikoshi procession.

15 *Funa-hiki Matsuri* (Boat-pulling Fest), Bandai-cho temple, Fukushima; giant tug-o-war with 3 bales of rice on wooden boat.

21, Equinox, *Ohigan* marked by unusual shishi-mai lion dance. Dancers' headgear more like deer, troupes of 3 perform front of castle, each keeping time to own drum.

April

2-3 *Yachi-hina* Doll Fete, Kahoku town, NW of Yamagata airport; roadside stalls sell beauts of traditional dolls.

2nd half of month, triple spring of Miharu simultaneous blossoming plum, peach, cherry; Miharu City, Fukushima.

Last weekend, *Ningen-shogi* Human Chessmen matches, Tendo Onsen, Yamagata; peak of cherry blossoms.

24 *Memorial for Byakko-tai*, Aizu Wakamatsu; sword dance offered in front of their graves on Iimori-yama hill.

25 *Hana-matsuri* (Flower Fete), Shiogama City, Miyagi; colorful mikoshi parade.

29-May 3, *Uesugi Festival* Yonezawa. Best 29-1st shrine, temple fairs in town. 2nd parade armies in feudal garb, Uesugi force muster at nite 3rd recreate decisive Battle Kawanakajima vs Takeda Shingen *(see* Kai), Matsukawa River cuts town.

May

3-7 All Japan *Kokeshi Festival*, Shiroishi City, Miyagi; vendors from all Japan.

5 Jion-ji temple, Sagae City, NW of Yamagata City, hosts Buddhist sects in 12 century-old tradition to recite sutras together. Ancient court music, dance done.

12 Rural Kabuki Hinoemata Village, Aizu *(see* p.969).

Mid-May, all week from first Snake Day, *Koganeyama Shrine Festival*, Kinka-zan Isle, Miyagi.

25 *Bakemono Matsuri*, (Monster Festival) Tenmangu Shrine, Tsuruoka C, Yamagata; people in fancy costumes and red cloths over face parade around handing out sake from gourd to passersby; costume contest.

June

5 Ohyama *Inu Matsuri* (Dog Fete), Shigiyo Jinja S, Tsuruoka C, Yamagata; after local tale of how certain dog got rid of evil spirit to lift local drought and plague. Various floats, mikoshi shaped like or somehow related to dogs paraded around town, also *diamyo-gyoretsu* feudal parade.

July

1 Start of Aizu Wakamatsu *Hi-ichi* fest; all local shrines, temples honored. Every day for several weeks, find neighborhood fetes somewhere in town, entertainment, food stalls and assorted dances.

2 *Bange* (Mid-summer) *Festival*, Ouchijuku hamlet, Aizu, Fukushima; 400-year-old festival begins morning with shishi-mai lion dance, followed by dashi float parade and *daimyo-gyoretsu* feudal procession.

12 *Ota-ue* Ceremonial Transplanting of first rice crop, at Isasumi Jinja shrine, Aizu Takada; this one of best in Japan.

Sometime first half of month, *kagura* dances by rural troupes, *shishi-mai* lion dance; Yuzusame Jinja shrine Yutagawa Onsen, near Tsuruoka City, Yamagata.

15 Parade of flower-covered mikoshi, Haguro Jinja, Dewa Sanzan Yamagata.

19-21 Aizu Tajima *Gion Festival*, Tajima-cho, Fukushima; 700-year-old festival based on Kyoto's Gion, 20th parade of colorful decorated giant floats.

25-26 Fireworks festival, Inawashiro Lake, Fukushima; follows memorial floating of lanterns for victims 1888 eruption of Mt Bandai. Torch parade, outline character for 'fire' on hillside.

23-25 Noma-oi Wild Horses, Soma City, Fukushima; best 23-4 (*see* p.972).

24-26 *Kumano Taisha Festival*, Kumano Shrine, Nanyo C, Yamagata; yamabushi ascetics end purification period with ritual 24th nite, ancient version *hishi-mai* lion dance 25th am.

4th Weekend, *Dashi Matsuri* Parade, Kurikoma town, Miyagi; lively event, colorful *dashi* floats paraded around town.

Last Weekend, Shizugawa Bay Summer Fest, north coast Miyagi; offering for good catch, safety at sea; fireworks at nite.

August

1st Sunday, *Seto-ichi* ceramic market at Aizu Hongo.

1-2, Fukushima *Waraji* (sandal) *Festival*.

— *Kawa-biraki* 'River Opens' with one of largest fireworks, Ishinomaki C, Miyagi.

2-4 Koriyama *Uneme Festival*; dancers wind thru streets between 30,000 lanterns.

4 *Kujira* (Whale) *Festival*, Ayukawa T on Oshika Peninsula, Miyagi; relives glory as major whaling center with whale parade thru town, fireworks over water at nite.

5 *Minato Matsuri* Port Festival of Shiogama City, Miyagi; two mikoshi from Shiogama Jinja shrine are carted down to harbor, then loaded onto 2 gaudily decorated phoenix boats and paraded all around Matsushima Bay, followed by all fishing boats equally colorfully decorated – Kessen-numa Port Festival, Miyagi.

5-8 *Tanabata-sai*. Sendai's is largest '7th Nite' Star Festival in all Japan, city trademark with city and fete as one; also among Tohoku's Top 3 events, with coloful streamers hanging down along major streets. (*see* p.985).

6 *Sugisawa Hiyama Bangaku*, ancient form of noh, originally performed by yamabushi, at Yuza, north of Sakata, Yamagata. Repeated August 15 and 20.

6-8 Yamagata City's grand *Hanagasa Matsuri* (Flower-hat) *Fest*, one of Tohoku's Top 3 summer events, 1000s of synchronized dancers wind thru city streets. Began as celebration of safflower, which is represented on flower hats.

10 *Masamune Festival*, Iwadeyama T, Miyagi; 'sparrow' dances, samurai parade recreating Date Masamune's departure for Korean invasion.

13-20 Giant *bon dance* at Higashiyama Onsen, Aizu Wakamatsu.

15-16 *Toro-nagashi* Floating Lanterns, fireworks Matsushima Bay, Miyagi.

15-16 Summer Festival, Kitakata City, Aizu, Fukushima.

18 Rural Kabuki, Hinoemata,Aizu (p.l000).

24-26 *Shinjo Fete* Shinjo C, Yamagata; main day **25th**, 20 giant colorful floats roll thru town. Originated mid-18th cent when local lord ordered all neighborhoods to ready float for ceremony as offering to rid area of famine. Seems to have worked, for next harvest was bumper crop.

27-28 *Hanagasa Matsuri* Obanazawa town.

31–1st, *Hassaku Festival*, *yamabushi* just finished with 7 days purification rites, Haguro Jinja S, Dewa Sanzan, Yamagata.

31–1st, *Fujin Matsuri* Wind God Fest, Asahi-cho, Yamagata; prayers offered for good harvest and to ward off any crop-damaging typhoon.

September

7-9 All-Japan *Kokeshi Fete* Narugo Onsen Miyagi *kijishi*, carvers from all over show

8-16 All-Japan *Kakashi* Scarecrow Contest Tsukioka Park, Kami-no-Yama Onsen, Yamagata; all sorts of entrants in traditional, modern categories scarecrows.

14-17 *Yachi Donga Festival*, Kahoku town, NW of Yamagata airport; 8th century court dance Hayashike performed at Yachi Hachiman-gu Shrine; parade thru town of floats carrying musicians.

22-24 Aizu Wakamatsu *Byakko Fest*, big samurai procession 23rd and lots more (*see* p962) nite fireworks 10,000 *O-bon* dancers

October

1 thru Nov 23, *Kiku-ningyo* Chrysanthemum doll) *Fete* Kasumiga-jo Park, Nihonmatsu,Fukushima; life-size floral figs.

1st, 2nd weekend + 10th, Ritual cut deer antlers, Kinka-zan Isle, Miyagi. Done at mating season avoids injuries. Any horn found around any other time is yours.

4-6 *Nihonmatsu* (Lantern) *Festival;* main event 4th nite, 7 giant floats supporting drum teams, covered with lanterns, parade thru town. One of top lantern fetes.

November

3 *Shonai Hyakuman-goku Festival*, Tsuruoka City, Yamagata; citywide thanksgiving for good harvest.

2nd Sun *Haiku* fans gather from all Japan for contests at Matsushima, Miyagi.

December

4 *Horoha-do Toshikoshi* Year End Fete, Yonezawa City 300-year-old festive thanks for good harvest, citizens gather Sengan-ji temple's Horoha-do Pavilion, pound *mochi* out of newly reaped rice.

II: IWATE, AOMORI, AKITA

January

3-5 Miyako *Shake* (salmon) Festival, Miyako City, Iwate, salmon season is celebrated with food stalls around town, visitors join in salmon grabbing contests.

5 Kite-flying contests, Noshiro C, Akita.

6 *Amahage* demons (from Oga's famed *Namahage*) visit backwoods villages of south Akita to scare laziness out of kids.

14 *Hadaka-mairi* Naked Fest to ward off sickness and fires, Kyojo-ji, Morioka C; repeat following day Hachiman-gu Shrine.

13-15 *Mochitsuki Odori*, dancers carrying mochi-tsuki (rice cake pounding) tools make rounds of all homes performing their rhythmic mochi making skills and offer finished products as New Year's gift, Ouchi district, Mutsu City, Aomori.

15-20 Tono, Iwate, farmers pray for good year enacting year's worth of farm chores.

16 Ceremonial changing of clothes of oshirasama sacred stick figures, Tono Town, Iwate.

16 *Hadaka-mairi*, Arayama Jinja, Honjo City, Akita, loincloth-clad youths in cold water purification rites charge up snowy mount to be first to offer to local kami.

17 *Bonten Fes,* participants in pushy contest vie to be first to offer special tablets to shrine's kami, Miyoshi Jinja, Akita City.

Lunar 7 7th Day Rites of ancient offertory for good year of harvest, Iwakisan Jinja Shrine, Iwaki Town, Aomori.

20 *Hatsuka-ya* (20th nite) *Fete* at Motsu-ji Temple's Jogyo-do Hall has centuries old *Ennen-no-mai* dance; Hiraizumi C, Iwate.

26 *Hadaka-mairi*, Sakurayama Jinja S, Morioka City.

Lunar 15 (full moon Feb) giant tug-o-war as townspeople face off on 300m long rope, Kawano village, Akita.

February

Mid-winter blues are kept away in north Tohoku with countless festivals, of which *-marked are Top 5 Winter Festivals.

***2-13** Iwate Snow Festival*, Koiwai Farm, giant *kamakura* igloos of various shapes become settings for Genghis Khan BBQ feasts. Assorted games and contests every day are open to all, night sky is background for laser-sound shows.

***4-13** Hirosaki Snow Sculpture Fete*, *kamakura* igloos, long slides are put up around castle park, games, contests, shows daily, Hirosaki City, Aomori.

4 Offertory rites for good harvest of crops and fish and for safety at sea, at main shrine of Kaneura Town, Akita.

11 Ohara *Mizu-kake* (Water-splashing) Festival, men purified at local Hachiman shrine race about town splash people with water to purify them, Daito Town, Iwate.

11 All-Japan *Wanko-soba* Eating Contest, at various places around town participants from all over Japan race to see who can eat most helpings of *wanko-soba* noodles in 5min, Hanamaki City, Iwate.

11-12 *Amekko* Fete, colorful old floats, dancers wind thru Ohdate City, Akita, stalls sell assorted candy on these 2 days as 400-year-old belief says eating sweets at this time prevents colds.

***13-15** Namahage Demon Dances*, late nite 13 & 14 teams of demons blowing conches go around with purifying sacred torches, main event 15th day is dances by 20 *namahage*, Shinzan Jinja, Oga City, Akita. Buy set ticket (*setto-ken*) at shrine, includes admission, some *mochi*, beans, soup, and bamboo cup which lets you drink as much sacred shrine sake as can.

15 Tug-o-war between two halves of town, Omagari City, Akita.

15 *Take-uchi* (Bamboo-hitting) between 2 armies, Suwa Jinja, Rokugo Town, Akita.

15-16 Inukko figures molded out of powdered rice are offered by children to spirits enshrined in igloos for safety from illness and fire, Yuzawa City, Akita.

*15-16 *Kamakura Igloo Fete*, Yokote C, Akita, best known of Tohoku's many. Altar local deity set up in each *kamakura*, children spend eve in drinking *ama-zake* non-alchohol sweet sake, roasting mochi, snacks. 500+ about town, mainly around Yokote Park, Futaba-cho, Yokka-machi.

16-17 Yokote City's fun continues as rough-and-tumble *Bonten Festival* at Asahioka-yama Jinja (sometimes at Kita Elementary School near Yokote Park).

17 Spirit of Izusan Jinja is ferried across river to sister shrine for annual visit, Omagari City, Akita.

*17-20 *Enburi Festival*, 800-year-old offertory dances for good harvest, Hachinohe City, Aomori. 17th sees troupes all around town, and teams compete 17-18 at Kokai-do Town Hall.

April

2nd Monkey Day of Lunar Calendar, brides married past year make pilgrimage to Hiyoshi Jinja, Noshiro City, Akita.

3rd Sun Annual festival of Kabushima Isle, Hachinohe City, Aomori.

22 Colorful float procession to Hidaka Jinja for offerings to shrine for protection from fire; Mizusawa City, Iwate.

Late – open cherry blossom season usually lasting about two weeks. Following are best-known places for fetes: 20-May 5 at Kitakami City, Iwate, tunnel of 10,000 sakura; 24-May 7, 5,000 trees bloom at Hirosaki City park, Aomori; similar dates feudal Kakunodate Town, Akita.

25-May 5 Lord Tsugaru mummy shown at Chosho-ji, Hirosaki City, Aomori.

May

1-5 Gala *Fujiwara Festival*, 1st parade, 3rd reenact Yoshitsune's flight from wrath of brother Shogun Yoritomo; 5th has noh dances at Chuson-ji and ancient *Ennen-no-mai* at Motsu-ji; Hiraizumi Town, Iwate.

3-4 Folk Dance parades, Esashi C, Iwate.

15 *Takamura Fete* honors poet TAKAMURA Kotaro, poetry readings historic Takamura-sanso house, Hanamaki C, Iwate.

15-16 *Oshira-sama* shamanistic stick figures (seen in Tono) offered as charms against evil, Kudoji, Hirosaki C, Aomori.

Mid– wknd, Apple Fete, Hirosaki apple orchards reputed Japan best, Aomori.

June

10 Memorial rites for 'true' Jesus Christ at his supposed grave, Shingo Vill, Aomori.

15 *Chagu-chagu* Horse Festival, decked-out horses bear kimonoed women, feudal retainers parade Takizawa village outside Morioka C → Hachiman Shrine Morioka; ringing of bells marking their approach.

15 Lesser Horse Festival at Tono, Iwate.

20 Heian Period songs and dances by veiled kimonoed women at Komachi-do Hall, Okachi Town, Akita.

4th Sat, *Kashima-nagashi Fest*, Kashima warrior dolls float down river as charm against evils, Omagari City, Akita.

Lunar 22-24 Itako shamans contact dead, Kawakura Jizo-son, Kanagi T, Aomori.

July

20-21 Tosaki Harbor Fete, giant wheeled floats with puppets atop roll around town, Tosaki Shinmeisha Shrine, Akita City.

20-24 Mt. Osore Grand Festival, *Itako* shamanesses gather for believers to contact departed ones, Aomori.

3rd Sat-Sun Lake Towada Water Fete, local folk dances and fireworks, Aomori. Same days, similar at Lake Tazawa dedicated to dragon spirits of Hachirotaro and Takko-hime, Akita.

26-28 Harbor Festival, parade of bannered boats and fireworks, Kuji City, Iwate.

Last Weekend Summer Gala, mikoshi-bearers charge into sea as gaily decorated boats fill harbor; various folk dances in town, Miyako City, Iwate.

31-Aug 3 *Sanja Taisai*, 3-Shrine Grand Fete of Hachinohe, Morioka, feudal parade, 30 floats, contests on horseback. Best parade 31st nite, all gather; 8/2 old form of polo rarely seen elsewhere (*see* Tours).

August

1-7 *Nebuta Festival*, Hirosaki City, Aomori, floats of fan-shaped giant paper lanterns are decorated with ornate paintings and wheeled thru town. Wildly colorful festival based on:

2-7 *Nebuta Festival*, Aomori City, floats more ornate, paper-on-bamboo-frame shaped into assorted wild figures. Climax nite of–7th when floats rushed to sea, set afloat; design new every year (*see* Tours).

3-7 Rid insects rite, Goshokawahara vil, Tsugaru Pen, Aomori, giant serpentine straw figure carted thru fields then tossed into river, beaten with sticks.

5 Gala Harbor Fete, Kessen-numa, Iwate.

5-7 *Kanto Festival* Akita City, top Tohoku fete. *Kanto* 10m-bamboo pole of 9 tiers on which 46 giant lanterns–60kg carried by one man–balance, bounce hip to shoulder to knee, to music. Display many *kanto* front Hirano Museum festival days 10:00-16:00, at nite become part of colorful procession of 160 *kanto* and 50 wheeled floats; kids carry smaller; (*see* Tour)

6-7 *Nebu-nagashi,* cart giant paper lantern in castle shape around Noshiro C, Akita.

6-7 300 Tanabata Lantern floats of varying sizes with Ukiyo-e paintings of women are pulled thru town, Yuzawa City, Akita.

7-8 *Kenka* (Fighting) Tanabata, wheeled floats with colorful streamers pulled thru town, crash against each other to drums & flutes, Rikuzen Takada City, Iwate.

7-9 Kitakami Folk Arts Fest has over 70 groups of unique local dancers–160-man squad *oni-ken-mai* demon-sword-dancers, *shika-odori* deer-dancers, Kitakami City Iwate.

9 Thousands of lanterns float downstream as fireworks burst, Kitakami City, Iwate.

14 Takigi Noh torch-lite performances, Hakusan Pavilion, Chuzon-ji, Hiraizumi.

14-16 Ancient style *Bon dance* nitely shore Lake Jusan-ko, Tsugaru Pen, Aomori.

14-18 Ohyu Giant Drum Contest, over 40 squads of drummers compete in loud but fun event, Kazuno City, Akita.

14-20 *Yosare* Bon Dance, Kuroishi City, Aomori, 3,000 synchronized dancers wind thru narrow streets of town in what was once one of best known O-bon events, ranks with Shikoku's crazy *Awa-odori.*

15 *Hachiro Festival* Showa-machi Town, Akita, commemorates dragon-spirit of Hachirotaro of nearby Lake Hachiro-gata (*see* Tazawa-ko), parade dragon thru town.

16 Marks end of *O-bon* festival, on which day guide visiting spirits back to other world. Every city, village celebrates now. Some popular ones: candles in mini *yakata-bune* covered boats floated down stream at Yokote City, Akita; straw boats ignited and sent downstream at Kuroishi City, Aomori; 1000s of lantern boats float thru Morioka City; giant character *dai* is lit on Mt Tabashine at Hiraizumi, Iwate; similar flaming *dai* Mt Ho-o, Odate City, Akita, preceded by afternoon dance of 10,000 forming *dai. Bon* dance festivities.

16-18 Nishimonai district of Hago-cho Town nr Yuzawa City, Akita, Bon dances in which dancers cover heads in black veil.

18-20 Summer Fete Noheji City, Aomori, colorful floats paraded thru town, *mikoshi* go around harbor by boat, kagura dances.

3rd Sat-Sun Summer Fest of Moritake Onsen, near Lake Hachiro-gata, Akita.

25-29 Horse Fair at Kizukuri T, Aomori, retains little old wildness of main horse mart, but still fun with horse shows and contests, countless food and game stalls.

4th Sat-Sun All-Japan Fireworks Contest draws top 'pop' masters whose works lite up skies of Omagari City, Akita.

4th Sun *Daimyo-gyoretsu* parade Satake lords en route old Edo, Yuzawa C, Akita.

Lunar 14-16, *Shishi-mai* Lion Dancers of all Tohoku compete at Saruga Jinja, Okami-machi, Aomori.

September

1-5, Mt Osore Autumn Festival draws *itako* shamanesses and people hoping to contact departed ones, Aomori (*see* p.1021).

5-7 *Hanamaki City Festival,* Iwate, dozen gaudy floats wheeled around town.

7-9 *Oyama-bayashi,* Kakunodate C, Akita, colorful floats with moving puppets on stage parade thru town afternoon into nite, climax in combat as they ram each other.

8 Shishi-mai dances, red-lion replaced by warrior horse, Fujisato-cho Town, Akita.

10 Fest of Shinmei Jinja Ohdate C, Akita.

14-15 *Folk Dance Fete* Hachiman Shrine, Tono, Iwate, flute & drum *Nanbu-bayashi,* rhythmic *shishi-mai,* 2 types old *Kagura,* Tiger Dances, *yabusame* horse archery; + station-front plaza, Shimin (Peoples') Ctr.

14-16 Morioka City's Hachiman Shrine Gala Fete *yabusame* usually on 15th.

21 Poems read at memorial flame for poet Miyazawa Kanji, Hanamaki City, Iwate.

October

All month Tohoku sees changing colors of maple and flowering chrysanthemum and of many festivals, Hirosaki City, Aomori, boasts top display *kiku-ningyo* chrysanthemum dolls and fair display of maples.

15-19 Tigers dance on boats in Kamaishi City harbor, Iwate.

November

1-3 Autumn *Fujiwara Festival,* Hiraizumi, 1st parade for Yoshitsune, 3rd noh dances Chuzon-ji, *Ennen-no-mai* dance Motsu-ji.

December

31 *Namahage* demons visit houses of Oga Peninsula to scare evil out of children.

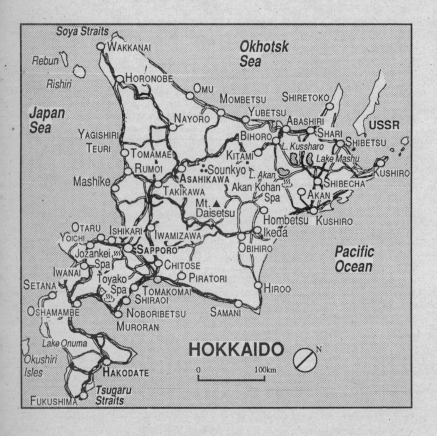

Soya Straits
WAKKANAI
Rebun
Rishiri
Japan
Sea
YAGISHIRI
TEURI
Mashike
HORONOBE
OMU
NAYORO
TOMAMAE
RUMOI
OTARU
YOICHI
Jozankei
Spa
IWANAI
SETANA
Toyako
Spa
OSHAMAMBE
Lake Onuma
Okushiri
Isles
FUKUSHIMA
Tsugaru
Straits
HAKODATE
MOMBETSU
YUBETSU
BIHORO
KITAMI
Sounkyo
ASAHIKAWA
TAKIKAWA
Mt.
Daisetsu
ISHIKARI
IWAMIZAWA
SAPPORO
CHITOSE
PIRATORI
TOMAKOMAI
SHIRAOI
NOBORIBETSU
MURORAN
SAMANI
HIROO
OBIHIRO
Ikeda
Hombetsu   KUSHIRO
Akan Kohan
Spa
AKAN
L. Akan
SHIBECHA
L. Kussharo
Lake Mashu
SHIBETSU
KUSHIRO
ABASHIRI
SHARI
SHIRETOKO
Okhotsk
Sea
USSR
Pacific
Ocean
HOKKAIDO
0   100km
N

He who travels far will often see things
far removed from what he believed was truth...
— Herman Hesse, Journey to the East

HOKKAIDO 北海道
JAPAN'S PIONEER FRONTIER

HOKKAIDO IS STRANGE. Japanese language travel books call it *e-ki-zo-chikku* (exotic), 'Wild West of Japan'. Modern Japan's love of cowboy flicks has even spawned simulated hoss-operas set in wild Hokkaido, in so many ways resembling America's West. Hokkaido has 22% of all arable land in country, 25% each of forest and fish catch with 1/50th land costs and 30% lower utility bills due to no need for cool air conditioning.

Hokkaido's 'indians', indigenous Ainu, who call themselves **Yutari**, were decimated by encroaching Yamato Japanese, especially during Japan's modern era, and now barely subsist on tourist-oriented reservations. Until this century island was, like early America and Australia, settled by country's defeated outcasts: Takeda clan refugees in early 1600s and pro-Tokugawa clans of Tohoku after Meiji Restoration. With Shogunate's fall, travel restrictions were lifted and poor farmers and ex-convicts 'went north' to start new lives in this virgin territory far from meddling government. This post-Restoration freedom lasted only few short years until 1875 and coming of *Tonden-hei,* government marshalls whose roles were similar to those of their U.S. wild-west counterparts.

Tho its wild and woolly days are long past, we still find interesting mixes of Japanese here, who have come from all over Japan to start anew. But whether farmers starting businesses or frustrated businessmen taking up natural farming, Hokkaido's residents are proud of their new home and they often go to great lengths to help us enjoy our visit to their lovely land.

Hokkaido looks different because it is different. Its flora and fauna are different. Gnarled and twisty pines of Honshu give way to stately poplar. Instead of ghostly, finely sculpted hills, these of Hokkaido show complete disregard for any urgency of landscape gardening to fit limited area and roll on as if they had all the space in the world. Misty silhouette is replaced by sharp clear outline, and gorgeousness gives way to grandeur. Air is dry, feeling spacious—one even sees expanses of undeveloped shrub land. Both weather and geography are continental. Winter is severe but crisp; summer hot but dry. Ideal escape from southern humidity. Straits of Tsugaru which we cross is in fact border between Asia and Oceania. Hokkaido is geologically one with Siberia and Manchuria, lies outside Japan island plate formed by great tectonic upthrusting from Pacific floor, which Japanese myth refers to as drippings from creator god Izanagi's thrust spear.

Japanese tourists come here to see on smaller scale what Americans go to Far West states to see—scenery on grand scale. Tho there are no Grand Canyons or expanses of Painted Desert, Hokkaido possesses its own natural wonders. Dozens of volcanic lakes, all accompanied by indoor and outdoor onsen-spas, dot island; coastal salt-water lakes sprout red carpets of coral in spring; and year-round at Shiretoko hot water river cascades over into natural pool. Daisetsuzan Mountains soar majestically in island's center.

Scattered thru all this natural beauty, enormous ranches, dairy farms and wineries provide changes of pace for wanderers.

WHEN TO GO: Best time to visit is late spring or fall. All blooms— cherry, iris, lily-of-valley, azalea—burst out at once in late May. Late September-October is lovely with cool, crisp evenings; ideal. Mountains, like those in America, have dry, hot days and crisp evenings. Fine skiing in winter (nothing like coming in from full day on staves to plop right into onsen); good **hiking** and **camping** in summer in clear mountain air, lake **swimming**, fair fishing; and numerous budget inns and government-run camp sites with cabins and tents for rent all make your back-country excursions easy. In short, not what most tourists come halfway around world to see, but something for old time residents looking for new adventure. And it is all best by **car**, whether your own, rent-a-car, or **hitching**.

Of course, this is not to say that all Hokkaido has to offer is its scenery, tho that is frontier island's main attraction. Its towns and cities have much to see. No abundant shrines and temples like southern Japan, but many fine examples of early modern Japanese architecture—interesting amalgam of Victorian and Oriental. Or you can visit Ainu in their *kotan*-villages at Asahikawa or elsewhere; ruins of Ainu fort at Kushiro; or infamous Abashiri maximum security prison—like Alcatraz surrounded by water, icy arctic water—part of which is now museum.

Whether visiting Hokkaido for few days or weeks, visitors find it well worth their effort, and experience part of Japan often missed by tourists— mainly because its 'un-Japaneseness' excludes it from most tour itineraries.

GETTING THERE: Train & plane most common, **plane** best for time— economical airline tours, individual or group (*see* below)—using Sapporo as base; with **train** or coastal ferry for adventurer coming up thru TOHOKU, or even from TOKYO/Shinagawa (dep midnite, 30hr-up, 28hr-ret Kushiro, p1111) or MAIZURU on Japan Sea N of Kyoto. SAPPORO has its own Okadama airport 15min bus from town mostly for intra-isle, nearby CHITOSE (1hr bus) gets most longer inter-island flights.

Plane: several daily JAL & ANA flights to CHITOSE from TOKYO (Haneda), NAGOYA, OSAKA, FUKUOKA, SENDAI. JAS also flies from Haneda as well as from northern cities of MISAWA & AOMORI; ANA from NIIGATA. Internal runs also CHITOSE-HAKODATE, KUSHIRO, ASAHIKAWA & ABASHIRI (Memanbetsu). JAS and ANK are main intra-isle carrier servicing HAKODATE, ASAHIKAWA, OBIHIRO, WAKKANAI, MONBETSU, ABASHIRI, KUSHIRO, NEMURO, NAKASHIBETSU. Inter-island flight times (fares o.w.) to CHITOSE from: HANEDA 1hr25min (¥23,850), OSAKA 1hr45min (¥31,750), SENDAI 1hr10min (¥19,250). Rates as of summer '91 for 7-day excursion slightly less. Competition air–JR heating up, promises better package deals.

Train: direct from TOKYO takes 12hrs using Tohoku Shinkansen to MORIOKA, 3hrs, change to old line for AOMORI (2hr30min) and change again thru new **Seikan Tunnel**, world's longest, to HAKODATE (2hrs), change again for SAPPORO (3hr40min); 16 daily– only 4x-day run Morioka-Hakodate non-change. 2nd class train fare approximates airfare (unless using Skymate standby, NG hi-season). **Rail Pass** is valid on JR ferries, buses, so if taking train to HOKKAIDO Rail Pass really pays. For leisurely luxe train-o-philes TOKYO → SAPPORO has **Hokuto-sei #1, 3, 5** w/private compartment on regular line non-change, cheaper than air for couple, w/toilet, shower (in sgle), video: ¥13,180 basic (Rail Pass covers) +¥6,180sgl, ¥12,360dbl. For those with time, makes sense as arrive refreshed, save hotel bill. Only 3x-daily, dep TOKYO/Ueno 16:50 (arr Hakodate 4:24, Sapporo 8:53), 17:17 (arr 30min later), 19:03 (Sapporo 10:57), few cars, demand high so should increase. Trains #3 & 5 have 'Lobby Car', no extra.

Traversing **Seikan Tunnel**, train stops at undersea stn midway at which you may detrain and visit exhibition of construction, then get on next train thru.

Drivers & hitchhikers have several choices crossing to Hakodate. Coming up Japan Seacoast or thru central TOHOKU, use AOMORI city departures on Seikan Renrakusen, or Higashi Nihon Ferry out of ABURAKAWA 5km W of town—used by trucks, ideal hitch. Coming up Pacific coast use Noheji also good hitch, saves time by skirting Aomori. Also from OMA on tip of Shimokita Peninsula NE Aomori Prefecture to HAKODATE. On TSUGARU PENINSULA (NW Aomori Pref), **ferry** from northernmost main isle MIUMAYA to OSHIMA-FUKUSHIMA nr Matsumae, 45 km SW of Hakodate. Ferry to HIGASHI-MURORAN from AOMORI (7hr), HACHINOHE (8hr); to TOMAKOMAI from HACHINOHE (9hr), SENDAI (16hr), TOKYO (28hr), NAGOYA (40hr). OTARU links Japan Sea cities: NIIGATA (21hr), MAIZURU & TSURUGA (either 31hr) at rates from ¥6,590-2nd to ¥25,230 cabin or in car.

GETTING AROUND: Is as varied as getting here. **Trains** between cities excellent, not as extensive as on mainland and recently greatly reduced so we use buses (many old rtes JR, use **Rail Pass**, but new lines pvt) to see most of Territory's natural wonders. With expense of train up to Hokkaido—even recent reduction of JR lines on isle—Rail Pass (buy before leaving home) pays off, even used only for and validated at start of this frontier escapade. In Japan check JR *shuyu-ken*, similar to Rail Pass for limited area; new rail packages. Short-term visitor can experience cross-section of all Hokkaido has to offer on variety of bus tours out of Sapporo (*see*). Our Hokkaido trek begins at Hakodate circling isle clockwise. 3 main areas lack trains–across central Daisetsuzan mts, easternmost Shiretoko peninsula (part newly privatized), and newly discontinued lines paralleling N Japan and Okhotsk Seas. **Budgeteer** has extensive if infrequent **bus**es; or use thumb. **Bicycles** find flat open roads. Rent-a-car economical for circle route.

Tours available from Tokyo (next page), or around various areas once there. To see all takes more time than visitor has—for whom we offer this condensed Hokkaido:

TILT: Basic is 4-day/3-nite: fly → SAPPORO 2nites (prefer 2nd Jozankei) → OTARU → NISEKO → TOYA-KO overnite or at NOBORIBETSU; see Shiraoi Ainu Village → SAPPORO; or if train backtrack HAKODATE for ferry–train down HONSHU with stops. Can be done by rent-a-car, or local trains/buses. See our itineraries for day units.

CAR enjoyable way to see Hokkaido, cheapest for couple. Main means of transport. Roads well maintained, under constant improvement. Reasonably well-posted in Latin lettering (*romaji*), highway numbering agrees with maps. During Garet's '84 visit found excellent paved roads where only dirt lanes existed 5 years prior. Completed (as of '89) between Otaru via Sapporo S to Muroran, & E almost to Asahikawa, Dochu Expressway will eventually link all Hokkaido major cities. Reliance on trucking is boon to hitchers.

Rent-a-car widespread. **Nippon** Rent-a-car (**Hertz** link) ubiquitous, all airports and cities where usually located in JR stn plaza. Common is **Toyota Rental**. Red-logo of **Eki-mae Rent-a-car** (stn-front rental) in most small-town stns but mostly to tour immediate vicinity–advise long distance rental requiring drop-off thru Nippon or Toyota. Unlike US, rate differences between companies insignificant, tho Hokkaido rates lower than mainland. Besides 3 classes of cars, campers are now available. Drop-off fees are high, so plan circular routes returning to point of origin.

TOURS Ace-JTB has 2 good ones listed here as example from dozens of courses available, of air plus **rent-a-car** with hotels & main meals (which we pioneeringly recommended in our 1964 edition and do so even more now)—can extend for reserved hotel travel or just open-end for car alone, open air return to Tokyo. They also list Driver and car "hire car" offerings. **Drop-off** system improved: leave at designated hotels, airports. JTB ☎(03)-3276-7777, your agent anywhere. They plan more, cheaper to compete w/Hawaii.

Hokkaido-East 5-day ¥149,000 each for 2, drops to ¥137,000 ea for 4, (air alone ¥43,100), incl rsvd hotels, bkfsts, dinners, you pay lunches, parking, tolls, gas, admissions: fly Haneda → Asahikawa, get car, drive Shirogane Onsen → Tokachi-dake →

overnite Furano; **–day 2** drive Akan-ko lake district → Teshikaga, Mashuko → overnite at Lake Kussharo; **–day 3** Bihoro Pass → Iou-zan → L. Shireto-ko → Genseikaen → o'nite Saroma-ko on Okhotsk Sea; **–day 4** Onne-yu → Sounkyo-gorge → Asahikawa Ainu village Kamui-kotan → o'nite Sapporo **–day 5** roam Sapporo → bus to Chitose airport, ret Haneda or other desired destination.

Hokkaido-South 4 day ¥120,000ea for 2, to ¥107,000ea for 4; fly Haneda Hakodate then car, Haneda → see Hakodate → Onuma Park, overnite; **–day 2** long drive thru lovely countryside down → Matsumae castle → Esashi → overnite Niseko; **–day 3** to our favorite Otaru, nearby mystery cave we introduced to tourism → Yoichi brewery → overnite in Sapporo; **–day 4** see some of Sapporo and bus → Chitose for return to Haneda or other destination.

Catches to above are surcharges high season 'East'-¥9,000 and 'South'-¥8,000 during 4/26-5/6, 6/1-7/23, 9/1-9/30; and whopper 7/20-8/31 when youth move like lemmings and not even mad dog nor Englishman should be on road, of 'East'+¥15,000 & 'South' +¥12,000. Also, up to 5 per car at above rates and all share one room. (Children discounted about 20%). But 2 couples at ¥90,000-ish per person for 5-days/4-nites runs low season only ¥45,000-net (plus airfare), or ¥11,000 per overnite w/2 meals & car, and at hi-season worst when flights and rooms are at premium, ¥18,000 each per day — which are great bargains, competitive with Rail Pass plus minshuku.

JTB Sunrise Tour 4days/3nites Apr 15-Oct 31 from Chitose airport → Sapporo Nite → Mt Moiwa → Nakayama Pass → Mt Yotei → Lake Toya N → Noboribetsu N → Shiraoi → Chitose; ¥199,000 incl bkfsts, 1 lunch, 2 dinners; land only +airfare extra.

JAL tour seems better buy. **JR** regularly announcing new package deals, which watch for at main travel agents or JR info booths in main stns, or thru your private travel agent.

Special Tours for Winter Snow Sculpture Festival, Autumn Colors, are run annually. Check JTB, JAL, ANA.

Nature Tour small group, Mark Brazil *Japan Times*, PO Box 144, Tokyo 200-91.

KAMCHATKA (Sakhalin) in Russia, J-group tours of several days start '92, fly out of Niigata (other airports later likely) → Khabarovsk Siberia thence → Kamchatka capital of Petropavlovsk, noted for volcano, hot springs (expect further development by Jpn) and crater lakes; thru Sapporo's **Times Kanko** ☎(011) 241-2381.

slapping armor, bowstrings' concert
sounds of our captains' warriors
falling to their drill
—Empress Gemyo, on Ainu Wars
Manyoshu, 708 AD

AINU ABORIGINES
PERSONAL ORIENTATION

WHAT WE WANT TO SEE most in this Wild West of North Japan are *Ainu,* or *Yutari.* There are few 'real injuns' left, displayed like reservation Indians for tourists. However, state protection assures that all Ainu affairs are self-managed and -owned. Ainu are full citizens, tho under 'Law to protect Primitive People' they are not allowed to freely buy and sell land without special permit. This law is under fire now with demand to rescind it as it is condescending, thus prejudiced. Easiest to get to and best 'staged' is display village in Shiraoi near Noboribetsu located on our inner routing for short-term visitors; on our outer-circle routing are somewhat more interesting, tho really little different, small colony in Asahikawa, village at lake Akan and Piratori's largest concentration. Family of KAWAKAMI Hiroshi in Asahikawa, great-grandson of great chief Konosa, with whom Jay and Sumi spent pleasant and personally oriented afternoon in 1959, still head community in mid '80s.

Before we take you anywhere in Hokkaido, let's pause for bit of...

PERSONAL ORIENTATION: We got ours from: Batchelor's classic book *The Ainu of Japan*; from firsthand conversations on our first 1959 trip with Father Gerhardt Huber Austrian priest who taught in Otaru and Sapporo; Prof KODAMA Sakuzaemon of Sapporo U amid his fabulous then-private museum of Ainu artifacts; with such Ainu friends as Kawakamis of Chikabumi village 'where birds live' and long-bearded *Otema*, Chief, Miyamoto of Shiraoi village; then Garet's several subsequent trips in '70s and '80s, and mid-'80s heavy press attention to problems of prejudice.

Census records (1986) show 24,331 Ainu in 7,168 households, anyone with any recent Ainu ancestry, little changed from first record of 1804: 23,797 (low point 1902, 17,000). Full-blooded estimate at 200 with zero pure births. Ainu prefer to wed *shamo* (their term for Japanese) to speed assimilation and social acceptance, tho there has been in this last generation some slight upsurge in pride in language and return to their heritage, helped by sympathetic NHK TV mini-series in early '80s. Still, Ainu women prefer *shamo* mates, who may climb higher in society than Ainu counterparts. Ex-Prime Minister Nakasone attributed his hairiness and thick brows to possible Ainu antecedants—which remark Ainu did not appreciate. They have recently become vociferous in bringing attention to heavy discrimination by Yamato (or Wa) neighbors.

Ancient Ainu were hunter-fishers. Now roughly 40% are farmers (down from 50% 1960 while national ratio has dropped from 47% to 16%) mostly subsistence; 20% fishermen; balance mainly laborers. While few of last generation made it to college, nor many even to high school, 78.4% present generation (vs 94% Wa) continue beyond compulsory jr high with only 8.1% (but improving) advancing to college and prospects of well-paying jobs. Thus with increasing numbers becoming businessmen or merchants lured by life in cities, few return to ancestral homes. But even with equal education income is often substandard (Hokkaido ¥800,000 annual, vs national ¥1,900,000). There still exists, albeit to lessening degree, college-entry and job discrimination, as even Minister of Justice admitted late '86.

Few postwar Ainu speak any Ainu at all, few young adults know much. Even those in large Ainu communities speak Japanese at home. Of monolingual Ainu, sole survivor 1984 was 98-year-old Piratori woman. Ainu on Kuril isles relocated to Hokkaido during WWII, those in Sakhalin were 'repatriated' to Japan at war end. Hundreds remain in Soviet Kamchatka. As separate entity, Ainu are all but extinct, with only shadow of their former culture kept alive in tourist communities. While 22 years ago in 1964 edition we predicted cultural extinction within three decades, this has not occurred, and does not seem any more imminent now, perhaps less so.

Yet Ainu influence on Japanese culture has been profound. Defeated Ainu usually settled around Shinto shrines of victors as serfs to this spiritual fulcrum of Wa (Japanese) society. Ainu influence in Shinto is fundamental. Japanese word 'god', *kami*, literally 'above', is probably from Ainu *kamui*, itself eventually traceable back to some Siberian or Central Asian concept of half-man, half-deity as in Persian term for god-like man, *kamil*. Ainu rites of sacred directions, paraphernalia and of representing presence of deity as bundle of paper shavings (*inao*) have become intrinsically Japanese. Other influences can be catalogued and many more, far subtler, be surmised.

Ainu conservatism which preserves them as people apart (much like that of mainstream Wa) can be traced back to their great culture hero Oina-kamui. This demigod taught all cultural basics, proscribed future change, like plot in sci-fi novel. Breaking this commandment meant immediate excommunication from society. This set Ainu apart from their neighbors, despite fact they have no terms to differentiate themselves from others, tho of late they are taking to calling themselves **Yutari**, 'fellow man'. 'Ainu' simply means 'man', indicating both adult male and our species, came to mean this one people by Japanese usage only century ago. 'Others', whether Ainu of other area, or other ethnic groups, are called by name of place they inhabit. But this is true with most languages. Many non-Wa peoples other than Ainu, native or immigrant, have been absorbed into mainstream Japan, despite modern ignorance of it, but much because of millennial old imperial practice.

According to Father Huber, with whom we had unforgettable morning-long breakfast generation ago in Otaru, these other pre-Yamato people included Emishi, Tsuchigumo, Matagi and Koropguru; and we add Saeki/Saheki, now family name. Some scholars feel Emishi alternate name for Ainu. Ainu did inhabit as far south as Tokyo, which old name until 1867 was Edo, perhaps same as Ainu/Emishi name for Hokkaido: Ezo, Yezo. Emishi were in strength around Tokyo, but also around Nara, recruited en-masse as units of Palace Guard, as were Saheki, who may have been sub-group of Emishi. Emishi sites abound in north Kyushu, around Hiroshima. We go along with Father Huber, Ainu and Emishi were different.

Tsuchigumo, literally 'earth spiders', are of interest because of their place in folk literature and theater. Here before either Wa came up from south or even Ainu from north, but no match for either invader, they soon expired. Kyushu lore tells of their conquest by first shogun Tamura-maro. Some interpret name as referring to race of 'little men', much as slight Picts of Scotland mythologized into Pixies. No archaeological remains support this. More accepted surmise is that pre-Wa hunters lived in roofed-over pit dwellings, as we saw in Shizuoka and Hiroshima in reconstructed archaeological sites. These also common to pre-Columbian America, North China, Siberia, even Australia for, while ground might freeze to depth of several inches, subterranean floor below this level enjoys stored heat of deep earth.

Design-rich Ainu textiles never repeat pattern

Tsuchigumo are much maligned as demons and half-beasts, who snarl in speech, grovel before conquering heroes—common fiction in all cultures. *We* are always superior to any *them* we lick even when, as in India, Aryan savages of 1400 BC conquered 'demons' in Indus valley who had long been building brick cities with sophisticated plumbing likes of which world was not to see again for 33 centuries. Conquest of Tsuchigumo is popular motif in folk theater carrying over into kabuki. Some dramatic kagura plays recount it, as we saw near Hiroshima, where some of world theater's most magnificent costumes drape despicable monsters who probably dressed in animal skins or grass. Maybe clothes do make us man.

Koropguru were similar to Tsuchigumo, if not identical. But all pre-Wa lived in pit dwellings. (California, size of Japan, had hundreds of native American ethno-linguistic groups.) Matagi lived in northern Honshu and Hokkaido until century ago in hunting economy, providing bear livers for Chinese pharmacopoeia and 'Injun scouts' against Russians: still inhabit isolated mountains in Tohoku and live by hunting, speak incomprehensible dialect but are apparently Wa otherwise. Other tribes made incursions into Hokkaido. Tungus and Gilyaks came from Siberia. Eskimo migrated to America from Asia five to ten thousand years ago, remigrated on small scale to Hokkaido ten centuries ago. But various cultures constantly interchange, making moving back of history's limits by archaeologists fascinating game of detective work. Take comb-like boats carved in Fugope cave, Otaru (*see*). Similar boat is on cast bronze bell from Fukui, north Honshu, of perhaps second century AD; another incised on jar from Nara some 300-400 years earlier; and clay model found in tomb in Miyazaki, Kyushu, perhaps also second century, resembles them. Only one thing is certain about these boats: their upturned prow and stern aren't Ainu, which resemble southeast Asian hulls. Fugope's look Polynesian?

But back to our Ainu friends. Oinakamui's commandment has not been strictly followed. Father Huber believes Ainu only began burying their dead 1200 years ago, or their burials may not go back over three centuries, so far as indisputable Ainu burials can be traced. Skeletally, Ainu fall between Jomon and modern Japanese. Prior to this, whether 3 or 12 centuries back, Ainu set out their dead as did many Native Americans, Tibetans and early

Aryans, as still do Parsees. When they did take to burial they provided articles one might need in next world, as in this life. This Ainu grave furniture is always broken, 'to release its spirit' to accompany human spirit to next world. This Siberian custom, not Wa-Japanese nor Chinese, is also found in Norse lore. Ainu costume shares much with north Asia: men wear calf-length wrap-around, women ankle-length, both with narrow sash, status head gear. Ainu archery is primitive 'pinch', like most Amerind, drawing string of light, simple bow between thumb and forefinger, not Mongolian style draw with thumb, or European with fore- and middle-digit. Iron came to pre-neolithic level Ainu as trade goods via Sakhalin from Amu River basin of Siberia-Manchuria.

Ainu may first enter historical records not in Japan, but in China. Just before Christian Era Chinese annals mention people from far northeast called by them Mao-min, 'Hairy Men'. But this pejorative may also refer to possible Yeti and Wild Men today and to 'monkey men' in south Chinese folklore (wait till pro-wrestling invades China: ideal villain gimmick). It is just this hairiness that sets our Ainu off from relatively hairless Mongol neighbors and which is his most obvious physical link with white man: Japanese writers on Ainu love to use 'hirsute'. But what clinches 'white man' label is his blood type, fingerprint, foot pattern and skin pigmentation, lack of mongol's subcutaneous arctic fat. Incidence of blood types have been compared with Japanese, Chinese, Europeans, Oceanians, Siberians:

BLOOD TYPE -	O	A	B	AB	
AINU: percentiles of	37	47	11	5	almost identical to...
EUROPEAN	39	43	12	6	but quite different from...
JAPANESE	28	39	19	14	

...and other neighbors so there can be little mistake.

Fingerprint and footprint ratios show similar parallels. Ainu skin has little yellow pigmentation, carotin. He is hairy and this curly; Mongoloids are straight-haired, 'pure Mongolian' Eskimo are beardless. Eye color is 90% brown (Mongol=100%) but with some grey-blue. Ainu eyes are sunken relative to pronounced brow, cheek bones and nose bridge, while Mongol is rather flat-faced. Nor do Ainu children have *Mongolian spot*— dark bruise-like birthmark low on spine found on children in Asia until around age five: and often in Europeans, like Hungarians, where Mongols have mixed in.

Father Huber, studied their language in many dialectics, finds clues that link Ainu with our own Aryan tongues, as well as with pre-Aryan Western languages. Ainu for mother is *mat, ham* or *hambe* is father, as Sanskrit *ham* 'being who was in beginning'. Ainu cosmology, their concepts of gods, beings and heavens, resembles ancient Sumerian. *Fuchi*, Ainu fire (perhaps French *feu*) may be root of name of that ancient fire-spitter, Mount Fuji. Other scholars add heavy Ural-Tungusic structural-linguistic ties. Such clues indicate origins in west Siberia, perhaps near birthplace of Hungarians, as Ainu word neighbor, *ungar*, hints at former proximity.

Were they then pressed eastward by expansionist Indo-Aryans? Place names across Siberia are Ainu, tho no one in recent time speaks any Ainu-related tongue. Newcomers often keep original place names, meanings long forgotten, as we did in America with Indian names and was done in Europe as in such extreme cases as *Wor-cester-shire*, for three successive names meaning same 'our place'. Note also there is no Ainu word for north: only south, east, west. North is phrased 'going out to Ocean': Arctic Ocean? But Hokkaido has ocean in all four directions. Kuril Isles, occupied by Russia since 1945 and claimed by Japan, is Ainu *kurimse*. Kamchatka is Ainu for 'meat-drying rocks'. Coincidentally, only two US Aleutian islands occupied during WWII by Japan, Attu (Attush) and Kiska, are Ainu names.

Classic Japanese theory has Ainu original inhabitants of archipelago with Mongoloid Wa invading from south. Professor Kodama of Sapporo U holds to this majority, if simplistic, view. He spent his life studying Ainu with sympathy, his physical anthropologist-son specializes in Ainu crania, his wife was, daughter is, expert in Ainu costume, decoration. His fabulous collection became **Sapporo University Museum**–which don't miss.

Oldest human habitation of Hokkaido is 40-50,000 years ago, by Carbon-14 dating, and Kodama believes this to be Ainu. Oldest skeletal remains and flint tools are 30,000, but not clearly typed. First pottery, resembling squat ice cream cones with patterns scratched in with sea shells, dates back at least 7,000 years. It resembles that common from earlier sites throughout Japan, as do most subsequent ceramic evidence. About 2,000 BC 'agricultural goddess' figurines emerge, but with no clear evidence of agriculture. In 500 AD beautiful carved bone daggers and snow slicers may show Eskimo incursions at Moyoro, east Hokkaido. Nothing of this is definitely, even particularly, Ainu. Huber's idea that Ainu started eastward trek from west Siberia second millennium BC agrees with commonly accepted modern thought that Ainu arrived in north simultaneously to Wa in south, just before Christian era, and that both are mixed cultures.

Eighth century AD south-moving Ainu and north-advancing Imperial Japanese met head on. Previous small scale meetings had led to intermingling, and many 'Ainu barbarians' of Japanese official records were Japanese draft- and tax-dodger frontiersmen with Ainu families. In 784 Kyoto sent large army to quell Ainu, cutting off taxes by playing Geronimo with Wa settlers between Tokyo and Sendai. It had taken five years to raise army of 52,000 horse and foot—handful who made it back did so in their birthday suits. Next army sent in 794 had 30,000 armored in leather, 3,000 in iron under general, Saka-no-ue no Tamura-maro first to be named *Sei-i Tai-Shogun*, Western-Barbarian Subduing Generalissimo (this 'west' meant west-Japan, Kyushu). Successive shogunal dynasties eventually usurped power from emperor till Perry arrival triggered overthrow of last Tokugawa dynasty shogun. Meanwhile, multitude of troops maintained to repel Ainu came to form privileged, tax-exempt professional warrior class: *samurai*, numbering 2,000,000 tax-freeloaders by 1854.

Campaign of 795 succeeded, due mostly to shogun Tamura-maro. His exploits became favorite subject of kagura folk theater and children's tales, in which Ainu in north and Tsuchigumo elsewhere, including southwest, are thoroughly mixed up. Many conquered Ainu were forcibly resettled in west and south Japan to assimilate. Free Ainu, augmented by constant flow of refugees from exiled Yamato clans, continued making trouble, as well providing lucrative market for Wa manufactures. Great lacquer bowls, which Ainu villages at Shiraoi and Asahikawa boast, were popular Ainu status symbols. Some of best, oldest common lacquer, even 14-15th century, is preserved thanks to it being treasured by Ainu as heirlooms.

Warfare, almost class-struggle, between Wa-samurai and 'barbarian' Ainu may have almost Oedipal sidelight. According to one US anthropolgist, samurai as social, almost racial, class are descended from Ainu. When first samurai troops were levied on frontier to fight Ainu, they were of course chosen from residents–most of whom were Ainu or mixed Ainu-Wa ('mixed bloods' or 'half-breeds'). True Wa, he claims, are more Han-

Korean in feature, that is slight-boned, hairless bodies. Samurai class tend more toward Ainu features of hairiness, etc. 'Naturally' modern Japanese prefer not to discuss this theory. But it is interesting.

Most action took place not in Hokkaido, but on main isle. Honshu town names of number plus suffix-hé (like Hachi-no-hé, 'camp #8') mark garrisons built during Yamato march north. Shogun Saka-no-ue no Tamura-maro's final victory over Ainu chief Akuro took place in 802 near Hiraizumi, Iwate prefecture, north Honshu. Tamura-maro in silent salute to his valiant foe, built temple to Bishamonten, Buddhist deity of war (one of popular 'Lucky 7'), in cave used as fort by Akuro.

Late 16th century reapportionment of estates accompanying unification of Japan under Nobunaga, Hideyoshi and Tokugawa Ieyasu sent displaced to Yezo to carve out new domains. Lordship of frontier in 1604 was granted to Takeda branch family, Matsumae, who effectively ruled Sapporo-Hakodate and gradually extended eastward. In 1868 admiral of overthrown Tokugawa fleet steamed north to storm Matsumae and Hakodate, setting up short-lived republic. After republic defeated, Yezo was put under special department of colonization, now for first time considered part of Japan proper, renamed Hokkaido, North Sea Circuit or Northern Territory.

SUM UP: Ainu basic Tungusic with southern mix, not unlike Wa-Japanese but in different proportions. Wa are racially-linguistically more complex, that is 'mixed'—not just samurai-warrior class, but all.

Huber, as we, thinks best Ainu **book** still Batchelor classic, tho only discusses one group: Etter's book not as good. Fosco Maraini writes intelligently, as expected, if on smaller scale. Donald Philippi translated Yukar epics as *Songs of Gods, Songs of Humans*. Kodansha *Encyclopedia of Japan* has good biblio of modern studies.

Passing of Ainu may be, understandably, regretted by romantics, but they more than left their mark. It may also be, as we have found, rudely premature to note it.

HAKODATE 函館
SOUTHERN GATEWAY

OUR TRAIN CONNECTING with Tsugaru Straits ferry winds out of
Hakodate for Otaru and Sapporo, 7 hours away, twisting and turning up
Oshima Peninsula to give passengers either side of cars repeated and varied
views of Mount Ezo-Fuji, locally Yoteizan, but more properly called in Ainu
Shiribeshi. Half height of Honshu's Fuji, more squat, they bear physical
but not aesthetic similarity. Fuji dominates in atmosphere of contrast: Ezo-
Fuji is lost in one of similarity. **Drivers** parallel this on Rte5.

But before racing up island to Sapporo, let us spend some time in...

HAKODATE: Hokkaido's key port since early times—when it appears in
annals as 'Hakodadi'. City first appears similar to any large port-town, but
under coarse facade lies long history of foreign commerce, particularly with
Tzarist Russia, memorialized by many turn-of-the-century W-style buildings, more numerous and better examples, better utilized, than Nagasaki or
Kobe. Also several interesting Tokugawa period structures in outskirts date
to chaotic days near end of Shogunate. Of 89 protected private historical
structures, in 1989-90 13 unilatterally renounced status in order to demolish
to build condos, most of which built so far are absentee-owned by
Tokyoites for investment and stand empty. Fun but crowded time to visit is
first week Aug when all Hakodate comes to life for *Minato Matsuri* **Port Festival**
with 10,000-dancer chain winding way thru streets, one main event of dozens of parades,
fireworks displays and whatever might come to mind that year. Parks and streets fill with
stalls selling food, drink, gifts, trinkets, games providing fun for all in this gala event.
Festival started 1926 to celebrate 70th anniversary of March 31, 1854 Kanagawa Treaty of
Amity between Commodore Perry and Edo Shogunate 'opening' Shimoda immediately and
'Hakodadi' 1855 as first two ports available to foreign traders in addition to Nagasaki.

However, on May 18, 1854, while Perry's flotilla was still in port, first
tourists arrived in Japan: first American woman 31-year-old Abigail Vincent
Jernegan with 9-year-old son Holmes aboard hubby's whaler *Eliza F Mason*
of New Bedford. They spent nite ashore, impressed by inquisitiveness and
kindness of people after troublesome return, suitably ritually wrapped, of
some common pin she'd left behind. She did no shopping.

WHERE TO STAY: Porttown traditionally caters to *less-affluent*, but
recent tourist boom adds new lodgings ranging to ¥-L. Minshuku and ¥-B
ryokan mostly outside downtown center, business hotels near stn. Town
hotels in **DAIMON DISTRICT** E of stn, most ¥-L in eastern outskirts at...
YUNOKAWA ONSEN, literally 'hot river baths', only 25min tram, 5x-mtr taxi
from stn, for relaxing change from busy downtown and preferable to town lodgings.
Flanked by two rivers which converge into Tsugaru Straits, onsen offers beautiful view in
summer when multitude of lights from squid-boats fill horizon. Over 60 hotels & ryokan
from ¥-B–LL cluster here. Recommended of better lodgings are: **Yunokawa Kanko**
(Tourist) Hotel ☎(0138)-57-1188; **Yunokawa Grand** Hotel ☎57-9161; and more
traditional **Hanabishi** Hotel ☎57-0131. Yunokawa also has only YH in Hakodate area,
Hokusei-so YH ☎57-3212. All rooms can be arranged thru **Ryokan Info Center**
(*Ryokan annai-jo*) at Hakodate stn, or **Yunokawa Ryokan Cooperative** (*Yunokawa
onsen ryokan kumiai*) ☎57-0166.

GETTING AROUND:
Most of city's attractions are
concentrated in old district of
town, easy to see on **foot**.
Two old forts and Trappistine
convent outside town reachable by **tram**, **bus**, or short
taxi run. Several **bus tours**
stop Goryokaku fort and
convent–but expensive, spend
too much time at other
uninteresting places. City-run
tram system reaches all sites
around town—fun to ride old
trolleys; ¥900 **all-day pass**,
ichi-nichi joshaken, for all
intra-city buses and trams;
single fares ¥180. Buy passes
at stn, bus or tram offices.
Late April thru early Nov
tours in horse-drawn cart
start at stn for 9km, 2hr
circular course, stop Hakodate
Koen, ropeway, Haristos
Greek Orthodox Church, ex-
Assembly Hall, Foreigners'
Cemetery: departures *10:00,
11:00, *13:00, 14:00. ('*' by
Hakodate Kanko Horobasha,
☎52-3077; other 2 by Kanko
Horobasha, ☎42-0421): fares
¥1,800 adult, child ¥800.

Hakodate is located on
small peninsula with
335m Hakodate-yama at
western tip. Older section
of town was built at base
of hill, and spread inland.
Take **tram** to last stop
Yachigashira, from where
road heads N along hill base to
various sites. Yachigashira
is small onsen tucked into
hillside, few budget inns
and public baths drawing
from hot spring waters
originating from within
Hakodate-yama.

HAKODATE

0 —— 1km   N

19 ✈ AIRPORT

1. Yachigashira Tram
2. Yachigashira Baths
3. Hakodate Park, Mus.
4. Gokoku Jinja
5. Hakodate-yama
6. Haristos Church
7. Ex-ward Hall
8. Ex-tsarist consulate
   Youth Ctr.
9. Jikko-ji
10. Shomyo-ji
11. Koryu-ji
12. Yamakami Shrine
13. Foreign Cemetery
14. Dock Tram Stop
15. History Museum
16. Chinese Merchants
    Hall
17. Goryo-kaku Fort
18. Trappistine Convent
19. Airport
20. Yunokawa Spa
21. Station
22. Daimon St.
23. Jujigai St.
∴ Morning Market
•—• Tram Line

TO AOMORI

Cable Car

Near Yachigashira tram stop...
Hakodate Koen, park, popular for cherry viewing early May. On park
grounds is **Municipal Museum**, *Shiritsu Hakodate Hakubutsukan*, with
large collection of Ainu artifacts: ¥100, X-mon.

North past...
GOKOKU JINJA (dedicated to war-dead) is ropeway leading to top of
Hakodate-yama, best at evening, as sun sets on one side and city begins to
light up on other. Summit also reached by **bus** in 30min from stn.

Beyond lower ropeway terminal across from Catholic church & Higashi Honganji is...
HARISTOS Greek Orthodox Church, oldest of its sect in country, originally constructed 1859, completely rebuilt after 1916 fire. Interior is all Byzantine grandeur. Locals jokingly refer to it as *Gangan-dera* (clanging temple) for sound of its European-style bells, harsh in comparison to mellow gongs of Japanese temples. Original bells, cast in Greece, were transferred to senior St Nikolai Cathedral in Kanda, Tokyo upon its completion 1874.

Continue on to...
Ex-Hakodate Ward Meeting Hall, *Kyu Hakodate-ku Kokaido*, Western-style two storey wood structure, most handsome of any Meiji building we know, built 1909 by local millionaire SOMA Teppei. Modeled after Tokyo's late famous Rokumeikan dance hall, subject of many woodblock prints. Used as much for upper-class social affairs as for official meetings.

2nd L from here leads to...
Prefectural Youth Center, *Donan Seinen-no-Ie*, 1860 red brick structure was Tzarist Russia's Consulate until Bolshevik Revolution and subsequent severance of diplomatic relations. Altho interior still in original condition, furniture unfortunately is not. This old ex-Consulate is surrounded by several temples:

JIKKO-JI to E; behind, N is SHOMYO-JI and to its W KORYU-JI built 1609 by displaced Takeda clan.

At end of street is ...
YAMAKAMI DAI-JINGU, Grand Shrine also built by Takeda.

Few hundred mtrs down road W from Koryu-ji is...
Foreign Cemetery, *Gaijin Bochi*, final resting place for forty-odd early foreigners, many of whom were Russian sailors and residents. Large early Russian presence in Hakodate was due to frequent use by Russian fishing and whaling fleets, even before official opening of port to foreigners. Smattering of other nationalities make for interesting mix of Greek Orthodox, Catholic, Protestant and Chinese markers. Closest point of official contact with Tzarist Government, Hakodate's other visitors were few Yankee and British-Canadian whalers landing for supplies.

Back about 1km from cemetery on same road is Hakodate Dock tram terminus. Two stops to Suehiro-cho lets you off in front of...
Local History Museum, *Kyodo Shiryokan* built 1880 as Kanamori Imported Goods Store, Japan's first fireproof building exhibits mostly Meiji, Taisho era mementos of Hakodate; 2nd Annex of Municipal Mus. X-mon, hols. Also reach by bus from KORYU-JI, off at Hakodate Byoin-mae, main hospital.

Chinese-style red brick structure N of bus stop is...
Chinese Overseas Merchant Hall, *Chuka Kaikan*, was local Chinese-financed built by labor imported from Shanghai and Fukien, China.

Road Chuka Kaikan, museum leads to harbor & 2 historic monuments...
Stone marker L is where NIIJIMA Jo(-seph) set sail secretly for Amherst College in Massachusetts in June 1864 on 'fact-finding trip' which led him to found Kyoto's prestigious Doshisha University in 1875—especially valiant act, since violation of still-valid old Tokugawa ban on any overseas travel was punishable by death, and then always enforced. R big white bear marks location of first, only, pier for boats from Honshu. All pioneer settlers set first foot on Ezo-Hokkaido here.

5 km NE of town is...
Goryo-kaku star-shaped fortress built in 1861 by Tokugawa shogunate to protect N frontier from foreign–particularly Russian–forces. First W-style fortress in Japan, built to withstand heavy artillery, it saw action, tho, not against expected foreign invader but government forces attacking instead of defending it. In 1868 large anti-restoration force led by ENOMOTO Takiaki and other disgruntled samurai excluded from Meiji government, sailed into Hakodate and nearby Matsumae in Tokugawa fleet to establish short-lived independent republic. In this group was French Captain Jules Brunet, formerly of French Military training mission to Tokugawa shogunate, who upon fall of Tokugawa held loyalty to them required he desert with several compatriots to follow them to Hakodate. Here he helped improve fortifications. Half-year later rebels were chased out of Matsumae by superior Imperial government forces and holed up in Goryo-kaku. Unable to take star-fortress by force, government built another fort, four-sided...

Shiryo-kaku to N from which rained shells down on rebels. Out-gunned and out of supplies, Enomoto's rebels were defeated May 1869. In true samurai spirit, they made do-or-die charge into surrounding army. (Brunet and gang got aboard French ship and escaped to Yokohama, samurai glory be damned); small museum within park exhibits 1869 battle relics. Mid-May 'liberation' of fort celebrated in **Goryo-kaku Matsuri**, in which men costumed as opposing forces (Japanese only) parade as part of larger **Hakodate Cherry-Blossom Festival** (*Sakura Matsuri*) celebrated at Goryo-kaku and Hakodate Parks. Bus or tram to Goryo-kaku Koen-mae and 5min walk from either, 2x-mtr taxi from Haristos church: if by cab don't keep it as many can be found here. Park now stands within remaining fortifications; tower has great view but not really worth ¥500 fee. SHIRYO-KAKU reached by bus from Goryo-kaku Koen-mae stop: 9min to Kamiyama-dori stop and 20min walk beyond: not especially interesting.

For past century Hakodate has been haven of...
Trappists: Convent, *Torapischine Shudoin* founded 1898 by 8 nuns from Normandy, France. Sisters of Order still operate convent taking in novices from all over Japan. Entering main gate you come to statue of Saint Michael, to R is kiosk behind which is replica of Virgin Mary at Lourdes. Up steps lies red brick convent fronted by massive statue of Virgin Mary. We can't enter convent, but next to kiosk exhibit room offers glimpse of lifestyle. Bus from stn 50min to Yukawa Danchi Kitaguchi stop at apartment complex, 15min walk; or bus from Matsukaze-cho (5min walk E of stn at tram intersection) 30min to Trappist-shita, 10min walk. From Goryo-kaku, bus from tram stop 30min to Trappist-shita; taxi 2x-mtr.

Two years before nuns' arrival, French monks opened **Trappist Abbey,** *Torapisto Shudoin*, on Tobetsu Maruyama Mountain in Esashi 25 km SW of Hakodate: This Gothic-style Abbey can be visited en route Matsumae and Esashi. Noted for fine cheeses, dairy products, candies, available only here and one shop in Hakodate, **Jujiya** gift store near Jujigai tram stop. Highly appreciated all over Japan as visiting gift. JR Matsumae line to OSHIMA TOBETSU and 30min walk. On H.E.M. bus tour.

CHOPSTICKS: Back in town, main food and entertainment sections are DAIMON near stn and central JUJIGAI. Daimon better at nite than Jujigai, greater range in variety and prices; more cheap but good drinking places. Centered around Daimon St, main street heading E from stn, are most of more famous restaurants. As old port town, Hakodate saw first foreign-owned bar when on June 2, 1855 two Italian and one French carpetbaggers passing as Americans (Italy and France had no treaties) landed 'in transit' with stock of 'grog' to try and operate, which they did to extent of getting US Naval Squadron gobs drunk and disorderly enough to rile Japanese authorities. On June 26 they were loaded aboard first would-be US free-trader *Caroline E Foote* carrying back disappointed ships-chandlers and families rejected at Shimoda and here. As port it boasts *best seafood*.

From stn, up third street on L 100 m is **Tototei** Chinese restaurant specializing in Peking Cuisine since 1941. Can't miss it, outside looks like gaudy Chinese palace; but food is superb, over 200 items to choose from at moderate prices. **Sushi-gin Honten** one of best sushi bars in town is on Daimon street at end of third block on R: annex **Sushi-gin** (young brother's) among best in Japan; up one alley earlier on the L. Tokyo prices, and if $30 dinner is too much, Hakodate has over 300 other sushi establishments in all price ranges: turn R just past Sushi-gin Honten and half block down on L is **Irikawa** 93-year-old local cuisine restaurant specializing in eel and other fresh-water fish. Back on Daimon street at end of first block on R past large intersection is **Yaoyacho** serves all sorts of Japanese food: another hard-to-miss place, outside is wood lattice-work, traditional wood tablets list menu, two large lanterns flank entrance. Up street on other side of Daimon from Yaoyacho is **Rengatei** local cuisine, specialty charcoal-broiled fish. These are but sampling of city's tastier eateries.

Budgeteers will have little trouble finding equally good food for less. Numerous robata-yaki and local drinking establishments–all serve lots of good, cheap food, are lots of fun and great way to party with locals, whether you speak Japanese or not, just pick ones that look (or sound) fun.

If in need of good late-nite snack head to stn plaza for *Asa-ichi* **open-air market** 4:00 to noon daily, X-sun. Farmers and fishermen sell their goods and run several 'red-lantern' push-cart food stalls all nite 3:00am to 15:00 offering good, cheap snacks. Even if not buying *Asa-ichi* is enjoyable to wander thru, as some vendors peddle rural folkcraft, assortments of gifts, antiques, prewar and J- Army Occupation money, and almost anything else. Similar nearby pm **Jiyu-ichiba** and 250 stalls **Nakajima Renbai**.

With full stomachs, those with time can begin to explore...

OFFBEAT SOUTH LONG WAY TO SAPPORO

ADVENTURERS with time on their hands have several alternate routes up to Sapporo that take you thru parts of Hokkaido where even out-of-town Japanese visitors are rare sight. Yet, this lack of traffic in no way indicates lack of hospitality—rather the opposite.

Alternate routes head up either coast, rejoining main line to Sapporo.

GETTING AROUND: HAKODATE-ESAN-ONUMA Hot Spring Route: takes you around eastern of two peninsulas sandwiching Hakodate, thru series of secluded onsen villages with little to offer other than beautiful natural surroundings and therapeutic baths. Budget lodgings abound on this run, also several campsites open in summer. Infrequent buses along this route can be supplemented with **hitching**; and **drivers** will find good roads, but some back-tracking necessary as road around point not yet completed. Rte278 can be used much of this route.

Buses for Esan leave Matsukaze-cho bus stop (E end of Daimon). Hakodate Bus Co runs to Esan Tozan-guchi and Ishida Onsen, 1hr30min and 1hr40min each. Passing thru Yunokawa Onsen bus hugs coast-line on Rte278.

10min walk N up side road from Tozan-guchi stop...
ESAN ONSEN has 2 ryokan and Minshuku Esan tapping hot water from Mt Esan, unusual active conitroide volcano rising 620m. Small museum here has prehistoric clay and stone artifacts from area as well as local folk items; 9:00-17:00 closed mon, ¥100. Known spot for alpine plants, 630 varieties found.

Few km past Tozan-guchi stop along coast is...
ISHIDA ONSEN, sea-side outdoor bath and beach, served by one and only **Ishida Onsen Ryokan**.

1064   HOKKAIDO FRONTIER

ESAN MISAKI, our next stop, is only 2km away, but road ended just beyond Ishida and only way across is to **hike** over or around Mt Esan.

Drivers must back-track to Rte278, passing N of Mt Esan to coast where R (S) on local road to Esan Misaki. Shortest trail starts from end of road beyond Ishida, crossing base of mountain to end on coast road just above Esan Misaki. Longer second trail begins at Esan Onsen and takes you past *crater*, thru flower-covered fields to end same place as first. Esan Misaki cape is known for Mizunashi Kaigan Onsen, no-water beach baths, hot spring beaches which at low tide have pools of hot water. One ryokan, Kokumin-shukusha, and campsite here.

From cape occasional buses make 1hr run up Rte278 to...
KAKKUMI ONSEN in wooded hills near source of Kakkumi River. Gorge and picturesque waterfall fills with *azaleas* late spring.

From Kakkumi local road heads back to Hakodate (75min bus) for those planning to go up E coast; or continue up this coast thru more isolated onsen ending at **Onuma National Park** recreational mecca. N and slightly further inland of Kakkumi Onsen is **OFUNA KAMINOYU**; N and near seacoast is...

OFUNA SHIMONOYU—Upper and Lower Ofuna baths. Few km beyond to even more rustic **ISOYA ONSEN**; beyond which is **KABE ONSEN** from where local road cuts inland to Onuma. Area around Isoya and Kabe noted for many old minka, traditional folk houses.

ONUMA: As three lakes here are collectively called, declared National Park 1958, formed when nearby volcanic Komagatake erupted sealing rivers which pooled into lakes. Lake Onuma largest of three boasts 81 islets, with slightly smaller **KONUMA** separated from it by narrow natural (except for bridge at end) causeway; smallest Junsui-numa (water-shield pond) so called for water-shields growing there. Larger two lakes have fishing, boating during warm months, ice skating in winter. Park itself lies between two lakes with dozen or so wooded isles interconnected by small bridges; *Ezo-shika*, **Hokkaido Deer Farm**, and groves of imported trees.

Most lodgings concentrated in park and nearby Onuma Koen stn. Coming by train on Hakodate main line (25min express Hakodate) can also get off at Onuma stn, half km before main stop Onuma Koen. Horse-drawn carts meet all incoming trains at Onuma Koen for 40min ¥800 r.t. of park.

WHERE TO STAY: Up street from stn is **Kanko-annai** Tourist Info Center which can arrange rooms for any pocket from Youth Hostel to luxe hotel. Next door is **bicycle rental**: ¥500/2hr. Several large ryo-tels as well as more traditional ryokan such as **Kita-no-yado** ☎(0138)-67-2158 and **Satsuki-kan** ☎67-2036 in park grounds. Best located is **Chikusen** ☎67-2316 on small cove in middle of park. All above inns ¥-mid-T class. Several cheaper ryokan around stn, with dozen minshuku scattered in area; **Ikusanda YH** near Onuma stn.

About 800 meters E of stn is old public onsen (no one quite remembers when it first opened): L (E) on road from stn, ask for **Tomenoyu** Detaining Waters. Old wooden building in grove of trees charges ¥250 for bath. Great place to 'be detained' to steam loose sore muscles after climbing **Mt Komagatake**, 4hr hike each way from Choshiguchi stn. Park's symbol, Komagatake, actually three peaks together, all active volcanos (highest 1133m). Fantastic view from peaks overlooking lakes below; on clear day can see Aomori's Shimokita peninsula across Tsugaru Strait, and across Uchiura Bay to volcanic Toya's plumes. Uchiura Bay itself formed when massive prehistoric volcanic eruption blew off eastern rim thru which ocean flowed in to form bay, taking out chunk of peninsula between Hakodate and Sapporo.

Ideal cycling country—when tired take bike on train, or plop into hot spring bath.

UP WEST COAST HAKODATE–MATSUMAE to YOICHI

LONGER ROUTE offers variety of places: castle-towns, onsen, quiet farms, mountains; and secluded island in Japan Sea. First two stops, MATSUMAE and ESASHI, with some interesting sites relating to days of feudal rule, can be done in full day out of Hakodate: worth visit even if not planning to do rest of this run before heading to Sapporo.

One-day **bus tour** out of Hakodate takes in major sites: HOKKAIDO–ESASHI MATSUMAE GO: Leaves HAKODATE stn 8:10 → Trappist Abbey (above) → KIKONAI → MATSUMAE (castle and museum) → ESASHI (Kyodo Shiryo-kan, Kamome isle, Yokoyama House, Nakamura House) → ret HAKODATE 17:30; ¥4,660 adult, ¥2,330 child, all adm fees incl.

Non-return JTB bus **The Hokkaido** course dep HAKODATE stn 8:00 → Onuma pickup Park Hotel 9:40 → Oshamambe (crabs) → Showa Shinzan–Lake Toya (cruise) → Jozankei → reach **Sapporo** Grand Hotel 18:00; ¥8,800. All sites cited in this book. JR Esahi bus line & Rte228 head W HAKODATE → MATSUMAE, S-most pt Hokkaido.

MATSUMAE: After Sekigahara battle, 1600, Matsumae branch of defeated Takeda clan was sent by Tokugawa Ieyasu to carve out new domain in northern island. Largely ignored by central government, distant Matsumae lord was exempted from annual 'visit' to Edo (sole such case), not even permitted to build castle. Matsumae lived on in quiet anonymity until mid-18th century when it became important source of marine products for Tokugawa, primary trade item with Chinese at Nagasaki. Some Osaka merchants got shipping rights between Matsumae and Nagasaki, bringing first influx of cash. Only news of Russian moves into Kurils aroused Edo interest in Matsumae, or for that matter, Hokkaido.

In 1792, Russian envoy from Catherine II's court arrived at Matsumae to open trade talks, but was informed that all foreign dealings had to be done in Nagasaki–polite way of telling them get lost and gain time to re-enforce hitherto ignored territory against foreign incursions. This led to active colonization of Hokkaido via Matsumae which soon was full of Tokugawa bureaucrats and samurai. By 1802 real control of Hokkaido was shifted from Matsumae to newly formed government Ezo Bugyo (Commissioner of Ezo) in Hakodate responsible for colonization and defense. After several skirmishes with Russian adventurers in Sakhalin and north Hokkaido permit was finally granted to build castle in Matsumae. In 1854, year Perry arrived off Yokohama, 17th lord MATSUMAE Takehiro completed Japan's last, and Hokkaido's only, traditional...

Castle is 15min walk E of stn along Rte228. Donjon restored 1961, now local history **museum**; main gate also restored then.

Rear portion of castle grounds is...
Matsumae Koen park, traditional cherry-viewing garden, now expanded, boasting some 2,350 sakura trees of more than 200 different species.

Continue short distance thru wooded area N of castle to reach...
TERA-MACHI TEMPLE DISTRICT, with several temples dating to early 1600s. Far back (5min from castle) nestled among ancient cryptomeria and gingko is Matsumae Clan's burial plot. 25min walk takes you to top of Shogun-zan hill overlooking castle-town.

Town is small but has over two dozen mostly inexpensive lodgings: ryokan mainly around stn and castle entrance, minshuku all over. Continue along Rte228 few hundred meters past castle to YH Yano Ryokan. Next to it is **Kanko-annai** tourist info, which can get rooms for you, or just try any place you pass.

Ikeda Toen ceramic kiln, here 30+ years is down across Rte228 from Kanko-annai.

CHOPSTICKS: Several eateries here, but you may want to try *Daimyo-nabé*, seafood and mountain herb combination platter (sukiyaki-style) at **Sampei-zushi**: 100m past castle on Rte228 take R, street curves L, 150m beyond on L is shop. Good, quick noodles try **Maruni** across Rte228 before Kanko-annai.

WHERE NEXT: From MATSUMAE one can **bus, drive, hitch** up coastal Rte228 60km to ESASHI; Hakodate **H.E.M. bus tour**; or **train** back towards Hakodate changing at KIKONAI to Esashi Line. **Driving** from Hakodate, take local road branch-off at KIKONAI for...

ESASHI: Once major fishing source for Matsumae clan, Esashi is now area's commercial and agricultural center. Modern, yet town still retains authentic rural atmosphere of feudal days, preserved in old homes, temples, shrines.

30min walk N from stn is...
KAMOME-SHIMA (seagull isle) connected to mainland by man-made causeway. Leeward side, sea often dotted with myriads sheltering gulls, thus its name, while windward side is beaten dramatically by high seas. Only 2.6km around and 20m above sea level, isle offers swimming and camping in summer. At S end lie remains of artillery bunker first set up in 1859 against any Russian Perry and enlarged during WWII. Mainland side of causeway is Esashi harbor with its terminal for OKUSHIRITO-bound ferries (below).

Immediate area was called *Esashi no Oiwake* (parting of roads at Esashi) as one road (now Rte228) led S to MATSUMAE, other (now Rte227) headed N into wilds. From Kamome-shima we head up Rte227 (as does bus tour) to two old mansions dating to days when Esashi thrived as Matsumae clan trading port.

400m beyond isle is...
Yokoyama House, *Yokoyama-ke*, which belonged to village head-man and leader of herring fleet 160 years ago. Main house and storerooms show tools of trade. Important Cultural Asset, section of house was rebuilt in 1893, rest is original: representative of style of homes once abundant in area. In partial use as Youth Hostel.

500m beyond is...
Nakamura House, *Nakamura-ke*, built 1872 for local shipping merchant, differs from Yokoyama House as represents 'upper class' architecture. Built of cypress in rare *sokai-zukuri* style; ICA.

Across from Nakamura House is Town Hall: street to its E (L, facing Hall) 400m...
HOKKE-JI: originally built nearby Kaminokuni 1572, this Nichiren sect temple was moved here in 1665; famous for $7m^2$ painting of fierce dragon in its main hall.

Little beyond Hokkeji, street joins another along which backtrack L to...
Matsushiro Koen in which park is **GOKOKU JINJA** shrine and local **museum** exhibiting mostly marine-related items, tools of herring trade, day-to-day items of past century, objects from Tokugawa first warship *Kaiyo-maru* which sank nearby.

Back at fork in road, little beyond is intersection at which R (N) leads to...
UBAKAMI DAIJINGU, Grand Shrine, oldest shrine in Hokkaido dating back over 500 years, located behind Yokoyama House. **Aug 9-11**, shrine's 3-day, 300-year-old festival, highlighted by procession of 13 massive floats.

WHERE TO STAY: Esashi has dozen inexpensive ryokan in harbor area; sole minshuku **Terakoya** ☎(01395)-2-0855, located mainland side of Kamome-shima causeway.

Interesting side trip out to...

KAMINOKUNI-CHO and **JOKOKUJI.** Built 1568, Momoyama style temple, at 400+ oldest in Hokkaido, still mostly in original shape and good condition. Kaminokuni area was settled by Yamato Japanese in early Heian period, probably exiles from Court. Besides temple, there are few other remains of area's past inhabitants: such as foundations of **Hanazawa Mansion**, *Hanazawa Yakata-ato.* JOKOKUJI 10min bus from Kaminokuni stn on Esashi line, back towards Hakodate 5km. If **driving**, Kaminokuni is on road before reaching Esashi. *Then out to sea...*

OKUSHIRI-TO isle 61km from ESASHI in Japan Sea and 84 km around, for those going nowhere seeking nothing in particular. **Ferries** for 2hr30min crossing leave ESASHI at 6:50 and 12:50 during May-Oct, and at 12:50 only Nov-Apr. Return 9:40 and 15:40 May-Oct, and only 8:40 Nov-Apr. Boats use Okushiri harbor half-way up E coast. For sleepy Okushiri-to's residents, arriving boats have always been major event, even to this day. While in earlier days boats brought supplies and only news from outside world, they still greet boats which now bring tourists–and their money–to isle. Each boat greeted with beating of large drums, flashy welcome but fun. Coming into Okushiri harbor, boat passes seaward of giant dunking donut rock, *Nabetsuru Iwa*, pot-handle stone, protruding 19 meters out of water. Beach leeward of rock has good swimming and campsite. Large stone marker at Aonaé-misaki dedicated to imperial Prince Taruhiko (Arisukawa-no-miya) who while training on British Naval vessel landed here for repairs after storm in 1880. Nearby **airport** has several flights weekly to and from Hakodate on ANK airlines.

AONAE has 4 ryokan, 3 at Okushiri; also 2 dozen minshuku scattered around island, mostly concentrated in towns. Kokumin-shukusha Horonai-so at **HORONAI ONSEN** on W coast is sole lodging at Horonai. Only way to Horonai is 35min taxi or hitch, but call ☎(01397)-2-2975 as they may now run shuttle service. Road may not yet go all way around isle. Buses from Okushiri go counter-clockwise around N tip to stop just beyond Inaho Point, swimming beach.

Buses also go around S tip via Aonaé, and half-way up W side to...

KAMUIWAKI ONSEN. Halfway to Kamuiwaki is **Muen-jima Kaigan** beach, good swimming, fishing. Just off coast is tiny Muen-jima 'uninhabited isle'; 1 km N is small 'floating' rock formation, Hoya-ishi; and Hoya-ishi no taki waterfall just up river there: get off at MONAI stop. From KAMUIWAKI, 3km seaside path leads up to...

HORONAI ONSEN, tho by now road may be completed Kamuiwaki to Horonai. Okushiri-Aonaé-Kamuiwaki bus dep Okushiri 6:10, 9:15, 12:40, 15:35; 30min to Aonaé, 30min beyond to Kamuiwaki. Returns from Kamuiwaki dep 7:10, 10:40, 13:50 and 17:00. N-bound buses from Okushiri dep 9:15, 12:40, 15:40; return from last stop **Nonamae** 9:55, 13:30, 16:20.

May 1 thru Sept 15, **ferries** run between OKUSHIRI port and SETANA back on main island, 2hrs away. June thru Aug, boats dep Okushiri at 7:40 & 12:20; only at 8:00 during May and Sept 1-15. SETANA → OKUSHIRI boats dep 10:00 and 14:40 June-Aug; 14:30 May and Sept 1-15. *Back on mainland...*

SETANA: Sleepy little farm community feels loss of cancelled JR Setana line (80km up coast from Esashi); now served by bus from Hakodate main line at Kunnai. From Setana, it is about 150km up coastal Rte229 to Iwanai where JR used to have line to Hakodate line. In between are several small villages, all with inns and several rural hot springs. Setana is one of poorer farming areas, started by people from all over Japan for interesting mix of people. Students from Tokyo and Kansai international high schools (and recent grads like Garet) for several weeks in summer, usually mid-June to early July, come to work on farms, paying few thousand yen to cover lodging (in Youth Center) and food (breakfast and dinner) per week. Lunches are on farms with always enough food to feed twice as many people as at table. Program begun by **Tokyo Union Church** thru which apply, ✍**T.U.C.**, Jingu-mae 5-chome 7-7, Shibuya-ku, Tokyo-150. Or if already here in Hokkaido, head farmer in charge of program (Oidé-san) lives about 15min walk from town, and he *may* be able to arrange something. Most farmers will exchange room and board, no cash either way, for work in fields.

SHIMAMAKI village (about 50 km up coast) has two backwoods onsen. Bus stops in village center Town Hall *Shimamaki-son yakuba*, whence 4 km inland to...
GUNAI ONSEN. Three km upstream is picturesque **Tomarikawa gorge**. Few km down Rte229 towards Setana another road branches inland which leads to...
CHISO ONSEN. Few km upstream from here is one of Hokkaido's more famous falls **Karo-no-taki falls**, Shimamaki YH ☎(01367)-4-5264 just outside Shimamaki village. **Gunai Onsen Ryokan** at Gunai, ☎5-6320. 15 minshuku between Shimamaki–Gunai–Chiso.

Hour bus up Rte229 from Shimamaki is **RAIDEN ONSEN** on coast in Raiden Kaigan National Park, with campsite and swimming. Only 22min bus from Iwanai, this onsen attracts many visitors and is built-up in comparison to what we just passed thru, with 10 ryokan ranging budget to moderate. 1km inland from coastal Raiden onsen is **ASAHI ONSEN**, smaller, part way up volcanic Mt Raiden, from where hot spring water is piped down to other two onsen.

From Iwanai bus to Kozawa to rejoin JR to Sapporo via Yoichi; or same but with optional stop Kutchan to visit Niseko Kogen Plateau & Yoteizan. Also special **Steam Locomotive** all rsved run OTARU-NISEKO in season, dep Otaru 9:55, arr Niseko 11:37, ret dep 13:52 arr 16:02; fare ¥1,560 but Rail Pass users pay only ¥300, **rsve well ahead!**

NISEKO KOGEN, large year-round resort centered around 1309m Mt An'nupuri main peak of volcanic chain extending to Raiden coastline. Separated by narrow valley to E is Yoteizan (Mt Ezo-Fuji). Four JR stns serve Niseko area, starting from Hakodate direction: Konbu, Niseko, Hirafu, Kutchan. From Niseko & Kutchan are further buses to various onsen and ski resorts.

Mountains are popular in summer with several **hiking** trails: starting from Weiss ski ground one trail takes N approach to Goshiki Onsen; 2nd trail starts at Hirafu ski ground up E slope of Mt An'nupuri to summit on down to **GOSHIKI ONSEN** main trailhead to surrounding peaks (2 hrs to An'nupuri summit). 35min bus from Kutchan or 50min bus from Niseko, onsen has 2 inns: **Goshiki Onsen Ryokan** ☎(0136)-58-2707, and JR-run **Niseko Yama-no-Ie** ☎58-2611. From here, 4hr trail takes you up 1118m Mt Iwaonupuri, past several lakes ending at **YUMOTO ONSEN** with ryokan: **Niseko Sanso** ☎58-2103; minshuku **Orikasa** ☎58-3063; Kokumin-shukusha **Yukichichibu** ☎58-2328. Yumoto is 25min bus from Niseko stn on road to Goshiki. Other trail-heads at **KONBU ONSEN** and **NIIMI ONSEN**. Yoteizan can be climbed in 5 hours from Hirafu stn or shave off hour by starting from TOZAN-GUCHI bus stop, 25min bus from KUTCHAN; campsite near bus stop there.

Usual **ski season** is Nov thru May. Of seven separate ski areas, largest is **Niseko Kokusai Hirafu Ski-jo**, 20min bus from Kutchan, with **14 lifts** on E face of An'nupuri. Most runs here are 1-1.5km long; 4.5km run from top to base lodge. Has nite skiing on lower slopes until 21:00; **lessons** also offered. **Niseko An'nupuri Kokusai Ski-jo** with 8 lifts covering An'nupuri's southern slope is used by National Ski Team and offers some difficult runs. Between these two resorts is smaller Higashiyama ski ground from where gondola climbs to top of An'nupuri for long runs. 2km W of An'nupuri Kokusai's slopes is Moiwa Ski-jo, 5 lifts with nite skiing. **Weiss Ski-jo** (30min bus from Kutchan) has 3 lifts serving many runs on 1046m mt. Weisshorn, including 4km run from summit to base. YUMOTO ONSEN has one lift serving quiet runs thru wooded slopes of Mt Chisenpuri. Passed up by many people for larger resorts on An'nupuri, relaxing escape from crowds. All resorts have dozens of minshuku, pensions and ryokan, but if coming to ski, book well ahead, especially weekends and hols.

Out of NISEKO, we have two routes to Sapporo. Shorter and more common way is train via Yoichi and Otaru; other is train S from Kutchan to Lake Toyako, around NOBORIBETSU and SHIRAOI to SAPPORO.

We cover second route out of Sapporo, and now take first route on train or driving Rte5, cutting across Shakotan Peninsula to...
YOICHI, home of **Nikka Whiskey Distillery** established 1934 by MASATAKA Taketsuru, son of sake brewer of Hiroshima, when he returned from studying Waters of Life in Scotland and found this area with similar

clime of right temperatures, ozone content and with year-round constant
humidity, available peat and good water to make malt liquor. Ishikari Plain
sets on innumerable layers of pure peat thru which Ishikari River filters.
Ozone drifting in from Japan Sea is so dense one can smell it. Before bot-
tling, 'sacred waters' are stored up to 20 years in barrels of Japanese oak.
Second largest whiskey maker in Japan after Suntory, also produce here
score of drinks like apple-brandy, apple-wine, dry gin etc. Hootch sold on
trains in Hokkaido is exclusively Nikka, at prices starting cheaper than
mineral water up to top Scotty-Scotch tags.

Also worth look-in is Hokkaido Marine Products Experimental Station. Also in town
is restored merchant's home built in 1830s exhibits farming and daily life implements of
its time. **First weekend July**, Yoichi hosts *Hokkai Soran Matsuri* with folk-dances,
fireworks and wine-tasting. *From stn, buses leave for...*

MYSTERY CAVE FUGOPE DOKUTSU

HOKKAIDO is dotted with Continental links: stone circles, inscriptions. All
testify to minor invasions other than those principal migrations from north,
south, center. Intriguing to archaeology buffs like us are these cave glyphs.
Second such cave found, one in Temiya park in Otaru first discovered when
excavating railroad coal yards nearby. Denounced as fraud, further rail construction unearthed Ranshima cave and they were taken seriously.

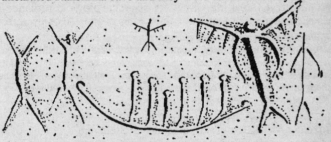

Montage of inscriptions in Fugope caves

GETTING THERE: **Bus** YOICHI–OTARU stops front of cave. Alternatively,
walk from RANSHIMA JR out stn only exit to hiway L 2km down coast thru tunnel
along beach, white wood sign R marks cave up side road R. (If no one around, **keys**
100m at first house seaside; ¥150).

According to *JTB Official Guide*, inscription is in "ancient Turkish characters
...believed written by Tungus from N.E. Asia" and are translated by Prof Nakane
as "Leading my army, I crossed great sea...fought...entered this cave." Hogwash.
While such scenario is valid, these glyphs cannot be read at present or even
guessed at except wildly.

Father Huber queried elder Ainu extensively about these caves, searched
their oral literature came up blank. Ainu-Tungus fought. Ainu had fort at
cave from which said Huber, they beat back Tungus viking raids. Chinese
annals note Tungus had form of writing, probably no more than record
keeping, since lost. From this surmise that inscription may be 'lost'
Tungus, Nakane conjures his 'Turkish' translation.

Once within cave it is apparent we do not have one continuous inscription
but some galactic hodge-podge over two converging walls of triangular cell.
No one style of 'writing', if that is what it is, but at least two, possibly five.
Our 'definite' two are quickly differentiated. One style deeply cut into wall,
few in number and near cave entry on left at ground level, made by better
masons with better tools, could be some intelligible glyphs. Style #2, raised

above face of rock by cutting away background, is true relief sculpture. All resemble hordes of praying mantids, walking sticks, daddy-long-legs and other bugs from some child's dream of being lost in demonic glades with sprinkling of humanoid stick figures.

Possible type #3 is like #2 in form, but incised like #1, simpler, its figures more human than bug, limbs end in precise spheres as with #1. Some resemble skeletal forms of 'winged goddess' or perhaps bird perched on stick-man's shoulder. Perhaps of this type also, or type #4, are numerous incised figures resembling combs, teeth set upwards, like canoes laden with stick men and like incised pottery elsewhere. There are other variants, both incised and raised, some of which may be water-worn or otherwise damaged main types. Many degenerate, being perhaps later imitations by inhabitants of different origin who imitated earlier markings for pleasure or assumed magic use. Most figures are 5 to 10 cm, some 15cm/6ins. Some faded painted abstract figures. No evidence of continuity or story construction: no action, no hunters, no combat. Certainly nothing to support JTB's literary translation. Educated guesses include: genealogical records, tribal census of group on hunting, fishing or marauding expeditions. Or educated doodles by men who, knowing of Chinese script, experimented. Glyphs continue below long-time ground level. There has been formal excavation since 1959 visit, with publication telling little more than here, in detail.

Whatever, it's exciting. Readers of archaeological romance may find brief visit provide for many dull winter nites of fireside conjecture.

Of further interest to archaeology-buffs is...
Otani Shell Mound. Few kilometers back toward RANSHIMA just as sea came into view before road made R along coast was another hard-R cutoff. Follow that back 6km to *Otani-chikai Zuka*. Were habitation sites for Jomon Japanese, old stone age clamgatherers. Little to see except for those with archaeologically-trained eyes.

Continue by bus into OTARU.

Also between Otaru–Yoichi towards Otaru from caves is...
Oshoro Kanjo Resseki stone circle, Stonehenge-like ring of monoliths of unknown origin. Man-made archaeological mystery resembling oversized sun-dial, central post stone at hub of radiating stone spokes, but no apparent astronomical significance. Cultural continuity exists with other such sites across North Asia and Europe, thru England down into North Africa. Most famous, westerly and oldest exemplar is Stonehenge; most refined, newest probably Temple of Heaven Beijing. Unknown who built them in Japan, or when, but Jomon man, 2,-1,000 BC is assumed. They extend down into Honshu, reportedly as far as Rokko behind Kobe.

GETTING THERE: Bus from OTARU stn 25min to **Oshoro Shogakko** elementary school and 15min walk beyond. Also reached by 20min walk from **Ranshima** JR stn opp direction from Fugope cave, 40min from Fugope.

OTARU, in Ainu means 'sand road' but has cobble streets to look like pleasantly decrepit north European port town. Sidewalks are everywhere, if narrow, and in general town has gone to seed, however genteelly—but more like do European towns than Oriental, effect being more what one might expect of some not-too successful graft of Chinatown onto England's northeast coast. With its natural harbor and closeness to Sapporo two were linked 1880 by first railroad in Hokkaido. Major port thru first half of century for northeast Asian trade and fishing fleets, supplying Sapporo with mainland goods. Loss of local coal mines and international trade crippled town, then with coming of larger truck-bearing ferries and improved roads, Otaru gradually was replaced in inter-island shipping by southern port of

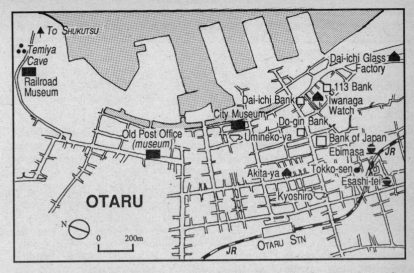

Tomakomai closer to mainland roads. Otaru linked by **ferry** to Japan Sea cities of Niigata, Tsuruga and Maizuru (last 2 are down near Kyoto) for alternate way to Hokkaido for sea-faring types. Ferries ('91) to Kholmsk on Russian Sakhalin and Vanino near Khabarovsk on Siberian coast: inquire agents, JTB or Intourist.

City's charm lies in abundance of Meiji and Taisho era Europeanesque buildings and canal, reminiscent of its past importance. From stn go down main road three blocks to Kaen-Ginza main street, turn R, then L at next big road (past Daikokuya Department Store) takes you to Otaru branch of **Nippon Ginko** (Bank of Japan) built 1912. Downhill from here is early **Meiji canal** *Shokunai Unga* lined with stone and red brick warehouses. Some 15 buildings have been restored and put to modern use: *kura*-store houses and churches, now beerhalls and coffee shops. Across canal on Pier 3 (far L) are old offices of Hokkai and Kyodo Shipping firms. Just inland from canal N end is **Municipal Museum**, *Shiritsu Haku-butsukan*, originally built as branch Post Office in 1906. Inside this two-storey English-style building (Important Cultural Asset) are exhibits on local history and art. Open 9:30-16:00, X-mon, hols; ¥50 adm; 10min bus to stn.

Half km N...
Temiya Koen with still undeciphered glyphs of Temiya caves *Temiya Dokutsu* like those in Fugope cave, above. Next to park is **Hokkaido Railroad Museum**, *Tetsudo Kinenkan* showing some of oldest steam locomotives and trains of Japan. Building constructed 1885 as office for American engineer Joseph Crawford who headed Horonai Rail Construction Co. Bronze statue in front is Crawford. May–Oct 9:30-16:00, X-mon, hols; free. SL Star of RR Museum has been C62-3, vintage 1956-71 which was polished and oiled in '88 to go back into service (p1068) between Otaru (dep 9:57) and Niseko (arr 11:37) returning 13:52 to arrive Otaru 16:02, about 25 days per year, sat-sun-hol between Apr 29–Nov, 320 rsvd seats ¥1,560 o.w., at all JR counters. May extend frequency—thus change times—and season and extend to NISEKO.

10min bus from Temiya Park (25 from stn) is small fishing village of...
SHUKUTSU, site of **Marine Park Shukutsu** and **Otaru Aquarium**. Next to aquarium is **Nishin Goten** Herring Palace, so named because original owners, Tanaka family, made their fortune from herring in early

1800s. Of many old merchant homes of this style, this is one of few in such good condition, easily accessible. Open mid-Apr thru Nov, 9:00-17:00, closed 3rd of every month; adm ¥100.

SOEN-JI temple (few km SW of Otaru stn is), on which grounds are rows of 511 stone images of Buddha's '500' disciples (*gohyaku-rakan*) with unusual comical expressions. Carved 400 years ago, originally at Matsumae castle were moved here 1901. Bus from stn 10min to Ryutokuji-mae & 5min walk, or 20min walk from Minami-Otaru stn.

CHOPSTICKS: Otaru restaurants mostly around JR stn and along Kaen-Ginza, but better known are at S end of town. S on Kaen-Ginza past New Ginza Dept Store on R is **Tokkosen** robatayaki grill. Past that on L is **Ebimasa Sushi**, one of many in town using famed fresh local catch. Just beyond rail overpass, on R **Esashi-tei** specializes in seafood; **Kasube** next door local specialties.

Otaru also boasts Hokkaido's oldest restaurant, **Kaiyo-tei** outside town in Sumiyoshi-cho, slightly expensive, full-course traditional meals from ¥10,-15,000. Was also site of celebration following signing of Treaty of Portsmouth incorporating Karafuto peninsula, southern half of Sakhalin, into Empire in 1905; treaty ended Russo-Japan war giving Russ ports in China and Manchuria to Japan as well as Sakhalin, which was split. Russians got south back in 1945, taking Kuril Isles with it, still contested. Taxi from stn, drivers all know it: ☎(0134)-23-0021.

Old 19th century warehouses have been converted into coffee shops: **Umine-koya** near Ryugu Bridge W-bank of canal, and **Kyoshiro** in front of stn. Several times monthly Umine-koya sponsors traditional dancers who perform on their small inside stage, other times local jazz bands show their stuff.

Out in *Shukutsu area,* interesting noodle shop **Yabuhan** in reconstructed annex of fishing fleet 'commodore's' home: tiled entry gate and storehouses all original; prices slightly higher than run-of-mill noodleries, but food excellent as is setting. Hokkaido justly famed for its noodles—Sapporo Ramen all over Japan, Hokkaido noodleries all over New York as Oriental quick-lunch. Other local specialties widely available—*Kamome-Ramen*, seagull-noodles—not gull meat but dish of steaming delicious local noodles topped by seafood delicacies loved by gulls: crableg, squid, scallops, sea urchin, etc, and about ¥800 meal-size portion.

Interested in local arts and crafts visit **Exhibit Hall,** *Sangyo Kaikan*—displays, gift counters. R at street in front of stn, 300m to end of long block, L. Glass-blowing is new craft in Hokkaido at *Kita-ichi Garasu* gifts, 300m beyond Sangyo Kaikan, also on L just past overpass.

WHERE TO STAY: Most hostelries cluster near stn, inexpensive. **Green, New Green** and **New Minato Hotels** are ¥-B located along main road from stn to canal. Good ryokan is **Akitaya** ☎(0134)-22-5181, off Kaen-Ginza; road from stn to Kaen-Ginza turn R, then first L. Many minshuku, but all located outside of town at Shukutsu, Oshoro and Ranshima. All arrangements can be made thru **Station Tourist Information Booth**. On Tengu-yama hill W of stn is **Tengu-yama YH** ☎34-1474. Another option head to **ASARIKAWA ONSEN** 30min bus from stn, secluded hot spring in mountains, far more quiet and cheaper than famous **JOZANKEI ONSEN**, 40min bus down same road en route Sapporo.

DATEBOOK: During last weekend of July OTARU hosts one of Hokkaido's main summer fetes *Ushio Matsuri:* 200+ boats sport banners circle harbor start off festival, ends 2 days later with 20,000 dancers around pier and Temiya Park. Smaller festival at Shukutsu same time. Late October, *Autumn Festival* at Asarikawa & Shukutsu. Also *Tsutsuji Matsuri* late May Temiya Park for blooming azaleas.

From OTARU only short run to SAPPORO: JR Hakodate main line, Rte5 and recently opened Dochu Expressway follow coast before cutting inland. Mountain route via ASARIKAWA and JOZANKEI hot springs takes you thru scenic mountains, but time-consuming so should be attempted only if staying at either onsen. **Drivers** may want to spend nite in JOZANKEI luxury accommodations before heading down into bustling...

*land of my childish fantasies, thy dark green forest
is where my soul goes to seek comfort...*
—Garrison Keillor, *Lake Woebegone Days*

SAPPORO 札幌
BEER & SNOWMEN

BROAD, CLEAN AND MODERN, unlike any other in Japan with its open spaces, parks and wide streets laid out in geometric grid. City was begun in 1869 with idea to create cultural, economic, governmental center of Hokkaido—plan similar to Heian Kyoto's founding eleven centuries earlier. In its single century Sapporo has grown impressively to 1.6 million people —who host 11 million tourists—spreading far beyond its original groundplan. As 'natural' result, in suburbs these well-planned city roads become typical Japanese mazes, but wider.

Limited time travelers will find Sapporo ideal base for short trips around S Hokkaido. In spite of its size, you can 'do' city in one day. If taking time to see whole island, city offers pleasant change of pace — its abundant entertainment makes it great place to let loose. As with other Hokkaido cities, Sapporo historic attractions are Meiji-Taisho era buildings with little else antique for sightseers. But brewery tours, active nite-life can keep us busy during our stay in this easy-to-live-in metropolis.

GETTING AROUND: Tips before starting tour of Sapporo: Streets prefixed *Kita* (north), 北 *Minami* (south), 南 *Higashi* (east), or 東 *Nishi* (west) 西 numbered. N-S division is Ohdori (Big Street) half km S of stn; E-W division is Rte231-Narikura River 300m E of stn. Most downtown is in W half and S of stn. All streets running N-S bear E or W name and are called *chomé*, E-W are *jo*. Main street running from stn down to Nakajima Koen is Nishi Yon-chome (west fourth, W4) under which runs...

Subway-blissfully quiet on rubber tires—has N-S line (*nan-boku-sen*) and E-W line (*to-zai-sen*) which meet in middle of downtown at Ohdori and Nishi Yon-chome/W4. Tram line circles western section of town, starting just south of Ohdori subway stn and ending at Susu-kino stn, on subway stop south. Buses, unless headed for specific destination such as airport or Jozankei, are marked by direction and number, E16 or W14. Distances are easy to figure in town since each major block is 100m each side (thus 16 per mile). May thru Nov, **bicycles** available free of charge from Toyohiragawa rentals *Toyohiragawa Jitensha Taishussho*, Minami Ku-jo Nishi It-chome (S9-W1) where Minami Kujo meets Toyohira river. If cycling not your thing, Sapporo abounds with **taxis**, rates slightly less than main Honshu cities.

Much of area north of stn is taken up by **University of Hokkaido**; established 1872, but really dating to 1876 when Dr William S Clark, then president of Massachusetts Agricultural College (now U. Mass) was invited for one year to set up Ag School and, if nothing else, left behind his famed admonition 'Boys be Ambitious'—since obeyed with frontier vengeance.

Most things to see and do are **south** of stn. Ohdori (Big Street) is over 100m wide with green belt **Ohdori Koen** park running across middle for 1.5km/one mile. Common gathering spot, Ohdori Koen is main site of *Sapporo Snow Festival*. All summer it is world's biggest beer garden. Thruout year, push-cart vendors in park sell corn-on-the-cob, noodles and other snacks. Stone tablet inscribed with favorite local poet ISHIKAWA Takuboku (d.1912): " In broad streets and still autumn nite comes aroma of roasting ears of corn". Ah, Sapporo. At E end of Ohdori Koen is local 'Eiffel Tower' of TV companies, observation platform overlooking city.

Three blocks S of stn and two W is ex-**Prefectural Office** *Hokkaido Kyu-Chosha* built 1888. Modeled after Massachusetts State Legislature building, red brick structure's octagonal dome represents frontier spirit of

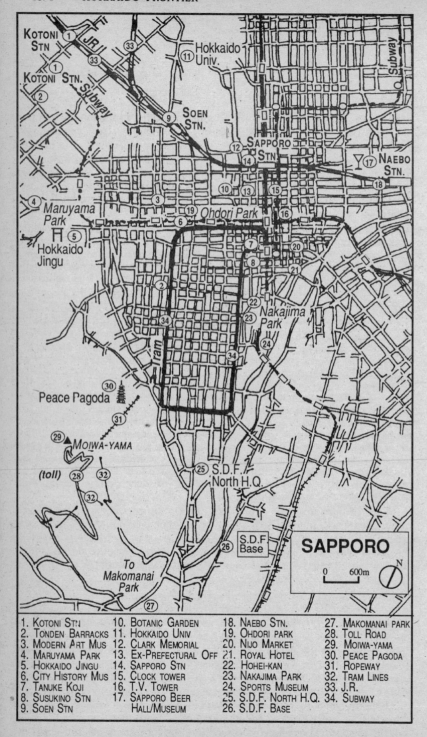

SAPPORO

0   600m   N

1. Kotoni Stn
2. Tonden Barracks
3. Modern Art Mus
4. Maruyama Park
5. Hokkaido Jingu
6. City History Mus
7. Tanuke Koji
8. Susukino Stn
9. Soen Stn
10. Botanic Garden
11. Hokkaido Univ
12. Clark Memorial
13. Ex-Prefectural Off
14. Sapporo Stn
15. Clock Tower
16. T.V. Tower
17. Sapporo Beer Hall/Museum
18. Naebo Stn.
19. Ohdori park
20. Nijo Market
21. Royal Hotel
22. Hohei-kan
23. Nakajima Park
24. Sports Museum
25. S.D.F. North H.Q.
26. S.D.F. Base
27. Makomanai park
28. Toll Road
29. Moiwa-yama
30. Peace Pagoda
31. Ropeway
32. Tram Lines
33. J.R.
34. Subway

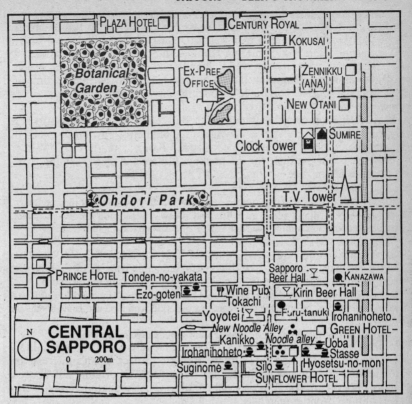

early settlers spreading in 'all 8' directions, inside are pictures of those settlers. 9:00-17:45 weekdays (-13:00 sat). With completion of new Prefectural Office in 1968, old one was preserved as memento of Hokkaido early history. Building is in present government complex including Prefectural Assembly, Police HQ, Administrative Center.

One block W is...
University **Botanical Garden**, 140,000m² park contains over 5,000 species of plants. Open 9:00-16:00, ¥400.

Also...
Batchelor Memorial Museum, *Batchelor Kinen-kan*, dedicated to Batchelor who taught at University, author of *Ainu of Japan*, with its Northerly Peoples' Exhibition Hall (*Hoppo Minzoku Shiryo-shitsu*); and...
University Museum, *Hokudai Hakubutsukan*, both of which have collections of Ainu arts and other tribal artifacts.

About 10min walk SW, to W end of Ohdori Koen is...
City Historical Museum, *Sapporo-shi Shiryokan*, was old Court of Appeals built 1892. **Horse-drawn** wagons circle Ohdori Koen, start-end here: ¥1,500/adults, half-rate child.

At Kita Ichijo Nishi Sanchome (N1-W3)–5min walk from TV tower is city symbol...
Clock Tower atop two-storey wood building constructed 1878. Originally auditorium for Sapporo School of Agriculture, predecessor to Hokkaido U; now **Sapporo History Museum**, *Sapporo Rekishi-kan* of 400+ items tracing area history; 9:00-16:00, X-mon. Clock is American-made Howard, specially ordered and imported in 1878. Is and has been faithfully wound every third day since 1939, rain or shine, by volunteer Mr Igami.

S end of town reached by subway Nanboku/NS line, to stop of same name is...
Nakajima Koen park bounded on W by Kuranari river, is full of ponds,
large Japanese garden also rose garden. On park grounds is two-storey
western style white wood building **Hohei-kan** built 1880 as public meeting
and dance hall, now city-run wedding hall. Hidden in Japan garden is century-old tea house **Hasso-an** built Kobori Enshu style, by master himself.
Apt name '8-window hermitage' as opening any one of 8 windows exposes
viewer to one of 4 seasons to drink tea against natural setting.

City's fixation on '72 Olympics can be seen at **Sports Museum** at S
end of park exhibiting Winter Olympics related items. Few km S to end of
Nanboku subway line is **Makomanai Koen** site of 1972 Winter
Olympics' Main Stadium for ice hockey, figure- and speed-skating. Nation's best indoor rink, now public.

3km NW is...
Moiwayama hill offering great nite view of city below: toll road up S side,
ropeway up N. Hiking summer; 3 lifts and ropeway serve runs for skiers winter.
Ropeway terminal reached by tram from Ohdori or Susukino (ea, 15min).

On western fringe of town is...
Maruyama Koen largest zoo north of Tokyo. Nearby is **HOKKAIDO
JINGU**, primary shrine of island, constructed same time as city. Favorite
cherry viewing spot in spring when its 500 wild Ezo-sakura blossom. *Jingu
Matsuri* **Jun 14-17** is largest shrine festival in area, highlighted by mikoshi and feudal
costume procession. Maruyama and Nakajima parks fill with food and game booths for
festival.

Tozai/EW line subway to western terminus Kotoni, and 5min walk to...
Kotoni Tondenhei-oku barracks. Tondenhei were some 956 special law
officers sent in 1875 as paramilitary force to protect Japan's interests on
frontier and provide law and order among settlers. Of original 208 houses,
this is only one restored to original condition. Also exhibited day-to-day
tools of these frontier marshals.

Back in town **open-air morning market**, *Asa-ichi* daily at Nijo-ichiba
on W bank of Kurinari River between Minami Nijo and Sanjo/N2-3 streets
...5min walk from TV tower.

45min bus from Clock Tower is...
Nopporo Koen, Prefectural Park opened 1968 commemorating 100th
anniversary of opening of Hokkaido as full-fledged territory. Covers 2,000
hectares of virgin forest, has new three-storey museum dedicated to
Hokkaido's history since gaining 'statehood'; 9:00-16:00, X-mon/hols, ¥150.
Striking **100m high tower** next to museum also commemorates 1968
centennial. Viewing platform atop looks out over forest and Ishikari Plain,
stretching 150km to Daisetsuzan Mountains in central Hokkaido.

No visit would be complete without seeing...
Sapporo Brewery. First brewery opened 1876, no longer in operation,
about 1km SE of stn. Kita Sanjo Higashi Yon-chome (N3-E4); now located 2+km from
stn at Kita-shichijo, 9-chome/N7-S9: take Higashi/E #3 or #16 buses; taxi 1.5x-mtr.

Sales boomed, another brewery was soon built in NE suburbs, expanded
to cover output from closed first. Free tour of brewery (in J- with E- pamphlet)
outlining process: arrange at booth inside main gate. No set times, guide starts once
small group set, usually few mins. Some E-spkg guides, prearrange ☎(011)-741-9191.

Tour ends at red brick 1890 brewery museum of antique mugs (mostly
German, another great beer society), other beer paraphernalia, old Sapporo
Beer labels, coasters, awards; photos of Imperial visit. On walls are posters
since 1876 which show prevalent styles and moods. Starting out in traditional kimono, to mostly women models of Japan's 'Roaring Twenties' and

obsession with West who dress like their Yankee counterparts, only to return to kimono on posters during military rule of 1930s-40s. Modern posters reflect Japan's balance of old and new: New Wave and kimono-clad models, discos and cool country inns. After this, sample freshly brewed beer, or their O.J. for nondrinkers. Daily 12:00–21:00, X-sun, hol and some sats.

Brewery building is century old. Massive red brick with large red stars– company logo, emblazoned everywhere, looks more like something you'd expect in Peking or Moscow. Gift stalls sell everything from beer mugs to T-shirts with company labels. Long line of waiting taxis suddenly made sense when we staggered to one after more than breaking even in 'Viking'. Freshly brewed beer is incredibly delicious... and potent!

Three beer-halls (1 outdoor) offer assorted meals from salad to Genghis Khan BBQ lamb and vegetables. Ye of large appetite, try 'Viking' eat-and-drink-all-you-want in 2hrs for ¥3,000: platters of Genghis Khan and beer, whiskey or juice, but don't count on doing anything else that day–each person must eat at least one platter and drink 5 mugs to break even.

Similar arrangement of tour and sampling at ice cream factory of...
Yukijirushi Snow Brand, one of nation's top dairy producers, also started in Hokkaido. Located 1.5km E of Sapporo Brewery at Naeho-cho 6-chome; daily May-Oct 9-11:00, 13-15:30, others sat, sun, hols, advise phoning ☎704-2817. Across from Yukijirushi is JR construction plant.

For different factory visit, try...
Toyohira Garasu Kojo, main workshop for *hand-blown* Sapporo glass found in shops all over island: at far southern end of town, easiest way there is by taxi, all know place.

City-run **bus tour** *Sangyo* (business) *course* includes both **Sapporo Brewery** and **Yukijirushi**: runs May 1 thru Oct 15 weekdays, 4hr ¥1,600; tour also stops at Makomanai and **Clock Tower**, starts and ends at stn bus terminal.

WHERE TO STAY: Sapporo has everything from Youth Hostels to luxury hotels comparable to any in Tokyo. Most modern W-style hotels clustered around stn: **Keio Plaza** (011)-271-0111, **Century Royal** ☎221-2121, **Sapporo Kokusai** ☎222-3811, **Zennikku** ☎221-4411, **New Otani** ☎222-1111. With mostly all tatami rooms are **Sumiré**, **Koei** and **Sapporo Dai-ichi**. Business Hotels are all over town: one we found convenient & cheap (¥-P) was **Center Park Hotel** ☎231-5651 N of Ohdori Koen on Nishi Hatchome (W8): room small but clean; best of all is its fabulous top floor—all baths and saunas, great after long day walking town. SUSUKINO area has several budget business hotels: **Hotel Sunflower** ☎512-5533 (S5-E3); **Hotel Stasse** ☎531-7111 one block E; **Green Hotel** one block N of Stasse. Sunflower is favorite for young Japanese, with clean, cheap rooms, and great 50-item spread buffet meals. **Mets** ☎726-5511 by N 18 subway stn; washer, dryer, mini-kitchen, ¥-T.

Only 4 Youth Hostel in town, 2 convenient are **Sapporo House** 2 blocks W of stn on N side and **Lion's YH** in Miyanomori. Many ryokan, but Sapporo is one place where budgeteer may want to pass up usual room w/2-meals to experience city's eateries. Many hotels, notably cheaper ones, have free breakfast coupons (at most ¥300).

CHOPSTICKS: Centers in TANUKI KOHJI (Badger or Coon-Dog Alley) and SUSUKINO areas with 3,500 eat-'n-drinkeries. Tanuki Kohji runs between Minami Nijo and Sanjo streets/S2-3, extending 6 blocks. Susukino is even larger, centered around Susukino subway stop. Susukino has more classy eateries, Tanuki Kohji is more relaxed with cheaper places.

TANUKI KOHJI, starting at eastern end: on L just past Ni-chome/S2 is **Kanazawa** specializing in robatayaki grill. On S side of block (San-jo/S3) is **Furu-tanuki**, Old Badger, one of more popular robatayaki places, inside full assorted folkcrafts. Back on

Tanuki Kohji past Kanazawa on R is **Sapporo Beer Hall** on 4th floor specializes in Genghis Khan lamb BBQ. Street is lined with stores, at W end past Roku-chome/S6 are: **Tonden-no-Yakata** for local cooking, owner is grand-daughter of Tondenhei marshal. Next door is **Nishin Goten** for seafood, and next to that in Grand Bldg. is **Ezo Goten** also local cuisine. If you'd like to try some local wine but can't make it out to Ikeda-Hokkaido's wine country–head to **Wine Pub Tokachi** run by Ikeda folks, financed by wine-town; on Minami San-jo/S3 (1 blk S of Tanuki Kohji) btwn Rokuchome/S6 and Go-chome/S5; steak dinner also served. But for Matsuzaka beef, the kind that dies drunk, **Ohtemon** at Minami Ju-jo, Nishi Itchome/S10-W1, sukiyaki, charcoal-broil ¥7,000.

SUSUKINO AREA is two blocks S. Before heading into its heart, places on N side of Minami Yon-jo/S4: corner of Go-chome/S5 is **Yoyotei** Genghis Khan restaurant, ¥2,800 eat-and-drink-all-u-can. Next door is **Toritei** sake and yakitori local hangout. Along Go-jo on corner of San-chome/S5-W3 is fine king crab place **Hyosetsu-no-Mon**, next door **Uoba** assorted seafood. *Next alley on R is known as...*
RAMEN YOKOCHO (Noodle Alley), 90 noodle stalls offering 20 kinds of famed Sapporo noodles combined with everything imaginable for near-infinite choice. Across from entrance to Ramen Yokocho is **Robatayaki Silo**, famous for its skewers of Ezo-shika venison. NW corner intersection of Go-jo and Yon-chome/S5-W4 is **Kanikko** crab restaurant, cheaper and more youth-oriented than Hyosetsu-no-Mon. You'll not be disappointed with crab in Hokkaido. Giant crabs caught in Uchiura Bay are shipped fresh daily to Sapporo. If you drove from Hakodate up Rte5, you passed dozens of roadside stalls selling crab, especially near Oshamambe.

Just W of Ramen Yokocho is Robatayaki **Irohanihoheto** with fantastic interior, budget but high quality food. Primarily oriented to Japanese in mid-twenties, plays music from popular shows and TV serials when this generation was growing up. Nationwide chain; **another** is block-and-half N of Hyosetsu-no-Mon. *Next is...*
SHIN RAMEN YOKOCHO, New Noodle Alley, N end **Anpon** saké stall. Block-and-half past Irohanihoheto on L side Gojo is **Suginome** one of best local cuisine houses since before war; slightly more expensive–good full-course meals from ¥5,000. **Anna**, Russian cuisine ☎231-1209, near Ohdori Sbwy stn. Branch Khabarousk restaurant; 11:00-22:00.

For natural food try **Sapporo Kitchen Horenso** catty-corner from Hokkaido U. Hospital. Home-like atmosphere with teishoku from ¥780. 11:30-20:00, no X, ☎747-7317. Also **Natural-Tei**, using all organic foods, has Genmai (brown rice) teishoku ¥700. 9:00-21:00 X-2nd & 4th sun, ☎251-1102.

SHOPPING: Tanuki Kohji also good, with 300+ shops. Across street from diner Tonden-no-yakata are: **Maruwa Mingei Center** and **Tondensha** for wood carvings and such folkcrafts as Sapporo blown glass. Next to Tonden-no-yakata is **Kotan** run by chief of Ainu village at Lake Akan; upstairs at nite is bar-restaurant.

PERSONAL DATEBOOK: Since extensive coverage during '72 Winter Olympics, Sapporo's *Yuki Matsuri* Snow Festival has become internationally famous event. Every year **Feb 5-11**, Ohdori and Makomanai Parks are filled with over 180 snow and ice sculptures, some up to 10m tall using over 500 truck-loads, 3,000 tons of snow. 1984 fest saw half-scale replica of Buckingham Palace and Okinawa's Shuri Castle donjon! Festival began in 1950 when hi-school students made 6 sculptures in Ohdori Koen, little realizing it would grow into world event drawing over 1.8 million people in 1984. Ohdori Koen is main site with sculptures lit up nites. During day folk dances, Snow Queen contest, capped with nitely fireworks fun continues late nite. Last day great as cranes demolish near-full scale snow castles like mischievous kids breaking up sand castles. *White Illumination* in Sapporo Plaza early **Dec** thru New Year holidays.

Not as spectacular but more colorful is *Lilac Festival* at Ohdori Koen W4 to W8 in **late May** with concerts, puppets etc. Brought over from France 1890 to line city's streets, lilac became city's official tree in 1959, now hundreds of trees fill city, covering streets in white and purple flowers in spring. Saplings given away at festival.

Summer attitude is beery while city wallows in its favorite product. **HOKKAIDO JINGU** at Maruyama Park end of Ohdori Ave **mid-June** annual big fete, Mikoshi towed on horse cart; market stalls, the works. Elsewhere most of town joins in, shopping streets have small fetes, department stores put out local Mikoshi and in Nakajima Park there's small circus and usual stalls. Then with *Summer Festival* from last mon in **July** for four weeks, first two weeks stressing beer gardens almost length of Ohdori Ave, with final week *Bon Dance Festival*. Last weekend July thru **first sun Aug** is *Northern Regions Festival* at Mt Okura Ski jump and including **Sapporo Carnival** street from JR stn to Nakajima Park full of street dances, from Samba to Bon-odori, everything. Sapporo is always Carni.

As mentioned earlier, Sapporo is base for numerous quick visits to sights of south Hokkaido.

But before heading out, let us pay visit to...

JOZANKEI ONSEN: Aptly called 'Back room of Sapporo', best known of Hokkaido's hot springs. Unfortunately, fame beckons large ferroconcrete hotels to accommodate hordes of annual visitors. Prices high, tho' still some moderate places. Hour bus or ¥9,000 taxi (18x-mtr) from Sapporo (drivers take Rte230), Jozankei is relaxing alternative to downtown Sapporo hotels, made all more worthwhile with its hot baths. Most bus tours out of Sapporo for Toya-ko, Noboribetsu and Shiraoi first pick up at Jozankei.

WHERE TO STAY: Lodgings all located along 1.5km of Toyohira River, with best there on river bank, smaller ones little way back tho no more than 200m. Most are upper-class hotels and ryokan starting ¥-lo-T: At W end of town is **Jozankei Grand Hotel** ☎(011)-598-2214 (where we stayed 1959), and annex **New Grand** across river. Hotel **Shikanoyu** ☎598-2311 central, on N bank which is more traditional, but still large. Several high-class smaller ryokan along bank. Cheaper (¥-Bw/2) is JR-run **Shiraito-so Hokenjo** at E end. **YH Nakayama-togé**, inconveniently located Nakayamatogé 40min bus down Rte230 towards Toya-ko lake. Can make all arrangements at Sapporo stn's **Ryokan-annai**, or **Kanko-annai** by Jozankei Bus Center.

150m N of Jozankei Hotel is...

IWATO KANNON-JI in which temple grounds is **Kannon cave**. Dug out by hand, tunnel extends 120m into hill, its walls lined with 33 carved **Goddesses of Mercy** to which are offered prayers for good luck on exams and in love. Legend has it *kappa* (water-imps) used to inhabit river at E end of onsen in **Kappa-fuchi Pool** which is still marked. Tho they no longer appear, in their memory festival **first weekend of August** 1,000 Kappa-masked dancers wind thru streets. Grab mask and join in, or at least partake of food and drink at street stalls.

20min bus from Jozankei towards Otaru at Asari-toge pass is Jozankei Kogen Sapporo **Kokusai Ski-jo**, International Ski-Run. Recently opened (1978), 4 lifts and one gondola take skiers on dozen runs, from beginner to expert.

About 15km NE of Sapporo is...

TEINE, year-round recreation ground spread over Teine-yama mt. Site of '72 Olympic alpine skiing and bob-sled races, one of Hokkaido's largest ski resorts, tho no long expert runs. In addition to down-hill, also 5km cross-country course and nite runs. Downhill and cross-country lessons, equipment rental. Ski season mid-Dec to late Apr; from May 3 amusement park with golf course, heated pool open. Lots of lodgings in area all price ranges, but during ski season book ahead thru **Teine Olympia Info Center** ☎(011)-681-3191; or Sapporo City's branch office ☎681-2131. Several hiking trails on mountain, most popular is Heiwa-no-taki to summit.

Heiwa-no-taki (Peace Waterfall) reached by bus from To-zai subway Kotoni stn to Heiwa-no-taki Iriguchi and 20min walk: waterfall often used by followers of Nichiren Buddhism for meditation. From here trail follows Hassamu River to Menoshiki-no-taki waterfall, whence 5km hike up back trail to 1024m summit of Mt Teine; 40min hike (5min ropeway) down to base ropeway stn where JR buses year-round 1hr to Sapporo stn.

Ski season, JR has special 45min bus runs from stn to Teine Olympia stop.

INNER CIRCLE SOUTHERN LAKES

COVERS WHAT MOST short-term visitors to Hokkaido will experience: touristized but nonetheless offering cross-section of Hokkaido's natural beauties. Dominated by **Shikotsu-Toya National Park**, area between Sapporo – Uchiura Bay has 4 major places of interest, each with own lake. **Shikotsu-ko** and **Toya-ko** two main lakes, attractions themselves; **Kuttara-ko** better known for nearby bubbling hell; **Poroto-ko** with its Shiraoi Ainu village (p.1122) and newly discovered onsen and waterfalls.

GETTING THERE: **Bus tours** out of SAPPORO and CHITOSE cover area in one or two days, more if taking in other places. Same routes can be done easily solo by bus, train, driving or hitching. **Train** is best if taking lakes in between SAPPORO → HAKODATE. If planning to circle entire island, suggest taking this area in reverse order at end of trip on way back to Hakodate to avoid back-track.

Usual run is JOZANKEI → TOYA-KO → NOBORIBETSU → SHIRAOI → SHIKOTSU, return by way of SAPPORO or CHITOSE.

Ace Travel, affiliate of JTB has best tours—all include lunch:

One-day THE HOKKAIDO SAPPORO-HAKODATE course departs SAPPORO 8:30 → Jozankei → Showa Shinzan (via Nakayama pass) → Toya-ko (lunch)→ Oshamanbe → Onuma Park → HAKODATE 18:00. Reverse course leaves HAKODATE 8:00, ends SAPPORO 18:30; runs 6/1-10/20, ¥7,500-8,500.

In Hakodate, can extend with **Hakodate one-day tour:** dep HAKODATE Bus Center 8:30 → Tobetsu Trappist Shudoin Abbey → Kikonai Stn → Seikan Tunnel Museum → Matsumae Castle → Esashi → HAKODATE 17:45; runs 7/1-9/30, ¥4,660. Hakodate Bus ☎(0138)-51-3136. Also **Hokuto Kotsu** ☎57-7555 has several courses.

One-day THE HOKKAIDO SAPPORO-OTARU: dep SAPPORO 8:40 → OTARU (via Asari-toge pass) → Hokkaido Rail Museum → Municipal Museum, followed by 90min free time, then → glass-blowing studio, returning SAPPORO 15:00. ¥5,500, ¥5,000, lunch included.

Other one day tours by Chuo Bus are:
One-day SHIKOTSU course: dep SAPPORO 8:15 → Hitsujigaoka → Lake Okotanpe → Lake Shikotsu (cruise) → Chitose airport → SAPPORO stn 15:20; runs 6/1-10/10, ¥4,050.

NISEKO SHAKOTAN course: dep SAPPORO 8:00 → Nakayama pass → Niseko → Iwanai → Furubira → Otaru → SAPPORO stn 17:50; runs daily 7/1-10/1, hol 6/4-10/29, ¥5,500. Chuo bus ☎(011)-221-5161.

Ace-JTB also has large selection of pre-set and 'you-make' tours by hired **cab**, again which make much sense for 4 travelers together.

All tours arrangeable thru JTB offices (at stn in Sapporo) anywhere in Japan or overseas, some Sapporo major hotels also can arrange for you.

Pilgrim use local buses, prices: Sapporo-Jozankei-Toya ¥2,550 time 2hr45min; Toya-Noboribetsu ¥1,350 1hr25min; Noboribetsu-Shiraoi ¥590 42min; Tomakomai-Shikotsu ¥540 45min; Shikotsu-Chitose ¥620 40min; Shikotsu-Sapporo ¥990 80min.

TOYA-KO: Lake 15km across, 40km/25mi around almost circular, 183m deep, in volcanic caldera with large central island which was ex-mountain peak. Along S bank, Toya-ko and Sobetsu Onsens are main lodging areas. Lake cruises available.

GETTING THERE: With cancellation of JR Kutchan-Datemonbetsu, lake inconvenient from North route. Buses from Kutchan to **SOBETSU ONSEN** and **TOYA-KO ONSEN** 100min. From SAPPORO on JR is roundabout, via Noboribetsu on S route. Bus more expensive but quicker, 2hr40min via **JOZANKEI ONSEN**. All nontour buses are Donan Bus Co, except from Sapporo which is also serviced by Jotetsu Bus Co. **Drive** from Sapporo Rte230.

LEG I:
HAKODATE TO SAPPORO
& INNER CIRCLE ROUTE

0   30km

WHERE TO STAY: The most major hotels and ryokan are located in Toya and Sobetsu Onsen, there are budget minshuku and campsites also around lake. Toya-ko Onsen has built itself up to third rank onsen area in Japan, full of luxury hotels and ryokan each boasting spacious bath-halls and excellent service. Best known is **Toya Park Hotel Sun Palace** with its giant 3,000m² hall containing 27 assorted baths, ☎(01427)-5-4126. **Manseikaku Hotel** with all rooms facing lake, ☎5-2171.

SOBETSU ONSEN is only 2km E of Toya-ko, but being more recent is about one-third size and somewhat quieter. Good hotel here **Kawanami** ☎5-2715. Most hotels and ryokan in both areas from ¥10,000, tho you may find rooms as low as ¥8,000 especially off-season. Handful of ryokan in both, more in Toyamura village N end of lake. At Sobetsu Onsen is **Showa Shinzan YH** ☎5-2283. Stretching up E shore are four **campsites**: Nishi-kotan Camp-jo between Toya and Sobetsu, Takinokami Camp-jo 3km beyond Sobetsu (1 bus stop to Takinokami), Naka-Toya Camp-jo halfway up E shore (Naka-Toya stop), 5km further to Kita-kotan at Iwaya Kannon stop. If camping, highly recommend dip in local sento in Toya-ko Onsen, ¥260.

Boats leave from both Toya and Sobetsu Onsen to central **Oshima Island**, Ezo-shika deer sanctuary. Across from island's pier is white building, **Forest Wildlife Museum** *Nakanoshima Shinrin Hakubutsu-kan*, 8:30-16:30, ¥200, closed Nov-Apr. Opened 1955 as wildlife research center, now exhibits most plant and animal life found in Hokkaido. Boat stops at two smaller isles: **Kannon-shima**, with Buddhist Kannon Hall; and **Benten-jima**. R.t. beginning and ending at Toya or Sobetsu 90min, ¥970. Assorted watercraft from paddleboats to motorboats can be rented, fishing tackle.

While most people come here just for baths, those with time may want to spend some of it at volcanoes from which hot spring water is drawn. More famous Usuzan with two openings just behind Toya-ko Onsen. In Aug, 1977 massive explosion shot fire and ash out of two craters damaging portions of two onsen. Lesser eruptions followed for year spreading ash to Sapporo and as far as Asahikawa. Ropeway ascended E face, but since '77 it and whole mountain **off-limits**. 5min walk from Toya-ko Onsen bus stop is **Volcanic Science Hall**, *Kazan Kagaku-kan* outlining life of nearby Showa Shinzan and photos of Usuzan's eruptions. Hi-lite is Experience Room where eruption realistically simulated – whole theater shakes rather violently – after which is 20min film of recent volcanic activity. Open daily Apr thru Oct 9:00-17:00; sat, sun and hols Nov thru Mar, ¥400. Showa Shinzan (Showa New Mt), 1km E of Usuzan, is so named because in Showa 18 (1943) mt suddenly rose out of what were once wheat fields. Still only 400m (1300ft) high, no one here doubts but that it will grow larger in near future. At base (from where now-halted cablecar rose to Usuzan's peak) is small **Ainu Exhibit Hall**, *Ainu Kinen-kan* open 8:00-17:00, free; **Volcanic Museum**, *Kazan Hakubutsu-kan* same hours, ¥400; **Bear Farm**, *Kuma Bokujo;* Tropical **Botanical Garden** ¥500.

PERSONAL DATEBOOK: Weekend End-Aug, *Toya-ko Lake Festival*, mikoshi and other parades, *Toro-nagashi* paper lanterns float in lake, fireworks all 3 nites.

WHERE NEXT: Bus for 1hr40min ride from Toya-ko to bubbling hells of NOBORIBETSU. En route is Muroran, dull industrial city with ferry connections to Aomori. At Noboribetsu stn, 15min bus to hot springs. Bus scenic, especially at halfway Orofure-toge Pass where you munch fresh corn-on-cob while looking on gorgeous view of hills below.

NOBORIBETSU

NOBORIBETSU is Ainu for 'wonderful river' (*Enclyopedia Japan* says 'mud river')–or rather Japanese mispronunciation of Ainu *Nupurpet*. Popular jumping off place for forlorn youths who want literally to go to hell; suicides from steep crater edge of hellishly bubbling **Jigoku-dani** (Valley of Hell) do occur. 300m behind (N) of Jigoku-dani is **Oyunuma** boiling sulphur pond. Surface about 40° Celsius (same as good, hot country public bath, which most foreigners find unbearably hot)–but subsurface temperature reaches 130°C. Sulphur content stains surrounding area deep yellow. Spa itself is in broad hollow above Jigoku-dani.

Arriving by bus, runners from various hotels and inns cluster around bus stop to take your luggage or book any who haven't yet reservations. This is one place where we recommend biggest, splashiest places:

WHERE TO STAY: Noboribetsu Grand Hotel or Daiichi Takimotokan at both you've choice of W- or J-style rooms and food, in dining room or own room, any combination. Daiichi and Grand outdo each other in their baths. **Daiichi** boasts biggest bath hall (it can't be called 'room'): **Grand** biggest single 'tub'. Daiichi has 16 tubs and pools of various sizes, shapes and temperatures; Grand has several pools of varying degrees of privacy, but their main is gigantic *coeducational* 'Roman' vat which it is hard to see across for steam and size. Each have dance hall, bar, shopping arcade, you name it.

If staying at less-expensive places, you can still experience their baths for small fee, usually ¥500. **Grand** ☎(0143)-84-2101, just across river from main bus terminal; whence 300m to Jigoku-dani **Daiichi Takimoto-kan** ☎84-2111, both ¥-hi-Tw/2. Some cheaper inns in village: minshuku **Kikusui** ☎84-2437, **Noboribetsu-so** ☎84-3352. 4 Youth Hostel: **Noboribetsu Kannon-ji** ☎84-2359 E of Yuzawa Jinja; **Akashiya-so** ☎84-2616 bit S of bus terminal; **Ryokan Kinfuku** ☎84-2565 500m S; **Ryokan Noboribetsu Ekimae** ☎83-1039 at stn. *See also* SHIRAOI, *below*.

To E is...
Mt Shihorei, 549m, at top of which is **Bear Farm**. Hokkaido Brown Bear nearing extinction with 1985 census down to 1,900, of which 10%, 180 here; with 330 born annually but 350 hunted (uncontrolled) for annual net loss of 20-30. Larger than Honshu species, may attack man when riled.

Also atop mt is...
Yukara-no-Sato reconstructed Ainu houses of early Meiji era, under one thatch-roof exhibit Ainu folkcrafts made of miscanthus reed, other displays *Yukara* Ainu fabrics, 3rd has tools used in day-to-day life.

Twice daily May thru Oct (more often if groups show up) at Bear Farm you can see Iyomanté *Ainu Bear Festival*. Tho not as lively as real Iyomanté, this well-staged version is worth it, particularly since real one is hard to see, set at different locations thru year. Open 6:00-20:10 June-Aug (times vary rest of year), ¥2,100 *kyotsu-ken* combi-ticket includes round-trip on ropeway, Bear Farm and Yukara-no-Sato. Pilgrims can save: hike up 1.2km path parallel to ropeway, continuing down other side of mt 1.5km to lake **Kuttara-ko** with camping, boating, swimming and fishing. Kuttara-ko can also be reached by 5km scenic road which loops N from onsen area.

NITELIFE: Consists of several 'live-houses' and mini discos along main streets. But if looking for something more Japanese, head into side alleys for cheap robatayaki joints which we find more enjoyable. Older locals head to these, extremely hospitable. Usually quite lively, streets really jump **last weekend Aug** for *Jigoku Matsuri* (Hell Festival), starting friday evening visitors and locals alike don red or green demon masks and dance thru streets accompanied by eerie, fast-paced drum and flute music.

SHOPPING: Streets of Noboribetsu lined with usual gift stores mostly selling Ainu wood carvings and fabrics. Carvers work outside several Ainu-run stores, some have 'good-luck' live bear cubs caged or on leashes out front. Also good selection of hand-woven elm-fiber and mass-produced cotton print happi. If you came up to Hokkaido thru Tohoku you couldn't have missed *kokeshi* carved dolls. Noboribetsu has its own *kokeshi*, made & sold at **Ezochi Mingu Komatsu** oldest store in area: from ¥800.

Before heading on, word on shopping: Japanese friend bought some 'authentic' souvenirs bought on U.S. Indian reservation, labeled 'Made in Japan'. In Tehran turquoise bazaar 1976 we found silversmiths making Navajo designs, ordered by New Mexico tribal reservation! Ainu of old imported most of their trinkets and consumer goods; but crafts Ainu offer tourists today are genuine Ainu-made. Non-Ainu shops peddle Taiwan-made. Carved bears, bark-cloth novelties are modern Ainu specialties.

Carved bears never had any place in old Ainu culture, but wood carving has always been Ainu tradition and bear main object of veneration. Thus wedding of craft and ritual subject resulted in legitimate offspring: handsome and life-like wooden bears of Hokkaido curio counters. Carving no longer limited to bears, and everything from practical items, plates, cups, eating utensils to all sorts of decorations are made. Noboribetsu offers best carvers on inner circle route. Most carvers here are 2nd or 3rd generation with great pride in their work. Their carving is done on spot and you can commission any special carvings—rest assured they will send as promised.

Shiraoi (*below*) has good selection of usual carvings but stores there are merely outlets for carvers thruout Hokkaido, so it's more difficult to find top work. On outer circle route fine carvers can be found at Asahikawa's Chikabumi Ainu village and Akan-ko village. Setup similar to Noboribetsu, can also commission work from these artists.

AINU TEXTILES:

True and distinctive Ainu art is textile design, doomed to extinction until recently discovered that others beside Ainu appreciate it, and that applied to accessories rather than costume it fills practical as well as aesthetic use. Ainu costumes can still be bought—but truly authentic complete couture start from ¥100,000, tho new made-for-tourist outfits can be pieced together for about ¥28,000 for lady's full-length kimono-like robe, narrow obi, leggings, happi-coat, head-band or hat. (Men's robe is calf-length). Full length robe with leggings harder to come by. Two stores at Shiraoi always carry them; sometimes found at Chikabumi or Akan-ko. At Akan they will search out your requirements and send on when available; pay in advance, absolutely reliable.

No one knows how long Ainu have been weaving. Chinese records tell of Ainu 2,000 years ago before they mention Yamato-Wa-Japanese. China's annals first century AD record that Wa, Mongoloid Japanese, had hemp and silk mulberry, knew weaving and made rough cloth. Ainu and Wa lived in close proximity on Honshu. If so, we can assume Ainu have been weaving as long as Wa. Ainu *attush* (Aleutian Isle name) cloth woven from inner fiber of elm. Ainu woman never repeats pattern, thus any duplication of pattern is accidental. Basic design element is 'parenthesis', thus '}'and '{}'; and subsidiary element is spiral or whorl. These are blended in minor variations and combinations on basic ground in patterns so complex that they allow almost infinite permutations and combinations of these elements. Dyed in natural vegetable restrained pastels of which one never tires.

Cloth is almost as coarse as burlap, stiff. It is not practical for modern use and was being edged out by superior and cheaper modern textiles. Recent research however has shown how to make it finer. Sometimes fiber is combined with strand of modern fiber for strengthening, or warp may be another fiber other than elm. Result is distinctive textile which makes up into excellent men's ties and shirts. Pure elm is somewhat stiff and makes ideal purses and wallets. Weaving techniques are unchanged and patterns are traditional, merely scaled down to fit smaller objects.

30km up coast from Noboribetsu on Muroran Main Line or Rte36 is Shiraoi stn, 400m E of which on Rte36, road branches L passing under unattractive front 'gate'.

SHIRAOI: Main Ainu tourist *kotan*, or village, once largest Ainu community, declined into small hamlet till revived by postwar tourist boom. Tourism has again made Shiraoi prosperous, but it has also come to dominate villagers' lives so that place lacks any soul. Nor has it any sense of community like Akan's village, only atmosphere of novelty show.

Shiraoi has truly prospered off tourist trade. On our first visit in 1959 it was just small corral; at Garet's first visit here 1974 simple wood fence enclosed village and dirt parking lot served cluster of quaint, individual wooden shops. Now even villages beyond stores have more authentic rustic air about them.

Across large parking lot is large modern building with permanent stores. Once past gauntlet of almost identical shops small turnstile lets you in to reconstructed village.

At entrance 16m statue is of...

Kotankolkul, guardian deity of this *kotan*. Carving center and several houses exhibit Ainu treasures (usually early Tokugawa lacquerware), weapons, hunting, fishing and herb-gathering tools, other day-to-day items. Hourly or so, village chief explains background of these, then traditional Ainu dance, songs. Several times daily ceremonial dances outside in compound center. Dance authentic, but dancers (especially younger ones) seem apathetic. Alas, Shiraoi is sole inner circle spot to offer dances. Outer circle CHIKABUMI (p.1087) & AKAN (p.1115) have more pleasantly energetic dances. 8:00-17:00 May-Oct; 8:30-16:30 Nov-Apr; ¥510.

But we don't say one should pass up Shiraoi. It still offers good glimpse of Ainu culture; fine, small **Folk History Museum**, *Minzoku Shiryokan* alone makes visit well worth it. One of best-done exhibits on Ainu life using authentic items, panoramic scenes and photos. Notably, has good English pamphlet on all items shown, recounts Ainu history, ¥400.

PERSONAL DATEBOOK: Best time to visit Shiraoi is last weekend **Jul**, *Dosanko Matsuri*, when *kotan* area celebrate old *Ainu festival*–with added Japanese festival touches. Ceremonial fire offered to Ainu Fire Goddess Kamui-fuchi (from whom onceflaming Mt Fuji gets name); *Iyomante Bear Festival* performed as well as Ainu *Dosanko Odori* folk dance. For two days fete really adds spice to place. Another smaller festival is *Yu Matsuri* held early **Feb** (dates vary, but usually first or 2nd weekend). If you think February is cold time to be watching unclothed festival imagine how participants feel: youths clad in nothing but skimpy loin-cloths run around in snow 'purifying' each other with buckets of water, typical of Japanese Hadaka Matsuri 'naked' festival common thruout country.

200m W of parking lot on road past skating rink lie...

Remains of non-Ainu history nearby: **Sendai clan mansion** in Shiraoi. Stone markers next to it are graves of clan samurai; was branch family of powerful Daté clan from Tohoku's Sendai area. Defeated in post-Restoration Boshin Wars, clans given option of remaining in home territory (with loss of status), or colonizing newly-opened Hokkaido. Daté branch families chose latter, settling around Cape Muroran between Toya–Shiraoi. Main town established in area dedicated to clan, named Daté-Mombetsu.

SHOPPING: Interesting **antique** store to browse on Rte36 across from entrance to village. Besides usual knick-knacks, has some Ainu items, Daté memorabilia.

WHERE TO STAY: Noboribetsu or Shikotsu were long-recommended until recent discovery of onsen wells nr stn, leading to new hotels and minshukus along beach. Best is **Hotel Izumi**, ¥-hi-T-lo-Sw//2, ☎(0144)-87-2621, Kojo-hama 321, is closer to Noboribetsu along beach overloooking Ocean. More convenient to Ainu village opp (W) at lake bottom end is **Hotel Poroto**, Wakakusa-machi 2-2 ¥-Tw//2, ☎(0144)-82-2165. **Shiraoi Onsen Hotel** ☎85-2725, E of Shiraoi stn ¥-T (J-); next door **YH** ☎82-2302. Several minshuku near stn: **Izumiya**, Shadai 284, ☎82-2428; **Ogita** ☎82-2330; & **Kuretaka** ☎87-2333 heads association of 15 minshuku, can book any if need. **Campground** N end of lake in woods. **Golf** at Shiraoi CC, arrange thru hotel.

Due N of SHIRAOI half hour drive (no bus as of '91)...

GREAT WATERFALLS discovered only in late '80s, '90; within 2 km radius of MORINO are 15, all gorgeous, range from spectacular Oboshisawa 100m tall, to most recently-found Miebashi-no-taki at 12m. Reach only by car or taxi, then walk 30-60min. Many more in wider area, great hiking; 10km drive E of Morino then 25min walk is best (one of 5 most beautiful in country) 50m-tall Inkura-no-taki: E-info at SHIRAOI **city office** ☎82-2216 Ms GOTO Miyuki, who can make arrangements for you, provide maps, intro to discovery group under Mr SATO Masanori, also of City Office.

Several km N...

SHIKOTSU-KO: 40km around by 360m deep this volcanic caldera lake
is second deepest in Japan, next to Akita's Tazawa-ko.

GETTING THERE: **Bus**: SHIRAOI 30min to Tomakomai Terminal, change
to SHIKOTSU bus, 45min. **Train** to TOMAKOMAI and 3min walk to bus terminal, as
above. **Drive**: Rte36 to Tomakomai, whence Rte276 to Shikotsu.

WHERE TO STAY: 4 ryo-tels here, best is **Kanko Hotel** ☎(0123)-25-2211.
Cheaper: **People's Rest Village**, *Kokumin Kyuka Mura* ☎25-2201; and Gov't-run
Friendship Center–both in woods on lake S of Shikotsu bus stn. Minshuku nr kotan.

Main Ainu village, **SHIKOTSU-KOTAN** E end of lake also has newest
of 3 onsen here. Village is old, but hot spring waters not tapped till 1974.

Tho roads lead around lake to other two older onsen, boats also available...

MARUKOMA ONSEN N shore is oldest at lake, tapped 1915. Quieter than
kotan, has *outdoor bath*. 15min bus from Shikotsu-kotan to Eniwa Tozanguchi stop
& 10min walk, or 25min boat. 3 ryokan, best **Marukoma Onsen Ryokan** ☎25-2341

4km SW of Narukoma is...

OKOTAN ONSEN: Small onsen in woods had moment of glory when some
downhill events were held on Eniwa-daké during 1972 Winter Olympics.
Only reachable by lake boat, 45min from Shikotsu-kotan or 20min from Marukoma.
Sole lodgings here are **Grand Hotel**, new annex, ☎25-2636.

In Ainu lore god Kotankara-kamui in shaping Hokkaido dug this lake to
keep all his fish in one place. Even gods goof, he dug too deep, connecting
with ocean (says tale, water is fresh tho it never freezes). Fish escaped into
sea except for species of trout–still sole fish here. Fishing for delicious trout
is main recreation; smaller ryokan, minshuku will prepare catch for dinner.

PERSONAL DATEBOOK: **Early Dec thru New Year**, *White Illumination*
in Sapporo Plaza. **Feb 5-11** *Yuki Matsuri* (Snow Fest), gigantic snow sculptures &
architecture, Sapporo. **May (late)** *Lilac Fete*, O-dori Park, Sapporo. **June 14-17**
Hokkaido Jingu shrine *Festival* mikoshi & costume parade, Miyagaoka. **July last Mon**
for 4 wks, *Summer Fete*, Sapporo. **Aug first weekend** 1,000 *kappa*-masked dancers in
streets of Jozankei. **Mid-**, *Bon Dances*, everywhere, especially O-dori Park—horrid pun:
odori in o-dori park.

People from old Honshu think we're naive,
we believe we're just more open-minded
—Hokkaido miss in *FE Economic Review*

ASAHIKAWA 旭川
'HUB' OF HOKKAIDO

'HUB' OF HOKKAIDO is centrally located Asahikawa. Modern city of 360,000 set in middle of Kamikawa basin where quartet of major rivers—Chubetsu, Ishikari, Biei, Ushubets—converge, making area ideal for agriculture and bountiful in fish. Ainu settled along river bank thousands of years ago and still retain small colony at Chikabumi, with their sacred offering grounds 15km downstream. With post-Restoration influx of Wa-Japanese, Asahikawa's location made it only natural, first as HQ for Tondenhei contingent and eventually army camp (still SDF force here), to become outer Hokkaido's political, economical, cultural and transportation center second only to Sapporo. Despite this, Asahikawa is small, clean, wears its modernity with reluctance. Behind new stores and bright lights lies quiet rustic town; beyond center area city looks frontier-like, as whole did generation ago on our first visit, rugged and weathered. Summer is refreshing, winter bitterly cold as moist winds from Siberia sweep in to be blocked in by Daisetsuzan mountains east of city.

GETTING THERE: By train, ASAHIKAWA is 2hrs from SAPPORO, 4hrs from WAKKANAI, 4hr40m ABASHIRI → and 3hr OBIHIRO →. By **air** 2hr TOKYO →, under 40min ↔ any other city on HOKKAIDO. Rte12 from SAPPORO, Rte40 N, 39 E, 40 to 38 S are all fine roads. For outdoor types, Asahikawa ideal base to explore natural wonder **Daisetsuzan National Park** by foot, bus or rent-a-car. Tho part of our OUTER CIRCLE Asahikawa can be done overnite from Sapporo—well worth trip out.

From stn, 15min bus (#24), or cab 1.5x-mtr to our first stop...
CHIKABUMI 'where birds live', Asahikawa's prime attraction is this Ainu community in NW outskirts of town. Roughly 2,000 Ainu still live here, tho most are at least half mongoloid Japanese by blood.

Our first stop is...
KAWAMURA AINU VILLAGE, *Kawamura Ainu Kinenkan*, Hokkaido's first organized display of Ainu culture, 7th generation Ainu chieftain KAWAMURA Kaneto used his own money to set up this village in late 1920s, peak of Japanese interest in Ainu culture. By this time Ainu way of life was changing drastically, anthropologists were busy recording what remained. Most Ainu collections and photos date to this time. Present village chief is Kaneto's son Kenichi (Wa-name but full-Ainu), who when not working at village operates his **jazz coffee-shop** at bus stop. Compound of stores, reconstructed Ainu houses, museum and stage worked entirely by Kawamura clan; except for packaged machine-made happi, goods sold here all made by local Ainu, mostly by Kawamuras. Full traditional costumes lent here for photos, no charge. Kaneto's museum, which he stocked himself, covers all aspects of Ainu life; also lists of Ainu words with Japanese meanings. On stage next door, several short dances and songs performed for groups of 10 or more calling ahead ☎(0166)-51-2461.

If not in group, wait till daily tour comes at 14:30 and follow them. Store owners are helpful, let you know if tour coming. We followed group of SDF cadets, good responsive audience made performances even better.

Tho performances here similar to Shiraoi's, repertoire is greater, more variations for performers to choose from. Also each dance and instrument is explained—in Japanese, alas. Most interesting is *mukkul*, wood Jews' Harp-like instrument. Originally portable instrument for hunters, later used only by women for tribal rites. With assimilation into Japanese society *mukkul* was becoming obsolete until revived by tourism. Now hand-mass-made and found at almost any store with Ainu goods.

West 2km is...

Chikabumi Ainu Cemetery, *Chikabumi Ainu Bochi*, ancestral burial ground. Grave markers are simple wood posts devoid of names, sole differences are rounded tip on female marker, pointed on male.

2km SW of cemetery, **Bus** #3 or #4 from stn (also catch at Kitamon 15-chome stop 500m W on road from Kawamura) to Chikabumi 25-chome stop. Cemetery 20min walk N, Arashiyama 15min S. **Cab** Kawamura via cemetery → Arashiyama 2x-mtr.

Arashiyama Koen park, several km/sq of thick woods; view from hilltop of nearby Daisetsuzan mts. At base is Ainu Cultural Forest, *Ainu Bunka no mori* reconstructed Ainu village. Unlike Kawamura complex this was built later with municipal financing. Several traditional Ainu *chise* (bamboo houses) are set up, showing various arts and crafts—embroidery, carving, basketry—performing ceremonial dances. Wood long-house exhibits hunting and fishing paraphernalia, one of few with original hollowed log boats. Naturally, staffed only by local Ainu; best over-all representation of Ainu culture. No fee, 9:30-16:30; X-mon, hols.

Tho more Ainu artifacts can be seen at municipal museum, there is one more actual site to visit—sacred ceremonial grounds of *Kamui-kotan*, 'gods' living place', downstream of Asahikawa. Only way there is by **cab** or 30min bus from stn, or bicycle. On Ishikari river north bank, was used to offer thanks to river gods and pray for bountiful fish, safe passage on rivers and to mountain gods for good hunting. Mountain south of Kamui-kotan is called Kamui-zan, Japanized Ainu for 'mountain of gods'. Not that this particular mountain was special, just near, thus representative of all mountains. During much of year it is just another scenic spot, but early October (usually around 10th) it hosts major Ainu festival *Kamui Matsuri*. Traditional age-old offerings to gods; dances, songs performed, including elusive *Iyomante bear rite*. Truly non-tourist Ainu event. This is still serious affair, they couldn't care less if they have outside audience or not, but appreciative audience is welcome.

Cycling road runs 19km from Asahi Nishi-bashi bridge at W end downtown to Shino-bashi bridge 3.5km beyond Kamui-kotan, along old abandoned section Hakodate RR thru tunnels and stns with no rails. **Bicycles** are loaned free May-Oct at **City Gymn**, *Shiritsu Taiku-kan*, Tokiwa Koen 1.5km N of stn. Full day, easily cover all city sights.

N end of town, 20min bus #5 or #6 from stn; 2x-mtr cab is...

Municipal Museum, *Asahikawa Kyodo Hakubutsu-kan* in two-storey W-style building built 1902 as Officer Training School for Imperial Army. Displays relate to Hokkaido history, mostly Ainu and Tondenhei marshals stationed in nearby Toma beginning modern age. Daily 9:30-16:30, X-mons, hols; token fee used for restoration.

If interested in *Tondenhei*, several restored barracks in **Toma** 10km NE; 20min train (5 stops) Sekiboku Main Line for Abashiri. Barracks scattered round town center. 25min bus from Toma stn gets you to **Toma stalactite caverns**, ¥300, X-winter.

Last must-see in town (6km W on Rte12) is...

Yuukara Weaving Center, *Yuukara-ori Kogei-kan*. Palatial North European building houses workshop-museum, center of Yuukara weaving found thruout, and unique to, Hokkaido. Wool weave uses natural dyes from island's many flowers and trees, developed over 100 years ago by Kazuhiro family from Honshu, has become Hokkaido's main souvenir, if

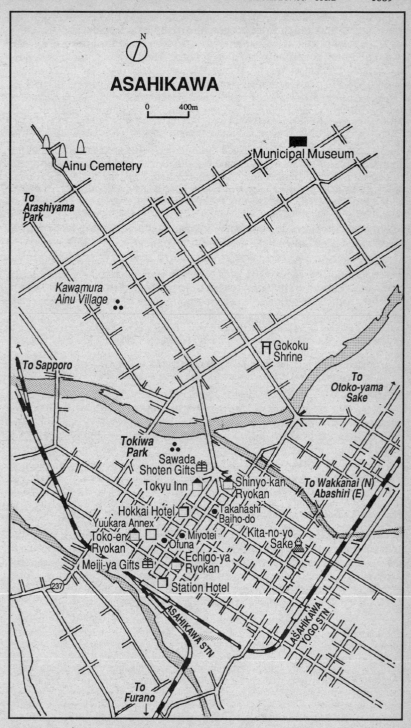

N

ASAHIKAWA

0   400m

Ainu Cemetery

Municipal Museum

To Arashiyama Park

Kawamura Ainu Village

To Sapporo

Gokoku Shrine

To Otoko-yama Sake

Tokiwa Park

Sawada Shoten Gifts

Tokyu Inn

Shinyo-kan Ryokan

To Wakkanai (N) Abashiri (E)

Hokkai Hotel

Takahashi Baiho-do

Yuukara Annex

Toko-en Ryokan

Miyotei

Ofuna

Kita-no-yo Sake

Meiji-ya Gifts

Echigo-ya Ryokan

Station Hotel

237

ASAHIKAWA STN

ASAHIKAWA YOGO STN

To Furano

expensive, high-class gift, surpassing now harder-to-find Ainu traditional weaving. Colors range from grey, white, deep blue (representing winters here) to brilliant greens, reds, yellows (represent springtime burst of color). Fashioned into almost anything: bags, purses, ties, wallets, kimono, vests, placemats. Prices high: from ¥1,200 purses, wallets; ¥2,500 ties; vests, other garments over ¥20,000; ¥100,000 for larger masterpieces. Best prices and selection at CENTER, or ANNEX in town, altho Yuukara sold almost everywhere. Not only is weaving representative of Hokkaido's natural beauty, three-floor museum itself represents island, built solely of local material: brick and tile from Hokkaido soil, each room different indigenous wood, white walls represent island's most common sight—snow. Each room covers different subject, style or theme; workshops show all phases from wool-spinning and dying to weaving, with fine final products available here. Easiest, cheapest way here is via Annex in town whence hourly **free bus** shuttles to main store: **Annex Yuukara-ori Kogei-bunkan** 1km NW of stn is showroom/store.

Next door is...

Dyeing-art Museum housing superb world textile collection of UEMURA Rokura, late prexy of Kyoto's prestigious art college.

With pure mountain water from snowy Daisetsuzan and abundant rice (best in island) Asahikawa is **sake capital** of Hokkaido. Of eight stills here, best known nationally (exports to US) is **Otoko-yama**: small museum of distilling tools, drinking paraphernalia of late Edo period. N of town 15min bus stn → Nagayama Nijo Roku-chome lets off nr distillery. **City bus-tours** go here: SHINAI course: dep stn 13:00 → Heison Kinenkan → Otoko-yama distillery → Municipal Museum → Ainu Kinenkan → Yuukara Weaving Center → hilltop Kannon → Mihonrin, Forest of trees of the world → stn 17:25; runs 6/10-9/10, ¥2,350/adult, ¥1,230/kid: by **Asahikawa Denki Kido** ☎(0166)-32-2161.

No set **taxi tours**, but can be easily arranged thru taxi stand at stn. **Half-day tour** of all major sites done at basic hourly rate of 7x-mtr.

SHOPPING: Island's second largest commercial center, Asahikawa has anything you may want to buy concentrated in one area. Easiest place to shop is Heiwa-dori street running N from stn, shoppers' paradise, 1km of shops lining narrow park. Several good gift-shops but best buy Yuukara at **Center**, Ainu goods **Kawamura**, tho **Meiji-ya** L-side first block has big selection of Ainu-pattern happi. Others sell local folkcrafts. **Takahashi Baiho-do**, R-side Heiwa-dori 6 blocks past Meiji-ya, top-rated items incl pottery of 10 local kilns. **Tomiya Sawada Shoten** end of Heiwa-dori W-side of rotary, folkcrafts from every corner of Hokkaido, local ceramics, Yuukara and somewhat similar *Atsushi-ori* weaving.

CHOPSTICKS: And with good trade comes good food: fish from its rivers and north sea, crab from Oshamambe; beef, pork, venison, bear, boar and fowl from nearby farms and mountains; all served with best rice, vegetables, mountain herbs. Local specialties in two categories: seafood and (most often) meat, tho true Asahikawa dishes rely heavily on pork. Heiwa-dori area is also center for eating establishments; Sanjo-dori (3rd main E-W street from stn) known as '**Neon Alley**', *Neon-gai*, is heart of city's nite-life. W-end Neon-gai has more of cheaper local *izakaya* and robatayaki places: **Ofuna** 2 blocks from Heiwa-dori on Sanjo is especially popular with visitors—owner Baba-san worked at City Tourist Bureau until 1973 when he opened, knows just about anything about city. He gave us lots of help when hitching thru Hokkaido in '79. Next door **Hanamarutei**, excellent local seafood specialties. **Bateren-chaya**, one shop down is another robata-yaki which gets fresh, pure saké from Kita-no-yo saké company. Kita-no-yo has old *kura* (storehouse) distillery 2km E at Rokujo 15-chome. Gorge yourself on Genghis Khan barbeque at **Miyote** on Heiwa-dori and Sanjo. Next door **Kabuto** for local meat dishes.

WHERE TO STAY: No shortage of lodgings in town either. Best hotel is **New Hokkai** ☎(0166)-24-3111, corner of Rokujo and Showa-dori (one block W of Heiwa-do); singles from ¥-hi-B+. **New Tokyu Inn** ☎26-0109 at N end of Showa-dori has heated pool and athletic facilities, singles ¥-B+. **Station Hotel** ☎23-9288, singles ¥-P+; business hotels near stn from ¥3,500. Better traditional ryokan relatively cheap, room w/2 from ¥6,500: **Seiseikan** ☎22-1488, 3min walk N of stn and **Echigoya** ☎23-2237, one block E and two N of stn. With over 50 inns and hotels to choose from, you should have no problem matching your wallet. **Joguji**, quiet, rustic temple, 20min bus from stn, ¥2,-3,000 w/2, 1 Kamui Ichijo,☎61-6134. All can be easily booked thru **Stn Information Center**, far L corner from wickets. **Campers** set up in **Kaguraoka Park**, 1.5km SE of stn along S bank of Chubetsu River, with simple, beautiful Kamikawa Jinja in N end of park.

PERSONAL DATEBOOK: *Kotan Matsuri (above)* most interesting; 2 other big festivals here: *Fuyu Matsuri*, Winter Festival is held same time as Sapporo Snow Festival but is similar, only 150-odd snow and ice sculptures on Heiwa-dori and in Tokiwa Park 1.5km N of stn. Tho festival itself lasts only 5 days, entire town spends over month preparing. *Natsu Matsuri* Summer Festival **early Aug** sees over 100 homemade boats float down Ishikari River, later to engage in 'combat'.

Now we head further E to Abashiri passing thru spectacular Daisetsuzan Mountains, countless backwoods hot springs. If you don't have time to head out that way but are in search of onsen, there's small one 50min train N of Asahikawa at Shiokari on Soya Main Line: **Shiokari Onsen** found by grazing cows early this century. Changed little since, single inn draws from spring. Also onsen Youth Hostel.

OUTER CIRCLE NORTH SPOKE WAKKANAI
FROM HERE ON is strictly for **hardy adventurer** with loads of time. Central Asahikawa is major cross-road, where one heads north to Wakkanai and west to Abashiri, or south to Obihiro. We take north first, continuing clock-wise around Hokkaido's hinterland.

North 'spoke' of Hokkaido called *Dohoku*, or Northern Region, offers little for tourist except scenery: small hot springs up middle, good beaches on W coast. But main 'attractions' are offshore islands and Japan's north-ernmost city Wakkanai—whose main redeeming quality when not snowed-in is its locale. Upper half of peninsula is **Rishiri-Rebun-Sarobetsu National Park**, which encompasses Rishiri and Rebun Islands, Sarobetsu-genya Primeval Marsh.

GETTING THERE: Short of flying, quickest to WAKKANAI from SAPPORO is about 8hr JR express via ASAHIKAWA up spine on Soya Main Line. Up Japan Sea Coast: FUKAGAWA 1hr25min from Sapporo change to Rumoi Main Line then bus from Rumoi. **Drivers** take Rte12 to ASAHIKAWA, then Rte40 N; or coastal Rte231 from SAPPORO. Halfway at RUMOI (where JR hits coast) Rte231 becomes Rte232, joining Rte40 at HORONOBE for last 60km to WAKKANAI. **Hitchhikers** make better time via ASAHIKAWA on central route. **Steamer** departs every other day from OTARU → RISHIRI (9hr30min) and REBUN (10+hr).

JAL has 5-day tour to north: **1st day** TOKYO → CHITOSE → SAPPORO overnight; **2nd day** → WAKKANAI by train overnight; **3rd day** → REBUN ISLE → RISHIRI ISLE overnight; **4th day** → WAKKANAI → SOYA PENINSULA → LAKE SAROMA overnight; **5th day** → ABASHIRI → SAPPORO → CHITOSE. Runs even numbered days 6/13-7/31, 9/1-17; odd numbered days 8/2-30, from ¥102,600.

RUMOI small but modern thriving fishing town with good swimming at Kogane-misaki, rocky point said 'most scenic in Hokkaido' (decided probably by same people who chose Amanohashidate in top 3).

From here JR Rumoi Line heads S 35km to end...

MASHIKE from where 1hr15min steamer or 50min bus down coast to **OFUYU**. Quiet fishing village's attraction is good beach. Daily steamer (¥1,180) hugs Ofuyu Kaigan coastline, 26km of sheer cliffs punctuated by occasional waterfalls cascading into sea. 3x-daily buses start RUMOI, 40min (¥400) → MASHIKE, 50min more (¥1,340) → OFUYU. Direct from SAPPORO 2hr45min bus (4x-daily) → RUMOI. OFUYU has 2 budget ryokan, ll minshuku—most operate summer only.

If **Island-crazy** take coastal route (JR Haboro Line or road) RUMOI → HABORO and boat → Yagishiri and Teuri islands.

Between two towns is...

ONISHIKA ONSEN, nr which **Nishin Banya** herring fishery watch-tower. No problem pulling into Haboro too late for boat; many budget ryokan in town, minshuku **Jinya** 100m down from stn. Pier for steamer to isles is 15min walk from stn; 5min by bus in July–Aug only. Nothing special on either isle other than primitive scenery and quiet living; Yagishiri more so than Teuri. Haboro 3hr train from Fukagawa via Rumoi; 75min (¥1,170) boat to Yagishiri, 20min further (¥1,710) to Teuri, ¥520 between isles. Steamers vary seasonally: dep HABORO May 2x-daily abt 8:00 and 13:00; Jun–Aug 3x-daily am, one early pm; Extras 7/20-8/15 early am: HABORO → TEURI direct 80min; TEURI → YAGISHIRI → HABORO usual 100min; Sept abt same as May; Oct–Apr once daily abt 9:00. Returns TEURI → YAGISHIRI → HABORO on turn-arounds abt 15min later. Purchase tickets at **Ryoto Unyu** company.

YAGISHIRI-TO: More secluded of pair, much of 12km circumference is wooded natural park criss-crossed by streams, dotted with occasional ponds. Narrow road circles it; **rent bicycles** at steamer terminal, ¥600/2hr which is about how long one round takes. Hills on old bikes take time pushing; you can walk it in 3hrs. Path cuts lengthwise across isle, at western end of which you may come across flock of sheep, raised for wool. S shore Shirahama beach fine swimming, **campsite**: 40min walk from port. 10 ¥-B minshuku at **Yagishiri** village. 2 more at **Nishiura** village N shore, beaches. Both isles abound in shrimp, sea urchin, abalone, other shell-fish, sold at stalls along beach; inns serve these delicacies for dinner.

TEURI-TO: Roughly same size and only 4km W of Yagishiri, Teuri is more barren—less trees and fresh water tho higher elevation, yet attracts more visitors (still not many). N shore lined with sheer cliffs and rock, great formations of screeching sea-birds. Few times every day, **sightseeing boat** circles island to view these rocks, stopping at four villages on E shore. ¥760/80min, no set schedule—leaves when full or boatman feels like. Here, too, road circles island but unlike Yagishiri, Teuri has motorized vehicles—2 **cabs**. 17 ryokan from ¥-Bw/2 and 10 minshuku from ¥-Pw/2 mostly Teuri village; best **Ryokan Aoi Tori** with fabulous dinners—owner runs restaurant downstairs famous for *hama-nabe*, sea-food platter done sukiyaki style. Interesting place to stay is minshuku-style **Nishin-banya YH**, ☎(01648)-35158, 2.5km from village on S shore. Built over 80 years ago, once home of prosperous local herring fisher. House parent Obachan Ikeda grew up here during its heyday and will entertain during meals with stories of 'good ole days'. Few hundred meters down road from her hostel is Kurosaki beach with **campsite**. Water around Teuri, especially N shore, is clearest in all of Japan Sea.

Back on mainland 100km upcoast from Haboro, rejoin main inland route at Horonobe, 20km beyond which is...

TOYOTOMI ONSEN: 6km E of Toyotomi stn (15min bus) and Rte40. Once Japan's northernmost hot spring, this sleepy village lost that distinction when in 1978 fissure spouted hot water in Wakkanai. Toyotomi was 'discovered' in early 1930's while searching for now-depleted oil, yet water is not oily. Dozen ryokan ¥-B+w/2, few minshuku and town-run **New Hotel Sarobetsu** ☎(0162)-82-1211, ¥-Tw/2. 6km N is Japan's largest dairy farm with over 3,500 head of cattle on 14km^2; small by U.S. standards, but something Japanese like to say 'only in Hokkaido' to. **Rest House** there serves steak, fresh milk from ranch.

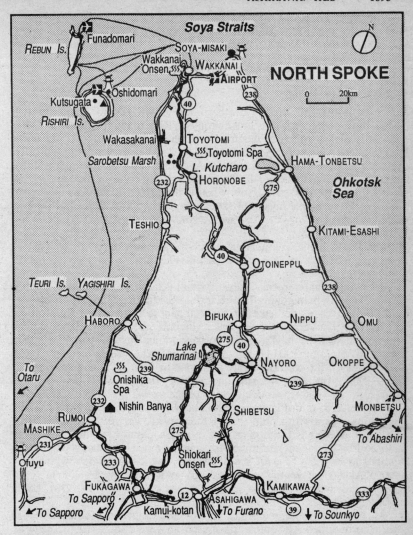

W of Soya Main Line and Rte40 is 230km² ...

SAROBETSU-GENYA marsh where over 100 different species of wild flowers bloom in July. Stretches almost 40km between Horonobe and Kabuto-numa stns; any of six local stops inbetween serve marsh, but Toyotomi is best. Beyond this sea of color volcanic Mt Rishiri-Fuji floats out of sea.

Bordering marsh on W (in Toyotomi area) is ...

Wakasakanai Kaigan coast where you can **camp** and fish. Once bare expanse of sand dunes, it now is bordered by line of 108 ponds with ancient pine and oak around them. One particularly massive pine is over 1,200 years old. 25min bus from Toyotomi cuts across Sarobetsu marsh (with 1 stop) to Wakasakanai. Buses infrequent; rent bikes at **TOYOTOMI** ¥300/hour. Most buses start at TOYOTOMI stn heading to onsen or Sarobetsu, also two round-trips daily to each from WAKKANAI stn (leaving from Soya bus terminal): Stn to hot spring (15min) deps 7:35, 8:40, 9:25, 12:09, 14:50, 15:50, 18:04 (12:09 and 18:04 originate Wakanai 11:15 and

17:10 respectively). Returns leave hot spring 7:56, 9:12, 9:51, 12:28, 15:17, 16:11, 18:31 (9:12 and 15:17 end Wakkanai 10:19 and 16:24 resp). Stn to Wakasakanai departs 6:30, 8:35, 10:30, 12:10, 14:53, 15:05, 17:00 (6:30 and 10:30 June thru Sept only). Returns dep Wakasakanai 7:00, 9:00, 10:58, 12:40, 15:16, 17:25 (7:00 and 10:58 June thru Sept only). Both courses operate all year, but 2 fewer runs each in winter, 11/1-5/31.

WAKKANAI 稚内

DISTINGUISHED AS Japan's northernmost town, yet not major tourist mecca, most people just pass thru en route to Rishiri and Rebun isles—still, tourism is major source of income close behind its thriving fishing fleet. Best in early August for South Pole Festival—they're not geographically dyslectic: commemorates Japan's 1st Antarctic expedition which trained here. Banner-draped ships fill harbor and equally colorful food and game stalls fill streets. Port also lively when fishing fleets head out with much fanfare. JR **express** 6hr from SAPPORO, 4hr from ASAHIKAWA, WAKKANAI also reached by hour **plane** from CHITOSE and SAPPORO; **airport** is 25min bus from town.

Main attraction is its...
Hilltop Park. 20min walk from stn, short cablecar shaves 10min off uphill climb. Down main road from stn, R one block past Rte40 to ropeway; *keep on this road if walking up...*

Park is full of monuments—town symbol is large, white statue of pair of prongs flanking man gazing N to Karafuto/Sakhalin island: *Hyosetsu-no-mon*, 'Frozen Gate', dedicated to those Japanese stranded on Karafuto at end of WWII, overrun by Soviets. Unclaimed 'no-man's land', Japan gained control 1905 by Treaty of Portsmouth as Russo-Japan War spoil; populated solely by 300,000 Japanese by 1945 when 'reclaimed', renamed Sakhalin by USSR who say treaty as signed by Tzar is invalid so island is theirs. Major obstacle to formal peace treaty to end WWII between two nations, tho in 1956 it was declared that state of war no longer existed and USSR offered to return Habomai-Shikotan (*see*). On clear day you can see mountains where Ainu used to 'dry their meat', *karafuto*, till moved to Hokkaido. Abounds in good fishing in rivers, natural resources and was main source of Japanese lumber for paper pulp. Now boasts airfields, missile silos as main base for Soviet Far East Tactical Air Force, which shot down KAL 007. Ferry to Soviet Sakhalin port of **KHOLMSK** 180km, from Spring '89, non-sched, 6-8hrs abt ¥98,000r.t. Check Taimus Kanko ☎(011)-241-2381, USSR consulate Sapporo.

Nearby marker commemorates visit by late Emperor; another honors 9 girls who operated Karafuto's transmitter at war's end. Last message as Red Army approached engraved on rock: 'This is end, good-bye everyone, good-bye...' Pagoda, statue nearby dedicated to team of Karafuto huskies trained here for Antarctic expedition and abandoned at Pole: story made all-time money making Japanese cinematic tear-jerker '83. Tower marks centennial of Hokkaido's 'statehood', with small museum inside, viewing platform on top. Memorial to victims of '83 downing of Korean Air 747.

Wakkanai and its park are halfway up Noshappu-misaki peninsula, at which tip is aquarium and science exhibit hall. Also two small museums: **Herring Museum**, *Nishin Shiryokan* on history of trade here, and **Local History Museum**, *Kyodo Shiryokan*, 10min bus from stop at post office, corner of Rte40 and main street. Small ex-US Army weather station now sophisticated SDF radar station for monitoring Soviet Sakhalin activity. Americans warmly welcomed here as many locals (especially elders) are thankful for General MacArthur's refusal to partition Japan into occupation zones—Hokkaido would have come under Soviet rule.

W coast of Noshappu-misaki has new northernmost hot spa...
WAKKANAI ONSEN, 20min bus from stn (10min from Noshappu) to Fujimi Yonchome stop. Can stay at city-run **Onsen Health Center**, *Shimin Onsen Hoya Center* or 3 other new inns. More in town: **Katsumi** near stn, ☎(0162)-23-5595; **Kinokuniya** by port, ☎23-3071; **Kanno** ☎23-3587, is old two-storey W-style building operating for 70 years, near town hall, L 2 blocks on Rte40 from stn. Over 40 inns to choose from, all in ¥-Bw/2 range; also dozen minshuku and two Youth Hostels, all bookings can be made at **information center** outside stn.

CHOPSTICKS: As can be expected, Wakkanai has dozens of excellent seafood houses in all price ranges. Most clustered along **Nakadori Street**—3 blocks from stn, turn R one block puts you in heart of Nakadori at Chuo-Nichome. If you've had too much fish lately, try **Kohran** on L as Nichome begins. Sole outlet for beef (steaks or sukiyaki) from nearby Tenboku Ranch: full meals start ¥2,500. Best, inexpensive for assorted seafood is **Ezo-no-sato** on R in Nichome; gathering place for local fishermen, master is fleet leader. Few doors beyond is **Kurumaya** best in city: full-course traditional meals—immense platters of beautifully arranged, variously prepared shellfish and shrimp from ¥5,000. Excellent crab at **Toriyoshi**, also on this block. Everything else from budget soba and ramen to Korean BBQ can be found along street.

If in Wakkanai early spring, 2hr cruises (¥2,500) take you **ice-floe viewing** in Soya straits: **Feb 5-28** then every **sat-sun** thru mid-Mar, 1 cruise daily unless canceled by poor weather—book thru Higashi Nihonkai Ferry office in port terminal. **Ferries →** Rebun, Rishiri leave from here; also occasionals → KORSAKOV on USSR Sakhalin, but what's there of interest—check JTB re visa, which may be waived?

Since you've made it this far N, only hour more by bus E on Rte238 to...
SOYA MISAKI, 45°31'13" N lat, postwar Japan's northernmost point marked by granite monument, only 43km here to Karafuto—return of Habomai-Shikotan by Russia will negate this distinction. Memorialize your visit with ¥100 certificate sold at gift stores here and in town.
20min before tip is...
Soya Park, on site of Tokugawa era garrison. In closing years of Tokugawa Shogunate samurai from Aizu and Akita clans were sent here to guard against Tzarist Russia's southward expansion. On grounds of Gokoku Shrine are graves of 13 samurai who died here: boredom?

WHERE NEXT: From Soya, Rte238 continues down E coast to ABASHIRI 280km thru dozens of secluded fishing villages on OKHOTSK SEA COAST, passing Lake Kutcharo-ko. JR discontinued Soya-Abashiri coast line as well as inland Tenboku and Nayoro-Okoppe-Monbetsu lines. Private buses service these routes on which JR Rail Pass not valid. Buses run between major towns about 5-7x-daily. 45min on down coast → KITAMI ESASHI, or inland by bus on adjoining Tenboku Line → OTOINEPPU to rejoin Rte40. If already Asahikawa seen, try longer scenic backwoods route to ABASHIRI: take bus alongside old Soya Main Line (1hr express) → NAYORO, then Nayoro Main Line which hits E coast at OMU/OKOPPE and on down → ABASHIRI.
Coming down middle is SHIBETSU, 1hr before Asahikawa, site of large sheep farm with over 500 head of these wool producers.

ISLAND HOP: Before leaving Wakkanai, we head out to volcanic **RISHIRI and REBUN ISLES**. One can fly from WAKKANAI → RISHIRI (¥5,880) and REBUN (¥6,710); ANK daily 20min flight. 2-2hr30min crossing by **steamer** far cheaper (less than 1/3 of airfare), and more relaxing. WAKKANAI → OSHIDOMARI: May 7:20, 13:05, 14:20; June-Aug 7:10, 7:50, 11:30, 15:40; Sept 7:10, 13:55, 16:15; Oct 7:30, 14:05; Nov 7:30, 13:40; Dec-Apr 8:30. Return OSHIDOMARI → WAKKANAI: May 8:45, 12:00, 17:50; June-Aug 9:20, 10:30, 13:40, 18:20; Sept 9:20, 11:25, 16:25; Oct 9:40, 11:35, 16:40; Nov 9:40, 16:10; Dec-Apr 12:20; ¥1850 o.w. OSHIDOMARI → KABUKA: May 9:45, 15:25, 16:35; June-Aug 11:40, 14:30; Sept 15:00, 18:30; Oct 15:20; Nov 154:20; Dec-Apr 10:50; ¥720 o.w. Direct to Funadomari Rebun northern point June-Aug 13:05; Sept 10:35; ¥2,270.

RISHIRI-TO: Visible from Wakkanai, volcanic Mt Rishiri—fondly called Rishiri-Fuji, looms larger as you pull into OSHIDOMARI or KUTSUGATA harbors. Considered by some to be Hokkaido's **foremost scenic spot**, it dominates island, soaring 1719m from isle center; main activity on island is climbing it. Not too difficult, three trails make for wonderful summer hikes. Each starts from three main towns of OSHIDOMARI, ONIWAKI, KUTSUGATA to **summit**. Each trail is about 7hr round-trip, so 7hr from any town to another. Oshidomari course is longest but *easiest*, most common. Oniwaki trail is *hardest* but most scenic way up; near summit is large flat *senjo-jiki* '1000-mat rock'. Late spring-early summer, summit bursts out in rainbow of colors as thousands of mountain flowers bloom; and near base at Kutsugata hundreds of chishima-zakura cherry trees flower bright pink.

Main town...
O SHIDOMARI has airport and most ferries ↔ Wakkanai and Rebun. Town has bulk of Rishiri's lodgings: 9 ryokan, try ¥-T **Tanaka-ya** ☎(01638)-2-2190; ¥-B Kokumin-shukusha **Kitaguni-so** ☎2-1362; **Rishiri-Oshidomari** YH ☎2-1577; and 8 minshuku, of which try ¥-B **Himenuma-so** ☎2-1531, near Himenuma pond 1km SE of town. **Campsite** 1km W of town, trail up Rishiri-Fuji begins behind town temple.

Oshidomari has little special to see but how people here live. Thruout isle rooftops of simple homes covered with boulders against strong winds, small rice fields carved out of volcanic slopes, equally small fisherman's huts all attest to frugal life. There is no trace of once great whaling center. Most young people work on mainland, tho increased tourism prompts some to remain. Near airport, stone monument marks graves of Aizu clan samurai, detachment from force stationed at Soya.

On W coast is secondary harbor...
KUTSUGATA with connections to REBUN summer only: June-Aug two ferries daily dep 6:50 and 7:35 arr at Rebun's KABUKA 16:40 arr 17:25. KUTSUGATA → KABUKA ¥720. Ferries from OTARU stop at KUTSUGATA before continuing on to KABUKA: Schedules vary according to month, July on odd-numbered days, Aug even-numbered days. Apr-Jun, Sept, Oct every mon, wed, fri. Nov-Mar 5, 10, 15, 20, 25, 30. Dep OTARU 21:00, arr KUTSUGATA 6:10 next morning, dep 7:20 for KABUKA, arr 8:10. Return dep KABUKA 8:30 (16:30 summer) arr KUTSUGATA 9:40 (17:20), dep 10:20 (21:00) to OTARU arr 19:30 (6:10 next morning). All seats must be reserved July-August, rest of year no reservations needed 2nd class. All schedules have held for years and should not change much.

WHERE TO STAY: Kutsugata has 4 ryokan; dozen minshuku of which try **Nagori-so** ☎(01638)-4-2233, and **Kutsugata-so** ☎4-2038; Kokumin-shukusha **Rishiri** ☎4-2001; YH **Rishiri-cho** ☎4-2523. **Campsite** slightly inland on trail to Rishiri-Fuji. Good beach just outside town.

10km down the coast from Kutsugata (25min bus) small town...
SENHOSHI with **Nature Museum**, *Rishiri-to Hakubutsu-kan*, exhibits on isle's past whaling and herring fishing trades, tools, and island flora and fauna. 5km on is **Otadomari-numa pond**, largest on island, was formed by small volcanic eruption, minerals from which give water dark-red tint. Nearby beach is quite good swimming. 4km up E shore to fourth town **ONIWAKI** with sporadic steamers to Wakkanai. 3km up trail to **campsite** atop summit.

GETTING AROUND: There are several ways other than hiking over mountain. Regular **sightseeing bus** circles isle in 3hrs June-Sept; 6 non-tour **buses** circle in 2hrs; **rent-a-car** agencies at Oshidomari and Kutsugata; **bicycle** rentals also Oshidomari and Kutsugata. You can 'do' isle in half-day, heading on to Rebun, but attraction here is its quiet, relaxed atmosphere and it would be shame not to stay at inn and try curative dose of fresh seafood which all serve copiously.

REBUN-TO: Rishiri's oblong, squat twin lies 10km N. Rebun's W coast is barren, mostly sheer rock cliffs with only three small fishing hamlets at N end. In winter, ice fills their bays and hamlets abandoned till spring; residents move to Funadomari, Kabuka, or mainland villages. Middle hamlet of Nishiuendomari has particularly beautiful rugged coast. Population is concentrated on protected N and E shores.

Most **ferries** come into southernmost KABUKA, 2hr30min ↔ WAKKANAI, 50min ↔ OSHIDOMARI or KUTSUGATA: deps WAKKANAI 7:30, 11:20, 14:20* in May; and June-Aug 7:30, 10:35, 15:50*; Sept 7:30, 11:30, 16:15*; Oct 7:40, 11:50, 14:40; Nov 7:40, 11:50; Dec-Apr 8:00. Returns to WAKKANAI May 7:30*, 10:20, 17:45; June-Aug 8:00, 12:55, 18:15; Sept 8:00, 10:10*, 16:15; Oct 8:00, 10:20*, 16:35; Nov 10:30, 16:35; Dec-Apr 12:05. One-way WAKKANAI → KABUKA ¥2,060. *-boats stop at OSHIDOMARI. KABUKA → OSHIDOMARI May 7:30, 10:50, 16:35; June-Aug 10:25, 13:25; Sept 10:10, 13:50; Oct 10:20, 14:10; Nov 14:10; Dec-Apr 10:20. During May, one ferry daily at 14:15 to KUTSUGATA. One-way KABUKA → OSHIDOMARI, or → KUTSUGATA ¥720. Ferries to/from Otaru _see_ Kutsugata, p1096.

KABUKA is this island's main town and thriving fishing port with 10 ryokan, 22 minshuku in town, all budget. 4km S at Shiretoko, road ends (3 buses daily, 4 July-August, cover it in 15min) and trail goes up W coast to **Moiwa Plateau**, colorful field of wild flowers covering what was once battle field between Rebun Ainu and Teshio Ainu from mainland (home team won). **Moiwa** is also reached by bus from Kabuka cutting across island in 10min, ending at Motochi 2km up coast. Coastal trail continues from **Motochi** 34km to **Sukoton-misaki point**, northmost tip; easily done in 8hrs. Shave off 6km by taking dirt road from **Nishiuendomari**, 40min to **Hamanaka** bus stop, 20min to **Funadomari** main town on north shore. Funadomari is 35min bus up E coast from Kabuka, 20min beyond to Sukoton-misaki. Tho smaller, airport located here, 10min walk from town. 2 ryokan, 6 minshuku in town; **campsite** at Lake Kushu-ko 1km SW of town open June-September also rents tents ¥300/day.

Road between Kabuka and Funadomari runs six buses daily, each way. If timed right you can bus from Funadomari to Nairo, climb to summit of 490m **Rebun-dake peak** and down to Kitousu 2km down road and rejoin later bus to Kabuka. Climb can be done round-trip in 3-4hrs.

PERSONAL DATEBOOK: Best time to visit these islands is June, especially latter half when villages and hamlets hold their summer festivals. None are singularly spectacular, but all fun, and spaced out so none overlap. On Rishiri, thanksgiving for field and sea harvests **Jun 24-25** Kutsugata, **Jun 27-29** Oniwaki, **Jun 30-Jul 2** Oshidomari. **3rd sunday Jun** is Rebun's main festival celebrated Funadomari and Kabuka (to a lesser degree). Late summer festivals (combined with O-bon) mostly on Rishiri: Hokkai Island Festival **Aug 2-3** Oshidomari, and after day rest festivities move on to Kutsugata for Rishiri Floating Island Festival **Aug 4-5**.

Back on mainland we continue our trek around Hokkaido, stopping at Asahikawa for those who passed it on way up, or head straight to...

DAISETSUZAN NATIONAL PARK 大雪山

'ROOF OF HOKKAIDO' as it is commonly called, Daisetsuzan (Great Snowy Mountain) National Park covers 230,000 hectares of rugged peaks criss-crossed by trails starting and ending at backwoods onsens. Japan's largest National Park includes **Daisetsu** *volcanic chain* centered around 2290m **Asahi-daké** peak, **Tokachi** *volcanic chain* centered on 2077m **Tokachi-daké** to south, **Ishikari Mountains** north.

Numerous routes into park from ASAHIKAWA; most lead to secluded 'dead-end' spas tucked away in scenic wonderlands. Experienced out-doorsman can continue on across park, camping en route, to another 'dead-end' from which to exit. Majority are difficult trails; not dangerous but not to be taken lightly either. Guides are not necessary, but suggested and can be easily arranged for. Many groups heading out will often be willing to take you in. Your Japanese companions will be armed with latest detailed Japanese info. If you have done much camping out in America, Europe or elsewhere they will want to know all you can tell them about how we do it. You may find them some-what over-burdened as Japanese prefer old style Alpine frameless packs, tho Western light-framed backpacks are coming more into use. If you prefer soloing, fairly accurate maps can be picked up at most trail-head onsen or at stn information centers. Supplies and maps available in sporting sections of Asahikawa's many department stores clustered near stn: best are **Seibu**, nearest stn, and next door **Marui**.

Longest trails begin from Shirogané and Tokachi-daké spas in SW corner of park, following Tokachi chain to join main group of central mountains.

25min train from Asahikawa S on Furano Line to Biei stn from whère 35min (¥620) JR Bus 7-9 daily to...
SHIROGANE ONSEN. As you near Shirogane, bus passes thru several kilometers of white birch forest in midst of which is **Hokkaido Siberian Tiger Park**, where handful of these rare cats roam free in something close to their natural Siberian habitat. Onsen sits along Biei River gorge; in spite of modern inns (from ¥-hi-Bw/2) and 'gift- store plaza', it lets you enjoy spectacular Tokachi mountains: northernmost Biei-Fuji to smoking Tokachi-dake. Trails traversing these peaks boast some fine waterfalls, rock formations and craters still spouting smoke. Trail starts end of road 5km S of Shirogane; five buses daily to Hogaku-dai viewing platform,1km before trail-head. Start Shirogane for 8-hour hike across Tokachi chain to Tokachi onsen, but hardcore hikers planning to take long trek thru park will find better start...

20min train Biei → Kami Furano stn and 35min bus (Kami Furano Bus Co) to...
TOKACHI-DAKE ONSEN: Buses dep Kami Furano stn 9:15, 13:25 (Nov-May sat, sun), 16:35; ¥490. Tokachi-dake more 'back-woods' than Shirogane, used mostly by hikers. Start of official climbing season celebrated here in small ceremony second sunday June; similar but larger one held same time at Shi-rogane. Depending on condition of trails you can climb earlier than this date. Two full days' hike N into heart of Daisetsuzan chain whence one day to any of several other trail-head onsen. Lodgings here are cheap: ryokan **Ryoun-kaku** ☎(0167)-45-2572, annex ¥-B; Kokumin-shukusha **Kamihoro-so** ¥-B.

Before exploring other routes, visit wine and perfume center of...
FURANO: 15min train beyond Kami Furano; 1hr from Asahikawa. Winery is 10min cab N of stn; **tours** offered or just enjoy their wine at Wine House there, also

juicy steaks from nearby ranch. 7km N is **Tomita Lavender Farm**, several acres of lavender used in perfume. Mid-July blooms fill area with their aroma.

Yet, it is not wine and perfume for which Furano is known. Affectionately called *heso-no-machi*, **belly-button town**, Furano is geographical center of Hokkaido. Plaque marks exact center—on grounds of Furano Elementary School 10min walk W of stn. Town's summer fete, *Hokkai Heso Matsuri* (belly-button festival), **July 28-9** commemorates this fact with crazy dances and partying; at HOKUSHIN JINJA 'North Central Shrine' SW of stn. Nearby **Furano Ski Resort** offers excellent runs.

We now follow more common route thru park on sole road across park. 3 trail-heads start at dead-end onsen on western edge of park, used most commonly are TENNINKYO and ASAHI-DAKE, each reached by 90min bus from Asahikawa stn on Asahikawa Denki Kido Bus. **Bus** for Tenninkyo deps 9:00, 13:00 (July 1-Oct 15), 15:00: free. Asahi-daké deps 11:00, 15:00 (July 1-Oct 15), 17:00: ¥1,130.

TENNINKYO 'Angels Gorge' at half-mile altitude sits part way up rugged gorge lined with fantastic rock formations. Upstream from onsen are two fabulous waterfalls: 10min walk up L fork of river is one of Japan's most famous falls, *Hagoromo-no-taki*, 'Angel's Robe Falls', cascading down 250m in seven levels, flanked by sharp rocky peaks eliciting grace of long flowing robes. 20min up R fork is *Shikishima-no-taki*, equally spectacular but completely different—river here wider, more powerful, thundering over 60m wide, 20m high falls. Typical Japanese fashion comparing with famous foreign sights, this is 'Hokkaido Niagara' for slight similarity in shape. Tho onsen itself is popular it has managed to remain relatively unspoiled, only 4 ryokan, all from ¥-B. Trail heads S joining trail from Tokachi-dake.

Short 2-hour trail heads N thru giant fir forest to Yukomanbetsu Onsen, now better known as...

ASAHI-DAKÉ ONSEN: On same road from Asahikawa as to Tenninkyo, but take branch road to L 10km before Tenninkyo. In days when known as Yukomanbetsu it was more natural and backwoods, but has become more popular, especially as main western trail-head to Asahi-dake peak—thus its new name. Half-dozen ryokan, town-run **Ezomatsu-so** Lodge ☎(0166)-97-2246 ¥-T+. ¥-Pilgrims stay at Daisetsuzan **Shirakaba-so YH**, big onsen bath; good place to meet other hikers. Small **Visitors' Center** opp Ezomatsu-so offers info on trails.

Even if not planning to trek across park, you can enjoy mountains in short treks out of onsen. Trail to summit of Asahi-dake (highest peak on Hokkaido) 8hrs r.t.; halfway up is **Sugatami-no-ike** pond in what was once volcanic crater. Scarred by successive eruptions, area from pond to summit is barren, smoking wasteland appropriately called *jigoku-dani*, Hell Valley. From summit you can continue across volcanic peaks of Daisetsuzan chain, ending at any of several onsen on E edge of park. First two hours of trail can be done in 12min using new **ropeway** (o.w. ¥1,300) with aerial view of Tennyoga-hara plain from halfway station there. Ropeway much used in winter by skiers flocking to long runs thru quiet woods. From Sugatami-no-ike another 8hr trail heads north thru **Numa-no-daira** 'Plateau of Ponds' marsh ending at third trail-head at...

Most natural of three...
AIZANKEI ONSEN is quiet wooded onsen 1,000m above sea-level surrounded by forest of red Ezo pine, more commonly reached in hour by bus from Kamikawa stn, 55min from Asahikawa on Sekiboku Main Line. Popular base for hikers has only town-run ¥-B hostel **Aizankei Seishonen-no-Ie** ☎(01658)-2-3887. Here too are several short trails into surrounding mountains as well as long treks. Numa-no-daira marshes in area sprout flowers most of year even at this altitude; waters warmed by volcanic activity. Trekking across park, can break at any of several natural onsen pools bubbling out of rocks. Buses from Kamikawa operate only 7/1-9/30, dep 10:05 & 15:30.

Heading W across park, most hikers end at...
SOUNKYO ONSEN, most popular spa in park and only one on thru road. Hokkaido's longest river, Ishikari-gawa, carves way across 24km of Daisetsuzan's NE forming spectacular...
SOUNKYO (Layered Cloud) **GORGE**; sheer cliffs at points soaring 160m either side, dozens of graceful waterfalls breaking thru rock. Rte39 from Asahikawa heads upstream thru gorge — Direct **bus** almost hourly from Asahikawa, 2hrs to onsen; or 1hr train Sekiboku Main Line to Kamikawa whence bus for 35min run to onsen. All buses run by Dohoku Bus Co. Stop ASAHIKAWA, KAMIKAWA, front either stn ASAHIKAWA–SOUNKYO ¥1,750 (direct expresses ¥200 surcharge), KAMIKAWA–SOUNKYO ¥650. Fewer winter runs; extra buses July 1-Oct 10.

WHERE TO STAY: Town itself has flourished off gorge's visitors into fair sized community complete with elementary school and Red Cross hospital. Latter nestles in woods outside town near valley of maples, popular in autumn. Vale's natural beauty somewhat marred by half-dozen modern ferro-concrete luxury hotels, but town has managed to escape gross commercialization found in most other popular resorts. All large hotels boast excellent service, spacious baths (used by non-guests for small fee, set according to season, run to ¥500 at peak July-August). These mostly J-style ryotels are ¥-T+w/2 luxurious meals; usually local specialties fish, quail or Aberdeen Angus steaks from nearby ranch. For around ¥6,000 you can stay at smaller, more personal ryokan like **Ginsen-kaku** ☎(01658)-5-3003 where we stayed, also runs minshuku and youth hostel. Budgeteers choose from dozen minshuku and two Youth Hostels in town. Two good minshuku are **Kitakawa** and **Tsuchiya**; latter runs *bike rental*. Runners meet all incoming buses and if their establishment is out of your price range they will make you better deal or refer you to another runner. Or if you want to compare prices, see Tourist Information booth, **Kanko-annai**, by bus terminal. **Campsite** located on opposite bank of Ishikari River kilo E of town. *Budgeteers* and campers who want big bath without hotel fee will find *Furo-no-yu* ('Bath of Immortality') public *bath-house* at N end of town: ¥100 per dip and open 'til late.

S end of town has reconstructed Ainu house, as **Ainu Museum**. 100m further S is **Sounkyo Natural Museum** with displays on Daisetsuzan history, fauna and flora. Other side of stream there, beyond shrine is lower station of cable car to 1250m level of Kuro-dake peak (¥1,390 r.t.) whence chair-lift (¥390 r.t.) to 1400m level and hour hike on to 1984m summit. Good skiing in winter down Kuro-dake. Hike from bottom without mechanical help takes about 2hr30min. If taking long treks thru park from here, sign in at park office at top chair-lift platform.

• **PERSONAL DATEBOOK**: Sounkyo hosts *hi-matsuri* **Fire Festival**, one of Hokkaido's top summer onsen fetes, last weekend of July. Tho J-style offerings are given to kami enshrined here, it is predominantly Ainu event with ceremonies, dances and music dedicated to Ainu gods of Fire and Mountain. Japanese added sacred fire 'relay' and spectacular fireworks nitely.

Most people come to SOUNKYO ONSEN to see **gorge**; most spectacular along 6km stretch of road from onsen W to Obako; best seen on foot or bike from TSUCHIYA. For first few kilos river is flanked by steep cliffs with several spectacular falls. As you near first tunnel, gorge narrows, flanked now by sheer rock cliffs that look like rows of upright logs. Pass thru second tunnel to Obako rock formation, split by river. Atmosphere of what could be beautiful, serene spot is destroyed by bus loads of tourists unloading, clump of tacky gift-shops selling junky trinkets. From here, sheer cliffs continue several more kilos. Buses between Sounkyo and Rubeshibe on JR Sekiboku Line (2hr, ¥1,850) do not stop here. To visit Obako take Sounkyo-Obako bus.

En route Rubeshibe on Rte39 are two small backwoods onsens...
TAKI-NO-YU and **SHIOBETSU**, both near Taki-no-yu bus stop, just over hour from Obako.

Few km beyond is...
ONNEYU ONSEN town. Once quiet village with few inns has profited by being on route to Sounkyo, is now gaudy town full of multi-storey ferroconcrete 'shoe-boxes' offering little for tourist unless interested in freshwater fish in Mount Aquarium, or azalea—on hill behind town over 100,000 purple azalea bloom early May.

20min bus on to...
RUBESHIBE from where 3 alternate routes lead to Abashiri Direct via **KITAMI**, Rte39 or Sekiboku Line; north (on Rte242 or rail) to **YUBETSU** on Okhotsk Sea Coast and E on coast via **SAROMA** and **NOTORO** lakes; or bus direct Saroma (1hr55min), quicker than second option if not too long wait for bus.

But before heading that way, another backwoods detour for adventurer with time. About 45min from Obako on Rte39 at FUJIMI village, local road follows Tokoro-gawa River taking you thru some rural onsen which Japanese call *rampu no yado*, 'lamp-light inns', because hamlets have no electricity. Some friends passing thru found it still so relaxing escape from modern stress, with incredibly hospitable hosts. No buses run this road, hitching only way thru (they had no trouble). About 10km from Fujimi is **SHIKA-NO-YU** Onsen; another 10km to **SHIKA-NO-KO** (deer lake) Onsen both deep in woods with hiking trails, spectacular waterfalls. 8km from Shika-no-ko at GASSAN, infrequent buses cover 10km to **OKETO** on JR Chihoku Line whence 40min → **KITAMI** rejoining Sekiboku Line; another hour on to Abashiri.

*Craftsmanship to be artistic must be "loving",
it must care deeply for the subject matter...*
—John Dewey, *Art as Experience*

EASTERN SPOKE
ABASHIRI — SHIRETOKO — UTORO —
NEMURO —KUSHIRO — AKAN — OBIHIRO — PIRATORI

EMERGING from Daisetsuzan Mountains, we enter Abashiri Plains,
northern portion of what Japanese refer to as *Doto*, or 'Eastern Region' of
Hokkaido, where you will be spending most of your time in back-country.
Region has 2 main bases: ABASHIRI city, heart of Abashiri National Park,
many natural and historic attractions, east to rugged SHIRETOKO
PENINSULA, and Akan National Park lakes to south...*beyond which...*
KUSHIRO at far south, another popular jumping off point for NEMURO and
AKAN, has several remains of Ainu sites and fortifications.

GETTING AROUND: Best seen on your own personally-oriented, leisurely
trip—tho several BUS TOURS take in major sites for those on limited time, but mix-
and-match for full coverage takes almost as long as soloing. Tho somewhat expensive,
tours have added benefit of hassle-free transportation and prearranged lodging. Once again
we turn to JTB-Ace for best tours which still require mix-and-match for full coverage.
Best combinations: SAPPORO → ABASHIRI → SHIRETOKO + SHIRETOKO → AKAN →
KUSHIRO, with boat, train or plane from KUSHIRO, or reverse course; do same start but
end first day at AKAN, covering AKAN → KUSHIRO → NEMURO → AKAN next day;
SAPPORO → across south 'spoke' → AKAN + AKAN → SHIRETOKO + SHIRETOKO →
ABASHIRI → SAPPORO.

'THE HOKKAIDO: SHIRETOKO-AKAN' dep UTORO 8:00 → Shiretoko-Goko five
lakes → Abashiri (lunch) → Abashiri Tento-zan (Okhotsk ice floe exhibit hall) → Bihoro
pass → Sunayu (sand baths) → Mt Iouzan → Lake Mashu → Lake Akan (18:30, overnite
Akan View Hotel) runs daily 7/22-8/28, even-numbered days 6/11-7/21, 9/1-10/19; from
¥16,400 adult, ¥13,500 child. Without hotel, ¥7,900.

'THE HOKKAIDO: SAPPORO-AKAN' dep SAPPORO 11:19 across south spoke →
SHINTOKU via Chitose airport by deluxe resort train JTB Panorama Express → Ikeda wine
brewery → AKAN 18:50; runs daily 6/10-10/20; from ¥18,900 adult, ¥16,200 child.
Without hotel, ¥10,400.

'THE HOKKAIDO: NEMURO-AKAN' dep NEMURO 8:00 → Nossapu-misaki
peninsula → Kirittapu-misaki → Akkeshi (lunch) → Kushiro-Shitsugen marshlands →
Tawa ranch → AKAN 18:00; runs daily 7/22-8/20, even-numbered days 7/2-7/20, 9/8-
10/20, odd-numbered days 8/21-8/31; from ¥15,900 adult, ¥13,200 child. Without hotel,
¥7,400.

'THE HOKKAIDO: SHIRETOKO-NEMURO' dep UTORO 8:30 → Shiretoko-goko
five lakes → Nogami pass → Kawayu (lunch) → Lake Mashu → Hakucho-dai swam-
viewing platform → NEMURO 18:00; runs daily 7/22-8/19; odd-numbered days 7/1-7/21,
9/7-10/19; even-numbered days 8/20-8/30; from ¥15,900 adult, ¥13,200 child.

Similar tour 'THE HOKKAIDO: AKAN-SHIRETOKO' from LAKE AKAN–dep 8:00
→ Lake Mashu → Tawa ranch → Odaito (lunch) → Todowara → Rausu → Shiretoko pass
→ UTORO 17:30; runs dailty 7/21-8/27; even-numbered days 6/12-7/20, 9/2-10/20; from
¥15,900 adult, ¥13,200 child. Without hotel ¥7,400

'DAISHIZEN HOKKAIDO' Comprehensive 5-day/4-nite nature tour, 1st day dep
CHITOSE airport 17:00 → Noboribetsu Onsen (o'nite); 2nd day dep 8:30 → Jigoku-dani
→ Bear ranch → Takikawa (lunch) → Asahikawa → Kamikawa → Sounkyo 17:30
(overnite); 3rd day dep 8:00 → Onneyu → Bihoro pass → Sunayu → Kawayu (lunch) →
Mt Iouzan → Lake Mashu → Lake Akan (cruise, overnite); 4th day dep

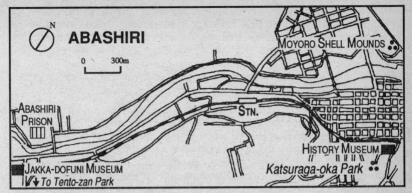

8:30 → Ashoro → Ikeda wine brewery (lunch) → Shintoku → SAPPORO on JTB panorama Express dep 14:21 arr 17:13 (overnite); **5th day** free; from ¥80,700 adult, ¥63,900 child; runs even-numbered days 8/2-8/30 occasionally in July and Sept. Room and board, all admission fees incl.

ABASHIRI 網走

PRIMARY FISHING CENTER of Okhotsk Sea, locked in by ice floes all winter but thrives off of bountiful sea spring thru autumn. Of interest to archaeology buffs, city preserves sites, artifacts of many societies who once inhabited area from stone-age pit dwellers to Ainu. There is infamous Abashiri Jail exhibit hall, not to mention many lakes that make up Abashiri National Park.

GETTING THERE: Just over 6hrs **train** from SAPPORO, ABASHIRI also reached by **plane** from CHITOSE in 55min, & TOKYO in 3hr. **Memambetsu airport** is 20min train or bus S of town. Stn is at western edge of town, 1km to center. Not large town, can easily be 'done' in half-day, giving option of staying nite here or heading out to more interesting Akan or Shiretoko-misaki.

WHERE TO STAY: Lodgings in town all ¥-B-lo-T, better hotels and ryokan at **Abashiri Kohan** Onsen 3km S on Abashiri-ko lake. Most ryokan in town start from minshuku rate; and minshuku are cheaper than national norm. No outstanding inns, but all have good service, baths, clean rooms. Handful of inns around stn, rest in town. **Book** thru **Information Center** at stn plaza.

Shell Mounds of Moyoro is our first stop in town, kitchen garbage of Stone Age dwellers, where large quantity of pottery, stone, bone and wood tools, some artistically carved, as well as skeletons have been excavated and housed in museum. Over 2000 years ago Moyoro tribe settled here on coast, living in pit-dwellings similar to Tsuchigumo and other pre-Ainu tribes. Within 4 hectares of wooded land covering their village, over 20 of these dwellings have been excavated and some restored. Museum here exhibits much of what was found, rest went to other museums in Hokkaido. Mus/mound 5min bus from stn to **Moyoro Kaizuka**; X-mon, hol; 9:00-17:00, ¥50.

Walk this road S across Abashiri-gawa River into town...
Katsuraga-oka Koen at S end town has more archaeology. Coming from stn, take bus into town 10min to Higashi Nichome stop, 5min walk S. From Moyoro, down road to main street (Rte244), and L 3 blocks to same Higashi Nichome bus stop.

Historic Museum, *Kyodo Hakubutsukan* in park devoted solely to artifacts of tribes which once inhabited area—Moyoro, Orokko, Siberian Gilyak, Koropguru. Open daily X-mon, hols; 9:00-17:00. Near museum are remains of Ainu *shachi*, fortress, built burrowing into earthwork mound.

Jakka-dofuni Museum, *Shokugyo Kunrenjo-mae* stop nr prison, big collection of Orokko artifacts. In Orokko language *jakka-dofuni* means 'house where valuables are kept'; fitting name for museum, hands-on exhibits in addition to folkcrafts, tools, clothing of Orokko people. Daily X-mon, 9:00-16:00, ¥200.

Hour bus W from Abashiri, 20min from Tokoro stn 6 stops W to:
Sakae-ura on E shore of Saroma-ko, for Tokyo University research center **Museum of Prehistoric Cultures**, *Todai Hokkai Bunka Shiryo-kan*.

PERSONAL DATEBOOK: With such rich store of ancient cultures, seems only natural that city's main summer fete has origins in ways of area's early inhabitants. **Fire Festival**–Orochon *Hi-matsuri* is said to have originated by Siberian Orokko and Gilyak tribes; offer ritual fire, so rising smoke will carry their prayers up to heavens. **4th weekend July** main event sat nite sacred fire procession Moyoro Shell Mounds thru town to Katsuraga-oka Park where pre-Ainu, Ainu songs, dances around bonfires till late.

Abashiri Keimusho maximum security prison has made city famous. Here nation's worst criminals, many on death sentences for 'extended execution', but including political undesirables from Meiji era rebels 1880-on, to 1940's guest communist leader Tokuda were sent, in Siberia-like project to use cheap prisoner/slave labor to build frontier (to buffer Czarist expansion) no free men would come to. Now no longer reserved for them. At height of notoriety had Devil's Island reputation: only ways out were surviving one's sentence, or feet first. Survival no easy feat; inmates built most Hokkaido early roads, rails under inhuman conditions, meager rations. When winter exceptionally harsh they were given second blanket—if guards felt kind. Inmates now not hardened criminals, conditions more normal for prison, high walls and moat reminisce its past. Only prisoners' visitors can enter compound, to new prison erected in center, but outer arched redbrick gate popular spot to be photographed. For 'reality' *see* next paragraph. **Gift shop** sells *Nipopo* (Ainu for 'little people') carved dolls, Ainu charms for hunting or anything else gods might be able to help, carved by inmates —hint that early inmates included disproportion of Ainu 'rebels'. Specially marked: similar sold in town shops are without prison mark, thus fakes.

Prison is 10min bus W from stn, nr Jakka-dofuni Museum, *see above.*

From prison 30min walk, mtr-plus cab S...to Park, where...
Abashiri Prison Museum, *Hakubutsu-kan Abashiri Kangoku*, relocated and reconstructed 5 actual Meiji period cell blocks of prison plus main gate, prison chapel. Has scenes of prison labor and conditions using dummies, featuring skylight escape of SHIRATORI Yoshihide, murderer and frequent escapee 1936-46 (chewed out of shackles and thru bars, then released 1961), and historic relics such as crippling 'crab' shackles, ball-and-chain. 9:00-17:00, ¥1,000—bit expensive but good set-up. Also reached by 10min walk from Ko-no-guchi bus stop, 10min bus from Abashiri stn, just beyond prison.

Main attraction in park is...
Tentozan hill for great view of lakes and ocean below; summer hiking courses and winter skiing. First floor of observatory is **Okhotsk Ice Floe Exhibit Hall** with films and simulated floes, for summer-time visitors. Exhibit is closed winter when real thing can be seen: giant sheets of ice float in during January sealing off harbor until early April when they float back to northern Okhotsk Sea. During ice floe season **boat tours** take you out; can also get aerial view February thru March on **helicopters** leaving from Abashiri Pier—no set scheds, arrange thru **Central Japan Air Service**, *Naka-Nihon Koku* ☎(0152)-43-0299. For 4 days early Feb city hosts *Ryuhyo Matsuri*, **Ice Floe Festival** similar to Sapporo's Snow Festival but sculptures carved out of chunks of sea ice. At nite dances of **Orochon Fire Festival** and Ainu performed in front of sculptures; **fireworks** burst overhead as macho Okhotsk *taiko* great drums thunder across frozen bay.

ABASHIRI NATIONAL PARK covers 100km of coast from Yubetsu E to Shari, encompassing several lakes and marshes. W-most lake **Saromako** is largest in Hokkaido, salt-water separated from Okhotsk Sea by narrow spit of land broken in one spot. Mid-September this lake and **Notoro-ko** to E myriads of coral-like plants suddenly break thru surface, carpeting both lakes in red. *Sango-kusa* 'coral-grass' is National Natural Object, celebrated **Sept 15** in *Sango-kusa Matsuri* at **Ubaranai** on Notoro S shore. Both lakes have several campsites, dozens of minshuku. Summer seas off Notoro-misaki point full of seals returning to Karafuto for winter. E-most Lake **Tofutsu-ko** fills with Siberian swans spring and autumn, migrating between Siberia and winter haven near Nemuro Shibetsu. Abashiri National Park lakes are each beautiful in their own way, it would be better to use time spent at them at places offering more—lakes of Akan National Park, or...

SHIRETOKO PENINSULA 知床半島

GETTING AROUND: SHIRETOKO with AKAN is one route where you may prefer to **rent car** to save time and take full advantage of all area has to offer. Driving, you can cover Utoro (N) coast of Shiretoko, cross over to Rausu (south) coast and head out to Akan National Park. If three or more traveling, rental fees match or better public transport; JR Rail Pass not much good as most of area has no rail lines and only one not-too-useful JR-run bus line. **Hitching** often quicker than infrequent back-country buses, especially from Utoro to Rausu on to Akan. No matter what transportation used, having hitched, bussed and driven we've found this area offers best memories of Hokkaido.

Peninsula (name is from Ainu *shirietoku*, 'world's end') juts into Okhotsk Sea, separating it from Pacific. Natural wonderland, its central mountains and coastline past Utoro is protected from encroaching civilization as **Shiretoko National Park.** Several trails cross peninsula thru what is perhaps foremost natural wildlife habitat in Japan. Of 2,-3,000 wild bears in Hokkaido, some 200 live in these mountains; relatively harmless, just take usual precautions while hiking. Hills also full of *kita-kitsune*, reddish-brown northern foxes which come down to road at dusk. Unafraid of men, they are quite friendly, often approach for handout. One nite while driving from Utoro to Yu-no-taki hot-water falls we saw over 30 of these friendly critters in less than two hours. Became popular last few years thanks to fine, full-length film docu-drama, *Kita-kitsune Monogatari* (North Fox Tale). Countless other animals inhabit area: rare eagles, hawks and owls; seals bask in sun along rugged coast.

GETTING THERE: From Abashiri, 40min express train on Senmo Main Line and 70min **bus** on Rte244 head E to SHARI where rail heads S to KUSHIRO. Rte224 cuts across base of Shiretoko peninsula to NEMURO; just beyond Shari Rte334 branches L off Rte244, heading out to UTORO, 55min bus. ABASHIRI → SHARI buses (¥980) dep ABASHIRI stn about every hour. SHARI → UTORO (¥1,340) 8:00, 8:50, 10:50, 12:00, 14:40, 16:30, 18:10. Buy tix before boarding Abashiri, get one thru to Utoro and save few hundred yen over two fares combined.

Drive Abashiri → Utoro takes you thru constantly changing scenes: coastal lakes and flower-filled marshes, to wide open plains dotted with farms and cattle ranches. Then pass close to Shari mountains and thru rugged coastline. Around Shari dozens of roadside ads for several ranches boast fine meals of steak or Korean-style *yaki-niku* BBQ, budget. Those who want to familiarize themselves with Shiretoko, or just have time to blow at Shari, visit **Shiretoko Museum**, *Shiretoko Hakubutsukan* 10min walk from stn: tools and pottery of pre-Ainu and Ainu folk; farm tools; household goods of last century used by early settlers; displays and background on Shiretoko flora, fauna. 8:30-17:00, X-mon, hols, last of month; ¥200.

10km out of Shari on Rte334, upstream of first river you come across is mystery...
Stone circle made by some early tribe; similar Oshoro Stone Circle,
Otaru. Quite ways down coast road you come to Shiretoko's unofficial
entry-point, **Oshinkoshin-no-taki**, dynamic many leveled waterfall split
into two before thundering thru trees into Sea. You can't miss it; right along
road, with bus stop expanded for tour buses.

From here only few more km to...

UTORO:

Main town here, draws hot-spa water from nearby mountain onsen source.
Became more modern between our '79 & '84 visits, with Rte334 all paved,
few more stores and big modern ryokan in town, more since. Despite ever-
increasing tour buses, Utoro's backwoods nature has changed very little.
Even old-time classic hotels like **Shiretoko Grand** ☎(01522)-4-2021, ryokan **Kaiyo**
near harbor are still moderately priced, from ¥-T+. Dozen smaller ryokan start ¥-B; 16-
plus minshuku are ¥-lo-B, mostly near main bus stop and around harbor. Good ones
Shiretoku-Peleke near bus stop, **Shucho-no-Ie** and **Kaisan-so** near port. Summer
'79, we camped at town-run **campsite** (¥200 fee) and 'borrowed' large onsen bath at Hotel
Shiretoko, another ¥200. During peak season July-Aug, easiest is to have information
booth at bus terminal find open rooms. **Utoro Kokimin-Shukusha** on road to tour-
boat pier open Feb-Mar, Jun-Oct 10; **Shiretoko YH** (all year) Eastern fringe of town;
Iwaobetsu YH (Jun-Oct) 6km E of town in middle of woods near Iwaobetsu.

Several **boat tours** follow coast-line out towards tip of peninsula for
view of rock formations and long stretches of cliffs. In some spots,
mountain streams cascade over cliffs into sea; most famous is Kamuiwakka-no-taki Waterfall which steams on cold days from hot-spring water.
More waterfalls and rock formations at tip; clinging to base of these cliffs
are several small huts used by locals for salmon fishing and kelp gathering.
90min **tours** (¥1,900) run Apr-Oct, dep 8:15, 10:30, 14:30, summer extras at 12:30
(Jun-Sep) and 16:30 (Jun-Aug). These go as far as Kamuiwakka before returning. June
thru Sep, special 3hr45min (¥4,910) ride leaves 12:10, covers entire length of peninsula.
Tour boat pier is 10min walk from bus terminal, at far end of harbor after passing thru
Oronko-iwa rock. 172 stone steps lead to top for clear view of coastline and mountains.

You can spend more time floating around, and get some fishing in.
Local fishermen take you out on combination *fishing-sightseeing* outings,
turbots and some other fish caught are prepared as sashimi onboard while
they point out coastal sights. Other catches will be prepared for dinner at
your inn: arranged thru minshuku Peleke, usually early morning departures.
During summer it's possible to hitch ride out to point with fishermen
heading out to huts there. May end up staying nite out there with them, or
hitch ride back with someone else; ask before you get on if they're staying.
Just hang out near fishing fleet and ask around for ride.

Now for sights on land. Most popular is...

Shiretoko Goko, group of five small lakes 12km (35min bus) E; well
worth visit. Trail circles lakes thru woods, giving varied spectacular views of each lake,
their smooth surfaces reflecting perfect mirror images of mountains, capped with snow
until florid May—photograper's dream come true. Can easily pass relaxing hour here,
barely noticing bus tours which rush thru every so often. **Buses** for Goko dep UTORO
7:00*, 8:55, 11:45, 12:55, 15:35*. Returns dep GOKO 10:25, 13:10, 14:25, 17:40*.
O.w. Utoro-Goko ¥570. Sched for summer 5/1-10/31; winter usually no buses go past
Utoro; *=run only 6/1-9/15. Buses continue to Shiretoko O-hashi Bridge 6km past Goko.

Stop for...

Hot-water falls of Yu-no-taki, alias translated from Japanized-Ainu
Kamuiwakka-no-taki. From O-hashi stop backtrack on road few min to
small red metal bridge over stream. We were there in '84 road was still dirt,
but was slightly widened to park few cars; also trail-head leading into

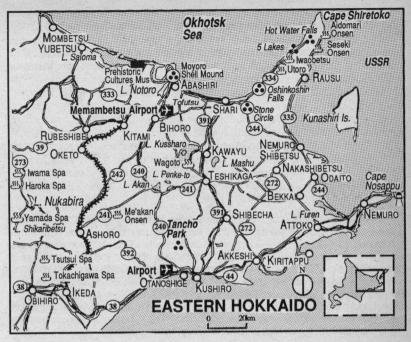

Okhotsk Sea
Cape Shiretoko
EASTERN HOKKAIDO
0   20km

mountains. Wood sign points to trail (near dumpster), follow it and then cut right to stream. Water is warm (barefeet or sandals, you'll spend lot of time walking in river) and gets hotter as you head upstream, 30min to natural outdoor bath. You'll know when you're near – use ropes to traverse steep slope on river's left (watch it, some of those rivulets are boiling hot!). You finally see bath large, deep basin carved out of rock by waterfall behind. Water is hot! Great massage under hot or cold water as alternate streams of both come over falls. Best time early morning before 9:00 or late eve, as it's popular spot for young Japanese, many of whom come to Shiretoko just for this fantastic experience. Great way to end day, perhaps after hiking thru mountains, but pick up flashlight in town if going to be here evening.

3km from Iwaobetsu bus stop up side road into foothills is...

IWAOBETSU ONSEN (one inn, Chi-no-hate ☎901522]-4-2831). Less spectacular than Yu-no-taki, it is indoor onsen in quiet forest surroundings; completely different but equally relaxing. From here trail crosses mountains to **Rausu Onsen** (abt 6 hrs); or follow peaks NE to **Yu-no-taki** (abt 9 hrs). Lone peak to south is tallest, **Rausu-daké** (1661m) reached by dead-end trail; cutting across peaks to Yu-no-taki takes you over 1508m **Mitsuminé** and 1564m **Sashirui-daké**, 1464m **Ochikaba-daké**, trail curving NE to 1663m Iouzan before finally heading down to Yu-no-taki. View from peaks gorgeous; Okhotsk Sea one side, other side looks down over Nemuro Bay, middle of which is Kunashiri, southernmost isle of...

Soviet-occupied **Kurils**, disputed territory mid-19th century. Japanese built outpost early as 1811 when they captured Russian Naval officer there. Japanese settlers moved into uninhabited Kurils and Sakhalin, recognized as Japan 1855 by first Shimoda treaty, setting border mid-archipelago between Russian Urup and Iturup Japan. Treaty of Petrograd, 1875, gave all Kurils to Japan including outermost Paramusir off Kamchatka tip thus recognized as Russian, as was Sakhalin. Treaty of Portsmouth N.H. after Russo-Japan war 1905 gave Japan then-uninhabited south Sakhalin. Soviets 'reclaimed' all 1945, tho offered back tiny seaweed-encrusted Habomai-Shikotan group 1956 as peace offering. Japan government might have accepted, but out-doing Liberal-Democrats, nationalistic blackshirts along with Socialist & Communist parties claim all Kurils to Kamchatka are Japan. There it stands as Perestroika rises. Expect some some mid-ground will be found early '90s —perhaps phased sharing economic development. And if Russ return isles, what will Japan do about 1000s of Russ living there? Countries are made of people, not real estate and emotions. Give them resident status?...recognize their occupancy rights—negotiable asset in Japan almost as valuable as real estate itself. Doubtful, chauvinism reigns. But binational-rights solution could revolutionize diplomacy. Anyway, check to see if this backdoor to poorest part of Russia has opened yet to enlightenment of tourism.

Just before Iouzan another trail branches R, heads down to **Rusa** (3hr30min) on S coast, whence 6km up coast to **Seseki Onsen**.

GETTING THERE: Only 2 buses come as far as IWAOBETSU ONSEN: between 6/1-9/15, dep UTORO 7:00 arr 7:25. Returns dep here 7:17 (6/1-9/15 only) direct UTORO arr 7:35. Rest of time must hitch or walk from Iwaobetsu bus stop where buses UTORO → GOKO stop 9:10, 12:00, 13:10, 15:50 May-Oct. GOKO → UTORO stop IWAOBETSU 10:31, 13:16, 14:31. UTORO-IWAOBETSU ¥540, GOKO-IWAOBETSU ¥220.

From UTORO you can take quick way (3-4hrs) to AKAN via SHARI, or laze thru other side of peninsula. Hiking is no longer only way across, Rte334 cuts across to RAUSU 20km (1hr bus) on opposite coast. Halfway across road hits highest point at Shiretoko-toge Pass, all buses stop here 5min, for much same view as from peaks. From here 2hr round-trip hike cuts W into hills to Rausu-ko Lake, source of Chisaibetsu River.

RAUSU ONSEN, 2km before Rausu, pleasant rural spa along Rausu River. Mountain trail from Iwaobetsu ends here; onsen waiting for sore muscles to plop in. Campers bathe at **KUMA-NO-YU ONSEN** outdoor bath up-side stream just above main onsen. Several moderate, budget ryokan and campsite here; **Shiretoko Kanko Hotel** ☎(01538)-7-2181, ¥-T, is ryokan. Nearby Kanketsu-sen hot *geyser*: spouts hourly for 3min, to heights of 20m, that's 7 storeys.

Just down road is...
RAUSU, nothing but wonderfully rustic port town. Not as popular as Utoro, most travelers just pass thru en route other coast. Has true feeling of small village with relaxed-relaxing friendly folk. Many ¥-B and ¥-T minshuku, ryokan and Rausu Youth Hostel. Two particularly nice ryokan are **Takashimaya** and neighbor **Shiga**, both from ¥-lo-T, old establishments in great location along shore looking out over bay, just S of Rausu River. Few **buses** go to Rausu: Akan Bus Co serves Utoro-Rausu 7/1-10/15 only 4x-daily, leaving Utoro Onsen and Rausu for hour trip about 11:00, 14:20, noonish and mid-afternoon stops Utoro Onsen → Shiretokotoge-Iriguchi → Shiretoko-togé → Rausu Onsen → Rausu, return. Thru bus between Rausu and Nemuro Shibetsu runs all year.

Shiretoko-togé Iriguchi (Shiretoko-pass entry) bus stop is halfway between Iwaobetsu and Utoro, used going to or coming from Goko, Yu-no-taki or Iwaobetsu onsen. Utoro → Shiretoko-toge ¥650; Utoro → Rausu ¥1,180.

If time, full-day trip takes you to end of peninsula past moss cave, two onsen. 'Glowing Cave' of *Hikari-goké Dokutsu*, called *makkausu* by Ainu, has traces of stone-age dwellers but sea-worne cave's attraction is *luminescent moss* on its walls–species found only in few places in Japan and northern Norway. Cave just 2km N of town, so save bus ride (only two a day) for SESEKI ONSEN 20km up coast. No inns here, just handful of fishing huts. At low tide hot waters form pools in sand for outdoor baths on beach. 2km beyond road's end is AIDOMARI ONSEN with few small budget inns. From here you can walk 20km (4-5hr) along beach to

Shiretoko-misaki Point. Two buses make round Aidomari-Rausu only 7/15-9/12, leave Rausu 6:10 and 16:00, arriving Aidomari under hour later to head right back.

From Rausu mainline buses follow Rte335 across rivers with salmon, trout hatcheries hour and half to Nemuro Shibetsu, whence train to Teshikaga in **Akan National Park**. Buses leave **Rausu** 6:55-every 2hrs-16:20; returns dep **Nemuro Shibetsu** same betw 8:30-18:05; ¥1,650. Before heading to Akan Park we continue back-country loop around Nemuro Plains to Japan's Easternmost point at **Nossappu-misaki**–not to be confused with another Noshappu-misaki which is Northernmost point.

Enter Akan from Kushiro to its S...

NEMURO COAST TO KUSHIRO 根室湾　釧路

THIS ROUTE takes us down Nemuro Seacoast past beautiful salt-water lakes, leading us to delicious, freshly caught ocean treats in summer; thousands of swans in winter. Our main goal is Japan's easternmost point **Nosappu-misaki**. Bypass coast on buses replacing JR Shibetsu Line trains from **Nemuro Shibetsu** to **Nemuro**; or follow it on Rte244, taking in all sights to end at Nemuro at day's end. Bus down coast joins rail at Bekkai or Attoko.

NEMURO SHIBETSU, just another port town, only thing there is small 'Northern Territories' Museum, *Hokuho Reido-kan* across from stn. Mostly exhibits photos and wildlife; serves as constant reminder that nearby Kunashiri and sister isles are occupied by Soviet Union. Japanese still call them *Chishima-retto* chain. Few Kuril Ainu and such indigenous islanders lived there, and many relocated in Ainu area of Piratori, which we visit later. Commercial value to Russians was mainly for their seals, long since hunted to extinction. To Japanese, islands valuable for edible seaweed. Constant fog, which 19th century editions of *China Sea Directory* warn of, and treacherous currents make navigation difficult.

20km S is main attraction of...

ODAITO 'pond'. Actually shallow bay, only 3m/10ft at its deepest, almost completely circled by hook-shaped Nozuki-hanto peninsula. Marshy peninsula makes for pleasant strolls, you can bus along most of it to **Todowara Iriguchi** half-hour from Nemuro Shibetsu and catch boat back across mainland to **Odaito** town. *Boats* dock at **Todowara** (5 daily), barren remains of forest, and **Ippon-matsu** (2 daily) at tip: 1.5km and 6km respectively, from Todowara Iriguchi. Bay floor is treasure trove for shrimp, clams and other shellfish; in summer, triangular-sailed fishing boats will take you out to catch these delicious ocean treats. January thru March, pond E end fills with over 10,000 giant swans; world's largest wintering spot, see from *Hakucho-dai*, **swan viewing platform**. Salmon also flock to rivers here, encouraging several fish-farms. Buses run **Nemuro Shibetsu** → **Odaito** → **Hakucho-dai Swan View** → **Bekkai** → **Attoko**.

PERSONAL DATEBOOK: All major festivals dedicated to local fauna: Early **Jan** *Swan Festival*, mostly drinking fete; *Shrimp Festival* late **Jul**, lots cheap seafood mark start shrimp season; *Salmon Festival* **mid-Oct** great sales assorted salmon dishes.

WHERE TO STAY: If in Nemuro Shibetsu area late in day, better to stay out here than in town. Half-dozen minshuku, several budget ryokan and Youth Hostel in Odaito town. Best is **Kusunoki Ryokan** ☎(01538)-6-2417, ¥-B, serves seafood cornucopia of every available catch of season. Friends passed thru in summer, were served 17 different types fish & shellfish for dinner.

BEKKAI is halfway between Nemuro Shibetsu and Attoko on discontinued JR line, now only bus; Hakucho-dai is 3km S of Odaito, modern tower w/ enclosed viewing deck.

GETTING AROUND: **Bus** cuts inland at Hon-Bekkai. Nemuro Shibetsu →
Odaito (¥570), → Hakuchodai (¥710), → Bekkai (¥1,050), Odaito → Bekkai (¥1,620);
Odaito → Attoko (¥2,070). Nemuro Shibetsu → Todowara Iriguchi 30min (¥800).
Summer only dep Nemuro Shibetsu 10:15, 12:40; dep Todowara 11:45, 14:10. Down-
coast on Rte244 or buses 100min to **ATTOKO**; change to Rte44 or Nemuro Main Line,
both lead to Nemuro & easternmost **Nosappu-misaki** point At peninsula base is
Furenko Lake–another swan wintering spot for over 12,000 Siberian swans. Buses run
all year between **ATTOKO** and **NEMURO**, under half-hour either direction (either abt
¥600), stop here: from NEMURO stops 7-ish, 1pm, after 4pm, down return hour later.

*From Attoko Rte44 follows unpopulated N coast via Furenko, while JR passes thru
several small towns on S shore. One such rural hide-away 3 stops beyond Attoko is...*
OCHI-ISHI: Located on Ochi-ishi-misaki point, this fishing village has
only one minshuku. On point grow rare species of azalea found only here
and in Manchuria. Stn is half-hour walk from town; can train or bus 40min
along coast to Nemuro. 5km before Nemuro is fishing fleet port base
Hanasaki, holds several hundred boats during warmer months when town
transformed by bustle of activity. Good fishing, delicacy is *Hanasaki-gani*,
red 'hairy' crabs served at most inns, tourist places on peninsula. Hanasaki-
misaki point is unusual rock *Kuruma-ishi* **wheel-rock**, 6m tall semi-circle.

And on to...
NEMURO: Here too, town has little to offer besides surrounding scenery.
Way off normal tourist route, it is quiet, relaxing place to just sit around;
outlying towns are better, Nemuro itself is becoming slightly more popular—built first resort, **Hotel Nemuro Grand** ☎(01532)-4-6611, complete with sky-
restaurant, twin from ¥-T; also lots of ¥-B ryokan and minshuku in Nemuro; one out at
Nosappu-misaki. If in town early June, go cherry-blossom viewing at
SEIRYU-JI temple 5min walk from stn. Several dozen trees blossom white,
rare type of cherry, *Chishima-zakura* also called *Kunashiri-sakura*, grown
from seed brought over from Kunashiri while still under Japanese control.

Half-hour walk NE of town up N coast is...
KOTOHIRA JINJA, affiliated shrine of Shikoku's famed Kotohira. Not as
spectacular as Shikoku's, nonetheless fine shrine taking into account that it
was built by small fishing village. Just goes to show how much faith fishermen have in Kompira-san, as it's affectionately called, worshipped for
safe sailing, good catch. Major *Shrine Festival* **Aug 9-11** is flamboyant affair of
dancing, partying and food, originally started as prayer and offering for bountiful catch and
safety; since 1945 it has also come to include prayers offered for return of Chishima isles.

45min bus from Nemuro takes you to...
NOSAPPU-MISAKI; once quiet hamlet of fishermen, now touristized as
being Japan's easternmost point. Except for large cafeteria and parking lot,
Nosappu is still same. Couple of *konbu* kelp-farmers' houses at point.
They harvest this special kelp from rocks below, spreading them out in
fields behind to sun-dry into marketable delicacy. Just inland of drying
fields are two minka used by fishermen; old wood building next to them is
now local police box, but served in past as light-house with flame burning
in tower to guide fleet back. Stalls here sell cooked *Hanasaki-gani* crabs to
munch while walking around. Small islet just off point is **Habomai**, another Soviet-occupied, formerly Japan. From Nemuro we head back west
along Rte44 or Nemuro Main Line towards Kushiro.

60km west is...
KIRITAPPU town, another small fishing village. Nothing special here,
but good place to spend nite. 7 minshuku from ¥-lo-Bw/2, dinners with virtually
unlimited servings of sushi using fresh catches of day. To get here, get off at Hamanaka
stn and 20min bus into town.

Instead of back-tracking to Hamanaka, bus 30km along coast to...
AKKESHI. Only thing here of note is **KOKUTAI-JI** temple 2km S of stn, built 1804, one of 3 temples constructed by Tokugawa government in attempt to 'enlighten' Ainu with Buddhism. From KIRITAPPU take Kushiro bus (8:15 and 15:50 only) straight to AKKESHI stn (1hr20min). On these get off at Akkeshi Ohashi bridge and backtrack on branch road 1km to Kokutai-ji. Between Akkeshi stn and Kokutai-ji temple (15min) Kushiro bus and JR buses take turns running every hour from 6:11 weekdays. Ret from temple starts about 6:25.

From Akkeshi hour train or Toho Kotsu bus on Rte44 W, to...
KUSHIRO, as southern gateway to Akan National Park, city has grown into modern center, with some of country's most exciting modern architecture by ex-local boy MOZUNA Kiko whose **Fisherman's Wharf** celebrates largest fishing port in all Hokkaido and Tohoku, mountains of fish piled up every morning at market. Linked to Tokyo by 30hr-up/28hr-return ferry (¥43,260 for car and driver 2nd cl) & 1hr40min plane, also by air to all other major Hokkaido cities. Boasts some fine hotels: Castle (0154)-43-2111 midtown, ¥-T, is by Mozuna; Tokyu Inn next to stn, Oriental 500m down main Odori St from stn; both ¥-T. Almost 100 other hotels & ryokan make it easy to fit your budget.

Here we visit remains of two **Ainu forts**, Moshiriya and Charanke. **Moshiriya** is 1km E of stn across Kushiro-gawa River, 10min bus from stn to Shiroyama Jujiro: once large fort protecting fair-sized community outer walls and central keep on 15m high earth mound. Around outer walls are remains of over dozen semi-subterranean dwellings. 10min bus E of Moshiriya is second fortification of **Charanke-shachi**; actually neutral meeting place for tribal chieftains, *charanke* is Ainu for 'negotiation'; *shachi* is term used for house, rather than fort. Its neutrality held also in times of war, and was often used to resolve conflicts by talks.

In **Harutori Koen** park, Charanke-shachi is on small point jutting into N end of Harutoriko lake. Buses stop either Harutori Koen-mae stop or in front of Youth Hostel, closer to Charanke-shachi. Short walk S along lake shore takes you past Science Exhibit Hall to **Local History Museum**, *Hakubutsu-kan* exhibit on artifacts excavated at 2 fortifications; X-mon, hols; 10:00-17:00, ¥350.

For modern architecture buff, other Mozu buildings are **City Museum**, looking like small town version of Bucky Fuller integrated amphitheater city; nearby **Higashi Middle School**; and midtown **Fisherman's Wharf** shopping-complex (1989) which promises more exciting eateries. Just W of Youth Hostel bus stop is minshuku **Charanke**, one of only two in town. Town has little else for visitor, but fun place to visit first weekend Aug for *Port Festival*, commemorates official opening of port on August 4, 1899.

Those passing thru Kushiro on way out of Akan National Park can cut across central Hokkaido back to Sapporo-Hakodate or circle S 'spoke' of Erimo-misaki point.

GETTING THERE: From Kushiro 2 ways to **Akan National Park**: Bus E along coastal Rte38 to **Otanoshike** and inland on Rte240 direct to **Akan-ko lake**; Kushiro airport is on Rte240. Halfway (1hr15min bus) is **Tancho-no-sato** park of *red-crested crane*, symbol of Japan and sacred bird almost extinct as natural habitats destroyed by man. 50,000m² park conserving cranes' natural habitat opened '76 in attempt to breed in captivity now has 30+ year-round residents. Winter 100+ wild cranes migrate here.

Other way up is Kushiro Main Line and Rte391. No buses make this run until midway Shibecha. Train follows Kushiro River along W fringe of Kushiro marsh half-hour to Toroko lake. Lake is abundant source for water chestnuts, Ainu staple (as for all Japanese in Jomon pre-rice agriculture era), once had large Ainu community on shores, remaining artifacts at nearby **Shibecha Museum**, *Shibecha Kyodo Shiryokan*.

Bus from Kushiro stn from 7-ish almost every 2 hrs (May thru Oct) via Airport (45min), Tsuru Koen (most midday stop to see cranes 10min) to Akan-kotan after 2hrs.Heading to airport, special bus leaves Kushiro stn 80min before each flight.

PERSONAL DATEBOOK: **Mid-Sep** Ainu from all Hokkaido gather for *Pekanpé* (Ainu for water chestnut) *Festival*; one of their more secretive events—not publicized, it is nonetheless open to anyone passing thru. If in area around festival time, exact dates can be gotten thru Ainu community at Akan-ko, or Kushiro stn info booth. Lake is 5min walk from Toro stn, 3 stops from Kushiro.

AKAN NATIONAL PARK 阿寒国立公園

LINKING DAISETSUZAN and Shiretoko-Shari mountains is another cluster of volcanic peaks among which are nestled several lakes surrounded by now common virgin forest. This is Akan National Park, heart of *Doto*–Hokkaido-East region and crown jewel of Hokkaido. Three big lakes **Akan-ko, Mashu-ko, Kussharo-ko**, each special in its own way, can be done in two days (**bus** tour or solo), but one could just as easily spend week in park. Kussharo-ko and Mashu-ko, both volcanic caldera lakes, are close to each other, Akan-ko is 30km west. Between Kussharo-ko and Mashu-ko are Teshikaga and Kawayu onsen towns, both in-park bases for exploring area. We have come here three times, have only scratched what park has to offer: outdoor types will find many mountain trails and 'hidden' lakes; hot-spring lovers will find many different, unique baths; luxury travelers will have no trouble finding suitable facilities. On top of all this natural beauty is warm hospitable legacy of Ainu who have lived in here for countless generations.

GETTING THERE: Numerous routes into park from all sides. Most common, best for those limited in time are ABASHIRI → south or KUSHIRO → north. Less used are W from NEMURO, E from ASHORO. Following our clockwise circle around Hokkaido, ABASHIRI is best gateway with two main routes. Quickest is JR Line 30min S → BIHORO & Akan Bus 75min → Kussharo-ko's WAGOTO ONSEN; continue → MASHU-KO via Kawayu then AKAN-KO via Teshikaga; another route outlined below is down coast by JR.

Several buses leave BIHORO daily (meet Abashiri train arrivals): 8:40 and 12:40 (5/1-10/10). These are **AKAN PANORAMA COURSE TOURS** but can be boarded or left at any stop. BIHORO-WAGOTO ¥1,950; BIHORO-KAWAYU ¥2,580; BIHORO-MASHU ¥3,350; BIHORO-TESHIKAGA ¥3,810; BIHORO-AKAN ¥5,360; KAWAYU-AKAN ¥3,140; TESHIKAGA-AKAN ¥1,950. Halfway between Bihoro-Wagoto is **Bihoro-toge Pass** where buses stop 15min to view **Kussharo-ko**. If taking this tour to whiz thru much of park on short schedule, buses also stop briefly at other scenic spots en route . 8:40 and 11:00 departures from BIHORO take 45min lunch break (buy your own) at KAWAYU ONSEN. 15:00-BIHORO departures end at KAWAYU, which also has 8:40, 11:00, 12:40 departures covering MASHU and AKAN; also 7:20, 9:00, 11:30 departures for Bihoro via KUSSHARO-KO.

Or you can hit AKAN-KO first, taking Akan Bus from Bihoro, since JR cancelled direct to Akan-ko (start 7:30, 70min). Return buses dep 9:25, 12:15, 15:05, 17:25. Buses stop at Kitami Aioi 5min walk W of old train stn on Rte240; run 5/1-10/31. BIHORO-KITAMI AIOI ¥1,030; KITAMI AIOI → AKAN-KOHAN ¥830. Those coming direct from SOUNKYO in Daisetsuzan National Park take bus to Rubeshibe then JR to BIHORO.

Other route from ABASHIRI is Senmo Main Line 1hr45min → KAWAYU or 15min beyond → TESHIKAGA. **Drivers** from ABASHIRI best to take Rte39 → BIHORO then Rte243 over Bihoro Pass → WAGOTO; or Rte240 via KITAMI AIOI to AKAN.

Those coming from UTORO join this route mid-way at Shari. Coming from RAUSU, take Shibetsu Line from NEMURO SHIBETSU 1hr40min to SHIBECHA, change to Senmo Main Line 30min → TESHIKAGA. Coming up from KUSHIRO, Senmo Main Line 1hr30min → TESHIKAGA, which **drivers** parallel on Rte391. 2hr bus from KUSHIRO direct → AKAN-KOHAN on Rte240; **Kushiro Airport** is along road 45min from town. Last-least used way is 75min bus W from ASHORO → AKAN-KOHAN. We use this to exit park, heading to Ikeda wine country, Shikaribetsuko, and Obihiro.

Before visiting the lakes themselves, a quick introduction to...
KAWAYU ONSEN and TESHIKAGA. Both pale in comparison to lakes which we prefer to stay at, and tho Kawayu has high-class luxury accommodations, we find no real reason to stay at either unless coming in late at nite after all lake-bound buses have stopped.

TESHIKAGA, park hub where roads from all directions converge, with easy bus access to all three lakes: 1hr to Akan-ko, 20min to Mashu-ko, 2hr to Kussharo-ko. If you must stay here, many inns of all price ranges cluster S of stn at Mashu Onsen: made up of two onsen 1km apart; TOBETSU ONSEN near bus road (10min bus from stn) has mostly government-run inns; TESHIKAGA ONSEN E along Kushiro River (10min walk from stn) has everything from minshuku to hotels. What you least expect in this neck of woods is this **European Folkcrafts Museum**, *Yoroppa Mingeikan*, 15min walk NW from stn along river. Inside this north European-style folk house (capped with witch-on-broom weather vane) are furniture and other household items of 18-19th century Europe. Prize possession here is orchestrina, organ-like instrument producing sounds of small orchestra. Restaurant serves French cuisine, full-course lunch from ¥1,500. Museum (¥500) and restaurant 9:00-18:00, X-wed. W of town *sightseeing airport*, Teshikaga Hikojo has short flights over lakes: Mashu or Kussharo course 25min each, ¥8,240; combined Kussharo-Mashu course 35min ¥11,540; Akan course 45min ¥42,490 (for 3). July-Oct, arrange by calling ahead ☎(01548)-2-2576.

10min bus from Kawayu stn sandwiched between Mashu and Kussharo is...
KAWAYU ONSEN, area's oldest established onsen resort. Tour and local buses to lakes stop here rather than stn. Despite many ferro-concrete buildings, it is quiet, surrounded by forest. Name, 'Warm River', comes from geothermally heated water mixing with river causing it to steam. They say it's best here late fall to early spring when snow blankets area and mist from steaming river wafts thru town. Three streams start middle of town pool into small pond before flowing down to Lake Kussharo. Area is strong in volcanic activity; 510m **Mt Iouzan** S of town is active volcano spouting forth sulphurous smoke. 360m **Mt Ponponzan** west of town has been hollowed out by underground activity. Sulphur gases in cavity spout out of numerous surface fissures; grass withers in summer and autumn to explode to life in winter nourished by snow melting as it hits hot mountain, only to wilt again with spring. Stomp on ground around fissures lets out hollow sound (*pon-pon*) giving hill its name.

Two dozen modern hotels and ryokan, 6 minshuku serve as base for day trips to lakes. Best ones are W, separated from town along Yukawa River: **Kawayu Grand** ☎(01548)-3-2311, closest to town, and **Yunokaku** ☎3-2011 at far W have rooms from ¥-Tw/2.

Near which is...
Ezo Wood-Carving Museum, *Ezo Fuzoku Kibori Bijutsukan* with various old and new Ainu carvings. At nite May thru September, Ainu dances are performed here. Between Grand and Yunokaku are several more ryotels, budget minshuku Wagaya and **Tourist Information Center** to book rooms. Cheap but large public bath E of Grand. Near central bus terminal is **Akan National Park Visitors' Center**, 100m E is start of Iouzan nature trail 30min to barren crater summit Ainu call Atosanepur 'naked mountain'.

Continue 1hr hike to Ponponzan, 20min on to Nibushi Onsen at...
KUSSHARO-KO: Second largest of Hokkaido's lakes after Saromako this crescent moon-shaped caldera lake was formed eons ago by massive

volcanic eruption, peaks ringing lake are all that remain of crater, long since dead. Some folks claim prehistoric creature akin to Loch Ness monster, and unimaginatively named *Kusshie* lives within its murky depths occasionally roaming wooded shores. Thanks to that eruption, lake boasts several unique onsen on east shore. Subsequent mini eruption off S shore formed Wagoto-hanto peninsula, linked to land by flowing magma thru which seep wisps of sulphur-tinged smoke.

Centered around peninsula is...

WAGOTO ONSEN, main recreation center for lake. Water around peninsula is heated by subterranean volcanic activity; small coves form two natural outdoor baths, *rotemburo*, to warm up in after swim in cold lake. All manner of water craft can be rented here. You can't help but notice shrill chorus of *minmin-zemi* cicadas which have been blissfully absent so far in Hokkaido. For some reason they flourish only at this one spot; declared National Natural Treasure. Small campsite operates here in summer. Several lodgings draw onsen water from peninsula-mostly small budget:

WHERE TO STAY: Wagoto Ryokan ☎(01548)-4-2236, & Wagoto-so ☎4-2206, both ¥-B minshuku rate. Most luxurious is Prince Hotel 2km up W shore with its own bus stop, W- and J-style rooms from modest ¥-T.

From Wagoto 55min bus follows E shore to Kawayu. 10min up road is...

Kussharo Ainu Kotan, one of oldest on Hokkaido. It is small community now, but well-stocked museum and *chisé* preserves its history. 10min further is Inasé Land, up-and-coming family-oriented leisure land with arboretum, zoo, amusement park and Health Center boasting spacious onsen-fed Jungle Bath. Rent cabin at Rokuen-so in summer: 5-person size ¥3,000/person, ¥5,000w/2. If this is not your style, two lakeside onsen have budget inns: Akayu and Ikenoyu outdoor bath frequented by cranes in winter. 1km beyond Akayu (10min bus from Inasé Land) are lake-side sand-baths of Sunayu. Dig few feet into beach here and hole fills with hot water. Only campsite here summer. More inns at NIBUSHI ONSEN 4km on at lake's eastern tip. Leisurely walk along shore from Nibushi to Goishiga-hama, 'Go-stones Beach' covered in myriads of white and black stones resembling Go pieces.

MASHU-KO: Also crescent-moon caldera lake, *most beautiful* of Akan's lakes, 500m higher in elevation than Kussharo-ko, ringed by white birch forest it is easy to see why the Ainu revered this place calling it Kamuito, sacred 'Lake of Gods'. Mist enshrouded much of year, oft making 'invisible' gods' home of tiny Kamuisshu island floating in middle. Other times, clouds cover sacred Kamuinepur 'Gods' Peak'. It rarely clears up for complete view of lake and mountain, but is breathtaking when it does.

Mashu's water ranks second in world for clarity, next to Lake Baikal in Russia. At one time Mashu was first, but rainbow trout released in it have murkied water and visibility is now down to still impressive 36m. Lake has sheer sides down to water continuing another 200m to bottom, deepest at 212m. Of our three visits to Mashu-ko, two were blessed with fine weather; spectacular view, but lacking that certain mysteriousness as when seen on misty days. Most of year, you're lucky to get clear day or two per month, chances in summer are good, late August best with mostly clear days. Fortunately, mankind has not marred lake's beauty—no buildings of any kind; nearest inns at Kawayu, and Mashu-ko Youth Hostel halfway to Teshikaga. Road detouring off Rte391 heads to two viewing platforms on W shore. Buses spend 10-15min at each. From southernmost Dai-ichi Tenbodai 5km trail circles S around lake to summit of 855m Kamuinepur; popular climb on full moon nites. Another viewing platform on E shore is accessible only by car or summer-bus from Shari (1hr15min).

From Dai-ichi Tenbodai 20min bus to Teshikaga and 2hrs further to...
AKAN-KO: Garet's personal favorite. Sandwiched between *O'akan-daké* (male) and *Me'akan-daké* (female) peaks, Akan-ko is famous for its Ainu and *marimo*, strange spherical green free-floating weed *cladophora sauteri* found only in Akan-ko, one lake on Russian Sakhalin and one in Switzerland. Grow mostly around Churui-to isle and mouth of Kinetanpe River at lake's N end, its lazy bobbing depends on water temperature and light intensity. Brownish variety called *marikoge* found at Kussharo-ko is not as rare as *marimo*.

PERSONAL DATEBOOK: For 3 days **(Oct 8-10) Akan-kohan** Ainu community celebrates *Marimo Matsuri* festival started after war when authorities became alarmed at rate *marimo* were disappearing and facing extinction, taken home by sightseers. Ainu living in this area regard *marimo* as incarnation of their local god, *genus locii*, and lead ceremonies of returning *marimo* to lake, event they helped start. Dates coincide with old Ainu ritual and Ainu gather from all over Hokkaido for one of largest festivals. Most takes place at Akan-ga-oka Jinja tho dances are also held at their *kotan*. Festival highlights **10th** at *bokké*, bubbling 'mud volcano' 10min walk E along shore from town: *marimo* brought from Churui-to are blessed, then put back in lake, carried out by two Ainu in hollowed-log boat as those on shore offer prayers. Many marimo are allowed to be sold, ¥400-¥5,000 each depending on container size: easy to care for, change water (15-20° C) twice monthly, keep out of direct sunlight.

Of more interest to us than *marimo* are Ainu who revere them. Lake's populace (both Ainu and Wa-Japanese) is concentrated on S shore at **AKAN-KOHAN**, once major Ainu settlement. Ainu have maintained their own *kotan* few hundred meters west of main Japanese town. Tho Ainu families also live in town, most live in *kotan* around cluster of two dozen stores selling usual Ainu gift items. Most here are skilled carvers, at least second or third generation; few have moved here from other less prominent *kotan* to bask in high reputation of Akan craftsmen. Most live behind store: some in modern prefab houses, some in traditional wooden ones. Others operate small restaurants around *kotan* serving semi-Ainu fare of venison and bear meat with mountain herbs. People we have met here are wonderfully friendly and have made each of our visits memorable.

In '79 Garet was passing thru *kotan* heading to campsite at W-end when carver offered to put him up for nite in return for few hours work polishing his finished carvings. TOKO Nepuri-san, whom friends affectionately call Ainu Rodin, is full-blood Ainu. Fourth generation woodcarver and one of best, has won acclaim at numerous national and international events, exports to France and Spain. Works range from enormous animal-filled landscapes carved out of massive tree trunks, to small white birch figurines with movable parts, as well as common, but oh-ever so life-like bear. Favorite subjects are Ainu gods, in particular his *kotan*'s guardian deity Kotankamui represented as watchful owl, and slender Ilessh'u-sapo, sun goddess.

Toko-san has several masterpieces done by his late father. We talked with him late into nite at their well-stocked personal bar. Thru him, we were introduced to SHITOMI Sosaku-san, *kotan* elder chieftain, unassuming, humorous man with taste for fine brandy and old, worn clothing. He also owns gift store **Kotan** in Sapporo Tanuki-koji district which doubles as pub at nite. Toko-san's wife heads Ainu Women's Dance Troupe. To cap that perfect evening, he invited us to traditional hunting dances around *kotan* bonfire.

People were all equally hospitable and willing to share their homes (we were again offered lodgings in '83), but it is no guarantee that you will get similar offer: two buddies passing thru week earlier were offered same, but another pair later weren't. Nor is language criterion. Year before, our hosts had taken in three young American tourists who spoke only few words of Japanese. Toko-san's store **Yuukarado** is halfway up right hand row of stores. He will undertake special orders and mail to you when done. No stores here specialize in Ainu weaving or clothing, but most carry some stock, and some will order and send specific items when available: reliable.

When we returned to Akan in '83 it had changed little, but had become more tourist-oriented. Large traditional *chisé* now sits in compound center; enclosed stage where Ainu dances are performed daily (¥500) at 11:00, 13:00, 15:00, 20:00, 21:00, 22:00. Best are evening shows, more crowded with better response: on rare occasion performed outside by firelight. On our first visit they had no indoor stage and performed randomly about monthly, more for themselves than for show. But demand (and money) made them regular staged event, but still good and spirited. Good thing about regular assured audience is it allows nightly performance of 30-person *pirika* deer dance. Ainu dances contain many vestiges of their hunting and fishing past, many dances dedicated to hunt stem from their belief that game animals take on human form in other world, come to this world as animals to be hunted and eaten by people. If man pays sufficient homage to their spirits they return to their own world satisfied and bearing 'gifts' from hunters. If pleased, animal-spirits return next year to reciprocate favor by providing more food. Ainu blame diminishing wildlife on our modern negligence of homage. Celestial 'potlatch' idea is shared by many other tribes in Eurasia and thru North America, especially Pacific Northwest.

Ainu of Akan are most conscious of their heritage and have set up special group *Yukara-za,* to preserve Ainu folklore, myths, traditions, language. Located in Ainu Information Center, modern two-storey structure uphill of *kotan.* Also cheap dining hall. Dance troupes under aegis of *Yukara-za* perform around world at international folk-tribal expositions as well as solo engagements. Tho still planning, *Yukara-za* hopes to publish Ainu-Japanese dictionary before it inevitably becomes dead language.

During our '83 visit another carver offered to put us up (had to decline), then directed us to one of several good **Ainu restaurants** for our first taste of *bear meat.* Cooked, it's like oily venison; raw, reputed to be delicacy started by Japanêse hunters in search of new unusual sashimi, which Ainu think crazy, aware that uncooked bear can cause severe pains if not properly cleaned. After one fatality (probably *trichinosis?*) government banned serving of bear-sashimi.

We found another interesting store **Rakan** on Rte240 between *kotan* and town run by Nishiyama Chuji-san, fellow expatriate from our hometown of Kobe. His Akan-Ainu mother married *shamo* (Japanese) and moved to Kobe after war. Tired of subtle but constant discrimination by Wa, he came 'home' in early '70's to open his workshop-store, budget pension-style inn **Guest House Koropkul** (Ainu, unlike Japanese, uses 'L'), and steak restaurant **Bordeaux.** Large statue of short fat 'man' in front is *Koropkul*; mystical magical 'little folk' of Ainu myth who live under leaves of edible butterbur plant. Sprouting fragrant white and purple flowers, its furry stem and leaves which form natural umbrella can grow to three meters in height— largest in Japan grow at nearby Onneto lake. Nishiyama-san's wood renditions of *Koropkul* range from palm-size midgets to bear-size giant which can sit you on its lap. Favorite childhood story character, his Koropguru (Jpn), have regenerated interest in this forgotten Ainu myth, prompting other carvers to follow him.

Akan-ko was once much larger until volcanic O'akan-daké burst thru its middle, breaking it up into several lakes and moving main body of water west of original location. Now-dormant O'akan-daké is Akan-ko's east shore. On its other side are two smaller lakes once part of greater Akan-ko and now connected to it by Ibeshibetsu River circling N around O'akan-daké: Penketo and Panketo, Ainu for Upper and Lower Lake.

View these cobalt lakes from...
Sokodai 'Twin Lakes' viewing platform, 20min bus E of Akan-kohan. Buses between Akan-Teshikaga stop here 10min. 5hr round-trip trail from Taki-guchi leads to summit of 1,371m O'akan-daké. On clear day can see all eastern Hokkaido: from Okhotsk Sea to Pacific and Nemuro Straits to Daisetsuzan's peaks. 20min up trail from Taki-guchi are two more mini lakes, **Taro-ko** and **Jiro-ko** also separated from Akan in big blast. Few people come this way; perfect for relaxing afternoon in woods, deep blue water refreshingly cold. **Taki-guchi**, 5min bus (45min walk) from Akan-kohan along Rte240 towards Teshikaga. Small but spectacular waterfall at confluence of streams from Akan and Taro becomes Akan-gawa River winding way to Pacific near Kushiro. Sightseeing boats on Akan come to falls for much touted view 'Akan's best' of Jukyu-retto '19 isles' stretching across lake.

WHERE TO STAY: Several dozen inns and hotels draw onsen water from within O'akan-daké. Large luxe hotels are geared towards tour-groups; solo travelers will find it more quiet at equally fine family-oriented ones like **Ichikawa** ☎(0154)-67-2011, or **New Daito** ☎67-2031. Both on lake-front, separated from main hotel cluster and closer to Ainu kotan, with rooms from ¥-Tw/2. Smaller ryokan start around ¥-lo-B; over two dozen minshuku; 3 Youth Hostels in town. Large public bath next to Kumaya Hotel near sightseeing boat pier.

GETTING AROUND: Sightsee cruises dep Akan-kohan every 30min 7:00-17:00 mid-June to Aug; hourly 9:00-15:00 thru Oct; 9:30, 11:00, 13:00, 15:00 May. 85min (¥600) cruises stop Churui-to island for **Marimo Exhibition Hall** where you see these aquatic plants.

Row-boats and **motor-boats** can be rented near Akan-kohan pier. Feel energetic, 2km row quarter way up E shore to partially submerged cave burrowing into base of O'akan-daké, formed by secondary volcanic vent–can enter by boat. Row 3km more up E shore to Ibeshibetsu River; leave boat in cove, 3km easy hike along river or dirt road along N bank to pine surrounded Panketo. In winter Akan freezes, forms natural ice-skating rink–but watch out for holes chopped in ice by smelt fishers. **Skiers** will find several runs (2 lifts) at **Kokusetsu Akan-kohan Ski-jo** 2km S of lake.

ONNETO, 'Ancient Lake' in Ainu, one of 'hidden' lakes included in Akan-ko cluster tho never part of Akan-ko. Off beaten path this lake is must for those with extra day. Especially popular with hikers as base for climbing Me'akan-daké as hot-waterfall nearby to soak in. Road from Akan *kotan* crosses Rte240 heading S to ski ground (no bus) whence 3hr trail to 1503m summit of still active Me'akan-daké: in crater 2 small ponds *aka-numa* (red) & *ao-numa* (blue). From summit, hour down to Me'akan Onsen, or cross over to adjacent 1476m Akan-Fuji and down to Onneto (2hr).

ME'AKAN ONSEN can also be reached by half-hour bus from Akan-kohan. Onsen, also called Nonaka, 'Middle of Fields', is just that: small backwoods onsen with three small inns. **Akan-Fuji-so** ☎(01562)-9-7211 ¥-B; Kokumin-shukusha **Nonaka Onsen** ☎9-7321; Nonaka Onsen **Youth Hostel** ☎9-7454 ¥-P. 40min walk from onsen to Onneto, usually cobalt blue it is also called 'Five-color Lake' as it dramatically changes hues of blue or green depending on sunlight and geothermal activity. S beyond lake is government-run **Youth Center** *Onneto Seinen-no-Ie* ☎9-7061, bunks ¥-Pw/2; runs campsite nearby. Hot waterfall **Yuno-taki** upstream near campsite; not large but constant 45°C. Buses come to S end of Onneto:

Tokachi Bus: 4x-daily only 6/1-10/31 from abt 7:30am; 4 extra 7/24-8/16 some early buses require change to shuttle at **Tozan-guchi** (dep Me'akan Onsen 8:35 arr Tozan-guchi 8:40). Tozan-guchi on Rte241 to Ashoro at local road branch-off to Onneto. Akan-kohan → Onneto ¥1,130. Stops with time between: Akan-kohan on 20min → Tozan-guchi 10min → Me'akanOnsen 10min → Onneto—same return.

WHERE NEXT: We now leave Akan National Park. Following our route exit park S or W. Those pressed for time best to bus two hours from **AKAN-KOHAN** to KUSHIRO from where 7hr express train to **SAPPORO**; 1hr45min flight or 33hr steamer to **TOKYO**. Buses for Kushiro dep Akan-kohan at 7:30, 9:45, 11:00, 14:40, 17:30. One-way fare ¥2,000. En route Sapporo is **wine country of Ikeda**. Two short detours off this course lead to Shikaribetsu-ko lake on southern fringe of Daisetsuzan National Park; and **Piratori Ainu settlement** near coast. Those who took our leisurely route around Shiretoko (Utoro-Rausu) down to Nemuro, up here thru Kushiro can head direct Shikaribetsu-ko by 3hr bus from Akan-kohan, optional detour to **IKEDA**.

OBIHIRO 帯広   EAST SPOKE

HEADING WEST from Akan National Park or Kushiro we leave *Do-to* region, enter south portion of *Do-o* Central Region of Hokkaido. 2hr30min from Kushiro is area's main city OBIHIRO (**Horse Museum**,*Uma-no Shiryokan* new '90, hors eas worker and racer, bus from JR stn) with easy access to Ikeda and two more mountain lakes to N, before continuing to Sapporo, or Hakodate. 2hrs express on Nemuro Main Line from Kushiro is our first stop.

IKEDA, center of Tokachi wine country. In wine business since 1961, already won several gold medals at international wine tastings. That Ikeda lives off of winery is apparent from moment you get off train. Eront of stn is fountain with monstrous, perpetually overflowing wine glass in center. Resembling white wine by day, light at nite turns it into red wine. Road to winery is wine-colored asphalt, appropriately called '**Wine Road**'.

Summer horse-carts carry people to *Makiba-no-Ie* '**Meadow House**' for out-door BBQs, accompanied of course by Tokachi wine. Beef fresh from surrounding pastures. Prize-winning rosé served here is specially bottled for townspeople, sold only at restaurants and inns in town nor can you buy bottle to take out. *Makiba-no-Ie* is massive 3-storey white birch A-frame modeled after turn-of-century folk houses, of which few remain, and in turn modeled after ages-old *gassho-zukuri* farmhouses of central Honshu (*see* HIDA TAKAYAMA), whence many of Tokachi's early settlers originate. *Makiba-no-Ie* is also inn mid-April to mid-November.

Winery, called *Wine-jo* or **Wine Castle**, 10min walk from stn. Can't miss massive concrete structure somewhat resembling old European castle with corner turrets. Wine aged in cellars, tour fermentation process first and second floors. Third floor restaurant serves tender Tokachi steaks and wine, topped off by bottle-shaped wine *yokan* (bean jelly) dessert.

PERSONAL DATEBOOK: **Mid-May** cherry-viewing *Sakura Matsuri* at Kiyomi-ga-oka Koen 15min walk from stn; over 2,000 Ezo yama-zakura trees bloom here. Usual sake parties under trees replaced by wine parties. **Mid-Sep** *Wine Matsuri* is town affair, wine tastings, general festivities at Kiyomi-ga-oka, Makiba-no-Ie and winery. Unless here for these fetes, half-day should do it, head on to Obihiro and up to lakes, 2hr30min train & bus. Or take your time, spend nite at any of 4 nearby onsen, all within short bus distance from Obihiro. Best are 3 btwn Ikeda–Obihiro, N of Tokachi-gawa.

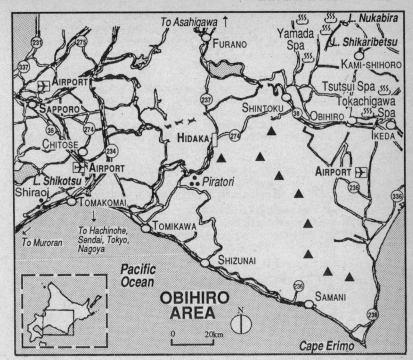

OBIHIRO
AREA

Most popular of 4 nearby Onsen is...

TOKACHI-GAWA ONSEN 30min bus from Obihiro, 25min from Ikeda; 13x-daily btwn 7:00-19:50 from Obihiro and Ikeda; also reached from **Akan-kohan** direct 2hr50min bus via Ashoro, dep 8:00 (6/1-10/31), 13:00 (7/24-8/16), and 14:00 (all year). ¥490 from Obihiro, ¥370 from Ikeda, ¥3,350 Akan-kohan. On N bank of Tokachi River, onsen is mix of luxury hotels and small inns; relatively 'backwoods' in spite of modern hotels. Best is giant **Tokachi-gawa Onsen Hotel** with spacious bath-hall, cheap at ¥-B+. Budgeteers have usual run of minshuku. Anglers find good *fishing* here, Tokachi River is spawning ground for Pacific salmon.

Chiyoda Entei Weir, few km towards Ikeda is special area for myriads of *salmon* which swim up in autumn. Nearby is smaller **CHIYODA ONSEN**.

Area's other two spas...

TSUTSUI ONSEN N of Tokachi, and **MAKUBETSU ONSEN** south, can only be reached by 30min ¥600 bus from Obihiro. But if you've made it that far we suggest head straight to lakes. We've not been to either, but if in mood for exploring, they might be worth it if stuck late in Obihiro. Tsutsui is by far most backwoods of four; buses leave Obihiro stn all year at 15:40, 17:45. Returns leave Tsutsui 7:21, 16:10, 18:24. Larger, more popular Makubetsu at base of small vulcan hill middle Tokachi Plains on Rte242 which continues S to Erimo-misaki Point.

OBIHIRO is region's main agricultural, industrial, business, transportation hub, but with little to offer budget-tourist other than few parks to while away hours between trains or buses.

1.5km SW (10min JR bus) of stn is sprawling...

Midoriga-oka Koen 420,000m^2 of woods, municipal athletic facilities, small **Museum of Local History**. More relaxing is **Suikoen** garden, 2km (10min bus) E of stn. Quiet, landscaped park with trout fishing on pond marks spot where Yoda Benzo 'Father of Obihiro' and band of settlers planted Obihiro's first crops. Few hundred meters up main road stone marks city's first settlement. Or bus15min S of town, as we did, to **Manabe Teien** traditional Japanese landscape garden, to sit under large red paper umbrellas among rhododendrons.

CHOPSTICKS: Only other 'activity' in town while waiting to get out is eating; which city seems to have anticipated, placing almost all good eateries near stn. Making small clockwise circle around few blocks fronting stn we passed several attractive places: noodlery **Ippuku** at bend in road L from stn, **Kiyo-zushi** at corner beyond. R at intersection block and half to robatayaki **Akari**. Just in front of stn is tempura house **Hagé-ten**. We gorged ourselves at **Heiwa-en** *yaki-niku*, R from stn, R at intersection.

Now head up to lakes:

70min straight N on Shihoro Line or bus on Rte273 is...
KAMI-SHIHORO, gathering spot for hot-air balloonists from around Japan with over 70 participants early August & mid-January competitions.

Half-hour further up Rte273 (bus) is...
NUKABIRA-KO man-made lake formed by damming Nukabira River. Rail ends at Nukabira Onsen, but road, closed in winter, winds over eastern Daisetsuzan mountains 2hrs to Sounkyo. All-year buses dep Obihiro 8x-daily 7:10-19:30, returns dep onsen 8x-daily 6:10-20:10; 100min, ¥1,100.

WHERE TO STAY: Onsen is at southern end of lake with nine large ryotels around central park, all from ¥7,000. Also **Youth Hostel**, one **minshuku** and **campsite**. Nukabirako is year-round recreation area, water sports and 8hr round-trip hike to summit of 870m Upepesanke mountain in summer. In winter lake freezes over into large outdoor skating rink, and three lifts service expansive ski resort–slopes only 15min walk from onsen.

25km N of Nukabira onsen (20min JR shuttle-bus) is...
HOROKA ONSEN, isolated mountain spa. Station-master Nukabira told us it is ideal place to escape summer crowds who prefer to stay by lake. Horoka gets few summertime visitors; most people go there in winter just to bathe, returning to Nukabira lodgings. 2 inns at Horoka: **Horoka Onsen** ☎(01564)-4-2167 and **Shika-no-Tani** ☎4-2163, both room w/2 ¥-P-B.

But we passed up both Nukabira and Horoka going direct to...
SHIKARIBETSU-KO nestled in southern foothills of Daisetsuzan National Park is its only natural lake; all others dam-made within past half-century. 16km around and 108m deep, 810m above sea-level and misty; surrounding forest marches right to water line giving this beautiful lake more intimate feeling. Only way to really see is by small **sightseeing boat** which rounds lake in 50min daily from May 20 to Oct 31–first and last 2 weeks only 4x-daily; 7x-daily beween 7:00–16:30 all June to Oct 15; peak season July-Aug hourly between 7:00-18:00. Easy full day hike takes you over two peaks on S shore of lake; 90min to 1187m Haku'unzan and hour more to 1174m Tenbozan. From Tenbozan trail continues on 30min to small Shimonome-ko lake following stream flowing to Shikaribetsu-ko, then along S shore. Trail starts & ends 1.5km S of Shikaribetsu-kohan Onsen where road crosses Toumabetsu-gawa River. For avid hikers, another trail from Shimonome-ko leads from/to Kami-shihoro 15km E. Needless to say Shikaribetsuko area abounds in wildlife: Deer roam mountains sometimes wandering down to road; sole habitat of rare short-eared rabbit, live fossil. Several rare fish found in high-altitude lakes.

SHIKARIBETSU-KOHAN ONSEN south end of lake has 2 fine hotels: **Royal Hotel Fukuhara** ☎(01566)-7-2301, and **Shikaribetsu-kohan Onsen Hotel** ☎7-2211 with rooms from ¥-T. Budgeteers have Youth Hostel or campsite N of hotels. There are some cheaper lodgings N end of lake which you pass coming from Nukabira-ko. about 1km before we reach Shikaribetsu-ko is **YAMADA ONSEN** mountain hot-spring, **Hotel Fukuhara** ☎7-2301 with rooms at ¥-B. On northern lake shore is cabin-style **Central Lodge Kogetsuen** ☎7-2559, ¥-B. Next to it, another **campsite**.

Shikaribetsu-ko also directly from Obihiro by 2hr bus all year: Dep **Obihiro** 5x-daily 7:20-16:30 (4/29-11/3); 2x-daily 8:30, 13:30 (11/4-4/28). Returns dep Shikaribetsu-ko 6x-daily 8:40-18:40 (4/29-11/3); 2x-daily 11:10, 16:00 (11/4-4/28); o.w. ¥1,600.

WHERE NEXT: From Shikaribetsu-ko we head back to **OBIHIRO** to rejoin rail to **SAPPORO**, 4hr30min (3hr by express) circling N via Takigawa. Or head to **HAKODATE** taking our inner circle around Shikotsu-ko, Noboribetsu, Toya-ko. To do so, take Nemuro Main Line N (towards Takigawa) hour to **SHINTOKU** changing to Sekisho Line which ends Chitose, from where bus to Shikotsu-ko. But if you have some time, 2hr30min JR bus out of Obihiro cuts across majestic Hidaka Mountains to **HIDAKA-CHO** rejoining rail down to coast & **Ainu settlements of Piratori**. One bus daily (only 7/22-10/1) at 10:20. Bus stops briefly at 2 platforms en route for views of mountains. **Hidakacho**, small town with nothing in particular, but if you get in late at nite, like we did driving, ryokan will take in latecomers if you get your own food.

PIRATORI:

Prof Chamberlain 1903 referred to this as largest Ainu settlement in south, if not all, Hokkaido. Prof Kodama also said area still today most legitimately Ainu. 1961 partial preservation was undertaken by local Donan Bus which occasionally runs direct **tours** 7hr r.t. from Sapporo. But following our route around Hokkaido, best is bus (or drive) 1hr15min down Rte237 from Hidakacho; can do first leg rail to Furenai or Horokeshi, but all bus better.

Along east bank of Sarugawa River are three large Ainu villages of...
SHIUNKOTSU, **NIOI**, **NIPUTANI** which make up Piratori. Villages consist of 20 to 30 *kotan*, Ainu term for their main social unit approximating extended family living together in group of huts. **NIPUTANI** has small **Museum of Ainu Ways**, *Ainu Bunka Shiryokan*, occasional dances for groups. Few small stores sell usual Ainu items; even fewer inns: half-dozen budget and moderate country ryokan here at ¥-B-lo-Tw/2. Even cheaper, minshuku at ¥-P like **Chisé** ☎(01457)-2-2559 whose owner carves Ainu figures, bears and beautiful furniture sold at adjacent **Mingeihin-ten** folkcrafts store.

Interesting non-Ainu site is...
YOSHITSUNE JINJA small shrine dedicated to 12th century warrior-lord Yoshitsune. We met him in Tohoku's Hiraizumi (*see*) fleeing wrathful brother shogun Yoritomo of Kamakura (*see*) who eventually had him killed. To 'validate' romantic accounts of his miraculous escape to Hokkaido and beyond, locals claim that in Ainu tales Yoshitsune spent several years in area 'with Ainu princess', to disappear into wilderness. Ainu say possible occasional 'stray' wandered up from Honshu, but no stories tell of any great Wa warrior, much less one married to any Ainu princess. Likely romanticized version of some early wanderer started by later-relocated samurai from Hiraizumi. Whatever, visit remains of Yoshitsune's abode **Bankan-yakata** at mouth of Niikappu River, few km W from **SHIZUNAI** stn. Supposed Ainu 'legends' also claim after Yoshitsune's departure his heart-broken princess threw herself off cliff onto rocks below this spot.

Half-hour walk N of Shizunai stn are...
Shibechari fort remains. Late 1600s Ainu chieftain Shakushain holed up here in his final battle against northward moving Matsumae samurai. This chieftain died here in last stand of so-called 'Ainu Rebellion', but invaders were later decimated by other Ainu, discouraging further major attempts to move northward until early 1800's. Statue of chief Shakushain in nearby park.

From Shizunai, 25min bus W to...
TOMIKAWA on coast and S of Piratori; on alternate route from Obihiro, circling S around Erimo-misaki Point. 2hr Tokachi Bus from Obihiro to last stop **HIRO'O**, catching JR bus 2hr (¥2,140) → **SAMANI** start of Hidaka Main Line up W

coast. Buses 7-8x-daily all year follow rugged coastline past waterfalls, rock formations and trail crossing Hidaka-Erimo Mountains National Park; passing thru several villages, most with ¥-budget country inns. Several kilos S of Samani is **Apoi-daké peak**, sacred to Ainu. Early Aug, *Ainu Fire Festival* at nearby park. Peak popular climb, 4hr round-trip from **TOZAN-GUCHI** bus stop 15min S of Samani.

Mountainous Furenai and coastal Samani districts in Piratori area are most fertile grounds for deer, seen descending to villages across shallow streams. Some get killed straying on roads. Estimated 3,-5,000 live in this region. Polygamous, during breeding season from May, multiply at prolific rate of 2,000 yearly. Not always happy with deer, however, are farmers whose crops are devastated by their ravaging fields for food. Thus deer hunting is allowed in November. Hunters take roughly 1,000 annually.

Hunter coming here for first time would find it advisable to hire guides or beaters (*seko*) familiar with area, since deer hunting involves beating around bush in circular advancement. Peak of season is December when leaves start to fall. Obtaining **gun license** is complicated, to put it mildly—check JNTO at home well before departure. Don't try to bring hunting gun in unlicensed, you'll lose it!

From **TOMIKAWA** it is 3hr train to Tomakomai entrance to **SHIKOTSUKO**, 30min beyond to **Shiraoi Ainu tourist village** (p1084). If you have already visited Shikotsu-Toya National Park, ferries out of Tomakomai for Aomori pick up our route in reverse down Tohoku's Japan Sea (W) coast, or continue with us down Pacific Ocean (E) coast. If using **Rail Pass**, choose your ferry at Tomakomai from those run by JR.

PERSONAL DATEBOOK: HOKKAIDO

(* = detailed in location text)

January

15-Apr 15 Exotic, boat thru ice floes, Abashiri. ☎0154-48-2120.

25-27 Ice Fete, huge ice sculpture, fireworks, dog-sled race, Obihiro.

February

Early – Winter Festival. 50 teams vie in ice sculpture contest. Asahikawa.

3–Mar 17 Boat thru ice floes. Wakkani.

First Wknd *Dosanko Matsuri* Shiraoi.

8-11 Ainu Fire Fete; ice sculpt, Abashiri.

April

End – Kite-flying; largest 24-tatami size (18x24ft), Samani-cho. ☎01463-6-2111.

May

Mid – *Goryu Kaku Matsuri*, overthrow of Hakodate Republic memorial, Goryu Fort Park Hakodate; & Cherry Blossom Fete.

Mid – *Ezo-yamazakura festival*, 1,000 cherry trees special to Hokkaido. Abashiri.

Late – *Azalea Fete*, Otaru Park, Otaru.

June

Early – Spectacular 15 hectares of lilies-of-valley. Hiratori-cho, ☎01457-2-2221.

Mid –*Work for room/bd on farms, Setana.

19 Gala fireworks, Lake Akan.

End –Wild *Hiogi-ayame* iris, 100ha,Gensei Kaen, Akkeshi-cho. ☎0153-52-3131.

July

First Weekend *Hokkai Soran Matsuri*, dances, fireworks, wine tasting; Yoichi.

2nd Fri-Sun 200km International Cycling Rally along Okhotsk coast road, Omu. ☎0152-44-7171.

24-25 *Hi-matsuri* (Fire Festival), Ainu dances, rituals, Soun-kyo, Kimikawa-cho.

27 Ainu *Orochon* fire festival, Abashiri.

Last Wknd (usually), *Dosanko* Ainu Matsuri, Shiraoi Ainu Village.

Last Wknd *Ushio Matsuri* big fete Otaru.

End–Ice floe dances, yacht races. Abashiri.

August

1-7 *Port Festival*, 10,000 dancers Hakodate.

Early – Lantern Floating fete, Niseko-cho.

7-8 Onneyu *Onsen Festival*, carry Mikoshi back–forth across Mukagawa R from spa to spa at hour per l00m; huge fireworks at Onneyu Onsen betw Daisetsu–Akan.

9-11 *Summer Festival* with market, float parade Ubagami Daijingu, Esashi.

Mid – *Hachiman Festival*, Mikoshi, costume parades daily, Hakodate.

End – *Toya-ko Lake Festival* 3 nites.

September

Full Moon, *Kangetsu-e* Moon Viewing on Lake Mashu; Ainu *Iyomanté* sacred Bear Festival held, Akan-machi.

15 Races 100 horses, ponies, Ashoro-machi, ☎01562-5-2141.

October

8-10 *Marimo Festival* Akan-ga-oka Jinja on Lake; in postwar consternation over extinction floating Marimo as souvenirs. To Ainu, plant apotheosis of deity, Bihoro chief in dugout canoe leads rite return Marimo to lake. Sat nite Ainu dance.

10 Kotan Matsuri, Ainu dances, rituals. Kami-kotan, Asahikawa.

During my travels I have seen much of pomp and ceremony.
I had thought Turks masters in that sphere, but never did
I behold a sight to equal the parade from Yedo to Kyoto.
— Robert Lund, *Daishi-san*

It gets worse all the time...much nicer 20-30 years ago.
—Edward Seidenstecker, *Japan Times*, 1990

TOKYO 東京
EAST WEST, -EST IS BEST

THIS GREAT METROPOLIS celebrated its 500th anniversary generation ago with our first edition by becoming our world's most populous city. Some lists, notably *The 1991 World Almanac*, still give Tokyo-Yokohama metropolitan area that rank at 26,952,000. In 1990, 400th anniversary of Ieyasu's move here, 13,000,000 slept in Tokyo itself. But population density is twice as heavy in Seoul, ten times in Hong Kong, even 10% worse in greener Osaka-Kobe. In '64 oxcarts had only recently disappeared from heart of town (banned for Olympics), while in suburbia they—or their replacement, even more cantankerous garden-size tractors—still choked traffic as limousine vied with ricksha for limited parking space in downtown geisha quarters. Buckets on shoulder-yokes, H-frames, barrows, swarming dragon-smoky minivans with motorcycle engines carried goods to stations of world's fastest, most punctual rail system. Rockette-like chorus lines dazzled us few doors away from 'licensed' area of Yoshiwara pictured century or two ago by woodblock-print artists. Downtown next to chrome-plated, neon-lit cafeteria one old geisha ran traditional sweet shop right out of Hiroshige print. Hoard of ancient gold coins was turned up by workmen digging foundation in main street Ginza. In school yard archaeologists dig up 8,000-year-old village and reconstruct its prehistoric shanties alongside new housing tract. That was just one generation ago.

Today, tho cyclists juggling stacks of noodle trays overhead have given way to 30-minute pizza scooters, American movie and baseball stars still get tickertape receptions few alleys over from where some festival is being held —so hoary in format that it's unknown elsewhere in Asia for generations. Sounds of Tokyo nite are still symphonic—pule of chow-mein peddler's haunting *charumella* flute, clock of wooden *geta* sandals on pavement, clack of fire watch's 'all's clear' sticks and his soft song, and occasional operatic voice of summer's goldfish vendor, staccato roll of wooden shutters being closed, morning roar of guns of popped-rice man who pops your rice from cannon, drums of paper-theater man calling children to buy candy and view his ancient pre-electronic TV, crazy quilt music of farce-faced *chindonya*-band advertising sales. On entertainment street, cat-skin *samisen* banjo wails under its flailing like some feline ghost, punctures moaning of sick jazz sax across street (vogue here again for 1950s styles). At *kabuki* theater with 11-hour daily schedule, world's most exacting drum solo riffs to accompany phantom dance or facial contortions of mourning mother, and within snare drum-hearing distance, jazz drummer rattles and rolls on drums given him generation back by Krupa in recognition of his excellent performance.

All these were sounds of old still current generation ago at first edition—ah, nostalgia, we do so agree with Seidenstecker, above. We loved that raucous post-Occupation era until razing-cum-rape of city for '64 Olympics. We know few, foreign or native, who disagree. But wandering older residential districts, especially Yanaka-sh'tamachi (p1177–), we are surprised to hear these sounds yet: sometimes, as with our toodle of noodle man's floodle, from casette tape on minitruck rather than high-piping *charumella* played by him standing by pushcart—but still with same meaning, same spine-tingling magnetism. (It's hard to accept that this flute originated in China to communicate during battle—tho one can see how it carried over war din as it does over traffic).

Tokyo then was all only two-storeyed, except for cluster of 8-storeyed around Ginza and Palace, some few taller rising above then-newly rescinded earthquake height limits. Now most of downtown is skyscraper, if with tiny cottages huddled here or there in shadow. Still taller islands dot skyline at satellite 'centers' Ikebukuro and Shinjuku. Elevated hiways, multi-layered straight out of 1930s Flash Gordon comic strip, soar over same old narrow pedestrian alleys choked with vehicular traffic. Our conglomerate of villages now accounts for 12% of national population, 33% wholesale sales, 43% bank loans (rising), 62% major companies of ¥5billion+ capital ($40million) in only 0.6% of land area. Crowded: only 2.2m2 public space per person vs Europe's most-crowded Paris (half-again Tokyo's population density) 12+m2, or airy Washington DC's 45m2. Living space average for family of 4 is 700ft2/70m2 for income $30,000 per capita! Population influx up again. But there's room aplenty: 15,000 'farm' acres, area equivalent of Chicago!

Mid-Edo era, 1695, population was 1 million, world's largest preindustrial city. Near end of era, 1858, Oliphant reckoned it at 2 million, slightly more than London, double Paris. Emperor Meiji, borne in gilt black lacquer palanquin on broad shoulders of bearers and with Court all afoot, moved his establishment from Kyoto east 550 km and renamed Edo as Tokyo, 'Eastern Capital'. Pedestrian traffic jam on old Tokaido highway drained old Kyoto. City was over 4 million when burned (with Yokohama) by 'quake of 1923, and by 1940 its 7 million ranked it with New York and London. War's end saw it down 50%, but rebuilding began while still smoldering. Now it has 13 million residents, plus daytime 2.5 million commuters from neighboring metro-suburbia for total population of 30-35 million within 20mi/32km. Most spend 2-4 hours daily on trains or buses, leaving nest at dawn, returning on last train to sleep.

Old city was centered on filled-in flats of downtown *shitamachi* around Ueno till postwar boom. Now population growth west of Shinjuku makes sense of move of city hall out to that area, while downtown converts to what master architect TANGE Kenzo calls "world city-Tokyo". City, long spreading onto landfill in bay since 17th-century shogun leveled hill in Ueno for fill, is again heading that way even tho most shallows were filled long ago. New buildings rent p.a. at 1-2% of cost vs mortgage interest of 3-5% (rising '90-91), rental payback runs to 150 years. Land is valued not for income but appreciation, already astronomical, for its value as collateral to borrow money to develop it, or buy real estate overseas. Foreign firms can't find office space. Nor can local residents find apartments, new leases are awarded by lottery with hundreds of applicants per key. Smaller nations share embassies or close to commute from Seoul or Peking. Tange estimates need by millennium-end at fully 40 more urban monsters like Kasumigaseki's largest building. Yet except for center and Shinjuku, it is still low rise city with sunlight common-law inhibiting upward growth.

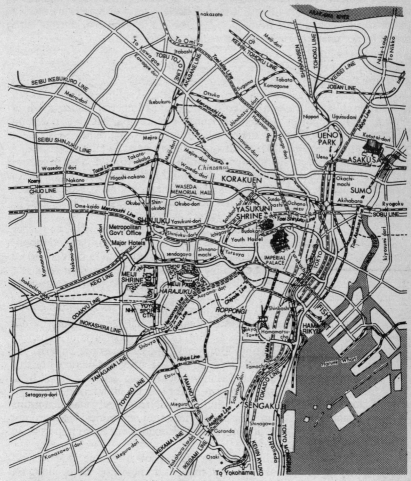

PERSONAL ORIENTATION

THUS THIS city was *never* planned, no checkerboard was laid out in wilderness as in ancient Nara, Kyoto or modern Sapporo, nor atop postwar rubble as in Hiroshima and Nagoya. It all just growed, following paths and contours between rice fields and pedestrian tracks linking villages, or *kaido* dyke-top 'main' roads to such frontier towns as Shinjuku. (There is small checkerboard area around Ginza thru Marunouchi to Imperial Palace, result of British laying out 'Little London' for Mitsui, etc, in 1880s). Result was narrow pedestrian-pathed human warren with no separations on roads for pedestrian and vehicular traffic—there was none of latter and goods were hauled by barge thru old moat-canal system, mostly filled in postwar with express roads. Then on top of this maze for 1964 Olympian rebuilding of city, multi-level high-speed, high-volume elevated super-toll road (more often, super-tolls for 2-lane parking lots) system was superimposed with no basic street structure to carry off increased input of vehicles. Chaos.

Architect MAKI Fumihiko sees Tokyoites "experiencing exciting moment that doesn't come often in history…ascendant, flourishing, money, opportunity, tradition", and like other candidate as world capital, Los Angeles, it "has no center, no downtown, it is chaotic labyrinth of small, interesting inner spaces, constructed from light, fragile materials and connected to each other by complex network of grids, radials and spirals".

Main half of this megalopolis, 'downtown' we refer to as Tokyo—its modern, bustling half—we can further split into two as well:

1: area around Imperial Palace, old nerve center of Tokugawa shogun, as so for present-day Japan, with most major financial and trade institutions in **Marunouchi** area between Tokyo station, east of Imperial Palace to Ginza Street, while south of palace are central government offices, including ziggurat-top Diet bldg (parliament): all this is on our first route. Beyond are posh **Azabu**, **Roppongi**, **Hiro** districts hosting most foreign embassies.

2: then come west side centers of **Harajuku**, **Shibuya**, **Shinjuku** and far west which, once satellite 'villages' of old Edo, represent New Tokyo. We dwell lightly on these sections of town next, giving you feel of each place, leaving exploring to you. It's worth full day by bus or cab or hoof'n-subway—perhaps your second day, after...

But we now dwell more on our secondary half, fast-disappearing older residential quarters on bay, which we took for granted for their common-ness in 1964, revisit now (pp 1189-1223) for warm glow of nostalgia—to be able to understand attitude of everyday Japanese that has made one of area's fictional denizens, Tora-san, into star of Guinness world record-continuing series of films.

As you see, this is no sightseeing town. There are few sights or sites to arrest one long, to consume days of trekking. But there is much to do. There is no single great museum despite, or perhaps because of, Japanese hoary penchant for collecting. But small museums, some superb, are plentiful and small art galleries (with no high-security locked doors or live *nio*-guardian-grimacing faces) are as numerous as bars in other cities. Check your morning paper or *Tokyo Journal–TJ* for special shows, or offerings in other fields. What this town does offer is theater, from hoary classical forms to hairy avant garde. Again your local prints are your guide. Seats are not that expensive compared with other capitals, except for those imports you didn't come here to see anyway.

Tokyo is over 500 years young. In many ways it is more modern than US cities, in other ways more ancient than Asia's hoariest. Come along on our leisurely tour of her high seas, back alleys, canals and boulevards.

After all, you're only 500 years—half millennium—old once.

GETTING THERE

FOLLOWING OUR original historical itinerary from landing here then heading down Tokaido has brought us thru entire country from most ancient areas back into Tokyo, that peculiar anarchy of which you will now better appreciate. Or, at great risk of repeating ourselves, having flown in direct via Osaka International Airport from Honolulu, Los Angeles, San Francisco, New York or Hong Kong or even Europe, into Osaka airport you treat Tokyo as side trip on Shinkansen bullet train. If you did brave that hassle of Narita airport's fortress and hour-plus train-cab transfer or hundred-fifty-dollar-plus taxi into town, you will perhaps now appreciate our seemingly odd suggested national itinerary.

Note: TOKYO ☎ NUMBERS Paris/London-like increase to 8 digits. 1991 all 7-digit phone numbers added 8th digit—prefix '3'—so if you have old 7-digit number on file, add '3' in first place; or when dialing from out of town, after area code '03'.

sick wild duck
falling in evening cold, oh
those traveler's lodgings !
—Basho

WHERE TO STAY
HOTELS & RYOKAN

HOTELS in Tokyo are like those in its sister city New York: overpriced and overbooked. But you get what you pay for and most of Tokyo's pricey parlors produce, especially for visiting international businessmen for whom they are intended. Tourists pay for all those expensive extra business amenities we don't need. Thus Kyoto hotels, which cater to tourists, are cheaper for same R&B—and Kobe's should be but are not. Also, tourists pay their own bills, businessmen sign for someone else or write off.

Whatever, hotels in Tokyo proliferate. Higher and higher property costs, world's dearest, boost construction costs even at world's cheapest bank interest. Rooms available increase, at higher room rates. Still there are not enough. This is not just gripes of this trio of cantankerous travel writers, but published opinion generation ago before our first edition ('expensive' hotels ran $10) by international hotel executives and even then-president of Japan Travel Bureau. And it's gotten far worse. Tokyo has often led in various trends and here she led as other cities emulated in inflating hotel rates beyond other costs, like food and transport.

But in all fairness, you will have little if any complaint with excellent service and fine restaurants at top-rate ¥-L international hotels—and conversely for budgeteers at in-town minshuku (mostly fun *sh'tamachi*–downtown) and budget inns. Mid-ranges offer decidedly less despite economies in reducing high manpower costs by cutting service, still seem especially overpriced, tho improving slowly. Some ¥-L/S hostels are top solely in price, tho generally you do get what you pay for.

If here on business you will have made reservation. Tourists at luxury (¥-L) and standard (¥-S) levels will have reservations, at least for first few nites or so. If visiting mid-February thru October this is obligatory. Spring is local travel time, with lull in rainy June, so again is summer, then boom in crisp autumn. Thus, arriving without reservation for your first few days is stuff of which adventure is made. In February 1987 Jay and Sumi to their great surprise trod streets, used up telephone card, futilely trying to find ¥-S or -T hotel to stay in and review, to be saved only by falling back on available-room guarantee of our New Otani Hotel membership (¥-L). February, it now turns out, sees hotels of all ranks packed with high school seniors and recent grads (and many with moms) in town to cram for and take college entrance exams. It may well now be worst time to try to get room at any level, millionaires' kids take tests, too.

Reserve thru your travel agent. Or if booking your airline direct, most of their computers are linked in to handle this as well as your air tix. JTB had invaluable service, which we referred friends to—who after drawing blanks elsewhere tried it, it worked. We later checked ourselves and drew blanks: some numbers had changed, some had clerks who couldn't understand us— testifying to changeable nature of tourist services. For ¥-S and -L tourists, best bet for onward bookings are agencies in your hotel lobby.

HERE THEN is our brief hotel review to assist you in making advanced plans. From our preferred ¥-L-up hostels, then by major areas:

Seiyo Ginza: Ginza 1-ch-11-2, ☎3535-1111; small, quiet 80-room, more staff than guests; quiet, distinguished dining; combines best of all worlds from personal concierge with personalized service even Okura and Imperial suites lack (next check-in they remember pillow and liquor preferences, dietary foibles incl kosher—first time specify), to VCR, 2 PC-usable phone lines each room. Short walk from Ginza at end of Ginza-dori St, minimal taxi from financial center. Japan's first true posh hotel—¥-LL, runs for couple, w/bkfst, svce, tax, ¥50,000+ for roomy basic with bathroom as big as many another hotel room and tub solid marble to stretch full length. Up for suites. World's richest multi-billionaire TSUTSUMI Seiji, president of Saison Group, 'Dallas-like' archrival-brother of Seibu-Prince hotel-RR prexy, dissatisfied with impersonal Tokyo hotels built one he could stay at. Now developing hotels in USSR with Intourist, which should test his personal perestroika.

Seiyo isn't sole hotel in Tokyo where you can spend one way trans-Pacific fare for single nite's lodging. All of what we once simply called **International Standard** we now call ¥-L **Luxe**, with accommodations on up in amenities and price thru ¥-LL–limited-access executive membership floors, suites. Two top hotels by general acclaim are Okura and Imperial, tho we'd pass on latter. Jay has stayed in their respective Royal and Presidential suites, far prefers Okura's, fabulous bath tub, calm service—Imperial always seems imperiously up-tight. Most have sealed windows, many old wings open, few newest, so specify if you need fresh air.

'64 we rated top 3 as Okura, Hilton, Tokyo Prince; runners up close-heat of Palace, Otani, Imperial. Still think ¥-S Palace under-rated. Now prefer:

Okura Toranomon 2ch-10-4, Minato-ku, ☎3582-0111, ¥-LL; always to us unparalleled top, we're proud to see it now acclaimed one of best in world, its pioneering modern Japanese decor is by occidental designers.

Tho Garet's generation find clientele old fogeyish, rather rates as top...
Century Hyatt Nishi Shinjuku 2ch-7-2, ☎3349-0111; ¥-hi-S; flashy for fun and frolic in youthful Shinjuku for which it sets tone, we fogies like it too.

(New) Otani Kioi-cho-4, Chiyoda-ku, ☎3265-1111; no 'Old-O', 'New' added to make name numerologically auspicious; city in itself, monstrous size but holding quality. (Money-saving *New Otani Club Golden Membership* cuts 10% plus free $20 bkfst, guarantees room even if 'full'; branches nationwide, membership avail NY, LA, London Otanis). '64 we saw its potential, said needed long shake-down—it's it had; grown worldwide, tho no branches match main house quality; ¥-L.

Tokyo Prince Shiba Koen 3ch-3-1, ☎3432-1111; next to shogun's temple Zojoji and Tokyo Tower. Seibu RR group, chain evolved from converting palatial manses of old nobility of princes and barons, and still noble despite modern high rise. Several around Tokyo, others nationwide, all well run.

Hilton in US to us were always large business hotels, but here since their '-International' inception they're tops; new Tokyo HI- after 23 years downtown is in new Shinjuku area, Nishi Shinjuku 6ch-6-2, ☎3344-5111—(oldie now Capitol Tokyu). Architecturally not as interesting as old, rooms bit smaller but amenities and kitchens same, as is singular, thrifty family plan for kids.

Imperial Uchisaiwai-cho 1-1-1, Chiyoda-ku, ☎3504-1111; ¥-LL; has world rep we can't second, tho fine it is and location is like its address, #1-1-1 no question.

Meguro Gajoen newly restored to old grandeur, now all suite, *see* p.1131.

```
                    OUR RANKING: 1992 EDITION
Ryokan: per person                    Hotel: twin/dbl room
¥50,000+                pricey-princely    'LL'   ¥35,000+%
¥25,000-50,000w/2       international luxe  'L'    ¥20,000-35,000+%
¥13,000-25,000w/2       standard           'S'    ¥12,000-20,000+%
¥7,000-13,000w/2        tourist/business   'T'    ¥7,000-12,000
¥4,400-7,000w/2         budget             'B'    ¥7,000-under
¥4,500-under            pilgrim            'P'

Under ¥5,001 per person (¥10,001 dbl) rm chge add 3% tax; ¥5,001-up 6%;
rm w/ meal/s to ¥10,001 per person tax +3%, ¥10,001-up 6%, with any service chge
incl in taxable base.
 Abbreviated in text as: ¥-LL, ¥-L, ¥-S, ¥-T, ¥-B, ¥-P; "+" = higher end; ¥-lo-hi-T
= lo to hi end T; ¥-S-L = basic overlap main price range, tho most inns & hotels
also range higher. Minshuku all = ¥-B. W/2 indicates two meals are included.
```

BY AREA

From ¥-T+ (up) all incl air-conditioning, pvt bath, color TV, most CNN.

MARUNOUCHI PALACE TO SHIMBASHI STN:

Imperial above ¥-LL, opp Imperial Palace; taxis know in Japanese as *Teikoku hoteru*.

Palace Marunouchi 1ch-1-1, Chiyoda-ku, ☎3211-5211; can't beat scenic locale facing palace gate and turret, cross street to start our first IMPERIAL route; walkable to Ginza shopping. ¥-hi-S, far superior all around to many so-called ¥-L.

Dai Ichi straddles Shimbashi stn–original **Shimbashi**, Shimbashi 1-2-6 ☎3501-4411 & newer **Ginza-** Ginza 8ch-13-1 ☎3542-5311; ¥-S; always full due location.

Mitsui Urban Ginza 8-6-15, ☎3572-4131 ¥-S, other similars this area, usually full.

Ginza Nikko (JAL) Ginza 8ch-4-21 ☎3571-4911; ¥-S; oldest of chain, newer are better.

Ginza Daiei Ginza 3-12-1 ☎3545-1111, ¥-T

Shiba Park Shiba Koen 1ch-5-10, ☎3433-4141, ¥-S, nr TOKYO PRINCE.

Urashima bit E at Harumi 2ch-5-23, Chuo-ku ☎3533-3111, ¥-hi-T; W- & J-, walkable to Tsukiji Fishmarket's fabulous sushiya, Kabuki theater, sh'tamachi-walks and Ginza.

AROUND TOKYO STATION JR

Marunouchi Marunouchi 1ch-8-3, ☎3215-2151 ¥-hi-S.

Tokyo Station Marunouchi 1ch-9-1, ☎3231-2511, ¥-T, old high ceilings echo.

Holiday Inn Hatchobori 1ch-13-7, ☎3553-6040, ¥-lo-S.

Other side of Stn, Yaesu-guchi outside Shinkansen arrivals, many Business Hotels:

Kokusai Kanko ☎3215-3281, first, ¥-S.

Yaesu Fujiya ☎3273-2111, ¥-hi-T.

Ryumeikan ☎3271-0971, ¥-hi-T.

Terminal ☎3281-3771, ¥-lo-S.

PALACE TO KANDA

Grand Palace Iidabashi 1ch-1-1, ☎3264-1111, ¥-S; annex of fine PALACE.

Hilltop Kanda Surugadai 1ch-1, Chiyoda-ku, ☎3293-2311 tell taxi *Yamano-ue Hotel* or end up across town at Hilton. ¥-S. Long time favorite of ours. Convenient to Kanda bookshops, Yasukuni shrine.

YMCA Hotel Kanda Mitoshiro-cho-7, ☎ 3293-1911, ¥-lo-T.

YMCA Asia Youth Center Suidobashi (on JR Chuo line), ☎3233-0611, ¥-lo-T

New Kanda nr Ochanomizu stn (JR chuo line), ☎3258-3911; ¥-hi-T.

YWCA Hostel Kanda Surugadai 1ch-1-1, ☎3268-7313, family use ¥-B.

OTHER SIDE OF PALACE

Fairmont Kudan Minami-2ch-1-17 ☎3262-1151, ¥-lo-S; friends like it, cozy.

Diamond — ¥-T but only if desperate

Kayu Kaikan Sanbancho 8-1, ☎3230-llll; ¥-S, OKURA-operated no guarantee quality 10% svce–carry own bags, hard to get taxi.

AKASAKA OLD AFTER-DARK POLITICAL CAPITAL

New Otani (*above*), ¥-L, dominates like feudal castle, while playing court are:

Akasaka Prince Kioi-cho 1-2, ☎3234-1111; ¥-L; handsome skyscraper snuggled against it on rear is its old princely manse now dining and weddings.

Capitol Tokyu Nagata-cho 2-10-28, ☎3581-4511; ex-Hilton, still good thanks to Hilton staff holdovers especially chief chef, but not what it was. Time will tell.

L'Ermitage opp Hie Shrine, ☎3583-9111; ¥-L+; *TJ* ranks tops, we say vulgar, no E-.

Akasaka Tokyu nearby, same Tokyu chain we abhor; **Ginza Tokyu** branch not to be taken seriously; 'economical' **Tokyu Inns** undersize rooms for oversize tabs.

ANA Hotel Akasaka 1-12-33 ☎3505-llll; ¥-hi-L—back to sensible hotels, tho high.

ROPPONGI

Ibis Roppongi 7ch-14-4 ☎3403-4411, nice but grossly overpriced, jumped ¥-T to ¥-L!

Asia Center Akasaka 8-10-32, ☎3402-6111, ¥-T, old favorite of our young days.

AOYAMA

President Minami Aoyama 2ch-2-3, ☎3497-0111, ¥-T, worth more.

TAKANAWA-SHINAGAWA

Takanawa Prince Takanawa 3ch-13-1, ☎3447-1111, ¥-hi-S; great restaurants.

Shinagawa Prince Takanawa 4-10-30 opp JR stn, ☎3451-1111, top buy ¥-T-S.

Pacific Meridien Takanawa 3ch-13-3, ☎3445-6711, ¥-hi-S.

Miyako Inn Mita 3ch-7-8, ☎3454-3111, ¥-S. *Several other similar.*

SHINJUKU NEW CITY CENTER & YOUTHFUL FUN TOWN

Hilton International, ☎3344-5111, ¥-L; *see* best 8, above. Great budget bkfst across street at ROYAL HOST.

Century Hyatt ☎3349-0111; *see* best 8, above; ¥-hi-S.

Keio Plaza Intercontinental Nishi Shinjuku 2ch-2-1, ☎3340-0111; ¥-L.

Shinjuku Prince Kabuki-cho 1ch-30-1, ☎3205-llll, ¥-S, princely slumming nr stn.

Listel Shinjuku 5ch-3-20 well E of stn nr Gyoen-mae subway ☎3350-0123, ¥-lo-T; rates by wk, mo; 'deluxe sgl' = dbl bed.

Star Nishi Shinjuku 7-10-5, ☎3361-1111.

Washington Nishi Shinjuku 3ch-2-9, ☎3343--3111, ¥-S, overpriced....*also...*

New City ☎3375-6511, ¥-T;

Town ☎3365-2 211, ¥hi-T;

Central ☎3354-6611, ¥-S.

Several 'Business' hotels both sides stn and towards Hilton-Hyatt area.

Okubo House Hyakunincho 1-11-32, ☎3364-2534; ¥-B.

BEHIND HILTON remains of old-style neighborhood, nice stroll; small inns, hotels.

TCAT HAKOZAKI, NEWLY DEVELOPING TRANSPORT-HOTEL CENTER

Royal Park Nihonbashi Kakigara-cho 2-1-1 opp TCAT, ☎3667-1111, ¥-lo-L; lovely.

Universe Nihonbashi Kayabacho 2-13-5, ☎3668-7711; ¥-T.

Pearl Shinkawa 1-2-5 nr Kayabacho subway, ☎3553-2211; ¥-T.

BMC Koto-ku Hirano 1-2-20 Monzennakacho –subway Tozai line ☎3643-2131, ¥-lo-T

DISNEYLAND & MAKUHARI MESSE CONVENTION CTR [Area code ☎(0473)-]

Newly developing ¥-L,-S hotel complex—more to come (6 a-building with 3,500 rooms) on Wangan Expwy btwn Narita-Tokyo, surprisingly convenient to downtown, 20min by Tozai line subway then 1x-mtr taxi; bus subway terminal   Disneyland stops at hotels. Free shuttle hotels   D-land and small entry discount.

Hilton International ☎(0473)-55-5000, ¥-hi-L, worth it, gorgeous.

Dai-Ichi Tokyo Bay, Maihama 1-8; ☎55-3333, ¥-hi-L (and Shinbashi Dai-Ichi orignally gained fame for its very low rate!), J-style family bath.

Bay Sheraton ☎55-5555, Ginza office ☎(03)3562-6131,¥-LL, featuring immense hot-spa pool-bath with picture window on Bay as in tourist PR but rarely experienced, for those who won't get to 'real' onsen.

Sun Route Plaza ☎55-1111, ¥-lo-S; pool.

MISCELLANEOUS But Within JR Loop-Line

Meguro Gajoen Kanko Shimo Meguro 1ch-8-1, ☎3491-0111; ¥-LL-70,000up all-suite, great domed atrium-garden setting, dining rooms monuments to prewar opulence, sight in itself for fine affordable lunch stop; *see* p.1153.

Metropolitan Nishi Ikebukuro 1ch-8-1, ☎3980-1111, ¥-lo-S; immense, good rep.

Four Seasons, Bunkyo-ku Sekiguchi 3-10-8, ☎3943-2222, ¥-L 'European Classic' tops; part of great restaurant-cum-tourist sight **Chinzan-so**; *see* p.1164

Sun Route, 2 in Shibuya ☎3375-3211 & ☎3464-6411; Ikebukuro ☎3980-1911, ¥-T; fine nationwide chain intelligently-run at fair-price, always good inexpensive coffee shop.

RYOKAN JAPANESE INN

FOR ¥-L or ¥-S travelers who wish to sample J-style and not going to Kyoto or onsen spas, last fine J-garden-inn in town, plus some lesser.

All charges incl bkfst/dinner, at top level usually J-cuisine—best chance for gourmet *kaiseki*-dinner. Room only, or w/bkfst can be arranged, usually only 20-25% less than full service. Usual 10% svce, 6% tax. Most inns of '64 edition closed or rebuilt as hotels:

Fukudaya Ryokan Kioi-cho 6, ☎3261-8577, betw Sophia U and New Otani, few min walk from JR Yotsuya stn, perhaps last true classical garden- full service-ryokan in town left over from '64 edition; ¥-L-LL w/bkfst only, or w/full-service *kaiseki* formal dinner; prefers introduction so say you saw it here and book thru agent or previous hotel or inn.

Migusa Sendagaya 4-7-7 Shibuya-ku, 5min from JR Sendagaya stn, Meiji-dori katty-corner Harajuku police, ☎3401-5187; old moss garden, nice folks; ¥-L w/bkfst.

Seifuso Fujimi 1-12-16, nr Iidabashi stn JR Chuo lne, ☎3263-0681, pool bath ¥-T, pvt bath ¥-S, rm only or full svce w/2; 'used to foreign clientele'.

Sadachiyo Asakusa 2-20-1 off Kokusai-dori nr Asakusa View Hotel 10min from Asakusa stn, ☎3842-6431, ¥-lo-S incl-up; nice folks, real sh'tamachi (*see* below).

LONGER TERM STAY

VISITORS using ¥-S or ¥-L accommodations who plan to stay over one week in Tokyo, especially if searching for digs for long-term or residence, should consider **APARTMENT HOTELS**. One chain of 9, all located in prime residential downtown Azabu, Roppongi, Akasaka etc, is operated by **Asahi Homes Ltd**-Apt Hotel Management Div, ☎(03)-3583-7551, or FAX 3583-7545. Single BR, roomy kitchen-dining, all home facilities, fully furnished from cable TV, VCR, full kitchen to cutlery, utilities, weekly hotel-style maid svce, ¥130,000 weekly to ¥370,000 monthly, one week deposit (one month for 1-3mos at lower rate). Two BR ¥700,000; parking extra. Advise advance international phone or fax to have apt/flat ready on arrival. Other companies similar, check agents.

Usually 24-hr 'convenience store' (mini-super) like **Lawson** nearby.

BUDGETEERS

WE HIGHLY recommend several JIG and other ¥-B–lo-T ryokans in old 'downtown'-*sh'tamachi* of Ueno and Asakusa–we deal with these inns in separate WHERE TO STAY paragraph (*following*). For less adventurous who prefer sleeping elevated, we advise as second best, any of numerous 'business hotels' usually concentrated around stations–and remember in these you pay in advance, all room service amenities are available from hall vending machines, from drinks and snacks to toiletries and prophylactics. JNTO-TIC Yurakucho **Welcome Inn Reservation Center** books rooms at ¥8,000 per person, apply in person only.

Another budget ploy for *males only*, especially if having hitched into town, or unable to find digs, is to go to neon-lit entertainment area and to **24-hr sauna** where you can steam, bathe (massages end midnite), eat and usually flop for nite in TV lounge in stuffed easy chair, draped in bath towel with beer and bites beside. These serve mostly young boozy office workers who missed last train home. Have full fast-laundry services at fair price.

For young couples or young at heart, any gender combination or count, this is where using love hotels pays off—remember that check-in before 10pm or -out after 10am costs additional time charge, and again usually payable in advance with reckoning of refrigerator withdrawals at check-out. These usually garishly-lit emporia are found most commonly around drinking districts and more and more, convenient to main expressway interchanges. Dark back alleys (safe) of liquory-lanes often have older ones, shabby but clean and safe, usually ¥-B or even ¥-P, ¥3,500+ dbl, old J-style house with sign, old fashioned pictograph for 'hot bath':

TEMPLE EXPERIENCE

Grand Hotel Shiba, ☎3454-0311 [E-mgr SAITOH Akira], originally inn for priests visiting capital—who get priority—to their taste and low budget; tatami or bed. J-room with top vegetarian fare abt ¥15,000 each; other w/ or w/out meals from ¥-B--up, excellent J-restaurant open to all. Zazen available, publish E-*Zen Quarterly*. [Jean Pearce].

HACHIOJI CITY, Tokyo suburb, YAKUO-IN; rsv 3 days ahead ☎(0426)-61-1115. 40min walk to mountain retreat from Takao-zan-guchi stn, wild birds, plants, trees. Attend 5:00am full Shingon (tantric) rites compulsory, worth waking for. ¥6,500w/2.

CAPSULE HOTELS

FOR TEMPORARY entombment of train-missers; fun as single-shot experience, but no solution to tourist's woes. Most admit any time 24hrs. Rates are single ¥3,200 (¥-B) to ¥4,100 (¥-T); Ueno lower end, Shimbashi mid, Shinjuku ¥4,000 and seemingly rising. Provide soap, toothbrush, shampoo, sleeping gear, shower and sometimes sauna. **Note**: no women nor double occupancy. Some:

SHIMBASHI

Capsule Hotel Shimbashi 1min walk from Shimbashi stn, ☎3434-0022.

Fast Inn Shimbashi 5min walk from JR stn E-exit, ☎3436-0036.

SHINJUKU

Capsule Green Plaza Shinjuku by Seibu RR stn, 660rms, free sauna baths, ☎3207-5411.

Kuyakusho-mae Capsule opp Kuyakusho (ward office), in Trebi-no-Izumi bldg 6min walk from stn, ☎3232-1110.

Space Inn, 2min from stn, near Seibu line N exit; ☎3232-9456.

UENO-ASAKUSA cheaper in keeping with sh'tamachi thrift...

Ueno Capsule 1min walk from Ueno stn, big bath, ☎3836-5858.

Capsule Hotel Azuma, 3min Ueno stn, ☎3831-4047, 24hr svce.

Capsule Sauna Tochigiya behind Senso-ji temple N-side Kototoi-dori ave, ☎3841-1851; 24hr sauna, yet cheapest of any Capsule (*see* following).

SH'TAMACHI   TOKYO'S LOWER EAST SIDE

IF YOU don't mind passing prestige of names like Okura, Hilton, Imperial and such, or their prices, we highly recommend tourists to stay in Tokyo's east side, to see old Edo part of Tokyo. However, those here on business may find it slightly off beat, no business services. Budgeteers have great selection. One good thing about ryokan in sh'tamachi is that with so many good eating places around, they almost expect you to eat outside. So inn rates are evenly distributed between room and meals, unlike most rural ryokan which give you feasts at cut-rate. That's not to say that dinners in sh'tamachi ryokan are not good, it just means that money saved going room only or with breakfast only will get you as good meal outside—another example of sh'tamachi frugality and practicality. We also recommend passing inn dinners so as to enjoy various sh'tamachi treats. Some inns are used to catering to Westerners, which makes life easier all around especially just trying to get room on one's own. Most are members of nationwide Japanese Inn Group, JIG; (*see* INTRO WHERE TO STAY, p.131), all have English flyers at TIC which show updated rates, map, address bilingual. JIG has 3 inns in Asakusa, 2 in Ueno area—convenient if planning trip up to Nikko area with its two JIG inns, which your inn in sh'tamachi can book for you at cost of out of town phone call, no extra. Asakusa TIC will help you find rooms almost anywhere in sh'tamachi.

Many cheaper inns have shared J-style baths–no, not at same time, bath is reserved for you exclusively just as in European hotels with hall baths.

ASAKUSA

Asakusa View Hotel ☎3842-2111, Nishi-Asakusa 3-17-1, ¥-L tops list, comparable to international luxe hotels in town in service as well as price, tho smallness unfairly gives air of fancy business hotel. Some staff speak English. 3 levels basement parks 220 cars, topped by 28 floors with 350 rooms–24th is private access concierge floor, 25th suites, 6th floor is all J-style rooms and suites. Also has huge J-style *hinoki* (cedar) bath– ¥500 fee no matter what room you stay in. If you do use it, and it's well worth it after long day of walking, get free ticket for *asa-buro* morning extra bath. Great view from top floor lounge bar **Belvedere**; dining French, Italian, Chinese and Japanese; several bars and coffee shop; full gym, all season indoor pool & jaccuzzi; two floors shopping arcade. One side, rooms look out over Asakusa temple complex and Sumida River, other sees distant green of Ueno Park, and on rare clear day, Mount Fuji. 8-10min walk from Tawaramachi or Asakusa stns; cab basic-mtr+ from Ueno stn, 3x-mtr from TCAT.

Several other W-style hotels, mostly business class, of which ¥-T and good is **Asakusa Plaza Hotel**, ☎3851-2621. Rooms small, somewhat spartan, but convenient, clean: red brick building R of Kaminari-mon Gate.

Less discriminating budgeteers try **Capsule Sauna Hotel Tochigiya** (*men only*) ¥2,600 for cheapest Capsule, includes 24hr sauna baths; behind Senso-ji Kannon temple, N-side of Kototoi-dori Ave;☎3872-8897.

Adventuresome bachelor may want to head up to old Yoshiwara and try those business hotels (¥-T), there for late-nite turkish bath visitors.

RYOKAN in Asakusa mostly behind temple, off Hisago-dori covered shopping street. Heading N, past Yonekyu sukiyaki shop is intersecting alley where on L red awning with English sign **Hotel Koromo**, ☎3844-1646, ¥-B room-only. L at this intersect, next corner far R is **Sadachiyo** ☎3842-6431, ¥-T rm-only, bkfst ¥1,500; top ryokan, new building but old-fashioned hospitality. On-the-ball staff wearing traditional *hanten* top and *patchi* pantaloons greet you; rooms nice, but lack homey feel of rural inn. Some upper rooms have small verandah. Old annex, **Sadachiyo Bekkan** (same phone #) traditional architecture and better 'feel' to it; same rates. To get to Bekkan, go R at Koromo intersection (if coming up Hisago-dori) and it's halfway on R. Sadachiyo can also arrange for dinner out on their roofed *yakata-bune* boat afloat on Sumida River.

One door beyond and across from Bekkan was great 'find' **Namiju** where Jay stayed 1954 and Garet 1986, in lovely old room looking out on small garden, had certain rustic charm to it which made it hard to believe we were in Tokyo. Well it closed, alas.

But if you want to really soak and stretch, good old-fashioned neighborhood *sento* bathhouse two doors down.

Around Bekkan and along next parallel alley N, are handful of ¥-B mostly room-only inns which also offer few hours of 'rest' time. Most allow evening check-in time to avoid extra 'rest' time fee; usually after 8pm. Rates posted outside, lesser is 2hr rest; other, usually followed by check-in time, is overnite. Some offer choice of bath, + ¥500-1,000. With hassle of this time constraint (tho some may store your luggage during day), we don't recommend for several day stays, but good in pinch. Being in most part for trysters, space-taking single's room differs little from couples. If you've shown up at Sadachiyo and no rooms, their people can usually help you find something. Of several around here, most promising looking was **Edo-ya** ☎3841-3350 (next to Sadachiyo Bekkan), its quaint entrance and overall appearance add touch of class. Posted rates: w/o bath (check-in 6pm), pair ¥4,940; w/bath +¥210 (check-in 8pm).

There are some more 'regular' inns just off of main Nakamise shopping street: **Mikawaya Bekkan annex** ☎3843-2345; Asakusa 1-31-11, another JIG ryokan; short way down last L off of Nakamise street before temple (at corner is traditional sweet shop Umezono). 12 J-style rooms w/o private baths (communal tub); ¥-lo-T, bkfst ¥700–W- or J-, dinner ¥2,000. New main **Mikawaya Honkan** ☎3841-8954; Asakusa 1-30-12, one alley towards Kaminari-mon, at slightly higher.

Kikuya ☎3841-6404; Nishi-Asakusa 2-18-9—third JIG ryokan here. Bit far, on quiet residential street betw temple and Kappa-bashi plastic food street (closer to latter, 6min walk from Tawaramachi stn). Rates similar to Namiju, w/ or w/o bath; continental bkfst.

While we find Asakusa is more fun, many people find it bit too 'local' and head to...

UENO

Favored lodging location, bit more central with larger selection. Lodgings within short walk of Keisei Narita and JR, thus convenient from Narita. Also within cab 3x-mtr from TCAT or JR Tokyo Central stn. One of best known is **Takara Hotel** ☎3831-0101; Ueno 2-18-9, few min walk S of JR stn along Showa-dori Ave. All one expects of good W-hotel, ¥-S—*rebuilding*, open 1993.

Area between Takara and station have dozen-plus ¥-B–¥-S lodgings of all sorts; business hotels abound also along Theater Row, road between Ueno Park and station. Budgeteers will also find 2 all-nite saunas along same road where you get room for cheap.

Hotel Parkside ☎3836-5711; Ueno 2-11-18, S side Shinobazu Pond, good new ¥-S 'family rate' hotel ¥-mid-S, also offers fine J-style rooms ¥-mid-S; extra 7-8% for larger room facing park; Japanese, Chinese, Western restaurants, cafe. Along W side of Shinobazu Pond is **Ikenohata Hokke Club** ☎3822-3111; Ikenohata 2-1-48 of nationwide chain. We have stayed at several in other parts of Japan and found service good, rooms small but clean. ¥-T, incl bkfst.

Perhaps best deal at paired Hotels of J-style **Suigetsu** ☎3822-4611, Ikenohata 3-3-21 and W-style **Ohgai-so** ☎3828-3181, where foreigners get special discount on already low rates. J-style rooms give choice of w/private bath and toilet (nicer rooms), or cheaper room-only which shares communal baths, toilets. Latter are in older bldg and bit faded looking. Unique feature of Suigetsu's baths is their murky water—not dirty, real hot spa water from drilled well. W-style rooms all private bath toilet. If order J-dinner (tempura, sukiyaki, sashimi, etc), ask it be served in lovely traditional wooden cottage between two hotels. Once home of MORI O(h)gai (1862-1922), prominent Meiji era writer. House open to visitors during day. Several restaurants between two. Either hotel can arrange for demonstrations of ikebana or chanoyu for groups of 10 or more. Suigetsu and Ohgai-so 7min walk from Ikenohata exit of Keisei Ueno stn (few min more from JR): head N along Theater Row road between Ueno Park and Shinobazu Pond and they are on L beyond monorail track. Nezu stn of subway Chiyoda (Green) line only 4min walk NE.

Few hundred meters beyond on R is...
Yamanaka Ryokan ☎3821-3189; Ikenohata 4-23-1,¥-Budget...and further down on L is **Ryokan Katsutaro** ☎3821-9808; Ikenohata 4-16-8, 20% cheaper, JIG member.

Still further, across main Kototoi-dori Ave is...
Sawanoya Ryokan ☎3822-2251; Yanaka 2-3-11, JIG, 25min walk from Ueno stn, or cab 1x-mtr; only 6min walk from Yanaka exit subway Nezu stn. Amid quiet very sh'tamachi Yanaka, homey and comfortable; good place to meet other foreign travellers. Another Yanaka inn ready to take in Westerners, but one we've not checked out ourselves, **Suzuki Ryokan** ☎3821-4944; Yanaka 7-15-23, nr Nippori stn (Keisei and JR). Rates similar to JIG inns, rooms w/ or w/o bath.

GETTING AROUND TOWN
DO IT YOURSELF SIGHTSEEING

B Y TAXI or public transport. Cab offers two choices: air-conditioned hotel-, or Hato, 'hire' limo, abt ¥5-7,000 by hour (longer less); or taxi, air-conditioned compact 5 psgr ¥4,500 (9x-mtr) per hr on negotiation, smaller 4 psgr 10-15% less, sometimes ¥3,000 as in Osaka. For limo contact hotel desk, or Hato Bus ☎3201-2725, or travel agent if using one, specify English-speaking driver (no extra cost if available) and save price of guide you don't need carrying us.

Most Tokyo taxi drivers long ago outgrew *kamikaze* suicide pilot rep. But many are straight from farms and can't cross Imperial Palace Plaza unless you point. It stands to reason such is of no use to equally innocent-ignorant 'deaf-mute' non-Japanese-speaking tourist. However, several thousand highly experienced taxi drivers in Tokyo own and drive their own cabs, at exactly same rate fleet drivers get. Desk clerk might have one of these *kojin*-cabbie friend, some speak some English. *Kojin* taxi simply means private, owner-driver—own boss.

If your desk cannot be of help, go out to taxi line in front of your hotel —assuming major hotel for we assume that desk at smaller hotel will help— walk along taxi line and look for two large *ko-jin* ideographs (*see* p.110) on side of taxi door or on roof light, usually on lite-green car. Hotel doorman can help negotiate with driver, (tho it isn't easy to pick cabby before his time comes on queue) who may very well have heard about our suggestion thru independent owner-driver's association. Drivers themselves suggest ¥4,500 ('91) per hour for running and waiting in town, or meter charge, whichever comes out higher—and meter will rarely approach this flat charge. **Hato** for large 'hire' car w/4psgrs within Tokyo averages ¥5,500 per hr 3-4hrs, ¥5,000 per abt 8hr course (¥48,000). For out-of-town, straight meter, or prior negotiate; Hato tours to Kamakura, Fuji, Nikko etc by big US car ¥60,000 for 9+hrs to ¥90,000 for 13+hrs, incl tolls and admissions. Budgeteers find taxi for 4 usually cheaper than tour bus and twice as fast—Hato 'hire' limo competitive, with convenience of freedom of itinerary, etc.

Taxis usually plentiful and easy to get, even suburbs and small towns, unless rain, or late nite in main entertainment areas of Shinjuku, Roppongi, Shibuya or Akasaka. At such times, especially if last train has gone, it's free-for-all, with cab drivers picking up who they feel will be big fare. Foreigners don't count since you will only go short ride to some nearby hotel, not be fat-cat run to suburbia. Bad weather and year-end party season make cab catching even harder. Our solution to long late waits is either to hole up in some cafe until after 2am when rush to get home is over, or walk to nearest luxury hotel where cabs are queued up. You will not be taken for ride, and if you are asked for more than meter fare, it's because of toll incurred and cabbies always ask before going on toll road so you will expect surcharge at cost. Most taxis now issue printed receipt—take it in case you forget something in car as it has his registry number and company phone. Anything forgotten in cab will likely be returned if driver can tie it to you when he finds it or later passenger points it out to him.

TRAVEL AIDS

SUPPLEMENT US with fine freebie city maps available TIC or hotel. Tops by far is pocket magazine *Tokyo Walking Map*, mostly ads and puff articles, with map insert which rip out as fits inside us–smallest, phenomenal detail, neighborhood insets, subway color code map.

Close 2nd is similar pocketable *Sightseeing-Shopping Map of Tokyo* by Hato Bus, Airport Transport and JAL. Also fine is taller pocket-size *Escort Tokyo & Yokohama* 'monthly handy guide map'. All have subway map, detail insets. For more serious Tokyo trekkers, longtime visitors, residents–*Japan Times Tokyo Transit Book*, ¥800; or KI's*TOKYO–A Bilingual Atlas* ¥1,850 or *Tokyo Bilingual Map*, ¥850, both alphabet & Japanese; *Bird's Eye View of Tokyo* picture maps by ISHIHARA Tadashi, of Nihonbashi, Kohkyo (Palace), Ginza, Shinjuku, others due: ¥580 each.

Books: *Tokyo Journal*'s excellent detailed individual Tokyo Area Guides now superceded by editors Don Morton & Naoko TSUNOI's *The Best of Tokyo* (Tuttle ¥1,350 in Japan, $12.95 overseas). Additional guide material for residents when you run out of us: anything by Jean Pierce,

especially her *Footloose in Tokyo* series, publ Japan Times. Or for serious gourmet or gourmand *Good Tokyo Restaurants* 'tasted and compiled' by Rick Kennedy [KI] ¥1500, eatery expert for *TJ* and *Japan Times*. Best of many city-wide guidebooks is *Tokyo City Guide* by Judith Connor & YOSHIDA Mayumi, ¥2,600, 30 top maps. Background: Waley *Tokyo, City of Stories*.

Hikes in and out of town: Sh'tamachi old town guided walking tours, Mr OKA Nobuo **monthly walks** all day 3rd sat ¥1,000 each plus lunch: ☎(0422)-51-7673. Take pvt groups walking anywhere in town min 5hrs/¥10,000, phone rsvtn, *see* text.

Out of town nature hikes often, by *Friends of the Earth*, at cost–usually advise bring own brown bag or bento–plus ¥1,000 or so contribution; suns-hols; check TIC bulletin board, or *Japan Times* notices, or ☎(03)-3770-6308 for info.

PUBLIC TRANSPORTATION

ALMOST REASONABLY PRICED and perhaps world's most efficient, tho writing system makes understanding routes somewhat tricky. It's easiest on ever-growing network of subways and interlinked JR lines–any place in Tokyo is within fair walk of some station. Equally extensive network of private rail and JR serves suburbs and many sites within day-trip distance. Bus routes all-encompassing, but hard to figure out for uninitiated. Taxis can almost always be found without too much trouble, but crosstown runs get expensive, usually thru excruciatingly slow traffic. As big as Tokyo may look on map, interesting old-town area really isn't that big, walking is pleasant budget alternative allowing you to see much more on side streets, shop fronts, open doors, etc.

Bus universally ¥180 per ride, and no free transfers; much beyond JR-Yamanote loop run on graduated zone system; as too subways and elevated JR.

JR ¥120 basic for 1-2 stns, rising so that JR Yamanote loop costs ¥180 to opp side, more to suburbs on branches. Main routes in town are: Yamanote (var Yamate) 'loop' circles city, *soto-mawari* 'outer round' clockwise, *uchi-mawari* inner round counter Cutting across circle from Shinjuku–Kanda is Chuo Line, continuing on beyond either to suburbs. Keihin tangent runs parallel Tokyo–Shinagawa where Yamanote loop turns and Keihin continues down Tokaido for Yokohama. Plan is to rebuild whole system 50m underground, with loop-hiway at 30m, freeing valuable surface real estate. **JR InfoLine** ☎(03)3423-0111, English scheds, fares, discounts, weekdays 10–6.

Subway fine, clean, fast, not crowded except at rush hours. Presently 10 lines–3 municipal (Toei) & 7 private Teito Rapid Transit Authority (TRTA) **color-coded**: Ginza Line (orange or gold), Marunouchi (red), Hibiya (grey or white), Tozai (light blue), Chiyoda (green), Yurakucho (yellow), Hanzomon (purple), Toei Asakusa (pink), Toei Mita (blue), Toei Shinjuku (light green). Scheduled 1995 completion is outer-loop Junigo-sen (magenta) Line, to circle beyond JR Yamanote el-loop. Eng route maps available almost anywhere, companies use wallet-sized maps for PR.

Ticket-vending machine has map above, more often with latin-alphabet names. Figure above destination name is total fare (smaller, about half, is for child), you figure out own transfer points. But it's not that simple as government lines have

different ticketing and their own machines–
if puzzled, someone, station-staff or
passenger, is sure to help even during rush
hour. Even we native out-of-towners get
confused–if so, buy minimum fare and
when exiting hand in ticket and wait for
charges on difference, no penalty. Some
suggested public transportation itineraries
are charted for you, and access to main
locations by public transportation is
indicated. Map color-coded by line is on
whatever freebie city map you use: if not,
up-to-date pocket-size copy can be obtained
at any subway kiosk, ask for *chikatetsu ro-
sen-zu*, free. Pick up English one at TIC,
most hotel lobbies, also in *Tokyo Tour
Companion* and *Tokyo Journal*. Narita TIC
has best–laminated wallet-size, folds in half
to name-card size, put out by NTT, cover
has phone numbers for basic English info.
If print too small, you can get bigger about
size of paperback book page. Subway map,
especially in English, is valuable tool for
getting around Tokyo on your own. Not
only shows all subway lines and junctions,
but also xfer points to JR. Most every train
has map of its route inside, above door.

If subway journey involves **transfer**
from Toei to Teito (also called Eidan) lines,
you pass thru transfer wicket where show
your ticket but keep until final destination.
You cannot do joint use of both lines if
you are using any of special free use passes
(below) put out by Toei or TRTA, unless
you have both–then not so economical.

Free-use Pass: TRTA has one-day
free pass (*ichi-nichi josha-ken*) valid on any
of their 7 lines. Valid stamped date only,
but you can buy it up to one month ahead
thru *teiki-ken uriba*, advance ticket sellers,
of 27 main subway stops incl Ikebukuro,

Shinjuku, Shibuya, Shinbashi, Ginza, Ueno
–¥620 adult, child ¥310. Also *teiki*
commuter passes valid 1-month (¥14,110),
3-month (¥40,220), take one day to order.

Toei has several pass choices: ¥650 one-
day *joshaken* good for 3 Toei subway lines,
all city buses (except double-decker between
Ueno–Asakusa), Arakawa Tram (p.1164).
Ideal for you who will stay in sh'tamachi,
Asakusa Line covers most of our
sh'tamachi stops along Sumida River, and
Shinjuku Line crosses town. Sold at most
Toei station ticket windows, purchasable
from one month prior till same day.

Toei and JR combined JR-Toei Free
Pass (¥1,400) includes all JR lines within
Tokyo. Railpass is valid of course inside
Tokyo (JR elevated rail only), but don't
validate it just for this Tokyo sightseeing,
use only if already validated.

Budgeteer do-it-yourself sightseer will
probably find it most convenient to make
his way to section of town by subway and
there go out, hoof it, and play it by ear.

Factory Visit: Nissan Auto, 90min
outside Tokyo, train or cab, prior contact
PR International div ☎3543-5523 xt 2355
Mr Miyanishi; Oppama plant every Tue
10:00, Murayama plant Wed 10:15–noon.
(For Toyota cars *see* Nagoya p300; Mazda
see Hiroshima p655; motorcycles *see*
Hamamatsu p288 on opening leg Tokaido
Yokohama–Nagoya). *See* JTB-Sunrise
Industrial tours (*next*) for Isuzu auto.

TIC Tokyo, ☎3502-1461, at Yurakucho
across Harumi-dori S-side from JR stn;
Japan Minshuku Ctr, reservations, also
Yurakucho JR stn, NE to Kotsu Kaikan
bldg, basement, ☎3216-6556.

City Bus Tours subject to change—1985 thru '92 changed annually, dropping
variants as true tourists declined; E-spkg guides, book direct or thru hotel desk; all offer
earlier free pickup major hotels; tax incl.

HATO Bus ☎3595-1083: co-sponsor with
JTB following **Sunrise** tours daily.

Japan Gray Line ☎3436-6881, after
8pm 7days all 24hrs ☎3433-5745:
Ohayo-good-morning Fish Market
tour, 5:15-8:45am, pickup earlier; coffee on
bus Shimbashi Dai-Ichi hotel to Tsukiji,
don water-proof overshoes see auctions,
wander 56-acre world's largest fish mkt; eat
J-bkfst: soup, sashimi, egg, or W/ham'n-
eggs; ¥4,900 /¥3,500 no bkfst.
Discontinued '89 but too good to believe
won't offer again: check, or hop cab and do
it yourself just as easily.

Morning tour 8:45: Tokyo Tower, Palace
Plaza, Asakusa Kannon, stroll Nakamise,
drive Ginza, ret 12:30; ¥3,910.

Afternoon tour 13:20: Diet bldg, pearl
gallery, Meiji Memorial gallery, Meiji
Shrine, Olympic complex, NHK Center,
drive Ginza, ret 17:30; ¥4,330.

Full Day, w/lunch, 17:30; ¥9,170.

Imperial Nite tour 17:00; kabuki, geisha
house for entertainment w/sukiyaki or steak
then to modern revue, ret 23:45; ¥15,800.

Nite tour 18:30: steak or sukiyaki dinner,
then same above, ret 23:15; ¥14,000.

Samurai Nite tour 18:30: Kabuki, Geisha w/drink, 22:00; ¥10,200.

Fuji-Hakone tour 8:45; bus to 5th stn Mt at 8,000'/2450m, lunch hotel, cable-car, boat ride L Hakone, ret 18:00; ¥14,320.

SUNRISE-JTB ☎3276-7777: with Hato.

Morning tour 9:00; Tokyo Tower view, Asakusa Kannon, drive–Kasumigaseki gov't ctr–Diet–Ginza–Marunouchi visit Imperial Palace East Gdn, Tasaki Pearls for ikebana and pearl demo, 13:00; ¥3,910.

Afternoon 14:00; same, –18:00; ¥4,450.

Full Day 9:00 Tokyo Tower view, tea ceremony at Happo-en garden, lunch at Chinzanso Garden Restaurant, Asakusa Kannon, Imperial Palace East Garden, Meiji-jingu shrine, 17:30; abt ¥10,000.

Disneyland 9:00; bus r.t., entry, full day free w/tix to 'big-10' attractions, ret 18:30; ¥8,630, kids/tots less by age.

Village Life & Crafts full day, 9:00; papier-mache Daruma-doll maker, bamboo fishing rod maker, farmers' Co-op, W-lunch, doll-making town, Bonsai cultivator, 18:00; wed-only ¥10,300.

Industrial full day 9:00-17:30; sites vary with day: several of Isuzu auto, stock exchange, JAL maintenance, robot ctr, electronics, w/lunch; ¥9,980.

Kabuki Nite 6:00pm X-25-31 monthly; sukiyaki at Suehiro J-restnt (shoes off squat –alt steak avail), Kabuki theater with Eng usually simultaneous xlation earphone (no photos), Geisha show Matsubaya in old red light Yoshiwara-Asakusa w/drinks (pix OK) ret 11:00pm; ¥13,000.

Bright Nite 6pm; Tokyo Tower view, tempura dinner, Geisha at Matsubaya, ret 9:30pm, ¥9,000.

Fascinating Nite 6pm; opt'l dinner of *kushiage* deep-fried skewers of seafood, meat, etc, at **Kushinobo** stage show at nitery New Latin Quarter or cabaret Shogun, ret 11pm; ¥11,000 w/dinner.

Sumo in season, 4+hrs, incl 3hrs sumo w/ drinks, lunch elsewhere; *masu* tatami box ¥23,780, or chair ¥17,780; off'n on.

Bay Cruises thru Hato or JTB; all out of Hinode pier short walk from JR loop Hamamatsucho stn; prices shown, first is cruise, +2nd/3rd cheapest meal/top course, top plus cruise & odd ¥200-300 discounted:

Morning cruise 10:00, 90min; ¥3,200+ ¥800/1,500; around harbor isle.

Lunch cruise 12:00, 90min; ¥3,200+ ¥8,000/10,000 varying; same rte.

Afternoon cruise 14:30, 50min; ¥2,000+ ¥800/1,500; innermost harbor pool.

Sunset cruise 17:00, 90min; ¥3,200+ ¥10,/13,000; same rte as morning, lunch.

Dinner cruise 19:00, 2hr30min, ¥4,300+ ¥13,/15,000; above rte plus outer harbor.

Helicopter course 9:30,12:30, 4hrs, daily summer, often others; to heliport, 5-6min fly over town, drive science museum, cruise bay 30min; ¥7,690, child ¥4,930. Off'n on annually, check.

KAMAKURA, FUJI-HAKONE, NIKKO: all above companies run day or longer tours, as well as several-day tours to farther points; check brochures available all hotels.

PLANNING TO STAY

INTERNATIONAL associations to meet bilingual Japanese of similar interests: **Japan-American Soc**, binational, mostly businessmen; or culture-oriented **Japan-British**, **Maison Franco-Japonaise**, **Goethe Society**, other relevant binationals, charity-aiding women's auxiliary. Watch dailies for announcements or phone your embassy or consulate for info. Business men/women have likes of **ACCJ**, American Chamber of Commerce in Japan–sadly, self-enwalled ghetto restricts self to staff of US companies in Japan, while allowing guest membership to other nations, ignores local-incorporated, self-employed, professionals. JALT (Japan Association of Language Teachers) self-explanatory worthwhile, branches in most cities. **Asiatic Society of Japan** (Tokyo only) intellectual oasis in cultural desert of foreign ghetto life–good monthly lectures 3rd-mon. Wives have binational ladies groups, like **Tokyo Women's Club** with good program for newcomer, and **FEW** (Foreign Executive Women). plus larger but exclusive **ILBS**, International Ladies Benevolent Society: good activities, great annual formal ball. College Women's Assoc worthwhile activities, annual print show-sale. Floraphiles have I.I., **Ikebana International**, chapters in big cities. Watch daily newspapers, *TJ*, *KTO*, etc. **Tokyo American Club** 'home away from home'-like, invites all: inquire ☎3583-8381. **Foreign Correspondents Club** admits almost anyone who can hold pencil and drink at same time, good bar but long waiting list: ☎3211-3161.

Tokyo-resident expats read weekly *Weekender*, free at hotels, TAC. For businessmen: *Tokyo Business Today*, or *Business Tokyo*, M. Several local mags bear looking into.

Having been able to safeguard and maintain the structure of the Imperial State, We are always with ye, Our good and loyal subjects...
— Emperor Hirohito, *Rescript on Surrender*

One of two most powerful cities of modernity...built around an opaque ring of walls...whose own center is no more than an evaporated notion...to give the entire urban movement the support of its central emptiness. —Roland Barthes, *Empire of Signs*

IMPERIAL PALACE
& ENVIRONS

AREA OF PRESENT-DAY TOKYO has been settled for several thousand years, but it never amounted to much more than hick hamlet until 500 years ago when OTA Dokan, local lord, chose to build his fort on site of present Imperial Palace. In 1590 Hideyoshi assigned Kanto (half of country east, *-to*, of Fuji-Hakone mountain barrier, *kan-*) as fief to Tokugawa Ieyasu who took over Ota estate, began its development as great castle. 1603 this became de facto center of empire's administration when Ieyasu officially took title as Shogun: Generalissimo or Dictator. Further developed under his dynasty of 15 shoguns. During this era bayside castle first overlooked swamps, which were filled in by leveling hills of Ueno to make both areas suitable for urban development, pushing population of Edo over 2 million by end of era 1860s. Fall of house of Tokugawa with Imperial Restoration 1868 ended schizoid government (tho military-civil schizophrenia surfaced again in 1930s, as worldwide, to bring about calamity of 1941-45). Imperial forces under young emperor Meiji deemed it more practical to move imperial de jure capital to Tokyo than move de facto administration to Kyoto.

WALKING TOUR

WE START around Imperial Palace. Back in '64 we pioneered what is now basis for JNTO (and others') walking tour. Best stations to start from are JR Yurakucho, or subways Yurakucho, Hibiya, or Nijubashi-mae; JR and subways at Tokyo Central are only few minutes further away. Yurakucho good station to keep in mind, convenient to TIC, and nearby American Pharmacy stocked with hard-to-get home items.

IMPERIAL PALACE, *Kohkyo*, was never what we consider true palace. Edo castle was primarily fortified administration center, altho principal apartments were palatial, especially when compared to then-dull, stone castles of Europe. Immense in comparison with European castles, only our castle-towns or walled cities can really be compared with its 1,090,000 square meters of fortification. Very imposing in its heyday, accounts of Dutch tribute missions from Nagasaki and early European traders and diplomats who entered precincts are florid in praise of its grandeur. It is today only shadow of former self, its real estate value equals State of California. Most old inner buildings were wood, suffered greatly from periodic fires, biggest of which aerial bombings of World War II. Sole surviving original building is one moved in 1630s to Kita-In Temple, in suburban Kawagoe (p.1221).

There was move to rebuild palace after war, but late emperor Hirohito-Showa would not permit it. Moved family into remaining outbuildings such as his library, determined not to allow use of scarce material on him until terrible housing problem beyond walls had been decently alleviated. 1960 plans finalized to start construction of palace, partly with government funds, partly contributions—accepted only if voluntary and after submitting appli-

cation for permission to give cash or presents, to minimize if not prevent
gifts accumulated by pressure groups, or reject donations from blackshirt
groups we still see roving around in cage-like black sound trucks, *hino-
maru* sun flags crackling in slipstream. Showa's widow lives there now,
ground broken October '91 for Akihito's new **Fukiage Palace** 150m to S.
To be 4,500m², cost ¥5,000,000,000, move in summer '93.

Public is admitted en-mob thru outer fringe of palace twice yearly, at
New Year and for *Emperor's Birthday* **December 23**. You may also enter to
witness *bugaku* performances (*see* ON STAGE, p 1248) in **Imperial Music
Hall** or on palace lawn. There are also arrangements to tour new palace,
except for private apartments. These were rather complicated but are now
greatly simplified—seem secret in travel trade. Here is procedure:

   Application: Japanese organized groups (considered 2 or more, solo tourist must
await group forming or get friend) need write Imperial Household Agency (below) 10 days
ahead (due to mass of applications by rural groups to do voluntary labor on grounds), but
day before for foreigners phone ☎3213-1111 ext 485 with names of all in small
group (large only group leader name, general info on group, exact number), professions,.
ages (must be over 20). Then go before 4:30 to **Kikyo-mon** to pick up permit for next
day, learn time appointed. Entering hours 10-11:30am & 1:30-3pm may vary. Group
planning ahead advised to write in advance with responsible person's data, number and
some general facts on members, give 2 alternate dates for your projected visit in event
your first choice not practical, enclose stamped self-addressed postcard or envelope, or
advise what day you will phone for confirmation after arrival in Tokyo, hotel you'll be at.
✍ Sanka-bu, **Imperial Household Agency**, Chiyoda-ku, Tokyo-100, w/ group info.

   For **Bugaku** court dance performances: May, restricted to organizational, diplomatic
etc invitation; but **Mid-October** (fri-sat-sun) open, write using double return postcard
self addressed, or self-addressed postcard enclosed in your letter, pertinent data as above,
✍ Shiki-bushoku, Imperial etc. Always pre-advertised in English press (p 1248).

   Hato Bus **Historical Tokyo** tours visit East Garden daily, they can arrange for you
privately to visit palace if you hire car or bus thru them for sightseeing—takes 10 days.
Closed to public some holidays, several days around **Dec 23** for court functions.

   Appointed group present selves at *Kikyo-mon* gate at appointed time and Imperial
Household guide will lead thru fringe of palace grounds. Visit takes under hour.

Palace is deceptive. Looks flat, heavily wooded, far from impregnable.
Once inside you'll see it quite differently. Ground within is raised quite bit,
presents lovely vista of city. Trees disguise heights, camouflage inner buildings. Walls marvelously designed for defense with numerous *culs de sac*,
walls beyond walls that cannot be seen until what would have been too late
for any enemy breaching outer wall.

INNER MOAT CIRCLE: *Maru-no-uchi*, 'circle-within', so called as it
was just within bounds of outermost moat and castles—like ships and
swords—are referred to by special term *maru* (not because any are round or
make round trips, but because *maru* is honorific, probably from Syriac—
Jesus' language—for saint). Area housed mansions of Matsudaira daimyo,
sub-clan of Tokugawa. Now name applies to whole neighborhood between
Palace and Tokyo Station (*following*). Moats not only defensive but served as
canals for heavy barge traffic, trucks of that era. Outer moat long ago filled
in and paved over to become Sotobori-dori 'Outer-moat Ave', remaining
postwar moats filled in with overhead or sunken highways. Innermost moat
remains; part home to swans & ducks, part rowboat ponds.

   To retain impressive aura of mystery one feels towards palace after
seeing it from plaza park—Japanese turrets, German steel-arched *Niju-bashi*
bridge—recommend you take taxi ride or brisk walk thru and around outer
grounds. We suggest take circular course, counter clockwise, from main
Hibiya intersection cutting thru Palace East Garden, which President Carter

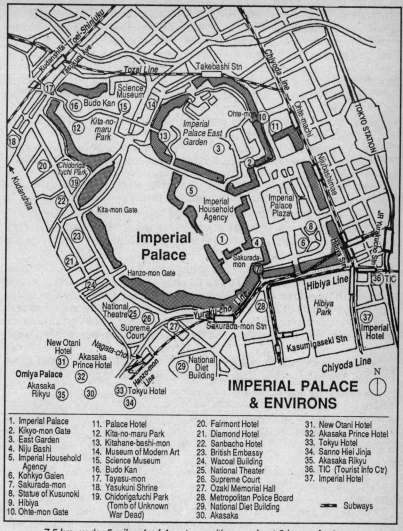

IMPERIAL PALACE & ENVIRONS

1. Imperial Palace
2. Kikyo-mon Gate
3. East Garden
4. Niju Bashi
5. Imperial Household Agency
6. Kohkyo Gaien
7. Sakurada-mon
8. Statue of Kusunoki
9. Hibiya
10. Ohte-mon Gate
11. Palace Hotel
12. Kita-no-maru Park
13. Kitahane-bashi-mon
14. Museum of Modern Art
15. Science Museum
16. Budo Kan
17. Tayasu-mon
18. Yasukuni Shrine
19. Chidorigafuchi Park (Tomb of Unknown War Dead)
20. Fairmont Hotel
21. Diamond Hotel
22. Sanbacho Hotel
23. British Embassy
24. Wacoal Building
25. National Theater
26. Supreme Court
27. Ozaki Memorial Hall
28. Metropolitan Police Board
29. National Diet Building
30. Akasaka
31. New Otani Hotel
32. Akasaka Prince Hotel
33. Tokyu Hotel
34. Sanno Hiei Jinja
35. Akasaka Rikyu
36. TIC (Tourist Info Ctr)
37. Imperial Hotel

━━━ Subways

—7.5 km, under 5 miles, taxi 4x-mtr + waiting, or about 2 hrs on foot—

jogged mornings establishing jogging course now published as pamphlet by nearby hotels. From Hibiya corner, follow moat either direction crossing first bridge to *Kohkyo Gaien*, Imperial Palace Outer Garden, wide pine tree-covered plaza which was to serve as open kill-zone against attacking forces. Till 1860s area housed mansions of top Honda, Matsudaira, Sakai, other clans whose lords were most trusted original inner circle of Ieyasu during his bid for shogun. Then turn up toward obvious main entrance to Palace, *Nijubashi* **double iron bridge**. Your taxi may approach to within few hundred feet of it, and you may walk right up to it.

Facing, at far back L of plaza is hoary, historic **Sakurada-mon** Gate. Our walking tour ends thru that gate, but if you don't plan full circle, see it now.

Facing, we go R, continue across park to...

Kikyo-mon gate thru which tour groups normally enter. Moat blocks your continuing straight and you must now turn R, follow moat then L to

Ohte-mon Gate (opp PALACE HOTEL), main entrance to *Kohkyo Higashi Gyoen*, **Imperial East Garden** (Ohte-machi stn of several subways). Cross moat thru gate by 3pm. No entry fee, but must keep ticket given to you by gate guard, return it when you leave, any gate. Now in innermost Tokugawa era castle; site of *honmaru* **central keep**, of which stone foundations remain from whose top is fabulous view of city. Ninomaru Garden, landscaped by 3rd shogun Iemitsu 1630 (when he moved some buildings to Kawagoe), has pond and tea house. Park also contains **Imperial Music Hall**, seasonal performances of bugaku and gigaku court music, dance can be seen. Park open daily 9:00-16:00 X-mon, fri.

Exit via northern **Hirakawa-mon** Gate–(turn in ticket)–for Takebashi stn, Tozai (lite blue) subway line. At western corner is **Kitahane-bashi-mon** Gate and bridge across to Kita-no-maru Park, with Budo-kan and museums (*next*).

Alternate- cross wide street 90° from moat under hiway, go 6-700m (10min) to Yasukuni-dori, Jinbocho intersection for **Bookshop Detour** (*see* KANDA, p.1174).

North-of-keep Park, *Kita-no-maru Koen*, crossing via Kitahane-bashi-mon Gate to our right (SE corner of park) is **National Museum of Modern Art** (10:00-17:00, X-mon, ¥600), focusing on post-Meiji Japanese art on top floors, rotating loan exhibits on Ist. To our far L is **Crafts Gallery** of museum housed in 19th century home of Imperial Palace Guards. Central is **Science & Technology Museum** (9:30-17:00, ¥500), large, square honeycomb type structure, showing how everything from plows to space-ships function; lots of hands-on exhibits. At N end is 'tradition-in-concrete' **Hall of Martial Arts**, *Budo-kan*, (*see* INTRODUCTION–SPORT p.68) built for '64 Olympic martial arts events and since used for such, but perhaps better known to Westerners as site of great live concerts. You may enter either of these or continue past Budokan snaking thru double **Tayasu-mon** Gate, only one thru which public automotive travel is permitted...

This leads us back out across moat for detour of only few dozen paces to...

YASUKUNI SHRINE: Dedicated to some 2.5million military war dead since first battle for imperial restoration, 1853—but for winners only, loyal Tokugawa samurai are not enshrined. Originally founded 1879 as TOKYO SHOKON JINJA shrine: its concept is of no greater antiquity than this. Until end of war all Japanese were considered, by jingoist-government at least, to be Shinto so all war dead were enshrined here. Not operated under Home Ministry as other shrines, but directly under military. Actual ashes returned here from battle when practical, otherwise spirit-souls alone made trek. Flip 'GI' good-bye: "See you in Yasukuni". Since 1945 only those who voluntarily adhere to Shintoism recognize this spiritual interment. Shrine is now denationalized and, we hope, entombs dead carcass of Bushido Jingoism.

Royal family as Shintoists may visit officially. PM, Cabinet visit as individuals. But recent tries by Cabinet,to officialize visits as 'respect to war dead' (does not include civilian air-raid victims) caused hullabaloo with China, Korea, etc, as well as Japanese who do not recognize shrine—including not only most native Christians, but many Buddhists and sects of 'folk-shinto', some of whom suffered bloody government pogroms prewar for their beliefs. China, Korea objected as war criminals who pillaged them are enshrined here. Problem of shrine is not simply to recognize Shintoism—that was done in 1950s by Christian PM Hatoyama resuming historical 'reporting to Ise Grand Shrine'. It is forced 'spiritual interment' of all who died whether their survivors want such. It is 'worship' of war criminals as Enshrined Spirits, much to chagrin of most of East Asia today. See, but no call to show respect. Politico-military tone set by insipid bronze statue of OMURA Masujiro, insignificant first modern War Minister 1860s.

Your visit will be most scenic early morning as clog-clad priests and shrine maidens shuffle on duty. **Treasure house** *Yushukan* war relics 1870-1945 incl Pearl Harbor, kamikaze pilots; (more in Kyoto, p.503).

PERSONAL DATEBOOK: Gala spring & autumn festivals to enshrined military dead. Gay with vendors, outdoor stalls, displays of flower arrangements. Varied offerings of song, dance at main hall. **Apr 21-23**, *Grand Spring Festival* (p.1267 details); **August 15** rites for end of World War II. **Oct 17-19** *Autumn Festival* (p.1270 details).

Continuing L, counterclockwise, 500 meters around moat we pass...
Chidorigafuchi Aquatic Park and **Fairmont** fine tourist class Hotel. Facing us in moat point, there is dock for rowboat rental.

Point of land we must now turn R around, is park containing...
TOMB of Unknown War Dead (nondenominational) was raised at *Chidorigafuchi*, obviously without knowledge of US Embassy protocol section who tried to send then-VP Nixon, and later Ike on his never-realized 1960 state visit to Yasukuni to lay usual unknown-soldier wreath. Quiet park, strikingly simple open pavilion with protohistoric-type stone sarcophagus. Drop coin in box and take flower, place it before Tomb of Unknown War Dead—with no war criminals enshrined—as you would at Arlington, Arc de Triomphe or Westminster Abbey.

L again w/ moat, on btwn Chidorigafuchi Park–British Embassy 15min to great gate–
Hanzo-mon and most dramatic outer view of Palace. At this point we realize we have been circling slowly uphill and we stand at edge of moat looking down on great ravine several stories deep by football field wide. From here, and top of Asakusa View Hotel, are our favorite views of Capital. Looking away from Palace, you notice interesting **Wacoal Bldg**, architect KUROKAWA Kisho—fine exhibits and art deco theater, cafe lounge.

Hanzomon subway station is about 200m W, downhill from Hanzo-mon Gate.

National Theater (traditional kabuki and bunraku stages, *see* pp1246-7); next to which is striking cubist **Supreme Court**.

It's easy (mostly downhill) 2km from here back to our starting point, but rather than going whole way, we recommend turn-off—continue down from Hanzo-mon Gate about one km to second large road coming in from our R, Aoyama-dori Ave.

We are now at...
Ozaki Memorial Hall erected in memory of founder of Japanese Parliamentarism, OZAKI Yukio (1859-1954), lovely example of modern memorial architecture. From here back to our starting point (Hibiya intersection) is another 1km; we have come 6.5km/4mi not taking bookstore detour, 7.5km with bookstores. 5min along moat is **Sakurada-mon** which we noted at start beyond Nijubashi bridge main entry, and facing it is new **Police Headquarters** skyscraper on site of old brick drumtower HQ and jail, in which Doolittle's airmen captured in Shangri-la raid were held in pie-slice-shape cells until executed.

At this point one may continue back down to Hibiya, but we would suggest you turn R here to stroll or drive thru...
Capitol, Kasumigaseki political center **National Diet**, *Kokkai-Gijido* – homonymous Japanese nickname 'ziggurat'–beyond which is residence of PM (who may refuse to live in its 1-BR) and in neighboring 'Downing' (or 'Georgetown') streets, of Speaker of House and President Upper House.

Short walk W of Diet Bldg, via Sanno Hie Jinja shrine, is...
Akasaka-mitsuke intersection with main offices of Tokyo Broadcasting System. This area has many fine restaurants of enough variety to fit any palate or pocket (¥-L hotels **New Otani**, **Akasaka Prince**, **Tokyu**, nearby Capitol; major subway xfer stn red, orange lines, underground walkway to yellow line).

SANNO HIE JINJA, one of top shrines of Edo, built 15th century by Ohta Dokan and later adopted by Tokugawa as tutelary shrine. Later associated with safe childbirth, proper upbringing of children—for which now best known. Present structure 1959. *DATEBOOK*: **June 10-16** *Sanno-sai* ranks among Top Three Edo Festivals (with Kanda and Asakusa). Gala parade was cancelled at time of our first edition then revived, with giant affair alternating years (1992,'94,'96,'98). Over 300 costumed participants and main floats, drums, carriages and 50-odd mikoshi put out by districts around Palace, which outermost grounds parade circles (over 20km).

If **taxiing** you have consumed perhaps one hour, allowing for stops for snapshots; **walk** consumed 2hrs rounding Palace, 3 w/ bookshop detour. Probably ready for lunch — suggest continue to Akasaka Mitsuke. **Taxi** tourist still has 1-2 hours till lunch.

Garden buffs take tea break here in...
Hotel New Otani, former Edo Era daimyo estate, formal gardens remain. If not guest, advise combine garden stroll with snack in **Garden Lounge**, or for best long view in town 40th fl Top of Tower **Grill** (bottomless buffet bkfst). Budgeteers might splurge on grand bkfst in Garden Lounge then, before or after, stroll. Or go up to Tower-top for meal and great view.

AKASAKA RIKYU Detached Palace, *Geihin-kan*, imitation Versailles built by public subscription 1909 for emperor Meiji, who by one legend humbly turned it down, another more likely is he ordered it for crown prince Taisho. Housed National Diet Library until 1962, then '64 Olympic HQ, now palace at last for state guests. Recent past, could enter outer grounds at all times, and see inside palace when not in official use, but now can only visit garden on specially appointed days which are random and announced in English papers. Otherwise, peer in thru fence—tho sympathetic guard allowed Garet quick snapshot-view from inside side gate.

10min walk uphill along right (facing) leads past walled **Togu Palace** of all members of Imperial Family, left, within immense wooded park of **Omiya Palace** in which other royals have palaces, rather less palatial than good-size US wealthy mansion— Japanese Imperial family not imperious—and on via **Meiji Kinen-kan Hall** to **Jingu Outer Garden** (next chapter WEST).

Geihin-kan 7min walk Yotsuya Stn (JR, red subway), beyond moat is steeple of ...
St. Ignatius Church and **Sophia International University**, which offers degree programs in English and Japanese, with very international student body.

OUTER MOAT CIRCLE

Filling in few details on areas just beyond moat, great complex of modern buildings to your right along front of Palace is, as noted above...
MARUNOUCHI, economic heart of Tokyo, area between Palace and Tokyo Stn includes: Central Post Office, old Marunouchi Building (popularly *Maru-biru*—till '50s biggest structure in nation, commercial predecessor of Pentagon in labyrinthine plan), next-door Shin (new) Marunouchi Building housing like its neighbors, Japan and US banks. Marshland when Ieyasu took over Castle 1603, he had mountain that stood at adjoining Kanda leveled for fill. Kanda became residential area for samurai retainers, filled-in portions nearest bay became city proper with Nihonbashi, Nippon Bridge (Meiji era balustrade still runs under highway) as center from which all road distances were, and are, measured—but way it has been cluttered is amazing. Marunouchi (modern business area beyond protective ring of most-trusted lords' mansions, which are now palace plaza) was infantry drill field and good place to hunt ducks.

When emperor Meiji moved in 1869 to newly renamed Tokyo (Eastern Capital), empty field on his front door became problem. Mitsubishi were pressured into "doing something about it", and they dutifully, if regretfully took over blight. Architecture of few square blocks mirrors its subsequent history. They invited British architect, Webster, to put up "little bit o'London" of 4-storey brick business buildings in 1894. These were only torn down in '60s to make better use of now fabulously expensive land, one temporarily preserved as architectural monument—but Mitsubishi, as unhappy about leaving it up as they were about putting it up, moved it to Meiji Mura near Nagoya. Webster extemporized floating foundations so buildings were earthquake-proof and survived 1923 cataclysm, as did most modern steel-reenforced buildings tho only Frank Lloyd Wright's Imperial Hotel was publicized (by Wright himself)—and it suffered damage. Front section of hotel also at Meiji Mura. Fire was great killer in '23.

Buildings immediately lining Palace and boulevard leading to Tokyo Station (including Maru-buildings), were limited in height to 8 storeys out of combination of aesthetics and respect for emperor to avoid looking down on him. Thus presented unified front of variety of structures of level height, projecting firm national image. This arrangement collapsed with hassle in recent years about new red fake brick-front 24-storey Tokyo Kaijo (again insurance) building. Insurance moguls say to hell with aesthetics or respect, king cash-flow reigns. Image of resolve degenerated to one more accurately reflecting present business greed.

First spike for railroad in Japan was laid in 1870, Year of Iron Horse in 60-year calendar of 12 celestial beasts and 5 elements. Ran from Yokohama to Shinagawa in 1872, later extensions brought it to Shimbashi, then to Marunouchi where present **Tokyo Station** was built, 1914, modeled after Amsterdam Station. 1988 saw it saved from wrecking ball thanks to citizen movement—to be restored, old domes burned in air raids to be rebuilt and nondescript new skyscraper will be raised over track area behind brick Marunouchi (north) entry. Most JR stations are buildings thru which you pass between getting off train and getting into cab. Old Tokyo Station Marunouchi side (exiting from Shinkansen wicket go R) gives you old-fashioned impression of having arrived at some place of substance. Architect was TATSUNO Kingo, pioneer westernist, student of Josiah Conder—who, ladies, wrote first English book on ikebana, major art of manipulating space like architectire.

At *Babasaki-mon* on Hibiya-dori facing Palace, on corner of ave to Tokyo Station is **Meiji Seimei** (insurance) bldg (1934) characteristic of 'New England Greco-Roman' school of Japanese architecture, molded cement front imitating Grecian pillars. It covers spot woodblock print artist Ando Hiroshige was born—no monument marks. This standard bank design created new ideograph: bank ads often show stylized pair or trio of Greek pillars—now as set trademark as occidental three balls. (Architecture buffs may want to visit another Greco-Roman built 1896, by Tatsuno, **Bank of Japan**, *Nihon Ginko*, with its **Money Museum** [enter 9:30-4:00, free, rsve advance ☎3279-1111, need passport] other side of Tokyo Stn, nr world's oldest DS **Mitsukoshi** and its stone lions). Other buildings reflect faceless anonymity of western architecture of past several decades. Romantic antique W-style block L of Meiji Seimei is 3-storey, cupolaed **Bankers' Club**, red brick with wrought iron carriage cover. May kiss wrecker's ball. **Dai-ichi** Bldg, was MacArthur's GHQ, overlooks Imperial Palace as it seems only insurance companies could then, as now, dare. Shogun Mac personally used only half private office of prewar prexy ISHIBASHI Taizo. Mac's spartan office and marble staff john (loo) preserved on 6th floor.

Tokyo Stock Exchange, *Tokyo Shoken Torihikijo,* now world's 2nd biggest; fronted by sculptor Kuwahara's 'Hommage to the Sun'. Tozai subway Kayabacho stn nr exit 10,11; mon-fri 9-11, 1-3; go to 2nd fl Visitors' Center for info, printed guide, etc, phone link explaining action in English and French, video in Jpn. Fish-bowl view of floor where 1500 traders semaphore trades: finger under (*shita*) eyelid (*matsuge*) is 'moving Matsushita', etc. B1,2 bond trading.

... *down from Babasakimon, just before JR overhead tracks, is...*

Ex-Tokyo Metropolitan Government Bldg (City Hall), internationally modern yet classically Japanese. Ferroconcrete-glass construction prevalent worldwide today, but overcame problem wall of glass created before special glass invented—washing it, cooking of inhabitants sunny days, protecting pedestrians from falling glass in 'quake (due soon?)—by adapting traditional Japanese design. Each glass area within skeletal frame is set back behind small veranda. Floor of one above is sun shade, window washer can step out to work, any falling glass falls only on its own veranda. And recessed glass areas create play of shadows, as in ancient Persian architecture, which sooth eyes. Architect inimitable Tange who also did Hiroshima Peace Park and Olympic stadia across town in Yoyogi, new super City Hall in Shinjuku and planning new 'World Tokyo'. But as in Peace Park, landscape artist fouled him up. For short while initiated new era in Japanese architecture, before new type glass made possible glass slab high rises. (Extant **NTT** bldg 2nd S of Imperial Hotel emulates). As in Peace Park, concrete did not age well. Fell to wrecker's ball '91 after city gov't moved to Shinjuku high rise.

Adjoining W is...

YURAKUCHO, in area called Nishi (West) Ginza, has newest addition to area, grand Yurakucho Mullion Bldg, alias **Center Bldg**—half Seibu Dept Store, other half Hankyu DS, with 3 floors underground parking, top floors movie theaters which in former incarnation monopolized site. Still drawing gawkers is huge clock on outside wall which rises up at every hour between 10:00-21:00 to have dancing dolls emerge to announce time. For one decade before war and three after, this was most-photographed corner in Japan, its round-fronted Nichigeki theater put forth as epitome of modernization. Adjoining overhead highway was until 1960s one of palace outer moats-cum-freight canal, spanned by Sukiya-bashi bridge, now just name for underpass thru expressway. Bridge was favorite place for locals separated by war to find each other again—legend being that if you stood at bridge long enough you would meet everyone in world or someone who knew someone who.... Then during US Occupation also grew as trysting spot.

Still place to meet everyone who comes to Japan—with main office of **TIC** JNTO Tourist Info Center, S across main ave from kooky clock.

Center of Tokyo where ministries and big department stores are is abominable. Ugly skyscrapers next to booths...only on the vertical alleys left and right of Ginza can you enjoy old Japan—porcelains, silk fabrics, umbrellas, wooden sandals, kimonos, dolls, and window displays with genuine (-appearing) food, real paintings by Cezannne or Matisse...
— Nikos Kazantsakis, *Japan and China*

GINZA

PERHAPS BEST known site in Japan after Fuji-san, glittery shopping street on some of most expensive property on earth aptly named 'Silver Site'. Exclusive district was once marshlands, and when Ieyasu had this whole area reclaimed it became first *shitamachi*, (pron sh'ta-machi) downtown district of Edo, home to merchants and craftsmen. Got name after first silver mint built here in 1612. Main shopping strip is right above subway Ginza line's

Ginza station along Chuo-dori Ave, 'center street'—name given early '60s when Tokyo's unnamed streets were christened tho no one, certainly no taxi driver, knows these names, all addresses go by -chome subdivisions like Chinese boxes within boxes. It was to be called Ginza-dori (street) until merchants of central strip Ginza from 1-chome at Kyōbashi 'capital bridge' (where overhead expressway crosses over former bridge, behind ¥-LL Seiyo Hotel) to 8-chome (near Shimbashi expwy overpass) claimed exclusive right to historic name, denying lower class shopkeepers beyond of Kanda and elsewhere, even posh Mitsukoshi at Nihonbashi. Chuo-dori it may be on street-signs, but to everyone it's Ginza. Narrow alleys either side are neon-drenched Nishi-West- (toward palace, see Chopsticks) and Higashi-, East-Ginza.

Several subway lines meet at center of Ginza-4-chome, just E of JR Yurakucho stn.

One remnant of old sh'tamachi days is **Kabuki-za Theater**, 100m E of main 4-chome intersection (see p.1246).

Old Timer visiting for first time since Occupation days would have hard time recognizing street—except for its charisma. Main intersection 4-chome has changed little, still dominated SW & SE (despite larger, brasher new glass towers on N corners, less attractive) by Mitsukoshi-Ginza branch DS and facing **Wako** DS. Former has fine teashop 2nd fl overlooking fascinating intersection, ideal for mid-trek break), while grand show windows of latter display some of country's most interesting decorative art in their mannequin compositions—so good they stay up for 40-day stints, nine annually, premiering sundays. Window display in Japan is major art form, Wako is its Old Master.

First time Jay took *gin-bura* (Ginza-stroll) was Xmas nite, 1951. Then trolleycars rattled down center and curbs were lined with kerosene-lamped pushcarts selling *Made in Occupied Japan* junk—souvenirs, cheap box cameras, toys, especially tin windups, stuffed dolls ("How will resource-poor Japan ever survive in this modern peaceful world?" we all wondered) —like any carny-strip, but with willow trees whispering overhead. There was barely room for one lane of intermittent traffic either side—mostly Army of Occupation-tagged big US cars and charcoal-burning, clinker-putt-putting taxis. New Year 1952 saw street stalls moved off-avenue to roofed-over Ginza-kan Mart, eventually to be absorbed by burgeoning arcades, like **International Arcade** behind Imperial Hotel where ever-popular Hayashi kimono is vestige. Meanwhile, willow trees of old woodblock print-Edo were cut down at insistence of 'tradition-conscious' shops because they concealed their signs. In '70s it looked for while like Ginza would fade away to secondary status after ring-towns Shibuya, Shinjuku, Ikebukuro. But while these may surpass Ginza in daily traffic, concentrations of shops or gross sales—tho statistics vary annually showing Ginza repeatedly rebounds—they are just commuter hubs and class trade gradually returned to Silver Site. Land here is too expensive to sustain normal business and small shops here are usually name-promotional flagships for chains of counter-size concessions in larger shops and DS nationwide, or build office and shop rental blocks upstairs.

Gin-bura, stroll-Ginza. Shop-see even if you don't buy anything. Would you visit New York and miss Fifth Avenue, or Paris and Champs Elysee? Sundays or national holidays boulevard is mile-long **Pedestrian Paradise** with no vehicular traffic and lots of parasolled tables and chairs set out, lots of refreshments available, all shops open, sometimes sidewalk sales.

*The Battery (N.Y.) still seems like the entrance to the city
and the New World. Shinjuku seems like a point of egress,
it turns its back upon the old city and its eye upon the suburbs,*
— Edward Seidenstecker, *Never the Twain*

WESTSIDE GARDENS
AND BACK INTO TOWN

WEST EDGE of city loop boasts three large parks, each with own singular character: **Shinjuku Gyoen** (Imperial) **Garden** with seasonal displays of chrysanthemum and iris; **Meiji Shrine** magnificent shinto shrine in gigantic glade; **Meiji Shrine Outer Garden** with Olympic athletic stadia complex.

SHINJUKU

OFTEN CALLED *Shin To-shin*, New Capital, vibrant new heart of Tokyo, far from olde Edo—incorporated into city in 1932, 44-storey Billion Dollar **City Hall** (observatory top) moved here April Fool '91. Astounds country folk with superlatives, like electric bill equal to 20,000 homes. Shinjuku stn at heart is busiest in Tokyo with over 2 million transiting daily—in addition to main junction of JR and 2 subways it is terminus for Odakyu, Keio and Seibu private lines. EAST (inside Yamanote Loop) of station are entertainment and shopping districts; WEST (outside Loop, *see* p1151) out from labyrinthian multi-level West Exit is new commerce center, its ever-growing skyline called Tokyo's Manhattan, including beyond those office giants several of Tokyo's best ¥-L hotels: **Hilton, Hyatt, Keio Plaza** and several good ¥S-T-up such as **Shinjuku Prince, Washington**, with more rising.

EAST: Outside smaller East Exit is old area, where action is, mainly for *sarariman*, younger office worker types. Sprawling Shinjuku station confuses, but at least main directional signs are in English. Easiest way around is move underground as far as possible, but here most guiding signs are Japanese only. Spreading E, 1.5km underground shopping street called **Sub-nadé**, named from Japanese habit of creating their own 'Western' words, this from **Sub**(terranean Prome)**nadé**. East exit landmark at ground level is **My City**, several floors of restaurants, boutiques, and such. North across plaza is easy to spot **Studio Alta**, another everything-store, with giant TV screen façade. East along wide Shinjuku-dori Ave front of Alta is main shopping strip; closed to traffic Sundays to create *Hokosha-tengoku* 'Pedestrian Heaven' or—Hell depending on how you feel about crowds. You find long-famed department store branches like **Isetan, Mitsukoshi**, credit king **Marui** (red logo OIOI) which so far has three separate buildings —*Sports, Young* and *Fashion*—and **Techno**, which tries to outdo **Alta** thru blaring music videos out front.

Kinokuniya bookstore has huge selection of foreign language books and magazines. **Sakuraya Camera**, at nearest corner, is loaded with discount cameras, watches, calculators, portable cassettes and such; but you may want to compare to **Doi** and our favorite **Yodobashi** camera shops at West exit—but first of all with US or hometown discounters. You will also find numerous clothing stores, many of which sell good quality at low prices. Sidewalk merchants sell American junk from yuppie buttons to LA souvenirs. We found Chinese art student working his way thru Japanese language school, selling his traditional ink paintings at prices nostalgic of our '64 edition, and bought several.

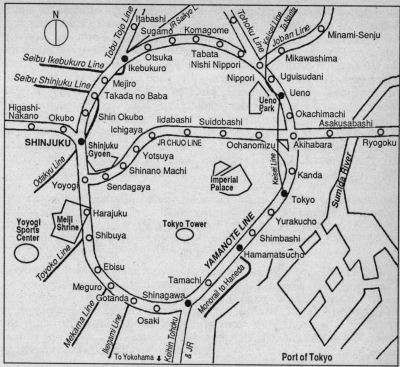

Kabuki-cho playground for adult entertainment; neon jungle SE of E-exit
—one place that could just as well be passed over, but should see once, if
briefly. Facing Studio Alta, take shopping street to its L, cross next, wide Yasukuni-dori
and you're there. By day, main strip looks like any street, but at nite crawls
with people looking for action. Daytime population of 3,000 or so swells to
400,000 after dark. Many large, cheap drinking joints make area popular
with college crowd (crazed but fun madhouse after final game of college
baseball series). Sidestreets are same day or nite, lined with countless 'Peep
Rooms', 'No-pants coffee shops', strip shows, rooms for rent by hour, no
questions. You rarely get what you pay for—posted prices usually just get
you inside, after which you might get more, but for more money. Some
enterprising touts have some English, but on whole visitors to these back
alleys would do better to go with Japanese-speaking friend.

Despite its appearance and reputation (vernacular press sensationalizes as
'Tokyo's Hell'), Kabuki-cho is safe; no fear getting rolled, or even harassed
unless you do something to warrant it, and even then most problems will be
dealt with simply at nearby police box. Worst is you may be overcharged in
strip joints, as expected anywhere. Kabuki-cho roared 24hrs 'round clock
until latest of half-hearted police attempts to crack down on porn led to most
places shutting down around midnite. Last trains out of Shinjuku as bad as
morning rush, except everyone is quite drunk. It may be quiet for while, but
sooner or later everything will reappear again, just under different names.
Citizen-supported cleanup won't work until developers level area.

Grander scale than Asakusa, Kabuki-cho does not discriminate against
age. Game corners are full of kids daytime, with evening curfew crowd ages
to collegiates and businessmen. Newest US movies in some theaters, others

show period dramas for older Japanese, or feature length cartoons for junior
—but most prevalent are porno flicks. Japanese censors make sure you
don't 'see' much in these flicks (taboo-pubic hair blotted out), but then one
can always hit side streets of Kabuki-cho for live-anything goes and more-
shows. Look around tho, and you will also find many interesting joints
which do *not* exploit sex trade. Many play jazz, another specializes in 'Big
Band' sounds, while yet another embraces California surf sounds of '60s.
Many are run by aging student radicals of '60s—Jay taught at radical
campus then, finds them some of most interesting folks in Japan. In another
corner are two odd but interesting looking Gothic 'castles' which started out
as proper piano bar-coffee lounges, went 'no-pants', now talk of returning
to original format. Anything we particularize will change by time you get
here. Some good restaurants are listed later in Tokyo CHOPSTICKS, p1256.

GOLDEN GAI, elegant name for rabbit-warren of alleys lined with 150
hole-in-wall eateries, bistros—most good, some super...all fun, safe,
cheap. Many denizens are E-spking intellectuals. Alas, steadily falling to
wrecking ball, which may moderate their frequent antagonism to outsiders,
'non-clubmembers'—whether club sexual preference or 'attitude'.

GET THERE: NW of Kabuki-cho up Yasukuni-dori in low-rise block facing Ward
Office, from Kabuki-cho up L side Yasukuni-dori. Scenic approach is up Yasukuni to big
intersection with Meiji-dori, turn L 3 small streets to torii on L, enter this to well-lit
HANAZONO JINJA Shrine, on to warrens, turn in any of 200+ that
sound or look good. Most have specialty crowds: Nabe-san (short for
owner Watanabe-san, '60s student radical refugee), just W behind shrine,
no name on door up to 2nd fl ¥-B soba-house, gets film crowd from pros to
celluloid addicts. Bar Maeda, (abt dead center of maze, one alley R/N of Nabe, up
nr end on L-side), gets stage folks and cartoonists. Daijin door has one of our
favorite English signs: "Run by guy who wants to keep busy. No smiles,
but our food is cheap and good"; alley straight up from rear of shrine, first L of
Nabe, or coming in curving lane Shinjuku Yuhodo from Yasukuni-dori, 2nd on R, down.
     Rick Kennedy's *Good Tokyo Restaurants* for rathole-by-rathole description of GG.

SHINJUKU NI-CHOME, largest gay district in country, few blocks from
Kabuki-cho past Golden-Gai. East end of Toei Sanchome subway stn, E on either
Shinjuku-dori or Yasukuni-dori to next main street and try bars around there; you'll
find many fun ones, straight or gay. Early in AIDS scare some discouraged
white-trade, but this changed—could change again. Longtime favorite
watering spot for young foreign Tokyo gays and 3rd worlders is Club 69
reggae bar run by pair of Japanese rastas—intentionally ratty inside fits
mood perfectly; all drinks ¥600. E on Yasukuni-dori cross next big street marked by
circular Isetan parking bldg, take alley to its R, first R and notice small red 69 sign—
basement of new, red Daini Seiko Bldg, Shinjuku 2-18-5. Kinsmen, int'l gay but
welcomes foreigners and women; in neighboring Oda Bldg, 2-18-5 block at corner,
9-5am X-tue. Few doors up alley on L is Sazae, for real low-life. Up alley to next
street, turn R, go on 2 alleys and in to L, to Peter Pan, relatively posh, live
shows midnite and 3am, cover chge ¥7,000, drinks ¥1,000up; Shinjuku 2-13-
6 cellar Koa Bldg, 10pm-5am X-sun. Many others in area, explore!
     Shinjuku known as entertainment center since feudal times when it lay
just outside Edo proper. Jumping off point for Tokaido and Koshu-kaido
pedestrian hiways, busy Shinjuku had all 'services' any traveller might
require. Reputation got so bad that early 18th century saw it completely shut
down for half century. It was back in fine form not long after being allowed
to reopen. First rail station put here in 1880s and Shinjuku was never same,

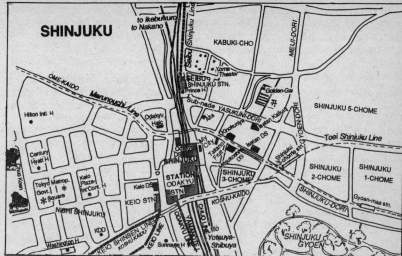

suddenly finding itself hub for western reaches of Tokyo. 'Entertainment' grew even more. Shinjuku also didn't suffer as badly during Kanto Quake.

Kabuki-cho name coined postwar as initial plan to rebuild Kabuki-za Theater (fire-bombed) had new theater here. Kabuki ended up at old spot off Ginza, but Shinjuku kept name and built giant **Koma Theater** in its place.

As if to emphasize Shinjuku's undesirability, it was site for sprawling sewage treatment plants processing all of Tokyo's waste. Spread of city later helped Shinjuku by forcing out these odiferous pits. In ambitious reclamation project saw pits emptied, cleaned, reshaped, so that these former sewage pits are now prime property of Shinjuku's new fertile center of commerce, as pricey as Ginza...

WEST SIDE OF SHINJUKU. Bird's eye view of this area—from one of its skyscraper lounges—shows enormous uniform blocks, rare sight in Tokyo's usually haphazard maze of streets. Walking among them you notice elevated roads on what were dividing walls between sewer pits, from which grow respectable skyscrapers of financial giants Nomura, Sumitomo, KDD, Mitsui, with Washington, Hilton, Century Hyatt, Keio, Prince Hotels. Prince first up in '71; since then dozen high-rises sprouted with room for more. W end is **Shinjuku Chuo Park**, oasis of green for quarter of million people who work in these dozen Manhattany high-rises.

Many of these buildings offer great views of city, best on clear days, especially winter when Mt Fuji is in plain view. Bell-bottomed **Yasuda Kasai Bldg** (43fl, 200m) has observatory on 42nd floor, part of small gallery exhibiting works of painter TOGO Seiji whose pasty art-deco style reminds of French hair oil labels of 1920s; ¥300, 9:30-16:30, X-weekend, hol. Next door **Nomura Bldg** (50fl, 210m) has shops 1st, 2nd floors; while brown **Center Bldg** (54fl, 223m) has many fine moderate-priced restaurants in basement, branch of Tsukiji sushiya Tama-zushi 53rd floor. Has underground link to **Mitsui Bldg** (55fl, 224m) which has red brick 55 Plaza in front with outdoor tables. Next is three-faced **Sumitomo Bldg** (52fl, 210m) with restaurants on top floors, metal and stone sculptures outside and prize-winning pieces from Nitten Art Exhibit hang 1st floor hollow innard; then matched paired towers **Dai-ichi Seimei** and **Century Hyatt** hotel. Far corner is 'S'-shaped new ¥-L **Hilton International**. Facing Mitsui is ¥-L

Keio Plaza Hotel; behind is **KDD Bldg**, communications satellite displayed in lobby. Next to KDD is most interesting hulk here, square **N-S Bldg**: far from tallest at 121m, but 'hollow' inside offers toe-tingling bird's eye view from 30th floor 'bridge' to lobby below, with its giant pendulum water clock. It, too, has many restaurants and coffee shops on top floors.

Lining station WEST EXIT is **Odakyu** DS, with **Keio** Dept store facing (corresponding private rail stns under each); fashion plaza **Lumine** at south end. Arched glass walkway connects Odakyu to annex, **Odakyu Halc**, with carillon clock which has dancing animals come out hourly 10:00-17:00. If you end up at underground West Exit, you can walk along tunnel road from/to business center. Despite giant fans, pollution from trapped auto exhaust poses great health hazards for those who must trudge (or work in) this route every day. And sheltered from elements down here are boxpeople, scores of Tokyo's 'non-existent' homeless living out of their cardboard box shelters. Watching over them is giant wall sculpture **Eye of Shinjuku** by MIYASHITA Yoshiko.

North of Odakyu, along tracks, are narrow lanes with many fun secondhand clothing stores. Just beyond are paired mini lanes lined with dozens of budget food stalls. What you get at these stalls is good, tho alley has unflattering name of *Shomben-yokocho*, or 'Pisspot-Alley.' Recently, name was changed to *Yakitori* (barbecue) *Yokocho*, since one lane is almost all yakitori joints; other assorted mix. These alleys also easily reached from E side of Shinjuku: facing Studio Alta go L, thru first low tunnel and R on other side.

SHINJUKU GYOEN Garden, reach best from subway Shinjuku Gyoen-mae stn, red Marunouchi line. Exit either end of stn, follow concrete-pillared outer wall in either direction to either **Shinjuku-mon Gate** or **Okido-mon Gate**: former closer to Japanese half of garden, latter to Western half. Garden 583,000 m² was daimyo's during Edo era, taken by State 1872 as Imperial, redone 1899-1904 by French Henri Martinet, first to combine E-W elements. During war grew vegetables and fruits for Palace. Best if cherry (April), iris, (June) or chrysanthemum (Nov 1-15) in bloom. If not bloom season, casual tourist may want to skip it. Japanese half has **Taiwan-kaku** Pavilion in one corner, given by Taiwan (then richest colony) for late Showa emperor's wedding—funeral here Feb 24,'89. Unfortunately neglected, half-heartedly boarded up, can no longer view garden from inside—may refurbish it in his honor. Around it are beautiful silver pine from Taiwan. Wonderful escape any time of year from city sounds and crowds for those stuck in Tokyo, rare public park where one may actually sit on grass. **Late Sept** *Takigi noh.*
Alt **bus** #71 from Shinjuku via palace ring road → Ginza → waterfront → Harumi Pier.

> For fascinating **detour** before Meiji Outer Garden and Shrine, or Meiji Jingu; between 2 continue out from Shinjuku 2x-mtr taxi → Suginami-ku Wada Honmachi, or subway 4 stops → Honan-cho terminus of Marunouchi red line.

Short walk or bus #86 from Meguro el-loop stn or in-town Nihonbashi Mitsukoshi...
DAI SEI DO (Great Sacred Hall) 30,000-capacity cathedral of major new faith Rissho Kosei Kai, offshoot of folk-Buddhist Reiyukai founded 1925 based on Lotus Sutra reciting, faith healing, still 3,000,000 strong. Rissho Kosei Kai cofounded 1938 by present president NIWANO Nikyo, then milkman, with NAGANUMA Miyoko, revered as female living Buddha, d.1957. In 1941 boasted 1,000 followers, by end of war 3,000, 1954 over million, '64 edition 2,500,000 and now over 5,000,000. Still based on simplified Lotus Sutra, no formal link to Nichiren, no clergy. Gigantic center was built by public subscription of over 10 million dollars, completed in May 1964—

8 storeys plus spirals, domes, turrets and towers with great central hall like opera house on 3rd floor. Atop 8-storey structure is dome 37m/120ft across topped by central spire 16m/50ft high. Surrounding 8 small spires represent 8-fold path of enlightenment which Buddha taught, while roof tower numerology symbolizes 4 noble truths, 12 chains of causation and 6 transcendental virtues. Materials Swedish granite, Italian marble, Mexican agate all superbly, often intricately worked by Japanese craftsmen. From entrance we proceed directly into large hall enshrining Shakyamuni Buddha.

Teenage reader of first edition mid '70s, fascinated by building, climbed outside to pinnacle—then went on spree climbing other buildings in town.

Aside from Soka Gakkai—Value-Creating Society—Rissho Kosei Kai is one of main modern offshoots of Japanese protestant Nichiren sect of Buddhism. These modern sects differ from traditional Buddhism in their worship of historic Buddha, Prince Saint Shakyamuni, whom they also regard as being earthly form of ultimate-eternal Buddha (*see* ORIENTATION ON BUDDHISM p23). Credo of sect is based on Lotus Sutra and they share with other Nichiren Buddhists ritual recitation *"Namu myoho renge-kyo"* or "Adore Lotus of Perfect Law". But whereas other Nichiren offshoot, Soka Gakkai, recruits and expands thru militant policy known as 'break & subdue', Rissho Kosei Kai is more traditionally Buddhisticly pacific.

Gajoen, 'Garden of Lyric Elegance' built 1931 after 'quake by great restaurateur HOSOKAWA Rikizo to enshrine by use best of contemporary arts and crafts, including 'colonial' Korean (fantastic rreception hall of black lacquer inlaid with mother-of-pearl, 3 years to recreate 1980s). Murals covered all 100 rooms, halls, toilets. Best 35 of 1200 not preserved in situ in 7 still-functioning halls are now in attached **museum**, ¥500. Dine in ornate Chinese or J-restaurants as they were 1930s. **Hotel**, *see* p.1131.

OFFBEAT STUDENT SIDETRACK

SHIMOKITAZAWA, or just 'Shimokita', quiet neighborhood rapidly becoming new youth hangout. Ideal location with station junction of private Inokashira (from Shibuya 4 stops on way to Kichijoji, follows) and Keio (6 from Shinjuku) lines. Recent emergence from rice paddy-cheap rents hospitable to shops just starting; with area's youth also encourages rash of health food restaurants—Indian vegetarian curry to macrobiotic, p1261. Young hangout.

KICHIJOJI, not really Tokyo, one of her satellite cities (20min JR Chuo line from Shinjuku; cheaper alternate is Inokashira Line from Shibuya via Shimokita, above) in Musashino plain far W of town. Cheap shopping: mostly clothes, odds'n-ends. Of course, has its share of overpriced department stores (all recent), but as long as you stick to older side streets and covered shopping lanes N of station, you find great buys. Many inexpensive shops in station building, basement of which numerous good eateries. In old part of town near station, section of several narrow lanes is much like Ueno's Ame-yoko packed with stalls, inexpensive-fashionable clothiers next to fish or fruit stands. One side of station also has large section for budget nitelife, mostly student-oriented.

Inokashira Koen Park few minutes walk south, pleasant wooded area centered around Inokashira Pond, fed by seven natural subterranean springs which become Kanda River. Hard to believe now, but until modern era crystal clear waters of pond used to supply drinking water to whole area. Now it's full of fowl and boats. Springs feeding pond have been here for millennia, as remains of prehistoric settlements have been found in one corner of park. Another corner houses **Benten-do** Pavilion, originally built by MINAMOTO Yoritomo in 12th century, last rebuilt 1927.

CHOPSTICKS: En route Park on main street 2min S of stn, great old yakitori joint **Iseya**, shown Garet by Tokyo chum, longtime wanderer of Kichijoji alleys. Your nose will spot it blocks away, you see white smoke billowing from ancient-looking, sturdy wood 2-storey shop. Wide open 1st floor has long counter and tables, *zashiki* tatami rooms upstairs; or get batch of skewers-to-go for park picnic. Fine chicken comes from butcher next door. ¥70-80 per stick: *kashira* (head), *tan* (tongue), *hatsu* (heart), *reba* (liver), *nankotsu* (cartilage), *shiro* (intestine), *hinadori* (chicken), *negi* (with scallions); ¥300 for *wakadori-no-momoyaki* (roast leg), ¥180 *tomorokoshi* (corn-on-cob), priced between last two are sit-down dishes *maguro* (tuna) *sashimi*, *hiyashi* (cold) *tomato*, *edamame* beans, *nama-yasai* (raw veggies), beer, *sake, shochu*, sodas; sukiyaki, other meals ¥1,200-1,500.

JINDAI-JI, (several km SE of Kichijoji), is one of those lovely out-of-way temples to spend those extra hours. Its pavilions are spread among ancient cryptomeria trees, many house treasured figures of Buddha. Part of its grounds (300,000 m2) has been converted into *Jindaiji Shokubutsu Koen*, **Metropolitan Botanical Garden** (¥300), of 25 various flower fields so that visit any time of year will reveal some color. All trees and plants native to Musashino Plain. Approach to temple lined with shops selling famed Jindaiji soba buckwheat noodles which regularly graced tables of shoguns.

25min from Kichijoji stn on Jindai-ji– or Chofu-bound bus. Returns from temple to Kichijoji, Mitaka (one JR stop beyond), or Chofu stations on JR, all about 25min; or 12min to Tsutsuji-ga-oka stn on private Keio line.

Chofu Airport sends Air Nihon flights to Isles of Izu (*see* SOUTH SEA p.1234).

MITAKA on way in from Jindai-ji, pass **I.C.U. International Christian University** with degree programs in English and Japanese; neighboring *Chu-kin-to-Bunka Sentah*, **Middle East Culture Center**, best museum in Japan for that region, houses Idemitsu Oil's collection, director HIH Prince Mikasa—main Far East and European are upstairs of Imperial Theater in downtown Hibiya, opp Imperial Palace. Also nearby in ICU is **Archaeological Collection**–YUASA Heihachiro Memorial, record and site of most important ongoing excavation in Japan.

Between Shinjuku and Kichijoji on JR Chuo Line are neighborhoods of budget...
KOENJI and quietly classy **ASAGAYA**, both lately heralded as 'new' playgrounds for Tokyo youth. Explorer will find many interesting eating and party places in narrow shopping alleys around either station.

Back on Yamanote loop line, 3 stops S of Shinjuku is...

SHIBUYA

HERALDED AS new center of Tokyo at time of our first edition; prototype of Tokyo's bustling terminal centers, sub-center of mammoth metropolis. Station area was to be, and is, inexpensive paradise for rank-&-file pleasure seekers in contrast to Ginza, nestling place of fashionable folk. Since then it has been out-stripped by Shinjuku, salaryman's heaven since advent of Asian 'Manhattan Complex' while in turn its old student horde shifted here to Shibuya. Its streets day-long rush hour, Shibuya has almost as many people passing thru station as Shinjuku. Shibuya is Tokyu territory: giant station complex **Tokyu DS** and interrelated **Culture Village** flanks, joins over JR stn of Yamanote line. Besides sprawling station complex serving suburbia, they have set up E of stn *Tokyu Bunka Kaikan* **Culture Hall** with plush restaurants, reception halls, movie theaters, mammoth beauty parlor with most up-to-date equipment, planetarium, romantic meeting place for young couples. '89 added *Bunkamura* CULTURE VILLAGE with two superb halls: 2,150-seat Orchard, home of Tokyo Philharmonic, and 747-

seat **Theater Cocoon**–both state of art accoustically near-perfect. Tokyu giant main store is 700m NW of station; few blocks E is new, equally large **Tokyu Hands** specializing in hobbies and other do-at-home projects. Midway to main store is **Fashion Plaza 109** (10-9 in Jpns reads *to-kyu*); its prominent almost windowless tower front was first to break away from typically stodgy department store architecture to lead in new wave of futuristic buildings.

Also terminus to Inokashira and Toyoko private lines; Shin-Tamagawa line becomes subway Hanzomon line here; subway Ginza line starts 3rd floor of station bldg. Toyoko line runs between Shibuya & Sakuragicho in Yokohama City thru better residential areas such as Denen-chofu and Jiyugaoka. Tamagawa line links Shibuya & Futako-Tamagawa on Tama River, and branch lines with Shimotakai-do and Kinuta. Inokashira line runs from Shibuya to Kichijoji Stn of JR (*above* p.1153). Narby **Tokyu Inn**, one of their tourist rate nationwide hotel chain, but tiny ¥-T-class rooms overpriced at ¥-S.

Keeping Tokyu on its toes is some formidable competition. NW across from stn is 2-building complex of **Seibu D S**, beyond which sit 2 **Maruis**; in back streets near Hands are 3 buildings of innovative **Parco** 1, 2, 3 plus new #4 **Quattro**—all owned by world's richest multi-billionaire TSUTSUMI Seiji, rival-brother of Seibu hotel-RR prexy. Then countless smaller shops.

Shibuya is relatively inexpensive, tho it has its fair share of pricey places. It has long been primarily for students and young businessmen looking for something notch above tastes of Shinjuku's Kabuki-cho, but new cultural expansion by Tokyu and Seibu are widening area's appeal. For those who have stayed too late in Shibuya, or just looking for cheap room, dozens of purple-lighted love hotels jam narrow streets W of main drag. Some look quite fancy, but late niters find room often far cheaper than cab across town. From symphony hall, theaters, movie houses, nite clubs, cabarets, bars, discos, restaurants, coffee shops to myriads of small drinking places, almost all kinds of establishments for leisure and pleasure line slopes of...

DOGEN-ZAKA, once residential district of samurai, is ideal for strollers; starts from plaza front of Shibuya station, at its most famous spot **statue** of *Chuken Hachiko*, **Faithful Hachiko**, pet dog of Tokyo University prof. Dog habitually saw off and welcomed back master at station. After prof's death, faithful dog continued to await his return at station daily for 10 years. Image of Hachiko was erected in 1934, year before his death; rededicated after last war (original melted down for war scrap) and deeply respected by Tokyo citizens, is long-famous rendezvous for young people. Just try to find anyone here on any given nite or sunday afternoon and you can easily waste day. If you understand Japanese, keep yourself amused listening to tirades of various extremist groups who gather here to spout their doctrines. One day communists, next day fascists in black vans with Rising Sun flags ...and never twain shall meet; no matter how radical, all demonstrators have precious police permits.

CHOPSTICKS: Longing for bit of 'American' food, but had enough of fast food and steaks? You can find yuppie-esque food plaza with all sorts of good little counters serving what many people here feel is California cuisine. Head to modern food plaza for **The Prime**, next to Fashion Plaza 109; bit to W is Chinese **Toutou** lunch ¥1,000. All-You-Can-Eat at **Shaburi**, Parco I, on 7th fl, ¥3,200. 2 blocks E by tracks, Koream BBQ **Texas**, 2d-3d fls, ¥1,550-1,800

Far (NW) corner behind 109, city's sole whale restaurant **Kujiraya**. Most Westerners, particularly Americans, find eating whale morally if not physically repulsive. But in Japan there is no moral taboo against it. Matter of fact, it was one of few sources for red-meat protein in Buddhist-dominated antiquity when eating of any 4-legged creatures forbidden. After war, seas still teemed with great mammals, major source of cheap meat for starving Japan. But as stock depleted market price of whale by 1984 exceeded even artificially inflated pork or veal. If you have open mind and stomach, Kujiraya is excellent. Prices moderate and portions substantial. Their freezer has few years' stock. Popular dishes *sukiyaki*, steak, *geijisukan* (whale Genghis-khan BBQ); particularly sought after is sashimi, which many compare to finest *toro* cut of tuna. Lunch specials featuring one of above with extras is under ¥1,100-1,500; special set (¥4,000) gets you geijisukan and sashimi. Store hours 11:30-22:30, X-1st, 3rd mon.

Atop Dogen-zaka hill (taxi suggested) is unique J-restaurant **Furusato** in centuries-old dwelling brought to present site from Shirakawa-go Gifu Prefecture (*see* p.907). Meals wholesome cooking of mountainous Gifu, but sea specialties like Ise lobster, Hokkaido king crab also. Summer, enjoy country-style *nagashi somen*, thin white noodles rinsed in ice-cold flowing water from garden. Furusato is J-word describing that ancestral home in country, as soothing psychically as its reality is physically. Also feature folk dances.

Japan Folkcraft Museum, *Nihon Mingei-kan*, founded by YANAGI Soetsu and now run by son, grew out of same *mingei*, or folk art revival philosophy as did English *Crafts*, and California *Craftsman* movements. (10:00-17:00, X-mon) beyond Furusato—easier reached from Shibuya on Inokashira Line

2 stops to Komaba Todai-mae and few minutes walk W then N. Nearby...
Museum of Modern Literature, *Kindai Bungaku-kan*, housed in grand European style former-mansion of Marquis Maeda. Postwar elimination of peerage forced many de-titled nobles to sell off land to pay taxes; Maedas preserved their home by donating it to Tokyo University. During US Occupation manse residence of MacArthur's successor General Ridgeway.

Back in heart of Shibuya you may want to visit 23-storey...
NHK Broadcast Center for **guided tour** (about 1hr) of working studios; daily 10:00-17:00, X-4th mon. Plaza in front of adjacent NHK Hall is site of **flea mart** sun.

In addition, Shibuya has numerous movie houses showing J- and W- films, incl **Shibuya Shochiku, Shibuya Toho, Shibuya Nikkatsu, S- Scalaza, S-Takarazuka, Pantheon, Milano-za,** and plain **Theater Shibuya...**

Between station and NHK on Koen-dori Ave is...
Tobacco & Salt Museum, *Tabako to Shio no Hakubutsu-kan*; 10:00-18:00 X-mon, ¥100. Regular exhibits center around tobacco (woodblocks prints of-) & salt; temporary exhibits are always quite interesting (check papers). If wondering how anybody came up with combining salt and tobacco—both were till early 1980s government monopolies, offices just down street. Next door is Communication, Sound, Visual music store. CSV hosts live band every weekend. Look across to **Tobu Hotel** which left side is waterfall. Few blocks east of T&S Museum is Tokyo Electric Co, with *Denryokukan* **Electric Energy Museum** (no charge) showing wonders of electricity, latest hi-tech gimmicks, promises; X-wed.

Between Denryokukan and JR tracks parallel street is lined with fun second-hand clothing stores. To S is **Tenmi** natural foods, X-2d,3d wed. From NHK, only minute to graceful 1964 Olympics buildings (*below*) designed by TANGE Kenzo, and beyond which is station for...

HARAJUKU
WHERE TOKYO youth come to spend parents' hard earned money on all sorts of fashion recording past few decades of US and London scenes. Here, find everything from most exclusive Japanese and foreign designer fashions at exorbitant prices, to Brand-X duds for peanuts. You will also find numerous good foreign restaurants.

Coming out front of train (from Shinjuku direction), view from pedestrian overpass is of Tange's 2 space-age **Olympic stadia**, occupying corner of **Yoyogi Park**...also home of weekend street dancers: troupes of James

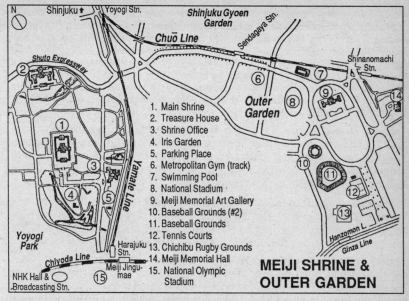

Meiji Shrine and its Outer Garden

Dean look-alikes with pony-tailed gals in ankle socks and saddle shoes; countless Elvis Presleys; assorted 'Yankee' groups; and colorful antics of *Takenoko-zoku* 'bamboo-shoot tribe'—sprout anywhere, grow to bend with winds of today, peel off outside any number of layers to find what really lives within. Best time to come see them is Sunday. If such pseudo '60s Americana seems 'unJapanese' to you, know that such is hoary tradition—paintings of late 1500s show stylish fops in wild kimonos with Portuguese frill collars, hairdos mixed European locks and topknot, wide-brim floppy hats...and it was probably same at many unrecorded eras. This is 'real Japan' in one of her varied realities, as valid as Fuji and geisha. Main road at that intersection is Omote Sando Ave; heading E is shopping area which still caters to foreigners as much as to today's youth.

This was residential area for Occupation forces, but this road wasn't made intentionally wide for Americans; Omote Sando is main approach to...

MEIJI JINGU where emperor Akihito's great-grandfather is enshrined. Grand but simple shrine stands in sharp contrast to smaller but gaudy Shogunal mausoleum in Nikko. Favorite first-pilgrimage-of-year spot draws over 3,000,000 visitors during first few days. Its enormous wooded grounds are popular getaway for Tokyo-ites. If you look north (towards Shinjuku) from platforms at Harajuku stn, notice small station platform—special for emperor only, when imperial entourage boards at private Tokyo stn platform for pilgrimage.

PERSONAL DATEBOOK: Garden, pond lovely setting for iris **mid-June**, followed by water lilies, lotus, then trained chrysanthemums in **Oct-Nov**. Shrine itself most popular first-pilgrimage-of-year spot with 3,00,000+ visitors first few days. Principal fete: **Feb 17** *Grain Petitioning*, **Apr 11** *Empress Shoken Memorial*, **Apr 29-May 5** *Grand Spring Festival*: Apr 29 10am rites, bugaku court dances and 2pm service; Apr 30 10am and 2pm services, 11:30 *noh* dances; May 2 11:30am trad music, dances, May 3 9am martial arts, 11:30 music, 1pm *biwa* lute; May 5 *Boys' Day* fete. **June 30** *Great Exorcism* absolves human sins. **July 30** *Meiji's Death* commemorated, compound filled with flower arrangements, enchanting evening with cages of singing crickets on trees along shrine approach lit by bonfires, entertainment 7-9pm, fireworks. **November** *Culture Week* salutes Meiji's birthday **Nov 3** with *Grand Autumn Festival*, **Nov 1-3:** Nov 1 10:30 am *bugaku* music-dance, 12:30 ancient polo; Nov 2 10:30 *noh*, 12:30 Japanese dance; Nov 3 archery 9am, 11 *aikido*, 12:30 old martial arts, 1 pm *yabusame* archery on horseback; Nov 5 ceremonial tea by head of one of Senke schools, alternating. During Culture Week, **Seinen-Kan** (young men's hall) in Meiji Park is locale for 2 days of best rural folk theater from all over Japan. **Nov 23** *Thanksgiving* rite for harvest. **Dec 23** *Emperor Akihito's Birthday.* **Dec 31** *Great Rite of exorcism* ends year.

Jingu Homutsu-kan, **Treasure House** in back displays various items used by emperor Meiji. Jingu lower gardens (Occupation era Washington Heights residential and barracks enclosure) is now **Yoyogi Sports** grounds (not to be confused with other Olympic stadia at Meiji Outer Garden) with Tange's Olympic covered gym.

Few minutes walk W of Treasure House, outside of park is...
Yo-ken Hakubutsu-kan, **Sword Museum** with several hundred swords and suits of armor, including 30 National Treasures (9:00-16:00, X-mon; ¥500). Also reached in short walk from Sangu-bashi stn on private Odakyu rail from Shinjuku.

Back out on Omote Sando Ave, first big block from Harajuku stn is not too shop-oriented yet but next few to next intersect with Aoyama-dori Ave (subway Omote Sando stop) has almost every fashionable outlet. There's 5-storey toy emporium **KiddyLand** just beyond which is **Oriental Bazaar** where you can still get good real antiques as well as copies and other Japanese goods at fair price, silver at **Mori Silver** where *showing this book earns discount.* More antiques in basement of **Hanae Mori Bldg** (at far end)—most over-priced, except for one good woodblock print shop.

Harajuku also has its share of discos and partying joints (for which update, as for all areas of Tokyo, see *Tokyo Journal's* CITYSCOPE), of which perhaps unique is **Oh! God** with its large screen showing recent popular movies. In basement of Jingu-bashi Bldg, at end of alley station-wards of KiddyLand. Under same ownership are nearby **Crocodile** (New Sekiguchi Bldg, B1) which plays music, and 'log cabin' motif **Backwood** (Yamaji Bldg, B1).

Takeshita-dori street, for inexpensive clothes. Actual alley, Takeshita-dori is lined with dozens of holes-in-wall peddling everything imaginable. You can outfit yourself like any of those street dancers, or pick up latest fashion. If you come out of 'back' of station, cross street and Takeshita-dori is just in front of you branching off perpendicular from train tracks. It's only one long block to Meiji-dori Ave, where R takes you past some new 'fashion' buildings to Omote Sando. Left (N) on Meiji-dori short ways to **Dyna**(mic)**Audio** shop on R, just after road takes sharp L. It specializes in lo-price hi-quality used audio equipment as well as discontinued new models at rates below Akihabara.

Midway down Takeshita-dori, on your left is tiny glade-oasis of...
TOGO JINJA, shrine dedicated to admiral TOGO Heihachiro who trounced Imperial Russian Navy off Tsushima in 1905, thus effectively ending Russo-Japanese War, and inciting Hearst's 'Yellow Peril' scare in USA. Small museum displays some of his belongings. Photo and letter of US WWII Fleet Admiral Nimitz are here, 'Bull' was admirer of Togo, met him as young ensign when given invitation to reception for Admiral our 'remittance man' gentlemen-admirals snubbed, Nimitz was sole yank that day to speak to Togo (who, British-trained, spoke fluent English). Bull later helped save Togo flagship *Mikasa* from scrap, now preserved in Yokosuka (*see* KAMAKURA p236). Big flea mart here 1st and 4th sundays.

L off Omote-sando Ave few minutes from stn is excellent...
Ohta Kinen Bijutsu-kan, Memorial Museum (10:30-17:30, X-mon and 25th to end month, ¥500), huge collection woodblock prints of Hiroshige, Sharaku— 12,000+ prints and sketches, exhibit rotates monthly to varying themes.
Omote Sando subway stn Chiyoda, Hanzomon, Ginza lines—access to rest of town.

Following Aoyama-dori on foot, only 1.4km/0.9 mi to Shibuya, p1154; you pass...
Spiral Wacoal gallery-theater (p1143), **Kinokuniya** supermart, **Aoyama Gakuin** Univ started by US Methodist, **Sushi Daigaku** (Sushi U, learn art of sushi chef in few months, foreigners accepted–not traditional apprenticeship, but it serves its purpose. Across from Aoyama Gakuin is modern **Children's Castle**, 7 floors of assorted computers, A-V, playroom, etc. Space age sculpture in front may look familiar to any who saw Expo 70's theme plaza moon-faced idol by OKAMOTO Taro—this is also his.

Interesting detour is, after crossing Aoyama-dori, to continue along narrowed-down Omote Sando. Several minutes on, where road curves left, on R is...
Nezu Art Museum, for fine Japanese paintings, ceramics, lacquer, etc. (9:30-16:30, X-mon, ¥500) in beautiful hillside garden with paths, streams, tea house.

Road continues E thru **Aoyama Cemetery**, top sakura viewing. *15min walk to...*
NOGI ZAKA, with subway stn of same name on Chiyoda Line, or 10min walk north of Roppongi Intersection. **NOGI JINJA**, shrine dedicated to General NOGI Maresuke (in whose honor area is named Nogi-hill), also of Russo-Japanese War fame. Unlike admiral Togo, general Nogi did not face easy victory on land. His siege of Port Arthur was long bloody campaign, and despite final victory, general Nogi always felt humiliation at terrible loss of life which included his own infantry sons. When emperor Meiji died in 1912, Nogi followed his lord in true samurai spirit, committing *seppuku*, ritual suicide as cannons marking emperor's death boomed in distance. Nogi's wife, as true wife of samurai, followed him, slitting her throat. You can also visit their modest small house, preserved as monument. **Flea market** 2nd sun.

From Omote Sando in other direction, townward, along Aoyama-dori leads to...
MEIJI SHRINE Outer Gardens, sports complex. Wind thru stadia and grounds built originally by public subscription, expanded for never-held 1940 Olympics, used at last, much extended with Tange's exciting new architecture for '64 Olympics. **Meiji Memorial Art Gallery**, gothic domed structure north end, Victorianized Japonica including 80 large murals recording life of that revolutionary emperor. Incidentally right across Gaien-higashi-dori Ave at Shinano-machi stn you might catch Shinto wedding at **Meiji Kinen-kan** for shrine weddings. Formal Shinto wedding is social invention of Meiji period, before which everyone just met at groom's house for drunken bash set off by bride and groom sipping from formal sake cups.
Here continue E 10min past Togu Palace grounds to Akasaka Detached Palace to end of IMPERIAL PALACE WALKING TOUR, p1144, which you can then join in reverse.

Or exit Outer Garden go L on Aoyama-dori, townwards 700m, pass fine new architecture Honda and New Aoyama bldgs at corner facing Omiya Palace compound, cross to—
Place Canada, city's most beautiful embassy, half public space, fabulous internal rock gardens, etc; Japanese-Canadian architect Raymond MORIYAMA expounds best of both cultures as true bridge; fine gallery 4th fl.

Two short blocks E, past small **Takahashi Memorial Park**, *is striking...*
Sogetsu Kaikan exquisite TANGE-designed HQ of Sogetsu school ikebana (flower arranging)—no artist has finer concept of space than ikebana master, which is what architecture is...architect ought study ikebana. Lobby gallery, upstairs museum of Sogetsu collection, rotating exhibits. Visitor arrange at reception for flower arrangement lessons in English. Whole thing lives.

ROPPONGI

DISCO DISTRICT, playground of Japanese youth, and gathering spot for obnoxious foreign models who figure anyone not Japanese is competition and treat you accordingly. Some spots exclusive (no foreigners, thank you) expensive, most basic Tokyo rates, others inexpensive without losing classiness. Most younger visitors find themselves here at some point, tho this is not exactly what one comes half way around world for. It's loud, crowded, bright, vibrant, and lots of fun. But turn corner and you'll find quiet residential area, with light seeping out from sole ramen shop's door. In Roppongi are branches of **Hard Rock Cafe**, **Spago's**, and **Tony Roma** (all in one building), **Victoria Station**, **Henry Africa's**, and more. With literally hundreds of bars you'll find almost any type of music, live and taped: blues, jazz, country, reggae, rock, calypso, but keep in mind 'live houses' take table charge, music charge and 2 drink minimum, at least. If not posted, *ask*—tho we have never been, or heard of, anyone being taken for ride. Once, waiting in vain in rain for cab, tout offered drinks for cheap. Following with some misgivings, we had time of our lives as it turned out 'tout' was bored owner who only wanted people to talk to. Later, he called enough cabs to get us all home. That's traditional Edo-Tokyo.

Daytime, Roppongi is 'fashion center', scores of over-priced boutiques peddling latest styles. Popular shopping plazas **Axis Bldg** (interior decor), **Wave** (music related), **Roi Bldg** (clothes). Surfacing from Roppongi subway stn puts you at busy intersection. Notice **Almond** (pron *Amondo* in J-), popular old time rendezvous spot, as attested to by hordes gathered in front. Running E-W is overhead expwy; main strip of nitelife is south. **Roppongi Information Center** is between Almond and Roi Bldg, info on local shops and what's on. Streets of Roppongi and neighboring Azabu are full of fine restaurants, ¥-T to ¥-L, representing almost every national cuisine, and with all those embassies around, guaranteed to be good.

For all its popularity, Roppongi is hard to get to on public transport, lacking usual multiple choices one expects in Tokyo. New subway under construction will link directly with other main areas of town, but so far only Hibiya grey line services this station; which W-end terminus before joining with, to serve suburbia, Toyoko private line is...

EBISU, (one stop S of Shibuya on Yamanote loop), may be of interest for drinkers, especially in heat of summer. Here is **Sapporo Brewery**, where Yebisu Beer is brewed. Once reserved mostly for budget drinkers, Yebisu Beer has become popular with all types in past few years as it was long sole totally natural beer brewed in Japan—new malts break this monopoly. Can tour their brewery, or just go direct to their converted railroad car pubs and eat and drink all you want for few thousand yen. Area to be developed mid-'90s into great culture hub with theater, museum, etc.

IKEBUKURO

4 STOPS N of Shinjuku on Yamanote line, yet another terminus of several lines: subways Yurakucho & Marunouchi lines, Seibu Ikebukuro Line, Tobu Tojo Line which we take out to old Edo town of **Kawagoe** (p 1216). Like other centers around Tokyo, department stores play major role, and here bosses are **Seibu** and **Tobu** chains. Outshining both is **Sunshine City**, soaring all-purpose community center built on site of former Sugamo Prison. Sunshine City is multi-building complex dominated by 60-storey (240m) **Sunshine 60** which has top floor observatory (¥600). Other attractions are top floor planetarium and aquarium, international bazaar, three floors of specialty shops, **Ancient Orient Museum** (mostly Middle East),

theaters and man-made gardens. Quiet, oddly placed empty courtyard in back marks spot where gallows in 1948 hanged 7 Class A war criminals (Tojo et al) whom UN Tribunal judged most responsible for war. Someday it will become sepulcher; we predict semi-centennial '95 (end of war), or '97 (of hangings) if too much stink raised on first date. In typical Japanese style when building planned feelers were already put out for memorial, public outcry too strong. Given enough years of subtle pressure anything can get done here, as we saw in PM's official visit to Yasukuni—tho that not soon repeated, urge to do so still itches ruling party (ruled unconstitutional '91). One of buildings here is **Prince Hotel**.

Convenient to those living in N-outskirts of Tokyo, Ikebukuro has countrified air to it, despite all this new glitter. Won't find anything here that you can't get in 'center' of Tokyo, but it's change of pace and worth dawdling. Good place to jump on ARAKAWA TRAM (see p1164) for leisurely ride thru N-side of Tokyo, retaining much of old Edo village atmosphere.

And it boasts one of country's best sake bars, **Sasashu** (see p.149).

SHINAGAWA, S-most on Yamanote loop, has little to draw sightseer, but you could end up here because of numerous fine ¥-L hotels near station: **Shinagawa Prince**, **Takanawa** and **New Takanawa Prince**, **Pacific Tokyo** etc. Bit out of way but excellent **Miyako Hotel**, which runs ¥-T **Miyako Inn** in nearby Tamachi. There is also new fashion plaza, **Wings** at Shinagawa stn. Area rapidly being built up so you don't really have to head to any other part of town for shopping. End your day here, dine at bayside —car park has lotsa daddies' dough—many good eateries ¥-L to ¥-B, most post menu outside.

Latest trend in Tokyo real estate is pumping life back into **warehouses** of Tokyo Bay, especially Shinagawa–Tamachi–Hamamatsucho, all known as **Shiba-ura**. Cheap rent and lots of space have drawn many of trendiest artists and restaurateurs to what many label Tokyo's SoHo. 1987 opened media blitz on Shiba-ura centered on trendy Roppongi joint **Ink Stick**'s **Shibaura Factory**, noted for its drums. Many following suit—**Venice**, **Tango**—in this 'Roppongi-by-Bay' or other nicknames. New Wave bands. Inventive experiment **Terada Soko** 'Art of Living' exemplar of modern art gallery-disco. Dance 9pm-5am midst art installations, be part of them, ☎3740-0030. Menus in French-i or Supanishi are as funny as local Engrish. Small cruise boats at pier for Edo's 'Grand Canal'.

SENGAKU-JI temple (Takanawa, nr Shinagawa Stn, or just around corner from subway stop of same name on Asakusa line), is site of climax of one of more romantic, dramatic paradoxes of Japan's paradoxical past: graves of 47 *ronin* (masterless samurai). Used by jingoists before war to exemplify patriotism and blind loyalty, postwar purge of old thought control sent them into temporary eclipse. But without doubt their story is one of great romances of history. Certainly before it became cultified it appealed to British sense of principle in Victorian era, Teddy Roosevelt admired them. (See foe Kira's mansion remains in ASAKUSA, p1203). Many modern Japanese respect 47 as men who were willing to die for their principles and judge them in rational light realizing that feudal object of their loyalty and sacrifice could not or should not attract such emotion today, but that similar spirit of determined principle applied to modern loyalties should be valued. That, in any event, is how we evaluate loyal 47 and how some of our more mature Japanese friends do. That, to us, is also subtle message their story carries, if it carries any at all.

They are favorite subject of artists and movie producers and their story, *Chushingura* in kabuki and bunraku is one of classics of world theater, performed annually. June 1986 saw premiere of *The Kabuki*, fantastic ballet version choreographed by Maurice Bejart with international cast. After rave tour thru Europe, it returned for February '87 Tokyo run, repeated. Generation ago when Japan was being revived, almost every December as many as 3 movie companies each released new version of epic for peak movie season straddling Xmas-tide anniversary of their famous vendetta. Adjoining graves is small museum of relics. At shops by temple gate buy picture-strips illustrating story, replica of drum that sounded final attack with famous design of three spiraling commas.

Vendetta of 47 Ronin—to make long story short, were retainers of lord Asano who had been driven by insults from protocol instructor lord Kira to force him to point of drawing sword within Edo castle, 'sin' punishable by death. As Kira had hoped, Asano was sentenced to commit *seppuku* alias *harakiri*, his land confiscated, family and followers disgraced. Led by OISHI Yuranosuke, Asano's trusted men, denied official permit for vendetta, plotted revenge in secret. Went to great lengths to throw off spies of Kira, convince all that nothing was planned—drunken Oishi even publicly berating Asano name on his death anniversary. At long last, lunar **December 15**, 1702 (W-Jan 31, 1703), 47 stormed Kira's palatial manse to find him cowering in storage shed. They lopped his head off, paraded it to Asano's grave here at Sengaku-ji. They had avenged their master's death, but had violated law in doing so—as they feared they might, but were sure wouldn't (even their jailers were surprised at severity of Shogunal judgement) they had to commit seppuku, to disembowel selves. Teddy Roosevelt loved story, realized Japanese were losing Russo-Japan War (tho winning Pyrrhic victories) so intervened to get peace before Russians woke up to reality. Our intelligence in WWII analyzed story, surmised Japan would not surrender but fight on desperately—so we decided to use A-Bomb. Tho US Admiral Zacharias (Japan linguist) pointed out that of almost 400 retainers of Asano only 47 remained loyal, thus Japan would surrender except for few hard-heads. He was ignored, correct as we now realize he was, and most of his predicted 1945 holdouts died at Atago hill (next page) near Shimbashi in mass grenade-suicide just before US landed.

Drive on down Dai-ichi-Keihin to Sakura-dori past Keio University and Shiba Park (or Dai-ichi-Keihin to Hibiya-dori...direct 2.5km taxi to...

ZOJO-JI temple's red gate [NT] sole structure in area to survive great fire raids of World War II thanks to civilian fire brigades who saved it at expense of their own homes. Lovely illuminated garden behind is not antique: it's golf driving range built over old graveyard of former Tokugawa Shoguns—fitting shrine to new cult of Japan. Adjoining this, swimming pool and summer beer-garden of ¥-Luxe **Tokyo Prince Hotel**.

Towering up behind all this is...

Tokyo Tower, well worth ascent for view—if queue, go to special entry reserved for foreign guests. ¥600 to reach 150m main observatory, ¥400 extra to 250m/75ft platform; about as much for aquarium, wax museum, science museum; major sight on most bus tours, day and nite. Many locals seem proud of announcing that they are too modest to mention to French fact that Tokyo Tower at 333m, is taller than Eiffel in Paris (neither matches Warsaw antenna). If France seriously wants honor of owning 6th or 7th highest structure, DeGaulle-ish beaked francophile can stand atop Eiffel, look up and balance tri-color on his nose. Eiffel is far more imposing structure: Tokyo Tower isn't much advance for 60 years. 'American origin' of Tokyo Tower eludes Japanese. Admittedly modeled on Eiffel—as are several smaller ones in Tokyo, Osaka, Sapporo, Nagoya and dozens of miniscule antenna atop

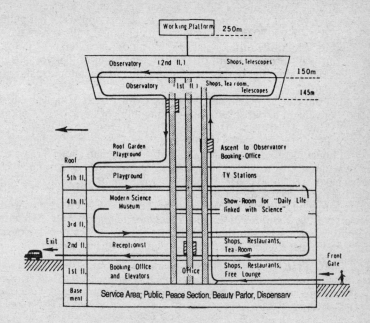

Tokyo Tower Plan; bus stop for most Sightseeing buses

small-town broadcasting stations. But Eiffel reputedly originates in construction scaffolding French set up to build Statue of Liberty. Perhaps symbolically, Japan's 'Liberty Structure' was financed by TV companies. Only well-informed public can support liberty.

N on ave btwn Tower and Prince Hotel, 2 main blocks, then at foot of hill left to...
ATAGO HILL, site of original NHK studio and antenna, and of Occupation era FEN, US Far East Network, now **NHK Broadcast Museum**. 86 stone steps built 17th century. August 1945 word got out that emperor was to broadcast Rescript on Surrender, hard-head junior officers tried to capture record disc or otherwise prevent broadcast. They failed and broadcast was made, war ended. When subsequent request for suicide charge against US landing parties was rejected, group vowing 'honorable way out' formed circle in open area by studio atop hill as each pulled pin on his hand grenade —held against belly of neighbor to help him keep faith.

Taxi-tourist may now be ready for **lunch**. You may want to eat while you drink in view. Otherwise there are many good W-style restaurants, especially around nearby Roppongi intersection. L at base of tower 100m brings you back to Sakura-dori whence up hill. From here to Roppongi, next intersection, is 1km long choice of moderate-priced restaurants, many foreign-run foreign-specialty houses: Chinese, Italian, etc. **Tokyo Prince** has good array of restaurants, moderate to luxe, and along Hibiya-dori within 5min walk of Prince are several of Tokyo's best Chinese restaurants. If you've planned ahead, enjoy true *shojin-ryori* Buddhist priest fare at nearby **Misho-an, ☎3454-0311.**

1 km E of Shiba Park is Hamamatsu-cho, from which 600m SE is...
Hinode Pier for ocean bus ferry cruises around bay, ships to IZU ISLES (*see*) & **river bus** boat to Asakusa—some of latter stop at nearby **Hama Rikyu Detached Palace Garden** 800m NE of Hamamatsucho stn and better place to get boat for ASAKUSA (p1189).

ARAKAWA TRAM LINE

MEANDERING 13km across N side of Tokyo since 1907, sole remnant of once extensive web of trolley lines. It, too, was almost ripped up, but public outcry saved it—now, 70,000+ people ride its blue and yellow cars daily. This relaxing 50min ride thru 29 stations, most not much longer than tram itself, is fun way to cross town, offers different view of Tokyo as tram passes thru old-style neighborhoods of shopping streets, temples, shrines, folk's backyards.

We start our ride at W end near **Waseda Univ**, end at Minowabashi N of Ueno, convenient to our sh'tamachi walking tours of Iriya, or to Asakusa thru ex-Yoshiwara district. At several places en route tram stops near subway or JR stn for those who want shorter ride. Or spend anywhere from few short hours to full day exploring this off-beaten-path route. Trams run every few minutes from 6:00 to after 22:00 so no worry about getting stuck. '91 fares ¥140 (¥70 child); ¥1,000 for *kaisu-ken* book of 8 tix; OK use Toei bus-rail pass (*see* GETTING AROUND TOKYO, p1136).

There is much to see around Waseda even before we board tram, starting with University's *Tsubouchi Engeki Hakubutsu-kan* **Theater Museum** in memory of prof who translated all Shakespeare's works into Japanese. Exhibits on various aspects of Japanese, Asian and Western theater.

GETTING THERE: Tozai (lite blue) subway line to Waseda, best back of train if from Takadanobaba direction. Coming up, you'll be at intersect with Mr Donuts and MacDonalds. Surfacing across street from Mr Donuts go R down narrower road. Pass high school on L; about 150m down will be mosaic-ed, Gaudi-esque building on corner hard to miss its stained-glass windows and hideous tilework faces—no displaced Love Hotel, just ordinary apartment building. Down narrow hallway is small dead-end room, giant tile hand pointing to upstairs corner good coffee shop. L at intersect leads to Waseda U main gate, past Theater Museum to tram stn.

Alternately, at gaudy apartment, straight to next large intersect (Mejiro-dori Ave) which cross, go L. Tram stop is just down road but we take R down first alley, leads to...
Site of poet Basho's house along Kanda River which here is still full of giant carp, and egret or other birds will probably be wading there. It doesn't take much imagination to mentally block out cement banks of river and concentrate on stretch of old buildings here to visualize what it must have been like when only feudal lords lived in this area. Basho's house didn't make it thru WWII, but compound has lovely old houses sometimes open to public.

Stately wall continues on to another giant gate; special entrance to...
Chinzan-so, grand garden complex with traditional houses for weddings. You can see garden, but main entrance is around front. We entered thru side door reached by going thru adjacent apartment complex. Chinzan-so hosts receptions, modern main building handles few thousand people, with more in new '92 ¥L hotel **Four Seasons**. Lunch stop for several Eng bus tours. Or can arrange small party, or just regular meal. There is W-style **Camellia**, J-style **Miyuki**, **Kaizan-do** for sukiyaki, and first floor **tea lounge-bar** overlooking garden. Prices reasonable for top-class establishment; run by Fujita Group. Hill long famed for its beauty, Prince YAMAGATA Aritomo, prime mover of early Meiji Japan, bought what is now Chinzan-so for his own. Various notables, including emperor Meiji, feasted here. Next owner Baron FUJITA Heitaro brought treasured structures here to enhance garden and began restaurant business. Meals at Camellia, Miyuki, lounge can be had on spot, no rsv; for parties ☎3943-1101. Fireflies brought in from countryside in summer when 1,000s are released to bring nostalgic woodblock-print era air to this old garden.

If rear closed, go uphill narrow alley next to Basho house, right when it hits main road to main gate to Chinzan-so (*See also* CHOPSTICKS p.1257)..

Across from it note modern but graceful steel-concrete...
St Mary's Cathedral, beaut by Tange, worth visit by architecture buffs.

Part way up this alley on your L will be somewhat rundown Western-style building...
Eisei Bunko archives, housing mixed but superb 150,000-piece art collection of Hosokawa family (their old feudal manse garden is on other side of wall) spanning over dozen generations. Only 50 or so pieces displayed at one time, admission ¥500; X-weekends.

If you don't have time or energy to visit Chinzan-so, can still take in traditional landscape garden with entrance here along Kanda River.

Upstream of Basho's house is...
Shin-Edogawa Koen Park, once second Edo residence of Hosokawa clan, lord of Kyushu's Kumamoto fief. This is one of Tokyo's 'forgotten' parks, and makes for great escape. Can take quick stroll around ponds, or hide up in wooded hillside away from noise of giant metropolis. Roomy house there built post-Meiji for children of Hosokawa; later, all donated to Tokyo which handed control of it to local ward which made it 'people's park' and building is now ward public hall. Tho not as well manicured, we find almost unkempt airs of Shin-Edogawa more relaxing than Chinzan-so. Garden open daily 9:00-17:00, no fee (just walk thru small gate there), tho there is small donation box.

From here, upstream to next intersect, L is thru old neighborhood shopping street to tram stn. Basho house and Shin-Edogawa side-trip only add 600m/5min; Chinzan-so another 1km.

Between Waseda and next tram stop Omokage-bashi is yet another...
Sweet Spring Garden, *Kansen-en*. Once part of another daimyo manse, name comes from spring in nearby **MIZU INARI SHRINE** which bubbles forth cool, sweet water favored by tea masters. In October fete, mounted archers race down shrine's pathway firing arrows at small wooden targets as *yabusame* is performed.

Tram next stops...
Gakushu-in Univ, where royalty goes and Sumi spent Jr year abroad.

Next is Kishibojin-mae, near...
KISHIBOJIN TEMPLE, dedicated to guardian spirit of children and pregnant women. Child-devouring demoness Kishimojin was rehabilitated by Buddha who gave her pomegranites to munch on instead of kids. Thus pomegranites around her temple; fruit also old fertility symbol. Want to get pregnant?—ask priest to bless. Tram runs next to **Zoshigaya cemetery**, final resting place of Lafcadio Hearn, Natsume Soseki, host of notables, then stops at Higashi Ikebukuro 4-chome, just under elevated expressway. Optional embarkation point, with subway Yurakucho (yellow) Line stn.

Or short walk to Ikebukuro's soaring...
Sunshine-60 complex [*see* p1160] which occupies site of once infamous Sugamo Prison for major war criminals. Between tram stop and Sunshine-60 is Tokyo branch of government mint where only ¥5 (brass wth hole in center) and ¥10 (copper) coins are minted; visit by first calling ahead to ☎3987-3131, ext-207.

2 stops to Ohtsuka, JR Yamate station of same name; half dozen stops further is...
OHJI, also with JR station, this one on Tohoku Main Line and Keihin Tohoku Line (both go to Ueno, where latter links with Yamate Line). You can get off one stop earlier at Asuka-yama and stroll across small park to Ohji. We disembark at Ohji to visit...
Paper Museum, *Kami-no-Hakubutsukan*, (9:00-17:00, X-mon, ¥200), with fascinating exhibits of endless varieties of *washi* (Japan-paper), various

paper products from parasols to fire-retardant firemen's clothes, utensils used in paper making, English language books on Japanese 'rice' paper. Locomotive in front was used within compound to cart pulp and trees to make paper. Red brick museum only 150m from tram stop, easiest to continue along tracks and cross over. From museum look back toward tram line and if timing right, you'll see tram running ground level, regular JR train slightly elevated, and passing above both is bullet train.

15min side-trip from Asukayama stop takes us to interesting...
Furukawa Garden *Kyu-Furukawa Tei-en*, semi-Edwardian, part Japanese landscaped. Head SE (R if facing Asukayama Park) from tram stop along main road and park will come into view on your R. Grand Edwardian house was home of late Meiji industrialist FURUKAWA Ichibei, designed by Dr Josiah Conder who also designed St Nikorai Cathederal at Ochanomizu and wrote first English book on Ikebana. Garden was reputedly all English-style with large lawns, flowerbeds, well-kept hedges, but Japanese touches later added so that now we have interesting mix of 'scaping. Garden is slightly closer to JR Komagome stn of Yamanote Loop, or Kami-Nakazato on Keihin Tohoku.

Your tram may end few stops beyond Ohji, at Arakawa Shako-mae, where all trams are serviced and cleaned. Office here is also only place where you can get *Japanese map of sights* along Arakawa tram line. You are now about 2/3rds along tram line, and from here to Minowa-bashi is mostly thru quiet residential areas. You come to one slightly busy shopping area... **Machiya**, where one can change to subway Chiyoda (green) Line, or Keisei private line to Ueno (preferred). If staying with your tram for 4 more stops and as many minutes to Minowa-bashi terminus, you can also take subway Hibiya (grey) Line from nearby Minowa stn: when you get off tram, go R down shopping street, pass under JR tracks to wide street where L and you see subway sign at next intersect.

Depending on how much time you spent on tram, how much walking you have done, there are several options which merge with our various **SH'TAMACHI WALKING TOURS**:
1) Subway Hibiya Line is 2 stops to UENO, p1167;
2) or just go one stop to IRIYA for our IRIYA tour, p1176;
3) 6 stops to NINGYO-CHO for many good lunch choices, p1206;
4) or another 3 stops to TSUKIJI fish market for freshest sushi, p1206;
5) last is walk to ASAKUSA, p1189, via Yoshiwara ex-gay quarters— which, while probably least interesting, however does take you past some great old restaurants for true Edokko-style *tempura* or *sakura-nabe* meals in photogenic shops that look like stage sets out of old movies.

If like us, you've gotten here around lunch time, take slight detour along first part of our YOSHIWARA course, p1186, for lunch at **Iseya**.

*...the place where the populace of Edo goes for pleasure
and to hike the hills which overlook immense ricefields.
There are a number of men, women and small children
running as quickly as possible in order to see us, crying
sometimes 'Americans', but more often 'Tojin'.*
— Henry Heusken, *Japan Journal*, 1885

UENO 上野
FAR-EAST SIDE

UENO, LITERALLY 'UPFIELD', was pleasant hill village overlooking great reed marshes of Musashi-Edo Plains, and is today lovely park with variety of entertainment and cultural facilities.

GETTING THERE: Taxi 3x-mtr from Ginza, Tokyo Stn or TCAT; or Yamanote Loop → Ueno Stn (regular JR & Tohoku Shinkansen to/from N); or Ginza yellow or Hibiya blue subways → Ueno; or Keisei terminus from Narita Airport.

Ieyasu, first Tokugawa shogun, noting that Ueno stood to northeast or demon gate direction from his Edo castle, decided to build temples to negate evil luck from that direction, as was done atop Mount Hiei in relation to Kyoto. He renamed Ueno To-Eizan or East Eizan after Kyoto demon-quelling temple complex, Hieizan. He resettled his retainers' residences in Ueno nearer in at Kanda (p.1173). His main Ueno temple was Kanei-ji which with Zojo-ji in Shiba became largest in Edo and where Tokugawa Shoguns were buried. Name To-Eizan never took hold, however. In 1868 Shogi-Tai, or supporters of shogun numbering some 3,000 die-hards, entrenched themselves against army of emperor Meiji's supporters. Imperial Army headquarters was set up at site of present Matsuzakaya Department Store on Ginza. This 'War of Ueno' saw shogunal army totally destroyed and Kanei-ji temple razed but for seven small structures, including park pagoda. In 1873 at suggestion of Dutch medical advisor Dr AF Baldwin, temple's land was designated Ueno Public Park, and temple was rebuilt in corner of its former property 1877. Bronze statue of bull-necked Saigo Takamori, clad in kimono, accompanied by his favorite hunting dog, was erected 1899 to commemorate his having been leader of government forces—tho he died leading second rebellion soon after. Ueno Park, for period of 'Ueno War' thru Japan's own 'Gay Nineties', is locale of many popular short stories and woodblock illustrations, especially of sakura-viewing.

Ueno TOSHOGU SHRINE in park is where Ieyasu is enshrined—he died in hometown Shizuoka, later reburied in great Nikko mausoleum (*see* preceding), but Ueno Toshogu was established in 1651 as being more convenient for descendants to pay daily homage. It's one of Tokyo's few architectural relics of Edo era. Great stone gate at entrance of *Sando* was boated from Himeji on Inland Sea and 300-odd stone and bronze lanterns donated by feudal lords. Lovely 5-storeyed pagoda survived wars, dates from 1651. Commanding view of Shinobazu Ike (pond–actually 3 contiguous ponds) is **Kiyomizu-do**, built 1698 in imitation of larger Kiyomizu Temple in old imperial capital of Kyoto (p.492).

Park one of few places in Tokyo left that is still worthwhile for cherry blossoms. Summer dawn folks come to hear lotus blossoms in pond open with pop like 'clap of one hand'. During seasonal migrations over 10,000 wild birds take sanctuary here—tho both may have to make way for underground car park and concrete lotus and water-bird pool.

Ueno National Museum, *Kokuritsu Hakubutsukan.* Hour or so in this museum is rewarding, especially their **Horyu-ji Treasure House** annex, but keep in mind daily X-at 4pm and all day mon. Unfortunately displays receive nowhere near attention they deserve. We think they would do better to ship most treasures back to their home temples, for many temples are today building fine private museums (combination art gallery-fireproof store-house) for treasures; some built with local bus or tourist company financial support, for tourist companies then promote package tours to see temples and their collections. Wise policy for all concerned. Old **gate** near museum entrance belonged to Edo mansion of Ikeda clan; dates to early 1800s. Originally located in Palace foregarden in Marunouchi, moved to Shiba park where it survived airraids, then moved here 1951.

Check daily newspapers for any special exhibitions in National Museum, or nearby **Art Gallery,** *Tokyo-to Bijutsu-kan* mostly modern Japanese art or **National Museum of Western Art,** *Kokuritsu Seiyo Bijutsu-kan* older of its two buildings by leCorbusier, 1959. Modern European masters.

From museum, stroll thru...
Ueno Park and around Shinobazu Pond (especially during **July-Aug** evenings when outdoor *bon* dances are held every nite) for pagoda, shrines, temples, General Grant's cypress and magnolia trees and fascinating slice of life in what has been Tokyo's favorite pleasure gardens for over century.

Good for lunching and dining are:
Seiyo-ken ☎3821-2181 in park, or inns S and W of pond. If you've always wanted to make own sushi, try our find, friendly comfortable **Iroha-zushi,** 3min walk S of Ueno stn, on L as you enter Ame-yoko-cho alley. Prices below standard for good quality fish; also serve tempura as well as small orders of *tsumami* snacks. But what has made it popular with young crowd is their new 'invention', *Omakase temaki,* make-it-your-way rolls: ¥300 per item with enough rice and seaweed to roll own. Order bunch at once and comes carefully arranged on tray. Counter and tables 1st floor, or semi-private *zashiki* rooms upstairs.

Also some restaurants in...
OKACHIMACHI, considered part of Ueno by most people, and might as well be, for there's only 500m separating their two stations. Yet, within these few city blocks is amazing assortment of mostly "I can get it for you wholesale"-type stores. South of Shinobazu Pond is one short shop street Nakamichi-dori (*see* p.1170) worth browsing, retains much of its old Edo airs with odd mix of architecture representing traditional, Meiji era Western, and modern. And if you are one of those people who needs destination, this is good route to YUSHIMA TENJIN, shrine to scholars (p.1171).

Easy starting point...
Shitamachi Museum (9:30-16:30, X-mon & 12/29-1/3, ¥200) SE corner of Shinobazu pond. Dedicated to preserving historic *Shitamachi*-'downtown', small, but excellent coverage representing Meiji thru Taisho eras (1867-1925). All 45,000+ items displayed donated by Shitamachi-ites and collection is always growing. English brochure (free), and E-books on sale. 1st floor has reconstructed old neighborhood: candy shop, coppersmith's workshop, merchant home, tenement house, all with appropriate utensils and such. Each has good, descriptive English flyer. Upstairs, assorted displays of everyday items, crafts, toys, war memorabilia and photos. Also reconstructed Milk Bar, popular 'Western' hangout in prewar days. On our visit, bus tour of old folks came and their joy in seeing all this nostalgia was overpowering. Some displays change seasonally; occasional special shows and demonstrations add further color. 'Must' for understanding Shitamachi; great intro for our Shitamachi walking tours.

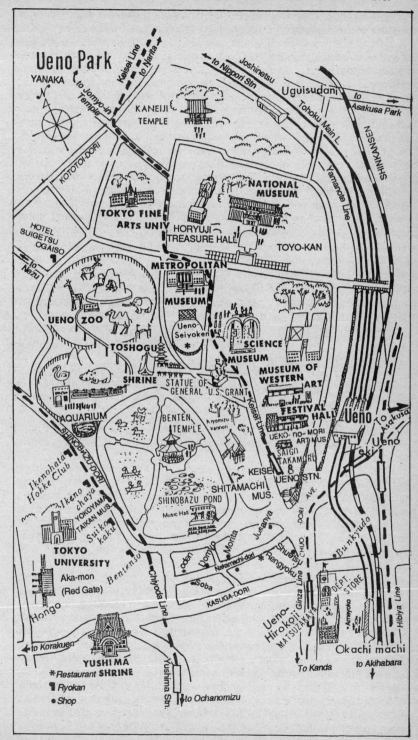

From museum, cross big street S to solitary old fashioned wood building like those in museum. You have found **Jusanya**, 250-year-old, 14th generation comb maker. Founder in 1736 chose name of Jusan-ya '13-shop', as word for comb, *kushi*, is phonetically 9 (*ku*) + 4 (*shi*). Present master and wife spend their days here carving everything you see. Material is strong but supple *tsuge* boxwood; not too abundant, so prices bit high. Jusanya uses only finest *tsuge* from south Kyushu or Izu Isles, cured over time. Combs made here go thru 18 different phases of carving and polishing. Their handmade combs pass thru hair much more easily than similar machine-mades which only polish outsides of teeth leaving insides rough. Jusanya also has old-style wood *kanzashi* hair pins. These don't need suppleness of combs, and carving one leaves much waste wood so mostly used is less expensive (and not as good) imported boxwood, darker in color than local boxwood. Jusanya's owners are hospitable, enjoy sharing their work with interested customers. Will custom-make to any design using local or imported boxwood (your choice); mailed upon completion (please pay in advance). Fun just to watch, you'll probably find it hard to resist buying some great gifts for folks back home. Follow their recommended care and your comb will last for generations: wipe with lightly oiled cloth (camellia, olive, or hair oil), twice weekly at first, then every other week, then once monthly.

From here, head towards Okachimachi stn, R & next R to head down **Nakamachi-dori** shopping alley (entrance arch has '2' in blue circle with '2') on back side of block.

Japanese pickle fanatics might want to keep going S along main street here for half block to **Shu-etsu**. Here since early 1600's, 15th generation owner, NODA Kiyoemon, invented now-popular *fukujin-zuke* pickle back in early Meiji (1870s). About 50m on L as you go down Nakamachi shopping alley is lovely little soba shop **Rengyoku-an** known for past 140 years for its great homemade noodles. If full or closed there's another highly recommended noodle shop further down this street. Little further along on R is 2-storey wood Taisho era (1920s) building, **Kyoya Lacquer** and Furniture shop; exquisite traditional pieces made of sturdy *kiri* paulownia wood.

You'll find some turn-of-century Meiji buildings further down: liquor and tobacco shop and next door **Morita Hotan** Pharmacy. Brick building may only be 80 years old, but shop has been here for over 300. In addition to modern medicines and cosmetics, Morita Hotan sells many herbal medicines tried and proved true over centuries, like powdered *hotan* for headaches, *morimyo* for colds and *rikkogan* for coughs. R at this corner towards Shinobazu Pond takes you to **Shinseido Honbo**, 250-year-old art supply store with finest brushes, ink, paper and such.

Corner facing Morita Hotan is kimono store, next to which is **Domyo**, only shop left in Tokyo specializing in *kumi-himo* braided cords. Domyo has been creating colorful masterpieces by hand for 300 years, since first master commissioned by shogunate. Finest silk thread used, all hand-colored using only natural dyes. Originally used on sword hilts and scabbards, armor, and harnesses, *kumi-himo* are now mostly used with kimono. But as kimono fast disappear from everyday use, we leave it to your imagination to come up with some new fashion using *kumi-himo*. Shouldn't be too difficult, with endless possibilities of color and patterns. Present master, 8th generation Mr KAWASHIMA Takeichi (50 years experience knows 100+ braids), has branched out to keep art alive: beautiful man's necktie ¥16,000.

Across alley from Hotel Parkside's rear entrance is...
Ikenohata Yabu Soba, discriminating soba connoisseurs rank one of best noodle shops in Tokyo; 11:30-14:00, 16:30-20:00 (no break sun). Past next corner **Kikuya** samisen store is marked by its white plectrum-shape sign. Beyond **Kiya** is another old art supply store which has branched out to include more modern office supplies in its inventory. This may not be busiest of shopping streets around Ueno, but probably has most interesting array of old stores.

At next wide street, cross, go L, cross next big street Kasuga-dori (corner is entrance to Chiyoda Line's Yushima subway stn) and R at next light. Long flight of steps at end leads up to Yushima Tenjin shrine. This straight up approach is called *otoko-zaka* (man's slope); winding one to its R is *onna-zaka* (woman's hill), both known for abundant plum blossoms Jan. Base of steps is tiny **SHINJO-IN** guardian temple of Yushima tenjin —If you don't want meal but rather just place to sit and sip, then step in to next-door cozy tea house **Shino**; few hundred yen buys coffee, *ko-cha* W-style tea, *ama-zake* sweet sake, *sen-cha* leaf tea, or *konbu-cha* powdered kelp tea, little more for cocoa, orange juice, *oshiruko*, ¥700 for *matcha* whisked thick green tea with sweet cakes.

YUSHIMA TENJIN SHRINE: Dedicated 1355 to Sugawara Michizane, apotheosis of wisdom. *Ennichi* festive market **monthly 25**, sat-sun during *Ume Matsuri* **Feb 15-Mar 15** and **May 25** for year's main *ennichi* (*see* DATEBOOK). Famed for *ume* plum blossoms which bloom February to March, about which time students swarm to offer prayers for success in upcoming entrance examinations. Many will be trying to get in to nearby most prestigious Tokyo University, and every little bit of extra help is called on. Amulets sold here reputedly good for retaining knowledge, overall luck in studies; can even buy pens and pencils blessed at shrine. Some pilgrims coming here may seem little too young to be worrying about college, or even high school—kids dragged here by their Japanese media-dubbed 'education monster moms' (Ori-Yental Yiddisher mommas). Driven to succeed from as early as kindergarten, many children deal with academic failure by most Japanese of solutions—suicide among youth is one of Japan's growing problems, as also in US, Australia and Europe.

In Tokugawa days, parents would come to look for lost children, leave notes on giant rock here hoping to be reunited with children separated during fire or other catastrophe. Many of modern Japan's early writers lived in Ueno area, and this Tenjin shrine is especially popular with writers.

You can leave thru shrine front entrance; about 15min walk straight S to...
KANDA MYOJIN SHRINE established 1,200 years ago by migrant tribe from Izumo, enshrines Okuninushi-no-Mikoto, earthy earth god, and his folk counterpart Ebisu as well as Daikoku. Enter typical *ryobu-shinto* gate, mixed Buddhist-Shinto style—that is, instead of fierce nio-wrestlers in gate flanks, there are ornately colored seated formal warriors with long-bows, *udaijin* and *sadaijin*, ministers of right and left, both tight lipped. On inside of gate are similarly lacquered white horses, in place of live ones, mouths open to accentuate their active friskiness. Beyond gate in court center is vertical hoop of straw, passage thru is good luck, symbolizing rebirth. To far L is immense stone statue of Daikoku on his scrotal rice bags. Since 1923 3rd deification worshipped here has been Taira no Masakado, popular rebel killed 940, whose nearby shrine nearby was destroyed in quake.

Kiosk sells wine gourd talismans, keyholder fobs of Daikoku- & Ebisu-head bells. Tiny turtle charms testify to primeval antiquity of Okuninushi as fertility deity.

Gorgeous interior of Shrine, restored 1934 after quake, survived bombs and is typical *ryobu-Shinto* all in red lacquer and ornate Chinese decor. Main interest is that they will perform *miko-mai* (sacred shrine maiden dance, done usually only for regular supporters), on request, four dancers for *sanpai* 'shrine offering' of ¥100,000 – reasonable if for whole tour group; ☎3255-8871 *shamusho*, shrine office week ahead. Main festivals: *spring*, **May 15** is grand *Kanda Matsuri*, among Edo Top Trio; *autumn* **Oct 25**. On way out, between shrine and outer *torii* on L, are shops selling attractive little bottles and pottery barrels, few hundred yen and up. These contain Jizo *ame* (candy) and *ama-zake* (tasty drink). For latter, add contents, about pound, to 5 cups of boiling water, half teaspoon salt; drink hot as toddy. Other attractive packages on view are *nasubi-no-karashizuke* (pickled eggplant in mustard) and other such condiments. **Amanoya**, old-looking shop at outer *torii*, serving ama-zake to visitors since 1597, hot in winter, cold in summer, either way with portion of their specialty *Hisakata-miso*. Just to L is **Mikawaya** senbei cracker shop.

Downhill of shrine, L 10min walk **Akihabara** wholesale electronics market (p.l176). One stop JR beyond which is **Asakusa-bashi** wholesale doll, etc, market.

Exit shrine, L on Hongo-dori Ave, L again next big street, up 2 alleys on L old house **Kandagawa Hontenn**, old favorite *unagi-ya*, eel restaurant as old-fashioned as can be, pvt rooms on garden with great stone lanterns. Best *shiroyaki*, plain w/pinch of *sansho*-herbs (¥2,000) and best w/*reishu* cooled sake, 2 get by ¥10,-12,000; ☎3251-5031, X-sun.

YUSHIMA SEIDO, Shrine to Confucius—Confucianism in Japan is one big anachronism even among anachronisms. Importance of Confucian influence in Japan is gravely underrated (except in book *Sources of Japanese Tradition*, Columbia Univ Press) tho its end results were very antithesis of sage-ruled Republic theorized by itinerant savant of 2,500 years ago. Seems odd that only fertile ground upon which true seeds of Master Kung fell were Virginian, its sole lasting fruit US Declaration of Independence. Teachings of Kung Fu-tze recognized people as ultimate repository of power thru their inalienable right, even duty, to replace emperor-son-of-heaven (by analogy, any state system or government) who gave evidence of losing mandate of heaven, 'divine right', thru failure to provide for their well-being. Yet his teachings in Japan were usurped to perpetuate totalitarian status-quo which for two and half centuries suspended natural laws of evolution. Confucius ranked military lowest class of humankind: in Japan it was this very military who adopted and worshipped him. Confucius considered merchant not much better: merchandising for years supported his only shrine in Japan. Until recently it maintained self by art & curio gallery.

Enter outer gate, follow path past...
Great standing **sculpture** of Master Kung, a.k.a. Confucius, to great black gate *Nyu-toku-mon*, sole survivor of first 1799 restoration. Yushima Seido is not old building. Shrine was founded 1609, burned and restored 1799, destroyed by great 1923 quake, rebuilt 1935, being restored '89-93. Noble, as Chinese building can be, shape is Chinese grand, but material is concrete. **Taiseido** enshrines statue of Confucius. Building is on occasion school, bookshop, antique shop, restaurant, office. Compound open daily 10:00-16:00, only as far as Nyutoku-mon gate until restoration complete, main shrine is atop stairs. **4th sun April** at 9:30 & 10:15 am sees performance of Japan's sole Confucian rite.

But it is more confusion than Confucian. Sage of Reason seems to have been forgotten, except that he still attracts student or two who sits in his aura to study or think in peace. There is no cult of Kung Fu-tse to maintain it— no longer important educational institution (was 'university' that first US Ambassador Townsend Harris asked to see) as it was under Tokugawa until century ago when its function was absorbed by nearby Tokyo University.

GETTING THERE: On block down to back of...or from foot of Ueno Park 10-15 min walk, if you don't get lost, across river from Ochanomizu Stn. Tho immense building with 'cock's tail' roof ridge visible for miles, entrance is hard to find—at bottom of hill below and away from bridge leading to Nicorai-do Orthodox Cathedral opposite (and from which bridge on side away from Shrine, stairs down to Shrine are blocked off).

Saint's Bridge, *Hijiri-bashi*, 1928, purposely at odd angle (especially noticeable from JR platform) to connect Yushima Seido over JR and river to....

Nikorai-do Orthodox Cathedral, popular name honoring founder but properly Cathedral of Holy Resurrection, Byzantine style, 1891. Founding monk Nikolai, later archbishop, saint—born 1836, came to Hakodate 1861, Tokyo 1872 before prohibition of Christianity lifted, died 1912. Once boasted largest Christian congregation in Japan. Defeat in Russo-Japanese war saw following plummet—not because it was enemy faith (Nikorai developed mostly native clergy, insisted parishioners' loyalty was to their homeland and not to tsar), but because it lost, so, obviously, didn't work.

Area just W of Nikorai-do is **Meiji Univ** *with two interesting specialty museums...*
Criminal Museum, *Meiji Daigaku Keiji Hakubutsu-kan* with Edo period police paraphernalia and modern ones such as guillotine onward; and **Archaeological Collection**, *Meiji Daigaku Kokogaku Chinretsu-kan*, with primarily Chinese (prehistoric to T'ang) and Japanese (Jomon to Kofun) objects. Both museums free, daily 10:00-16:30 (till noon sat) X-mon, Univ and Nat hols. Opposite direction (E) from Nikorai-do some 500m is TRANSPORTATION MUSEUM (*see* KANDA, below, p1175).

Downhill (S) from Nikorai-do 400m to main Yasukuni-dori Ave, where R takes you thru **sporting goods market** specializing in surf, skii, climbing; prices 30% discount.

Continue on and you soon enter...
Jimbo-cho, commonly known as **Kanda used-book street**, lining both sides of which are scores of fine old bookshops, many of which also specialize in old woodblock prints and block-printed books. Bookstores sprang up here early Meiji era to supply then-new Imperial University (now Tokyo U). More schools followed, and 60% of Tokyo's (50% of national) publishing house offices set up around here. Several centered around Jimbo-cho intersection of Yasukuni-dori and Hakusan-dori (under which is subway stn on Toei Mita and Shinjuku lines) specialize in foreign language books and particularly on books in English on Oriental subjects. You'll find most on S side of Yasukuni-dori; subway exit A-6 puts you at main intersect. Top for old and new is **Kitazawa** Bookstore in new white building about 200m W of intersect. Same distance E is **Tuttle** books, beyond which is **Isseido** (☎3292-0071) and paired **Ohya Shobo** (☎3291-0062), one for used English and other for woodblocks—great selection at fair prices.

Continue W on up Yasukuni-dori Ave till you cross bridge, then 50m or so on at wide street, Uchibori-dori or Kudanshita intersect (subway stn, Toei Shinjuku, Tozai) turn L at foot of large **Kudan Hall** (¥-B hostel), greenery up Yasukuni-dori is Yasukuni Shrine, or continue to main moat to reverse our IMPERIAL PALACE route (p.1142) at bridge across moat, which you may cross to **Science & Technology Museum**.

700 to 1,000mtrs between Jimbo-cho–Nikoraido (depending on how you twist thru] is maze of alleys of college-town, buildings of several major univerities, student bookstores, noodleries, mahjong parlors and all trappings of Japanese student life. Interesting route to meander thru.

Koishikawa Koraku-en, *Garden of Other World Pleasures*, lies about 1km W of Yushima Tenjin. Designed by, and for sole use of, Mito lords construction begun 1629 by first Mito Yorifusa, youngest son of Ieyasu; finished 30 years later by son Mitsukuni. (Mito lords had knack for gardens, one of Japan's Top 3, their Kairaku-en is in Mito city, p.253) Started Japanese style, Mitsukuni had Chinese scholar Chu Sun-shui create Sino-Japanese amalgam, replicating famed scenes from Japan and China, notably latter's West Lake, Hangzhou—on which other fine Japan gardens are also modeled. 18 acres crisscrossed with paths to and around ponds, streams, pavilions and bridges (best known arched Full Moon Bridge) provide great escape from busy Tokyo. Tho among Tokyo's best traditional gardens, it is relatively unknown and visitors are usually rather sparse.

Daily 9:00-16:30, X-mon, year-end, ¥200; short walk from Suido-bashi stn (JR Loop; subway Toei Mita–blue) or closest Koraku-en (subway Marunouchi-red).

Overshadowed by its modern neighbor of This World Pleasures...
Korakuen *Yuenchi* **Amusement Park** and *Domu* **Baseball Stadium** with baseball Hall of Fame. Former (¥800, daily peak Aug, X-mon rest of year) dominated by roller-coaster and other rides. Latter is site of National Baseball Series, new domed diamond (first in Japan) opened 1988 series— old open air one making way for giant new hotel. **Kodokan** Judo *dojo* is block N; E across street is **Hosho Nohgaku-do** Noh theater.

1km N is...
Koishikawa *Shokubutsu-en* **Botanical Garden**, on site of 2nd shogun Hidetada's manse. Later shoguns created medicinal herb garden, post-Meiji Restoration saw it given to new Tokyo Imperial University, which now, as Tokyo University still owns. Part of original garden remains, modern additions are hot-houses, flower beds, etc; old building was old Main Hall of Tokyo U's Med school. 9:00-16:30, X-mon, year-end, ¥250.

Enthusiasts find another fine landscape strolling garden 1.5km N of Botanical Garden...
Rikugi-en, *Garden of Six Principles* (-of poetry), easier reached from (5min S of) JR Komagome stn on Yamate Loop. Hours 9:00-16:00, ¥200, X-mon. Rikugi-en, created 1695-1702 by lord YANAGISAWA Yoshiyasu, noted literator who recreated 88 famed spots of Chinese and Japanese poetry. Meiji Restoration saw decline of Yanagisawa wealth, garden bought by IWASAKI Yataro (founder of Mitsubishi zaibatsu) 1878 who improved it; donated to city by family in 1934. Bit larger than Koraku-en, Rikugi-en is less known, thus much more quiet. Wandering thru woods, ponds, streams, hills and tea houses, easy to see how poet Yoshiyasu found it ideal to contemplate.

Perhaps, that's why city set up...
Research Library of East Asia, *Toyo Bunko* across street, houses half million books & periodicals (many early 20th Cent).

Few minutes walk N of Komagome stn is mixed Edwardian-Japanese *Kyu-Furukawa Tei-en* (see ARAKAWA TRAM, *preceding*, p.1164).

KANDA, 'God's Field', now busy family-run shop and restaurant district, got its name since this area used to belong to Ise Grand Shrine (thus, many shops this area have names Ise-something, chosen by early merchants to honor their hometown). Then, it was big hill, but Ieyasu had it flattened to fill in marshlands near his Edo castle. As aside, progressive warriors were attracted to Kanda as it was just next to Surugadai, cultural center of Edo— attracting poets like Basho, artists such as Hokusai, Hiroshige, Utamaro, and playwrights, scholars, sculptors, centers of education as evidenced in school-shrine of Confucius. This dual tradition of culture and progress are reflected in present-day composition of whole area: YMCA and YWCA are here, Meiji, Chuo, Dental and Kyoritsu Women's Universities as well as Nihon U, Japan's biggest campus. Tokyo U (Todai) began here and was moved over short distance to its present locale, as also Gakushuin Peers School. It is still book center of Japan, for both publishers and shops (estimated 150), important art center and dynamic part of dynamic town. It's fun area to walk thru (p.1173), which you do from JR Kanda stn, en route to electronic Akihabara, or Ochanomizu with Nikorai-do and Yushima shrines. Countless wholesale markets have come and gone over centuries here— **stone marker** memorializes produce mart which disappeared in '23 quake; Yanagi-hara, 'poor man's Yoshiwara', and Edo period gangster hangout. Now, you'll find many interesting shops, especially along main Chuo-dori Ave which during good weather will have numerous stalls set up.

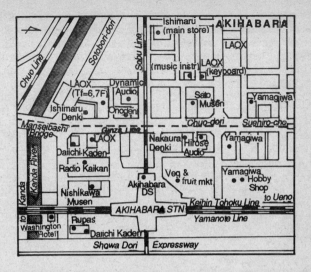

We leave exploring to you, and head to ....
Transportation Museum, *Kotsu Hakubutsu-kan* (9:30-16:30 X-Mon, ¥250),
8min walk N of Kanda stn, or 500m E from Nikorai-do. You can't miss it, poking
out of building (part of which red brick was used in railway bridge) is nose
of bullet train and old black steam locomotive; and it's fun, worth visiting.
Outlined is history of modern transportation in Japan, mostly trains, like
Engine #1 which ran first Tokyo-Yokohama run; but also some cars,
Japan's first domestically made bus (1930), and first airplane in which
Japan's first flyer, TOKUGAWA Yoshitoshi, flew for 70mtrs on December 19,
1910; his statue sits in Yoyogi Park near Meiji Shrine. From here N across
Mansei-bashi Bridge, one of Edo's earliest bridges, is only 5min to Akihabara.

   LUNCH TIME: Many good eateries which have been around since Edo times, of
which, try: **Kanda Yabu Soba** (☎3251-0287)Awajicho-2 block E of Kanda PO, old
house surrounded by bamboo with large square lantern in front, original of now-famous
yabu-soba restaurants in Ueno and other parts of Tokyo; also **Shoei-tei** for budget
'Western' food, i.e. *tonkatsu*...
   Ise-gen in antique architectural treasure for *anko-nabe*, 'one pot' sukiyaki-like
cooking of fish especially (Nov-Mar) meter-long catfish-like *anko*, usually not considered
edible; abt ¥2,000; lunch-9pm, X-sun. Across from which is traditional sweets shop
Takemura (specialty *age-manju*, deep-fried bean paste cake, comes with Japanese tea; get
Western cakes and must pay for coffee); **Botan** for chicken dishes (recommend *tori-suki*
chicken sukiyaki) served in what looks like old house, eating around tiny *hibachi* table.
All nr Ochanomizu JR el, or Marunouchi subway Awaji-cho, Shinjuku line Ogawamachi.

   *Back in Ueno...following overhead JR tracks between Ueno–Okachimachi stns is...
perhaps most interesting market in Tokyo...*
AME-YOKO, *American Alley*, so named since this was biggest black
market area after war where Japanese were exposed to cornucopia of US
goods which had somehow made their way over from military PX's. And
so its postwar alias of Ueno PX, once notorious and still fabulous Tokyo
black market area (now tattle-tale grey), and candy and cookie wholesalers.
During and after Korean War Ame-yoko became outlet for surplus goods,
much like side alleys of Okinawa's Naha during '70s. You'll still find
'surplus' goods, but much of it is imitation, as is everything sold in
countless 'gun' shops. But Okachimachi was known for its cheap goods

even prior to Yanks. Just after war it was place to get what little fresh produce, rice, and other basic foods were available, tho at exorbitant prices. After New Year 1987 big clean-up of alley was announced and police moved out pushcarts so shops can 'upgrade' to boutiques ubiquitous elsewhere in town. Let's see what it becomes—will it lose more than gain?

OKACHIMACHI seems to have been fated to become Shitamachi marketplace, tho pre-Meiji inhabitants were of samurai class. Name means town of *kachi* (with honorific O), foot-soldiers of shogunate. 'Grunts' of those days, they were samurai of low-rank, and with Meiji Restoration were for most part unneeded extras who didn't fit into new bureaucracy. Some joined new conscript army, others set out to settle northern lands. Many who stayed started businesses, but unskilled in dealing with money, many had to sell out to business-minded merchants from Shitamachi.

Nowadays, as in past, economical Tokyo-ites come here to stock up on cheap foodstuffs. In addition to fresh edibles, you'll find clothing, sporting goods (reputedly cheapest place for golf gear), and anything else you might or might not be looking for.

Area just E of Okachimachi station is...
Jewelry town, over 2,000 wholesalers clumped together. Granted, much of what you find here will be more akin to costume jewelry, but then again, you can find fine pieces at bargain prices.

Motorcycle enthusiasts will want to hit Showa-dori street, running N towards Iriya, on other (E) side of Ueno stn. Called **Kita-Ueno**, probably largest motorcycle market in world, long known as biker's heaven since dozens of repair shops opened their doors here after war. Now there are hundreds of bike-related shops. Not only for repairs or bikes themselves, you can outfit you and your bike in newest and wildest of accessories and fashion clothing. In most cases, you'd still do better to get US or European goods in America for lower prices, but then again, creators of Yamaha, Kawasaki, Suzuki and Honda don't do badly in accessories department either.

From Okachimachi it's not far (only one stop JR or Hibiya subway) down road to...
AKIHABARA, long famed as one of cheapest places in world for electronic goods...alas *en-daka* rising yen. Sprawling beneath this station is Tokyo wholesale and cut-rate electronics parts district, 'Canal and Sixth' of Orient, with sometimes terrific bargains even in these days of distorted exchange rates, tho with strong yen you can get most things cheaper in US. What Akihabara does offer is much greater selection of gadgets and new 'toys' not offered in overseas markets. If looking for portable ghetto blaster that has 3 cassette players, CD player, maybe small color TV, this is place. Then there is maze of packed lanes under tracks which sell every electronic part imaginable, as well as many you've never seen. Even if you don't plan to buy, it's fun to browse to see what newest craze is going to be.

Akihabara's JR station is giant '+'; junction of N-S-running Yamanote Line & E-W Sobu Line. Under tracks are shoebox-sized parts stores; most of big electronics department stores are clustered W of station. As matter of fact, W spoke of station is itself one such store. **LAOX** is probably best known of giant stores, first to have exclusive for-export floor with knowledgeable multilingual staff. Others followed suit, so you should have little problem getting across language barrier. For **duty-free purchases**, remember to take along passport; in most big places, foreign currency and travelers cheques accepted, with exchange rate being official that-day rate quoted by Bank of Japan, no 'handling charges'.

NORTH UENO WALKS IRIYA,YANAKA,YOSHIWARA

IRIYA: Northeast of Ueno, is another one of those quiet little neighborhoods reminiscent of old Edo; nothing very special here, but pleasant place to stroll thru. (Ex-Yoshiwara gay quarters is few minutes' walk NE of here.)

Our walking tour starts Iriya subway stop of Hibiya (grey) Line and ends Kanei-ji temple N end Ueno Park—1.5km (almost mile) and we give it about one hour, tho easily spend more, especially if taking in lunch at any of several fine restaurants. We came midmorning; perfect timing for early 'health food' lunch of tofu dishes at **Sasa-no-yuki** conveniently located near end of our tour. This of course left enough time to add on our next leg of Yanaka, but to do so is up to you and how much walking you're ready for...

Surfacing Iriya stn you're at intersect of Showa-dori (N-S) and Kototoi-dori Aves. W on Kototoi-dori, short way down, across street is steep roof of Iriya's...
KISHIBOJIN SHRINE, within precincts of **SHINGEN-JI** temple—worth detour during July 6-8 *Asagao-ichi* **Morning Glory Market**, over 200 stalls show and sell all sorts of these flowers from 7am.

We keep going, R at next intersect (Fuji Bank on corner) and we head up Yanagi-dori. Short way on R, narrow lane marked by red banners leads to simple black gate of...
EISHIN-JI temple. Better known around here as *San-men* (3-faced) *Daikoku*, you'll see why if you go look at their Daikoku statue in glassedoff area L of temple. Reputedly carved by Saint Kobo-daishi, it is Daikoku, but sprouting aside his head are those of muse Benten on L and warrior Bishamon R. Glass door to your L leads to temple office where you can get copy of prints shown on glass of Daikoku (¥100 for small, ¥1,000 large), *ema-e* votive plaque ¥500 or interesting painting of all Seven Lucky Gods (¥500 plain, ¥5,000 framed). Pilgrims can visit all Seven at their own temples or shrines (including solo Benten and Bishamon) by wandering back alleys around here. As you leave, look up at roof of temple—two petrified pigeons up there are unique tile decorations.

Other side of Yanagi-dori is row of ancient shops, at far end of which is...
Igarashi, century-old *chochin* (paper lantern) shop. Here, old man Igarashi and son deftly decorate their delicate lanterns, just as has been done here for 4 generations. Old man is true master; his most recognized work being calligraphy on great red lantern at Asakusa's Kaminari-mon Gate. Choose among their stock, or have lantern custom painted, perhaps your name in homonymic ideographs; either way, rates reasonable.

Next intersection, on far side is lovely old building with sloping tiled roof, intricately carved wood crane hanging above entrance: **Hosen-yu**, public bath where you can duck in to warm up for few hundred yen. Used to be several more such baths around here, but most homes now have baths and these old neighborhood *sento* are disappearing—tho 1988 *Shitamachi* mag reports new apartment houses have on ground floor. L at Hosen-yu takes us down short street of old shops, ends at perpendicular street where we run smack into...
SENJU-IN temple with 1,000-armed Kannon figure.

Facing Senju-in, L down street takes us back to Kototoi-dori, passing some oldfashioned snack shops. Several doors from Senju-in is...
Miyuki (blue awning and noren) serving such summer delights as *mitsumame* (fruits and gelatin), *an-mitsu* (same, with sweet red beans) and homemade ice cream, and winter snacks such as *shiruko* or *ozoni* (types of mochi and red beans in warm soup). Here, everything is served all year, along with various drinks: sodas, tea and coffee. Further down on L are two old *sembei* shops, **Azumaya & Daikokuya**, where you can get fresh handmade rice crackers; much better than anything you'll find at market, and at such low prices.

Backtrack to Senju-in intersect and this road split—in 'V' is another old sembei shop...
Tejina, best known one around here. Wider fork (L) takes us past some more little neighborhood temples; and for no reason in particular we decided to wander up narrower lane branching off R. Houses along here have signs in front stating that they are qualified teachers for everything from piano and English to flower arrangement and tea.

We come to...
SEISON-JI temple on R, boasting large gate and new building. As you enter, on L is slatted-front shed which has two stone jizo inside believed to have power over child rearing, many little gilt jizo lining inside walls left as offerings by parents wishing for healthy children (each figure bears name of child). Beyond is mountain formed of 500 rakan, saints, Buddha atop. On R as you enter is big shed with stone slab, on which is etched 6 beautiful figures, reputedly of Kobo-daishi himself. Wooden wheel to its R is used to keep track of number of prayers recited here; each rotation marks 50. Not everyone comes here offering prayers for healthy children. Some pray at shiny bronze figure surrounded by toddlers in middle of courtyard: *mizuko jizo*, for spirits of aborted infants. Seison-ji is one temple which has managed to prosper, but not all are able to as you will see just up street.

On L is squat blue-grey concrete box with parking lot below...
SAINEN-JI temple, which, like many shrines and temples around Japan, has been forced to supplement income by other means. This is probably one of most extreme cases we have seen.

LUNCH TIME: Soon, we come to intersection with stop light; those who took L fork will hit this road little to W (L) of here. Along this street are several choices:
Soba shop at this light; little to E is grand entrance to sushi bar **Takase** (good but pricey); across from Takase is red white and blue awning of...
Kamiya one of Tokyo's oldest Western food (French, here) restaurants. Present owner's grandfather started back in 1925, and since has served all sorts of people while retaining sh'tamachi prices and atmosphere. Choose from various dishes, or go for daily lunch special—11:30-21:00 daily X-wed.
If saving lunch for Sasa-no-Yuki (p.1179), go L at this soba shop corner.
Walking on, R is **Ebiya** *somé-kojo* family-run cloth dying workshop. Across from it is **Okano Eisei**, another family-run shop here for generations, makes delicate cakes used for tea ceremony, as well as other 'regular' tea cakes—for one-stop shopping, excellent tea store next door. If you want tea and cakes ready served, follow us around corner (R at next intersection) to...
Shiguré Chaya tea house—also generations old, but rather than old tea house, look for modern glass-fronted building with low stone tables in front. Go in, point to which ever piece of mochi or cake you want, and eat it there, washed down with tea, coffee or juice. They have matcha and sweets set for ¥500; about same for *an-mitsumamé* with lots of fruit. Also light fried rice with herbs dish which comes with soup.

Just N of Shigure Chaya is...
Tiny temple, its real name mostly forgotten, just known as *Ogyo-no-Matsu*, or **Great Pine**...once enormous pine tree here, famed landmark of Edo you can see in one of Hiroshige's *100 Views of Edo* prints—recreated on wrapping paper used at Okano Eisei (*above*). Cool stream flowing under branches of pine tree in print was filled in during early Meiji expansion of Tokyo, and not long after stately tree withered. Another pine tree grows here now struggling to survive, but without stream it will never get as large as original. All that remains of Hiroshige's pine is part of its trunk, mounted on stone pedestal behind.

Back at Shigure Chaya intersect, we go W, street narrows and we take first L (up 3 steps), then R at end. Take next L which is winding alley. Just when you think you are lost (tho it's only 50m or so), you see another temple on your R...

ENKO-JI, bit hard to find but worth seeking out, for it gives glimpse of how some deal with Japan's greatest vice. Anyone in Japan for one nite will notice that vast majority of men on late trains are drunk—easy escape from pressures of life here; chance to break strict social bonds. Enko-ji, divine Schick Center of sorts, people come here to pray for help if they or someone they know is too snared by booze. Enter temple (thru small door R side of locked main gate) and make your way to rear. There, Daikoku, depicted here sitting on barrel of sake (instead of bushel of rice), symbolically keeping evil of over-indulging safely locked away. In spring you get full effect of temple's second name, *Fuji-dera*, or Wisteria Temple, well-manicured small garden is in full bloom, with great strands of wisteria winding all over.

Leaving Enko-ji, R (W) takes us past some hole-in-wall diners on one side and Negishi primary school on other, and we come out on busy street, Otakebashi-dori. (If you think our route to Enko-ji will get you lost, another way is to stay on same road going W from Shigure Chaya until you hit Otakebashi-dori, then L; alley to Enko-ji has huge blue and white 'Suginami-ku' sign at its entrance.) Facing out on this intersection here.

Far L corner is our lunch destination...
Sasa-no-Yuki, tofu specialty restaurant here since Genroku era (1680s), boasts being first in Edo to serve finer *kinugoshi* (silk strained) tofu. Present modern structure has lovely interior and inner garden, creating such relaxed atmosphere that you forget where you are. Everything served here is tofu in some form or another; recommend lunch special combination of six assorted types bit over ¥2,000; 11:00-21:00, X-mon; **July 6-8** Morning Glory Fair, open 5am —next big street S is Kototoi-dori, about 500m to Kishimojin. Full but not over-stuffed, ready to continue our walk, our choices are many:

Short detour...about 150m W of Sasa-no-Yuki in back streets: go W along big street, take 2nd L then first R, down bit on R is fine...
Calligraphy Museum, *Shodo Hakubutsu-kan*, in Meiji era house of painter-calligrapher NAKAMURA Fusetsu. Famed as W-style painter, also learned in Oriental styles. This is his collection, in which history of calligraphy is outlined thru such as ancient inscribed pottery and stone, how early ideograms and various writing styles developed. (10:00-16:00, X-mon and mid-June–mid-July; pricey at ¥600). Across from museum is another old house, belonged to popular Meiji era haiku poet MASAOKA Shiki.

If you cut down S along any of these alleys, you will end up on Kototoi-dori, just before bridge which takes us over JR rails and to KANEI-JI temple.

If passing up museum, head S to Kototoi-dori, cross it and go R to steps up to bridge crossing railroad; about 8min walk from Sasa-no-Yuki to Kanei-ji. If you keep going S down narrow street once across Kototoi-dori, you end at JR Uguisu-dani stn. For those continuing on, rather than going to Kanei-ji to begin our Yanaka tour, we have optional route taking us via Nippori stn. After Calligraphy Museum, return to big street, go W. Shortly it forks, take L. Few short blocks on L corner is...

Habutae Dango, mochi dumpling shop since 1819: *habutae* is fine silk cloth, *dango* are dumplings. Back when shop opened, had reputation for dango as smooth as habutae, so its name. You can munch on stick of *dango* for under ¥200, or pay just bit more and enjoy them with cup of tea, in their tea room overlooking small garden: open 9:00-17:30, X-tue.

Turn down alley here and bridge crosses tracks to park-like **Yanaka Cemetery**; or continue few more minutes W to Nippori station for alternate bridge crossing. Nippori stn is fun area to walk around; wholesale district specializing in fabrics and sewing goods, and

cheap toys and candies—types Cellin and Garet grew up with, sold by neighborhood
grandma-run shops, which you don't see too often nowadays. Most shops here close on
3rd Tuesday every month—old style monthly sabbath, not weekly.

Those tired of walking, or who have other plans for rest of day, hop train at Nippori.
Otherwise, strong of calf, we cross over to...

YANAKA

NORTHWEST of Ueno Park, in many ways best preserved area of old Edo.
Survived all great fires, including flames of Great Quake and WWII, thanks
to heavy greenery of this giant cemetery. This is heart of area also known as
YANESEN, combining Yanaka-Nezu (*follows*)—Sendagi, one of last of old
style low-rise *nomiya-sento* (drinking house and public bath) centered areas.
It started its art-literary refugee reputation with painters like YOKOYAMA
Taikan and authors MORI Ogai and NATSUME Soseki (who wrote fantasy *I
am a Cat* here), and continues it with modern expatriate (from Roppongi and
points West) authors Donald Keene, Edward Seidensticker, Donald Richie,
others. It is borderline Shitamachi (*follows*).

When Ieyasu chose Edo for his capital, he had most temples built in this
area because this was NE of castle, traditionally unlucky. But main reason
to cluster temples together was to more easily keep tabs on them. He was
not about to let them meddle in government affairs and bring about ruin as in
Nara, Kyoto, Kamakura. Whatever his reasons, we've been left with grand
tera-machi **temple-town** to wander in. Early Meiji map of Yanaka had 68
temples, of which most remain—not spectacular, but you never know what
you'll come across. Some have been known as places to view things, like
full moon, sakura in bloom, or snow. Not only do we find countless
temples, but more interesting are equally numerous shops here. They too
have survived Tokyo's modernization, retain strong sh'tamachi air.

Yanaka is on high ground, with maze of quiet narrow lanes winding up
and across this hill. Streets here have names like *Hebi-michi* 'Snake Lane';
Koyo-zaka 'Autumn Maple Hill' with its fiery fall colors, connects to
Sakura-namiki 'Cherry Blossom Lane', while nearby *Ginnan-yokocho* is
lined with majestic gingko trees, *ginnan*; *Kiyomizu-zaka* 'Clear Water Lane'
used to have quiet stream flowing nearby, was also called *Kurayami-zaka*,
'Hill of Darkness', for there used to be so many trees around here that it
was cool and dark even on midsummer's day (can see Ueno's pagoda from
here); and *Fujimi-zaka*, between Nippori and Nishi Nippori stations, got its
name 'Fuji View Hill', because this was only high ground in crowded old
Edo for unobstructed view of Mt Fuji. If you've been looking for *sento* to
jump into to warm up or just relax, you'll come across many fine old
bathhouses in back streets of Yanaka.

If starting out from Kanei-ji, exit at its far back L. Cross street there (this is Kototoi-
dori after crossing over tracks; note fine old houses along here) and go W.

After crossing Kototoi-dori, you will see...
JOMYO-IN temple on L, grounds full of rows of stone jizo figures. When
Jomyo-ji started in 1850, head priest Osho set goal of 1,000 jizo to be put
here thru offerings. Took almost 30 years to reach goal, then he aimed for
84,000. So far, there are about 14,000 and each successive head priest will
keep collecting until magic number is reached.

Take 1st or 3rd L, 200m to next busy street where R. Shortly, road forks: R goes via
scattering of old shops to main path thru Yanaka Park to Nippori stn, L is main street
Sansaki-zaka hill with lots of fun shops, which we follow. There is tiny, interesting
coffee shop, **Kawashima** tucked into 'V' of this fork, looking like something out of set
for Meiji era movie.

You can also start from Nippori station, which is where our walk from Iriya left us. Nippori is 2 stops from Ueno on JR; same if by Keisei Private Rail. This is best during sakura season, for you are immediately exposed to canopied walkway of blooming trees. This place comes alive then, with hordes of merrymakers camped out under trees for full day of picnicing and partying. Walk along here then will surely find you 'eating grass along road', which Japanese like to say when something distracts you from your original goal, as some group of revelers will surely call you over to join them.

Coming here in spring gives good idea of what Yanaka was like during Edo days, when countless tea houses (and as many less 'noble' houses) lined approaches to...
TENNO-JI temple, with shadow of its former self standing at station end of Cherry Tree Lane, mere fraction of what stood here during Tokugawa days, when it prospered as caretaker for all graves around here. One rather fine work of art that remains is large sitting bronze Buddha there, cast in 1690. Tenno-ji was chosen as site of first government lottery in 1732, with head priest drawing lucky numbers; grand prize was 100-ryo (1,500g gold). with time, prize money grew, as did crowds, and lottery was cancelled little over century later. For rough idea of what it must have looked like, walk to end of cherry trees, where Yanaka Park ends and becomes street, and you are among few remaining old shop/houses. These now just serve tea to passers-by, some sell fresh flowers to those visiting graves. As we have mentioned thruout our travels, Japanese cemeteries afford some of most pleasant strolls thru beautiful scenery. There also used to be lovely pagoda here at Tenno-ji. It survived Great Quake and War, but in 1957, young couple committed double-suicide by using it as funeral pyre. Halfway along sakura lane is police box; behind it is geometric stone foundations of pagoda. Perhaps someday replica will rise up here, faithful in design to original but most probably concrete.

R at end of cherry trees, and R again at end takes you to...
Sculpture Museum, *Asakura Choso-kan* (¥300, 9:00-16:00), using studio home of sculptor ASAKURA Fumio (1883-1964) and displaying his works. Even if sculpture doesn't interest (mostly portraits of famous people 1st fl, and favorite animal, cats, on 2nd) house and garden are well worth seeing, and 3rd fl gives great view of Yanaka. You can't miss this modernistic black building on R. Garden not large, but so well laid out as to defy spatial limits, its lavish use of water creates relaxing sense of timelessness, especially in heat of summer. Adjacent is teahouse where Asakura spent his time contemplating his art. Open only sat-sun-mon, but plans call for more regular days, which probably means open daily, X-mon.

Continuing past Asakura Museum, on L is...
Dokiku, old copper goods shop; items sold here so finely finished they look machine-made but are actually pounded out by hand. Passing some more small shops, we come to next intersect, where R (back towards station) few doors is **Yanaka Sembei**, hand-frying rice crackers for 80 years. This street we are now on is called Yanaka Ginza, and was once active shopping street; slowly coming back to life, you will find some interesting shops here. We go L (W) here toward main drag of Yanaka Ginza, shortly after you come to stairs, after which is intersect, go R;

5th shop on R is....
Buseki Hanakago, workshop-home of Mr Buseki, maker of finely woven bamboo flower baskets, *hana-kago*. Notice that all of his baskets are fine dark brown color...from years of being aged by smoke from hearths in old thatch-roof farm houses. Bamboo he uses is bought from farmers when they re-thatch roof; but with times changing supply is getting harder to replenish. So he has gone out and bought great quantities at once, but his son, who works next door, may not be so lucky in years to come. With this

natural ageing his bamboo stands up extremely well, and is yet supple enough to fashion into delicate baskets found here. Once you have seen some of his prices tho, you will probably just settle for watching him at work. Most of his work is pre-commissioned, by such as imperial family members or flower arrangement masters.

Returning to Yanaka Ginza, we cross it and go S down narrow lane.

Few minutes' walk and on your L is small park with small shrine, site of...
Japan Arts Institute, founded here 1898 by OKAKURA Tenshin. Any student of Japanese art will be familiar with his *Book of Tea*, published under name of OKAKURA Kakuzo: Tenshin was his artistic name. He greatly influenced development of early modern art in Japan, and we see works of one of his best pupils near Ueno at Yokoyama Taikan Memorial Museum (p.1184). Okakura and Dr E.F. Fenollosa, his mentor at what is now Tokyo Univ were among few people to advocate development of traditional arts as opposed to then-mainstream thought of totally adopting Western styles. By tradition they meant before mid-Tokugawa, from which time, they felt (as did Langdon Warner) Japanese art had become too formalized and lost its living spirit. Inside small shrine is gilt bust of Okakura, by same sculptor who did giant wood lion dancer in foyer of National (kabuki) Theater.

Take L at this little park and we are on yet another narrow lane, called *Hotaru-zaka* **Firefly Hill**; but these bright insects have faded away, along with clear stream they used to live around. There is talk of re-introducing fireflies from countryside. This zig-zagging lane gives excellent view of Yanaka's home life. After few turns, you should come out on street with Asakura Museum, just near turnoff you took from sakura lane. Museum to L, we go R. Past more temples, look out on L for **Akazuka Bekko**, small shop making *bekko*, tortoise-shell goods. Further on, this lane hits busy road, where L for 50m or so takes us to **Kawashima** coffee shop.

Let's now work our way down Sansaki-zaka hill from Kawashima. Across street is **Makino Ivory** (English sign), which sells replicas of old netsuke, as well as other ivory goods. Buying here cuts out middleman and you will find prices about one-third below most stores. Japan long ignored most international strictures limiting ivory trade, is world's largest market. Japan outlawed trade in ivory—but we'll see.

Back on Kawashima side of street, just after turnoff from/to Asakura Museum, we find stonecutters, next to which is little grandma-run candy shop sure to arouse nostalgia in any who spent childhood in Japan.

Ratty-looking joint next door, all sorts of junk hanging out in front is...
Izakaya **Chonin**, meaning 'townsfolk' or 'commoner'. If afternoon, shutter will be up to expose deliberately patched shoji door. They don't start serving until 5pm or so, but you can stick your head in to look to discover that inside is as unorganized as outside. But their food is good, sake is plentiful, and those that speak some Japanese looking for adventure will find it here. Their sign says it all: under English...   "This is sake" is pseudo-mathematical formula substituting letters for numerals, and which reads...   "Life – sake = 0".

As we go on, next stop is...
Taguchi Ningyo-ten, easily spotted by masks and other carvings in front window. Here, Mr Taguchi and helpers carve orders from all over Japan. Pop in for look, and you may even pick up some of those elaborate fire-men's standards, black and white tasseled 'pom-poms' that Edo fire brigade leader waved while standing over hottest part of fire to show where to direct water. Hoary temple next door is **KANCHI-IN**, which runs kindergarten on other side of Taguchi. Two doors down is **Ogino**, mochi shop which has excellent *sakura-mochi*; so

is their *yaki-dango* (skewered, with sweet sauce) and *kusa-dango* (with thick sweet red bean paste). Next to Ogino is antique shop **Kunitomi**.

Next stretch is all temples, on both sides of street; in all sizes and shapes, from hoary old wood ones to new concrete and everything in between.

Take first L after temples, and short walk to...
Daimyo Tokei Hakubutsu-kan, **Clock Museum**, in interesting old house are over 100 assorted timepieces of Edo period. (¥300, 9:00-16:00, X-mon and all July–Sept and end-Dec–mid-Jan). Just bit down street is **Sawanoya ryokan** (*see* SH'TAMACHI WHERE TO STAY, p.1133).

Back on Sansaki-zaka, pass temples, at next corner on L is...
Isé-tatsu, selling all sorts of items of handmade *washi* 'rice'-paper. You can also get beautifully decorated sheets of washi; just look on shelves for what you want. All reasonably priced. If you go L down alley by Ise-tatsu you shortly come to lovely old folkcraft shop **Chiga**, literally overflowing with fun odds and ends. Few doors below Ise-tatsu is **Asahi-yu**, recently restored neighborhood bath house, boasts saunas and bubble baths.

Crossing back to R side of Sansaki-dori, pass more shops; among them are...
Noike sushi, and **Oshimaya** noodles, and **Osawa** eyeglass shop with their specialty of bekko shell frames. Little beyond is lovely old building, home of century-old **Kikumi Sembei** rice cracker shop. Next is **Bunshichi**, workshop making bunraku 3-man puppets.

At next alley, you will see fronts of various trains: old steam locomotive, electric train, and nose piece of Shinkansen bullet train. Then come assorted RR station signs, and at far end under Station Master sign is entrance to **Setouchi**—menu lists various seafood dishes and name reminds us of our old ancestral village on Inland Sea, but alas, we must have missed last train, for Setouchi was closed and we never got to see ourselves how good it was. Later learned that it is good, cheap, and very popular.

Across street from Setouchi alley is...
Ise-ichi, folk toy store. Owner is woodblock carver himself, is outlet for neighborhood craftspeople. Look up at its eye-catching sign, giant mural of armed Bishamon (of Lucky 7) riding tiger and chasing demons.

You now come to big intersection: Shinobazu-dori leading to Ueno's Shinobazu Pond. Even with detours to Asakura and Daimyo Clock Museums, you have walked barely 2km (1.3mi) from Kanei-ji; tho with much to see it feels like more. At this crossing is Sendagi subway station of Chiyoda (green) Line. It's two stops to Yushima, at SW corner of Shinobazu Pond. You can walk this 2km stretch if your feet are up to it, and there are enough places en route to refresh yourself, be it with coffee, juice, food, sake, or hot bath. There are two places worth visiting if you choose to walk: Nezu Shrine, & Yokoyama Taikan Museum.

About 7min walk from Sendagi station, taking Shinobazu-dori to 4th stop light (3-way intersect) where go R, then turn in L at gate beyond torii of...
NEZU JINJA shrine. Note forest of red torii covering hillside; in spring is coated in colorful azalea. All looks very shrine-like, but on L is fenced compound of main hall, and at once, anyone with some knowledge about shrines and temples will find something out of whack here. Everywhere you look are *manji*, 'other-way' swastikas of Buddhism (actually it was nazi swastika that was 'evil' backwards) decorating tiles, posts and mandala Wheels of Life on sides of main steps. Nezu one of Edo's top ten shrines, held in great veneration for centuries as major center of *ryobu Shinto* (Buddhist-Shinto amalgam). Symbols so intertwined here that nationalist zealots advocating forced separation of Buddhism and Shinto in early Meiji, 1860s, decided best way to deal with Nezu was just ignore it. Thankfully, it escaped destruction, survived Quake and War. It is now ICA.

We exit via its front torii: note stone temple dogs—one with face upturned howling at 'moon', which here is glass light globe protruding from its mouth. Immediate L down narrow lane brings us back to Shinobazu-dori, which, if cross and keep going straight up another narrow lane, we end up at Daimyo Clock Museum. Next main intersect on Shinobazu-dori is its meeting with by now familiar Kototoi-dori. Here, you will find entrance to Nezu subway stn on Chiyoda Line.

YOKOYAMA Taikan *Kinen-kan*, Memorial Hall, (midway Nezu–Yushima stns, across street from Shinobazu Pond); was house where Taikan (1868-1958) spent his last 50 years. Most of Taikan's works are in major museums, but you do get to see some fine paintings and pottery of his. Garden and house well worth visit: 10:00-16:00, X-mon, tue, wed; ¥300.

If you walked all this way (especially following us all way from Iriya), you should be ready for dinner and hot bath (whatever order). Luckily, restaurant-lined alleys of Ueno-Okachimachi are few mins away and if, like us, you stay at inn in sh'tamachi, hot bath isn't far. Or there are respectable saunas between Ueno Keisei & JR stns.

YOSHIWARA

EVEN TODAY, mention Japan and most people (especially men) ask "whereza geesha girls?" For one thing, it's almost impossible for casual tourist (or even resident) to see geisha, so few left; as for services most bachelors seem to expect, better to roam streets of Shinjuku's Kabuki-cho— (*see* INTRODUCTION, GOING IT ALONE–FOR HIM). Actual geisha is entertainer skilled in various arts, not prostitute. Geisha of modern Japan developed from skilled courtesans of old. In old Edo there were never more than few dozen true geisha, and only few ever retained coveted top rank of oiran. But there were plenty of other equally talented and beautiful women to take care of lonely merchant or samurai in this most famous of licensed quarters. Both classes of men came to Yoshiwara, where money not bloodline spoke.

Yoshiwara of today is nothing like Yoshiwara of old, now found only in antique Kabuki plays and woodblock prints. Stag can still come here, but it would be to that classic Japanese institution *toruko,* or Turkish Bath, with embellishments no Turk could ever dream up. Actually, recent protests by Turkish Embassy lead to change in terminology to more diplomatic, if asinine 'soapland'. Are New York gay Turkish baths truer Turk?

Here is that Japan we probably all first met in woodblock prints and cheapy movies, so it's time for some...

PERSONAL ORIENTATION: Yoshiwara was ultimate product of Tokugawa pseudo-Confucian fanaticism for order. If you can't clean it up (who can clean up organized vice?) then sweep it under your best carpet, put carpet in side room and control door. And make carpet so fine you don't notice ugly reality of that lump. Shogun established licensed quarters in *yoshi-wara*, 'reed plains', downtown where Nihonbashi is now. Most of Tokyo is land-fill. After great fire of 1657 it was rebuilt further out from burgeoning downtown in present location, renamed *Shin* (new) Yoshiwara, with 'reed'-*yoshi* ideograph changed to homonym meaning 'auspicious'. 8hectare(20acre) area, slightly elevated fortress-like with wall, moat and single sturdy, guarded ornate gate closed at 10pm. No man left without paying or clearing credit, no woman left at all. Inside streets were laid out in grid, unlike chaotic Edo outside which just grew along cow paths.

It was no simple prostitution stable. Girls earned ranks, from quick-job *teppo* (gun) to high courtesan, names for which (*taiyu, oiran, yobidashi* etc) changed periodically as rising standards of gals and stricter tax-office control of customers, caused inflation and 'bracket creep' pricing top out of business. Top gals were choosey: usually took three visits to get down to basics, and only if she accepted suit. Courtesans suavely swished around in fabulously ornate kimono teetering atop elevated geta-clogs, accompanied by court of little *kamuro* page-girls and teenage male *shinzo*. *Oiran dochu* or periodic processions of top courtesans (relived today on Asakusa stage and in Kyoto Shimabara-quarter fetes) were star parades which drew audiences from town. Lesser ranks sat behind wooden grills, like mannequins in fashion boutique windows, waiting to be rented. And beyond gate, unlicensed free-lancers risked free enterprise where they could, periodically getting rounded up with bath-girls and dumped into this brocade stockade, this aesthetic concentration camp.

Edo connoisseurship, *tsu*, in this era, especially late 1700s, evolved-revolved about these courtesans based on art and literature of this gaudy quarter and many of its denizens were highly cultured. Subject of art (ukiyoe prints sold to men nationwide as pinups, their wives and daughters admired them as fashion plates) by great names Kiyonaga, Koryusai and later Utamaro; of popular literature *sharebon* (smart books), *ki-byoshi* (yellow-covers) mass-produced paperbacks, often illustrated in color.

Yoshiwara was big business. Early 1600's records note daily gross of 1,000 ryo (gold coin then 15 grams 84% pure), about ¥50,000,000 or $333,000 1990 rate. Matched only by Theater District (kabuki and satellite restaurants etc) and main fish market (now at Tsukiji). Yoshiwara and kabuki spun off consumer society much like today's, social rank based on dollar-democracy in that no class ranks (and Edo Japan was one big social concentration camp) carried beyond its moat except ability to pay, and perhaps ability to play with some dilettantism. Main houses were for millionaires.

Census of May 1787 showed Edo population at 1,285,300, Yoshiwara at 1% or 14,500—6,300 of these female, of whom 2,500 courtesans, prostitutes and *kamuro*-child attendants. Courtesans were actually down from peak 3,907 in 1737 and superstar *tayu* and even next rank *koshi* had disappeared, due to closer scrutiny of big spenders by tax office. Top gal inherited name 'Takao of Maison Miuraya', of whom 11 between 1610-1741 when last one had her freedom bought by Lord Masamune—who was "demoted for this cavalier act". Still this 1787 list included 37 top class who earned one nite's tip equivalent to annual salary for seamstress or man-servant (posted fee went to house, her 'share' paid room and board).

Several attempts were made to stamp it out, squelch procurers from time to time to stop kidnapping, minimize slavery aspects of indenture. By modern times gloss was off, geisha of other quarters had more renown, Meiji Christians, liberals campaigned, Taisho democracy abhorred, US Occupation recognized it, with severe limits. But Korean War GIs needed safety valve tho language barrier, alternate standards of appreciation and short leaves worked against developing new connoisseurs or literary salon.

Then came April Fool's Day, 1957. Japan, on its feet as never before, passed anti-prostitution law that turned ancient traffic back to baths. Soon after, turkish baths arrived, with apparently innocent facades, but bathhouse girls carrying on same services of old. Some houses transformed (some would say reformed) into *minyo-sakaba*, restaurant-drinking joint for common folk of sh'tamachi, where they could eat, drink and be merry. Entertainment was innocent enough, mostly folk dance troupes from country, and such. But alas, even these places have now faded out of being. Now, all you find here are well-dressed young 'advertising executives' out in front of their establishments propositioning prospective clients. But trade of yore now prefers 'Sex Tour' to SE Asia to tune of 1.5 million annually.

TOURING YOSHIWARA: Using large intersection as your **starting point**; coming from tram station, cross big street to subway sign and go L, take first R just beyond tiny hat shop. This spot commemorates darker side of Yoshiwara:

JOKAN-JI temple, also known as *Nagekomi-dera*, or 'toss-in temple', where women too old to cook or clean were abandoned. Small, quiet compound; behind temple is monument dedicated to those hapless women left here to die. Plaque in front claims over 20,000 women met their fates here since 1664.

Back at main intersection, we go E, along Meiji-dori street.

After short while road forks; while we take R, L takes us to site of old...
'Bridge of Tears', *Namida-bashi* across which convicts went to Kotsukappara execution grounds. Just beyond is Ekoin temple, with *Kubikiri* (**headless**) *Jizo*, dedicated to 200,000-plus heads lopped here in 300 years thru 1877. Site of first autopsy, verifying Dutch medical book, March 4, 1771. Now busy intersection with no trace of bridge or stream— tho execution grounds long gone, area beyond, **Sanya**, is home to some of Tokyo's most desperately unemployed, discriminated-against day laborers. Early '80s crusader tried to organize union to improve conditions and was killed by yakuza on 'contract' to labor contractors.

Lunch Time: Continue along R fork several mins to some old shops—our lunch destination, 15min walk from Minowabashi tram or subway, or cab basic-mtr. Of several choices, we pick classic not-as-old-as-it-looks (60+ yrs) wooden tempura joint **Iseya** on corner (easy landmark is pachinko Ikoi diagonally across) by old entrance to Yoshiwara quarter. If can't read sign, look for shrimp etched on windows. Satisfying diners since 1874, almost always busy 11:30-14:30, 17:00-20:00, X-tue. Worth trip just to see shop interior, food good. Tempura not typical light airy shrimp-vegetable mix, but true sh'tamachi style shrimp— only with thick batter in sesame oil. Menu basic ('91 prices), good portions: *tendon* ¥950-1700, *tenju*-tempura ¥1200, ¥1400; miso soup ¥150-200.

Other choices: Next door...
Nakae in equally lovely old building, *kanban* sign is red cherry blossom enclosing character for meat—specialize in *sakura*, as horse-meat used to be called, serving *sakura-nabe* (sukiyaki) and *ba-shashi* (raw fillets). We save our horse experience for later, at rustic **Minoya** in Ryogoku (*see* p.1204). **Chibaya** meat shop few doors before, stocks top sakura. Corner facing Iseya is old-timer soba shop **Omura**, for reasonably priced homemade noodles; 2 doors beyond is **Atsumiya**, another sakura-nabe shop.

After lunch, you can walk back to Minowa subway stop, cab to Ueno (2x-mtr), or to Iriya for preceding walking tours (p.1177). If Asakusa destination it's short cab or 20min walk thru heart of **ex-Yoshiwara**. One street E of Iseya, R (S) at intersect leads down what was main street of Yoshiwara.

Just past 'S'-curve, you see hoary gate & walls of...
Matsubara, sole remnant of geisha houses of yore—now tamely for tours (J- & foreign) who come here to glimpse old Yoshiwara, see geisha shows, folk dances. Many nite tours (*see*) stop here for dinner and show. Group 50+, show ¥72,000, dinner ¥6,-25,000ea; duo join group, E-show 9pm, ¥2,500 w/drink.

Note covered **pushcarts** along wall like rickshaws of old waiting for someone inside. Come to life at nite to make rounds of town peddling old-time favorites *oden*-stew, *ramen*-noodles, sweet spuds. Continue down street, past modern pleasure palaces of Yoshiwara—Turkish baths. Well-dressed men approach with various offers for 'bath break'. Some with names **Stardust, Monaco**, others like **Miuraya & Kado-ebi** kept old names, but once inside, services are much alike.

As Toruko fade from view, on R is...

YOSHIWARA JINJA shrine, once patronized by Yoshiwara courtesans. Like any old neighborhood Yoshiwara has own pilgrimage of *Shichi-fukujin* 7 Lucky Gods. Shrine belongs to Benten, sole woman of 7, patron of music and arts, geisha prayed here. But Benten is jealous, women would remain single for fear of arousing Benten's wrath, lose new-found skills.

Another of '7', Ebisu, is enshrined at **SHOBO-IN** temple on side street behind Yoshiwara Jinja. Modern jet-setter may well seek this temple out, for its better known main deity is flying Fudo figure. Commonly known as *Tobi-fudo dera*, or **Flying-Fudo Temple**, as local legend credits Fudo with flying from his original home on Nara's Mt. Ohmine to Edo in one giant leap to help out against some local disaster. Enterprising priest decided this fudo was great traveller's guardian especially in this flying era. *Omamori* sold here do just that, and you can get cover-all traffic safety (one with car), or one only to keep you safe up in air (tiny silver 747 attached).

Large street W is Kokusai-dori...10min walk N back to Minowa stn; same S to Asakusa View Hotel.

Few blocks S of Tobi-Fudo, along busy Kokusai-dori street is...

OTORI JINJA, another sh'tamachi main shrine. New concrete version not-too-interesting stop most days, but you may want to come on days of cock (one of 12 zodiacal critters), at least twice monthly—any November with 3 is thus lucky month. Name reads 'Eagle Shrine', but actually dedicated to cock, and coming here cock days assures good fortune. On November cock days, this is one of places where Tokyo-ites come to buy *kumade* (bear paw) lucky rakes—gaily decorated, to 'rake' in good luck, especially if bought right after midnite in wee hours of cock day. Kids love kiddy types.

Across Kokusai-dori from Otori fair-size street runs W towards Iriya stn, 2 blocks along it is **Bon**, restaurant serving authentic *shojin-ryori* vegetarian priests' fare. Out of way but worth trip, since it's one of few in Tokyo for shojin-ryori without too much trouble, tho rsvtns necessary. Served in semi-private J-style room, plate after plate beautifully arranged. Choice of 3 courses, served in 2-hour shifts from noon, 3 & 6pm, X-tue: 1-2-11 Ryusen, Taito-ku; ☎3872-0375.

Short walk beyond Yoshiwara Jinja is another small shrine compound on L...

Rocky mound here with sad-faced Kannon statue on top is dedicated to all Yoshiwarans who perished in Great Quake and WWII bombings. Plot used to be part of Yoshiwara Jinja but need for space and loss of offerings from no-longer-existent geisha forced shrine to sell most of its land.

Further, intersect of 6 streets; 2nd L (90°) E to Senzoku-dori shop-street next crossing S 2 blocks cross Kototoi-dori, become Hisago-dori, main shop-street of **ASAKUSA**...

DETOUR: DOLL-MAKING TOWN & BONSAI

Simplest doll in ancient times was wooden shingle or peg, carved & painted—then thrown into river as scapegoat to carry off illness and ill-luck. Doll-making evolved here into craft and even art, noted worldwide. Cheap dolls were mass-produced in sweatshops, fine dolls crafted in ateliers. Iwatsuki town has over 500 shops making doll parts from eyeballs (at **Sanoya** ☎0487-58-0001), heads, arms etc, to final assembly of full dolls, from cuddlies to mantelpiece masterpieces (at hospitable **Nakajima** ☎56-1244).

For best sightsee-shopsee, contact city tourist section ☎(0487)-56-1445. No TIC but big map facing station notes other sights: 25min walk to **park** on remains of castle **gate** 1457 by OHTA Dokan (built Tokyo Castle–now Imperial Palace). Nearer stn are *Toki-no Kane* bell-tower, 1720; **Senkyokan School**, 1799. Doll masquerade parade July 29.

Combine with nearby **Bonsai** at Omiya: JR Keihin Tohoku light blue train at any JR stn Yokohama-Tokyo-Ueno-Omiya line, to end of line Omiya, transfer to Tobu-Noda pvt line 2 stops to Omiya-koen, **Bonsai Village**. Then continue Noda-line 3 stops to Iwatsuki, above. See other dollmakers & **Bonsai** at Omiya, JTB tour, ¥10,300.

DETOUR: MOVIE BUFF *Guinness Book of World Records* list for Japan includes consecutive series of movies with same story line and cast— record held by *Otoko-wa Tsurai-yo*, 'Being a Man is Rough', starring ATSUMI Kiyoshi as Tora-san which started 1969 with semi-annual releases, 44 to end 1991. Series has single master plot repeated with different love interests, new 'other' settings.

Ever-smiling, itinerant fairground huckster, born loser Tora-san (name means 'tiger' which he is anything but) always falls in love but loses gal who usually doesn't realize his 'brotherly' help is affection, so he either runs home or, if in love while at home runs away again. Home is SHIBAMATA, archetypical sh'tamachi old Edo working class neighbor-hood, where location shoot takes place. Brilliant low-key acting, under-stated cinematography, fine naturalistic writing by creator YAMADA Yoji keep humorous series from degenerating into cloying soap opera. #42 brought in second generation elements, bright young 'new faces'.

Excellent socio-anthropological documentary material for Japanologues, would make good PhD study. Occasionally on Japanese TV in US, or JAL in-flight flicks, brilliantly dubbed. Shown only once on Japan's commercial bilingual TV (often on monolingual), which set off torrent of letters to editors begging for more—and which stations studiously ignore.

GETTING THERE: From Ueno Stn, Keisei line to Takasago, change to Kanamachi-bound one stop to Shibamata—for help, say 'Shibamata' or just 'Tora-san'.

Exit Shibamata station to...
Old-style gate with red lanterns to Monzen-machi (temple-gate-front-street) few blocks-long shop-lined mall. Many shops sell *senbei* crackers, *kusa* dumplings, etc in bags bearing Tora-san's smiling visage, along with other souvenirs of local hero who has brought them prosperity. Just inside gate two stone markers spell out local faith—on L bears name of temple, Shibamata Taishakuten (Indra), R one quotes 'living Indra' Tora-san's boast, "Born and bred in Katsushika Shibamata". 40+ meters along on R is open-front teahouse **Toraya**, original location for films, where Tora-san's loving sister lives, always eager to take him in. This is traditional small town 'teahouse' serving light snacks of soba (order some), cold drinks, unimproved since film brought it fame except for collection of posters of all Tora-san films.

Down MALL, *where street fair every other month, is handsome, ornate tall gate of...*
TAISHAKUTEN, highly photogenic Nichiren (commoners' sect) temple, with large courtyard and full set of attendant buildings typical of founding in 1629. Image, lost for decades, miraculously reappeared 1779, after which temple prospered. Fine modern (1920-30s) carved-wooden frieze of scenes of Buddha's life indicates Buddhist art doesn't have to be antique to be worth our attention.

Exit via main gate, R to last natural riverbank in Tokyo, popular playground—beware baseballs. Follow crowd to...

Yagiri Ferry is last feudal era oared, wooden boat across Edo River. Daylight daily Mar thru Nov; but only weekends, hols Dec-Feb; 150m 5min ride ¥100; cross over to Chiba Pref, whence 15min walk to JR-Sobu line, Ichikawa or Koiwa stns, for easy return to Tokyo.

The time to see Yoshiwara to best advantage
is just nightfall, when the lamps are lighted.
Then it is that the women...
— A. B. Mitford, 1906

SHITAMACHI - I
ASAKUSA OF OLDE TIME

IT'S ALWAYS FUN to ride to end of some line, especially when, as with Ginza (yellow) subway, it is as much trip back in time as it is thru space. This is heart of *shitamachi* (first "i" silent), 'downtown' merchant district, lining Sumida River's bank from here down to Ningyo-cho; in many ways still as it was during old Edo times when it was faraway neighborhood of little interest to uptown city folk. Here, you still find stubborn spirit of born and raised Edokko, and they're just as happy to remain ignored by mainstream Tokyo. Craftsmen work in their homes practicing skills perfected by their ancestors generations ago, and you can see these people at work; just walk down any side street in sh'tamachi. Here, too, is Greenwich village of Tokyo, home of artists and characters, and just as deceptive. Others equate it with Soho or Pigalle. It is all these and more of its own. *If you have only one day in Tokyo, spend it here.* If you have week to spend in one place, you could spend it all here exploring endless side streets, watching countless master craftsmen creating everything from tatami mats (with its unmistakable odor) and portable shrines to plastic food. This is old Edo of woodblock prints: rest of Tokyo, while fun, is just another modern metropolis.

Third generation lower eastside Manhattanite Jay fell in love with sh'tamachi at first sight 1952. In our mid-'50s guide magazine *Anoné* we pioneered introducing area, as in this first edition. Even then excellent volunteer group in town office offered us great info —as now at TIC oppositee gate. Garet, sent to check it out, wandered back streets as we had and ended up with virtual new book in itself. Other authors discovered 'downtown', have good books—interested get Enbutsu's *Discover Shitamachi*, Jean Pearce writes about it in her fine *Footloose–* books; K Itsuo drew several sets of post cards *Old Tokyo Today* one shouldn't miss. Explorers who prefer guided tours sh'tamachi-phile OKA Nobuo takes **monthly walks** all day 3rd sat ¥1,000 each plus lunch. Take special groups walking anywhere in town ¥1,000 per person/hr, min 5hrs ¥10,000—nonwalkers can do same by cab+cost, limit trio, but prefers walk; phone rsvtn 2 days ahead: ☎(0422)-51-7673. Course similar to ours, he is walking encyclopedia human-history; *highly recommended.*

ASAKUSA KANNON-DERA temple, properly SENSO-JI, is reason for Asakusa's uniqueness. All shops, craftsmen, restaurants, residents, were drawn here by this temple. Asakusa-dera owes start to two fisher-brothers, HINOKUMA Hamanari and Takenari, who, March 18, 628AD fishing nearby Sumida River drew up in their net small gold figure of Kannon. Their master HAJI-no-Nakatoshi saw it as sign to follow Buddha's path, enshrined figure in his own house. Years later, Saint Shokai passed thru village here, hearing about Kannon figurine, completed temple to house it in 645 (which makes it oldest in Tokyo). As its fame grew, so did complex, and by mid-tenth century had dozen pavilions, many lesser halls. It fared well, in 1590 shogun-to-be Tokugawa Ieyasu made Senso-ji official clan temple, allotting it stipend of 500 koku of land. Hit by many fires and quakes, great fire of 1865 drastically reduced number of buildings to about present count. Main hall collapsed in Great Kanto 'Quake of 1923, rebuilt March 10, 1933 only to be destroyed again exactly 12 years later, March 10, 1945 fire-bombings of Tokyo spread to Asakusa, little survived. All main structures have been rebuilt faithfully following Edo era plans, but tired of doing it so often, pragmatic merchants of Asakusa decided this time to use less traditional but more practical concrete. Like many temples (alas, not all), Senso-ji returns most income to its parishioners—behind temple is Senso-ji Hospital which began as aid station after devastating 1910 flood, as after '23 quake, is now general hospital with 150 beds. In addition to other social work Senso-ji operates kindergarten under watchful eye of chief abbot adjacent to Denpo-in sanctuary and pagoda.

Coming up from Ginza Line's Asakusa subway station, head short distance W (or N if from Asakusa Line station), aiming for...
Thunder-gate, *Kaminari-mon* with its great red lanterns, leads to temple —guarding on R is *Fu-jin*, Wind God, holding wind sack; on L is *Rai-jin*, Thunder God, holding rolling-thunder drums.

But before entering, look over your back, across street, to ...
Asakusa TOURIST INFORMATION CENTER, all-volunteer group of Taito-ku (name of this ward) workers. Their sincere desire to help and to inform foreign visitors of wonders of sh'tamachi more than make up for occasional lack of fluent English speakers. Entire staff works here on own free time, yet it is open every day of year 9:00 to 17:00; ☎3842-5566. Good selection of brochures and maps of Taito-ku area, constantly being updated, upgraded, expanded. Also, as 2nd floor of Matsuya Department Store (just N of subway stn) is Tokyo terminus of zippy, cheaper private Tobu Rail to Nikko–Kinugawa Onsen area, Asakusa TIC has much info on those areas as well. Can help find lodgings around here for all budgets, from cheap-clean inns and Business Hotel next to Kaminari-mon, to '85-opened Luxe **Asakusa View Hotel**, 27 storeys, 400 mostly W-style rooms, its rates one place sh'tamachi tradition of budget lost out to uptown splash.

This most recent plan to revitalize Asakusa, has, alas, led to demolition of classic theater, Kokusai, near infamous Rokku theater row. New hotel and nearby ultra-modern ROX Bldg, typical urban-fashion clothing store has met with mixed reactions from sh'tamachi-ites. Friend covering area for *Shitamachi Catalog* magazine found many older stores unreceptive to publicity, which they claim would only draw bratty rich kids of Tokyo and make area no different from Shibuya or any other central Tokyo shopping mall. But they cooperated when English edition was proposed. Conclusion: tourists more than welcome, but "keep young brats away, who needs their money anyway". As if to emphasize difference between uptown and sh'tamachi, metallic tubular ROX Building with its grossly overpriced items sticks out like sore thumb amid theaters (often porn)...and never twain shall meet. We agree with folks of sh'tamachi—if you want hi-fashion, stay 'in town' and leave Asakusa alone. Many attempts to modernize Asakusa, as you see have not fared well except new Kabuki theater and OTB horse race betting center, proletarian pleasures. Here folks still live in low houses, bonsai shelves by doors which are never locked, often wide open to pass breezes, allowing one to peep inside. Even love hotels are old style.

Asakusa TIC is convenient place to rest feet for those who walked from Ueno or once flowery Yoshiwara. In winter, your bench-mate, also sipping tea (provided gratis), or taking nap, may be one of less fortunate under-employed people of sh'tamachi. Nobody minds that they stay, after all it's public building, people of sh'tamachi have always cared for their own.

So armed with English explanations of Asakusa & Ueno, map of nearby Kappa-bashi plastic food shops, we plunge headlong into pulsing, colorful world of sh'tamachi old Edo. Taito Ward puts out magazine *Shitamachi Catalog* since 1985, scaled down (but still packed with lots of great info). Eng-edition available. Get copy at Asakusa & Narita TIC; ask for it at Yurakucho TIC; also *Yanesen Magazine* (YAnaka, NEzu-SENdagi areas), ¥400; good maps, eating and shopping tips.

Passing thru Asakusa's unofficial symbol, Kaminari-mon gate, we enter...

SHOPPING LANE colorful **Nakamise-dori**, lined both sides with red ancient-style 2-storey stalls right out of famed woodblocks (which, alas, were 'modernized' to glass and chrome uniformity for '64 Olympics) has changed little in nature over past few centuries. As Edo grew during Ieyasu's reign and more people came to Senso-ji, locals set up shop along temple main approach to peddle souvenirs and food to tourists. And now it becomes apparent why Senso-ji plays such major role in lives of Asakusa's folks, and why after each temple-flattening disaster (of which there have been over 20) it has been quickly, lovingly rebuilt with donations by locals. Here, you will find all sorts of knickknacks: all fun but cliché Japanese gifts—silk boxer shorts with ukiyo-e prints are down first alley to L; cheap toys which 20 years ago were 'made in Japan' but now 'made in China'; wigs, masks, stage props, electronics and cameras are just some of samplings here. Behind this first row of shops is another, with lots of eateries in all budgets. If by chance you can't find that certain gift here, branch off on numerous shopping streets around temple and you're sure to find it. Being sh'tamachi, prices reasonable, if not downright cheap.

At far end can be seen gigantic sloping roof of Asakusa Kannon Temple of goddess of mercy with its giant paper lanterns, ever-present hordes of worshippers. Working our way towards it we pass numerous old shops which still handle traditional merchandise difficult to find elsewhere. Lovely gift ideas for milady fill these shops, which once furnished fine silks and rich accessories to geisha of neighboring Yoshiwara: *hakoseko*, ornate brocade bag carried with their elaborate outfits makes fine evening bag, or lightweight silk-floss-lined *haori-shita* as bed jacket. Shops specializing in traditional hair ornaments abound. They do rushing business at year-end with increasing (re)popularity of kimono here, if not Kyoto, and elaborate hairdos...now usually wigs. **Matsuzaka**, halfway up on L, has *kanzashi*, charming hair pins with bangles or tiny bells, gay trinkets mounted on fine springs that quiver with every little movement, clever imitation tortoise-shell combs like those worn by Utamaro's woodblock print beauties. Real tortoise shell, *bekko*, at **Tsuruya**—L on Denpo-in dori alley (where shops end on L side)—keep in mind importing tortoise shell into US is illegal. At large wig-makers **Komachiya** Honten, you can have perfectly matched switch, chignon, or any style hairpiece in genuine hair, as well as wigs; even brunettes or blondes. Halfway is toy store **Koyama Shoten**, close inspection reveals specializes in theatrical supplies: huge basket hats about 24" across worn by samurai wanting to be incognito; comical masks from around ¥1,000 for papier mache, to several thousand for hand-carved wood; comfortable *waraji* (straw sandals); exclusive array of all styles of sword reproductions, for they were once sole manufacturer and supplier of swords for TV and movie samurai flicks.

Almost last shop on R is our favorite for third of century, little treasure house, **Sukeroku**. Master clay craftsman's miniatures have delighted Edokko and uptown Tokyoites alike for generations. What's so wonderful is that most of his pixy-like pieces and other novel clay originals are so affordable. Enchanting artisans, dancers, minstrels and common folks in everyday scenes of old Japan are realistically reproduced in these charming, oft-times humorous works.

We mentioned that alleys immediately behind Nakamise are mostly food, which is true, but three more interesting shops are hidden here, back side of Sukeroku. This lane, E of Nakamise, is called **Metro-dori**. Closest to temple is **Nakaya**, displaying mostly kids' items in front but loaded with interesting things for all ages once inside, like kabuki-type full body tattoo T-shirts. Stage make-up (particularly for Kabuki), various natural facial ointments, creams available **Hyakusuke** on corner. Little further down is **Fujiya**, for *tenugui*, printed hand-towels, used for almost everything from dressy headbands to wash-cloths, tho most here are so beautiful that it would be shame to use; with time, can have your own pattern custom-made.

Matsuya Dept Store has 'Gifting Studio' 6th floor, numerous outlets of Edo merchants—you'll find regular supply of traditional crafts made by sh'tamachi artists.

Nakamise ends here at great *Hozo-mon,* **Treasure storage gate** (reconstructed 1964), so called since its 2nd floor used for storage of 14th century sutras brought from China. **5-tiered pagoda** to L completed '73, replacing 17th century original (NT) lost in war. Relic of Buddha presented by Sri Lanka is kept in top tier, odd in that most such are kept at bottom level. Walled compound on L is **Denpo-in pavilion**, living quarters of Senso-ji's head priest and other official halls. Built 1777, but magnificent **garden** it is set in dates to early 1600's and landscaped by famed Kobori Enshu. Unfortunately, casual visitor cannot always enter to see building; you must be invited for tea or some other special ceremony—as good as saying don't bother trying (tho worth asking at Asakusa TIC and see what, if anything, can be done). Garden enthusiast, however, can usually get in to see garden by asking at *shomuka* office at pagoda (3rd door on L). Sign in and get free entry ticket. If for some reason you can't enter, or want just quick look, follow our lead and get rather good glimpse of garden over wall of...

CHINGO-DO temple, L down along Denpo-in street with all tent-stall booths selling kimono, old clothes and various bric-a-brac. Keep eyes peeled to your R for **main gate** to Chingo-do, and if closed use smaller entrance to L (facing it). Good view of Denpo-in garden over back fence. Notice numerous colorful pinwheels here, and perhaps somber people offering prayers. This little compound is temple for aborted children, and pinwheels, along with bibs, hats, strings of *senba-zuru* (1,000 cranes) and other items left as offerings for spirits of lost children. While abortion is legal, and Christian taboos absent, that does not make loss any less painful for those parents-to-have-been. Note also numerous tiny figures of *tanuki* (badger-dog). This often mischievous critter is temple's guardian—can purchase one of his miniatures and leave it here with your prayer to be answered.

Stretching up R side of temple complex, first is...
Benten-do pavilion (rebuilt 1983) and its small **bell tower**, which bell used to mark every hour daily but now only rings out at 6am, and for 108 bongs of New Year. Tiny mound it sits upon is said to be Kofun (tumulus) period burial mound. Next up **Yogo-do hall**, dedicated to Amida, survived flames of war and served as temporary main hall. At far R is **Niten-mon gate**, dating to 1819 and declared ICA.

Also in this corner you will notice shinto **torii**, and may wonder what shrine is doing in middle of temple complex. This is ASAKUSA JINJA **shrine** dedicated to two brothers who found Kannon, and their master who first honored it. Dates 1649, survived numerous fires that swept thru. Locals refer to it as Sanja-sama (Sacred Trinity), and sh'tamachi's biggest festival, held mid-May, is *Sanja-matsuri*, Trinity-Fete. Gigantic smoking **cauldron** front of main hall is healing vat. Devout, to take advantage of Kannon's curative powers, fan incense smoke onto selves in prayer. Add your own bundle of incense to pile for better luck.

Up into **main hall**. Three giant hanging **lanterns** were offered by geisha representing main districts, L to R Yanagibashi, Asakusa, Akasaka; once 1,000-strong, 1991 only 75—but new geisha school hopes to reverse decline, if under new name tho in kimono. Ceiling painted with temple's dragon and angel by contemporary artists DOMOTO Insho and KAWABATA Ryushi. Within inner sanctum, largest gilt altar in middle contains diminutive Kannon figure, flanked by two smaller altars: L Aizen Myo-o, god of love and wealth, R fiery Fudo Myo-o of justice and might. Most people offer their prayers in front, tossing coins into big box, but devout, or those in particular need of help can, for larger offering of at least ¥3,000, enter.

Now you've made pilgrimage to temple, go back out to shopping streets some more.

PERSONAL DATEBOOK: **January** sees usual beginning of year rituals. **February 3**, *setsubun* bean scattering, dances follow. **8th**, *hari-kuyo*, memorial for broken needles at Awashima-do pavilion. **March 18** marks day of Senso-ji's Kannon's appearance, and highlight is *Kinryu-no-mai* (Golden Dragon Dance). No one is sure when it began, but this style, with dragon atop several poles carried by men, is Chinese. Like Nagasaki's grand festival, possible Chinese merchants settling area did this offertory dance. For whatever reason, it was abandoned centuries ago, revived to commemorate postwar reconstruction of Senso-ji, now one of main events for Senso-ji. **April 8**, rites mark birth of Gautama Buddha. **May 5** Boy's Day mark by *Takara-no-mai* Treasure Dance, thank for offspring. **3rd weekend**, *Sanja-matsuri*, one of top three Edo festivals, sees about 100 mikoshi portable shrines carted around streets of Asakusa.

June 18 is *Yoji-josui*, ritual in which sacred water is sprinkled on visitors with willow twig to ensure health for rest of year. **July 9-10** *Hozuki-ichi*, colorful red Chinese lantern plant mart, and *Shiman-rokusen-nichi*, 46,000-day festival marks Kannon's most benevolent days, and one's visit during this time is most definite plus. **August 15**, lanterns offered to memory of war dead. Sometime late August streets of Asakusa come alive with *Asakusa Samba Carnival*. Usually **last weekend** is outdoor *Takigi Noh*—check TIC. **Last Sat** huge *fireworks* on Sumida River.

October 18, *Kiku Kuyo*, offering of chrysanthemums to Kannon, Golden Dragon Dance repeated. For next month until November 15, chrysanthemums displayed. **November 3**, *Shirasagi-no-mai* White Heron Dance, depicts ancient agricultural rite; women in stylized bird costumes portray herons eating harmful worms. This graceful dance, accompanied by slow music, can be seen thruout rural Japan, with most famous at Tsuwano near western tip of Honshu. **15th** is *shichi-go-san* 7-5-3 festival when children of those ages are brought to local temples for blessings. **December 17-19**, *year end market*, see lots of *hago-ita* paddles on sale.

CHOPSTICKS: Asakusa is for all budgets and tastes—hard to go wrong no matter where you enter. Dine on full course *kaiseki-ryori* traditional meals at **Kuremutsu** or **Tatsumiya** on Metro-dori (alias Kannon-dori), or slurp down quick bowl of noodles for almost nothing in back alleys. If craving good ol' Yankee fast-food, there is ever present xenophobic McDonald's (going towards temple, 1st covered alley to R) and Kentucky Fried Chicken (continue past Mac to next big road). Some better known, locally recommended restaurants follow. One thing you will notice is sh'tamachi people go to bed early; few places stay open after 22:00, some close hour between lunch–dinner.

ON METRO-DORI: at top end, btwn Nakaya and Hyakusuke is **Kuremutsu**, typical *izakaya* drinking-eating spot for late lunch or dinner when you have no time constraints; lots of *ippin-ryori* (ala carte) few hundred yen each to wash down with sake. Full course *kaiseki* from ¥8,000. Open 16:00-22:00 (X-thur)—not particularly cheap, but you won't go broke either and atmosphere is great. Shop itself is traditional old farmhouse moved here from country.

2 short blocks down (on near corner) also on R, is centuries-old deluxe...
Tori Kaneda: Chicken sukiyaki and mizutaki. Its *noren* (entrance curtain) bears ancient Chinese pictograph for bird; front has been rebuilt as typical Japanese farmhouse. Full *sukiyaki* or *mizutaki* dinner ¥6,000 and up; sit around beautiful lacquered table specially made with built-in *hibachi*; cook as you eat. A la carte with *kara-age* (chicken in basket), *yaki-tori* (BBQ chicken), and tempura, ¥700-2,000; X-tue.

Block E of Tori Kaneda to big street and L is sushi...
Miyako, since 1866 and as popular now as then. Reasonable prices for top quality. 12-3, 5-9pm, X-mon, 4th Sun.

Kujyu-ichi, another good sushi joint, but better known for *fugu* (blowfish), is block down from **Tori Kaneda**. Next corner on L is **Towada** serving excellent *te-uchi soba* (hand-made buckwheat noodles) at very reasonable prices.

Next to Towada is...
Tatsumiya in old folk house brought here from central Japan and full of antiques (run by brother of Kuremutsu owner); front looks more like that of antique store and not at all like restaurant, easy to mistake. Lunch (noon-2pm) and dinner (5-9pm) feature good ol'

home-style cooking at good prices: multi-course sets ¥4,200; delicious *gyu-rosu bento* (teriyaki beef lunch, w/rice) for mere ¥900; X-mon.

Where bottom of Metro-dori hits main Kaminari-mon-dori Ave, go R towards Kaminari-mon gate and you pass **Sansada**, popular old-time tempura shop; their many voluminous and well-priced set meals displayed in front. Theirs is excellent, light batter tempura, but if you want real Edo-style tempura we suggest that you try...

Daikokuya, catering to satisfied customers for over century. Batter here bit heavier, but their magical touch makes it light on your stomach, and they still use dab of sesame oil in their vat for that special flavor. *Ten-don* is filling, with 4 giant pieces of tempura shrimp (one hidden under rice in bowl) and veggies with special sauce, bargain at ¥1,600. Across from Denpo-in temple; (11:30-20:30, X-wed).

Facing L of Kaminari-mon gate is old...
Chinya, founder bred Chin dogs for Shogun, switched to restaurant at Meiji Restoration. No, doesn't serve dog meat. Serves beef exclusively in grand 7-storey building, own meat shop in front boasts finest Matsuzaka beer-fed beef. 11:30-21:30, X-wed; basement budget served at tables, upper floors = upper-class, in tatami-matted zashiki private rooms. Sukiyaki or shabu-shabu teishoku dinners from ¥2,900; only ¥1,800 in basement.

Down street from Chinya is pretty little budget tempura house **Kawamatsu**, lately well known for its *unagi* (grilled eel), delicious and energy-laden. Another great *unagi* house is 200-year-old **Yakko** (11:30-22:00, X-tue), 3 blocks beyond, corner of Kaminari-mon-dori and Kokusai-dori streets. Prices at both similar, ¥1,300 for *kabayaki teishoku* (eel on bed of rice, w/pickles, soup). Yakko lunch special ¥1,000 from 11:30 to 16:00. Turn up Kokusai-dori and half-way to Asakusa View Hotel, on L, is **Asakusa Imahan**, another top sukiyaki restaurant with great bargain lunch specials.

Next corner beyond Kawamatsu, small building with black grill front is...
Owari-ya, old-line noodle restaurant serving such favorites (of ours) as *kamo-namban* buckwheat noodles in broth with 'duck' (now chicken) and veggies, or *niku-soba* w/ beef.

Turn down this narrow alley, Koen-dori, better name...
Hors d'oeuvres Alley. First, there's **Haru** (on L, middle of 2nd short block), for *kama-meshi*-rice steamed with seafood and meat specialties cooked especially for you in mini iron *kama*-pot with wooden lid: best to start with yaki-tori tidbits and bottle of sake. Spacious air-conditioned place with glass front, complete Japanese atmosphere with tatami floors; and wondrously budget. Just across street is **Sakefuji**, advertising *hormone* foods, which means *yaki-tori* and other *kushi-yaki* (cooked-on-stick), especially various tripe. On corner is **Matsu-kaze** (alias Sake-no-mise), workers' sake bar serving oden, yaki-tori and almost any brand of local sake desired from anywhere in Japan: *tokkyu* (special grade), *ikkyu* (first), *nikyu* (second) for two basic tastes, *ama-kuchi*, sweet, and *kara-kuchi*, dry. All food and drink ¥-B.

Next alley over, or...
Sushiya-dori, sushi-shop alley, and you will find just that in fourth alley W (L if facing temple) of Nakamise. Old time favorite of ours (but haven't been to lately) is **Sushi-sei**, 2nd shop in and on L if entering sushi alley from main Kaminari-mon-dori. Actually, only few short blocks at bottom (S) end make up Sushiya-dori; middle portion (where it widens) is Rokku, Theater Row. Another great (some say greatest) old sushiya **Kibun-zushi**, is 2 alleys to E, or from Kaminari-mon first alley W and up to 2nd L corner {12-3pm, 5-9:30; X-wed, no E); wooden interior and pebble floor unchanged since 1902 except for TV set and prices still appeal to local shopkeeper-tourist.

At top of Rokku, marked by Toei theater, street zigzags slightly R, to become...
Hisago-dori, another of numerous shopping lanes. Covered, continues N about 100m to main Kototoi-dori Ave. Halfway, on L are red and white lanterns of top *sukiyaki* house **Yonekyu**, since 1885, airy tatami rooms; filling meals run basic ¥2,400 to luxe ¥3,600. 2 interesting *izakaya* local drinking joints are just across Kototoi-dori Ave...

For those who speak, or are with Japanese speaker...
Ichi-mon gets its name from 1-*mon*, lowest denomination copper coin in Edo era. Cross Kototoi-dori and go up Senzoku-dori shopping street, first L, just past first alley on L is lovely house with willow tree, and giant wooden tub over entrance. When you enter, buy store's 'currency', wood chips of 1, 5, or 10-*mon* at ¥100 per *mon*—50 mon is

enough for great time, and leftovers are re-converted to real yen when you leave. Interior is like something out of some old Kurosawa film. Food is great, huge selection of *ji-zake* (local brew sake) from all over Japan. Choose from album menu—served cold but can be heated in private heating units built into walls. **Bansho** is simpler version of Ichi-mon; food as good but atmosphere not as fun. To find Bansho, take 2nd L off of Senzoku-dori shopping street and it's on second short block on L. Watch for bamboo in front.

We backtrack south of Kototoi-dori for
HISAGO-DORI shops are fun, being geared for locals and not tourists. One particular shop is **Adachiya**, on L, half block before Kototoi-dori street. Festival specialty store, stocked with headbands to *waraji* (straw sandals) and everything in between, including colorfully hand-dyed *hanten* short (happi) coats. They also have wide array of everyday workers' clothes which can often equal or outdo latest fashions at fraction of cost. Across from it is **Hanato**, specializing in *chochin* paper lanterns, which you can have custom-made. Few doors before Yonekyu is **sword shop** which deals mostly in real swords, and their ornamental replicas are fine. You may want to mark E-W alleys btwn Yonekyu and Adachiya, as they have bulk of ¥-B lodgings in Asakusa (*see*).

Hisago-dori is optional way out of Asakusa for sh'tamachi walker: only 10min N to Otori Shrine and old pleasure quarters of **YOSHIWARA** (p.1184) now mostly *toruko-buro*, Turkish baths; or W along Kototoi-dori to Ueno via **Kappa-bashi** plastic food shops (DATEBOOK big bargain mart around Oct 9).

KAWAKIN was next to View Hotel, S side just down alley, whose claim to fame it was to have invented ever-so-popular *katsu-kare* dish, alas is no more.

Asakusa View Hotel 27th floor is French restaurant boasting fine food, view; but if pilgrim looking only for view, 28th (top) floor coffee lounge.

Two final fine eating places for those who want ultimate in novel Japanese food...
Komagata Dojo and **Mugitoro**, serving what are considered delicacies—but only to those whose palates have gotten acclimated. **Komagata Dojo** serves *dojo* (loach, or mud-fish) prepared various ways. In general, uninitiated diners find taste little bitter (Japanese eat it as source of 'stamina', which translates virility) especially when prepared traditional *dojo-shiru*: slim little loach fish cooked in tofu by putting live fish in soup with tofu squares, slowly bring to boil so fish burrow into cooler tofu to escape heat, only to be cooked when it, too, reaches boiling point. *Dojo-nabe* is stew with vegetables; *dojo-no-kabayaki* is most acceptable to Westerners: broil over charcoal, serve with thick sweet-ish sauce used for unagi (eel). Dojo season June thru Sept; rest of year they serve other seafood like *kujira-nabe*: fillets of tender whale-meat cooked in broth with veggies. Komagata Dojo around since 1801 and their way of serving has changed little since. It's one large room, few tables, but most eat on bamboo slat floor with board for table. Komagata is straight down from Kaminari-mon gate, 4th block on F, just S of Asakusa subway stn of Toei Asakusa Line (pink). Building itself is well worth visit, attractive old Edo wood structure next to majestic weeping willow, looking like something out of samurai flick, especially when tree silhouetted by shop lights.

Mugitoro is back towards temple, on far R side (river-side) of intersection at Komagata-bashi Bridge, next to small park. All dishes contain *yama-imo*, type of mountain yam served *oroshi* (grated) or *kizami* (sliced) when by itself. Both are quite good, but somewhat 'slimy' consistency of *oroshi* takes some getting used to. Popular dish, also found at most izakaya-type drinking establishments, is *maguro-no-yama-kake*: chunks of maguro (tuna) sashimi mixed into *yama-imo* paste, strips of *nori* (dried seaweed), *wasabi* (horse radish), soy sauce and sometimes *uzura-no-tamago* (yolk of quail egg). Mix whole concoction together and slurp down. Recommended are their course meals, every dish down to green tea ice cream dessert (take-home 2-liter case for ¥2,000) has some form of *yama-imo* in it. Top course *Asakusa Komagata* (¥13,000) is grand feast of dozen dishes; *Shirasagi* (¥5,000) is almost as sumptuous. Store hours daily 11:30-21:00. Can poke your head into this attractive little shop just for dessert; also sell traditional waxed-paper umbrellas, folkcrafts and packaged *yama-imo*. There is branch behind this where only budget lunch ¥1,100 is served 11:30-14:30.

Arrange private dinner party, or join large one, cruising on Sumida River–*see* below.

Next bridge upstream is...

Azuma-bashi—extension of main Kaminari-mon street. Main dock for *Yakata-bune* party boats (*see below*). Cross Sumida river here over to **Azumabashi Beer Hall**, open daily 13:00-21:30; spacious old hall serves regular draft, black, and whatever is this year's fashion, straight from nearby Asahi brewery.

Kamiya Bar is Japan's first W-style bar, opened 1881 by winery owner Kamiya Denbei. Immediately catching on with sh'tamachi-ites, ithas appeared in numerous Meiji era novels, and seeing those people who frequent this comfortable, homey bar, you can almost picture yourself back century in time. Try their *denki-bran* (electric brandy), slightly sweet cocktail concocted by Kamiya Denbei. Prices reasonable, but Kamiya keeps old-fashion early-to-work sh'tamachi hours: 11:30am to only 10pm.

ENTERTAINMENT: Asakusa has for centuries been entertainment center of Edo and later Tokyo. Kabuki and other forms of commoners' theater flourished here, and until recent-past wandering troupes from countryside could always find *minyo-sakaba* (folk song sake shops) to perform at. Alas, they too have disappeared (one left in nearby Yoshiwara, **Matsubaya**, *see* p.1186), along with *onna-kengeki* (female sword play), local version of Annie Oakley, and amateur kabuki. All that remains is well-staged oiran shows at Matsubaya, and mixed bag of performances at...

Kaminari Goro-goro Center on Kototoi-dori Ave just N of temple. Here you *could* catch performances of *Kappore*-old Edo era street dancing, *Edo Kagura* lion dance with comic hermaphrodite dancer, samisen perfor-mances and geisha dances. (*Closed* 'late '91, but hopefully to be revived?) Evening show (8-9pm) was all four; early show (6-6:30pm) had shorter performances and replaced one of four pieces with either movie on Asakusa or some performance piece. Now, 3rd and 4th floors are **Okuyama Chaya** restaurant (once on own near temple), 2nd flr is shopping arcade.

And with grand gay quarters of Yoshiwara just up street, Asakusa was long associated with sensual. While much of old folksy shows have died out, programs in good old girly-burly tradition continue. Most obvious are many theaters which advertise porn flicks, tho strict Japanese censorship always shows strategically placed smears, and never any pubic hair. These run-down movie houses were once center stage to many interesting live shows. Alas, greatest of them all, Kokusai, featuring shows comparable to any in Paris was closed down in spring of 1982 with teary farewell, torn down for new hotel. Chances are that next to steamy looking porno theater, another will be showing latest popular US release, while yet another will feature children's animation festival. There is something here for all tastes.

KABUKI tradition has kept stronghold here, tho old theater of wood-block print days replaced by soulless modern **Asakusa Kokai-do** Public Hall, S of Dempo-in. In front, local version Grauman's Chinese Theater with embedded-in-concrete hand prints of famed entertainers of sh'tamachi. Kabuki here several times yearly, and since mid '70s much-loved Ichikawa Danjuro puts on New Year series in January. Kabuki-za's repertoire may be better, but you can't beat sh'tamachi audience. When not used for kabuki, performances range from symphonies to children's recitals, traditional dance to *manzai* and *rakugo*–traditional vaudeville. Other theaters around here also feature *manzai* and *rakugo* comics known for swift tongue and word-play. **Mokuba-kan** near temple is long-standing theater, oft features local variety shows. In true sh'tamachi fashion of mimicking their idols, one regular actor here dubs self sh'tamachi's Tamasaburo, after top kabuki *onna-gata*. **Tokiwa-za** (1877) reopened 1988 after years closed, musicals, imported jazz festivals etc hope to revive area, closed again late '91—reopen (? TIC).

After war, Asakusa's entertainment continued to bloom as *onna-kengeki* traditional swordplay-strip shows were quickly replaced with another Western import—strip tease. Some theaters here still do strip, touts outside. Live sex shows also exist, but constant police crackdowns keep them on move with no set address—'PR agents' keep mobile on street. It's all pretty harmless; real sleaze moved to new section of town: Kabuki-cho Shinjuku.

BOOKIE: Amid theaters, *pachinko* parlors, game centers & bowling alley of **Rokku** district (not Japlish, contraction of *roku-ku*, 6th-district) is enormous, utilitarian structure on R side of top end of street. This caters to another, perhaps most popular vice of sh'tamachi, **horse-racing**. Off-track betting is legal, organized by Japan Racing Assoc, branch of Agriculture, Fisheries and Forestry Ministry. Easy to spot, at least on race days. Since only bets are taken inside, and with no TV set up to watch races (prevents over-crowding), bettors wait outside. On first passing, you may think some important yakuza is about to pass by, what with dozens of surly looking men standing around, listening intently to inconspicuous earphones; and several police hanging around corner. All around this central betting area, *Jogai Baken Uriba* (OTB) are dozens of sidewalk fast-food stalls set up to feed bettors with, not burgers, but classic Japanese fast-food: *oden*, noodles and such, at cheapest prices in town. Enterprising vendors bring along TV sets for guaranteed crowd. Building has 3 floors, each for set bets: one on top takes only ¥1,000 bets, middle floor for ¥500 wagers, and street floor for most common ¥100 bets which make up over half total bets placed. Compulsive bettor can do all by phone: have your voice recorded into computerized voice-printer, then all you have to do is call in your bet. Your bank account is automatically credited or debited depending on your luck. How to Bet (*see* INTRODUCTION-SPORTS, p 75).

KIDDIES aren't neglected in Asakusa, luckily, for there are many here. Diagonally across from OTB is **Hanayashiki Amusement Park** with its miniature roller coaster, rockets and sputniks and elephant merry-go-round, swings and many try-your-luck games. Everything in this country-fair park is cheap; ¥50 or ¥100. During 1970s it was run-down and almost torn down, but locals decided to fix it up, and 'new' park (with same attractions) opened in 1984. Here, kids can still find age-old favorites and scoop for tadpoles or goldfish, or fish for water balloons in heat of summer, with incessant cry of its resident cicadas taking you back to much simpler time of old sh'tamachi—even Jay hunted crickets in Manhattan's east-side.

Massage parlor Turkish baths (recently renamed *Soaplands* due to official gripe from Turkish embassy—do they have embassy in New York or Frisco?) are all in what was Yoshiwara gay quarters. **Asakusa Kannon Onsen**, is real hot spring bathhouse where one goes to soak, perhaps watch show. This classic *sento* public bath house draws water from hot spring, and temperature is always kept at ideal 45° C, 113° F. After-bath shows are harmless, usually traditional dances. Relaxing dip in tub costs ¥500, daily 6:30-18:00; show on 3rd floor is ¥500 (10:00-17:00); get private bath and massage (legit) for ¥4,000 10:00-18:00. If your *tenugui* hand towel from Fujiya is too nice but for souvenir, pick up cheapie for ¥100 or so at any pharmacy. Kannon Onsen is on one of streets fanning E from temple main hall and S of Hanayashiki Park, anyone will direct, just ask by its name.

Bright Red Double-decker Buses make frequent **sightseeing run** Asakusa ↔ Ueno. Daily 10:00-19:30, weekday every 30min, weekend-hol every 20min; one-way 10min: ¥200 adult, ¥100 kids, one-day subway-bus pass not valid. Asakusa boarding spot is at Kaminari-mon in front of Chinya butcher shop, Ueno boarding front of

Suzumoto Engeki theater, across from fashion plaza ABAB. Quick departures can get off at stop right in front of JR Ueno stn. Several other stops around Ueno and Asakusa, but buses only stop to pick up if seats available, so best wait at boarding points.

CRUISING SUMIDA RIVER

ANOTHER ROUTE from/to Asakusa is **river bus** plying Sumida River. Asakusa terminus is Hinode-sanbashi pier by Azuma-bashi Bridge near Matsuya Dept Store. Downstream terminus Takeshiba (short walk from JR Hamamatsucho stn), from where you can catch **ocean bus** for short hop across Tokyo bay to **Maritime Museum** and remnants of anti-Perry 'floating' fortresses (*odaiba*) still in bay. One of these battlements can be reached by ocean bus; linked to main man-made isle by artificial sandy beach, packed with swimmers in summer, wind-surfers all year. But check timetable before boarding for some connections at Hinode pier are long wait. We highly recommend **Hama-rikyu Detached Palace Garden**, 5min upstream of Takeshiba, for lovely stroll (*see* Shinbashi Shiba area, p1215). It is not particularly attractive ride with much of river banks walled in, but it gives whole new perspective of Tokyo, refreshingly cool summer. Between Asakusa ↔ Hinode 11 r.t. daily weekdays and 15 sun and hols till 7:30pm; 4 extra daily in summer. *Warning*, Hama-rikyu closes early (at 16:00) so last boat from Asakusa that allows you to get off at Hama-rikyu is 14:45 departure, last out of Hama-rikyu 16:05; Hama-rikyu 35min → Asakusa. In our 1964 edition, this was true river commuter bus with several stops en route, and ran every 15min or so; now o.w. ¥560.

Dine and Cruise down river, around bay and back for ¥7,800 per person (¥5,200 for kids), your choice of several meals. **Sunset Cruises** offer W-style buffet or J-dinners; **Barbecue Cruises** offer meals of freshest fish, taken from fishing boats that day. Prices include all you can drink of beer, wine, sake and soft drinks. During July and August, 3 or more persons can get private small boat; large group can reserve entire boat, in which case set own times. For more info and/or reservations call **Tokyo Kanko Kisen** (Tour Boats) ☎3433-5591: 6:30pm, late Jun–early Sept, other times 15 minimum charter. Also regular day cruise around Tokyo harbor from Hinode.

Sumida-gawa Koen, Park stretches upstream both sides of river from Azuma-bashi bridge. Lined with cherry trees, has been favorite sakura viewing spot for centuries. Many trees planted in recent beautification plans. In early April when they bloom *yabusame* mounted archery is held along W (Asakusa side) bank, with samurai on horseback racing among pink-petalled trees (check papers, *TJ*). Makes for pleasant strolling, especially in sakura season...as beautiful in autumn 'turning'.

If you've few extra hours, go up to next bridge, Kototoi-bashi, cross over to...
MUKO-JIMA in Edo times famed for its sakura (these now here are even younger than Asakusa side's). Area you are standing in was detached manse of Tokugawa, now long gone.

Little further up on your R is...
USHIJIMA JINJA, Cow Shrine, its small compound has several such beasts. **Stone bull** in compound with red bib is main deity here, rubbing it fulfills your wishes: particularly good for curing ills of mind and body, just touch what ails you then rub same spot on bossie.

Continuing upstream, pass another shrine, dedicated to **kitchen gods** fish-carrying Ebisu and Daikoku with his scrotal rice bales and foreskin hat, two of *Shichi-fuku-jin*, Seven Lucky Gods.

Further on we come to...
KOFUKU-JI zen temple, dedicated to another of Lucky Seven, jolly rolly Hotei with his never-emptying bag of good fortune. This rather impressive temple is post-1923 Earthquake structure. Notice lovely **sculptured garden** rear, covered bridge linking main hall and head priest's quarters.

Just beyond is...
CHOMEI-JI temple, dedicated to Benten, sole female of Lucky 7, goddess of beauty and music. If you want to make local pilgrimage to other 3 of Lucky Seven, ask at any we've just visited for **map**, *Sumida-gawa Shichifuku-meguri no annai*, noting each shrine and temple.

Since you've come this far you should try *Chomei-ji sakura-mochi* of Mr Yamamoto. His store **Yamamoto** is next to Chomei-ji. Thin sheet of mochi (glutinous rice cake) is wrapped around ball of *anko* (sweet been paste), and whole wrapped in three leaves (of course edible) from Chomei-ji temple's sakura trees; delectable treat has been favorite of customers for over 260 years. It was started early 18th century by first Yamamoto, gate-keeper at Chomei-ji. After sakura blossomed, he would gather up fallen leaves and pickle them in salt water mix, recipe still in use. Most of year, you should have no problem getting taste; 2 sakura-mochi and tea for ¥250 in little shop (note old Ukiyo-e prints used as advertisements). But they're hot item during cherry viewing season, and Yamamoto-san warns that advance orders are so numerous that by time first tiny blossoms bud, he will be sold out for next week—about as long as flowers bloom. *Kototoi-dango* are as famous—or perhaps more so since nearby bridge and street named after—at nearby **Kototoi-dango** store run by Mr Toyama. Dango are rice dumplings often served 3-on-a-skewer, broiled or with special sauce. Toyama-san sells 3 different kinds, unskewered.

You can retrace your steps—alternately, nearby is X-shaped pedestrian...
Sakura-bashi Bridge back across to Asakusa side of river to stroll back down this side of Sumida-gawa Park. *Or* those with wanderlust can meander thru streets here, visit countless old temples and shrines tucked away in quiet neighborhoods, and perhaps end up in what was once Yoshiwara, about 1km NE.

On W side of Kototoi Bridge is small...
MATSUCHIYAMA SHOTEN temple in small glade of trees. Its symbols are paired, intertwined *daikon* radish and coin purses. Former believed to be good for sexual stamina, latter for wealth—also symbolize male-female. Understandably, this temple was popular with those in sex trades of old Edo's nearby Yoshiwara Gay Quarters.

While our MUKO-JIMA WALKING TOUR is more for those with no particular goal, shorter, if not more unique **walking tour** from Asakusa takes you toward Ueno for those who prefer to have particular destination.

Let us thus head to...
KAPPA-BASHI, wholesale district for kitchenware, restaurant supplies where you can pick up that neat plastic-model food, colorful banners and paper lanterns (or hardier waterproof plastic imitation) advertising anything under sun. Have just about anything custom made here to fit your taste. Asakusa TIC has simple map showing how many and location of each type of store along this Kappabashi Dogu-gai, 'equipment street'. *DATEBOOK*: Giant clearance-sale in 188 shops for 50-80% discounts, lots of fun events, 4-5 days centered on Oct 9 (homonyms for 'equipment' and 10-9=*do-gu* in Jpn); for exact dates ☎3844-1255 in Japanese.

Several routes from Asakusa: basically just go W for about 10min and you run into Dogu-gai street, next major street after Kokusai-dori. If you are on Kototoi-dori, passing N of Asakusa you hit Dogu-gai top end and Kappabashi **Yo-kagu-ten** furniture store at near corner and **Azuma Shokai** restaurant kitchen utensil store on other side. Just turn L here, walk entire length and let your eyes take it all in.

Most common route—head W on Kaminari-mon-dori, which suddenly becomes two narrow alleys as you hit Kokusai-dori. Notice distinctive **Jintan-to** tower advertising jintan breath fresheners at that spot—classic landmark of Asakusa, it was modeled after similar mid-Meiji period landmark, now long gone, once towering 12-storey Ryoun-kaku. Near base of Jintan-to is most interesting clock shop **Mitoya**. Actually it sells much more than regular antique clocks: various older 'timepieces', lanterns, lights and other odds'n ends.

Just N of tower is **Miyamoto Unosuke Shoten**, shop specializing in portable shrines, drums, and other festival paraphernalia including clothes. More than welcome to browse here, you may find some rather interesting gift. In addition to drums, shop has various ancient instruments used in Gagaku and Bugaku. See their **Drum Museum**. Also, beautifully carved Noh masks, to ties embroidered with Noh mask designs. (Another such shrine specialty store is **Miyashi Miyajima** on S side Kaminari-mon-dori across from Sushiya-dori sign; next to which is interesting old-time cutlery shop.) W on alley by Miyamoto Unosuke few min walk, past local branch of Kyoto's Higashi Hongan-ji temple on L, to Dogu-gai which you hit near bottom end.

More interesting route is to branch W off Kokusai-dori few blocks further N at Kappabashi-dori street (Imahan sukiyaki house on corner) which takes you to...

Asakusa Kogei-kan **museum** dedicated to local craftsmen. Sh'tamachi is long proud of its artists who carefully hand-make almost everything imaginable. But such traditional arts are slowly dying out as automation takes over, or as certain products become obsolete, so local tourism office has set up this little museum to record some of Asakusa's crafts. Displays some crafts and photos of others, odd assortment of old Asakusa memorabilia, prints & such, some of which have been reproduced for sale. 2nd floor of Tokyo Electric's service center; open daily but only until noon sat, X-sun, hol, no fee. Kappabashi-dori hits Dogu-gai almost in center, and just before reaching it on R are two interesting shops (one is **Tsubaya**) specializing in all sorts of knives. If you keep going on Kappabashi-dori, quiet street, you pass various local workshops. Note nostalgic (for us anyway, and Japanese) 'green' aroma from tatami mat makers on your R. Further on is traditional sign makers shop; pass 2 small temples...

When you come to old brown gate and barber pole turn R for you are at...
SOGEN-JI, better known as Kappa-dera, namesake of this area. Tale has it back in early Edo times there was canal here which always flooded in rain. Finally local maker of *kappa* (straw raincoats), decided to build bridge (*hashi* or *bashi*), thus Kappa-bashi. Like all good stories, this one has been built on; especially easy when given name and location. Kappa, beside meaning raincoat, is also name of mythical water imp—part man, part frog, with turtle-like shell and bowl atop head which must always be kept full of water or creature will die. Kappa can be nasty, but they are also very polite, so tried and true method of dealing with troublesome one is to bow. It bows back, loses water from scalp-bowl and must jump back into river. Anyway, living in nearby Sumida River were some particularly friendly kappa who helped build bridge. Folks now come to this temple and offer prayers to kappa for help in some endeavor. Purchase kappa figure at temple office, place it on special altar and toss few coins into money box (marked with kappa) to get kappa's attention, then make your wish.

Kappabashi's Dogu-gai by subway–yellow Ginza Line to Tawaramachi, head one big block W. Can't miss giant cook's head at intersection; marks **Niimi** kitchen goods store, traditional and modern.

KAPPA-BASHI TO UENO is interesting walk if along main Asakusa-dori Ave for that street is also lined with dozens of shops dealing in religious paraphernalia. While above-mentioned Miyamoto is probably best single store, this strip has many to browse thru. Largest religious wholesale district in Japan. Start at subway Tawaramachi stn and head W, shops thin out as you approach subway Inaricho stn, from where it's only 8min to Ueno. Just past Inaricho subway's steps on R sign points to tiny **EISHO-JI** temple, where Kodokan school of Judo was originally founded.

Little further on down alley on L is...
SHITAYA JINJA, main Inari (foxy fox rice god) shrine of sh'tamachi. Many festivals held here (*see* DATEBOOK, p.1265).

KURAMAE, ASAKUSABASHI, RYOGOKU

JUST KILOMETER S of Kaminari-mon, and we enter another unique area of sh'tamachi, one stop from Asakusa on subway Toei Asakusa Line (pink).

We have seen wholesale entertainment and wholesale kitchen supplies; now we see **wholesale toy district** of Kuramae, which used to be rice warehouse area of old Edo. Kuramae was also 'temporary' home to sumo's Kokugikan arena. Shortly after WWII, new Kokugikan was erected along Sumida River (between river and Kuramae stn), but sumo's rightful place is across river at Ryogoku, to which it has recently returned. In 1985, newest Kokugikan hosted its first New Year tournaments.

S from Kuramae stn at first intersection, L takes across to Ryogoku (following), and R takes you in few minutes to...

TORIGOE JINJA shrine on your R. If here **January 8** *dondo-yaki* fire festival, pick up one of mochi cakes roasted over sacred flame and it will keep you healthy for whole year. But this shrine is best known for its summer grand festival, *Torigoe Yoru matsuri* nite festival, **2nd sunday June** –with wild climax at dark when giant mikoshi, which takes over 100 people to carry, is paraded thru this part of town by lantern-light.

Around Kuramae are lots of stores selling plastic cherry and maple tree branches and such decorations often seen lining Tokyo's neighborhood shopping streets. Continue down Edo-dori Ave towards Asakusa-bashi, you find almost anything sold here, but especially toys, models, novelty items, dolls. Notably, around Asakusa-bashi are some of better known dollmakers, hand-creating those exquisite Japanese dolls in black lacquer glass boxes—southern belle Western dolls in finest Scarlett O'hara style. In summer, you find delicate paper *chochin* lanterns used in O-bon festivities to guide back spirits of lost loved ones. Visitors pressed for time would do well to limit selves to Asakusa-bashi area; it's only 800m or so between Kuramae and Asakusa-bashi, but with many great little shops to explore.

Also on same subway (pink) line, as well as on JR Sobu Line (one stop W is electronics center of **Akihabara**).

Asakusa-bashi, 'Bridge to Asakusa', got its name as popular departure spot for river boats heading up to entertainment in Asakusa-Yoshiwara. Rendezvous was S of present stations, between Asakusa-bashi and Yanagibashi bridges, which span Tokyo's 'other' river, Kanda, flowing into Sumida here. Kanda starts from lake at Inokashira Koen Park (*see*) on other side of Tokyo, is for most part little more than canal until it gets near Iidabashi, N of Palace. From here to Sumida, Kanda was artificially enlarged by Tokugawa shogun to make it more useful for transportation. If you are on JR Chuo Line cutting across Tokyo, you follow river, and most acclaimed view of it is from high ground around Ochanomizu.

Back to Asakusa-bashi—we take Edo-dori down to Kanda, but rather than cross here, head L along river past more family-run shops like generations-old...

Baika-tei traditional pastries. For different but equally popular Japanese snack of sweet bean and mochi concoctions try **Ninkiya**, quiet little shop on street behind Baika-tei and closer to Edo-dori. They have *anmitsu*, refreshingly cool dish of not-too-sweet gelatin cubes, fruits and scattering of sweet red beans; *oshiruko*, soup of finely whipped sweet red bean with mochi served warm; and *zenzai*, similar to oshiruko but with some whole red bean added and also served hot; all few hundred yen each. Turn L one street before canal-side alley, and it's on your R; looks almost like house, but not, with small blue *noren* split-curtain at entrance, few potted bonsai trees in front, and small glass display window; easy landmark is new red brick **Business Hotel Yanagibashi**. Just before Ninkiya and across street is good little **coffee shop** for W-style refreshments. Narrow green and white 2-storey building (next to barber Imai) looks bit North European, which is translation of its Japanese name, **Kita-Oshu**.

Take R towards Kanda River at next alley by classier white **Business Hotel** **Belmonte** *and you are at...*

Ami-haru, just one of several **boat rental** houses along here, but one we found to be most hospitable and ready to accommodate foreign guests. With modernization, most of boats used to ferry people up to Asakusa and Yoshiwara turned to more profitable business of fishing, as seen by many fishing boats docked here; but some of old *funa-yado* (boat-houses) transformed into *ryotei*, top class dining establishment. Several still survive, and you can charter traditional covered *yakata-bune* boat to take you out on private dinner-party-cruise, with free-flowing drinks and freshly prepared seafood feasts as you float thru summer eve. Like pleasures of old floating world of Edo, such pleasures do not come cheap, as many such outings are on expense accounts. Husband and wife team of Ami-haru really go out of their way to please, and rates are lower. While other such *funa-yado* use converted fishing boats with roof stuck on over *goza* straw mat, Ami-haru has had special *yakata-bune* boats made with wider, longer cabin with real *tatami*, more deck space, and lavatory in back can be used without fear of falling overboard like on some other boats. Boat boom of '87-'88 saw fleets increase to over 120 bottoms from dozen-odd, surpassing limit of 100 set in Edo era. Also built slightly wider than usual to reduce rocking. Their new *yakata-bune* for foreigners features *teppan* grill so they can cook dozen steaks as well as seafood; middle row of *tatami* under tables lifts out to plop legs down so one doesn't have to sit Japanese style, with special vent system in floor space to provide heat in winter and cool air in summer; slightly enlarged (but still tight for you six-footers) bathroom is W-style and others are expected to emulate.

They are also thinking about combining with one of Tokyo Nite Tours. Minimum number of guests 10, and can squeeze up to 40, tho they don't recommend over 30 at once. If all their good boats are full, they can sometimes get another and if not as nice as their's, Ami-haru will drop charge accordingly. Basic 2hr30min course is about ¥7,-15,000 (1992) per head and includes full course meal with sashimi and tempura as main; replace with, or add, soon-to-come steaks; price will also vary slightly on type and amount of drink. Good audio system for cassettes or *kara-oke* available, or can have troupe of geisha entertain at about ¥18,000 per geisha for 2hrs30min. Ami-haru arranges all. Best dinner with geisha will run about ¥15,000 each. Tho Ami-haru is not busy every nite, best to call and reserve as early as possible to ensure. They ask for at least one day advance so they can get supplies and arrange for any extras you may want. ☎(03)-3866-5878; if unavailable at night, try ☎(0484) 71-5291. Also **Amisei**, ☎3844-1869, min-charter 22, ¥10,300ea tax incl, tempura dinner. Not quite as classy but cheaper at ¥7,800, are BBQ dinner cruises of **Tokyo Kanko Kisen** (*see* CRUISING SUMIDA, p.1198).

End of canal, by Yanagibashi Bridge, modern red brick apt house has restaurant...

Kamesei-ro on first floor. Used to be sprawling geisha house (*see* woodblock print in store brochure, which also has pictures of your menu choices) where Sumo officials met. Still gather here for their decision-making, but minus geisha. As departure point for Yoshiwara, Asakusa-bashi was colorful in its own way, and many pleasure-seeker never made it up river, for women of Asakusa-bashi were reputedly among finest for hospitality. You may want to try Kamesei-ro's famed *Yanagibashi bento* box lunch– 'box' of fine lacquer containing exquisite set features their best delicacies. Not cheap, but you get more than you pay for. Budget version in simple pine box good; lunch service features mini *kaiseki* set ¥4,500.

Here, we cross Sumida River on great...
Ryogoku-bashi '2-country' Bridge, so called since it linked old provinces of Musashi and Shimofusa. There didn't used to be bridge here, as bridge building was restricted by government to hamper attack on Edo. People wanting to cross waited for boatman. However, in 1657, Edo was hit by great Furisode Fire which swept thru most of city killing almost 110,000 people—world record till WWII air raids. Multitudes perished along river banks waiting for boats (Japanese were notoriously bad swimmers) and first bridge to span Sumida River was put here in 1659. Great fires, poetically called *Edo-no-hana* 'flowers of Edo', swept thru city on many occasions. Since 1733 this bridge, and others spanning Sumida, is popular place to watch another sort of Edo-no-hana—controlled flames of Sumida-gawa **Fireworks** (*hanabi*–flower-fire) spectacle. Begun as part of festival to ask gods for deliverance from plague sweeping city. Seemed to work and grateful Edokko have carried on fete ever since. One of largest such in Japan, last weekend of July, fired off from Sumida Koen near Asakusa.

Across river (on R past 2nd Crossing) is...
EKO-IN temple, dedicated to those who perished in Furisode Fire and subsequent disasters, including latest two which even temple did not survive —1923 'quake and WWII fire-bombing. Also known as final resting place for Edo's Robin Hood, Nezumi-kozo ('ratsy') Jirokichi.

Few short blocks E of Eko-in (use side exit) is...
Stone Wall, marks site of mansion of KIRA Kozukenosuke, villain of 47 Ronin saga. Here, on December 15, 1702, 47 loyal retainers of Lord Asano avenged their master's death by beheading Kira, cause of Asano's forced suicide (*See* translation of play in our book *You Mean to Say You Still Don't Know Who We Are* ?). All that remains of Kira's palatial manse is miniscule park with tiny shrine, dedicated not to Kira but to his 20 retainers who perished carrying out their duty to serve him. After washing Kira's head (well is still here), 47 walked to Lord Asano's grave at Sengaku-ji temple in Shinagawa (*see* p 1161) where, after presenting it to their lord, submitted themselves to arrest and were sentenced to commit *seppuku*, ritual self-disembowelment. They carried out vendetta without proper authorization and so committed illegal act. They had principles to uphold. This is perhaps best known story in Japan, epitomizing true sense of loyalty. Teddy Roosevelt read it and intervened in Russo-Japanese war on Japan's behalf (were winning all battles but would surely lose war on logistics), led others to expect some sneak attack December 15, 1941; while contending US intelligence groups late WWII used story to prove respective viewpoints that Japan would not surrender and needed A-Bomb (predominated) *vs* Japanese-speaking Admiral Zaccarius who contended they would surrender without Bomb.

CHOPSTICKS: Before continuing to N side of JR Ryogoku stn you may want to pick up some old traditional sh'tamachi food, **Momonji-ya** for boar, wild fowl, badger, other game. On R just as cross Ryogoku Bridge; can't miss large picture of boar above entry. Guests of once-hoary inn (alas, rebuilt modern since our last edition) started over 240 years ago when only 'barbarians' ate meat, known in days of Buddhist prohibition as *yama-kujira* (mountain whale). Owner Yoshida is 9th generation. Main dishes served in season– *inoshishi* (wild boar) sukiyaki, abt ¥3,800 (no matter how hot won't burn tongue, but beware onions); *shika* (deer) ¥1,800 for sashimi, also steaks; *tanuki* (badger) usually served as *tanuki-jiru* thick meat-vegetable broth; *kuma* (bear) steak; *saru* (monkey). You may get other seasonal surprises, as such places are wont to get. For example, past few years saw imported kangaroo meat from Australia where they are hunted to control overpopulation, so you may find *kanzashi* (kangaroo-sashimi) on your menu—thinly sliced fillets are surprisingly tender with strong, but not unpleasant, oniony flavor. Open noon-9pm, daily in winter, X-sun in summer; ☎3631-5596.

Bozu-shamo nearby noted for *shamo* fighting-cock meat. Must rsve, ☎3631-7224.

Another typically Japanese dish is horse meat, or *sakura* (cherry) as sometimes called. One of best in Tokyo is near here, **Minoya**, reminds one of scenes from samurai movies of old Edo, with its large tatami room. Turn shoes in at entrance, grab zabuton cushion and pick spot at either of two low, long tables running full length of shop. Real sh'tamachi atmosphere. Start out with appetizer of *basashi*, thin fillets of horse-meat sashimi, or head into main dish. Guests enjoy their *sakura-nabe* (horse meat and vegetables) or *buta-nabe* (pork with vegetables) cooking their own nabé-pot over old-fashioned charcoal braziers. It's about 10min walk from Ryogoku Bridge: head E on main road to first big X-ing (about 500m) past police station, turn R and go another 300m or so. If coming here just to eat, easiest is to take subway Toei Shinjuku Line (light green) to Morishita stn, and it's 2min walk from there. We ate here after Ningyo-cho area (see), for which board Shinjuku Line at Hamacho stn front of Meiji-za Theater and 1 stop to Morishita. ¥1,000 for basashi or sakura-nabe, appetizers of *hiya-yakko* (cold tofu), *yaki-dofu* (cooked tofu), *yaki-tamago* (omelette) few hundred each, beer and sake at usual rates.

To Momonjiya's R is narrow block with 3 restaurants. Middle one is...
Kariya serves *chanko-nabe* steaming cauldron of stew to beef up sumo wrestlers. Run by ex-sumo wrestler of Dewanoumi stable, and while almost anything can be and often is tossed into chanko-nabe, he adheres to old Shinto taboo of original sumo against four-legged meat and his specialty is traditional chicken, full courses around ¥5,000—too much for normal mortal? If Kariya closed (sun & hols) or you're too early (doesn't open until 5pm), several other chanko-nabe restaurants are nearby all run by ex-sumo wrestlers. **Tomoegata**, on main street just past Iko-in other side of street; another is **Kawasaki**, L up big street between Tomoegata and river. **Chanko Dojo** is nr opposite, E, end of station nr intersect of Keiyo-doro and Kiyosumi-doro.

You will probably come across some *sumo-tori* wrestlers around here. **Kokugi-kan** sumo stadium (N side of Ryogoku stn—2nd from Akihabara on Sobu line—5min walk from here) with in this area 13 individual *sumo-beya* ('**stables**' where they practice in environment that makes marine boot camp seem like nursery school). If you come across one, and it would be hard not to, most allow you in to watch, free (5:30-11:00am, upper ranks 9ish-on). Just few minutes makes it clear that these are not just giants throwing their weight around, but highly disciplined, trained and muscular (not flab), devoted athletes. Jay drew cartoons of sumo for Japanese sports daily in mid-50s, one showing 'impossible' situation of wrestler whirling another around by his topknot—then over quarter century later saw just this act in 'comic sumo' and learned it is done to mid-rank wrestlers by their stable master at their daily practice. N of stn around arena are sumo-beya **Miyagino** ☎3624-9957 and **Kataonami** ☎3625-6807; S-side are **Dewanoumi** ☎3631-009, **Isenoumi** ☎3631-3066, **Izutsu** ☎3633-8920, **Kasugano** ☎3631-1871, **Mihogaseki** ☎3631-3067, **Nishonoseki** ☎3631-0719, **Takashima** ☎3631-1241, **Tatsudagawa** ☎3631-9336, **Tatsunami** ☎3632-1138, **Tokitsukaze** ☎3635-0015, **Wakamatsu** ☎3631-3847— advise phone ahead in Japanese to check hours, availability.

New Kokugi-kan is quite impressive structure which can accommodate up to 11,500 spectators—Albert Hall where London sumo held seats 5,500. Inside, *dohyo*-ring and *sajiki*-overhanging roof can be cleared by push of button, allowing use for concerts and exhibitions. Tournaments held here every **Jan, May, Sept** for 15 days starting Sun closest to **10th**, tickets go on sale 3 weeks before. Cheapest-furthest bleacher-seats ¥500, better ones ¥1,000 for 'C', ¥3,700-'B' and ¥6,000-'A'. Up-front tatami-matted box sections (sit 4 people) run ¥26,-34,000 per box. Can usually get in and see inside Kokugi-kan other than during tournament. Flat roof collects rain water which is used for airconditioning and flushing toilets. Part of building set aside as *Sumo Hakubutsu-kan* **Museum** with thousands of sumo-related items. *Free*, 9:30-16:30, X-wknds, hols; during tournament fortnites only those with sumo bout admission tickets may enter museum. *See* INTRODUCTION-SPORT, p.62.

N of Kokugi-kan is...

Landscape garden, *Yasuda Tei-en,* of Yasuda lords, among finest in Edo. Even now, tho just shadow of its former self, it is fine garden. 1922 Baron Yasuda presented garden to ward to be enjoyed by public.

NE of Baron Yasuda garden is another...

Park: Sept 1,1923, **Great Kanto Quake** struck. Thousands fled here and to surrounding open spaces, carting what possessions they could. Sparks from encircling inferno ignited their belongings and with escape routes cut off 30,000-odd people burned to death. Area was turned into giant burial ground. Initial Big One struck at 11:58 when most families had just started cooking lunch, and as flimsy wooden buildings collapsed, flames spread rapidly. First word heard around world about disaster was broadcast from ship in Yokohama harbor:

"Conflagration subsequent to severe earthquake at Yokohama noon today. Whole city practically ablaze with numerous casualties."

This was eight hours after initial quake, and no one was really sure about Tokyo. Dominating park is imposing hall topped by **three-tiered pagoda,** contains ashes of some 58,000 people—in addition to those who perished here '23 are remains of those who met similar fate in fire-bombings WW II.

Bell tower presented by Chinese Buddhists in 1925. *Doai Kinen Byoin,* **Fraternity Memorial Hospital** next door built with contributions from US following quake (less than 2 decades earlier, after 1906 San Francisco quake, Japan gave most aid of any foreign country).

Back corner of park is...

Earthquake Memorial Museum exhibits effects of quake, reminiscent of Hiroshima A-bomb memorial; part also devoted to fire-bombing. Last but not least, it shows what to do in case of another quake. With narrow roads, sub-standard building conditions and crowding, nobody in Tokyo doubts that when that next Big One hits, sh'tamachi will certainly suffer most again—but at least it won't have falling glass-guillotines of high rise business districts..

Big street N of us is Kuramae-dori, go W: we're back at Kuramae stn in under 10min.

Earthquake!

*To see a shop girl wrap a package
or a factory worker assemble a bike is
to see routine work developed to fine art.
This...may be Japan's greatest tradition.*
　　　　　　　—Ian Buruma

SHITAMACHI - II
DOWNTOWN INTO TOWN
(Along Sumida River—Ningyo-cho—Tsukiji—Tsukuda-jima—Fukugawa)

NINGYO-CHO, or 'Doll Town', as name translates, is yet another of those odd corners of Tokyo often skipped by visitors. Those who do come this way are more than likely to be budgeteers making way on foot from or to Tokyo City Air Terminal (TCAT), 10min walk S: arriving, you just want to get to your lodgings; leaving, you're usually pressed for time. But it would be worth spending even one hour strolling around this area. You will find many interesting shops, **SUITENGU SHRINE**, hoary **Meiji-za** theater and nearby **Hamacho Park** leading to Sumida River.

In its early days, this area was called Yoshiwara, where pleasure quarters first established in 1617 by order of Shogun Ieyasu who decided all Edo's nite ladies should be kept in one place. But Tokugawa officials soon felt it too close to heart of Edo, and after great Furisode fire of 1657, moved entire operation, and area name, to fields near Asakusa. Other forms of entertainment remained here, such as bunraku puppet theater, and since most of dolls used were made here name Ningyo-cho stuck. Those artists who didn't make bunraku dolls capitalized off theater crowd by selling souvenir dolls and such. Some doll makers created beautiful porcelain dolls as well— cheapies back then but now collector's items if you find one. Annual Ceramics Fair **1st or 2d wknd August** no longer has these dolls being unloaded at cut rate. Now all Bunraku theaters are gone too, as are all shops which used to make regular ornamental dolls—that trade moved upstream to Asakusa-bashi. Two of Edo's main kabuki theaters also thrived here, but of once- abundant theaters only Meiji-za remains. Nonetheless, several blocks of Ningyo-cho retains flavor of old Edo, providing for short step back in time. You will find lots of places for great lunch or dinner at some of sh'tamachi's better-known shops; and if date is right, fit it all in with kabuki performances at Meiji-za (X-till '93). So let's take hour away from Tokyo's hectic pace and see some more of sh'tamachi.

GETTING THERE: **Ningyo-cho** stn is on subways Hibiya Line (grey) & our faithful Toei Asakusa (pink). Coming from TSUKIJI breakfast (*next*), come Hibiya from Tsukiji stn, head for exit for TCAT (posted). This surfaces at intersection of main N-S road and Amazake-yokocho lane. (Other 3 possible exits from underground put you at main intersection 200m N.) We use this intersection as base, as *Amazake-yokocho* - Sweet-saké Alley is main shop street, many great old shops along it, on alleys to N. Main stretch E toward Meiji-za theater, with some good restaurants W of intersection. **Hamacho** stn, near Meiji-za, is on Toei Shinjuku Line (light green). Those who toured previous ASAKUSA-BASHI-RYOGOKU and lunched at **Minoya**, that restaurant is near Morishita stn, one stop E of Hamacho.

SUITEN-GU fertility shrine, Ningyo-cho's main attraction, (short walk S of Amazake-yokocho just past next big intersect); ¥3,000 be blessed for pregnancy, **monthly 5** market. Shrine is replete with water symbols—dragon and wave motif on giant lanterns, pair of anchors in front. Name means Celestial

Palace of Sea. Tho area was reclaimed from bay, Suiten-gu is not here to protect from sea. Originally dedicated to child-emperor Antoku who, along with Imperial Regalia Sword, was plunged into depths of Dan-no-Ura at west tip of Honshu (*see*) by empress-mother as ships of victorious Genji swept thru Heike remnants in 1185. Association with water and infant emperor eventually lead to its becoming popular to offer prayers and thanks for safe birth, and health of mother and child. Visitors increase every 12th day on day of Dog, which animal is envied for its easy birthing. (Sumi was advised to put on her pregnancy support by English-speaking, American-trained Japanese doctor on Day of Dog at Hour of Dog, "No, not superstitious, but why take chances?")

Locals say that many cake and candy shops around here owe their existence to traffic to Suiten-gu, and child would find it hard to resist colorfully hand-colored sweets of **Tenka-do**, at entrance to shrine.

Heading back to Amazake alley go R (E) at intersect just N of shrine & 2nd L.
Further down, web of overhead expressways under which nestle Tokyo City Air Terminal, **Royal Park Hotel**, other new hotels (p.1130).

Walking towards Suiten-gu on corner of 2nd alley past Amazake-yokocho is tiny **Kotobuki-do** confectionery, making those delicately intricate traditional *Kyo-gashi* (Kyoto-style *vs* sickly sweet Tokyo type) cakes one gets with matcha tea. Usual long line in front shows how popular it is. Few doors beyond is old-fashioned *sembei* shop **Kofuji-ya**, samples in front help you choose from among their budget-priced excellent rice crackers. If these snacks don't hit spot, try local specialty *ningyo-yaki*, brown airy cake with red or white bean paste fill: find these at next corner **Shigemori Eisei-do**, since 1922. At these and most other local shops you can see workers making whatever it is they sell, and if not crowded, you may be hosted to some special demonstration. As in all sh'tamachi, we find folks of old Ningyo-cho open and friendly.

Few doors down on R is tiny...
MATSUSHIMA JINJA, dedicated to *Daikoku* of 7 Lucky Gods. Facing is **Nishiura Honbo** pottery shop, direct outlet for rural *Mino-yaki* pottery of central Japan since 1878.

Back at Amazake intersection...
Kaisei-ken, you can break at popular coffee shop opened in 1875 as first teahouse in Japan to serve English-style tea: 2 doors W of X-ing, look for small bronze cow's head over door, and red cow-bell-like *mokugyo*, clapperless Buddhist bell beat during chants. Prices low, coffee good, and placed about spacious inside are family heirlooms. If lunchtime, 2 doors W **Tamahide**, chicken specialists since 1760. You may run into line here during lunch (11:30-13:00) when people come from all over for their lunch special, *oyako-donburi*, chicken with cooked egg on rice (¥600). Tamahide is recognized as birthplace of this now popular lunch dish, first served 1880s. Lunch *teishoku* portions are substantial and prices low. Original owner of Tamahide used to prepare special bird (most often cranes) dishes for shogun. Serve special meals for dinner (16:00-21:00) where, too, portions huge and prices reasonable; *sukiyaki, mizutaki*, soups and assorted bird dishes for ¥6,000 up.

Between Kaisei-ken and Tamahide interesting little budget diner...
Mifuku-tei advertises 'Western-style food'—in this case Japan-naturalized dishes such as assorted *katsu* (cutlet) and deep-fried foods, hamburger, curry and such. Between Kaisei-ken and subway exit is tempura shop **Tentoku**, moderate rates with picture menu, prices, out front.

KOAMI JINJA shrine, dedicated to *Fukuroku-ju*, God of Longevity & Wealth of Lucky 7, just another neighborhood shrine seemingly forgotten.

That is, as long as you don't come here on **Nov 28**, when it comes to life in 500-year-old *Doburoku Matsuri*. Ancient kagura dances performed during am, at noon, *doburoku* (unrefined 'sacred' sake made from first rice of year) is ladled out to everyone attending.

Go 2 intersections W of Tamahide then R...

AMAZAKE-YOKOCHO 'sweet sake alley' fun to stroll, most shops crammed into first 2 short blocks. As we head east towards Meiji-za (10min if direct), few doors down on left is tea store which also sells teapot-cup sets from normal size down to something more fitting in doll house. Next door is tofu shop **Futaba Shoten** which handmakes various types of tofu. Reputation for quality is enhanced by daily orders from top restaurants in Ginza and Roppongi. On far corner lovely old **Toshina-ya** serves good cheap noodles, various rice dishes. Facing it next corner is **Iwai Tsuzura-ten**, where you can see old Mr and Mrs Iwai weaving *tsuzura*, lightweight bamboo storage baskets—lacquered in red, black, or brown—common means of storing clothes until recent advent of cardboard or plastic cases. Latter can't compare for usefulness, as well as being less attractive: *tsuzura* has open weave to allow for air-flow, thus preventing mildew, major problem in humid Japan. Being flexible, they're much stronger than newer cases; cheaper unlacquered *tsuzura* used to be popular way of shipping by airline check-in luggage. Iwais work here every day 8am to after dark, gladly show off their work. They'll custom make with *mon* family crest, initials or any other design, painted on. Large from ¥20,000, small ones ¥5,000up.

Beyond that is another old craft shop...

Bachi-ei, samisen specialty store marked by white plectrum-shaped sign and huge *noren*. Samisen master-owner makes everything he sells. Next to it is take-out sushi stall **Shinoda-zushi**, selling freshly made *inari* and assorted sushi rolls. Across street, **Yanagiya**, reputedly one of best shops in Tokyo specializing in *tai-yaki*, fish-shaped pastries filled with bean paste —almost always long line here as people wait to get them hot off griddle.

Continuing towards Meiji-za, on same side of street as Yanagiya, we come to...

Machinaga bamboo and woodcraft shop where you can get lovely handmade trays, boxes, baskets for just few thousand yen. Nearby budget **Hotel Kitcho**, small clean rooms, business hotel rates.

Cross narrow green belt, cross back over to other side and short way down is red brick Tokyo branch of...

Museum of Japanese Pottery, *Kurita Bijutsu-kan* (10:00-17:00, X-last 3 days Dec, ¥500). Leave shoes at first floor, pay admission 2nd floor and take elevator to 4th and 5th floors. Displayed here are several hundred pieces of Mr Kurita's personal collection; mostly Imari, Nabeshima and Kakiemon porcelains from Kyushu. Exhibit here is only fraction of what is kept at main museum in Ashikaga City, Tochigi Pref in several buildings-full of Imari Nabeshima. 2hr drive; by rail, take private Tobu Isezaki line from Asakusa to Ashikaga (1hr 40min) and 20min bus or cab basic-mtr+.

Next to Kurita Museum is old style black wood wall and small gate leading to classy luxe **Hamacho Tempura**.

Just beyond is...

Meiji-za theater, so named since it was first opened in Meiji 6 (1873). (X-for Rebuilding thru 1993). First called Kishu-za; renamed after emperor Meiji's death. Regularly scheduled kabuki performances, but much of time shows will be non-kabuki period pieces or fast-talking comic monologue *rakugo*. Park in front, **Hamacho Koen**, extends to Sumida River where, in pre-concrete days, Tokyo-ites strolled sakura-lined riverbank. Under park is Hamacho subway stop on Toei Shinjuku (lite green) Line.

If you've already seen all of Ningyo-cho and want something different for dinner, do as we did and jump on Shinjuku Line one stop east to Morishita, and 2min walk to **Minoya** (*see* RYOGOKU, p.1204) for excellent sakura-nabe.

BACK STREETS OF NINGYO-CHO: Saving best for last, we now explore back streets, running north off Amazake, area that somehow escaped fires of war and which offers glimpse of what this whole area must have looked like architecturally. Some are of durable *kura*-style thick-walled houses which we see dozens of on our out-of-town old Edo tour of KAWAGOE (*follows*) or any countryside. Down alley between Toshina-ya & Iwai Tsuzura we come to **Imahan**, branch of famed Asakusa sukiyaki house. 2nd fl *zashiki* tatami rooms for sukiyaki dinners (¥3,800), 1st fl has Western dishes, steak, thin sukiyaki beef cooked in sherry. Lunchtime *teishoku* served until 16:00–*sukiyaki* or *shabu-shabu*.

Continuing past Imahan, first R leads to...
Homi-tei restaurant; look out for faded English 'restaurant' sign on your right. With its very Japanese façade of potted plants, wood-slat door, you would be hard pressed to tell that this is one of Tokyo's oldest W-style restaurants. Started century ago by cook from Yokohama's New Grand Hotel. While meals served on low tables in tatami rooms, choices are such as steak, beef or tongue stew, shrimp croquettes, or pork cutlets. For Meiji atmosphere and taste, Homitei is great. Prices inexpensive, and daily lunch specials substantial. Hours 11:00-14:00, 17:00-21:00, X-mon and last sun monthly.

If you go straight without turning off to Homi-tei, L at next intersection leads to...
Hiyama, one of Tokyo's earliest and best meat shops featuring beer-fed Matsuzaka beef from Ise area (note their many delivery trucks); their restaurant is around corner on main street. 2nd shop past intersection is **Ise-tatsu** old store specializing in *tabi* split-toed Japanese socks, tho they now also sell trophies as tabi are losing popularity. Near end of alley R is **Hinode**, speciality *cha-soba* green tea noodles; samples-prices in case.

Take next parallel alley N from Amazake-yokocho (L after Bachi-ei), you come to...
Misaku, handmade noodle shop where chef pounds and stretches fresh noodles in front of you. Further down this alley, and you will come to row of several old shops. One, **Yoneyama** rice dealer, over century old. Next door used to be geisha house; now dentist. Just few doors farther on old fashioned **Obase Orimono** sells bolts of silks for kimono. Two more shops N of main Ningyo-cho intersect (where 3 of 4 subway exits surface): R on corner is **Ise-ryu** pottery shop, marked by large blue *noren*-curtain.

You may have noticed many shops around here, for that matter all thru sh'tamachi, are named ISE-something. When Ieyasu began expanding Edo, he needed people to set up services in his new capital so volunteers where sought to settle. Large number of first settlers came from Ise area, and kept home ties in their names.

Few doors N of it is...
Ubuke-ya, well-known cutlery shop here since 1783. From intersection, it is only short walk back to our starting point at Amazake-yokocho.

TSUKIJI

COMMON NAME for Tokyo Central Fish Market, interesting place to start very early day—or end very late one. During nite nuzzling into nearby wharves to tie up there come little Viking-size tubs which may have been fishing off coasts of Japan or may have just come in from months-long journeys into Indian Ocean or seas off Antarctica or just outside American coastal limits. At 5am most of city's 14,000 fish retailers, restaurateurs appear in rubber boots, swathed like hybrid of Eskimo and mummy, heads wrapped in towels and caps bearing names of their shops. Flashlights peer into open bellies of great fish to judge quality of meat. At 5:45 bells sound, auctions begin, hoarse growls of auctioneers' voices elicit dumb-talk replies from fingers of buyers. Stroll thru but be light on your feet, for great fish and gritty men on opposite ends of giant grappling hooks easing themselves onto pushcarts and tiny truck-vans move in familiar anarchy governed by their own laws of motion. Heavy shoes or rubber boots advised.

Name Tsujiki means 'Reclaimed Land', and it is just that. From Palace to present shore was all giant feudal reclamation project to make Edo habitable. Tsukiji was created after great Furisode fire of 1657. In Meiji era it was residential area for foreigners. Market moved here 1935 from Nihonbashi. Also boasts restaurants noted for superior fish offerings which, as most any Englishman or Scandinavian will testify, make superb breakfast.

TSUKIJI HONGAN-JI temple is closer to town, but if coming for fish auction and breakfast, you do better to take it on way out, so we cover it after....

CENTRAL FISH MARKET. Straight ahead is wholesale area of 1,677 stalls for individual storekeepers to shop for 450 types of sea produce; curving to its L is main unloading area, auctions held behind. Wholesale area separated from retail by canal, with blue bridge at tuna auction end, where single blue-fin air-lifted from New York or Boston can fetch $10,000. Area grosses over $5-billion annually. At this bridge is small *Nami-yoke Inari Jinja* **Wave Repelling Fox Shrine**, guardian spirit for Tsukiji. At almost any time you see people going in to offer quick prayer: fishermen for calm seas, local merchants for continued business. Everyone gives thanks to fish who have given themselves to feed mankind, as you enter several monuments dedicated to sea animals line left side of shrine grounds. One is even dedicated to sushi in general.

Drawback about coming here for crack-of-dawn fish auctions is that you are too early for most good sushi joints which open between 10:00-11:00. But you can eat good, inexpensive noodles, oden, curry and like hot dishes at several stalls frequented by fishmongers. Time your arrival depending on what you want to see. Auctions begin 5am, various locations depending on what fish being sold (largest tuna sale begins 5:50 at far SE corner), continue few hours. Wholesale fish market section winds down 10-ish, retail markets outside main compound slow down by 11:00 or so, tho they stay open all day. Retail here runs at least 20% below supermarkets.

Earlier better, most shop hours are 6:00-14:00, but many close around noon. Wander thru spacious outdoor market area to find your own sushi-ya, and notice many assorted food and cooking supply shops here, sushi chef's dream-come-true. For sushi shop to survive down here, it's got to be better-than-good, and about any that you wander into will be—but here we mention some old-time favorites.

Facing out from shrine we go straight, along shops selling bamboo goods (now also disposable tins), cups, dishes and such. Little way down, right, is small wood shack with ratty white lantern and blue *noren*: **Takagi** serving surprisingly good budget tempura dishes. Continuing on to 2nd alley (1st after crossing short bridge) R, few doors down on L at Tsukiji-Ginza 7-3-15, is *best sushi-ya anywhere*: **Sushi-sei**, ☎3541-7720, 10:00-14:00 & 17:00-21:30 X-sun and almost always full. But don't despair, they cram you in, seats open up quickly. If first floor is full they have another bar upstairs: 2 doors to right of main shop go up steps, bigger, also some tables. Since each chef has many customers to serve, wait until he addresses you then order several at once so that you can hold out until next round. Tongue-tied?–hold up fingers for as many as you want and say *mori-awasé*, 'mixed'. Needless to say, fish is fresh. While you could easily spend fortune trying to eat like this at city or hotel sushi bars, expect unbelievably low prices–'89 visit per person ¥2,150 got beer, 13 portions of pricey choices. Woman there said: "we have reputation for good and cheap that we have to uphold". ·

Continue along Sushi-sei alley, pass knife shops on L and almost at far end on R is...
Kibun sushi, good combination dishes of sushi ¥1,-2,000.

In these back lanes you come across several tiny temples. Notice that all are of Jodo Shinshu, Pure Land sect. People in Tsukiji, like most common folk in old Edo, were attracted to no-nonsense approach to salvation that Jodo called for, didn't have time for elaborate rituals of more esoteric sects.

Another popular sushi shop is **Edo-gin**, across Shin-Ohashi-dori Ave. Cross at Segawa, L at other side and first R down alley. Edo-gin is much larger; can eat leisurely meal here. Also serve other seafood dishes besides sushi, for which picture menus make for easy ordering. Open straight thru 11:00-21:30, X-sun.

Heading S on Harumi-dori along retail shops, just past first alley is coffee shop...
Yonemoto with many types of fresh strong coffee, to-go is ¥50 cheaper than drink-it-there. Continuing on, we cross canal and after 2nd alley is **Totoya,** excellent little yakitori stall open only 9:00-13:00, X-sun. If your eyes miss blue noren with bird pictograph, your nose won't miss delicious aroma of chicken sizzling in teriyaki sauce. Next shop over is traditional sweets shop. Between it and end of block is narrow alley; down R leads to **Takeno,** excellent budget diner where you can fill up on assorted sashimi & tempura along with usual tidbits. Best deals for quantity and variety of fish are *mori-awase*, or assortments. About ¥800 for either *tempura mori-awase* or *sashimi mori-awase* rounded out with rice, pickles and soup; and add beer at rock-bottom rates. Open 11:00-20:30 (last order). Takeno will be first eatery on your right; next two shops are also budget diners, serving *ippin-ryori* one-dish snacks to go with beer or sake.

Back on Harumi-dori, we cross to other side and left (east) one block to...
Minatoya, traditional sweets shop since 1809. Few short blocks down Harumi-dori on left side is **Tentake**, one of better known restaurants specializing in *fugu* (blow- or puffer-fish). Photographers looking for old buildings should check alley behind Tentake for row of well-kept wooden houses reminiscent of old Edo prints. Further S on Harumi-dori takes us to Kachidoki Bridge, across which is our TSUKUDA-JIMA TOUR, *next.*

TSUKIJI HONGAN-JI temple across Harumi-dori from Tsukiji is large, modern ferroconcrete pinnacled structure in pseudo-Indian-Southeast Asian-Gothic architecture which inter-war style thankfully did not take hold. Main Tokyo temple of active Nishi Hongan-ji sect and because large following among Japanese-Americans, weekly service sunday 10:30am is in English followed by discussion meeting. Leading group is nisei former New Yorker Rev YAMASHITA Kiyoshi, now in Berkeley, Cal. Center for inter–national Buddhist studies and information group is generous to interested foreigners, helping them establish desired individual contacts: **Misaku** ☎3541-1131 xt3214 for someone to speak English, mon-wed-fri 10am-3pm, sat 10am-noon, or ask for at worship hall. Regular Japanese services daily, 10:30am & 1:30pm.

Main intersection by Hongan-ji temple is meeting of avenues Harumi-dori (roughly N-S from town) and Shin-Ohashi-dori (E-W paralleling river). N- leads via **Kabuki-za** Theater to heart of Ginza district (15min walk) intersection marked on L by tall glass cylindrical **Sanai Building;** S goes out to new man-made isles with **Tokyo International Trade Fair** and **Antique Furniture Museum,** one route to TSUKUDA-JIMA WALK. W, street continues past Central Fish Market, curving to entrance of **Hama Rikyu Detached Palace Garden** (15min walk).

This about finishes our tour of Tsukiji. Anyone interested in history of early foreign settlement of Tokyo might stroll **St Luke's Hospital** area (soon to be levelled to redevelop) which housed Tokyo's first foreigners. First here were Americans, under Japan-US Commerce Treaty. Only few decorative stones from 2nd US Legation remain, displayed in garden of St Luke's. Garden also contains **Teusler House**, once home of hospital's founder Dr Rudolph Teusler who came here in 1901. Garden open only saturday afternoon, and permission to visit must be gotten ahead of time; call ☎3541-5151.

WHERE NEXT: To go on from Tsukiji, two options are: TSUKUDA-JIMA, and HAMA RIKYU. Latter is not too far to walk, former about 2km (1.25mi, 30min), taxi basic meter, but St Luke's, *below*, is 1/3 way there. In keeping with sh'tamachi theme, let's take step back in time to what is probably as close to fishing village as one will get in heart of one of world's largest cities...`

TSUKUDA-JIMA

ONE OF THOSE rare places which escaped devastations of 20th century Tokyo. It made it thru post-quake flames of 1923 (for some reason their houses didn't fall either), got unscathed thru fire-bombings of 1945. Locals attribute it to divine intervention (as we will soon see), but perhaps, that this is island may have had something to do with it. Or rather was island—now it is just part of much greater man-made island which in turn is bridge-linked to several others filling mouth of Sumida River. But these land-fill projects are postwar, and people of Tsukuda-jima have had time to brace against encroaching 'progress', which, as you can see, means hideous high-rise apartment complexes and heavy industry. Matter of fact, Tsukuda-jima-ites cherish their quiet little neck of woods and over 90% of people have created formidable group whose members have agreed not to sell their land. And as long as they stick together, we will have this escape into old Edo.

Most of Tsukuda-jima's early settlers—for that matter, much of Edo's—were 'imported' from Osaka's Nakano-shima village by shogun Ieyasu who favored hard-working Kansai folk to get his new capital going. During Edo era Tsukuda-jima served as halfway house for petty criminals who were thought able of re-assimilating into society after having done time on penal isles off Edo. Here they were taught trades, then sent off to earn their keep. Tsukuda-jima didn't have to worry about too many ex-cons running around since few were lucky enough to be released. But isle became haven for poor wretched and outcasts who came hoping to do well; Ellis Island of sorts, but with nowhere further to go. As fishermen, Tsukuda-jima-ites didn't do too badly and, if anything, they are remembered for having perfected way to preserve fish for their long journeys—*tsukudani*—simmer fish or meat in soy sauce mix until fully absorbed; salty soy preserves against rot.

Tsukuda-jima's fate was forever changed in 1853 when Mito lords (main Tokugawa branch) built shipyard here. With Meiji Restoration and need to modernize, this firm, Ishikawajima Heavy Industries (IHI), became leader in field. In 1960 they merged with Hyogo's Harima Industries to create Ishikawajima-Harima Heavy Industries, famed worldwide for revolutionizing shipbuilding. Ishikawa-jima (Ishikawa's Island) was formal name for Tsukuda-jima, given to one ISHIKAWA Hachiemon in 1630s by Tokugawa—by no small coincidence he was in shipping. Factory is again changing fate as site now under construction as high rise Okawabata River City 21.

GETTING THERE: Calls for some walking. Most direct is 15min walk from Shintomicho stn, terminus of Yurakucho Line (yellow); Tsukiji stn of Hibiya Line (grey) is few hundred meters further W of Shintomicho. From Shintomicho go SE along big street to Tsukuda Ohashi Bridge, cross it and Tsukuda-jima is there on your L. You'll cross on Tsukuda Bridge if wandering thru from St. Luke area or if like us, you've just breakfasted on superb sushi at markets of **Tsukiji** before seeing Tsukuda-jima—we offer slightly different course starting out along Harumi-dori Ave. But beware, it's bit of hike, almost 2km (30min) from oriental-gothic-deco **TSUKIJI HONGAN-JI** temple near fish market. From Tsukiji stn we advise this as more interesting, as only 100m stn–temple.

Further out Harumi-dori is Harumi Pier...

International Trade Fair Complex, *Tokyo Kokusai Boeki Center* where there is permanent exhibition of manufactured goods, machine goods; in spring of odd-numbered years, site of *International Trade Fair* which alternates Osaka; October *Automobile Show* moved to **Makuhari Messe**. Nearby are **Antique Furniture Museum,** *Kagu no Hakubutsu-kan* (10:00- 16:00, X-wed) displays old Occidental and Oriental furniture; **Hotel Urashima**.

South on Harumi-dori from Tsukiji, cross Sumida River on...

Kachidoki Bridge. Note towers; bridge was completed after 10 years in 1940, said to be largest drawbridge in Asia. Middle portion used to be raised five times daily, but nowadays with river traffic limited to low barges (too many other low fixed bridges) and formerly non-existent road traffic now more important, it no longer draws up. Cross Kachidoki on its L side, down stairs at far end, where for change of pace can take narrow shopping alley parallel to road. Next street go L after crossing canal, it becomes typical old neighborhood shopping street. At far end is another Jodo temple. Cross big road (Tsukuda Ohashi Bridge is to L) and keep going another block along old shops and first L. Down short way street jogs L then R to small red bridge cross which to Tsukuda-jima. **(Public rest room** by bridge.)

Not really island anymore, just few blocks of old neighborhood separated from rest of surrounding man-made island by L-shaped canal which shelters handful of fishing boats. This few blocks hidden away here is among few parts of Tokyo with houses dating back to Taisho era, 1920s. Won't take much time to explore quiet back alleys here, some barely wide enough for one person. Tho old, houses here are kept in immaculate condition, and this whole area is clean. Walking down main street, part way down on left is **Nakajima** lacquer shop, where owner Mr Nakamura is 3rd generation to do this *Edo shikki* style of lacquer, *urushi*.. His works are in clear lacquer, as well as common red and black. All beautifully done, relatively inexpensive.

We come to small playground at end with stone marker in corner commemorating site of old boat crossing (similar marker NW on other side of Sumida River). Regular boat crossed until 1964 when Tsukuda Ohashi Bridge completed just in time for Olympics. High concrete walls not here before then, either. Along this 'water-front' lane are three old shops selling island's specialty of *tsukudani*: **Ten-yasu** and **Tanaka-ya** across from boat landing marker ...

Going R, follow lane to end and another R which takes you to...

SUMIYOSHI JINJA, guardian shrine of Tsukuda-jima, also 'imported' from Osaka by Ieyasu during his early years here. Enshrined *kami* is same as Osaka grand merchant-oriented Sumiyoshi Shrine's. Dragon and Tiger carvings here are credited with protecting Tsukuda-jima thru various fires which have plagued Tokyo. Every 3 years (1992,'95,'98, 2001, –) for 3 days around **Aug 7**, shrine is honored in gigantic festival with special octagonal mikoshi carted around town, dancing in streets, enormous 20m long banner hoisted up on 25m pole. For some special reason, only this shrine was granted rights to such show under anti-sumptuary laws of Tokugawa Shogunate. Festival is immortalized in one of Hiroshige's prints of *100 Views of Edo*. Isle's **mid-July** *Nembutsu odori* dance is capital's ICA.

There really isn't too much to Tsukuda-jima, but it does offer glimpse of old Tokyo. First-time visitors on limited time may want to pass it up, but anyone who has spent much time here will find this another pleasant escape from everyday mobs. It is not expected to last, high rise apartments throw shadows across bordering canals, land worth ¥350,000 per tsubo (36ft² 3.3m²) in 1983 was attracting real estate agents' bids of ¥10–20-million per tsubo by '87, doubling again quickly.

To return, go up steel stairs climbing up to big bridge, cross it and short walk to intersection with Shintomicho stn on Yurakucho (yellow) subway line. Hibiya Line Tsukiji stn is just few minutes walk W of Shintomicho, taxi basic-meter.

To continue pleasant detour for hardy of calf. From bridge head back into isle on wide street (SE) to big intersection of Kiyosumi-dori St, L across bridge to Etchujima isle straight 3 blocks across stream to...(or from town, Tozai subway to Monzen-nakacho stn)

FUKAGAWA

EDO ERA 'temple town', starting with short block above stn is FUDO TEMPLE, branch of mob-drawing Narita Fudo, postwar rebuilding of little interest except to witness supplicants who devoutly believe in this deity of contracts.

Before gate R, famed manju-cake shop Miyagetsudo. Block E is...
TOMIOKA HACHIMANGU is home of one of Tokyo's 3 big festivals; Aug 15 carriers run 100 huge omikoshi to shrine while onlookers toss water on them. Major fete every 3rd year (1992, '95, '98, 2001, '04, '07...). Home of big-time sumo wrestling, in 1600s site of big meets for farmer sumo, originally local shrine rite for luck and divination, developing for own sake in prosperous times. From 1684 its formal spring-autumn meets started present tournament tradition. Sumo moved to temple in Ryogoku then to own arena nearby. 1900 erected **Yokozuna Rikishi stele** here, 3.5m tall, 3m wide and 20 tons inscribed with names of all yokozuna from first Akashi 1624 to 45th Wakanohana 1958; 46-Asashio-on continue on second slab adjoining.

Back toward subway and Eitaidori St for fine soba shop Hoseian, X-thur & 3-4pm. Back to Kiyosumi-dori and R, cross bridge, walk 10+min to...
Kiyosumi Teien garden, built by fabulous KINOKUNIYA Bunzaemon Edo era mandarin orange mandarin of Wakayama, great playboy and patron of artists and artistes, as 'culmination of Edo landscape gardens'. Bought by Baron Iwasaki and 1924 gifted to city (as above RIKUGI-EN). Large pond of 10,000 carp up to 1m/40in length; noted for collection of water-worn and otherwise naturally beautiful large stones. 9:00-16:30, X-mon.

15min walk to...
Emma-do Hall enshrining 3.5m tall, 4m wide, 1.5 ton gaudy arabesque on red King of Hades, judge of those who pass over river of no return. Favorite temple of sh'tamachi masses in Edo era, razed in Quake of '23, rather than simply rebuild structure, rebuilt tradition 1988 with gaudy icon (how much else was so when new?–witness Nikko) and hi-tech accessories —toss coin in either of two boxes for 'household safety' or 'business prosperity' to set off computer-controlled multi-light show and tape-recorded music. Other offerings bring choice of sermons of 20-40 seconds, 'TV ad length' for today's short attention spans; English and Spanish promised. Most supplicants ask forgiveness for lies, plenty of business— kids are told Emma pulls out tongue of liar. Emma full showing monthly 15-16.

Return to Monzen-nakacho stn; or bus 33 in front of garden back to Tsukuda-jima.
From **Asakusa** we followed Sumida River thru much of sh'tamachi. You can retrace your steps, perhaps even another day, but this time by river bus, more memorable as

you glimpse now-familiar sights: **Kokugikan** sumo hall's new roof poking above river walls to L, boat-lined Kanda river on R; little bit on, tree tops of **Hamacho Park** peer over concrete walls; and still further on river splits, you take R fork and Tsukuda-jima will soon appear, hints of Tsukiji's great market not far behind. This is near end of our ride, soon boat enters gate in formidable wall and suddenly grey concrete gives way to greenery of...(in reverse, to board river-bus from town, take JR Keihin or Loop elevated line to Hamamatsu-cho stn, exit bayside and walk 10min, or basic taxi).

HAMA-RIKYU, DETACHED PALACE GARDENS: Much perked up since our first edition warning to bypass, is usually taken in as part of Sumida River cruise as most river boats end or start here. As you enter, left path leads directly to boat pier. But it is not too long to walk from Tsukiji, and worth visit if interested in relaxing stroll in garden. This used to be one of outside residences of Tokugawa shogunate, but its many lovely old buildings were lost in firebombing. Recently one has been rebuilt, 'floating' tea house in largest pond, exact replica of original in which President Ulysses Grant was guest of Emperor Meiji in 1879. Parts of garden fenced off as natural habitat for ducks: ¥200, 9:00-16:00, X-mon.

WHERE NEXT: Walk from Hama-rikyu back to Tsukiji stn, or follow curving overhead expressway (R if facing out from Garden) to **Shinbashi** with JR loop or subways Toei Asakusa (pink) and Ginza (orange) Lines. Halfway, on L, is **Shiodome Freight Yards**, site of JR's zero kilometer mark; not interesting in itself, but being developed as extension to Ginza business district. Another choice is to follow expressway other direction (along side of Hama-rikyu) almost 2km to **Hinode pier** for cruise around Tokyo Bay or out to fortified remains of anti-Perry cannon isles and **Maritime Museum**. Or, after passing corner of Hama-rikyu, small garden with pond (ex-**Shiba Palace Garden**, 9:00-16:00 X-mon, ¥100) is on your R. Behind it JR **Hamamatsucho station** and end of monorail from/to Haneda airport. Tall building there is **World Trade Center**, 40 floors –152m tall. 38-9th floors have restaurants with fine view of Hama-rikyu and Tokyo Bay; or take direct elevator to 40th floor observatory (¥500) for panoramic view of bay, entire city. And of course you see another high vantage point, **Tokyo Tower** (*see* WEST SIDE, p.1162).

*Tokyo...no claim to magnificence...does not
advertise its true self, but yields its secret only
to loving and sympathetic acquaintance.*
— Zoe Penlington, *The Times*, 1922

KAWAGOE 川越
HIDDEN BIT OF OLD EDO

WHILE WE recommend our walking tours of sh'tamachi to get feel of
what old Edo was like, they fill up few hours of spare time. But with day to
spare **KAWAGOE** City is must, especially if you don't have time to go far
into Japan's countryside. Kawagoe is one of better preserved old towns we
have come across, and only short ride from Tokyo; much of town resembles
what old Edo must have looked like, with dozens of sturdy kura houses
lining narrow merchant-town streets. **Kita-in** is sole extant original building from Edo castle dating to 1638-40, screens of 500 rakan.

Kawagoe lies in agriculturally rich area and long prospered, even before
OHTA Dokan set up castle here in 1457. Became main center of trade, further
enhanced in 1600s when Tokugawa made Edo their capital. Kawagoe
became primary center of commerce where produce and materials from
surrounding areas were gathered, loaded on boats for Edo via Shingashi
River passing thru north end of town—where Ohta put his castle, later
expanded on by Tokugawa-appointed lords of Matsudaira clan. Merchants
set up in front of castle and as near to river as possible to make for easy
transport. It was nicknamed *ko-Edo*, 'Little Edo', even during Tokugawa
rule, and today's residents try to live up to name. Here, you will experience
that woodblock print street of Edo, something you can just barely taste in
sh'tamachi, even in back streets of Ningyo-cho. With Meiji Restoration and
soon-to-follow rail and roads, Kawagoe began to spread south of present
tracks, leaving old part of town alone but still flourishing. And thanks to
sturdy fireproof kura houses, we are able to step back in time and trod
streets of old Kawagoe.

As you will see, kura have almost 1-foot thick packed-earth walls with
supports holding up tiled roof. Windows will have equally thick 'shutters'
which make them almost airtight to stop spread of fire. Yet, despite their
stodgy appearance, rooms get lots of light, and most had small garden in
back (as seen in one house/museum). Kawagoe was not always full of kura
houses—actually developed in Edo early 18th century, under orders of
shogun who got tired of having Edo burn down every few years. It wasn't
long for Kawagoe to pick up *kura-zukuri* style of architecture. Oldest such
house in Kawagoe dates to 1792, many more rose in following decades, but
about half of what we see dates after great inferno of 1893 which leveled
one third of town. You will see some use of red brick in those buildings;
experimenting with 'new' import. Nit-pickers claim that only about half are
real kura *dozo-zukuri* (dirt wall style) while rest fit under category of
nurikabe-zukuri (plastered wall style). Let them rant on about fine points,
both are equally attractive; you'd be hard pressed to distinguish. As if to
show Kawagoe's transition thru time, you will come across occasional
Western style buildings from Taisho era, graceful wood ones as well as
gothic stone, even little red brick church. So let's start on our walking tour.

GETTING THERE: 3 separate rail lines, choice of 3 stns. *Quickest & cheapest*
is Tobu Tojo private line out of Ikebukuro. Not counting locals (black on timetable), dep
roughly every 10min; *junkyu* semi express (blue) most frequent, takes 35min, *kyuko*

express (red) is few minutes quicker, and even more so is rare *tokkyu* ltd express (green). '92 cost ¥400. Line gives you choice of 2 stns, **Kawagoe** or **Kawagoe-shi**, 1.5km apart. Also to Kawagoe stn is JR-Saikyu Line from **Shinjuku** via **Ikebukuro** and **Ohmiya**, slower, costs double; RailPass choices are 1hr by local (5-6 hourly), 52min by *kaisoku* (red, 1-2 hourly), or 46min on *tokubetsu kaisoku* (green, only morning 8-ish, & evening rush). And from **Ueno**, take any of JR Tohoku Main Line trains to Ohmiya (25-30min) and change to Kawagoe Line (23min) which has relatively frequent runs—recommended for those stuck in Tokyo looking for quick ride on bullet train. All trains on both JR Tohoku and Joetsu Shinkansen Lines stop at Ohmiya, mere 25min from Ueno costing under ¥1,500, but at least you got to go on. Our 3rd choice is Seibu Shinjuku private rail line from **Shinjuku**; fairly frequent but fastest express takes 65min as line meanders to Kawagoe, but **Hon-Kawagoe** stn, located between and slightly N of others, is most convenient to old part of town, saves 10-15min walk over other 2 stns.

Walking map of Kawagoe—pick up at any 3 stations. Best (Jpn) is single folded sheet of tan paper with drawings on front; also City Hall's English pamphlet, less detailed map, use together. Just follow dark-shaded route as our tour is based on it, with some variations and options. This route will be shown on any tourist map of Kawagoe, be it on hand-outs, or on giant signboards. Another pamphlet found at stations is accordion-like brochure with color photo front. This also has small map with route marked, but not as good as tan one which shows most old buildings and other sites such as temples, shrines and part of old castle. Both maps should be found on wall racks just before passing out thru ticket takers at all stations. If they are empty, ask station staff for *'Kawagoe no chizu'* or head to Tobu Kanko **travel center** around corner from Kawagoe or Hon-Kawagoe stations and they have them. **Note**: while this marked course covers almost everything Kawagoe has to offer, it is just over 6km/3.8mi, 2hr walk—only using Hon-Kawagoe as base, and so may not be for everyone. But there are many good coffee shops for breaks, or you can always cut accordingly, so just wear comfortable shoes—but *don't pass up this lovely little town.*

GETTING AROUND: Directions simple here; town is pretty much set up north-south, with stations S of old part of town. Using intersection at Hon-Kawagoe stn as focus: 900m E is Kita-in temple compound, N leads to main strip of kura shops (about 500m up); Kawagoe-shi stn is 600m SW, Kawagoe stn is 1km SE.

Coming on Tobu, pass thru modern looking Kawagoe stn and get off at next stop, Kawagoe-shi. From here, direct route to Hon-Kawagoe is: take station-front diagonal street R, L at end, R at next light. But first 4-500m N from Hon-Kawagoe is not too interesting (regular shopping street), so can try: L from Kawagoe-shi stn, first intersect has old Western building, **first post office**—now shops. R (N) at this intersect, and next R takes you past another Western oldie, **Kawagoe Catholic Church** (across from it is Girls' Hi-school, covered with sakura in April). Or keep going N on road from PO, old buildings coming into view after 1st intersect; R (E) at 2nd big intersect (with several kura) and next L takes you to 100-year-old **soy sauce factory** of Matsumoto family; buildings date at least to 1820's. Back at that intersection is **Shiono**, which has been selling sembei rice crackers for over 100 years out of this same shop. It is still made old-fashioned way, kneaded and shaped by hand, dried in sun, then slowly roasted over special charcoal.

Going E, next intersect puts you at start of main strip of kura marked on NE corner...
Yamazaki Museum (9:30-16:30 X-wed, last 2 days of month unless former holiday or latter weekend, ¥400) displays family treasures, antiques, and tools of their trade; has operated their *wagashi* (Japanese sweets) shop, **Kameya**, since 1783. You can't see most of house, but 3 storerooms have been converted, with first one as you enter displaying various molds used to create wagashi shapes, as well as some sample arrangements of ornate sweets. 2nd store-room contains family heirlooms; 3rd (thru auto door) contains scrolls, great screen paintings, and other art pieces, rotated every 2 months. Those who have walked here will appreciate complimentary tea & sweets at low tables (floor heated in winter) with video of Kawagoe's grand autumn festival.

You can **taxi** here basic-mtr from Kawagoe stn, cut out 1.5km of not too exciting walk. Or cover it in 8min bus. If walking from Kawagoe, we suggest alternate to marked route: L out of stn-front and N up shopping street (one marked with all coffee cups on tan map). At first big intersect, instead of going L to Hon-Kawagoe stn, keep going straight. Quieter way than parallel main street from Hon-Kawagoe to Yamazaki Museum. It ends just E of Yamazaki Museum.

Just before 'T', on L is row of several old kura-zukuri shops, ending with lovely...
Unagi restaurant, marked by blue noren 'curtain' hanging at entrance. Pillared stone giant on corner dates to early Taisho era, is gathering spot for local merchants' association.

Few doors E (on N side) is...
Kameya tea store; and if you're wondering why name and logo is same as Kameya confectioner, its because second son in 1869 branched off into tea business. You will notice many stores selling tea in Kawagoe—high quality of Kawagoe's Sayama-cha tea has been legendary since 14th century, ranking with best. Look to far E end of this street and remember that church for we visit it later.

Back at Yamazaki Museum corner, we head N into...
Main group of kura shops, which, we see, sell everything from tea to sporting goods. As we go up, keep eye on on your R for 100-year-old **Kurazukuri Chaya**, another traditional sweet shop, with logo of two linked circles—fine tea house in back where you can lunch on light rice dishes for ¥750, or just have tea (Japanese and Western), coffee, juice or their famed sweets. Rice dishes come in two choices: *sansai-meshi*, cooked with seasonal vegetables and herbs, or *kura-meshi*, which has some type of seasonal meat as well; both come with miso soup. Next to it is semi-Western turretted 2-storey stone 'castle' built Taisho era for Saitama Bank.

Few doors further on R is...
Folklore Museum, *Hattori Minzoku Shiryokan* which at first glance inside looks like poorly supplied candy shop. Used to be old footwear shop, and displayed along one wall are many types of *geta* (clogs); back set up as shop would have been. It is town-run museum and **information center**, daily 10:00-16:30, no fee. They have some English brochures and pamphlets (in back, ask for), but none with good maps. Of many books and brochures sold here (all in Japanese), two with superb photos are: *Kawagoe no Kura-zukuri* with cover shot of kura windows, photos of finest kura houses here; *Kawagoe Matsuri*, front photo of wood wheel, pictures of all floats used in Kawagoe's grand festival. Few hundred yen each.

Across street are...
Four 100-year-old shops: **Yamawa pottery** store, **Miyazaki knife** shop (now also selling other hardware items), **Fukazen art gallery** (English sign), and **Hiraiwa house**, split into book store and barber shop. R (E) down alley here to 16m tall *Toki-no-kane*, **Bell Tower**, first built 350 years ago, often fixed but still rings every day at 6:00, 12:00, 15:00 and 18:00. Liquor shop on corner, despite its modern beer, juice and ice cream vending machines, is almost 100 years old. Best view of Bell Tower is seeing it rising above tiled roofs, looking out second storey windows of...

Museum, *Kura-zukuri Shiryokan* (10:00-16:30, X-mon), well worth ¥100 entry, for it allows you to explore inside of kura house. Few doors N of Toki-no-kane turn-off, on L side; watch for wood-slat doors along entire front, bare except for one wood and one paper sign and poster or two, string of blue noren has logo of character with triangular "roof" over it. This shop belonged to Koyama family, tobacco and smoking paraphernalia dealers since late 1600s (introduced to Japan shortly after Sir Raleigh brought to Europe). This shop dates to April, 1893, rebuilt in only one and half months after great fire. You enter spacious front and pay, this is area where shop was set up. Stairs go (shoes off) to 2nd floor storage space. Pass thru to backyard with part of living quarters and 3 kura storehouses intact. Doors to store connected to main house, which used to have several more rooms and bathtub room on S side. Hallway now-gone between house and first kura led to bathrooms (now modern out-houses), and entire space between first and second kura (now partially filled with mini kura) used to be kitchen. 1st and 3rd kura stored records, some valuables; largest middle kura kept their supply of tobacco. #1 kura displays old fire-fighters' tools and outfits; #2 has displays of festival items and *wagashi* candy molds; #3 shows how these houses are made, and some tools used. We enter house from back (shoes off) and follow arrows upstairs. Only sure-footed slender folks try coming down back corkscrew stairs, under 2-feet wide, slippery.

Few doors up on L is...
Osawa family house, alias Komatsuya footwear and gift shop. Oldest house here, one of oldest folk houses in Kanto dating to 1792. Many of these old houses are known by two names, _-ke which uses family name, and _-ya as their *yago* shop name: Yamazaki-ke are owners of Kame-ya. Most yago from favorite animals, plants or old home town; or some aspect of their work, can be humorous, such as Taguchi family's shop Mukade-ya, or Centipede-ya (nextpage). Characters for *mukade* read '100-legs', and Mukadeya's business is dealing in fine threads, yarns, embroidered cords.

Around next corner from Osawa house is great place to eat, but first, quick detour...
Candy Shop Lane, *Kashiya-yokocho*, narrow lane where SUZUKI Tozaemon opened his candy shop in late 19th century, and by 1930's there were over 70 such shops here. Some 10 still left, sell old-fashion common folks' sweets. Note how little they resemble fancy wagashi sweets of Kameya. Take first narrow alley L (W) past Kura-zukuri Museum, R at wider street and quick L to another alley and you're on Kashiya-yokocho, which is well worth few minutes' detour it takes. Kashiya-yokocho curves, then ends on main street where we deviate from map course. It has you going L across river and around to TOMEI-JI temple at far N end, then back along river to HIKAWA SHRINE.

Nearing lunch time, join us at great restaurant; (R/E at end of Kashiya-yokocho, back to that intersection near Osawa house). See modern butcher shop **Yoshinoya**, intersection, funny little English sign on wall. We're looking for **Tsuji-no-soba** noodle shop, which would be hard to miss since it has 2 dummies sitting outside second floor window. Their soba and udon are handmade, as is their special *cha-soba* 'tea-noodles'. Also serve unagi, tempura, curry and katsu-curry for non-noodle eaters. In addition to usual choice of noodle dishes, they have several combo meals (photos on wall) which are quite good: *Toki-no-kane* (¥2,300) gives you taste of everything, with sashimi, unagi, tempura, udon, cha-soba, rice, soup, salad, pickles. *Fuda-no-tsuji* (¥1,800) is same, except minus udon, unagi, salad. *Una-soba* (¥1,500) is tray of cold zaru-soba with side of grilled unagi-eel and pickles. *Kama-age* (¥1,500) is bucket of steaming udon which you dip in small sauce bowl, with side of tempura. *Tempura-moriawase*, assorted tempura meal, ¥1,000.

Now that you have filled up, its time for more walking; distance covered so far from Hon-Kawagoe is about 2km, half-hour.

You can follow map course to visit several temples and shrines; we found most to be historically interesting but not really worth trekking to see, except for...
HIKAWA JINJA shrine and KITA-IN temple. So back at intersection near Osawa house, we go N past few more old shops, to next big street R which takes us in about 10min to Hikawa Shrine.

Hikawa Shrine dates to mid-7th century, tho it wasn't until early 1600s when it was made Kawagoe's guardian shrine, that it became important. Main hall quite small, but loaded with beautifully intricate carvings.

TOMYO-JI temple, N end, was site of fierce night battle of 1546 when Hojo forces defeated Uesugi army to take strategic Kawagoe castle.

S from Hikawa shrine to next intersect where L (E) past tennis courts then R to...
Honmaru Goten Palace, sole remnant of Kawagoe castle, now only main entrance and waiting rooms to lord's residence, rest of mansion dismantled after Meiji Restoration. No admission fee, there is little to see once inside: some pottery from nearby archaeological digs, ancient dug-out canoe, and photos of old Kawagoe. Their pamphlet superimposes used-to-be castle over present town; 2nd diagram is how complete Honmaru Palace was, with shaded part showing what we are now standing in.

Just E of here is...
MIYOSHINO SHRINE, now almost forgotten, but one time famed thruout Japan. Often has huge straw ring hanging inside of main torii, passing thru which was auspicious. With expansion of castle, shrine became enclosed within castle ramparts. Approach was limited to one narrow path which followed along inner moats, and town folks wishing to visit had to go thru typically officious Japanese officialdom (*ah*, tradition). Combining arduous process of admission with passing thru straw ring, local children developed game called *toryanse*, London-Bridge-falling-down of sorts, which spread over Japan—any kid even now should know it, lovely song.

From here we go S (hillock on R was old Fujimi-yagura turret) to next road where R/W to end, where L, follow curve in road to next intersect.

R (N) here few doors to...
Mukade-ya 100-year-old string shop, with red postal box in front;

L leads to...
Kawagoe Christian Church, quaint little red brick church built 1921, funds for building mostly donated by Petersens, husband-wife teaching team at New York University. Feel free to enter; Reverend Francis Toshiaki MORI lives out back.

Continuing S, we pass more shops, then on R at corner of shopping street is...
Imoju, black kura shop marked by English sign stating "antique shop and confectionary". And it is just that. Sweets here local specialty, made from variety of sweet potato which grows in abundance locally. Some typical types of this *imo-kashi* (potato sweets) are: *imo-yokan*, gelatinous cake of pureed sweet-potato; *imo-natto*, candied sweet potato slices; *imo-karinto*, deep-fried fingers of sweet-potato a la french fry; *imo-sembei*, sweet-potato crackers. Found all over Kawagoe—good, inexpensive.

Next intersection, go L (E); corner is excellent...
Ichinoya, unagi restaurant satisfying customers for over 150 years. Few doors beyond is **antique shop Okahira**, with stone temple dogs and jizo figures out front. This is busy road we have turned on, but many fun neighborhood shops. Cross to S side street at yellow pedestrian overpass; old wooden shop at base is **Tsugahara**, for *dango* skewered rice dumplings. These here, called *yaki-dango*, are occasionally dipped into soy sauce mixture while being slow-roasted over charcoal, best eaten hot off grill.

Next to Tsugahara is...
NARITA-SAN BETSU-IN, annex of Narita's great **Fudo temple**; built 1850 by local merchant who went to Narita's temple and returned with his eyesight cured (if you can distinguish Narita's Fudo out of surrounding dark, you have good eyes). Incidentally, Narita is not all airport, its old part

of town is cross between Asakusa and Kawagoe, and we visit it later. But back to this Narita-san (also affectionately called Ofudo-san). We have entered thru its side gate, and tucked into corner is miniature garden with pond full of turtles; lone stream of water fountaining up. Although only wall separates it from busy street out front, it is peaceful, sitting here rejuvenates. This usually quiet compound is full of people on **28th of every month**, when *nomi-no-ichi* "flea market" draws peddlers and buyers from Tokyo and elsewhere. Main hall enshrines Fudo figure; facing it, R of coin offering box sits red cross-legged jolly old man with bib—*Obinzuru-sama*, cure-all man: leave your offering in box in front of him, say little prayer and rub him where you ail, then rub self.

We exit out of front gate, R, and we are at...

KITA-IN, one temple which is *must* on visit to Kawagoe. Not only historically important, you can enter 400-year-old living quarters and guest house, as well as inside of main hall. Kita-in is head Tendai sect temple in all Kanto, flourished under Tokugawa patronage. It got its start back in 830 AD when Saint Jikaku enshrined figurines of Amida Buddha, Fudo Myo-o and Bishamon-ten. Torched in 1205, emperor Fushimi in 1296 had priest Sonkai (later Saint Jie) rebuild, in 1301 ranked foremost of Kanto's 580 temples. Again torched in 1537 battle, left in sorry state until 1588 when Tenkai became 27th head priest, most responsible for continued prosperity of Kita-in. Tenkai met shogun Ieyasu when latter was falconing here in 1611, and strong bond was formed between them, resulting in fabulous complex completed in one year, Tenkai becoming head abbot of Ueno's Kanei-ji—Edo's top Buddhist temple, directly patronized by shogun. Tho Ieyasu officially retired title and office of shogun to his son, he did much policy-making and Tenkai was major advisor. March 1617 when Ieyasu's remains were moved from Kunozan (Shizuoka) to Nikko, entourage stopped here, which Tenkai commemorated by building small Toshogu shrine in honor of Ieyasu; ranked among top trio of Toshogu shrines, with home-town Kunozan and Nikko.

Tenkai's links with shogunate did not end with Ieyasu, and when all but Sanmon Gate/bell-tower of Kita-in burned to ground in 1638, 3rd shogun Iemitsu immediately had local lord Hotta Masanori rebuild Kita-in, even had part of his palace in Edo moved here. Tenkai almost outlived even Iemitsu; 'attained Nirvana' at Ueno Kanei-ji in 1643 at ripe old age of 108. Tenkai succeeded in preserving his beloved temple, and so far, Kita-in has survived without any fires, and almost every structure here dates to 1638-40, classified as Important Cultural Assets.

KITA-IN is bit out of way, and those who want to cut out some walking can **cab** here to start tour of Kawagoe, doing our route in reverse. It's 1km from HON-KAWAGOE, 1.7km from KAWAGOE-SHI, 2km from KAWAGOE, thus basic-mtr cab from any station.

From Narita-san, we enter Kita-in's side gate; we stand in middle of complex facing main hall. Wandering into Kita-in complex in mid-January, we were surprised to see half-dozen fire engines parked here, and man on telescoping ladder poised high above Kita-in Main Hall's lovely bark roof. Expecting worst, it turned out local fire-fighters were just practicing for **January 26th** exhibition—every year to show how quickly they'd arrive in case of dreaded flame. Kawagoe-ites take much pride in their architectural heritage, banding together to preserve kura-zukuri houses as well as temples and shrines. When you visit, there may still be huge open plot near city hall, flanked with huge banners with red letters, protesting, so far successfully, to prevent construction of high-rise apartments in heart of old Kawagoe.

You can get good feel of **Main Hall** just by walking around it, but notice lightly arched, long, roofed hallway linking back of Main Hall—go to that building, enter (shoes off), and pay our ¥300. We are now in buildings Iemitsu had moved here from Edo castle—*sole* extant original structure from Edo castle of prime Tokugawa days—with Nishi Honganji temple in Kyoto, sole true palace architecture that so awed early visitors to Japan. You are treated to spectacular views of Kita-in's **garden**—could distract for hours, various treasures, series of wonderful *byobu* **painted screens**. One set of rather scruffy monks contemplating in various positions. Another is called *Shonin Tsukushi-e*, Scenes of Craftsmen: 24 panels depicting 25 different kinds of artists at work, from Buddhist statue carvers to tatami mat weavers—late 16th century. Room usually displaying armor is where Iemitsu was born. Next, we cross **bridge** to enter Main Hall from its rear. Look out for small sign barring way, as sometimes (as on one visit during early New Year busy season), not open to public if temple busy with rites.

Keep your ticket, for you will need it to go see...
Gohyaku-rakan, **500 disciples** of Buddha, in walled off area behind gift shop: If no one at booth show your ticket to salesperson there. Actually 540 stone figures, and you could spend as many minutes here, for all have different expressions and poses. Rakan are often shown as crotchety old men broadcasting in their facial expressions that "we have it made": having attained qualities of buddhas and ready to be elevated to nirvana. One sleeps; one reads, laughing; another stares off to side, arms crossed looking bored, yawning; yet another is rubbing his head with all-knowing grin on his face in oh-so-Japanese gesture; then there are pairs sharing some sly secret or joke, or sharing great jugs of sake, another gets massage. Sitting in middle, high above all of this are three Buddhas meditating in lotus flowers. It took from 1782 to 1825 to carve all. (Photographers don't worry, gift shop sells film).

Next we head up to small red... **Jigen-do pavilion**, on top of hillock. Peek thru front slit. Pale hawkish looking old man in flowing red robes sitting on lacquer throne is said to be exact likeness to Tenkai, carved two years after he passed on. Posthumously proclaimed Saint Jigen.

TOSHOGU, shrine to Ieyasu, is on another rise, S. It is more often than not locked in, offering only view from afar, but if there when you can enter, do so. You'll get close-up of its intricate carved work, may even get to see series of *e-ma* offeratory plaques with paintings of falcons; Ieyasu was avid falconer. There is also another set of '36 greatest Poets', painted by IWASA Matabei, originator of ukiyo-e woodblock prints. These, other treasures special display Golden Week **April 27–May 6**, matcha green tea served in garden 10am-3pm.

This ends our tour of Kawagoe, truly pleasant day and still be back in Tokyo for early dinner. Those who want to keep this feel of old Edo long enough for dinner, follow us back to Tokyo, but across to its E side for sh'tamachi dinner *sakura-nabe* at **Minoya** in Ryogoku's Morishita area, perhaps preceded by excellent inexpensive sushi appetizer at **Sushi-sei** in Tsukiji fish market. We return, satisfied, to our old wood ryokan in back streets of Asakusa. Whoever said nothing remains of old Edo?

While out this far, art-loving museum hunters should take in...
Toyama Museum *Toyama Kinenkan* out in rural Kawajima-machi Shiroinuma 675; ☎(0492)-97-0007. Fine pvt coll J-, Chin, W-Asia, Inca art, 10-4:30, X-Jul 21-Aug 31; Dec 21-Feb-end. ¥500. From Kawagoe, short taxi only. *See* MUSEUMS, p.1241.

New 1990, we haven't seen for ourselves......
Kawagoe Museum: take Shinmei Shako-bound bus from any of 3 stns, off at Shiyakusho-mae, walk E 7-8mins. New bldg shows much same as old converted houses, thus in less romantic setting; standing exhibits Crafts, Festivals etc, main gallery rotating shows; ¥200, X-mon; ☎0492-22-5399.

Kawagoe Museum: take Shinmei Shako-bound bus from any of 3 stns, off at Shiyakusho-mae, walk E 7-8mins. New bldg shows much same as old converted houses, thus in less romantic setting; standing exhibits Crafts, Festivals etc, main gallery rotating shows; ¥200, X-mon; ☎0492-22-5399.

TRADITIONAL INDUSTRY TOUR of Kawagoe can be fit into your walking tour. While most craftsmen will gladly show off their skills if you catch them at work, here are cottage-industries who encourage visitors:

Tamariki Seika **confectionary**, on R as you enter Kashiya-yokocho; in business 70 years, will show you how these traditional candies are made; 9:00-19:00, X-mon.

Matsumoto Shoyu Shoten **soy sauce** shop (*see* text) will guide you around their factory daily 8:00-19:00; they ask that you call prior, ☎22-0432.

Kagamiyama Shusaku **sake brewery** (also call, ☎22-0113), shows factory, daily 13:00-17:00, x-mon and hols; it's NE of Hon-Kawagoe station, go R 2nd street N of stn and it's on your R next block, can't miss grand old building.

Kikyo-ya Tansu **cabinet-maker**, visit 9:00-18:00 but first call ☎22-0347. Factory and main shop few blocks S of Church, at intersect w/unagi restaurant Ichinoya; showroom few blocks N of Hon-Kawagoe stn. If not able to call (in Japanese) before coming out, person at **Hattori Museum** may help make call. Or just show up and see what happens, most times you'll find them hospitable even with language barrier.

WHERE TO STAY: Kawagoe—minimal but adequate, as most see as day trip. Best ryokan is **Sakuma**, ☎(0492)-24-0012, in business since 1894. J- and W- style, new wing or old wing, various rates ¥-S-L. Meals sumptuous, Sakuma is also topclass restaurant. Conveniently located, central; E down street from Yamazaki Museum, across from Kawagoe Christian Church. **Budgeteers** try **Hoshino Ryokan** ☎22-0264, at entrance to Kita-in. Several other inns; if in Tokyo, have Japanese speaker call **Kawagoe City Tourism Bureau** at ☎24-8811, ext-451, or if already in town, maybe people at Hattori Folkcraft Museum can help. Consider spending monthly 27th nite here to get head start at flea-market. Book well ahead for October's *Kawagoe Festival*.

PERSONAL DATEBOOK KAWAGOE ENVIRONS

January

3 *Daruma-ichi* Kita-in (p.1221) many stalls sell roly-poly Daruma dolls, eyeless; paint in 1st eye with wish at project start, paint in 2nd eyeball when you attain goal.

15 *Tsutsu-gayu no Shinji*, divine coming year's weather and harvest, early AM at Fuji-no-Miya Jinja shrine. Head priest counts how many rice grains end up in bamboo tube after complex ritual. Once done all around area, now only here. More lively event later same day is *Mochi-tsuki odori*, mochi pounding dance, Saifuku-ji temple's coming-of-age rite; usual mochi-tsuki livened up by antics of pounders.

February

3 *Setsubun* bean tossing, Kita-in (p.1221).

11 *Yumitori-shiki* and *amazake* festival at Hikawa shrine (p.1220). 5-6-year-old boys shoot 3 arrows each at target, coming harvest divined by positions of arrows; clear skies if arrows land in white, rain if in black. Afterward, *amazake* (sweet sake) and oden passed out to all.

March

21 *Fusegi festival* at Ozaki Jinja equinox, exorcising begun 1721. AM, locals gather at Ozaki shrine, with mikoshi preceded by drum, make rounds of houses.

April

Early *Sakura festival (O-goma)*, Kita-in temple; Burning Goma votive prayer sticks

11 Hikawa shrine (p.1220) hosts *mansaku*, dances and traditional skits handed down generations of local peasants. I.C.A.'s, these shows used to be performed all around countryside heralding spring, being done at any open plot or room in house.

14-15 *Ashi-odori* 'foot-dances' at Minami-Tajima Hikawa shrine (p.1220). Odd form of puppet plays, puppeteers lie on backs, legs extended up, each foot covered by mask and appropriate clothing, hands manipulate props. Low wall hides puppeteers from audience, and in back is usually group of child musicians.

Mid *Matsuri-bayashi* festival drums at Sugawara Jinja shrine stars local Imafuku troupe. Repeat mid-Jul, Oct 15. Similarly, Nakadai troupe struts their stuff on

18 *Matsuri-bayashi* festival drums at Yakumo Jinja shrine; will repeat **Aug 1** & **Nov 27**. Both troupes perform **Oct 14-15** grand autumn Kawagoe Festival.

19 *Kagura* dances, Nakafuku Inari Jinja S. It's real stuff; most often Shindai-mono, or Age-of-Gods pieces, Susano-O slaying gigantic 20m dragon.

3rd weekend has *sasara shishi-mai* lion dances, at Ishihara Kannon-ji temple; for interesting rural style of lion dance, sasara are bamboo percussion instruments played by young girls bedecked in floral head gear; lion is sometimes single, sometimes paired, or even menage a trois.

May

Last sun plant fair at Kita-in (p.1221).

June

30-July 1 nites, at. Hachiman Jinj, pass thru straw circle to get rid of all first half-year's ills; commemorates having safely passed thru mid-summer.

July

13 Senba Sengen Jinja shrine celebrates start of Mt. Fuji climbing season; it is affiliated with Sengen Shrine at base of Fuji which enshrines spirit of mountain.

14 Kami-Terayama's Yata Jinja shrine site of *Manguri*, primitive version of present-day portable mikoshi which is paraded thru town exorcising summer's evil spirits. Mikoshi is actually ten-foot tall, thick green bamboo trunk; straw bale skewered on top has decorative colored cloth, paper offerings pinned to it. This is carted down to river, purified, then taken back to shrine and presented.

Mid Big drums repeat of mid-April, above.

Last weekend & Fri-Mon straddling is *Hyakuman-to chochin Natsu-matsuri* ' 1,000,000-Lantern Summer Festival'. Classic O-bon festival for dead, honoring particularly benevolent, capable lord, Matsudaira Naritsune, who died 1849—he must have been very popular indeed, for at following year's O-bon, people of Kawagoe put out special lantern to guide their lord back to home. Tradition stuck, today, Kawagoe's O-bon is spectacularly colorful. Various parades all day, from samba and homemade new mikoshi to lanterns and ancient mikoshi.

August

1 Great drums, repeat of April 18, above.

September

1 Suzume-no-mori Sengen Jinja has *fire festival* praying to Mt. Fuji for safety at home and prosperity in business. Bigger fire is better as prayers carried up mountain on rising smoke, and thus festival's name

of Taki-age, or Rising Flame.

15 *Horokake-matsuri,* Furuoya Hachiman Jinja, Furuoya-hongo district. Procession of four youths wearing elaborate giant umbrella-like flowered ornaments on their backs; to Hachiman shrine to offer thanks. Origins were martial; now, mostly just colorful attraction. *Horokake* means 'wearing *horo*', medieval form of armor protecting backs of mounted samurai from arrows; came here to pray for strength from Hachiman, God of War.

Mid-Sep-mid-Oct sweet potato harvesting season, sold hot from carts.

October

14-15 *Kawagoe Matsuri,* annual fete of Hikawa Jinja (p.1220), guardian shrine of Kawagoe. To us, one of best nationwide! Main event is procession of enormous wheeled floats colorfully decorated and loaded with musicians. All boast beautiful carved work, most shine in black lacquer and metal fittings. Tier above stage supports large doll of famous character (many made by top Edo craftsmen). 24 such wagon-floats; 10 date Tokugawa era, half-dozen to early Meiji fix ups, rest added as town grew, some post-WWII. Each neighborhood fields own float, which mostly stays in home turf **14th**. On **15th**, all make their way to spot in town, parade some, then scatter all over town. When two meet at intersection, contest starts to see who has better show and so gets to pass first. Platform of 'wagon' rotates freely from wheeled base so musicians face each other and masked beings dance on stage. By nite, some floats have bogged down in sea of people, while others try to compete across and over pedestrian hordes, and all keep gliding thru town, illuminated by hundreds of lanterns. High-pitched wild and something to definitely join. This is how Tokyo's grand summer festivals used to be till they lost their floats from earthquake and war.

November

1-23 Kawagoe *Chrysanthemum Fair,* show thousands of plants, Kita-in (p.1221).

27 Great drums, repeat of April 18.

December

3 Kumano Jinja *Tori-no-ichi festival,* sale of good fortune rakes, other lucky charms.

Monthly

8 Renkei-ji temple's outdoor market.

28 Ofudo-san flea mart, Narita-san temple.

One ought to begin at Kyoto, but one lands at Tokyo.
Unpleasant surprises occur thick and fast.
— Robert Guillain, *Japan*

NARITA'S FUN ENVIRONS
AT COMING IN OR GOING OUT

NARITA doesn't conjure up pleasant memories of Japan for most visitors, which is understandable if one has only passed thru airport there—or worse yet had interminable layover due to notoriously bad interline connections between domestic and non-JAL international. Tokyo newspaper headlined it "World's worst airport". Yet, short cab or bus ride away is Narita city, wonderfully rural with lots to see and experience, especially burial mounds, as area has about 1000, and is as important as Nara's Kashihara complex.

Narita is worthy day trip from Tokyo. Edo era J- guidebook to Narita describes Edo-Narita trip as 3 nites/4 days. Topping list, now as then, is **Narita-san Fudo temple** which all should make effort to see; hour enough for rush visit, at least two to take in quick meal and shop bit; easy to pass more time to take in all museums, beautiful park behind, and shops. Other sites: **Sogo Mausoleum**, **Fudoki-no-oka** hill, **ex-Imperial guest house**, Shibayama temple's **Haniwa Museum**. But all this takes full day cab or U-drive (rent at airport), so unless staying at any of several fine inns at Narita city (or airport hotel) you won't have time but for 1 or 2.

If late flight, do as Garet on recent visit: go airport early and leave luggage at temporary bag check (only 1st floor arrival area) or coin locker (all floors) and head for town; or early check in at airline counter at Hakozaki Air Terminal; Tokyo and Shinjuku JR stns plan similar early check-in. Or from anywhere in country ship luggage by *takkyu-bin* to office in airport terminal —but first confirm which terminal, North or South, you leave from.

GETTING THERE: DEPARTING JAPAN, if splurging on **taxi** from Tokyo hotel to Narita airport, add hour or two meter and use cab to sightsee Narita town. Fast **trains** to Narita city incl JR from TOKYO stn, *tokkyu*, *Ayamé & Suigo* (¥2,530) in 1hr every 2-3hrs bet 06:45-20:45 doesn't go to airport; airport trains from YOKOHAMA or SHINJUKU don't stop in city; *Kaisoku* 80min (¥1090) abt hourly bet 05:02-21:09 ends at airport; from UENO JR is Joban/Narita Line via Abiko, better than hourly 07:00-09:00 and after 16:00 direct *kaisoku* express, 1hr20min, ¥880, frequent in-between 09:00-16:00 require change at Abiko. Also from UENO area is pvt (no rail pass) Keisei RR 83min *kyuko* (exp) every 10-15min from 06:21, 64min *tokkyu* (ltd exp) every 20min, 55min *Sky Liner* (super-express rsve only) every half hour, 8:40 thru 14:00 OK to city, earlier and later are non-stop into airport terminal; *tokkyu* or *kyuko*.¥730, *Liner* ¥1450; last dep Ueno 23:11, arr 0:43.

In Narita city, Keisei stn is about 100m from JR stn; airport bus stops front of JR.

ARRIVING from o'seas (*see* p210) from airport to Narita town **taxi**, under 4x-mtr; cheapest and as quick (10min) is Keisei Rail from airport basement (all except for *Sky Liner* super-express stop at Narita town), for which ticket vending machine at 1st floor Keisei counter or pay as you board. JR trains also in basement, railpass OK, but rsv-only *Narita Express* non-stops don't stop in town. **Bus**: Chiba Kotsu to JR Narita City stn in town from #1 bus stop, every 50min, take 25min.

Kanko-annai JR city stn has English-speaking staff, good E-maps and brochures, so let's use it as **starting point**: Facing out, follow along L side (note airport bus stops #1 Chiba Kotsu; #7 across street is for Sogo Mausoleum), L at intersection with lights (Mac on far corner) and we're on main pilgrim approach to Narita-san Fudo.

WHERE TO STAY: Those who decide to spend their first or last (or any) nite in Japan at Narita instead of Tokyo, have several choices right along bustling shopping street (quiet from late afternoon thru morning). Best rated, most used to Western clients is **Wakamatsu Honten** ☎(0476)-22-1136, at temple gate; room w/2 ¥-S, 20% off if no dinner, 10% off no bkfst, so room only from ¥7,000. 14 rms all w/toilet; 2 w/pvt bath (40% more), others use communal bath open 24hrs for luxurious soak. As good in service and food is oldest (350 yrs) **Ume-ya** ☎22-0003, just up street. Rates similar tho most rooms lack pvt bath. If you can't spend nite, can still see inside rooms of this classic inn; **lunch** (reasonable) of tempura, unagi, sashimi, served in private room. Ume-ya also gets their share of foreign guests, as too neighbor **Ohno-ya** ☎22-0007, prominent bell tower.

Tourist rate (¥-T) is **Ohgi-ya** ☎22-1161 (from ¥5,000 room only), another old-timer with relatively new building around small garden (not on main street, take L fork at Yakushi-do and 2min walk, on L). Several other ryokan in lo-Tw/2 range, look more like restaurants at first glance, but rooms are fine, service good, and food is needless to say excellent: just before Ohgi-ya on opp side is **Naruge-ya** ☎22-0239. On main street near Ume-ya: **Ohmi-ya** ☎22-0119 (on R), opp is **Kona-ya** ☎22-1083, between two old classics is **Daikoku-ya** ☎22-0130 and closest to temple is **Hishi-ya** ☎22-0112. Just around corner from temple entrance are **Hama-ya** ☎24-1285, lovely old **Tamaru-ya** ☎22-0045, **Azuma-ya** ☎22-0039. Cheapest in town is **Business Hotel Teradai**, new, clean all J-style rooms, ¥-B room only, extra for dinner (¥1,000), bkfst (¥500).

These and other lodgings including business hotels, can be booked thru E-speaking **kanko-annai** at JR Narita stn, just mention price range, preferred location; if at airport, ask at **TIC** office on 1st floor, north end of Central Bldg. JR kanko-annai open daily 8:30-16:30; TIC 9:00-20:00 weekdays, until noon sat, X-sun and hols. We recommend room w/2, or at least dinner, for it will be feast of local specialties, usually crispy tempura, fresh sashimi, succulent unagi and various side dishes of vegetables, herbs, rice, soup, pickles and such. You can't get same for anything close price-wise at regular restaurants. If going **budget** and want *sudomari* (room-only), make sure you eat early as most restaurants along main street close early evening. Budgeteers will find cheap ramen or soba stalls around either station where you can fill up for few hundred yen. W-style room at Narita, try family-style **Hotel Let's Narita** ☎23-0222, ¥-hi-T (¥9,000 single).

Western-style hotels at standard international rates, clustered between airport and town are (from cheapest to highest): **Holiday Inn** ☎32-1234; **Hotel Nikko** ☎32-0032; **Tokyu Inn** ☎33-0109; **Narita View Hotel** ☎32-1111; **Prince Hotel** ☎33-1111. All are under 10min cab from either town or airport. Newly joining this crowd is **Airport Rest House** ☎32-1212, rates fraction cheaper, and truly for those just passing thru Narita on lay-over. Almost within airport complex, only 2min by 24hr hotel shuttle bus service from terminals; monitors in lobby keep track of all arrivals–departures. For any interested in such, rooms boast view of airport, but don't worry, hotel soundproof.

TILT: Good English color map from TIC, *Welcome to Narita*. Get cab after seeing **Fudo** temple (or at airport) then → **Sogo Mausoleum** → **Makata Shrine** & **Sogo's house** → **Fudoki-no-Oka** → **Narita stn** is about 15x-mtr incl wait time; extra 8x-mtr if start/end airport. Cut out Fudoki-no-Oka, makes it about 6x-mtr r.t. from Narita Stn, about 15x-mtr if from airport, *see* p.1229. Ex-Imperial guest house and Shibayama are opp direction, add 7x-mtr to include former, or 14x-mtr to include both. Alt add **National History Museum**

Narita for Hotel Guests: Airport Passenger Service (APS) for years did **AM tour** to Narita-san Fudo and Sogo Mausoleum. Discontinued '91. Was good deal if you could fit into time slot, but you can do it on your own: 3 adults by cab for little less than old bus tour ¥3,000, and 4-5 people can cover much more for less, and time is your own. If returning to hotel after check-out, take bags down early, they will hold for you. Check on taxi thru hotel front.

SHOPPING: Near station is busiest shopping area in Narita with countless stores peddling to millions of pilgrims as they have done for centuries. Many old buildings are well-preserved, giving street look which even most unimaginative can recognize as something from old woodblock print. Here, you'll find all sorts of typical gifts, specialty foods, 'life-prolonging' sake, as well as numerous places to eat (most with plastic food and prices shown). We note some here.

Short way down on left is **Kurauchi folkcrafts** and snack shop; few doors down at corner, **Fujiya** sells fresh packaged *wasabi* (green horse-radish used in sushi), and next door **Takatoku** sells assorted pickles, followed by tiny *unagi* (eel) and tempura shop. Little further, road curves left and on left is impressive kura-style building **Yamada cutlery** shop which has been going for generations. Old woman in stall set up in front sells wooden gourd-shaped 'bottles' containing *karashi, hichimi* (mustard, red pepper). Across street in lovely wood building is **Kagaya noodle** shop serving excellent *te-uchi* (handmade) soba at reasonable prices. Inside is as traditional as outside, simple yet ornate; and one of those rare places that automatically gives *soba-yu* (broth) with orders of *zaru* or *seiro*. Next to Yamada knife shop is outlet for **Chomei-sen sake**, which characters read Spring of Long Life—small collectible pottery jugs with cup make great gifts. Next is pricey but excellent classic tempura, unagi, sashimi restaurant **Anamiya**. Across is another classic, **Sakuraya** *sembei* (rice cracker).

Little further on right, rambling...
Fujikuraya restaurant serves similar to Anamiya in price but ranked bit higher in quality. Across is centuries-old **Yoneya** selling *yokan*, sweet bean paste cakes. Beyond, on left, we come to **Aji-yokocho**, or 'flavor-alley', large space with many tiny stalls where rushed pilgrims can buy all different local specialties under one roof. Next, squat old wood building is **Gotoh-ya**, old-style refreshment shop selling inexpensive *dango* (dumplings on stick), *mochi, oden* and such. Now, street splits into two, and as you begin to go towards right fork, pagoda and soaring tiled roof of temple's main hall come into view. Looking R is **Yanagiya** another traditional sweets store; note small tea-shop tucked away in corner (L if facing), we stop here on return for refreshing rest and drink: *matcha* with cakes (¥450); other teas are *gyokuro* (¥450) or *sencha* (¥350), both with sweets, Western *kocha* red-tea or coffee (¥300). Models with prices at entrance.

Back at intersection **Yakushi-do** Pavilion dedicated to Yakushi-nyorai, healing Buddha. If prayers here don't seem to cure your ills, try **Shimoda Kenseido**, old-fashioned medicine shop selling *kampo-yaku* (Chinese style medicine) few doors down on L as we start downhill. Looks more like taxidermist, with all sorts of stuffed, dried, and pickled animals and herbs displayed. You probably won't know what most of these cures are good for, but if you can get your symptoms across, he'll get you appropriate dose. Some two-thirds of W- style Japanese doctors use *kampo-yaku*, both because they are often effective (at least as often as Western, if for specifics) and have no side effects even whether or not ineffective. (Few doors down is regular drugstore for those in search of more 'conventional' or W-style medicines.)

Bamboo and wood crafts store **Fujikura** next door has all sorts of old style everyday items which make great gifts, even if you can't figure out what something is really meant for. Now are more eateries, halfway down on right is old-timer **Kikuya**, with E- menu and often times E- speaker around. Like most restaurants in area, they specialize in unagi, tempura, sashimi. On this last stretch to temple, many eateries double as ryokan, while others are ryokan doubling as restaurants. Of latter, most eye-catching are two rambling old-timers **Ume-ya** (first on left) and **Ohno-ya** (with its bell tower); much newer, but built to look old is **Wakamatsu Honten** across from temple entrance (*see* WHERE TO STAY for more).

Straight walking, no shopping, takes under 15min from either station to...

NARITA FUDO TEMPLE: SHINSHO-JI temple, or as commonly called, **Narita-san**. Dates to 940 AD, founded by priest Kanjo of esoteric Shingon sect, dedicated to fiery Fudo Myo-o, deity of Immovable Wisdom. Legend has it this Fudo decided temple was needed here. Image was carved by saint Kukai (Kobo-daishi) founder of Shingon, late 8th–early 9th centuries, who sat at Kyoto's Jingo-ji temple. In 939, local warlord Taira-no-Masakado led revolt proclaiming self emperor, based here. Meanwhile, emperor (Suzaku, #61) in Kyoto wasn't too happy about this upstart, and his troops sent to subdue Masakado fared poorly. So Suzaku sent priest Kanjo, bearing Fudo statue, to better odds. Kanjo underwent 3-week sacred fire ritual praying for defeat of Masakado. It seems to have worked, for on last day of prayers, Masakado fell in battle and revolt collapsed. Work done, Kanjo readied to return, but Fudo statue wouldn't move, becoming heavier as more people tried to lift it. Taking it as sign, Kanjo set up shop here—ever since, Narita-san has blossomed into greatest temple to Fudo, now with over 13 million annual visitors—over 3 million in first 2 weeks of January.

Winding thru final maze of trinket-peddlers (stalls in compound are seasonals set up for peak times), you come to impressive **Nio-mon Gate** with its giant hanging lantern, rebuilt 1831. Flanking entrance are two by-now-familiar Nio guardian kings, keeping out any evil. Up to next level, and in front is majestic *Dai-Hondo*, **Great Hall**, built 1963; ferroconcrete but traditional in proportions and looks. Fudo is in there, but only eagle-eyes will be able to pick it out of surrounding gloom. If lucky, you will be here for one of five *goma* sacred fire rituals held daily. All-knowing Fudo of purifying fire is here to rid us of our earthly passions, weaknesses and anxieties. His sword cuts off binding evils, his rope ties them up to prevent return. Goma fire ritual symbolizes destruction of roots of carnal desire; purification of soul by burning *goma-gi*, flat wood prayer sticks. Write your prayer on board (purchase for ¥3,000, or ¥30,000 for better luck), piles of goma-gi are burned at each ceremony. Note vending machines along sides, they dispense *omikuji* fortunes and *omamori* amulets; all have been appropriately blessed before being loaded into these vendors. Narita-san gets so crowded at times that this is needed to help speed up process of being saved.

Facing main hall, to R is...

Three-tiered **pagoda**, tiers represent Buddha, Law, Priesthood. Recently fixed up but most of it still dating to 1803 restoration. R corner is smaller *Sho-ro*, **Bell Tower**, 1701, still rings daily. Building next is *Issai-kyodo*, **Sutra storage** containing complete set of Buddhist sutras, presented by Dalai-Lama in 1731. Here too, you earn enlightenment equivalent to reading each and every scroll just by one revolution of giant rotating cabinet they are kept in. To our left is glassed in rest area, behind which is path leading to **Korin-kaku Pavilion**, giant new structure which serves as guesthouse for pilgrims and visitors. We enter thru glass door to small but good **museum** *free* displaying temple treasures, exhibits rotated 3-4 times yearly. As you enter door, man gives you plastic bag for your shoes, which you remove and carry with you. Museum is first door on right.

Back outside and facing main hall again, we look to far left at...

Shaka-do housing wood statue of Oshaka-sama, historic Sakyamuni-Gautama founder of Buddhism. Lovely pavilion used to be main hall 1858-1964 when moved here to make room for present one. This is *must-see*; walk around outer veranda to get close look at intricate carvings on sides and back walls—of *gohyaku rakan*, 500 disciples of Buddha, each with different expression. You could lose yourself here for hours just studying variety of faces; easy to see how it took master carver MATSUMOTO Ryozan 10 years to do. Other carvings by SHIMAMURA Shunpyo depict *Niju-shiko*, or 24 Paragons of Filial Piety. Buddha figure encased in back is of Dainichi, Great Buddha of Light. This is as far as most people short on time get.

But others follow us up steps between main hall and Shaka-do, to...
Gaku-do, **Offertory Hall**, on left. Prized picture offerings and such are hung here, built 1861 to take overflow from first Gaku-do (burned 1964). Seated man of stone is Danjuro 7th of Kabuki; Narita-san is family temple of Ichikawa clan of actors. Old globe next to Danjuro was offered 1909, but it appears to be much older. Smaller building opposite it is *Kaisan-do*, or **Founder's Pavilion**, built 1938 for millennium of temple's foundation. Kanjo is enshrined here; only in spirit, not in body. Largest hall is **Komyo-do**, which once served as main hall, now is Oku-no-in, or inner-sanctum, housing statue of Dainichi Buddha. Little behind and to its side is **Seiryu Gongen-do**, built 1732 to house Seiryu Gongen guardian spirit of Narita.

Looming up behind all this is shiny new...
Daito Grand Pagoda of Narita-san. Completed 1983, just in time for 1984 1,150th anniversary of St Kukai's attainment of Nirvana. First floor is gallery exhibiting paintings, calligraphy, *ema-e* (votive plaques) and other temple offerings. Keep ticket, for it also gets you into *Reiko-kan* **History Museum**, far R corner—one room on temple history, with good E- signs; second room is on history of town (mostly shopping street leading to temple).

Narita-san Park is lovely landscaped garden created around 3 linked ponds—truly worth detour at any time of year, but especially for plum blossoms (**Feb-Mar**), cherry (**April**) and wisteria (**May**), then fiery hues of fall. You can go down giant stairs at Great Pagoda, but we prefer dirt path or steps by Seiryu Gongen-do...puts us at *Senshin-do*, **Spirit Cleansing Pavilion**, where priests would come to meditate, then stand under two waterfalls nearby. High-ground areas of park are full of stone markers and monuments creating surreal landscape. Upon closer examination, what look like giant gravestones are mostly signs noting how much certain person donated to temple...put up until early this century, when labor still cheap. How times have changed. Great monoliths credit donations of ¥500 or so; quite fortune during Taisho era, when most of these date. Many also date specifically to Taisho 7 (1918) and pray for 'victory at war'. Japan was ally.

You can head back to stn same way, or instead, go L leaving temple then next R and you come to taxi stand and stop for buses to **Sogo Mausoleum**. If headed back to JR stn, there is 'short cut' of sorts: between Aji-yokocho and children's clothing shop Tokuri (red neon sign in Eng) is alley cutting R. This lets you out by stn; not so much savings in distance (not much over 100m saved), saves time by-passing shops so you can't linger.

SOGO REIDO MAUSOLEUM also called *Sakura Reido*, is common name for **TOSHO-JI** temple. Tosho-ji dates back to mid-8th century, erected by first imperially-appointed shogun Sakanoue Tamuramaro. Sent here by emperor Kanmu to subdue 'northern barbarians', Ainu, major battle for control of Boso Peninsula was waged here, and after defeating Ainu, Tamuramaro dedicated temple to fallen on both sides. (He appears to have had more regard for his foes than later Japanese, for he erected such temples at all his major battlefields, as we see at Tohoku's Hiraizumi.) But Sogo Mausoleum has nothing to do with that battle; in fact, this temple is famed for event which occured centuries later, in 1652.

Our hero is KIUCHI Sogoro (alias Sakura Sogo), village headman. Usually verdant Boso Peninsula had experienced bad harvests for some years, and yet local lords, Sakura clan, kept up heavy taxes, forcing many

to starvation. Sogoro took unheard of bold step, directly petitioned shogun
in Edo for help, knowing full well that such act by peasant was punishable
by death. Shogun Ietsuna relaxed local taxes, but also had to uphold law so
Sogoro was crucified and his four children beheaded. Tosho-ji was their
ancestral temple, and all five are buried here.

Behind and to left of main hall is...
Reiho-kan Museum, semi-Western 2-storey stone building, containing
various Sogoro memorabilia, records of his trial, temple treasures, odds and
ends left by visitors over centuries, and artifacts excavated around here.
Further back is modern, squat, round building housing **Sogo Memorial
Hall,** series of 13 panoramas depicting scenes of Sogoro's epic.

2km down street...
Sogoro's house, *Sogo kyu-taku* still stands, past lovely Makata shrine—
traditional dirt-floored farmhouse, with new tin roof covering old thatch,
modern appliances tucked away in corners. Present occupant is 16th
generation descendant of Sogoro who will show you at least part of their
house. Beyond his house **Imba-numa** lake which also fits in Sogoro's
story. It seems Sogoro rushed out on his mission at night, and this lake
stood in his way, but shogunal edict put dusk-to-dawn curfew on boat
crossings, enforced by death of boatmen who were caught doing so. Well,
Sogoro needed to get across, so his friend Jimbei boatman decided to ferry
him, after which, Jimbei drowned himself in lake to prevent capture by
officials. Small **stone monument** marks site of Jimbei's crossing.

Sogo Reido is 4km SW of Narita, 15min bus from stn, or cab 2x-mtr. If **cab**, keep,
as road to Sogo's house continues on N to **Fudoki-no-Oka**. Some special **buses** go to
Sogo Reido from bus stop near Narita-san's entrance. You can also take Keisei Line one
stop to Sogo Sando stn, from where under 10min walk: out stn front street about 400m
to end, go R, and you'll hit straight on.

Fudoki-no-oka Hill, or Boso Historical Park, (8km NW of Narita; 15min
cab at 4x-mtr, or JR Joban Line one stop to Shimofusa-Manzaki stn and 30min walk).
Recommend doing this by **cab** and keeping it. Boso area is full of clusters
of *kofun* burial mounds and park is no exception, with about 120 mounds
of all sizes identified. One giant one is shaped like squat pyramid, 80m sides
but only 15m tall. Called **Iwaya kofun**, two chambers were discovered
inside but occupants not identified. Middle of park is **Prefectural
Museum** containing various excavated items from around Chiba
Prefecture; best place in Kanto to see lots of pottery and *haniwa* tomb
figurines. Semi-colonial house we pass near entrance used to sit on
Gakushuin University campus in Tokyo. Two old farmhouses follow.
Closer **Hirano-ke house** was brought from nearby fishing village; next
one, **Mikogami-ke house,** came from mountain village and was built
1779. Park hours 9:00-16:30, X-mon.

Sanrizuka Ex-Imperial Guest House, *Goryo Bokujo Kinen-kan* (9km
S of town, almost along side of airport perimeter). As noted in our intro blurb on
Narita airport, runways now cover what were imperial pasture grounds.
This half-Western half-Japanese guest house was moved to its present site
and opened as museum of sorts, open 9:00-16:30, X-mon. You can get taste of
what it must have been like, looking at old photos of emperor visiting
'ranch', carriage he used, and other memorabilia.

SHIBAYAMA NIOSON TEMPLE (about 7km down road from Sanrizuka) was
founded 781; once as popular as Narita-san, pilgrims came here to pray for
success in business. In old days, it was just another day of walking, but
now everyone rushes and with no bus (can be reached by not-too-frequent

JR bus from Narita stn) or train nearby, Nioson has faded quietly. It carries its age well, and you may find it well worth trek to spend time in quiet nature without anyone around. We visited on overcast day which further muffled sound, covering land with small pockets of mist. Approaching, suddenly we saw temple rising out of mist. Steep mossy stairs lead up to grand **Nio-mon Gate**, its black lacquered guardian Ni-O image reputedly brought over from India. Credited with putting out great fire in old Edo, so is most famous part of temple—even more so than 11-faced kannon figure kept in main hall. Temple's full name is actually Shibayama Kannonkyo-ji, but most folks know it as, simply, Nioson.

This area is also loaded with *kofun,* and you find here **small museum**, *Haniwa Hakubutsu-kan* (9:00-16:30, X-mon), exhibiting items excavated from kofun here; mostly *haniwa* (terra-cotta figures of animals, houses and people) which accompanied rulers into life after. There are almost 1,000 kofun around here, and while most are simple little burial mounds, two most impressive are 88m long **Tono-zuka** and 55m long **Hime-zuka**, both moated, and with many relics intact.

Avid history buffs may find it well worth their while to spend some time at new... **National Museum of Japanese History,** *Kokuritsu Rekishi Minzoku Hakubutsu-kan* at nearby Sakura city. Building up fine research center of antiquities. 2-storey museum occupies site on hill where Sakura Castle once stood. Basic history of Japan is displayed chronologically, using authentic artifacts and scale models of villages. Hours 9:30-16:30 (no entry past 16:00), X-mon. It is 15min walk from Keisei Sakura stn which is 5 stops (15min) from Narita.

Across town from museum (2.8km), while in Sakura, you may want to pass by... **Sakura Juntendo Hospital** Japan's first private hospital, set up in 1843. This classic old building still stands, part of new Juntendo Hospital. Juntendo began as center for Dutch medical studies and hit such high point that sayings of time went 'Nagasaki of West, Sakura of East', east and west referring to Kanto and Kansai.

This pretty much ends our quick tour of Narita. There are many other sites around Boso Peninsula which can be done as day trips out of Tokyo. In back-country mountains of Boso Peninsula at southern tip pointing into Pacific are several hidden hot springs, feudal town of **Ohtaki,** and women ama divers of coastal **Shirahama**, while eastern coast is bow-shaped sandy **Kujukuri-hama**, 99 League Beach stretching for 50km and crowded in summer. From Choshi Point, eastern coastline curves back in, almost reaching Mito City (*see*), one of our entrances to Tohoku.

We leave most of this area to adventurer with lots of time, but have picked out just one more spot for unique day trip...

SAWARA & ITAKO   FEUDAL TOWN AND RIVER RIDES

GETTING THERE: **Sawara** is just 30min JR express from Narita; **Itako** is 3 stops (15min) beyond. If by car, Higashi Kanto Expwy continues past Narita, to end at Sawara I.C., 5km from town, quick 30min drive. From Tokyo, 2hrs by Narita line rail.

SAWARA was depot for rice, soy sauce; boats laden with either used to ply Tone River. Connecting Sawara to Tone River is Onogawa River along which banks are many old buildings reminiscent of days gone by. Stone steps still lead down to river where goods used to be loaded onto boats, and many white, mud-walled kura storehouses flank willow-lined river.

From Sawara stn, take first L and after about 5min walk we come to **Onogawa River**; take your pick of which side to walk along, both are as fun, we went down far side. Pass many interesting stores and workshops, with enough great shots to keep any photog happy along this 700m stretch of old Japan.

At far upstream end on far side is...
House of INO Tadataka (1745-1818), noted geographer-cartographer who lived here until 50 years old. He began map-charting at age 56 when on trip around northern Japan, he charted precise map of Tohoku and southern Hokkaido for shogunate. They were so impressed that they ordered him to make similar map for all Japan. For next 16 years Tadataka took ten separate journeys to all parts of Japan, finally coming up with three maps of different scales. He barely outlived his project, but his maps remained in use until early 1920's. **Memorial Museum** displays his various tools, maps, notes and other memorabilia. House and Museum *no fee*, X-mon.

Nearest bridge is...
Chukei-bashi; standing there facing downstream, L takes you to **Koboriya Honten**, 250-year-old noodle shop, with great handmade soba. Next is bookstore in equally old building. Continue on, and 2nd R leads back to stn. See **large torii** by stn, it leads to **Suwa Shrine** with statue of Tadataka; good cherry viewing. R at Chukei bridge takes you past **Nakamura-ya** grocery store in 190-year-old bldg to Meiji period red brick structure, **Mitsubishi Bank**.

Few kilometers down this road leads to...
KATORI JINGU shrine, 15min bus from Sawara stn (which stops Chukei-bashi, but ask to make sure right one), about 30min walk from Chukei-bashi, or quick on bikes which can be rented at stn for few hundred per hour. Katori Jingu is one of most celebrated shrines in this eastern quarter of Japan. Along with nearby Ikisu and Kashima Jingu shrines, they make up Tokoku Sansha, or Three Great Shrines of Eastern Kingdom. **Ikisu** is about 10km due east and hard to reach; **Kashima** (*follows*) is 30min beyond at end of JR Kashima Line.

Katori has been here for as long as most records go back, long popular with warrior class. 12th century Minamoto Yoritomo and 14th century Ashikaga Takauji among noted warriors to make offerings here. Present structures date to 1700, when Tokugawa shogun Tsunayoshi rebuilt all, basing it on Gongen-zukuri style of Nikko's Toshogu.

From bus stop, up main sakura-lined approach and we soon come to...
So-mon gate, natural light tan color. Next is bright vermilion-lacquered **Ro-mon gate**, behind which **Honden main hall**, black building in sharp contrast to bright gates. Yet, it melds in well with surroundings and it all seems to balance out. *Homutsu-den* **Treasure Hall** (daily 9:00-16:00, ¥300) exhibits various treasures offered here. Tea houses in back offer grand view of this area.

ITAKO is where we get on tiny wooden skiffs for tourist poster **cruise** along flower-lined canals. 6km wide area between Sawara and Itako has several rivers and canals, all branching off Tone River or from Kasumi-ga-ura Lake west of here. Women clad in *kasuri* tie-dyed kimono pole these skiffs thru canals meandering thru rice paddies, especially beautiful in May-June when irises line waterways. Classic run on this tour is called *Suigo Juni-kyo meguri*, 12 Bridges of Suigo, which passes thru most scenic of these canals. Departure point is 5min walk from Itako station, 3 basic courses offered: **'A'** does '12 Bridges' only, in 30min; **'B'** continues to Yota-ura Bridge, 50min; **'C'** circles entire area in 1hr 10min. May-June, all rides are 'C'. Can also get on at *Suisei Shokubutsu-en*, **Botanical Garden** specializing in water plants, which is 25min bus from Sawara or 10min bus from Itako. Boats take 5 people, ¥600-1,000 per head if full load, depending on course; must pay for full boat if not 5 people.

Those who come out here on overnite trip have many inns to choose from. Most of big tourist-oriented ones are in Itako. Sawara has several small ryokan among old houses along Onogawa River, and atmosphere there is more interesting. Most are moderate rate.

KASUMI-GA-URA LAKE, second largest fresh-water lake next to Biwa-ko, popular escape for Tokyo-ites. Long famed for graceful *hobiki-sen*, kite-fishing-boats, with enormous billowing white sails which used to drag nets across lake in early trawler-fishing. With advent of modern fishing boats, they were being edged out till enterprising locals converted to tour cruising. Come here in summer, and once again see graceful craft skimming over lake surface. Visitors may want to base themselves in feudal town of **Tsuchiura** at west end—many old buildings of Edo days; merchant shops, and ex-samurai mansions around old castle grounds. Some sight–seeing boats cross lake bet Itako–Tsuchiura. Town itself worth fun half-day stroll; Tsuchiura on JR Joban Line, 30min beyond Abiko turn off for Narita

KASHIMA, (end of JR Kashima Line, 25min from Sawara), shrine of same name was patronized by famed samurai, enshrined deity is Takemikazuchi-no-mikoto, guardian of warriors. Most structures here date *ca* 1620 when 2nd Tokugawa shogun Hidetada restored it. Under 10min walk from stn. Beyond huge vermillion **Ro-mon Gate,** on R is **Main hall,** giant 2,000-year-old **sacred tree** soaring behind. On left past shrine office is *Homutsu-kan* **Treasure House** (9:00-16:00, ¥300), mostly martial offerings left by passing dignitaries, as Minamoto Yoritomo. Among them, 2.7m/8.5-ft long sword of mid-Nara period. Path leads behind to low-walled compound where archery once practiced. **Mid-May** see yabusame here, mounted and feudal-costumed archers gallop down stretch between next gate and Oku-no-In pavilion, shooting at small targets. Far back is 'bottomless' Mitarashi pond.

For adventurer continuing on, private Kajima Rinkai Tetsudo rail line chugs up-coast, 75min to MITO (p.253); few stops before which is OO-ARAI, port for ferries up to Tomakomai (Nihon Enkai Ferry Co) & Muroran (Higashi Nihon Ferry Co) on Hokkaido.

PERSONAL DATEBOOK: Like any rural corner wandering around Boso Peninsula we come across festivals at almost every town, especially Apr, Aug, Oct. Here are some of major ones, easily reached from Tokyo:

February 3, *Setsubun* bean toss at Narita-san and Sogo Reido, both jammed as hordes vie to catch good luck tokens.

Late Feb-early March, *Plum Blossom* festival at Narita-san Park. Outdoor tea ceremonies, haiku contests every sunday and national holiday in March, leading to–

April 3, traditional dances start off *cherry-blossom* viewing season, leading ...

1st Sun, flower parade,....

8 *Hana-matsuri,* gala fete in temples mark Birthday of Buddha.

Early, *sakura festival* in Tsuchiura, best in castle park, along river in town.

14 *spring festival* Katori Jingu shrine.

May, 3rd Sun, *Takigi Noh* outdoor Noh performance by torch-light, Narita-san

June *iris bloom* best time to boat Itako

July, 7-9, *Gion Festival* of Narita-san temple; great wheeled floats, musicians and large puppet on roof parade town, best 9th.

10-12th more dashi appear in streets of Sawara for great Yasaka Jinja Gion Festival. Again, usually...

Last weekend, dashi at Tsuchiura's Gion Festival.

20-22, *Ama* (Women divers) *Festival* at Nojima-zaki Point, Shirahama; divers go out at nite by torch-lite in thanks to sea. **31**st is Makata Shrine's *summer fete.*

August, 1st wknd Choshi *Port Fete* mikoshi parades on land & sea; fireworks & dancing. Several days around 7th large *Tanabata* Star Fete, dancing Tsuchiura.

16-22, *Dara-dara* Fest Chiba City Shrine.

23-24, *Bon dance* Narita-san.

Sept 2-3, Sogoro Memorial, SogoReido.

23-24, *hadaka-matsuri,* naked-fest, coastal Ohara city; 100s loincloth-clad youths charge around with lanterns, mikoshi.

October, 2nd wknd and Fri preceding, Sawara's dashi reappear on streets for Suwa Jinja's *autumn fest,* 14 floats (10 in summer) parade around town—some of Sawara's floats date back to 1830s.

20, Funabashi Daijingu fete amateur *sumo.*

November is *chrysanthemum season* and great flower shows all month at Narita-san, Sogo Reido, and Sanrizuka.

December 25, for change from usual Xmas fireplace yule log, Narita-san has its grand yearend *goma fire rite.*

*...lying off Tokyo, of which I have read and re-read
of anko or island girls who ...have fair skins and
reddish hair, the result of rubbing it with camellia oil,
the chief product of the island.*
— Sacheverell Sitwell *Bridge of the Brocade Sash*

TOKYO'S SOUTH SEA ISLES

NEW YORK may boast world's longest 'bus-fare' sea voyage (to Staten
Isle), but Tokyo can claim longest intra-city ocean voyage. From downtown to farthest flung island under Tokyo City administration is 145km, 90
miles—halfway to battlefield of Iwojima. Seven isles of Izu (with eighth
never mentioned because inhabited only by monkeys) Oshima and outer six
of Toshima, Nii-jima (Shikine-jima), Kozushima, Miyake-jima, Mikurajima
and Hachijo-jima, stretch from entrance to Tokyo Bay where Oshima's
Mount Mihara beckons frustrated lovers to leap into its smoldering crater,
past isles no more than peaks of sea-floor mountains, Shikine-jima and its
houses of pure pumice and lava stone, to distant Hachijo-jima or #8-Isle,
isle of exiles and pirates, Pitcairn Isle of many Japanese *kabuki* plays.

OSHIMA: Largest, nearest to Tokyo and most popular, isle with its two
main ports of Motomachi and Okada. Population November 1986 was
10,316, as that many evacuated when great eruption-'quake nite of Nov 21
alone blew 2,000,000 tons of ash—and not off top of mount in usual eruption
pattern but from new side vents. Lava flowed to within 200m of Motomachi
and quakes registered Richter-4, with 3 in Tokyo-Yokohama.

Most liners dock at Motomachi's pleasant village, over-niters dock at
more primitive Okada; but weather may cause port switch.

Ship leaves Takeshiba pier, near Hamamatsu-cho JR/monorail stn, nitely 10pm for
OSHIMA; rates steerage ¥2,840 (shoes-off for tatami, blankets available extra), double for
cabin, better cabins up. Arrives OKADA on Oshima Isle 6am; dep → TOKYO 2:50pm-
arr Tokyo 7:10 pm. Air Nihon flies from Haneda am, early pm 3x-daily 40min; return
on turn-around; fare ¥6,550 o.w.; Air Nihon → MIYAKE-JIMA 50min ¥8,210; →
HACHIJO-JIMA 6x-daily, 1hr, ¥11,110. Shorter 2hr daylight hydros from Izu Peninsula:
ATAMI 9:10am → ITO 10am → OSHIMA; addit runs direct ATAMII → OSHIMA 10am,
2:30pm Sept-Nov only; Shimoda 9:20am. Daily liner up from southern isles. Further
info: Tokai Kisen Takeshiba port Tokyo ☎3432-4551.

Cycling: younger Tokyo residents often cycle Oshima, other Izu Isles, rentals
available: if have your own, carry on ship dissembled in carrying bag for few hundred yen,
or as is ¥750 Tokyo → Oshima, less other short legs, Tokyo → Hachijo-jima as is
¥1000, but on fast hydrofoil Izu → isles must be broken down. Bikes can be rented at
Senzu park, also Miyake-jima and Hachijo-jima isles. Circle Oshima half-day, good
surfaces, few cars; best counterclockwise. Don't take bike up volcano, leave it in port, at
inn you will stay at or at restaurant where you lunch, hike to crater and return. Or as we
did, hike volcano—as far as they now permit since eruption—bus → Senzu and rent bike.

Overnite liners arrive early, as did ours. Oshima was something out of
Hiroshige woodblock print. Stars shone brightly, their absence in one area
outlining deep purple void in classical volcano shape. Orange ovals with
black Chinese characters on them bobbed along dock, faintly illuminating in
red outline kimono-clad damsels carrying them. *Anko* girls, as costumed
local belles are known, snatched our bags, heaved them onto entoweled
heads (no tip) and hobbled off down pier to taxi and bus stands. Our bus made
short stopover for connection with boat from Ito on Izu mainland at Okada—town worth
missing—and we returned to bus. On Oshima everything is done by numbers—reach bus
first, you get number and you sit first, even if you stroll off just tell driver you'll be back.

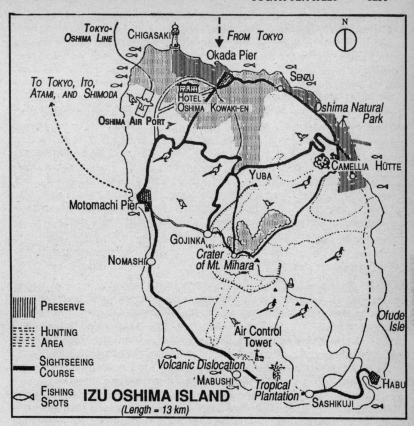

IZU OSHIMA ISLAND
(Length = 13 km)

Main feature of isle is **Mount Mihara**, local tourist literature calls it at 758m world's 3rd tallest island volcano after Etna, Stromboli—but we note Miyake-jima's Oyama volcano to be 814m. Of many routes up volcano bus from either Okada or Motomachi (depending on where boat docks) are easiest. For adventurous souls full walk up from Motomachi recommended: they say it takes 45 minutes but unless you are Olympic marathoner, allow 2 hours with breaks for sightseeing; on clear day look back for country's best view of Fuji. Buy walking stick; there are refreshment houses along way. Lava flow of '86 stopped at very edge of town, now attracts reverse flow of viewers. Old man in small shop about third of way up carves little souvenir *kokeshi* dolls out of native camellia wood. Also sells odd-shaped roots and branches debarked and polished, that make good decorations or ikebana props—but since volcano? Camellia, azalea, rhododendron, hydrangea, mountain cherry flank our route up according to season. One third of trees on isle are *tsubaki*, camellia, of which there are 1,500 varieties here.

About 8th stn up from Motomachi is...
JIZO SHRINE is for easy births which expectant mothers visit. Isle's main industry with tourism is camellia oil, many houses crush oil from seeds by stone press. On sale everywhere, as hair oil, cosmetic and fine tempura deep-fry oil: isle's *meibutsu*.

Bus from Okada stops at steam bath that first gave isle right to claim hot-spring title. Dungeon-like affair and being more of Tokyo Onsen sport type, we passed it up. More appetizing spa is in Motomachi at **Umino-ye** 'Sea-House' overlooking docks, which boasts island's only true hotspring. It stands to reason that live volcano should offer source of natural hot springs but only owner of Umino-ye took trouble to drill well for one. (Others since followed suit). Bathe, dine, rest in clean Japanese room, dine and watch giant sea turtles, small manta rays sport in indoor pool. 180-year-old mamma-turtle may have some eggs ready for hatching as she did when we were there. Food excellent, budget.

By bus or foot, mountain top is reached. On edge of desert of black sand and weird lava rocks, we watched television, sipped tea while our horses were saddled for last leg of journey up to crater. For ¥5,000 'or so' (dicker off season—after 1988 eruption horse trail off limits, now back in business) guide takes you up crater and back, he hangs on to tail. Business was slow, guides lived other side of isle so for little extra they'd take us up and down other side to fishing village of Habu, where we spent nite, good advice.

Crater is less interesting now than before eruptions of '51, '86 when it was deeper and steeper so lovers bought one-way tickets to Oshima to jump in—practice frowned upon by locals as such twosomes usually spent few nites in *ryokan* running up fat tabs before taking plunge. Suicide rate was drastically reduced when shipping company refused one-way tickets to young couples: non-refundable round-trip or nothing. 1954, being popular for foreigners to go native, one romantically-frustrated mixed couple jumped in. Custom hasn't ceased completely, but we hadn't time to wait around. Crater after '86 off limits, reopened '88 with new observatory.

30min of slow rolling gait brought us to crater where we stood in some of fuming blowholes for photos. Over far fringe, en route to Habu great fallen cement *torii*; simple wood one in front, was knocked down by locals during war as American bomber pilots found it excellent marker for Tokyo express run. Route down lava slopes, thru ravines, between great misshapen blobs of lava takes about two hours. Odd strips of yellow vegetation were first signs of plant life just before we entered lush greenery characteristic of vulcan isle—islanders advancing vegetation line in attempt to control erosion.

After tea stop and odd-hundred 'hellos' to children along way in small hamlets, we came upon harbor town of...
HABU, (little affected by big '86 eruption) snuggled in horse-shoe of mountains ringing inlet. Islanders carved gap in wall of crater lake in late Tokugawa period to let in sea, later earn fame in popular song, became locale for famed story *The Izu Dancer*, translated in most modern anthologies. Today, Habu busy in summer with Tokyo yachts for fishing, swimming, sailing.

We made our way thru pleasant narrow alleys on far side of harbor to minshuku Minato-ya where we stayed before to find it converted to mini-**museum** with memorabilia and dolls related to *The Izu Dancer*; *free*. Found 2 minshuku nearby: **Yoshimura** with 4 room, ☎04992-4-0009,` and next door **Habu-ya**, ☎4-0675, both ¥-Bw/2 (¥5,000). Needless to say, supper is several courses of delicious sea food. Dinner for us climaxed with luscious whole lobster each. *Biftekky* available.

Almost 300° around isle and some 1hr30min by bus (we sat up front this time) is...
Senzu Park. Fascinating hike thru, and don't forget to close gate on your way in so animals don't get out. Bikes available. If in flower season Oct-Feb, pedal or walk thru camellia tunnel. Taiwan deer released during war as food now roam island, much increased in number. Said to be good hunting —saw hunters returning with pheasant, no deer. Released Taiwan monkeys few years back—smaller, more playful than native—thriving.

SOUTH SEA ISLES   1237

Thru maze of woodland paths we hiked to long beautiful beach of coal black sand. (Only other such black beach we know is in south Wakayama). We crossed this and it ended in cave in great lump of lava, cave shrine to 7th century Buddhist ascetic En-no Gyoja. Eerie place, damp and foreboding, natural stone altar, wall lined with miniature stone shrine houses. Deathly silence hung over all, waves outside could not be heard within.

OUTER ISLES

WITH DAWN we headed for isles beyond. JTB long listed seven isles of Izu as Oshima and outer sextet Toshima, Nii-jima, Kozushima, Miyake-jima, Mikurajima and Hachijo-jima. But Shikine-jima our destination, situated between Nii-jima and Kozushima, population 900, was then evidently unknown to JTB. Numbering may be off as Nii-jima and Shikine were once one; or because Hachijo being so far out was not counted thus just called Hachi- or #8. Popularity with young lady tourists for its famous outdoor baths has restored Shikine to septet: Hachijo is again #8. While lovely liner now plies route, we made our way down quay to tub that made *African Queen* look like luxury cruiser: *Chomatsu Maru*–MS Long Pine.

We hopped aboard with two girl passengers...aged engine coughed, crewmen pushed, we were off. As we left inlet, crewmen bowed to seaman's shrine and said their prayers. We asked where cabin was. Salty old captain just grinned.
"But we were told there would be nice warm cabin."
"Oh, that's on regular big boat," he smiled. "...we're not regular big boat...sea's too.rough today for them."
As beautiful Oshima Isle sank from view beyond horizon, our hearts sank with it.

But it wouldn't be fair to recount our voyage on *SS Long Pine,* for you take regular liner, *Camellia*, with comfy cabin-lounge where you eat your picnic lunches (packed in advance by your inn), drinking in seascape and glimpses of almost Polynesian life on jewel-like beaches at which ship stops on its mail-freight-passenger run. Only sugarloaf monkey-isle is by-passed, for no one sends them mail—but you can see them.
Warning: summer hols has each isle crowded with over 5,000 youths!

Run takes between 2 and 4 hours depending upon boat or winds to...
SHIKINE-JIMA where we berthed in lovely fisher harbor and were taken to simple minshuku. Most houses here are made of volcanic pumice stones which islanders also shape into characteristic boat-shaped cakes for export to bathrooms of world. We bathed that evening in **Junata Onsen** hot spring discharging into volcanic stone pools at beach edge, cooled to near perfection from near-boiling temperature by lapping waves of sea—one of 2 *kai-chu* (in sea) onsen here noted for healing powers of their natorium. We had written ahead to junior-hi English teacher HAYAKAWA Hideo, welcomed us in superb English, got us lovely budget-rate inn then invited us to his school, as he assures us he would gladly do for our readers. ✍ c/o **Shikine-jima Junior High School**, Izu, Tokyo-to; students hope for pen pals.

TILT: Boats most everyday: continue on down → MIYAKE-JIMA or return → Oshima. Ships go on down → HACHIJO-JIMA, regularly scheduled run is overniter dep Tokyo Hinode pier abt 10pm arr MIYAKE-JIMA 5am, Tokyo city limits 8:30; daily, X-tue **Rates**: o.w. ¥4,280 (Jul-Aug ¥5,980) public 2nd class; also 2-bunk cabin available. Popular short time run is liner or plane → HACHIJO and on return leg, take off → SHIMODA on Izu Peninsula; or vice versa. Ships connect with other isles from Shimoda with increased new services: Mon, thur, sat 9:20am → KOZUSHIMA (3hrs) then → SHIKINE-JIMA (60min) and NII-JIMA (1hr). These link with ships plying isles out of Tokyo; latest scheds, **Tokai Kisen** ☎3432-4551.

For more rushed, frequent flights → OSHIMA, → MIYAKE-JIMA (¥8,210 o.w.), HACHIJO-JIMA (¥11,110 o.w.) pair with o.w. sea trip enable you see Hachijo in half-day: leave HINODE PIER 10:10pm, arr HACHIJO next 8:20am. See bull fight and local dances. Fly back: ret flights 13:50, 15:25, 17:15 arrriving Tokyo within 1hr; or ship → Hachijo, arr 8:20am and leave 9:30am next day. Alternately, plane both ways, nite on isle.

Unfortunately, no plane Oshima–Hachijo-jima to do all in one trip. But could change as Air Nihon now flies Tokyo-Oshima.

NII-JIMA, (ten minutes boat ride), was joined to Shikine until great quake of early Edo era. First thing you'll see are numerous funny-face sculptures, *moyai-zo*. Much of year surf pounds beach at foot of cliffs as this is where warm Black Current hits cold Pacific. In summer isle swarms with average of 5,000 surfers, hang-gliders. Nii-jima Ginza is like movie-set of false-front shanties, which off-season gives it appearance of ghost town.

WHERE TO STAY: Several minshuku *only*, advance reservation necessary in school holiday, also advised in off-season as most closed.

MIYAKE-JIMA, (180km from Tokyo and 35km around), is another new summer playground—good scuba diving, good fishing year-round. Bird sanctuary with over 250 varieties complicates US Navy plan to build practice nite-landing strip for carrier planes at southwestern Ako on lava bed from disastrous 1983 eruption. This buried 40 houses and 3-storey primary school, left moonscape of burned out forests, lost lake which evaporated. *Ten-en* (natural) *sauna*, in which you squat, *clothes on* or you'll get burned by 70-80° steam jets. Other blows Meiji 7 (1874), 1940 left lava fields, 1962 whole new hill. Rent bike at inn, pedal around ruins to lovely **Ako beaches** of (S→N) Sabigahama, Imazaki, Yukehama noted for weird rock formations and pastures at foot of 814m **Mt Oyama**. Other fine beaches ring isle. Sunsets pure Polynesia.

KAMITSUKI in north has camp, minshuku, and oldest house in isles— feudal government office of early 1500s: to be open to public, eventually, check.

Facing is...
OSHAKU SHRINE, built 1516, displays ancient mirrors of same era. Cycle or hike (5-6hrs) from here across center of isle over HACHODAIRA for good view of other isles, along west side of mountain to **Sonei Bokujo** (cow pasture), alt 400m, fresh milk available, on to AKO.

GETTING THERE: Via our island hop as above, or direct **Tokai Kisen** ☎(03)-3432-4551 liner from Hinode pier daily X-tue, 10pm, ¥4,280 deck, 2nd class double, also cabins; or **Air Nihon** (☎3780-7777) from Haneda, 2x-daily, 50min ¥8,210. Airport at SE corner of isle. Bicycles available, isle flat, easy pedal.

CHOPSTICKS: Isle specialty is 'stamina' *Umigamé Ryori*, sea-turtle dinner, best at **Yashi-en**. Flappers run 1-1.5mtr; dinner is sashimi red meat, soup, *nabe*-stew and red-meat steaks on which side dish of fat is delicacy: ¥4,000 per.

WHERE TO STAY: Hotels, plenty of minshuku, campsites. School hols rsvtn advised. Miyake-jima **Kanko Kyokai** (Tourist Association) ☎04994-6-1144 can arrange.

HACHIJO-JIMA is 108 mountainous km^2 (42mi^2) with 2 volcanic peaks which our plane (7x daily Air Nihon from Tokyo-Haneda, ¥11,110 o.w.) lands at foot of higher of pair, 860m/2,800ft Hachijo-Fuji, in saddle formed by lava flow. Some 13,000 folks live simple lives even by rural Japanese standards. Many are fishermen using South Sea outrigger canoes. Island gardeners do good export of ornamental plants to mainland. Products of isle of interest to us are coral jewelry and *Kihachijo*, taffeta-like silk textiles in black and yellow combinations, available in bolts for kimono or made up into simple but lovely handbags, men's ties and such: expensive, but worth it. Old weaver says one *tan* or bolt long enough for kimono, 12-13m, now takes 10 days, in old days took 2—no mention of hours worked then.

Roads, buses since our first edition, when bus drivers wore motorcyclist abdominal supports, now improved. Alas, can no longer hire pack-oxen.

WHERE TO STAY: Dozens of budget inns, minshuku rates, camps on E coast; **Hachijo View Hotel** on hillside, W- & J- styles, ☎(04996)-2-3221, ¥-Tw/2 as all non-minshuku. **Hotel Royal** (☎2-0441) ¥-Tw/2; special local dish giant shrimp, stone crab. **Marushima**, in woods, J, ☎2-2411; and **Nangoku Onsen Hotel** ☎8-0211, J-. **Hachijo Onsen Hotel** (☎7-0111) natural baths, one of which is outdoor *roten-buro*, all rooms overlook sea; some W-, but best buy is J-room with private hot-spring bath, or one of two private honeymoon bungalows. Oddly, kitchen specialty is not seafood but Genghis Khan pork BBQ, served in your room or terrace or beneath banana trees in ornamental plant greenhouse. Live-wire staff run place in typical J- family fashion. They'll help you hire car (¥5,000 per hr, or taxi ¥20,000 per 5hrs) or *baiku* motorbike (Mobil ☎2-0148, ¥2,300 per hr) or bicycle (¥550 1-hr, ¥2,050 all day), or take bus to see weavers or men-divers (diving profession female monopoly elsewhere) who go in nude after abalone, or flying-fishermen—who don't fly, they catch flying fish.

He can also arrange for bull-*sumo*, South Seas variety bull fight pits two bulls against each other until one backs down or draws blood. Bouts short but exciting and true sport (not gaudy sacrifice) for loser, as in human-*sumo*, rarely suffers injury (*See* also SHIKOKU, p.694). Often done for tourists so ask about this or other forthcoming programs.

Folk dancing and thrilling variety of *Hachijo-taiko* drum beating round out isle offerings and should be asked for. If not already scheduled, modest fees for special show are worth it and vary, of course, according to number of spectators. Good bar beneath banana trees.

AOGA-SHIMA, south of Hachijo-jima, less island than block of sheer cliffs rising straight out of sea. Single monthly Hachijo-jima steamer goes on down, its school declares holiday so kids can pile into outrigger canoes, launched from steep cliffs like lifeboats from mother ship, and help unload. Hundred island families live by making charcoal, raising cattle in scrub-jungle. Houses are thatched on stilts like Stone Age buildings in earliest Japanese pictures. Hospitable, negotiate—stay is whole month, no escape.

OGASAWARA ISLANDS, *still farther S...*

GETTING THERE: Island-hopping as above or direct from Tokyo by **Ogasawara Kaiun** ☎(03)-3451-5171 in 28hrs for ¥22,140 2nd cl (add 10% Jul-Aug), every 5-6 days from Takeshiba pier (WWF-J says enquire of them re whale watching)...

CHICHI-JIMA isle off which President Bush was shot down March '44 — actually his first 'visit' to Tokyo. Once there you can go **whale watching** (only **Feb–Apr**) on boat, 2hrs, abt ¥4,000 each if running, or charter boat ¥35,000 with knowledgeable J-spkg guide: phone in J- Mr Shibuya or his replacement at Ogasawara village office-*mura yakuba*, ☎04998-2-2823, or prearrange in Tokyo **Ogasawara Kaiun** Ship Co, ☎(03)-3451-5171. He can also arrange minshuku or inn to your budget; advises avoid Golden Week. 1,000 cats here and another horde on HAHA-JIMA descended of house pets left behind by US Occupation, threaten easy-going local rare birds.

Farther S is...

IO-JIMA, better known to US marines by older spelling IWOJIMA where on its tragic sands and flag-raising mount, we finally, near 24° N Lat, reach southern limits of Metropolitan Tokyo.

> Are these artists trying to tell us that
> just as Tokyo has no spiritual center, no agora,
> there is nothing at the core of Tokyo's spirit?
> —Nick Palevsky, *The New Republic*

MUSEUMS & GALLERIES

THAT ATTITUDE of impermanence which has long characterized Edo personality has naturally not fostered any urge to lay things away for posterity. City has been spared great losses of land to cemeteries, but similarly it has been deficient in museums. This is no great loss as it first seems and is perhaps some gain. Edoko have always wanted to possess art or curiosities themselves, if even only temporarily. They have always had insatiable curiosity, as their love of theater shows. While great mausolea-cum-museums may be lacking, there are numerous commercial galleries which exhibit for sale, or (as with department stores) for self-promotion or paid admission, or (as with individually-, company- or sect-owned halls) out of some inner urge to educate, communicate or simply show off.

Following is partial survey of main permanent or rotating collection display centers, from *Kokuritsu Bijutsukan,* **National Museum of Art** to specialized hobby houses. Besides these lanes off Ginza, Roppongi, Omote Sando and Shinjuku are lined with small galleries, every department store has galleries and exhibit halls. Our '64 edition was probably first comprehensive list of museums of Tokyo and we have since been updated by other publications, including specialized museum-only guides in both languages.

English dailies list special shows at department stores, private galleries or museums as also *Tokyo Journal.* Several big museums on drawing boards.

FINE ARTS ORIENTAL & WESTERN

CLOSED MONDAYS unless otherwise noted; most close last few days of year and first few; additional closings noted X-, etc; admission to most ¥300-500, special exhibits more; hours mostly 10-5, most deny entry 30min before closing.

Asakura Sculpture Museum, *Asakura Choso-kan,* 9-4 on sat,sun, mon, ¥300; studio of ASAKURA Fumio (1883-1964) displays his works, *see* UENO, p1181.

Azabu Museum of Arts & Crafts, *Bijutsu Kogeikan,* 4-6-9 Roppongi, ☎5474-1371; rotating modern art-crafts.

Bridgestone Gallery Kyobashi 1-10-1 Ginza; ☎3563-0241, private coll of tire tycoon Ishibashi (literally Stone-Bridge): art by Occidental masters, contemporary Japanese; special exhibits of modern artists. Corner Ginza–Yaesu-dori; 10-5:30.

Gajoen Hotel coll, Shimo Meguro 1-8-1, ☎3491-0111; 1200 murals etc, fabulous '30s J-art ex-hotel's decor; ¥500, *see* p11••.

Gotoh Museum of Art, bit far in Kaminoge 3-9-25 on Oimachi line, ☎3703-0661; var rare Orient antiques.

Grand Gallery 11fl Odakyu DS Shinjuku stn; ☎3342-1111; fine loan shows o'seas & local, mostly modern.

Hara Museum, Kita-Shinagawa 4-7-25, ☎3445-0651; art deco pvt home shows modern art, holography; top shop; 11-4:30.

Idemitsu Collection—EUROPE, CHINA *Idemitsu Bijutsukan* 3-1-1 Marunouchi, ☎3213-9402 top Imper'l Th'ter opp Palace.

Idemitsu Collection—MIDDLE EAST CULTURE CENTER, *Chukinto Bunka Sentah,* HIH Prince Mikasa, director; out JR line from Tokyo or Kanda stns to 8th stn, Mitaka, p1154, bus or taxi to nr Int'l Christian University; ☎(0422)-32-7111.

See also ARCHAEOLOGY–YUASA COLL.

Isetan Art Museum in Isetan DS annex 8fl, Shinjuku stn; ☎3352-1111; fine loan shows mostly modern.

Ishiguro Collection, Mid-East archaeo-art; Crescent Bldg (opp Tokyo Prince H), Shiba Koen 1-8-20, ☎3436-3211; w/ Crescent French restn't & Mikazuki Gall'y for its clients; advise pre-dinner, interested welcome; smaller objects, all exquisite.

Itabashi Museum 5-34-27 Itabashi, ☎3979-3251; loan shows artcrafts.

Matsuoka Museum 5-22-10 Shinbashi, nr Onarimon, ☎3437-2787; fair China, Persia, India; fine J lacquer boxes.

Mid East Art & Archaeology *see* above Idemitsu & Ishiguro colls; foll Tenri Gal, Toyama Mus, West Asian Archae Mus.

Mitsukoshi Mus in their Shinjuku DS, ☎3354-1111, X-mon; hi-profile market-oriented shows, usually top W- (Dali, etc).

Modern Art National Museum, Kitanomaru Koen-3, Chiyoda-ku facing Palace; ☎3214-2561; 10-5, ¥400, p1139.

Modern Crafts Nat'l Mus 1-Kitanomaru Koen ☎3211-7781; p1119, 10-5.

National Mus, *Kokuritsu Bijutsukan,* Ueno Koen, Taito-ku, ☎3822-1111; heart of Ueno Park museum complex, Oriental bldg (L), Jpn (Ctr), Horyuji Hall treasures beyond those still in Nara monastery, *see* p.357; (thur only). Nt'l Treasures, ICA, espec J-archaeology; top book, museum shop; ¥-var; 9-4:30. *See* UENO, p1167.

New Otani Art Mus, in Hotel Garden Court; 10-6 X-mon; ¥500, hotel guest free

Nezu Mus, Omote Sando; ☎3400-2536, rare antiquities of Japan & Orient, in great garden; 9:30-4:30, ¥500, p1159.

Ohta *Kinen Bijutsu-kan* **Memorial Mus**; nr Omote Sando subway stn; 10:30-17:30, X-25th to end month, ¥500, huge coll ukiyoe woodblock prints, p1159.

Ohara Espace Minami Aoyama 5-7-17 in basement Ohara bldg, ☎3499-1200; irregular shows pvt coll (esp pre-Inca txtls) of flower-master and major aesthetician OHARA Houn (*see* KOBE p594).

Okura Museum *Okura Shukokan*; ☎3583-0781; Far East art from man who made world's best porcelain, built Orient's best hotel; opp Okura Hotel nr Toranomon back US Embassy; 10-4, ¥400.

Riccar Museum Ginza 6-2-3, ☎3571-3254 fabulous collection Ukiyoe woodblock prints (fine shops for on street facing), 2 blocks E, back, of Imperial Hotel.

Saitama Modern Art Museum suburban Urawa City 9-30-1 Tokiwa; ☎(048)-824-0111; fine loan shows mostly modern, import & domestic theme mixes.

Seibu [aka Sezon] Art Museum adjoins Ikebukuro Seibu DS, 1-2fls; top antique, modern art from o'seas museums, fine presentation, top art book-catalog shop.

Seibu Art Forum & Gallery in DS 6fl, Ikebukuro stn; ☎5992-8920; top artists of sculpture, painting, artcrafts; art goods floor; X-tues.

Setagaya Art Museum Kinuta Koen 1-2, Setagaya-ku, ☎3415-6011; major loan shows [British Museum, Japonisme, etc]; occasional music shows out front.

Sogetsu Museum of Sogetsu coll, rotating exhibits; in **Sogetsu Kaikan** Aoyama-dori, exquisite Tange-designed HQ of Sogetsu school of ikebana, p1159.

Spiral Garden 'art space' often theater, often gallery; Spiral Bldg, Omote Sando; deco & avant garde; ☎3498-1171, free.

Station Gallery in Tokyo's great old JR main stn Marunouchi, great space for loan shows, photos on antique brick walls.

Suntory Museum, *Suntory Bijutsukan,* special show on single theme as, *Summer in Old Edo, Sea & Jpn Life,* specific area of Japan, etc: consistently best presented, best organized, most beautiful shows in town. Owned, housed by Suntory Whisky, 5th fl ☎3470-1073; Akasaka-mitsuke opp hotels Otani, A-Prince, A-Tokyu; .

Teien Metropolitam Art Museum var shows in one of world's most beautiful art deco buildings, exquisite detail prime exhibit itself; Minato-ku Shirokanedai 5-21-9, 5min walk E JR loop Meguro stn E exit; ☎3443-0201; 10-6, X-2d, 4th wed, day after hol, exhibit prep; ¥-var.

Tenri Gallery Tenri Kyokan Bldg, Kanda Nishiki-cho 1-9; ☎3292-7025, excerpts from main Collection (*see* TENRI p352); Asian antiquities, archaeo-, fine- & folk arts; mon-fri 10-6, sat, sun –4pm.

Tobu DS Gallery DS 8fl; ☎3981-2211; loan shows, domestic & import.

Toguri Museum of Art pvt collection 1,500+ Oriental ceramics, show on rotation by theme; 1-11-3 Shoto, Shibuya, ☎3465-0070; 10-5:30, ¥1,000.

Tokyo Metropolitan Art Mus Ueno Park ☎3823-6921, rotating modern.

Tomioka Tessai Museum, paintings by -in Omori, ☎3771-1054; 10-4, ¥300.

Touko Museum of Contemporary Art 3-5-28 Kita Aoyama, ☎3404-1791, loan shows, mostly imports. (Closed for renovation till '95)

Toyama Museum *Toyama Kinenkan* in suburban Saitama-ken, Kawajima-machi Shiroinuma 675; go Ikebukuro Tobu-Tojo line 40min to Kawabiki stn/ JR Takasaki line from Ueno 50min to Okegawa stn; then taxi 5x-mtr, or bus to Ushigaya-do; ☎(0492)-97-0007. Fine pvt coll J-, Chin, W-Asia, Inca art. ¥500, 10-4:30, X-Jul 21-Aug 31; Dec 21-Feb-end. See p1223.

West Asian Archaeology Museum, *Kodai Orient Hakubutsukan* in Sunshine City, subway stn before Ikebukuro, rear elevator to 5fl; overview standing exhibit with special rotations; ¥-var. *See* p1161. ☎3989-3491.

Western Art National Museum, *Kokokuritsu Seiyo Bijutsukan,* 7-7 Ueno Koen, Taito-ku; ☎3828-5131, of museum complex in UENO PARK, p1167, built on

remnant of fabled Matsukata collection of European art, return of which took top diplomatic talks for several years postwar. Yamanote loop el or Ginza yellow or Shibuya blue subway to Ueno; -4:30.

Yamatane Museum of Art, Nihonbashi Kabuto-cho 7-12,☎3669-4056

Yokoyama Taikan *Kinen-kan* Memorial, Ueno, midway Nezu–Yushima stns across from Shinobazu Pond; in house Taikan (1868-1958) spent his last 50 yrs. Garden, house, collected paintings, pottery, together well worth visit: 10-4, X-tue, wed; ¥300; p1184.

SPECIALIZED EXHIBITS

Archaeological Collection, *Meiji Daigaku Kokogaku Chinretsu-kan,* China (prehistory to T'ang), J- (Jomon to Kofun); w/ Criminal Mus (*see*) in Meiji Univ nr JR Chuo line Ochanomizu stn; free, daily -4:30, X-Univ, Nat hols, noon sat; p1173.

Archaeological Collection–Yuasa Heihachiro Memorial, International Xtian Univ in Mitaka;p1154. Nr Idémitsu Mid East Coll (*see*), record and site of most important ongoing excavation in Japan; ☎(0422)-33-3340; 10-5, X-sun, hol; free.

Asakusa Kogei-kan, museum of local craftsmen of Sh'tamachi, 2nd fl Tokyo Electric svce ctr; daily X-sun, hol, pm sat, no fee. Kappabashi-dori Asakusa, p1200.

Baseball Hall of Fame, Museum 1-3-61 Koraku, Bunkyo-ku; ☎3811-3600; in Tokyo Dome just outside Yamate loop at Suidobashi stn or Korakuen stop Marunouchi red subway; p1174.

Bicycle Culture Center Akasaka opp US Embassy police box, exhibits history, intro to Japan 1870, info on bike travel.

Bunkamura (Culture-village), Dogen-zaka 2-24-1, ☎3477-9111, exhibit-performance complex of Tokyu DS/Stn Shibuya N-side Shibuya JR/subway Stn; w/ Seibu makes promising complex, true to its name.

Calligraphy Museum 1-3 Tokiwadai, Itabashi-ku; ☎3965-9611;*see* UENO p1179

Canada Embassy: exhibit itself; p1159.

Cartoons: antique art form; count 'em, 3--
-**Modern C'toon Library** *Gendai Manga Toshokan*: Yurakucho subway line to Edogawabashi stn, 5min walk; 12-7pm, X tue, fri; ☎3203-6523.

-**Kawasaki City Mus,** ☎(044)754-4500, Fgn & J, 9:30-5, thur-8, X-mon.

-**Omiya City Cartoon Art Museum** in hometown of first modern cartoonist Racten-Kitazawa, founder of *Tokyo Puck* 1903; Tobu Narita line, Omiya Koen stn, 5min wlk; 9-4, X-mon; ☎(048)663-1541.

Children's Hall, *Tokyo-to Jido Kaikan,* 2nd signal E of Shibuya stn; ☎3409-6361 -museum for children, w/ elaborate robots, car driving, airplane piloting simulators, regional dolls of world, designed to aid boys and girls gain knowledge of scientific technology and enrich international cultural sentiments; 9-4pm, X-2nd mon. *See* AND BRING YOUR KIDS, p162.

Classic Cars *see* HATA MUSEUM of–

Clock Museum,*Daimyo Tokei Haku-butsu-kan,* in interesting old house 100+ assorted timepieces of Edo era. (¥300, 9-4; X-all Jul-Sep & end Dec–mid-Jan), p1183.

Communication Museum Otemachi 2-3-1, Chiyoda-ku; ☎3244-6811; history of post, telephone and telegraph in Japan; first Morse telegraph key presented by Commodore Matthew C Perry 1854, most other significant 'firsts' since; 250,000 postage stamps incl all J-; nr Iidabashi stn Yamate loop el. (9-4)

Criminal Museum, *Meiji Daigaku Keiji Hakubutsu-kan,* Edo era and modern police gear; with Archaeology Museum (*above*) in Meiji University nr JR Chuo line Ochanomizu stn; free, daily 10-4:30 X-Univ, Nat hols, noon sat; p1173.

Designers' Space Open Gallery Hanae Mori bldg 1fl terrace, Omote-sando, ☎3587-2007; 12-7pm, X-sun, hol; p1158.

Doll Mus, *Togyoku Ningyo no Kuni,* Iwatsuki, Tobu Noda line, ☎(0487)-56-llll immense coll J-, foreign, dolls & puppets;

live puppet shows, kids see how dolls are made, make own on spot; 10-7, X-tue.

Drum Museum, Asakusa opp police box, Kokusai-dori st block below Asakusa View hotel in Nishi Asakusa-ten bldg 4fl; 10-5, X-mon, tue, ¥200; world & J- drums made by major festival drum maker, major reference library of books & videos p1200.

Earthquake Memorial Museum N of Kokugikan Sumo arena Asakusa; p1205.

Edo-Tokyo Outdoor Museum of old urban architecture: relocated Edo era Shitamachi & Meiji era W-style Yamanote bldgs; Koganei Park *1992*.

Folk Architecture Garden, *Minka-en*; 20-odd classic houses, rural kabuki stage; E- & J-material. Newer, better preserved than Osaka's architecture coll. Odakyu line Shinjuku to Mukogaoka then 15min walk, 9:30-4 X-mon, ¥300, ☎(044) 922-2181.

Folkcraft Museum, *Mingei-kan*; post-war modern after traditional J-storehouse; changing show J-, East Asian folk items, furniture, ceramics, house goods, textiles; periodic special import shows European, South American, African or Asian folk art. Little unity to exhibits; small unexciting coll folk prints, folksy items designed for tourists on sale. KURASHIKI p628 better, not worth special trip unless special show; Komaba Todai-mae stn Inokashira line 3rd stn from Shibuya, short walk; or taxi from Shibuya p1156; ☎3467-4527; 10-4, X-all Jan, Feb, Aug; ¥700. Just as interesting collection for sale nr, to E of Shimbashi stn at **Takumi Folkcraft Shop**.

Forty-seven Ronin Museum Sengaku-ji temple, Shinagawa; *see text* p1161.

Furniture Museum, *Kagu no Hakubutsukan* on Harumi Pier nr International Trade Center; displays antique Occidental and Oriental furniture, *see* SH'TAMACHI-TSUKIJI, p1213; 10-4, X-wed.

Hata Museum of Classic Cars from JR Ueno stn Keihin-Tohoku or Shinkansen to Omiya stn, out E exit 7min walk S; ☎(048)-648-0065; ¥1,200, 11am-8pm all year, 90 foreign classics 1900-'70s; '50s-style ¥-T diner -10pm.

Hearn (Lafcadio) Library, housed in Irish Embassy (he was Irish-Greek), nr Yasukuni shrine; ☎3263-0695 for appt.

Industrial Safety Mus, *Sangyo Anzen Kenkyujo*, Shiba 5-35-4, ☎3455-3202; at Tamachi stn Yamate loop el, 2nd stn from Shimbashi, before Shinagawa; X-sat, sun.

Kite Museum, *Tako-no Hakubutsukan*, behind Nihonbashi Tokyu DS, Taimeikan bldg 5fl, ☎3275-2704; 11-5, X-sun, hol; ¥100, kites of Japan & world.

Kurita Bijutsukan, museum of J-pottery 10-5, X-end 3 days Dec-¥500. *see* TSUKIJI p1208; Kurita's personal collection mostly Nabeshima, Kakiemon, Imari porcelains from Kyushu; (main museum in Ashikaga City, Tochigi Pref in several buildings-full; 2hr drive; by rail, take private Tobu Isezaki line from Asakusa to Ashikaga 1hr 40min and 20min bus, or cab 1.5x-mtr).

Laforet Museum Akasaka in Akasaka Twin Towers, var modern commercial arts; 11-8, ¥300; also live, *see* STAGE, follows.

Laforet Museum Espace in Laforet part 2, Harajuku stn, ☎3486-9891; 11-8, ¥300 Modern or in modern taste.

Maritime Museum 3-1 Higashi Yashio, Shinagawa-ku, ☎3528-1111; *see* p1138.

Matsushita P/N, Human Electronics Environment for computer nuts or kids, OA or future home gadgetry, by makers of National, Panasonic etc, owners of MCI. Hands-on educational fun, ☎5568-0461; E of Shimbashi stn; no-X 11am-10pm, *free*.

Meiji Memorial Picture Gallery *Meiji Kinenkan*, Yoyogi Kamizono-cho, Shibuya; ☎3379-5511, pictorial history & mementos of Meiji Era, 1867-1912, which saw Emperor Meiji lead Japan into modern international community of nations: in Meiji Park, (*see* WEST SIDE, p1159) 9-4.

Middle East Art & Archaeology *see* Fine Arts above: Idemitsu and Ishiguro collections, Tenri Gallery, West Asia....

Miyagi Michio Memorial Hall, 35 Nakamachi, Shinjuku-ku; ☎3269-0208; mementoes (1894-1956) of blind primary modern virtuoso of koto who greatly expanded its scope w/ Korean import; wed, sat, #1 & 3 sun (10-4), free E-earphone; short walk NE JR Chuo el Idabashi stn.

Modern Literature Museum, *Kindai Bungaku-kan*, in grand European style mansion of Marquis Maeda, donated to Tokyo University. *See* WESTSIDE p1156; nr Folkcraft Museum, Komaba stn from Shibuya, Komaba 4-3-55, ☎3468-4181

Paper Museum 1-1-8 Horifune, Kita-ku; ☎3911-3545, fascinating exhibits endless varieties of *washi* (Japanese paper), paper products:parasols to firemen's clothes, utensils for paper making, English books on Japanese paper: Oji-machi in Kita-ku nr

Oji stn on Omiya line, taxi 4x-mtr from center; 10-4; X-sun, national hols, p1166.

Photo Museum, temporarily till '93 nr Ebisu stn showing 5,000 pix by top local & world photogs, move to permanent quarters nearby in '93 to display 10,000 pix, movies and videos; ☎3280-0031.

Planetarium & Gotoh Museum of Astronomy, 2-21-12 Shibuya, Shibuya-ku; ☎3407-7409.

Planetarium, Sunshine Building Ikebukuro; ☎3989-3466; 11-5 mon-fri, -7 sat, sun, hol; ¥1400, kids ¥700; p1161.

Radio Broadcasting Museum, 2-1-1 Atago, Minato-ku; ☎3433-5211, atop Atagoyama Hill (up 86 17th century stone steps) site of Japan's first radio transmitter, and where last young hot-bloods held out against surrender 1945 committing mass suicide, and where US Forces Far East Network long had main transmitter during US Occupation & after; 9:30-4:30; p1163.

Science Museum, 2-1 Kitanomaru Koen, Chiyoda-ku; ☎3212-8471, lavish funds provide this 6-storey handsome modern bldg displays chronicling Japan's technological advances: working rocket models, robots, models of earthquake resistant architecture, magic hands to handle radioactive, model buildings for future techno complexes and endless push-button educational exhibits. Nippon Electric Co has computer on which you design own tours pushing buttons indicating purpose of trip, budget, preferred locale, desired effect: suggestion flashes on panel. Imperial Palace grounds next to Budo-kan; 9-4:30; p1139.

Shinjuku Historical Museum, nr Marunouchi-subway Yotsuya 3-chome stn, ☎3359-3741; 9-5, ¥200; archaeology to feudal shops, literary (Hearniana etc).

Shitamachi Museum 9:30-4:30, ¥200, X-12/29-1/3; SE corner Shinobazu pond, Ueno. Dedicated to preserving historic *Shitamachi*-'downtown', p1168, *see also* EDO-TOKYO MUSEUM.

Sony Building, Harumi St W of Ginza nr Yurakucho stn; showplace for Sony, fascinating *free* gallery of future products.

Sumo Museum *see* p1204; in Kokugikan Sumo Arena nr Kuramae stop of Tokyo Met subway grey line, ☎3622-0366 –hall of fame of singularly J- spectator sport: costumes, portraits, statues, palm prints, other exotica associated with its history.

During tournament for audience only; otherwise OK, X-sat, sun, hol.

Sword Mus, *To-ken Hakubutsu-kan*, 100s swords, suits of armor incl 30 NT. 9-4pm, ¥500. W of Meiji Park Shrine Treasure house or few min walk of Sangu-bashi stn Odakyu rail from Shinjuku, ☎3379-1386.

Telecommunications-Postal Service Museum Ote-machi 2-2-2, Chiyoda-ku, ☎3241-8080; 9-4.

Theater Museum, Tsubouchi Memorial of Waseda Univ 1-6-1 Nishi Waseda, Shinjuku-ku; ☎3203-4141, theater items of world; mainly superb collection J-costumes, masks, props, set in reproduct'n Shakespeare theater. Within Waseda University grounds, Totsuka; 9-4; p1164.

Tobacco & Salt Museum, *Tabako to Shio no Hakubutsu-kan*; on Koen-dori up from Shibuya stn; 10-6; ¥100. Changing, permanent exhibits on art around tobacco & salt (check papers); tobacco-salt gov't monopolies till privatized 1980s, p1156.

TOGO Heihachiro Memorial in Togo Shrine (*see* p1159); small museum of admiral's belongings; must for naval buffs.

Toy Museum, *Nihon Gangu Shiryokan* bus from Asakusa to Kiyokawa 2-chome, ☎3874-5133; 9:30-5, X-tue, wed, ¥200, J-toys of great tin era of '50s-70s.

Toy Museum, worldwide collection, JR Nakano stn 8min walk to Arai 2-12-10 ☎3387-5461, 10:30-5, X-fri, ¥500

Transportation Mus 1-25 Kanda Suda-cho, Chiyoda-ku, located downtown-side of Chuo line el, block from Manseibashi; ☎3251-8481. Preserves historic locomotives, equipment tracing history of J-RRs since introduction in 1872 (Chinese zodiac Year of Iron Horse) to Shinkansen, world's fastest train, first Tokyo–Osaka, now spreading. RR men adventurous, and this was medieval center of intellectual samurai, is now also center of publishing, and it borders main college quarter—all types noted for their tastes in good solid food—alleys facing townwards from museum within triangle formed by two streets are lined with some of town's tastiest ¥-B–T small traditional restaurants; p1175.

War Mus *Yushukan* in Yasukuni Shrine to War Dead (p.1143); no E- except on kamikaze corps 'peace' hypocrisy.

Woodblock Prints : top moderns annual College Women's Assoc show at Tokyo American Club, ☎3444-2167, late Oct.

*life is a lying dream, he only wakes
who casts this world aside......*
— Seami, *Atsumori*

ON STAGE

TOKYO is one city where bad weather should not prove anything but minor inconvenience to visitors. Main attraction, almost exclusive offering of metropolis, is its fabulous theater. *Kabuki* should best be seen in Tokyo: only *kao-mise*, face-showing, performance of Kyoto in December is worthwhile outside of Tokyo, and Osaka *kabuki* theater might be passed over unless it is only opportunity you have to see this flamboyant stage art.

Noh makes its best and most numerous offerings in Tokyo. Originally Kyoto art, it made its greatest advancement as medium of education for Tokyo warrior class. Democracy inherent in much of its philosophy was not compatible with thought-police state and *noh* was controlled under Tokugawa dynasty, under whom there was some degree of meritocracy but limited to warrior caste. Subsequent police state which fell in 1945 almost totally proscribed *noh*—but, to avoid martyring art subsidized it heavily to obviate reliance on paying public, restricting audience to brain-washed officer class and powerless, aristocratic intelligentsia.

Less traditional arts of girls' reviews and girlie shows, not to be confused, are also best seen in Tokyo. These include famed and fabulous Takarazuka All Girl Opera, and Asakusa strip-tease houses, Lady Sword plays, night club reviews and floor shows and their kimono counterparts in geisha-show restaurants, as well as live music at *minyo-sakaba* (folk-music sake bars) and sheer theatricalism of its streets by nite. (Alas, those longest-in-world chorus lines are gone as also girlie shows of Nichigeki Music Hall) All these are best seen on this great floating revolving stage, modern, timeless Tokyo.

Internationally acclaimed, (locally not so) avant garde *buto* may be seen almost only in Tokyo, rarely Kyoto. What bodes best for whole stage scene is '80s boom in building fine smaller theaters and halls, many by successful manufacturers like Wacoal (ladies' undies), Suntory (whisky to biotech), other building planned.

At Waseda University, start of ride on Arakawa tram (*see* p 1164) is *Tsubouchi Engeki Hakubutsu-kan,* **Theater Museum** in memory of prof Tsubouchi who translated all Shakespeare's works into Japanese. Exhibits on various aspects of Japanese, Asian and Western theater.

PROGRAM INFORMATION, *see* English dailies, especially *Mainichi Daily News* mon special, or monthly magazine *Tokyo Journal*, weekly hotel-handouts *Tour Companion & Tokyo Weekender* (ask at desk if not obvious). *Japan Times* has top theater reviews of notable offerings, usually tue in Entertainment, sometimes saturdays with What's On. Have your hotel desk phone theaters listed below for specifics, except **Kabuki-za** which you phone direct in English ☎3541-3131. **PlayGuide** agencies at which tickets for all theatrical, musical and sports events can be obtained: PlayGuide Building, 1st floor Mitsubishi Denki Show Room, Ginza 2ch-6-4, ☎3561-8821 & 5011; Harajuku ☎3401-9395 till 9pm; Shibuya ☎3462-0011; Shinjuku ☎3352-4080. Branches most dept stores, usualy main floor unless store has theater. Also **Ginza Kyukyodo Ticket Service** till 8pm, no-X, ☎3571-0401. **Japan Times Ticket Ctr**, mail order, ☎3769-4134 M-F 10–17:30, expanding their services, worth trying. Most theaters have ticket booth for others. Basic English often spoken. Hotel desks will handle for you, some travel agents.

KABUKI

ONE OF GREAT performing arts of mankind, noteworthy more for its staging than its literature. It is rare for entire play to be performed (every several years entire *Chushingura*, vendetta of 47, may be performed over entire day, or in parts over several performances)—program usually consists of several fragments, assembled into esthetically balanced multi-course feast for eyes. Language of plays is formal dialect of three centuries ago, even tho play may be but century old, of period when its greatest writers wrote: men like Chikamatsu Monzaemon, usually referred to as 'Shakespeare of Japan'. Language more foreign to modern Japanese than Shakespeare to us, your lack of comprehension of dialogue may well be matched by that of your Japanese neighbor. He, however, is probably theater-buff and knows story (or probably wouldn't be here). You can bring yourself fairly up to his level by buying fine English program, which gives you entire story outline and then details portion being played. Thanks to great stylization and exaggeration of emotion and expression, once you have read story you will usually find it easy to follow action. Usually wireless earphones for rent providing intelligent English running translation, explanatory notes.

Even if you cannot follow story, it is still worth taking in, for costumes, music, action, stage setting and fantastic use of mechanical gadgetry blend into one fabulous surrealistic potpourri of color, cacaphony and continuous motionx (*see* p.56).

Kabuki-za is adventure in itself even without show. It includes several restaurants and bars, frequented by audience during intermissions or when sitting out play-portion they don't care to see. *Tachimiseki* (standing-room), unfortunately do not have access to main area (entering segregated peanut gallery by side-entry) so can't use restaurants. All others do, however, regardless of ticket. Planning meal during main intermission, make sure you reserve in advance at counter indicated by both English and Japanese signs inside to left of main entrance, or miss either food or next play. Top price seats bring waitress to you with menu, your box lunch is served in your seat box (*see* p.1147).

Kabuki runs year around, with three or four different troupes performing at either Kabuki-za, *Kokuritsu Gekijo* (National Theater), Meiji-za, or Shimbashi Embujo, and sometimes one in Asakusa. **Kabuki-za** is main theater, two performances daily from begining month running 25 days straight—except July-August when sometimes mix kabuki and modern drama (hot weather programs traditionally include ghost plays to chill spines, so perhaps include modern plays to chill fervor for theater?). One of other troupes may be performing at another theater simultaneously.

First performance starts about 11 or 11:30am running till about 4pm; PM usually 4:30 or 5 till 10pm or so. 1986 experiments with 3 shows daily promise lower prices, easier access, as almost no one goes for whole show anyway, makes for more efficient use of seats, greater turnover. Usually 4 plays, several acts to main. AM program is entirely different from PM. At **Kabuki-za** you can buy *tachimiseki*, standing room only for one play, enter 'stage door' to L of main entry to truly peanut (4th) gallery, ¥600-1,000, with topside ticket booth in case you want to extend. Regular tix ¥2,000 top balcony, ¥3,500 front balcony (preferred overall view), to ¥7,-15,000 main floor & loges with extra for main floor-side tatami-mat boxes for 4; available **Playguides** other theaters, or thru hotel, or go bit early for limited number sold hour prior performance. Kabuki-za phone ☎3541-8597 for general info in English; box office to rsve seats, all clerks speak E- (pay & pick up ahead) ☎3541-1151. **National** 1x daily, varies noon or 4:30; ¥1,300-7,800.

Introduction to—fine demonstrations dress, tricks etc all June am, pm shows.

Kabuki-za, Chuo-ku, Ginza 4-chome 12-15, ☎3541-3131 or -8597 (English info).
Meiji-za, Chuo-ku, Hamacho 2-chome 31-1, ☎3667-5151.   Hibiya subway line to
Ningyo-cho stn, exit #1, walk 5-min thru old theater area p1206. Rebuilding, X-till 1993.
National Theater, Chiyoda-ku, Hayabusa-cho 4-1, ☎3265-7411.
Shimbashi Embujo, Chuo-ku, Ginza 6-chome 18-2, ☎3541-2211.

NOH (var: No, Nô)

DISCUSSED IN greater detail in INTRODUCTION, p.54. Even older, more
abstract and aristocratic esoteric theater, great literary as well as performing
art, much translated since Ezra Pound rewrote draft translations of late E. F.
Fenollosa. Two outstanding schools, Hosho with their **Suidobashi Noh
Theater**, Kanze with **Kanze Kaikan** are over 500 years old. Numerous
other schools each with its own noh theater, noted *. Each school has sub-
groups that give performances occasionally, principal performers taking part
in one or two main performances monthly.   With major and minor performances, look at *Nohgaku Times* monthly J-circular, shows that there's
some performance almost daily, majors every weekend. Tickets average
¥3-4,000. **Suidobashi Noh Theater** special seats for foreigners, ¥-high,
which budgeteers may forego. National Noh Theater ¥2,000up, mixes
troupes, has school for lesser actors, state financed—all other theaters are
private enterprises.   No mere tourist fossil, Umewaka expounds philosophy
of late master who pioneered introduction overseas, that it spread to
influence as well as be open to influence in order to remain viable living
form. Tradition must stay alive as tradition in spirit as well as in form. 1987
saw premier of latest UMEWAKA, Soraya, 3-year-old daughter by Syrian
mother...will she become first lady noh-pro? '80s saw expanded experiments in noh, support for English plays, translation as well as original.
UMEWAKA Naohiko, son Cellin's classmate, played in E- to rave reviews.

Noh may be seen at:
Ginza Nohgaku-do (own bldg 9fl), Chuo-ku, Ginza 6 chome-5-15, ☎3571-0197.
Hosho* Suidobashi Nohgaku-do, Bunkyo-ku, Hongo 1ch-5-9, ☎3811-4843.
Kanze* Kaikan, Shibuya-ku, Shoto 1ch-16-4, ☎3469-5241.
Kita* Roppeita Noh-butai, Shinagawa, Kami-Osaki 4ch-6-9, ☎3491-7773.
National Noh Theater, Shibuya-ku, Sendagaya 4ch-18-1, ☎3423-1331.
Tessen-kai Nohgaku Kennshu-jo, Minami Aoyama 4ch-21-29, ☎3401-2285.
Umewaka* Nohgaku-do, Nakano-ku, Higashi Nakano 2ch-16-4, ☎3363-7748.
Yarai* Nohgaku-do, 60 Yarai-cho, Kagurazaka Shinjuku, ☎3268-7311.
—Kamakura Noh Butai in Kamakura, ☎(0467)-22-5557.

Watch daily papers, *TJ*, especially for *Takigi Noh*, lit by real torchlight, late Aug in
Senso-ji temple at Asakusa (p.1189); late Sept in Shinjuku Gyoen-Park (p.1152); varies
1st-2nd week Oct, on special stage **Hibiya City** nr Uchisaiwai-cho subway, outdoors,
but if rain few days later at nearby theater; (☎3595-0295); ¥3,-4,000.

BUNRAKU

REFERS TO school of puppetry developed to its best in Osaka, uses gigantic
puppets manipulated on stage each by 3 puppeteers: one for head and right
arm, one for body and left arm, one for legs. Master puppeteer will be
gaudily dressed in direct proportion to his ability to bring puppet to life and
distract your attention from puppeteers.   Other two dress in black with mask
like little man in kabuki who isn't there either. Puppet eyes, mouths, hands
move, facial expressions also effected by gimmicks (*see* p.55).

Declining in its home town of Osaka (new National Theater there may encourage
revival), it has made steady comeback in Tokyo, where its new main theater now in
National Theater complex. Also occasionally in **Mitsukoshi DS** little theater, and
Shimbashi Embujo. Check papers or **Playguides**—and if on boards, don't miss it.

BUGAKU
STATELY, HIGHLY charged court ballet, costumes as flamboyant as *kabuki*, masks wilder than *noh*. Oldest theater in Japan, origins in 8-9th century China, India, Persia, Cambodia, other sources. Past century preserved in Imperial Court. Music alone called *Gagaku*. Also performed in Osaka, Nara, Kyoto, Miyafima.. (*See* p.51).

Performance Apr & Oct **Imperial Music Hall**, Imperial Palace Garden, *see* p.1140, also INTRODUCTION–ON STAGE (p.50). If Court performance off, public show usual, watch *Tokyo Journal*—also for **National Theater** dates. Also **Meiji Shrine May 3** at 10am & **Nov 1**, 10am; **Yasukuni Shrine Apr 23**, 1pm. Gagaku practice at **Onoterusaki Shrine**, Taito-ku Shitaya 2-13-14, ☎3872-5514 , monthly 6th, 7:30pm, free. For other cities *see* local ON STAGE.

FOLK THEATER
FREQUENTLY STAGED here as are Korean & Chinese. For *kagura*, folk theater, *see* DATEBOOKs, watch dailies for *Japan Folkloric Dance Group* (Eng sched ☎3582-9171). Korean rarely advertised due local prejudices, ask Korean restaurants. Chinese performed by visiting troupes from either China, advertised. *Geijitsu-sai*, Culture Week of **Nov 3** sees special performances of all forms and special assembly of folk troupes from all parts of nation, with month previous seeing city-wide warm-ups in many theatrical forms vying for final consideration for annual awards: DATEBOOK.

REVUES
FEATURING ROCKETTE-TYPE lines of beautiful girls, once world's grandest have almost become extinct since Nichigeki (now Mullion Bldg) and Kokusai (now Asakusa View Hotel) theaters succumbed to developers' wrecking balls. Koma Dancers (Shinjuku), most recent casualty; but theater still puts on regular grand musicals in old flamboyant style; Japanese movies share program as in prewar Broadway houses. Famed Takarazuka girls have two-part programs; one-half Japanese in lively tempo, other Western dancing-pseudo opera. Former usually earlier half of each show, excellent, but latter, tho main attraction to young and middleage gals (mommas and daughters, but not together) who weep profusely at gay-90s melodrama, usually too saccharine for occidental tastes (high school drama club quality at best, but great stage effects) except for you theater buffs eager to see how our classics get staged.

Revues may be seen at:
Koma Theater, Kabuki-cho 1-ch 19-1, Shinjuku, ☎3202-0131; showtimes 11:30, 5.
Takarazuka Theater, Yuraku-cho 1ch-1-3, ☎3591-1711; daily 5:30, Sat-Sun noonish, extra performance; ¥2,500top. Share bill with first-run movie a la classical B'way formula (Occupation vet on nostalgia tour recognizes old **Ernie Pyle** Theater).

GEISHA DANCES
PREDECESSORS of reviews, Spring and Autumn, *see* DATEBOOK. Main *Asakusa Odori*, **Kabuki-za** late April; *Azuma Odori* (classic synonym for Tokyo) **Shinbashi Embujo** late May. Private party-scale on Evening Tours at **Matsubaya** (☎3874-9401) in YOSHIWARA, antique red light town (*see* p.1186), or drop in direct about 9ish for drink and show (¥2,000), or sukiyaki dinner and show (¥7,700+). Geisha-Oiran parade in Spring (3rd weekend May) and autumn Asakusa festivals.

MUSIC HALLS
PRESENT GIRLIE shows, strip and burlie. Alas, Nichigeki Music Hall, is no more. **Shinjuku Koma Gekijo** now stage-musical/movie formula, above.

DRAMA
WESTERN STYLE, both translations from European languages and original Japanese plays, showing strong resurgence in 80s. 1965 experiment

importing US cast and show took root. Broadway musicals now come regularly—translated or original cast—Japanese *Fiddler on Roof* top record-breaker. *Cats* had own tent theaters built Tokyo, Osaka. Modern Japanese plays were verbose, staging dull, until Gaudi-esque **Nissei Theater** upgraded technique and audiences.

AVANT GARDE
MOSTLY IN Tokyo with numerous small troupes, many holding together from college clubs, taking advantage of rash of excellent, small theaters abuilding in 80-90s. Satellite towns Shibuya, Shinjuku house many. *See programs in TJ.*

ENGLISH LANGUAGE STAGE
LIGHT but variety. Kabuki etc have English by earphone. Kyogen comic noh by Don Kenny, with traditional actors of ancient families. Umewaka Noh school carrying on its crusade to export noh to keep contemporary. English slapstick **Albion Za** satirized life in Japan to both visitor and large Japanese following—successor group, **Za Gaijin** (☎3281-7270). Regular shows. **TIP**-Tokyo International Players perform abt semi-annually, US-UK standard plays.

CONCERTS
IN SOLID diet of symphony to soloists, classic to modern, local and top import. Name performers covered in press, but often not what is most exciting for music-loving visitor: experimental music using traditional Japanese and other Oriental instruments, or mixtures of Oriental-Occidental instruments, forms—often called 'fusion' but not to be confused with modern indistinct pseudo-jazz of same name (which is perhaps better called 'con-fusion'). Mostly Tokyo.

RESIDENTS keep in mind that top-quality imports sell out months in advance to theater-hungry natives, well before major news in newspapers gets published. Avoid disappointment by subscribing to *Forecasts*, fortnitely X-Jul, Aug; one year (20 issues) ¥7,500 incl postage, or 6 mos/16x ¥4,000; also encyclopedic *Directory* of theaters and halls, only ¥1,500; from **International Music Arts** Svce, Nishi Azabu 3ch-21-2, Minato-ku Tokyo 106, ☎3400-3386.
    Subscriber service includes mail order rsvtns at mere 5% svce chge: must for any resident music buff.

TOKYO INTERNATIONAL FILM FESTIVAL late September, from 1988 and long overdue; held in several theaters in Shibuya, expect welcome accent on Asian films as pioneered by frequent NHK TV series. Alas, hotels theaters far apart. We bet it grows into major world event; watch dailies, *TJ* for program details. Amazingly, co-host is Tokuma, country's leading publisher of anti-Jewish books—just who does he deal with in Hollywood and Broadway?

STAGES
Theater critics opened 1992 with snide remarks about theaters being built in every rice field and station plaza, but with no 'software' available except grandmothers doing bon dances. Bodes well for theater revival outstriping classical Genroku era. Expect more modern dance, experimentals, quality fusion experiments and more imports—not to mention, music.
    DIRECTORY follows overleaf —

DIRECTORY

PlayGuides for full, up-to-date lists. Or have Japanese speaker ☎- following:

Asakusa Engei Hall, (rakugo stand-up comics) Asakusa 1-43-12, ☎3841-8126.

Asakusa Kokaido, reviving area's theater tradition; occasional kabuki; ☎3841-8221.

Budokan Kitanomaru Koen 2-3 in outer Palace, ☎3216-0781, monster music events.

Bunkamura (Culture-village) ☎3477-9111 hall complex of Tokyu DS/Stn Shibuya, N-side Shibuya Stn; which with Seibu composes promisiing cultural complex, true to its name.

Geijitsu-za, ☎3591-7633, opp. Imperial Hotel annex (rear).

Ginzaa Saison, ☎3535-0555; Ginza-1, Kyobashi; notably advanced experimental.

Globe-za Shin-Okubo, Isozaki's masterful-fun recreation of Shakespeare classic of 1599; W-theater & experiments in near-perfect acoustics; ☎3360-1151.

Hibiya Kokaido (Public Hall), in Hibiya Park, ☎3591-6388.

Honmoku-tei (rakugo) Ueno 2-6-7, ☎3831-6137.

Haiyu-za, Actors' Theater, Roppongi 4-9-2, ☎470-2880.

Ikebukuro Engeijo (rakugo) Nishi Ikebukuro 1-23-7, ☎3971-4545.

Imperial Theater, Marunouchi 3-1-1, ☎3213-7221.

International House Hall, Roppongi 5-11-16, ☎3470-4611.

Kinikuniya Hall, Shinjuku, ☎3354-0131.

Kosei Nenkin Hall, Banshucho, Shinjuku-ku 5-3-1, ☎3356-1111.

Kyoritsu Hall, Kanda Hitotsubashi, ☎3237-2464.

LaForêt Asakusa, under Asakusa Twin Towers, ☎3582-9255.

" **Museum**, Harajuku, ☎3475-0411.

" **800/500-IKURA**, Mori #39 Azabu-dai, ☎3433-6801.

Metropolitan Art Space, Ikebukuro, great architecture housing 4 halls: for concerts 1,500-seat w/ 8,300-pipe organ; medium 850-seat for ballet, drama, etc; 2 smaller 450 and 300; public *free space* out front.

Mitsukoshi Theater, in Dept Store, Nihonbashi, ☎3ß241-5366, pioneer.

Mokuba-kan (rakugo) Asakusa 2-7-5, ☎3842-0709.

NHK Hall, Shibuya, ☎3465-1111.

Nikkei Hall (Nihon Keizai daily) Ohtemachi 1-9-5, ☎3270-0251.

Nissei Theater, great architecture facing Imperial Hotel rear, ☎3503-3111.

Orchard Hall, 2,159 seat hall of Bunkamura (*see*) in Shibuya; Tokyo Phil home.

Parco, Shibuya Udagawa-cho 15-1, ☎3477-5858. Occasional kabuki (new year).

Puc Puppet, Shibuya Yoyogi 2-12-3, ☎3379-0234.

Seibu Theater, Shibuya Parco (*above*), ☎3477-5858.

Setagaya Art Museum (p.1241), Kinuta Koen 1-2 Setagaya-ku, ☎3415-6011; occasional outdoor concerts out front.

Shinjuku Koma Stadium, Kabuki-cho 1-19-1, ☎3202-8111.

Sogetsu Art Center Hall, Asakusa, ☎3405-0246.

Space Den, mini-stage avant garde J with E-explanation, in Golden Gai, Shinjuku; ☎3208-7498.

Spiral Theater (Wacoal) Minami Aoyama, ☎3498-1171,experimental space, interesting presentations, late show.

Suehiro-tei (rakugo), Shinjuku 3-6-12, ☎3351-2974.

Sunshine Theater, Sunshine 60 skyscraper in Ikebukuro, ☎3987-6345.

Suzumoto Engeijo (rakugo) Ueno 2-7-12, ☎3834-5906.

Suntory Hall Akasaka 1-13-1, ☎3505-1001, fitting number like delights it gives

T-2, avant garde Tenkei troupe nest, Ikebukuro Hikawa-dai, ☎3993-9486.

Takarazuka (revue/movie) Yurakcho1-1-3, backside of Imperial Hotel, ☎3591-1711.

Teikoku (**Imperial**) **Theater**, Chiyoda-ku, Marunouchi 3-1-1, ☎3213-7221.

Theater Cocoon smaller theater (747 seats) of Bunkamura, Shibuya (*see*).

Tokyo Bunka Kaikan (Metropolitan Festival Hall), Ueno Park, ☎3828-2111.

Yamaha Hall, Ginza 7-9-14, ☎3572-3111, especially piano concerts.

Yomiuri Hall, Yurakucho, Sogo Dept Store 7th fl, ☎3231-0551.

For programs above or other halls, see daily newspapers or *Tokyo Journal*.

*....let me boldly state what any
experienced world traveler already knows:
Tokyo is a Great Eating City.*
    —Rick Kennedy *Good Tokyo Restaurants*

CHOPSTICKS

Eᴀᴛ is one thing Edo-ko, or children of Tokyo, have always done well. Kennedy reflects his predecessor first US Ambassador Townsend Harris's interpreter Henry Heusken who wrote in 1855:

> Every day we have excellent very fresh oysters, geese, ducks—open your eyes, be all ears you celebrated gastronomes... true canvasback is served at our table as are quails, wild boar...

Edo-ko still prefer their theater spectacular, geisha flashy, rice-wine baby bottle warm and myriad varieties of exotic food always within hail Any Tokyo-ite has his choice of foods of every land–except perhaps Arab–and often cooked by native chefs. From Indonesian curries, Madrasi soup, Mongol barbecue, borscht and Shanghai style jellyfish to Old English roast beef with ale, and hamburger with milk shake. Edo-ko will frequently mix them all up for full course United Nations feast. As for infinite choice of coffees and teas, only kind not readily available is tasteless American drugstore variety–tho airline coffee is close approximation.

For most tourists, dining in your hotel will be your mainstay simply out of convenience, and their offerings are fabulous if expensive. For tourists especially, Tokyo is nocturnal and your most satisfying tourist adventuring will be done at and after dinner. You will not be able to take Tokyo to your heart unless it gets there thru your stomach.

For flavor of olde Edo and bright lights and color and action and scenes that should have (but for some strange reason have not) inspired new woodblock or genre painters, for that atmosphere you came half way round world to experience, stroll Ginza's Suzuran-dori and nearby alleys of Shimbashi, or subway out to end of line at gay and bright Asakusa. For more classical Japanese atmosphere try garden or geisha restaurants. And for way-out sort of stuff which weirdo magazine articles are made (and regularly at that) there really are restaurants to which octopus or sea-slug as too bourgeois compared with their menus of embalmed bees, pickled pig's foetus, raw snake washed down with glass of blood. Or just some good old-fashioned apeman specialities like monkey and wild boar.

First consideration of those dining out will be, of course, geographic convenience: either to your hotel, or to where you plan to spend your after-dinner hours. Or if shopping, where to lunch or snack convenient to shops —so we suggest places in some itineraries for light lunch. Most dining areas are concentrations not only of restaurants, but of nitespots and shops as well which tend to cluster around and among main hotels or attract new ones, so that shopper or night-crawler always finds good choice of restaurants handy.

Ginza our first area, here refers to maze of streets and alleys W of actual Ginza street (Chuo-dori) between Harumi-dori and Shimbashi, strolling-convenient to Imperial, Ginza Tokyu, Nikko, Dia-Ichi Hotels ringing area.

Shiba-Shimbashi continues on beyond Shimbashi, far side of Dai-Ichi Hotel, strolling-convenient to Dai-Ichi, Nikko, Imperial Hotels and contains numerous tiny alleys with woodblock print atmosphere, lined with small bars and nibbling shops and some fine restaurants.

Roppongi Strip, Iikurazaka–Roppongi, stretches between Shiba Park behind Tokyo Prince Hotel to Roppongi intersection, short taxi ride but too much to walk from Tokyo Prince, and minimal taxi from Okura, Capitol and Otani Hotels. Late Hours.

Akasaka Strip, concentration of nite life, especially late-hours restaurants virtually at foot of Capitol, Otani, ANA, Akasaka Prince Hotels and near Okura.

But by far most fun, most rewarding for culinary adventurer, as much for Garet in past few years as for Jay and Sumi generation ago (and still)...

Shitamachi old Edo downtown, which we think done best as walking tour dropping into eateries for snack-lunch or nomadic course-by-house dinner, so refer to Asakusa and Tsukiji–downtown chapters *preceding*, p1189 —tho our brief NOVELTY DIRECTORY, p.1259–, highlights some.

For those hoping to satisfy particular culinary urge, we follow our geographic coverage with directory of various Japanese and other kitchens.

GINZA

AFTER SUNSET, 'Ginza' refers to checkerboard of narrow streets and alleys W of Ginza Ave between Harumi-dori and Shimbashi. This area is reputed to have highest land values in world, tho Shinjuku may now match: some ¥35,000,000 per square meter ($250,000, £170,000), which breaks down to further absurdity of about ¥2,800,000 or US$20,000 for area under your shoes. And this is only tax assessment value, no land will change hands at this 'give-away' price.

Despite these astronomical land prices and obvious uneconomical use of land–most buildings off main street are still two-storey shanties–budgeteer can find some of cheapest eating of good quality, epicure find full delight. And we note that while declared real estate prices since '64 edition are up 20x (more like 50x market price) dinners in this area rose average fourfold, some posh exceptions 8x. Every street is dotted with little restaurants: here we've chosen one street that has always seemed to have bit of almost any kind of food one might want: located between Ginza Tokyu and Imperial Hotels, thus short stroll from them or minimal taxi from Akasaka hotel area.

SUZURAN-DORI (Lily-of-Valley Street) name given first street west of Ginza Ave, but **Gourmet Alley** may be more apt, for its 4 blocks, starting with 5-chome at Harumi-dori, working S to 8-chome near Shimbashi stn, has about anything from budget to gourmet with tops in Japanese dinners.

Using well-known Ando Cloisonne Store on Harumi-dori as landmark, we find arch across street with English SUZURAN STREET and in Suzuran-dori on R **Munchen Beer Hall**–snacks, Sapporo draft steins, beery type sausage & sandwiches in real beer hall atmosphere. Any place with 'beer hall' or 'beer garden' will have inexpensive dishes to go with *nama-beeru* (draft) or *bin* (bottle), and 'draft' now comes in bottles. Next comes **German Bakery** with wonderful pies. Then modern front, E-sign **Nanbantei** of Kobe for *yakitori*, by stick or dish of 10vars for ¥3,000. Bit further on same R side is **Nakata** *sushi*, excellent, suggest *mori-awase* (mixed plate) ¥1,500up.

Few words about ordering *sushi*. There are two ways to do it. One, sit at counter and just pick or point out what you'd like. This preferred way can get out of fiscal control tho. Other, order by plate of assorted, which come in three prices *nami* (ordinary), *jo* (top), and *tokubetsu* (special), from ¥600 to ¥1500 at cheap places, ¥2,500-¥4,000up at top.

Typical of top Japanese restaurants in downtown Tokyo, most are tiny, having counter and from 4 to 10 tables downstairs, upstairs 4 to 8 small *tatami* rooms. Chef-owner watches over his guests, most of whom are regulars. Appointments having been made in advance (tho not always necessary), he knows just who is coming when. As he cooks, he chats with his guests, cozy personal atmosphere. Many top restaurants in Ginza are offshoots of well-known *itamae-ryoriya* restaurants of Kyoto or Osaka. *Ita-mae* refers to chef's 'board in front' of you: as one Tokyo kabuki star put it early, "they show you back stage and have nerve to take your money".

We cross st btwn flanking branches of Eikoku-ya, fine old tailor for 6-chome...
Bunmei-do famed *castera* cake shop and then run-of-mill Chinese restaurant, opp on L **Ginza Lion Brasserie**, ¥-B, and **O-Edo Tempura** behind old wood-slatted front.
Ton-tsu *kushi-katsu*, moderate, with **Tori-shige** *yakitori* upstairs–but for this suggest novice hold out till **Tori-gin**.
Nakajima, ☎3571-2600, ground floor of its own bldg, last before **Almond**, another top counter-style J-restaurant, dinners from ¥20,000.
Matsukawa with Japanesey front serves budget W- *ton-katsu* pork cutlet.
Pilsen Beer Hall, old-time hangout, Asahi draught, snacks, cheap, good.
Tenkin (English sign) near end of block, R, noted moderate-price *tempura* house.
Hamasaku Honten, ☎3571-2031 (on R), one of best Japanese restaurants; branch next door. Introduced Kansai cookery to Tokyo 60-odd years ago. 9-course dinner ¥26,000.

Ginza 8-chome, is gold mine for it has several of Tokyo's best restaurants...
Maruya tiny *soba* shop at start of block. Best for cold season are hot dishes, budget. (There are some fine *soba* specialty houses such as **Sunaba** in Muromachi; **Yabu** in Ueno nr pond and Kanda nr Transport museum (*see*) ¥500-¥2,100; **Izumo** in Jimbo-cho Kanda book street, famed for taste and setting, all dishes ¥800-¥1,500).
Uemoto (☎3571-3387), first of fine houses, owner-chef trained at famed Tsuruya in Osaka; refined atmosphere, all *tatami* rooms, lunch or 10-course dinner ¥25,000+.
Hamamura, ☎3571-2233 ¥18,000+, tables & chairs downstairs, specialty *nabe* cookery —duck, quail, vegetable and terrapin dinners.
Okuma is across street, ☎3571-0721; small but exquisite; 3 black lacquered tables, counter seats 5; dinners ¥15,000+. Rsve advised.

Countless eateries in many tiny alleyways that cut across adjoining streets...
Tsuyuki, ☎3571-7208, opp Jiro's and Senbikiya, miniscule; only *tendon* ¥800, delicious and filling.
One thing we missed on this street is *yakitori* (meat tidbits skewered and barbecued) and *kamameshi* (paella-type rice dish); while another is *unagi* (eel). But luck is with us as best *yakitori* house is in next block W:
Tori-gin, ☎3571-333, at 5-chome–easiest to find is to enter from Namiki-dori alley by **Ketel's German Restaurant** (fine old-style) back towards Ginza. Actually two separate shops adjoining, easily identified by effusing tantalizing odors of barbecuing chicken. English sign, always packed, turnover quick. *Kamameshi* cooked in old-fashioned individual metal pot with large wooden lid; enough for 2, ¥650-1,000. E-menu.
Isehiro, ☎3571-7295, 7-chome on same street next to Ishi Pharmacy; fine, counter and tables; small room upstairs. Order 'set' 7–8 courses of barbecued tidbits, some w/ soy sauce others just plain salt; incl sashimi, barbecued mom, duck, quail eggs; ¥4,500 per.

Complete dinners at exclusive *tempura* or *sukiyaki* houses, as well as first-class hotels (lower fare in their coffee shops only), range ¥1,000 to ¥5,000 lunch, dinners ¥8,000 to over ¥25,000. Here are: *sukiyaki, tempura, sushi*:

SUKIYAKI
Okahan, conveniently located on Namiki-dori Ginza Nishi 7-6-16, ☎3571-1417. Ranks at top with top rates, dinner ¥25,000up.
Suehiro, popular original US beef house, Ginza 6-11-2 E-side of Ginza behind Matsuzakaya DS, ☎3571-9271; *sukiyaki*, ¥4,000up, char-broil US steak from budget lunch ¥500 (3rd fl), to 300g tenderloin ¥6,000.
Hasejin, started about 130 years ago by present owner's grandfather, among first to serve W-dishes. Unfortunately, original restaurant no longer exists, replaced by one in Iikura-zaka Azabu-dai 3-3-15, ☎3582-7811. Lunch ¥1,000+; dinner ¥5,-10,000.

Zakuro good restaurants for simple Japanese meals, all w/ charming folkcraft decor, clean and well-organized. Beef *mizu-taki* or *shabu-shabu*, *sukiyaki* or *oil-yaki*. Lunch ¥1,500-¥4,000; dinners abt ¥6,800up. Main store upper Ginza, S of Takashimaya DS back entrance, ☎3271-3791; best known is branch opp US Embassy at Akasaka. Another branch in Ginza-Kyobashi, ☎3535-5031, in block S of Bridgestone building.

BUDGET is in all arcades, as in smaller restaurants. Tell by plastic dishes in windows.

TEMPURA
TEMPURA HOUSES abound, of two basic types. Exclusive ones, dealing in seasonal delicacies and specialities, with their own shrimp farms, revolving stages and fancy atmosphere. These serve you at their counters or in special rooms where tempura is cooked especially for you; usually 'cheap' dinner is ¥8,000; most from about ¥12,000up and up. Other is for general public, with modest prices, usually best is their *teishoku* dinner with soup, rice, pickles for about ¥3,000; *tendon* (shrimp tempura on rice) ¥1,200up. These top serve only seasonal delicacies and best shrimp and sea food. Their secret is in oil–mixture of rape seed oil and sesame or whatever 'secret' they use, and that they change it for every party of customers, resulting in light crispy *tempura* we cannot reproduce.

Leaving Imperial Hotel, go out towards Ginza in street before Sotobori-dori, turn R...
Tempachi, ☎3571-0783, one of top *tempura* houses. ¥8,000 to ¥20,000 per person. (While you're on this street, there's Misono steak house, but you might be more interested in Iwashiya, fine place serving sardines in countless ways.)
Ten-ichi, ☎3571-1949, another good *tempura* place, in 6-chome on Namiki-dori just S of Miyuki-dori. One of oldest of these fancy *tempura* houses, building was designed by owner-chef, rabid art collector. Delicious food in pleasant surroundings. Lunch ¥5,000+, dinner ¥7,-12,000.
Further into town are 3 well-known places...
Hana-cho by Meiji-za theater, ☎3666-6271. *Tendon* for ¥3,500, dinners start ¥9,000.
Inagiku, ☎3669-5501, at Kayaba-cho 2-9-8, Nihonbashi has dramatic trap-door stage upon which master chef appears from downstairs in center of circular *tempura* bar Lunch starts ¥7,000, dinner ¥13,000; branch in Keio Plaza Hotel. These places have chairs, but some have pit in floor so you sit comfortably on *tatami* floor, and chef cooks right in front of you, lovely garden open to your back.

SUSHI
In Nishi Ginza is...
Nakata, ☎3571-0063, (open sun) bit cheaper, ¥3,000+.
Near Nikko Hotel is...
Kyubei, Ginza Nishi 5-23, ☎3572-3704, famed for originality, expensive, 20 at counter seats, branch Okura Hotel. Next block E in alley by Watanabe Woodblock shop is tiny **Sushi-sen**, ☎3571-3288; delicious, best go with Japanese as few foreigners go there.

BUDGET SUSHI: E beyond Ginza Tokyu Hotel is Tsukiji Fish Market with loads of *sushi-yas*, inexpensive are those bordering Harumi-dori across from Kabuki-za Theater.
Edo-Gin, Tsukiji 5-1, ☎3543-4401, in alley E of Tokyo Theater. Popular with foreigners. Colorful tiny original shop always crowded, two annexes across street. Safe bet is *nigiri hitori-mae* (one person portion) in beautiful lacquer trays. For best see TSUKIJI —DOWNTOWN, p.1210.

Downtown area has budget Japanese in pretty little places all thru...
Teishoku lunches from ¥750; ¥1,200-¥2,500 includes old-time favorites of *tempura*, *sukiyaki*, *yose-nabe*. Or simple lunches of *soba* noodles ¥450-¥1,000 in ordinary to ¥2,000 in deluxe; *sushi* assorted per order of two pats for ¥150-250 cheap places, way up. Collection of these shops are found in any shopping arcade, and every department store prides itself on its *noren-gai*, gourmet shops of long repute all gathered in one section, sometimes called *aji-no-noren-gai*, referring to noted 'tasty' shops. Walk along any street and you'll see plastic models of real thing in window with price. However, corner of Harumi-dori and Sotobori-dori has cluster of interesting Japanese.

*We mentioned **Tori-gin**, chicken tidbits shop. Across street from **Ketel's** is block full of budget places...*

Owada, on corner of small alley, eel restaurant, branch of chain, order *unagi teishoku.*

Yasu-koı, R of Owada towards Harumi-dori, with picturesque sliding doors draped with *noren* curtain, with large white characters reading oden shop, has vegetables, meats, eggs, fish on bamboo skewers stewing in delicious broth, each ¥70-¥100; just peek over counter and point. Drink sake with this.

Otako, similar shop, is around corner from eel house with similar *noren* over doorway.

At intersection of Ginza and Showa-dori...

Hashi-zen, Shimbashi 1-1-11, ☎3571-2700. Another old *tempura* house budget diners will enjoy knowing about, popularly priced and delicious enough to make most gourmet guide books. Suggest *kakiage* (crispy big one, with mixed seafood), or *teishoku*, ¥2,200; 11:30-8pm.

Up Ginza Street, just across old Shimbashi bridge, now underpass...

Tenkuni on corner of 8-chome, ☎3571-0686. As good as Hashizen with budget prices starting at ¥2,500; great *tendon* lunch, ¥-T.

Hage-ten at Ginza 3-chome, ☎3561-1668, behind Matsushima optical goods store. Rather interesting budget place *tempura* cook comes to your booth with wagon and equipment and cooks for you. Features light course from ¥1,200; 'heavy' ¥10,000. Private *tatami* rooms upstairs dinner ¥5,000up; 11am-2pm, 5-9pm; X-sun.

SHIMBASHI-SHIBA

THIS IS continuation of Downtown Ginza and has two distinct areas. First is extension of Ginza Street, south of Sotobori-dori and west of JR Shimbashi stn; second is down Hibiya-dori to Tokyu Prince Hotel.

Our Shimbashi stroll starts across from Dai-ichi Hotel. On one end of plaza here, is circular building. Look across at big *pachinko* parlor on corner, then to left down into gaily colored area which beckons with its twinkling neons. But first head straight in front on street with *pachinko* parlor (actually second small alley from Sotobori-dori).

Tiny building with giant red paper lantern, willow by door is...

Hanaya, ☎3580-0878, our favorite Japanese sweet shop. For many years, Hanaya was run by retired geisha, whose daughter now manages it, serves customers, taking your order in song and relaying it back by singing part from *kabuki* play, which mentions your dish—easily done in Japanese where there are so many homonyms for punning. But size is not *kabuki*, just 5 tables and two Japanese *tatami* booths. Japanese (especially Tokyo) sweets are sickly-sweet to our taste—as ours are too richly-sweet to theirs. We recommend *fruits mitsumame*, fruit salad with Japanese gelatin, ¥700, or *Shiraume*, which is same with ice cream and banana slices added. Plain vanilla ice cream is called *koriyama* (ice mountain). When she sprinkles sugar (*o-sato*) on dish, with grand, *kabuki*-controlled flourish, she sings "Ato-kara tobi-komu no wa O-sato", translating as "and follows by leaping in love suicide is our heroine O-sato". *Dojoji-no-tsuri gane* (Bell of Dojoji Temple) is sung as she tinkles your change into your hand—*tsuri-gane* means both 'hanging bell' and 'small change'.

Our fondest delight is to stroll these alleys, especially next two parallel to this and away from Dai-ichi Hotel. Enchanting at night with neon signs filling little passageways, lined with tiny stalls serving *sushi*, *yaki-tori*, *oden*, and all kinds of tidbits in some shops so tiny that guests eat standing. But fun it is. Some years back this area was rundown and hoodlums were beginning to destroy free, friendly atmosphere; then local shopkeepers cooperated with each other and police to control things, and once again Shimbashi is safe to stroll and play in, clip-joints having been cleaned out.

Hidden in tiny alleys just beyond is...

Bubu-ya, medieval time machine trapped in back alley. Most exquisitely Japanese (in highest aesthetic sense) restaurant we have come across. Not for tourist who wishes only to observe and say he has been there, but only for aesthete who wishes sublime

experience. We were introduced by KAWAI Takeshi, photographer supreme, whose
office is nearby, and even with his detailed map it took us hour to find it—there is tiny
sign, no light, no indication that it is anything but private house and perhaps abandoned
at that. When we did discover its three-by-one inch name plate, hidden under eaves of
low entrance way, we had to identify our introduction as if we were entering speakeasy
and then, only because they had no one there under prior reservation, could we get in.
There is single counter behind which proprietor master chef and his assistant work,
chatter and gab with customers sitting at four stools facing bar between. For larger
groups of perhaps seven or eight total, there is tiny table-alcove extension of bar.
Flower arrangement is single flower in hanging vase under corner eaves, low spotlight
playing on it, sort of arrangement one reads about in medieval art chronicles—exquisite,
quintessential. Illumination is of candlelight intensity, and enigma to match setting.
You must assure chef "*nandemo tabemasu*" (I eat everything), then just sit back and see
what comes. To begin with, crockery will be selected to fit both food and guest, and
couple will note that his and hers are all different services. Sake is must with this,
karakuchi (dry) preferable here. Food varies according to season and if you or anyone in
your party is Japanese, banter will be light, witty and somewhat at your expense. We
stress–do not go unless you are willing for experience that may be somewhat trying if
not exasperating for anyone not hankering after extreme aesthetic adventure.
☎3431-0901 in J- for mandatory rsve, mention us as reference. Expensive.

AKASAKA STRIP

LIKE TBS (Tokyo Broadcasting System) tower that dominates scene here, TBS building
takes over in culinary field with restaurant **Shido**, ☎3582-5891, reigned over by Shido-
san, chef supreme, whose magic touch was earned thru years of work in kitchens of top
European hotels and restaurants and perfected on his own at former **Maison Shido** and
Hananoki. Combine Shido's art with flair that President Katsura has shown in elegant
decor and table setting which he painstakingly chose in months abroad and we are set for
gastronomic experience. Basement of same building has **Tops**, with hamburgers, toasted
sandwiches deluxe and other snacks; **Saxon** serves only curry dishes with trimmings; and
Zakuro another folk restaurant. Striking resemblance of smartness in decor in all these
places is due to they're all owned by Shido's Katsura.

Akasaka Misono, Akasaka 2-14-31, ☎3583-3389; nearby steak house; room overlooking small garden; not related to other Misono, but similar fare, rather high prices.

Yamano-chaya, up by Capitol, L of back door; fairy-tale setting of 'mountain tea
houses' (as its name translates) set in hillside garden. It's top *unagi* (eel) house; phone
for reservations ☎3581-0585 in Japanese; luncheons from ¥12,000; dinners ¥14,000.

Nearby, towards Nogi-zaka and next R...
Plaza Mikado, which Jean Pearce dubs 'Oriental Trump Tower', full of boutiques,
galleries and good restaurants; Akasaka 2ch-14-44.

Little triangle between Akasaka Detached Palace grounds and moat by New Otani is...
Tamahan, ☎3408-2628, tiny *tonkatsu* (pork cutlet) place, block from Toyokawa Inari
Shrine, set in lovely bamboo garden, has sign in English outside, tiny rooms and
counter. Delicious tenderloin *katsu* (cutlets), ¥1,850; *sirloin-katsu*, ¥1,600. E-menu.

Following street around Palace grounds you'll find...
Kikutei, branch of one of finest Japanese restaurants on Suzuran-dori in Ginza; dinners
¥33,000+; reservations necessary, ☎3408-3029, Moto-akasaka 1-7-18.

SHINJUKU

Kurumaya, ☎3232-0301, Kabuki-cho 2 chome behind (N) Koma stadium opp police
box; no-X till 10pm; lovely J-style house, upper floors kaiseki, basememt art deco with
Zen stone garden, serves 'French kaiseki', nouvel cuisine, by whatever name it's
fabulous; each course based on J- or Chinese w/ Frankified sauce served on progression
of museum quality Arita, Royal Dalton, Danske etc tableware in classical kaiseki taste.
Fixed menu ¥8,-10,-12,000 but choose smaller unless devoted trencherman as very rich.
Rsve advised; chef is formally introduced, as is each course and its china.

Suzuya, ☎3209-4480, two blocks from front of Shinjuku stn. Veritable folkcraft museum with interesting Tudor-type exterior. *Mashiko-yaki* plates are by HAMADA Shoji and textiles by Serisawa, special cherrywood furniture. Budget snack is J-*ocha-zuke* (home-style rice dish w/pickles), mostly Western a la carte (abt ¥1,000), some Thai.

Shinjuku is loaded with good places to eat at all budgets, just roam. Cheaper places have posted menus or plastic samples; posh like Kurumaya look it, no sign of prices.

IIKURA-ZAKA to ROPPONGI

BACK AT Roppongi directly across from U.Goto, florist, in small alley Roppongi 3-13-2, Seryna, ☎3403-6211, Japanese place in modern decor; both table and *tatami*; steaks and beef specialities, menu in English, lovely folk pottery from Mashiko used. Popular is *shabu-shabu* (beef *mizutaki*), ¥8,500+. They even have glass display case with inviting samples of what to expect. A la carte and dinners ¥800+.

From intersect head NW past police box towards Nogi-zaka, fourth alley on R is...
Inakaya, Roppongi 7-8-4, ☎3405-9866; as we say in introduction it's top robatayaki-ya in country, in quality of food and especially price—unless prudent and expert, figure on ¥10,000 each, enough to feed and booze quartet in common robata-ya. But there's no denying their quality. Open 5pm-5am, so one way for budgeteer to swing it is not take hotel one nite and check bags at station locker and gorge here till dawn. Branch Akasaka.

Straying some from Roppongi strip down towards Akasaka strip, from Roppongi head down toward Tameike past Haiyuza Theater and we come to Fukiyoshi-cho bus stop. Little further up and on L we approach famed Akasaka geisha area, with loads of lovely restaurant-inn or private apt-looking buildings. L area to stroll. Here is well-known...
Akahane, ☎3585-3534, wild game restaurant. We first discovered it in our ancient *Anone Magazine* days and wrote about it when it was one of those charming oriental buildings. Alas, it has completely new look, now being inside hotel built on its site. Still well-appointed, but mood is different. Still serve honeyed walnuts with baby bees, barbecued sparrows, broiled quail, and main dish of *Takasho-nabe*, ¥13,000+.

From here, just walk up hill to road leading R to Akasaka driving school, 2nd alley...
Muryoan, ☎3583-5829, vegetarian; lovely quiet surroundings; complete *fucha ryori* (vegetarian meal of dozen or so dishes), or combine this with their *tempura* dinner, ¥8,000+. Rsve necessary. From here, you're not far from Capitol Hotel.

OUTLYING

MOST OF restaurants of note have been covered in novel section, but we list some here that have not been listed and are worth visit, if out of way.
Tsunahachi, delicious *tempura* (choose your own fish from tank) at moderate prices. Has counters just like expensive *tempura* houses; branch in Shinjuku stn bldg, 5th floor; also Matsuya DS on Ginza. *Tempura teishoku* with soup, rice and pickles, ¥1,080. 31-8, 3-chome, Shinjuku, ☎3352-1011.
Genghis Khan unique huge Mongolian tents in garden where guests dine around circular table. Genuine lamb; one of first to feature this type of cookery from ¥2,000. Phone for reservations, ☎3314-0291, Koenji 2-chome, Suginami-ku.

GARDEN RESTAURANTS

ARE FEWER now, but our chosen top trio each represent certain type: **Hannya-en**, luxury dining in elegant fashion; **Chinzan-so** largest, most beautifully landscaped and easiest to go to with varied menu from ¥-T–¥-L; **Happo-en** smaller and more personal (with owner's collection of *bonsai* potted trees on view), and which is also from reasonable ¥3,000-up now.

How would you like to rent public garden for yourself after gates close to public? It's custom here for parks to do catering for wedding receptions, class reunions or just plain moon viewing. So we cover these briefly, too.

Chinzan-so, largest, 17-acre garden built by Meiji era statesman, further improved by baron, greatly reconstructed post-war. Now unbelievably beautiful oasis in bustling Tokyo. Stroll before or after dinner is must to properly appreciate landscape of rolling 'hills', suggesting deep ravines, and enhanced by 1,000-year-old pagoda. Seasonal attractions include 1,000s of fireflies released nitely in June; country fair *ennichi* recaptured with goldfish scooping, candy and toy booths and plant stalls; maple viewing in fall. Suggest *wafu* (J- style) lunch ¥3,500+; or J- style barbecue ¥6,000+; meals in J- rooms (Rsves) ¥15,000+, ☎3943-1111, 2-10-8 Sekiguchi, Bunkyo-ku. (*See* p.1164).

Hannya-en's garden is not as large; but more lavish. Garden is beautifully kept, architecture exciting and interiors sumptuous. Formerly estate of one of powerful feudal lords of Kyushu, not having suffered destruction during war, it gives us picture of extravagance of Tokugawa period. We see fabulous old buildings—one guest house brought all from Nara and assembled for visit of Emperor Meiji, another old *noh* stage, still used. Each room is appointed to carry out special theme. Ultimate in Japanese dinners can be enjoyed here for about ¥38,000 for which Geisha entertainment is also included. Reservations necessary, ☎3441-1256, Shiba, Shirogane-dai 2-20-10.

Happo-en larger private garden, 100s of *bonsai* dwarf trees on display, 100s of years old. Elegant *kaiseki*, ¥6,500+; Japanese *makuno-uchi* lunch ¥2,000+; 1-1-6 Shirokanedai ☎3443-3111. (Branch at Ginza Nishi 6-chome 4.)

Horikiri-en most charming of public gardens. Lovely in May, loveliest in June and July when iris for which it is famous are in bloom. Here you can see bridge paths that artist OGATA Korin painted among hundreds of purple iris. Tiny huts in garden, rent for ¥800 1-4pm, ¥1,300 5:30-9pm. Take your own lunch or order thru **Isogai**, ☎3691-0339, for meals ¥2,000+. Located in Katsushika-ku, taxi from Monami Senju on subway Hibiya line; or Keisei Line from Ueno stn to Horikiri-en stn.

Rikugi-en Garden up N at Hon-Komagome, is rated best among older gardens (lain out in late 1600's). Huts rented in two sessions: 9am-12pm and 12:30-4pm; ¥4,000 for each room. Garden open to public daily 9am-4:30pm. Dining reservation necessary, ☎3941-2222, crowded in spring and autumn.

THEATER RESTAURANTS

TIME-HONORED geisha party is best, but because of complications and prices, contact with geisha in Tokyo is best left to guided tours. If private geisha party is must for you, we suggest it for Kyoto where it is easier to arrange (fewer Japanese expense-accounters competing) and held in more traditional atmosphere anyway. It is more that anything setting that makes geisha party, and Kyoto has settings. But if Kyoto is out, head for Asakusa —where most of old woodblock prints of geisha were made. However, there are several restaurants which provide entertainment along with dinner. Most elaborate being grand *oiran* (queen bee of geisha house) show presenting her large retinue of geisha as she sizes up prospective customer for evening. But for us *minyo sakaba* (folk song *sake* wine shops) hit spot: **Oiwake**, Nishi-Asakusa 3-28, ☎3843-4092. 'Supper club' for working class and local residents, who go there to enjoy songs and dances from their native prefectures, along with their local *ji-sake* or beer—informal and friendly. Watch your waitress quick-change and become star on stage. You may even be called upon to sing and dance. Unless you're heavy drinker, you'll have lots of fun fairly inexpensively; beer usually ¥600, *sake* ¥500 per *choshi* (small bottle); *sashimi* ¥1,800+, full entree *nabe-mono* ¥3,500+, and a la carte.

Oiran Show:

Matsubaya: *Oiran*, top geisha of Edo, in elaborate hairdo and kimono with sleeves so heavy they are carried by assistants, screens candidates (someone from audience) for her favors tonite. Also folk dances. Excellent show 7pm (Japanese) and 9:10pm (English) is included in ¥7,950 *sukiyaki* or *tempura* dinner, which starts 8pm. Show & drink only ¥1,500-2,000; (included in nite tour); ☎3872-1937, 4-33-1 Senzoku, Asakusa, rsve.

Folk Dances

Mokuba-kan near Asakusa Kannon Temple near Nishi Sando Street; at *Minyo Sakaba* (*see* ASAKUSA, p.1196).

Furusato, in 800-year-old farmhouse of unusual Shirakawa construction, which we visited in Samurai Offbeat, with steep slanting roof, set up in Shibuya, features country cuisine in rustic setting for elderly, unadventurous; slightly expensive, lunch ¥2,000+; dinner ¥8,500+ plus svce chge 15%. Open 11:30-14:00, 17:30-22:00; X-sun, hol; Aobadai 3-4-1, Meguro-ku, ☎3463-2310. *See* WEST, p.1156.

OKINAWAN RESTAURANTS: With their tradition of entertainment received kick-off to their renaissance from movie *Tea House of the August moon* in late '50s. We stress 'renaissance' and 'comeback' for they are not new to Japan scene as they are origin of geisha, having introduced her from Okinawa in 16th century, and her traditional instrument, *samisen* (banjo-like with cat's belly stretched over body as resonator) is refinement of Okinawan *jamisen* (which uses snake skin). Okinawan food has somewhat heavier body than Japanese with, like its music, ever so slight tendency toward Korean flavoring. However, Japanese taste and Japanization of Okinawa have brought food here closer to plainer local.

Shima-no-hito, ☎3350-5098, Shinjuku 2-13-7, home cooking, a la carte ¥500+.

Miyarabi, ☎3261-3453, owned by Ms Reiko, head of Kwansen Ryu School Okinawan dance, serves Okinawan pork dishes as specialty; top dinner of 8 courses about ¥5,000 including dance presentation. Located nr Yasukuni Shrine 2nd block in from Hitokushi-zaka busstop between Kudanshita and Ichigaya.

KOREAN Infinite, ubiquitous, but highly recommended are...
Kusa-no-ie, Azabu-juban, ni-no-hashi (#2) bridge. Dinner ¥7,000+ for 2; a la carte ¥600+; ☎3455-8356.

Senei, Azabu-juban, ichi-no-hashi (#1) bridge. Course min 4, ¥8000+; a la carte ¥600+; ☎3452-1714.

IKEBUKURO has many, and we've never hit bad one yet in almost 40 years.

FRENCH Numerous, from **Maxim**'s, **Tour d'Argent** down, but our favorite is...
Crescent, Shiba-koen 1-8-20, ☎3436-3211; L 11:30-14:30 ¥4,500, D 17:30-22:30 ¥15,000up; X-sun Jul-Aug only; opp Tokyo Prince hotel and Daimon stn subway Asakusa line. Finest French-a la-Japonaise served for nostalgia buffs in recreated Meiji era brick building with grand dining room, and each small (private by rsvtn) room different theme atmosphere complete with furnishings and table settings of its own. Basement bar, snacks can be ordered. No one else can match owner ISHIGURO Kojiro's exquisite taste. For atmosphere-plus-palate we have always ranked this uncontested No.I W-style restaurant. Go early [pre-6pm] and see his antiquities gallery (shop, 4th fl) and ask to see private Ishiguro Collection of Near Eastern ancient art, all small but all eye-treasures, secreted away upstairs behind vault doors in superb private museum.

NOVEL
ANGLER Ise-gen specializes in *anko-nabe* (*anko*, according to Webster's is 'angler', looks like mammoth catfish with loads of antennae, and like catfish lies partly 'buried on bottom' growing 3 to 5 ft/1-1.8m in length). J- generally don't consider this ugly monster fit for humans, Ise-gen one of few to serve it. Cleaned and cut in cubes, you'd never know what it came from: cooked on charcoal before you, in soup min 2, ¥2,500. Two blocks from Transport'n Museum, Kanda Suda-cho 1-ll-l, ☎3251-1229.

EEL Chikuyotei Honten in Shimbashi, one of best restaurants serving this delicacy. Unlike most *unagi* (eel) shops that serve only various *unagi* dishes, serves fish *sashimi*, regular soups and seasonal salads, limiting *unagi* to entree *shira-yaki* charcoal-broil with salt only, and *kabayaki* charcoal broil in soy-base sauce. Lovely *sukiya*-style building; beautiful pottery and lacquerware almost as important as food itself; serve on lustrous individual raised tray, rather than at table. 7 courses from ¥10,000. Rsve only. Ginza 8-chome, ☎3542-0787, block E of Showa-dori. 11:30-2pm, 4:30-8pm; X-sun, hol.

Kandagawa Honten perhaps best eel house in town, lovely Meiji era wood home, pvt rms, 5-8pm only, rsve ☎3251-5031; p.1172 nr Kanda Myojin shrine and Akihabara.

Miyagawa Tsukiji, another of our favorites; next to Tsukiji Post Office. *Una-ju* simple box lunch ¥1,500, dinner ¥3,000+; 11am-2pm, 5-8:30pm, X-sat, ☎3541-1292.

FISH **Rikyu** Whoever heard of cooking in paper pots? They do here at Rikyu, for specialty is about 60 different types of fish in *kami-nabe* cooked in 14in-square pots made of hand-made *washi* paper; formula by owner keeps it from burning. Dinner of *zenzai* (antipasto), *kami-nabe* (chicken, clams, 3 or 4 different fish and various vegetables in soup), rice, pickles and fruit. Dinners ¥10,000, open 12-11pm. Reservations necessary, 2-2-7 Yanagibashi, Taito-ku, ☎3851-5075.

LOACH For dash of fish course we stop at **Komagata Dojo**, 1-7-12, Asakusa, Komagata-cho (☎3842-4001), for *dojo-nabe*, ¥1,100, slim little loach fish are cooked in *tofu* (bean curd cakes) by putting live fish in soup with curd squares and bringing to boil slowly, causing fish to burrow into cooler curd to escape heat, only to be cooked when it, too, reaches boiling point. Open lunch till 9pm, X-3rd tue.

ROBATAYAKI **Inakaya,** *see* Roppongi, p.1257; open 5pm-5am; also branch in Akasaka 3-12-7, foot of Capitol Hotel, ☎3586-3054, open 5-11pm. Excellent but hotel-expensive, worth every yen, did for plebian robatayaki what Paris did for starving peasants' frogs' legs; budgeteers find fine cheap robata-ya in low-down areas.

SARDINE **Iwashiya** large menu lists only *iwashi* (sardines). Try their specialities, *sashimi, shioyaki* (charcoal broiled), even sardine burgers, or old standby *tempura*; about ¥700. From 12-2pm lunchtime special *miso* soup, rice, pickles and one of many sardine dishes (differs daily) for ¥1,000. Popular with office workers, Nishi-Ginza, 7-chome, block in from express highway. Open eves 5-8:30pm, X-sun, hol, ☎3571-3000.

WHALE **Kujira-ya** translates to 'whale house' and only that is served there. Dishes are results of headmaster of Hattori Advanced Cooking School's efforts to make former postwar poor-man's food, *kujira*, interesting and delectable. Small, ordinary restaurant with walls covered with all kinds of whaling pictures and artifacts. Try *tempura*-like *kara-age* (¥1,050) or *Geijisukhan-nabe* (¥1,900), his adaptation of Mongolian barbecue mutton dish. Budget, popular with office workers. No longer kills whales, has store-house of frozen meat. Sakae-dori 1-1, ☎3461-9145, few min walk from Shibuya stn.

GAME **Momonji-ya**, 10-2-chome Ryogoku, across Ryogoku Bridge, ☎3631-5596. Hoary house started over 260 years ago when only 'barbarians' ate meat, disguised boar as *yama-kujira* (mountain whale). Owner Yoshida is 9th generation. Served here **in season** are *inoshishi* (wild boar) *sukiyaki*, about ¥3,800; *shika* (deer), *tanuki* (badger), *kuma* (bear) and *saru* (monkey). Butcher shop next door: try deer salami sausages.

HORSE MEAT **Minoya,** ☎3631-0748, reminds of scenes from samurai movies of old Edo, with its large *tatami* room. Enjoy *sakura-nabe* (horse meat & vegetables) or *buta-nabe* (pork & vegetables), both ¥1,200, cook your own *nabe* over old-fashioned charcoal braziers. Across Shin-ohashi bridge in Koto-ku, 2-19-9 Morishita-cho.

SNAKE **Bunkyu-do** is one of many snake restaurants. In Ueno, Opposite Ueno Matsuzakaya Department Store, few doors from Ginza towards Yamate el tracks. Window full of poisonous vipers, harmless snakes, and *kanpo-yaku* (Chinese medicines) such as dried monkeys' heads, sea horses, eight-eyed eels, herbs, bears' livers. Try their one-week treatment of dried silver-fox tongue brewed with white bark of mulberry which is good for high blood pressure; for headache try dried embryo of deer or broiled monkey head at ¥20,000+ per. Snake bar and restaurant towards back of shop, snake wine special three-year-old rice brandy in which vipers have been pickled.

VEGETARIAN

Tsukiji Tamura one of best known old-line *kaiseki* restaurants. Lunch ¥6000+; dinner ¥8,000+. Lunch starts 12pm and dinner starts 5:30; X-sun. Tsukiji 2-12-11, reservations necessary, ☎3541-2591/2. *See* TEMPLE FOOD, facing

BUDGET DINING

¥-PILGRIM TIP, true for all cities but surprisingly so for rich modern Tokyo: search out pushcarts. Usually around outer loop stations, but some of best and oldest are off Ginza at E-end of Yurakucho stn, or opp Dai-Ichi Hotel under tracks—old favorites of Jay 35 years ago as of Garet and pals now.

Cater to late 'working' or 'bibing' salarymen, once hangout for journalists in newspaper-row formerly centered here; still some, so, good, cheap and safe in all ways, nothing not well-cooked; just think of it as gourmet version of New York hot dog or kebab pushcarts—and whatever happened to those luscious oyster and clam carts in Greenwich Village, but here no raw food is allowed to be served in non-permanent eatery.

NATURAL & TEMPLE FOOD RESTAURANTS

DOWNTOWN MINATO-KU

Tofuya Akasaka 3-5-2, San Akasaka-biru 1F, ☎3582-1028, 11:30-13:30, 17:00-23:00, X-sat, sun, hol. Tofu cookery, extremely reasonable prices, misc dishes ¥100-450, teishoku ¥600, complete full meal ¥800.

Muryo-an *fucha-ryori* Chinese temple cuisine, Akasaka 6-9-17, ☎3583-5829, ¥8,000up

Daigo in Seisho-ji temple garden, lovely small place featuring *shojin ryori* as prepared for priests and nuns. Partake here in this lovely restful environment, ¥11,000+. Rsve necessary 2-3 days ahead ☎3431-0811; noon-3pm, 5-9pm, X-thur; Atago 2-4-2.

SETAGAYA-KU

Many natural food restaurants in Shimokitazawa area, few mins from Shimokitazawa Stn on Inokashira line out of Shibuya:

Ashun Kitazawa 32-26-2, Shimokitazawa credit bldg 2F; ☎3465-7653; 16:00-01:00 (sat, sun 14:00-01:00) X-1st, 3rd wed. Indian dishes w/ brown rice, whole-wheat chappatti; most dishes ¥500.

Goodie: Kitazawa 3-22-11, ☎3466-0090, 12:30-21:00; desserts & drinks, under ¥500.

Alicia Kitazawa 2-9-23, Daini Suzuki Biru, 2F; ☎3485-3681; 11:00-21:30, X-tue.

Gu Kitazawa 2-26-8, ☎3485-2187, 11:00-24:00, X-wed; new, spacious; teishoku under ¥1,000, tofu cake, homemade bread.

SUGINAMI-KU

Aruporan Asagaya-kita 2-11-2, ☎3350-8341; 17:00-02:00, X-2nd & 4th wed, 3min from JR Asagaya stn., N exit. Super budget, great food, natural beers, sake.

SHINJUKU

Manna Nishi Shinjuku 1-16-5 Kikusui Biru, ☎3344-6606, 11:00-21:00, X-15:00 on fri, sat, sun, hol. Seventh Day Adventists owner, food varied, Lunch Service best buy under ¥1000, other teishoku around ¥1800.

See also various walk itineraries in passing for recommended convenient lunch stops, exotic or otherwise.

Get book by Rick Kennedy *Good Tokyo Restaurants*. Also *Tokyo Journal* editors Don Morton and Naoko TSUNOI's *Best of Tokyo* (Tuttle ¥1,350/$12.95). Both have great maps, are encyclopedically thorough–but we are proud to note not as much so as our original 1964 edition. We think we were too complete, tho—perhaps to point of confusion. We have dropped more-obvious W-style, many ¥-B J-style apparent by their plastic window displays (unless something special), and hotel dining. Latter in Tokyo is to our experience above world average, and of great variety from economical coffee house to expensive gourmet W- (our pet Palace Hotel is topped by superb French-style **Crown**, rsve ☎3211-5211), var J-specialties, Chinese. For residents good reference is E-phone book *City Source*, free from NTT.

Some years back friend who wholesales gourmet supplies let us in on pricing policies: good restaurants take price of raw food and triple to arrive at menu price, but hotel dining rooms quadruple. So all other things equal, you're better off adventuring out. But what you pay for in hotel is unquestioned convenience and, in Tokyo anyway, assured quality, vastly improved since our first 1964 edition.

I will go back to see Tokyo by night,
when its ugliness is transformed
into a fairylike pattern.
—Robert Guillain, *Japan*

TOKYO BY NITE

NITE LIFE IN TOKYO can be more varied than *Thousand and One Nites*. It can be thrilling evening for mere few thousand yen or some few hundred thousand yen—just find your right focus in this ever-changing ever-revolving kaleidoscope that is Tokyo after dark. This magic world of glittering lights hides its grey buildings as neons come on one by one. Ginza Street itself fades out rather early as large stores start closing around six and by nine, just hollow shells remain framed by lights. However, Ginza is one district and just one block on either side of its central Ginza Street (Chuodori) it's different world. Gayest is Nishi (west) Ginza, few square blocks between Shimbashi stn and Sony bldg on Harumi-dori Ave. This used to be 'it'…still tiny cozy 'joints' vie with brassy palaces with hostesses galore attracting office clerks, while at others svelte doorgals greet Mr Big and guests in his expense-account limo.

Before going into these, let's familiarize ourselves with local setup. First of all are top international hotels with bars, cocktail lounges and annex clubs with bands or revolving combos for dinner-dancing, quality shows, or just relaxing piano music. For quiet evening out, of dancing and *tete-a-tetes*, old-time residents prefer hotels, most of which till 11:30pm or 12:00am. There are occasional 'spectacular' shows, with whopping cover charge. All restaurants in Japan have beer, most have bartender who can whip up basic mixed drinks. Big place and international hotel bartenders are as good as any and once-expensive imported brand prices now match or better locals. Some late-hour restaurants feature entertainment in their lounges.

Popular for dinner-dancing is IMPERIAL'S **Rainbow Room**. Of cocktail lounges and bars around town, we prefer **Starlight Lounge** (midnite) at HOTEL OKURA, excellent atmosphere, reasonable, terrific view makes us homesick for Frisco's Top-of-the-Mark. HILTON **St George Bar** till 1 am.

Besides colorful Ginza with neighboring Shimbashi, of friendly small bars and eateries, there are **five areas**, each with its distinctive air:

AKASAKA always has been expensive as home of exclusive Akasaka geisha who rank tops with politicos. Modern entertainment world has entrenched itself here slowly and definitely, until now area is referred to as 'the Strip', home of top W-style niteries. But these are giving way to more profitable high rise offices now, Just try to hail cab past 11:30pm when Akasaka clubs let out—taxis pass you by like Indianapolis speedway racers.

ROPPONGI once quiet residential area, Jay was PR for first nitery to spoil silence in 1954—burned down opening nite. Long famed for reasonable international dining, now fast becoming mecca for all-nite clubs and after-showtime hangouts. Particularly popular with young international set, with long-limbed models galore, language students and stock brokers. *See* p1160

SHINAGAWA wharves, full of spacious old warehouses ideal for noisy nite-club or quiet day-gallery (*see* p.1161). Being restored in with some inventive experiments. Menus in Furench-i or Supanish-i are as funny as local Engrish. Small cruise boats at pier for Edo's 'Grand Canal'.

SHINJUKU now lively, colorful and gaudy area where Tokyo's students and masses live it up; best enjoyed with someone familiar with native haunts and who can steer you away from nasty 'no foreigners' dives—fewer every year but still some. But its fascinating back alley commercial hi-rise 'rabbit hutches' house some of Japan's most exciting joints. *See* p1149—.

ASAKUSA: rowdy, bawdy, giddy, teems with *sh'ta-machi*downtown tradesmen, merchants, fun-loving youth, and country bumpkins, all out to enjoy this living theater-Tokyo, especially here in Asakusa. Revellers here accept us as just another novelty part of tonite's act, and not as unwanted intruders as in some upper-class areas, or parts of Shinjuku. New trend, sure to be aped, is marked by giant inverted pyramid of **Asahi Beer bldg** across river, visible from KANNON TEMPLE,

NITE-CLUBBING

IN TOKYO it is exciting and expensive and surprisingly quite early-closing at better class clubs concentrated in Akasaka strip. There's midnite curfew on nite clubs, cabarets and bars that employ hostesses, but intimate little places abound in Roppongi, Shibuya and Shinjuku (some language recommended) which stay open till all hours, all nite. Old-timers or hostesses-can guide you after curfew to some clubs where doormen greet you with flashlights and guide you from your car down inside. Some key clubs exist with closed membership, so don't be disappointed if you are refused entrance— assuming you could find one. In fact, many bars are actually private clubs, too. We list top places where foreigners are welcome. Cover (or 'music' at jazz houses) charge at first-class nite clubs usually ¥2,000 to ¥10,000, but differs with quality of show, or in other words what they think your pocket can stand, and it's always best to check on this before going. Tendency at hostess club is to include her charge on bill, averaging about ¥3,-5,000 per hour, but tip is in order if you've been there all evening or plan to return. Even girls in first-class clubs will pad your bill by guzzling. 'Teetotaling' hostess is rare—tho her 'cocktail' may be only 1% alky, 'homeopathic'. Chinese or French cuisine are their fare, but dining beforehand is recommended. Hotel desk can stear you to nearby reputable club.

Nite out at top cabarets will run about ¥30,000up for solo who heads back to his hotel alone to sleep it off. Couple out on big posh places should figure on same if keeping close tab, to way up. Thus for dinner-dancing and nice show, safe hotel supper clubs can't be beat, more than make up for their hotel room rates. But if couple wants to go out clubbing, best is to eat light, take in spot with floor show, or jazz 'live house', and head for Roppongi (if not already there for supper and/or follow-up jazz-club) for late-hours spots for midnite supper and drinks.

Cabarets and youthful *arbeit salons* (meaning 'part-time' and supposed to indicate that hostesses are non-pro office gals, thus less hardened, less demanding?) feature hundreds of girls, and similar smaller places, usually charge by '*setto*' (so many bottles of beer or whiskey-waters, and hors d'oeuvres for 'set' price) and girls are furnished 'free of charge'; whole package at price posted at door—multiple prices apply for different times. Kabuki-cho (pp1150, 1256) has imported Osaka system of ¥10,-12,000 whereby one can eat, drink, sing, dance and fondle unlimited all nite till closing time at this prix-fixé. Some offer unrestricted 'take-out' service after hours at another ¥20,-50,000. Exclusive clubs that cater mostly to expense account crowd charge exhorbitant prices.

BUDGET OUTING best with Japanese friend, for there are loads of tiny friendly bars where plain folks gather. It would pay to invite reasonably-knowledgeable colleague out on your treat. But alone, your safe bet for inexpensive drink is popular **Suntory Bars** (signs in English) that feature ¥500 highballs, as posted outside—chain, affiliated with Japan's leading whiskey distiller—and now importer of Scotch and Boubon whiskeys at similar prices—Suntory. Or poke head in any noisy joint with *noren*-curtain over entry, workman's joint, and if greeted with raucous chorus of laughter and *irrasshaimasseh*, go on in. And those with red folding lantern especially cheap. Usually good places to eat, too, just point and smile and never have fear of clip. Best slumming (*see* KABUKI-CHO p1149, GOLDEN-GAI p1150) where reverse discrimination often against fancy outsiders, so relax.

Summer sees rooftop beergardens flowering like penthouse gardens atop most buildings on main drags or near stations. All about same ¥ for reasonably priced mugs of draft and simple dishes, mostly W-style-a la J.

Real treat is *minyo sakaba*, Japanese style beer and *sake* drinking house where guests divested of shoes sit on cushions on *tatami* and are entertained with folk dances and songs by kimono-clad country gals accompanied by *samisen*, flute and drum...house master is accomplished dancer-musician and takes over often. **Oiwake** (*see* p.1258), Nishi-Asakusa 3-28, ☎3843-4092; inexpensive, beer usually ¥600, *sake* ¥500 per *choshi* (small bottle), *sashimi* ¥1,800+, full entree *nabe-mono* ¥3,500+, and a la carte; **Matsubaya** (*see* pp.1186, 1258), 4-33-1 Senzoku, Asakusa ☎3872-1937 (visited in nite tour) in YOSHIWARA old gay quarter are last ones left in town and enjoy popularity with company presidents rubbing elbows with day laborers, all drinking and joining in folk singing—tho this aspect is fading fast with rising popularity of its Oiran shows, 7pm (Jpn) and 9:10pm (Eng). It's difficult to spend much each even with food unless one takes his drinking seriously. Best bet is to go for show (itself only, ¥2,000) and buy its 'set', which seems to change often, varying from ¥1500 for drink-&-show to full sukiyaki or tempura dinner from 8pm for 9:10 show, ¥7,950. Interpreter not necessary, late show is translated, but would be handy to translate reason for crowd laughter at ribald songs.

Music salons and tea shops cater to younger crowd of office workers and students who can enjoy nite out for few thousand yen. Our original edition had Shimbashi-Ginza and Shinjuku areas peppered with jazz-*kissa* tea shops with Japan's first hi-fi sets supported by superb record collections from Jazz to orchestral big-band and classics. Some evolved into live music tea salons ranging from dozen tables with classical soloists to jazz combos and chamber quartets to nite-club size CANDLE [one set valid as long as your personal candle burned—long gone] which hosted three different jazz bands daily with no repeats for whole month.

Hi-fi (usually on CD) salons are still common, tho we can't find any near Ginza. *TJ* notes several survivors which alternate with live performances in Shinjuku, one in Roppongi and some scattered around town elsewhere: **Bird Land**, 2-12-4 Shinjuku, ☎3352-3692; **Dug** 3-17-15 Shinjuku, ☎3354-7776, and **New Dug**, 3-15-12 Shinjuku, ☎3354-7776, 4 floors each with its individual ambience; **Romanisches Café**, Court Annex Roppongi B-1, 3-2-13 Nishi-Azabu, ☎3405--1622.

LIVE HOUSES, also mainly in Roppongi and Shinjuku, are similar to above except that they offer hard drinks and usually food. They may take cover charge, covering one basic drink (usually beer, sometimes choice of simple *mizuwari* highball), or if decent menu and drink list just add 'music charge' of ¥2,000 to ¥7,000 depending on price of talent on stage. Some *TJ* referals which we checked out and second:

SHINJUKU:
Pit Inn [A], 3-16-4 Shinjuku, ☎3354-2024; with differnet band lunch, afternon, eve, sometimes foreign artists; usually deserted between gigs.
The Carnival, 1-19-2 Kabuki-cho Shinjuku, Koma Theater basement, ☎3200-1291; features female J-vocalists, most of whom have lollypop fixation on mike.
Peter Pan, live shows midnite and 3am, cover chge ¥7,000, drinks ¥1,000up; Shinjuku 2-13-6 in basement Koa Bldg, 10pm-5am X-sun. For others nearby *see* pp1150-51.

ROPPONGI-AOYAMA:
Pit Inn [B], 3-17-7 Roppongi, ☎3585-1063; eve show only, 7:30pm.
Body & Soul, 7-14-12 Roppongi, ☎3408-2094; live till midnite, close at 2am; menu plus music charge abt ¥2,000; visiting foreign artists often drop by late to sit in.
Satin Doll, 4-9-2 Roppongi, ☎3401-3080; "Jazz et Cuisine Française", latter off-key.
Cay, 5-6-23 Minami Aoyama, ☎3498-5790; Thai restn't-bar (Thai king is fine jazz musician); often live imports.
Blue Note, 5-13-3 Minami Aoyama, ☎3407-5781; US musicians only, ¥7,000-up one set only incl drink.
　　HARAJUKU center for discos, *see* p1158. SHINAGAWA warehouses, *see* p.1161.

SHIMBASHI threatens return to life with opening summer '90 of psychadelic...
Pax †heater Psycher town's biggest concert-disco danced 3,000, cost $50,000,000 and looked it—but bombed, as did follow-ups. However, with all that hot investment money floating around, and appetite of nite-owls...watch for imitators, new technologies.
　　Nearby *Nishi-Ginza*: opposite end of cultural spectrum for traditional geisha is...
Club Maiko, ¥8,000 incl for 3 real drinks, hors d'oeuvres, souvenirs of color photo with gals, gourd sake hip-flask; full meals *kaiseki* extra, ¥-S. *Maiko*, novice geisha more ornately dressed, and *geiko*, young geisha, join you at table, welcomes with your national flag which she flutters with dancing fan, pours, serves, all give 20min dance show 7:40,8:40,9:40,10:30. *Ginza*, Aster Plaza Bldg 4fl, Ginza 7ch-7-6, ☎3574-7745.

　　New discos and inexpensive dance halls by whatever name open from time to time. Politicians even seem to have stopped passing special laws to close them—either they grew up or got tired of every new fad popping up calling for new laws few months later. Hanging in for few years now are...

KARA-OKE BARS (have seen *kara-oke kissa*-teashops, resort hotels and new luxe cruise-liners have them, you may have seen those horrid gimmicks advertised mail-order in such as Sharper Image in US) Name means literally 'empty *oke*stra' or orchestra without vocalist—where you come in. Hostess will jam mike into your hand and songbook (usually only in Japanese but more and more have English) and ask you to choose song. They'll have what you want, as tape library that comes with amp is immense (do they pay royalties?). Then they play your tape—or slide in CD-Laser video disc to give you scenic background on large projection TV—orchestral part only. Then you sing... and worser is better-appreciated. Everyone is too polite, aware of his own limitations, to mind tin-eared (*on-shi*) crooners, built-in echo effect conceals much. Everyone will say you are *umai-umai*, 'very good', clap like mad. And if you can croon middle-aged salaryman's anthem *I Did it My Way* you'll be greeted like you was Franky his-sel'.

VIRTUAL REALITY computer graphics, used in US for esoteric medical research, developing here as dressmaking tool, customer-design of kitchens, for coin-operated game centers and thrill theaters (karaoke scenery next?) in places like Kabuki-cho. This will pay to develop serious hard-/software for medical, school, home use the way war and space have for US in past. Watch for 'em, and watch Japan dominate another production technology— tho possibly more advanced in UK. Play arises as "substitute for war"?

*Everyone in Tokyo appeared to be
going somewhere....*
—Brooks Atkinson, *The Cingalese Prince*,1934

PERSONAL DATEBOOK

January

1-5 *New Year* celebrations: 31-1st midnite ships in harbor sound horns; temple bells rung. Pilgrimages to various shrines and temples. Best time to photo families in kimono, girls with elaborate hairdos. Most popular shrines: Asakusa-, Meiji-, Yasukuni-, Kanda Myojin-, from midnite but especially First day from dawn.

2 Imperial family greets nation hourly 9am-3:30pm from balcony as citizens visit Imperial Palace, Niju-bashi Bridge.

5 *Ganzan Daishi*, Kanei-ji temple, Ueno Park honors saint of pregnant women.

6 *Dezome Shiki*, annual firemen's demonstration dressed in Edo period firemen's happi-coats & costumes, carrying ancient streamers & emblems; perform tricks and acrobatics on tall bamboo ladders. Contrasting display of modern aerial, marine, ground firefighting equipment. From 10:00 at Harumi Pier. Smaller scale in Asakusa.

7 *Daikon Matsuri*, Matsuchiyama Shoten Shrine, Asakusa; 11:30-14:30, daikon (symbol of fortune), and other vegetables, sake, dumplings, handed out to visitors.

7 *Jinganna-sai*, Daijo-ji Temple (Adachi-ku, NE of Tobu Isezaki line Take-no-zuka stn), early am burning of 6m long straw snake to ward off ills and call for good harvest; one of few such primitive agricultural rites continuing in 20th century Tokyo.

7 *Children's Yabusame*, Rokugo Jinja Shrine, Ohta-ku; kids shoot arrows at demon eyes targets.

8 Visit to Iriya Kishimojin on this day said to be especially effective for safe birth, healthy upbringing of children.

8 *Dondo-yaki*, burn New Year's decorations, Torigoe Jinja, Asakusa-bashi. Weenie-roast-like campfire actually *mochi* cooked over flame, eating of which said wards off ills for new year. Noon-3pm.

12 *Manaita-biraki*, ritual blessing of chef's cutting boards, Ho-on-ji Temple Inaricho; gaily dressed priest performs ceremonial slicing of two carp.

Sun nearest 10th *Hatsu-basho*, first sumo tournament, Kokugikan Sumo arena, Kuramae; 15 days, ends on Sunday (p.62).

2nd Sun *Kagami-biraki* marks end of New Years celebrations. *Kagami-mochi* (2-tier rice cake) section of New Years decorations is cut up and served in *oshiruko* red bean soup. at most homes. Kodokan Judo Hall in Korakuen Park hosts special match 10am after which priest cuts up mochi, passes out to all.

15 21-yr olds celebrate coming of age with rituals nationwide. Meiji Shrine at Harajuku Stn holds traditional ritual for men (*genpukushiki*), l0:30am. Colorfully dostumed archers of Ogasawara join in.....

15 *Momote-shiki*, Meiji Jingu Shrine, Ogasawara-ryu school of archers shoot.

15-16 *Boro-ichi* flea mart, Boroichi-dori st, Setagaya-ku. Over 600 stalls sell everything in 400-year-old mart. Repeated **Dec 15-16**. Nearby is preserved manse of lord who started it, now museum. Near Tokyu Setagaya Line's Setagaya stn.

18 *Moja-okuri* torchlite prayer service wards off ills and fires, Senso-ji Temple. From 6pm.

25 *Uso-kae* (Bullfinch) *Festival*, popular date at Tenjin Shrine at Kameido for on that day you can be forgiven past lies; *uso* is both "lie" and "bullfinch" in Japanese. People bring last year's Uso bird talisman and exchange for new one. Last year's takes with it last year's lies, get new bird in which to store this year's.

February

3 or 4 *Setsubun* bean-throwing exorcises ills of past year. Nothing spectacular as Kyoto or Nara; mostly geisha, prominent folk and stars throwing parched beans in public rites at such places as Kabuki-za Theater, Zojoji Temple, Tokyo Tower, Hibiya Public Hall. Asakusa Senso-ji temple features ancient Fukuju-no-mai dance; Gojo Tenjin Shrine in Ueno Park has *Ukera-no-Shinji*, old version, much more effective double-whammy in ridding evil) when *oni wa soto* "out with demon" shouted, good spirit shoots arrow at demon.

4 *Memorial Rites for 47 Ronin*, Sengaku-ji Temple, commemorates their deaths by seppuku on this day 1703; *see* p.1161.

8 *Hari-kuyo*, memorial service for broken needles. Women give thanks, appreciation for broken needles' long faithful service and deposit them at temples. Best rites seen at Awashima-do Temple, precincts of Asakusa Kannon Temple, Asakusa.

11, 13 *Ta-Asobi*, ancient ritual offering and prayer for good harvest. Two shrines, Kitano-Jinja (11) & Suwa Jinja (13), both in Itabashi-ku, still observe. Rice is steamed and pounded into rice cakes. Instead of traditional round shape, these are formed into spades, plow shares, farming tools, then used in drama, depicting hardships and joys of entire, year-round rice cycle.

1st Day of Horse, *Hatsu-uma*, all Inari Shrines marks day main Inari Shrine, Kyoto, was founded. Best in Tokyo are: Toyokawa Inari near Akasaka Mitsuke & Akasaka Detached Palace; and festival at Inari Shrine at Ohji in NW Tokyo is popularly dubbed *tako-ichi* because merchants selling huge *tako* (kites) hold market here

25 *Hakubai-sai White Plum Blosssom Festival* at Yushima Shrine, Bunkyo-ku.

Mid-month marks start of *Hina-doll Fair*, sales and special displays at doll stores around Asakusa-bashi; large stores have elaborate setups as each tries to outdo other: child's dream and parents' nitemare come true. Ends with—

March

3 *Hina Matsuri*, national observance of Dolls' Festival. Dolls of entire court and retinue are displayed in many homes; fine displays all DS during preceding weeks.

1st Sunday *Fire-walk*: Nagatoro Saitama Pref, Fudo-ji Temple, 1-4pm; info town office *cho yakuba* ☎0494-66-3111

3-4 *Daruma-ichi* fair, Jindai-ji Temple, Chofu; hundreds of stalls sell red, roly-poly daruma.

2nd Sun *Fire-walking*, 11am-noon. Crowded so go early; starts with yama-

bushi mountain ascetics, then anyone who wants to try—like you. Kotsu Anzen Kitosho, Yakuo-in, ☎0426-61-1115. Takao-guchi stn, Keio line from Shinjuku

18 *Kinryu-mai*, Gold Dragon Dance, Senso-ji Temple; legend says dragons flew up to heaven when Senso-ji's gold Kannon image found. Revived to mark postwar resurrection of Senso-ji, golden dragon dances around temple; big floats in later parade feature geisha musicians.

Late thru mid-April, *Sakura Festival*, Ueno Park is best known in Tokyo from old woodblock prints, where today over 1,500 cherry trees bloom. Sumida Park's cherry viewing gets better every year as newly planted trees get bigger; fun day.

April

Early *Kanda Myojin Spring Festival*, all day dances, stalls. Famous *ama-zake* (sweet rice wine), which is somewhat like our hot toddy, is sold by traditional old grog shop at temple front gate.

1st Sat *Yabusame* archery by mounted horsemen galloping under sakura trees by Sumida River, near Senso-ji.

1 - 7 2nd set of *Memorial Rites for 47 Ronin*, at Sengaku-ji Temple.

8 *Hana-Matsuri*, observance of Buddha's birthday with parade of *chigo*, children dressed as heavenly messengers of Buddha. Best Tsukiji Honganji Temple, Asakusa Kannon Temple and Gokoku-ji Temple.

8 *Memorial for dog Hachiko*, at his Shibuya station-front statue.

2nd Sun *Kanamara Phallic Fete*. 11am light fire by flint, 1pm parade in phallic masks, 2:30 forge iron phalli (*kana-mara*) to break castrating teeth of maiden who has hers in wrong orifice, 3-5pm dancing, partying. Red Keihin *kyuko* Shinagawa → Kawasaki stn, xfer for Kawasaki Daishi stn, block walk to Kanayama Jinja in Wakamiya Hachiman. Sole phallic fete *not* of agricultural origin, but of Freudian castration phobia; said started early 1600s by prostitutes to ward off rampaging syphilis; also called *Utamaro Festival* after great erotic woodblock print artist.

13-15 *Spring Festival* at Zojoji Temple in Shiba Park—one of few lovely old Edo era gates left in Tokyo; by Tokyo Tower in front of Palace Hotel.

15 *Fire-walking*, Saitama Pref Takayama Fudo-san, noon. Seibu Chichibu line to Agano, then bus; **info** ☎0429-78-0027.

15 *Tata Kagura* at Shingawa Jungu, Shinagawa-ku.

End-month Waseda U *vs* Keio U Regatta on Sumida River; good viewing from Asakusa bridges or riverbanks.

17 Main Festival of Ueno Toshogu.

21-23 Yasukuni Shrine *Spring Festival*, varied program thruout 3 days. Old schedule gives good example of events: 21st 11am—noh dances; 4-7pm *kendo* (fencing), *biwa* (lute) music, ballet, folk dances. 22nd, 1pm—noh and kyogen: 23rd, 1pm—bugaku, with sumo wrestling at some time during day.

24-25 *Tenjin Festival*, Hiraga Shrine, Chiyoda-ku. Kagura 5:30.

25 Ueki-ichi Plant market at Ikegami Honmonji Temple, Ota-ku.

4th Sun *Confucius Festival*, Yushima Seido Temple, Kanda.

4th Sun *Yabusame* archery on horseback at Mizu Inari Jinja, Shinjuku-ku.

Mid-Apr to early 5, *Tsutsuji* azalea bloom in Ueno Park, while *botan* peonies last until mid-May.

Mid-Apr to May 5, Asakusa-bashi's doll shops hold another *fair*—for boys.

End April *Tokyo Trade Fair* Harumi Pier, or alternate Makuhari Messe.

29 *Birthday* late emperor Showa (Hirohito) 1901-89, now *Green Day*, ecological.

29-May 5 Golden Week, most offices closed at least some of week, schools out. *Warning* — don't travel anywhere without reservations.

May

3 *Kenpo Kinen-bi* Constitution Day, National Holiday with public offices, banks, schools closed; no fetes.

4 Day off linking 3rd & 5th hols.

5 *Kodomo-no-hi* Children's Day, marked nationwide with flying carp streamers outside homes, helmets & warrior dolls inside. Meiji Shrine has varied program of classical music, dances, traditional sports on outdoor stages. Ancient *Takara-no-mai* Treasure Dance at Senso-ji Temple.

5 Main Festival of Suitengu Shrine (Ningyo-cho), kagura dances, *mikoshi* and float parade, best noon to 3pm.

5 *Kurayami Matsuri* Festival-in-the-Dark, outside of town at Chofu's Okunitama Jinja Shrine, wild *mikoshi* parade starts 4pm, festivities go on late nite.

Sun nearest 10th *Natsu-basho* Summer Grand Sumo Tournament, for 15 days, Kokugi-kan, Ryogoku; (*see* Sports, p.62).

Sun nearest 11th *Shitaya Jinja Fete*, Inaricho, Ueno; main fete even years, parade features giant *mikoshi* palanquins of 4 tons.

15 *Spring Festival*, Kanda Myojin Shrine, carry portable shrines thru streets in Kanda area, other activities.

3rd wknd *Sanja-sai Festival*, one of Tokyo's biggest fetes, Asakusa Shrine in Asakusa Park. 3-day fete starts fri, best 1–4pm sat and 5-7pm sun as 100 portable shrines carried by children's, girls' & mens groups. Colorful parade includes men with grotesque (or artistic) tattoos over whole body.

3rd Sun *Ono Terusaki Jinja Grand Festival* in Iriya, sh'tamachi.

21-23 *Osuna-fumi* 'Sand-stomping', visit Tamagawa Daishi Temple (Setagaya-ku) these days is equal merit to visiting all 88 of Shikoku's pilgrimage temples. Temple dedicated to Saint Kobo-daishi who founded those 88.

22 *Spring Festival* at Toyokawa Inari Shrine nr Akasaka Detached Palace.

22 *Kasamori Inari Festival*, Daien-ji temple, Sendagi Yanaka.

25 *Spring Festival*, Yushima Tenjin; *mikoshi* portable shrine procession.

28 *Fudo Ennichi* observed nationwide: in Tokyo at Fukagawa Fudo in Koto-ku, shitamachi; Meguro Fudo Meguro-ku.

25 *Gojo Tenjin Grand Festival* Ueno Park.

Last Sat Takigi Noh, at Zojoji Temple in Shiba, Onarimon subway stn; 5:30, ¥3,000 non-rsve.

End Gojo Tenjin Shrine *Summer Festival* of mikoshi & other dances; Ueno Park.

End — *Azuma Odori*, annual performance gorgeous dances by Tokyo's top geisha: 2 performances daily 11am, 2:30 pm; tickets ¥3,-7,000 at Shimbashi Embujo, for 4 days.

31-Jun 1 Sengen Jinja *Plant Fair* converts Senzoku-dori area Asakusa into huge nursery garden, stalls line street after street of morning glory, gardenia, bonsai dwarfed plants. (Again July 30-Aug 1).

June

1-7 Display azaleas from all Japan around Shinobazu Pond, foot of Ueno Park.

7-Jul 14 *Firefly Festival* Chinzanso Restaurant, Bunkyo-ku; 30,000 fireflies released. Dinner: ☎✓943-1111.

1st Sat, day before and after. *Kappa Matsuri* 3-day water fete, Ebara Shrine with climax Sunday as young men carry large portable shrine into sea at Odaiba-Kaihin Koen, Minato-ku.

1st Sun (full scale even years, 1992, '94) Sakaki Jinja *Grand Festival*, Kuramae; parade of *mikoshi*, Kagura dances. Same time, Suga Jinja *Grand Festival* in nearby Asakusa-bashi parades giant wheeled floats in place of *mikoshi*, also Kagura.

2nd Sun *Torigoe Shrine Festival* in Kuramae Asakusa-bashi features one of largest *mikoshi* (portable shrines) in town over 4 tons/4,000kg, carried about by youth group. When it finally gets back to shrine after sunset it's dark, hundreds of paper lanterns light up nite, which earns it its other name of Nite Festival.

10-12 (3 days, incl. 10th) *Main Festival* of Tsukiji's Namiyoke Inari Shrine, last day wild *mikoshi* parade.

14-16 *Sanno Festival* at Hie Shrine, Nagata-cho near Capitol Hotel. Grand mikoshi parade thru parish, varied program from 10am: sacred Shinto ritual music and dancing, *bugaku*, and **14th** at 1pm worshipers pass thru ring of wisdom made of miscanthus leaves. Similar 16th, flower arrangements .

18th *Yoji-Josui* water purification rites Senso-ji to cure or ward off illness; holy water sprinkled with willow branch. Double your insurance at . . .

30-Jul 1 Plant Fair as Sengen Jinja converts Senzoku-dori area of Asakusa into huge nursery, stalls lining streets sell all sorts potted plants--flowers to bonsai.

30-Jul 1 *Water Festival*, Torigoe Shrine. Life-sized paper cutouts of human beings brought to shrine in evening offered on altar, while worshipers pray for good luck, then passed thru 'ring of wisdom' made of reed. At 9 am, **July 1** these are all placed in 60 boats near Ryogoku Bridge and cast into sea off Shinagawa with prayer for purification.

Final wknd (date varies, also 5 times yearly) Largest *antique fair* in country held Fri-Sun 10:00-18:00, over 250 dealers, free. Haneda Monorail from Hamamatsu-cho to Heiwajima Ryutsu Center-mae.

July

All month most shrines, something on.

1 *Mt Fuji Festival*, Ono Terusaki Jinja; start of Mt Fuji climbing season celebrate with pilgrims climbing mini (12m tall) version of Fuji here, Iriya, Taito-ku.

1 *Suijo Matsuri* Water Festival of Torigoe Jinja Shrine sees hodgepodge boat procession from Asakusa-bashi Bridge to Shinagawa.

River Fireworks

(Vary +1 or +7 days later if rain). .
Last Sat Jul (+1) original Sumida River flash famed in woodblock prints, greatest such in Tokyo since 1733, discontinued during war, reinstated 1977 as competition for fireworks mfrs. Best seen from boats on river, for which book well ahead; or Sakurabashi bridge, or betw Komagata & Umayabashi bridges 10min walk from Tobu line Asakusa Stn. .
Last Thur Jul (+1) at Adachi, Arakawa-ku Senjushin-bashi & Nishi Araibashi bridges; Chiyoda subway to Kitasenju Stn and walk 20 minutes.
1st Sat Aug (+1) incl biggest single shot 1 km Niagara; Itabashi-Toda, Toei-Mita sub to Nishidai Stn, walk 20min.
— Shinozaki Park, Toei Shinjuku subway to Shinozaki Stn, walk 12min.

Suburbs

Early Aug in Chofu, Keio line to Tamagawa Stn; 7pm.
1st Sat Aug (+7) Chiba City plus around park lasers from port tower; Keiyo line to Chiba Minato Stn.
2nd Sat (+7) Matsudo, Chiba-ken, Joban line to Matsudo Stn, walk 5+min.
Aug 10 (+1) Kamakura beach, fired from offshore boat; JR Yokosuka line to Kamakura Stn, walk 15min.

6-8 *Asagao-ichi Morning Glory Market*, carefully grown morning glory plants in pots, skillfully trained to bear many blooms. Tokyo-ites look forward to this 3-day affair at Iriya Kishimojin.

9-10 *Shiman-rokusen-nichi* or 46,000-day rites at Kannon Temple, Asakusa. One pilgrimage this day worth 46,000 times; same day *hozuki* ground cherry plant mart, Kannon Temple.

13-15 *Bon Dancing* in streets or compounds: 5,000 lanterns illuminate Yasukuni Shrine, and Shinobazu Pond in Ueno Park; nitely lighting of bonbori lanterns, plant fairs, entertainment on outdoor stages, *bon* dances (thru rest of month till mid-August). *Kusa-ichi Food Mart* around Tawaramachi stn; selling not plastic foods of this supply area, but specialized food used for offerings to spirits of deceased during O-bon.

13-15 Tsukuda-jima's *Bon Dances* are special combo of prayers and dance; 300-year-old, Intangible Cultural Asset.

Mid-July marks start of month-long *Ueno Summer Festival,* almost nightly shows at Ueno Park outdoor stage, food and game booths set up all over, bon dancing nitely, lots of fun. Grand parade, usually last weekend of month.

Latter part month *Tohoku Joetsu Furu-sato* (hometown) *Festival,* Ueno; recreates Tohoku & Joetsu regions' main fetes.

August

Early (date varies) *Hama-cho Ondo* folk, geisha, folk dances mark Park founding.

1st or 2nd wknd *Seto-mono-ichi* Ceramics Fair, Ningyocho, bargain sales ceramics.

4 *Hashi-kuyo,* memorial rites for chopsticks Torigoe Jinja shrine Asakusa-bashi.

5 (date varies) *Kanto-sai* Lantern Fest, along Chuo-dori shopping st to Ueno Park, area commemorates Satake clan of Akita (mansion occupied present entire Satake area) by recreating gala giant lantern fest of lord's home. Tall bamboo poles festooned with tiers of lanterns.

6-8 *Tsukuda Festival* at Sumiyoshi Shrine, Tsukuda-jima; large scale every 3 years, otherwise small; large 1992, '95, '98...

Early-Mid sometime, outdoor Takigi Noh by light of *bonbori* torches, Hie Jinja Shrine, Akasaka-mitsuke; 17:30 to 20:30.

15 In past (maybe again), *Float Paper Lanterns,* with reciting of Buddhist sutras at Kototoi-bashi Bridge by Asakusa Senso-ji, 7pm, in memory of war dead & others. Now major bon fete.

– *Fukagawa Festival,* Fukagawa Hachiman Shrine across Sumida River at Tomioka-cho, Koto-ku, with 100 huge *omikoshi.* Carriers run to shrine while watchers toss water on them. Major fete every 3 years (1992, '95, '98, 2001, '04, '07 etc...)

16 (every 3rd year, 1993, '96, '99, 2002...) *Omen-kaburi* at Kuhonbutsu Temple sees procession of *Mask Wearing* priests masquerade as Bodhisattvas who follow Amida. Near Kuhonbutsu stn on Tokyu Oimachi Line.

26-28 *Koenji Awa Odori,* modeled after famed Awa dance of Shikoku Isle, whence

more and more participants come every year, making this most rapidly growing summer fun festival of Tokyo. Held around Koenji JR station plaza.

End Summer end marked as flashy Samba Carnival Parade winds around Asakusa. Prizes to best dancers, most original costume, etc; teams from Brazil also show. You can join in parade if your group is larger than 5 people and you have informed parade committee by mail: Asakusa Samba, Taito-kuyakusho Tokyo,

Latter part month, *Takigi Noh,* outdoor noh play illuminated by torchlight, Senso-ji Asakusa.

September

1 *Earthquake Memorial Day,* memorial service is held for those who died in great Tokyo Earthquake and Fire of 1923, Memorial Hall, right across Kuramae Bridge on Sumida River.

11 *Dara-dara Matsuri* at Shiba Daijingu Shrine, Shiba Minato-ku, features vendors of fresh ginger in shrine compound along with other festive stalls. Thru 21st. Fete name means "to drag on". Best **16th**.

Sun nearest 10, *Akibasho,* fall sumo tournament, Kuramae Kokugikan for 15 days; starts & ends sun; best from 3pm, end abt 6pm. *See* Sports, p.62.

14 *Daija oneri* 'Taming of Giant Snake' at Okuzawa Jinja Shrine (nr Tokyu Toyoko Jiyu-ga-oka stn) sees men of town cart around giant straw snake—10m long, 1m around with 2m head, total 100kg—which ends wrapped around main tori. Begun 1754 to rid village of plague .

18-19 Hikawa Jinja Shrine (Meguro-ku, Yagumo) Grand Fete feature *Swords Dance* kagura piece in which Susa-no-O defeats Great Snake and gets sacred sword from its tail.

20 Matsuchiyama Shoten shrine *Grand Festival* marks its founding. Blessing of coin purses and *daikon,* symbols of good business and health.

20-21 *Nezu Gongen-sai,* dedicated to guardian spirit of Nezu Shrine; colorful festival features *mikoshi* parade, stalls.

25 *Ningyo-kuyo,* Memorial Rite for Old Dolls, mothers with daughters flock, Kiyomizu-do pavilion Ueno Park.

Sun nearest 27th (odd years, '93, '95..), *Teppo-gumi Hyaku-nin-tai* '100-musketeers' parade of Edo era gunners around Kaichu Inari Shrine, near Shin-Ohkubo stn, Shinjuku-ku.

Late *–Takigi Noh* by torches, Shinjuku Pk.

Late - *Film Festival*, Shibuya (p.1250), sponsored by Japan's principle publisher of Jew bait books.

October

1 *Citizen's Day* observed by Tokyo-ites, various events scheduled thruout city; check *TJ* or *Japan Times* for events.

1st Sat *Kiba-no-kakunori*, log rolling contests among Edo's lumberjacks. Dressed in traditional garb, logs are floated down from mountain areas. Main water-sport near Kurofune-bashi Bridge, Koto-ku. Lumberjacks welcome. Strength contest at nearby Fukagawa Koen park, anyone welcome to join.

1st Sun *Ekoda Shishi-mai*, 700-year-old Lion Dances, Nakano-ku Hikawa Jinja Shrine.

1st or 2nd Sun All-Tokyo *Mikoshi Festival* in Asakusa, parade of all main *mikoshi* palanquins from all sections of Tokyo.

1st-2nd week, *Takigi Noh* on special stage Hibiya City nr Uchisaiwai-cho subway, outdoors, but if rain few days later at nearby theater; (☎3595-0295); ¥3,-4,000.

9-10 *Ryusen Kiku* Chrysanthemum Fair at Tobi-Fudo Temple, ex-Yoshiwara.

11-13 *Oeshiki* at Honmonji Temple in Ikegami Ohta-ku as Nichiren Buddhists celebrate Nichiren's birthday with mammoth parade beating drums, carrying huge umbrella-shape poles with long streamers & lanterns—1000s converge on temple from various parts of city.

14-15 Yanaka *Chrysanthemum Fair* Daien-ji temple in Sh'tamachi Yanaka.

17-19 *Autumn Festival*, Yasukuni Shrine, all-day entertainment, colorful stalls selling toys, masks, souvenirs.

18 *Rite for Chrysanthemums* at Senso-ji, followed by repeat of Golden Dragon Dance; display of dolls and figures using chrysanthemum on show until mid-Nov.

19-20 *Ebisu Matsuri*, at Takarada Jinja shrine, Nihonbashi; throngs blessed by Ebisu, god of fortune, buy talismans.

19-20 *Bettara Ichi*, annual fair where radish pickled rather sweet are sold by peddlers from all over at Takarada Shrine in Kodenma-cho, Chuo-ku.

Mid-Oct–Mid-Nov Chrysanthemum show at various spots; Shinjuku Gardens best collection grown for Imperial Family, open to public. Also *kikuningyo-*'mums wire-linked in shapes of life-size dolls, best Tamagawa-en; train from Shibuya.

Late – odd-number years only, 2 weeks, world's biggest *International Auto Show*, Makuhari Messe starring latest dream cars.

November

1 *Azuma-Odori*, geisha program, from Sunday nearest 1st, Tokyo top geisha of Shimbashi area numbering 350, present annual autumn show, Shimbashi Embujo Theater 11am, 4pm. **Note:** Festival has not been performed over the past several years, with remodelling of the theater as the excuse. It will hopefully be revived.

3 *Culture Day*, formerly known as Emperor Meiji's birthday and still main festival at Meiji Shrine. All-day program includes *yabusame* (archery on horseback), *noh*, Japanese dances and sports. (*See* Meiji Shrine, p.1157, & On Stage, p.52).

7 *Fire-walk*, Akiba Shrine, Matsugaya Taito-ku, 15min walk Inari-cho stn.

3 *Shirasagi-no-mai*, White Crane Dance, Senso-ji Temple; women in stylized bird costumes dance, depicting cranes eating bugs harmful to crops.

15 *Shichi-go-san*, annual celebration for families with daughters of 7 and 3 and sons aged 5. These children with their parents, all dressed in their best kimono go on pilgrimage to their local shrine to give thanks for having reached these ages in good health. Popular shrines are Meiji, Suiten-gu, Asakusa.

All three Fowl days on zodiacal calendar celebrated with *Tori-no-ichi* (Fowl Fair). On these days, O-tori Shrines (grandest at ex-Yoshiwara) dedicated to Fowl hold special festivals, at where merchants and businessmen go to buy *kuma-de* rake decorated with symbols of wealth to hang up in their place of business, each year buying bigger rake in order to rake more in. Unbelievable unless you see it, over-sized 6-foot rakes are sold at stalls filled with all sizes. Fowl Days: 1992–2,14,26; '93–9, 21; '94–4, 16, 28; '95–11, 23; '96–7, 19, 31; '97–2, 14, 26; '98–9, 21; '99–4,16,28; 2000–11,23; '01–6,18,30.

Oct 19-20 *Ebisu Matsuri* at Takarada Jinja, Nihonbashi. Throngs come for blessings from Ebisu, god of fortune, buy shrine talismans.

December

5 *Osame-no Suitengu* Suitengu Shrine, Nihonbashi in downtown Ginza; street stalls amid fine old shops, nr Hakozaki airport bus terminal, or Hibiya subway to Ningyo-cho.

Early *Daimyojin Matsuri*, Owashi Shrine Ajiki, Sakae-cho Chiba: procession of 2.5-meter sacred phallus, men dressed as women in *Okame* masks, pudenda-faced fertility maid (whose name is used to mean transvestite) ride Tengu float, pulled by real women dancing; (Narita line to Ajiki Stn, walk 15min).

14 *Memorial Service* for 47 loyal ronin who avenged their master then committed mass hara-kiri. At Sengakuji Temple in Takanawa nr Shinagawa Stn, Minato-ku.

15-16 *Boro-ichi* Flea Market, Setagaya-ku (*see* Jan 15-16); this one features more plants and trees than antiques.

17-19 *Hagoita-ichi* Battledore Market, in compound of Senso-ji Temple, Asakusa; stalls sell beautifully decorated battledore, used as paddle in badminton-like game, somewhat like oversized elongated ping-pong paddle, comes in all sizes. This event is combined with *Gasa-ichi* (**14-27**) selling New Year decorations.

23 Emperor Akihito's Birthday (b.1933), HIM salutes well-wishers on inner plaza from bullet-proof-glassed-in Palace porch; enter via Nijubashi bridge.

25 Last *Tenjin Festival* of year held at Kameido Tenjin Shrine, Kameido, Sumida-ku. Stalls sell New Year decor for shops and homes.

28 Last *Fudo Festival*, Fudo temples thru-out city: best seen at Fukagawa Fudo, Koto-ku across Sumida River, and at Meguro Fudo.

31 Pilgrimages start to various shrines and temples (latter ring bell 108 times) 31st midnite and continue thru New Year holidays. Four million-plus visit Meiji Shrine; best time midnite for fairs, fun.

we meet to part
I ask my heart
part we to meet
?

— Sir Richard Burtom
Qasidah of Abdu'ulYezdi

*...best introduction to modern Japanese life
is a visit to a department store...*
—Jean Pearce, *Foot-loose in Tokyo*

TOKYO MARKET PLACE
FOR OUR HURRIED SHOPPER

SHOPPING IN TOKYO is lifetime pastime. Sumi did first book on this subject alone back in '54. Tokyo has largest selection in most modern goods, traditional items adapted to Western tastes, and with influx of foreign company personnel resident for 2 to 3 years, more things oriental are on local shelves today. In our first edition we advised to shop in hotel arcades, but they have changed in character, now catering to affluent natives as their main clientele and so carry mostly foreign label goods (which are much cheaper back home). You still find small souvenir shops with tasteful selections, as well as old standbys like Mayuyama and Odawara in Imperial Hotel carrying fine arrays of Japanalia.

ORIENTAL MARKETPLACE (pp.168-174) has basic information useful for Tokyo (children p171, fashions p174). As we cover routings in town, shopping is mentioned in passing, especially Asakusa and Kawagoe. We all look for bargains and *Tokyo Journal* lists sales at various shops each month.

We run thru alphabet with ideas for our hurried traveler-shopper, we mark our best choice shops with *.

ANTIQUES, CURIOS, ART

Japan is natural museum of entire Far East, being geographically end of all old trade roads. Past cultural invasions into Japan and Japanese invasions onto continental mainland have brought untold art goods to Japan. "It's cheaper back home" won't hold here, for you can't find many of these curios, antiques back home—unless lucky enough to stumble on Occupation era loot making way onto market as old GIs die off.

You're lucky if you're here for huge all-Japan antique fair *Heiwa-jima Kotto Matsuri—over 200 dealers' booths at Heiwa-jima (Ryutsu Center stop of Monorail to Haneda). Started only few years ago, now held 5 times yearly in Mar, May, Jun, Sep and Dec, 3-day weekends around middle or 20th of month: from tiny netsuke to huge staircase chests. No entry fee. Kottoh Ichi office (ask for Mr Takehi) ☎3980-8228 or *Tokyo Antique News* ☎3950-0871 (both in Japanese). If avid collector, get *News* (¥300) for current dates (have someone read Japanese). Other places with regular monthly antique markets (AM) are listed below. If raining, fair may be called off, so check in Japanese. Handy numbers for checking antique marts: ☎3226-6800 (in Japanese), tape after 5pm; for flea markets and occasional fairs are ☎3258-6029 or ☎3258-6000 (also in Japanese).

1st sun: **Arai Yakushiji** Arai Yakushi-mae, Seibu Shinjuku Line, ☎3386-1355.
1st & 4th sun: **Togo Jinja** Harajuku JR stn. Large grounds, ☎3403-3591.
2nd sun: **Nogi Jinja** Roppongi (Hibiya L). If rain cancel, ☎3402-2181.
2nd&3rd sun: **Hanazono Jinja** Shinjuku 3-chome (Maru L/TSL) ☎3402-2181.
4th thu & fri: **Roppongi** in front Roa Bldg (Hibiya L) 8am-8pm, ☎3583-2081.
1st sat: **Iidabashi** AM, Central Plaza, Ramia Sq, Iidabashi (Tokyo Metro subway line), 6am-dusk, ☎3260-8211.
3rd sat: **Aoyama**, at C1 Plaza, Gaien-mae (Ginza line) 6am-dusk. ☎3597-7972.

Note: ☎ nos as of 1991 are 8-digit; if you have old 7-digit no, add extra '3' in first place.

For other nearby out-of-town, irregular or small local flea markets see *Tokyo Journal's* thoro list in *Cityscope*, which includes nearby Yokohama.

In London, antique shops are clustered along Davies St or New Bond. Tokyo is no exception, and even goes one better with one whole street, **KOTTO-DORI** 'Antique St' from Aoyama-dori (Kinokuniya Mkt) to Roppongi-dori (Fuji Film Bldg) boasting over 60 antique shops. Start from Kinokuniya end (Ginza-line subway to Omotesando stn, walk 5min W) and work towards Roppongi. At time of original edition shops were just moving into this area from Toranomon and numbered about 15: Toraya and Yanagawa (now gallery of W paintings) still exist. Select sampling of shops:

*Komingei Morita (classic folkcrafts), opp Ohara Kaikan, ☎3407-4466, no X.
Wada Bijutsuten (contemporary arts), same side st next block, ☎3409-5292, X-sun.
Toraya (well-known to decorators) S of Wada, ☎-3400-8121, X-sun, hols.
Kottoya Karakusa (old blue and white Imari-ware only), ☎3499-5858, X-sun, hol.
Matsushita Dojinsha (woodblock prints), on L side ☎3407-4966, X-sun, mon.

Shops run by expatriates may be bit more expensive, but compensate by feeling of familiarity as they cater to our tastes (such as folding screens) and to satisfy which is usually cheaper than catering to natives. Shops of old-timers like Mildred Warder (her former mgr carries on in Hotel Okura), or Pat Salmon are sorely missed, but others fill gap as they upgrade their merchandise. Conveniently located near each other in Roppongi are three:

*Kurobune, John Adair keeps supply of fine antiques incl folding screens, ceramics, old prints, texiles, chests, folkcrafts. Original 3 rooms has grown to 7 with 3/4 devoted to furniture (abt 80 chests alone). l0am-6pm; X-sun, hols. 7-7-4 Roppongi. ☎3479-1552.

Kathryn Milan, relatively new since 1983, specializes in furniture. porcelains, Chinese and some Korean paintings. In old Japanese home with garden, her baskets, hibachi, paintings, decorative accessories set out beautifully. Weekday & eve by app't only; but sat, sun, natl hols open 10:30am-6pm. ☎3408-1532; 3-1-14 Nishi Azabu, Minato-ku.

Harumi, Harumi Yoshizawa, 7 years in USA and many years with US firm as secretary, manages shop which she and ex-husband David Rose started. Now she has other specialty shops join her for greater variety of kimono, scrolls, screens and art work, porcelains, folkcrafts, and lots of hibachi in huge space. 9-6-14 Akasaka, next (L) of Self Defense Min. l0am-6pm; ☎3403-1043, X-sun when open by appointment.

Other old-line local shops are:
*Bingoya, folkcraft shop with 6 floors of fascinating items, and being one owner there's huge assortment, unlike others with different shops duplicating. *New York Times* supplement ran feature on their collection of handmade kites large and small. They have toys in basement; pottery and glass, hand-woven and -dyed textile goods, stenciled textiles; articles of bamboo, wood, lacquer and straw (farmer's sandals, boots and rain wear), pottery, handmade papers and paper products, with top floor gallery rotating living artists. Bit out of way, in Shinjuku Wakamatsu-cho 10-6, near Kawada-cho bus stop, 10-7pm; ☎3202-8778. Taxi about ¥-2x-mtr from Shinjuku JR.

*Antique Mart, more than 30 shops, over half carrying Japanese items, in Hanae Mori Bldg basemt on Omote-Sando off Aoyama-dori. ☎3406-1021, no-X, 11-8pm

Old favorites of foreign community for good mixture of general antiques:
*Oriental Bazaar also on Omote Sando, 2nd floor has better collection and prices than first floor or basement of second-hand kimonos, traditional folkcrafts, festival banners, lamps, woodblock prints, bronzes for garden, ceramics. 5-9-13 Jingumae. X-thu, ☎3400-3933. **Mori Silver** run by Sandra Mori who helped update this section, with good buys in pearls, jewelry, silver coffee sets also here; ☎3407-7010.

Fuso old advertiser from our *Anone* (1954-55) Tokyo Guide mag days has changed hands since, runs 'Warehouse Sale' sat, sun, 11:00-18:00 at 2-38-1 Ebisu, ☎3442-1945 sales day only. Main shop in Kamata btwn 2 Kamata stns of JR & Keikyu Line, ☎3730-6530. General antiques, chests, screens. No-X, occasionally when out buying.

Old-time antique fans may wonder what happened to great 5-storey Jimbo-cho's Komingu Kottoh Kan (Japan Old Folkcrafts Center) building in Kanda, full of antiques. Few years back that closed down, split into 2 groups with some joining to become two markets:

*Tokyo Ochanomizu Antique Hall** in basement of Kenkyusha Bldg with 9 shops, selling folding screens, tansu chests, swords, imari ceramics, clocks. 11am-7:00pm, ☎3295-7110/8; some English spoken. 1 block from JR Ochanomizu Stn.

*Tokyo Komingu Kottoh Kan**, Satomi Bldg, IF, 5-min walk from Ikebukuro Stn and Seibu DS east exit on Meiji-dori just beyond Musashino Gakuen and across from Inakaya Restaurant, Kanda's Kottoh Kan new location, run by Mr. Takehi, organizer of Heiwa Jima Antique Fair. ☎3295-7112 (Mr. Miura).

Hinata Antiques, chests, screens, hibachi, etc, Odakyu Line exp from Shinjuku to Seijogakuen-mae, left exit. Open sat, sun & hols; by appt week days ☎3417-8514.

ARCHERY

Mr Onuma (*see* p70) is proprietor of **Asahi Archery Shop** (about 400m along Kasuga-dori from Shin-Otsuka stop of red Marunouchi subway line, or Toden tram from Waseda to Mukohara stop); at Minami-Otsuka 3-23-3, Toshima-ku; ☎3986-2301.

Contact English-speaking in-house *deshi* assistant, Dan Deprospero, for supplies or to see or take lessons nearby at dojo with English instruction. Equipment are works of art—full set of 7+ft bow, yard-plus bamboo arrows, deer-skin arrow glove, wicker quiver, string roll and outfit of kimono-fold blouse, split skirt and belt runs from about ¥50,000. Bows alone start at ¥15,500 in fiber glass, ¥25,000 traditional compound bamboo-&-yew, while masterpieces of lacquered bows run to artware prices. Bow is off-center, short bottom arc, long top (usable from horseback as in *yabusame*); called compound recurve, made of sandwich of several strips of bamboo & yew, that curves back on itself when strung—modern cheap practise bows of glass fiber. Too long to mail; must, and can, take as baggage, set weighs 1.5 kg, goes on as check-in or even carry-on baggage as we've done often—it's too unwieldy to use for hijacking, so won't be challenged. Lay it down alongside seat against outer wall.

BAMBOO

In late spring to late summer **DS** have large selection of *sudare* blinds, *kago* baskets, traditional housewares made of this wonder grass. (Kyoto is best place for artistic bamboo wares.) Out of season try:

Kamiyama Sudareten, 1-8-8 Kyobashi, ☎3561-0945, 8-8pm, no-X. Orders take about 3 weeks.

Iwai-shoten makes traditional storage boxes lacquered black, dark brown or vermilion in a nest of 3, often embellished with family crest. 2-10-1 Ningyocho Nihonbashi near far east end of Ningyocho subway exit. 8-8:30pm, X-sun, hols. ☎3668-6058.

CAMERAS

If you must buy one here, best discount shops are in Shinjuku with branches at both east and west exits. East (Higashi): son Cellin's favorite

Yodoyabashi Camera ☎3356-1010, 9:30-9pm, no-X;

Sakuraya, 2 doors away and next door to Takano fruit store, ☎3352-4711, 10-8pm;

Yodoyabashi Camera on opposite side, west (Nishi) of JR-complex station closing 30min earlier ☎3346-1010, **Sakuraya** 10-8pm; at 2-Gokan ☎3348-2241, 8:30-9pm, sun & hols 10-8:30pm.

Incidentally, if you've lost your camera, our Tokyo Shopper Sandra Mori suggests buying 2nd-hand. She got buy for ¥5,000.

Good shop is...
Matsuzakaya Camera near Takanawadai by Meiji Gakuin-mae stop of bus from
Shinagawa stn. Amazing array of cameras from just point and shoot idiot boxes to
whole floor of foreign-made cameras; 1-27-34 Takanawa; 10-7pm (sun, hol-5pm),
☎3443-1311.

CERAMICS
Ceramics fall into 3 groups: antique (covered above), folkcraft (covered
below) and contemporary utilitarian covered here. Choose *DS at all times
for best assortment of gift and practical use items of latter two groups.
Regional ware specialty shops downtown are:

Kyoto Center (*Kyoto Noren*) carries Kiyomizu-yaki among their elite selection of
products of Kyoto (*see* CRAFTS below). Across from Nikko Hotel in Kyoto Shimbun
Bldg lF, 8-2-8 Ginza, 11-7pm, X-sun, hol. ☎574-6484.

Tachikichi Kyoto maker of Kiyomizu-yaki porcelains in excellent taste, is in Nishi
Ginza on 2nd street W of Ginza, little N of Miyuki-dori; 11-7pm, X-sun; ☎3571-2924.

Koransha, magnificent porcelains of Kyushu's Arita ware, at far E end of Miyuki-dori
extended beyond Ginza almost at Showa-dori. ☎3543-0951, 9:30-6:30pm, X-sun, hol.

CRAFTS
We list shops that have bit of everything in contemporary or recent folk–
crafts—others carrying primarily antique crafts are listed under 'ANTIQUES'.
Interesting visit would be to stop in at **Prefectural product display** and
sales rooms run by various prefectures which are conveniently clustered
together in two buildings at Yaesu side of Tokyo Stn in Tetsudo Kaikan (9th
fl. of Daimaru DS) ☎3231-0953, 10-5pm, X-sun, hols; and next door on 1st thru
4th floors of Kokusai Kanko Kaikan ☎3215-1181. If you're not going to
Kyoto, there's **Kyoto Center** (Kyoto Noren) with independent stalls for
dolls, incense (Shoeido), Kiyomizu pottery, textiles incl Tatsumura
brocades, and bamboo baskets large and small in Kyoto Shimbun Bldg lF, Ginza
8-2-8 on Sotobori-dori opposite Nikko Hotel, ☎3572-6484, 11-7pm, X-sun, hol.

*Bingo-ya** in Shinjuku (taxi lx-mtr from Waseda stn, Tozai subway) worth visit. Has
basement of folk toys, dolls, and 5 fls full of usual crafts plus lots of kites, masks,
drums, straw coats, no large tansu. 10-7pm, 69 Wakamatsu-cho, ☎3202-8561.

Japan Traditional Craft Center, excellent selection, also holds exhibitions of
various top artisans or high quality crafts, in Plaza 246 2fl, Aoyama-dori & Aoyama 1-
chome. Has fine library, videos (Eng.) of many crafts. ☎3403-2460, X-thu.

*Takumi**, one of first folkcraft shops in Tokyo. Has superb quality textiles, pottery,
paper & paper products, etc. Owner led in folk art movement with Yanagi Soetsu &
Bernard Leach. 4-25 Ginza 8-chome on Sotobori-dori. ☎3571-2017, X-sun.

KITES made by artisan at home, colorfully hand-painted by:

Teizo Hashimoto. Ueno, 2-2-5 Higashi Ueno, Taitoku. ☎3841-2661, call for appt.
Standard size 45x40cm, one warrior, ¥5,000; 55x80cm, 2 warriors, ¥15,000+.
Bingoya has fine selection available (which *see*, p1274, and above).

CARP STREAMERS (*koinobori*) put up on Boy's day, around May 5.

Yoshitoku Doll Co has them year round and available at DS April-June, (*see* Dolls).
Mostly nylon fabrics now. Small size set includes 2 carps (1 red, 1 black), decorative
wheel ¥20,000, 3m ¥30,000, 5m ¥67,000, 10m ¥200,000.

HERO BANNERS (*hata-nobori*) tall banners, formerly for samurai, now Boy's Day
decoration, made at **Musashiya Shoten**. Battle scenes with 3-5 warriors, 5m tall
¥50,000, 7m ¥80,000. Order filled in 2 weeks, usually family crest is added. Carp
streamers here: 1 red 5m is ¥17,000. Blk is usually 1m longer. 1-7-1 Kuramae near

Kuramae-dori. 9-6pm, X-sun, hol. ☎3851-5817. If going out to Mashiko pottery center in Tochiki Pref not far from Nikko, visit **Musha-e-no-Sato Ohata** and watch banners being made. Maker's prices one-half. JR Hamamachi stn, Haga-gun, Ichigai-machi, Tanobe 701-2. ☎(0285)-68-0108. JTB had good tour covering them and paper maker.

DEPARTMENT STORES

First of all, department stores (DS) are described in MARKETPLACE (p169), but we'll list here bringing out their special characteristics by location.

Downtown few blocks from Imperial Hotel, by Yurakucho stn is Mullion bldg, with movie theaters and two chic new DS carrying unique quality merchandise and limited utilitarian sections of select foods, furniture: **Seibu** (X-thu, foreign liaison section on 3rd fl ☎3286-0111) and **Hankyu** (X-thu, ☎3575-2233) both catering more to well-heeled younger. Then bit N across el tracks is **Sogo** (X-tue); S across ave older **Hankyu** (X-thu) mostly clothing—both standard DS.

Few blocks east is Ginza 4-chome intersection with massive sprucing up and facelifting in maneuver to attract affluent younger women to shop where until now mostly wealthy matrons frequented, such as: **Wako** (X-sun, hol, ☎3562-2111) more specialty shop than DS, with smart clothes, exquisite gift items–fashionably expensive. To S is **Sanai** haven for young women, clothes and accessories relatively inexpensive. **Mitsukoshi** branch of old prestigious DS (X-mon, ☎3562-1111) is E across Ginza with **Matsuya** (X-tue, ☎3567-1211) bit north, both more for fashion, smart accessories than housewares. **Matsuzakaya** (X-wed, ☎3572-1111) down S few blocks on Ginza is large sprawling with just about anything you want.

Up north on Ginza near Tokyo Stn are two DS whose wrappers, bags are status prizes like NY Tiffany's:
Mitsukoshi Nihonbashi (X-mon, ☎3241-3311), branches at JR stns in Ikebukuro ☎3982-1111, Shinjuku ☎3368-1111; and **Takashimaya** (X-wed, ☎3211-4111). Nearby is **Tokyu** (X-thur, ☎3273-3111) and **Daimaru** (X-wed, ☎3212-8011) at Stn.

These standard DS all have handy section for tourists—yukata out of season, washi paper products, crafts, kimono, touristy items, souvenirs.

SHIBUYA area in 1964 had only Tokyu **Toyoko** DS at end of Toyoko Ry, later **Tokyu Plaza**, **Tokyu** DS and **Tokyu Bunka Kaikan**, but then **Seibu** (X-wed, ☎462-0111) moved in confidently with their **A-Kan** (Bldg A), **B-Kan** and **C-Kan** followed by modern idea conglomerate of boutiques in **Parco Part I** (fashions for all), **II** (designer clothes), **III** (fashions plus some furniture and 'interior' goods), all no-X. Seibu with excellent merchandising brings new vista to department stores, which until then were mostly all of same pattern catering to same upper-middle classes and tastes. **Tokyu Hands** then appeared with something for everyone and Hands means 'do it yourself' with their supplies for home, garden, garage, etc, and more important 'let us do it for you'–repair, sew, make customized most anything you need, services now badly needed (X-2nd & 3rd wed) ☎3476-5461. **Seed** Seibu's latest touts newest ultra-fashion items. Tokyu came back with **109** series, geared for young crowd and **Loft**. Shibuya is exciting for resident or those with plenty of time (*see* p1154) but hurried shopper can skip.

SHINJUKU, major hub for suburban lines has had **Isetan** (X-wed, ☎3352-1111) and **Mitsukoshi** (X-mon, ☎3354-1111) for years; all-purpose DS, but Isetan Shinkan 'new'-annex is favored by foreign residents for clothing section carrying large sizes for both men and women plus foreign-staff Int'l counter, 5 fl. Watch for their super designer clothes sales. In station **Keio** (X-thu, ☎3342-2111) and **Odakyu** (X-thu, 3342-1111) typical terminal DS.

While in Shinjuku we mention couple of shops from our original edition:
Takano, fruit shop (listed by tax office as sitting on most expensive piece of land in
Shinjuku, Tokyo, Japan, perhaps world); bldg houses designer boutiques, incl great shop
for handbags (next door to famous discount electronic and camera shops **Sakuraya** and
Yodobashi Camera);
Okadaya (no-X, ☎3352-5411) from Shinjuku stn on L 2nd blk up on street leading to
Koma Theater in Kabuki-cho, now multi-storeyed stocking ribbons, buttons, lingerie,
and all your sewing needs and related items.

IKEBUKURO further out has huge sprawling 12-story **Seibu**, forerunner in
new ideas, with everything any DS offers, including art, plus probably
largest selection of unusual local and imported goods—was probably largest
DS in world, and enlarged further in October 1989 with connecting annex
known as **SMA** incorporating **Sezon**, new spelling of their Saison group,
with 2 basements devoted entirely to books, 1st fl Art gallery well-known
for its world-class exhibitions, and 2nd fl Museum (☎3981-0111, 10-4pm, X-
thu). Across street another new annex **Wave** (*Eizo-kan*), 6 fls entirely of
audio-visual, hi-tech equipment incl robots. Main store fls 9-12 is sports,
including yachts. Main store 10-7pm; Wave 10-8, SMA 10-8pm. X-tue, ☎981-0111.

DOLLS
More to be looked at than played with. Ningyo-cho by Mitsukoshi DS was
center for dolls. Now best are:
Yoshitoku 1-9-14 Asakusabashi, ☎3851-0165; & *Kyugetsu** nearby 20-4
Yanagibashi ☎3861-5511. Both experienced in shipping overseas. Beautiful refined
classic dolls by **Beishu Hara**, designated 'Intangible Cultural Asset', 5-9-13 Ginza, N of
Matsuzakaya DS in Ginza, ☎3572-1397. Tiny figurines at **Sukeroku** at end Nakamise-
dori arcade leading to Asakusa Kannon (*see* Asakusa, p1191).

HANKO (SIGNATURE SEALS)
Signature Seals or 'chops': have your own signature seal carved in *kanji*,
ideographs fitting your name phonetically. You'll have to have someone
choose appropriate ideographs to fit your name. Most commonly made of
ivory, now banned, but summer '90 Japan bought deep-sea-salvaged cache
of ancient ivory, enough for years of legal seal-making.
Haibara in Marunouchi Arcade just W facing old Tokyo Stn has been carving them for
years. Seals in *tsuge* boxwood ¥1,133 for plain small ovals with 2-3 characters and
¥8,240 for larger *jitsu-in hanko* of 4-5 ideographs of last and first names. Allow 4 days.
☎3212-4771.

KIMONO
Kimono can be divided into two groups: worn by Japanese in Japan, and
for use by foreigners. First, basically kimono for special occasions, which
are exquisite, different for weddings, formal affairs, visiting or casual home
wear now not often seen. Seasonal, fashions change regularly subtlely so
uninitiated should be advised that kimono may be kimono, but it might not
be right one. And proper accessories make wearing kimono quite expensive
hobby. DS have large kimono floors and specialty kimono shops abound.
Best kimono are all sewn to order from rolls of textiles rolled up into 15-
inch rolls, or better still designed or handpainted or woven from scratch just
for you. I chose textured white roll and had it dyed to my favorite lilac for
use as special Chinese dress.
Can't resist bringing in shop recutting old kimono textiles for modern wear:
Boutique Yuya on TV Asahi-dori across from Chinese embassy. Spacious showroom
filled with wearable chic outfits at reasonable prices. Yuya Nagahata collection of skirts,
blouses from ¥30,000 with dressy outfits from ¥60,000. Margot Yuki, able assistant,
stands by to help; ☎5474-2097, 11-8pm, X-sun, hol.

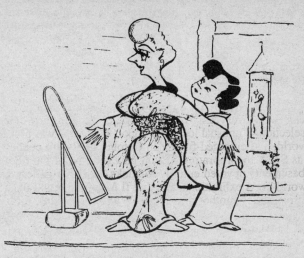

Somehow, Sumi, it doesn't look the same on me

But what interests most of us is **used**, that is mostly semi-antique, kimono. There are shops selling these with basically inexpensive new and secondhand kimono, including elaborate wedding robes. Shops mentioned under "popular with foreigners" in ANTIQUE, CURIO above carry good line. Monthly antique markets have stalls with secondhand kimono and obi, usually cheaper and lesser quality goods. First three shops below are easy to get to with good selection.

*Hayashi Kimono, we've known them from postwar occupation days in Kanda. Now in easy-to-find INTERNATIONAL ARCADE ☎3591-9826 by Imperial Hotel, and across street in other part of Int'l Arcade; large selection, experienced staff. No-X, 9:30-7pm.

George Silk, kimono new, old; painted screens 2x4ft (¥30-40,000), 3x6ft (avg ¥60,000); ceramics, pearls ☎3580-5350, Akasaka nr Hie Shrine and Tokyu Capitol Hotel, X-sun.

*Oyama upstairs in Oriental Bazaar on Omote-Sando, ☎3498-3291, large stock, ¥3,000 up, bridal robes about ¥10,000; 9:30-6:30pm, X-thu.

Akariya, 5-57-11 Yoyogi, Shibuya-ku ☎3467-0580 (X-thu), 11-7 pm.

Doi, Antique Gallery Meguro, 2fl, 2-24-18-201, Kamiosaki, Shinagawa-ku, X-mon, hol, ☎3493-1971

Omoshiroya, old main shop is bit out in suburb Kichijoji (*see* p1153), huge selection, inexpensive; ☎(0422)-22-8565, 1-11-101 Kichijoji Higashi-cho, Musashino-shi; but new branch in Asakusa in Asakura bldg 2fl, Asakusa 1-chome 6-3, on Koen-dori 4 blks W of Kaminarimon gate; ☎3847-8380, 11-7pm, no-X.

If you're lucky to be here when **DS** hold semi-annual used kimono sales of *kashi-isho* rental kimono, ¥5,000 up; with *uchi-kake* bridal robes ¥5-10-15,000—you'll find great buys since kimono are not so old:

Takashimaya DS, Ginza, (☎3211-4111) schedules 3-6 day periods in Jan, Mar, Apr, July, Oct, Dec.

Daimaru Tokyo stn Yaesu side (☎3212-8011) has Feb/Mar and Aug/Sept for 1-6 days; similar in branches in other cities.

Isetan (☎3352-1111) is fun with spring 1wk show usually April combined with Kyoto antique shops; Aug is 1wk kimono sale.

KIMONO ACCESSORIES
Fine accessories are chosen discriminately, especially footwear as *zori* slippers are left in foyer as one enters local home. (This holds for shoes, too, hence popularity of top brand shoes for men and women, who place shoes—neatly pointing outward—so as to show off brand-name on insole). Best shops are in Ginza because that was and still is, *the* place to shop. Try specialty shops:

Zenya whose master invented an easy to dance in *zori* . Their oiled paper & silk bamboo ribbed umbrellas are wonderful. Ginza 8-8-1, ☎3571-3468.

Awaya, Ginza 8-4-23, ☎3571-0722, also top quality; can get men's large sizes. Normally 28cm is considered large, but...

*Okada-ya in Ryogoku has *zori* and *geta* in gigantic sizes as they supply sumo wrestlers from nearby Kokugikan sumo arena. 9:30-8pm, X-sun, hol. ☎3631-2002.

BAGS, *TABI*: *Tabi*, neat split-toe sox, worn with kimono are usually white or black (for men), but...

*Myogaya with tradition of 330 yrs catering to elite and dancers of Hayanagi School, makes custom-made tabi in plain colors or beautiful theatrical prints. Jean Cocteau was one of their foreign clients. Ginza 8-6-6, ☎3571-3670.

Onoya at 2-2 Shintomi-cho, just E of Showa-dori, ☎3551-0896, 10-8pm, X-sun. Fine shop I covered in 1953 as a columnist for local English paper.

Kikuya carries similar goods; also caters to sumo-tori, 1-9-3 Midori, Sumida-ku; ☎3631-0092, 9-7pm, X-sun.

Workmen's *jika-tabi* split-toe canvas shoes with flexible rubber soles, and being slip-proof ideal for working on tile roofs or for climbing) at...

*Isogai Tetsuzo Shoten, shop for laborer's gear, 1-10-2 Narihira, Sumida-ku, ☎3622-2665, 8-8pm; also carries cotton or wool jodhpur-like trousers and other exotica.

Kunoya on Ginza for bags10-8pm, X- , ☎3571-2546; Kaname, bags, accessories for hair, Ginza 8-7-18, ☎3571-1715.

LACQUERWARE
DS have excellent selection of *Urushi* or 'Japaning'. Specialty shops best:

*Inachu is from Wajima, where ware is epitome of exquisite, shibui, classic lines. Akasaka &Tameike intersection, ☎3582-4451, 10-7pm, X-sun.

Heiando, 3-ch Nihonbashi behind Takashimaya DS, ☎3272-2871; 9-6pm, X-sun, hol.

Kuroeya, 1-2-6 Nihonbashi, in front of Tokyu DS. ☎3271-3356, 9-5pm.

NOH MASKS
Fine noh masks of performance quality, old or new, are difficult to find. Most DS have small selection on art floor, but...

Wanya Shoten is affectionately called "DS where anything connected with noh can be found or arranged for." Noh mask signed by artist from ¥150,000; ceramic, papier mache around ¥11,000; fans, drums, accessories. Exquisite shop, on Konparu-dori, 1 block W of Ginza from Shiseido bldg. 10-6pm, X-sun, hols, 1st & 3rd sat; 8-7-5 Ginza, ☎3571-0514. Main store at Kanda Jimbo-cho 3-9, 9:30-5:30pm, X-sun, hols. ☎3263-6771.

PAPER, PAPER PRODUCTS
Infinite variety in *washi* handmade papers—mistakenly called "rice" paper, but actually made from *kozo* mulberry or other vegetable fibers, etc. Papers thin as angel's hair, white or pastels and shibui colors, all natural dyes, others flecked with gold, silver, leaves, folkcraft stenciled paper, and wallpaper incl silk and grasscloth.

Most craft shops carry good line, but few primarily paper shops are:

Haibara old reputable shop has all these and more in new bldg, lst fl, same location as before at S-exit of Tokyu DS, 2-7-6 Nihonbashi, ☎3272-3801, X-sun, hols.

*****Washikobo**, devoted to *washi* from all parts of Japan, all sizes up to fusuma-door size and hundreds of folkcraft articles—masks, kites, boxes, chests, lanterns. Near Jiyu Theater on wide st from Roppongi to Shibuya, ☎3405-1841, X-sun, hols.

Kyukyo-do, easy to find on Ginza just S of round Sanai Bldg at Ginza 4-chome & Harumidori intersection. Elegant *washi*-paper stationery and paper products along with fine paraphernalia for artists, seasonal ceramic seals to embellish paintings, incense, fans, bit of old Kyoto refinement transported from Kyoto main shop, so different from souvenir shops. 10-8pm; 11-7pm sun, hol, no-X. ☎3571-4429.

Origami Kaikan has 2 floors filled with every conceivable type of paper for folding-origami animals, gift wrapping, covering boxes, stationery. 1-7-14 Yushima, Bunkyo-ku. 9-5pm, X-sun, hol. ☎3811-4025.

PEARLS

Judged on natural combination of color, luster, size, coating, shape and flaws (see p326). Pinks in greatest demand, whites follow, with yellows last and cheapest. Limited and expensive blue-grays are known as black pearls. Luster is depth of glow created by numerous layers of translucent "pearl" which grew on irritant. Perfectly round flawless are best; tear-drops are in demand for pendants, earrings; baroque, misshapen and bluish-gray, were worthless till fashion dictates gave them considerable value. *Mabe* half-pearl grows on oyster shell itself. Quality of fresh-water pearls has greatly improved.

Better imitation pearls now have same shell center for weight (thus same heft) and are coated with crushed powdered pearl for 'genuine' look—known as 'shell pearl' and hard to tell from real at ordinary level except, obviously, on price tag. However, recently becoming difficult to find available on market.

Present $ exchange makes shopping difficult, but still for top quality pearls you will get better buy here. Hongkong offers good buys in inexpensive fresh-water and lower quality pearls.

We must bring out **Mikimoto**, whose founder developed cultured pearls. For years Mikimoto was world pearl king. Branches found everywhere; main Ginza shop is worth visit. They maintain highest standards of quality and design with commensurate prices. Ginza 4-chome few doors N of Wako, 10:30-6pm, X-wed. ☎3535-4611.

Foremost dealers from Kobe—known as Pearl City, capital of pearl wholesalers—have opened showrooms in Tokyo:

*****Yamakatsu Pearl** claims most expanse of own farms including Ise, Ehime, Saga, Kumamoto and Kagoshima prefectures. Their gallery is in 8-storey red brick bldg at Toranomon across from original wing of Okura Hotel. Sales on lst fl; can ask to see their factory workshop on 8th fl. ☎437-3320, 10:00-6:30, X-sun, hol. Branches: Akasaka 8-5-32, ☎3470-0222; Shinjuku, Hilton Hotel Hiltopia arcade, 11-7pm, no-X, ☎3345-9251.

*****Tasaki Pearl**'s main shop, l-chome Akasaka, near NCR bldg has 5 fl (3, 4 devoted to intricate process of cultured pearls; lst fl, pendants, brooches, men's accessories; 2 finer pearl necklaces; 5 pearls combined with other stones). They recently developed so-called South Sea pearls at their farm at Amami Oshima. ☎5561-8880, 10-6:30pm, no-X.

Our favorite shops:

*****Mori Silver** in ORIENTAL BAZAAR, 2nd fl (*see* pp1158, 1328) carries good selection of quality inexpensive pearls, jewelry, netsuke.

*Takane Pearl located under Yamate el-line behind Imperial Hotel, way back at end of INTERNATIONAL ARCADE, is run by artistic family. Mother's keen eye has kept quality and styling above all. Large selection and very moderate prices. Daughter WATANABE Nobuko who spent years in Paris, keeps up tradition. ☎3591-2764.

Imperial Hotel Arcade has old stolid standbys, 10-7pm, no-X:
Mikimoto Pearl, ☎3591-5001; ***Mayuyama Antique** ☎3591-6655, **K.Uyeda Jewelry**, ☎3503-2587, **Asahi Shoten** ☎3503-22528 & **Okubo Bros** ☎3504-0088.

WOODBLOCK PRINTS

Most antique and curio shops carry good selection of reproductions, as well as some old prints. Originals may still be found on general market, tho usually lower quality prints of popular Hokusai, Hiroshige landscapes. But fine originals from storybooks are still available at reasonable prices—keep eye open for old woodblock-printed books with colored pictures.

Two old favorite specialty shops are:
Sakai Kokodo we've known them since 1952, and they still have affordable original Hiroshige, etc; now in new shop same location across from N-side Imperial Hotel (maintain own print museum *Nihon Ukiyoe-kan* in Matsumoto, Nagano), 10am-7pm, ☎3591-4678, X-sun, hol.

Nakazawa next door with equally interesting supply. Neighboring second-hand book stores carry good selection.

Oldtimers in Jimbo-cho in Kanda (see p.1173) are:
Oya Shobo where years ago we bought old sets of hilarious 15 vol *Hokusai Manga*, now priceless, ☎3291-0062, 10-6:30pm, X-sun; and
Hara Shobo prints, few doors away.

MODERN PRINTS
Tolman Collection: Norman and Mary Tolman, since his USIS days have built fine collection of prints by modern artists sold from their beautiful Japanese house near Zojoji Temple by Tokyo Prince Hotel in Shiba; 2-2-18 Shiba Daimon, nr Shibakoen stn on Mita subway, or Hamamatsu stn on JR Loop; 11am-7pm, advise phone to enquire what's on special show, ☎3434-1300.

Japan Print, contemp, nr Iikura-Katamachi intersection, ☎3582-5679, X-sun, hol.

SWORDS

Embodied spirit of samurai and were sacred, thus special rituals of purification attended forging of new blade. Sword blade itself is of interest only to special collectors (tho British or Germans often outbid Japanese when good swords come up at London auction), but decorative fittings, *menuki* clasps on hilt; *tsuba* metal sword guards and small throwing knives are exquisite examples of carved metalwork. *Menuki*, tho only 1.5 inches long, have overpowering designs in miniature, miniscule sculpture that also make up as exceptional cufflinks, earrings, brooches.

Japan Sword, is best, with English-speaking INAMI Tomio, owner-smith-expert, ready to help you choose finest swords, helmets, and armor; 3-8-1 Toranomon–drop in on walk p.1162–☎3434-4321, X-sun, hols. Selection of modern accessories in sword motifs.

*Every man carries within himself a world made up of
all that he has seen and loved; and it is to this world
that he returns incessantly, though he may pass through
and seem to inhabit, a world quite foreign to it.*
— Chateaubriand, *Voyage en Italie*

PEBBLES CARRIED HOME
UNDER OUR SANDLE THONGS

WHETHER TRAVELING Japan on shoestring, oops, sandal thong, or finest Bonwit Teller seven-league boots, we find pebbles in them when we get home: each another memory relived in aftertaste, its recollection keyed while unpacking some trifle or getting back snapshots and transparencies. Little things will stand out to be savored, recalled in flashback by some strange trigger: smell, word. That pigeon in Central Park wiggles in to land like that one in Higashi Hongan-ji in Kyoto and momentarily bell of park Good Humor man and prayer bell of white-robed Buddhist pilgrim are one.

We've jotted down our aftertastes of numerous departures and share them, as Sydney Clark did his of Italy in book we once enjoyed using.

Strolling alleys of weaver's section, Nishijin, unable to tell it from any other old Kyoto quarter, same grillfront dark houses low hanging tiled roofs ...until we hear clack and clatter of what we learn to be brocade looms.

Suspension-shattering road over spine of Japan from Himeji to Tottori, too steep and winding and bumpy to allow enough calm for looking at scenery until very top and dark, dank tunnel through peak and out into light, wide spot roadside and on knoll like apparition from some ancient painting stood this moon-viewing pavilion with bench facing breath-taking view of mountain upon mountain down to far distant Japan Sea.

Living masks of *noh* dance-drama which when in full possession of actor-wearer flush and perspire like living flesh.

Sheet of heavy paper, unrolled, reveals intricately scaled and shaded writhing dragon in black and colored ink interworked; we picked it up at country shrine fair where old man painted them, each different, each completed with one single unbroken stroke of brush dipped in several shades and colors of inks.

Weird trees along Hozu River rapids near Kyoto bring to mind old haiku: *Seen from moving boat even mountains move...but do those pines know*.

Hot summer night in country inn, lying flat on *tatami* mats making book on race of gekko house lizards across ceiling after emerald lace-wings.

Dripping faucet at home keeps us awake all night while purposeful drip into garden pond outside our Japanese inn window lulled us to sleep.

Late summer sun setting behind mountain; glitter of rubies and sapphires in air — *tombo* dragonflies over paddy, pirouetting higher and higher above line of rising dark to stay in sun's last light.

Indigo silence of air calmed during still 'eye' of typhoon.

Birdhouse-size stone roadside shrine, fresh flowers set before door just inch ajar, inquistive, just one peak, open and ...oops, fertility idol.

Jay slumming red light and bar alleys of Hiroshima with fellow *gaijin sensei* (foreign teacher): nymphet dashes from bar, arms wide, screaming, "Hey, my Engrish professer!"

Our honeymoon morning, since-lost inn in Hakone, Hokusai-red sun rising in vale between two mammary mountains enshrouded in purple mist.

Midnite in city, eerie silence broken?...deepened?...by lonely toodle of noodle man's floodle, hollow clop of *geta* clog footsteps on pavement.

Skyscraper inns of Kinugawa entered as single-storey and walked thru to find we're 8 floors up in gigantic wasps' hive against chasm wall, every room with full unencumbered view of public baths of inns across canyon.

Hill between Kyoto and Osaka where two famous folklore frogs met: one coming from each city to visit other, exhausted, propped each other up to see where they were going and disappointedly saw city just like his own so turned home, unaware their eyes were in backs of their heads — as modern tourists frog-hop from imitation American hotel to imitation American hotel, eating tasteless imitation American foodless food.

First faltering steps into giant mixed bath, flustered, worrying "What do I do if ..." and before you know it you're out there in public...there's nothing to it— and no one grinning "Sir, or madame, may I speak Engrish?"

Winter in Japanese *hori-kotatsu*, feet in hole-in-floor getting warmed, smell of smouldering nylon ...ouch!

Sunrise on Inland Sea like developing color film as misty world transforms from greys and shadows subtly thru pastels into living colors.

Skitter and slap of *shoji* panels sliding open in your ryokan room, *suru-suru* of breeze in bamboo outside, crickets lamenting their loneliness.

Summer dining out on stage set out over "Duck River" in downtown Kyoto for natural air conditioning — concert of itinerant 'samurai' flutist on *shakuhachi* (¥100 or 500 coin in order), clowning of female impersonators of hobo kabuki troupe taking "net profit" with their ten-foot butterfly net.

Smell of handmade paper recalls healthy cows and New England hayloft.

Sad looks on faces of group tourists trudging from imitation American hotel to imitation French restaurant or rooftop imitation Rathskeller (*sic*), with every step despair deepening of ever seeing any piece of that Japan tourist brochures advertised or of meeting any Japanese beyond bamboozle curtain of their mercenary Judas Goat: this sight saddens us, thus Japanesely deepening our own smug savoring of our present fact.

Take things as they come, one step at time, epitomized by sumo grand champion when interviewed 1990, "Chiyonofuji, you have set all-time record of 1,000 victories; what is your next big goal?" He smiled, "1,001".

Peace Dome ruins of Hiroshima, pile of charred rubble barren but for giant sunflower growing wild — one snapshot we did get.

"...in centuries to come, when another traveller visits this same place, he too may groan aloud at the disappearance of much that I should have set down, but cannot. I am victim of a double infirmity: what I see is affliction to me; and what I do not see, a reproach." Claude Levi-Strauss wrote that in *Tristes Tropiques* and it haunts every writer, as it will haunt you when you make up your snapshot album and curse shots you forgot to take.

STREET SCENES

THINGS TO WATCH FOR IN PASSING: Those few pedlars who still ply their trades with traditional whistles and cries, etc, of morning scrap-paper buyer exchanging for toilet paper or tissues, yodel of *nato*-bean paste man, steam whistle of baked sweet potato hawker, to late-nite clack of sticks punctuating cautioning chorus of volunteer firewatch, and toot of noodle man's flute–now played on tape thru amp run off his truck battery. Noiseless fixed-time visit of fishmonger in open-sided truck laden with fresh seafood, some of it still flopping. Tiny truck hawking cupcake-balls of minced octopus, *tako-yaki*. Photogenic flower carts in cities, selling fine blooms fit for ikebana.

School uniforms, JrHi and Hi-schoolboys in tight high celluloid-lined collars of Bismarck's Prussia, recently giving way to British-style blazer and contrasting slacks — but thankfully no beany-cap. Girls in middy and shin-length pleated skirt. Many schools have draconian dress codes forbidding hair or skirt length variation of single inch, no makeup, nor accessories beyond school badge.

Dress code or not, on days off young girls wear some of best readiing in Japan: T-shirts with Japlish or arbitrarily (mis-)quoted Engrish, some of it unintentionally risque. Makes for good excuse to stare at chests — but turn aside to snicker. Shopping bags are second fun source of such surrealist literature.

Stroll residential areas and note gates and wall textures of varied aged-and scorched-woods or freestone masonry evolved of ricepaddy terracing. Gate, word for which is homonym with that for family crest, *mon*, was mark of status from olden times — emperor is Mikado, 'Illustrious Gate'. Note gate (whether tile-roofed J-style or side-pillared W-style) often has two doors, one large car-size central double door rarely opened except at new year or special occasions (actual garage is in new box off to side), other for daily use is usually to left, narrow and low enough to have to stoop thru in humility.

At base of residence walls, especially along narrow alleys, we often see small torii some 10-12"/25-30cm tall, sometimes just in red paint, others actual wooden torii, also red. Such touching faith, one thinks to oneself, fine example of folk religion…then we learn that such 'sanctification' of place is to discourage passersby from urinating.

Department stores, from just before 10am opening with troops of girls in uniform lined up outside, along inner corridors, at escalators and elevators, bowing in Rockettes-unison and chorusing welcome and news of day's specials. Helpful sales-persons who never impose but help and usually stick with you till satisfied—so different from '64 edition when they were well-intentioned but hopelessly inept because untrained. Basement food section (open later than upstairs), true oriental bazaar of scents and tastes with food and drink bars galore and most counters decorated with screaming hawkers welcoming you to platters full of toothpick-handled free samples of every sort of exotic dish one can imagine, washed down with paper shot-glass of wine or juice–where budgeteer can smilingly cadge light lunch, or true-shopper make surprisingly tasty discoveries worth buying. Store usually adjoins rail station, linked thru subterranean market-maze of small shops and boutiques and pilgrim- to budget-rate eating and drinking alleys, such as Tokyo-Shinjuku or Osaka-Umeda, virtually towns in themselves.

Restaurants here or along streets have front window or showcase full of food plates, 3-D menu of offerings with prices in Arabic numerals (sometimes in Sino-Japanese characters)—their presence marks affordable place from pilgrim rate to comfortable tourist. Hint: if plastic decoy looks clean and 'fresh', so is their food.

Young men, swaggering theatrically in broad pantaloons or knicker-bockers, usually with putties and black rubber sneakers with separate mitten-like big toe (WWII sniper shoes, or 'ninja boots'). Pants and usually matching shirt, often with vest, range from business-suit somberness to wild chartreuse and such. Still feudal craft-costume of construction gangs, Japanese navvies. Great guys, who respond heartily to greetings.

Japan-Basher James Fallows mellowed after residing here on research fellowship. Told interviewer Mike Millard of *Japan Times Weekly*: "Japan has given me a new zest for life...shown me that the world is bigger than I thought, that the world has more twists and turns than I thought. It gives me more reason to live".

Memories of childhood and Japanese toys; dry, sweet pungent odor of "Japan'd" (lacquered) miniature chiffonier whose tiny drawers we loved to open, noses near crack to catch first waft of its special aroma. Japanese shops in New York (especially favorite Katagiri's on 59th st) all smelled that way; little miniature garden pagodas did — ah, smell of Japan. For years here we hunted for it in vain, in old shops, musty temples, even in lacquer factory. Nowhere. Then home to America, unpacking gifts, opening trunk sent as unaccompanied and mother exclaims, "Smell it, smell Japan. How lovely it must be to live in such an aura...." Smell of Japan, that olefactory Holy Grail.

Reading Joseph Brodsky's warning: "Bearing in mind that every observation suffers from the observer's personal traits — that is, it too often reflects his psychological state rather than that of the reality under observation..."

But rereading Bernard Berenson: "I encountered fellow men singularly like ourselves. Culturally, this is the best recommendation for travelling."

Sayonara ... which translates literally, "If it must be..."

                                        ...then *mata irasshai* "...come again".

GLOSSARY

FOR GUIDE to Japanese pronunciation, useful conversation and handy expressions see SAY IT IN NIHON-GO, p.175. For local foods, *see* CHOPSTICKS, p.139. For easier recognition, long 'o' is, here only, written 'oh', as also 'ah', 'uh'(uu).

NUMBERS	*bangoh*
one	*ichi; hitotsu*
two	*ni; futatsu*
three	*san; mittsu*
four	*shi; yottsu*
five	*go; itsutsu*
six	*roku; muttsu*
seven	*hichi; nana; nanatsu*
eight	*hachi; yattsu*
nine	*kyu; kokonotsu*
ten	*juu; toh*
eleven	*juu-ichi*
twenty	*ni-juu*
thirty	*san-juu*
forty	*yon-juu*
hundred	*hyaku*
2 hundred	*ni-hyaku*
3 hundred	*san-byaku*
4 hundred	*yon-hyaku*
5 hundred	*go-hyaku*
6 hundred	*rop-pyaku*
7 hundred	*nana-hyaku*
8 hundred	*hap-pyaku*
9 hundred	*kyu-hyaku*
thousand	*sen*
2 thousand	*ni-sen*
10 thousand	*ichi-man*
20 thousand	*ni-man*
million	*hyaku-man*
10 million	*sen-man*
100 million	*oku*

MONEY	(O) *kane*
1 yen, 5 yen	*ichi en, go en*
10 yen, 60 yen	*juu en, roku-juu en*
5,000 yen	*go-sen en*
5,800 yen	*go-sen hap-pyaku en*
10,000 yen	*ichi-man en*
15,000 yen	*ichi-man go-sen en*

EVERYDAY words	*nichijyoh yohgo*
when	*itsu*
where, whither	*doko, dochira*
why	*dohshite, naze*
what, what is	*nani, nan desuka*
how long	*dono gurai*
how many	*ikutsu*
which	*dochira*
north (comb-)	*kita, hoku-*
south "	*minami, nan-*
west "	*nishi, -sai or sei-*
east "	*higashi, toh-*
SE, NE	*toh-nan, toh-hoku*

SW, NW	*nan-sei, hoku-sei*
right, left	*migi, hidari*
straight	*massugu*
next	*tsugi no*
before	*mae*
beside	*tonari*
little (amt)	*sukoshi*
many (amt)	*takusan*
big, small	*ohkii, chiisai*
narrow, wide	*hosoi, hiroi*
thin	*usui*
new	*atarashii, shin-*
old	*furui*
long, short	*nagai, mijikai*
late, early	*osoi, hayai*
fast, slow	*hayai, osoi*
here, there	*koko, asoko*
this	*kore*
that (near)	*sore*
that (afar)	*are*

GREETINGS	*aisatsu*
good morning	*ohayoh gozaimasu*
good afternoon	*konnichiwa*
good-evening	*konbanwa*
good-night (before sleep)	*oyasumi nasai*
good-bye	*sayonara*
nice to meet you	*hajime mashite*
how are you?	*o'genki desu ka?*
thank you	*arigato gozaimasu*
you're welcome	*doitashimashite*
please (giving)	*dozo*
please (asking)	*onegai shimasu, kudasai*
please excuse me	*shitsurei shimasu, sumimasen*
after you	*dozo osaki-ni*
is this alright?	*ii desu ka?*
Yes, it's fine	*hai, kekko desu*
I'm sorry	*gomen nasai*
let's meet again	*mata ai masho*
please take care	*ki o tsukete kudasai*
please wait	*chotto matte kudasai*
I don't understand	*wakarimasen*

TRAVEL	*ryokoh, tabi*
address	*juusho*
airplane	*hikohki*
airport	*kuhkoh*
bank	*ginkoh*
bicycle	*jitensha*
boat	*fune*

car, automobile	*jidohsha, kuruma*
entrance, exit	*iriguchi, deguchi*
excursion ticket	*shuyuken*
fare	*ryohkin*
station (*abbr* stn)	*eki*
electric train	*densha*
- bullet train	*Shinkansen*
- special express	*tokkyu*
- express	*kyuhkoh*
- semi-express	*junkyuh*
- regular	*futsuu*
- local	*kaku eki teisha*
- rapid	*kaisoku*
- sleeper car	*shindai-sha*
- green car	*gureen-sha*
- reserved seat	*shitei seki*
- unreserved	*jiyuh seki*
map	*chizu*
police station	*kohban*
policeman	*keisatsu*
public telephone	*koshu-denwa*
round trip, one way	*ohfuku, katamichi*
subway	*chikatetsu*
taxi	*takushi*
telephone (no.)	*denwa,(bangoh)*
ticket	*kippu*
toilet	*toire, benjo*
- wash room	*ote arai*
tourist info office	*kankoh annai-jo*
Where is the train station?	*eki wa doko desu ka?*
Which is the track for Kyoto	*Kyoto wa nan ban sen desu ka?*
Does this train stop in Kyoto?	*kono densha wa Kyoto ni tomarimasu ka?*
Is this Kyoto?	*Kyoto wa koko desu ka?*

SIGHTS

bath (*see* p121)	*(o) furo*
- hot spring, spa	*onsen*
- outdoor bath	*rotenburo*
- mixed bathing	*kon-yoku*
- mud bath	*doroyu*
bridge	*hashi, -bashi*
Buddhist temple 卍	*tera, -dera, -ji, -in*
countryside	*inaka*
cherry tree	*sakura*
church	*kyohkai*
festival	*matsuri*
- lantern float fest.	*tohro nagashi*
Japanese inn (p140)	*ryokan*
- family run inn (")	*Minshuku*
- gov't run inn (")	*Kokumin-shukusha*
- temple stay (")	*Shukubo*
garden	*niwa, tei-en*
house	*uchi, ie*
island	*shima, -jima*
library	*toshokan*

mountain	*yama, -san, -zan*
museum (art,)	*bijutsukan*
museum (other)	*hakubutsukan*
park	*koen*
- amusement park	*yuuenchi*
plum tree	*ume*
lake, pond	*ike, -ko*
river	*kawa, -gawa*
school	*gakko*
college, university	*daigaku*
sea	*umi, -kai*
storehouse	*kura, sohko*
street	*michi, tohri, -dohri*
Shinto shrine 卄	*jinja*
- shrine gate	*torii*
theater	*gekijoh, (name+) -za*
- movie theater	*eiga-kan*
town	*machi*
village	*mura*
zoo	*dohbutsu-en*
zen meditation	*zazen*

BODY/health   *karada/kenkoh*

ache	*itai*
cold	*kaze*
cough	*seki*
fever	*netsu*
dentist	*ha-isha*
doctor	*(o) isha*
hospital	*byoh-in*
illness	*byohki*
medicine	*kusuri*
pharmacy	*kusuri-ya, yakkyoku*
eye, ear, nose	*me, mimi, hana*
throat	*nodo*
mouth, tooth/teeth	*kao, ha*
face, head	*kao, atama*
hair (on head)	*(kami no) ke*
finger , hand	*yubi, te*
arm	*ude*
foot/leg	*ashi*
hip/lower back	*koshi*
back	*senaka*
stomach	*onaka*

WEATHER/season   *tenki/kisetsu*

sun, moon, star(s)	*taiyoh, tsuki, hoshi*
sunny /clear	*hare*
cloud(y)	*kumo(ri)*
rain	*ame*
snow	*yuki*
wind	*kaze*
cold, cool, hot	*samui, suzushii, atsui*
hot & humid	*mushi atsui*
rainy season (Jun)	*tsuyu*
typhoon (Sept)	*taifuu,* or *bohfuu*
earthquake	*jishin*
spring, summer	*haru, natsu*
autumn, winter	*aki, fuyu*

SHOPPING	kaimono
store, -shop	mise, -ya, -ten
department store	depahto, hyakka-ten
shopping street	shohten-gai
sales kiosk	bai-ten
book(shop)	hon(-ya)
- newspaper	shinbun
- magazine	zasshi
dictionary	jibiki
cigarette(shop)	tabako(-ya)
camera(shop)	kamera(-ya)
- photo	shashin
- film	firumu
- battery	denchi
clothes	fuku
- Japanese style	wa-fuku, kimono
- summer kimono	yukata
- Western style	yoh-fuku
fan (folding)	sensu
fan (round)	uchiwa
folding screen	byohbu
folk art	mingei
gold; silver	kin; gin
lacquer	shikki, urushi
lantern	chohchin
umbrella	kasa
Japanese umbrella	ban-gasa
scroll	kake-jiku
business card	meishi
pottery	yaki-mono, tohki
price	nedan
how much does this cost?	kore wa ikura desu ka?
expensive, inexpensive	takai, yasui

COLOR	iro, -shoku
black	kuro, koku-
blue	ao, buruu
brown	cha-iro
green	midori
orange	orenji
purple	murasaki
red	aka
white	shiro, haku-
yellow	kii-iro

POST OFFICE (p189)	yubin kyoku
air mail	kokuh bin
letter	tegami
money order	yubin gawase
parcel	kozutsumi
post card	hagaki
sea mail	funa bin
stamps	kitte
commemorative-	kinen-kitte
P.O. savings acct.	yuubin chokin
savings pass book	chokin tsuuchoh
withdraw, take out	shukkin, dasu (simple)
deposit, put in	furikomi, ireru (")
telegram	dempoh

ANIMAL	dohbutsu
bird, cat, dog, horse	tori, neko, inu, uma
cow, rabbit, monkey	ushi, usagi, saru

PEOPLE	hito, hitobito (pl)
I, me, my	watakushi (m). watashi(f)
you / plural	anata / anata-gata
he	kare
she	kanojo
we	watashitachi
they	karera
boy	otoko-no-ko, boya
girl	onna-no-ko, gyaru
child, also plural	kodomo
female (person)	onna-(no-hito)
male (person)	otoko-(no-hito)
foreigner	gaijin, gaikokujin
foreign country	gaikoku
person	hito, (-bito); -jin
friend	tomodachi
white person	haku-jin
black person	koku-jin
father	otohsan, papa
mother	okaasan, haha, mama
grandfather, old man	ojiisan
grandmother, old lady	obaasan
elderly people	toshiyori, rohjin
husband	(go-) shujin
wife (another's)	okusan
" (one's own)	kanai
sibling (M or F)	kyodai
older brother	ani, o-nisan
older sister	ane, o-neisan
younger brother	otohto
younger sister	imohto
relative	shinseki

TIME	jikan, -ji, -kan
one o'clock	ichi-ji
two o'clock	ni-ji
ten o'clock	juu-ji
twelve o'clock	juuni-ji
What time is it?	nan ji desu ka?
I don't have time	jikan ga nai
span of time	-kan as in ...
one hour	ichi jikan
two hours	ni jikan
morning	asa, gozen
afternoon	gogo
evening	yuugata
night, late night	yoru, shinya
dawn, sunrise	yo-ake, hi-no-de
twilight, sunset	yuu-yake, nichi-botsu
day time	hiruma
day	nichi, hi, -bi, -jitsu
today	kyoh, hon-jitsu
tomorrow	ashita, yoku-jitsu
day after tomorrow	asatte
yesterday	kinoh, saku-jitsu
day before yesterday	ototoi

MONTH	tsuki/-gatsu
Jan, Feb	ichi-gatsu, ni-gatsu
March, April	san-gatsu, shi-gatsu
May, June	go-gatsu, roku-gatsu
July, August	shichi-gatsu, hachi-gatsu
Sept, Oct	ku-gatsu, juu-gatsu
Nov, Dec	juuichi-gatsu, juuni-gatsu
one month ('s time)	ikka-getsu(-kan)
two months	ni ka-getsu
1st day of month, 2nd	tsuitachi, futsuka
3rd 4th	mikka, yokka, itsuka
6th, 7th, 8th	muika, nanoka, yohka
9th, 10th	kokonoka, tohka
eleventh day	juu ichi nichi
fourteenth day	juu yokka
twentieth day	hatsuka
New Year	(o)shoh-gatsu, shin-nen
New Year's Day	Gan-tan
this week	konshuu
next week	raishuu
last week	senshuu
this month	kon-getsu
next week	rai-getsu
last week	sen-getsu
this year	kotoshi
next year	rainen
last year	kyonen, sakunen

DINING/ FOOD	shokuji /tabemono
menu please	menyu onegai shimasu
bill	kanjo, o-aiso
I would like ____,	watakushi wa _____
please	o kudasai
before meal (grace)	itadakimasu
thank you for	gochiso-sama
this meal	deshita
delicious (past tense)	oishii (oishikatta)
breakfast	choshoku, asa gohan
(morning set)	mohningu sahbisu
lunch	chuhshoku, hiru gohan
(set lunch)	ranchi setto
dinner	yuushoku, yoru gohan
restaurant	resutoran, shokudoh
dining room, diner	shokudoh
box lunch	(o-) bentoh
bread	pan (Port.pano)
sandwich	sandoitchi, or just sando
chopstick(s)	(o-) hashi
bowl	(o-)chawan
Japanese tea cup	yu-nomi
cup, glass	koppu. gurasu
fork	fohku (hohku)
knife	naifu
spoon	supoon
miso soup	(o-)miso shiru
moist towelette	o-shibori
plate	(o-) sara
rice (uncooked)	(o-) kome
rice (cooked)	gohan, raisu

curry rice	karei raisu
salt, pepper	shio, koshoh
soy sauce	(o-) shohyu
sugar	satoh
japanese sweet	okashi
MEAT	niku
beef	gyuu niku
chicken	tori; chikin
- egg	tamago
pork	buta niku
steak	sutehki, teki

VEGETABLES	yasai
bamboo shoot	takenoko
bean curd	(o-) tohfu
beans	mame
eggplant	nasu
onion	tamanegi
Japanese pickles	(o-)tsukemono
spinach	hohrensoh
turnip, radish	daikon

FRUITS	kudamono
apple	ringo
banana	banana
grapes	budoh
melon	meron
pear, 'pear-apple'	nashi
persimmon	kaki
strawberry	ichigo
tangerine	mikan
watermelon	suika

FISH	sakana
crab	kani
eel	unagi
lobster	robusutah, ise ebi
oyster	kaki
red snapper	tai
salmon	sake, or shake
sardine	iwashi
shrimp, prawn	ebi, kuruma-ebi
tuna	maguro
octopus; squid	tako; ika

DRINKS	(o) nomimono
alcohol in general	(o) sake, arukohru
rice wine	(o) sake, Nihon-shuu
-warmed	atsu-kan, or just kan
-cold	rei-shuu, or hiya
beer	biiru
coffee	kohi; hotto (or aisu)
cola	kohra
cold water	mizu; o-hiya
hot water	o-yu
japanese tea	o-cha, in sushiya agari
" whisked, formal	(o) matcha
western (black) tea	koh-cha
juice (carbonate)	sohda, juusu
juice (fresh fruit-)	furuutsu juusu
milk	gyuu nyuu, miruku

Ashimori, 634
Ashiya, Hyogo, 595, 603
Ashuku, 394
Asia Institute School for
  Asian Studies, 361, 470
Asia Society, NYC, 82
- of Japan, 1138
Aso, Mount, 742, 748-49
Asuka (552-645), 10, 312
- Shrine, 409
- Asuka-dera Great Bronze
  Buddha, 349
Asuka-Nara era, 346, 360
Asuke Village, 301
Asuras, 27
Atago Hill, 1163
Atami, 243
Atomic Dome. See
  Hiroshima
Atomic Era, 645
Atsumi Peninsula, 293
Atsumori, 614
Atsumori-zuka, 598
Atsuta Shrine, 298
ATT access, 189
Avant-garde. See Theater
Awa-no-Jurobei House, 681
Awa-odori, 680
Awaji Island, 682
- puppets, 55, 681, 682
Awase 'comparison party', 484
Awata Palace, 490
Awazu Onsen, 854
Aya Tribe, 8
Azuchi-Momoyama Era
  (1573-1613), 440, 445, 489
        B
Baby products, svces, 164
Baggage & Checking, 184
- allowance, 168
Baijo-dake, Mount, 850
Bakufu, 215
Bamboo, baskets, 598
- crafts, 302
Bamian, Afghanistan, 339
Bandai Kogen Plateau, 971
- Mount, 962, 971
Bando Tamasaburo, 57
Bangai, 679
Bankers' Club, 1145
Bank of Japan, 1145
Banshu Ako, 621
Barbarian & Geisha, 248
Baseball, 73, 578, 1242
Basho, Matsuo (1644-94),
  49, 279, 286, 332, 336, 489,
  947, 960, 984, 1164
- Memorial Hall, 334
Basket-making, 302

Batchelor Ainu Mus, 1075
Bath. See Hot Springs
- bathhouses, 157
- goemon-buro, 490
- iwa-buro, rock bath, 123
- kamaburo, steam, 519
- mud-, 769, 911
- ofuro, 121, 122
- rotenburo outdoorr, 121,
  124, 923
- sand -, 758
- sento, public, 124
- Turkish, 157, 1197
Battle,-of Kawanakajima, 973
- of Nagashino, 273
- of Seki-ga-hara, 973
- of Tsushima, 236
Bay Cruises, Tokyo, 1138
Bear-sashimi, 1116
Beauty Shops, 161
Beer-fed cows, 308
Bejart, Maurice, 1162
Bekkai, 1109
Bekku attached shrine, 313
Ben Daisan, 39
Bengara red dye, 637
Benkei, 216
Benten, goddess/muse, 30,
  212, 230, 234, 288
Bentenjima, 289
Benten-kozo, 234
Bento, 'box' lunch, 516
Benzaiten, 1032
Beppu, 742, 766, 769
Bessho Onsen, 941
Bicycle, 75, 117
- racing, 578
Big bang, 31
Big Buddha, Daibutsu. See
  Buddha
Bijin-ga, 43
Bike license, 117
Bingata, 777, 779
Bird Museum, 915
Birdwatchers, 81
Bishamonten, 30, 236, 1032
Biwa Lake of Lute, 496-500
Bizen, 615, 621-25
- bizen ware, 621
Blacksmithing, 302
Blood-lake Hell, 769
Blood type, 1056
Blue/white porcelain, 46
Boar, 618
- hunting, 415
- sukiyaki, 521, 618
Bodai-ji temple, 1021
Bodhidharma. See Daruma
Bodhisattva. See Bosatsu

Bodhisattva of medicine. See
  Yakushi Nyorai
Bon dance capital, 933
Bon odori dancing, 198, 306
  See also local Datebooks
Bonfire noh, see Takigi
Bonotsu, 760
Bonsai, 13, 684, 1187
- village, 740
Bonseki, 412
Bosatsu, 23, 25, 359, 382
Boshin Wars, 962, 1003,
  1020, 1085
Boston Museum, 42, 297
Botan-nabé, 521, 618
Bowling, 74
Boxing, 74
Bridal kimono, 448
Bridge of Brocade Sash, 674
British, 798
- fleet, 14
Bronze Age, 6
Brunet, Capt. Jules, 1062
Bubbling hells, 1082
Bucket-shops, agents, 84
Buddha, 10, 28, 412, 452
- Coming Buddha, 25
- Daibutsu, Great Buddha
  - of Kamakura, 231
  - of Kyoto, 492
  - of Nara, 376
- Dainichi 'Sun' Buddha, 24,
  368, 399, 985, 994-5
- 500 disciples of-. See Go-
  hyaku Rakan
- Hotei laughing-, 30, 463
- Lacquered Buddha, 307
- Medicinal. See Yakushi
- Roshana, of light-, 368, 379.
  See Dainichi above
- Ten Great Disciples, 382
- Tibetan, 402
- Ultimate Buddha, 23
Buddhism, 8, 23, 397, 1029
Buddhism - Shinto, 984
Buddhist(s), 474
- art, 850
- icons, 23, 995
- sects, 474
Budo-kan, 68
Bugaku, 51, 233, 583, 611, 668,
  709, 1143, 1158, 1200
Buke-yashiki, samurai house
  634, 710, 716, 731, 766, 770,
  798, 810, 826, 827, 933, 964,
  975, 1000, 1010
Bullet train. See Shinkansen
Bullfight, 693, 782, 843, 949
Bunkyu era (1861-3), 15

Index covers Datebooks only incidentally; see also FESTIVAL CALENDAR, p.xx.

TERMS, ABBREVIATIONS & SYMBOLS

Ryokan	Japanese Inn	JR	Japan Rail (former JNR)
Minshuku	Family-run People's Inn	Bullet Train	High-speed Shinkansen
Kokumin-shukusha	Gov't-run Budget Inn	stn	Station
Shukubo	Temple Stay - usually ¥-B	xfer	Transfer
YH	Youth Hostel	o.w. / ow	One way
J- style, J-	Japanese style	r.t. / rt	Round trip
W- style, W-	Western style	JT	*Japan Times* daily newspaper
E-	English [-spoken, etc]	MDN	*Mainichi Daily News* daily
¥-LL	Very expensive	KTO	*Kansai Time Out* monthly
¥-L	Luxe (International) rate	KVG	*Kyoto Visitors Gyide* monthly
¥-S	Standard rate	TJ	*Tokyo Journal* monthly
¥-T	Tourist rate	NT	National Treasure (art)
¥-B	Price at Budget rate	ICA	Important Cultural Asset "
¥-lo-B	Lo-end Budget rate	TILT	Traveling in Limited Time
¥-lo-B-hi-S	Price range from lo	TIC	Travel Information Center
	Budget to high Standard	JNTO	Japan National Tourist Org
¥-B+	Budget (or other) rate and up	JTB	Japan Travel Bureau
¥-P	Room price at Pilgrim rate	X-mon	Closed monday, etc
¥-Bw/2	Rate includes 2 meals	no-X	No closing days
+%	Plus tax and svce chge	basic meter	Basic cost of taxi for 2km
bkfst	Breakfast	2x-mtr	2x (etc) above basic rate
W, E, N, S	West, East, North, South	☎ (#)	Telephone number (area code)
		✍	Write for info to following –
		卍	Buddhist temple
		开	Shinto shrine
		♨	Hot spring, spa, onsen

* Complete Ryokan & Hotel price range
abbreviations used throughout this book,
see Chart any of pages 431, 564 or 1129.

Field research and first drafts by Garet recorded on Epson laptop,
transferred to Macintosh (-128 to -Plus to -SE) for
editing and page design in Microsoft Word-3, by Jay.
Final formatting, standardizing, compiling of INDEX and CONTENTS by Amy Sacks.
Cover design by Cellin Gluck.
Calligraphy on frontispiece in antique seal style, brushed by Prof OWYANG Keliang.